CALIFORNIA

HANDBOOK DIVISIONS

THE NORTHERN MOUNTAINS AND MODOC

THE NORTH COAST

THE WINE COUNTRY

THE GOLD COUNTRY

THE SAN FRANCISCO BAY AREA

THE SIERRA NEVADA

MONTEREY BAY AREA

THE GREAT VALLEY AND DELTA

THE CENTRAL COAST

THE DESERTS

GREATER LOS ANGELES

SAN DIEGO AND VICINITY

ORANGE COUNTY

GREATER LOS ANGELES DIVISIONS

HOLLYWOOD AND VICINITY

PASADENA AND VICINITY

THE L.A. COAST

BEVERLY HILLS AND VICINITY

DOWNTOWN AND AROUND

© AVALON TRAVEL PUBLISHING, INC.

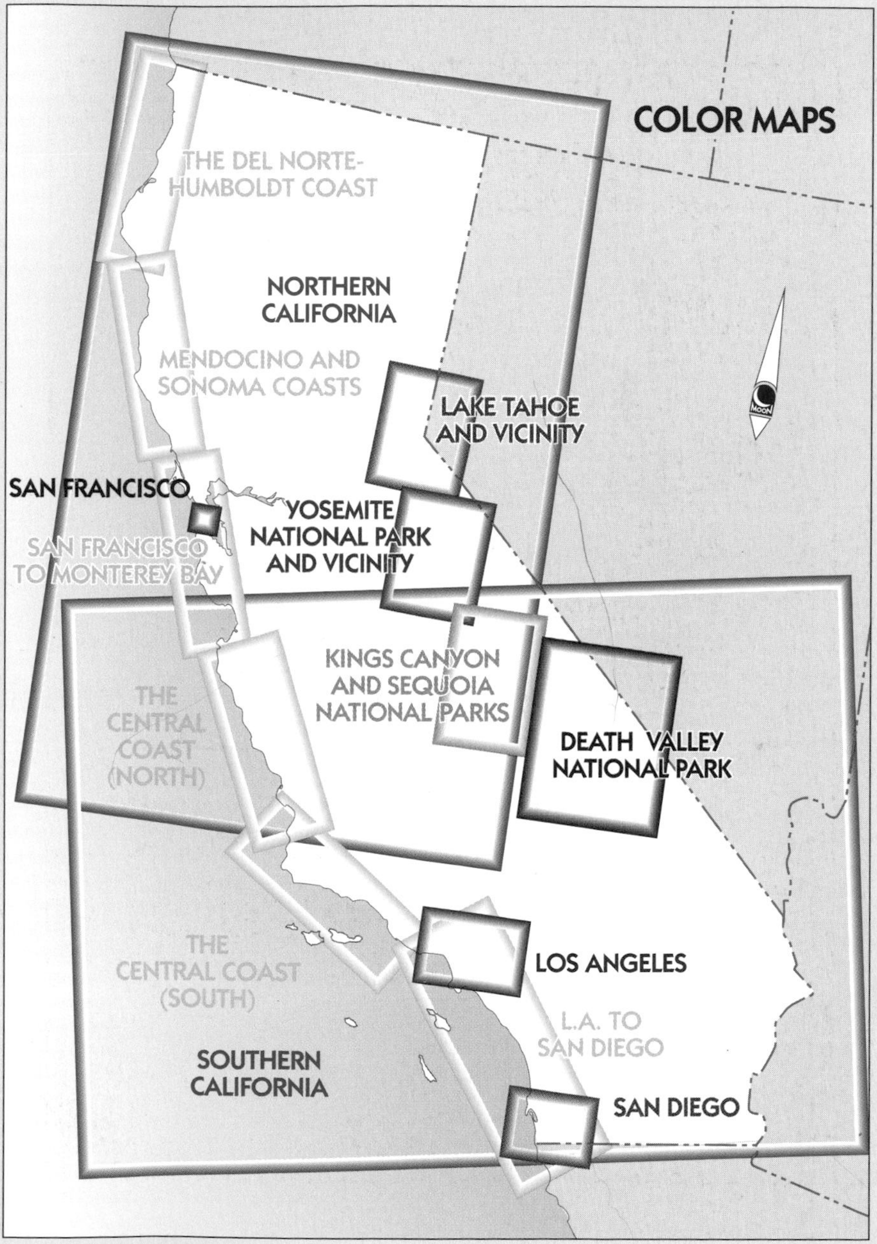

COLOR MAPS

THE DEL NORTE-
HUMBOLDT COAST

**NORTHERN
CALIFORNIA**

MENDOCINO AND
SONOMA COASTS

**LAKE TAHOE
AND VICINITY**

SAN FRANCISCO

SAN FRANCISCO
TO MONTEREY BAY

**YOSEMITE
NATIONAL PARK
AND VICINITY**

**KINGS CANYON
AND SEQUOIA
NATIONAL PARKS**

THE
CENTRAL
COAST
(NORTH)

**DEATH VALLEY
NATIONAL PARK**

THE
CENTRAL COAST
(SOUTH)

LOS ANGELES

L.A. TO
SAN DIEGO

**SOUTHERN
CALIFORNIA**

SAN DIEGO

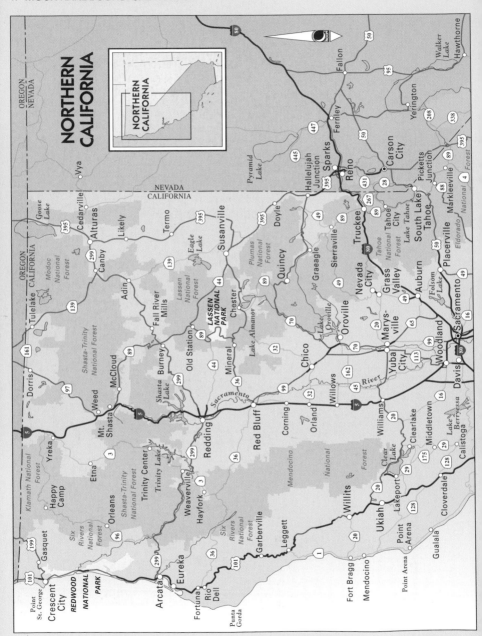

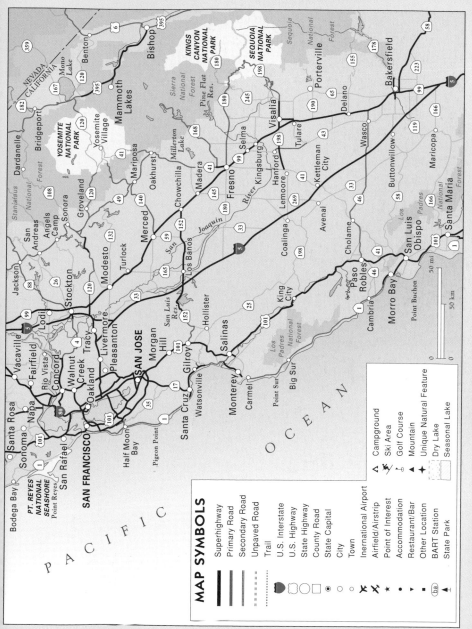

MAP SYMBOLS

▬▬▬	Superhighway
▬▬	Primary Road
───	Secondary Road
-----	Unpaved Road
········	Trail
🛡	U.S. Interstate
⬭	U.S. Highway
◯	State Highway
▢	County Road
◉	State Capital
◯	City
○	Town
✈	International Airport
✶	Airfield/Airstrip
•	Point of Interest
▸	Accommodation
▪	Restaurant/Bar
⬭a	Other Location
🅱	BART Station
▲	State Park

△	Campground
🎿	Ski Area
⛳	Golf Course
▲	Mountain
✚	Unique Natural Feature
	Dry Lake
░	Seasonal Lake

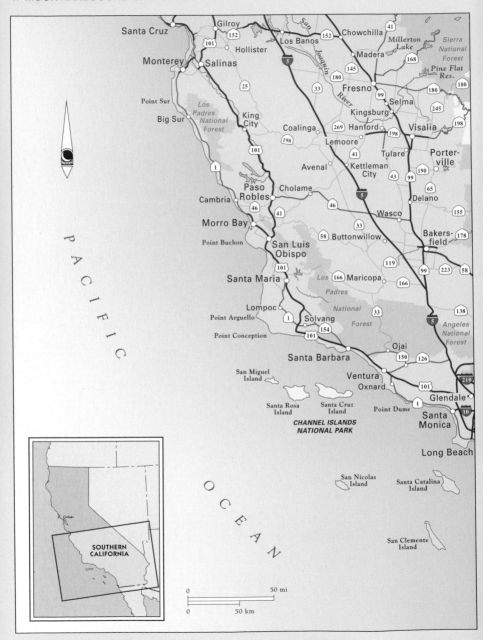

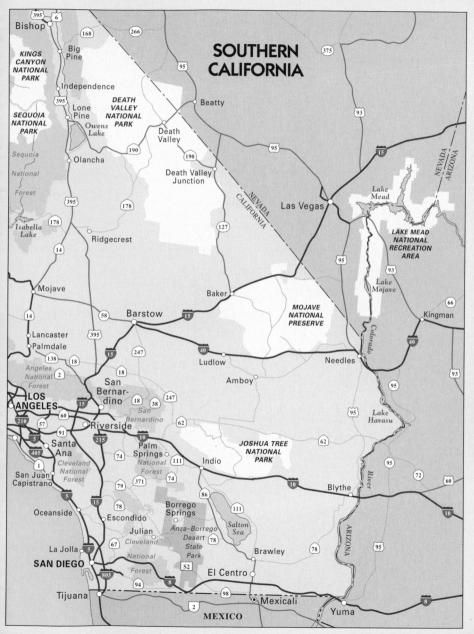

SOUTHERN CALIFORNIA

Bishop · 395 · 6

168

266

KINGS CANYON NATIONAL PARK

Big Pine

95

375

Independence

DEATH VALLEY NATIONAL PARK

Beatty

93

395

Lone Pine

Owens Lake

SEQUOIA NATIONAL PARK

190

Death Valley

190

Death Valley Junction

15

Lake Mead

Sequoia

National

Olancha

95

NEVADA

Forest

178

Las Vegas

CALIFORNIA

LAKE MEAD NATIONAL RECREATION AREA

NEVADA ARIZONA

Isabella Lake

395

178

127

178

Ridgecrest

95

93

Lake Mojave

14

MOJAVE NATIONAL PRESERVE

66

Mojave

14

58

Baker

Kingman

Barstow

15

Colorado

Lancaster

395

15

247

40

40

95

Palmdale

138

18

18

Ludlow

Needles

93

Angeles National Forest

2

San Bernardino

18

38

247

Amboy

95

Lake Havasu

LOS ANGELES

15

San Bernardino

62

210

60

Riverside

57

91

215

10

JOSHUA TREE NATIONAL PARK

62

95

Santa Ana

5

405

Palm Springs

111

Indio

Cleveland National Forest

74

National Forest

74

10

Blythe

72

60

1

San Juan Capistrano

79

371

86

River

10

5

Oceanside

15

78

Borrego Springs

111

Salton Sea

ARIZONA

Escondido

Julian

Anza–Borrego Desert State Park

95

La Jolla

5

67

Cleveland National Forest

78

Brawley

78

SAN DIEGO

805

S2

El Centro

8

Tijuana

94

98

Mexicali

Yuma

8

2

MEXICO

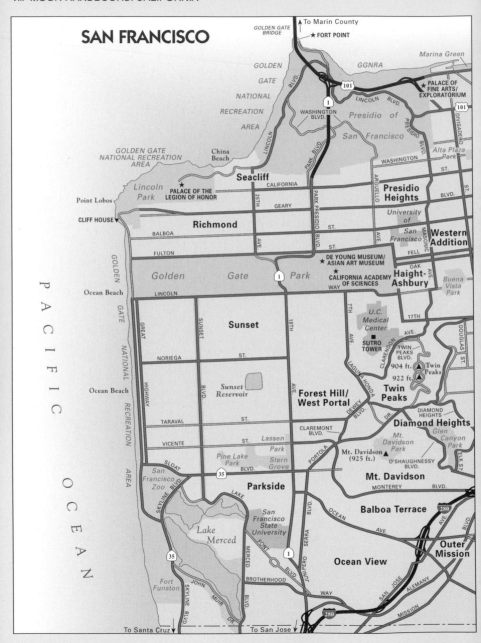

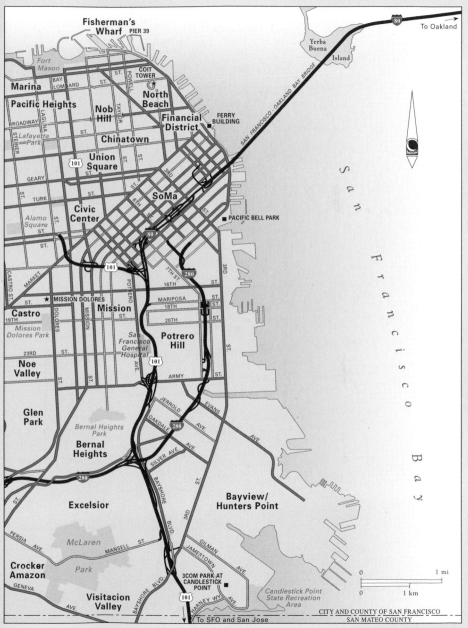

To Oakland

Yerba Buena Island

San Francisco Bay

Fisherman's Wharf
PIER 39

Fort Mason

BAY
LOMBARD ST.
ST.

COIT TOWER

Marina

Pacific Heights

Nob Hill

North Beach

Financial District

FERRY BUILDING

BROADWAY

LAGUNA
STEINER

Lafayette Park

Chinatown

POWELL ST.
TAYLOR ST.

Union Square

101

GEARY

TURK

3RD ST.

SoMa

ST.

6TH ST.
7TH ST.

PACIFIC BELL PARK

Alamo Square
ST.

Civic Center

ST.

80

MARKET
101

280

CASTRO ST.

ST.

POTRERO AVE.

16TH

MARIPOSA ST.
18TH
20TH

ST.
ST.
ST.
ST.

3RD ST.

★ MISSION DOLORES

Castro
19TH

Mission Dolores Park

DOLORES ST.
MISSION ST.

Mission

San Francisco General Hospital

Potrero Hill

23RD

Noe Valley

ST.

101

ARMY

ST.

ST.

Glen Park

Bernal Heights Park

JERROLD
OAKDALE

EVANS AVE.

AVE.
AVE.

Bernal Heights

280

SILVER AVE.

BAYSHORE

Bayview/ Hunters Point

280

Excelsior

3RD ST.

BLVD.

PERSIA AVE.

McLaren Park

MANSELL ST.

GILMAN AVE.

JAMESTOWN AVE.

Crocker Amazon

GENEVA

Visitacion Valley

BAYSHORE BLVD.

101

HARNEY WY.

3COM PARK AT CANDLESTICK POINT ■

Candlestick Point State Recreation Area

AVE.

0   1 mi
0   1 km

CITY AND COUNTY OF SAN FRANCISCO
SAN MATEO COUNTY

To SFO and San Jose

© AVALON TRAVEL PUBLISHING, INC.

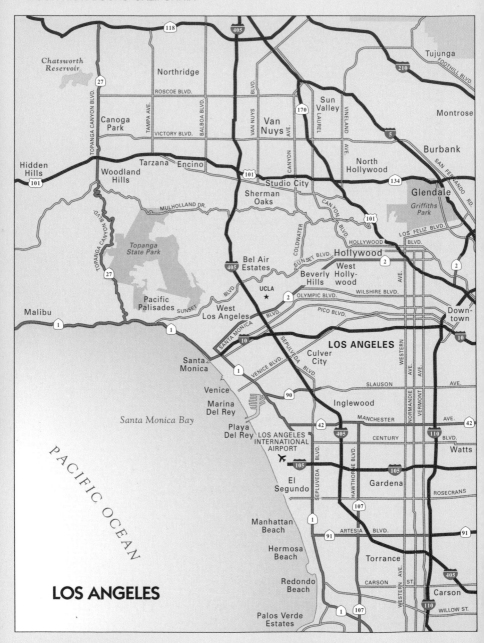

LOS ANGELES

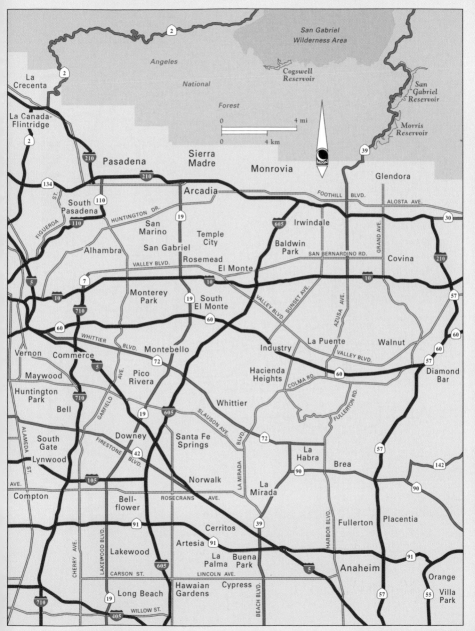

© AVALON TRAVEL PUBLISHING, INC.

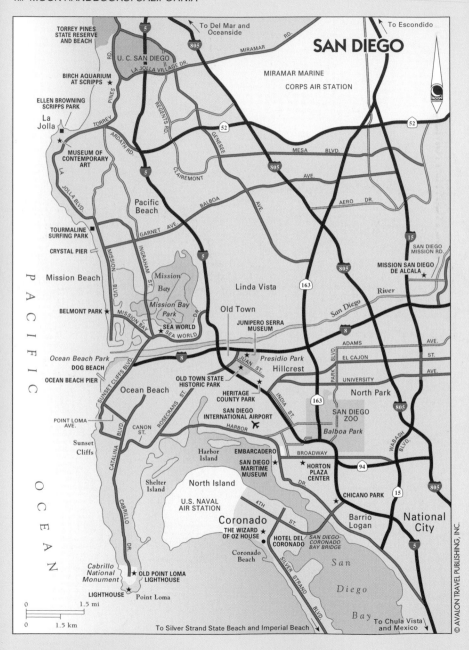

TORREY PINES
STATE RESERVE
AND BEACH

To Del Mar and
Oceanside

To Escondido

SAN DIEGO

MIRAMAR MARINE
CORPS AIR STATION

U. C. SAN DIEGO

BIRCH AQUARIUM
AT SCRIPPS

ELLEN BROWNING
SCRIPPS PARK

La
Jolla

MUSEUM OF
CONTEMPORARY
ART

Pacific
Beach

MESA   BLVD.

AERO   DR.

SAN DIEGO
MISSION RD.

TOURMALINE
SURFING PARK

MISSION SAN DIEGO
DE ALCALA

CRYSTAL PIER

Mission Beach

Mission
Bay

Linda Vista

River

San Diego

Mission Bay
Park

BELMONT PARK

SEA WORLD
SEA WORLD

Old Town

JUNIPERO SERRA
MUSEUM

ADAMS   AVE.

EL CAJON   ST.

UNIVERSITY   AVE.

Presidio Park

Ocean Beach Park

DOG BEACH

OCEAN BEACH PIER

Hillcrest

North Park

Ocean Beach

OLD TOWN STATE
HISTORIC PARK

HERITAGE
COUNTY PARK

SAN DIEGO
INTERNATIONAL AIRPORT

SAN DIEGO
ZOO

POINT LOMA
AVE.

Balboa Park

Sunset
Cliffs

HARBOR

Harbor
Island

EMBARCADERO

SAN DIEGO
MARITIME
MUSEUM

BROADWAY

HORTON
PLAZA
CENTER

Shelter
Island

North Island

U.S. NAVAL
AIR STATION

Coronado

CHICANO PARK

Barrio
Logan

National
City

THE WIZARD
OF OZ HOUSE

HOTEL DEL
CORONADO

SAN DIEGO
CORONADO
BAY BRIDGE

Cabrillo
National
Monument

Coronado
Beach

San

OLD POINT LOMA
LIGHTHOUSE

Diego

LIGHTHOUSE

Point Loma

Bay

0   1.5 mi

0   1.5 km

To Chula Vista
and Mexico

To Silver Strand State Beach and Imperial Beach

PACIFIC   OCEAN

© AVALON TRAVEL PUBLISHING, INC.

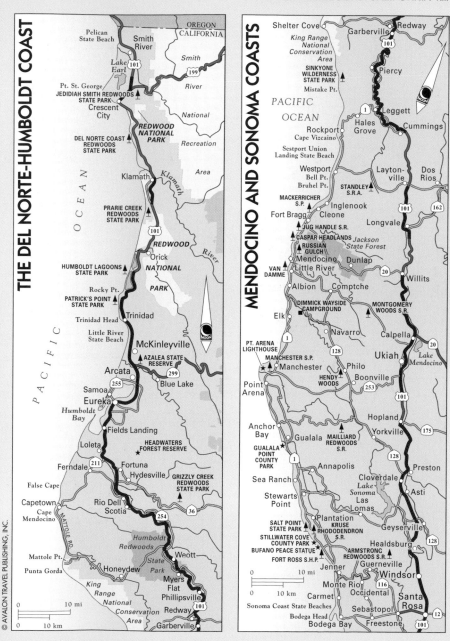

THE DEL NORTE-HUMBOLDT COAST

OREGON
CALIFORNIA

Pelican
State Beach

Smith
River

Smith

Lake
Earl

101

Smith

199

Pt. St. George
JEDIDIAH SMITH REDWOODS
STATE PARK

River

Crescent
City

National

REDWOOD
NATIONAL
PARK

DEL NORTE COAST
REDWOODS
STATE PARK

Recreation

Klamath

Klamath

PRAIRIE CREEK
REDWOODS
STATE PARK

Area

101

REDWOOD

River

Orick

NATIONAL

HUMBOLDT LAGOONS
STATE PARK

PARK

Rocky Pt.
PATRICK'S POINT
STATE PARK

Trinidad Head   Trinidad

Little River
State Beach

McKinleyville

AZALEA STATE
RESERVE

Arcata

299

Samoa   Blue Lake

255

Eureka

*Humboldt
Bay*

Fields Landing

Loleta   HEADWATERS
FOREST RESERVE

Ferndale   211   Fortuna

False Cape   Hydesville

Capetown   GRIZZLY CREEK
REDWOODS
STATE PARK

Cape   Rio Dell
Mendocino   Scotia   254   36

*Humboldt
Redwoods*

Mattole Pt.   State
Punta Gorda   Park   Weott

Honeydew   Myers
Flat
Phillipsville

*King
Range
National
Conservation
Area*   Redway   101

Garberville

O C E A N

P A C I F I C

© AVALON TRAVEL PUBLISHING, INC.

MATTOLE RD.

0   10 mi

0   10 km

MENDOCINO AND SONOMA COASTS

Shelter Cove   Garberville   Redway

*King Range
National
Conservation
Area*   101

SINKYONE
WILDERNESS
STATE PARK   Piercy

Mistake Pt.

PACIFIC
OCEAN   Leggett

1

Hales   Cummings
Grove

Rockport
Cape Vizcaino

Sestport Union
Landing State Beach   Layton-   Dos
ville   Rios

Westport
Bell Pt.   STANDLEY   101   162
Bruhel Pt.   S.R.A.

MACKERRICHER
S.P.   Inglenook   Longvale

Fort Bragg   Cleone

JUG HANDLE S.R.   *Jackson
State Forest*

CASPAR HEADLANDS   Dunlap
RUSSIAN
GULCH   Mendocino   20   Willits
VAN   Little River
DAMME

Albion   Comptche

DIMMICK WAYSIDE
CAMPGROUND   MONTGOMERY
WOODS S.R.

Elk   Navarro   Calpella

20

PT. ARENA
LIGHTHOUSE   128   Ukiah   Lake
Mendocino

MANCHESTER S.P.   Philo
Manchester   Boonville

Point   HENDY   253
Arena   WOODS   101

Anchor   Hopland
Bay   Gualala   Yorkville   175

GUALALA   MAILLIARD
POINT   REDWOODS   128
COUNTY   S.R.
PARK

Annapolis   Preston

Sea Ranch   *Lake   Asti*
Cloverdale   *Sonoma*
Stewarts   Las
Point   Lomas   Geyserville

SALT POINT   Plantation
STATE PARK   KRUSE   128
STILLWATER COVE   RHODODENDRON   Healdsburg
COUNTY PARK   S.R.
BUFANO PEACE STATUE   ARMSTRONG   Windsor
FORT ROSS S.H.P.   REDWOODS S.R.   Guerneville
Jenner

Monte Rio   Occidental   116   Santa
Carmet   Rosa
Sonoma Coast State Beaches   Sebastopol
Bodega Head   12
Bodega Bay   Freestone   101

0   10 mi

0   10 km

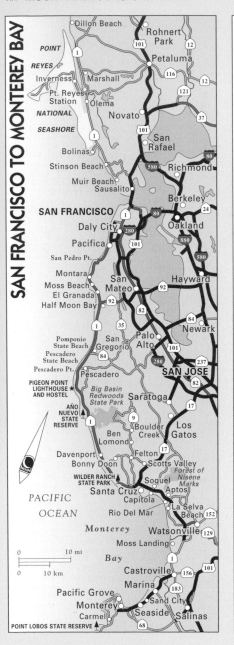

SAN FRANCISCO TO MONTEREY BAY

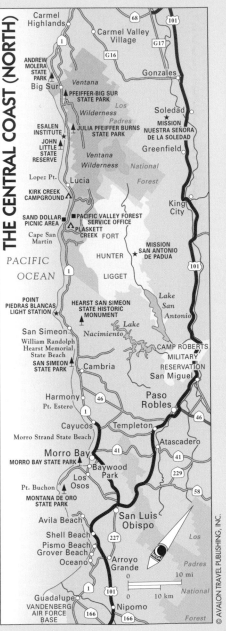

THE CENTRAL COAST (NORTH)

© AVALON TRAVEL PUBLISHING, INC.

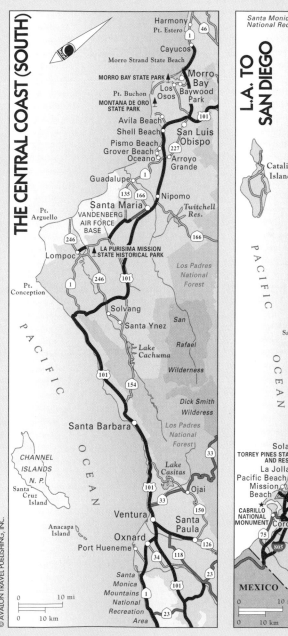

THE CENTRAL COAST (SOUTH)

Harmony
Pt. Estero
Cayucos
Morro Strand State Beach
MORRO BAY STATE PARK
Morro Bay
Los Osos
Baywood Park
Pt. Buchon
MONTANA DE ORO STATE PARK
Avila Beach
Shell Beach
San Luis Obispo
Pismo Beach
Grover Beach
Oceano
Arroyo Grande
Guadalupe
Pt. Arguello
Santa Maria
VANDENBERG AIR FORCE BASE
Nipomo
Twitchell Res.
LA PURISIMA MISSION STATE HISTORICAL PARK
Lompoc
Pt. Conception
Los Padres National Forest
Solvang
Santa Ynez
San Rafael Wilderness
Lake Cachuma
Dick Smith Wilderness
Los Padres National Forest
Santa Barbara
Lake Casitas
CHANNEL ISLANDS N. P.
Santa Cruz Island
Ojai
Anacapa Island
Ventura
Santa Paula
Oxnard
Port Hueneme
Santa Monica Mountains National Recreation Area
PACIFIC OCEAN

© AVALON TRAVEL PUBLISHING, INC.

0   10 mi
0   10 km

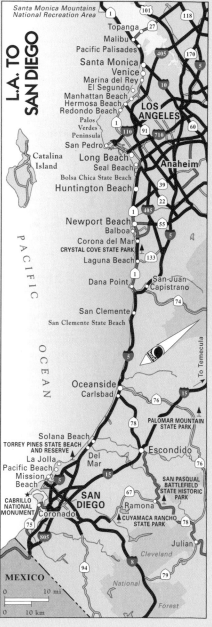

L.A. TO SAN DIEGO

Santa Monica Mountains National Recreation Area
Topanga
Malibu
Pacific Palisades
Santa Monica
Venice
Marina del Rey
El Segundo
Manhattan Beach
Hermosa Beach
Redondo Beach
LOS ANGELES
Palos Verdes Peninsula
San Pedro
Catalina Island
Long Beach
Seal Beach
Anaheim
Bolsa Chica State Beach
Huntington Beach
Newport Beach
Balboa
Corona del Mar
CRYSTAL COVE STATE PARK
Laguna Beach
Dana Point
San Juan Capistrano
To Temecula
San Clemente
San Clemente State Beach
Oceanside
Carlsbad
PALOMAR MOUNTAIN STATE PARK
Solana Beach
TORREY PINES STATE BEACH AND RESERVE
La Jolla
Pacific Beach
Mission Beach
Del Mar
Escondido
SAN PASQUAL BATTLEFIELD STATE HISTORIC PARK
Ramona
CABRILLO NATIONAL MONUMENT
SAN DIEGO
Coronado
CUYAMACA RANCHO STATE PARK
Julian
Cleveland
MEXICO
National Forest
PACIFIC OCEAN

0   10 mi
0   10 km

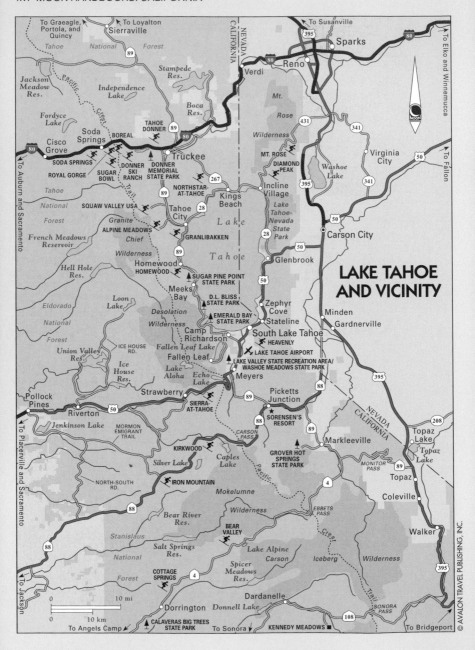

To Graeagle, Portola, and Quincy
To Loyalton
Sierraville
To Susanville
Sparks
To Elko and Winnemucca

Tahoe
National
Forest
89
Stampede Res.
Reno
Verdi
80
80
395

Jackson Meadow Res.
Independence Lake
Boca Res.
Mt.
Rose
Wilderness
431
341
To Fallon

Fordyce Lake
Soda Springs
Tahoe Donner
89
MT. ROSE
DIAMOND PEAK
Washoe Lake
Virginia City
50

Cisco Grove
Boreal
80
Truckee
395
341

SODA SPRINGS
ROYAL GORGE
DONNER SKI RANCH
SUGAR BOWL
DONNER MEMORIAL STATE PARK
89
267
NORTHSTAR-AT-TAHOE
Incline Village
Lake Tahoe-Nevada State Park
Carson City

To Auburn and Sacramento
80

SQUAW VALLEY USA
89
28
Tahoe City
Kings Beach
L a k e

Tahoe
National
Forest
Granite Chief
ALPINE MEADOWS
GRANLIBAKKEN
28
50
Glenbrook

French Meadows Reservoir
Wilderness
89
Homewood
HOMEWOOD
T a h o e

Hell Hole Res.
Loon Lake
Meeks Bay
SUGAR PINE POINT STATE PARK
D.L. BLISS STATE PARK
Zephyr Cove
Stateline
Minden
Gardnerville

Eldorado
National
Forest
Desolation
EMERALD BAY STATE PARK
Camp Richardson
South Lake Tahoe
HEAVENLY

Union Valley Res.
ICE HOUSE RD.
Wilderness
Fallen Leaf Lake
Fallen Leaf
LAKE TAHOE AIRPORT
LAKE VALLEY STATE RECREATION AREA/ WASHOE MEADOWS STATE PARK

Ice House Res.
Lake Aloha
Echo Lake
Meyers
Picketts Junction
88

Pollock Pines
Riverton
50
Strawberry
89
SIERRA-AT-TAHOE
SORENSEN'S RESORT
89
Markleeville
395

To Placerville and Sacramento
Jenkinson Lake
MORMON EMIGRANT TRAIL
88
CARSON PASS
GROVER HOT SPRINGS STATE PARK
208
Topaz Lake

KIRKWOOD
Silver Lake
Caples Lake
89
Topaz Lake

NORTH-SOUTH RD.
IRON MOUNTAIN
Mokelumne
4
MONITOR PASS
Topaz

88
Wilderness
EBBETS PASS
Coleville

Bear River Res.
BEAR VALLEY
Lake Alpine
Carson
Walker

Stanislaus
Salt Springs Res.
Iceberg
Wilderness

National
Forest
COTTAGE SPRINGS
Spicer Meadows Res.
4
395

10 mi
10 km
Dorrington
Donnell Lake
Dardanelle
SONORA PASS

To Jackson
CALAVERAS BIG TREES STATE PARK
To Angels Camp
To Sonora
KENNEDY MEADOWS
To Bridgeport
108

CALIFORNIA
NEVADA

LAKE TAHOE AND VICINITY

© AVALON TRAVEL PUBLISHING, INC.

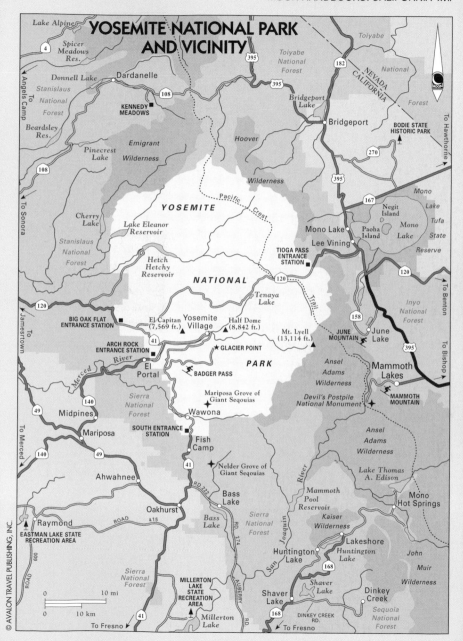

YOSEMITE NATIONAL PARK AND VICINITY

Lake Alpine

Spicer Meadows Res.

4

Donnell Lake

Dardanelle

108

Stanislaus National Forest

KENNEDY MEADOWS

Beardsley Res.

Pinecrest Lake

Emigrant Wilderness

108

To Angels Camp

To Sonora

Cherry Lake

Lake Eleanor Reservoir

Stanislaus National Forest

YOSEMITE

Hetch Hetchy Reservoir

NATIONAL

120

120

To Jamestrown

BIG OAK FLAT ENTRANCE STATION

El Capitan (7,569 ft.)

Yosemite Village

ARCH ROCK ENTRANCE STATION

41

El Portal

Merced River

Sierra National Forest

Half Dome (8,842 ft.)

★ GLACIER POINT

PARK

BADGER PASS

Mariposa Grove of Giant Sequoias

Wawona

SOUTH ENTRANCE STATION

140

49

Midpines

Mariposa

49

To Merced

140

Ahwahnee

Oakhurst

ROAD A15

RD 222

Fish Camp

41

Nelder Grove of Giant Sequoias

Bass Lake

Bass Lake

RD 274

RD 222

Raymond

EASTMAN LAKE STATE RECREATION AREA

ROAD 600

Sierra National Forest

MILLERTON LAKE STATE RECREATION AREA

Millerton Lake

41

AUBERRY RD.

To Fresno

Toiyabe

Toiyabe National Forest

395

182

NEVADA

CALIFORNIA

Bridgeport Lake

395

Bridgeport

National

Forest

To Hawthorne

BODIE STATE HISTORIC PARK

270

Hoover

Wilderness

395

Mono

167

Negit Island

Mono Lake

Lee Vining

Paoha Island

Mono Lake

Tufa State Reserve

120

Pacific

Crest

120

Tenaya Lake

TIOGA PASS ENTRANCE STATION

Trail

158

Inyo National Forest

To Benton

Mt. Lyell (13,114 ft.)

JUNE MOUNTAIN

June Lake

395

To Bishop

Ansel Adams Wilderness

Mammoth Lakes

Devil's Postpile National Monument

MAMMOTH MOUNTAIN

Ansel Adams Wilderness

Lake Thomas A. Edison

Mono Hot Springs

San Joaquin River

Mammoth Pool Reservoir

Kaiser Wilderness

Lakeshore

Huntington Lake

John Muir Wilderness

Huntington Lake

168

Shaver Lake

Dinkey Creek

Shaver Lake

168

DINKEY CREEK RD.

Sequoia National Forest

To Fresno

0   10 mi

0   10 km

© AVALON TRAVEL PUBLISHING, INC.

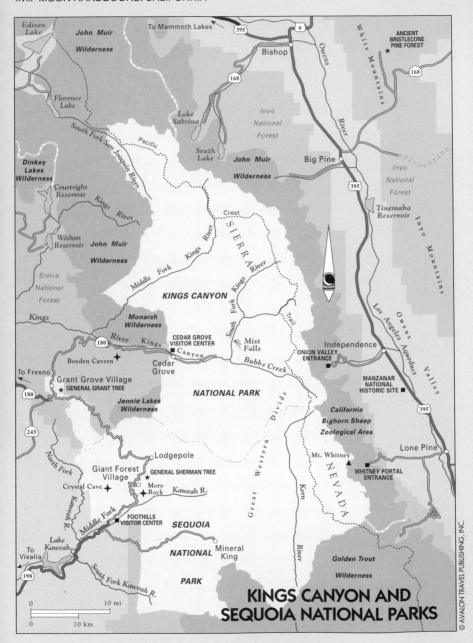

KINGS CANYON AND
SEQUOIA NATIONAL PARKS

© AVALON TRAVEL PUBLISHING, INC.

DEATH VALLEY NATIONAL PARK

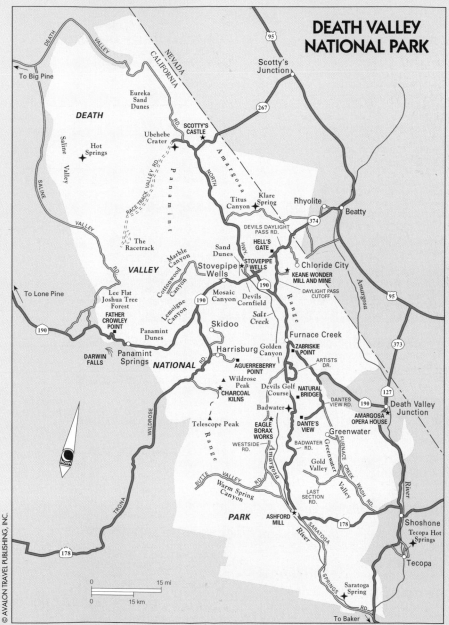

To Big Pine

DEATH

Eureka Sand Dunes

Saline Valley

Hot Springs

SALINE

VALLEY

DEATH

VALLEY

CALIFORNIA

NEVADA

95

Scotty's Junction

267

Ubehebe Crater

SCOTTY'S CASTLE

RACE TRACK VALLEY RD.

The Racetrack

VALLEY

Panamint

NORTH

Amargosa

Titus Canyon

Klare Spring

Rhyolite

Beatty

374

DEVILS DAYLIGHT PASS RD.

HWY.

HELL'S GATE

Marble Canyon

Sand Dunes

Cottonwood Canyon

Stovepipe Wells

STOVEPIPE WELLS

Chloride City

KEANE WONDER MILL AND MINE

Lee Flat Joshua Tree Forest

To Lone Pine

190

FATHER CROWLEY POINT

Panamint Dunes

Lemoigne Canyon

Mosaic Canyon

Devils Cornfield

190

Skidoo

DAYLIGHT PASS CUTOFF

Range

Salt Creek

Furnace Creek

190

DARWIN FALLS

Panamint Springs

NATIONAL

Harrisburg

Golden Canyon

ZABRISKIE POINT

ARTISTS DR.

AGUERREBERRY POINT

Wildrose Peak

CHARCOAL KILNS

Devils Golf Course

NATURAL BRIDGE

DANTES VIEW RD.

DEATH

WILDROSE

RD.

Telescope Peak

EAGLE BORAX WORKS

Badwater

DANTE'S VIEW

AMARGOSA OPERA HOUSE

Death Valley Junction

127

373

95

Amargosa

Range

WESTSIDE RD.

Amargosa

Greenwater

BADWATER RD.

Greenwater Valley

FURNACE CREEK WASH RD.

TRONA

BUTTE

VALLEY

Warm Spring Canyon

Gold Valley

River

178

PARK

ASHFORD MILL

LAST SECTION RD.

178

Shoshone

Tecopa Hot Springs

River

178

Saratoga Spring

Tecopa

SARATOGA SPRINGS RD.

To Baker

MOON

0   15 mi

0   15 km

© AVALON TRAVEL PUBLISHING, INC.

MAPS

MOON HANDBOOKS

CALIFORNIA

FIRST EDITION

KIM WEIR

AVALON
TRAVEL

MOON HANDBOOKS:
CALIFORNIA
FIRST EDITION
Kim Weir

Published by
Avalon Travel Publishing
5855 Beaudry St.
Emeryville, CA 94608, USA

ISBN: 1-56691-126-5
ISSN: 1533-354X

Please send all comments,
corrections, additions,
amendments, and critiques to:

**MOON HANDBOOKS:
CALIFORNIA
AVALON TRAVEL PUBLISHING
5855 BEAUDRY ST.
EMERYVILLE, CA 94608, USA
email: info@travelmatters.com
www.moon.com**

Printing History
May 2001
5 4 3 2 1

Editor: Kate Willis
Series Manager: Erin Van Rheenen
Copyeditor: Leslie Miller
Graphics Coordinator: Erika Howsare
Production: Carey Wilson, Amber Pirker, Alvaro Villanueva
Cartographers: Chris Folks, Ben Pease, Mike Morgenfeld, Kat Kalamaras
Cartography Editors: Mike Ferguson, Naomi Dancis, Michael Balsbaugh
Index: Leslie Miller
Front cover photo: © 1995 Rankin Harvey

Distributed in the United States and Canada by Publishers Group West

Printed in USA by Worzalla

"I have come where I was going."
—URSULA K. LE GUIN

CONTENTS

Hostels and Other Cheap Sleeps; Inexpensive to Moderate Hotels;
Moderate to Premium Hotels; Boutique Hotels; Top of the Line Hotels;
City-Style Bed-and-Breakfasts

The Avenues: Richmond, Seacliff, Sunset; Union Square and Nob Hill;
The Financial District and Embarcadero; Civic Center and Vicinity;
Haight-Ashbury and Vicinity; The Mission District and the Castro; South
of Market (SoMa); Fisherman's Wharf and Ghirardelli Square; The
Marina District, Cow Hollow, and Pacific Heights; Chinatown; Jackson
Square, North Beach, and Russian Hill

Useful Information; Transportation: Getting To and From Town;
Transportation: Getting Around Town

SPECIAL TOPICS

SPECIAL TOPICS

THE NORTHERN MOUNTAINS AND MODOC 292-325

SPECIAL TOPICS

THE GREAT VALLEY AND DELTA 424-481
One Sweet Bee Garden

Sacramento and Vicinity. 427
The Big Tomato; Seeing Old Sacramento; Seeing Downtown
Sacramento; Staying in Sacramento; Eating in Sacramento: Capital
Ingredients; Eating in Sacramento: Downtown and Vicinity; Eating in
Midtown; Eating in East Sacramento and "Gourmet Gulch"; Sacramento
Information; Sacramento Transportation; Near Sacramento: Folsom and
Vicinity; Near Sacramento: Davis

From Sacramento. 462
The Sacramento Valley; Red Bluff and Vicinity; The San Joaquin Valley;
The Sacramento–San Joaquin Delta

SPECIAL TOPICS

MONTEREY BAY AREA 482-533
One Bay, Many Worlds 482
Monterey Bay by Land and by Sea; The Monterey Bay Story: California Firsts
Santa Cruz and Vicinity 488
Seeing and Doing Santa Cruz; Outdoors in Greater Santa Cruz; Staying
in Santa Cruz; Staying near Santa Cruz; Eating in Santa Cruz; Eating
near Santa Cruz

WELCOME TO L.A. 592-610

Land of Endless Sunshine. 593
Los Angeles as Place; Dusty Pueblo Days; Oranges, Water, Oil—and
Autos Everywhere; Hollywood's Heyday; Barbies and Bombers: Los
Angeles After World War II; Los Angeles in the New Age

Practical Los Angeles 602
Getting Informed; Getting There: By Freeway; Getting There: By Bus,
Boat, Train, and Plane; Getting Around

SPECIAL TOPICS

PASADENA AND VICINITY 611-641

Crowned by Agriculture—and Culture; The Craftsman Crown

Seeing and Doing Pasadena. 617
Old Pasadena; The Arroyo Seco; The Gamble House and Vicinity;
Downtown Again

Artful, Entertaining Pasadena 621
Museum-Quality Pasadena; Entertaining Pasadena; Shopping as
Entertainment

Practical Pasadena 626
Staying in Pasadena; Eating in Pasadena; Getting Oriented, Getting
Around

Near Pasadena 632
South Pasadena; San Marino and "The Huntington"; Highland Park: El
Alisal et Alia; The Arboretum of Los Angeles County; Santa Anita Park

Toward the Desert: The Inland Empire. 637
Riverside: Navel of the Inland Empire; San Bernardino: Birthplace of
McDonald's; Into the Mountains: Big Bear and Vicinity

SPECIAL TOPICS

SPECIAL TOPICS

SAN DIEGO AND VICINITY 836-883

SPECIAL TOPICS

EXPRESS YOURSELF

Not on just any topic, though. This being California, most things change faster than traffic lights. Because of this unfortunate fact of life in the fast lane of travel writing, comments, corrections, inadvertent omissions, and update information are always greatly appreciated. Though every effort was made to keep all current facts corralled and accounted for, it's no doubt true that *something* (most likely, a variety of things) will already be inaccurate by the time the printer's ink squirts onto the paper at press time.

Just remember this: whatever you divulge may indeed end up in print—so think twice before sending too much information about your favorite hole-in-the-wall restaurant, cheap hotel, or "secret" world's-best swimming hole or hot springs. Once such information falls into the hands of a travel writer, it probably won't be a secret for long. Address all correspondence to:

Moon Handbooks: California
c/o Avalon Travel Publishing
5855 Beaudry Street
Emeryville, CA 94608
E-mail: info@travelmatters.com
(Please put Moon California in subject line.)

ACCOMMODATIONS RATINGS

Accommodations in this book are rated by price category, based on double-occupancy, high-season rates. Categories used are:

Budget	$35 and under
Inexpensive	$35-60
Moderate	$60-85
Expensive	$85-110
Premium	$110-150
Luxury	$150 and up

ACKNOWLEDGMENTS

I am immensely grateful to my editor, Kate Willis, who cleverly managed to leap over the big pond from England and land at Avalon Travel Publishing, here in California, just in time to polish up this particular tome. To make certain her corporate initiation was sufficiently challenging, or so I imagine, someone in editorial added to the assignment: "Oh, and could we have that the day after tomorrow?" That day has arrived, and with it this book. Congratulations, Kate, and I hope they assign you an easy one—maybe even a short one—next time. My heartfelt thanks as well to editors Pauli Galin and Ellen Cavalli (now my honorary herbalist), who also helped round up these chapters, and to Editorial Director Krista Lyons-Gould, who guided our galloping pace with good humor and grace.

Always at the top of my thank you list is Bill Newlin, publisher at Avalon Travel Publishing. I still appreciate his original efforts to "make it work" so I might complete my longer-term task—telling the entire California story in travel book form. Now that the all-California book is finished at last, perhaps we should think up some new overwhelming challenge.

As always, I reserve a special category of gratitude for the many Moon Handbooks authors who helped me learn the ropes, particularly now-departed Joe Bisignani ("Mr. Hawaii"), Jane King, Steve Metzger, and Bob Nilsen.

Once again I extend heartfelt thanks to Pat Reilly, my assistant on San Francisco Handbook (now known as Moon Handbooks: San Francisco), who also helped spruce up the Southern California chapters of this book. Pat, a talented wordsmith in her own right, has a real job at San Francisco's own *Wired* magazine—one that pays considerably better than this one does—so I'm particularly grateful for her enthusiasm, good-natured determination, and graciousness in the midst of all the hard work it takes to make an easy read. I am also eternally grateful to fellow graduate student, college instructor, and writer Kyle McDowell, who helped me hack some of the wordier sections down to size. I offer my appreciation, too, to Ed Aust, Taran March, and Tim Moriarty for their contributions to this book's editorial content.

It takes so many people to make a good book. My thanks to everyone who helped turn my words into the book you now hold in your hands. It's a bit confusing to correctly call the roll—and to give appropriate credit where it is due—now that Moon's administrative (and part of its editorial) staff are subsumed within the greater whole of Avalon Travel Publishing, in Emeryville. But at last report hard-working bookmakers, of both the editorial and production persuasions, were still in the Chico office, bravely flailing away at the immense tasks before them.

Snapping off a few dozen rolls of fascinating photographs would be the best way to express my gratitude to the production crew. Words will have to suffice at the moment, though I promise to dust off the old Pentax next time I hit the road. Thanks to layout artist Carey Wilson, for his keen sense of balance, design, and overall visual aesthetics as well as patient attention paid to all those picayune graphic details. Special thanks to Cartography, for such fine work on the maps, and to Erika Howsare for her artistic contributions and dedication in organizing all of the book's graphic elements.

A hearty "Welcome Back" to Associate Publisher Donna Galassi—long-running Moon marketing inspiration and a friendly face from the good ol' days. After having worked her magic at both Foghorn and John Muir, now that all three companies have been joined together as Avalon Travel Publishing it's particularly appropriate, and pleasing, to have Donna at the helm once again. Many thanks also to Marketing Director Amanda Bleakley, as well as all those promotion and sales wizards—Mary Beth Pugh, Keith Arsenault, Stacy Johnson, Becky Owston, and Alannah Kern—for doing everything possible to help us all make a living in this business.

My special thanks to photographer friends and sympathizers who have contributed their work to this work, including Tom Myers, Bob Nilsen, and Aislinn Race, not to mention the California Department of Parks and Recreation.

Reaching back into my past, I am still indebted to many of my environmental studies instructors at the University of California at Santa Barbara and to my biology professors at California State University, Chico—particularly Doug Alexander, Wes Dempsey, Roger Lederer, Rob Schlising, and Tom Rodgers—for teaching me to see the living world. As I recall, that subject was never included on any class syllabus.

Arriving in the present, I also extend my heartfelt thanks to Fred Sater, media relations manager for the California Division of Tourism. I appreciate his personal encouragement and support, not to mention that refreshing sense of humor. I am also grateful for so many gracious introductions to travel industry pros at chambers of commerce and visitors bureaus throughout California. Their contributions and thoughtful suggestions have greatly improved this book's practical focus and (I hope) its overall usefulness.

—Kim Weir

PREFACE

INVENTING CALIFORNIA, THAT WELL-MAPPED MYSTERY

California is a myth, as the following Introduction to *Moon Handbooks: California* explains. To understand California, it's important to understand its mythic nature—the reason, still, that people are drawn to its mystery and magic.

Yet California is also a massive and well-mapped geographical fact, some 158,693 square miles of territory spanning 10 degrees of latitude. A meandering, 1,264-mile-long coast creates its western edge at the Pacific Ocean. To the east, the southern Cascade Range, the 500-mile-long mountain serpent known as the Sierra Nevada, and three inhospitable deserts separate California from the rest of the United States.

The scale of California the place is awesome for even native Californians, so it's no surprise that the sheer size of the state often overwhelms first-time visitors. Travel industry professionals collect favorite traveler tales to illustrate this bafflement. Like the one about the dapper Englishman who stepped off the 747 in San Francisco at noon and inquired at the rental car counter: "If I leave right now for Disneyland, can I be back in San Francisco in time for tonight's opera?" Fat chance, fella, since it takes a solid day of driving just to *get* to Disneyland from San Francisco. (Such an estimate assumes that, on the way, you don't get hopelessly snarled in Silicon Valley and L.A. freeway traffic, not typically a safe assumption.) People who haven't visited California often can't comprehend its vastness—the great distances between one place and another—until they've actually experienced it. Traveled it.

Visitors can be equally befuddled by how the culture works, and what it all means. Despite its relative youth, California is culturally complicated. As of the 2000 census, some 34 million people lived here— a figure that doesn't include the millions of visitors also wandering the state at any given time. California's undaunted population is not only the largest of any state in the union, it's also the most ethnically diverse, representing just about every place on the globe.

As huge and complex as California is, it's also an endless adventure. The aim of *Moon Handbooks: California* is to enhance that adventure, to introduce travelers to the amazing totality of California—from the far north near Oregon all the way south to the Mexican border—and to explain the surprising cultural circus as well, all as succinctly as possible.

With this book as one's congenial companion, first-time visitors and seasoned California travel hands alike will easily discover the essence and all essential current details about a given locale—who goes there and why, what to see and do, where to stay and eat, and when to come (though by and large California as destination is a year-round amusement). Whether one develops a specific day-by-day itinerary or prefers to navigate by a more general, drifting timeline, *Moon Handbooks: California* is designed for reader convenience and "easy access," with all destinations, attractions information, and abundant practical facts carefully organized by neighborhood, city, and region.

In addition to its accessible and detailed practical information, *Moon Handbooks: California* also offers another travel essential: perspective. Perspective on California the place—its unique natural history, its impatient history, its essentially sunny outlook—and on California the destination. Must-see-and-do draws include the cities of Los Angeles, San Diego, and San Francisco, with their vibrant arts, entertainments, and amusements. The breathtaking and expansive Death Valley, Redwood, and Yosemite National Parks, not to mention other natural wonders: sapphire-blue Lake Tahoe, abundant Monterey Bay, and eccentric, inaccessible Big Sur. Increasingly, California's cultivated agricultural nature—particularly its many "wine countries," including the famed Napa and Sonoma Valley region—also makes the list.

But there is more, so much more, to experience in California, and to know about California—more than can easily fit in any one volume. *Moon Handbooks: California* covers more of that mysterious "more" than any other available book, from offbeat and out-there destinations and unusual events to frank, sometimes funny essays about the state's people, places, and popular culture. More than enough to get any traveler well started on the life-long adventure of appreciating California.

So. Get started. Take a peek at this book's Table of Contents to get an idea of the possibilities that beckon, then start reinventing your personal conceptions of California—and inventing your own adventures.

—*Kim Weir*

TOM MYERS PHOTOGRAPHY

INTRODUCTION
CALIFORNIA AS MYTH

California is a myth—a myth in the sense of a traditional tale told to impart truth and wisdom, and in the fanciful sense of some extravagant storybook fiction. Californians happen to like the quirky character of the state they're in. Whether or not they realize it, California as myth is exactly why they're here—because in California, even contradictions mean nothing. In California, almost everything is true and untrue at the same time. In California, people can pick and choose from among the choices offered—as if in a supermarket—or create their own truth. Attracted to this endless sense of creative possibilities—California's most universal creed, the source of the ingenuity and inventiveness the state is so famous for—people here are only too happy to shed the yoke of tradition, and traditional expectations, that kept them in harness elsewhere.

Californians tend to think life itself is a California invention, but "lifestyle" definitely is: people come to California to have one. Coming to California, novelist Stanley Elkin observes, "is

a choice one makes, a blow one strikes for hope. No one ever wakes up one day and says, 'I must move to Missouri.' No one chooses to find happiness in Oklahoma or Connecticut." And according to historian Kevin Starr, "California isn't a place—it's a need." Once arrived in California, according to the myth, the only reason to carry around the baggage of one's previous life is because one chooses to.

But it would be naive to assume that this natural expansiveness, this permission to be here now, is somehow new in California. It may be literally as old as the hills. Native peoples, the first and original laid-back Californians, understood this. Busy with the day-to-day necessities of survival, they nonetheless held the place in awe and managed to honor the untouchable earth spirits responsible for creation. The last remembered line of an ancient Ohlone dancing song—"dancing on the brink of the world"—somehow says it all about California.

As a place, California is still a metaphor, for

Shakespeare's "thick-coming fancies" as well as for those awesome mysteries that can't be taken in by the five senses. People come here to sort it all out, to somehow grasp it, to transform themselves and the facts of their lives—by joining in the dance.

CALIFORNIA AS EUROPEAN MYTH

Native peoples had many explanations for how the land and life in California came to be, almost as many stories as there were villages. But it's a stranger-than-fiction fact that California as a concept was concocted in Europe, by a Spanish soldier turned romance writer.

The rocky-shored island paradise of California, according to the 1510 fictional *Las Sergas de Esplandían* by Garcí Ordóñez de Montalvo, overflowed with gold, gems, and pearls, was inhabited by griffins and other wild beasts, and "peopled by black women, with no men among them, for they lived in the fashion of Amazons" under the great Queen Calafia's rule. With such fantastic images seared into the European imagination, it's no wonder that Cortés and his crew attached the name California to their later territorial claims from Baja California north to Alaska.

THE MYTH OF NORTHERN AND SOUTHERN CALIFORNIA

While California is still a destination of the imagination and a rich land indeed, its true wealth is (and always was) its breathtaking beauty, its cultural creativity, and its democratic dreams.

The primary political fact of life here is that California is one state. Technically indisputable, this fact is nonetheless widely disputed. Californians themselves generally view the state as two distinct entities: Northern California, centered in sophisticated San Francisco, and the continuous sprawl of Southern California south of the Tehachapi Mountains, its freeways spreading out from its Los Angeles heart like the spokes of a bent and broken wheel.

According to the myth that successfully populated Southern California, simple, neighborly, nature-oriented living amid sunny gardens and citrus groves would save civilization from the

mass-production mind-set of industrialism—almost shocking to contemplate now, when one sees what's become of that idea. Yet this is also the land of the American dream made manifest, where the sun always shines—on the degenerate and deserving alike, the ultimate in California-style social democracy—and where even the desert itself is no limitation since, thanks to the wonders of modern engineering, water can be imported from elsewhere. In the newer Southern California myth, style is more important than substance and image is everything, cultural truths shaped in large part by Hollywood and the movies. Life itself is defined by humanity—by an artificial environment of pavement and plastic technologies manufactured by human need and vanity, by the worship of physical beauty in human form, and by the relentless search for the ultimate in hedonistic diversion and novelty. An engineered Eden ruled by Midwestern social and political mores, Southern California worships everything new—from new beliefs and ideas and commercially viable images transmitted via its own film and media industries to art and innovation for their own sakes—and rarely questions the intrinsic value of cosmetic change. The main moral question in the southstate is not "Is it important?" or "Is it right?" but: "Is it new?"

Northern California's mythic soul is represented by nature in all its contradictions—the rugged outdoors in tandem with the rugged individualist struggling for survival, the simple beauty of humanity in nature as well as more complicated relationships that result from humanity's attempts to change and control nature's inherent wildness. The collective and personal histories of Northern California suggest secessionism, rebellion, and the high-technology innovations largely responsible for today's global culture. Northern California is also about human awareness in nature, and a modern consciousness seemingly sprung fully formed from nature worship: holistic health and get-in-touch-with-yourself psychological trends; mandatory physical fitness, as if to be ready at a moment's notice to embark upon ever more challenging outdoor adventures; natural foods and a regionally focused appreciation for fresh produce and fine wines. Life in Northern California is defined by outdoor-oriented, socially responsible narcissism—and symbolized by an upwardly mobile young professional couple nudging their new, gas-guzzling four-wheel drive onto well-engineered highways leading out of the city and into the wilderness.

Yet in many ways the two ends of the state are becoming one. Despite regional chauvinism, southstate-style growth, with all its attendant problems, is fast becoming a fact of life in the north; within several decades, almost as many people will live in Northern California as in Southern. In all parts of the state, growth is moving away from major cities and into the suburbs—a fact that is influencing political trends as well. Northern California, traditionally more liberal than Southern California, is becoming more Re-publican, while the southstate's increasing concerns over health and environmental issues are liberalizing urban political trends. And though Northern California politicians tend to openly oppose any increased water shipments to Southern California (unless their districts are paid well for private water sales), most are much quieter about supporting water engineering feats designed to meet the needs of the northstate's own suburban growth.

Californians themselves still see most statewide social, political, and "style" differences in terms of north versus south regionalism. The time-honored historical issue of politically splitting California into two separate states—an idea now

SCHRÖDINGER'S SURFBOARD

Deep in his or her heart, every surfer believes that the act of riding a wave is somehow different from anything else a person can do. Not better, necessarily, just different. Something you can't understand until you've tried it. Of course, the same could be said of skiing, or skydiving, or jamming a screwdriver up your nose. But I am convinced, as are most surfers, that there is something truly special about our sport, something that goes beyond the sun and the water and the babes on the beach. It has to do with the waves themselves.

When you catch a wave, you are being propelled by a phenomenon that plays a fundamental role (perhaps *the* fundamental role) in the way the universe works. Waves sit at the heart of the ninety-year-old debate that defines quantum mechanics. Should the subatomic world be regarded as matter or energy? Albert Einstein realized at the turn of the twentieth century that light waves sometimes behave like particles. Thirty years later another physicist, Louis de Broglie, alternately reasoned that electrons, always thought to be particles, sometimes behave like waves. But it was Erwin Schrödinger, an Austrian, who eventually won the hearts of surfers everywhere when he worked out the equation that accurately predicted the motion of de Broglie's electron waves.

"The electron is not a particle, [Schrödinger] argued, it is a matter wave as an ocean wave is a water wave," Heinz R. Pagels, the theoretical physicist, wrote in 1982. "According to this interpretation . . . all quantum objects, not just electrons, are little waves—and all of nature is a great wave phenomenon."

All of nature is a great wave phenomenon. If you're a surfer, you have to like the sound of that.

In theory, the swells we surf are no different from the light waves that travel from Alpha Centauri to your eyeball. Once the wind kicks up a swell, ocean waves move with the predictability of billiard balls, abiding by the same mathematical principles that govern all waves. Like their high-speed counterparts, our waves come in a variety of frequencies and amplitudes. The can be focused, diffracted, refracted. They decay.

Of course, measured against other waves with which humans are familiar, surfable swells move like lumbering beasts. They are the Schrödinger equation writ large—abstract mechanical principles magnified from the subatomic to a scale even the Beach Boys could grasp. While sound waves travel 760 miles per hour and light waves at 186,000 miles per second, surfable ocean waves move a little faster than the average person can run.

With sound and light waves, we detect only a byproduct of their oscillations. In the case of sound, a barrage of waves beats against your eardrum; your eardrum activates your auditory nerve; your auditory nerve sends a signal to your brain; your brain tells you to dance. Out in the surf, no such translation is needed. You can feel each undulation, each pulse of energy, as it moves through the universe. With a little practice, you can ride it.

by Steve Hawk

at least rhetorically quite popular in the rural north, though the state's first secessionism arose in the south—still comes up regularly. But the actual facts about modern-day California suggest a different reality. Life here is, and will continue to be, defined by the conflicting cultures of minority-dominated urban areas, more conservative Sun Belt suburbs created by "white flight," and declining, truly rural resource-based communities.

CALIFORNIA AS "FIRST IN THE NATION"

California's most obvious "first" is its population. Half of the people living in the West, the fastest-growing region of the nation, live in California. Number one in the nation now—with more than 34 million people—California's population at current growth rates will be nearly 40 million by the year 2005, nearly 50 million by 2030 (some say 2020 or 2025), and 60 million by 2040. Or more. The state has been growing so rapidly during the past decade, largely because of legal and illegal immigration, that demographers can't keep up. Keeping tabs on Californians has been complicated further by their increasing migration, in recent years, to other states; more than 1.1 million left in the early 1990s, though with the state's recent economic recovery that trend has slowed.

The sheer heft of California humanity makes it first in the nation in immigration (both legal and illegal), first in bomb threats and investigations, first in firearm-related violent crime, and first in prison budgets. Largely because of Southern California population pressures, California also ranks shockingly high for endangered and threatened species. Yet California boasts more Nobel Prize laureates than any other state, more engineers and scientists, and more research labs, colleges, and universities.

California is also number one in construction-related business contracts and leads the nation in number of millionaires, though it no longer tops the nation's lists for livable cities or average personal incomes. Despite the crush of its urban population, California usually makes more money in agriculture than any other state, and produces—and consumes—most of the country's wine.

The land has its own firsts-and-bests, since California boasts the highest point in the contiguous United States (Mt. Whitney) and the lowest (Death Valley). California is also home to the world's largest living thing, the Sequoia big tree; the world's tallest, the coast redwood; and the world's oldest, the bristlecone pine. Depending upon how one defines individuality, however, two of the latter records may fall. One particular subterranean fungus in Michigan, sprouting multiple mushrooms, spans at least 37 acres, is estimated to weigh 220,000 pounds, and may have been alive since the end of the last Ice Age.

Common wisdom in the United States holds that "as California goes, so goes the nation." As with most California legends, there is at least some truth to this. California is quite often the national trendsetter, from fads and fashions in political or social beliefs to styles in cars and clothes. In its endless pursuit of style, California searches for its identity, for some explanation of itself. California is constantly inventing and reinventing its own mythology. Yet California was among the last states in the United States to emerge from the latest recession, and few states so far are following California's lead in eliminating affirmative action programs and attempting to withhold public services from immigrants.

The Free Speech Movement, the philosophical foundation supporting both civil rights and anti–Vietnam War activism, took root in California. But so did the New Republicanism (best represented by Richard Nixon and Ronald Reagan), a reactionary trend toward social control that arose at least as an indirect result. California is usually first in the nation for new religious and spiritual trends, too, from New Age consciousness to televangelism.

California is the birthplace of the motel, the climate-controlled shopping mall, suburban sprawl, and a lifestyle almost entirely dependent upon cars and elaborately engineered highway and freeway systems. But California is also first in the nation in car thefts and in marijuana cultivation. It's home to the back-to-the-land culture and spawning ground for the philosophy of bioregionalism, too, decrying all things homogenized, unnatural, unnecessarily imported, and plastic. For every action in California, there is also a reaction.

CONTEMPORARY CALIFORNIA FACTS AND FANCY

Among common misconceptions about the state is the one the rest of the world tenaciously clings to—that everyone in California is laid-back, liberal, blond, rich, and well educated.

California as Laid-Back

California may be casual, but it's not exactly relaxed. Despite the precedents set by native peoples and early Californios (those of Spanish descent born in the pre-U.S. period), most of the state's modern residents are hardly content to live in leisure. In their frantic rush to accumulate, to stay in style, to just keep up with the state's sophisticated survival code and incredible rate of change, Californians tend to be tense and harried. And now that Californians have remembered—and reminded the rest of the world—that rest and relaxation are necessary for a well-rounded life, people here pursue recreation with as much determination as any other goal. Just sitting around doing nothing isn't against the law in California, but it's definitely déclassé.

California as Liberal

If people in California aren't particularly laid-back, they aren't particularly liberal either. After all, California created both Richard Nixon and Ronald Reagan. The truth is, California has never committed itself to any particular political party, though lately the state has become notably Democratic. As of 2000 Democratic legislators strongly dominate in California's Senate and Assembly—a trend that started as a surprise in 1996, considering the general Republican drift elsewhere in the United States—and Democrats, after losing ground in 1994, regained strength in the state's U.S. House of Representatives by 1996 and dominance by 2000. Some blame former Republican governor Pete Wilson, described by national columnist Anthony Lewis as "the premier gutter politician of our day," for the Grand Old Party's almost overnight decline in California, since Wilson's reactionary anti-immigrant re-election campaign of 1994 and his activist anti–affirmative action stance in 1996 made Latino citizens—and other voters—angry enough to vote Democratic in a big way. Perhaps it was

only fitting that Fresno's Cruz Bustamante, the first Latino speaker of the state Assembly, took office in 1996. Subsequently, there was a similarly rapid decline in the Republicans' race-baiting politicking—but not enough to slow the shocking statewide drop in Republican influence.

In November 1998, California elected a Democratic governor, Gray Davis, by a whopping 20-point margin, though the state has supported only Republicans in that office since the departure of "Governor Moonbeam," Jerry Brown, in the late 1970s. And Cruz Bustamante was elected lieutenant governor, the first Latino in the 20th century elected to statewide office. In the same election, the previously ascendant Christian conservatives in the Republican Party lost big—and the state also elected its first Green Party candidate, Audie Bock, to the state Assembly. (Bock subsequently lost that seat to a Democrat.)

Even in 1992, when Republicans otherwise dominated state politics, California was first in the nation to elect women—both Democrats, Barbara Boxer and Dianne Feinstein—to fill its two U.S. Senate seats, outdoing all other states, cities, and municipalities in paying homage to "the year of the woman." (Boxer and Feinstein both still serve.) And California overwhelmingly supported Gov. Bill Clinton, a Democrat, in the 1992 presidential election (by a lesser margin in 1996), and Vice President Al Gore in 2000. Yet the Democrats' previous electoral declines and Republican dominance on the national level have diminished the state's traditional political clout in the United States, at least in the short term, because of the loss of key committee chairs and committee rankings once held by California Democrats.

Occasional flamboyant public figures and long-standing double-edged jokes about the land of "fruits and nuts" aside, predicting the direction in which political winds will blow here is difficult. Until recently, pollsters detected a steady trend toward increasing identification with the Republican Party among the state's voting-age population. Generally speaking, the political labels of Democrat and Republican mean little in California. People here tend to vote on the basis of enlightened economic interest, personal values, and "political personality."

If Compassionate Conservatism (New Republicanism's new brand name) is quite comfortable in California, so is the orthodoxy of no orthodoxy. Values, political and social, are discarded as easily as last year's fashions. (Californians don't oppose tradition so much as they can't find the time for it.) The state's legendary liberalness is based on the fact that, like social voyeurs, Californians tolerate—some would say encourage—strangeness in others. Rooted in the state's rough-and-tumble gold rush history, this attitude is almost mandatory today, considering California's phenomenal cultural and ethnic diversity.

California as Blond

Despite the barrage of media and movie images suggesting that all Californians are blond and tan and live at the beach, not much could be further from the truth. Though Caucasians or "Anglos" predominate ethnically, California's population has represented almost every spot on the globe since the days of the gold rush. More than 240 identified cultures or ethnicities have been identified in California. Blacks, Asians, and those of Hispanic descent have the highest numbers among the state's diverse minority populations. Already, California's collective "minority" populations have become the majority. This has long been true in major cities, including Los Angeles, East Los Angeles, Fresno, Oakland, and San Francisco, and in many public school classrooms.

California's Asian population, now representing over 12 percent of the total, will grow slightly. Its Latino population, now approximately 32 percent, will increase to 50 percent by the year 2040 (some say this demographic event will occur much sooner). Blacks in California will remain at a fairly stable population level, demographers project, at near 7.5 percent of the population, as will Native Americans at around 1 percent.

No matter what color they started out, people in paradise have been getting a bit gray; throughout the 1980s, retirees were California's fastest-growing age group. But just as it seemed the Golden State's stereotypical golden glow of youth was on the wane came the news that the population is actually getting younger, helped along by the arrival of millions and millions of preschools. According to U.S. census results released in 2000, the state's median age is now 33 years—on the young end of the national spectrum.

California as Rich

Though California is the richest state in the union, with a bustling economy of nation-state status and an average per-capita personal income of $22,000, the gap between the very rich and the very poor is staggering—and shocking to first-time visitors in major urban areas, since the despair of homelessness and poverty is very visible on city streets.

The news in 1995 that the United States is now the most economically stratified of all industrialized nations—with the top 20 percent of the population controlling 80 percent of the nation's wealth—barely raised an eyebrow in California. Neither did the word in 1996 from the Public Policy Institute of California that, with the state's economy once again booming, California has the largest gap between rich and poor in the world because of precipitous declines in wages and income among the working poor. That income gap was still growing in 1999, with the widest income disparities in Los Angeles.

Interpretations of U.S. census data suggest that California is becoming two states—or at least two states of mind. One California is educated, satisfied, and safe. The other is young, uneducated, immigrant (many do not speak English), restless, and impoverished. The ranks of the upper-income professional class (household income $50,000 or above) increased almost 10 percent between 1980 and 1990, to 33 percent—a phenomenon partly attributed to greater numbers of working women. (It's also striking to note that 18 percent of all U.S. households with an annual income of $150,000 or more are in California.) During that same decade, the state's middle-income households shrank from 35 percent to 33 percent, and the number of low-income households also declined, from 41 percent to 34 percent. But the numbers of the actual poor increased, from 11.4 percent to 12.5 percent.

Contradicting the skid row–alcoholic image of street life, nearly one-third of the homeless in California are under age 18. But almost more disturbing is California's unseen poverty. Not counting those who are turned away because there isn't enough to go around, more than two million people—almost one in every 10 Californians—regularly require food from public and private charitable organizations just to survive; on any given day in the Golden State, half a million people stand in line to get a free meal at a soup kitchen or commodity pantry. Minors, again, are California's largest class of hungry people. More than one in every four children in the Golden State live in poverty.

California as Well Educated

California has long been committed to providing educational opportunity to all citizens—a commitment expressed in once-generous public school funding as well as public financing for the nine (soon 10) campuses of the prestigious University of California, 23 California State University (CSU) campuses (CSU recently acquired the Maritime Academy), and the 106 independent California Community College (CCC) campuses. But because of the obvious educational impacts of increased immigration—80 separate languages are spoken at Los Angeles schools, at least 40 at Hollywood High alone—and the unofficial reality of socially segregated schools, uneven early educational opportunities are a fact of life even in well-intentioned California. Until recently the situation has been steadily worsening, with California spending $900 less per public school student than the national average; ranked 40th in per-pupil spending; and burdened with the nation's highest student-teacher ratios. Faced with a projected 18 percent enrollment increase in elementary and high schools by 2006, California has lately turned its attention to improving public schools—both with increased levels of funding and increased performance testing.

Previous declines in public school performance, coupled with increasingly stringent entrance requirements at both University of California and California State University campuses, have led critics such as former state Assemblymember (now Senator) Tom Hayden of Santa Monica to suggest that California's current public education policies are creating a "de facto educational apartheid." Though California's two-year community colleges are providing more four-year college preparation courses and are increasingly encouraging students to transfer to state universities, most minority groups in California are vastly underrepresented even in public universities.

The state's recent budget crisis meant significant cuts in public financial support for education; fees at public universities (California educators and legislators never say "tuition") have increased rapidly. Student fees jumped 40 percent at the University of California in 1992 alone, for example. Fees at CSU have also increased radically since 1990; CSU trustees plan to increase undergraduate student fees until they reach at least $2,500 annually, or about one-third the per-student education cost. Yet even with the general public financing a diminishing share of the cost of each student's college education, there still isn't enough opportunity to go around. Just to keep pace with current and anticipated demand early in the coming century, the University of California needs three new campuses, the California State University system

University of California
at Berkeley

needs five, and the California Community Colleges need 28. According to a gloomy 1996 report by the nonprofit RAND think tank in Santa Monica, all three levels of California public higher education will be in deep financial crisis yet challenged to absorb a record 2.3 million potential students by 2010.

Overall trends in education, economics, and employment patterns suggest that California is evolving into a two-tiered society dominated by an affluent and well-educated Anglo-Asian "overclass." Those who make up the underclass and who compete for relatively low-paying service jobs will increasingly be immigrants or the functionally illiterate. According to Bill Honig, former state superintendent of public instruction, about 60 percent of California's public school students leave school without being able to read well enough to compete in California's increasingly complex, technology-oriented job market.

THE LAND: AN ISLAND IN SPACE AND TIME

California's isolated, sometimes isolationist human history has been shaped more by the land itself than by any other fact. That even early European explorers conceived of the territory as an island is a fitting irony, since in many ways—particularly geographically, but also in the evolutionary development of plant and animal life—California was, and still is, an island in both space and time.

The third-largest state in the nation, California spans 10 degrees of latitude. With a meandering 1,264-mile-long coastline, the state's western boundary is formed by the Pacific Ocean. Along most of California's great length, just landward from the sea, are the rumpled and eroded mountains known collectively as the Coast Ranges.

But even more impressive in California's 158,693-square-mile territory is the Sierra Nevada range, which curves like a 500-mile-long spine along the state's central-eastern edge. Inland from the Coast Ranges and to the north of California's great central valley are the state's northernmost mountains, including the many distinct, wayward ranges of the Klamaths— mountains many geologists believe were originally a northwesterly extension of the Sierra Nevada. Just east of the Klamath Mountains is the southern extension of the volcanic Cascade Range, which includes Mount Shasta and Lassen Peak.

This great partial ring of mountains around California's heartland (with ragged eastern peaks reaching elevations of 14,000 feet and higher) as well as the vast primeval forests that once almost suffocated lower slopes, have always influenced the state's major weather patterns— and have also created a nearly impenetrable natural barrier for otherwise freely migrating plant and animal species, including human beings.

But if sky-high rugged rocks, thickets of forest, and rain-swollen rivers blocked migration to the north and east, physical barriers of a more barren nature have also slowed movement into California. To the south, the dry chaparral of the east-west Transverse Ranges and the northwest/southeast-trending Peninsular Ranges impeded northern and inland movement for most life forms. The most enduring impediment, however, is California's great southeastern expanse of desert—including both the Mojave and Colorado Deserts—and the associated desert mountains and high-desert plateaus. Here, only the strong and well adapted survive.

EARTHQUAKES, VOLCANOES, AND CRUSTY PLATES

Perched along the Pacific Ring of Fire, California is known for its violent volcanic nature and for its earthquakes. Native peoples have always explained the fiery, earth-shaking temperament of the land quite clearly, in a variety of myths and legends, but the theory of plate tectonics is now the most widely accepted scientific creation story. According to this theory, the earth's crust is divided into 20 or so major solid rock (or lithospheric) "plates" upon which both land and sea ride. The interactions of these plates are ultimately responsible for all earth movement, from continental drift and landform creation to volcanic explosions and earthquakes.

Most of California teeters on the western edge of the vast North American Plate. The adjacent

Lake Tahoe

Pacific Plate, which first collided with what is now California about 250 million years ago, grinds slowly but steadily northward along a line more or less defined by the famous San Andreas Fault (responsible for the massive 1906 San Francisco earthquake and fire as well as the more recent shake-up in 1989). Plate movement itself is usually imperceptible: at the rate things are going, within 10 million years Los Angeles will slide north to become San Francisco's next-door neighbor. But the steady friction and tension generated between the two plates sometimes creates special events. Every so often sudden, jolting slippage occurs between the North American and Pacific Plates in California—either along the San Andreas or some other fault line near the plate border—and one of the state's famous earthquakes occurs. Though most don't amount to much, an average of 15,000 earthquakes occur in California every year.

A still newer theory augments the plate tectonics creation story, suggesting a much more fluid local landscape—that California and the rest of the West literally "go with the flow," in particular the movement of hot, molten rock beneath the earth's crust. "Flow" theory explains the appearance of earthquake faults where they shouldn't be, scientists say, and also explains certain deformations in the continental crust. According to calculations published in the May 1996 edition of the journal *Nature,* the Sierra Nevada currently flows at the rate of one inch every three years.

CALIFORNIA CREATION: WHEN WORLDS COLLIDE

In ancient times, some geologists say, the American Southwest was connected to Antarctica. This new theory, presented in 1991 by researchers at the University of California at Davis and the University of Texas, suggests that 500–700 million years ago a "seam" connected the two continents; Antarctica's Transatlantic Mountains were contiguous with the western edge of the Sierra Nevada, parts of Idaho, and the Canadian Rockies. The geological similarities between the now far-flung rock formations are unmistakable. Yet at that time the North American continent was missing California. Some geologists theorize that California came along later; certain rock formations now found south of the equator match those of California's Coast Range.

Wherever its raw materials originally came from, California as land was created by the direct collision, starting about 250 million years ago, of the eastward-moving Pacific Plate and the underwater western edge of the North American Plate—like all continents, something like a floating raft of lighter rocks (primarily granite) attached to the heavier, black basalt of the earth's mantle. At first impact, pressure between the two plates scraped up and then buckled offshore oceanic sediments into undulating ridges of rock, and an eventual California shoreline began to build.

But the Pacific Plate, unable to follow its previous forward path against such North American resistance, continued on its way by first plunging downward, creating a trough that soon began filling with oceanic basalts, mud, and eroded sediments from what is now Nevada. Sinking (or subducting) still farther beneath the North American Plate, some of these trench sediments slipped into the hot core (or athenosphere) beneath the earth's lithosphere and melted—transformed by heat into the embryonic granitic backbone of the Sierra Nevada and other metamorphic mountains that slowly intruded upward from the inner earth.

Approximately 140 million years ago, the northern section of what would later be the Sierra Nevada started to shift westward along the east-west tectonic fault line known as the Mendocino Fracture, the genesis of the Klamath Mountains. The Pacific Ocean, sloshing into the area just north of the infantile Sierra Nevada, brought with it the sediments that would create California's northeastern Modoc Plateau—a high-plains landscape later transformed by volcanic basalt flows and "floods."

About 60 million years ago, California's modern-day Sierra Nevada was a misshapen series of eroded ridges and troughs sitting on the newly risen edge of the continent. The violent forces generated by continuing plate confrontation, including sporadic volcanism and large-scale faulting, pushed the state's mountains slowly higher. Remaining ocean sediments later rose to create first the Coast Ranges, as offshore islands about 25 to 30 million years ago, and eventually an impressive, 450-mile-long inland sea, which, once filled with sediment, gradually evolved into the marshy tule wetlands recognizable today as California's fertile central valley.

Though California's creation has never ceased—with the land transformed even today by volcanic activity, earthquake shifts, and erosion—the landscape as we know it came fairly recently. According to the widely accepted view, about 10–16 million years ago the Sierra Nevada stood tall enough (approximately 2,000 feet above sea level) to start changing the continent's weather patterns: blocking the moisture-laden winds that had previously swept inland and desiccating the once-lush Great Basin. Then, one million years ago, the Sierra Nevada and other fault-block

ranges "suddenly" rose to near their current height. By 800,000 years ago, the mountains had taken on their general modern shape—but fire was giving way to ice. During the million-year glaciation period, particularly the last stage from 100,000 to 30,000 years ago, these and other California landforms were subsequently carved and polished smooth by slow-moving sheets of ice. Vestigial glaciers remain in some areas of the Sierra Nevada and elsewhere.

A "countercultural" view of Sierra Nevada creation is emerging, however. According to this theory, based on research done in the southern Sierra Nevada, the range reached its zenith about 70 million years ago—massive mountains, as tall as the Andes, looming large during the last days of the dinosaurs. The height of the Sierra Nevada, once reaching 13,000 feet, has been declining ever since—a loss of about a quarter-inch in the course of a single person's lifetime—because erosion has proceeded faster than the forces of ongoing creation.

Though vegetation typical of the late ice age has largely vanished and mastodons, saber-toothed cats, and other exotic animals no longer stalk the land, the face of the California landscape since those bygone days has been transformed most radically by the impact of humanity—primarily in the past century and a half. Building dams and "channeling" wild rivers to exploit water, the state's most essential natural resource; harvesting state-sized forests of old-growth trees; hunting animals, to the edge of extinction and beyond, for fur and pelts; digging for, and stripping the land of, gold and other mineral wealth; clearing the land for crops and houses and industrial parks: all this has changed California forever.

FROM FIRE TO ICE:
THE CALIFORNIA CLIMATE

California's much-ballyhooed "Mediterranean" climate is at least partially a myth. Because of extremes in landforms, in addition to various microclimatic effects, there are radical climatic differences within the state—sometimes even within a limited geographic area. But California as a whole does share most of the classic characteristics of Mediterranean climates: abundant sunny days year-round, a cool-weather coast, dry summers, and rainy winters. California, in fact, is the only region in North America where summer drought and rainy winters are typical.

Between the coast and the mountains immediately inland, where most of the state's people live, temperatures—though cooler in the north and warmer to the south—are fairly mild and uniform year-round. Because of the state's latitudinal gradation, rain also falls in accordance with this north-south shift: an average of 74 inches falls annually in Crescent City, 19–22 inches in San Francisco, and less than 10 inches in San Diego. When warm, moist ocean air blows inland over the cool California Current circulating clockwise above the equator, seasonal fog is typical along the California coast. Summer, in other words, is often cooler along the coast than autumn. (Just ask those shivering tourists who arrive in San Francisco every June wearing Bermuda shorts and sandals.)

Inland, where the marine air influence often literally evaporates, temperature extremes are typical. The clear, dry days of summer are often hot, particularly in the central valley and the deserts. (With occasional freak temperatures above 130°F, Death Valley is aptly named.) In winter, substantial precipitation arrives in Northern California—especially in the northwest "rain belt" and in the northern Sierra Nevada—with major storms expected from October to May. California's northern mountains "collect" most Pacific Ocean moisture as rain; in the High Sierra, the average winter snowpack is between 300 and 400 inches. Wrung out like sponges by the time they pass over the Sierra Nevada and other inland mountains, clouds have little rain or snow for the eastern-slope rainshadow.

Since the 1970s, California's climate patterns have been increasingly atypical—which may be normal, or may be early local indications of global warming. The reason no one knows for sure is because the state's "average" weather patterns were largely defined between the 1930s and the 1970s, a period of unusually stable weather conditions, it now appears. Complicating the question further is new scientific research suggesting that California climate has been characterized, since ancient times, by alternating cycles of very wet and very dry weather—200- to 500-year cycles. Epic droughts have been traced to the Mid-

dle Ages, and just 300 years ago California experienced a drought lasting 80–100 years. California's last century and a half, it turns out, represents one of the wettest periods in the past 2,500 years.

The increasing scientific consensus is that global warming is indeed having a major impact on California weather. Since the late 1970s, El Niño "events" have increased noticeably, bringing warmer offshore waters and heavy storms in California and the Southwest. But in other years—drought times for California—"La Niña" occurs, with colder offshore waters and storms tracking into the Pacific Northwest. Being whipsawed between periods of torrential rains and flooding (yet subnormal snowpack) and devastating drought seems to be California's future—a future almost certain to feature disrupted water supplies, even without a 100-year drought.

CALIFORNIA FLORA: BLOOMING AT THE BRINK

"In California," observed writer Joaquin Miller, "things name themselves, or rather Nature names them, and that name is visibly written on the face of things and every man may understand who can read." When explorers and settlers first stumbled upon California's living natural wonders, they didn't "read" landforms or indigenous plants and animals in the same way native peoples did, but they were quite busy nonetheless attaching new names (and eventually Latin terminology) to everything in sight. From the most delicate ephemeral wildflowers to California's two types of towering redwoods, from butterflies and birds to pronghorns, bighorn sheep, and the various subspecies of grizzly bear, the unusual and unique nature of most of the territory's life forms was astonishing. California's geographical isolation—as well as its dramatic extremes in landforms and localized climates—was (and still is) largely responsible for the phenomenal natural divergence and diversity found here.

Former president Ronald Reagan, while still governor of California and embroiled in a battle over expanding redwood parks, unwittingly expressed the old-and-in-the-way attitude about the state's resources with his now-famous gaffe, widely quoted as: "If you've seen one redwood,

ROBERT HOLMES/CALTOUR

poppies, the state flower of California

you've seen 'em all." (What Reagan actually said was: "A tree is a tree—how many more do you need to look at?") But his philosophy, however expressed, is the key to understanding what has happened to California's trees, other native flora, and animal species.

Even today, the variation in California's native plantlife is amazing. Nearly 5,200 species of plants are at home in the Golden State—symbolized by the orange glow of the California poppy—and more than 30 percent of these trees, shrubs, wildflowers, and grasses are endemic. (By comparison, only 13 percent of plantlife in the northeastern United States, and 1 percent of flora in the British Isles, are endemic species.) In fact, California has greater species diversity than the combined totals of the central and northeastern United States and adjacent Canada—an area almost 10 times greater in size.

But to state that so many plant species survive in California is not to say that they thrive. The economic and physical impacts of settlement have greatly stressed the state's vegetative

wealth since the days of the gold rush, when the first full-scale assaults on California forests, wetlands, grasslands, and riparian and oak woodlands were launched. The rate of exploitation of the state's 380 distinct natural communities has been relentless ever since. Half of the state's natural terrestrial environments and 40 percent of its aquatic communities are endangered, rare, or threatened.

Some of the state's most notable natural attractions are its unique trees—entire forests nearly toppled at the edge of extinction. California's *Sequoiadendron giganteum,* or giant sequoia, grows only in limited surviving stands in the Sierra Nevada—saved as much by the brittleness of its wood as by the public outcry of John Muir and other enlightened 19th-century voices. But the state's remaining virgin forests of *Sequoia sempervirens,* the "ever-living" coast redwoods, are still threatened by clear-cutting, a practice that also eliminates the habitat of other species. The same conservation-versus-economic expediency argument also rages over the fate of the few remaining old-growth outposts of other popular timber trees. And decades of fire suppression, logging, grazing, and recreational development in California's vast forests of ponderosa pines, combined with increasing air pollution and the state's recent drought, have led to insect infestations, tree disease, and death—and a tinder-dry, fuel-rich landscape more vulnerable than ever to uncontrollable fires. Even trees without notable economic value are threatened by compromises imposed by civilization. Among these are the ancient bristlecone pines near the California-Nevada border—the oldest living things on earth, some individuals more than 4,000 years old—now threatened by Los Angeles smog, and the gnarled yet graceful valley oak. An "indicator plant" for the state's most fertile loamy soils, even the grizzled veteran oaks not plowed under by agriculture or subdivision development are now failing to reproduce successfully.

And while the disappearance of trees is easily observed even by human eyes, other rare and unusual plants found only in California disappear, or bloom at the brink of extinction, with little apparent public concern. A subtle but perfectly adapted native perennial grass, for example, or an ephemeral herb with a spring blossom so tiny most people don't even notice it, are equally endangered by humankind's long-standing laissez-faire attitude toward the world we share with all life.

Only fairly recently, with so much of natural California already gone for good, have public attitudes begun to change. No matter what Ronald Reagan says, and despite the very real economic tradeoffs sometimes involved, most Californians—and usually the state's voters—strongly support conservation, preservation, and park expansion proposals whenever these issues arise. Yet urban and suburban sprawl and commercial development continue unabated throughout California, with little evidence that the general public connects its personal and political choices with a sense of shared responsibility for the state's continued environmental decline.

CALIFORNIA FAUNA: A LONELY HOWL IN THE WILDERNESS

The Golden State's native wildlife is also quite diverse and unique. Of the 748 known species of vertebrate animals in California, 38 percent of freshwater fish, 29 percent of amphibians, and 9 percent of mammals are endemic species; invertebrate variation is equally impressive. But with the disappearance of quite specific natural habitats, many of these animals are also endangered or threatened.

One notable exception is the intelligent and endlessly adaptable coyote, which—rather than be shoved out of its traditional territory even by suburban housing subdivisions—seems quite willing to put up with human incursions, so long as there are garbage cans to forage in, swimming pools to drink from, and adequate alleys of escape. Yet even the coyote's lonely late-night howl is like a cry for help in an unfriendly wilderness.

The rapid slide toward extinction among California's wild things is perhaps best symbolized by the grizzly bear, which once roamed from the mountains to the sea, though the wolf, too, has long since vanished from the landscape. The Sierra Nevada bighorn sheep, the San Joaquin kit fox, the desert tortoise, and the California condor—most surviving birds maintained now as part of a zoo-based captive breeding program—are among many species now endangered. Upward of 550 bird species have been recorded in California, and more than half of these breed here. But the vast flocks of migratory birds (so abundant they once darkened the midday sky) have been thinned out considerably, here and elsewhere, by the demise of native wetlands and by toxins.

The fate of the state's once-fabled fisheries is equally instructive. With 90 percent of salmon spawning grounds now gone because of the damming of rivers and streams, California's commitment to compensatory measures—fish hatcheries and ladders, for example—somehow misses the point. Now that humans are in

the northern
elephant seal

ROBERT NILSEN

WATCHING THE CALIFORNIA GRAYS

A close-up view of the California gray whale, the state's official (and largest) mammal, is a life-changing experience. As those dark, massive, white-barnacled heads shoot up out of the ocean to suck air, spray with the force of a fire hose blasts skyward from blowholes. Watch the annual migration of the gray whale all along the California coast—from "whale vistas" on land or by boat.

Despite the fascination they hold for Californians, little is yet known about the gray whale. Once endangered by whaling—as so many whale species still are—the grays are now swimming steadily along the comeback trail. Categorized as baleen whales—which dine on plankton and other small aquatic animals sifted through hundreds of fringed, hornlike baleen plates—gray whales were once land mammals that went back to sea. In the process of evolution, they traded their fore and hind legs for fins and tail flukes. Despite their fishlike appearance, these are true mammals: warm-blooded, air-breathing creatures who nourish their young with milk.

Adult gray whales weigh 20–40 tons, not counting a few hundred pounds of parasitic barnacles. Calves weigh in at a hefty 1,500 pounds at birth and can expect to live for 30 to 60 years. They feed almost endlessly from April to October in the arctic seas between Alaska and Siberia, sucking up sediment and edible creatures on the bottom of shallow seas, then squeezing the excess water and silt out their baleen filters. Fat and sassy with an extra 6–12 inches of blubber on board, early in October they head south on their 6,000-mile journey to the warmer waters of Baja in Mexico.

Pregnant females leave first, traveling alone or in small groups. Larger groups make up the rear guard, with the older males and nonpregnant females engaging in highly competitive courtship and mating rituals along the way—quite a show for human voyeurs. The rear guard becomes the frontline on the way home: males, newly pregnant females, and young gray whales head north from February to June. Cows and calves migrate later, between March and July.

Multiple places along the California coast, north and south, are noted whale-watching vistas; most of these are mentioned elsewhere in this book's travel chapters. Many locales also offer winter whale-watching charters and tours (weather permitting).

---

charge of natural selection, the fish themselves are no longer wild, no longer stream-smart; many can't even find their way back to the fisheries where they hatched out (in sterile stainless steel trays). California's once-fabled marine fisheries are also in dire straits because of the combined effects of overfishing, pollution, and habitat degradation, a subject of only very recent political concern.

However, some California animals almost wiped out by hunters, habitat elimination, and contamination are starting out on the comeback trail. Included among these are native elk and the antelope-like pronghorn populations, each numbering near 500,000 before European and American settlement. Also recovering in California is the native population of desert bighorn sheep. Among marine mammals almost hunted into oblivion but now thriving in California's offshore ocean environments are the northern elephant seal and the sea otter. And in 1994 the California gray whale was removed from the federal endangered species list—the first marine creature ever "delisted"—because its current population of 21,000 or so is as high, historically speaking, as it ever was.

Until recently, California's predators—always relatively fewer in number, pouncing from the top of the food chain—fared almost as poorly as their prey, preyed upon themselves by farmers, ranchers, loggers, and hunters. Though the grand grizzly hasn't been seen in California for more than a century, California's black bear is still around—though increasingly tracked and hunted by timber interests (for the damage the bears inflict on seedling trees) and poachers out to make a fast buck on gall bladders popular in Asian pharmacology. Of California's native wildcats, only the mountain lion and the spotted, smaller bobcat survive. The last of the state's jaguars was hunted down near Palm Springs in 1860.

THE HISTORY OF THE GOLDEN DREAM

Europeans generally get credit for having "discovered" America, including the mythic land of California. But a dusty travel log tucked away in Chinese archives in Shenshi Province, discovered in the 19th century by an American missionary, suggests that the Chinese discovered California—in about 217 B.C. According to this saga, a storm-tossed Chinese ship—misdirected by its own compass, apparently rendered nonfunctional after a cockroach got wedged under the needle—sailed stubbornly for 100 days in the direction of what was supposed to be mainland China. (The navigator, Hee-li, reportedly ignored the protests of his crew, who pointed out that the sun was setting on the wrong horizon.) Stepping out into towering forests surrounding an almost endless inlet at the edge of the endless ocean, these unwitting adventurers reported meetings with red-skinned peoples—and giant red-barked trees.

Conventional continental settlement theory holds that the first true immigrants to the North American continent also came from Asia—crossing a broad plain across the Bering Strait, a "bridge" that existed until the end of the ice age. Archaeologists agree that the earliest Americans arrived more than 11,500 years ago, more or less in synch with geologists' belief that the Bering bridge disappeared about 14,000 years ago. Circumstantial support for this conclusion has also come from striking similarities—in blood type, teeth, and language—existing between early Americans and Asians, particularly the northern Chinese. But recent discoveries have thrown all previous American migration theories into doubt.

In 1986, French scientists working in Brazil discovered an ancient rock shelter containing stone tools, other artifacts, and charcoal that was at first carbon-dated at approximately 32,000 years old. (A subsequent announcement, that the discovery was actually more than 45,000 years old, shocked archaeologists and was widely discredited.) Wall paintings suggest that cave art developed in the Americas at about the same time it did in Europe, Asia, and Africa. Preliminary evidence of very early human habitation (possibly as long ago as 33,000 years) has also been found in Chile. Subsequent Chilean finds at Monte Verde, dated authoritatively to 10,900 to 11,200 years ago, were announced in 1997—setting off a flurry of searches for still earlier sites of human habitation.

So the question is: if migration to the Americas was via the Bering Strait, and so long ago, why hasn't any similar evidence been discovered in North America? The mummified, mat-wrapped body of an elderly man discovered in 1940 in Spirit Cave near Fallon, Nevada, has subsequently been dated as 9,415 years old—making this the only Paleonoid (more than 8,500 years old) ever found in North America; the body was particularly well preserved by the desert climate. And a human skull dated as 9,800 years old has been discovered on Canada's Prince of Wales Island. But both of these finds are thought to bolster the Bering Straits land bridge theory—as does the Monte Verde discovery in Chile, if the first American arrivals were fishing people who worked their way down the continental coastline to settle, first, in South America. Some suggest that signs of earlier human habitation in North America have been erased by climatic factors, or by glaciation. But no one really knows. One thing is certain: most archaeologists would rather be buried alive in a dig than be forced to dust off and reexamine the previously discredited "Thor Heyerdahl theory" of American settlement: that the first immigrants sailed across the Pacific, landed in South America, and then migrated northward.

CALIFORNIA'S FIRST PEOPLE

However and whenever they first arrived in California, the territory's first immigrants gradually created civilizations quite appropriate to the land they had landed in. "Tribes" like those typical elsewhere in North America did not exist in California, primarily because the political unity necessary for survival elsewhere was largely irrelevant here. Populations of California native peoples are better understood as ethnic or kinship or community groups united by common experience and shared territory.

Though no census takers were abroad in the land at the time, the presettlement population (about 500 groups speaking 130 dialects) of what is now California is estimated at about 250,000—a density four to eight times greater than early people living anywhere else in the United States. Before their almost overnight decimation—from settlement, and attendant disease, cultural disintegration, and violence—California's native peoples found the living fairly easy. The cornucopia of fish, birds, and game, in addition to almost endlessly edible plantlife, meant that hunting and gathering was not the strict struggle for survival it was elsewhere on the continent. Since abundance in all things was the rule, at least in nondesert areas, trade between tribal groups (for nonlocal favorite foods such as acorns, pine nuts, or seafood and for nonlocal woods or other prized items) was not uncommon. Plants and animals of the natural world were respected by native peoples as kindred spirits, and a deep nature mysticism was the underlying philosophy of most religious traditions and associated myths and legends.

Most California peoples were essentially nonviolent, engaging in war or armed conflict only for revenge; bows and arrows, spears, and harpoons were used in hunting. The development of basketry, in general the highest art of native populations, was also quite pragmatic; baskets of specific shapes and sizes were used to gather and to store foods and for cooking in. Homes, boats, and clothing were made of the most appropriate local materials, from slabs of redwood bark and animal hides to tule reeds.

Time was not particularly important to California's first immigrants. No one kept track of passing years, and most groups didn't even have a word for "year." They paid attention, however, to the passage of the moons and seasons—the natural rhythm of life. Many native peoples were seminomadic, moving in summer into cooler mountain regions where game, roots, and berries were most abundant, and then meandering down into the foothills and valleys in autumn to collect acorns, the staff of life for most tribes, and to take shelter from winter storms.

But there was nowhere to hide from the whirling clouds of change that started sweeping into California with the arrival of early explorers and missionaries, or from the foreign flood that came when the myth of California gold became a reality. Some native peoples went out fighting: the 19th-century Modoc War was one of the last major Indian wars in the United States. And others just waited until the end of their world arrived. Most famous in this category was Ishi, the "last wild man in America" and believed to be the last of his people, captured in an Oroville slaughterhouse corral in 1911. Working as a janitor as a ward of the University of California until his death five years later from tuberculosis, Ishi walked from the Stone Age into the industrial age with dignity and without fear.

FOREIGNERS PLANT THEIR FLAGS

The first of California's official explorers were the Spanish. Though Hernán Cortés discovered a land he called California in 1535, Juan Rodríguez Cabrillo—actually a Portuguese, João Rodrigues Cabrilho—first sailed the coast of Alta California ("upper," as opposed to "lower" or Baja California, which then included all of Mexico) and rode at anchor off its shores.

But the first European to actually set foot on California soil was the English pirate Sir Francis Drake, who in 1579 came ashore somewhere along the coast (exactly where is still disputed, though popular opinion suggests Point Reyes) and whose maps—like others of the day—reflected his belief that the territory was indeed an island. Upon his return to England, Drake's story of discovery served primarily to stimulate Spain's territorial appetites. Though Sebastián Vizcaíno entered Monterey Bay in 1602 (18 years before the Pilgrims arrived at Plymouth), it wasn't until 1746 that even the Spanish realized California wasn't an island. It wasn't until 1769 and 1770 that San Francisco Bay was discovered by Gaspar de Portolá and the settlements of San Diego and Monterey were founded.

Though the Spanish failed to find California's mythical gold, between 1769 and 1823 they did manage to establish 21 missions (sometimes with associated presidios) along El Camino Real or "The Royal Road" from San Diego to Sonoma. And from these busy mission ranch outposts, maintained by the free labor of "heathen" natives, Spain grew and manufactured great wealth.

THE FIRST CALIFORNIA MISSION AND "THE ROYAL ROAD"

Though Spain claimed ownership of California in 1542, it settled the territory only after Russians were poised, from their trapping and trading colonies farther north, to challenge such absentee ownership. San Diego—and Father Junípero Serra's **Mission San Diego de Alcalá,** built in 1769 atop the city's Presidio Hill—thus became California's first Spanish outpost. But it was far from the last. Working northward along the coast—steadily adding new missions and adjunct presidios, or military outposts—the Spanish had constructed 21 missions in the territory by 1823, when the new nation of Mexico laid claim to California.

From San Diego in the south to Petaluma and Sonoma north of San Francisco Bay, California's missions were linked by **El Camino Real,** "the Royal Road," one of four dusty routes known by that grand title that radiated from Mexico City—Spain's capital city in the New World—and, by political extension, from the Spanish throne. The actual route of California's El Camino Real was fairly fluid, shifting to accommodate weather conditions, terrain changes, and available modes of transportation. But by 1900, with California's population growing—and California roadways expanding and changing accordingly—El Camino Real was almost lost. Through the efforts of the statewide Camino Real Association, starting in 1904 city, county, and state roads along the original Royal Road were identified and marked with mission-bell signposts—some of which, including four in front of San Diego's mission, still stand.

But even at its zenith, Spain's supremacy in California was tenuous. The territory was vast and relatively unpopulated. Even massive land grants—a practice continued under later Mexican rule—did little to allay colonial fears of successful outside incursions. Russian imperialism, spreading east into Siberia and Central Asia, and then to Alaska and an 1812 outpost at Fort Ross on the north coast, seemed a clear and present danger—and perhaps actually would have been, if the Russians' agricultural and other enterprises hadn't ultimately failed. And enterprising Americans, at first just a few fur trappers and traders, were soon in the neighborhood.

As things happened, the challenge to Spain's authority came from its own transplanted population. Inspired by the news in 1822 that an independent government had been formed in Baja California's Mexico City, young California-born Spanish ("Californios") and independence-seeking resident Spaniards declared Alta California part of the new Mexican empire. By March 1825, when California proper officially became a territory of the Republic of Mexico, the new leadership had already achieved several goals, including secularizing the missions and "freeing" the associated native neophytes (not officially achieved until 1833), which in practice meant that most became servants elsewhere. The Californios also established an independent military and judiciary, opened the territory's ports to trade, and levied taxes.

During the short period of Mexican rule, the American presence was already prominent. Since even Spain regularly failed to send supply ships, Yankee traders were always welcome in California. In no time at all, Americans had organized and dominated the territory's business sector, established successful ranches and farms, married into local families, and become prominent citizens. California, as a possible political conquest, was becoming increasingly attractive to the United States.

General John C. Frémont, officially on a scientific expedition but perhaps acting under secret orders from Washington (Frémont would never say), had been stirring things up in California since 1844—engaging in a few skirmishes with the locals or provoking conflicts between Californios and American citizens in California. Though the United States declared war on Mexico on May 13, 1846, Frémont and his men apparently were unaware of that turn of events and took over the town of Sonoma for a short time in mid-June, raising the secessionist flag of the independent—but very short-lived—Bear Flag Republic.

With Californios never mustering much resistance to the American warriors, Commodore John C. Sloat sailed unchallenged into Monterey Bay on July 7, 1848, raised the Stars and Stripes above the Custom House in town, and claimed California for the United States. Within two days, the flag flew in both San Francisco and Sonoma, but it took some time to end the statewide skirmishes. It took even longer for official Americanization—and statehood—to proceed. The state constitution established, among other things, California as a "free" state (but only to prevent the unfair use of slave labor in the mines). This upset the balance of congressional power in the nation's antislavery conflict and indirectly precipitated the Civil War. Written in Monterey, the new state's constitution was adopted in October 1849 and ratified by voters in November.

GOLD IN THEM THAR HILLS

California's legendary gold was real, as it turned out. And the Americans found it—but quite by accident. The day James Marshall, who was building a lumber mill on the American River for John Sutter, discovered flecks of shiny yellow metal in the mill's tailrace seemed otherwise quite ordinary. But that day, January 24, 1848, changed everything—in California and in the world.

As fortune seekers worldwide succumbed to gold fever and swarmed into the Sierra Nevada foothills in 1849, modern-day California began creating itself. In the no-holds-barred search for personal freedom and material satisfaction (better yet, unlimited wealth), something even then recognizable as California's human character was also taking shape: the belief that anything is possible, for anyone, no matter what one's previous circumstances would suggest. Almost everyone wanted to entertain that belief. (Karl Marx was of the opinion that the California gold rush was directly responsible for delaying the Russian Revolution.) New gold dreamers—all colors and creeds—came to California, by land and by sea, to take a chance on themselves and their luck. The luckiest ones, though, were the merchants and businesspeople who cashed in on California's dream by mining the miners.

Sutter's Mill

Because of the discovery of gold, California skipped the economically exploitive U.S. territorial phase typical of other western states. With almost endless, indisputable capital at hand, Californians thumbed their noses at the Eastern financial establishment almost from the start: they could exploit the wealth of the far West themselves. And exploit it they did—mining not only the earth, but also the state's forests, fields, and water wealth. Wild California would never again be the same.

Almost overnight, "civilized" California became an economic sensation. The state was essentially admitted to the union on its own terms—because California was quite willing to go its own way and remain an independent entity otherwise. The city of San Francisco grew from a sleepy enclave of 500 souls to a hectic, hell-bent business and financial center of more than 25,000 within two years. Other cities built on a foundation of prosperous trade included the inland supply port of Sacramento. Agriculture, at first important for feeding the state's mushrooming population of fortune hunters, soon became a de facto gold mine in its own right. Commerce expanded even more rapidly with the completion of the California-initiated transcontinental railroad and with the advent of other early communications breakthroughs such as the telegraph. California's dreams of prosperity became self-fulfilling prophecies. And as California went, so went the nation.

SOUTHERN CALIFORNIA'S GOLDEN AGE

There was gold in Southern California, too—and it was actually discovered first, at Placerita Canyon not far north of Mission San Fernando. But the subsequent discovery at Sutter's Mill soon dwarfed Southern California's gold rush–era mining finds. The bonanza here came from inflated beef prices and otherwise supplying the booming northstate gold fields. The boom went bust in the mid-1850s, and depression came to California. Only the arrival of the railroads awakened Southern California from its social and economic slumber. Lured by well-promoted tales and photographs of the salubrious sunny climate—a place where oranges grew in people's backyards, where even roses bloomed in winter—migrants arrived by the trainloads, particularly from the Midwest, throughout the 1880s. Soon agriculture, with orchards and fields of crops stretching to every horizon, became Southern California's economic strength. Real estate developments and grand hotels, often built on land owned by the railroad barons, soon boomed as well. In the late 1800s oil was discovered throughout the greater Los Angeles basin, creating still more regional wealth.

As a land with little annual rainfall, its vast underground aquifers already well on the way to depletion because of agricultural irrigation and urban use, by the early 1900s Los Angeles was quickly running out of water. Yet the inventiveness of self-taught water engineer William Mulholland, soon an international celebrity, eliminated any prospect of enforced limits on growth. When the floodgates of the famed Los Angeles Aqueduct first opened, to great public acclaim, in 1913, Southern California had made its first monumental step toward eliminating the very idea of limits. Mulholland's engineering miracle, which successfully tapped into Owens Valley water supplies that originated 250 miles to the north, also tapped into the southstate's social imagination. In no time at all the "desert" was in full bloom, landscaped with lush lawns, ferns, roses, and palm trees and populated by happy, healthy families frolicking in the sunshine.

That image, translated to the world's imagination via Hollywood's movie industry in the 1920s and subsequent years, essentially created the Southern California of today. Massive growth followed World War II, when Los Angeles began to create itself as an industrial and technological superpower—one soon beset by traffic, pollution, and social problems befitting its size.

Yet for all its current challenges Southern California is still a surprisingly optimistic place. For every problem there is a solution, according to traditional southstate thinking.

DREAMING THE NEW GOLD DREAM

California as the land of opportunity—always a magnet for innovation, never particularly respectful of stifling and stodgy tradition—has dictated terms to the rest of the country throughout its modern history. Even with the gradual arrival of what the rest of the world could finally recognize as civilization, which included the predictable phenomenon of personal wealth translated into political power, California's commitment to prosperity and change—sometimes for its own sake—has never waned.

From the founding of the Automobile Club of Southern California in 1900 to the construction of Yosemite's Hetch Hetchy Dam (to slake San Francisco thirst) in 1923; from the establishment of the first Hollywood movie studio in 1911 to the 1927 transmission, from San Francisco, of the first television picture; from the completion in 1940 of the world's first freeway to the opening of Disneyland in 1955; from the 1960s' Free Speech Movement, the rise of Black Power in the wake of the Watts riots in 1965, and the successes of César E. Chávez's United Farm Workers Union to the Beat poets, San Francisco's

Summer of Love, and the oozing up of New Age consciousness; from California's rise as leader in the development of nuclear weapons and defense technology to the creation of the microchip and personal computer: California history is a chronicle of incredible change, a relentless double-time march into the new.

"All that is constant about the California of my childhood," writes Sacramento native Joan Didion in an essay from *Slouching Towards Bethlehem,* "is the rate at which it disappears."

CALIFORNIA GOVERNMENT: THE BEST THAT MONEY CAN BUY

California's political structure is quite confusing, with thousands of tax-levying governmental units—including special districts, 58 county governments, and hundreds of cities both large and small—and a variety of overlapping jurisdictions. Based on the federal principle of one person, one vote and designed with separate executive, judicial, and legislative (Assembly and Senate) branches, the game of state-level California government is often quite lively, almost a high form of entertainment for those who understand the rules. The use and abuse of public resources is the ultimate goal of power-brokering in the Golden State, affecting statewide and local economies as well as the private sector and creating (or abandoning) commitments to social justice and various human rights issues many Californians still hold dear.

The popularity of unusually affable, charismatic, and highly visible California politicians, from Ronald Reagan to Jerry Brown, would suggest that Golden State politics generally takes place in the entertainment arena. Nothing could be further from the truth. Though Californians are committed to the concept of public initiatives and referenda on major issues—politicians be damned, basically—most decisions affecting life in California are still made in the time-honored behind-the-scenes tradition of U.S. politics, with backroom deal-making conducted something like a poker game. In order to know the score, you must know the players and what cards they hold.

Those in the know contend that the California Legislature, considered the best state-level legislative body in the nation as recently as 1971,

has steadily been careening downhill, in terms of effectiveness and ethics, ever since—largely because of "juice," or the influence of lobbyists and special interest money. According to veteran *Sacramento Bee* political reporter and columnist Dan Walters: "Votes are bought, sold, and rented by the hour with an arrogant casualness. There are one-man, one-vote retail sales as well as wholesale transactions that party leaders negotiate for blocs of votes."

Though from some perspectives California voters—and nonvoters—are largely responsible for the seemingly insoluble problems the state now faces, polls indicate that Californians increasingly distrust their politicians. From his years observing the species from the 19th-century Washington, D.C., press gallery, Mark Twain offered this fitting summary, a quote from a fictitious newspaper account in his novel, *The Gilded Age:* "We are now reminded of a note we received from the notorious burglar Murphy, in which he finds fault with a statement of ours that he had served one term in the penitentiary and one in the U.S. Senate. He says, 'The latter statement is untrue and does me great injustice.'"

Given California voters' current penchant for taking matters into their own hands, no matter how disastrously, it came as no surprise in 1992 when California became one of the first states in the nation to pass a "term limitations" law, restricting its Assembly members to maximum six-year terms in office and limiting the terms of governor, state senators, and other constitutional officers to eight years. Another initiative, put before the voters in 1990 as Proposition 140, cut the Legislature's operating budget by $70 million, about 38 percent. It has been upheld as constitutional by the state supreme court.

THE GLITTER OF THE GOLDEN STATE ECONOMY

If the lure of gold brought pioneers to California, the rich land, its seemingly endless resources, and the state's almost anarchistic "anything goes" philosophy kept them here. The Golden State has essentially become a nation-state—an economic superpower, the fifth-largest (or sixth or seventh, depending on the comparison data) economy in the world. A major international player in the game of Pacific Rim commerce, California's cry is usually "free trade," in contrast to the philosophy of high-tariff trade protectionism typically so strong elsewhere in the United States. And with so much financial clout, California is often the tail that wags the dog of U.S. domestic and foreign economic and political policy. No one ever says it out loud, but California could easily secede from the union, only too happy to compete as an independent entity in the world market. This seems especially true in the early 21st century, as California emerges stronger than ever after its recent economic slump, buoyed by booming exports to both Japan and Mexico.

Though industry of every sort thrives in California, agriculture has long been the state's economic mainstay. ("The whole place stank of orange blossoms," observed H. L. Mencken on a Golden State visit.) Though most Southern California citrus groves have long since been paved over for parking lots and shopping malls—those disturbed by California's proclivity for bulldozing the past in the name of progress have coined a verb for it: "to californicate"—agriculture in pockets of Southern California and in Northern California is still going strong. Because of the large size and concentrated ownership of farm and ranch lands, helped along by public subsidies of irrigation engineering projects, agriculture in California has always been agribusiness. In its role as agricultural nation-state, California produces more food than 90 percent of the world's nations, a $25 billion annual business.

The economic spirit of the northstate, suggested philosopher George Santayana in a 1910 Berkeley speech, is best summed up by the immense presence of nature in Northern California—nature in tandem with engineering and technology. Now that the roughshod, rough-and-tumble days of man against nature are no longer widely condoned, Californians increasingly expect technology to respect nature's standards. In Northern California particularly, but increasingly in Southern California, information is the cleanest industry of all. It seems no coincidence that both the microchip and the personal computer were born here.

Yet California, northern and southern, is industrious in all ways. Travel and tourism is a major industry—now promoted, since California has started to lose ground in the tourist sweeps to other Western states—with annual revenues in the $52 billion range. Growth itself is a growth industry in California, with all aspects of the construction trade generating an average $30 billion in business annually. Revenues generated by California's top 100 privately held companies—including Bechtel Group, Hughes Aircraft, USA Petroleum (and other oil companies), Twentieth-Century Fox Films (and other media giants), Purex Industries, Denny's Inc., Raley's, both the AAA-affiliated Automobile Club of Southern California and the California State Automobile Association, and a long string of agricultural cooperatives as well as health- and life-insurance companies—approach $100 billion annually.

A U.S. capital of finance and commerce, the state is also the world's high-technology headquarters. Helped along by state-supported University of California labs and research facilities, California has long been a leader in the aerospace and weapons development industries, though that role was diminished in the 1990s with the closure of many military bases and federal cuts in defense spending.

THE PEOPLE— ALWAYS ON THE MOVE

Everyone is moving to California and vicinity, it seems. According to *American Demographics,* the geographic center of the U.S. population moves 58 feet farther west and 29 feet to the south every year. (Bad times in the early 1990s slowed that trend temporarily, as Californians left to find jobs elsewhere, but state population jumped—with previous losses eclipsed by ongoing increases—when boom times arrived in the late 1990s.) Be that as it may, some people consider Californians among the most obnoxious people on earth, and this is not necessarily a new phenomenon.

To some, the state is a kind of cultural purgatory, settled (in the words of Willard Huntington Wright) by "yokels from the Middle West who were nourished by rural pieties and superstitions." Others consider, and have always considered, Californians as somehow inherently unstable. "Insanity, as might be expected, is fearfully prevalent in California," Dr. Henry Gibbons stated before San Francisco's local medical society in 1857. "It grows directly out of the excited mental condition of our population, to which the common use of alcoholic drink is a powerful adjunct." The general outside observation today is that if Californians aren't talking about themselves—and about accomplishing their latest career, financial, fitness, or psychospiritual goals—they talk about California. New Englander Inez Hayes Irwin defined those afflicted with Californoia in her 1921 book *Californiacs:*

The Californiac is unable to talk about anything but California, except when he interrupts himself to knock every other place on the face of the earth. He looks with pity on anybody born outside of California, and he believes that no one who has ever seen California willingly lives elsewhere. He himself often lives elsewhere, but he never admits that it is from choice.

There may be more than a shred of truth in this, even today; pollsters say one out of every four Californians would rather live elsewhere—for the most part, either in Hawaii or Oregon. But many who live and work in California are not native Californians. This is almost as true today as it ever was; at least one-third of contemporary Californians were born somewhere else. Somehow, California's amazing cultural and ethnic diversity is the source of both its social stability and its self-renewal.

Perhaps because of misleading portrayals of California's past, in the media and the movies as well as the history books, a common misconception is that the impact and importance of California's ethnic populations is relatively recent, a post–World War II phenomenon. But many peoples and many races have made significant contributions to California culture and economic development since the days of the gold rush—and since the decimation of native populations.

Blacks and Hispanics, despite attempts (official and otherwise) to prevent them from dreaming the California dream, were among the first to arrive in the gold fields. The Chinese, who also arrived early to join the ranks of the state's most industrious citizens, were relentlessly persecuted despite their willingness to do work others considered impossible—including the unimaginable engineering feat of chiseling a route over the forbidding Sierra Nevada for the nation's first transcontinental railroad. And when the state's boom-bust beginnings gave way to other possibilities, including farming, ranching, and small business enterprises, California's minorities stayed—helping, despite the realities of subtle discrimination and sometimes overt racism, to create the psychological pluralism characteristic of California society today.

DOING THE DREAM: PRACTICALITIES

California is crowded—both with people trying to live the dream on a permanent basis and with those who come to visit, to re-create themselves on the standard two-week vacation plan. Summer, when school's out, is generally when the Golden State is most crowded, though this pattern is changing rapidly now that year-round schools and off-season travel are becoming common. Another trend: "mini-vacations," with workaholic Californians and other Westerners opting for one- to several-day respites spread throughout the year rather than traditional once-a-year holidays. It was once a truism that great bargains, in accommodations and transport particularly, were widely available during California's non-summer travel season. Given changing travel patterns, this is no longer entirely true. Early spring and autumn are among the best times to tour the Northern California coastline, for example. And winter is "peak season" at Lake Tahoe, Mammoth Lakes, and other ski and winter-sport areas—as well as in Palm Springs. Yet winter travel can be less expensive.

Spontaneous travel, or following one's whims wherever they may lead, was once feasible in California. Unfortunately, given the immense popularity of particular destinations, those days are long gone. Particularly for those traveling on the cheap and for travelers with special needs or specific desires, some of the surprises encountered during impulsive adventuring may be unpleasant. If the availability of specific types of lodgings (including campgrounds) or eateries, or if transport details, prices, hours, and other factors are important for a pleasant trip, the best bet is calling ahead to check details and/or to make reservations. (Everything changes rapidly in California.) For a good overview of what to see and do in advance of a planned trip, including practical suggestions beyond those in this guide, also contact the chambers of commerce and/or visitor centers listed. Other good sources for local and regional information are bookstores, libraries, sporting goods and outdoor supply stores, and local, state, and federal government offices.

BEING HERE: BASIC TRUTHS

Conduct and Custom:
Smoking, Drinking, and General Truths
Smoking is a major social sin in California, often against the law in public buildings and on public transport, with regulations particularly stringent in urban areas. People sometimes get violent over other people's smoking, so smokers need to be respectful of others' "space" and smoke outdoors when possible. Smoking has been banned outright in California restaurants and bars, and smoking is not allowed on public airplane flights, though nervous fliers can usually smoke somewhere inside—or outside—airline terminals. Many bed-and-breakfasts in California are either entirely nonsmoking or restrict smoking to decks, porches, or dens; if this is an issue, inquire by calling ahead. Hotels and motels, most commonly in major urban areas or popular tourist destinations, increasingly offer nonsmoking rooms (or entire floors). Ask in advance.

The legal age for buying and drinking alcohol in California is 21. Though Californians tend to (as they say) "party hearty," public drunkenness is not well tolerated. Drunken driving—which means operating a vehicle (even a bicycle, technically) while under the influence—is definitely against the law. California is increasingly no-nonsense about the use of illegal drugs, too, from marijuana to cocaine, crack, and heroin. Doing time in local jails or state prisons is not the best way to do California.

English is the official language in California, and even English-speaking visitors from other countries have little trouble understanding California's "dialect" once they acclimate to the accents and slang expressions. (Californians tend to be very creative in their language.) When unsure what someone means by some peculiar phrase, ask for a translation into standard English. Particularly in urban areas, many languages are commonly spoken, and—even in English—the accents are many. You can usually obtain at least some foreign-language brochures, maps,

WHAT TO BRING

Generally speaking, bring what you'll really need—but as little of it as possible. A good rule of thumb: select everything absolutely necessary for your travels, then take along only half. Remember, you'll be bringing back all sorts of interesting tokens of your trip, so leave space. Remember, too, that camera equipment is heavy; bring only what you'll really use. (Try carrying your packed luggage around for 15 or 20 minutes if you need motivation to lighten the load.) Standard luggage is adequate for most travelers, especially those traveling by bus or car. For those planning to be without personal wheels, and therefore destined to cover more ground on foot, a backpack—or convertible backpack-suitcase—may be more useful, since you can also carry the load on your back as needed. For any traveler, a daypack may also come in handy, for use on day hikes and outings, and as an extra bag for toting home travel trinkets.

In characteristically casual California, clothing should be sensible and comfortable. Natural and certain high-tech fibers are preferable because they "breathe" in California's variable climate. Cotton is the most fundamental California fiber—quite versatile,

too, when layered to meet one's changing needs. Shorts, jeans, T-shirts, and sandals or sport shoes are the standard tourist uniform (swimming suits at the beach). Dark or bright colors, knits, and durable clothing will keep you presentable longer than more frivolous fashions, though laundry services and coin-operated laundromats are widely available. Even for summer travel—and especially along the coast—always bring a sweater or light jacket, since summer fog can cool daytime temperatures, and evenings can be cool in coastal or foothill areas. A heavier jacket is advisable for summers in the mountains—and quality cold-weather gear for winters in the mountains, where the climate can be quite severe. Northern California's cold and rainy season usually begins in October or November and continues into March or April (sometimes June), so pack clothing and raingear accordingly. Except in the mountains and the high desert, milder temperatures in winter are the norm in Southern California. Those planning to participate in California-style high life should pack dress clothes, of course, but the most universally necessary thing to bring is a decent (preferably broken-in) pair of walking shoes.

and other information from city visitor centers and popular tourist destinations. (If this is a major concern, inquire in advance.)

Californians are generally casual, in dress as well as etiquette. If any standard applies in most situations, it's common courtesy—still in style, generally speaking, even in California. Though "anything goes" just about anywhere, elegant restaurants usually require appropriately dressy attire for women, jacket and tie for men. (Shirts and shoes—pants or skirt too, usually—are required in any California restaurant.)

By law, public buildings in California are wheelchair-accessible, or at least partially so. The same is true of most major hotels and tourist attractions, which may offer both rooms and restrooms with complete wheelchair accessibility; some also have wheelchairs, walkers, and other mobility aids available for temporary use. Even national and state parks, increasingly, are attempting to make some sights and campgrounds more accessible for those with physical disabilities; to make special arrangements, inquire in

advance. But private buildings, from restaurants to bed-and-breakfasts, may not be so accommodating. Those with special needs should definitely ask specific questions in advance.

Conduct and Custom: Tipping

For services rendered in the service trade, a tip is usually expected. Some say the word is derived from the Latin *stips,* for stipend or gift. Some say it's an 18th-century English acronym for "to ensure promptness," though "to ensure personal service" seems more to the point in these times. In expensive restaurants or for large groups, an automatic tip or gratuity may be included in the bill—an accepted practice in many countries but a source of irritation for many U.S. diners, who would prefer to personally evaluate the quality of service received. Otherwise, 15–20 percent of the before-tax total tab is the standard gratuity, and 10 percent the minimal acknowledgment, for those in the service trade—waitresses and waiters, barbers, hairdressers, and taxi drivers. In fine-dining circumstances, wine stewards should be acknowledged personally, at the rate of $2–5 per bottle, and the maître d' as well, with $5 or $10. In very casual buffet-style joints, leave $1 each for the people who clear the dishes and pour your coffee after the meal. In bars, leave $1 per drink, or 15 percent of the bill if you run a tab. At airports, tip skycaps $1 per bag (more if they transport your baggage any distance); tip more generously for extra assistance, such as helping wheelchair passengers or mothers with infants and small children to their gates.

At hotels, a desk clerk or concierge does not require a tip unless that person fulfills a specific request, such as snagging tickets for a sold-out concert or theater performance, in which case generosity is certainly appropriate. For baggage handlers curbside, $1 tip is adequate; a tip of at least $1 per bag is appropriate for bell staff transporting luggage from the lobby to your room or from your room to the lobby. For valet parking, tip the attendant $2–3. Tip the hotel doorman if he helps with baggage or hails a cab for you. And tip swimming pool or health club personnel as appropriate for extra personal service. Unless one stays in a hotel or motel for several days, the standard practice is not to tip the housekeeper, though you can if you wish; some guests leave

CALIFORNIA DREAMIN', CALIFORNIA STYLIN'

Visitors often mistakenly assume that anything goes in California style—that it's okay to be seen just about anywhere wearing the I'm-on-vacation-so-sue-me tourist look: sunglasses, sandals, ill-fitting shorts, and theme park T-shirt. Wrong, wrong, wrong. Stylin' it in California is actually an applied science, albeit social science. California even has a dress code—actually, a variety of dress codes—though it's fairly simple to fathom the rules. There are only two.

First Rule of California Fashion: Form does follow function, so dress appropriately for the occasion. Anyone donning shorts and sandals in fog-bound San Francisco summers will nearly freeze to death, for example. Summertime shorts also scream "tourist!" (Locals dress warmly when it's cold outside.) And people in Southern California still snicker over the now-mythic memory of Richard Milhous Nixon—an Orange County homeboy, mind you—strolling on the beach in suit, tie, and wingtips during his presidency.

Second Rule of California Fashion: Figure out whether you're in Northern or Southern California, and then dress accordingly.

The fashion focal point of the north is San Francisco, birthplace of internationally renowned Levi's blue jeans. Excepting artists, students, and sundry eccentrics—categories that include just about everyone in San Francisco—blue jeans and more out-there wear are strictly reserved for weekends and casual activities. (Sightseeing in the city qualifies as a casual activity, in most circumstances, as does traveling almost anywhere else in Northern California.) Still, San Franciscans like to see themselves as

tuned in to European and East Coast sensibilities (if a bit self-consciously), and they like to be seen as sophisticated. Tailored suits, for women as well as men, are de rigueur for business, or at least for the business establishment. On some San Francisco streets, both sexes even wear hats. It was no coincidence that the first official act of Mayor Willie Brown, known for his handmade Italian suits and fedoras, involved establishing a strict dress code for city staff. San Francisco can get quite serious about stylin' it for dinner and the theater, too.

Both geographically and in a fashion sense, Los Angeles is all over the map. But achieving a fashionable L.A. "look" is deceptively complicated. The basic trés-L.A. hip wardrobe, for both men and women, centers on the "incognito movie star" look—blue jeans with an understated blazer or casual jacket tossed over a T-shirt, sweater, or natural-fiber sport shirt. (Never, *ever* iron your jeans in California—utter blasphemy in Levi's country.) Cotton and natural fibers are almost mandatory; polyester, whether or not it's been reduced to its petroleum essence, is viewed as suitable only for fuel tanks. Ethnic "attitude" is always in. And though they might seem more appropriate in the north, so are cowboy boots (the western was born in L.A., after all). So are running shoes and stylish athletic wear. Anything associated with youth, fitness, and perfect body tone—including spandex and those poured-on Latex dresses—works in L.A., so long as one's body also fits the mold. No matter how seemingly outlandish the get-up, in L.A. you can get away with it if, in your manner and bearing, you manage to convince everyone around you that you're more cool than they are.

$1–2 each morning for the housekeeper and $1 each evening for turn-down service.

Entertainment, Events, Holidays

Not even the sky's the limit on entertainment in California. From air shows to harvest fairs and rodeos, from symphony to opera, from rock 'n' roll to avant-garde clubs and theater, from strip shows (male and female) to ringside seats at ladies' mud-wrestling contests, from high-stakes bingo games to horse racing—anything goes in the Golden State. Most communities offer a wide variety of special, often quite unusual, annual events; many of these are listed by region or city elsewhere in this guide.

Official holidays, especially during the warm-weather travel season and the Thanksgiving-Christmas–New Year holiday season, are often the most congested and popular (read: more expensive) times to travel or stay in California. Yet this is not always true; great holiday-season bargains in accommodations are sometimes available at swank hotels that primarily cater to businesspeople. Though most tourist destinations are usually jumping, banks and many businesses close on the following major holidays: New Year's Day (January 1); Martin Luther King Day (the third Monday in January); Presidents' Day (the third Monday in February); Memorial Day (the last Monday in May); Independence Day (July 4); Labor Day (the first Monday in September); Veterans Day (November 11); Thanksgiving (the fourth Thursday in November); and Christmas (December 25). California's newest state holiday is César E. Chávez Day, in honor of the late leader of the United Farm Workers (UFW), signed into law in August 2000 and celebrated each year on the Friday or Monday closest to March 31, Chávez's birthday. In honor of the nation's most famous Latino civil rights leader, all state offices close but banks and other businesses may not.

Shopping Standards

Most stores are open during standard business hours (weekdays 8 A.M.–5 P.M. or 9 A.M.–5 P.M.) and often longer, sometimes seven days a week, because of the trend toward two-income families and ever-reduced leisure time. This trend is particularly noticeable in cities, where shops and department stores are often open until 9 P.M. or later, and where many grocery stores are open 24 hours.

Shopping malls—almost self-sustaining cities in California, with everything from clothing and major appliances to restaurants and entertainment—are the standard California trend, but cities large and small with viable downtown shopping districts often offer greater variety and uniqueness in goods and services. Also particularly popular in California are flea markets and arts-and-crafts fairs, the former usually held on weekends, the latter best for handcrafted items and often associated with the Thanksgiving-through-Christmas shopping season and/or festivals and special events. California assesses a 7.25 percent state sales tax on all nonfood items sold in the state, and many municipalities levy additional sales tax.

PLAYING HERE: OUTDOOR RECREATION

With its tremendous natural diversity, recreationally California offers something for just about everyone. Popular spring-summer-fall activities include hiking and backpacking; all water sports, from pleasure boating and water-skiing to sailing, windsurfing, and swimming; whitewater rafting, canoeing, and kayaking; mountain and rock-climbing; even hang gliding and hunting. In most years, winter activities popular in Northern California can also be enjoyed in Southern California, at least to a certain extent. These include both Alpine and Nordic skiing, snowshoe hiking, sledding and tobogganing, and just plain snow play. Also high on the "most popular" list of outdoor California sports: bicycling, walking, and running, and coastal diversions from beachcombing to surfing. The most likely places to enjoy these and other outdoor activities are mentioned throughout this book.

And where do people go to re-create themselves in the great outdoors? To Northern California's vast public playgrounds—to the rugged coast and almost endless local, regional, and state parks as well as national parks and forest lands. In Southern California, where wide-open spaces are fast disappearing, outdoor recreation still centers on local beaches, some nice local and regional parks as well as state parks and beaches, national forests—and the vast expanse of the state's deserts. For more information on the national parks, national forests, and other state- and federally owned lands (including Bureau of Land Management wilderness areas) mentioned in this book, contact each directly.

National Parks Information and Fees

For those planning to travel extensively in national parks in California and elsewhere in the United States, a one-year Golden Eagle Passport provides unlimited park access (not counting camping fees) for the holder and family, for the new price of $50. Though the Golden Eagle pass has recently doubled in price, it can still be worth it in California, where fees at certain national parks have recently increased; admission to Death Valley is now $10 (for up to a one-week stay) and Yosemite is $20. Those age 62 or older qualify for the $10 Golden Age Passport, which provides free access to national parks, monuments, and recreation areas, and a 50 percent discount on RV fees. Disabled travelers are eligible for the $10 Golden Access Passport, with the same privileges. You can buy all three special passes at individual national parks or obtain them in advance, along with visitor information, from: **U.S. National Park Service,** National Public Inquiries Office, U.S. Department of the Interior, 1849 C St., P.O. Box 37127, Washington, DC 20013, www.nps.gov. For regional national parks information covering California, Nevada, and Arizona, contact:

Western Region Information Office, U.S. National Park Service, Fort Mason, Bldg. 201, San Francisco, CA 94123, 415/556-0560 (recorded) or 415/556-0561.

Campgrounds in some national parks in California—including Sequoia–Kings Canyon and Whiskeytown National Recreation Area, along with Southern California parks including Channel Islands, Death Valley, and Joshua Tree—can be reserved (with MasterCard or Visa) through the **National Park Reservation Service,** reservations.nps.gov, or by calling toll-free 800/365-2267 (365-CAMP) at least eight weeks in advance. The total cost includes both the actual camping fee plus an $8–9 reservations fee. From California, call 7 A.M.–7 P.M. (10 A.M.–10 P.M. Eastern time). If you're heading to **Yosemite,** make campground reservations via the Internet (see address above) or by calling toll-free 800/436-7275 (436-PARK). And to cancel your reservations, call toll-free 800/388-2733. To make national park camping reservations from outside the United States, call 619/452-8787.

To support the protection of U.S. national parks and their natural heritage, contact the nonprofit **National Parks and Conservation Association** (NPCA), 1776 Massachusetts Ave. NW, Washington, DC 20036, 202/223-6722, fax 202/659-0650, www.npca.org/home/npca. Both as a public service and fundraiser, the NPCA publishes a number of comprehensive regional "overview" guides to U.S. national parks—Alaska, the Pacific, the Pacific Northwest, the South-

Rafting is one popular outdoor sport in California.

ROBERT HOLMES/CALTOUR

west included—that cost less than $10 each, plus shipping and handling. To order one or more titles, call toll-free 800/395-7275.

National Forests and Other Federal Lands
For general information about U.S. national forests, including wilderness areas and campgrounds, contact: **U.S. Forest Service,** U.S. Department of Agriculture, Publications, P.O. Box 96090, Washington, DC 20090, 202/205-1760. For a wealth of information via the Internet, try www.fs.fed.us. For information specifically concerning national forests and wilderness areas in California, and for maps, contact: **U.S. Forest Service, Pacific Southwest Region,** 630 Sansome St., San Francisco, CA 94111, 415/705-2870. Additional California regional offices are mentioned elsewhere in this guide.

Some U.S. Forest Service and Army Corps of Engineers campgrounds in California can be reserved through ReserveAmerica's **National Recreation Reservation Service** (with Master-Card or Visa) at www.reserveusa.com, or call toll-free 877/444-6777 (TDD: 877/833-6777), a service available 5 A.M.–9 P.M. (8 A.M.–midnight Eastern time) from April 1 through Labor Day and otherwise 7 A.M.–4 P.M. (10 A.M.–7 P.M. Eastern time). From outside the United States, call 518/885-3639. Reservations for individual campsites can be made up to eight months in advance, and for group camps up to 360 days in advance. Along with the actual costs of camping, expect to pay a per-reservation service fee of $8–9 for individual campsites (more for group sites). In addition to its first-come, first-camped campgrounds, in some areas the U.S. Forest Service offers the opportunity for "dispersed camping," meaning that you can set up minimal-impact campsites in various undeveloped areas. For detailed current recreation, camping, and other in-

COASTWALKING: THE CALIFORNIA COASTAL TRAIL

Californians love their Pacific Ocean coastline. Love of the coast has inspired fierce battles over the years concerning just what does, and what does not, belong there. Among the things most Californians would agree belong along the coast are hiking trails—the reason for the existence of the nonprofit educational group **Coastwalk,** which sponsors group walks along the **California Coastal Trail** to introduce people to the wonders of the coast.

The California Coastal Trail seems to be an idea whose time has come. Now a Millennium Legacy Trail, honored at a special White House ceremony in October 1999 recognizing 50 unique trails in the United States, Washington, D.C., Puerto Rico, and the Virgin Islands, in March 2000 the California Coastal Trail also received a special $10,000 Millennium Trails Grant from American Express.

Yet in some places, the trail is still just an idea. It doesn't yet exist everywhere along the California coastline—and changing that fact is the other primary purpose of this unique organization. Since 1983, Coastwalk's mission has been to establish a border-to-border California Coastal Trail as well as preserve the coastal environment.

Guided four- to six-day trips offered in 1999, typically covering 5–10 miles each day, included in the far north the Del Norte coastline, Redwood National Park in Humboldt County, the rugged Mendocino shoreline, the "Lost Coast" of Sonoma County, and Marin County. In central California, hikes were offered near San Francisco Bay, along the San Mateo and Santa Cruz coasts, in Monterey and San Luis Obispo Counties, and along the Santa Barbara and Ventura coasts. Southern California coast walks in 1999 covered Los Angeles (the Santa Monica Mountains) and Catalina Island, Orange County, and San Diego County. Always popular, too, is the eight-day Lost Coast Backpack in Humboldt and Mendocino Counties.

Accommodations, arranged as part of the trip by Coastwalk, include state park campgrounds and hostels with hot showers. "Chuckwagon" dinners, prepared by volunteers, are also provided; bring your own supplies for breakfast and lunch. All gear—you'll be encouraged to travel light—is shuttled from site to site each night, so you need carry only the essentials as you walk: water bottle, lunch, camera, and jacket.

At last report, daily "coastwalk" fees were $39 adults, $21 full-time students, and $16 children ages 12 and under—all in all a very reasonable price for a unique vacation.

For more information and to join Coastwalk—volunteers are always needed—contact Richard Nichols, Coastwalk, 1389 Cooper Rd., Sebastopol, CA 95472, 707/829-6689 or toll-free 800/550-6854, www.californiacoastaltrail.org or www.coastwalk.org/coastwalk.

formation, contact specific national forests mentioned elsewhere in this book.

Anyone planning to camp extensively in national forest campgrounds should consider buying U.S. Forest Service "camp stamps" (at national forest headquarters or at ranger district stations) in denominations of $.50, $1, $2, $3, $5, and $10. These prepaid camping coupons amount to a 15 percent discount on the going rate. (Many national forest campgrounds are first-come, first-camped; without a reserved campsite, even camp stamps won't guarantee one.) Senior adults, disabled people, and those with national Golden Age and Golden Access recreation passports pay only half the standard fee at any campground and can buy camp stamps at half the regular rate as well.

For wannabe archaeologists, the U.S. Forest Service offers the opportunity to volunteer on archaeological digs through its **Passport in Time** program—certainly one way to make up for stingy federal budgets. To receive the project's newsletter, which announces upcoming projects in various national forests, contact: Passport in Time Clearinghouse, P.O. Box 31805, Tucson, AZ 85751.

Some Northern California public lands and vast expanses of Southern California are managed by the **U.S. Bureau of Land Management** (BLM). For general information, contact: U.S. Bureau of Land Management, Public Affairs Office, 1849 C St. NW, LS 406, Washington, DC 20240, 202/452-5125, www.blm.gov. For infor-mation specifically related to California, contact: **California BLM,** 2800 Cottage Way, Room W1824, Sacramento, CA 95825, 916/978-4400, www.ca.blm.gov. If you plan to camp on BLM lands, be sure to request a current *California Visitor Map,* which includes campgrounds and other features; the BLM also allows "dispersed camping" in some areas (ask for details). For detailed information on all 69 of the BLM's new desert wildernesses, contact the BLM's **California Desert District Office,** 6221 Box Springs Rd., Riverside, CA 92507, 909/697-5200 or toll-free 800/446-6743, www.ca.blm.gov/cdd.

For information on national wildlife reserves and other protected federal lands, contact: **U.S. Fish and Wildlife Service,** Division of Refuges, 4401 N. Fairfax Dr., Room 640, Arlington, VA 22203, toll-free 800/344-9453, www.fws.gov.

California State Parks

California's 275 beloved state parks, which include beaches, wilderness areas, and historic homes, have recently been going through bad times—the unfortunate result of increasing public use combined with budget cuts. That trend was dramatically reversed in 2000, as Governor Gray Davis decided to share with the state parks—and, indirectly, the public—some of the revenue wealth generated by booming economic times. State park support has increased, park day-use fees cut in half, and camping fees reduced.

Day-use fees for admission to California state parks now range from free (rare) to $2 or $3 per

ROBERT HOLMES/CALTOUR

Anza-Borrego State Park

STATE PARK FEES REDUCED BY HALF

In recent years California's state parks have struggled just to survive, challenged both by budget cuts and relentlessly escalating visitor use. Fee increases—and new types of fees—were adopted as part of the park system's survival strategy.

But suddenly the state's coffers are overflowing, a side effect of economic boom times, and the state park system has a powerful new friend in Sacramento. In May 2000 Governor Gray Davis proposed a radical reduction in most visitor fees now charged at California state parks—a move designed, he announced at a press conference, "to make sure our parks are accessible to all Californians."

As a result of these across-the-board fee cuts, since implemented, day-use and most other state park fees have been reduced by half. Previously, admission and day-use fees at historic sites, museums, and 109 of the state's parks were reduced by 50 percent (cut in half then rounded down to the nearest dollar).

The price of admission to the **California State Railroad Museum** in Sacramento, for example, dropped from the current $6 adults, $3 children to $3 adults, children free (age 16 and under). Day-use fees at most state parks and beaches were $5–6 and have been reduced to $2–3.

Camping fees have also been reduced, primarily by eliminating extra fees previously charged for premium, peak season, and weekend camping reservations. Current camping fees—now $24 per night, on average, all fees considered—will drop to $12 for most people (lower for seniors). Fees for trail camps and "hike and bike" camps, once $3 per person, are now just $1. Fees for state cabin rentals, previously $20–30 per night, are now $10–15.

Fees for most tours offered at California state parks remain the same. One notable exception is **Hearst Castle,** where tour fees were reduced from $14 adults, $8 children to $10 adults, $5 children (age 16 and under).

Annual fees for certain passes—parking and boat passes in particular—have been eliminated, and the Annual Day Use Parking Pass has been cut from $75 to $35. Prices for special state parks passes—the Golden Bear Pass, the Disabled Discount Pass, and the Disabled Veteran/POW Pass—will stay the same.

For more information about the state park system, see California State Parks elsewhere in this chapter or try the website, www.cal-parks.ca.gov. Individual state parks, lakes, and beaches are listed in this book under relevant regional chapters.

---

vehicle, with extra fees charged for dogs (if allowed), extra vehicles, and other circumstances. In highly congested areas, state parks charge no day-use fee but do charge a parking fee—making it more attractive to park elsewhere and walk or take a bus. For information on special assistance available for individuals with disabilities or other special needs, contact individual parks—which make every effort to be accommodating, in most cases.

Annual passes (nontransferable), which you can buy at most state parks and at the State Parks Store in Sacramento (see below), are $35 for day use. Golden Bear passes, for seniors age 62 and older with limited incomes and for certain others who receive public assistance, are $5 per year and allow day-use access to all state parks and off-road vehicle areas except Hearst/San Simeon, Sutter's Fort, and the California State Railroad Museum. For details on income eligibility and other requirements, call 916/653-4000. "Limited

use" Golden Bear passes, for seniors age 62 and older, allow free parking at state parks during the nonpeak park season (usually Labor Day through Memorial Day) and are $20 per year; they can be purchased in person at most state parks. Senior discounts for state park day use ($1 off) and camping ($2 off, but only if the discount is requested while making reservations) are also offered. Special state park discounts and passes are also offered for the disabled and disabled veterans/POWs (prisoners of war). For more information, contact state park headquarters (see below).

Detailed information about California's state parks, beaches, and recreation areas is scattered throughout this guide. To obtain a complete parks listing, including available facilities, campground reservation forms, and other information, contact: **California State Parks,** Public Information, P.O. Box 942896, Sacramento, CA 94296, 916/653-6995 (recorded, with an endless multiple-choice menu), www.cal-parks.ca.gov.

State park publications include the *Official Guide to California State Parks* map and facilities listing, which includes all campgrounds, available free with admission to most state parks but available by mail, at last report, for $2; send check or money order to the attention of the Publications Section. Also available, and free: a complete parks and recreation publications list (which includes a mail order form). Other publications include the annual magazines *Events and Programs at California State Parks,* chock-full of educational and entertaining things to do, and *California Escapes,* a reasonably detailed regional rundown on all state parks.

For information about the state parks' Junior Ranger Program—many parks offer individual programs emphasizing the state's natural and cultural heritage—call individual state parks. For general information, call 916/653-8959. Also available through the state parks department is an annually updated "Sno-Park" guide to parking without penalty while cross-country skiing or otherwise playing in the snow; for a current Sno-Park listing, write in care of the program at the state parks' address listed above or call 916/324-1222 (automated hotline). Sno-Park permits (required) cost $3 per day or $20 for the entire season, Nov. 1–May 30; you can also buy them at REI and other sporting goods stores and at any AAA office in California. Another winter-season resource, free to AAA members, is the annual *Winter Sports Guide* for California, which lists prices and other current information for all downhill and cross-country ski areas.

California state parks offer excellent campgrounds. In addition to developed "family" campsites, which usually include a table, fire ring or outdoor stove, plus running water, flush toilets, and hot showers (RV hookups, if available, are extra), some state campgrounds also offer more primitive "walk-in" or environmental campgrounds and very simple hiker-biker campsites. Group campgrounds are also available (and reservable) at many state parks. If you plan to camp over the Memorial or Labor Day weekends, or the July 4th holiday, be sure to make reservations as early as possible.

Make campground reservations at California state parks (with MasterCard or Visa) through **ReserveAmerica,** www.reserveamerica.com, or call toll-free 800/444-7275 (444-PARK) week-days 8 A.M.–5 P.M. For TDD reservations, call toll-free 800/274-7275 (274-PARK). And to cancel state park campground reservations, from the United States call toll-free 800/695-2269. To make reservations from Canada or elsewhere outside the United States, call 619/638-5883. As in other camping situations, before calling to make reservations, know the park and campground name, how you'll be camping (tent or RV), how many nights, and how many people and vehicles. In addition to the actual camping fee, which can vary from $7 for more primitive campsites (without showers and/or flush toilets) to $8–12 for developed campsites, there is an $8–9 reservations fee. Sites with hookups cost $6 more. You can make camping reservations up to seven months in advance. Certain campsites, including some primitive environmental and hiker/biker sites (now just $1) can be reserved only through the relevant state park.

To support the state's park system, contact the nonprofit **California State Parks Foundation,** 800 College Ave., P.O. Box 548, Kentfield, CA 94914, 415/258-9975, fax 415/258-9930, www.cal-parks.org. Through memberships and contributions, the foundation has financed about $100 million in park preservation and improvement projects in the past several decades. Volunteers are welcome to contribute sweat equity, too.

Other State Recreation Resources

For general information and fishing and hunting regulations, usually also available at sporting goods stores and bait shops where licenses and permits are sold, call the **California Department of Fish and Game** in Sacramento at 916/653-7664; for license information, call 916/227-2244, www.dfg.ca.gov. For additional sportfishing information, call toll-free 800/275-3474 (800/ASK-FISH).

For environmental and recreational netheads, the California Resources Agency's CERES website, a.k.a. the California Environmental Resources Evaluation System at ceres.ca.gov, offers an immense amount of additional information, from reports and updates on rare and endangered species to current boating regulations. The database is composed of federal, state, regional, and local agency information as well as a multitude of data and details from state and national environmental organizations—from REINAS, or the Real-time Environmental Information Network and Analysis System at the University of California at Santa Cruz, The Nature Conservancy, and NASA's Imaging Radar Home Page. Check it out.

Worth it for inveterate wildlife voyeurs is the recently revised *California Wildlife Viewing Guide* (Falcon Press, 1997), produced in conjunction with 15 state, federal, and local agencies in addition to Ducks Unlimited and the Wetlands Action Alliance. About 200 wildlife viewing sites are listed—most of these in Northern California. Look for the *California Wildlife Viewing Guide* at local bookstores, or order a copy by calling toll-free 800/582-2665. With the sale of each book, $1 is contributed to California Watchable Wildlife Project nature tourism programs.

To support California's beleaguered native plantlife, join, volunteer with, and otherwise contribute to the **California Native Plant Society** (CNPS), 1722 J St., Ste. 17, Sacramento, CA 95814, 916/447-2677, fax 916/447-2727, www.cnps.org. In various areas of the state, local CNPS chapters sponsor plant and habitat restoration projects. The organization also publishes some excellent books. Groups including the **Sierra Club, Audubon Society,** and **The Nature Conservancy** also sponsor hikes, backpack trips, bird-watching treks, backcountry excursions, and volunteer "working weekends" in all areas of California; call local or regional contact numbers (in the telephone book) or watch local newspapers for activity announcements.

STAYING—AND EATING— IN THE GOLDEN STATE

Camping Out

Because of many recent years of drought, and painful lessons learned about extreme fire danger near suburban and urban areas, all California national forests, most national parks, and many state parks now ban all backcountry fires—with the exception of controlled burns (under park supervision), increasingly used to thin understory vegetation to prevent uncontrollable wildfires. Some areas even prohibit portable camp stoves, so be sure to check current conditions and all camping and hiking or backpacking regulations before setting out.

ACCOMMODATIONS RATINGS

Accommodations in this book are rated by price category, based on double-occupancy, high-season rates. Categories used are:

Budget.	$35 and under
Inexpensive	$35-60
Moderate	$60-85
Expensive	$85-110
Premium	$110-150
Luxury	$150 and up

To increase your odds of landing a campsite where and when you want one, make reservations (if reservations are accepted). For details on reserving campsites at both national and state parks in California, see relevant listings under Playing Here: Outdoor Recreation, immediately above, and listings for specific parks elsewhere in this book. Without reservations, seek out "low-profile" campgrounds during the peak camping season—summer as well as spring and fall weekends in most parts of California, late fall through early spring in Southern California desert areas—or plan for off-season camping. Some areas also offer undeveloped, environmental, or dispersed "open camping" not requiring reservations; contact relevant jurisdictions above for information and regulations.

Private campgrounds are also available throughout California, some of these included in the current *Campbook for California and Nevada,* available at no charge to members of the American Automobile Association (AAA), which lists (by city or locale) a wide variety of private, state, and federal campgrounds. Far more comprehensive is Tom Stienstra's *California Camping: The Complete Guide* (Foghorn Outdoors), available in most California bookstores. Or contact **California Travel Parks Association,** 530/823-1076, fax 530/823-5883, www.campgrounds.com/ctpa, which features a great online campground directory. Request a complimentary copy of the association's annual *California RV and Campground Guide* from any member campground, or order one by mail—send $4 if you live in the United States, $7 if outside the United States—by writing to: ESG Mail Service, P.O. Box 5578, Auburn, CA 95604.

For a Cheap Stay:
Hostels, YMCAs, YWCAs

Among the best bargains around, for travelers of all ages, are the **Hostelling International-American Youth Hostels** (HI-AYH) scattered throughout California—in major urban areas, at various scenic spots along the coast, and in other appealing locations. Most are listed separately throughout this guide, but the list continually expands (and contracts); the annual HI-AYH *Hostelling North America* guide, available free with membership (or for $6.95 plus tax at most hostels), includes updated listings. Most affiliated hostels offer separate dormitory-style accommodations for men and women (and private couple or family rooms, if available), communal kitchens or low-cost food service, and/or other common facilities. Some provide storage lockers, loaner bikes, even hot tubs. At most hostels, the maximum stay is three nights; most are also closed during the day, which forces hostelers to get out and about and see the sights. Fees are typically $10–16 for HI-AYH members, usually several dollars more for non-members. Since most hostels are quite popular, especially during summer, reservations—usually secured with one night's advance payment—are essential. Contact individual hostels for details (or see listings elsewhere in this book), since reservation requirements vary. Guests are expected to bring sleeping bags, sleep-sacks, or sheets, though sheets or sleepsacks are sometimes available; mattresses, pillows, and blankets are provided.

For membership details and more information about hostelling in the United States and abroad, contact: Hostelling International-American Youth Hostels, 733 15th St. NW, Ste. 840, Washington, DC 20005, 202/783-6161, fax 202/783-6171, www.hiayh.org. For more information on Northern California hostels, contact the **HI-AYH Golden Gate Council,** 425 Divisadero St., Ste. 307, San Francisco, CA 94117, 415/863-1444 or 415/701-1320, fax 415/863-3865, www.norcalhostels.org, and the **HI-AYH Central California Council,** P.O. Box 3645, Merced, CA 95344, 209/383-0686, www.hostelweb.com/centralcalifornia. For details about Southern California hostels, contact the **HI-AYH Los Angeles Council,** 1434 2nd St., Santa Monica, CA 90401, 310/393-6263, fax 310/393-1769, www.hostelweb.com/

losangeles, headquartered at the Santa Monica hostel, and the **HI-AYH San Diego Council,** 437 J St., Ste. 301, San Diego, CA 92101, 619/338-9981, fax 619/525-1533, www.hostelweb.com/sandiego, newly located in downtown's historic Gaslamp Quarter.

You'll find other reputable hostels in California, some independent and some affiliated with other hostel "chains" or umbrella organizations (such as the Banana Bungalow group, now well represented in Southern California). For current comprehensive U.S. listings of these private hostels, contact: **BakPak Travelers Guide,** 670 West End Ave., Ste. 1B, New York, NY 10025, 718/626-1988, fax 718/626-2132, bakpakguide.com, and **Hostel Handbook of the U.S. and Canada,** c/o Jim Williams, 722 St. Nicholas Ave., New York, NY 10031. Copies of both these guides are also usually available at affiliated hostels.

Particularly in urban areas, the **Young Men's Christian Association** (YMCA) often offers housing, showers, and other facilities for young men (over age 18 only in some areas, if unaccompanied by parent or guardian), sometimes also for women and families. **Young Women's Christian Association** (YWCA) institutions offer housing for women only. Life being what it is these days, though, many of these institutions are primarily shelters for the destitute and the homeless; don't steal their beds unless absolutely necessary. For more information, contact: **Y's Way International,** 224 E. 47th St., New York, NY 10017, 212/308-2899 (Mon.–Fri. 9 A.M.–5 P.M. Eastern time), or contact local YMCA outposts. Another low-cost alternative in summer is on-campus housing at state colleges and universities; for current information, contact individual campuses (the student housing office) in areas you'll be visiting.

Modern "Motor Hotels": Motels and Hotels

California, the spiritual home of highway and freeway living, is also the birthplace of the motel, the word a contraction for "motor hotels." Motels have been here longer than anywhere else, so they've had plenty of time to clone themselves. As a general precaution, when checking into a truly cheap motel, ask to see the room before signing in (and paying); some places look much more appealing from the outside than from the inside. Midrange and high-priced motels and hotels are generally okay, however. In addition to the standard California sales tax, many cities and counties—particularly near major tourism destinations—add a "bed tax" of 5–18 percent (or higher). To find out the actual price you'll be paying, ask before making reservations or signing in. Unless otherwise stated, rates listed in this guide do not include state sales tax or local bed taxes.

Predictably reliable on the cheaper end of the accommodations scale, though there can be considerable variation in quality and service from place to place, are a variety of budget chains fairly common throughout California. Particularly popular is **Motel 6,** a perennial budget favorite. To receive a copy of the current motel directory, from the United States and Canada call toll-free 800/466-8356, which is also Motel 6's central reservations service. Alternatively, reserve on the website at www.motel6.com. (To make central reservations from outside the United States, use the website; call 614/601-4060; or reserve by fax at 937/325-4095.) You can also make reservations, by phone or fax, at individual motels, some listed elsewhere in this book. Other inexpensive to moderately priced motels are often found clustered in the general vicinity of Motel 6, these including **Comfort Inn,** toll-free 800/228-5150, www.comfortinn.com; **Days Inn,** toll-free 800/329-7466, www.daysinn.com; **Econo Lodge,** toll-free 800/553-2666, www.econolodge. com; **Rodeway Inn,** toll-free 800/228-2000, www.rodewayinn.com; and **Super 8 Motels,** toll-free 800/800-8000, www.super8.com. You can also pick up a current accommodations directory at any affiliated motel.

You'll find endless other motel and hotel chains in California, most of these more expensive—but not always, given seasonal bargain rates and special discounts offered to seniors, AAA members, and other groups. "Kids stay free," free breakfast for families, and other special promotions can also make more expensive accommodations competitive. Always reliable for quality, but with considerable variation in price and level of luxury, are **Best Western** motel and hotel affiliates, toll-free 800/780-7234 in the United States, www.bestwestern.com. Each is independently owned and managed, and some are listed in this guide. Though there are many upmarket hotels and chains in California—the gold rush is over, but the West's amenities rush is in full swing—the **Four Seasons,** www.fshr.com, and **Ritz-Carlton,** www.ritzcarlton.com, hotel and resort chains top most people's "all-time favorite" lists of luxurious places to stay in California if money is no object.

For members of the American Automobile Association (AAA), the current *Tourbook for California and Nevada* (free) includes an impressive number of rated motels, hotels, and resorts, from inexpensive to top of the line, as well as some recommended restaurants, for nearly every community and city in both Southern and Northern California. Nationwide, AAA members can also benefit from the association's reservations service, toll-free 800/272-2155; with one call, you can also request tour books and attractions information for any destination. Other travel groups or associations offer good deals and useful services, too.

Bargain Room Rates and Bed-and-Breakfasts

Even if you don't belong to a special group or association, you can still benefit from "bulk-buying" power, particularly in large cities—which is a special boon if you're making last-minute plans or are otherwise having little luck on your own. Various room brokers or "consolidators" buy up blocks of rooms from hoteliers at greatly discounted rates and then broker them through their own reservations services. In many cases, brokers still have bargain-priced rooms available—at rates 40–65 percent below standard rack rates—when popular hotels are otherwise sold out. For great hotel deals, try **Hotel Discounts,** toll-free 800/715-7666, www.hoteldiscount.com. Particularly helpful for online reservations is the discounted **USA Hotel Guide,** toll-free 888/729-7705, www.usahotelguide.com. For other bargain hotel prices in San Francisco, Los Angeles, San Diego, and sometimes also Santa Barbara and Palm Springs, contact **Hotel Reservations Network,** toll-free 800/715-7666, www.180096hotel.com, and **Room Exchange,** toll-free 800/846-7000, www.hotelrooms.com. If you're willing to bid for a hotel bargain, try **Revelex,** www.revelex.com.

Another hot trend, particularly in Northern California, is the bed-and-breakfast phenomenon. Many bed-and-breakfast guides and listings are

Bed-and-breakfasts, like the Pacific Grove B&B on the Monterey Peninsula, are a burgeoning phenomenon in California.

ROBERT HOLMES/CALTOUR

available in bookstores, and some recommended B&Bs are listed in this book. Unlike the European tradition, with bed-and-breakfasts a low-cost yet comfortable lodging alternative, in California these inns are actually a burgeoning small-business phenomenon—usually quite pricey, in the $100–150+ range (occasionally less expensive), often more of a "special weekend getaway" for exhausted city people than a mainstream accommodations option. In some areas, though, where motel and hotel rooms are on the high end, bed-and-breakfasts can be quite competitive.

For more information on what's available in all parts of California, including private home stays, contact **Bed and Breakfast California,** P.O. Box 282910, San Francisco, CA 94128, 650/696-1690 or toll-free 800/872-4500, fax 650/696-1699, www.bbintl.com, affiliated with Bed and Breakfast International, the longest-running bed-and-breakfast reservation service in the United States. Or contact the **California Association of Bed and Breakfast Inns,** 2715 Porter St., Soquel, CA 95073, 831/462-9191, fax 831/462-0402, www.cabbi.com.

The Land of Fruits and Nuts and California Cuisine

One of the best things about traveling in California is the food: they don't call the Golden State the land of fruits and nuts for nothing. In agricultural and rural areas, local "farm trails" or winery guides are often available—ask at local chambers of commerce and visitor centers—and following the seasonal produce trails offers visitors the unique pleasure of gathering (sometimes picking their own) fresh fruits, nuts, and vegetables direct from the growers.

This fresher, direct-to-you produce phenomenon is also quite common in most urban areas, where regular farmers' markets are *the* place to go for fresh, organic, often exotic local produce and farm products. Many of the most popular California farmers' markets are listed elsewhere in this book—but ask around wherever you are, since new ones pop up constantly. For a reasonably comprehensive current listing of California Certified Farmers' Markets (meaning certified as locally grown), contact: **California Federation of Certified Farmers' Markets,** P.O. Box 1813, Davis, CA 95617, 707/753-9999, fax 707/756-1853, farmersmarket.ucdavis.edu.

Threaded with freeways and accessible on-ramp, off-ramp commercial strips, particularly in urban areas, California has more than its fair share of fast-food eateries and all-night quick-stop outlets. (Since they're so easy to find, few are listed in this guide.) Most cities and communities also have locally popular cafés and fairly inexpensive restaurants worth seeking out; many are listed here, but also ask around. Genuinely inexpensive eateries often refuse to take credit cards, so always bring some cash along just in case.

The northstate is also famous for its "California cuisine," which once typically meant consuming tastebud-tantalizing, very expensive food in very small portions—almost a cliché—while oohing and aahing over the presentation throughout the meal. But the fiscally frugal early 1990s restrained most of California's excesses, and even the best restaurants offer less-pretentious menus and slimmed-down prices.

THE CALIFORNIA CUISINE SCENE

Some people assume California cuisine is expensive, exotic, and odd—or worse, as if the very combination of these two words could only produce a dining experience too far out there to be taken seriously. Yet culinary creations categorized as "California cuisine" aren't necessarily expensive or odd. The phrase simply refers to the most notable new trend in conscious, and health-conscious, eating, a phenomenon quite popular in every corner of California.

The basic requirement of California cuisine is that all ingredients be as fresh and natural as possible—including salad greens, other vegetables, herbs, dairy products, meat, fish, and seafood. Naturally enough, this emphasis on food freshness and quality has spawned a substantial and profitable agricultural sub-genre in an era otherwise dominated by corporate farms and ranches: the small specialty grower, whether that specialty be raspberries, organic grains, or beef. Not to mention the related phenomenon of certified farmers' markets—"certified" referring to foods and other products guaranteed to be grown by those who are selling them, though organic produce is also available—which are now found almost everywhere in the Golden State.

Beyond freshness, California cuisine encompasses any and all influences—French, Italian, Asian, Mexican, South American, regional American, and more. The unassuming epicenter of California's culinary earthquake was in Northern California—at **Chez Panisse** in Berkeley, innovator Alice Waters's original restaurant—though Wolfgang Puck's original **Spago** helped establish the Southern California standard. It's now possible to find "California cuisine" in all parts of the state—and in many other states as well.

There's another school of thought about "California cuisine," of course, which suggests that the fancy-restaurant routine is a decades-long joke on the world, some conspiracy largely launched by unemployed European chefs. *Real* California cuisine—surf 'n' turf, humongous hamburgers, date milkshakes, bean sprouts and brown rice, Mexican, Asian, and soul-food takeout—is served forth from beach shacks and mom-and-pop shops everywhere. Always has been, always will be. We Californians were just kidding about the rest.

The region's culinary creativity is quite real, and worth pursuing (sans pretense) in many areas. Talented chefs, who have migrated throughout the region from Los Angeles and San Francisco as well as from France and Italy, usually prefer locally grown produce, dairy products, meats, and herbs and spices as basic ingredients. To really "do" the cuisine scene, wash it all down with some fine California wine.

OTHER DETAILS

Visas for Foreign Visitors

A foreign visitor to the United States is required to carry a current passport and a visitor's visa plus proof of intent to leave (usually a return airplane ticket is adequate; find passport information on the Web at travel.state.gov). Also, it's wise to carry proof of one's citizenship, such as a driver's license and/or birth certificate. To be on the safe side, photocopy your legal documents and carry the photocopies separately from the originals. To obtain a U.S. visa (most visitors qualify for a B-2 or "pleasure tourist" visa, valid for up to six months), contact the nearest U.S. embassy or consulate. Should you lose the Form I-94 (proof of arrival/departure) attached to your visa, contact the nearest local U.S. **Immigration and Naturalization Service** (INS) office. Contact the INS also for a visa extension (good for a maximum of six months). To work or study in the United States, special visas are required; contact the nearest U.S. embassy or consulate for current information. To replace a passport lost while in the United States, contact the nearest embassy for your country. Canadian citizens entering the United States from Canada or Mexico do not need either a passport or visa, nor do Mexican citizens possessing a Form I-186. (Canadians under age 18 do need to carry written consent from a parent or guardian.)

Time

California, within the Pacific time zone (two hours behind Chicago, three hours behind New York) is on daylight saving time (a helps-with-harvest agricultural holdover), which means clocks are set ahead one hour from the first Sunday in April until the last Sunday in October. Without this seasonal time adjustment, when it's noon in California, it's 10 A.M. in Hawaii, 8 P.M. in London, midnight in Moscow, and 4 A.M. (the next day) in Hong Kong.

Business Hours, Banking, Money

Standard business hours in California (holidays excepted) are Mon.–Fri. 9 A.M.–5 P.M., though many businesses open at 8 A.M. or 10 A.M. and/or stay open until 6 P.M. or later. Traditional banking hours—10 A.M. until 3 P.M.—are not necessarily the rule in California these days. Particularly in cities, banks may open at 9 A.M. and stay open until 5 or 6 P.M., and may offer extended walk-up or drive-up window hours. Many banks and savings and loans also offer Saturday hours (usually 9 A.M.–1 P.M.) as well as 24-hour automated teller machine (ATM) service; you'll even find ATMs at most theme parks and, increasingly, inside most grocery stores. Before traveling in California, contact your bank for a list of California branches or affiliated institutions.

For the most part, traveling in California is expensive. Depending on your plans, figure out how much money you'll need—then bring more. Most banks will not cash checks (or issue cash via ATMs) for anyone without an account (or an account with some affiliated institution). Major cred it cards (especially Visa and MasterCard) are almost universally accepted in California, except at inexpensive motels and restaurants. Credit cards have become a travel essential, since they are often mandatory for buying airline tickets, renting cars, or as a "security deposit" on bicycle, outdoor equipment, and other rentals. The safest way to bring cash is by carrying traveler's checks. American Express traveler's checks are the most widely recognized and accepted.

Domestic (U.S.) travelers who run short of money, and who are without credit lines on their credit cards, can ask family or friends to send a postal money order (buyable and cashable at any U.S. Postal Service post office); ask your bank to wire money to an affiliated California bank (probably for a slight fee); or have money wired office-to-office via Western Union, toll-free 800/325-6000 (800/225-5227 for credit-card money transfers; 800/325-4045 for assistance in Spanish). Use the local phone book to find Western Union offices. In each case, the surcharge depends upon the amount sent.

International travelers should avoid the necessity of wiring for money if at all possible. With a Visa, MasterCard, or American Express card, cash advances are easily available; get details about affiliated U.S. banks before leaving home, however. If you must arrange for cash to be sent from home, a cable transfer from your bank (check on corresponding California banks before leaving), a Western Union money wire, or a bank draft or international money order are all possible. Make sure you (and your sender) know the accurate address for the recipient bank, to avoid obvious nightmarish complications. In a pinch,

Vineyards provide one celebrated component of the California dining experience.

ROBERT HOLMES/CALTOUR

consulates may intervene and request money from home (or your home bank) at your request—deducting their cost from funds received.

Measurements, Mail, Communications

Despite persistent efforts to wean Americans from the old ways, California and the rest of the union still abide by the British system of weights and measures (see measurements chart in the back of this book). Electrical outlets in California (and the rest of the United States) carry current at 117 volts, 60 cycles (Hertz) A.C.; foreign electrical appliances require a converter and plug adapter.

Even without a full-fledged post office, most outback California communities have at least some official outpost of the U.S. Postal Service, usually open weekdays 8 A.M.–5 P.M., for sending letters and packages and for receiving general delivery mail. At last report, basic postal rates within the United States, which may soon increase, were $.20 for postcards, $.34 for letter mail (the first ounce). Rates for international mail from the United States were $.50 cents for postcards, $.60 cents for letters (the first half-ounce), except to Canada and Mexico. The postal code for any address in California is CA. For mail sent and received within the United States, knowing and using the relevant five- or nine-digit zip code is important. Mail can be directed to any particular post office c/o "General Delivery," but the correct address and zip code for the post office receiving such mail is important—especially in cities, where there are multiple post offices. (For zip codes and associated post office information, refer to the local phone book, call toll-free 800/332-9631, or go to www.usps.com.) To claim general delivery mail, current photo identification is required; unclaimed mail will be returned to the sender after languishing for two to four weeks. At larger post offices, **International Express Mail** is available, with delivery to major world cities in 48–72 hours.

Telephone communication is easy in California (always carry change in your pocket in case you need to make an emergency call). Local calls are often free (or inexpensive) from many motel and hotel rooms, but long-distance calls will cost you. Some hotels add a per-call surcharge even to direct-dialed or credit card calls, due and payable when you check out. And the anything-goes aspect of deregulation has also re-sulted in a spate of for-profit "telephone companies" that generate most of their income through exorbitant rates charged through the hotels, motels, and miscellaneous pay telephones they serve. Using your own long distance carrier (usually with a personal phone card) is typically a better deal. If in doubt about what long-distance services are available on a given phone system, what rates they charge, and whether a hotel or motel surcharge will be added to your bill, ask *before* making your phone call(s). Collect and person-to-person operator-assisted calls are usually more expensive than direct-dial and telephone company (such as AT&T or Sprint) credit-card calls, but in some cases they could save you a bundle.

Telephone communication in California has been further complicated, almost overnight, by a mushrooming number of area codes, those three-digit parenthetical regional prefixes preceding seven-digit local telephone numbers. This chaotic change in California, as elsewhere, is directly related to the proliferating numbers of people, phones, fax machines, pagers, and online computer connections. Between about 1990 and 2000, every telephone area code in California has "split" (usually into two, the previous code plus a new one) at least once, and some more than once. This book has made every effort to keep up with area code changes, and has noted upcoming changes that were known at the time of publication. But during the useful life of this guide, it's likely that a few new area codes will present themselves nonetheless, or that area codes and/or phone numbers associated with areas outside this book's immediate scope will change. So—when in doubt, call the local operator and check it out.

IN THE KNOW: SERVICES AND INFORMATION

Basic Services

Except for some very lonely areas, even backwater areas of California aren't particularly primitive. Gasoline, at least basic groceries, laundries of some sort, even video rentals are available just about anywhere. Outback areas are not likely to have parts for exotic sports cars, however, or 24-hour pharmacies, hospitals, and garages, or natural foods stores or full-service supermarkets, so you should take care of any special needs or problems before leaving the cities. It's often cheaper, too, to stock up on most supplies, including outdoor equipment and groceries, in urban areas.

General Information

Visitors can receive free California travel-planning information by writing the **California Division of Tourism,** P.O. Box 1499, Dept. 61, Sacramento, CA 95812-1499, or by calling toll-free 800/462-2543, ext. 61. Or try the Internet site, www.visitcalifornia.com, which also includes an accommodations reservation service. California's tourism office publishes a veritable gold rush of useful travel information, including the annual *California Official State Visitors Guide* and *California Celebrations.* Particularly useful for outdoor enthusiasts is the new 16-page *California Outdoor Recreation* guide. The quarterly *California Travel Ideas* magazine is distributed free at agricultural inspection stations at the state's borders. For travel industry professionals, the *California Travel and Incentive Planner's Guide* is also available.

Most of these California tourism publications, in addition to regional and local publications, are also available at the various roadside volunteer-staffed **California Welcome Centers,** a burgeoning trend. The first official welcome center was unveiled in 1995 in Kingsburg, in the San Joaquin Valley, and the next four—in Rohnert Park, just south of Santa Rosa; in Anderson, just south of Redding; in Oakhurst in the gold country, on the way to Yosemite National Park; and at Pier 39 on San Francisco's Fisherman's Wharf—were also in Northern California. There are others in Northern California, too, including the fairly new one in Arcata, and several in Southern California. Eventually the network will include virtually all areas of California; watch for signs announcing new welcome centers along major highways and freeways.

Most major cities and visitor destinations in California also have very good visitor information bureaus and visitor centers, listed elsewhere in this book. Many offer accommodations reservations and other services; some offer information and maps in foreign languages. Chambers of commerce can be useful, too. In less populated areas, chambers of commerce are something of a hit-or-miss proposition, since office hours may be minimal; the best bet is calling ahead for information. Asking locals—people at gas stations, cafés, grocery stores, and official government outposts—is often the best way to get information about where to go, why, when, and how. Slick city magazines, good daily newspapers, and California-style weekly news and entertainment tabloids are other good sources of information.

Special Information for the Disabled

Twin Peaks Press, P.O. Box 129, Vancouver, WA 98666, 360/694-2462, or toll-free 800/637-

---

BEING HERE: RIGHT ATTITUDE

Whenever you arrive and wherever you go, one thing to bring along is the right attitude—bad attitude, strangely enough, being a particular problem among American travelers (including Californians) visiting California. One reason visitors become annoyed and obnoxious is because, often without realizing it, they started their trip with high, sometimes fantasy-based expectations—akin, perhaps, to being magically cured of all limitations at a Lourdes-like way station along life's freeway—and, once arrived in California, reality disappoints. Even the Golden State has traffic jams, parking problems, rude service people, and lowlifes only too happy to make off with a good time by stealing one's pocketbook—or car. Be prepared.

Visitors also bring along no-fun baggage when they go to new places and compare whatever they find with what they left behind "back home." This is disrespectful. The surest way to enjoy California is to remain open-minded about whatever you may see, hear, do, or otherwise experience. It's fine to laugh (to one's self) at California's contradictions and cultural self-consciousness—even Californians do it—but try to view new places, from sophisticated San Francisco to the most isolated and economically depressed backwater, from the perspective of the people who live and work there. Better yet, strike up conversations with locals and ask questions whenever possible. These experiences invariably become the best surprises of all—because people, places, and things in California are often not quite what they first appear to be.

2256 for orders only, publishes particularly helpful books, including *Wheelchair Vagabond, Travel for the Disabled,* and *Directory of Travel Agencies for the Disabled.* Also useful is the *Travelin' Talk Directory* put out by **Travelin' Talk,** P.O. Box 3534, Clarksville, TN 37043, 615/552-6670, a network of disabled people available "to help travelers in any way they can." Membership is only $10, a bargain by any standard, since by joining up you suddenly have a vast network of allies in otherwise strange places who are all too happy to tell you what's what. Also helpful: **Mobility International USA,** P.O. Box 10767, Eugene, OR 97440, tel. and TDD 541/343-1284, fax 541/343-6812, www.miusa.org, which provides two-way international leadership exchanges. Disabled people who want to go to Europe to study theater, for example, or British citizens who want to come to California for Elderhostel programs—anything beyond traditional leisure travel—should call here first. The individual annual membership fee is $25 for individuals, $35 for organizations.

Special Information for Seniors

Senior adults can benefit from a great many bargains and discounts. A good source of information is the *Travel Tips for Older Americans* pamphlet published by the U.S. Government Printing Office, 202/275-3648, www.gpo.gov, available for $1.25. (Order it online at www.pueblo.gsa.gov/travel.) The federal government's Golden Age Passport offers free admission to national parks and monuments and half-price discounts for federal campsites and other recreational services; state parks also offer senior discounts. (For detailed information, see appropriate recreation listings under Playing Here: Outdoor Recreation, above.) Discounts are also frequently offered to seniors at major tourist attractions and sights as well as for many arts, cultural, and entertainment destinations and events in Southern California. Another benefit of experience is eligibility for the international **Elderhostel** program, 75 Federal St., Boston, MA 02110, 617/426-7788 or toll-free 877/426-8056, www.elderhostel.org, which offers a variety of fairly reasonable one-week residential programs in California.

For information on travel discounts, trip planning, tours, and other membership benefits of the United States' largest senior citizen organization, contact the **American Association of Retired Persons** (AARP), 601 E St. NW, Washington, DC 20049, 202/434-2277 or toll-free 800/227-7737, www.aarp.org. Despite the name, anyone age 50 and older—retired or not—is eligible for membership. Other membership-benefit programs for seniors include the **National Council of Senior Citizens,** 8403 Colesville Rd., Ste. 1200, Silver Springs, MD 20910, 301/578-8800, fax 301/578-8999, www.ncscinc.org.

Not Getting Lost: Good Maps

The best all-around maps for California, either in the city or out in the countryside, are those produced by the **American Automobile Association,** which is regionally organized as the California State Automobile Association (CSAA) in Northern and Central California, and as the Automobile Club of Southern California in the southstate. The AAA maps are available at any local AAA office, and the price is right (free, but for members only). In addition to its California state map and Southern California map, AAA provides urban maps for most major cities, plus regional maps with at least some backcountry routes marked (these latter maps don't necessarily show the entire picture, however; when in doubt about unusual routes, ask locally before setting out). For more information about AAA membership and services in Northern California, contact the **California State Automobile Association;** the main office address is 150 Van Ness Ave., P.O. Box 1860, San Francisco, CA 94101-1860, 415/565-2012 or 415/565-2468, www.csaa.org, but there are also regional offices throughout the northstate. Members can also order maps, tour books, and other services online. If you'll also be visiting Southern California, the AAA affiliate there is the **Automobile Club of Southern California,** 2601 S. Figueroa St., Los Angeles, CA 90007, 213/741-3686, www.aaa-calif.com. For AAA membership information, from anywhere in the United States call toll-free 800/222-4357, or try www.aaa.com.

The best maps money can buy, excellent for general and very detailed travel in California, are the **Thomas Bros. Maps,** typically referred to as "Thomas guides." For the big picture, particularly useful is the *California Road Atlas & Driver's Guide,* but various other, very detailed spiral-bound book-style maps in the Thomas guide street atlas series—San Francisco, Monterey County, Los Angeles, Orange County, San Diego—are the standard block-by-block references, continually updated since 1915. Thomas guides are available at any decent travel-oriented bookstore, or contact the company directly. In Southern California, you'll find a major Thomas Bros. Maps store at 603 W. 7th St., Los Angeles, CA 90017, 213/627-4018; the map factory and another store is in Orange County, at 17731 Cowan in Irvine, 949/863-1984, fax 949/852-9189. In Northern California, stop by Thomas Bros. Maps, 550 Jackson St., San Francisco, CA 94133, 415/981-7520. Or order any map by calling, from anywhere in California, toll-free 800/899-6277— or by trying, from anywhere in the world, www.thomas.com.

When it comes to backcountry travel—where maps quickly become either your best friend or archenemy—the going isn't nearly as easy. U.S. Geological Survey quadrangle maps in most cases are reliable for showing the contours of the terrain, but U.S. Forest Service and wilderness maps—supposedly the maps of record for finding one's way through the woods and the wilds—are often woefully out of date, with new and old logging roads (as well as disappearing or changed trail routes) confusing the situation considerably. In California, losing oneself in the wilderness is a very real, literal possibility. In addition to topo maps (carry a compass to orient yourself by landforms if all else fails) and official U.S. maps, backcountry travelers would be wise to invest in privately published guidebooks and current route or trail guides for wilderness areas; the Sierra Club and Wilderness Press publish both. Before setting out, compare all available maps and other information to spot any possible route discrepancies, then ask national forest or parks personnel for clarification. If you're lucky, you'll find someone who knows what's going on where you want to go.

Aside from well-stocked outdoor stores, the primary California source for quad maps is: **U.S. Geological Survey,** 345 Middlefield Rd., Menlo Park, CA 94025, 650/853-8300 (ask for the mapping division); an index and catalog of published California maps is available upon request. Or try the USGS website, info.er.usgs.gov, or call toll-free 888/275-8747. Also contact the U.S. Forest Service and U.S. National Park Service

(see Playing Here: Outdoor Recreation, above). The best bet for wilderness maps and guides is **Wilderness Press,** 1200 5th St., Berkeley, CA 94710, 510/558-1666 or toll-free 800/443-7227 (for orders), fax 510/558-1696, www.wildernesspress.com. Most Wilderness Press titles are available in California bookstores.

Not necessarily practical for travelers are the beautiful yet utilitarian maps produced by **Raven Maps & Images,** 34 N. Central, P.O. Box 850, Medford, OR 97501, 541/773-1436, or (for credit-card orders) toll-free 800/237-0798, www. ravenmaps.com. These beauties are big, and—unless you buy one for the wall and one for the road—you'll never want to fold them. Based on U.S. Geological Survey maps, these shaded relief maps are "computer-enhanced" for a three-dimensional topographical feel and incredible clarity—perfect for planning outdoor adventures. Raven's *California* map measures 42 by 64 inches, and *Yosemite and the Central Sierra* is 34 by 37 inches. Wonderful for any California-lover's wall is the three-dimensional, five-color *California, Nevada, and the Pacific Ocean Floor* digital landform map, which offers three aerial oblique views: now, five million years ago, and five million years in the future. Fabulous. All Raven maps are printed in fade-resistant inks on fine quality 70-pound paper and are also available in vinyl laminated versions suitable for framing.

SURVIVING: HEALTH AND SAFETY

Emergencies, Medical Care, and General Health

In most places in California, call 911 in any emergency; in medical emergencies, life support personnel and ambulances will be dispatched. To make sure health care services will be readily provided, health insurance coverage is almost mandatory; carry proof of coverage while traveling in California. In urban areas and in many rural areas, 24-hour walk-in health care services are readily available, though hospital emergency rooms are the place to go in case of life-threatening circumstances.

To avoid most health and medical problems, use common sense. Eat sensibly, avoid unsafe drinking water, bring along any necessary prescription pills—and pack an extra pair of glasses or contacts, just in case. Sunglasses, especially for those unaccustomed to sunshine, as well as sunscreen and a broad-brimmed hat can help prevent sunburn, sunstroke, and heat prostration. Drink plenty of liquids, too, especially when exercising and/or in hot weather.

No vaccinations are usually necessary for traveling in California, though here as elsewhere very young children and seniors should obtain vaccinations against annually variable forms of the flu virus; exposure, especially in crowded urban areas and during the winter disease season, is a likelihood.

As in other areas of the United States and the world, the AIDS (Acquired Immune Deficiency Syndrome) virus and other sexually transmitted diseases are a concern. In mythic "anything goes" California, avoiding promiscuous or unprotected sex is the best way to avoid the danger of contracting the AIDS virus and venereal disease—though AIDS is also transmitted via shared drug needles and contaminated blood transfusions. (All medical blood supplies in California are screened for evidence of the virus.) Sexually speaking, "safe sex" is the preventive key phrase, under any circumstances beyond the strictly monogamous. This means always using condoms in sexual intercourse; oral sex only with some sort of barrier precaution; and no sharing sex toys.

City Safety

Though California's wilderness once posed a major threat to human survival, in most respects the backcountry is safer than the urban jungle of modern cities. Tourism officials don't talk about it much, but crimes against persons and property are a reality in California (though the state's overall crime rate has dropped sharply in recent years). To avoid harm, bring along your street-smarts. The best overall personal crime prevention includes carrying only small amounts of cash (inconspicuously, in a money belt or against-the-body money pouch); labeling (and locking) all luggage; keeping valuables under lock and key (and, in automobiles, out of sight); being aware of people and events, and knowing where you are, at all times; and avoiding dangerous, lonely, and unlighted areas after daylight, particularly late at night and when traveling alone. If you're not sure what neighborhoods are considered dangerous or

unsafe, ask locals or hotel or motel personnel—or at the police station, if necessary.

Women traveling alone—not generally advisable, because of the unfortunate fact of misogyny in the modern world—need to take special care to avoid harm. For any independent traveler, self-defense classes (and/or a training course for carrying and using Mace) might be a worthwhile investment, if only to increase one's sense of personal power in case of a confrontation with criminals. Being assertive and confident, and acting as if you know where you are going (even when you don't), are also among the best deterrents to predators. Carry enough money for a phone call—or bus or taxi ride—and a whistle. When in doubt, don't hesitate to use it, and to yell and scream for help.

General Outdoor Safety

The most basic rule is, know what you're doing and where you're going. Next most basic: whatever you do—from swimming or surfing to hiking and backpacking—don't do it alone. For any outdoor activity, be prepared. Check with local park or national forest service officials on weather, trail, and general conditions before setting out. Correct, properly functioning equipment is as important in backpacking as it is in hang gliding, mountain climbing, mountain biking, and sailing. (When in doubt, check it out.)

Among the basics to bring along for almost any outdoor activity: a hat, sunscreen, and lip balm (to protect against the sun in summer, against heat loss, reflective sun, and the elements in winter); a whistle, compass, and mylar "space blanket" in case you become lost or stranded; insect repellent; a butane lighter or waterproof matches; a multipurpose Swiss Army–type knife; nylon rope; a flashlight; and a basic first-aid kit (including bandages, ointments and salves, antiseptics, pain relievers such as aspirin, and any necessary prescription medicines). Hikers, backpackers, and other outdoor adventurers should bring plenty of water (or water purification tablets or pump-style water purifiers for long trips), at least minimal fishing gear, good hiking shoes or boots, extra socks and shoelaces, "layerable" clothing adequate for all temperatures, and a waterproof poncho or large plastic garbage bag. (Even if thunderstorms are unlikely, any sort of packable and wearable plastic bag can keep you dry until you reach shelter.) The necessity for other outdoor equipment, from camp stoves to sleeping bags and tents, depends on where you'll be going and what you'll be doing.

Poison Oak

Poison oak (actually a shrublike sumac) is a perennial trailside hazard, especially in lowland foothill areas and mixed forests; it exudes oily chemicals that cause a strong allergic reaction in many people, even with only brief contact. (Always be careful what you're burning around the campfire, too; smoke from poison oak, when inhaled, can inflame the lungs and create a life-threatening situation in no time flat.) The best way to avoid the painful, itchy, often long-lasting rashes associated with poison oak is to avoid contact with the plant—in all seasons—and to immediately wash one's skin or clothes if you even suspect a brush with it. (Its leaves a bright, glossy green in spring and summer, red or yellow in fall, poison oak can be a problem even in winter—when this mean-spirited deciduous shrub loses its leaves.) Learn to identify it during any time of year.

Once afflicted with poison oak, never scratch, because the oozing sores just spread the rash. Very good new products on the market include Tecnu's **Poison Oak-n-Ivy Armor** "pre-exposure lotion," produced by Tec Laboratories, Inc., of Albany, Oregon, toll-free 800/482-4464 (800/ITCHING). Apply it before potential exposure to protect yourself. Another excellent product, quite helpful if you do tangle with poison oak, is Tecnu's **Poison Oak-n-Ivy Cleanser,** the idea being to get the toxic oils off your skin as soon as possible, within hours of initial exposure or just after the rash appears. The cleanser—which smells suspiciously like kerosene—also helps eliminate the itching remarkably well. (But do *not* apply after oozing begins.) Various drying, cortisone-based lotions, oatmeal baths, and other treatments can help control discomfort if the rash progresses to the oozing stage, but the rash itself goes away only in its own good time.

Lyme Disease and Ticks

Even if you favor shorts for summer hiking, you had better plan on long pants, long-sleeved shirts, even insect repellent. The weather may be mild, but there's an increasing risk—particularly in California coastal and foothill areas, as in other states—that you'll contract Lyme disease, transmitted by ticks that thrive in moist lowland climates.

A new ailment on the West Coast, Lyme disease is named after the place of its 1975 discovery in Old Lyme, Connecticut. Already the most common vector-transmitted disease in the nation, Lyme is caused by spirochetes transmitted through blood, urine, and other body fluids. Research indicates it has often been wrongly diagnosed; sufferers were thought to have afflictions such as rheumatoid arthritis. Temporary paralysis, arthritic pains in the hands or arm and leg joints, swollen hands, fever, fatigue, nausea, headaches, swollen glands, and heart palpitations are among the typical symptoms. Sometimes an unusually circular red rash appears first, between three and 30 days after the tick bite. Untreated, Lyme disease can mean a lifetime of suffering, even danger to unborn children. Treatment, once Lyme disease is discovered through blood tests, is simple and 100 percent effective if recognized early: tetracycline and other drugs halt the arthritic degeneration and most symptoms. Long-delayed treatment, even with extremely high doses of antibiotics, is only about 50 percent effective.

Outdoor prudence, coupled with an awareness of possible Lyme symptoms even months later, are the watchwords when it comes to Lyme disease. Take precautions against tick bite: the sooner ticks are found and removed, the better your chances of avoiding the disease. Tuck your pants into your boots, wear long-sleeved shirts, and use insect repellent around all clothing openings as well as on your neck and all exposed skin. Run a full-body "tick check" daily, especially checking hidden areas such as the hair and

poison oak

scalp. Consider leaving dogs at home if heading for Lyme country; ticks they pick up can spread the disease through your human family.

Use gloves and tweezers to remove ticks from yourself or your animals—never crush the critters with your fingers!—and wash your hands and the bitten area afterward. Better yet, smother imbedded ticks with petroleum jelly first; deprived of oxygen, they start to pull out of the skin in about a half hour, making it easy to pluck them off without tearing them in two and leaving the head imbedded.

GETTING HERE, GETTING AROUND

By Bicycle
Many parts of California are not much fun for cyclists. Let's face it: cities are car country. Cycling on public roadways here usually means frightening car traffic; brightly colored bicycle clothing and accessories, reflective tape, good lights, and other safety precautions are mandatory. And always wear a helmet. Only the brave would pick this part of the world—or at least the urban part of this world—for bicycle touring, though some do, most wisely with help from books such as *Bicycling the Pacific Coast* (The Mountaineers) by Tom Kirkendall and Vicky Spring. Yet there are less congested areas, and good local bike paths here and there, for more timid recreational bikers; rental bike shops abound, particularly in beach areas. For those who hanker after a little two-

wheel back-roads sightseeing, many areas along the central and north coasts, throughout the Sonoma and Napa County "wine countries," and in the Sierra Nevada foothills, are still sublime. Southern California has bicycling possibilities, too, including paved beachfront bike paths and reasonably untraveled backcountry routes.

Various good regional cycling guides are available, though serious local bike shops—those frequented by cycling enthusiasts, not just sales outlets—and bike clubs are probably the best local information sources for local and regional rides as well as special cycling events. For upcoming events, other germane information, and referrals on good publications, contact: **California Association of Bicycling Organizations** (CABO), P.O. Box 26864, Dublin, CA 94568. The **Adventure Cycling Association,** P.O. Box 8308, Missoula, MT 59807, 406/721-1776 or toll-free 800/755-2453, fax 406/721-8754, www.adv-cycling.org, is a nonprofit national organization that researches long-distance bike routes and organizes tours for members. Its maps, guidebooks, route suggestions, and *Cyclist's Yellow Pages* can be helpful. For mountain biking information via the Internet, also try the **International Mountain Bicycling Association** at www.greatoutdoors.com/imba.

By Bus
Most destinations in California are reachable by bus, either by major carrier, by "alternative" carrier, or in various combinations of long-distance and

Monterey Bike Trail

ROBERT HOLMES/CalTour

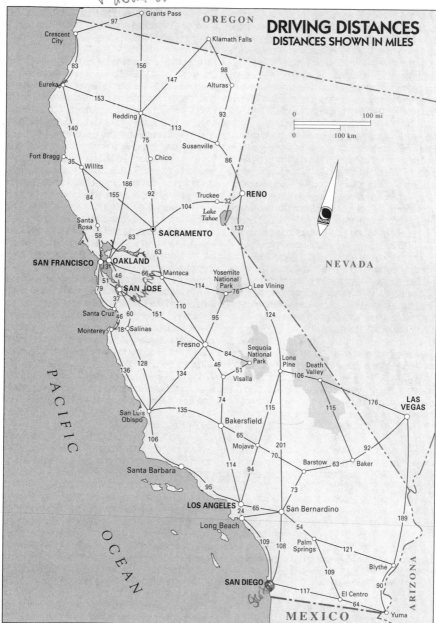

DRIVING DISTANCES
DISTANCES SHOWN IN MILES

OREGON

NEVADA

PACIFIC OCEAN

MEXICO

ARIZONA

Grants Pass
Crescent City
Eureka
Fort Bragg
Willits
Santa Rosa
SAN FRANCISCO
OAKLAND
SAN JOSE
Santa Cruz
Monterey — Salinas
San Luis Obispo
Santa Barbara
LOS ANGELES
Long Beach
SAN DIEGO

Klamath Falls
Alturas
Redding
Chico
Susanville
RENO
Truckee
Lake Tahoe
SACRAMENTO
Manteca
Yosemite National Park
Lee Vining
Fresno
Sequoia National Park
Visalia
Lone Pine
Death Valley
Bakersfield
Mojave
Barstow — Baker
San Bernardino
Palm Springs
El Centro
Yuma
Blythe

LAS VEGAS

97
156
147
98
83
140
153
35
84
155
186
92
75
113
93
86
58
83
63
104
32
137
46
51
79
37
66
114
76
124
110
95
60
151
18
46
84
136
128
134
46
51
74
135
106
65
201
115
70
94
114
73
54
109
108
121
109
117
64
90
189
176
92
63
24
65

© AVALON TRAVEL PUBLISHING, INC.

0   100 mi
0   100 km

local bus lines. And if you can't get *exactly* where you want to go by bus, you can usually get close. **Greyhound** is the universal bus service. Obtain a current U.S. route map (see contact information below), but check with local Greyhound offices for more detailed local route information and for information about "casino service" to Reno and other local specials. Greyhound offers discounts for senior adults and disabled travelers, and children under age 12 ride free when accompanied by a fare-paying adult (one child per adult, half fare for additional children). The **Ameripass** offers unlimited travel with on-off stops for various periods of time, but it is usually more economical for long-distance trips with few stopovers. International travelers should inquire about the **International Ameripass.** For more information, in the United States contact Greyhound Bus Lines, Inc., at toll-free 800/232-2222, www.greyhound.com.

Then there are alternative bus options, most notably **Green Tortoise,** the hippest trip on wheels for budget travelers, combining long-distance travel with communal sightseeing. Sign on for a westbound cross-country tour to get to California, an eastbound trip to get away—seeing some of the most spectacular sights in the United States along the languid, looping way. As the motto emblazoned on the back of the bus says: "Arrive inspired, not dog tired." Unlike your typical bus ride, on Green Tortoise trips you bring your sleeping bag—the buses are converted sleeping coaches, and the booths and couches convert into beds come nightfall. And you won't need to stop for meals, since healthy gourmet fare (at a cost of about $10 a day) is usually included in the freight; sometimes the food charge is optional, meaning you can bring your own. But Green Tortoise also offers a weekly three-day **California Coast Tour,** with departures from both Los Angeles and San Francisco, making it easy—and fairly entertaining—to get from one end of the state to the other. From San Francisco, you can also get to Southern California on the Green Tortoise **Death Valley National Park** tour; dropoffs can be arranged in either Bakersfield or Mojave, and Greyhound can get you to Los Angeles. For more information, contact: Green Tortoise Adventure Travel, 494 Broadway, San Francisco, CA 94133, 415/956-7500 or, from anywhere in the United States and Canada, toll-free 800/867-8647, www.greentortoise.com.

By Train

An unusually enjoyable way to travel the length of the West Coast to California, or to arrive here after a trip west over the Sierra Nevada or across the great desert, is by train. Within Northern California, travel along the coast on Amtrak's immensely popular and recently spiffed up **Coast Starlight,** which now features more comfortable tilt-back seats, a parlor car with library and games, and California-style fare in its dining cars. (From the south, the two-way route continues north to Oakland, across the bay from San Francisco, and eventually continues all the way to Seattle.) If you'll eventually arrive in Southern California, from grand Union Station near downtown L.A. you can head east to New Orleans on the **Sunset Limited,** to San Antonio on the **Texas Eagle,** and to Chicago on the **Desert Wind** and the **Southwest Chief.** Regional trains operated by Amtrak within California include the **Pacific Surfliner** (formerly the San Diegans) along the state's central and south coasts, and the **San Joaquins** connecting Sacramento with the greater San Francisco Bay Area.

For **Amtrak** train travel routes (including some jogs between cities in California by Amtrak bus), current price information, and reservations, contact a travel agent or call Amtrak at toll-free 800/872-7245 (USA-RAIL), www.amtrak.com or amtrakwest.com. For the hearing impaired, Amtrak's toll-free TTY number is 800/523-6590 or 91.

By Automobile

This being California, almost everyone gets around by car. Urban freeway driving in California, because of congestion and Californians' nononsense get-on-with-it driving styles, can inspire panic even in nonlocal native drivers. If this is a problem, plan your trip to skirt the worst congestion—by taking back roads and older highways, if possible, or by trying neighborhood routes—but only if you know something about the neighborhoods. Alternatively, plan to arrive in San Francisco, other Bay Area destinations, Sacramento, and anywhere in Southern California well after the day's peak freeway commute traffic, usually any time after 7 or 8 P.M.

A good investment for anyone traveling for any length of time in California is a membership in the American Automobile Association (see above) since—among many other benefits, including excellent maps and trip-planning assistance—a AAA card entitles the bearer to no-cost emergency roadside service, including five gallons of free gas and at least limited towing, if necessary.

Gasoline in California is typically more expensive than elsewhere in the United States, up to $.40 per gallon more, only in part because of California's new cleaner-burning "reformulated" fuels, the world's cleanest gasoline. The effect of using the new gasoline is roughly equivalent to the effect of taking 3.5 million cars off the road on any given day—or sucking about three million pounds of toxins and particulate matter out of the air. The clean fuels are designed to reduce vehicle emissions and improve air quality, which seems to be working, but a new concern is that clean fuel residues (particularly from the additive MTBE) are polluting California's water. Though MTBE will soon be banned, the Golden State's pollution solutions are, clearly, ideas that still need work.

To check on current **California road conditions** before setting out—always a good idea in a state with so much ongoing road construction and such variable regional weather—call **Caltrans** (California Department of Transportation) from anywhere in California at toll-free 800/427-7623, and from outside California at 916/445-7623. The road-condition phone numbers are accessible from touch-tone and pay phones as well as cellular phones. Or check road conditions for your entire trip route on the regularly updated Caltrans website, www.dot.ca.gov.

Though every municipality has its own peculiar laws about everything from parking to skateboarding or roller skating on sidewalks, there are basic rules everyone is expected to know and follow—especially drivers. Get a complete set of regulations from the state motor vehicles department, which has an office in all major cities and many medium-sized ones. Or contact **California Department of Motor Vehicles**, 2415 1st Ave., P.O. Box 942869, Sacramento, CA 94269, www.dmv.ca.gov. Foreign visitors planning to drive should obtain an **International Driver's License** before leaving home (they're not available here); licensed U.S. drivers from other states can legally drive in California for 30 consecutive days without having to obtain a California driver's license. Disabled travelers heading for California can get special handicapped-space parking permits, good for 90 days, by requesting applications in advance from the DMV and having them signed by their doctors (there is an application fee). If you'll be renting a car, ask the rental car agency to forward a form to you when you make reservations.

Among driving rules, the most basic is observing the posted speed limit. Though many California drivers ignore any and all speed limits, it's at their own peril should the California Highway Patrol be anywhere in the vicinity. The statewide speed limit for open highway driving varies, typically posted as somewhere between 55 and 70 miles per hour; freeway speeds can vary at different points along the same route. Speed limits for cities and residential neighborhoods are substantially slower. Another avoidable traffic ticket is *not* indulging in what is colloquially known as the "California stop," slowing down and then rolling right through intersections without first making a complete stop.

Once arrived at your destination, pay attention to parking notices, tow-away warnings, and curb color: red means no parking under any circumstances; yellow means limited stops only (usually for freight delivery); green means very limited parking; and blue means parking for the disabled only. In hilly areas of California—and most necessarily in San Francisco—always turn your front wheels into the curb (to keep your car from becoming a rollaway runaway) and set the emergency brake.

Driving while under the influence of alcohol or drugs is a very serious offense in California—aside from being a danger to one's own health and safety, not to mention those of innocent fellow drivers and pedestrians. Don't drink (or do drugs) and drive.

By Rental Car

Renting a car—or a recreational vehicle—in California usually won't come cheap. Rates have been accelerating, so to speak, in recent years, especially when consumers put the kibosh on mileage caps. Turns out people really liked the idea of unlimited "free" mileage. So now the average car rental price is just above $50 a day (lower for subcompacts, higher for road hogs).

Still, bargains are sometimes available through small local agencies. Among national agencies, National and Alamo often offer the lowest prices. But in many cases, with weekly rentals and various group-association (AAA, AARP, etc.) and credit-card discounts ranging from 10–40 percent, you'll usually do just as well with other major rental car agencies. According to the *Consumer Reports* June 1996 national reader quality survey, **Hertz, Avis,** and **National** were rated highest by customers for clean cars, quick and courteous service, and speedy checkout.

Beware the increasingly intense pressure, once you arrive to pick up your rental car, to persuade you to buy additional insurance coverage. In some companies, rental car agents receive a commission for every insurance policy they sell, needed or not, which is why the person on the other side of the counter is so motivated (sometimes pushy and downright intimidating). Feel free to complain to management if you dislike such treatment—and to take your business elsewhere. This highly touted insurance coverage is coverage you probably don't need, from collision damage waivers—now outlawed in some states, but not in California—to liability insurance, which you probably don't need unless you have no car insurance at all (in which case it's illegal to drive in California). Some people do carry additional rental-car collision or liability insurance on their personal insurance policies—talk to your agent about this—but even that is already covered, at least domestically, if you pay for your rental car with a gold or platinum MasterCard or Visa. The same is true for American Express for domestic travelers, though American Express recently rescinded such coverage on overseas car rentals; it's possible that Visa and MasterCard will soon follow suit. (Check your personal insurance and credit-card coverage before dealing with the rental car agencies.) And bring personal proof of car insurance, though you'll rarely be asked for it. In short—buyer beware.

For current information on options and prices for rental cars in Northern California, Southern California, and elsewhere in the United States, contact **Alamo,** toll-free 800/327-9633, www.alamo.com.; **Avis,** toll-free 800/831-2847, www.avis.com; **Budget,** toll-free worldwide 800/527-0700, www.budget.com; **Dollar,** toll-free 800/800-4000, www.dollar.com; **Enterprise,** toll-free 800/736-8222, www.enterprise.com;

Hertz, toll-free worldwide 800/654-3131, www.hertz.com; **National,** toll-free 800/227-7368, www.nationalcar.com; and **Thrifty,** toll-free 800/847-4389, www.thrifty.com. You can also make rental car arrangements online, either directly through individual home pages or through virtual travel agencies and reservations systems such as **Travelocity,** www.travelocity.com, and **The Trip,** www.thetrip.com.

Though some rental agencies also handle recreational vehicle (RV) rentals, travelers may be able to get better deals by renting directly from local RV dealers. For suggestions, contact area visitor bureaus—and consult the local telephone book.

By Airplane

Airfares change and bargains come and go so quickly in competitive California that the best way to keep abreast of the situation is through a travel agent. Or via the Internet, where major U.S. airlines regularly offer great deals—discounts of up to 90 percent (typically not *quite* that good). Popular homepages include **American Airlines,** www.aa.com; **Continental,** www.flycontinental.com; **Delta,** www.delta-air.com; **Northwest,** www.nwa.com; **TWA,** www.twa.com; **United,** www.ual.com; and **US Airways,** www.usairways.com. Also look up the people's favorite, **Southwest,** at www.iflyswa.com. Have your credit card handy. To find additional websites, know your computer—or call any airline's toll-free "800" number and ask. Fueling travel agents' fears that online airline ticket sales will doom them (and independent online agencies) is the news that five airlines—American, Continental, Delta, Northwest, and United—plan to launch their own "independent" online travel service, **Orbitz,** by mid-2001.

But the online agencies may be able to fight back: **Travelzoo,** www.travelzoo.com, searches the 20 major airline websites for the deep-discounted fares and posts them, so you don't have to spend hours looking for the best deals. Relative newcomer **Hotwire,** www.hotwire.com, offers airline tickets at a 40 percent discount (though with limited consumer routing control), with hotel rooms and rental car discounts added to the mix in late 2000. For possibly great deals on last-minute departures, try **Savvio,** www.savvio.com.

Another good information source for domestic and international flight fares: the travel advertisements in the weekend travel sections of major urban newspapers. Super Saver fares (booked well in advance) can save fliers up to 30–70 percent and more. Peak travel times in and out of California being the summer and the midwinter holiday season, book flights well in advance for June–August and December travel. The best bargains in airfares are usually available from January to early May.

Bargain airfares are often available for international travelers, especially in spring and autumn. Charter flights are also good bargains, the only disadvantage usually being inflexible departure and return-flight dates. Most flights from Europe to the United States arrive in New York; from there, other transcontinental travel options are available. Reduced-fare flights on major airlines from Europe abound.

Keep in mind, too, if you're flying, that airlines are getting increasingly strict about how much baggage you're allowed to bring with you. They mean business with those prominent "sizer boxes" now on display in every airport. Only two pieces of carry-on luggage are allowed on most carriers—some now allow only one—and each must fit in the box. Most airlines allow three pieces of luggage total per passenger. (Fortunately for parents, diaper bags, fold-up strollers, and—at least sometimes—infant carrier seats don't count.) So if you are philosophically opposed to the concept of traveling light, bring two massive suitcases—and check them through—in addition to your carry-on. Some airlines, including American, charge extra for more than two checked bags per person. Contact each airline directly for current baggage guidelines.

SAN FRANCISCO CONVENTION & VISITORS BUREAU/MICHAEL MOESON

SAN FRANCISCO
LIFE ON THE EDGE

"When I was a child growing up in Salinas we called San Francisco 'The City,'" California native John Steinbeck once observed. "Of course it was the only city we knew but I still think of it as The City as does everyone else who has ever associated with it."

San Francisco is The City, a distinction it wears with detached certitude. San Francisco has been The City since the days of the gold rush, when the world rushed in through the Golden Gate in a frenzied pursuit of both actual and alchemical riches. It remained The City forever after: when San Francisco started, however reluctantly, to abandon its Barbary Coast ways and conceive of itself as a civilized place; when San Francisco fell down and incinerated itself in the great earthquake of 1906; when San Francisco flew up from its ashes, fully fledged, after reinventing itself; and when San Francisco set about reinventing almost everything else with its rolling social revolutions. Among those the world noticed this century, the Beatniks or "Beats" of the 1940s and '50s publicly shook the

suburbs of American complacency, but the 1960s and San Francisco's Summer of Love caused the strongest social quake, part of the chaos of new consciousness that quickly changed the shape of everything.

Among its many attributes, perhaps most striking is The City's ability, still, to be all things to all people—and to simultaneously contradict itself and its own truths. San Francisco is a point of beginning. Depending upon where one starts, it is also the ultimate place to arrive. San Francisco is a comedy. And San Francisco is tragedy.

As writer Richard Rodriquez observes: "San Francisco has taken some heightened pleasure from the circus of final things. . . . San Francisco can support both comic and tragic conclusions because the city is geographically *in extremis,* a metaphor for the farthest flung possibility, a metaphor for the end of the line." But even that depends upon point of view. As Rodriquez also points out, "To speak of San Francisco as land's end is to read the map from one direction only— as Europeans would read or as the East Coast has always read it." To the people living on these hills before California's colonialization, before the gold rush, even before there was a San Francisco, the land they lived on represented the center, surrounded on three sides by water. To Mexicans extending their territorial reach, it was north. To Russian fur hunters escaping the frigid shores of Alaska, it was south. And to its many generations of Asian immigrants, surely San Francisco represented the Far East.

The precise place The City occupies in the world's imagination is irrelevant to compass points. If San Francisco is anywhere specific, it is certainly at the edge: the cutting edge of cultural combinations, the gilt edge of international commerce, the razor's edge of raw reality. And life on the edge is rarely boring.

THE LAND: NATURAL SAN FRANCISCO

Imagine San Francisco before its bridges were built: a captive city, stranded on an unstable, stubbed toe of a peninsula, one by turns twitching under the storm-driven assault of wind and water, then chilled by bone-cold fog.

The city and county of San Francisco—the two are one, duality in unity—sit on their own appendage of California earth, a political conglomeration totaling 46.4 square miles. Creating San Francisco's western edge is the Pacific Ocean, its waters cooled by strong Alaskan currents, its rough offshore rocks offering treachery

to unwary sea travelers. On its eastern edge is San Francisco Bay, one of the world's most impressive natural harbors, with deep protected waters and 496 square miles of surface area. (As vast as it is, these days the bay is only 75 percent of its pre–gold rush size, since its shoreline has been filled in and extended to create more land.) Connecting the two sides, and creating San Francisco's rough-and-tumble northern edge, is the three-mile-long strait known as the Golden Gate. Straddled by the world-renowned Golden Gate Bridge, this mile-wide river of seawater cuts the widest gap in the rounded Coast Ranges for a thousand miles, yet is so small that its landforms almost hide the bay that balloons inland.

Spaniards named what is now considered San Francisco Las Lomitas, or "little hills," for the landscape's most notable feature. Perhaps to create a romantic comparison with Rome, popular local mythology holds that The City was built on seven hills—Lone Mountain, Mt. Davidson, Nob Hill, Russian Hill, Telegraph Hill, and the two Twin Peaks, none higher than 1,000 feet in elevation. There are actually more than 40 hills in San Francisco, all part and parcel of California's Coast Ranges, which run north and south along the state's coastline, sheltering inland valleys from the fog and winds that regularly visit San Francisco.

City on a Fault Line

The City has been shaped as much by natural forces as by historical happenstance. Its most

beautiful San Francisco

SAN FRANCISCO SIGHTS

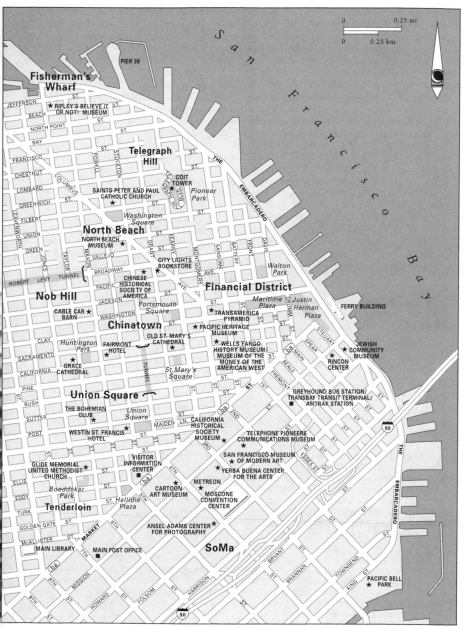

spectacular event involved both. More than any other occurrence, San Francisco's 1906 earthquake—estimated now to have registered 8.25 on the Richter scale—woke up residents, and the world, to the fact that The City was built on very shaky ground. California's famous, 650-mile-long San Andreas Fault, as it is now known, slips just seaward of San Francisco. In the jargon of tectonic plate theory, The City sits on the North American Plate, a huge slab of earth floating on the planet's molten core, along the San Andreas earthquake fault line. Just west is the Pacific Plate. When earth-shaking pressure builds, sooner or later something has to give. In San Francisco, as elsewhere in California, a rumble and a roar and split-second motion announces an earthquake—and the fact that an interlocking section of the earth's crust has separated, a movement that may or may not be visible on the earth's surface. San Francisco's most recent major quake, on October 17, 1989, reminded us that The City's earthquake history is far from a finished chapter.

City in a Fog
San Francisco's second most famous physical feature is its weather—mild and Mediterranean but with quite perverse fog patterns, especially surprising to first-time summer visitors. When people expect sunny skies and warm temperatures, San Francisco offers instead gray and white mists, moist clouds seemingly filled with knife-sharp points of ice when driven by the wind.

Poets traditionally call forth all nine muses to honor the mysteries of fog. Scientists are much more succinct. Summer heat in California's central valley regions creates a low-pressure weather system, while cooler ocean temperatures create higher atmospheric pressure. Moving toward equilibrium, the cool and moist coastal air is drawn inland through the "mouth" of the Golden Gate and over adjacent hills, like a behemoth's belly breath. Then, as the land cools, the mists evaporate. So even during the peak fog months of July and August, wool-coat weather dissipates by midafternoon—only to roll back in shortly after sundown. Due to microclimates created by hills, certain San Francisco neighborhoods—like the Mission District, Noe Valley, and Potrero Hill—may be quite sunny and warm when the rest of the city still shivers in the fog.

San Francisco Weather
The coast's strong high-pressure system tends to moderate San Francisco weather year-round:

PREPARING FOR SAN FRANCISCO

San Francisco's weather can upset even the best-laid plans for a frolic in the summertime California sun. For one thing, there may not be any sun. In summer, when most visitors arrive, San Francisco is enjoying its citywide natural air-conditioning system, called "fog." When California's inland areas are basting in blast-furnace heat, people here might be wearing a down jacket to go walking on the beach. (Sometimes it does get hot—and "hot" by San Francisco standards refers to anything above 80°F.) Especially during the summer, weather extremes even in the course of a single day are normal, so pack accordingly. Bring warm clothing (at least one sweater or jacket for cool mornings and evenings), in addition to the optimist's choice of shorts and sandals, and plan to dress in layers so you'll be prepared for anything. The weather in late spring and early autumn is usually sublime—balmy, often fog-free—so at those times you should bring two pairs of shorts (but don't forget that sweater, just in case). It rarely rains May–Oct.; raingear is prudent at other times.

Most buildings in San Francisco and most public-transit facilities should be accessible to people in wheelchairs and those with other physical limitations; many hotels, restaurants, and entertainment venues will make special accommodations, given some advance notice.

All of San Francisco's (and California's) public buildings and restaurants are nonsmoking. Most motels and hotels have nonsmoking rooms, and many have entire floors of nonsmoking rooms and suites.

Unless otherwise stated on a restaurant menu, restaurants do not include a gratuity in the bill. The standard tip for the wait staff is 15 percent of the total tab, though truly exceptional service may merit 20 percent.

The average tip for taxi drivers is 15 percent. It's also customary to tip airport baggage handlers and hotel porters ($1 per bag, one way, is an acceptable standard), parking valets, and other service staff. When in doubt about how much to tip, just ask someone.

expect average daytime temperatures of 54–65°F in summer, 48–59°F in winter. (Usually reliable is the adage that for every 10 miles you travel inland from the city, temperatures will increase by 10 degrees.) September and October are the warmest months, with balmy days near 70 degrees. The local weather pattern also prevents major rainstorms from May through October. Despite the water-rich imagery associated with the San Francisco Bay Area, the region is actually semiarid, with annual (nondrought) rainfall averaging 19–20 inches. Snow is a very rare phenomenon in the region.

HISTORY AND CULTURE: HUMAN SAN FRANCISCO

At its most basic, the recorded history of San Francisco is a story of conquest and curiosity. The region's original inhabitants, however, were generally content with the abundant riches the land provided quite naturally. Descendants of mysterious nomads who first crossed the Bering Strait from Asia to the North American continent some 20,000 or more years ago, California's native peoples were culturally distinct. The language groups—"tribes" doesn't serve to describe California Indians—living north of the Golden Gate were classified by anthropologists as the Coast Miwok people. Though the barren and desolate site of San Francisco attracted few residents, the dominant native population throughout the greater Bay Area was called Costanoan ("coast people") or Ohlone by the Spanish, though the people called themselves Ramaytush.

In precolonial days, the region was the most densely populated on the continent north of Mexico, with a population of 10,000 people living in 30 or more permanent villages. Though each village considered itself unique, separated from others by customs and local dialect, the Ohlone intermarried and traded with other tribes and shared many cultural characteristics. Though dependent on shellfish as a dietary staple, the Ohlone also migrated inland in summer and fall to hunt game, fish, and collect acorns, which were valued throughout California for making bread and mush. Thousands of years of undisturbed cultural success created a gentle, gracious, unwarlike society—a culture that quickly passed away with the arrival of California's explorers and colonizers.

Early Explorations
Discoveries of dusty manuscripts, ancient stone anchors, and old coins now suggest that Chinese ships were the first foreign vessels to explore California's coastline, arriving centuries before Columbus bumbled into the New World. The Portuguese explorer Juan Cabrillo (João Cabrilho) was the coast's first official surveyor, though on his 1542 voyage he failed to discover the Golden Gate and the spectacular bay behind it. In 1579 the English pirate Sir Francis Drake took the first foreign step onto California soil, quite possibly near San Francisco, and claimed the land for Queen Elizabeth I. (Where exactly Drake landed is a subject of ongoing controversy and confusion. For a further discussion, see Point Reyes National Seashore, San Francisco Bay Area chapter.) And even Drake failed to see the Golden Gate and its precious natural harbor, perhaps due to the subtle subterfuge of landforms and fog.

The Arrival of Spain, Mexico, Russia, and America
In 1769, some 200 years after Drake, a Spanish scouting party led by Gaspar de Portolá discovered San Francisco Bay by accident while searching for Monterey Bay farther south. After Monterey was secured, Captain Juan Bautista de Anza was assigned the task of colonizing this new territorial prize. With 35 families plus a lieutenant and a Franciscan priest, de Anza set out on a grueling trip from Sonora, Mexico, arriving on the peninsula's tip on June 27, 1776, just one week before the American Revolution. The first order of business was establishing a military fortress, the Presidio, at the present site of Fort Mason. And the second was establishing a church and mission outpost, about one mile south, on the shores of a small lake or lagoon named in honor of Nuestra Señora de los Dolores (Our Lady of Sorrows). Though the mission church was dedicated to Saint Francis of Assisi, it became known as Mission Dolores—and the name "San Francisco" was instead attached to the spectacular bay and the eventual city that grew up on its shores.

Though Spain, then Mexico, officially secured the California territory, underscoring ownership

HISTORIC TRANSPORTATION: RIDING THE CABLE CARS

With or without those Rice-a-Roni ads, Muni's cable cars are a genuine San Francisco treat. (Don't allow yourself to be herded onto one of those rubber-tired motorized facsimiles that tend to cluster at Union Square, Fisherman's Wharf, and elsewhere. They are not cable cars, just lures for confused tourists.) San Francisco's cable cars are a national historic landmark, a system called "Hallidie's Folly" in honor of inventor Andrew S. Hallidie when these antiques made their debut on August 2, 1873. The only vehicles of their kind in the world, cable cars were created with the city's challenging vertical grades in mind. They are "powered" by an underground cable in perpetual motion, and by each car's grip-and-release mechanism. Even though maximum speed is about nine mph, that can seem plenty fast when the car snaps around an S-curve. (They aren't kidding when they advise riders to hold onto their seats.) After a complete $67.5 million system overhaul in the early 1980s, 26 "single-enders" now moan and groan along the two Powell Street routes, and 11 "double-enders" make the "swoop loop" along California Street. (New cars are occasionally added to the city's collection.)

To get a vivid education in how cable cars work, visit the reconstructed Cable Car Barn and Museum on Nob Hill.

by means of vast government land grants to retired military and civilian families, the colonial claim was somewhat tenuous. By the 1830s, Americans were already the predominant residents of the settlement at Yerba Buena Cove (at the foot of what is now Telegraph Hill), the earliest version of San Francisco. Yerba Buena was first a trading post established by William Anthony Richardson, an Englishman who married the Presidio commandant's daughter. In the early 1800s, Russian fur hunters established themselves just north along the coast, at the settlement of Fort Ross. They sailed south to trade. English, French, and American trading ships were also regular visitors. By the 1840s, Yankees were arriving by both land and sea in ever greater numbers, spurred on by the nation's expansionist mood and the political dogma of "Manifest Destiny!" The official annexation of the California territory to the United States, when it came in mid-1846, was almost anticlimactic. After the 13-man force at the Presidio surrendered peacefully to the Americans, the citizens quickly changed the name of Yerba Buena to that of the bay, San Francisco—a shrewd business move, intended to attract still more trade.

The World Rushes In:
The Gold Rush and the Barbary Coast

Events of early 1848 made the name change all but irrelevant. San Francisco could hardly help attracting more business, and more businesses of every stripe, once word arrived that gold had been discovered on the American River in the foothills east of Sacramento. Before the gold rush, San Francisco was a sleepy port town with a population of 800, but within months it swelled to a city of nearly 25,000, as gold seekers arrived by the shipload from all over the globe. Those who arrived early and lit out for the goldfields in 1848 had the best opportunity to har-

ROBERT HOLMES/CALTOUR

vest California gold. Most of the fortune hunters, however, arrived in '49, thus the term "forty-niners" to describe this phenomenal human migration.

As cosmopolitan as the overnight city of San Francisco was, with its surprisingly well-educated, liberal, and (not so surprisingly) young population, it was hardly civilized. By 1849 the ratio of men to women was about 10 to one, and saloons, gambling halls, and the notorious red-light district—known as the Barbary Coast—were the social mainstays of this rootless, risk-taking population. Though early San Francisco was primarily a tent city, fire was a constant scourge. The city started to build itself then burned to the ground six times by 1852, when San Francisco was recognized as the fourth largest port of entry in the United States. And though eccentricity and bad behavior were widely tolerated, unrestrained gang crime and murder became so commonplace that businessmen formed Committees of Vigilance to create some semblance of social order—by taking the law into their own hands and jailing, hanging, and running undesirables out of town.

More Barbarians and Big Spenders
By the late 1850s, the sources for most of California's surface gold had been picked clean. Ongoing harvesting of the state's most precious metal had become a corporate affair, an economic change made possible by the development of new technologies. The days of individualistic gold fever had subsided, and fortune hunters who remained in California turned their efforts to more long-lasting development of wealth, often in agriculture and business.

The city, though temporarily slowed by the economic depression that arrived with the end of the gold rush, was the most businesslike of them all. A recognizable city and a major financial center, no sooner had San Francisco calmed down and turned its attentions to nurturing civic pride than another boom arrived—this time silver, discovered in the Nevada territory's Comstock Lode. Silver mining required capital, heavy equipment, and organized mining technology; this was a strictly corporate raid on the earth's riches, with San Francisco and its bankers, businesses, and citizenry the main beneficiaries. Led by the silver rush "Bonanza Kings," the city's nouveau riche built themselves

a residential empire atop Nob Hill and set about creating more cultured institutions.

Confident California, led by San Francisco, believed the future held nothing but greater growth, greater wealth. That was certainly the case for the "Big Four," Sacramento businessmen who financed Theodore Judah's dream of a transcontinental railroad, a development almost everyone believed would lead to an extended boom in the state's economy. Soon at home atop Nob Hill with the city's other nabobs, Charles Crocker, Mark Hopkins, Collis Huntington, and Leland Stanford also set out to establish some political machinery—the Southern Pacific Railway—to generate power and influence to match their wealth.

Bad Times and Bigotry
But the transcontinental railroad did little to help California, or San Francisco, at least initially. As naysayers had predicted, the ease of shipping goods by rail all but destroyed California's neophyte industrial base, since the state was soon glutted with lower-cost manufactured goods from the East Coast. A drought in 1869—a major setback for agricultural production—and an 1871 stock market crash made matters that much worse.

Legions of the unemployed, which included terminated railroad workers all over the West, rose up in rage throughout the 1870s and 1880s. They attacked not those who had enriched themselves at the expense of the general populace but "outsiders," specifically the Chinese who had labored long and hard at many a thankless task since the days of the gold rush. Mob violence and the torching of businesses and entire Chinese communities, in San Francisco and elsewhere, wasn't enough to satisfy such open racist hatred. Politicians too bowed to anti-Chinese sentiment, passing a series of discriminatory laws that forbade the Chinese from owning land, voting, and testifying in court, and levying a special tax against Chinese shrimp fishermen.

A near-final bigoted blow was the federal government's 1882 Oriental Exclusion Act, which essentially ended legal Asian immigration until it was repealed during World War II. San Francisco's Chinese community, for the most part working men denied the opportunity to reunite with their families, was further damaged by the

WALKING ON WATER
ACROSS THAT GOLDEN GATE

Nothing is as San Francisco as the city's astounding **Golden Gate Bridge,** a bright, red-orange fairy pathway up into the fog, a double-necked lyre plucked by the wind to send its surreal song spiraling skyward. The bridge stands today as testimony to the vision of political madmen and poets, almost always the progenitors of major achievements. San Francisco's own **Emperor Norton**—a gold rush–era British merchant originally known as Joshua A. Norton, who went bankrupt in the land of instant wealth but soon reinvented himself as "Norton I, Emperor of the United States and Protector of Mexico"—was the first lunatic to suggest that the vast, turbulent, and troublesome waters of the Golden Gate could be spanned by a bridge. The poet and engineer **Joseph Baermann Strauss,** a titan of a man barely five feet tall, seconded the insanity, and in 1917 he left Chicago for San Francisco, plans and models in hand, to start the 13-year lobbying campaign.

All practical doubts aside, San Francisco at large was aghast at the idea of defacing the natural majesty of the Golden Gate with a manmade monument; more than 2,000 lawsuits were filed in an effort to stop bridge construction. California's love of progress won out in the end, however, and construction of the graceful bridge, designed by architect Irwin F. Morrow, began in 1933. As Strauss himself remarked later: "It took two decades and 200 million

words to convince the people that the bridge was feasible; then only four years and $35 million to put the concrete and steel together."

Building the Golden Gate Bridge was no simple task, rather, an accomplishment akin to a magical feat. Some 80,000 miles of wire were spun into the bridge's suspension cables, a sufficient length to encircle the earth (at the equator) three times, and enough concrete to create a very wide sidewalk between the country's West and East Coasts was poured into the anchoring piers. Sinking the southern support pier offshore was a particular challenge, with 60-mile-an-hour tidal surges and 15-foot swells at times threatening to upend the (seasick) workers' floating trestle. Once the art-deco towers were in place, the *real* fun began—those acrobats in overalls, most earning less than $1 an hour, working in empty space to span the gap. Safety was a serious issue with Strauss and his assistant, Clifford Paine. Due to their diligence, 19 men fell but landed in safety nets instead of in the morgue, earning them honorary membership in the "Halfway to Hell Club." But just weeks before construction was completed, a scaffolding collapsed, its jagged edges tearing through the safety net and taking nine men down with it.

When the Golden Gate Bridge was finished in 1937, the world was astonished. Some 200,000 people walked across the virgin roadbed that day,

TOM MYERS PHOTOGRAPHY

just to introduce themselves to this gracious steel wonder. At that time, the bridge was the world's longest and tallest suspension structure—with a single-span, between-towers distance of 4,200 feet—and boasted the highest high-rises west of New York's Empire State Building. Its total length was 1.7 miles, and its 746-foot-tall towers were equivalent in total height to 65-story buildings. Even now, the bridge's grace is much more than aesthetic. As a suspension bridge, the Golden Gate moves with the action of the immediate neighborhood. It has rarely been closed for reasons of safety or necessary repairs, though it *was* closed, in 1960, so French president Charles de Gaulle could make a solo crossing. Even in treacherous winds, the bridge can safely sway as much as 28 feet in either direction, though standing on a slightly swinging bridge of such monstrous dimensions is an indescribably odd sensation.

Perhaps the best thing about the Golden Gate Bridge, even after all these years, is that people can still enjoy it, up close and very personally. Though the bridge toll is $3 per car (heading south), for pedestrians it's a free trip either way. The hike is ambitious, about two miles one-way. For those who don't suffer from vertigo, this is an inspiring and invigo-rating experience, as close to walking on water as most of us will ever get. (But it's not necessarily a life-enhancing experience for the seriously depressed or suicidal. The lure of the leap has proved too tempting for more than 900 people.) Parking is available at either end of the bridge.

Though the Golden Gate Bridge is the Bay Area's most royal span, credit for San Francisco's propulsion into the modern world of commerce and crazy traffic actually goes to the **Bay Bridge** spanning San Francisco Bay between downtown San Francisco and Oakland/Berkeley. Completed in 1936, and built atop piers sunk into the deepest deeps ever bridged, the Bay Bridge cost $80 million to complete, at that time the most expensive structure ever built. And in recent history, the Bay Bridge has made front-page and nightly news headlines. The whole world watched in horror when part of the bridge collapsed amid the torqued tensions of the 1989 earthquake, a pre-rush-hour event. There were deaths and injuries, but fewer casualties than if the quake had come during peak commuter traffic. Despite the quake, the bridge still remained structurally sound, and the more critically necessary repairs have been made. A new span for the Bay Bridge is in the planning stages.

Geary Act of 1892, which declared that all Chinese had to carry proper identification or face deportation. The failure of American society to support traditional Chinese culture led to rampant crime, gambling, and prostitution—acceptable diversions of the day for bachelors—and a lawless reign of terror by competing tongs who fought to control the profits. Only the gradual Americanization of the Chinese, which minimized tong influence, and the disastrous events during the spring of 1906 could change the reality of Chinatown. But the year 1906 changed everything in San Francisco.

The World Ends: Earthquake and Fire

By the early 1900s, San Francisco had entered its "gilded age," a complacent period when the city was busy enjoying its new cosmopolitan status. San Francisco had become the largest and finest city west of Chicago. The rich happily compounded their wealth in downtown high-rises and at home on Nob Hill and in other resplendent neighborhoods. The expanding middle class built rows of new Victorian homes, "painted ladies" that writer Tom Wolfe would later call "those endless staggers of bay windows," on hills far removed from the lowlife of the Barbary Coast, Chinatown, and the newest red-light district, the Tenderloin. But the working classes still smoldered in squalid tenements south of Market Street. Corruption ruled, politically, during the heyday of the "paint eaters"—politicians so greedy they'd even eat the paint off buildings. The cynical reporter and writer Ambrose Bierce, sniffing at the status quo, called San Francisco the "moral penal colony of the world." But the city's famous graft trials, a public political circus that resulted in 3,000 indictments but shockingly little jail time, came later.

Whatever was going on in the city, legal and otherwise, came to an abrupt halt on the morning of April 18, 1906, when a massive earthquake hit. Now estimated to have registered 8.25 on the Richter scale, the quake created huge fissures in the ground, broke water and gas mains all over the city, and caused chimneys and other unstable construction to come tumbling down. The better neighborhoods, including the city's

Victorian row houses, suffered little damage. Downtown, however, was devastated. City Hall, a shoddy construction job allowed by scamming politicians and their contractor cohorts, crumbled into nothing. Though a central hospital also fell, burying doctors, nurses, and patients alike, the overall death toll from the earthquake itself was fairly small. Sadly for San Francisco, one of the fatalities was the city fire chief, whose foresight might have prevented the conflagration soon to follow.

More than 50 fires started that morning alone, racing through the low-rent neighborhoods south of Market, then into downtown, raging out of control. The flames were unchecked for four days, burning through downtown, parts of the Mission District, and also demolishing Chinatown, North Beach, Nob Hill, Telegraph Hill, and Russian Hill. The mansions along the eastern edge of Van Ness were dynamited to create an impromptu firebreak, finally stopping the firestorm.

When it was all over, the official tally of dead or missing stood at 674, though more recent research suggests the death toll was more than 3,000, since the Chinese weren't counted. The entire city center was destroyed, along with three-fourths of the city's businesses and residences. With half of its 450,000 population now homeless, San Francisco was a tent city once again. But it was an optimistic tent city, bolstered by relief and rebuilding funds sent from around the world. As reconstruction began, San Francisco also set out to clean house politically.

Modern Times
By 1912, with San Francisco more or less back on its feet, Mayor James "Sunny Jim" Rolph, who always sported a fresh flower in his lapel, seemed to symbolize the city's new era. Rolph presided over the construction of some of San Francisco's finest public statements about itself. These included the new city hall and Civic Center, as well as the 1915 world's fair and the Panama-Pacific International Exposition, a spectacular 600-acre temporary city designed by Bernard Maybeck to reflect the "mortality of grandeur and the vanity of human wishes." Though the exposition was intended to celebrate the opening of the Panama Canal, it was San Francisco's grand announcement to the world that it had not only survived but

thrived in the aftermath of its earlier earthquake and fire.

During the Great Depression, San Francisco continued to defy the commonplace, dancing at the edge of unreal expectations. Two seemingly impossible spans, the Golden Gate Bridge and the Bay Bridge, were built in the 1930s. San Francisco also built the world's largest man-made island, Treasure Island, which hosted the Golden Gate International Exposition in 1939 before becoming a U.S. Navy facility. (In 1997, the Navy abandoned ship and ceded the island to the city of San Francisco; now it's a venue for occasional concerts and a regular flea market.)

No matter how spectacular its statements to the world, San Francisco had trouble at home. The 1929 stock market crash and the onset of the Depression re-ignited long-simmering labor strife, especially in the city's port. Four longshoremen competed for every available job along the waterfront, and members of the company-controlled Longshoremen's Association demanded kickbacks for jobs that were offered. Harry Bridges reorganized the International Longshoremen's Association, and backed by the Teamsters Union, his pro-union strike successfully closed down the waterfront. On "Bloody Thursday," July 5, 1934, 800 strikers battled with National Guard troops called in to quell a riot started by union busters. Two men were shot and killed by police, another 100 were injured, and the subsequent all-city strike—the largest general strike in U.S. history—ultimately involved most city businesses as well as the waterfront unions. More so than elsewhere on the West Coast, labor unions are still strong in San Francisco.

Other social and philosophical revolutions, for iconoclasts and oddballs alike, either got their start in San Francisco or received abundant support once arrived. First came the 1950s-era Beatniks or "Beats"—poets, freethinkers, and jazz aficionados rebelling against the suburbanization of the American mind. The Beats were followed in short order by the 1960s, the Summer of Love, psychedelics, and rock groups like the legendary Grateful Dead. The Free Speech Movement heated up across the bay in Berkeley, not to mention anti–Vietnam War protests and the rise of the Black Panther Party. Since then, San Francisco has managed to make its place at, or near, the forefront of almost every change in social awareness, from women's rights to gay pride. And in the 1980s and '90s, San Franciscans went all out for baby boomer and Gen X consumerism; young urban professionals have been setting the style for quite some time. But there are other styles, other trends. You name it, San Francisco probably has it.

SEEING SAN FRANCISCO: COASTING THE PACIFIC

Coastal travelers might start a San Francisco tour at the Golden Gate Bridge, which stretches between San Francisco and Marin County and dramatically spans the Golden Gate, the entry to San Francisco Bay. Just beyond the bridge Highway 1 splits off from Highway 101 and dashes south through the Presidio of San Francisco, just one highlight of the Golden Gate National Recreation Area. The national park also hugs much of the coastline heading south, all the way to Pacifica. Notable features along the way include the Cliff House, Fort Funston, and Thornton Beach—not to mention San Francisco's famed Golden Gate Park.

GOLDEN GATE NATIONAL RECREATION AREA

One of the city's unexpected treasures, in San Francisco the Golden Gate National Recreation Area (GGNRA) starts in the north amid the pilings of the Golden Gate Bridge. Along the coast the park also follows a narrow strip of land adjacent to Hwy. 1, taking in the Cliff House, Fort Funston, Thornton Beach, and other milestones before reaching Sweeney Ridge near Pacifica. The GGNRA also includes Alcatraz Island, one of the nation's most infamous prison sites, and state-administered Angel Island, "Ellis Island of the West" to the Chinese and other immigrant groups. In late 1995, the historic Presidio—1,480 acres of forest, coastal bluffs, military outposts, and residences adjacent to the Golden Gate Bridge—was converted from military to domestic purposes and formally included in the GGNRA. Vast tracts of the southern and western Marin County headlands, north of the bridge, are also included within GGNRA boundaries, making this park a true urban wonder. Much of the credit for creating the GGNRA, the world's largest urban park, goes to the late congressman Phillip Burton. Established in 1972, the recreation area as currently envisioned includes more than 36,000 acres in a cooperative patchwork of land holdings exceeding 114 square miles. The GGNRA is also the most

The views from the Cliff House are spectacular.

THE PRESIDIO AND FORT POINT

A national historic landmark and historic military installation, San Francisco's **Presidio** is the nation's newest national park. In 1994, Congress closed the Presidio to the Sixth Army Command, and the Golden Gate National Recreation Area (GGNRA) gained 1,446 acres of the multimillion-dollar real estate.

Among other proposals for putting the buildings here to good public use, it's quite possible that 23 acres on the Presidio's eastern border will house studios for filmmaker George Lucas's Industrial Light & Magic, as well as facilities for other Lucas enterprises, on the site of the old Letterman Army Hospital.

The Presidio lies directly south of the Golden Gate Bridge along the northwest tip of the San Francisco Peninsula, bordered by the Marina and Pacific Heights districts to the east and Richmond and Presidio Heights to the south. To the west and north, a coastal strip of the Golden Gate National Recreation Area frames the Presidio, which boasts some 70 miles of paths and trails of its own, winding along cliffs and through eucalyptus groves and coastal flora. The 1,600 buildings here, most of them eclectic blends of Victorian and Spanish-revival styles, have housed the U.S. Army since 1847.

Founded by the Spanish in 1776 as one of two original settlements in San Francisco, the Presidio had a militaristic history even then, for the area commands a strategic view of San Francisco Bay and the Pacific Ocean. The Spanish garrison ruled the peninsula for the first 50 years of the city's history, chasing off Russian whalers and trappers by means of the two cannons now guarding the entrance to the Officer's Club. After 1847, when Americans took over, the Presidio became a staging center for the Indian wars, a never-used outpost during the Civil War, and more recently, headquarters for the Sixth Army Command, which fought in the Pacific during World War II.

Today the Presidio is open to the public, and visitors may drive around and admire the neat-as-a-pin streets with their white, two-story wood Victorians and faultless lawns or trace the base's history at the **Presidio Army Museum** (one of the oldest buildings, originally the hospital) located near the corner of Lincoln Blvd. and Funston Ave., 415/561-4131. Pick up a map there showing the Presidio's hiking trails, including a six-mile historic walk and two ecology trails. Museum hours are Wed.–Sun. noon–4 P.M., admission free.

Ranger-led GGNRA guided tours include the **Natural History of the Presidio,** an exploratory

popular of the national parks, drawing more than 20 million visitors each year.

One major attraction of the GGNRA is the opportunity for hiking—both **urban hiking** on the San Francisco side, and **wilderness hiking** throughout the Marin Headlands. Get oriented to the recreation area's trails at any visitor center (see below), look up the National Park Service website at www.nps.gov/prsf, or sign on for any of the GGNRA's excellent guided hikes and explorations. The schedule changes constantly. A particularly spectacular section of the GGNRA's trail system is the 2.5-mile trek from the St. Francis Yacht Club to Fort Point and the Golden Gate Bridge. This walk is part of the still-in-progress **San Francisco Bay Trail,** a 450-mile shoreline trail system that will one day ring the entire bay and traverse nine Bay Area counties. Ambitious hikers can follow the GGNRA's **Coastal Trail** from San Francisco to Point Reyes National Seashore in Marin County. Once on the north side of the Golden Gate, possibilities for long hikes and backpacking trips are almost endless.

San Francisco-Side GGNRA Sights
The GGNRA includes the beaches and coastal bluffs along San Francisco's entire western edge (and both south and north), as well as seaside trails and walking and running paths along the new highway and seawall between Sloat Blvd. and the western border of Golden Gate Park.

The original Cliff House near Seal Rocks was one of San Francisco's first tourist lures, its original diversions a bit on the licentious side. That version, converted by Adolph Sutro into a family-style resort, burned to the ground in 1894 and was soon replaced by a splendid Victorian palace and an adjacent bathhouse, also fire victims. Ruins of the old **Sutro Baths** are still visible among the rocks just north. Aptly named **Seal Rocks** offshore attract vocal sea lions.

The current **Cliff House,** across the highway from Sutro Heights Park, dates from 1908 and lesson in the San Francisco Peninsula's geology, geography, and plant and animal life, featuring an enchanted forest and the city's last free-flowing stream; **Presidio Main Post Historical Walks;** and the **Mountain Lake to Fort Point Hike.**

For more information about the Presidio and scheduled events and activities, look up the National Park Service's website at www.nps.gov/prsf, or call the **Presidio Visitor Center,** at 415/561-4323.

More businesslike in design but in many respects more interesting than the Presidio, **Fort Point,** off Lincoln Blvd. is nestled directly underneath the southern tip of the Golden Gate Bridge and worth donning a few extra layers to visit. Officially the Fort Point National Historic Site since 1968, the quadrangular redbrick behemoth was modeled after South Carolina's Fort Sumter and completed in 1861 to guard the bay during the Civil War. However, the fort was never given the chance to test its mettle, as a grassroots plot hatched by Confederate sympathizers in San Francisco to undermine the Yankee cause died for lack of funds and manpower, and the more palpable threat that the Confederate cruiser *Shenandoah* would blast its way into the bay was foiled by the war ending before the ship ever arrived.

Nonetheless, military strategists had the right idea situating the fort on the site of the old Spanish adobe-brick outpost of Castillo de San Joaquin, and through the years the fort-that-could was used as a garrison and general catchall for the Presidio, including a stint during World War I as barracks for unmarried officers. During the 1930s, when the Golden Gate Bridge was in its design phase, the fort narrowly missed being scrapped but was saved by the bridge's chief design engineer, Joseph B. Strauss, who considered the fort's demolition a waste of good masonry and designed the somewhat triumphal arch that now soars above it.

Fort Point these days enjoys a useful retirement as a historical museum, open daily 10 A.M.–5 P.M., admission free. While the wind howls in the girders overhead, park rangers clad in Civil War regalia (many wearing long johns underneath) lead hourly tours, 11 A.M.–4 P.M., through the park's honeycomb of corridors, staircases, and gun ports. Cannon muster is solemnly observed at 1:30 and 2:30 P.M., and two side shows are also offered, at 11:30 A.M. and again at 3:30 P.M. A fairly recent addition is the excellent exhibit and tribute to black American soldiers. At the bookstore, pick up some Confederate money and other military memorabilia. For more information about tours and special events, call Fort Point at 415/556-1693.

by Taran March

still attracts locals and tourists alike. The views are spectacular, which explains the success of the building's Cliff House Restaurant, 415/386-3330, as well as the building's Phineas T. Barnacle pub-style deli and the Ben Butler Room bar. The stairway outdoors leads down the cliff to the GGNRA **Cliff House Visitor Center,** 415/556-8642, a good stop for information, free or low-cost publications and maps, and books. Open daily 10 A.M.–5 P.M. Also down below just behind the Cliff House is the **Musée Méchanique,** 415/386-1170, a delightful and dusty collection of penny arcade amusements (most cost a quarter)—from nickelodeons and coin-eating music boxes to fortune-telling machines—and the odd **Camera Obscura & Hologram Gallery.** The gallery's "camera" is actually a slow revolving lens that reflects images onto a parabolic screen—with a particularly thrilling fractured-light image at sunset.

Wandering northward from Cliff House, Point Lobos Ave. and then El Camino del Mar lead to San Francisco's **Point Lobos,** the city's westernmost point. There's an overlook, to take in the view. Nearby is the **USS *San Francisco* Memorial,** part of the city's namesake ship. Also nearby is **Fort Miley,** which features a 4-H "adventure ropes" course. But the most spectacular thing in sight (on a clear day) is the postcard-pretty peek at the Golden Gate Bridge. You can even get there from here, on foot, via the **Coastal Trail,** a spectacular city hike that skirts Lincoln Park and the California Palace of the Legion of Honor before passing through the Seacliff neighborhood, then flanking the Presidio. From Fort Point at the foot of the Golden Gate, the truly intrepid can keep on trekking—straight north across the bridge to Marin County, or east past the yacht harbors to Fort Mason and the overwhelming attractions of Fisherman's Wharf.

For some slower sightseeing, backtrack to the Presidio's hiking trails and other attractions. The GGNRA's **Presidio Visitor Center,** 102 Montgomery St. (that's a *different* Montgomery

SAN FRANCISCO CONVENTION & VISITORS BUREAU/KERRICK JAMES

the Palace of Fine Arts

St. than the one downtown), 415/561-4323, can point you in the right direction. It's open year-round, daily 9 A.M.–5 P.M. One possible detour: the **Presidio Army Museum** at Lincoln and Funston, 415/561-4331.

Or spend time exploring the coast. At low tide, the fleet of foot can beach walk (and climb) from the Golden Gate Bridge to **Baker Beach** and farther (looking back at the bridge for a seagull's-eye view). Though many flock here precisely because it is a de facto nude beach, the very naked sunbathers at Baker Beach usually hide out in the rock-secluded coves beyond the family-oriented stretch of public sand. Near Baker Beach is the miniature **Battery Lowell A. Chamberlin** "museum," a historic gun hold, home to the six-inch disappearing rifle. Weapons aficionados will want to explore more thoroughly the multitude of gun batteries farther north along the trail, near Fort Point.

For More Information

For information on the GGNRA included elsewhere in this chapter, see also the special topic The Presidio and Fort Point in this section; the

Avenues, immediately below; and Fort Mason and Touring the Real Rock under Seeing San Francisco: Coasting the Bay. For more information on the Marin County sections of the GGNRA, see Point Reyes National Seashore and the special topic Angel Island in the San Francisco Bay Area chapter.

For current information about GGNRA features and activities, contact: **Golden Gate National Recreation Area,** Fort Mason, Building 201, 415/556-0560, www.nps.gov/goga. To check on local conditions, events, and programs, you can also call the GGNRA's other visitor centers: **Cliff House,** 415/556-8642; **Fort Point,** 415/556-1693; **Marin Headlands,** 415/331-1540; **Muir Woods,** 415/388-2596; and **Presidio,** 415/561-4323.

For a set of maps of the entire San Francisco Bay Trail ($10.95) or detailed maps of specific trail sections ($1.50 each), contact the **San Francisco Bay Trail Project,** c/o the Association of Bay Area Governments, 510/464-7900, or order the maps online at www.abag.org. About 215 of the Bay Trail's 450 total miles of trails are completed, with planning and/or construction of the rest underway. Call the Association to volunteer trail-building labor or materials, to help with fundraising, or to lead guided walks along sections of the Bay Trail.

Also of interest to area hikers: the **Bay Area Ridge Trail,** a 400-mile ridge-top route that one day will skirt the entire bay, connecting 75 parks. For information, contact the **Bay Area Ridge Trail Council,** 26 O'Farrell St., 415/391-9300, www.ridgetrail.org. You can order a book about the trail ($14.95) by calling the office.

THE AVENUES

Richmond District and Vicinity

Originally called San Francisco's Great Sand Waste, then the city's cemetery district—before the bones were dug up and shipped south to Colma in 1914—today the Richmond District is a middle-class ethnic sandwich, built upon Golden Gate Park and topped by Lincoln Park and the Presidio. White Russians were the first residents, fleeing Russia after the 1917 revolution, but just about everyone else followed. A stroll down **Clement Street,** past its multiethnic eaties and shops, should bring you up to speed on the subject of cultural diversity.

The area between Arguello and Park Presidio, colloquially called "New Chinatown," is noted for its good, largely untouristed Asian eateries and shops. Russian-Americans still park themselves on the playground benches at pretty **Mountain Lake Park** near the Presidio. And the gold-painted onion domes of the Russian Orthodox **Russian Holy Virgin Cathedral of the Church in Exile,** 6210 Geary Blvd., along with the Byzantine-Roman Jewish Reform **Temple Emanu-El** at Arguello and Lake (technically in Pacific Heights), offer inspiring architectural reminders of earlier days.

Highlights of the Richmond District include the **University of San Francisco** atop Lone Mountain, an institution founded by the Jesuits in 1855, complete with spectacular **St. Ignatius** church, and the **Neptune Society Columbarium,** 1 Loraine Ct. (just off Anza near Stanyan), 415/221-1838, the final resting place of old San Francisco families including the newspaper Hearsts and department store Magnins. With its ornate neoclassical and copper-roofed rotunda, the Columbarium offers astounding acoustics, best appreciated from the upper floors. The building is open to the public weekdays 9 A.M.–5 P.M., weekends 10 A.M.–2 P.M.

Seacliff, an exclusive seaside neighborhood nestled between the Presidio and Lincoln Park, is the once-rural community where famed California photographer **Ansel Adams** was raised.

West of Seacliff, **Land's End** is the city's most rugged coastline, reached via footpath from Lincoln Park and the Golden Gate National Recreation Area. **China Beach,** just below Seacliff, was probably named for Chinese immigrants trying to evade Angel Island internment by jumping ship, all a result of the Exclusion Act in effect from the 1880s to World War II. During the Civil War, this was the westernmost point of the nation's antislavery "Underground Railroad." You can swim here—facilities include a lifeguard station plus changing rooms, showers, and restrooms—but the water's brisk. Northeast is **Baker Beach,** considered the city's best nude beach.

California Palace of the Legion of Honor

The area's main attraction, though, just beyond Lincoln Park's Municipal Golf Course, is the **California Palace of the Legion of Honor,** on Legion of Honor Dr. (enter off 34th and Clement), 415/750-3600 (office) or 415/863-3330 (visitor hot line), www.famsf.org. Established by French-born Alma de Bretteville Spreckels, wife of the city's sugar king, this handsome hilltop palace was built in honor of American soldiers killed in France during World War I. It's a 1920 French neoclassic, from the colonnades and triumphal arch to the outdoor equestrian bronzes. Intentionally incongruous, placed out near the parking lot in an otherwise serene setting, is George Segal's testimony to the depths of human terror and terrorism: the barbed wire and barely living

*California Palace of
the Legion of Honor*

bodies of *The Holocaust.* Also here are bronze castings from Rodin, including *The Thinker* and *The Shades* outdoors, just part of the Legion's collection of more than 70 Rodin originals. Inside, the permanent collection was originally exclusively French, but now includes the M. H. de Young Museum's European collection—an awesome eight-century sweep from El Greco, Rembrandt, and Rubens to Renoir, Cézanne, Degas, Monet, and Manet. Take a docent-led tour for a deeper appreciation of other features, including the Legion's period rooms.

Special events include films, lectures, and painting and music programs, the latter including Rodin Gallery pipe organ concerts as well as chamber music, jazz, and historical instrument concerts in the Florence Gould Theater. The Legion of Honor also features a pleasant café and a gift shop. Museum hours are Tues.–Sun. 9:30 A.M.–5 P.M., and until 8:45 P.M. on the first Saturday of every month. Admission is $7 adults, $5 seniors, $4 youths 12–17, free for everyone on the second Wednesday of each month. Admission may be higher during some visiting exhibitions.

The fit and fresh-air loving can get here on foot along the meandering **Coastal Trail**—follow it north from the Cliff House or south from the Golden Gate Bridge.

Sunset District

Most of San Francisco's neighborhoods are residential, streets of private retreat that aren't all that exciting except to those who live there. The Sunset District, stretching to the sea from south of Golden Gate Park, is one example, the southern section of the city's "Avenues." In summertime, the fog here at the edge of the continent is usually unrelenting, so visitors often shiver and shuffle off, muttering that in a place called "Sunset" one should be able to see it. (To appreciate the neighborhood name, come anytime *but* summer.) For beach access and often gray-day seaside recreation, from surfing and surf fishing to cycling, walking, and jogging (there's a paved path), follow the **Great Highway** south from Cliff House and stop anywhere along the way.

Stanyan Street, at the edge of the Haight and east of Golden Gate Park, offers odd and attractive shops, as does the stretch of **9th Avenue** near Irving and Judah. Just south of the park at its eastern edge is the **University of California at San Francisco Medical Center** atop Mt. Sutro, the small eucalyptus forest here reached via cobblestone Edgewood Ave. or, for the exercise, the Farnsworth Steps. From here, look down on the colorful Haight or north for a bird's-eye view of the **Richmond District,** the rest of the city's Avenues.

Stern Grove, at Sloat Blvd. and 19th Ave., is a wooded valley beloved for its Sunday concerts. Just off Sloat is the main gate to the **San Francisco Zoo,** which offers an Insect Zoo, a Children's Zoo, and the usual caged collection of primates, lions, tigers, and bears. (Mealtime for the big cats, at the Lion House at 2 P.M. every day except Monday, is quite a viewing treat.) Large **Lake Merced** just south, accessible via Skyline Blvd. (Hwy. 35) or Lake Merced Blvd., was once a tidal lagoon. These days it's a freshwater lake popular for canoeing, kayaking, nonmotorized boating (rent boats at the Boat House on Harding), fishing (largemouth bass and trout), or just getting some fresh air.

The Lake Merced area offers one of the newer sections of the **Bay Area Ridge Trail,** a hiking route (signed with blue markers at major turning points and intersections) that one day will total 400 miles and connect 75 parks in nine Bay Area counties. Farther south still is **Fort Funston,** a one-time military installation on barren cliffs, a favorite spot for hang gliders and a good place to take Fido for an outing (dogs can be off-leash along most of the beach here). East of Lake Merced are **San Francisco State University,** one of the state university system's best—noted for its **Sutro Library** and **American Poetry Archives**—and the community of **Ingleside,** home of the 26-foot-tall sundial.

GOLDEN GATE PARK

Yet another of San Francisco's impossible dreams successfully accomplished, Golden Gate Park was once a vast expanse of sand dunes. A wasteland by urban, and urbane, standards, locals got the idea that it could be a park—and a grand park, to rival the Bois de Boulogne in Paris. Frederick Law Olmsted, who designed New York's Central Park, was asked to build it. He took one look and scoffed, saying essentially that it couldn't be done. Olmsted was wrong,

AISLINN RACE

The Japanese Tea Garden beckons those in search of serenity.

as it turned out, and eventually he had the grace to admit it. William Hammond Hall, designer and chief engineer, and Scottish gardener John McLaren, the park's green-thumbed godfather, achieved the unlikely with more than a bit of West Coast ingenuity. Hall constructed a behemoth breakwater on the 1,000-acre park's west end, to block the stinging sea winds and salt spray, and started anchoring the sand by planting barley, then nitrogen-fixing lupine, then grasses. Careful grading and berming, helped along in time by windrows, further deflected the fierceness of ocean-blown storms.

"Uncle John" McLaren, Hall's successor, set about re-creating the land on a deeper level. He trucked in humus and manure to further transform sand into soil, and got busy planting more than one million trees. And that was just the beginning. In and around walkways, benches, and major park features, there were shrubs to plant, flowerbeds to establish, and pristine lawns to nurture. McLaren kept at it for some 55 years, dedi-

cating his life to creating a park for the everlasting enjoyment of the citizenry. He bravely did battle with politicians, often beating them at their own games, to nurture and preserve "his" park for posterity. He fought with groundskeepers who tried to keep people off the lush lawns, and he attempted to hide despised-on-principle statues and other graven images with bushes and shrubs. In the end he lost this last battle; after McLaren died, the city erected a statue in his honor.

McLaren's Legacy

Much of the park's appeal is its astounding array of natural attractions. The botanic diversity alone, much of it exotic, somehow reflects San Francisco's multicultural consciousness—also transplanted from elsewhere, also now as natural as the sun, the moon, the salt winds, and the tides.

The dramatic **Victorian Conservatory of Flowers** on John F. Kennedy Drive, 415/641-7978, was imported from Europe and assembled here in 1878. A showcase jungle of tropical plants also noted for its seasonal botanic displays, the Conservatory was heavily damaged in a December 1995 storm and has been closed pending reconstruction. Call for an update.

The 55-acre **Strybing Arboretum and Botanical Gardens,** Ninth Ave. at Lincoln Way, 415/661-1316, features more than 7,000 different species, including many exotic and rare plants. Noted here is the collection of Australian and New Zealand plant life, along with exotics from Africa, the Americas, and Asia. Several gardens are landscaped by theme, such as the Mexican Cloud Forest and the California Redwood Grove. The serene Japanese Moon-Viewing Garden is a worthy respite when the Japanese Tea Garden is choked with tourists. Quite a delight, too, is the Fragrance Garden—a collection of culinary and medicinal herbs easily appreciated by aroma and texture, labeled also in Braille. Any plant lover will enjoy time spent in the small store. The arboretum is open weekdays 8 A.M.–4:30 P.M., weekends 10 A.M.–5 P.M.; admission is free, donations appreciated. Guided tours are offered on weekday afternoons and twice a day on weekends; call for tour times and meeting places. Next door is the **San Francisco County Fair Building,** site of the annual "fair"—in San Francisco, it's a flower show only—and home to the

Helen Crocker Russell Library, containing some 18,000 volumes on horticulture and plants. The **Japanese Tea Garden** on Tea Garden Dr. (off Martin Luther King Jr. Dr.), 415/752-4227 (admission information) or 415/752-1171 (gift shop), a striking and suitable backdrop to the Asian Art Museum, is an enduring attraction, started (and maintained until the family's World War II internment) by full-time Japanese gardener Maokota Hagiwara and his family. Both a lovingly landscaped garden and tea house concession—the Hagiwaras invented the fortune cookie, first served here, though Chinatown later claimed this innovation as an old-country tradition—the Tea Garden is so popular that to enjoy even a few moments of the intended serenity, visitors should arrive early on a weekday morning or come on a rainy day. The large bronze "Buddha Who Sits Through Sun and Rain Without Shelter," cast in Japan in 1790, will surely welcome an off-day visitor. The Japanese Tea Garden is most enchanting in April, when the cherry trees are in bloom. Open daily Mar.–Dec. 8:30 A.M.–6 P.M., Jan.–Feb. 8:30 A.M.–dusk. The tea house opens at 10 A.M. Admission is $3.50 adults, $1.25 seniors and children 6–12.

Also especially notable for spring floral color in Golden Gate Park: the **Queen Wilhelmina Tulip Garden** on the park's western edge, near the restored (northern) **Dutch Windmill,** and the **John McLaren Rhododendron Dell** near the Conservatory of Flowers. The very English **Shakespeare Garden,** beyond the Academy of Sciences, is unusual any time of year, since all the plants and flowers here are those mentioned in the Bard's works. Poignant and sobering is the expansive **National AIDS Memorial Grove,** at the east end of the park between Middle Drive East and Bowling Green Drive. Regardless of whether or not you personally know anyone with AIDS, this is a good place to wander among the groves of redwoods and dogwoods, quietly contemplating the fragility of life and your place in it. The grove is maintained by volunteers; to volunteer, or for more information, call 415/750-8340.

Even the **San Francisco Zoo,** 1 Zoo Rd. (Sloat Blvd. at 45th Ave.), 415/753-7080, has its botanical attractions. The main reason to come, though, is to commune with the 1,000 or so animals in captivity. The zoo is open 365 days a year, 10 A.M.–5 P.M.; admission is $9 adults, $6 youths 12–17 and seniors 65 and over, $3 children 3–11, free on the first Wednesday of every month.

M. H. de Young Memorial Museum

Though closed for renovations until Spring 2005, when the new De Young will open on the same site in Golden Gate Park, programming for the museum continues at the De Young's sister museum, the Legion of Honor (located in San Francisco's Lincoln Park). Call the 24-hour hotline at 415/863-3330 for more information. Now merged administratively with the California Palace of the Legion of Honor into the jointly operated Fine Arts Museums of San Francisco, the de Young Museum, 75 Tea Garden Dr. (at 9th Ave.), 415/750-3600, www.thinker.org or www.famsf.org, is one of the city's major visual arts venues. The museum, with its Spanish-style architecture, honors San Francisco newspaper publisher M. H. de Young.

The de Young's specialty is American art, from British colonial into contemporary times, and the collection here is one of the finest anywhere. Examine the exhibits of period paintings, sculpture, and decorative and domestic arts; the 20th-century American realist paintings are almost as intriguing as the textile and modern graphic arts collections. Also included in the de Young's permanent collection are traditional arts of the Americas, Africa, and Oceania. Come, too, for changing special exhibits, like "San Francisco's Old Chinatown: Photographs by Arnold Genthe."

Prior to closing, admission was (which included access to the Asian Art Museum) $7 adults, $5 seniors, and $4 youths 12–17. For current information on exhibits, call 415/863-3330; for information on becoming a museum member, call 415/750-3636.

Asian Art Museum

Scheduled to move to the site of the old downtown library in 2001, the astounding Asian Art Museum, 75 Tea Garden Dr. (at 9th Ave.), 415/379-8801, www.asianart.org, currently shares a wing and the admission charge with the de Young Museum. The museum got its start in 1966 when the late U.S. diplomat Avery Brundage donated his collection to the city. Since then it has expanded greatly. Today, in addition to its vast collections of Chinese and Japanese

THE CITYPASS

The money-saving **CityPass** provides admission to six of San Francisco's top attractions—the Exploratorium, California Palace of the Legion of Honor, de Young Museum, Museum of Modern Art, California Academy of Sciences/Steinhart Aquarium, and a San Francisco Bay Cruise—for a price, at last report, half of what the individual admissions would cost: $27.75 adults, $19.75 seniors, $17.25 youths 12–17. It's good for seven days and is available at any of the participating attractions or any of the city's visitor information centers.

art, the museum holds masterpieces from some 40 other Asian cultures, including India, Tibet, Nepal, Mongolia, Korea, and Iran. The total collection—more than 12,000 objects in all, spanning 6,000 years of history—is so large that only about 10 percent can be displayed at any one time. Among the treasures here: the oldest known dated sculpture of Buddha, from China, circa A.D. 338 in Western time; earthenware animals from the Tang Dynasty; and an astounding array of jade artifacts. Special changing exhibits are presented periodically; call for current exhibit schedule.

The Asian Art Museum is open Tues.–Sun. 9:30 A.M.–5 P.M., except on the first Wed. of each month, when it's open 10 A.M.–8:45 P.M. Admission (which includes access to the adjacent M. H. de Young Museum) is $7 adults, $5 seniors, $4 youths 12–17 (free for everyone on the first Wed. of each month). Admission is sometimes higher during special exhibitions. Call for information about docent-led tours.

California Academy of Sciences

At home on the park's Music Concourse (between Martin Luther King Jr. and John F. Kennedy Dr.), 415/750-7145, www.calacademy.org, the California Academy of Sciences is a multifaceted scientific institution, the oldest in the West, founded in 1853 to survey and study the vast resources of California and vicinity. In the academy's courtyard, note the intertwining whales in the fountain. These were sculpted by Robert Howard and originally served as the centerpiece of the San Francisco Building during the Golden Gate International Exposition of 1939–40.

Natural History Museum: Dioramas and exhibits include **Wild California**, the **African Hall** (with a surprisingly realistic waterhole), and **Life Through Time**, which offers a 3.5 billion-year journey into the speculative experience of early life on earth. At the **Hohfeld Earth & Space Hall**, the neon solar system tells the story of the universe and the natural forces that have shaped—and still shape—the earth. Especially popular with children is **Earthquake**, a "you are there" experience that simulates two of the city's famous earthquakes. The **Wattis Hall of Human Cultures** specializes in anthropology and features one of the broadest Native American museum collections in Northern California, with an emphasis on cultures in both North America and South America. The **Far Side of Science Gallery** includes 159 original Gary Larson cartoons, offering a hilarious perspective on humanity's scientific research. The **Gem and Mineral Hall** contains some real gems, like a 1,350-pound quartz crystal from Arkansas.

Morrison Planetarium: This 65-foot dome simulates the night sky and its astronomical phenomena; Sky Shows are offered daily, at 2 P.M. on weekdays, and hourly from 11 A.M.–4 P.M. on weekends. The associated Earth & Space Hall features a moon rock, a meteorite, and other exhibits. Admission (over and above Academy admission) is $2.50 adults, $1.25 seniors/youths, children under six free. For more information, call 415/750-7141. But the planetarium is most noted for its weekend evening **Laserium** shows, 415/750-7138, where blue beams from a krypton/argon gas laser slice the air to the rhythm of whatever's on the stereo—classical music as well as rock. Tickets are $7 adults, and are available through BASS (415/478-2277) or at the Academy one-half hour before show time.

Steinhart Aquarium: The oldest aquarium in North America, the 1923 Steinhart Aquarium allows visitors to commune with the world's most diverse live fish collection, including representatives of around 600 different species (including fish, marine invertebrates, and other sealife). The stunning glass-walled, 100,000-gallon Fish Roundabout here puts visitors right in the swim of things, as if they were standing in the center of the open ocean; it's especially fun at feeding time (daily at 2 P.M.). Altogether there are 189 exhibits here, but some of the most dramatic include: Sharks of the Tropics; the Penguin Environment, featuring an entire breeding colony of black-footed penguins; and The Swamp, featuring tropical critters like alligators, crocodiles, snakes, lizards, and frogs. Fun for some hands-on wet and wild exploring is California Tidepool.

The Academy of Sciences, 415/221-5100 or 415/750-7145 (24-hour recorded information), is open daily 10 A.M.–5 P.M. (extended hours from Memorial Day weekend through Labor Day). Admission is free the first Wed. of the month (when hours are extended until 8:45 P.M.), otherwise $8.50 adults; $5.50 youths 12–17, seniors, and students with ID; and $2 children ages 4–11.

Park Activities, Events, and Information
Kennedy Dr. from 19th Ave. to Stanyan is closed to automobile traffic every Sunday; enjoy a walk, bike ride, or rollerblade (bicycle and rollerblade rentals on Stanyan). **Friends of Recreation and Parks,** 415/750-5105, offers free guided tours throughout the park May–Oct. But even more active sports fans won't be disappointed. Golden Gate Park action includes archery, baseball and basketball, boating and rowing, fly-casting, football, horseback riding and horse-shoes, lawn bowling, model yacht sailing—there's a special lake for just that purpose—plus polo, roller skating, soccer, and tennis. In addition to the exceptional Children's Playground, there are two other kiddie play areas.

Free **Golden Gate Band Concerts** are offered at 2 P.M. on Sunday and holidays at the park's Music Concourse. The **Midsummer Music Festival** in Stern Grove, Sloat Blvd. at 19th Ave., is another fun, and free, park program. Scheduled on consecutive Sundays from mid-June through August, it's quite popular, so come as early as possible. (For exact dates and program information, call the park office,

listed below.) A variety of other special events are regularly scheduled in Golden Gate Park, including **A la Carte, a la Park,** San Francisco's "largest outdoor dining event." This gala gourmet fest, with themed pavilions, showcases the wares of Bay Area restaurants and Sonoma County wineries, the talents of celebrity chefs, and a wide variety of entertainment. It's a benefit for the San Francisco Shakespeare Festival, which offers an annual schedule of free public performances in August. A la Carte, a la Park is usually scheduled in late summer, over the three-day Labor Day weekend. Call 415/458-1988 for information.

To save money on visits to multiple park attractions, purchase a **Golden Gate Explorer Pass** for $14 at the park office, downtown at the visitors information center at Hallidie Plaza, or at TIX Bay Area in Union Square, 415/433-7827. For more information about park events and activities (maps are $2.50; other items are free), contact the **San Francisco Recreation and Park Department** office (which is also Golden Gate Park headquarters) in ivy-covered McLaren Lodge, 501 Stanyan (at Fulton, on the park's east side), 415/831-2700, open weekdays 8 A.M.–5 P.M. The park's official website is www.civiccenter.ci.sf.ca.us/recpark/.

Light meals and snacks are available at various concessions or at **Cafe de Young** inside the de Young Museum; at the Academy of Sciences; and at the **Japanese Tea Garden Teahouse** (fortune cookies and tea). There is also great choice in restaurants near the intersection of 9th Ave. and Irving, or along Haight and Stanyan Streets.

To reach the museums and tea garden via public transportation, board a westbound #5-Fulton bus on Market St., climbing off at Fulton and 8th Avenue. After 6 P.M. and on Sun. and holidays, take #21-Hayes to Fulton and 6th. Call 415/673-MUNI for other routes and schedule information.

SEEING SAN FRANCISCO: DOWNTOWN AND OTHER DISTRICTS

In other times, San Francisco neighborhoods and districts had such distinct ethnic and cultural or functional identities that they served as separate cities within a city. It wasn't uncommon for people to be born and grow up, to work, to raise families, and to die in their own insular neighborhoods, absolutely unfamiliar with the rest of San Francisco.

For the most part, those days are long past. Since its inception, the city has transformed itself, beginning as a sleepy mission town, then a lawless gold-rush capital that gradually gained respectability and recognition as the West Coast's most sophisticated cultural and trade center. The process continues. The city's neighborhoods continue to reinvent themselves, and California's accelerated economic and social mobility also erase old boundaries. Just where one part of town ends and another begins is a favorite San Francisco topic of disagreement.

For more information about city attractions, see Delights and Diversions below. For complete practical information, including how to get around town and where to stay and eat, see the concluding sections of this chapter.

AROUND UNION SQUARE

Named after Civil War–era rallies held here in support of Union forces (California eventually spurned the Confederacy), San Francisco's Union Square is parking central for downtown shoppers, since the square also serves as the roof of the multilevel parking garage directly below. (Other garages within walking distance include the Sutter-Stockton Garage to the north, the Ellis-O'Farrell Garage two blocks south, and, across Market, the huge and inexpensive Fifth & Mission Garage.)

The landmark **Westin St. Francis Hotel** flanks Union Square on the west, its bar a time-honored retreat from nearby major stores like **Saks Fifth Avenue, Tiffany, Bullock & Jones, Macy's,** and **Neiman-Marcus** (which also has its own popular **Rotunda** restaurant for après-shop dropping; open for lunch and afternoon tea).

Immediately east of Union Square along Post, Maiden Lane, and Geary, you'll find an unabashed selection of expensive and fashionable stores, from **Cartier, Dunhill,** and **Wilkes Bashford** to **NikeTown USA, Eddie Bauer,** and **Brooks Brothers.** Or dress yourself up at **Ralph Lauren, Versace, Chanel, Laura Ashley,** and several other designer emporiums. **Gumps** at 135 Post is the elegant specialist in one-of-a-kind and rare wares, where even the furniture is art. Don't miss a stroll down traffic-free, two-block **Maiden Lane,** a one-time red-light district stretching between Stockton and Kearny, chock-full of sidewalk cafés and shops. Here stands the Circle Gallery building, most ogled for its architecture. Designed in 1949 by Frank Lloyd Wright, with its spiral interior this building is an obvious prototype for his more famous Guggenheim Museum in New York. **Crocker Galleria,** at Post and Montgomery, offers still more shopping.

DEFINING DOWNTOWN

In San Francisco, "downtown" is a general reference to the city's hustle-bustle heart. Knowing just where it starts and ends is largely irrelevant, so long as you understand that it includes Union Square, much of Market Street, and the Civic Center government and arts buildings. The Financial District and the Waterfront are also included. Six or seven blocks directly west of the Civic Center is the Alamo Square Historic District, one among other enclaves of gentrified Victorian neighborhoods in the otherwise down-and-out Western Addition, which also includes Japantown. Though purists will no doubt quibble, for reasons of proximity these are included with downtown. And while more "uptown" parts of the South of Market Area (SoMa) are essentially downtown too, as are Nob Hill and Chinatown, those areas are covered in more depth elsewhere below.

SAN FRANCISCO ON STAGE

Geary Street near both Mason and Taylor is the official center of the theater district, and the 400 block of Geary serves as the epicenter of the mainstream theater scene. These days the concentration of upscale Union Square hotels downtown roughly duplicates the theater district boundaries. With so many fine theaters scattered throughout the city, it's something of a New York affectation to insist on that designation downtown. But San Francisco, a city that has loved its dramatic song and dance since gold rush days, definitely insists. Poetry readings, lectures, opera, and Shakespeare were integral to the 1800s arts scene. Superstar entertainers of the era made their mark here, from spider-dancer Lola Montez and her child protégé Lotta Crabtree to Lillie Langtry, opera star Luisa Tetrazzini, actress Helena Modjeska, and actor Edwin Booth. Today, out-of-towners flock to big musicals like *Phantom of the Opera* and evergreens like the murder mystery *Shear Madness*. Luckily, the best shows are often less crowded. Most shows begin at 8 p.m., and the majority of theaters are closed on Monday.

Theater Information

Finding information on what's going on in the theater is not a difficult task. Listings are printed in the *San Francisco Bay Guardian*, the *SF Weekly*, and the Sunday edition of the *San Francisco Chronicle*. Or check out the arts online at www.citysearch7.com. And wherever you find it, pick up a free copy of *Stagebill* magazine, www.stagebill.com, for its current and comprehensive show schedules.

Getting Tickets

Theater tickets can be purchased in advance or for half price on the day of the performance at **TIX Bay Area,** on Stockton St. at Union Square, 415/433-7827, www.tix.com. Payment is cash only, no credit card reservations. A full-service BASS ticket outlet as well, TIX also handles advance full-price tickets to many Bay Area events (open Tues.–Sat. noon–7:30 P.M.). You can get a catalog for ordering advance tickets at half price by calling **TIX by Mail,** at 415/430-1140. To charge BASS arts and entertainment tickets by phone or to listen to recorded calendar listings, call 415/478-2277 (BASS). Order full-price tickets in advance with a $2.50 service charge from Ticketmaster, 415/421-8497 or toll-free 800/755-4000, www.ticketmaster.com.

Other ticket box offices include: **City Box Office,** 415/392-4400; **Entertainment Ticketfinder,** 650/756-1414 or toll-free 800/523-1515; and **St. Francis Theatre and Sports Tickets,** a service of the Westin St..Francis Hotel, 415/362-3500, or www.premiertickets.com.

Heading south from Union Square on Stockton, between O'Farrell and Market, you'll pass the famous **F.A.O. Schwarz** (full of adult-priced toys and still fun for kids); **Planet Hollywood;** and the **Virgin Megastore,** where music lovers can find just about anything to add to their CD collection. At Market St. is the new **Old Navy,** as well as a cheap thrill for shoppers—the eight-story circular escalator ride up to **Nordstrom** and other stores at **San Francisco Centre,** 5th and Market, which was built in the late 1980s with the hope of attracting suburbanites and squeezing out the homeless.

Just down a ways from the theater district and skirting the Tenderloin at 561 Geary (between Taylor and Jones) is the odd **Blue Lamp** bar—note the blue lamp, a classic of neo-neon art. Once just a hard-drinkers' dive, now the Blue Lamp is a campy, hipsters', hard-drinkers' dive, most interesting late at night when the neighborhood gets a bit scary. But the real reason to come here is live music, just-starting band badness. Just a few blocks away, near Union Square at 333 Geary (between Powell and Mason), is another world entirely—**Lefty O'Doul's,** a hofbrau-style deli and old-time bar stuffed to the ceiling with baseball memorabilia. Lefty was a local hero, a big leaguer who came back to manage the minor-league San Francisco Seals before the Giants came to town.

The Tenderloin

Stretching between Union Square and the Civic Center is the Tenderloin, definitely a poor choice for a casual stroll by tourists and other innocents. A down-and-out pocket of poverty pocked these days by the city signposts of human misery—drug dealing, prostitution, pornography,

Theater District Venues

For Broadway shows, the **Curran Theatre,** 445 Geary (between Mason and Taylor), 415/551-2000 (information), 415/478-2277 (BASS) for tickets, is the long-running standard. The repertory **American Conservatory Theater** (ACT), 415/834-3200 or 415/749-2228 (box office), performs its big-name-headliner contemporary comedies and dramas in the venerable **Geary Theatre,** 415 Geary (at Mason).

Other neighborhood venues include the **Mason Street Theatre,** 415/982-5463, at 340 Mason (near Geary); the **Cable Car Theatre,** 415/255-9772, at 430 Mason (between Post and Geary); the **Golden Gate Theatre,** 415/551-2000, at 1 Taylor (at Golden Gate), longtime home of the Pulitzer Prize and Tony Award–winning *Rent;* and the **Marines Memorial Theater,** 415/551-2000, at 609 Sutter (at Mason). All are good bets for off-Broadway shows. Unusual small theaters include the **Theatre on the Square,** 415/433-9300, sharing space with the Kensington Park Hotel at 450 Post (between Powell and Mason), and the **Plush Room Cabaret,** 415/885-2115, inside the York Hotel at 940 Sutter (at Leavenworth).

Performance Spaces Elsewhere

San Francisco is also home to a number of small, innovative theaters and theater troupes, including the **Magic Theatre, Cowell Theater,** and **Young Performers Theatre** at Fort Mason, and the **Asian Amer-** ican Theatre in the Richmond District, mentioned in more detail in The Avenues section of this chapter. The **Actors Theatre of San Francisco,** 533 Sutter (between Powell and Mason), 415/296-9179, usually offers unusual plays. Also popular for progressive dramatic theater is SoMa's **Climate Theatre,** 252 9th St. (at Folsom), 415/978-2345. Another innovator in the realm of performance art is **Theater Artaud,** 450 Florida St. (at 17th), 415/621-7797. **Theatre Rhinoceros,** 2926 16th St. (between Mission and S. Van Ness), 415/861-5079, is America's oldest gay and lesbian theater company, established in 1978.

The long-running **Eureka Theatre Company,** 215 Jackson (between Front and Battery), 415/788-7469 (box office and information), is noted for its provocative, politically astute presentations. **Intersection for the Arts,** 446 Valencia St. (between 15th and 16th), 415/626-2787 (administration) or 415/626-3311 (box office), the city's oldest alternative arts center, presents everything from experimental dramas to performance and visual art and dance. One-time "new talent" like Robin Williams, Whoopi Goldberg, and Sam Shepard are all Intersection alumni. **George Coates Performance Works,** 110 McAllister (at Leavenworth), 415/863-8520 (administration) or 415/863-4130 (box office), offers innovative multimedia theater presentations in a repurposed neo-Gothic cathedral.

by Pat Reilly and Kim Weir

---

and violent crime—the densely populated Tenderloin earned its name around the turn of the century, when police assigned to patrol its mean streets received additional hazard pay—and, some say, substantial protection money and kickbacks. (The extra cash allowed them to dine on the choicest cuts of meat.) The Tenderloin's historic boundaries are Post, Market, Van Ness, and Powell. In reality, however, the city's designated theater district (with accompanying cafés and nightspots), many newly gentrified hotels, even the St. Francis Hotel and most Civic Center attractions fall within this no-man's land, which is especially a no-woman's land. More realistic, better-safe-than-sorry boundaries are Larkin, Mason, O'Farrell, and Market, with an extra caution also for some streets south of Market (especially 6th) as far as Howard. As a general rule, perimeters are safer than core areas, but since

this is San Francisco's highest crime area, with rape, mugging, and other assaults at an all-time high, for tenderfeet no part of the Tenderloin is considered safe—even during daylight hours. Ask local shopkeepers and restaurant or hotel personnel about the safety of specific destinations, if in doubt, and travel in groups when you do venture any distance into the Tenderloin.

But the area has its beauty, too, often most apparent through the celebrations and ministries of the Reverend Cecil Williams and congregation at the renowned **Glide Memorial United Methodist Church,** which rises up at 330 Ellis (at Taylor), 415/771-6300, www.glide.org. Glide sponsors children's assistance and other community programs, from basic survival and AIDS care to the Computers and You program, which helps the economically disadvantaged learn computer skills. The Glide Ensemble choir sings an uplifting mix of gospel, freedom songs, and rock at its celebrations, held each Sunday at 9 and 11 A.M. And some neighborhoods are cleaning up considerably, the indirect influence of commercial redevelopment and the influx of large numbers of Asian immigrants, many from Cambodia, Laos, and Vietnam. The annual **Tet Festival** celebrates the Vietnamese New Year. The Tenderloin also supports a small but growing arts community, as the 'Loin is one of the few remaining pockets of affordable housing in San Francisco. Among the neighborhood's many bars, the **Edinburgh Castle** at 950 Geary (between Polk and Larkin), 415/885-4074, stands out, drawing an interesting crowd of Scottish expatriates and young urbanites. The pub specializes in single malt Scotch, lager, and some of the best fish 'n' chips in the city.

MARKET STREET AND THE FINANCIAL DISTRICT

The Financial District features San Francisco's tallest, most phallic buildings, perhaps suggesting something profound about the psychology of the global capitalist thrust. When rolling into town on the river of traffic, via the Golden Gate Bridge or, especially, Oakland's Bay Bridge, this compact concentration of law offices, insurance buildings, investment companies, banks, brokerages, and high-brow businesses rises up from the sparkling waters like some fantastic illusion, the greenback-packed Emerald City of the West Coast. Even if wandering on foot and temporarily lost, to get back downtown one merely looks up and heads off toward the big buildings.

COCKTAIL TIME

Sometimes you just need to cast off the flannel shirt and Doc Martens and join what used to be known as the "jet set" to toast the high life. The following establishments offer a sample of that old San Francisco sparkle.

Entering the magnificent art-deco **Redwood Room**, 495 Geary St. (at Taylor) at the Clift Hotel, 415/775-4700, in the heart of the theater district and just two blocks from bustling Union Square, makes you feel like you've been transported to an earlier era. Romantic lighting, gleaming redwood walls, and a baby grand appeal to WASPy types and businesspeople in search of a quiet drink. And the drinks, especially martinis, are top-notch.

The **Tonga Room** at 950 Mason St. (between California and Sacramento), 415/772-5278, opened its exotic doors in 1945 inside the Fairmont Hotel—the lobby recognizable by American TV addicts as the one in the short-lived series *Hotel*—to bring the Pacific Islander theme to San Francisco. Polynesian decor and thatch-roofed huts surround a deep blue lake, where simulated tropical rainstorms hit every half hour. The lethal Bora Bora Horror tops the list of intriguing frozen cocktails, combining rum, banana liqueur, and Grand Marnier with a huge slice of pineapple. Rum also features in the Hurricane, Lava Bowl, and the Zombie. Happy hour offers the most economical visit possible. Normally pricey drinks cost $5, and you can graze on a buffet of edible treats (egg rolls, pot stickers, and dim sum) while listening to the house band's forgettable elevator music.

The drinkery at the **Top of the Mark,** 999 California St. (at Mason), 415/392-3434, is the city's most famous view lounge, an ideal place to take friends and dazzle them with the lights of San Francisco. Large windows take in a panorama of San Francisco's landmarks, from the Twin Peaks Tower to the Transamerica Pyramid and the Golden Gate Bridge. There's live music every night, and given the ritzy setting, a $7–10 cover charge doesn't seem all that steep. Classic cocktails—Manhattans, sidecars, and martinis—are the libations of choice. The bar food is upscale and excellently prepared, with selections ranging from a Mediterranean platter to Beluga caviar.

The word "cocktail" practically whispers from behind the ruby red silk curtains at the glamorous **Starlight Room** at 450 Powell St. (between Post and Sutter), 415/395-8595, perched on the 21st floor of the 1928 Sir Francis Drake Hotel. Polished mahogany fixtures, luxurious furnishings, and a 360-degree view of the city make the Starlight Room one of the nicest cocktail experiences going. The spacious bar embraces the retro swing theme, and a mahogany dance floor and live music by Harry Denton's Starlight Orchestra attract young swing fans and older couples from out on the town. Light supper options range from pan-roasted crab cakes to oysters on the half-shell. All of this dazzle is surprisingly affordable, with a small evening cover charge and cocktails from $7–10.

by Pat Reilly

The actual boundaries of the Financial District, built upon what was once water (Yerba Buena Cove), are rather vague, dependent upon both personal opinion and that constant urban flux of form and function. In general, the district includes the entire area from the north side of Market St. to the Montgomery St. corridor, north to the Jackson Square Historic District. Market Street is anchored near the bay by the concrete square of **Justin Herman Plaza** and its either loved-or-hated **Vaillancourt Fountain,** said to be a parody of the now-demolished freeway it once faced.

Embarcadero Center

Above and behind the plaza is the astounding and Orwellian Embarcadero Center complex, the high-class heart of the Golden Gateway redevelopment project. Here is the somewhat surreal **Hyatt Regency Hotel,** noted for its 17-story indoor atrium and bizarre keyboard-like exterior, as well as the **Park Hyatt Hotel.** But the main focus is the center's four-part shopping complex, **Embarcadero One** through **Embarcadero Four,** stretching along four city blocks between Clay and Sacramento. Inside, maps and information kiosks can help the disoriented. Atop One Embarcadero is San Francisco's equivalent to the Empire State Building observation desk, here called **SkyDeck,** 415/772-0590 or toll-free 888/737-5933. This attraction couples basic bird's-eye viewing with art and artifact exhibits, interactive touch screens providing historical and cultural information about the city, and free docent "tours." SkyDeck is open year-round (except major holidays), daily 9:30 A.M.–9 P.M.; admission is $7 adults, $4 seniors/students, $3.50 children 5–12. Wheelchair accessible.

For a hands-on lesson in the **World of Economics,** including the chance to pretend you're president of the United States or head of the Fed, stop by the lobby of the **Federal Reserve Bank,** 101 Market (at Spear), 415/974-2000, open weekdays 9 A.M.–4:30 P.M., to play with the computer games and displays. The **World of Oil** in the Chevron USA Building, 555 Market (at 2nd), 415/894-4895, open weekdays 9 A.M.–3:30 P.M., is a small museum with industry-oriented facts, including a computerized "Energy Learning Center." **Robert Frost Plaza,** at the intersection of Market and California, is a reminder that New England's poet was a San Francisco homeboy.

Heading up California St., stop at the **Bank of California** building at 400 California (between Sansome and Battery), 415/445-0200, for a tour through its basement **Museum of the Money of the American West,** everything from gold nuggets and U.S. Mint mementos to dueling pistols. The **Wells Fargo History Museum,** in Wells Fargo Bank at 420 Montgomery (near California), 415/396-2619, features an old Concord Stagecoach; a re-created early Wells Fargo office; samples of gold, gold scales, and gold-mining tools; and a hands-on telegraph exhibit, complete with telegraph key and Morse code books. It's open Mon.–Fri. 9 A.M.–5 P.M.; admission free. **Bank of America** at California and Kearny also has historical exhibits. In the 1905 **Merchants Exchange** building at California and Montgomery, the bygone boat-business days are remembered with ship models and William Coulter marine paintings. For a look at more modern mercantile action, climb to the visitors gallery for an insider's view of the action at the **Pacific Stock Exchange** at Pine and Sansome, the largest in America outside New York City.

THE BAWDY BARBARY COAST

Designated these days as the **Jackson Square Historical District,** the section of town stretching into North Beach across Washington St. was once called the Barbary Coast, famous since the gold rush as the world's most depraved human hellhole. Pacific St. was the main thoroughfare, a stretch of bad-boy bawdy houses, saloons, dance halls, and worse—like the "cowyards," where hundreds of prostitutes performed onstage with animals or in narrow cribs stacked as high as four stories. Words like "Mickey Finn," "Shanghaied," and "hoodlum" were coined here. Local moral wrath couldn't stop the barbarity of the Barbary Coast—and even the earthquake of 1906 spared the area, much to everyone's astonishment. Somewhat settled down by the Roaring '20s, when it was known as the International Settlement, the Barbary Coast didn't shed its barbarians entirely until the 1950s. Today it's quite tame, an oddly gentrified collection of quaint brick buildings.

the Transamerica Building: once outrageous, now a landmark

AISLINN RACE

People were outraged over the architecture of the **Transamerica Pyramid** at Montgomery and Washington, the city's tallest building, when it was completed in 1972. But now everyone has adjusted to its strange winged-spire architecture. Until recently it was possible to ride up to the 27th floor, to the "viewing area," for breathtaking sunny-day views of Coit Tower, the Golden Gate Bridge, and Alcatraz. These days, you'll get only as far as the lobby and the popular new **Virtual Observation Deck,** with its four monitors connected to cameras mounted at the very tip of the Pyramid's spire. What's fun here is the chance to zoom, tilt, and pan the cameras for some fairly unusual views. Back down on the ground, head for Transamerica Center's **Redwood Park** on Friday lunch hours in summer for "Music in the Park" concerts.

CIVIC CENTER AND VICINITY

Smack dab in the center of the sleaze zone is San Francisco's major hub of government, the Civic Center, built on the one-time site of the Yerba Buena Cemetery. (See cautions mentioned under the Tenderloin above, which also apply to almost any section of downtown Market St. after dark.) A sublime example of America's beaux arts architecture, the center's **City Hall,** 401 Van Ness (at Polk), 415/554-4858, www.ci.sf.ca.us/cityhall, was modeled after St. Peter's Basilica at the Vatican, in the belle

epoque style, complete with dome and majestic staircase. Renaissance-style sculptures state the city's dreams—the not necessarily incongruous collection of Wisdom, the Arts, Learning, Truth, Industry, and Labor over the Van Ness Ave. entrance, and Commerce, Navigation, California Wealth, and San Francisco above the doors on Polk Street. After sustaining severe damage in the 1989 earthquake, the building was repaired and meticulously refurbished, and its interior stylishly redone, on the watch of equally stylish Mayor Willie Brown, a project with a price tag of several hundred million dollars. Former state senator Quentin Kopp, never a Brown fan, has called this the "Taj Mahal" of public works projects. See it yourself—free 45-minute tours are available daily.

The **War Memorial Opera House,** 301 Van Ness (at Grove), 415/865-2000, www.sfopera. com, is the classical venue for the San Francisco Ballet Company as well as the San Francisco Opera, the place for society folk to see and be seen during the September to December opera season. Twin to the opera house, connected by extravagant iron gates, is the **Veterans Memorial Building.** The **Louise M. Davies Hall** at Van Ness and Grove, which features North America's largest concert hall organ, is the permanent venue for the **San Francisco Symphony.** If in the neighborhood, performing arts aficionados should definitely head west one block to the weekdays-only **San Francisco Performing Arts Library and Museum** at Grove and Gough.

San Francisco's **Main Library,** 100 Larkin (at Grove), 415/557-4400, is worth a browse, especially for the free Internet access offered at computer stations throughout the library. Free volunteer-led City Guides tours are headquartered here, 415/557-4266, and some depart from here. Civic Center Plaza, across Polk from the library, is home to many of the area's homeless, and also forms the garden roof for the underground **Brooks Hall** exhibit center and parking garage. **United Nations Plaza** stretches between Market St. and the Federal Building at McAllister (between 7th and 8th), commemorating the U.N.'s charter meeting in 1945 at the War Memorial Opera House. On Wed. and Sun., the plaza bustles with buyers and sellers of fish and unusual fruits and vegetables when the **Heart of the City Farmers' Market** is in bloom. Across Market St., technically in SoMa but allied in spirit with the Civic Center, is the stunningly refurbished former San Francisco Post Office and **U.S. Courthouse,** at 7th and Mission. This gorgeous 1905 granite masterpiece, full of marble and mosaic floors and ceilings, was damaged in the 1989 earthquake, but it's now back and better than ever after a $91 million earthquake retrofit and rehabilitation. The post office is gone, replaced by an atrium, but the courts are back in session here. The third-floor courtroom is particularly impressive.

In addition to the area's many cafés, restaurants, and nightspots, the **California Culinary Academy,** 625 Polk St. (at Turk), 415/771-3500 or toll-free 800/229-2433, is noted for its 16-month chef's training course in Italian, French, and nouvelle cuisine. For the curious, the academy is also an exceptionally good place to eat wonderful food at reasonable prices. The academy operates a bakery and café, the basement **Tavern on the Tenderloin** buffet, 415/771-3536, and the somewhat more formal **Careme Room,** 415/771-3535, a glass-walled dining hall where you can watch what goes on in the kitchen. Call for hours and reservation policies, which vary.

WESTERN ADDITION

These central city blocks west of Van Ness Ave. and south of Pacific Heights are certainly diverse. Settled in turn by Jewish, Japanese, and African

Americans, the neighborhood's historical associations are with the Fillmore's jazz and blues bars, which hosted greats like John Coltrane and Billie Holiday in the 1950s and '60s.

The area is remarkable architecturally because so many of its 19th-century Victorians survived the 1906 earthquake, though some subsequently declined into subdivided apartments or were knocked down by the wrecking ball of redevelopment. The Western Addition's remaining Victorian enclaves are rapidly becoming gentrified. The most notable—and most photographed—example is Steiner St. facing **Alamo Square** (other pretty "painted ladies" with facelifts stretch for several blocks in all directions), though countrylike **Cottage Row** just east of Fillmore St. between Sutter and Bush is equally enchanting.

Today most of the Western Addition is home to working-class families, though the area south of Geary, considered "The Fillmore," was long composed almost exclusively of heavy-crime, low-income housing projects. Many of those boxy projects have been demolished, and redevelopment here is generally improving the aesthetics of the neighborhood.

The Western Addition's intriguing shops, restaurants, and cultural attractions reflect the neighborhood's roots. For an exceptional selection of African-American literature, check out **Marcus Books,** 1712 Fillmore (at Post), 415/346-4222, which also hosts occasional readings. Until quite recently, on Sunday mornings jazz emanated from **St. John Coltrane's African Orthodox Church** on Divisadero at Oak, a tiny storefront ministry devoted to celebrating the life of St. John Coltrane. Sadly, due to rapidly rising rents, the congregation has been forced to find a new church. For current information and church updates, check out www.saintjohncoltrane.org. Fancy dressing like a member of Run DMC? You'll find one of the country's biggest selections of Adidas clothing at **Harput's,** 1527 Fillmore (between Ellis and Geary), 415/923-9300. And **Jack's Record Cellar,** 254 Scott St. (at Page), 415/431-3047, is the perfect place to browse through obscure jazz and blues records.

Fillmore St. also creates the western border of **Japantown,** or Nihonmachi, an area encompassing the neighborhoods north of Geary, south of Pine, and stretching east to Octavia. This very

American variation on Japanese community includes the old-style, open-air **Buchanan Mall** between Post and Sutter, and the more modern and ambitious **Japan Center,** a three-block-long concrete mall on Geary between Fillmore and Laguna. It's inaccessibly ugly from the outside, in the American tradition, but offers intriguing attractions inside, like karaoke bars and the **Kabuki Hot Springs,** 415/922-6000, a communal bathhouse on the ground floor.

Lined with boutiques selling clothing from small labels, sidewalk restaurants, and oddball furniture stores, **Hayes Street** between Franklin and Laguna is an oasis of funky charm. Stroll over to **560 Hayes,** 560 Hayes St. (at Laguna), 415/861-7993, for an excellent selection of 1960s and '70s evening wear, including vintage items from top designers like Chanel and Gucci. Find vintage timepieces and watches at **Zeitgeist Timepieces and Jewelry,** 437 Hayes St. (between Gough and Octavia), 415/864-0185.

HAIGHT-ASHBURY

Aging hippies, random hipsters, and the hopelessly curious of all ages are still attracted to San Francisco's Haight-Ashbury, once a commercial district for adjacent Golden Gate Park and a solid family neighborhood in the vicinity of Haight Street. The Golden Gate's block-wide Panhandle (which certainly resembles one on a map) was intended as the park's carriage entrance, helped along toward the desired ambience by neighboring Victorian-age Queen Annes. Once abandoned by the middle class, however, Haight-Ashbury declined into the cheap-rent paradise surrounded by parklands that became "Hashbury," "hippies," and headquarters for the 1967 Summer of Love.

Drawn here by the drum song of the coming-of-age Aquarian Age, some 200,000 young people lived in subdivided Victorian crash pads, on the streets, and in the parks that summer, culturally recognizable by long hair, scruffy jeans, tie-dyed T-shirts, granny glasses, peace signs, beads, and the flowers-in-your-hair style of flowing skirts and velvet dresses. Essential, too, at that time: underground newspapers and unrestrained radio, black-lights and psychedelia, incense, anything that came from India

(like gurus), acid and mescaline, hashish, waterpipes, marijuana and multicolored rolling papers, harmonicas, tambourines, guitars, and bongo drums. A Volkswagen van was helpful, too, so loads of people could caravan off to anti–Vietnam War rallies, to wherever it was the Grateful Dead or Jefferson Airplane were playing (for free, usually), or to Fillmore West and Winterland, where Bill Graham staged so many concerts. It was all fairly innocent, at first, an innocence that didn't last. By late 1967, cultural predators had arrived: the tourists, the national media, and serious drug pushers and pimps. Love proved to be fragile. Most true believers headed back to the land, and Haight-Ashbury became increasingly violent and dangerous, especially for the young runaways who arrived (and still arrive) to stake a misguided claim for personal freedom.

"The Haight" today is considerably cleaner, its Victorian neighborhoods spruced up but not exactly gentrified. The classic Haight-Ashbury head shops are long gone, runaway hippies replaced by runaway punks panhandling for quarters (or worse). But Haight St. and vicinity is still hip, still socially and politically aware, still worth a stroll. The parkside Upper Haight stretch has more than its share of funky cafés, coffee shops, oddball bars and clubs, boutiques, and secondhand stores. If this all seems stodgy, amble on down to the Lower Haight in the Western Addition, an area fast becoming the city's new avant-garde district.

Seeing and Doing Haight-Ashbury

Aside from the commercial versions, there are a few significant countercultural sights in the Upper Haight, like the old Victorian **Dead House** at 710 Ashbury (near Waller), where the Grateful Dead lived and played their still-living music (and possibly where the term "deadheads" first emerged for the Dead's fanatic fans), and the **Jefferson Airplane's** old pad at 2400 Fulton (on the eastern edge of Golden Gate Park at Willard). Definitely worth a stop, for organic juice and granola, art to meditate by, and New Age computer networking, is **The Red Victorian** at 1665 Haight (near Belvedere), 415/864-1978, www.redvic.com, also a fascinating bed-and-breakfast complex that successfully honors the Haight's original innocence. Do climb on up the steep paths into nearby **Buena Vista Park,** a shocking tangle of anarchistically enchanted forest, just for the through-the-trees views. Otherwise, the scene here is wherever you can find it. **Bound Together,** 1369 Haight St. (at Masonic), 415/431-8355, is a collective bookstore featuring a somewhat anarchistic collection: books on leftist politics, conspiracy theories, the occult, and sexuality. **Pipe Dreams,** 1376 Haight (at Masonic), 415/431-3553, is one place to go for Grateful Dead memorabilia and quaint drug paraphernalia, like water pipes and "bongs," but **Distractions,** 1552 Haight (between Clayton and Ashbury), 415/252-8751, is truest to the form; in addition to the Dead selection, you can also snoop through head shop supplies, an ample variety of Tarot cards, and Guatemalan clothing imports.

Style is another Haight St. specialty. Though secondhand clothing stores here tend to feature higher prices than elsewhere, three of the best are **Wasteland,** 1660 Haight (at Belvedere), 415/863-3150; the **Buffalo Exchange,** 1555 Haight (between Clayton and Ashbury), 415/431-7733; and **Aardvarks,** 1501 Haight (at Ashbury), 415/621-3141. For old-style music bargains—and actual albums, including a thousand hard-to-find ones—head to **Recycled Records,** 1377 Haight (at Masonic), 415/626-4075. For thousands of used CDs and tapes, try **Reckless Records,** 1401 Haight (at Masonic), 415/431-3434. Housed in a former bowling alley, **Amoeba Music,** 1855 Haight (between Stanyan and Shrader), 415/831-1200, is huge and offers an encyclopedic collection of new and used sounds.

Shops of interest in the Lower Haight include: **Zebra Records,** 475 Haight (near Webster), 415/626-9145, a DJ supply store that's the place to find cutting-edge hip hop, acid jazz, and Latin House; the **Naked Eye,** 533 Haight (between Fillmore and Steiner), 415/864-2985, which specializes in impossible-to-find videos; and **Used Rubber U.S.A.,** 597 Haight (at Steiner), 415/626-7855, which makes durable, hip, high-style handbags out of otherwise unrecycled car tires (a bit expensive). Well respected in the neighborhood for more organic personal decoration is **Erno's Tattoo Parlor,** 252 Fillmore (between Haight and Waller), 415/861-9206. Shop the Lower Haight, too, for stylish used clothing stores with good pickings, low prices, and zero crowds.

MISSION DISTRICT

Vibrant and culturally electric, the Mission District is one of San Francisco's most exciting neighborhoods. The fact that most tourists never discover the area's pleasures is a sad commentary on our times. To the same extent people fear that which seems foreign in America—a nation created by foreigners—they miss out on the experience of life as it is. And the country becomes even more hell-bent on mandating social homogenization despite ideals and rhetoric to the contrary.

On any given day in the Mission District, especially if it's sunny, the neighborhood is busy with the business of life. The largely Hispanic population—Colombian, Guatemalan, Mexican, Nicaraguan, Peruvian, Panamanian, Puerto Rican, Salvadorean—crowds the streets and congregates on corners. Whether Mission residents are out strolling with their children or shopping in the many bakeries, produce stores, and meat markets, the community's cultural energy is unmatched by any other city neighborhood—with the possible exception of Chinatown early in the morning. This remains true, even now, though gentrification has also arrived in the Mission.

Even with onrushing gentrification, the Mission's ungentrified modern attitude and still relatively low rents have also created a haven for artists, writers, social activists, and politicos. The Latino arts scene is among the city's most powerful and original. This is one of San Francisco's newest New Bohemias, a cultural crazy quilt where artists and assorted oddballs are not only tolerated but encouraged. Businesses catering to this emerging artistic consciousness are becoming prominent along Valencia St., already considered home by the city's lesbian community.

Technically, the Mission District extends south from near the Civic Center to the vicinity of Cesar Chavez (Army). Dolores or Church St. (or thereabouts) marks the western edge, Alabama St. the eastern. Mission St., the main thoroughfare (BART stations at 16th and 24th), is lined with discount stores and pawnshops. Main commercial areas include 16th St. between Mission and Dolores, 24th St. between Valencia and York, and Valencia St.—the bohemian center of social life, lined with coffeehouses, bars, bookstores, performance art venues, and establishments serving the lesbian and women's community. For the latest word on feminist and lesbian art shows, readings, performances, and other events, stop by the nonprofit **Women's Building,** 3543 18th St. (just off Valencia), 415/431-1180.

Mission Dolores

The city's oldest structure, completed in 1791, Mission San Francisco de Asis at Dolores and 16th Sts., 415/621-8203, open daily 9 A.M.–4:30 P.M., is the sixth mission established in California by the Franciscan fathers. A donation of $2 or more is appreciated. (The best time to arrive, to avoid busloads of tourists and the crush of schoolchildren studying California history, is before 10 A.M.) Founded earlier, in 1776, the modest chapel and outbuildings came to be known as Mission Dolores, the name derived from a nearby lagoon and creek, Arroyo de Nuestra Señora de los Dolores, or "stream of our lady of sorrows."

And how apt the new shingle proved to be, in many ways. In the peaceful cemetery within the mission's walled compound is the "Grotto of Lourdes," the unmarked grave of more than 5,000 Ohlone and others among the native workforce. Most died of measles and other introduced diseases in the early 1800s, the rest from other varieties of devastation. After California became a state, the first U.S. Indian agent came to town to take a census of the Native American population. It was an easy count, since there was only one, a man named Pedro Alcantara who was still grieving for a missing son. Near the grotto are the vine-entwined tombstones of pioneers and prominent citizens, like California's first governor under Mexican rule, Don Luis Antonio Arguello, and San Francisco's first mayor, Don Francisco de Haro.

The sturdy mission chapel—the small humble structure, not the soaring basilica adjacent—survived the 1906 earthquake due largely to its four-foot-thick adobe walls. Inside, the painted ceilings are an artistic echo of the Ohlone, whose original designs were painted with vegetable dyes. And the simple altar offers stark contrast to the grandeur next door. For a peek at the collection of mission artifacts and memorabilia, visit the small museum.

Mission District Murals

The entire Mission District is vividly alive, with aromas and sounds competing everywhere with color. And nothing in the Mission District is quite as colorful as its mural art. More than 200 murals dot the neighborhood, ranging from brilliantly colored homages to work, families, and spiritual flight to boldly political attacks on the status quo.

Start with some **"BART art,"** at the 24th St. station, where Michael Rios's columns of humanoids lift up the rails. Another particularly impressive set is eight blocks down, off 24th St.

California's sixth mission: Mission Dolores and the adjacent basilica

AISLINN RACE

Mission District mural

SAN FRANCISCO CONVENTION & VISITORS BUREAU/CAROL SIMOWITZ

on the fences and garage doors along **Balmy Alley,** and also at **Flynn Elementary School** at Precita and Harrison. At 14th and Natoma is a mural honoring Frida Kahlo, artist and wife of Diego Rivera.

Walking tours of the neighborhood murals (with well-informed guides) are led by the **Precita Eyes Mural Arts Center,** a charming gallery at 2981 24th St. (at Harrison), 415/285-2287, www.precitaeyes.org. The tours are offered every Sat. at 11 A.M. and 1:30 P.M., Sun. at 1:30 P.M.; $7 general, $4 seniors, $1 youths 18 and under. Call for information on the center's many other tours.

Other good art stops in the area include the nonprofit **Galeria de la Raza,** 2857 24th St. (at Bryant), 415/826-8009, featuring some exciting, straight-ahead political art attacks; the affiliated **Studio 24** gift shop adjacent, with everything from books and clothing to religious icons and Day of the Dead dolls; and the **Mission Cultural Center for Latino Arts,** 2868 Mission (between 24th and 25th Sts.), 415/821-1155, a community cultural and sociopolitical center that can supply you with more information on area artworks.

Potrero Hill

East of the Mission District proper and southeast of the SoMa scene is gentrifying (at least on the north side) Noe Valley–like Potrero Hill, known for its roller-coaster road rides (a favorite spot for filming TV and movie chase scenes)

and the world-famous **Anchor Brewing Company** microbrewery, 1705 Mariposa St. (at 17th), 415/863-8350, makers of Anchor Steam beer. Join a free weekday tour and see how San Francisco's famous beer is brewed. If you drive to Potrero Hill, detour to the "Poor Man's Lombard" at 20th and Vermont, which has earned the dubious honor of being the city's second twistiest street. This snakelike thoroughfare is not festooned with well-landscaped sidewalks and flowerbeds, but instead an odd assortment of abandoned furniture, beer bottles, and trash. Not yet socially transformed is the south side of the hill, which is close to **Bayview-Hunters Point;** these once-industrialized neighborhoods were left behind when World War II–era shipbuilding ceased and are now ravaged by poverty, drugs, and violence.

Levi Strauss & Co. Factory

If you're curious about how the West's most historic britches evolved, stop by Levi Strauss & Co., 250 Valencia St. (between Clinton Park and Brosnan), 415/565-9100, for a free tour (Tues. and Wed. only, at 9 A.M., 11 A.M., and 1:30 P.M., reservations required—and make them well in advance). This, Levi's oldest factory, was built in 1906 after the company's original waterfront plant was destroyed by earthquake and fire. The company is the world's largest clothing manufacturer, and most of its factories are fully automated. But at this site you can hear the riveting story of how Levi's 501's were originally made, and see it, too. Skilled workers cut, stitch, and assemble the button-fly jeans, as in the earlier days of the empire that Bavarian immigrant Levi Strauss built. During the boom days of the California gold rush, miners needed very rugged pants, something that wouldn't bust out at the seams. Strauss stitched up his first creations from tent canvas; when he ran out of that, he switched to sturdy brown cotton "denim" from Nimes, France. Levi's characteristic pocket rivets came along in the 1870s, but "blue jeans" weren't a reality until the next decade, when indigo blue dye was developed. After the tour, you can shop in the on-site company store.

Mission District Shopping

Clothes Contact, 473 Valencia (just north of 16th), 415/621-3212, sells fashionable vintage clothing for $8 per pound. (Consumer alert: those big suede jackets in the back weigh more than you might imagine.) Worth poking into, too, is the **Community Thrift Store,** 623-625 Valencia (between 17th and 18th), 415/861-4910, a fundraising venture for the gay and lesbian Tavern Guild. It's an expansive, inexpensive, and well-organized place, with a book selection rivaling most used bookstores. (The motto here is "out of the closet, into the store.") Cooperatively run **Modern Times Bookstore,** 888 Valencia (between 19th and 20th), 415/282-9246, is the source for progressive, radical, and Third World literature, magazines, and tapes.

If you're down on your luck, head up to **Lady Luck Candle Shop,** 311 Valencia (at 14th), 415/621-0358, a small store selling some pretty big juju, everything from high-test magic candles and religious potions (like St. John the Conqueror Spray) to Lucky Mojo Oil and Hold Your Man essential oil. **Good Vibrations,** 1210 Valencia (at 23rd), 415/974-8980, home of the vibrator museum, is a clean, user-friendly, liberated shop where women (and some men) come for adult toys, and to peruse the selection of in-print erotica, including history and literature.

More common in the Mission District are neighborhood-style antique and secondhand stores of every stripe. Bargains abound, without the inflated prices typical of trendier, more tourist-traveled areas.

CASTRO STREET AND VICINITY

The very idea is enough to make America's righteous religious right explode in an apoplectic fit, but the simple truth is that San Francisco's Castro St. is one of the safest neighborhoods in the entire city—and that's not necessarily a reference to sex practices.

San Francisco's tight-knit, well-established community of lesbian women and gay men represents roughly 15 percent of the city's population and 35 percent of its registered voters. Locally, nationally, and internationally, the Castro District epitomizes out-of-the-closet living. (There's nothing in this world like the Castro's Gay Freedom Day Parade—usually headed by hundreds of women on motorcycles, the famous Dykes on Bikes—and no neighborhood throws a better street party.) People here are committed to protecting their own and creating safe neighborhoods. What this means, for visitors straight or gay, is that there is a response—people get out of their cars, or rush out of restaurants, clubs, and apartment buildings—at the slightest sign that something is amiss.

Who ever would have guessed that a serious revival of community values in the United States would start in the Castro?

Actually, there have been many indications. And there are many reasons. The developing cultural and political influence of the Castro District became apparent in 1977, when openly gay Harvey Milk was elected to the San Francisco Board of Supervisors. But genuine acceptance seemed distant—never more so than in 1978, when both Milk and Mayor George Moscone were assassinated by conservative political rival Dan White, who had resigned his board seat and wanted it back. White's "diminished capacity" defense argument, which claimed that his habitual consumption of high-sugar junk food had altered his brain chemistry—the "Twinkie" defense—became a national scandal but ultimately proved successful. He was sentenced to a seven-year prison term.

The community's tragedies kept on coming, hitting even closer to home. Somewhat notorious in its adolescence as a safe haven for freestyle lifestyles, including casual human relationships and quickie sex, the Castro District was devastated by the initial impact of the AIDS epidemic. The community has been stricken by the tragic human consequences of an undiscriminating virus. But otherwise meaningless human loss has served only to strengthen the community's humanity. Just as, after Milk's assassination, greater numbers of community activists came forward to serve in positions of political influence, Castro District organizations like the Shanti Project, Open Hand, and the Names Project have extended both heart and hand to end the suffering. And fierce, in-your-face activists from groups like Act Up, Queer Nation, and Bad Cop No Donut have taken the message to the nation's streets.

So, while Castro District community values are strong and getting stronger, the ambience is not exactly apple-pie Americana. People with pierced body parts (some easily visible, some not) and dressed in motorcycle jackets still stroll in and out of leather bars. Its shops also can be somewhat unusual, like **Does Your Mother Know,** a seriously homoerotic greeting card shop on 18th St. near Castro.

Seeing and Doing the Castro

The neighborhood's business district, both avant-garde and gentrified Victorian, is small, stretching for three blocks along Castro St. between Market and 19th, and a short distance in each direction from 18th and Castro. This area is all included, geographically, in what was once recognizable as **Eureka Valley.** (Parking can be a problem, once you've arrived, so take the Muni Metro and climb off at the Castro St. station.) Some people also include the gentrifying **Noe Valley** (with its upscale 24th St. shopping district) in the general Castro stream of consciousness, but the technical dividing line is near the crest of Castro St. at 22nd Street. Keep driving on Upper Market St., and you'll wind up in the city's geographic center. Though the ascent is actually easier from Haight-Ashbury (from Twin Peaks Blvd. just off 17th—see a good road map), either way you'll arrive at or near the top of **Twin Peaks,** with its terraced neighborhoods, astounding views, and some of the city's best stairway walks. More challenging is the short but steep hike to the top of Corona Heights Park (at Roosevelt), also noted for the very good **Josephine D. Randall Junior Museum,** 199

Museum Way (at Roosevelt), 415/554-9600, a youth-oriented natural sciences, arts, and activities center open Tues.–Sat. 10 A.M.–5 P.M. Admission free; donations welcome.

Down below, **A Different Light,** 489 Castro St. (between Market and 18th Sts.), 415/431-0891, is the city's best gay and lesbian bookstore, with literature by and for. Readings and other events are occasionally offered; call for current information. Truly classic and quite traditional is the handsome and authentic art deco **Castro Theater,** 429 Castro (at Market), 415/621-6120, built in 1923. San Francisco's only true movie palace, the Castro is still a favorite city venue for classic movies and film festivals. Another highlight is the massive house Wurlitzer organ, which can make seeing a film at the Castro a truly exhilarating experience. **Cliff's Variety,** 479 Castro (at 18th), 415/431-5365, is another classic, a wonderfully old-fashioned hardware store where you can buy almost anything, from power saws to Play-Doh. Retro kitsch **Uncle Mame,** 2241 Market (between Noe and Sanchez), 415/626-1953, is another Castro gem. Packed to the rafters with 1950s, '60s and '70s pop culture ephemera, this is the place to shop for vintage board games, lunch boxes, and Barbies.

Also stop by **The Names Project,** 2362 Market (between 16th and 17th), 415/863-1966, a museum-like memorial to those felled by AIDS. It's also the original home of the famous AIDS Memorial Quilt, each section created by friends and family of someone who died of the disease. Adjacent (in the same building) is **Under One Roof,** 415/252-9430, a cool and classy little gift shop with Act Up votive candles, artwork, T-shirts, and more. All money earned goes to support some 50 AIDS service organizations.

SOUTH OF MARKET (SoMa)

Known by old-timers as "south of the slot," a reference to a neighborhood sans cable cars, San Francisco's South of Market area was a working- and middle-class residential area—until all its homes were incinerated in the firestorm following the great earthquake of 1906. Rebuilt early in the century with warehouses, factories, train yards, and port businesses at **China Basin,** these days the area has gone trendy. In the style of New York's SoHo (South of Houston), this semi-industrial stretch of the city now goes by the moniker "SoMa."

As is usually the case, the vanguard of gentrification was the artistic community: the dancers, musicians, sculptors, photographers, painters, and graphic designers who require low rents and room to create. Rehabilitating old warehouses and industrial sheds here into studios and performance spaces solved all but strictly creative problems. Then came the attractively inexpensive factory outlet stores, followed by eclectic cafés and nightclubs. The Yerba Buena Gardens redevelopment project sealed the neighborhood's fate, bringing big-time tourist attractions including the Moscone Convention Center, the San Francisco Museum of Modern Art, the Yerba Buena Center for the Arts, and The Rooftop at Yerba Buena Gardens, a multi-facility arts and entertainment complex.

Now the city's newest luxury hotel, the 30-story **W San Francisco,** towers over 3rd and Howard. Sony's futuristic new Metreon holds down 4th and Mission. Even near the once-abandoned waterfront just south of the traditional Financial District boundaries, avant-garde construction like **Number One Market Street,** which incorporates the old Southern Pacific Building, and **Rincon Center,** which encompasses the preserved Depression-era mural art of the Rincon Annex Post Office, have added a new look to once down-and-out areas. More

massive high-rises are on the way, and land values are shooting up in areas where previously only the neighborhood homeless did that. The starving artists have long since moved on to the Lower Haight and the Mission District, and in SoMa, the strictly eccentric is now becoming more self-consciously so.

San Francisco Museum of Modern Art

SoMa's transformation is largely due to the arrival of the San Francisco Museum of Modern Art (SFMOMA), 151 3rd St. (between Mission and Howard), 415/357-4000, which moved from its cramped quarters on the 3rd and 4th floors of the War Memorial. Many consider the modern, Swiss-designed building to be a work of art in itself. Love it or hate it, you're not likely to miss the soaring cylindrical skylight and assertive red brick of the new $60-million structure rising above the gritty streets south of Market.

The museum's permanent collection includes minor works by Georgia O'Keeffe, Pablo Picasso, Salvador Dali, Henri Matisse, and some outstanding paintings by Jackson Pollock. Mexican painters Frida Kahlo and her husband, Diego Rivera, are represented, as are the works of many Californian artists, including assembler Bruce Connor and sculptor Bruce Arneson. The museum also hosts excellent temporary exhibitions showcasing world-renowned individual artists. There's a hip little café, the **Cafe Museo,** 415/357-4500, and the **SFMOMA Museum Store,** well stocked with art books and postcards.

San Francisco Museum of Modern Art, seen from adjacent Yerba Buena Gardens

JEFF MYERS/TOM MYERS PHOTOGRAPHY

CLEAN UP YOUR ACT AT BRAINWASH

No doubt the cleanest scene among SoMa's hot spots is BrainWash at 1122 Folsom, 415/861-FOOD, 415/431-WASH, or www.brainwash.com, a combination café, smart bar, nightclub, and laundromat in a reformed warehouse. The brainchild of UC Berkeley and Free Speech Movement alumna Susan Schindler, BrainWash ain't heavy, just semi-industrial, from the beamed ceilings and neon to the concrete floor. The decor here includes café tables corralled by steel office chairs with original decoupage artwork on the seats. (Admit it—haven't you always wanted to sit on Albert Einstein's face?) BrainWash also features a small counter/bar area, and bathrooms for either "Readers" (lined with *Dirty Laundry Comics* wallpaper) or "Writers" (with walls and ceiling of green chalkboard, chalk provided for generating brainwashable graffiti). Since literary urges know no boundaries in terms of gender, of course both are open to both basic sexes. And others.

The small café at BrainWash offers quick, simple fare—salads, spinach and feta turnovers, pizza, and decent sandwiches (vegetarian and otherwise)—plus pastries and decadent pies, cakes, and cookies. Try a BrainWash Brownie, either double chocolate or double espresso. There's liquid espresso too, of course, plus cappuccinos and lattes, fresh unfiltered fruit or carrot juice, teas, beer, and wine.

Behind the café (and glass wall) is the BrainWash washhouse, a high-tech herd of washers and dryers ($1.50 per load for a regular wash load, $3.50 for a jumbo washer, and a quarter for 10 minutes of dryer time). Ask about the laundromat's wash-and-fold and dry-cleaning services. The whole shebang here is open daily 8 A.M.–midnight (until 1 A.M. on Fri. and Sat. nights). "Last call" for washers is 10 P.M. nightly. Call ahead to make sure, but live music is usually scheduled after 9 P.M. on Tues.–Thurs. and Fri. or Sat. nights, jukebox available otherwise. BrainWash also sponsors community events, such as the "Take the Dirty Shirt Off Your Back" benefit for the STOP AIDS Project. The place can also be rented for private parties.

So come on down, almost anytime, for some Clorox and croissants.

The Museum of Modern Art is open 11 A.M.–6 P.M. daily except Wed. Additionally, it's open until 9 P.M. on Thurs., and opens at 10 A.M. instead of 11 A.M. from Memorial Day weekend through Labor Day. The museum is closed on July Fourth, Thanksgiving, Christmas, and New Year's Day. Admission is $8 adults, $5 seniors, and $4 students with ID (children under 12 free). Admission is free for everyone on the first Tues. of each month, and half price Thurs. 6–9 P.M. Admission charge is sometimes higher during special exhibitions.

Yerba Buena Center for the Arts

Opposite the museum on the west side of 3rd St. is the Yerba Buena Center for the Arts, 701 Mission St. (at 3rd), 415/978-2700 or 415/978-2787 (ticket office), www.yerbabuenaarts.org, a gallery and theater complex devoted to showcasing the works of experimental, marginalized, and emerging artists. A YBC classic was the exhibition of a century of drawings for tattoos, *Pierced Hearts and True Love,* featuring drawings by prominent tattoo artists Sailor Jerry and Ed Hardy. A five-acre downtown park surrounds the complex, where a waterfall dedicated to the memory of Martin Luther King Jr. reads: "We will not be satisfied until 'justice rolls down like a river and righteousness like a mighty stream.'" Amen. The Center for the Arts galleries are open 11 A.M.–6 P.M. daily except Mon. (until 8 P.M. on the first Thurs. of each month). Admission is $5 adults, $3 seniors/students; children 12 and under free. Everyone gets in free on the first Thurs. of every month, 6–8 P.M.

The Rooftop at Yerba Buena Gardens

Cleverly built atop the Moscone Center along 4th, Howard, and Folsom Sts., this park-cum-entertainment complex is the latest addition to the Yerba Buena Gardens redevelopment project. It holds a 1906 carousel, a full-size indoor ice rink with city-skyline views, a bowling center, and **Zeum,** 415/777-3727, an interactive art and technology center for children ages 8–18. Hours are Wed.–Fri. noon–6 P.M., Sat.–Sun. 11 A.M.–5 P.M., and admission is $7 adults, $5 youths ages 5–18. The **Ice Skating Center,** 415/777-3727, is open for public skating daily, 1–5 P.M. Admission is $6 adults and $4.50 seniors and children ($2.50 skate rental).

Metreon

Anchoring the corner of 4th and Mission Sts. like a sleek spacecraft, the block-long, four-story-tall **Metreon,** 415/537-3400, www.metreon.com, is the latest icon of pop culture to land in San Francisco's SoMa district. The Sony Entertainment–sponsored mall features a 15-screen cinema complex, a 600-seat IMAX theatre with 2-D and 3-D capability, and fashion-forward shopping options including a Sony Style store and MicrosoftSF.

Interactive exhibits include **Where the Wild Things Are,** based on Maurice Sendak's magical children's book; an interactive 3-D show titled **The Way Things Work,** based on David Macaulay's book of the same name; and **Airtight Garage,** a futuristic gaming area based on the images of French graphic artist Jean "Mobius" Giraud. The mall's food court features offshoots of several popular local restaurants: LongLife Noodle Co., Buckhorn, Sanraku, and Firewood Café, gathered under the umbrella "a taste of San Francisco." Technically admission to Metreon is free, but doing anything will cost you. For a family of four the "all attractions" option is a bit pricey at $20 per person (children age 2 and under free), and even that doesn't include Airtight Garage games, movie or IMAX admission, restaurants, or shopping. There are multiple options, though; for admission prices, hours, and other current information, see the website or call Metreon at 415/537-3400.

Other SoMa Sights

The **Ansel Adams Center for Photography,** 655 Mission St. (between Montgomery and Third St.), 415/495-7000 or 415/495-7242, is a major presence in San Francisco's art scene, with five galleries dedicated to the photographic art, one set aside exclusively for Adams's own internationally renowned black-and-white works. Open daily 11 A.M.–5 P.M. (until 8 P.M. on the first Thurs. of every month). Admission is $5 adults, $3 students, $2 seniors/youths.

Less serious is the **Cartoon Art Museum,** 814 Mission (between 4th and 5th Sts.), 415/227-8666, which chronicles the history of the in-print giggle, from cartoon sketches and finished art to toys and videos. Open Wed.–Fri. 11 A.M.–5 P.M., Sat. 10 A.M.–5 P.M., Sun. 1–5 P.M. Admission is $5 adults, $3 seniors/students, $1 children.

The **California Historical Society Museum,** 678 Mission St. (between 2nd and 3rd Sts.), 415/357-1848, displays rare historical photographs and includes exhibits on early California movers and shakers (both human and geologic), Western art of California, and frontier manuscripts. The museum bookstore features a great selection of books by California authors. The museum and bookstore are open Tues.–Sat. 11 A.M.–5 P.M. Small admission.

SPORTING SAN FRANCISCO

As of April 2000, the **San Francisco Giants** major-league baseball team plays ball on the bay at the city's new 42,000-seat Pacific Bell Park, 415/468-3700, www.sfgiants.com. (To betray the city's baseball heritage, zip across the bay to the Network Associates Coliseum and the Oakland A's games, 510/430-8020, www.oaklandathletics.com.) Still at home at 3Com Park—once known as Candlestick Park—are the **San Francisco 49ers,** NFL footballers made famous by their numerous Super Bowl victories. For 49er tickets and information, call 415/656-4900 or check www.sf49ers.com.

San Franciscans are big on participatory sports. Some of the city's most eclectic competitive events reflect this fact, including the famous *San Francisco Examiner* **Bay to Breakers** race in May, 415/777-7770, which attracts 100,000-plus runners, joggers, and walkers, most wearing quite creative costumes—and occasionally nothing at all. It's a phenomenon that must be experienced to be believed. (Request registration forms well in advance.)

San Francisco's outdoor and other recreational opportunities seem limited only by one's imagination (and income): hot-air ballooning, beachcombing, bicycling, bird-watching, boating, bowling, camping, canoeing, kayaking, hang-gliding, hiking, horseshoes, fishing, golf, tennis, sailing, swimming, surfing, parasailing, rowing, rock climbing, running, windsurfing. Golden Gate National Recreational Area and Golden Gate Park are major community recreation resources.

For a current rundown on sports events and recreational opportunities, or for information on specific activities, consult the helpful folks at the San Francisco Convention & Visitors Bureau (see Useful Information under Practical San Francisco).

Actually closer to the waterfront and Financial District, the **Jewish Community Museum,** 121 Steuart St. (at Mission), 415/543-8880, features changing, usually exceptional exhibits on Jewish art, culture, and history. (The museum is scheduled to move to the Yerba Buena Gardens area in 2000, so call before going.) The **Telephone Pioneers Communications Museum,** 140 New Montgomery (at Natoma), 415/542-0182, offers electronic miscellany and telephone memorabilia dating to the 1870s.

SoMa Shopping

Shop-and-drop types, please note: serious bargains are available throughout SoMa's garment district. The garment industry is the city's largest, doing a wholesale business of $5 billion annually. Most of the manufacturing factories are between 2nd and 11th Sts., and many have off-price retail outlets for their own wares. But you won't necessarily shop in comfort, since some don't have dressing rooms and others are as jam-packed as the post office at tax time. Major merchandise marts, mostly for wholesalers, are clustered along Kansas and Townsend Streets. Some retail discount outlets for clothing, jewelry, and accessories are here, too, also along Brannan St. between 3rd and 6th Streets. If at all possible, come any day but Saturday, and always be careful where you park. The parking cops are serious about ticketing violators.

Yerba Buena Square, 899 Howard St. (at 5th), 415/543-1275, is an off-price factory mall. **Tower Outlet,** 660 3rd St. (at Townsend), 415/957-9660, offers discounted CDs and tapes. Some of the best places have to be hunted down, however. **Esprit Direct,** 499 Illinois (at 16th), 415/957-2500, is a warehouse-sized store offering discounts on San Francisco's hippest women's and children's wear. (Try lunch—weekdays only—at **42 Degrees,** tucked behind the outlet at 235 16th St., 415/777-5558.) Neighborhood anchor **Gunne Sax,** 35 Stanford Alley (between 2nd and 3rd, Brannan and Townsend), 415/495-3326, has a huge selection of more than 25,000 garments (including dress-up dresses); the best bargains are way in the back. Nearby, at the border of South Park, **Jeremy's,** 2 South Park (at 2nd), 415/882-4929, sells hip designer clothes for one-third or more off retail. Consumer alert: because some of the items are returns, be sure to check garments for snags or other signs of wear before buying. **Harper Greer,** 580 4th St. (between Bryant and Brannan), 415/543-4066, offers wholesale-priced fashions for women size 14 and larger.

Since shopping outlets open, close, and change names or locations at a remarkable rate, consult the "Style" section of the Sunday *San Francisco Examiner and Chronicle,* which lists discount centers and factory outlets in SoMa and elsewhere around town.

SoMa Nightlife

Many SoMa restaurants (see Eating in San Francisco below) do double-duty as bars and club venues. You won't go far before finding something going on. The classic for people who wear ties even after work is **Julie's Supper Club,** 1123 Folsom (at 7th), 415/861-0707, though **Hamburger Mary's,** 1582 Folsom St. (at 12th), 415/626-5767, has achieved an almost mythic status among the alternative crowd.

Catch touring and local rock bands at **Slim's,** 333 11th St. (between Folsom and Harrison), 415/522-0333, the cutting edge for indie rockers; pretty steep cover. Before braving the lines, fill up across the street at the **20 Tank Brewery,** 316 11th (at Folsom), 415/255-9455, a lively brewpub run by the same microbrewery folks who brewed up Triple Rock in Berkeley.

The **Caribbean Zone,** 55 Natoma (between 1st and 2nd, Mission and Howard), 415/541-9465, has a mezzanine cocktail lounge created from an airplane fuselage, so you can sit and down a few while porthole-window television screens and sound effects simulate takeoff (and crash landings). Artistically and genetically expansive, in a punkish sort of way, is the **DNA Lounge,** 375 11th St. (between Harrison and Folsom), 415/626-1409, serving up dancing nightly after 9 P.M., cover on weekends.

But don't miss the **Paradise Lounge,** 1501 Folsom St. (at 11th), 415/861-6906, marvelously mazelike and sporting several bars, four separate live stages, and an upstairs pool hall. Upstairs is **Above Paradise,** featuring more music—often acoustic—and occasional poetry readings. Next door is the **Transmission Theatre,** 415/621-4410, an 800-seat venue for live music and performing arts built in an old auto shop. And all of this adventure for a reasonable cover charge.

Since SoMa in the 1970s was a nighttime playground for the bad-boys-in-black-leather set, the gay bar scene here is still going strong. The original gay bar is **The Stud,** 399 9th St. (at Harrison), 415/252-7883, formerly a leather bar, now a dance bar. For dancing in the gay, country-western style, try the **Rawhide II,** 280 7th St. (at Folsom), 415/621-1197. But the hottest gay nightclub in the neighborhood, some say in the entire city, is the **Endup** ("you always end up at the Endup"), 401 6th St. (at Harrison), 415/357-0827, famous for serious dancing—"hot bodies," too, according to an informed source—and, for cooling down, its large outdoor deck. Saturday nights are lesbian.

Other SoMa clubs to explore (if you dare) include: **El Bobo,** 1539 Folsom (between 11th and 12th), 415/861-6822, an elegant supper club open late for nightcaps and midnight munchies; the mostly lesbian **CoCo Club,** 139 8th St. (between Mission and Howard), 415/626-2337; **Covered Wagon Saloon,** 917 Folsom (between 5th and 6th), 415/974-1585, favored by bike messengers; **Holy Cow,** 1535 Folsom (between 11th and 12th), 415/621-6087; the **Hotel Utah Saloon,** 500 4th St. (at Bryant), 415/421-8308, featuring eclectic live music; and the dance club **1015 Folsom,** 1015 Folsom (at 6th), 415/431-1200.

SEEING SAN FRANCISCO: COASTING THE BAY

San Francisco's waterfront stretches some six miles along the wide, seawall-straddling **Embarcadero,** which runs from China Basin south of the Bay Bridge to Fisherman's Wharf in the north. Remnants of bygone booming port days, the docks and wharfs here are today devoted as much to tourism as to maritime commerce. The area is much improved, aesthetically, now that the elevated, view-blocking Embarcadero Freeway is gone (it was razed after being damaged in the 1989 earthquake). Today the Embarcadero is lined with nonnative Canary Island palm trees—a landscaping strategy that initially angered botanical purists who dismissed the trees as being "too L.A."

Rising up at the foot of 2nd St. is the new **Pacific Bell Park,** www.sfgiants.com, which replaced 3Com Park (better known by its original name—Candlestick Park) as the home of the San Francisco Giants in April 2000. Pac Bell Park sits right on the waterfront and seats 42,000 fans, offering sweeping views of the bay and the city skyline. Designed by Hellmuth, Obata & Kassabaum architect Joe Spear, the fellow responsible for Coors Field in Denver and Camden Yards in Baltimore, the park aims to combine the feel of an old-time ballpark with modern amenities. Quite modern is the potential traffic nightmare of 40,000 fans trying to drive and find parking downtown, so smart fans may find that public transportation—including BART and ferries from surrounding Bay Area communities—is a better option. The ballpark is a fairly short walk from downtown.

In China Basin is **South Beach Marina Pier,** a public fishing pier with a good skyline view of the South Beach Marina. Next along the Embarcadero are various new developments housing such varied tenants as the **Bayside Village** restaurant and the world-renowned drug rehabilitation program **Delancey Street.** Next is **Hills Plaza,** a fairly new commercial-and-apartment development with a garden plaza, incorporating the shell of the old Hills Brothers Coffee building.

Across from the updated 1889 Audiffred Building at 1 Mission is city-within-the-city **Rincon**

Center, incorporating the former Rincon Annex Post Office, which was saved for its classic New Deal mural art. Note, too, the **36,075-pound brass screw** from a World War II tanker at 100 Spear St., introducing the waterfront exhibits inside. More than elsewhere in the city, except perhaps Nob Hill, the ironies of Financial District art are indeed striking.

At the foot of Market St. is the **Ferry Building,** completed in 1898. Formerly the city's transportation center, the Ferry Building today is largely office space, including the **World Trade Center.** But the building still features its 661-foot arcaded facade, triumphal entrance arch, and temple-style clock tower echoing the Giralda tower of Spain's Seville cathedral. During commute hours, the area bustles with suits disembarking ferries from Marin. Hop one of the high-speed boats to Sausalito for lunch and you'll get there in about half an hour. Boats leave frequently during the day, with extended hours in summer. Tickets $1.35–4.70 one-way.

The **Waterfront Promenade** stretches from the new Giants ballpark to the **San Francisco Maritime National Historic Park** at the foot of Hyde Street. The promenade, built in stages over the last few years, replaces the waterfront's old piers 14 through 22. Named **Herb Caen Way** (complete with three dots) in 1996, for the late *San Francisco Chronicle* columnist, the seawall walkway features grand views of the bay. It's a favorite spot for midday runners and office brown-baggers; literary types enjoy the poems embedded in the sidewalk.

Just south of Broadway is the city's only new pier since the 1930s; 845-foot-long **Pier 7** is an elegant public-access promenade for dawdlers and fisherfolk, complete with iron-and-wood benches, iron railings, and flanking colonnades of lampposts, the better for taking in the nighttime skyline.

FISHERMAN'S WHARF

San Francisco's fishing industry and other port-

Fisherman's Wharf

TOM MYERS PHOTOGRAPHY

related businesses were once integral to the city's cultural and economic life. Fisherman's Wharf, which extends from Pier 39 to the municipal pier just past Aquatic Park, was originally the focus of this waterfront commerce. Early on, Chinese fishermen pulled ashore their catch here, to be followed in time by Italian fishermen who took over the territory. After World War II, however, the city's fishing industry declined dramatically, the result of both accelerated pollution of San Francisco Bay and decades of overfishing. Today, Fisherman's Wharf has largely become a carnival-style diversion for tourists. Nevertheless, beyond the shopping centers, arcade amusements, and oddball museums, a small fishing fleet struggles to survive.

Pier 39

At Beach St. and Embarcadero, Pier 39 offers schlock par excellence. If you don't mind jostling with the schools of tourists like some sort of biped sardine, you're sure to find *something* here that interests you. But this place really isn't about San Francisco—it's about shopping and otherwise spending your vacation wad. And you could have done that at home.

Shopping possibilities include the **Disney Store,** selling licensed Disney merchandise; the **Warner Bros. Studio Store,** selling meepmeeps, cwazy wabbits, and the like; the **NFL Shop,** offering official 49er jerseys and other pigskin paraphernalia; the **City Store,** selling actual bits of San Francisco—old street signs, old

bits of cable-car cable, old bricks from Lombard St.—all to benefit San Francisco social-services programs; and **Mel Fisher's Sunken Treasure Museum Store,** displaying artifacts collected by Fisher on his shipwreck dives.

At **Turbo Ride Simulation Theatre,** 415/392-8872, you'll be thrown around in your spastic, hydraulically controlled seat in perfect time with what's happening on the big screen before you; think armchair Indiana Jones (and three similar adventure scenarios). Open daily. Summer hours are Sun.–Thurs. 10 A.M.–9:30 P.M., Fri. 10 A.M.–11 P.M.; Sat. 10 A.M.–midnight. The rest of the year, it's open Sun.–Thurs. 10:30 A.M.–8:30 P.M., Fri.–Sat. 10 A.M.–10 P.M. Admission is $8 general, $5 seniors/children under 12. And at **UnderWater World,** 415/623-5300, you can travel through a 300-foot-long acrylic tube on a moving walkway, looking out on schools of glittering anchovies, stingrays, leopard sharks, and other sea creatures swimming through the 700,000-gallon Pier 39 Aquarium. UnderWater World is open daily 10 A.M.–6 P.M.; extended summer hours. Admission is $12.95 adults, $9.95 seniors, $6.50 children 3–11.

No, you won't lack for attractions to take your money at Pier 39. But for free you can spend time watching the lolling **sea lions** out on the docks, a fairly recent invasion force. The docks once served as a marina full of pleasure boats—until the sea lions started making themselves at home. It turned out to be a futile effort trying to chase them off, so the powers that be decided to abandon the marina idea and let the pinnipeds

ROBERT HOLMES/CALTOUR

Pier 39 and its residents

(up to 600 of them in the peak Jan.–Feb. herring season) have their way, becoming a full-time tourist attraction. Score: Sea Lions 1, Yachties 0.

Most shops at the pier are open daily 10:30 A.M.–8:30 P.M. Hours are longer in summer. For more information, call 415/981-7437, or look up www.pier39.com online. The **Blue & Gold Fleet** ferries to Alcatraz and elsewhere around the bay also depart from here.

Along Jefferson Street

A culinary treat on the Wharf, especially in December or at other times during the mid-November-to-June season, is fresh **Dungeness crab.** You can pick out your own, live or already cooked, from the vendor stands, or head for any of the more famous Italian-style seafood restaurants here: **Alioto's, Castagliona's, Sabella's,** or the excellent and locally favored **Scoma's,** hidden slightly away from the tourist hordes on Pier 47 (near the intersection of Jones and Jefferson), 415/771-4383.

If you're in the mood for still more entertainment, Fisherman's Wharf offers a wacky variety.

Ripley's *Believe It Or Not!* **Museum,** 175 Jefferson St. (near Taylor), 415/771-6188, features both beautiful and bizarre items—including a two-headed cow, a shrunken head, and other grotesqueries—collected during Robert L. Ripley's global travels. Open Sun.–Thurs. 10 A.M.–10 P.M., Fri.–Sat. 10 A.M.–midnight. Admission $8.50 adults, $7 children and seniors.

Around Ghirardelli Square

You can also shop till you drop at elegant **Ghirardelli Square,** 900 North Point (Beach and Larkin), 415/775-5500, a complex of 50-plus shops and restaurants where you can get one of the best hot fudge sundaes anywhere, or **The Cannery,** 2801 Leavenworth (at Beach), 415/771-3112, another huge theme shopping center, this one offering outdoor street artist performances as well as the **Museum of the City of San Francisco,** 415/928-0289; **Cobb's Comedy Club,** 415/928-4320; and **Quiet Storm,** 415/771-2929, a jazz club also serving Pacific Rim cuisine. Beer lovers will be in hops heaven at the Cannery, checking out the house-made offerings of **Beach Street Brewhouse,** 415/775-5110, and the 83 different beers on tap at **Jack's Cannery Bar,** 415/931-6400. Time-honored for imports and the occasional bargain is the nearby **Cost Plus,** 2552 Taylor (at North Point).

Quieter, less commercial pleasures are also available along Fisherman's Wharf—a stroll through **Aquatic Park** perhaps, or fishing out on **Municipal Pier.**

San Francisco Maritime National Historical Park

Historic ships and a first-rate maritime museum make up the core of this national park on the west end of Fisherman's Wharf. To get oriented, first stop by the park's **National Maritime Museum of San Francisco** in Aquatic Park at Beach and Polk, 415/556-3002, open daily 10 A.M.–5 P.M., free admission. The double-decker building itself looks like an art deco ocean liner. Washed ashore inside are some excellent displays, from model ships and figureheads to historic photos and exhibits on fishing boats, ferries, and demonstrations of the sailor's arts. The affiliated **J. Porter Shaw Library,** 415/556-9870, housed along with the park's administrative offices west of Fisherman's Wharf in Building E

TOURING THE REAL ROCK

Visiting Alcatraz is like touring the dark side of the American dream, like peering into democracy's private demon hold. At Alcatraz, freedom is a fantasy. If crime is a universal option—and everyone behind bars at Alcatraz exercised it—then all who once inhabited this desolate island prison were certainly equal. Yet all who lived on the Rock were also equal in other ways—in their utter isolation, in their human desperation, in their hopelessness.

Former prison guard Frank Heaney, born and raised in Berkeley, is now a consultant for the Blue & Gold Fleet's exclusive Alcatraz tour. When he started work as a correctional officer at age 21, Heaney found himself standing guard over some of America's most notorious felons, including George "Machine Gun" Kelly, Alvin "Creepy" Karpis, and Robert "The Birdman of Alcatraz" Stroud. Heaney soon realized that the terrifying reality of prison life was a far cry from Hollywood's James Cagney version.

The job was psychologically demanding, yet often boring. There was terror in the air, too. Inmates vowed—and attempted—to "break him." But he ignored both death threats and too-friendly comments on his youthful appeal. Guards were prohibited from conversing with the inmates—one more aspect of the criminals' endless isolation—but Heaney eventually got to know Machine Gun Kelly, whom he remembers as articulate and intellectual, "more like a bank president than a bank robber." Creepy Karpis, Ma Barker's right-hand man and the only man ever personally arrested by FBI Director J. Edgar Hoover, was little more than a braggart. And though the Birdman was considered seriously psychotic and spent most of his 54 prison years in solitary confinement, Heaney found him to be "untrustworthy" but rational and extremely intelligent. Many of Heaney's favorite stories are collected in his book *Inside the Walls of Alcatraz,* published by Bull Publishing and available at Pier 39 and the National Park Store gift shop.

Others who remember the Rock, both guards and inmates, are included on the **Alcatraz Cellhouse Tour,** an "inside" audio journey through prison history provided by the Golden Gate National Park Association and offered along with Blue & Gold Fleet tours to Alcatraz.

Among them is Jim Quillen, former inmate, who on the day we visit is here in person. He leans against the rusted iron doors of Cell Block A. His pained eyes scan the pocked walls and empty cells, each barely adequate as an open-air closet. Quillen spent the best years of his life on Alcatraz. "Ten years and one day," he says in a soft voice. "The tourists see the architecture, the history—all I see are ghosts. I can point to the exact spots where my friends have killed themselves, been murdered, gone completely insane."

That's the main reason to visit Alcatraz—to explore this lonely, hard, wind-whipped island of exile. The ghosts here need human companionship.

Alcatraz

ROBERT HOLMES/CalTour

There is plenty else to do, too, including the ranger-guided walk around the island, courtesy of the Golden Gate National Recreation Area (GGNRA), and poking one's nose into other buildings, other times. National park personnel also offer lectures and occasional special programs. Or take an **Evening on Alcatraz** tour, to see the sun set on the city from the island. For current information, contact the Golden Gate National Recreation Area at 415/556-0560 or www.nps.gov/goga, stop by the **GGNRA Visitors Center** at the Cliff House in San Francisco (415/556-8643), or contact the nonprofit, education-oriented Golden Gate National Park Association, 415/561-3000. (For more information about the recreation area in general, see that section elsewhere in this chapter and also Point Reyes National Seashore in the San Francisco Bay Area chapter.)

If you're coming to Alcatraz, contact the **Blue & Gold Fleet,** Pier 41, Fisherman's Wharf, 415/773-1188, www.blueandgoldfleet.com, for general information. To make charge-by-phone ticket reservations—advisable, well in advance, since the tour is quite popular, attracting more than one million people each year—call 415/705-5555, or make reservations through the Blue & Gold Fleet's website (with seven days' advance notice). At last report, round-trip fare with audio was $12.25 per adult, $7 per child, plus a $2.25-per-ticket reservation surcharge if you reserve your ticket by phone/Internet; there's also a $1 day-use fee in addition to the ferry price. (Be sure to be there 30 minutes early, since no refunds or exchanges are allowed if you miss the boat.) The entire audio-guided walking tour takes more than two hours, so be sure to allow yourself adequate time. (The audiotape is available in English, Japanese, German, French, Italian, and Spanish.) If at all possible, try to get booked on one of the early tours, so you can see the cellblocks and Alcatraz Island in solitude, before the rest of humanity arrives. Pack a picnic (though snacks and beverages are available), and bring all the camera and video equipment you can carry; no holds barred on photography. Wear good walking shoes, as well as warm clothes (layers best), since it can be brutally cold on Alcatraz in the fog or when the wind whips up.

In the past, the island's ruggedness made it difficult to impossible for those with limited mobility, with moderate to strenuous climbing and limited access for wheelchairs and strollers. Now wheelchair users and others with limited mobility who can't "do" the Alcatraz tour on foot can take SEAT (Sustainable Easy Access Transport) up the 12 percent grade hill one-quarter mile to the prison. Contact the Blue & Gold Fleet information line for details.

If you're not coming to Alcatraz in the immediate future, you can still take a comprehensive virtual tour, on the web at www.nps.gov/alcatraz/tours.

by Tim Moriarty and Kim Weir

---

at Fort Mason (a reasonable walk away along a bike/pedestrian path), holds most of the Bay Area's documented boat history, including oral histories, logbooks, photographs, and ship-building plans.

Not easy to miss at the foot of Hyde St. are the **Hyde Street Pier Historic Ships,** 415/556-3002 or 415/556-6435, an always-in-progress collection that is also part of the national park. Admission is $5 adults, $2 youths 12–17, free for children. Here you can clamber across the decks and crawl through the colorfully cluttered holds of some of America's most historic ships.

The Hyde Street fleet's flagship is the three-masted 1886 **Balclutha,** a veteran of twice-annual trips between California and the British Isles via Cape Horn. Others include the side-wheel **Eureka** (the world's largest passenger ferry in her day, built to ferry trains), the ocean-going tugboat **Hercules,** the British-built, gold rush–era paddlewheel tug **Eppleton Hall,** the scow schooner **Alma,** and the three-masted lumber schooner **C. A. Thayer.** Also among the collection, but berthed at Pier 45, is the **U.S.S. Pampanito,** a tight-quarters Balao-class World War II submarine that destroyed or damaged many Japanese vessels and also participated in the tragic sinking of the Japanese *Kachidoki Maru* and *Rayuyo Maru,* which were carrying Australian and British prisoners of war.

Tagging along on a ranger-led tour (complete with "living history" adventures in summer) is the best way to get your feet wet at this national park. Call for tour schedule (guided tours are usually offered daily). But self-guided tours are available anytime the pier is open, which is daily 9:30 A.M.–5 P.M. year-round (until 5:30 P.M. in summer); closed Thanksgiving, Christmas, and New Year's Day. Special activities give you the chance to sing sea chanteys, raise sails, watch the crews "lay aloft," or participate in the Dead Horse Ceremony—wherein the crowds heave a horse doll overboard and shout "May the sharks have his body, and the devil have his soul!"

SS *Jeremiah O'Brien*

Berthed at Pier 45 in summer, Pier 32 the rest of the year, this massive 441-foot-long World War II Liberty Ship made 11 crossings from England to the beaches of Normandy to support the Allied invasion. In 1994, it returned to Normandy for the 50th anniversary of D day. The ship is still powered by its original engines. In fact, the engine-room scenes in the movie *Titanic* were filmed here.

The historic ship is open for self-guided tours year-round, daily 10 A.M.–7 P.M.; admission is $5 adults, $4 seniors/military, $3 children. In addition, the ship makes several daylong cruises each year; you can come along for $100 per person. For more information or for cruise schedule and reservations, call 415/441-3101.

FORT MASON

Headquarters for the Golden Gate National Recreation Area, Fort Mason is also home to **Fort Mason Center,** a complex of one-time military storage buildings at Marina Blvd. and Buchanan St., now hosting surprisingly contemporary nonprofit arts, humanities, educational, environmental, and recreational organizations and associations.

Since the 1970s, this shoreline wasteland has been transformed into an innovative multicultural community events center—perhaps the country's premier model of the impossible, successfully accomplished. Several pavilions and the Conference Center host larger group events, though smaller galleries, theaters, and offices predominate. The variety of rotating art exhibits, independent theater performances, poetry readings, lectures and workshops, and special-interest classes offered here is truly staggering.

Expansion plans include the establishment of a marine ecology center, another theater, more exhibit space, and another good-food-great-view restaurant. All in all, it's not surprising that Fort Mason is being studied by the Presidio's national park transition team, and even by other nations, as a supreme example of how urban eyesores can be transformed into national treasures.

Fort Mason Museums

The **San Francisco African American Historical & Cultural Society,** in Bldg. C, Room 165, 415/441-0640, is a cultural and resource center featuring a library, museum (small admission), speaker's bureau, and monthly lecture series. Open Wed.–Sun. noon–5 P.M.

The **Mexican Museum,** Bldg. D, 415/202-9700 or 415/441-0404, www.folkart.com/~latitude/museums, is devoted exclusively to exhibitions of, and educational programs about, Mexican-American and Mexican art. Its permanent collection includes 9,000 items from five periods, including pre-Hispanic and contemporary Mexican art, and rotating exhibits attract much public attention. The changing exhibits typically focus on one particular artist or on a theme, such as "100 Years of Chroma Art Calendars." Open Wed.–Sun. 11 A.M.–5 P.M.; admission $4 adults, $3 students and seniors. The museum plans to move downtown to the Yerba Buena Center in the not-too-distant future, so call or check with the website before setting out.

Exhibits at the **Museo ItaloAmericano,** in Bldg. C, 415/673-2200, foster an appreciation of Italian art and culture. Open Wed.–Sun. noon–5 P.M. Small admission. Definitely worth a detour is the **San Francisco Craft & Folk Art Museum,** Bldg. A-North, 415/775-0990, www.sfcraftandfolk.org, which features rotating exhibits of American and international folk art. Open Tues.–Fri. and Sun. 11 A.M.–5 P.M.; Sat. 10 A.M.–5 P.M. Free on Sat., 10 A.M.–noon, otherwise there's a small admission fee.

In addition to any free hours listed above, all of the museums at the center are free (and open until 7 P.M.) on the first Wed. of every month.

Fort Mason Performing Arts

Fort Mason Center's 440-seat **Cowell Theater,** 415/441-3400, is a performance space that hosts events ranging from the acclaimed Solo Mio Festival and the New Pickle Circus to guest speakers such as Spalding Gray and unusual video, musical, and theatrical presentations. Among its showstoppers is the **Magic Theatre,** Bldg. D, 415/441-8001 (business office) or 415/441-8822 (box office), which is internationally recognized as an outstanding American playwrights' theater, performing original plays by the likes of Sam Shepard and Michael Mc-Clure as well as innovative new writers.

Other Fort Mason performing arts groups include the **Performing Arts Workshop,** Bldg. C, 415/673-2634, and the **Young Performers' Theatre,** Bldg. C, 415/346-5550, both for young people. The **Blue Bear School of American Music,** Bldg. D, 415/673-3600, offers lessons and workshops in rock, pop, jazz, blues, and other genres. **Bay Area Theatresports** (BATS) is an improv comedy group that performs at the **Bayfront Theater,** Bldg. B, 415/474-8935, and **World Arts West,** Bldg. D, 415/474-3914, promotes and produces world music and dance festivals.

Fort Mason Visual Arts

The **Fort Mason Art Campus** of the City College of San Francisco, Bldg. B, 415/561-1840, is the place for instruction in fine arts and crafts. Works of students and faculty are showcased at the **Coffee Gallery,** in the Bldg. B lobby, 415/561-1840. The 10-and-under set should head to the **San Francisco Children's Art Center,** Bldg. C, 415/771-0292. One of the most intriguing galleries here is the **San Francisco Museum of Modern Art Rental Gallery,** Bldg. A-North, 415/441-4777, representing more than 1,300 artists and offering, in addition to rotating exhibits, the opportunity to rent as well as buy works on display.

Fort Mason Environmental Organizations

The **Endangered Species Project,** Bldg. E, 415/921-3140, works to protect wildlife and habitat and to prevent illegal poaching and trade of endangered animals. **Friends of the River,** Bldg. C, 415/771-0400, supports efforts to protect and restore the West's waterways and riparian areas. The **Fund for Animals,** Bldg. C, 415/474-4020, is an animal-rights organization. The **Oceanic Society,** Bldg. E, 415/441-1106, offers environmental education programs including whale-watching trips, cruises to the Farallon Islands, and coral-reef and rainforest expeditions. The **Resource Renewal Institute,** Pier 1 North, 415/928-3774, promotes integrated environmental planning—"Green Plans"—at every level of government, both domestically and internationally. The **Tuolumne River Preservation Trust,** Bldg. C, 415/292-3531, focuses its efforts on protecting and preserving the Tuolumne River watershed.

Glorious Grazing

No one will ever starve here, since one of the country's best vegetarian restaurants, the San Francisco Zen Center's **Greens,** is in Bldg. A-North, 415/771-6222. It's open Mon.–Sat. for lunch and dinner and Sun. for brunch. The restaurant also offers **Greens-To-Go** take-out lunches Tues.–Sun.; call 415/771-6330.

Other Fort Mason Services and Information

Book Bay Bookstore, Bldg. C-South, 415/771-1076, is run by friends of the San Francisco Public Library. Book sales are regularly held to benefit the city's public-library system.

For more complete information on Fort Mason, including a copy of the monthly *Fort Mason Calendar of Events,* contact the **Fort Mason Foundation,** Bldg. A, Fort Mason Center, 415/441-3400, www.fortmason.org, open daily 9 A.M.–5 P.M. For recorded information 24 hours a day, call 415/979-3010. To order tickets for any Fort Mason events, call the **Fort Mason box office** at 415/441-3687.

MARINA DISTRICT

The neat pastel homes of the respectable Marina District, tucked in between Fort Mason and the Presidio, disguise the fact that the entire area is essentially unstable. Built on landfill, in an area once largely bay marsh, the Mediterranean-style Marina was previously the 63-acre site of the Panama-Pacific International Exposition of 1915—San Francisco's statement to the world that it had been reborn from the ashes of the 1906 earthquake and fire. So it was ironic, and fitting, that the fireboat *Phoenix* extinguished many of the fires that blazed here following the 1989 earthquake, which caused disproportionately heavy damage in this district.

The Marina's main attractions are those that surround it—primarily the neighborhood stretch of San Francisco's astounding shoreline Golden Gate National Recreation Area, which includes the **Fort Mason** complex of galleries, museums, theaters, and nonprofit cultural and conservation organizations. (For more information, see Golden Gate National Recreation Area and Fort Mason above.) If you're in the neighborhood and find yourself near the yacht harbor, do wander out to see (and hear) the park's wonderful **Wave Organ** just east of the yacht club on Bay Street. Built of pieces from an old graveyard, the pipes are powered by sea magic. (The siren song is loudest at high tide.) Then wander west toward the Golden Gate Bridge on the **Golden Gate Promenade,** which meanders the three-plus miles from Aquatic Park and along the Marina Green—popular with kite fliers, well-dressed dog walkers, and the area's many exercise freaks—to Civil War–era **Fort Point.** (Be prepared for wind and fog.) The truly ambitious can take a hike across the bridge itself, an awesome experience.

Exhausted by nature, retreat to more sheltered attractions near the Presidio, including the remnants of the spectacular Panama-Pacific International Exhibition of 1915, the Bernard Maybeck–designed **Palace of Fine Arts,** and the indescribable **Exploratorium** inside, fun for children of all ages and a first-rate science museum. (For more area information, see the special topic The Presidio and Fort Point.) The Marina also boasts its own version of Cow Hollow's chic Union Street shopping and eating district: **Chestnut Street.**

Exploratorium: Sophisticated Child's Play
Scientific American considers this the "best science museum in the world." *Good Housekeeping* says it's the "number one science museum in the U.S." It's definitely worth spending some time here. Inside the Palace of Fine Arts, 3601 Lyon St. (at Bay), 415/397-5673, www.exploratorium.edu, the Exploratorium is billed as a museum of science, art, and human perception, and ostensibly designed for children. But this is no mass-marketed media assault on the senses, no mindless theatrical homage to simple fantasy. The truth is, adults also adore the Exploratorium, a wonderfully intelligent playground built around the mysterious natural laws of the universe.

The Exploratorium was founded in 1969 by physicist and educator Dr. Frank Oppenheimer, the original "Explainer" (as opposed to "teacher"), whose research career was abruptly ended during the blacklisting McCarthy era. Brother of J. Robert Oppenheimer (father of the atomic bomb), Frank Oppenheimer's scientific legacy was nonetheless abundant.

"Explaining science and technology without props," said Oppenheimer, "is like attempting to tell what it is like to swim without ever letting a person near the water." The Exploratorium was the original interactive science museum and influenced the establishment of hundreds of other such museums in the United States and abroad. Its 650-some three-dimensional exhibits delve into 13 broad subject areas: animal behavior, language, vision, sound and hearing, touch, heat and temperature, electricity, light, color, motion, patterns, waves and resonance, and weather. Everything can be experienced—from a touch-sensitive plant that shrinks from a child's probing hand, to strategically angled mirrors that create infinite reflections of the viewer; from tactile computerized finger painting to the wave-activated voice of the San Francisco Bay, as brought to you by the "Wave Organ." The extra special **Tactile Dome,** 415/561-0362 (reservations recommended), provides a pitch-black environment in which your vision is of no use, but your sense of touch gets a real workout.

Stock up on educational toys, games, experiments, and oddities at the Exploratorium Store. Especially worth purchasing, for teachers and brave parents alike, is the Exploratorium Science Snackbook, which includes instructions on building home or classroom versions of more than 100 Exploratorium exhibits.

The Exploratorium is open in summer daily 10 A.M.–6 P.M. (Wed. until 9 P.M.). The rest of the year, hours are Tues.–Sun. 10 A.M.–5 P.M. (Wed. until 9 P.M.). On the first Wed. of each month, admission is free. Otherwise it's $9 adults, $7 seniors/students with ID, $5 youths 6–17, and $2.50 children 3–5. Admission to the Tactile Dome is $12 per person, which includes museum admission.

SEEING SAN FRANCISCO: NEAR THE BAY

A total tour of San Francisco has to include a spin through the north-of-downtown neighborhoods near or overlooking the bay, including Nob Hill, Chinatown, North Beach, and Telegraph Hill. All are easily accessible from the Embarcadero and other points along the waterfront, so walk if possible. Parking can be impossible.

COW HOLLOW AND PACIFIC HEIGHTS

Separating the Marina District from high-flying Pacific Heights is the low-lying neighborhood of Cow Hollow, a one-time dairy farm community now noted for its chic **Union Street** shopping district—an almost endless string of bars, cafés, coffeehouses, bookstores, and boutiques stretching between Van Ness and Steiner. Other chic areas have included upper **Fillmore Street** near the Heights (and near the still-surviving 1960s icon, the **Fillmore** concert hall, at Geary and Fillmore), and outer **Sacramento Street** near Presidio Avenue. **Pacific Heights** proper is the hilltop home pasture for the city's well-shod blue bloods. Its striking streets, Victorian homes, and general architectural wealth are well worth a stroll (for personal guidance, see Walking Tours, under Delights and Diversions, below). Especially noteworthy here is the **Haas-Lilienthal House,** 2007 Franklin (at Jackson), 415/441-3004, a handsome and huge Queen Anne Victorian, a survivor of the 1906 earthquake and the city's only fully furnished Victorian open for regular public tours. Tours are conducted Wed. and Sun.; call for times. Admission is $5 adults, $3 seniors and children.

In the Cow Hollow neighborhood, don't miss the unusual 1861 **Octagon House,** 2645 Gough (at Union), 415/441-7512, owned by the National Society of Colonial Dames of America; it's now restored and fully furnished in colonial and Federal period antiques. Open only on the second and fourth Thurs. and the second Sun. of each month (closed in Jan. and on holidays). Call to request special tour times. Donations greatly appreciated.

NOB HILL

Snide San Franciscans say "Snob Hill" when referring to cable car–crisscrossed Nob Hill. The official neighborhood name is purported to be short for "Nabob Hill," a reference to this high-rent district's nouveau riche roots. Robert Louis Stevenson called it the "hill of palaces," referring to the grand late-1800s mansions of San Francisco's economic elite, California's railroad barons most prominent among them. Known colloquially as the "Big Four," Charles Crocker, Mark Hopkins, Collis Huntington, and Leland Stanford were accompanied by two of the "Irish Big Four" or "Bonanza Kings" (James Fair and James Flood, Nevada silver lords) as they made their acquisitive economic and cultural march into San Francisco and across the rest of California.

Of the original homes of these magnates, only one stands today—James Flood's bearish, square Connecticut brownstone, now the exclusive **Pacific-Union Club** (the "P-U," in local vernacular) at 1000 California Street. The rest of the collection was demolished by the great earthquake and fire of 1906. But some of the city's finest hotels, not to mention an exquisite Protestant place of worship, have taken their place around rather formal **Huntington Park.** Huntington's central memorial status atop Nob Hill is appropriate enough, since skinflint Collis P. Huntington was the brains of the Big Four gang and his comparatively simple home once stood here.

Facing the square from the corner of California and Taylor is the charming, surprisingly unique red-brick **Huntington Hotel** and its exceptional **Big Four** bar and restaurant. The **Mark Hopkins Hotel** ("the Mark," as it's known around town) was built on the spot of Hopkins' original ornate Victorian, at 1 Nob Hill (corner of California and Mason). Take the elevator up to the **Top of the Mark,** the bar with a view that inspired the city's song, "I Left My Heart in San Francisco," and perhaps its singer, Tony Bennett, as well. Straight across the street, facing Mason between California and Sacramento, is the famed **Fairmont Hotel,** an architectural extrav-

HOBNOBBING WITH SPIRIT: GRACE CATHEDRAL

At the former site of Charles Crocker's mansion is Grace Cathedral, facing Huntington Park from Taylor St., an explosion of medieval Gothic enthusiasm inspired by the Notre Dame in Paris. Since the lot *was* cleared for construction by a very California earthquake, Grace Cathedral is built not of carefully crafted stone but steel-reinforced concrete.

Most famous here, architecturally, are the cathedral doors, cast from Lorenzo Ghiberti's Gates of Paradise from the Cathedral Baptistry in Florence, Italy. The glowing rose window is circa 1970 and comes from Chartres. Also from Chartres: Grace Cathedral's spiritual **Labyrinth**, a roll-up replica of an archetypal meditative journey in the Christian tradition. Since Grace is a "house of prayer for all people," anyone can walk the Labyrinth's three-fold path, just part of the cathedral's multifaceted **Veriditas** program. The Labyrinth is open to the public during church hours weekdays and Sun. 7 A.M.–6

P.M., Sat. 8 A.M.–6 P.M. Music is another major attraction at Grace Cathedral, from the choral evensongs to pipe organ, carillon, and chamber music concerts. Mother church for California's Episcopal Diocese, Grace Cathedral hosts endless unusual events, including St. Francis Day in October, which honors St. Francis of Assisi—the city's patron saint—and the interconnectedness of all creation. At this celebration, all God's creatures, large and small—from elephants and police horses to dressed-up housepets, not to mention the women walking on stilts—show up to be blessed. For more information about Grace Cathedral's current calendar of odd and exhilarating events, call 415/749-6300. And while you're in the neighborhood, take a peek into the modern **California Masonic Memorial Temple** at 1111 California, with its tiny scale model of King Solomon's Temple and colorful mosaic monument to Freemasonry.

aganza built "atop Nob Hill" by James Fair's daughter Tessie (the lobby is recognizable to American TV addicts as the one in the short-lived series *Hotel*). Inside, the Tiki-inspired Tonga Room is straight out of *Hawaii Five-O*. Kick back, enjoy a frozen cocktail, and soak in the strange ambience. Simulated rainstorms interrupt the tropical calm every half hour.

The **Stanford Court Hotel** at California and Powell, one of the world's finest, occupies the land where Leland Stanford's mansion once stood. For an artistic rendering of local nabobery, stop for a peek at the Stanford's lobby murals.

As for ascending the neighborhood's spiritual heights, on Taylor St. across from Huntington Park—where Charles Crocker's Nob Hill Mansion once stood—is Gothic **Grace Cathedral.** For details, see Hobnobbing with Spirit: Grace Cathedral.

The **Bohemian Club** on the corner of Taylor and Post is a social club started by some of California's true bohemians, from Jack London, Joaquin Miller, and John Muir to Ambrose Bierce, Ina Coolbrith, and George Sterling. Though for old-time's sake some artists are invited to join, these days this very exclusive all-male club has a rank and file composed primarily of businessmen, financiers, and politicians. In July each

year, these modern American bohemians retreat to the Russian River and their equally private Bohemian Grove all-male enclave for a week of fun and frolic.

Nob Hill's Invention and the Cable Car Barn

Not just material wealth and spiritual high spirits are flaunted atop Nob Hill. Technical innovation is, too, and quite rightly, since this is where Andrew Hallidie launched the inaugural run of his famous cable cars, down Clay Street. A free stop at the **Cable Car Barn,** 1201 Mason (at Washington), 415/474-1887, open daily 10 A.M.–5 P.M. (until 6 P.M. during the summer), tells the story. No temple to tourist somnambulism, this is powerhouse central for the entire cable car system, energized solely by the kinetic energy of the cables. Electric motors turn the giant sheaves (pulleys) to whip the (underground) looped steel cables around town and power the cars. The idea is at once complex and simple. Feeding cable around corners is a bit tricky; to see how it works, hike down to a basement window and observe. But the "drive" mechanism is straightforward. Each cable car has two operators, someone working the grip, the other the brake. To "power up," heading uphill, the car's "grip" slides through the slot in the street to grab onto the cable, and the cable does the rest. Heading downhill, resisting gravity, the brake gets quite a workout. Also here: a display of historic cable cars and a gift shop.

CHINATOWN

The best time to explore Chinatown is at the crack of dawn, when crowded neighborhoods and narrow alleys explode into hustle and bustle, and when the scents, sounds, and sometimes surreal colors compete with the energy of sunrise. Due to the realities of gold rush–era life and, later, the Chinese Exclusion Act of 1882, this very American variation on a Cantonese market town was for too long an isolated, almost all-male frontier enclave with the predictable vices—a trend reversed only in the 1960s, when more relaxed immigration laws allowed the possibility of families and children. The ambitious and the educated have already moved on to the suburbs, so Chinatown today—outside of Harlem in New York, the country's most densely populated neighborhood—is home to the elderly poor and immigrants who can't speak English. It's still the largest community of Chinese anywhere outside China. And it's still a cultural and spiritual home for the Bay Area's expanding Chinese community. Even those who have left come back, if only for a great meal and a Chinese-language movie.

To get oriented, keep in mind that Stockton St. is the main thoroughfare. Grant Ave., however, is where most tourists start, perhaps enticed away from Grant's endless upscale shops and galleries by the somewhat garish green-tiled Chinatown Gate at Bush, a 1969 gift from the Republic of China. As you wander north, notice the street-sign calligraphy, the red-painted, dragon-wrapped lampposts, and the increasingly unusual roofscapes. Grant goes the distance between Market St. and modern-day Pier 39. This happens to be San Francisco's oldest street and was little more than a rutted path in 1834, when it was dubbed Calle de la Fundación (Foundation St. or "street of the founding") by the ragtag residents of the Yerba Buena pueblo. By the mid-19th century, the street's name had been changed to Dupont, in honor of an American admiral—a change that also recognized the abrupt changing of California's political guard. But by the end of the 1800s, "Du Pon Gai" had become so synonymous with unsavory activities that downtown merchants decided on another name change, this time borrowing a bit of prestige from Ulysses S. Grant, the nation's 18th president and the Civil War's conquering general. Despite the color on Grant, the in-between streets (Sacramento, Clay, Washington, Jackson, and Pacific) and the fascinating interconnecting alleys between them represent the heart of Chinatown.

Since traffic is horrendous, parking all but impossible, and many streets almost too narrow to navigate even sans vehicle, walking is the best way to see the sights. If you haven't time to

The Chinatown Gate was a gift from the Republic of China.

AISLINN RACE

wander aimlessly, taking a guided tour is the best way to get to know the neighborhood.

Seeing and Doing Chinatown

At the corner of Grant and California is **Old Saint Mary's Cathedral,** the city's Catholic cathedral from the early 1850s to 1891, still standing even after a gutting by fire in 1906. On Saint Mary's clock tower is sound maternal advice for any age: "Son, Observe the time and fly from evil." (Saint Mary has a square, too, a restful stop just east and south of California St., where there's a Bufano sculpture of Dr. Sun Yat-sen, the Republic of China's founder.) Also at the Grant/California intersection is the **Ma-Tsu Temple of the United States of America,** with shrines to Buddha and other popular deities.

Packed with restaurants and tourist shops, Grant Ave. between California and Broadway is always bustling. Of particular interest is the unusual and aptly named **Li Po Bar** at 916 Grant, a former opium den and watering hole honoring the memory of China's notoriously romantic poet, a wine-loving warrior who drowned while embracing the moon—a moon mirage, as it turned out, reflected up from a river.

The **Chinese Historical Society of America,** 644 Broadway (between Stockton and Grant), Ste. 402, 415/391-1188, is the nation's only museum specifically dedicated to preserving Chinese-American history. Chinese contributions to California culture are particularly emphasized. Some unusual artifacts in the museum's huge collection: gold-rush paraphernalia, including a "tiger fork" from Weaverville's tong war, and an old handwritten copy of Chinatown's phone book. Open Mon. 1–4 P.M., Tues.–Fri. 10:30 A.M.–4 P.M.; closed weekends and major holidays. Admission is free, but donations are appreciated.

The **Pacific Heritage Museum,** 608 Commercial (between Montgomery and Kearny, Sacramento and Clay), 415/399-1124, is housed in the city's renovated brick 1875 U.S. Mint building. The museum features free rotating exhibits of Asian art and other treasures; open Tues.–Sat. 10 A.M.–4 P.M. To place it all in the larger context of California's Wild West history, head around the corner to the **Wells Fargo History Museum,** 420 Montgomery, 415/396-2619.

Portsmouth Square—people still say "square," though technically it's been a plaza since the 1920s—on Kearny between Clay and Washington is Chinatown's backyard. Here you'll get an astounding look at everyday local life, from the city's omnipresent panhandlers to early-morning tai chi to all-male afternoons of checkers, *go,* and gossip—life's lasting entertainments for Chinatown's aging bachelors. Across Kearny on the 3rd floor of the Financial District Holiday Inn is the **Chinese Culture Center,** 750 Kearny (between Clay and Washington), 415/986-1822, which has a small gallery and gift shop but otherwise caters mostly to meeting the needs of the local community.

The further actions and attractions of Chinatown's heart are increasingly subtle, from the Washington St. herb and herbalist shops to Ross Alley's garment factories and its fortune cookie company, where you can buy some instant fortune, fresh off the press—keeping in mind, of course, that fortune cookies are an all-American invention. Intriguing, at 743 Washington, is the oldest Asian-style building in the neighborhood, the three-tiered 1909 "temple" once home to the Chinatown Telephone Exchange, now the **Bank of Canton.** But even **Bank of America,** at 701 Grant, is dressed in keeping with its cultural surroundings, with benevolent gold dragons on its columns and doors, and some 60 dragons on its facade. Also putting on the dog is **Citibank** at 845 Grant, guarded by grimacing temple dogs.

Both Jackson and Washington Sts. are best bets for finding small and authentic neighborhood restaurants. **Stockton Street,** especially between Broadway and Sacramento and especially on a Saturday afternoon, is where Chinatown shops. Between Sacramento and Washington, **Waverly Place** is referred to as the "street of painted balconies," for fairly obvious reasons. There are three temples here, open to respectful visitors (donations appreciated, picture-taking usually not). **Norras Temple** at 109 Waverly is affiliated with the Buddhist Association of America, lion dancing and all, while the 4th-floor **Tien Hau Temple** at 123 Waverly primarily honors the Queen of Heaven, she who protects sojourners and seafarers as well as writers, actors, and prostitutes. The **Jeng Sen Buddhism and Taoism Association,** 146 Waverly, perhaps offers the best general introduction to Chinese religious tolerance, with a brief printed explanation (in English) of both belief systems.

For a delightfully detailed and intimate self-guided tour through the neighborhood, bring along a copy of Shirley Fong-Torres's *San Francisco Chinatown: A Walking Tour,* which includes some rarely recognized sights, such as the **Cameron House,** 920 Sacramento, a youth center named in honor of Donaldina Cameron (1869–1968), who helped young Chinese slave girls escape poverty and prostitution. Fong-Torres's marvelous and readable guide to San Francisco's Chinese community also covers history, cultural beliefs, festivals, religion and philosophy, herbal medicine (doctors and pharmacists are now licensed for these traditional practices by the state of California), and Chinese tea. It includes a very good introduction to Chinese food—from ingredients, cookware, and techniques to menus and restaurant recommendations.

Shopping Chinatown

To a greater extent than, say, Oakland's Chinatown, most shops here are aware of—and cater to—the tourist trade. But once you have some idea what you're looking for, bargains are available. Along Grant Ave., a definite must for gourmet cooks and other kitchen habitués is the **Wok Shop,** 718 Grant (between Sacramento and Clay), 415/989-3797, the specialized one-stop shopping trip for anything essential to Chinese cooking (and other types of cooking as well). The **Ten Ren Tea Company,** 949 Grant (at Jackson), 415/362-0656 or toll-free 800/543-2885, features more than 50 varieties of teas, the prices dependent on quality and (for blends) content. There's a private area in back where you can arrange for instruction in the fine art of a proper tea ceremony. (Notice, on the wall, a photo of former president George Bush, who didn't quite get it right when he tried it.) For unusual gifts, silk shirts, high-quality linens and such, **Far East Fashions,** 953 Grant, 415/362-0986 or 415/362-8171, is a good choice.

Finally, musicians and nonmusicians alike shouldn't miss Clara Hsu's **Clarion Music Center,** 816 Sacramento St. (at Waverly Place), 415/391-1317 or toll-free 888/343-5374, a treasure trove full of African drums, Chinese gongs, Tibetan singing bowls, Indian sitars, Native American flutes, Bolivian panpipes, Australian didgeridoos, and other exotic instruments from every corner of the world. The store also offers lessons,

workshops, and concerts to promote awareness of world musical culture. Open Mon.–Fri. 11 A.M.–6 P.M., Sat. 9 A.M.–5 P.M.

NORTH BEACH AND VICINITY

For one thing, there isn't any beach in North Beach. In the 1870s, the arm of San Francisco Bay that gave the neighborhood its name was filled in, creating more land for the growing city. And though beatniks and bohemians once brought a measure of fame to this Italian-American quarter of the city, they're all gone now, priced out of the neighborhood. Nowadays, North Beach is almost choking on its abundance—of eateries, coffeehouses, tourist traps, and shops. Forget trying to find a parking place; public transit is the best way to get around.

Adding to neighborhood stresses and strains—and to the high costs of surviving—is the influx of Asian business and the monumental increase in Hong Kong–money property investment, both marching into North Beach from Chinatown. Old and new neighborhood residents tend to ignore each other as much as possible, in that great American melting-pot tradition. (Before the Italians called North Beach their home turf, the Irish did. And before the Irish lived here, Chileans did. In all fairness, Fisherman's Wharf was Chinese before the Italians moved in. And of course Native Americans inhabited the entire state before the Spanish, the Mexicans, the Russians, and the Americans.) Like the city itself, life here makes for a fascinating sociology experiment.

What with territorial incursions from Chinatown, the historical boundaries of North Beach increasingly clash with the actual. Basically, the entire valley between Russian Hill and Telegraph Hill is properly considered North Beach. The northern boundary stopped just short of Fisherman's Wharf, now pushed back by rampant commercial development, and Broadway was the southern boundary—a thoroughfare and area sometimes referred to as the "Marco Polo Zone" because it once represented the official end of Chinatown and the beginning of San Francisco's Little Italy. The neighborhood's spine is diagonally running Columbus Ave., which begins at the Transamerica Pyramid at the edge of the Financial District and ends at the Cannery near

Fisherman's Wharf. Columbus Avenue between Filbert and Broadway is the still-beating Italian heart of modern North Beach.

Seeing and Doing North Beach

Piazzalike **Washington Square**, between Powell and Stockton, Union and Filbert, is the centerpiece of North Beach, though, as the late *San Francisco Chronicle* columnist Herb Caen once pointed out, it "isn't on Washington Street, isn't a square (it's five-sided) and doesn't contain a statue of Washington but of Benjamin Franklin." (In terms of cultural consistency, this also explains the statue of Robert Louis Stevenson in Chinatown's Portsmouth Square.) There's a time capsule beneath old Ben; when the original treasures (mostly temperance tracts on the evils of alcohol) were unearthed in 1979, they were replaced with 20th-century cultural values, including a bottle of wine, a pair of Levi's, and a poem by Lawrence Ferlinghetti. In keeping with more modern times, Washington Square also features a statue dedicated to the city's firemen, yet another contribution by eccentric little old Lillie Hitchcock Coit. **Saints Peter and Paul Catholic Church** fronts the square at 666 Filbert, its twin towers lighting up the whole neighborhood come nightfall. Noted for its rococo interior and accompanying graphic statuary of injured saints and souls burning in hell, the Saints also offers daily mass in Italian and (on Sunday) in Chinese.

Two blocks northeast of Washington Square is the **North Beach Playground**, where boccie ball is still the neighborhood game of choice, just as October's **Columbus Day Parade** and accompanying festivities still make the biggest North Beach party. Just two blocks west of the square are the stairs leading to the top of **Telegraph Hill**, identifiable by **Coit Tower**, Lillie Coit's most heartfelt memorial to the firefighters. (More on that below.)

For an overview of the area's history, stop by the free **North Beach Museum**, 1435 Stockton St. (near Green, on the mezzanine of Bayview Bank), 415/626-7070, open Mon.–Thurs. 9 A.M.–5 P.M. and Fri. until 6 P.M., which displays a great collection of old North Beach photos and artifacts in occasionally changing exhibits.

The North Beach "experience" is the neighborhood itself—the coffeehouses, the restaurants, the intriguing and odd little shops. No visit

NORTH BEACH BOHEMIA

Quite a number of American poets and writers grubbed out some kind of start in North Beach: Gregory Corso, Lawrence Ferlinghetti, Allen Ginsberg, Bob Kaufman, Jack Kerouac, Gary Snyder, Kenneth Rexroth. By the 1940s, North Beach as "New Bohemia" was a local reality. It became a long-running national myth.

Otherwise sound-asleep America of the 1950s secretly loved the idea of the alienated, manic "beat generation," a phrase coined by Jack Kerouac in *On the Road*. The Beats seemed to be everything no one else was allowed to be—mostly, free. Free to drink coffee or cheap wine and talk all day; free to indulge in art, music, poetry, prose, and more sensual thrills just about any time; free to be angry and scruffy and lost in the forbidden fog of marijuana while bopping along to be-bop. But Allen Ginsberg's raging *Howl and Other Poems,* published by Ferlinghetti and City Lights, brought the wolf of censorship—an ungrateful growl that began with the seizure of inbound books by U.S. Customs and got louder when city police filed obscenity charges. The national notoriety of an extended trial and Ginsberg's ultimate literary acquittal brought busloads of Gray Line tourists. And the Beats moved on, though some of the cultural institutions they founded are still going strong.

is complete without a stop at Lawrence Ferlinghetti's **City Lights Bookstore,** 261 Columbus (between Broadway and Pacific), 415/362-8193, on the neighborhood's most literary alley. City Lights is the nation's first all-paperback bookstore and a rambling ode to the best of the small presses; its poetry and other literary programs still feed the souls of those who need more nourishment than what commercial bestsellers can offer. A superb small museum, **Lyle Tuttle's Tattoo Museum and Shop,** is a few blocks up the way at 841 Columbus, 415/775-4991.

You can shop till you drop in this part of town. And much of what you'll find has something to do with food. For Italian ceramics, **Biordi Italian Imports,** 412 Columbus (near Vallejo), 415/392-8096, has a fabulous selection of art intended for the table (but almost too beautiful to use). For a price—and just about everything is pricey—the folks here will ship your treasures, too.

While you're wandering, you can easily put together a picnic for a timeout in Washington Square. Italian delicatessen and meat market **Prudente & Company,** 1460 Grant (at Union), 415/421-0757, is the place to stop for traditionally cured pancetta and prosciutto. Head to landmark **Molinari's,** 373 Columbus (between Broadway and Green), 415/421-2337, for cheeses, sausages, and savory salads, or to the Italian and French **Victoria Pastry Co.,** 1362 Stockton St. (at Vallejo), 415/781-2015, for cookies, cakes, and unbelievable pastries. Other good bakery stops nearby include **Liguria Bakery,** 1700 Stockton (at Filbert), 415/421-3786, famous for its focaccia, and the **Italian French Baking Co. of San Francisco,** 1501 Grant (at Union), 415/421-3796, known for its french bread. If you didn't load up on reading material at City Lights—for after you stuff yourself but before falling asleep in the square—stop by **Cavalli Italian Book Store,** 1441 Stockton (between Vallejo and Green), 415/421-4219, for Italian newspapers, magazines, and books.

North Beach Hangouts
Caffe Greco, 423 Columbus (between Vallejo and Green), 415/397-6261, is the best of the neighborhood's newish coffeehouses. But for that classic beatnik bonhomie, head to what was once the heart of New Bohemia, the surviving **Caffe Trieste,** 601 Vallejo (at Grant), 415/392-6739. Drop by anytime for opera and Italian folk songs on the jukebox, or come on Saturday afternoon for jazz, opera, or other concerts. Also-been-there-forever **Vesuvio Cafe,** 255 Columbus Ave. (at Broadway), 415/362-3370, across Kerouac Alley from the City Lights bookstore (look for the mural with volcanoes and peace symbols), is most appreciated for its upstairs balcony section, historically a magnet for working and wannabe writers (and everyone else, too). It was a favorite haunt of Ginsberg and Kerouac, as well as an in-town favorite for Welsh poet Dylan Thomas. And Francis Ford Coppola reportedly sat down at a back table to work on *The Godfather.* A painting depicts *Homo beatnikus,* and there's even an advertisement for a do-it-yourself beatnik makeover (kit including sunglasses, a black beret, and poem).

Another righteous place to hide is **Tosca,** 242 Columbus (between Broadway and Pacific),

415/391-1244, a late-night landmark with gaudy walls and comfortable Naugahyde booths where the hissing of the espresso machine competes with Puccini on the jukebox. Writers of all varieties still migrate here, sometimes to play pool in back. But you must behave yourself: Bob Dylan and Allen Ginsberg got thrown out of here for being unruly. **Cafe Malvina,** 1600 Stockton (at Union), 415/391-1290, is a good bet, too, especially for early-morning pastries with your coffee.

Serious social history students should also peek into the **Condor Cafe,** Columbus (at Broadway), 415/781-8222, the one-time Condor Club made famous by stripper Carol Doda and her silicone-enhanced mammaries, and now a run-of-the-mill sports bar. Still, the place offers a memory of the neighborhood's sleazier heyday. Other neighborhood perversion palaces, survivors of the same peep-show mentality, are becoming fewer and farther between, and in any event aren't really all that interesting.

Telegraph Hill and Coit Tower
The best way to get to Telegraph Hill—whether just for the view, to appreciate the city's hanging gardens, or to visit Coit Tower—is to climb the hill yourself, starting up the very steep stairs at Kearny and Filbert or ascending more gradually from the east, via either the Greenwich or Filbert steps. Following Telegraph Hill Blvd. as it winds its way from Lombard, from the west, is troublesome for drivers. Parking up top is scarce; especially on weekends you might sit for hours while you wait—just to park, mind you. A reasonable alternative is taking the #39-Coit bus.

Lillie Hitchcock Coit had a fetish for firemen. As a child, she was saved from a fire that claimed two of her playmates. As a teenager, she spent much of her time with members of San Francisco's all-volunteer Knickerbocker Engine Company No. 5, usually tagging along on fire calls and eventually becoming the team's official mascot; she was even allowed to play poker and smoke cigars with the boys. Started in 1929, financed by a Coit bequest, and completed in 1933, Coit Tower was to be a lasting memorial to the firemen. Some people say its shape resembles the nozzle of a fire hose, others suggest more sexual symbolism, but the official story is that the design by Arthur Brown was intended to look "equally artistic" from any direction. Coit

COIT TOWER'S
REVOLUTIONARY ART

Aside from its architectural oddity, another reason to visit Coit Tower is to appreciate the marvelous Depression-era Social Realist interior mural art in the lobby, recently restored and as striking as ever. (At last report, seven of the 27 total frescoes, those on the 2nd floor and along the narrow stairway, weren't available for general public viewing, since quarters are so close that scrapes from handbags and shoes are almost inevitable. You can see these murals on the Saturday guided tour.) Even in liberal San Francisco, many of these murals have been controversial, depicting as they do the drudgery, sometimes despair, behind the idyllic facade of modern California life—particularly as seen in the lives of the state's agricultural and industrial workforce. Financed through Franklin Roosevelt's New Deal–era Public Works Art Project, some 25 local artists set out in 1934 to paint Coit Tower's interior with frescoes, the same year that Diego Rivera's revolutionary renderings of Lenin and other un-American icons created such a scandal at New York's Rockefeller Center that the great Mexican painter's work was destroyed.

In tandem with tensions produced by a serious local dock worker's strike, some in San Francisco almost exploded when it was discovered that the new art in Coit Tower wasn't entirely politically benign, that some of it suggested something less than total support for pro-capitalist ideology. In various scenes, one person is carrying *Das Kapital* by Karl Marx, and another is reading a copy of the Communist-party *Daily Worker;* grim-faced "militant unemployed" march forward into the future; women wash clothes by hand within sight of Shasta Dam; slogans oppose both hunger and fascism; and a chauffeured limousine is clearly contrasted with a Model T Ford in Steinbeck's

Whatever its symbolism, Coit Tower offers great views and houses a striking collection of Depression-era frescoes.

Joad-family style. Even a hammer and sickle made it onto the walls. Unlike New York, even after an outraged vigilante committee threatened to chisel away Coit Tower's artistic offenses, San Francisco ultimately allowed it all to stay—everything, that is, except the hammer and sickle.

Tower was closed to the public for many years, due to damage caused by vandalism and water leakage. After a major interior renovation, the tower is now open in all its original glory, so come decide for yourself what the tower symbolizes. Or just come for the view. From atop the 180-foot tower, which gets extra lift from its site on top of Telegraph Hill, you get a magnificent 360-degree view of the entire Bay Area. Coin-op telescopes allow you to get an even closer look. Coit Tower, 415/362-0808, is open daily 10 A.M.–5 P.M., until 9 P.M. in summer. Ad-

mission is free, technically, but there is a charge for the elevator ride to the top: $3.75 adults, $2.50 seniors, $1.50 children ages 6–12.

Another Telegraph Hill delight: the intimate gardens along the eastern steps. The **Filbert Steps** stairway gardens are lined with trees, ivy, and garden flowers, with a few terraces and benches nearby. Below Montgomery St., the Filbert stairway becomes a bit doddering—unpainted tired wood that leads to enchanting Napier Ln., one of San Francisco's last wooden-plank streets and a Victorian survivor of the city's 1906 devastation. (Below Napier, the stairway continues on to Sansome Street.) The brick-paved **Greenwich Steps** wander down to the cliffhanging Julius' Castle restaurant, then continue down to the right, appearing to be private stairs to the side yard, weaving past flower gardens and old houses to reach Sansome. If you go up one way, be sure to come down the other.

Russian Hill

Also one of San Francisco's rarer pleasures is a stroll around Russian Hill, named for the belief that Russian sea otter hunters picked this place to bury their dead. One of the city's early bohemian neighborhoods and a preferred haunt for writers and other connoisseurs of quiet beauty, Russian Hill today is an enclave of the wealthy. But anyone can wander the neighborhood. If you come from North Beach, head up—it's definitely up—Vallejo St., where the sidewalks and the street eventually give way to stairs. Take a break at **Ina Coolbrith Park** at Taylor, named in honor of California's first poet laureate, a woman remarkable for many accomplishments. A member of one of Jim Beckwourth's westward wagon trains, she was the first American child to enter California by wagon. After an unhappy marriage, Coolbrith came to San Francisco, where she wrote poetry and created California's early literary circle. Many men fell in love with her, the ranks of the hopelessly smitten including Ambrose Bierce,

Bret Harte, and Mark Twain. (She refused to marry any of them.) Librarian for both the Bohemian Club and the Oakland Free Library, at the latter Coolbrith took 12-year-old Jack London under her wing; her tutelage and reading suggestions were London's only formal education. Up past the confusion of lanes at Russian Hill's first summit is **Florence Street,** which heads south, and still more stairs, these leading down to Broadway (the original Broadway, which shows why the city eventually burrowed a new Broadway under the hill). Coolbrith's last home on Russian Hill still stands at 1067 Broadway.

To see the second summit—technically the park at Greenwich and Hyde—and some of the reasons why TV and movie chase scenes are frequently filmed here, wander west and climb aboard the Hyde-Powell cable car. Worth exploration on the way up: Green St., Macondray Ln. just north of Jones (which eventually takes you down to Taylor St.), and **Filbert Street,** San Francisco's steepest driveable hill, a 31.5-degree grade. (To test that thesis yourself, go very slowly.) Just over the summit, as you stare straight toward Fisherman's Wharf, is another wonder of road engineering: the one-block stretch of Lombard St. between Hyde and Leavenworth, known as the **Crookedest Street in the World.** People do drive down this snake-shaped cobblestone path, a major tourist draw, but it's much more pleasant as a walk.

DELIGHTS AND DIVERSIONS

WALKING TOURS

San Francisco is a walking city par excellence. With enough time and inclination, exploring the hills, stairways, and odd little neighborhood nooks and crannies is the most rewarding way to get to know one's way around. Helpful for getting started are the free neighborhood walking-tour pamphlets (Pacific Heights, Union Square, Chinatown, Fisherman's Wharf, the Barbary Coast Trail, and more) available at the Convention & Visitors Bureau Information Center downstairs at Hallidie Plaza (Powell and Market Sts.), 415/391-2000.

Even with substantially less time, there are excellent options. A variety of local nonprofit or-

ganizations offer free or low-cost walking tours. Commercial tours—many unusual—are also available, most ranging in price from $15 to $40 per person, more for all-day tours.

Free and Inexpensive Walking Tours

Gold rush–era San Francisco is the theme behind the city's **Barbary Coast Trail,** a four-mile self-guided walking tour from Mission St. to Aquatic Park, marked by 150 bronze plaques embedded in the sidewalk along the way. Among the 20 historic sites en route are the oldest Asian temple in North America, the western terminus of the Pony Express, and the Hyde Street historic ships. Two guides to the trail are sold at the Hallidie Plaza visitor information center (Powell and Market).

The **City Guides** walking tours offered by Friends of the San Francisco Public Library, headquartered at the main San Francisco Public Library (Larkin and Grove), include many worthwhile neighborhood prowls. Call 415/557-4266 for a recorded schedule of upcoming walks (what, where, and when) or try www.walkingtours.com/CityGuides. Most walks include local architecture, culture, and history, though the emphasis—Art Deco Marina, Pacific Heights Mansions, Cityscapes and Roof Mansions, the Gold Rush City, Victorian San Francisco, Haight-Ashbury, Mission Murals, Japantown—can be surprising. City Guides are free, but donations are definitely appreciated.

Pacific Heights Walks are sponsored by the **Foundation for San Francisco's Architectural Heritage,** headquartered in the historic Haas-Lilienthal House at 2007 Franklin St. (between Washington and Jackson), 415/441-3000 (office) or 415/441-3004 (recorded information), and offer a look at the exteriors of splendid pre–World War I mansions in eastern Pacific Heights.

Friends of Recreation and Parks, headquartered at McLaren Lodge in Golden Gate Park, Stanyan and Fell Sts., 415/263-0991 (for upcoming hike schedule), offers guided flora, fauna, and history walks through the park May–Oct., Sat. at 11 A.M. and Sun. at 11 A.M. and 2 P.M. Group tours are also available.

Precita Eyes Mural Arts Center, at 2981 24th St. (at Harrison), 415/285-2287, www.precitaeyes.org, offers fascinating two-hour mural walks through the Mission District on Sat. starting at 11 A.M. and 1:30 P.M., and Sun. at 1:30 P.M. Admission is $7 adults, $4 seniors, $1 youths 18 and under. Call for information on the center's many other tours. In addition to its self-guided Mission murals tour, the **Mexican Museum** at Fort Mason, 415/441-0404 (recorded) or 415/202-9700, sponsors docent-led tours of San Francisco's Diego Rivera murals.

The San Francisco Symphony Volunteer Council, San Francisco Opera Guild, and San Francisco Ballet Auxiliary combine their services to offer a walking tour of the three **San Francisco Performing Arts Center** facilities: Davies Symphony Hall, the War Memorial Opera House, and Herbst Theatre. The tour takes about an hour and 15 minutes; cost is $5 adults, $3 seniors/students; and is offered every Mon., hourly from 10 A.M. to 2 P.M. Purchase your ticket at the Davies Symphony Hall box office (main foyer) 10 minutes before tour time. For more information, call 415/552-8338.

Commercial Walking Tours
Helen's Walk Tours, P.O. Box 9164, Berkeley, CA 94709, 510/524-4544, offers entertaining walking tours, with a personal touch provided by

SAN FRANCISCO AS EVENT

Even more kaleidoscopic than the city's arts scene, San Francisco events include an almost endless combination of the appropriate, inappropriate, absurd, inspired, and sublime. Museums, theaters, neighborhood groups, and other cultural institutions usually offer their own annual events calendars. Even most shopping centers sponsor a surprising array of entertainment and events.

Among the city's most famous events are the two-week **San Francisco International Film Festival** in late April, featuring more than 100 films and videos from some 30 different countries; the mid-May **Bay to Breakers** race, when some 100,000 participants—many decked out in hilarious and/or scandalous costumes—hoof it from the Embarcadero out to Ocean Beach; and late May's **Carnaval San Francisco,** featuring an uninhibited parade with samba bands, dancers, floats, and hun-

dreds of thousands of revelers. Typically in June, coinciding with the **San Francisco International Lesbian and Gay Film Festival,** comes the annual **Lesbian-Gay-Bisexual-Transgender Freedom Day Parade and Celebration,** one huge gay-pride party usually led by Dykes on Bikes and including cross-dressing cowboys (or girls), gay bands and majorettes, cheerleaders, and everyone and everything else.

Among the city's most intriguing events otherwise are galas such as the February 14 **Valentine's Day Sex Tour** at the San Francisco Zoo, where people let their animal passions run wild; the April 1 **St. Stupid's Day Parade,** a no-holds-barred celebration of foibles and foolishness; and the annual **Bay Area Robot Olympics** at the Exploratorium in September. Consult local newspapers for more complete information on what's going on when you're in town.

ROBERT HOLMES/CALTOUR

*Chinese
New Year parade*

personable Helen Rendon, tour guide and part-time actress. Tour groups usually meet "under the clock" at the St. Francis Hotel (Helen's the one with the wonderfully dramatic hat) before setting off on an entertaining two-hour tour of Victorian mansions, North Beach (want to know where Marilyn Monroe married Joe DiMaggio?), or Chinatown. Other options: combine parts of two tours into a half-day Grand Tour, or, if enough time and interested people are available, request other neighborhood tours. Make reservations for any tour at least one day in advance.

Dashiell Hammett Literary Tours, 510/287-9540, are led by Don Herron, author of *The Literary World of San Francisco and its Environs.* The half-day tours wander through downtown streets and alleys, on the trail of both the writer and his detective story hero, Sam Spade. They're usually offered May–Aug., and other literary themes can be arranged. Shelley Campbell's **Footnotes Literary Walk,** 415/381-0713 or 415/721-1763 (recorded), takes guests on a stroll through North Beach, past the former haunts of great writers.

Roger's Custom Tours, 650/742-9611, offers unusual adventures and custom tours of San Francisco tailored to your specifications. German spoken.

The personable Jay Gifford leads a **Victorian Home Walk Tour** (including a scenic bus trolley ride) through Cow Hollow and Pacific Heights, exploring distinctive Queen Anne, Edwardian, and Italianate architecture in the neighborhoods.

You'll see the interior of a Queen Anne and the locations used for *Mrs. Doubtfire* and *Party of Five.* While also enjoying spectacular views of the city, bay, and gardens, you'll learn to differentiate architectural styles. Tours meet at 11 A.M. daily in the lobby of the St. Francis Hotel on Union Square and last about 2.5 hours. For reservations and information, call 415/252-9485 or visit www.victorianwalk.com.

Cruisin' the Castro, historical tours of San Francisco's gay mecca, 415/550-8110, www.webcastro.com/castrotour, are led by local historian Trevor Hailey and offer unique insight into how San Francisco's gay community has shaped the city's political, social, and cultural development. Everyone is welcome; reservations are required. Tours are offered Tues.–Sat., starting at 10 A.M. at Harvey Milk Plaza, continuing through the community's galleries, shops, and cultural sights, then ending at the Names Project (original home of the AIDS Memorial Quilt) around 2 P.M. Brunch included.

San Francisco's coffeehouse culture is the focus of **Javawalk,** 415/673-9255, www.javawalk. com, a stroll through North Beach haunts starting at 334 Grant Ave., Sat. at 10 A.M.

OTHER CITY TOURS

Tours by Land
Gray Line, 415/558-9400 or toll-free 800/826-0202, www.grayline.com, is the city's largest tour

operator, commandeering an impressive fleet of standard-brand buses and red, London-style double-deckers. The company offers a variety of narrated tours touching on the basics, in San Francisco proper and beyond. Unlike most other companies, Gray Line offers its city tour in multiple languages: Japanese, Korean, German, French, Italian, and Spanish. Much more personal is the **Great Pacific Tour Company,** 518 Octavia St. (at Hayes), 415/626-4499, www.greatpacifictour.com, which runs 13-passenger minivans on four different tours, including half-day city tours. **Tower Tours,** 77 Jefferson (at Pier 43½), 415/434-8687, is affiliated with Blue & Gold Fleet and also offers city tours; all tours leave from their office at Fisherman's Wharf.

Quality Tours, 5003 Palmetto Ave., Pacifica, 650/994-5054, www.qualitytours.com, does a San Francisco architecture tour and a "whole enchilada" tour in a luxury seven-passenger Chevy suburban. **Three Babes and a Bus Nightclub Tours,** 415/552-CLUB, www.three-babes.com, caters to visiting night owls, who hop the bus and party at the city's hottest nightspots with the charming hostesses. Many firms create personalized, special-interest tours with reasonable advance notice; contact the Convention & Visitors Bureau for a complete listing.

Though both are better known for their ferry tours, both the Blue & Gold Fleet and the Red & White Fleet (see below) also offer land tours to various Northern California attractions.

AN OPEN-MINDED GUIDE TO NIGHTCLUBBING IN SAN FRANCISCO

First, ask the basic questions: Who am I? What am I doing here? Where do I belong? To go nightclubbing in San Francisco, at least *ask* the questions. The answers don't really matter; your political, social, sexual, and musical preferences will be matched somewhere. Techno, disco, new wave, house, fusion, industrial, world beat—whatever it is you're into, it's out there, just part of the creative carnival world of San Francisco nightclubbing. Everything goes, especially cultural taboos, leaving only free-wheeling imaginations and an unadulterated desire to do one thing and only one thing—dance with total abandon. In the city, heteros, gays, lesbians, blacks, whites, Asians, and Latinos all writhe together, unified in a place where all prejudice drops away: the dance floor.

The hottest dance clubs come and go considerably faster than the Muni buses do, so the key to finding the hippest, most happening spot is to ask around. Ask people who look like they should know, such as young fashion junkies working in trendy clothing shops, used-record stores, or other abodes of pretentious cool. If you're seeking one of those infamous "warehouse" parties, then look for small invitational flyers tacked to telephone poles or posted in the above-mentioned and other likely places (particularly in the Haight, lower Haight, and Castro neighborhoods). The flyers announce a party and list a phone number to call. When you call up—ooh, the intrigue—you'll get directions to that night's secret

dance locale. Warning: these roving, nonlicensed dance clubs tend to put on quite crowded parties, very expensive to boot.

Throbbing together with hundreds of other euphorics, experiencing ecstasy en masse, may be the closest we'll ever really get to living in one united world. Still, San Francisco nightclub virgins tend to avoid their initiation, somehow intimidated by the frenzied cosmic collision of electrifying lights, thumping dance tunes, and sweat-drenched bodies. But be not afraid. There are answers to even the three most common worries:

Worry: I can't dance. *Answer:* It wouldn't matter even if you could. The dance floors are so crowded, at best it's possible only to bounce up and down.

Worry: I'm straight (or gay) and the crowd seems to be predominantly gay (or straight). *Answer:* Since the limits of gender and sexuality are hopelessly blurred in San Francisco, and since nobody would care even if they weren't, just dump your angst and dance.

Worry: I'm afraid I'll look like a fool (feel out of place, be outclassed, fall down, throw up, whatever). *Answer:* As we said, nobody cares. You're totally anonymous, being one of more than 728,000 people in town. And no matter what you do, nobody will notice, since narcissism in San Francisco's clubs is at least as deep as the Grand Canyon.

by Tim Moriarty

Tours by Sea

The **Blue & Gold Fleet** is based at Piers 39 and 41, 415/705-8200 (business office), 415/773-1188 (recorded schedule), or 415/705-5555 (information and advance ticket purchase), www.blueandgoldfleet.com. Blue & Gold offers a narrated year-round (weather permitting) **Golden Gate Bay Cruise** that leaves from Pier 39, passes under the Golden Gate Bridge, cruises by Sausalito and Angel Island, and loops back around Alcatraz. The trip takes about an hour. Fare: $17 adults, $13 seniors over 62 and youths 12–18, $9 children 5–11. The justifiably popular **Alcatraz Tour** takes you out to the infamous former prison (see the special topic Touring the Real Rock for more information). Fare is $12.25 adults with a self-guided audio tour, or $8.75 adults without the audio. Day-use fee on the rock is $1. (Also available is an evening "Alcatraz After Hours" tour, $19.75 adults, which includes a narrated guided tour.) Blue & Gold ferries also can take you to **Sausalito, Tiburon, Oakland, Alameda, Vallejo,** and **Angel Island.**

The **Red & White Fleet,** at Pier 43¹/2, 415/447-0597 or toll-free 800/229-2784 (in California), www.redandwhite.com, offers one-hour, multilingual Bay Cruise tours that loop out under the Golden Gate and return past Sausalito, Angel Island, and Alcatraz ($17 adults, $13 seniors/youths, $9 kids 5–11, not including the $1 day-use fee). Other offerings include weekend Blues Cruises in summer; an excursion across the bay to Alameda to tour the aircraft carrier USS *Hornet;* and a variety of land tours in Northern California.

Hornblower Cruises and Events, 415/788-8866, www.hornblowercruises.com, has boats at Pier 33 and elsewhere around the bay. The company offers big-boat on-the-bay dining adventures, from extravagant nightly dinner dances and weekday lunches to Saturday and Sunday champagne brunch. Occasional special events, from whodunit murder mystery dinners to jazz cocktail cruises, can be especially fun. And Hornblower's Monte Carlo Cruises feature casual Las Vegas–style casino gaming tables (proceeds go to charity) on dinner cruises aboard the M/V *Monte Carlo.*

Oceanic Society Expeditions, based at Fort Mason, 415/474-3385, www.oceanic-society.org, offers a variety of seagoing natural history trips, including winter whale-watching excursions, usually late Dec.–Apr., and Farallon Islands nature trips, June–Nov. Reservations are required. Oceanic Society trips are multifaceted. For example, only scientific researchers and trusted volunteers are allowed on the cold granite Farallon Islands, but the Society's excursion to the islands takes you as close as most people ever get. The Farallons, 27 miles from the Golden Gate, are a national wildlife refuge within the Gulf of the Farallones National Marine Sanctuary, which itself is part of UNESCO's Central California Coast Biosphere Reserve. The nutrient-rich coastal waters around the islands are vital to the world's fisheries, to the health of sea mammal populations, and to the success of the breeding seabird colonies here. Some quarter million birds breed here, among them tufted puffins and

San Francisco Bay tour boat

TOM MYERS PHOTOGRAPHY

POETIC AMUSEMENTS

There's probably only one thing better than reading a good poem in a quiet room by yourself. And that's listening to an impassioned poet reading a poem out loud in a small coffee-scented café full of attentive writers, lawyers, bikers, teachers, computer programmers, divinity students, musicians, secretaries, drug addicts, cooks, and assorted oddball others who all love poetry and are hanging onto every word being juggled by the poet behind the microphone. The only thing better than *that* is to read your own poems at an open-mike poetry reading.

One of the wonderful things about San Francisco and vicinity is that this kind of poetic melee takes place in some café, club, or bookstore almost every night, for those who know where to look. No one revels in the right to free speech like Bay Area denizens, and open poetry readings are as popular as stand-up comedy in many cafés and clubs, with sign-up lists at the door. Bring your own poetry, or just kick back and listen to some amazing musings.

The following suggested venues will get you started. Since schedules for local poetic license programs do change, it's prudent to call or otherwise check it out before setting out. Current open readings and other events are listed in the monthly tabloid *Poetry Flash*, P.O. Box 4172, Berkeley, CA 94704, 510/525-5476, the Bay Area's definitive poetry review and literary calendar, available free at many bookstores and cafés.

**Open-Mike Poetry
Readings in San Francisco**
Café du Nord, 2170 Market St., 415/861-5016, Sun. at 5 P.M.
Elbo Room, 647 Valencia (at 17th), 415/552-7788, Fri. at 9 P.M.
Paradise Lounge, 1501 Folsom St. (at 11th), 415/861-6906, Sun. at 8 P.M. (upstairs).
Keane's 3300 Club, 3300 Mission St. (at 29th), 415/826-6886, poetry readings on the second and fourth Tues. of each month since 1993.

In the East Bay
Diesel—A Bookstore, 5433 College (between Lawton and Hudson) in Oakland's Rockridge district, 510/653-9965, hosts fiction, nonfiction, and poetry readings three times a week.
La Val's Pizza and Subterranean Theatre, 1834 Euclid Ave. (at Hearst) in Berkeley, 510/843-5617, housed poetry readings and Free Speech Movement gatherings in the 1960s. Poetry readings Tues. at 7:30 P.M.

by Ed Aust

THEATER AS CIRCUS

Worth seeing whenever the group is in town is the much-loved, always arresting, and far from silent **San Francisco Mime Troupe,** 855 Treat Ave. (between 21st and 22nd), 415/285-1717, a decades-old institution true to the classic Greek and Roman tradition of theatrical farce—politically sophisticated street theater noted for its complex simplicity. In addition to boasting actor Peter Coyote and the late rock impresario Bill Graham as organizational alumni, and inspiring the establishment of one-time troupe member Luis Valdez's El Teatro Campesino, the Mime Troupe was repeatedly banned and arrested in its formative years.

In 1966, the state Senate Un-American Activities Committee charged the group with the crime of making lewd performances, the same year troupe members were arrested in North Beach for singing Christmas carols without a permit. More recently, the Mime Troupe has won a Tony Award and three Obies.

A tad more family-oriented, "the kind of circus parents might want their kids to run away to," according to NPR's Jane Pauley, is the **Pickle Family Circus,** another exceptional city-based theater troupe, which performs at Fort Mason's Cowell Theatre, 415/441-3400.

Bizarre cabaret-style **"Beach Blanket Babylon,"** playing at Club Fugazi, 678 Green St. (between Powell and Columbus) in North Beach, 415/421-4222, is the longest-running musical revue in theatrical history. The story line is always evolving. Snow White, who seems to be seeking love in all the wrong places, encounters characters who strut straight off the front pages of the tabloids.

rhinoceros auklets (bring a hat). The Oceanic Society trip to the islands takes eight hours, shoving off at 8:30 A.M. (Sat., Sun., and select Fridays) from Fort Mason. The 63-foot Oceanic Society boat carries 49 passengers and a naturalist. Contact the nonprofit Oceanic Society for other excursion options.

SAN FRANCISCO PERFORMING ARTS

San Francisco's performing arts scene offers everything from the classics to the contemporary, kitsch, and downright crazed. Find out what's going on by picking up local publications or calling the San Francisco Convention & Visitors Bureau information hot lines (see Useful Information, below). Tickets for major events and performances are available through the relevant box offices, mentioned below.

Low-income arts lovers, or those deciding to "do" the town on a last-minute whim, aren't necessarily out of luck. **TIX Bay Area,** on Stockton St. at Union Square, 415/433-7827, www.tix.com, offers day-of-performance tickets to local shows at half price. Payment is cash only, no credit card reservations. Along with being a full-service BASS ticket outlet, TIX also handles advance full-price tickets to many Bay Area events. Open Tues.– Sat. noon–7:30 P.M. You can get a catalog for ordering advance tickets at half price by calling **TIX by Mail** at 415/430-1140. To charge BASS arts and entertainment tickets by phone or to listen to recorded calendar listings, call 415/478-2277 (BASS). Another helpful information source: KUSF 90.3 FM's **Alternative Music and Entertainment News (AMEN)** information line, 415/221-2636.

Other ticket box offices include: **City Box Office,** 415/392-4400, **Entertainment Ticketfinder,** 650/756-1414 or toll-free 800/523-1515, and **St. Francis Theatre and Sports Tickets,** a service of the Westin St. Francis Hotel, 415/362-3500, www.premiertickets.com.

STAYING IN SAN FRANCISCO

San Francisco is an expensive city, for the most part. A first-time visitor's first impression might be that no one is welcome here unless they show up in a Rolls Royce. The normal system of price categories used throughout this book isn't too useful here, either, when probably 90 percent of the lodgings fall into the "Luxury" category. To counterbalance this, price ranges for Luxury accommodations have been provided where possible.

ACCOMMODATIONS RATINGS

Accommodations in this book are rated by price category, based on double-occupancy, high-season rates. Categories used are:

Budget.	$35 and under
Inexpensive	$35-60
Moderate	$60-85
Expensive	$85-110
Premium	$110-150
Luxury	$150 and up

Mind you, this is for the "standard" room, two persons, one bed, in peak summer season. (Many offer off-season and weekend deals; always ask about specials before booking.) Most also have higher-priced suites, and if you feel the need to drop $500 or $1,000 (or more) per night on a suite, you'll find plenty of places in town that will be more than happy to accommodate you. If you can afford these prices ("tariffs," actually), you'll not be disappointed. And some of the city's four- and five-star hotels also rank among its most historic, survivors—at least in part—of the great 1906 earthquake and fire.

That said, a little looking will uncover plenty of accommodations suitable for the rest of us. San Francisco offers two hostels affiliated with Hostelling International (American Youth Hostels), in addition to other hostels and inexpensive options. Other than the hostels, some dirt-cheap fleabags can be found, but they're often in seedy areas; budget travelers with city savvy, street smarts, and well-honed self-preservation skills might consider these establishments, but women traveling solo should avoid them. (In the

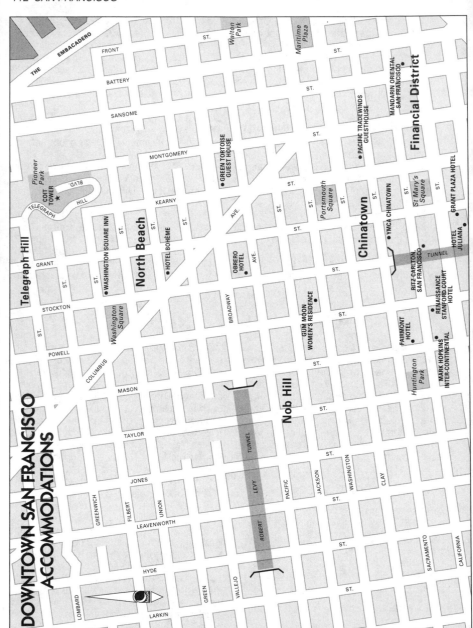

© AVALON TRAVEL PUBLISHING, INC.

context of truly low-budget accommodations, "European-style" generally means "the bathrooms are in the hallway.")

City-style motels offer another world of possibilities. Some reasonably priced ones are scattered throughout the city, though Lombard St. (west of Van Ness) is the place to go for overwhelming concentrations of motel choice. The city also supports a wide variety of bed-and-breakfast inns, with ambiences ranging from Haight-Ashbury-style funk to very proper Victoriana.

In general, San Francisco offers great choices in the midrange hotel market, including a number of "boutique" hotels. Many of these attractive and intimate hotels—old-timers and aging grand dames now renovated and redecorated for the modern carriage trade—are well located, near visitor attractions and public transit. Lack of convenient off-street parking is rarely a drawback, since most offer some sort of valet parking arrangement. Very good to exceptional restaurants—and room service—are often associated with boutique hotels. When travel is slow, most notably in winter, off-season and package deals can make these small hotels (and others) genuine bargains. Do check around before signing in. Also check at the visitors center on Market St., since some establishments offer special coupons and other seasonal inducements. Many boutique and fine hotels also offer substantial discounts to business travelers and to members of major "travel-interested" groups, including the American Automobile Association (AAA) and the American Association of Retired People (AARP). The visitor center is located at Benjamin Swig Pavilion on the lower level of Hallidie Plaza at Market and Powell Streets. Open weekdays 9 A.M.–5:30 P.M., Sat. until 3 P.M., Sun. 10 A.M.–2 P.M. Or call 415/391-2000. You can also call 415/391-2001 24 hours a day for a recorded message listing daily events and activities.

Reservation Services

If you're unable to make an accommodations choice well in advance, or if you'd rather let someone else do the detail work, contact a local reservations service.

San Francisco Reservations, 22 2nd St., 4th Floor, San Francisco, CA 94105, 415/227-1500 or toll-free 800/677-1550, offers a no-fee reservations service for more than 200 hotels, most of these in San Francisco, and keeps current on discounts, specials, and packages. The company offers preferred rates for business travelers at some of the city's finest hotels, including many of the boutiques. With one call, you can also take advantage of their free best-deal airline ticketing and car rental reservations service. Reservation lines are open daily 7 A.M.–11 P.M. If you have access to a computer, you can make reservations (three or more days in advance) through their website at www.hotelres.com.

Discount Hotel Rates/California Reservations, 165 8th St., Ste. 201, San Francisco, CA 94103, 415/252-1107 or toll-free 800/576-0003, also no-fee, represents more than 200 hotels in San Francisco and beyond. Subject to room availability, the firm offers rates at quality hotels for 10–50 percent less than posted rates.

Bed & Breakfast California, P.O. Box 282910, San Francisco, CA 94128-2910, 650/696-1690 or toll-free 800/872-4500, offers referrals to a wide range of California bed-and-breakfasts—everything from houseboat and home stays to impressive Victorians and country-style inns—especially in San Francisco, the Napa-Sonoma wine country, and the Monterey Peninsula. Rates: $70–200 per night (with two-night minimum). Similar, and often without the mandatory two-night stay, is **Bed and Breakfast San Francisco,** P.O. Box 420009, 415/899-0060 or toll-free 800/452-8249, www.bbsf.com.

HOSTELS AND OTHER CHEAP SLEEPS

San Francisco is full of shoestring-priced hostels renting dorm-style bunks for around $12–20 per person per night. Many also have higher-priced private rooms. Some hostels are open to everybody; others, as noted below, are open only to international travelers. Most have group kitchen facilities, laundry facilities, and helpful staff to give you hot tips on seeing the city.

Hostelling International

The **San Francisco Fisherman's Wharf HI-AYH Hostel** is just west of the wharf at Fort Mason, Bldg. 240, 415/771-3645, fax 415/771-1468, www.norcalhostels.org. It's a local institution—located on a hill overlooking the bay and occupying part of the city's urban national park, the

Golden Gate National Recreation Area. Close to the "Bikecentennial" bike route and the cultural attractions of the Fort Mason complex, the hostel is within an easy stroll of Fisherman's Wharf and Ghirardelli Square, as well as Chinatown and downtown (you could take the cable car).

The hostel itself is one of HI-AYH's largest—and finest—offering a total of 160 beds in clean rooms; one chore a day expected. Popular with all age groups and families, amenities include lots of lounge space, a big kitchen, plenty of food storage, laundry facilities, and pay lockers for baggage. No lockout or curfew. Family rooms are available, as is parking, and it's wheelchair accessible. The ride board here is helpful for travelers without wheels. Guests can also participate in hostel-sponsored hikes, tours, and bike rides. Reservations are essential for groups and advisable for others—especially in summer, when this place is jumping. Rates include linen and free breakfast; 14-day maximum, no minimum stay. To reserve by mail, send one night's deposit (address above) at least three weeks in advance; by phone or fax, call at least 48 hours in advance and confirm with a major credit card (Visa, MasterCard).

Near all the downtown and theater district hubbub is the **HI-San Francisco Downtown Hostel,** 312 Mason St. (between Geary and O'Farrell), 415/788-5604, fax 415/788-3023, www.hiayh.org, another good choice for budget travelers. This hotel-style hostel offers double and triple rooms—most share a bathroom—and amenities from kitchen to baggage storage and vending machines. Laundry facilities are nearby. The desk is essentially open for check-in 24 hours; no lockout, no curfew, no chores. Family rooms available. Groups welcome, by reservation only, and reservations for summer stays are essential for everyone and should be made at least 30 days in advance. Reserve by phone or fax with Visa or MasterCard. Rates include linens, but bring your own towel. Ask about the best nearby parking.

Other Hostels

The excellent **Green Tortoise Guest House,** 494 Broadway, 415/834-1000, fax 415/956-4900, www.greentortoise.com, sits on the corner of Broadway and Kearny, where Chinatown runs into North Beach. It offers a kitchen, laundry,

sauna, free internet access, and complimentary breakfast. No curfew.

The **Interclub Globe Hostel,** 10 Hallam Place (south of Market near the Greyhound station, just off Folsom), 415/431-0540, is a fairly large, lively place with clean four-bed hotel rooms, a private sundeck, community lounge, pool table, café, and laundry room. The Globe is specifically for foreign guests, usually students, but can also include Americans who present passports with stamps verifying their own international travels. Open 24 hours, no curfew. Also in the area and strictly for international travelers ("operated by students for students" and affiliated with the American Association of International Hostels) are two other SoMa budget outposts: the **European Guest House,** 761 Minna (between 8th and 9th Sts.), 415/861-6634, and the affiliated **San Francisco International Student Center,** 1188 Folsom (near BrainWash), 415/487-1463 or 415/255-8800, both offering dorm-style accommodations and basic amenities.

North of Market, the **San Francisco Globetrotter's Inn,** 225 Ellis St. (at Mason, one block west of Powell), 415/346-5786 (or 415/673-4048 to reach guests), offers daily and weekly rates. In the Chinatown area, the lively **Pacific Tradewinds Guest House,** 680 Sacramento St., 415/433-7970, is in a prime spot near the Transamerica Pyramid. The hostel offers eight-bed rooms or larger dorm rooms, and rates include free tea and coffee all day, use of a fully equipped kitchen, Internet access, free maps, laundry service, fax service, long-term storage, and (I quote) "an extremely friendly, helpful, and good-looking staff." No curfew. You can make arrangements to stay through their website at www.hostels.com/pt.

A good budget bet in the Mission District is the **San Francisco International Guest House,** 2976 23rd St. (at Harrison), 415/641-1411, an uncrowded Victorian popular with Europeans. Accommodations include two- to four-bed dorm rooms, as well as four couples rooms; five day minimum stay. It's geared toward longer-term stays and usually full.

Boardinghouses

The **Mary Elizabeth Inn,** 1040 Bush (between Jones and Leavenworth), 415/673-6768, is a women's residence, part of a mission program sponsored by the United Methodist Church. Tourists are welcome when space is available. Facilities include private rooms (shared baths) with linen service, laundry facilities, a sundeck and solarium, and two meals daily (except Sunday). Weekly rate: $155. An even better bet, though, for a longer visit in San Francisco is the **Harcourt Residence Club**, 1105 Larkin, 415/673-7720, where a stay includes two meals a day, Sunday brunch, and access to TV. Unlike most other residence hotels, this one attracts international students—a younger clientele. Weekly rates: $150–250 per person.

INEXPENSIVE TO MODERATE HOTELS

Close to Nob Hill is the very nice **James Court Hotel**, 1353 Bush St. (between Polk and Larkin), 415/771-2409, with European-style accommodations and basic amenities plus kitchen. Some rooms have kitchenettes and some have private baths. All have color cable TV and phone. Amenities include complimentary coffee and coin laundry.

Perhaps the epitome of San Francisco's casual, low-cost European-style stays is the **Adelaide Inn**, 5 Isadora Duncan Ct., (in the theater district, off Taylor between Geary and Post), 415/441-2261. Reservations are advisable for the 18 rooms with shared baths. Rates include continental breakfast. Inexpensive-Moderate. Also in the area, **The Ansonia**, 711 Post, 415/673-2670, is a real find. This small hotel has a friendly staff, comfortable lobby, nice rooms, a laundry, and breakfast and dinner (except on Sunday). Inexpensive-Moderate (depending upon the bathroom arrangement). Student rates for one month or longer.

A budget gem in the Chinatown area, the **Obrero Hotel**, 1208 Stockton, tel. 415/989-3960, offers just a dozen cheery bed-and-breakfast rooms with bathrooms down the hall. Full breakfast included. Inexpensive-Moderate. Another best bet is the **Grant Plaza Hotel**, 465 Grant Ave. (between Pine and Bush), 415/434-3883 or toll-free 800/472-6899, where amenities include private baths with hair dryers, telephones with voice mail, and color TV. Group rates available. Inexpensive-Moderate.

MODERATE TO PREMIUM HOTELS

A few blocks north of the Civic Center between Hyde and Larkin, in a borderline bad neighborhood, is the justifiably popular **Essex Hotel**, 684 Ellis St., tel. 415/474-4664 or toll-free (800) 443-7739 in California, 800/453-7739 from elsewhere in the country. The hotel offers small rooms with private baths and telephones; some have TV. Free coffee. It's especially popular in summer—when rates are slightly higher—with foreign tourists, particularly Germans. Moderate-Expensive. Weekly rates, too. **Pensione International**, 875 Post St., tel. 415/775-3344, lies at the gentrifying edge of the Tenderloin just east of Hyde St. and offers attractive rooms with either shared or private bath. Breakfast included. Moderate-Expensive.

Noteworthy for its antiques, comfort, and fresh flowers, is the small **Golden Gate Hotel**, 775 Bush St. (between Powell and Mason), 415/392-3702 or toll-free 800/835-1118. Sixteen of the rooms have private bath; the other seven, with shared bath, are less expensive. Rates include complimentary breakfast and afternoon tea. Moderate-Expensive. Unpretentious and reasonably priced (private bathrooms) is the **Union Square Plaza Hotel**, 432 Geary (between Powell and Mason), 415/776-7585. Expensive.

Located right across from the Chinatown gate just off Union Square, the bright and comfortable **Baldwin Hotel**, 321 Grant Ave. (between Sutter and Bush), 415/781-2220 or toll-free 800/622-5394, www.baldwinhotel.com, offers comfortable, newly renovated guest rooms with TV and telephones with modem hookups. Expensive-Premium.

A relative of the Phoenix Inn, the new **Abigail Hotel**, 246 McAllister St., 415/861-9728 or toll-free 800/243-6510, www.sftrips.com, offers spruce British-style charm and antiques, even down comforters, all just a hop, skip, and a jump from City Hall, the Civic Auditorium, and nearby arts venues. The on-site vegan restaurant, Millennium, is purportedly superb. Discounts for artists, government employees, and groups; other deals when the town slows down. Weekly and monthly rates also available. Continental breakfast included. Expensive-Premium.

Styled after a 1920s luxury liner, the **Com-**

modore Hotel, 825 Sutter St., 415/923-6800 or toll-free 800/338-6848, www.sftrips.com, is a fun place to stay downtown. All of the rooms are spacious, with modern bathrooms and data ports on the phones. Downstairs, the **Titanic Café** serves California-style breakfast and lunch, and the Commodore's **Red Room** is a plush cocktail lounge decorated with rich red velvets, pearlized vinyl, and red tile. Expensive-Premium. Nearby, and also between the theater district and Nob Hill, the newly refurbished 1909 **Amsterdam Hotel,** 749 Taylor St. (between Bush and Sutter), 415/673-3277 or toll-free 800/637-3444, features an attractive Victorian lobby and clean, comfortable, spacious rooms, all with contemporary private bathrooms. All rooms have color cable TV, radio, and direct-dial phones. Rates include complimentary breakfast. Expensive-Premium.

Near Union Square, the **Sheehan Hotel,** 620 Sutter St. (at Mason), 415/775-6500 or toll-free 800/848-1529, is a real find—a surprisingly elegant take on economical downtown accommodations. Rooms have cable TV and phones; some have private baths, others have European-style shared baths. Other facilities include an Olympic-size lap pool, a fitness and exercise room, and a downstairs tearoom and wine bar. The hotel is close to shopping, art, BART, and other public transportation. Discount parking is available. Rates include continental breakfast, and children under 12 stay free with parent(s). Moderate-Premium.

Quite charming, between Union Square and Nob Hill, is the **Cornell Hotel,** 715 Bush St. (at Powell), 415/421-3154 or toll-free 800/232-9698, where rates include breakfast and all rooms are nonsmoking. Expensive-Premium.

BOUTIQUE HOTELS

San Francisco's bouquet of European-style boutique hotels is becoming so large that it's impossible to fit the flowers in any one container. In addition to those mentioned above, the following sampling offers an idea of the wide variety available. Most of the city's intimate and stylish small hotels are included in the annual San Francisco Convention & Visitors Bureau Lodging Guide, listed among all other accom- modations options, by area, and not otherwise distinguished from more mainstream hostelries. Two clues to spotting a possible "boutique": the number of rooms (usually 75 to 150, rarely over 200) and prices in the Premium or Luxury category.

Near Union Square and Nob Hill
The 111-room **Hotel Diva,** 440 Geary (between Mason and Taylor, right across from the Curran and Geary Theaters), 415/885-0200 or toll-free 800/553-1900, is a chrome-faced contemporary Italian classic, awarded "Best Hotel Design" honors by *Interiors* magazine. Special features include a complete business center—with computers, modems, you name it—daily newspaper, complimentary breakfast delivered to your door, meeting facilities, and a 24-hour fitness center. Monday through Friday, Diva offers complimentary limousine service to downtown. Premium-Luxury ($159–199 for standard rooms, $179–219 suites).

Cable cars roll right by the six-floor **Hotel Union Square,** 114 Powell St., 415/397-3000 or toll-free 800/553-1900, one of the city's original boutiques, with an art deco lobby and 131 rooms decorated in a blend of contemporary California and old-brick San Francisco. Multiple amenities, including continental breakfast and on-site parking. Wonderful rooftop suites with gardens. Premium.

The one-time Elks Lodge #3 is now the 87-room **Kensington Park Hotel,** 450 Post St., 415/788-6400 or toll-free 800/553-1900, just steps from Union Square. Its parlor lobby still sports the original hand-painted Gothic ceiling and warm Queen Anne floral decor. Guests enjoy all the amenities, including Financial District limo service, a fitness center, complimentary continental breakfast, and afternoon tea and sherry. Premium-Luxury ($175–205). (Inquire about hotel/theater packages, since Theatre On The Square is also located here.)

The century-old **King George Hotel,** 334 Mason (at Geary), www.kinggeorge.com, is a cozy and charming stop near Geary St. theaters and Union Square. Breakfast and afternoon tea served daily in the traditional English **Windsor Tearoom.** Ask about seasonal discounts and other specials, with rates as low as $85. Moderate-Premium.

SOME HIP SAN FRANCISCO STAYS

Every city has its style, reflected in how things appear, of course, but mostly in how they feel. The following establishments offer just a sample of that inimitable San Francisco attitude.

The Phoenix Inn at 601 Eddy St. (on the corner of Eddy and Larkin at the edge of the Tenderloin), 415/776-1380 or toll-free 800/248-9466, www.sftrips.com, is more than just a 1950s motel resurrected with flamingo pink and turquoise paint. It's a subtle see-and-be-seen art scene, first attracting rock 'n' roll stars and now attracting almost everybody—*the* place in San Francisco to spy on members of the cultural elite. This is, for example, the only place Sonic Youth ever stays in San Francisco. Just-plain-famous folks like Keanu Reeves and Ben Harper can also be spied from time to time. Like the trendy, on-site California-style restaurant, **Backflip**, even the heated swimming pool here is famous, due to its Francis Forlenza mural, "My Fifteen Minutes—Tumbling Waves," the center of a big state-sponsored stink over whether it violated health and safety codes (since public pool bottoms are supposed to be white). "That's how it is up at Eddy and Larkin, where the limos are always parkin'," according to the inn's complimentary *Phoenix Fun Book*, a cartoon-style coloring book history illustrated by *Bay Guardian* artist Lloyd Dangle. (Also as a service for guests, the Phoenix sporadically publishes its own hippest-of-the-hip guide to San Francisco, *Beyond Fisherman's Wharf*.)

Accommodations at the Phoenix—the inn named for the city's mythic ability to rise from its own ashes, as after the fiery 1906 earthquake—are glass-fronted, uncluttered, pool-facing '50s motel rooms upscaled to ultramodern, yet not particularly ostentatious, with handmade bamboo furniture, tropical plants, and original local art on the walls. Phoenix services include complimentary continental breakfast (room service also available), the "Phoenix Movie Channel" on in-room cable—with 15 different made-in-San Francisco movies (plus a film library with 20 "band on the road" films)—and a complete massage service, including Swedish, Esalen, Shiatsu, even poolside massage. In addition to concierge services, the Phoenix also offers blackout curtains, an on-call voice doctor (for lead vocalists with scratchy throats), and free VIP passes to SoMa's underground dance clubs. Regular rates: $89–109, and $139 for each of the three suites, including the

Tour Manager Suites. Ask about deals, including the "special winter rate" for regular customers (subject to availability), with the fourth night free.

Awesomely hip, too, is the playful **Hotel Triton** on Grant, in the heart of the city's downtown gallery district. The one-time Beverly Plaza Hotel just across from the Chinatown Gateway has been reimagined and reinvented by Bill Kimpton, the man who started the boutique hotel trend in town in 1980. The Triton's artsy ambience is startling and entertaining, boldly announcing itself in the lobby with sculpted purple, teal, and gold columns, odd tassle-headed, gold brocade "dervish" chairs, and mythic Neptunian imagery on the walls. Rooms are comfortable and contemporary, with custom-designed geometric mahogany furniture, sponge-painted or diamond-patterned walls, original artwork by Chris Kidd, and unusual tilework in the bathrooms. Each guest room reflects one of three basic configurations: a king-size bed with camelback upholstered headboards, similar double beds, or oversized daybeds that double as a couch. Imaginative guest suites include the kaleidoscopic J. Garcia suite, furnished with swirls of colorful fabrics and a self-portrait of Jerry next to the bed. All rooms include soundproof windows, same-day valet/laundry service, room service, color TV with remote (also cable and movie channels), in-room fax, voice mail, and two-line phones with long cords and dataports. Basic rates: $159–179, $229–305 for deluxe rooms and suites. A nice feature of this and other Klimpton-owned hotels, too, is the fully stocked honor bar—unusual in that items are quite reasonably priced. For more information or reservations, contact: Hotel Triton, 342 Grant Ave., San Francisco, CA 94108, 415/394-0500 or toll-free 800/433-6611, www.hotel-tritonsf.com.

Affordable style is apparent and available at other small San Francisco hotels, including Klimpton's Prescott Hotel, home to Wolfgang Puck's Postrio Restaurant. But there's nothing else in town quite like Haight-Ashbury's **Red Victorian Bed and Breakfast Inn**, a genuine blast from San Francisco's past. This 1904 survivor is red, all right, and it's a bed-and-breakfast—but except for the architecture, it's not very Victorian. The style is early-to-late Summer of Love. Downstairs is the Global Village Bazaar, a New Age shopper's paradise. (The Global Family also offers a coffee house, computer networking services, meditation room, and gallery of meditative art with calligraphic paintings to help you program yourself, subliminally and otherwise, with proper consciousness.) Everything is casual and *very* cool—just two blocks from Golden Gate Park and its many attractions.

Upstairs, the Red Victorian's 18 guest rooms range from modest to decadent, with sinks in all rooms; some have private baths, others share. (If you stay in a room that shares the Aquarium Bathroom, you'll be able to answer the question: "What happens to the goldfish when you flush the toilet?") The Summer of Love Room features genuine '60s posters on the walls and a tie-dyed canopy over the bed. The Peace Room has an unusual skylight, though the Skylight Room beats the band for exotica. Or get back to nature in the Japanese Tea Garden Room, the Conservatory, or the Redwood Forest Room. Expanded continental breakfast (with granola and fresh bakery selections) and afternoon popcorn hour are included in the rates, which range from $75–120 (with specials if you stay over three days, two-night minimum on weekends). Spanish, German, and French spoken. No smoking, no pets, and leave your angst outside on the sidewalk. Well-behaved children under parental supervision are welcome. Make reservations for a summer stay well in advance. For more information, contact: The Red Victorian Bed and Breakfast Inn, 1665 Haight St., San Francisco, CA 94117, 415/864-1978, www.redvic.com.

Fairly reasonable, near the theater scene, is the cheerful and colorful **Clarion Hotel Bedford,** 761 Post St., 415/673-6040 or toll-free 800/252-7466, a 17-story 1929 hotel featuring florals and pastels. There's a café adjacent, but don't miss the tiny mahogany-paneled Wedgwood Bar just off the lobby, decorated with china gifts from Lord Wedgwood. Luxury ($179–199). Another good choice in the vicinity is the **Maxwell Hotel,** 386 Geary, 415/986-2000, or toll-free 888/734-6299. Luxury (rates run $155–205, though specials can drive the price as low as $119). Also close to the theaters is the 1913 **Savoy Hotel,** 580 Geary, 415/441-2700 or toll-free 800/227-4223, a taste of French provincial with period engravings, imported furnishings, and goose down featherbeds and pillows. Amenities include complimentary afternoon sherry and tea. Premium-Luxury ($149–229). Downstairs is the Brasserie Savoy.

Closer to Nob Hill and Chinatown is the nine-floor **Hotel Juliana,** 590 Bush St., 415/392-2540 or toll-free 800/372-8800 in California, 800/328-3880 elsewhere in the United States. The 107 rooms and suites have in-room coffeemakers, hair dryers, and irons and ironing boards. Other amenities include complimentary evening wine, morning limo service to the Financial District (just a few blocks away), and the on-site **Oritalia** restaurant (MediterrAsian). Premium-Luxury (singles and doubles $179, suites $235; great deals in the low season).

Also within an easy stroll of Nob Hill: the elegant art deco **York Hotel,** 940 Sutter St., 415/885-6800 or toll-free 800/808-9675, used as the setting for Alfred Hitchcock's *Vertigo.* The York offers the usual three-star comforts, including limousine service and complimentary breakfast. Expensive-Premium.

The **Villa Florence Hotel,** 225 Powell St., 415/397-7700 or toll-free 888/501-4909 in California, 800/553-4411 elsewhere in the U.S., www.villaflorence.com, features a 16th-century Tuscany/Italian Renaissance theme, and American-style European ambience. The colorful and comfortable guest rooms feature soundproofed walls and windows—a good idea above the cable cars and so close to Union Square—as well as in-room coffeemakers and all basic amenities. The hotel has a beauty salon and features the adjacent (and outstanding) NorCal-NorItal **Kuleto's Restaurant** and antipasto bar, 415/397-7720. Premium-Luxury ($155–215).

For an all-American historical theme, consider the **Monticello Inn,** 127 Ellis (between Powell and Cyril Magnin), 415/392-8800 or toll-free 800/669-7777, www.monticelloinn.com. Its cool colonial-style lobby holds Chippendale reproductions and a wood-burning fireplace. Rooms feature early-American decor, soundproofed walls and windows, refrigerators, honor bars, phones with data ports and voice mail, and other amenities. Complimentary continental breakfast is served in the lobby. Premium-Luxury ($115–175). The inn's adjacent **Puccini & Pinetti,** 415/392-5500, is a highly regarded Cal-Italian restaurant well patronized by theatergoers.

Between Union Square and Nob Hill is **Hotel Rex,** 562 Sutter (between Powell and Mason), 415/433-4434 or toll-free 800/433-4434, www.sftrips.com, furnished in 1930s style and "dedicated to the arts and literary world." Rates include a complimentary evening glass of wine. Premium-Luxury (as high as $250). Also reasonable by boutique hotel standards is the **San Francisco Carlton Hotel,** 1075 Sutter (at Larkin), 415/673-0242 or toll-free 800/922-7586, www.carltonhotel.com, placed on *Condé Nast Traveler*'s 1999 Gold List and offering 165 comfortable rooms with Queen Anne–style chairs and pleasant decor, as well as the on-site Oak Room Grille. Expensive-Luxury ($115–175).

Moving into San Francisco's trendsetting strata, the gleeful **Hotel Triton,** 342 Grant Ave., 415/394-0500 or toll-free 800/433-6611, is the talk of the town—and other towns as well—attracting celebrities galore as well as comparisons to New York's Paramount and Royalton Hotels. (For more information, see the special topic Some Hip San Francisco Stays.)

The city has more classical class, of course. The four-star **Prescott Hotel,** 545 Post St. (between Taylor and Mason), 415/563-0303 or toll-free 800/283-7322, www.prescotthotel.com, elegantly combines earthy Americana—most notable in the lobby—with the feel of a British men's club. Rooms and suites come complete with paisley motif, overstuffed furniture, and every imaginable amenity—from honor bar and terry robes to shoe shines and evening wine and cheeses. Not to mention room service courtesy of Wolfgang Puck's downstairs **Postrio** restaurant, where hotel guests also receive preferred dining reservations (if rooms are also reserved well in advance). Services for guests on the Executive Club Level include express check-in (and check-out), continental breakfast, hors d'oeuvres from Postrio, personal concierge service, and even stationary bicycles and rowers delivered to your room on request. Luxury ($185–215, suites run $235–255).

Among other exceptional small hostelries in the vicinity of Union Square is the wheelchair-accessible, 80-room **Warwick Regis Hotel,** 490 Geary St., 415/928-7900 or toll-free 800/827-3447, www.warwickregis.com, furnished with French and English antiques and offering exceptional service. Amenities include hair dryers and small refrigerators in every room, plus cable TV, complimentary morning newspaper, and onsite café and bar. Premium-Luxury ($135–205).

Another best bet, and a bargain for the quality, is the **Chancellor Hotel,** 433 Powell (on Union Square), 415/362-2004 or toll-free 800/428-4748, www.chancellorhotel.com, offering elegant rooms within walking distance of just about everything. (Or hop the cable car.) Expensive-Luxury ($100–230). Truly exceptional is **The Donatello,** 501 Post St. (at Mason, a block west of Union Square), 415/441-7100 or toll-free 800/227-3184, noteworthy for its four-star amenities and its restaurant, **Zingari** (415/885-8850). Luxury ($189–210). Quite refined, too, with the feel of a fine residential hotel, is **Campton Place Hotel,** 340 Stockton St. (just north of Union Square), 415/781-5555 or toll-free 800/235-4300 in California, 800/426-3135 elsewhere. The hotel has all the amenities, including the superb, critically acclaimed (and AAA five diamond) **Campton Place Restaurant,** featuring impeccable contemporary American cuisine (415/955-5555). Luxury ($230–345).

Other Areas

The Embarcadero YMCA south of Market near the Ferry Building now shares the waterfront building with the **Harbor Court Hotel,** 165 Steuart St. (at Mission), 415/882-1300 or toll-free 800/346-0555, www.harborcourthotel.com, a fairly phenomenal transformation at the edge of the Financial District—not to mention near Pac Bell Park—and a perfect setup for Giants fans and business travelers. The building's Florentine exterior has been beautifully preserved, as have the building's original arches, columns, and vaulted ceilings. Inside, the theme is oversized, Old World creature comfort. The plush rooms are rich with amenities, including TV, radio, direct-dial phones with extra-long cords, and complimentary beverages. The penthouse features a Louis XVI–style bed and 18-foot ceilings. Business travelers will appreciate the hotel's business center, Financial District limo service, and same-day valet laundry service. And to work off the stress of that business meeting, head right next door to the renovated multilevel YMCA, where recreational facilities include basketball courts, aerobics classes, an Olympic-size pool, whirlpool, steam room, dry sauna, and even stationary bicycles with a view. Rates include complimentary continental breakfast and valet parking. Luxury ($220 for a Bay view room, $205 courtyard room, specials as low as $175). Affiliated Victorian saloon–style Harry Denton's Bar & Grill here has predictably good food and becomes a lively dance club/bar scene after 10 P.M. Adjacent and also worthwhile is the **Hotel Griffon,** 155 Steuart St. (at Mission), 415/495-2100 or toll-free 800/321-2201, www.hotelgriffon.com, with amenities like continental breakfast, complimentary morning newspaper, and a fitness center. Luxury ($220–270).

Two blocks from Pier 39 at Fisherman's Wharf, the **Tuscan Inn,** 425 North Point, 415/561-1100 or toll-free 800/648-4626, though part of the Best Western hotel chain, has been reinvented by hotelier Bill Kimpton. The hotel features an Italianate lobby with fireplace, a central garden court, and 221 rooms and suites with modern amenities. Rates include morning coffee, tea, and biscotti, and a daily wine hour by the lobby fireplace. Premium-Luxury ($118–228). Just off the lobby is a convenient Italian trattoria, **Cafe Pescatore,** specializing in fresh fish and seafood, pastas, and pizzas (baked in a wood-burning oven) at lunch and dinner. Open for breakfast also.

Near Civic Center cultural attractions is the exceptional small **Inn at the Opera,** 333 Fulton, 415/863-8400 or toll-free 800/325-2708, featuring complimentary breakfast and morning newspaper, in-room cookies and apples, free shoeshine service, available limousine service, and an excellent on-site restaurant, **Ovation.** The guest list often includes big-name theater people. Rooms were immaculately refurbished in 1999. Premium-Luxury (singles $140, doubles $180).

In Pacific Heights, west of Van Ness and south of Lombard, the **Sherman House,** 2160 Green St. (between Fillmore and Webster), 415/563-3600, is among the city's finest small, exclusive hotels. Once the mansion of Leander Sherman, it now attracts inordinate percentages of celebrities and stars. The ambience here, including the intimate dining room, exudes 19th-century French opulence. Luxury ($305–415). In the same neighborhood is a somewhat cheaper option for a "boutique stay": the **Laurel Inn,** 444 Presidio Ave. (at California), 415/567-8467 or toll-free 800/552-8735, www.thelaurelinn.com. Comfortable if a bit trendy—in 1960s style—and within walking distance of the Presidio, the Laurel features 49 rooms, 18 with kitchenettes. Ask about their pet-friendly policy. Premium ($120–150).

TOP OF THE LINE HOTELS

In addition to the fine hotels mentioned above, San Francisco offers an impressive selection of large, four- and five-star superdeluxe hotels. The air in these establishments is rarefied indeed. (Sometimes the airs, too.) Many, however, do offer seasonal specials. Business-oriented hotels often feature lower weekend rates.

The Ritz

Peek into **The Ritz-Carlton, San Francisco,** 600 Stockton (between California and Pine), 415/296-7465 or toll-free 800/241-3333, www.ritzcarlton.com, to see what a great facelift an old lady can get for $140 million. Quite impressive. And many consider the hotel's Dining Room at The Ritz-Carlton among the city's finest eateries. (For more information, see the special topic Puttin' on the Ritz.) Luxury (singles and doubles run $335–385, suites $525–3,500).

The Palace

Equally awesome—and another popular destination these days for City Guides and other walking tours—is that grande dame of San Francisco hostelries, the recently renovated and resplendent 1909 **Sheraton Palace Hotel,** 2 New Montgomery St. (downtown at Market), 415/512-1111 or toll-free 800/325-3535, www.sfpalace.com. Wander in under the metal grillwork awning at the New Montgomery entrance, across the polished marble sunburst on the foyer floor, and sit a spell in the lobby to appreciate the more subtle aspects of this $150 million renovation. Then mosey into the central Garden Court restaurant. The wonderful lighting here is provided, during the day, by the (cleaned and restored) 1800s atrium skylight, one of the world's largest leaded-glass creations; some 70,000 panes of glass arch over the entire room. It's a best bet for Sunday brunch. Note, too, the 10 (yes, 10) 700-pound crystal chandeliers. The Pied Piper Bar, with its famous Maxfield Parrish mural, is a Palace fixture, and adjoins **Maxfield's** restaurant. Tours of the hotel are available; call for schedules and information.

In addition to plush accommodations (rooms still have high ceilings), the Palace offers complete conference and meeting facilities, a busi-

PUTTIN' ON THE RITZ

Serious visiting fans of San Francisco, at least those with serious cash, tend to equate their long-running romance with a stay on Nob Hill, home base for most of the city's ritzier hotels. And what could be ritzier than the Ritz?

The Ritz-Carlton, San Francisco, 600 Stockton at California St., 415/296-7465 or toll-free 800/241-3333, www.ritzcarlton.com, is a local landmark, San Francisco's finest remaining example of neoclassical architecture. At the financial district's former western edge, and hailed in 1909 as a "temple of commerce," until 1973 the building served as West Coast headquarters for the Metropolitan Life Insurance Company. Expanded and revised five times since, San Francisco's Ritz has been open for business as a hotel only since 1991. After painstaking restoration (four years and $140 million worth), this nine-story grande dame still offers some odd architectural homage to its past. Witness the terra-cotta tableau over the entrance: the angelic allegorical figure ("Insurance") is protecting the American family. (Ponder the meaning of the lion's heads and winged hourglasses on your own.)

The Ritz offers a total of 336 rooms and suites, most with grand views. Amenities on the top two floors ("The Ritz-Carlton Club") include private lounge, continuous complimentary meals, and Dom Perignon and Beluga caviar every evening. All rooms, however, feature Italian marble bathrooms, in-room safes, and every modern comfort, plus access to the fitness center (indoor swimming pool, whirlpool, training room, separate men's and women's steam rooms and saunas, massage, and more). Services include the usual long list plus morning newspaper, child care, VCR and video library, car rental, and multilingual staff. Rates run $335–385 for rooms, $525–3,500 for suites. (The Ritz-Carlton's "Summer Escape" package, when available, includes a deluxe guest room, continental breakfast, valet parking, and unlimited use of the fitness center.) The Ritz-Carlton also provides full conference facilities.

The Courtyard restaurant here offers the city's only alfresco dining in a hotel setting—like eating breakfast, lunch, or dinner on someone else's well-tended garden patio. (Come on Sunday for brunch—and jazz.) Adjacent, indoors, is somewhat casual **The Restaurant.** More formal, serving neoclassical cuisine, is **The Dining Room.**

---

ness center, and a rooftop fitness center. The swimming pool up there, under a modern vaulted skylight, is especially enjoyable at sunset; spa services include a poolside whirlpool and dry sauna. Luxury (rooms $255–320, suites $760–2,800).

The St. Francis

Another beloved San Francisco institution is the **Westin St. Francis Hotel,** 335 Powell St. (between Post and Geary, directly across from Union Square), 415/397-7000 or toll-free 800/228-3000, www.westin.com, a recently restored landmark recognized by the National Trust for Historic Preservation as one of the Historic Hotels of America. When the first St. Francis opened in 1849 at Clay and Dupont (Grant), it was considered the only hostelry at which ladies were safe, and was also celebrated as the first "to introduce bedsheets to the city." But San Francisco's finest was destroyed by fire four years later. By the early 1900s, reincarnation was imminent when a group of local businessmen declared their intention to rebuild the St. Francis as "a caravansary worthy of standing at the threshold of the Occident, representative of California hospitality." No expense was spared on the stylish 12-story hotel overlooking Union Square—partially opened but still under construction when the April 18, 1906, earthquake and fire hit town. Damaged but not destroyed, the restored St. Francis opened in November 1907; over the entrance was an electrically lighted image of a phoenix rising from the city's ashes. Successfully resurrected, the elegant and innovative hotel attracted royalty, international political and military leaders, theatrical stars, and literati.

But even simpler folk have long been informed, entertained, and welcomed by the St. Francis. People keep an eye on the number of unfurled flags in front of the St. Francis, for example, knowing that these herald the nationalities of visiting dignitaries. And every longtime San Franciscan knows that any shiny old coins in their pockets most likely came from the St. Francis; the hotel's long-standing practice of washing coins—to prevent them from soiling ladies' white gloves—continues to this day. Meeting friends "under the clock" means the Magneta Clock in the hotel's Powell St. lobby, this "master clock" from Saxony a fixture since the early 1900s. Both the Tower and Powell St. lobbies were freshened up by 1991 restorations. Highlights include three 40-foot trompe l'oeil murals by Carlo Marchiori depicting turn-of-the-20th-century San Francisco, new inlaid marble floors and central carpet, and gold-leaf laminate applied to the ornate woodwork in the Powell St. lobby. Restoration of the original building's Colusa sandstone facade was finished in 1997.

After additions and renovations, the St. Francis today offers 1,200 luxury guest rooms and suites (request a suite brochure if you hanker to stay in the General MacArthur suite, the Queen Elizabeth II suite, or the Ron and Nancy Reagan suite), plus fitness and full meeting and conference facilities, a 1,500-square-foot ballroom, five restaurants (including elegant Victor's atop the St. Francis Tower), shopping arcade, and valet parking. Luxury (rooms $255–320, suites $760–2,800).

Others Downtown

The **Clift Hotel,** 495 Geary St. (at Taylor), 415/775-4700 or toll-free 800/652-5438, www.clifthotel.com, is a five-star midsize hotel offering every imaginable comfort and service, including free Financial District limo service, transportation to and from the airport (for a fee), and a good on-site restaurant. Luxury ($240–1,260).

Also within easy reach of downtown doings is the sleek, modern, four-star **Pan Pacific Hotel,** 500 Post St. (at Mason, one block west of Union Square), 415/771-8600, toll-free 800/533-6465 or 800/327-8585, www.panpac.com. The business-oriented Pan Pacific offers three phones with call waiting in each room, personal computers delivered to your room upon request, notary public and business services, and Rolls Royce shuttle service to the Financial District. It's also luxurious; bathrooms, for example, feature floor-to-ceiling Breccia marble, artwork, a mini-screen TV, and a telephone. Luxury ($199–309). "The Pampering Weekend" special starts at $139 and includes breakfast in your room or at the 3rd-floor **Pacific** restaurant (California-fusion cuisine), 415/929-2087.

Other worthy downtown possibilities include the contemporary Japanese-style **Hotel Nikko,** 222 Mason, 415/394-1111 or toll-free 800/645-5687, www.nikkohotels.com, which boasts a glass-enclosed rooftop pool (Luxury, $195–255). The exquisite **Mandarin Oriental San Francisco,** 222 Sansome, 415/276-9888, 415/885-0999, or toll-free 800/622-0404, www.mandarinoriental.com, is housed in the top 11 floors of the California First Interstate Building in the Financial District. The 160 rooms boast great views (even from the bathrooms) and all the amenities, including wonderful **Silks** restaurant, 415/986-2020. Luxury (rooms $295–520, suites $800–1,650).

Other comfortable hotel choices near the Financial District and the booming new media companies south of Market include the super-stylish, granite-faced **W Hotel,** 181 3rd St. (at Howard), 415/777-5300 or toll-free 877/946-8357, www.whotels.com, which is as sleek as its next-door neighbor, the San Francisco Museum of Modern Art. This business-oriented hotel also offers boutique touches: plush down comforters and Aveda bath products in all rooms. Downstairs, the XYZ restaurant and bar serves creative fusion cuisine. Luxury (starting at $175).

Also in the area, near the Moscone Center, is the **Argent Hotel,** 50 3rd St., 415/974-6400 or toll-free 877/222-6699, www.destinationtravel.com (Luxury, starting at $220).

Nob Hill

Some of the city's finest hotels cluster atop Nob Hill. Since judgment always depends upon personal taste, despite official ratings it's all but impossible to say which is "the best." Take your pick.

Across from Grace Cathedral and Huntington Park, the **Huntington Hotel,** 1075 California St. (at Taylor), 415/474-5400 or toll-free 800/652-1539 in California, 800/227-4683 from elsewhere in the U.S., www.huntingtonhotel.com, is the last surviving family-owned fine hotel in the neighborhood. It's a beauty, a destination in and of itself. Every room and suite (one-time residential apartments) has been individually designed and decorated, and every service is a personal gesture. Stop in just to appreciate the elegant lobby restoration. Dark and clubby, and open daily for breakfast, lunch, and dinner, the **Big Four Restaurant** off the lobby pays pleasant homage to the good ol' days of Wild

Mark Hopkins Hotel

West railroad barons—and often serves wild game entrées along with tamer continental contemporary cuisine. Luxury ($190–260).

Top-of-the-line, too, is the romantic, turn-of-the-20th-century **Fairmont Hotel,** 950 Mason St. (at California), 415/772-5000 or toll-free 800/527-4727, www.fairmont.com, noted for its genuine grandeur and grace. The Fairmont offers 596 rooms (small to large) and suites, all expected amenities, and several on-site restaurants. For a panoramic Bay Area view at Sunday brunch, the place to go is the hotel's **Crown Room** atop the hotel's Tower section. Locally loved, too, however, are the hotel's **Mason's,** for steak and seafood (also open for breakfast), and the Tiki-inspired **Tonga Room,** which specializes in Chinese and Polynesian cuisine and features a simulated tropical rainstorm every half hour. The Fairmont also offers full conference and business facilities (20 meeting rooms) and the Nob Hill Club (extra fee) for fitness enthusiasts. Luxury ($229 and up).

The five-star **Renaissance Stanford Court Hotel,** 905 California St. (at Powell), 415/989-3500 or toll-free 800/468-3571, www.renaissancehotels.com, boasts a 120-foot-long, sepia-toned lobby mural honoring San Francisco's historic diversity. On the west wall, for example, are panels depicting the hotel's predecessor, the original Leland Stanford Mansion, with railroad barons and other wealthy Nob Hill nabobs on one side, Victorian-era African Americans on the other. Other panels depict the long-running economic exploitation of California places and peoples, from Russian whaling and fur trading, redwood logging, and the California gold rush (with Native Americans and the Chinese looking on) to the 1906 earthquake and fire framed by the construction of the transcontinental railroad and California's Latinization, as represented by Mission Dolores. Stop in and see it; this is indeed the story of Northern California, if perhaps a bit romanticized.

The hotel itself is romantic, recognized by the National Trust for Historic Preservation as one of the Historic Hotels of America. The Stanford Court features a decidedly European ambience, from the carriage entrance (with beaux arts fountain and stained-glass dome) to guest rooms decked out in 19th-century artwork, antiques, and reproductions (not to mention modern comforts like heated towel racks in the marble bathrooms and dictionaries on the writing desks). Opulent touches in the lobby include Baccarat chandeliers, Carrara marble floor, oriental carpets, original artwork, and an 1806 antique grandfather clock once owned by Napoléon Bonaparte. Guest services include complimentary stretch limo service, both for business and pleasure. Luxury ($235–315). Even if you don't stay, consider a meal (breakfast, lunch, and dinner daily, plus weekend brunch) at the hotel's Mediterranean-inspired restaurant, **Fournou's Ovens,** 415/989-1910 for reservations, considered one of San Francisco's best.

Don't forget the Mark Hopkins Hotel, now the **Mark Hopkins Inter-Continental,** 1 Nob Hill (California and Mason), 415/392-3434 or toll-free 800/327-0200, www.interconti.com, another refined Old California old-timer. Hobnobbing with the best of them atop Nob Hill, the Mark Hopkins features 391 elegant guest rooms (many with great views) and all the amenities, not to mention the fabled **Top of the Mark** sky room, still San Francisco's favorite sky-high romantic bar scene. The French-California **Nob Hill Restaurant** is open daily for breakfast, lunch, and dinner. Luxury ($220–340).

CITY-STYLE BED-AND-BREAKFASTS

With most of San Francisco's European-style and boutique hotels offering breakfast and other homey touches, and many of the city's bed-and-breakfasts offering standard hotel services (like concierge, bellman, valet/laundry, and room service), it's truly difficult to understand the difference.

The eight-room **Chateau Tivoli** townhouse, 1057 Steiner St., 415/776-5462 or toll-free 800/228-1647, is an 1892 Queen Anne landmark with an astounding visual presence. "Colorful" just doesn't do justice as a description of this Alamo Square painted lady. The Tivoli's eccentric exterior architectural style is electrified by 18 historic colors of paint, plus gold leaf. Painstaking restoration is apparent inside, too, from the very Victorian, period-furnished parlors to exquisite, individually decorated guest rooms, each reflecting at least a portion of the city's unusual social history. (Imagine, under one roof: Enrico Caruso, Aimee Crocker, Isadora Duncan, Joaquin Miller, Jack London, opera singer Luisa Tettrazini, and Mark Twain. Somehow, it is imaginable, since the mansion was once the residence of the city's pre-earthquake Tivoli Opera.) Chateau Tivoli offers nine rooms and suites, all but two rooms with private baths, two with fireplaces. Premium-Luxury ($110–250).

One-time home to Archbishop Patrick Riordan, the **Archbishop's Mansion**, 1000 Fulton St. (at Steiner), 415/563-7872 or toll-free 800/543-5820, is also exquisitely restored, offering comfortable rooms and suites in a French Victorian mood. Some rooms have fireplaces and in-room spas, and all have phones and TV. Continental breakfast. Luxury ($159–419). The **Alamo Square Inn,** 719 Scott St., 415/922-2055 or toll-free 800/345-9888, www.alamoinn.com, is another neighborhood possibility, offering rooms and suites in an 1895 Queen Anne and an 1896 Tudor Revival. Expensive-Premium.

Petite Auberge, 863 Bush St. (near Nob Hill and Union Square), 415/928-6000, is an elegant French country inn right downtown, featuring Pierre Deux fabrics, terra-cotta tile, oak furniture, and lace curtains. All 26 guest rooms

here have private bathrooms; 16 have fireplaces. The "Petite Suite" has its own entrance and deck, a king-size bed, fireplace, and hot tub. Premium-Luxury ($110–225). Two doors down is the affiliated **White Swan Inn,** 845 Bush, 415/775-1755, with parlor, library, and 26 rooms (private baths, fireplaces, wet bars) decorated with English-style decorum, from the mahogany antiques and rich fabrics to floral-print wallpapers. Premium-Luxury ($145–250). Both these inns serve full breakfast (with the morning paper), afternoon tea, and homemade cookies, and provide little amenities like thick terry bathrobes. All rooms have TV and telephone.

Close to the Presidio and Fort Mason in Cow Hollow is the **Edward II Inn,** 3155 Scott St. (at Lombard), 415/922-3000 or toll-free 800/473-2846, an English-style country hotel and pub offering 24 rooms and six suites, all with color TV and phone, some with shared bathrooms. The suites have in-room whirlpool baths. A complimentary continental breakfast is served. Moderate-Expensive.

Peaceful and pleasant amid the hubbub of North Beach is the stylish and artsy 15-room **Hotel Bohème,** 444 Columbus Ave., 415/433-9111, offering continental charm all the way to breakfast, which is served either indoors or out on the patio. On-site restaurant, too. Premium (a good deal). Also in North Beach is the French country **Washington Square Inn,** 1660 Stockton St., 415/981-4220 or toll-free 800/388-0220, featuring 15 rooms (most with private bath), continental breakfast, and afternoon tea. Premium-Luxury ($125–210).

Near Lafayette Park in Pacific Heights and something of a cause célèbre is **The Mansions,** 2220 Sacramento St., 415/929-9444 or toll-free 800/826-9398, www.themansions.com, an elegant bed-and-breakfast-style hotel composed of two adjacent historic mansions filled with art. The 28 rooms and suites here are opulent and feature telephones, private bathrooms, and numerous amenities. Stroll the Bufano sculpture gardens, play billiards, or attend nightly music concerts or magic shows. Full breakfast is served every morning, in the dining area or in your room, and dinners are also available. Premium-Luxury ($139–250).

Not a B&B per se, but providing as intimate a lodging experience as you'll get, **Dockside Boat & Bed,** Pier 39, 415/392-5526 or toll-free

800/436-2574, www.boatandbed.com, contracts a stable of luxury yachts, both motor and sail, on which guests can spend the night. Guys, get a clue: You can't get much more romantic than moonlight champagne with your lovely in-amorata—lying on deck, admiring the city lights, and listening to the water lap, lap, lapping against the hull. Luxury ($165–270).

EATING IN SAN FRANCISCO

San Franciscans love to eat. For a true San Franciscan, eating—and eating well—competes for first place among life's purest pleasures, right up there with the arts, exercising, and earning money. (There may be a few others.) Finding new and novel neighborhood eateries, and knowing which among the many fine dining establishments are currently at the top of the trend-setters' culinary A-list, are points of pride for long-time residents. Fortunately, San Franciscans also enjoy sharing information and opinions—including their restaurant preferences. So the best way to find out where to eat, and why, is simply to ask. The following listings, which roughly follow the geographic drift of this chapter's Seeing San Francisco sections, should help fine-food aficionados get started, and will certainly keep everyone else from starving.

THE AVENUES: RICHMOND, SEACLIFF, SUNSET

A fixture in the midst of the Golden Gate National Recreation Area and a favorite hangout at the edge of the continent, the current incarnation of the **Cliff House,** 1090 Point Lobos Ave. (at Upper Great Hwy.), 415/386-3330, is also a decent place to eat. Sunsets are superb, the seafood sublime. As close to fancy as it gets here is **Upstairs at the Cliff House,** an Old San Francisco-style dining room. Decidedly more casual at this cliff-hanging complex are both the **Seafood and Beverage Company** and the **Phineas T. Barnacle** pub.

Heading south down the beachfront, on the opposite side of Great Hwy., is the **Beach Chalet Brewery and Restaurant,** 1000 Great Hwy. (between Fulton and Lincoln), 415/386-8439. This delightful renovation, upstairs (above a visitor center and City Store outlet) in the old 1925 Willis Polk–designed building, features wall-to-wall windows looking out on the surf (a great spot to watch the sunset), as well as creative California cuisine and a long list of house-made microbrews. The atmosphere is casual—don't come in your bathing suit, but you won't need the dinner jacket—and the service is friendly. Open daily for lunch and dinner.

Moving inland, exceptional ethnic fare is a specialty of Richmond District restaurants. The 100-plus eateries lining Clement St.—among them Asian, South American, Mexican, Italian, and even Russian restaurants and delis—are representative of the district's culinary and cultural mix.

Notable in the city's "new Chinatown," the modern **Fountain Court,** 354 Clement St. (at 5th Ave.), 415/668-1100, is a wonderful, inexpensive stop for northern-style dim sum and other Shanghai specialties. One of the few San Francisco restaurants serving spicy, sweet Singapore-style fare is **Straits Cafe,** 3300 Geary (at Parker), 415/668-1783, a light, airy, white-walled rendition complete with interior palm trees. For delicious (and cheap) Taiwanese food, head to the **Taiwan Restaurant,** 445 Clement (at 6th), 415/387-1789, which serves great dumplings. Good for Indonesian fare is **Jakarta,** 615 Balboa St. (between 7th and 8th Aves.), 415/387-5225, another airy and bright place featuring an extensive menu of unusually well-done dishes, plus an eye-catching array of artifacts, musical instruments, and shadow puppets. Some say that the romantic **Khan Toke Thai House,** 5937 Geary (at 23rd Ave.), 415/668-6654, is San Francisco's best Southeast Asian restaurant (and a good deal). Open daily for dinner only, reservations accepted. Another reliable neighborhood choice is **Bangkok Cafe,** 2845 Geary (at Collins), 415/346-8821.

For the whole Moroccan experience, including a belly dancer on some nights, try **El Mansour,** 3121 Clement (near 32nd Ave.), 415/751-2312. A bit more grand, **Kasra Persian & Mediterranean Cuisine,** 349 Clement (at 5th Ave.),

415/752-1101, is a very good choice for all kinds of shish kabobs.

Tiny, welcoming **Cafe Maisonnette**, 315 8th Ave., 415/387-7992, specializes in country-French cuisine. People rave about the rack of lamb. Monthly changing menu. **Café Riggio,** 4112 Geary (between 5th and 6th Aves.), 415/221-2114, is much appreciated for its antipasti, world-class calamari, and homemade cannoli for dessert.

Clement Street Bar & Grill, 708 Clement (at 8th Ave.), 415/386-2200, serves a mostly American menu featuring vegetarian fare, grilled seafood, and California-style pastas. Farther up Geary toward the beach, **Bill's Place,** 2315 Clement (between 24th and 25th Aves.), 415/221-5262, is an eclectic burger joint with presidential portraits on the walls and a Japanese-style garden. The culinary creations here are named in honor of local celebrities. Guess what you get when you order a Carol Doda burger: two beefy patties with an olive sticking out smack dab in the middle of each. **Tia Margarita,** 300 19th Ave. (at Clement), 415/752-9274, is a long-running family café serving American-style Mexican food.

Things are more than a bit gentrified in Presidio Heights. Just a few blocks south of the Presidio is the **Magic Flute Garden Ristorante,** 3673 Sacramento (between Locust and Spruce), 415/922-1225, which offers Italian and other continental specialties in a sunny French country atmosphere. Folks also sing the praises of nearby **Tuba Garden,** 3634 Sacramento (between Locust and Spruce), 415/921-8822, a cozy Victorian open just for lunch and brunch, serving up Belgian waffles, homemade blintzes, and eggs Benedict.

Out at the edge of the Sunset District, assemble everything for a memorable picnic from the delis and shops along Taraval. Or check out the diverse ethnic neighborhood eateries. **Leon's Bar-BQ,** in an oceanside shack at 2800 Sloat Blvd. (at 46th Ave.), 415/681-3071, is a great stop for chicken and ribs. (Leon's has outposts in the Fillmore and at Fisherman's Wharf.) **Brother's Pizza,** 3627 Taraval (near 46th Ave.), 415/753-6004, isn't much to look at, but the pizzas (try the pesto special), pastas, and calzone overcome that first impression in a big hurry. The colorful, always crowded **Casa Aguila,** 1240 Noriega (between

19th and 20th Aves.), 415/661-5593, specializes in authentic Mexican fare from Cuernavaca and offers lots of food for the money. **El Toreador Fonda Mejicana,** 50 W. Portal (between Ulloa and Vicente), 415/566-2673, is a homey place serving traditional Central and Southern Mexican food. Just down the way on the buzzing West Portal retail strip, **Cafe for All Seasons,** 150 W. Portal (between Vicente and 14th Ave.), 415/665-0900, is a popular stop for hungry shoppers. The California-American menu emphasizes light pastas, grilled fish, and big salads.

UNION SQUARE AND NOB HILL

A well-kept secret, perhaps downtown's best breakfast spot, is **Dottie's True Blue Cafe,** 522 Jones St., 415/885-2767, a genuine all-American coffee shop serving every imaginable American standard plus new cuisine, such as (at lunch) grilled eggplant sandwiches. Open daily for breakfast and lunch only, 7 A.M.–2 P.M. But those in the know say you haven't "done" the city until you've ordered breakfast—specifically, the 18 Swedish pancakes—at **Sears Fine Foods,** 439 Powell (at Post), 415/986-1160, a funky, friendly old-time San Francisco café.

Another area classic, if for other reasons, is **John's Grill,** 63 Ellis (just off Powell), 415/986-3274 or 415/986-0069, with a neat neon sign outside and *Maltese Falcon* memorabilia just about everywhere inside. (In the book, this is where Sam Spade ate his lamb chops.) Named a National Literary Landmark by the Friends of Libraries, USA, this informal eatery ode to Dashiell Hammett serves good continental-style American fare, plus large helpings of Hammett hero worship, especially upstairs in Hammett's Den and the Maltese Falcon Room. Open Mon.–Sat. for lunch and dinner; Sun. for dinner only. Live jazz nightly.

For excellent seafood, dive into the French provincial **Brasserie Savoy** at the Savoy Hotel, 580 Geary St. (at Jones), 415/441-8080, open for breakfast (until noon), dinner, and late supper. Gallic stodgy? *Mais, non!* How about a "Lobster Martini"? Or a fish soup described as "haunting" by one local food writer (perhaps she had one too many Lobster Martinis?).

SAN FRANCISCO RESTAURANTS

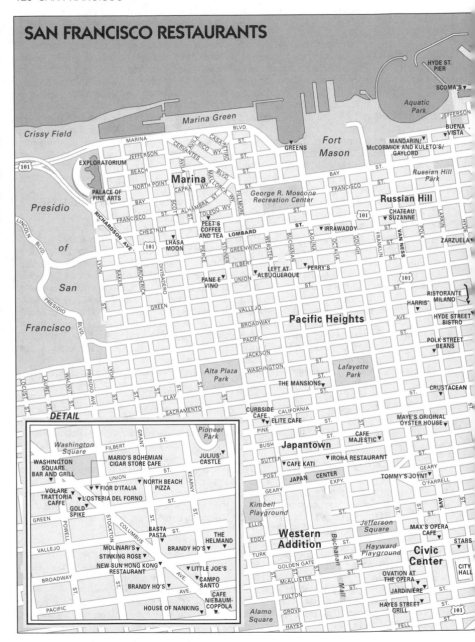

HYDE ST. PIER

SCOMA'S ▼

Aquatic Park

JEFFERSON

BUENA VISTA ▼

Crissy Field

Marina Green

Fort Mason

MARINA BLVD.

GREENS ▼

MANDARIN/▼ McCORMICK AND KULETO'S/ GAYLORD

Russian Hill Park

EXPLORATORIUM

JEFFERSON

BEACH

NORTH POINT

BAY

Marina

CAPRA

George R. Moscone Recreation Center

BAY

FRANCISCO

Russian Hill

PALACE OF FINE ARTS

Presidio

101

FRANCISCO

RICHARDSON AVE.

CHESTNUT

LHASA MOON

ST.

PEET'S COFFEE AND TEA

LOMBARD

▼ IRRAWADDY

CHATEAU ▼ SUZANNE

101

ZARZUELA ▼

of

San

Francisco

PRESIDIO BLVD.

GREENWICH

FILBERT

PANE E ▼ VINO

UNION

LEFT AT ▼ ALBUQUERQUE

▼ PERRY'S

101

RISTORANTE MILANO ▼

HARRIS ▼

HYDE STREET BISTRO ▼

VALLEJO

BROADWAY

Pacific Heights

POLK STREET BEANS ▼

PACIFIC

JACKSON

Alta Plaza Park

WASHINGTON

Lafayette Park

THE MANSIONS ▼

CRUSTACEAN ▼

CLAY

SACRAMENTO

CURBSIDE CAFE ▼ CALIFORNIA

▼ ELITE CAFE

MAYE'S ORIGINAL OYSTER HOUSE ▼

DETAIL

PINE

BUSH

Japantown

CAFE MAJESTIC ▼

SUTTER

▼ IROHA RESTAURANT

Pioneer Park

POST

▼ CAFE KATI

JAPAN CENTER

EXPY.

TOMMY'S JOYNT ▼

GEARY

Washington Square

FILBERT

GRANT ST.

JULIUS' ▼ CASTLE

MARIO'S BOHEMIAN CIGAR STORE CAFE

GEARY

O'FARRELL

WASHINGTON SQUARE BAR AND GRILL ▼

Kimbell Playground

Jefferson Square

MAX'S OPERA CAFE ▼

VOLARE TRATTORIA CAFFE ▼

▼▼ FIOR D'ITALIA

KEARNY

▼ NORTH BEACH PIZZA

ELLIS

Western Addition

STARS ▼

▼ L'OSTERIA DEL FORNO

GOLD ▼ SPIKE

EDDY

CITY HALL

GREEN

POWELL

STOCKTON

COLUMBUS

BASTA ST. PASTA ▼

TURK

Hayward Playground

Civic Center

VALLEJO

MOLINARI'S ▼

THE ▼ HELMAND

GOLDEN GATE

OVATION AT THE OPERA ▼

STINKING ROSE ▼

BRANDY HO'S ▼

McALLISTER

JARDINIÈRE ▼

BROADWAY

NEW SUN HONG KONG RESTAURANT

▼ LITTLE JOE'S

FULTON

HAYES STREET ▼ GRILL

101

BRANDY HO'S ▼

▼ CAMPO SANTO

Alamo Square

GROVE

PACIFIC

CAFE NIEBAUM-COPPOLA

HOUSE OF NANKING ▼

HAYES

FELL

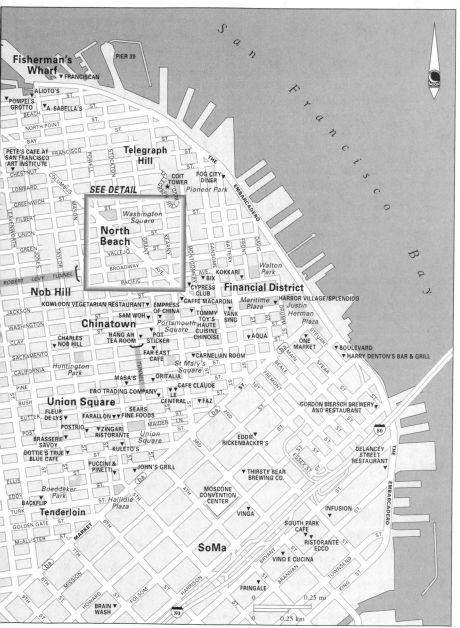

San Francisco Bay

Fisherman's Wharf
PIER 39
▼ FRANCISCAN
ALIOTO'S
ST.
▼POMPEI'S
GROTTO   ▼A. SABELLA'S
BEACH
NORTH POINT
ST.
BAY
PETE'S CAFE AT   FRANCISCO
SAN FRANCISCO
ART INSTITUTE   **Telegraph**
CHESTNUT   **Hill**
LOMBARD   COIT
TOWER
GREENWICH   FOG CITY
DINER
FILBERT   *Pioneer Park*

SEE DETAIL

Washington
Square
North
Beach
VALLEJO
BROADWAY
ST.
PACIFIC

ROBERT LEVY TUNNEL

Nob Hill

KOWLOON VEGETARIAN RESTAURANT▼
EMPRESS
OF CHINA   CAFFE MACARONI
Financial District

▼ KOKKARI
Walton Park
▼ BIX
CYPRESS
CLUB
*Maritime   Justin
Plaza   Herman
Plaza*
HARBOR VILLAGE/SPLENDIDO

JACKSON   SAM WOH ▼
WASHINGTON   **Chinatown**
CLAY   CHARLES
▼NOB HILL   HANG AH
TEA ROOM
SACRAMENTO
POT
STICKER
TOMMY
TOY'S
HAUTE
CUISINE
CHINOISE
YANK
SING
*Portsmouth
Square*
FAR EAST
CAFE
▼ AQUA
ONE
MARKET   ▼ BOULEVARD
▼ HARRY DENTON'S BAR & GRILL

CALIFORNIA   *Huntington
Park*
▼CARNELIAN ROOM
St Mary's
Square
PINE
BUSH   MASA'S
E&O TRADING COMPANY ▼
ORITALIA
CAFE CLAUDE
LE
CENTRAL   ▼ FAZ

Union Square

FLEUR
DE LYS ▼
FARALLON ▼▼
SEARS
FINE FOODS
GORDON BIERSCH BREWERY
AND RESTAURANT

SUTTER
POSTRIO
POST   BRASSERIE
SAVOY   ▼ZINGARI
RISTORANTE
*Union
Square*
MAIDEN
LN.
EDDIE
RICKENBACKER'S
DOTTIE'S TRUE ▼
BLUE CAFE   KULETO'S
DELANCEY
STREET
RESTAURANT
PUCCINI &
PINETTI   JOHN'S GRILL
ELLIS
EDDY   *Boeddeker
Park*
BACKFLIP
TURK   **Tenderloin**
St. Hallidie
Plaza
MOSCONE
CONVENTION
CENTER
▼ THIRSTY BEAR
BREWING CO.
INFUSION
GOLDEN GATE
McALLISTER   ▼
VINGA
SOUTH PARK
CAFE
RISTORANTE
ECCO
VINO E CUCINA
SoMa
▼ FRINGALE

0   0.25 mi
0   0.25 km

Farallon, 450 Post (near Powell), 415/956-6969, might be *the* place in town for seafood. And the unique Pat Kuleto–designed interior might make you feel like you're under the sea, in an octopus's garden, perhaps. Look for such intriguing specialties as truffled mashed potatoes with crab and sea urchin sauce, or ginger-steamed salmon. Open for lunch Mon.–Sat. and for dinner nightly.

Two blocks from Union Square, **Oritalia,** 586 Bush St. (at Stockton), 415/782-8122, offers an eclectic menu mixing Asian, American, and Mediterranean cuisine. Try the signature tuna tartare on sticky rice cakes, perhaps, or the potato gnocchi with Maine lobster and asparagus. Open daily for dinner.

Puccini & Pinetti, 129 Ellis (at Cyril Magnin), 415/392-5500, is a beautifully designed Cal-Italian restaurant popular with theater crowds. Menu highlights include bruschetta with arugula and roasted garlic, smoked salmon pizzas, and risotto with charred leeks and wild mushrooms. Prices are surprisingly reasonable—most entrées run $10–15. Open for lunch and dinner.

Worth searching for downtown is **Cafe Claude,** 7 Claude Ln. (between Grant and Kearny, Bush and Sutter, just off Bush), 415/392-3505, an uncanny incarnation of a genuine French café, from the paper table covers to the café au lait served in bowls. Good food, plus live jazz four nights a week.

A good choice downtown for pasta is **Kuleto's,** 221 Powell St., 415/397-7720, a comfortable trattoria-style Italian restaurant and bar at the Villa Florence Hotel. It's popular for power lunching and dinner, and it's also open for peaceful, pleasant breakfasts.

Better yet, though, is **Zingari Ristorante,** 501 Post St. (at Mason, in the Donatello hotel), 415/885-8850, justifiably famous for its Northern Italian regional dishes. This premier San Francisco restaurant, where the separate dining rooms are small and intimate, and dressing up is de rigueur, puts on a show as good as, or better than, almost anything else in the neighborhood.

People should at least pop into Wolfgang Puck's **Postrio,** 545 Post St. (at Mason, inside the Prescott Hotel), 415/776-7825, www.postrio .com, to appreciate the exquisite ribbon-patterned dining room designs by Pat Kuleto. The

food here is exceptional, with most entrées representing Puck's interpretations of San Francisco classics. Since the restaurant is open for breakfast, lunch, and dinner, try the Hangtown fry and some house-made pastries at breakfast, perhaps a pizza fresh from the wood-burning oven or Dungeness crab with spicy curry risotto at lunch. Dinner is an adventure. Great desserts. Make reservations well in advance, or hope for a cancellation.

Famous among local foodies, not to mention its long-standing national and international fan club, is **Masa's,** 648 Bush St. (at the Hotel Vintage Court), 415/989-7154, one of the city's finest dinner restaurants and considered by many to be the best French restaurant in the United States. Masa's serves French cuisine with a fresh California regional touch and a Spanish aesthetic. Reservations accepted three weeks in advance. Very expensive.

Fleur de Lys, 777 Sutter (between Jones and Taylor), 415/673-7779, is another local legend—a fine French restaurant that also transcends the traditional. Nothing is too heavy or overdone. Everything is elegant and expensive. Open Mon.–Sat. for dinner. Reservations. Also on Sutter is the **E&O Trading Company,** 314 Sutter (between Stockton and Grant), 415/693-0303, which serves up Pacific Rim cuisine with flavors borrowed from all over Southeast Asia: small plates include naan breads, satays, and Vietnamese rice paper rolls. The Dragon Bar offers tropical cocktails like mai tais and Singapore Slings, as well as house-made microbrews. An odd combination, perhaps, but it seems to work.

On Nob Hill, **Charles Nob Hill,** 1250 Jones St., 415/771-5400, is a neighborhood French restaurant featuring specialties like Hudson Valley foie gras and Sonoma duck. Open for dinner Tues.–Sat. Some of the city's finest hotels, on Nob Hill and elsewhere, also serve some of the city's finest food.

THE FINANCIAL DISTRICT AND EMBARCADERO

Harry Denton's Bar & Grill, 161 Steuart St. (across from Rincon Center, inside the Harbor Court Hotel), 415/882-1333, is a great bar, restaurant (hearty American cuisine), and club, usually crowded as a sardine can after 5 P.M. The food is

*Eat and shop at the Crocker
Galleria shopping center.*

AISUNN RACE

excellent. To hold a conversation, sink into a booth in the narrow dining room above the bar scene; to take in the great scenery, head for the back room (which doubles as a dance floor Thurs.–Sat. nights). Harry Denton's is open weekdays for lunch and nightly for dinner. Nearby **Boulevard,** 1 Mission St. (at Steuart), 415/543-6084, is a Franco-American bistro serving American classics—ribs, pork chops, mashed 'taters—in an art nouveau atmosphere. Nice views.

In the seafood swim of things, **Aqua,** 252 California St., 415/956-9662, is making a global splash among well-heeled foodies nationwide. Entrées include basil-grilled lobster, lobster potato gnocchi, and black-mussel soufflé. Open weekdays for lunch, Mon.–Sat. for dinner.

At **Delancey Street Restaurant,** 600 Embarcadero, 415/512-5179, the restaurant staff is composed of Delancey's drug, alcohol, and crime rehabilitees. The daily changing menu at this radical chic, sociopolitically progressive place is ethnic American—everything from matzo ball

soup to pot roast. And there's a great view of Alcatraz from the outdoor dining area. Open for lunch, afternoon tea, and dinner.

On the 52nd floor of the Bank of America building, the **Carnelian Room,** 555 California St. (between Kearny and Montgomery), 415/433-7500, is the closest you'll get to dining in an airplane above the city. On a clear night, you can see all the way to Detroit. The menu is upscale American, with specialties including Dungeness crab cakes, rack of lamb, and Grand Marnier soufflé. **Yank Sing,** 427 Battery, 415/781-1111, is popular with the Financial District crowd and noteworthy for the shrimp dumplings in the shapes of goldfish and rabbits. (There's another Yank Sing at 49 Stevenson St. between 1st and 2nd Sts., 415/541-4949.)

A good choice for Cantonese food is Hong Kong–style **Harbor Village,** 4 Embarcadero Center (at the corner of Clay and Drumm), 415/781-8833, serving everything from dim sum to Imperial banquets. Open daily for lunch and dinner. Straight upstairs (on the Promenade level), behind those old olive-wood doors, is splendid **Splendido,** 415/982-3222, a contemporary Mediterranean-style retreat for Italian-food fanatics. Everything here is fresh and house-made, from the breads and seafood soups to the pastas and unusual pizzas. Exceptional entrées include grilled swordfish and guinea hens roasted in the restaurant's wood-burning oven. Good wine list; save some space for dessert. Open for lunch and dinner daily; the bar serves appetizers until closing (midnight). Alfresco dining available in summer.

CIVIC CENTER AND VICINITY

Backflip, 601 Eddy (near Larkin), 415/771-3547, serves up California cuisine in an aquatically inspired setting that sits poolside at the Phoenix Hotel, another beacon of style in the seedy Tenderloin. Fountains and lots of blue have you thinking "fish" from the get-go, and sure enough, seafood is the specialty here. At night, the house turns into a nightclub with DJs and dancing.

North along Polk Gulch (roughly paralleling fairly level Polk St., from Post to Broadway) are abundant cafés, coffeehouses, and avant-garde junque and clothing shops. Worthwhile eateries include **Polk Street Beans,** 1733 Polk (at Clay), 415/776-9292, a funky Eurostyle coffeehouse serving good soups and sandwiches, and **Maye's Original Oyster House,** 1233 Polk, 415/474-7674, a remarkably reasonable Italian-style seafood restaurant that's been in business in San Francisco since 1867.

Tucked inside the Inn at the Opera, **Ovation at the Opera,** 333 Fulton St. (between Gough and Franklin), 415/305-8842 or 415/553-8100, is a class act noted as much for its romantic charms as its fine French-continental cuisine—a fitting finale for opera fans who have plenty of cash left to fan (this place is on the expensive side). Open nightly for dinner (until 10:30 or 11 P.M. Fri. and Sat. nights).

Max's Opera Cafe, 601 Van Ness, 415/771-7300, also pitches itself to the neighborhood's more theatrical standards. Like Max's enterprises elsewhere, you can count on being served huge helpings of tantalizing all-American standards. At least at dinner, you can also count on the wait staff bursting into song—maybe opera, maybe a Broadway show tune. Open daily for lunch and dinner, until late (1 A.M.) on Fri. and Sat. nights for the post-theater crowds.

Also by the Opera House is the elegant and superlative **Jardinière,** 300 Grove St. (at Franklin), 415/861-5555, a French restaurant created by the city's top restaurant designer and one of its top chefs. Open for lunch weekdays and for dinner nightly (late-night menu available after 10:30 P.M.).

The **Hayes Street Grill,** 320 Hayes (at Franklin), 415/863-5545, is a busy bistro serving some of the best seafood in town. Open weekdays for lunch, Mon.–Sat. for dinner.

Sometimes more like a moveable feast for fashion, judging from all the suits and suited skirts, the **Zuni Cafe,** 1658 Market (at Gough), 415/552-2522, is an immensely popular restaurant and watering hole noted for its Italian-French country fare in a southwestern ambience. (Expensive.) Still yuppie central, even after all these years, is somewhat immodest, barn-sized **Stars,** 555 Golden Gate Ave. (between Van Ness and Polk), 415/861-7827. It's strictly reservations-only beyond the bar.

At Chelsea Square, **Crustacean,** 1475 Polk St. (at California), 415/776-2722, is another one of those cutting-edge eateries enjoyable for ambience as well as actual eats. This place serves exceptional Euro-Asian cuisine (specialty: roast crab) and looks like a fantasy home to those particularly crunchy critters, with underwater murals and giant seahorses, not to mention hand-blown glass fixtures and a 17-foot wave sculpture. Open for dinners only, nightly after 5 P.M.; valet parking, full bar, extensive wine list. Reservations preferred.

Near Japan Center, **Cafe Kati,** 1963 Sutter (near Fillmore), 415/775-7313, is one of those casual neighborhood places serving surprisingly good food. **Iroha Restaurant,** 1728 Buchanan (at Post), 415/922-0321, is a great inexpensive stop for noodles and Japanese standards.

HAIGHT-ASHBURY AND VICINITY

On any afternoon, most of the restaurants and cafés lining the Haight will be filled to the gills with young hipsters chowing down on brunch specials or self-medicating with food to cure party-related hangovers.

Campy as all get out, what with those murals and all, **Cha Cha Cha,** 1805 Haight St. (at Shrader), 415/386-5758, is just a hop or skip from Golden Gate Park. A hip tapas bar, it features unforgettable entrées such as grilled chicken paillard in mustard sauce, shrimp in spicy Cajun sauce, and New Zealand mussels in marinara. It's one of the most popular places around, so it's sometimes hard to find a place to park yourself.

Love the Haight: you can fill up at hippie-ish prices (cheap!) at several places that serve all-day breakfasts or pizza by the slice. For monstrously generous omelettes and a hearty side of potatoes, slide on into **All You Knead,** 1466 Haight (between Ashbury and Masonic), 415/552-4550. You'll get just that. Always popular for pizza is **Cybelle's,** with two neighborhood outlets: one at 1535 Haight St. (near Ashbury), 415/552-4200; the other at 203 Parnassus (at Stanyan), 415/665-8088. When East Coast transplants get homesick, they escape to **Escape from New York Pizza,** 1737 Haight (between Cole and Shrader), 415/668-5577. (There's another Escape at 508 Castro, at 18th, 415/252-1515.)

In the Haight's heyday, **Magnolia Pub & Brewery,** 1398 Haight (at Masonic), 415/864-

7468, was occupied by the Drugstore Café and later by Magnolia Thunderpussy's, a way-cool dessert-delivery business. The place has retained much of its bohemian charm with colorful murals and sweeping psychedelic signs out front. The menu offers a twist on traditional pub fare—mussels steamed in India Pale Ale, mushroom risotto cakes, along with regular old burgers and house-cut fries. The formidable house-made beer list includes Pale Ales, Porters, and more offbeat selections like the Old Thunderpussy Barleywine, a tribute to the brewpub's most famous tenant.

The area referred to as "the lower Haight" is an avant-garde enclave sandwiched between seedy Western Addition and the Webster St. public housing, with nary a tourist attraction in sight. Without the homeless, runaways, and drug dealers notable in the upper Haight, this several-block area has become a fairly happy haven for artists and low-end wannabes, as well as the cafés, bars, and restaurants they inhabit. (Great people-watching.) **Kate's Kitchen,** 471 Haight (at Fillmore), 415/626-3984, is a small storefront diner where the emphasis is on down-home American food like buttermilk pancakes and scallion-cheese biscuits. A bit more boisterous, with sunny-day sidewalk tables, is the **Horse Shoe Coffee House,** 566 Haight (between Fillmore and Steiner), 415/626-8852, which also offers high-octane coffee and Internet access.

Most of the neighborhood's bars serve fairly decent food during the day and into the evening; try **Mad Dog in the Fog,** 530 Haight (between Steiner and Fillmore), 415/626-7279, a rowdy English-style pub, or just across the street, painfully hip **Noc Noc,** 557 Haight, 415/861-5811. Particularly off the wall, in the spirit of the neighborhood, is **Spaghetti Western,** 576 Haight, 415/864-8461, an earring-heavy reinterpretation of our collective cowboy heritage. Lots of food for the money.

THE MISSION DISTRICT AND THE CASTRO

The Mission District is known for its open-air markets. One of the best is **La Victoria Mexican Bakery & Grocery,** 2937 24th St. (at Alabama), 415/550-9292. Buy some homemade tamales, fruit, and a few *churros* (Mexican sugar-dipped doughnuts) and have a feast at the children's park (between Bryant and York on 24th) while studying the murals. Other ethnic bakeries worth poking into for impromptu picnic fixings include **Pan Lido Salvadoreno,** 3147 22nd St. (at Capp), 415/282-3350, and **Pan Lido Bakery,** 5216 Mission (at Niagra), 415/333-2140. An ethnic change-up, serving great sandwiches, is **Lucca Ravioli Company,** 1100 Valencia (at 22nd St.), 415/647-5581.

Among the Mission's inexpensive neighborhood joints is the justifiably famous **Taqueria Can-Cun,** 2288 Mission (at 19th), 415/252-9560, which serves jumbo-size veggie burritos, handmade tortilla chips, and scorching salsa. There are two other locations: 10 blocks south on Mission (near Valencia) and at 6th and Market. **Fina Estampa,** 2374 Mission St. (between 19th and 20th), 415/824-4437, is a nondescript Peruvian outpost featuring exceptional seafood, chicken, and beef entrées (humongous portions) and good service. At **La Rondalla,** 901 Valencia (at 20th), 415/647-7474, mariachi bands play while you eat. At **Pancho Villa Taqueria,** 3071 16th (between Mission and Valencia), 415/864-8840, you'll be hard-pressed to find anything over seven bucks. And the portions are huge, including the grand dinner plates of grilled shrimp. At **Los Jarritos,** 901 S. Van Ness Ave. (at 20th), 415/648-8383, the "little jars" add color to an already colorful menu of Jalisco specialties.

The line between the Mission and Castro Districts has distinct geographical and sociopolitical divisions elsewhere in the city, is often blurred. **Pozole,** 2337 Market St., 415/626-2666, has an almost religious south-of-the-border folk feel, what with the candlelit shrines, skull masks, and festive colors. But the food here isn't a literal cultural interpretation—especially comforting when one recalls that *pozole* originally was human flesh specially prepared as fight fuel for Aztec warriors.

The **Flying Saucer,** 1000 Guerrero (at 22nd), 415/641-9955, where the daily-changing menu is beamed over onto the wall, is a happy landing for mostly French culinary creativity—like an interplanetary marriage between Berkeley's Chez Panisse and the Zuni Cafe in a neighborhood burger stand. Three nightly seatings.

One more stop along the Mission's restaurant row (Valencia between 16th and 24th Sts.) is the bustling **Slanted Door,** 584 Valencia (at 17th), 415/861-8032, where the food is healthy, eclectic, and surprisingly reasonable. People flock from all over the city, so make a reservation or be prepared to wait. Menu changes weekly.

Another popular spot for Vietnamese is **Saigon Saigon,** 1132 Valencia (at 22nd), 415/206-9635, serving an astounding array of dishes, from majestic rolls and barbecued quail to Buddha's delight (vegetarian). Open for lunch on weekdays, for dinner nightly.

Both restaurant and tapas bar, **Esperpento,** 3295 22nd St. (at Valencia), 415/282-8867, is a great place for delectable Catalonian entrées, as well as tasty and sophisticated Spanish finger foods. Fairly inexpensive. Open Mon.–Sat. for lunch and dinner. **Cafe Nidal,** 2491 Mission (at 18th), 415/285-4334, is a long-standing neighborhood stop for falafel and other inexpensive Middle Eastern specialties. **Cafe Istanbul,** 525 Valencia (between 16th and 17th), 415/863-8854, occasionally has belly dancers.

A neighborhood classic in the retro diner genre is **Boogaloos,** 3296 22nd St. (at Valencia), 415/824-3211, famous for huge breakfasts, slacker crowds, and its signature dish, the Temple o' Spuds. **Cafe Ethiopia,** 878 Valencia (at 20th), 415/285-2728, offers all the usual espresso drinks plus Ethiopian cuisine, including poultry, beef, and vegetarian dishes from mild to spicy hot. Hugely popular and excellent value for the money, **Ti Couz,** 3108 16th St. (at Valencia), 415/252-7373, specializes in crepes—stuffed with everything from spinach to salmon to berries.

For real cheap eats in the Castro, head to **Hot 'n' Hunky,** 4039 18th St., 415/621-6365, for locally famous burgers and renowned French fries, not to mention excessive neon and Marilyn Monroe memorabilia. Very Castro is **Cafe Flore,** 2298 Market St. (at Noe), 415/621-8579, a popular gay hangout and café serving up omelettes and crepes, salads and good sandwiches, and current information about what's going on in the neighborhood. (Great for people-watching, especially out on the plant-populated patio.)

Missed by most tourists but popular for brunch is the **Patio Cafe,** 531 Castro (near 18th), 415/621-4640, a romantic hideaway where diners sit outside in a sunny, glass-domed patio sheltered from the wind. Another popular Castro destination is the **Bagdad Cafe,** 2295 Market St. (at 16th), 415/621-4434, offering a healthy take on American-style fare, plus great salads. Nearby, and wonderful for succulent seafood, is the **Anchor Oyster Bar,** 579 Castro (between 18th and 19th), 415/431-3990.

It's Tops, 1801 Market (at McCoppin), 415/431-6395, looks like a classic American greasy spoon—the decor hasn't changed since 1945—but the surprise is just how good the pancakes and other breakfast selections are. **Sparky's 24-Hour Diner,** 242 Church St. (between Market and 15th), 415/626-8666, got lost somewhere in the 1950s, style-wise, but the breakfast omelettes, burgers, and salads are certainly up to modern expectations.

The atmosphere at suave, contemporary **2223 Market** (at Noe), 415/431-0692, is cozy, and the food is down-home American. Excellent garlic mashed potatoes and onion rings.

SOUTH OF MARKET (SoMa)

San Francisco's answer to New York City's SoHo, the South of Market area, or SoMa, is post-hippie, post-hip, post-just about everything. Anything goes. Reality here ranges from streetpeople chic and chichi supper clubs to only-those-in-the-know-know-where-it's-at dance clubs. An exploration of the neighborhood reveals the same stunning cultural contrast as those encampments of the homeless in front of the White House. Many areas here are considered unsafe after dark—stay with a group.

Head toward the bay down 2nd St. to reach the delightful South Park neighborhood, home to photo studios and shops serving the multimedia and advertising industries, as well as trendy coffeehouses, restaurants, and the postage-stamp-size greensward of South Park itself (bordered by Bryant and Brannan, 2nd and 3rd). The design-and-dine crowd is attracted in spades by South Park's **Infusion,** 555 2nd St. (at Brannan), 415/543-2282, a busy, chic restaurant beloved for its innovative, spicy menu and fruit-infused vodka drinks. **Ristorante Ecco,** 101 South Park, 415/495-3291, is a trattoria-style California/Italian place with yellow sponge-painted walls; it's popular with the young professional crowd. Great desserts. Straight across the park is Ecco's slightly older sibling, the **South Park Cafe,** 108 South Park, 415/495-7275, an intimate French-style bistro whipping up espresso and croissants in the morning and more elaborate creations at lunch and dinner. Open daily. After exploring Moscone Center and Yerba Buena Gardens, drop in for a cold one at **Thirsty Bear Brewing Co.,** 661 Howard (at 3rd), 415/974-0905, where you can enjoy one of the seven house-made microbrews and outstanding Spanish and Catalan dishes. Marked by the huge tomato hanging outside, no-fuss **Vino e Cucina,** 489 3rd St. (at Bryant), 415/543-6962, offers fine Italian cuisine scene, including pastas, pizzas, and unusual specials. Exceptional **Fringale,** 570 4th St. (between Bryant and Brannan), 415/543-0573, is a bright and contemporary French/American bistro serving excellent food at remarkably reasonable prices—a place well worth looking for. Open for lunch weekdays and for dinner Mon.–Sat.

Continuing southwest through the district, you'll find good and pretty cheap, fast-as-your-laundry-cycle fare at **BrainWash,** 1122 Folsom (between 7th and 8th), 415/861-3663 (see the special topic Clean Up Your Act at BrainWash). It's by one of the area's sociocultural flagships, **Julie's Supper Club,** 1123 Folsom, 415/861-0707, a restaurant and nightclub/bar known for its combination of space-age-meets-the-'50s supper-club style and Old West saloon atmosphere. Not to mention the famous martinis. For spice and great atmosphere, **India Garden,** 1261 Folsom (at 9th), 415/626-2798, is well worth poking into for wonderful nans (flatbreads) and *kulchas* baked in a tandoor oven. Although most folks come for the fresh-brewed beer, the **20 Tank Brewery,** 316 11th St. (at Folsom), 415/255-9455, also serves respectable bar food. You can fill up on a plate of nachos, a tasty sandwich, or a bowl of chili—and almost nothing's over five bucks. For those stirred to the soul by the world burger beat, the top stop is **Hamburger Mary's,** 1582 Folsom (at 12th), 415/626-1985 (reservations) or 415/626-5767 (information), a cleaned-up bikers' bar easily mistaken for a downhome junque store. For deliciously spicy Thai food at bargain prices, you won't go wrong at **Manora's Thai Cuisine,** 1600 Folsom (at 12th), 415/861-6224, with a menu featuring well-prepared seafood and curries.

Night owls like to come here before hitting the nearby clubs.

Also a possibility (if only for the great view of the railroad tracks) is **42 Degrees,** 235 16th St. (at Illinois, along the waterfront in China Basin), 415/777-5558, serving "nouvelle Mediterranean" food. The menu offers cuisine from southern France, Italy, Spain, and Greece—all regions at 42° north latitude. This is one of the trendiest spots around, so sometimes you wait awhile. Open weekdays for lunch and Wed.–Sat. for dinner.

FISHERMAN'S WHARF AND GHIRARDELLI SQUARE

Fisherman's Wharf is both tourist central and seafood central. Most locals wouldn't be caught dead eating at one of the Wharf's many seafood restaurants—but that doesn't mean the food isn't good here. Pick of the litter is probably **Scoma's,** on Pier 47 (walk down the pier from the intersection of Jefferson and Jones Sts.), 415/771-4383. It's just off the beaten path (on the lightly pummeled path) and therefore a tad quieter and more relaxing than the others—or at least it seems so. The others would include: **A. Sabella's,** 2766 Taylor St. (at Jefferson), 415/771-4416; **Alioto's,** 8 Fisherman's Wharf (at Jefferson), 415/673-0183; the **Franciscan,** Pier 43½, The Embarcadero, 415/362-7733; **Pompei's Grotto,** 340 Jefferson St. (near Jones), 415/776-9265; and a large number of places at Pier 39. You can get a decent bowl of clam chowder and a slab of sourdough bread at any of them.

Ghirardelli Square, 900 North Point (at Larkin), though technically part of the same Fisherman's Wharf tourist area, houses some fine restaurants patronized by locals even in broad daylight. The **Mandarin,** 415/673-8812, was the city's first truly palatial Chinese restaurant and the first to serve up spicy Szechuan and Hunan dishes. The food here is still great. Stop by at lunch for off-the-menu dim sum (including green onion pie, spring rolls with yellow chives, and sesame shrimp rolls), served 11:30 A.M.–3:30 P.M. daily, or come later for dinner. You won't go wrong for seafood at **McCormick's and Kuleto's,** 415/929-1730, which features its own Crab Cake Lounge and 30 to 50 fresh specialties every day. Another much-loved Ghirardelli Square eatery is **Gaylord,** 415/771-8822, serving astounding Northern Indian specialties with a side of East Indies decor.

Elsewhere in the area, the Victorian-style **Buena Vista,** 2675 Hyde St. (at Beach), 415/474-5044, is notorious as the tourist bar that introduced Irish coffee. It's a great spot to share a table for breakfast or light lunch, and the waterfront views are almost free.

THE MARINA DISTRICT, COW HOLLOW, AND PACIFIC HEIGHTS

Perhaps San Francisco's most famous, most fabulous vegetarian restaurant is **Greens,** at Building A, Fort Mason (enter at Buchanan and Marina), 415/771-6222, where the hearty fare proves for all time that meat is an unnecessary ingredient for fine dining—and where the views are plenty appetizing, too. Open for lunch and dinner Tues.–Sat., and for brunch on Sun.; reservations always advised. The bakery counter is open Tues.–Sun. from 10 A.M. to mid- or late afternoon.

Left at Albuquerque, 2140 Union St. (at Fillmore in Cow Hollow), 415/749-6700, offers Southwestern ambience and an energetic, dining-and-drinking clientele. Modern-day Malcolm Lowrys could spend the rest of their tormented days here, sampling from among 100-plus types of tequila. (Stick with the 100 percent blue agave reposados.) Good food, too. Open daily for lunch and dinner.

Pane e Vino, 3011 Steiner St. (at Union), 415/346-2111, is a justifiably popular neighborhood trattoria that's unpretentious and unwavering in its dedication to serving up grand, deceptively simple pastas. If you tire of privacy, head over to **Perry's,** 1944 Union (between Buchanan and Laguna), 415/922-9022, one of the city's ultimate see-and-be-seen scenes and a great burger stop.

Irrawaddy, 1769 Lombard St. (between Octavia and Laguna), 415/931-2830, is a good spot for Burmese cuisine. **Curbside Cafe,** 2417 California, 415/929-9030, specializes in flavorful delights from all over—France, Morocco, Mexico, and the Caribbean (the crab cakes are justifiably famous). **Lhasa Moon,** 2420 Lombard (at

Scott), 415/674-9898, offers excellent, authentic Tibetan cuisine Thurs.–Fri. for lunch, and Tues.–Sun. for dinner.

Elite Cafe, 2049 Fillmore (between Pine and California), 415/346-8668, is a clubby pub serving Cajun and Creole food in a dark, handsome room. It's somehow appropriate to the neighborhood. **The Mansions,** 2220 Sacramento (between Laguna and Buchanan), 415/929-9444, serves wonderful food in a Victorian dining room, complete with unusual entertainment. Be sure to reserve in advance.

For people of modest means planning a special night out, **Chateau Suzanne,** 1449 Lombard, 415/771-9326, is a good choice, serving healthy and absolutely elegant French-Chinese entrées. Open Tues.–Sat. for dinner only; reservations advised.

Close to Japantown and adjacent to the Majestic Hotel (a one-time family mansion), the **Cafe Majestic,** 1500 Sutter St. (at Gough), 415/776-6400, is widely regarded as one of San Francisco's most romantic restaurants. The setting radiates old-world charm: ornate Edwardian decor, pale green and apricot decor with potted palms. It's sedate, yet far from stuffy and serves plentiful breakfasts on weekdays and brunch on weekends. Listen to a live classical pianist Fri.–Sat. nights and at Sunday brunch. Lunch is served Tues.–Fri., dinner nightly. Reservations are wise.

East of Pacific Heights, right on the stretch of Hwy. 101 that surface-streets its way through the city en route to the Golden Gate Bridge, is **Harris',** 2100 Van Ness Ave. (at Pacific), 415/673-1888, the city's best steakhouse, and unabashedly so. This is the place to come for a martini and a steak: T-bones, rib eyes, and filet mignon all star on a beefy menu. Open for dinner daily.

CHINATOWN

To find the best restaurants in Chinatown, go where the Chinese go. Some of these places may look a bit shabby, at least on the outside, and may not take reservations—or credit cards. But since the prices at small family-run enterprises are remarkably low, don't fret about leaving that plastic at home.

Very popular, and always packed, the **House of Nanking,** 919 Kearny (between Jackson and

Columbus), 415/421-1429, has a great location at the foot of Chinatown on the North Beach border. At this tiny restaurant, diners often sit elbow to elbow, but the excellent food and reasonable prices make it well worth the wait. For spicy Mandarin and the best pot stickers in town, try the **Pot Sticker**, 150 Waverly Place, 415/397-9985, open daily for lunch and dinner. Another possibility is the tiny turn-of-the-20th-century **Hang Ah Tea Room**, 1 Pagoda Place (off Sacramento St.), 415/982-5686, specializing in Cantonese entrées and lunchtime dim sum. Inexpensive and locally infamous, due largely to the rude waiter routine of Edsel Ford Wong (now deceased), is three-story **Sam Woh**, 813 Washington St. (at Grant), 415/982-0596, where you can get good noodles, jook (rice gruel), and Chinese-style doughnuts (for dunking in your gruel). **Empress of China**, 838 Grant Ave. (between Washington and Clay), 415/434-1345, offers a wide-ranging Chinese menu, elegant atmosphere, and great views of Chinatown and Telegraph Hill. They've been in business for three decades, so you know they're doing something right. Open daily for lunch and dinner.

Vegetarians will appreciate **Kowloon Vegetarian Restaurant**, 909 Grant Ave., 415/362-9888, which serves more than 80 meatless selections, including 20 types of vegetarian dim sum and entrées like sweet and sour or curried (faux) pork (with soybean and gluten substituting for meat). Open daily 9 A.M.–9 P.M.

JACKSON SQUARE, NORTH BEACH, AND RUSSIAN HILL

In and Around Jackson Square

"Like the Flintstones on acid," one local food fan says of the almost indescribable style of the **Cypress Club**, 500 Jackson St. (at Montgomery), 415/296-8555. This popular restaurant near the Financial District is named after the nightclub in Raymond Chandler's *The Big Sleep*. Snide types say: "Très L.A." Others have called doing lunch or dinner here "like sitting under a table" (those huge columns could be table legs) or "like going to a very expensive, very garish, catered carnival." You enter through a copper door, then push past the blood-red velvet speakeasy curtain. Curvaceous copper sectional "pillows," some-

thing like overblown landscaping berms, frame the dining room and separate the booths. At table, you sink into plush burgundy mohair seats or pull up a clunky chair, then relax under the familiarity of the WPA-style Bay Area mural wrapping the walls near the ceiling. (Finally, something seems familiar.) Then you notice the odd polka-dotted light fixtures. If the atmosphere is stimulating, so is the food—simple French cuisine reinvented with fresh local ingredients. Matching the decor, desserts are tantalizing "architectural constructs." The wine list is remarkable—and safe, since the 14,000-bottle wine cellar is downstairs in an earthquake-proof room. The Cypress Club is open daily for dinner, Mon.–Sat. for lunch, and Sun. for brunch.

If that's not enough otherworldly ambience, head around the corner and down an alley to **Bix**, 56 Gold St. (between Jackson and Pacific, Montgomery and Sansome), 415/433-6300, a small supper club and bar with the feel of a 1940s-style film noir hideout. At Kearny and Columbus, you'll find movie-magnate-turned-winemaker Francis Ford Coppola's **Cafe Niebaum-Coppola**, 916 Kearny St., 415/291-1700, which offers an Italian menu and a good wine bar (serving, among other selections, Coppola's own vintages).

One of the country's best Greek restaurants is **Kokkari**, 200 Jackson St. (at Front), 415/981-0983. Open weekdays for lunch and Mon.–Sat. for dinner. While in the Montgomery-Washington Tower, **Tommy Toy's Haute Cuisine Chinoise**, 655 Montgomery St. (between Washington and Clay), 415/397-4888, serves up classical Chinese cuisine with traditional French touches, called "Frenchinoise" by Tommy Toy himself. The restaurant itself is impressive enough; it's patterned after the reading room of the Empress Dowager of the Ching Dynasty, and the rich decor includes priceless Asian art and antiques. Open for dinner nightly and for lunch on weekdays; reservations always advisable.

North Beach Proper

Farther north in North Beach proper, you'll find an almost endless selection of cafés and restaurants. Historically, this is the perfect out-of-the-way area to eat, drink good coffee, or just while away the hours. These days, North Beach is a somewhat odd blend of San Francisco's Beat-era bohemian

a sidewalk café in North Beach

SAN FRANCISCO CONVENTION & VISITORS BUREAU/
DAWN STRANNE

nostalgia, new-world Asian attitudes, and other ethnic culinary accents. An example of the "new" North Beach: the **New Sun Hong Kong Restaurant,** 606 Broadway (at the sometimes-harmonic, very cosmopolitan cultural convergence of Grant, Broadway, and Columbus), 415/956-3338. Outside, marking the building, is a three-story-tall mural depicting the North Beach jazz tradition. But this is a very Chinatown eatery, open from early morning to late at night and specializing in hot pots and earthy, homey, San Francisco–style Chinese fare.

Also here are some of old San Francisco's most traditional traditions. The **Washington Square Bar and Grill,** 1707 Powell St. (at Union), 415/982-8123, is an immensely popular social stop-off for the city's cognoscenti—a place that also serves outstanding food with your conversation. The live jazz, too, is often worth writing home about. The venerable **Fior D'Italia,** 601 Union St. (at Stockton), 415/986-1886, established in 1886, is legendary for its ambience—including the Tony Bennett Room and the Godfather Room—and its historic ability to attract highbrow Italians from around the globe.

"Follow your nose" to the **Stinking Rose,** 325 Columbus (between Broadway and Vallejo), 415/781-7673, an exceptionally popular Italian restaurant where all the food is heavily doused in garlic. For exceptional food with a more elevated perspective, a dress-up restaurant on Telegraph Hill is appropriately romantic: **Julius' Castle,** 1541 Montgomery St. (north of Union), 415/392-

2222, for French and Italian, and beautiful views of the city. Not that far away (along the Embarcadero), renowned for its fine food and flair, is the one and only **Fog City Diner,** 1300 Battery St. (at Lombard), 415/982-2000. Though this is the original gourmet grazing pasture, Fog City has its imitators around the world.

But the real North Beach is elsewhere. **Campo Santo,** 240 Columbus Ave. (between Pacific and Broadway), 415/433-9623, is yet another cultural change-up: Latin American kitsch kicking up its heels with campy Day of the Dead decor. The food is lively, too, from mahimahi tacos to crab quesadillas. Open Mon.–Sat. from lunchtime through dinner (until 10 P.M.). For genuine neighborhood tradition, head to stand-up **Molinari's,** 373 Columbus (between Broadway and Green), 415/421-2337, a fixture since 1907. It's a good deli stop for fresh pastas, homemade sauces, hearty sandwiches, and tasty sweet treats. Or stop off for a meatball sandwich or cappuccino at landmark **Mario's Bohemian Cigar Store Cafe,** 566 Columbus (near Washington Square), 415/362-0536. The inexpensive sandwiches, frittata, and cannelloni here are the main menu attraction, but folks also come to sip cappuccino or Campari while watching the world whirl by, or while watching each other watching. Sorry, they don't sell cigars.

"Rain or shine, there's always a line" at very–San Francisco **Little Joe's,** 523 Broadway (between Kearny and Columbus), 415/433-4343, a boisterous bistro where the Italian food is authentic, the atmosphere happy, and everyone hale and hearty. The open kitchen is another main attraction. For faster service, belly up to a counter stool and watch the chefs at work.

Volare Trattoria Caffe, 561 Columbus (between Union and Green), 415/362-2774, offers superb Sicilian cuisine—try the exceptional calamari in tomato-garlic sauce. Owner Giovanni Zocca plants himself outside on Friday and Saturday nights and sings the restaurant's theme tune, "Volare, volare, volare, ho ho ho." Just up the street is **L'Osteria del Forno,** 519 Columbus, 415/982-1124, a tiny storefront trattoria with six tables. This place is a great budget bet for its wonderful Italian flatbread sandwiches.

For pizza, the place to go is **North Beach Pizza,** 1499 Grant (at Union), 415/433-2444, where there's always a line, and it's always worth standing in. Heading down toward the Financial District, **Caffe Macaroni,** 59 Columbus (between Washington and Jackson), 415/956-9737, is also a true blue—well, red, white, and green— pasta house in the Tuscany tradition: intimate, aromatic, and friendly.

Exceptional for Afghan fare is **The Helmand,** 430 Broadway (between Kearny and Montgomery), 415/362-0641. Here linguistics majors can enjoy ordering such dishes as *dwopiaza, bowlani,* and *sabzi challow.* Most entrées are oriented around lamb and beef, but vegetarian entrées are available and are separated out on the menu, making for easy selection.

Russian Hill

The **Hyde Street Bistro,** 1521 Hyde St. (between Jackson and Pacific), 415/292-4415, is one of those sophisticated little places where San Franciscans hide out during tourist season. It's quiet, not too trendy, and serves good French cuisine. Appreciate the breadsticks.

Ristorante Milano, 1448 Pacific Ave. (between Hyde and Larkin), 415/673-2961, is a happy, hopping little Italian restaurant with pastas—do try the lasagna—fresh fish, and sometimes surprising specials.

Not far away and a real deal for foodies who don't care one whit about the frills is **Pete's Cafe at San Francisco Art Institute,** 800 Chestnut St. (at Jones), 415/749-4567, where you can get a great lunch for $5 or less, along with one of the city's best bay views. The atmosphere is arty and existential, with paper plates and plastic utensils just to remind you that this is for students. Everything is fresh and wholesome: southwestern black bean/vegetable stew, white bean and escarole soup, even house-roasted turkey sandwiches. Good breakfasts, too. Open in summer Mon.–Fri. 9 A.M.–2 P.M., and during the school year Mon.–Fri. 8 A.M.–9 P.M., Sat. 9 A.M.–2 P.M. (hours can vary; it's best to call ahead).

PRACTICAL SAN FRANCISCO

USEFUL INFORMATION

The clearinghouse for current visitor information is the **San Francisco Convention & Visitors Bureau,** 900 Market St. (at Powell, downstairs—below street level—outside the BART station at Hallidie Plaza), P.O. Box 429097, San Francisco, CA 94142-9097, 415/391-2000, www.sfvisitor.org. Here you can pick up official visitor pamphlets, maps, booklets, and brochures about local businesses, including current accommodations bargains and various coupon offers. Multilingual staffers are available to answer questions. The Visitor Information Center is open for walk-ins weekdays 9 A.M.–5 P.M., Sat.–Sun. 9 A.M.–3 P.M.; closed Thanksgiving, Christmas, and New Year's Day.

If you can't make it to the Visitor Information Center or are planning your trip in advance and need information, you have a couple of options. To find out what's going on in town, from entertainment and arts attractions to major professional sports events, you can call the city's free, 24-hour visitor hot line, available in five languages. To get the news in English, call 415/391-2001; in French, 415/391-2003; in German, 415/391-2004; in Japanese, 415/391-2101; and in Spanish, 415/391-2122. The information is updated weekly. You can also write to the SFCVB to request current information on accommodations, events, and other travel planning particulars. For $3 postage and handling, you can get a copy of the SFCVB's semiannual *The San Francisco Book,* which contains thorough information about sights, activities, arts, entertainment, recreation, shopping venues, and restaurants, as well as a detailed map. (And then some.) If you'll be in town awhile, it's worth the money to request in advance.

Where-San Francisco is a slick, free magazine full of useful information on accommodations, dining, shopping, and nightlife. It's available at the Hallidie Square visitor center and elsewhere around town. You can also order a subscription ($30/year) by contacting: Where Magazine, 74 New Montgomery St., Ste. 320, San Francisco, CA 94105, 415/546-6101.

Even more real: the **San Francisco Bay Guardian** and **SF Weekly** tabloid newspapers, available free almost everywhere around town. The *Guardian*'s motto (with a hat tip to Wilbur Storey and the 1861 *Chicago Times,* as interpreted by Editor/Publisher Bruce Brugmann), "It is a newspaper's duty to print the news and raise hell," is certainly comforting in these times and also generates some decent news/feature reading, along with comprehensive arts, entertainment, and events listings. The *Guardian* also publishes **FYI San Francisco,** a tourist-oriented guide to the city with some of the same punchy, irreverent writing. It's free and widely available around town. The *Weekly* also offers what's-happening coverage and—to its everlasting credit—Rob Brezsny's "Free Will Astrology" column.

While roaming the city, look for other special-interest and neighborhood-scope publications. The **San Francisco Bay Times** is a fairly substantive gay and lesbian biweekly. For compre-

hensive events information, pick up a copy of the **Bay Area Reporter.** Widely read throughout the Sunset and Richmond Districts is **The Independent.** Other popular papers include the award-winning, hell-raising, **Street Sheet,** published by the Coalition on Homelessness in San Francisco and distributed by the homeless on San Francisco's streets; the **New Mission News;** and the **Noe Valley Voice.**

The city's major dailies are universally available at newsstands and in coin-op vending racks. Until quite recently the morning paper was the **San Francisco Chronicle,** and the afternoon/evening paper the **San Francisco Examiner,** two separate papers linked since the 1960s in a federally approved joint operating agreement. The two shared printing facilities (and classified ads) and also combined forces every week to produce the humongous Sunday paper. All that began to change in late 1999, when the *Chronicle* was sold to the Hearst Corporation. The *Examiner* was subsequently sold, and began publishing as a morning paper in late November 2000. The Chronicle's Sunday "The Pink" section is packed with readable reviews, letters from sometimes demanding or demented Bay Area readers, and the most comprehensive listing of everything going on in the coming week. San Francisco's major non-English and ethnic newspapers include the **Chinese Times,** the **Irish Herald,** and the African-American community's **Sun Reporter.**

If you don't feel obliged to buy what you need to read, the newish, high-tech, and highly

Don't miss a visit here: The landmark City Lights bookstore in North Beach.

AISUNN RACE

STAYING SAFE

San Francisco is a reasonably safe city. Definitely unsafe areas, especially at night, include the Tenderloin, some areas south of Market St., parts of the Western Addition, and parts of the Mission District (including, at night, BART stops). For the most part, drug-related gang violence is confined to severely impoverished areas. The increased number of homeless people and panhandlers, particularly notable downtown, is distressing, certainly, but most of these people are harmless lost souls.

Definitely not harmless is the national crime craze known as "carjacking." As the scenario usually goes, you're sitting in your car at an intersection or at a parking garage when an armed stranger suddenly appears and demands that you get out. Though there have been highly publicized cases involving successful driver heroism, the best advice is, don't try it. If a criminal demands that you get out of your car or give up your car keys, do it. Losing a car is better than losing your life. Though there is no sure-fire prevention for carjacking, locking all car doors and rolling up windows is often suggested. Another good idea: avoid dubious or unfamiliar neighborhoods.

If your own vehicle isn't safe, keep in mind that no place is absolutely safe. And sadly, in general it still holds true that female travelers are safest if they confine themselves to main thoroughfares. As elsewhere in America, women are particularly vulnerable to assaults of every kind. At night, women traveling solo, or even with a friend or two, should stick to bustling, yuppie-happy areas like Fisherman's Wharf and Union Street. The definitely street-savvy, though, can get around fairly well in SoMa and other nightlife areas, especially in groups or by keeping to streets with plenty of benign human traffic. (You can usually tell by looking.)

---

controversial **San Francisco Main Library,** downtown at 100 Larkin (at Grove), 415/557-4400, is a good place to start becoming familiar with the local public-library system. For better or worse, the old card catalogs are gone—replaced by a computerized system—and the computers here offer free Internet access. But many users decry the seemingly low percentage of space in the expensive, expansive building actually devoted to stacks of books. A complete listing of neighborhood branch libraries is offered in the white pages of the local phone book, under "Government Pages—SF City & County—Libraries."

Other Helpful Information Contacts
For current **weather information,** call 415/936-1212. For current San Francisco **time,** call that old-time favorite POPCORN (767-8900). For current **road conditions** anywhere in California, call toll-free 800/427-7623. The free **DOC** (Directory On Call) service, 415/808-5000, offers a prerecorded summary of local news, sports, stocks, entertainment, and weather information.

For special assistance and information on the city's disabled services, contact the **Mayor's Office of Community Development** (Attn.: Disability Coordinator), 25 Van Ness Ave., Ste. 700, San Francisco, CA 94102, 415/252-3100, or the helpful local **Easter Seal Society,** 6221 Geary Blvd., 415/752-4888. To understand the ins and outs of disabled access to local public transit, request a copy of the **Muni Access Guide** from Muni Accessible Services Program, 949 Presidio Ave., San Francisco, CA 94115, 415/923-6142 weekdays or 415/673-6864 anytime.

Emergency Assistance: Safety and Health
In any emergency, get to a telephone and dial 911—the universal emergency number in California. Depending upon the emergency, police, fire, and/or ambulance personnel will be dispatched. Runaways can call home free, anytime, no questions asked, by dialing the **California Youth Crisis Line,** toll-free 800/843-5200. Other 24-hour crisis and emergency hot lines include: **Helpline,** 772-HELP; **Rape Crisis** (operated by Women Against Rape, or WAR), 415/647-7273, the number to call in the event of any violent assault; **Suicide Prevention,** 415/781-0500; **Drug Line,** 415/834-1144 or 415/362-3400; **Alcoholics Anonymous,** 415/621-1326; **Narcotics Anonymous,** 415/621-8600; and **Poison Control,** toll-free 800/876-4766.

The San Francisco Police Department (general information line: 415/553-0123) sponsors several Japanese-style kobans—police ministation neighborhood kiosks—where you can get law-enforcement assistance if you're lucky enough to be nearby when they're open. The Hallidie Plaza Koban is in the tourist-thick cablecar zone at Market and Powell; open Tues.–Sat. 10 A.M.–6 P.M. The Chinatown Koban is on Grant between Washington and Jackson; open daily 1–9 P.M. The Japantown Koban is at Post and Buchanan; open Mon.–Fri. 11 A.M.–7 P.M. **San Francisco General Hospital,** 1001 Potrero Ave. (at 22nd St., on Potrero Hill), 415/206-8000 (911 or 415/206-8111 for emergencies), provides 24-hour medical emergency and trauma care services. Another possibility is **UCSF Medical Center,** 505 Parnassus Ave. (at 3rd Ave.), 415/476-1000. (The UCSF dental clinic is at 707 Parnassus, 415/476-1891 or 415/476-5814 for emergencies.) Convenient for most visitors is **Saint Francis Memorial Hospital** on Nob Hill, 900 Hyde St., 415/353-6000, which offers no-appointment-needed clinic and urgent-care medical services as well as a **Center for Sports Medicine,** 415/353-6400, and a physician referral service, toll-free 800/333-1355.

For nonemergency referrals, call the **San Francisco Medical Society,** 415/561-0853, or the **San Francisco Dental Society,** 415/421-1435.

**Post Offices, Banks,
Currency Exchanges, Et Cetera**
San Francisco's main post office is the Rincon Annex, 180 Steuart St. (just off the Embarcadero, south of Market), San Francisco, CA 94105. It's open weekdays 7 A.M.–6 P.M., Sat. 9 A.M.–2 P.M. For help in figuring out local zip code assignments, and for general information and current postal rates, call toll-free 800/275-8777 or log on to www.usps.gov. Regional post offices are also scattered throughout San Francisco neighborhoods. Some branches are open extended hours, such as 7 A.M.–6 P.M. weekdays, or with limited services some Saturday hours, and some have after-hours open lobbies, so customers can purchase stamps via vending machines. Public mailboxes, for posting stamped mail, are available in every area. Stamps are also for sale in major hotels (usually in the gift shop) and, increasingly, even in major grocery stores.

Branches of major national and international banks are available in San Francisco; most offer automated cash-advance facilities, often accessible through various member systems. Getting mugged while banking is a potential disadvantage of getting cash from an automated teller. Always be aware of who is nearby and what they're doing; if possible, have a companion or two with you. If the situation doesn't feel "right," move to another location—or do your banking inside.

Most currency exchange outlets are either downtown or at the San Francisco International Airport (SFO). **Bank of America Foreign Currency Services,** 345 Montgomery St., 415/622-2451, is open Mon.–Fri. 9 A.M.–6 P.M. Another possibility is the Bank of America at the Powell St. cable car turnaround, 1 Powell (at Market), 415/622-4498 (same hours). **Thomas Cook Currency Services, Inc.,** 75 Geary, 415/362-6271 or toll-free 800/287-7362, is open weekdays 9 A.M.–5 P.M., Sat. 10 A.M.–4 P.M. (Another location is at 1 Powell St.) To exchange currency at the airport, head for the International Terminal, where **Bank of America,** 650/615-4700, offers currency exchange for both in- and outbound travelers daily 7 A.M.–11 P.M.

For cardmembers, the **American Express Travel Agency** is another possibility for check cashing, traveler's-check transactions, and currency exchange. There are three San Francisco offices: 455 Market (at 1st), 560 California St. (between Kearny and Montgomery), and 333 Jefferson (at Jones); 415/536-2600 for all. In Northern California, the American Automobile Association (AAA) is known as the California State Automobile Association (CSAA). The San Francisco office is near the Civic Center at 150 Van Ness Ave., 415/565-2012. The CSAA office is open weekdays for all member inquiries and almost endless services, including no-fee traveler's checks, free maps and travel information, and travel agency services.

San Francisco's major hotels, and most of the midrange boutique hotels, have a fax number and fax facilities; some offer other communications services. For telex and telegrams, you can pop into one of the many **Western Union** branches throughout the city.

TRANSPORTATION:
GETTING TO AND FROM TOWN

At least on pleasure trips, Californians and other Westerners typically drive into San Francisco. The city is reached from the north via Hwy. 101

across the fabled Golden Gate Bridge ($3 toll to get into the city, no cost to get out); from the east via I-80 from Oakland/Berkeley across the increasingly choked-with-traffic Bay Bridge ($2 toll to get into the city, no cost to get out); and from the south (from the coast or from San Jose and other South Bay/Peninsula communities) via Hwy. 1, Hwy. 101, or I-280/19th Avenue. Whichever way you come and go, avoid peak morning (7–9 A.M.) and afternoon/evening (4–6 P.M.) rush hours at all costs. The Bay Area's traffic congestion is truly horrendous.

Major Bay Area Airports

About 15 miles south of the city via Hwy. 101,

San Francisco International Airport (SFO), 650/876-2377 (general information) or 650/877-0227 (parking information), perches on a point of land at the edge of the bay. (That's one of the thrills here: taking off and landing just above the water.) Each of the three terminals—North, Central (or International), and South—has two levels, the lower for arrivals, the upper for departures. San Francisco's is the fifth busiest airport in the United States and seventh busiest in the world; its 80 gates handle some 32 million passengers per year. More than 40 major scheduled carriers (and smaller ones, including air charters) serve SFO. There's protected parking for 7,000 cars, best for short-term car storage.

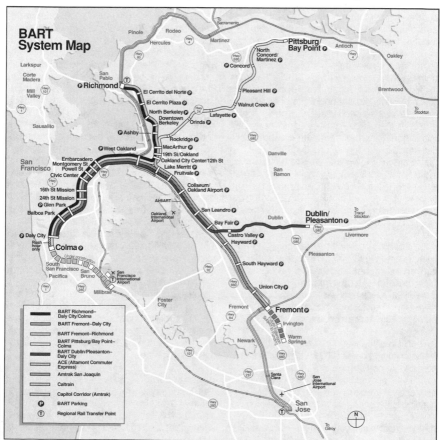

San Francisco International has its quirks. For one thing, its odd horseshoe shape often makes for a long walk for transferring passengers; the "people movers" help somewhat, but people seem to avoid the 2nd-floor intraterminal bus. (In all fairness, though, since SFO is primarily an origin/destination airport, for most travelers this isn't a problem.) And with such a high volume of air traffic—an average of 1,260 flights per day—delays are all too common, especially when fog rolls in and stays.

People complain, too, that the airport always seems to be under major construction. A multibillion-dollar expansion project has been underway, which has resulted in a new international terminal. If you've got some time to kill, check out the permanent "Images of Mexico" cultural display, with masks and such, in the South Terminal connector (beyond the security check) and the outstanding changing exhibits along United's North Terminal connector. Or you can make use of the AT&T Communications Center, upstairs in the International Terminal; it's open 8 A.M.–10 P.M. and offers special phone facilities to allow callers to pay the attendants (multilingual) in cash, as well as a six-person conference room set up for teleconferencing (fax, too). Other airport facilities include restaurants (the BayView Restaurant in the South Terminal, the North Beach Deli in the North), the South Terminal's California Marketplace (where you can get some wine and smoked fish or crab to go with that sourdough bread you're packing), and the North Terminal's Author's Bookstore, which prominently features titles by Bay Area and California writers.

Due to its excellent service record and relatively lower volume, many travelers prefer flying into and out of efficient, well-run **Oakland International Airport** just across the bay, 510/577-4000. It's fairly easy to reach from downtown San Francisco on either public transit or one of the convenient shuttle services.

Airport Shuttles

If flying into and out of SFO, avoid driving if at all possible. Airport shuttles are abundant, fairly inexpensive, and generally reliable. Most companies offer at-your-door pick-up service if you're heading to the airport (advance reservations usually required) and—coming from the airport—take you right where you're going. The usual one-

way fare, depending upon the company, is around $15 per person for SFO/San Francisco service. (Inquire about prices for other shuttle options.)

The blue-and-gold **SuperShuttle** fleet has some 100 vans coming and going all the time, 415/659-2547. When you arrive at SFO, the company's shuttle vans (no reservation needed) to the city are available at the outer island on the upper level of all terminals. To arrange a trip to the airport, call and make your pick-up reservation at least a day in advance. (And be ready when the shuttle arrives—they're usually on time.) Group, convention, and charter shuttles are also available, and you can pay on board with a major credit card. (Exact fare depends on where you start and end.)

SFO Airporter, 415/641-3100, offers nonstop runs every 20 minutes between the airport and the Financial District or Union Square. No reservations are required in either direction. **City Express Shuttle** in Oakland, 510/638-8830, offers daily shuttle service between the city of San Francisco and Oakland International Airport. **Bayporter Express, Inc.,** 415/656-2929, 415/467-1800, or toll-free 800/287-6783 (from inside the airport), specializes in shuttle service between most Bay Area suburban communities and SFO, and offers hourly door-to-door service between any location in San Francisco and the Oakland Airport. **Marin Airporter** in Larkspur, 415/461-4222, provides service every half hour from various Marin communities to SFO daily, 4:30 A.M.–11 P.M., and from SFO to Marin County daily, 5:30 A.M.–midnight.

San Mateo County Transit (SamTrans), call toll-free 800/660-4287, offers extensive peninsula public transit, including express and regular buses from SFO to San Francisco. It's cheap, too (about $1). Buses leave the airport every 30 minutes, starting very early in the morning and finishing just after midnight; call for exact schedule. The express buses limit passengers to carryon luggage only, so heavily laden travelers will have to take one of the regular buses—a 10-minute-longer ride.

Buses and Trains

The **Transbay Terminal,** 425 Mission St. (just south of Market St. between 1st and Fremont), 415/495-1551 or 415/495-1569, is the city's regional transportation hub. An information center on the 2nd floor has displays, maps, and fee-free phone lines for relevant transit systems. Bus companies based here include **Greyhound,** 415/495-1569, with buses coming and going at all hours; **Golden Gate Transit,** 415/455-2000, offering buses to and from Marin County and vicinity; **AC Transit,** 415/817-1717, which serves the East Bay; and **San Mateo County Transit** (Sam-Trans), toll-free 800/660-4287, which runs as far south as Palo Alto. Shuttle buses here also take passengers across the bay to the Amtrak station at 245 2nd St. in Oakland's Jack London Square, 510/238-4306 or toll-free 800/USA-RAIL, www.amtrak.com, where you can make train connections both north and south.

Primarily a regional commute service, **Cal-Train,** toll-free 800/660-4287 within Northern California, runs south to Palo Alto and the Amtrak station in San Jose, where you can get a bus connection to Santa Cruz. The San Francisco CalTrain depot is at 4th and Townsend Streets.

Bay Area Ferries

Since the city is surrounded on three sides by water, ferry travel is an unusual (and unusually practical) San Francisco travel option. Before the construction of the Golden Gate Bridge in 1937, it was the only way to travel to the city from the North and East Bay areas. Nowadays, the ferries function both as viable commuter and tourist transit services. (See Delights and Diversions for more about ferry tours and other oceangoing entertainment.)

The **Blue & Gold Fleet,** 415/773-1188 (recorded schedule) or 415/705-5555 (reservations and information), based at Fisherman's Wharf, Piers 39 and 41, offers round-trip service daily between San Francisco (either the Ferry Building or Pier 41) and Oakland (Jack London Square), Alameda (Gateway Center), Sausalito, Tiburon, Angel Island, and Vallejo (via high-speed catamaran). The company also offers bay cruises, tours of Alcatraz, an "Island Hop" tour to both Alcatraz and Angel Island, and various land tours (Muir Woods, Yosemite, Monterey/Carmel, Wine Country).

Golden Gate Ferries, headquartered in the Ferry Building at the foot of Market St., 415/923-2000, specializes in runs to and from Sausalito (adults $4.70) and more frequent large-ferry (725-passenger capacity) trips to and from Larkspur.

Family rates available, and disabled passengers and seniors (over age 65) travel at half fare.

Red & White Fleet at Fisherman's Wharf, Pier 43 1/2, 415/447-0597 or toll-free 800/229-2784, offers bay cruises and various land tours, as well as a commuter run to Richmond.

TRANSPORTATION: GETTING AROUND TOWN

San Francisco drivers are among the craziest in California. Whether they're actually demented, just distracted, insanely rude, or perhaps intentionally driving to a different drummer, walkers beware. The white lines of a pedestrian cross-walk seem to serve as sights, making people easier targets. Even drivers must adopt a heads-up attitude. In many areas, streets are narrow and/or incredibly steep. Finding a parking place requires psychic skills. So, while many people drive into and out of the Bay Area's big little city, if at all possible many use public transit to get around town.

But some people really want to drive in San Francisco. Others don't want to, but need to, due to the demands of their schedules. A possible compromise: if you have a car but can't stand the thought of driving it through the urban jungle yourself, hire a driver. You can hire a chauffeur, and even arrange private sightseeing tours and other outings, through companies like **WeDriveU, Inc.,** 60 E. 3rd Ave. in San Mateo, 650/579-5800 or toll-free 800/773-7483. Other local limousine companies may be willing to hire-out just a city-savvy driver; call and ask.

Though those maniacal bicycle delivery folks somehow manage to daredevil their way through downtown traffic—note their bandages, despite protective armor—for normal people, cycling is a no-go proposition downtown and along heavy-traffic thoroughfares. Bring a bike to enjoy the Golden Gate National Recreation Area and other local parks, though it may be easier to rent one. Rental outlets around Golden Gate Park include **Lincoln Cyclery,** 772 Stanyan (near Waller), 415/221-2415; **Start to Finish Bicycles,** 672 Stanyan (near Page), 415/750-4760; and **Avenue Cyclery,** 756 Stanyan, 415/387-3155. In Golden Gate Park, you can rent a bike, in-line skates, or a pedal-powered

TAKING A TAXI

Taxis from SFO to San Francisco cost around $30. Standard San Francisco taxi fare, which also applies to around-town trips, is $2.50 for the first mile, $1.80 per additional mile (plus tip, usually 15 percent). Among the 24-hour taxi companies available:

DeSoto Cab Co.	415/673-1414
Luxor Cab	415/282-4141
Veteran's Taxicab Company	415/552-1300
Yellow Cab	415/626-2345

surrey at **Golden Gate Park Bike & Skate,** 3038 Fulton, 415/668-1117.

Car Rental Agencies

Some of the least expensive car rental agencies have the most imaginative names. Near the airport in South San Francisco, **Bob Leech's Auto Rental** 435 S. Airport Blvd., 650/583-3844, specializes in new Toyotas, from $25 per day with 150 fee-free miles. (You must carry a valid major credit card and be at least 23 years old; call for a ride from the airport.) Downtown, family-owned **Reliable Rent-A-Car,** 349 Mason, 415/928-4414, rents new cars with free pick-up and return for a starting rate of $19 per day ("any car, any time"). That all-American innovation, **Rent-A-Wreck,** 2955 3rd St., 415/282-6293, rents out midsize used cars for around $29 per day with 150 free miles, or $159 per week with 700 free miles.

The more well known national car rental agencies have desks at the airport, as well as at other locations. Their rates are usually higher than those of the independents and vary by vehicle make and model, length of rental, day of the week (sometimes season), and total mileage. Special coupon savings or substantial discounts through credit card company or other group affiliations can lower the cost considerably. If price really matters, check around. Consult the telephone book for all local locations of the companies listed below.

Agencies with offices downtown include: **Avis Rent-A-Car,** 675 Post St., 415/885-5011 or toll-free 800/831-2847; **Budget Rent-A-Car,** 321 Mason, 415/775-5800 or toll-free 800/527-0700;

Dollar Rent-A-Car, 364 O'Farrell (opposite the Hilton Hotel), 415/771-5301 or toll-free 800/800-4000; **Enterprise,** 1133 Van Ness Ave., 415/441-3369 or toll-free 800/736-8222; **Hertz,** 433 Mason, 415/771-2200 or toll-free 800/654-3131; and **Thrifty Rent-A-Car,** 520 Mason (at Post), 415/788-8111 or toll-free 800/367-2277.

For a transportation thrill, all you wannabe easy riders can rent a BMW or Harley-Davidson motorcycle from **Dubbelju Tours & Service,** 271 Clara St., 415/495-2774. Rates start at $92 a day and include insurance, 100 free miles, and road service. Weekly and winter rates available. Open Mon.–Fri. 9 A.M.–noon and 4–6 P.M., Sat. 9 A.M.–noon, or by appointment. German spoken.

Parking Regulations and Curb Colors

If you're driving, it pays to know the local parking regulations as well as rules of the road—it'll cost you if you don't.

Curbing your wheels is the law when parking on San Francisco's hilly streets. What this means: turn your wheels toward the street when parked facing uphill (so your car will roll into the curb if your brakes and/or transmission don't hold), and turn them toward the curb when facing downhill.

Also, pay close attention to painted curb colors; the city parking cops take violations seriously. Red curbs mean absolutely no stopping or parking. Yellow means loading zone (for vehicles with commercial plates only), half-hour time limit; yellow-and-black means loading zone for trucks with commercial plates only, half-hour limit; and green-yellow-and-black means taxi zone. Green indicates a 10-minute parking limit for any vehicle, and white means five minutes only, effective during the operating hours of the adjacent business. As elsewhere in the state, blue indicates parking reserved for vehicles with a California disabled placard or plate displayed. Pay attention, too, to posted street-cleaning parking limits, to time-limited parking lanes (open at rush hour to commuter traffic), and avoid even a quick-park at bus stops or in front of fire hydrants. Any violation will cost $25 or more, and the police can tow your car—which will cost you $100 or so (plus daily impound fees) to retrieve.

Public Transportation: Muni

The city's multifaceted San Francisco Municipal Railway, or Muni, headquartered at 949 Presidio

PARKING AND PARKING GARAGES

If you're driving, you'll need to park. You also need to find parking, all but impossible in North Beach, the Haight, and other popular neighborhoods. San Franciscans have their pet parking theories and other wily tricks—some even consider the challenge of finding parking a sport, or at least a game of chance. But it's not so fun for visitors, who usually find it challenging enough just to find their way around. It's wise to park your car (and leave it parked, to the extent possible), then get around by public transit. Valet parking is available (for a price, usually at least $15 per day) at major and midsize hotels, and at or near major attractions, including shopping districts.

Call ahead to inquire about availability, rates, and hours at major public parking garages, which include: **Fisherman's Wharf,** 665 Beach (at Hyde), 415/673-5197; **Fifth and Mission Garage,** 833 Mission St., 415/982-8522; **Downtown,** Mason and Ellis, 415/771-1400 (ask for the garage); **Moscone Center,** 255 3rd St., 415/777-2782; **Chinatown,** 733 Kearny (underground, near Portsmouth Square), 415/982-6353; and **Union Street,** 1550 Union, 415/673-5728. For general information on city-owned garages, call 415/554-9805.

And good luck.

Ave., 415/673-MUNI weekdays 7 A.M.–5 P.M., Sat.–Sun. 9 A.M.–5 P.M., is still the locals' public transit mainstay. One of the nation's oldest publicly owned transportation systems, Muni is far from feeble, managing to move almost 250 million people each year. Yet even small glitches can wreak havoc when so many people depend on the system; heated criticism regularly crops up on local talk-radio shows and in the Letters to the Editor sections of local newspapers.

The city's buses, light-rail electric subway-and-surface streetcars, electric trolleys, and world-renowned cable cars are all provided by Muni. It costs $2 to ride the cable car. (It's odd that people stand in long lines at the Powell and Market turnaround, since it actually makes much more sense—no waiting, unless there's absolutely no space available—to grab on at Union Square or other spots en route.) Otherwise, regular Muni fare is $1 ($0.35 for seniors and

youths, children under 5 free), exact coins required, and includes free transfers valid for two changes of vehicle in any direction within a two-hour period. If you'll be making lots of trips around town, pick up a multitrip discount Muni Passport (which includes cable car transit), available for sale at the Muni office, the Convention & Visitors Bureau information center downtown, Union Square's TIX box office, the City Hall information booth, and the Cable Car Museum. A one-day pass costs $6, a three-day pass $10, a seven-day pass $15, and a monthly pass $35.

Muni route information is published in the local telephone book yellow pages, or call for route verification (phone number listed above). Better yet, for a thorough orientation, check out one of the various Muni publications, most of which are available wherever Muni Passports are sold (and usually at the Transbay Terminal). A good overview and introduction is provided (free) by the *Muni Access Guide* pamphlet and the useful, seasonally updated *TimeTables,* which list current route and time information for all Muni transit. Especially useful for travelers is Muni's *Tours of Discovery* brochure, which lists popular destinations and possible tours with suggested transit routes (including travel time) and optional transfers and side trips. But the best all-around guide, easy to carry in pocket or purse, is the official annual *Muni Street & Transit Map* ($2), available at bookstores and grocery stores in addition to the usual outlets. The Muni map explains and illustrates major routes, access points, frequency of service, and also shows BART and Muni Metro subway stops, along with the CalTrain route into San Francisco. As a city map, it's a good investment, too.

San Francisco's Muni buses are powered by internal-combustion engines, and each is identified by a number and an area or street name (such as #7 Haight or #29 Sunset). Similarly numbered local trolleys or streetcars are actually electrically operated buses, drawing power from overhead lines, and are most notable downtown and along the steepest routes. The summers-only Historic Trolley Festival is actually a do-it-yourself party, achieved by climbing aboard Muni's international fleet of vintage electric streetcars (F-Market) that start at the Transbay Terminal and run along Market St. to and from Castro.

The Muni Metro refers to the five-line system of streetcars or light-rail vehicles, often strung together into trains of up to four cars, that run underground along Market St. and radiate out into the neighborhoods. Metro routes are identified by letters in conjunction with point of destination (J-Church, K-Ingleside, L-Taraval, M-Oceanview, and N-Judah).

Public Transportation: BART

The Bay Area's space-age, 95-mile Bay Area Rapid Transit, or BART, system headquartered in Oakland, 510/464-6000 or 650/992-2278 (transit information), calls itself "the tourist attraction that gets people to the other tourist attractions." Fair enough. Heck, it is pretty thrilling to zip across to Oakland and Berkeley underwater in the Transbay Tube. And at least as far as it goes, BART is a good get-around alternative for people who would rather not drive. Currently, there isn't much BART service on the San Francisco side of the Bay, with 10 BART stations in San Francisco, the line ending at Colma. Some day in the not-too-distant future, a line will extend south to the airport; work is underway and is expected to be completed in 2001. But the system can take you to Oakland/Berkeley, then north to Richmond, south to Fremont, or east to Pittsburg or Pleasanton. (BART Express buses extend transit service to other East Bay communities.)

Helpful publications include the annual *All About BART* (with fares, travel times, and other details), *Fun Goes Farther on BART,* and the *BART & Buses* BART guide to connections with the bus system. BART trains operate Mon.–Fri. 4 A.M.–midnight, Sat. 6 A.M.–midnight, and Sun. 8 A.M.–midnight. Exact fare depends upon your destination, but it'll be $4.75 or less. For a special $3.90 "excursion fare," you can tour the whole system; just don't walk through the computerized exits, or you'll have to pay again before you get back on. Tickets are dispensed at machines based at each station. (Change machines, for coins or dollar bills, are nearby.) If you don't have a current Muni map, you can get your bearings at each station's color-keyed wall maps, which show destinations and routes.

THE SAN FRANCISCO BAY AREA

"Everything in life is somewhere else, and you get there in a car," writer E. B. White once observed. And so it is, for the most part, once outside San Francisco with one's sights set on the wilds, scrambling through the urban and suburban fringe surrounding the bay. Worth exploring in its almost endless urbanism, the Bay Area

also has its own wildness and wayside pleasures. As White also said: "I would feel more optimistic about a bright future for man if he spent less time proving that he can outwit Nature and more time tasting her sweetness and respecting her seniority." The San Francisco Bay Area offers ample opportunity for both.

SOUTH FROM SAN FRANCISCO

Sticking out into the Golden Gate like an aristocratic nose is the city and county of San Francisco, the northern tip of the San Francisco Peninsula. South of the city along the San Mateo County coastline is **Daly City,** its hillside neighborhoods almost immediately recognizable as the inspiration for Malvina Reynolds's "Little Boxes" lyrics: "And they're all made out of ticky tacky and they all look just the same." Smaller communities, including **Pacifica** and **Half Moon Bay,** pop up alongside the string of state beaches that continue down the coast as far as the

northern elephant seal refuge at Año Nuevo. Just inland from the coast near San Andreas Lake is Sweeney Ridge, a small nugget among the parks collected into the Bay Area's Golden Gate National Recreation Area.

South of the city along the shores of San Francisco Bay are **Brisbane** (which merges with Daly City) and undeveloped San Bruno Mountain County Park. Continuing south, you'll pass a stretch of the San Francisco Bay National Wildlife Refuge and a slew of bayside communities stretching into Santa Clara County. A bit farther is the heart of

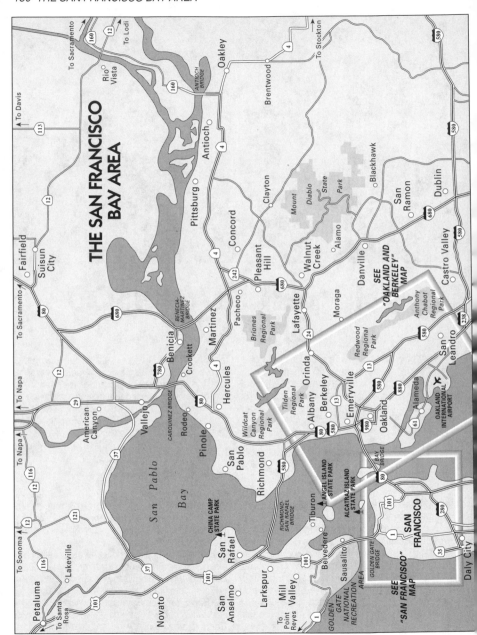

THE SAN FRANCISCO BAY AREA

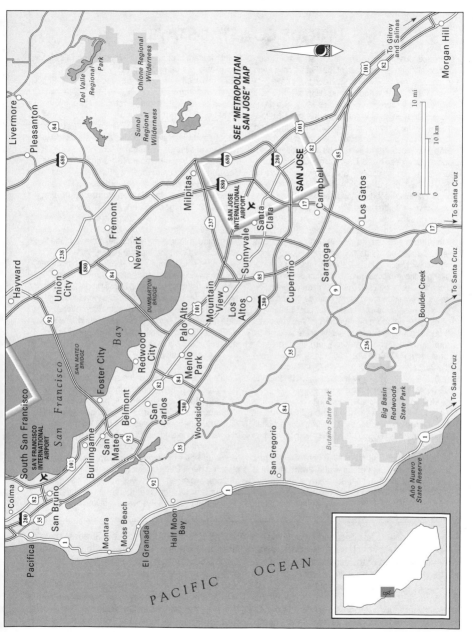

© AVALON TRAVEL PUBLISHING, INC.

UNIQUE COASTAL STAYS

Some serious creature comforts are establishing themselves along the coast south of San Francisco, a trend that was undeniable when Half Moon Bay's new, 261-room Ritz-Carlton resort—complete with two 18-hole golf courses—opened in December 2000. Also pretty "luxe"—and unusual in the nature getaway category—is the fairly new **Costanoa Coastal Lodge and Camp** on the coast near Pescadero, an hour south of San Francisco. In addition to its sophisticated 40-room lodge, deluxe traditional cabins, luxurious "camp bathroom" comfort stations, and gourmet-grub General Store, Costanoa also offers the nation's first "boutique camping resort." Though some RV and pitch-your-own-tent campsites are available, most of the camping provided is tent camping—in 1930s-style canvas "safari tents," complete with skylights, that range from economy to luxury. Deluxe tent cabins feature queen-size beds, heated mattress pads, nightstands with reading lamps, and Adirondack chairs for taking in the great outdoors. And nature is the main attraction. Costanoa itself, near Año Nuevo State Reserve, is linked to four nearby state parks and some 30,000 miles of hiking trails. Other possible adventures here include mountain biking, sea kayaking, tidepooling, whale-watching, elephant seal observation, and bird-watching. For more information, contact: Costanoa, P.O. Box 842, 2001 Rossi Rd. (at Hwy. 1), Pescadero, CA 94060, 650/879-1100 or toll-free 800/738-7477 for reservations, fax 650/879-2275, www.costanoa.com. Budget-Luxury.

Much more affordable—and quite appealing in a back-to-basics style—are the two lighthouse hostels offered in California by Hostelling International-American Youth Hostels (HI-AYH), both located on the coast south of San Francisco.

Just north of Half Moon Bay between Montara and Moss Beach is picturesque **Point Montara Lighthouse Hostel,** 16th St. at Hwy. 1 in Montara, 650/728-7177 (for phone-tree reservations, call toll-free 800/909-4776, #64), www.norcalhostels.org.

Point Montara is popular with bicyclists, and it's also accessible via bus from the Bay Area. The 1875 lighthouse itself is no longer in operation, and the Fog Signal Building here is now a roomy woodstove-heated community room. Hostel facilities include kitchens, dining rooms, laundry, bunkrooms, and couples' and family quarters. Volleyball court, outdoor hot tub, and bicycle rentals also available. Open to travelers of all ages. Reserve in advance: $12 AYH members, $15 nonmembers (extra charge for couples or family accommodations). Budget. Ask at the office for referrals to local restaurants.

Farther south is the **Pigeon Point Lighthouse Hostel,** 210 Pigeon Point Rd. (at Hwy. 1) in Pescadero, 650/879-0633 (for phone-tree reservations, call toll-free 800/909-4776, #73), www.pigeonpointlighthouse.org—the inexpensive place to stay while visiting the elephant seals. Named after the clipper ship *Carrier Pigeon,* one of many notorious shipwrecks off the coastal shoals here, the 1872 lighthouse is now automated but still impressive with its Fresnel lens and distinctive 10-second flash pattern. Lighthouse tours (40 minutes) are offered by state park staff every weekend year-round, and also on Fri. in summer; rain cancels. Small fee. For tour reservations, call 650/879-2120.

The hostel itself is made up of four former family residences for the U.S. Coast Guard—basic male or female bunkrooms, plus some spartan couples' and family rooms. The old Fog Signal Building is now a rec room; there's also a hot tub perched on rocky cliffs above surging surf. Fabulous sunset views, wonderful tidepools. Rates: $13 HI-AYH members, $16 nonmembers, kids half-price with own parent(s). Extra charge for couples'/family rooms and for linen rental (in lieu of bringing your own sleep sack or sleeping bag). Budget. Get groceries in Pescadero and prepare meals in the well-equipped communal kitchens, or ask for local restaurant suggestions. Very popular, so reserve well in advance.

high-tech Silicon Valley, its suburbs spreading out like printed circuits from hard-driving **San Jose.**

South from San Francisco along the peninsula's inland spine is **Colma,** an incorporated city inside Daly City where the dead outnumber the living by more than 2,000 to one, due to Colma's cemetery industry. Among the city of the dead's most famous residents are gunfighter Wyatt Earp,

riveted-blue-jeans creator Levi Strauss, sculptor Benjamin Bufano, and baseball batting champ Lefty O'Doul, whose gravestone lists his statistics and this comment: "He was here at a good time and had a good time while he was here."

After the one-time dairy town of **Millbrae** comes down-to-the-bayshore **Burlingame** (the West's first community dedicated to the country club

CALIFORNIA DEPARTMENT OF PARKS & RECREATION

the popular
Point Montara
Lighthouse Hostel

lifestyle) and very highbrow Hillsborough, founded in 1851 by a deserter from the British Navy, just north of **San Mateo.** San Mateo spreads into **Belmont,** which collides with **San Carlos** and the outskirts of **Redwood City,** named for its brisk business, historically, as a redwood-lumber port. **Atherton,** nearby **Menlo Park,** and **East Palo Alto** all stand in the intellectual shadow of **Palo Alto,** home of California's prestigious Stanford University and the contentious Hoover Institution.

PACIFICA TO HALF MOON BAY

The unstable wave-whipped coast south of San Francisco is all buff-colored bluffs and sandy beaches faced with rough rocks. Often foggy in summer, the coastline in winter is crowded with bird- and whale-watchers. But from late summer into autumn, the weather is usually good and the crowds minimal, making this the perfect time for a superb escape. Though wetsuit-clad surfers brave the snarling swells even in gale-force winds, swimming is dangerous even on serene sunny days due to treacherous undertows. Many of the region's beaches are officially accessible as state beaches or local beach parks; others are state-owned and undeveloped, or privately owned. Almost 20 miles of this 51-mile-long coastline are included as part of the **San Mateo Coast State Beaches,** 650/726-8819, starting with Daly City's **Thornton Beach** (popular for fishing and picnicking) in the north and ending with tiny **Bean Hollow State Beach** just north of Año Nuevo in the south. Though campgrounds are available inland, seaside public camping is possible only at Half Moon Bay State Beach, 650/726-8820.

Pacifica is the self-proclaimed Fog Capital of California, sometimes a dreary place. But the locals make up for the opaque skies with *attitude.* Come here in late September for the annual **Pacific Coast Fog Fest,** which features a Fog Calling Contest (almost everyone's a winner), the Phileas Fogg Balloon Races, high-octane alcoholic "fogcutters" (if drinking, *don't* drive off into the fog), plus a fog fashion show. When the weather's sunny, the town offers superb coastal views. And good food abounds here—fog or shine. At **Sharp Park State Beach** along Beach Blvd. (reached from Hwy. 1 via Paloma Ave., Clarendon Rd., or streets in between) is the **Pacifica Pier,** popular for fishing and winter whale-watching. For more information on the area, including places to stay and eat, call the **Pacifica Chamber of Commerce** at 650/355-4122, or try www.pacificachamber.com.

Farther south is sort-of-secluded **Rockaway Beach,** a striking black-sand beach in a small rectangular cove where the coast has backed away from the rocky bluffs. Hotels and restaurants cluster beyond the rock-reinforced parking lot. Long and narrow **Montara State Beach** offers hiking and rock-and-sand beachcombing. The state's tiny **Gray Whale Cove Beach** here is a concession-operated clothing-optional beach, open for all-over tans only to those 18

ELEPHANT SEALS AND
AÑO NUEVO STATE RESERVE

South from San Francisco via Hwy. 1 and about 20 miles north of Santa Cruz is the 4,000-acre Año Nuevo State Reserve, breeding ground and rookery for sea lions and seals—particularly the unusual (and once nearly extinct) northern elephant seals. The pendulous proboscis of a "smiling" two- to three-ton alpha bull dangles down like a fire hose, so the name is apt.

Hunted almost to extinction for their oil-rich blubber, northern elephant seals numbered only 20–100 at the turn of the 20th century. All these survivors lived on Isla de Guadalupe off the west coast of Baja California, Mexico. Their descendants eventually began migrating north to California. In the 1950s, a few arrived at Año Nuevo Island, attracted to its rocky safety. The first pup was born on the island in the 1960s. By 1975, the mainland dunes had slowly been colonized by seals crowded off the island rookery, and the first pup was born onshore. By 1988, 800 northern elephant seals were born on the mainland, part of a total known population of more than 80,000 and an apparent ecological success story. (Only time will tell, though, since the species' genetic diversity has been eliminated by their swim at the brink of extinction.) Though Año Nuevo was the first northern elephant seal rookery to be established on the California mainland, northern elephant seals are now establishing colonies elsewhere along the state coastline.

The Año Nuevo Mating Season

Male northern elephant seals start arriving in December. Since the males are biologically committed to conserving their energy for sex, they spend much of their time lying about as if dead, in or out of the water, often not even breathing for stretches of up to a half hour. Not too exciting for spectators. But when two males battle each other for the "alpha" title, the bellowing, often bloody nose-to-nose battles are something to see. Arching up with heads back and canine teeth ready to tear flesh, the males bellow and bark and bang their chests together.

In January, the females start to arrive, ready to bear offspring conceived the previous year. They give birth to their pups within the first few days of their arrival. For every two pounds in body weight a pup gains, its mother loses a pound. Within 28 days, she loses about half her weight, then, almost shriveled, she leaves. Her pup, about 60 pounds at birth, weighs 300–500 pounds a month later. Although inseminated by the bull before leaving the rookery, the emaciated female is in no condition for another pregnancy, so "conception" is actually delayed for several months, allowing the female to feed and regain her strength. Then, after an eight-month gestation period, the cycle starts all over again.

Año Nuevo Etiquette

The Marine Mammal Act of 1972 prohibits people from harassing or otherwise disturbing these magnificent sea mammals, so be respectful. While walking among the elephant seals, remember that the seemingly sluglike creatures are wild beasts and can move as fast as any human across the sand, though for shorter distances. For this reason, keeping a 20-foot minimum distance between you and the seals—especially during the macho mating season—is important.

Information and Tours

Official 2.5-hour guided tours of Año Nuevo begin in December and continue through March, rain or shine, though January and February are the prime months and reservations are necessary. The reserve is open 8 A.M. –sunset. Tour tickets are available only through ReserveAmerica's Año Nuevo and Hearst Castle reservations line, toll-free 800/444-4445. Reservations cannot be made before November 1. To take a chance on no-shows, arrive at Año Nuevo before scheduled tours and get on the waiting list. The reserve's "equal access boardwalk" across the sand makes it possible for physically challenged individuals to see the seals. For wheelchair access reservations, beginning Dec. 1 call 650/879-2033, 1–4 P.M. only, on Monday, Wednesday, and Friday. For more information, contact: Año Nuevo State Reserve, New Year's Creek Rd., Pescadero, CA 94060, 650/879-2027 (24-hour recorded information) or 650/879-2025 (reserve office, open weekdays 8:30 A.M. –4 P.M.), www.anonuevo.org.

and over. Just south of Montara proper is the cypress-strewn **Moss Beach** area, named for the delicate sea mosses that drape shoreline rocks at low tide. Best for exploration Nov.–Jan. are the 30 acres of tidepools at the **James V. Fitzgerald Marine Reserve** (open daily from sunrise to sunset), which stretches south from Montara Point to Pillar Point and Princeton-by-the-Sea. At high tide, the Fitzgerald Reserve looks like any old sandy beach with a low shelf of black rocks emerging along the shore, but when the ocean rolls back, these broad rock terraces and their impressive tidepools are exposed. For area state park information, call 415/330-6300. Nearby, along Hwy. 1 in Montara, are **McNee Ranch State Park** and Montara Mountain, with hiking trails and great views of the Pacific. Next south is **El Granada**, an unremarkable town except for the remarkable music showcased by the **Bach Dancing & Dynamite Society,** 311 Mirada Rd. (technically in Miramar), 650/726-4143, the longest-running venue for jazz greats in the Bay Area.

Known until the turn of the century as Spanishtown, Half Moon Bay was a farm community settled by Italians and Portuguese, and specializing in artichokes and brussels sprouts. Fast becoming a fashionable Bay Area residential suburb, these days Half Moon Bay is famous for its pumpkins and offers a rustic Main Street with shops, restaurants, and inns, plus pseudo–Cape Cod cluster developments along Hwy. 1. Come for the **Half Moon Bay Art & Pumpkin Festival** in October, where pumpkin-carving and pumpkin pie-eating contests as well as the Great Pumpkin Parade take center stage. For a complete list of area events, places to stay, places to eat, and other information, contact the **Half Moon Bay/Coast-side Chamber of Commerce,** 520 Kelly Ave., Half Moon Bay, CA 94019, 650/726-5202 or 650/726-8380, www.halfmoonbaychamber.org.

Just a few miles south of Half Moon Bay off Pillar Point and legendary among extreme surfers is **Mavericks,** home of the world's baddest wave. When surf's up here, during wild winter storms, Mavericks creates mean and icy 35-foot waves—mean enough to break bones and boards. Nearby **Burleigh Murray Ranch State Park** is still largely undeveloped, but the former 1,300-acre dairy ranch is now open to the public for day use and hiking.

FROM SAN GREGORIO SOUTH

On the coast just west of tiny San Gregorio is **San Gregorio State Beach,** with the area's characteristic bluffs, a mile-long sandy beach, and a

GOING COASTAL

From south of Half Moon Bay to Santa Cruz, people will be able to go coastal in perpetuity, thanks in large part to the recent land acquisition efforts of the Peninsula Open Space Trust (POST). Thousands and thousands of acres on and near the coast are now protected from the possibility of development; some parcels are under the jurisdiction of the California Department of Parks and Recreation or other agencies, and many are open to the public (or soon will be) for day use.

Among these is **Cowell Ranch Beach** just south of Half Moon Bay, 650/726-8819, where a half-mile trail leads out to the point, and stairs trail down to a well-protected sandy beach.

Gazos Creek Beach, 650/879-2025, with its abundant tidepools, is now included within Año Nuevo State Reserve. The reserve also includes the 2,914 acres of **Cascade Ranch,** which adjoins Big Basin and Butano State Parks. Only a dream in years past, it's now possible to hike from the redwoods to the sea via the associated **Whitehouse Ridge Trail.** The result of one of the largest land deals ever negotiated by POST, one day the hiking and equestrian trails within the 5,638-acre Cloverdale Coastal Ranch south of Half Moon Bay will also be included in the new coastal parks landscape.

Just north of Santa Cruz, the 2,305-acre **Gray Whale Ranch** now part of **Wilder Ranch State Park,** 650/426-0505, was donated by the Save-the-Redwoods League and the Packard Foundation. A key wildlife corridor, the new ranch lands offer hiking and mountain-biking trails.

sandbar at the mouth of San Gregorio Creek. San Gregorio proper is little more than a spot in the road, but the back-roads route via Stage Rd. from here to Pescadero is pastoral and peaceful.

Inland Pescadero ("Fishing Place") was named for the creek's once-teeming trout, not for any fishing traditions on the part of the town's Portuguese settlers. Both **Pomponio** and **Pescadero State Beaches** offer small estuaries for same-named creeks. The 584-acre **Pescadero Marsh Natural Preserve** is a successful blue heron rookery, as well as a feeding and nesting area for more than 200 other bird species. (To bird-watch—best in winter—park at **Pescadero**

State Beach near the bridge and walk via the Sequoia Audubon Trail, which starts below the bridge.) Rocky-shored **Bean Hollow State Beach,** a half-mile hike in, is better for tidepooling than beachcombing, though it has picnic tables and a short stretch of sand.

For a longer coast walk, head south to the **Año Nuevo State Reserve.** (Año Nuevo Point was named by Vizcaíno and crew shortly after New Year's Day in 1602.) The rare northern elephant seals who clamber ashore here are an item only in winter and spring, but stop here any time of year for a picnic and a stroll along Año Nuevo's three-mile-long beach.

Five miles inland from Año Nuevo State Reserve is **Butano State Park,** 650/879-2040, which offers 20 miles of excellent if strenuous hikes among redwoods, plus picnicking, camping, and summer campfire programs. Another worthy redwoods destination is **San Mateo Memorial County Park,** 9500 Pescadero Rd. (eight miles east of Pescadero), 650/879-0238, which features a nature museum, 200-foot-tall virgin trees, creek swimming, camping, and trails connecting with surrounding local and state parks. Adjacent **Pescadero Creek County Park** (same address and phone) includes the steelhead trout stream's upper watersheds—6,000 acres of excellent hiking. The Old Haul Rd. and Pomponio Trails link Pescadero to nearby Memorial and Portola Parks.

SILICON CITIES

Characteristic of the San Francisco region, most Peninsula and South Bay communities offer up culture in surprising, usually delightful ways. In Palo Alto, hometown of Stanford University, cultural creativity is concentrated and always accessible—making this a choice destination when climbing down out of the hills. This is the place, after all, where the Silicon Valley computer revolution started—where, in the 1930s, Bill Hewlett and Dave Packard, founders of modern-day Hewlett-Packard, started their spare-time tinkering with electronic bells, whistles, and other gadgetry in a garage on Addison Avenue. (Their first creation was the audio oscillator, a sound-enhancing system first used by Walt Disney in *Fantasia,* which catapulted the inventive duo

into the corporate big leagues.) Most people these days, however, think of San Jose and vicinity as the heart of Silicon Valley.

Seeing and Doing Palo Alto

The northernmost city in Santa Clara County, Palo Alto is not a typical tourist destination, which is in itself a major attraction for those tired of prepackaged community charm.

A major attraction is 9,000-acre **Stanford University,** once known as The Farm, formerly Leland Stanford's spacious spread for thoroughbred racehorses. Some people now refer to Stanford as The Idea Farm, since this is the place that spawned birth-control pills, gene splicing, heart transplants, the IQ test, the laser, the microprocessor, music synthesizers, and napalm—among other breakthroughs of the civilized world. Royalties from on-campus inventiveness earn private Stanford University millions of dollars each year. The sprawling Spanish-style campus, designed by famed landscape architect Frederick Law Olmsted (designer of New York City's Central Park), is much too large to tour on foot; use a bike or the free Marguerite Shuttle. A good place to start is the campus quadrangle, where undergraduate students mill around between classes (some perhaps still proudly wearing T-shirts announcing the student body's unofficial motto: Work, Study, Get Rich). Before arriving, get a campus map and other Internet information at www.stanford.edu; once arrived, try the 2nd floor of the Tresidder Student Union, 650/723-4311. For a fairly comprehensive one-hour general campus walking tour, contact **Stanford University Guide and Visitor Service,** Building 170, 650/723-2560. Finely focused tours of the **Stanford Linear Accelerator Center,** home of the quark, are led by graduate students; call 650/926-3300 or 650/926-2204 for information and appointments. Also visit the **Iris & B. Gerald Cantor Center for the Visual Arts,** Museum Way and Lomita Dr., 650/723-4177, home to the world's second largest collection of Rodin works, after only the Musée Rodin in Paris.

Palo Alto-Stanford (PASt) Heritage, 650/299-8878, offers guided one-hour walking tours of Palo Alto, either downtown or "Professorville." Both areas are included on the National Register of Historic Districts. It's also fun to just stroll around downtown. Some of Palo Alto's best attractions are its bookstores, from **Megabooks,** 444 University Ave., 650/326-4730 (good used books) and the **Stanford Bookstore** just down the street at 135 University, 650/614-0280, to **Chiméra Books and Records,** 165 University, 650/327-1122, noted for its great selection of new and used poetry. **Bell's Books,** 536 Emerson, 650/323-7822, is a Palo Alto classic—a time-honored book emporium stacked floor to ceiling with both new and used volumes. **Printers Inc.,** 310 California Ave., 650/327-6500, is a café and bookstore all in one.

Near Palo Alto, Menlo Park is home to the West Coast lifestyle-establishing institution of **Sunset** magazine, 80 Willow Rd. (at Middlefield), 650/321-3600. The gorgeous gardens at **Sunset** are open to the public weekdays 8:30 A.M.–4:30 P.M. Also in Menlo Park is the **U.S. Geological Survey map center,** 345 Middlefield Rd., 650/329-4390. For earthquake information, call the survey office at 650/329-4025 or visit their website at quake.wr.usgs.gov.

For more area information, including a current listing of member restaurants and accommodations, contact the **Palo Alto Chamber of Commerce,** 325 Forest Ave., 650/324-3121, www.batnet.com/pacc.

Seeing and Doing San Jose

Once thickly forested in oaks, the vast Santa Clara Valley was quickly converted to farmland by the early settlers. Even within recent memory, the valley was one continuous orchard of almonds, apples, apricots, peaches, cherries, pears, and prunes where blossom snow fell from February into April. Now unofficially known as Silicon Valley—in honor of the computer chip and its attendant industry—these fertile soils today grow houses, office buildings, and shopping malls—all tied together by frightening freeways.

Sunny San Jose, more or less in the middle of it all, though aptly described as "all edges in search of a center," is the biggest city in Northern California, and was the state's first capital following American territorial occupation. Typical of the Bay Area gentrification trend, the city's decrepit downtown—more or less defined as the plaza area near San Carlos and Market Sts.—has been swept clean of derelicts and the otherwise down-and-out.

IT WAS A DARK AND STORMY NIGHT . . . IN SAN JOSE

Though others in the Bay Area taunt San Jose for its all-too-contemporary concrete and its apparent lack of community, the area has many merits—one being a good sense of humor. While Palo Alto enshrines the memory of Ernest Hemingway, and Oakland honors its native-born Gertrude Stein, San Jose honors the badly written novel. Launched by professor Scott Rice, San Jose State University's Bulwer-Lytton ("It was a dark and stormy night . . .") Fiction Contest attracts 10,000 or more entries each year for its Worst Possible Opening Sentence competition. Among earlier entries: "She was like the driven snow beneath the galoshes of my lust" (Larry Bennett, Chicago) and "We'd made it through yet another nuclear winter and the lawn had just trapped and eaten its first robin" (Kyle J. Spiller, Garden Grove). The contest's 1999 Purple Prose Award winner, by David Hirsch of Seattle, describes a phenomenon he no doubt knows well: "Rain—violent torrents of it, rain like fetid water from a God-sized pot of pasta strained through a sky-wide colander, rain as Noah knew it, flaying the shuddering trees, whipping the white-capped waters, violating the sodden firmament, purging purity and filth alike from the land, rain without mercy, without surcease, incontinent rain, turning to intermittent showers overnight with partial clearing Tuesday."

For an anthology of the best of the contest's worst writing, look for Penguin's *It Was a Dark and Stormy Night: The Final Conflict.*

As a friendly destination for families and businessfolk alike, the new downtown San Jose is astounding. The unofficial and striking centerpiece is the towering 541-room **Fairmont Hotel,** part of the city's Silicon Valley Financial Complex, which also includes a 17-story office tower, an apartment complex, and a retail pavilion. Market Street's **Plaza de César Chávez,** the original center of the Pueblo of San Jose, is almost like the Fairmont's private front lawn, with walkways, benches, and a dancing-water fountain. Not far away, at Market St. and Viola Ave., is the city's downtown **San Jose McEnery Convention Center,** a 425,000-square-foot, $140 million project that augments existing convention facilities

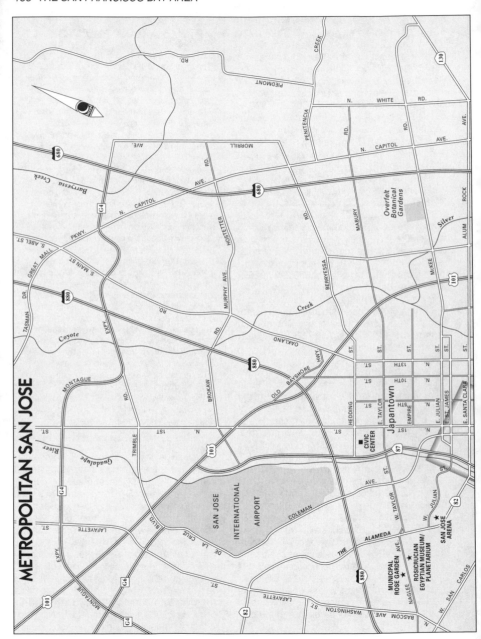

METROPOLITAN SAN JOSE

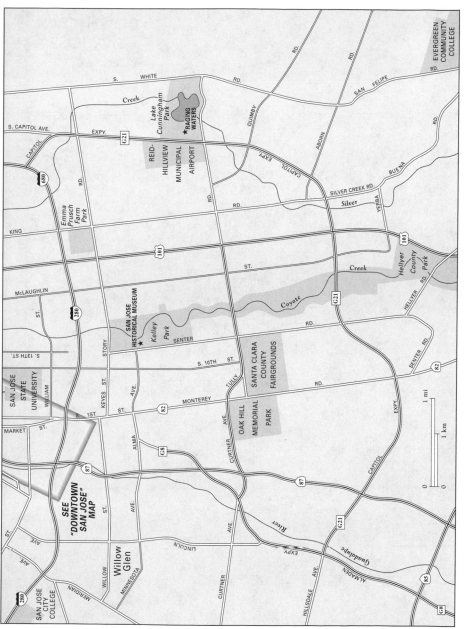

© AVALON TRAVEL PUBLISHING, INC.

DOWNTOWN SAN JOSE

W. JULIAN ST.

87

N. JULIAN ST.

SANTA CLARA COUNTY COURTHOUSE

THOMAS FALLON HOUSE

PERALTA ADOBE

San Pedro Square

HOTEL DE ANZA

W. SANTA CLARA

Confluence Point

POST

W. SAN FERNANDO

McEnery Park

CENTER FOR PERFORMING ARTS

SAN JOSE CONVENTION & VISITORS BEREAU

87

Guadalupe River Park

Discovery Meadow

CHILDREN'S DISCOVERY MUSEUM

E. ST. JAMES ST.

Saint James Park

E. ST. JOHN ST.

E. SANTA CLARA

ST. JOSEPH'S CATHEDRAL

SAN JOSE MUSEUM OF ART

FAIRMONT HOTEL

Plaza de César Chávez

TECH MUSEUM OF INNOVATION

CIVIC AUDITORIUM

CROWNE PLAZA

MARTIN LUTHER KING JR. LIBRARY

SAN JOSE HILTON

SAN JOSE MCENERY CONVENTION CENTER

E. SAN FERNANDO

MUSEUM OF QUILTS AND TEXTILES

DE SAN ANTONIO

PASEO

E. SAN CARLOS

HYATT SAINTE CLAIRE

SoFA District

SAN SALVADORE

E. WILLIAM ST.

Parque de los Pobladores

W. REED

SAN JOSE STATE UNIVERSITY

280

0   200 yds
0   200 m

280

87

VINE

ALMADEN

VIRGINIA

© AVALON TRAVEL PUBLISHING, INC.

and the **Center for Performing Arts.** Other hotels surrounding the Convention Center—including the Crowne Plaza San Jose, the San Jose Hilton and Towers, and the refurbished historic Hotel De Anza and Hyatt Sainte Claire—help make the area attractive to conventioneers.

Families and other travelers will enjoy downtown's variety of museums—including the **Tech Museum of Innovation,** 201 S. Market St. (at Park), 408/795-6100 or 408/294-8324, www.thetech.org; the **Children's Discovery Museum,** 180 Woz Way, 408/298-5437; and the **San Jose Museum of Art,** 110 S. Market St. (at San Fernando St.), 408/294-2787, www.sjmusart.org. Nearby **San Jose State University,** between E. San Fernando and E. San Salvador Sts. at

SARAH WINCHESTER'S MYSTERY HOUSE

Though somewhat expensive for voyeuristic time travel, at least once in a lifetime everyone should visit the beautifully bizarre **Winchester Mystery House,** 525 S. Winchester Blvd. (west of downtown San Jose at Hwy. 17 and I-280), 408/247-2101. A six-acre monument to one woman's obsession, built up from eight rooms by Sarah L. Winchester and now a state historic monument, this labyrinth of crooked corridors, doors opening into space, and stairs leading nowhere includes 40 stairways, some 2,000 doors and trapdoors in strange places, and 10,000 or so windows. (Though only 160 rooms survive, 750 interconnecting chambers once testified to Winchester's industriousness.)

A sudden widow and heir to the Winchester firearms fortune, the lady of the house was convinced by a medium that she was cursed by her "blood money" and the spirits of all those shot by Winchester rifles, but that she would never die as long as she kept up her construction work. So Sarah Winchester spent $5.5 million of the family fortune to create and re-create her Gothic Victorian, working feverishly for 38 years straight. But death eventually came knocking on her door anyway, and the around-the-clock racket of workers' hammers and saws finally ceased.

At least, that's the official version of the story, the one that draws the crowds to this amazing mansion. But others, including her personal attorney, recall Sarah Winchester as quite sane, a clear-headed businesswoman who actively managed her vast holdings and estate. According to a 1923 *San Jose Mercury News* interview with Roy F. Leib, Winchester reconstructed the house "due to her desire to provide accommodations for her many relatives who she thought would come to California to visit her." And she stopped work on the house long before her death; according to Leib's records, she hired no more carpenters after the 1906 earthquake. The wild stories about Winchester's eccentricities, Leib suggested, grew out of her extreme reclusiveness,

which may have been related to severe arthritis and limb deformities.

In any event, the lady of the house was quite a woman. People tend to focus on Sarah Winchester's craziness, but—once here—it's hard not to be impressed by her creativity and craft as an impromptu architect.

The estate is open daily except Christmas. In summer, it opens at 9 A.M., with the last tour departing at 7 P.M.; reduced hours the rest of the year. The Estate Tour costs $13.95 general, $10.95 seniors, $7.95 children ages 6–12. The Behind the Scenes Tour costs $10.95 adults, $9.95 seniors. A combined tour costs $21.95 general, $18.95 seniors. Children under 12 are not permitted on the Behind the Scenes or combined tours.

ROBERT HOLMES/CALTOUR

S. 4th St., is home to the unique **Center for Beethoven Studies and Museum.** Not far away is San Jose's artsy **SoFA** neighborhood, a blend of galleries, small theaters, and coffee joints located in the South of First (St.) Area.

San Jose's most popular tourist attraction is the **Rosicrucian Egyptian Museum,** 1342 Naglee Ave. (at Park Ave.), 408/947-3635, a temple of possibilities (in the California tradition) set up in a parklike setting open to all. The Egyptian Museum includes outdoor statuary and the largest collection of Assyrian, Babylonian, and Egyptian artifacts in the western United States: amulets and charms, mummies, musical instruments, a life-sized walk-through replica of a pyramid tomb (guided tours every half hour), and other artifacts in the mystical mode. Also here is the **Rosicrucian Planetarium,** built in 1936, which has been closed for major repairs; call to inquire about its reopening date.

For more information about the San Jose area, including food and lodgings as well as area wineries and other diversions, contact the excellent **San Jose Convention & Visitors Bureau,** downtown at 333 W. San Carlos St., Ste. 1000, San Jose, CA 95110, 408/295-9600, toll-free 800/800-7522 or 888/726-5673, www.sanjose.org. The visitors bureau also sponsors three Visitor Information Centers, one in the lobby of the San Jose McEnery Convention Center (408/977-0900), the others inside Terminal C and the new Terminal A at the San Jose International Airport.

Adventures Near San Jose
Distract the kids with the waterslides and pools at **Raging Waters** at Lake Cunningham Regional Park east of I-680 on Tully Rd. off Capitol Expressway. The 14-acre theme park has more than 30 waterslides in a tropical atmosphere. Admission is $21.99 general; $17.99 seniors over 60 and kids under 42 inches tall; $3 off after 3 P.M.; under 3 free. Call 408/654-5450 for more information.

Top gun wannabes swoop down on **Fightertown USA** just off Hwy. 101 in Mountain View, 1625 N. Shoreline Blvd., 650/254-7325, www.caladventures.com/fightertown, a virtual reality adventure complete with ersatz jet simulators, aircraft carriers, ready rooms, flight checks, and officers' clubs.

NASA's space-age **Ames Research Center** at Mountain View's Moffett Field, 650/604-6497, features the world's largest wind tunnel and—more modern and certainly appropriate to Silicon Valley—computer-simulated aircraft-safety test facilities. Tours are free; call for current information.

Several miles north of San Jose (via Hwy. 101) in Santa Clara is **Paramount's Great America,** 408/988-1776 (recorded information), www.pgathrills.com, one of the nation's largest family-style amusement parks, with more than 100 rides—some considerably more thrilling than the traditional roller coaster—plus kiddie diversions of all types, live entertainment, shops, and restaurants. Open daily from Memorial Day weekend to Labor Day, otherwise weekends only from late Mar. through May and early Sept. to mid-Oct.

On the western peak of Mount Hamilton to the east of San Jose—reached from downtown via Hwy. 130 (the Alum Rock Ave. extension of E. Santa Clara St., which connects with adventurous Mt. Hamilton Rd.)—is the **Lick Observatory,** 408/274-5061, which has been casting its 36-inch telescopic eye skyward since 1888. The telescope was named for its eccentric gold rush–millionaire benefactor James Lick, who was convinced there was life on the moon. At the time that it was dedicated as part of UC Berkeley's research facilities, the Lick telescope was the world's most powerful and the only one on the planet staffed permanently. Nowadays, the Lick Observatory is administered by UC Santa Cruz, and additional telescopes (including the 120-inch Shane Telescope, built in the 1950s and one of the world's most productive) have been added to this mountaintop astronomy enclave. Excepting major holidays, the observatory is open to the public Mon.–Fri. 12:30–5 P.M., Sat.–Sun. 10 A.M.–5 P.M. Fifteen-minute tours are offered every half hour, starting half an hour after opening and ending at 4:30 P.M.

Also fun for astronomy buffs—considerably farther away, at **Fremont Peak State Park** south of San Juan Bautista—is the 30-inch homemade Kevin Medlock telescope, available to the public for the actual eyes-on experience of stargazing on most new-moon or quarter-moon Sat. nights, Mar.–Oct., weather permitting. No reservations required. Call 831/623-2465 or 831/623-4255 for information. Medlock, a mechanical engineer at the Lawrence Berkeley Laboratory, scrounged up the necessary materials ($2,000 worth) for this project, an amazing accomplishment in itself. Well north of San Jose via I-680, then Mission Blvd. (Hwy. 238) is beautiful **Mission San Jose** at Mission and Washington Blvds. in Fremont, 510/657-1797, open daily 10 A.M.–5 P.M.

for self-guided tours (slide shows on the hour, in the museum). Painstakingly restored at a cost of $5 million, then reopened to the public in 1985, Mission San Jose was once the center of a great cattle-ranching enterprise—a successful Spanish outpost noted also for its Ohlone Indian orchestra. Very evocative, worth a stop.

EAST FROM SAN FRANCISCO

OAKLAND: FINDING "THERE" THERE

Since the job description requires them to say what needs to be said, writers tend to offend. Gertrude Stein, for example, apparently insulted her hometown until the end of time when she described Oakland with the statement "There is no there there"—most likely a lament for the city she no longer recognized. But Oakland later proved Stein wrong by erecting a sculpture to *There,* right downtown on City Square at 13th and Broadway where everyone can see it.

Long bad-rapped as crime-riddled and somehow inherently less deserving than adjacent Berkeley or San Francisco across the bay, Oakland has come a long way, with a booming economy, downtown redevelopment and neighborhood gentrification, and both a thriving port industry and waterfront district to prove it. In many ways, Oakland has become one with Berkeley, with some neighborhoods defined most strongly by shared cultural associations. And the city has become a respectable neighbor to San Francisco, that relationship integrated by accessibility. But Oakland still struggles with its own contradictions. It was the birthplace of the Black Power movement but also home base for the Hell's Angels. It's home to the World Series–winning Oakland A's but also home to one of the most troubled public school systems in the nation. The class distinctions here are obvious; Oakland houses its immigrants and low-income residents in the flatlands while those with money and power live up in the hills. There's definitely a there here, for those who can afford it.

The city was shaken to its roots by the October 1989 Bay Area earthquake, which collapsed a section of the Bay Bridge and flattened a double-decker section of the Nimitz Freeway (I-880) in

the flatlands. No sooner had the city made peace with that disaster than another struck; in October 1991, wildfires raged through the Oakland hills, killing 22 people, torching entire neighborhoods at a cost of some $2 billion, and stripping hills of the luxuriant growth so typical of the area. Though wildflowers and other sturdy survivors sprang back to life with the next spring's rains, these naked neighborhoods have been slow to rebuild. Times have been tough in many areas of Oakland.

And yet, Oakland abides. Blessed with fair weather year-round, excellent health-care services, a generally robust economy, and a good public transportation system, Oakland ranked 24th in *Money* magazine's 1997 survey of the best places to live in the United States. Even political life here seems destined to wake up: in January 1999, new urban visionary and former California governor Jerry Brown was sworn in as Oakland's mayor.

The **Oakland Community and Economic Development Agency,** 250 Frank Ogawa Plaza, Oakland, CA 94612, 510/839-9000 or toll-free 800/262-5526, publishes the slick annual *Destination Oakland,* a fairly comprehensive listing of where to go, eat, and sleep; it's also helpful with other information. The visitors bureau also publishes two newsletter-like tabloids: *Oakland Travel Monthly,* most useful for travelers; and *Oakland Monthly.* Worth the price wherever you find it is *Oakland—A Guide to the Cultural, Architectural, Environmental, and Historic Assets of the City,* a detailed map style guide to the city's major (and minor) attractions. Walk-in **visitor centers** are located in Jack London Square at Broadway and Embarcadero (in the same building as Barnes & Noble), at the **Oakland City Store,** 14th and Broadway, and at the **Oakland Black Chamber Convention & Visitor**

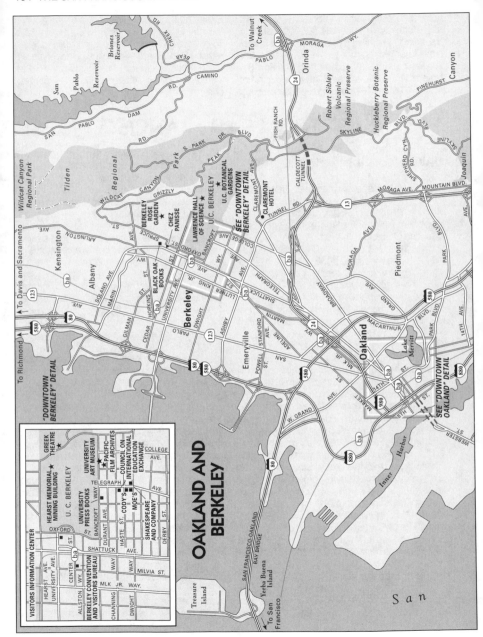

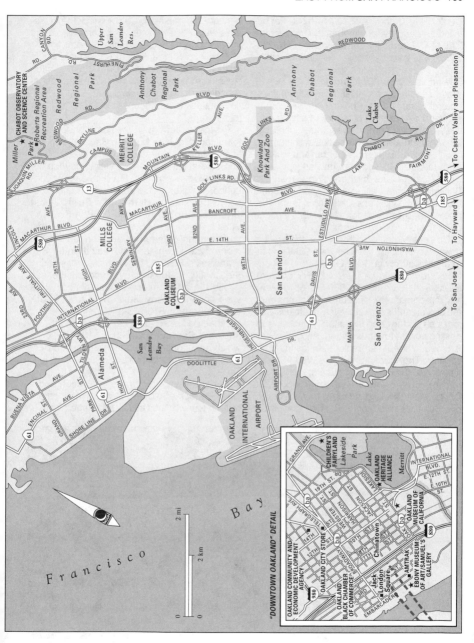

"DOWNTOWN OAKLAND" DETAIL

Center, 117 Broadway, 510/444-5741. For detailed arts and events information, contact the **City of Oakland, Visitor Marketing,** 510/238-2935, or try the city website: oaklandnet.com.

Seeing and Doing Oakland

Water seems to be Oakland's most prominent natural feature. Right downtown, wishbone-shaped **Lake Merritt** is a very unusual urban lake—actually an enclosed saltwater tidal basin. Merritt's **Lakeside Park** includes delightful gardens; the **Rotary Nature Center and Wildlife Refuge,** 552 Bellevue Ave. (at Perkins), a fine nature center and bird sanctuary featuring Buckminster Fuller's first public geodesic dome (now a flight cage); and **Children's Fairyland,** the original inspiration for all the world's theme parks (including Disneyland).

On Lake Merritt's harbor side is the jewel of downtown Oakland, the renowned **Oakland Museum of California,** 1000 Oak St. (at 10th, one block from the Lake Merritt BART Station), 510/238-2200 or toll-free 888/625-6873. Actually three separate museums under one roof, the Oakland Museum creatively examines California art, history, and the natural sciences, suggesting how all are interrelated. Altogether, this is probably the finest regional museum in the country. The museum is open Wed.–Sat. 10 A.M.–5 P.M. (until 9 P.M. on the first Fri. of every month), Sun. noon–5 P.M.; admission is $6 adults, $4 seniors and students, free on the second Sun. of every month. Parking is available

beneath the museum. Call or check the museum's website, www.museumca.org, for current information on special exhibits.

A walk up 10th St. from the Oakland Museum leads straight into thriving **Chinatown** (though "Asiatown" is actually more accurate) east of Broadway, its wide streets packed with authentic restaurants and shops but surprisingly few tourist traps.

On the waterfront where Jack London once toted cargo is **Jack London Square,** a collection of shops and restaurants the twice-defeated Socialist candidate for Oakland mayor probably would have ignored. (Take a peek into Jack London's Yukon Cabin and maybe quaff a couple at the classic **Heinhold's First & Last Chance Saloon,** 56 Jack London Square.) What a shame, for locals and visitors alike, that so many ignore nearby Jack London Village. It's a mystery why anyone would prefer San Francisco's Pier 39, for example, considering the quality of these shops and businesses housed in a former warehouse district. Here you'll find the **Ebony Museum of Art,** 30 Jack London Square, 510/763-0745, a museum and gift shop dedicated to African-American art, and adjacent **Samuel's Gallery,** 510/452-2059, which holds one of the nation's largest collections of African-American posters, original prints, cards, and graphics.

For some architectural appreciation and a close-up look at old and new Oakland, take a walking tour with the **Oakland Heritage Alliance,**

Oakland's lovely Lake Merritt

ROBERT HOLMES/CALTOUR

1418 Lakeside Dr., 510/763-9218. The organization offers various Oakland tours, including an Art Deco Tour, for a small fee—call for a descriptive brochure and to make reservations.

Oakland Outdoors: Into the Hills
Aside from regional parks offering hiking and recreation, the park in Oakland is **Knowland Park and Zoo,** 9777 Golf Links Rd. (off I-580, at 98th St.), 510/632-9523.

In the hills behind Oakland is large **Anthony Chabot Regional Park,** most noted for large Lake Chabot, a peaceful and popular spot for fishing and boating (rentals only). No swimming is allowed, since it's classified as an emergency local water supply. The vast backyard of this 4,700-acre park holds some hidden attractions, including a blue heron rookery and remnants of an old Chinese village. You can also camp here: 73 eucalyptus-shaded sites above Lake Chabot (including 35 walk-in sites), hot showers, flush toilets. To get here, take Castro Valley Blvd. east off I-580, then turn north onto Lake Chabot Boulevard. To reserve camping and picnic sites, call 510/562-2267.

Adjacent to Chabot Park on the north, mushroom-shaped **Redwood Regional Park** offers 1,800 acres of redwood serenity and forest meadows and creeks—wonderful hiking. To get here, take Hwy. 13 to the Redwood Rd. exit, then take Redwood uphill beyond Skyline for two miles to the main entrance.

West of Redwood Regional Park, smaller **Joaquin Miller Park** was named for the irascible writer who once lived on 80 acres here and hoped to establish an artists' colony. At the park's entrance, on the corner of Sanborn Dr. and Joaquin Miller Rd., you can see Miller's small home, The Abbey. The most lasting homage to the poet are the redwood trees here, planted by Miller and now integral to the park, which is said to be the world's only urban redwood forest. (Along with whiskey, women, and poetry, trees were a passion of Joaquin Miller's.)

Joaquin Miller Park is now home to the huge, 80-some-thousand-square-foot **Chabot Observatory and Science Center,** 10000 Skyline Blvd., which boasts several large telescopes, a 270-seat planetarium, a Challenger Center space mission simulation, the Tien MegaDome Science Theater, and three exhibition halls host-ing permanent and traveling exhibits focusing on the natural and physical sciences. For more information, call 510/530-3480 or try www.cosc.org. Other facilities at the park include picnic grounds and an amphitheater.

Nearly surrounded by Redwood and Joaquin Miller Parks is lush **Roberts Regional Recreation Area** off Skyline Blvd., which offers more hiking among the redwoods, as well as picnicking, baseball and volleyball, an outdoor dance floor, and a heated swimming pool equipped with a hoist to assist the disabled in and out of the water.

Just north of this multipark complex, in the hills behind Piedmont, are the wild surprises of **Huckleberry Botanic Regional Preserve.** Though the eucalyptus and logged-over redwoods here testify to the area's disturbance over time, most of the shrubs in this rare-plant community are natives—thriving in the park's unusually protective microclimate. Spring comes early every year, attracting hummingbirds, and autumn comes early too, with still more birds flocking in to harvest berries and nuts. The preserve's narrow path can be almost invisible amid the thickets, yet offers some scenic overviews in spots; more views are gained by looping back on the East Bay Skyline National Trail.

Farther north is **Robert Sibley Volcanic Regional Preserve,** actually the remnants of what was once the East Bay's dominant volcano. Exploring otherwise unimpressive Round Top Peak here is a favorite pastime for amateur and professional geologists alike. To find out why, follow the self-guided trail.

For more information about regional parks here and in nearby Berkeley, contact the East Bay Regional Park District office, 510/635-0135, www.ebparks.org.

Bayshore Parks near Oakland
A few areas along San Francisco and San Pablo Bays offer some respite from modern reality. In Alameda, **Crab Cove Marine Reserve,** McKay near Central, 510/521-6887, offers a nice beach and a visitor center with marine biology exhibits. And while you're in the area, head out to the former Alameda Naval Air Station to view the **USS Hornet,** a World War II–era aircraft carrier now serving as a museum; open daily 10 A.M.–6 P.M. in summer, 10 A.M.–5 P.M. the rest of the year.

Along the eastern edge of the South Bay, the **Don Edwards San Francisco Bay National Wildlife Refuge,** 1 Marshlands Rd. in Fremont, 510/792-0222, usually yields good bird-watching throughout its protected marshes and mudflats. The refuge was renamed in recognition of Congressman Don Edwards's 25-year effort to protect sensitive wetlands in southern San Francisco Bay. The refuge is open for day use only (free).

An intriguing if downcast monument to the past here is the 1876 ghost town of **Drawbridge** near the modern bridge. Once a popular bird-hunting resort (where rotating bridges across Coyote Creek and Warm Springs Slough permitted Southern Pacific trains to pass), Drawbridge died a slow death as both marshland and birds disappeared—the latter partly due to "market hunting," which involved loading and firing cannons with nails and shot to kill 1,000 birds or more with one attack. Today the old town site is accessible only on docent-led guided tours, usually offered May–Oct., Sat. at 10 A.M. Call for reservations.

In the midst of semi-industrial Fremont is an unusual Victorian-era farm park, the only one of its kind in the northstate. **Ardenwood Historical Farm,** 34600 Ardenwood Blvd. (off Hwy. 84), 510/796-0663, is a 200-acre remnant of a major mid-1800s ranch. The highlight here is historic Patterson House mansion, which has been restored by the East Bay Regional Park District to its original, upper-class ambience and features picket fences, period furnishings, and period-clothed character actors. Small admission fee. To get here: from I-880 take the Hwy. 84 (Decoto Rd./Dumbarton Bridge) exit, then exit at Newark Blvd. and follow Ardenwood/ Newark north to the park's entrance.

The bulk of the land once encompassed by the old ranch now makes up nearby **Coyote Hills Regional Park,** noted for its own living-history program—one that re-creates the daily life of the Ohlone people who lived in these salt-marsh grasslands ("Old Ways" workshops are also offered). For more information on ranger-led tours to area shell mounds and other archaeological sights, including a reconstructed Ohlone village, stop by the Coyote Hills Visitor Center, 8000 Patterson Rd. in Fremont, open daily 10 A.M.–5 P.M., or call 510/795-9385. Coyote Hills Regional Park is also a good place to start a

creekside trek along the Alameda Creek Bicycle Path, the longest (12 mile) paved bike trail in the East Bay. Pick up trail and park maps at the visitor center.

Farther north, undeveloped **Hayward Regional Shoreline** (in two separate sections along the bay just north of Hwy. 92) is not particularly appealing—but will be one day, because this is the largest salt-marsh restoration project underway on the West Coast. Though it's much more difficult to reestablish what was so easily destroyed through diking and other diversions of nature, the birds are already coming back.

North of San Pablo and jutting into San Pablo Bay is 2,000-acre **Point Pinole Regional Shoreline,** an area once dedicated to manufacturing dynamite—which explains why there has been no development here—and now an amazement: several miles of pristine bay frontage and salt marshes sheltering rare birds, meadows, and peace.

BERKELEY: BISHOP BERKELEY'S EMPIRE

Berkeley is too casually dismissed as "Berserkley" or the "People's Republic of Berkeley," epithets deriding fairly recent historical trends. Berkeley, after all, was named for evangelist Bishop Berkeley of Ireland, who crossed the great waters to save wild America from itself with the cry: "Westward, the course of empire takes its way." The course of empire in Berkeley, however, veered off to the left. That trend began in the 1930s, was sparked anew in the '60s with Mario Savio and the Free Speech Movement, and ignited during years of anti–Vietnam War protests and activism on behalf of minorities, women, the politically downtrodden worldwide, and the beleaguered environment. Still the star at the city's center, the prestigious University of California at Berkeley has become the somewhat reluctant mother ship in the ever-expanding universe of ideas swirling around it.

For basic Berkeley information, contact the **Berkeley Convention and Visitors Bureau,** 2015 Center St., 510/549-7040 or toll-free 800/847-4823, www.berkeleycvb.com, though budget travelers will find the **Council on International Education Exchange,** 2486 Channing Way (at Telegraph), 510/848-8604, much more helpful.

The University of California

Despite the existence of many other campuses in the University of California system, UC Berkeley—by virtue of its history and preeminence—is the one often referred to simply as "Cal." Despite town-gown tensions, most everything in Berkeley radiates from the Frederick Law Olmsted–designed campus. Before wandering around this sprawling 1,232-acre institution, get oriented at the **visitors information center** in University Hall Room 101, 2200 University Ave. (at Oxford St.), 510/642-5215. The center offers maps and pamphlets for self-guided tours in addition to other information. Or take a guided tour, also offered through the visitors center.

Behind Sather Gate is Sproul Plaza, where Mario Savio and others spoke out against university policies in the 1964 genesis of the Free Speech Movement. Fronting the plaza is Sather Tower, still known as the Campanile, which holds 61 fully chromatic carillon bells that are usually played weekdays just before 8 A.M., at noon, and at 6 P.M.; the bells can be heard from almost anywhere on campus. (To watch the bell players at work, take a ride to the top.)

To soak up some of the university's powerfully impersonal seriousness, spend time in any of

---

BERKELEY'S GOURMET GHETTO

Do eat in Berkeley. The Shattuck Ave. and Walnut St. area between Rose and Virginia Sts. is known as Berkeley's Gourmet Ghetto (or Gourmet Gulch) in wry recognition of the fine delis, food shops, gelato stops, and upscale restaurants so prominent here—a phenomenon started by the internationally renowned **Chez Panisse,** 1517 Shattuck, 510/548-5525 for dinner reservations, 510/548-5049 for café information. The entire neighborhood offers poor parking possibilities but wonderful opportunities for trend-watching. And the trend has spread far beyond its original geographical limits—onto University and San Pablo Aves., along 4th St., even onto Telegraph Avenue. Gourmet grazing is also available along Hopkins St., between Monterey and McGee.

---

its 25 libraries, a total information collection second only in size and prestige to Harvard's. The **Bancroft Library,** 510/642-3781 or 510/642-6481, is the most immediately impressive; its stacks are open to the public, and its excellent exhibits change frequently. Also worth a stop: the **UC Earth Sciences Building,** home of the Berkeley Seismographic Station, the Museum of Paleontology (510/642-1821), and the Museum of Geology (510/642-4330); and the **Phoebe Apperson Hearst Museum of Anthropology** in Kroeber Hall, once known as the Lowie Museum of Anthropology (510/643-7648), which boasts the finest collection of anthropological artifacts in the western United States, including many of A. L. Kroeber's contributions.

Another on-campus monument to the memory of William Randolph Hearst and clan is the **Hearst Memorial Mining Building.** Also donated by Hearst: UC's gorgeous outdoor **Greek Theatre,** 510/642-0527. The **University Art Museum,** 2626 Bancroft Way, 510/642-0808, also runs the **Pacific Film Archives,** 2625 Durant Ave., 510/642-1124 or 510/642-1412, a cinema collection with screenings of oldies but goodies. The films are presented on campus at the PFA theater, Bancroft at Bowditch (tickets available at either the theater or the Durant Ave. box office).

Modest **Le Conte Hall** on campus has been the birthplace of some of the university's most striking achievements: physical and nuclear science breakthroughs that have changed the course of history. The university was already internationally renowned as a leader in the field of physics by 1939, when Ernest Lawrence won the Nobel Prize for inventing the cyclotron. By 1941, as a result of cyclotron experiments by Glenn Seaborg and others, plutonium had been discovered. In that same year, Lawrence, Edward Teller, and J. Robert Oppenheimer began planning the development of the atomic bomb, at the behest of the U.S. government. For development and testing, that project was transferred from Berkeley to New Mexico—the world saw the result in 1945 when the first A-bombs were dropped on Nagasaki and Hiroshima—the swan song of World War II and the birth of our brave new world.

The exceptional **Lawrence Hall of Science** on Centennial Dr. (at Grizzly Peak), 510/642-5132 or 510/642-5133, pays postmodern homage. A top contender for the title of Northern

California's best science museum, Lawrence Hall holds hands-on exhibits (and the opportunity to try some freestyle physics experiments in the Wizard's Lab) and includes Holt Planetarium. Outside are fabulous giant wind chimes and a Stonehenge-style "solar observatory." Open daily 10 A.M.–5 P.M. Admission is $6 general, $4 seniors, $2 children 3–6. Nearby, on UC's eastern fringe, is the Strawberry Canyon **UC Botanical Garden,** 200 Centennial Dr. (above Memorial Stadium), 510/643-2755. The garden's 30 acres of native plants and exotics include some 17,000 species, one of the world's biggest and best botanic collections. Open daily 9 A.M.–7 P.M. in summer, 9 A.M.–5 P.M. the rest of the year. Small admission, free on Thurs. Free guided tours are offered on weekends. Pleasant picnicking. Across the way is the university's **Mather Redwood Grove,** open daily.

Berkeley by the Bookstore
More famous during its Free Speech heyday and later anti-war riots is the Telegraph Ave. and Durant area south of the university. From Dwight Way to Bancroft, it's one busy blur of bookstores, boutiques, cheap clothing shops, record shops, ethnic restaurants, and fast-food stops—plus street people and street vendors, Berkeley's version of a year-round carnival. One wag has called Telegraph Ave. "a theme park with no theme"—an astute observation about much of California. Among the incredible numbers of bookstores in the area, **Cody's,** 2454 Telegraph (at Haste), 510/845-7852, has been a haven for poetry (readings once a week) and prose since the days of the Beats.

Bookstores are almost as necessary to maintaining community consciousness as coffee. Older hipsters may remember **Moe's,** 2476 Telegraph, 510/849-2087, from the film *The Graduate.* The store holds four floors of used books, including antiquarian and art sections. Literature and art lovers should also meander through **Shakespeare and Company,** 2499 Telegraph, 510/841-8916, and, if you're in the Gourmet Ghetto, **Black Oak Books,** 1491 Shattuck, 510/486-0698 or 510/486-0699, where they actually hope you'll sit down and start reading. Popular contemporary authors, from Ursula K. Le Guin and Toni Morrison to Salman Rushdie, are often on the guest lecture circuit here. **University**

Press Books, 2430 Bancroft Way, 510/548-0585, carries the largest selection of university press regional titles in the West.

Berkeley Outdoors
Back up in the Berkeley Hills, **Tilden Regional Park** and adjacent **Wildcat Canyon Regional Park** are the area's major parks. The trend at Tilden over the years has been toward recreational development, so this is the place for getting away from it all city-style: swimming in Lake Anza and sunning on the artificial beach; picnicking with family and friends; stopping off at Little Farm and riding the miniature train, merry-go-round, and ponies with the kiddies; or playing tennis or 18 holes at the golf course.

Tilden Park's popular **Native Plant Botanic Garden** (not to be confused with the university's), 510/841-8732, shelters 1,500 varieties of native California plants and wildflowers. Open 10 A.M.–5 P.M. daily, with free tours offered on weekends June–Aug. The park's Environmental Education Center, 510/525-2233, is a good stop for trail brochures and other park information, as well as the starting point for a self-guided nature walk around little Jewel Lake on the Wildcat border. Though Tilden has some trails, for full-tilt hiking, Wildcat Canyon is preferable—no paved roads and not many hikers or runners on its fire roads, which contour through grazing lands and foothill forests.

Right in town on the southeast side of the university is **Claremont Canyon Regional Preserve,** consisting of 200 steep, secluded acres suitable for deer-path wandering. **Indian Rock Park** on Indian Rock Ave. at Shattuck is popular with practicing rock climbers. But for just smelling the roses, stop by **Berkeley Rose Garden** on Euclid Ave. at Eunice, 510/644-6530, open May–Sept.

EAST BAY OUTBACK

The eastern expanse of the Bay Area is best known for its Berkeley-Oakland metropolis and surrounding suburban communities. But natural areas in the East Bay's outback offer snippets of silence and serenity in the midst of suburban sprawl, and an occasional glimpse of life as it once was in these hilly former farmlands. Many of the East Bay's treasures are collected into the **East Bay Regional Park District,** 510/635-0135 or 510/562-7275 for 24-hour information and to request brochures, www.ebparks.org. The East Bay's regional parks include more than 91,000 acres of parklands in Alameda and Contra Costa Counties—90 percent of it "natural"—with 1,000 miles of trails.

East Bay Parks

Between Lafayette and Martinez, **Briones Regional Park** offers wonderful hiking up hillsides, down valleys, and across meadows. For more information, call the park office at 925/370-3020. **Las Trampas Regional Wilderness** west of Danville is more than 3,000 acres of wilderness—home to mountain lions, wildcats, skunks, foxes, weasels, and golden eagles. The developed Little Hills Ranch area near the park's entrance offers picnic areas, a swimming pool, playground, and stables. For more information, call East Bay Regional Parks at 925/837-3145.

Mount Diablo State Park is a wonder, one which some half-million people enjoy each year. Peak experiences here include the view from the summit, the Mitchell Canyon hike to the summit (the park has a total of 50 miles of trails), rock climbing, fabulous spring wildflower displays, and Fossil Ridge (don't touch). Mountain bikers may ride unpaved roads to the west of North Gate and South Gate Roads. A wonderful visitor center occupies the beautiful 1939 stone Summit Building built by the WPA. For more information, call the park at 925/837-2525 (information) or 925/673-2893 (administration). Reserve campgrounds in advance through ReserveAmerica, toll-free 800/444-7275.

One way to beat the heat in summer is by heading underground for a stroll through the cool sandstone caverns deep within the six-level Hazel-Atlas Mine—part of the former Mount Diablo coal-mining district (the state's largest) and later, prime underground fields for harvesting high-grade silica sand. Included as part of the **Black Diamond Mines Regional Preserve,** the mine is open for two-hour tours by advance reservations only. For safety reasons, children under age 7 are not allowed. For more information, call 925/757-2620; for tour reservations, call East Bay Parks headquarters in Oakland at 510/562-2267 or 510/562-7275.

A great place for spring hiking is the **Morgan Territory Regional Preserve** on remote eastern ridge tops beyond Mount Diablo—quiet and almost inaccessible due to the wild one-lane road winding up the mountain. For those looking for solitude, here it is. For more information, call 925/757-2620 or 510/562-7275.

Other large area parks include **Ohlone Regional Wilderness,** encompassing some 7,000 acres of wild high ridges on the south end of Alameda County, accessible only via the Sunol Regional Wilderness to the west or the Del Valle Regional Recreation Area to the north. **Sunol Regional Wilderness** is rich in oak woods and remoteness as well as developed family picnic

Mount Diablo's stone Summit Building, now a visitor center, under a rare blanket of snow

facilities, and backpack and walk-in camping; **Del Valle Regional Recreation Area** is popular for swimming and windsurfing on Lake Del Valle, picnicking and camping around the shore, and rugged spring hiking. For more information on all these parks, call East Bay Regional Parks at 510/562-7275.

Some Outback Communities

Just north of the Benicia-Martinez Bridge via I-780 is **Benicia,** the onetime capital of California. Take a quick tour of the town's historic architecture (most buildings aren't open to the public) and stop at the restored **Benicia Capitol State Historic Park,** 115 W. G St. (at 1st St.), 707/745-3385, which preserves the 1852 brick building that housed the California Senate, Assembly, and Treasury for 13 months in 1853–54. Also part of the park is the 1850 Fischer-Hanlon House next door, with its Victorian-era furnishings and displays of period clothing. Admission to the park is free. Benicia's **Camel Barn Museum,** 2024 Camel Rd. (in the town's onetime military arsenal complex, now an industrial park), 707/745-5435, is named for a short-lived 1860s experiment—using camels to transport military supplies across the Southwest. The cranky creatures were once stabled here, but the barn is now home to local memorabilia. Open Wed.–Sun. 1–4 P.M.; small admission. The **Benicia Fire Museum,** 900 E. 2nd St. (at E. J St.), 707/745-1688, exhibits rare firefighting equipment and a collection of historical photos. It's open on the first and third Sat. of each month, noon–4 P.M., or by appointment. Or just wander. Benicia proper is experiencing an art-community boom and overall revitalization, with interesting cafés and shops popping up everywhere.

Martinez, on the other end of the Benicia bridge, was settled by Italian fishing families and is historic home to both the martini and New York Yankee baseball great Joe DiMaggio. A modern-day attraction is the **John Muir House National Historic Site,** 4202 Alhambra Ave., 925/228-8860, which preserves the naturalist's 1882 Victorian home and grounds. Home to Muir and his wife during the last 24 years of his life, this is where he did most of his conservation writing. In addition to becoming an astute businessman, orchardist, inventor, pioneer of factory automation, patron of the arts, and magazine editor, the inde-

fatigable Scot explored California and Alaska, established the U.S. Forest Service and five national parks, and co-founded the Sierra Club. Collected here are many of Muir's books and writings, along with exhibits chronicling his amazing influence. Muir House is open Wed.–Sun. (except major holidays) 10 A.M.–4:30 P.M.; small admission. Also on the grounds is the **Martinez Adobe,** the 1844 home of Don Vincente Martinez, part of the old Rancho Las Juntas. Nearby **Crockett** is most famous for the C&H sugar refinery, but it's also something of an artsy-industrial enclave, like a smokestack-style Sausalito.

Worthwhile in **Danville** is a stop at **Eugene O'Neill's Tao House National Historic Site,** a two-story Spanish-style home and national historic landmark where O'Neill wrote some of his last plays, including *The Iceman Cometh, Long Day's Journey into Night,* and *A Moon for the Misbegotten.* Two tours per day are offered Wed.–Sun. at 10 A.M. and 12:30 P.M., with buses leaving from downtown Danville. Every spring, in the restored barn, the acclaimed **Playwright's Theatre** performs works by O'Neill and playwrights he influenced. Call 925/838-0249 for more information and advance reservations (required) or try www.nps.gov/euon. Also in Danville, the opulent **Blackhawk Automotive Museum,** 3700 Blackhawk Plaza Circle, 925/736-2277, is a showcase for a $100 million collection of classic cars, including the 1924 torpedo-shaped Tulipwood Hispano Suiza built for Andre Dubonnet of French aperitif fame; Clark Gable's 1935 Duesenberg convertible; and Rudolph Valentino's 1926 Isotta Fraschini. Visit the ground floor **Automotive Art Gallery.** Open Wed.–Sun. 10 A.M.–5 P.M.; admission is $8 adults, $5 seniors and students, free for children 6 and under. Free guided tours offered weekends at 2 P.M.

Pleasanton in the Livermore Valley seems to be the face of California's future: corporate business parks mixed with backyard barbecues. But the surrounding hills provide some great hiking opportunities, particularly at 1,800-acre **Pleasanton Hills Regional Park. Livermore** is home of **Lawrence Livermore National Laboratory,** 7000 East Ave. (follow the signs), 925/423-3272 (visitor center), 925/422-4599 (public affairs), or 925/422-1100 (main operator), which was developing the X-ray laser for the U.S. "Star Wars" defense system before the world changed. The surrounding Livermore Valley, home of the Livermore Rodeo every June, is noted for its wineries—some of the oldest in the state. The historic Cresta Blanca vineyard has been resurrected as **Wente Vineyards,** 5050 Arroyo Rd., 925/456-2400, which offers a restaurant open daily for lunch and dinner. Also in the neighborhood: **Concannon Vineyards,** 4590 Tesla Rd., 925/456-2500; award-winning **Fenestra Winery,** 83 E. Vallecitos Rd., 925/447-5246, which offers limited wine-tasting in summer, otherwise only quarterly by invitation (call for information); and the traditional **Wente Estate Winery,** 5565 Tesla Rd., 925/456-2300, where picnicking is possible on the grounds.

A wine-related stop in the area is **Ravenswood Historic Site,** 2647 Arroyo Rd. (south of Superior), 925/373-5708, an early winery estate open to the public only on free guided tours given by costumed docents on the second Sun. of each month. Two Victorian homes preside over 33 acres of apple orchards and vineyards; one of the old Vics is filled with period furniture and functions as a museum.

Beyond Livermore on the way to Tracy via I-580 is the **Altamont Pass** area, open foothill grazing land best known for the thousands of wind turbines in the power-generating "wind farms" here—an alternative energy source with the nasty negative side effect of chopping airborne birds into bits.

NORTH FROM SAN FRANCISCO

POINT REYES NATIONAL SEASHORE

Some 71,000 acres of fog-shrouded lagoons, lowland marshes, sandy beaches, coastal dunes, and ridge-top forests, Point Reyes National Seashore also features windy headlands and steep, unstable cliffs, populations of tule elk and grazing cattle, and a wonderful lighthouse all too popular for winter whale-watching. A dramatically dislocated triangular wedge of land with its apex jutting out into the Pacific Ocean, Point Reyes is also land in motion: this is earthquake country. Separated from mainland Marin County by slitlike Tomales Bay, the Point Reyes Peninsula is also sliced off at about the same spot by the San Andreas Fault. When that fault shook loose in 1906—instantly thrusting the peninsula 16 feet farther north—the city of San Francisco came tumbling down.

Seeing and Doing Point Reyes

Get oriented at the park's barnlike **Bear Valley Visitor Center,** 415/663-1092, just off Bear Valley Rd. (off Hwy. 1 near Olema), which, in addition to natural history and fine arts exhibits, includes a seismograph for monitoring the earth's movements. Take the short **Earthquake Trail** loop (wheelchair accessible), which demonstrates the San Andreas seismic drama. Also

THE MYSTERY OF SIR FRANCIS DRAKE

Though named by Sebastián Vizcaíno in 1603 while he was passing the rocky headlands on the 12th day of Christmas, or the Feast of the Three Kings, Point Reyes was actually explored earlier by the privateer Sir Francis Drake. Tired of pursuing Spanish ships around the world, he beached the *Pelican* (later known as the *Golden Hinde*) and came ashore at "a fit and convenient harbour" somewhere in California in June 1579. Naming the land Nova Albion, here he made repairs, rested his tired crew, and claimed the area for Queen Elizabeth I with "a plate of brasse, fast nailed to a great and firme post." This much most historians agree on. The rest of the story is contentious at best.

Where exactly did Drake land? Since the main estuary at Point Reyes is named after Drake, as is the bay, the simple answer is that he came ashore here, some 20 nautical miles north of San Francisco. But some contend that Drake actually landed at Bolinas Lagoon or explored San Francisco Bay and landed near Point San Quentin or Novato, near an old Olompali village site where a 1567 English silver sixpence was discovered in 1974. A more recent quest for remnants of Drake's visitation centers on Bodega Bay. Others say he stumbled ashore on Goleta Beach near Santa Barbara, where five cast-iron British cannons similar to those missing from the *Golden Hinde* were unearthed in the 1980s. But 70 pieces of antique Ming porcelain have been found near Point Reyes—proof enough, say true believers of the Point Reyes theory, since four chests of Chinese porcelain, which Drake stole from the Spanish, never arrived in England. (Unbelievers counter that the porcelain washed ashore instead from the wreckage of the *San Agustin* off Drakes Bay.)

Other related questions remain unanswered. Is the infamous brass plate found on a beach near Point San Quentin in 1936 genuine or a clever forgery? After years of controversy, in the 1970s the British Museum declared the corroded placard an "undoubted fake" despite the olde English ring of its language, and metallurgists say the plate is no more than 100 years old. (To judge for yourself, the brass plate is on display at UC Berkeley's Bancroft Library.)

What became of Drake's journal, which supposedly documented this journey as well as Drake's discovery of the Northwest Passage? What happened to the gold, gems, and silver Drake stole from the Spanish ship *Cacafuego* and others, estimated in today's currency values as worth $50 million? Some say no treasure was buried along the California coast, that Drake would have jettisoned cannons, china, and other goods instead to lighten his ship's load. Drake, they say, took all his loot back to England, where he and his crew became millionaires, and the queen retired some of the national debt and started the East India Company. Others, however, are still looking.

POINT REYES AND MARIN

To Bodega Bay

Freestone

To Eureka

Santa Rosa

HWY.

Sebastopol

12

BODEGA

HWY.

Valley Ford

116

Bodega Bay

Dillon Beach

Bloomfield

Rohnert Park

101

STONY POINT RD.

LAWSON'S LANDING

TOMALES-PETALUMA RD.

Cotati

ADOBE RD.

PETALUMA VALLEY FORD RD.

CHILENO VALLEY RD.

BODEGA AVE.

Tomales Bay

Marshall

Laguna Lake

Petaluma

To Sonoma

MARCONI STATE HISTORIC PARK

MARSHALL-PETALUMA RD.

PETALUMA RD.

POINT

TOMALES BAY STATE PARK

Soulajule Reservoir

116

PACIFIC

DRAKE BLVD.

Inverness

PT. REYES

101

Lakeville

POINT REYES LIGHTHOUSE AND VISITOR CENTER

REYES

SIR FRANCIS

Drakes Beach

Pt. Reyes Station

Nicasio Reservoir

NOVATO BLVD.

To Vallejo

Limantour Beach

POINT REYES HOSTEL

Stafford Lake

37

Drakes Bay

BEAR VALLEY VISITOR CENTER

Olema

G.G.N.R.A.

Nicasio

Novato

NATIONAL

Samuel P. Taylor State Park

LUCAS VALLEY RD.

101

OCEAN

SEASHORE

1

Lagunitas

Woodacre

Agate Beach

Kent Lake

SIR FRANCIS DRAKE BLVD.

Marinwood

China Camp State Park

San Pablo Bay

G.G. N.R.A.

Alpine Lake

Fairfax

San Anselmo

Bolinas

AUDOBON CANYON RANCH

Ross

San Rafael

Kentfield

Stinson Beach

Mt. Tamalpais (2,571 ft.)

Mt. Tamalpais State Park

Greenbrae

Larkspur

Corte Madera

RICHMOND-SAN RAFAEL BRIDGE

San Francisco Bay

MUIR WOODS N.M.

Mill Valley

101

Red Rock Beach

RING MOUNTAIN PRESERVE

580

To Sacramento

Muir Beach

Golden Gate National Recreation Area

131

Belvedere

Richmond

80

Rodeo Beach

FORT BARRY

FORT CRONKHITE

Tiburon

POINT BONITA LIGHTHOUSE

Sausalito

POINT DIABLO LIGHTHOUSE

San Francisco

0   5 mi

0   5 km

GOLDEN GATE BRIDGE

Bay

80

SAN FRANCISCO

To Oakland

580

© AVALON TRAVEL PUBLISHING, INC.

Marin Headlands

TOM MYERS PHOTOGRAPHY

near the Bear Valley Visitor Center are the short, self-guided **Woodpecker Nature Trail;** the **Morgan Horse Ranch,** where the Park Service breeds and trains its mounts; and **Kule Loklo,** an architectural re-creation of a Coast Miwok community.

Limantour Estero near Drakes Estero and Drakes Beach is great for bird-watching; **McClures Beach** is best for tidepooling; and both **North Beach** and **South Beach** north of Point Reyes proper offer good beachcombing but treacherous swimming. Protected **Drakes Beach** and **Limantour Beach** along the crescent of Drakes Bay are safe for swimming.

For astounding views when the fog lifts above the ship graveyard offshore, head out to Point Reyes proper and the **Point Reyes Lighthouse and Visitor Center,** 415/669-1534 (open daily 9 A.M.–5 P.M. during whale-watching season, more limited hours at other times). The **Chimney Rock Trail** is wonderful for spring and summer wildflowers and, if you head west, is also a roundabout way to reach the lighthouse. On all Point Reyes hikes, carry water, wear proper walking shoes, and dress for sudden, unpredictable weather changes.

To experience the sound and fury of Coast Creek hurling itself into the Pacific via the "sea tunnel" at the **Arch Rock Overlook,** dress warmly, wear raingear and slip-proof shoes, and come (via the popular Bear Valley Trail) during a storm. For safety's sake, stay well back from the spectacle, and don't attempt to walk through the tun-

nel under any circumstances—though people often do in calm weather.

To make the most of a full moon at Point Reyes, head to the **Wildcat Beach Overlook** via the Bear Valley Trail from the visitor center, then south via the Coast Trail to the area overlooking the beach, **Alamere Falls** (most spectacular after heavy rains), and the southern stretch of Drakes Bay. An alternate route to Alamere Falls, about one mile south of Wildcat Camp, is via the Palomarin Trail from Bolinas or the Five Brooks Trail. For the best panoramic vista of Drakes Bay, take the Bear Valley, Sky, then Woodward Valley Trails to the bay (alternatively, take the Coast Trail from Coast Camp to the Woodward Valley Trail), then climb up the small hill overlooking the bay, just northwest of the trail.

The **Randall Spur Trail,** created by the Civilian Conservation Corps, connects the Bolinas Ridge Trail with the various Inverness Ridge and Olema Valley trails—making Point Reyes's southern stretches more accessible for day hikers. Worth a stop on the way to the Palomarin trailhead in south Point Reyes is the **Point Reyes Bird Observatory,** 415/868-1221, established in 1965 as the first bird observatory in the country. Though it's a full-fledged research facility, the Palomarin observatory is open to the public, with educational classes (call ahead for information), interpretive exhibits, and a nature trail. To get here by car, take the unmarked turnoff to Bolinas (near highway marker 17.00 at

THE FARALLON ISLANDS

Visible from Point Reyes on a clear day are the Farallon Islands to the southwest. The largest seabird rookery south of Alaska, these islands are one of the five most ecologically productive marine environments on earth and now part of an international UNESCO Biosphere Reserve. Some 1,235 square miles of nearshore and offshore waters from Bodega Head to Rocky Point are included in the Gulf of the Farallones National Marine Sanctuary, which was established in 1981. These rugged granite islands 27 miles west of San Francisco are actually the above-sea-level presence of the Farallones Escarpment, which parallels the coast from the tip of Point Reyes to south of the Golden Gate. The natural but rare phenomenon of upwelling around the islands, with warm offshore winds drawing cold, nutrient-rich ocean water to the surface in spring, creates the phenomenal algae and plankton populations that support the feeding frenzies and breeding successes of animals farther up the food chain.

In recent centuries, life was almost undone at the Farallones. In the 1800s, "eggers" exploited the rookeries here to provide miners and San Francis-cans with fresh eggs at breakfast. The islands have also survived assaults from sealers, whalers, gill netters, bombers, ocean oil slicks, and radioactive waste dumping.

In the summer, more than 250,000 breeding birds—from tufted puffins and petrels to auklets and murres—consider the Farallones home. Sea lions and seals, including the northern fur seal and the once-almost-extinct northern elephant seal, also breed here, and gray and humpback whales are often spotted in the area. The nonprofit, member-supported **Point Reyes Bird Observatory** in Stinson Beach, 415/868-1221, staffs a scientific study center at the Farallones (in addition to its center at Point Reyes). Otherwise people are not allowed on the islands, though ocean-going educational expeditions around the Farallon Islands are offered June–Nov. and during the winter whale-watching season. (Bring binoculars.)

For more information about the Farallon Islands and the surrounding marine sanctuary, contact: **Gulf of the Farallones National Marine Sanctuary,** 415/561-6622, www.gfnms.nos.noaa.gov.

---

the north end of Bolinas Lagoon), continue two miles or so to Mesa Rd., then turn right and continue four miles to the observatory's bird-banding station.

Practical Point Reyes

Seasonally, dogs are specifically restricted at Point Reyes—and people must also restrain themselves—because the northern elephant seals have returned to area beaches and established a breeding colony. To protect the elephant seals during the winter breeding and pupping season, no dogs are allowed on South Beach and beaches to the south Nov.–Apr. Only leashed dogs are allowed on North Beach, Kehoe Beach, and the southern part of Limantour Beach. Contact the park office for current details.

For information about Point Reyes, including current trail maps, and to obtain permits for camping and backpacking, stop by any of the park's three visitor centers: **Bear Valley Visitor Center** at the park's Bear Valley entrance; **Kenneth C. Patrick Visitor Center** at Drakes Beach; or **Point Reyes Lighthouse Visitor Center.** Or contact: Point Reyes National Seashore, Point Reyes, CA 94956, 415/663-1092, www.nps.gov/pore. For advance or additional information about the area, contact the **West Marin Chamber of Commerce,** P.O. Box 1045, Point Reyes Station, CA 94956, 415/663-9232, www.pointreyes.org.

GOLDEN GATE NATIONAL RECREATION AREA AND VICINITY

Beginning immediately adjacent to Point Reyes near Olema is the Golden Gate National Recreation Area (GGNRA), which wraps itself around various state and local parks inland, then extends southeast across the Marin Headlands and the Golden Gate Bridge to include the Presidio and a thin coastal strip running south to Fort Funston. The GGNRA also includes two prominent tourist attractions in San Francisco Bay: Angel Island and Alcatraz. Most notable is the dramatic natural beauty of the Marin Headlands—sea-chiseled chilly cliffs, protected valleys, and grassy wind-combed hills rich with wildlife and wildflowers, all opening out to the bay and the Pacific Ocean. Protected at first by the Nature Conservancy until coming under national management in 1972, the vast Marin Headlands feature trails for days of good hiking and backpacking (stop by the headquarters for a current trail map). Backcountry and group camps are scattered across the area.

Aside from the GGNRA's natural beauty, here also is historic scenery, from the 1877 Point Bonita Lighthouse to four military installations— Forts Barry, Cronkhite, Baker, and Funston— that protected the Bay Area beginning in the 1870s and continuing through World War II.

For more information about the GGNRA, contact: **Golden Gate National Recreation Area** headquarters, Building 201, Fort Mason, San Francisco, CA 94123, 415/556-0560, www .nps.gov/goga. Or stop for maps and other information at the **Marin Headlands GGNRA Visitor Center** at Fort Barry (near Rodeo Lagoon and Fort Cronkhite), 415/331-1540, open daily 8:30 A.M.–4:30 P.M., or the **Muir Woods Visitor Center** at Muir Woods, 415/388-2595 or 415/388-2596. Pick up trail maps and events calendars and ask about backcountry camping at the visitor centers.

Point Bonita Lighthouse

The Point Bonita Lighthouse, 415/331-1540 for hours and tour information, was one of the first lighthouses ever built on the West Coast and is still operating. Technically, though, this isn't really a lighthouse—there's no house, just the French-import 1855 Fresnel lens with protective glass, walls, and roof, with gargoyle-like American eagles guarding the light. Getting here is as thrilling as being here—meandering along the half-mile footpath to the rocky point through hand-dug tunnels and across the swaying footbridge, in the middle of nowhere yet in full view of San Francisco. Especially enjoyable are the sunset and full-moon tours conducted by GGNRA rangers. The tours and admission to the lighthouse are free.

Fort Barry

Just north of Point Bonita, Fort Barry includes an intact 1950s missile launch site and underground bunkers not usually open to the public; one of the bunkers is still home to a Nike Hercules missile.

"Guardians of the Gate" military-history tours, offered twice-monthly by park personnel, 415/331-1540, include the various batteries in the area and end at the Nike site. Also at Fort Barry: an **HI-AYH youth hostel,** the **Headlands Center for the Arts,** and the **Marin Headlands Visitor Center.**

Fort Cronkhite

Just north of the visitor center is Fort Cronkhite, home of the **California Marine Mammal Center** (just above Cronkhite Beach), 415/289-7325. Established in 1975, this hospital for wild animals returns its "patients," once fit, to their native marine environments. The center, with more than 400 active volunteers and popular hands-on environmental education programs for children, is open to the public daily 10 A.M.–4 P.M. Also at Fort Cronkhite: the **Pacific Environment and Resources Center,** 415/332-8200, which offers teacher training, special elementary and secondary school programs, and exhibits on local and global environmental issues.

Other Marin GGNRA Sights

The hands-on **Bay Area Discovery Museum** at East Fort Baker, 415/487-4398, is designed for children ages 2–12 and their families. It offers a great variety of special programs year-round—"In the Dream Time" children's art workshops, for example. Open Wed.–Sun. 10 A.M.–5 P.M. Two miles north of Muir Beach is the **Slide Ranch** demonstration farm and family-oriented environmental education center, 2025 Hwy. 1, 415/381-6155, which offers special events (such as "Family Farm Day") year-round. Reservations are required for all events.

Tomales Bay State Park

Among the half-moon beaches and secret coves along the steep cliffs and shores of Tomales Bay are those protected within fragments of Tomales Bay State Park. One section is just north of Inverness, via Pierce Point Rd. off Sir Francis Drake Blvd., and others are scattered along Hwy. 1 north of Point Reyes Station on the east side of the bay. One of the prime picnic spots at Tomales Bay is **Heart's Desire Beach,** popular for family picnicking and swimming, and usually empty on weekdays. Hiking the forested eastern slope of Inverness Ridge is also worth

STAYING FOR CHEAP IN WESTERN MARIN

Among best bets for noncamping budget travelers is **HI-AYH Point Reyes Hostel** on Limantour Rd., P.O. Box 247, Point Reyes Station, CA 94956, 415/663-8811. Pluses here include the well-equipped kitchen (get food on the way). Advance reservations advisable, particularly on weekends. For information on getting to Point Reyes and taking public transit, call the hostel or Golden Gate Transit, 415/923-2000. The hostel's office hours are 7:30–9:30 A.M. and 4:30–9:30 P.M. daily. Considerably closer to urban Marin but also an excellent choice is the hostel within the Golden Gate National Recreation Area.

Point Reyes camping is another inexpensive way to go, but the state's quite reasonable **Steep Ravine Environmental Cabins** on Rocky Point at Mount Tamalpais State Park, looking out to sea from near Stinson Beach, are quite the budget find. These small redwood-rustic homes-away-from-home come with just the basics: platform beds (bring your own sleeping bag and pad), woodstoves, separate restrooms with pit toilets. But such a deal: $15 per cabin per night (each sleeps five) and an almost-private beach below in a spectacularly romantic setting. Before the state wrested custody of these marvelous cabins from the powerful Bay Area politicians and other clout-encumbered citizens who held long-term leases, photographer Dorothea Lange wrote about

staying here in *To a Cabin,* co-authored by Margaretta K. Mitchell. Even the walk down to the bottom of Steep Ravine Canyon is inspiring, Lange noted, with "room for only those in need of sea and sky and infinity." One cabin (there are only 10) is wheelchair accessible; none have electricity, but they do have outside running water. Bring your own provisions. Budget. To reserve (up to eight weeks in advance), contact ReserveAmerica, toll-free 800/444-7275, and request an application form. You can also make reservations online; point your browser to www.cal-parks.ca.gov.

Best bet for budget travelers in eastern Marin County is the **HI-AYH Marin Headlands Hostel,** in Building 941 at Fort Barry, 415/331-2777, urban enough—just five minutes from the Golden Gate Bridge—but also rural, 103 beds in a 1907 building in an otherwise abandoned fort in the midst of Golden Gate National Recreation Area. Basic dorm-style accommodations with hot showers (family room available by advance reservation), but facilities also include a great kitchen, dining room, common room with fireplace, even laundry facilities, game room, tennis court, and bike storage. Quite popular in summer and on good-weather weekends, so reservations advised. Budget, with an extra fee for linen rental—or bring a sleeping bag.

it—especially in early spring. Unique is the park's fine virgin forest of Bishop pines. Along the eastern edge of Tomales Bay, the **Marconi Conference Center,** 415/663-9020, occupies the 1914 Marconi Hotel once owned by Guglielmo Marconi, inventor of the wireless. This onetime communications center facility—taken over by the U.S. Navy during World War I, later operated by RCA, and more recently home to the much-praised then pilloried Synanon alcohol and drug abuse program—is now a state-owned conference center operated on the model of Asilomar on the Monterey Peninsula.

For more information about the park, call Tomales Bay State Park at 415/669-1140.

Samuel P. Taylor State Park

East of Point Reyes National Seashore and hemmed in by the Golden Gate National Recreation Area is Samuel P. Taylor State Park, 2,600

acres of redwoods, mixed forests, and upcountry chaparral reached via Sir Francis Drake Boulevard. The park offers an extensive hiking and horseback trail system, a paved bicycle path running east-west, no-frills camping (including hiker/biker camps), picnicking, and swimming. For more information, call the park at 415/488-9897 or 415/893-1580.

Bolinas Lagoon and Audubon Canyon Ranch

Well worth a visit is the Bolinas Lagoon, as serene as a Japanese nature print, especially in spring, when only the breeze or an occasional waterfowl fracas ruffles the glassy blue of this long mirror of water surrounded by a crescent-moon sandspit. Reflected above is wooded Bolinas Ridge, the northwestern extension of Mount Tamalpais. In autumn, the lagoon is much busier, temporary home to thousands of waterfowl migrating south along the Pacific Flyway as well as

*the view from
the summit of
Mt. Tamalpais*

ROBERT HOLMES/CALTOUR

the salmon offshore waiting for a ferocious winter storm to break open a pathway through the sandbars blocking their migratory path. At minus tide any time of year, the surf side of the sandspit offers good beachcombing.

Facing out into the Bolinas Lagoon several miles north of Stinson Beach is the Audubon Canyon Ranch, a protected canyon offering a safe haven and rookery for great blue herons and common egrets in particular, though more than 50 other species of water birds arrive here each year. By quietly climbing up the canyon slopes during the Mar.–July nesting season, visitors can look down into egret and heron nests high atop the redwoods in Schwartz Grove and observe the day-to-day life of parent birds and their young. Other hiking trails lead to other discoveries; picnic facilities also available.

The white Victorian farmhouse here serves as ranch headquarters and bookstore/visitor center, and participants in weekend seminar programs bed down in the bunkhouse, which features wind-powered toilets (God's truth) and solar-heated water. (Bring your own bedding, food, and other necessities.) The ranch is wheelchair accessible and generally open to the public mid-March through mid-July only on weekends and holidays, 10 A.M.–4 P.M., admission free, though donations are always appreciated. Large groups can make tour arrangements for weekdays, though the ranch is always closed Mondays. For more information, contact: Audubon Canyon Ranch, 4900 Shoreline Hwy. (Hwy. 1), Stinson Beach, CA 94970, 415/868-9244, www.egret.org.

Mount Tamalpais State Park

Though the park also stretches downslope to the sea, take in the views of Marin County, San Francisco Bay, and the Pacific Ocean from the highest points of Mount Tamalpais. This long-loved mountain isn't particularly tall (elevation 2,600 feet), but even when foggy mists swirl everywhere below, the sun usually shines atop Mount Tam. And the state park here has it all: redwoods and ferns, hillsides thick with wildflowers, 200 miles of hiking trails with spectacular views (plus access to Muir Woods), beaches and headlands, also camping and picnicking. The best way to get here is via Hwy. 1, then via the Panoramic Hwy., winding up past Pan Toll Ranger Station and park headquarters (stop for information and a map) to near the summit. From the parking lot, it's a quarter-mile hike up a steep dirt road to the fire lookout on top of Mount Tam.

The best way to explore Mount Tamalpais is on foot. Take the loop trail around the top. For the more ambitious, head downslope to the sea and the busy public beaches at Stinson Beach, still noted for its annual Dipsea Race held on the last Sunday in August, a tradition since 1904. Rugged cross-country runners cross the still more rugged terrain from Mill Valley to the sea at Stinson Beach; the last stretch down the footpath is known as the Dipsea Trail. Or hike into the park from Marin Municipal Water District lands on the east (for information, call the Sky Oaks

Ranger Station in Fairfax, 415/459-5267) and head upslope, via the Cataract Trail from just off Bolinas Rd. outside of Fairfax and past Alpine Lake—something of a steep climb but worth it for the waterfalls, most dramatic in winter and early spring but sublime for pool-sitting in summer.

Via the Matt Davis Trail, or the Bootjack Camp or Pan Toll Ranger Station routes, hike to the charming old (1904) **West Point Inn**, 1000 Panoramic Hwy., 415/388-9955, for a glass of lemonade and a rest in the porch shade. Four miles away is the **Tourist Club**, 30 Ridge Ave., 415/388-9987, a 1912 chalet where overnight stays are available only to members and their families, but hikers arriving via the Sun, Redwood, or Panoramic Trails can get snacks, cold imported beer, sodas, and juices. More accessible for a picnic or snack stop (bring your own) is Mount Tam's Greek-style **Mountain Theater,** a 5,000-seat outdoor amphitheater on Ridgecrest Blvd., the site each spring of a major musical stage production.

Mount Tamalpais State Park (admission free, though parking may cost you) is open daily from 7 A.M. to sunset. Limited primitive camping and other accommodations are available. For more information, contact park headquarters at 801 Panoramic Hwy., Mill Valley, CA 94941, 415/388-2070. For current information on Mount Tam's Mountain Theater productions, call the **Mountain Play Association** at 415/383-1100 or 415/383-0155.

Muir Woods National Monument

Muir Woods is peaceful and serene but quite a popular place—not necessarily the best destination for getting away from them all. Lush redwood canyon country surrounds Redwood Creek within the boundaries of Mount Tamalpais State Park, with a short trail system meandering alongside the stream, up to the ridge tops, and into the monument's main Cathedral and Bohemian redwood groves. For an easy, introductory stroll, the Muir Woods Nature Trail wanders through the flatlands, identifying the characteristic trees and shrubs. Fascinating at Muir Woods, the first national monument in the United States, are the dawn redwood from China and the park's albino redwood, the shoots from this freak of nature completely chlorophyll-free. But to avoid the crowds imported in all those tour buses clogging the parking lot, get away from the visitor center and the trails near the parking lot. Muir Woods is open daily 8 A.M.–sunset, $1 day-use fee, no picnicking or camping. No dogs. For more information, contact: Muir Woods National Monument, Mill Valley, CA 94941, 415/388-2595 or 415/388-2596, www.nps.gov/muwo.

EASTERN MARIN AND VICINITY

Though the marshlands and open areas fringing the northern and eastern portions of San Pablo Bay could almost be included, the San Francisco Bay's northernmost boundary is actually Marin County. More than just the structural anchor for the other side of San Francisco's Golden Gate Bridge, eastern Marin has somehow become the psychological center for "the good life" Californians pursue with such trendsetting abandon. This pursuit costs money, of course, but there's plenty of that in Marin County, which boasts one of the highest per-capita income levels in the nation. Jaguars, Porsches, and more exotic automobiles are among Marin folks' favored means of transport, and BMWs are so common here that the late *San Francisco Chronicle* columnist Herb Caen long referred to them as Boring Marin Wagons.

Jokes about Marin County change, but other things stay the same. The weather here is unusually pleasant, mild in both summer and winter. Also, Marin au naturel is incredibly diverse. From Mill Valley west to the Bolinas Lagoon near Point Reyes, seven different ecological communities are typical: chaparral, grassland, coastal scrub, broadleaf forest, redwood and mixed evergreen forest, salt marsh, and beach strand. Almost one-third of the county is public parkland—national, state, and local.

CITIES AND SIGHTS

Sausalito
Sausalito is a community by land and by sea, a hillside hamlet far surpassed in eccentricity by the

highly creative hodgepodge of houseboaters also anchored here. Aside from the pleasures of just being here, stop in Sausalito at the U.S. Army Corps of Engineers' **San Francisco Bay Model,** 2100 Bridgeway, 415/332-3870, a working 1.5-acre facsimile of the Bay and Delta built by the Corps to study currents, tides, salinity, and other natural features. We should all be grateful that the ever-industrious Corps realized it couldn't build a better bay even with access to all the bulldozers, landfill, and riprap in the world and settled, instead, for just making a toy version. Interpretive audio tours are available in English, Russian, German, Japanese, French, and Spanish. Guided group tours (10 or more people) can be arranged by calling 415/332-3871 at least four weeks in advance. Open in summer Tues.–Fri. 9 A.M.–4 P.M., weekends and holidays 10 A.M.–5 P.M.; the rest of the year, Tues.–Sat. 9 A.M.–4 P.M. Free.

For more information about Sausalito attractions and practicalities, contact: **Sausalito Chamber of Commerce,** 29 Caledonia St., Sausalito, CA 94965, 415/331-7262, www.sausalito.org, open weekdays 9 A.M.–5 P.M.

Tiburon

Tiburon ("shark" in Spanish), once a ramshackle railroad town, is an affluent bayside community most noted for the Audubon Society's 900-acre **Richardson Bay Audubon Center and Sanctuary,** 376 Greenwood Beach Rd. (in the Belvedere Cove tidal baylands), 415/388-2524. Wonderful for bird-watching and nature walks, also picnicking (pack out your trash); day-use fee $2. Tiburon is also home to Dr. Gerald Jampolsky's **Center for Spiritual Healing,** 415/435-2281, a well-respected organization that emphasizes the emotional and spiritual aspects of healing in the face of catastrophic illness and events. The wooded 24-acre **Tiburon Uplands Nature Preserve,** south of Paradise Beach Park on Paradise Dr., 415/499-6387, includes a natural history loop trail and great bay views from higher ground. Absolutely spectacular for spring wildflowers, though, are the few acres surrounding the 19th-century gothic church at **Old St. Hilary's Historic Preserve,** 201 Esperanza (at Mar West), 415/435-2567, open to the public Wed. and Sun. 1–4 P.M. Apr.–Oct., otherwise by appointment only. Nearby Belvedere is one of the nation's 10 most expensive outposts of suburbia.

For more information about Tiburon attractions and practicalities, contact: **Tiburon Chamber of Commerce,** 96 Main St. #B, Tiburon, CA 94920, 415/435-5633.

Mill Valley

Mill Valley is another affluent North Bay bedroom community, this one rooted on the eastern slope of Mount Tamalpais. The big event here every autumn is the **Mill Valley Film Festival,** the biggest little film festival outside Telluride, Colorado, with screenings of local, American independent, international, avant-garde, and various premier films. For more information about the festival, contact the festival office at 38 Miller Ave., 415/383-5256. For information on other Marin art events, contact the **Marin Arts Council,** 251 N. San Pedro Rd., Building O, San Rafael, CA 94903, 415/499-8350, which publishes a free monthly *Marin ArtsGuide* and the quarterly *Marin Review* (available free to council members but also often available at local chambers of commerce).

Area Nature Preserves

Inland on the Tiburon Peninsula near Corte Madera is the **Ring Mountain Preserve,** another Nature Conservancy success story. A protected tract of native California grasslands around a 600-foot-tall hill known for its unusual serpentine soils and rare endemic plants, geological peculiarities, and Native American petroglyphs, Ring Mountain is known particularly for the rare Tiburon mariposa lilies—they grow nowhere else—that now thrive here, in a population estimated at 32,000 plants. To get to Ring Mountain, take the Paradise Dr. exit from Hwy. 101, then continue east to the preserve's entrance, 1.75 miles down the road. For more information, contact Marin County Open Space, 3501 Civic Center Dr., Room 415, San Rafael, CA 94903, 415/499-6387. Also in Marin is the **Spindrift Point Preserve** near Sausalito; for more information, call the Nature Conservancy at 415/777-0487.

San Rafael

San Rafael is Marin's biggest little city and the county seat, a Modesto-like community where scenes from George Lucas's *American Graffiti* were shot (on 4th St., restaurant row). San

ANGEL ISLAND STATE PARK

Still sometimes called the "Ellis Island of the West," at the turn of the 20th century Angel Island was the door through which Asian immigrants passed on their way to America. Japanese and other "enemy aliens" were imprisoned here during World War II, when the island's facilities served as a detention center. Explore the West Garrison Civil War barracks and buildings at the 1863 site of Camp Reynolds—built and occupied by Union troops determined to foil the Confederacy's plans to invade the bay and then the gold country. Among the buildings, the largest surviving collection of Civil War structures in the nation, note the cannons still aimed to sea (but never used in the war because Confederate troops never showed up). On weekends, volunteers in the park's living history program—with the help of apparently willing visitors—fire off the cannons, just in case the South rises again.

Though most visitors never get past the sun and sand at Ayala Cove (where the Cove Cafe offers lunch, coffee, and beer), also worth a stop are the 1899 Chinese Immigration Center, quarantine central for new Asian arrivals, and World War II–era Fort McDowell on the island's east side near the Civil War battlements. Often sunny in summer when the rest of the Bay Area is shivering in the fog, outdoorsy types consider Angel Island's hiking trails its chief attraction. (The eucalyptus trees being felled on Angel Island are nonnatives first planted in the 1860s and now being removed so natural vegetation can be reintroduced.) On a clear day, the view from the top

of Angel Island's Mount Livermore is spectacular—with three bridges and almost the entire Bay Area seemingly within reach.

For unbeatable scenery (and sometimes brisk winds), picnic atop Mount Livermore. The intrepid can even camp on Angel Island, which features nine hike-in environmental campsites. Call park headquarters for information and reservations. (Campstove or charcoal cooking only—no fires.) If you're coming, come light, since you'll have to manage it on the ferry and pack it all into camp, at least a mile hike. The **Tiburon-Angel Island State Park Ferry,** berthed at the pier on Main St. in Tiburon, 415/435-2131, is available to island-bound hikers, bikers, and backpackers daily during summer (and often into autumn, weather permitting), but only on weekends during the rest of the year. The **Blue & Gold Fleet,** 415/773-1188, also offers Angel Island runs from San Francisco's Pier 41.

For more information about island hikes and docent-led tours of historic sites, also current ferry schedules, contact: **Angel Island State Park headquarters,** 1455 E. Francis Blvd., San Rafael, CA 94501, or P.O. Box 866, Tiburon, CA 94920, 415/ 435-1915. For information on tram tours of the island, as well as mountain-bike and kayak rentals there, call 415/897-0715. For information about island tours for the disabled and about fundraising and other volunteer work to continue the island's restoration, contact: **Angel Island Association,** P.O. Box 866, Tiburon, CA 94920, 415/435-3522.

CALIFORNIA DEPARTMENT OF PARKS & RECREATION

Angel Island State Park, once the Ellis Island of the West

THE BAY BEYOND MARIN

San Pablo Bay National Wildlife Refuge
Also along the shores of San Pablo Bay—to the northeast, between the Petaluma and Napa Rivers south of Hwy. 37—are the salt marshes, mudflats, and open waters of the San Pablo Bay National Wildlife Refuge, a winter refueling stop for migrating shorebirds and waterfowl, also permanent home to two endangered species: the California clapper rail and the salt marsh harvest mouse. Largely undeveloped but accessible—under certain strict conditions—for boaters and hunters, the only easy access for the general public is at **Tubbs Island**, originally acquired by the Nature Conservancy. To get here, park (well off the road) along Hwy. 37 just east of its intersection with Hwy. 121 (and just east of Tolay Creek) and walk. It's almost three miles (one-way) to these marsh ponds and nature trails on the northern edge of San Pablo Bay. Open during daylight hours only, no restrooms available, bring your own drinking water. For more information, contact: San Pablo Bay National Wildlife Refuge, P.O. Box 2012, Mare Island, CA 94592, 707/562-3000.

Six Flags Marine World and Vicinity
Vallejo sprawls across the point where the Napa River flows into San Pablo Bay, near the Mare Island Naval Shipyard. Vallejo is also home to Six Flags Marine World, a big-time theme park next to the Solano County Fairgrounds. A popular venue for family-style fun, Marine World features some 30 rides—including Boomerang, Hammerhead Shark, Kong, Roar, and Voodoo—and 35 marine and land animal exhibits. Among the most intriguing experiences are the tamest, including strolls through the fluttering **Lorikeet Aviary** and the glassed-in **Butterfly Habitat.** Trained-animal performances and other shows round out the action here. Marine World is open daily in summer, weekends only in fall and spring, and is closed entirely Nov.–Feb.; call or see the website for current days and hours. At last report, admission was $34 adults, $25 seniors, and $17 children (under 48 inches tall). There's a parking fee, too. For more information, contact: Six Flags Marine World, Marine World Parkway, Vallejo, CA 94589, 707/644-4000, www.sixflags.com/marineworld. For more information about Vallejo and vicinity, contact: **Vallejo Chamber of Commerce,** 2 Florida St., Vallejo, CA 94590, 707/644-5551, www.vallejochamber.com.

Northeast of Vallejo and north of Suisun Bay is Fairfield and adjacent Travis Air Force Base with its **Travis Air Force Base Heritage Center Museum,** 707/424-5605, www.travis.af.mil/, open 9 A.M.–5 P.M. weekends and 9 A.M.–4 P.M. weekdays, an impressive indoor-outdoor collection of old aircraft—including a handmade 1912 wooden biplane, cargo planes, jet fighters, and bombers.

Rafael is known for its downtown mansion district; for the 1947 replica of the **Mission San Rafael** (second to last in California's mission chain), 1104 5th Ave., open daily 11 A.M.–4 P.M.; and most of all for the **Marin Civic Center** just off Hwy. 101, Frank Lloyd Wright's last major architectural accomplishment. The center, home to the county's administrative complex and quite the tour de force, exemplifies Wright's obsession with the idea that all things are (or should become) circular. Surrounded by 140 acres of lovingly groomed grounds, the county fair is held here on the fourth weekend of July.

The **Marin Civic Center/Marin County Certified Farmers' Market,** toll-free 800/897-3276, takes place here Thurs. and Sun. 8 A.M.–1 P.M., year-round, rain or shine; this is as good a place as any to sample public opinion on recent proposals to abandon the civic center. Docent-led civic center tours are available, but call 415/499-6646 at least several days in advance. The center is wheelchair accessible, open weekdays 8 A.M.–5 P.M. (excepting legal holidays). To find out about major events and entertainment programs, request a current copy of the quarterly civic center arts magazine, *Marin Center.*

For more information about the area, contact the **San Rafael Chamber of Commerce,** 817 Mission Ave., San Rafael, CA 94901, 415/454-4163, www.localcommunities.com, open weekdays 9 A.M.–5 P.M.

Nearby Greenbrae is neighbor to **San Quentin State Prison,** California's first prison, home since the mid-1800s to sociopaths and other criminals; early prisoners wore balls-and-chains fashioned from surplus Civil War canon balls. Not all inmates were necessarily criminals; more than 100 union members and organizers of the Industrial

Workers of the World were also imprisoned here after World War I. Fascinating here: the prison museum (new in 1985) and the Boot Hill prison cemetery (not usually accessible to visitors), posthumous home to a veritable Who's Who of Very Bad Guys. Head on through the entrance to visit the **California State Prison Museum,** just inside the main gate, with its artifacts, memorabilia, historical photographs, and records documenting the prison's history. Stop by the prison gift shop for inmate-made arts and crafts—from San Quentin T-shirts and hats to belt buckles, rings and other jewelry, artwork, and novelties. For hours and information on both, call 415/454-8808.

ASK MR. JELLY BELLY

A particularly sweet treat in Fairfield is the tour of the Herman Goelitz Candy Company and adjacent **Jelly Belly Visitors Center,** where the phrase "bean counter" takes on immense new meaning—especially just before Easter, when the factory here produces more than a million jelly beans every hour. These aren't just any jelly beans. Former President Ronald Reagan made them internationally famous, when he started to eat Jelly Belly beans to help kick his pipe-smoking habit. And a Jelly Belly was the first jelly bean in space. These are the original "gourmet jelly beans." The company boasts 40 flavors on its regular roster—buttered popcorn, root beer, pink bubble gum, jalapeño, and many fruit flavors among them—and produces many more for its seasonal lists. Jelly Belly is always experimenting with new possibilities, these known as "rookies," which each get a one-year tryout.

At the end of the factory tour, you'll probably meet up with a few rookies. But first you'll follow the **Jelly Belly Candy Trail,** looking down on the production floor to see how the beans are made. You'll also find out how the company comes up with all those flavors. You'll even get to sample the merchandise. There's a fully stocked Jelly Belly store and a Jelly Belly restaurant.

Free tours are offered several times daily (except major holidays, April 1, and two weeks in summer). For current information, call 707/428-2838. To take a virtual Jelly Belly tour, the website is www.jellybelly.com. Mr. Jelly Belly will happily answer all your questions.

China Camp State Park

After the gold rush, many of California's Chinese turned to fishing as a way to make ends meet. Chinese fishing camps were common all along the northstate's coast, and 30 or more flourished on the more remote edges of San Francisco Bay. The Chinese were quite successful at plying their trade in the state's waters—so successful that by the 1900s enforcement of anti-Chinese, anti–bag netting fishing laws essentially killed these Asian communities. Partially restored China Camp, once the Bay Area's largest Chinese shrimp center, is the last of these old fishing villages. The community, where John Wayne's *Blood Alley* was filmed, survives now as a memory complete with history museum, renovated buildings, and rebuilt rickety piers. The only actual survivor is **Frank Quan's bait and sandwich shop,** which serves up fresh bay shrimp when available (put in your order early, especially on weekends). The park's 1,600 acres of oak forest, grasslands, and salt marshes also offer hiking, picnicking, and walk-in developed campsites. Reserve through ReserveAmerica, toll-free 800/444-7275.

China Camp State Park is open daily, sunrise to sunset; day-use fee is $3. The museum is open daily 10 A.M.–5 P.M. year-round. To get here, take the San Pedro Rd. exit from Hwy. 101 and continue for several miles past the Marin Civic Center. For more information, contact: China Camp State Park, Rte. 1 Box 244, San Rafael, CA 94901, 415/456-0766.

Novato

Two museums in Novato are worth a stop: **Novato History Museum,** 815 De Long Ave., 415/897-4320, a monument to the town's pioneer past, open Wed.–Thurs. and Sat. noon–4 P.M. (free), and **Marin Museum of the American Indian** and park at 2200 Novato Blvd., 415/897-4064, a small but fascinating place with friendly staff and hands-on exhibits and other displays about Coast Miwok and Pomo culture. Open Tues.–Sat. 10 A.M.–3 P.M., Sat. noon–4 P.M., closed Sunday. Free.

Just north of Novato is **Olompali State Historic Park,** P.O. Box 1016, Novato, CA 94948, 415/892-3383, a 700-acre ranch with broad historic significance. At one time it was a major Miwok trading village, a fact archaeological finds have verified. Sir Francis Drake and his men

HEAR YE, HEAR YE~WHERE'S THE FAIRE?

To experience the Middle Ages modern style, head for the long-running **Renaissance Pleasure Faire,** sponsored by the Bay Area's Living History Center, toll-free 800/523-2473 for current details and tickets. Held almost forever in Novato's Black Point Forest just off Hwy. 37, of late the Faire has been on the move—looking for a new permanent home. In 1999, the Faire's 33rd year, it settled into the old Nut Tree spread in Vacaville. Wherever it is these days, Northern California's own Renaissance Pleasure Faire is held on weekends from September through mid-October, 10 A.M.–6 P.M.

During the Faire, life in the local shire features an authentic return trip to 16th-century England, on the world's largest stage—a mile-long Elizabethan village with 16 separate neighborhood villages inhabited by thousands of corporate executives, computer programmers, housewives, and other amateur medievalists (including paying guests) dressed and acting in historical character and speaking only "Basic Faire Accent."

In keeping with Northern California history, Sir Francis Drake himself presides over each day's opening ceremonies; the queen leaves the shire by late afternoon. But in between, the activity never ends. There are madrigal groups and musical processions; games, juggling, singing, and dancing; full-contact fighting and jousting; feasts of broiled beef, beer, and fresh-baked bread, mixed inimitably with other aromas—incense and herbs and flower essence—in the air. At last report, admission was $17.50 adults, $15 seniors and students with current ID, and $7.50 children ages 5–11 (under 5 free). Call for current details and directions.

---

may have passed through, since a silver six-pence circa 1567 was discovered here. A Bear Flag Revolt skirmish occurred at the Olompali Adobe in the mid-1800s. Olompali's tenure as a ranch is obvious, given the weathered barns and the Victorian home of the onetime ranch manager. Restoration and park development are still underway, but the public is welcome to stop for a picnic and a hike to the top of Burdell Mountain, offering some good views of San Pablo Bay. Olompali is open daily 10 A.M.–7 P.M. Small day-use fee. Getting here is easy from the north; from Hwy. 101, just take the marked exit (north of Novato proper). From the south via Hwy. 101, exit at San Antonio Rd. and head west, then backtrack to the park on Hwy. 101.

ROBERT HOLMES/CalTour

THE WINE COUNTRY
SMALL IS BEAUTIFUL

The inland valleys of Napa, Sonoma, Mendocino, and Lake Counties have become known as California's wine country—this despite the fact that a fairly small percentage of California wines are produced in this region. Quality, not quantity, is the point here, an area home to some of the state's (and the world's) finest small wineries.

Yet California's small-is-beautiful wine country secret has definitely been shared. Millions of visitors each year squeeze through the Napa Valley alone. The foothills and valleys, cooled by north coastal weather patterns yet usually fog-free, snap to life with lush greenery in spring when the vines and foothill trees leaf out. On warmer summer weekends—and on weekends generally—wine-tasting traffic is bumper-to-bumper. By late September and early October, most of the summer's tourists have evaporated, though the sweet harvest heat still hangs in the air and the vineyards flame with autumn colors. This is the best time to come, particularly on weekdays. Whenever you arrive, stick to back-road routes (and destinations) whenever possible to avoid the worst of the wine-country crush.

"Bottled Poetry" and other Appreciations

For many, a first-time trip to the wine country is overwhelming. Particularly in the Napa Valley, the first impression is one of pleasure-seeking pretension: too few people have too much money and all arrive at the same place (at almost the same time) to spend it on themselves. Yet these first impressions aren't lasting. California's wine country is actually dedicated, consciously and otherwise, to an appreciation of the appetites—and to an understanding of how we human beings go about satisfying them.

Writer Robert Louis Stevenson hinted at modern wine-country trends in his *Silverado Squatters* when he described the 19th-century Schramsberg wines as "bottled poetry." Closer to the modern-day mark, though, is Sonoma Valley resident M. F. K. Fisher, food writer extraordinaire, who died in June 1992. Fisher was America's finest

THE WINE COUNTRY

To Laytonville
Mendocino
National Forest
To Willows

To Fort Bragg
Willits
Lake Pillsbury

Russian River
Eel River
Snow Mountain Wilderness

Potter Valley
Redwood Valley

To Hwy. 1
Lake Mendocino
Ukiah
Cow Mtn. Recreation Area
Talmage
Mendocino National Forest

HENDY WOODS STATE PARK
Philo

Boonville
Upper Lake
Nice

MAILLIARD REDWOODS STATE RESERVE
Hopland
Lakeport
Clear Lake
Lucerne

Yorkville
Kelseyville
Clearlake Oaks
To Williams

Mt. Konocti (4200 ft.)
CLEAR LAKE STATE PARK
Indian Valley Reservoir

Preston
Clearlake
ANDERSON MARSH STATE HISTORIC PARK

Lake Sonoma Recreation Area
Cloverdale
Lake Sonoma
Asti
Cobb
BOGGS MOUNTAIN STATE FOREST

Austin Creek State Recreation Area
Geyserville
Harbin Springs
Rumsey

Cazadero
Jimtown
Middletown
Knoxville
Guinda

Armstrong Redwoods State Reserve
Lytton
Healdsburg
Kellogg
ROBERT LOUIS STEVENSON STATE PARK
Tancred

Guerneville
Rio Nido
Windsor
Brooks

Duncans Mills
Jenner
Monte Rio
Forestville
Graton
Fulton
Calistoga
Pope Valley
Lake Berryessa
Capay

BOTHE-NAPA VALLEY STATE PARK
BALE GRIST MILL S.H.P.
Angwin
Deer Park
Lake Hennessey
To I-505 and Woodland

Occidental
Freestone
Santa Rosa
St. Helena

Bodega Bay
Bodega
Sebastopol
Annadel State Park
Rutherford
Kenwood
To I-5
Winters

Valley Ford
Bloomfield
Rohnert Park
JACK LONDON S.H.P.
Glen Ellen
SONOMA VALLEY REGIONAL PARK
Oakville
Yountville

Dillon Beach
Cotati
Penngrove
SONOMA STATE HISTORIC PARK
PETALUMA ADOBE S.H.P.

Point Reyes National Seashore
Marshall
Petaluma
Vineburg
Schellville
Sonoma
Napa
Vacaville

PACIFIC OCEAN
Lakeville
To San Francisco
To Vallejo
To San Francisco
To Sacramento

0   7 mi
0   7 km

© AVALON TRAVEL PUBLISHING, INC.

prose writer according to W. H. Auden, and "poet of the appetites" to John Updike. More than anyone else, Mary Frances Kennedy Fisher is responsible (in America) for newly nonpuritanical and unaffected attitudes about the pure pleasures of good regional foods and wines. That she settled in California's wine country is no accident.

Indulgence and Overindulgence

Notably, but not exclusively, American is the blurred line between indulgence and overindulgence, particularly as applied to alcohol and other mood-altering drugs. When the appearance of pleasure is actually a self-administered remedy of "spirits" to alleviate personal spiritual pain, addiction shows up, the shadow side of the pleasure principle. Alcohol abuse and alcoholism aren't more prevalent in the wine country than elsewhere in California, but the opportunities for their more open expression are almost endless.

Perhaps it's also no coincidence that the phenomenally successful adventure novelist Jack London, whose alcohol-related death at age 40 shocked the world, lived here with his second wife, Charmian, for many otherwise charmed (if compulsive) years on their Glen Ellen ranch north of Sonoma. He lived by following the boldly defiant creed:

I would rather be ashes than dust! I would rather that my spark should burn out in a brilliant blaze than it should be stifled by dry rot. I would rather be a superb meteor, every atom of me in magnificent glow, than a sleepy and permanent planet. The proper function of man is to live, not to exist. I shall not waste my days trying to prolong them. I shall use my time.

AREA CODES
THEY ARE A CHANGIN'

In late December 2000, and then again in October of the following year, Northern California will suffer yet another change in telephone area codes—the direct result of residents' red-hot relationship with communications technology and the proliferating numbers of cellular phones, fax machines, and online computer connections that go with it.

The old 707 area, which covered much of the northern part of the Bay Area and the Wine Country, as well as the entire north coast, will get two new codes—369 and 627—in late December 2000. In affected areas to the south—including Dixon, Rio Vista, Vacaville, Fairfield, Suisun City, Benicia, and Vallejo—you can use either 707 or 369 beginning December 2000, but you must use 369 by June 2001. The second phase, introducing the 627 code, affects Cloverdale, Geyserville, Healdsburg, Sea Ranch, Bodega Bay, Guerneville, Forestville, Sebastopol, Santa Rosa, Calistoga, St. Helena, Rohnert Park, Sonoma, Yountville, and Napa. "Permissive dialing"—meaning you can use either area code—begins in October 2001, but 627 will be mandatory by April 2002.

In addition to these changes in telephone area codes, it's likely that more will occur during the useful life of this book. If you have trouble using any area codes listed in this book, dial 0 and ask the operator for current information.

London also died by his personal creed. A noted barroom orator and people's philosopher who wrote of his struggles with alcohol, he died officially of gastrointestinal uremic poisoning in 1916. Whether his death was actually due to a morphine overdose is still disputed by his biographers.

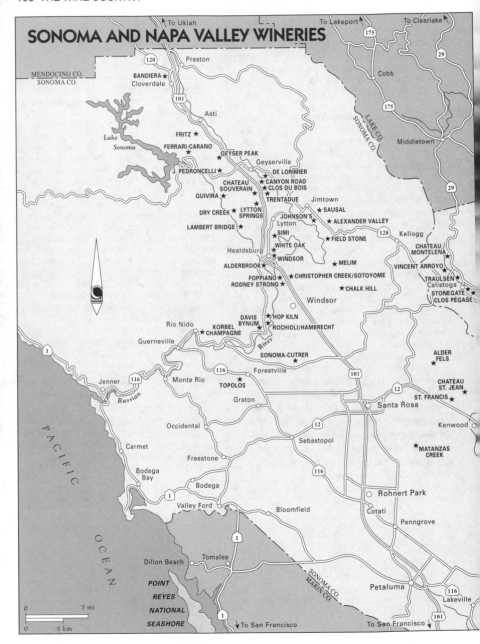

SONOMA AND NAPA VALLEY WINERIES

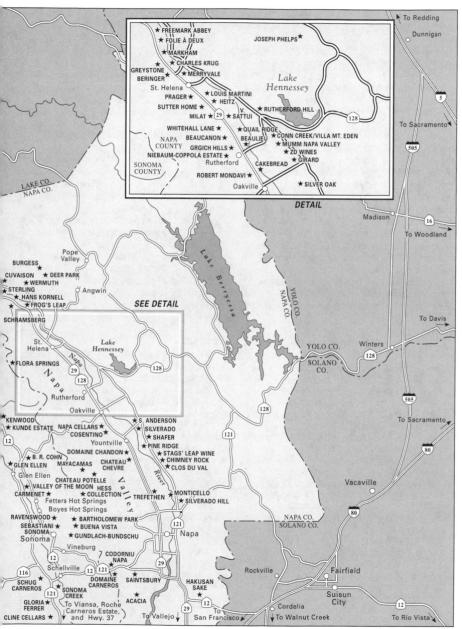

© AVALON TRAVEL PUBLISHING, INC.

NAPA AND VICINITY

A cozy 35 miles long and framed by rounded rolling hills, the Napa Valley is the nation's most famous vineyard and winery region. Though the town of Napa is more prosaic than Sonoma, the valley itself has seasonally changing charm, hill-hugging vineyards, world-renowned wineries, and famous spas—experiences available, for the most part, even to budget travelers. Disappointed refugees from the goldfields helped build the city of Napa, working in lumber mills, orchards, and on cattle ranches. Napa in the 1850s was already a rowdy town of hotels, saloons, and money. But the "silver rush" of the late 1870s brought more of all these, plus mine shafts throughout the county. The hottest currency nowadays? Wine and rumors of wine, tourists and rumors of tourists. But since 1996, Napa has been the preseason training-camp home to the **Oakland Raiders,** the bad boys of Bay Area football, a fact that has generated rumors of celebrity, sports, and sports celebrities.

For information on the entire Napa Valley, in addition to what's available from individual community chambers of commerce, contact the **Napa Valley Conference and Visitors Bureau,** 1310 Napa Town Center, Napa, CA 94559, 707/226-7459, www.napavalley.com.

CITY OF NAPA AND VICINITY

Most Napa wineries aren't *in* Napa but are farther north, scattered among the more picturesque Napa Valley towns. Napa itself is a blue-collar town, where most of the winery farm workers live, yet well on its way to becoming a permanent upscale bedroom community for San Francisco and the Bay Area—and an unabashed anchor for the fleets of wine tasters sloshing northward. More than half of the valley's 100,000-plus population is concentrated here. Despite the grape-stained march of progress, Napa's small townness lives on in older, shady neighborhoods (some dignified and stately Victorians preside

WINE-TASTING

Though there *are* other things to do, tasting superior wines—and finding out how they're made—is where the action is for most wine-country travelers. In preparation for wine-tasting, *don't* feel obliged to memorize lines like "rich, bold, unassuming," "light but perspicacious," and "flushed with heroic tonalities." Pretense is passé; an honest personal response is all that's required. To get up to speed on the sensory awareness skills and wine knowledge necessary for informed appreciation, buy a copy of *The University Wine Course,* an excellent self tutorial and comprehensive text by Dr. Marian Baldy available through the Wine Appreciation Guild in San Francisco, 800/231-9463.

Courtesy, however, is never out of style. Because too many wine-country visitors still assume wine-tasting is primarily an opportunity to get drunk for free, most wineries now charge a tasting fee or offer wine-tasting only after tours. And because still too many people come, some wineries also require advance reservations even for tasting. Keep in mind, too, that small, independent wineries are often family operations: tasting rooms and tours tend to shut

down when everyone's out in the fields or busy in the wineries. So, always call before going.

For the sake of wine art appreciation, beginners should start at the established larger wineries—many give educational and informational tours—before venturing into the small winery avant-garde. Focus on one variety of wine or wine grape while tasting, or start with a white, proceed on to a rosé or red wine, then finish with a dessert wine. Do ask questions whenever possible, particularly at smaller wineries where hands-on experience *creates* the experience. People here love what they do and (generally) like to talk about it.

While wine-tasting, be selective about stops—try to visit only a handful of wineries each day—and, if traveling by car, choose a nondrinking designated driver in advance. Tasting rooms are dangerously close together as you head north on Hwy. 29 through the Napa Valley, so the unwary can easily be seeing double before getting as far as St. Helena. Wineries are also quite cozy in the Sonoma Valley. Drunk driving is not only dangerous, it's illegal—a serious offense in California.

over Division, Randolph, and 5th Sts.), which can be toured in more detail with an assist from the local walking tour brochure.

Napa has its share of intriguing shops (lots of antique stores) and galleries, including the **Napa County Historical Society Museum and Gallery,** 1219 1st St. (in the library building downtown), 707/224-1739, open Tues. and Thurs. noon–4 P.M. To power up for further shopping and wine-tasting, stop by the "ABC"—**Alexis Baking Company**—not far away at 1517 3rd St., 707/258-1827, for a good cup of coffee and a piece of cake.

For more information about Napa and environs, including free maps, winery information, suggested bike routes and picnic stops, contact: **Napa Chamber of Commerce,** 1556 1st St., P.O. Box 636, Napa, CA 94559, 707/226-7455, www.napachamber.com. For valley-wide information, contact the nearby **Napa Valley Conference and Visitors Bureau,** listed above.

A Garden of Modern Art: The di Rosa Art and Nature Preserve

The 200-acre di Rosa Art and Nature Preserve, 5200 Carneros Hwy. (Hwy. 12/121), 707/226-5991, fax 707/255-8934, www.dirosapreserve.org, a onetime winery right across the road from Domaine Carneros, is a fascinating destination on the Napa end of the Carneros region. This 40-year-old labor of love by Rene di Rosa and his late wife Veronica, open to the public since March 1997, blends art into the landscape in surprising ways.

The motto of the eclectic collection here is: "Divinely regional, superbly parochial, wondrously provincial—an absolute native glory." More than 1,600 works by emerging Northern California artists, most of them from Davis, Sacramento, and the San Francisco Bay Area, have the run of the place—having taken over the winery building, multiple galleries, and the large meadow and lake. A wooden horse pulls a cart, cows inhabit the lake, sheep guard the dam, and a rooster hangs from a tree—but the only living, breathing animals in the collection are the peacocks. A vehicle that once belonged to di Rosa's mother, refashioned with horse head and saddle and otherwise surprisingly redecorated, is among several reimagined car mosaics on display. If you expect the label on each work to explain

what you're looking at, you're out of luck—no labels here, because di Rosa wants people to look at the *art.*

So, come and look—at the Robert Arneson bust at the door in the main gallery, Ray Beldner's *Nature Remains,* the Mark Di Suvero, the Robert Hudson, the Viola Frey, and all the others. The di Rosa Preserve is open for tours (two-plus hours) year-round, and they are conducted rain or shine. Call for tour times and reservations (required). The cost is $10 per person.

Coming Soon: The American Center for Wine, Food & the Arts

Coming soon to a 13-acre site on the banks of the Napa River is the $44-million American Center for Wine, Food & the Arts, scheduled to open its doors around Thanksgiving in the year 2001. Brainchild of Robert Mondavi, the Napa Valley's visionary winemaker, this unique museum—the first in the world devoted exclusively to food and wine—will be dedicated to "the American passion for living well," in Mondavi's words, and to elevating America's cultural image worldwide. Centered in a two-story, 75,000-square-foot main pavilion with working kitchens, interactive exhibits, art galleries, performance space, seminar and education facilities, café, and gift shop surrounded by seven acres of flower, vegetable, and herb gardens, this new food and wine mecca will also include a 500-seat outdoor amphitheater for live music and theater performances. For current information, contact the center at 707/257-3606, fax 707/257-8601, www.theamericancenter.org.

Napa Area Wineries: Silverado Trail

Escape the crush by avoiding Hwy. 29 as much as possible. Instead, head up the **Silverado Trail** from Napa to Calistoga on the valley's east side. (Cut across the valley to Hwy. 29 and westside wineries via several main crossroads.) Near Napa on the Silverado Trail is **Silverado Hill Cellars,** 3105 Silverado Trail, 707/253-9306, open for retail sales Mon.– Fri. 10 A.M.–4:30 P.M. (tasting and tours by appointment only). A bit farther north, turn left on Oak Knoll Ave. to reach a couple of other good tasting options. **Monticello Cellars,** 4242 Big Ranch Rd. (off Oak Knoll), 707/253-2802 or toll-free 800/743-6668, offers tasting and picnicking daily 10 A.M.–4:30 P.M., tours three times daily. The immense three-story redwood winery at **Trefethen Vineyards,** 1160 Oak Knoll Ave., 707/255-7700, produces four premium varietals; open for tasting daily 10 A.M.–4:30 P.M., tours by appointment.

Back on Silverado Trail, north of the Big Ranch turnoff (in the hilly Stags' Leap area), **Clos du Val,** 5330 Silverado Trail, 707/259-2225, is open daily 10 A.M.–5 P.M. for tasting (European-style wines) and shady picnics (tours by appointment only). Next door is **Chimney Rock Winery,** 5350 Silverado Trail, 707/257-2641 (tasting daily 10 A.M.–4 P.M., tours by appointment only). A bit farther north (about six miles north of Napa) is modern **Stags' Leap Wine Cellars,** 5766 Silverado Trail, 707/944-2020, noted for its chardonnay, sauvignon blanc, merlot, and its particularly popular cabernet sauvignon. Open for tasting (fee) daily 10 A.M.–4 P.M. (tours by appointment only).

Continuing north up Silverado Trail from Stags' Leap, you'll pass several other worthy wineries. Tiny **Pine Ridge Winery,** 5901 Silverado Trail, 707/253-7500 (administration) or 707/252-9777 (tours and tasting), produces 85,000 cases of its several premium wines annually and is open daily 11 A.M.–4 P.M. for tasting and picnicking (tours by appointment). **Silverado Vineyards,** 6121 Silverado Trail, 707/257-1770, is known for its chardonnay, cabernet, and herb-scented sauvignon blanc; tasting is offered daily 11 A.M.–4:30 P.M. in the visitor center (tours by appointment). Nearby is **Shafer Vineyards,** 6154 Silverado Trail, 707/944-2877, noted for its cabernet sauvignon. Shafer is open for retail sales Mon.–Fri. 9 A.M.–4 P.M. (tasting and tours by appointment only).

Mayacamas Mountains Wineries

Well worth the adventurous side trip is **Mayacamas Vineyards,** 1155 Lokoya Rd., 707/224-4030, established here atop Mt. Veeder since 1941. Mayacamas is so *period,* in fact, that it was selected as a 1940s' location for the film *A Walk in the Clouds.* Low-tech and intriguing, Mayacamas makes some excellent wines— rich, earthy chardonnay that ages exceptionally well, cabernet sauvignon, some zinfandel and pinot noir—and the original 1889 stone winery is still used for winemaking. Closed weekends. Tours only by appointment.

NAPA VALLEY WINE TRAIN

Ever popular with tourists is the *Napa Valley Wine Train,* which rolls along 18 miles of railroad from Napa to St. Helena, paralleling Hwy. 29. Passengers ride in luxuriously renovated vintage 1915–47 Pullman cars, which feature plush touches such as burnished mahogany woodwork, overstuffed chairs, and marble-and-brass bathrooms. The basic *Wine Train* tour includes food (brunch, lunch, or dinner—all cooked up fresh onboard) and costs $57–70 plus gratuity. You can also opt to ride in the deli car (not available on the dinner trains), where you'll pay around $27.50 train fare and can purchase light food and beverages at additional cost, à la carte. In addition to a huge array of fine wines, full cocktail service is available. Trains run daily, and a full calendar of special events is offered. For information and reservations (required), contact: Napa Valley Wine Train, 1275 McKinstry St. (1st and Soscol), Napa, CA 94559, 707/253-2111 or toll-free 800/427-4124 (in California) or check it out on the web at www.winetrain.com.

TOM MYERS PHOTOGRAPHY

Napa Valley Wine Train

WINE COUNTRY BY CRUISE SHIP

You can't actually *do* Napa Valley and Sonoma wineries by cruise ship, of course—but you can get there by boat from San Francisco, certainly a memorable way to launch a wine country group adventure. The 82-passenger *Spirit of Alaska* offers two fall and spring small-ship cruises from San Francisco, the four-day/three-night **Weekend Escape for the Senses** and the five-day/four-night **Premium Wine Country Experience.** The four-day trip departs from San Francisco, spends the next day sightseeing and wine-tasting in Sonoma, and the following full day wine-tasting in the Napa Valley before the return trip to San Francisco. The five-day trip includes the same basic itinerary with an additional mid-trip excursion through the Sacramento–San Joaquin Delta to Old Sacramento for sightseeing and an overnight. Wineries visited each year change, but tend to include those not typically open for drop-in tastings and tours.

Four-day cruises start at $495 per person, double occupancy, and five-day cruises start at $695 per person, but more generous staterooms—with double beds, sofa, TV/VCR, and in-room refrigerator—and suites cost considerably more. For current details or to book a trip, contact: **Cruise West,** 4th & Battery Blvd., Ste. 700, Seattle, WA 98121, 206/441-8687 or toll-free 800/426-7702, fax 206/441-4757, www.smallship.com.

The remote, stone **Hess Collection Winery** in the Mayacamas hills just west of Napa, 4411 Redwood Rd., 707/255-1144, is noted for its chardonnay and cabernet sauvignon. But many people also come for the collection itself—very abstract contemporary American and European art dramatically showcased as part of the self-guided tour. The remodeled Christian Brothers winery also includes a small theater for watching a short slide show about growing grapes here on Mt. Veeder. Open daily 10 A.M.–4 P.M. for tasting and self-guided tours.

Napa-Carneros Wineries
Four miles southwest of Napa off Hwy. 12/Hwy. 121, **Saintsbury Vineyards,** 1500 Los Carneros Ave., 707/252-0592, produces pinot noir and chardonnay exclusively. Open Mon.–Fri. 9:30 A.M.–4:30 P.M. by appointment only. Exclusive is the word for **Acacia Winery,** 2750 Las Amigas Rd., 707/226-9991, which took almost immediate bows for its pinot noir and chardonnay. Open daily by appointment only. As striking as the wine is the avant-garde architecture of **Codorniu Napa,** 1345 Henry Rd., 707/224-1668, a sparkling wine venture by Spain's Codorniu clan; tasting is offered daily 10 A.M.–5 P.M. Also in the heart of the Carneros district, **Domaine Carneros,** 1240 Duhig Rd. (four miles southwest of town just off Hwy. 121/12), 707/257-0101, produces *méthode-champenoise* sparkling wine from Carneros grapes. Established in 1987 and already considered a regional landmark, Domaine Carneros is architecturally inspired by the historic 18th-century Champagne residence of the founding Taittinger family, as in Champagne Taittinger of Reims, France. Open daily 10:30 A.M.–6 P.M. for tours and tasting.

Not really "Carneros" but definitely different in the Napa Valley: **Hakusan Sake Gardens,** 1 Executive Way, at the southern junction of Hwy. 12 and Hwy. 29 (enter from N. Kelly Rd.), 707/258-6160 or toll-free 800/425-8726, which is open for sake tasting and sales daily 10 A.M.–5 P.M.

For wineries in the Sonoma area of the Carneros region, turn to Sonoma-Carneros Wineries in the Sonoma Valley section of this chapter.

Staying in Napa
The **Napa Valley Budget Inn,** 3380 Solano Ave. (formerly Motel 6, north of Napa proper via the Redwood Rd. exit off Hwy. 29), 707/257-6111 or toll-free 877/872-6272, is a small motel with air-conditioning and a pool, offering free local phone calls and continental breakfast. Moderate-Expensive. The **Discovery Inn,** 500 Silverado Trail (near Soscol Ave.), 707/253-0892, offers 15 clean units with small kitchens and TV. Expensive. **Napa Valley Travelodge,** 853 Coombs St. (at 2nd), 707/226-1871, is across from the courthouse (limited parking), four blocks from the *Wine Train.* Premium. The **Napa Valley Marriott,** 3425 Solano Ave., 707/253-7433 or toll-free 800/228-9290, is a full-service hotel with some country-inn charms—from lovely rooms to a scenic courtyard with heated pool and hot tub—as well as lighted tennis courts and a restaurant and lounge. Luxury.

NAPA VALLEY MUSTARD FESTIVAL

Spring in the Napa Valley is heralded by fields of blooming wild mustard—and the annual Napa Valley Mustard Festival, a seemingly endless calendar of events stretching from late January or early February through March. The Mustard Festival entertains visitors, celebrates mustard—and the arts, culture, and agriculture of the Napa Valley—and simultaneously serves local businesses, whose wares are on parade in myriad venues. But proceeds from the festival also support many local nonprofit organizations, including the Napa Valley Museum, the Sharpsteen Museum, Dreamweavers Theatre, and music and drama programs in local high schools. The program varies each year, but in 1999 the Mustard Festival started with January's **Mustard Magic—Une Soirée Française** at the Culinary Institute of America at Greystone, where the Grand Cask Room became a gallery and theater with trapeze artists dangling from the ceilings, accompanied by live opera, and the three-story atrium a Parisian café. The signature two-day **Napa Valley Mustard Festival Marketplace** in mid-March featured mustards from around the world, cooking demonstrations, arts and crafts, children's events, and live music on three stages. Other main events in 1999 included the **Valley Chef of the Year Mustard Recipe Competition** and the **Napa Valley Mustard Festival Photography Contest,** though endless other events—from Calistoga's **Yellow, Blues & All That Jazz** and **Savor St. Helena** to golf benefits, marathon runs, mountain biking, and Domaine Chandon's **Blessing of the Balloons**—completed the calendar. For current information—or to become a sponsor—contact the **Napa Valley Exposition,** headquartered at 575 3rd St. in Napa, 707/259-9020, www.mustardfestival.com.

Staying at Napa Bed-and-Breakfasts

Characteristic of the region, Napa has many bed-and-breakfasts, none particularly inexpensive. And Napa's historic homes have become the belles of the bed-and-breakfast ball. A notable Napa landmark is the 1902 **Beazley House,** 1910 1st St., 707/257-1649 or toll-free 800/559-1649, Napa's first bed-and-breakfast and still one of the best, with 11 guest rooms; all have private baths, six feature fireplaces, and five have whirlpools. Rates include full breakfast and complimentary tea and cookies. Premium-Luxury.

Arbor Guest House, 1436 G St., 707/252-8144, has five antique-filled rooms (three with fireplaces, two with double-wide spa tubs). Full breakfast. Two-night minimum on weekends. Premium-Luxury. An excellent choice is the 1899 Queen Anne Victorian **Napa Inn,** 1137 Warren St., 707/257-1444 or toll-free 800/435-1144, with six rooms (private baths), full breakfast, and evening dessert and refreshments. Premium-Luxury. The wheelchair-accessible **Candlelight Inn,** 1045 Easum Dr. (west of Hwy. 29 off 1st St.), 707/257-3717, a 1929 English Tudor on verdant, one-acre grounds, offers 10 rooms (all with private bath), a large swimming pool, full gourmet breakfast, and evening wine, sherry, and hors d'oeuvres. Premium-Luxury.

La Belle Époque, 1386 Calistoga Ave., 707/257-2161 or toll-free 800/238-8070, is an 1893 Queen Anne Victorian with many-gabled dormers and period antiques, vintage and contemporary stained glass, and a wine-tasting room and cellar. All six guest rooms have private baths, several have fireplaces. Rates include full breakfast, wine-tasting, and appetizers. From here it's a short walk to the *Wine Train* and the local opera house. Luxury.

Historic **Churchill Manor,** 485 Brown St., 707/253-7733, is a three-story Second Empire mansion built in 1889 and offering 10 guest rooms (some with fireplaces, one with spa, all with private bath) and full breakfast, on an acre

ACCOMMODATIONS RATINGS

Accommodations in this book are rated by price category, based on double-occupancy, high-season rates. Categories used are:

Budget.	$35 and under
Inexpensive	$35-60
Moderate	$60-85
Expensive	$85-110
Premium	$110-150
Luxury	$150 and up

LAKE BERRYESSA

One of the state's big reservoirs and the county's eastern "escape" route since 1957 when the Monticello Dam was completed, Lake Berryessa is one place to avoid the wine-country crunch—arid oak foothills in summer, gorgeous greenery in spring—though it, too, is also popular on weekends. Berryessa has the usual lake action—good trout fishing, swimming, sailing, water-skiing, even houseboats—plus private campgrounds. Camp at **Spanish Flat** (call Spanish Flat Resort at 707/966-7700), or **Putah Creek** (call Putah Creek Resort at 707/966-0794). For more information about the lake, call the Bureau of Reclamation at 707/966-2111. **Lake Solano** below the dam is a Solano County park with 90 campsites ($18 RVs, $15 tents)—and peace and quiet (no motorboats); call 530/795-2990 for information.

of gardens. Expensive-Luxury. Down the street is **Blue Violet Mansion,** 443 Brown, 707/253-2583 or toll-free 800/959-2583, a striking 1886 Queen Anne Victorian with antiques, a heated pool on the one-acre grounds, and vintage Napa atmosphere. It offers 14 rooms with private bath; depending on the room, additional amenities include balconies, in-room spas, and gas fireplaces. Rates include full breakfast and refreshments (picnic baskets and dinner also available). Luxury.

Staying at Bed-and-Breakfasts near Napa
For non-Victorian ambience, consider a stay at **Tall Timbers Chalets,** 1012 Darms Ln. (off Hwy. 29), 707/252-7810, a collection of country-style cottages, some with decks or porches. Continental breakfast. Premium-Luxury. A pleasant change-up, too, is **La Residence Country Inn,** 4066 St. Helena Hwy. (two miles north of Napa), 707/253-0337, which has grown from a bed-and-breakfast into a luxurious yet casual country inn. La Residence offers 20 rooms (most with private bath) in an 1870 Gothic Revival farmhouse and French-style barn. Full breakfast, pool, and hot tub, too. Luxury. Also outside town is the 1984 **Oak Knoll Inn,** 2200 E. Oak Knoll Ave., 707/255-2200, a French country-style inn built of stone. It has just four guest rooms, all with king-size beds and fireplaces. Other amenities include a hot tub, heated pool, croquet, and a generous full breakfast served on the deck or in rooms. Luxury.

For more Napa area bed-and-breakfast choices, contact **Accommodations Referral/Bed and Breakfast Exchange,** 1407 Main St., Ste. 102., St. Helena, CA 94574, 707/942-5900, 707/942-2924, 707/963-8466, toll-free 800/499-8466 inside California or 800/240-8466 outside California (open Mon.–Fri. 9 A.M.–5 P.M.); **Napa Valley Reservations Unlimited,** 1819 Tanen, Napa, 707/252-1985; or the **Napa Valley Tourist Bureau,** 6488 Washington, Yountville, 707/258-1957 or 707/944-1558.

Eating in Napa: The Basics
Time your visit to take advantage of the local farmers' markets. The **Napa Chef's Certified Farmers' Market** is held May–Sept. on Fri., 2–9 P.M., at 1st and Coombs Sts.; for more information, call 707/255-8073. The **Napa Downtown Certified Farmers' Market,** 707/252-7142, is held May–Nov. on Tues. 7:30 A.M.–noon, downtown at West and Pearl.

The **Curb Side Cafe,** 1245 1st St., 707/253-2307, serves good sandwiches and decent breakfasts. You can't beat the huge made-to-order burgers at **Nation's Giant Hamburgers,** 1441 3rd St., 707/252-8500—very reasonable. But no trip to Napa is quite complete without a stop at **Downtown Joe's Restaurant and Brewery,** 902 Main St., 707/258-2337, where a specialty is sausage marinated in Tail Waggin' Ale.

Eating in Napa: Fancier Fare
Talk of the town for food lovers is the exceptional but decidedly unfussy **Bistro Don Giovanni,** 4110 St. Helena Hwy. (Hwy. 29 just north of Napa), 707/224-3300, brought to you by the folks behind Scala Bistro at San Francisco's Sir Francis Drake Hotel. Expect delicious Italian bistro fare with the occasional French accent at lunch and dinner daily, whether served forth from the wood-fired pizza oven or mesquite grill.

Well worth seeking out is the casual, whimsical **Foothill Café,** in a shopping center at 2766 Old Sonoma Rd. (west of Hwy. 29), 707/252-6178, where hearty vegetarian, seafood, poultry, and meat selections (try the baby-back ribs) star at dinner.

La Boucane, 1778 2nd St., 707/253-1177,

offers classical but friendly French dining in a dressed-up Victorian, everything from poached salmon to roasted duck. Impressive wine list. (In pricier Napa Valley restaurants, call first for reservations and ask about corkage fee policies. It may not be worth it to bring your own bottle of local wine to dinner.) Open Mon.–Sat. for dinner only.

YOUNTVILLE AND VICINITY

George Yount built the first house in the valley—a fortified log cabin—and planted the valley's first vineyard in the 1830s. But Yountville's humble beginnings are none too apparent these days. Yountville has gone—and is still going—yupscale. The **Veterans Home of California** here, 707/944-4541, now run by the state, first opened its doors in 1884, started by veterans of the Mexican War and members of the Grand Army of the Republic. The doors are still open at this, the largest facility of its kind in the nation—the kind of place always in need of some Compassionate Conservatism, even Loving Liberalism. If you have time, spend some here, visiting those who would appreciate a visitor. The attached **Armistice Chapel Museum,** 707/944-4919, is stuffed with military memorabilia, some items on loan from San Francisco's Presidio Army Museum. Open Fri.–Sun. noon.–2 P.M. Free. New here in 1998, the **Napa Valley Museum,** 55 Presidents Circle (off California Dr. at the entrance to the Veterans Home), 707/944-0500, offers an alternative to all-day shopping and wine-tasting—including a permanent high-tech interactive exhibit on the entire winemaking process, the "industry gallery," as well as changing exhibits on the art, culture, and land of Napa Valley. The museum is open Wed.–Mon. 10 A.M.–5 P.M. (until 8 P.M. on the first Thurs. of every month). Admission is $4.50 adults, $3.50 seniors/students, $2.50 children 7–17, and free for everyone 5–8 P.M. on the first Thurs. of every month.

For most people, though, the town's main event is browsing through the tony clothing, jewelry, and art and antique shops. After doing the town, try a simple picnic in **Yountville City Park** at Washington and Lincoln. Nearby is the fascinating cemetery where George Yount and other valley pioneers are buried.

For information, contact the **Yountville Chamber of Commerce,** 6516 Yount St., Yountville, CA 94599, 707/944-0904 or toll-free 800/959-3604, www.yountville.com. Rent bikes at **Yountville Bicycle Rentals,** in the Vintage 1870 center at 6525 Washington, 707/944-9080.

Domaine Chandon
The modern $42 million Domaine Chandon facility is just west of Hwy. 29, 1 California Dr., P.O. Box 2470, Yountville, CA 94599, 707/944-2280, www.dchandon.com. Owned by France's Moet-Hennessey cognac and champagne producers (the Dom Perignon people), Domaine Chandon is renowned for its sparkling wines. (Never say "champagne" in public in the wine country; by custom, that term is reserved exclusively for bubbly produced in the Champagne region of France.) Foodies come for the restaurant, but the winery is striking architecturally, sporting fieldstone walls with barrel-arched vaulted roofs over terraced stair steps. Inside you'll find a champagne museum and a fine, fairly expensive, fairly formal California-style French restaurant. Call 707/944-2892 at least two weeks in advance for reservations. Tours here (full "operations" tours only on weekdays) are among the best in the valley and can be given in any of several languages with advance notice. A wide variety of cultural events are also scheduled year-round. The winery is open May–Oct., Wed.–Sun. 10 A.M.–8 P.M., Mon.–Tues. 10 A.M.–6 P.M.; the rest of the year Wed.–Sun. 10 A.M.–6 P.M., closed Mon.–Tuesday.

Other Yountville
Area Wineries
Cosentino Winery, 7415 St. Helena Hwy. (next to Mustard's Grill), 707/944-1220, www.cosentinowinery.com, is a local innovator, known for its pioneering merlot and its sparkling blanc de noir. Open daily 10 A.M.–5 P.M. Just north (technically in Oakville) is **Napa Cellars,** 7481 St. Helena Hwy., 707/944-2565 or toll-free 800/535-6400, open for sales and tastings ($5 fee, refundable with wine purchase) daily 10 A.M.–6 P.M. and for tours by appointment.

Across the valley, **S. Anderson Winery,** 1473 Yountville Cross Rd. (near the Silverado Trail), 707/944-8642, is a small family-owned

NAPA VALLEY BALLOONING

An 18th-century diversion of the French aristocracy, ballooning somehow seems appropriate here, though local residents and many wineries alike have long since tired of the sight and sound of ballooners in the skies. For most people, too, this is an outrageously expensive airborne experience, at about $180 an hour and up. Reservations are required. **Napa Valley Balloons Inc.,** P.O. Box 2860, Yountville, CA 94599, 707/944-0228 or toll-free 800/253-2224 (in Northern California), offers dawn balloon trips launched from Domaine Chandon, followed by brunch and sparkling wines.

Also well known among local high-but-slow floaters are a trio of affiliated companies headquartered at the Vintage 1870 complex (6525 Washington) in Yountville: **Balloon Aviation of Napa Valley,** 707/252-7067 or toll-free 800/367-6272; **Adventures Aloft,** 707/944-4408 or toll-free 800/944-4408; and **Above the West Hot Air Ballooning,** 707/944-8638 or toll-free 800/627-2759, which is the most expensive but for its base rate offers either complimentary shuttle service from San Francisco or a trip guaranteed at just four passengers. All three of these companies make single flights instead of multiple hops, offer preflight coffee and pastries and postflight champagne, and have the same mailing address: P.O. Box 2500, Yountville, CA 94599.

In Rutherford, the **Bonaventura Balloon Company,** 707/944-2822, is headquartered at the Rancho Caymus Inn; ask about the "Stay and Fly" package.

producer of sparkling wines. The facility itself is a fascination; its 18-foot-high wine-aging caves tunnel into a rhyolite hillside and boast peaked ceilings, cobblestone floors, and a stage. Special wine-tastings and concerts are held in the caves. Open daily 10 A.M.–4:30 P.M. (tours by appointment).

Chateau Chevre, 2030 Hoffman Ln. (one mile south of Yountville off Hwy. 29), 707/944-2184, is small, offering tasting and tours by appointment only. The winery building was once a goat-milking barn, hence the name, "Goat Castle."

Staying in Yountville

Once a bordello, **Maison Fleurie,** 6529 Yount St., 707/944-2056, is now a fine bed-and-breakfast offering 13 rooms (six with fireplace, all with private bath) in a luxuriously restyled 1873 brick-and-fieldstone lodge (plus a cottage). All rooms are furnished in French country style and amenities include a pool, whirlpool, and full breakfast. Premium-Luxury. Next door is the **Petit Logis Inn,** 6527 Yount St., 707/944-2332 or toll-free 800/944-2332, www.petitlogis.com, offering just five rooms, each with a fireplace and a two-person spa tub, and more contemporary European style. Luxury.

The California-hacienda-style **Napa Valley Lodge,** 2230 Madison St. (at Hwy. 29), 707/944-2468 or toll-free 800/368-2468, www.woodside-hotels.com, has very nice rooms, a heated pool and spa, a fitness center, and a complimentary champagne breakfast buffet. Luxury. Built in the mid-'80s, the **Vintage Inn,** 6541 Washington St., 707/944-1112, www.vintageinn .com, is a first-rate place for a great grape escape. All rooms have wood-burning fireplaces, whirlpool baths, and wine bars. Most also have either a balcony or patio, not to mention other cushy wine-country comforts. Many of the upstairs rooms have very high ceilings. A canal runs through the grounds, which also feature a heated pool and spas situated here and there. Rates include a champagne-and-pastry breakfast and afternoon tea. Luxury.

ROBERT HOLMES/CALTOUR

Eating in Yountville

Good restaurants cluster along Washington Street. **The Diner,** 6476 Washington, 707/944-2626, is a wonderful roadside diner *very* popular (even with locals) for its inexpensive food. At lunch and dinner, choose from American and Mexican standards—everything from burgers accompanied by buttermilk milkshakes to burritos washed down with Dos Equis—but breakfast is the meal of the day here; to get in, come very early or very late. Stick with the simple—perfect scrambled eggs with bacon or ham, good huevos rancheros—or go wild with banana-walnut waffles. Great place. Open Tues.–Sun. 8 A.M.–3 P.M. for breakfast and lunch, and 5:30–9:30 P.M. for dinner. Fun, too, is **Gordon's Café & Wine Bar,** 6770 Washington St., 707/944-8246.

The original **Ristorante Piatti,** 6480 Washington St., 707/944-2070, is an offbeat pasta place also offering grilled chicken, rabbit, and daily risotto specials. (There's another Piatti in Sonoma.) Open daily for lunch and dinner. Also reasonably high on the local restaurant scale is **Compadres,** 6539 Washington, 707/944-2406, a festive and friendly Mexican bar and grill inside a brick vintner's mansion built in 1872.

"Napa Valley Goes Hawaiian" could be the theme at **Brix,** 7377 St. Helena Hwy. (just north of town on Hwy. 29), 707/944-2749, where the fare includes such things as seared ahi and smoked salmon pizza with Maui onions. Full bar. Open daily for lunch and dinner.

Practically next door is that venerable foodie mecca **Mustards Grill,** 7399 St. Helena Hwy., 707/944-2424, an unassuming upscale bistro serving forth much of its frisky fare from the wood-burning oven—the kind of place you could easily dawdle the day away ordering one tasty tidbit after another. Appetizers, grilled vegetables and meats, good desserts, extensive wine list, microbrews. Full bar. Open daily for lunch and dinner.

Still hot after all these years, too, is the exceptional **French Laundry,** 6640 Washington, 707/944-2380, at home in a charming old ivy-covered 1890s stone house, a onetime laundry. Absolutely nothing else here qualifies as blue-collar, however, since this particular laundry is near the top of the wine-country charts these days in both price and quality for fixed-price French. Daily changing menu, beer and wine only. Reservations accepted up to two months ahead, which gives you some idea how popular this place is. Four-course lunch served Fri.–Sun., choice of five- or seven-course tasting menu at dinner.

Also exceptional is the California-style French at **Domaine Chandon,** 1 California Dr. (just off Hwy. 29), 707/944-2892, where stylish high-season lunch is the high point of many a foodie's wine country adventure. After superb roasted chicken or grilled fish, make sure to leave room for dessert. Changing menu. Wine only, naturally enough. Open for lunch daily May–Oct. (Wed.–Sun. the rest of the year) and dinner Wed.–Sun. year-round. Closed the first two weeks in January.

NORTHERN NAPA VALLEY: ST. HELENA AND VICINITY

The next town to speak of "up valley," small St. Helena is surrounded by historic vineyards and wineries. Increasingly, the town is an elite enclave catering to the moneyed minions from the city, though the area was originally settled by German, Italian, and Swiss farm families. If possible, park on the east side of the highway—so you don't have to try to cross it—then stop by the St. Helena Chamber of Commerce office on the main drag, 1010 Main St., Ste. A, St. Helena, CA 94574, 707/963-4456 or toll-free 800/799-6456, fax 707/963-5396, www.sthelena.com, to get oriented. Ideally, *leave* your car parked and avoid the local traffic snarls by renting mountain or touring bikes ($7 an hour or $25 a day) at **St. Helena Cyclery,** 1156 Main St., 707/963-7736. Staff recommend local tour routes.

SEEING AND DOING ST. HELENA

St. Helena Diversions

Like Yountville, St. Helena is becoming something of a hoity-toity shopping mecca, though some utilitarian farm-town businesses still survive. At **Hurd Beeswax Candles,** inside the old Freemark Abbey Winery, 3020 St. Helena Hwy. N, 707/963-7211, visitors can watch the process of handmade candle making. **Napa Valley Grapevine Wreath Company,** 8901 Conn Creek Rd., 707/963-8893, specializes in gorgeous handwoven wreaths, baskets, and other functional and decorative vine sculpture. **Main Street Books,** 1315 Main St., 707/963-1338, carries both fiction and nonfiction, and provides a children's book corner. A further stroll down Main St. in either direction leads visitors through the heart of St. Helena's high-priced, tasteful consumerism. If nothing else is going on come nightfall (and, due to local preference, nightlife here is quiet), take in a movie at the local **Cameo Cinema,** 1340 Main St., 707/963-9779.

Bale Grist Mill State Historic Park

Dr. Edward T. Bale, a surgeon originally from London who became General Vallejo's medical officer and his nephew by marriage, owned a substantial portion of the Napa Valley in the 1830s, due to Vallejo's largesse. A physician with a sense of humor, Bale named his spread Carne Humana Rancho—perhaps to suggest that we are all grist for the mill of life. Bale himself was ground up early, at the age of 38. But in 1846, he built a small state-of-the-art flour mill—powered by a 20-foot waterwheel—on Mill Creek just north of modern-day St. Helena. The original grist for the mill was locally grown wheat, but later corn was ground into highly prized cornmeal.

The wooden waterwheel (today's massive 36-footer a 19th-century improvement) and three-story mill were first restored in the 1920s, at a cost of nearly $1 million; a 10-year restoration project to reachieve the mill's fully operational 1850 status was completed in 1988. Lucky visitors may get to see the whole works in operation.

The park is a few miles north of St. Helena on Hwy. 29. Small admission. To get to the waterwheel and millworks, follow the shaded, paved path downhill from the parking lot—a good stretch for car-cramped legs, and ramps make the area wheelchair accessible. Better yet, hike in on the mile-long History Trail from Bothe-Napa Valley Park just to the north. For more information, contact: Bale Grist Mill State Historic Park,

3801 St. Helena Hwy., Calistoga, CA 94515, 707/963-2236.

Bothe-Napa Valley State Park

This is not exactly wilderness, but it's the only place to really camp in the valley. Its 100 acres of pleasant wooded valley and Coast Range ridges stretch from four miles north of St. Helena to three miles south of Calistoga. Hiking is a major attraction here, given the abundance of trails. You can even hike to the park from **Sugarloaf Ridge State Park** near Santa Rosa on the California Riding and Hiking Trail (sometimes a hot trek in summer but usually tolerable). Guided hikes and campfire programs are offered in summer.

Included within the park's boundaries are Ritchey Creek, the foundation ruins of Napa Valley's first church, and a pioneer cemetery with Donner Party gravestones. Near the cemetery (and the speeding highway traffic) are a pleasant maple-shaded picnic area, a group camp, and a rarity in state parks—a swimming pool, complete with dressing rooms and showers. The pool is open mid-June through Labor Day, noon–6 P.M., lifeguard on duty (small admission).

Park day use is $2 per car. **Ritchey Creek Campground** features 40 fairly private family campsites tucked into wooded thickets. Restrooms have laundry tubs, flush toilets, drinking fountains, and hot showers. No RV hookups here, but a dump station is available. The park also has 10 walk-in (tents only) campsites, one reserved for hikers and bikers. Camping reservations are wise in spring, summer, and fall. For camping reservations, call ReserveAmerica toll-free at 800/444-7275. For more information, contact: Bothe-Napa Valley State Park, 3801 St. Helena Hwy. N, Calistoga, CA 94515, 707/942-4575.

WINERIES NEAR ST. HELENA

Oakville Area Wineries

Most famous of all is the **Robert Mondavi Winery,** 7801 St. Helena Hwy. in Oakville, 707/963-9611, www.mondavi.com, with decent wines, a never-ending schedule of Napa Valley entertainment, and the best free tour available for the untutored. Drop by early or call first for reservations; tours are limited and fill up fast, especially

REMEMBERING ROBERT LOUIS STEVENSON

Well worth a visit is the world-renowned **Silverado Museum** collection of Robert Louis Stevenson memorabilia, housed in its own wing at the St. Helena Public Library Center, 1490 Library Ln., P.O. Box 409, St. Helena, CA 94574, 707/963-3757 or 707/963-3002 (open daily noon–4 P.M. except Mondays and holidays). Stevenson's honeymoon story is the stuff of true romance. He met his bride-to-be (Fanny Osbourne, a married American woman) at an artists' colony in France, fell in love with her, then left his Scotland home for California in hot pursuit. Critically ill and poverty-stricken—living briefly in Monterey, San Francisco, and Oakland while awaiting Fanny's divorce—Stevenson managed to survive until his marriage to Fanny in May 1880. Too poor to afford the $10 a week for room and board in Calistoga, the two honeymooned in an abandoned bunkhouse at the Old Silverado Mine on Mt. St. Helena above the Napa Valley. Almost overnight, Robert Louis Stevenson regained his health, won his parents' approval of his new marriage, and returned to Scotland with his beloved Fanny to write his masterworks (*Treasure Island* and *The Strange Case of*

Dr. Jekyll and Mr. Hyde among them).

On display at this red-carpeted "jewel box" museum—which offers something for everyone—are more than 8,000 items related to Stevenson's life and literary career: first editions and variant editions of almost all his works, more than 100 books from his library in Samoa, original manuscripts and letters, as well as paintings, photographs, sculptures, and drawings. The collection here includes some of the first words he ever wrote, in the form of childhood letters, as well as his last written words. Also here: his wedding ring, his work desk, and the lead soldiers he played with as a boy. The Silverado Library is free, though voluntary contributions to the library's Vailima Foundation are always welcome.

Next door in the public library, the fine **Napa Valley Wine Library**, 1492 Library Ln. (at Adams St.), 707/963-5244, shelves 3,000 or so wine-related books, journals, and magazines—one of the largest collections of libation literature on the West Coast. Wine-appreciation seminars, wine-tastings, and other events are regularly scheduled, primarily during summer months.

---

in summer. The modernesque mission-style buildings here were designed by Cliff May, spiritual father of the Western ranch-style house. Open May–Oct., daily 9 A.M.–5 P.M., otherwise 10 A.M.–4:30 P.M. Robert Mondavi co-owns the nearby Opus One winery with the Baroness Philippine de Rothschild; this Franco-American partnership has produced expensive progeny. It's even expensive to taste here. North of Mondavi, **Cakebread Cellars**, 8300 St. Helena Hwy., 707/963-5221, www.cakebread.com, is a fine, small family winery noted for chardonnay, cabernet sauvignon, and sauvignon blanc, housed in an abstract-style barn. Open daily 10 A.M.–4 P.M. for tastings (tours by appointment).

East of Oakville, **Silver Oak Cellars**, 915 Oakville Cross Rd., 707/944-8808, www.silveroak.com, produces only cabernet sauvignon,

aged five years before release. Silver Oak is open for wine sales Mon.–Fri. 9 A.M.–4 P.M. and Sat. 10 A.M.–4 P.M., and for tours by advance appointment only weekdays at 1:30 P.M. (visitors on tours can taste). The **Girard Winery/Rudd Estate**, 500 Oakville Cross Rd. (on the valley's east side), 707/944-8577, is small but plays in the big leagues: Girard wines found an appreciative place on the White House dinner table during the Reagan years. Try the chardonnay. Open for tasting daily 11 A.M.–4:30 P.M.

West of Oakville is **Chateau Potelle Winery**, 3875 Mt. Veeder Rd. (off Oakville Grade), 707/255-9440, www.chateaupotelle.com, open Thurs.–Mon. noon–5 P.M. Chateau Potelle wines were served at George Bush's inaugural dinner. Also in the neighborhood is the **La Famiglia di Robert Mondavi**, up on the hill at 1595 Oakville

Grade (at the onetime Vichon Winery), 707/944-2811 or toll-free 888/453-9463, which features an "Italian Marketplace" selling wine, gifts, clothing, and gourmet food items. Lovely picnic area, also a boccie ball court. Open daily 10 A.M.–4:30 P.M. (call for current tour information).

Rutherford Area Wineries

Vine-covered **Beaulieu Vineyard,** 1960 St. Helena Hwy. S, 707/967-5200 (main number) or 707/967-5230 (visitor center), www.beaulieu-vineyard.com, an old family winery founded by Georges de Latour in 1900, survived Prohibition by producing altar wines. Beaulieu is known for its vintage-dated sparkling wines and table wines; BV (as it's often called) is also credited with making cabernet sauvignon "king of the California wines." Open daily 10 A.M.–5 P.M. (excellent guided tour and tasting).

Continuing north, tiny **Grgich Hills,** 1829 St. Helena Hwy., 707/963-2784, offers some of the valley's finest chardonnay and zinfandel. Open daily 9:30 A.M.–4:30 P.M. for tastings (tours by appointment only). The most famous place around these days, though, is the **Niebaum-Coppola Estate Winery,** now headquartered at 1991 St. Helena Hwy., 707/963-9099, www.niebaum-coppola.com, the former chateau of the Inglenook Winery, acquired along with the vineyards in 1994. But filmmaker and screenwriter Francis Ford Coppola (*The Godfather, Apocalypse Now,* and Bram Stoker's *Dracula,* among many others) and his wife have been making wine at their original Napa Valley estate (adjacent) for years. Tastings are offered daily (tours by appointment), but most people get no farther than the museum-style gift shop, where Coppola's and Inglenook's histories are on display along with wine, books, movie-themed gifts, sweatshirts, T-shirts, even F. F. Coppola's own line of pastas, vinegars, olive oils, candies, and cigars. Keep an eye out for copies of another Coppola enterprise, the literary magazine *Zoetrope.*

Quail Ridge, 1155 Mee Ln., 707/963-9783, is noted for the sauvignon blanc, chardonnay, merlot, and cabernet sauvignon produced from its 200-acre vineyard. Nearby **Beaucanon,** 1695 St. Helena Hwy. S, 707/967-3520, is also exceptional, open daily 10 A.M.–5 P.M. Just north, family-operated **Whitehall Lane Winery,** 1563

the harvest

ROBERT HOLMES/CALTOUR

St. Helena Hwy., 707/963-9454 or toll-free 800/963-9454, a modern redwood winery that produces both varietals and dinner wines, welcomes visitors in a friendly tasting room. Open daily 11 A.M.–6 P.M. (tours at 1 and 4 P.M.).

East of Rutherford, Rutherford Cross Rd. leads to more wine-tasting. **Frog's Leap,** 8815 Conn Creek Rd., 707/963-4704 or toll-free 800/959-4704, www.frogsleap.com, seemingly an amphibious takeoff on Stags' Leap Winery, produces premium chardonnay, cabernet sauvignon, sauvignon blanc, and zinfandel varietals, as well as, ahem, Leapfrogmilch. The winery is very small and open for retail sales Mon.–Sat. 10 A.M.–4 P.M. (tours and tastings by appointment only).

Continue on to Silverado Trail and turn north (left) to reach the well-known **Rutherford Hill Winery,** 200 Rutherford Hill Rd. (at Silverado Trail), 707/963-1871 (office) or 707/963-7194 (visitor center), www.rutherfordhill.com. The winery looks like an old-fashioned hay barn perched on the hill—but there's nothing really "country" here except the straw-colored white wines and flowery picnic grounds. Noted for its award-winning merlot, sauvignon blanc, and several other varietals, Rutherford Hill's wine-aging caves are the largest in the world, the tunnels and cross-tunnels capable of storing 6,500 small oak barrels. (These caves, like most throughout the region, were dug by Alf Burtleson using a Welsh coal-mining machine with carbide teeth.) Open daily 10 A.M.–5 P.M. for tastings and public picnicking, with cave tours offered three times daily starting at 11:30 A.M.

Head south on Silverado Trail to find several other wineries. **Conn Creek/Villa Mt. Eden,** 8711 Silverado Trail, 707/963-9100, is low-key and lovely, with wine-tasting offered daily 10 A.M.–4 P.M. (closed on major holidays, tours by appointment only). Also worth a stop is **Mumm Napa Valley,** 8445 Silverado Trail, 707/942-3434 or toll-free 800/686-6272, www.mumm.com, open daily in peak visitor season 10:30 A.M.–6 P.M. for tasting and tours (last tour at 4 P.M.) and 10 A.M.–5 P.M. Nov.–April. Of special note here is the art gallery, which features a permanent exhibit of Ansel Adams photographs and also hosts visiting exhibitions. **ZD Wines,** 8383 Silverado Trail, 707/963-5188, makes fine pinot noir and chardonnay. Open daily 10 A.M.–4:30 P.M.

Wineries South of St. Helena

Among the closest wineries to town, **Merryvale Vineyards,** 1000 Main St. (next to Tra Vigne), 707/963-7777, www.merryvale.com, is noted for its award-winning wines, antique cask collection, and boccie ball court. Merryvale offers a worthwhile free wine seminar on weekends (call ahead for reservations). Open daily 10 A.M.–5:30 P.M.

Heading south from St. Helena toward Rutherford on Hwy. 29, it almost seems that every road and driveway off the highway leads to a different winery. Just south of town is **Louis Martini Winery,** 254 St. Helena Hwy. S (Hwy. 29), 707/963-2736 or toll-free 800/321-9463, www.louismartini.com, open daily 10:30 A.M.–4:30 P.M. for tastings, tours, and picnicking. Nearby is **Sutter Home Winery,** 277 St. Helena Hwy. S, 707/963-3104, www.sutterhome.com, famous for its white zinfandel and chardonnay. The tasting room is open daily 10 A.M.–6 P.M. (no tours, accommodations available). Next door, off the highway, **Prager Winery and Port Works,** 1281 Lewelling, 707/963-7678 or toll-free 800/969-

7678, is open daily 10:30 A.M.–4:30 P.M., tours only by appointment. Prager also offers bed-and-breakfast accommodations at the winery.

Continuing south, the small family-owned **V. Sattui Winery,** White Ln. at Hwy. 29 (1.5 miles south of St. Helena), 707/963-7774, www.vsattui.com, is as renowned for its fabulous 1885 stone-and-beam construction as it is for its award-winning wines. Also here: a Euro-style deli stocking some 200 local and imported cheeses, and a pleasant two-acre picnic area. Open daily 9 A.M.–6 P.M. most of the year, until 5 P.M. Nov.–Feb. (tours by appointment). Noted for its Martha's Vineyard cabernet sauvignon is the family-owned **Heitz Wine Cellars,** 436 St. Helena Hwy. S (Hwy. 29), 707/963-3542, open daily 11 A.M.–4 P.M. (tours by appointment only). **Flora Springs Wine Company,** 677 St. Helena Hwy. S, 707/967-8032 or 707/963-5711, www.florasprings.com, specializes in estate-grown chardonnay, sauvignon blanc, cabernet sauvignon, and merlot. The winery's tasting room and visitor center is open Mon.–Sat. 10 A.M.–6 P.M. (winery tours by appointment). Just south, another family enterprise well worth a stop is **Milat Vineyards,** 1091 St. Helena Hwy. S, 707/963-0758 or toll-free 800/546-4528, www.milat.com, open daily 10 A.M.–6 P.M.

Wineries North of St. Helena

North of St. Helena, you'll find yet more tasting opportunities. Small **Markham Vineyards,** 2812 St. Helena Hwy. N (in the 1876 St. Helena Cooperative Winery building), 707/963-5292, is open daily 10 A.M.–6 P.M., with "sensory evaluation" of its several premium varietals and tours by appointment only. **Freemark Abbey Winery,** 3022 St. Helena Hwy. N (two miles north of St. Helena on Hwy. 29), 707/963-9694, www.freemarkabbey.com, occupies an 1895 building filled with new winery technology. The specialties here are chardonnay, riesling, and cabernet sauvignon. Open daily 10 A.M.–4:30 P.M., tours at 2 P.M. only.

A favorite for those with a similarly peculiar sense of humor is **Folie à Deux,** 3070 St. Helena Hwy. N, 707/963-1160, www.folieadeux.com. Two psychiatrists started this "shared fantasy or delusion," believing that people are crazy to go into the wine business but also believing that wine and life go together. Share their fantasy and taste the award-winning chardonnay and dry chenin blanc. Open daily 10 A.M.–5 P.M., with public picnicking (group tours by advance arrangement only).

Wineries East of St. Helena

Across the valley, **Joseph Phelps Vineyards,** 200 Taplin Rd. (off Silverado Trail), 707/963-2745, offers retail sales Mon.–Sat. 9 A.M.–5 P.M., Sun. 10 A.M.–4 P.M. (tours, tasting, and picnicking by appointment).

In the Deer Park area, **Deer Park Winery,** 1000 Deer Park Rd., 707/963-5411, www.deerparkwinery.com, doesn't have any deer—despite the antlers on the winery label—but does have a tiny vineyard, a century-old "gravity flow" stone wine cellar, and a collection of antique winemaking machinery. Also here is a guest cottage for bed-and-breakfasters. The winery is open for tasting Fri.–Sat. 10 A.M.–5 P.M. or by appointment. Nearby, **Burgess Cellars,** 1108 Deer Park Rd., 707/963-4766, www.burgesscellars.com, is another rare old stone and woodframe winery, this one also producing premium varietals: cabernet franc, cabernet sauvignon, zinfandel, and chardonnay (open for tasting and tours by appointment).

FAMOUS AREA WINERIES

In the tourist sweeps, the biggest St. Helena wineries are Beringer and Charles Krug. At **Beringer Vineyards,** 2000 Main St. (Hwy. 29), 707/963-7115 (main office) or 707/963-4812 (retail sales and tours), www.beringer.com, the famous wine-aging caves were hand-dug in 1876 by Chinese laborers hired by Frederick and Jacob Beringer. Open for business ever since, Beringer is the oldest Napa Valley winery in continuous operation. The winery's strikingly ornate 17-room Victorian **Rhine House,** comfortably at home on the National Register of Historic Places, is a study in stained glass and oak paneling surrounded by lovely gardens. Thirty-minute tours of the winery—which include a peek into the wine caves—end at Rhine House, where a good time is had by all tasting award-winning wines. (It's a mob scene here in summer; to avoid the crowds, head up to Beringer's Reserve Room on the 2nd floor of Rhine House, where generous samples of better wines are poured). Open daily 9:30 A.M.–5

P.M. Closed on major holidays. Group tours by appointment only.

At the Charles Krug Home Ranch, the **Charles Krug Winery,** 2800 Main St. (Hwy. 29), 707/963-5057, was founded in 1861, making it the valley's oldest working winery. Now another Mondavi enterprise noted for its consistently good California cabernets (among the best anywhere), Krug also offers fine, quite popular tours. The regular "tour and tasting" is a free 45-minute facility tour covering everything from the ancient 30,000-gallon redwood aging tanks to a review of new computer-assisted winemaking technology, followed by a 15-minute tasting session (no charge, no reservations required). The "select tasting" option, possible in addition to the tour, offers visitors eight premium wines (including vintage reserve cabernets) for leisurely tasting, no reservations needed. Call for other tour information. Complimentary tasting on Wednesday. Sales shop open daily 10:30 A.M.–5:30 P.M.

The beautiful, three-story stone structure on the north end of town is the famed former 1888 Christian Brothers' **Greystone Winery,** now the Napa Valley campus of the **Culinary Institute of America** (CIA), 2555 Main St., St. Helena, CA 94574, 707/967-1100 or toll-free 800/333-9242, www.ciachef.edu. Foodies, stop by for a superlative lunch or dinner at the **Wine Spectator Greystone Restaurant** on the 1st floor of the original winery, 707/967-1010 (reservations essential in summer). While you're here, wander through the museum of winemaking memorabilia (open daily 10 A.M.–6 P.M.), which includes a collection of unique corkscrews.

Historic Sparkling Wine

Two noted sparkling wine producers are at home midway between Calistoga and St. Helena. The historic family-owned weathered-wood-and-oldstone **Hanns Kornell Champagne Cellars,** 1091 Larkmead Ln. (east of Hwy. 29, north of St. Helena), 707/942-0859, makes fine sparkling wines in the *méthode champenoise* (and brazenly calls them champagnes), as well as chardonnay, cabernet, sangiovese, and zinfandel. Tours here are a treat, since visitors walk through the winery itself rather than peeking into the action from a visitors' gallery. Open daily 10 A.M.–5 P.M. for tasting, tours, and sales.

Schramsberg Vineyards, 1400 Schramsberg

Rd., 707/942-4558, www.schramsberg. com, established in 1862 by Jacob Schram, is four miles south of Calistoga and five miles north of St. Helena off Hwy. 29. It was the first hillside winery in Napa Valley and was immortalized by Robert Louis Stevenson in his *Silverado Squatters* ("... and the wine is bottled poetry"). Jacob Schram was one of the first to successfully export American wines to Europe. So it should have come as no surprise when Schramsberg produced the "California champagne" President Nixon took along on his first trip to China in 1971. No tasting offered, and tours and sales are by appointment only (closed Sundays and holidays).

STAYING IN AND NEAR ST. HELENA

St. Helena Motels and Hotels

In general, there's not much room at the inn in St. Helena for people without *money,* though well-located camping with hot showers is available at Bothe-Napa Valley State Park (see listing above). Predictably, bed-and-breakfast establishments are the rule in and around St. Helena. A surprise, though, is the simple art deco **El Bonita Motel,** 195 Main St. (on the south end of town), 707/963-3216 or toll-free 800/541-3284. Once a darker (and cheaper) 1950s motel, now the El Bonita is pure 1930s down to the last detail—the kidney-shaped swimming pool. Some rooms are smallish (and the walls are thinnish), but all come with TV, phone, alarm clock, wall heaters, and window air-conditioners. Expensive-Luxury. An updated version of 19th-century St. Helena is presented by the 1888 **Hotel St. Helena,** 1309 Main St., 707/963-4388 or toll-free 888/478-4355, an 18-room inn that feels as much like a B&B as a hotel. The rooms are all furnished with antiques and most have private baths. Rates include continental breakfast in the lobby. Premium-Luxury.

Exceptional among uptown motels is the English Tudor–style **Harvest Inn,** 1 Main St. in downtown St. Helena, 707/963-9463 or toll-free 800/950-8466, www.harvestinn.com, featuring 54 luxurious rooms graced with antiques; many have wood-burning fireplaces. Endless amenities include in-room refrigerators, wet bars, vanities, and patios or balconies. Rental bikes available. Luxury, but winter rates are more affordable. An-

other possibility is the all-suite, Old World–style **Vineyard Country Inn,** 201 Main St., 707/963-1000, fax 707/963-1794, where all 21 rooms feature wood-burning fireplaces and many new-world comforts. Heated pool and spa. Generous breakfast. Luxury.

A swank newcomer right downtown is the 17-room **Inn at Southbridge,** 1020 Main St., 707/967-9400 or toll-free 800/520-6800, www.placestostay.com, sister inn to the Meadowood Resort. Simplicity is the key to the relaxed elegance here, from the French-doored private patios to cotton piqué comforters. Luxury. On-site extras include **Tomatina,** 707/967-9999, in the courtyard, for great pizza, and the **Health Spa Napa Valley**—though guests here also have spa privileges at the Meadowood Resort.

South of St. Helena, the **Rancho Caymus Inn,** 1140 Rutherford Rd. (one block east of Hwy. 29) in Rutherford, 707/963-1777 or toll-free 800/845-1777, is a fine, contemporary Old California–style hotel, its 26 suites a marvel of skilled craftsmanship, from the adobe walls and fireplaces (wood-burning), hand-thrown pottery sinks, and hand-hewn beams and furnishings to south-of-the-border wall hangings and evocative stained glass. Luxury.

St. Helena Area Bed-and-Breakfasts

Bed-and-breakfasters could stay for weeks in St. Helena alone, just keeping up with the new inns. Most have lower off-season rates.

Outside town, the cedar-shingled **Deer Run Inn,** 3995 Spring Mountain Rd., 707/963-3794, has four rooms (three with fireplace) and a swimming pool. Full breakfast; hiking trails nearby. Premium-Luxury.

Ambrose Bierce House, 1515 Main St., 707/963-3003, www.ambrosebiercehouse.com, is the crotchety cynic's former residence, an 1870 Victorian with four guest rooms, all with private bath. Luxury. The **Cinnamon Bear Bed and Breakfast,** 1407 Kearney St. (two blocks off Main), 707/963-4653 or toll-free 888/963-4600, the first B&B in the Napa Valley, offers four rooms in a 1904 craftsman bungalow. Amenities include a hearty breakfast, as well as wine or coffee and cookies in the afternoon. Premium-Luxury. Just north of town, the **Wine Country Inn,** 1152 Lodi Ln., 707/963-7077, www.winecountryinn.com, is a large New England–style inn with a swimming pool and whirlpool. Many of the 24 guest rooms (including three suites) have fireplaces. Premium-Luxury. **Shady Oaks Country Inn,** 399 Zinfandel Ln., 707/963-1190, www.shadyoaksinn. com, features four rooms in a 1920s country house and converted winery. Gourmet champagne breakfast. Luxury. **Bartels Ranch and Country Inn,** 1200 Conn Valley Rd., 707/963-4001, www.bartelsranch.com, offers a secluded 60 acres and four "California country" rooms. Full breakfast. Luxury.

Oliver House Bed and Breakfast Inn, 2970 Silverado Trail, 707/963-4089 or toll-free 800/682-7888, offers four antique-furnished rooms (with private baths) in a 1920s Swiss-style chalet overlooking valley vineyards. Full breakfast. Expensive-Luxury. Near the Silverado Trail on a 600-acre thoroughbred horse ranch in the Chiles Valley hills is **Rustridge Ranch,** 2910 Lower Chiles Valley Rd., 707/965-9353 or toll-free 800/788-0263, www.rustridge.com, offering three rooms in a 1940s Southwestern ranch-style house. Full breakfast. Premium-Luxury.

Hilltop House, 9550 St. Helena Rd., 707/944-0880, has four rooms, all with private bath. The ranch house, built circa 1980, is furnished with antiques and boasts a big deck with a panoramic view of the mountains. Rates include a full breakfast and use of the hot tub. Premium-Luxury.

For more bed-and-breakfasts in the area, contact the local chamber of commerce or the various regional inn referral services.

Auberge du Soleil

This 33-acre elite but relaxed retreat among the olive trees on Rutherford Hill above the Silverado Trail evokes the sunny south of France, from the country-village cottages on the terraced hillside to the panoramic valley views. Each of the 11 rough-walled two-story cottages features four large rooms and suites, each with a private entrance, private terrace with French doors, and plenty of privacy. The basics include tiled floors, fireplaces, large and luxurious bathrooms with every imaginable amenity, and refrigerators stocked with wine, cheese, and snacks. Luxury. Facilities at Auberge du Soleil include a swimming pool with hot tub, sauna, massage room, well-supplied exercise room, full spa services, and three tennis courts. If the tab for an overnight here would put a serious dent in the monthly budget, don't let that keep you from a marvelous meal at the exceptional on-site restaurant, where breakfast, lunch, and dinner are served daily. Reservations advised.

For more information or to make reservations, contact: Auberge du Soleil, Rutherford, CA 94573, 707/963-1211 or toll-free 800/348-5406, www.aubergedusoleil.com.

Meadowood Napa Valley Resort

Also tops for hotel-style resort luxury in St. Helena is the 256-acre **Meadowood Napa Valley Resort,** which looks out on St. Helena and vicinity from just above the Silverado Trail. Guest rooms and suites inside the gray New England-desque mansions and lodges are scattered around the wooded grounds along with tennis courts, two croquet lawns, a nine-hole golf course, lap pool, and complete spa facilities. Luxury, with rooms starting at $400 per night. Nonguests with reservations can enjoy the two excellent on-site restaurants—the **Restaurant at Meadowood,** for fine dining overlooking the golf course, and the more casual **Grill at Meadowood,** for its breakfast buffet, lunch, and Sunday brunch.

For more information or to make reservations, contact: Meadowood Resort, 900 Meadowood Ln., 707/963-3646 or toll-free 800/458-8080, fax 707/963-3532, www.meadowood.com or www.placestostay.com.

EATING IN ST. HELENA

The Basics

For the absolutely freshest local produce, show up for the **St. Helena-Napa Valley Certified Farmers' Market,** 707/252-2105, held Fri. 7:30–11:30 A.M. at St. Helena Hwy. (Hwy. 29) and Grayson-Crane Park May–October. South of St. Helena and Rutherford in Oakville, **Oakville Grocery Co.,** 7856 St. Helena Hwy., 707/944-8802, is actually an upscale deli featuring items like country hams, salmon jerky, pâtés, truffles, imported caviar and cheeses (and an endless array of imported curds, butters, chutneys, and marmalades), decadent desserts, pastries, and premium wines and beers. Adjacent is the deli's expansion, the **Oakville Grocery Café,** on the site of the former Stars restaurant, where you can have granola, an omelette, or a country frittata for breakfast, and exceptional salads, soups, and wood-fired pizzas for lunch. Open daily 7 A.M.–4 P.M.

In St. Helena, **Guigni's Deli**, 1227 Main St., 707/963-3421, is a local institution making hefty sandwiches for about $4 (including salad). It's a good, unpretentious place for putting picnic fixings together. In bad picnic weather, you can even eat in the back. Or get picnic supplies at **Napa Valley Olive Oil Manufacturing Company**, hidden away at 835 Charter Oak Ave. south of town (at Allison Ave.; call 707/963-4173 for hours and directions), a real find for wonderful sausages, cheeses, and other reasonably priced, authentic Italian deli fare, even extra-virgin California olive oil. Picnic tables, too. A mecca for olive oil connoisseurs is the **St. Helena Olive Oil Company**, 345 La Fata St., 707/967-1003, which also features balsamic vinegars.

The **Model Bakery** in St. Helena, 1357 Main St., 707/963-8192, is one of the best anywhere, specializing in European country-style breads—and still using its 1920s brick-and-sand ovens (without thermostats). Practically next door is **Gilwoods**, 1313 Main St., 707/963-1788, a sit-down restaurant and bakery famous for its herb rolls.

Sunny **Sunshine Foods**, 1115 Main St., 707/963-7070, is the place to stop for just about anything else. For stocking up on less exotic supplies, there's also a **Safeway** market in town (open until midnight), at 1026 Hunt Ave., 707/963-3833.

Good St. Helena Fare

Surprisingly good food is almost everywhere around town, so poke around to see what's new. For a casual meal, try **Gail's Cafe**, 1347 Main St., 707/963-3332, basically a breakfast and lunch place but, this being St. Helena, one that offers champagne and mimosas on the breakfast menu (dinner is also offered Fri.–Mon. Apr.–Oct.). Or get your frijoles fix at **Armadillo's**, 1304 Main St., 707/963-8082, which offers CalMex cuisine for lunch and dinner daily.

For something stylish yet family-friendly and casual, head for **Tomatina** inside the Inn at Southbridge, 1020 Main St., 707/967-9999, where the menu runs to pasta, imaginative pizza, and *piadine,* or open-faced flatbread sandwiches. Open daily for lunch and dinner.

Fancier Fare

Finding fine food—to accompany the area's fine wines—seems to be a favorite pastime in and around St. Helena. Reservations at the region's best restaurants are almost mandatory. The exceptional, simple, and previously too popular **Tra Vigne**, 1050 Charter Oak Ave., 707/963-4444, offers a stunningly serene setting and Italian fare in the Napa Valley style but the Tuscany tradition: simple sauces, fresh and hearty food, just about everything house-made. Some people make a meal out of the appetizers or pastas and pizzas. Great desserts. All this in a refurbished old stone building with sky-high ceilings and a relaxed, breezy atmosphere, refreshingly unaffected. Open daily for lunch and dinner. For something lighter or less expensive at lunch—or to grab something delicious to go—try **Cantinetta Tra Vigne** in front, 707/963-8888.

At home in its earthy (and historic) stone surroundings is **Terra**, 1345 Railroad Ave., 707/963-8931, which some people say is still one of the Napa Valley's best restaurants. The fare here is Northern Italian and Southern French, regionalized with subtle East-West flair along with local produce, meats, and fish—and of course wines. Open Wed.–Mon. for dinner only. **Pairs Parkside Cafe**, 1420 Main St., 707/963-7566, offers Cal-Asian-eclectic cuisine for lunch and dinner Wed.–Monday. At lunch, alliteration lovers can linger over the pine nut parmesan penne pasta. At dinner, try the Japanese braised yellowtail, grilled peppered sirloin steak, or sea scallops with herbes du Provence olives.

Routinely raved about is **Brava Terrace**, 3010 St. Helena Hwy. N (next to the Freemark Abbey), 707/963-9300, a Mediterranean restaurant serving exceptional food—some of it from the restaurant's own gardens—in a friendly atmosphere. Weather permitting, enjoy your meal out on one of the large namesake outdoor terraces. Open for lunch and dinner daily most of the year, Thurs.–Tues. in winter.

Trilogy, 1234 Main, 707/963-5507, is a tiny restaurant with a dedicated following, serving French-California fare considered among the valley's best. Changing fixed-price menu, excellent wine list. Open for lunch and dinner Tues.–Fri., also for dinner on Saturday. The Southern California restaurant heritage of

Joaquim Splichal, known for L.A.'s famed Patina restaurant and its various Pinot siblings, has arrived in the Napa Valley. Splichal's French bistro-style **Pinot Blanc,** 641 Main St., 707/963-6191, serves both hearty fare and lighter selections, either in the dining room or out on the patio. Open for lunch and dinner daily.

Don't leave town before trying out the Culinary Institute of America's **Wine Spectator Restaurant at Greystone,** at home on the first story of the historic onetime Greystone Winery north of town, 2555 Main St. (at Deer Park), 707/967-1010, email: wsgr@culinary.edu, website: www.ciachef.edu. The menu changes constantly—for starters and full lunches or dinners—but expect just about anything Mediterranean, from vegetarian gnocchi to fresh seafood. Open daily in summer for lunch (call for off-season days and times) and daily year-round for dinner. Full bar. Reservations essential in summer—call, email, or use the online reservation request form.

CALISTOGA AND VICINITY

Despite the Napa Valley's hectic hubbub, there's something fun and funky about Calistoga. It's genuinely *hot,* for one thing, built atop a boiling underground river. Industrious Sam Brannan officially laid out the town in 1859 on the site of the natives' Colaynomo, or "oven place." Brannan's dream was to make the area the "Saratoga of California." So his original hotel and 20 cottages were christened "Calistoga"—an awkward combination of the state's name and the well-known resort spa in New York. The main stop nowadays (besides the spas and nearby wineries) is **Sharpsteen Museum** and the adjacent **Sam Brannan Cottage,** 1311 Washington St., 707/942-5911. The modern brick museum, next to public restrooms and the senior center, features a well-designed diorama of 1865 Calistoga plus antique dolls, clothing, and quilts. The cottage itself is furnished in wealthy San Franciscan, circa late 1800s. Open daily 10 A.M.–4 P.M. in summer and noon–4 P.M. the rest of the year. In recent years, special tours of Calistoga's **Villa Ca'Toga House,** home of the artist Carlo Machiori, featuring trompe l'oeil murals, have been offered in mid-May, in conjunction with the Sharpsteen Museum; call for current details.

Get oriented at the **Calistoga Chamber of Commerce,** 1458 Lincoln #9 (in the back of the Depot building), Calistoga, CA 94525, 707/942-6333, www.calistogafun.com.

Calistoga Area Wineries
Several wineries lie along Dunaweal Ln., which intersects Hwy. 29 just south of Calistoga. **Stonegate Winery,** 1183 Dunaweal, 707/942-6500, is a small winery with a big reputation for its premium cabernet sauvignon, sauvignon blanc, and chardonnay. Open daily 10:30 A.M.–4 P.M. for tasting and sales (tours by appointment only). Stop at Seagram's **Sterling Vineyards,**

Sam Brannan's Cottage

CALISTOGA'S SPAS

Bathe in a volcano—or at least the bubbling springs and murky mud generated by one. The combinations available for curing yourself of whatever ails you are almost endless, but the basic routine is this: a soak in a mud bath usually followed by a mineral bath and whirlpool (with or without steam bath and blanket sweat), finished with a massage. Some new twists: herbal facials, herbal wraps, eucalyptus steams, and Japanese-style enzyme baths (heat-generating tubs full of cedar, bran, and fiber).

Nance's Hot Springs, 1614 Lincoln, 707/942-6211, is a good place to take the mud cure. The basic program includes hot springs mineral bath, steam bath, black volcanic mud bath, and blanket sweat; extra for massage. (Nance's is also a clean and fresh downtown motel with nice mountain views). Sam Brannan's original resort site is now completely renovated at nearby **Indian Springs Spa and Hot Springs Resort,** 1712 Lincoln, 707/942-4913, which boasts a huge 1913 geyser-heated mineral swimming pool. The spa menu includes mud baths (100 percent volcanic ash) with mineral bath, eucalyptus steam, and blanket wrap (all about one hour), with half-hour massage extra. Reservations are nec-

essary for **Dr. Wilkinson's Hot Springs,** 1507 Lincoln, 707/942-4102 for reservations, which offers a bathhouse, and no-nonsense complete physical therapy package, and 1950s-style accommodations (Moderate-Premium). **Calistoga Spa Hot Springs,** 1006 Washington, 707/942-6269, is family-oriented, with use of outdoor mineral pools, mud baths, and massage extra.

Housed in an old bank building, **Lincoln Avenue Spa,** 1339 Lincoln, 707/942-5296, offers a mineral hot tub, acupressure face lifts, herbal facials, manicures and pedicures, mud wraps, and massage. Open daily 9 A.M.–9 P.M. At **Lavender Hill Spa,** 1015 Foothill Blvd. (Hwy. 29), 707/942-4495, 707/942-6122, or toll-free 800/528-4772, www.lavenderhillspa.com, you can get a unique type of low-viscosity mud bath ("like a sango bath without the salicyl"), an herbal facial, herbal blanket wrap, massage, acupressure, or reflexology. Bathhouses are designed for couples, and the massage is about the best around. Open daily 9 A.M.–9 P.M. The **Golden Haven Spa,** 1713 Lake St., 707/942-6793, is open daily 8 A.M.–9 P.M. and also offers accommodations (Moderate-Premium).

1111 Dunaweal Ln. just south of Calistoga, 707/942-3345, www.sterlingvineyards.com, for a gondola-car ride up to this majestic and modern monastic-style Martin Waterfield palace ($6 adults, $3 ages 3–18; fare good for $2 off on the purchase of your first bottle of wine). Great valley views. Open for tasting and tours (self-guided with visual aids) daily 10:30 A.M.–4:30 P.M., and picnicking May–October. Nearby, the postmodern terra-cotta **Clos Pégase Winery,** 1060 Dunaweal, 707/942-4981, www.clospegase.com, designed by architect Michael Graves and conceived as a tribute to mythology, art, and wine, produces cabernet sauvignon, sauvignon blanc, chardonnay, and merlot. Big attractions here are the underground wine caves—featuring their own art collection—and the occasional "Wine in Art" slide show. Open daily 10:30 A.M.–5 P.M. Call for current tour information.

Continuing on to Silverado Trail from Dunaweal, you'll find **Cuvaison,** 4550 Silverado Trail, 707/942-6266, www.cuvaison.com, an-

other of the region's elite small wineries. Here wine lovers find some of the best cabernet, chardonnay, merlot, and zinfandel produced anywhere. Open daily 10 A.M.–5 P.M. for tastings, sales, and picnicking (tours by appointment). South down the Silverado Trail from Cuvaison is small **Wermuth Winery,** 3942 Silverado Trail, 707/942-5924, open weekends 11 A.M.–5 P.M. (irregular hours on weekdays, so call first).

Heading north from Dunaweal on the Silverado Trail leads to **Traulsen Vineyards,** 2250 Lake County Hwy., 707/942-0283, a zinfandel-only winery open Fri.–Sun. 10 A.M.–4:30 P.M. and by appointment (tours by appointment only); **Vincent Arroyo Winery,** 2361 Greenwood Ave., 707/942-6995, open weekdays 9 A.M.–4:30 P.M., weekends 10 A.M.–4:30 P.M. (tours by appointment); and **Chateau Montelena,** 1429 Tubbs Ln., 707/942-5105, www.chateaumontelena.com. Chateau Montelena is noted for its cabernet sauvignon, which has appeared on White House menus, *and* its intriguing medieval French chateau surrounded by Chinese gardens. Somehow it's all very American. Open daily 10 A.M.–4 P.M. (tours by appointment only).

Then, if Napa Valley's wineries still haven't quenched that vineyard thirst, head northwest on Hwy. 128 through the mountains above Calistoga into the Alexander Valley area near Healdsburg—such a pleasant, peaceful contrast that you'll wonder why you spent so much time in the Napa Valley.

"Old Faithful" and Petrified Forest

Northwest of town is California's **Old Faithful Geyser,** 1299 Tubbs Ln., 707/942-6463, one of just three in the world that erupt on schedule. Lately, Old Faithful has been erupting about every 13 minutes for about 60–90 seconds a shot. That's much more frequently than the 25-year average of about once every 30–45 minutes; the blast once lasted four minutes. Geologists think these and other irregularities indicate seismic changes within the earth. The blasts of hot water and steam shoot up 75–100 feet into the air, creating rainbows if the sun is right. Open daily year-round, 9 A.M.–6 P.M. in summer and 9 A.M.–5 P.M. the rest of the year. Admission is $6 general, $5 seniors, $2 kids 6–12.

Turn west off Hwy. 29 onto Petrified Forest Rd. (just north of downtown Calistoga) to take the back-roads route to Santa Rosa. About five miles down this road is the **Petrified Forest,** 4100 Petrified Forest Rd., 707/942-6667, a California historic landmark of volcano-flattened, fossilized remains of ancient redwoods along a quarter-mile, wheelchair-accessible trail, with fossils in the small museum. Picnicking possible. Open daily 10 A.M.–6 P.M. in summer, 10 A.M.–5 P.M. in winter (small fee).

Robert Louis Stevenson State Park

Twisting north up Mt. St. Helena like a corkscrew, Hwy. 29 out of Calistoga leads to an easy-to-miss sign at the pass marking essentially undeveloped 3,200-acre Robert Louis Stevenson State Park (about seven miles out of Calistoga, with parking pullouts on both sides of the road). Particularly pleasant in spring and fall, the open mixed woodland offers good hiking and freestyle picnicking (no camping, no fires) and blissful quiet. Stevenson honeymooned on the cheap in the old bunkhouse here in 1880 with his American bride. There's a monument on the site of the old Silverado Mine, already abandoned when the couple spent two happy months here. Stevenson wrote parts of *Silverado Squatters* while here and generated notes for some of his later, greater works. He called Mt. St. Helena (the 4,500-foot peak named after a visiting Russian princess) "the Mont Blanc of the Coast Ranges," and, some say, modeled *Treasure Island* scenes from his impressions. Most of the

---

WINE COUNTRY SAFARI

Here's something you won't see on every wine country tour—a herd of zebras and Saharan desert antelopes. Not a zoo or animal park, **Safari West** is a 400-acre private wildlife sanctuary dedicated to conserving and propagating African plains species in particular. Its endangered-species breeding programs have earned Safari West membership in the American Zoo and Aquarium Association, a rare feat for a private enterprise.

Though animal protection is the primary emphasis here, visitors are welcome—by appointment only—on naturalist-guided small-group jeep tours through the sanctuary. Guests are invited to dress for the experience (comfortable walking shoes, sun hat, and sunscreen) and to bring their cameras, because the photo ops are close to unbelievable on this 2.5 hour trip. Sunset tours available, too.

Since late August 1999, **The Tent Camp at Safari West** has also welcomed guests at its safari-style accommodations—canvas tents with hardwood floors, king-sized beds, and separate bathrooms (with showers)—up close to the animals. A guest cottage and lodge, both with private kitchen and bath facilities, are also available. Rates are Expensive (tent cabins) to Luxury (lodge), with a two-night minimum stay on weekends. Weekly rates available. Continental breakfast served to tent-cabin guests.

For more information and tour reservations, contact: Safari West, 3115 Porter Creek Rd., Santa Rosa, CA 95404, 707/579-2551, fax 707/579-8777, www.safariwest.com. Safari West is located between Santa Rosa and Calistoga; ask for directions when you make your tour reservations.

trail to the summit follows an abandoned roadbed, but it's well worth the five-mile effort for panoramic views of the Sonoma and Napa Valleys, San Francisco to the south, and even (on rare clear and cool smogless days) mighty Mt. Shasta far to the northeast. Naturalist-led hikes are occasionally offered. For information, call 707/942-4575.

Staying in Calistoga:
Camping, Cabins, Motels

It's first-come, first-camped at the **Napa County Fairgrounds,** 1435 Oak St., 707/942-5111, offering fairly cool campsites with electricity and hot showers. In town is the friendly landmark **Calistoga Inn,** 1250 Lincoln Ave., 707/942-4101, a clean and cozy old hotel with genuine nicks in the down-home furniture. Rates include continental breakfast. Bathrooms are down the hall. Inexpensive-Moderate.

Otherwise, the cheapest lodging choices are well out of town. A great deal is **Triple S Ranch,** 4600 Mountain Home Ranch Rd., 707/942-6730, www.triplesranch.com, a collection of tiny, rustic redwood cabins open Apr.–December. Moderate. The restaurant here is popular with locals, good food for a good price. (To get there from Calistoga, head west on Petrified Forest Rd., then north on Mountain Home Ranch Road.) **Mountain Home Ranch,** 3400 Mountain Home Ranch Rd., 707/942-6616, has a lake, creek, pools, and accommodations ranging from rustic cabins to deluxe cottages. Moderate-Premium. Another rarefied rustic possibility is the **Rainbow Ranch Group Retreat,** 3975 Mountain Home Ranch Rd., 707/942-5127, atop the Mayacamas Mountains on 80 acres of foothill woodlands, with a huge redwood lodge, swimming pool, spring-fed lake, and hot tub. Guests can choose A-frame sleeping cabins, cottages, or high-beamed motel rooms. Group rates only.

Even if you're not doing the spa scene, you can stay at the historic **Indian Springs Resort,** 1712 Lincoln Ave. (between Brannan St. and Wappo Ave.), 707/942-4913, where the family-friendly cottages with kitchens are a main attraction—along with the marvelous swimming pool, fed by natural hot springs (open only to hotel and spa guests). Expensive-Premium.

Staying in Calistoga:
Bed-and-Breakfasts

Calistoga boasts a dozen or more bed-and-breakfasts. The art-deco **Mount View Hotel,** 1457 Lincoln Ave., 707/942-6877 or toll-free 800/816-6877, www.mountviewhotel.com, is a beautifully restored 1917 hotel-style bed-and-breakfast with a hot tub, pool, and spa facilities. Accommodation options include 20 guest rooms (all with private bath), nine suites, and three cottages (each with private patio and hot tub). Continental breakfast is delivered to your room, and the excellent on-site **Catahoula** restaurant, 707/942-2275, serves fare inspired by the Louisiana bayou. Premium-Luxury.

Among the area's other historic offerings, the restored Greek Revival **Brannan Cottage Inn,** 109 Wapoo Ave. (near downtown), 707/942-4200, is one of the original Sam Brannan guesthouses. It offers two suites and four guest rooms, all with private entrances, private baths, and queen beds. Full breakfast. Luxury. Also included on the National Register of Historic Places is **The Elms,** 1300 Cedar St., 707/942-9476 or toll-free 800/235-4316, www.theelms.com, an 1871 home in the French Second Empire style, with six rooms plus a carriage house (all with private bath), afternoon wine and cheese, and full breakfast. Luxury. Across the street is **La chaumière,** 1301 Cedar St., 707/942-5139 or toll-free 800/474-6800, www.lachaumiere.com, a 1932 Cotswald cottage offering two guest rooms and a honeymoon cottage (all with private bath), along with a hot tub, full breakfast, afternoon wine and cheese, and evening sherry. Luxury. Also close to town is **Eurospa and Inn,** 1202 Pine St., 707/942-6829, www.eurospa.com, a 1930s-vintage ranch house and full-service spa with 12 rooms, buffet-style continental breakfast, pool, and whirlpool. Call for rates.

Quite special is small **Scott Courtyard,** 1443 2nd St., 707/942-0948 or toll-free 800/942-1515, fax 707/942-5102, www.scottcourtyard.com, featuring three suites—two with an interconnecting living area, perfect for couples traveling together—and three bungalows, all with unique 1940s and 1950s decor, private bathrooms, and private entrances. Rooms are cheerful and inviting, featuring amenities including in-room coffeemakers, refrigerators, irons, and hair dryers; half have wood-burning fireplaces and kitchens.

Scott Courtyard also includes a pool, hot tub, art studio, and gardens, and a sunny central bistro-style social area. Generous buffet-style breakfast, afternoon wine and cheese. Luxury. The 16 luxurious bed-and-breakfast cabins at the **Cottage Grove Inn,** 1711 Lincoln Ave., 707/942-8400 or toll-free 800/942-1515, fax 707/942-5102, www.cottagegrove.com, just about have it all, starting with soundproofing, recycled hardwood floors, tasteful decor, wood-burning fireplaces, vaulted ceilings, and front porches with their own white wicker rockers. Creature comforts include the deep two-person whirlpool tub, stereo system with CD, cable TV and VCR, refrigerator, wet bar, in-room coffeemaker, and phone with modem jack. Not to mention cozy down comforters and pillows, an ironing board and iron, and dressing robes. Expanded continental breakfast, afternoon wine and cheese. Luxury.

Inquire at the local chamber of commerce for a more complete listing of accommodation options.

Eating in Calistoga

Almost everything is on Lincoln Ave., Calistoga's main drag. **Nicola's Delicatessen,** 1359 Lincoln Ave., 707/942-6272, is open daily 7 A.M.–5 P.M. and makes a good stop for inexpensive breakfast, lunch, or picnic fixings. Another picnic put-together possibility is the stylish **Palisades Market,** 1506 Lincoln, 707/942-9549. **Pacifico,** 1237 Lincoln, 707/942-4400, offers a wide-ranging Mexican menu (try the mole del pueblo). If barbecue suits your fancy, head to the **Smokehouse Cafe,** 1458 Lincoln Ave. (in the Depot building), 707/942-6060, which does a fine breakfast and lunch, too, but specializes in finger-lickin' hickory- or mesquite-smoked pork or beef ribs smothered in a choice of barbecue sauces. Brave vegetarians can attempt the smoked barbecue tofu plate.

Hipper by far than most local restaurants is the relaxed **Calistoga Inn,** 1250 Lincoln Ave., 707/942-4101, home of the **Napa Valley Brewing Company** pub, serving its own lagers and ales, and a spicy contemporary menu—like grilled gulf prawns with red-curry Thai sauce, or a home-smoked turkey sandwich with double-cream jack cheese on rye. Meals are served outside (in season) on a relaxed backyard patio.

The **All Seasons Market and Cafe,** 1400 Lincoln, 707/942-9111, is something of a wine country destination these days—boasting one of the most impressive, and reasonably priced, wine lists anywhere. California-style wine country fare (changing menu) is served at lunch and dinner. Beloved locally is the **Wappo Bar & Bistro,** 1226-B Washington St. (near Lincoln), 707/942-4712, named for local Native Americans. The style, though, is craftsman-like, and the fare is an eclectic regional take on global cuisine—everything from duck carnitas, chiles rellenos with walnut-pomegranate sauce, and Moroccan lamb stew to chicken pot pie. Open Wed.–Mon. for lunch and dinner.

Also quite enticing is the **Catahoula Restaurant** at the Mount View Hotel, 1457 Lincoln Ave., 707/942-2275, rather cheekishly named after Louisiana's state dog. Yet Catahoula definitely fits a place serving up creative interpretations of dishes from Louisiana and the Deep South, from oyster Bienville cakes and pan-fried catfish to pizza with andouille sausage and crayfish. Try the brown-butter fruit tarts for dessert. Open for lunch and dinner Wed.–Mon., dinner daily in summer (reservations recommended, especially at dinner).

LAKE COUNTY

Suffocated by the sophisticated air of the wine country? Too mellowed by Mendocino? Lake County has the cure. The area supported various world-class health spas from the late 1800s through the early 1900s, but now it's a friendly, frumpy, working people's resort and retirement area, as familiar as an old sneaker. Things are fairly inexpensive in the tiny towns around Clear Lake, there are no parking meters, and nobody seems to mind the noise that comes packaged as children. People have been coming here for a long, *long* time. The Clear Lake Basin is one of California's oldest known areas of human habitation: petroglyphs and artifacts found here in recent years date back 10,000 years or more.

The trip from the Napa Valley to Clear Lake via narrow Hwy. 29 (the old Calistoga-Lakeport stage route) is slow but beautiful. Thickly forested hillsides hug the old road, soft green in spring, hazy with blazing color in fall. The only settlement of any size in Loconomi Valley along the way to Clear Lake, **Middletown** isn't particularly exciting but *is* aptly named: it's exactly halfway between Calistoga and Lower Lake. Close to Middletown is the historic **Harbin Hot Springs Retreat Center,** P.O. Box 92, Middletown, CA 95461, 707/987-2477 or toll-free 800/622-2477 (reservations only), a clothing optional place welcoming anyone not drunk or "terribly psychotic." Camp here and do the baths for a very reasonable fee plus yearly membership. Or stay in lodge or dormitory rooms, or try a tepee for two. Just east of Middletown is Lillie Langtry's winery, she being the state's first celebrity winemaker. **Guenoc & Langtry Estate Vineyards and Winery,** 21000 Butts Canyon Rd., 707/987-2385 or 707/987-9127 (tasting room and weekends), was once owned by Langtry—friend of Oscar Wilde and mistress of the Prince of Wales (later King Edward VII). The winery welcomes visitors 11 A.M.–5 P.M. daily. On special occasions, Langtry's house is open to the public for group tours (call in advance to arrange a visit), and her likeness is included on every Guenoc wine label.

For more information on the area's attractions—including Clear Lake, Clear Lake State Park, Anderson Marsh State Historic Park, and other area wineries—contact the **Lake County Visitor Information Center,** 875 Lakeport Blvd., Lakeport, CA 95453, 707/263-9544 or toll-free 800/525-3743, or try www.lakecounty.com.

SONOMA VALLEY

VALLEY OF THE MOON

According to the native Miwok, when they walked at night through the valley between the Mayacamas and Sonoma Mountains, the moon rose seven times—thus the name Sonoma, or many moons. Dubbed the "Valley of the Moon" by writer Jack London, a romantic but off-key translation, the narrow 17-mile-long Sonoma Valley is as rich in history as it is in natural beauty and agricultural wealth. Often called "the cradle of California history," surprisingly serene Sonoma has been ruled by many flags—English, Russian, Spanish, Mexican, and of course, the U.S. Stars and Stripes—and much colonial fervor. But no other ruling power was quite as colorful as the Bear Flaggers, a seedy band of several dozen American freelance landgrabbers.

The land is still the primary local focus, and these days it's grabbed up most frequently for vineyards and wineries. From the historic town of Sonoma, fine wine estates, fruit and nut orchards, and livestock and poultry farms scatter out in all directions.

TOWN OF SONOMA

Picturesque Sonoma, protected from progress today only by strict zoning laws, still survives the troops of tourists massing in the plaza for their wine country assault in spring, summer, and fall. A California-style Spanish town built around an eight-acre central plaza, Sonoma's center is surrounded by carefully preserved old adobes and historic buildings, stately trees, rose gardens, and picnic tables. Many of the superb stone buildings here were crafted by Italian masons. Many of the trees comprise a California botanical native garden, including some of the state's most impressive species—Monterey pine and cypress, coast redwood, giant sequoia, California live oak, California bay laurel, foothill pine, and sycamore.

The **Sonoma Valley Visitors Bureau,** 453 1st St. E (in the old library building on the plaza), Sonoma, CA 95476, 707/996-1090, www.sonomavalley.com, offers the free monthly *Sonoma Valley Visitors Guide*—a complete listing of sights, galleries, wineries, events, accommodations, and restaurants, also available elsewhere around town—and abundant free brochures and flyers. The visitors bureau also helps arrange accommodations. Very helpful staff, worth a stop. There are public restrooms out back, too.

Sonoma State Historic Park
This spread-out collection of historic buildings includes the Sonoma Mission itself (properly known as **Mission San Francisco Solano de Sonoma**), the Sonoma Barracks, the remnants of Vallejo's La Casa Grande, the Blue Wing and Toscano Hotels, and Lachryma Montis ("Mountain Tears"), Vallejo's adobe-insulated Gothic retirement home just outside town. Pick up basic

information and a walking tour guide at park headquarters on the plaza, 20 E. Spain St., Sonoma, CA 95476, 707/938-1519. A small fee covers admission to all historic attractions open to the public (10 A.M.–5 P.M. daily, except major holidays). The fee here also covers admittance to uncrowded **Petaluma Adobe State Historic Park,** west of town in Petaluma, where Vallejo's ranch headquarters still stands.

Sonoma Mission, on the corner of E. Spain St. and 1st St. E, was an upstart enterprise founded in 1823 by Father José Altimira, who didn't bother to ask his superiors for permission. The Russians at Fort Ross on the coast apparently weren't threatened by the mission's presence: they sent bells and other gifts in honor of its dedication. Now a museum with a restored chapel (Vallejo built the church for the pueblo in 1840) and adjacent padres' quarters (constructed in 1825, the oldest building in town), the mission also houses historic exhibits, displays on adobe-building techniques and restoration, and mission art. The impressive and unrestored **Blue Wing Inn** across the street at 217 E. Spain St., built in the 1840s, was the first hotel north of San Francisco.

The two-story adobe and redwood **Sonoma Barracks** building dates from the mid-1830s, when it provided troop housing and headquarters for Mexico's far northern frontier and later headquarters for the boisterous Bear Flaggers. In 1860, Vallejo started his winery here, next door to his home. Now a state-run history museum with exhibits on Sonoma-area Native Americans, Sonoma's rancho era, and the early U.S. years, the dusty courtyard and corral—complete with fowl underfoot—add even more historic authenticity. **La Casa Grande,** Mariano Vallejo's first home in Sonoma, stood near the barracks. The main house was destroyed by fire in 1867, but the servants' wing still stands in the dooryard of the **Toscano Hotel,** which offers free tours.

Just as California moved from a Mexican to an American national identity, Vallejo modified his house style in later years. Named "Mountain Tears" by Vallejo (after nearby natural hot and cold springs), this seemingly un-Spanish two-story New England mansion at the end of the tree-lined lane was built in 1851—the wooden walls wisely layered over adobe brick, traditionally appreciated for its insulating qualities. **Lachry-ma Montis,** at W. Spain St. and 3rd St. W, is finely furnished with many of the general's family belongings, as if waiting for Vallejo himself to return. The grounds, too, are unusual, planted with prickly pear cacti, magnolia trees, even some of Vallejo's original grape vines. The white cast-iron fountains in front and back are part of the original garden decor of Vallejo's 17-acre homesite.

Seeing and Doing the Rest of Sonoma

Start at the plaza—the largest in California, intended as the center of community life—for a downtown walking tour. Shady green and inviting today, the plaza was a dusty, barren piece of ground in Sonoma's early years, trampled by Vallejo's marching troops and littered with animal skeletons left over from communal feasts. (The town still burns the bull here during the annual Ox Roast in early June.) The small duck pond adds noise and feathers to the spacious gardens and picnic grounds, and the bronze **Bear Flag Republic sculpture** to the northeast is a reminder of the region's short-lived political independence. The impressive stone **Sonoma City Hall** and courthouse in the center of the plaza is post-Spanish, added by Americans in 1906. The **Swiss Hotel** near the Toscano Hotel was built by Mariano Vallejo's brother Salvador and now houses the Swiss Hotel restaurant. Down 1st St. is the 1846 **Jacob Leese House,** home of California's military governor (and Vallejo's brother-in-law) in 1849.

SONOMA VALLEY CYCLING

Though Napa Valley is touted as the area's bicycling mecca, Sonoma County is better in many respects—not nearly as trammeled (yet) with treacherous traffic and offering many more backcountry routes. Far better for cyclists than Hwy. 12, for example, is the parallel Arnold Dr.–Bennett Valley Rd. route through the Sonoma Valley toward Santa Rosa. An excellent casual cyclist's guide to the region (including Sonoma and the Sonoma Valley) is *Sonoma County Bike Trails* by Phyllis L. Neumann, available in many local shops and bookstores. In Sonoma proper, where many people start their wine country adventure, rent bikes at **Sonoma Valley Cyclery,** 20093 Broadway, 707/935-3377.

*Bodega Church,
Sonoma County*

ROBERT HOLMES/CALTOUR

While wandering through downtown Sonoma, stop by the local historical society's **Depot Park Historical Museum,** 285 1st St. W (in the small building between the free parking lots and the bike path), 707/938-9765, for a look at annually changing local heritage exhibits. Open Wed.–Sun. 1–4:30 P.M.; donations always appreciated. Ask here, or at the visitors bureau, about historical walking tours.

CALIFORNIA'S FIRST AND FINAL FLAG

William Todd, a nephew of Mary Todd Lincoln, designed the flag that flew over Sonoma for less than a month in 1846 on behalf of the Bear Flag Republic. The grizzly bear became the primary symbol—reverse psychological warfare, since the rowdy Americans were nicknamed *osos* (bears) by the Mexicans. Like the republic's one star, the grizzly was drawn with blackberry juice; so clumsy was the original artwork that the Sonorans called the flat-faced bear a pig. A strip of red flannel was stitched along the bottom, below the words "California Republic." The same basic (but artistically improved) design, with a red star in the upper corner, was officially adopted as the state's flag in 1911. Charred fragments of the original flag (destroyed by fire in San Francisco's 1906 earthquake) are still on display in the Sonoma Mission museum.

Staying in Sonoma

Forget about camping in Sonoma, but not far north is **Sugarloaf Ridge State Park,** 2605 Adobe Canyon Rd. (above Kenwood), 707/833-5712, which offers RV and tent camping, as well as good hiking (see listing below for more information). If headed toward the Napa Valley, consider camping at **Lake Berryessa** or **Bothe-Napa Valley State Park.** Otherwise, low-rent accommodations are hard to find. There's one **Motel 6** in Petaluma to the west and three more near Santa Rosa to the north (one in Rohnert Park). A best bet in Sonoma is **El Pueblo Inn,** 896 W. Napa St., 707/996-3651 or toll-free 800/900-8844 in California, which is well located (about a mile from the plaza) and features comfy rooms, garden, pool, and spa. Moderate.

The contemporary **Best Western Sonoma Valley Inn,** near the plaza at 550 2nd St. W, 707/938-9200 or toll-free 800/334-5784, www. bestwestern.com, has all the amenities—from pool, whirlpool, and fitness center to fireplaces (in most rooms), in-room coffee and refrigerators, hair dryers, and complimentary continental breakfast. On-site restaurants. Two-night minimum stay on weekends in the high season. Premium-Luxury.

Staying in Sonoma: Bed-and-Breakfasts

Many area bed-and-breakfasts require a two-night minimum stay on weekends. The restored 1872 **Sonoma Hotel,** 110 W. Spain St., 707/996-2996, is right on the main plaza. Maya Angelou wrote *Gather Together in My Name*

THE GROWLING OF THE BEAR FLAG REPUBLIC

Mexican fears of Russian territorial incursions weren't put to rest by the 1823 establishment of California's last missionary outpost, Mission San Francisco Solano de Sonoma, in what was then Mexico's far northern territory. So General Mariano Vallejo was sent to Sonoma to found a frontier pueblo for Alta California. Due to hostilities with Native American populations, Vallejo failed to establish colonies at both Santa Rosa and Petaluma. His third try, the town of Sonoma, was laid out near the mission in 1835. Troops rode out to subdue northern natives on many occasions, but General Vallejo further secured the town through his alliance and friendship with the chief of the Suisun, baptized "Solano."

Peace reigned until June 14, 1846, when a scruffy band of armed gringos rode into town and took over. Taking orders from Captain (later General) John C. Frémont, these Yankee trappers had camped out near Marysville on a "scientific expedition" while awaiting the opportunity to conquer California (or at least acquire some large tracts of land). Fearing expulsion by Mexican authorities, the ragtag revolutionaries decided to launch their own war for acquisition and independence, unaware that the United States had already declared war against Mexico in May.

There was no battle. Frémont and his freedom fighters met with Vallejo, who peacefully surrendered after offering the Americans some wine. The whole town surrendered, seemingly amused. To justify their theft of the township with a greater purpose, the Americans declared California a new republic, and quickly fashioned an appropriate banner and ran it up the flagpole in the plaza. (Almost no one saluted.) The banner of the Bear Flag Republic flew over Sonoma for just a few weeks, though, before U.S. Navy Commodore John Sloat sailed into Monterey Bay and on July 9 raised the American flag over the Alta California capital, ending Frémont's dream of an independent western republic.

As for Vallejo, after two months' imprisonment at Sutter's Fort, he went on to become the district's first state senator, and later Sonoma's mayor. Though Vallejo owned more than 175,000 acres of California lands at one time, his holdings shrank to a mere five acres by the time he died in 1890. But he wasn't bitter, despite the wild swings in his fate and fortune. "I had my day," he said, "and it was a proud one."

---

while staying in room 21. All rooms have private bath. Rates include continental breakfast and afternoon wine. Premium-Luxury. A real gem is the elegantly restored yet unfussy **El Dorado Hotel,** 405 1st St. W, 707/996-3030 or toll-free 800/289-3031, www.hoteleldorado.com, with 26 rooms (private baths, balconies overlooking the plaza), courtyard, heated lap pool, and the wonderful on-site **Piatti Ristorante** (707/996-2351). Luxury. Also convenient is the charming and relaxed turn-of-the-century Victorian **Thistle Dew Inn,** 171 W. Spain St., 707/938-2909 or toll-free 800/382-7895, www.thistledew.com, offering full breakfast, complimentary hors d'oeuvres, a spa, and use of bicycles. Premium-Luxury. The 1870 farmhouse **Victorian Garden Inn,** 316 E. Napa St. (near the plaza), 707/996-5339 or toll-free 800/543-5339, http://victoriangardeninn.com, has just four rooms, three with private entrance, and offers an expanded continental breakfast and swimming pool. Marvelous garden. Expensive-Luxury. The equally special **Sonoma Chalet,**

18935 5th St. W, 707/938-3129 or toll-free 800/938-3129, www.sonomachalet.com, offers relaxed country charms quite close to town, and features a suite and three rooms in a chalet-style farmhouse (two share a bath and living room) plus three outlying cottages with private baths and a fireplace or woodstove. Amenities include a hot tub and expanded continental breakfast. Expensive-Luxury. **The Hidden Oak Inn,** 214 E. Napa St., 707/996-9863, is a 1913 Craftsman offering three rooms (private baths) and full breakfast. Premium-Luxury.

Definitely different is **Ramekins,** 450 W. Spain St., 707/933-0452, fax 707/933-0451, www.ramekins.com, where the six rooms (all feature private baths) are upstairs, above the cooking school of the same name. Everything is so strongly food-themed here—even the staircase resembles asparagus—that you're grateful that there are so many restaurants in and near the Sonoma Plaza (the General's Daughter restaurant is right next door). Continental breakfast. Luxury, with slightly lower off-season rates.

The California mission-style **Vineyard Inn,** 23000 Arnold Dr., 707/938-2350 or toll-free 800/359-4667, www.sonomavineyardinn.com, offers 24 bungalows with private baths and entrances, a pool, and both expanded continental breakfast and English tea. Premium-Luxury.

At least two dozen bed-and-breakfast inns are scattered throughout the Sonoma Valley, some in Kenwood, Glen Ellen, and Santa Rosa. Contact the visitors bureau for a fairly comprehensive current listing, or see what's available through the **Bed & Breakfast Association of Sonoma Valley,** 707/938-9513, www.sonomabb.com.

Sonoma Mission Inn & Spa

The public hot springs are long gone at Boyes Hot Springs, but the old hotel still stands. The peachy-pink **Sonoma Mission Inn and Spa,** 18140 Sonoma Hwy., 707/938-9000 or toll-free 800/862-4945 (in California), www.sonomamissioninn.com, is the best spa in the world, according to recent *Gourmet* magazine reader surveys. And what's not to like? Swank and contemporary yet somewhat old-fashioned at the same time, Sonoma Mission Inn facilities—"10 acres of pure indulgence"—include a luxury

---

FAMILY FUN

A mile south of Sonoma's plaza on Broadway, the miniature **Sonoma Traintown Railroad,** 20264 Broadway, 707/938-3912, is a quarter-scale model of the 1875 diamond-stack locomotive—the same size as everything else here. You can take the 20-minute ride through the Lilliputian landscape mid-June through Labor Day daily (the rest of the year Fri.–Sun. and holidays only). Also here are a carousel, petting zoo, gift shop, and picnic facilities. Open 10 A.M.–5 P.M. (small fee, babes-in-arms free).

A great spot for a picnic, **Agua Caliente Mineral Springs** is a summertime family spa just outside Sonoma at 17350 Vailetti Dr., 707/996-6822, featuring hot mineral pools and a cold pool. Usually open Apr. 15–Sept. 30, weekends and holidays 10 A.M.–7 P.M., Mon., Thurs., and Fri. 10:30 A.M.–6 P.M. (call ahead to make sure). Admission fee. Another possibility, farther north near Kenwood, is **Morton's Warm Springs,** 1651 Warm Springs Rd., 707/833-5511.

---

hotel, exceptional restaurants, and an incredible 27,000-square-foot spa offering Roman baths, individual baths and whirlpools, herbal steam, and everything from aromatherapy and shiatsu massage to seaweed or herbal body wraps. Even the inn's swimming pool is filled with mineral water. Other active diversions include exercise classes and tennis. Luxury.

Eating in Sonoma: The Basics

The best food is the simplest. With a current *Sonoma County Farm Trails* brochure and map in hand (available here at local shops and the visitors bureau, or try www.farmtrails.org)—and by visiting one of the popular local farmers' markets—hunting down local produce in season is easy as pie. The **Sonoma Certified Farmers' Market** is held Fri. year-round, 9 A.M.–noon, at the Arnold Field parking lot, 1st and Spain Streets. The Sonoma **Tuesday Certified Farmers' Market,** held Apr.–Oct. on Tues., 5:30–8:30 P.M., and the **Sonoma Saturday Certified Farmers' Market,** held Nov.–Dec. on Sat., 1–4 P.M., both take place at Sonoma Plaza (at Napa Street). For information on all three markets, call 707/538-7023.

Or combine a walking tour with the pleasure of putting together a homegrown picnic. An excellent cheese stop on the way up the hill and off the usual tourist track is the **Vella Cheese Company,** 315 2nd St. E, 707/938-3232. Vella has been in the cheese business since 1931, much of that time in this same sturdy stone building. Famous for its sweet, nutty-tasting "dry" Monterey cheeses, Vella also makes garlic, onion, and jalapeño jack varieties, tasty raw milk cheddar, and an Oregon blue cheese.

The **Sonoma Cheese Factory,** 2 W. Spain St., Sonoma, CA 95476, 707/996-1000, is known for its famous Sonoma Jack cheeses. Take a peek at the cheese makers, try some homemade salads or good basic sandwiches, and browse through the awesome array of deli and gourmet items while you wait.

Next stop is the **Sonoma French Bakery,** 470 1st St. E, 707/996-2691, for good Basque yeastless sourdough bread (people line up for it). The **Home Grown Baking Co.,** 122 W. Napa St., 707/996-0166, makes fresh bagels, salads, and soups. (A second location is at 19161 Sonoma Hwy., 707/996-0177.) For upscale Italian deli fare, brought to you by the Viansa Winery folks, head for **Lo Spuntino,** 400 1st St. E, 707/935-5656. The **Cherry Tree,** 1901 Fremont Dr., 707/938-3480, is a combination fruit stand/deli with wonderful black cherry cider. Other delis abound.

Eating in Sonoma: Fairly Inexpensive

Absolutely superb is **Siena Red Brewery and Bistro,** 529 1st St. W, 707/938-1313, which features a bright Mediterranean interior, a beautiful garden patio out back, some truly fine microbrews—seven or eight to choose from—and a great menu of gourmet pub fare. You can't go wrong here. Open daily for lunch and dinner.

Best bet for barbecue and killer fries is **Rob's Rib Shack,** next to the driving range at 18709 Arnold Dr., 707/938-8520. Open daily for lunch and dinner. For inexpensive and very good Mexican (Yucatecan) food, try the **Ranch House Cafe,** 20872 Broadway (Hwy. 12), 707/938-0454. Open daily 11 A.M.–10 P.M. The long-running **La Casa** restaurant and bar, 121 E. Spain St. (right across from the mission), 707/996-3406, is a good midpriced choice for dinners, specializing in traditional Mexican food (very good enchiladas suizas). **Little Switzerland,** just west of town in El Verano at the corner of Grove St. and Riverside Dr., 707/938-9990, offers steak, chicken, bratwurst, and sauerbraten dinners, as well as ballroom dancing on Sun. 5–9 P.M.

Eating in Sonoma: Fancier Fare

Good for dinner is the small, locally popular **Sonoma Hotel** restaurant at 110 W. Spain St., 707/996-2996 for reservations. The lunch menu is seasonal, the dinner menu changes twice each month, and the Sunday brunch is worth getting up for. Always featured: fresh local produce and fine local products, including area wines. The quite reasonable **Depot Hotel,** 241 1st St. W, 707/938-2980, is a regular winner of *Wine Spectator* magazine's Award of Excellence, serving Northern Italian and Mediterranean fare Wed.–Fri. for lunch and Wed.–Sun. for dinner. Another local classic is **Della Santina's,** now at home at the onetime site of the Eastside Oyster Bar & Grill, 133 E. Napa St., 707/935-0576, with a wonderful outdoor patio. You can't go wrong with the house-made pastas.

SONOMA COUNTY FARM TRAILS

Best and cheapest for quality wine-country eating is stocking up on the basics—local wines and fresh baked bread, cheese from Sonoma, area fruits and veggies—then picnicking around. To find your own fresh local produce, pick up a current copy of the *Sonoma County Farm Trails* map and brochure at local visitor centers or at chamber offices. Or contact: Sonoma County Farm Trails, P.O. Box 6032, Santa Rosa, CA 95406, 707/571-8288 or toll-free 800/207-9464, fax 707/571-7719. You can also visit the website: www.farmtrails.org. (Most Farm Trails stops are near Sebastopol and Forestville, though there are good choices also in the Sonoma Valley.)

Open daily for lunch and dinner. The light and airy **Piatti Ristorante** at the El Dorado Hotel, 405 1st St. W, 707/996-2351, is absolutely wonderful for chic Italian, but far from stuffy—great for handmade pastas, pizzas, and calzones. Open for lunch and dinner daily.

According to a 1997 *Gourmet* magazine survey, the **General's Daughter,** 400 W. Spain St., 707/938-4004, is among Sonoma's finest restaurants. Housed in the 1864 Victorian home General Mariano Vallejo built for his daughter Natalia, the General's Daughter serves everything from andouille sausage pizza to grilled game hens. Open Mon.–Sat. for lunch, Sun. for brunch, and dinner nightly.

Another contender, though, is eclectic **Babette's Restaurant & Wine Bar,** 464 1st St. E (on an alley between Spain and Napa Sts.), 707/939-8921, serving contemporary French, the fixed-price menu including at least one vegetarian entrée. For less expensive bistro fare, head for the wine bar. Open for lunch and dinner daily.

Prices at **The Grille** at the Sonoma Mission Inn in Boyes Hot Springs, 18140 Hwy. 12, 707/938-9000, are high, and the food certainly holds its own. Good Sunday brunch. But if you must eat at the big pink, try **The Café** instead, popular for its hearty breakfast selections (like apple oatcakes) and California-style Mediterranean fare, from pastas and pizzas to grilled chicken.

SONOMA AREA WINERIES

Wineries near Sonoma

Sonoma is the birthplace of California's wine industry. The local mission planted the state's first vineyards in 1824. Part of the Sonoma Mission's original vineyards are living history at **Sebastiani Sonoma Cask Cellars,** 389 4th St. E, Sonoma, CA 95476, 707/938-5532 or toll-free 800/888-5532, www.sebastiani.com, open daily 10 A.M.–5 P.M. for tours, tasting, and sales. The winery was one of the few open during Prohibition, producing altar wine and a potent "wine tonic" patent medicine.

Green Hungarian is bottled in the Sonoma Valley (as elsewhere) in honor of "Count" Agoston Haraszthy, the aristocratic Austrian-Hungarian immigrant who convinced California's governor to send him to Europe in 1861 to collect vinifera vines. He returned with 100,000 or so, which he distributed throughout the area. The striking stone **Buena Vista Winery,** a mile east of town at 18000 Old Winery Rd., 707/938-1266 or toll-free 800/926-1266, www.buenavistawinery.com, open daily 10:30 A.M.–4:30 P.M., is the Hungarian's original winery and a state historic landmark. Though the winery's focal point these days is its Carneros estate, stone cellars here (some tunnels collapsed during the 1906 earthquake) are the oldest in California and are also the headquarters for the only wine brotherhood in the United States, the Knights of the Vine. Take the self-guided tour, which emphasizes the life and times of Haraszthy, then head to the original tile-floored press house for a free taste. (Lift a glass of Green Hungarian in a toast to the count, then hike up to the art gallery on the 2nd floor.) Buena Vista's picnic grounds are quite inviting.

Noted for its merlot and other fine wines is the prestigious but small **Gundlach-Bundschu Winery,** 2000 Denmark St., 707/938-5277, www.gundlach-bundschu.com, a family-run operation since the mid-1800s yet the kind of place you're more likely to hear vintage rock than classical music. The winery's 400-acre Rhinefarm Vineyards were originally established in 1858 by Jacob Gundlach and Charles Bundschu. Tasting is offered daily 11 A.M.–4:30 P.M.; tours are offered, as well as outdoor picnicking. The winery also sponsors an immensely popular summer

Sonoma's Buena Vista Winery

Shakespeare series. Take a short hike to the top of Towle's Hill for the view of San Francisco and San Pablo Bays.

At **Carmenet Vineyard,** 1700 Moon Mountain Dr., 707/996-5870, the aging caves are large, with room for stacking wine barrels as well as daily hand-racking and washing. Specialties here are cabernet sauvignon and sauvignon blanc, wines made using traditional French techniques, including barrel fermentation. Tours by appointment only.

Also worth visiting near Sonoma is **Ravenswood,** 18701 Gehricke Rd., 707/938-1960, most appreciated for its zinfandel, open daily 10 A.M.–4:30 P.M. for tasting and picnicking (tours by appointment).

Bartholomew Park Winery, located at the former site of the Hacienda winery, 1000 Vineyard Ln., 707/935-9511, www.bartholomewparkwinery.com, emphasizes wine education. The **Museum of Wine** here displays vintage winemaking equipment, period clothing, and local history—including Pomo Indians, Agoston Haraszthy, and

Kate Johnson and her 2,000 angora cats, whose Victorian castle became a work farm for "wayward women." Open daily 10 A.M.–4:30 P.M. for tasting, self-guided tours, and picnicking.

Sonoma-Carneros Wineries

Taking in the southern reaches of both Sonoma and Napa Valleys is a distinct wine area—the relatively uncrowded Carneros region, generally defined by Highway 12/121, renamed the Carneros Highway in 1992 and the only U.S. highway named after a wine-growing region. Formerly sheep grazing land—"carneros" is Spanish for sheep—the unique climate here, often windy or foggy and cold, but moderated by proximity to San Pablo Bay, provides a longer growing season perfect for persnickety pinot noir grapes. For that reason, the Napa-Sonoma Carneros region is known for its rich, sweet pinot noir wines. But chardonnay also does exceptionally well under the Carneros appellation, as do sparkling wines. In fact, most of California's top sparkling wine makers are either located here or buy their grapes here. With grape demand much greater than supply, most Carneros wines are on the pricey side.

Though southern Napa County boasts an impressive roster of Carneros wineries (see Napa-Carneros Wineries under the City of Napa and Vicinity, above), Sonoma's is equally prestigious. And from Sonoma proper, it's just a short, straight shot south on Broadway to reach the Carneros region.

The Spanish have returned to Sonoma County. About six miles north of Sears Point Raceway in the Sonoma Valley section of the Carneros wine region are the **Gloria Ferrer Champagne Caves**, 23555 Carneros Hwy. (Hwy. 121), 707/996-7256, www.gloriaferrer.com, the American winemaking arm of Barcelona's 600-year-old Ferrer family enterprise, Freixenet S.A.—the world's largest producer of *méthode champenoise* sparkling wines (called *cava* in Spain, after the aging caves). While the "caves" here at Gloria Ferrer are not much to explore, the champagnery itself is as elegant in its genteel, understated way as the Napa Valley's Domaine Chandon is opulent—a Mediterranean-style villa with a terrace and "Hall of Tasters" for wine-tasting (fee for the wines, snacks provided free). Tasting and tours available daily 10:30 A.M.–5:30 P.M.

A bit farther south on the opposite side of the highway, the **Viansa Winery and Italian Marketplace**, 25200 Hwy. 121, 707/935-4700 or toll-free 800/995-4740, www.viansa.com, occupies a hilltop perch overlooking the Carneros region, a popular destination these days (watch out for those tour buses). Founded by Sam and Vicki Sebastiani, the winery features beautiful Mediterranean-inspired grounds, a Tuscan villa perfect for a picnic. Inside the tasting room, you'll find one of the valley's best selections of delectable finger foods—olives, cheeses, crackers, pestos, etc.—for sale or sample (after you try, you'll *want* to buy). Open daily 10 A.M.–5 P.M. The Viansa Winery has also become something of a wildlife refuge, thanks to the 90-acre restored wetlands here—an effort that won the winery a National Wetlands Award in 1995. Even novice bird-watchers can identify migrating winter waterfowl from the winery's terrace; Jan., Feb., and Mar. are the best months to try.

Nearby **Cline Cellars,** 24737 Arnold Dr. (Hwy. 121), 707/935-4310 or toll-free 800/546-2070, www.clinecellars.com, got its start in Oakley, in the Sacramento-San Joaquin Delta. Cline's intriguing wines include viognier, zinfandel, and Carneros syrah. The grounds are particularly inviting, from the 1850s farmhouse tasting room and deli/gift shop to the old rock-walled ponds and wood-plank bathhouse. Open daily 10 A.M.–6 P.M. for tasting, sales, and picnicking in the eucalyptus grove (tours by appointment).

Also well worth visiting in Sonoma's Carneros region are the **Schug Carneros Estate Winery,** 602 Bonneau Rd., 707/939-9363 or toll-free 800/966-9365, www.schugwinery.com, where German winemaking styles have been transplanted to American soil (open daily 10 A.M.–5 P.M.); **Sonoma Creek Winery,** 23355 Millerick Rd., 707/938-3031, www.sonomacreek.com; and **Roche Carneros Estate Winery,** 28700 Arnold Dr. (Hwy. 121), 707/935-7115, www.rochewinery.com. Roche—the white barn at the top of the hill—sells its wines only here.

Glen Ellen Area Wineries

The **Benziger Family Winery,** 1883 London Ranch Rd., 707/935-4085, www.benziger.com, offers a tractor-drawn tram tour through the vineyards—quite informative, covering subjects such as root grafts, covercrops, trellising, terracing, and crushing. Tram tours are offered daily (call for current information), and a self-guided tour of the demonstration vineyard is available, too. The art gallery displays original wine label art. Open for tastings—sauvignon blanc, zinfandel, syrah—daily 10 A.M.–5 P.M.; picnic area in the cedars.

Before they opened their current winery enterprise, the Benzigers owned the popular **Glen Ellen Winery** nearby, which now operates its tasting room and history center at 14301 Arnold Dr. (in Jack London Village), 707/939-6277. The winery produces good everyday chardonnay and cabernet sauvignon marketed as its Proprietor's Reserve line for a very affordable price. Open daily 10 A.M.–5 P.M. for tasting (try the sauvignon blanc), tours, and picnicking.

The **B. R. Cohn Winery,** 15140 Sonoma Hwy., 707/938-4064, www.brcohn.com, is also noteworthy for its gourmet vinegars and olive oil—French picholine olive oil pressed from the olive trees here (more than 120 years old) for the Olive Hill Oil Company. Come in spring for the annual **California Olive Oil Festival,** a day full of olive oil tastings, olive oil cooking demonstrations by Bay Area gourmet chefs, and more. Proceeds benefit local charities. The B. R. Cohn Winery is open daily 10 A.M.–5 P.M. for tasting, guided tours, and picnicking.

Or try the white zinfandel at **Valley of the Moon Winery,** 777 Madrone Rd. (four miles west of Hwy. 12, near Arnold Dr.), 707/996-6941, www.valleyofthemoonwinery.com. Founded by General "Fighting Joe" Hooker and including part of Senator George Hearst's 19th-century vineyards, Valley of the Moon is open 10 A.M.–5 P.M. daily.

Kenwood Area Wineries—and Beyond

Taste buds still willing, visit **Chateau St. Jean,** 8555 Sonoma Hwy. (Hwy. 12), Kenwood, CA 95452, 707/833-4134, www.chateaustjean.com. The 1920s chateau sits on a wooded 250-acre estate. Open for tastings (try one of the justly famous chardonnays), sales, and self-guided tours daily 10 A.M.–4:30 P.M. Also worth some time in the neighborhood is **St. Francis Vineyards,** 8450 Sonoma Hwy., 707/833-4666 or toll-free 800/543-7713, open daily 10 A.M.–4:30 P.M. for tours and tasting (call for tour details).

Stop at the **Wine Room,** 9575 Sonoma Hwy. (Hwy. 12, at Warm Springs Rd.) in Kenwood, 707/833-6131, open 11 A.M.–4 P.M. daily, to taste wines produced by six different local vintners. The excellent **Kenwood Vineyards** nearby, 9592 Sonoma Hwy., 707/833-5891, www.kenwoodvineyards.com, has exclusive rights to Jack London's vineyards, and bottles a special wine in his honor each year. (According to *The Wine Journal,* Kenwood consistently produces one of California's best sauvignon blancs.) Open daily 10 A.M.–4:30 P.M.

The **Kunde Estate Winery,** 10155 Sonoma Hwy., 707/833-5501, www.kunde.com, features a half mile of hillside caves. Cave tours are offered frequently Fri.–Sun., otherwise by appointment. Open daily 11 A.M.–5 P.M. for tours (call for details), sales, and tastings of its chardonnay and unusual viognier, made from a French grape. If you're lucky, Kunde may even have some of its immensely popular zinfandel, produced from ancient vines (more than a century old).

Technically in Santa Rosa but overlooking the Sonoma Valley from its perch in the Mayacamas Mountains is the excellent but very small **Adler Fels Winery,** 5325 Corrick Ln., 707/539-3123, www.adlerfels.com, known for its chardonnay, sauvignon blanc, and Mélange à Deux sparkling wine. Open for tours, tasting, and sales daily, but only by appointment. You can also taste Adler Fels at the Wine Room, mentioned above.

Also quite close to Santa Rosa is the **Matanzas Creek Winery,** 6097 Bennett Valley Rd., 707/528-6464 or toll-free 800/590-6464, www.matanzascreek.com, known for its merlot and chardonnay. Matanzas Creek also grows lavender—and lots of it. Open daily 10 A.M.–4:30 P.M. for tasting and sales (tours by appointment).

JACK LONDON STATE HISTORIC PARK

When Jack London first saw the soft primeval forests sprawling up the sides of Sonoma Mountain in 1905, he knew this was his new home. The canyons and grassy hills separated by streams and natural springs, the mixture of redwoods, firs, live oaks, and madrones all spoke to him. This was his escape from city life, which he called "the man-trap." So here, at his beloved Beauty Ranch, Jack London lived with his second wife Charmian for 11 years, "anchoring good and solid, and anchoring for keeps," except for a two-year sail through the South Seas. The Londons' former ranch, now an 800-acre state historic park near Glen Ellen, is a must-do destination, a strangely silent monument to one person's grand spirit.

Once out of the city, London became a hardworking, forward-looking farmer—eventually expanding his holdings from 130 to 1,400 acres. He raised horses, cattle, and pigs, and grew innovative and unusual crops (a passion shared by his Santa Rosa contemporary and friend, "Mr. Arbor Day," horticulturist Luther Burbank). London also wrote here, voluminously—he sometimes scrawled away for 19 hours straight.

To get to the park, take London Ranch Rd. (up the hill from Arnold Dr. at the curve in "downtown" Glen Ellen), then follow the signs. The park is open daily 9:30 A.M.–7 P.M., and the park's museum, in the House of Happy Walls on the park's east end, is open daily 10 A.M.–5 P.M. The London Cottage—where Jack London lived and wrote from 1911 until his death in 1916—has been restored and is at the west end of the park, open weekends only noon–4 P.M. No camping is allowed in the park, and the day-use fee is $3 per car. For more information, contact: Jack London State Historic Park, 2400 London Ranch Rd., Glen Ellen, CA 95442, 707/938-5216. Fortunately for future visitors, restoration of Beauty Ranch is still underway. Contributions are welcomed.

Seeing and Doing Beauty Ranch

The park's once-overflowing museum collection has been slimmed down substantially. At home in the two-story stone **House of Happy Walls**, which Charmian London built from 1919–22, the museum is still well worth the short hike uphill from the main parking lot. The impressive collection of rejection slips should comfort any writer (as will the meticulously worked page proofs), and much of London's correspondence is hilarious. In addition to the Londons' array of South Pacific paraphernalia, Jack London's study—too neat for a working writer—is quite evocative. A well-done display on his social life and socialist political adventures and polemics (London ran twice, on the Socialist ticket, for mayor of Oakland) is upstairs.

It's an easy half-mile downhill walk to the still-standing rock ruins of the Londons' dream home, **Wolf House,** a magnificent 15,000-square-foot mansion of carefully carved maroon lava and natural unpeeled redwood logs on an earthquake-proof concrete slab. Built with double-thick concrete walls to make it fireproof, Wolf House was nonetheless burned to the ground by unknown arsonists, just before the Londons planned to move in.

Take the **Beauty Ranch Trail** through the other side of the park to see what remains of London's experimental farm, which raised Shire draft horses and grew for feed the spineless cacti developed by London's friend, Luther Burbank. The circular, stone **Pig Palace** is London's original design. Tucked among vineyards on the rolling gold and green hills is the simple white wood-frame **London Cottage** where Jack and Charmian lived and worked, and where Jack died. Adjacent are the ruins of the old winery (severely damaged by the 1906 earthquake) where the Londons' many guests usually stayed.

London Ranch Horseback Rides

"I am a sailor on horseback!" Jack London once proclaimed. "Watch my dust!" Though elsewhere horseback rides seem like a mere tourist diversion, at Jack London State Park the trip is a real treat—and an opportunity to see parts of London's ranch just as he and Charmian did (though hikers can cover the same terrain for free, of course). The **Sonoma Cattle Company,** P.O. Box 877, Glen Ellen, CA 95442, 707/996-8566, offers small group rides (for either novice or experienced riders) through the park's hinterlands, past London's vineyards, his onetime irrigation lake and bathhouse, abandoned ranch buildings, London's disappointing experimental forest of eucalyptus—even up the steep slopes of Sonoma Mountain. One- to four-hour rides are available, as are box lunch, moonlight, and other specialty trips, $35 and up. Reservations required. The same company also offers rides in nearby Sugarloaf Ridge State Park and in Bothe-Napa Valley State Park.

Sugarloaf Ridge State Park

It's several steep and narrow miles via Adobe Canyon Rd.—mud or rockslides may close the road in winter—up to Sugarloaf Ridge State

CALIFORNIA DEPARTMENT OF PARKS & RECREATION

JACK LONDON

A phenomenally successful and prolific author (the first writer ever to earn $1 million with his pen), Jack London (1876–1916) completed more than 50 books and hundreds of short stories and articles between 1900 and 1916.

Colorful and controversial, Jack London was just as celebrated for his other activities: socialist lecturer, political activist, barroom orator, war correspondent, world traveler, sailor, and outdoorsman. Part of London's public appeal was the essential contradiction he represented: the rugged individualist in search of universal justice. The illegitimate Irish son of an astrologer, primarily self-educated through public libraries (his formal schooling ended at age 14 when he went to work in the factories of West Oakland), Jack London became a founding member of the original Bay Area Bohemian Club (then an artists' club, now an elite social clique).

Park, a fine 2,700-acre wine-country park in the Mayacamas Mountains. Camping is available, and the park also invites hiking, horseback riding, fishing, and rock climbing. In spring, the air is cool, the hillsides are green and thick with wildflowers, and trout swim up Sonoma Creek's seasonal waterfall below the campground. On any clear day, the views from the park's ridge tops are worth the hike. (The **Sonoma Cattle Company,** 707/996-8566, offers ridge-top rides for small groups.) Twenty-five miles of trails lace the park, which is connected via **Goodspeed Trail** to **Hood Mountain Regional Park,** 707/527-2041, open for day use only on weekends and holidays, closed during the fire season. Starting from the campground on the meadow, Sugarloaf's **Creekside Nature Trail** introduces native vegetation and area landforms.

The campground at Sugarloaf has flush toilets but no showers, reservations usually required late Mar.–October. Hiker and biker campsites are also available. Day-use fee: $2 per car. Trail map available at the entrance or at the visitors center near the campground. For more information, contact: Sugarloaf Ridge State Park, 2605 Adobe Canyon Rd., Kenwood, CA 95452, 707/833-5712. For camping reservations, call ReserveAmerica toll-free at 800/444-7275.

PETALUMA AND SANTA ROSA

PETALUMA

You can't always tell a town by its freeway. Petaluma, for example, is hometown America. Though inspired by the mores of Modesto, *American Graffiti* was filmed here, as were *Peggy Sue Got Married* and the forgettable *Howard the Duck* (not to mention *Basic Instinct.*) Petaluma means "beautiful view" (or by some accounts, "flat back," a reference to local Miwok people). Once promoted as the World's Egg Basket, the area still has plenty of chicken ranches and once even had a Chicken Pharmacy downtown, which dispensed poultry medicines. Dairy farming is another major area industry, as are its 30-plus antique shops.

Get oriented at the **Petaluma Visitors Center,** 799 Baywood Dr., Ste. 1, Petaluma, CA 94954, 707/769-0429 or toll-free 877/273-8258, www.petaluma.org. To get there, take the Washington St. exit off Hwy. 101, go west on

Washington and turn left (south) on Lakeville; Baywood intersects Lakeville. Free parking is available downtown in the city garage at Keller and Western, as well as along the riverfront on Water Street.

Seeing and Doing Petaluma

Petaluma is something of a garden spot, home to an incredible number of prime gardener destinations—including the rose-lover's mecca **Garden Valley Ranch,** 498 Pepper St., 707/795-0919; **Cottage Garden Growers of Petaluma,** 4049 Petaluma Blvd., 707/778-8025, and the **North Coast Native Nursery,** 2710 Chileno Valley Rd., 707/769-1213.

Worth a quick stop in Petaluma is the free **Petaluma Historical Library and Museum,** 20 4th St., 707/778-4398, open Mon. and Thurs.–Sat. 10 A.M.–4 P.M., Sun. noon–3 P.M. Also downtown, along the Petaluma River, is the redeveloped **historic district**—shops, restaurants, yacht harbor, and 65 structures listed on the National Register of Historic Places—described by the good walking-tour brochure available at the visitors center. Free **guided walking tours**—docents dress in Victorian attire—are offered May–Oct., Sat. and Sun. mornings at 10:30 A.M.

Head east via Hwy. 116 to **Petaluma Adobe State Historic Park,** 3325 Adobe Rd., 707/762-4871, open daily (except major holidays) 10 A.M.–5 P.M. The park's centerpiece is Vallejo's Casa Grande, a huge two-story adobe hacienda that was once headquarters for the old Rancho Petaluma. The site, atop a low hill, is almost as stark today as it was in its prime; the landscape was intentionally left barren, the better to spy potential interlopers. Vallejo's "big house" was originally a quadrangle, with a traditional interior courtyard and massive front gates. Only a U-shaped section remains, protected then as now by a wide redwood veranda and overhanging roof.

Practical Petaluma

Get more comprehensive listings of area accommodations and eateries at the visitors bureau. The **Cavanagh Inn,** 10 Keller St., 707/765-4657 or toll-free 888/765-4658, www.cavanaghinn.com, offers a total of seven bed-and-breakfast rooms in a 1912 Craftsman cottage and a 1902 Georgian Revival mansion; two rooms share a bath, one has a whirlpool tub. Amenities include a VCR and assorted movies,

as well as a full breakfast. Moderate-Premium.

A great choice downtown is **Dempsey's Restaurant & Brewery** in the Golden Eagle Center at 50 E. Washington, 707/765-9694. This microbrewery features excellent beer and food; everything is homemade, down to the hand-cut fries and bar snacks like spicy nuts and jerky. Grab a table outside, overlooking the Petaluma River. **Washoe House,** at the corner of Roblar and Stony Point Rd., 707/795-4544, is California's oldest roadhouse, still open for lunch and dinner daily—a good place to pull over for steaks, prime rib, chicken in a basket, even buffalo burgers. A best bet for breakfast—blue corn pancakes and omelettes—is **New Marvins,** 145 Kentucky St., 707/765-2371. For art deco atmosphere and Italian food, try **Fino Cucina Italiana,** 208 Petaluma Blvd. N (at E. Washington), 707/762-5966. Other upscale possibilities include **Buona Sera,** 148 Kentucky St., 707/763-3333, and the **River House,** 222 Weller St., 707/769-0123. A long-running local favorite for country French is bustling **De Schmire,** 304 Bodega Ave., 707/762-1901, serving dinner nightly.

McNear Building, Petaluma

PETALUMA CONVENTION & VISITORS BUREAU

Santa's tour of Petaluma

SCOTT HESS

SANTA ROSA AND VICINITY

A sprawling Bay Area bedroom community and one of the fastest-growing towns in Northern California, Santa Rosa, with its suburban malls and housing developments, is fast spreading into rich Sonoma County farmlands. The most prominent citizen historically was horticulturalist Luther Burbank; California celebrates Arbor Day on his birthday, March 7. But Robert "Believe It or Not!" Ripley was a local boy who also made good, and famed *Peanuts* cartoonist Charles Schulz (who died February 2000), a long-time local whose family owns the ice-skating rink, is still revered by the citizenry.

For current information about Santa Rosa and vicinity, contact: **Santa Rosa Convention & Visitors Bureau,** 9 4th St., Santa Rosa, CA 96401, 707/577-8674, fax 707/571-5949, www.visitsantarosa.com, which publishes its own visitor guide to Santa Rosa and Sonoma County. The **Sonoma County Wineries Association and California Welcome Center,** 707/586-3795 or toll-free 800/939-7666, fax 707/586-1383, http://sonomawine.com, is located south of Santa Rosa at 5000 Roberts Lake Rd. in Rohnert Park (take the Country Club Dr. exit from Hwy. 101).

Seeing and Doing Santa Rosa
Santa Rosa looks so thoroughly modern—i.e., ordinary—to the casual observer that it's tempt-

ing to assume there's nothing much worth seeing. Not so. Though Santa Rosa lost most of its would-have-been historic heart to the 1906 San Francisco earthquake, head downtown to experience Santa Rosa's true character—much disguised but definitely *there,* at least where the renovation wrecking balls were held back.

Railroad Square, west of Hwy. 101 along 3rd, 4th, and 5th Sts. downtown, is now part of a restored 1920s-style shopping district with gift and antique shops, cafés, restaurants, and concentrated nightlife. The depot here, built of locally quarried stone, was among the few local buildings still standing in 1906 when aftershocks from the big quake subsided. (Alfred Hitchcock fans will recognize it as the train station in *Shadow of a Doubt.*) Other nearby quake survivors are **Hotel La Rose;** the **Western Hotel** (Santa Rosa's first luxury hotel), and the **Railroad Express** building. Also here is the little oasis of **Railroad Park,** where the trees were planted by Luther Burbank.

The building housing the **Sonoma County Museum,** 425 7th St., 707/579-1500, was once Santa Rosa's post office. This 1,700-ton Renaissance revival building was moved to its present site, from deeper downtown, in 1979 (a slow trip, just 25 feet per day on railroad ties and rollers). The museum features changing exhibits on local history, culture, and the arts. Open limited hours, small fee. The **Jesse Peter Memorial Museum** at Santa Rosa Junior College, 1501 Mendocino Ave., 707/527-4479, features rotating exhibits of local interest, particularly Native American art and artifacts. Visit the **Luther Burbank Home and Memorial Gardens** on Santa Rosa Ave. at Sonoma Ave., 707/524-5445, where the gardens (free) are open year-round, daily 8 A.M.–7 P.M. Also take a trip through the Burbank Home adjacent, now a free museum with original furnishings and memorabilia, open Tues.–Sun. 10 A.M.–4 P.M. from Apr. through early October. In Burbank's dining room, the 1946 edition of the Webster's dictionary is opened to the word burbank, a verb meaning: "to modify and improve plant life." Outside is Luther Burbank's greenhouse—his beloved tools still inside—where he burbanked his way to fame if not fortune. The "plant wizard" is buried just a few steps away beneath a large cedar of Lebanon. Guided tours include the house, carriage house, gardens, and greenhouse. Originally built in downtown Santa Rosa and now at home in **Julliard Park,** 492 Sonoma Ave.

ANNADEL STATE PARK

A good cure for the Santa Rosa shopping mall syndrome is a day hike through Annadel State Park, 5,000 acres of steep canyons, rolling foothills, woodlands, grassland meadows, and marshland (also poison oak) on the city's eastern edge. No camping, but good hiking. Most of the trail ascents here—except **Steve's S Trail**—are gradual. To beat the heat, come in spring or fall. Small **Lake Ilsanjo,** less than a half mile from the parking lot, is popular with fisherpeople (black bass, bluegill). More than 130 bird species have been spotted, primarily near **Ledson Marsh** along Bennet Ridge. In spring, appreciate the wildflowers: wild iris, lupine, shooting stars, poppies, buttercups, goldfields. *Don't* pick the delicate white fritillaria—it's endangered.

Annadel State Park is open daily from an hour before sunrise to an hour after sunset. To get to Annadel from Santa Rosa or from the Sonoma Valley area, head south on Los Alamos Rd., turn right on Melita Rd., then take a quick left onto Montgomery Dr. and left again on Channel Dr., which leads to the park office and the parking lot beyond. From Spring Lake, take Montgomery Dr. east. For more information, call 707/539-3911 or 707/938-1519. Trail map available.

(across from the Burbank Gardens), is the Church of One Tree, an unusual Gothic church—70-foot spire and all—built entirely from 78,000 board feet of lumber contributed by a single coast redwood felled near Guerneville in 1875. Robert L. Ripley made the onetime First Baptist Church famous in his syndicated *Believe It or Not!* cartoon strip. Julliard Park also makes a nice place for a picnic.

Also worth some time in Santa Rosa, especially for fans of historic flight, is the **Pacific Coast Air Museum,** 2330 Airport Blvd., 707/575-7900, fax 707/545-2813, pacificcoastairmuseum.org. This nonprofit group acquires, restores, operates, and displays some classics. The museum is open Tues. and Thurs. 10 A.M.–2 P.M. and on Sat. and Sun. 10 A.M.–4 P.M., but also sponsors a wide variety of special events and activities.

Staying in Santa Rosa

Motels are abundant in Santa Rosa. Look for relatively inexpensive choices downtown along Santa Rosa Ave. or north along Mendocino Ave., actually an extension of Santa Rosa Ave., north of Sonoma Avenue. Always a best bet, with lower winter rates, is the **Best Western Garden Inn,** 1500 Santa Rosa Ave., 707/546-4031 or toll-free 800/929-2771, www.hotelswest.com. Moderate-Expensive. The **Vintners Inn,** 4350 Barnes Rd., 707/575-7350 or toll-free 800/421-2584, fax 707/575-1426, www.vintnersinn.com, is an upscale place with plush amenities set amid a 45-acre vineyard. All 44 rooms are furnished in a country-French style, and most have fireplaces. Amenities include a spa, gorgeous grounds, continental breakfast, and concierge service. Next door is **John Ash & Co.** restaurant, one of the county's finest. Premium-Luxury.

Santa Rosa even has a genuine old-time but updated hotel, this one listed on the National Register of Historic Places. Quite classy is the 1907 cobblestone **Hotel La Rose** and associated carriage house, 308 Wilson St. (on Railroad Square), 707/579-3200 or toll-free 800/527-6738, fax 707/579-3247, www.hotellarose.com, with English country-house atmosphere and all the modern comforts. The staircase here came from San Francisco's Cable Car Barn. Decent restaurant, too. Premium-Luxury, with lower rates in the off-season.

LUTHER BURBANK

An astoundingly successful, self-taught horticulturist, Luther Burbank (1849–1926) was also quite pragmatic. His primary aim in 50 years of work here was producing improved varieties of cultivated plants. Joaquin Miller wrote that Burbank was "the man who helped God make the earth more beautiful." And he did, with the help of Santa Rosa Valley's rich soils and mild climate. More modest, Burbank himself said: "I firmly believe, from what I have seen, that this is the chosen place of the earth, as far as nature is concerned."

Have you ever admired a showy bank of Shasta daisies or giant calla lilies? Ever bitten into a Santa Rosa plum, tried plumcots, or been grateful for stoneless prunes? These are just a few of the 800 or so "new creations" spawned at the Burbank Experimental Gardens here and in Sebastopol, whose alumni also include the Burbank cherry, gold plums, Burbank potatoes, asparagus, edible and thornless cacti, paradox walnuts, and countless other fruits, nuts, vegetables, trees, flowers, and grasses.

A calm and colorful but controversial figure and a student of Charles Darwin, Burbank openly advocated eugenics and outraged the general population with his heterodox religious views. Luther Burbank's long work days were often interrupted by visitors: his good friend Jack London, William Jennings Bryan, Thomas Edison, Henry Ford, Helen Keller, John Muir, and King Albert and Queen Elizabeth of Belgium. Others (via some 10,000 personal visits per year plus 2,000 letters each week) sought his advice on everything from marigolds and mulch to mysticism.

Eating in Santa Rosa

A real treat for beer lovers is downtown's **Third Street Ale Works**, 610 3rd St., 707/523-3060, an extremely well-designed brewpub that produces a fine repertoire of ales—from light wheat to oatmeal stout and even a barleywine (try the sampler)—and offers a full menu of classy pub fare as well. The bright interior is enlivened by good blues pouring out of the sound system. Or sit outside on the courtyard patio and people-watch. Open Sun.–Thurs. 11:30 A.M.–midnight, Fri.–Sat. 11:30 A.M.–1 A.M.

Fourth Street is Santa Rosa's hip-restaurant hotspot. New haute spots come and go here at near the speed of light—walk the neighborhood to see what's new—though some manage to stay awhile. The **Moonlight Restaurant and Bar,** 515 4th St., 707/526-2662, serves pizza and drinks Mon.–Sat. noon–2 A.M., Sun. 3 P.M.–2 A.M. Across the way, **The Cantina,** 500 4th St., 707/523-3663, serves California-style Mexican food and is a definite see-and-be-seen scene. The **Sonoma Coffee Company,** 521 4th St., 707/573-8022, offers good coffee and coffeehouse atmosphere.

Casual **Mixx,** 135 4th St., 707/573-1344, serves an inventive, constantly changing menu that mixes it all up—Mediterranean standards with Indian, Southwestern, and other influences. Good sandwiches, fresh seafood, pastas, and house-made desserts round out the menu. Reservations advisable. Open for lunch Mon.–Fri. only, for dinner daily.

Surprisingly reasonable **Mistral** at Parkpoint, 1229 N. Dutton, 707/578-4511, is brought to you by the same folks behind Santa Rosa's beloved but departed Matisse. Located in an office complex, Mistral offers Mediterranean fare with French and Italian flair—such things as duck breast with blueberries, pasta al greco with artichoke hearts, and an exceptional Caesar salad. Very good wine list, emphasizing local fruit of the vine. Open for lunch Mon.–Fri. and for dinner nightly. Reservations advised.

Also hiding out in a mall-like setting is excellent **Lisa Hemenway's,** at its new location, 1612 Terrace Way, 707/526-5111, where an expansive East-West menu includes everything from vegetable tamales to chutney burgers. Takeout counter, too, for the perfect picnic. Open for lunch Mon.–Sat., brunch on Sun., dinner nightly. Reservations a must.

Wonderful on the way to Guerneville is the very reasonable, roadhouse-style **Willowside Café**, 3535 Guerneville Rd. (at Willowside), 707/523-4814, where fresh flowers on the tables and an amazing wine list welcome you once inside. The country French menu changes weekly. Don't miss dessert. Open Wed.–Sun. for dinner.

The acclaimed **John Ash & Company** sits amid the vineyards near the Vintners Inn, 4330 Barnes Rd., 707/527-7687. The romantic setting seems to stimulate the appetite, while the

KIM WEIR

*vineyards in the
Alexander Valley
north of Santa Rosa*

menu features local California cuisine with Asian overtones (seafood cake with sole, shrimp, and crab, or Sonoma chicken breasts with corn and chives), served with imaginative French flair. Reservations required. **La Gare,** in Railroad Square, 208 Wilson St., 707/528-4355, is a legend in Santa Rosa (and beyond), known for its French-Swiss cuisine, decadent desserts, and elegant white-linen atmosphere.

Sebastopol

Due west from Santa Rosa, perched on Sonoma County's "Gold Ridge" and famous for its early-ripening, reddish-yellow Gravensteins, Sebastopol was once part of the original Analy Township. An early Irish settler, inspired by the British and French siege of the Russian seaport of Sebastopol, named the California town when one of two feuding local residents barricaded himself inside a store. Stop off at **Ives Memorial Park** next to the Veterans' Memorial Building on High St., the center of Sebastopol's April **Apple Blossom Festival.** Or head west to

Ragle Ranch Park, where the Sonoma County Farm Trails' **Gravenstein Apple Fair** is held every August at the beginning of harvest season. Gravensteins, the best all-purpose apples anywhere, don't keep, which explains all the apple-processing plants in the area. (In the United States, you can't get these red or green beauties beyond the Bay Area.) For a complete listing and map of the area's fruit, nut, and vegetable (even fresh goat cheese) vendors, pick up the current *Sonoma County Farm Trails* brochure at the chamber office. If the sight of all those apples starts making you think of Mom and apple pie, stop in at **Mom's Apple Pie,** 4550 Gravenstein Hwy. N (toward Forestville), 707/823-8330. Mom bakes apple and other assorted pies fresh daily.

For current information about the area, contact the **Sebastopol Chamber of Commerce,** 265 S. Main, P.O. Box 178, Sebastopol, CA 95473, 707/823-3032 or toll-free 877/828-4748, www.sebastopol.org. The office is open weekdays during business hours, and also on Sat. in summer.

ALONG THE RUSSIAN RIVER

Most people think of the Russian River as the cluster of rustic redwood-cloistered resort villages stretching from Guerneville west along Hwy. 116 to Jenner-by-the-Sea, about an hour-and-a-half drive north from San Francisco. It's a mistake, though, to view the Russian River as strictly a Guerneville-to-Jenner phenomenon. The river's headwaters are far to the north, just southeast of Willits, though it's not much of a river until it reaches Cloverdale. The Russian uncoils slowly through Sonoma County's northern wine country, and multiple small wineries cluster like grapes along most of its length. To find them—representing the Alexander Valley, Chalk Hill, Dry Creek Valley, Green Valley, and Russian River Valley appellations—pick up a free map and brochure at area chamber of commerce offices. Or contact **Russian River Wine Road**, P.O. Box 46, Healdsburg, CA 95448, 707/433-4374 or toll-free 800/723-6336, www.wineroad.com. Come on the first weekend in March for the annual **Russian River Wine Road Barrel Tasting,** the big annual event at all member wineries.

RUSSIAN RIVER RESORT AREA

Once arrived in **Guerneville,** *don't* say "Gurneyville." The name's GURNville—and any other pronunciation pegs people straight away as tourists. On the eastern outskirts of town is **Armstrong Redwoods,** a 750-acre redwood reserve with first- and second-growth *Sequoia sempervirens* and a study of nature's moods in various shades of green. Beyond Armstrong to the north, reaching up into the surrounding coastal mountains, is 4,200-acre **Austin Creek State Recreation Area,** home of some huge madrones and the primitive, sky-high **Redwood Lake Campground.** For information about both parks, contact: Armstrong Redwoods State Reserve, 17000 Armstrong Woods Rd., Guerneville, CA 95446, 707/869-2015, 707/869-2958, or 707/865-2391 (district office). Small day-use fee. Dominating the big vineyard-hugging curve on River Rd. a few miles east of Rio Nido near Guerneville is the vine-covered red brick 1886 **Korbel Champagne Cellars,** well worth a stop for tastes of Korbel

champagne and wines, a snifter of brandy, or even a glass of beer—microbrewed here by the **Russian River Brewing Company.** Open May–Sept., daily 10 A.M.–5 P.M. (shorter hours in the off-season); tours (of the winery and brewery) and tastings are offered hourly. For more information, contact: Korbel Champagne Cellars, 13250 River Rd., Guerneville, CA 95446, 707/824-7000, www.korbel.com.

Monte Rio west of Guerneville is a gracefully sagging old resort town, with a big faded Vacation Wonderland sign stretching across the highway. Most of the redwood used to build San Francisco was shipped south from **Duncans Mills,** next west, and Duncan Landing. A lumber-loading depot during the region's redwood-harvesting heyday—the original mills were constructed in 1860—Duncans Mills is now a newly built old-looking collection of buildings and businesses: crafts and gift shops, galleries, two very good restaurants (Blue Heron and Cape Fear), a coffee house-cum-kayak-rental shop, candy store, barber shop, and Wine & Cheese Tasting of Sonoma County (just what it sounds like).

The **Russian River Rodeo** is held here in June, as is the big **Russian River Blues Festival** at Johnson's Beach. The biggest deal of all, though, is the **Russian River Jazz Festival** in September—quite the event, featuring big-name talent from everywhere. In addition to its popular rustic resorts and gay-friendly resorts, the lower Russian River also boasts a number of nice bed-and-breakfasts—including the elegant Mission revival-style **Applewood Inn** in Guerneville, 707/869-9093, www.applewoodinn.com. For current events, accommodations, restaurant, and other information, contact: **Russian River Chamber of Commerce,** 16209 1st St., P.O. Box 331, Guerneville, CA 95446, 707/869-9000, www.russianriver.com. The chamber has a complete business directory of gay-oriented establishments, available for reference.

HEALDSBURG AND VICINITY

Though most people head to Napa or Sonoma for wine-country tastings and tours, an increasingly

THE BOHEMIAN GROVE

Monte Rio's real claim to fame is the infamous Bohemian Grove on the south side of the river, the all-male elite enclave where the rich and powerful come to play. These 2,700 acres of virgin redwoods—the largest remaining stand in the Russian River region—are enjoyed exclusively by members and guests of San Francisco's Bohemian Club, founded (an irony only in retrospect) by anarchist-socialist journalist types like Ambrose Bierce and Jack London.

Once each year, during their two-week Annual Summer Encampment, 1,500 or so Bohemians and guests get together in this luxurious grown-up summer camp "to celebrate the spirit of Bohemia." According to local lore, what that amounts to is getting drunk, urinating on trees, and staging silly skits and plays. The traditional summer encampment—which President Herbert Hoover once called "the greatest men's party on earth"—was held for the first time in 1869. Bohemian Grove guests include U.S. presidents and cabinet members, members of Congress, captains of industry and finance, plus diplomats and foreign dignitaries. In 1999, reported encampment guests included former President George Bush, President-elect George W. Bush, former House Speaker Newt Gingrich, General Colin Powell, and Dow Chemical Chairman Frank Popoff.

According to encampment rules, Bohemian Club members and guests *never* discuss business or politics, and *never* make deals. (Each summer's Lakeside Talks, however, sometimes come awfully close to being "private" public policy talks.) It's difficult to verify these official facts, however. Double chain-link fences, guardposts, and highly sensitive security systems provide ample protection from riffraff. Unless invited, no one—and never a woman—gets inside the compound. But judging from the very visible, very professional imported prostitutes doing a brief, brisk local business during the week, each year at least some from inside manage to "jump the river" and get out.

At the right time in July, during the Bohemian Grove encampment, it's an astoundingly absurd sight: caravans of Rolls-Royces and black stretch limos jockeying for highway position among the ranks of one-eyed VWs and battered Ramblers. Most Bohos (a favorite local epithet) step down from their private Lear jets at the airport in Santa Rosa, then travel to the Grove under the cover of darkness, to avoid unnecessary visibility. The real bigwigs usually arrive by helicopter.

Among Russian River residents, there's at least begrudging acceptance of these ruling-class Bohemians, since locals do work at the Grove as waiters, carpenters, and repairmen. But there is also resentment, if rarely expressed openly. On the Russian River, for example, there are no hospitals or emergency health-care facilities, but the Bohemian Grove has a fully staffed emergency hospital and cardiac care unit—open year-round yet rarely used—completely off-limits to the community. In the event of a heart attack or drowning accident, for residents it's a half-hour ambulance ride to Santa Rosa.

In the recent past, outside-the-gates "people's encampments" like the Bohemian Grove Action Network kept 24-hour vigils when the Bohos came to town, with banners ("See You in Hell!"), placards, and arrests for civil disobedience in protest of the incestuous relationship of business and government. But some years, all's quiet on the Bohemian front. Except for the limos and the highly visible high-priced hookers, it's hard to know when the party's going on.

---

popular destination in Sonoma County is Healdsburg, the urban convergence of three well-known wine regions: the Alexander, Dry Creek, and Russian River Valleys. A onetime trading post founded by Harmon Heald, downtown Healdsburg is built around a sublime Spanish-style plaza.

The **Healdsburg Area Chamber of Commerce,** 217 Healdsburg Ave., Healdsburg, CA 95448, 707/433-6935 or toll-free 800/648-9922 (in California), fax 707/433-7562, www.healdsburg.org, offers free winery and *Farm Trails* pro-

duce maps, plus current information about events, accommodations, and food. For more information about the Windsor area, just south, contact the **Windsor Chamber of Commerce,** 8499 Old Redwood Hwy., Ste. 202., P.O. Box 367, Windsor, CA 95492, 707/838-7285.

Seeing and Doing Healdsburg

Shaded by citrus trees, palms, and redwoods, **Healdsburg Plaza** is "community central"—home to summer concerts and celebrations, pleasant for picnics, and surrounded by shops and shoppers.

Unique in Healdsburg is the **Sonoma County Wine Library** in the Healdsburg Regional Library, 139 Piper St. (at Center), 707/433-3772. This collection of wine and winery information includes the thousand-volume Vintner's Club Library of San Francisco. The exceptional **Healdsburg Museum,** 221 Matheson in the 1910 stone Carnegie Library, 707/431-3325, features north-county history displays. Wine connoisseurs, the **Russian River Wine Company,** 132 Plaza St., 707/433-0490, stocks top vintages from more than 60 small wineries, including hard-to-find labels. In season, stop by **Sonoma Antique Apple Nursery,** 4395 Westside Rd., 707/433-6420, for flavorful apples from yesteryear, even bareroot trees to grow your own. *The* place for a movie, artsy fare as well as new releases, is the **Raven Theater,** 115 North St., 707/433-5448, also a performing arts venue.

Practical Healdsburg

Healdsburg offers some nice motels, but Victorian accommodations are the "inn thing" here. Downtown is the wonderful Victorian **Healdsburg Inn on the Plaza,** 110 Matheson St., 707/433-6991 or toll-free 800/431-8663, www.healdsburginn.com, a bed-and-breakfast with 10 rooms (several with fireplace) furnished in antiques. Full breakfast buffet is served in the rooftop solarium, and champagne brunch is offered on weekends. Luxury. The new Victorian in town, quite exceptional, is **The Honor Mansion,** 14891 Grove St., 707/433-4277 or toll-free 800/554-4667, fax 707/431-7173, www.honormansion.com. This 1883 Italianate Victorian features five rooms in the house (some with fireplaces and decks), two luxury suites, and the Squire's Cottage out back near the koi pond. Luxury.

Refreshingly free of Victoriana are the French country-style cottages at **Belle de Jour Inn,** across from Simi Winery at 16276 Healdsburg Ave., 707/431-9777, fax 707/431-7412, www.belledejourinn.com. All feature either a wood-burning stove or fireplace, refrigerator, and air-conditioning. Great breakfast. Luxury.

For simple bakery specialties and snacks approaching perfection, try the **Downtown Bakery and Creamery,** on the plaza at 308-A Center St., 707/431-2719, an enterprise launched by pastry chef Lindsey Shere of Berkeley's Chez Panisse and her daughters. Nothing fancy, but everything is excellent, from the fresh-baked breads (try the sourdough French and the sourdough wheat-rye), light pastries, and sticky buns to *real* ice cream milkshakes and sundaes. Also a surprise is **Costeaux French Bakery & Café,** 421 Healdsburg Ave., 707/433-1913, where you'll have to buy at least one loaf of the whole-wheat walnut-rosemary bread. There's also an outlet of the **Oakville Grocery** in Healdsburg, in the onetime city hall at 124 Mathesen St., 707/433-3200.

A best bet for American bistro fare is the tiny **Ravenous Café** at the Raven Theater, 117 North St., 707/431-1770, open Wed.–Sun. for lunch and dinner. For Sonoma County–fresh Mediterranean, the place is **Restaurant Charcuterie,** 335 Healdsburg Ave., 707/431-7213, open Mon.–Sat. for lunch and nightly for dinner. Reservations advised.

Trendier restaurants come and go, but **Bistro Ralph,** 109 Plaza St. E, 707/433-1380, is a keeper—one of the best restaurants in Sonoma County. The menu at this all-American bistro changes constantly, ranging from Szechuan pepper calamari and duck breast with baked pears and rosemary potatoes to spring lamb stew. Expect salads and stylish sandwiches at lunch. Beer and wine only. Open for lunch Mon.–Sat., for dinner nightly.

Microbrew aficionados, hunt down the **Bear Republic Brewing Co.,** 345 Healdsburg Ave., 707/433-2337. Bear flag ales include Pale, English ESB, Red Rocket, and Big Bear Dark.

WINERIES NEAR HEALDSBURG

Visiting the 60-plus wineries near Healdsburg is challenge enough for any wine lover. Start in town. **Windsor Vineyards**—which won the California State Fair's coveted Golden Winery Award in 1997—sells its wines directly to consumers only. But the winery offers tastings in Healdsburg, at 308-B Center St., 707/433-2822, www.windsorvineyards.com. Open weekdays 10 A.M.–5 P.M., weekends 10 A.M.–6 P.M. **White Oak Vineyards,** 7505 Hwy. 128, 707/433-8429, is open daily 11 A.M.–5 P.M. Just west of town,

Alderbrook Winery, 2306 Magnolia Dr., 707/433-5987 or toll-free 800/405-5987, www. alderbrook.com, is open daily 10 A.M.–5 P.M. for tasting and sales (tours only by appointment). The remote **Hop Kiln Winery,** 6050 Westside Rd., 707/433-6491, is award-winning and well respected, known for its rustic Old World wines. Hop Kiln's meticulously restored 1905 stone hop-drying "barn" houses the working winery, with wine-tasting (try the zinfandel) in the more typical barn adjacent. Nice views of the vineyards, pond, and picnic area. Small deli, too. Open for tasting and sales 10 A.M.–5 P.M. daily (tours by appointment only). The excellent **Davis Bynum Winery,** 8075 Westside Rd., 707/433-5852, tasting room toll-free 800/826-1073, www.davisbynum.com, produces small quantities of some winning wines, including gewˌrztraminer. Open daily 10 A.M.–5 P.M. Look for private wines by **Gary Farrell,** Davis Bynum's winemaker, at premium wine outlets.

Also in the same general neighborhood and well worth a visit: **Rochioli Vineyards and Winery,** 6192 Westside Rd., 707/433-2305, open daily 10 A.M.–5 P.M. (chardonnay, sauvignon blanc, and pinot noir) and **Hambrecht Vineyards and Wineries,** 4035 Westside Rd., 707/433-8236 (main office) or 707/431-4442 (tasting room, open daily 10 A.M.–4:30 P.M.). Hambrecht also has a tasting room on Healdsburg Plaza, 250 Center St., 707/431-4430.

The 1896 **Foppiano Vineyards** winery, 12707 Old Redwood Hwy., 707/433-7272, www.foppiano.com, is one of California's oldest family-owned wineries, open for tasting and picnicking daily 10 A.M.–4:30 P.M. Just north of town, the 1876 hand-hewn stone and modernized **Simi Winery,** 16275 Healdsburg Ave., 707/433-6981, www.simiwinery.com, once specialized in bulk wines. But now—like most Napa-Sonoma establishments—it produces premium wines, available for sampling in the redwood-and-stone tasting room. Open daily 10 A.M.–4:30 P.M., with half-hour guided tours at 11 A.M., 1 P.M., and 3 P.M. It's a wonderful spot for picnics.

Wineries West of Healdsburg

The ivy-covered stone winery at **Dry Creek Vineyard,** 3770 Lambert Bridge Rd. (four miles north of Healdsburg, just off Dry Creek Rd.), 707/433-1000, www.drycreekvineyard.com, is known for its cabernet sauvignon, sauvignon blanc, fumé blanc, dry chenin blanc, and other fine wines produced in very limited quantities. Pleasant picnic grounds. Open daily 10:30 A.M.–4:30 P.M. for tasting and tours. Wine critics also can't stop raving about **Quivira Vineyards,** 4900 W. Dry Creek Rd., 707/431-8333 or toll-free 800/292-8339, noted in particular for its cabernet sauvignon, sauvignon blanc, and zinfandel. Open daily 11 A.M.–5 P.M. for tasting (tours only by appointment). The **Lambert Bridge Winery,** 4085 W. Dry Creek Rd., 707/431-9600, www.lambertbridge.com, resembles an old barn but is actually contemporary in all respects, including the view of the winemaking process from the tasting room. Open for tasting (chardonnay, merlot, cabernet sauvignon) daily 10 A.M.–4:30 P.M. The **Lytton Springs Winery,** 650 Lytton Springs Rd. (three miles north of Healdsburg off Hwy. 101), 707/433-7721, produces a traditional fruity zinfandel from the well-seasoned vines of the old Valley Vista Vineyards. Open 10 A.M.–4 P.M. daily.

Wineries Northeast of Healdsburg

Johnson's Alexander Valley Wines, a small premium winery at 8333 Hwy. 128 (seven miles southeast of Geyserville), 707/433-2319, is open daily 10 A.M.–5 P.M. for tasting. (Write to receive the winery's regular newsletter.) The small but impressive **Alexander Valley Vineyards,** 8644 Hwy. 128, 707/433-7209 or toll-free 800/888-7209, on the old Cyrus Alexander homestead, is known for its estate-bottled varietal wines—including a very good chardonnay, though "Sin Zin" is a popular choice. Picnic facilities available. Open daily 10 A.M.–5 P.M. (very complete guided tours offered by appointment).

Sausal Winery, 7370 Hwy. 128, east of Healdsburg, 707/433-2285, www.sausalwinery.com, produces three different zins, as well as cabernet sauvignon, sangiovese, and a house white. The small family winery has been making wine here for three generations. Open for tasting and picnicking daily 10 A.M.–4 P.M. (tours by appointment only).

The earthy simplicity of the aptly named **Field Stone Winery,** 10075 Hwy. 128 (near the Chalk Hill Rd. intersection), 707/433-7266, is striking yet deceptive. Literally a back-to-the-land bunker of concrete faced with fieldstone and sliced into this hillside, Field Stone as a winery is actually contemporary. Noted for its spring cabernet, petite sirah, rosé of petite sirah, and other fine wines, Field Stone Winery also sponsors special events in summer—everything from concerts to Shakespeare. Wine-tasting daily 10 A.M.–4:30 P.M. (tours by appointment only). The **Chalk Hill Estate**, 10300 Chalk Hill Rd., 707/838-4306, is noted for its chardonnay. Open by appointment only. Also highly regarded, **Melim Vineyards**, 15001 Chalk Hill Rd., 707/433-4774, is open only by appointment.

Wineries South of Healdsburg

Two miles south of Healdsburg just off Old Redwood Hwy., the small **Christopher Creek Winery**, 641 Limerick Ln., 707/433-2001, www.christophercreek.com, occupies part of the original Rancho Sotoyome and produces chardonnay and petite sirah. Open Fri.–Mon. 11 A.M.–5 P.M. (or by appointment) for tasting and tours. Near Windsor is **J Wine Company**, 11447 Old Redwood Hwy., Healdsburg, toll-free 888/594-6326 (call for tasting-room hours), www.jwine.com. Nearby is **Sonoma-Cutrer Vineyards**, toward Santa Rosa at 4401 Slusser Rd., 707/528-1181, which produces premium chardonnay. Open for tasting and tours Mon.–Sat. by advance appointment only.

Founder Rodney Strong of **Rodney Strong Vineyards**, 11455 Old Redwood Hwy., 707/431-1533 or toll-free 800/678-4763, www.rodneystrong.com, was recognized by the *Los Angeles Times* as Winemaker of the Year way back in 1983. Today the company produces a full complement of fine wines, including cabernet sauvignon, pinot noir, zinfandel, merlot, chardonnay, and sauvignon blanc. Open for free tasting, tours, and picnicking 10 A.M.–5 P.M. daily.

GEYSERVILLE AND VICINITY

The tiny town of Geyserville lies at the heart of the Alexander Valley at the foot of Geyser Peak. Geyserville hosts a **Fall Color Tour** on the last Sunday in October—a good time to enjoy the autumn blaze of red, gold, and russet grape leaves.

For more information about Geyserville and vicinity, contact the **Geyserville Chamber of Commerce**, P.O. Box 276, Geyserville, CA 95441, 707/857-3745, www.geyserville.com.
Geyserville Area Wineries

Clos du Bois, 19410 Geyserville Ave., 707/857-3100 or toll-free 800/222-3189, www.closdubois.com, has won so many awards since its inception in 1974 for its various fine varietal and vineyard-designated wines that even most of the winery's fans have stopped counting. Open daily 10 A.M.–4:30 P.M. for tasting (no tours).

Also among the best wineries in the area is **Chateau Souverain**, with its kiln-like modern architecture, 400 Souverain Rd. (Hwy. 101 at Independence Ln.), 707/433-3141, 707/433-8281 or toll-free 888/809-4637, www.chateausouverain.com. In addition to its fine wines—chardonnay, cabernet sauvignon, sauvignon blanc, merlot—Souverain offers chamber music and jazz concerts during the summer months, other special events, and a nice little café. Open for tasting and sales daily 10 A.M.–5 P.M.

A mile north of town, the family-owned **J. Pedroncelli Winery & Vineyards**, 1220 Canyon Rd., 707/857-3531 or toll-free 800/836-3894, sold grapes to home winemakers during Prohibition, then specialized in producing bulk wines. The winery now offers award-winning Alexander Valley and Dry Creek Valley premium varietal wines (tasting and sales daily 10 A.M.–5 P.M.). A onetime bulk winery, the 1888-vintage **Canyon Road Winery**, 19550 Geyserville Ave., 707/857-3417, www.canyonroadwinery.com, now sells young age-them-yourself wines directly to consumers. Open for tasting and sales only, 10 A.M.–5 P.M. daily.

The **Ferrari-Carano Vineyards and Winery,** 8761 Dry Creek Rd., 707/433-6700, www.ferrari-carano.com, open daily 10 A.M.–5 P.M., is brought to you by the same folks behind the landmark El Dorado Hotel-Casino in Reno, the Don Carano family. At the center of this stunning and serene place is the overwhelming Villa Fiore, the tasting center, a virtual Florentine estate surrounded by five acres of gardens, streams, waterfalls, and ponds. Open 10 A.M.–5 P.M. daily for tasting and sales (tours by appointment).

Other worthwhile Geyserville-area stops include **Geyser Peak Winery**, 22281 Chianti Rd. (Canyon Rd. exit from Hwy. 101), 707/857-9463 or toll-free 800/255-9463, www.geyserpeakwinery.com, open for tasting daily 10 A.M.–5 P.M.; **Trentadue Winery**, 19170 Old Redwood Hwy., 707/433-3104, www.trentadue.com, also featuring a gourmet food and gift shop, open daily

LAKE SONOMA

A mammoth recreation area created by the U.S. Army Corps of Engineers, Lake Sonoma offers swimming, fishing, boating, camping, and 40 miles of hiking and horseback trails over the tinder-dry wooded grasslands. Lake Sonoma's construction was controversial; the flooding of popular hot springs, sacred Native American sites, and rugged scenic valleys led to court battles and public protests in the 1970s. But Sonoma County voters really wanted a lake, and approved the construction of Warm Springs Dam in two separate elections. Near the dam are a fish hatchery and a visitor center/museum emphasizing Native American culture, the area's early history, and natural history.

For secluded camping, hike, ride, or boat in to primitive lakeside campgrounds equipped with tables and portable restrooms. Various other "primitive" campgrounds are near the lake. Or car camp at first-come, first-camped **Liberty Glen** developed campsites (both individual and group), which offer flush toilets and hot showers. All campsites are available only by reservation. Reserve five days or more in advance by calling the National Recreation Reservation Service at toll-free 877/444-6777. For more information, contact: **Lake Sonoma Recreation Area,** 3333 Skaggs Springs Rd., Geyserville, CA 95441, 707/433-9483.

10 A.M.–5 P.M.; and **De Lorimier Vineyards and Winery,** 2001 Hwy. 128, 707/857-2000 or toll-free 800/546-7718, open daily 10 A.M.–4:30 P.M.

CLOVERDALE AND HOPLAND

Surrounded by oak-dotted foothills and usually free of summer's chilly coastal fog, Cloverdale was once an infamous traffic bottleneck on Hwy. 101, where local police made a killing on speeders trying to quickly slip through town. But now the freeway has been rerouted to the east, and travelers on 101 can bypass Cloverdale altogether. Tourist revenues may be down as a result, but the townfolk can once again hear birds singing in the trees. And Cloverdale is sprucing up its downtown, which is much more pleasant without all the big-rig traffic. The **Cloverdale Historical**

Museum, 215 N. Cloverdale Blvd., 707/894-2067, is a worthwhile stop. Also check out the new (since May 2000) **Cloverdale Wine and Visitor Center,** 105 N. Cloverdale Blvd., 707/894-4470, www.cloverdale.net, open daily—the place to stop for general area information. On the north side of town begins back-roads Hwy. 128, a winding route that wends through the **Anderson Valley** on the way to the Mendocino coast.

If you're looking for a burger-and-fries fix, everyone loves the **World Famous Hamburger Ranch and Pasta Farm,** up on the hill north of downtown at 31195 Redwood Hwy., 707/894-5616, just about the best in Sonoma County for all-American burgers and fries for more than half a century. Fresh pastas and blues, too, not to mention brews from the Anderson Valley Brewing Company. Open daily for breakfast, lunch, and dinner.

Cloverdale Wineries

The vineyards and wineries thin out considerably near Cloverdale, though several local wineries have tasting rooms here. Check at Cloverdale wine sellers for the tulip-labeled bottles of local **Bandiera Winery,** 707/894-4295 (no tasting room). The **Fritz Winery,** 24691 Dutcher Creek Rd., 707/894-3389, www.fritzwinery.com, features a picnic area and patio with vineyard views (wine-tasting daily 10:30 A.M.–4:30 P.M., tours by appointment only).

Hopland and Vicinity

If you continue north on Hwy. 101 instead of heading out to the coast, you'll soon come to tiny Hopland. Named for the brewery hops once raised throughout the area, Hopland returned to tradition—at least in a small way—with the 1980s opening of the first brewpub in California since Prohibition. The **Hopland Brewery Pub & Restaurant,** 13351 Hwy. 101 S, 707/744-1015, www.mendobrew.com, is owned and operated by the Mendocino Brewing Company, maker of (among others) Red Tail Ale—one of the state's original microbrews and still among the best. Though the main brewery facility is now in Ukiah, the brewpub here features a Beer Garden out back, a big patio draped with trellised hops and furnished with long tables—a super place to spend some time in the sun, enjoying good brew. Good food, too, from burgers to that famous

Red Tail Chili. Open for lunch and dinner daily (the restaurant's usually open until 9 P.M.), and frequent live entertainment.

For the most part, hop fields have been replaced with vineyards. The **Fetzer Vineyards** tasting room and visitor center at Valley Oaks, 13601 Eastside Rd. (three-quarters of a mile east of Hopland off Hwy. 175), 707/744-1250 or toll-free 800/846-8637, www.fetzer.com, is open daily 9 A.M.–5 P.M. The complex offers wine-tastings, vineyard tours, a "wine library" offering select tastings and sales of wines available nowhere else, a deli, picnic grounds by the lake, a five-acre organic garden, and a very nice 12-room B&B (Premium-Luxury). Fetzer, official winemaker for the 1996 Summer Olympics, also produces a Bonterra line of organic wines—try the North Coast Cabernet Sauvignon—as well as the Bel Arbors label, which boasts an excellent modestly priced chardonnay.

Other wineries near Hopland include **McDowell Valley Vineyards,** 3811 Hwy. 175 (between Old Toll and Ukiah Boonville Rds.), 707/744-1053, fax 707/744-1826, www.mcdowellsyrah.com, the nation's first (and probably only) solar-integrated winery. The specialties here are California-grown Rhône varietals, including syrah, grenache, viognier, marsanne, and roussanne. McDowell Valley's syrahs are consistently rated "best buys" by *Wine Spectator* magazine. The **Milano Winery,** where the tasting room is at home in an old hop kiln at 14594 Hwy.

REAL GOODS

Attractions beyond Hopland's surrounding vineyards, pastures, and rolling hills include the **Real Goods Solar Living Center,** 13771 Hwy. 101 S, 707/744-2100, www.realgoods.com, the 12-acre outgrowth from a previous smaller operation in Willits. Started as a service primarily for off-the-gridders, Real Goods has grown exponentially. At this big new center, see the latest in solar-, wind-, and water-powered generators; study an impressive array of environmentally friendly and "sustainability" products; wander the grounds, past the ponds and through the botanical garden; or just hang out and picnic. Real Goods is a classroom as much as an outlet. Open daily. Free tours.

---

101 (near Mountain House Rd.), 707/744-1396, specializes in chardonnay, cabernet sauvignon, and dessert wines. Open daily for tasting; tours only by appointment. **Duncan Peak Vineyards,** 14500 Mountain House Rd., 707/744-1129, makes only one wine—a cabernet sauvignon, of which only 500 cases are produced each year. Tasting and tours only by appointment.

For more information on regional wineries and a virtual winery map, contact: **Mendocino Wineries Alliance,** P.O. Box 1409, Ukiah, CA 95482, 707/468-9886, fax 707/468-9987, www.mendowine.com.

ANDERSON VALLEY, UKIAH, AND BEYOND

Anderson Valley

Traveling northwestward into the Anderson Valley via Hwy. 128—people make the trip more quickly from Ukiah—is an enjoyable if slow and snaking road trip. In addition to several appealing parks, the Anderson Valley boasts some excellent wineries—**Greenwood Ridge** (home to the annual California Wine Tasting Championships), **Navarro, Husch, Roederer, Scharffenberger,** and **Handley Cellars** among them, outposts of the new north coast economy. The valley also boasts seasonal roadside produce stands and the intriguing small town of **Boonville,** home to the exceptional **Boonville Hotel,** 707/895-2210, www.boonvillehotel.com; the rabble-rousing *Anderson Valley Advertiser,* one of the state's most intriguing newspapers; and the refreshingly noncommercial **Mendocino County Fair and Apple Show,** held in mid-September.

For more information on the Anderson Valley area, contact the **Anderson Valley Chamber of Commerce,** P.O. Box 275, Boonville, CA 95414, 707/895-2379, or the **Greater Ukiah Chamber of Commerce,** 200 S. School St., Ukiah, CA 95482, 707/462-4705, www.ukiahchamber.com.

Ukiah

Back on Hwy. 101, Ukiah is a sprawling old lumber town in the center of the inland Yokayo Valley. This rowdy and rough-edged place is populated by just plain folks: rednecks, redwood loggers, even redwood-loving tree huggers. The most interesting thing about Ukiah is its name:

"haiku" spelled backward, but derived from the Pomo word Yu Haia, meaning either "south" or "deep." The town itself isn't necessarily backward. Most astonishing in Ukiah is the **Grace Hudson Museum** on Main (see the special topic in this chapter), but there are other attractions. Now a state historical landmark, once host to literary lions and U.S. presidents, the restored **Vichy Hot Springs Resort & Inn** mineral baths are at 2605 Vichy Springs Rd., 707/462-9515, fax 707/462-9516, www.vichysprings.com. The day-use fee ($35 per person) covers all-day use of the mineral baths, Olympic-size swimming pool (summer only), hot pool, and hiking trails on the 700-acre property. But all that and full breakfast comes with an overnight stay here, in either motel-style rooms or private cabins (Premium-Luxury). Massage and facials are also available. Secluded, clothing-optional **Orr Hot Springs Resort,** 13201 Orr Springs Rd., 707/462-6277, historically accessible only by stagecoach, is still remote. Facilities include a large redwood hot tub, four private hot tubs (Victorian porcelain), plus a tile-inlaid natural rock mineral pool (cool), steam room, dry sauna, large mineral water swimming pool, and massage room. Overnight accommodations are available in private rooms or cottages, a communal sleeping loft, and campsites.

Ukiah also has some intriguing restaurants, including **Ellie's Mut Hut & Vegetarian Café,** 732 S. State St., 707/468-5376, where you can get hot dogs as well as omelettes, tofu dinners, and fruit smoothies.

For more information about the area, contact: **Greater Ukiah Chamber of Commerce,** 200 S. School St., Ukiah, CA 95482, 707/462-4705, www.ukiahchamber.com.

Ukiah Area Wineries

Near Ukiah are some fairly well known Mendocino County wineries and some up-and-comers. **Parducci Wine Cellars,** 501 Parducci Rd. (a few miles north of town), 707/463-5357 or toll-free 888/362-9463, www.parducci.com, has been in business since 1931. Its modern-day emphasis is on producing premium varietals from Mendocino County grapes. Open for tasting and picnicking daily 10 A.M.–5 P.M. (Sun. until 4 P.M.). Family-run **Jepson Vineyards,** 10400 S. Hwy. 101, 707/468-8936, offers tasting daily 10 A.M.–5 P.M.

Some say the handmade brandy produced by the Franco-American partnership of Ansley Coale and Hubert **Germain-Robin** is the country's best, and a challenge to the finest French cognacs. For a taste, stop by at 3001 S. State St. #35, 707/462-0314. Open Mon.–Fri. 9 A.M.–3 P.M. To get more information, write: **Alambic Inc.,** P.O. Box 1059, Ukiah, CA 95482.

For more information about these and other area wineries, contact the **Mendocino Winegrowers Alliance,** P.O. Box 1409, Ukiah, CA 95482, 707/468-1343.

Willits

Continuing north from Ukiah on Hwy. 101, you'll cross Ridgewood Summit, the divide that effec-

Hendy Woods State Park

BOONTLING: A SLIB OF LOREY

Until recently, the friendly people here in Boonville regularly spoke Boontling, a creative local dialect combining English, Scottish-Irish, Spanish, French, Pomo, and spontaneous, often hilarious words with strictly local significance. This private community language, locals say, was originally created by people now in their "codgiehood" (old-timers) to "shark the bright lighters" (confuse outsiders) and befuddle children—a word game started by men toiling for endless hours in the hop fields. Outsiders still get confused. Local kids learn some of the lingo in school, but at last report, the number of locals fluent in Boontling—all well into their codgiehood—was down to three.

Bright lighters, by the way, are people from the city. A *walter levy* is a telephone, because Walter was the first person in town to have one. A more modern variation, *buckey walter* (pay phone), refers to the old-time nickel phone call and the Indian head, or "buck," on the nickel's face. There's a buckey walter, so labeled, right outside the Horn of Zeese (coffee) café in town. Another sign in downtown Boonville—and a sign of the times, over a realtor's office—is a facsimile of a clock with the phrase *A teem ta hig, a teem ta shay,* meaning: "A time to buy, a time to sell."

A *featherleg,* in Boontling, is a cocky, arrogant person (because everyone knows banty roosters have feathers down their legs). *Shovel tooth* means "doctor," because the valley's physician had buck teeth. A *jeffer* is a big fire, since old Jeff built a huge fireplace into his house. A *madge* is a house of ill repute (in honor of Madge, who ran one of the best in Ukiah).

Burlappin' is a very active sexual verb (there are others in Boontling) referring to the time a shop clerk was caught in the act atop a pile of burlap sacks in

the storeroom. *Skrage* means "to make love." *Charlie-ball* is a verb meaning "to embarrass," a direct reference to a local Pomo who was easily embarrassed.

But the ongoing creativity behind Boontling's evolution (and the community's insularity) started to get confused after World War I, with the coming of roads, telephones, and other inroads of civilization. To pick up whatever is left of the language, tutor yourself with the animated, sometimes outrageous, and impeccably written *Anderson Valley Advertiser* or the local language dictionary, *A Slib of Lorey.*

KIM WEIR

---

tively separates red wine from redwood. With the last of the vineyards behind you, you're on the road to the land of *Sequoia sempervirens,* or coast redwoods, tallest trees in the world. At Leggett, coastal Hwy. 1 reaches its end at a T junction with Hwy. 101. (See The North Coast chapter for coverage of Hwy. 1 and Hwy. 101 north of Leggett.) Between Ukiah and Leggett—on the north side of Ridgewood Summit—are some worthwhile stops.

Winsome little **Willits** is a friendly frontier town among the ranches and railroads of Little Lake Valley north of Ukiah, a slice of life whittled from

the Old West: Black Bart used to love it here. Besides the horse shows, rodeos, and other regular town hoedowns, the best thing about this place is the **Willits Station** train depot, 299 E. Commercial St., 707/459-5248, the eastern terminus of the old Union Lumber Company logging line (now the California Western Railroad's *Skunk Train* route)—a little dowdy these days, but it was (and is) an astounding architectural achievement, carefully crafted from clear heart redwood. Downtown, the restaurant of choice is the casual but elegant **Tsunami,** 50 S. Main St., 707/459-4750, which serves first-class Japanese and "Mendonesian"

GRACE HUDSON MUSEUM AND SUN HOUSE

Sometimes the most amazing people and things turn up in the most unlikely places. Unconventional Grace Carpenter Hudson and her physician-turned-ethnologist husband John lived in Ukiah in a modest custom-created redwood home they affectionately called "Sun House." She was nationally recognized for her striking, sensitive paintings of Pomo Indians; he was a scholar and collector of Native Americana. Their former home is now part of the city of Ukiah's extraordinary museum complex honoring the contributions of both.

The large Grace Hudson Museum and gallery at 431 S. Main St. (between Perkins and Gobbi Sts.), 707/467-2836, www.gracehudsonmuseum.org, exhibits an impressive collection of Grace Hudson's paintings and John Hudson's artifacts and research. Until recently only selected works—including some fine and rare examples of intricate and delicate Pomo basketry, essentially a lost art—are on display at any one time, but that should change with the spring 2001 debut of the museum's million-dollar **Ivan B. and Elvira Hart Wing.** In addition to the museum's permanent collection, special exhibits of local artists are also featured.

It is astounding that Ukiah (Lumbertown U.S.A.) hosts such a rare and valuable collection of lost Americana. But the *quality* of the museum itself is even more astounding. The building's interior design creates a powerful awareness of the cycle of birth and rebirth that speaks to the *truth* at the heart of this place. An impressive accomplishment.

Adjacent Sun House—note the Hopi sun symbol over the entrance—and the museum are open Wed.–Sat. 10 A.M.–4:30 P.M., Sun. noon–4:30 P.M. (closed on major holidays). Suggested donation: $2 per person, $5 families. Docent-led tours of Sun House are available Wed.–Sun. noon–3 P.M. on the hour.

cuisine in a tranquil atmosphere. Good microbrews and fine wines are available.

For more information about what's in and around Willits, contact the **Willits Chamber of Commerce,** 239 S. Main St., Willits, CA 95490, 707/459-7910, www.willits.org.

TOM MYERS PHOTOGRAPHY

THE NORTH COAST
LAND OF MAGIC

Fog created California's north coast, and still defines it. Fog is everywhere, endless, eternal, *there*. Even on blazing, almost blinding days of sunshine when the veil lifts, the fog is still present somehow, because life here has been made by it. Stands of sky-scraping coast redwoods need fog to live. So do many other native north coast plants, uniquely adapted to uniformly damp conditions. The visual obscurity characteristic of the coast also benefits animals, providing a consistent, year-round supply of drinking water and, for creatures vulnerable to predators, additional protective cover.

Fog even seems to have political consequences. As elsewhere in the northstate, the secessionist spirit is alive and well on the north coast, but the fog makes it seem fuzzy, and the urge is taken less seriously here than it is elsewhere. When, in the mid-1970s, for example, some Mendocino County citizens banded together to form their own state (they called it Northern California), the response from Sacramento was off-the-cuff and casual: "The county's departure, if it ever goes, would scarcely be noticed, at least not until the fog lifted."

People often find fog disquieting, depressing. Some almost fear it. If only momentarily, in fog we become spatially and spiritually bewildered. Our vision seems vague; we hear things. We fall prey to illusions; we hallucinate: trees walk, rocks smile, birds talk, rivers laugh, the ocean sings, someone unseen brushes our cheek. All of a sudden, we don't know where we are and haven't the foggiest notion where we're going. Life as we know it has changed. We have changed.

Dense coastal fog occurs along this cool-weather coast, according to meteorologists, as a result of shoreward breezes carrying warm, moist oceanic air over colder offshore waters. The air's moisture condenses into fog, which rolls in over the coastal mountains in cloudlike waves. As the marine air moves inland and is warmed by the sun, it reabsorbs its own moisture and the fog dissipates.

But science doesn't really explain fog at all—not fog as change, as creator, as fashioner of fantastic forms, as shape-shifting summoner of strange sounds, or protector of the primeval purpose. Fog, in the mythic sense, is magic.

THE SONOMA COAST

Northern California beaches are different from the gentler, kinder sandy beaches of the south-state. The coast here is wild. In stark contrast to the softly rounded hillsides landward, the Sonoma County coast presents a dramatically rugged face and an aggressive personality: undertows, swirling offshore eddies, riptides, and deadly "sleeper" or "rogue" waves. It pays to pay attention along the Sonoma coast. Since 1950, more than 70 people have been killed here by sleepers, waves that come out of nowhere to wallop the unaware, then drag them into the surf and out to sea.

October is generally the worst month of the year for dangerous surf, but it is also one of the best months to visit; in September and October the summertime shroud of fog usually lifts and the sea sparkles. Except on weekends, by autumn most Bay Area and tourist traffic has dried up like the area's seasonal streams, and it's possible to be alone with the wild things.

BODEGA BAY AND VICINITY

Alfred Hitchcock considered this quaint coastal fishing village and the inland town of Bodega perfect for filming *The Birds,* with its rather ominous suggestion that one day nature will avenge itself. But people come to Bodega Bay and vicinity to avoid thinking about such things. They come to explore the headlands, to whale-watch, to kayak, to beachcomb and tidepool, to catch and eat seafood (including local Dungeness crab), to peek into the increasing numbers of galleries and gift shops, and to *relax.* Just wandering through town and along the harbor is fascinating. While keeping an eye on the sky for any sign of feathered terrorists, watch the chartered "party boats" and fishing fleet at the harbor—particularly at six each

evening, daily catch arrives at the Tides Wharf. Bodega, just inland, is where visitors go to reimagine scenes from Hitchcock's movie, most particularly **St. Teresa of Avila Church** and **Potter Schoolhouse.**

Most people don't know, though, that Hitchcock's story was based on actual events of August 18, 1961, though they occurred in Capitola, Rio Del Mar, and other towns on Monterey Bay, farther south. That night, tens of thousands of crazed shearwaters slammed into doors, windows, and hapless people; the next morning these birds, both dead and dying, stank of anchovies. In 1995, researchers at the

---

NORTH COAST AREA CODES ARE A CHANGIN'

In late December 2000, and then again in October of the following year, parts of Northern California will suffer yet another change in telephone area codes—the direct result of residents' red-hot relationship with communications technology and the proliferating numbers of cellular phones, fax machines, and online computer connections that go with it.

The old 707 area, which covered much of the northern part of the Bay Area and the Wine Country, as well as the entire north coast, will get two new codes—369 and 627—in late December 2000. In affected areas to the south—including Dixon, Rio Vista, Vacaville, Fairfield, Suisun City, Benicia, and Vallejo—you can use either 707 or 369 beginning December 2000, but you must use 369 by June 2001. The second phase, introducing the 627 code, affects Cloverdale, Geyserville, Healdsburg, Sea Ranch, Bodega Bay, Guerneville, Forestville, Sebastopol, Santa Rosa, Calistoga, St. Helena, Rohnert Park, Sonoma, Yountville, and Napa. "Permissive dialing"—meaning you can use either area code—begins in October 2001, but 627 will be mandatory by April 2002.

In addition to these changes in telephone area codes, it's likely that more will occur during the useful life of this book. If you have trouble using any area codes listed in this book, dial 0 and ask the operator for current information.

See **color maps** of the **Del Norte-Humboldt Coast** and the **Mendocino** and **Sonoma Coasts** at the front of the book.

BODEGA HEAD

Hulking Bodega Head protects Bodega Bay from the heavy seas, a visible chunk of the Pacific plate and also bulwark for the area's state beaches. Good whale-watching from here. Nearby is the University of California at Davis's **Bodega Marine Lab**, 2099 Westside Rd., 707/875-2211, a marine biology research center open to the public every Friday. Hike on and around the head on well-worn footpaths, or head out for an invigorating walk via hiking trails to **Bodega Dunes.** Five miles of hiking and horseback riding trails twist through the dunes themselves (access at the north end of the bay, via W. Bay Road). To get to Bodega Head, take Westside Rd. and follow the signs past **Westside Park.**

Doran County Park, on the south side of the bay, 707/875-3540, looks bleak, but its windswept beaches and dunes provide safe harbor for diverse wildlife and hardy plants. Swim at these protected beaches; also good clamming. Small day-use fee. Or visit the water-filled sump once destined for the nuclear age—called "hole in the head" and "the world's most expensive duckpond" by bemused locals. With Hitchcock's nature-vengeance theme in mind, we can only shudder at what might have been if PG&E had built its proposed nuclear power plant here, just four miles from the San Andreas Fault.

Institute of Marine Sciences at UC Santa Cruz suggested that a lethal "bloom" of a natural toxin produced by algae—domoic acid—present in Monterey Bay anchovies was probably responsible for the birds' bizarre behavior. Toxic amounts of domoic acid cause amnesia, brain damage, and dementia.

Other than the beautiful landscape, one of the few sights in Bodega Bay is the **Children's Bell Tower**, next to the Community Center on the west side of Hwy. 1, about a mile and a half north of the visitors center. This moving monument was inspired by seven-year-old Nicholas Green of Bodega Bay, who in 1994 was shot and killed while traveling with his family in Italy. His parents, Maggie and Reg Green, decided to donate Nicholas's organs to needy Italian recipients—a decision all but unheard of in Italy at that time. Near Bodega Bay and stretching north to Jenner are the slivers of collectively managed **Sonoma Coast State Beaches,** which include **Bodega Head** and **Bodega Dunes** near the bay itself. Inland are a variety of small spots-in-the-road, some little more than a restaurant or boarded-up gas station at a crossroads, all connected to Bodega Bay by scenic roller-coaster roads.

For more information on Bodega Bay and environs, stop by the **Bodega Bay Area Visitor Information Center**, 850 Hwy. 1, P.O. Box 146, Bodega Bay, CA 94923, 707/875-3866, www.bodegabay.com. Or call the **Bodega Bay Area Chamber of Commerce** at 707/875-3422.

Staying in and near Bodega Bay

In town, the hotspot is the fairly pricey **Bodega Bay Lodge & Spa**, 103 Hwy. 1 (off the highway at Doran Beach Rd.), 707/875-3525 or toll-free 800/368-2468, www.woodsidehotels.com, which offers full luxury amenities, including an ocean-view pool, spa, fitness center, and an exceptional restaurant, The Duck Club. Luxury. It's also adjacent to the **Bodega Harbour Golf Links**, 21301 Heron Dr., 707/875-3538, an 18-hole Scottish links–style course designed by Robert Trent Jones Jr.

Another possibility is the **Inn at the Tides,** 800 Hwy. 1, 707/875-2751 or toll-free 800/541-7788, fax 707/875-3285, www.innatthetides.com. Rates include full amenities (pool, sauna, whirlpool, TV and movies, and many rooms with fireplaces), great views, and continental breakfast. Premium. The Inn at the Tides also features a casual in-house restaurant and the very good Sonoma-style continental **Bay View** restaurant, and sponsors a **Dinner with the Winemaker** series of monthly dinners and wine-tastings. Also nice is the **Bodega Coast Inn,** 521 Hwy. 1, 707/875-2217 or toll-free 800/346-6999, www.bodegacoastinn.com (Premium), and the old-fashioned, small **Bodega Harbor Inn,** 1345 Bodega Ave., 707/875-3594 (Moderate-Luxury), which also rents out cottages and houses.

People often knock at the door of the Queen Anne Victorian **Bay Hill Mansion**, 3919 Bay Hill Rd., P.O. Box 567, 707/875-3577 or toll-free 800/526-5927, www.bayhillmansion.com, to ask if it was featured in *The Birds*. (It wasn't.) But you can pretend. Five comfortable rooms (some share bath), great views of Bodega Bay. Luxury.

The **Chanslor Guest Ranch,** 2660 Hwy. 1

(just north of Bodega Bay), 707/875-2721, is a working horse and sheep spread that also boards people. Suites available, including one with two private balconies and a whirlpool tub. Rates include continental breakfast; horseback riding is extra. Moderate-Premium.

Eating in Bodega Bay

The **Breakers Cafe,** 1400 Hwy. 1, 707/875-2513, is a good choice for breakfast (waffles, Benedicts, omelettes, breakfast burritos), lunch (good sandwiches like portobello mushroom or cold shrimp and crab), and dinner (pastas, soups, salads, steaks). The wholesome **Sandpiper Dockside Café & Restaurant,** 1410 Bay Flat Rd. (take Eastshore Dr. off Hwy. 1 and go straight at the stop sign), 707/875-2278, is a casual locals' place open daily for breakfast, lunch, and dinner. The **Whaler's Inn,** 1805 Hwy. 1, 707/875-2829, is the town's "country kitchen," open daily for breakfast, lunch, and dinner, and serving fresh American-style specialties, from seafood and chicken-fried steak to barbecued ribs. No checks or credit cards.

Get fresh fish and chips, even hot seafood to go, at popular **Lucas Wharf Deli and Fish Market,** 595 Hwy. 1 (on the pier at the harbor), 707/875-3562. Or pick up a delicious seafood sandwich and microbrew, and take it out to one of the benches and tables overlooking the working dock. The adjacent sit-down **Lucas Wharf Restaurant and Bar,** 707/875-3522, is open for lunch and dinner daily and is known for its pastas

---

DINUCCI'S

To drive somewhere in order to totally enjoy sitting down again, head south on Hwy. 1 to Valley Ford, the town made famous by Christo's *Running Fence.* The frumpy white frame building is Dinucci's, 14485 Valley Ford Rd., 707/876-3260, a fantastically fun watering hole and dinner house. Study the massive rosewood bar inside, shipped around Cape Horn, while waiting for a table (folks are allowed to linger over meals). The walls in the bar are almost papered in decades-old political posters, old newspaper clippings, and an eclectic collection of lighthearted local memorabilia. The dim barroom lighting reflects off the hundreds of abalone shells decorating the ceiling.

---

and steaks as well as seafood. Great clam chowder, fisherman's stew, and sourdough bread.

A bit more spiffy—and a *lot* more pricey—is the recently renovated **The Tides Wharf Restaurant,** 835 Hwy. 1 (just north of Lucas Wharf), 707/875-3652, which also overlooks the bay (and has its own dock and video arcade) and was featured as a backdrop in *The Birds.* The Tides is popular for breakfast, and you can count on fresh seafood at lunch and dinner. Open daily; there's a fresh fish market and bait shop here, too. The finest dining in town, though, is available at **The Duck Club** at the Bodega Bay Lodge, 103 Hwy. 1, 707/875-3525, famous for its Sonoma County cuisine—everything from

Bodega Bay

Petaluma duck with orange sauce and Hagemann Ranch filet mignon to grilled Pacific salmon with sweet mustard glaze. Open daily for breakfast and dinner (picnic lunch available).

SONOMA COAST STATE BEACHES

Most of the spectacular 13 miles of coastline between Bodega Bay and Jenner is owned by the state. The collective Sonoma Coast State Beaches are composed of pointy-headed offshore rock formations or "sea stacks," natural arches, and a series of secluded beaches and small coves with terrific tidepools. Don't even think about swimming here (though diving is possible in certain areas), since the cold water, heavy surf, undertows, and sleeper waves all add up to danger. But for beachcombing, ocean fishing, a stroll, or a jog—perfect. Rangers offer weekend whale-watching programs from mid-December through mid-April.

Sprinkled like garnish between the various state beaches from Bodega Bay north to Jenner are a variety of public beaches. North of Bodega Bay, first among the state beaches is **Salmon Creek Beach,** part of which becomes a lagoon when sand shuts the creek's mouth. (If you must swim, try the lagoon here.) **Portuguese Beach,** best for rock fishing and surf fishing, is a sandy beach surrounded by rocky headlands. Plan a picture-perfect picnic near **Rock Point** on the headland (tables available). **Duncans Landing,** midway to Jenner, is also referred to as **Death Rock;** a former offshore lumber-loading spot during the redwood harvesting heyday, today it's one of the most dangerous spots along the Sonoma coast. Farther north is **Shell Beach,** best for beachcombing and seaside strolls, with some tremendous tidepools and good fishing.

It's a spectacularly snaky road from Hwy. 1 down to dramatic Goat Rock, popular **Goat Rock Beach,** and the dunes just east. The craggy goat itself is an impressive promontory but illegal to climb around on: more than a dozen people have drowned in recent years, swept off the rocks by surging surf. In the **Willow Creek** area, near the mouth of the Russian River on the east side of Hwy. 1, are hiking trails and simple campground facilities; this area is popular with local bird-watchers.

For a great hike, take the three-mile **Dr. David Joseph Trail,** starting at the Pomo Canyon Campground just off Willow Creek Rd., south of the mouth of the Russian River (see below). The route threads through the redwoods into the ferns, then on through the oak woodlands and grassland scrub down to the Pacific Ocean at Shell Beach.

Practical Sonoma Coast Beaches

Along this stretch are plentiful pulloffs for parking cars, with access to beach trails and spectacular views. The day-use fee for the Sonoma Coast State Beaches is $2. Camp at **Wright's Beach,** with 30 developed campsites (but no showers) just back from the beach, or **Bodega Dunes,** a half mile south of Salmon Creek, with 98 developed sites secluded among the cypress-dotted dunes, hot showers, an RV sanitation station, and a campfire center. Developed Sonoma Coast campsites are reservable in advance through ReserveAmerica, toll-free 800/444-7275. Primitive walk-in camping is available Apr.–Nov. at 11-site **Willow Creek Campground** along the banks of the Russian River (first-come, first-camped, no dogs). Register at the trailhead, up Willow Creek Rd. (turn right at the Sizzling Tandoor restaurant). The walk-in **Pomo Canyon Campground** is reached via the same route. About five minutes after turning off Hwy. 1, you'll reach the gravel parking lot marked Pomo Canyon Campground. From here, two trails run into the redwoods to the 21 walk-in sites, which feature a picnic table, fire grill, and leveled tent site.

For current conditions and other information on the Sonoma Coast State Beaches, call the Bodega Dunes campground at 707/875-3483, or contact the **Salmon Creek Ranger Station,** 3095 Hwy. 1 (just north of town), Bodega Bay, CA 94923, 707/875-2603.

FORT ROSS STATE HISTORIC PARK

A large village of the Kashia Pomo people once stood here. After the Russian-American Fur Company (Czar Alexander I and President James Madison were both company officers) established its fur-trapping settlements at Bodega Bay, the firm turned its attention northward to what, in the spring of 1812, became **Fort Ross,** imperial Russia's farthest outpost. Here the Russians grew

Fort Ross State
Historic Park

grains and vegetables to supply Alaskan colonists as well as Californios, manufactured a wide variety of products, and trapped sea otters to satisfy the voracious demand for fine furs.

The First Fort, the Reconstructed Fort

The weathered redwood fortress perched on these lonely headlands, surrounded by gloomy cypress groves, was home to Russian traders and trappers for 40 years. The original 14-foot-high stockade featured corner lookouts and 40 cannons. Inside the compound were barracks, a jail, the commandant's house, warehouses, and workshops. Perhaps due to the Russian Orthodox belief that only God is perfect, the fort was constructed with no right angles. At the fort and just outside its walls, the industrious Russians and their work crews produced household goods plus saddles, bridles, even 200-ton ships and prefabricated houses.

A good place to start exploring Fort Ross is at its million-dollar **visitor center** and museum, which includes a good introductory slide program (shown throughout the day in the auditorium), as well as Pomo artifacts and basketry, other historic displays, period furnishings, and a gift shop. The free **audio tour** of the fort is itself entertaining (balalaika music, hymns, and Princess Helena Rotchev—namesake of Mt. St. Helena near Calistoga—playing Mozart on the piano).

The fort's only remaining original building (now restored) is the commandant's quarters.

Other reconstructed buildings include the barracks—furnished as if Russians would sail up and bed down any minute—an artisans' center, and the armory.

Practical Fort Ross

The park's boundaries also encompass a beach, the ridge-top redwoods behind the fort, and other lands to the north and east. Thanks to the Coastwalk organization, hiking access (including a handicapped-accessible trail) has been added to the Black Ranch Park area south of the fort. Ask at the visitors center for current hiking information. Just 12 miles north of Jenner along Hwy. 1, Fort Ross is open to the public 10 A.M.–4:30 P.M. daily (except major holidays), day-use fee $3 per car. On **Living History Day** in July or August, the colony here suddenly comes back to life circa 1836. History buffs can have fun questioning repertory company volunteers to see if they know their stuff.

For those who want to rough it, first-come, first-served primitive camping is possible at **Fort Ross Reef State Campground,** tucked into a ravine just south of the fort (20 campsites, no dogs). For more information, contact: Fort Ross State Historic Park, 19005 Hwy. 1, Jenner, CA 95450, 707/847-3286 or 707/865-2391.

Those who want to "smooth it" can instead try **Fort Ross Lodge,** 20705 Hwy. 1, Jenner, CA 95450, 707/847-3333 or toll-free 800/968-4537, which offers all modern amenities and great ocean views. Moderate-Luxury.

TIMBER COVE TO SEA RANCH

Hard to miss even in the fog, the landmark eight-story **Benjamin Bufano** *Peace* sculpture looms over **Timber Cove**. Once a "doghole port" for lumber schooners, like most craggy north coast indentations, Timber Cove is now a haven for the reasonably affluent. But ordinary people can stop for a look at Bufano's last, unfinished work. From the hotel parking lot, walk seaward and look up into the face of *Peace,* reigning over land and sea. To stay a while, consider the **Timber Cove Inn,** 21780 N. Hwy. 1, 707/847-3231 or toll-free 800/987-8319, fax 707/847-3704, which offers fairly luxurious lodgings on a 26-acre point jutting out into the Pacific. Premium-Luxury.

Salt Point State Park

This 3,500-acre park is most often compared to Point Lobos on the Monterey Peninsula, thanks to its dramatic outcroppings, tidepools and coves (this is one of the state's first official underwater preserves), wave-sculpted sandstone, lonely wind-whipped headlands, and highlands including a pygmy forest of stunted cypress, pines, and redwoods.

Though most people visit only the seaward side of the park—to dive or to examine the park's honeycombed *tafuni* rock (sculpted sandstone)—the best real hiking is across the road within the park's inland extension (pick up a map to the park when you enter).

Among Salt Point's other attractions are the dunes and several old Pomo village sites. In season, berrying, fishing, and mushrooming are favorite activities. Park rangers lead hikes and sponsor other occasional programs on weekends, and are also available to answer questions during the seasonal migration of the gray whales. The platform at Sentinel Rock is a great perch for whale-watching.

Among its other superlatives, Salt Point is also prime for camping. The park has tent and RV campsites with hot showers, as well as walk-in, bike-in, and environmental campsites. Make reservations, at least during the summer high season, through ReserveAmerica, toll-free 800/444-7275. Pleasant picnicking here, too. Day-use fee: $2 per carload. For more information, contact: Salt Point State Park, 25050 Hwy. 1, Jenner, CA 95450, 707/847-3221 or 707/865-2391.

Kruse Rhododendron Preserve

Adjoining Salt Point State Park, the seasonally astounding Kruse Rhododendron Preserve is an almost-natural wonder. Nowhere else on earth does *Rhododendron californicum* grow to such heights and in such profusion, in such perfect harmony—under a canopy of redwoods. Here at the 317-acre preserve, unplanted and uncultivated native rhododendrons up to 30 feet tall thrive in well-lit yet cool second-growth groves of coast redwood, Douglas fir, tan oak, and madrone. The dominant shrub is the *Rhododendron macrophyllum,* or California rosebay, common throughout the Pacific Northwest. Also here is the *Rhododendron occidentale,* or western azalea, with its cream-colored flowers.

Most people say the best time to cruise into Kruse is in April or May, when the rhododendrons' spectacular pink bloom is at its finest. (Peak blooming time varies from year to year, so call ahead for current guestimates.) For bloom predictions, preserve conditions, and other information, contact: Salt Point State Park, 25050 Hwy. 1, Jenner, CA 95450, 707/847-3221 or 707/865-2391.

Sea Ranch

Almost since its inception, controversy has been the middle name of this 5,200-acre sheep ranch-cum-exclusive vacation home subdivision. No one could have imagined the ranch's significance in finally resolving long-fought battles over California coastal access and coastal protection. It was here in the 1970s that much of the war over beach access took place, ending with the establishment of the California Coastal Commission.

Sea Ranch architects get rave reviews for their simple, boxlike, high-priced condominiums and homes, which emulate weatherbeaten local barns. The much-applauded cluster development design allowed "open space" for the aesthetic well-being of residents and passersby alike, but provided no way to get to the 10 miles of state-owned coastline without trespassing. Now there's access, but Sea Ranch charges a day-use fee. Make it worth your while. From the access at Walk-On Beach, you can link up with the Bluff Top Trail that winds along the wild coastline to Gualala Point Regional Park some miles to the north.

On the northern edge of the spread is the gnomish stone and stained-glass **Sea Ranch Chapel** designed by noted architect James Hubbell. Consider an overnight stay at the 20-room **Sea Ranch Lodge,** 60 Seawalk Dr., 707/785-2371 or toll-free 800/732-7262, fax 707/785-2917, www.searanchlodge.com. Its pretty and plush accommodations look out over the Pacific, and some rooms have fireplaces and private hot tubs. Other amenities include pools, saunas, and an 18-hole links-style golf course (707/785-2468). Luxury, though ask about specials in the Premium range. Vacation home rentals are also available. Inquire at the lodge for current info.

THE SOUTHERN MENDOCINO COAST

The Gualala River forms the boundary between Sonoma and Mendocino Counties. Travelers heading north will find that most of the Bay Area weekenders have by now tailed off, leaving Mendocino County's stretch of coast highway for the locals and long-haul travelers. It's a little greener (and wetter) here than in Sonoma County, but the crescent coves and pocket beaches you appreciated along the wild Sonoma Coast continue north across the county line, one after the next, like a string of pearls.

Beachcombers and hikers, to get properly oriented along the Mendocino coast, a travel essential is Bob Lorentzen's *The Hiker's Hip Pocket Guide to the Mendocino Coast,* which keys off the white milepost markers along Hwy. 1 from the Gualala River north. The book provides abundant information about undeveloped public lands along the southern Mendocino coast, such as the state's Schooner Gulch and Whiskey Shoals Beach. Also worthwhile to carry anywhere along the coast, though a bit unwieldy, is the *California Coastal Resource Guide* by the California Coastal Commission, published by the University of California Press.

GUALALA AND VICINITY

Though people in the area generally say whatever they please, Gualala is supposedly pronounced Wah-LA-la, the word itself Spanish for the Pomos' *wala'li* or "meeting place of the waters." Crossing the Gualala River means crossing into Mendocino County. Gualala and vicinity is also known as the north coast's "banana belt," due to its relatively temperate, fog-free climate.

The fine-dining restaurant of choice in Gualala these days is the **Oceansong Pacific Grille,** 39350 S. Hwy. 1, 707/884-1041, which enjoys a splendid location overlooking the beach and Gualala River. Seafood is one specialty, but you'll also find steaks, pastas, rack of lamb, and other entrées, all expertly done. For "downhome gourmet," try **The Food Company** just north of

St. Orres, Gualala

town at Robinsons Reef Rd., 707/884-1800, a combination café, deli, and bakery serving up fresh, wholesome fare. Sit outside on the sunporch or in the garden area, or pack your goodies to go. Open daily for breakfast, lunch, and dinner. Gualala and nearby Anchor Bay also boast many nice inns. North of town is the **Old Milano Hotel,** 38300 S. Hwy. 1, 707/884-3256, fax 707/884-4249, a fine Victorian-style bed-and-breakfast listed on the National Register of Historic Places. Six rooms share two baths, but seven others (including six cottages) have private baths. One room features the canopied bed where Cathy (Merle Oberon) lay before Heathcliff (Laurence Olivier) carried her to the window for one last look at the moors. The unique "caboose" cottage not far from the main house has a woodstove, terrace, and observation cupola, and the Iris Cottage features ocean views. Rates include a full breakfast and use of the hot tub. Moderate-Luxury. The Old Milano also serves delightful dinners in its Victorian dining room.

Continuing north from Gualala, you'll soon come upon a local landmark—the ornate onion-domed inn and restaurant of **St. Orres,** 36601 S. Hwy. 1, 707/884-3303 or 707/884-3335 (restaurant), fax 707/884-1840, www.saintorres.com. Some rock 'n' roll–literate wits refer to a sit-down dinner here as "sitting in the dacha of the bay." Dazzling in all its Russian-style redwood and stained-glass glory, St. Orres is also a great place to stay. For peace, quiet, and total relaxation, nothing beats an overnight in one of the 11 handcrafted redwood cabins (some rather rustic) or one of the eight lodge rooms (shared bathrooms). Come morning, breakfast is delivered to the door in a basket. Moderate-Luxury. Even if they don't stay here, people come from miles around to eat at St. Orres, known for its creative French-style fare. Wonderful desserts, and good wines (beer and wine only). No credit cards. Reservations are a must, a month or more in advance.

reka in the 1870s. When the local pier was wiped out by rogue waves in 1983, the already depressed local fishing and logging economy took yet another dive. But today Point Arena has a new pier—folks can fish here without a license—and a new economic boon: the sea urchin harvest, to satisfy the Japanese taste for *uni*.

A monument to the area's historically impressive ship graveyard, the Coast Guard's six-story, automated 380,000-candlepower **Point Arena Lighthouse** north of town is open to visitors (limited hours, small donation requested). To help protect the lighthouse and preserve public access (no government support has been available), local volunteer lighthouse keepers maintain and rent out "vacation rental homes" (U.S. government-issue houses abandoned by the Coast Guard)—Premium-Luxury, a good deal for families. For more information and reservations, contact **Point Arena Lighthouse Keepers, Inc.,** 45500 Lighthouse Rd., P.O. Box 11, Point Arena, CA 95468, 707/882-2777, www. mcn.org/1/palight/lodging.html.

Besides the lighthouse cottages, more conventional digs are also available in town. **La Bou's Sea Shell Inn,** 135 Main, 707/882-2000, has decent rooms with cable TV, phones, and morning coffee. Inexpensive. The **Coast Guard House Historic Inn,** 695 Arena Cove, 707/882-2442 or toll-free 800/524-9320, is a 1901 Cape Cod with six guest rooms (two share a bath), queen or double beds, and an expanded continental breakfast. Premium-Luxury.

Don't miss dinner at **Pangaea,** 250 Main St., 707/882-3001. This self-proclaimed "café" boasts an arty, elegant interior and advertises its fare as "eclectic cuisine: global, local, organic." What that means exactly varies from night to night, but might include such mouthwatering temptations as pan-roasted Chilean sea bass with anise-scented black beans, or mahimahi with Lebanese couscous tabbouleh, lentils, greens, and a cumin-scented lemony tahini sauce. Outrageous.

POINT ARENA

Farther north is remote Point Arena, "discovered" by Capt. George Vancouver in 1792. Another good spot for whale-watching, Point Arena was the busiest port between San Francisco and Eu-

TO MENDOCINO

Manchester State Park
This 5,272-acre park just north of Point Arena and the burg of Manchester is foggy in summer and cold in winter, but it presents dedicated

beachcombers with a long stretch of sandy shore and dunes dotted with driftwood. Five miles of beaches stretch south to Point Arena. A lagoon offers good birding, and excellent salmon and steelhead fishing in both Brush and Alder Creeks. Also interesting here is the opportunity for some walk-in environmental camping, about a mile past the parking area. (Making an overnight even more thrilling is the knowledge that here at Manchester is where the San Andreas Fault plunges into the sea.) For more information about Manchester and a camping map, contact the Mendocino state parks office, 707/937-5804, or call the park directly at 707/882-2463. More private and protected is the **KOA** campground at 44300 Kinney Ln. (adjacent to the park office), 707/882-2375.

Elk

The tiny town of Elk perches on the coastal bluffs farther north. Elk was once a lumber-loading port known as Greenwood, hence **Greenwood Creek Beach State Park** across from the store, with good picnicking among the bluff pines. The park is also a popular push-off point for sea kayakers. If you're just passing through and looking for a bite to eat, note that the nondescript store beside the highway—the **Elk Store,** 6101 Hwy. 1, 707/877-3411—whips up some of the best deli sandwiches in the known universe, and also carries gourmet cheeses and an impressive selection of wines and microbrews.

The all-redwood Craftsman-style 1916 **Harbor House,** 5600 S. Hwy. 1, 707/877-3203 or toll-free 800/720-7474, www.theharborhouse inn.com, is a sophisticated Elk bed-and-breakfast noted for its stylish, classic accommodations (recently refurbished) and fine dining. Rates include full breakfast, fabulous four-course dinner, and access to a private strip of beach. Luxury. Dinners emphasize Sonoma County seafood, meats, poultry, and produce, à la Tuscany or Provence. Open for dinner daily, at least most of the year. Beer and wine. No credit cards. Limited seating, and advance reservations required— and be sure to request a window table.

The **Greenwood Pier Inn,** 5928 S. Hwy. 1, 707/877-9997 or 707/877-3423, fax 707/877-3439, www.greenwoodpierinn.com, is a complex of upscale cottages perched at the edge of the cliffs above the sea. Homey and romantic, most cottages feature wood-burning fireplaces or wood-

stoves, and some also have in-room spa tubs. Premium-Luxury. Continental breakfast is delivered to your room; other meals are available at the on-site **Greenwood Pier Café,** where the house-baked breads and fresh garden veggies and herbs make even a simple meal quite delightful. Open daily mid-May through Oct. for breakfast, lunch, and dinner, Fri.–Mon. in the off-season.

Also charming are the cottages at **Griffin House at Greenwood Cove,** 5910 S. Hwy. 1, 707/877-3422, www.griffinn.com. The "house" is now **Bridget Dolan's Irish Pub & Dinner House,** serving pub grub, soups and salads, Gaelic garlic bread, and hearty main dishes such as Irish stew, bangers and mash, and "very, very veg" specials. Out back are the flower gardens and cozy 1920s cottages; three feature sun decks and ocean views, and all have private baths (most with clawfoot tubs) and woodstoves. One includes a full kitchen, and is a best bet for families. A hearty full breakfast is served in your room. Expensive-Luxury.

MENDOCINO AND
THE MENDOCINO COAST

People just love Mendocino. They love it for a variety of reasons. Some are smitten by the town's Cape Cod architecture, admittedly a bit odd on the California side of the continent. The seaside saltbox look of the 19th-century wood-frame homes here, explained by the fact that the original settlers were predominantly lumbermen from Maine, is one of the reasons the entire town is included on the National Register of Historic Places. Others love Mendocino for its openly artistic attitude. Of course, almost everyone loves the town's spectacular setting at the mouth of Big River—and at the edge of one of the most sublime coastlines in California.

Everybody loves Mendocino—and as a result, people tend to love Mendocino to death, at least in summer. Not even 1,000 people live here, yet the community is usually clogged with people, pets, and parked cars. Mendocino-area rental homes are inhabited in summer and at other "peak" times, but in the dead of winter, locals can barely find a neighbor to talk to. Besides, almost no one who actually *lives* here can afford to now. Exactly when it was that things started to change for the worse—well, that depends on whom you talk to.

In the 1950s, when nearby forests had been logged over and the lumbermill was gone, and the once bad and bawdy doghole port of Mendocino City was fading fast, the artists arrived. Living out the idea of making this coastal backwater home were prominent San Francisco painters like Dorr Bothwell, Emmy Lou Packard, and Bill Zacha, who founded the still-strong Mendocino Art Center in 1959. Soon all the arts were in full bloom on these blustery bluffs, and the town had come alive. But even back then, as *Johnny Belinda* film crews rolled through Mendocino streets and James Dean showed up for the filming of *East of Eden,* old-timers and retirees could see what was coming. The town's possibilities could very well destroy it.

In the decades since, the costs of living and doing business in Mendocino have gotten so high that most of Mendocino's artists have long since crawled out of town with their creative tails between their legs—pushed out, locals say, by the more affluent "culture vultures" who consume other people's creativity. Though many fine artists, craftspeople, performers, and writers (including Alice Walker) work throughout Mendocino County, most art, crafts, and consumables sold in Mendocino shops are imported from elsewhere. Even finding a local place to park is nearly impossible in Mendocino, a town too beautiful for its own good.

a Mendocino home and garden

TOM MYERS PHOTOGRAPHY

MENDOCINO AT ITS BEST

Thankfully, in postage-stamp-size Mendocino, cars are an unnecessary headache. You can stroll from one end of town to the other and back again—twice—without breaking a sweat. So leave your car parked at the village lodging of choice. If you're staying elsewhere, take the bus. Or hike here, or ride a bike. Mendocino is at its best when seen on foot or from the seat of a bike. Note, however, that street addresses in Mendocino can be either three digits or five digits, all in the same block. Fortunately, the town is small and beautiful. So just find the street you need by name and wander along it until you find what you're looking for.

To stroll the streets of Mendocino or explore the headlands at the moodiest, most renewing time, come when most people don't—in November or January. This is the season when Mendocino is still itself, and seems to slip back to a time before this New Englandesque village was even an idea. A sense of that self blasts in from the bleak headlands, come winter, blowing rural reality back into town. In winter you can meet the community—the fishermen, fourth-generation loggers, first-generation marijuana farmers, apple and sheep ranchers, artists and craftspeople, even city-fleeing innkeepers and shopkeepers as they, too, come out of hiding.

The Mendocino Coast: Greater Mendocino
Given Mendocino's proximity to, and dependence on, a number of nearby coastal communities, any visit to Mendocino also includes the coastline for about 10 miles in either direction. The Mendocino Coast business, arts, and entertainment communities are so intertwined that they share a single visitors bureau.

Not counting Garberville, **Fort Bragg** north of Mendocino is the last community of any size before Eureka. Mendocino's working-class sister city to the north was named after a fort built there in 1855 for protection against hostile natives. Unpretentious home now to working (and unemployed) loggers and mill workers, an active fishing fleet, and many of Mendocino's working artists and much of their work, friendly Fort Bragg offers an array of relatively urban services and amenities not found in the smaller Mendocino. Just north of Fort Bragg is tiny **Cleone,** and at the south end of Fort Bragg is **Noyo Harbor,** with its bustling fishing fleet. Approximately halfway between Mendocino and Fort Bragg lies the little hamlet of **Caspar,** which makes Mendocino look like the big city.

Just a few miles south of Mendocino, near Van Damme State Park, is **Little River,** a tiny burg boasting its own post office but most famous for the long-running Little River Inn. A bit farther south is **Albion,** a miniscule coastal hamlet straddling the mouth of the Albion River—a natural harbor supporting a small fishing fleet. From just south of Albion and inland via Hwy. 128 is the attractive Anderson Valley and Boonville (for more information, see the Wine Country chapter).

SEEING AND DOING MENDOCINO

Start your Mendocino explorations at the state park's **Ford House interpretive center,** near the public restrooms on the seaward side of Main, 707/937-5397. The center features a model of Mendocino as it looked 100 years ago, historical photos, exhibits on lumbering and the Pomo Indians, wildflower displays, local art, lots of brochures, free apple cider, and a store selling books and postcards. It's open year-round, daily 11 A.M.–4 P.M. (longer hours if volunteers are available).

Across the street is the 1861 **Kelley House** (entrance around the front at 45007 Albion), 707/937-5791, now housing the Mendocino region's historical society museum and library. The museum is open June–Sept., daily 1–4 P.M. (small admission). Sign up here for a guided walking tour of Mendocino (nominal fee).

When you're ready to head off around town, a good first destination is the nonprofit **Mendocino Art Center,** 45200 Little Lake Rd. (between Williams and Kasten), 707/937-5818 or toll-free 800/653-3328, fax 707/937-1764, www.mendocinoartcenter.com, open daily 10 A.M.–5 P.M. This place is a wonder—a genuine *center* for countywide arts awareness and artistic expression. Whatever artistic endeavor is happening in Mendocino County, someone at the center knows about it.

The number of art galleries in and around Mendocino is staggering. A veritable fine furniture and woodworking emporium in town is the three-story **Highlight Gallery,** 45052 Main, 707/937-3132, which also displays handwoven textiles. The **William Zimmer Gallery,** Ukiah and Kasten, 707/937-5121, offers a large, eclectic collection of highly imaginative, contemporary fine arts and crafts. **Panache Gallery,** 10400 Kasten, 707/937-1234, specializes in fine art, glassware, and gold jewelry (a second location on Main St. stocks sterling silver jewelry). **Gallery One,** at Hwy. 1 and Main, 707/937-5154, features fine painting, photography, and works in a variety of other media.

ARTFUL MENDOCINO COAST

On the first Friday evening of the month, don't miss Fort Bragg's **First Friday** local gallery and shop "event," 5:30–8:30 P.M., sponsored by the Fort Bragg Center for the Arts. For the latest on other art events, stop by the Fort Bragg Center or the Mendocino Art Center.

At home in Mendocino is the **Mendocino Theatre Company,** 45200 Little Lake Rd., 707/937-4477 or 707/937-2718, which begins its performance season in March. An eclectic mix of one-night or short-run acts—anything from local school plays to comedy troupes to touring world-beat bands—are presented at Mendocino's **Crown Hall,** 45285 Ukiah St. (down at the west end), a delightfully intimate venue with reasonably good acoustics as well.

Fort Bragg is also quite theatrical. The **Gloriana Opera Company,** 721 N. Franklin St., 707/964-7469, offers a six-week run in summer and special events throughout the year. The **Footlighters Little Theatre,** 248 E. Laurel St., 707/964-3806, features Gay Nineties melodrama; performances occur Wednesday and Saturday from Memorial Day through Labor Day. Fort Bragg's **Warehouse Repertory Theater,** 319-A N. Main St., 707/961-2942 (admin.) or 707/ 961-2940 (box office), www.warehouserep.com, the regional repertory company, sponsors the annual **Mendocino Shakespeare Festival.**

Fort Bragg is also home to the fine **Symphony of the Redwoods,** 707/964-0898, which presents several major concerts each year along the Mendocino coast, leading up to its season-capping performance in mid-July at the annual Mendocino Music Festival.

One of Mendocino's earliest buildings (1852) is its joss house, the **Temple of Kwan Ti,** a half block west of Kasten on Albion (between Kasten and Woodward), 707/937-4506 or 707/937-5123, open to the public by appointment only. Though the old wooden temple boasts a bright red, well-maintained paint job, you can't help but get the feeling that the whole thing might well collapse in a strong wind.

Make sure to drop by **Crown Hall,** 45285 Ukiah St. (toward the west end), to see what's going on. The intimate theater hosts everything from local comedy troupes and community plays to big-name touring bands.

SEEING AND DOING FORT BRAGG

Fort Bragg is the western terminus of the California and Western Railroad's *Skunk Train,* a sightseeing railroad that winds inland along the redwood-thick and rugged Noyo River gulch and over the mountains to Willits, about 40 track miles away. The train stops at Northspur, the halfway point, where a little tourist village offers food booths, souvenir stands, and restrooms. You can return to Fort Bragg from here, a half-day round-trip, or continue on the rest of the way to Willits for a full-day round-trip. The longer ride offers some cliff-hanging nonoceanic scenery and on-board camaraderie. In Willits, the end of the line is the historic Willits railroad station, a small marvel of redwood craftsmanship.

The railroad's "Old No. 45" steam engine, *Super Skunk* diesel locomotives, or *Skunk* Motorcars (resembling city-style trolley cars), chug out from the station at Laurel St. in Fort Bragg; call or see the website for current schedule details. Train fare is $35 full-day, $27 half-day or one-way for adults; $18 and $14, respectively, for children 3–11. For information and advance reservations (highly recommended, especially to secure a place on one of the steam-engine runs), contact: The Skunk Train, P.O. Box 907, Fort Bragg, CA 95437, 707/964-6371 or toll-free 800/777-5865, www.skunktrain.com.

The nonprofit 47-acre **Mendocino Coast Botanical Gardens,** 18220 N. Hwy. 1 (two miles south of downtown), 707/964-4352, www.gardenbythesea.org, features native plant communities as well as formal plantings of

EVENTFUL MENDOCINO COAST

For most people, just being here along the Mendocino coast is entertainment enough. But if that's too quiet for you, the **Caspar Inn** between Mendocino and Fort Bragg, 707/964-5565, is a venerable rock 'n' roll hot spot; this boisterous roadhouse-style tavern draws packed houses for dancing to big-name touring bands.

Community events offer something for just about everyone. New in 2000 was the **Mendocino Wine & Crab Days** event, held from the last weekend in January through the first week in February. Everyone celebrates the return of the California gray whale. The **Mendocino Whale Festival,** on the first weekend in March, celebrates the annual cetacean migration with wine and clam-chowder tastings, art exhibits, music and concerts, and other special events. The **Fort Bragg Whale Festival,** held the third weekend in March, happily coincides with the arrival of spring. Festivities include chowder tasting and beer tasting (the latter courtesy of Fort Bragg's own North Coast Brewing Company), a "whale run," doll show, car show, lighthouse tours, and more. On both weekends, **whale-watching tours** are offered from Noyo Harbor, and **whale-watch talks** are offered at area state parks.

On or around July Fourth, Fort Bragg hosts the **World's Largest Salmon Barbecue** down at Noyo Harbor. And Mendocino holds its old-fashioned **Fourth of July Parade.** Starting in mid-July, Mendocino hosts the noted, two-week **Mendocino Music Festival,** 707/937-2044, www.mcn.org/a/music. At this gala event, held in a 600-seat tent set up next to the Ford House, the local Symphony of the Redwoods joins with talented players from Bay Area orchestras to perform classical works that might include symphonies, opera, and chamber music, as well as less highbrow fare. At Greenwood Ridge Vineyards in the Anderson Valley, come in late July or early August for the annual **California Wine Tasting Championships.**

Usually held the first weekend in August is the Mendocino Art Center's **Summer Art Fair.** Also in August is the Mendocino Coast Botanical Gardens' **Art in the Gardens** event. Fort Bragg's biggest party every year is **Paul Bunyan Days,** held over Labor Day weekend and offering a logging competition, parade, and crafts fair. The following September weekend, the **Winesong!** wine-tasting and auction takes place at the Mendocino Coast Botanical Gardens.

December brings the **Mendocino Christmas Festival,** which includes tree lighting, candlelight inn tours, and other festivities. In Fort Bragg, the yuletide spirit extends to special programs by the Symphony of the Redwoods, the Gloriana Theater Company, and Warehouse Repertory—and the **Holiday Gift Show** at the restored Union Lumber Company Store, not to mention the **Hometown Christmas & Lighted Truck Parade.** This particular community party includes music, tree lighting, and truck lighting—a yuletide parade of logging trucks and big rigs all lit up for the holidays.

---

rhododendrons, azaleas, fuchsias, and other regional favorites. Also here—in addition to some smashing views of the crashing coast—are a native plant nursery, picnic tables, the fine **Gardens Grill** restaurant, and summertime music concerts. A year-round calendar of special events and workshops are offered, too, from bird-watching tours to organic gardening classes. Wheelchair accessible. The gardens are open daily 9 A.M.–5 P.M. Mar.–Oct., and 9 A.M.–4 P.M. the rest of the year. Admission is $6 general, $5 seniors (60 and up), $3 youths (ages 13–17), and $1 children (ages 6–12).

For the local version of redwood logging history, as told through photos, artifacts, and tree-mining memorabilia, stop by the **Guest House Museum,** 343 N. Main St., 707/961-2840, in an attractive 1892 redwood mansion that was once used as a guest house for friends and customers of local Union Pacific Lumber execs. Small admission. The only remaining **fort building** from the original Fort Bragg stands a block east of the Guest House on Franklin Street.

Noyo Harbor, Fort Bragg's tiny fishing port, lies at the south end of town, at the mouth of the Noyo River. It's a safe harbor for fisherfolk during stormy seas and shelters several fish restaurants popular with tourists, but fairly ho-hum in terms of cuisine and ambience. Don't miss Noyo's **Salmon Barbecue** festivities every July. It's a must-attend event for delicious fresh salmon and an intimate encounter with the local populace. Good folks, good food, big tradition.

MENDOCINO AREA PARKS

Mendocino Headlands State Park

The headlands and beach are subtle, more a monument to sand sculpture than an all-out ode to hard rock. The impressive stony sea stacks here and elsewhere are all that remain of sandstone headlands after eons of ocean erosion. Curving seaward around the town from Big River to the northern end of Heeser Dr., the park includes a three-mile hiking trail, a small beach along the mouth of Big River (trailheads and parking on Hwy. 1, just north of the bridge), sandstone bluffs, the area's notorious wave tunnels, offshore islands and narrows, and good tidepools. *The* peak experience from the headlands is whale-watching. (Whether watching the waves or whales, stand back from the bluff's edge. Sandstone is notoriously unstable, and the ragged rocks and wicked waves below are at best indifferent to human welfare.) For a map and more information, get oriented at Ford House or contact: Mendocino State Parks, P.O. Box 440, Mendocino, CA 95460, 707/937-5804. You can easily walk here from town—it's just an invigorating and spectacular stroll away. Pick up the path at the west end of Main Street.

Van Damme State Park

This small state park just south of Mendocino is not famous but, despite the considerable competition, is one of the finer things about this stretch of the coast. The excellent and convenient camping here midway between Mendocino and Albion is secondary. Van Damme State Park is an 1,831-acre, five-mile-long preserve around Little River's watershed, pointing out to sea. A new 1.5-mile trail offers a self-guided tour of the coho salmon's life cycle. Squeezed into a lush ravine of second-growth mixed redwood forest, Van Damme's pride is its **Fern Canyon Trail**, a 2.5-mile hiking and bicycling trail weaving across Little River through red alders, redwoods, and ferns. Though the Fern Canyon Trail is easy, the going gets tougher at the east end as the path climbs the canyon and connects with the loop trail to Van Damme's **Pygmy Forest**, a gnarly thicket bonsaied by nature. (It is possible to drive most of the way to this green grove of miniatures via Airport Rd. just south of the park, and the forest is wheelchair accessible.) Van Damme's tiny beach is a popular launch point for scuba divers and is usually safe for swimming, though no lifeguards are on duty. The 1996 addition of Spring Ranch added more beach, and some spectacular tidepools.

RECREATIONAL SIGHTSEEING

For sightseeing afloat practically in Mendocino, catch a canoe (or kayak) from among the **Catch a Canoe and Bikes Too!** fleet, at the Stanford Inn by the Sea (on the south bank of Big River), 44850 Comptche-Ukiah Rd., 707/937-0273 or toll-free 800/320-2453. Birders especially will enjoy the serene estuarine tour of Big River. Catch a Canoe also rents bicycles and can offer tips on the best area rides. **Dive Crazy Adventures** in Albion, 707/937-3079, also offers kayaks and tours, dive charters, and other adventures. **North Coast Divers Supply**, 19275 S. Harbor Dr. in Fort Bragg, 707/ 961-1143, also offers diving supplies and expertise. **Lost Coast Adventures,** 707/937-2434, offers Sea-Cave Tours at Van Damme State Park in sit-on-top ocean kayaks. At last report **free, ranger-guided canoe trips** (for age 6 and older) were still offered in summer at **Navarro River Red-** woods State Park south of Mendocino. For details, call 707/937-5804.

Near Fort Bragg, MacKerricher's Haul Rd. is a cycle path par excellence. Rent mountain bikes, 10-speeds, and two-seaters at **Fort Bragg Cyclery,** 579 S. Franklin St., 707/964-3509.

Ricochet Ridge Ranch, 24201 N. Hwy. 1, located north of Fort Bragg in Cleone, across the highway from the entrance to MacKerricher State Park, 707/964-7669, offers a daily horseback trail ride along the beach at MacKerricher, as well as other rides (English/Western) by advance arrangement. **Back Kountry Trailrides,** about 14 miles east of Fort Bragg, 707/964-2700, www.bktrailrides.com, offers guided rides along redwood trails. For a guided llama trip, contact **Llama Treks,** 707/964-7120, www.lodgingandllamas.com.

Van Damme's redwood-sheltered campground area is protected from winds but not its own popularity. A small group camp is also available. For more information, contact the regional state parks office (see above) or: Van Damme State Park, Little River, CA 95456, 707/937-5804. Reserve campsites in advance through ReserveAmerica, toll-free 800/444-7275. The park's day-use fee is $2.

Russian Gulch State Park

Just north of Mendocino on the site of another days-past doghole port, Russian Gulch State Park is 1,200 acres of diverse redwood forests in a canyon thick with rhododendrons, azaleas, berry bushes, and ferns; coastal headlands painted in spring with wildflowers; and a broad bay with tidepools and sandy beach, perfect for scuba diving. Especially fabulous during a strong spring storm is the flower-lined cauldron of **Devil's Punch Bowl** in the middle of a meadow on the northern headlands. A portion of this 200-foot wave tunnel collapsed, forming an inland blowhole, but the devil's brew won't blast through unless the sea bubbles and boils. After a picnic on the headlands, take a half-day hike upcanyon. Make it a nine-mile loop by combining the southern trails to reach 36-foot **Russian Gulch Falls** (best in spring), then loop back to camp on the North Trail.

Camping at Russian Gulch is itself an attraction, with 30 family campsites tucked into the forested canyon. The separate group camp accommodates about 40 people. (This close to the coast, campers often sleep under a blanket of fog, so come prepared for wet conditions.) Reserve campsites in advance through ReserveAmerica, toll-free 800/444-7275. For more information, contact the Mendocino State Parks headquarters here, 707/937-5804. The park's day-use fee is $2.

Caspar Headlands State Beach and Reserve

Just north of Russian Gulch, and reached via Pt. Cabrillo Dr., are the Caspar Headlands, hemmed in by housing. Miles of beaches are open to the public, though, from sunrise to sunset—perfect for whale-watching. The headlands are accessible only by permit. A particular point of interest is the historic 300-acre **Point Cabrillo Light Station and Preserve.** The big news lately is that 19th-century technology replaced that of the 20th century in 1998, thanks to the restoration efforts of dedicated volunteers. The light station's original Fresnel lens once again casts its light seaward. Though access to buildings is not allowed during restoration, which continues, guided walks of the area are offered May–Sept. on Sun. at 11 A.M.

For details about headlands access, call 707/937-5804. For information on whale-watching weekends and guided 1.5-mile walks at the preserve, call 707/937-0816 or try www.pointcabrillo.org.

Jug Handle State Reserve

For serious naturalists, the "ecological staircase" hike at this reserve just north of Caspar is well worth a few hours of wandering. The staircase

Jug Handle State Reserve

KIM WEIR

itself is a series of uplifted marine terraces, each 100 feet higher than the last, crafted by nature. The fascination here is the *change* associated with each step up the earth ladder, expressed by distinctive plants that also slowly change the environment.

The only way to get to the staircase trail is by heading west from the parking lot to Jug Handle Bay, then east again on the trails as marked, hiking under the highway. The trail was in some disrepair recently, so heads up. For more information about Jug Handle State Reserve, contact the Mendocino area state parks headquarters at Russian Gulch State Park, 707/937-5804.

MacKerricher State Park

This gorgeous stretch of ocean and forested coastal prairie starts three miles north of Fort Bragg and continues northward for seven miles. Down on the beach, you can stroll for hours past white-sand beaches, black-sand beaches, remote dunes, sheer cliffs and headlands, offshore islands, pounding surf, rocky outcroppings, and abundant tidepools. Or you can stay up atop the low bluff paralleling the shore, where you'll revel in great ocean views and, in spring, an abundance of delicate, butterfly-speckled wildflowers.

The park's usage is de facto separated into two areas: the tourist area (crowded) and the locals' areas (desolate). Tourist usage centers around the park's little **Lake Cleone**, a fishable freshwater lagoon near the campground and picnic area. Nearby are a picturesque crescent beach pounded by a thundering shore break, and the **Laguna Point** day-use area (wheelchair accessible), a popular place for watching whales offshore and harbor seals onshore. (Another good local spot for whale-watching is **Todd's Point,** south of the Noyo Bridge, then west on Ocean View). That's the tourist's MacKerricher. Not bad. And most visitors to the park don't venture far from it.

Which leaves the locals and savvy passersby to enjoy in blissful, meditative solitude the extensive areas to the south and north, which are connected to the lake/campground area by the eight-mile-long **Old Haul Road.** Once used by logging trucks, the now-abandoned haul road parallels the shore from **Pudding Creek Beach** in the south to **Ten Mile River** in the north. Only a short stretch of the road is open to vehicles, so

it's a great path for bicyclists and joggers. North of the campground area, the asphalt road gradually deteriorates until it gets buried completely by the deserted and exquisite Ten Mile Dunes; if you venture up the coast this far, you'll likely have it all to yourself. South of the campground, the road passes a few vacation homes and a gravel plant before ending up just past a parking lot and a phalanx of beachfront tourist motels. (If you wander far enough south, you'll end up at Fort Bragg's **Glass Beach** just north of town, where if you're lucky you might find a Japanese fishing float or an occasional something from a shipwreck.) Either way, you'll get magnificent ocean views and plenty of solitude.

The fine campgrounds at MacKerricher are woven into open woods of beach, Monterey, and Bishop pines. Campsites are abundant (no hookups), with the usual amenities. It's a popular place, so reservations are wise; call ReserveAmerica toll-free, 800/444-7275. No day-use fee. For more information, call MacKerricher at 707/964-9112 or the Mendocino state parks headquarters at 707/937-5804.

STAYING IN AND NEAR MENDOCINO

The battle of the bed-and-breakfasts in and around Mendocino is just one aspect of the continuing local war over commercial and residential development. The conversion of homes to bed-and-breakfast establishments means fewer housing options for people who live here, but a moratorium on B&Bs means higher prices for visitor accommodations.

ACCOMMODATIONS RATINGS

Accommodations in this book are rated by price category, based on double-occupancy, high-season rates. Categories used are:

Budget.	$35 and under
Inexpensive	$35-60
Moderate	$60-85
Expensive	$85-110
Premium	$110-150
Luxury	$150 and up

LITTLE RIVER INN

In "downtown" Little River, the classic stay is the family-owned **Little River Inn,** just south of Van Damme State Park at 7751 N. Hwy. 1, 707/937-5942 or toll-free 888/466-5683, fax 707/937-3944, www.littleriverinn.com, originally just one rambling old mansion built by lumberman Silas Coombs in the area's characteristic Maine style. The old inn itself is still a slice of Victorian gingerbread. Upstairs are two small and affordable rooms—and really the best, in terms of period charm: quilt-padded attic accommodations illuminated by tiny seaward-spying dome windows. In addition to its classic fireplace cottages and updated lodging annex, the inn now includes romantic luxury suites just up the hill—complete with gigantic hot tubs, wood-burning fireplaces, view decks and patios, and every imaginable amenity. Expensive-Luxury (but inquire about specials and packages). Two-night minimum stay on weekends, three-night on holiday weekends.

Little River also offers an 18-hole golf course—the only one on the Mendocino Coast—and tennis facilities. (For tee times, call 707/937-5667.) In addition to full meeting and small-conference facilities, new is **The Third Court** day spa, with a full menu of men's and women's body and facial massages, skin treatments, and hair and nail care. (For spa reservations, call 707/937-3099.) Tucked in behind appealing **Ole's Whale Watch Bar** (good bar menu) is the Little River Inn's **Garden Dining Room.** The restaurant serves great food, including simple and excellent white-tablecloth breakfasts with Swedish pancakes, absolutely perfect eggs, and fresh-squeezed orange or grapefruit juice. The inn's restaurant is just about the only room in sight without an ocean view, but it does feature many windows—these opening out into lush and inviting gardens.

Avoid contributing to the problem altogether by camping. There are almost endless choices among the state parks nearby, and some very enjoyable, very reasonable alternatives inland along Hwy. 128 toward Ukiah (see Anderson Valley in the Wine Country chapter). More than 2,000 commercial guest rooms are available in and around Mendocino, but that doesn't mean there's room at the inn (or motel) for spontaneous travelers. Usually people can find last-minute lodgings of some sort in Fort Bragg, though the general rule here is plan ahead or risk sleeping in your car or nestled up against your bicycle in the cold fog.

To stay in style in Mendocino, there are some great places to choose from. Reservations are absolutely necessary at most places on most weekends and during summer, preferably at least one month in advance (longer for greater choice). Most bed-and-breakfasts require a two-night minimum stay on weekends (three-night for holiday weekends) and a deposit.

A number of the inns listed below, in both Mendocino and Fort Bragg, are members of the **Mendocino Coast Innkeepers Association,** P.O. Box 1141, Mendocino, CA 95460, and if one inn is full, it's possible that another can be accommodating. (Request a current brochure for full information.) **Mendocino Coast Reservations,** 1000 Main St., P.O. Box 1143, Mendocino, CA 95460, 707/937-1000, 707/937-5033, or toll-free 800/262-7801, www.mendocinovacations.com, offers 60 or so fully furnished rentals by the weekend, week, or month, from cottages and cabins to homes and family reunion–size retreats.

Mendocino Hotel

The grand 1878 **Mendocino Hotel & Garden Suites,** 45080 Main St., 707/937-0511 or toll-free 800/548-0513, fax 707/937-0513, www.mendocinohotel.com, is one of those Mendocino experiences everyone should try at least once. All 51 of its meticulous rooms and suites—24 Victorian rooms and two suites in the historic building, and 25 one- and two-story garden rooms and suites—are furnished in American and European antiques; many have fireplaces or wood-burning stoves and views of Mendocino Bay or the one-acre gardens, plus such not-like-home little luxuries as heated towel racks, fresh flowers from someone else's garden, and chocolate truffles on the pillow at bedtime. Victorian rooms with in-room washbasins and shared baths (across the hall) are Moderate. Other rooms are Premium-Luxury—but inquire about off-season specials, which can be quite attractive.

Bed-and-Breakfasts in the Village

Selecting "the best" bed-and-breakfasts in an area like Mendocino is like asking parents which of their children they love best. A new star in

STANFORD INN BY THE SEA

How organic can you get? To find out, head for the comfortably luxurious yet outdoorsy Stanford Inn by the Sea (known in a previous incarnation as the Big River Lodge), 44850 Comptche-Ukiah Rd. (at Hwy. 1, on the south bank of Big River), 707/937-5615 or toll-free 800/331-8884, fax 707/937-0305, www.stanfordinn.com. This is an elegant but friendly lodge in the country tradition, with big gardens. But here, the working certified organic garden and farm—Big River Nurseries—dominate the setting. The swimming pool, sauna, and spa are enclosed in one of the farm's greenhouses. The on-site **The Ravens** restaurant is strictly (and deliciously) vegetarian and/or vegan, even serving organic wines. The inn may be organic, but it's not overly fussy—pets are welcome, for a fee, and "guest-friendly" dogs, cats, llamas, and swans are available for those who arrive petless. The Stanford Inn also provides exercise facilities and complimentary mountain bikes; canoe and kayak rentals are available.

The 33 guest rooms and suites are inviting and outdoorsy, paneled in pine and redwood, and decked out with big four-poster or sleigh beds and decent reading lights. Each features a wood-burning fireplace or Irish Waterford stove, as well as houseplants and original local art. Amenities include in-room coffee makers and refrigerators, TV with cable and Cinemax, and stereos with CD players (on-site CD library, or bring your own). Luxury, complimentary gourmet breakfast included, but ask about the Stanford Inn's Health Kick and other special packages.

town, and amazingly elegant even for Mendocino, is **The Whitegate Inn,** 499 Howard St., 707/937-4892 or toll-free 800/531-7282, fax 707/937-1131, www.whitegateinn.com. This classic Victorian itself served as a star vehicle—in the classic *The Russians Are Coming* as well as Julia Roberts's *Dying Young* and Bette Davis's *Strangers*. But visitors don't stay strangers for long, once they step past that white gate and succumb to the Whitegate's charms. The entire inn, including the seven guest rooms, is impeccably decorated in French, Italian, and Victorian antiques. Amenities include fireplaces, European featherbeds and toiletries, down comforters, TVs, and clock radios—not to mention fresh-baked cookies and bedtime chocolates. Breakfast is also sumptuous. But don't forget to smell the roses—and all the other flowers—in the spectacular cottage garden. Premium-Luxury.

The charming **MacCallum House,** 45020 Albion St., 707/937-0289 or toll-free 800/609-0492, www.maccallumhouse.com, is the town's most venerable bed-and-breakfast. This 1882 Victorian and its barn rooms and garden cottages, lovingly restored, still have a friendly quilts-and-steamer-trunk feel—like a fantasy weekend visit to Grandma's farm, if Grandma had some sense of style. MacCallum House features a total of 19 rooms, all with private baths. Six are in the main house, some of these named after members of the MacCallum family. Another six are in the barn, including the very special Upper Barn Loft. Of the seven cottages, the Gazebo Playhouse is most affordable, and the Greenhouse Cottage is wheelchair accessible. Rates include a creative continental breakfast. Expensive-Luxury, but ask about the Winter Whale Watch Special and other packages. Also on the premises are the excellent **MacCallum House Restaurant** and the **Grey Whale Bar & Café,** 707/937-5763, www.maccallumhousedining.com, owned and overseen by Chef Alan Kantor, a graduate of the Culinary Institute of America. Both serve regional cuisine (seasonally changing menu), including fresh seafood and shellfish, meats and poultry, organic produce, and north coast wines. And don't miss the house-made ice creams. Reservations recommended.

The fine **Joshua Grindle Inn,** 44800 Little Lake Rd., 707/937-4143 or toll-free 800/474-6353, www.joshgrin.com, is a New England country-style inn with 10 exquisite rooms furnished with Early Americana. The historic main building, surrounded with stunning cypress, was built in 1879 by local banker Joshua Grindle. All have private bathrooms; most feature wood-burning fireplaces or woodstoves; and some have deep soak tubs or other special features. Particularly inviting, for a little extra privacy, are the two large rooms in the converted water tower out back and the two "saltbox cottage" rooms. Rates include a sumptuous full breakfast. Premium-Luxury, but ask about the inn's various off-season packages. Joshua Grindle also offers an ocean-view guesthouse, located near the Point Cabrillo Light Station, north of Russian Gulch State Park.

For something more contemporary and "country," try the **Agate Cove Inn,** just north of downtown at 11201 N. Lansing St., 707/937-0551 or toll-free 800/527-3111, fax 707/937-0550, www.agatecove.com, which offers two rooms in an 1860s farmhouse (built by Mathias Brinzing, founder of Mendocino's first brewery) and a cluster of eight cottages, all on an acre and a half of beautifully landscaped grounds. Most rooms have fireplaces and ocean views; all have private baths, country decor, and beds with Scandia down comforters. Enjoy a fabulous full country breakfast (cooked on an antique woodstove) of omelettes or other entrées with country sausage or ham, homebaked breads, jams and jellies, and coffee or tea. Premium-Luxury. The **Sea Rock Bed and Breakfast Inn,** 11101 Lansing St., 707/937-0926 or toll-free 800/906-0926, www.searock.com, is also a collection of country cottages and guest rooms, most of these with Franklin fireplaces; a few have kitchens, and all have private bath, queen bed, cable TV, and VCR. Breakfast buffet served in the lobby. Premium-Luxury.

The **John Dougherty House Bed & Breakfast,** 571 Ukiah St., 707/937-5266 or toll-free 800/486-2104, www.jdhouse.com, is a Mendocino classic. This 1867 Saltbox, surrounded by English gardens and filled with Early American antiques, is included on the town's historic house tour. Its two light, airy suites and six rooms all have private baths, and some have spa tubs and woodstoves. There's also a charming cabin in the garden. Bountiful hot breakfast. Premium-Luxury.

Bed-and-Breakfasts near the Village
Rachel Binah is a creative cook and caterer also noted for her **Rachel's Inn,** 8200 N. Hwy. 1, 707/937-0088 or toll-free 800/347-9252, www.rachelsinn.com, with five rooms in the Victorian farmhouse and four suites in the adjacent barn. Just north of Van Damme State Park, the inn abuts an undeveloped strip of the park just two miles south of Mendocino. Each room has its own bathroom, a big bed, fresh flowers and personal amenities, plus individual charm: a view of the ocean or gardens, a balcony, or a fireplace. If you rent all or a combination of rooms for a casual conference or family gathering, special dinners can be arranged. Any day of the week, a good full breakfast is served in the dining room. Premium-Luxury.

HERITAGE HOUSE

South of Little River proper, the **Heritage House,** 5200 N. Hwy. 1, 707/937-5885 or toll-free 800/235-5885, www.heritagehouseinn.com, was once a safe harbor for that notorious gangster Baby Face Nelson, though things are quite civilized and serene these days. Heritage House itself is an old Maine-style farmhouse (now the inn's dining room, kitchen, and office) and the center of a large complex of antique-rich luxury cottages and suites—the best looking out to sea. Premium-Luxury. Another major attraction is the exceptional yet reasonably relaxed **Heritage House Restaurant,** with its stunning domed dining room, open nightly for dinner—except when the entire establishment is shut down in winter, usually from Thanksgiving through Christmas and again January 2 to President's Day in February. The gardens (and garden shop) at Heritage House are also quite impressive.

Across the highway is **Glendeven,** 8221 N. Hwy. 1, 707/937-0083 or toll-free 800/822-4536, fax 707/937-6108, www.glendeven.com, a part-inn, part-art gallery featuring quilted paper and other textile works, abstract art, and handcrafted furniture. Declared one of the 10 best inns in the United States by *Country Inns* magazine, Glendeven's charms start with the New England Federalist farmhouse, continue into the secluded and luxurious Carriage House, and also surround the Stevenscroft annex. Many rooms and suites feature fireplaces and ocean views. Not to mention every imaginable amenity and a sumptuous breakfast. Premium-Luxury.

South of Mendocino are several other options. Notable among them is **Cypress Cove** on Chapman Point, 45200 Chapman Dr., 707/937-1456 or toll-free 800/942-6300, www.cypresscove.com, quite the place to get away from it all. The property's two luxury suites look out on Mendocino and the bay. Amenities include queen beds, fireplaces, and two-person hot tubs. Among the plush extras: in-room coffee, tea, brandy, chocolate, fresh flowers, and bathrobes. One suite has a full kitchen, the other a kitchenette. Luxury.

In Little River, folksy **The Inn at Schoolhouse Creek,** 7051 N. Hwy. 1, 707/937-5525 or toll-free 800/731-5525, www.binnb.com, features restored

1930s country-style garden cottages looking downslope to the ocean. All have a fireplace, private bath, and a TV and VCR. Rates include full breakfast, access to the welcoming lodge (books, games, and breakfast), and a chance to jump into that hot tub. Premium-Luxury.

Farther south and right along the highway is the beautiful **Albion River Inn**, 3790 N. Hwy. 1, Albion, 707/937-1919 or toll-free 800/479-7944, www.albionriverinn.com, offering 22 rooms in bluff-top cottages, each one unique. Fireplaces, decks, and ocean views are par for the course here, and the inn's elegant and très-gourmet restaurant draws locals south from Mendocino and Fort Bragg. Rates include full breakfast, wine, coffee and tea, and morning newspaper. Luxury.

The unusually charismatic **Fensalden Inn**, seven miles south of Mendocino and then inland, at 33810 Navarro Ridge Rd., Albion, 707/937-4042 or toll-free 800/959-3850, www.fensalden.com, is a restored two-story stage station circa 1880, still straddling the ridge top among open fields and forests. Under new ownership, the eight charming rooms feature exquisite antiques; all have fireplaces. For the more rustically inclined, there's also a Rustic Bungalow. Hors d'oeuvres, wine, and full breakfast are complimentary. Premium-Luxury.

STAYING IN FORT BRAGG

Bed-and-Breakfasts

The boxy, weathered, clear-heart redwood **Grey Whale Inn**, 615 Main St., 707/964-0640 or toll-free 800/382-7244, fax 707/964-4408, www.greywhaleinn.com, was once the community hospital. If you're one of those people who don't think they like bed-and-breakfasts—under any circumstances—this place could be the cure for what ails you. The two-story whale of an inn offers peace and privacy, very wide hallways, 14 individually decorated rooms and suites (some quite large) with myriad amenities, a basement pool table and rec room, fireplace, and an award-winning breakfast buffet of hot dish, cereals, coffeecakes, fresh fruits and juices, yogurt or cheese, and good coffee. (And if you don't feel too sociable in the morning, load up a tray in the breakfast room and take breakfast back to bed with you.) A truly exceptional stay—and some of the rooms are quite affordable. Expensive-Luxury. From here it's an easy walk to the *Skunk Train* depot and downtown, to Glass Beach, and to area restaurants.

For fans of Victoriana, a particularly inviting local bed-and-breakfast is the 1886 **Weller House Inn**, 524 Stewart St., 707/964-4415 or toll-free 877/893-5537, fax 707/964-4198, www.wellerhouse.com—the only Mendocino Coast inn listed on the National Register of Historic Places. The seven Victorian guest rooms all have private baths; some have a fireplace or woodstove, hot tub, or clawfoot bathtub. "Very full" breakfast is served in the 900-square-foot ballroom, completely paneled in exquisite old redwood. Expensive-Luxury.

The two-story **Noyo River Lodge**, 500 Casa del Noyo Dr., 707/964-8045 or toll-free 800/628-1126, www.mcn.org/a/noyoriver, is a redwood Craftsman-style mansion (circa 1868) on a hill with harbor and ocean views, rooms and suites with private baths (some with fireplaces), a restaurant and lounge, big soaking tubs, skylights, and gardens. Premium. The **Avalon House**, 561 Stewart St., 707/964-5555 or toll-free 800/964-5556, is a 1905 Craftsman with six rooms (three with in-room spas, three with fireplaces). Moderate-Premium. The newly restored **Old Coast Hotel**, 101 N. Franklin St., 707/961-4488, has 16 rooms and a hot tub; its adjoining bar and grill is a pleasant place for dinner or a cocktail. Expensive-Luxury.

Motels and Lodges

Mendocino has most of the bed-and-breakfasts, but Fort Bragg has the motels—in general the most reasonable accommodations option around besides camping. Most places have cheaper off-season rates, from November through March or April. Pick up a current listing of area motels at the chamber office (see Mendocino Coast Information and Services, below).

The **Anchor Lodge** in Noyo (office in The Wharf Restaurant), 780 N. Harbor Dr., 707/964-4283, has 19 rooms. Inexpensive-Expensive. The **Fort Bragg Motel** is at 763 N. Main St., 707/964-4787 or toll-free 800/253-9972. Inexpensive-Expensive. The **Surf Motel** is at 1220 S. Main St. (just south of the Noyo River Bridge), 707/964-5361 or toll-free 800/339-5361, fax 707/964-3187, www.surfmotelfortbragg.com.

Moderate-Expensive. The **Surrey Inn** is just north of the bridge at 888 S. Main, 707/964-4003 or toll-free 800/206-9833. Inexpensive-Moderate. **Harbor Lite Lodge,** 120 N. Harbor Dr., 707/964-0221 or toll-free 800/643-2700, overlooks Noyo Harbor from just off the highway. Moderate-Expensive.

You'll find a cluster of places on the beach side of the highway, just north of town past the Pudding Creek trestle. These places provide easy access to the Haul Road and beach. Try the very friendly **Beachcomber Motel,** 1111 N. Main St., 707/964-2402 or toll-free 800/400-7873, www.thebeachcombermotel.com (Moderate-Luxury), which sometimes welcomes pets, or the **Surf 'n Sand Lodge,** 1131 N. Main (Hwy. 1), 707/964-9383 or toll-free 800/964-0184 (Moderate-Luxury). Across the highway is the newish **Beach House Inn,** 100 Pudding Creek Rd., 707/961-1700 or toll-free 888/559-9992, www.beachinn.com. Moderate-Expensive.

EATING IN MENDOCINO

Mendocino Basics
For the **Mendocino Certified Farmers' Market,** which runs May–Oct., show up on Fri., noon–2 P.M., at Howard and Main Sts.; for details, call 707/937-2728. Otherwise stock up on natural foods, for here or to go, at **Corners of the Mouth,** 45015 Ukiah St., 707/937-5345, and get general groceries at **Mendosa's,** 10501 Lansing St., 707/937-5879.

For a hefty slice of pizza or quiche, a bowl of homemade soup, or just a good danish and a cafe latte, head for the **Mendocino Bakery,** 10485 Lansing, 707/937-0836. It's the locals' coffee house of choice and offers outdoor seating when the weather's nice. Open 7:30 A.M.–7 P.M. weekdays, 8:00 A.M.–7 P.M. weekends. The **Mendo Juice Joint,** on Ukiah a half block east of Lansing, 707/937-4033, specializes in fresh juices, smoothies, and healthy snacks.

Mendo Burgers, 10483 Lansing, 707/937-1111, is open 11 A.M.–7:30 P.M. and serves beef-, turkey-, fish-, and veggie-burgers. For that sweet tooth, try the famous ice cream (including quarter-pounder cones) at the **Mendocino Ice Cream Company,** 45090 Main, 707/937-5884; and the definitely decadent

chocolates at **Mendocino Chocolate Company,** 10483 Lansing, 707/937-1107.

Simple and Good
Herbivorous visitors will be right at home at **Lu's Kitchen,** 45013 Ukiah St., 707/937-4939, which serves "organic cross-cultural vegetarian cuisine" in a casual atmosphere. Look for salads, quesadillas, and burritos in the $4–7 range. One of the best views in town is from the big deck at the **Mendocino Café,** 10451 Lansing St., 707/937-2422 or 707/937-6141, which has a great menu of Pacific Rim–inspired cuisine (try the Thai burrito) and a good beer selection. Another place for great views—but in a slightly more upscale atmosphere—is the **Bay View Cafe,** 45040 Main St. (upstairs), 707/937-4197, which enjoys unobstructed views of the coast from its bay-window-lined, second-story perch.

Cafe Beaujolais
No one should come anywhere near Mendocino without planning to eat at least one meal at the noted Cafe Beaujolais, 961 Ukiah St., 707/937-5614, now under new ownership. The fresh-flower decor inside and on the deck of this old house is as refreshingly simple and fine as the food itself. Some of us still haven't gotten over the fact that Cafe Beaujolais is no longer open for breakfast. (Beaujolais granola, pancake mix, and other take-home items are available.)

Dinner is a fixed-price French-and-California-cuisine affair featuring such things as local smoked salmon and roast duck with a puree of apples and turnips. Cafe Beaujolais is open nightly 5:45–9 P.M., though the restaurant is closed from late November through January. Reservations are necessary. Bring cash or personal checks; no credit cards accepted. The restaurant's bakery, called The Brickery, produces breads and pizzas from a wood-fired brick oven. It's open daily, 11 A.M. to 4 or 5 P.M.

Other Worthy Restaurants
Neighbor to the much-more-famous Cafe Beaujolais is **955 Ukiah St.,** 707/937-1955, difficult to find in the fog despite its numerically straightforward attitude. (The entrance is 100 feet off the street around a few corners.) The dining room itself is a former art studio, and dinners feature excellent fresh seafood, unforgettable

bread sticks, and Navarro and Husch wines from the Anderson Valley. No credit cards. Open Wed.–Sun. from 6 P.M. Also quite good in town is the **MacCallum House Restaurant,** 45020 Albion, 707/937-5763, open nightly for dinner, and the **Moosse Café,** 390 Kasten St., 707/937-4323, featuring an eclectic menu of north coast fare—and sumptuous chocolate desserts reminiscent of its original local incarnation as the Chocolate Moosse Café. Open for lunch and dinner daily, and brunch on Sunday.

For prime rib, steaks, and seafood in a semi-formal Victorian setting, consider the crystal-and-Oriental-carpet ambience of the **Mendocino Hotel,** 45080 Main St., 707/937-0511. The hotel's Garden Court restaurant and bar (the ceiling almost one immense skylight to keep the garden going) serves more casual lunch fare, good salads, sandwiches, and specials. Open daily for breakfast, lunch, and dinner.

EATING NEAR MENDOCINO

You can always find a good meal at the **Little River Inn,** which is particularly noted for its breakfasts and brunches but also offers fine American-classic dinners emphasizing steak and seafood. Another restaurant in town well worth seeking out is the elegantly simple **Little River Restaurant** (unaffiliated with the Little River Inn), 7750 N. Hwy. 1 (tucked away behind the post office), 707/937-4945. Don't miss it. Only 14 people can squeeze in here at any one time, but what they sit down to is a perfect meal, soup through excellent dessert, with entrées like roast lamb in mustard sauce. Reservations essential, especially on weekends. For fine dining, another top area destination is the **Heritage House Restaurant,** 5200 Hwy. 1 south of Little River, 707/937-5885, with its seasonally changing menu of superb north coast cuisine.

At the intimately elegant **Ledford House,** 3000 N. Hwy. 1 (south of "downtown" Albion), 707/937-0282, even vegetarians can try the excellent soups because none are made with meat bases. Entrées include pasta picks like ravioli stuffed with ricotta cheese in sorrel cream sauce, and some definitely nonstandard seafood and meat specialties.

EATING IN FORT BRAGG

Finding a meal in Fort Bragg is a more relaxed task than in Mendocino, with less confusion from

---

SHOPPING MENDOCINO

Despite its small size, Mendocino is stuffed with shops and stores, enough to keep shopping addicts happy for an entire weekend. **Alphonso's Mercantile,** 520 Main St. (between Kasten and Osborne), is a classical music store and smokeshop (even though Alphonso doesn't smoke anymore) with a million-dollar view of the coast. Music lovers should stroll into **Lark in the Morning,** 10460 Kasten St., 707/937-5275, with its trove of hand drums, unique stringed instruments, and even accordions. If you forgot to pack some summer reading, plan to spend some quality time at the **Gallery Bookshop & Bookwinkle's Children's Books** at Main and Kasten Sts., 707/937-2215, www.gallerybooks.com, a truly impressive independent bookstore.

Wind & Weather, in the Albion St. water tower (at Kasten), sells all kinds of devices bearing some sort of meteorological relevance—from rain gauges to anemometers to weathervanes, wind chimes, and sundials. Much of the stuff is downright fun. For a complete catalog, call toll-free 800/922-9463. Also fascinating and very Mendocino is **Mendosa's Merchandise and Market,** 10501 Lansing (at Little Lake), 707/937-5879, one of those rare *real* hardware stores long gone from most California communities. Quite the contrast but equally wonderful (with its "food for people, not for profit" slogan) is the collectively run **Corners of the Mouth** natural food store, 45015 Ukiah (between Ford and Lansing), 707/937-5345.

Venerable **Dick's Place,** 45070 Main St., 707/937-5643, with few concessions to the changing times, is still Mendocino's real bar. Inside, the locals drink beer, plug the jukebox (lots of good Patsy Cline), and play darts. Outside, the bar's sign (a distinctly un-P.C. neon 50s-style martini glass grandfathered in under local anti-neon ordinances) is visible from miles away through the regularly dense coastal fog. Next door, and a sign of changing times, is the **Fetzer Wine Tasting Room,** 707/937-6191, open daily 10 A.M.–6 P.M.

SHOPPING FORT BRAGG

People think first of Mendocino when they think of art galleries, but Fort Bragg has at least as many—and more of the "working artist" variety. Not to be missed is the nonprofit **Northcoast Artists Collaborative Gallery,** 362 N. Main St., 707/964-8266, with everything from wearable art (weavings and handpainted silk scarves) and handcrafted jewelry to original art, prints, pottery, photographs, and greeting cards made by member artists. A very impressive enterprise. Also drop by the **Fort Bragg Center for the Arts,** 337 N. Franklin St., 707/964-0807, to see what's going on. The center is within Fort Bragg's **Gallery District**—between Main and Franklin, and Redwood and Fir—so while you're in the area, see what else looks interesting. North Franklin St. be-tween Laurel and Redwood boasts a number of **antique shops.**

Also unique in Fort Bragg is **Adirondack Design,** 350 Cypress St., P.O. Box 656, Fort Bragg, CA 95437, 707/964-4940 or toll-free 888/643-3003 (orders only), www.adirondackdesign.com. Founded by a group known as Parents and Friends, Inc., Adirondack Design provides jobs and services for the area's developmentally disabled adults. And what a job this crew does—crafting a high-quality line of redwood garden furniture and accessories, everything from Adirondack chairs, loveseats, rockers, and swings to garden benches and planters, cold frames, and a charming "bird chalet." Adirondack even produces a small footbridge.

the madding crowds. Most restaurants are casual. For farm-fresh everything, show up for the **Fort Bragg Certified Farmers' Market,** held May–Oct. on Wed., 3:30–6 P.M., at Laurel and Franklin. Call 707/964-0536 for details. For something unusual to take home as a memento, stop by Carol Hall's **Hot Pepper Jelly Company,** 330 N. Main, 707/961-1422 or toll-free 800/892-4823, an inviting shop that sells some intriguing jams and jellies, fruit syrups, mustards, herb vinegars, and unusual food-related gift items. For a sweet treat, **Goody's,** 144 N. Franklin St., 707/964-7800, is the town's old-time malt shop and soda fountain, complete with checkerboard counter (open weekdays and Saturdays). Another possibility is the **Mendocino Chocolate Company,** 542 N. Main St., 707/964-8800 or toll-free 800/722-1107 (for orders), which serves up everything from edible seashells and Mendocino toffee to an amazing array of truffles and chews—including Fort Bragg 2x4s (peanut butter–flavored fudge "veneered" with dark chocolate) and Mr. Peanut Coastal Clusters. Though this is their headquarters, there's another company outlet in Mendocino.

Breakfast and Lunch

The venerable **Egghead Omelettes of Oz,** 326 N. Main St., 707/964-5005, is a cheerful diner with booths, the whole place decorated in a Wizard of Oz theme. (Follow the Yellow Brick Road through the kitchen to the restrooms out back.) Equally unforgettable, on the menu, are fried potatoes and omelettes with endless combinations for fillings, including avocado and crab. Good sandwiches at lunch. Open daily 7 A.M.–2 P.M. For picnic fixin's or a special gift for that hard-to-please carnivore, just north is the **Round Man's Smoke House,** 412 N. Main, toll-free 800/545-2935, which specializes in all kinds of meat-eater's delights, from smoked chinook or pepper salmon and salmon jerky to Canadian bacon and turkey apple sausage; Round Man's also sells some delightful cheeses.

Around the corner is the charming **Headlands Coffeehouse,** 120 E. Laurel St., 707/964-1987, an artsy place with an interesting crowd of locals, all the usual espresso drinks, delicious healthy food (for breakfast, try the Belgian waffle with fruit and yogurt), and regular live acoustic music. Also a best bet for coffee, bakery items, and simple lunch is the **Thanksgiving Coffee Café,** 120 Main St., 707/964-5767, open daily 7:30 A.M.–4 P.M.

At lunch, locals line up for the Dagwood-style sandwiches at **David's Deli,** 450 S. Franklin St., 707/964-1946, but breakfast here is pretty special, too. For a unique atmosphere, head just south of town to the Mendocino Coast Botanical Gardens, where you can dine with garden views at the **Gardens Grill,** 18220 N. Hwy. 1, 707/964-7474. It's open for lunch Mon.–Sat., for dinner Thurs.–Sat., and for Sunday brunch.

American-Style and Special

When locals want a special dinner, they often head to the **Rendezvous Inn & Restaurant,** just down the street from the Grey Whale Inn at 647 N. Main St., 707/964-8142 or toll-free 800/491-8142. This gorgeous homey bungalow with warm wood interiors serves marvelous crab cakes, jambalaya, vegetarian pasta and "beggar's purses," civet of venison, and other unusual entrées, starting from the freshest local ingredients. Open Wed.–Sun. for dinner. Upstairs are several guest rooms, each with private bath (Moderate-Expensive). Another good choice is **The Restaurant,** 418 N. Main St., 707/964-9800, where the California-style fare might include delectable entrées such as poached halibut, calamari, scallops, shrimp, steak, and quail. Open for lunch and dinner (call for current schedule) and Sunday brunch. Children's menu. Reservations wise.

Fort Bragg's favorite fancy seafood restaurant, open for dinner only, is **The Cliff House,** just south of the Harbor Bridge, 1011 S. Main St., 707/961-0255. Overlooking the jetty and the harbor, The Cliff House serves wonderful seafood and pastas—try the smoked salmon ravioli—and steaks, along with specialties including chicken mushroom Dijon and pepper steak. On Fri. and Sat. night, prime rib is also on the menu.

In a little less rarified atmosphere, good food is also available at **North Coast Brewing Co. Taproom and Restaurant,** 444 N. Main, 707/964-3400, a brewpub and grill pouring award-winning handmade ales to accompany pub grub (including Route 66 chili), pastas, steaks, seafood, and Cajun-inspired dishes. On a sunny day, the outside beer garden—a genuine garden, quite appealing—can't be beat. Beer lovers take note: North Coast is among the finest of North American microbreweries, consistently producing brews that always satisfy and frequently astonish even the pickiest connoisseurs. All the offerings are outstanding, but don't miss the unique Belgian-style Pranqster or the positively evil Rasputin imperial stout. Open noon–11 P.M. daily except Monday. Across the street (at 455 N. Main) is the brewery itself, 707/964-2739, www.ncoast-brewing.com, offering free tours on weekdays, along with some memorable memorabilia and gift items.

Relatively new in town but promising is **Mendo Bistro,** 301 Main (at Redwood, upstairs in the Company Store), 707/964-4974. Here you pick a meat or seafood entrée and a style of preparation, then get it served just the way you like it. Prices are low. The restaurant at the restored **Old Coast Hotel,** 101 N. Franklin, 707/961-4488, is another possibility, with a steak and seafood menu. Open for lunch and dinner daily.

Outstanding Ethnic Options

Yes, Fort Bragg has outstanding ethnic food. **Viraporn's,** on S. Main St. at Chestnut (across the street from PayLess), 707/964-7931, serves great Thai food, while **Samraat,** 546 S. Main St., 707/964-0386, specializes in the tastes of India. Both of these restaurants, humble as they may appear from the outside, are worth seeking out.

Just north of town in Cleone, the legendary **Purple Rose,** 24300 N. Hwy. 1, 707/964-6507, prepares delicious and locally famous Mexican food in a bright, spacious, and casual atmosphere. The veggie burrito here is a work of culinary art. Open Wed.–Sun. for dinner. Mexican fare is also available in town at **El Sombrero,** 223 N. Franklin, 707/964-5780.

For Italian, everyone's favorite is **D'Aurelio's,** 438 S. Franklin St., 707/964-4227, which offers outstanding pizzas, calzones, and the like in a comfortable, casual atmosphere. Another possibility is **Bernillo's,** 220 E. Redwood Ave., 707/964-9314.

Fishing for Food in Noyo

Noyo Harbor is where the tourists go for fish. True, you'll find a "school" of inexpensive seafood eateries here amid the comings and goings of fishing boats. But none of the restaurants are memorable for either cuisine or decor. If you don't need the "down on the docks" atmosphere, you'll probably do better satisfying your seafood cravings at one of the "American-style" restaurants listed above.

That said, **The Wharf,** 780 N. Harbor Dr., 707/964-4283, serves a creamy clam chowder and crispy-outside-tender-inside fried clams, and the prime rib sandwich here is nothing to throw a crab pot at. For dinner, specialties include seafood and steak. The specialty at the plastic-tableclothed **Cap'n Flint's,** 32250 N. Harbor, 707/964-9447, is shrimp won tons with

Fishing is a way of life in Noyo Harbor.

cream cheese filling. Open 11 A.M.–8:30 P.M. **El Mexicano,** 701 N. Harbor Dr., 707/964-7164, serves up authentic Mexican food, down to the fresh-daily tortillas. Open daily 10 A.M.–8:30 P.M.

MENDOCINO COAST INFORMATION AND SERVICES

The **Fort Bragg-Mendocino Coast Chamber of Commerce,** 332 N. Main St., P.O. Box 1141, Fort Bragg, CA 95437, 707/961-6300 or toll-free 800/726-2780, fax 707/964-2056, www.mendocinocoast.com, is an incredible resource. It's open Mon.–Tues. and Thurs.–Fri. 9 A.M.–5 P.M., Sat. 11 A.M.–4 P.M. (closed Wednesday and Sunday). Among the free literature published by the chamber is the regularly updated *Mendocino* brochure and map (mostly a shop listing), the *Walking Tour of Historic Fort Bragg* guide, and the new *Something to Bragg About* brochure. Also available here and elsewhere is the free annual *Mendocino Visitor* tabloid, the coast guide to state parks, the *Guide to the Recreational Trails of Mendocino County,* and the Mendocino Art Center's publications. For an "advance packet" of information, send a self-addressed, stamped, legal-size envelope.

For books on the region—and just plain great books—plan to spend some quality time in **Gallery Bookshop & Bookwinkle's Children's Books** in Mendocino at Main and Kasten Sts., 707/937-2215, www.gallerybooks.com, a truly impressive independent bookstore.

The **Fort Bragg post office** is at 203 N. Franklin, 707/964-2302, open weekdays 8:30 A.M.–5 P.M. The **Mendocino post office** is at 10500 Ford St., 707/937-5282; open weekdays 8:30 A.M.–4:30 P.M. The **Mendocino Coast District Hospital,** 700 River Dr., 707/961-1234, offers 24-hour emergency services.

Mendocino Coast Transportation
The **Mendocino Transit Authority** (MTA), based in Ukiah, 707/462-1422, runs one bus each weekday between Ukiah and Gualala via the Navarro River bridge. At the bridge, you can transfer to or from the smaller vans of **Mendocino Stage,** 707/964-0167, which run weekdays between Fort Bragg and Navarro, with stops in Mendocino. The MTA also makes round-trips between Point Arena and Santa Rosa. Connect with **Greyhound** in Ukiah.

Near Little River, a few miles inland from the coast, is the **Little River Airport,** the closest airfield to Mendocino. Private pilots flying into the airport can get a ride into Little River or Mendocino by calling Mendocino Stage.

closed to motorized vehicles, rebel off-roaders are becoming a problem.

Most people come here to "beach backpack," hiking north to south in deference to prevailing winds. The trail saunters along miles of sandy beaches, around some tremendous tidepools, and up onto headlands to bypass craggy coves where streams flow to the sea. Make camp on high ground well back from the restless ocean, and always adhere to the backpacker's credo: if you pack it in, pack it out. There are worthwhile inland trails as well.

The camping fee for the various campgrounds is $5–8 per night, and the day-use fee is $1 per day. Permits are required for building fires and using camp stoves in the backcountry. All organized groups also need BLM permits. For more information, contact: **King Range National Conservation Area,** U.S. Bureau of Land Management, 1695 Heindon Rd., Arcata, CA 95521, 707/825-2300, www.ca.blm.gov/arcata/king_range.html; or the **BLM Ukiah Field Office,** 2550 N. State St., Ukiah, CA 95482, 707/468-4000. For more information on accommodations, restaurants, and services available at Shelter Cove, call the **Shelter Cove Information Bureau** at 707/986-7069, or try the online **Shelter Cove Business Directory** at www.sojourner2000.com.

SINKYONE WILDERNESS STATE PARK

Sinking into Sinkyone is like blinking away all known life in order to finally *see*. Named for the Sinkyone people, who refused to abandon their traditional culture and hire on elsewhere as day laborers, this place somehow still honors that indomitable spirit.

More rugged than even the King Range, at Sinkyone Wilderness State Park jagged peaks plunge into untouched tidepools where sea lions and seals play. Unafraid here, wildlife sputters, flutters, or leaps forth at every opportunity. The land seems lusher and greener, with dark virgin forests of redwoods and mixed conifers, rich grassland meadows, waterfalls, and fern grottos. The one thing trekkers won't find (yet) among these 7,367 wild acres is a vast trail system. Many miles of the coast are accessible to hikers, and much of the rest of the 40-mile main trail system includes a north/south trail and some logging roads.

The trail system connects with trails in the King Range National Conservation Area around the Wailaki area, but you can't reach Sinkyone from Shelter Cove by hiking south along the coast.

Sinkyone Wilderness State Park is always open for day use. The park also offers limited camping at more than 22 scattered and primitive environmental campsites that are rarely full. To get oriented, stop by the park's **visitor center** at **Needle Rock Ranch House.**

Campsites are first-come, first-camped; small per-car day-use fee. Solitude seekers, please note that Sinkyone is particularly crowded on summer holiday weekends. For more information, contact: **Sinkyone Wilderness State Park,** P.O. Box 245, Whitethorn, CA 95589, 707/986-7711 (recorded), or the regional state parks office at **Richardson Grove State Park,** 1600 Hwy. 101 #8, Garberville, CA 95542, 707/247-3319. You can also pick up a park map at the **Humboldt Redwoods State Park Visitor Center,** on the Avenue of the Giants in Weott, north of Garberville.

EEL RIVER COUNTRY

North of Fort Bragg, Hwy. 1 continues up the coast until it's deflected inland by the rugged King Range; details on exploring that landscape are included above under The Lost (and Found) Coast section of this chapter. The highway ends at Leggett, where it merges into Hwy. 101. Here, continue north to enter the realm of the coast redwoods. From Leggett north to just beyond Fortuna, the scenic highway winds alongside the aptly named Eel River, past many redwood groves and riverbank beaches. Among attractions between Leggett and Garberville are Leggett's Drive-Thru-Tree Park, 707/925-6363 or 707/925-6446, and a number of small redwood reserves, including the **Standish-Hickey State Recreation Area,** the **Smithe Redwoods State Reserve,** and **Richardson Grove State Park.** Along the way, too, is **Confusion Hill Fun Center,** 707/925-6456, one of those places where gravity is defied and water runs uphill, etc. North of Richardson Grove is **Benbow Lake State Recreation Area,** 707/923-3238, a summers-only lake created by a temporary dam on the Eel River's south fork. To reserve campsites at Benbow and other area state campgrounds, call ReserveAmerica at toll-free 800/444-7275.

Also at Benbow is the elegant four-story Tudor-style Benbow Inn, 445 Lake Benbow Dr., 707/923-2124 or toll-free 800/355-3301, fax 707/923-2122, www.benbowinn.com. Designed by architect Albert Farr, the **Benbow Inn** first opened its doors in 1926 and over the years has welcomed travelers including Herbert Hoover, Charles Laughton, and Eleanor Roosevelt. A National Historic Landmark, the inn has been restored to a very English attitude. Premium-Luxury, but ask about off-season specials. Complimentary scones and tea are served in the lobby, and the dining room serves a good breakfast, lunch during the summer only, and staples like steak-and-kidney pie for dinner.

the sinsemilla cultivation capital of the world, an honor most locals are fed up with. The general belief today is that the big-time Rambo-style growers have gone elsewhere. But don't expect people here to share their knowledge or opinions on the subject, pro or con. With annual CAMP (Campaign Against Marijuana Production) invasions throughout the surrounding countryside, discretion is the rule of tongue when outsiders show up.

In June, the annual **Rodeo in the Redwoods** is the big to-do in these parts, followed in July or early August by the West Coast's largest and usually most impressive reggae festival—the **Reggae on the River** concert—which attracts top talent from Jamaica and America. For concert information, contact the **Mateel Community Center,** 59 Rusk Ln. in Redway, 707/923-3368.

The locally famous **Woodrose Café,** 911 Redwood, 707/923-3191, is beloved for its fine omelettes, good vegetarian sandwiches, and like fare, everything locally and/or organically grown. Open daily for breakfast, for lunch only on weekdays. A good choice for wheat-bread-and-sprouts-style Sunday champagne brunch. Just northwest of Garberville, across the highway in Redway, is the **Mateel Cafe,** 3344 Redwood Dr., 707/923-2030, a fine-food mecca that lures folks even from San Francisco. With a French chef and an owner who is a nutritionist, count on gourmet fare done right—everything from Thai tofu to seafood linguine and stone-baked pizza. Vegans, carnivores, low-protein or high-protein dieters—all will find something to satisfy and delight. And check out that Jazzbo Room. Open Mon.–Sat. for lunch and dinner.

For more information about the area, contact: **Garberville-Redway Chamber of Commerce,** 773 Redwood Dr., P.O. Box 445, Garberville, CA 95542, 707/923-2613 or toll-free 800/923-2613, open daily 9 A.M.–5 P.M. in summer, and weekdays 9 A.M.–5 P.M. in winter.

GARBERVILLE AND VICINITY

A former sheep ranching town, Garberville is *not* an outlaw enclave paved in $100 bills by pot-growing Mercedes Benz owners, as media mythology would have it. The town was once considered

HUMBOLDT REDWOODS STATE PARK

This is the redwood heart of Humboldt County, where more than 40 percent of the world's redwoods remain. The Save-the-Redwoods League and the state have added to the park's holdings grove by grove. Most of these "dedicated groves," named in honor of those who gave to save the trees, and many of the park's developed camp-grounds are along the state-park section of the Avenue of the Giants parkway.

Humboldt Redwoods State Park is one of the largest state parks in Northern California, with

ICE AGE SURVIVORS: COAST REDWOODS

Though they once numbered an estimated two million, California's native population of coast redwood trees has been reduced through logging and agriculture to isolated groves of virgin trees. The tallest trees in the state but only the fourth oldest, *Sequoia sempervirens* are nonetheless ancient. Well established here when dinosaurs roamed the earth, redwood predecessors flourished throughout the Northern Hemisphere 60 million years ago. Isolated from the rest of their kind by thick ice sheets a million years ago, the redwoods made their last stand in California.

The elders among today's surviving coast redwoods are at least 2,200 years old. These trees thrive in low, foggy areas protected from fierce offshore winds. Vulnerable to both wind and soil erosion, shallow-rooted redwoods tend to topple over during severe storms. Redwoods have no need for deep taproots since fog collects on their needle-like leaves, then drips down the trunk or directly onto the ground, where the equivalent of up to 50 inches of rainfall annually is absorbed by hundreds of square feet of surface roots.

Unlike the stately, individualistic Sierra big trees or *Sequoiadendron giganteum,* the comparatively scrawny coast redwoods reach up to the sky in dense, dark-green clusters—creating living, breathing cathedrals lit by filtered flames of sun or shrouded in foggy silence. The north coast's native peoples religiously avoided inner forest areas, the abode of spirits (some ancestral). But in the modern world, the sacred has become profane. A single coast redwood provides enough lumber for hundreds of hot tubs, patio decks, and wine vats, or a couple of dozen family cabins, or a hefty school complex. Aside from its attractive reddish color, pungent fragrance, and water- and fire-resistance, redwood is also decay-, insect-, and fungus-resistant—and all the more attractive for construction.

Yet coast redwoods never really die. Left to their own devices, redwoods are capable of regenerating themselves without seeds. New young trees shoot up from stumps or from roots around the base of the old tree, forming gigantic woodland fairy rings in second- or third-growth forests. And each of these trees, when mature, can generate its own genetically identical offspring. Sometimes a large, straight limb from a fallen tree will sprout, sending up a straight line of trees. In heavily logged or otherwise traumatized forest areas, tiny winged redwood seeds find room to take root, sprout, and eventually flourish, blending into a forest with stump-regenerated trees.

Coast redwoods never really die, but regenerate in a variety of ways.

CALIFORNIA DEPARTMENT OF PARKS & RECREATION

more than 51,000 acres of almost unfrequented redwood groves, mixed conifers, and oaks. The park offers 35 miles of hiking and backpacking trails, plus 30 miles of old logging roads—and surprising solitude so close to a freeway. Down on the flats are the deepest and darkest stands of virgin redwoods, including Rockefeller Forest, the world's largest stand of stately survivors.

Humboldt Big Trees

At almost 13,000 acres, **Rockefeller Forest** is the main grove here and among the most valuable virgin stands of redwood remaining on the north coast (and yes, it was donated to the world by the John D. Rockefeller family). In **Founder's Grove,** the Founder's Tree was once erroneously known as the World's Tallest Tree; the park's Dyerville Giant is—or was—actually the park's tallest at 362 feet, when last measured in 1972 (the Giant toppled over in a 1991 storm and now lies on the forest floor), and even taller trees reach skyward in Redwood National Park north of Orick. But the Founder's Tree and Dyerville Giant are two mindful monuments to the grandeur of the natural world. After exploring Founder's Grove, consider the nearby **Immortal Tree,** which has withstood almost every imaginable onslaught from both nature and humanity—a testament to this tree's tenacity, and perhaps the forest's.

Not the largest tree or most martyred but a notable one nevertheless is the ***Metasequoia,*** which you can see near Weott (and south down the highway at Richardson Grove State Park). It's a dawn redwood native to China, kissing cousin of both species of California redwoods.

Practical Humboldt Redwoods

Camping is easy at Humboldt Redwoods, which offers hundreds of campsites and four picnic areas. **Burlington Campground** near Weott is fully developed (hot showers, restrooms, tables—the works for outdoor living). Ditto for the **Albee Creek Campground** not far to the south, and **Hidden Springs Campground** near Miranda. All three of these campgrounds are popular, so make advance reservations in summer through ReserveAmerica, toll-free 800/444-7275.

Unusual at Humboldt Redwoods State Park are five backcountry backpackers' camps, reservable in advance (first-come) at park headquarters. In addition to the outback pleasures of these backcountry camps, the park features two walk-in environmental campgrounds: **Baxter** and **Hamilton Barn** (pick apples in the old orchard), both with convenient yet secluded campsites; sign up at park headquarters, where you can get the particulars. Group camps and horse camps are also available. Should all the state

---

AVENUE OF THE GIANTS

This scenic 33-mile drive on the old highway, a narrow asphalt ribbon braiding together the eastern edge of Humboldt Redwoods, the Eel River, and Hwy. 101, weaves past and through some of the largest groves of the largest remaining redwoods in Humboldt and Del Norte Counties. Get off the bike (the avenue's very nice for cycling, but wear bright clothing) or out of the car and picnic, take a short walk, and just *appreciate* these grand old giants.

The part-private, part-public Avenue is dotted with commercial attractions—tourist traps offering redwood knickknacks and trinkets manufactured overseas and trees transformed into walk-in or drive-through freaks of nature. But the curio shops and commercial trappings barely distract from the fragrant grandeur of the dim, dignified forest itself, sunlit in faint slivers and carpeted with oxalis and ferns.

Among the tiny towns dwarfed still more by the giants along the Avenue are **Redcrest, Meyers Flat,** and **Phillipsville.** In Redcrest you'll find the **Eternal Tree House,** 26510 Avenue of the Giants, 707/722-4262 (gift shop) or 707/722-4247 (café), a 20-foot room inside a living tree. Meyers Flat boasts one of the state's oldest tourist attractions, the **Shrine Drive-Thru-Tree & Gift Shop,** 13078 Avenue of the Giants, 707/943-3154. Wagon-train travelers heading up and down the Pacific coast once pulled *their* vehicles through it. The tree stands 275 feet tall, measures 21 feet in diameter, and people can see the sky if standing inside the eight-foot-wide tree tunnel. Food is available at the **Drive-Thru-Tree Cafe,** 707/943-1665. Phillipsville is home to the **Chimney Tree,** 707/923-2265, open 8 A.M.–8 P.M. from May to mid-October, and the Tolkienesque **Hobbitown U.S.A.** (currently closed, but ask at the Chimney Tree about possible reopening).

STORY WITHOUT END:
THE POLITICS OF HARVESTING REDWOODS

Along the north coast, the politics of logging are as universally explosive as the issue of offshore drilling. The battle to preserve redwoods, especially the remaining first-growth stands, has been going on for decades. So strong are the economic forces in support of logging and related industry that without the untiring efforts of the private Save-the-Redwoods League, Sierra Club, and other environmental organizations, most of the coast redwood groves now protected from commercial "harvesting" would be long gone. The fact that Redwood National Park north of Eureka was established at all, even if late, is something of a miracle. And the recent battle over the old-growth Headwaters Forest echoes all the wars that came before.

Environmentalists adamantly oppose the accelerating practice of clear-cutting, the wholesale denuding of hillsides and entire watersheds in the name of efficiency and quick profits. "Tree huggers" have argued for years that anything other than sustained yield timber harvesting—cutting no more timber than is grown each year—not only destroys the environment by eliminating forests, wildlife habitat, and fisheries but also ultimately destroys the industry itself. Someday, they've been saying for several decades, the forests will be gone and so will logging and lum-

ber mill jobs. "Someday" has arrived. The timber business has harvested its own industry into oblivion.

The failure of both the 1990 "Green" and Forests Forever initiatives, statewide ballot propositions in favor of forest protection, has only served to increase local furor. Earth First! and other activist groups subsequently took on Pacific Lumber Company and other timber firms—taking the battle into the forests and surrounding communities, as in 1990's "Redwood Summer." Timbermen and truckers have themselves taken to the streets defending their traditional livelihoods with community parades and other events accented by yellow solidarity ribbons. The fight has become so intense, philosophically, that the Laytonville school board was publicly pressured to ban *The Lorax* by Dr. Seuss because of the book's anti-clear-cutting sentiments. (The book banning failed, ultimately.)

A further blow to business as usual came with a 1990s admission by the California Board of Forestry that the state has allowed timber companies to cut down so many mature trees—old growth and otherwise—that there now looms a serious "timber gap," a substantial reduction in future forest harvests. The "statewide emergency" is due to "past failure" to regulate industrial timberlands and "has resulted in long-

---

facilities be full, the area also includes a number of private campgrounds and RV parks.

The day-use fee at Humboldt Redwoods is $2 per car. For maps and more information about the park, stop by or contact: Humboldt Redwoods State Park headquarters (at the Burlington Campground), P.O. Box 100, Weott, CA 95571, 707/946-2409. The **Humboldt Redwoods Interpretive Association Visitor Center,** between headquarters and Burlington Campground, 707/946-2263, is open daily 9 A.M.–5 P.M. (until 8 P.M. in July and August).

SCOTIA AND VICINITY

Scotia is a neat-as-a-pin town perfumed by the scents of apple pie, family barbecues, and redwood sawdust. A company town built (to last) from redwood and founded on solid economic

ground created by sustained-yield logging, picture-perfect Scotia is one of California's last wholly owned company towns. Generations of children of Pacific Lumber Company (PALCO)

SCOTIA INN

While in Scotia, consider a stop or a stay at the spruced-up **Scotia Inn,** 100 Main St. (at Mill), 707/764-5683, fax 707/764-1707, www.scotia inn.com, a classic 1923 redwood bed-and-breakfast-style hotel with a very good restaurant—the **Redwood Room,** serving American and international fare—plus separate café and several bars, one known as the **Steak and Potato Pub.** The inn has eight rooms and two suites, all with private baths (one with a hot tub and whirlpool). Continental breakfast included. Expensive-Luxury.

term overharvesting, drastically reducing both the productive capability of the land and maintenance of adequate wildlife habitat." This new crisis has further shocked the California timber industry, long accustomed to the board's regulatory sympathies.

The most recent chapter in the redwood wars began when the north coast's Pacific Lumber Company (PALCO) was acquired in a junk bond–financed deal by Maxxam Corporation. The original PALCO was well regarded by environmentalists as a responsible, sustained-yield logger, but with Maxxam CEO Charles Hurwitz at the helm, PALCO began clear-cutting on its 202,000 acres in Humboldt County, for the first time in its history—to pay the price of Hurwitz's purchase. Among PALCO's holdings: the 60,000-acre Headwaters Forest, the largest remaining stand of privately owned old-growth redwoods in the world.

When the PALCO chainsaws threatened to fell the roadless 3,000-acre Headwaters Grove at the heart of the vast old-growth redwood forest, environmentalist activists went to war with Hurwitz. For more than 10 years, Earth First! and other environmental groups stopped at nothing—public protests, guerrilla theater, tree-sitting, lawsuits—to prevent the harvesting of the Headwaters Forest. After years of forest warfare and hot tempers in nearby north coast communities, a deal brokered in 1998 by U.S. Senator Dianne Feinstein seemed destined to provide the political solution. Feinstein's compromise allowed the federal and state governments to purchase the core Headwaters acreage and a surrounding watershed buffer—a total of 7,500 acres—and required a "habitat conservation plan" for the remaining PALCO acreage, in an attempt to balance logging and wildlife protection.

But Hurwitz balked. The federal funding authorization was set to expire, negotiations were stalled, and the Headwaters' future looked grim. Yet on March 1, 1999—with just *seven minutes* left on the funding clock—the deal was struck and signed, and the Headwaters Forest became public property—for a hefty price tag of $480 million.

After the dramatic conclusion to the Headwaters conflict, most area residents were relieved. At least some of the Headwaters Forest is now preserved, the state and federal governments will regulate logging and wildlife habitat protection on the remaining acreage, and PALCO loggers can return to work.

Some environmentalists, though, say it was a bad deal—not going far enough to protect the Headwaters ecosystem as a viable whole. They are particularly concerned about the probable loss of several pristine old-growth groves, and the threat to the coho salmon run due to damage to the Elk River watershed. They promise further court battles. The saga continues.

---

loggers happily grew up in Scotia, then went to work in the mills—or went away to college on PALCO-paid scholarships before returning to work as middle managers in the mill offices.

Scotia's serenity was obliterated in 1985, when PALCO was taken over in a Michael Milken–related stock raid by the Maxxam Group. Maxxam's Charles Hurwitz began his tenure at PALCO by clear-cutting old-growth redwoods on the company's land. More recently, when Hurwitz directed his chainsaws toward the Headwaters Grove—in the midst of PALCO's 60,000-acre Headwaters Forest, one of the last privately held stands of virgin redwoods left in the country—it sparked an environmental and political battle that has taken a decade to resolve, to less than unanimous satisfaction.

As if such multiplex stresses weren't enough, the town's business district was lost in April 1992, when fires started by a massive north coast earthquake destroyed the entire business district and damaged many area homes. (The mill was saved.) The quake's total regional price tag: somewhere in the neighborhood of $61 million.

The big event in Scotia is taking a tour of the **Pacific Lumber Company redwood sawmill,** 125 Main St., 707/764-2222, the largest in the world. Visitors are welcome to observe the operation on the company's self-guided Mill B tour (free). Also stop by PALCO's **Scotia Museum** and visitor center on Main St., 707/764-2222, ext. 247, housed in a stylized Greek temple built of redwood, with logs taking the place of fluted columns. (Formerly a bank, the building's sprouting redwood burl once had to be pruned regularly.) Open summers only.

The **Rio Dell/Scotia Chamber of Commerce** is at 715 Wildwood Ave., Rio Dell, CA 95562, 707/764-3436, www.101chamber.org.

FORTUNA AND HIGHWAY 36

The largest city in southern Humboldt County, Fortuna (pop. around 10,000) was originally called Springville and established in 1875. Logging is still the major industry in these parts. Come in March for a big **Daffodil Show;** in July for the long-running **Fortuna Rodeo** and parade; in October for the **Apple Harvest Festival;** or in December for the **Christmas Music Festival.**

The **Fortuna Depot Museum,** 4 Park St., 707/725-7645, occupies the old 1893 rail depot and houses a collection of area artifacts from the local railroad, logging, and fishing industries. It's open in summer, daily 10 A.M.–4:30 P.M.; the rest of the year, Wed.–Sun. noon–4:30 P.M. Admission is free (donations appreciated).

Clendenen's Cider Works, 96 12th St. (next to the freeway), 707/725-2123, open daily Aug.–Feb., is *the* place for half-gallons of homemade apple cider and fresh local produce. The **Eel River Brewing Company,** 1777 Alamar Way, 707/725-2739, offers around half a dozen homemade beers, including Ravensbrau Porter and Climax Amber. To go with the brew, you can order from a fine menu of steaks and seafoods, pastas, and burgers. Justifiably popular with locals, and quite a find, is **Savannah's Steak & Seafood** (next to Safeway in the shopping center), 703 S. Fortuna Blvd., 707/725-7056.

For more information about Fortuna and vicinity, contact the **Fortuna Chamber of Commerce,** 735 14th St., Fortuna, CA 95540, 707/725-3959, www.sunnyfortuna.com/~chamber.

Attractions east from Hwy. 101 along Hwy. 36 include **Van Duzen County Park,** 707/445-7651 for information, Humboldt's largest county park, and **Grizzly Creek Redwoods State Park** near Carlotta, 707/777-3683.

FERNDALE AND VICINITY

Ferndale is the kind of place Disneyland architects would create if they needed a new movie set. Ferndale, however, is the real thing, a thriving small town where people take turns shuttling the kids to Future Farmers of America and 4-H meetings, argue about education at PTA meetings or ice-cream socials, and gossip on street corners.

Lovers of Victoriana, take the walking tour; for a free guide to historic buildings (almost everything here qualifies), pick up the souvenir edition of the *Ferndale Enterprise* at the Kinetic Sculpture Museum or at most main street shops, or contact the **Ferndale Chamber of Commerce,** P.O. Box 325, Ferndale, CA 95536, 707/786-4477, www.victorianferndale.org/chamber.

Most of the historic commercial buildings are concentrated on three-block-long Main Street. The **Kinetic Sculpture Museum,** 580 Main St. (no phone, but inquire at Hobart Galleries, 707/786-9259), displays a decidedly eclectic collection of survivors of the annual kinetic sculpture

Ferndale's Gingerbread Mansion

KIM WEIR

race, as well as works in progress. The Kinetic Sculpture Museum is usually open weekdays 10 A.M.–5 P.M., shorter hours on weekends. Worth a stop, too, is the 1892-vintage **Golden Gait Mercantile,** 421 Main St., 707/786-4891, a squeaky-floored emporium of oddities and useful daily items, from sassafras tea and traditional patent medicines to butter churns, bushel (and peck) baskets, and treadle sewing machines. There's a museum on the 2nd floor. Travelers will be relieved to find that Ferndale has public restrooms (next to the post office on Main).

Once off Main, most people head first to the famous 1899 **Gingerbread Mansion,** 400 Berding St., 707/786-4000 or toll-free 800/952-4136, http://gingerbread-mansion.com, a Victorian built in a combination of Queen Anne, Eastlake, and stick styles. Tucked into its formal English gardens at 400 Berding and virtually dripping with its own frosting, the Gingerbread is one of the most photographed and painted buildings in Northern California. In order to fully appreciate the town, take a quick visit to the **Ferndale Museum,** 515 Shaw Ave. (just off Main at the corner of 3rd), 707/786-4466. **Centerville County Park** at the end of Ocean is small (pass **Portuguese Hall** on the way) but provides access to the 10 miles of beaches between False Cape and the Eel River lagoon.

Picnickers can stop in at the **Ferndale Meat Company,** 376 Main, 707/786-4501, to pick up handmade smoked sausages and other meats from the two-story stone smokehouse, as well as cheeses and other surprises. For a sit-down meal, try immensely popular **Curley's Grill,** 460 Main St., 707/786-9696, open daily for lunch and dinner, and the small **Stage Door Café,** 451 Main, 707/786-4675, open for breakfast and lunch. Other possibilities include the **Victorian Inn** restaurant, 400 Ocean St., 707/786-4442, which is open for breakfast, lunch, and dinner and features a popular sushi and oyster bar, and **The Ivanhoe,** 315 Main St., 707/786-9000, offering Italian cuisine for dinner Tues.-Sunday.

EUREKA AND VICINITY

When James T. Ryan slogged ashore here from his whaling ship in May of 1850, shouting (so the story goes) *Eureka!* ("I have found it"), what he found was California's largest natural bay north of San Francisco. Oddly expansive and naked today, huge Humboldt Bay was once a piddling puddle at the edge of the endless redwood forest. Early loggers stripped the land closest to town first, but the bare Eureka hills were soon dotted with reincarnated redwoods—the buildings of pioneer industry, and the stately Victorians that still reflect the community's cultural roots.

No matter how vibrant the colors of the old homes here, at times it seems nothing can dispel the fog in these parts. When the fog does finally lift, in wet years the rains come, washing away hillsides and closing roads, trapping the locals behind what they jokingly call the Redwood Curtain. That sense of isolation from the rest of the human world—something harried visitors from more urban locales long for—and the need to transform life into something other than *gray* may explain why there are more artists and performers per capita in Humboldt County than anywhere else in the state. Sunshine is where one finds it, after all.

For more local sunshine, contact the **Eureka Chamber of Commerce,** 2112 Broadway, Eureka, CA 95501, 707/442-3738 or toll-free 800/356-6381, www.eurekachamber.com, or the **Eureka Main Street Information Bureau,** 123 F St. #6, 707/442-9054. The **Eureka-Humboldt County Convention and Visitors Bureau,** 1034 2nd St., 707/443-5097, toll-free 800/338-7352 (in California), or toll-free 800/346-3482 (outside California), www.redwoodvisitor.org, is the central source for countywide visitor information.

SEEING AND DOING EUREKA

Humboldt Bay

Eureka's 10-mile-long Humboldt Bay was named for the German naturalist Baron Alexander von Humboldt. So it's fitting that the extensive, if almost unknown and largely neglected, **Humboldt Bay National Wildlife Refuge** was established on the edge of the bay's South Jetty to protect the black brant, a small migratory goose, and more than 200 other bird species. The refuge headquarters, 707/733-5406, is on Beatrice Flat, 10 miles south of Eureka off Hwy. 101, between Loleta and Fields Landing.

Fields Landing, where the last Northern California whaling station operated until 1951, is the bay's deep-water port, the place to watch large fishing boats unload their daily catch; the rest of the fleet docks at the end of Commercial St. in downtown Eureka.

The **Samoa Bridge** connects the city of Eureka with the narrow peninsula extending south from Arcata (almost across Humboldt Bay) and the old company town of **Samoa,** the name inspired by the bay's resemblance to the harbor at Pago Pago. The **Samoa Cookhouse,** 707/442-1659, is a noted rustic restaurant and the last logging camp cookhouse in the West; it also serves as a fascinating museum. The **Eureka City Airport** and **U.S. Coast Guard** facilities occupy the fingertip of Samoa Peninsula, near county-owned fishing access.

Old Town Eureka

Part of Eureka's one-time skid row—the term itself of north coast origin, referring to the shantytowns and shacks lining the loggers' "skid roads" near ports—has been shoved aside to make room for Old Town. Most of the fleabag flophouses, sleazy sailors' bars, and pool halls along 1st, 2nd, and 3rd between C and G Sts. were razed and others renovated to create this bayside concentration of new cafés, art galleries, and trendy shops.

Most people stop first for a look at the gaudy, geegawed Gothic **Carson Mansion,** 143 M St., at the foot of 2nd St. (locals say "Two Street"),

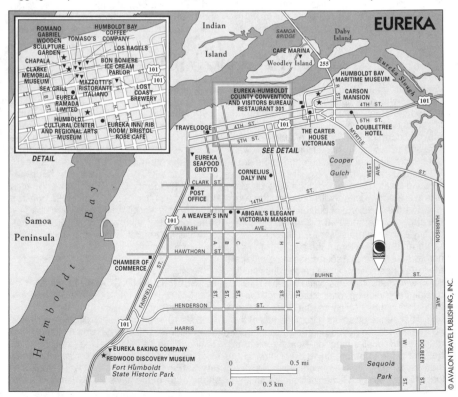

HEADING FOR HEADWATERS

So intense was public interest in visiting the 7,500-acre Headwaters Grove after its 1999 purchase by California and the United States that state officials decided to limit initial access. Only those willing to hike a rugged 10 miles got an early look.

Botanists fear that tourism will threaten the fragile old-growth redwood ecosystem. No trail leads into the reserve's 3,000-acre core, but visitors can drive to the north edge of the forest, just south of Eureka, via Elk River Rd., then hike in some five miles along an abandoned logging road to reach an overlook into the unperturbed heart of the Headlands. Limited visitor access is also available from southeast of Fortuna. That logging-road route, via Newburg and Felt Springs Rds., leads to a 10-vehicle parking area at Salmon Pass. Guided hikes are also offered.

For current information on Headwaters access and guided hikes, contact the **U.S. Bureau of Land Management's Arcata Field Office,** 1695 Heindon Rd. in Arcata, 707/825-2300, fax 707/825-2301, www.ca.blm.gov. The website includes basic maps of the area.

For background information on the battle to protect the Headwaters Grove, updates on current skirmishes, and details on other regional environmental issues, contact: **Environmental Protection Information Center (EPIC),** P.O. Box 397, Garberville, CA 95542, 707/923-2931, fax 707/923-4210, www.wildcalifornia.org.

once the home of lumber baron William Carson. Those in the know say this is the state's—perhaps the nation's—finest surviving example of Victoriana. Now it's home to the exclusive all-male (how Victorian) Ingomar Club, and even unescorted men are not welcome inside.

Fine and friendlier is the **Clarke Memorial Museum,** 240 E St. (at 3rd), 707/443-1947, where you'll feel as though you're stepping into a 19th-century parlor. The museum was founded in 1960 by Cecile Clarke (a history teacher at Eureka High 1914–50), who personally gathered most of the impressive collection of Victoriana, which includes a signed first edition of *The Personal Memoirs of General Grant.* The museum building, the Italian Renaissance onetime **Bank of Eureka,** listed on the National Register of Historic Places, is itself a collector's item with its stained-glass skylight and glazed terra-cotta exterior. Open Tues.–Sat., noon–4 P.M. Admission is free.

The **Humboldt Bay Maritime Museum,** 1410 2nd St., 707/444-9440, is a block east of the Carson Mansion in a replica of the George Mc-Farlan home, originally built here in 1852. The museum, opened in 1984, chronicles the area's contributions to Pacific seafaring heritage. Open daily 11 A.M.–4 P.M. Admission is free (donations welcomed).

The museum also owns and runs the **MV Madaket,** a former Humboldt Bay passenger ferry now providing sightseeing tours of the bay, daily May–October. Built in 1910, the *Madaket* is the oldest passenger vessel in continuous use in the United States. The harbor cruises leave from the foot of C St. in Old Town. Fare is $9.50 adults, $8.50 seniors/juniors, $6.50 children. Cocktail and bird-watching cruises are also available. For more information, call 707/445-1910.

BLUE OX MILLWORKS

Not really a tourist attraction but endlessly compelling is Eureka's time-honored Blue Ox Millworks complex, located at the foot of X St., 707/444-3457 or toll-free 800/248-4259 (for tour reservations). The antithesis of all things high-tech, the Blue Ox pays hands-on homage to the beauty of craftsmanship, and particularly the craft of old-fashioned woodworking. In this going concern—a de facto living history environment, the only mill of its kind remaining in the United States—the machines date from 1850 to the 1940s. There's an aromatic whirl of sawing, chipping, turning, grinding, and sanding as custom orders are filled. Customers include the National Park Service—which once ordered 400 custom planters for the White House—and endless couples in the midst of Victorian restorations. Victorian replication is the specialty here, though the Blue Ox can duplicate or restore just about anything. Mill tours—visiting the main shop, sawmill, moulding plant, blacksmith shop, "logging skid camp," and more—occur Mon.–Sat. (usually closed Sun.) 9 A.M.–4 P.M. Weekday tours are usually more action-packed, if you want to see the craftsmen at work, and Saturday tours are more personally guided.

the Eureka home
of a lumber baron

TOM MYERS PHOTOGRAPHY

In the old Carnegie Library at 636 F St. (7th and F), the Humboldt Arts Council's **Humboldt Cultural Center and Regional Arts Museum,** 636 F St., 707/442-0278, www.thepalette.com, hosts concerts and performances during much of the year as well as major art exhibits, and offers the work of local artists for sale.

Fort Humboldt and Sequoia Park
Interesting but not necessarily worth writing home about is Eureka's **Fort Humboldt State Historic Park,** 3431 Fort Ave., 707/445-6567. Admission is free to this essentially unrestored site of the U.S. military's 1850s' Indian Wars outpost, onetime stomping grounds of the young U.S. Grant. As depressed in Eureka as elsewhere in California, Grant reportedly spent much of his six months here in saloons, then resigned his commission to go home and farm in Missouri. The fort does have an excellent (and wheelchair-accessible) indoor/outdoor museum display of early logging technology, along with picnic tables (with a good view of Humboldt Bay) and restrooms. Call for actual directions—it's tricky to find.

Sequoia Park is the last significant vestige of the virgin redwood forest that once fringed Humboldt Bay. The park is situated southeast of downtown at Glatt and W Sts., 707/443-7331, and is open Tues.–Sun. 10 A.M.–8 P.M. May–Oct., until 5 P.M. the rest of the year. It's melancholy here, despite the peace of these dark woods laced with walking paths, a rhododendron dell, and duck pond. The five-acre **Sequoia Park Zoo,** 3414 W St., 707/441-4263, incarcerates animals from six continents, though the native river otters are best. The zoo is open Tues.–Sun. 10 A.M.–5 P.M. (until 7 P.M. in summer). Admission is free.

STAYING IN EUREKA

Broadway is "motel row," and you'll also find reasonable motels on 4th Street. Most Eureka motels offer substantially cheaper rates Oct.–Apr.,

---

ROMANO GABRIEL'S GARDEN

Fabulous folk art "grows" at the **Romano Gabriel Wooden Sculpture Garden** in Old Town Eureka at 315 2nd St., a blooming, blazing, full-color world of delightful plants, people, and social commentary, crafted from packing crates with the help of a handsaw. This is "primitive art" (snobs say "poor taste") on a massive scale, one of two pieces of California folk art recognized internationally (the other is Watts Towers in Los Angeles). Gabriel, a gardener who died in 1977, said of his work: "Eureka is bad place for flowers—the salty air and no sun. So I just make this garden." He worked on this garden, which includes likenesses of Mussolini, the Pope, nosy neighbors, and tourists amid the fantastic flowers and trees, for 30 years. After Gabriel's death, it was restored, then transplanted downtown from his front yard.

and even the cheapest places usually have color TV and cable and/or free HBO. Eureka's **Travelodge**, 4 4th St. (at B St.), 707/443-6345 or toll-free 800/578-7878, has a pool and cable TV with HBO (Inexpensive-Moderate). The **Eureka Ramada Limited**, 270 5th St., 707/443-2206, toll-free 800/233-3782, or toll-free 800/272-6232, features a sauna and indoor hot tub. Moderate. The large and attractive **Doubletree Hotel**, 1929 4th St. (between T and V Sts.), 707/445-0844 or toll-free 800/222-8733, includes amenities such as a swimming pool and spa, laundry and valet service, and a good restaurant (Pacific Grill & Smokehouse).

Two Noteworthy Lodgings
Very "old Eureka" is the excellent **Eureka Inn**, 518 7th St. (at F St.), 707/442-6441 or toll-free 800/862-4906, fax 707/442-1663, www.eurekainn.com. First opened in 1922, this imposing 1920s Tudor-style hotel is listed on the National Register of Historic Places. Among the luminaries who have wandered its halls and dined at its famous **Rib Room**—the locals' favorite seafood-and-steak restaurant—are Sir Winston Churchill, Bobby Kennedy, Mickey Mantle, Steven Spielberg, Ronald Reagan, and Shirley Temple. In addition to its spectacular clear-heart redwood interiors, the Eureka Inn features abundant amenities, including a sauna, whirlpool, year-round heated pool, three restaurants (including the **Bristol Rose Café**), three bars, "live hot jazz," a shoe-shine stand, and free transportation to and from the airport. Expensive-Luxury. Or stay at the Eureka Inn's associated **Downtowner Motor Inn**, where rates start at Inexpensive.

Definitely "new Eureka" but also emanating more contemporary Victorian charms are **The Carter House Victorians**, 301 L St., 707/444-8062, 707/445-1390, or toll-free 800/404-1390, fax 707/444-8067, www.carterhouse.com. What has become known as The Carter House is actually a complex of four properties—The Hotel Carter, The Carter House Inn, The Carter Cottage, and Bell Cottage—under unified management. The hotel and inn are vintage-1980s facsimiles, while the cottages are renovations of the original 19th-century structures. Rates at any of The Carter House Victorians—Premium-Luxury—include luxurious amenities and a

breathtaking full breakfast, evening wine and hors d'oeuvres, and before-bed cookies and tea. The outstanding restaurant here, **Restaurant 301**, is a 1998 recipient of the coveted *Wine Spectator* magazine Grand Award. Restaurant 301 is supported by the extensive, organic **301 Gardens**—guests can help harvest vegetables, fruits, and herbs before dinner—and the **301 Wineshop**. Quite special, too, are the **Winemakers Dinners at Restaurant 301**.

Eureka Bed-and-Breakfasts
Eureka's showplace inn, a destination in its own right for connoisseurs of high-Victorian style, is the award-winning **Abigail's Elegant Victorian Mansion**, 1406 C St., 707/444-3144, fax 707/442-5594, www.eureka-california.com. This elegant Victorian mansion offers more than just four comfortable rooms (two shared baths and a Finnish sauna), fabulous breakfasts, and vintage auto tours. Guided by the inn's irrepressible innkeepers, Doug ("Jeeves") and Lily Vieyra, visitors could easily spend an entire day just touring *this* eclectic place, which is a spectacular de facto museum of authentic Victorian substance and style. Old movies and music add yet another delightful dimension to a stay here. And once you're done inside, don't miss the Victorian flower garden. Expensive-Luxury.

The 1905 **Cornelius Daly Inn**, 1125 H St., 707/445-3638 or toll-free 800/321-9656, offers three antiques-furnished rooms (two share a bath) and two suites in a 1905 colonial revival. Guests enjoy a spectacular full breakfast, afternoon tea, phones, TV, a library, and gardens with a fishpond. But don't miss the 3rd-floor Christmas Ballroom. Expensive-Premium.

A Weaver's Inn, 1440 B St., 707/443-8119 or toll-free 800/992-8119, is an impressive 1883 Queen Anne Victorian featuring three rooms (two share a bath) and one suite, antiques, cottage gardens, and full breakfast. Two rooms have fireplaces, one has a two-seat soaking tub. Moderate-Premium.

EATING IN EUREKA

Eureka's fishermen's wharf is the real thing, not a tourist trap like San Francisco's. The **Eureka Seafood Grotto** at 6th and Broadway, 707/443-

2075, is the locals' choice for seafood. The retail outlet for Eureka's fisheries as well, the Grotto is a tremendous place to slide into seafood stupor, with immense quantities of everything, all quite reasonable. The **Cafe Marina** on Woodley Island, 707/443-2233, is another popular fish house (open daily for breakfast, lunch, and dinner), as are the **Café Waterfront,** 102 F St., 707/443-9190, and the **Sea Grill,** 316 E St., 707/443-7187.

For just about the best bagels anywhere, try **Los Bagels,** 403 2nd St. (at E), 707/442-8525, open daily for breakfast and lunch. (The original Los Bagels is in Arcata.) The **Eureka Baking Company,** 3562 Broadway (Hwy. 101), 707/445-8997, is wonderful for croissants, muffins, sourdough baguettes, and other fresh-baked fare. **Ramone's Bakery & Cafe,** 209 E St., 707/445-2923, is excellent for pastries and fresh breads, not to mention espresso and other good coffees. A great choice, too, for fresh-ground coffees (by the pound or by the cup) is **Humboldt Bay Coffee Company,** 211 F St., 707/444-3969, which offers live music on Friday and Saturday nights and outdoor seating in good weather. An-

other good stop for soup and sandwiches—and quite possibly the best ice cream anywhere on the north coast—is **Bon Boniere Ice Cream Parlor,** 215 F St. in Old Town, 707/268-0122.

The **Lost Coast Brewery,** 617 4th St., 707/445-4480, is the place to go for locally hand-crafted ales like Alley Cat Amber and 8-Ball Stout, as well as good pub fare (served until midnight).

Justifiably famous for its tomato and spinach pies, calzones, and other straightforward selections—one slice of the Sicilian pizza makes a meal—**Tomaso's,** 216 E St. (between 2nd and 3rd), 707/445-0100, is open for lunch and dinner weekdays and Saturday. Expect a wait, which will be worth it. For decent pasta and quiet atmosphere, try **Mazzotti's Ristorante Italiano,** 305 F St., 707/445-1912. Mexican food is the cuisine of choice at **Chapala,** 201 2nd St., 707/443-9514.

The locals' longtime choice for fine dining is the **Rib Room** at the Eureka Inn, 7th and F Sts., 707/442-6441, noted for its steaks, seafood, and great wine list. For breakfast or lunch, try the inn's **Bristol Rose Café.**

Eureka's new culinary star is elegant and small **Restaurant 301** at The Hotel Carter, 301 L St., 707/444-8062, open nightly for candle-light, classical music, and superb dining. In fact, Restaurant 301 has become something of an international dining destination, since it won *Wine Spectator* magazine's coveted Grand Award in 1998. Fewer than 100 restaurants in the world have been so honored. Menus here are created from fresh, local ingredients, from Humboldt Bay seafood to the fresh vegetables, fruits, and herbs harvested daily from the restaurant's own extensive organic gardens. The exceptional wine list represents a cellar of more than 23,000 bottles. Reservations are a must. The Hotel Carter also offers a famous four-course breakfast.

ARCATA AND VICINITY

Arcata is Eureka's alter-ego, no more resigned to the status quo than the sky here is blue. In 1996, Arcata made national news when a majority of Green Party candidates was elected to the city council. Far-from-the-mainstream publications

---

SAMOA COOKHOUSE

At least once in a lifetime, everyone should eat at the **Samoa Cookhouse** on the Samoa Peninsula, 707/442-1659 ("open after 0600" but no reservations taken). All major credit cards are accepted, and there's a gift shop next door. The Samoa is a bona fide loggers' cookhouse oozing redwood-rugged ambience. The phrase "all you can eat" takes on new meaning here: portions are gargantuan. Good ol' American food—platters of thickly sliced ham, beef, turkey, and spare ribs (choices change daily), plus potatoes, vegetables, fresh-baked bread—is passed around among the checkered oilcloth-covered tables. Soup and salad are included in the fixed-price meal ($11.45 when last we checked), not to mention homemade apple pie for dessert. Hearty breakfasts and lunch, too. Come early on weekends, particularly in summer, and be prepared to wait an hour or so. To get there, head west from Eureka over the Samoa Bridge, turn left, then left again at the town of Samoa (follow the signs).

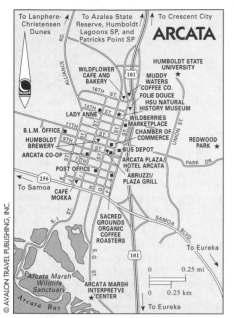

are available even at the visitor center. In addition to Arcata's world-famous **Cross-Country Kinetic Sculpture Race** on Memorial Day weekend, popular annual events include the **April Fools Income Tax Annual Auction,** a benefit for the North Coast Environmental Center, and the **North Country Fair,** one of the West Coast's premier craft fairs. A relaxed and liberal town, Arcata is determined to make a difference.

The helpful **Arcata Chamber of Commerce** is in the new California Welcome Center at 1635 Heindon Rd., Arcata, CA 95521, 707/822-3619, open weekdays 10 A.M.–5 P.M. in tourist season, and 10 A.M.–3 P.M. in winter (hours may be expanded; call for current schedule).

Seeing and Doing Arcata

The presence of **Humboldt State University** keeps things in Arcata lively. Humboldt State, east of town on Fickle Hill near 14th St. and Grant Ave., 707/826-3011, emphasizes the study of forestry practices, fisheries and wildlife management, and oceanography. On campus, worthwhile sights include the **arboretum, fish hatchery,** and **art gallery.** Off campus, the HSU Nat-

ural **History Museum,** 1315 G St., 707/826-4479, features local natural history displays, an impressive fossil collection, and lots of hands-on exploration. Open Tues.–Sat. 10 A.M.–4 P.M. Admission is free (donations appreciated).

Arcata Plaza downtown, with its memorial statue of President McKinley and out-of-place palm trees, is custom-made for watching people come and go from surrounding cafés and shops, or for resting up after a tour of local Victorian homes—if you don't mind hangin' out with the hang-out crowd. Several of the historic buildings framing the plaza are worth a look, including the **Jacoby Storehouse** on the south side, a stone-and-brick beauty with iron shutters (now housing woodwork, glass, and other fine local crafts), and the quite pleasant **Hotel Arcata.**

The 30-acre **Azalea State Reserve** just north of Arcata on North Bank Rd. (Hwy. 200) is famous for its cascading, fragrant pinkish-white western azalea blooms (usually best around Memorial Day) and other wildflowers, all in the company of competing rhododendrons. Good steelhead fishing can be found in the area along North Bank Rd. near Hwy. 299's Mad River bridge. For more information, call Patrick's Point State Park at 707/677-3570.

Walk **Arcata Bay** to appreciate the impromptu scrap wood sculptures sometimes in bloom. The most fascinating bayside sights, though, are at the **Arcata Marsh and Wildlife Preserve** at the foot of I Street. This was one of the first wildlife preserves in the United States to be created from an old landfill dump and "enhanced" by treated sewage water. The aesthetic settling ponds offer excellent bird-watching. For more information, stop by or call the **Arcata Marsh Interpretive Center,** 600 S. G St., 707/826-2359; open daily 1–5 P.M.

Just east of Arcata, on the Samoa Peninsula near the Mad River Slough, is the 300-acre **Lanphere-Christensen Dunes Preserve,** managed by the U.S. Fish and Wildlife Service. It's open to the public by permit, obtained from the office at 6800 Lanphere Rd., Arcata, CA 95521, 707/822-6378. No camping is permitted. This fragile ecosystem is noted for its many well-preserved plant communities, from vernal pools and salt marsh to forest. The area is unique for another reason. At this latitude, the northern and southern dune floras overlap, meaning rare and typical plantlife from both are present as well as more than 200 species of birds and other animals.

Practical Arcata

Quite pleasant, and right on the plaza, is the refurbished and welcoming 1915 **Hotel Arcata,** 708 9th St., 707/826-0217 or toll-free 800/344-1221, fax 707/826-1737. Moderate. If you'd prefer a B&B, try the **Lady Anne,** 902 14th St., 707/822-2797, which features five rooms (some with fireplaces, all with abundant antiques and plush guest robes) in an 1888 Queen Anne Victorian, plus full breakfast and bicycles to borrow. Expensive. Many motels are fairly inconveniently located along Valley West Blvd., off Hwy. 101 north of town; take the Giuntoli Ln./Janes Rd. exit and turn right.

First stop for those just passing through should be **Arcata Co-op,** 8th and I Sts., 707/822-5947, a natural-foods store with an abundance of organic everything, open 9 A.M.–9 P.M. (until 8 P.M. on Sunday). Healthy groceries, vitamins, and health-care products, as well as a juice bar and deli/café, are also available at **Wildberries Marketplace,** at the top of G St. (at 13th), 707/822-0095. Wildberries is also the site of the **Arcata**

Certified Farmers' Market, held June–Oct. on Tues., 3–6 P.M. The **Arcata Plaza Certified Farmers' Market** is held May–Oct. on Sat., 9 A.M.–1 P.M., at the Arcata Plaza (8th and G Streets). For details on both, call 707/441-9999.

The **Wildflower Cafe and Bakery,** 1604 G St., 707/822-0360, has fresh bakery items, veggie food, homemade soups and salads, and "macrobiotic night" every Wednesday. Open Mon.–Sat. for breakfast, lunch, and dinner, and Sun. for brunch. **Café Mokka,** 495 J St. (at 5th), 707/822-2228, has decadent, incredibly good pastries, good coffee, and excellent espresso (as well as private outdoor hot tubs and sauna cabins for rent out back). Another good java joint is **Muddy Waters Coffee Co.** at 1603 G Street. But don't miss **Sacred Grounds Organic Coffee Roasters,** 686 F St., 707/822-0690.

Abruzzi, 791 8th St. (in Jacoby's Storehouse, facing the plaza), 707/826-2345, is a slice of real Italiana here in the foggy north. Fresh daily are the baguettes, breadsticks, and tomato-onion-and-fennel-seed bread, along with Humboldt-grown veggies and seafood specialties. Good calzones, wonderful pastas. And do try the 14-layer torte. Upstairs, the **Plaza Grill,** 707/826-0860, offers steak—seafood, salads—even gumbo—along

---

A MOVING TRIBUTE TO "FORM OVER SUBSTANCE"

If you're in the area for Memorial Day weekend, don't miss Arcata's sight-of-all-sights—the exuberant 38-mile, three-day trans-bay **World Championship Great Arcata to Ferndale Cross-Country Kinetic Sculpture Race.** Founded in 1969 by Ferndale artists Hobart Brown and Jack Mays, the race is a moving display of "form over substance." It's an almost-anything-goes tribute to unbridled imagination, but it does have a few rules.

The mobile "sculptures" must be people-powered (though it is legal to get an assist from water, wind, or gravity), amphibious, and inspired by the event's high moral and ethical standards—"cheating is a privilege, not a right." (Kinetic cops patrol the course and interpret the rules.) Otherwise, anything goes—and rolls, floats, and flounders, through sand, saltwater, and swamp slime—in this ultimate endurance contest, also known at the Triathlon of the Art World.

Coming in first, even dragging in last, is not the point of this race. The contest's most coveted award is the Aurea Mediocritas, for the entry finishing closest to dead center—because, as the founders explain, winning and losing are both extremes, therefore "perfection lies somewhere in the middle." However, losing has its virtues, too, so the much-coveted Loser Award has been reinstated. Even spectators are part of the competition, thanks to the Most Worthy Fanatical Spectator Award.

Favorite entries have included Brown's own floating bus-boat, the ever-popular Pencilhead Express, the man-eating Hammerhead Cadillac, and the Chicken-and-Egg Mobile. Some race survivors are on display at the sculpture museum in Ferndale. Prerace festivities include the **Kinetic Kickoff Party** and the **Rutabaga Queen Pageant** at Eureka's Ritz Club. For information about the race, call Hobart Galleries in Ferndale at 707/786-9259.

with great views of Humboldt Bay. **Folie Douce,** 1551 G St., between 15th and 16th, 707/822-1042, is regionally famous for its exotic and stylish wood fire–baked pizzas—everything from Thai chicken to goat cheese and wild mushroom. Reservations wise.

For homegrown brew and good basic food (a bit heavy on the grease) to go with it, try the **Humboldt Brewery,** 856 10th St., 707/826-2739, also a hot local nightspot attracting big-name blues, country, and folk talent. Open Mon.–Wed. 11:30 A.M.–11 P.M., Thurs.–Sat. 11:30 A.M.–1 A.M. Closed Sunday.

Patrick's Point State Park

The Yuroks who for centuries seasonally inhabited this area believed that the spirit of the porpoises came to live at modern-day Patrick's Point State Park just before people populated the world—and that the seven offshore sea stacks that stretch north to south like a spine were the last earthly abode of the immortals. Most impressive of

Patrick's Point in wintertime

CALIFORNIA DEPARTMENT OF PARKS & RECREATION

these rugged monuments is **Ceremonial Rock,** nicknamed "stairway to the stars" by fond rock climbers. Fine forests grew here until the area was logged and cleared for farming and grazing. Now the surrounding meadows are spectacular with wildflowers every spring, and the parks people are holding forest succession at bay.

The Port Orford cedars, Sitka spruce, shore pines, azaleas, and abundant berry bushes are returning. Both here and just north at Big Lagoon, you'll be in the right place for those "fungus among us" jokes. During the rainy season, duff from spruce trees produces delicious mushrooms—also fantastically fatal ones, so be sure you're an expert (or in the company of one) before you go rooting through forest detritus for dinner. Take the easy, self-guided **Octopus Grove** nature trail near Agate Beach Campground for an introduction to life's hardships from a spruce tree's viewpoint. Old trails once walked by native peoples lead to and beyond rocky **Patrick's Point,** one of the finest whale-watching sites along the coast. Stroll the two-mile **Rim Trail** for the views, but stay back from the hazardous cliff edge. Sea lions are common on the park's southern offshore rocks near **Palmer's Point.** The short trail scrambling north from near the campground (steep going) leads to long, sandy, and aptly named **Agate Beach,** noted for its many-colored, glasslike stones.

Patrick's Point has three developed campgrounds, with 123 naturally sheltered tent or trailer sites and hot showers. In addition, there are two group camps, 20 hike-and-bike campsites, a cabin, and a yurt. For camping reservations (essential in summer), call ReserveAmerica at toll-free 800/444-7275. The park's day-use fee is $3. For more information, contact: Patrick's Point State Park, Trinidad, CA 95570, 707/677-3570.

Humboldt Lagoons State Park

The community of **Big Lagoon** just off the highway north of Patrick's Point is also the site of Big Lagoon County Park with its dirty sand beaches and camping. Humboldt Lagoons State Park includes Big Lagoon itself (and the miles-long barrier beach separating it from the sea) and three others, a total of 1,500 beachfront acres best for beachcombing, boating, fishing, surfing, and windsurfing (swimming only for the hardy or foolhardy). The **Harry A. Merlo State**

Recreation Area, 800-plus acres named for a noted Louisiana-Pacific executive, entwines throughout the lagoon area.

Boat-in and hike-in campsites are available. There is no day-use fee. The small **Humboldt** **Lagoons Visitors Center** is at Stone Lagoon, open summers only. For more information and to reserve campsites, contact **Humboldt Lagoons State Park,** 15336 Hwy. 101, Trinidad, CA 95570, 707/488-2041.

DISCOVERING "OLD TOWN" TRINIDAD

A booming supply town of 3,000 in the early 1850s and later a whaling port, Trinidad is now a tiny coastal village recognized as the oldest incorporated town on California's north coast. Impressive **Trinidad Head** looms over the small bay, with a white granite cross at the summit replacing the first monument placed there by Bodega y Cuadra for Spain's Charles III.

The **Trinidad Memorial Lighthouse** on Main St. was the village's original light tower and was relocated to town as a fishermen's memorial. It features a giant two-ton fog bell. The **Trinidad Museum,** 529-B Trinity St., 707/677-3883, offers displays about the region's natural and cultural history. It's open in summer, Fri.–Sun. noon–5 P.M. Humboldt State University's **Fred Telonicher Marine Laboratory,** 570 Ewing St., 707/826-3671, has an aquarium open to the public, as well as a touch tank for getting intimate with intertidal invertebrates. It's open year-round, weekdays 9 A.M.–5 P.M., and also weekends 10 A.M.–5 P.M. when school is in session.

Besides solitary beachcombing on **Trinidad State Beach** (day-use only, good for moonstones and driftwood), surfing at rugged **Luffenholtz Beach** two miles south of town, and breathtaking scenery, the area's claim to fame is salmon fishing. Commercial and sportfishing boats, skiffs, and tackle shops line Trinidad Bay.

For more information on the area, contact: **Trinidad Chamber of Commerce,** Main St. and Patrick's Point Dr., P.O. Box 356, Trinidad, CA 95570, 707/677-1610.

Staying in Trinidad

For the most reasonable accommodations, head north on Patrick's Point Dr. to the state park and its excellent camping (see p. 283). Nice for cabins (most have kitchens) is the recently refurbished **Bishop Pine Lodge,** 1481 Patrick's Point Dr., 707/677-3314, fax 707/677-3444, also featuring two-bedroom units and cottages with hot tubs. Playground area, well-equipped exercise room. Moderate-Expensive. Another possibility is the **Shadow Lodge,** 687 Patrick's Point Dr., 707/677-0532, offering cottages furnished with antiques. Moderate-Expensive. In town, across from the lighthouse, the **Trinidad Bay Bed and Breakfast,**

560 Edwards St., 707/677-0840, fax 707/677-9245, www.trinidadbaybnb.com, is a Cape Cod–style home circa 1950. It offers two standard rooms and two suites, all with king or queen beds and private baths (one suite with fireplace). Closed Dec.–January. Premium-Luxury. About five miles north of Trinidad proper and adjacent to the state park is the **Lost Whale Bed and Breakfast Inn,** 3452 Patrick's Point Dr., 707/677-3425 or toll-free 800/677-7859, fax 707/677-0284, www.lostwhaleinn.com, a contemporary Cape Cod with eight guest rooms (all with private bath), full breakfast, hot tub, and afternoon refreshments. Luxury. Ask about the **Farmhouse,** a two-bedroom house on five acres, also available for rent. Nearby is the relatively new and tastefully decorated **Turtle Rocks Inn B&B,** 3392 Patrick's Point Dr., 707/677-3707, www.turtle-rocksinn.com, which offers six guest rooms on three oceanfront acres. Each room has a private bath, private deck, and modern amenities. Rates include a gourmet hot breakfast. Premium-Luxury (lower rates in the off-season).

Eating in Trinidad

In April or May each year, the town hosts a massive **crab feed** at Town Hall. Otherwise, *the* place to eat in Trinidad is the very relaxed and rustic **Seascape Restaurant** (once the Dock Cafe) at the harbor, 707/677-3762, which serves hearty breakfasts, excellent omelettes, and seafood specialties (good early-bird specials). Open 7 A.M.–9 P.M. daily. Reservations are a good idea at dinner. Also here, just north of town, is the excellent **Larrupin Cafe,** 1658 Patrick's Point Dr., 707/677-0230, a friendly and fine place noted for things like barbecued cracked crab, barbecued oysters, steamed mussels, and chicken breast wrapped up with artichokes and cream cheese in phyllo dough. Or try the mesquite-grilled portobello mushroom on slices of Spanish cheeses and potato bread. Excellent desserts, too. No credit cards. Other dining choices include the **Trinidad Bay Eatery & Gallery,** at Trinity and Parker, 707/677-3777, open Wed.–Sun. for breakfast and lunch, and **Merryman's Dinner House,** 100 Moonstone Beach Rd., 707/677-3111, noted for its sunsets as well as its food.

REDWOOD NATIONAL PARK AND VICINITY

Pointing north to Oregon like a broken finger is Redwood National Park, California's finest temple to tree hugging. Although well-traveled Hwy. 101 passes through the park, away from the highway much of the park is remote and often empty of worshipers. Those visitors just passing through to the Trees of Mystery are likely unaware that they're witnessing a miracle—forests being raised (albeit slowly) from the dead. Redwood National Park is complete, yet unfinished. Standing in the shadow and sunlight of an old-growth redwood grove is like stepping up to an altar mindful only of the fullness of life. But elsewhere in the park—out back toward the alley, looking like remnants of some satanic rite—are shameful scars of sticks and scabbed-over earth, the result of opportunistic clear-cutting during the political wrangling that accompanied the park's formation. Today, these areas are still in the early stages of healing. Yet Redwood National Park features some magnificent groves of virgin old-growth redwood. Three of the world's 10 tallest trees grow here—one of the reasons for UNESCO's 1982 declaration of the area as a World Heritage Site, the first on the Pacific coast. Redwood National Park is also an international Man in the Biosphere Reserve.

Though federal and state lands within the boundaries of Redwood National Park are technically under separate jurisdictions, as a practical matter the national and its three associated state parks—the **Prairie Creek Redwoods, Del Norte Coast Redwoods,** and **Jedediah Smith Redwoods State Parks**—are cooperatively managed. In general, the visiting weather is best in late spring and early autumn. August and September are the busiest times here (the salmon fishing rush), but September after Labor Day offers fewer crowds and usually less fog.

SEEING AND DOING REDWOOD NATIONAL PARK

The main thing to do in Redwood National Park is simply *be* here. Sadly, "being here" to many area visitors means little more than pulling into the parking lot near the 49-foot-tall Paul Bunyan and Babe the Blue Ox at Klamath's Trees of Mystery, buying big-trees trinkets, or stopping for a slab or two at roadside redwood burl stands in Orick.

Paul Bunyan and Babe the Blue Ox

TREES OF MYSTERY

The site of old Klamath is now overgrown with blackberries. New Klamath is dominated by the Trees of Mystery, 5500 Hwy. 101, 707/482-2251 or toll-free 800/638-3389, made famous by Robert Ripley's *Believe It or Not!* Chainsawed redwood characters are the featured attraction along Mystery's Trail of Tall Tales. The free End of the Trail Indian Museum is worth some time, though, with its end-of-the-line artifacts from everywhere in the United States and Canada.

Just south of Klamath is the **Tour-Thru-Tree,** 430 Hwy. 169, 707/482-5971, this one chainsawed in 1976. To get there, take the Terwer Valley exit off Hwy. 101 and go east a quarter mile on Hwy. 169.

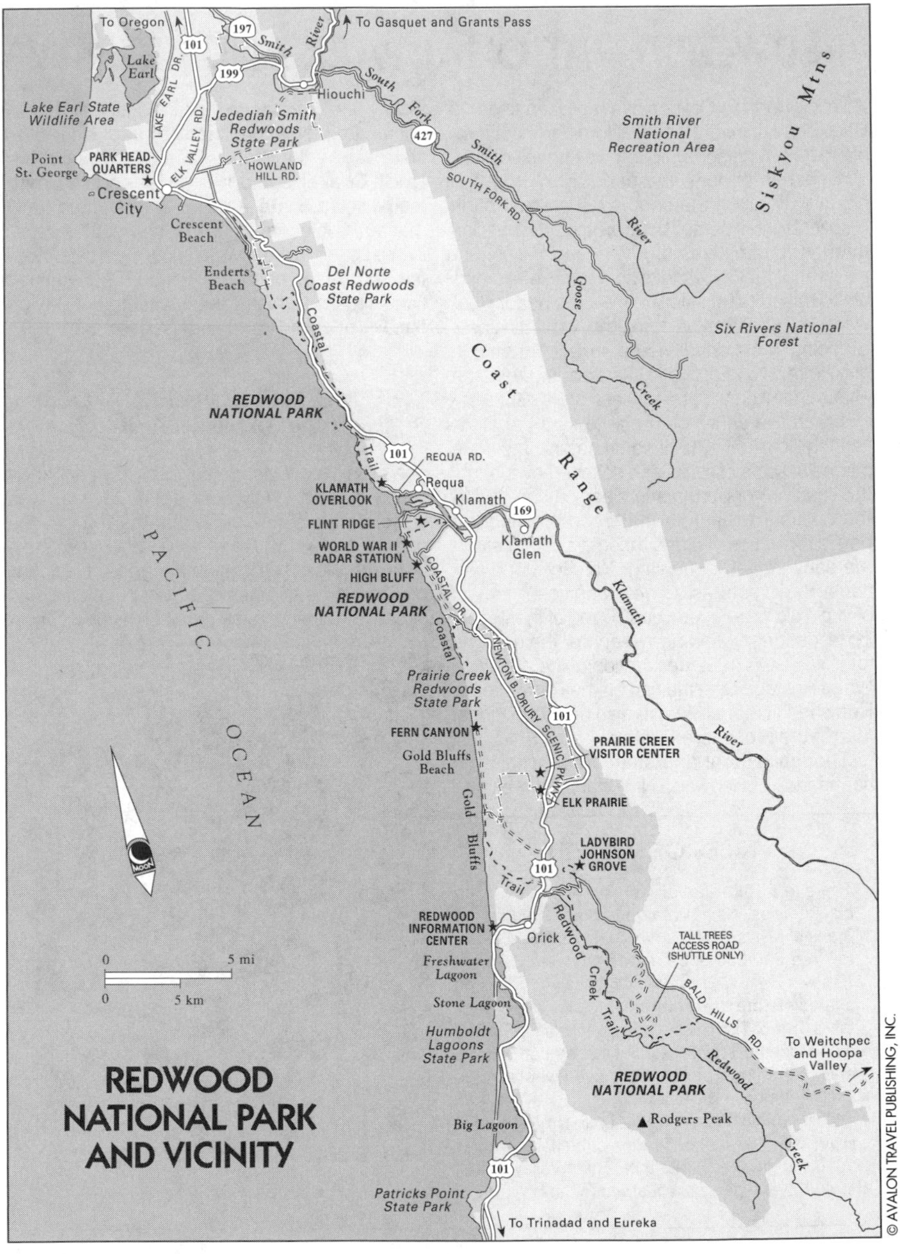

To Oregon
To Gasquet and Grants Pass
197
101
199
Smith River
South Fork
Hiouchi
Lake Earl
Lake Earl Drive
Elk Valley Rd.
Lake Earl State Wildlife Area
Jedediah Smith Redwoods State Park
427
Smith River National Recreation Area
Siskyou Mtns
Point St. George
PARK HEADQUARTERS
HOWLAND HILL RD.
SOUTH FORK RD.
Smith River
Crescent City
Goose Creek
Six Rivers National Forest
Crescent Beach
Enderts Beach
Del Norte Coast Redwoods State Park
Coast Range
REDWOOD NATIONAL PARK
Coastal Trail
101
REQUA RD.
KLAMATH OVERLOOK
Requa
FLINT RIDGE
Klamath
169
WORLD WAR II RADAR STATION
Klamath Glen
Klamath River
HIGH BLUFF
REDWOOD NATIONAL PARK
Coastal Dr.
PACIFIC OCEAN
Coastal Trail
NEWTON B. DRURY SCENIC PARKWAY
Prairie Creek Redwoods State Park
101
FERN CANYON
PRAIRIE CREEK VISITOR CENTER
Gold Bluffs Beach
ELK PRAIRIE
River
LADYBIRD JOHNSON GROVE
Gold Bluffs Trail
101
REDWOOD INFORMATION CENTER
Orick
Redwood Creek
TALL TREES ACCESS ROAD (SHUTTLE ONLY)
BALD HILLS RD.
Freshwater Lagoon
Stone Lagoon
To Weitchpec and Hoopa Valley
Humboldt Lagoons State Park
Redwood Creek Trail
REDWOOD NATIONAL PARK
Redwood Creek
Big Lagoon
101
Rodgers Peak
Patricks Point State Park
To Trinidad and Eureka

0   5 mi
0   5 km

MOON

REDWOOD NATIONAL PARK AND VICINITY

© AVALON TRAVEL PUBLISHING, INC.

KIM WEIR

Lady Bird Johnson Grove

Though fishing, kayaking, surfing, and rafting are increasingly popular, nature study and hiking are the park's main recreational offerings. For those seeking views with the least amount of effort, take a drive along Howland Hill Rd. (one-lane dirt road) through some of the finest trees in Jedediah Smith Redwoods State Park. (Howland Hill Rd. transects the park and can be reached via South Fork Rd. off Hwy. 199 just east of the park or via Elk Valley Rd. south of Crescent City.) Or try a sunny picnic on the upland prairie overlooking the redwoods and ocean, reached via one-lane Bald Hills Rd., eight miles or more inland from Hwy. 101. Among sights along the primarily unpaved **Coastal Drive,** which starts on the south side of the Klamath River—great views on a sunny day— is a World War II–vintage early-warning radar station cleverly disguised as a farmhouse (with false windows and dormers) and barn.

Park Hiking Trails

The together-but-separate nature of the park's interwoven state and federal jurisdictions makes everything confusing, including figuring out the park's trail system. Pick up a copy of the ***Trails*** brochure published by the Redwood Natural History Association available at any of the state or national park information centers and offices in the area. *Trails* divides the collective system north and south, provides corresponding regional trail maps, describes the general sights along each trail, and classifies each by length and degree of difficulty. Fifty cents well spent.

Among the must-do walks is the easy and short self-guided nature trail on the old logging road to **Lady Bird Johnson Grove.** Near the grove at the overlook is an educational logging rehabilitation display composed of acres of visual aids—devastated redwood land clear-cut in 1965 and 1970 next to a forest selectively logged at the end of World War II. At the parking lot two miles up steep Bald Hills Rd., you'll find a picnic area and restrooms.

The traditional route for true tree huggers, though, is the long (but also easy) 11.5-mile round-trip hike (at least five hours one-way, overnight camping possible with permit) along **Redwood Creek Trail** to the famous **Tall Trees Grove.** The grove's **Howard Libby Redwood** was once 368 feet tall and claimed the title of the world's tallest tree. But in 1999, a storm blew off the top 10 feet, and the tree lost its tallest-tree crown, as it were, to another redwood (unmarked, for its own protection) in Montgomery Woods State Reserve in Mendocino County. There is also a shuttle to the grove from the information center near Orick.

The longest and most memorable trek in Redwood National Park is the 30-mile-long **Coastal Trail,** which runs almost the park's entire length (hikable in sections) from near Endert's Beach south of Crescent City through Del Norte Redwoods State Park (and past the HI-AYH hostel there), inland around the mouth of the Klamath River, then south along Flint Ridge, Gold Bluffs Beach, and Fern Canyon in Prairie Creek Redwoods State Park. A summers-only spur continues south along the beach to the information center.

If the entire coast route is too much, the **Flint Ridge Trail** section from the east end of Alder Camp Rd. to the ocean (primitive camping) is wild and wonderful, passing beavers and beaver dams at Marshall Pond. Easy and exquisite is the short **Fern Canyon Trail,** just off the Coastal

Trail in Prairie Creek Redwoods State Park; it's less than a mile round-trip through a 60-foot-high "canyon" of ferns laced up the sides of Home Creek's narrow ravine. To get there by car, take Davison Rd. from near Rolf's west over the one-lane bridge—watch for cattle being herded home—for six miles to the Gold Bluffs Beach Campground, then continue 1.5 miles to the parking lot. Even better is the four-mile hike west on the **James Irvine Trail** from the visitor center (or via the **Miners Ridge Trail,** which connects to Irvine by means of the **Clintonia Trail**). However you get there, the trip is worth it for the jeweled greenery—sword, deer, five-fingered, chain, bracken, lady, and licorice ferns—clinging to the canyon's ribs along the chuckling stream.

The **Revelation Trail,** just south of the visitors center in Prairie Creek Redwoods State Park, is a short self-guided nature trail for blind and sighted people, with rope and wood handrails the entire length and "touchable" sights. Trailside features are described on signs, in brochures also printed in Braille, and on cassette tapes available at the visitor center. Also special, rarely visited, and especially rich in rhododendrons is the short **Brown Creek Trail,** east of Hwy. 101 and north of the Prairie Creek visitors center.

PRAIRIE CREEK REDWOODS STATE PARK

An almost dangerous feature at Prairie Creek is the permanent and photogenic herd of Roosevelt elk usually grazing in the meadow area right along Hwy. 101. Drivers tend to screech to a halt at the mere sight of these magnificent creatures. A separate herd of elk grazes in the coastal meadows along 11-mile **Gold Bluffs Beach,** also noted for its excellent whale-watching, sand dunes carpeted in wild strawberries, and a primitive campground with solar showers.

Elsewhere in 14,000-acre Prairie Creek Redwoods State Park, heavy winter rainfall and thick summer fog produce rainforest lushness. Redwoods rub elbows with 200-foot-tall Sitka spruce, Douglas fir, and Western hemlock above an amazing array of shrubs, ferns, and groundcover, not to mention 800 varieties of flowers and 500 different kinds of mushrooms. **Fern Canyon** is unforgettable. Also particularly worthwhile at

Prairie Creek: beachcombing, surf fishing, nature walks and photography, picnicking, and camping.

Near the visitors center/museum are some fine family campsites with flush toilets and hot showers. The more primitive beach campsites are first-come, first-camped, as are the adjacent hike-and-bike sites. Walk-in campsites are available at **Butler Creek Primitive Camp.** Register first with the office at Prairie Creek. The park day-use fee is $2. For more information on Prairie Creek Redwoods, stop by the visitors center here or other park visitors centers.

DEL NORTE COAST REDWOODS STATE PARK

Del Norte is a dense and foggy coastal rainforest composed of 6,400 acres of redwoods, meadows, beaches, and tidepools. It's so wet here in winter that the developed campgrounds close. The **Damnation Creek Trail,** crossing Hwy. 1 en route, leads through magnificent old-growth Sequoias, spruce, Oregon grape, and seasonal wildflowers to a tiny beach with offshore sea stacks and tidepools. Or, take the **Coastal Trail** from Wilson Creek to the bluffs. Easier is the short walk to the north coast's finest tidepools (and the Nickel Creek Primitive Camp) at the end of **Enderts Beach Trail,** accessible from Enderts Beach Rd. south of Crescent City. To see the park's second-growth redwoods, and for exceptional bird-watching, take the almost four-mile **Hobbs Wall Trail.**

JEDEDIAH SMITH REDWOODS STATE PARK

Though the competition is certainly stiff even close by, this is one of the most beautiful places on earth—and almost unvisited. Few people come inland even a few miles from Hwy. 101 near Crescent City.

Historic **Howland Hill Rd.,** once a redwood-paved thoroughfare, is now graveled and meanders like a summer river through the quiet groves. The **National Tribute Grove,** a 5,000-acre memorial to veterans of World Wars I and II, is the park's largest. Tiny **Stout Grove** includes the area's largest measured redwoods. For an easy two-mile loop, walk both the **Simpson** and **Peterson Trails** through primeval redwoods and ferns. Even shorter is the combined walk along the **Leiffer** and **Ellsworth Trails,** something of a Jedediah Smith sampler. The 30-minute **Stout Grove Trail** offers trees and access to some of the Smith River's excellent summer swimming holes (complete with sandy beaches). Take the **Hiouchi Trail** for rhododendrons and huckleberries. More ambitious are hikes along both forks of the **Boy Scout Tree** and **Little Bald Hills Trails.** Also among the Smith River redwoods are excellent developed campsites.

PRACTICAL REDWOOD NATIONAL PARK

Public Camping in Redwood National Park
Each of the three state parks in the area offers developed family-type camping, with hot showers and such. Disposal stations for RVs are available but hookups are not. These campgrounds are popular in summer, so advance reservations are advised; call ReserveAmerica at toll-free 800/444-7275. Though the Del Norte Campground is closed off-season due to very wet conditions (sometimes washouts), winter drop-in camping at the other campgrounds is usually no problem. Primitive sites are also available throughout the park. Obtain the required permits at information centers or at park headquarters in Crescent City. Primitive camping at the national park sites is free, though there is a small fee for environmental campsites within the state parks.

Staying in Redwood National Park
Accommodation prices in and around Orick are reasonable, partly because Redwood National Park is too far north for most visitors to California, but also because it's foggy here during peak tourist season. Most people follow the sun. Choice in area motels is meager, but **Rolf's Motel,** next to Rolf's Park Café in Orick, 707/488-3841, is certainly convenient. Inexpensive. The **Orick Motel and RV Park,** 121381 Hwy. 101, 707/488-3501, has rooms (Budget, but often full), tent spaces, and RV hookups.

Also within national park boundaries but right on the coast—about 12 miles south of Crescent City at the Hwy. 101 junction with Wilson Creek Rd.—is the fabulous HI-AYH **Redwood Hostel,** 14480 Hwy. 101 N, 707/482-8265, known locally as the DeMartin House. This is the grandly restored onetime home of one of Del Norte County's pioneer families. The 30-bed hostel is perfect even for small group retreats, with a dining room, small dorm rooms, a common room cozied up with a woodstove, outdoor redwood decks with fine views, and good kitchen facilities. The hostel is wheelchair accessible. Couple and family rooms are available with adequate advance notice. The rate is $13 per night, members and nonmembers alike. Advance reservations are advisable in summer.

The **Motel Trees,** 15495 Hwy. 101 S (across from Trees of Mystery) in Klamath, 707/482-3152, offers amenities including a tennis court, in-room color TV with movies, and an adjacent restaurant. Inexpensive. The historic **Klamath Inn** (formerly the Requa Inn), 451 Requa Rd., Requa, 707/482-1425 or toll-free 888/788-1706, is an English-style country inn first opened in 1885. Some rooms have great views. Moderate. The inn's **dining room** is open to guests and nonguests alike. Reservations advised.

Eating in Redwood National Park
Most people camp, and bring their own provisions—the Eureka-Arcata area being the last best supply stop before heading north. Supplies are also available in Crescent City, just north of the park.

Best bet for a fascinating meal in Orick, not to mention friendly people, is **Rolf's Park Café,** 123664 Hwy. 101, 707/488-3841, on the highway north of Orick proper (take the Fern Canyon exit). Rolf Rheinschmidt is known for his exotic dinner specialties, like wild turkey, elk and buffalo steaks, wild boar and bear roasts, even antelope sausage, plus chicken and pasta dishes, vegetarian dishes, and forest fare like fiddlehead ferns and wild mushrooms. Rolf also cooks up some great breakfasts and wholesome lunches. Wash it down with beer or wine, and have some linzertorte for dessert. Great place.

Other possibilities include the basic diner fare and good cream pies at the **Palm Cafe** in Orick, 121130 Hwy. 101, 707/488-3381, or a quick grocery stop at the **Orick Market,** 121175 Hwy. 101, 707/488-3501. Or eat at the somewhat pricey but quite good **Klamath Inn,** 451 Requa Rd., Requa, 707/482-1425 (reservations advised).

Redwood National Park Visitor Information
In addition to the national park proper, three state parks—Prairie Creek, Del Norte, and Jedediah Smith, all covered above—are included within the larger park boundaries, protecting more redwoods (160,000 acres total for the four parks) and offering additional recreation and camping possibilities. The centralized information source for all the parks is: **Redwood National and State Parks Information Center,** 1111 2nd St. (at K St.), Crescent City, CA 95531, 707/464-6101, www.nps.gov/redw/. The center's telephone number includes recorded information on each of the individual parks in the system, and you can also reach a human during office hours. There is no fee for admission to Redwood National Park, but the day-use fee for each state park is $2. This and other park visitors centers are closed on Thanksgiving, Christmas, and New Year's Day.

In addition to the main visitors center in Crescent City, several other visitors centers are available. The **Orick Redwood National Park Information Center,** near Orick at the old lumber mill site at the mouth of Redwood Creek (north of Freshwater Lagoon and west of the highway), 707/464-6101, ext. 5265, is an imposing, excellent interpretive museum. The enthusiastic staff is very helpful. Open mid-June to Labor Day, daily 8 A.M.–7 P.M., and the rest of the year, daily 9 A.M.–5 P.M. Pick up a map for the park's 200-mile trail system. Sharing the same building is the **Orick Chamber of Commerce,** P.O. Box 234, Orick, CA 95555, 707/488-2885.

Another good visitors center is **Hiouchi,** on Hwy. 199 at Jedediah Smith Redwoods State Park, 707/464-6101, ext. 5067. Open mid-June to Labor Day, daily 8 A.M.–7 P.M.; until 5 P.M. the rest of the year. The **Prairie Creek Visitor Center,** 127011 Newton B. Drury Scenic Parkway in Prairie Creek State Park, 707/464-6101, ext. 5301, is usually open 8 A.M.–dusk in summer and 9 A.M.–5 P.M. in winter.

And feel free to explore farther afield. California's only completely undammed river system, the three-fork Smith River and its tributaries are the focal points of the **Smith River National Recreation Area,** a 305,337-acre preserve. For maps and other information, contact the **Gasquet Ranger District** of Six Rivers National Forest, on Hwy. 199, P.O. Box 228, Gasquet, CA 95543, 707/457-3131, open daily 8 A.M.–4:30 P.M. in travel season, weekdays only mid-October to April. Also abutting Redwood National Park are almost one million acres of other public forest lands, extending in a long, fairly narrow block from the Oregon border to southeast of Garberville in **Six Rivers National Forest.** For a $4 forest map—definitely advisable—and current river, trail, and camping information, contact **Six Rivers National Forest Headquarters,** 1330 Bayshore Way, Eureka, CA 95501, 707/442-1721, or any of the area ranger district offices.

Park Transportation
Most people drive—and the immense size of the park makes a personal vehicle quite handy. **Greyhound,** 1603 4th St. in Eureka, 707/442-0370, or 500 E. Harding in Crescent City, 707/464-2807, stops on its way between those two cities at the Shoreline Deli just south of Orick, at Paul's Cannery in Klamath, and at the AYH hostel north of Klamath. To fly into the area, nearest is the **Eureka-Arcata Airport** in McKinleyville, 3561 Boeing Ave., 707/839-1906. Rental cars are available there.

CRESCENT CITY AND VICINITY

Most of the world's Easter lilies, that ultimate modern-day symbol of resurrection, are grown north of Crescent City, the only incorporated city in Del Norte County. A proud if historically downtrodden town laid out in 1853 along the crescent moon harbor, Crescent City is a grim weatherbeaten gray, pounded so long by storms it has become one with the fog. Grim, too, is life for prisoners locked up just outside town at **Pelican Bay State Prison,** the state's largest maximum-security prison. The prison primes the community's economic pump with some $40 million per year and was the focus of California senator Barry Keene's Name That Prison contest. Among the unselected but otherwise superior suggestions from clever north coast minds: The Big Trees Big House, Camp Runamok, Dungeness Dungeon, Saint Dismos State (a reference to the patron saint of prisoners), and Slammer-by-the-Sea.

Crescent City still suffers from the 1964 tsunami

ROBERT HOLMES/CALTOUR

Crescent City Harbor

that tore the town off its moorings after the big Alaska earthquake, as well as a freak typhoon with 80-mile-an-hour winds that hit in 1972. Life goes on, however; the once devastated and denuded waterfront is now an attractive local park and convention center. Crabbing from the public **Citizens' Wharf,** built at Crescent Harbor with entirely local resources and volunteer labor when government rebuilding assistance fell through, is especially good. The French-design harbor breakwater is unique, a system of interlocking, 25-ton concrete "tetrapods."

The **Crescent City-Del Norte County Chamber of Commerce Visitor Center** is at 1001 Front St., 707/464-3174 or toll-free 800/343-8300. For web information, try the **Del Norte County website,** www.delnorte.org.

Seeing and Doing Crescent City

See the **Battery Point Lighthouse** near town. Weather and tides permitting, walk out to it on a path more than 100 years old and visit the island museum, 707/464-3089, open Wed.–Sun. 10 A.M.–4 P.M. (small donation). Decommissioned in 1953, though it was 12 more years before they turned the light out, the Battery Point Lighthouse was restored in 1981 by Craig Miller, with local donations of materials. The Del Norte Historical Society has operated the light as a private navigational aid since 1982. Stop by the **Del Norte County Historical Society Museum,** 577 H St., 707/464-3922, to appreciate its collection of Native American artifacts, quilts and kitchenware, and logging and mining paraphernalia. Open

Mon.–Sat. 10 A.M.–4 P.M. (admission by donation). Stop by the historic **McNulty House** nearby, 710 H St., 707/464-5186, to take in exhibits of antiques, old clocks, and works of area artists.

Practical Crescent City

Motel rates in Crescent City drop markedly in winter. The **Curly Redwood Lodge,** 701 Hwy. 101 S (a half mile south of town on the highway, near the marina), 707/464-2137, fax 707/464-1655, has large rooms, color TV with cable, and coffee available in the lobby. Moderate. Also across from the marina is the top-of-the-line **Best Western Northwoods Inn,** 655 Hwy. 101 S, 707/464-9771 or toll-free 800/557-3396. Amenities here include in-room hair dryers and coffeemakers, along with a guest laundry and spa. On-site restaurant, free breakfast. Moderate-Expensive.

For cheese (and a plant tour), head for the north coast's noted **Rumiano Cheese Company,** at 511 9th St. (at E St.), 707/465-1535, open Mon.–Sat. 8:30 A.M.–3:30 P.M. Many local restaurants don't take credit cards, so bring cash. Basic for breakfast is **Glen's Bakery & Restaurant,** 722 3rd St., 707/464-2914, where you can also get a mean bowl of clam chowder, fresh fish dishes, and good baked goods. Beer lovers will want to head for **Jefferson State Brewery,** 400 Front St., 707/464-1139, for handcrafted ales and decent food. Open Sun.–Thurs. 11 A.M.–11 P.M., Fri.–Sat. 11 A.M.–midnight. For seafood, head for the **Beachcomber Restaurant,** on Hwy. 101 at South Beach, 707/464-2205, right on the beach.

KIM WEIR

THE NORTHERN MOUNTAINS AND MODOC

The northern mountains are too far north for most travelers, and despite the economic benefits of tourism, most people living here prefer it that way. Here in the Klamaths and Cascades, mountains tower like monuments to the gods, and lava badlands pocked with mud pots and fumaroles create nightmare scenes from hell. Here is "the heart of the great black forests" described by badman poet Joaquin Miller, remnants of the virgin old-growth forests that once defined the land from here to Canada. Here also are craggy mountain peaks under cobalt blue skies, rushing rivers, crystal-clear lakes, and delicate meadows where dainty wildflowers bloom during very short summers. The glacial high-country terrain is as spectacular as the Sierra Nevada.

Almost as wild as the land is the area's settlement history, a stream of rebellions, secessions, and regional wars. Trappers first came to the northern mountains in the late 1820s, traversing the territory from Oregon to San Francisco via the Siskiyou Trail until the 1840s. In

1842, English pirates discovered gold at Sailors Bar on the Trinity River, and in 1849 one of Frémont's men, Major Pierson Barton Reading, likewise found nuggets at Big Bar near his namesake town, modern-day Redding. New gold dreams brought a new gold rush, and the fever soon spread north; nuggets were found at Scott Bar near the mouth of the Scott River and farther north in the Siskiyous and Rogue River country. But if gold brought settlers to these mountains, the lure of lumber kept them here.

To the east of California's northern mountains is remote Modoc County, a high-country volcanic plateau that remains a rugged remnant of the Old West. California's outback, Modoc County is a popular pit stop for migrating birds along the Pacific Flyway.

States of Rebellion

In 1852, a bill to form the separate State of Shasta was introduced in the California legislature, with the intent of providing more military protection, better roads and mail service, and lower taxes for northstate territory. That bill died in committee, but it was hardly the end of the idea. In 1853 came the call for the formation of the State of Klamath, an area running roughly from Cape Mendocino to the Umpqua River. The following year, a meeting in Jacksonville, Oregon, was convened to plan the statehood convention for Jackson; in 1855, the issue came up again.

Those who sought separate statehood during the mid-1800s did so because they felt isolated and victimized, complaining about the area's inadequate roads and lack of protection against angry, militant native peoples. The widespread support among settlers toward secession was also reflected locally, resulting in the eventual creation of Modoc and Lassen Counties from Siskiyou County and the Nevada Territory, respectively.

Organized acts of rebellion weren't confined to settlers. Attacks by native warriors were expressions of their rage over decimation due to disease and violence. Notable among these "unwritten histories," as Joaquin Miller would call

THE STATE OF JEFFERSON

Possibly only half seriously during this century, the issue of secession came up again. On Nov. 27, 1941, the State of Jefferson officially seceded from Oregon and California. Citizens of the new "state" put up roadblocks on Hwy. 99 and stated their intent "to secede each Thursday until further notice"—or until they got good roads into the copper belt between the highway and the sea. The short-lived state of Jefferson extended from the Pacific over to the high plateau in Nevada, north to Roseburg, Oregon, and south to Redding, California. The new state's capital was Yreka, and its symbol was a gold pan. In the center of the state seal was "XX," indicating just how the people here felt about California and Oregon: double-crossed.

On December 4, Judge John L. Childs of Crescent City was selected as acting governor of the new U.S. state, and his inauguration ceremony took place on the lawn of the courthouse in Yreka. "Our roads are not passable, barely jackassable; if our roads you would travel, bring your own gravel" read signs posted for the benefit of *Time, Life,* and film crews. Plans to release film footage of that event, the formation of what was to be America's 49th state, were foiled on December 8 by the greater news of Japan's attack on Pearl Harbor the day before. If it weren't for World War II, California travelers today would cross Jefferson on the way to Oregon. But the rebellion wasn't ineffective. Roads *were* finally paved in the far north, the construction of a major interstate freeway was inspired, and Stanton Delaplane of the *San Francisco Chronicle* won a Pulitzer Prize for his news coverage.

THE STATE OF JEFFERSON

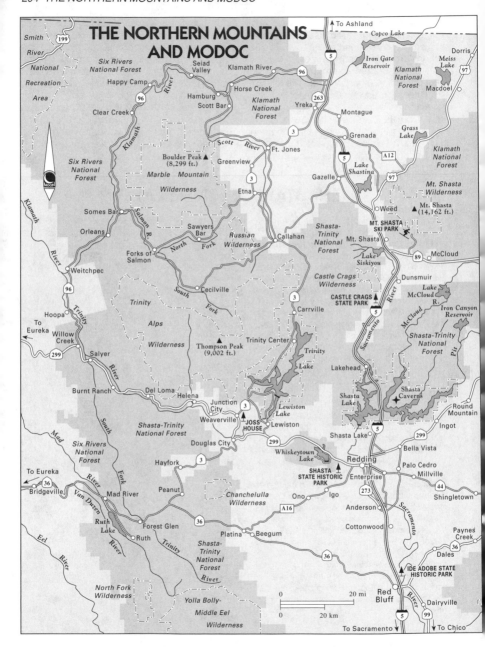

THE NORTHERN MOUNTAINS AND MODOC

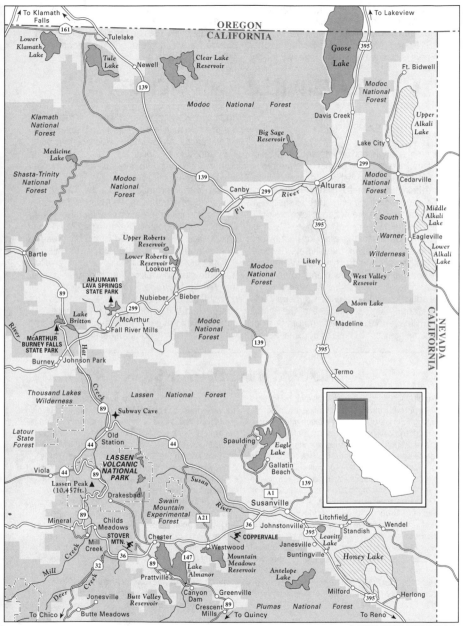

© AVALON TRAVEL PUBLISHING, INC.

them, was one actually written—the long-running Modoc War of "Captain Jack" and his band, among the last major Indian Wars fought by U.S. troops. Modoc's Lava Beds National Monument is also a monument to the war fought in and among its lava caves. Another well-written history of California's northern mountains is the story of Ishi, "the last wild man in North America," though his was a tale of grief and acceptance, rather than defiance.

WEAVERVILLE AND VICINITY

WEAVERVILLE

There's not a single parking meter or traffic signal in Trinity County. And people here are proud of that. *Wild* is the word in this landscape. White-water rafting is good on the Trinity River, as are salmon and trout fishing along quieter stretches. Early in summer, before hot days take their toll, mountain wildflowers are everywhere. Cycling, hiking, and backpacking are worthwhile endeavors. In the Trinities, the ultimate destination is the glacier-carved Trinity Alps Wilderness to the north, though there's plenty to see and do elsewhere. And don't miss Weaverville.

The county seat, Weaverville is a friendly little city of around 4,000 at the base of the Trinity Alps. In Weaverville, cottages and old brick or wood-frame homes are corralled by picket fences and covered with creeping vines. Notable here are the gold rush–era buildings with exterior spiral staircases. An inventory of local historic buildings and sights is included in the free walking tour brochure and map, available at the chamber of commerce.

For more information about the Trinity Alps area and its attractions, including community events and lake recreation, contact the **Trinity County Chamber of Commerce,** 211 Trinity Lakes Blvd. (Hwy. 3), P.O. Box 517, Weaverville, CA 96093, 530/623-6101 or toll-free 800/487-4648, www.trinitycounty.com. In addition to the downtown walking-tour brochure, ask for the *Trinity Heritage Scenic Byway* auto-tour pamphlet and map of the Hwy. 299 corridor; it's jam-packed with useful details. Ask here, too, for fishing information, guide services, and area white-water rafting companies.

KLAMATH MOUNTAINS

"Klamath Mountains" is the collective name for several separate ranges in northwestern California reaching 6,000–9,000 feet in elevation and oriented in all different directions. The Klamaths include some of the wildest, least-known, and most fragile wilderness areas in California. The fresh, clear streams are still important for salmon and steelhead spawning because few roads cut into these areas. And the timber industry hasn't yet cut out all the heart of the wilds here.

Close to Oregon, the **Siskiyou Mountains** are one of several California coastal ranges milking airborn moisture from storms headed inland from the ocean. The Siskiyous, averaging 5,000–6,000 feet in elevation, run mostly east-west along the Oregon border from the Pacific Ocean to the Rogue River Valley. But the western end of the range runs north-south, forming the divide between the Smith and Klamath Rivers.

South of the Siskiyous are the towering peaks, meadowlands, and glacial lakes of the rugged **Marble Mountains,** laced by interconnecting trails, and the nearby **Russian Mountains.** The **Salmon** and **Scott Mountains** (to the south and southeast, respectively) form the northerly fringe of the **Trinity Alps,** which include the Trinity Wilderness and the easterly Trinity Mountains. Most notable in the Trinities is evidence of ancient glacial activity: scoured mountain lakes, serrated ridges, and high, sloping meadows. One glacier remains on Thompson Peak, the highest point in northwestern California.

The **Yolla Bolly Mountains** (named from the Wintu Yo-la Bo-li, meaning "high, snow-covered peak") include the **Yolla Bolly-Middle Eel Wilderness** and are the most southerly of the Klamaths. Near Mt. Shasta, the **Castle Crags** area (now a state park) is technically part of the Klamath range, forming its eastern boundary.

For information and campfire permits for the Trinity, Lewiston, and Whiskeytown Lakes areas—and for wilderness permits and maps—contact the U.S. Forest Service **Weaverville Ranger District** office, 210 Main St. (Hwy. 299), P.O. Box 1190, Weaverville, CA 96093, 530/623-2121, open weekdays 8 A.M.–5 P.M. (daily in summer), or the **Coffee Creek Ranger Station** at the north end of Trinity Lake on Hwy. 3, Coffee Creek, CA 96091, 530/266-3211. Though open only weekdays 8 A.M.–5 P.M., these places will leave a permit outside for campers arriving after hours (with advance notice).

For details on all regional national forest recreation and wildernesses, contact: **Shasta-Trinity National Forest** headquarters, 2400 Washington Ave., Redding, CA 96001, 530/242-2360, www.r5.fs.fed.us/shastatrinity.

Seeing and Doing Weaverville

The **Weaverville Drug Store,** 219 Main St., 530/623-4343, is the oldest drugstore in California—a 1950s-feeling Rexall that's been in business since 1852—complete with pill-rolling machines. Across the street is the old *Trinity Journal* newspaper office, 218 Main, 530/623-2055, home of one of the state's oldest newspapers. The **Weaverville Firefighters Museum,** 100 Bremer St. (in the Weaverville Volunteer Fire Station), 530/623-6156, still features a hand pumper, a hose cart, and other old-time equipment on display. In the 1850s, half the town's population was Chinese, so it's not surprising that the old firehouse is a Chinese rammed-earth adobe.

A fine old Taoist temple is the focal point at **Weaverville Joss House State Historic Park.** ("Joss" is a corruption of the Spanish word *dios,* meaning "god.") Originally built in 1853, then torched 20 years later, the temple was rebuilt in 1874—the oldest Chinese temple in continuous use in California. Inside the brightly painted wood-frame are three ornately carved wooden canopies. The ancient altar, more than 3,000 years old, embraces candles, incense, an oracle book and fortune sticks, and glass-painted pictures of Immortals. In front are a table and urn for food and alcohol (usually whiskey) offerings to the gods. The joss house, known as "The Temple of the Forest Beneath the Clouds," is closed to the public when Taoists come to worship. Otherwise, tours (small fee) are scheduled on the hour when the park is open. For a current schedule of operating hours and more information, contact: Weaverville Joss House State Historic Park, P.O. Box 1217, Weaverville, CA 96093, 530/623-5284.

Across the parking lot from the joss house is the county historical society's excellent **J. J. "Jake" Jackson Memorial Museum,** 508 Main St., 530/623-5211, a handsome brick building with an extensive collection of firearms, mining equipment, Native American basketry, Chinese artifacts, and other documentation of California's development. Also on the grounds of this "historical park" are an original miner's cabin from La Grange; a working two-stamp mill (once used by miners to crush rock and extract gold) housed in a replica of the original building; and a facsimile blacksmith and tin shop. Admission is free but donations are much appreciated. For current hours, contact: **Trinity County Historical Society,** P.O. Box 333, Weaverville, CA 96093.

Staying in and near Weaverville

Public campgrounds abound in the area; get details at the local Forest Service office. A Weaverville motor-court motel with classic mountain ambience is the **Red Hill Motel** on Redhill Rd. right across from the U.S. Forest Service office, 530/623-4331, with 14 one- and two-bedroom cabins under the pines. Inexpensive. The large **Best Western Weaverville Victorian Inn,** 1709 Main St. (Hwy. 299), P.O. Box 2400, 530/623-4432, is actually a contemporary motel with modern conveniences ranging from satellite TV to in-room spas. Inexpensive-Moderate.

Unique among the Weaverville area's more outdoorsy lodging options are the **Ripple Creek**

ACCOMMODATIONS RATINGS

Accommodations in this book are rated by price category, based on double-occupancy, high-season rates. Categories used are:

Budget.	$35 and under
Inexpensive	$35-60
Moderate	$60-85
Expensive	$85-110
Premium	$110-150
Luxury	$150 and up

Cabins, HCR 2, Box 4020 (on the Eagle Creek loop off Hwy. 3), Trinity Center, CA 96091, 530/266-3505 or 510/531-5315, www.ripplecreekcabins.com. The beautifully restored cabins (with both woodstoves and electric heat) are casually scattered through the woods near a meadow, along Ripple Creek and the Trinity River. Each cabin features "basics" like garlic presses, colanders, corkscrews, and wineglasses, not to mention outdoor Weber barbecues and picnic tables. There's even a playground. Children and pets welcome. Expensive-Premium.

Bed-and-breakfasts near Weaverville include the casually elegant and historic **Carrville Inn Bed & Breakfast** on Carrville Loop Rd. just off Hwy. 3 north of Trinity Lake, HCR 2, Box 3536, Trinity Center, CA 96091, 530/266-3511, just about the area's most popular phenomenon since the arrival of paved roads. The inn is open mid-Apr. through Oct.; advance reservations are strongly advised. Premium. In the historic sector of Lewiston—and complete with prime fishing frontage along the Trinity River near the old bridge—is the **Old Lewiston Inn** Bed and Breakfast, P.O. Box 688, Lewiston, CA 96052, 530/778-3385 or toll-free 800/286-4441, fax 530/778-0309. This completely refurbished tin-roofed gold rush–era building is "as romantic as all get out," as the innkeepers say. A hot tub overlooks the river. Rates include full breakfast. Expensive.

Or try one of the Weaverville area's famed rustic resorts. Most of the area's truly rustic accommodations are veritable family-vacation traditions, usually booked at least a year in advance with one-week minimum stays during the peak summer season. The 1920s-style **Trinity Alps Resort,** 1750 Trinity Alps Rd., Trinity Center, CA 96091, 530/286-2205, is the oldest around, with rustic cabins along the Stuart Fork River. The cabins come in various sizes, sleeping anywhere from four to 10 people. Activities here include good fishing and river rafting, horseback riding, a pool hall and game room, and bingo and Ping-Pong at the resort's General Store. Open mid-May through Sept., the resort books one-week minimum stays from Memorial Day weekend through Labor Day, and a three-night minimum the rest of the season. Moderate. For other possibilities, inquire at the chamber of commerce (see above).

Eating in and near Weaverville
Absolutely organic eaters don't need to starve in Trinity County. The **Trinity Organic Growers Association** sponsors weekly **farmers' markets** in Weaverville and Hayfork, and the **Mountain Marketplace Natural Foods Grocery,** 222 Main St., 530/623-2656, sells organic fruits, vegetables, and bulk grains.

Quite popular is the **Pacific Brewery,** 401 S. Main (across from the joss house in the 1855

OTTER BAR LODGE

Just so you'll know where you are: The Salmon Mountains snaggle toward the southeast from the Siskiyous into both the Trinity Alps and Marble Mountain Wildernesses. The Scott Mountains snake down from the north, the two ranges never quite intersecting but coming close just south of the Marble Mountains. The north and south forks of the wild, undammed Salmon River flow west to their confluence at Forks of Salmon, then northwest to Somes Bar, where they merge with the Lower Klamath River.

The cultural highpoint of Forks of Salmon—not for budget travelers, except those willing to save up for a supreme white-water experience—Otter Bar Lodge is a world-class kayaking school and wilderness resort on the banks of the river. Though nothing here is particularly fancy or fussy, to describe Otter Bar as "rustic" is to suggest that Hearst Castle is a tract home. But it is 100 miles from any place you've ever heard of, and more than two hours from the nearest store.

Accommodations are available in three cabins and a four-bedroom lodge with a library. All rooms have down comforters, and antiques are peppered throughout the complex. Other amenities include great food (raved about in *Bon Appétit*) and an outdoor sauna and hot tub. When you're not kayaking, you can borrow a mountain bike to explore local trails, or go fishing—particularly pleasant in fall. The standard program is a week-long stay including everything—kayak instruction, use of equipment, lodging, and food. With adult classes grouped by experience, from beginners to "adventure travel," beginning and intermediate kids' kayaking camp is also offered.

For current information or reservations, contact: Otter Bar Lodge, Forks of Salmon, CA 96031, 530/462-4772, www.otterbar.com.

Pacific Brewery building), 530/623-3000, as appreciated for its food—everything from chicken fajitas to lasagna, seafood, and steaks—as its great selection of microbrews on tap and eclectic decor. Open daily for breakfast, lunch, and dinner. Or try the cheery **Garden Café,** 252 Main St., 530/623-2058, where the Austrian strudel is a specialty. Seasonally changing menu. Open for dinner on Fri. and Sat. year-round, for breakfast and lunch Tues.–Sat. during summer.

The place for creative yet comforting local cuisine—pastas, poultry, beef, fish, and game—is the **La Grange Cafe,** 315 N. Main, 530/623-5325, open Mon.–Sat. for lunch and dinner.

Best bets near Weaverville include the **Airporter Inn,** on Airport Rd. (at the airport), 530/266-3223—the overall ambience not particularly enticing, but the food quite good—European and American fare, primarily fish and meat selections. Another possibility, if you're willing to backtrack along Hwy. 299 toward Redding, is the attractive and historic **French Gulch Hotel,** 530/359-2112, a bed-and-breakfast also usually open Thurs.–Sat. nights for dinner and Sun. for brunch.

NEAR WEAVERVILLE

Trinity Alps Wilderness

Revel in these glacier-gouged goliaths looming over sapphire lakes. Though not as tall as major Cascade or Sierra Nevada peaks, these mountains, likened to the Swiss Alps, are snow-covered even in summer and thickly forested on lower slopes. The Trinity Alps are rocky and rugged, intimate and close. Depending upon snowpack and trail conditions, late June to late July is generally the ideal hiking time here, when wildflowers are best. But the Trinity Alps are also nice in fall, when crowds are absent.

California's Trinity Alps Wilderness is second in size only to the John Muir Wilderness in the Sierra Nevada. The area takes in more than a half-million acres, the headwaters of both the Salmon and Trinity Rivers, and more than 400 miles of trails, including a stretch of the Pacific Crest Trail and the New River area to the west. Before planning even a day trip into the wilds here, check locally on current conditions (see U.S. Forest Service contacts, above).

Trinity Lake and Trinity Center

Once officially known as **Clair Engle Lake** in honor of the senator behind the damming of the Trinity here, locals have long refused to recognize that name. People here call the lake "Trinity," after the river that once roared through the valley past the gold rush towns of Minersville and Stringtown (now underwater). With 150 miles of forested shoreline, the lake is warm enough for swimming in summer. Fishing for catfish, bass, trout, and salmon is popular, as are all types of boating.

Trinity Center, the main town near the lake, was founded in the 1850s and named for its original location at the center of the Shasta-Yreka Trail; the town was relocated to its present

KIM WEIR

Trinity Lake

site due to dam construction. Visit the **Scott Museum** here for its outstanding collection of historical material, including 500 types of barbed wire; the museum is on Airport Rd. and open only mid-May to mid-Sept., Tues.–Sat. 1–5 P.M.

Lewiston Lake and Lewiston

Just south of Trinity Lake, Lewiston Lake is a cold lake just below the dam. The cooler water means excellent fishing for rainbows and browns in the upper channels. Picnicking is good here, and since boat speeds are restricted to 10 mph, you won't hear any roaring engines. Camping is also good, and often less crowded than at Trinity. The most automated salmon and steelhead hatchery anywhere, worth seeing (to believe), is the California Department of Fish and Game's **Trinity River Fish Hatchery,** just south of the Lewiston Dam, 530/778-3931. Steelhead fishing is good along this stretch of the Trinity River.

The tiny town of Lewiston, south of the lake and about five miles from Hwy. 299 via Rd. 105, is just three miles upriver from where the first gold dredger was built. Among other shops, a real find for antique lovers is **The Country Peddler,** 530/778-3325 or 530/778-3876, along Deadwood Rd. in historic downtown. The town's **Sons of Temperance** meeting hall was erected in 1862 and still stands. Near Lewiston, **Limekiln Gulch** was once an active gold-mining area, now mostly visited by river-runners, hunters, and hikers. A restored cabin here was built in a style reminiscent of the French Colonial architecture common in the Mississippi River delta.

YREKA

Yreka is the only city to speak of in the central far north. People here (all 7,200 of them) are proud of their pioneer history. The town boasts a good local-history museum, a gold nugget display (in the courthouse), well-preserved old Victorians and brick gold-rush buildings, and a historic steam excursion train.

Visitor information, maps, and walking-tour brochures are available at the **Yreka Chamber of Commerce,** 117 W. Miner St., Yreka, CA 96097, 530/842-1649 or toll-free 800/669-7352 (recorded message), www.yrekachamber.com. At **Klamath National Forest** headquarters, 1312 Fairlane Rd., Yreka, CA 96097, 530/842-6131, www.r5.fs.fed.us/klamath, pick up regional camping, recreation, and wilderness information plus topo maps and wilderness and campfire permits.

Seeing and Doing Yreka

Most of the town's gold rush–vintage buildings, included in the National Register of Historic Places, are concentrated between Oregon and Main, and W. Lennox and Miner Streets. Horsehead hitching posts rear up out of modern-day sidewalks. (Pick up a free walking guide to Yreka's historic district at the chamber of commerce.)

downtown Yreka

ROBERT HOLMES/CalTour

The **Siskiyou County Museum,** 910 S. Main St., 530/842-3836, is an indoor-outdoor collection of historical relics, Native American and gold mining exhibits, firearms, and paraphernalia left behind by trappers and pioneers. Historical publications are available during normal museum hours, Mon.–Fri. 9 A.M.–5 P.M. (plus evenings and Sun. 1–5 P.M. in summer), closed Sun.–Mon. in winter. Free.

Eye-opening are the gold displays in the foyer of the **Siskiyou County Courthouse,** 311 4th St., 530/842-8340. The exhibit shows off a fortune in gold nuggets—the largest such collection south of Anchorage, Alaska—taken from local mines and placers. The museum is open Mon.–Fri. 8 A.M.–5 P.M. (also free). Worth a stop, too, is the **Klamath National Forest Interpretive Museum,** part of the headquarters complex at 1312 Fairlane Rd., 530/842-6131. Here you'll find an extensive collection of historical and natural history exhibits—one of the most impressive offered at any U.S. Forest Service outpost. Step into the lookout and check out the "firefinder." Admission is free.

Blue Goose

Yreka's pride and joy is the Yreka Western Railroad and its *Blue Goose* steam excursion train. When the *Goose* is in full flight, the 1915 black Baldwin locomotive pulls the art deco-vintage cars and an open-air passenger flatcar on a sightseeing trip through the Shasta Valley to Montague and back, about 15 miles round-trip. Trains run May–Sept., and fares are $12.25 adults, $10.75 seniors, $5.25 children (ages 3–12). For more information, stop by the historic depot (jog east from I-5's Central Yreka exit) or contact: **Yreka Western Railroad,** 300 E. Miner St., P.O. Box 660, Yreka, CA 96097, 530/842-4146 or toll-free 800/973-5277, www. yrekawesternrr.com.

Staying and Eating in Yreka

Get information on nearby Klamath National Forest campgrounds at forest headquarters here (see above). Yreka has a number of inexpensive motels, most of these clustered along "motel row" on Main. Top of the mark for Yreka-area motels is the **Best Western Miner's Inn,** 122 E. Miner (near I-5), 530/842-4355 or toll-free 800/528-1234. Inexpensive-Moderate. The attractive **Wayside Inn,** 1235 S. Main St. (about a mile south of town), 530/842-4412 or toll-free 800/795-7974, offers a few units with kitchens as well as one deluxe suite. Inexpensive-Moderate.

Charming **Nature's Kitchen** inside the old Bottling Works Mall on Main St., 530/842-1136, serves great salads and soups, house-made breads and rolls, even carrot juice and espresso. The **Miner Street Bakery,** 328 W. Miner, 530/842-6770, offers good coffee, espresso drinks, doughnuts, and pastries—a great place to get your morning sugar/caffeine rush; open Mon.–Sat. mornings. Across the way and housed in the city's old meat market is the **Miner Street Deli,** 319 W. Miner, 530/842-1854, with original mining-era art on the walls. **Lalo's,** 219 W. Miner, 530/842-2695, is popular at lunch and dinner for its Mexican fare. Quite good is the continental-American **Old Boston Shaft Restaurant,** 1801 S. Main, 530/842-5768, where the menu features seafood, beef, and wonderful Old World desserts. Open Mon.–Fri. for lunch and Mon.–Sat. for dinner. Reservations are a good idea.

Those in the know say downtown's **Rex Club,** 111 S. Main, 530/842-2659, is the best local bar.

MOUNT SHASTA AND VICINITY

"Lonely as God and white as a winter moon"—so Joaquin Miller described California's most majestic mountain in the 1800s. And so it still is. Mount Shasta is California's sixth-highest peak but more awesome than any other—perpetually snow-covered, glowing orange, pink, and purple at sunset, casting shadows on the lava lands below. Area Indians revered Shasta as the abode of the Great Spirit.

Sometimes clearly visible from as far away as 150 miles, close up Shasta is more mysterious and obscure. Mount Shasta is the highest point in California's Cascades. Though Mt. Whitney is taller by 332 feet and other mountains are bigger by different degrees of measurement, their grandeur is lost among ranks of lofty peaks. Not so Shasta, which stands alone at 14,162 feet and towers 10,000 feet above the surrounding countryside. But height isn't everything. Shasta is the largest volcano in the contiguous 48 states, and with a diameter of more than 20 miles, it is perhaps in sheer volume the largest mountain as well.

MOUNT SHASTA CITY

Perpetually in the mountain's shadow, this tiny town popped up in the 1850s and was first called Sisson after J. H. Sisson, John Muir's friend and guide (also the local postmaster and innkeeper). With the growth of tourism here in the 1920s came the more marketable moniker.

Taste the mountain's (and the town's) pure sweet water at the public water fountain downtown. The **Sisson Fish Hatchery,** 1 N. Old Stage Rd. (follow W. Jessie west from town), 530/926-5508, is the state's first successful hatchery. Located here because of the pure water and the railroad (for fish transport), the century-old hatchery is still in operation, birthing new generations of rainbow trout for planting as far afield as New Zealand. The facility is capable of producing millions of fish per year. On the grounds are a well-manicured park (with oaks, cedars, and 50 ponds for the small fry) and a museum covering all aspects of local history, also featuring a decent selection of books on the Mt. Shasta region. The museum includes a new major exhibit each year and is open daily, in summer 10 A.M.–5 P.M., in winter noon–4 P.M.

For more area information, contact the very helpful **Mt. Shasta Convention and Visitors Bureau,** at the local chamber office, 300 Pine St., Mt. Shasta, CA 96067, 530/926-4865 or toll-free 800/397-1519, www.mtshastachamber.com, open weekdays 9 A.M.–6 P.M., weekends 10 A.M.–4 P.M. The bureau provides brochures and other information about local services and special events, and also offers guided bus tours.

At the office of Shasta-Trinity National Forest's **Mt. Shasta Ranger District,** 204 W. Alma (a block and a half west of Mt. Shasta Blvd., across the railroad tracks), 530/926-4511, stop for camping and climbing information; fire permits; forest,

---

SHASTA WEATHER

It's frigid here in winter, and always cool but sometimes cold in summer. The weather at the summit is changeable and often severe. Even in summer, sudden storms—wicked icy winds, thunderstorms, sometimes snow or hail—are possible, so always be prepared. Shasta, in a sense, creates its own weather and affects the Sacramento Valley as well, blocking the wet Canadian north winds in winter and, in summer, turning the north valley into a bake oven—the primary reason Redding is often among the hottest spots in the nation.

Nothing about Mt. Shasta weather is stranger, though, than the sudden flying saucer–shaped cloud formations generating intense greenish-blue beams of light—evidence, to many, of UFOs or celestial spirit-beings of one sort or another. Scientists, however, explain it like this: cold, fast-moving northerly winds push cold dry air over the top of Shasta and also around and up the mountain's sides. Wind shear is created where these winds meet and, between 6,500 and 10,000 feet, icy, almond-shaped lenticular clouds form. The sun's reflection off the miniscule ice particles creates the mountain light show.

SHASTA ADVENTURING

The Fifth Season Sports, 300 N. Mt. Shasta Blvd., 530/926-3606 or 530/926-2776, rents ice axes and crampons and also offers hiking, backpacking, and other recreation supplies. For Fifth Season's **24-hour climbing report,** call 530/926-5555. **Shasta Mountain Guides,** 1938 Hill Rd., Mt. Shasta, CA 96067, 530/926-3117, offers mountaineering, ice and rock-climbing, and glacier travel instruction, and leads guided Shasta and Castle Crags climbs. Among popular nontechnical climbs is the two-day "Traditional John Muir Route," following the famed naturalist's favored ascent. Custom climbs are easily arranged. Unusual, too, is Shasta Mountain's wilderness program for the physically disabled.
Turtle River Rafting Company, P.O. Box 313, Mt. Shasta, CA 96067, 530/926-3223 or toll-free 800/726-3223, offers a tremendous selection of fun runs (inflatable kayaks and rafts) spring through fall, on the Klamath, Upper Sacramento, Scott, Salmon, and Trinity Rivers. Turtle River has an exceptional safety record, is fully insured, leaves its schedule "open" to a remarkable degree (to accommodate travelers' particular needs), and happily works with schools, churches, and other groups. Many raft trips are appropriate for children ages 4 and up; families are welcome. Contact the company for current rates, reservations, and further information.
For an aerial view of the mountain aboard a hot-air balloon, contact **Shasta Valley Balloons,** 316 Pony Trail, Mt. Shasta, 530/926-3612. Four-hour excursions are offered Fri.–Mon. and include a dawn launch, one-hour flight, open-air brunch, and a champagne toast; $160 per person.

wilderness, and some topo maps; wilderness permits; and trailhead parking and summit-climb passes (which can be self-issued after hours and at the trailheads). Not to mention some friendly advice. Alternatively, for Mt. Shasta information contact the **McCloud Ranger District,** 2019 Forest Rd., P.O. Box 1620, McCloud, CA 96057, 530/964-2184.

Staying in Mt. Shasta City
Ask about area camping options—abundant—at both the visitors bureau and the Forest Service office. Otherwise, the best choice for an amicable, low-budget Shasta stay is the independent **Alpenrose Cottage Hostel,** 204 E. Hinckley St., 530/926-6724. This homey two-story place boasts magnificent views of the mountain, and options include separate dorm-style rooms for men and women (three bunk beds in each) plus a couples room. Clean and inviting, with a communal kitchen and living area with woodstove. Budget.
Inexpensive-category motels include the **Evergreen Lodge,** 1312 S. Mt. Shasta Blvd., 530/926-2143; **Pine Needles Motel,** 1340 S. Mt. Shasta Blvd., 530/926-4811; and the **Strawberry Court Motel,** 305 Old McCloud Rd., 530/926-4704, which is off the main drag and usually has rooms available.
The **Best Western Tree House Motor Inn,** 111 Morgan Way (next to I-5 at the Central Mt. Shasta exit), 530/926-3101 or toll-free 800/528-1234 for reservations, offers typical top-of-the-line Best Western amenities, here including an indoor heated pool. Moderate-Expensive.
Or try a bed-and-breakfast. Quite wonderful in town is the **Strawberry Valley Inn,** 1142 S. Mt. Shasta Blvd., 530/926-2052, fax 530/926-0842, a onetime motor court transformed into a welcoming 15-room inn with plenty of privacy, attractive gardens, and oak trees. A lovely stone home serves as the inn's lobby—the fireplace particularly inviting in winter. Moderate. Also quite nice is the **Dream Inn,** 326 Chestnut St., 530/926-1536 or toll-free 877/375-4744, offering four rooms with shared bath and one with private bath in a 1904 Victorian. Moderate-Expensive.
The **Mt. Shasta Ranch Bed and Breakfast,** 1008 W. A. Barr Rd., 530/926-3870, is truly something special—a classic in the Dutch Gambrel tradition. Some people would say it's a barn, albeit a barn with covered veranda and unobstructed views of Mt. Shasta. But the atmosphere here is actually like a 1920s lodge—tasteful, almost formal, from the 1,500-square-foot living room with original oak floors and huge stone fireplace to the huge upstairs suites. Rooms in the separate Carriage House share two bathrooms, and the "cottage" is a completely equipped two-bedroom home with woodstove and electric heat. Unusual for B&Bs these days, children are genuinely welcome. Moderate-Expensive.
North of Weed, in Gazelle, is the impressive **Hollyhock Farm Bed and Breakfast,** 18705

Old Hwy. 99, 530/435-2627, a charming stone farmhouse dressed up in antiques and lace—also serving up spectacular views of Mt. Shasta. Moderate-Expensive. An excellent choice in the vicinity of Mt. Shasta is the exquisitely restored 1915 **McCloud Hotel.** For details, see McCloud, below.

Eating in Mount Shasta

A traditional post-Shasta-climb stop is **Willy's Bavarian Kitchen,** 107 Chestnut, 530/926-3636. Sit out in the sun and slurp a pint of good German beer with the local hip-oisie, and if you're hungry, get German and vegetarian food to go with it.

Lalo's, 520 N. Mt. Shasta Blvd., 530/926-5123, serves decent Mexican food and in summer offers outdoor dining. Very good and reasonable is **Michael's,** 313 N. Mt. Shasta Blvd., 530/926-5288, locally famous for its homemade pastas (including *pelemy,* or Russian ravioli), sauces, and soups. A big hit at lunch is Michael's "rancho burger," a half-pound slab of fresh hamburger cooked to order and served on french bread with good fries on the side.

Lily's, across the street from the Strawberry Valley Inn at 1013 S. Mt. Shasta Blvd., 530/926-3372, is fabulously popular for its ethnically spiced California cuisine at breakfast, lunch, and dinner. Mexican entrées are available at every meal, and the menu features abundant vegetarian choices. Open daily.

Truly fine dining in these parts (dinners only) means making a reservation at **Serge's Restaurant,** located a block east of Mt. Shasta Blvd. at 531 Chestnut, 530/926-1276. Serge's, which got its start at Stewart Mineral Springs, features classical French cuisine (seasonally changing menu) accented with a few Thai, Cajun, and vegetarian dishes, and finished with wonderful house-made desserts. Closed Monday and Tuesday.

NEAR MOUNT SHASTA CITY

The trouble with climbing Mt. Shasta is that you can't see it if you're on it. So hike up nearby **Mt. Eddy** (elev. 9,025 feet) and along adjacent stretches of the **Pacific Crest Trail** for majestic Mt. Shasta views.

Stewart Springs and Vicinity

Scenic **Stewart Mineral Springs Therapeutic Mountain Retreat,** seven miles north of Weed, was founded in 1875 by the near-dead Henry Stewart, who was brought here by local Indians and healed by the waters. Facilities include a bathhouse with 13 individual mineral baths, three massage rooms (separate fee for massage), a sauna, sun deck, gift shop, and restaurant. Accommodations include cabins, motel rooms, tepees, campsites, and a three-level A-frame for large groups. Inexpensive-Moderate. Nearby is the trail to the **Deadfall Lakes,** some of the prettiest on the Trinity Divide.

For more information, contact: Stewart Mineral Springs Therapeutic Mountain Retreat, 4617 Stewart Springs Rd., Weed, CA 96094, 530/938-2222. To get there from I-5 north of Weed, take the Edgewood exit and head west four miles on Stewart Springs Road.

Mt. Shasta Board & Ski Park

Shasta's downhill ski area has three triple-chair lifts for novice to advanced skiers, a poma lift for beginners, and 425 acres (27 trails) of excellent skiing. A snowmaking system offers protection against drought years. Snug in a valley at lower elevations and protected from wicked winter winds, the Ski Park is family-oriented and friendly, reached via Hwy. 89 near McCloud. Half-day rates are available starting at noon, and night skiing is offered Wed.–Sat. 4–10 P.M. "Learn to ski" packages including equipment and either one or two lessons are available. Disabled skiers and snowboarders are welcome. Lifts run daily 9 A.M.–4 P.M. for all-day skiing (noon–4 P.M. for half-day), and 4–10 P.M. Wed.–Sat. for nighttime skiing. Other facilities include a lodge, cafeteria, rental shop, and an adjacent Nordic ski area with miles of machine-groomed trails.

In the off-season, hitch a ride on the ski lift for hiking access, or partake in nature hikes and mountain bike tours. Increasingly popular is the annual **State of Jefferson Micro Brewery Festival,** held on a Saturday in early September. For more information, contact: **Mt. Shasta Ski Park,** 104 Siskiyou Ave., Mt. Shasta, CA 96067, 530/926-8610 (lodge), 530/926-8600 or toll-free 800/754-7427 (business office), or 530/926-8686 (snow and weather conditions), www.skipark.com.

RIDING THAT TRAIN

The **McCloud Railway Company,** P.O. Box 1199, McCloud, CA 96057, 530/964-2142 or toll-free 800/733-2141, www.mctrain.com, offers the opportunity to relive the glory days of rail onboard the **Shasta Sunset Dinner Train,** a white-linen-and-fine-china ride through the area's magnificent mountain scenery. The immaculately restored vintage rail cars feature enough deep mahogany and polished brass to satisfy even the most earnest woulda-been rail barons. Whippersnappers with no appreciation for history will still enjoy the constant clickety-clack of the cars over the track, the scrumptious grub, and the million-dollar views. Trains leave from the McCloud station on Main St. year-round except January; the $70 fare ($50 for lunch trains) includes nonalcoholic beverages (beer and wine are extra). Dress as if you were dining with the Hearsts, if you'd like, but most folks are reasonably casual.

For a less ostentatious train tour of Mt. Shasta, opt instead to jostle with the masses on a day trip for just $10 (diesel locomotive) or $15 (for the occasional steam-locomotive excursion). The ride lasts a little over an hour and the views are just as priceless. Call or visit the website for current schedule information and reservations.

McCloud

Head east on Hwy. 89 into McCloud country. The McCloud River is an excellent trout fishing stream, but only short stretches are open to the public (lots of lumbering, difficult access). For more information about camping and area recreation, stop by the office of the **McCloud Ranger District,** 2019 Forest Rd., 530/964-2184.

Aside from fishing, McCloud is most famous for the 60,000-acre Wyntoon estate, a private retreat designed by architect Julia Morgan for mythic American media magnate William Randolph Hearst. The estate's buildings still stand after being charred in a 1992 fire, but the retreat is (and always has been) closed to the public. Otherwise, even today the town reflects its more humble mill town history, from the general store to the variations on camp-town architecture. Stop by the massive **Mercantile Building** downtown on Main to sample the wares at the **McCloud General Store** and the **Milky Way Trad-**

ing **Company;** for a thick old-fashioned milkshake, the place is the **McCloud Soda Shop and Café** adjacent.

If at all possible, stay in McCloud. The painstaking restoration of the 1915 **McCloud Hotel** has created quite a buzz in the neighborhood. The three-story restored hostelry, now an exceptional bed-and-breakfast listed on the National Register of Historic Places, offers 14 "standard" guest rooms exquisitely decorated in 1930s style and four hot tub–equipped suites, all with private bath. After the complimentary full breakfast in the lobby, get out and enjoy the mountain scenery—the *Shasta Sunset* departs from the small public park across the street—or relax and read a book. Moderate-Luxury. For more information and to make reservations, contact: **McCloud Hotel,** 408 Main St., P.O. Box 730, McCloud, CA 96057, 530/964-2822 or toll-free 800/964-2823, www.mchotel.com.

CASTLE CRAGS

A foreboding granite formation created by volcanic forces some 170–225 million years ago, Castle Crags towers over I-5 40 miles north of Redding. Marking the southeastern edge of the Klamath Mountains, the Crags offer challenging rock-climbing, easy and difficult hikes, good camping (but within earshot of the freeway), and picnicking.

At 6,000-acre **Castle Crags State Park,** the **Pacific Crest Trail** swings through, making this a good spot for trekkers to arrange a supply drop and pick up mail. The impressive silver-gray crags snaggle upward at an elevation of 6,000 feet. Rock-climbing here is only for the experienced. The strenuous **Crags/Indian Springs Trail** to Castle Dome (which resembles Yosemite's Half Dome) is worthwhile for hikers, especially with the side trip to the springs. (High-country hikers, don't wander off the trail: cliffs have sudden 2,000-foot drop-offs and no warning signs.) Easier is the one-mile **Root Creek Trail,** which offers views of the crags and picnicking at Root Creek (soak your feet). The pleasant, one-mile **Indian Creek Nature Trail** loops over the creek and passes old mining paraphernalia.

Park headquarters is at the park's entrance in Castella (follow the signs from I-5), **Castle Crags**

Castle Crags

KIM WEIR

State Park, 20022 Castle Creek Rd., P.O. Box 80, Castella, CA 96017-0080, 530/235-2684. The state campground offers attractive campsites, some large enough for 21-foot trailers. Reserve in summer through ReserveAmerica, toll-free 800/444-7275. In the off-season, campsites are first-come, first-camped. The park's day-use fee is $2.

Dunsmuir and Castella

Dunsmuir, six miles to the north of Castle Crags, is a good supply stop. For area information, contact the **Dunsmuir Chamber of Commerce and Visitors Center,** toll-free 800/386-7684, www.dunsmuir.com.

Train fanatics, consider a stay at **Railroad Park Resort,** 100 Railroad Park Rd. (just off I-5) in Dunsmuir, 530/235-4440 or toll-free 800/974-7245 (motel, main office), www.rrpark.com. In keeping with area history, this unique establishment is a modern motel composed almost entirely of refurbished railroad cars (there are also a few cabins). Moderate. The good American-style dinner house and bar here, 530/235-4611, is a successful meshing of nine separate railroad cars. Campers can stay at the resort's RV park and tent campground, 530/235-0420. In addition, area accommodations options include the four stone cottages at the **Castle Stone Cottage Inn** in Castella, 530/235-0012. Moderate.

Dunsmuir offers one of the region's best restaurants, the tiny dinner-only **Café Maddalena,** 5801 Sacramento Ave. (a block west of Dunsmuir Ave.), 530/235-2725. Open only Thurs.–Sun. nights from mid-May to mid-Dec., Café Maddalena serves exceptional Southern Italian fare with the Sardinian accent of proprietor Maddalena Sera.

SHASTA DAM

The Sacramento River is one of the most channelized, diverted, and dammed rivers in the world, and Shasta Dam is its ultimate diversion. The mainstay of the federally funded Central Valley Project (CVP), Shasta Dam was constructed between 1938 and 1945. Flooding the canyons and holding back the waters of the Sacramento, Pit, and McCloud Rivers in addition to Squaw Creek, Shasta Dam is the second-largest concrete dam in the country. Enough concrete to build a three-foot-wide sidewalk around the world created this backwater behemoth, which is 602 feet high, 3,460 feet long, and 883 feet across at its base. The cost of construction: $182 million (in World War II–era dollars), 14 workers' lives, and the taming of the northstate's most impressive river. Public discussion of a possible expansion of Shasta Dam—increasing its height in an effort to store more water and quench the state's endless thirst—began again in 1997.

Walk or drive across the top of the dam for an above-water-level view of this technological tour de force. From here and from the vista point, see "the three Shastas" at once: dam, lake, and mountain. **Shasta Dam tours** are available year-round, on the hour from 9 A.M.–4 P.M. in summer and at 10 A.M., noon, and 2 P.M. in winter. The **visitors center** tells at least some of the story, with exhibits and a short film. It's open 7:30 A.M.–4 P.M. daily April–Oct. (closed weekends in winter).

For more information about Shasta Dam, contact: **U.S. Bureau of Reclamation,** Northern California Area Office, 16349 Shasta Dam Blvd., Shasta Lake, CA 96019, 530/275-4463 or 530/275-1554. To reach the dam, from I-5 take the Shasta Dam Blvd. exit (about 10 miles north of Redding).

SHASTA LAKE

When full, super-size Shasta Lake has around 370 miles of shoreline—one-third more than San Francisco Bay—and a surface area of 30,000 acres. Despite its gigantic girth, Shasta is not always the best place for those seeking complete solitude; two million or so people come here each year to camp, picnic, fish, swim, sail, and water-ski. And those in search of natural beauty might be disappointed in drought years or at other times when the lake's water level is down—the ugly swath of bare-naked red dirt above the water line looks like a giant-sized bathtub ring. But when the lake is full, Shasta is dazzling.

By virtue of its sheer size, Shasta Lake is water-skiing heaven. Houseboating is particularly popular here, too; with so much lake (and so many coves and inlets to tie up in), houseboaters either party Shasta-style or drift off alone for some peace and quiet. Shasta's rental houseboat fleet is probably the state's finest, some units featuring every amenity imaginable. Warmwater fishing is another big draw (spring is best), with anglers going primarily after small and largemouth bass, but also casting for crappie, and brown and rainbow trout.

Shasta Lake has five recreation areas connected to its "arms": **Jones Valley** (near the Pit and Squaw arms), **Gilman Rd.** (upper McCloud River arm), **O'Brien** (lower McCloud River arm), **Salt Creek** (Salt Creek inlet off the Sacramento arm), and **Lakehead** (upper Sacramento River arm). For information on all U.S. Forest Service campgrounds at Shasta Lake, call the **Shasta Recreation Company** at 530/238-2824; only group campgrounds are reservable, the rest are first-come, first-camped. For other recreation information, contact the **Shasta Lake Ranger District** office, 14225 Holiday Rd. (just south of the lake at the Mountain Gate exit off I-5), 530/275-1589.

For more information about Shasta Lake, from restaurants and accommodations to houseboat rentals, contact the excellent **Shasta-Cascade Wonderland Association,** 1699 Hwy. 273 (in the Shasta Factory Outlets mall, I-5 at Deschutes Rd.) in Anderson, 530/365-7500 or toll-free 800/474-2782, www.shastacascade.org, or the **Redding Convention and Visitors Bureau,** 777 Auditorium Dr., Redding, CA 96001, 530/225-4100 or toll-free 800/874-7562.

Lake Shasta Caverns

Only the out-and-out adventurous had access to these ancient caverns until 1964, when a tunnel was driven into the mountain below the original

Lake Shasta Caverns

entrance. Now, even armchair adventurers visit these natural wonders where California's Coast and Cascade Ranges, Sierra Nevada, and Klamath Mountains come together. The 60-foot-wide, 20-foot-tall drapolite "draperies" of the Cathedral Room were formed from calcium carbonate crystals in a stalactite waterfall. Elsewhere, stalagmites reach up from the cave floor and, fusing with stalactites, create multicolored fluted columns. In the Spaghetti Patch, gravity-defying masses of straw-thin helictites seem to swirl and swarm. Though the tour route itself is well lighted, with concrete steps and guardrails, fit purists can still go spelunking through the dank darkness and primal ooze (by reservation).

Two-hour tours of Lake Shasta Caverns start at O'Brien and cost $15 for adults, $7 for children (under age 3 free). Spelunking tours are four hours long. Either way, it's a 15-minute ferry trip by catamaran, then a thrilling bus ride up an 800-foot hill to the lower cave entrance. Bring a sweater or sweatshirt even in summer: the temperature inside is a constant cool 58°F. Open year-round, with tours offered May–Sept., hourly 9 A.M.–3 P.M., and Oct.–Apr. at 10 A.M., noon, and 2 P.M. Special group and spelunking tours are available by advance reservation only. For more information, contact: Lake Shasta Caverns, 20359 Shasta Caverns Rd., P.O. Box 801, O'Brien, CA 96070, 530/238-2341 or toll-free 800/795-2283.

REDDING AND VICINITY

A boomtown that never busted, this is The City of the northern mountains, with a total metropolitan-area population of more than 115,000. Redding perches just beyond the northern edge of the Sacramento Valley on the banks of the Sacramento River, which is joined here by 14 tributaries. Early explorer John C. Frémont described the Redding area as "fertile bottom lands watered by many small streams." Still watered by streams, the fertile bottom lands have become lucrative subdivisions and malls. Intersected by I-5 and Highways 44 and 299, well served by bus and even Amtrak, Redding is the northern getaway gateway.

Though it's got its share, Redding still isn't widely known for cultural attractions and it's easy to understand why. The breathtaking landscape surrounding the town tends to draw people away, into nearby mountains and beyond. Entering or leaving the wilderness, stop here for supplies and almost-urban sustenance.

The **Redding Convention and Visitors Bureau** is at 777 Auditorium Dr. (take Park Marina Dr. east, then turn north on Auditorium or, from I-5, follow the signs), 530/225-4100 or toll-free 800/874-7562; open Mon.–Fri. 8 A.M.–5 P.M., Sat.–Sun. 9 A.M.–5 P.M. An unbeatable information source is the **Shasta-Cascade Wonderland Association,** 1699 Hwy. 273 in Anderson (south of Redding alongside I-5, at the Shasta Factory Outlets mall), 530/365-7500 (from Redding, call 275-5555 or 275-9711) or toll-free 800/474-2782, www.shastacascade.org; open Mon.–Sat. 9 A.M.–6 P.M., Sun. 10 A.M.–6 P.M.

Headquarters for **Shasta-Trinity National Forest** is at 2400 Washington Ave., 530/242-2360, www.r5.fs.fed.us/shastatrinity. The office offers information about regional recreation areas—from Whiskeytown and Trinity Lakes to the Trinity Alps Wilderness Area and the Mt. Shasta Wilderness—and supplies the necessary permits. The **BLM Redding Resource Area** office, 355 Hemsted Dr., 530/246-5325, offers information about recreation on BLM lands.

Turtle Bay Museums and Arboretum on the River

A multimillion-dollar museum and outdoor education complex along the Sacramento River west of I-5, Turtle Bay, 530/243-8850, is a work in progress. The complex will eventually grow to some 300 acres in size—and perhaps into one of the state's finest museums. So far, Turtle Bay includes **Paul Bunyan's Forest Camp,** a replica of a logging camp and interactive children's center complete with a model of Mt. Shasta and the Sacramento River; the 200-acre **Redding Arboretum by the River;** and (in Caldwell Park, on Quartz Hill Rd.) both **Carter House Natural Science Museum,** 530/243-5457, featuring wildlife endemic to Northern California, and the **Redding Museum of Art & History,** 530/243-8801. The museums are open year-round, Tues.–Sun. 10 A.M.–5 P.M.; the arboretum is open daily, dawn to dusk. A small admission fee covers all sites except the Butterfly House (extra admission); the arboretum is free. To get here, take Hwy.

299 west off I-5 and exit at Auditorium Dr. (turn right on Auditorium); Paul Bunyan's Forest Camp—a good place to start your explorations—is just past the Convention Center at the northeast corner of the parking area.

Shasta State Historic Park

About three miles west of Redding is the town of Shasta, in its heyday the leading gold mining center of the northstate and "Queen City of the Northern Mines." Originally known as Reading Springs (named for Redding's Reading, who found gold here in 1848), Shasta in the early 1850s was a lively little city by all accounts, with up to 100 freight wagons, 2,000 pack mules, and countless drunken miners in the streets on any day of the week. Old Shasta became an overnight ghost town when area mines played out and it was bypassed by both stage and rail routes, but it was remembered again in 1950 with its designation as a state historic monument. For more information, contact: Shasta State Historic Park, Hwy. 299 W, P.O. Box 2430, Shasta, CA 96087, 530/243-8194 or 530/244-1848.

Whiskeytown National Recreation Area

Miners on the trail to Oregon settled the original Whiskeytown near Whiskey Creek (so christened when a mule fell off a cliff and spilled its precious cargo). That town is now underwater, but its spirit lives on in the brick store north of Hwy. 299 in the new Whiskeytown. The **Whiskeytown Dam,** connecting the waters of the Trinity River with the Sacramento, is another link in the Central Valley Water Project's chain of reservoirs.

Whiskeytown Lake is pretty but packed in summer, subject to water levels. Recreation is the big attraction: boating, water-skiing, swimming, scuba diving, horseback riding, hiking, gold panning, fishing, and deer and duck hunting in season. Whiskeytown's day-use fee is $5. Camp in backcountry areas ($10 per night, including park day-use fee; get required wilderness permits at the information center) or at **Oak Bottom Campground,** 14 miles west of Redding on Hwy. 299, which has abundant campsites and hot showers ($14–18). Sites at Oak Bottom are reservable; call toll-free 800/365-2267.

For more information, contact: Whiskeytown National Recreation Area, P.O. Box 188, Whiskeytown, CA 96095-0188, 530/241-6584, www.nps.gov/whis, or stop off at the lake's visitor information center, just off Hwy. 299 at Kennedy Dr., 530/246-1225.

Staying in Redding

Most motels in Redding are clustered along Hwy. 299 or Hilltop Dr., but some cheaper places are available south of town on Market St. (Hwy. 273).

THE SHINGLETOWN WILD HORSE SANCTUARY

Western culture fans, come rendezvous with mustangs. At this preserve near Manton (southeast of Redding, northeast of Red Bluff), get up close and personal with the wildest of free-ranging horses. Dianne and Jim Clapp started adopting mustangs more than a decade ago. At the time, their effort was the only private project in America dedicated to protecting wild horses from domestication or destruction. Today, the herds here number around 150 horses, as well as dozens of wild burros. The sanctuary office opens to the public Tues.–Wed. 10 A.M.–4 P.M., but visitors are welcome to hike the horse trails any time.

More exciting, though, are the guided horseback trips and two- or three-day overnight rides, complete with hearty campfire fare and a sleeping-bag stay in rustic kerosene-lit cabins. Mustang lovers, you can even "adopt" a wild horse, through regular financial contributions. For more information, contact: Wild Horse Sanctuary, P.O. Box 30, Shingletown, CA 96088, 530/222-5728.

Shingletown also offers a couple of stores and, for sit-down meals, the **Big Wheels Loggers Lounge & Cookhouse,** 32776 Hwy. 44, 530/474-3131. Open daily 7 A.M.–8 or 9 P.M., bar open until 2 A.M. If roughin' it in and around Lassen National Park has left you (or will soon leave you) a tad rough around the edges, the perfect place to ease the transition back into polite society is the hilltop **Weston House** bed-and-breakfast, P.O. Box 276, Shingletown, CA 96088, 530/474-3738, which offers three comfortable rooms and one suite (with a private entrance); three rooms have private bathrooms, two feature woodstoves and balconies. Swimming pool, fruit trees, vineyard, gardens. Expensive-Premium.

Redding, a northstate convention center, also has a number of higher-priced large motels, most of these along Hilltop Dr. and including the **Doubletree Hotel**, 1830 Hilltop Dr., 530/221-8700 or toll-free 800/222-8733 (Expensive-Premium); **Best Western Hilltop Inn**, 2300 Hilltop Dr., 530/221-6100 or toll-free 800/336-4880 (Expensive); **Grand Manor Inn**, 850 Mistletoe Ln. (just off Hilltop), 530/221-4472 (Moderate-Expensive); **La Quinta Inn**, 2180 Hilltop Dr., 530/221-8200 or toll-free 800/687-6667 (Moderate); and **Oxford Suites**, 1967 Hilltop Dr., 530/221-0100 or toll-free 800/762-0133 (Moderate).

Or try a bed-and-breakfast. The gabled, hilltop **Tiffany House Bed & Breakfast Inn**, 1510 Barbara Rd., Redding, CA 96003, 530/244-3225, is the town's first showplace inn, with enticing views of the area, spacious living areas and deck, and four appealing rooms. Other amenities include a swimming pool, deck, and full gourmet breakfast. Expensive-Premium. At the newish **Apple's Riverhouse Bed and Breakfast**, 201 Mora Ct., 530/243-8440, alongside the Sacramento River Trail next to Elks City Park, guests can borrow bikes to ride the trail. The B&B's two large rooms both have private bath and balcony, and other amenities include a spa, great views, and an expanded continental breakfast. Expensive.

For something fantastically escapist, consider **Brigadoon Castle**, 9036 Zogg Mine Rd. in Igo, 530/396-2785 or toll-free 888/343-2836, about 15 miles southwest from Redding off Placer Rd. (County Rd. A16). Brigadoon holds down the fort on 86 acres of forest and meadow. The four rooms inside the ivy-draped, turreted castle are all unique, while the separate Cottage guesthouse sits streamside and features a fireplace, four-poster bed (with a view), and private hot tub. Midweek, rates include breakfast; on weekends, rates include breakfast and dinner. Luxury.

Eating in Redding

Redding has its share of farmers' markets. Open year-round is the **Redding Certified Farmers' Market** held Sat. 7:30 A.M.–noon at Pine St. and Eureka Way, 530/246-0761; ask locally about others, offered seasonally.

Year-round, get good fresh seafood at funky **Buz's Crab Stand**, 2159 East St., 530/243-2120, a fish market and popular cheap eatery where you can get everything from snapper and Dungeness crab (in season) to fish and chips, charbroiled swordfish, seafood burritos, and much more. Started as a home-based wholesale cheesecake enterprise, **Cheesecakes Unlimited & Cafe**, 1344 Market St. (just north of the Downtown Redding Mall), 530/244-6670, is a cozy café serving lunch Mon.–Fri., everything simple and fresh. And don't miss the cheesecake, everything from lemon or lime to Dutch chocolate almond.

For the best steaks in town, head downtown to **Jack's Grill**, 1743 California St., 530/241-9705, a funky 1930s tavern where people start lining up outside at 4 P.M. in order to get a table. Closed Sunday.

For elegant ambience and exceptional food, the place is **De Mercurio's**, 1647 Hartnell Ave., Ste. 21, 530/222-1307, which offers fine French, Italian, and American fare nightly. Specialties include gourmet preparations of veal, duck, rack of lamb, and fresh seafood, but De Mercurio's "special event" nights—with Chef Cal cooking up everything from Thai cuisine to St. Patrick's Day surprises—are always fun. De Mercurio's won a gold medal in the 1996 Culinary Olympics in Berlin. Open nightly for dinner (senior specials, too).

LASSEN VOLCANIC NATIONAL PARK AND VICINITY

Visitors to Lassen Volcanic National Park and its backcountry wilderness should cultivate a better sense of direction than the park's namesake, Danish immigrant and intrepid traveler Peter Lassen. According to a journal entry by his friend, General John Bidwell, Lassen "was a singular man, very industrious, very ingenious, and very fond of pioneering—in fact, of the latter, very stubbornly so. He had great confidence in his own power as a woodsman, but, strangely enough, he always got lost." This almost led to his lynching on at least one occasion, when he confused Lassen and Shasta peaks while guiding a party of immigrants westward, inadvertently taking them more than 200 miles out of their way. More recently, one of the best-known seasonal residents of the Lassen area was Ishi, "the last wild man in North America." In 1916,

the year Ishi died and a year after Lassen Peak finished blasting its way into the 20th century, Lassen was designated a national park.

Lassen's Volcanic History

In the early 1900s, area residents, including the "experts," believed Lassen to be extinct. The naked 10,457-foot peak had stood mute for eons. Though the immediate area was pocked with volcanic scars and various thermal sinks, Lassen as an *event* was considered a thing of the past.

But in late May 1914, preceded by a small earthquake, columns of steam and gases began spewing forth, littering Lassen's upper slopes with small chunks of lava. During the next year, Lassen blew more than 150 times, spitting dust and steam and spraying the surrounding area with cinders and small boulders. Curious spectators were thrilled but generally unconcerned.

Following an unusually heavy snowfall during the winter of 1914–15, the volcanic activity intensified. Snow in the crater melted almost instantly and, seeping into the earth, contributed large volumes of liquid to the volcanic brew. Then, on May 19, 1915, molten lava bubbled up to the rim of the crater, spilled over on the

TOM MYERS PHOTOGRAPHY

Mount Lassen

FINDING LASSEN

If Peter Lassen got disoriented in his time, contemporary travelers could easily do the same if they fall prey to the commonsense notion that Lassen Peak should be located within Lassen County. It's not. When plotting your journey, look for Lassen Peak, and much of Lassen Volcanic National Park, in Shasta County. The usual routes to Lassen are east on Hwy. 44 out of Redding (to the park's north entrance) or east from Red Bluff on Hwy. 36 or from Chico on Hwy. 32 (to enter the park from the south). If the weather is bad in winter, Hwy. 36 is safer than Hwy. 32. Westbound travelers can get to Lassen only via Highways 89 and 44 from the north, or Highways 44 or 36 out of Susanville.

MOUNTAIN-RIPPED-APART

Native peoples knew Lassen Peak by various names: Little Shasta, Water Mountain, Broken Mountain, Fire Mountain, and Mountain-Ripped-Apart. Now named after intrepid pathfinder Peter Lassen, the peak is the southernmost outpost of the Cascade Range, which runs almost due north from here to British Columbia. Much of Lassen Peak is cradled within a huge caldera formed by the volcano's collapse 300,000 years ago. Of the four types of volcanoes found in the world, Lassen Park has three: cinder cones, shield volcanoes, and dome volcanoes. (An example of the fourth type of volcanic mountain, a composite or stratovolcano—and a classic Cascades version, at that—is Mt. Shasta.)

Lassen's unimaginatively named Cinder Cone is also a classic one, composed entirely of pyroclastic, or "fire-broken," rock (molten fragments that solidify before they hit the ground). Prospect Peak is a shield volcano, formed from lava flows. Lassen Peak itself is a dome volcano formed by a "plug," a single, solid mass of rock squeezed up through the vent of a previous volcano. Relatively recent volcanism here—pumice showers, lava flows, and mudflows—has buried most evidence of earlier glacial action, but the scouring of the Warner, Blue Lake, and Mill Creek valleys suggests ancient ice sheets more than 1,000 feet thick.

Bumpass Hell, Lassen National Park

JEFF MYERS/TOM MYERS PHOTOGRAPHY

southwestern side, and flowed 1,000 feet down the mountain slope before cooling into a solid mass. On the peak's north side, lava poured over the rim, steam shot from a vent near the peak, and chunks of lava fell like hard spring rain. Boiling mud flows peeled off tree bark 18 feet above ground and submerged meadows with six feet of debris as the ooze flowed into the valleys of Hat and Lost Creeks.

But the Big One came three days later, when billowing smoke shot five miles into the air, catapulting five-ton boulders skyward. Steam blasted out again, this time horizontally, flattening trees and anything else in its path. After a few more minor eruptions in following years, Lassen was officially declared asleep (again) in 1921, after seven years of volcanic activity.

Lassen's fiery nature is in part responsible for its present-day beauty. By the early 1900s,

demand for lumber meant that lumberjacks threatened Lassen's magnificent forests, and in an effort to protect the area, Lassen Peak and Cinder Cone were declared national monuments. Lassen's volcanic eruptions of 1914–15 created such a national stir that the area was granted full national park status in 1916—at first in name only, since funding for actual park protection was delayed for years.

SEEING AND DOING LASSEN

Unlike other wilderness areas, many of Lassen's more notable features—including major volcanic peaks and glacial lakes like **Emerald** and **Helen**—are easily visible and/or accessible from the one paved road that traverses the park, making a tour of Lassen enjoyable for families with small children as well as for anyone with physical limitations. The *Road Guide to Lassen Park* (available at park headquarters and visitors centers) gives a useful overview of what you'll

IN SEARCH OF ISHI

For years it was believed that the last of the Yahi people were wiped out in a massacre by settlers at Kingsley Cave in Tehama County. But in 1908, power-company surveyors in the Deer Creek foothills south of Lassen came across a naked Indian man standing near the stream, poised with a double-pronged fishing spear. The next day a stone-tipped arrow whistled through the underbrush past other members in the same party. The surveyors pushed on and stumbled onto the camp of a middle-aged Yahi woman and two elders, a man and a woman. To prove their find, the interlopers carried off blankets, bows, arrows, and food supplies. They returned the next day (reputedly to make reparations), but the camp and the Yahi were gone. Anthropologists searched the area to no avail.

Ishi's Journey: From Chaparral to City Life
In August 1911, butchers at a slaughterhouse in Oroville were awakened by barking dogs at the livestock corral. There they found a near-naked man crouched in the mud, surrounded by snarling dogs. The man's only clothing was a piece of dirty, torn canvas hanging from his shoulders. He was emaciated and suffering from severe malnutrition. His skin was sunburned a copper brown, his hair burnt close to his skull (a Yahi sign of mourning). But the oddest thing was the man's speech, a language no one in the area had ever heard. People tried to communicate with him in English, Spanish, and several local Native American dialects, to no avail. Finally, for lack of a better place to put him, the sheriff locked him in a cell usually reserved for mental cases.

The "Wild Man of Oroville" made good newspaper copy, but news of his appearance caused even more excitement in the anthropology department at the University of California. Befriended by anthropologist Alfred L. Kroeber and others, Ishi (as he was called, though he never revealed his true Yahi name) moved to San Francisco, where he lived for almost five years in the old UC Museum of Anthropology. On trips through his people's lands with Kroeber and others, Ishi shared his knowledge of his own and other tribes' beliefs, customs, crafts, and technology. *Ishi in Two Worlds: A Biography of the Last Wild Man in North America* by Theodora Kroeber tells this fascinating story. Ishi died of tuberculosis in 1916 but not before sharing with a friend his observation that whites were "smart but not wise, knowing many things including much that is false."

Ishi Comes Home
Illustrating Ishi's astute perception was the scandalous discovery in the late 1990s that not only was his body autopsied after death, against his express wishes, but Ishi's brain was removed, stored in a jar of formaldehyde, and shipped by Alfred Kroeber and the University of California to the Smithsonian Institution, where it was stored for years at a Maryland facility. The University of California had long insisted that Ishi's brain was cremated following the autopsy, along with the rest of his remains. But an investigation launched by the Butte County Native American Cultural Committee, aided by UC San Francisco medical historian Nancy Rockafellar and Duke University professor Orin Starn, traced Ishi's brain to the Smithsonian. As it turns out, the Smithsonian knew all along that it possessed the brain; it just didn't seem to know anyone was looking for it.

But people were looking, and quite seriously, since many Native Americans—including those now considered Ishi's closest relatives, Yahi-Yana descendants—believe that a person's spirit is not free unless his or her remains are all buried together. In May 1999, the Smithsonian announced that it was repatriating the brain to the Redding Rancheria and the Pit River Tribe—which both claim Yana descendants, determined to be Ishi's closest kin—so it could be reunited with Ishi's bodily remains for a proper burial in his homeland. As a result, Ishi is finally free—and freed from association with the whites who had befriended him. Ishi's legacy is also freed from the notion that he was the last of his kind, since as a Yana (Ishi means "man" in Yana), or a Yahi-Yana, he has 100–200 living relatives.

see along the park road, whether walking, biking, or driving.

See examples of Lassen's explosive personality at **The Sulphur Works, Little Hot Springs Valley, Bumpass Hell** (where the unfortunate Mr. Bumpass lost a leg to a mud pot), **Devil's Kitchen, Boiling Springs Lake, Terminal Geyser,** and **Drakesbad.**

Hiking Lassen

Lassen's 150 miles of interconnecting hiking trails—including 19 miles of the Pacific Crest Trail—offer both short easy strolls and rigorous backcountry treks. Bring water on all walks, and pack a lunch or high-energy snacks on longer hikes. Mountain bikes are not allowed on any trails.

Among less strenuous Lassen hikes are those to the volcanic "hot spot" **Bumpass Hell** and to **Paradise Meadows,** the best place to see midsummer wildflowers. The mostly downhill hike from Kings Creek Meadows to impressive **Kings Creek Falls** is not difficult—though what goes down does have to come back up. Extend the hike by continuing to Cold Boiling Lake and eventually Bumpass Hell, or to Crumbaugh Lake and the Sulphur Works. Two trails—the quarter-mile **Devastated Area Interpretive Trail** (wheelchair accessible) and the mile-long **Lily Pond Nature Trail** into the Chaos Jumbles area—offer public access to remnants of Lassen's disruptive past. Or try the three-mile **Devil's Kitchen Trail,** which begins and ends at the Warner Valley Picnic Area and explores thermal features. Hikers can get closer to the volcanic action here than at Bumpass Hell, so stay on the trail and keep a close watch on the kids.

More challenging trips include the steep switchback climb up **Lassen Peak** on the wide and well-graded trail. Bring water and a jacket or sweater. From the summit, see majestic Mt. Shasta to the north, Brokeoff Mountain to the southwest, and Lake Almanor ("Little Tahoe") just south. On a clear day (most likely in spring or fall), the broad Sacramento Valley and the Sutter Buttes are also visible. To hike the Lassen stretch of the **Pacific Crest Trail,** which traverses Drakesbad and Twin Lakes, start at Little Willow Lake at the park's far southern border.

Three-fourths of the park is designated wilderness. Instead of hiking in from the main park road, enter the park's wilderness areas from the southeast or northeast and backpack. Wilderness permits are required for backcountry camping, and no campfires are allowed in wilderness areas, so pack a camp stove and fuel. Remember also that backcountry camping is a privilege; leave the area as clean as you found it (if not cleaner).

Lassen in Winter

Only the southwestern part of the road into Lassen is snowplowed in winter and only as far as the old ski area chalet. (The highway *to* the park at Manzanita Lake is also plowed in winter, allowing northern park access for Nordic skiers and snowshoe hikers.) Most of the park's main snowshoe and ski-touring routes start from the unplowed road and are well marked during the season. **Lassen Peak, Brokeoff,** and **Bumpass Hell** are difficult treks, but trips from the chalet to **Lake Helen, Kings Creek Meadows,** and **Summit Lake** are possible even for beginners. The entire main road through Lassen Park is available in winter for cross-country ski touring (stunning views). For safety reasons, registration is necessary for both day and overnight trips. Day-trippers can sign in at trail registers outside the chalet or the Manzanita Lake office, as can overnighters. Free **ranger-guided cross-country ski tours** are also offered from Jan. to early Apr. on Sat. at 1:30 P.M.; bring your own skis and poles and meet at the Loomis Ranger Station.

In addition, winter camping is allowed at the **Southwest Campground** near the chalet. Overnight campers can also register at park headquarters in Mineral (see Lassen Area Information below).

NEAR LASSEN

Lovely **Lake Almanor** is a man-made reservoir but otherwise like a tiny Tahoe—a very pretty deep blue—adjacent to the mountain town of Chester. Almanor is still surprisingly lonely, despite being so close to major valley cities. Its attractions include clean cool air, clear water at a near-perfect 65–70°F in summer, good fishing, swimming, sailing, and water-skiing. Yet even in summer, there are days when not a single outboard motor disturbs the silent waters—though sailboats appear quickly whenever the wind's up. The lake's west side is more rustic and relaxed; the east side is newer, mostly private subdivisions and upscale resorts. **Chester** is a rustic logging town in the shadow of Lassen Peak on Almanor's north shore. The town has some reasonably priced motels, fast-food joints, decent restaurants, gas stations, and various places to pick up sporting goods and outdoor equipment. It also has a genuine old-time soda fountain—one of the best anywhere—inside the **Lassen Drug Co.** on Main, where the soda jerks err on the side of generosity. The best place to get miscellaneous outdoor supplies and sundries is fascinating **Ayoob's Department Store,** 201 Main St., 530/258-2628, a general store with a quirky array of merchandise. A best bet for cycling and canoeing supplies in summer and snowshoe and cross-country ski rentals in winter is **Bodfish Bicycles & Quiet Mountain Sports,** 152 Main St., 530/258-2338. Stop here, too, for suggested local trails and tips. The **Chester/Lake Almanor Museum,** 200 1st Ave., 530/258-2742, displays historical photographs of the area, as well as artifacts from the area's early Maidu people and later pioneer industry. For Chester visitor information, see Lassen Area Information, below.

In **Westwood,** the **Westwood Museum,** 315 Ash St., 530/256-2233, tells the story of the old Red River Lumber Company, which is credited with creating the story of **Paul Bunyan** and **Babe the Blue Ox** as a promotional gimmick. So it's only appropriate that a carved statue of both mythic figures stands near the western end of the nearby Bizz Johnson Trail. (For trail details, see Susanville, below.) For information on the **Paul Bunyan Mountain Festival,** held the weekend after July Fourth, call the **Westwood Chamber of Commerce** at 530/256-2456.

PRACTICAL LASSEN

Camping in and near Lassen Park

Campsites are abundant in the park. Because Lassen is the most "unvisited" of all national parks, campground reservations aren't taken. But there *is* a 14-day limit (seven days only at popular **Lost Creek Group Campground** and at both **Summit Lake** campgrounds). The camping fee is $12–14 per night. The best way to land a campsite within Lassen Park is to arrive early in the day, preferably midweek but otherwise early Friday for weekend camping, and Sunday for the following week.

DRAKESBAD: A TRUE MOUNTAIN HIGH

Comfortably rustic simplicity at its finest, but only for those with the urge (and resources) to splurge, the unusual **Drakesbad Guest Ranch** complex sprouts up seemingly out of nowhere in the Warner Valley, actually part of Lassen Volcanic National Park. The resort is named for trapper and guide Edward Drake, who claimed to be a descendant of Sir Francis.

Now a 19-room guest ranch that could pass for a B&B, Drakesbad offers a unique resort *experience.* Soak in the ancient hot springs, now a crystal-clear 116°F swimming pool, and snuggle under quilts in kerosene-lit rooms in the simple pine lodge or cabins (no electricity, though a generator runs the kitchen). In addition to "country basic" lodge rooms, bungalows and other units with private baths are available. Rates are on the American plan (meals are included), and meals—announced with a clang of the chow bell—are generous. Enjoy big ranch breakfasts, hot lunches (sack lunches for hikers are available with advance notice), and full dinners with fine wines and beers (alcohol extra). Vegetarian meals are available by request. Open June to early October (varies depending on the length of winter); reservations are often booked a year in advance. Luxury.

Drakesbad is accessible by car only via the Chester-Warner Valley Rd. from Chester (heading east on Hwy. 36, turn left at the firehouse, then left again when the road forks), about 17 miles. For a special treat, hike in—from the Pacific Crest Trail, from Bumpass Hell, Kings Creek Meadows, or from the Summit Lake area. All routes are basically downhill.

For more information and to make reservations, contact: **California Guest Sevices, Inc.,** 2150 N. Main St. #5, Red Bluff, CA 96080, 530/529-9820 or 530/529-1512, www.drakesbad.com. To contact the resort in season, call the AT&T long-distance operator and ask for area code 530, Drakesbad toll station no. 2.

If the park's campgrounds are full, there are many fine campgrounds throughout Lassen National Forest; the region's 43 U.S. Forest Service campgrounds include a total of about 1,000 campsites. Most are open May 1–Nov. 1 and are fairly primitive. For details, contact area national forest offices (see Lassen Area Information, below).

There are various private campgrounds with RV hookups in and around Chester, including fun and funky **Wilson's Camp Prattville Resort,** 2932 Almanor Dr. W on the lake's west shore, 530/259-2464, which also includes a pleasant lake-view front lawn, picnic area, grocery store, and restaurant. For a complete listing of Almanor area camping facilities, public and private, contact the Chester/Lake Almanor Chamber of Commerce (see Lassen Area Information, below).

Staying at Lassen Area Cabin Resorts
Numerous reasonably priced, often rustic "resorts" with cabins ring Lassen. Ever popular on the north side of Lassen Park is **Adams' Hat Creek Resort,** 13 miles north of Manzanita Lake on Hwy. 44 in Old Station, 530/335-7121, with both cabins and motel units. Inexpensive. Weekly rates available. Under new ownership and now a year-round resort, **Childs Meadow Resort,** southwest of Lassen Park on Hwy. 36 in Mill Creek, 530/595-3383, offers motel units and housekeeping chalets (with basic kitchen facilities), RV sites, tent camping, and amenities including laundromat, bathhouse, group picnic facilities, and regulation tennis courts. Inexpensive-Moderate. Quite nice, too, are the 10 cabins at **Mill Creek Resort,** in the woods along Hwy. 172 just a few miles off Hwy. 36/89, 530/595-4449—rustic but comfortable, and prices are consistent year-round. Cabins have kitchens and one or two bedrooms. Some have sitting rooms, and one sleeps six and has a cozy fireplace. Other facilities include RV spaces, campsites, a small grocery store, and a restaurant with a breakfast and sandwich menu. Inexpensive-Moderate. **Fire Mountain Lodge,** on the west side of Hwy. 36/89, just north of the Hwy. 32 junction, 530/258-2938, features motel rooms and cabins (one, two, or three bedrooms, some with kitchens). A big draw here is the main lodge and its huge stone fireplace, featuring a bar and restaurant. Inexpensive-Moderate.

BIDWELL HOUSE

Close to Lake Almanor and Lassen, the historic Bidwell House country inn at 1 Main St. in Chester, 530/258-3338, www.bidwellhouse.com, was once the summer home of noted California pioneers John and Annie E. K. Bidwell. When the Bidwells first started retreating from the valley's summer heat to the cool mountain meadow below Mt. Lassen, the trip took three days (one-way) by wagon caravan, and "home," once they arrived, was a massive circus tent. But after 30 years of this summertime tradition, Annie apparently tired of the tent and insisted upon a cabin. John built this lovely two-story home instead. First located in a meadow along the Feather River, the house was rolled into town on logs in 1919.

As perfect now as ever for summer retreats—and a great choice in winter, too, given the area's exceptional cross-country skiing and other attractions—the impressive, completely renovated Bidwell House offers a total of 14 guest rooms, most with private baths, some with in-room hot tubs, and three with woodstoves. A separate cottage is perfect for two couples or families. Scrumptious full breakfast is included. Moderate-Premium. With advance reservations for breakfast (daily) and dinner (Thurs.–Sat.), you can eat here even if you don't stay.

Eating near Lassen
A fairly complete listing of area eateries (and available lodgings) is included in the seasonal tabloid newspaper handed out to park visitors. People once went well out of their way to eat at the **Black Forest Lodge,** 10 miles west of Chester on Hwy. 36/89, 530/258-2941, an unassuming, simple place noted for its excellent German food. Unfortunately, family health issues have curtailed operations for the time being; call ahead to see if it's reopened.

For a good cuppa joe in Chester, try **Three Beans Coffee House & Bakery,** 150 Main St., 530/258-3312, also good for a quick breakfast and tasty lunch, or **Ernest and Jessie's Coffee Lounge and Tea Room,** 346 Main St., 530/258-2238, where you can count on waffles at breakfast and quiche or chowder at lunch. **The Evergreen Company Pizza and Pub** at the Hwy. 36/89 junction, 530/258-3240, offers 20 different pizzas as well as sandwiches, a salad bar, and ice-cold beer. Closed Tuesday. The **Chester Saloon,** 159 Main St., 530/258-2887, has decent Italian food, including exceptional calamari.

The regional hot spot, at last report, was the **Creekside Grill,** 278 Main St., 530/258-1966, which offers fresh California-style cuisine—pastas, meats, fish, salads, soups, and great desserts—in a creekside setting. Enjoy a choice of microbrews or fine wines by the glass. Closed Tues.–Wednesday. **Benassi's,** 118 Watson Rd., 530/258-2600, is a best bet for tasty specialties at lunch—salads, sandwiches, and burgers—and fairly sophisticated fare at dinner, from pastas to chicken and seafood. Closed Monday. Distinctive dinners are served Thurs.–Sat. at **The Bidwell House,** 1 Main St., 530/258-3338; reservations are essential.

Famous in Chester is the **Timber House Lodge** restaurant at 1010 Main St. (at 1st St.), 530/258-2989 or 530/258-2729. The Timber House is an anomaly built into an enigma—Sam Harreld's creation of huge quarried stone and "forest duff and storm fall," massive timbers hauled into town in the back of an old Studebaker. Inside, tree trunks (cut into sections, then reassembled with cement), carved wooden bars, bar stools, tables, and even light fixtures suggest a cave-dweller ambience. Check it out. Open for lunch and dinner daily.

Lassen Area Information

A park admission pass, good for one week, costs $10 for cars, $2 for hikers or bikers. Pick up the pass and a free *Lassen Park Guide* (with a complete calendar of seasonal park activities, maps, and other pertinent information) upon arrival at the north or south park entrance, or at **Lassen Park Headquarters,** 38050 Hwy. 36 E, P.O. Box 100, Mineral, CA 96063, 530/595-4444, www.nps.gov/lavo, open Mon.–Fri. 8 A.M.–4:30 P.M. year-round. Visitor information is also available at the Southwest Information Station (SWIS), a booth in the parking lot of the chalet. The SWIS booth is open 9 A.M.–4 P.M. weekends from Memorial Day weekend to mid-June; daily through Labor Day, then weekends only through the rest of September.

The **Loomis Museum** at Manzanita Lake, 530/335-7575, has natural history and geology exhibits, and also sells books and other publications about the area. The museum is open 9 A.M.–5 P.M. on weekends from Memorial Day weekend to mid-June, then daily through the end of September. (Loomis Museum Association publications are also available at park headquarters.) Adjacent is the similarly intriguing stone home of B. F. Loomis, the photographer who captured on film Lassen Park's extraordinary early-1900s explosions. Loomis's home has been refurbished and was reopened in late 1997 as Lassen Park's **winter visitor center.**

Free wilderness permits, required for backcountry trekking in Lassen, can be obtained at park headquarters in Mineral, at the park entrance stations, at the seasonal SWIS visitor center, or by mail (contact park officials at least 14 days before you plan to arrive).

For information about camping and recreation in surrounding **Lassen National Forest,** contact forest headquarters at 55 S. Sacramento St., Susanville, CA 96130, 530/257-2151, www.r5.fs.fed.us/lassen, or any of the individual ranger districts: **Almanor,** 900 Hwy. 36, P.O. Box 767, Chester, CA 96020, 530/258-2141; **Eagle Lake,** 477-050 Eagle Lake Rd., Susanville, CA 96130, 530/257-4188; and **Hat Creek,** P.O. Box 220, Fall River Mills, CA 96028, 530/336-5521. A visitor's guide (including information on campgrounds and the Thousand Lakes and Caribou Wildernesses); a wilderness areas map ($4); and a forest map ($4) are available.

For regional visitor information, contact the **Chester/Lake Almanor Chamber of Commerce,** 529 Main St., P.O. Box 1198, Chester, CA 96020, 530/258-2426 or toll-free 800/350-4838, and the **Plumas County Visitors Bureau** in Quincy, located a half-mile west of town on Hwy. 70 (next to the airport), P.O. Box 4120, Quincy, CA 95971, 530/283-6345 or toll-free 800/326-2247, www.plumas.ca.us.

SUSANVILLE AND VICINITY

On the dry eastern slope of the Sierra Nevada, Susanville is the Lassen County seat and a rough 'n' tumble lumber town full of history, lumber mills, loggers, and cowboys. Pioneer Isaac Roop built the first home here in 1854, naming the town and the river after his daughter Susan. Roop's cabin became **Fort Defiance,** capital of

Nataqua ("woman") Territory and headquarters for the Sagebrush War of the early 1860s. Peter Lassen struck gold here, though area mining quickly petered out. Cattle and timber have dominated the local economy for years; one lumber mill and a door factory are still in operation, survivors of recent hard times. But the biggest employer in Susanville is the California Department of Corrections, providing well over 1,000 jobs at the two minimum-security prisons just outside town.

Stop off at Susanville's **Historic Railroad Depot,** 601 Richmond Rd., 530/257-3252, now a visitors center and local-history museum. The depot also marks the start of the **Bizz Johnson Trail,** a scenic 25.4-mile path to Westwood via the old Fernley & Lassen Railroad route through Susan River canyon. The trail is open to hikers, mountain bikers, and horseback riders, and makes a great cross-country ski trip in winter. The railroad depot is open May to mid-Oct., Fri.–Sun. 9 A.M.–5 P.M.

The **Lassen Historical Museum,** 75 N. Weatherlow, 530/257-3292, features historical photographs plus Native American and lumbering artifacts. Next door is **Roop's Fort,** which was originally constructed in 1854.

The **Grand Café,** 730 Main St. (near Gay St.), 530/257-4713, has been a local institution since the 1920s. Slide into a smooth wooden booth or belly up to the Formica counter for buckwheat hotcakes at breakfast, all-American burgers or soup and fresh bread at lunch. Open Mon.–Sat. for breakfast and lunch. The place for dinner is the **St. Francis Café** at the St. Francis Hotel, 830 Main (at Union), 530/257-4820, which pays proud homage to the area's cattle ranching heritage. Prime rib—get here early on weekend nights—and hefty New York steaks are specialties. Open Mon.–Sat. for lunch and dinner.

Annual Susanville events include the **Lassen County Fair** in late July, and **Wild West Days** in mid-August. For more information, contact the **Lassen County Chamber of Commerce,** 84 N. Lassen St., P.O. Box 338, Susanville, CA 96130, 530/257-4323, www.lassencounty-chamber.org.

Eagle Lake

Bordering Lassen National Forest, five miles wide and 14 miles long, Eagle Lake is no jewel at

CLEARWATER HOUSE

A comfortable full-service anglers' inn, in the style of an English fishing lodge, Clearwater House is especially appropriate for fly-fishing aficionados. Tucked into the town of Cassel (between Burney and Fall River Mills), on the banks of Hat Creek, a premier wild trout stream, the inn's location is heaven for fly fishers. Hat Creek is internationally renowned for its stream-bred, wild trout, but it's not alone here; five designated wild trout streams are all within minutes of the inn, and the expert guide staff takes guests to all of them. Clearwater House offers an extensive array of fishing programs, from weekend instruction (at all levels) to five-day "Mastering the Art of Fly Fishing" and "Big Trout Tactics" courses.

Clearwater House opens to the public from late Apr. through mid-Nov. (but available for private groups in the off-season). Rates are on the American plan (meals are included). Luxury. Reservations mandatory. For information and reservations, contact: Clearwater House on Hat Creek, P.O. Box 90, Cassel, CA 96016, 530/335-5500.

first glance. Its deep waters are fed from below by hundreds of springs. Eagle Lake is noted for its excellent fishing—especially for the unusual Eagle Lake trout (very good eating). Uniquely capable of surviving in highly alkaline waters, the Eagle Lake trout is evolutionary testament to the area's isolation over the eons. Another special thrill here: watching birds of prey fishing. Bald eagles (most numerous in winter) remain remote even while fishing and hunting, but ospreys also fish here and in greater numbers. It's humbling to watch one of these awesome birds work the waters, scooping prey from the lake and winging homeward, trout writhing in its talons. Brown pelicans and other waterfowl are also abundant at Eagle Lake.

For camping and other information about Eagle Lake, contact the **Eagle Lake Ranger District** office, 477-050 Eagle Lake Rd. in Susanville, 530/257-4188, or Lassen National Forest headquarters in Susanville, 530/257-2151. To get to Eagle Lake, turn north on Rd. A-1 two miles west of Susanville. The turnoff is marked by a sign and by a long-destroyed gas station on the south side of the highway.

NORTH AND WEST OF LASSEN

Old Station is the closest thing to a town you'll find immediately north of Lassen Park. Gas is available. Most of the "town" is **Uncle Runt's Place,** 530/335-7177, a cheap, cozy burger palace, restaurant, and bar offering good dinner specials (open Tues.–Sun. noon–8 P.M., no credit cards).

Considered one of the best trout-fishing streams in the United States, **Hat Creek** is a destination in its own right. The season usually opens May 1, but the two-trout 18-inch-length limit is meaningless to many fishing enthusiasts here, as most throw their catch back. At Cassel—consisting of a general store and PG&E campground (800/743-5000)—Hat Creek is joined by Rising River. Heading downstream, you'll pass the **Crystal Lake Fish Hatchery,** Crystal Lake, and Baum Lake. Farther on, below the Hat Creek II Powerhouse and before the creek empties into Lake Britton, are the Lower Hat Creek waters of the **Hat Creek Wild Trout Project,** with big, wily fish (catch-and-release only).

Burney Falls and Vicinity

Halfway between Lassen Peak and Mt. Shasta, 15 miles northeast of Burney, is one of the state's oldest parks, **McArthur-Burney Falls Memorial State Park.** That Teddy Roosevelt called Burney Falls "The Eighth Wonder of the World" is a notorious and lingering misattribution; Roosevelt actually said the waterfall here was a "wonder." Wonder that it still is, Burney Falls is fed by spring flows of 100 million gallons daily and thunders down a moss-covered 129-foot cliff into emerald-green water before flowing into Lake Britton. The porous volcanic basalt makes for some fascinating water action. Easy walks here include the half-mile **Headwaters Trail** to Burney Creek above the falls (for the best view), and the 1.2-mile self-guided **Nature Trail** circuit into the gorge. For a longer trip, follow the **Burney Creek Trail** all the way down to Burney Creek Cove (and beach) at Lake Britton, then climb back up on the **Rim Trail.**

The park is especially popular in summer but open year-round. Two state park campgrounds include a total of 128 sites and feature hot showers;

CALIFORNIA DEPARTMENT OF PARKS AND RECREATION

Burney Falls, Teddy Roosevelt's "wonder"

AHJUMAWI LAVA SPRINGS STATE PARK

A lovely lava springs area of pine, juniper, and chaparral, Ahjumawi ("Where the rivers meet") is a good place to get away from it all—especially since you can only get there by boat. This remote state park is 6,000 acres of wilderness fringing the lakes at the north end of Fall River Valley. Park highlights include fascinating basalt formations, many freshwater springs, and incredible views. Facilities include tent campsites (30-day maximum stay), tables, and an outhouse. Waterfowl and bald eagles nest here.

To get there, from head north on Main St. past the Intermountain Fairgrounds and turn onto Rat Ranch Rd. (dirt road, unlocked gate—please close) and continue four miles through PG&E's McArthur Swamp (known locally as "the Rat Farm") to the boat launch area. For more information, including suggestions about where to rent boats or canoes and where to camp, contact the rangers at McArthur-Burney Falls State Park.

make reservations for the busy summer months through ReserveAmerica, toll-free 800/444-7275. The park day-use fee is $2 per car. For more information, contact: McArthur-Burney Falls Memorial State Park, 24898 Hwy. 89, Burney, CA 96013, 530/335-2777.

Highway-straddling **Burney** is making a comeback after years of declines in the timber industry (and in local fortunes). Nearby **Fall River** is noted for its outcroppings of white diatomaceous rock; its attractions include the **Fort Crook Museum,** 530/336-5110, and the noted **Fall River Valley Golf Course,** 530/336-5555. For more information on the area, contact the **Burney Basin Chamber of Commerce,** 37477 Main St., P.O. Box 36, Burney, CA 96013, 530/335-2111.

MODOC COUNTRY

Native peoples called the high Modoc Plateau area "the smiles of God," a strangely fitting name for this rugged remnant of the Old West. To the west, mysterious Mt. Shasta presides over the lava-topped tableland. Sister volcano Lassen Peak, the southernmost sentry of the Cascade Range, looms up from the south. Shasta and Lassen stand out visually, but the dividing line between the Cascades and the Modoc Plateau is obscure. Defining the area's plateau-ness is also difficult; this high country is both the southern tip of the vast Columbia Plateau and part of the Great Basin, which extends from the Sierra Nevada through Nevada and into Utah, Idaho, Oregon, and Washington.

One of those rare places in California where local folks still wave to strangers passing on back roads, the Modoc Plateau is dramatic in its desolation. Even in the thick of winter's tule fog, accompanied by the lonely musings of migrating waterfowl, cowboys still ride the range here—and belly up to the bar in local saloons on Saturday nights. Here in Modoc country, California's outback and site of one of the last major Indian wars in the United States, distrust between native peoples and settlers still lingers. The hundreds of lava caves and craggy outcroppings at what is now Lava Beds National Monument enabled charismatic "Captain Jack" and his Modoc warriors to hold out against hundreds of U.S. Army troops (with superior arms) for more than three months before being starved into defeat in 1873. A 19th-century domestic Vietnam, the Modoc War cost U.S. taxpayers $40,000 for every Native American killed. The other costs cannot be counted.

LAVA BEDS AND VICINITY

Technically part of Siskiyou County, the 72 square miles of **Lava Beds National Monument** is dry,

Modoc's melancholy beauty

KIM WEIR

FINDING MODOC

Arriving in middle-of-nowhere Modoc is rarely accidental. (Without a car—better yet, a pickup truck—forget it.) Hwy. 139 from Klamath Falls in Oregon provides the most direct access, cutting through the plateau between the Lava Beds/Klamath wildlife area and Clear Lake. Also get here from the south via Hwy. 299 from Red Bluff, Hwy. 139 from Eagle Lake (then Hwy. 299), or Hwy. 395 as it winds north from Susanville and the farthest reaches of the Sierra Nevada.

inhospitable, and rugged—a tumble of lava caves, craggy volcanic chimneys, and cinder cones dusted by sagebrush and tumbleweed. Fog is common, especially in winter, adding to the landscape's eeriness. Somehow this desolate patch of plateau became the perfect staging ground for the most expensive war ever launched against native peoples by the U.S. government—the only full-blown Indian war ever waged in California. During the presidency of Ulysses S. Grant, the U.S. government spent more than a half-million dollars in a relentless six-month war against Chief Kentipoos (or Kentapoos or Keintpoos) and his mixed band of freedom fighters. Known also as "Captain Jack," Kentipoos gained notoriety both for his strategic shrewdness and his style, particularly the habit of wearing brass buttons and military insignia. The Modoc Indian War was not only costly in money and human lives, it also caused cultural disintegration when the surviving Modocs were shipped off to a reservation in the Midwest.

Fascinating background reading is *Life Amongst the Modocs: Unwritten History* by Joaquin Miller, written at the time of the Modoc War. This visionary 1873 based-on-fact fiction is drawn from Miller's personal experiences in Shasta and Siskiyou Counties during the gold rush, among settlers and native peoples alike. His protagonist eventually learns that at the edge of the frontier, that all-American symbol of democratic hope and justice, treachery and self-betrayal are just as likely.

Seeing and Doing
Lava Beds National Monument
This is where it all happened, the bleak scene of Captain Jack's last stand. Especially when the black lava and death-gray sagebrush are shrouded in drifts of tule fog, unquiet ghosts seem to dwell here. Scrambling into lava caves and up cinder cones, it's apparent how clever the Modocs were. Captain Jack's battlements were perfect: a lava fortress surrounded by deceptively "easy" terrain almost impossible to cross without being vulnerable to sniper fire.

Even those uninterested in the bloody march of history will enjoy Lava Beds National Monument, however. Two separate, high-desert wilderness areas (no fires, bring water, camping by permit only) offer hiking and some arid vistas. The area's volcanic history—and the area is still considered volcanically active—is everywhere apparent. Cinder cones, spatter cones, stratovolcanoes, shield volcanoes, chimneys, flows of both smooth *pahoehoe* and rough and chunky *a'a* lava, and lava tubes abound. Lava tubes, formed when the outer "skin" on streams of superheated magma cools and hardens, are not unusual in volcanic areas, but the sheer quantity (almost 200) found at Lava Beds is.

Caving is particularly instructive here, starting with **Mushpot Cave,** in the Indian Well parking lot, which is lighted and comes complete with

MODOC WAR SITES

About a mile past Boulevard and Balcony Caves, between Black Crater and Hardin Butte, is the **Thomas-Wright Battlefield.** Here, on April 26, 1873, two-thirds of Captain Evan Thomas's troops met their maker during the Modoc War. The park road crosses over it, then continues past Gillem's Bluff for four miles to **Gillem's Camp,** which was the U.S. Army's field headquarters during the six-month Modoc War. **Canby's Cross,** a white wooden marker erected by U.S. troops, marks the spot where General Canby, the U.S. Army's field operations commander, was gunned down during the last session of the Peace Commission negotiations. At the park's northeast corner near Tule Lake Sump is the complex maze of caves, lava trenches, and natural rock battlements of **Captain Jack's Stronghold,** the center of the war zone. Wounded U.S. Army soldiers were sheltered at **Hospital Rock,** another natural fortification nearby where the cavalry camped in 1873.

good interpretive displays and a film. A loop road from Indian Well toward the south offers access to most of the other park caves that can be visited without passes. (People are allowed to explore these and other caves alone, but that's not wise.) For serious spelunking, inquire at park headquarters.

Or head out on a hike to appreciate the landscape. **Schonchin Butte,** named for a Modoc chief, is the largest of the area's 11 scoriaceous cinder cones. A three-quarter-mile trail climbs to the fire tower on the summit, where you'll get great views of the monument. Other cones—Mammoth, Hippo, Bearpaw, Modoc, and Whitney—are across the road in the wilderness area. **The Castles** are two large groups of fumaroles or chimneys of gas-inflated lava, similar to the fire fountains on Kilauea in Hawaii.

Practical Lava Beds

Come with a full tank of gas and bring food and water as well as hard-soled shoes and warm- and cool-weather clothes. It can snow here any season, though it can also get quite hot in summer. (But even in summer heat, it stays cool in the lava caves.) If you plan to explore the caves, bring two flashlights (in case one dies in the darkness), or get flashlights (free, but they must be returned) and buy protective hardhats ($3.25) at headquarters. The 43 campsites at **Indian Well,** near park headquarters, are open year-round; $6–10. The day-use fee at Lava Beds is $4 (good for seven days). Freestyle camping in nearby national forest areas is free (permit necessary for motorized vehicles).

For basic information and a map, contact **Lava Beds National Monument,** P.O. Box 867, Tulelake, CA 96134, 530/667-2282, www.nps.gov/labe. Park headquarters is at Indian Well (reached most easily via the southeast entrance) and offers a good selection of books on the area and its history plus cultural and historical exhibits. Ranger-led interpretive programs are offered in summer.

The park's northeast entrance is about eight miles from Tulelake. The southeast entrance is 30 miles south of Tulelake (or 58 miles from Klamath Falls) on Hwy. 139, then Tionesta Rd. (follow the signs from the highway). The south entrance is 47 miles from Canby via Hwy. 139. Major airlines serve Medford and Klamath Falls, where rental cars are available.

Medicine Lake Highlands

About 14 miles south of the monument by gravel road, the Medicine Lake region truly qualifies for the "lunar landscape" label so often used to describe volcanic areas. In 1965, astronauts came here to study the highlands in preparation for the first moon landing. In late 1988, the rumble of earthquakes beneath Medicine Lake attracted the attention of geologists, who believe an eruption from one of the state's most powerful volcanoes is due. Snows close this national forest area for general use from Nov. to mid-June, though the popular "trail" from Mammoth Crater, 26 miles round-trip, provides off-season access for cross-country skiers and snowmobilers. **Medicine Lake,** its deep crystal-blue water filling an old volcanic crater, is fringed with lodgepole pines and has sandy beaches and good swimming, picnicking, and camping. The area also offers birding opportunities, good fishing, and water-skiing. "Big medicine" rites were traditionally held here—and still are—by various Native American peoples.

Above the lake is the black jumble of **Burnt Lava Flow,** a "virgin area" because virgin forests form islands within these 14 square miles of very young (300–500 years old) lava. Five miles northeast just off Medicine Lake Rd. is **Medicine Lake Glass Flow,** a square mile of stone-gray dacite formations 50–150 feet tall. **Glass Mountain** is a 1,400-year-old flow of black obsidian and glassy dacite, ending suddenly in a stark contrast of white pumice. Pumice rock is so light an average person could toss huge boulders with ease. (But don't: all of the area's natural features and any artifacts or archaeological sites within the area are protected.) Otherwise, wear proper shoes and be careful here. Native peoples used these flint-edged obsidian stones for making arrowheads, and a fall can cause puncture wounds and lacerations.

The three developed camping areas at Medicine Lake (elev. 6,700 feet)—**Hemlock, Medicine Camp,** and **Headquarters**—feature a total of 72 sites. All campgrounds close by Oct. 15. (To get away from it all, head to **Bullseye Lake, Blanche Lake,** or **Paynes Springs;** campfire permits required.) For Medicine Lake information and permits, contact the Modoc National Forest's **Doublehead Ranger District** office in Tulelake,

530/667-2246, or **Modoc National Forest headquarters,** 800 W. 12th St. in Alturas, 530/233-5811, www.r5.fs.fed.us/modoc. The **McCloud Ranger District** office, 2019 Forest Rd. in McCloud, 530/964-2184, can also answer general questions about the Medicine Lake area.

KLAMATH BASIN WILDLIFE REFUGES

The Klamath Basin was once an almost endless expanse of shallow lakes and marshes. But things have changed. Reclamation has vastly diminished the region's wetlands, and the one-time autumn bird population of 10 million or more dropped to six or seven million by the 1960s and has since been reduced to one or two million. Central to the decline of this, the hub of the Pacific Flyway, is an ongoing war over water between environmentalists and Native Americans on one side of the issue, and farmers and algae growers on the other. This water war continues to boil because, in the latter days of the 20th century, the basin's Tule Lake—once centerpiece of the Klamath Basin refuges—has become little more than an agricultural wastewater sump, and increased water alkalinity due to low water levels and agriculture runoff threatens the ecological health of the entire refuge system. Despite some positive local intervention—The Nature Conservancy, beginning with the Williamson River Delta Preserve, has started to buy up farmland within the Klamath Basin for wetlands restoration—the area remains deeply troubled. Still a critical habitat for most of North America's migratory birds and one of the top birding spots in the nation, as things stand it may not continue to be.

Klamath Bird-Watching
Since hunting is as close to big business as Tulelake and like towns ever get—and also because the battle between the refuges and farmers over scarce water (farmers have first dibs) is increasing in rancor—bird-watchers aren't as popular as hunters in these parts. That could change, though, here as elsewhere, once beleaguered rural economies realize the positive local-business benefits of birding and other low-impact outdoor activities. Spring (early March through early May) is good for birders, but fall is

the best—usually phenomenal, in fact, when the largest concentration of migrating waterfowl in North America converges on the Klamath Basin. Until the refuge crisis of the 1990s, Lower Klamath and Tule Lakes in particular were famous for their bird populations. For birding here, the best observation blind is your car (while traveling the dike-road tour routes). But if there's enough water to float a canoe, lake canoe routes offer the chance to get up-close and personal.

Seventy to eighty percent of the birds on the Pacific Flyway come together here—more than 250 species. Among them: snow, white-fronted, cackling, Canada, and Ross geese; avocets and egrets; swans and sandhill cranes; grebes and herons; pelicans, ospreys, and eagles. In addition, ducks abound. Redhead, gadwall, cinnamon teal, canvasback, shoveler, mallard, and pintail ducks nest near the lakes, hatching tens of thousands of ducklings each year. (The duck population usually peaks in late October, geese two to three weeks later.) Besides wintering bald eagles and hawks, many shorebirds, songbirds, falcons, and owls can also be spotted here.

The Klamath Basin National Wildlife Refuges include six separate refuge areas. Farthest north is the **Klamath Forest** area; also in Oregon, just south of Crater Lake and north of Klamath Falls, is the **Upper Klamath.** Newest, established in 1978, is the **Bear Valley** refuge between the Oregon towns of Keno and Worden; it's a winter nighttime roosting area for bald eagles. Straddling the California-Oregon border is the large **Lower Klamath** refuge, the first U.S. waterfowl refuge, created by President Teddy Roosevelt in 1908. Just east are the **Tule Lake** and **Clear Lake** refuge areas.

Klamath Information
The Klamath Basin refuges are open to the public during daylight hours only. Birders: bring warm (and water-resistant) clothing, comfortable walking shoes, extra wool socks, and binoculars. For current information about refuge access and the natural rhythms of bird migration, contact: **Klamath Basin National Wildlife Refuges,** 4009 Hill Rd., Rte. 1, Box 74, Tulelake, CA 96134, 530/667-2231, www.klamathnwr.org. The **visitors center** at refuge headquarters (at the Tule Lake reserve, reached via Hill Rd. from Hwy. 61 or from Lava Beds National Monument) has

excellent wildlife exhibits and a museum, as well as information on birding, hunting, upcoming events, and road and weather conditions.

ALTURAS AND VICINITY

With several thousand people, a few restaurants and motels, and the county's only two traffic lights, Alturas is the biggest city around. Situated in the dry, sparsely vegetated landscape in the western shadow of the Warner Mountains, Alturas is predictably hot in summer and cold in winter. The roads in town weren't even paved until 1931, about the same time talking pictures arrived. Some crotchety old buildings still stand, among them a fine museum and the **Elks Hall,** 619 N. Main, onetime headquarters of the old Narrow, Cantankerous, and Ornery Railroad and now on the National Register of Historic Places. But the center of social life here is the wild and woolly Old West **Niles Hotel & Saloon,** 304 Main St., 530/233-3261, a museum in its own right and the most popular restaurant in Alturas.

For information about area accommodations and sights, stop in at the **Alturas/Modoc County Chamber of Commerce,** 522 S. Main St. (next to the historical society museum), 530/233-4434. Open 9 A.M.–4:30 P.M. weekdays.

Seeing and Doing Greater Alturas
Pick up a free Alturas **historic tour** guide and Modoc County historic homes brochure at the local chamber office, 522 S. Main St., 530/233-4434. Next door to the chamber is the **Modoc County Museum,** 600 S. Main St., 530/233-2944, housing 400 vintage firearms and other antiques; a collection of arrowheads, knives, and spears; 500 woven baskets and other Native American artifacts; and photo and oral-history archives. Open May–Oct. (and two weeks at Christmas). Check out the works of local artists at the Alturas **Art Center,** 317 S. Main St., 530/233-2574, which occupies a vintage 1877 or '78 building fashioned of locally quarried stone.

The 6,800-acre **Modoc National Wildlife Refuge** extends for miles along Hwy. 395 south of Alturas proper, with access via County Roads 56 and then 115. Part and parcel of the semiarid landscape surrounding Dorris Reservoir and

open during daylight hours Mar.–Sept., the refuge hosts migrating waterfowl in fall and spring, and is a major summer nesting area. Bird-watching is especially good near headquarters, where a general map/guide, bird list, and hunting brochures are available. For more information, contact: Modoc National Wildlife Refuge, P.O. Box 1610, Alturas, CA 96101, 530/233-3572.

Dominating Alturas and vicinity is **Modoc National Forest,** almost two million acres of volcanic plateaus, lakes, and mountains, offering recreational opportunities for hikers, backpackers, hunters, photographers, and rock hounds. Many campgrounds are free, as are picnic areas. Forest headquarters is at 800 W. 12th St., Alturas, CA 96101, 530/233-5811. Available publications include forest and off-road vehicle maps, camping and recreation listings, and brochures/maps for Modoc National Forest, the South Warner Wilderness, and the Medicine Lake Highlands areas. Very helpful and friendly staff.

Practical Alturas
No public campgrounds are nearby, but you can try the **Brass Rail Campground,** on Hwy. 299 adjacent to the Brass Rail Basque Restaurant, 530/233-4185, complete with laundromat and hot showers; around $15 per night. Motels in Alturas include **Drifter's Inn,** on Hwy. 395, 530/233-2428 (Inexpensive), and **Best Western Trailside Inn,** 343 N. Main, 530/233-4111, where a few units have kitchens (Moderate). The **Dorris House** bed-and-breakfast on Parker Creek Rd., P.O. Box 1655, Alturas, CA 96101, 530/233-3786, borders Modoc Wildlife Refuge on the shores of Dorris Reservoir (and even offers accommodations for horses). Rates include expanded continental breakfast. Inexpensive.

Alturas has fast food restaurants and coffee shops, but the best thing going is at home in a former burger palace—**Nipa's California Cuisine,** 1001 N. Main, 530/233-2520, which actually serves Thai food. What could be better after a brutal weekend backpack than a plate of pad Thai and a tall Thai iced tea? Open daily for lunch and dinner. Good for Basque food at lunch or dinner is the **Brass Rail,** on Lakeview Hwy. (Hwy. 299 a few blocks east of the intersection with Hwy. 395), 530/233-2906. Closed Monday. Locals highly recommend the **Niles Hotel and**

Saloon, 304 S. Main, 530/233-3411, for American fare, open for lunch Wed.–Fri. and for dinner nightly; look for good meat-and-potatoes meals and a veritable Buffalo Bill Cody Wild West Show atmosphere. *Don't* miss the saloon. (Rooms are also available at the Niles.) For special lunches and dinners, also breakfast on weekends, head to the northern end of Surprise Valley and the surprisingly good **Fort Bidwell Hotel and Restaurant,** at Main and Garrison in Fort Bidwell, 530/279-2050, a bed-and-breakfast and cozy eatery.

South Warner Wilderness Area

The **Warner Mountains** were named for William H. Warner, who was killed here by Paiutes while mapping the upper reaches of the Pit River. Widespread lava flows containing quartz crystals (now called Warner basalt) oozed up from the earth several million years ago and covered much of the Modoc Plateau. The later Warner Mountains, a remote spur of the Cascades but technically part of the plateau, are typical of ranges in the Great Basin. Pine forests, clear blue glacial lakes, and good fishing streams are characteristic at higher elevations, with chaparral and juniper below.

Most of the Warner Range is included in Modoc National Forest, which also contains the South Warner Wilderness Area. Eagle Peak is almost 10,000 feet tall, but most of the range stands at half that height—a green, gently rolling highland area wonderful for walking. Hiking and backpacking in the South Warner Wilderness are best from late June to Labor Day, with peak wildflowers in late July and August. When exploring the remote Warners, bring water or water-purification tablets/filter and a backpacking stove and fuel, since firewood is in short supply. Also bring a topo map and good compass; trails sometimes seem to disappear. Otherwise, come prepared for anything. Predictable for the South Warner Wilderness is its unpredictable weather, with freezing temperatures, thunderstorms, and brutal winds possible anytime, though less likely in July and August. Wilderness permits are necessary for backcountry camping.

For wilderness permits and more information, including forest, wilderness, and trail maps, contact **Modoc National Forest** headquarters in Alturas (see above) or Modoc's **Warner Mountain Ranger District** office in Cedarville (385 Wallace St., just one block north and west of the main intersection), 530/279-6116.

KIM WEIR

THE SIERRA NEVADA
RANGE OF LIGHT

Though the many ancient peoples who once shared California's vast Sierra Nevada territory would surely be puzzled by his comparative historical prominence, John Muir has become California's preeminent mountain man. Long before his fame as freedom fighter for the wilderness and Great White Father of the modern American conservationist ethic, Muir began to act on his then-heretical belief that the orderly beauty of nature was the highest revelation of the One Mind. Unyoked from his heavy sense of social duty by an industrial accident that temporarily blinded him, Muir finally set out to see God. His decade-long, 19th-century wanderings led him to the Sierra Nevada's "sunbursts of morning among the icy peaks," to its "noonday radiance on the trees and rocks and snow," and to its "thousand dancing waterfalls." But the solitary naturalist, by then also a Civil War draft dodger, renamed the mountains even before personally meeting them, as he looked upward from Pacheco Pass. "Then it seemed to me the Sierra should be called not the Nevada, or Snowy Range, but the Range of Light . . . the most divinely beautiful of all the mountain chains I have ever seen."

The young run-amok Mark Twain, too, was smitten with these mountains and their magic: "Three months of camp life on Lake Tahoe would restore an Egyptian mummy to his pristine vigor, and give him an appetite like an alligator," he wrote. "The air up there in the clouds is very pure and fine, bracing and delicious . . . the same the angels breathe."

Yet something about his experience in this near-vertical expanse of the Old West upset Twain's otherwise refined sense of common humanity. Starting with the acceptable sanctimony of the day—"If we cannot find it in our hearts to give these poor naked creatures our Christian sympathy and compassion, in God's name let us at least not throw mud at them"—he then flung invective with both hands. In *Roughing It,* Twain rejected the "mellow moonshine of romance" about noble red men, whom he found "treacherous, filthy, and repulsive." And though he derided one tribe in particular, he managed, by inference, to include all Native Americans. His comments reflect perfectly the prejudices of his time—precursors to the cultural cataclysm that occurred when gold seekers and settlers swept into California—which was, perhaps, Twain's point:

[They are] a silent, sneaking, treacherous looking race; taking note of everything, covertly . . . and betraying no sign in their countenances; indolent, everlastingly patient and tireless . . . prideless beggars—for if the beggar instinct were left out of an Indian he would not "go," any more than a clock without a pendulum; hungry, always hungry, and yet never refusing anything that a hog would eat, though often eating what a hog would decline; hunters, but having no high-

er ambition than to kill and eat jackass rabbits, crickets and grasshoppers, and embezzle carrion from the buzzards and cayotes [sic]; savages who, when asked if they have a common Indian belief in a Great Spirit, show a something which almost amounts to emotion, thinking whiskey is referred to. . . .

Cataclysm or no, the Old Spirits, some of the Old Ways, even some of the Old Ones survive still in the secrecy of lost and lonely places. Among the survivors, there are now new traditions. Followers of the Tipi Way, scattered members of the Washoe Nation from the eastern slopes of the Sierra Nevada, worship the Great Spirit and seek collective salvation with the relatively new sacrament of the Medicine (hallucinogenic peyote buttons), a religious practice first borrowed from the Paiute people in the 1920s and '30s. Warren L. Azevedo's *Straight*

HAPPY MOUNTAIN HIGH: BASIC HEALTH AND SAFETY

All Sierra Nevada travelers—backpackers, cyclists, day hikers, even car campers and those who plan no outdoor trips—should be reasonably prepared for anything, for despite the Sierra Nevada's recreational popularity, there may be no one around to help if something goes wrong. Though snowstorms are common in winter, these and other freak storms also occur in summer. Drivers should always carry tire chains, blankets, basic first aid supplies, and some water and food in case they become stranded. To help avoid that possibility, have some sort of itinerary and get current destination, weather, and road information before setting out.

Even casual hikers need to remember that the air is thin at high elevations and it takes a day or two to adjust. Plan outdoor excursions and exertions accordingly; altitude sickness and hyperventilation are not fun.

In otherwise pristine backcountry areas, drinking water also poses a problem. Sadly, because of the widespread presence of a single-celled intestinal parasite called *Giardia lamblia*, it's no longer safe to dip that tin Sierra Club cup into marshy mountain meadows for a drink of the world's best-tasting water. Backpackers and hikers far from water faucets should boil all drinking water (for at least five min-

utes), carry water purification tablets, or invest in a portable purification pump—by far the best option.

For backpackers and hikers, adequate food is the next most important necessity. Always bring more than you think you'll need (avoid canned or bottled items if backpacking), including high-energy trail snacks, but not so much that you can't carry the load comfortably. Also essential are good, broken-in, and waterproofed hiking boots; plenty of cotton and wool socks (packed accessibly); long pants; cold-weather clothing; and rain and wind gear—including a tarp or small waterproof tent, a poncho large enough to keep most of one's body and pack dry, and waterproof matches. (Even for day hikes, a handy item is an inexpensive and lightweight Mylar "space blanket," to help stay dry and warm if lost or unexpectedly stranded.) A whistle, good compass, and topographic maps are also wise. It's not uncommon for even experienced woodspeople to accidentally stray from established trails; be sure to learn how to use your compass and topo map before setting out. Insect repellent is another essential—voracious mosquitoes are usually worse in marshy meadow or lake areas—as are sunscreen, sun hat, and sunglasses. Other basics include a flashlight or headlamp (extra batteries can't hurt) and a first-aid kit.

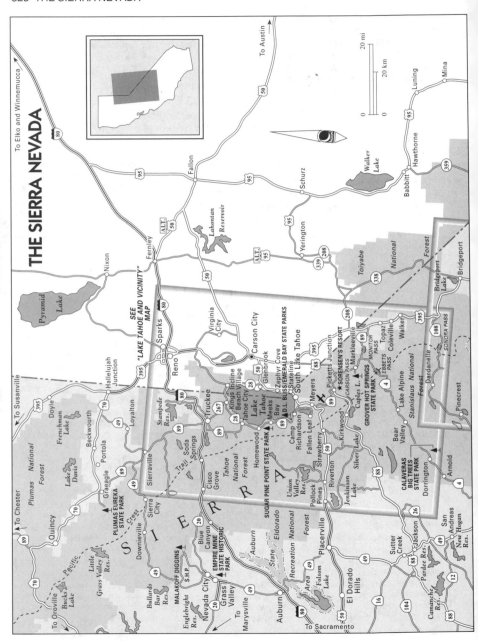

THE SIERRA NEVADA

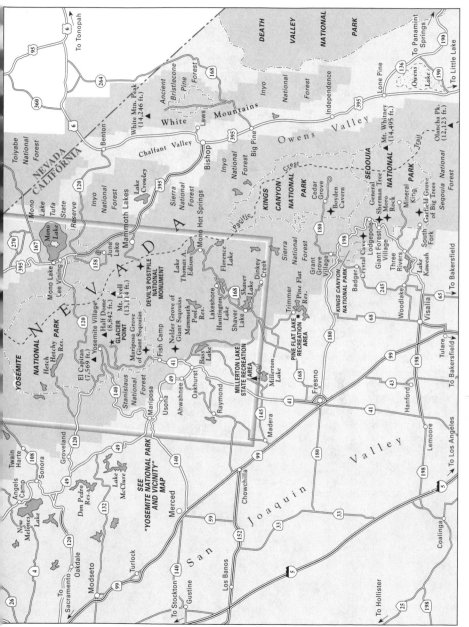

Like other Sierra
Nevada regions,
Yosemite Valley was
carved and polished
by glaciers.

CALIFORNIA DEPARTMENT OF PARKS & RECREATION

with the Medicine: Narratives of Washoe Followers of the Tipi Way shares the truth about
these survivors' spiritual depth:

*How can an Indian pray like a white man?
The white man gets his prayers out of books
. . . old books about things maybe thousands
of years ago. He don't even have to think
about it. He just says it and it is supposed to
do him some good. He can be a drunk bum
for a long time, do all kinds of no good
thing, think all kinds of bad thoughts about
people. But then he can walk right into that
Church and pray one of them prayers and he
gets away with it. Anybody can go into them
Churches anytime and walk out without
anything happening to him. . . .*

*The way a man sing shows you what kind
of person he is. If he sings good, he can help
people. His song goes through them and the
Medicine is working. Singing is like praying
. . . it's the same thing. When we sing here it
is for a reason. . . . So when I sing, it ain't
like on the radio or to pass the time. I'm
trying to get myself up good as I can. I don't
just sing a song . . . I'm taking a trip. When
I'm singing I'm praying in the Tipi and
going on that trip over that Road.*

Many who visit California's astounding Sierra
Nevada come for essentially the same purpose: to take a dose of the mountains' Medicine,
to sing praises to the spirits, to get "up good
as I can," to embark on a seriously joyous trip.

LAKE TAHOE AND VICINITY

Like a vast oval mirror laid across the California-Nevada border reflecting both states back on themselves, sapphire-blue Lake Tahoe is North America's largest alpine lake. Mark Twain described Lake Tahoe as "a noble sheet of blue water . . . walled in by a rim of snow-clad mountain peaks. . . . As it lay there with the shadows of the mountains brilliantly photographed upon its still surface I thought it must surely be the fairest picture the whole earth affords." If you ignore modern-day condo-to-condo encroachments and the area's unsightly strip development, the lake itself is still some picture.

Lake Tahoe exists by the grace of geologic accident. Despite the area's later glacial scouring, the Tahoe Basin was created by the earth's faulting; as the land sank, the Sierra Nevada rose on the west and the Carson Range on the east. Over the eons, snow melt and rain filled this great basin, and kept on filling it: volcanic lava flows then glacial debris plugged the lake's original outlets. (Today, Tahoe's only outlet is the

THE LAND: CARVED BY FIRE AND ICE

A massive block of granite some 450 miles long and 60 to 80 miles wide, the Sierra Nevada range starts in the north, just south of Lassen Peak, shimmies down to the southeast toward Walker Pass east of Bakersfield, then dribbles off into the desert where it meets the Tehachapis. Tilting gracefully to the west, the range's underlying rock foundation gives the broad western side its very gradual slope. Most of the mountains' drama is reserved for the eastern ascent—where spectacular peaks rise in dizzying degrees from the flat high-desert plateaus—and for the range's craggy high country, natural anarchistic architecture of the highest order.

From average elevations of 6,000–8,000 feet near the Feather River in the north, Sierra Nevada summits increase in altitude toward Yosemite, Sequoia, and Kings Canyon National Parks. Mount Whitney, the tallest mountain in the continental United States (excluding Alaska) and the range's triumph, pierces the sky at 14,495 feet. Near Mt. Whitney almost a dozen other peaks stand taller than 14,000 feet, and more than 500 throughout the Sierra Nevada exceed 12,000 feet. But the High Sierra, technically speaking, refers to the 150-mile-long, 20-mile-wide stretch of near-naked glaciated granite peaks, icy blue alpine lakes, and relatively level highlands above tree line from just north of Yosemite south to Cottonwood Pass.

The calm, cool facade of the Sierra Nevada range almost succeeds in hiding the region's deep fiery nature—almost, but not quite. Ancient calderas, old volcanic rock formations (basalt and andesite), young volcanoes, and quite contemporary earthquakes and hot springs—all common throughout the eastern Sierra—verify the fire below. Some say the region's abundant hot springs are evidence of decreasing volcanic vigor along the eastern Sierra Nevada; others suggest that the earth's fire is merely sleeping.

The creative fire underlying these massive mountains is usually unseen, but water, the other great shaping force, is everywhere. Like John Muir, everyday mortals are overwhelmed here by the aesthetics of this elixir of life: the crystalline mountain rivers and streams, waterfalls crowned with misty rainbows, and 1,500 or so lakes (including the breathtaking "lake of the sky," Lake Tahoe) in glacier-ground basins. (Most of the glacial scouring and earthquake faulting responsible for the range's spectacular scenery occurred during the past one million years.) For the most part, rivers and streams flow to the southwest. Many of the west side's 11 major river systems—from the Feather and Yuba Rivers in the north to the Kings, Kern, and Kaweah Rivers in the south—flow first through glacier-scoured gorges, then through V-shaped unglaciated canyons before reaching California's great central valley. On the Sierra Nevada's steep eastern flank, the waters of the few major rivers—among them the Truckee, Carson, and Walker—fly downhill in liquid freefall before settling into alkaline lakes or drying up in the desert. Dramatic waterfalls, though, are more common in western river valleys with glacier-created "hanging valleys," especially in Yosemite National Park and vicinity.

Truckee River, which begins at Tahoe City and flows north and east to Reno and Nevada's Pyramid Lake.) Surface measurements alone—Tahoe is 22 miles long, 12 miles wide, and has a 72-mile shoreline—still don't do the great lake justice. Tahoe's depth averages 989 feet; it plunges down 1,645 feet at its deepest point. And the lake usually contains 122 million acre-feet of water, enough to cover the entire state of California to a depth of about 14 inches. More important than quantity is the *quality* of the lake's waters. Even today, though there are water quality problems, Lake Tahoe water is some of the purest in the world, with dissolved gases, salts, minerals, and organic matter rivaling the ratios found in distilled water. Tahoe water is so clear that, despite measurable increases in algae growth and sedimentation during the past 30 years, objects can be spotted to depths of 75 feet or so. One of the lake's stranger characteristics is that, because of its great depth, it never freezes. As surface water gets colder it sinks, forcing warmer, lighter water upwards. Though Emerald Bay—a natural beauty created by glacial moraine—and other shallow inlets may occasionally freeze over, the lake itself is ice free because of its own gentle temperature-controlled dance.

SEEING AND DOING GREATER TAHOE

Lake Tahoe has a monster, people say. This is a modern phenomenon, swimming along with Tahoe's trend toward cable TV, condos, and casinos. But so many people claim to have seen the Unidentified Swimming Object now casually referred to as Tahoe Tessie that in 1984 a USO Hotline was set up to take the flood of calls. The more scientifically oriented suggest that those who spot Tahoe's monster are actually seeing a "standing wave," a phenomenon that occurs when separate boat wakes traveling miles and miles across the lake's still surface cross each other and collide. Tessie is described as a 10-foot-long (or longer) dark humpbacked creature, undulating along the water's surface fast enough to leave a wake of its own. Old-timers hope the monster is at least some sort of mutant sturgeon—though no one's ever seen one here—or giant trout.

One definite place to *see* gigantic trout, though—except in drought years when the river has died—is at **Fanny Bridge** on the Truckee River in Tahoe City, named for the fascinating collection of derrieres on display as fish fans lean over to get a good look. (No fishing allowed.) In 1995, the U.S. Fish and Wildlife Service stocked the Truckee River with Lahontan cutthroat trout—a species that hasn't been seen in its native waters here for more than 50 years, when introduced brown and rainbow trout eliminated them.

Most sights on Lake Tahoe proper are easily accessible, even for bicyclists enjoying the bike lanes that help keep cyclists off the highway (50 miles paved). Along Hwy. 28 just northeast of Tahoe City, on the lake, is tiny **Tahoe State Recreation Area,** 530/583-3074 or 530/525-7982, popular for summer camping and beach fun. Farther on, near the Nevada border, is day-use-only **Kings Beach State Recreation Area,** 530/546-7248, popular in summer for swimming, sunning, and volleyball. In the mountains directly north of Tahoe City is 2,000-acre **Burton Creek State Park,** 530/525-7232, which offers forested hikes and (in winter) short cross-country ski trails.

In Tahoe City is the **Gatekeeper's Museum/ Marion Steinbach Basket Museum,** 130 W. Lake Blvd., 530/583-1762, a reconstruction of the original log cabin—once the residence of the dam's attendant—at Lake Tahoe's Truckee River outlet, part of a several-acre park with picnic area and restrooms. Museum displays include local geology and fossils, Washoe and Paiute artifacts (including arrowheads and grinding stones more than 8,000 years old), and some 800 baskets from the late artist Marion Steinbach's lifetime collection. A real hit with most folks is the dachshund-sized dog sled. Also popular: special film and lecture programs. Usually open May 1–Oct. 1 (daily 11 A.M.–5 P.M. from mid-June through Labor Day, otherwise Wed.–Sun. only). Also worth a peek in Tahoe City is the 1909 **Watson Cabin Museum,** 530/583-8717, the oldest building in town.

North from Tahoe City via Hwy. 89 (or via Hwy. 237) is the down-home community of Truckee, a relaxed old railroading town. South from Tahoe City are houses and condominiums and a string of fine state parks: Sugar Pine Point between Tahoma and Meeks Bay, and the run-together

THE TRAGIC FATE OF THE DONNER PARTY

California's most chilling migration story is that of the Donner Party, an ill-fated group of wagon train travelers who split off from the main train in Utah in the spring of 1846 to try the more southerly, supposedly easier, and shorter Hastings Cutoff to California. But the shortcut, which passed through the alkaline deserts of Utah and Nevada and over difficult mountain ranges, was much too long. Nevertheless, led by George and Jacob Donner, the group decided to cross the rugged Sierra Nevada in late October. Despite some early snows, the Donner Party almost made it up and over the California Emigrant Trail pass—almost, but not quite. Having found the pass and prepared for the passage, the group decided to sleep and then set out at sunup, and this delay of one day sealed their fate. New snowfall during the night obliterated the trail, and a decision to wait for a break in the weather meant still more snow.

Most of the group's oxen were lost in the ensuing storms, due to carelessness and panic, and the Donner Party—without adequate provisions and huddled in flimsy tents, makeshift cabins, and snow caves along Alder Creek—settled in for a horrible winter. As the elderly and babies started to sicken and die, the Donner Party's "forlorn hope" group of men and women set out on foot toward the Sacramento Valley to get help. Thirty-two days later, after great privation and misery, the survivors (who cannibalized their fallen travel companions and killed and ate their Indian guides) finally reached Wheatland, and a rescue party of expert mountaineers immediately set out to save the others. Several successive rescue parties carted out those most capable of making the trip, but only about half of those who set out from the eastern side of the Sierra Nevada—reduced to eating mice, sticks, shoes, and even their own dead just to survive—ever made it to the west side. An 1840s medallion found recently on the archaeological excavation site of Murphy's Cabin contained the inscription: "Blessed Virgin Mary Pray for Us." Even more recent excavations suggest that the actual "last camps" of both George and Jacob Donner have finally been found.

For the most evocative human account of the story, read the powerful *The Donner Party*, a lyrical book-length poem by California writer George Keithley—perhaps not coincidentally, considering the lasting American fascination with this story, the only poetry book ever featured as a Book-of-the-Month Club selection.

monument to the ill-fated Donner Party

CALIFORNIA DEPARTMENT OF PARKS & RECREATION

D. L. Bliss and Emerald Bay farther south—all filled to the gills in summer; see below for more information on all of these parks. Still farther south is the Pope-Baldwin Recreation Area and Tallac Historic Site near Camp Richardson and Fallen Leaf Lake.

Worth a stop in South Lake Tahoe is the **Lake Tahoe Historical Society Museum,** 3058 Hwy. 50, 530/541-5458, containing the area's best collection of native cultural artifacts and Tahoe area pioneer relics; call for current days and hours. Relatively new is the year-round **South Tahoe Ice Center** (STIC), 1180 Rufus Allen Blvd., 530/542-4700, a professional-size facility for recreational skaters, figure skaters, and ice hockey leagues. South Lake Tahoe's **Lake**

Valley State Recreation Area, 530/525-7277, offers an 18-hole golf course in summer and snowmobiling and cross-country skiing in winter. (For golf course information, call 530/577-0802.) Adjacent are the undeveloped forests and meadows of 620-acre **Washoe Meadows State Park** on Lake Tahoe Blvd., 530/525-7232.

Truckee and Vicinity

The once wicked tin-roofed town of Truckee, which grew up here during construction of the transcontinental railroad, also once had a thriving Chinatown. The Wild West ambience, still intact today despite gentrification, inspired Charlie Chaplin to film *The Gold Rush* here. Even during Prohibition, Truckee's saloons did a blatantly brisk business, and Truckee's red-light district lasted well into this century—not cleaned up, locals say, until the 1960 Olympics in Squaw Valley. The shops, restaurants, and bars along block-long Commercial Row (off I-80) is where most of Truckee's action is these days, though "new Truckee" boasts shopping centers, a Starbucks, and astounding levels of development. The combination of tourists rolling down off I-80, minimal parking, train traffic, and Truckee's famous southern-right-of-way three-way stop makes for some exciting local traffic jams—a problem that may soon be minimized with a three-story parking structure as well as a new road and "roundabout" linking Donner Pass Rd. and West River St. at the west end of town. Truckee's first motel, the old Gateway, is now a museum sponsored by the local historical society. (To round up more information on Truckee, see Tahoe Area Events and Information below.)

Donner Memorial State Park, 12593 Donner Pass Rd. (at Donner Lake south of Truckee, just two miles off I-80 via old Hwy. 40), Truckee, CA 96161, 530/582-7892, is a choice summertime spot for picnicking, camping, short hikes, and water recreation. Most notable here, though, is the park's **Emigrant Trail Museum,** which tells the stories of the Donner Party's nightmarish winter of 1846–47, the construction of the Central Pacific Railroad, and the Sierra Nevada's natural history. Open daily 10 A.M.–noon and 1–4 P.M., small admission fee (but free to campers and picnickers who show their receipts). Rangers often offer free guided hikes to interpret the Donner story. Day-use fee for the park is $2. The park's campground is open late May–Oct. and quite popular, so reservations are essential. For campsites, call ReserveAmerica, toll-free 800/444-7275.

Sugar Pine Point State Park

A main attraction at Tahoe's Sugar Pine Point State Park is the baronial **Ehrmann Mansion,** probably Tahoe's finest example of a rich person's summer home, built here in 1903 by San Francisco banker Isaias W. Hellman. An amazing shoreline fortress of all-native stone and fine woods—Hellman called the place Pine Lodge—the mansion-cum-interpretive center is open only in summer for tours, but poke around the estate's spacious grounds anytime. Worth a look, too, are the old ice house and the Phipps cabin. Down by the lake, at one of the estate's boathouses, peek through the window for a bit of local boat racing history. Boathouses are usually open to the public over the July Fourth weekend.

Also at Sugar Pine Point: almost two miles of mostly rocky lake frontage for sunbathing and swimming, plus hiking and biking trails, picnicking, and good year-round camping at the **General Creek Campground** (175 very nice campsites, hot showers only in summer). Also appreciate the **Edwin L. Z'Berg Natural Preserve** (walk to the point here to see Tahoe's only operating lighthouse). In winter, cross-country skiing is popular, and the heated restrooms serve as de facto warming huts. The park day-use fee is $2. For more information, stop by the area's state park headquarters at D. L. Bliss or call 530/525-7982.

D.L. Bliss and Emerald Bay State Parks

Managed as one unit, these two contiguous state parks on Lake Tahoe's southwest shoreline offer camping—268 family campsites, 20 accessible only on foot or by boat—and swimming, fishing, boating, and hiking (day-use fee is $2). Sandy **Lester Beach** at Bliss is packed by noon on summer weekends. Even if you're not up for the longer haul south to Emerald Bay, hike to **Rubicon Point** to get a good, deep look into Tahoe's clear waters. Or take the short **Balancing Rock Nature Trail.**

Emerald Bay offers one of Tahoe's best brief hikes—a very scenic one-mile downhill scramble to 38-room **Vikingsholm,** a Scandinavian-style

A LAND UNDER SIEGE

The Sierra Nevada is in serious trouble. Its beauty and utility have bred a familiar plague—popularity with humans—that threatens its very survival. According to an exhaustive three-year environmental study released in 1996 by a 100-member scientific consortium that prepared the report for the U.S. Congress, the region's human population will treble by the year 2040—it doubled between 1970 and 1990—and will far outpace the state's overall growth. That estimate doesn't take into account the millions just visiting each year.

Population growth, with its consequential development pressures, has had a direct impact on the Sierra Nevada's decline, along with overgrazing, logging, mining, soil erosion, water projects, and increasing air and water pollution. In a sense, the cities are making themselves at home in the wilderness. Subdivisions and strip malls are popping up all over, and software firms are the latest Sierra Nevada industry.

At last count, according to the Sierra Nevada Ecosystem Project Report, 69 species of wildlife are now considered "at risk," the predominant cause the loss of essential habitat—particularly foothill woodland, riparian, and late successional forests. If present trends continue, the extinction of many Sierra Nevada fish species and all amphibians is predicted within the next 50 years.

The report also challenged common California forestry practices and beliefs—especially the belief that logging "mimics" the ecological functions of fire—and stated that logging has increased the risk and severity of forest fires. The Sierra Nevada's remaining 15 percent of old-growth forests—the oldest, largest trees, which support a complex community of other plants and animals—represent the last stand of a once-healthy ecosystem. And unregulated grazing has created "widespread, profound and, in some places, irreversible ecological impacts."

Urban-class air pollution plagues highly populated areas, including Truckee and Mammoth in winter, due to the twin scourges of vehicle exhaust and wood-burning stoves. The Sierra Nevada also suffers from environmental damage that originates elsewhere, particularly ozone pollution blown in from Los Angeles, the San Francisco Bay Area, and the great central valley. Jeffrey and ponderosa pines on west-facing slopes are increasingly debilitated and dwarfed, as ozone settles onto their leaves and accelerates both defoliation and vulnerability to insects and fire. Drifting pollution is also partially responsible for clouding the waters at Lake Tahoe, which loses about one foot of its once-mythic transparency each year—and will resemble a fairly typical, murkier lake in about 40 years.

Remedies to the Sierra Nevada's problems are available, however, according to the report's authors—assuming that there is sufficient political will. Air pollution could be reduced almost instantaneously, and forest complexity could be restored within a century. Revitalizing degraded watersheds would take considerably longer.

---

summer mansion on the bay's fjordlike shore. (People claim it's at least two or three miles climbing back out, however.) The trail heads downhill from the Emerald Bay overlook, where there's a fairly small parking lot, so arrive early. You can also get here the long way, via the easy 4.5-mile Rubicon Trail from D. L. Bliss State Park just north. Considered the Western Hemisphere's finest example of Scandinavian architecture, Vikingsholm seems inspired by all things Norwegian and Swedish—11th-century castles, churches, forts, even sod-roofed homes—and was built in 1928–29. Its half-million-dollar original price tag included the now-ruined stone teahouse on tiny Fannette Island. Access to Vikingsholm is by guided tour only (small admission fee). In summer—mid-June through Labor Day—tours are offered daily 10 A.M.–4 P.M., every half-hour; tours are usually also offered in spring and fall, on weekends only. Call the park at 530/525-7277 for further details.

Unusual is the **Emerald Bay Underwater Park,** established here to allow scuba divers a chance to explore the bay's boat boneyard. Also unique is the 20-site **Emerald Bay Boat Camp,** at the onetime site of the Emerald Bay Resort on the north side of the bay (first-come, first-camped). To reserve other campsites, call ReserveAmerica toll-free at 800/444-7275.

For more information about these two parks, contact: California State Parks, Sierra District office, P.O. Box 266, Tahoma, CA 96142,

CALIFORNIA DEPARTMENT OF PARKS & RECREATION

Emerald Bay

530/525-7277. Or stop by the central state parks headquarters off the highway at D. L. Bliss.

Tallac Historic Site and
Pope-Baldwin State Recreation Area

An enclave of peace preserving the past, the Tallac Historic Site is a 74-acre monument to Tahoe's social heyday, when Lake Tahoe was the elite retreat for California's rich and powerful. Though the Tallac Hotel Casino is long gone, undergoing gradual restoration here under U.S. Forest Service supervision are several impressive summer estates featuring distinct architectural affectations, including "Mr. Santa Anita" Lucky Baldwin's **Baldwin Estate** (now an educational center) and the lavish **Pope-Tevis** and pine-pillared **Valhalla** Mansions (summers-only interpretive center and community events center, respectively). **Thursday Night Jazz** and other events at Valhalla take full advantage of the great hall downstairs, most notable for its massive stone fireplace. With a boost from the nonprofit Tahoe Tallac

Association, a cultural arts organization that also raises funds for restoration, the estate boathouse has now opened its doors as the **Valhalla Boathouse Theatre.**

And that's the point about Tallac. Though it is indeed a monument to Tahoe's past, the complex is fast becoming a cultural and fine arts center. The Tallac Association's "Artists in Action" program, for example, showcases local artists and their talents in various on-site open studio settings, including former guest cottages and cabins. The twin cabins near Valhalla house the **Cultural Arts Store,** featuring (for sale) arts and fine crafts created by Tallac artists. Almost all summer long, Tallac hosts a refreshingly uncommercial arts and music festival, well worth several trips, and other creative culture.

The Tallac Historic Site is part and parcel of the Pope-Baldwin Recreation Area near Camp Richardson and popular southwestern Tahoe beaches. Just north of Tallac is a **picnic area,** a **multiagency visitors center** open only in summer, 530/544-5050, and some **self-guided nature trails.** Particularly worthwhile is the **Rainbow Trail,** which dips down below Taylor Creek into a glass-walled "stream profile chamber" for observing creek life, particularly the October run of Kokanee salmon. For a longer walk, take the trail to **Fallen Leaf Lake.**

Summer tours of Tallac are conducted by the U.S. Forest Service. If you come here just to wander—and the dock at the boathouse is often empty, a great spot for sunbathing—there is no on-site parking, though visitors can park just north at the Kiva Picnic Area or south at Camp Richardson. For more information about the area, contact: **Tahoe Tallac Association,** P.O. Box 19273, South Lake Tahoe, CA 96151, 530/541-4975 (year-round), 530/542-2787 (summer only), or 530/542-4166 (winter only).

HIKING TAHOE

Local state parks offer nature trails and longer hikes, plus sponsor a full schedule of guided hikes—including winter snowshoe and Nordic ski treks—throughout the Tahoe area. Popular short hikes include the trip to seasonally swimmable **Five Lakes** (the trailhead is two miles off Hwy. 89 on Alpine Meadows Rd.), a steep six-mile round-

NORTH OF TAHOE-TRUCKEE

The northernmost reaches of the Sierra Nevada are north of Lake Tahoe and I-80—scattered forested lakes, reservoirs, and rivers among still more scattered small towns. **Quincy,** on Hwy. 70/89 south of Lake Almanor and Indian Valley, is a picturesque mountain town with a longtime lumber history. The main attraction here is the impressive indoor-outdoor **Plumas County Museum,** 500 Jackson St., 530/283-6320, open weekdays 8 A.M.–5 P.M., on weekends and holidays 10 A.M.–4 P.M. (small admission). Museum exhibits here are "living," which means they rotate periodically. Yet they typically include area natural history, Maidu basketry, cultural and home art displays, and pioneer weaponry. New since 1999, with the museum's expansion, is the Industrial History Wing, which offers exhibits on gold mining, railroading, and early logging. Find refreshment at the **Morning Thunder Cafe,** 557 Lawrence, 530/283-1310, with Mexican and American fare, fine desserts, and an espresso bar, or **Moon's,** 497 Lawrence, 530/283-0765, serving Italian-American food, including hand-spun gourmet pizzas.

For more information about Quincy and vicinity, contact the **Plumas County Visitors Bureau,** located a half-mile west of town on Hwy. 70 (next to the airport), P.O. Box 4120, Quincy, CA 95971, 530/283-6345 or toll-free 800/326-2247, www.plumas.ca.us, or the **Quincy Main Street Chamber of Commerce,** 1905 E. Main St., P.O. Box 3829, Quincy, CA 95971, 530/283-0188.

Highway 70 east from the Blairsden-Graeagle area passes through Portola before lurching up over Beckwourth Pass, then hooking up with Hwy. 395 at Hallelujah Junction in the high desert—the official end of the **Feather River National Scenic Byway** that starts some 130 miles away in Oroville. Mount Ina Coolbrith south of the pass was named for California's first poet laureate, who met James Beckwourth while an 11-year-old girl traveling westward by wagon train through his same-named pass. Beckwourth described himself as a Crow Indian war chief, trapper, trader, and explorer; today he is also credited with being an African-American pioneer and trailblazer. A once dilapidated two-story cabin believed to be Jim Beckwourth's 1852 hotel and trading post, on Rocky Point Rd. east of Portola near the town of Beckwourth (old maps carry the distorted "Beckwith"), has been painstakingly restored by volunteers and is now known as **Beckwourth's Cabin,** 530/832-4888, open only by appointment.

In **Portola,** the most popular attraction is the **Portola Railroad Museum** (cross the river and follow the signs), an all-volunteer effort sponsored by the Feather River Rail Society, P.O. Box 608, Portola, CA 96122, 530/832-4131. The quantity and quality of in-process and already-restored iron stock on display at the railway yard here is impressive (admission is free, but donations are appreciated). For more information about Portola and vicinity, contact the **Plumas County Visitors Bureau** (see above) or the **Eastern Plumas County Chamber of Commerce,** 73136 Hwy. 70 (at Delleker Rd.), P.O. Box 1379, Portola, CA 96122, 530/832-5444 or toll-free 800/995-6057, www.psln.com/ep.

---

trip with great scenery. Or take the **Shirley Lake** hike from the Squaw Valley tram building, a five-mile round-trip of granite and waterfalls.

The **Donner Summit** area offers exceptional hiking, some routes quite challenging (and therefore least traveled). A complete listing of longer trails in the Tahoe National Forest suitable for hiking and backpacking, including lonely routes like the **Hawley Grade** trek from near Meyers, and the **Tucker Flat** and **Duck Lake–Lost Lake** hikes, are available locally from national forest headquarters. Ask, too, about progress on the **Tahoe Rim Trail,** a volunteer-powered effort to complete a 150-mile-long trail around the lake through two states, six counties, and three national forests. At last report, the Rim Trail was expected to be completed in 2001.

For more information about long hikes and Tahoe area backpacking, contact U.S. Forest Service headquarters for the Lake Tahoe Basin Management Unit year-round (see Tahoe Area Events and Information below) or, in summer, stop by the visitors center on the highway near Camp Richardson.

The best available guidebook to Tahoe area hiking and backpacking is *The Tahoe Sierra* by Jeffrey P. Schaffer, published by Wilderness Press, though Schaffer's *Desolation Wilderness and the South Lake Tahoe Basin* and Thomas and Jason Winnett's *Sierra North:*

backpackers near Meiss Lake

KIM WEIR

100 Back-Country Trips (also published by Wilderness Press) are also good.

With its glaciated High Sierra scenery, the **Desolation Wilderness** straddling the Sierra Nevada divide on Tahoe's southwestern side is far from desolate. In fact, this rugged 63,475-acre wonderland is so popular that the wilderness permit system is actually a quota system to minimize human impact in the wild. Permits are required for both day-use and overnight trips. Half of all wilderness permits for the backpacking season (mid-June through early Sept.) are issued up to 90 days in advance of planned trips, the other half reserved for entrance dates. At last report, permits were $3 for day use, $5 for one night, and $10 each for two or more nights; 80 percent of the revenues stay at Tahoe, to pay for maintenance and new services. To obtain advance permits to enter from the east, contact the U.S. Forest Service office in South Lake Tahoe (see Tahoe Area Events and Information below). To enter from the west, contact the Eldorado National Forest Information Center, 3070 Camino Heights Dr., Camino, CA 95709, 530/644-6048.

Usually better for privacy on backpacks and longer hikes is the **Granite Chief Wilderness** to the west of Tahoe City, established in 1984 to protect the headwaters of the American River. Also not yet subject to visitor rationing and within easy reach of Tahoe is the 105,165-acre **Mokelumne Wilderness** between Hwy. 88 and Hwy. 4—meadows, lakes, and mountains dominated by Mokelumne Peak and the canyon of

the Mokelumne River. Farther south still but almost adjacent to Mokelumne is the **Carson-Iceberg Wilderness** between Hwy. 4 and Hwy. 108 and—south of Hwy. 108—the 112,000-acre **Emigrant Wilderness** on the edge of Yosemite, another glaciated lakes-and-meadows volcanic landscape, quite accessible. The Sierra Nevada stretch of the Pacific Crest Trail either skirts (on other national forest lands) or climbs through all of these wilderness areas.

SKIING TAHOE

See all the latest in Alpine ski wear on Tahoe's flashier fashion slopes, and maybe overhear conversations about investments and stock market risks and whether this is the year to get a new cover for the hot tub. For most, making the Tahoe ski scene is a fairly expensive escape from city life—bringing most of that urban baggage along for the ride. But purists are here just *for* the ride—straight down some of the finest downhill slopes in North America.

Most Tahoe-area resorts have seriously upgraded their setups and services in recent years, in an attempt to garner worldwide attention for its world-class skiing. Snowboarding and snow tubing are among the new trends. Almost all resorts offer ski schools and ski shops, equipment rentals, day lodges, and some sort of accommodations and food. (A few offer spectacular facilities.) Many also provide children's ski instruction and good programs for disabled skiers. Also popular here are private Nordic ski resorts—sometimes affiliated with downhill facilities—offering great cross-country ski access and/or groomed trails, and low-key but much-appreciated amenities like trailside warming huts.

Due to the possibility (and fairly recent reality) of extended drought in California, most resorts have invested in snowmaking equipment—so good skiing is possible even when the weather refuses to cooperate.

Alas for thrift-conscious skiers, discounted midweek skiing is a thing of the past. But you can find special bargains if you're willing to hunt them down (often as easy as checking in with the relevant website), from frequent skier programs and family packages to free lessons, two-for-one days, and other special bargain-ticket days or half-days.

Donner Summit and North Tahoe Resorts

Closest and most accessible to San Francisco and the Bay Area are the four major ski resorts along Donner Summit and two others near Truckee. Farthest west and just off I-80 is small, family-oriented **Soda Springs Ski Area,** 19455 Boreal Ridge Rd., open to the public weekends and holidays but otherwise rentable by groups on an advanced-reservation-only basis. Often uncrowded and oriented to beginners and intermediates, advanced skiers still get a good workout on the upper slopes. Snowboarding is allowed—and snow tubing is also popular, assisted by lifts and groomed runs. Three lifts, 16 runs. Located on old Hwy. 40, one mile off I-80 via the Norden/Soda Springs exit. For more information, contact: Soda Springs Ski Area, P.O. Box 39, Truckee, CA 96160, 530/426-1010 (in season) or 530/426-3666 (off season), www.skisodasprings.com. Next east and affiliated with Soda Springs is **Boreal** (named for Boreas, Greek god of the north wind), 530/426-3666, www.borealski.com, an intermediate-advanced resort with plenty of beginners' opportunities—and Friday Night Expression Sessions for snowboarders. They also make snow at Boreal when nature won't cooperate. Nine lifts, 38 runs. Located just off I-80 via the Castle exit.

Three miles off I-80 via the Norden/Soda Springs exit is **Donner Ski Ranch,** 19320 Donner Pass Rd., an unpretentious place by Tahoe standards, with a cozy down-home lodge, inexpensive dormitory-style accommodations, and impressive terrain most suited to intermediate and advanced Alpine skiers (beginners' slopes too). Snowboarders enjoy three terrain parks and a halfpipe. Six lifts, 45 runs. With so much corporate consolidation among Tahoe ski areas determined to become luxury visitor destinations, Donner Ski Ranch is just about the last holdout for pure, relatively inexpensive skiing. For more information, contact: Donner Ski Ranch, P.O. Box 66, Norden, CA 95724, 530/426-3635, www.donnerskiranch.com.

Nearby 1,500-acre **Sugar Bowl,** 11260 Donner Pass Rd., offers some of California's best Alpine skiing, emphasizing advanced slopes more than any other resort along I-80—though intermediates and beginners also have plenty to do here: Sugar Bowl is nothing if not family-friendly. New in 1999 was a High Speed Quad Chair, a beginner's Quad on the Mt. Judah side, and more terrain on the Mt. Judah Express Quad. Advanced skiers head for the Silver Belt and Disney chairlifts. When necessary, resort-made snow is available on at least three main runs. Twelve ski lifts, 80 runs. Sugar Bowl also features a new 20,000-square-foot main lodge, at the base of the Mt. Judah and Jerome Hill Quads. For more information, contact: Sugar Bowl Ski Resort, P.O. Box 5, Norden, CA 95724, 530/426-9000, www.sugarbowl.com.

Small **Tahoe Donner,** northwest of Truckee on Northwoods Blvd. off Donner Pass Rd. (take Donner State Park exit from I-80) is primarily for beginners and intermediates, excellent for first-timers and children, with a special Snowflakes Ski School for children ages 3–6. Three lifts, 14 runs. For more information, contact: Tahoe Donner, P.O. Box 11049, Truckee, CA 96162, 530/587-9400. **Northstar-at-Tahoe,** between Truckee and Lake Tahoe on Hwy. 267, is a convenience- and family-oriented resort—featuring a cluster of condominiums and creature comforts. It offers excellent advanced and intermediate Alpine as well as Nordic ski opportunities. Fairly new at Northstar is snow tubing and night skiing, the latter at Polaris Park, at the base lodge. Twelve lifts, 63 runs. For more information, contact: Northstar-at-Tahoe, P.O. Box 129, Truckee, CA 96160, 530/562-1010 or toll-free 800/466-6784, www.skinorthstar.com.

Not far across the Nevada border is **Diamond Peak at Ski Incline,** 1210 Ski Way, Incline Village, NV 89451, 775/832-1177, www.diamondpeak.com, also noted for its snowboarding, cross-country skiing, moonlight tours, and sleigh rides. Three express quads, 30 runs, two natural glades (for advanced skiers).

More North Shore Resorts

The most famous of all Tahoe ski resorts, offering some of the world's finest, most challenging Alpine skiing, is **Squaw Valley USA,** 1960 Squaw Valley Rd. (off Hwy. 89 northwest of Tahoe City), P.O. Box 2007, Olympic Valley, CA 96146, 530/583-6985 or toll-free 888/766-9321, www.squaw.com. Squaw Valley has gained a fairly negative reputation in environmental circles in recent years, due to its ongoing legal skirmishes with Placer County and the Sierra Club over its environmental violations and attempts to develop Shirley Canyon—popular with hikers—for still more ski runs. Squaw Valley has lost its legal cases to date. But this is still heaven to truly competitive skiers; Squaw Valley's 4,000 acres of skiable terrain include some of the steepest steeps in the West. It's also one of the most popular and crowded resorts around—a ski-oriented city in its own right. Squaw Valley offers slopes for advanced, intermediate, and beginning skiers; night skiing; snowboarding; and restricted access for disabled skiers. Thirty lifts, open-bowl terrain. Snowboarding options include two terrain parks and two halfpipes (one of each is lighted) and a boardercross facility.

Even nonskiers show up just to ride the Cable Car tram up the mountain for the views—a year-round pleasure, especially now that the cabins are heated. A **climbing wall** in the tram building, 530/583-7673, offers fun and exercise while you wait. An increasing array of summer recreational opportunities includes the astounding **Bath and Tennis Club** atop the mountain at High Camp, which features the stunning **Olympic Ice Pavilion,** spas, a swimming lagoon, tennis courts (heated for winter play), and restaurants. If that's not enough adventure for you, sign up for a 75-foot freefall with **Bungee Squaw Valley,** 530/583-4000, also at High Camp and open year-round. Opened in late 1998 at Squaw Valley is its $20 million **Funitel,** a double-cable gondola running from the base up to Gold Coast, Squaw Valley's other mid-mountain facility—a ride that's all but immune to high winds that otherwise shut down the mountain. The six-passenger **High Camp Pulse** shuttles back and forth between High Camp and Gold Coast.

Scheduled for a Christmas 2001 opening is the first phase of Squaw Valley's $250 million pedestrian-friendly **The Village**—North Lake Tahoe's largest development ever, a 13-acre complex of lodging, restaurants, entertainment venues, and shops done in "California alpine" architectural style.

Relatively new in the valley is the deluxe **Resort at Squaw Creek,** a hotel and conference/convention center with three restaurants, fitness center, shopping, and a winter-only outdoor ice rink—more urban luxury in the middle of the wilderness. For more information, contact: Resort at Squaw Creek, P.O. Box 3333, Olympic Valley, CA 96146, 530/583-6955 (recorded information), 530/583-6985 (office), toll-free 800/327-3353 or 800/545-4350 (Squaw Valley central reservations), www.squawcreek.com.

Closer to the lake is the **Alpine Meadows** ski area off Hwy. 89 (via Alpine Meadows Rd.), still one of the West's best ski resorts, now owned by Utah-based Powdr Corp. (which also owns Boreal and Soda Springs). With six bowls, steep glades, and exceptional runs and views, Alpine is expansive yet low-key, a fine family-oriented alternative to Squaw Valley. (This is where locals ski.) Busy on weekends, Alpine Meadows also offers one of the state's superior disabled ski programs and is excellent for spring skiing. Twelve lifts, 100-plus runs. For snowboarders, Alpine offers two terrain parks (one just for children) and one halfpipe. For more information, contact: Alpine Meadows, P.O. Box 5279, Tahoe City, CA 96145, 530/583-4232 or toll-free 800/441-4423, www.skialpine.com.

West Shore Resorts

More resort than ski area is **Granlibakken** just south of Tahoe City (off Hwy. 89 via Tonopah Rd., at the end of Granlibakken Rd.), mostly a beginners' hill perfect for families. For more information, contact: Granlibakken Resort and Conference Center, P.O. Box 6329, Tahoe City, CA 96145, 530/583-4242 or toll-free 800/543-3221, www.granlibakken.com. The **Homewood**

Mountain Resort, 5145 W. Lake Blvd. (six miles south of Tahoe City), P.O. Box 165, Homewood, CA 96141, 530/525-2992, www.skihomewood.com, is unassuming and small, with stunning Tahoe views, perfect slopes for intermediate skiers—but also some good advanced runs, beginner and family ski possibilities, even a child care center. Kids age 10 and under ski free. Snowboarders enjoy the "Shredwood Forest" terrain park. Good spring skiing. In 1996, *Outside* magazine named Homewood the best tree-skiing resort in the United States.

South Shore Resorts
Heavenly, "America's Largest Ski Resort," on the California-Nevada border near South Lake Tahoe, is geared toward advanced and high-intermediate skiers. Its 20 square miles of ski terrain offers great opportunities—and views—for intermediates. A children's ski center and a reasonable number of beginners' slopes make Heavenly heavenly for families, too. Courageous skiers head for Motts Canyon, Killebrew's, and the legendary Gunbarrel. Snowboarders enjoy a halfpipe on each side, a permanent boardercross trail, and additional terrain. Heavenly, now owned by the conglomerate American Skiing

Co., has expanded ambitiously during the last decade—and that expansion continues, in conjunction with South Lake Tahoe redevelopment plans. A high-speed gondola from urban South Lake Tahoe, new hotels, remodeled base facilities, seven new lifts, and new trails are all coming soon; at last count Heavenly sported 27 lifts and 82 runs. In relatively dry years, snowmaking saves the day. Get here via Ski Run Blvd. from Hwy. 50 in South Lake Tahoe. For more information, contact: Heavenly Ski Resort, P.O. Box 2180, Stateline, NV 89449, 775/586-7000, www.skiheavenly.com.

A few miles west of Echo Summit off Hwy. 50 is impressive **Sierra-at-Tahoe Ski & Snowboard Resort,** sister resort to Northstar-at-Tahoe, offering something for everyone: open bowls and tree-lined runs for experts and intermediates, snowboarding, also plenty of fun for beginners and families—including a tubing hill with a lift. The emphasis here on better access and options for beginning skiers continues, but Sierra-at-Tahoe also offers free lessons for intermediates and above. The Ranchhouse restaurant up top is a worthy destination, just for the views. For more information, contact: Sierra-at-Tahoe Ski & Snowboard Resort, P.O. Box 3501, Twin Bridges, CA

SKI RESORTS IN SUMMER

As elsewhere, ski resorts in and around the Tahoe area have been transformed into year-round vacation destinations. Formerly winter-only resorts now offer everything from guided hikes (sometimes with llamas), mountain biking, mountain boarding, and horseback riding to tennis and fly-fishing.

During summer months, for example, **Northstar-at-Tahoe** near Truckee, 530/562-1010 or toll-free 800/466-6784, www.skinorthstar.com, offers hiking and mountain biking (rentals available) on 1,700 acres of diverse trails, not to mention full use of its recreation center with swimming pool, tennis courts, exercise room, and hot tubs. Golfing—including golf school—and horseback riding available, too, as well as organized programs for children. Special events in summer are almost endless. Vacation packages, featuring rodeos to romance, can be very good deals. Nearby **Squaw Valley,** 530/583-6985 or toll-free 888/766-9321, www.squaw.com, also dedicates itself to endless summers, offering everything from

Alpine mountain biking, ice skating, tennis, horseback riding, bungee jumping, and swimming at its **High Camp Bath & Tennis Club** (elev. 8,200 feet) to a full roster of special events.

Near Tahoe, **Sorensen's Resort** on Hwy. 88, 530/694-2203 or toll-free 800/423-9949 for reservations (see Hope Valley and Sorensen's under Southeast from Picketts Junction, below, for more information on the resort), is perhaps the epitome of resort creativity any time of year, with summer activities including fly-fishing instruction, historical hikes, stargazing, photography workshops, and other educational adventures. In the off-season, **Kirkwood** on Hwy. 88, 209/258-6000 or toll-free 800/967-7500, www.skikirkwood.com, offers private tennis courts, golf, a mountain bike park (open weekends and holidays), mountain bike trails, a climbing wall, a disc golf course, hiking, horseback riding (and pony rides for children), nearby fly-fishing, and occasional special events.

95735, 530/659-7453, www.sierratahoe.com. South of Tahoe via Hwy. 89 then Hwy. 88, but close enough for Tahoe skiers, are Iron Mountain and Kirkwood (see Near Tahoe below).

Nordic Skiing: Public Trails

Fun is the three-mile **Castle Peak Trail,** a Sno-Park site near Boreal (exit I-80 at Castle Peak/Boreal), which also offers unmarked backcountry cross-country access and a nearby ski hut. (There are other backcountry huts in the area as well.) A variety of other marked and unmarked Nordic ski trails near Tahoe are maintained in winter by the U.S. Forest Service, including those at Donner Memorial State Park (easy), Martis Lookout (moderate), Tahoe Meadows (easy), and Spooner Lake (easy) in the north and east. Cross-country ski trails along the lake's west shore include Five Lakes (strenuous), Paige Meadows and Blackwood Canyon (both moderate), Sugar Pine Point State Park and Meeks Creek (both easy), and McKinney/Rubicon (moderate).

The **most strenuous Nordic trails** near the south shore are at Angora Lookout and Trout Creek/Fountain Place. The Taylor Creek/Fallen Leaf trail is **moderately difficult** but good for beginners. There are **moderate trails** at the Echo Lakes area (which also offers good ski camping access into Desolation Wilderness), Benwood Meadows, and Big Meadow/Round Lake. The **easiest trails** are at the Lake Tahoe Visitor Center and at Grass Lake and Hope Valley.

For more information about the area's national forest ski trails, and to find out about ranger-led interpretive ski tours—usually scheduled Jan.–mid-Mar.—contact the U.S. Forest Service (see Tahoe Area Events and Information below).

South and southwest from Tahoe are other good public Nordic ski areas, including the Loon Lake area north of Hwy. 50 (reached via Ice House Rd.) and Strawberry Canyon near Strawberry and Twin Bridges; the invigorating Leek Springs Loop and Winnemucca Lake Loop off Hwy. 88; various sites along Hwy. 4 (including—a good workout—skiing the highway beyond Bear Valley's Hwy. 4 closure gate to Ebbetts Pass); and Pinecrest (24 miles of trails) above Sonora on Hwy. 108.

Nordic Skiing: Private Resorts

Nordic skiing is big news at Tahoe ski resorts. Closest to Sacramento (off I-80 at Yuba Gap) is **Eagle Mountain Resort,** offering 86 km of trails groomed for both skating and striding, both a day lodge and a wilderness lodge, lessons, and special events. The resort becomes a mountain-biking mecca in summer. For more information, call 530/389-2254 or toll-free 800/391-2254, or write: Eagle Mountain Resort, P.O. Box 1566, Nevada City, CA 95959.

Among the best in the country—and largest, most complete in the nation—is immensely popular, 9,000-acre **Royal Gorge** in Soda Springs, with 88 trails and 204 miles of track, warming huts, Eurostyle wilderness lodge (small rooms but large

skiing in Tahoe

MICHAEL J. NEVINS/TOM MYERS PHOTOGRAPHY

SKI TOURING AND WINTER MOUNTAINEERING

Among instructors and guides offering back-country ski trips in the Sierra Nevada are **Alpine Skills International (ASI),** on Donner Summit near Truckee and North Lake Tahoe, P.O. Box 8, Norden, CA 95724, 530/426-9108, www.alpineskills.com; **Sierra Ski Touring,** serving the South Lake Tahoe area, P.O. Box 176, Gardnerville, NV 89410, 775/782-3047; and **Yosemite Mountaineering School,** Yosemite National Park, Yosemite, CA 95389, 209/372-1244, www.yosemitepark.com. Alpine Skills International offers a full range of mountain-climbing, rock-climbing, ice-climbing, and other special outdoor skills instruction. Sierra Ski Touring leads ski trips and also offers avalanche seminars and dog sled trips. Yosemite Mountaineering offers backcountry ski instruction, as well as the world's finest "office" for rock-climbing instruction.

common areas), day lodge, cafés, and rental-retail ski shops. Royal Gorge's lifts offer easier access to upper slopes; steeper slopes are good for practicing downhill cross-country. Guided snowshoe hikes and ski clinics are also offered. And there are hot tubs, for soaking those screaming muscles. For more information, contact: Royal Gorge Cross-Country Ski Resort, P.O. Box 1100, Soda Springs, CA 95728, 530/426-3871 or toll-free 800/500-3871, www.royalgorge.com. The Sierra Club's volunteer-built 1934 **Clair Tappaan Lodge,** 19940 Donner Pass Rd. in nearby Norden, 530/426-3632—one of the best inexpensive places to stay near Tahoe, any time of year—offers cross-country lessons, rentals, and a few miles of track. (Discounts offered for Sierra Club members.) The **Tahoe Donner Cross Country Center,** 11509 Northwoods Blvd., 530/587-9484, features 37 trails and 56 miles of track (with some night Nordic skiing). **Northstar-at-Tahoe,** 530/562-2475 or 530/562-1010, has 38 trails and 40 miles of cross-country and telemarking track; **Squaw Valley** also offers Nordic skiing. See listings above for more information on both. Popular for beginners is **Diamond Peak at Ski Incline,** 1210 Ski Way, Incline Village, NV 89451, 775/832-1177, www.diamondpeak.com, is the Vista View Loop, which offers sweeping Tahoe views.

The **Lakeview Cross Country Ski Area,** 938 Country Club Dr. near Tahoe City, 530/583-3653, offers 18 trails and plenty of track, moonlight ski tours, daytime tours, warming hut, rest areas, and clinics. Resort areas south of Tahoe also offer good cross-country skiing opportunities. Just south of the airport is the **Lake Tahoe Winter Sports Center,** 3071 Hwy. 50, 530/577-2940, with many miles of groomed trails. The center also offers snowmobiling on groomed tracks adjacent to its cross-country ski trails.

STAYING AT TAHOE: NORTH

North Tahoe Camping
State park campgrounds at Lake Tahoe (see Seeing and Doing Greater Tahoe above) are popular. Reservations through ReserveAmerica, toll-free 800/444-7275, www.reserveamerica.com, are necessary May–early Sept.—though all campgrounds may be open considerably later in the year, weather permitting, on a first-come, first-camped basis—and Sugar Pine Point is open to campers year-round. Nearby state parks with campgrounds include Donner Memorial State Park and Grover Hot Springs State Park, the latter also open year-round. Most U.S. Forest Service campgrounds—there are plenty near the lake, and dozens throughout the greater Tahoe area—are first-come, first-camped, but popular campgrounds like **Fallen Leaf** can be reserved in advance ($12–14 per night) through the National Recreation Reservation Service, toll-free 800/280-2267. One of the area's best-kept camping secrets is near South Lake Tahoe across the Nevada border, at **Nevada State**

ACCOMMODATIONS RATINGS

Accommodations in this book are rated by price category, based on double-occupancy, high-season rates. Categories used are:

Budget . . . . $35 and under
Inexpensive $35-60
Moderate $60-85
Expensive $85-110
Premium $110-150
Luxury . . . . $150 and up

Beach, with open, pine-shaded lake frontage camping just a stone's throw from the beach and an easy walk to Safeway and other signposts of civilization. Ask about other regional campground choices at ranger stations, chambers of commerce, or visitors centers.

Clair Tappaan Lodge and Rainbow Lodge

The Sierra Club's Clair Tappaan Lodge, 19940 Donner Pass Rd., Norden, 530/426-3632, www.sierraclub.org, is a time-honored skiers' tradition—rustic dormitory-style rooms, family rooms, and tiny two-person rooms (all with bunk beds) in a rambling cedar shake–sided three-story lodge complete with hot tub, library, kitchen, and dining facilities. Three family-style meals per day are included in the rates—as is the necessity to do at least one simple housekeeping chore each day. Inexpensive (five- and seven-day rates available). Extra fee for cross-country ski rentals, ski school, and hot tub. But Clair Tappaan is a year-round treat, also popular with hikers and those who just need to get away for a while. Call to request a current brochure.

Also a particular pleasure, but more of the simple-but-comfort-conscious variety, is the **Rainbow Lodge,** about six miles west of Soda Springs on old Hwy. 40 (take the Rainbow Rd. exit from I-80), Soda Springs, 530/426-3871, 530/426-3661, or toll-free 800/500-3871, www.royalgorge.com. Now affiliated with the Royal Gorge Nordic ski resort—cross-country trails connect it with Royal Gorge's Wilderness Lodge—Rainbow Lodge was originally built in the late 1800s of granite and hand-hewn timbers, then expanded in 1928. It features a log-beamed ceiling and knotty pine interiors, 32 homey rooms (20 with private baths), and one suite. Those in the know say the Rainbow Lodge also features a ghost named Mary, who lives on the 3rd floor. Expensive-Premium, breakfast included. The fine **Engadine Cafe,** 530/426-3661, is on the premises—serving breakfast, lunch, and dinner daily—as well as a tavern with live weekend entertainment.

Other Stays near Truckee and Donner Summit

Get complete accommodations listings from local visitors bureaus. Most ski resorts in and around the Tahoe-Truckee area (see above) and elsewhere offer restaurants and various accommodations options, but unusually interesting inns are also scattered throughout the greater Tahoe area.

A real treat in downtown Truckee is the **Truckee Hotel** at Commercial and Bridge Sts., 530/587-4444 or toll-free 800/659-6921, an old 1868 lumberjack hotel spruced up to suit the modern world, with 37 rooms (but only eight with private bath). Bargain basement rooms are in the Inexpensive range; rooms with private baths are Premium. Includes continental breakfast buffet, and features a good restaurant, **Passages,** and bar downstairs.

Motels in the Truckee area include the **Donner Lake Village Resort Hotel & Marina,** 15695 Donner Pass Rd. (about six miles west of town on old Hwy. 40 at the west end of Donner Lake), 530/587-6081 or toll-free 800/621-6664, www.donnerlakevillage.com, with studios and one- and two-bedroom units. Expensive-Luxury. The simple, small, and quiet **Loch Leven Lodge** on Donner Lake, 13855 Donner Pass Rd., 530/587-3773, features eight motel-style units with kitchens and queen beds, also a townhouse that sleeps eight, complete with fireplace. Extras here include a 5,000-square-foot redwood deck, rowboat, barbecue, picnic tables, and spa. Moderate-Expensive. (No credit cards.) Just over a mile outside town is the **Best Western Truckee Tahoe Inn,** 11331 Hwy. 267, 530/587-4525 or toll-free 800/824-6385. Expensive-Premium.

Overlooking Truckee is the elegant 1881 Victorian **Richardson House** bed-and-breakfast, 10154 High St. (at Spring), 530/587-5388 or toll-free 888/229-0365, www.richardsonhouse.com, with period decor and abundant amenities. Wonderful breakfast. Expensive-Premium. Another excellent choice, also quite reasonable, is the 11-room **The Swedish House Bed & Breakfast** in the heart of town adjacent to the Truckee River, 10009 E. River St., 530/587-0400 or toll-free 888/302-0400. All rooms feature private bathrooms with new claw foot tubs and pedestal sinks, and custom furnishings. And who can pass on those Swedish pancakes at breakfast? Expensive-Premium.

Staying on the North and West Shores

Overall best bets for travel bargains are seasonal vacation packages—suited to all interests and income levels—offered in the north shore area (including Truckee) through the North Lake Tahoe Resort Association, 950 N. Lake Blvd., Tahoe City, 530/583-3494 or toll-free 800/824-6348, www.tahoefun.org. The visitors bureau will also recommend (and make) lodging reservations based on budgetary and other preferences.

The **Cedar Glen Lodge**, 6589 N. Lake Blvd. (Hwy. 28), just a few miles west of the Nevada border, 530/546-4281, toll-free 800/500-8246 or 800/341-8000, www.cedarglenlodge.com, has motel rooms, housekeeping cottages, sauna, whirlpool, pool, and playground. Inexpensive-Premium. Farther from the madding crowds as well is the **Charmey Chalet Resort** (pronounced shar-MAY) in Tahoe Vista at 6549 N. Lake Blvd., 530/546-2529, where the highway widens into four lanes. A hot tub, pool, and other relatively recent renovations have jazzed up this hill-climbing motel with tall trees and outdoor patios, sliding glass doors, in-room refrigerators, TV, and phones. Coffee and sweet rolls at breakfast. Moderate. Nearby are other decent midrange motels. In Tahoe City, the **Tahoe City Inn**, 790 N. Lake Blvd., 530/581-3333 or toll-free 800/800-8246 for reservations, has rooms with waterbeds and in-room spas. Moderate-Premium. Also an off-season bargain, especially for AAA members, is the **Tahoe City Travelodge**, 455 N. Lake Blvd., 530/583-3766, comfortable and attractive, near the lake, with golfing adjacent. Moderate-Premium.

Very Tahoe Stays

Always a best bet among area motels is the **Franciscan Lakeside Lodge**, 6944 N. Lake Blvd. (Hwy. 28), 530/546-6300 or toll-free 800/564-6754, which also features lakefront cottages. The simple rooms and cottages are either one- or two-bedroom and include full kitchens. The lodge offers a private beach and pier, swimming pool, volleyball, croquet, horseshoes, and children's play area. Moderate-Luxury.

A popular après-ski spot, fun in summer for riverside dining, and a great choice year-round for lodgings is the **River Ranch Lodge** on the Truckee River just off Hwy. 89 at Alpine Meadows Rd., 530/583-4264, www.riverranchlodge.com. Originally established in 1888 as the Deer Park Inn, the old building was replaced in 1950

with this woodsy shingle-sided lodge overlooking the Truckee River. All 19 rooms feature antiques and modern amenities, and some offer private river-view balconies. Continental breakfast. Premium. Another attraction here is the very good **River Ranch Lodge Restaurant.**

For updated Old Tahoe ambience, a great choice is the refurbished 1908 **Sunnyside Lodge**, 1850 W. Lake Blvd., 530/583-7200 or toll-free 800/822-2754, on the lake south of town. Some of the 23 rooms feature stone fireplaces, and many have lake views. Luxury, continental breakfast included. For good California-style fare, try Sunnyside's **Chris Craft** restaurant. Among cabin choices, those at the **Tahoma Lodge**, 7018 W. Lake Blvd., 530/525-7721, are quiet and comfortable. Three-night minimum. Premium.

Swanker North Shore Stays

Particularly appealing to skiers are the many area resorts, which also offer options in the summer. For a complete listing of the possibilities, see the Resorts sections above. An upscale newcomer at Squaw Valley is the 60-room **Plumpjack Squaw Valley Inn**, 1920 Squaw Valley Rd., 530/583-1576 or toll-free 800/323-7666, a sophisticated and stylish hotel offering all the understated urban comforts, great views, swimming pool, spas, and room service from the excellent on-site **Plumpjack Café.** Otherwise, swankest of the swank in the north shore area is the nine-story, 450-room **Resort at Squaw Creek**, 400 Squaw Creek Rd. in Squaw Valley, 530/583-6300 or toll-free 800/327-3353, www.squawcreek.com, which, from the outside, resembles Darth Vader's corporate headquarters. The super-luxury resort offers every imaginable amenity, with extras including children's programs, shopping promenade, three excellent restaurants, three swimming pools, fitness center and spa, ice-skating rink, cross-country ski trails, and ski-in, ski-out access to Squaw Valley lifts. In summer, there's the Robert Trent Jones Jr. 18-hole golf course, equestrian center, and Peter Burwash International Tennis Center. Luxury, but ask about midweek packages—sometimes a good deal.

For current information on Nevada-side accommodations, as well as suggestions on condominium and cabin rentals, contact the Incline

Village/Crystal Bay Visitors Bureau, listed below under Tahoe Area Events and Information.

North Tahoe Bed-and-Breakfasts

The north shore boasts B&B accommodations in addition to those near Donner Pass and Truckee (listed above).

A popular lakefront newcomer is **The Shore House at Lake Tahoe,** 7170 N. Lake Blvd., 530/546-7270 or toll-free 800/207-5160, www.inntahoe.com, where all nine refreshingly outdoorsy rooms feature custom-built log furniture, Scandia down comforters and feather beds, and gas fireplaces. All have private bathrooms, private outdoor entrances, and unique features. Private pier. Wonderful breakfast. Premium-Luxury.

An excellent choice, and a Tahoe classic, is the 15-cabin **Cottage Inn,** 1690 W. Lake Blvd. (Hwy. 89, just south of town), 530/581-4073 or toll-free 800/581-4073, a cluster of cozy knotty-pine bed-and-breakfast cabins; full breakfast is served in guest rooms or in the dining room. Beach access and sauna. Premium-Luxury.

A half mile north of the Hwy. 28/89 intersection and just blocks from the lake, the **Mayfield House** bed-and-breakfast inn, 236 Grove St., 530/583-1001, www.mayfieldhouse.com, is the former cottage home of Norman Mayfield, a contractor who worked closely with architect Julia Morgan. Five rooms plus a cottage, all with private bath; full breakfast served. Expensive-Luxury.

Five miles south of Tahoe City proper, the lakefront **Chaney House** bed-and-breakfast in Homewood at 4725 W. Lake Blvd., 530/525-7333, www.chaneyhouse.com, is a striking 1920s-vintage stone house complete with Gothic arches and massive fireplace, four rooms or suites with private baths, private beach and pier, wonderful full breakfast. Premium-Luxury. Quite popular (two-week notice required for cancellations). An elegant choice is the **Rockwood Lodge** bed-and-breakfast, 5295 W. Lake Blvd., Homewood, 530/525-5273 or toll-free 800/538-2463, www.rockwoodlodge.com, which offers antique furnishings in a plush, 1930s-vintage Tahoe rock-and-pine home. Full breakfast. Expensive-Luxury.

Quite reasonable and welcoming is the **Tahoma Meadows Bed & Breakfast,** 6821 W. Lake Blvd. in Tahoma, 530/525-1553 or toll-free 800/355-1596, www.tahomameadows.com,

where the 11 cabins all feature private baths, comfortable beds—king, queen, or twin—TV, and framed watercolors. One cabin sleeps six—perfect for families. Moderate-Luxury. Full breakfast is served in the main lodge, which is upstairs from the separate Stoneyridge Cafe. Also near Sugar Pine Point State Park is the **Norfolk Woods Inn,** 6941 W. Lake Blvd., Tahoma, 530/525-5000, www.norfolkwoods.com, a collection of five self-contained cottages with full breakfast, pool, and whirlpool. Moderate-Luxury.

STAYING AT TAHOE: SOUTH

The **Lake Tahoe Visitors Authority,** 1156 Ski Run Blvd. (at Tamarack), South Lake Tahoe, CA 96150, 530/544-5050 or toll-free 800/288-2463 (reservations only), www.virtualtahoe.com, maintains a current listing of South Lake Tahoe accommodations and is happy to help with reservations. Also helpful is the **South Lake Tahoe Chamber of Commerce,** 3066 Lake Tahoe Blvd., 530/541-5255.

Ski bums on a budget can try the **Monaco Blu-Zu Hostel,** 4140 Pine Blvd., South Lake Tahoe, 530/542-0705, where dorm bunks go for $16 per day, $80 per week. Budget. Two good motels outside town are both great bargains. The **Lazy S Lodge,** 609 Emerald Bay Rd., 530/541-0230, is a quiet find, featuring quaint cottages with kitchens and Swedish wood-burning fireplaces or motel-style rooms, as well as barbecues, picnic tables, lots of lawn, pool, and deck. Moderate-Expensive. Closer still to Sierra Ski Ranch and Kirkwood is the **Ridgewood Inn,** 1341 Emerald Bay Rd., 530/541-8589, a small motel (12 units), some adjoining rooms perfect for families. Moderate.

Rustic South Shore Resorts

The 83-acre **Camp Richardson Resort,** 1900 Jameson Beach Rd., 530/541-1801 or toll-free 800/544-1801, www.camprichardson.com, is a wonderful 1930s-style rustic respite among the pines located a few miles south of Emerald Bay on Hwy. 89. The circa-1923 lodge includes a rugged stone fireplace, log rafters, and 30 rooms with private baths. Expensive-Premium. Out back are Camp Richardson's 42 cabins, complete with kitchens and bathrooms, available by the week in summer. Moderate-Luxury. The resort's campground across the highway features 112 campsites with amenities like hot showers for $17–22 per night. Camp Richardson also offers a beach, marina, and other recreational attractions, including Nordic skiing in winter.

South on Hwy. 50, the granite-and-log **Echo Chalet**, 9900 Echo Lakes Rd., 530/659-7207, is quiet and isolated, with 10 rustic, woodsy summer cabins that sleep two to four. Moderate. (Take the chalet's water taxi service across the lake to Desolation Wilderness). Also special, winter or summer, is the refurbished **Strawberry Lodge** roadhouse, 17510 Hwy. 50 in Strawberry, 530/659-7200, www.strawberry-lodge.com. Tucked under the granite cliffs beyond Echo Summit, about 20 miles west of South Lake Tahoe via Hwy. 50, it's the first genuine ski lodge in the Sierra Nevada, originally built in the 1850s. Smack dab in the middle of the popular Strawberry Canyon cross-country ski area, lodge rooms—either in the main lodge or the annex across the highway—are Inexpensive-Premium (shared or private bath). Also here: a dining hall with stone fireplace, hearty restaurant fare (open-air deck dining in summer), and even an ice cream shop.

Swanker South Shore Stays

South Lake Tahoe has a seemingly endless supply of motels and hotels—with more on the way—but is still short on bed-and-breakfasts. **The Christiania Inn** ("The Chris" to its fans), 3819 Saddle Rd. (off Ski Run Blvd.), 530/544-7337, www.christianiainn.com, has been around just about forever—a European-style country inn almost under Heavenly's main chairlift. Two rooms and four unique suites—popular with honeymooners—all with private baths, plus lounge and excellent continental restaurant. Continental breakfast. Two-night minimum on weekends. Expensive-Luxury.

Right on the California-Nevada border, the **Embassy Suites Resort**, 4130 Lake Tahoe Blvd., 530/544-5400, toll-free 800/988-9820 or 800/362-2779, is an example of South Tahoe's new redevelopment style, a modern take on the traditional early-1900s architecture on display at Tallac and elsewhere. Luxury. Another nice hotel close to the casinos (which are also housed in four-star hotels) is the **Best Western Station House Inn**, 901 Park Ave.,

530/542-1101, www.stationhouseinn.com. Luxury. Another best bet, if you want to stay condostyle, is **Lakeland Village Beach & Ski Resort**, 3535 Lake Tahoe Blvd., 530/544-1685 or toll-free 800/822-5969, www.lakeland-village.com, a townhouse resort where the appeal includes the lakefront beach, two swimming pools, and tennis courts. Expensive-Luxury.

Top-flight farther up the hill is the **Tahoe Seasons Resort** at Heavenly Valley, 3901 Saddle Rd. (at Keller), 530/541-6700 or toll-free 800/540-4874, www.tahoeseasons.com, featuring comfortable suites with in-room spas, kitchenettes (refrigerators, sink, microwave), TVs and VCRs, and fold-out sofa bed in a sitting room, all with adequate privacy for families or two couples traveling together. Valet parking. Luxury. Exceptionally elegant and with every imaginable resort amenity is **The Ridge Tahoe**, 400 Ridge Club Dr., Stateline, NV, 775/588-3553 or toll-free 800/334-1600, www.ridge-tahoe.com, a resort complex at an elevation of 7,300 feet—just a gondola lift to the slopes. Luxury.

EATING WELL AT TAHOE: NORTH

Eating in Truckee

Most everything is along Commercial St. or within a block or two. For cheap eats in Truckee, try the **Squeeze In**, 10060 Donner Pass Rd. (Commercial Row), 530/587-9814, noted for its 22 kinds of sandwiches, 57 varieties of omelettes, and city-style pizzas with toppings like artichoke hearts and prosciutto. Open for breakfast and lunch daily. After lunch, stop off at **Bud's Fountain**, 10043 Donner Pass Rd. (inside the sporting goods store), 530/587-3177, for that old-fashioned ice cream soda. **Andy's Truckee Diner**, 10144 W. River St. (at Hwy. 267), 530/582-6925, does a good job with all the American standards at breakfast, lunch, and dinner. For somewhat fancier fare, try **O.B.'s Pub and Restaurant**, 530/587-4164 (fabulous Sunday brunch).

For contemporary Italian, the place to go in Truckee is **Pianeta**, 10086 Donner Pass Rd. downtown, 530/587-4694, open nightly for dinner. **Cottonwood**, 10142 Rue Hilltop, off Hwy. 267 heading toward Northstar, 530/587-5711, enjoys a nice perch overlooking Truckee—great views, pleasant atmosphere, upscale American cuisine. Still quite fine after all these years is **The Passage** downstairs in the Truckee Hotel, 530/587-7619, a consistent *Wine Spectator* magazine award-winner. Open nightly for dinner, weekdays for lunch, and weekends for brunch. Also quite wonderful is dinner—any meal, actually—at the Rainbow Lodge's exceptional **Engadine Cafe,** on Rainbow Rd. in Soda Springs, 530/426-3661, featuring pastas, seafood, and more eclectic selections. Open daily, if the roads are open.

Eating on the North and West Shores

Much-loved is **Rosie's Cafe,** 571 N. Lake Blvd. in Tahoe City, 530/583-8504, for reasonably priced and tasty American favorites like ham and eggs for breakfast, burgers at lunch. *The* thing for dinner in ski season is the Yankee pot roast, though the Southern-fried chicken holds its own. Open daily for breakfast, lunch, and dinner. Full bar. Very "Tahoe" and a genuine locals' hot spot is the **Fire Sign Cafe** two miles south of Tahoe City at 1785 W. Lake Blvd. in Tahoe Park (near the Cottage Inn), 530/583-0871—wholesome homestyle cooking in a casually eclectic atmosphere, fabulous for a morning meal—fresh-squeezed juices, homemade muffins and coffeecake, omelettes, eggs Benedict, and other hearty fare—and open seven days a week (until 3 P.M.) for both breakfast and lunch. In good weather, sun yourself out on the deck. But expect a wait on weekends. Another local hangout, **Hacienda del Lago,** 760 N. Lake Blvd., 530/583-0358, is open daily for lunch and dinner—*the* place for Mexican food and great margaritas.

Especially at lunch, another good spot to soak up local atmosphere—pool tables, Jägermeister on tap, and all—is the **Bridgetender,** 30 West Lake Blvd. (on the south side of Fanny Bridge) in Tahoe City, 530/583-3342, best for burgers (including veggie burgers). Best bet for pizza and Italian is tiny, casual **Za's,** 395 N. Lake Blvd., 530/583-1812, open daily for dinner. For seafood and steaks on the lake, the place is **Jake's on the Lake,** downtown at 780 N. Lake Blvd., 530/583-0188. Open for dinner daily year-round, and in summer for lunch Mon.–Sat. and Sunday brunch. Full bar. The **Tahoe House** restaurant and bakery, 625 W. Lake Blvd. (a half-mile south of Tahoe City's Y intersection on Hwy. 89), 530/583-1377, serves European fare (spe-cializing in Swiss-German and Swiss-French entrées at dinner), also pastas and fresh seafood specials. Children's menu, takeout available.

A locals' favorite for breakfast and lunch in Carnelian Bay is the **Old Post Office Cafe,** 5245 N. Lake Tahoe Blvd., 530/546-3205. The casual **Boulevard Café & Trattoria** in Tahoe Vista at 6731 N. Lake Blvd., 530/546-7213, serves great house-made pastas and breads, filet mignon, and changing seafood specials. Beer and wine. Open daily for dinner. Fun and quite good for hot and spicy Cajun food in Tahoe Vista is **Colonel Claire's,** 6873 N. Lake Blvd., 530/546-7358. *The* breakfast and lunch place in Kings Beach is the **Log Cabin Caffe,** 8692 N. Lake Blvd., 530/546-7109, where everything is fresh and tasty—from the Belgian waffles to the turkey, cranberry, and cream cheese sandwiches.

North Shore Fine Dining

Area resorts are starting to outdo themselves in the foodie destination sweepstakes. At Squaw Valley alone you can enjoy a midday meal at top-of-the-tram **Alexander's,** 530/583-2555, and an exceptional dinner at the **Plumpjack Café**—sister restaurant to the one in San Francisco—at the new Plumpjack Squaw Valley Inn, 530/583-1576. Or head to Squaw Valley's Resort at Squaw Creek, 530/583-6300, for any of its three restaurants—the exceptional contemporary French-American **Glissandi** (brought to you by the former La Cheminée folks), the continental **Cascades,** and the **Ristorante Montagna.**

For more fine dining—reservations always recommended—North Tahoe choices include very romantic, very expensive **Christy Hill** in the Lakehouse Mall, 115 Grove St. in Tahoe City, 530/583-8551, noted for its California cuisine, views, and fireplace. Also quite famous in Tahoe City—and unforgettable for its excellent if high-priced vegetarian fare—is **Wolfdale's,** 640 N. Lake Blvd. in Tahoe City, 530/583-5700, noted for Japanese-flavored California cuisine. Everything served here is made here. Good wine list, full bar. Still considered one of the best French restaurants in the West is **Le Petit Pier** in Tahoe Vista at 7238 N. Lake Blvd., 530/546-4464, where the sunset views are part of the fixed-price experience. Open nightly for dinner in summer, more limited days the rest of the year. Impressive wine list, full bar. Also time-honored in the high-priced dinner category is the **Swiss Lakewood Restaurant,** 5055 W. Lake Blvd., 530/525-5211, unstuffy yet elegant (dining room dress code), which first opened its doors here in 1920. Full bar. Open Tues.–Sun. for dinner. The stylish newcomer in the neighborhood is **Sunsets on the Lake** in Tahoe Vista, 7320 N. Lake Blvd., 530/546-3640, serving exceptional California-style Northern Italian and, yes, sunsets. Heated outdoor deck. Full bar. Open for dinner nightly, for lunch daily in summer.

EATING WELL AT TAHOE: SOUTH

The cheapest eats of all are available in the casinos in Nevada's Stateline; the big hotels are happy to serve breakfast for a couple of bucks just to get folks within reach of those one-armed bandits. In South Lake Tahoe, fast-food eateries, small cafés, and some very decent restaurants manage to coexist. For an incredibly generous breakfast, try **Red Hut Waffles,** 2723 Hwy. 50, 530/541-9024, noted for its huge waffles and good omelettes. (There's another Red Hut across the border in Nevada, on Kingsbury.) Another local favorite, quite casual in the lunch and dinner fast food tradition, is **Izzy's Burger Spa,** 2591 Hwy. 50, 530/544-5030. The rockin' burger joint, though, is **Planet Hollywood** just across the Nevada border in Stateline at Caesars, Hwy. 50 at Lake Pkwy., 702/588-7828, open daily 11 A.M.–2 A.M. Immensely popular **Sprouts Natural Foods Café,** 3123 Harrison St., 530/541-6969, offers some great burger alternatives, from turkey and tuna-veggie sandwiches to burritos and fruit smoothies.

For fancier fare, **Nephele's,** 1169 Ski Run Blvd., 530/544-8130, has excellent daily specials, also pastas, baby back ribs, and scampi. Private hot tubs on the premises. **Scusa! on Ski Run,** 530/542-0100, features imaginative pizzas and calzones, great pastas (try one of the specialties), and select chicken, fish, seafood, and steak entrées, all in an inimitable Tahoe atmosphere. Also raved about: the exceptionally fine dining room at the **Christiania Inn,** 3819 Saddle Rd., 530/544-7337.

Popular for European cuisine (mostly German and Swiss) and fairly casual is the **Swiss Chalet Restaurant,** four miles west of Stateline at 2540 Tahoe Blvd. (Hwy. 50 at Sierra Blvd.), 530/544-3304. Probably the best for American-style seafood is **The Dory's Oar,** 1041 Fremont, 530/541-6603, a New England–style restaurant and lounge with fresh seafood from both coasts plus a selection of steaks, though the Japanese **Samurai,** 2588 Hwy. 50, 530/542-0300, is the best bet for sushi and other seafood specialties.

The Edgewood Terrace at the Edgewood country club, 775/588-2787, offers great food and good views. Sometimes a meal here is a real bargain, too, with two-for-one coupons available in winter and at other slower times. The **Zephyr Cove Resort** is also quite good, the dining room cozied up in winter by wood heat. Worth it, Nevada-side, is **Primavera,** the Italian restaurant at Caesars Tahoe, 55 Hwy. 50, 775/588-3515. Also exceptional is **Llewelyn's,** on the 19th floor at Harvey's on Hwy. 50 at Stateline, 775/588-2411. The wonderful view is unveiled, on sunny days, by light-sensitive electronic shades that raise automatically at sunset.

For fine dining, *the* place to eat in South Lake Tahoe is still eclectic **Evan's American Gourmet Cafe,** 536 Emerald Bay Rd., 530/542-1990, a tiny restaurant (just 12 tables) raved over by repeat guests—and by *Bon Appétit.* Great wine list. Reservations essential. Open nightly for dinner.

TAHOE AREA EVENTS AND INFORMATION

There's always something going on, from North Tahoe's winter **Snowfest** and the summer **Truckee-Tahoe Air Show** to South Tahoe's **Valhalla Summer Arts & Music Festival** at the Tallac Historic Site and the **Lake Tahoe Shakespeare Festival** at Sand Harbor. To get current information on the entire Tahoe area and its events and attractions, contact *all* area visitors bureaus, since each represents a limited geographical area.

The best source for South Lake Tahoe information is the **Lake Tahoe Visitors Authority,** 1156 Ski Run Blvd. (at Tamarack), South Lake Tahoe, CA 96150, 530/544-5050 or toll-free 800/288-2463 (reservations only), www.virtualtahoe.com. Request a copy of the annual *Lake Tahoe Travel Planner* and, if you stop by, be sure to pick up the *Tahoe Resource Brochure,* an all-around Lake Tahoe-at-your-fingertips guide produced in conjunction with the Nevada Commission on Tourism and the Tahoe-Douglas Chamber of Commerce. Another helpful option is the **South Lake Tahoe Chamber of Commerce,** 3066 Lake Tahoe Blvd., 530/541-5255. The **North Lake Tahoe Resort Association,** 950 N. Lake Blvd., P.O. Box 5578, Tahoe City, CA 96145, 530/583-3494 or toll-free 800/824-6348 (for accommodations, rates, special package information, and reservations), www.tahoefun.org, shares office space with the **Greater North Lake Tahoe Chamber of Commerce,** 530/581-6900. Visitors arriving after business hours can use the light-up "locator map" and free reservations phone for lining up last-minute lodgings, plus rifle the racks for brochures and free local publications. To take advantage of Tahoe North's aggressive marketing of vacation packages, from ski weekends to honeymoon and wedding specials, advance planning is necessary—and usually well worth it.

For more regional information, contact the **Truckee-Donner Chamber of Commerce,** 10065 Donner Pass Rd. (inside the train station), Truckee, CA 96161, 530/587-2757 or toll-free 800/548-8388 (central reservations), www.truckee.com, and the **Incline Village/Crystal Bay Visitors Bureau,** 969 Tahoe Blvd., Incline Village, NV 89451, 775/831-4440, fax 775/832-1605 or toll-free 800/468-2463, www.laketahoechamber.com. For Reno visitor information and assistance, call toll-free 800/367-7366.

Headquarters for the U.S. Forest Service's **Lake Tahoe Basin Management Unit** are at 870 Emerald Bay Rd., P.O. Box 8465, South Lake Tahoe, CA 96158, 530/573-2600, and open year-round. Regional ranger district offices are another good source for camping, hiking, recreation, and other national forest information. Local outdoors and recreation stores are always good sources for information, as well as rental equipment. Summers-only information centers, at the Pope-Baldwin visitors center and at the west shore's William Kent campground, can be useful. Stop by or contact the local state parks headquarters (see the D. L. Bliss and Emerald Bay State Parks listing, above) for current information about state parks camping, hiking, and other activities. Another helpful resource is the Forest Service **Truckee Ranger District** office, 10342

Hwy. 89 N, Truckee, CA 96161, 530/478-6254.

One of the most useful publications around is the *Lake of the Sky Journal* published jointly by the U.S. Forest Service and California and Nevada state parks offices. Another great free publication is *North Tahoe/Truckee Week,* available everywhere around the north shore. For very comprehensive and updated regional tourist information, everything from recreation and sightseeing to area accommodations and select restaurant menus in magazine-style, buy *The Guide to Lake Tahoe,* available locally for around $5.

TAHOE AREA TRANSPORTATION

At last report, the **South Lake Tahoe Airport,** 530/542-6180, was served by **Tahoe Air,** toll-free 888/824-6324, and **Allegiant Air,** toll-free 877/202-6444. Many travelers prefer flying into the **Reno-Cannon International Airport,** served by a half-dozen major carriers (including American, Southwest, and United), then renting a car or taking the local "luxury shuttle"—the latter quite a good deal. For $17 per person one-way ($30 round-trip), the **Tahoe Casino Express,** 775/785-2424 or toll-free 800/446-6128, offers nonstop transportation to and from the Reno airport and south shore destinations (skiers and noncasino guests welcome, with room for ski gear and luggage). The feasibility of offering inexpensive Casino Express–type bus service (about $15 one-way) from the greater Sacramento area to South Lake Tahoe was being investigated by the Tahoe-Douglas Visitor Authority in 1999; for an update, contact the Lake Tahoe Visitors Authority.

TART (Tahoe Area Regional Transit) buses, 530/581-6365, run year-round, serving northwest Placer County and the Incline Village area, stopping only at TART signs (exact fare only, $1.25 per ride, commuter passes available). **STAGE** (South Tahoe Area Ground Express) buses, 530/542-6077, provide 24-hour service around South Lake Tahoe, more limited routes elsewhere, fare $1.25 (a 10-trip pass is $10).

To take a taxi ride anywhere around the lake, any time of day or night, call **Yellow Cab,** 775/831-8294 (Incline Village area), 530/546-9090 (North Lake Tahoe), or 775/588-5555

(South Lake Tahoe). An unusual Tahoe-style transportation option is the sternwheeler *Tahoe Queen,* 530/541-3365, which runs from South Lake Tahoe to the north shore regularly and—in combination with a bus shuttle system—even carries skiers to Northstar, Squaw Valley, and Alpine Meadows in winter. For more information—tours and dinner-dance cruises are also offered—contact: **Hornblower Cruises,** 900 Ski Run Blvd., P.O. Box 14292, South Lake Tahoe, CA 96151, 530/541-3364 or toll-free 800/238-2463. For other Tahoe tour information, contact local chambers of commerce and visitor bureaus.

If you're not cycling, driving, flying, or hitch-hiking, **Greyhound,** toll-free 800/231-2222, www.greyhound.com, can get you to Lake Tahoe. Buses leave daily from South Lake Tahoe (1000 Emerald Bay Rd.) to San Francisco and Los Angeles, also to Las Vegas, Reno,

and other Nevada destinations. (Or connect with Greyhound in Truckee at the train station, 10065 Donner Pass Road.)

Best bet for sights and serenity, though, is riding the rails on **Amtrak,** which stops at Truckee's restored train depot. There's no office or ticket sales here, however; call toll-free 800/872-7245 or try www.amtrak.com or www.amtrakwest.com for fare and route information. Coming from Oakland, Amtrak's *California Zephyr* rolls through Berkeley backyards, over the Benicia-Martinez Bridge, through the Suisun Marsh (good bird views in winter and a look at the Mothball Fleet), then across farmland and fields to Sacramento. From there to Tahoe, riders are treated to some fine, rare views: a cliff-hanging peek into the yawning canyon of the American River's north fork, the Yuba River, Sugar Bowl's slopes, then through the Judah Tunnel and Coldstream Valley to Truckee.

SOUTH FROM TAHOE

Instead of heading east to the South Lake Tahoe strip and the Stateline casino wilderness, jog due south into the rock-hard heart of true wildness. Highway 50 veering west toward Placerville and Sacramento is a major mountain thoroughfare that shoots past pretty little Echo Lake (fishing, picnicking, and boating; no camping but good access to the Desolation Wilderness) and up and over Echo Summit for some fine high-mountain scenery.

Off in the other direction from just south of Meyers, Hwy. 89 leads into big-sky country, including both the Mokelumne and Carson-Iceberg Wilderness Areas. Heading west on Hwy. 88 from Picketts Junction leads to Carson Pass and its gorgeous granite high lakes. South of fun and funky Markleeville and nearby Grover Hot Springs State Park, Hwy. 4 also cuts west, this time over Ebbetts Pass and the Pacific Grade Summit, dipping slightly into the Bear Valley–Lake Alpine high country before sliding down the Sierra Nevada's western slope to Calaveras Big Trees State Park, then Angels Camp and vicinity. And here's a thought, while you admire the scenery: Archaeologists working near Ebbetts Pass have unearthed evidence of a Native American campsite some 10,000 years old—one of the oldest ever found in the Sierra Nevada—and the clay floor and hearth of an ancient hunting hut, the oldest prehistoric structure ever found in North America.

Southeast from the Hwy. 4 junction, Hwy. 89 heads up and over Monitor Pass—special in autumn, with fiery fall-colored aspens and an unusual autumn fishing season at Heenan Lake for rare Lahontan cutthroat trout (strict limits, current fishing license necessary). At Hwy. 395, the eastern Sierra Nevada's only major roadway, head north to windy Topaz Lake straddling the California-Nevada border for trophy-sized trout, camping, and (once across the state line) that omnipresent casino scene. Or roll south past the lonely towns of Topaz, Coleville, and Walker to Sonora Junction, then on into Bridgeport, the nearby Mono Lake Basin, and the breathtaking beauty of the Sierra Nevada as experienced from the backside (see Mono Lake and Vicinity, below). But heading west on Hwy. 108, past the U.S. Marine Corps' Mountain Warfare Training Center, then up and over incredible Sonora Pass (closed in winter), can prove equally enticing.

NEAR CARSON PASS

Highway 88 from Picketts Junction—where a roadside monument marks the old Pony Express route—climbs to an elevation of 8,573 feet at Carson Pass. Quite serene, with fine national forest campgrounds (some operated by concessionaires) open in summer, are the alpine lakes just off the highway west of Carson Pass. Small **Woods Lake** a couple of miles south of Hwy. 88 offers a quiet wooded campground (water, no showers), nice lakeside picnicking (wheelchair accessible), fishing, also a nice hike

the stunning High Sierra

ROBERT HOLMES/CALTOUR

to the old Lost Cabin Mine. Large **Caples Lake** farther west and right on the highway, like tiny **Kirkwood Lake** nearby, also offers good camping, picnicking, swimming, fishing, and boating. (No motorboats are allowed at Kirkwood; larger RVs also discouraged.) From near the dam at Caples Lake, hike south into the Mokelumne Wilderness. Near the highway maintenance station close to Caples Lake is the trailhead for **Round Lake** and relatively remote **Meiss Lake.** For more information about these lakes, trails, and campgrounds, contact the **Amador Ranger District** office in Pioneer, 209/295-4251.

Popular here in winter is the excellent **Kirkwood Ski and Summer Resort,** P.O. Box 1, Kirkwood, CA 95646, 209/258-6000 or toll-free 800/967-7500, 209/258-3000 for ski conditions, and 209/258-7000 for resort lodgings, www.skikirkwood.com, a modern ski complex once beloved for its frontier feel and relative lack of urban-style amenities. The fact that the Telluride Ski and Golf Co. now owns a hunk of Kirkwood hasn't changed the fact that this area receives Tahoe's biggest snowfalls. Adding a bit of luxury is the new 43,000-square-foot **Lodge at Kirkwood,** a four-story condominium hotel.

About six miles west of the Caples Lake–Kirkwood area is **Silver Lake,** another popular granite-and-blue water recreation lake along Kit Carson's trail. For more information about Silver Lake and vicinity, contact the **El Dorado National Forest Information Center,** 3070 Camino Heights Dr., Camino, 530/644-6048, or **forest headquarters,** 100 Forni Rd. in Placerville, 530/622-5061.

Between Silver Lake and the Bear River Reservoirs, at the junction of Hwy. 88 and the Mormon Emigrant Trail, is **Iron Mountain Ski Resort,** oriented primarily to intermediate Alpine skiers, with a ski school, ski shop, rentals, lodging, and food. For more information, contact: Iron Mountain, P.O. Box 1500, Pioneer, CA 95666, 209/258-4400. There's good national forest cross-country skiing in the area, too.

SOUTHEAST FROM PICKETTS JUNCTION

Sorensen's Resort

On Hwy. 88/89 south of Lake Tahoe—a half mile east of Picketts Junction in Hope Valley—

Sorensen's Resort is *the* local institution, with a café, cozy cabins, and roadside serenity far removed from the Stateline casino scene. Most cabins have kitchens and woodstoves; all have gas heaters and bathrooms. Otherwise, each cabin is unique, with distinct features. Rates are complicated (two-night minimum on weekends), calculated on a per-cabin basis, rates lower midweek, everything higher on holiday weekends. Group cabins and private homes are also available. (To make an enlightened choice, see the website.) Expensive-Luxury. General amenities include a sauna (small fee), wedding gazebo, hammocks, and a kid's catch-and-release trout pond.

Besides good food (breakfast, lunch, and dinner served at the café) and reasonably priced lodging, Sorensen's also offers a variety of special events, from historical tours of the Mormon Emigrant Trail over Carson Pass to river rafting on the East Fork of the Carson River, from watercolor painting and photography workshops to cross-country ski tours and sleigh rides. In the works: plans for a new bed-and-breakfast lodge and dozens more cabins. For more information, contact: Sorensen's Resort, 14255 Hwy. 88, Hope Valley, CA 96120, 530/694-2203 or toll-free 800/423-9949, www.sorensensresort.com. The **Hope Valley Cross-Country Ski Center,** with 60 miles of trails, is also affiliated with Sorensen's.

Markleeville and Vicinity

Up on the hill above town is the **Alpine County Historical Museum** complex, 530/694-2317, open Thurs.–Mon. 11 A.M.–4 P.M. from Memorial Day through October (free, but donations greatly appreciated). Here stands the white clapboard **Old Webster School,** restored to its one-room 1882 ambience, and the county's unusual **Old Log Jail,** with hand-riveted iron jail cells imported north from the original Silver Mountain City building in 1875. Also here: miscellaneous farming, mining, and lumbering artifacts. The modern museum itself has an impressive display of local historical memorabilia, including some beautiful Washoe basketry used for gathering then winnowing pine nuts, a dietary staple.

A fascinating feature in downtown Markleeville is the redneck **Cutthroat Bar** inside the Alpine Hotel and Cafe. Typical are the D.A.M.M. (Drunks Against Mad Mothers) bumper sticker on the pool table, brand-name beer mirrors, and animal heads on the walls. Unusual, though, are the "trophies" hanging from the ceiling—an impressive but somehow empty collection of women's bras. The standing deal is that any "gal" can trade in her bra for a free Cutthroat Saloon T-shirt, as long as she makes the trade right then and there. Despite the lingerie on display, there aren't that many takers.

Just west of Markleeville via Hot Springs Rd. is **Grover Hot Springs State Park,** the perfect hot-soak antidote for weary high-country hikers. Tucked into a mountain meadow near the northeastern edge of the Mokelumne Wilderness, the hot and cool natural spring-fed pools at Grover Hot Springs aren't particularly aesthetic—caged with cement and nonclimbable fence like public swimming pools, but complete with changing rooms and presoak showers (bathing suits required). Yet who cares? The water feels so *good*. (Mineral purists, walk up the hill to the spring's source to find out the water's exact mineral content.) Except for two weeks in Sept. when the pools are closed for their annual cleaning, Grover Hot Springs is open all year—if you can get here—and popular in winter for hardy souls hankering for a hot soak and a roll in the snow. Developed campsites, just outside the valley, are in an open forested area, none too private—but tired hikers and well-soaked hot springs aficionados rarely complain. ReserveAmerica reservations, toll-free 800/444-7275, are usually necessary in summer. Small day-use fee. For more information, contact: Grover Hot Springs State Park, P.O. Box 188, Markleeville, CA 96120, 530/694-2248 or 530/525-7232.

For more information about the area, contact: **Alpine County Chamber of Commerce/U.S. Forest Service office,** at the corner of Main and Webster, P.O. Box 265, Markleeville, CA 96120, 530/694-2475 (chamber) or 530/694-2911 (Forest Service), www.alpinecounty.com.

EBBETTS PASS AND VICINITY

Another impressive after-the-snows climb is up and over Ebbetts Pass via Hwy. 4 (on very narrow roads with hairpin turns) and down the other side to Bear Valley, Calaveras Big Trees, Murphys, and ultimately Angels Camp in the Sierra Nevada foothill gold country. The **Highland**

MUSIC AT BEAR VALLEY

For some musical Ebbetts Pass rambling in summertime, come to Bear Valley and the tent pavilion set up outside the Bear Valley Lodge for the annual **Bear Valley Music Festival** concert series—a long-standing tradition usually scheduled from late July through mid-August, featuring everything from classical music and opera to Rodgers and Hammerstein and pop. For more information, contact: Bear Valley Music Festival, P.O. Box 5068, Bear Valley, CA 95223, 209/753-2574 or 209/753-2334. Season tickets and single-event tickets are available. You can also arrange accommodations with ticket purchase, but plan well ahead.

Lakes area off the highway just west of Ebbetts Pass offers good trout fishing and primitive camping (no drinking water), as do the tiny, very picturesque **Mosquito Lakes** beyond Hermit Valley on the Pacific Grade Summit.

The sky-high **Lake Alpine** area northeast of Bear Valley features backpacking trailheads into both Mokelumne and Carson-Iceberg Wilderness Areas, spring and early summer white-water rafting on the North Fork of the Stanislaus River (usually from Sourgrass to Calaveras Big Trees downriver), and lake recreation: canoeing, kayaking, and sailing in addition to fishing for rainbows, swimming, picnicking, and casual hiking.

For more information about Lake Alpine and vicinity, including area campgrounds, contact the **Calaveras Ranger District,** 5314 Hwy. 4, P.O. Box 500, Hathaway Pines, CA 95233, 209/795-1381, or stop by the ranger station on the north side of the highway just west of the Silver Tip and Lodgepole (overflow) campgrounds.

Though Hwy. 4 is closed just east of Bear Valley by winter snows, the **Bear Valley Ski Area,** P.O. Box 5038, Bear Valley, CA 95223, 209/753-2301 or 209/753-2308 (snow conditions), www.bearvalley.com, is accessible from the gold country even in winter. Surrounded by a condominium city complete with mall, Bear Valley is otherwise a medium-sized mellow alternative to the Tahoe ski scene. The resort offers an uncrowded but top-notch downhill ski slope with a comfortable lodge; good beginning, intermediate, and advanced ski runs; an excellent restaurant; and a well-developed program for disabled skiers. Bargain prices on weekdays and for groups. The resort's affiliated **Bear Valley Cross Country Ski & Adventure Company,** 1 Bear Valley Rd., 209/753-2834, offers impressive Nordic-ski facilities, from trails to warming huts, in winter.

Even more accessible than Bear Valley in winter is **Cottage Springs Ski Area,** a snowplay and learn-to-ski center on Hwy. 4 at Beatrice Dr., Camp Connell, just above Dorrington, 209/795-1209 or 209/795-1401.

SONORA PASS AND VICINITY

Though the old Sonora & Mono Toll Rd. has been a state highway since 1901, the stomach-churning, switchback slither over shoulderless Sonora Pass, where the granite meets the clouds above timberline at an elevation of 9,626 feet, is unforgettable. Assuming he or she survives, anyone attempting the pass in an RV or pulling a trailer of any kind up this lonely stringlike stretch of Hwy. 108, onetime film location of *For Whom the Bell Tolls,* should check into the nearest mental health clinic immediately. But otherwise, don't hesitate—especially if you're cycling. It's beautiful, and literally breathtaking. Stop near the top for a picnic or to camp.

Sliding down the western slope from Sonora Pass, just south of the Carson-Iceberg Wilderness and north of the 107,000-acre Emigrant Wilderness of alpine meadows, high lakes, and granite adjacent to Yosemite National Park, the road leads to **Kennedy Meadows** (trailhead and pack station) and **Dardanelle,** with a string of national forest campgrounds between the two. (For off-highway camping, head northeast on Clark Fork Rd. west of Dardanelle to the campgrounds on the way to **Iceberg Meadow** just outside the wilderness area.)

About 20 miles southwest beyond Dardanelle are the tiny towns of Strawberry and Pinecrest near **Pinecrest Lake,** quite popular in summer for lake recreation—swimming, canoeing, and boating (no water-skiing) to fishing and horseback riding—and family camping.

Also at Pinecrest is the casual, gold rush–flavored **Dodge Ridge** ski and snowboarding resort, with exceptional but underrated downhill skiing for beginner, intermediate, advanced, and skiers with disabilities, as well as a ski school—all the better after a $3.5 million 1999 terrain expansion. In summer, mountain biking is a draw. For more information, contact: Dodge Ridge, P.O. Box 1188, Pinecrest, CA 95364, 209/965-3474, www.dodgeridge.com.

Get local camping, hiking, horseback riding, and nature trail information, national forest and wilderness maps, as well as wilderness permits, topo maps, and updates on trail conditions for both Emigrant and Carson-Iceberg Wilderness Areas at the **Summit Ranger Station** at the Y intersection on Hwy. 108 near Pinecrest, 1 Pinecrest Lake Rd., Pinecrest, CA 95364, 209/965-3434.

MONO LAKE AND VICINITY

Calling it "one of the strangest freaks of Nature found in any land," Mark Twain was particularly impressed by his mid-1800s visits to Mono Lake, then commonly referred to as the Dead Sea of California:

Mono Lake lies in a lifeless, treeless, hideous desert. . . . This solemn, silent, sailless sea— this lonely tenant of the loneliest spot on earth—is little graced with the picturesque. It is an unpretending expanse of grayish water, about a hundred miles in circumference, with two islands in its centre, mere

upheavals of rent and scorched and blistered lava, snowed over with gray banks and drifts of pumice-stone and ashes, the winding sheet of the dead volcano whose vast crater the lake has seized upon and occupied.

Mono Lake's water was so alkaline, Twain quipped, that "the most hopelessly soiled garment" could be cleaned simply by dipping it in the lake then wringing it out. He also noted the peculiarity of a sky full of seagulls so far from the sea, and the region's predictable two seasons: "the breaking up of one winter and the beginning of the next."

tufa formation at Mono Lake

While some characteristics of modern-day Mono Lake are still as Twain described them, the depth, size, and very nature of this high-desert sea have changed greatly. Mono Lake today is the victor in one of the hardest-fought environmental wars of the century, a preeminent political hot potato pitting Los Angeles water consumers against lovers of the land and landowners in the eastern Sierra Nevada.

MONO LAKE NATURAL HISTORY TOUR

Despite the craters-of-the-moon look, highly alkaline waters, and surrounding day-old stubble of sage, life abounds at 750,000-year-old Mono Lake, now protected as both the **Mono Basin National Forest Scenic Area** and the **Mono Lake Tufa State Reserve.** Though early settlers considered the lake "dead," since it was too salty to support even fish life, native peoples knew better. They observed the huge seagull popula-

tions nesting here in spring—85 percent of the total California gull population—and some 300 other bird species, including migrants like phalaropes and eared grebes, and knew they depended on lake shrimp and brine flies for survival. (The word *mono* means "fly" in Yokut. The Kutzadika'a Paiutes who lived near Mono Lake harvested the brine fly grubs, a protein-rich delicacy, and traded them to the Yokuts for acorns.)

Still a vast gray-blue inland sea despite Los Angelenos' long-term water predation, Mono Lake's saline waters make for fun, unusually buoyant swimming. Old-timers claim a good soak in Mono Lake's medicinal waters will cure just about anything. But Mono's most notable features are its surrounding salt flats and peculiar tufa formations—strangely beautiful salt-white pillars of calcium carbonate (limestone). Naturally created underwater when salty lake water combines with calcium-rich fresh spring water bubbling up from below, these 200- to 900-year-old "stone" spires are now less exposed than in recent years, due to rising water levels. (Since 1941, the first year that water from four of Mono Lake's feeder streams was shipped south to L.A., the lake's level dropped an average of 18 inches per year, a total drop of about 45 feet. In the 1990s, however, with area streams now flowing into the lake once again, that trend is reversing.) The best place to see and wander through these fantastic tufa formations—no climbing or souvenir-taking allowed—is in the **South Tufa Area** off Hwy. 120 ($3 fee), which features basic visitor facilities, including flush toilets. Here and elsewhere, due to deceptively soft pumice "sand," heed warnings about driving on less-traveled roads—particularly on the lake's east side—without a four-wheel-drive vehicle.

Mono Lake has two major islands: the yin-yang twins of white **Paoha** and black **Negit;** until recently the latter was the gulls' preferred nesting spot. (The islands, and the lake itself within one mile of them, are closed to the public from April through July to protect nesting birds.) Environmentalists fighting for Mono Lake's right to life pointed out that L.A.-bound water diversions, made worse by natural disasters like drought, created the land bridge that connected the islands to the mainland, allowing coyotes and other bird and egg predators to reach nesting seagull

THE WAR WAGED FOR MONO LAKE

The war of politics and power waged on behalf of Mono Lake and its water has been so contentious, convoluted, and long-running, and has involved so many public agencies and public hearings, so many lawsuits and compromises, that the simple facts are virtually impossible to separate from the details. Central to the saga, though, is the Los Angeles Department of Water and Power. "If we don't get the water," said self-taught engineer and water czar William Mulholland in 1907, "we won't need it." To get water to the L.A. desert, Mulholland and his DWP proposed an aqueduct that would carry the eastern Sierra Nevada's water south from the Owens Valley (and the towns of Bishop, Big Pine, Independence, and Lone Pine) to Los Angeles. To gain support (and municipal bond funding) for "Mulholland's ditch," even the *Los Angeles Times* helped fudge on the facts—convincing the public in the early 1900s that a drought existed, a deception unchallenged until the 1950s.

After buying up nearly all private land in the Owens Valley (usually dishonestly, by condemning the land and water rights by lawsuit to drive down the price), Mulholland and his water people had their finest day in November 1913, when the first Owens Valley water flowed into the aqueduct: 30,000 people showed up for the event.

Commenting on the subsequent, permanent desolation of the once lush, quarter-million-acre Owens Valley, the cowboy comedian Will Rogers said soberly: "Los Angeles had to have more water for its Chamber of Commerce to drink more toasts to its growth."

As L.A.'s thirst grew ever more unquenchable—by 1930, the city's population had grown from 200,000 to 1.2 million—violence over eastern Sierra Nevada water rights became commonplace. Denied use of the land as abruptly as their forebears had denied the native Paiutes, outraged ranchers "captured" and controlled the aqueduct on many occasions, and dynamited it 17 times. But urban growth was seemingly unstoppable, and in 1930, L.A. voters approved another bond issue—to extend the aqueduct north into the Mono Lake Basin.

Following completion of this northern stretch in 1941, runoff from Rush, Lee Vining, Walker, and Parker Creeks was diverted into the ditch-tunnel drilled under the Mono Craters and into the Owens River and aqueduct. Even worse for Mono Lake—with its water level dropping and its delicate aquatic ecology suffering almost instantaneously—Los Angeles completed a second aqueduct in 1970, to "salvage" runoff otherwise lost to the lake. Until quite recently, Mono Lake had been shrinking ever since. In 1990, it was estimated that about 17 percent of Los Angeles water came from Mono Lake. California's Dead Sea had nearly died as a direct result.

Central to the present-day chapter of Mono Lake's story is David Gaines, longtime Lee Vining resident, biologist, and founder of the Mono Lake Committee—killed, along with committee staffer Don Oberlin, in a January 1988 car accident near Mammoth Lakes. Though he surely would have loved to see Mono Lake's waters rise again, at the time of his death, Gaines had already made major progress toward that eventual result. Starting in the 1970s, he and his growing, loosely organized band of Mono Lake lovers began taking on the Los Angeles Department of Water and Power and anyone else involved, even through passive inaction. From guerrilla theater and educational "events"—such as public picketing, protests, and volunteer bucket brigades hand-carrying water from Lee Vining Creek to Mono Lake—to press conferences and political confrontations, the Mono Lake Committee was untiring in its war against water diversions.

As a result, the Interagency Mono Lake Task Force—including representatives from Mono County, the L.A. Department of Water and Power, the California Departments of Water Resources and Fish and Game, the U.S. Forest Service, the U.S. Fish and Wildlife Service, and the federal Bureau of Land Management—was convened. The group agreed, by 1980, that the only way to protect the natural resources of the Mono Basin was by curtailing water diversions and raising the lake's level. An almost endless round of lawsuits against the DWP and state and federal regulatory agencies (along with countersuits) in both the state and federal court systems has subsequently helped implement the task force recommendations.

A state Supreme Court decision in 1983—specifically related to Mono Lake but setting the California legal precedent that now protects all state waters—declared that lakes, rivers, and other natural resources are owned by all the people and must be protected by the state for the public trust. Though competing needs are undeniable, the right to divert water from any ecosystem depends upon that system's continued

(continued on next page)

THE WAR WAGED FOR MONO LAKE

(continued)

health—and if harm occurs, water rights must be adjusted accordingly, throughout time.

But though the tide finally turned in Mono Lake's favor, at least legally, skirmishes have continued over how much water must be released into the Mono Lake Basin to ensure the health of that ecosystem— how much water will protect island-nesting gulls from coyote predation, how much water will protect the lake's brine shrimp, how much water will protect the region's stream fisheries. Needless to say, the opinions of Mono Lake Committee members and other environmentalists differ from those of L.A.'s Department of Water and Power. Actual cutbacks in diversions—under court order—didn't begin until 1989.

Political pundits contend that recent state legislation to make peace at Mono Lake merely pays the city of Los Angeles, with public funds, to strike a rather vague deal with the Mono Lake Committee— and encourages L.A. to increase groundwater pumping from Inyo County's Owens Valley, all at California taxpayers' expense. "If this is what peace looks like for Mono Lake and the Owens Valley," commented the *Sacramento Bee's* Bill Kahrl, "it's hard to understand what anyone thought was worth fighting for in the first place."

Members of the Mono Lake Committee answered that even successful lawsuits have not yet protected Mono Lake, and that state legislative action at least opens the door for a lasting peace. The committee also noted that new state and federal water reclamation and conservation projects would more than compensate for L.A.'s loss of Mono Lake water.

But despite L.A.'s impressive progress in water conservation, the city's Department of Water and Power has indeed increased its groundwater pumping in the Owens Valley, directly south, to the great detriment of that environment—a crisis without a committee to speak on its behalf.

The war over eastern Sierra Nevada water goes on.

---

colonies on Negit Island. But lack of freshwater also increased the lake's salt levels by two or three times, threatening both Mono Lake's brine shrimp and brine fly populations—a more subtle but long-term threat to gulls and other bird species dependent on these creatures for food. Other problems as well may have affected area life. Long-term measurements of the levels of radioactive carbon in Mono Lake, for example, showed notable increases in the 1950s and 1970s. For a time there was worry that nuclear waste may have been dumped here, but more recent information suggests that the carbon increase came from U.S. Navy munitions testing.

Now the lake's future—and future water levels—are less clouded by human politics. But in a sense, life had already "returned" to the Mono Lake Basin by 1985, when bald eagles came back to the area's stream canyons.

PRACTICAL MONO LAKE

No developed camping is available at Mono Lake, but independent camping—"dispersed camping"—is allowed in certain areas near Mono Lake, so long as campsites are staked out above the 1941 waterline. For more information, and for details on developed area campgrounds, ask at the Mono Basin National Forest Scenic Area Visitor Center or the Mono Lake Committee Information Center (see below).

Staying at Mono Lake

Lee Vining is "town" for Mono Lake, a pleasant roadside collection of motels, gas stations, and supply stops on Hwy. 395 just north of the junction with Tioga Rd./Hwy. 120 from Yosemite. Usually the cheapest motel around (pets allowed) is the **King's Inn,** two blocks off the highway at 45 2nd St., 760-647-6300, with small, cozy rooms, kitchen units extra. Moderate. Also reasonable and small-pet friendly is **Murphey's Motel,** on the highway, 760/647-6316. Moderate-Expensive. The **Gateway Motel,** 85 Main St. (Hwy. 395), 760/647-6467, has comfortable rooms with queen beds, coffee, and TV. Expensive (rates lower from Nov. through mid-May). Pretty uptown in this town is the **Best Western Lake View Lodge,** 30 Main St.,

760/647-6543, complete with coin-op laundry and putting green. Moderate-Expensive.

Eating Out at Mono Lake

Folks here will tell you *the* place to eat in town is **Nicely's Restaurant** ("real nicely people") on Main, 760/647-6477, open daily for good café fare—breakfast, lunch, and dinner. A more stylish option, just north of town about four miles in the otherwise long-gone town of Mono Lake, is exquisitely restored **The Mono Inn** restaurant and bar, 760/647-6581, www.adamsgallery.com, and the affiliated third outlet of the **Ansel Adams Gallery,** all owned and operated by descendants of famed photographer Ansel Adams. What you'll get here in addition to the elegantly rustic farmhouse ambience and great California-style American fare (be sure to save room for the chocolate pecan pie) are some great lake views and an up-close look at some Ansel Adams originals. Restaurant open for Sunday brunch and Tues.–Sun. for dinner in summer; call for gallery and winter hours. The **Virginia Creek Settlement** near the turnoff to Bodie (see below) is worth the drive, if what you're hungry for is whole wheat–crust pizza and other wholesome yet reasonably sophisticated fare.

Mono Lake Committee Information and Events

Stop by the **Mono Lake Committee Information Center and Bookstore** (a onetime dance hall, now renovated) on Hwy. 395 at 3rd St., P.O. Box 29, Lee Vining, CA 93541, 760/647-6595, www.monolake.org. Committee headquarters also houses the **Lee Vining Chamber of Commerce,** www.leevining.com, making this the all-purpose Lee Vining visitors center—providing the latest information on Mono Lake politics; schedules of lake hikes, tours, and canoe trips;

THE DEMISE OF THE SIERRA BIGHORN?

The ragged beauty and rugged agility of Sierra Nevada bighorn sheep, John Muir's "bravest of all Sierra mountaineers" and Native Americans' "white buffaloes," can still sometimes be appreciated firsthand by mountain visitors. Though bighorn hunting was banned in California in 1878, the law provided little real protection from domestic sheep ranchers, who viewed bighorn as grazing competition, and from diseases transmitted by domestic herds, particularly bacterial pneumonia. The state's Sierra Nevada bighorn population dropped off steadily until the 1970s, when new bighorn reserves were established and relocation efforts began in earnest to increase the population. The Sierra bighorn sheep may still be spared the fate of California's wolves and grizzly bears, both extinct.

But no one's too sure. Now numbering as few as 100, this genetically distinct bighorn population has been all but wiped out. In early 1999, both the state and federal governments officially listed the Sierra Nevada bighorn as an endangered species.

As alive, alert, and independently ingenious as domestic sheep are simple and herd-bound, these magnificent creatures historically have taken in stride whatever tough territory the Sierra Nevada offers. Bands of bachelor rams or small family groups of ewes and lambs, watched over by a wary old ram with massive curved horns, can sometimes be spotted in spring and summer in Lee Vining Canyon west of Mono Lake, scrambling up impossibly steep and unstable inclines or leaping across ravines.

Yet Lee Vining Canyon is the last viable range of the Sierra bighorn. Due to the recent harsh winters, mountain lion predation, mountain lion population increases—which have forced the bighorn to winter (and die) in high elevations—and disease transmitted by contact with domestic sheep grazing on wild lands, even these sheep are under great stress. Several other bighorn populations, relocated elsewhere in the Sierra Nevada in the hopes of increasing total numbers, have virtually disappeared.

As a last-resort effort to guard against species extinction until range management and other political decisions can be made to protect more effectively the surviving wild populations, state biologists plan to capture at least some Sierra Nevada bighorn sheep, pen them, and begin a captive breeding program. Based on the successful captive breeding of Peninsular bighorn near Palm Springs—those sheep quick to revert to their wild ways upon release from captivity—the hope is that the numbers of Sierra Nevada bighorn can be increased fairly rapidly, to establish new relocated populations in the wild.

NORTH FROM MONO LAKE: BODIE AND VICINITY

Evocative even these days is the published 19th-century response of a young girl when told her family was moving to this bad, brawling, desolate frontier town on the lonely, wind-sheared plateau: "Goodbye, God, we are going to Bodie." In defense of this godless Gomorrah, a gold mining town with a population of more than 10,000 employed at 30 mines in its heyday, a Bodie newspaper editor claimed the child had been misquoted—that what she actually said was: "Good, by God, we are going to Bodie." But the town's own citizenry boasted that Bodie had the widest streets, wickedest men, and worst climate and whiskey in the West.

What remains of the busted boomtown of Bodie—California's largest ghost town, which actually persisted as a town until 1942—is now protected as part of **Bodie State Historic Park.** A strangely silent place still standing (more or less) in the shadow of the old Standard Mine, where the sage-whistling winds speak loudest of days gone by, Bodie still somehow evokes the spirit of the truly wild Wild West. Preserved in its entirety in a state of arrested decay, what's here is certainly worth at least a half-day's exploration, but only about 5 percent of Bodie's well-weathered 1860s and 1870s wood-frames still stand, the rest destroyed over the decades by fire and the elements.

Pick up a self-guided tour brochure at the small museum (in the old Miner's Union Hall) or at the ranger's office/residence on Green St., one of the few occupied buildings in town. Visitors are free to wander at will through godless, lawless, treeless Bodie. Peek through tattered lace curtains into general stores, restaurants, saloons, livery stables, and miners' shacks abandoned for more than a century, and peer into dusty rooms furnished with cracked and peeling wallpaper and woodstoves, sprung bedframes, banged-up wash basins, even battered old shoes and clothing.

For obvious reasons, beyond the parking lot no smoking is allowed in Bodie. Camping is also prohibited, but picnicking is okay (no shade, just tables and pit toilets). Pack a lunch and bring your own drinking water—Bodie is a ghost town, with no stores or services. The park is open daily 9 A.M.–7 P.M. in summer, until just 4 P.M. the rest of the year—hours strictly enforced (the rangers close and lock the road gates). Small day-use fee. For more information, contact: Bodie State Historic Park, P.O. Box 515,

Bridgeport, CA 93517, 760/647-6445. Call for current hike, tour, and history talk schedules.

A half-mile north of the turnoff to Bodie is the best little dinner house (and overnight stop) for miles around—**Virginia Creek Settlement** on Hwy. 395, 760/932-7780, www.virginiacrksettlement.com. A windmill out front marks the spot. The settlement was once part of Dogtown, the region's first gold-rush mining camp, though nearby Bodie surpassed it in reputation and longevity. These days, Virginia Creek Settlement serves a variety of good American-style dinners and nightly specials, from steaks and chicken to pastas, but the real prize here is the pizza. The restaurant is open for dinner Wed.–Sat. in spring and fall, Tues.–Sun. in summer. An equally great deal is a stay in the large suite directly above the restaurant, the only historically authentic rooms remaining from the building's past as a boardinghouse

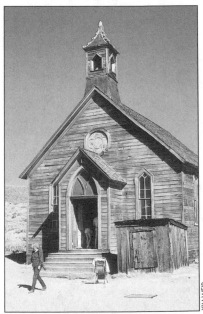

Bodie was the wickedest Old West mine camp of them all, locals boasted, but there were a few churches in town.

KIM WEIR

for Bodie miners. Behind the restaurant and well back from the highway are a few log cabin–style motel units. Even more intriguing is an overnight in one of Virginia Creek's "Tent Town" cabins; campsites are also available. Budget-Moderate. Farther north is **Bridgeport,** the place to get groceries, parts for emergency car repairs, and outdoor equipment—as well as to rest one's head in a real bed. For information about the area, contact **Bridgeport Chamber of Commerce,** 85 Main St. (the highway), P.O. Box 541, Bridgeport, CA 93517, 760/932-7500, www.cabiz.com/bridgeportchamber. Another good information source, especially for national forest maps, wilderness permits, and area campground and hiking information, is the Toiyabe National Forest's **Bridgeport Ranger Station,** P.O. Box 595, 760/932-7070.

suggestions about what else to see and do in the area—including where some of the best hot springs are—and practical guidance on visiting the eastern Sierra Nevada. In addition, many educational field seminars are held annually by the Mono Lake Foundation (P.O. Box 153, Lee Vining, CA 93541), primarily from late spring to early fall. Most weekend workshops run $75–150.

Other Mono Lake Information
Easy **naturalist-guided walks** of Mono Lake are offered year-round, daily in summer—usually at 10 A.M., 1 A.M., and 6 P.M.—and every Sat. and Sun. from mid-Sept. through mid-June, in the South Tufa Area, 10 miles southeast of Lee Vining via Highways 395 and 120. Off-season hikes usually meet at 1 P.M. There's no charge for the walk, but there is a $3 admission fee for the South Tufa Area. Even if you've hiked the lake before, be sure to come again; now that Mono Lake's water level is rising, the landscape is surprisingly *different.*

For guided walk details and more Mono Lake information, stop by the impressive **Mono Basin National Forest Scenic Area Visitor Center** just north of town off the highway, P.O. Box 429, Lee Vining, CA 93541, 760/647-3044, TTY 760/647-3045, www.r5.fs.fed.us/inyo/vvc/mono, open daily 9 A.M.–5 P.M. most of the year, until 8 P.M. from mid-June through Labor Day. Call for winter days and hours. An impressive contemporary museum overlooking the lake, it features an information center, a good bookstore, and very well done natural history exhibits.

The Mono Basin Visitor Center is also a good source for regional U.S. Forest Service information, including area day hikes, forest and wilderness maps ($4), topo maps, wilderness permits, and regional campground information. Ask too about surrounding national forest areas—including the eastern Sierra Nevada's Hoover Wilderness adjacent to Yosemite north of Hwy. 120 and the Ansel Adams Wilderness south of the highway.

MAMMOTH LAKES AND VICINITY

The Mammoth Lakes area offers surprising contrast to the sagebrush scrub along the main highway—and good summer hiking among the geological wonders, mountain lakes, hot springs, and cool conifers of this otherwise hot shot winter ski area.

For information about Mammoth Lakes and vicinity, contact the **Mammoth Visitor Center and Ranger Station,** on Hwy. 203 as you come into town, P.O. Box 148, Mammoth Lakes, CA 93546, 760/924-5500, TTY 760/924-5501, where you can pick up information on the town as well as surrounding national forest lands, wilderness maps ($4), wilderness permits, and current information on hiking, backpacking, and camping. The *Mammoth Trails Hiking Guide,* available for $3, is worth the investment if you're staying awhile. Also contact the **Mammoth Lakes Visitor Bureau,** 437 Old Mammoth Rd., Ste. Y (in the Minaret Village Mall), P.O. Box 48, Mammoth Lakes, CA 93546, 760/934-2712 or toll-free 888/466-2666, www.visitmammoth.com, which is helpful for phone queries but is no longer set up as a walk-in visitor center. Another good information source can be found at www.mammothweb.com, offering a visitor's guide with useful topics such as lodging, food, weather, attractions, events, and road conditions.

MAMMOTH LAKES AND THE MAMMOTH LAKES BASIN

Aside from the area's lovely lakes and streams, the star attraction of the Mammoth Lakes Basin is **Devil's Postpile National Monument,** a seemingly pile-driven vertical collection of three- to eight-sided basalt columns formed by slowly cooling lava flows (getting there involves an easy day hike, after a national forest shuttle ride). Nearby is colorful **Rainbow Falls,** complete with mountain pools for invigorating swimming. Near Devil's Postpile is **Fish Creek Hot Springs,** with no facilities, no fees, no restrictions, reached from Reds Meadow by hiking south on the Fish Creek Trail past the Sharktooth Creek Trail (about 100 yards along the path beyond the campground).

But the area's all-time favorite hot soak is at **Hot Creek,** three miles east of Hwy. 395 via Long Valley Airport Road. Officially "not recommended" for swimming or soaking by the Forest Service, people hop in happily nonetheless. The steaming Hot Creek experience is created by a *very* hot spring bubbling into an ice-cold stream—so the trick is finding a spot that's not so hot that you'll get scalded. (Most people manage.) Swimsuits required. Open daily from sunrise to sunset, free.

To get an eagle's-eye view of the area, in summer take a tram ride up **Mammoth Mountain** (open daily 11 A.M.–3 P.M., fee) and stop halfway for a snack or cup of coffee. Do explore some of the area's 100-plus lakes. The only one noted for swimming is **Horseshoe Lake,** also the trailhead for the Mammoth Pass Trail. For shorter hikes, there are many ways to get to **Lake George.** Picture-perfect for picnicking is **Lake Mamie.** Diehard trout fishing enthusiasts may want to visit **Lake Crowley,** some 15 miles south of Mammoth Lakes.

Mammoth Mountain Inn, 1 Minaret Rd., 760/934-2581 or toll-free 800/228-4947, attracts mountain bikers in summer to its **Mammoth Mountain Bike Park,** 760/934-0706, which offers 75 miles of trails, climbing rock, and chairlift rides; almost a religious experience for adventure cyclists is flying down the Kamikaze Trail on Mammoth Mountain. The inn is home base, too, for **Mammoth Adventure Connection,** 760/924-5683, which offers mountain-bike tours, mountain climbing, and a variety of other adventures year-round.

Winter Sports at Mammoth

At the center of the area's winter ski scene is the **Mammoth Mountain Ski Area** just past town, P.O. Box 24, Mammoth Lakes, CA 93546, 760/934-2571 or toll-free 800/626-6684, www.mammoth-mtn.com. The area's 2,500 acres of great skiing and snowboarding are far from everywhere but particularly popular with the L.A. crowd. To cope with drought conditions, the resort also has snowmaking capabilities. Some $25 million in recent improvements at Mammoth

Devil's Postpile
National Monument

KIM WEIR

MAMMOTH SHUTTLES

The Mammoth Lakes area is so popular in winter that public transit is almost mandatory. The **Mammoth Shuttle System**, 760/934-3030, is a taxicab company operating year-round. **Mammoth Area Shuttle**, 760/934-0687, is Mammoth Mountain ski area's local shuttle-bus service, which operates only during the ski season; the "red line" connects the main lodge and the village, another line serves Tamarack (760/934-2442) in winter for cross-country skiing, and other lines connect to base chairlifts.

In summer, it's almost necessary to take the Forest Service shuttle to reach the Agnew Meadows, Red's Meadow, and Devil's Postpile areas beyond Mammoth Lakes. Backpackers *must* ride the shuttle, because wilderness permits prohibit driving into the valley or parking at trailheads. Car campers, however, *can* drive in—assuming they first get a camping permit—but during the summer high season, anyone opting to drive must do so either before 7:30 A.M. or after 5:30 P.M. Board shuttles at the Mammoth Mountain Inn near the ski slopes; buses leave every half hour between 8 and 10 A.M., between 3:30 and 5 P.M., and every 15 minutes from 10 A.M. to 3:30 P.M. (Returning to Mammoth Mountain, the last bus leaves Red's Meadow at 6:15 P.M.) Round-trip fare: $9 adults, $7 ages 13–18, $5 ages 5–12, age 4 and under free.

Mountain include eight-person cars on the Panorama gondola, new high-speed quad chairs, the new Mill Café—complete with 6,000-square-foot deck—at the foot of Stump Valley, and the remodeled Canyon Lodge with sundeck and new food court. To avoid the parking crunch at Mammoth Mountain's slopes, take the shuttle from the village. If the crowds seem unbearable, remember a lift ticket for Mammoth's slopes is also good, on the same day, at June Mountain.

Mammoth also offers good cross-country skiing. The **Tamarack Cross-Country Ski Center** at Tamarack Lodge, P.O. Box 69, 760/934-2442 or toll-free 800/237-6879, offers extensive backcountry trails (children under age 12 free), telemarking, tours, rentals, and lessons. The **Sierra Meadows Ski Touring Center** at Sherwin Creek Rd. off Old Mammoth Rd., P.O. Box 2008, Mammoth Lakes, CA 93546, 760/934-

6161, has groomed trails and set track plus lessons, rentals, and warming hut.

Forest Service cross-country ski trails include the **Obsidian Dome Trail**, which begins at the junction of Hwy. 395 and Glass Flow Rd. (south of June Lake Junction), as well as several near Mammoth Lakes, such as the **Earthquake Fault Trail** to Inyo Craters. Winter camping is available, too, at the national forest's Shady Rest campgrounds.

June Lake Loop

Some 20 miles north of Mammoth and five miles south of Lee Vining off Hwy. 395 is Hwy. 158, the northern end of the June Lake Loop, leading to a high-country collection of lakes and summer cabins eerily shadowed in late afternoon by the sawtoothed snowy peaks looming up from the Ansel Adams Wilderness just to the west. Particularly worthwhile in summer is the short hike to **Obsidian Dome,** a poetically poised mountain mass of once-molten black- and color-streaked glass; the trailhead is reached via dirt road 1.5 miles south of June Lake Junction. Worth it in winter is the excellent, usually uncrowded **June Mountain Ski Area** (now owned by Mammoth Mountain, which is now partially owned by Intrawest), P.O. Box 146, June Lake, CA 93529, 760/648-7733 or toll-free 888/586-3686, www.junemountain.com. June Mountain often has better snow and ski conditions than Mammoth—and is more sheltered—but year after year the big guy gets all the glory. In theory, you can buy same-day lift tickets at one place and ski at both. June Mountain also offers cross-country skiing.

For more information about the June Lake area and its recreation possibilities, accommodations, and restaurants, contact the **June Lake Loop Chamber of Commerce,** P.O. Box 2, June Lake, CA 93529, 760/648-7584, visitjunelake.com.

PRACTICAL MAMMOTH

Staying at Mammoth: Budget to Moderate

The best bet in summer is camping. There are numerous **Inyo National Forest campgrounds** in the Mammoth Lakes Basin. Some of these campsites can be reserved in advance through the National Recreation Reservation Service, toll-free 800/280-2267. For complete listings of regional camping choices, contact the Mammoth Visitor Center and Ranger Station (see above). **Camp High Sierra** just west of New Shady Rest Campground, operated by the L.A. Department of Recreation, 760/934-2368, has nice tent sites, rustic cabins, hot showers, even a lodge.

In winter and summer Mammoth does offer other budget accommodations, generally most appropriate for travelers on their own. Most inexpensive are lodges that provide dorm-style bunks for around $15–25 per person (lower summer rates). These include the homey, smoke-free **Davison St. Guest House** (formerly the Asgard Chalet), 19 Davison St., 760/924-2188, fax 760/544-9107, which also rents rooms or the entire lodge, and **Ullr Lodge,** on Minaret Rd., 760/934-2454.

Motel 6 is at 3372 Main St. (Hwy. 203), 760/934-6660 or toll-free 800/466-8356. Moderate. The **Executive Inn** is at 54 Sierra Blvd., 760/934-8892. Moderate-Expensive. The **White Stag Inn** is west of town on the highway, 760/934-7507. Moderate. Other midrange motels include the **Econolodge Wildwood Inn,** 3626 Main St., 760/934-6855 (Moderate); the **Swiss Chalet Motel,** 3776 Viewpoint Rd., 760/934-2403 (Moderate); and the **North Village Inn,** 103 Lake Mary Rd., 760/934-2525 (Moderate-Expensive).

Staying at Mammoth: Rentals, Hotels, Major Motels

People who plan to stay awhile often opt for comfort on the group living plan—renting condominiums, cabins, or homes by the week and cooking most meals "at home." For information on reputable area rental agencies, contact the Mammoth Lakes Visitors Bureau or stop by the visitors center (see above).

The **Sierra Lodge,** 3540 Main, 760/934-8881 or toll-free 800/356-5711, www.sierralodge.com, is a completely nonsmoking and contemporary hotel. Rooms include kitchens and microwaves, refrigerators, TV and cable, access to spa. Children under age 12 stay free. Free breakfast. Premium. Nice, too, is the **Alpenhof Lodge,** 6080 Minaret Rd. (a mile west of town on Hwy. 203), 760/934-6330 or toll-free 800/ 828-0371 (reservations only), mini-suites (some with fireplaces) close to the slopes, with spa, sauna, and pool in summer. Expensive. Another good choice is the **Quality Inn,** 3537 Main St. (just west of town on the highway), 760/934-5114. Moderate-Premium. The all-suites **Shilo Inn,** 2963 Main (on the highway east of Old Mammoth Rd.), 760/934-4500, has rooms with kitchens, refrigerators and wet bars, continental breakfast, free access to complete fitness center and sauna, whirlpool, indoor pool, and steam room. Premium.

Time-honored and very traditional, though, for a ski-in, ski-out stay on the slopes is the ski resort's very nice, bustling, and mammoth **Mammoth Mountain Inn,** 1 Minaret Rd., 760/934-2581 or toll-free 800/228-4947 for reservations, www.mammoth-mtn.com. Premium-Luxury.

Staying at Mammoth: Bed-and-Breakfasts

The **Rainbow Tarns** bed-and-breakfast, 760/935-4556, south of Mammoth Lakes at 505 Rainbow Tarns Rd. off Crowley Lake Dr., a mile north of Tom's Place, offers three B&B rooms, unusual serenity, access to cross-country skiing, hiking, and horseback trails, and a full country breakfast. Premium. Visit on the web at www.rainbowtarns.com.

There are other good choices, though. Near town is the **White Horse Inn Bed & Breakfast,** 2180 Old Mammoth Rd., 760/924-3656, which offers several theme rooms in a private home. The Emperor's Room, for example, pays homage to the area's mining-era Chinese influence. All rooms (except one kids' room) have private baths; a full breakfast is served every morning, wine and cheese in the afternoon. Two-night minimum stay required. Premium-Luxury. The **Mammoth Country Inn** bed-and-breakfast,

---

ACCOMMODATIONS RATINGS

Accommodations in this book are rated by price category, based on double-occupancy, high-season rates. Categories used are:

Budget	$35 and under
Inexpensive	$35-60
Moderate	$60-85
Expensive	$85-110
Premium	$110-150
Luxury	$150 and up

75 Joaquin Rd., 760/934-2710 or toll-free 800/358-2710, www.mammothcountryinn.com, has a VCR and goose-down comforter in every room, a shared lounge with huge stone fireplace and indoor diversions, and an upstairs guest kitchen. Seven themed rooms, one with private bath. Moderate-Expensive. Another good choice—noted for the great breakfasts and casual yet cozy ambience—is the **Snow Goose Inn**, 57 Forest Trail, 760/934-2660 or toll-free 800/874-7368. Moderate-Luxury. The **Cinnamon Bear Bed & Breakfast**, 113 Center St., 760/934-2873, fax 760/934-2873, offers 14 rooms (some with four-poster beds), weekly rates, and packages.

Staying at Mammoth:
Rustic Regional Resorts
The special **Tamarack Lodge** a few miles beyond town on Lake Mary Rd. (the extension of Hwy. 203), 760/934-2442 or toll-free 800/237-6879, www.tamaracklodge.com, is a 1920s mountain lodge on Twin Lakes at the foot of Mammoth Mountain featuring a fine restaurant—the Lakefront—and a fireplace-anchored lobby, plus knotty pine-paneled lodge rooms (only four have private baths). Outlying housekeeping cabins—studios and cabins with one, two, or three bedrooms—are more rustic but nice, and feature kitchens, bathrooms, some fireplaces. Moderate-Luxury. Fish for trout in summer, try Nordic skiing in winter—also ice skating, when the lakes freeze over.

Also recommended in the area: the summers-only **Red's Meadow Resort** near Devil's Postpile and Rainbow Falls, next door to a hot springs and practically in the middle of the Pacific Crest Trail. Trout fishing is popular here, but so is hiking: the Ansel Adams Wilderness is one mile away, and the John Muir Wilderness is two miles away. Facilities include lodging, café, and store, also a large string of horses and mules for wilderness rambling. Open mid-June to the end of September. Inexpensive (two motel rooms)-Moderate (cabins). For more information and reservations, contact: Red's Meadow Resort, 760/934-2345 in summer, 760/873-3928 in winter, www.mammothweb.com/redsmeadow.

Rock Creek Lodge, 7497 Rock Creek Rd. in Little Lakes Valley, halfway between Mammoth Lakes and Bishop (take the Rock Creek Rd. turnoff at Tom's Place on Hwy. 395), is heaven for

anglers and hikers. A home-style restaurant is close to the small rustic cabins. Two-bedroom cabins have completely equipped kitchens (but no bathrooms: showers and flush toilets a short walk away), or rent two-story A-frames with the works. In winter, cross-country skiing and guided tours are offered—with the added attraction of backcountry trailside huts for overnights. Moderate-Premium. For more information and to make reservations, contact: Rock Creek Lodge, 760/935-4170, www.rockcreeklodge.com.

Another great choice, in lush meadows and Jeffrey pine forests along the Owens River, is the **Alper's Owens River Ranch**, Rte. 1, Box 232, Mammoth Lakes, CA 93546, 760/648-7334 in summer, 760/647-6652 in winter, a collection of simple cabins on a one-time cattle ranch.

Eating at Mammoth
Though fast-food stops have popped up in this forested town like mushrooms after the first fall rains (there's a Safeway here, too), Mammoth Lakes' attractions include its restaurants, a better selection of good eateries than anywhere else along the Sierra Nevada's eastern slope. Excellent is **Blondie's Kitchen**, 3599 Main St., 760/934-4048, noted for its exceptional all-day breakfasts—including breakfast burritos—and daily specials. Also good for brunch, lunch, and dinner is the casual **Mountain Cafe**, in Minaret Village Shopping Center on Old Mammoth Rd., 760/934-9316.

For bakery goods, deli fare, and decent sandwiches, including some veggie choices, stop off at the **Gourmet Grocer & Co.** in the Village Center West mall off Main, 760/934-2997, open daily 8 A.M.–6 P.M. The **Mammoth Stonehouse Restaurant**, 360 Old Mammoth Rd., 760/934-6196, offers good beer and pub grub. Live music scheduled regularly.

Grumpy's Saloon & Eatery, 37 Old Mammoth Rd., 760/934-8587, is most famous for its bacon-avocado burger and other simple favorites, but **Berger's** on Minaret Rd. (at Canyon) on the way to the slopes, 760/934-6622, also has good burgers and other American fare, excellent fries, and great homemade desserts. **Perry's Pizza and Italian Cafe** in the Village Center West on Main, 760/934-6521 or 760/934-3251, serves it Sicilian style, along with good all-you-can-eat specials Tues. and Wed. nights.

ANCIENT BRISTLECONE PINE FOREST

Anthropologists have recently retrieved some 24,000 artifacts from two peoples who lived, from 1300 B.C. to the 14th century, high in the White Mountains. But today's most notable old-timers are the gnarled and gristly *Pinus longaeva* trees, still thriving here in the Ancient Bristlecone Pine Forest, apparently unperturbed by summer drought and heat, severe winters, or the passage of time—though smog may now be doing them in. Bristlecones growing in this stark, dry, and dramatic mountain range have been alive longer than anything else on earth, many for more than 4,000 years.

Along the **Schulman Grove**'s short **Pine Alpha Trail** and 4.5-mile **Methusaleh Trail,** home turf of the Methusaleh Tree, the planet's oldest living being (unidentified for its own protection), there's a strange sense of timelessness. Life and death, past and future are almost indistinguishable. Eleven miles and 40 minutes farther up the road, another 1,000 feet higher in elevation, the moonscape at the **Patriarch Grove** (home of the biggest known bristlecone) is even bleaker, with just scattered specimens of firm-rooted, living driftwood.

A visit to the White Mountains' Bristlecone Pine Forest is at least an all-day journey—one usually not possible in winter, when the road is closed by snow. Start out with a full tank of gas and bring food, water (none is available), good walking shoes, and sun protection as well as warm clothing, since even in summer it's cool at higher elevations and the weather changes constantly. To get here, head northeast on Hwy. 168 from Big Pine to near Westgard Pass, about 13 miles, then head north on White Mountain Rd.—the highest auto route in California, reaching an elevation of 10,500 feet. Picnic near the fossil area beyond Cedar Flat; family campsites are available in summer at **Grandview Campground** on the way to Schulman Grove.

To get oriented to these trees and their significance, pick up a brochure/map at the Cedar Flat entrance station. Better yet, spend some time at the

bristlecone pine

handsome new **Ancient Bristlecone Pine Visitor Center** at Schulman Grove, open from mid-June to Nov. 1, and study the interpretive displays. The Schulman Grove center also hosts other visitor programs and is the starting point in summer for naturalist-led hikes.

For more information about the 100-million-year-old White Mountains—home also to ghosts of mining history, mustangs, and golden eagles—stop by or call the **White Mountains Ranger Station** in Bishop, 760/873-2500 (recorded info after hours).

Whiskey Creek on Hwy. 203 (Main at Minaret), 760/934-2555, is the locals' choice for steaks, prime rib, and barbecued ribs. Just as good, others say, smaller and usually less crowded, is **Mogul,** 1528 Tavern Rd., 760/934-3039.

The **Ocean Harvest** restaurant, just south of Hwy. 203 on Old Mammoth Rd., 760/934-8539, is noted for its fresh mesquite-grilled seafood. **Restaurant Skadi,** in Sherwin Plaza on Old Mammoth Rd. (at Chateau Rd.), 760/934-3902, serves upscale California/Alpine cuisine, along with fine California wines, champagnes, and a full bar. Open for dinner nightly except Tuesday.

The very small (10-table) **Lakefront Restaurant**

at Tamarack Lodge Resort at Twin Lakes, 760/934-3534 or 760/934-2442, serves salmon and other fresh fish plus such classics as rack of lamb and beef Wellington, "excellent meals that will satisfy both the heartiest of appetites and the most finicky," according to *Bon Appétit*. At the top of the local food chain is lively American **Nevados** on Minaret Rd. at Main St., 760/934-4466, open nightly for dinner. Reservations recommended.

FROM BISHOP TO INDEPENDENCE

Some 40,000 people descend on **Bishop** over the Memorial Day weekend for kick-over-the-traces celebrations of native mulishness—mule races, mule-drawn chariot races, and braying contests for people who (apparently) would rather be mules—during the town's annual **Mule Days Celebration.** Also worth showing up for is the **Millpond Bluegrass Festival** in late September. Bishop itself is pleasant in the neon-and-highway category, with a few parks and swimming pools scattered among the markets, motels, and cowboy cafés. The **Inyo Country Store,** 177 Academy Ave., 760/872-2552, open for breakfast and lunch Mon.–Sat., for dinner Thurs.–Sat. nights, is *the* place for fine coffee, cappuccino, and espresso, not to mention American bistro fare and gourmet picnic items. For a truly fine sit-down dinner, head for **The Restaurant at Convict Lake** at Convict Lake, 760/934-3803, where the seasonal menu might include fresh-caught local trout and beef Wellington. Full bar. Open daily for dinner.

For more information about Bishop and vicinity, stop by the **Bishop Chamber of Commerce & Visitors Center** at City Park, 690 N. Main St., Bishop, CA 93514, 760/873-8405, www.bishopvisitor.com. And visit the **Inyo National Forest headquarters,** 873 N. Main, 760/873-2400 (also the Bishop area BLM office, 760/872-4881), www.r5.fs.fed.us/inyo, though the national forest's **White Mountains Ranger Station** nearby at 798 N. Main, 760/873-2500, TTY 760/873-2501, is actually better for national forest and wilderness maps ($4), wilderness permits, and information on area hikes, sights, and campgrounds. Bookstore and gift shop, too. The ranger station is open daily from mid-June to mid-Sept., otherwise only on weekdays.

Heading south from Bishop, it's hard to notice anything except the awesome Sierra Nevada looming ever higher. Rolling into **Big Pine,** next south, note the Palisade Glaciers looming above Big Pine Canyon to the west—small but distinguished, being the continent's southernmost "living" glaciers (which means they melt, break off, and otherwise diminish at the low end

WINNEDUMAH HOTEL

The 1926 Winnedumah Hotel on the highway, 211 N. Edwards St. in Independence, 760/878-2040, fax 760/878-2833, www.qnet.com/~winnedumah, has been transformed into a creative bed-and-breakfast perfect for fans of affordability—folks without SUVs full of cash but who'd still like to stay long enough to revel in the wonders of the eastern Sierra Nevada. Though the hotel's style has changed considerably since the 1920s, this venerable hostelry actually has quite a history. It was once a popular place to stay for movie stars and film crews during the region's Hollywood heyday, and a favorite stopover for that desert myth-maker, Death Valley Scotty. These days the Winnedumah features a fireplace in the casual lobby, lots of colorful overstuffed furniture, a grand piano, plenty of games and books, classical music, and a relaxed Western-outdoors ambience that invites adventurers. The 26 guest rooms are simple but charming and eclectic, furnished with hand-painted 1920s furniture and handmade quilts. Some share baths. There's even air-conditioning when the weather gets hot—and a lovely garden to enjoy balmy evenings. Inexpensive-Moderate. For breakfast—cereal, fruit, and such—the café is just off the lobby. Hearty, wholesome fixed-price dinners normally cost about $10.

Usually a sweet deal at the Winnedumah Hotel are its **Winnedumah Weekends** special-events packages, ranging from mountain-biking tours and Manzanar photography to watercolors. And ask about the off-season Three for Two special. Even sweeter, for true budget travelers, is the fact the Winnedumah is also an affiliated HI-AYH hostel, with hostel beds available at $18 per person, including breakfast and linen. Hostel beds are Budget. Other hotel rooms are Inexpensive-Moderate.

while new snowpack-turned-to-ice replenishes them on the high side). Big Pine itself offers no comparable experiences or sights. For a High Sierra meal, head out to **Glacier Lodge,** 11 near-vertical miles west of town at Big Pine Creek, 760/938-2837, usually open for breakfast 7:30–9 A.M., for dinner 6–10 P.M. (but call first). The historic Glacier Lodge, built in 1917, is most popular,

RETURN TO MANZANAR

The land itself says little about the devastating experience of Japanese Americans imprisoned during World War II at Manzanar some six miles south of Independence. Now, as then, Manzanar is bleak and desolate, dust and sagebrush surrounded by barbed wire and remnants of chain-link fencing. Two pagoda-style stone guardhouses, sans doors and windows, stand near what was once the entrance to the internment camp; remnants of building foundations seem like skeletons exposed by shifting sands. A new monument, white and austere, honors those who lived here during the post–Pearl Harbor days of the war. The Eastern Sierra Nevada Museum in Independence, worth a stop despite its too-modern facade, tells some of the story in exhibits and artifacts. Museum staff also offer occasional guided tours of Manzanar. The collected photographs of both Ansel Adams and Dorothea Lange tell more.

Executive Order 9066, signed by President Franklin Roosevelt, created Manzanar and other isolated Pacific Coast internment camps. That decree meant that some 100,000 people of Japanese descent—men, women, and children—were immediately removed from their communities and imprisoned by the U.S. Army. Ten thousand people, most of them U.S. citizens, many with sons in the military, were herded into tarpaper shacks at Manzanar ("apple orchard" in Spanish). The name of the place seemed inappropriate, but not for long. Allowed irrigation water and the opportunity to work the land, internees soon transformed their arid section of valley into lush, productive farm acreage and a tight-knit community. In addition to its orchards, gardens, and hog and chicken ranches, Manzanar once boasted a Bank of America branch, an orphanage, a Boy Scout troop, baseball teams, pools, a nine-hole golf course (with oiled sand for greens), and a swing band called the Jive Bombers.

The U.S. Supreme Court struck down Roosevelt's executive order in 1944, ruling it unconstitutional, and Manzanar was closed. Its legacy lived on, however. Upon returning to their hometowns, former internees often found themselves facing blatant racism and discrimination from former neighbors—and, this time, facing it largely alone.

Every year, camp survivors and their families and friends make the pilgrimage to Manzanar, to remember. In April 1992, the Owens Valley **Manzanar Pilgrimage** attracted some 1,500 people, to formally celebrate the establishment of the **Manzanar National Historic Site** by the U.S. Congress. (In the hope that we'll all remember.) And restoration has begun, albeit slowly, on this vast and empty monument to a nightmarish political past.

Though at present there are no visitor facilities at Manzanar—funding could flow a little faster from Washington, D.C.—stop to explore the site from the stone guardhouses; from there you can stroll Manzanar's old roads and orchards. About eight-tenths of a mile north of the gate houses on Hwy. 395 is an (unmarked) dirt road heading west. At its end is Manzanar's cemetery, and the somber white Buddhist "tower of memory" monument.

For more information about this place and its history, contact: Manzanar National Historic Site, P.O. Box 426, Independence, CA 93526, 760/878-2932, fax 760/878-2949, www.nps.gov/manz/. Expect to leave a message, and receive one, because staffing to date is intermittent. For current information on walking tours offered by the nearby Eastern California Museum, call 760/878-0258.

KIM WEIR

though, for its modest accommodations—a pleasant lodge and rustic, fully equipped cabins near the Palisades. No phones, no TV, no swimming pool, and—since Glacier Lodge generates its own electricity—absolutely no extra appliances (hair dryers, etc.) are allowed.

The next town south is **Independence,** the Inyo County seat. Worth a side trip just north of Independence is the **Mt. Whitney Fish Hatchery,** 760/878-2272, possibly the most beautiful in the world—an Old World–style fish monastery with a Tudor tower, built in 1917 of native stone. (Pleasant pond, park, and picnic facilities.) Near the turnoff are the ruins of old **Fort Independence.** The World War II–vintage **Manzanar Relocation Center** stood southeast of Independence, one of California's internment camps, temporary "home" to 10,000 Japanese Americans (see the special topic Return to Manzanar).

Stop for a look at the **Mary Austin Home** in town (follow the signs), designed and built under the supervision of the very independent author of *Land of Little Rain,* an ode to the once-beautiful Owens Valley. Also worthwhile is time spent at the modern, wheelchair-accessible **Eastern California Museum,** 155 N. Grant St., 760/878-0258 or 760/878-0364. Open Sun.–Mon. and Thurs.–Fri. noon–4 P.M., Sat. 10 A.M.–4 P.M. Free, but donations always appreciated.

MOUNT WHITNEY AND LONE PINE

Mount Whitney and the Alabama Hills

A climb up Mt. Whitney, California's highest point, is not an experience for solitude seekers. It seems everyone wants to do it—though it's a strenuous vertical walk, most people can—and they all want to hike the 10-mile trail at the same time, during the snow-free period from mid-July (sometimes as early as mid-May) into early October. Mount Whitney is the most frequently climbed peak in the Sierra Nevada—and possibly the United States. For this simple reason, a trail quota is in effect May 22–Oct. 15. Ascending Mt. Whitney requires a permit. Plan ahead, and contact the local Wilderness Reservation Service in Lone Pine. If you *don't* plan ahead, cancellations are divvied up on Friday afternoons. See Hiking Mount Whitney below.

Savvy hikers can put quick distance between themselves and the crowds, however, by continuing on from the summit along the John Muir Trail—but again, plan ahead, as permits are required for all backcountry travel in Sequoia and Kings Canyon National Parks and associated wilderness areas.

For those cycling or driving up and back via 13-mile Whitney Portal Rd., take the dirt-road detour through the area's Alabama Hills (follow the signs), a sparse desert sage landscape most people have seen before as the jumbled, round-bouldered granite backdrop for countless movies (*High Sierra, Red River, Bad Day at Black Rock,* and *They Died with their Boots On*) and TV westerns including *Bonanza, Have Gun—Will Travel,* and *Tales of Wells Fargo.*

Hiking Mount Whitney

For national forest and wilderness maps and regional recreation and camping information, contact the **Mount Whitney Ranger District** office, 640 S. Main St., P.O. Box 8, Lone Pine, CA 93545, 760/876-6200, TTY 760/876-6201. There is a Whitney Trail daily hiker quota in place from May 22 until mid-October—and permits are required in order for you to be on the trail. To apply for wilderness permits—including free day-hike permits for Mt. Whitney—contact the **Inyo National Forest Wilderness Reservation Service** inside the Big Pine Chamber of Commerce, 126 S. Main St., P.O. Box 430, Big Pine, CA 93513, 760/938-1136 or toll-free 888/374-3773, fax and TTY 760/938-1137. The reservation service office is open Mon.–Fri. 8 A.M.–4:30 P.M. until March 31, and daily April 1 to mid-September. Or get current information from the Inyo National Forest website, www.r5.fs.fed.us/inyo. Wilderness and day-hike permits are free, but there is a $15 reservation fee. Cancellations for the Mt. Whitney Trail are filled only on Friday afternoons, 1–3 P.M.; call the local Wilderness Reservation Service between those hours—and good luck!

Camp at the scrub-shrouded national forest **Lone Pine Campground** on the way to Mt. Whitney, with water, picnic tables, and stoves (but not showers) for $10 per night—with the extra free thrill of waking up at dawn to see Mt. Whitney bathed in the orange glow of morning's first light. More probable for early arrivals (or in spring or fall), try the **Whitney Portal** or **Whitney Portal Trailhead campgrounds**—the latter with just 11 walk-in sites, one-night limit—near the trailhead to the top of California (trailers are not recommended). Other camping possibilities include the county's **Portagee Joe** campground just outside town (off Whitney Portal Rd.); the **Diaz Lake county campground** south of Lone Pine, with 300 campsites; and the BLM's free **Tuttle Creek Campground.**

Lone Pine and Vicinity

Lone Pine, below Mt. Whitney, has abundant motels, restaurants, and other services. It also has a Hollywood past and presence. More than 300 movies have been shot near here, including *High Sierra, Gunga Din,* and *Star Trek V.* Movie stars and their antics are also an important part of local lore. Stop by the **Indian Trading Post,** 137 S. Main St., 760/876-4641, to see "the wall"—even movie stars have tried to buy it, or steal it, for the priceless autographs. For more information about the area's cinematic history, pick up *The Movies of Lone Pine* brochure at the chamber of commerce, or point your browser to the chamber's website. To really celebrate, show up in October for the annual **Lone Pine Film Festival.**

For more information about Lone Pine and vicinity, including events and activities sponsored by the Inyo County Arts Council, contact the **Lone Pine Chamber of Commerce,** 126 S. Main St., P.O. Box 749, 760/876-4444, www.lone-pine.com. Especially fun, and free, is the chamber's ***Southern Inyo Self-Guided Tours*** brochure (with map). If available, also pick up the ***Campground Guide*** put out by the Inyo County Parks and Recreation office. Just south of Lone Pine, at the Hwy. 395/Hwy. 136 junction, is the excellent **Eastern Sierra Interagency Visitor Center,** 760/876-6222, with in-depth information about hikes, sights, and practicalities; wonderful books; and public bathrooms and picnic area.

YOSEMITE AND VICINITY

Somewhere in Yosemite National Park there should be a placard that reads: "This is the spot where John Muir fell in love with life" because this *is* the spot. When Muir found Yosemite (from the native *uzumati,* or "grizzly bear"), he found his spiritual home, a place where even this notable traveler was "willing to stay forever in one place like a tree." He also found himself. His passion for this high holy place became the impetus behind a lifelong commitment to preserving this and other great works of wildness. Though even John Muir couldn't save Hetch Hetchy Valley (from the native *hatchhatchie,* or "grass,") from the water engineers, he did manage to achieve U.S. National Park protection for most of his beloved Yosemite country.

Despite the chiselings of progress, Yosemite is still a wild wonder of granite, gorges, and silent godlike peaks with names that only hint at their true presence: El Capitan, Half Dome, Royal Arches, Cathedral Rock, Clouds Rest, Three Brothers. Even the trees, the ancient giant sequoias, are larger than life. The sky itself can barely keep the area's grandness down to earth. But the laws of gravity hold true even in Yosemite—witness the waterfalls. Cascading from a height of 2,425 feet, Yosemite Fall is the highest waterfall in North America and the fifth highest in the world. Other park waterfalls—which often seem to shoot out from nowhere, sometimes right off the edge of glacier-scoured hanging valleys—include Yosemite Valley's equally famous Bridalveil, Vernal, and Nevada Falls, plus many of the park's lesser-known liquid gems. The abundance of water in Yosemite also sustains the subtle, flower-rich summer lushness of its meadows, the mountain-fringed and massive Tuolumne Meadows still among the loveliest in the Sierra Nevada.

The pitfalls of John Muir's enthusiastic promotion of Yosemite Valley and vicinity are all too apparent these days. Once word of its wonders got out, people from around the world started coming to see Yosemite for themselves, and what was once a tourist trickle has now become a rampaging torrent. With its increasing all-season popularity, well over four million people visit the park each year. Three-fourths are day-use visitors. In summer, a virtual city—complete with rush-hour traffic, litter, overflowing garbage cans, smog, juvenile delinquency, and crime—sprawls out across the valley floor. Despite the Park Service's commitment to "de-develop" Yosemite for the sake of saving the place from its own overwhelming popularity, congestion is still the rule. Visitors who relish even some semblance of solitude in the wilds should plan a Yosemite visit in early spring, late fall, or winter—and anytime of year, come on weekdays if at all possible.

CALIFORNIA DEPARTMENT OF PARKS & RECREATION

Yosemite Falls

YOSEMITE HIKES AND BACKPACKS

Like its campgrounds, the overall level of activity on Yosemite trails relates directly to the distance traveled from Yosemite Valley. Some of the short, easily accessible trails to the valley's most famous sights can resemble pedestrian freeways in summer and on peak visitor weekends. The best way to avoid the crowds, on any hike, is to start out very early in the morning. Except on the park's shortest strolls, bring water on all excursions.

For casual short-distance hikers, the Park Service's trail map is adequate for getting oriented. For backcountry hiking and backpacking, more detailed maps (including topo maps), a compass, and a good guidebook are advisable. Wilderness permits are required for overnight camping in the Yosemite outback (see below). Those planning an extensive backpacking trip should inquire, too, about access into adjacent and nearby federal wilderness areas—including the Emigrant, Hoover, Ansel Adams, and John Muir wildernesses—also limited by national forest permit. There are many good books of use to Yosemite-area hikers and backpackers. Among the best: the *Tuolumne Meadows* hiking guide by Jeffrey B. Schaffer and Thomas Winnett; Schaffer's *Yosemite National Park;* and *Sierra North* by Thomas Winnett and Jason Winnett, all published by Wilderness Press.

Shorter Yosemite Hikes

Among Yosemite's most popular trails are the easy half-mile, half-hour hikes to Lower Yosemite Fall and to Bridalveil Fall, called Pohono or "puffing wind" by native people. Also fairly easy, and noted for its magnificent view of Half Dome, is the two-mile round-trip to Mirror Lake (trailhead accessible only by shuttle), though you can make the walk longer by circling the lake. With some assistance, all the paved trails are wheelchair accessible. Along Glacier Point Rd. is the one-mile trail to **Sentinel Dome,** a fairly easy hike, the last 200 yards strenuous. The nearby Taft Point Trail offers great views of El Capitan and Yosemite Fall. Though often quite crowded, the stroll to the scenic splendor of Glacier Point should not be missed.

Longer Yosemite Hikes

Strenuous but short is the Inspiration Point Trail that starts at the park's **Wawona Tunnel,** offer-

SIERRA BIG TREES

Ancient and unique is the Sierra Nevada's "big tree" or *Sequoiadendron giganteum,* a species of redwood quite distinct from California's coastal redwoods and surviving in substantial numbers only in Yosemite and neighboring national parks and at Calaveras Big Trees State Park. Also called giant sequoias, these massive forest monarchs are botanical dinosaurs, living relics that first evolved some 160 million years ago—15,000 times older than Yosemite Valley.

Sierra Nevada big trees are indeed big—so gigantic that few people can escape an overwhelming feeling of awe when looking (up) at them. The everyday, garden-variety giant sequoia measures 10 to 15 feet in diameter at maturity and stands some 250 feet tall. The true giants, including the most massive trio, the General Sherman, General Grant, and Boole trees in or near Sequoia and Kings Canyon National Parks, are almost 30 feet across well above ground level. The lowest limb branching off from General Sherman is seven feet thick and would create a canopy for a 12-story office building. During California's pioneer past, people hollowed out big trees for cabins or barns. Though they live to a ripe old age (the oldest verified mature tree is about 3,200 years old), they also grow vigorously and rapidly throughout their life spans. Theoretically, Sierra big trees could live forever, but sooner or later, too-heavy winter snow and brutal winds topple otherwise healthy elders.

Adapted to fire, insect pests, and just about every other natural scourge, the Sierra Nevada big trees were not at first able to escape loggers' saws. Not counting John Muir's advocacy on their behalf and the accompanying public outcry, one major difference between coast and mountain redwoods eventually saved the big trees' skins: the wood of the giant sequoia is brittle and weak. After a big tree is toppled—a task that once took four men sawing by hand up to a month to achieve—it tends to shatter. Though industrious lumber crews still managed to market giant sequoias as shingles, fenceposts, and such, the difficulty of felling big trees and hauling them off to lumber mills slowed the destruction of old-growth groves. Unfortunately, government protection of today's 70 surviving groves of Sierra Nevada sequoias still came too late to save most of California's ancient big trees.

YOSEMITE MOUNTAINEERING

Yosemite is a natural magnet for rock-climbers, ice-climbers, and mountaineers of every persuasion. The **Yosemite Mountaineering School,** Yosemite National Park, CA 95389, 209/372-8344, www.yosemitepark.com, is the place to leave behind one's fear and scale the heights.

Headquartered in Yosemite Valley with a summers-only outpost on the highway at Tuolumne Meadows, this mountaineers' mountaineering school offers exceptional training and outings for beginners, intermediates, and the expert let's-go-hang-off-the-edge-of-the-world granite-hugging Yosemite subculture. All climbing students must be at least 14 years of age.

Basic and intermediate rock-climbing classes are offered daily from April to mid-October. Spring and fall classes are held in Yosemite Valley, and summer sessions adjourn to the heights near Tuolumne Meadows. The basic class starts off with ground school followed by some hands-on experience in bouldering and rappelling. Also available are advanced seminars and private guiding, big walls included. (Even amateur mountaineers must be "in reasonably good condition" and need to bring lunch and water.) Reservations are advisable, though drop-ins sometimes find space available. Yosemite Mountaineering also offers backpacking instruction and guided backpack trips, and rents outdoor equipment—the obvious plus backpacks, sleeping bags, and ski mountaineering necessities.

ing good views. For a panoramic view of Yosemite Valley, the seven-mile round-trip hike to **Upper Yosemite Fall** starts from Sunnyside Campground—a steep trail with many switchbacks, hot in summer; quite a vigorous workout, allow an entire day. The **Vernal Fall** hike from Happy Isles via the Vernal Fall Mist Trail (closed in winter) is less strenuous but a three-mile, half-day round-trip nonetheless. It's a seven-mile hike up and back on the Nevada Fall Horse Trail to take in both **Vernal and Nevada Falls,** a day's outing for most people.

But unforgettable—and only for the determined and fit—is the 10–12 hour "hike" from Happy Isles up the back side of **Half Dome,** a 17-mile round-trip with hang-on-for-dear-life assistance at the end from steel cables anchored in granite (the cables are usually taken down in mid-October).

Also challenging: the five-mile Four Mile Trail from the valley up to **Glacier Point** (trail closed in winter), easily a full-day round-trip. Easier but longer is the 8.5-mile, half-day (one way) downhill route from **Glacier Point to Yosemite Valley** via the park's Panorama Trail. (A popular all-day excursion is hiking up via the Four Mile Trail then back down on the Panorama route.) Another option entails starting from Glacier Point and taking the all-day, 13-mile (one way) Pohono Trail hike to Wawona Tunnel—well worth it for the rim-hugging views.

Backcountry Backpacking and Camping

The best way to get away from it all is to head into the Yosemite backcountry for camping, long-distance hiking, and backpacking. Because of the popularity of this option, and to protect the park from overuse, access to each trailhead is by wilderness permit only. Permits are free, and wilderness-conscious camping is permitted anywhere along the trail (beyond a minimum radius away from Yosemite Valley). Reserve Yosemite wilderness permits well in advance—or take your chances come summer. Half of the season's permits are issued by mail Feb.–May ($3 processing fee), the others are available in person up to 24 hours in advance from visitors centers and ranger stations (free). For advance reservations, write to **Yosemite Wilderness Center,** P.O. Box 545, Yosemite National Park, CA 95389. Call 209/372-0200 for general information, 209/372-0740 for reservations. You can also visit www.nps.gov/yose/wilderness.

OTHER YOSEMITE DIVERSIONS AND RECREATION

Yosemite manages to offer something for just about everyone. Dedicated people-watchers can have a field day in Yosemite Valley. Guided **horseback rides** (either from Yosemite Valley, Tuolumne Meadows, or Wawona) are available for time periods of two hours, a half-day, or a full day; call 209/372-8348 (Valley), 209/372-8427 (Tuolumne), or 209/375-6502 (Wawona) for information and reservations. **Bike rentals** are available Apr.–Oct. at Curry Village, 209/372-8319, or year-round at Yosemite Lodge, 209/372-1208. A two-hour open-air **tram tour** of Yosemite Valley, leaving from Yosemite Lodge, costs $17.50, and several other tours—to Mariposa Grove, Glacier Point, and elsewhere, as well as a hikers' shuttle to Tuolumne Meadows—also depart from the Lodge. For more information, call the Lodge Tour Desk at 209/372-1240.

Other entertaining diversions include free classes offered spring through autumn and over Thanksgiving and Christmas holidays (painting, photography, sketching), sponsored by the **Art Activity Center** in Yosemite Village. Next to the Valley Visitor Center are the **Museum Gallery,** where bits and pieces of Yosemite's history are on display in rotating exhibits, and the **Indian Cultural Museum,** featuring excellent exhibits on the Miwok and Paiute peoples as well as native arts demonstrations. (Behind the visitors center is a self-guided trail through a reconstructed native village.) Also worth exploring is the revitalized **Happy Isles Nature Center,** complete with nature shop, open daily in summer (through September).

At the park's south end on Hwy. 41 is the **Pioneer Yosemite History Center,** a walk-through collection of historic buildings (self-guided trail), which includes an introduction to U.S. national parks history. For a 10-minute thrill, take a summer-through-September stagecoach ride from the Gray Barn near the covered bridge (fare $3 adults, $2 children). The center's buildings are open daily 9 A.M.–5 P.M., usually from June through Labor Day, but you can wander around outside anytime.

In the same general neighborhood, from summer into early fall, the **Big Trees** open-air tram ride into the Mariposa Grove leads to Grizzly Giant (considered the oldest surviving Sierra big tree) and on to the Mariposa Grove Museum, the old Wawona drive-through tree (now toppled and known as the Fallen Tunnel Tree), and Wawona Point. Tram fare is $8.50 adults, reduced fare for seniors and children.

Just outside the park's south gate near Fish Camp is the **Yosemite Mountain Sugar Pine Railroad,** 56001 Hwy. 41, 559/683-7273, which offers four-mile scenic steam and "Model A"–powered rail rides into Sierra National Forest daily from late Mar. through Oct. (call for winter schedule), $7.25–11 adults, $3.75–5.75 children

3–12. Special Saturday-night moonlight tours include steak dinner late May through early Oct., $33 adults, $18 children 3–12.

Yosemite in Winter
Winter in Yosemite is the hot new trend for park visitors, though it's not *really* new, since Badger

---

PLANNING FOR PRESERVATION AND POPULARITY

Though it's been slow going, Yosemite National Park is now completing its master planning—a process in progress for some 20 years as Yosemite continues to search for practical ways to protect the park's unique character and natural features while managing the increasing numbers of visitors who crave a satisfying Yosemite experience. Most park visitors are categorized as day-use visitors—and most of that day use takes place in summer, in overcrowded Yosemite Valley.

In the late 1990s, planning efforts stalled out due to the fairly radical Yosemite Valley mass-transit proposition that would have required outside-the-park public parking and shuttle bus "staging" areas. Surrounding communities, concerned about increased local congestion, never quite warmed up to the idea, though in the summer of 2000 the Yosemite Area Regional Transportation System (YARTS) began a two-year demonstration program offering bus service along the Hwy. 140 corridor (Merced to El Portal), with adult fares $7–15 ($20 park admission included) to Yosemite Valley. However it is ultimately achieved, the goal is to reduce auto traffic by 50 percent in the congested valley area—and to replace auto traffic with state-of-the-art, low-emission shuttle buses, bicyclists, and pedestrians.

Other major changes the National Park Service hopes to include in its final Yosemite Valley plan—and to begin implementing as soon as the year 2001—include reducing overnight lodging in Yosemite Valley by 20 percent. Planners also propose moving park headquarters and Yosemite Concessions Services administrative offices to El Portal; removing the Ahwahnee Hotel's tennis courts; removing existing roads through Cook's, Stoneman, and Ahwahnee Meadows; and eliminating 2,300 existing day-use parking spaces at the valley's east end.

Pass was California's first ski area. Skiing, snowshoe hiking, ice skating in the rink at Curry Village, and just plain snow play are popular. For those who want to get around and see the sights without too much winter exercise, inquire about open-air snow-cat tours. Ranger-led snowshoe tours are popular, with a token equipment maintenance fee.

A half-hour drive up from Yosemite Valley via the park highway then Glacier Point Rd. is **Badger Pass Ski Area,** Yosemite National Park, CA 95389, 209/372-1446 (year-round information), 209/372-1000 (ski conditions and park activities), noted for its emphasis on beginning and intermediate downhill skiing—especially fun for families. Badger Pass features four chairlifts and one cable tow. Skiers with disabilities are welcome at Badger Pass (call for particulars). Babysitting is available in the **Badger Pups Den,** and children can also have a good time participating in the park's various naturalist-led wintertime children's programs. Special Badger Pass events include the 17-km **Nordic Holiday Race** in March, April's **Yosemite Springfest,** and the **Ancient Jocks Race,** for antique skiers (over age 30). The Badger Pass Midweek Ski Package is usually a good deal, but see if the Ski Free offer is still on—one free day's skiing for every night you stay at either the Ahwahnee or Yosemite Lodge. Yosemite's ski season runs from Thanksgiving through Easter Sunday, daily 9 A.M.–4:30 P.M.

The **Yosemite Cross-Country Ski School** at Badger Pass offers telemarking and Nordic ski instruction, overnight ski trips to the Glacier Point Hut, instructional snow-camping trips, and trans-Sierra ski excursions. Use of the groomed track from Badger Pass to Glacier Point and the park's 90 miles of marked cross-country ski trails (map available) is free. (To avoid the parking crunch at Badger, and to enjoy Yosemite's winter views without worrying about the adequacy of one's winter driving skills, take the free park service shuttle from Yosemite Lodge.)

Yosemite boasts two ski huts for cross-country skiers, in the European tradition. Beyond Badger Pass—available only on guided cross-country ski tours—is the hip new **Glacier Point Hut.** With its cathedral ceiling, timber beams, and impressive stone fireplace, the hut stands on the site of the original Glacier Point

Hotel as positive testament to the park's recent $3.2 million Glacier Point restoration. In summer, it's a snack bar and gift shop. But in winter, out go the shelves and in go the bunk beds—and voilà, the hut becomes a cozy overnight lodge. Deeper into the wilderness, some nine miles from Badger Pass—the last four miles definitely uphill—is Yosemite's rustic 25-bunk **Ostrander Hut,** built in 1940 of oak and stone, and a favorite destination for intermediate to advanced cross-country skiers. Visitors (selected by lottery) pack in their own food (by tradition, gourmet fare), stoves, and sleeping bags. The cost is $20 per night. For more information, contact: **Ostrander Reservations,** P.O. Box 545, Yosemite, CA 95389, 209/372-0740.

Just outside Yosemite's eastern entrance—and reached after a one- to six-mile uphill ski to Tioga Pass on Hwy. 120, depending on the year's snow levels—is the **Tioga Pass Winter Resort,** P.O. Box 307, Lee Vining, CA 93541, 209/372-4471, where cozy heated log cabins and hearty lodge fare support spectacular backcountry skiing into Yosemite's high country.

STAYING IN YOSEMITE

Ahwahnee Hotel

In a setting like the Yosemite Valley, even a peek out the window of a Motel 6 would be inspirational. But Yosemite's Ahwahnee Hotel, just a stone's throw from Yosemite Fall under the looming presence of the Royal Arches, is *the* place to bed down in Yosemite. The Ahwahnee is as much a part of the changeless Yosemite landscape as the surrounding stone,

ACCOMMODATIONS RATINGS

Accommodations in this book are rated by price category, based on double-occupancy, high-season rates. Categories used are:

Budget	$35 and under
Inexpensive	$35-60
Moderate	$60-85
Expensive	$85-110
Premium	$110-150
Luxury	$150 and up

sky, and water—and quite possibly the most idyllic (and most popular) hotel in all of California.

Open to the public since 1927, except for a short two-year commission as a U.S. Navy hospital during World War II, this plush six-story hotel handcrafted of native stone combines art deco and Native American flourishes with that Yosemite sense of *vastness*. The impressive fireplace in the ruggedly comfortable Great Lounge, the downstairs floor-to-ceiling windows, and the 130-foot-long dining hall with open-raftered ceiling trussed with unpeeled sugar pine logs all reinforce the idea that at the Ahwahnee, the outdoors is welcome even indoors. For an extra taste of the hotel's ambience, try the Ahwahnee Bar.

Stay either in the palatial stone lodge, with its large, comfortable public rooms and recently redecorated guest rooms, or in the cottages. Fresh from a $1.5 million makeover in 1997, rooms have all been restyled and refurnished, with unique, specially made headboards, armoires, and storage chests. Fabrics, designs, and colors reflect the hotel's original Native American motif. Make reservations early; unless there are cancellations, the hotel will be booked. (Reservations are accepted a year and a day in advance.) Luxury.

For more information about the Ahwahnee Hotel—and all other concessionaire-operated accommodations at Yosemite—and to make reservations, contact: Yosemite Concession Services, 559/252-4848, TTY 559/255-8345, fax 559/456-0542, www.yosemitepark.com. To contact hotel guests, call 209/372-1407.

Wawona Hotel

Set amid the lush summer meadowlands of one-time Clark Station near the park's southern entrance, the wood frame Wawona Hotel is the Ahwahnee's rustic kissing cousin. Here, at the main hotel and its adjacent wings (known as "cottages"), sit out on the veranda and imagine that the next stagecoach full of tourists will be arriving any minute. Time seems forgotten, judging from some interior touches, too. Rooms (half have private baths) feature brass doorknobs, push-button light switches, steam radiators, and claw-foot bathtubs. Other pleasures here include the swimming pool, golf course, and tennis court—all these in season—and the dining room

and lounge. You can go on a guided horseback ride from the stables. Or wander through the **Pioneer Yosemite History Center,** explore the **Mariposa Grove** of big trees nearby, or hike to Chilnualna Falls. Expensive-Premium. Open year-round. For reservations, call 559/252-4848.

Other Yosemite Stays

At **Curry Village,** two miles east of park headquarters, you can choose from among canvas tent cabins (no food or cooking allowed; Inexpensive); basic back-to-back cabins, with or without private bath (Moderate); or a standard room (Expensive). Summer-only tent cabins are also available at **White Wolf Lodge** on Tioga Rd. and at **Tuolumne Meadows Lodge,** just a half-mile from the visitors center at Tuolumne Meadows. Inexpensive.

The **Yosemite Lodge** near the foot of Yosemite Fall, on the site of the U.S. Army Cavalry's Fort Yosemite, now include standard and deluxe motel rooms—deluxe rooms including a deck or patio—and European-style rooms with a central shared bath. Yosemite Lodge cabins, damaged in the floods of 1997 along with some of the motel rooms, are temporarily closed and may be relocated. Expensive-Premium.

Accommodations not affiliated with Yosemite Concession Services include **Yosemite West Condominiums** six miles from Badger Pass, 209/372-4240. **The Redwoods,** 8038 Chilnualna Falls Rd., 209/375-6666, are very nice, fully equipped one- to five-bedroom cabins (houses, actually) with picture windows, fireplaces, and cable TV. Quite comfy, laundry facilities available, close to the Merced River. Expensive-Luxury.

Yosemite Campgrounds

Except for backcountry tent pitching—see Yosemite Hikes and Backpacks above—camping outside designated campgrounds is not allowed. Reservations for developed year-round valley campgrounds are advisable from April into November. Most Yosemite National Park campsites can be reserved through the National Park Reservation Service's Yosemite-only number, toll-free 800/436-7275, up to three months in advance. In the mid-September through May off-season, the maximum campground stay is 30 days, but the summertime limit is seven days for Yosemite Valley campgrounds,

HIGH SIERRA HIKERS' CAMPS

Definitely plan ahead for one of Yosemite's finest pleasures—an overnight or longer "luxury" camping trip with stays at backcountry hikers' **High Sierra Camps**—a trail-connected loop of tent cabins complete with two-person bunks, clean sheets, and showers (breakfast and dinner also included). The trip is not necessarily a piece of cake, though, even without the burden of a heavily laden pack: the route is strenuous, and hikers must cover up to 10 miles of ground each day to get to camp.

Most people start at the Tuolumne Meadows Lodge (one of the "camps") and loop either north or south, but you can start and end elsewhere.

Getting to **Glen Aulin** beside the White Cascades and near Waterwheel Falls (spectacular in spring) involves leaving Tuolumne Meadows into the Grand Canyon of the Tuolumne. The climb to **May Lake** to the southwest offers good views of Mount Hoffman, and the camp is a good base for climbers. **Sunrise** is in the high-lake Sunrise Lakes country south of Tenaya Lake, a splendid setting. From there, it's downhill back

into the forest and **Merced Lake**—then either a further descent to Yosemite Valley alongside the Merced River or a climb up to **Vogelsang**, the highest of the high, rooted in an alpine meadow, the last stop before trekking back to Tuolumne Meadows.

Yosemite's High Sierra Camps are usually open from late June through Labor Day, but the actual dates vary from year to year, depending on snowpack and weather conditions. Not surprisingly, they're immensely popular. Reservations are booked by lottery. Submit your request for an application anytime, either by phone or on the website; applications are mailed out in September for the following year's hiking season. Backpackers following the same camp loop but sleeping under the stars can lug substantially less food and gear by arranging for meals (breakfast and dinner) at the encampments.

For more information, contact: High Sierra Reservations, Yosemite Concession Services, 5410 E. Home Ave., Fresno, CA 93727, 559/454-2002, www.yosemitepark.com.

---

14 days for camping outside the valley. Yosemite also has five group campgrounds, reservable in advance through the National Park Reservation Service.

One problem with camping for any length of time at Yosemite is that campgrounds here have no showers. To get cleaned up, from spring into fall, buy yourself a shower at Curry Village in the valley, at Curry's housekeeping cabin complex, or at the lodges at White Wolf and Tuolumne Meadows in summer.

For those committed to a stay in the valley, the **Lower River** and **Upper River campgrounds** a mile east of Yosemite Village, open May through mid-Oct., are urban zoos in summer, with water and flush toilets, $15 per night. The same facilities and prices apply to the **Lower Pines, Upper Pines,** and **North Pines campgrounds** another half mile east. Lower Pines is open year-round, Upper Pines is open Apr.–Oct., and North Pines is open May-October.

More peaceable in general is the very basic walk-in **Backpackers Camp** behind North Pines, open summer through mid-Oct., with running water and toilets, $3 per person per night, available without reservation but only to campers car-

rying wilderness permits, two-night limit. The year-round **Sunnyside** walk-in campground (also known as Camp Four) near Yosemite Lodge is also $3 per person, no reservations, with a seven-day limit in summer; this is *the* rock climbers' camp, collecting climbers from around the globe in season. Contention has been hot over the park's plans to close Sunnyside for the construction of Yosemite Lodge accommodations, to replace units lost in the disastrous 1997 flooding.

In general, the quantity of peace available while camping out is directly proportional to distance removed from Yosemite Valley. One exception to this rule, though, is the **Tuolumne Meadows Campground** about 55 miles northeast on Tioga Rd., with 314 family campsites, $15 per night. The campground is usually open from early June to mid-Oct.; half the campsites are reservable through the National Park Reservation Service, the others are first-come, first-camped. The walk-in campsites here are strictly for backpackers with wilderness permits, one-night limit, $3 per person.

Both **Porcupine Flat** and **Yosemite Creek Campgrounds** farther west are peaceful and primitive—no drinking water, pit toilets only, but cheap at just $6 per night. The **White Wolf Campground** a few miles west of Yosemite Creek, does have water, and thus a higher price: $10.

The year-round **Hodgdon Meadow Campground** is close to Yosemite's Big Oak Flat entrance on Big Oak Flat Rd., $15 per night for the usual amenities, limited facilities in winter, National Park Reservation Service reservations required through October. The **Crane Flat Campground** is spread out and fairly serene, open late May–Sept., and reservable through the National Park Reservation Service's Yosemite toll-free number, 800/436-7275, $15 per night. More remote and more primitive in the same general vicinity is **Tamarack Flat Campground,** reached via Old Big Oak Flat Rd. heading south from Tioga Rd., $6 per night.

Heading south from Yosemite Valley, very nice for a summer stay is the **Bridalveil Creek Campground** halfway to Glacier Point on Glacier Point Rd., with the usual facilities, $10 per night. The **Wawona Campground** on Old Wawona Rd. north of the park's south entrance is open all year, $15.

Staying near Yosemite

Just outside the park's southern entrance is the very nice cottage-style **Apple Tree Inn,** 1110 Hwy. 41, 559/683-3200 or toll-free 888/683-5111, www.moonstonemgmt.com. The 53 cheerful yellow units, a collection of two-story duplexes and triplexes scattered in the woods, feature a fireplace, microwave, refrigerator, coffeemaker, and TV with VCR; kitchenettes are available. Also here: an indoor pool, spa, and racquetball court. Great breakfast buffet. Moderate-Luxury.

Another good choice in Fish Camp, a couple miles west, is **The Narrow Gauge Inn,** 48571 Hwy. 41, 559/683-7720 or toll-free 888/644-9050, www.narrowgaugeinn.com, especially for fans of railroading nostalgia. Families and "well-behaved pets" welcome, open Apr.–October. Moderate-Luxury. Features a decent restaurant, too, serving "Old California ranch cuisine" specials, beef, chicken, and fish.

Also in Fish Camp is the **Tenaya Lodge at Yosemite,** 1122 Hwy. 41, 559/683-6555 or toll-free 888/514-2167, fax 559/683-8684, www.tenayalodge,com, an outpost of urban-style rusticity with heirloom and antique accents and all the amenities (including work stations and in-

room movies and Nintendo). Includes three on-site restaurants, swimming pools, fully equipped fitness center, and full-service spa. Full conference facilities available. Luxury, with rates usually substantially lower in the spring, fall, and nonholiday winter seasons.

Barely more than a mile from Yosemite and just off Hwy. 41 in Fish Camp, **Yosemite Fish Camp Bed & Breakfast Inn,** 1164 Railroad Ave., 559/683-7426, is a 1940s cabin-style mountain home with just three guest rooms (one has private bath), a small shared sitting room with woodstove, and full country breakfast. Moderate. Practically next door and cozy in a more contemporary sense is two-story **Karen's Yosemite Bed and Breakfast,** 1144 Railroad Ave., 559/683-4550 or toll-free 800/346-1443, where all three rooms have private baths and rates include full breakfast and afternoon tea or refreshments with homemade pastries and such. Expensive.

Other good choices are available in Mariposa and vicinity—an area overflowing with bed-and-breakfasts these days. Budget travelers will particularly appreciate the HI-AYH **Yosemite Bug Hostel, Lodge, & Campgrounds,** 6979 Hwy. 140, Midpines, 209/966-6666, fax 209/966-6667, www.yosemitebug.com, just 25 miles from Yosemite Valley on the way to Mariposa, and just $15 a night for a dorm-style bunk. Inexpensive private rooms and campsites are also available, not to mention the camaraderie—and the on-site bistro. Open year-round. At the other end of the scale is the very elegant, very pricey **Chateau du Sureau** farther south in Oakhurst, 48688 Victoria Ln., 559/683-6860 (Luxury).

EATING IN YOSEMITE

If you're backpacking, camping, staying in tent cabins, or otherwise trying to do Yosemite and vicinity on the cheap, bring your own food. Groceries are available in Yosemite Village at the **Village Store,** open daily 8 A.M.–10 P.M. in summer, just 9 A.M.–7 P.M. otherwise, but it's more expensive to stock up at the park than in a major town en route.

The **Village Grill** next door to the Village Store is just a snack bar serving basic breakfasts and burgers, the most inexpensive place around. The village's **Degnan's Deli,** fast-food stand,

and ice cream parlor are other options, but **Degnan's Pasta Palace** is the place to carbo-load. The **Yosemite Lodge** features a **cafeteria** open for breakfast, lunch, and dinner (they put together box lunches here for picnickers if you

remember to order the day before); the new family-friendly **Garden Terrace** restaurant—an all-you-can-eat, serve-yourself buffet with soups, salads, pastas, and hand-carved meats; and the all-new, dinners-only **Mountain Room**

EDUCATIONAL ADVENTURES IN THE SIERRA NEVADA

Among the many groups in California offering educational experiences and seminars in the Sierra Nevada is the University of California at Berkeley's **Cal Adventures,** 5 Haas Clubhouse, Strawberry Canyon Recreation Area, Berkeley, CA 94720, 510/642-4000, fax 510/642-3730, www.strawberry.org. This outdoor education program is largely tailored to Bay Area residents, but some programs—particularly its summer backpacking, white-water rafting, and white-water guide school workshops—are held in the Sierra Nevada. Call for a current program. Registration is strictly first-come, first-served, so either call in your registration or fax it after downloading the form from the website. **Field Studies in Natural History,** San Jose State University, One Washington Square, San Jose, CA 95192, 408/924-2625, offers interdisciplinary natural history field seminars, open to the public, as part of its continuing education program. Some focus on the Sierra Nevada. Check with other UC and CSU campuses for similar programs.

A particular boon for adventurous seniors (age 55 and older) is **Elderhostel,** 75 Federal St., Boston, MA 02110, toll-free 877/426-8056, www.elderhostel.org, which offers an abundance of low-cost environmental and educational adventures in California's Sierra Nevada, many of these sponsored by various state colleges and universities. The 1999 summer schedule, for example, included programs based at the Lost Valley Pack Station (for burro backpacking), Mammoth Lakes, Meadow Valley near Quincy, Oakhurst near Yosemite, Sierra National Forest, and Wonder Valley Ranch near Sequoia and Kings Canyon National Parks. Most trips cost less than $500 per week.

The **Yosemite Association,** P.O. Box 230, El Portal, CA 95318, 209/379-2646, www.yosemite.org, sponsors a variety of excellent college-level field seminars, from bird studies and botany weekends to backpacks and family day hikes. Even specialized day hikes are offered, such as On the Trail of Gourmet Delights. Seminars on Yosemite in winter, basketry, geology, and ecology are also offered, along with photography, poetry, writing, painting, and drawing. Most seminars are in the $150-and-up range.

The **Mono Lake Committee** in Lee Vining, 760/647-6595, www.monolake.org, sponsors naturalist-led tours and seminars on an endless variety of topics. A typical year's roster of courses might include Prehistoric Peoples and Their Environments, Mono-Bodie Historical Tour, Mono Basin Photography, Geology of the Mono Basin, Survival of the Sierra Nevada Bighorn, Birds of the Mono Basin, California Gull Research, High Country Wildflowers, and the Paoha Island Kayak Tour. Usually starting in June, guided Mono Lake canoe tours are also offered. Volunteers are needed, too, for ongoing bird counts and environmental restoration work. Most weekend workshops are $75–150.

At the group, chapter, and national level, the Sierra Club and the Audubon Society also offer hikes and treks—some free, some almost free (like working wilderness outings), and some guided trips with fees. For bird-watching trips, typically offered at the chapter level, contact **Audubon California,** 555 Audubon Pl., Sacramento, CA 95825, 916/481-5332, www.audubon-ca.org. (For eastern Sierra Nevada bird-watching in particular, try the chapter website: lnr.dragonfire.net/ESAS.) For information about all Sierra Club trips, including those in and near the Sierra Nevada, contact: **Sierra Club Outing Dept.,** 85 2nd St., San Francisco, CA 94105, 415/977-5630 (24-hour voice mail), www.sierraclub.org/outings. Be sure to inquire, too, about current—and very affordable—hikes, outings, and educational programs offered at the Sierra Club's **Clair Tappaan Lodge** near Lake Tahoe.

The **Nature Conservancy of California,** 201 Mission St., San Francisco, CA 94105, 415/777-0487, www.tnc.org/infield/State/California, offers no-cost or low-cost natural history expeditions and restoration work parties throughout the state, though that information is typically only available at the local or regional levels. (Ask for a list of preserves open to the public, and contact these directly.) Inquire for current schedules—and also ask about major trips and tours, which have included expeditions tracing the footsteps of John Muir and Ishi.

Restaurant, a striking rough-sawn-cedar-walled restaurant featuring fantastic views of Yosemite Fall. In addition to steaks, seafood, and poultry, the menu includes pastas, salads, and such things as duck quesadillas.

Curry Village has a **cafeteria** (closed in winter) and a seasonal hamburger deck, coffee and ice cream corners, and the **Terrace Meadow** deck for lunch, pizza, and light dinner. There's also a seasonal snack stand at **Happy Isles.** Both **Tuolumne Meadows Lodge**—there's also a separate grill—and **Whitewolf Lodge** serve meals (breakfast and dinner) until the snow flies. Sandwiches, salads, pizza, and such are available at **Badger Pass Lodge** (open winters only), and in summer, the new **Glacier Point Hut** serves as a snack stand.

For a good breakfast and decent lunch in Yosemite Valley's priciest price range, or for those who simply must dress for dinner (no jeans allowed), try the **Ahwahnee Hotel Dining Room,** 209/372-1488 or 209/372-1489 (dinner reservations), open 7–10:30 A.M. for breakfast, 11:30 A.M.–3:30 P.M. for lunch, and 5:30–9 P.M. for dinner. (Hours may change slightly from season to season.) A snack service is available in the afternoons between mealtimes, and a late-night menu is available in the Ahwahnee's lounge. Less expensive and more casual is the Victorian-style dining room in the **Wawona Hotel** near the park's southern entrance, open 7:30–11 A.M. for continental and American breakfasts, noon–1:30 P.M. for lunch, and just 6–8 P.M. for dinner. Sunday brunch is a special treat here, 7:30 A.M.–1:30 P.M.

YOSEMITE INFORMATION AND TRANSPORTATION

Yosemite Information and Services

The $20-per-car park entry fee is good for one week, though the fee is only $10 for walk-in and bike-in visitors and those who arrive by bus. Except hiking, backpacking, and free park-sponsored activities, almost everything else in

---

ENTERTAINING YOSEMITE

A mythic event in Yosemite Valley is the annual Christmas season **Bracebridge Dinner** in the Ahwahnee Hotel, the 1927 brainchild of photographer Ansel Adams and cohorts. Modeled after the Yorkshire feast of Squire Bracebridge as portrayed in *The Sketch Book of Geoffrey Crayon, Gent* by Washington Irving, the three-hour medieval pageant includes a full-dress, seven-course processional English feast of fish, "peacock pie," boar's head, baron of beef, and more, accompanied by music, song, and great merriment. The Lord of Misrule and his pet bear provide still more entertainment. Because of the event's great popularity, there are five dinner seatings these days, but even so, it's almost impossible to get tickets—and those who get them (by lottery) find it quite an expensive experience.

Also incredibly popular is Yosemite's other great holiday tradition, the **New Year's Eve Dinner-Dance.** To attend either event, contact Yosemite Concession Services (see Yosemite Information and Services below) in November to request ticket-lottery applications. A separate application is necessary for each event. Applications—for the *following* year's festivities—are accepted Dec. 15–Jan. 15.

Other Ahwahnee-centered events include the very popular **Vintners' Holidays,** wines-among-the-pines appreciation offered from November into December, and the equally popular **Chefs' Holidays** offered from January into February. During Yosemite's Vintners' Holidays, some 30 California winemakers are invited to bring samples of their best vintages to these special tastings, seminars, and dinners, which are usually scheduled Sunday–Thursday. Chefs' Holidays feature some of California's most innovative chefs sharing their culinary secrets, food demonstrations, and banquet finales. For more information, contact Yosemite Concession Services.

Not park-sponsored but a great party nonetheless is the **Strawberry Music Festival** held at Camp Mather, usually each spring and fall. Expect a parking lot full of VWs with fading Grateful Dead bumper stickers along with BMWs and Volvos, everyone assembled for a long weekend of folk music, bluegrass, and big-time good times. Plan ahead if you're going—the event often sells out well in advance due to headliners like Emmylou Harris, Vassar Clements, and the David Grisman Quartet.

Yosemite—camping and other lodging, food, and park-related services of all kinds—is extra.

Tracking down information about Yosemite is an adventure in itself, considering the number of separate agencies involved. The all-purpose clearinghouse for information about the park itself and about current activities is the National Park Service. For general information, contact: **Yosemite National Park,** P.O. Box 577, Yosemite National Park, CA 95389, 209/372-0200 or 209/372-0264, TTY 209/372-4726, www.nps.gov/yose/.

Though the current edition of the *Yosemite Guide* tabloid and a park map are included in the "package" passed out to visitors at all park entrances, the **Yosemite Valley Visitors Center** in Yosemite Village (at the west end of Yosemite Village Mall), 209/372-0200, open 9 A.M.–5 P.M., is the place to get oriented. The displays here are good, also the various park-sponsored special programs, but the visitors center also offers maps, hiking and camping information, do-it-yourself trip planning assistance, and wilderness permits. Foreign-language pamphlets and maps are also available.

Next to the visitors center in Yosemite Valley is the park's **Valley Wilderness Center,** P.O. Box 545, Yosemite, CA 95389, 209/372-0745 for wilderness information, 209/372-0740 for reservations—the essential stop for those seriously setting out to see Yosemite. Other park visitor information centers are at **Big Oak Flat** near Crane Flat, and at **Wawona.**

A good selection of books about Yosemite, including *Yosemite Wildflower Trails* by Dana C. Morgenson, *Birds of Yosemite, Yosemite Nature Notes,* and other titles published by the Yosemite Association, is available in the visitors center bookstore. Worth it, especially for first-time visitors, is the *Yosemite Road Guide,* a key to major sights throughout Yosemite. To get a publications list and/or to obtain books and pamphlets in advance, contact: **Yosemite Association,** P.O. Box 230, El Portal, CA 95318, 209/379-2646, www.yosemite.org. For information on ongoing park restoration projects—or to make a contribution—contact: **The Yosemite Fund,** 155 Montgomery St., Ste. 1104, San Francisco, CA 94104, 415/434-1782, www.yosemitefund.org.

For information about noncamping accommodations and most other facilities and services available at Yosemite, contact the concessionaire's headquarters: **Yosemite Concession Services,** 5410 E. Home Ave., Fresno, CA 93727, 559/252-4848, fax 559/456-0542, www.yosemitepark.com. The company's general in-park phone number is 209/372-1000.

For **Yosemite area travel information,** brought to you by a consortium of surrounding counties also via touch-screen kiosks, message signs, and highway radio advisories, the website is www.yosemite.com.

As an urban outpost in a wilderness setting, Yosemite National Park offers most of the comforts of home. The main post office (open even Saturday mornings) is next to the visitors center in Yosemite Village. There's another at Yosemite Lodge, and a stamp vending machine at Curry Village. To contact the local lost-and-found bureau, call 209/372-4357 or 209/379-1001. For both regular appointments and 24-hour emergency care, the **Yosemite Medical Group,** 209/372-4637, is located near the Ahwahnee Hotel in Yosemite Village. Other valley services include the laundry facilities at Housekeeping Camp, an auto repair garage, 24-hour tow service, even warm-weather-only dog kennels. The gas station in Yosemite Valley has closed permanently—be sure to gas up outside the park—though gas is available at Wawona, Crane Flat, and (in summer only) Tuolumne Meadows.

Yosemite Transportation

Coming from most places in Northern California, Hwy. 140 through Merced and Mariposa is usually the best route into Yosemite—especially in winter—though Hwy. 41 from Fresno is more convenient when coming from the south. The only trans-Yosemite road, Hwy. 120 or Tioga Rd., is usually open between Groveland and Yosemite Valley (via New Big Oak Flat Rd.), but the high-country stretch from beyond Crane Flat to Mono Lake and the eastern Sierra Nevada is closed in winter. When driving Yosemite roads in spring, fall, and winter, come prepared for frosty road conditions (use snow tires or chains).

You can't get to Yosemite by train, but **Amtrak,** toll-free 800/872-7245, www.amtrak.com, does come close. From the Amtrak stop in Merced, buses take you the rest of the way. Greyhound doesn't serve the park directly either, but **Yosemite Via,** 300 Grogan Ave. in Merced,

209/722-0366, makes four daily bus trips between Merced's Greyhound station and Yosemite via Mariposa and Midpines, $20 one-way (or $11 from Mariposa). A better deal, if it's still going, is the Yosemite Area Regional Transportation System (YARTS) bus service along Hwy. 140 from Merced to Yosemite Valley. Fares vary depending on distance, $7–15 round-trip—and that figure "includes" the park's $20 entrance fee. For more information call 209/372-4487 or toll-free 877/989-2787, or try www.yosemite.com/yarts.

Most people drive to Yosemite. Gas stations are available on the way. (Be sure to fill the tank, too, because there are no longer any gas stations in Yosemite Valley.) Because of the park's immense popularity, getting around on the park's free **shuttle bus system** is the best option during summer and other "peak" popularity periods; this holds true, to avoid slick snowy and icy roads, for getting to Badger Pass and elsewhere in winter. And the only way to get to Mirror Lakes Junction and Happy Isles is via shuttle. Though the shuttle schedule changes with the seasons, in summer buses run every five minutes 9 A.M.–10 P.M.

SEQUOIA AND KINGS CANYON NATIONAL PARKS

Separate but equal, contiguous Sequoia National Park and Kings Canyon National Park are Yosemite's less-popular redwood country cousins—which means privacy seekers can more easily find what they're looking for here. Connected by the big tree-lined, closed-in-winter Generals Hwy., both parks offer limited winter access—via Hwy. 198 from Visalia, Sequoia's southern entrance, and via Hwy. 180 from Fresno into Kings Canyon's Grant Grove Village area. But because of the ruggedness and haughty height of eastern Sierra Nevada peaks, including Mt. Whitney, no road connects west to east—so vast areas of both parks are inaccessible to casual sightseers, perfect for hiking and backcountry trekking. The Pacific Crest Trail threads its way north through both parks, and through adjacent wilderness areas, to Yosemite.

Making a Sequoia–Kings Canyon visit even more expansive is the adjacent 328,000-acre **Giant Sequoia National Monument,** created in 2000 by President Bill Clinton to protect the watersheds of 34 ancient Sierra big trees groves.

Seeing and Doing Sequoia

No tree cathedral on earth is as awesome as the **Giant Forest** in Sequoia National Park, a silent stand of big trees threaded with some 40 miles of footpaths. The easy, one-mile Hazelwood Nature Trail loop tells the story of the giant sequoias, but the two-mile Congress Trail loop leads to the famous **General Sherman** and other trees strangely honored with military and political titles (General Lee, Lincoln, McKinley, House, Senate, etc.). Fortunately, the National Park Service stopped naming trees after presidents and politicians after World War II.

drive-through tree in Sequoia National Park

ROBERT HOLMES/CALTOUR

GIANT SEQUOIA NATIONAL MONUMENT

An ancient yet new presence on the western flanks of Sequoia–Kings Canyon National Park is 328,000-acre Giant Sequoia National Monument, created by executive order of President Bill Clinton in April 2000. This new national monument, created from lands previously included within Sequoia National Forest, protects 34 groves of ancient sequoias. Giant Sequoia National Monument and nearby national parks together encompass the area first identified by naturalist John Muir in 1901 as crucial for adequate protection of these massive trees.

Though these groves were already protected from logging, national monument status ends commercial timber harvest within the groves' respective watersheds. Environmentalists have long contended that logging within the big trees' watersheds is detrimental to their survival. Off-road vehicles and motorcycles are banned from trails in the new national monument, but hiking, backpacking, horseback riding, fishing, river rafting, and camping are all permitted.

Giant Sequoia National Monument, which is managed by Sequoia National Forest, contains two separate units. The **northern section** straddles Hwy. 180 just west of the national parks. Of particular note is **Converse Basin,** logged in the late 1800s and early 1900s. The basin's **Stump Meadow** is something of a big tree graveyard. For maps and other information, contact the **Hume Lake Ranger District** office in Dunlap, 559/338-2251.

The monument's **southern section,** reached from Hwy. 190 east of Porterville, borders the national parks on the south. Highlights include the half-mile **Trail of the 100 Giants** loop and the more challenging **Freeman Creek Trail.** For more information and maps, contact the **Tule River Ranger District** office in Springville, 559/539-2607.

For more information about Giant Sequoia National Monument and surrounding national forest lands, contact headquarters for **Sequoia National Forest,** 900 W. Grand Ave., Porterville, CA 93257, 559/784-1500, www.r5.fs.fed.us/sequoia.

Even better are some of the longer, more lyrical loops: the moderately challenging, six-mile Trail of the Sequoias and Circle Meadow trip through the eastern forest (some of the finest trees) and adjacent meadows; the five-mile Huckleberry Meadow journey into the heart of the redwoods; and the Crescent Meadow and Log Meadow walk around the forest's fringe—since sometimes a view of these giants from afar is the best way to really *see* them. Near Giant Forest Village is the Moro Rock and Soldier's Loop Trail to the impressive granite dome **Moro Rock**—famous for its views of the Kaweah River's grand middle fork canyon.

Hiking in the park's impressive **Mineral King** area—all trails start at an elevation of near 7,500 feet—is only for fit fans of fantastic scenery. Steep but very scenic is the White Chief Trail, a four-mile round-trip through luscious summer meadow flowers to and from the old White Chief Mine. (Mineral King was named for the Nevada-generated silver mining mania that stormed through the area in the 1870s.) For unforgettable views of the southern Sierra Nevada, take the Monarch Lakes Trail to Sawtooth Pass, a challenging round-trip of just over four miles. Other worthwhile trails lead through dense red fir forests to Timber Gap; to the alpine granite of Crystal Lake; to sky-high Franklin Lake; and to Eagle and Mosquito Lakes.

Most spectacular, though, are Sequoia's high-country trails, some of the finest in the nation and the only way to appreciate the land's grandeur once the park's big trees have been honored. Most popular is the High Sierra Trail, which connects with the John Muir (Pacific Crest) Trail and eventually arrives at hiker-congested Mt. Whitney.

Seeing and Doing Kings Canyon

The **Grant Grove** trails are easiest, pleasant strolls through Kings Canyon's impressive giant sequoias; most trails start near campgrounds. Also easy are fairly short trails to waterfalls, including the very easy one-mile round-trip River Trail on the way to Zumwalt Meadow, the longer Hotel Creek Trail, and the lovely Sunset Trail. The Paradise Valley Trail offers a fairly easy day trip to **Mist Falls** and back, a longer (and more challenging) journey to Paradise Valley.

Indeed, Kings Canyon National Park, which includes most of the deep middle and south fork canyons of the Kings River, celebrates the height and majesty of the High Sierra and its rushing waters to the same degree that Sequoia honors its trees. Most of this park is true wilderness, seemingly custom-made for backpacking and backcountry camping, with more than 700 miles of trails. The Copper Creek Trail is one of the park's most strenuous day hikes, quickly leading into the Kings Canyon backcountry. Also beginning at Roads End is the 43-mile, one-week round-trip trek to Rae Lakes, a lake basin as lovely as any in the Sierra Nevada. For suggestions on other good backcountry routes (wilderness permit required), contact park headquarters or any visitor information center.

Boyden Cavern between Grant Grove Village and Cedar Grove on Hwy. 180, 559/736-2708, www.caverntours.com, offers a 45-minute guided tour of crystalline stalactites and stalagmites (fee).

Staying and Eating
in Sequoia–Kings Canyon

Campgrounds at Sequoia and Kings Canyon are reservable through the National Park Reservation Service, toll-free 800/365-2267. Both parks have a 14-day camping limit (in summer). Among the most popular in Sequoia is **Lodgepole Campground,** an enclave with its own visitors center and organized activities. Popular Kings Canyon campgrounds cluster near Grant Grove: **Azalea, Sunset, Swale,** and **Crystal Springs Campgrounds.**

For information and reservations on lodging options in Kings Canyon National Park, contact:

Sequoia-Kings Canyon Park Services Company, Grant Grove, P.O. Box 909, Kings Canyon National Park, CA 93633, 559/335-5500. The company's offerings include **Cedar Grove Lodge,** about 30 miles north of Grant Grove at the end of Hwy. 180, a small 18-room lodge open only from late May into Sept.; the impressive new 30-room **John Muir Lodge,** offering stylish motel-style rooms and suites in Grant Grove; **Grant Grove Cabins,** which range from rustic to deluxe; and **Stony Creek Lodge,** between Giant Forest and Grant Grove in Sequoia National Forest. Rates at these accommodations vary widely, from Inexpensive to Premium.

In Sequoia, the attractive new timber-and-stone **Wuksachi Lodge,** with 102 rooms in three separate buildings, toll-free 888/252-5757 or www.visitsequoia.com for information and reservations, has replaced Giant Forest Village as the center of park lodging—so the trampled forest area can take a rest and return to a more natural state. Wuksachi is six miles north of Giant Forest, offers no TV (at last report), and is open year-round. Premium-Luxury. Very nice casual restaurant, too, serving such things as pasta, vegetarian entrées, and baked trout.

Sequoia's **Bearpaw Meadow High Sierra Camp** offers tent cabins and clean sheets, hot showers, and home-style meals. It's an 11.3-mile hike in (figure anywhere from four to eight hours depending on your speed). Bearpaw is usually open from some time in June to early Sept., depending on weather and snowpack.

After the exciting trip via paved cowpath over Kaiser Pass, a summer stay at rustic Mono Hot Springs is quite refreshing.

KIM WEIR

MONTECITO-SEQUOIA LODGE

The private **Montecito-Sequoia Nordic Ski Center and Family Vacation Camp** between Sequoia and Kings Canyon on Hwy. 180, nine miles south of Grant Grove, offers convenient access to miles and miles of marked and groomed ski trails (trail map available), warming huts, also private and group lessons and equipment rentals. Fun too in winter is the naturally frozen skating rink with Zamboni grooming, where at night you can skate to music under the stars, then warm yourself with hot chocolate in front of the bonfire. Nice here are the old-fashioned lodges, offering cozy accommodations (private baths) and good home-style food (buffet meals), reasonable rates, also holiday packages. Moonlight photo tours, ski football, igloo building, and other activities are also sponsored. With summer comes a program of weeklong summer camps for families (singles and couples welcome, too). For more information, contact: Montecito-Sequoia Lodge, P.O. Box 858, Grant Grove, Kings Canyon National Park, CA 93633, 559/565-3388, www.montecitosequoia.com. For reservations, call 650/967-8612 or toll-free 800/227-9900.

Luxury rates include breakfast and dinner. Reservations are taken beginning at 7 A.M. January 2 for the following summer, and the camp is usually booked out for the whole season by 7:30 A.M. If you snooze, your only hope is a subsequent cancellation. For more information, call toll-free 888/252-5757 or visit www.visitsequoia.com.

Sequoia–Kings Canyon and Area Information

The $10-per-car entrance fee is good for one week, in either park. (If you walk, cycle, or arrive by motorcycle or bus, it's $5.) For more information, especially current trail conditions, contact: **Sequoia and Kings Canyon National Parks,** Ash Mountain, 47050 Generals Hwy., Three Rivers, CA 93271, 559/565-3341 or 559/335-2856, www.nps.gov/seki. For road and weather information, call 559/565-3341, then press 4 (message updated after 9 A.M. daily). The **Grant Grove Visitor Center** is the main information stop in Kings Canyon, open daily 8 A.M.–5 P.M.; the **Cedar Grove Visitor Center** is open only May–October. In Sequoia National Park, the former Ash Mountain Visitor Center near the park's southern entrance has been expanded into the **Foothills Visitors Center**—still the best stop for books, maps, wilderness permits, and information, along with natural history exhibits. The summer-season-only **Lodgepole Visitor Center** also features history and natural history exhibits.

For more information about surrounding public lands, including national forest and wilderness maps ($4 each), and to obtain backcountry wilderness permits, contact local ranger stations or regional U.S. Forest Service headquarters: **Sierra National Forest,** 1600 Tollhouse Rd., Clovis, CA 93611, 559/297-0706; **Sequoia National Forest,** 900 W. Grand Ave., Porterville, CA 93257, 559/784-1500; and **Inyo National Forest,** 873 N. Main St., Bishop, CA 93514, 760/873-2400.

CALIFORNIA DEPARTMENT OF PARKS & RECREATION

THE GOLD COUNTRY
OLD–AND NEW–GOLD DREAMS

When James Marshall found flakes of gold in the tailrace of Sutter's sawmill on the American River in 1848, hundreds of thousands of fortune hunters—a phenomenal human migration—soon set sail for California. Some came by boat, making either the brutal voyage around South America or a shorter two-leg sailing involving a treacherous overland crossing at the Isthmus of Panama. Others chose to lurch across the North American plains in landlubbing prairie schooners. The money-hungry hordes who soon arrived swept aside everything—native populations, land, vegetation, animals—that stood between them and the possibility of overnight wealth. The California gold rush was largely responsible for the Americanization of the West.

Though the region's native peoples were obliterated by the gold rush, the wildness of the life and land they loved lived on through a colorful cast of characters who came pouring in from around the world. In search of adventure, freedom, and overnight wealth, the stampeding gold seekers also unwittingly created a new collective cultural identity; without the old social restraints

that once bound them, men and women in the gold camps made up new rules. From principled bandits like Black Bart and Joaquin Murrieta to literary scalawags like Mark Twain, from the gambling Madame Moustache to the railroad barons who controlled California politics, from scandalous Lola Montez and her "spider dancing" to her innocent young song-and-dance protégé Lotta Crabtree (the first U.S. entertainer ever to become a millionaire)—somehow these and other creative individualists combined into one great psychological spark that became the essence of the modern California character.

Mark Twain wryly observed that "a gold mine is a hole in the ground with a liar at the entrance." There were, and still are, many gold mines here, and some say there's at least as much gold remaining in the ground as has been taken out. Today, recreational gold panners and more serious miners are increasingly common. And just as tourists flooded into the gold-laced Sierra Nevada foothills in the mid- to late 1800s (the literate ones lured in part by the tall tales of writers like Twain and Bret Harte), so they come today,

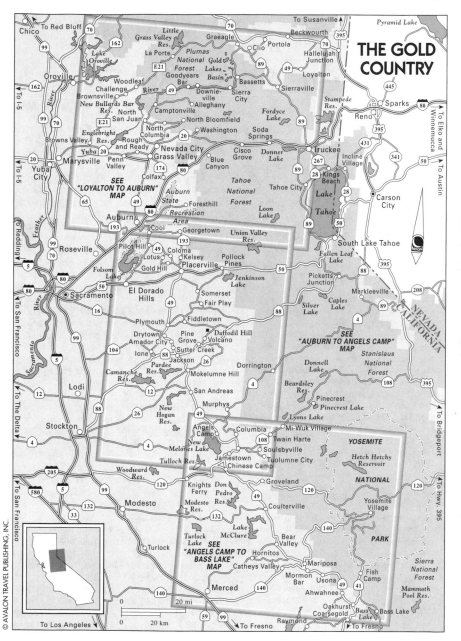

THE GOLD COUNTRY

Pyramid Lake

To Red Bluff · Chico · To Susanville · Beckwourth · Sparks · Reno · To Elko and Winnemucca · To Austin

Oroville · Little Grass Valley Res. · Graeagle · Clio · Portola · Hallelujah Junction · Loyalton · Sierraville · Carson City

Marysville · Nevada City · Grass Valley · Truckee · Kings Beach · Lake Tahoe · South Lake Tahoe

SEE "LOYALTON TO AUBURN" MAP

Auburn State Recreation Area · Tahoe National Forest

Roseville · Sacramento · Placerville · El Dorado Hills

SEE "AUBURN TO ANGELS CAMP" MAP

NEVADA · CALIFORNIA

Lodi · Stockton · Modesto

SEE "ANGELS CAMP TO BASS LAKE" MAP

YOSEMITE NATIONAL PARK

Yosemite Village

To Los Angeles · Merced · To Fresno

Sierra National Forest · Mammoth Pool Res. · Bass Lake

© AVALON TRAVEL PUBLISHING, INC.

0   20 mi
0   20 km

inheritors of a landscape systematically scarred and transformed by greed. But while strolling through the relics of an era, gold country travelers can witness the evidence that some scars do heal, given a century or two.

NEVADA CITY AND VICINITY

NEVADA CITY

In this small, sophisticated mountain town near the beloved San Juan Ridge of earth poet Gary Snyder, ghost-white Victorians cling to the hillsides, most streets are little more than paved crisscrossing cow paths, and the creekside trees downtown blaze with New England color in autumn. Officially populated by only a few thousand these days, Nevada City once competed with Sonora for recognition as California's third-largest city. It was first called Deer Creek Dry Diggins and Caldwell's Upper Store, but after the particularly brutal winter of 1850, the Spanish *nevada* ("snow covered") seemed more fitting. When the state of Nevada stole that name about 15 years later, the town took today's name of Nevada City.

Start exploring at the **Nevada City Chamber of Commerce,** 132 Main St. (the old office of the South Yuba Canal Company), 530/265-2692 or toll-free 800/655-6569, where you can pick up free guides and maps to local sights, almost endless information on arts, entertainment, and New Age happenings, and a copy of the exhaustive *Compleat Pedestrian's Partially Illustrated Guide to Greater Nevada City* ($7). The **Tahoe National Forest** office is at 631 Coyote St. (by the Hwy. 49/20 junction), 530/265-4531; stop by for forestwide recreation and camping information, or send $4 to request a forest map in advance.

Seeing and Doing Nevada City

Though the town nestles into steep hills, downtown Nevada City, primarily along Broad and Commercial Sts., is fairly level. Stroll first to Firehouse No. 1, now the small **Nevada County Historical Society Museum,** 214 Main, 530/265-5468. Inside the tall, thin gingerbread you'll find a dusty collection of Donner Party relics, fine Maidu basketry, and the altar from Grass Valley's original Chinatown joss house. Open daily 11 A.M.–4 P.M. in summer, Thurs.–Sun. the rest of the year. Small fee. On gaslamp-lit Broad St. is the handsome stone-and-brick **Nevada Theatre,** 401 Broad, 530/265-6161, where Mark Twain launched his career as a lecturer. One of the oldest theaters in the state, it was built in 1865 and renovated a century later. Nearby, you can stroll through the lobby of the green and white **National**

HISTORIC NEVADA CITY

Nevada City began as a placer mining camp. But due to only seasonal natural water supplies, local miners soon developed unique mining techniques allowing them to work year-round; the long tom, ground sluice, and hydraulic mining were all Nevada City "firsts." More than $400 million in gold was unearthed in the area.

Bold and brazen women were (and still are) a fact of life in and around the town; the lives of Nevada City's infamous gambler, Eleanor "Madame Moustache" Dumont, as well as precocious Lotta Crabtree and outrageous Lola Montez of Grass Valley, all intersected here. Appropriately enough, the U.S. senator who introduced legislation eventually leading to women's suffrage lived in Nevada City. Other famous Nevada City natives included world-class soprano Emma Nevada and cable car inventor Andrew Hallidie.

Nevada City's Baptist church stands on the site of a joint session of the Congregational Association of California and the San Francisco Presbytery, a meeting that eventually led to the establishment of the University of California. Water barons created by the conglomeration of capital necessary for mining-related water engineering also met here to create Pacific Gas and Electric Company (PG&E), the world's largest utility. Not so successful was the railway connecting Nevada City and Grass Valley, built in 1901; service on the notoriously unreliable "Never Come, Never Go" railroad stopped for good after a harsh 1926 snowstorm.

MINING MODERN GOLD: TRAVEL AND RECREATION

No matter how you go, several separate trips to the gold country are advisable, since the abundance of museums, old hotels, and other attractions is almost overwhelming on one long trip. Towns along Hwy. 49, the much-ballyhooed "Golden Chain Mother Lode Highway," are the most touristy yet also essential to a California gold country tour. If you're allergic to commercially tainted quaint, keep in mind that there *is* historic, scenic, and actual gold to be mined here.

Travel off the beaten track is not easy without a car or bicycle. If you're planning to explore most of the gold country's major towns on wheels, take the interconnecting old highways and county roads roughly paralleling Hwy. 49 whenever possible. Bicycle tours of the Mother Lode are great fun, assuming

you plan ahead—and stay off the main highway as much as possible.

Historical exploration, gold seeking, hiking, camping, fishing, swimming and tubing, boating, and waterskiing are other popular gold country pursuits.

River-running offers even more thrills, since most rivers that begin in the Sierra Nevada flow westward—and down through the gold country's foothills on their way to the valley. April and May are usually the "high water" months, though in some years even June is wet and wild. Summer and fall offer a tamer experience. Pick up a copy of *California Whitewater* by Fryar Calhoun and Jim Cassady—a worthwhile investment for fans of the inland wave. Get current listings of the many reputable rafting companies in the region from chambers of commerce or national forest offices.

TOM MYERS PHOTOGRAPHY

panning for gold

Hotel, 211 Broad St., 530/265-4551. Open continuously since 1856, despite a few fires, the National is one of several gold rush hotels claiming to be the state's oldest hostelry. Not content with just that honor, it also claims to be the oldest hotel in continuous operation west of the Rockies.

A quarter mile west on E. Broad lies a stone monolith known locally as Nevada City's first hospital; the area's early Maidu people, believing the sun healed all, climbed atop this im-

pressive sunning rock and nestled into the hollow to take the cure.

The **Miners Foundry Cultural Center,** 325 Spring St., 530/265-5040, is a meandering 1856 machine works, now the town's de facto arts center. Part of the building is devoted to a mining museum with historical displays. The center's huge free-span Old Stone Hall features a large pipe organ and a stage, making it a popular venue for local drama and music performances, occasional banquets, and other events. Open

ELEANOR DUMONT, "MADAME MOUSTACHE"

Eleanor Dumont arrived in Nevada City in 1854, a 25-year-old woman with a vague past and a French accent. Within 10 days of her arrival, she held a gala opening for her new gambling house, the ultimate in respectability by gold camp standards. She was an overnight sensation and fabulously successful. Miners, all dusted off for the occasion, came from far and wide to bask in her genteel presence and lose their hard-earned gold dust.

But, almost as suddenly, her fortune faded. After a business partnership soured and before hardrock mining took hold, she grew restless and drifted out of Nevada City in 1856 into less amiable gold camps. Twenty-one years later she turned up in Eureka, Nevada—a harder, stouter, and older woman nicknamed "Madame Moustache" by a California wit. Dumont's new establishment in Eureka offered entertainments other than gambling, and though the Wild West was fast becoming tamed, mining camps had become Dumont's life.

In September 1879, in the desolate High Sierra town of Bodie, she committed suicide and was buried and forgotten. The last line of her obituary, printed in the 1880 *History of Nevada County, California,* read: "Let her many good qualities invoke leniency in criticising her failings."

Mon.–Fri. 10 A.M.–4 P.M. Docent-led tours are available by appointment, but a thorough self-guided-tour pamphlet is always available.

Railroad buffs will enjoy the short narrow-gauge **Nevada County Traction Company** railway ride, 402 Railroad Ave. (next to the Northern Queen Inn), 530/265-0896. A joint project of the Northern Queen and the local historical society, the narrated rail tour winds through woods to the old Chinese cemetery and back. Open 10 A.M.–4 P.M. daily June 1–Sept. 30, Fri.–Tues. the rest of the year. Fare is $6 adults, $3 children.

To play tourist to the hilt, take a carriage tour with **Nevada City Carriage Company,** 431 Uren, 530/265-8778, boarding in front of the National Hotel. Options include a short saunter downtown, custom taxi rides to and from dinner, and various tours. One of these—the Car-

riage House and Stable Tour—heads out to the stunning company stable at the east end of town, home to the company's 20-some draft horses. The carriage house really is something—a 12,000-square-foot replica of a 19th-century gentleman's stable, complete with cobblestone floors and ornate stall dividers. Free walking tours of the carriage house are offered Mon., Fri., and Sat. at 10 A.M. sharp.

Staying in Nevada City

Camping possibilities abound; for public campground information, contact the local **Tahoe National Forest** office, 530/265-4531. Among private tent-pitching and RV possibilities near Nevada City is private **Scotts Flat Lake Recreation Area,** 23333 Scotts Flat Rd. (second gate), 530/265-5302 or 530/265-8861. To get there, head five miles east on Hwy. 20, then four miles south on Scotts Flat Road. This very nice campground offers year-round campsites in the pines near the lake, as well as a beach, swimming, fishing, a playground, hot showers, and a coin laundry. Budget, for up to four persons. Reservations advisable in summer.

If you're in the area to enjoy the great outdoors—kayaking, rock-climbing, mountain biking, or whatever—you'll love the concept behind the **Outside Inn,** 575 E. Broad St., 530/265-2233. Manager and inveterate outdoorswoman Natalie Karwowski has taken a fine old motor court–style motel and turned it into an outdoor-lover's home away from home. Each of the 11 rooms has been remodeled in a specific outdoor-sport theme, and the staff can tell you all the best local places to pursue your particular passion. Very hip. Moderate.

ACCOMMODATIONS RATINGS

Accommodations in this book are rated by price category, based on double-occupancy, high-season rates. Categories used are:

Budget. . . . . $35 and under
Inexpensive $35-60
Moderate $60-85
Expensive $85-110
Premium $110-150
Luxury . . . . $150 and up

THE INN THING

Nevada City offers a stunning selection of bed-and-breakfasts, a real draw for the inn crowd. For an advance online tour of local bed-and-breakfasts, you'll find most listed under www.virtualcities.com. **Grandmere's Inn**, 449 Broad St., 530/265-4660, is generally considered Nevada City's downtown showplace, a grand colonial revival home built in 1856 by former U.S. senator Aaron Sargent—who first introduced women's suffrage legislation—and his wife, Ellen. Premium-Luxury. The 1856 **Emma Nevada House,** 528 E. Broad St., 530/265-4415 or toll-free 800/916-3662, is the childhood home of opera star Emma Nevada—painstakingly restored and transformed into a romantic six-room inn. Scrumptious full breakfast. Premium-Luxury, with a two-night minimum stay on weekends May–December.

Also artistically, architecturally, and historically fascinating, in a more eclectic sense, is the wonderful **Red Castle Inn,** 109 Prospect St. (on the south side of the highway and up the hill; call for directions), 530/265-5135 or toll-free 800/761-4766.

This towering four-story brick home, painted barn red and dripping with white icicle trim, is one of only two genuine Gothic Revival mansions on the West Coast. And the Red Castle has been in business since 1963—well in advance of America's bed-and-breakfast trend—making this perhaps the oldest U.S. hostelry of its type. Vegetarians happily accommodated. Premium.

Surprisingly free of the typical bed-and-breakfast Victoriana is the 1869 **Downey House,** 517 W. Broad St. (atop Nabob Hill), 530/265-2815 or toll-free 800/258-2815, a bright and airy, pale yellow Eastlake Victorian with a very contemporary inner attitude. Each of six large rooms features pastel contemporary decor, a private modern bathroom, and even an aquarium (fish provided). Moderate-Expensive.

For a current listing of the region's historic bed-and-breakfasts or a referral, contact: **Historic Bed and Breakfast Inns of Grass Valley & Nevada City,** P.O. Box 2060, Nevada City, CA 95959, 530/477-6634.

The **Northern Queen Inn,** 400 Railroad Ave., 530/265-5824 or toll-free 800/226-3090, offers modern and clean motel rooms as well as cottage units, all on 34 wooded acres. Amenities include a pool, spa, restaurant, and an affiliated **narrow-gauge railroad** offering free mile-long train rides to guests (nonguests pay $6 adults, $3 children). Moderate-Expensive. For more information on the railroad, contact **Nevada County Traction Company,** 402 Railroad Ave., 530/265-0896.

Nevada City also boasts an impressive number of excellent bed-and-breakfasts. For details, see the special topic The Inn Thing.

Eating in Nevada City

How can a town with barely 2,500 people have so many restaurants, most of them very good? **Cowboy Pizza,** 315 Spring St., 530/265-2334, is the locals' favorite for fast food and quite a find. Cowboy's slogan—"Small children cry for it, mothers ask for it by name"—becomes believable once you pass the "Free Tibet" bumper sticker and open the door. The aroma of garlic is almost overwhelming—garlic blended with traditional gourmet pizza toppings and some very

untraditional ones (like Danish feta cheese, spinach, pine nuts, and onions). Pizzas here take a while, so either call ahead or sit down and enjoy some of California's best microbrews (Red Tail, Sierra Nevada, St. Stan's) while studying the oddball collection of decorative cowboy kitsch, from the Gene Autry: Singing Cowboy poster to the official emblem of Manure Movers of America. Stop by the **Nevada City Bakery Cafe,** 316 Commercial St., 530/470-0298, for great morning pastries and potent coffee, sandwiches and hot specials for lunch, and creative entrées for dinner.

Harder to find (not a tourist joint) but worth it for all-American café fare is the **Northridge Inn,** 773 Nevada St., 530/478-0470. On the menu are fabulous burgers and home fries, café standards like BLT and grilled-cheese sandwiches, *real* milkshakes, and more than 100 beers to choose from, including local Nevada City brews. Dinner entrées include barbecued chicken or ribs, fresh trout, and daily specials. The Northridge is a few minutes' drive from downtown, off Uren at the Hwy. 49/20 junction; ask locally for directions.

Peter Selaya's **New Moon Cafe,** 203 York St., 530/265-6399, Nevada City's bright new bistro, is sure to please even citified connoisseurs. Serving imaginative California-style Mediterranean for the most part—such things as grilled duck and smoked salmon—the New Moon also offers lighter choices, including some outstanding vegetarian fare. And everything's fresh—even the breads and ice cream served here are housemade. Open Tues.–Fri. for lunch and Tues.–Sun. for dinner. Reservations advised.

Romantic creekside atmosphere is the trademark of **Kirby's Creekside Restaurant & Bar,** 101 Broad St., 530/265-3445, one of the best restaurants for miles around. Specializing in international fare—pastas, seafood, steaks, and more—Kirby's is open daily for lunch (brunch on Sunday) and dinner.

NORTH OF NEVADA CITY

Six miles north of Nevada City, before the Hwy. 49 South Yuba River crossing and along Rush Creek, is the **Independence Trail,** constructed *in* a hill-hugging flume to provide wilderness access for people in wheelchairs. The trail provides a nice view of the canyon, and along the way you'll see waterfalls and, in spring, wildflowers. There's even a ramp, with seven switchbacks, leading down to a fishing pool.

The highway snakes on toward **San Juan Ridge.** The Yuba River, called Rio de las Uvas ("River of the Grapes") by the Spanish for the vines woven along its rocky banks, squeezes rugged San Juan Ridge from both sides. During and since the gold rush, the Yuba and its tributaries have yielded more gold than any other U.S. river system. A spot in the road worth a wander, **North San Juan** mixes gold rush memorials with new accomplishments like the lovingly hand-crafted **North San Juan School** built by local people and parents. The long-running Ananda commune near North San Juan, fairly well accepted even by redneck mountain folk, is a notable presence. To the southwest (via Pleasant Valley Rd.) is what's left of **French Corral,** the oldest town on San Juan Ridge, named after a mule pen. The **North San Juan Certified Farmers' Market** convenes every Sat. at 29190 Hwy. 49, 9 A.M.–noon; for information, call 530/292-3458.

To the north is **Bullards Bar Reservoir,** a steep-sided recreation lake with campsites reached from this area via either Moonshine or Marysville Roads. Wandering the narrow back roads from here into the far northern gold camps is only for those with time to get thoroughly lost. But if you have the time and inclination, head out in search of 365-acre **Renaissance Vineyard & Winery,** 12585 Rices Crossing in Oregon House (northwest of Nevada City and northeast of Marysville), 530/692-2222 or toll-free 800/655-3277, sponsored by the Fellowship of Friends, devotees of P. D. Ouspensky and George Gurdjieff. Renaissance's 1985 Special Select Late Harvest Riesling was ranked among the world's top 10 dessert wines by the *Gault Millau* wine journal.

Just north of the bridge over the Yuba River is the turnoff to the **Oregon Creek Day Use Area,** nice for picnicking, swimming, and some shallow wading. The area is popular with nude sunbathers.

Malakoff Diggins

North and then east of Nevada City (about 26 miles) is 3,000-acre Malakoff Diggins State Historic Park, an unforgettable, ecologically horrifying, yet strangely seductive monument reminding one that positive thinking may move mountains, but greed can do it too. Here's the proof—a ghoulish moonscape created by 1870s "high-tech" mining. Hydraulic mining at the Malakoff Mine scoured the area into barren, colorful spires now haunted by the lonely spirit of Utah's Bryce Canyon. You can wander below San Juan Ridge along 16 miles of trails that cut through otherworldly terrain. The park's **North Bloomfield** is a ghost town on the site of old Humbug City, so named and then abandoned by disgusted miners (though rich claims were later found), all part and parcel of the park. Old **Cummins Hall** is the park's interpretive center, with an impressive display of simulated gold plus a working hydraulic mine model and other exhibits.

Camp at **Malakoff Diggins State Historic Park,** which features 30 individual sites plus a group camp, but no showers; sinks with running water in the bathrooms make sponge baths feasible, though. Or stay in one of three restored, original cabins "in town"—rustic, historically evocative, and only $20–30 per night (reservations required at least five days in advance). To reserve campsites or cabins in summer, con-

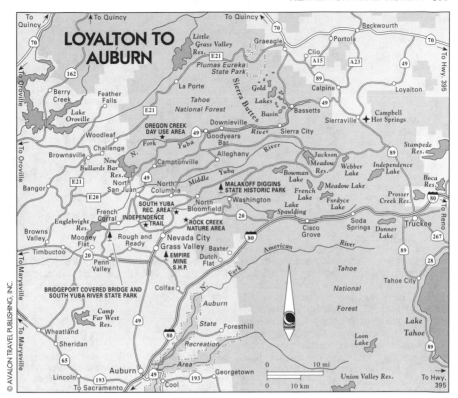

tact ReserveAmerica, toll-free 800/444-7275; otherwise, just show up. The park's interpretive center and other exhibits are open daily 10 A.M.–4:30 P.M. in summer, but in other seasons you may have to track down the ranger to get in. For information: **Malakoff Diggins State Historic Park,** 23579 N. Bloomfield Rd., Nevada City, CA 95959, 530/265-2740.

INTO THE SIERRA NEVADA

Past North San Juan and the intriguing dance of light and shadow on the canyon walls, Hwy. 49 starts climbing to the northernmost reaches of the gold country, up past Loyalton. **Camptonville,** just off the highway, with its old-fashioned flower gardens, was once a booming way station. Lester Alan Pelton, the millwright who invented the tangential waterwheel, lived here before moving to Nevada City. Special in Camptonville is the cowboy continental **Mayo Restaurant,** 15315 Cleveland (the town's main street), 530/288-3237, with creatively prepared soups, salads, and entrées served in a vintage Western saloon. Open for lunch Mon.–Sat., for dinner Wed.–Sat., and for brunch on Sunday.

Downieville is a tidy, tiny brick-and-tin-roof town squeezed into the cool canyon at the confluence of the Yuba and Downie Rivers. **Downieville Heritage Park** (a.k.a. Lions Park), near the river forks downtown, has picnic tables and a rusty outdoor collection of mining mementos; you can pan for gold here, right in town. In the trees near the jailyard of the **Sierra County Courthouse** is the state's only remaining original gallows, used for the first and last time in 1885 to hang convicted murderer James O'Neal.

Modern-day travelers can visit what remains of North Bloomfield, now part of the historic legacy of hydraulic mining preserved at Malakoff Diggins.

CALIFORNIA DEPARTMENT OF PARKS & RECREATION

Another tiny mountain town, **Sierra City** is the kind of place where fathers play football with their small sons—right on the highway—on a Saturday morning in autumn. It's also the reputed birthplace of The Ancient and Honorable Order of E Clampus Vitus, hog Latin meaning "from the handshake comes life." Worth a stop is **Kentucky Mine Park and Museum,** at the Kentucky Mine just north of town. Thanks to the efforts of Sierra County citizenry, the old Kentucky Consolidated Gold Mining Co. hardrock mine is now a beautifully restored historical park, its original machinery still intact. The park is open Wed.–Sun. 10 A.M.–5 P.M., from Memorial Day through Sept., then on weekends only in Oct.; tours of the stamp mill are usually offered at 11 A.M., 1 P.M., and 3 P.M. Closed the rest of the year. For information, call the Sierra County Historical Society at 530/862-1310.

To reach **Lakes Basin,** beyond the Kentucky Mine turn north at Bassetts onto Gold Lakes Highway. The Sierra Buttes area is a dramatic, seemingly unspoiled glacial landscape and a locally popular spot for fishing, swimming, hiking, and backpacking in summer and cross-country skiing in winter. For a map and guide to the Lakes Basin area, as well as recreation and other information, contact the **Eastern Plumas Chamber of Commerce,** toll-free 800/995-6057, www.psln.com/epluchmb, and the **Plumas County Visitors Bureau,** P.O. Box 4120, Quincy, CA 95971, 530/283-6345 or toll-free 800/326-2247, www.plumas.ca.us.

Popular, semirustic resort-style stays in the area include **Gold Lake Lodge,** 530/836-2350 or 530/836-2751, with 11 charming but rustic cabins (portable heaters), some with shared baths. Premium, breakfast and dinner included. Or sim-

E CLAMPUS VITUS

Members of a gold rush fraternity established in 1857, the Clampers were and are a parody of brotherhoods like the Masons and Odd Fellows. The organization's stated purpose was assisting and comforting orphans and "widders"—especially the latter. In addition to this vital public service, and the many worthwhile community activities the group actually *did* support, Clampers spent most of their time holding drunken initiation ceremonies and thinking up overblown titles to recognize all members' equality. Throughout the gold country, E Clampus Vitus met in their "Halls of Comparative Ovations" (the Latin motto over the door meaning "I believe because it is absurd").

Revived in San Francisco in 1931 by historian Carl Wheat, E Clampus Vitus thrives today, its primary modern mission marking historical sites and otherwise bringing early California history to life. But the order's debauched traditions continue to this day, with drunken annual celebrations still sometimes causing consternation for Sierra City citizenry.

ply plan to eat at the pleasant restaurant (call ahead if you're not a resort guest). An all-time favorite but a bit farther away is the **Gray Eagle Lodge,** on Gold Lake Rd. in Blairsden, 530/836-2511 or toll-free in Northern California 800/635-8778, www.grayeaglelodge.com. Cabins are basic but comfortable. Luxury, breakfast and dinner included. Gray Eagle's pine-log-walled **Firewoods** restaurant is noted at dinner for fresh fish, prime rib, and fine wines (reservations necessary). The **High Country Inn,** 100 Greene Rd. (some distance north of town at Bassetts and the junction with Gold Lakes Rd.), HCR 2, Box 7, Sierra City, CA 96125, 530/862-1530 or toll-free 800/862-1530, is a modern mountain home in an astounding setting—and a welcoming bed-and-breakfast. Moderate-Premium.

From the Gold Lakes area, head to Graeagle and nearby Johnsville (turn at Rd. A14). One of those almost-undiscovered outdoor gems, **Plumas-Eureka State Park,** a ghost town mining camp in steep canyon country crowned by thick pines and firs, offers good hiking, fine summer camping, a ski-tour trail in winter, and even limited, low-key downhill ski facilities. When the land was owned by the Sierra Buttes Mining Co. in the 19th century, one of the area's old mining trams served as the world's first ski lift when snowbound miners organized, promoted, and wagered on high-speed downhill ski competitions. For more information, contact: Plumas-Eureka State Park, 310 Johnsville Rd., Blairsden, CA 96103, 530/836-2380.

GRASS VALLEY

Some people, including many who live here, think of Grass Valley as a redneck alternative to the effete egghead ambience of neighboring Nevada City. It's hometown working-class America, complete with fast food, but Grass Valley has a charm all its own, especially downtown, where a sidewalk stroll takes you straight into the '50s (of both the 1800s and the 1900s).

In 1850, George McKnight discovered gold-laced quartz here, and Grass Valley, a company town of former copper miners and their kin from England's Cornwall, quickly became a hardrock mining capital. It's estimated that nearly a billion dollars in gold was deep-mined in and around

---

THE NOTORIOUS LOLA MONTEZ AND LITTLE LOTTA CRABTREE

Most fascinating of all Grass Valley's characters were two women: Lola Montez and Lotta Crabtree. The infamous Lola Montez was a charming Irish actress from Galway who reinvented herself as a Spanish dancer. The mistress of pianist Franz Liszt, but pursued by Honoré de Balzac, Alexandre Dumas, and Victor Hugo, Montez (Liza Gilbert) was eventually run out of Europe and came to California during the gold rush, where she single-handedly created more excitement than the completion of the transcontinental railroad. Montez's notorious "spider dance" (the arachnids may have been imaginary, but the kick-off-your-knickers dance routine was real) was too popular in sophisticated San Francisco. After about three days in any city venue, the fire department had to be called in to hose down the overheated all-male crowd.

Finally run out of the City, Lola moved to the goldfields, where her spider dance was jeered by miners. So Montez retired to Grass Valley with her husband, a bear, and a monkey. She stayed long enough to scandalize respectable women, send her hubby packing after he shot her bear, and encourage the career of schoolgirl Lotta Crabtree before setting sail for Australia, where she continued her career and lectured in theosophy.

Little Lotta Crabtree sang and danced her way into the hearts of California's miners and later the world. The darling of the gold camps, Lotta began her career at age six and was the first entertainer ever to become a millionaire. When she died in 1924 at age 77, she left $4 million to charity.

Grass Valley during the gold rush. The high cost of underground mining meant capital investment and consolidation: the Idaho-Maryland, North Star, and Empire Mines soon became the area's main operations. The Empire Mine, now a state park but once the largest of these 19th-century mining conglomerates—some say the richest gold mine in the United States—operated profitably until the 1950s.

The **Grass Valley/Nevada County Chamber of Commerce,** 248 Mill St., Grass Valley, CA 95945, 530/273-4667, toll-free within Cali-

the Bourn "cottage" at
Empire Mine State
Historic Park

KIM WEIR

fornia 800/655-4667, occupies the rebuilt Lola Montez home. The staff is very helpful, providing maps, a walking-tour guide, and information on current events, accommodations, and eateries. For additional information, contact the **Grass Valley Downtown Association**, 151 Mill St., 530/272-8315.

Seeing and Doing Grass Valley

The **Lola Montez House,** 248 Mill St. (a replica of the original building condemned and demolished in 1975), now houses the chamber of commerce and a small one-room museum displaying some of Lola's belongings. The town's first election was held here in November 1850. Two doors down at 238 Mill is **Lotta Crabtree's House** (now private apartments), where Lola Montez taught the six-year-old redhead to dance and sing.

Down the street, the **Grass Valley Public Library,** 207 Mill St., 530/273-4117, was built in 1916 with Carnegie funds on the site of Josiah Royce's birthplace. Mark Twain slept at the impressive **Holbrooke Hotel,** 212 W. Main Street. The site originally housed two separate buildings, but both were later destroyed by fire. The saloon was rebuilt immediately (gold-country priorities) and the later hotel incorporated it, so now the hotel has two separate bars. At the end of Main St. is **Lyman Gilmore's airfield** (now a school), where he reportedly flew his 20-horsepower steam-powered aircraft on or before May 15, 1901—more than a year and a half before the Wright brothers took off from Kitty Hawk.

Grass Valley's main attraction is **Empire Mine State Historic Park,** 10791 E. Empire St., 530/273-8522 or 530/273-7714. It's easy to find by following the signs around town. English miners from Cornwall, called "cousin Jacks," worked this mine complex on Gold Hill, one of the oldest and most profitable hardrock mines in the state. In business for more than 100 years, the Empire's 367 miles of tunnels reluctantly yielded millions of ounces of gold. The mine closed for business in 1956 and is now a 784-acre state park. The **Bourn "Cottage,"** an elegant epistle to wealth tucked into the estate's impressive gardens, was designed by San Francisco architect Willis Polk for mine owner William Bowers Bourn II. It was built from mine tailings and stone, paneled inside with hand-rubbed heart redwood, and finished with leaded stained-glass windows. Take the tour and appreciate the original furnishings. See the mining and geology displays at the **visitors center** and museum. Down the hill are the well-preserved mine offices, machine shop, retort room and furnaces, and hoist house. Most of the mine shafts are now flooded, so forget about an underground hike—though you can get a feeling for life in the tunnels by taking the stairs down into the one open shaft as far as it goes. The **Hardrock Trail,** a two-mile walk through the forest past mining relics and old shafts, loops up into the hills for a peek at the remains of the Betsy, Daisy Hill, and Prescott Mines.

The park is open daily year-round, 10 A.M.–5 P.M. (9 A.M.–5 P.M. in May, and 9 A.M.–6 P.M.

June–August). Films and slide shows are offered regularly, tours of the "cottage" and grounds usually depart at 1 P.M., and tours of the mine typically start at 2 P.M. (Hours and schedules for all events vary considerably with the seasons, so call ahead.) Small admission. Other area mines include the **North Star Mining Museum** on Allison Ranch Rd., near the intersection of Mill St. and McCourtney Rd., 530/273-4255, where mining technology displays include the 10-ton Pelton wheel—the world's largest—used to harness water power and later to generate power for the mines with air compressors. The museum is open May through mid-Oct., daily 10 A.M.–5 P.M.; admission by donation. The docents do an exceptional job.

A restored 1863 convent, orphanage, and school behind imposing brick walls, the Old Mount St. Mary's Academy (and St. Joseph's Chapel), 410 S. Church St. (at Chapel St.), 530/273-5509, is home to the **Grass Valley Museum,** where exhibits include period memorabilia, a music room, parlor, doctor's office, some fine old lace, and a collection of glass slippers, all on the convent's 2nd floor.

Staying in Grass Valley

Contact the chamber of commerce for complete listings of local accommodations. For something truly unique, consider the **Sivananda Ashram Yoga Farm,** 530/272-9322, where outdoor options include tent camping and tepees, and farmhouse choices include both dorm and private rooms (Budget-Inexpensive).

Top of the mark is the fine **Holbrooke Hotel and Restaurant,** downtown at 212 W. Main St., 530/273-1353 or toll-free 800/933-7077, where rich green colors and fine wood interiors create an atmosphere of seasoned elegance. The 28 authentic gold rush–era rooms have been completely restored and are named for luminaries and famous lunatics who once snored here. This historic landmark is one of a few truly fine gold country hotels, and its rates are remarkably reasonable. Moderate-Premium.

For casual artsy surroundings, try the **Swan-Levine House,** 328 S. Church St., 530/272-1873, an 1867 Queen Anne Victorian that's a home away from home for the artistic soul (both owners are artists). Moderate-Expensive. Most elegant is the legendary 1866 **Murphy's Inn,** 318 Neal

THE MUSEUM OF ANCIENT AND MODERN ART (MAMA)

Worth looking into in Penn Valley is the Museum of Ancient and Modern Art, located in the Wildwood Business Center, one mile north of Hwy. 20 at 11392 Pleasant Valley Rd., Penn Valley, CA 95946, 916/432-3080, www.mama.org, a volunteer-run organization of "dedicated, zany, zealous artists." MAMA's mainstay of ancient art is a collection of Western Asiatic artifacts excavated at Amarna in the 1920s and '30s under the auspices of the Egypt Exploration Society, including the largest collection of 18th Dynasty Egypt in North America. Masks, pottery, and statues collected here also come from Greece, Rome, Alexandria, Carthage, Mesopotamia, Assyria, Sumer, and other significant sites of antiquity. Also impressive are the African masks and statues from 20 tribes and eight countries. Particularly appropriate to its location in the gold country is the museum's collection of ancient gold jewelry—examples from Neolithic to historical times, many of the more spectacular pieces part of the Theodora Van Runkel Collection of Ancient Gold.

The modern art here includes works on paper spanning the 15th to 20th centuries, from an extensive and exquisite collection of Rembrandt etchings to works from many schools, including Manet, Renoir, Goya, Picasso, Chagall, Miró, and Matisse. Also at home at MAMA: historical art books that document the history of printing as well as art. Major exhibits, from the museum's rotating collection, change every few weeks.

The museum also supports research, cataloging, documentation, and conservation/preservation programs related to its collection. Donations of art and money are welcome. A tax-exempt nonprofit educational organization, MAMA raises funds primarily from memberships and special events. The museum also sells books and educational toys through its gift shop, and offers art education classes, art-collecting classes, and free Saturday morning art workshops for children.

The Museum of Ancient and Modern Art is open daily 10 A.M.–5 P.M., Sat. until 7 P.M. Docent-led tours are available for groups. Admission is free. If you can't get here in person, one of these days MAMA's cyber museum will be available online.

St. (at School St.), 530/273-6873 or toll-free 800/895-2488, once the personal estate of North Star and Idaho mine owner Edward Coleman. This Victorian-era inn has eight large opulent rooms, all with private baths and four with fireplaces. Outside are exquisite gardens, a comfortable ivy-trimmed porch, and a 140-year-old redwood tree towering over the large outdoor deck. Breakfast is a feast. Expensive-Luxury.

Eating in Grass Valley

Grass Valley has the certified farmers' markets. The **Grass Valley Friday Market** is held downtown at Mill and Main Sts. on Fri., July–Oct. 5:30–9 P.M. The **Grass Valley-Nevada County Certified Farmers' Market** convenes at the Nevada County Fairgrounds (Gate #4), 11228 McCourtney Rd., May–Oct. 9 A.M.–noon.

While in town, sample the local specialty: Cornish pasties—historical fast food. These hot turnover-like pies with various spicy meat and vegetable fillings were favored by early miners. The best ones are found at **Mrs. Dubblebee's,** 251-C S. Auburn St., 530/272-7700, but you also won't go wrong at **King Richard's Pasties,** 217

Colfax (near the freeway), 530/273-0286, and **Marshall's Pasties,** 203 Mill St., 530/272-2844.

A local landmark is cozy brick-and-oak **Tofanelli's,** 302 W. Main St., 530/272-1468; open daily for breakfast, lunch (brunch on weekends), and dinner. Every breakfast you can imagine is on the menu, or dream up your own egg specialty with their design-your-own omelettes. At lunch, you'll find sandwiches, salads, lots of burger choices (including veggie burgers). Good dinner specials and reasonable "early-bird" dinners.

The **Holbrooke Hotel Restaurant,** 212 W. Main St., 530/273-1353, is excellent for continental and American lunches and dinners (written up in *Bon Appétit,* no less), as well as a famous weekend brunch. If you pass up the onion rings, you might have room for a piece of the Holbrooke's locally famous Chocolate Hazelnut Cake. Weather permitting, dine out on the patio. Open for lunch weekdays, for dinner Mon.–Sat., and for brunch on Sunday. Just across the street from the Holbrooke is another contender in the fine food sweeps: the **Main Street Saloon & Eatery,** 213 W. Main, 530/477-6000, contemporary and casual.

SOUTH FROM GRASS VALLEY

AUBURN

Hill-hugging Auburn, once a tent city called North Fork Dry Diggins, then Wood's Dry Diggins, was one of the first towns in the gold country. In the spring of 1848, Frenchman Claude Chana, a friend of James Marshall, found three gold nuggets here while panning in the north fork of the American River. Auburn today has a small Old Town, a homey downtown, shady old streets lined with Victorian homes, and some fine restaurants. The Auburn *Journal* has published regularly since 1852, its longevity (and the town's) assured by the construction of the transcontinental railroad through here. These days both Hwy. 49 and I-80 provide most of the traffic.

The **Auburn Area Chamber of Commerce,** 601 Lincoln Way, Auburn, CA 95603, 530/885-5616, is housed in the attractive and restored railroad depot, open weekdays 9 A.M.–5 P.M. Stop by to pick up the local walking-tour brochure and other visitor information. The helpful **Placer County Visitor Information Center,** 13464 Lincoln Way, Auburn, CA 95603, 530/887-2111, is open Wed.–Sun. 9 A.M.–4 P.M.—though you can peruse the racks outside at other times, or call or write for information in advance.

Seeing and Doing Auburn

Downtown Auburn, the business district along Lincoln Way, is distinctly Midwestern; visitors feel more like neighbors than suckered tourists. Old Town, a national landmark, is nearby but separate—a five-square-block area at the intersection of Lincoln and Sacramento Streets. The stately **Placer County Courthouse** on Lincoln, its impressive arcaded dome looming above Old Town, was built in 1849, entirely of local materials. The town's volunteer fire department, established in 1852, is the state's oldest. But the odd four-story, red-and-white **Hook and Ladder Company Firehouse** in Old Town was built in 1893. Inside is California's first motorized fire engine. Antique hunters like the area for its antiquities and junk shops. Take a peek inside the **Shanghai Bar,** 289 Washington St., Auburn's oldest bar, almost a museum.

Actual area museums include the fine **Gold Country Museum** at the fairgrounds, 1273 High St., 530/887-0690, open Tues.–Sun. 10 A.M.–4 P.M., closed holidays (small fee). Nearby is the **Bernhard Museum Complex,** 291 Auburn-Folsom Rd., 530/888-6891, actually an annex of the main museum (same hours, one ticket admits you to both), an old Auburn family home furnished with Victorian antiques typical of the 1800s' middle class. Do stop by the grandly domed, meticulously restored Placer County Courthouse, 101 Maple, on a rise above Old Town. Now home to the free **Placer County Museum,** 530/889-6500, displays emphasize local history, including the Placer County Gold Collection (inside the gift shop). Open Tues.–Sun. 10 A.M.–4 P.M. Then appreciate the courthouse itself—its fine wood, marble stairways, and terrazzo floors. The prettiest picture of all, though, may be from outside at night.

Staying in Auburn

Camping is least expensive. The **Auburn KOA,** 3550 KOA Way (exit I-80 at Hwy. 49 or Bell Rd.), 530/885-0990, has all the usual KOA amenities, and in this location a pool, pond, and playground. Tent sites (all prices for two people) are $21, RV spots $28 (water and electric only), $30 (full hookups), and $32 (prime hookups). In town, a good deal for tent campers is **Bear River Park** on Plum Tree Rd., 530/889-7750, $6 per night per vehicle.

Most of Auburn's motels line the I-80 freeway north of town near the Foresthill turnoff. Take your pick. Auburn's showplace bed-and-breakfast inn, the **Powers Mansion Inn** downtown at 164 Cleveland Ave., 530/885-1166, is a luxurious, pastel pink Victorian beauty built by gold rush millionaire Harold T. Powers at the turn of the century. It offers 15 unique rooms with antique touches yet with modern private baths. The suites are something special, with a heart-shaped hot tub big enough for two in the Honeymoon Suite. Breakfast is served in the dining room downstairs. Expensive-Premium.

Other choices in the area include the **Auburn Valley Ranch,** 11300 Lone Star Rd., 530/269-0160, which has a pool, spa, and mountain views

AUBURN TO ANGELS CAMP

(Moderate-Premium), and two B&Bs in Loomis: the **Old Flower Farm,** 4150 Auburn-Folsom Rd., 916/652-4200, offering three rooms plus a country cottage (Expensive-Premium), and **Emma's,** 3137 Taylor Rd., 916/652-1392 or toll-free 800/660-5157, with four suites and a cottage (Premium).

Eating in Auburn

The **Auburn Certified Farmers' Market** convenes every Sat., 8 A.M.–noon, at the intersection of Lincoln Way and Auburn-Folsom Rd.; for information, call 530/823-6183. But if you're not here on a Saturday, stop instead at family-owned-and-operated **Ikeda's** just off I-80 at 13500 Lincoln Way, 530/885-5243, a wonderful full-service food emporium that's been an Auburn institution, in one form or another, since 1950. Ikeda's includes a dynamite burger bar, espresso bar, fresh-fruit pie shop, fruit smoothie counter, and impressive fresh produce and gourmet food shop. If coming from Sacramento, take the Foresthill exit from I-80; from Tahoe/Reno, take the Bowman exit. Fast fooderies line the freeway frontage. Best of the bunch is **In-N-Out Burger,** located close to downtown at the junction of I-80 and Hwy. 49.

Bootleggers Old Town Tavern & Grill, at home in Auburn's old-brick original city hall, 210 Washington St., 530/889-2229, looks something like a boardinghouse cum barn, yet the food here is far from bumpkin fare—great rib eye steak and barbecued baby back ribs, sure, but also grilled shrimp, fried oysters, vegetarian spring rolls, Indonesian satays, chicken strudel, baked Brie—everything surprisingly consistent. Wine and beer are available, including some 50 bottled beers, both imported and domestic. Open Tues.–Sat. for lunch, Tues.–Sun. for dinner.

Exceptional **Latitudes,** in the White House at 130 Maple (across from the county courthouse in Old Town), 530/885-9535, serves healthful and intriguing international cuisine in serene historic surroundings. Much of the fare here is vegetarian—a flavorful and risk-taking, ever-changing "world cuisine" menu, from chilled fruit soups, spicy curried tofu, and fettuccine Alfredo to gingered prawns and filet of salmon. Full bar downstairs with plentiful beer—including Sierra Nevada Pale Ale and Deschutes' Obsidian Stout on tap—and wine selections. Open for lunch weekdays only, dinner Wed.–Sun., and brunch on Sunday.

French-country regional fare in these parts means a reservation at tiny **Le Bilig French Cafe,** 11750 Atwood Rd. (look for the "Bail Bonds" sign), 530/888-1491, which features a changing menu of hearty dishes. Beer and wine only. Open Wed.–Sat. for dinner. But for something truly special, reserve a table on the second Sunday of the month—a fixed-price feast.

COLOMA

Birthplace of the Gold Rush

Coloma was the site of a former Cullooma Maidu village but is most notable for its historic role as birthplace of the California gold rush. By 1849, more than 10,000 miners populated this tiny valley, but just two years later the town was "golddry" and dull (at least by miners' standards). Most of Coloma is now part of the 240-acre **Marshall Gold Discovery State Historic Park.**

EVENTFUL COLOMA

In May, Coloma hosts its **Art in the Park** weekend arts and crafts festival in conjunction with El Dorado County's Celebrate the Arts week. For drama and melodrama on weekend nights (May–Sept.), try the Crescent Players' performances at the **Olde Coloma Theatre,** 380 Monument Trail (just up the hill off Cold Springs Road). Tickets are $10 ($5 for children 12 and under); call 530/626-5282 for reservations. Come in mid-June for **Historic Demonstration Day,** when costumed docents display all kinds of ancient arts, from rope making to pine-needle basketry. **Gold Rush Days** and the **U.S. National Goldpanning Championship** (in some years Coloma hosts the World Goldpanning Championships) are scheduled concurrently in late Sept./early Oct., a tent-city circus including goldpanning lessons, a market, parade, live music, and living history demonstrations. Big doin's here in winter include the **Christmas in Coloma** festivities each December and **Discovery Day,** January 24. Tours of the town's **Pioneer Cemetery** are offered on weekends, subject to the availability of docents. For current information on local events, contact the state park office.

Sutter's Mill in Marshall Gold Discovery State Historic Park

ROBERT HOLMES/CALTOUR

The park is open 8 A.M.–sunset year-round. The day-use fee is $3 per vehicle ($2 for seniors). For information on the park or special events, contact: **Marshall Gold Discovery State Historic Park,** 310 Back St., P.O. Box 265, Coloma, CA 95613, 530/622-3470.

Seeing and Doing Coloma

The park's main attraction, with summer tourists buzzing around it like wasps, is the full-size replica of **Sutter's Mill** near the river. Demonstrations and lectures about how it works are held daily at 2 P.M. Adjacent is a restored miners' cabin.

The park's **Gold Museum** and visitors center, across the highway from the mill, is first-rate and a good place to start exploring. Here are a rare collection of Maidu artifacts, history exhibits, some of James Marshall's memorabilia, plus dioramas and films. Open daily 10 A.M.–5 P.M., except on major holidays.

Also explore the stone-and-shuttered **Wah Hop Store and Bank,** a revivified Chinese general store; on display are herbs and animal parts for medicinal potions, an altar and ancestral portraits, business desk, tea cups, and rice bowls. Another store—and you can shop at this one— is the **Argonaut,** a soda fountain and candy shop with home-brewed root beer. Farther south, note the freestanding steel jail cell and crumbling old stone jailhouse ruins. Nearby is the new **Papini House Museum,** a turn-of-the-20th-century home complete with antique garden

tools. Other sights and activities include mining technique demonstrations, stagecoaches, and the old "Mormon Cabin" (a reconstruction of Marshall's cabin, downhill from his final resting place near the Catholic church). Art lovers should peek into the 1855 **Friday House,** the gallery home of the late artist George Mathis. On the hill behind Coloma is a monumental **statue of James Marshall,** erected in belated gratitude by the state after his death.

Practical Coloma

Home base for area **hot-air ballooning**—ask about combined balloon-and-bed packages—is the fine and friendly **Coloma Country Inn,** 345 High St. (just a two-block stroll from Sutter's Mill), 530/622-6919. This Cape Cod–style home with sitting porch and gardens has been painstakingly restored, with five quilt-cozied guest rooms (two with shared bath) in the main house, and two suites in the carriage house. Expensive-Premium.

More rustic is the **American River Resort,** 6019 New River Rd., 530/622-6700, on the banks of the American River near where James Marshall discovered gold. Cabins are Moderate-Expensive and campsites are $18–24 (open year-round). The American River Resort has a swimming pool, fishing pond, and a miniature animal farm for the kiddies.

For a sit-down meal try the **Coloma Club Cafe,** on Hwy. 49 at Marshall Rd., 530/626-6390, where you'll get Western humor and generous helpings (the lasagna is particularly good). The club is open daily, with live C&W music on weekend nights. If it's pizza you crave, head to **Yosum's Pizza,** 7312 Hwy. 49, 530/622-9277.

Vicinity of Coloma

"Mr. Gold Rush" James Marshall, reclusive blacksmith, lived in nearby **Kelsey** from 1848 until he died, penniless, in 1885. His blacksmith shop still stands just outside town, though most of Marshall's memorabilia is in the museum at Coloma. Also here in the far north of the mythic Mother Lode, on the divide between the American River's north and south forks, **Georgetown** is like a tiny New England hill town with pretty Victorians and fragrant rose gardens. It was once called Growlersburg, because the nuggets found here were so large they "growled" in the gold pans. The balconied **Georgetown Hotel,** 6260 Main St., 530/333-2848, is a reasonably priced place to hang your hat. Inexpensive. Even if you're just passing through, stop by to eat here and to appreciate the rough stone bar and fireplace, rich woodwork, and eclectic furnishings: tractor seat barstools, decorative farm equipment, cowboy boots dangling from the ceiling. Live music, usually on weekends. The 1853 **American River Inn,** at Main and Orleans, P.O. Box 43, Georgetown, CA 95634, 530/333-4499 or toll-free 800/245-6566, was once a Wells Fargo office and a mining camp boardinghouse. Today it offers nothing but elegant country-style luxury, with a pool, spa, lovely gardens, an aviary, and yes, an antique shop. Breakfasts here are fabulous. Expensive.

PLACERVILLE AND VICINITY

HANGTOWN

Hangtown and Oak Tree Justice

Known at one time or another as Dry Diggins, Ravine City, and Hangtown—in honor of the locals' enthusiastic administration of oak tree justice—Placerville was a wild town in bygone days. Today the seat of El Dorado County and the historical heart of the gold country, Placerville was strategically located on the old Overland Trail (now Hwy. 50) and the road to Coloma. The town prospered during the rush to Nevada's Comstock Lode; it was a chief way station en route, boasting telegraph, Pony Express, and Overland Mail service.

A few industrial kingpins got their start here. Railroad magnate Mark Hopkins set up shop on Main St., peddling groceries from Sacramento. Canned meat king Philip Armour ran a small butcher shop here. John Studebaker built wheelbarrows for miners, one-wheeled predecessors of his later automobiles. And Leland Stanford, progenitor of Stanford University, ran a store in nearby Cold Springs.

These days, Placerville is losing much of its charm to progress and is often crowded to overflowing with a fast-growing local population and Tahoe traffic. Placerville has a huge, free parking garage downtown. The **El Dorado County Chamber of Commerce,** 542 Main St., Placerville, CA 95667, 530/621-5885, www.eldoradocounty.org, offers information on what's going on plus free maps and guides.

The county boasts about 35 wineries, most of these near Placerville. A complete list of them is available at the chamber office; from the **El Dorado Wine Grape Growers Association,** P.O. Box 248, 530/626-4329, www.atasteofeldorado.com, and from the **El Dorado Winery Association,** P.O. Box 1614, toll-free 800/306-3956, www.eldoradowines.org.

Seeing and Doing Hangtown

The town's pride and joy is the 60-acre **Gold Bug Mine** in Gold Bug Park (about a mile north of town on Bedford Ave.), 530/642-5232, www.goldbugpark.org, the only city-owned gold mine in the country. Take a tour of the well-lit Gold Bug, one of 250 gold mines once active within the park's perimeter; bring a sweater. Open daily 10 A.M.–4 P.M. from mid-Apr. through Oct., and only on weekends noon–4 P.M. from mid-Mar. to mid-Apr. and in Nov. (closed Dec. through mid-March). Small admission.

The **El Dorado County Historical Museum,** 104 Placerville Dr. at the county fairgrounds two miles west of town, 530/621-5865, is worth a stop. Exhibits in the yard full of aged vehicles and equipment include a restored Concord stagecoach, one of Studebaker's wheelbarrows, Pony Express paraphernalia, and a pair of Snowshoe Thompson's skis. Open Wed.–Sat. 10 A.M.–4 P.M., Sun. noon–4 P.M. Admission free.

In downtown Hangtown, 305 Main marks the spot where Hangtown's old hangin' tree once grew; a doomed dummy strung up from the second story of the Hangman's Tree Bar offers graphic testimony to the reality of the bad ol' days. Hangtown's old fire bell, used to summon both vigilantes and volunteer firefighters, also hangs—from an 1898 steel tower up the street at Main and Center. The narrow, rugged old firehouse is now **Placerville City Hall,** at Main and Bedford Streets. The local **courthouse,** circa 1912, is flanked by two Civil War cannons. The classic brick **Cary House,** which replaced the old Raffles Hotel at 300 Main, is worth a looksee; today it's an elegant hostelry also housing professional offices.

Staying in Hangtown

The best bet, really, is a stay at the refurbished and cheerful 19th-century **Historic Cary House Hotel,** downtown at 300 Main St., 530/622-4271 or toll-free 800/537-8438, with fresh but simple rooms, all with private baths and many with kitchenettes. Moderate-Premium.

Or try a B&B. The elegant **Chichester-McKee House,** 800 Spring St., 530/626-1882 or toll-free 800/831-4008, is an 1892 Victorian featuring four guest rooms with fireplaces, a parlor, library, conservatory, and large porches. A full breakfast is served in the dining room. Moderate-Expensive. The spectacular **Combellack-Blair House,** 3059 Cedar Ravine Rd., 530/622-3764, is another lovely local Victorian with four rooms, all with private bath. The porch swing adds to the old-days ambience, as do the gardens. Premium. North of town near Chili Bar, the **River Rock Inn,** 530/622-7640, has four rooms all opening onto the deck (with hot tub) above the American River. Two rooms have half baths. Children are genuinely welcome, and a full breakfast is served. Moderate-Expensive. For a current regional bed-and-breakfast brochure, send a self-addressed, stamped envelope to: **Historic Country Inns of El Dorado County,** P.O. Box 106, Placerville, CA 95667; call toll-free 877/262-4667; or try www. comspark.com/eldoinns.

Eating in Hangtown

The **Placerville Certified Farmers' Market** convenes May–Oct. on Sat., 8 A.M.–noon, at Main St. and Cedar Ravine Road. For information, call 530/622-0262.

Placerville is the hometown of "Hangtown Fry," a surprisingly tasty creation of oysters and bacon wrapped up in an omelette, first concocted during the days of the gold rush. To try it, stop downtown at the **Bell Tower Café,** 423 Main St., 530/626-3483, or head for **Chuck's Restaurant,** 1318 Broadway, 530/622-2858. A best bet at breakfast and lunch is **Sweetie Pies,** 577 Main, 530/642-0128, where coffee and a pecan roll (or two) will sweeten you up at breakfast. For lunch, order quiche and a green salad or house-made soup and sourdough bread. Don't pass up the olallieberry pie.

The **Hangtown Grill,** 423 Main, 530/626-4431, offers traditional American fare for breakfast, lunch, and dinner. Open daily except Wednesday. For more American café fare, try **Cafe Sarah's,** 301 Main (across from the Cary House Hotel), 530/621-4680, which serves basic breakfasts and burgers and such at lunch. A new culinary star in town is inventive California-style **Café Luna,** on the creek at 451 Main St., 530/642-8669, where the fare often takes on a European accent. The menu changes weekly, but expect everything from vegetarian fusion and pastas to marinated flank steak. Open Mon.–Sat. for lunch, Wed.–Sat. for dinner.

Eating near Hangtown

Still a fine-dining find east of Diamond Springs just south of Placerville is the exceptional **Zachary Jacques,** 1821 Pleasant Valley Rd., 530/626-8045, noted for its seasonal French-country wonders, from cassoulet to King Salmon in puff pastry. Wine and beer only (excellent wine list). Full dinners are served Wed.–Sun., with a light menu available in the wine bar after 4:30 P.M. Reservations advised, especially on weekends.

APPLE HILL APPLES~AND WINES

On the ridge east from Placerville to near Camino, the Apple Hill "tour" follows a path originally blazed by Pony Express riders—a great bike ride when the roads aren't choked with cars. It's hard to believe that half a million people visit this suburban ranch region each autumn, but they do; weekend traffic then is a nightmare. The reason for the influx? In late summer and fall, farms along the way sell tree-fresh apples and delectable, decadent homemade treats—apple pies and strudel, cheesecake, other fine baked goods, apple cider, spicy apple butter, and even caramel and fudge apples. Earlier in the year you can get cherries, strawberries, plums, peaches, and pears; natural honey is available year-round. A year-round calendar of events, from the **Father's Day Cherry Festival** to the **Harvest Festival**, keep the crowds coming. People also come up to Apple Hill in November and December to cut their own locally grown yule trees.

Get a free Apple Hill growers map and other information at the **Apple Hill Visitor Center**, 2461 Larsen Dr. in Camino, 530/644-7692, www.applehill.com, or receive the map in the mail by sending your name, address, and $1 for postage and handling to: **Apple Hill Growers Association**, P.O. Box 494, Camino, CA 95709. Just a half block from Apple Hill's visitors center is the **Camino Hotel Bed and Breakfast**, 4103 Carson Rd., 530/644-7740, a fully renovated historic hotel (The Seven Mile House) along the old Carson Trail. Moderate-Expensive.

Fruit of the vine is also a hot item around Apple Hill. Get winery information here or in Placerville (see above), then set out to explore—a wine tasting adventure that takes you as far south as **Fair Play** and **Somerset**. If what you need is a *beer,* though, head for the **Jack Russell Brewing Co.**, 2380 Larsen Dr. (off Carson Rd.) in Camino, 530/644-4722. This microbrewery doggedly produces three British-style ales using finishing hops grown right here on the farm. Tours, tasting, and picnicking are available. Open daily 11 A.M.–5 P.M.

AMADOR WINE COUNTRY

Heading south from Placerville on Hwy. 49 toward Jackson, the rolling foothills become the steep canyon sides of the Cosumnes River—the Sierra Nevada's only undammed river—and suddenly Amador County visitor information becomes useful. **Plymouth,** formerly Pokerville

then Puckerville, was a late-in-the-game but lucrative mining center.

The action these days is at area wineries. To the east, the Shenandoah Valley flourishes with foothill vineyards and winemakers—impressive California zinfandel country. But it's been California zin country for more than 150 years; the region's winemaking history reaches back to the days of the gold rush. Most wineries can be reached from Plymouth via Plymouth-Shenandoah Rd. (Rd. E-16). Most famous for a taste and a tour is the **Sobon Estate,** just northeast of town at 14430 Shenandoah Rd., 209/245-6554. Sobon took over the old D'Agostini winery, the fourth-oldest winery in California and a state historic landmark. The **Shenandoah Valley Museum** here offers free self-guided tours that include the vintage (1856) stone cellar, old casks made from local oak, coopering equipment, old farm equipment, and old-fashioned household items—something like a historical overview of the entire area. The winery and museum are open daily 9:30 A.M.–5 P.M. except holidays.

FIDDLETOWN

Bret Harte immortalized this rowdy placer mining town in "An Episode of Fiddletown," though today it's considerably calmer. A friendly, slightly down-at-the-heels spot in the road, Fiddletown was reportedly named by a Missourian who noted the townspeople's fondness for "fiddlin'" (though what he meant is still a matter of speculation, since he didn't mention violins). Center of social life here is the old **Fiddletown General Store,** where locals loiter on the front porch and gossip. Walk down Oleta Rd. to see most of the town's older buildings. Rare in California is the 1850s Chinese rammed-earth adobe **Chew Kee Store,** now a museum on Main Street. A medicinal herb shop run by the doctors Yee (father and son), it was in remarkably good shape even before its relatively recent restoration. The tiny museum is open for a couple of hours each Saturday in summer. Nearby is the brick-and-stone Chinese "gambling hall," next to the old blacksmith shop (complete with original forge). During the gold rush, Fiddletown was home to the state's largest Chinese population outside San Francisco.

To get oriented, pick up free wine-tour pamphlets locally or send a stamped, self-addressed business-size envelope to **Amador Vintners' Association,** P.O. Box 667, Plymouth, CA 95669, 209/245-4309, www.amadorwine.com. Celebrate local winemaking heritage and tour the wineries in mid-February, at the annual **Amador County Vintners' Barrel Tasting,** which usually starts at the Shenandoah Valley Schoolhouse on Shenandoah School Rd. just outside Plymouth.

Interesting area stays include **Amador Harvest Inn,** 209/245-5512, the only bed-and-breakfast in the Shenandoah Valley, at home at the now-famous **Deaver Vineyards,** 12455 Steiner Rd., 209/245-4099. The intriguing 1932 **Indian Creek Bed & Breakfast,** 21950 Hwy. 49 (several miles north of Plymouth proper), 209/245-4648, is a stucco-sided lodge with hidden log-cabin spirit. A grand design with cathedral ceilings and two-story fireplace, the house was built here in the woods by a Hollywood producer and was known locally as the John Wayne House, since America's mythic cowboy was a frequent guest. Premium.

AMADOR CITY AND SUTTER CREEK

Mines along the "Amador strip" between Amador City and Plymouth produced half the $300 million in gold yielded by the gold country's Southern Mines. The state's smallest incorporated city, Amador City today is just one block long, but it's as pretty as Sutter Creek. The town's main events are strolling up and down the block, dodging cars while trying to cross the highway, and poking into shops.

John Sutter passed up Sutter Creek as a possible site for his lumber mill, but he did set up a lumber camp along the creek, hence the name. Never much of a placer mining town, though Leland Stanford started amassing his fortune by means of the hardrock Lincoln Mine here, Sutter Creek grew slowly as a supply center. The area's Central Eureka Mine became one of the state's richest, finally shutting down in 1958, leaving behind a legacy of toxic wastes. Today a tiny town of a few thousand souls, Sutter Creek is among the most attractive and authentic gold rush towns, its cheerful, spiffed-up Main St. a

blend of aged wood-frames and solid brick-and-stone buildings. A favorite pastime here is browsing through the excellent antique and other shops; pick up a walking-tour guide at the local civic auditorium.

A beloved local attraction is the historic **Knight & Co., Ltd. Foundry and Machine Shop,** on the creek just east of Main at 81 Eureka St., rescued at last from the vagaries of fate—or so the community hopes. A state historical landmark also included on the National Register of Historic Places, the Knight Foundry is the only water-powered foundry in the nation. Ask locally for tour details.

For current area information, contact the **Sutter Creek Visitors Center,** P.O. Box 1234, Sutter Creek, CA 95685, 209/267-1344 or toll-free 800/400-0305, www.suttercreek.org.

Staying in Amador City and Sutter Creek

The **Imperial Hotel,** a reincarnated red brick gold-rush hotel boldly embracing the big curve as Hwy. 49 snakes through Amador City, is a delightful surprise upstairs and down. Downstairs is an intimate bar and great restaurant (dinners and Sunday brunch). Upstairs, the six guest rooms are all artistically eclectic, some with a fun, almost folk-art feel. All feature modern private bathrooms (with "extras" like hair dryers and heated towel racks); several have balconies or access to the back upstairs patio. Best of all,

Imperial Hotel in Amador City

Sutter Creek

though, a stay here also includes a full breakfast. Expensive. For more information and to make reservations, contact: Imperial Hotel, 14202 Hwy. 49, P.O. Box 195, Amador City, CA 95601, 209/267-9172 or toll-free 800/242-5594, www.imperialamador.com.

Motels are *out* in Sutter Creek—fine bed-and-breakfasts are definitely in. The pick of the litter is probably **The Foxes Inn,** 77 Main St., 209/267-5882 or toll-free 800/987-3344, www.thefoxesinn.com. Premium-Luxury. The two-story **Grey Gables Inn,** 161 Hanford St., 209/267-1039 or toll-free 800/473-9422, www.greygables.com, features eight guest rooms named after British literary lights, from Brontë and Byron to Tennyson.

At the popular **Sutter Creek Inn,** 75 Main St. (between Keyes and Hayden), 209/267-5606, www.suttercreekinn.com, proprietor Jane Way is a legend in her own time among B&Bers. Hers is one of the first bed-and-breakfasts established in California. Rooms at this "country estate" are romantic and relaxed, and the grounds feature spacious gardens. Of the inn's 17 rooms, most are tucked away in remodeled outbuildings. A lavish full breakfast is served at oak tables in the sunny country kitchen. Expensive-Luxury.

Eating in Amador City and Sutter Creek
The **Sutter Creek Certified Farmers' Market** is held June–Oct. on Sat., 8–11:30 A.M., at the intersection of Eureka St. and Hwy. 49.; for information, call 209/296-5504. **Zinfandels,** 51 Hanford St. (Hwy. 49), 209/267-5008, has filled-in admirably for long-gone Pelargonium—pouring out contemporary California-style cuisine, from pastas and risotto to charbroiled chicken, in wine country–inspired surroundings. The wine list emphasizes regional wines. Open Thurs.–Sun. for dinner only. The **Sutter Creek Palace,** 76 Main St., 209/267-1300, offers freshly remodeled Victorian decor and fine continental cuisine—fish, pastas, seafood, all fresh as fresh can be. Prime rib is available on Fri. and Sat. nights. Open for lunch and dinner Fri.–Tuesday.

If at all possible—call ahead for reservations—do have at least one meal at **The Imperial Hotel** in Amador City (hotel details above).

JACKSON AND VICINITY

JACKSON

Though it wasn't the wildest of the gold rush settlements, Jackson was nonetheless a rambunctious place on the Sacramento-Stockton branch of the old Carson Pass Emigrant Trail. Not a classic boomtown—Jackson had a surprisingly stable population for more than 100 years—the town has remained lively even in recent times, with local bordellos and gambling halls operating until the 1950s and card parlors still dotting Main Street. Plan on spending some time in and around Jackson if you're not already museumed, ghost-towned, Victorian gingerbreaded, and gift "shoppe"ed out.

Get a walking-tour map from the **Amador County Chamber of Commerce & Visitors Bureau,** 125 Peek, Ste. B (at the southern juncture of Hwys. 49 and 88, next to the Chevron gas station), P.O. Box 596, Jackson, CA 95642, 209/223-0350, www.amadorcountychamber.com.

Seeing and Doing Jackson

Stone buildings with iron doors and shutters are the architectural rule in downtown Jackson. Main St., with its high wooden sidewalks, is narrow, crooked, and intersected by hill-climbing, alleylike streets. Many intriguing old homes are sprinkled around town, easily enjoyed on foot. (The entire town is better for walking than either biking or driving, and parking is just about impossible.) Tucked in between trees and terraced tombstones, the tiny white **St. Sava Serbian Orthodox Church,** 724 N. Main St., is the "mother church" of the Serbian Orthodox faith in the United States. The imposing **National Hotel,** 2 Water St. (down at the end of Main), 209/223-0500, is another California hostelry claiming the oldest-in-continuous-operation title. A peek into the National's saloon is almost like peering into a black hole—but one with brassy crystal light reflected from the bar mirror and absorbed by the honkytonk piano and fake red velvet wallpaper.

The best thing to see in town is the intriguing **Amador County Museum,** 225 Church St., 209/223-6386, which occupies an 1850s red-

brick house at the top of the hill. Out back, scale models of several historic local mining structures—the (working) North Star Stamp Mill, the Kennedy Mine headframe, a tailing wheel—provide a clear explanation of what gold mining was and is. Tours are offered every hour if enough people show up, otherwise at 10 A.M. and 2 P.M. (small fee). The museum is open Wed.–Sun. 10 A.M.–4 P.M. (admission by donation). To get to what remains of the famed **Kennedy Mine,** take Jackson Gate Rd. up the hill from Main St.—and ask at the visitors center about guided tours.

Staying in and near Jackson

El Campo Casa Resort Motel, 12548 Kennedy Flat Rd., 209/223-0100, is a pleasant, middle-aged Spanish-style establishment northwest of town near the intersection of Hwys. 49 and 88. Amenities include a pool and wonderful

Kennedy tailing wheel in Jackson

gardens. Inexpensive. But bed-and-breakfasts are the "inn thing" here. The 1872 **Court Street Inn,** 215 Court St., 209/223-0416, is an elegant state historic monument also listed on the National Register of Historic Places. Appreciate the tin ceilings, marble fireplace, and stunning redwood staircase. The inn offers seven rooms, a suite, and a two-bedroom cottage with a big-screen TV and souped-up stereo system, all with private baths. Expensive-Premium. East of town, quite special is a stay at Greek Revival–style **The Heirloom** bed-and-breakfast, 214 Shakeley Ln., Ione, CA 95640, 209/274-4468 or toll-free 888/628-7896—and also quite a bargain. Staying here is like taking in some of the charms of the antebellum South, what with the building's rambling verandas and sweet magnolias and wisteria vines. The main house features four delightful guest rooms (named for the four seasons), and an adjacent rammed-earth, sod-roofed adobe boasts two more—pleasantly cool in summer, heated in winter with wood-burning stoves. All have private baths. Moderate-Expensive.

If you're not that fussy about every little creature comfort, don't miss a stay at the venerable brick **St. George Hotel** in the fascinating foothill town of **Volcano** to the east, 209/296-4458, fax 209/296-4457, www.stgeorgehotel.com. Included on the National Register of Historic Places, with a straight-laced exterior accented by vine maple twining down from the overhanging balconies, this was once the most elegant hotel in the gold country. The St. George is still quite a character—recently spruced up with an art salon. At last report, all 14 rooms in the hotel, recently redecorated, shared five bathrooms. Less intriguing lodgings are available in the motel annex next door. Inexpensive-Moderate, including continental breakfast. Even if you're just passing through, do plan to eat here. The dining room now serves creative California-style fare. Open to nonguests for breakfast and lunch on weekends, and for dinner Thurs.–Sun.; call ahead for reservations.

Eating in Jackson

The **Jackson Certified Farmers' Market** is held June–Oct. on Wed. 3:30–6:30 P.M. at the intersection of Church and California Sts.; for information, call 209/296-5504. A local hot spot is **Mel and Faye's Drive-in,** 205 N. Hwy. 49, 209/223-0853, which serves chili, "mooburgers," and daily specials (takeout). **Rose-**

bud's Classic Cafe, 26 Main, 209/223-1035, is a good American-style café open daily for breakfast, lunch, and dinner. The **Upstairs Restaurant and Sidestreet Bistro,** 164 Main, 209/223-3342, offers contemporary gourmet American dinners in the fancy exposed-brick dining room, as well as creative sandwiches, salads, and such at lunch in the downstairs bistro. Local wines by the glass and bottle. Out of town a bit are two locally popular Italian-American restaurants: very good **Teresa's Place,** 1235 Jackson Gate Rd., 209/223-1786, a fixture since World War II—serving hearty homestyle fare and such things as Bisteca Florentina and braised swordfish in pine nut–basil cream sauce—and **Buscaglia's,** 1218 Jackson Gate Rd., 209/223-9992.

Indian Grinding Rock State Historic Park

Tucked into the foothills east of Jackson and just north of Pine Grove on the road to Volcano, Indian Grinding Rock State Historic Park features more than 1,100 ancient mortar holes *(chaw'se)* and petroglyphs on a flat limestone plateau. Miwok women used the holes as mortars in which to grind acorns and other seeds. This is the largest grinding rock in the United States; a replica is on display at the Smithsonian Institution. Also here: a reconstructed native village, with roundhouse, or *hun'ge,* bark tepees, a granary, and a Miwok ball field (the traditional game was similar to soccer). The **Chaw'se Regional Indian Museum** features a good collection of artifacts from 10 area tribes plus other displays (open daily except holidays).

The state park includes 23 year-round campsites (coin-op showers, no reservations). Or you can live like the Miwok in one of five bark houses—an "environmental camping" experience with a seven-day limit. The park's day-use fee is $2. For more information, contact: Indian Grinding Rock State Historic Park, 14881 Pine Grove-Volcano Rd., Pine Grove, CA 95665, 209/296-7488.

Volcano and Vicinity

There's not a volcano in sight in **Volcano,** but early settlers thought the landscape resembled a crater and abandoned the original name, Soldier's Gulch. Sleepy Volcano is a ghost town that wouldn't die, these days refreshingly free of tourist lures and alive with history, including a number of cultural "firsts." The **Miner's Library Association** here was the state's first lending library. California community theater was born here, too, with the formation of the 1845 **Volcano Thespian Society** and the subsequent construction of two local theaters. The state's first literary and debating society also thundered up from Volcano. On **Observatory Hill** two miles away sat California's first observatory. Volcano also once had a law school. A new area attraction, expected to open one of these years, is the **Black Chasm Cavern** on Volcano-Pioneer Rd.; for details, call 209/736-2708 or try www.caverntours.com.

Take Ramshorn Grade Rd. north from Volcano to reach **Daffodil Hill,** where the mid-March through mid-April daffodil bloom (300 varieties) on this six-acre farm is spectacular. The McLaughlins started planting daffodils here in 1887, when the area was a stage stop; their descendants have continued the tradition to this day.

BLACK BART

South across the Mokelumne River, the infamous Black Bart tossed and turned at least a little while in the San Andreas jail (now a museum). The "gentleman bandit" robbed 28 stagecoaches of their gold shipments, on foot and with the aid of an unloaded shotgun, before his capture in 1883. Black Bart (a.k.a. Charles Bolton or Charles Boles of San Francisco), a lover of the finer things in life, was characteristically polite, if commanding, and left quaint rhyming poetry with his unhappy victims. One of his finer efforts read: "I've labored hard and long for bread, for honor and for riches. But on my corns too long you've tred, you fine haired sons of bitches. Let come what will, I'll try it on, my condition can't be worse. And if there's money in that box, 'tis munney in my purse." Black Bart was something of a New World Robin Hood, since he stole nothing from the passengers—just money from Wells Fargo.

As successful as he was, the "PO-8" of the placers violated the never-return-to-the-scene-of-the-crime rule of criminology and was finally undone. Wounded in a holdup at Funk Hill near Copperopolis, the scene of his first and last known robberies, Black Bart dropped a handkerchief before he fled. Wells Fargo detective Harry Worse traced the hankie's laundry mark to an apartment house on Bush St. in San Francisco, and Charles Bolton's days of highway robbery were over. Arrested and returned to San Andreas, the county seat, Black Bart confessed to only the Funk Hill holdup and was sentenced to six years in San Quentin. Freed for good behavior after four years, Bolton then disappeared. An old rumor has it that Wells Fargo pensioned him in exchange for his promise to cease his stage (robbing) career, a suggestion dismissed by historians.

San Andreas and Vicinity

Once a Mexican town with a few adobes, San Andreas is now the Calaveras County seat, a bustling metropolis with a touristy downtown. The block-long historically interesting part of town is perpendicular to the highway. Still standing: both the courthouse where Black Bart finally faced justice and the jailhouse cell he called home before doing time in San Quentin. A walk through the pioneer cemetery west of town is sobering—so many young men, such short lives.

The brick county Hall of Records complex, beautifully restored, now houses the outstanding **Calaveras County Museum and Archives,** 30 N. Main St., 209/754-3910. Also a de facto visitors center, the museum's exhibits include a Miwok bark tepee, artifacts, and basketry; legal papers, including a black-bordered public hanging invitation signed and sealed by the sheriff; and fine mining displays. The jail is downstairs in the courtyard, which is planted with native flora. The museum is open daily 10 A.M.–4 P.M. Small admission.

The one-time resort town of Cave City has long since bitten the dust, but the **California Caverns,** 9565 Cave City Rd. (reached from Mountain Ranch Rd.; follow the signs), 209/736-2708 or 209/754-1849, www.caverntours.com, are still going strong. First opened in 1850 and now a state historic landmark, the caverns ain't what they used to be, due to visitor overload and vandalism. But they're still worth a peek. Open May–Dec. (variable, depending on the winter)—daily in the peak summer season, on weekends otherwise. Call for current details.

ANGELS CAMP AND VICINITY

Originally a simple trading post, Angels Camp became a jumping mining camp after Bennagar Rasberry accidentally shot the ground while cleaning his muzzleloader, murdering a manzanita bush and revealing an impressive chunk of gold-seamed quartz dangling from its roots. Placer gold was found here by either Henry Angel or George Angell, depending on the story, but the pans soon came up empty. The town boomed again, though, with help from later hardrock mining companies.

Though not a vintage gold rush town these days, Angels Camp is not yet overrun by corporate America. Main St. isn't too touristy, but it *is* an amphibian's paradise. Frogs leap from store windows, perch atop monuments, hang from balconies, swing from shop signs, and decorate sidewalks. The **Angels Camp Museum,** 753 S. Main, 209/736-2963, is open daily 10 A.M.–3 P.M. from Apr. to Thanksgiving, Wed.–Sun. otherwise (small

fee). Stop by if you're interested in horse-drawn wagons, buggies, and rock collections.

Dave's Diner, 451 Hwy. 49, 209/736-8080, does a mean breakfast and lunch. Dave's vies for local favor with **Sue's Angel's Creek Cafe,** 1246 S. Main St., 209/736-2941. The popular **B of A Cafe,** inside the onetime Bank of America at 1262 Main St., 209/736-0765, offers good coffee, bistro lunches, and gourmet dinners. For the fanciest dining in town, head for **Greenhorn Creek,** 676 McCauley Ranch Rd. out at the golf course, 209/736-8181, which offers gourmet fare and an extensive wine list.

For more area information, contact the **Calaveras County Lodging & Visitors Association,** 1211 S. Main St., P.O. Box 637, Angels Camp, CA 95222, 209/736-0049 or toll-free 800/225-3764, www.visitcalaveras.org, which publishes the use-

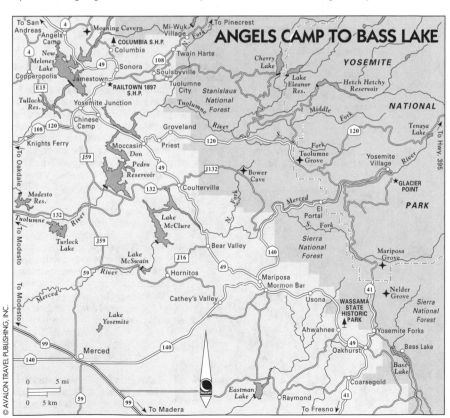

ful *Calaveras County Visitor's Guide* and serves as a reservations and information service for lodging, skiing and other recreation, and area events.

Murphys

Nice place to stay put awhile, old Murphys. Only recently discovered by the tourist trade, this one-street town is shaded by locust trees, cotton-woods, sycamores, and elms. Known affectionately as "Mountain Queen" and "Queen of the Sierra" by locals, down-home Murphys has hosted its share of Hollywood outsiders filming Westerns. These days area wineries are a main attraction. For a complete list, contact the **Calaveras Wine Association,** 209/736-6722, www.calaveraswines.org.

The restored **Murphys Hotel,** 457 Main St., 209/728-3444, was once considered the state's finest lodging outside of San Francisco, despite its Wild West reputation (genuine bullet holes decorate the doorway). And it's still an interesting overnight. Wonderful Western bar. Moderate. Nearby is the grand **Dunbar House 1880** bed-and-breakfast inn, 271 Jones St., 209/728-2897 or toll-free 800/692-6006, www.dunbarhouse.com, one of the best around. Premium-Luxury. Most popular for sophisticated fare in Murphys is **Grounds,** 402 Main St., 209/728-8663, open Thurs.–Mon. for breakfast, lunch, and dinner.

Mercer Caverns and Moaning Cavern

About one mile north of Murphys, the **Mercer Caverns** at 1665 Sheep Ranch Rd., 209/728-2101, were formed from an earthquake-caused fissure. There are unusual aragonite crystals in these limestone formations, and good examples of "flowstone," stalagmites, and stalactites. Open daily year-round, 10 A.M.–4:30 P.M. (expanded hours in summer). Admission is $7 adults, $3.50 children. More pristine is **Moaning Cavern,** 5350 Moaning Cave Rd. (off Hwy. 4 between Vallecito and Douglas Flat), 209/736-2708, www.caverntours.com, reportedly the largest hidden hole in the ground in California. Don't be put off by the hype. Moaning Cavern is really a vertical cave with a main cavity large enough to hide the Statue of Liberty (if anyone could ever figure out how to get it down the staircase). Thrill-seekers (over age 12) can rappel down into darkness on a special tour. Admission for the regular tour is $7.75 adults, $4 children. Open daily 9 A.M.–6 P.M. (10 A.M.–5 P.M. in winter).

Calaveras Big Trees State Park

The first grove of *Sequoiadendron giganteum,* or Sierra redwoods,

---

JUMPING FROGS AND OTHER CELEBRATIONS

Mark Twain once hung out in the Hotel Angels bar and pool hall in Angels Camp, where he first heard the miners' tall tale about the jumping frogs—inspiration for his first successful story, "The Celebrated Jumping Frogs of Calaveras County," published in 1864. When the roads in Angels Camp were finally paved in 1928, someone jokingly suggested holding a jumping frog contest to commemorate the fictional athletic humiliation of that now-famous toady, Dan'l Webster. And so the town's **Jumping Frog Jubilee** was hatched.

The event is now staged for tourists every May at Frogtown (the fairgrounds just south of Angels Camp) in conjunction with the Calaveras County Fair (rental frogs available). It's all considered serious sport by some, so don't kiss or otherwise distract the frogs until after the $1,500 prize has been awarded.

For information on the jumping frog contest and other events at the fairgrounds, contact the **Calaveras County Fairgrounds,** P.O. Box 96, Angels Camp, CA 95222, 209/728-2561.

TOM MYERS PHOTOGRAPHY

MARK TWAIN

After staying for a time in Carson City, Nevada, with his brother Orion, the governor's secretary, Samuel Clemens wandered through western Nevada in the early 1860s, suffering from a severe case of gold fever. Deeply in debt after his prospecting attempts repeatedly failed, in 1862 he walked 130 miles from Aurora to Virginia City to accept a $25-a-week job as a reporter on the *Territorial Enterprise.* Later, in San Francisco, Twain became part of the city's original Bohemia, mixing with Prentice Mulford, Ina Coolbrith (California's first poet laureate), Cincinnatus Heine "Joaquin" Miller, and Bret Harte. He defamed the city police in print, then decided to leave town after another bad turn of affairs, escaping in 1865 to the Mother Lode and an isolated cabin on the Stanislaus River's Jackass Hill near Angels Camp.

Surrounded by a few remaining pocket miners, Twain was content with wandering through the abandoned town and nearby settlements, symbols of the vagaries of fate and fortune. Most of the locals bored him, but he enjoyed the company of his more well read cabin mates. Twain's laziness was legendary—his unwillingness to draw one more bucket of water later meant his friend lost out on a $20,000 gold find—but the period here was productive nonetheless. Many of the stories shared by his imaginative friends ended up in Twain's later books, and it was here that he first heard the miner's tale of a local frog-jumping competition. "The Celebrated Jumping Frog of Calaveras County" was an overnight success with the Eastern literary establishment.

ever discovered by white explorers was noted by northstate pioneer John Bidwell in 1841. These trees grow only on the western slopes of the Sierra Nevada and are more plentiful in the Yosemite, Sequoia, and Kings Canyon areas to the south. Here, about four miles east of Arnold, there are relatively few "big trees," and these grow in isolated groves. But Calaveras Big Trees is a good spot for a summer escape (it's cool up here). It's also nice for uncrowded autumn campouts and wintertime snowshoe hikes or cross-country skiing. Camp at the **North Grove Campground** or at **Oak Hollow.** The pleasant campsites have wonderful hot coin-op showers and piped drinking water (reservations a must in summer). To reserve, call ReserveAmerica, 800/444-7275. For park information, contact: **Calaveras Big Trees State Park,** P.O. Box 120, Arnold, CA 95223, 209/795-2334.

JOAQUIN MURRIETA: ROBIN HOOD OF THE PLACERS

The notorious bandit Joaquin Murrieta reportedly ranged from San Andreas to Murphys and beyond, but may have been more legend than reality, a composite of many "Joaquins" forced into crime by the racism of the day. There's hardly a town in the gold country without tunnels, cellars, or caves supposedly frequented by him, or nearby hills where he gunned someone down. According to some versions, Murrieta was a bright, handsome young man who settled on the Stanislaus River with his bride and his brother. Primarily interested in farming, the Murrietas nonetheless took the liberty of panning for a little gold, ignoring the prohibition against Mexican miners until accosted by drunken whites. His brother was gunned down (or lynched), his wife assaulted or killed. Horsewhipped and left for dead, Murrieta survived and assembled a bandit band, and one by

one, those who had murdered his wife and brother eventually met death at Joaquin's hands.

Settling just north of Marysville, Murrieta and his men became accomplished horse thieves and stagecoach robbers. According to legend, much of Joaquin's booty went to poor Mexican families, who considered him a modern-day Robin Hood. (Others claim that Murrieta committed nearly 30 murders, usually victimizing unarmed men, including many Chinese.) Pursued by vigilantes, he moved farther north to Mt. Shasta (where writer "Joaquin" Miller borrowed the name for his nom de plume), then south to San Jose and various San Joaquin Valley towns. Turned in by a former lover, Murrieta was eventually tracked down in the Tehachapis by bounty hunters and state rangers—or so at least one version of the story goes.

COLUMBIA AND SONORA

COLUMBIA

Drunken bar brawls, shady ladies, and muddy, manure-filled streets once defined daily life in Columbia. The "Gem of the Southern Mines," Columbia served as capital city to an area population of more than 15,000 in its prime. But in 1854, the town lost the sensitive scuffle for state capital to Sacramento by just two legislative votes. It was a devastating political loss for the biggest, richest, and wickedest gold town of them all. When the mines declined in the 1870s, more than $87 million in gold had been stripped from the earth. Much of the land near Columbia has been laid waste by hydraulic mining.

Even before its painstaking restoration, the former American Camp was the most beautifully preserved of all gold country towns. Quite a few Westerns, including *High Noon,* have been filmed here. Now a state historic park, downtown Columbia is a fine outdoor "museum"; no cars are allowed in the historic sector, only tourists—about a half million each year. Most of the town's attractions and shops are open daily 10 A.M.–5 P.M. To get oriented, pick up a free guide at the visitors center, then wander through blocks of fire-resistant brick and iron buildings in the Greek Revival style, built following devastating fires in 1854 and 1857.

For more information, including details on Columbia's intriguing events, contact: **Columbia State Historic Park,** P.O. Box 151, Columbia, CA 95310, 209/532-4301 or 209/532-0150.

Seeing and Doing Columbia
The tiny **William Cavalier Museum** at Knapp's Corner, Main and State Sts., makes a good first stop. The museum's collection includes real gold and plentiful Western paraphernalia. Displays chronicle the massive town-wide restoration, and slide shows and films add historical context. The **Museum of the Gold Rush Press,** in the old *Columbia Gazette* building, features a collection of old-time newspapers and a rogue's gallery of gold rush journalists. The two-story red brick **Columbia Grammar School** on Kennebec Hill was used from 1860 to 1937 and is in excellent condition. The seedy **miner's cabin** at the end of Main is a bleak, definitely unromantic reminder of prospectors' real lives.

About $55 million in gold bullion and nuggets passed through Columbia's authentically furnished **Wells Fargo office** here. Notice the beautiful scales. The **D. O. Mills Building** next door was one of the first branches of the later Bank of California. Another authentic touch is the town's ample supply of saloons; before the first big fire, about one-fifth of Columbia's business establishments were bars.

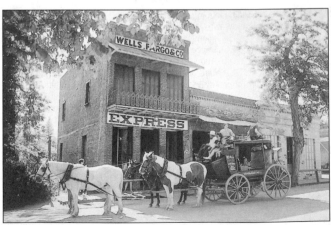

Columbia

TOM MYERS PHOTOGRAPHY

The fine **Fallon Hotel**, 11175 Washington St., with its elegant theater and restaurant, has been righteously restored. No matter what else you do, stop here to appreciate the careful craftsmanship. The **City Hotel**, on Main St., is less ostentatious but still impressive. **Papeete**, Columbia's first and most extravagant fire pumper (originally destined for the Society Islands), is now just for show, used only during the annual Firemen's Muster festivities.

With the right attitude—and here, there's nothing wrong with being one more tourist among the multitude—anyone can enjoy Columbia's family-focused emphasis. Get a glimpse of gold-bearing quartz on a guided tour of a nearby working gold mine (daily in summer, otherwise usually on weekends only). For information, contact: **Hidden Treasure Gold Mine**, 209/532-9693. Or stop by the **Matelot Gulch Mining Co.**, in Columbia proper, on Main at Washington, 209/532-9693. If you're going, bring a sweater.

Staying in Columbia

The clean, old-fashioned **Columbia Gem Motel**, 22131 Parrotts Ferry Rd., 209/532-4508, is pleasant, offering tiny barn-and-white 1940s-style cottages with mini sitting porches, plus a few standard motel rooms. This "gem" has just a handful of units, so be sure to reserve in advance.

The once-opulent **City Hotel**, on Main St. (between Jackson and State Sts.), 209/532-1479 or toll-free 800/532-1479, www.cityhotel.com, has regained its gloss. Period furniture and marble-topped tables accent the authenticity of the Victorian parlor. The 10 guest rooms have half-baths and share showers down the hall (bathrobes, slippers, and toiletries provided). Rates include generous continental breakfast, served in the central parlor. Expensive-Premium.

The ornate lobby of the **Fallon Hotel**, 11175 Washington St. (just off Broadway), 209/532-1470 or toll-free 800/532-1479, also on the web at www.cityhotel.com, features almost-too-perfect vintage wallpapers, green velvet drapes, oak furnishings, and Oriental rugs—all in all an over-statement of Old West luxury; when this was a miners' lodging house, the accommodations were much more spartan. (No wandering through the elegant hallways unless you're a paying customer.) The 14 exquisitely redone Victorian rooms—quite small, excepting the balconied rooms—feature chain-pull toilets and porcelain basins in the half-baths (showers are shared here, too). Continental breakfast. Moderate-Premium.

Hotel management students from the local junior college, dressed in 1850s attire, assist staff in attending to your every need at both the City and Fallon Hotels.

Eating in Columbia

Eat, at least once, at the **City Hotel** dining room, 209/532-1479 or toll-free 800/532-1479, another community college "project." Expect contemporary American regional cuisine with classic French touches: light sauces, intriguing appetizers (including that '49er favorite, oysters on the half shell), crisp linen and fresh flowers, and fine service. Open Tues.–Sun. 5–9 P.M. for dinner, and also Sun. 11 A.M.–2 P.M. for brunch; reservations are necessary. Also in the hotel is the **What Cheer Saloon**, a historic bar with a comfortable Western atmosphere.

The **Columbia House** on Main, 209/532-5134, is a relaxed and reasonably priced place for breakfast and lunch. Closed Wed. in the off-season. The **Lickskillet Cafe**, 11256 State St., 209/536-9599, serves good American fare: sandwiches and salads for lunch, and pastas, chicken, duck, steak, scampi, and other upscale preparations for dinner. Open Wed.–Sunday.

SONORA

Sonora, the "Queen of the Southern Mines" and old-time Columbia rival, is today something of a suburban octopus, its tentacles of one-acre ranchettes flailing out in all directions. No wonder people want to live here: this *is* a pretty town (downtown).

Mexican miners founded the town during a particularly nasty period of Yankee us-firstism. Greedy gringos eventually forced the first Sonorans off their claims here, too, creating considerable outlaw backlash. The novel *The Last Californian* by modern-day Sonora resident and schoolteacher Feliz Guthrie spins the story of the infamous Rancheria Massacre, a telling tale about anti-Hispanic racism in the Mother Lode. After the Latino "lawbreakers" were eliminated, the rich placer fields near Sonora harvested, and the pocket mines turned inside out and emptied, lumber became the area's main industry, spurred by the arrival of the railroad in 1898. Orange crates for packaging California citrus were manufactured here by the millions. The helpful **Tuolumne County Visitors Bureau,** 55 W. Stockton St., 209/533-4420, 209/984-4636 (Chinese Camp office), or toll-free 800/446-1333, www.thegreatunfenced.com, dispenses information on just about everything. There's even a photograph flip-book on area bed-and-breakfasts, so you can see how they look. The **Sonora Chamber of Commerce** is at 222 S. Shepherd St., 209/532-4212. Public camping, trail, and outdoor recreation information and permits are available at the **Stanislaus National Forest** headquarters, 19777 Greenley Rd. (across from the fairgrounds), 209/532-3671.

Seeing and Doing Sonora

Washington is the town's main street, an identity shared with Hwy. 49 and Hwy. 108 as both squeeze through Sonora's central ravine. Travelers flow in fits and spurts through a mother lode of boutiques, specialty shops, and eateries, all tucked into and around some noteworthy architecture. Pick up a free local guide at the county museum and elsewhere around town.

The elegant and unusual red **Saint James Episcopal Church** at Washington and Snell is still a place of worship, but also maintains a museum (in the rectory). Open weekdays 9 A.M.–5 P.M. Next door is the **Bradford Building,** complete with copper doors and an elaborate dome. It was constructed by local lumber baron S. S. Bradford, who also built the impressive, very San Francisco **Street-Morgan Mansion,** across from the church at 23 W. Snell.

The original 1850 **Gunn Adobe,** 286 S. Washington, later grew a balcony and new wings, becoming the Hotel Italia and today a motel. The **Tuolumne County Courthouse,** 2 S. Green St., is a bizarre yet stately building constructed from local materials: green sandstone, yellow pressed bricks, Columbia marble, and Copperopolis copper (for the Byzantine clock tower and doors). Inside, the **County Recorder's office** features a pre-dam photo of Hetch Hetchy Valley—second only to Yosemite Valley in natural beauty, according to John Muir—and a good collection of old newspapers.

At home in the town's former jailhouse, the **Tuolumne County Museum and History Center,** 158 W. Bradford, 209/532-1317, is worth some time. Inside are paintings by William West and some fascinating Western photography. The jailhouse setting itself lends an intriguing atmosphere, with local gold rush relics and other historical items exhibited in a "cell by cell" arrangement. Picnic in the jailyard. Open daily 10 A.M.–3:30 P.M. in summer (otherwise closed Sunday).

Staying in Sonora

Right downtown (and worth it for the "feel" of local history) is the **Sonora Days Inn,** 160 S. Washington, 209/532-7468, 209/532-2400, or toll-free 800/580-4667, a beige Spanish California beauty with tile roof, pool, hot tub, saloon, and restaurant. Moderate-Premium. **The Gunn House Motor Hotel,** 286 S. Washington, 209/532-3421, incorporates the original two-story adobe house into a pleasant inn-like motel oozing local charm. All rooms have private baths, and rates include continental breakfast. Inexpensive-Moderate. Ask for a room in the back, off the street.

Close to downtown but quiet is the small **Ryan House 1855 Bed & Breakfast Inn,** 153 S. Shepherd St., 209/533-3445 or toll-free 800/831-4897, www.ryanhouse.com, where all four rooms (the attic is a three-room suite) feature handmade quilts and private baths. Expensive-Luxury. The **Barretta Gardens Inn,** 700 S. Barretta St., 209/532-6039 or toll-free 800/206-3333, www.goldbnbs.com, overlooks the town from an acre of lovely lawns and gardens. Five guest rooms, private baths. Rates include a full breakfast. Expensive-Luxury. Pleasant yet unstuffy **Lulu Belle's Bed and Breakfast,** 85 Gold St. (downtown, off Washington), 209/533-3455 or toll-free 800/538-3455, features five rooms—three in a quiet, renovated carriage house—and a lively music room, where guests are encouraged to pick an instrument and join in. Full country-style breakfast. Moderate-Expensive. Families genuinely welcome.

There are also some fine inns beyond Sonora proper. For a current regional bed-and-breakfast brochure, reservations, and referrals, contact **Gold Country Bed and Breakfast Inns of Tuolumne County,** P.O. Box 462, Sonora, CA

95370, 209/533-1845 or toll-free 888/465-1849, www.goldbnbs.com.

Eating in Sonora

The **Sonora Certified Farmers' Market** is held May–Oct. on Sat., 8 A.M.–noon, at Theall and Stewart Streets. For information, call 209/532-4820. **Wilma's Cafe,** downtown at 275 S. Washington, 209/532-9957, is locally famous for its hickory-smoked barbecue. Open daily. **Sonora Joe's,** 1183 Mono Way (at Hwy. 108), 209/533-3327, is the best local steakhouse.

More sophisticated, in the culinary sense, is **Good Heavens,** in the old Yo Semite Hotel at 49 N. Washington, 209/532-3663, specializing in gourmet California-style fare at lunch and dinner—starting with those famous cheese-herb biscuits and select homemade jams. Open for lunch daily and for dinner Wed., Fri., and Saturday. And though the decor is nothing to write home about, almost everything else is at **Banny's,** 83 S. Stewart St., 209/533-4709, from the marinated rack of lamb to the bacon ragout. Open for lunch Mon.–Sat., for dinner nightly. **Coyote Creek Cafe & Grille,** 177 S. Washington, 209/532-9115, serves contemporary everything, from just about everywhere—from the Zuni black bean plate, Szechuan chicken salad, and The Bayou (chicken breast sandwich with Cajun spices) at lunch to daily changing dinner specials like BBQ Korean pork and chicken Thai curry. **La Torres' North Beach Cafe,** 14317 Mono Way, 209/536-1852, serves exceptional Italian and American fare. Open daily for lunch and dinner.

Hemingway's Cafe, 362 S. Stewart St., 209/532-4900, is an unusual and enjoyable place serving contemporary international cuisine in a ranch-style home dressed up like a European café. Open Tues.–Sat. for lunch and dinner (reservations wise).

JAMESTOWN AND VICINITY

Once a supply station for area mines and now pretty as a tintype photograph, Jamestown (also known as Jimtown) gained attention as the site of the Crocker family's Sierra Railroad Company, the main line running from here through Sonora and on to the mill at Fasler—rails you can still ride today, now part of Railtown 1897 State Historic Park. Countless movies, including *High Noon, The Virginian, Dodge City,* and *My Little Chickadee,* not to mention TV westerns like *The Lone Ranger, Tales of Wells Fargo,* and *Little House on the Prairie,* have been filmed at least partially in Jamestown.

Seeing and Doing Jimtown

Main St. is a bustling quarter-mile-long cowboy alley lined with pickup trucks. Hold down a bench in Jamestown Park on Main and just watch the summer sideshow pass by, or brave the streets and explore the stores. Gold rush–oriented stores and jewelry shops abound.

Jamestown Hotel

If you're a serious gold-lover, try finding some of your own. **Gold Prospecting Expeditions,** in the old livery stable at 18170 Main, 209/984-4653, can tell you how to go about it. Kids pan for free in the horse trough outside the stable, but basic placer mining, "rafting for riches," high-tech helicopter gold trips, and classes for grownups cost money.

Otherwise, Jimtown's main attraction is **Railtown 1897 State Historic Park,** headquartered at the old Sierra Railway Depot on 5th at Reservoir (just above Main, off the highways), 209/984-3953 (main office) or 209/984-1600 (recorded train and events information). With its expanse of cool green lawn, tables, barbecues, and running water, the park is pleasant for picnics. The 26-acre site includes a collection of venerable railroad cars—be sure to see the parlor car from the *California Zephyr*—and the Sierra's massive old roundhouse, still in use for locomotive and railroad car repairs and restorations. Self-guided roundhouse and blacksmith shop tours are available daily; guided tours are offered only on weekends. The park is open year-round, daily 9:30 A.M.–4:30 P.M. (closed Thanksgiving, Christmas, and New Year's Day). Small admission.

On weekends Apr.–Oct. (and Sat. only in Nov.), you can take a 45-minute, six-mile trip on the steam-powered *Mother Lode Cannon Ball*. Special-event trains are also offered. Call for details.

Staying in Jimtown

The fine **Jamestown Hotel,** 18153 Main St., 209/984-3902 or toll-free 800/205-4901, www.jamestownhotel.com, features 11 modern Victorian-style rooms with brass beds. Full breakfast included. Moderate-Premium. Here, too, the remodeled bar and contemporary **Café on the Patio** are open to the public.

Most bed-and-breakfasts in Jimtown are called "hotels." The elaborate, eye-catching balcony and wooden boardwalk at the exquisitely restored **National Hotel,** 77 Main St., 209/984-3446 or toll-free 800/894-3446, www.nationalhotel.com, mark this authentic gold rush relic, now a bed-and-breakfast with some original furnishings and pull-chain toilets. Continental breakfast; restaurant and bar open to the public. Moderate-Expensive.

The **Royal Hotel** on Main St., 209/984-5271, is one of those local institutions that attracts mostly regulars, at least in the hotel itself. (Great bookshop downstairs.) Best bet for travelers are the rooms and suites in the secluded cottages out back. Inexpensive-Moderate.

Eating in Jimtown

At **Kamm's Chinese Restaurant,** 18208 Main St., 209/984-3105, you can get a five-course Cantonese meal for next to nothing. Even better and still reasonable is **The Smoke Cafe,** 18191 Main St., 209/984-3733, which serves good margaritas and decent Mexican dinners, such as *chile verde* and *pollo de poblano*, in a tin-walled Western atmosphere. The specials here are usually enticing. Closed Monday.

Both the Jamestown Hotel's **Café on the Patio,** tel. 209/984-3902, and the **National Hotel Restaurant,** 209/984-3446, offer contemporary American cuisine at lunch and dinner, along with a full bar. The food at the National is usually more exciting. Popular with locals is **The Willow Steakhouse and Saloon,** in the old hotel at Main and Willow, 209/984-3998. Open for lunch weekdays and for dinner nightly (reservations usually necessary on weekends).

Around Jamestown

Just 12 miles west of Jamestown toward the valley, **Knights Ferry,** with a historic district of old brick and pine-frame buildings along the banks of the Stanislaus River, is a haven for swimmers, picnickers, and campers in summer. Stop by the Knights Ferry Covered Bridge, reportedly the longest of its type in the United States, designed by U. S. Grant; there's also a fine small museum and visitors center. Good for a meal in town—and almost as enjoyable for its riverside setting—is the **Knights Ferry Resort** restaurant, 17525 Sonora Rd., 209/881-3349. Open Tues.–Fri. for breakfast, lunch, and dinner (full bar), and Sat.–Sun. for champagne brunch and dinner (reservations suggested).

Chinese Camp, near the junction of Hwy. 49 and Hwy. 120 and east of Yosemite Junction, today consists of a volunteer-staffed **visitor information center,** post office, aged adobes, creaky wood-frames, and crumbling brick buildings hidden by trees of heaven along Main

Street. There's obviously not much happening here today, but this was once one of the largest U.S. Asian settlements.

Past Moccasin Creek Fish Hatchery and the brutal climb up Hwy. 120 to Priest (locals say the old road was worse) is **Groveland.** Founded by the gold rush, Groveland boomed again during the construction of Hetch Hetchy Reservoir, and is now a pine-woodsy, pleasant resort community. The 1920s **Hotel Charlotte** on Main St. (Hwy. 120), 209/962-6455 or toll-free 800/961-7799, built to house the men working on Hetch Hetchy Dam construction, is now a nothing-fancy bed-and-breakfast (Inexpensive-Moderate) serving good prime rib, chops, chicken, and other American fare. A real '49er old-timer, the gracious adobe **Groveland Hotel,** 18767 Main St., 209/962-4000 or toll-free 800/273-3314, www.groveland.com, recently received a million-dollar facelift. The Groveland offers 17 refurbished rooms and suites—furnished in attractive antiques, all with private baths—here and in the adjacent Queen Anne Victorian, along with continental breakfast. The wood-rich dining room serves dinner nightly. Premium-Luxury.

If you're traveling to or from Yosemite, a time-honored stop for a country-style breakfast is **Buck Meadows Lodge,** 7647 Hwy. 120, 209/962-5281, with restaurant, saloon, and motel.

COULTERVILLE

Coulterville is unpocked by progress and is, in its entirety, a state historic landmark (Main St. is included on the National Register of Historic Places). The second-largest town in Mariposa County, fringed by barren oak and chaparral slopes, Coulterville is safe (so far) from the stylized rusticity that's raking in the tourists elsewhere. From Coulterville, take Greeley Hill Rd. (J20) east, then follow Old Yosemite Rd.—the locals' route—into **Yosemite National Park.**

Contact the **North County Visitor Center,** 5007 Main St., P.O. Box 33, Coulterville, CA 95311, 209/878-3074, for current visitor information, or stop by the local history center.

Seeing and Doing Coulterville

Not to be missed in Coulterville is the **Northern Mariposa County History Center,** 10301 Hwy. 49, 209/878-3015. Enter this aged stone museum complex, the old Wells Fargo and Mc-Carthy's Store buildings, through the roofless shell of an open-air "courtyard" with cascading vines and flowers. Inside are well-done displays of Victorian Americana, the apothecary's art, surface mining, Wells Fargo boxes and gold scales, a well-preserved antique gun collection, and the old Studebaker buckboard Grace Kelly graced in *High Noon.* The center is open Apr. 1–Sept. 1, Tues.–Sun. 10 A.M.–

weeds and weather-beaten wood near Coulterville

KIM WEIR

4 P.M.; just weekends and holidays the rest of the year. Outside by the town's hangin' tree is a small steam engine locals call *Whistling Billy.* Bill once pulled ore carts to the stamp mills from the nearby **Mary Harrison Mine** along a snaking, nearly vertical route. Then take a walk. Since most of the town's old saloons, cafés, storehouses, and homes have neither been restored nor vandalized, you can peer in windows and see original, faded wallpapers, heavy old doors with ancient handles, and miscellaneous old-time oddities. Two original buildings still stand in Chinatown just off Main, one of them the old adobe **Sun Sun Wo Company Store**—not open to the public. Next door is the town's time-honored wood-frame whorehouse, **Candy's Place.** The ancient rosebush out front was harvested by Candy, who handed out the blooms to "gentlemen callers."

Practical Coulterville

Definitely imposing is the tin-sided, pine-green-and-tan **Hotel Jeffery,** 1 Main St., 209/878-3471 or toll-free 800/464-3471, a natural summer hideout with thick original adobe walls built in 1851. Legend has it that, among others, Ralph Waldo Emerson, Teddy Roosevelt, and Carrie Nation once slept here. There's no air-conditioning, but with adobe walls and ceiling fans, summer heat rarely poses a problem. Rates include continental breakfast. Moderate. A small restaurant downstairs, 209/878-3473, is open for breakfast, lunch, and dinner.

Swing open the batwing doors of the **Magnolia Saloon** right next door and step into another century: tintype photographs, mineral collections, dusty memorabilia, even a wooden Indian. There's one concession to life in the 20th century: a jukebox. (Come by Saturday nights for live music.) Also next to the Jeffery is a cool and pleasant park hosting local events like barbecues, bluegrass festivals, and the annual **Coyote Howl** and **Gunfighters Rendezvous.** The **Coulter Cafe,** 5015 Main St., 209/878-3947, is a good choice for no-frills country-style American food: barbecue ribs, pork chops, and fried chicken.

To Bear Valley

The stretch of "highway" between Coulterville and Bear Valley is beautiful but brutal, with hairpin turns, steep ascents, and sudden descents— a reminder of the demanding terrain challenged daily by hardscrabblers forced to traverse Merced River Canyon (nicknamed "Hell's Hollow"). You'll notice many closed mines along the way, but resist the temptation to go exploring; abandoned mineshafts are dangerous, each for different reasons.

John C. Frémont, intrepid explorer, militarist, and California's first U.S. senator, established his empire's headquarters in Bear Valley. He once owned the entire area from Mariposa to Bagby (fudging on the eastern boundary by about 50 miles when gold was discovered outside his original holdings). Frémont's scout Kit Carson discovered the first gold at the main Mariposa Mine and made strikes at other Bear Valley sites. But high overhead, lawyers' fees, and claim jumpers—Frémont had the governor call in the state militia to forcibly oust them— gradually nibbled away at the mines' potential profits. In his later years, Frémont bragged ruefully that he came to California penniless, "but now I owe $2 million!"

Today, note the ruins of **Frémont's house,** poke into the **Oso House** museum (actually the old Odd Fellows Hall—the original Oso, Frémont's headquarters, was lost to fire), visit the jail, explore the graveyard. There's not much else here. If you feel drawn to this place, to the dust of Frémont's dreams, stay at **Granny's Garden Bed and Breakfast,** 7333 Hwy. 49, Bear Valley, CA 95223, 209/377-8342, a yellow-and-white Victorian where the rooms all have private baths and rates include breakfast, afternoon wine, and spa privileges. Moderate.

MARIPOSA TO BASS LAKE

MARIPOSA AND VICINITY

Mariposa (Spanish for "butterfly"), a woodsy town of 1,500 with old homes and wide, peaceful streets, was named by General John C. Frémont during his sneaky land grab. It's the southernmost of the major gold camps and one of the southern gateways to Yosemite. (The highway from here into the park is almost always open, even in winter.) The hills near here—like half of California, if you believe all the stories—were once Joaquin Murrieta's stomping grounds. Also in these hills are the remains of many ghost towns, most not marked by so much as a stone. Good luck.

To get oriented, stop by the **Mariposa County Chamber of Commerce** office and visitors center, 5158 Hwy. 140 (at Hwy. 49), P.O. Box 425, Mariposa, CA 95338, 209/966-2456.

Seeing and Doing Mariposa

Frémont's old **Mariposa Mine,** the first steam-powered quartz mining operation in California, is at the end of Bullion, though visitors aren't exactly encouraged. Nearby is the white-steepled landmark, **St. Joseph's Catholic Church,** at 4985 Bullion. The grizzled granite **Old Mariposa Jail,** on Bullion between 4th and 5th, has natural rock walls more than two feet thick and was used until 1960.

The **Mariposa County Courthouse** is California's oldest in continuous use. Built in 1854 with local white pine, it has original furnishings on the 2nd floor, including a potbellied woodstove and simple wooden benches. As elsewhere in the gold country, mineral wealth seems to be the holy grail. There's a large rock collection here, and a mineral collage monument outside. Since Mariposa County has no incorporated cities, this is where the governmental action—such as it is—is. The courthouse sits on Bullion between 9th and 10th Sts., open for business as usual weekdays 8 A.M.–5 P.M. and for tours on weekends. Call 209/966-2456 for more information.

The excellent **Mariposa Museum and History Center,** just one block off Hwy. 140 at Jessie and 12th Sts., 209/966-2924, shares space with the local library. In the outdoor courtyard, note the mule-powered Mexican *arrastra* used to grind ore (as well as corn for tortillas) and the full-scale model of a five-stamp mill. Push the button on the miniature version inside, and you'll see how gold-rich rocks were pulverized. Also here are displays of printing and mining equipment, an old-time apothecary, school rooms, Miwok dwellings and sauna, a lady's boudoir, a sheriff's office, and a miner's cabin—altogether a thoughtfully tended historical record. The museum is open Apr.–Oct., daily 10 A.M.–4:30 P.M.; Nov.–Mar., weekends 10 A.M.–4 P.M. Closed January. Small admission (by donation).

Also in Mariposa is the excellent **California State Mining and Mineral Museum,** 5005 Fairgrounds Dr. (at the county fairgrounds), 209/742-7625. Displays include a re-created assay office and mine tunnel, as well as some fine examples of the state's mineral riches. Open May–Sept., Wed.–Mon. 10 A.M.–6 P.M.; the rest of the year, Wed.–Sun. 10 A.M.–4 P.M. Small admission.

Staying in and near Mariposa

Budget travelers will particularly appreciate the HI-AYH **Yosemite Bug Hostel, Lodge, & Campgrounds,** 6979 Hwy. 140 in Midpines, 209/966-6666, fax 209/966-6667, www.yosemitebug.com, just 25 miles from Yosemite Valley on the way to Mariposa, and just $15 a night for a dorm-style bunk. Inexpensive private rooms and campsites are also available, not to mention the camaraderie—and the on-site bistro. Open year-round.

The renovated 1901-vintage **Mariposa Hotel,** right downtown at 5029 Hwy. 140 (at 6th St.), 209/966-4676 or toll-free 800/317-3244, mariposa.yosemite.net/hotel_inn, is a bed-and-breakfast-style inn with generously sized rooms boasting exceptional Victorian detail and modern amenities. Expensive. Closed in January.

Most other lodgings in town provide the usual motel ambience at comparable prices. (Except during slow times, scouting around for bargain discoveries in areas so close to Yosemite is almost a fruitless effort.) Some of Mariposa's better choices include the **E. C. Yosemite Motel,** 5180 Jones St. (at Bullion), 209/742-6800 (Moderate);

the imposing **Miners Inn,** across the highway at 5181 Hwy. 40 N, 209/742-7777 or toll-free 800/237-7277 (Moderate-Luxury); and the **Comfort Inn-Mariposa,** 4994 Bullion, 209/966-4344 (Moderate).

Visitors could spend an entire vacation just trying to count all of the area's bed-and-breakfast inns. For more information, at least about member inns, stop by or call the Mariposa County Chamber of Commerce (see above) or request a current brochure from the **Yosemite-Mariposa Bed and Breakfast Association,** P.O. Box 1100, Mariposa, CA 95338, 209/742-7666.

Eating in and near Mariposa

There are two **Mariposa Certified Farmers' Markets**—one held July–Oct. on Sun., 9 A.M.–11:30 A.M., at Darrah and Triangle Sts., the other June–Oct. on Wed., 5–6 P.M., at Mariposa Park on 6th Street. For information, call 209/742-7230. A great find for Mexican food—everything quite tasty, served in humongous portions—is inexpensive **Castillo's** up the hill from the highway at 4995 5th St., 209/742-4413. Open daily after 10 A.M. for lunch and dinner. The best local choice for Chinese food is **China Station,** 5004 Hwy. 140, 209/966-3889. Not counting Erna's Elderberry House in Oakhurst, the area's fine dining salon is the **Charles Street Dinner House,** 5043 Hwy. 140, 209/966-2366, which serves American fare with the area's inimitable Old West flair. Near Mariposa and unusual for its food is **Chibcha's Inn,** 2747 Hwy. 140 in Cathey's Valley, 209/966-2940, a bed-and-breakfast inn (Moderate) serving authentic Colombian cuisine in the restaurant next door.

Oakhurst

Oakhurst, a scrubby little foothill town in Madera County, is the tail end of the southern Mother Lode and the southernmost official route into Yosemite. The talking grizzly statue downtown at the intersection of Hwy. 41 and Rd. 426 is an unusual monument to extinction. The historical society's **Fresno Flats Historical Park,** 49777 Rd. 427 (on School Rd., just off Crane Valley Rd.), Oakhurst, CA 93644, 559/683-6570, is a park complex with a museum contained in two old schoolhouses and displaying old lace, quilts, and "Yosemite Sam" guns and memorabilia. There's also a jail, blacksmith shop, double "dog-

trot" log cabin, and several wagons and stagecoaches—everything here collected, restored, and maintained by local volunteers. Open Wed.–Sun. 10 A.M.–noon and 5–7 P.M. Small admission (by donation). Two miles north of town, Oakhurst's **Golden Chain Theatre,** P.O. Box 604, 559/683-7112, offers old-time melodramas in summer; reservations advised.

The hautest place around to eat—and stay—is elegant **The Estate by the Elderberries** just west of town, both excellent restaurant and sophisticated country inn. **Erna's Elderberry House,** 48688 Victoria Ln. (at Hwy. 41), 559/683-6800, serves up French- and European-influenced cuisine with a California sensibility in its Mediterranean-style villa. Reservations are all but essential, though passersby may luck out at slow times. But unbelievable meals are just half the point here. Lodgings offered just up the hill at the affiliated European-style **Chateau du Sureau,** 559/683-6860, fax 559/683-0800, www.elderberryhouse.com, match the exceptional quality of the food. Luxury.

For other local information, contact the **Eastern Madera County Chamber of Commerce,** 49015 Rd. 426, Oakhurst, CA 93644, 559/683-7766, or the **Yosemite Sierra Visitors Bureau** just north of town at 41729 Hwy. 41, Oakhurst, CA 93644, 559/683-4636, www.yosemite-sierra.org.

Bass Lake

Hunter S. Thompson immortalized Bass Lake's days as stomping grounds for bad-boy motorcyclists in his 1965 book *Hell's Angels*. But the scene these days is comparatively tame, the main draw being reservoir recreation amid evergreens and summer homes. At the lake, get information and trail brochures at the **Bass Lake Visitors Station** on the west shore. For other information, contact the **Bass Lake Chamber of Commerce,** 54432 Rd. 432, P.O. Box 126, Bass Lake, CA 93604, 559/642-3676, or the **North Fork Chamber of Commerce,** P.O. Box 426, North Fork, CA 93643, 559/877-2410.

Plush **Ducey's on the Lake,** 39255 Marina Dr., Bass Lake, 559/642-3131, was built on the site of classic Ducey's Bass Lake Lodge (which burned down in 1988) and is sister resort to **The Pines Resort in Pines Village,** 559/642-3121, www.basslake.com. For reservations at either, call toll-free 800/350-7463. Open all year. Luxury.

Best bet for dinner here is the **Pines Resort restaurant,** 559/642-3233, which offers decent American fare and an outdoor deck in summer. Eateries and weekend entertainment are nearby in **Old Town,** which is actually new and touristy; among its few authentic historical features is the horse-drawn hearse advertising funerals for $5 (with discounts if the family helps dig).

TOM MEYERS PHOTOGRAPHY

THE GREAT VALLEY AND DELTA

When John Muir wandered west out of the Sierra Nevada in the late 1800s, he was overwhelmed by California's great central valley. "When California was wild," he wrote, "it was one sweet bee garden throughout its entire length . . . so marvelously rich that, in walking from one end of it to the other, a distance of more than four hundred miles, your foot would press about a hundred flowers at every step." As if in Kansas, early immigrants to California's great valley gazed out upon green waves of vegetation washed clean by April rains but burnished to a golden brown by August. The *tulares,* or marshes, and shallow lakes rippled with birdsong, and ancient rivers meandered through woodland jungles of deciduous trees, riverside thickets that were home to the valley's most complex web of wildlife. Grassland prairies, stretching to the distant foothills on every horizon, buzzed with life.

Millions of ducks, geese, swans, and other waterfowl once flocked here in feathery winter clouds so thick that amazed explorers claimed their flight blotted out the sun. Vast herds of tule elk, pronghorn, and deer browsed through woodlands and prairies. Even grizzly bears galloped across valley grasslands just over a century ago. Supported by the land's natural richness, California's great valley was also home to one of the continent's densest native populations, the Maidu, Miwok, Wintu, and Yokut peoples. To the native Maidu who populated much of the north, California's great valley was the source of life itself.

ONE SWEET BEE GARDEN

California's great central valley forms a 50-mile-wide, 400-mile-long plain between the rugged Sierra Nevada and the gentler Coast Ranges, stretching north to near Redding and south to the Tehachapis. There is no other flatland area of comparable size in the United States west of the

THE GREAT VALLEY AND DELTA

Rocky Mountains. The great valley is the state's primary watershed basin, collecting almost half of California's precipitation.

Most of the valley today is slightly above sea level, excepting the Sacramento-San Joaquin Delta area near San Francisco Bay, which is *below* sea level and dry only due to an extensive system of levees and dikes. But more than 140 million years ago, the area was an inland sea complete with swimming dinosaurs. Geologists speculate that this great trough started to fill with sediments when it became an isolated oceanic arm; sedimentation accelerated when the newborn Sierra Nevada range was carved by glaciers. Though flecks of gold still wash down through the foothills to the valley, the region's real wealth is its rich loamy topsoil, up to thousands of feet deep. The only interruption of the steady soil- and valley-building process occurred about three million years ago, when a series of volcanic eruptions near what is now Yuba City and Marysville created a large volcano. Today its remains are the handsome and heavily eroded Sutter Buttes, the world's smallest mountain range and the only peaks on California's vast interior plain.

As recently as 200 years ago, great shallow lakes covered the southern San Joaquin Valley, and when Sierra Nevada snow melt transformed creeks into raging rivers, the entire central valley became an inland sea once more, this time with freshwater lapping against the Sutter Buttes and the valley's encircling foothills.

MAIDU CREATION MYTH

There was no sun, no moon, no stars. All was dark, and everywhere only water. A raft floated down from the north, carrying Turtle and Father of the Secret Society. Then a rope of feathers was let down from the sky, and down came Earth Initiate. When he reached the end of the rope, he tied it to the bow of the raft and stepped in. His face was never seen, but his body shone like the sun.

Earth Initiate wanted to make land so there could be people. Turtle said he would dive for some, then was gone for six years. When he came back, Earth Initiate scraped out the dirt from under Turtle's fingernails, rolled it into a ball the size of a pebble, then looked at it until it was as big as the world and they had run aground on it. All around it were mountains. Father of the Secret Society shouted loudly and the sun came up. Then he called out the stars, each by name. Then he made a giant tree with 12 different types of acorns. Earth Initiate called the birds from the sky and made all the trees and animals. Later, Coyote and Earth Initiate were at E'stobusin Ya'-mani (the Sutter Buttes). Earth Initiate decided to make people, mixing dark red earth with water to make two figures, the first man and woman, Ku'k-su and Morning-Star Woman.

Harvesting the Watershed

Water is life in California's great valley, a fact reflected in the words on the sign arched across the old highway in Modesto: Water Wealth Contentment Health. But land is likewise necessary for economic wealth—for cities, local industries, and agriculture—and during the past 150 years, the valley's marshes and lakes have been drained and "reclaimed" to obtain that land. Converting California's vast central valley to farmland has also meant taming the rivers within its watershed. All major rivers have been dammed, redirected, or "channelized." The Central Valley Project and other 20th-century feats of water engineering have made it possible to transport water from the rain-soaked north to the arid San Joaquin Valley in the south, transforming inland deserts into gardens—truck gardens.

Despite its almost complete remodeling by water engineers, the largest and longest California river is still the Sacramento, which flows south from near Mt. Shasta to its confluence with the Pit and McCloud Rivers at Shasta Lake, then snakes south through the Sacramento Valley, where it is joined by the American, Feather, and Yuba. The San Joaquin River, which lends its name to the southern reaches of the great valley, once flowed westward until pushed north by the Coast Ranges, fed along the way by the Merced, Tuolumne, Stanislaus, Mokelumne, and Cosumnes Rivers. Due to agricultural water diversions, the San Joaquin River has been dry since the 1940s. What remains of the valley's two dominant river systems converge in the delta region, now a predominantly unnatural maze of canals, sloughs, islands, and levees, before flowing through the Carquinez Strait into San Pablo and San Francisco Bays.

THE LAND AS FARMLAND

Given the region's rich loam soils and abundant water, it's no surprise that immigrants came—and still come—to the valley primarily to farm or work in the fields. The valley's first landed gentry were recipients of Mexican land grants who transformed wildlands into ranchos dedicated first to livestock grazing, then to more diversified agricultural enterprises. Disillusioned fortune hunters from California's goldfields, attracted to the fertile heartland and its more predictable wealth, were followed by generations of farmers from around the country and the globe.

Almost from the beginning, helped along by the completion in 1869 of the transcontinental railroad, California agriculture developed to suit the interests of large landholders. In California, Thomas Jefferson's ideal of the yeoman democrat and the romance of the family farm have primarily been fiction. Though the growing popularity of organic produce and farmers' markets is beginning to change things, agriculture in California's central valley is agribusiness—and it's big business. The enormous holdings of corporate agriculture dominate both the landscape and local economies.

SUMMERS LIKE A BAKE OVEN, WINTERS OF FOG AND ICE

John Muir noted that in California's great valley "there are only two seasons—spring and summer." Muir was slightly mistaken. Summers are long and hot, and "winter" in the valley, though often foggy, can be quite cold. Spring and fall are noticeable transitions between the two extremes. If less than hospitable for humans, the valley's intense summer heat is perfect for crops. In most areas, characteristic 100-degrees-plus summertime temperatures are unforgettable and virtually unlivable—a fact now happily ignored by most residents since the advent of air-conditioning. Winter, which coincides with the state's rainy season, is the only time of year this part of the Golden State is green without the assistance of irrigation.

Thick, ground-hugging tule fog is common between winter storms, insulating the valley from most winter freezes. (Sacramento is derisively known as the Tule Fog Capital of the World by its bone-chilled residents.) On clear nights after a good rain, blankets of mist form that the weakened winter sun can't burn through for days, sometimes weeks. When it settles in for a stay, California's valley fog creates one of the world's largest ground clouds, a moist, ghostly shroud often going the distance between Redding and Bakersfield and stretching across the farmland between the Coast Ranges and the Sierra Nevada foothills; fog ceilings usually reach 1,000 feet or more above the valley floor.

Without fog, valley winters become even colder, with subfreezing temperatures no surprise Dec.–February. A phenomenon colloquially known as "false spring" sometimes occurs in late January or February—unseasonably balmy weather that encourages people to believe, albeit briefly, in the promise of spring. To experience California's heartland at its best, try a sparkling day in early spring when snowcapped coastal mountains and Sierra Nevada peaks seem just within reach beyond the wildflower-thick foothills.

SACRAMENTO AND VICINITY

THE BIG TOMATO

People have long poked fun at Sacramento, California's capital city. Mark Twain himself was among the first. In Sacramento, he observed, "It is a fiery summer always, and you can gather roses, and eat strawberries and ice cream, and wear white linen clothes, and pant and perspire at eight or nine o'clock in the morning." Comparing it to New York, the Big Apple, people from Sacramento call their metropolis the Big Tomato—a wry reference to the area's agricultural heritage. Though Sacramento is often dismissed as an overgrown cowtown—an epithet linguistically more apt for Vacaville down the road, vaca meaning "cow" in Spanish—this rural hub of commerce and political wheeling and dealing is now a real city around which the county's nearly two million people revolve.

Sacramento has a respectable professional basketball team—the Sacramento Kings—and hopes to lure a pro football franchise, meanwhile dreaming still about major league baseball. It has one of the state's finest newspapers, a sky-scraping skyline visible from nearby rice fields, and reverberating rings of suburbs. It also has traffic congestion, air pollution, and the seemingly hopeless problem of human homelessness.

Lately, Sacramento has set its more personal sights on bodily fitness, stylish possessions, and "lifestyle." Writer Cob Goshen protests this new trend toward trendiness. "It's as if we've packed up and moved to the remotest suburbs of Eliot's Wasteland," he suggests, "[and] exchanged lives of quiet desperation for those of cheerful inconsequence. No more long hot days. No life and death struggle. It finally happened. We're in California now." Well, perhaps not quite yet. Despite its big-city ways, Sacramento is still somehow uniquely lovable. The town is stuffed with good restaurants, sparkles with unpretentious arts and entertainment, and still offers some evidence of its friendlier but wilder past at the edge of the frontier.

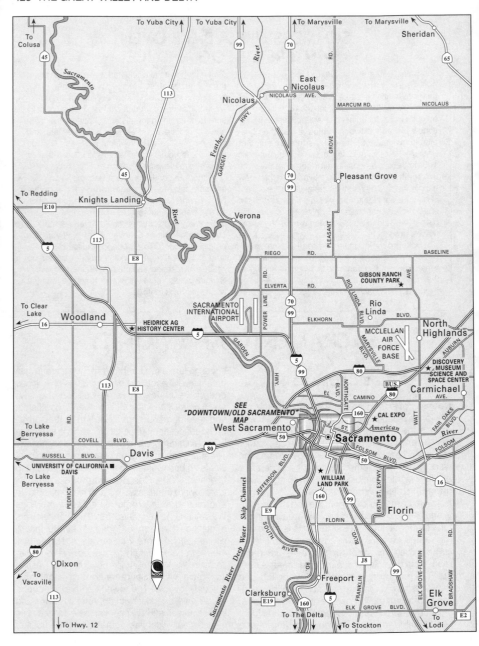

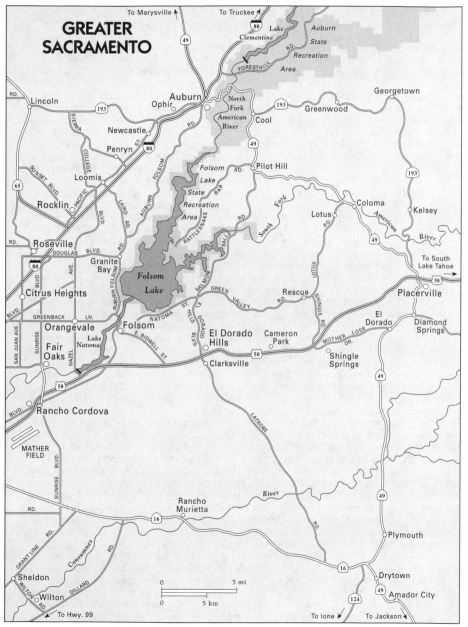

GREATER SACRAMENTO

© AVALON TRAVEL PUBLISHING, INC.

Unique in Sacramento is the opportunity to observe the antics of the state legislature up close and personal, as if at the zoo. There's nothing quite like sitting in on committee hearings or other wrangles to appreciate the absurd beauty of political fisticuffs, California style. Try exploring the Capitol building during the final days of budget battles before legislative recess in summer, when hallways are crowded with arm-twisting lobbyists, and exhausted politicians are most likely to call each other names in public or slip up and tell the truth to the press. All in all it's great fun—but only for those with strong constitutions.

SEEING OLD SACRAMENTO

The original gold rush boomtown of Sacramento boomed first as a tent city on the mudflats along the river, an area more or less defined these days by the intersection of Front and J Sts. downtown, just west of I-5. Mark Twain wrote here, Lola Montez danced here, and William Fuller painted here. These eight city blocks, appropriately called Old Sacramento and now both a state historic park and national landmark, almost capture the ambience of the Old West—especially on those low-key days when tourists are scarce. But, despite the careful restoration of the area's old buildings, the freeway looming overhead and the all-too-modern commercialism of the hundreds of shops and restaurants detract from the illusion.

Most worthwhile in Old Sacramento are the excellent history museums; plans are in the works for still more museums and an old-fashioned waterfront park. Another unusual attraction is the five-story *Delta King,* the last of California's original steam paddle-wheelers and a 1920s Prohibition-era pleasure palace. The *King,* now a floating hotel and restaurant/saloon, faithfully delivered passengers between San Francisco and Sacramento until the 1940s and World War II, when he and sister ship *Delta Queen* dressed up in battleship gray and transported Navy troops. (The *King* is docked these days. To paddle-wheel up and down the river, other boats are available. See Touring Old Sacramento below.) While wandering through Old Sacramento, note the elevated boardwalks and original streetside curbing, reminders of the

days when neighborhood rivers regularly rampaged through town in winter.

Touring Old Sacramento

Showing yourself the town is easy here, so pick up an *Old Sacramento Walking Tour Guide* at the visitor information center at 1101 2nd Street. Or, let the horses do the walking by hailing a **horse-drawn carriage** (various concessionaires, $10 and up, available daily except in bad weather). In addition, try the **self-guided historical audio tour** of Old Sacramento. A fairly skilled Mark Twain impersonator narrates the story, from nine sound stations (housed in redwood kiosks) set up throughout Old Sac; a map shows the particular buildings under discussion. Listen to all nine segments in exchange for a $4 bag of tokens—available at the visitor center, the Discovery Museum, and at participating merchants throughout Old Sac—or listen to individual segments for $.50 each.

With time and a little cash to spare, consider a one-hour paddle-wheel tour (spring, summer, and fall only) or a lunch or dinner cruise. Channel Star Excursions offers two boats: the very large *Spirit of Sacramento,* one-time star of the John Wayne movie *Blood Alley* (all cleaned up now), and the smaller *Matthew McKinley.* Sightseeing tours as well as brunch, lunch, happy hour, dinner, and dinner theater cruises are offered; private parties and charters are also possible. The company's office is at 110 L St., 916/552-2933 or toll-free 800/443-0263, but trips depart from the L Street Landing, across the way. Another possibility is **Exodus Boat Cruises** at 1115 Front St., Ste. 9, 916/447-0266, which offers steam paddle-wheel tours and a delta cruise to San Francisco.

Fairly new in the neighborhood but already immensely popular is the **River Otter Taxi Company,** part shuttle, part pleasure cruise, headquartered at 917 7th St., 916/448-4333. River Otter's happy yellow tug-like boats resemble river-size bathtub toys assigned the grown-up task of connecting Old Sac with marinas and waterfront restaurants just to the north along the Sacramento River. The River Otter water taxi, which holds a maximum of 24 people, makes at least six complete loops daily in season, typically from Apr. into fall (weather and river conditions permitting); charters are also available. At last report, regular round-trip river taxi fare was

$5 adults, $2 for children under 42 inches tall.

Full-steam-ahead train fans, take a ride on the **Sacramento Southern Railroad,** affiliated with the California State Railroad Museum. These 40-minute steam-powered excursions start from the railroad museum's reconstructed freight depot on Front St. and head south to the delta town of Hood. Trips run Apr.–Sept. on Sat. and Sun. only, with trains departing on the hour, 10 A.M.–5 P.M. "Theme" and dinner trains are also scheduled, on special weekends Oct.–December. For current information, call 916/445-6645.

If that's not enough train time, there's always the **Yolo Shortline Railroad Company.** On selected Saturdays May–Oct., steam train fans climb aboard the "Clarksburg Special" near the intersection of Jefferson Blvd. and S. River Rd. (there's no depot) across the river in West Sacramento and relax for a three-hour ride through surrounding farmland. (Watch out for those train robbers!) Trips also run from Woodland to West Sacramento on a more frequent schedule. For more information, call 916/372-9777.

California State Railroad Museum

Situated at the old terminus of Southern Pacific, the huge California State Railroad Museum at 111 I St. in Old Sacramento warehouses an exceptional collection of locomotives and railway cars that once rode the rails "over the hump," connecting California with more civilized areas of the United States. Stop just to appreciate the painstaking restoration of these fine old machines. Ever-popular is the *St. Hyacinthe,* a restored 1929 sleeping car that rocks and rolls in simulated nighttime travel. A relative newcomer is the elegant 1940s-style stainless steel *Cochiti* dining car, where a selection of Mary Colter's stunning 1937 Mimbre dinnerware (designed specifically for this car) is on display. The railroad museum's walk-through introductory diorama is well done, as are the films and interpretive exhibits. Docent-led tours are available daily. And don't miss the museum store.

Also part of the museum complex is the **Central Pacific Railroad Passenger Station** at Front and J, restored to its 1870s appearance. The museum's reconstructed old **Central Pacific Freight Depot** nearby, point of departure for steam train excursions, is also home to the **Old Sacramento Public Market.** The railroad museum is open daily 10 A.M.–5 P.M. Admission is $3 adults, free for children age 16 and under. (The same all-day ticket is good for admission to the passenger station.) For more information, stop by the museum at 125 I St., call 916/445-6645 (recorded), or try www.csrmf.org.

Sacramento Museum of History, Science, and Technology

Also worth a stop is Old Sac's **Discovery Museum** near the waterfront at 101 I St., 916/264-7057, fax 916/264-5100, www.thediscovery.org, more formally known as the Sacramento Museum of History, Science, and Technology—a merger of the original Sacramento History

*California State
Railroad Museum*

SACRAMENTO'S TRANSCONTINENTAL RAILROAD TIES

The Sacramento Valley's first railroad, completed in 1856, ran the 22 miles between Folsom and Sacramento. But the railroad's engineer, Theodore Judah, dreamed of a transcontinental railroad connecting California growers and merchants to the rest of the nation. Judah convinced four Sacramento business leaders that this east-west link over the treacherous Sierra Nevada could be built. With the help of California's "Big Four"—Charles Crocker, Mark Hopkins, Collis Huntington, and Leland Stanford—he founded the Central Pacific Railroad Company, which soon began lobbying the U.S. Congress for federal construction loans. In 1862, legislation finally authorized loans to construct a railroad route over Donner Pass—with the proviso that no money would be lent until 40 miles of track were laid.

In the spring of 1869, the Central Pacific and Union Pacific railroads were ceremoniously joined at Promontory Point, Utah. As Oscar Lewis noted in *The Big Four,* the slogan of the day was: "California Annexes the United States." Half in arrogance and half in the spirit of play, the wildest of the western colonies, he noted, "prepared to take its place (near the head of the table) with the family of states."

Soon after, railroad feeder lines connected Sacramento to Benicia and Oakland, and links were planned to Southern California and Oregon. As portrayed in the novel *The Octopus* by Frank Norris, Southern Pacific's tracks became tentacles reaching out in all directions to control the state's economy and political climate for more than 40 years, and Theodore Judah's financial backers became the richest, most politically powerful men in the state.

Museum with the Sacramento Science Center. Its exhibits emphasize education and fun. Local history is the first focus here, explored via artifacts, photos, and hands-on activities, but expect surprising special exhibits, too. The museum is open daily 10 A.M.–5 P.M. Admission is $5 adults, $4 seniors and youths, $3 children ages 6–12 (under age 6 free). Group tours are available. Call for information about the museum's Discovery Museum Science and Space Center (or see Capital Sights Farther Afield below).

California Military Museum
Among historical attractions in Old Sacramento is the four-story California Military Museum at 1119 2nd St., 916/442-2883, www.militarymuseum.org. Exhibits chronicle the early days of the California Militia, and the long-running history of the state's National Guard—first headquartered in the Pacific Stables building across the street. At home here are thousands of military relics, from rifles, World War I machine guns, and Civil War muskets and bayonets to uniforms predating the Civil War—even the sword that Major General Zachary Taylor carried into battle during the Mexican War. Military-oriented gift shop, too. Open Tues.–Sun. 10 A.M.–4 P.M. Admission is $3 adults, $1.50 se-

niors, $1 children ages 8 to 17 (under age 8 free) and military with ID.

Other Old Sacramento Sights
The **B. F. Hastings Building** at 2nd and J Sts. was once the original Wells Fargo office, rebuilt in 1852 after a fire destroyed most of the city. The small communications museum downstairs honors Sacramento's importance in Old West information flow. This was the end of the line for the original Alta Telegraph Company and the western terminus of the Pony Express, the place where trail-weary horses and dog-tired riders laid down their mailbag burdens after the last leg of the 10-day, 1,966-mile cross-country relay race against time. (From here, correspondence went on to San Francisco via steamboat.) Upstairs are the original chambers of the **California Supreme Court,** dignified courtroom and dark justices' chambers, the quality of pioneer jurisprudence perhaps polished by the passage of time.

The **Big Four Building** at 113 I St. between Front and 2nd, Central Pacific's original headquarters, actually stood on K St. when Theodore Judah made his bold pitch to the Big Four of California railroading fame; the building was moved to its present site to make way for the I-5 freeway.

Downstairs these days is an open-for-business re-creation of the original 1880s **Huntington & Hopkins Hardware Store** where visitors can gain recognition for themselves by correctly identifying samples of 19th-century hardware. Upstairs is a re-creation of the original Central Pacific Railroad boardroom, the general offices of the railroad museum, and the railroad museum's library reading room. Open Tues.–Sat. 1–5 P.M., 916/323-8073.

The tiny **Old Eagle Theatre** at 925 Front St. is a canvas reconstruction of the 1849 original, a venerable venue now thriving, theatrically speaking, under the auspices of the state's railroad museum. The dramatic repertoire includes gold rush–era classics and more contemporary productions such as *Seven Brides for Seven Brothers.* The Old Eagle also performs Storybook Children's Theatre weekend matinees. On weekdays, the theater sponsors interpretive and historical programs for schoolchildren. For information on upcoming events, call the theater directly at 916/323-6343. To arrange group tours, call 916/445-4209. For current information on live theatrical productions at the Old Eagle, call 916/445-6645.

Stop by the **Old Sacramento Schoolhouse Museum** at Front and L Sts. to reminisce on the romantic minimalism of one-room schools.

Practical Old Sac

Parking in Old Sacramento proper is often possible, with the fairly recent addition of new parking spaces along Front St. and elsewhere—

SACRAMENTO JAZZ JUBILEE

Things happen year-round in Sacramento. The withering summer heat does little to slow the pace of local activity, but winter can get a bit sluggish. For information about what's going on while you'll be in town, contact the Convention and Visitors Bureau or refer to local newspapers (see Sacramento Information).

But Sacramento's biggest party happens every year over Memorial Day weekend. Sacramento's original Dixieland Jazz Jubilee is now the Sacramento Jazz Jubilee, attracting 100,000 or more often outlandishly dressed but friendly fans and 100 or more bands from around the country and the world. Bridging the cultural divide between twentysomethings and their grandparents, swing bands joined the mix in 1999.

As the Jazz Jubilee has grown—it started out as a predominantly local event, staged in Old Sacramento—so has its need for space. These days, there are four additional event centers beyond Old Sacramento and miscellaneous venues nearby. Closest of these is the Sacramento Convention Center, but largest is Cal Expo (site of the annual state fair); two hotels near Cal Expo, the Radisson and the Sacramento Inn, complete the roster. Most concert and cabaret sites are clustered in and around Old Sacramento (from I to L Sts. between the river and I-5). For current details, contact **Sacramento Jazz Jubilee,** 2787 Del Monte St., West Sacramento, CA 95691, 916/372-5277, www.sacjazz.com.

Old Sacramento

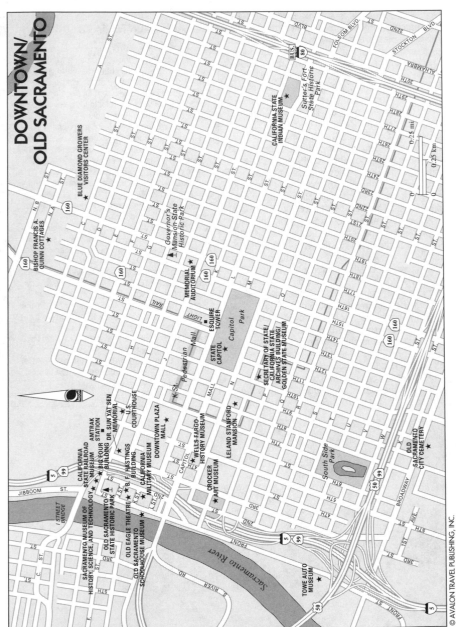

DOWNTOWN/
OLD SACRAMENTO

BLUE DIAMOND GROWERS
VISITORS CENTER ★

BISHOP FRANCIS A.
QUINN COTTAGES ★

CALIFORNIA STATE
INDIAN MUSEUM ★

Sutter's Fort
State Historic
Park ★

Governor's
Mansion State
Historic Park ★

MEMORIAL
AUDITORIUM ★

RAIL

LIGHT

ESQUIRE
TOWER ■

Capitol
Park

STATE
CAPITOL ★

SECRETARY OF STATE/
CALIFORNIA STATE
ARCHIVES BUILDING/
GOLDEN STATE MUSEUM ★

Pedestrian Mall

K St.

MALL

N

CALIFORNIA STATE RAILROAD
MUSEUM ★

AMTRAK
STATION

DR. SUN YAT SEN
MEMORIAL ★

BIG FOUR
BUILDING ★

U.S.
COURTHOUSE

B.F. HASTINGS
BUILDING ★

DOWNTOWN PLAZA
MALL ★

CALIFORNIA
MILITARY MUSEUM ★

WELLS FARGO
HISTORY MUSEUM ★

LELAND STANFORD
MANSION ★

CROCKER
ART MUSEUM ★

SACRAMENTO MUSEUM OF
HISTORY, SCIENCE, AND TECHNOLOGY ★

OLD SACRAMENTO
STATE HISTORIC PARK ★

OLD EAGLE THEATRE ★

OLD SACRAMENTO
SCHOOLHOUSE MUSEUM ★

OLD
SACRAMENTO
CITY CEMETERY ★

South Side
Park

I STREET
BRIDGE

JIBBOOM ST.

Sacramento River

S. RIVER RD

RIVER RD

TOWE AUTO
MUSEUM ★

FOLSOM BLVD.

STOCKTON BLVD.

ALHAMBRA

BROADWAY

FRONT ST.

0   0.25 mi
0   0.25 km

© AVALON TRAVEL PUBLISHING, INC.

though there's been talk about eliminating free parking. If that occurs—or if you're here at a busy time—the large public lots just to the east (under the freeway) and south are ample; from either, it's an easy stroll straight into the olden days. Or, if you've been exploring downtown, either stroll into Old Sac via the K Street Tunnel (a wide public walkway under the freeway) from the Downtown Plaza or take the inexpensive downtown shuttle buses.

For more information about Old Sacramento, pick up a current copy of the free tabloid *Old Sacramento Directory & Map* at local information kiosks, or contact the **Old Sacramento Visitor Information Center** at its newest location, 1101 2nd St. (below Carl's Jr.), 916/442-7644, which offers countless brochures, maps, and personable assistance. For still more info, try website www.oldsacramento.com. Find out what's going on by calling the Old Sacramento events line (recorded) at 916/558-3912.

SEEING DOWNTOWN SACRAMENTO

State Capitol

Painstakingly restored in the 1980s to its early 1900s ambience, California's spectacular state Capitol is hard to miss in its central Capitol Park location at 10th St. and the Capitol Mall (between L and N Streets). Constructed from 1860 to 1874, the Capitol and its magnificent gold-domed rotunda, bronze and crystal chandeliers, rich walnut woods, "Eureka tile," and marble mosaic floors speak of an era when buildings represented material yet high-flying ideals. The red-hued Senate and soft green Assembly chambers on the 2nd floor hint at Greco-Roman governmental tradition. Official declarations of these respective political bodies—"It is the duty of a Senator to protect the liberty of the people" and "It is the duty of the Legislators to pass just laws"—are inscribed in gold leaf but in Latin, perhaps so most citizens (including politicians) can't decipher them. Surrounding **Capitol Park** is an elegant 40-acre landscape of impressive and unusual trees also including the **Vietnam Veterans Memorial** and the new (1998) **California Veterans Memorial.**

The Capitol is open 9 A.M.–5 P.M. daily except Thanksgiving, Christmas, and New Year's Day. Free guided tours focus separately on the Capitol building's restoration, its history, the legislative process, and Capitol Park (weather permitting). For more information, or to arrange group (10 or more) or school tours, call 916/324-0333.

Golden State Museum

Open since summer 1998, the $10.8-million Golden State Museum tells the story of California since statehood through the themes of place, people, promise, and politics. (How could anyone launch a museum so near the Capitol *without* dabbling in politics?) But the perspective offered by this first-class museum, the brainchild of former Secretary of State March Fong Eu, is far

the State Capitol of California

from bureaucratic or institutional. Exhibits have been created from the paperwork of people's everyday lives, though the displays represent only a few file folders' worth of the 120 million documents collected in the State Archives.

For a fast-paced, intense tour, just let the audio program run and try to keep up. The museum's **Place** gallery explores the diversity of California's natural landscape, as well as the land's radical transformation by the gold rush and subsequent economic and social forces. In addition to the voices of resource management, a holographic ghost of John Muir also speaks. **People** introduces the astonishing diversity of new Californians, how and why they came as well as what it took to create a new collective homeland. Back downstairs, the overarching ceiling mural in the **Promise** gallery amplifies the historic and mythic themes that attracted settlers from around the globe. **Politics** makes one marvel that we've managed to pull it off this long. Since Sacramento's newest museum is self-supporting, be sure to seriously explore the stylish gift shop before strolling on.

Occupying the first two floors of the California Archives building at 1020 O St. (10th and O, just one block south of the state Capitol), 916/653-7524, fax 916/653-7134, the Golden State Museum is open Tues.–Sat. 10 A.M.–5 P.M. and Sun. noon–5 P.M. To schedule a group tour, call 916/653-3476 at least two weeks in advance. Admission is $6.50 adults, $5 seniors, $3.50 children ages 6–13 (under age 6 free). Student tours are $2.50 per person, adult tours $4 per person.

California State Indian Museum

Not far from the Capitol and sharing a city block with Sutter's Fort is the refurbished and updated California State Indian Museum at 2618 K St., 916/324-7405, open 10 A.M.–5 P.M. daily except Thanksgiving, Christmas, and New Year's Day. With its fine collection of artifacts and exhibits, selected and approved by Native American elders, the museum chronicles the material, social, and spiritual development of California native culture. Particularly fascinating is the significance of

JOHN SUTTER, "KING OF SACRAMENTO"

The Spanish claimed much of California's heartland from the 1540s until the early 1800s but never settled it. The first Europeans to see the Sacramento River were members of the Pedro Fages expedition of 1772, who discovered the confluence of the San Joaquin and Sacramento while exploring San Francisco Bay. Russian and Canadian fur trappers followed in the 1820s and '30s. First here, of course, were the Maidu and Miwok peoples. In 1839, when Johann August Suter (John Sutter) and his Hawaiian crew moored his ships near the future site of Sacramento's city dump on the American River, the native population had already been laid low by introduced diseases and straight-ahead slaughter.

John Sutter arrived at a fortunate time when he put down roots here in 1839. California's Mexican government was fretting over territorial invasions by trappers and mountain men, and Governor Alvarado happily granted the Swiss immigrant 50,000 acres— a move partially intended to thwart General Vallejo, his political rival. Sutter's fortunes increased again when the Russians abandoned Fort Ross and Alvarado's successor gave him still more land. Sutter's dream was to "civilize" the entire valley, and together with his small band of fellow travelers and

native workers, he built his adobe outpost in what is now downtown Sacramento—the center of his short-lived agricultural empire. By 1845, with fur trapping all but exhausted by the near extinction of both beavers and otters, Sutter had become the undisputed king of Sacramento.

Though essentially a blundering businessman, Sutter's empire was nonetheless becoming so large that his only limitation was lack of lumber. So, in 1848, he sent carpenter and wagon builder James Marshall to a site 40 miles east of Sacramento on the American River to build a lumber mill. With Marshall's discovery of gold, the end of Sutter's reign soon followed.

Within five years of Marshall's gold discovery, more than a half-million people arrived in the Sacramento area to seek their fortunes. But gold seemed to line everybody's pockets except Sutter's. Largely victimized by his own excess, he saw things differently. "I was the victim of every swindler that came along," he said. "These swindlers made the cornerstone of my ruin." In Washington, D.C., where he went to beg a pension for the services he rendered America prior to the gold rush, John Sutter died a bitter and broken man in 1880.

CALIFORNIA'S HOMELESS GOVERNORS

One of California's official peculiarities is the fact that the state has had no official governor's residence since 1967, when the old mansion was added to the state park system. It's a somewhat typical tale of California political throat-tearing.

In a way, it's all Ronald Reagan's fault. Preceding former governor Edmund G. "Pat" Brown's last campaign in the 1960s, land for a new governor's mansion had been cleared—at substantial expense—across from the Capitol near 14th, 15th, O, and N Sts., all part of the Capitol Master Plan. Mansion construction was delayed by design disagreements, however. Ultimately, a statewide contest was launched, and the winning Spanish-modern architectural design came from the San Francisco firm of Campbell & Wong. Though the mansion was privately estimated to cost less than $800,000, the official state estimate was $1.2 million. And the Ronald Reagan gubernatorial campaign suddenly had a hot populist issue—"Pat Brown's Million Dollar Mansion"—though Pat Brown had nothing to do with it.

Though it had been good enough for Pat Brown and family for all those years, when Reagan won the governor's race in 1966, he and Nancy refused to live in the old governor's mansion. It was probably time for the old residence to retire; in case of fire, for example, the Reagans would have had to shimmy down a rope ladder to escape its upper floors. California's new first family instead quietly moved into a private home on 45th St., in East Sacramento's Fabulous Forties.

But in the early 1970s, the idea of an official governor's residence reemerged. A group of influential businesspeople who the Reagans counted among their friends and political allies, including a number of lobbyists, bought an isolated 11-acre lot along the American River in Carmichael—out in the suburbs, adjacent to a golf course—for a new governor's mansion, and donated it to the state. After considerable partisan wrangling (Democrats felt coerced by the Republican land contribution), the state eventually paid $1.3 million to build an ostentatious but otherwise fairly ordinary home on the site. The Los Angeles Times described it as a giant roof suspended on poles; other critics compared its architecture to Safeway.

The mansion was not completed in time for the Reagans' benefit, however. Reagan's successor, then-governor Jerry Brown—picking up on the same issue that had pilloried his father, former governor Pat Brown—pointedly called the place a "Taj Mahal," partly to embarrass the Republicans, and refused to move into it.

Although Brown's successor, Republican governor George Deukmejian, wanted to move in, the Democrat-dominated legislature defied him and auctioned it off to the highest bidder in 1984. During his term, Deukmejian, and later Republican governor Pete Wilson, lived in another suburban home provided by a private foundation chaired by Republican anti-affirmative action activist Ward Connerly.

But California's governors may not be homeless forever. Governor Gray Davis, a Democrat, says he's committed to building an official California governor's mansion to house his successor.

---

basketry, a sacred survival art in which the basketmaker first offers thanks to the plant world for the materials gathered, then becomes part of that world and the basket itself, thereby guaranteeing abundant future harvests. Admission is $1 adults, age 16 and under free. Metered parking for both the museum and Sutter's Fort is available on K, L, 26th, and 28th Sts. nearby.

Sutter's Fort State Historic Park
Sutter's Fort, around the corner at 2701 L St., 916/445-4422, was Sacramento's—and the valley's—first nonnative settlement, the center of John Sutter's attempted agrarian empire. Many of Sutter's original furnishings and implements actually came from Fort Ross, which Sutter bought from the Russians in 1841. During the gold rush, unruly, rampaging '49ers plundered Sutter's storehouses, gardens, and fields, squatted on his territory, and even shot his cattle for food and sport. The "fort" was all but destroyed before restoration began in 1891, though the original adobe brick walls of the central building somehow survived.

Exhibits at the fort complex re-create the feel of daily life in 1846—an experience quite popular with school and tour groups. Take a self-guided audio tour, or show up for **Living History Days** and **Pioneer Demonstration Days.** Sutter's Fort is open daily 10 A.M.–5 P.M. except

Thanksgiving, Christmas, and New Year's Day (gift shop open till 4:30 P.M.). Admission is $1 adults, age 16 and under free; the price of admission increases on special-event days.

Governor's Mansion State Historic Park

Now part of the state park system, this 1877 Victorian home at 16th and H Sts., 916/324-7405, was one of the first houses in California to feature indoor plumbing, central heating, and other niceties of modern life. Home to 13 California governors—including Ronald Reagan, though he and Nancy moved out in 1967—the Governor's Mansion is now furnished with an eclectic collection of items including a 1902 Steinway piano owned by Governor George Pardee's family, Hiram Johnson's 1911 plum-colored velvet sofa and chairs, the state's official 1950s china, and a clawfoot bathtub off the master bedroom with each toenail painted red by former Governor Jerry Brown's younger sister Kathleen (more recently noteworthy as state treasurer) during their father Pat Brown's term in office. The mansion is open daily 10 A.M.–5 P.M. for guided tours only (last tour leaves at 4 P.M.). General admission is $1 adults, free for age 16 and under; fees are higher on special-event days. Tours start at the two-story Carriage House, now a gift shop and visitors center. Public parking is available in the lot at 14th and H Sts. if street parking is impossible.

Leland Stanford Mansion

That stunning presence at 800 N St. downtown (on the southeast corner of 8th and N) was once the home of Leland Stanford, one of California's "Big Four" railroad barons and Stanford University's founder. A fairly straightforward two-story house when Governor Stanford bought the place in 1861, as the Stanford Mansion it was destined to become the Golden State's de facto Capitol and "the most perfect specimen of a house in all of California." Said specimen soon grew from a fairly modest 1,700 to an astonishing 19,000 square feet. The original house was hoisted up off the ground to allow for construction of a new 1st floor and grand entrance stairway; on top of other additions came a new mansard-roofed 4th floor. A grab bag of architectural styles, including Italianate and Federalist, the Stanford Mansion is both a state and national

historic landmark featuring many of its original furnishings. Though restoration work was still underway, at last report, public tours (donation requested) are typically offered each week. For current details, call 916/324-0575; for group tour reservations, call 916/445-4209.

Crocker Art Museum

Among the oldest public art museums in the West, the Crocker Art Museum at 216 O St. (on the corner of 3rd and O, a short walk from Old Sacramento), 916/264-5423, www.crockerartmuseum.org, is very Victorian, and one of Sacramento's finest features. Built in 1869 by banker B. F. Hastings and later sold to E. B. Crocker (Charles "Big Four" Crocker's brother), the museum is listed on the National Register of Historic Places and is itself a work of art—High Italianate art, with twin curving stairways, ornate painted plaster, elaborate woodwork, and inlaid polychromed tile floors. The interiors echo San Francisco's early Nob Hill nuance. The Crocker family's original collection of predominantly 19th-century European paintings and drawings has been generously supplemented with new works over the years, including samples of Victorian decorative arts, Asian ceramics, and California landscapes and photography. A collector's coup came in late 1995, with Sacramento artist Wayne Thiebaud's gift of 68 original works; some of Thiebaud's legacy is usually on display. Cultural events are another Crocker claim to fame, from lectures to musical programs.

In addition to extra hours for special events and activities, the museum is open Tues.–Sun. 10 A.M.–5 P.M., until 9 P.M. on Thurs., closed Mon. and major holidays. Admission is $5.50 adults ages 18–64, $4.50 age 65 and older, $3 children ages 7–17, free for age 6 and under. Tours available. Wheelchair accessible. Parking is available at the nearby lot off 2nd Street.

Towe Auto Museum

The one-time Towe Ford Museum is now the Towe Auto Museum, following the traumatic 1997 car-by-car sale of the fabulous Towe Ford collection, to satisfy the Internal Revenue Service. Located just a few blocks south of the Crocker Art Museum, 2200 Front St. (corner of Front and V), 916/442-6802, www.toweautomuseum.com, the Towe (rhymes with "cow") was once the most complete collection of antique Fords anywhere—a stable of more than 100 of Ford's horseless carriages including Henry Ford's first successful production model, a rare 1906 Model N Runabout, which miraculously survived the IRS auction slaughter and is still on display. But for classic car enthusiasts the new collection is still quite fine, showcasing some 150 venerable vehicles in themed American "dream car" exhibits, including "The Dream of Cool" and "The Dream of Speed." Special monthly car club meets and other events are also scheduled. The Towe Auto Museum is open daily 10 A.M.–6 P.M.; admission is $6 adults, $2.50 youths ages 14–18, $1 children ages 5–13, free for age 4 and under. Gift shop. Free parking.

Other Capital Sights Downtown

New attractions downtown include an impressive number of new government buildings and office complexes adding still more vertical lift to the skyline. Most striking is the grand new 16-story **U.S. Courthouse** at 6th and I Streets. Inside there's an oval atrium and, if you take the elevator up, some spectacular views; outside, near the entrance, there's some intriguing interpretive art (do look down to appreciate the judicial aphorisms). Inspiring, too, is the new **Secretary of State/California State Archives Building** at 11th and O Streets. (Considerably less thrilling: the new **Department of Justice** and **California EPA** buildings on I Street.) But the state's not done yet. The mother of all government building booms is just beginning, near Capitol Park's east end—five new state office buildings and three parking garages between L and O and 14th and 17th Sts., 1.5 million square feet in all, scheduled for completion by 2003.

Fascinating at N. A and 15th Sts., near the railroad tracks, are the 60 tiny **Bishop Francis A. Quinn Cottages**, each just 375 square feet, one attempted local solution to the persistent problem of homelessness. Tenants have two-year leases, and pay one-third of their incomes for rent. The cottages were unveiled in mid-1998, and already there's a hopelessly long waiting list. Not far away, the modern brick **Blue Diamond Growers Visitors Center** of the California Almond Growers Exchange—the world's largest almond processing plant, whose nuts get around on Air Force One and the space shuttle—is located at 1701 C St., 916/446-8409, and offers a 20-minute informational video, free almond tasting, and on-site sales. Open Mon.–Fri. 10 A.M.–5 P.M., Sat. 10 A.M.–4 P.M.

Another unique downtown attraction is the **Dr. Sun Yat Sen Memorial** and museum honoring the "Father of China," in the Chinatown Mall near I-5, between 3rd and 5th and J and I Sts., open Tues.–Sat. 1–3 P.M. The mall stands on the site of Sacramento's **Old Chinatown**, "Yee Fow," and is notable for its Chinese language school, association halls, and shops. For some high-test consumerism and rocking cultural contrast, from here stroll south to K St. then east to the vast **Downtown Plaza** mall, where the **Hard Rock Cafe** is a main attraction. From the mall, stroll east along K St., downtown's central boulevard. There's big talk about an impending "K Street Comeback"—there's the new **Esquire Tower** and IMAX theater at 13th and K, near the convention center, and developers are

THE B STREET THEATER

Pretty big news in The Big Tomato is the arrival of serious (and seriously cheap) theater, thanks to Timothy Busfield—an actor most recently incarnated on TV as the pesky reporter on *The West Wing,* though baby boomers will also remember him as Elliot, the red-headed ad agency guy from *Thirtysomething*—and his brother Buck, founders of Sacramento's popular B Street Theater. At home in a midtown warehouse near the railroad tracks, the theater is strictly Manhattan basement, complete with subway-like rumble. Nothing posh. The emphasis here is on the plays and the performance. *Content.* The Busfields also run Sacramento's Fantasy Theater for children, performing professional plays in the public schools and sponsoring an annual play-writing contest, the eight winning plays becoming the Fantasy Festival. (If you're a celebrity hound—if you must have a taste of that glitz and glitter—plan to show up at the Fantasy Theater's annual black-tie fundraiser, which attracts some of the Hollywood crowd. Yup. Even to Sacramento.)

The B Street Theater is located at 2711 B St., 916/443-5300, with ticket prices usually in the $12–16 range. For information about the Fantasy Theater, which sometimes offers performances at B Street, call 916/442-5635.

otherwise fighting over turf—but empty storefronts predominate, still.

The Wells Fargo Center nearby at 400 Capitol Mall includes a **Wells Fargo History Museum**, 916/440-4161, in its five-story lobby. Exhibits range from an authentic Concord Stagecoach—imagine how nine passengers actually managed to fit—and a facsimile 19th-century Wells Fargo agent's office to a collection of gold ore samples from the Grass Valley area and a set of Howard & Davis gold balance scales, one of the museum's hottest attractions. Well worth a stop if you're in the neighborhood. Free. Open during regular business hours, Mon.–Fri. 9 A.M.–5 P.M., closed on bank holidays.

But for those with deep historical interests, the best museum in town could well be the immense **Old Sacramento City Cemetery** (once poetically known as the City of the Dead) founded by John Sutter in 1849 at Broadway and Riverside, where 20,000 pioneers from around the globe take their final rest; these marble monuments make good reading. Some of the city's most scandalous tales are also memorialized here, though to get the dirt you'll have to sign on for a weekend tour (free, but donations happily accepted). Regular tours are offered May–Sept., weather permitting Oct.–April. Themed evening tours are also quite popular; private tours can be arranged. Most tours depart from 10th St. and Broadway. For current information, call the Old City Cemetery Committee at 916/448-0811.

Land Park and Vicinity

William Land Park, a few miles south of the Capitol in the midst of one of the city's most appealing older neighborhoods, is home to the 15-plus-acre **Sacramento Zoo,** 3930 W. Land Park Dr. (Sutterville Rd. at Land Park Dr.), 916/264-5885, www.saczoo.com, which is itself home to hundreds of exotic animals, including 23 endangered species. Attractions include the Lake Victoria flamingos, a quarter-acre summer butterfly and hummingbird garden nearby, and the golden-headed lion tamarin monkeys. Open daily in summer 9 A.M.–4 P.M., though closing times vary with the season. On weekdays admission is $5.50 adults, $3.75 children ages 3–12, free for babies and toddlers; on weekends the fees are $6 and $4.25, respectively.

Free parking. Among Land Park's other attractions are a nine-hole golf course, athletic fields, picnic areas, the **FairyTale Town** kiddie playground (closed Dec.–Jan.), 916/264-5223, and the **Funderland Amusement Park** and pony rides also near the zoo, 916/456-0115.

Capital Sights Farther Afield

Though the military at McClellan Air Force Base is scheduled to clear out by 2001, even then the

BACK TO NATURE: THE COSUMNES RIVER PRESERVE

The Nature Conservancy has been quite busy in southern Sacramento County, particularly in the 1990s, determined to protect and preserve the Cosumnes River floodplain from development. The result is the massive—and ever-expanding—37,000-acre Cosumnes River Preserve, one of The Nature Conservancy's 75 "last great places," designed to protect the entire Cosumnes River watershed—wetlands, grasslands, woodlands, and agricultural lands—as safe haven for native plants and wildlife. The last undammed river originating in the Sierra Nevada, the Cosumnes River still nourishes flood-dependent valley oaks, which require deep alluvial soils; the oak stands here are among the most impressive remaining in California.

Walk along the preserve's 3.3-mile **Willow Slough Nature Trail** loop (naturally enough, the trail typically floods in winter) or the easier, mile-long **Lost Slough Trail,** where the boardwalk section is wheelchair accessible. Birdwalks are scheduled monthly, and on select winter and spring weekends you can kayak the Cosumnes on six-hour naturalist-led tours offered by **Blue Waters Kayaking,** 415/669-2600. Getting around by boat, in fact, is the best way to see the preserve, particularly now that old levees are being breached and the waterway is expanding in all directions. Free guided boat tours (BYOB) are sometimes scheduled. But you can also take a driving tour; see the website for directions.

For more information about the preserve and current activities, call 916/684-2816, try www.cosumnes.org, or stop by the visitors center, on the east side of Franklin Blvd. about 1.7 miles south of Twin Cities Rd., open most weekends 10 A.M.–4 P.M.

McClellan Aviation Museum will still be going strong. The impressive collection here includes 33 aircraft dating back to World War II (including a MiG-21 Soviet fighter and an F4-C Phantom II jet), a veritable Air Force fashion show of uniform and insignia changes over the years, and historical displays. Open Mon.–Sat. 9 A.M.–3 P.M., Sun. noon–3 P.M. Admission free. The museum is located at 3204 Palm St. (directly west of the gate) in North Highlands; the base is most easily reached via Watt Ave. (from I-80). For more information, call 916/643-3192. Equally fascinating at McClellan are its historic art deco buildings, most located quite near the museum on WPA-era McClellan Mall. At last report, 51 were listed on the National Register of Historic Places. Among the most striking: the 1938 Headquarters building (Building 1), where inside there's a multicolored floor map of North America done in terrazzo; the very-deco propeller and aviation-themed concrete castings decorating Building 250; the Officers Club; and the commander's house, among others.

If you've got restless kids in tow, consider a stop at the **Discovery Museum Science and Space Center** at 3615 Auburn Blvd., 916/575-3940 (recorded) or 916/575-3941, www.thediscovery.org, affiliated with Old Sac's Discovery Museum. Boasting the northstate's first Challenger Learning Center, a planetarium, science and history programs, nature trails, and hands-on exhibits are among its other notable attractions. At last report open daily in summer 10 A.M.–5 P.M., otherwise just noon–5 P.M. weekdays and 10 A.M.–5 P.M. weekends. A relief for kids and heat-stunned adults come summer is the **Waterworld USA Family Waterpark** at Cal Expo, 1600 Exposition Blvd., 916/924-3747 or 916/924-0556, with massive waterslides and Breaker Beach, the northstate's largest wave pool. The hillside Hook's Lagoon here, new in 1997, is something of an aquatic jungle gym. Adjacent **Paradise Family Fun Park,** 916/924-0757 or 916/924-3595, is raucous fun without the water, featuring attractions from a dragon roller coaster and bumper boats to 36-hole miniature golf and video and arcade games.

STAYING IN SACRAMENTO

Sacramento offers a reasonably good selection of accommodations in all price ranges—including an exceptional "new" hostel for budget travelers housed in a stunning Victorian right downtown, central to major attractions and the Midtown scene. The listings below are convenient to Old Sacramento, Downtown, and Midtown, though there are accommodations options flanking major freeways and thoroughfares throughout the greater metropolitan area. For a fairly complete and current listing of just about everything, contact the Sacramento Convention and Visitors Bureau (see Sacramento Information below). Camping is possible at various city-style RV campgrounds in the area—particularly at

Riverboat Delta King

JOHN POIMIROO/CALTOUR

ACCOMMODATIONS RATINGS

Accommodations in this book are rated by price category, based on double-occupancy, high-season rates. Categories used are:

Budget	$35 and under
Inexpensive	$35-60
Moderate	$60-85
Expensive	$85-110
Premium	$110-150
Luxury	$150 and up

the **Sacramento Metro KOA** in West Sacramento, 916/371-6771, and at the **Cal Expo RV Park,** 916/263-3187—but for those without wheels the nearest public camping is too far away for convenience.

Finding suitable accommodations in and around Sacramento is usually no problem, except when a large convention, the Jazz Jubilee, or other major event is underway. The newly incorporated warehouse district of West Sacramento, just across the Sacramento River from Downtown and Old Sacramento, also features reasonably priced lodgings.

A Capital Hostel

The stunning and spacious HI-AYH **Sacramento Hostel,** open since 1995, is proof positive that the Big Tomato finally has accommodating international flavor. Housed in the historic Llewellyn-Williams mansion (also known locally as Mory's Place, after previous owner Mory Holmes), the Sacramento Hostel sleeps up to 70 guests in its bunk-style dorms and private rooms. Aside from being an inexpensive and safe choice to hang one's hat, this is an unusually elegant place to hang out. There's no hostel quite like it anywhere in the United States. Meticulously restored to its 1885 Italianate Victorian grandeur at a cost of $2.1 million, thanks to financial support from American Youth Hostels, the National Trust for Historic Preservation, and the Sacramento City Council, the hostel features original stained glass, hand-carved oak staircases and decorative detail, parquet floors, original chandeliers, embossed wallpapers, period-style carpeting, and elegant marble fireplaces. Facilities also include modern shared baths and a sleek Euro-style kitchen.

The word in 2000 was that the hostel will be moving again, to accommodate city building plans—so call first to check on its status. At last report, the Sacramento Hostel was still located downtown just north of Sacramento City Hall, 900 H St. (at 9th), 916/443-1691, open daily (for check-out and check-in) 7:30–9:30 A.M. and 5–8 P.M. Budget.

Staying at Richards Boulevard and Vicinity

Most tourists are attracted to the big hotels downtown, but there is a local secret—the selection of inexpensive and moderately priced motels located along Richards Blvd. and Jibboom St., close to I-5 just north of Old Sacramento (Jibboom is west of the freeway, the extension of Richards). The neighborhood isn't all that special, decorated with overhead freeway, gas stations, and quik-stops, but the location is quite good—practically *in* Old Sacramento and downtown, at the confluence of the Sacramento and American Rivers, yet the last stop before both Arco Arena and the airport. Being able to gas up here is a plus, by the way, if you'll be returning a rental car to Sacramento International; at last report there was still no gas available at the airport.

Closest to Old Sacramento is the **Best Western Sandman Motel** at 236 Jibboom St., 916/443-6515, fax 916/443-8346, always a best bet. (Look for the Perko's restaurant—and the huge carved bison and other redwood sculptures outside.) Rooms are quite spacious and clean, with basic amenities plus HBO, in-room refrigerators, hair dryers, continental breakfast, swimming pool, and restaurant adjacent. Moderate. Other good midrange choices in the neighborhood include the new **Governors Inn** at 310 Richards Blvd., 916/448-7224, fax 916/448-7382, or toll-free 800/999-6689, with swimming pool, where children under 12 stay free; the **Super 8 Executive Suites,** 216 Bannon St. (off Richards), 916/447-5400, fax 916/447-5153, or toll-free 800/800-8000 (national), where all rooms have microwaves and refrigerators; and the very nice **Days Inn Discovery Park,** formerly the Discovery Inn, at 350 Bercut Dr. (off Richards), 916/442-6971, fax 916/444-2809, or toll-free 800/952-5516. Moderate. Another good value is the pleasant **La Quinta Inn Sacramento Downtown,** 200 Jibboom St., 916/448-8100, fax 916/447-3621, or toll-free 800/687-6667. Moderate.

Inexpensive in the same neighborhood: the small **Crossroads Inn** at 211 Jibboom St., 916/442-7777, with no swimming pool but in-room refrigerators and free movies, and the recently renovated **Motel 6** at 227 Jibboom, 916/441-0733, fax 916/446-5941, or toll-free 800/466-8356, with the basics plus swimming pool.

Even closer to the Sacramento River is the **Delta King River Boat Hotel** in Old Sacramento, 1000 Front St., 916/444-5464, fax 916/444-5314, or toll-free 800/825-5464. The real draw here is location, location, location—*in* Old Sacramento. Rooms are pleasant, if a bit small—but how often do you get the chance to sleep *on* a river? Beyond the on-board Pilothouse restaurant—even if you don't dine here, explore the stunning wood and brass decor—the shops and restaurants of Old Sac beckon. Very Expensive on weekends, Expensive on weekdays. For a truly swank stay, sign on for a night in the "Captain's Quarters" (Luxury).

Staying Downtown

Quite convenient among downtown motels and a good visitor choice when conventions aren't booked is the comfortable, ivy-covered **Clarion Hotel** at 700 16th St. (Hwy. 160), 916/444-8000, fax 916/442-8129, or toll-free 800/443-0880. On-site restaurant and bar. Expensive, but Moderate/Inexpensive with certain discounts and specials. Another best bet, just a few blocks from the Capitol, is the 98-room **Best Western Sutter House Motel** at 1100 H St. (between 11th and 12th), 916/441-1314, fax 916/441-5961, or toll-free 800/830-1314 in the United States. Moderate-Expensive. Also well located and nice in the neighborhood: the **Quality Inn** at 818 15th St., 916/444-3980, fax 916/444-2991, or toll-free 800/228-5151. Inexpensive-Moderate. Since summer in Sacramento can be sizzling, all have swimming pools.

For a truly special downtown stay, *the* place is the elegant 16-room **Sterling Hotel** at 1300 H St. (13th and H), 916/448-1300 or toll-free 800/365-7660, fax 916/448-8066. Once known as the Hale Mansion, it opened as the sophisticated boutique-style Sterling Hotel following an extensive $2-million renovation. During the week, the Sterling caters to business travelers—thus the new ballroom and other meeting facilities—but weekends are prime time for pleasure trav-

elers. All rooms feature Italian marble bathrooms with hot tubs, understated yet exquisite decor. In addition to the excellent on-site Chanterelle restaurant, the Sterling also features a small, stylish bar in the lobby. Luxury.

Not nearly so intimate but otherwise top drawer is the towering 500-room **Hyatt Regency Sacramento** right across from Capitol Park at 1209 L St. (12th and L), 916/443-1234, fax 916/321-6699, or toll-free 800/233-1234. The Mediterranean-style Hyatt can be crowded with conventioneers on weekdays—inquire, if it matters—but weekends are usually slow, a plus for vacationers. Swimming pool, two on-site restaurants, full business services, airport transportation. Luxury on weekdays, Premium on weekends.

Other popular downtown stays include the 16-story **Holiday Inn Capitol Plaza** across the freeway from Old Sacramento at 300 J St., 916/446-0100, fax 916/446-0117, or toll-free 800/465-4329, where children under age 18 stay free. In addition to the on-site restaurant and swimming pool, for inveterate shoppers the Holiday Inn has the added advantage of being a half-block stroll from the revitalized Downtown Plaza mall and all its attractions. Expensive-Premium. Also quite close to the downtown/Old Sac shopping scene is the **Vagabond Inn** adjacent to Sacramento's Chinese Cultural Center, 909 3rd St. (at J), 916/446-1481, fax 916/448-0364, or toll-free 800/522-1555. Expensive.

Staying in Bed-and-Breakfasts

These days, Sacramento's accommodating bed-and-breakfast inns are a mainstream lodging option, for business and pleasure. In general, prices compare favorably with much less personal hotels and motels. Inquire about weekday special rates and seasonal bargains.

A particularly fine Midtown choice is **Amber House Bed and Breakfast Inn,** actually three Craftsman houses headquartered at 1315 22nd St. (between Capitol Ave. and N St.), 916/444-8085, fax 916/552-6529, or toll-free 800/755-6526. Amber House started out as just one striking 1905 Craftsman under the elms, today's romanticized Poets' Refuge; the five rooms pay homage to Lord Byron, Chaucer, Dickinson, Longfellow, and Wordsworth. Then came the neighboring 1913 bungalow, Artists' Retreat, its three rooms dedicated to Degas, Renoir, and

Van Gogh. The most recent addition is the colonial revival Musician's Manor across the street, its five rooms dedicated to some classics: Bach, Brahms, Vivaldi, Beethoven, and Mozart (and yes, you can expect appropriate musical accompaniment). Rooms at Amber House are exquisitely decorated with antiques and appropriate artistic touches and boast abundant amenities; some rooms feature in-room spas, and all have private marble bathrooms with plush robes on hand. Cable-connected TVs with VCRs, CD players, and private phones with voice mail are also provided. Full gourmet breakfast, scrumptious cookies, and just plain hospitality make it feel like home (if not a tad better). Premium-Luxury.

Also reasonably close to the Capitol and the Sacramento Convention Center is **Hartley House,** around the corner from Abigail's at 700 22nd St., 916/447-7829, fax 916/447-1820, or toll-free 800/831-5806, once a 1906 colonial revival men's boardinghouse, now an accommodating five-room inn with all the comforts of home—cable TV, VCRs, clock-radio cassette players, and telephones. Not to mention private bathrooms, full breakfast, and homemade cookies. Building interiors are a study in the once commonplace grandeur of hand-carved redwood, including the grand two-landing "floating" staircase, and rooms are all English—Brighton (a one-time sunporch), Canterbury, Dover, Southampton, and Stratford. Premium-Luxury.

A pleasant find nearby in East Sacramento, particularly for fans of Gilbert and Sullivan, is the **Savoyard Bed and Breakfast** homestay at 3322 H St., 916/442-6709. Located right across from McKinley Park and its rose gardens, Savoyard is a 1925 Italian Renaissance home serving up two gracious guest rooms (private baths) and full breakfast. Moderate-Expensive.

A relative newcomer in Sacramento is the seven-room **Inn at Parkside** at 2116 6th St., 916/658-1818, fax 916/658-1809, or toll-free 800/995-7275, open as a bed-and-breakfast since 1994. An exquisite 1936 mansion originally built for the ambassador to China—which explains the art deco ballroom, complete with spring-loaded maple dance floor—these days the home has a decidedly romantic flair. All rooms, from the large Olympus Suite (with spa) to the cozy Florabunda room and library-style Scholars Corner, feature private baths. The basics here include full breakfast and TV, VCR, and telephone in every room. Guest kitchenette. Views of Southside Park. Moderate-Luxury.

Once known as the Driver Mansion Inn, **Vizcaya** on the edge of Midtown at 2019 21st St. (between T and U Sts.), 916/455-5243, fax 916/455-6102, or toll-free 800/456-2019, is a study in luxurious Italian marble and Victorian propriety, brought to you by the Sterling Hotel people. Catering to business execs during the week and hopeless romantics on weekends, Vizcaya features seven rooms and two suites—six in the main house, three in the carriage house—many with fireplaces and/or hot tubs. Full breakfast (small, private tables) and all the amenities. A fairly recent addition is Vizcaya's adjacent New Orleans–style events palace, quite appealing for weddings and other special events. Premium-Luxury.

EATING IN SACRAMENTO: CAPITAL INGREDIENTS

With Sacramento smack dab in the middle of a rich agricultural region, certified farmers' markets abound. Show up, in season, for farm-fresh fruit, vegetables, baked goods, flowers, and memorable cheap eats, such as homemade tamales. Most accessible for most visitors are those in and around central Sacramento, including the **Sacramento Chavez Plaza Certified Farmers' Market** held in downtown's César Chávez Plaza (still shown on some maps as Plaza Park) at 10th and J Sts., 10 A.M.–2 P.M. on Wed. May–Dec., and the **Downtown Plaza Certified Farmers' Market** (new in 1999) at 4th and L Sts. (between the mall and the Holiday Inn), held Fri. 10 A.M.–2 P.M. The **Sacramento Central Certified Farmers' Market** convenes every Sun. year-round, 8 A.M.–noon, beneath the Capital City Freeway at 8th and W Streets. For information on these and other area farmers' markets, call 916/688-0100.

Otherwise, cheapest and best for organic groceries is the recently remodeled **Sacramento Natural Foods Co-op,** 1900 Alhambra Blvd. (at S St.), 916/445-2667, with an incredible selection of herbs and teas, and natural foods in bulk. "Sac Natch" has a decent deli, too, serving such wonders as Kung Pao tofu, smoked tofu or roasted

EATING IN THE BIG TOMATO: GETTING ORIENTED

The elderly homes and Victorians of Midtown Sacramento have some pretty hip company these days. **Midtown** is the city's hottest, most happening and diverse dining and nightlife district, a neighborhood tucked neatly between downtown and high-rent East Sacramento. People quibble over Midtown's actual territory, but you'll surely find it if you head for the area just east of downtown's skyscrapers, bounded by 28th St. (and the Capital City Freeway soaring overhead) on the east, 16th St. on the west, P St. on the south, and H St. on the north. If you're veering off the freeway specifically in search of a good meal, just head for J St., which serves as Midtown's unofficial main drag.

Sacramento's "gourmet gulch," however, would have to be in upscale **East Sacramento,** particularly on or near Fair Oaks Blvd.—the extension of H St. east of the Capital City Freeway, just beyond CSU Sacramento—on the east side of the American River, more or less between Howe and Munroe Avenues.

As the listings reflect, **Downtown** and **Old Sacramento** also have a respectable selection of restaurants of all stripes, as do outlying **Folsom** and **Davis.** That's as far as this book goes, though there are many more worthy selections throughout the greater Sacramento region. Even if you find yourself at some mall or minimall in the vast suburban jungle, remember that good food is rarely far away. Ask around.

---

eggplant sandwiches, and various rice dishes, soups, and salads, including a very tasty Asiago cheese, basil, and chicken pasta salad. (Yes, veggie purists, chicken and turkey *are* served here.)

Greater Sacramento is also full of ethnic markets and nifty neighborhood groceries. If heading to the zoo or otherwise in the Land Park neighborhood, *the* place for essentials is been-thereforever **Taylor's Market** at 2900 Freeport Blvd., 916/443-6881, with fresh fish, meats, and poultry at the in-house butcher shop, a fairly impressive wine selection, and sundry grocery and deli items. (Safety note: It's hazardous getting into the parking lot here if you're heading north on Freeport; the easiest and safest way is to continue north until the first possible left turn over the railroad tracks, make the turn, then double back.) While you're in the neighborhood, don't miss the fabulous French-style **Freeport Bakery** just a few doors to the south, 2966 Freeport Blvd., 916/442-4256, a popular neighborhood pastry-and-coffee hangout and bakery where the fresh fruit tarts and cakes are starring attractions. (Special order fruit tarts to make sure one's waiting for you.) Nice selection of croissants, pastries, and specialty breads, too.

An equally beloved market in upscale East Sacramento, also not far from downtown, is charming **Muzzi & Sons** at 723 56th St. (near H St.), 916/736-3474, a tiny grocery and deli with a truly astonishing selection of seafood and fine meats.

In specialty food shops, some say the ultimate in upscale is served up at **David Berkley Fine Wines & Specialty Foods** at 515 Pavilions Ln., on the north side of Fair Oaks Blvd. between Howe and Fulton, 916/929-4422, a deli that has also become a popular take-out dinner destination (menu changes weekly). Others swear by **Corti Brothers** at 5810 Folsom Blvd., 916/736-3800 (deli: 916/736-3801), which carries every gourmet menu item imaginable, excellent meats, fine produce, cheeses and deli items, and a wide selection of fine wines. But Sacramento also has its **Trader Joe's,** at 2601 Marconi in the Town and Country Village shopping center, 916/481-8797, much cheaper for eclectic staples and gourmet fare. Another Trader Joe's is planned for East Sacramento.

EATING IN SACRAMENTO: DOWNTOWN AND VICINITY

Old Sacramento

Pleasant for a quick cuppa and scones or a light lunch is **Steamers Coffee Roasting Co.** at 101 K St. (Front and K Sts.), 916/448-9404, where a few tables outside offer great people-watching.

Something of a neighborhood old-timer, **California Fats** at 1015 Front St., 916/441-7966, still makes a splash with its bright neon, granite, and indoor-waterfall interior and East-West standards such as honey-glazed duck salad. The signature dish here, though, is rack of lamb. The **Fat City Bar and Cafe** at 1001 Front, 916/446-6768, is a more relaxed relative with casual café style.

A fairly new star in Old Sacramento is the laid-back Southwestern-Asian-European fusion **Rio City Cafe** near the Tower Bridge, housed in an open, airy, and inviting replica of a gold rush–era freight warehouse on the river at 1110 Front St., 916/442-8226. Bright lights on the menu here include such things as pasta with chipotle cream sauce and pecans, Chinese nachos, and mesquite-broiled New York steak with mushrooms and salsa. Wonderful house-made desserts. Full bar, sophisticated California wine list. Open for lunch Mon.–Sat., dinner nightly, and brunch on Sunday. Reservations wise. According to end-of-the-millennium rumors, new restaurants were destined for riverside sites both north and south of Rio City.

Still fine for fine dining Old Sac–style is **The Firehouse,** a local landmark at 1112 2nd St., 916/442-4772, reservations wise. Known for decades as the place to go for rococo atmosphere and rich, heavy American and French fare, under new ownership the Firehouse is now becoming a stylish, very imaginative Californian—at home in a venerable brick Victorian once home to Sacramento's Engine Company No. 3. Open for dinner Tues.–Sat, for lunch weekdays

CAPITAL ROAD FOOD

Picture yourself speeding through the Big Tomato, racing to or from Tahoe, San Francisco, or L.A., and suddenly in need of fuel—road food—a truly good hamburger, say, or memorable pizza. Sacramento has some exceptional pit-stop possibilities, none all that far from a major freeway.

Probably the best burger stop around is **Ford's Real Hamburgers** at 1948 Sutterville Rd. (just a few blocks east of I-5, on the south side of Land Park near the zoo, at Freeport Blvd.), 916/452-6979. Since everything's cooked to order, you may have to sit down on the patio and wait awhile. The toasted sourdough buns are slathered in Ford's sweet special sauce. Depending on your cholesterol count, choose between the humongous one-pound burger, hefty third-pound burger, and kid-sized burger. All are a bit pricey but worth the money; cheese (Swiss, cheddar, or American) and other additions (such as bacon) cost extra. And here, even a small order of fries is pretty large. Open daily (for lunch only on Sunday).

Also locally beloved, if you find yourself anywhere near Broadway and the Tower Records neighborhood (just north of Land Park), is **Willie's Hamburgers** at 2415 16th St. (on the alley, a half-block north of Broadway), 916/444-2006, something of a stylistic River City hybrid of L.A.'s legendary Tommy's Original World Famous Hamburgers (noted for its dripping chiliburgers) and the In-N-Out chain. Prices here are quite reasonable. You'll know these juicy, cooked-to-order burgers (hammers), chiliburgers (slammers), and killer fries mean business once you see the napkin dispensers—actually, industrial-strength paper towel holders—on the walls. Open daily 10 A.M. to at least midnight (until 2:30 the next morning on Fri. and Sat. nights). If you'll be in Folsom, there's another Willie's there—at 823 Wales Dr., 916/983-6755—but gussied up, what with the wine bar, juice bar, and Brie appetizers.

Legendary in these parts, and particularly popular on sizzling summer days, is **Merlino's Orange Freeze** at 6200 Folsom Blvd. (at 62nd St., near CSU Sacramento), 916/731-8266, where Sacramentans from all walks of life line up to slurp down the fresh-squeezed orange freezes (lemon, strawberry, and pineapple also available). Heftier fuel is served in the form of burgers, veggie burgers, deli sandwiches, fries, and onion rings. In summer, there's a Merlino's outpost in Old Sac, too.

A local pizza hot spot, typically at or near the top of the annual "Best of Sacramento" lists, is **Original Pete's** in Midtown at 2001 J. St., 916/442-6770. Also a Midtown classic is **Zelda's Original Gourmet Pizza** at 1415 21st St., 916/447-1400, *the* place for fantastic Chicago-style pizza accompanied by abundant attitude and somewhat bizarre charm, what with the multicolor year-round Christmas lights. Another Midtown possibility, open even late at night, is **Pieces Pizza by the Slice** at 1309 21st St., 916/441-1949, where you can get pesto with sun-dried tomatoes and feta cheese, say, or good ol' fashioned pepperoni. Popular for fancy pizza is **Paesano's** at 1802 Capitol Ave. (at 18th), 916/447-8646, where tagliatini puttanesca and grilled eggplant also star. Stylish California cuisine-style pizzas are culinary standards, too, at upscale local eateries such as Paragary's.

only; lunch in the lovely patio courtyard when the weather's balmy.

Over the River and up the River
If you crave culinary adventure in West Sacramento, just across the river, the best place anywhere for garlic steak sandwiches is **Club Pheasant**, 1822 Jefferson Blvd., 916/371-9530, a folksy family-style Italian restaurant (and unofficial community center) two miles south of I-80 on Jefferson Boulevard. There are other possibilities on this side of the river, too, including family-owned **Carol's** at 1201 W. Capitol Ave., 916/372-4631, where breakfast—french toast, pancakes, and bacon and eggs—is the best part of the day (breakfast and lunch served), and **Huey's Diner** at 805 Harbor Blvd., 916/372-1958, a retro 1950s diner that actually lives up to nostalgic expectations about happily gorging on chili cheeseburgers, home-style meatloaf, potato salad, and milkshakes (with real ice cream and buttermilk). Not to mention Sam Cooke, Nat King Cole, and the Coasters on the jukebox.

Just a hop, skip, and a jump north from Old Sac via I-5 and the Garden Highway takes you to the Sacramento River Complex—a hard-partyin' collection of riverside restaurants and bars including enormously popular **Chevy's Fresh Mex** and the river-themed **Crawdad's River Cantina** and the **Virgin Sturgeon**. For truly good food, *the* foodie place is the **Jammin' Salmon** at 1801 Garden Hwy., 916/929-6232, a sibling to Bailie's in Folsom. Not your run-of-the-mill restaurant on a barge, Jammin' Salmon is noted for its exceptionally well-prepared salmon and other fish and seafood dishes. The ambience is a bit rustic—and who wants the onboard scenery to detract from the riverside voyeur experience?—yet the food is tony and creative at both lunch and dinner. Reservations advisable.

Near Downtown
Strict vegetarians need not despair once arrived in the Big Tomato. In addition to some of the possibilities listed in this section, there's tiny **Mums Gourmet Vegetarian** in the Land Park neighborhood at 2968 Freeport Blvd., 916/444-3015—a best bet for globetrotting vegetarian fare at lunch (weekdays only) and dinner, not to mention full-blown brunch on Sunday. Once strictly a purist's food sanctuary, these days eggs and dairy products crop up fairly frequently

---

CAPITAL COFFEE AND DESSERT

One of the best stops for coffee and gelato around is in Midtown: **Java City**, 1800 Capitol Ave., 916/444-5282, open 6:30 A.M.–11 P.M. or so, an endlessly popular local hangout. You'll find Java Citys all over the place. Among other worthies is the time-honored and low-key **Weatherstone Coffee & Tea Company,** also in Midtown at 812 21st St., 916/443-6340, another see-and-be-seen destination. Whether anybody sees you or not, be sure to try those chocolate-dipped macaroons and Key West bars. Open 7 A.M.–11 P.M.

New Helvetia Roasters & Bakers at 1215 19th St., 916/441-1106, is another open-late, hang-loose coffee house, this one boasting one of the best selections of baked goods in town—go ahead, have that cinnamon roll—not to mention killer cappuccino. If you find yourself near the Sacramento Zoo or anywhere near the Land Park neighborhood, don't miss the fabulous French-style **Freeport Bakery** just south of the Freeport Market at 2966 Freeport Blvd. (Hwy. 160), 916/442-4256, a popular daytime neighborhood coffee-and-pastry hangout where the fresh fruit tarts—if they still have any—are a starring attraction. Nice fresh-baked bread selection, too. If you find yourself craving caffeine in Gourmet Gulch, Sacramento even has a **Peet's**, Berkeley's fabled java joint, at 2580 Fair Oaks Blvd. (near Blockbuster) between Watt and Howe, 916/485-7887.

Classic for ice cream in Sacramento, *the* local tradition, is **Gunther's**, 2801 Franklin Blvd. (just east of the Hwy. 99 freeway), 916/457-6646, famous for its 1940s neon and its unconcerned-about-cholesterol 16 percent butterfat ice creams, shakes, sundaes, and banana splits. The other local classic is on the other side of the Land Park neighborhood—**Vic's** at 3199 Riverside Blvd., 916/448-0892. **Rick's Dessert Diner,** 2322 K St., 916/444-0969, offers truly decadent desserts and great coffees in a 1950s-retro atmosphere—apple and other fresh-baked pies, carrot cake, and the infamous midnight torte. And there's another Rick's in Old Sac. Wonderful desserts are available all around town, though. See restaurant listings for ideas.

on the menu. But many of the soups, salads, and ambitious entrées will satisfy anyone.

The **Tower Cafe**, 1518 Broadway, 916/441-0222, next to the movie theater and otherwise a prominent part of the "trendy triangle" of Towers at Land Park and Broadway, isn't really known as a fine dining spot. It's a decent restaurant, though, with coffee house style, evening dress and dreadlocks okay. People come here to people-watch, to grab a bite (pre- or post-movie), and to talk—about films, about ideas, about what's going on. That's the idea, anyway, and the staff, menu, and decor reflect a one world/global village attitude. Cultural artifacts and oddities are prominent. During decent weather, the patio outside is packed until the wee hours—the better to take in all those Broadway traffic fumes.

Despite the proliferation of good Chinese restaurants well south, Broadway is still considered Sacramento's Little Asia, *the* place to go for very good, usually inexpensive meals. A long-running local favorite for Vietnamese is **Andy Nguyen's** at 2007 Broadway (20th and Broadway), 916/736-1157, where rice noodle soup, five-spice chicken, and sautéed clams star. Open daily for lunch and dinner, 10 A.M.–10 P.M. There's a small parking lot out back, accessible from the alley; otherwise, jockey for a spot on a side street. Even more venerable, here for more than 30 years, is the wonderful Japanese **Fuji** at 2422 13th St. (at Broadway), 916/446-4135, where the lunch specials—bento boxes available—are a particularly good deal. Lunch served weekdays only, dinner every night (holidays included). **Fortune House** a block away at 1211 Broadway, 916/443-3128, is popular for inexpensive Cantonese.

Downtown at the Mall

For some Big Tomato flash, try Sacramento's own **Hard Rock Cafe** at Downtown Plaza (7th and K Sts.), 916/441-5591—just look for the 36-foot-tall revolving neon guitar out front. The 78th link in the hard-rockin' Hard Rock chain, open since late 1997, this one is decked out in memorabilia including an Elton John patchwork denim overcoat, one of Elvis Presley's knit shirts (embroidered with peacocks), and one of Bob Dylan's harmonicas, complete with holder. Not to mention the World War I German/Prussian iron cross once worn by Jimi Hendrix. If you're here to eat, expect mostly meat-and-potatoes diner fare, from burgers and ribs to chicken and T-bone steaks. There are a few culinary alternatives, though, such as the veggie burger, grilled fajitas, and Chinese chicken salad. But who really comes here for the food, eh?

For more burgers and such, there's **Johnny Rockets** at the west end of the mall, 916/444-3404. It's hard to miss with the burgers here—the St. Louis, with swiss cheese, bacon, and grilled onions, is ever popular—but there's more, from veggie burgers to egg salad sandwiches.

Just downstairs, immensely popular, and quite good is the semi-industrial **River City Brewing Co.**, 916/447-2739, serving eclectic European-influenced fare along with its sandwiches, salads, and oak-oven-fired pizzas. Favorites inspired by the American Southwest include the Santa Fe snow crab cakes. Great desserts, too, along with a bevy of award-winning brews. Open for lunch and dinner daily; after 10 or 10:30 P.M., the dining room closes but a late-night menu is still available at the bar. Early birds, River City also opens for coffee and pastries from 7 A.M. on weekdays, 9 A.M. on weekends.

Inexpensive Downtown

Good for Thai downtown and open daily for both lunch and dinner, been-there-forever **Amarin Thai Cuisine** at 900 12th St. (12th and I Sts.), 916/447-9063, features an amazingly varied menu with such things as spicy eggplant and angel wings. Open 11 A.M.–9 P.M. on weekdays, from noon on weekends.

Closer to Midtown but also wonderful for vegetarian lunch—Middle Eastern, this time—is long-running **Juliana's Kitchen** at 1401 G St. (14th and G), 916/444-0966, open weekdays only, 11 A.M.–3 P.M. Falafel sandwiches (or pita with fried cauliflower, fried zucchini, or hummus) and the combination plate are best bets, but don't pass up the soups and salads. For the less adventurous, mainstream deli-style sandwiches are available.

Downtown offers other great deals. Popular for breakfast or lunch on the run and on the cheap is **Bagful of Bagels** at 1607 10th St., 916/446-6010; some say they serve the best in town. Messy and marvelous at lunch, for example, is the avocado, tomato, and cheese sandwich on an onion bagel. Two blocks from Sacramento's popular Fox & Goose pub is another find—**Hitomi Restaurant** at 1201 R St., 916/443-7870, serving very good, very inexpensive Japanese.

Fancier Fare Downtown

Not all that expensive for lunch, if you order wisely, is the popular and always-packed **4th Street Grille** near Downtown Plaza at 400 L St. (at 4th), 916/448-2847, serving not-too-trendy bistro fare, from grilled specialties to pastas, pizzas, and salads. Another possibility, in an absolutely stunning and stylish setting, is Sacramento's outpost of **Il Fornaio Cucina Italiana** on the ground floor of the Wells Fargo Building, 400 Capitol Mall, 916/446-4100, though sometimes the yellow terrazo floor and marble countertops outclass the fare. Open for lunch and dinner weekdays, for dinner nightly. With both places a brisk stroll away from the Capitol, don't be surprised to find yourself surrounded by pods of earnest politicos and policy wonks.

If you happen to be downtown and looking for politicians, though, don't overlook stunning, museum-like **Frank Fat's,** 806 L St., 916/442-7092, a success in Sacramento since 1939 and a local showplace almost as revered as the Capitol itself. The fact that lawmakers almost live here doesn't detract at all from the ambience, from the good Cantonese fare, or from the very American New York steaks. Open for lunch on weekdays only, for dinner every night. Full bar, California wine list. Reservations advised.

Top Tomatoes Downtown

For pricey and clubby fine-dining ambience, not to mention unabashed meat consumption, the place is Sacramento's own **Morton's of Chicago** at Downtown Plaza, 521 L St. (between 5th and 6th Sts.), 916/442-5091, another place you might find politicos. Steaks and chops are the featured attractions—select your own, from the presentation tray—along with lobster, swordfish, and chicken. Full bar, California wine list. Open nightly for dinner.

Long a favorite downtown and recently restyled is **Dawson's American Bistro and Martinis** at the Hyatt Regency, 1209 L St., 916/443-1234, ext. 59, a high-class chop house with broader appeal, California flair, and all-American and continental roots. Full bar, California wine list. Open weekdays only for lunch, Mon.–Sat. for dinner. Valet parking advisable.

And then there's **Chanterelle** at the Sterling Hotel, 1300 H St., 916/442-0451, a fairly formal but far from stuffy restaurant tucked into Sacramento's own upscale Victorian hotel. Serving contemporary fare with French and other international accents, Chanterelle is open for breakfast and lunch on weekdays only, for brunch on Sun., and for dinner nightly. Full bar, pricey wine list. Since this is another of Sacramento's favorite special-occasion restaurants, reservations are advisable.

Sunday Brunch at the Sterling Hotel

TOM MYERS PHOTOGRAPHY

EATING IN MIDTOWN

Fairly Inexpensive in Midtown
Midtown has some great inexpensive Mexican restaurants, quite popular. For contemporary Mexican—great flavor without the unhealthy fats—best bet is **Una Mas!** at 19th and J Sts., 916/448-2900, where the fish tacos, steak tacos, chicken tostadas, and hefty burritos are among the shining stars. Wash 'em down with a glass of strawberry lemonade. Also happening: **Tres Hermanas** at 2416 K St. (at 24th), 916/443-6919, beloved for its pozole and pork tamales as well as health-conscious selections. At **Taqueria Taco Loco** at 2326 J St. (at 23rd), 916/447-0711, people go crazy for chile verde burritos and generous

---

BIG TOMATO BREWPUBS

No matter what's for dinner, sometimes beer's the main attraction. Local brewski fans and fanatics, Sacramento's **Rubicon Brewing Co.** at 2004 Capitol Ave., 916/448-7032, may be the city's favorite brewpub, with brews including Summer Wheat and Irish Red. It's a tough contest, though. Worthy newcomers include the **Hopstreet Bistro & Brewery** at 6300 Folsom Blvd., 916/451-4677, where you can have some "brown bag salmon" or baby back ribs with your custom brews, and the snazzy **River City Brewing Company** at the Downtown Plaza mall, 916/447-2739. The **Hogshead Brewpub** down in the basement at 114 J St. in Old Sac, 916/443-2739, is Sacramento's oldest brewpub, a no-frills rock and blues bomb shelter with Old Sac's only pool table. For genuine German-style lagers, you don't need to drive all the way to Davis anymore: Sacramento now has its own Sudwerk, in this case the **Sudwerk Brewery & Grill,** 1375 Exposition Blvd., 916/925-6623, voted "Best Watering Hole" in 1997 by the Northern California Restaurant Association. A hot spot in Citrus Heights is the **Red Tomato** brewpub at 7217 Greenback Ln., 916/721-6668, where two pale ales, a brown ale, an Irish red, an oatmeal stout, and a raspberry-blackberry wheat beer—they call it "Screaming Chuck and the Berrytones"—are all on tap. For lunch or dinner, consider pasta, wood-fired pizza, fish and chips, country fried steak, or Mississippi catfish dinner. Live music Fri. and Sat. nights.

---

tacos (try the carnitas, or charbroiled chicken). There's another Loco downtown at 1122 11th St., and one at 7850 Stockton Boulevard.

Another Midtown possibility is **Pescado's Mexican Restaurant** at 2801 P St. (28th and P Sts.), 916/452-7237, the place for shrimp or fish tacos, beloved also for its machaco burrito, not to mention burritos, tostadas, and veggie and other specials. The combination plates here are a real treat. To find Pescado's, just look for the line snaking down the sidewalk. Needless to say, come early for lunch.

Casual **Cafe Bernardo** at 2726 Capitol Ave., 916/443-1180, is not the unbelievably cheap, tasty, and hip counterculture hot spot it used to be. But it is still inexpensive and pretty darn good, and open both early and late for coffee and lighter fare. Winners here include the potato–red pepper soup, the grilled salmon BLT, and the well-prepared salads. Open daily 7 A.M. to 10 P.M. (til 11 P.M. on weekend nights). Separating Cafe Bernardo from the youthful **Monkey Bar** scene is **Juice-O-Rama,** perfect for something orange, green, or purple to wash it all down with.

Ever popular for burgers and good brewskis—always packed at lunch, and most other times—is the **Rubicon Brewing Co.** at 2004 Capitol Mall, 916/448-7032. Everybody comes here. Before or after sampling local favorites on the beer menu—watch the brewing process through the glass walls—chow down on Rubicon wings, chicken fajitas, fish and chips, crisscross fries, sandwiches, or any of the daily specials. Breakfast served on weekends. If you really like the beer, you can get a Rubicon "box"—a full gallon (refillable) to go.

There are plenty of Midtown pizza joints, too. For some suggestions, see the special topic Capital Road Food.

Still Reasonable in Midtown
Sliding slightly up the affordability scale on the Midtown food chain—though here as elsewhere, the tab depends on what you order—at **Tapa the World,** 2115 J St. (at 21st St.), 916/442-4353, Spanish tapas are the main attraction, natch, but paella mixta, empañada specials, and occasional flamenco guitar add to the menu. Open daily 11:30 A.M.–midnight. For nuevo Latino there's also **Habañero Cava Latina,** also at 2115 J, 916/492-0333, a cave-like wine cellar

believably "of Havana." Here, you can get the wonderful spices, sauces, and citrus-based dressings of life in the far south with a lighter, contemporary touch—and without all that artery-hardening lard, since olive and other cooking oils are used instead. Marvelous chicken mole, very imaginative tamales, and other hearty selections star on the entrée menu. But don't neglect the starters, which alone could make a memorable meal. Beer and wine; takeout available. Open Mon.–Fri. from lunch until late (11 P.M. or midnight), and Sat.–Sun. from 5 P.M. Reservations advisable. An older sibling to Habañero is **Aioli Bodega Española** at 1800 L St. (at 18th), 916/447-9440, which serves wonderful regional Spanish in stylish surroundings—such things as seafood stew, rib eye steak with anchovy glaze, and vegetarian paella. Or make a meal out of the exceptional tapas, both hot and cold. Full bar. Lunch served Mon.–Sat., dinner nightly. Reservations wise.

Surprisingly reasonable for sophisticated pan-Asian fare is 1999's **Bamboo** at 2431 J St., 916/442-7200, the fortunate culinary child of David SooHoo (of Chinois East/West fame) and Elaine Corn. Here you can eat your way through China, Thailand, Malaysia, Indonesia, and beyond without cashing in a single CD (nothing over $10), sampling along the way such things as Hainese chicken, spicy Japanese eggplant, sweet and spicy green Thai chicken curry, and beefy "laughing buns." Open for dinner Mon.–Sat., for lunch weekdays only. Beer and wine.

More Expensive in Midtown

Centro Cocina Mexicana, 2730 J St., 916/442-2552, is another of local restaurant mogul Randy Paragary's creations, this one serving imaginative and unbelievably hip California-chic Mexican fare. On a hot day people suck down Cocina's margaritas, made with various fresh fruit juices, like mineral water, and hardly ever complain about paying $2 for chips and salsa. Favorites in the food department include the appetizers and contemporary yet authentic takes on regional Mexican fare. Daily seafood specials, wonderful desserts. Full bar. Open weekdays for lunch, Fri.–Wed. for dinner. If you seek some post-feast fun among Sacramento sophisticates, head upstairs to Paragary's **Blue Cue**, 916/442-7208, a stylish pool hall. Another making-the-scene

possibility quite nearby is Paragary's hip **Monkey Bar** at 2730 Capitol Ave. (28th and Capitol), 916/442-8490, where the entertainment comes with no cover charge.

City Treasure Restaurant at 1730 L St., 916/447-7380, started out as a relaxed deli and has evolved into a sophisticated eatery—a city treasure all decked out in local art, hand-painted fabrics, and fresh flowers. The menu, once fairly eclectic, now speaks Mediterranean with a Greek accent. Desserts are delightful. Reservations wise. Open weekdays for lunch, Sun. 10 A.M.–2 P.M. for brunch, nightly for dinner.

Casual **Virga's** restaurant and bar at 14th and O (1501 14th St.), 916/442-8516, is a small, sunny place serving big meals—robust California-style Italian, Roman fare with some lighter Asian touches. Before you sink your teeth into the Venetian lasagna or the day's ravioli, for example, consider the possibilities of Italian potstickers. Good food, great desserts, good value. Open for lunch weekdays, for dinner Tues.–Sat. nights. Street parking available, also a public lot across O.

How 'bout a Californian with New York attitude? One of the best places in town for hefty, home-style meatloaf, pot roast, lasagna and other upscale comfort food is **Moxie,** inside the onetime Burger Basket at 2028 H St. (between 20th and 21st Sts.), 916/443-7585, named after a tangy late 1800s soft drink marketed in Maine as nerve medicine, to prevent softening of the brain. The brain won't go soft here, whether you try the homey entrées or the bold California-style selections. Daily specials at lunch and dinner, good desserts. Beer and wine. Open weekdays for lunch, Tues.–Sun. for dinner.

A best bet in Midtown for a quick, tasty meal is **Michelangelo's** at 1725 I St., 916/446-5012, where one of the first things you'll notice is a Sacramento version of *The Creation of Adam.* The fare here runs to muscular East Coast–style Italian, from spaghetti and meatballs to steak Michelangelo. Open Tues.–Sun. for dinner, Tues.–Sat. for lunch.

Another Midtown option is Gothic art deco–style **Harlow's Restaurant and Nightclub** at 2708 J St., 916/441-4693, where the surviving stained glass window from the old Alhambra Theater is still a local celebrity. Historically, Harlow's has been known for its hearty Italian, but these days "modern American" and other eclectic selections set the standard at lunch and dinner (lunch served Tues.–Fri. only, dinner Tues.–Sunday). Entertainment, on Harlow's centerpiece live-music stage, kicks in about 9:30 P.M. and ranges from reggae and rockabilly to salsa and swing (cover). Upstairs is the **MoMo Lounge,** a cigar bar.

Top Tomatoes in Midtown

The onetime brick machine shop at 2000 Capitol Ave. (20th and Capitol), previously the popular Italian restaurant Americo's, is now a sunnier, more stylish bistro, but the muralistic monument to Bacchus remains. **The Waterboy,** 916/498-9891, adjacent to the Rubicon Brewing Company, cheerfully serves up sophisticated French provincial and American fare. One of Sacramento's best restaurants, the Waterboy is beloved for its pizzettas, daily fish and seafood specials, and entrées such as chicken with prosciutto and chard. Monthly changing menu, beer and wine only.

Beloved **Paragary's Bar & Oven** at 1401 28th St. (28th and N), 916/457-5737, is known for its exceptional California-style northern Mediterranean entrées, seafood, brick-oven pizzas, and fairly artsy, sophisticated San Francisco atmosphere. As at all Paragary's, the entrée menu changes regularly. A new star here is the Starlight Courtyard, a onetime parking area transformed into a Mediterranean paradise, complete with fountains and olive trees—a truly marvelous patio dining setup. Lunch served weekdays only, dinner nightly. Full bar, good wine list. Free valet parking (plenty of lots nearby). There's another Paragary's in East Sacramento at 2384 Fair Oaks Blvd., 916/485-7100—under separate ownership, though considered the local social and culinary standard bearer—a third in Folsom, a fourth in Gold River, and a fifth planned for Roseville.

The one-time Capitol Grill, another of Randy Paragary's culinary institutions, right across from the Midtown Paragary's at 28th and N, is now **Twenty Eight,** 916/456-2800. No longer a populist people-watching café cluttered with campaign mementos, the place is as sleek and shiny as a lobbyist's coin. In keeping with its new prestige near the top of the local food chain, Twenty Eight specializes in more sophisticated variations on the Capitol Grill's regional American, Californian, and Mediterranean themes. Try

some grilled spiced quail, butternut squash ravioli, or lobster potstickers. Twenty Eight is beloved for its desserts, including the memorable chocolate truffle cake, served warm with a scoop of malted milk chocolate ice cream. Full bar, expansive wine list, valet parking (public lot across N Street). Open weekdays for lunch, daily for dinner. Reservations advised.

The most elegant and extravagant night out for Big Tomato residents must include dinner at the exceptional **Biba,** in Midtown at 2801 Capitol Ave. (28th and Capitol), 916/455-2422, noted for its Tuscan tilt but also quite respectful of Southern Italian traditions—and easily the most cosmopolitan restaurant for many miles around. The menu changes with the seasons, and proprietor Biba Caggiano—she of the popular *Biba's Italian Kitchen* cooking show on The Learning Channel, and the author of a multitude of Italian cookbooks—is always introducing new wonders. Specialties include gnocchi, tortelloni (giant tortellini) in cream tomato sauce, smoked-salmon fettuccine, and carefully prepared (in-house) desserts. Full bar, excellent wine list. Open weekdays for lunch, Mon.–Sat. for dinner. Reservations all but mandatory. Public parking adjacent.

EATING IN EAST SACRAMENTO AND "GOURMET GULCH"

Fairly Inexpensive in East Sac

Casual neighborhood eateries are quite popular throughout East Sacramento. Even if you arrive at beloved **Queen of Tarts Bakery & Cafe** in the McKinley Park neighborhood, 3608 McKinley Blvd. (at 36th St.), 916/451-3102, with the intention of limiting yourself to a savory salad or soup and sandwich at lunch, in no time you'll be drooling over the delectable sweets on display. So you may as well give in and order a lemon tart, some shortbread, or a cinnamon roll to go. Great stop for coffee and breakfast pastries, too. Open weekdays 6:30 A.M.–7 P.M., weekends 6:30–3 P.M. Or try the tiny neighborhood **Nopalitos Southwest Cafe** near CSU Sacramento at 5530 H St. (near 55th St.), 916/452-8226, open weekdays only for breakfast and lunch; show up early for lunch, or plan on takeout. For lots of food at a fair price, try the taco plate, the smothered burrito—six kinds to choose from, including veggie, swimming in either green chile or ranchero sauce—or the chile verde, which is served up in various incarnations, including "tamale in a bowl." Java City coffee, great chocolate chip cookies.

Another budget saver, great for Lebanese, is **Byblos** south of the American River at 8887 Folsom Blvd., 916/857-0931, where fresh fruit drinks—including "Byblos Juice," a blend of strawberry, mango, kiwi, and lime—also star. Vegetarians can do well here with the falafels and other pita sandwiches, but lamb specials and rotisserie-roasted chicken choices are also available. Open daily. For inexpensive Vietnamese, try been-there-forever **Bo Bo Cafe** at 5412 Madison Ave., 916/348-1750, where menu stars include ginger beef and lemon grass chicken with chili.

Cafe East Meets West at Alta Arden and Howe, next to Cost Plus and Eat Your Vegetables, 916/483-7062, serves up intelligent European-Asian fusion, such things as grilled rib eye (marinated in Korean barbecue sauce) with eggplant and mashed potatoes, and seared salmon with shiitake mushrooms and sweet corn. The salads here, including a vegetarian rice salad, can also make a meal.

A long-running vegetarian favorite way out there in Fair Oaks Village is the **Sunflower Drive-In** at 10344 Fair Oaks Blvd., 916/967-4331, where the specialty nutburgers, nutty tacos, and falafels have kept folks lining up in the parking lot for two decades and counting. And do try the yogurt shakes. Open just 11 A.M.–3 P.M. on Mon. and 11 A.M.–5 P.M. Sun., but otherwise 11 A.M.–8 P.M.

More Expensive in East Sac

East Sacramento's **33rd Street Bistro** at 3301 Folsom Blvd. (the extension of Capitol Ave., separated from Midtown by the freeway), 916/455-2233, is bright, bold, relaxed, and natural, something of a culinary transplant from the Pacific Northwest specializing in reasonably priced seafood, he-man sandwiches, and impressive salads, though you'll find the see-and-be-seen Sacramento crowd also digging into other contemporary cuisine styles. Unlike most restaurants in town, 33rd Street is open daily for breakfast, lunch, and dinner. Reservations not taken, so muscle your way in.

For what may be the best baby back ribs in town, these marinated in red-gold ale and even-

tually dressed up in apple cider barbecue sauce, head for the **Hopstreet Bistro and Brewery,** just off Hwy. 50 near CSU Sacramento at 6300 Folsom Blvd., 916/451-4677. Other hearty regional American specialties dominate the menu, from Cajun blackened beef tips to grilled lamb chops. And here's a special treat for dessert: Hopstreet's surprisingly good "beer float," wherein the award-winning oatmeal stout floats the vanilla ice cream. Brewski fans will also want to sample the rest of the wares here (including a pale ale and honey ale), which can be done without DUI complications if you opt for the sampler set (seven three-ounce pours). Open for lunch and dinner daily, special brunch on weekends.

Italian-American **Andiamo,** at home in the homey brick digs of Sacramento's beloved but long departed Rosemount Grill at 3145 Folsom Blvd., 916/456-0504, serves both contemporary and honest, wholesome Italian specialties alongside fresh-faced all-American favorites. Something for everyone—from grilled eggplant, housemade pastas, and seafood to juicy steaks and other poultry, pork, beef, and lamb specialties. Changing daily specials add still more variety. Happily—and almost uniquely among Sacramento's better restaurants—Andiamo also serves breakfast. Full bar, largely Californian but varied wine list (many served by the glass). Open daily for breakfast, lunch, and dinner.

Long popular for Thai in Sacramento is contemporary, fresh, and fairly reasonable **Thai Palms** at 943 Howe Ave., 916/929-5915, open daily for dinner, weekdays only for lunch. Nothing here disappoints, from the shellfish stirfries and curries to delectable deep-fried stuffed chicken wings. There's also a special vegetarian menu. Beer and wine only. Lunch served weekdays, dinner nightly. Reservations advisable.

One of Sacramento's best Indian restaurants, way out there in East Sac is **Star of India,** 8121 Madison Ave., 916/967-1550. Most of the selections here hark back to northern India, from the tasty curried chicken vindaloo and spicy lamb *samosas* to creamy *aloo mutter* (potatoes and peas). Open daily for lunch and dinner. Another best bet is **Kaveri Madras Cuisine** at 1148 Fulton Ave., 916/481-9970, which serves specialties from southern India as well as the north, such things as the crepe-like *dosas,* filled with vegetable curry. Also open daily for lunch and dinner.

Fairly Inexpensive in Gourmet Gulch

If you're on a budget but craving something spectacular from Gourmet Gulch, try **Ettore's** at 2376 Fair Oaks Blvd., 916/482-0708, a European-style café well worth it for marvelous soups, salads, sandwiches, and such. But the real claim to fame here is dessert—elaborate and exceptional cakes, fruit tarts, and other bakery items. Don't leave without a bag-full. Open most days 6 A.M.–9 P.M. (until 10 P.M. Fri.–Sat.), and Sun. 8 A.M.–2 P.M.

Another best bet is **Cafe Napoli**, just off Fair Oaks behind Loehmann's Plaza at 535 Fulton Ave., 916/971-9090, where wonderful calzones, lasagna (even veggie), and pizzas star. Open weekdays only for lunch (served cafeteria-style), Mon.–Sat. for dinner. Closed Sundays.

Exceptional and affordable is **Danielle's Creperie** at Arden Town Center (Fair Oaks and Watt), 916/972-1911, where French onion soup, crepe Normande, ham and artichoke crepe, and some half-dozen veggie crepes are worth serious consideration. Open most days 9 A.M.–9 P.M., Sun.–Mon. 9 A.M.–3 P.M.

More Expensive in Gourmet Gulch

The second in the Mace family restaurant chain (for the original Mace's, see Top Tomatoes in East Sac below), casual **Mace's Grill and Wine Market** in the Almond Orchard shopping center, 11773 Fair Oaks Blvd. (at Madison), 916/863-0400, serves fresh and flavorful New American, Mediterranean, and Asian fare. Open weekdays only for lunch, nightly for dinner. Reservations advised.

A midrange favorite is dinner-only **Bandera** at 2232 Fair Oaks Blvd., 916/922-3524, where hearty regional American stars—such things as pork tenderloin and beef ribs. A real treat at Bandera is the spit-roasted chicken. Reservations not taken. Beer and wine, some liquor.

One of the Gulch's relative newcomers, **Amadeus** at 2310 Fair Oaks Blvd., 916/922-7070, serves up sophisticated, classical Mediterranean, from pastas to grilled lamb, King salmon, and filet mignon. Full bar. Dinner served nightly, lunch weekdays only. For rustic yet modern, boisterous Italian, the place is **Ristorante Piatti** at the Pavilions shopping center, 571 Pavilions Ln., 916/649-8885. The ever-changing seasonal menu ranges from grilled and rotisserie-roasted chicken to pizzas, pastas, and calzones. Full bar. Open

daily for lunch and dinner. Another popular possibility is **Bravo Ristorante Italiano** behind Swanson's Cleaners at 2333 Fair Oaks Blvd., 916/568-0494, a relaxed trattoria serving excellent pastas, veal scaloppini, and fresh fish. Full bar, good California and Italian wine list. Open Tues.–Fri. for lunch, Tues.–Sun. for dinner.

Chinois City Wok in the Arden Town Center, 3535 Fair Oaks Blvd., 916/485-8690, is a casual but sophisticated "fusion" descendant of Sacramento's Chinois East/West, launched by Terry and Alvin SooHoo. (The third Chinois E/W sibling, David, was busy in Midtown, at last report.) Particularly beloved here: honey-walnut prawns with crisp red and green peppers, prawn pot stickers, the "phoenix and dragon" stir fry, and the Mongolian beef "laughing buns" of East/West yore. Open for dinner nightly, for lunch weekdays only.

New in 1999, simple but stylish **Cafe Nikko** in Lyon Village at 2580 Fair Oaks, 916/485-2299, is a very good and fairly traditional sushi bar and Japanese restaurant. Here, even vegetarians can join in; there's a veggie roll composed of grilled vegetables with soy sauce and wasabi. Or try the Oriental Caesar salad. Entrées include fish, seafood, and chicken sukiyaki. Full bar, short California wine list. Open for lunch Mon.–Sat., dinner nightly (full menu available 11 A.M.–9 P.M. Saturday).

Top Tomatoes in East Sac

Classy **Lemon Grass Restaurant** at 601 Munroe St. (just north of Fair Oaks Blvd., near Loehmann's Plaza), 916/486-4891, is Sacramento's reigning Vietnamese-Thai restaurant—not to mention one of the region's best, period. Particularly wonderful for vegetarians here is the monk's curry—tofu and veggies bathed in a sweet and sour coconut-milk curry garnished with fresh basil. Other signature entrées keep everyone coming back for more, including the catfish in clay pot. Full bar, good wine list. Open for lunch on weekdays only, for dinner nightly. Quite reasonable, really.

Ever-popular **Paragary's Bar & Grill** at 2384 Fair Oaks Blvd., 916/485-7100, is incredibly hip, incredibly good, and incredibly fun, consistently one of the best restaurants in town. Paragary's changing menu emphasizes New American with Mediterranean flair (such things as crab or mushroom lasagna in winter), though the wood-fired pizzas and salads are reliable standards year-round. Reservations advisable (taken for any group at lunch but only for six or more at dinner). Full bar, good California wine list. Open for dinner nightly, lunch weekdays only.

Locally beloved and one of Sacramento's best restaurants, **Mace's** at the Pavilions shopping center, 2319 Fair Oaks Blvd., 916/922-0222, is very American, very "Western," the bold New American fare ranging from Northwestern to Southwestern and beyond. Lunch is served Mon.–Sat., dinner nightly, and brunch on Sun. 10 A.M.–2 P.M.

There's an excellent **Scott's Seafood Grill & Bar** in town, too, in Loehmann's Plaza at 545 Munroe St. (at Fulton), 916/489-1822, where diners people-watch while digging into an internationally accented array of seafood specialties. Full bar, California wines (heavy on the chardonnays). Open nightly for dinner, Mon.–Sat. for lunch.

The Terrace at Pavilions at 544 Pavilions Ln. (near the rear of the shopping center), 916/488-7285, once known as Mitchell's Terrace, is another good, fairly pricey favorite. The menu here emphasizes stylish California cuisine artistically elevated by European and Asian fusion—such as tiger prawns and papaya salad, shrimp dumplings, and grilled scallops in coriander sauce. Full bar, California and French wine list. Open daily for dinner, weekdays only for lunch, and Sunday for brunch.

In an era of California cuisine, sophisticated **La Boheme** at 9634 Fair Oaks Blvd., 916/965-1071, proudly serves duck a l'orange, steak Diane, crepe suzette, and other continental classics. European and California wine list. Full bar. Open weekdays only for lunch, Mon.–Sat. for dinner. Reservations wise.

Another East Sac classic—a local fine dining favorite—is dress-up continental **Aldo's** in the Town & Country Village shopping center at 2916 Pasatiempo Ln. (Fulton and Marconi), 916/483-5031, where the romantic menu runs from lobster Hungarian, filet medallion Diane, and herb-roasted rack of lamb to tableside flambés. These days they offer lighter choices, too, including pastas and seafood. For dessert, try the crepes suzette. Full bar. Open for lunch Mon.–Sat, for dinner nightly. Reservations wise.

A unique Sacramento foodie experience is **The Kitchen** at 2225 Hurley Way, 916/568-7171, which is certainly not guilty of false advertising. More kitchen and catering business than restaurant, here you show up and practically participate in the demonstration dinners so marvelously staged by Randall Selland and Nancy Zimmer. The evening's many pleasures will cost you—$75 per person, at last report—but you can keep the tab at that by bringing your own wine (no corkage). Wine list available, otherwise. Make reservations well ahead, because dinners here are booked months in advance.

SACRAMENTO INFORMATION

If you're downtown, find out what you need to know at the **Sacramento Convention and Visitors Bureau** at 1303 J St., Ste. 600, Dept. 100, Sacramento, CA 95814, 916/264-7777, fax 916/264-7788, 916/442-7644 on weekends. On the Internet it's www.sacramentocvb.org. The visitors bureau is open Mon.–Fri. 8 A.M.–5 P.M. Open on weekends *and* weekdays, the **Old Sacramento Visitor Information Center** is no longer on Front St.; it's been relocated to 1101 2nd St., 916/442-7644. For general Old Sacramento business, contact the **Old Sacramento Historic District** office at 111 2nd St. (3rd floor), 916/264-7031, fax 916/264-7286, www.old-sacramento.com. For current recorded info on special events in Old Sac, call 916/558-3912.

The best all-around source of local information is the award-winning *Sacramento Bee,* main link in the valley's Gannett newspaper chain, noted for its political coverage, reasonably enlightened editorials, and mainstream but informative features. Still the new kid in town after all these years, vying for community loyalty, is the free weekly *Sacramento News & Review,* especially strong on news features and entertainment coverage and attracting the younger crowd.

SACRAMENTO TRANSPORTATION

Getting Here: Air

Sacramento International Airport, 12 miles northwest of town via I-5, 916/929-5411, www.sacairports.org, is served by major airlines plus a few connector services. Airport traffic has definitely picked up since no-frills Southwest Airlines has carved out a major section of Sacramento airspace. But the name change (adding the "International") preceded a more dramatic transformation—the decision to build toward the day Sacramento would be adding nonstop flights to both Mexico and Canada. The first step in that airport building program was completed in 1998, when the airport's size was doubled with the addition of new $58 million Terminal A, dominated by Southwest Airlines but also including Delta and America West. When international flights do begin at Sacramento International Airport, anticipated for the year 2002, customs and immigration will also be housed in Terminal A.

Visitor facilities in light, airy Terminal A include a snazzy new food court—with Starbucks, Cinnabon, California Pizza Kitchen, and Capitol Brewing Co., among others—not to mention the Marketplace Deli, the Home Turf sports bar, and Java City, See's Candies, and newsstand kiosks

one of the many ways to get around Sacramento

JOHN POIMIROO/CalTour

elsewhere. There are also retail shops, selling everything from golf duds and luggage to gourmet California food items. Sacramento's Art in Public Places project has been busy here, too. Brian Goggin's *Samson* sculptures near the baggage claim area are particularly amusing in an airport setting—two towers of luggage from around the world piled high—some 23 feet— and rammed into the ceiling.

Terminal B (once known as Terminal B and C) is also getting a substantial facelift, everything from new carpets and ceilings, remodeled snack bars, and renovated elevators to improved restrooms, lighting, heating, air-conditioning, and security systems. Major airlines housed here include Alaska, American, Northwest, TWA, and United.

The bad news is, even with recent expansion, the airport is barely adequate to handle current use, let alone anticipated future growth in air travel—which means it's still hectic and crowded here. But there have been substantial practical improvements, including altered traffic flow that directs airport arrivals into lots designated for either Terminal A or B; both lots include hourly and daily parking. Near the rental car terminal (well south of the flight terminals) is an overflow lot (served by shuttle), and a multi-level 4,500-space parking garage was scheduled to open at the airport in 2000 or so.

As you can judge from the airport parking lots, most Sacramentans drive to catch their flights. A viable alternative is **Supershuttle Sacramento,** headquartered at 520 N. 16th St., toll-free 800/258-3826 for reservations or 916/557-8370. Better regional hotels and motels also offer airport transport. Cab service is available, too, through a variety of companies including **Yellow Cab** at 900 Richards Blvd., 916/444-2222 or toll-free 800/464-0777 (in California), which has been here since 1917, and **Sacramento Independent Taxi,** an association of independents contracted by the airport and headquartered at 555 Capitol Mall, Ste. 1440, 916/457-4862.

Getting Here: Trains

The **Amtrak** depot, in the shadow of the I-5 freeway at 4th and I Sts., is a wonderful remnant of Sacramento's railroading heyday. Well worth it on Amtrak is the climb over the Sierra Nevada to Reno (ultimately Chicago) onboard the *California*

Zephyr, a particularly appropriate opportunity to honor the unimaginable difficulty of building the nation's first transcontinental railroad. Amtrak's *Coast Starlight* also connects here, to Seattle/Vancouver in the north and Los Angeles/San Diego in the south. And for the first time in 28 years, beginning in 1999 Amtrak passengers could also get from Sacramento to Bakersfield (and points in between)—without having to first take a bus to Stockton—now that at least one *San Joaquin* train is routed directly to Stockton (call for details).

Now more viable, too, is train service connecting Sacramento to the Bay Area—thanks to the *Capitol* trains, a system initiated by Amtrak but now managed by the Capitol Corridor Joint Powers Authority and operated by Bay Area Rapid Transit (BART). Each day, seven trains connect Sacramento with Emeryville and Oakland, passing through Davis, Fairfield, Martinez, and Richmond on the way. "Feeder" bus links continue on to destinations including San Francisco, Hayward, Fremont, and San Jose.

For more information on Amtrak's "Capitol Corridor" train service, write to the Capitol Corridor Joint Powers Authority, 800 Madison St., P.O. Box 12688, Oakland, CA 94604-2688, or call Amtrak at toll-free 800/872-7245 (USA-RAIL), www.amtrakwest.com. Make advance reservations through Amtrak or your travel agent—or take your chance on a space-available trip; Amtrak station agents accept cash and major credit cards. The terminal is open daily 5:15 A.M.–10 P.M. (At last report no snacks, even vending-machine fare, was available here, so bring your own to munch while you wait.) At least limited food service is available on the trains, however.

Getting Here: Bus and Car

The **Greyhound Bus** terminal in downtown Sacramento, 715 L St. between 7th and 8th Sts., 916/444-7270 or toll-free 800/231-2222 for route and fare information, is open 24 hours and centrally located in a dicey part of downtown. From here, buses head out to Reno, L.A., San Francisco, Portland, and just about everywhere in between and beyond.

Since this is California, most people drive. Traffic throughout the greater Sacramento area can be hellish—particularly during peak weekday commute hours—though it's usually not that bad in central Sacramento. To keep abreast of traffic snarls (usually worse during the morning commute), tune in to local radio stations or watch morning TV news broadcasts. For general regional **road conditions,** call 916/445-7623. To rent a car for delta or gold country day trips and other adventures afield, contact the visitors bureau for a listing of reputable local companies.

Getting Around: Shuttle, Bus, and Light Rail

Quite popular downtown and in Midtown, since their routes expanded recently, are the vivid orange, violet, and yellow **Downtown Area Shuttle** (DASH) buses, operated by Sacramento Regional Transit, which travel in a loop linking Old Sacramento, the Downtown Plaza, and the Sacramento Convention Center on J St. with CSU Sacramento in East Sacramento. The loop runs east on J St.—passing major attractions in Midtown—and returns to downtown on L Street. Shuttle stops are signed with the same bright colors, and if you miss the bus, another will be along in 10–15 minutes. Depending on how far you're going, the fare costs $.50 to $1.50. Regular shuttle operating hours are Mon.–Sat. 11 A.M.–7:30 P.M. and Sun. noon–6 P.M. Other public transit bus routes link downtown with other destinations and provide service 5 A.M.–10 P.M. daily.

Always fun, though, especially to get out into the northeastern and eastern suburban sectors, is the city's new **RT Metro light rail** trolley system. Two separate links (roughly paralleling I-80 and Hwy. 50) connect downtown with the suburbs, primarily to get people to work without their cars. As of 1999, the light rail system extended only as far as Watt Ave. on the I-80 route and to Mather Field on the Hwy. 50 route. But by 2002, light rail will extend all the way to Folsom, and a third link will extend from downtown through the Land Park neighborhood near Freeport Blvd. to Meadowview Rd., eventually extending all the way to Elk Grove. Possible future extensions will reach to Roseville, Davis, and Sacramento International Airport. The light rail system runs 4 A.M.–midnight daily with trolleys every 15 minutes. To buy a light rail ticket, (1) select the appropriate fare (push button), (2) deposit the exact change ($1.50 or six quarters at last report, no change given), then (3) take your ticket, which you'll have to show to RT fare inspectors. If you bought your ticket in advance, you'll have to validate it in the ticket machine before boarding.

For more information on DASH shuttles and bus and light rail routes, stops, and fares, contact Regional Transit headquarters at 1400 29th St., P.O. Box 2110, Sacramento, CA 95810, 916/321-2877 or 916/321-2800, www.sacrt.com, or stop by the RT Downtown Service Center at 818 K Street. Request a copy of the current *Regional Transit Bus & Light Rail Timetable Book.*

NEAR SACRAMENTO: FOLSOM AND VICINITY

Some 25 miles east of Sacramento, Folsom's **Sutter Street** is center of the town's old-brick historic district—a popular regional destination for getting away from it all without going far. Museums in Folsom include the **Folsom History Museum,** 916/985-2707, the **Ashland Station** railroad depot, and the original **Powerhouse.** Also in the neighborhood: the well-sung slammer immortalized by Johnny Cash in his "Folsom Prison Blues," where the **Folsom Prison Museum** cum art gallery, 916/985-2561, ext. 4589, or toll-free 800/821-6443, is oddly inviting.

At the edge of the gold country is the 18,000-acre **Folsom Lake State Recreation Area,** the Sacramento area's biggest outdoor draw. It begins some 20 miles east of Sacramento where the American River Parkway ends near Folsom. The oak woodlands surrounding Folsom Lake and its campgrounds and picnic areas are threaded with hiking and horseback-riding trails, but the area's main attraction is summertime water recreation, everything from sailboarding to jet-skiing. The 150 campsites are quite popular during summer (reserve well in advance). For current Folsom Lake information, contact: **Folsom Lake State Recreation Area,** 7806 Folsom-Auburn Rd., Folsom, CA 95630, 916/988-0205. For camping reservations, necessary from Memorial Day to Labor Day, call toll-free 800/444-7275.

Tiny **Lake Natoma** behind Nimbus Dam is Folsom's forebay—more idyllic for rowing and sailing because the speed limit prohibits speedboats and water-skiing. Just downriver from Natoma's Nimbus Dam is the **Nimbus Fish Hatchery** in Rancho Cordova, a salmon and steelhead farm adjacent to the **American River Trout Hatchery** at 2001 Nimbus Road. For tour information, call 916/358-2020.

Folsom has some great restaurants, too. For starters, *the* breakfast place is the wonderfully homey **Lake Forest Cafe** in a venerable old house at 13409 Folsom Blvd. (at Park Shore), 916/985-6780, open just for breakfast and lunch, Wed.–Sun. only. Fairly inexpensive and excellent, next door to Folsom's branch of Paragary's in the Lakes Pavilion shopping center, is tiny **Thai Siam,** 705 Gold Lake Dr., Ste. 360, 916/351-1696, which serves fresh Thai specialties fit for royalty. Open nightly for dinner, Mon.–Sat. for lunch. Also a particularly good value is **Bailie's Restaurant & Bar** on the edge of old Folsom at 312 E. Bidwell Ave., 916/983-3093, sibling to the Jammin' Salmon on the river near Sacramento. A bit of the Wild West on the outside, inside Bailie's is strictly contemporary Californian—a casual, simple, yet earthy bistro.

For current events and other area information, call the **Sutter Street Merchants Association** at 916/985-7452 (info and events hotline) or contact the **Folsom Chamber of Commerce and Visitor Center,** 200 Wool St., 916/985-2698, www.folsomchamber.com.

NEAR SACRAMENTO: DAVIS

Northwest of Sacramento via I-80 but close enough to be socially connected is Davis, primarily home to the University of California, Davis, and its student body. People in self-consciously casual Davis, the self-proclaimed Bicycle Capital of the World and an intellectual oasis amid the fields of beans and tomatoes, are quite conscious of their environmental and global responsibilities—this despite the fact that some in California still dismiss the campus as strictly an agricultural school. Among its many other distinctions, UC Davis is one of the top 25 research universities in the nation. Yet Davis does shine in agriculture. Wine lovers should note that UC Davis has the largest enology department in the nation, with hundreds of students dedicated to the study of winemaking, and a distinguished program in viticulture. Davis also supports less glamorous crops, too, as befits a university so

ADVENTURING NEAR DAVIS

The **Jepson Prairie Reserve** near Dixon, purchased for protection in 1980 by The Nature Conservancy and now managed by the Solano County Farmlands and Open Space Foundation, includes 1,556 acres of native bunchgrass—grasslands that have never been tilled. Spectacular on a small scale at Jepson is the concentric-ring bloom progression of vernal pool wildflowers that grow in rainwater-collecting "hog wallows." Starting in early spring, the subtle show changes almost weekly. Other stars of the vernal pool ecosystem protected here include three species of fairy shrimp protected under the U.S. Endangered Species Act. There's a short self-guided nature trail at Jepson Prairie, but otherwise access is offered only on guided tours—offered every Sat. and Sun. during peak wildflower season, mid-Mar. to mid-May (small donation requested). For groups of five or more, call 707/421-1351 to make a reservation. To get to Jepson Prairie, head south on Hwy. 113 from Dixon, then dogleg left onto Cook Ln. (dirt road). Cross the railroad tracks and continue on to the parking area.

Another way to get to Jepson Prairie is by train—the Spring Wildflower Train offered by Solano County's **Western Railway Museum,** located between Suisun and Rio Vista, 707/374-2978, www.wrm.org. The museum itself, a project of the Bay Area Electric Railroad Association, offers unlimited rides on its rickety streetcars and "interurbans." But for the Jepson Prairie excursion, it enlists a diesel locomotive and Pullman parlor car coaches. For additional information and reservations (required) for the **Spring Wildflower Train** to Jepson Prairie and the holiday **Santa Train,** call toll-free 800/900-7245.

The **Yolo Shortline Railroad,** P.O. Box 724, West Sacramento, CA 95691, 916/372-9777, www.ysrr.com, offers a great train ride along the original Sacramento Northern route, with trains departing variously from Woodland, Raley's Landing, and West Sacramento on Sat. and Sun. from Mother's Day through Columbus Day. The refurbished 1940s-vintage trains are fun for family outings; Murder Mystery trains and other special events are also scheduled. On the third weekend of the month, the railroad usually gives its diesel a weekend off—and conscripts its World War I-vintage steam engine for all trips.

North from Davis via Hwy. 113 is **Woodland,** once a sleepy farm town but now a fast-growing commercial center with little of its hayseed history intact. Until 1997, that is, when the 130,000-square-foot **Heidrick Ag History Center** opened at 1962 Hays Ln. (just off I-5 adjacent to the County Road 102 offramp), 530/666-9700, fax 530/666-9712, www.aghistory.org. Stars of this collection of more than 170 farm machines include a number of Fordson tractors—not to mention the 150 trucks of the **Hays Antique Truck Museum,** all-American trucks from more than 100 manufacturers (like Graham Brothers, Old Reliable, and Oshkosh), also collected here. Open most days 10 A.M.–5 P.M. (until 6 P.M. on Sat., 4 P.M. on Sun.), admission $6 adults, $5 seniors, and $4 children under age 12. A real attention-getter immediately adjacent, in the fall of 1999, was the museum's amazing **MAiZE**—a 10-acre field of corn shaped like a map of California and pruned into a very challenging maze (you need the map to get out).

Also worth a look in Woodland is the Gibson House at 512 Gibson Rd., a restored 1872 farmhouse and gardens, prime for picnicking, now the **Yolo County Museum** and open Mon. and Tues. 9 A.M.–5 P.M., weekends noon–4 P.M. John Phillip Sousa and Sidney Greenstreet once performed at the **Woodland Opera House,** the only 19th-century theater in California to survive without being put to other uses; call 530/666-9617 for info. To fully appreciate local architecture, though, come for the annual **Stroll Through History** in September. For details about the area and its events and attractions, contact the **Woodland Chamber of Commerce,** 307 1st St., 530/662-7327 or toll-free 800/843-2636, www.woodland.org.

Since *vaca* in Spanish means "cow," impolite passersby have attached the literal "cowtown" to **Vacaville** as a modern epithet, though the community is one of the valley's oldest and was actually named for the area's original landowner, Don Manuel Vaca. Though the California Medical Facility at Vacaville is the place mass murderer Charles Manson now calls home, the town itself was most noted as that stretch of freeway perfumed by the overpowering aroma of onions. Now that the local dehydrating plant has closed its doors, even Vacaville's annual Onion Festival is defunct. And so is **The Nut Tree,** Vacaville's famous restaurant—originally a humble roadside fruit stand when it opened for business in the 1920s. People still hope someone will buy the Nut Tree and resurrect it. In the meantime, alternative rest stops include

(continued on next page)

ADVENTURING NEAR DAVIS
(continued)

the **Vacaville Museum,** 213 Buck Ave., 707/447-4513, and the **Animal Place** animal sanctuary just off Laguna Creek Trail, 707/449-4814.

Though new subdivisions are popping up among the tomato fields and fruit and nut orchards, **Winters** on Hwy. 128 (near Lake Berryessa as you head north off the 505 cutoff) is still an outpost of California's Western ethos. Winters' attractions include one of California's last working blacksmith shops (Anderson Iron Works); the elegant white terra-cotta First Northern Bank of Dixon, with its antique opaque glass and marble floors and counters; and a well-known trout stream, Putah Creek, running right through town. Otherwise, the biggest excitement in

Winters is at the **Buckhorn Steak & Roadhouse** inside the onetime DeVilbiss Hotel at 2 Main St., 707/795-4503, decorated with a mountain lion pelt over the bar and omnipresent mounted heads everywhere: bucks, rams, goats, antelopes, even a moose. Without reservations, it's a long wait playing liar's dice at the mahogany bar or sitting on "the horny bench" built of bullhorns and cowhide. The food is vegetarian nightmare fare—three kinds of prime rib, excellent steaks, and combos—though the daily specials usually offer some worthy alternatives. Full saloon, too. For breakfast or lunch—even cappuccino—try the nearby **Putah Creek Café,** at Main and Railroad Streets.

---

conveniently located between the Napa-Sonoma wine country and the Big Tomato. Speaking of tomatoes, those "love apple" aphrodisiacs all but banned by the Puritans are a specialty in and around Davis—more publicly since the local biotech firm, Calgene, Inc. (now owned by Monsanto) debuted its "Flavr Savr" variety in 1994. Ready or not, Calgene has also patented red and blue cotton varieties.

But Davis is more than agriculture, which is surely why UC Davis's unofficial poet-in-residence **Gary Snyder,** who won the Pulitzer Prize in 1975, was awarded the prestigious Bollingen Prize in Poetry in 1997.

For incredibly eclectic indoor entertainment any time, *the* place is **The Palms Public Playhouse,** a drafty 150-seat barn southeast of town on Drummond Ave. off Chiles Rd., 530/756-9901, its folk music ambience attracting homegrown regional talent as well as some of the top acts ever to make it to Northern California. Lots of good restaurants around, too. **Murder Burgers** ("Burgers so Good, They're to Die For") at 978 Olive Dr., 530/756-2142, serves very good burgers, and has the additional distinction of making the *National Lampoon* list of perverted restaurants. Always popular is the Davis branch of Sacramento's **Cafe Bernardo** bistro, here at home inside the Palm Court

UC Davis Library

Hotel at 3rd and D Sts., 530/750-5101, open for breakfast, lunch, and dinner. Quite special, tucked away in a solar-powered subdivision—the first in the United States—is **The Plumshire Inn** at 2557 Portage Bay E (call for directions), 530/758-1324, the spiritual descendant of Davis's popular French-country Colette. Open Tues.–Sat. for lunch and dinner—very popular, reservations advised.

For more information about UC Davis, or to arrange a campus tour, contact the **UC Davis visitor center** at 530/752-0539 or point your web browser to www.ucdavis.edu. For more information about the larger community, contact the **Davis Chamber of Commerce,** 130 G St., Davis, CA 95616, 530/756-5160, www.davischamber.com.

FROM SACRAMENTO

THE SACRAMENTO VALLEY

Heading north from Sacramento through the rice fields and orchards, up ahead near Yuba City loom the unusual midvalley mountains known as the Sutter Buttes, the world's smallest mountain range. The sacred, spiritual center of the world to the Maidu, the buttes were included in John Sutter's original New Helvetia land grant and also provided safe haven for General John C. Frémont and his ragtag ruffians before they launched their Bear Flag Republic invasion of Sonoma to the southwest.

Beyond the Buttes are some impressive wildlife refuges—Pacific Flyway stopovers for migrating waterfowl. Interwoven with fruit and nut orchards and laser-leveled rice fields are a number of valley towns and recreation destinations well worth a stop.

Sutter Buttes

Rising like some natural fortress from the surrounding flatlands, the circular Sutter Buttes include 20 or so separate peaks anchored by deep volcanic roots to the bedrock below. In the 1920s, UC Berkeley geologist Howel Williams first likened the buttes to a castle, with the surrounding low hills the ramparts, the small interi-

or valleys the moat, and the cluster of peaks and rocky spires at the center the castle itself. Because the volcanic buttes aren't connected to either the Sierra Nevada or California's coastal ranges, some geologists speculate that the Sutter Buttes are a volcanic extension of the Cascade Range—especially since similar but belowground buttes lie near Colusa.

To get an above-ground view, take a hike. The buttes themselves are privately owned and off-limits to the public, and the only way to explore the area is on a guided tour conducted with the cooperation of landowners. Though every trip has a particular emphasis, each also shares the story of the Sutter Buttes' human and natural history. For more information and for trip reservations, contact: **Middle Mountain Foundation,** 530/634-6387, www.middlemountain.org.

Twin Cities: Yuba City and Marysville

Yuba City, which sprawls like a fast-food jungle beyond the southeastern edge of the Sutter Buttes, has been the butt of north valley humor since 1985, when mapmaker Rand McNally, in its *Places Rated Almanac,* listed the town as the worst place to live in the entire United States. Community leaders decided to sidestep the notoriety Yuba City had accidentally earned for all it doesn't have by focusing attention on one thing it

Agriculture is the mainstay of the Central Valley.

ROBERT HOLMES/CALTOUR

THE SACRAMENTO VALLEY

does have—prunes, about two-thirds of the nation's annual crop. The new September **Prune Festival,** designed to celebrate Yuba City's uniqueness, makes the most of the noble dried plum—with samplings of pitted and whole prunes, prunes dipped in chocolate, prune-spiced chili and hamburgers, and chicken barbecued in prune sauce.

Just across the Feather River from Yuba City is Marysville, a gold rush–era town founded by Chilean miners and named after Mary Murphy, a survivor of the Donner Party disaster. If most people in Yuba City work in the prune orchards or at the Sunsweet processing plant, most people in Marysville are somehow affiliated with Beale Air Force Base, an aerial reconnaissance facility home to the U-2 and the now-decommissioned SR-71 spy planes. Stop in at the two-story brick **Mary Aaron Museum,** 704 D St. (at 7th), 530/ 743-1004, to see historical furniture, art, photographs, and artifacts from late 19th- and early 20th-century Marysville; open Tues.–Sat. 1:30–4:30 P.M. Also worthwhile is the **Bok Kai Temple,** on the levee at the foot of D St. (call 530/742-5486 for permission to visit). Built to honor the Chinese river god of good fortune, it's the only such temple in the country. Particularly pleasing is the town's tiny **Ellis Lake,** a piece of peace and quiet (picnic with ducks and geese) amid the traffic threading through downtown via the confusing conjunctions of Hwys. 20 and 70. (Hwy. 20 heading east is a pretty route to Grass Valley and Nevada City.)

Marysville's entertainment

© AVALON TRAVEL PUBLISHING, INC.

WILBUR HOT SPRINGS

West from Colusa and past Williams, an overgrown I-5 rest stop, Hwy. 20 winds up into the eastern foothills of the coast range. A surprise pleasure for bone-tired travelers there is Wilbur Hot Springs, Williams, CA 95987, 530/473-2306 or 530/473-2326, a clothing-optional, relaxed resort and spa tucked back in the hills. To get there the official way, turn north at the intersection of Hwy. 20 and Hwy. 16 (onto an unpaved old stage road) and continue for four miles, then turn left at the silver bridge; the elegant old Victorian hotel and spa are about a mile farther. There's no on-the-grid electricity, no traffic (park in the lot and walk the quarter mile in), and no particular concern with the concerns of the outside world. When you get here, take your shoes off—

once inside the lodge, no shoes allowed. (Strip off everything else at the bathhouse.)

Though Wilbur Hot Springs offers massage, yoga classes, volleyball, the option of sleeping under the stars, and a community kitchen (bring your own food; cooking and eating utensils supplied), the main attraction is the rustic bathhouse itself. The four covered mineral-water pools run warm to hot. Outside below the sundeck is a larger mineral pool—cold in summer, warm in winter. Overnight guests can camp in one of two campsites, or stay in one of 20 private rooms or an 11-bed dormitory (Premium). Day use (10 A.M.–5 P.M.) costs $25–30. Children are welcome, pets are not. Advance reservations required.

---

repertoire was radically expanded in 2000 with the opening of Bill Graham Presents' $25 million, 20,000-seat open-air **Sacramento Valley Amphitheatre** nearby, about five miles north of Wheatland on Forty Mile Rd. between Hwy. 65 and Hwy. 70, www.sacvalleyamp.com.

For more information about the area, contact the **Yuba-Sutter Chamber of Commerce,** 10th and E Sts., P.O. Box 1429, Marysville, CA 95901, 530/743-6501.

North Valley Wildlife Refuges

Unless the tule fog is thick, even beginning birders will have little trouble spotting ducks, geese, cranes, egrets, and swans—a total of 236 identified species—at the state's 9,150-acre **Gray Lodge Wildlife Area** just west of Gridley. On hunting days (three days a week during the season) up to a half-million birds huddle together at one end of the reserve while hunters hunker down in the cold water and mud elsewhere. Named for the old gray duck club once on the property, Gray Lodge is open daily to bird-watchers; small fee, best winter bird show from late Nov. into February. For more information, contact Gray Lodge Wildlife Area, 3207 Rutherford Rd., P.O. Box 37, Gridley, CA 95948, 530/846-3315.

Scattered to the south, north, and west of the Sutter Buttes are six separate areas that make up the **Sacramento Valley National Wildlife Refuges.** Of these, four are open to the public.

The largest refuge, Sacramento National Wildlife Refuge, includes 10,783 acres first set aside in 1933 to provide feeding and resting areas for migrating waterfowl. As valley farming expanded and the natural wetlands disappeared, waterfowl damage to crops increased—the reason behind

VALLEY OAKS: GRACEFUL GIANTS

Of all the tree species native to the region, most impressive—for its sheer size and gnarled grace—is California's valley oak, *Quercus lobata,* now endangered partly because early farmers soon realized that the most fertile and deepest soils (along with high natural water tables) were found wherever it grew. The largest oaks in North America, these light-barked, gray-green giants can grow to more than 100 feet in height, with a trunk diameter of up to eight feet. In addition to agriculture and the woodcutter's axe, encroaching development projects also threaten the valley oak. For reasons still incompletely understood (though livestock grazing, reduction of river flooding, and competition from introduced grasses are among the suspected problems), for decades valley oaks have not been successfully reproducing. This fact alone presents the most permanent threat to the species' survival, since many remaining trees are now dying of old age.

creating the smaller Colusa and Sutter Refuges (named after the nearby towns to the east and north, respectively) toward the end of World War II. In 1962, the Delevan Refuge was established southwest of Princeton and east of Maxwell. Though birds are present at all refuges year-round, the best time to come is in winter, usually Nov. and December. Areas available for public use are open daily during daylight hours, though these access hours are sometimes modified during hunting season. The **Sacramento National Wildlife Refuge**, flanking I-5 between Willows and Maxwell, offers a short hiking trail, a photography blind for birders, and a six-mile auto-tour route. Day-use fee here is $3. The **Sutter Refuge** is open seasonally to hunters and fishing enthusiasts. The **Colusa Refuge** (entrance south off Hwy. 20, just west of town) features a five-mile auto tour and abundant ducks and geese. The **Delevan Refuge**, with more than 5,600 acres of marsh and croplands, is another prime waterfowl wallow.

For more information—including current fishing and hunting regulations and schedules—contact headquarters at Sacramento National Wildlife Refuge, 752 County Road 99, Rt. 1, Box 311, Willows, CA 95988, 530/934-2801 or 530/934-7774 (recorded information), www.r1.fws.gov/sacnwrc.

Chico and Vicinity

Though the up-valley university town of Chico has been on the map for quite some time, it took the late *San Francisco Chronicle* columnist Herb Caen to remind the rest of California. Caen's original 1970s comment on Chico, that it was "the kind of place where you find Velveeta in the gourmet section at the supermarket," didn't offend anyone. In fact, good-humored locals started sending him similar examples of high culture, Chico-style—enough to keep Caen busy printing punchy one-liners for well over a decade.

Chico is equally famous for the local university's onetime ranking by *Playboy* magazine as the nation's number-one party school, a dubious

---

HIGH-MINDED MAVERICKS: THE BIDWELL LEGACY

That Chico has been known for its bad behavior and beer consumption is quite the irony, since city founders General John Bidwell and Annie E. K. Bidwell were politically progressive, active prohibitionists. It's no accident that "Lincoln" and "Frances Willard" are among the streets laid out directly north of the adobe-pink Bidwell Mansion. The Bidwells greatly admired the moral fiber of President Abraham Lincoln, much-vilified commander in chief of the Union troops during the Civil War, as well as that of Frances Willard, a well-known prohibitionist and suffragette. Chico's founding couple was also civic-minded on the local level: they laid out the city's streets and at one point gave lots away to anyone who wanted one. To start a teacher's college, they donated land for the Chico Normal School (now California State University, Chico). And they preserved the most beautiful creekside acres of their massive landholdings in a natural state, land Annie deeded to the city as a park after John's death. Even Chico's abundant street trees are part of the Bidwells' legacy.

Among the first party of overland settlers to arrive in California in 1841, John Bidwell first worked for John Sutter as his bookkeeper and business manager (leaving temporarily to join Frémont and the

bear flaggers at Sonoma). He then helped confirm the Sutter's Mill gold find, later discovering gold himself on the Feather River. With his gold rush earnings, Bidwell started a new career as an innovative farmer and horticulturist on his 28,000-acre Rancho del Arroyo Chico—the most admired agricultural enterprise in the state—where he grew wheat and other grains, nuts, olives, raisins, and more than 400 other varieties of fruit.

Always active in politics yet considered a high-minded maverick, Bidwell met the serious-minded Annie Ellicott Kennedy while serving a term in the U.S. Congress from 1865 to 1867. Bidwell's first bid for the California governorship was derailed by the state's powerful railroad lobby, and despite his incredible public popularity, he lost again in the 1870s. The Bidwells' farsighted beliefs, including support for election reforms, control of business monopolies, and women's rights, were quite controversial during the 19th century but have proved their worth to subsequent generations. Some of John Bidwell's biographical reminiscences (including "Life in California before the Gold Discovery," first published in 1890 in *The Century Illustrated* magazine) are available in the state parks' facsimile reprint, *Echoes of the Past.*

honor indirectly connected to the drunken debauchery of CSU Chico's now-dead Pioneer Days celebration. Over the years, the students' "fun" ceased to amuse the rest of the community, concerned with increased alcohol-related deaths and violence. When notified in 1987 of yet another round of national party-school notoriety, former university president Robin Wilson—a onetime CIA operative and part-time writer—said he was "appalled, horrified, disgusted." Trying to make the best of a bad situation, he added: "It's nice to be number one at something." But Wilson's most quoted remark was his warning that if Pioneer Days continued true to form he would personally "take it out in the backyard and shoot it in the head." He kept his word. Mission accomplished, he retired in 1993.

Though it's strictly a coincidence, Chico is also the proud home of the fine **Sierra Nevada Brewing Company,** 1075 E. 20th St., 530/893-3520 (brewery office) or 530/345-2739 (tap room/restaurant), progenitor of Sierra Nevada Pale Ale (among many other good beers) and now the 10th-largest brewing company in the country. If you'd like a close-up look at the facilities, free tours are scheduled Tues.–Fri. at 2:30 P.M., and on Sat. every half-hour from noon to 3 P.M. The pub also serves some of the best food in town, and the new stage is a popular venue for jazz and other performers. In fact, the accomplished creativity of Chico's business community is worth exploring at greater length, particularly throughout the vital downtown district.

Yet another irony is the fact that the town was founded by dedicated prohibitionists John and Annie E. K. Bidwell. **Bidwell Mansion,** now a state historic park at 525 Esplanade, 530/895-6144, was the center of valley social life from the 1860s until the turn of the 20th century. An elegant three-story Victorian designed by Henry W. Cleveland (later architect of San Francisco's Palace Hotel) in the style of an Italian villa, it was outfitted in the finery of the day and boasted newfangled technology—including the first indoor bathroom ever installed in California. The mansion is open daily 10 A.M.–5 P.M. for docent-led tours (last tour at 4 P.M.). Small fee. Well worth a stop.

Even more impressive is 3,600-acre **Bidwell Park,** now the second-largest city park in the nation following a recent 1,380-acre land acquisition. The untamed beauty of wooded Bidwell

Park prompted Warner Brothers to come to town in 1937 to film *The Adventures of Robin Hood,* starring Errol Flynn and Olivia de Havilland. The small **Chico Museum,** 141 Salem St. (at 2nd St., in the old Carnegie library), 530/891-4336, sometimes features memorabilia of that particular event, along with other locally focused rotating exhibits; open Wed.–Sun. noon–4 P.M.

In the narrow creekside section known as Lower Park, closest to downtown, are the **Chico Creek Nature Center,** 1968 E. 8th St., 530/891-4671, and both the **One-Mile** and **Five-Mile** Chico Creek public swimming areas, with shade trees, cool lawns, picnic tables, and playground facilities. (The creek is dammed for "pool" use during summers only.) The popular municipal **Bidwell Park Golf Course,** 530/891-8417, is in the otherwise undeveloped foothill wildness of Upper Park, known for its fine natural (sometimes *au naturel*) swimming holes and trails for hiking, horseback riding, and mountain biking. Except for golfing fees, access to Bidwell Park is free. For more information about Bidwell Park, stop by the Chico Creek Nature Center (see address above), which also serves as the park's visitor information center, or call the city parks department at 530/895-4972.

For more information about Chico and environs, contact the **Chico Chamber of Commerce** office downtown at 300 Salem St., 530/891-5556 or toll-free 800/852-8570, www. chicochamber.com, a good source for maps and brochures, open weekdays 9 A.M.–5 P.M. Particularly worth picking up are the chamber's "Butte County Spring Blossom Tour" and "Winter Migratory Waterfowl Tour" brochures. Otherwise, the best source of information, bar none, is the *Chico News & Review,* published on Thursdays and available free in distribution racks all over town.

Near Chico: Sights and Outings

South of town are almond orchards, scattered rice fields, and farm communities, including down-home, almond-happy **Durham,** founded as a 1931 California Land Act colony; rice-rich **Richvale,** where the **Richvale Cafe** serves as unofficial community center; and, farther east, the boom-and-bust town of Oroville, with its own unique sights (see listing below). Closer to Chico and pleasant for picnicking is the restored 1887 **Honey Run Covered Bridge** in Butte Creek

INN AT SHALLOW CREEK FARM

Well worth the drive, both for the price and the country-style quiet, is the Inn at Shallow Creek Farm, about three miles west of I-5 at 4712 County Road DD, Orland, CA 95963, 530/865-4093 or toll-free 800/865-4093. Shallow Creek is a small ivy-covered farmhouse surrounded by orchards and fields—and an impressive flock of poultry. Rooms are restful and tastefully decorated. The suite in the main house is large, with private bath; the two upstairs rooms share a bath. Downstairs there's a sunporch, a roomy living area with well-worn leather sofas in front of the fireplace, and a welcoming formal country dining room. Perhaps the best escape of all, though, and a real bargain by B&B standards, is the Cottage near the barn—the onetime groundskeeper's quarters with four rooms, fully equipped kitchen, sunporch, and wood-burning stove. Moderate.

Canyon to the southeast, restored by local volunteers and reached via Humbug Rd. (nice bike ride for the brave—narrow road, fast traffic) from the Skyway. This bridge is unique primarily because of its trilevel roofline, one roof for each interconnected span. From the bridge, snaking Honey Run Rd. climbs almost vertically up the craggy canyon walls, the hair-raising back-door route to **Paradise,** a large ridge-top retirement and residential community. Humbug Rd., which forks to the left from the covered bridge, continues up the canyon to the remains of old Centerville and the small **Colman Museum,** 13548 Centerville Rd., 530/893-9667 (open weekends 1–4 P.M.), displaying Native American and pioneer artifacts next to the Centerville School and pioneer cemetery.

About 13 miles north of Chico via Hwy. 99 is The Nature Conservancy's **Vina Plains Preserve,** noted for its native grasslands and fine springtime display of vernal pool wildflowers. For more information on guided tours and for specific directions, contact: **The Nature Conservancy,** California Regional Office, 201 Mission St., 4th Fl., San Francisco, CA 94105, 415/777-0487.

The **Our Lady of New Clairvaux Trappist Monastery** and farm along the Sacramento River 17 miles north of town near Vina, on part of Leland Stanford's onetime vineyard and ranch, has some guest facilities for spiritual seekers; call 530/839-2161 for information.

If you happen to be in the Los Molinos vicinity on a Sunday in April or May, and if you happen to be a miniature or steam train aficionado, call ahead to find out if the **Humann Ranch** on Holmes Road near Gerber, 530/385-1389, still offers public tours of its genuine blast from the past. Located in Godfrey Humann's farmhouse basement is the **South Shasta Model Railroad Museum,** a remarkably detailed model of the steam-train era route of the South Shasta between Gerber and Dunsmuir in the 1940s. From Hwy. 99E in Los Molinos, turn onto Aramayo Way and follow the signs—or call ahead for directions.

Oroville

The first thing most people notice about Oroville is the assortment of desolate gravel heaps surrounding the town—remaining dredge piles from placer miners who literally stripped away the fertile Feather River floodplain in search of gold. Still something of a rough-and-tumble foothill town, Oroville's historic boom-and-bust economic cycle has hounded the community into this century. When Oroville got a 20th-century boost in the form of state money and jobs for constructing the massive earth-filled Oroville Dam that created Lake Oroville, things were almost rosy for a while. When the job was done, though, the town was busted flat again. Yet the town has some worthwhile attractions, so stop and take a look around.

A reminder that many of those who created California's Old West were non-Western is Oroville's **Liet Sheng Kong,** the Temple of Assorted Deities (or "Many Gods"), 1500 Broderick St. (off 1st, at Elma), 530/538-2496. The temple was built by local Chinese (with financial support from the Chinese emperor) in 1863 for worshipers of three different faiths: Confucianism, Buddhism, and Taoism. A state historic landmark also listed on the National Register of Historic Places, Oroville's Chinese temple is both a place of worship and a museum. Call for current hours. Small fee.

Outdoors types, head for **Lake Oroville State Recreation Area.** Completed in 1967, the **Oroville Dam** created a large, many-fingered lake—and the necessity for the state's downstream

the Temple of Assorted Deities in Oroville

CALIFORNIA DEPARTMENT OF PARKS & RECREATION

Feather River Fish Hatchery, 5 Table Mountain Blvd., 530/538-2222, to artificially perpetuate the salmon and steelhead spawn. In addition to good views from the 47-foot observation tower, the **Lake Oroville Visitor Center and Museum,** atop Kelly Ridge at 917 Kelly Ridge Rd., 530/538-2219, offers films and exhibits on gold rush history, natural history, and the development of the California Water Project. Open daily 9 A.M.–5 P.M. New at Lake Oroville: the 41-mile **Bradford B. Freeman Mountain Bike Trail** across Oroville Dam and around the Thermalito Forebay, the Thermalito Afterbay, and the Oroville Wildlife Area. The lake itself, with a receding summertime waterline, is popular for boating, fishing, and houseboating. Camping facilities abound. Reserve campsites in advance through ReserveAmerica, toll-free 800/444-7275. For more information, contact: Lake Oroville State Recreation Area, 400 Glen Dr., Oroville, CA 95965, 530/538-2200.

And hike to **Feather Falls,** just above Lake Oroville in Plumas National Forest—the highest waterfall in California (outside Yosemite) and the sixth highest in the continental United States. Best for day hiking from March through May, the new trail is much improved. Wear good walking shoes and layered clothing—and bring plenty of drinking water, a picnic lunch, and any valuables (since vandalism and theft are an occasional problem in the parking lot). For more information, contact Plumas National Forest's Challenge Ranger District office (mail to: Chal-

lenge Visitor Center, 875 Mitchell Ave., Oroville, CA 95965), 530/675-1146 or 530/675-1629.

For more information about the area, contact the **Oroville Visitor & Tourism Bureau,** 1675 Montgomery St., Oroville, CA 95965, toll-free 888/676-8455.

RED BLUFF AND VICINITY

Named for the color of the riverbanks, Red Bluff often gains national notoriety in summer for being the hottest spot in the nation—with an all-time high temperature of 121 degrees in 1981. Besides the heat, the town is famous locally for the annual **Red Bluff Bull and Gelding Sale** in January, the **Red Bluff Round-Up** parade and rodeo in April, and the downtown **Cowtown Shopping Center.**

The **Kelly-Griggs House Museum,** 311 Washington, 530/527-1129, offers historical exhibits of local interest in an 1880s Italianate Victorian. Open Thurs.–Sun. 1–4 P.M. Taking the local Victorian House walking tour is also worthwhile. The **William B. Ide Adobe State Historic Park,** 21659 Adobe Rd. (two miles northeast of town on the Sacramento River), Red Bluff, CA 96080, 530/529-8599 or 530/895-6144, features remnants of the rustic adobe homestead of the first (and only) president of the Bear Flag Republic plus picnic tables and fishing. Open 8 A.M.–sunset daily. Free. **Ide Adobe Day** in August includes demonstrations of adobe

THE SAN JOAQUIN VALLEY

brick-making, candle-making, and old-time log sawing.

For more information about the north valley's hot spots, particularly recreation opportunities, contact the **Red Bluff-Tehama County Visitors Bureau,** 100 Main St., P.O. Box 850, Red Bluff, CA 96080, 530/527-6220 or toll-free 800/655-6255, www.discoverredbluff.com.

THE SAN JOAQUIN VALLEY

Californians may make fun of Sacramento, but they insult the San Joaquin Valley. Here, truly, is the Other California. The Kingston Trio made the insult public with: "How many of you are from San Francisco? How many are from someplace else? How many are from Modesto and don't understand the first two questions?" A San Francisco newspaper columnist once quipped that Fresno is "just like Modesto but without all the glitter." Most travelers pass by the long, hot landscape between Los Angeles and parts north with barely a blink.

Yet people in Modesto, Fresno, and Bakersfield enjoy life in California's salad bowl. By way of explanation, Fresno's most famous son, William Saroyan, says, "We made this place of streets and dwellings in the stillness and loneliness of the desert." And Sacramento native Joan Didion says: "Valley towns understand one another, share a peculiar spirit." But the best explanation to date is still inscribed on the Modesto Arch stretched across the old highway: Water Wealth Contentment Health.

Modesto and Vicinity

The biggest thing in Modesto is giant **Gallo Winery,** which produces millions of gallons of wine each year. But this is also the town that inspired George Lucas's film *American Graffiti,* which explains the bronze monument to Saturday night cruising at George Lucas Plaza. Nearby Turlock is most famous for its long-time "Turkeys from Turlock" slogan, a radio advertising jingle stuffed

into California's consciousness decades ago, though Livingston is Foster Farms headquarters.

Despite the jokes, there *is* high culture in and around Modesto, including the Modesto Civic Theatre's "Shakespeare in the Park" performances and concerts by the Modesto Symphony and the Townsend Opera Players. Increasingly popular is the annual **Central Valley Renaissance Festival** held each year in May at Laird

CALIFORNIA'S GRAPES OF WRATH

During the Great Depression of the 1930s, California's fertile valley was flooded with the down-and-out from the Midwest's dust bowl. Almost overnight the valley, which historically relied on migrant farm labor, became center stage for a real-life drama of human abuse and exploitation in the fields and squalid migrant labor camps. The story was best told by John Steinbeck in his Pulitzer Prize–winning *The Grapes of Wrath;* Steinbeck researched the novel while working as a journalist for the *San Francisco News.* Befriended by government worker Tom Collins, the two wandered up and down the valley, tending to people living in unimaginable poverty and despair. Steinbeck's many articles, illustrated by the wrenching photographs of Dorothea Lange, are now collected in Heyday Books' *The Harvest Gypsies: On the Road to the Grapes of Wrath.*

Thus, in California we find a curious attitude toward a group that makes our agriculture successful. The migrants are needed, and they are hated . . . for the following reasons, that they are ignorant and dirty people, that they are carriers of disease, that they increase the necessity for police and the tax bill for schooling in a community, and that if they are allowed to organize they can, simply by refusing to work, wipe out the season's crops. . . . Wanderers in fact, they are never allowed to feel at home in the communities that demand their services.

Despite the surprising popularity of Steinbeck's work, salvation for the migrants came only with the arrival of World War II. Most Dust Bowl refugees moved into the cities, getting well-paying jobs in mu-

nitions factories and other war-related industry. Desperate for cheap labor once again, California farmers turned to Mexico with the aid of the federal government's "bracero" (laborer) program. With Anglo workers removed from the picture, most Americans remained unconcerned about worsening agricultural labor conditions until 1965, when the Delano Strike, César E. Chávez and his fledgling United Farm Workers union, and long-running lettuce and table grape boycotts began to focus worldwide attention on the same story Steinbeck had told—illustrated now with different faces.

There have been some improvements in the lives, wages, and working conditions of at least some farm laborers since the 1960s, but abuses continue. In 1975, the California Legislature acted on one of Steinbeck's ideas and established its strife-torn Agricultural Labor Relations Board, though critics contend it's ineffective and politically stacked in favor of growers. Yet no matter what legal protections exist for farm workers, the continuing flood of illegal aliens into California's fields almost guarantees exploitation at the hands of the unscrupulous, since those avoiding deportation rarely speak out about even the most basic human rights (such as drinking water and sanitation facilities). Growers insist that workers' rights are being protected, but all evidence suggests that this is no truer now than it ever was.

Though few people even in California were paying attention, at the time of his death in 1993, Chávez and his supporters were still boycotting table grapes, this time primarily over the issue of worker protection against pesticide poisoning. Some former supporters contend the union has become ineffective, beset by infighting and not seriously concerned about the welfare of farm workers, and embittered growers claim the UFW has become "a boycott looking for an issue." But almost no one else is speaking out on behalf of farm workers.

Park. More typical of the area, though: the **Ripon Almond Blossom Festival** in February, and the **Oakdale Rodeo** in April, followed in late May or early June by the **Patterson Apricot Fiesta.**

Once arrived in Modesto, tour the **McHenry Mansion,** 906 15th St. (at I St.), 209/577-5341, an astounding restoration of the 1883 Italianate Victorian home of local banker Robert McHenry and his pioneering family. Open Sun.–Thurs. 1–4 P.M., Fri. noon–3 P.M.; admission is free (donations appreciated). The **McHenry Museum of Arts & History,** 1402 I St. (at 14th), 209/577-5366, offers a look at local history. It's free, and open Tues.–Sun. noon–4 P.M. The **Great Valley Museum of Natural History** at Modesto Junior College, 1100 Stoddard Ave., 209/575-6196, features exhibits, many interactive, on Central Valley animals, plants, and natural ecosystems. Open Tues.–Fri. noon–4:30 P.M., Sat. (and the first Sun. of each month) 10 A.M.–4 P.M.; small admission.

With extra time on your hands, taste your way around town, at places such as **Nick Sciabica & Sons Olive Oil Gift Shop,** 2150 Yosemite Blvd., 209/577-5067. Or take a trip to Oakdale and indulge yourself, starting at the **Bloomingcamp Apple Ranch,** 10528 Hwy. 120, 209/847-1412, open July through late Dec., and continuing on to the ever-popular **Hershey's Visitors Center,** 120 S. Sierra Ave., 209/848-8126, offering free chocolate-factory tours on weekdays. Then visit **Oakdale Cheese & Specialties** at 10040 Hwy. 120, 209/848-3139, noted also for its European

bakery goods and low-calorie "Quark" cheesecake. Open Mon.–Fri. 8:30 A.M.–5 P.M. Almond lovers, head to Salida and the **Blue Diamond Growers Store,** 4800 Sisk Rd., 209/545-3222.

A surprise in Modesto is **St. Stan's Brewery, Pub, & Restaurant,** 821 L St., 209/524-2337 or 209/524-4782, open daily for lunch and dinner. The main attraction at St. Stan's is the "alt bier," or old-style (pre-lager) beer, brewed and served here. (Since St. Stan's brews are high in alcohol content, in California they're considered malt liquors.) The Black Forest bar ambience includes 15-foot-tall faux fir trees. On the menu: plentiful pasta choices and dinner entrées from baked stuffed eggplant and Belgium beef stew to broiled New York steak. Jazz and dinner theater, too.

For a complete listing of restaurants, accommodations, and activities, as well as a current copy of the local harvest trails guide, contact the **Modesto Convention & Visitors Bureau,** 1114 J St., P.O. Box 844, Modesto, CA 95353, 209/571-6480 or toll-free 800/266-4282, http://modestocvb. org. Another good source of local information is the daily *Modesto Bee* newspaper.

Merced and Vicinity

The big news in Merced these days is that this is the chosen site for the University of California's 10th campus. Though construction details are still vague—despite recent state budget surpluses, funds are not yet available, and it seems there were a few environmental review oversights regarding vernal pools—the new $750-million

Castle Air Museum near Merced

KIM WEIR

University of California, Merced campus will one day serve 20,000 students.

Until that day, the area's pride and joy is the **Castle Air Museum** on Santa Fe Dr. (at Buhach Rd., adjacent to the former Castle Air Force Base just north of town), P.O. Box 488, Atwater, CA 95301, 209/723-2178. Castle's indoor museum features an impressive collection of wartime mementos, from vintage military uniforms and a Congressional Medal of Honor to a once-top-secret Norden Bomb Sight. The big show's outside, though—a meticulously restored open-air collection of World War II, Korean War, and Vietnam War aircraft. Also here, in the air base's onetime chapel, is the **Challenger Learning Center,** 209/726-0296, a space-and-science exhibit offering a two-hour space mission via simulator. Next door, for still more stimulating simulations, is **Aviation Challenge,** 209/726-0156, with state-of-the-art pilot training. The museum is open daily 9 A.M.–5 P.M. in summer, 10 A.M.–4 P.M. the rest of the year; closed major holidays. Admission is $5 adults, $3 seniors, $2 children age 12 and older. Guided tours are available with advance notice. Aviation buffs can also plan to show up for area air shows, including the **Antique Fly-In** in early June, held at the Merced Municipal Airport.

For more information about the area, contact the **Merced Conference and Visitors Bureau,** 690 W. 16th St., Merced, CA 95344, 209/384-7092 or toll-free 800/446-5353, www.yosemite-gateway.org.

Fresno and Vicinity

Johnny Carson joked that Fresno was the Gateway to Bakersfield, but the city prefers being recognized as the gateway to three Sierra Nevada national parks: Yosemite, Sequoia, and Kings Canyon. California's sixth-largest city, now larger than Sacramento, Fresno has become much more than the Raisin Capital of the World. Though it sprawls out in all directions, the city has a distinct and walkable downtown where the newer, taller buildings haven't yet crowded out the old. Fresno also boasts a full cultural calendar, a state university and city college, worthwhile sights, and culinary diversions. Quite fitting, when you consider the city's agricultural roots, Fresno now boasts the largest population of Hmong in the U.S., more than 30,000. Known for their own horticultural and agricultural traditions, Hmong growers are well represented here—and throughout California—at local farmers' markets.

The **Fresno Metropolitan Museum of Art, History, and Science** in the old *Fresno Bee* building, 1555 Van Ness (at Calaveras), 559/441-1444, www.fresnomet.org, features a permanent collection of (former Fresnoan) Ansel Adams's photographs, Dutch Old Masters, an Asian Gallery, plus rotating exhibits on local culture and natural history. The museum's Reeves Exploration Center offers 50 hands-on science exhibits. Open Tues.–Fri. 11 A.M.–5 P.M., weekends noon–5 P.M. Small admission fee. Among other local sights is the exceptional **Fresno Art Museum,** 2233 N. 1st St., 559/441-4220, which each year features

more than the Raisin Capital of the World

ROBERT HOLMES/CALTOUR

multiple exhibits—Mexican, American, French impressionist—in its contemporary galleries. Handicapped accessible. Open Tues.–Fri. 10 A.M.–5 P.M., Sat.–Sun. noon–5 P.M. Small admission fee, free for children under age 16. Guided group tours are available upon request. The **Discovery Center**, 1944 N. Winery Ave., 559/251-5533, is a hands-on museum offering exhibits on physical science and natural history. The center is surrounded by a six-acre park with a picnic area and a pond filled with turtles and

FORESTIERE UNDERGROUND GARDENS

Sicilian immigrant Baldasare Forestiere started his underground domestic sculpture, the beginnings of a somewhat fantastic underground retreat, in 1906. Determined to beat the heat of Fresno's searing summers, and utilizing the tunneling techniques he learned while working on New York subway construction, he worked steadily for 40 years—quickly carving out for himself a two-bedroom home with kitchen and library, and a multitude of patios, grottos, a fish pond, even an amazing glass-bottomed "walk-under" aquarium. But he didn't stop there. Forestiere's 10-acre underground labyrinth ultimately included more than 50 underground rooms, a ballroom complete with stage, a chapel, and interconnecting tunnels, arches, and stonework patterned after the catacombs of ancient Rome. To meet the needs of his changing world, he also added an 800-foot automobile tunnel, a "car corridor" for patrons of the underground restaurant and hotel Forestiere was building. Open in places to the sunlight above, the complex also included lush and exotic gardens with Moroccan grapevines, Chinese date trees, loquats, and citrus trees bearing multiple varieties of fruit.

Situated in the midst of strip development, only about 4.5 acres of Baldasare Forestiere's original domain remains. The Forestiere Underground Gardens, now a National Historic Landmark, are located two blocks east of Hwy. 99 at 5021 W. Shaw Ave. and are open weekends in spring (weather permitting) and Wed.–Sun. in summer. Four tours are offered daily; reservations are required. Admission is $6 adults, $5 seniors and teenagers, $4 children, $1 toddlers. For more information, call 559/271-0734.

EATING IN AND NEAR FRESNO

It's fair to say that Fresno offers something for every taste. For a quick meal, there's always **Fatburger,** 46 E. Herndon (at Blackstone), 559/439-2747. For inexpensive ethnic food, mostly Japanese and Mexican, head to old Chinatown, west of the railroad tracks in the vicinity of Kern and G Streets.

Basque is big in and around Fresno. Famous is the **Basque Hotel,** 1102 F St., 559/233-2286, with inexpensive and incredibly generous portions of peasant fare served up family style; entrées change nightly. Also traditional in Fresno is the old yellow-brick **Santa Fe Basque Restaurant,** 935 Santa Fe Ave. (at Tulare), 559/266-2170.

George's, 2405 Capitol St., 559/264-9433, has that California-cuisiney look but in fact dishes up wonderful Armenian authenticity, from peasant soup to shish kebab. Quite reasonable. Another George's is at 4452 W. Shaw, 559/276-1278. The **Butterfield Brewing Co. Bar & Grill,** 777 E. Olive, 559/264-5521, is open for lunch and dinner daily, serving its award-winning handcrafted Bridalveil, Tower Dark, and San Joaquin Ales, plus specialty beers. Also good at lunch and dinner is **Livingstone's Restaurant and Pub,** 831 E. Fern, 559/485-5198.

For exceptional French country classics with a San Joaquin touch, somewhat expensive by local standards, the place is the **Ripe Tomato,** 5064 N. Palm Ave., 559/225-1850. Also quite exceptional in town, and surprisingly reasonable, is the California-style **Echo Restaurant,** 609 E. Olive Ave., 559/442-3246, serving the best available produce simply and elegantly. Style-wise, the **Daily Planet,** 1211 N. Wishon, 559/266-4259, is out of this world—art deco and delightful, with a weekly changing menu featuring contemporary American cuisine, starting with lobster quesadillas for appetizers.

Out there in Hanford southeast of Fresno is another surprise, the impeccable **Imperial Dynasty,** adjacent to the Taoist Temple at 2 China Alley, 559/582-0196. The Dynasty is in the middle of nowhere, and not a Chinese restaurant (expect continental), but people jet in from everywhere for the gourmet fare. You can drop in for regular dinners but reservations are necessary well in advance for the daily changing seven-course dinners that run from $60 (food only).

goldfish. Open Tues.–Sat. 10 A.M.–4 P.M., Sun. noon–4 P.M. Small admission fee.

The **Shin-Zen Japanese Friendship Gardens** in Woodward Park (Audubon Dr. and Friant Rd.), 559/498-1551, are a wonderful respite for the road weary, with three acres of gardens, koi ponds, bridges, Japanese sculptures representing the four seasons, and a Japanese teahouse (open only on special occasions). Docent-led tours are available. Call for current hours. More mainstream and quite popular is Fresno's 157-acre **Roeding Park,** 894 W. Belmont Ave., a cool and green park that's also home to **Chaffee Zoological Gardens** (a.k.a. the Fresno Zoo), 559/498-2671 or 559/498-4692, as well as Playland (559/233-3980) and Storyland (559/264-2235) for the kiddies.

The **Kearney Mansion Museum** in Kearney Park seven miles west of downtown, 7160 W. Kearney Blvd., 559/441-0862, was once the center of M. Theo Kearney's Fruit Vale Estate. This 1900s mansion, listed on the National Register of Historic Places, has been lovingly restored—down to exact replicas of original wallpapers and carpets—and now honors the memory of "The Raisin King of California." Small admission fee. (No fee to use the surrounding 225-acre park if you tour the mansion.) Open for tours Fri.–Sun. 1–4 P.M.

For more information about the area, contact the **Fresno City & County Convention & Visitors Bureau,** 808 M St., Fresno, CA 93721, 559/233-0836 or toll-free 800/788-0836, www.fresnocvb.org. Check to see if the new tourist attraction and visitor information center—Fresno's historic **Water Tower**—has opened. The tower was patterned after a medieval German watch tower and built by George Washington Maher in 1894. Pick up the local historical society's free "A Guide to Historic Architecture—Tower District" to more fully appreciate the community's architectural heritage. For information on nearby Hanford—a worthwhile side trip—contact the **Hanford Chamber of Commerce/Visitor Agency,** 200 Santa Fe Ave., Ste. D, Hanford, CA 93230, 559/582-5024 or 559/582-0483.

Visalia

This, officially, is Middle America. Not only is Visalia (like Fresno) located near the state's geographic center, market researchers have discovered that the likes and dislikes of Visalians are a microcosm of West Coast consumer preference. To appreciate Visalia's homegrown, ask at the visitors bureau for a copy of the current *Tulare County Harvest Trail Guide,* which also lists locations of area farmers' markets. **Mearle's Drive-In,** 604 S. Mooney Blvd., 559/734-4447, no longer has carhops, but just hop inside for the 1950s ambience and burgers, fries, milkshakes, and 15 flavors

---

EATING IN BAKERSFIELD

Bakersfield has a notable Basque heritage, a fact reflected in its restaurants. One popular place for Basque fare is the **Wool Growers Restaurant,** 620 E. 19th St., 661/327-9584. Excellent but more expensive is **Chalet Basque,** 200 Oak St. (one block east of Hwy. 99 between Brundage and California), 661/327-2915, featuring seven-course dinners—choose from seafood, beef, chicken, or lamb—including wonderful sourdough bread, pink beans and salsa, well-spiced green beans, fabulous french fries (the potatoes peeled by hand), and Basque pudding for dessert. **Maitia's Basque Cafe,** 4420 Coffee Rd. (in Vons Shopping Center), 661/587-9055, is a relaxed, low-key Basque restaurant with a menu leaning more toward the contemporary than the traditional. Then there's the **Noriega Hotel,** 525 Sumner St., 661/322-8419, another good choice for family-style Basque dining. Everyone waits in the bar—fascinating place in its own right—until the dining room doors open and dinner begins. Call for current seating time.

For fine Italian food, good choices include **Mama Tosca's,** 6631 Ming Ave., 661/831-1242, and **Uricchio's Trattoria,** 1400 17th St., 661/326-8870. Another local favorite, for Mediterranean and California cuisine, is **Cafe Med,** 4809 Stockdale Hwy., 661/834-4433, which also offers a martini bar and live jazz. For fun and funky atmosphere and a heaping plate of thoroughly delectable Texas-style ribs, don't miss **Texas Tom's Barbeque,** 829 Chester St. (at 9th St.), 661/322-3355. If you're just flying by on the freeway, for good American fare try **Hodel's,** 5917 Knudsen Dr. (Olive exit off Hwy. 99), 661/399-3341; for pizza, visit **John's Incredible Pizza** at the Hwy. 178 (Rosedale) exit off Hwy. 99.

Dewar's, 1120 I St., 661/829-1882, is a candy and ice cream shop attracting people from far and wide, a Bakersfield tradition since 1909.

of ice cream. A classic in the genre. **Kat's Korner Cafe,** 1718 E. Mineral King Ave., 559/734-3119, is locally famous for its farm-style breakfast and hearty lunches. For Visalia-style fine dining the place is **Vintage Press,** 216 N. Willis St., 559/733-3033, with daily specials (predominantly seafood) and glorious desserts.

For more information about what's going on in Middle America, contact the **Visalia Convention & Visitors Bureau,** 301 E. Acequia St., Visalia, CA 93291, 559/734-3435 or toll-free 800/524-0303, www.cvbvisalia.com.

Bakersfield

Bakersfield is still prime agricultural country (grapes, citrus, and cotton are the top three crops), but it's also the center of the southern San Joaquin's oilfield development. Pumpjacks (oil-pumping derricks) march across the valley's landscape like industrial-age scarecrows. The city and its environs feature a symphony orchestra, theater troupes, country-western music and rodeos, and agricultural festivals celebrating everything from cotton and grapes to tomatoes and potatoes. The two-week-long **Great Kern County Fair** takes place here from late August into September.

The **Bakersfield Museum of Art,** 1930 R St., P.O. Box 1911, Bakersfield, CA 93303-1911, 661/323-7219, served as artistic headquarters for Christo's 1991 *The Umbrellas* environmental art extravaganza, which twirled up and over Tejon Pass. Other worthwhile stops include the **Kern County Museum,** 3801 Chester Ave., 661/852-5000, part of a complex that includes 14-acre **Pioneer Village** (an excellent outdoor "museum" of buildings and other history from the 1860s) and the hands-on **Lori Brock Children's**

COLONEL ALLENSWORTH STATE HISTORIC PARK

This park north of Bakersfield (west of Hwy. 99 near Earlimart) preserves the remnants of the only town in California founded by black Americans. Determined to develop a pragmatic yet utopian community, one dedicated to the values of education and economic independence and to the idea that blacks could live in equality with whites, Colonel Allen Allensworth (a former slave who won his freedom during the Civil War) arrived in the area in 1908 to stake a claim to a piece of the American dream. As the community grew, its early farming and other successes attracted more residents. In addition to the community schoolhouse (like some of the other buildings, beautifully restored), Allensworth dreamed of starting a major technical institute for black students—a proposal rejected by the state legislature. Soon after his accidental death in L.A. in 1914, Allensworth's dreams turned to dust, as agricultural development elsewhere in the valley created a water shortage that choked off community progress.

In May, come to the park for its annual **Allensworth Old Time Jubilee,** complete with living history programs, historic games, and special guided tours. The park's annual rededication ceremony is held in October. Camping is available. For more information, contact: Colonel Allensworth State Historic Park, 661/849-3433. To get there from Earlimart, turn right on J22 and take it five miles to Hwy. 43 (heading south)—two miles to Allensworth.

the schoolhouse at Colonel Allensworth
State Historic Park

KIM WEIR

Discovery Center. The museum is open Mon.–Fri. 8 A.M.–5 P.M., Sat. 10 A.M.–5 P.M., Sun. noon–5 P.M. Small admission. Kids who love dinosaurs will particularly enjoy the **Buena Vista Museum of Natural History,** 1201 20th St., 661/324-6350, open Wed.–Sun. 9 A.M.–5 P.M. Family-oriented, too, is the 13-acre **California Living Museum (CALM),** 10500 Alfred Harrel Hwy., 661/872-2256, open for up-close examination of native flora and also home to Central Valley indigenous fauna, animals all unreleasable into the wild for one reason or another.

Country-western music fans, don't miss **Buck Owens' Crystal Palace,** 2800 Pierce Rd., 661/869-2825 or toll-free 888/855-5005, a restaurant, museum, and theater complex bringing a bit of Nashville to the West. Call to find out who's playing. Please note that Buck Owens hisself ponied up the $175,000 required to rescue the historic but rusty 40-ton welcome sign that once stretched over Union Avenue. Bakersfield's famous sign now adorns Sillect Ave., across from the Crystal Palace.

For more information about the area, contact the **Kern County Board of Trade,** 2101 Oak St., P.O. Bin 1312, Bakersfield, CA 93302, 661/861-2367 or toll-free 800/500-5376, www.kerncountyonline.com. Popular Board of Trade brochures and booklets include *Birding, Ecotourism in Kern County, Harnessing Nature's Bounty, Watchable Wildlife,* and *Water World.* Or contact the **Greater Bakersfield Convention & Visitors Bureau,** 1325 P St., Bakersfield, CA 93301, 661/325-5051, www.visitbfield.com.

THE SACRAMENTO– SAN JOAQUIN DELTA

The ancient tule marshes created by the confluence of the Sacramento and San Joaquin Rivers are long gone in California's great delta. The Sacramento–San Joaquin Delta is the largest estuary on the West Coast, and the second largest in the country, overshadowed only by Chesapeake Bay. But by contemporary California standards there's really nothing to *do* in the delta—no world-class sights, amusement parks, or zoos, no big-name entertainment, nightclubs, coffeehouses. This fact is the main attraction of this lazy labyrinth of backwater sloughs, canals,

lakes, lagoons, and meandering rivers and streams. The personality and pace of the Deep South seep up throughout the delta; no one here was surprised when Samuel Goldwyn Jr. picked it as the filming location for *Huckleberry Finn.* People come here to drive along the levees and count great blue herons, to watch drawbridges go up and down, and ferries and freighters pass, to windsurf and sail and water-ski, or to houseboat like modern-day Huck Finns down unknown waterways in search of nothing in particular.

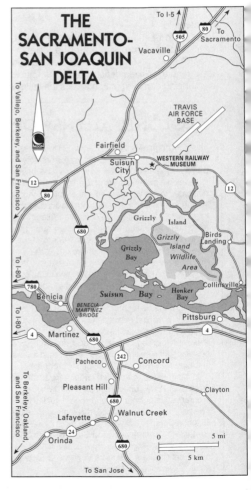

THE SACRAMENTO-SAN JOAQUIN DELTA

Only five of the delta's 70 major islands feature sizable development or towns. These include Bethel Island and its namesake subdivision; Byron Tract, home to Discovery Bay; Brannan-Andrus Island, with Brannan Island State Recreation Area and the town of Isleton; New Hope Tract and the town of Thornton; and Hotchkiss Tract and Oakley.

Many of the area's tiny towns and attractions are scattered around the delta's edges. The port city of Stockton, itself missable, is nonetheless a major jumping-off point for the southern delta. Rio Vista (via Hwy. 12) is a good place to start from in the north, Sacramento (via scenic Hwy. 160) in the east, and Antioch (over the Antioch Bridge via Hwy. 160) in the west.

Seeing and Doing Stockton

Billing itself as both "cosmopolitan and country," **Stockton** is mostly a bit strange, a hodgepodge of comfortable subdivisions and depressed ethnic neighborhoods, modern shopping centers, and a harbor district and partially devastated

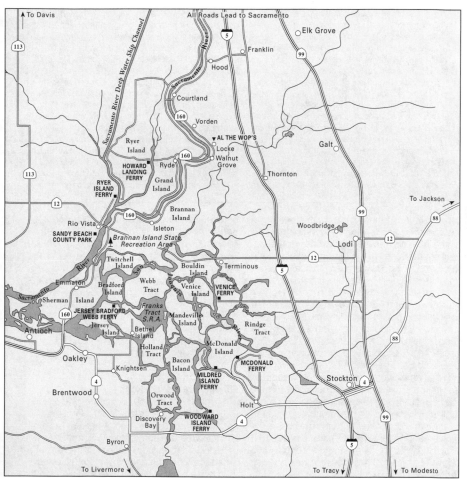

THE LAND: RECLAIMED JUNGLE

Since the last ice age and until the last century, the delta was a jungle of oaks, sycamores, willows, and vines punctuated by thickets of tules and teeming with life: herds of tule elk, pronghorn, and deer; beavers, river otters, and foxes; migrating waterfowl and songbirds; rivers of fish and the grizzlies who fished for them. Life went on, eon after eon, and however much water flowed through the delta—and then, as now, the mighty Sacramento River contributed 70–80 percent—it was always enough. But the situation soon changed, beginning in the 1860s when California leaders urged settlers to come and save the delta from its own wildness, to "reclaim" it for productive use. The wetlands were sold off for $1 an acre to anyone willing to dike and drain them.

The land in California's great delta—whether agricultural or recreational—isn't really *land,* not in the usual sense of the word. Before completion of the delta's complex system of levees and dredged canals, the annual winter-spring flooding of the area was as predictable as rain and Sierra Nevada snowmelt. Some islands emerged in summer and fall, or appeared only in dry years—a fact acceptable to the 30,000 or so native people who once lived off the region's natural bounty but too unpredictable for settlers determined to stake their ownership claims.

The delta is the largest water engineering network in the world, its century-old levee system built by Chinese laborers just finished with the transcontinental railroad. Before the advent of the clamshell dredge in the 1930s, hundreds of windmills once dotted the landscape, powering the pumps that first drained the area. Almost all Northern California river water eventually arrives in the delta; today up to 85 percent is channeled, diverted, and pumped south to irrigate farmland and to provide drinking water for some 20 million urbanites in the Bay Area and Los Angeles.

But even with levees and modern water-pumping stations in place, the struggle to control life and water here is difficult.

Out of that struggle has come innovation, such as snowshoe-like horseshoes for draft animals to keep them from sinking into mushy delta soils. With the arrival of agricultural machinery, the same problem called for an equally novel mechanical solution. Thus delta resident Ben Holt devised the caterpillar tread tractor shortly after the turn of the century, just in time for the British to buy the idea and convert it to military use, producing tanks that would roll ahead with ensuing world wars, mucky ground or no.

---

downtown now undergoing commercial redevelopment. But Stockton has its history. This place, after all, was the inspiration for the baseball poem "Casey at the Bat," first published in the *San Francisco Examiner.* Poetically speaking, this is Mudville. Whether or not that historic fact had anything to do with it, Stockton is now home to the **San Francisco 49ers** summer football training camp. Once known as Tuleberg, Stockton is also home to the **University of the Pacific,** which shares a campus with Delta College. The city is justifiably proud of its recently refurbished **Fox Theatre,** 242 E. Main, now drawing big-name entertainment downtown, and look for the multimillion-dollar Weber Point Events Center, coming soon. In addition to its community ballet, civic theater, chorale group, opera, symphony, and art galleries, the city also boasts the fine art-and-history **Haggin Museum,** 1201 N. Pershing Ave. in Victory Park, 209/462-4116 (open Tues.–Sun. 9 A.M.–5 P.M.). In nearby Lodi, at Micke Grove Regional Park, is the indoor-outdoor **San Joaquin County Historical Museum** (largely an ode to agriculture), 11793 N. Micke Grove Rd., 209/331-2055 or 209/953-3460 (open Wed.–Sun. 1–4:45 P.M.). Also at the park: a Japanese garden; the **Micke Grove Zoo,** 209/953-8840 or 209/331-7270; and **Funderwoods,** 209/369-5437 or 209/469-9654, a small children's amusement park (open daily May–September). Tykes will also like **Pixie Woods,** another kiddie park with train and boat rides and a merry-go-round, in Louis Park, west of I-5 at the Monte Diablo exit, 209/937-8220.

Seeing and Doing
Other Delta Destinations

The Chinese community of **Locke** sprang to life in 1915 shortly after nearby Walnut Grove's Chinatown burned to the ground. America's last rural Chinatown and listed on the National Register of Historic Places, today Locke has the look of a faded frontier town and consists of little more than levee-bound Main St., one block long, with weather-beaten wood frames leaning out over the narrow, pickup-lined street. But Locke in its prime was home to 2,000 or so Chinese and had general stores, herb shops, fish markets, a hotel, a dozen boardinghouses, even the Star Theatre, where Chinese opera was performed. In the roaring '20s and through the Depression, Locke was also known for its Caucasian brothels and speakeasies, and Chinese gambling houses and opium dens—attractive to both bone-tired field workers seeking escape from their dismal lives and big-city sophisticates out slumming.

Open on weekends only, the **Dai Loy Museum** on Locke's Main St. is a former gambling house that was in business from 1916 to 1950. Displays include gamblers' artifacts, old photos, and gaming tables set up for fan-tan and flying bull, as well as testimony to the vital role of the Chinese in delta development. The museum is usually open Thurs.–Sun.; for more information, call the **Sacramento River Delta Historical Society** at 916/776-1661. Almost a museum is **Al the Wop's** bar and restaurant, 13936 Main St., 916/776-1800, crammed with farmers, ranch hands, (and tourists), serving up local wisdom from behind the bar and jars of peanut butter and jelly on every table. The question people always ask: How *do* they get all those dollar bills up there on the ceiling?

Three miles from Ryde and a hop across the Delta Cross Channel from Locke is tiny **Walnut Grove,** the only town south of Red Bluff to occupy both banks of the Sacramento River. Reputed to be a lair for riverboat bandits in its early days, for decades the town has been serene and sleepy, a farm community with little left of its Japanese and Chinese past except a block-long strip of boarded-up bare-board buildings. One of Walnut Grove's contemporary claims to fame is football, since three NFL players—including Tony Eason, the New England Patriots' quarterback who got the team to the 1986 Super Bowl—grew up here, starting their football careers at Delta High School in Clarksburg. (Somewhat baffled about this, some people here say it's the delta water that grows so many big bruisers.) Another is the new **Walnut Grove Dock,** which has spurred a mini-boom in local business improvements.

Another delta town with a Chinatown past is **Isleton** on Andrus Island, today a tin-sided shadow of its former self. In the 1930s, Isleton billed itself as The Asparagus Center of the World, since 90 percent of the world's canned asparagus was grown and processed in the area. During post-fire rebuilding in the 1920s and '30s, Japanese-Americans also became an integral part of the community. The **Isleton Historical Museum,** 60 Main St., 916/777-6792, offers exhibits on the town's history, and staff can answer your questions about the area. Open May–Sept., weekends 1–4 P.M. Isleton only really comes to life these days during the community's famous and wildly popular **Crawdad Festival** in June. If

ROBERT HOLMES/CalTour

Sacramento river delta

you miss that, there's an annual **Spam Cook-Off** in February.

Rio Vista, a small town astride Hwy. 12 just across the drawbridge from Brannan-Andrus Island, is most famous for a 45-ton celebrity humpback whale named Humphrey, who swam into the delta and up the Sacramento River in the fall of 1985, apparently determined to become the first whale to tour the town. Lost for weeks in nearby backwaters and sloughs after taking a wrong turn through the Golden Gate on his way to Mexico, Humphrey was eventually herded back to sea by a flotilla of ships.

Sightseeing humans might peek into the **Rio Vista Museum,** 16 N. Front St., 707/374-5169, open 1:30–4:30 P.M. weekends only—a onetime blacksmith shop with several rooms of area memorabilia telling the story of Rio Vista. One wall is covered with old license plates and newspaper front pages. From May to October, world-class **windsurfing** is possible—and quite popular—in the open expanses of the Sacramento River near Rio Vista, at the **Sherman Island Public Access** just south of town via Hwy. 160.

Other local diversions include the Bay Area Electric Railroad Association's **Western Railway Museum** at the Hwy. 12-Rio Vista Junction, 707/374-2978 or 415/673-7774, featuring more than 100 streetcars and railroad cars, also a small looping track for 15-minute rides. Open Wed.–Sun. and holidays 11 A.M.–5 P.M. in summer, weekends only the rest of the year; admission is $6 adults, $5 seniors, $3 children 3–12, $18 families (two adults and up to three kids). Special rail excursions are frequently scheduled; call for information.

From Rio Vista, head north for a free ride on one of the delta's few remaining ferries, this one an authentic passenger ship requiring a licensed navigator at the helm. The **Ryer Island Ferry** *Real McCoy* navigates Cache Slough from Ryer Island Rd. off Hwy. 160 to Ryer Island. For another down-home delta crossing, turn right and follow the levee road to Steamboat Slough and the *J-Mack* cable-driven ferry, which runs to Grand Island and its landmark 1917 **Ryde Hotel,** 916/776-1318.

Brannan Island State Recreation Area

Not a natural environment by any means, open, often wind-blown Brannan Island State Recre-

RYDE HOTEL

Among the delta's most historically notorious stops is the **Ryde Hotel,** 14340 Hwy. 160 in Ryde, 916/776-1318, www.rydehotel.com, which housed a password-only speakeasy casino and dancehall in its basement during Prohibition. Later a popular bikers' bar and flophouse, the old Ryde Hotel was restored to its grand 1920s art-deco style—when people like Al Jolson and Herbert Hoover used to drop by—and renamed the Grand Island Mansion. Restored again in 1998—most rooms are now larger, with private baths—and once again named the Ryde Hotel, the soft peach hotel also features a river-view patio and popular restaurant. Suites available. Moderate-Luxury.

ation Area three miles south of Rio Vista nonetheless makes an ideal spot for picnicking, year-round camping, and recreational pursuits—from boating and windsurfing to fishing and swimming. Flanked on three sides by the Sacramento River, Seven Mile Slough, and Three Mile Slough and accessible via Hwy. 160, Brannan Island's facilities include two family camping areas; six group camps; 32 boat-in campsites with boat berths; boat-launching ramps; a public swimming beach and picnic area; and a rally site for RVs plus sanitation station (but no RV hookups). Learn more about area history and wildlife at the park's interpretive center.

Accessible only by boat across Piper Slough from Bethel Island, **Franks Tract State Recreation Area** five miles southeast of Brannan Island is now largely underwater due to levee breakage. The large "lake" here offers exceptional fishing. **Little Franks Tract** is a marsh area rich in natural vegetation and wildlife (no hunting, no fires) and still protected by the levees.

Camping reservations—through Reserve America, toll-free 800/444-7275—are usually necessary Mar.–October. The day-use fee for Brannan Island is $2. For more information, contact: Brannan Island/Franks Tract State Recreation Areas, 17645 Hwy. 160, Rio Vista, CA 95471, 916/777-6671.

Grizzly Island and Vicinity

Adjacent to privately owned portions of Solano

County's Suisun Marsh is Grizzly Island Wildlife Area. Now only semivast after a century of reclamation but still one of the world's richest estuarine marshes, the marsh has no grizzlies these days, but tule elk, "the little elk of the prairie," have come home again. Believed extinct more than 100 years ago, California's tule elk population is making quite a comeback everywhere the species has been reintroduced. March and April are the best months for observing the matriarchal tule elk during calving season, also for watching river otters.

Corraled by delta levees, the Grizzly Island area includes 1,887-acre Joice Island near the on-site headquarters and 8,600-acre Grizzly Island proper. Waterfowl hunting (by permit only, these issued at the headquarters on Wed. and weekends only in season) is popular here, as is fishing. With more than a million birds wintering here, bird-watchers and hikers rule the roost when hunters aren't afield.

The reserve is closed for extended periods each year. For exact dates and more information, contact: Grizzly Island Wildlife Area, Department of Fish & Game, 2548 Grizzly Island Rd., Suisun, CA 94585, 707/425-3828; or Department of Fish & Game, Region 3 Headquarters, 7329 Silverado Trail, Napa, CA 94558 (or P.O. Box 47, Yountville, CA 94599), 707/944-5500.

Lower Sherman Island Wildlife Area

This state reserve at the confluence of the Sacramento and San Joaquin Rivers is also popular with waterfowl hunters and fisherfolk. It's a delta island reclaimed by the forces of nature, with boat access only beyond the parking lot—fun to explore by canoe outside hunting season but only with great care, due to the area's strong tidal currents and sudden high winds (usually in the afternoon). For more information, call the Department of Fish & Game, Region 2 Headquarters at 916/358-2900 during regular business hours.

Delta Information

For more detailed area information, contact the **Stockton-San Joaquin Convention & Visitors Bureau,** 46 W. Fremont, Stockton, CA 95202, 209/943-1987 or toll-free 800/350-1987, www.visitstockton.org, or any of the chambers of commerce from the following locales: **Antioch,** 301 W. 10th St., Antioch, CA 94509, 510/757-1800; **Bethel Island,** P.O. Box 263, Bethel Island, CA 94511, 925/684-3220; **Brentwood,** 240 Oak St., Brentwood, CA 94513, 925/634-3344; **Byron,** 3926 Main St., Byron, CA 94513, 510/634-4460; **Isleton,** 308 2nd St., P.O. Box 758, Isleton, CA 95641, 916/777-5880; **Rio Vista,** 75 Main St., Rio Vista, CA 94571, 707/374-2700, www.riovista.org; and **Tracy,** P.O. Box 891, Tracy, CA 95376, 209/835-2131. Or, for the sake of efficiency, try the **California Delta Chambers & Visitors Bureau,** P.O. Box 6, Isleton, CA 95641, 916/777-5007, www.californiadelta.org, or the **Delta Loop Visitors Bureau,** 106 W. Brannan Island Rd., Delta Loop, CA 95641, 916/777-2233, www.deltaloop.com.

KIM WEIR

MONTEREY BAY AREA
ONE BAY, MANY WORLDS

The only remembered line of the long-lost Ohlone people's song of world renewal, "dancing on the brink of the world," has a particularly haunting resonance around Monterey Bay. Here, in the unfriendly fog and ghostly cypress along the untamed coast, the native "coast people" once danced. Like the area's vanished dancers, Monterey Bay is a mystery: everything seen, heard, tasted, and touched only hints at what remains hidden.

The first mystery is magnificent Monterey Bay itself, almost 60 miles long and 13 miles wide. Its offshore canyons, grander than Arizona's Grand Canyon, are the area's most impressive (if unseen) feature: the bay's largest submarine valley dips to 10,000 feet, and the adjacent tidal mudflats teem with life.

A second mystery is how two cities as different as Santa Cruz and Monterey could both take root and thrive on the shores of Monterey Bay.

Working- and dot-com-class Santa Cruz has the slightly seedy Boardwalk, sandy beaches,

good swimming, surfers, and—helped along by the presence of UC Santa Cruz—an intelligent and open-minded social scene. Nearby are the redwoods, waterfalls, and mountain-to-sea hiking trails of Big Basin, California's first state park, plus the Año Nuevo coastal area, until recently the world's only mainland mating ground for the two-ton northern elephant seal. The monied Monterey Peninsula to the south is fringed by shifting sand dunes and some of the state's most ruggedly wild coastline. Near Monterey is peaceful Pacific Grove (where alcohol has been legal only since the 1960s), Carmel-by-the-Sea (where Clint Eastwood once made everybody's day as mayor), and inland Carmel Valley (a tennis pro playground abounding in shopping centers). The Carmel Highlands hug the coast on the way south to Big Sur.

Just inland from the Monterey Peninsula is the agriculturally rich Salinas Valley, boyhood stomping grounds of John Steinbeck. Steinbeck's focus on Depression-era farm workers

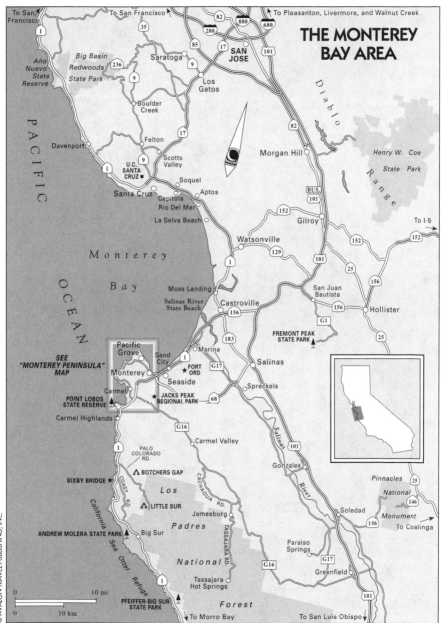

THE MONTEREY BAY AREA

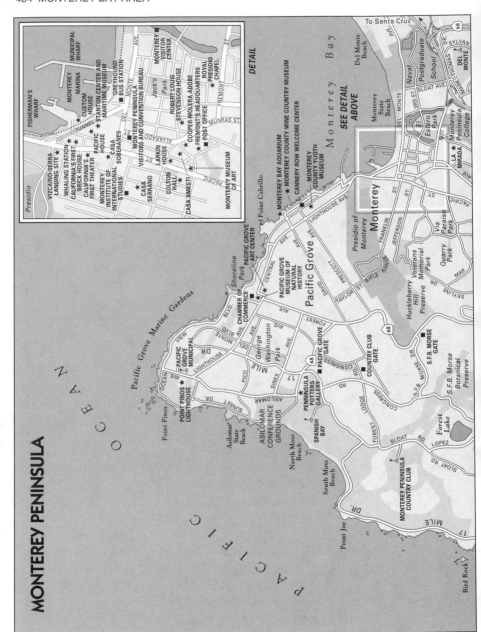

MONTEREY PENINSULA

DETAIL

FISHERMAN'S WHARF

MUNICIPAL WHARF

MONTEREY MARINA

MONTEREY VISITOR CENTER

Jack's Park

CUSTOM HOUSE

STANTON CENTER AND MARITIME MUSEUM

ROBERT LOUIS STEVENSON HOUSE

COOPER-MOLERA ADOBE

ROYAL PRESIDIO CHAPEL

GREYHOUND BUS STATION

VIZCAINO-SERRA LANDING SITE

WHALING STATION

CALIFORNIA'S FIRST BRICK HOUSE

PACIFIC HOUSE

MONTEREY INSTITUTE OF INTERNATIONAL STUDIES

CASA SOBERANES

CALIFORNIA'S FIRST THEATER

MONTEREY PENINSULA VISITORS AND CONVENTION BUREAU

LARKIN HOUSE

FREMONT'S HEADQUARTERS

POST OFFICE

CASA SERRANO

COLTON HALL

CASA AMESTI

MONTEREY MUSEUM OF ART

Presidio

To Santa Cruz

Monterey Bay

Del Monte Beach

Naval Postgraduate School

Monterey State Beach

SEE DETAIL ABOVE

Monterey Peninsula College

Estero Park

LA MIRADA

Via Paraiso Park

Quarry Park

Veterans Memorial Park

Huckleberry Hill Preserve

S.F.B. MORSE GATE

S.F.B. Morse Botanical Preserve

Forest Lake

Monterey

Presidio of Monterey

Point Cabrillo

MONTEREY BAY AQUARIUM

MONTEREY COUNTY WINE COUNTRY MUSEUM

CANNERY ROW WELCOME CENTER

MONTEREY YOUTH COUNTY MUSEUM

Pacific Grove Marine Gardens

PACIFIC GROVE ART CENTER

Shoreline Park

CHAMBER OF COMMERCE

PACIFIC GROVE MUSEUM OF NATURAL HISTORY

George Washington Park

Pacific Grove

COUNTRY CLUB GATE

PACIFIC GROVE MUNICIPAL

PACIFIC GROVE GATE

17 MILE

PENINSULA POTTERS GALLERY

SPANISH BAY

Point Pinos

POINT PINOS LIGHTHOUSE

Asilomar State Beach

ASILOMAR CONFERENCE GROUNDS

North Moss Beach

South Moss Beach

MONTEREY PENINSULA COUNTRY CLUB

17 MILE

Point Joe

Bird Rock

PACIFIC OCEAN

OCEAN

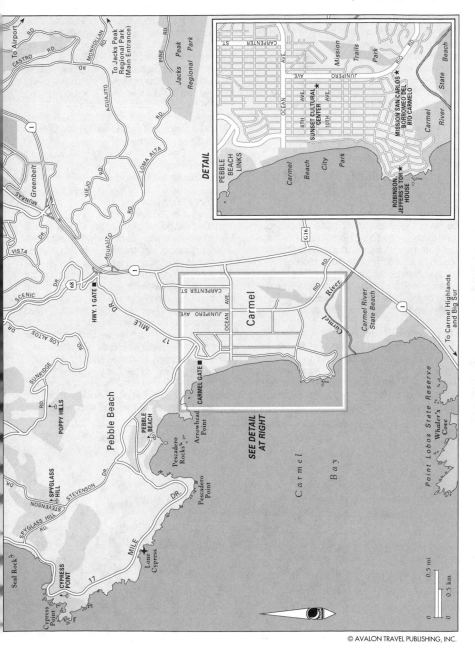

unleashed great local wrath—all but forgotten and almost forgiven since his fame has subsequently benefited area tourism. Not far north, right on the San Andreas Fault, is Mission San Juan Bautista, where Jimmy Stewart and Kim Novak conquered his fear of heights in Alfred Hitchcock's *Vertigo*. Also in the neighborhood is Gilroy, self-proclaimed garlic capital of the world. South of Salinas and east of Soledad is Pinnacles National Monument, a fascinating volcanic jumble and almost "the peak" for experienced rock climbers.

MONTEREY BAY BY LAND AND BY SEA

Much of the redwood country from San Francisco to Big Sur resembles the boulder-strewn, rough-and-tumble north coast. Here the Pacific Ocean is far from peaceful; posted warnings about dangerous swimming conditions and undertows are no joke. Inland, the San Andreas Fault menaces, veering inland as it heads north from the eastern side of the Coast Ranges through the Salinas Valley and on to the San Francisco Bay Area.

The Monterey Peninsula
Steinbeck captured the mood of the Monterey Peninsula in *Tortilla Flats*—"The wind . . . drove the fog across the pale moon like a thin wash of watercolor. . . . The treetops in the wind talked huskily, told fortunes and foretold deaths." The peninsula juts into the ocean 115 miles south of San Francisco

and forms the southern border of Monterey Bay. The north shore sweeps in a crescent toward Santa Cruz and the Santa Cruz Mountains; east is the oak- and pine-covered Santa Lucia Range, rising in front of the barren Gabilan ("Sparrow Hawk") Mountains beloved by Steinbeck. Northward are the ecologically delicate Monterey Bay Dunes, now threatened by off-road vehicles and development. To the south, the piney hills near Point Piños and Asilomar overlook rocky crags and coves dotted with wind-sculpted trees; farther south, beyond Carmel and the Pebble Beach golf mecca, is Point Lobos, said to be Robert Louis Stevenson's inspiration for Spyglass Hill in *Treasure Island*.

Monterey "Canyon"
Discovered in 1890 by George Davidson, Monterey Bay's submerged valley teems with sealife: bioluminescent fish glowing vivid blue to red, squid, tiny rare octopi, tentacle-shedding jellyfish, and myriad microscopic plants and animals. This is one of the most biologically prolific spots on the planet. Swaying with the ocean's motion, dense kelp thickets are home to sea lions, seals, sea otters, and giant Garibaldi "goldfish." Opal-eyed perch in schools of hundreds swim by leopard sharks and bottom fish. In the understory near the rocky ocean floor live abalones, anemones, crabs, sea urchins, and starfish.

Students of Monterey Canyon geology quibble over the origins of this unusual underwater valley. Computer-generated models of canyon creation suggest that the land once used to be

dramatically beautiful Point Lobos

near Bakersfield and was carved out by the Colorado River; later it shifted westward due to plate tectonics. More conventional speculation focuses on the creative forces of both the Sacramento and San Joaquin Rivers, which perhaps once emptied at Elkhorn Slough, Monterey Canyon's principal "head."

However Monterey Canyon came to be, it is now centerpiece of the 5,312-square-mile **Monterey Bay National Marine Sanctuary** which extends some 400 miles along the coast, from San Francisco's Golden Gate in the north to San Simeon in the south. Established in 1992 after a 15-year political struggle, this federally sanctioned preserve is now protected from offshore oil drilling, dumping of hazardous materials, the killing of marine mammals or birds, personal watercraft, and aircraft flying lower than 1,000 feet. As an indirect result of its federal protection, Monterey Bay now boasts a total of 18 marine research facilities.

Monterey Bay Climate

The legendary California beach scene is almost a fantasy here—almost but not quite. Sunshine warms the sands (between storms) from fall to early spring, but count on fog from late spring well into summer. Throughout the Monterey Bay area, it's often foggy and damp, though clear summer afternoons can get hot; the warmest months along the coast are August, September, and October. (Sunglasses, suntan lotion, and hats are prudent, but always bring a sweater.) Inland, expect hotter weather in summer, colder in winter. Rain is possible as early as October, though big storms don't usually roll in until December.

THE MONTEREY BAY STORY: CALIFORNIA FIRSTS

Cabrillo spotted Point Piños and Monterey Bay in 1542. Sixty years later, Vizcaíno sailed into the bay and named it for the viceroy of Mexico, the count of Monte-Rey. A century later came Portolá and Father Crespi, who, later joined by Father Junípero Serra, founded both Monterey's presidio and the mission at Carmel. Monterey would later boast the state's first capital, first government building, first federal court, first newspaper, and—though other towns also claim the honor—first theater.

The quiet redwood groves near Santa Cruz remained undisturbed by civilization until the arrival of Portolá's expedition in 1769. The sickly Spaniards made camp in the Rancho de Osos section of what is now Big Basin, experiencing an almost miraculous recovery in the valley they called Cañada de Salud (Canyon of Health). A Spanish garrison and mission were soon established on the north end of Monterey Bay.

By the end of the 1700s, the entire central California coast was solidly Spanish, with missions, pueblos, and military bases or presidios holding the territory for the king of Spain. With the Mexican revolution, Californio loyalty went with the new administration closer to home. But the people here carried on their Spanish cultural heritage despite the secularization of the missions, the increasing influence of cattle ranches, and the foreign flood (primarily American) that threatened existing California tradition. Along the rugged central coast just south of the boisterous and booming gold rush port of San Francisco, the influence of this new wave of "outsiders" was felt only later and locally, primarily near Monterey and Salinas.

Monterey: Capital of Alta California

In addition to being the main port city for both Alta and Baja California, from 1775 to 1845 Monterey was the capital of Alta California—and naturally enough, the center of much political intrigue and scheming. Spared the devastating earthquakes that plagued other areas, Monterey had its own bad times, which included being burned and ransacked by the French pirate Hippolyte Bouchard in 1818. In 1822, Spanish rule ended in California. In 1845, Monterey lost part of its political prestige when Los Angeles temporarily became the territory's capital city. When the rancheros surrendered to Commodore Sloat in July 1846, the area became officially American, though the town's distinctive Spanish tranquility remained relatively undisturbed until the arrival of farmers, fishing fleets, fish canneries, and whalers. California's first constitution was drawn up in Monterey, at Colton Hall, in 1849.

Santa Cruz and the Bad Boys of Branciforte

Santa Cruz, the site of Misión Exaltación de la Santa Cruz and a military garrison on the north end of Monterey Bay, got its start in 1791. But the 1797 establishment of Branciforte—a "model colony" financed by the Spanish government just across the San Lorenzo River—made life hard for the mission fathers. The rowdy, quasi-criminal culture of Branciforte so intrigued the native peoples that Santa Cruz men of the cloth had to use leg irons to keep the Ohlone home. And things just got worse. In 1818, the threat of pirates at nearby Monterey sent the mission folk into the hills, with the un-

derstanding that Branciforte's bad boys would pack up the mission's valuables and cart them inland for safekeeping. Instead, they looted the place and drank all the sacramental wine. The mission was eventually abandoned, then demolished by an earthquake in 1857. A small port city grew up around the plaza and borrowed the mission's name—Santa Cruz—while Branciforte, a smuggler's haven, continued to flourish until the late 1800s.

SANTA CRUZ AND VICINITY

Still in tune with its gracefully aging Boardwalk, Santa Cruz is a middle-class tourist town enlightened and enlivened by retirees and the local University of California campus. Here, people can exist even if they don't have lots of money, though it's getting harder—quite a different world from the affluent and staid Monterey Peninsula.

The Santa Cruz attitude has little to do with its name, taken from a nearby stream called Arroyo de Santa Cruz ("Holy Cross Creek") by Portolá. No, the town's relaxed good cheer must be karmic compensation for the morose mission days and the brutishness of nearby Branciforte. The Gay Nineties were happier here than anywhere else in Northern California, with trainloads of Bay Area vacationers in their finest summer whites stepping out to enjoy the Santa Cruz waterfront, the

Sea Beach Hotel, and the landmark Boardwalk and amusement park. The young and young-at-heart headed straight for the amusement park, with its fine merry-go-round, classic wooden roller coaster, pleasure pier, natatorium (indoor pool), and dancehall casino. Meanwhile, more decadent fun lovers visited the ship anchored offshore to gamble or engage the services of prostitutes.

Santa Cruz still welcomes millions of visitors each year, yet somehow manages to retain its dignity—except when embroiled in hot local political debates or when inundated by college students during the annual rites of spring. A tourist town it may be, but some of the best things to do here are free: watching the sunset from East or West Cliff Drives, beachcombing, bike riding (excellent local bike lanes), swimming, surfing, and sunbathing.

Santa Cruz beach boardwalk

TOM MYERS PHOTOGRAPHY

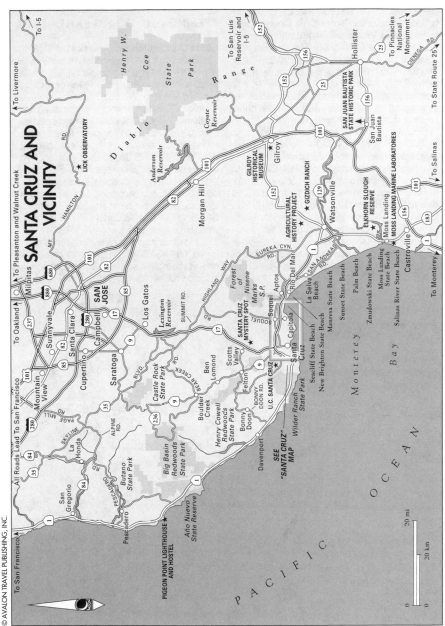

The best all-around source for city and county information is the **Santa Cruz County Conference and Visitors Council,** at its new location at 1211 Ocean St., Santa Cruz, CA 95060, 831/425-1234 or toll-free 800/833-3494, fax 831/425-1260, www.scccvc.org, open Mon.–Sat. 9 A.M.–5 P.M., Sun. 10 A.M.–4 P.M. Definitely request the current accommodations, dining, and visitor guides, and ask here about regional transportation options.

If you've got time to roam farther afield, also pick up a current copy of the **County Crossroads** farm trails map and inquire about area wineries. Cyclists should request the **Santa Cruz County Bikeway Map.** Antiquers, ask for the current **Antiques, Arts, & Collectibles** directory for Santa Cruz and Monterey Counties, published every June—not a complete listing, by far, but certainly a good start. If you once were familiar with Santa Cruz and—post-1989 earthquake—now find yourself lost, pick up the **Downtown Santa Cruz Directory** brochure.

SEEING AND DOING SANTA CRUZ

Santa Cruz Beach Boardwalk and Vicinity

The Boardwalk may be old, but it's certainly lively, with a million visitors per year. This is the West Coast's answer to Atlantic City. The original wood planking is now paved over with asphalt, stretching from 400 Beach St. for a half mile along one of Northern California's finest swimming beaches. A relatively recent multimillion-dollar facelift didn't diminish the Boardwalk's charms one iota. Open daily from Memorial Day to Labor Day each year, otherwise just on weekends, the Boardwalk's amusement park atmosphere is authentic, with 27 carnival rides, odd shops and eateries, good-time arcades, even a big-band ballroom. Ride the **Sky Glider** to get a good aerial view of the Boardwalk and beach scene.

None other than the *New York Times* has declared the 1924 **Giant Dipper** roller coaster here one of the nation's 10 best. A gleaming white wooden rocker 'n' roller, the Dipper's quite a

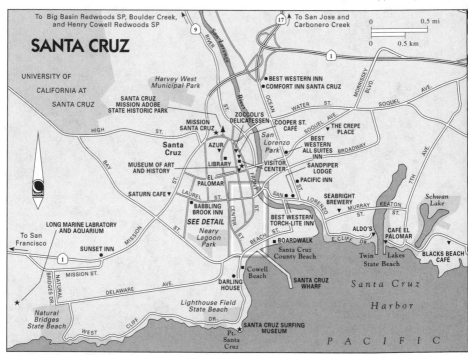

© AVALON TRAVEL PUBLISHING, INC.

sight any time, but it's truly impressive when lit up at night. The 1911 **Charles Looff carousel,** one of a handful of Looff creations still operating in the United States, has 70 handcrafted horses, two chariots, and a circa 1894 Ruth Band pipe organ—all now lovingly restored to the merry-go-round's original glory. (Both the Dipper and the carousel are national historic landmarks.)

New rides feature more terror, of course. The bright lights and unusual views offered by the Italian-made **Typhoon** are just part of the joys of being suspended upside down in midair. The **Hurricane** is the Boardwalk's modern high-tech roller coaster, providing a two-minute thrill ride with a maximum gravitational force of 4.7 Gs, and a banking angle of 80 degrees. There's only one other of its kind in the United States, on the east coast. Also state of the art in adrenaline inducement at the Boardwalk is the **Wave Jammer**—not to mention **Chaos, Crazy Surf, Tsunami,** and **Whirl Wind.**

To fully appreciate the Boardwalk then and now, pick up the **Walking Tour of the Historical**

Santa Cruz Boardwalk brochure, as well as a current attractions map/listing. Both will help you locate yourself, then and now.

Admission to the Boardwalk is free, though enjoying its amusements is not. The best deal is the all-day ride ticket, $19.95 at last report. Season passes are available. Height, age, and chaperone requirements are enforced. During **1907 Nights,** however, on certain Mon. and Tues. evenings in summer, ride prices revert to 1907 equivalents—$.50 per ride. For current complete information, contact the **Santa Cruz Seaside Company,** 400 Beach St., Santa Cruz, CA 95060-5491, 831/423-5590, www.beachboardwalk.com.

The **Santa Cruz Wharf,** the pier at the western end of Santa Cruz Beach, was once a good place to buy cheap, fresh fish, though today the place is packed instead with tourists. Still, the wharf's worth a sunset stroll. Peer down into the fenced-off "holes" to watch the sea lions.

Touring Santa Cruz

If over- or under-whelmed by the Boardwalk, take the Santa Cruz walking tour. This expedition is a lot quicker than it used to be, with so many of the city's unusual Victorians—with frilly wedding-cake furbelows and "witch's hat" towers on the Queen Annes—now departed to that great Historical Register in the Sky, after the 1989 earthquake. But some grande dames remain. To find them, stop by the visitors center and pick up a copy of the **Historic Santa Cruz Walking Tours and Museum Guide** brochure.

A sure sign that downtown Santa Cruz is almost done digging out from quake rubble is the **Museum of Art and History** at the McPherson Center, 705 Front St. (Front and Cooper), 831/429-1964, www.santacruzmah.org. Traveling exhibits and local artists get prominent play at the art galleries, and changing history exhibits include themes such as 1999's *Picks, Plows, and Potatoes: The Santa Cruz Region During the Gold Rush.* Open Tues.–Sun. noon–5 P.M. (until 7 P.M. on Fri.), small admission. The museum staff can fill you in on regional historical sites under their care, including the **Davenport Jail** (1917), up the coast in Davenport, and the **Evergreen Cemetery** (est. 1850) at Evergreen and Coral Sts., one of the oldest Protestant cemeteries in California.

The **Santa Cruz Mission Adobe State Historic Park,** restored and open to the public, is

GETTING ORIENTED TO GREATER SANTA CRUZ

Just east of Santa Cruz, along the south-facing coast here, are the towns of Soquel, Capitola, and Aptos—the Santa Cruz "burbs." High-rent **Soquel,** once a booming lumber town and the place where Portolá and his men were all but stricken by their first sight of coastal redwoods, is now noted for antiques and oaks.

The wharf in **Capitola** has stood since 1857, when the area was known as Soquel Landing. The name "Camp Capitola" was an expression of Soquel locals' desire to be the state capital—the closest they ever came. The city was, however, the state's first seaside resort. Nowadays, Capitola is big on art galleries and fine craft shops—take a stroll along Capitola Ave. from the trestle to the creek—but it's still most famous for its begonias. The year's big event is the **Begonia Festival,** usually held early

in September. Stop by **Antonelli Bros. Begonia Gardens,** 2545 Capitola Rd., 831/475-5222, to see a 10,000-square-foot greenhouse display of begonias, best in August and September.

Aptos, on the other side of the freeway, is more or less the same community as Capitola but home to Cabrillo College and the **World's Shortest Parade,** usually sponsored on the July Fourth weekend by the Aptos Ladies' Tuesday Evening Society.

Heading north on Hwy. 9 from Santa Cruz will take you through the Santa Cruz Mountains and the towns of **Felton, Ben Lomond,** and **Boulder Creek** before winding down the other side of the mountains into Saratoga on the flank of Silicon Valley. This route is also the road to several beautiful redwood state parks, including Henry Cowell, Fall Creek, Big Basin, and Castle Rock.

---

just off Mission Plaza at 144 School St., 831/425-5849. This is one of the county's last remaining original adobes, built by and for Native Americans "employed" at Mission Santa Cruz. Later a 17-unit "home for new citizens," only seven units remain, these now comprising a California history museum circa the 1840s. Call for current information about guided tours and "living history" demonstrations (usually offered on Sun., the latter just in March). Nearby, at 126 High St., is what's left of the original mission:

just a memory, really. It's open Tues.–Sat. 10 A.M.–4 P.M., Sun. 10 A.M.–2 P.M.; call 831/426-5686 for more information.

Cowabunga! Instead of a ribbon-cutting ceremony, they snipped a hot-pink surfer's leash when they opened the **Santa Cruz Surfing Museum**—the world's first surfing museum—here in May 1986. This historical exhibit reaches back to the 1930s and features displays like the evolution of surfboards—including the Model T of boards, a 15-foot redwood plank weighing 100

Santa Cruz
Surfing Museum

TOM MYERS PHOTOGRAPHY

pounds—and an experimental Jack O'Neill wetsuit made of nylon and foam, the forerunner to the Neoprene "shortjohn." The museum is located in the brick lighthouse on W. Cliff Dr. northwest of town and is open daily (except Tues.) noon–4 P.M.; admission is free. For more information, call 831/420-6289.

The much bumpersticker-ballyhooed **Santa Cruz Mystery Spot,** 465 Mystery Spot Rd., 831/423-8897, is a place where "every law of gravitation has gone haywire." Or has it? Trees, people, even the Spot's rustic shack and furnishings seem spellbound by "the force"—though people wearing slick-soled shoes seem to have the hardest time staying with the mysterious program. It's open daily 9 A.M.–8 P.M. in summer, 9 A.M.–5 P.M. in winter.

UC Santa Cruz

When the doors of UC Santa Cruz opened in the 1960s, few California students could gain admission to the close-knit, redwood-cloistered campus on the hill. The selection process (complete with essay) was weighted in favor of unusual abilities, aptitudes, and attitudes—to recruit students not likely to thrive within the traditional university structure. So many children of movie stars and other members of California's monied upper classes attended UC Santa Cruz at one time that it was often playfully dubbed California's public finishing school.

Once the Henry Cowell Ranch, the University of California regents set about transforming the redwood-forested rangeland here into California's educational Camelot in 1961. They hired some of the state's finest architects, whose designs ranged from modern Mediterranean to "Italian hill village" (Kresge College). The official explanation for the Santa Cruz "college cluster" concept was to avoid the depersonalization common to large UC campuses, but another reason was alluded to when then-governor Ronald Reagan declared the campus "riot-proof."

To truly appreciate this place, wander the campus hiking trails and paths (but not alone). Some of the old converted ranch buildings are also worth noting: the lime kilns, blacksmith's shop, cookhouse, horse barn, bull barn, slaughterhouse, workers' cabins, cooperage. For information and guided campus tours, stop by the wood-and-stone Cook House near the entrance. You can also obtain information by writing to UCSC Admissions Office, Cook House, Santa Cruz, CA 95064, or by calling 831/459-4008.

OUTDOORS IN GREATER SANTA CRUZ

At the Beach

Most of the outdoor "action" in Santa Cruz proper happens at local beaches; swimming, surfing, and

CRUISIN' SANTA CRUZ WINERIES

The coastal mountains near Santa Cruz are well known for their redwoods. But since the late 1800s, they have also been known for their vineyards. Regional winemaking is back, helped along since 1981 by the official federal recognition of the Santa Cruz Mountain appellation for wine grapes grown in the region defined by Half Moon Bay in the north and Mount Madonna in the south. More than 40 wineries now produce Santa Cruz Mountain wines.

The eclectic **Bonny Doon Vineyard,** north of Santa Cruz at 10 Pine Flat Rd., 831/425-4518, www.bonnydoonvineyard.com, specializes in Rhône and Italian varietals, though wine lovers and critics are also smitten with the winery's worldly, witty, and wildly footnoted newsletter (also available online). Open 11 A.M.–5 P.M. daily for tastings, except major holidays.

Nearby in Felton is the award-winning and historic **Hallcrest Vineyards,** 379 Felton Empire Rd. (call for directions), 831/335-4441, noted for its cabernet sauvignon, chardonnay, merlot, and zinfandel. Hallcrest is also home to **The Organic Wine Works,** producing the nation's first certified organic wines. Made from certified organically grown grapes, the winemaking process is also organic, without the use of sulfites. Open daily 11 A.M.–5:30 P.M. Also in Felton and open only by appointment is the small **Zayante Vineyards,** 420 Old Mount Rd., 831/335-7992.

For more information about Santa Cruz area wineries, including a current wineries map, contact: **Santa Cruz Mountains Winegrowers Association,** 7605 Old Dominion Ct., Ste. A, Aptos, CA 95003, 831/479-9463, www.wines.com/santa_cruz_mountains.

FOR A WHALE'S-EYE VIEW

For an unusual view of the Boardwalk and the bay, take a boat ride. One of the best going—definitely not just any boat—is the **Chardonnay II,** a 70-foot ultra-light sailing yacht offering special-emphasis cruises such as wine-tasting (usually on Saturdays), marine ecology (usually on Sundays), whale-watching (winter and spring)—even a Wednesday night Boat Race Cruise in the company of almost every other boat from the Santa Cruz Yacht Harbor. At last report, per-person fare for most scheduled trips was $39.95. For more information and to make reservations (required), call **Chardonnay Sailing Charters** at 831/423-1213 or inquire online at www. chardonnay.com.

The Santa Cruz area is big on ocean-going recreation. Contact the visitors center for current listings of local concerns offering sportfishing and whale-watching charters, sailing lessons, kayak rentals and tours, as well as surfboard, boogie board, and dive supply rentals.

fishing are all big, as are tamer pastimes like beachcombing, sandcastle-building, and sunbathing. The in-town **Santa Cruz Beach** at the Boardwalk, with fine white sand and towel-to-towel baking bodies in summer, is "the scene"—especially for outsiders from San Jose, locals say. For more privacy, head east to the mouth of the San Lorenzo River. Southwest of the pier, **Cowell Beach** is a surfing beach. Just before **Lighthouse Field State Beach** on W. Cliff is the Santa Cruz Surfing Museum, an eclectic lighthouse collection of surf's-up memorabilia keeping watch over the hotdoggers in churning Steamer Lane.

Natural Bridges State Beach, farther southwest at the end of W. Cliff Dr., attracts the mythic monarch butterflies each year from Oct. to May. Though Pacific Grove near Monterey proudly proclaims itself *the* destination of choice for these regal insects, Santa Cruz people claim they get the most monarchs. Sadly, generations of people walking across the sandstone "natural bridge" here finally caused the center arch to collapse. For information on guided butterfly walks and tidepool tours, stop by the visitors center or call 831/423-4609. The parking fee at Natural Bridges is $3 per car; walk-ins and bike-ins are free.

"Locals' beaches" include **Tyrell Park** and more inaccessible sandy beaches along E. Cliff Drive. **Twin Lakes Beach** near the Santa Cruz Yacht Harbor, on the eastern extension of E. Cliff before it becomes Portolá, is a popular locals' beach, usually quite warm. Beyond the Santa Cruz Yacht Harbor, various small, locally popular beaches line E. Cliff Dr.; the unofficially

WILDER RANCH STATE PARK

Open to the public since mid-1989, Wilder Ranch State Park is best summed up as "a California coastal dairy-farm museum," a remnant of the days when dairies were more important to the local economy than tourists. Before it was a dairy farm, this was the main rancho supplying Mission Santa Cruz. Though damaged by the 1989 earthquake, the old Victorian ranch house is open again, decked out in period furnishings. The grounds also include an elaborate 1890s stable, a dairy barn, and a bunkhouse-workshop with water-driven machinery. Seasoned vehicles and farm equipment, from a 1916 Dodge touring sedan to seed spreaders and road graders, are scattered throughout the grounds.

Almost more appealing, though, are the park's miles of coastline and thousands of acres of forest, creeks, and canyons. To help visitors take in the landscape, Wilder Ranch features 34 miles of hiking, biking, and equestrian trails.

General ranch tours, led by docents dressed in period attire, are offered every Sat. and Sun., usually at 1 P.M. Historical games are played on the lawn—hoop 'n' stick, bubbles, stilts—on weekends as well. A variety of other history- and natural history–oriented events are sponsored throughout the year, from demonstrations on making corn-husk dolls or quilts to mastering cowboy-style roping, plus guided hikes and bird walks. Usually on the first Sat. in May is the park's **annual open house,** a full day of old-fashioned family fun (and fundraising, for future park restoration work).

Wilder Ranch is two miles north of Santa Cruz on the west side of Hwy. 1 (1401 Coast Rd., about a mile past the stoplight at Western Dr.), 831/423-9703 or 831/426-0505, and is open for day-use only ($3 per car). To get here by bus, take Santa Cruz Metro No. 40 and ask the driver to drop you at the ranch.

named **26th St. Beach** (at the end of 26th St., naturally enough) is probably tops among them. Hot for local surfing is the **Pleasure Point,** E. Cliff at Pleasure Point Drive.

About six miles down the coast from Santa Cruz City Beach and just south of the Capitola suburbs is **New Brighton State Beach,** 1500 Park Ave., Capitola, 831/464-6330. Its 65 often-sunny acres are protected by wooded headlands that offer nature trails, good bird-watching, and a dazzling nighttime view of Monterey Bay. Several miles farther south, two-mile-long **Seacliff State Beach,** Park Dr., Aptos, 831/685-6442 (recorded information) or 831/685-6444 (visitors center), is so popular you may not be able to stop. It's nice for hiking, pelican-watching, fossil appreciating, swimming, and sunbathing. The wheelchair-accessible pier here reaches out to the pink concrete carcass of the doomed World War I–vintage *Palo Alto,* sunk here, now a long-abandoned amusement pier. As the name suggests, **Rio del Mar** beach is where Aptos Creek meets the sea. Here you'll find restrooms, miles of sand, and limited parking. It's free.

In the Redwoods
Just north of Santa Cruz, as the crow flies, is California's first state park. **Big Basin Redwoods State Park,** about 24 miles upcanyon from Santa Cruz, was created to save Big Basin's towering *Sequoia sempervirens* coast redwoods from loggers. To achieve that aim, 60-

some conservationists led by Andrew P. Hill camped at the base of Slippery Rock on May 15, 1900, and formed the Sempervirens Club. Just two years later, in September 1902, 3,800 acres of primeval forest were deeded to the state, the beginning of California's state park system.

The best time to be in Big Basin is in the fall, when the weather is perfect and most tourists have gone home. Winter and spring are also prime times, though usually rainier. Big Basin's **Nature Lodge** museum features good natural history exhibits and many fine books. Also here: more than 100 miles of hiking trails. Take the half-mile **Redwood Trail** loop to stretch your legs, and to see one of the park's most impressive stands of virgin redwoods. Or hike the more ambitious **Skyline-to-the-Sea** trail, at least an overnight trip. Another popular route is the **Pine Mountain Trail.** Thanks to recent land acquisitions along the coast north of Santa Cruz, the new 1.5-mile **Whitehouse Ridge Trail** now joins Big Basin with Año Nuevo State Reserve.

Big Basin's day-use fee is $3 per vehicle (walk-ins and bike-ins are free), and a small fee is charged for the map/brochure showing all trails and major park features. For park information, contact Big Basin Redwoods State Park, 21600 Big Basin Way, Boulder Creek, CA 95006, 831/338-8860. Big Basin features 190 campsites plus five group camps. Reserve all campsites through ReserveAmerica, toll-free 800/444-7275,

THE ROARING CAMP AND BIG TREES RAILROAD

F. Norman Clark, the self-described "professional at oddities" who also owns the narrow-gauge railroad in Felton, bought the Southern Pacific rails connecting Santa Cruz and nearby Olympia, to make it possible for visitors to get to Henry Cowell Redwoods State Park and Felton (*almost* to Big Basin) by train. During logging's commercial heyday here in the 1900s, 20 or more trains passed over these tracks every day.

Today you can still visit Roaring Camp and ride the rails on one of two different trips. Hop aboard a 100-year-old steam engine and make an hour-and-fifteen-minute loop around a virgin redwood forest ($14 general, $9.50 kids 3–12), or take a 1940s-

vintage passenger train from Felton down to Santa Cruz (round-trip fare $15 general, $11 kids 3–12). The year-round calendar of special events includes October's **Harvest Faire** and the **Halloween Ghost Train,** the **Mountain Man Rendezvous** living history encampment in Nov., and December's **Pioneer Christmas.**

The railroad offers daily runs (usually just one train a day on nonsummer weekdays) from spring through Nov., and operates only on weekends and major holidays in winter. For more information, contact: Roaring Camp and Big Trees Narrow-Gauge Railroad, P.O. Box G-1, Felton, CA 95018, 831/335-4484, fax 831/335-3509, www.roaringcamp.com.

up to seven months in advance. An unusual "outdoor" option: the park's tent cabins. For more information on tent camping, or to reserve backpacker campsites at the park's six trail camps, contact park headquarters.

Parks near Big Basin include **Henry Cowell Redwoods State Park** off Hwy. 9 in Felton, 831/335-4598 or 831/438-2396 (campground), featuring one of the most impressive redwood groves along the central coast. New in the summer of 1999 was the **U-Con Trail** connecting Henry Cowell to Wilder Ranch State Park on the coast—making it possible to hike, bike, or horseback ride from the redwoods to the ocean on an established trail. Henry Cowell has 150 campsites; reserve through ReserveAmerica, toll-free 800/444-7275.

In Aptos, **Forest of Nisene Marks State Park** is definitely a hiker's park. Named for the Danish immigrant who hiked here until the age of 96 and whose family donated the land for public use, this is an oasis of solitude. (This was also the epicenter of the 1989 earthquake that brought down much of Santa Cruz.) The park encompasses 10,000 acres of hefty second-growth redwoods on the steep southern range of the Santa Cruz Mountains, six creeks, lovely Maple Falls, alders, maples, and more rugged trails than anyone can hike in a day. Also here are an old mill site, abandoned trestles and railroad tracks, and logging cabins. The park is open daily 6 A.M.–sunset. For information and a trail map, contact: Forest of Nisene Marks State Park, Aptos Creek Rd., 831/763-7063. To reserve the trail camp (a six-mile one-way hike, just six sites, primitive), call 831/763-7064 or 831/763-7121.

STAYING IN SANTA CRUZ

Santa Cruz Area Camping
Camp in the redwoods at **Big Basin Redwoods State Park** and **Henry Cowell Redwoods State Park** (see above); to guarantee a spot, reserve well in advance. Best for tent camping at the beach is **New Brighton State Beach,** 1500 Park Ave. in Capitola, 831/464-6330. "New Bright" features 115 developed campsites (especially nice ones on the cliffs), some sheltered picnic tables, and a small beach. It's a good base camp

ACCOMMODATIONS RATINGS

Accommodations in this book are rated by price category, based on double-occupancy, high-season rates. Categories used are:

Budget	$35 and under
Inexpensive	$35-60
Moderate	$60-85
Expensive	$85-110
Premium	$110-150
Luxury	$150 and up

for the entire Santa Cruz area but quite popular, so reserve for summer at least six months ahead. Near Aptos, **Seacliff State Beach,** 831/685-6442 or 831/685-6444, has a better beach than New Brighton, but camping is a disappointment—unless you're an RVer, since these 24 sites are just for RVs. For more information about the area's state parks and beaches, contact the parks office in Santa Cruz, 600 Ocean St., 831/429-2850. For campground reservations, call ReserveAmerica toll-free at 800/444-7275 or try www.reserveamerica.com.

Private campgrounds and trailer parks are always a possibility; a complete current listing is available at the local chamber of commerce. Possibilities include **Cotillion Gardens,** 300 Old Big Trees Rd., Felton, CA 95018, 831/335-7669; **Carbonero Creek,** 917 Disc Dr., Scotts Valley, CA 95066, 831/438-1288; and the **Santa Cruz KOA,** 1186 San Andreas Rd., Watsonville, CA 95076, 831/722-0551 or 831/722-2377.

HI-AYH Santa Cruz Hostel
The Santa Cruz Hostel, 321 Main St., Santa Cruz, CA 95061, 831/423-8304, fax 831/429-8541, www.hi-santacruz.org, occupies a group of historic cottages downtown. The hostel is open year-round, is wheelchair accessible, and features an on-site cyclery, fireplace, barbecue, lockers, and a rose and herb garden. The fee is $13 for members, $16 for nonmembers, with family rooms and limited parking available (extra fee for both). Reservations strongly suggested.

Santa Cruz Motels and Hotels
As a general rule, motels closer to the freeway are cheaper, while those on the river are seedier.

There are some fairly inexpensive motels near the beach (some with kitchens, hot tubs, pools, cable TV, etc.). Off-season rates in Santa Cruz are usually quite reasonable, but prices can sometimes mysteriously increase in summer and on weekends and holidays—so ask before you sign in.

Inexpensive: The **Sandpiper Lodge,** 111 Ocean, 831/429-8244, is a small motel with rooms and suites. Rates include complimentary continental breakfast.

Moderate: The **Pacific Inn,** 330 Ocean St., 831/425-3722, fax 831/425-4983, has 36 rooms and a heated pool and spa. The attractive **Comfort Inn Santa Cruz,** 110 Plymouth St., 831/426-6224, fax 831/426-0923, offers 63 rooms with in-room coffee and refrigerators, color TVs and VCRs, and a heated pool and spa. Suites are available. Rates include continental breakfast. Quite reasonably priced are smaller rooms at the **Beach View Inn,** just a block from the beach at 50 Front St., 831/426-3575, fax 831/421-9218. Decent too are the **Best Western Inn,** 126 Plymouth, 831/425-4717, fax 831/425-0643, and the **Best Western Torch-Lite Inn,** 500 Riverside Ave., 831/426-7575, fax 831/460-1470, where smaller rooms fall into the Moderate category.

Expensive: The **Best Western All Suites Inn,** 500 Ocean St., 831/458-9898, 831/426-8333, or toll-free 800/528-1234, fax 831/429-1903, offers rooms with in-room whirlpools and microwaves, some gas fireplaces, an indoor heated pool, lap pool, and sauna, and other amenities. Also quite pleasant is the **Sunset Inn,** 2424 Mission St., 831/423-7500, fax 831/423-7500, where extras include free local phone calls and breakfast.

Luxury: For value, nothing in the motel/hotel category beats **Chaminade at Santa Cruz** up on the hill and overlooking Monterey Bay at 1 Chaminade Ln. (just off Paul Sweet Rd.), 831/475-5600 or toll-free 800/283-6569, fax 831/476-4948, www.chaminade.com. Occupying the old Chaminade Brothers Seminary and Monastery, this quiet resort and conference center offers a wealth of business amenities—but also personal perks, such as a health club (with massage, and men's and women's "therapy pools"), jogging track, heated pool, saunas, and whirlpools. Lighted tennis courts, too. Newly refurbished rooms and suites are scattered around the 80-acre grounds in 11 "villas" that include shared parlors with refrigerators, wet bars, and conference tables. Rooms feature king or queen beds, in-room coffee, irons and ironing boards, and two direct-line phones. Valet parking and airport transportation are available. Chaminade also boasts two good restaurants and a bar (with meal service), all open to the general public.

Adjacent to the wharf and across from Santa Cruz Beach Boardwalk, the imposing **WestCoast Santa Cruz Hotel,** 175 W. Cliff Dr., 831/426-4330 or toll-free 800/426-0670 (reservations), fax 831/427-2025, www.westcoastsantacruz.com, is right on the beach (the only beachfront hotel in Santa Cruz) and has 163 rooms and suites with balconies and patios, modern amenities, satellite TV, heated pool, and whirlpool.

Santa Cruz Bed-and-Breakfasts

Legendary is the been-there-forever local landmark, the **Babbling Brook Inn,** 1025 Laurel St., 831/427-2437 or toll-free 800/866-1131, fax 831/427-2457, www.cacoastalinns.com. Once a log cabin, this place was added to and otherwise spruced up by the Countess Florenzo de Chandler. All 14 rooms and suites are quite romantic, with private bathrooms, phone, and TV. Most are decorated to suggest the works of Old World artists and poets, from Cézanne and Monet to Tennyson. Most also feature a fireplace, private deck, and outside entrance. Two have whirlpool bathtubs. Full breakfast and afternoon wine and cheese (or tea and cookies) are included. Also here: a babbling brook, waterfalls, and a garden gazebo. Premium-Luxury.

Other Santa Cruz inns tend to cluster near the ocean. The 1910 **Darling House** seaside mansion at 314 W. Cliff Dr., 831/458-1958 or toll-free 800/458-1988, www.infopoint.com/sc/lodging/darling, is an elegant 1910 Spanish Revival mansion designed by architect William Weeks. In addition to spectacular ocean views, Darling House offers eight rooms (two with private baths, two with fireplaces), telephones, and TV on request. Hot tub in the backyard, robes provided. If you loved *The Ghost and Mrs. Muir,* you'll particularly enjoy the Pacific Ocean Room here—complete with telescope. Rates include breakfast and evening beverages. Expensive-Luxury.

Another good choice is the **Cliff Crest Bed and Breakfast Inn,** just blocks from both

COMPASSION FLOWER INN: HIGH-CLASS JOINT

One of the loveliest new B&Bs in Santa Cruz is actually the nation's first "BB&B," the first "bed, bud, and breakfast" in the United States. And "bud" in this case is not a marketing slogan for beer but a reference to high-quality marijuana.

The Compassion Flower Inn opened in March 2000 with the express purpose of being a hemp- and medical marijuana-friendly bed-and-breakfast. The establishment is "named for both the beauty of the passion flower and the compassion of the medical marijuana movement" to which the owners have dedicated themselves.

If you come, don't expect to find some tie-dyed weed-happy scene reminiscent of San Francisco's Haight-Ashbury during the Summer of Love. The proprietors have impeccably restored this Gothic Revival Victorian, at a cost of a half-million dollars. Tastefully and creatively decorated with antiques, hand-painted furniture, and custom tilework, the Compassion Flower Inn instead harks back to its historical roots as the onetime home of Judge Edgar Spalsbury, who made regular trips to a pharmacy downtown to buy opium as a pain medication for his tuberculosis.

Rooms range from the fairly simple **Hemp Room** and **Passionflower Room,** "twin" accommodations tucked under the eaves (these two share a bath), to the 1st-floor, fully wheelchair accessible **Canabliss Room** and the elegant **Lover's Suite.** Particularly striking in the suite is its bathroom, where exquisite tiled hemp designs wrap the two-person sunken tub.

Rates include full organic breakfast, including fresh-baked bread, and are $125–175 (Premium-Luxury). For all rooms, there is a two-night minimum stay.

For more information or to make reservations, contact: Compassion Flower Inn, 216 Laurel St., Santa Cruz, CA 95060, 831/466-0420, www.compassionflowerinn.com.

---

downtown and Main Beach at 407 Cliff St., 831/427-2609, fax 831/427-2710, www.cliffcrestinn.com, a Queen Anne by the beach and Boardwalk. Full breakfast is served in the solarium. Expensive-Luxury. The **Chateau Victorian,** 118 1st St., 831/458-9458, www.chateauvictorian.com, offers rooms with queen-sized beds, private tiled bathrooms and wood-burning fireplaces. Local Santa Cruz Mountains wines are served, as are generous continental breakfasts. Premium.

For more bed-and-breakfast choices in the greater Santa Cruz area, see listings below.

STAYING NEAR SANTA CRUZ

Staying in New Davenport

If you're heading up the coast from Santa Cruz, consider a meal stop or a stay at the **Davenport Bed and Breakfast Inn,** 31 Davenport Ave. (Hwy. 1), 831/425-1818 or toll-free 800/870-1817, fax 831/423-1160, www.swanton.com. The 12 comfortable rooms are upstairs, above the New Davenport Cash Store and Restaurant, where the food is very good at breakfast, lunch, and dinner. Rates include full breakfast. Moderate-Premium. Some of the pastries served here are made just up the road at **Whale City Bakery Bar & Grill,** 831/423-9803 or 831/429-6209, where the wide variety of homemade treats and very good coffee are always worth a stop.

Staying in Ben Lomond

For a bed-and-breakfast stay in Ben Lomond, consider the lovely and woodsy **Fairview Manor,** 245 Fairview Ave., 831/336-3355 or toll-free 800/553-8840, www.fairviewmanor.com, which features five rooms with private baths as well as a big deck overlooking the San Lorenzo River. Premium. Or try the 1879 Victorian **Chateau des Fleurs,** 7995 Hwy. 9, 831/336-8943 or toll-free 800/291-9966, www.chateaudefleurs.com, a bed-and-breakfast offering three rooms with private baths, along with a full breakfast. Expensive-Premium.

Staying in Soquel

The **Blue Spruce Inn,** 2815 S. Main St., 831/464-1137 or toll-free 800/559-1137, www.bluespruce.com, is a romantic 1875 Victorian farmhouse just a few miles from downtown Santa Cruz. Its six rooms all feature private baths and entrances, queen-sized featherbeds, and unique antique room decor color-keyed to the hand-made Lancaster County quilts. Five rooms have private spas; two have gas fireplaces. Great breakfasts. Expensive-Premium.

Staying in Capitola

A long-standing local jewel is the **Capitola Venetian Hotel,** 1500 Wharf Rd., 831/476-6471 or toll-free 800/332-2780, www.capitolavenetian.com—California's first condominium complex, built in the 1920s. These clustered Mediterranean-style stucco apartments are relaxed and relaxing, close to the beach. All have separate living rooms, kitchens with stoves, in-room coffee, and telephones with voice mail and data ports; some have balconies, ocean views, and fireplaces. Premium-Luxury (but Moderate-Premium in the off-season).

Almost legendary almost overnight, Capitola's **Inn at Depot Hill,** 250 Monterey Ave., 831/462-3376 or toll-free 800/572-2632, fax 831/462-3697, www.cacoastalinns.com, is a luxurious bed-and-breakfast (essentially a small luxury hotel) housed in the onetime railroad depot. Each of the eight rooms features its own unique design motif, keyed from international themes (the Delft Room, Stratford-on-Avon, the Paris Room, and Portofino, for example), as well as a private garden and entrance, fireplace, telephone with modem/fax capability, and state-of-the-art TV/VCR and stereo system. The private white-marble bathrooms feature bathrobes, hair dryers, and other little luxuries. Bathrooms have double showers, so two isn't necessarily a crowd. The pure linen bedsheets are hand-washed and hand-ironed daily. Rates include full breakfast, afternoon tea or wine, and after-dinner dessert. Off-street parking is provided. Luxury.

Staying in Aptos

The apartment-style **Rio Sands Motel,** 116 Aptos Beach Dr., 831/688-3207 or toll-free 800/826-2077, fax 831/688-6107, www.riosands.com, has a heated pool, spa, and decent rooms not far from the beach. The "kitchen suites" feature full kitchens and a separate sitting room, and sleep up to four. "Super rooms" sleep up to six and include a refrigerator and microwave. All rooms have two TVs. Extras include the large heated pool, spa, picnic area with barbecue pits, and expanded continental breakfast. Peak-season rates are Premium, with real deals available in winter.

Also a pleasant surprise is the **Best Western Seacliff Inn,** just off the highway at 7500 Old Dominion Court, 831/688-7300 or toll-free 800/367-2003. It's a cut or two above the usual motel, and an easy stroll to the beach. The rooms are large and comfortable, with private balconies, clustering village-style around a large outdoor pool and hot tub area. Suites have in-room spas. But the best surprise of all is the restaurant, **Severino's,** 831/688-8987, which serves good food both inside the dining room and outside by the koi pond.

Pigeon Point Hostel

ROBERT NILSEN

Great "sunset dinner" specials are served Sun.–Thurs. 5–6:30 P.M. Luxury.

On the coast just north of Manresa State Beach is the condo-style **Seascape Resort Monterey Bay,** 1 Seascape Resort Dr., 831/688-6800 or toll-free 800/929-7727, fax 831/685-0615, www.seascaperesort.com. Choices here include tasteful studios and one- and two-bedroom villas. Restaurant, golf course, tennis courts, and on-site fitness and spa facilities. Two-night minimum stay, late May through September. Luxury.

For a bed-and-breakfast stay, consider the elegant Southern-style **Mangels House Bed & Breakfast Inn,** 570 Aptos Creek Rd., 831/688-7982 or toll-free 800/320-7401, a landmark 1886 Italianate Victorian mansion on four secluded acres at the edge of Forest of Nisene Marks State Park. One room has a fireplace; some have balconies and shared bathrooms. The best thing, though, is the location—adjacent to the State Park and primo hiking. Premium-Luxury.

Nice, too, and also near the park, is the **Bayview Hotel Bed and Breakfast Inn,** 8041 Soquel Dr., 831/688-8654 or toll-free 800/422-9843, www.cacoastalinns.com, an 1878 Italianate Victorian hotel with 11 elegant rooms, all with private baths and some with fireplaces and two-person tubs. Downstairs is The White Magnolia restaurant, for good food California-style. Expensive-Luxury.

Another possibility is the **Inn at Manresa Beach,** 1258 San Andreas Rd., La Selva Beach, 831/728-1000 or toll-free 888/523-2244, www.indevelopment.com, built in 1897 as a replica of Abraham Lincoln's home in Springfield, Illinois. One grass and two clay courts are available for tennis, and guests can also play badminton, croquet, or volleyball on the lawn. The eight rooms and suites here feature king or queen beds, fireplaces, private bathrooms (most with two-person spa tubs), two-line phones, and cable TV, VCR, and stereo. From here amid the strawberry and calla lily fields, it's an easy walk to both Manresa and Sand Dollar State Beaches. Luxury.

EATING IN SANTA CRUZ

Farm Trails and Farmers' Markets
To do Santa Cruz area farm trails, pick up a copy of the **Country Crossroads** map and brochure, a joint venture with Santa Clara County row-crop farmers and orchardists. It's the essential guide for hunting down strawberries, raspberries, apples, and homegrown veggies of all kinds. Or head for the local farmers' markets. The **Santa Cruz Community Certified Farmers' Market,** 831/335-7443, is held downtown at Lincoln and Cedar every Wed. 2:30–6:30 P.M. There are many others in the area, too; inquire at the visitors center for a current listing.

Near the Beach in Santa Cruz
Unforgettable for breakfast or lunch is funky **Aldo's,** 616 Atlantic Ave. (at the west end of the yacht harbor), 831/426-3736. The breakfast menu features various egg and omelette combinations. Best of all, though, is the raisin toast, made with Aldo's homemade *fugasa* bread. Eat outdoors on the old picnic tables covered with checkered plastic tablecloths to enjoy the sun, sea air, and seagulls. At lunch and dinner, look for homemade pastas and fresh fish.

The Boardwalk alone features about 20 restaurants and food stands. The best Sunday brunch experience around is also here, at the historic **Cocoanut Grove,** 400 Beach, 831/423-2053, a veritable feast for the eyes as well as the stomach. In good weather, you'll enjoy the "sunny" atmosphere created by the sunroof. Nearby, along streets near the beach and Boardwalk, are a variety of restaurants, everything from authentic and casual ethnic eateries to sit-down dining establishments. Head to the municipal wharf to see what's new in the fresh-off-the-boat seafood department.

For romantic California-style and continental cuisine, the place is **Casablanca Restaurant,** 101 Main St. (at Beach), 831/426-9063, open for dinner nightly and brunch on Sunday. A lively newcomer for worldly American—and a surprising selection of vegetarian options—is **Blacks Beach Café,** E. Cliff at 15th, 831/475-2233, open Tues.–Sun. for dinner, on weekends for brunch.

Veggie Fare and Other Cheap Eats
The Crepe Place, 1134 Soquel Ave., 831/429-6994, offers inexpensive breakfasts, dessert crepes (and every other kind), good but unpretentious lunches, and dinners into the wee

hours—a great place for late-night dining. Open daily for lunch and dinner, on weekends for brunch. The **Saturn Cafe,** 1230 Mission, 831/429-8505, has inexpensive and wonderful vegetarian meals. Open daily for lunch and dinner, and until late for desserts and coffee.

For "natural fast foods," don't miss **Dharma's,** in Capitola at 4250 Capitola Rd., 831/462-1717, where you can savor a Brahma Burger, Dharma Dog, or Nuclear Sub sandwich (baked tofu, guacamole, cheese, lettuce, olives, pickle, and secret sauce on a roll).

But a vegetarian visit to Santa Cruz wouldn't be complete without feasting at the **Whole Earth Restaurant,** on the UC Santa Cruz campus (Redwood Blvd. next to the library), 831/426-8255. A quiet, comfortable place, this very fine organic eatery was the inspiration and training ground for Sharon Cadwallader's well-known *Whole Earth Cookbook* and its sequel. After all these years, the food is still good and still reasonable.

The **Santa Cruz Brewing Co. and Front Street Pub,** 516 Front St., 831/429-8838, is a local microbrewery (tours available) featuring perennial favorites like Lighthouse Amber, Lighthouse Lager, Pacific Porter, and handcrafted seasonal brews—14 different beers in all—plus homemade root beer. The **Seabright Brewery** brewpub, 519 Seabright Ave., Ste. 107, 831/426-2739, is popular for its Seabright Amber and Pelican Pale—not to mention casual dining out on the patio. If you're heading toward Boulder Creek, beer fans, stop by the **Boulder Creek Brewery and Cafe,** 13040 Hwy. 9, 831/338-7882.

The Santa Cruz Coffee Roasting Company at the Palomar Inn, 1330 Pacific Ave., 831/459-0100, serves excellent coffee and a bistro-style café lunch. Not far away and absolutely wonderful is **Zoccoli's Delicatessen,** 1534 Pacific Ave., 831/423-1711, where it's typical to see people lining up for sandwiches, salads, and genuine "good deal" lunch specials, usually under $5. Fresh homemade pastas. Open Mon.–Sat. 9 A.M.–5:30 P.M.

Best Bets Downtown

Downtown Santa Cruz is getting pretty uptown these days. A case in point: eccentric India Joze, 1001 Center St., serving up affordable Southeast Asian and Middle Eastern since 1971—and responsible for launching the famed Santa Cruz

International Calamari Festival—has been replaced by a sophisticated San Francisco–style Mediterranean, **Azur,** scheduled to open in late 2000. Quite stylish for European-style fare is the **Pearl Alley Bistro & Café,** 110 Pearl Alley, 831/429-8070, open daily for lunch (until 5 P.M.) and dinner. Full bar.

El Palomar at the Pacific Garden Mall, 1336 Pacific Ave., 831/425-7575, is a winner for relaxed Mexican—especially seafood—and for about a decade now has been just about everybody's choice for "best" south-of-the-border fare. Open daily for breakfast, lunch, and dinner. Full bar. (At the yacht harbor, there's **Café El Palomar,** 2222 E. Cliff Dr., 831/462-4248, open 7 A.M.–5 P.M. daily.) The **Cooper Street Café** at the back of the McPherson Center, Cooper and Front Sts., 831/423-4925, is a good choice for a tasty and reasonably priced lunch—serving everything from soup and salads to quiche and pastas. Open Tues.–Sun. from 11 A.M. to 9 or 11 P.M. (until just 6 P.M. on Sunday). Sit outside on the patio in nice weather, where there's live jazz on weekend afternoons.

Chaminade

The old Chaminade Brothers Seminary and Monastery, 1 Chaminade Ln. (just off Paul Sweet Rd.), 831/475-5600, is now the Chaminade Executive Conference Center and Resort. As part of the deal, the new owners had to include a public restaurant in their development plans. The **Sunset Dining Room at Chaminade** is the place to come on Friday nights for what is no doubt the best seafood buffet in Santa Cruz County—15 types of fish and seafood, an outdoor grill, and a spectacular view of Monterey Bay. It's worth every penny of the (fairly high) price. The Sunset Room also serves appetizing breakfast, lunch, and dinner buffets, and a popular Sunday brunch. Outdoor dining is available, weather permitting. Open daily; reservations wise. You can also sign on for a stay here (see Staying in Santa Cruz above).

EATING NEAR SANTA CRUZ

Eating in Soquel

The **Little Tampico,** 2605 Main St., 831/475-4700, isn't exactly inexpensive. A real bargain here, though, is the specialty "Otila's Plate": a mini-taco, enchilada, tostada, and taquito, plus rice and beans. Another good choice: nachos with everything. (Various Tampico restaurant relatives dot the county, too.) Another popular Mexican restaurant in town is **Tortilla Flats,** 4616 Soquel Dr., 831/476-1754. Open daily for lunch, dinner, and Sunday brunch.

If it's Italian you crave, try **Aragona's,** 2591 Main St., 831/462-5100, which serves house-made pastas and gourmet pizzas in a garden-like setting looking out on Soquel Creek. Open daily for lunch and dinner.

Eating in Capitola

Dharma's Natural Foods Restaurant, a Santa Cruz institution now at home at 4250 Capitola Rd., 831/462-1717, is purported to be the oldest completely vegetarian restaurant in the country. Open daily for breakfast, lunch, and dinner. Also classic in Capitola is **Mr. Toots Coffeehouse** upstairs at 221-A Esplanade, 831/475-3679, where you can get a cup of joe until late, and **Pizza-My-Heart,** 209-A Esplanade, 831/475-5714.

Casual in more upscale style and unbeatable for pastries and decadent desserts is **Gayle's Bakery and Rosticceria,** 504 Bay Ave., 831/462-1200. The "rosticceria" has a wonderful selection of salads and homemade pastas, soups, sandwiches, pizza, spit-roasted meats—even "dinners-to-go" and heat-and-serve casseroles. But the aromas drifting in from Gayle's Bakery are the real draw—heavenly pastries and apple crumb and olallieberry pies, not to mention the praline cheesecake. For decadence-to-go, try Grand Marnier truffles, florentines, éclairs, or Napoleons. Gayle's also sells more than two-dozen types of fresh-baked bread, and is open daily 7 A.M.–7 P.M.

If you're heading toward the Bay or San Jose the back way via Corralitos, stop by the **Corralitos Market and Sausage Co.,** 569 Corralitos Rd. via Freedom Blvd., Watsonville, 831/722-2633, for homemade sausages, smoke-cured ham and turkey breast, or other specialty meats—all great with Gayle's breads.

Near the beach, on or near the Esplanade, you'll find an endless variety of eateries. Among them, **Sea Bonne,** 231 Esplanade, 831/462-1350, is one of the area's better restaurants, serving up imaginative seafood and romantic views. Open for dinner nightly. Reservations wise. **Margaritaville,** 221 Esplanade, 831/476-2263, serves upscale Mexican fare and margaritas. Open for lunch and dinner daily and for brunch on weekends. The **Paradise Beach Grill,** 215 Esplanade, 831/476-4900, offers California cuisine as well as a variety of international dishes. Great views. Open for lunch and dinner daily. Also going for the California cuisine is **Zelda's on the Beach,** 203 Esplanade, 831/475-4900, which features an affordable lobster special on Thurs. night.

The most famous restaurant in Capitola is the **Shadowbrook Restaurant,** 1750 Wharf Rd. (at Capitola Rd.), 831/475-1511, known for its romantic garden setting—ferns, roses, ivy outside, a Monterey pine and plants inside—and the tram ride down the hill to Soquel Creek. The Shadowbrook is open for "continental-flavored American" dinners nightly. Extensive wine list. Brunch, with choices like apple and cheddar omelettes, is served on weekends. Reservations recommended.

Eating in Aptos

The **Bittersweet Bistro,** 787 Rio Del Mar Blvd., 831/662-9799, offers Mediterranean-inspired bistro fare featuring fresh local and organic produce—everything from Greek pizzettas and seafood puttanesca to garlic chicken and grilled Monterey Bay king salmon. Open Tues.–Sun. for "bistro hour" (3–6 P.M.)—half-priced pizzettas and drink specials—and for dinner. The best place around for Thai food, locals say, is **Bangkok West,** 2505 Cabrillo College Dr., 831/479-8297, open daily for lunch and dinner. For stylish and fresh Mexican, the place is **Palapas** at Seascape Village on Seascape Blvd., 831/662-9000, open daily for lunch and dinner, brunch on Sunday.

For a romantic dinner, splurge at the **Cafe Sparrow,** 8042 Soquel Dr., 831/688-6238, which serves pricey but excellent country French cuisine at lunch and dinner daily—a Santa Cruz County dining destination that's actually family friendly. Open Mon.–Sat. for lunch, daily for dinner. Extensive wine list. Or try the **White Magnolia,** downstairs at the Bayview Hotel, 8041 Soquel Dr., 831/685-1881, where everything is served up with a helping of the inn's historic 1878 charm.

NEAR SANTA CRUZ

Travelers heading north via Hwy. 1, on the way to San Francisco, will discover Año Nuevo State Reserve, breeding ground for the northern elephant seal—quite popular, so don't expect to just drop by—and two delightful hostels housed in former lighthouses. (For hostel details, see "Unique Coastal Stays" in the San Francisco Bay Area chapter.) Not far from Año Nuevo, as the crow flies, is spectacular Big Basin Redwoods State Park, California's first state park, and other spectacular redwood parks (see above). Those heading south on Hwy. 1 on the way to Monterey will pass through the towns of Watsonville, Moss Landing, and Castroville en route. Northeast from Watsonville via Hwy. 152 is Gilroy, famous for its annual Gilroy Garlic Festival. Southeast of Watsonville is historic San Juan Bautista, the mission and the town. Southeast from Moss Landing and Castroville via Hwy. 183 is Salinas, hometown of Pulitzer Prize–winning writer John Steinbeck. Southeast from Salinas is Pinnacles National Monument, heaven for rock climbers.

WATSONVILLE, GILROY, AND SAN JUAN BAUTISTA

Watsonville: Strawberries and Mushrooms
An agriculturally rich city of over 25,000, Watsonville is the mushroom capital of the United States, though the town calls this lovely section of the Pajaro Valley the "Strawberry Capital of the World," and "Apple City of the Ives." Get up to speed on local agricultural history at the **Agricultural History Project** at the Santa Cruz County Fairgrounds, 831/724-5898, museum exhibits and demonstrations open to the public on Fri. and Sat. noon–4 P.M. An almost mandatory stop, from May through Jan., is **Gizdich Ranch,** 55 Peckham Rd., 831/722-1056, www.gizdichranch.com, fabulous from late summer through fall for its fresh apples, homemade apple pies, and fresh-squeezed natural apple juices. Earlier in the season this is a "Pik-Yor-Sef" berry farm, with raspberries, olallieberries, and strawberries (usually also available in pies, fritters, and pastries). Also worth seeking in Wat-

sonville are Mexican and Filipino eateries, many quite good, most inexpensive.

The Watsonville area boasts some fine state beaches. At **Manresa State Beach,** 1445 San Andreas Rd., 831/724-3750, stairways lead to the surf from the main parking lot and Sand Dollar Dr.; restrooms, an outdoor shower, and tent camping are available. Rural San Andreas Rd. also takes you to **Sunset State Beach,** 201 Sunset Beach Rd., 831/763-7062 or 831/763-7063, four miles west of Watsonville in the Pajaro Dunes. Sunset offers 3.5 miles of nice sandy beaches, plus 90 campsites and 60 picnic sites, but also way too many RVs and not much privacy. Even so, after sunset the beach is open only to campers. Parking for pretty **Palm Beach** near Pajaro Dunes—a great place to find sand dollars—is near the end of Beach Street. Also here are picnic facilities, a par course, and restrooms. **Zmudowski State Beach** is near where the Pajaro River reaches the sea: good hiking and surf fishing, rarely crowded. Next, near Moss Landing, are **Salinas River State Beach,** Potrero Rd., 831/384-7695, and **Jetty State Beach.** To reserve campsites at all state beaches and parks, call ReserveAmerica toll-free at 800/444-7275.

For the local **Country Crossroads** farm trails map, and other visitor information, contact the **Pajaro Valley Chamber of Commerce,** 444 Main St., P.O. Box 470, Watsonville, CA 95077, 831/724-3900, www.pvchamber.com.

Gilroy and Garlic
It's chic to reek in Gilroy. Will Rogers supposedly described Gilroy as "the only town in America where you can marinate a steak just by hanging it out on the clothesline." But Gilroy, the "undisputed garlic capital of the world," dedicates very few acres to growing the stinking rose these days. The legendary local garlic farms have been declining due to soil disease since 1979—ironically, the first year of the now-famous and phenomenally successful **Gilroy Garlic Festival,** 408/842-1625, www.gilroygarlicfestival.com, held the last full weekend in July. Other attractions in Gilroy include the **Indian Motorcycle** production facility (call 408/847-2221 to arrange factory

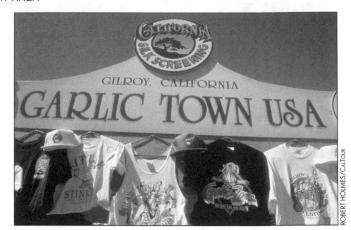

Gilroy celebrates its garlic-ness.

ROBERT HOLMES/CalTour

tours) and Goldsmith Seeds Gilroy's seasonal six-acre **Field of Dreams** experimental flower seed garden (call 408/847-7333 for tour information). Downtown Gilroy has its attractions, too. The best place to start exploring them is the **Gilroy Historical Museum** at 5th and Church, 408/848-0470, open weekdays 9 A.M.–5 P.M.

For more information about what's cookin' in and around Gilroy, contact: **Gilroy Chamber of Commerce,** 7471 Monterey St., Gilroy 95020, www.gilroy.org.

San Juan Bautista and Vertigo

The tiny town of San Juan Bautista is charming and charmed, as friendly as it is sunny. (People here say the weather in this pastoral valley is "salubrious." Take their word for it.) Named for John the Baptist, the 1797 Spanish mission of San Juan Bautista is central to this serene community at the foot of the Gabilan Mountains. But the historic plaza, still bordered by old adobes and now a state historic park, is the true center of San Juan—rallying point for two revolutions, onetime home of famed bandit Tiburcio Vasquez, and the theatrical setting for David Belasco's *Rose of the Rancho.* Movie fans may remember Jimmy Stewart and Kim Novak in the mission scenes from Alfred Hitchcock's *Vertigo,* which were filmed here.

In addition to history and celluloid celebrity, San Juan Bautista has galleries, antique and craft shops, and an incredible local theater troupe—**El Teatro Campesino,** established by

noted playwright Luis Valdez *(Zoot Suit* and *Corridos).* To get oriented, pick up a walking-tour brochure at the **San Juan Bautista Chamber of Commerce** office, 1 Polk St., 831/623-2454, or elsewhere around town. In June, experience mid-1800s mission days at **Early Days in San Juan Bautista,** a traditional celebration complete with horse-drawn carriages, period dress, music, and fandango. The barroom at the Plaza Hotel is even open for card games. The **Flea Market** here in August is one of the country's best. Later in the month, **San Juan Fiesta Day** is the most popular venue of the wandering **Cabrillo Music Festival.**

MOSS LANDING AND VICINITY

Near the mouth of Elkhorn Slough on the coast south of Watsonville, Moss Landing is a crazy quilt of weird shops and roadside knickknack stands, watched over by both a towering steam power plant (formerly under PG&E control and now owned by Duke Energy), built circa 1948, the second largest in the world, and a Kaiser firebrick-making plant. All of which makes for an odd-looking community.

First a Salinas Valley produce port, then a whaling harbor until 1930, modern Moss Landing is surrounded by artichoke and broccoli fields. The busy fishing harbor and adjoining slough are home to hundreds of bird and plant species, making this an important center for marinelife studies.

These days the area is also noted for its indoor recreational opportunities, with more than two-dozen antique and junque shops along Moss Landing Road. Show up on the last Sunday in July for the annual **Antique Street Fair,** which draws more than 350 antique dealers and at least 12,000 civilian antiquers.

Moss Landing Marine Laboratories

The laboratories here, at 895 Blanco Circle, 831/755-8650, are jointly operated by nine campuses of the California State Universities and Colleges system. Students and faculty study local marinelife, birds, and tidepools, but particularly Monterey Bay's spectacular underwater submarine canyons, which start where Elkhorn Slough enters the bay at Moss Landing. Stop for a visit and quick look around, but don't disturb classes or research projects. Better yet, come in spring—usually the first Sunday after Easter—for the big open house, when you can take a complete tour, explore the "touch tank" full of starfish, sea cucumbers, sponges, snails, and anemones, and see slide shows, movies, and marinelife dioramas.

Elkhorn Slough Reserve

Most people come here to hike and bird-watch, but the fish life in this coastal estuary, the second largest in California, is also phenomenal. No wonder the Ohlone people built villages here some 5,000 years ago. Wetlands like these, oozing with life and nourished by rich bay sediments, are among those natural environments most threatened by "progress." Thanks to The Nature Conservancy, the Elkhorn Slough (originally the mouth of the Salinas River, until a 1908 diversion) is now protected as a federal and state estuarine sanctuary and recognized as a National Estuarine Research Reserve—California's first. Elkhorn Slough is managed by the California Department of Fish and Game.

These meandering channels along an old, seven-mile-long river are thick with marshy grasses and wildflowers beneath a plateau of oaks and eucalyptus. In winter, an incredible variety of shorebirds (not counting migrating waterfowl) call this area home. Endangered and threatened birds, including the brown pelican, the California clapper rail, and the California least tern, thrive here. The tule elk once hunted by the Ohlone are long gone, but harbor seals bask on the mudflats, and bobcats, gray foxes, muskrats, otters, and black-tailed deer are still here. Come in fall for the annual **Monterey Bay Bird Festival.**

Though this is a private nature sanctuary, not a park, the public can visit. Some 4.5 miles of trails pass by tidal mudflats, salt marshes, and an old abandoned dairy. The reserve and visitors center, which offers a bird-watchers map/guide to the Pajaro Valley, are open Wed.–Sun. 9 A.M.–5 P.M. There's a small day-use fee to use the trails. Docent-led walks are offered year-round on Sat. and Sun. at 10 A.M. and 1 P.M. On the first Sat. of the month, there's also an Early Bird Walk at 8:30 A.M. Still, there's no better way to see the slough than from the seat of a kayak. Stop by the visitors center at the entrance to arrange a guided tour, or contact: **Elkhorn Slough Foundation,** 1700 Elkhorn Rd., P.O. Box 267, Moss Landing, CA 95039, 831/728-2822 or 831/728-5939, www.elkhornslough.org. Or arrange kayak tours through **Monterey Bay Kayaks,** 693 Del Monte Ave., Monterey, 831/373-5357 or 831/633-2211, or **Kayak Connections,** 831/724-5692. For a guided tour aboard a 27-foot pontoon boat, contact **Elkhorn Slough Safari** in Moss Landing, 831/633-5555, www.elkornslough.com.

Practical Moss Landing

Time-honored people's eateries abound, particularly near the harbor. Most serve chowders and seafood and/or ethnic specials. **Moss Landing Oyster Bay Restaurant,** 413 Moss Landing Rd., 831/632-0119, is well known for its exceptional fresh seafood and house-made pastas and desserts. (Enjoy outdoor patio dining in good weather.) Quite good, right on the highway, is **The Whole Enchilada,** 831/633-3038, open for lunch and dinner daily and specializing in Mexican seafood entrées. (The "whole enchilada," by the way, is filet of red snapper wrapped in a corn tortilla and smothered in enchilada sauce and melted cheese.) The Enchilada's associated **Moss Landing Inn and Jazz Club,** 831/633-9990, is a bar featuring live jazz on Sun. 4:30–8:30 P.M.

"En route camping" for self-contained RVs is available at **Moss Landing State Beach.**

Castroville and Artichokes

The heart of Castroville is Swiss-Italian, which hardly explains the artichokes all over the place. Calling itself "Artichoke Capital of the World," Castroville grows 75 percent of California's artichokes, though that delicious leathery thistle grows throughout Santa Cruz and Monterey Counties. Come for the annual **Artichoke Festival** every May; call 831/633-6545 or try www.artichoke-festival.org for information. It's some party, too, replete with artichokes fried, baked, mashed, boiled, and added as colorful ingredients to cookies and cakes. Nibble on french-fried artichokes with mayo dip and artichoke nut cake, sip artichoke soup, and sample steamed artichokes. Sometimes Hollywood gets in on the action: in 1947 Marilyn Monroe reigned as California's Artichoke Queen. If you miss the festival there are other artichoke options, including **Giant Artichoke Fruits and Vegetables** at 11241 Merritt St., 831/633-2778, and the **Thistle Hut,** just off Hwy. 1 at Cooper-Molera Rd., 831/633-4888. And the **Franco Restaurant,** 10639 Merritt, 831/633-2090, sponsors a Marilyn Monroe look-alike contest in June. But come by otherwise just to grab a burger—some say the best in the county—and to ogle the Marilyn memorabilia.

SALINAS AND STEINBECK

A long-running Salinas tradition (since 1911) is the four-day **California Rodeo** held on the third weekend in July, one of the world's largest, with bronco busting and bull riding, roping and tying, barrel racing, and a big Western dance on Saturday night. The rowdiness here—cowboy-style, of course—rivals Mardi Gras. But lately John Steinbeck's literary legacy has been giving the rodeo a run for the money.

Salinas is the blue-collar birthplace of novelist John Steinbeck, who chronicled the lives and hard times of California's down-and-out. Publication of *The Grapes of Wrath* in 1939 didn't do much for the writer's popularity in and around Salinas. Vilified here as a left-winger and Salinas Valley traitor, during his lifetime Steinbeck never came back to his hometown. Yet some people here have long been trying to make it up to Steinbeck. After all, he was the first American ever to

win both the Pulitzer and Nobel Prizes for literature. Efforts to establish a permanent local Steinbeck museum finally succeeded, and in summer 1998 the doors of the $10.3 million **National Steinbeck Center** opened to the public.

Billed as a "multimedia experience of literature, history, and art," the Steinbeck Center offers changing exhibits and seven themed permanent galleries—incorporating sights, sounds, and scents—to introduce Steinbeck's life, work, and times, with settings ranging from Doc Rickett's lab on Cannery Row and the replica boxcar of "ice-packed" lettuce to a (climbable) red pony in the barn. Seven theaters show clips from films derived from Steinbeck's writings. But some appreciations are strictly literal, including John Steinbeck's trusty green truck and camper Rocinante (named after Don Quixote's horse), in which the writer sojourned while researching *Travels with Charley.* The **Art of Writing Room,** with literary exhibits and all kinds of technical interactivity, explores the themes of Steinbeck's art and life. The 30,000-piece **Steinbeck Archives** are also here, open only to researchers by appointment. Quite accessible, though, are the sunny **Steinbeck Center Café** and the **museum store,** which features a good selection of books in addition to gift items. The center's new 6,500-square-foot wing, the **Salinas Valley Agricultural History and Education Center,** will showcase the Salinas Valley's agricultural heritage and is scheduled to open in late 2000.

The center is open daily 10 A.M.–5 P.M., but closed on Thanksgiving, Christmas, and New Year's Day. Admission is $7 adults, $6 seniors (over age 62) and students with ID, and $4 children ages 11–17 (under 10 free). For more information about the center and its events and activities, contact: National Steinbeck Center, 1 Main St., Salinas, CA 93901, 831/796-3833, fax 831/796-3828, www.steinbeck.org.

In Salinas John Steinbeck is not only a museum, but an event—and a dining destination. On the first weekend in August, come for the annual **Steinbeck Festival**—four days of films, lectures, tours, and social mixers. For information, call 831/796-3833. The Steinbeck family home—a jewel-box Victorian, located just two blocks from the National Steinbeck Center—was once described by the writer as "an immaculate and friendly house, grand enough, but not pretentious." And so it still is, though these days the Salinas Valley Guild serves up gourmet lunches for Steinbeck fans—featuring Salinas Valley produce and Monterey County wines and beer—at **Steinbeck House,** 132 Central St., Mon.–Sat. 11 A.M.–2:30 P.M. The menu changes weekly. Call 831/424-2735 for information and reservations.

For area visitor information, contact: **Salinas Valley Chamber of Commerce,** 119 E. Alisal, P.O. Box 1170, Salinas, CA 93902, 831/424-7611, www.salinaschamber.com.

PINNACLES NATIONAL MONUMENT

Exploring these barren 1,600 acres of volcanic spires and ravines is a little like rock-climbing on the moon. The weird dark-red rocks are bizarrely eroded, unlike anywhere else in North America, forming gaping gorges, crumbling caverns, terrifying terraces. Rock climbers' heaven (not for beginners), this stunning old volcano offers excellent trails, too, with pebbles the size of houses to stumble over. Visitors afraid of earthquakes should know that the Pinnacles sit atop an active section of the San Andreas Fault. Spring is the best time to visit, when wildflowers brighten up the chaparral, but sunlight on the rocks throughout the day creates rainbows of colors year-round. Climbers come during the cool weather.

Though it was Teddy Roosevelt who first utilized presidential decree on behalf on the Pinnacles—protecting it as a national monument in 1906—in early 2000 President Clinton announced plans to expand the park by some 5,000 acres. Some of that acreage, when acquired, may encourage gentler, family-oriented recreation.

Rock climbing is the major attraction, for obvious reasons. But you can also hike. Of Pinnacles' existing (pre-expansion) 16,000-plus acres, nearly 13,000 are protected as wilderness. Only hiking trails connect the park's east and west sides. Some trails are fairly easy, others are rugged; the fit, fast, and willing can hike east to west and back in one (long) day. No camping is offered (or allowed) within the park. The closest private camping is **Pinnacles Campground, Inc.** near the park's entrance on the east side, 2400 Hwy. 146, Paicines, CA 95043, 831/389-4462, www.pinncamp.com, which is quite nice—featuring flush toilets, hot showers, fire rings, picnic tables, swimming pool, some RV hookups, and group facilities. Basic supplies and some food are available at the campground's store.

As lasting testament to the land's rugged nature, there are two districts in the Pinnacles—west and east—and it's not possible to get from one to the other by road. If coming from the west, get visitor information at the **Chaparral Ranger Station,** reached via Hwy. 146 heading east (exit Hwy. 101 just south of Soledad). For most visitors, Pinnacles is most accessible from this route, but it's a narrow road, not recommended for campers and trailers. If coming from the east, stop by the **Bear Gulch Visitor Center,** reached via Hwy. 25 then Hwy. 146 heading west. From Hollister, it's about 34 miles south then about five miles west to the park entrance. Pinnacles is open for day use only; the vehicle entry fee is $5, valid for seven days. Within the monument, bicycles and cars may only be used on paved roads. For additional information, contact: Pinnacles National Monument, 5000 Hwy. 146, Paicines, CA 95043, 831/389-4485, www.nps.gov/pinn/index.htm.

MONTEREY: A NOSTALGIA, A DREAM

In his novel by the same name, local boy John Steinbeck described Monterey's Cannery Row as "a poem, a stink, a grating noise, a quality of light, a tune, a habit, a nostalgia, a dream," also a corrugated collection of sardine canneries, restaurants, honky-tonks, whorehouses, and waterfront laboratories. The street, he said, groaned under the weight of "silver rivers of fish." People here liked his description so much that they eventually put it on a plaque and planted it in today's touristy Cannery Row, among the few Steinbeck-era buildings still standing.

Local promoters claim that the legendary writer would be proud of what the tourist dollar has wrought here, but this seems unlikely. When Steinbeck returned here in 1961 from his self-imposed exile, he noted the clean beaches, "where once they festered with fish guts and flies. The canneries which once put up a sickening stench are gone, their places filled with restaurants, antique shops, and the like. They fish for tourists now, not pilchards, and that species they are not likely to wipe out."

In peak summer months, avoid feeling wiped out yourself—and worrying that you're contributing unduly to the city's visitor-induced chaos—by using Monterey's free WAVE public transit shuttles whenever possible.

The **Monterey Visitor Center,** 401 Camino El Estero, is staffed by the Monterey Peninsula Visitors & Convention Bureau and holds reams of flyers on just about everything in and around the region—including WAVE shuttles and other regional transportation options. It's open Apr.–Oct., Mon.–Sat. 9 A.M.–6 P.M., Sun. 9 A.M.–5 P.M.; Nov.–Mar., Mon.–Sat. 9 A.M.–5 P.M., Sun. 10 A.M.–4 P.M. The Visitor & Convention Bureau also co-sponsors the new **Monterey State Historic Park Visitor Center** at 5 Custom House Plaza, open seven days a week, 10 A.M.–5 P.M. For additional area information, including a current *Monterey County Travel & Meeting Planner,* contact: **Monterey County Convention & Visitors Bureau,** P.O. Box 1770, Monterey, CA 93942-1770, 831/649-1770, fax 831/648-5373, www.monterey.com. For additional information and accommodations reservations, call toll-free 877/666-8387 or try www.877monterey.com.

MONTEREY BAY AQUARIUM

The fish are back on Cannery Row, at least at the west end. Doc's Western Biological Laboratory and the canneries immortalized by Steinbeck may be long gone, but Monterey now has an aquarium that the bohemian biologist would love.

Just down the street from Doc's legendary marine lab, the Monterey Bay Aquarium on Cannery Row is a world-class cluster of fish tanks built into the converted Hovden Cannery. Luring 2.35 million visitors in 1984, its first year, Mon-

sea otter at the Monterey Bay Aquarium

terey's best attraction is the brainchild of marine biologist Nancy Packard and her sister, aquarium director Julie Packard. Much help came from Hewlett-Packard computer magnate David Packard and wife Lucile Packard, who supported this nonprofit, public-education endeavor with a $55 million donation to their daughters' cause. Not coincidentally, Packard also personally designed many of the unique technological features of the major exhibits here. Through the aquarium's foundation, the facility also conducts its own research and environmental education and wildlife rescue programs. The aquarium's trustees, for example, have allocated $10 million for a five-year unmanned underwater exploration and research project in the bay's Monterey Canyon.

The philosophy of the folks at the Monterey Bay Aquarium, most simply summarized as "endorsing human interaction" with the natural world, is everywhere apparent, once inside.

Seeing and Doing the Aquarium
Just inside the aquarium's entrance, serving as an introduction to the **Nearshore Galleries,** is the 55,000-gallon split-level **Sea Otter Tank.** These sleek aquatic clowns consume 25 percent of their body weight in seafood daily. If they're not eating or playing with toys, they're grooming themselves—and with 600,000 hairs per square inch on their pelts, it's easy to understand why otters were so prized by furriers (and hunted almost to extinction). To spot an occasional otter or two slipping into the aquarium over the seawall, or to watch for whales, head for the outdoor observation decks nearby, which include telescopes for bay-watching.

The three-story-tall **Giant Kelp Forest** exhibit, the aquarium's centerpiece and the first underwater forest ever successfully established as a display, offers a diver's-eye view of the undersea world. Dazzling is the only word for the nearby **Anchovies** exhibit, a cylindrical tank full of darting silver shapes demonstrating the "safety in numbers" group-mind philosophy. The 90-foot-long hourglass-shaped **Monterey Bay Habitats** display is a simulated underwater slice of sea life. Sharks roam the deep among the colorful anemones and sea slugs, bat rays glide under the pier with the salmon and mackerel, accompanied by octopi and wolf eels. The craggy-shored

indoor-outdoor **Coastal Stream** exhibit has a steady rhythm all its own and provides a small spawning ground for salmon and steelhead. In the huge **Marine Mammals Gallery** are models of a 43-foot-long barnacled gray whale and her calf, killer whales, dolphins, sea lions, and seals.

Unusual among the predominantly bay-related exhibits, but popular, is the live chambered nautilus in the **Octopus and Kin** exhibit. Also exciting here, in a spine-tingling way, is watching an octopus suction its way across the window. But to really get "in touch" with native underwater life, visit the **Bat Ray Petting Pool,** the **Touch Tidepool** of starfish and anemones, and the **Kelp Lab.** Visitors can stroll through the **Sandy Shore** outdoor aviary to observe shorebirds.

New exhibits are continually added to the Monterey Bay Aquarium. The stunning and relatively new $57 million **Outer Bay Galleries** nearly doubled the aquarium's exhibit space when this new wing opened in early 1996. Devoted to marinelife "at the edge," where Monterey Bay meets the open ocean, the centerpiece exhibit is a one-million-gallon "indoor sea" housing a seven-foot sunfish, sharks, barracuda, stingrays, green sea turtles, and schooling bonito—all seen through the largest aquarium window yet built, an acrylic panel some 15 feet high, 54 feet wide, and weighing 78,000 pounds. Quite visually arresting in the **Drifters Gallery** is the orange and deep-blue **Sea Nettles** jellyfish exhibit, where one might stand and watch the show—something like a giant, pulsing lava lamp—for hours. Equally mesmerizing, on the way into the Outer Bay, is the swirling, endlessly circling stream of silvery mackerel, directly overhead. The best way to watch—you'll notice that young children figure this out immediately—is by lying flat on your back, looking up. The new **Mysteries of the Deep** exhibit studies the often bizarre creatures that inhabit the murky depths.

New at the Monterey Bay Aquarium in spring 2000: the **Splash Zone: Rock and Reef Homes** exhibit designed particularly for families with small children.

Aquarium Tickets, Tours, Information, and Practicalities
Advance tickets are highly recommended, especially in summer. Tickets are available at any Northern California BASS outlet; call 510/762-

PUTTING THE BAY ON DISPLAY

The engineering feats shoring up the amazingly "natural" exhibits in the 322,000-square-foot Monterey Bay Aquarium are themselves impressive. Most remarkable are the aquatic displays, concrete tanks with unbreakable one-ton acrylic windows more than seven inches thick. The exhibits' "wave action" is simulated by a computer-controlled surge machine and hidden water jets. In the Nearshore Galleries, more than a half-million gallons of fresh seawater are pumped through the various aquarium tanks daily to keep these habitats healthy. During the day, six huge "organic" water filters screen out microorganisms that would otherwise cloud the water. At night, filtration shuts down and raw, unfiltered seawater flows through the exhibits— nourishing filter-feeders and also carrying in plant spores and animal larvae that settle and grow, just as they would in nature. The Outer Bay Galleries operate as a "semi-closed" system, with water from the main intake pipes heated to 68°F and recirculated through the exhibits. Wastes are removed by biological filters and ozone treatment, and a heat-recovery system recaptures energy from the water (cools it) before it is discharged into the bay.

In the event of an oil spill or other oceanic disaster, the aquarium's 16-inch intake pipes can be shut down on a moment's notice and the aquarium can operate as a "closed system" for up to two weeks.

2277 or toll-free 800/225-2277 from outside California. You can also order tickets directly from the aquarium, either via the website, www.mbayaq. org, a minimum of nine days in advance (tickets sent by mail), or by calling the aquarium directly toll-free 800/756-3737 or, from outside California 831/648-4888. You can also buy tickets at the aquarium on a just-show-up-and-take-your-chances basis—not advisable in summer.

The aquarium is open daily except Christmas, 10 A.M.–6 P.M. (from 9:30 A.M. in summer). At last report, admission was $15.95 for adults; $12.95 for youths ages 13–17, students with college ID, seniors, and active-duty military; $6.95 for children ages 3–12 and disabled visitors; free for tots under age three.

Free self-guided tour scripts with maps, also available in Spanish, French, German, and Japanese, are available at the aquarium's information desk, along with current "special event" details, including when exhibit feedings are scheduled. All aquarium facilities and exhibits are accessible to the disabled; an explanatory brochure is available at the information desk. Taped audio tours are available for rent (small fee). Docent-guided aquarium tours and tours of the aquarium's research and operations facilities are available, for a fee. (Guided tours for school groups are free, however.) For group tour information and reservations, call 831/648-4860. For additional information, contact: Monterey Bay Aquarium, 886 Cannery Row, Monterey, CA 93940-1085, 831/648-4800 (general switchboard) or 831/648-4888 (24-hour recorded information), fax 831/644-4810. Or visit the "E-Quarium" anytime, for virtual tours and information, at www.mbayaq.org.

To avoid the worst of the human crush, come in the off-season (weekdays if at all possible). If you do come in summer, avoid the traffic jams by riding Monterey's WAVE Shuttle, which operates from late May into September.

CANNERY ROW, FISHERMAN'S WHARF

Searching for Steinbeck on Cannery Row
Today the strip is reminiscent of Steinbeck's Cannery Row only when you consider how tourists are packed in here come summertime: like sardines.

Of all the places the Nobel Prize–winning author immortalized, only "Doc's" marine lab at 800 Cannery Row still stands unchanged—now owned and preserved as a historic site by the city, and open for guided public tours from time to time.

Wing Chong market, Steinbecked as "Lee Chong's Heavenly Flower Grocery," is across the street at 835 Cannery Row and now holds a variety of shops. The fictional "La Ida Cafe" cathouse still survives, too, in actuality the most famous restaurant and salon on the Monterey Peninsula, **Kalisa's** at 851 Cannery Row.

Inside the old Monterey Canning Co. cannery, 700 Cannery Row, wine enthusiasts can enjoy the **Monterey County Wine Country Museum,**

Cannery Row

SUSAN PHILLIPS

and perhaps follow their museum visit with wine-tasting, either at **A Taste of Monterey,** 831/646-5446, which offers tastings of regional wines as well as local produce to sample, or at **Bargetto Winery** downstairs, 831/373-4053.

Wine-tasting or no, adults might escort the kids to the nearby **Monterey County Youth Museum** (M. Y. Museum), 601 Wave St., 831/649-6444 or 831/649-6446, a hands-on adventure full of interactive exhibits on science, art, and more. The museum is open Mon.–Tues. and Thurs.–Sat. 10 A.M.–5 P.M., Sun. noon–5 P.M. (closed Wednesday). Admission is $5.50.

For more information about Cannery Row, or to seriously trace Steinbeck's steps through the local landscape, check in at the Cannery Row Foundation's **Cannery Row Welcome Center,** in the green railroad car at 65 Prescott Ave., 831/372-8512 or 831/373-1902. Guided tours of Cannery Row can also be arranged here. The free and widely available **The Official Cannery Row Visitors Guide** is well done, historically, and quite helpful.

Fisherman's Wharf

Tacky and tawdry, built up and beat up, Fisherman's Wharf is no longer a working wharf by any account. Still, a randy ramshackle charm more honest than Cannery Row surrounds this 1846 pier full of cheap shops, food stalls, decent restaurants, and stand-up bars indiscriminately frosted with gull guano and putrid fish scraps (the latter presumably leftovers from the

$.50 bags tourists buy to feed the sea lions). Built of stone by enslaved natives, convicts, and military deserters when Monterey was Alta California's capital, Fisherman's Wharf was originally a pier for cargo schooners. Later used by whalers and Italian-American fishing crews to unload their catch, the wharf today is bright and bustling, full of eateries and eaters. Come early in the morning to beat the crowds, then launch yourself on a summer sightseeing tour of Monterey Bay or a winter whale-watching cruise.

MONTEREY STATE HISTORIC PARK

Monterey State Historic Park, with headquarters at 20 Custom House Plaza, Monterey, CA 93940, 831/649-7118, www.mbay.net/~mshp, protects and preserves some fine historic adobes, most of which were surrounded at one time by enclosed gardens and walls draped with bougainvillea vines. Definitely worth seeing are the Cooper-Molera, Stevenson, and Larkin homes, as well as Casa Soberanes.

The park is open daily 10 A.M.–4 P.M. (until 5 P.M. in summer), and closed Christmas, Thanksgiving, and New Year's Day. A small all-day admission fee gets you into all buildings open to visitors. Guided tours of particular buildings are offered, as are general guided walking tours; schedules vary, so ask about current tour times. You can also design your own tours. Call for details. To poke around on your own, pick up the free *Path of His-*

Cannery Row

ROBERT HOLMES/CALTOUR

tory self-guided walking-tour map before setting out. Available at most of the buildings, the brochure details the park's adobes as well as dozens of other historic sights near the bay and downtown. Also stop by the Monterey State Historic Park Visitor Center at the Stanton Center.

Stanton Center and the Maritime Museum

A good place to start any historic exploration is the colossal Stanton Center at 5 Custom House Plaza. Inside you'll find the new **Monterey State Historic Park Visitor Center,** where staff can answer questions about the park. They'll also direct you to the center's **theater,** which screens a 17-minute park-produced film about area history—a good way to quickly grasp the area's cultural context. Most walking tours of the park (led by state park staff) also leave from the Stanton Center. Buy guided walking tour tickets here, as well as tickets for the adjacent maritime museum. The Stanton Visitor Center is open seven days a week, 10 A.M.–5 P.M. For state historic park information, call 831/649-7118 or try the web at www.mbay.net/~mshp. For visitor information, call 831/648-5373.

Don't miss the Monterey History and Art Association's **Maritime Museum of Monterey,** 831/375-2553 or 831/373-2469, which houses an ever-expanding local maritime artifact collection—compasses, bells, ship models, the original Fresnel lens from the Point Sur lighthouse, and much more—as well as the association's maritime research library, an acclaimed ship photography collection, and a scrimshaw collection. The museum's permanent exhibits, many interactive, cover local maritime history from the first explorers and cannery days to the present. Open daily 10 A.M.–5 P.M., closed Thanksgiving, Christmas, and New Year's Day. It's not technically part of the state park, so a separate admission is charged—$5 adults, $4 seniors/military, $3 youth, $2 children.

Custom House and Pacific House

On July 7, 1846, Commodore John Drake Sloat raised the Stars and Stripes here at Alvarado and Waterfront Sts., commemorating California's passage into American rule. The Custom House Building is the oldest government building on the West Coast—and quite multinational, since it has flown at one time or another the flags of Spain, Mexico, and the United States. Until 1867, customs duties from foreign ships were collected here. Today you can inspect typical 19th-century cargo and try to reason with the parrot in residence.

Once a hotel, then a military supply depot, the building at Scott and Calle Principal was called Pacific House when it housed a public tavern in 1850. Later came law offices, a newspaper, a ballroom for "dashaway" temperance dances, and various small shops. Today the newly renovated Pacific House includes an excellent museum of Native American artifacts (with special attention given to the Ohlone people) and interactive historical exhibits covering

MONTEREY'S DISTINCTIVE ARCHITECTURE

Monterey State Historic Park's **Larkin House,** a two-story redwood frame with low shingled roof, adobe walls, and wooden balconies skirting the 2nd floor, and the **Cooper-Molera Adobe** are both good examples of the "Monterey colonial" architectural style—a marriage of Yankee woodwork and Mexican adobe—that evolved here. Most traditional Monterey adobes have south-facing patios to absorb sun in winter and a northern veranda to catch cool summer breezes. On the 1st floor were the kitchen, storerooms, dining room, living room, and sometimes even a ballroom. The bedrooms on the 2nd floor were entered from outside stairways, a tradition subsequently abandoned. Also distinctive in Monterey are the "swept gardens"—dirt courtyards surrounded by colorful flowers under pine canopies—which were an adaptation to the originally barren home sites.

That so many fine adobes remain in Monterey today is mostly due to genteel local poverty; until recently, few developers with grandiose plans came knocking on the door. For an even better look at traditional local adobes and their gardens, come to the **Monterey Historic Adobe and Garden Tour** in April, when many private adobes are open for public tours.

the city's Spanish whaling industry, pioneer/logging periods, California statehood, and more.

Larkin House and Others

Built of adobe and wood in 1835 by Yankee merchant Thomas Oliver Larkin, this home at Jefferson and Calle Principal became the American consulate, then later military headquarters for Kearny, Mason, and Sherman. A fine pink Monterey adobe and the model for the local colonial style, Larkin House is furnished with more than $6 million in antiques and period furnishings.

The home and headquarters of William Tecumseh Sherman is next door; it's now a museum focusing on both Larkin and Sherman. Around the corner at 540 Calle Principal, another Larkin building, the **House of the Four Winds,** is a small adobe built in the 1830s and named for its weathervane. The **Gutierrez Adobe,** a typical middle-class Monterey "double adobe" home at 580 and 590 Calle Principal, was built in 1841 and later donated to the state by the Monterey Foundation.

Cooper-Molera Adobe

The long, two-story Monterey colonial adobe *casa grande* ("big house") at 508 Munras Ave. was finished in pinkish plaster when constructed

THE *CALIFORNIAN*

Sample some early California history before the mast. Though home port is now in Long Beach, the 145-foot **Tall Ship Californian,** the state's official tall ship, occasionally offers four-hour day sails on Monterey Bay. The trip includes lunch and lectures, and the fee is $75 per person. The *Californian* also offers private charters, five-day Cadet Cruises (for ages 14–19), and three- and four-day hands-on High Sea Adventures for adults, and spends part of each year in San Francisco, Long Beach, and San Diego. Crew positions are sometimes available.

The *Californian* is a re-creation of the first U.S. cutter to patrol the Pacific coast during the bad and bawdy gold rush, the 1848 **C. W. Lawrence** (in service to the U.S. Revenue Service, precursor of the U.S. Coast Guard), built in Washington, D.C. Since America's revenuers now typically enlist computers instead of ships to track down scofflaws, the *Californian* is free to serve as an international goodwill ambassador—circling the Pacific Rim each year, visiting Canada, Mexico, and closer ports, as well as occasionally (such as during the 1984 Olympics) leading the Tall Ships Festival parade and embarking on other international adventures. Appropriately enough, Queen Calafia, the imagined matriarchal monarch of the island paradise of California, is enthroned as the ship's figurehead.

For current details and advance reservations, contact: **The Nautical Heritage Society,** 1064 Calle Negocio, Unit B, San Clemente, CA 92673, 949/369-6773 or toll-free 800/432-2201 (reservations only), www.californian.org.

California's first theatre

TOM MYERS PHOTOGRAPHY

in 1829 by Captain John Bautista Rogers Cooper for his young bride, Encarnación (of California's influential Vallejo clan). The 2.5-acre complex, which includes a neighboring home, two barns, and a visitors center, has been restored to its 19th-century authenticity.

Robert Louis Stevenson House

The sickly Scottish storyteller and poet lived at the French Hotel adobe boardinghouse at 530 Houston St. for several months in 1879 while courting his American love (and later wife), Fanny Osbourne. The restored downstairs is stuffed with period furniture. Several upstairs rooms are dedicated to Stevenson's memorabilia, paintings, and first editions. Local rumor has it that a 19th-century ghost—Stevenson's spirit, according to a previous caretaker—lives upstairs in the children's room.

Casa Soberanes

This is an 1830 Mediterranean-style adobe with tile roof and cantilevered balcony, hidden by thick hedges at 336 Pacific. Home to the Soberanes family from 1860 to 1922, it was later donated to the state. Take the tour or just stop to appreciate the garden and abalone-bordered flower beds, some encircled by century-old glass bottles buried bottoms up.

California's First Theater

First a sailors' saloon and lodging house, this small 1844 weathered wood and adobe building at Scott and Pacific was built by the English sailor Jack Swan. It was commandeered by soldiers in 1848 for a makeshift theater, and later—with a lookout station added to the roof—became a whaling station. Today, a local theater troupe presents melodramas here year-round on Fri. and Sat. nights; for information and reservations, call 831/375-4916.

Casa del Oro

Built by Thomas Larkin at the corner of Scott and Olivier as part of his business empire, this two-story chalk and adobe building later served a number of purposes. At one time or another it was a barracks for American troops, a general store (Joseph Boston & Co.), a saloon, and a private residence. Rumors have it that this "house of gold" was once a mint, or that (when a saloon) it accepted gold dust in payment for drinks—thus the name.

Whaling Station

The old two-story adobe Whaling Station at 391 Decatur St. near the Custom House, now a private home, was a flophouse for Portuguese whalers in the 1850s. Tours are sometimes available (call the main state park number for information), and include access to the walled garden. Whale lovers, walk softly; the sidewalk in front of the house is made of whalebone.

California's First Brick House

This building nearby at 351 Decatur was started by

Gallant Duncan Dickenson in 1847, built with bricks fashioned and fired in Monterey. The builder left for the goldfields before the house was finished, so the home—the first brick house built in California—and 60,000 bricks were auctioned off by the sheriff in 1851 for just over $1,000.

OTHER MONTEREY SIGHTS

Colton Hall

The Reverend Walter Colton, Monterey's first American alcalde, or local magistrate, built this impressive, pillared "Carmel Stone" structure at 351 Pacific, 831/646-5640, as a schoolhouse and public hall. Colton and Robert Semple published the first American newspaper in California here, cranking up the presses on August 15, 1846. California's constitutional convention took place here during September and October of 1849, and the state constitution was drafted upstairs in Colton Hall.

Next door is the 1854 **Monterey jail** (entrance on Dutra St.), a dreary, slot-windowed prison once home to gentleman-bandit Tiburcio Vasquez and killer Anastacio Garcia, who "went to God on a rope" pulled by his buddies.

Monterey Museum of Art

This fine Monterey Museum of Art at 559 Pacific, 831/372-7591, is near many local historic sites and offers an excellent collection of Western art, including bronze cowboy-and-horse statues by Charles M. Russell. The Fine Arts collection includes photography and Asian art and artifacts. Also here: folk art plus high-concept graphics, photography, paintings, sculpture, and other contemporary art in changing exhibits. Open Tues.–Sat. 10 A.M.–4 P.M., Sun. 1–4 P.M., closed holidays. Free, technically, but a $2 donation is requested. Associated with the art museum is the amazing **La Mirada.**

Casa Amesti and La Mirada

If you're in Monterey on a weekend, be sure to tour **Casa Amesti,** 516 Polk St., a genteel Monterey colonial stylishly updated in the 1920s by Frances Adler Elkins, a noted West Coast interior designer whose other projects included the International House at UC Berkeley and the Royal Hawaiian Hotel in Honolulu. The sensibility here

is royal, relaxed, and European without the velvet and gilt. Open to the public on Sat. and Sun., 2–4 P.M. Small admission fee, children under age 12 free. For information, contact the Monterey History and Art Association, 831/372-2608.

Another impressive Monterey-style adobe also open to the public on a limited basis is **La Mirada,** the Castro Adobe and Frank Work Estate at 720 Via Mirada, 831/372-3689. Affiliated with the Monterey Museum of Art, the home is exquisite. The original adobe portion was the residence of Jose Castro, one of the most prominent citizens in California during the Mexican period. Purchased in 1919 by Gouverneur Morris—author/playwright and descendant of the same-named Revolutionary War figure—the adobe was restored and expanded, with the addition of a two-story wing and huge drawing room, to host artists and Hollywood stars. These days, the 2.5-acre estate overlooking El Estero still reflects the elegance of a bygone era. The house itself is furnished in antiques and early California art, and the gardens are perhaps even more elegant, at least in season. La Mirada is open Wed.–Sat. 11 A.M– 5 P.M., Sun. 1–4 P.M. Call for current tour information. Small admission, but free on the first Sun. of every month.

Monterey Institute of International Studies

This prestigious, private, and nonprofit graduate-level college headquartered at 425 Van Buren, 831/647-4100, specializes in foreign-language instruction. Students here prepare for careers in international business and government, and in language translation and interpretation. Fascinating and unique is the school's 200-seat auditorium, set up for simultaneous translations of up to four languages. Visitors are welcome Mon.–Fri. 8:30 A.M.–5 P.M., and most of the institute's programs—including guest lectures—are open to the public.

Presidio of Monterey

One of the nation's oldest military posts, the Presidio of Monterey is the physical focal point of most local history, though the original complex, founded by Portolá in 1770, was located in the area now defined by Webster, Fremont, Abrego, and El Estero Streets. Also here: incredible panoramic views of Monterey Bay. The **U.S. Army Museum,** in Building 113, 831/242-8414, once a tack house, is now filled with cavalry

Head to the harbor for a sport fishing excursion.

TOM MYERS PHOTOGRAPHY

artifacts, uniforms, pistols, cannons, photos, posters, and dioramas about the history of the army and the Presidio. Call before coming; the museum had been closed for a long period, but should be reopened by now. The main gate at Pacific and Artillery Sts. leads to the **Defense Language Institute,** 831/242-5000.

Royal Presidio Chapel

Originally established as a mission by. Father Junípero Serra in June 1770, this building at 555 Church St. near Figueroa became the Royal Presidio Chapel of San Carlos Borromeo when the mission was relocated to Carmel. The chapel was rebuilt from stone in 1791, and after secularization in 1835, it became the San Carlos Cathedral, a parish church. The cathedral's interior walls are decorated with Native American and Mexican folk art. Above, the upper gable facade is the first European art made in California, a chalk-carved Virgin of Guadalupe tucked into a shell niche. To get here, turn into Church St. just after Camino El Estero ends at Fremont—a district once known as Washerwoman's Gulch.

STAYING IN MONTEREY: MOTELS AND HOTELS

Monterey is so close to the neighboring communities of Pacific Grove, Carmel, and Carmel Valley, not to mention its own sand-dune suburbs, that peninsula visitors with cars can conveniently plan to stay and eat throughout the area. Current complete listings of accommodations (including prices) and restaurants in Monterey proper are available free from the convention and visitors bureau. Discounts of 50 percent or more are available at many inns, hotels, and motels during off-season promotions.

For assistance in booking midrange to high-end accommodations in and around Monterey, for individuals or groups, contact **Resort II Me Room Finders,** 2600 Garden Rd. #11, Monterey, CA 93940, 831/646-9250, 831/642-6622, or toll-free 800/757-5646, fax 831/642-6641, www.resort2me.com, a firm with a good track record in matching peninsula visitors with appropriate local lodgings. Also a best bet is **Time to Coast Reservations** 1855 Gateway Blvd. #630, Concord, CA 94520, toll-free 800/555-9283, fax 925/671-4044, www.timetocoast.com.

ACCOMMODATIONS RATINGS

Accommodations in this book are rated by price category, based on double-occupancy, high-season rates. Categories used are:

Budget.	$35 and under
Inexpensive	$35-60
Moderate	$60-85
Expensive	$85-110
Premium	$110-150
Luxury	$150 and up

CARMEL VALLEY AND PENINSULA WINERIES

Not surprising in such a moderate Mediterranean climate, vineyards do well here. So do wineries and wines, recognized as eight distinct appellations. To keep up with them all, pick up the free **Monterey Wine Country** brochure and map at area visitors centers, or contact the **Monterey County Vintners & Growers Association,** P.O. Box 1793, Monterey, CA 93942-1793, 831/375-9400, www.montereywines.org. Wine-related events well worth showing up for include the **Annual Winemakers' Celebration** in August and **The Great Wine Escape Weekend** in November. If you're short on touring time this trip, many Monterey County wines are available for tasting at **A Taste of Monterey,** 700 Cannery Row in Monterey, 831/646-5446, www.tastemonterey.com, open daily 11 A.M.–6 P.M.

The very small **Chateau Julien Winery,** 8940 Carmel Valley Rd., Carmel, CA 95923, 831/624-2600, www.chateaujulien.com, is housed in a French-style château and is open daily with tours on weekdays. The winery's chardonnay and merlot have both been honored as the best in the United States at the American Wine Championships in New York. Southwest of Carmel Valley and bordering Los Padres National Forest is the remote spring-fed "boutique" **Durney Vineyards,** owned by William Durney and his wife, screenwriter Dorothy Kingsley. The winery is not open to the public, but these organic wines are available for tasting in Carmel Valley Village at 69 W. Carmel Valley Rd., 831/659-6220 or toll-free 800/625-8466, and are widely sold in Carmel, Monterey, and vicinity.

Bernardus Winery's tasting room, 5 W. Carmel Valley Rd., 831/659-1900, www.bernardus.com, is open for tasting 11 A.M.–5 P.M. daily. Also look around for other premium small-production wines, such as **Joullian Vineyards** (cabernet sauvignon, sauvignon blanc, merlot, zinfandel, and chardonnay). Joullian's new winery visitors center, located at 20300 Cachagua Rd., 831/659-2800, is open for tasting and sales Mon.–Fri. 11 A.M.–3 P.M., excluding holidays.

Between Greenfield and Soledad along the inland Hwy. 101 corridor are a handful of good wineries. The 1978 private reserve cabernet sauvignon of **Jekel Vineyards,** 40155 Walnut Ave., Greenfield, CA 93927, 831/674-5522 or 831/674-5525 (tasting room), washed out Lafite-Rothschild and other international competitors in France in 1982. Tasting daily 10 A.M.–5 P.M. (appointments needed for tours or for groups of six or more). **Smith & Hook Winery-Hahn Estates** 37700 Foothill Blvd., Soledad, CA 93960, 831/678-2132, www.hahnestates.com, is known for its cabernet sauvignon—also for the amazing view across the Salinas Valley to the Gabilan Mountains. Open daily 11 A.M.–4 P.M., tours by appointment. Also in the area: **Chalone Vineyard** on Stonewall Canyon Rd. (Hwy. 146), 831/678-1717, www.chalonewinegroup.com, the county's oldest vineyard and winery, known for its estate-bottled varietals; and noted **Paraiso Springs Vineyard,** 38060 Paraiso Springs Rd., 831/678-0300, www.usawines.com/paraiso, open for tasting Mon.–Fri. noon–4 P.M., Sat.–Sun. 11 A.M.–5 P.M. (tours by appointment).

Farther north is small **Cloninger Cellars,** 1645 River Rd., Salinas, CA 93908, 831/675-9463, www.usawines.com/cloninger, which offers chardonnay, pinot noir, and cabernet sauvignon in its tasting room. Open for tasting Fri.–Mon. 11 A.M.–5 P.M., Tues.–Thurs. by appointment. Also worth popping into in Salinas is **Morgan Winery,** 590 Brunken Ave., 831/751-7777, www.morganwinery.com, which has garnered a glut of gold medals and other recognition for its chardonnays. Winners here, too, are the cabernet, pinot noir, and sauvignon blanc.

True wine fanatics must make one more stop—at America's most award-winning vineyard, **Ventana Vineyards,** 2999 Monterey-Salinas Hwy. (near the Monterey Airport just outside Monterey on Hwy. 68), 831/372-7415, www.ventanawines.com. Open daily 11 A.M.–6 P.M.

Inexpensive and Moderate Stays

Not many motel choices in Monterey are truly inexpensive. You might try the 15-room **Driftwood Motel,** 2362 N. Fremont, 831/372-5059, where pets are possible, and the **Econo Lodge,** 2042 Fremont St., 831/372-5851, fax 831/372-4228, with pool and spa, free continental breakfast, and some rooms with kitchenettes. Both are basic but pleasant, quite comfortable for anyone sticking to the family budget, and real deals in the off-season.

Most lower-priced motels fall into the Moderate category, including the **Motel 6,** 2124 N. Fremont, 831/646-8585, which is clean, has a pool, and isn't far from the downtown action. As a result, it's popular; make reservations six months or more in advance or stop by at 11 A.M. or so to check for cancellations. Another Motel 6 in the same price range (just a bit less expensive) is just outside Monterey proper, at 100 Reservation Rd. in Marina, 831/384-1000.

Quite nice, quite reasonably priced, and surprisingly homey are the locally owned Comfort Inns on Munras Avenue. **Comfort Inn-Carmel Hill,** 1252 Munras Ave., 831/372-2908, fax 831/372-7608, features just 30 cheery rooms with the usual amenities and electronic door locks. Adjacent is the **Comfort Inn-Munras,** 1262 Munras, 831/372-8088, fax 831/373-5829. Both are Moderate-Expensive, and both are close enough—but not too close—to local attractions, especially if you're looking forward to some vigorous walking. Directly across the way, flanking Munras all the way back downtown to its junction with Abrego, is long, narrow **Dan Dahvee Park,** with its pleasant trees, flowers, birds—and walking paths.

Other Moderate motel options include the 15-room **El Dorado Inn,** 900 Munras, 831/373-2921; the **West Wind Lodge,** 1046 Munras Ave., 831/373-1337 or toll-free 800/821-0805, fax 831/372-2451, with an indoor heated pool; and the very nice **Best Western Park Crest Motel,** 1100 Munras, 831/372-4576 or toll-free 800/528-1234, fax 831/372-2317, where rooms include in-room coffee and refrigerators and extras include TVs with free HBO, pool, hot tub, and free continental breakfast. There are also a number of good motels off Fremont.

Expensive Stays

Centrally located, near Hwy. 1 within easy reach of all area towns, is the **Bay Park Hotel,** 1425 Munras, 831/649-1020 or toll-free 800/338-3564, fax 831/373-4258, featuring in-room coffeemakers and on-site extras including a restaurant, pool, and hot tub. The nonsmoking **Best Western Monterey Inn,** 825 Abrego, 831/373-5345 or toll-free 800/528-1234, fax 831/373-3246, is quite pleasant, with 80 spacious rooms, some with fireplaces, all with in-room coffeemakers and refrigerators. Seasonally heated pool, hot tub.

Best bets on Fremont include the **Scottish Fairway Motel,** 2075 Fremont St., 831/373-5551 or toll-free 800/373-5571, fax 831/373-4250, where kitchens and kitchenettes are available, and the **Travelodge-Monterey/Carmel,** 2030 N. Fremont, 831/373-3381, fax 831/649-8741.

Premium Stays

With a delightful Old World ambience, right downtown, the refurbished and fashionable **Monterey Hotel,** 406 Alvarado St., Monterey, CA 93940, 831/375-3184 or toll-free for reservations 800/727-0960, fax 831/373-2899, www.montereyhotel.com, comfortably combines the best features of hotels with a bed-and-breakfast feel. This graceful 1904 Victorian is classic yet contemporary, with custom-made armoires (with TV sets), telephones, private baths with tub showers, antiques, queen-sized beds, and tasteful yet subtle decorating touches. The only inconvenience presented by a stay at the Monterey Hotel is lack of on-site parking. But an inexpensive city lot (rarely full) is nearby. Rooms are Premium, suites are Luxury.

Offering good value in comfortable accommodations on acres of lovely landscape is the **Casa Munras Garden Hotel,** 700 Munras, 831/375-2411 or toll-free 800/222-2446 in California, 800/222-2558 nationwide, fax 831/375-1365, conveniently located close to historic downtown. Another good deal, right downtown, is the attractive and accommodating **Colton Inn,** 707 Pacific, 831/649-6500 or toll-free 800/848-7007, fax 831/373-6987, where extras include a sauna and sundeck. The comfortable **Doubletree Hotel at Fisherman's Wharf,** 2 Portola Plaza (adjacent to the Convention Center downtown at Pacific and Del Monte), 831/649-4511 or toll-free 800/222-8733 (reservations), fax 831/372-0620, boasts 380 rooms and is convenient to just about everything.

Luxury Stays

For definite bayside luxury, head for the 290-room, Craftsman-style **Monterey Plaza Hotel & Spa,** 400 Cannery Row, 831/646-1700, or toll-free 800/334-3999 in California, 800/631-1339 from elsewhere in the U.S., fax 831/646-5937, www.woodsidehotels.com. The Monterey Plaza's fine accommodations include Italian Empire and 18th-century Chinese furnishings and every convenience.

Also deluxe, downtown, is the contemporary,

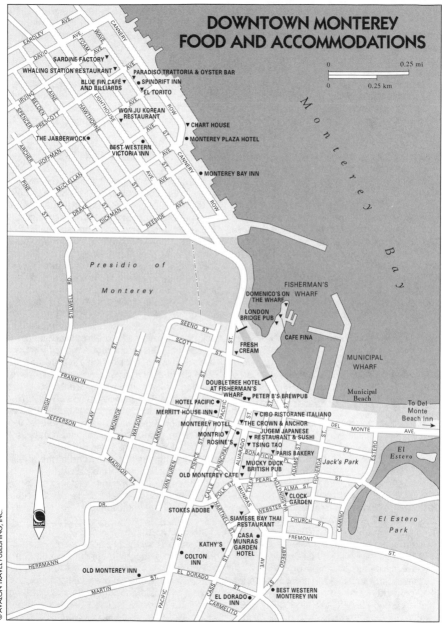

DOWNTOWN MONTEREY
FOOD AND ACCOMMODATIONS

faux-adobe-style **Hotel Pacific,** 300 Pacific, 831/373-5700 or toll-free 800/232-4141, fax 831/373-6921, www.hotelpacific.com. All rooms are suites and feature hardwood floors, separate sitting areas, balconies or decks, fireplaces, wet bars, in-room coffeemakers, irons and ironing boards—the works. Continental breakfast, afternoon tea, free underground parking.

Surprisingly appealing on Cannery Row is the **Spindrift Inn,** a onetime bordello at 652 Cannery Row (at Hawthorne), 831/646-8900, toll-free 800/841-1879, fax 831/646-5342, www.spindriftinn.com. Rooms feature hardwood floors, wood-burning fireplaces, TVs with VCRs, and every imaginable amenity—including a second telephone in the (tiled) bathrooms.

The huge (575-room) **Hyatt Regency Monterey Resort and Conference Center,** 1 Old Golf Course Rd., 831/372-1234 or toll-free 800/824-2196 or 800/233-1234, is definitely a resort; the spacious grounds here include an 18-hole golf course, six tennis courts (extra fee for both), two pools, whirlpools, fitness center—the works. The sports bar here, **Knuckles,** offers 200 satellite channels and 11 TV monitors.

MONTEREY BED-AND-BREAKFASTS

Monterey's showcase country inn is the gorgeous ivy-covered 1929 English Tudor **Old Monterey Inn,** 500 Martin St., 831/375-8284 or toll-free 800/350-2344, fax 831/375-6730, www.oldmontereyinn.com, featuring 10 elegant rooms and suites, most with fireplaces. All have sitting areas, featherbeds, CD players, a hot tub for two, and special touches such as skylights and stained glass. Marvelous full breakfasts, sunset wine hour. Luxury.

The Jabberwock, 598 Laine St., 831/372-4777 or toll-free 888/428-7253, fax 831/655-2946, www.jabberwockinn.com, is a seven-room "post-Victorian" with a Victorian name and an Alice-Through-the-Looking-Glass sensibility. Some rooms share baths. Rates include full breakfast (imaginative and good) plus cookies and milk at night. Premium-Luxury.

A classic in inimitable Monterey style is the historic **Merritt House Inn,** downtown at 386 Pacific St., 831/646-9686 or toll-free 800/541-5599, fax 831/646-5392, www.merritthouseinn.com.

The original adobe, built in 1830, features three suites with 19th-century sensibility and modern bathrooms. The 22 surrounding rooms are more contemporary. Premium-Luxury.

At the European-style **Del Monte Beach Inn,** 1110 Del Monte Ave., 831/649-4410, fax 831/375-3818, most of the rooms share baths—which means this place is affordable for people who don't normally do B&Bs. Rates include continental breakfast. Inexpensive-Expensive.

EATING IN MONTEREY

In Monterey, eating well *and* fairly inexpensively is easier than finding low-cost lodgings. Hard to beat is picnicking at the beaches or local parks. Happy hour, at the wharf and on "the Row" and elsewhere, is a big deal in the area. In addition to cheap drinks, many bars serve good (free) food from 4–7 P.M. With an abundance of reasonably priced (and generous) breakfast places, an inexpensive alternative to three meals a day is skipping lunch (or packing simple picnic fare), then shopping around for early-bird dinners, a mainstay at many local restaurants. Do-it-yourselfers can pick up whatever suits their culinary fancy at the open-air **Old Monterey Marketplace Certified Farmers' Market** on Alvarado St. at Pearl, held every Tues. night 3–8 P.M. year-round (until 7 P.M. in winter). Great food, great fun. For more information, call 831/665-8070.

No doubt helped along by the abundance of fresh regional produce, seafood, cheese and other dairy products, poultry, and meats, the Monterey Peninsula has also become a sophisticated dining destination. Some of the area's great restaurants are listed below (in various categories), but to get a true "taste" of the Monterey Peninsula, consider dining as well in nearby Pacific Grove and Carmel.

Monterey Standards

By "standard," we mean places people can happily—and affordably—frequent. The **Old Monterey Cafe,** 489 Alvarado, 831/646-1021, serves all kinds of omelettes at breakfast plus unusual choices like calamari and eggs, linguiça and eggs, and pigs in a blanket. Fresh-squeezed juices; espresso and cappuccino bar. Just about everything is good at lunch, too. Open daily for breakfast and lunch, 7 A.M.–2:30 P.M., breakfast served until closing. **Rosine's**, nearby at 434 Alvarado, 831/375-1400, is locally loved at breakfast, lunch, and dinner.

Still reasonable (and delicious) is **Kathy's**, 700 Cass St., 831/647-9540. Pick any three items for a fluffy omelette; includes home fries, cheese sauce, bran muffins, and homemade strawberry jam for around $5. Sandwiches, similarly priced, are best when eaten on the patio. For a casual lunch, dinner, or Sunday jazz brunch, the **Clock Garden**, 565 Abrego, 831/375-6100, is a popular place. Guests sit outside amid the antique clocks planted in the garden, weather permitting. Closed Sunday evening.

In Seaside, the **Fishwife Seafood Cafe**, 789 Trinity (at Fremont), 831/394-2027, offers quick and interesting seafood, pastas, and house-made desserts. (There's another Fishwife near Asilomar.) For exceptional ethnic eats, consider the Salvadoran **El Migueleño**, also in Seaside at 1066 Broadway, 831/899-2199. The house specialty, Playa Azul, combines six different kinds of seafood with ranchera sauce, white wine, and mushrooms, served with white rice and beans. For Chinese, there's **Yen Ching**, 1868 Fremont St., 831/899-7800. While you're in the general area—which also includes Marina, up the coast—scout around for other intriguing possibilities.

Back in Monterey, Thai food fanatics should try **Siamese Bay Thai Restaurant**, 131 Webster St., 831/373-1550. For Asian, two possibilities are quite close to each other—**Tsing Tao China Restaurant**, 429 Alvarado St., 831/375-3000, and **Jugem Japanese Restaurant & Sushi**, 409 Alvarado St., 831/373-6463. Both are open for lunch and dinner. Or head for **Won Ju Korean Restaurant**, 570 Lighthouse Ave., 831/656-0672.

Monterey Pubs

For fans of British pubs, the real deal in Monterey is **The Crown & Anchor**, 150 W. Franklin St., 831/649-6496, dark and inviting, with a brassy seagoing air, where the full bar features 20 beers on tap. But the food is pretty darn good, and reasonably priced—from the fish and chips or bangers and mash to spicy meatloaf, curries, and cottage pie. There's a special menu for the "powder monkeys" (Brit sailor slang for kids). Open for lunch and dinner daily. Also consider

the **London Bridge Pub**, Fisherman's Wharf #2, 831/655-2879, which specializes in authentic British cuisine and pours more than 60 different beers to wash it down with, and the **Mucky Duck British Pub**, 479 Alvarado, 831/655-3031.

With a logo depicting a one-eyed jack doing the proverbial 12-ounce curl, **Peter B's Brewpub**, 2 Portola Plaza (in the alley behind the Doubletree Hotel), 831/649-4511, offers 10 different Carmel Brewing Co. microbrews on tap and good pub grub.

Eating at the Wharf

Domenico's on the Wharf, 50 Fisherman's Wharf #1, 831/372-3655, is famous for its Southern Italian accent. The menu features fresh seafood, homemade pasta, chicken, steak, and veal dishes, and a long, very California wine list. Oyster bar open from 10 A.M. daily.

But **Cafe Fina**, 47 Fisherman's Wharf #1, 831/372-5200, is probably the best bet on the wharf—very Italian, and very lively and lighthearted. On the menu you'll find everything from mesquite-barbecued fish and beef to smoked salmon on fettuccine with shallot cream sauce and a goat cheese and black olive ravioli. People go crazy over Cafe Fina's "pizzettes," little eight-inch pizzas popped hot out of the restaurant's wood-burning oven.

Eating on Cannery Row

If you're spending most of the day at the Monterey Aquarium, try the **Portola Café and Restaurant** there. Or head out onto the Row. Many of the places along Cannery Row offer early-bird dinners, so if price matters, go deal-shopping before you get hungry.

Get your margarita fix and decent Mexican fare at **El Torito**, 600 Cannery Row, 831/373-0611. For something simple, an interesting choice for "views, brews, and cues" is the **Blue Fin Café and Billiards**, 685 Cannery Row, 831/375-7000. In addition to salads, sandwiches, and full dinners, the Blue Fin boasts a full bar emphasizing bourbons and scotches, and also serves some 40 beers, including 22 ales and lagers on tap. There's plenty to do besides eat and drink, too, thanks to 18 pool tables, snooker, foosball, darts, and shuffleboard.

Naturally enough, seafood is the predominant dinner theme along the Row. The **Chart House**,

444 Cannery Row, 831/372-3362, brings its trademark casually elegant, nautical-themed decor to the Row, serving primarily seafood, steaks, and prime rib—predictably tasty. Full bar.

A bit inland but still looking to the sea for inspiration is TV chef John Pisto's casual **Whaling Station Restaurant,** 763 Wave, 831/373-3778, another locally popular dinner house offering everything from seafood and house-made pastas to mesquite-grilled Black Angus steaks. Full bar. Open daily. Pisto's newest outpost is right on the Row: **Paradiso Trattoria & Oyster Bar,** 654 Cannery Row, 831/375-4155, open daily for lunch and dinner, serving fresh California-style Mediterranean. Full bar, and an extensive Monterey County wine list.

The exceptional, semiformal **Sardine Factory,** 701 Wave St., 831/373-3775, serves California-style regional fare, from seafood and steaks to pasta and other specialties. Full bar. Open daily for dinner.

Another upscale Row restaurant going for the nautical theme is **Schooners Bistro on the Bay,** 400 Cannery Row (at the Monterey Plaza Hotel), 831/372-2628, specializing in California cuisine at lunch and dinner. If a bistro isn't chi-chi enough for you, consider the hotel's renowned but still casual **Duck Club Restaurant,** 831/646-1706, which serves outstanding bay views and superb American regional cuisine for breakfast and dinner daily.

Stylish Dining

Fresh Cream, across from Fisherman's Wharf and upstairs at Heritage Harbor, 99 Pacific St., 831/375-9798, has wonderful French country cuisine lightened by that fresh California touch— one of the Monterey Peninsula's best restaurants, more formal than most. Great views of Monterey Bay are served, too. Expensive, but even travelers light in the pocketbook can afford dessert and coffee. Open for dinner only, menu changes daily. Call for information and reservations.

Still the contemporary dining hot spot downtown is the relaxed all-American bistro **Montrio,** 414 Calle Principal (at Franklin), 831/648-8880, *Esquire* magazine's new restaurant of the year in 1995. You might start with fire-roasted artichokes, terrine of eggplant, or Dungeness crab cakes, then continue with grilled gulf prawns, lamb tenderloins, or Black Angus New York steak. Vegetarians can dig into the oven-roasted portobello mushroom over polenta and veggie ragout. At last report, Monday was still cioppino night. Marvelous sandwiches at lunch and exquisite desserts. Full bar, great wine list. Open Mon.–Sat. for lunch, daily for dinner.

Equally stylish is the historic 1833 **Stokes Adobe,** 500 Hartnell St. (at Madison), 831/373-1110, its exteriors—including the gardens—preserving that Monterey colonial style, its interiors beautifully recast with terra-cotta floors, plank ceilings, and a light, airy ambience. But the food is the thing. On the menu here is rustic, refined, and reasonably affordable California-style Mediterranean, from savory soups and salads to seafood, chicken, lamb, and beef. Full bar, good wines. Open for lunch and dinner daily.

Serving up stylish "American country" fare, **Tarpy's Roadhouse** inside the historic stone Ryan Ranch homestead, three miles off Hwy. 1 on Hwy. 68 (at Canyon del Rey), 831/647-1444, is not to be confused with some cheap-eats-and-beer joint. The culinary challenge here is reinterpreting American classics—and that's no inexpensive task. Dinner includes such things as Indiana duck, Dijon-crusted lamb loin, baby back ribs, and grilled vegetables with succotash. Great desserts. Salads and sandwiches at lunch. Full bar. Open for lunch and dinner daily, brunch on Sunday.

PACIFIC GROVE AND VICINITY

Pacific Grove began in 1875 as a prim, proper tent city founded by Methodists who, Robert Louis Stevenson observed, "come to enjoy a life of teetotalism, religion, and flirtation." No boozing, waltzing, zither playing, or reading Sunday newspapers was allowed. Dedicated inebriate John Steinbeck lived here for many years, in the next century, but had to leave town to get drunk. Pacific Grove was the last "dry" town in California: alcohol has been legal here only since 1969.

Nicknamed "Butterfly City U.S.A." in honor of migrating monarchs (a big fine and/or six months in jail is the penalty for "molesting" one), Pacific Grove sparkles with Victorians and modest sea-

TOM MYERS PHOTOGRAPHY

Pacific Grove's surf

coast cottages, community pride, a rocky shoreline with wonderful tidepools, and an absolutely uncommercial Butterfly Parade in October. Also here is Asilomar, a well-known state-owned conference center with its own beautiful beach. Pacific Grove boasts more than 75 local art galleries, enough to keep anyone busy. The **Penin-** **sula Potters Gallery,** 2078 Sunset Dr., 831/372-8867, is the place to appreciate the potter's art; open Mon.–Sat. 10 A.M.–4 P.M. Also worth stopping for is the **Pacific Grove Art Center,** 568 Lighthouse, 831/375-2208.

For events, accommodations, restaurants, and other current information, stop by the **Pacific**

MONTEREY PENINSULA GOLFING

Golfers from around the globe make a point of arriving on the Monterey Peninsula, clubs in tow, at some time in their lives. The undisputed golf capital of the world, the Pebble Beach area between Carmel and Pacific Grove is the most famous, largely due to "The Crosby," which is now the AT&T Pebble Beach National Pro Am Golf Tournament. Making headlines in 1999 was news that the Pebble Beach Company and its four world-class courses had been sold to an investor group—Clint Eastwood, Richard Ferris, Arnold Palmer, and Peter Ueberroth—for $820 million.

It may cost a pretty penny—the greens fee at Pebble Beach Golf Links, for example, is more than $300—but the public is welcome at private **Pebble Beach Golf Links,** the **Links at Spanish Bay, Spyglass Hill Golf Course,** the **Peter Hay Par 3,** and the **Del Monte Golf Course** (in Monterey), all affiliated with The Lodge at Pebble Beach on 17 Mile Dr., 831/624-3811, 831/624-6611, or toll-free 800/654-9300. Also open to the public are the **Poppy Hills Golf Course,** 3200 Lopez Rd. (just off 17 Mile Dr.), 831/624-2035; the **Pacific Grove Municipal Golf** **Links,** 77 Asilomar Ave., 831/648-3177, which is great for beginners and reasonably priced ($14–35); the **Bayonet** and **Black Horse Golf Courses** on North-South at former Fort Ord, 831/373-3701; and the **Laguna Seca Golf Club** on York Rd. between Monterey and Salinas, 831/373-3701.

Though Pebble Beach is world-renowned for its golf courses and golf events, Carmel Valley and vicinity has nearly as many courses—most of them private in the country-club model, most recognizing reciprocal access agreements with other clubs. The **Rancho Cañada Golf Club,** about a mile east of Hwy. 1 via Carmel Valley Rd., 831/624-0111, is open to the public, however. As part and parcel of accommodations packages, nonmembers can golf at **Quail Lodge Resort,** 8000 Valley Greens Dr., 831/624-1581, and at **Carmel Valley Ranch,** 1 Old Ranch Rd. in Carmel, 831/625-9500 or toll-free 800/422-7635 (main switchboard), or 831/626-2510 (golf course), where two people can spend the night and play a round of golf for about $250 in winter, or $350 in summer.

THE MONARCH BUTTERFLIES AND BUTTERFLY TREES

Pacific Grove is the best known of the 20 or so places where monarch butterflies winter. Once partial to Monterey pine or cypress trees for perching, monarchs these days prefer eucalyptus introduced from Australia. Adults arrive in late October and early November, their distinctive orange-and-black Halloweenish wings sometimes tattered and torn after migrating thousands of miles. But they still have that urge to merge, first alighting on low shrubs, then meeting at certain local trees to socialize and sun themselves during the temperate Monterey Peninsula winter before heading north to Canada to mate in the spring and then die. Their offspring metamorphose into adult butterflies the following summer or fall and—mysteriously—make their way back to the California coast without ever having been here. Milkweed eaters, the monarchs somehow figured out this diet made them toxic to bug-loving birds—who subsequently learned to leave them alone.

Even when massed in hundreds, the butterflies may be hard to spot: with wings folded, their undersides provide neutral camouflage. But if fog-damp, monarchs will spread their wings to dry in the sun and "flash"—a priceless sight for any nature mystic.

KIM WEIR

Pacific Grove loves its monarch butterflies.

Grove Chamber of Commerce at Forest and Central, P.O. Box 167, Pacific Grove, CA 93950, 831/373-3304.

SEEING AND DOING PACIFIC GROVE

From Pacific Grove, embark on the too-famous **17-Mile Drive** in adjacent Pebble Beach. Not even 17 miles long anymore, the "drive" still skirts plenty of ritzy digs in the 5,300-acre, four-gated "town" of Pebble Beach. Most famous along the way is the landmark **Lone Cypress**—the official (trademarked) emblem of the Monterey Peninsula. From Pacific Grove (or other entrances), by bike the 17-Mile Drive is free, but by car "the drive" costs $7.75, refundable if you spend at least $25 on food or greens fees at The Lodge at Pebble Beach.

But better (and free), tour the surf-pounded peninsula as a populist. The city of Pacific Grove is one of few in California owning its own beaches and shores, all dedicated to public use. Less crowded and hoity-toity than the 17-Mile Drive, just as spectacular, and absolutely free is a walk, bike ride, or drive along Ocean View Boulevard. Or take the **Monterey Peninsula Recreation Trail** as far as you want; this path for walkers, joggers, bicyclers, skaters, and baby-stroller-pushers runs all the way from Marina to Pebble Beach—paved in places (right through downtown Monterey, for example), dirt in others. Along the way is the **Point Piños Lighthouse,** the oldest operating lighthouse on the Pacific coast. The lighthouse and the **U.S. Coast Guard Museum** inside are free and open Thurs.–Sun. 1–4 P.M.

Pacific Grove's **Museum of Natural History** at Forest and Central showcases *local* wonders of nature, including sea otters, seabirds (a huge collection with more than 400 specimens), rare insects, and native plants. For information, contact the museum at 165 Forest Ave., Pacific Grove, CA 93950, 831/648-3116. Open Tues.–Sun. 10 A.M.–5 P.M. Admission is free (donations greatly appreciated).

Asilomar

The ladies of the Young Women's Christian Association's national Board of Directors coined this Spanish-sounding nonword from the Greek *asilo* ("refuge") and the Spanish *mar* ("sea") when they established this as a YWCA retreat in 1913. **Asilomar State Beach** has tidepools, wonderful whitesand beaches, shifting sand dunes, and spectacular sunsets. Many of Asilomar's original buildings (designed by architect Julia Morgan, best known for Hearst's San Simeon estate) are now historical landmarks. Primarily a conference center with meeting rooms and accommodations for groups, Asilomar is now a nonprofit unit of the California state park system. Guest or not, anyone can fly kites or build sandcastles at the beach, stop to appreciate the forest of Monterey pine and cypress, and watch the wildlife. For information, contact: Asilomar Conference Center, 800 Asilomar Blvd., P.O. Box 537, Pacific Grove, CA 93950, 831/372-8016 or toll-free 800/881-7708 (reservations), fax 831/ 372-7227, www.asilomarcenter.com.

STAYING IN PACIFIC GROVE

To maintain its "hometown America" aura, Pacific Grove has limited its motel development. The local chamber of commerce provides accommodations listings. Bed-and-breakfast inns are popular in Pacific Grove—see separate listings below—and these comfortable, often luxurious lodgings compare in price to much less pleasant alternatives elsewhere on the peninsula.

Asilomar Stays

The state-owned **Asilomar Conference Center,** 800 Asilomar Ave. in Pacific Grove, 831/372-8016 or toll-free 800/881-7708, fax 831/372-7227, www.asilomarcenter.com, enjoys an incredibly beautiful 60-acre setting on the Pacific Ocean, complete with swimming pool, volleyball nets, and miles of beaches to stroll. When it's not completely booked with businesspeople, conferences, and other groups, it can be a reasonably priced choice for an overnight. Call ahead for reservations, up to 30 days in advance, or hope for last-minute cancellations. Moderate-Expensive, three meals a day included.

Moderate Stays

Especially if the monarchs are in town, consider a stay at the **Butterfly Grove Inn,** 1073 Lighthouse Ave., 831/373-4921. Butterflies are partial to some of the trees here. The inn is quiet, with pool, spa, some kitchens and fireplaces. Choose rooms in a comfy old house or motel units. Closest to the beach are the 1930s-style cottages at **Bide-a-Wee-Motel & Cottages,** 221 Asilomar Blvd., 831/372-2330. Some of the cottages have kitchenettes. Moderate-Premium. Also comfortable is woodsy **Andril Fireplace Motel & Cottages,** 569 Asilomar Blvd., 831/375-0994 (the cottages have the fireplaces).

Always a best bet for a quiet stay is the well-located **Pacific Grove Motel** near Asilomar, close to the ocean and just west of 17 Mile Dr. at Lighthouse Ave. and Grove Acre, 831/372-3218 or toll-free 800/858-8997, fax 831/372-8842. In addition to clean rooms with refrigerators, phones, and color TV (some have attractive patios), amenities include a heated pool, hot tub, BBQ area, and playground. Very low weekday rates in winter, two-night minimum stay on weekends. Moderate-Premium.

Premium Stays

Near Asilomar is the **Pacific Gardens Inn,** 701 Asilomar Blvd., 831/646-9414 or toll-free 800/262-1566 in California, www.pacificgardensinn.com, where the contemporary rooms feature wood-burning fireplaces, refrigerators, TVs, and phones—even popcorn poppers and coffeemakers. Suites feature full kitchens and living rooms. Complimentary continental breakfast and evening wine and cheese. Very nice. Right across from Asilomar is the all-suites **Rosedale Inn,** 775 Asilomar Blvd., 831/655-1000 or toll-free 800/822-5606, fax 831/655-0691, where all rooms have a ceiling fan, fireplace, large hot tub, wet bar, refrigerator, microwave, in-room coffee, remote-control color TV and VCR, even a hair dryer. Some suites have two or three TVs and/or a private patio.

Luxury Stays

Three superswank choices in adjacent Pebble Beach are definitely beyond the reach of most people's pocketbooks. At the **Inn at Spanish Bay,** 2700 17-Mile Dr. (at the Scottish Links Golf Course), 831/647-7500, rooms are definitely deluxe, with gas-burning fireplaces, patios, and balconies with views. Amenities include beach access, a pool, saunas, whirlpools, a health club, tennis courts, and a putting green. Also an unlikely choice for most travelers is **The Lodge at Pebble Beach,** another outpost of luxury on 17-Mile Drive, 831/624-3811. (If you don't stay, peek into the *very* exclusive shops here.) A recent addition is the elegant estate-style cottages at 24-room **Casa Palmero,** near both The Lodge and the first fairway of the Pebble Beach Golf Links. For still more pampering, the **Spa at Pebble Beach** is a full-service spa facility. For reservations at any of these Pebble Beach Resort facilities, call toll-free 800/654-9300, fax 831/644-7958, or try www.pebble-beach.com.

PACIFIC GROVE BED-AND-BREAKFASTS

Victoriana is particularly popular in Pacific Grove. The most famous Victorian inn in town is the elegant **Seven Gables Inn,** 555 Ocean View Blvd., 831/372-4341, which offers ocean views from all 14 rooms and an abundance of European antiques and Victorian finery. Rates include fabulous full breakfast and afternoon tea. Luxury. Sharing the garden and offering equally exceptional, if more relaxed, Victorian style is the sibling **Grand View Inn** next door, 557 Ocean View Blvd., 831/372-4341. The view from all 10 rooms, with their antique furnishings and luxurious marble bathrooms, is indeed grand. Full breakfast, afternoon tea. Luxury.

Another Pacific Grove grande dame is the pretty-in-pink 23-room **Martine Inn,** 255 Ocean View Blvd., 831/373-3388 or toll-free 800/852-5588, fax 831/373-3896, www.martineinn.com, a study in Victorian refinement and propriety masquerading, on the outside, as a Mediterranean villa. Full breakfast here is served with fine china, crystal, silver, and old lace. Also enjoy wine and hors d'oeuvres in the evening, a whirlpool, spa, game room, library, and a baby grand piano in the library. Luxury.

The lovely **Green Gables Inn,** 104 5th St., 831/375-2095 or toll-free 800/722-1774, fax 831/375-5437, is a romantic gabled Queen Anne seaside "summer house" with marvelous views, five rooms upstairs, a suite downstairs, and five rooms in the carriage house. Of these, seven feature private bathrooms. Rates include continental breakfast. The Green Gables, a Four Sisters Inn, was named the number one bed-and-breakfast inn in North America in 1997, according to the Official Hotel Guide's survey of travel agents. Premium-Luxury.

The **Gosby House Inn,** 643 Lighthouse Ave., 831/375-1287 or toll-free 800/527-8828, fax 831/655-9621, is another of the Four Sisters—this one a charming (and huge) Queen Anne serving up fine antiques, a restful garden, homemade food, and fresh flowers. All 20 rooms boast great bayside views, and most feature private bathrooms. Some have fireplaces, hot tubs, and TVs. Expensive-Luxury.

The 1889 **Centrella Inn,** 612 Central Ave., 831/372-3372 or toll-free 800/233-3372, fax 831/372-2036, www.centrellainn.com, a National Historic Landmark, offers 20 rooms plus a hot tub–equipped garden suite and five cottages with wood-burning fireplaces and wet bars. The cottage-style gardens are quite appealing, especially in summer. Rates include complimentary morning newspaper, full buffet breakfast, and a social hour in the afternoon (wine and hors d'oeuvres). Premium-Luxury.

The historic three-story (no elevator) **Pacific Grove Inn** is at 581 Pine (at Forest), 831/375-2825. Some rooms and suites in this 1904 Queen Anne have ocean views, most have fireplaces, and all have private baths and modern amenities like color TVs, radios, and telephones. Breakfast buffet every morning. Premium-Luxury.

But not every choice in Pacific Grove is Victorian. Perfect for aquatic sports fans—the proprietors can paddle you out to the best sea kayaking—is the **Inn at 213 Seventeen Mile Drive,** 981 Lighthouse Ave. (at 17 Mile Dr.), 831/642-9514 or toll-free 800/526-5666, fax 831/642-9546, www.innat213-17miledr.com. Guest rooms in this restored 1928 Craftsman home and affiliated cottages feature king or queen beds and essential comforts like down comforters, TVs, and phones. All rooms have private baths. Generous buffet at breakfast, hors d'oeuvres and wine in the evening. Premium-Luxury.

EATING IN PACIFIC GROVE

Breakfast and More

You can get marvelous crepes for breakfast or lunch, as well as good waffles and homemade soups, at **Toastie's Cafe,** 702 Lighthouse Ave., 831/373-7543, open daily 7 A.M.–2 P.M. Another cheap but good choice is the **Bagel Bakery,** 201 Lighthouse Ave., 831/649-1714, where you can fill up anytime for around $5. Specialties include fresh-baked bagels, homemade soups, and a salad bar for lunch or dinner. Open Mon.–Sat. 7:30 A.M.–9 P.M., Sun. until 7 P.M. Or try the vegetarian dishes and cheesecake at **Tillie Gort's Coffee House** and art gallery at 111 Central, 831/373-0335.

For lattes, cappuccinos, espressos, or just a good cuppa joe, head to **Caravali Coffee,** 510 Lighthouse Ave., 831/655-5633; **Juice and Java,** 599 Lighthouse Ave., 831/373-8652; or the dual-purpose **Bookworks,** 667 Lighthouse Ave., 831/372-2242, where you can sample the wares in the bookstore as well as the coffeehouse.

Lunch and Dinner

Thai Bistro, 159 Central Ave., 831/372-8700, is the place to go for outstanding Thai food. Those with a fireproof palate will love the restaurant's spicy dishes, and vegetarians will appreciate the large number of meatless entrées. Open for lunch and dinner daily. (There's another Thai Bistro in Carmel Valley at 55 W. Carmel Valley Rd., 831/659-5900.)

The **Crocodile Grill,** 701 Lighthouse Ave. (at Congress), 831/655-3311, offers eclectic and exotic decor along with fresh California-style Caribbean and Central-South American cuisine. Seafood is the specialty here—such things as red snapper Mardi Gras—but for dessert, don't miss the house-made Key lime cheesecake with mango syrup. Beer and wine. Open for dinner nightly except Tuesday.

Popular with locals (and a favorite of the late, great Ansel Adams) is **Pablo's,** 1184 Forest Ave., 831/646-8888, featuring *real* Mexican food, including *mariscos.* Open 11 A.M.–9 P.M. Locals say the homemade *chiles rellenos* at immensely popular **Peppers MexiCali Cafe,** 170 Forest Ave., 831/373-6892, are the best on the peninsula, but you also won't go wrong with the

tamales, seafood tacos, or spicy prawns. Beer and wine served. Closed Tues., but otherwise open weekdays and Sat. for lunch, nightly for dinner. Also popular for seafood is the relaxed and family-friendly **Fishwife** in the Beachcomber Inn, 1996 1/2 Sunset Dr., 831/375-7107, where Boston clam chowder and such things as grilled Cajun snapper fill out the menu. Beer and wine. Open for lunch and dinner Wed.–Mon., also brunch on Sunday.

Allegro Gourmet Pizzeria, 1184 Forest (near Prescott), 831/373-5656, offers innovative pizzas and exceptional calzones—people come from far and wide for the latter—but you can also enjoy pasta and risotto dishes, Italian-style sandwiches, and salads.

Favaloro's, 542 Lighthouse (at Fountain), 831/373-8523, is popular for traditional Italian, served in a bright location at street level in the Holman's Building. Try the gourmet specialty pizzas or the house-made pastas. Open for lunch Tues.–Sat. and for dinner Tues.–Sunday. Friendly **Pasta Mia Trattoria,** 481 Lighthouse Ave. (near 13th), 831/375-7709, open nightly for dinner, serves exceptionally creative and good house-made pastas. Beer and wine.

No longer the peninsula's best-kept secret, the exceptional **Taste Café & Bistro,** 1199 Forest Ave. (at Prescott), 831/655-0324, serves unique rustic variations on American, Italian, and French fare. Call well in advance for reservations. Beer and wine. Open Tues.–Sun. for dinner.

For boisterous Basque food, try **Fandango,** in the stone house at 223 17th St. off Lighthouse Ave., 831/372-3456. The restaurant serves up wonderful Mediterranean country fare—from mesquite-grilled seafood, steak, and rack of lamb to tapas, pastas, and paella—in several separate dining rooms warmed by fireplaces. Try the chocolate nougatine pie or *vacherin* for dessert. Sunday brunch here is superb. Formal dress prevails at dinner in the smaller dining rooms, but everything is casual in the Terrace Room. Open for lunch and dinner daily and for brunch on Sunday. Lunch is fairly inexpensive, dinners a bit pricier.

Upscale in more traditional continental style is gracious **Gernot's Victoria House,** at home in the 1892 Victorian Hart Mansion, 649 Lighthouse Ave., 831/646-1477, where fine Austrian and European fare stars. Beer and wine. Open

Tues.–Sun. after 5:30 P.M. (reservations advised). Truly exceptional for classical French is **Melac's** nearby at 663 Lighthouse (at 19th), 831/375-1743. Beer and wine. Open Tues.–Fri. for lunch, Tues.–Sun. for dinner. Still one of the best restaurants on the entire Monterey Peninsula, some say, is the **Old Bath House** at Lovers Point, 620 Ocean View, 831/375-5195. It's elegant and expensive but quite romantic, featuring lively northern Italian and French fare, exceptional desserts, and appetizing views. Full bar, extensive wine list. Open nightly for dinner.

CARMEL AND VICINITY

Vizcaíno named the river here after Palestine's Mount Carmel (probably with the encouragement of several Carmelite friars accompanying his expedition). The name Carmel-by-the-Sea distinguishes this postcard-pretty, almost too-cute coastal village of 5,000 souls from affluent Carmel Valley 10 miles inland and Carmel Highlands just south of Point Lobos on the way to Big Sur. Everything about all the Carmels, though, says one thing quite loudly: money. Despite its bohemian beginnings, these days Carmel crankily guards its quaintness while

Carmel Mission

cranking up the commercialism. (Shopping is the town's major draw.) Still free at last report are the beautiful city beaches and visits to the elegant old Carmel Mission. Almost free: tours of Robinson Jeffers's Tor House and fabulous **Point Lobos** just south of town.

In summer and on most warm-weather weekends, traffic on Hwy. 1 is backed up for a mile or more in either direction by the Carmel "crunch." Sane people take the bus, ride bikes, or walk to get here. This overly quaint community is so congested that parking is usually nonexistent. (Even if you do find a parking slot in downtown Carmel, you won't get to dawdle; parking is limited to one hour, and you'll risk a steep fine if you're late getting back.) Other scarce items in Carmel: streetlights, traffic signals, street signs, sidewalks, house numbers, mailboxes, neon signs, and jukeboxes.

The **Carmel Business Association** is upstairs in the Eastwood Building on San Carlos between 5th and 6th, P.O. Box 4444, Carmel, CA 93921, 831/624-2522. Its annual **Guide to Carmel** includes information on just about everything—from shopping hot spots to accommodations and eateries. The **Tourist Information Center,** Ocean and Mission, P.O. Box 7430, 831/624-1711, is quite helpful, and provides assistance with lodging reservations. The **Carmel Valley Chamber of Commerce** is in the Oak Building at 71 W. Carmel Valley Rd., P.O. Box 288, Carmel Valley, CA 93924, 831/659-4000.

SEEING AND DOING CARMEL

To get oriented, take a walk. Carmel has a few tiny parks hidden here and there, including one especially for walkers—**Mission Trails Park,** featuring about five miles of trails winding through redwoods, willows, and wildflowers (in season). **Carmel Walks,** 831/642-2700, www.carmel-walks.com, offers a great two-hour guided walk, with highlights including the town's original fairytale cottages, architecture by Bernard Maybeck and Charles S. Greene, onetime homes of the bohemians, and the local doings of photographers Edward Weston and Ansel Adams. Wellbehaved dogs (on leashes) are welcome, too, since the tour also visits Doris Day's petfriendly hotel, and notes local restaurants where dogs are permitted to dine with the family out on the patio. At last report walks—$15 per person, dogs free—were offered Tues.–Fri. at 10 A.M. and Sat. at 10 A.M. and 2 P.M. Reservations required.

And walk to the beach. The downtown crescent of **Carmel Beach City Park** is beautiful, but too cold and dangerous for swimming, and a tourist zoo in summer. (A winter sunset stroll is wonderful, though.) A better alternative is to take Scenic Rd. (or Carmelo St.) south from Santa Lucia off Rio Rd. to **Carmel River State Beach,** fringed with eucalyptus and cypress and often uncrowded (but dangerous in high surf). This is where locals go to get away.

The Carmel Mission, properly called **Mission Basilica San Carlos Borromeo del Rio Carmelo,** is wonderful and well worth a visit. California's second mission, it was originally established at the Monterey Presidio in 1770, then moved here the following year. Onetime headquarters and favorite foreign home of Father Junípero Serra, whose remains are buried at the foot of the altar in the sanctuary, the mission's magnificent vinedraped cathedral is the first thing to catch the eye. Most of the buildings here are reconstructions, painstakingly rebuilt and restored in the 1930s, since the Carmel Mission fell to ruins in the 1800s. The mission is just a few blocks west of Hwy. 1 at 3080 Rio Rd., 831/624-3600 (gift shop) or 831/624-1271 (rectory), and is open for self-guided tours Mon.–Sat. 9:30 A.M.–4:30 P.M., Sun. 10:30 A.M.–4:15 P.M. Admission is free, but donations are appreciated.

Robinson Jeffers's Tor House is a medieval-looking granite retreat on a rocky knoll above Carmel Bay—built by family-man poet Robinson Jeffers, who helped haul the huge stones up from the beach below with horse teams. Yet you can only begin to appreciate Tor House from the outside. Small-group guided tours are offered Fri.–Sat., advance reservations required. Write Jeffers's Tor House, 26304 Ocean View Ave., P.O. Box 1887, Carmel, CA 93921, or call 831/624-1813 or 831/624-1840, or try www.torhouse.org. Fee.

Point Lobos State Reserve

One of the crown jewels of California's state parks, Point Lobos is a 1,250-acre coastal wonderland about four miles south of Carmel. Pack a picnic; this is the best the Monterey area has to offer. The relentless surf and wild winds have pounded these reddish shores for millennia, sculpting six miles of shallow aquamarine coves, wonderful tidepools, aptly named Bird Island, and jutting points: Granite, Coal, Chute, China, Cannery, Pinnacle, Pelican, and Lobos itself. From here, look to the sea, as Santa Cruz poet William Everson has, "standing in cypress and surrounded by cypress, watching through its witchery as the surf explodes in unbelievable beauty on the granite below."

Because Point Lobos is beautiful, it's quite popular. It can be crowded in summer and sometimes on spring and fall weekends. Since only 450 people are allowed into the park at one time, come early in the day (or wait in long lines along Hwy. 1—not fun). Open for day use only (sunrise till sunset 9 A.M.–7 P.M. in summer, until 5 P.M. in winter), $4 per car, but free for walk-ins and bike-ins. Guided tours are offered daily. For more information, contact: Point Lobos State Reserve, Rt. 1 Box 62, Carmel, CA 93923, 831/624-4909.

STAYING IN CARMEL

Area Camping

Mary Austin's observation that "beauty is cheap here" may apply to the views, but little else in the greater Carmel area—with the exception of camping. **Carmel by the River RV Park,** 27680 Schulte Rd. (off Carmel Valley Rd.), 831/624-9329, fax 831/624-8416, is well away from it all—some 35 attractively landscaped sites right on the Carmel River, with full hookups, cable TV, laundromat, rec room, and other amenities. Budget-Inexpensive. Nearby **Saddle Mountain Recreation Park,** also at the end of Schulte Rd., 831/624-1617, fax 831/624-4470, offers both tent and RV sites, restrooms, showers, picnic tables, a swimming pool, playground, and other recreational possibilities—including nearby hiking trails. Budget.

Expensive Stays

Wonderful is the only word for the historic **Pine Inn,** downtown on Ocean between Monte Verde and Lincoln, 831/624-3851 or toll-free 800/228-3851, fax 831/624-3030, www.pine-inn.com. This small hotel offers comfortable "Carmel Victorian" accommodations and fine dining at the on-site **Il Fornaio** restaurant and bakery.

The **Carmel River Inn,** 26600 Oliver Rd. (south of town on Hwy. 1 at the Carmel River Bridge), P.O. Box 221609, Carmel, CA 93922, 831/624-1575 or toll-free 800/882-8142, fax 831/624-0290, www.carmelriverinn.com, is a pleasant 10-acre riverside spread with a heated pool, 24 cozy family-friendly cottages and duplexes (some with wood-burning fireplaces and kitchens), and 19 motel rooms. Two-night minimum stay on weekends. Pets welcome, $25 per pet. Expensive-Luxury.

Other above-average Carmel accommodations—and there are plenty to choose from—include the **Carmel Oaks Inn,** 5th and Mission, 831/624-5547 or toll-free 800/266-5547, fax 831/625-5908, attractive and convenient, a bargain by local standards, and the **Lobos Lodge,** Monte Verde and Ocean, 831/624-3874, fax 831/624-0135.

Premium and Luxury Stays

The **Sundial Lodge,** Monte Verde and 7th, 831/624-8578, is a cross between a small hotel and a bed-and-breakfast. Each of the 19 antique-furnished rooms has a private bath, TV, and telephone. Other amenities include lovely English gardens and courtyard, continental breakfast, and afternoon tea. Premium-Luxury.

The landmark 1929 **Cypress Inn,** downtown at Lincoln and 7th, 831/624-3871 or toll-free 800/443-7443, fax 831/624-8216, www.cypress-inn.com, is a charming, gracious, and intimate place—another small hotel with a bed-and-breakfast sensibility, recently updated. Pets are allowed—invited, actually, since actress-owner Doris Day is an animal-rights activist. Dog beds provided. And when hotel staff places a mint on your pillow at turn-down, they'll also leave a treat for your dog or cat. How's *that* for service? Premium-Luxury. Continental breakfast.

Très Carmel, and a historic treasure, is the Mediterranean-style 1904 **La Playa Hotel,** Camino Real and 8th, 831/624-6476 or toll-free 800/582-8900, fax 831/624-7966, where lush gardens surround guest rooms and cottages on the terraced hillside. Recently remodeled, rooms at La Playa feature evocative Spanish-style furnishings. The five cottages feature fireplaces, ocean-view decks, and separate living areas. Especially enjoyable when the gardens are in their glory is the on-site **Terrace Grill.** Premium-Luxury.

The luxurious **Adobe Inn,** downtown at Dolores and 8th, 831/624-3933 or toll-free 800/388-3933, features just about every amenity. Rooms include gas fireplaces, wet bars and refrigerators, patios or decks, color TVs, and phones; some have ocean views. Other amenities include a sauna and heated pool. Premium-Luxury.

Another option is the recently upgraded, 19-room Victorian-style **Chateau de Carmel** at 5th and Junipero, 831/624-1900, 831/624-8515 or toll-free 800/325-8515, fax 831/624-1571. Luxury.

Mission Ranch

Long the traditional place to stay, just outside town, is the Mission Ranch, 26270 Dolores (at 15th), 831/624-6436 or toll-free 800/538-8221, fax 831/626-4163. A quiet, small ranch now owned by Clint Eastwood, Mission Ranch overlooks the Carmel River and features views of the Carmel River wetlands and Point Lobos. And the mission *is* nearby. The Victorian farmhouse and its outbuildings have had an expensive makeover, and together now resemble a Western village—a total of 31 guest rooms decorated here and there with props from Eastwood movies. Lodgings are available in the main house, the Hayloft, the Bunkhouse (which has its own living room and kitchen), and the Barn. The newer Meadow View rooms feature, well, meadow views. Expensive-Luxury. Another attraction is the casual on-site **Restaurant at Mission Ranch,** 831/625-9040, which serves make-my-day American fare.

Bed-and-Breakfast Stays

Local inns offer an almost overwhelming amount of choice. (Keep in mind, what with the B&B craze, that "inn" in Carmel may be a code word for revamped motel.) Local bed-and-breakfast inns are comparable in price to most Carmel area motels, and they're usually much homier.

A Carmel classic is the ivy-draped **Stonehouse Inn,** 8th and Monte Verde, 831/624-4569 or toll-free 877/748-6618, www.carmelstonehouse.com, constructed by local Indians. All six rooms here are named after local luminaries, mostly writers, and all but two share bathrooms. Rates include full breakfast, wine and sherry, and hors d'oeuvres. Expensive-Luxury. The **Cobblestone Inn,** on Junipero near 8th, 831/625-5222 or toll-free 800/833-8836, fax 831/625-0478, is a traditional Carmel home with a cobblestone courtyard, gas fireplaces in the guestrooms, and English country-house antiques. Rates include a full breakfast buffet, complimentary tea, and hors d'oeuvres. Expensive-Luxury.

The **Green Lantern Inn,** 8th and Casanova, 831/624-4392, fax 831/624-9591, offers 18 rustic multiunit cottages, some with lofts, others with fireplaces or sunset-viewing porches, not far from town or the beaches. Generous continental breakfast with fresh-squeezed juices served in the morning, wine and cheese in the afternoon. Expensive-Luxury. The Victorian **Sea View Inn,** on Camino Real between 11th and 12th, 831/624-8778, is three blocks from the beach and offers eight rooms, six with private bath, and antique-filled decor. Rates include continental breakfast as well as afternoon tea and cookies or sherry. Expensive-Premium. **The Homestead,** Lincoln and 8th, 831/624-4119, rents rooms and cottages with private baths at easy-on-the-budget rates. Moderate-Expensive.

The pleasant **Carmel Wayfarer Inn,** 4th Ave. at Mission St., 831/624-2711 or toll-free 800/533-2711, fax 831/625-1210, is now a bed-and-breakfast. Some rooms feature ocean views and kitchens, most have gas fireplaces. Expensive-

Premium. Most rooms at the 11-room **Vagabond House Inn,** 4th and Dolores, 831/624-7738 or toll-free 800/262-1262, fax 831/626-1243, have fireplaces; some have kitchens. Continental breakfast is served in your room. Pets welcome. Expensive-Luxury.

Staying in Carmel Highlands

The swank and well-known 1916 **Highlands Inn,** along Hwy. 1 four miles south of Carmel, 831/620-1234, toll-free 800/682-4811 in California, or toll-free 800/233-1234 (Hyatt central reservations), www.highlands-inn.com, is indeed beautiful, though many people would have to forfeit their rent or house payment to stay long. That may not be a problem much longer, though, since the Highlands Inn is now beginning to sell off its luxurious rooms and suites as timeshares—a reality not too popular with long-time guests. Quite luxurious, with some of the world's most spectacular views, some suites feature wood-burning fireplaces, double spa baths, fully equipped kitchens, and all the comforts. Luxury. Those of more plebeian means can still enjoy a meal. The exceptional **Pacific's Edge** features stunning sunset views and was a top-10 winner in *Wine Spectator* magazine's 1998 Reader's Choice Awards. Open for lunch, dinner, and Sunday brunch. The more casual **California Market** is open daily 7 A.M.–10 P.M.

Staying in Carmel Valley

Robles del Rio Lodge, 200 Punta Del Monte,

ROBERT HOLMES/CALTOUR

Carmel Valley

831/659-3705 or toll-free 800/883-0843, fax 831/659-5157, www.roblesdelriolodge.com, perches atop a hill overlooking Carmel Valley and is reached via winding back roads—a bit hard to find the first time. Scheduled to reopen in late summer 2001 following an extensive remodel, Robles del Rio is destined to become a 59-room "luxury boutique spa," yet perhaps not the deluxe yet rustic down-home 1920s wonder it once was. Affiliated with the lodge is the excellent **The Ridge** restaurant, 831/659-0170. Call for current details and rates.

In the meantime, a popular local tradition is the historic **Los Laureles Country Inn,** 313 W. Carmel Valley Rd., 831/659-2233 or toll-free 800/533-4404, fax 831/659-0481, once part of the Boronda Spanish land grant and later a Del Monte ranch. Rooms here used to be horse stables for Muriel Vanderbilt's well-bred thoroughbreds. The inn has an excellent restaurant (American regional), pool, and conference facilities. Golf packages, too. Expensive-Luxury.

A great choice, too, is the **Carmel Valley Lodge** on Carmel Valley Rd. at Ford, 831/659-2261 or toll-free 800/641-4646 (reservations only), fax 831/659-4558, www.valleylodge.com. After all, who can resist "Come listen to your beard grow" as an advertising slogan? The Lodge features rooms fronting the lovely gardens plus one- and two-bedroom cottages with fireplaces and kitchens. Other amenities include a pool, sauna, hot tub, and fitness center. Dog friendly. Premium-Luxury.

Luxurious but still something of a new concept in Carmel Valley accommodations is the **Bernardus Lodge,** 831/659-3247 or toll-free 888/648-9463, fax 831/659-3131, www.bernardus.com, a luxury resort affiliated with the Bernardus Winery and open since August 1999. Crafted from limestone, logs, ceramic tiles, and rich interior woods, the nine village-style buildings feature suites for "discriminating travelers" and offer endless luxury amenities, including a different wine-and-cheese tasting every night at turn-down, a full-service spa, and special educational forums on gardening, the culinary arts, and viticulture. On-site ballroom and restaurants. Luxury.

Otherwise, for a super-luxury stay—and to avoid the country clubs and other "too new" places—the choice is the 330-acre **Stonepine Estate Resort,** 150 E. Carmel Valley Rd., 831/659-2245,

fax 831/659-5160, www.stonepinecalifornia.com, once the Crocker family's summer home. A Carmel version of a French château, Stonepine features luxury suites in the manor house, Chateau Noel, and others in Briar Rose Cottage, the Gate House, and—for horse lovers—the Paddock House. Luxury.

EATING IN CARMEL

Great at Breakfast and Lunch

For a perfect omelette with home fries and homemade valley pork sausage, try **The Cottage,** on Lincoln between Ocean and 7th, 831/625-6260. Another good choice for breakfast is **Katy's Place,** on the west side of Mission between 5th and 6th, 831/624-0199. Great eggs Benedict. Open daily. Also cozy and crowded is **Em Le's,** Dolores and 5th, 831/625-6780. Try the buttermilk waffles, available for lunch or dinner.

More Good Food, at Lunch and Dinner

Everyone tries the **Hog's Breath Inn,** former mayor Clint Eastwood's rather famous Carmel eatery on San Carlos between 5th and 6th, 831/625-1044, presided over by—you guessed it—a hog's head. Though it was hibernating for a year or so following a partnership dissolution, as of May 2000 the Hog's Breath was breathing again, and probably still serving up billboard-sized images of Clint Eastwood and Dirty Harry burgers, along with more serious menu choices.

The **Rio Grill,** 101 Crossroads Blvd. (Hwy. 1 at Rio Rd.), 831/625-5436, is a long-running favorite for innovative Southwestern-style American fare. Everything is fresh and/or made from scratch, and many entrées are served straight from the oakwood smoker. Open for lunch and dinner daily, great Sunday brunch. Interesting, too, is inexpensive **From Scratch** restaurant at the Barnyard Shopping Center, 831/625-2448, a casual and eclectic place with local art on the walls. Open for breakfast and lunch daily, for dinner Tues.–Sat., and for brunch on Sunday.

A great choice at lunch, dinner, and weekend brunch is the **6th Avenue Grill,** on 6th at Mission, 831/624-6562, serving California-style Mediterranean, from salads, sandwiches, and pastas at lunch to wild mushroom stew at dinner. The dinner specialty at the **Flying Fish Grill** at the Carmel Plaza shopping center, on Mission between Ocean and 7th, 831/625-1962, is Pacific Rim seafood—from yin-yan salmon to peppered ahi tuna served with angel hair pasta. Both establishments serve beer and wine only. Another possibility for seafood is **Flaherty's,** on 6th between Dolores and San Carlos, 831/625-1500 or 831/624-0311, which offers just-off-the-boat-fresh catch of the day, along with great chowders and cioppino.

Fine for takeout pastries and desserts or a light French-country lunch is **Patisserie Boissiere,** on Mission between Ocean and 7th, 831/624-5008. For good value and great food, the place is **Chez Christian Bistro & Restaurant,** on Ocean between Lincoln and Monte Verde, 831/625-4331, which offers a varied menu—everything from salads, pastas, fresh seafood, chicken, and steaks to the chef's specialty *confit de canard,* a classic French preparation of duck. French and California wines. Carmel boasts an outpost of **Ristorante Piatti,** too, on 6th at Junipero, 831/625-1766, open daily for lunch and dinner. Locally popular for Italian and unpretentious is **La Dolce Vita,** on San Carlos between 7th and 8th, 831/624-3667, open daily for both lunch and dinner. Beer and wine.

Downtown's **China Gourmet,** on 5th between San Carlos and Dolores, 831/624-3941, specializes in Mandarin and Szechuan cuisine, while **China Delight,** 133 Crossroads Blvd. (in the Crossroads Shopping Center), 831/624-3941, prepares Mandarin, Szechuan, and Cantonese dishes with no MSG.

Fine Dining

All the Carmels are crowded with "cuisine," some possibilities mentioned previously. Ask around if you're looking for the latest special dining experience. One of the more recent local stars is **Robert Kinkaid's Bistro,** an outpost of French-country atmosphere in the Crossroads Shopping Center, 217 Crossroads Blvd., 831/624-9626, brought to you by the chef behind Monterey's Fresh Cream. Open for lunch on weekdays, dinner daily. Friendly **Sans Souci,** on Lincoln between 5th and 6th, 831/624-6220, is an-

other fairly new French restaurant, this one serving both contemporary and classic fare. Full bar. The impressive **Crème Carmel Restaurant,** behind a liquor store on San Carlos between Ocean and 7th, 831/624-0444, showcases the abundance of fresh local produce, herbs, seafood, and poultry with a light French touch. Nightly vegetarian plate, wonderful chocolate soufflé. Full bar. The **French Poodle,** Junipero and 5th, 831/624-8643, still gets rave reviews for its light French cuisine, and the wine list is extensive. Those in the know say the venerable **L'Escargot,** Mission and 4th, 831/624-4914, is one of the finest French restaurants on the peninsula.

Casanova, 5th and Mission, 831/625-0501, serves both country-style French and Italian cuisine in a landmark local Mediterranean-style house (complete with heated garden seating for you temperature-sensitive romantics). House-made pastas here are exceptional, as are the desserts. Impressive wine list. Open daily for breakfast, lunch, and dinner. Equally popular, for its Northern Italian fare, is **Raffaello,** Mission between Ocean and 7th, 831/624-1541, where the decor is intimate and the pasta sublime. Extensive wine list. Open for dinner nightly except Tuesday. Sophisticated yet simple too is **La Boheme,** Dolores and 7th, 831/624-7500, a tiny, family-style place with French cuisine and European peasant fare for dinner. No reservations; call for the day's menu, or pick up the monthly calendar when you get to town. Open daily for dinner. Beer and wine. Elegant **Anton & Michel,** in the Court of the Fountains on Mission between Ocean and 7th, 831/624-2406, isn't really that expensive considering the setting and good continental fare.

Even if you can't afford to stay there, you can probably afford to eat at the Highlands Inn, on Hwy. 1 south of Carmel. The inn's **California Market** restaurant, 831/622-5450, serves California regional dishes with fresh local ingredients. Ocean-view and deck dining, fabulous scenery. Open for breakfast, lunch, and dinner daily. In the considerably pricier category at the Highlands is the elegant and renowned **Pacific's Edge** restaurant, 831/622-5445, open for lunch, dinner, and Sunday brunch.

CALIFORNIA DEPARTMENT OF PARKS AND RECREATION

THE CENTRAL COAST

Along this swath of coastline where north becomes south, the land itself is unfriendly, at least from the human perspective. Especially in the north, the indomitable unstable terrain—with its habit of sliding out from under whole hillsides, houses, highways, and hiking trails at the slightest provocation—has made the area hard to inhabit. Despite its contrariness, the central coast, that unmistakable pivotal point between California's north and south, successfully blends both.

The Great Transition

Though the collective Coast Ranges continue south through the region, here the terrain takes on a new look. The redwoods thin out, limiting themselves to a few large groves in Big Sur country and otherwise straggling south a short distance beyond San Simeon, tucked into hidden folds in the rounded coastal mountains. Where redwood country ends,

either the grasslands of the dominant coastal oak woodlands begin or the chaparral takes over, in places almost impenetrable. Even the coastline reflects the transition—the rocky rough-and-tumble shores along the Big Sur coast transform into tamer beaches and bluffs near San Simeon and points south.

Another clue that the north-south transition occurs here is water or, moving southward, the increasingly obvious lack of it. Though both the North and South Forks of the Little Sur River, the Big Sur River a few miles to the south, and other northern waterways flow to the sea throughout the year, as does the Cuyama River in the south (known as the Santa Maria River as it nears the ocean), most of the area's streams are seasonal. But off-season hikers, beware: even inland streams with a six-month flow are not to be dismissed during winter and spring, when deceptively dinky creekbeds can become death-dealing torrents overnight.

> **Note:** See **color maps** of the **Central Coast** at the front of the book.

BIG SUR

BIG SUR AND FALLING METEORS

The poet Robinson Jeffers described this redwood-and-rock coast as "that jagged country which nothing but a falling meteor will ever plow." It's only fitting, then, that this area was called Jeffers Country long before it became known as Big Sur. Sienna-colored sandstone and granite, surly waves, and the sundown sea come together in a never-ending dance of creation and destruction. Writer Henry Miller said Big Sur was "the face of the earth as the creator intended it to look," a point hard to argue. But Big Sur as a specific *place* is difficult to locate. It's not only a town, a valley, and a river—the entire coastline from just south of Carmel Highlands to some-

"That same prehistoric look. The look of always," Henry Miller said of Big Sur. "Nature smiling at herself in the mirror of eternity."

where north of San Simeon (some suggest the southern limit is the Monterey County line) is considered Big Sur country.

Once "in" Big Sur, wherever that might be, visitors notice some genuine oddities—odd at least by California standards. Until recently most people here didn't have much money and didn't seem to care. (This is changing as the truly wealthy move in.) They built simple or unusual dwellings—redwood cabins, glass tepees and geodesic domes, even round redwood houses with the look of wine barrels ready to roll into the sea—both to fit the limited space available but also to express that elusive Big Sur sense of *style*.

Because the terrain itself is so tormented and twisted, broadcast signals rarely arrive in Big Sur. In the days before satellite dishes there was virtually no TV; electricity and telephones with dial service have only been available in Big Sur since the 1950s, and some people along the south coast and in more remote areas still have neither.

Social life in Big Sur consists of bowling at the naval station, attending a poetry reading or the annual Big Sur Potluck Revue at the Grange Hall in the valley, driving into "town" (Monterey) for a few movie cassettes, or—for a really wild night—drinks on the deck at sunset and dancing cheek to cheek at Nepenthe. Big Sur is a very *different* California, where even the chamber of commerce urges visitors "to slow down, meditate," and "catch up with your soul."

It's almost impossible to catch up with your soul, however, when traffic is bumper-to-bumper. Appreciating Big Sur while driving or, only for the brave, bicycling in a mile-long coastline convoy is akin to honeymooning in Hades—a universal impulse but entirely the wrong ambience. As it snakes through Big Sur, California's Coast Highway (Hwy. 1), the state's first scenic highway and one of the world's most spectacular roadways, slips around the prominent ribs of the Santa Lucia Mountains, slides into dark wooded canyons, and soars across graceful bridges spanning the void. Though its existence means that a trip into Monterey no longer takes an entire day, people here nonetheless resent the highway that brings the flamed-out and frantic.

KIM WEIR

To show some respect, come to Big Sur during the week, in balmy April or early May when wildflowers burst forth, or in late September or October if you'd like to avoid the thick summer fog. Though winter is generally rainy, weeks of sparkling warm weather aren't uncommon. In April, Big Sur hosts the annual **Big Sur International Marathon,** with 1,600 or more runners hugging the highway curves from the village to Carmel.

CRUISING THE CENTRAL COAST

Just south of ruggedly aloof Big Sur is famous "Hearst Castle," now known formally as Hearst San Simeon State Historic Monument and one of the state's most popular visitor attractions. Always worth a stop, next south, is the scenic coastal town of Cambria, with its lush Monterey pines, galleries, and shops considered by some the Carmel of the southern Big Sur coast.

The biggest city immediately south from San Simeon is San Luis Obispo, a convenient stop halfway between L.A. and San Francisco along Hwy. 101 and most famous for inventing both the word and the modern concept of "motel," a contraction of "motor hotel." Agriculture is big business in and around San Luis Obispo. If you can time your trip right, roll into town on a Thursday evening to enjoy the Higuera Street Farmers' Market, one of the best anywhere (cancelled only in the event of rain).

Well worth going out of your way to discover is Mission San Antonio de Padua, north of San Luis Obispo and smack-dab in the middle of Fort Hunter-Liggett (security check at the base gate). Not the grandest or most spruced-up, San Antonio de Padua is perhaps the most genuinely evocative of all the California missions. Nearby Lake San Antonio is popular in winter for guided bald eagle–watching tours.

Off in the other direction, via Hwy. 58, is the Carrizo Plain Preserve, earthquake territory once sacred to the Chumash people and refuge to some of the state's most endangered animal species. In early 2001 President Clinton established the 204,107-acre Carrizo Plains National Monument, exercising his executive privilege under the 1906 Antiquities Act. One of 18 monuments created by Clinton in the last four years of his presidency, the establishment of the Carrizo Plains monument and seven similar end-of-term designations puts Clinton in the same league as Theodore Roosevelt—the only other U.S. president to use the Antiquities Act as often.

And if you head east from Paso Robles toward the San Joaquin Valley via Hwy. 46, you'll come to the shrine marking (almost) the spot where actor James Dean *(Rebel Without a Cause, Giant,* and *East of Eden)* died in a head-on car accident in 1955. Paso Robles itself and nearby Templeton anchor an increasingly popular—and increasingly impressive—wine region.

Morro Rock, California's little Gibraltar, spotted by Cabrillo in 1542, is the first thing people notice at Morro Bay on the coast west of San Luis Obispo. But the Morro Bay Chess Club maintains its giant outdoor chessboard downtown, and Morro Bay State Park, Montaña de Oro State Park, and area beaches are also worth exploring. The onetime port towns and piers along San Luis Obispo Bay to the south also have their attractions.

Santa Maria just over the border in Santa Barbara County is most noted for its own unique culinary heritage—"Santa Maria Barbecue," a tradition preserved since the days of the vaqueros. Near town is the Guadalupe-Nipomo Dunes Preserve, a coastal wildlife and plant preserve also protecting the remains of Cecil B. DeMille's *The Ten Commandments* movie set, buried under the sand here once filming was finished.

Lompoc is noted for its blooming flower fields—this is a major seed-producing area—and is home to Vandenberg Air Force Base as well as Mission La Purísima State Historic Park four miles east of town, California's only complete mission compound.

Farther south, Solvang is a Danish-style town founded in 1911 and now a well-trod tourist destination. If you've got time, worth exploring nearby are the towns of Los Olivos and Los Alamos, center of northern Santa Barbara County's impressive wine country.

Technically speaking, Point Conception just below Vandenberg marks the spot where California turns on itself—that pivotal geographical point where Northern California becomes Southern California, where rugged and rocky coastline gives way to broad white sandy beaches. The climatic and terrain changes are unmistakable by the time you arrive in Santa Barbara, a richly endowed city noted for its gracious red-tile-roofed California Spanish-style buildings and cultural attractions.

Continue south from Santa Barbara to Ventura to set off on whale-watching trips and guided boat tours of California's Channel Islands National Park, often visible from Santa Barbara and vicinity.

For general information about the area, contact the **Big Sur Chamber of Commerce,** P.O. Box 87, Big Sur, CA 93920, 831/667-2100,

HIGHWAY TO HEAVEN

The name Big Sur—"Big South" in Spanish, a reference point from the Monterey perspective—comes from Rio Grande del Sur, or the Big Sur River, which flows to the sea at Point Sur. The native Esselen people were long gone by the time the first area settlers arrived. California's native grizzly bears, long extinct, survived for much longer along the Big Sur coast than elsewhere in the state—and posed the greatest 18th-century threat to local settlement—since the terrain discouraged any type of travel and the usual wildlife predation that came with it.

Then, in the early 1900s came the highway, now a section of Hwy. 1, a hazardous 15-year construction project connecting Big Sur proper with San Simeon. Hardworking Chinese laborers were recruited for the job along with less willing workers from the state's prisons. The highway was completed in 1937, though many lives and much equipment were lost to the sea. Maintaining this remote ribbon of highway and its 29 bridges is still a treacherous year-round task. Following the wild winter storms of 1982–83, for example, 42 landslides blocked the highway; the "big one" near Julia Pfeiffer Burns State Park took 19 bulldozers and more than a year to clear.

Highway One is California's first scenic highway.

ROBERT HOLMES/CALTOUR

www.bigsurcalifornia.org. Combined headquarters for area state parks and the U.S. Forest Service is **Big Sur Station** on the south side of Pfeiffer-Big Sur on Hwy. 1, Big Sur, CA 93920, 831/667-2315. Open daily 8 A.M.–4:30 P.M., this is the place to go in search of forest and wilderness maps, permits, and backcountry camping and recreation information.

SEEING BIG SUR

Garrapata and Point Sur State Parks

Garrapata State Park stretches north along the coast for more than four miles from Soberanes Point, where the Santa Lucia Mountains first dive into the sea. Southward, the at-first unimpressive **Point Sur** and its lighthouse beacon stand out beyond 2,879-acre Garrapata State Park and beach, the latter named after the noble wood tick and featuring a crescent of creek-veined white sand, granite arches, caves and grottos, and sea otters. Ticks or no ticks, the unofficial nude beach here is one of the best in Northern California. Winter whale-watching is usually good from high ground. On weekends in January, ranger-led whale-watch programs are held at Granite Canyon. Or, if it's not foggy, take the two-mile loop trail from the turnout for the view.

Up atop Point Sur stands the Point Sur Lightstation, an 1889 sandstone affair still standing guard at this shipwreck site once known as the Graveyard of the Pacific. The lighthouse is now computer-operated and features an electrical aero-beacon, radio-beacon, and fog "diaphone." This 34-acre area and its central rocky mound (good views and whale-watching) is now a state park, though the Coast Guard still maintains the lighthouse. Guided three-hour lighthouse walking tours ($5) are offered five or six times a week in summer, three times weekly in winter. Current tour information is posted throughout Big Sur, or call 831/625-4419.

A few miles farther south on the highway is the famous **Rainbow Bridge** (now called Bixby Creek Bridge), 260 feet high and 700 feet long, the highest single-arch bridge in the world when constructed in 1932 and still the most photographed of all Big Sur bridges.

Andrew Molera State Park

Inland and up, past what remains of the pioneering Molera Ranch (part of the original Rancho El Sur), is marvelous Andrew Molera State Park, a 2,100-acre park first donated to The Nature Conservancy by Frances Molera in honor of her brother. There's no pavement here, just a run-down dirt parking lot and a short trail winding through sycamores, maples, and a few redwoods along the east fork of the Big Sur River to the two-mile beach and adjacent seabird-sanctuary lagoon below. The trail north of the river's mouth leads up a steep promontory to Garnet Beach, noted for its colorful pebbles. Except on major holiday weekends, it's usually uncrowded at Andrew Molera. The park also features a primitive yet peaceful 10-acre walk-in campground just one-quarter mile from the parking lot (three-night limit). For more information about the park, contact: Andrew Molera State Park, P.O. Box A, Big Sur, CA 93920, 831/667-2315.

Also at the park: **Molera Horseback Tours,** P.O. Box 111, Big Sur, CA 93920, 831/625-5486 or toll-free 800/942-5486, which offers regularly scheduled one- to three-hour rides along the beach and through meadows and redwood groves. Guides explain the history, flora, and fauna of the area. Private rides are also available by appointment. Rates are $25–35 an hour.

Pfeiffer–Big Sur State Park

Sunny Big Sur Valley, a visitor-oriented settlement surrounding picnic and camping facilities at 821-acre Pfeiffer–Big Sur State Park, adjoins the Ventana Wilderness. Take the one-mile nature trail or meander up through the redwoods to **Pfeiffer Falls,** a verdant, fern-lined canyon at its best in spring and early summer, then on up to **Valley View** for a look at the precipitous Big Sur River gorge below. The outdoor amphitheater at Pfeiffer–Big Sur (which hosts many of the park's educational summer campfires and interpretive programs) and lagoons were built by the Civilian Conservation Corps during the Depression.

The large developed year-round campground features more than 200 campsites with picnic tables and hot showers. To make reservations—advisable in summer, when the park is particularly crowded, and on good-weather weekends—call ReserveAmerica, 800/444-7275. The day-use fee for short park hikes and picnicking is $2. For more information, contact: Pfeiffer–Big Sur State Park, Big Sur, CA 93920, 831/667-2315.

About a mile south of the entrance to Pfeiffer–Big Sur is the road to Los Padres National Forest's **Pfeiffer Beach** (take the second right-hand turnoff after the park) and its cypresses, craggy caves, and mauve and white sands streaked with black. It's heaven here on a clear, calm day, but the hissing sand stings mercilessly when the weather is up. On any day, forget the idea of an ocean swim. The water's cold, the surf capricious, and the currents tricky; even expert divers need to register with rangers before jumping in. Pfeiffer Beach is open to the public 6 A.M.–sunset.

Urban Big Sur

Nowhere in Big Sur country are visitors really diverted from the land because big-time boutiques, gaudy gift shops, even movie theaters don't exist. But urban Big Sur starts at Big Sur Valley and stretches south past the post office to Deetjen's. This "big city" part of Big Sur includes the area's most famous inns and restaurants: the Ventana Inn, Nepenthe, and Deetjen's (see Practical Big Sur below). Fascinating about Nepenthe is the fact that although cinematographer Orson Welles was persona non grata just down the coast at San Simeon (for his too-faithful portrayal of William Randolph Hearst in *Citizen Kane*), when he bought what was then the Trails Club Log Cabin in Big Sur for his wife Rita Hayworth in 1944, he was able to haunt Hearst from the north. Welles's place became Nepenthe ("surcease from sorrows") shortly after he sold it in 1947.

South of Deetjen's is the noted **Coast Gallery** at Lafler Canyon (named for editor Henry Lafler, a friend of Jack London), 831/667-2301, open daily 9 A.M.–5 P.M. Rebuilt from redwood water tanks in 1973, the Coast Gallery offers fine local arts and crafts, from jewelry and pottery to paintings, sculpture, and woodcarvings. Nearby is the **Henry Miller Memorial Library,** a collection of

THE ESALEN INSTITUTE

The Esselen and Salinan peoples frequented the hot springs here, supposedly called *tok-i-tok,* "hot healing water." In 1939, Dr. H. C. Murphy (who officiated at John Steinbeck's birth in Salinas) opened Slate's Hot Springs resort on the site. The hot springs were transformed by grandson Michael Murphy into the famed Esalen Institute, where human-potential practitioners and participants including Joan Baez, Gregory Bateson, the Beatles, Jerry Brown, Carlos Castaneda, Buckminster Fuller, Aldous Huxley, Linus Pauling, B. F. Skinner, Hunter S. Thompson, and Alan Watts taught or learned in residential workshops.

Esalen is the Cadillac of New Age retreats, according to absurdist/comedian/editor Paul Krassner. Even writer Alice Kahn who, before arriving at Esalen, considered herself the "last psycho-virgin in California" and "hard-core unevolved," eventually admitted that there was something about the Esalen Institute that defied all cynicism.

Esalen's magic doesn't necessarily come cheap. The introductory "Experiencing Esalen" weekend workshop runs $485 or so, including simple but pleasant accommodations and wonderful meals ($230 if a sleeping bag is all you'll need). Five-day workshops are substantially more—in the $750-and-up range. But Esalen tries to accommodate even the less affluent with scholarships, a work-study program, senior citizen discounts, family rates, and bunk bed or sleeping bag options. You can also arrange just an overnight or weekend stay (sans enlightenment) assuming space is available.

Esalen offers more than 400 workshops each year, these "relating to our greater human capacity." Topics cover everything from the arts and creative expression to "intellectual play," from dreams to spiritual healing, from martial arts to shamanism. Equally mythic are Esalen's baths. In February 1998 a mudslide roared down the hill to demolish the previous bathhouse facilities, though an ambitious rebuilding project is now underway. The new, improved Esalen baths, scheduled to open in late 2000, will include a geothermally heated swimming pool and a handicapped-accessible hot tub and massage area. In the meantime, Esalen's "temporary baths" are available—but only to Esalen guests. When the new bathhouse opens, Esalen will again satisfy the California Coastal Commission's public access requirement, by allowing the general public access to the hot tubs (at the fairly unappealing hours of 1–3 A.M. daily). Call for details. The massages at Esalen are world-renowned, from $50 an hour. Nudity is big at Esalen, particularly in the hot tubs, swimming pool, and massage area, though not required.

Entrance to Esalen and its facilities is strictly by reservation only. For information on workshops and lodgings and to request a copy of Esalen's current catalog, contact: Esalen Institute, Big Sur, CA 93920, 831/667-3000, www.esalen.org. The website's online *In the Air* magazine offers a good sense of what Esalen is all about, and also includes a complete current workshop catalog (which you can download).

friendly clutter about the writer and his life's work, located on the highway about one mile south of the Ventana Inn but almost hidden behind redwoods and an unassuming redwood double gate. Henry Miller lived, wrote, and painted in Big Sur 1944–1962. The library is housed not in Henry Miller's former home but in that of the late Emil White. A good friend of Miller's, White said he started the library "because I missed him." Now a community cultural arts center, the library sponsors exhibits, poetry readings, concerts, and special events throughout the year. Original art and prints, posters, and postcards are available in the gallery. Miller's books, including rare editions, are also available. In summer the library is often open daily, but year-round is always open on weekends, 11 A.M.–6 P.M., and for special events. For current information, contact: **Henry Miller Library,** Hwy. 1, Big Sur, CA 93920, tel./fax 831/667-2574, www.henrymiller.org. Or call the county library at 831/667-2537.

Julia Pfeiffer Burns State Park

There's a stone marker at the park's official entrance, about seven miles south of Nepenthe. These spectacular 4,000 acres straddling the highway also include a large underwater park offshore. Picnic in the coast redwoods by McWay Creek (almost the southern limit of their range) or hike up into the chaparral and the Los Padres National Forest. After picnicking, take the short walk along McWay Creek (watch for poison oak) then through the tunnel under the road to **Saddle Rock** and the cliffs above **Waterfall Cove,** the only California waterfall that plunges directly into the sea. The cliffs are rugged here; it's a good place to view whales and otters. Only experienced divers, by permit, are allowed to scuba offshore. The park also features limited year-round camping at walk-in environmental sites and group campgrounds only. For more information about the park, including winter whale-watching programs held here on weekends, contact: Julia Pfeiffer Burns State Park, Big Sur, CA 93920, 831/667-2315.

Lucia and the New Camaldoli Hermitage

The tiny "town" of Lucia is privately owned, with gas station and a good down-home restaurant open after 7 A.M. until dark, when they shut off the generator. Try the homemade split pea soup.

South of Lucia (at the white cross), the road to the left leads to the New Camaldoli Hermitage, a small Benedictine monastery at the former Lucia Ranch. The sign says that the monks "regret we cannot invite you to camp, hunt, or enjoy a walk on our property" due to the hermitage's customary solitude and avoidance of "unnecessary speaking." But visitors *can* come to buy crafts and homemade fruitcake and to attend daily mass. In addition, the hermitage is available for very serene retreats of up to several days (few outsiders can stand the no-talking rules for much longer than that), simple meals included. Suggested offering is $45–55 per day, depending on the accommodation. For more information, contact: New Camaldoli Hermitage, Director of Vocations, Big Sur, CA 93920, 831/667-2456 or 831/667-2341, www.contemplation.com.

Limekiln State Park

About two miles south of Lucia is the newest Big Sur state park, open since 1995, 716 acres in an isolated and steep coastal canyon preserving some of the oldest, largest, and most vigorous redwoods in Monterey County. Named for the towering wood-fired kilns that smelted quarried limestone into powdered lime—essential for mixing cement—here in the late 1800s, Limekiln State Park offers a steep one-mile round-trip creekside hike through redwoods to the four kilns, passing a waterfall (to the right at the first fork), pools, and cascades along the way. Day-use area for pic-

nicking ($2 fee) and a very appealing 43-site family campground with minimal amenities but abundant ambience. To get here, take the signed turnoff (on the inland or landward side of the highway) just south of the Limekiln Canyon Bridge. For more information, contact: Limekiln State Park, 63025 Hwy. 1, Big Sur, CA 93920, 831/667-2403. See also Camping in Big Sur below.

DOING BIG SUR

The ultimate activity in Big Sur is just bumming around: scrambling down to beaches to hunt for jade and peer into tidepools or scuba dive or surf where it's possible, also cycling, sightseeing, and watching the sun set. Along the coastline proper there are few long hiking trails, since much of the terrain is treacherous and most of the rest privately owned, but the Big Sur backcountry offers good hiking and backpacking.

Ventana Wilderness

Local lore has it that a natural land bridge once connected two mountain peaks at Bottchers Gap, creating a window (or *ventana* in Spanish) until the 1906 San Francisco earthquake brought it all tumbling down. The Big Sur, Little Sur, Arroyo Seco, and Carmel Rivers all cut through this 161,000-acre area, creating dramatic canyon gorges and wildlands well worth exploring. Steep, sharp-crested ridges and serrated V-shaped valleys are clothed mostly in oaks, madrones, and dense chaparral. Redwoods grow on north-facing slopes near the fog-cooled coast, pines at higher elevations. The gnarly spiral-shaped bristlecone firs found only here are in the rockiest, most remote areas, their total range only about 12 miles wide and 55 miles long.

Most of all, the Ventana Wilderness provides a great escape from the creeping coastal traffic (a free visitor permit is required to enter), and offers great backpacking and hiking when the Sierra Nevada, Klamath Mountains, and Cascades are still snowbound—though roads here are sometimes impassable during the rainy season. Hunting, fishing, and horseback riding are also permitted. Crisscrossing Ventana Wilderness are nearly 400 miles of backcountry trails and 82 vehicle-accessible campgrounds (trailside camping possible with a permit).

The wilderness trailheads are at Big Sur Station, Carmel River, China Camp, Arroyo Seco, Memorial Park, Bottchers Gap, and Cone Peak Road. The Ventana Wilderness recreation map, available for $4 from ranger district offices, shows all roads, trails, and campgrounds. Fire-hazardous areas, routinely closed to the public after July 1 (or earlier), are coded yellow on maps.

For more Ventana Wilderness information, contact the Big Sur Station office (see above) or **Los Padres National Forest** headquarters, 6755 Hollister Ave., Ste. 150, Goleta, CA 93117, 805/968-6640, www.r5.fs.fed.us/lospadres.

Big Sur Hikes

The grandest views of Big Sur come from the ridges just back from the coast. The short but steep **Valley View Trail** from Pfeiffer–Big Sur State Park is usually uncrowded, especially midweek; there are benches up top for sitting and staring off the edge of the world. Those *serious* about coastal hiking should walk all the way from Pfeiffer–Big Sur to Salmon Creek near the southern Monterey County line. The trip from Bottchers Gap to Ventana Double Cone via **Skinner Ridge Trail** is about 16 miles one way and challenging, with a variety of possible campsites, dazzling spring wildflowers, and oak and pine forests.

Otherwise, take either the nine-mile **Pine Ridge Trail** from Big Sur or the 15-mile trail from China Camp on Chews Ridge to undeveloped Sykes Hot Springs, just 400 yards from Sykes Camp (very popular these days). Another good, fairly short *visual* hike is the trip to nearby Mount Manuel, a nine-mile round-trip. The two-mile walk to **Pfeiffer Beach** is also worth it—miles from the highway, fringed by forest, with a wading cove and meditative monolith.

PRACTICAL BIG SUR

Camping in Big Sur

In the accommodations category nothing but camping is truly inexpensive in Big Sur, so to travel on the cheap, make campground reservations *early* (where applicable) and stock up on groceries and sundries in Monterey up north or in San Luis Obispo to the south.

For up-to-date information on the area's national forest campgrounds and for free visitor permits, fire permits, maps, and other information about Los Padres National Forest and the Ventana Wilderness, stop by the **Big Sur Station** State Parks/U.S. Forest Service office at Pfeiffer–Big Sur State Park, open daily 8 A.M.–4:30 P.M., 831/667-2315; the Forest Service district office farther south at **Pacific Valley,** 805/927-4211; or the **Monterey Ranger District** office at 406 S. Mildred Ave., King City, CA 93930, 831/385-5434.

For secluded Big Sur camping, try **Andrew Molera State Park,** with 50 walk-in tent sites not far from the dusty parking lot, or **Julia Pfeiffer Burns State Park,** almost as nice, with two separate environmental campgrounds (far from RVs). More comforts (including flush toilets and hot showers) are available at the attractive redwoods-and-river family campground at **Pfeiffer–Big Sur State Park,** 200-plus tents-only campsites plus a regular summer schedule of educational and informational programs. For information about any of the area's state park campgrounds, stop by the office at Pfeiffer–Big Sur State Park or call 831/667-2315. For ReserveAmerica reservations (usually necessary May–early Sept. and on warm-weather weekends), call toll-free 800/444-7275.

Another possibility, just south of Lucia, is the postcard-pretty **Limekiln State Park,** 63025 Hwy. 1, 831/667-2403, which takes up most of the steep canyon and offers some good hiking in addition to attractive tent and RV sites (no hookups, but water, hot showers, and flush toilets). For reservations, call ReserveAmerica toll-free at 800/444-7275.

Big Sur also has some private campgrounds; for suggestions, contact the chamber of commerce (see p. 537).

ACCOMMODATIONS RATINGS

Accommodations in this book are rated by price category, based on double-occupancy, high-season rates. Categories used are:

Budget.	$35 and under
Inexpensive	$35-60
Moderate	$60-85
Expensive	$85-110
Premium	$110-150
Luxury	$150 and up

Affordable Big Sur Stays

Always a best bet for cabins and affordable for just plain folks is the charming **Ripplewood Resort** about a mile north of Pfeiffer–Big Sur, 831/667-2242, where the primo units, most with fireplaces and kitchens (bring your own cookware), are down by the Big Sur River (and booked months in advance for summer). Moderate-Expensive. Other options include the adobe **Glen Oaks Motel,** 831/667-2105, and the **Fernwood Resort,** 831/667-2422, both on Hwy. 1 and both Moderate-Expensive. The **Big Sur River Inn,** on Hwy. 1 in Big Sur Valley, 831/625-5255 or toll-free 800/548-3610, is a motel-restaurant-bar popular with locals and featuring views of the river and live music most weekends. Expensive-Luxury. The **Big Sur Lodge** nearby, just inside the park's entrance, 831/667-3100, is quiet, with pool, sauna, restaurant, and a circle of comfy cabins. Premium, but substantially lower in winter and early spring.

Deetjen's Big Sur Inn

Just south of the noted Nepenthe restaurant and the Henry Miller Library is the landmark Norwegian-style Deetjen's Big Sur Inn in Castro Canyon, 831/667-2377, a rambling, ever-blooming inn with redwood rooms—the experience now listed on the National Register of Historic Places. *Very* Big Sur. The 19 eccentric, rustic rooms chock-full of bric-a-brac—one's named Chateau Fiasco, after the Bay of Pigs invasion—have no TVs, no telephones, thin walls, front doors that don't lock, fireplaces, books, and reasonably functional plumbing. Forget about trendy creature comforts. People love this place—and have, ever since it opened in the 1930s—because it has *soul.* Private or shared bath. Reservations advised because rooms are usually booked up many months in advance. Expensive-Luxury. Eating at Deetjen's is as big a treat as an overnight. Wonderfully hearty, wholesome breakfasts are served 8–11:30 A.M., and dinner starts at 6:15 P.M. Reservations are also taken for meals.

Ventana Inn & Spa

Perhaps tuned into the same philosophical frequency as Henry Miller—"There being nothing to improve on in the surroundings, the tendency is to set about improving oneself"—in the beginning, when writer Lawrence A. Spector first built this place in 1975, the Ventana Inn people didn't provide distractions like TV or tennis courts. Though it's still a hip, high-priced resort, and there are still no tennis courts, things have

NEPENTHE

Nepenthe, about a mile south of the Ventana Inn, was built almost exactly on the site of the cabin Orson Welles bought for Rita Hayworth. So it's not too surprising that the restaurant is almost as legendary as Big Sur itself. A striking multilevel structure complete with an arts and crafts center, the restaurant was named for an ancient Egyptian drug taken to help people forget. Naturally enough, the bar here does a brisk business.

As is traditional at Nepenthe, relax on the upper deck (the "gay pavilion," presided over by a sculpted bronze and redwood phoenix) with drink in hand to salute the sea and setting sun. Surreal views. The open-beamed restaurant and its outdoor above-ocean terrace isn't nearly as rowdy as all those bohemian celebrity stories would suggest. Nonetheless, thrill-seekers insist on sitting on the top deck, though there's often more room available downstairs at the health food deli and deck. The fare here is good, but not as spectacular (on a clear day) as the views. Try the homemade soups, the hefty chef's salad, any of the vegetarian selections, or the world-famous Ambrosia burger (an excellent cheeseburger on French roll with pickles and a salad for a hefty price) accompanied by a Basket o' Fries. Good pies and cakes for dessert.

To avoid the worst of the tourist traffic and to appreciate Nepenthe at its best, come later in September or October. And although Nepenthe is casual any time of year, it's not *that* casual. Local lore has it that John F. Kennedy was once turned away because he showed up barefoot. Nepenthe is open for lunch and dinner daily, with music and dancing around the hearth at night. For more information or reservations, call 831/667-2345.

And if at the moment you can't be here in person, you can be here in spirit—much easier now that Nepenthe has an online weather camera pointing south over the back deck. To "see" what's happening along Nepenthe's coastline, try www.nepenthebigsur.com.

changed. Now the desperately undiverted *can* phone home, if need be, or watch in-room TV or videos. But the woodsy, world-class Ventana high up on the hill in Big Sur, 831/667-2331, 831/624-4812, or toll-free 800/628-6500, fax 831/667-2419, www.ventanainn.com, still offers luxurious and relaxed contemporary lodgings on 240 acres overlooking the sea, outdoor Japanese hot baths, heated pools, and a full-service spa. Family travelers, please note: Children are discouraged at Ventana, which is not set up to entertain or otherwise look after them.

If a stay here or a self-pampering spa session seem just *too rich,* try drinks-with-a-view or a bite of enticing California cuisine served in the lovely two-tiered **Cielo** restaurant overlooking the ocean, a pleasant stroll through the woods. The Ventana Inn is located eight-tenths of a mile south of Pfeiffer–Big Sur State Park; look for the sign on the left.

Post Ranch Inn

For good reason, new Big Sur commercial development has been rare in recent years. If further coastal development must come, the environmentally conscious Post Ranch Inn offers the style—if not the price range—most Californians would cheer. Perched on a ridge overlooking the grand Pacific Ocean, the Post Ranch Inn is a carefully executed nature study. The 30 redwood-and-glass "guest houses" are designed and built to harmonize with—almost disappear into—the hilltop landscape. The triangular "tree houses" are built on stilts, to avoid damaging the roots of the oaks with which they intertwine; the spectacular sod-roofed "ocean houses" literally blend into the ocean views; and the gracious "coast house" duplexes impersonate stand-tall coastal redwoods. Absolute privacy and understated, earth-toned luxury are the main points here. Priced for Silicon Valley whiz kids and Hollywood entertainment execs (like Ventana, in the $300 and up range), continental breakfast is included. Luxury. Guests can also enjoy the **Post Ranch Spa**—offering massage, wraps, and facials—and the exceptional California-style **Sierra Mar** restaurant, where the views are every bit as inviting as the daily changing menu. Full bar. Open for lunch and dinner.

The Post Ranch Inn is 30 miles south of Carmel on Hwy. 1, on the west (seaward) side of the road. As at Ventana, children are discouraged here. For more information, contact: Post Ranch Inn, P.O. Box 219, Big Sur, CA 93920, 831/667-2200, www.postranchinn.com. For inn reservations, call toll-free 800/527-2200. For restaurant reservations, call 831/667-2800.

Eating Well in Big Sur

Look for fairly inexpensive fare in and around the Big Sur Valley. Good for breakfast is the **Ripplewood Resort** just north of Pfeiffer–Big Sur near the tiny Big Sur Library, 831/667-2242, where favorites include the homemade baked goods and French toast. **Deetjen's,** 831/667-2377, is special for breakfast, wholesome and hearty fare is served in the open-beamed hobbit-style dining rooms. Dinner is more formal (fireplace blazing to ward off the chill mist, classical music, two seatings, by reservation only), with entrées including steaks, fish, California country cuisine, and vegetarian dishes. Tasty home-baked pies are an after-meal specialty at the casual **Trails Head Café** at the Big Sur Lodge, 831/667-3111, overlooking the river, also known for red snapper and California-style fare. Beer and wine.

Everyone should sample the view from **Nepenthe** at least once in their lifetime. A culinary hot spot is the **Glen Oaks Restaurant** next door to the Ripplewood Resort, 831/667-2264 or 831/667-2865, with fine music, flowers, and elegance à la Big Sur. Entrées emphasize what's local and fresh, and include crepes, good vegetarian, and seafood. Open for dinner Wed.–Mon. nights. The Glen Oaks also serves a fine Sunday brunch, with omelettes, eggs Benedict, and cornmeal hotcakes. A quarter-mile north of Palo Colorado Rd. on Hwy. 1 is the **Rocky Point Restaurant,** 831/624-2933, a reasonably well-heeled roadhouse overlooking the ocean. Open for breakfast, lunch, and dinner daily.

The finest of local fine dining is served at the area's luxury-hotel restaurants—at **Cielo** at the Ventana Inn & Spa, and **Sierra Mar** at the Post Ranch Inn—which both serve lunch and dinner daily. For information, see listings above.

SAN SIMEON AND VICINITY

Hearst San Simeon State Historic Monument ranks right up there with Disneyland as one of California's premier tourist attractions. Somehow that fact alone puts the place into proper perspective. Media magnate William Randolph Hearst's castle is a rich man's playground filled to overflowing with artistic diversions and other expensive toys, a monument to one man's monumental ego and equally impressive poor taste.

In real life, of course, Hearst was a wealthy and powerful man, the subject of the greatest American movie ever made, Orson Welles's 1941 *Citizen Kane.* "Pleasure," Hearst once wrote, "is worth what you can afford to pay for it." And that attitude showed itself quite early; on his 10th birthday, little William asked for the Louvre as a present. One scene in the movie, where Charles Foster Kane shouts across the cavernous living room at Xanadu to attract the attention of his bored young mistress, endlessly working jigsaw puzzles while she sits before a fireplace as big as the mouth of Jonah's whale, won't seem so surreal once you see San Simeon.

Designed by Berkeley architect Julia Morgan, the buildings themselves are odd yet handsome hallmarks of Spanish Renaissance architecture. The centerpiece La Casa Grande alone has 115 rooms (including a movie theater, a billiards room, two libraries, and 31 bathrooms) adorned with silk banners, fine Belgian and French tapestries, French fireplaces, European choir stalls, and ornately carved ceilings—some from continental monasteries, churches, and castles. The furnishings and art Hearst collected from around the world complete the picture, one that includes everything but humor, grace, warmth, and understanding.

TOURING HEARST CASTLE

Following his parents' death, William Randolph Hearst decided to build a house at "the ranch," partly as a place to store his already burgeoning art collection. Architect Julia Morgan, a family favorite, signed on for the project in 1919—for her, the beginning of a 28-year architectural collaboration. Morgan and Hearst planned the ever-evolving Enchanted Hill as a Mediterranean hill town, with La Casa Grande, the main house, as the "cathedral" facing the sea. Three additional palaces were clustered in front, the whole town surrounded by lavish terraced gardens.

In spring when the hills are emerald green, from the faraway highway Hearst's castle appears as if by magic up on the hill. (Before the place opened for public tours in the 1950s, the closest view commoners could get was from the road, with the assistance of coin-operated telescopes.) One thing visitors *don't* see on the shuttle up the enchanted hill is Hearst's 2,000-acre zoo—"the largest private zoo since Noah," as Charles Foster Kane would put it—once the country's largest. The inmates have long since been dispersed, though survivors of Hearst's

on Hearst's enchanted hill

CITIZEN HEARST

The name San Simeon was originally given to three Mexican land grants—40,000 acres bought by mining scion George Hearst in 1865. George, the first millionaire Hearst, owned Nevada's Comstock Lode silver mine, Ophir silver mine, and the rich Homestake gold mine in South Dakota, and also staked-out territory in California's goldfields. George Hearst later expanded the family holdings to 250,000 acres (including 50 miles of coastline) for the family's "Camp Hill" Victorian retreat and cattle ranch. With his substantial wealth, he was even able to buy himself a U.S. Senate seat.

But young William Randolph had even more ambitious plans—personally and for the property. The only son of the senator and San Francisco schoolteacher, socialite, and philanthropist Phoebe Apperson, the high-rolling junior Hearst took a fraction of the family wealth and his daddy's failing *San Francisco Examiner* and created a successful yellow-journalism chain, eventually adding radio stations and movie production companies.

Putting his newfound power of propaganda to work in the political arena, Hearst (primarily for the headlines) goaded Congress into launching the Spanish-American War in 1898. But unlike his father, William Randolph was unable to buy much personal political power. Though he aspired to the presidency, he had to settle for two terms as a congressmember from New York.

exotic elk, zebras, Barbary sheep, and Himalayan goat herds still roam the grounds.

Hearst Castle Tours

There are four separate day tours of the Hearst San Simeon State Historic Monument, each taking approximately two hours, plus an evening tour of the same duration. Theoretically the San Simeon tours could all be taken in a day, but don't try it. So much Hearst in the short span of a day could be detrimental to one's well-being. A dosage of two tours per day makes the trip here worthwhile yet not overwhelming. Visitors obsessed with seeing it all should plan a two-day stay in the area or come back again some other time. Whichever tour or combination of tours you select, be sure to wear comfortable walking shoes. Lots of stairs.

Tour One is a good first-time visit, taking in the castle's main floor, one guest house, and some of the gardens—a total of 150 steps and a half mile of walking. Included on the tour is a short showing in the theater of some of Hearst's "home movies." Particularly impressive in a gloomy Gothic way is the dining room, but the billiards room and mammoth great hall, with Canova's *Venus,* are also unforgettable. All the tours include both the Greco-Roman Neptune Pool and statuary, and the indoor Roman Pool with its mosaics of lapis lazuli and gold leaf. It's hard to imagine Churchill, cigar in mouth, cavorting here in an inner tube.

Tour Two requires more walking, covering the mansion's upper floors, the libraries, kitchen, and Hearst's Gothic Suite (from which he ran his 94 separate business enterprises), with its rose-tinted windows. The delightfully lit Celestial Suite was the nonetheless depressing extramarital playground of Hearst and Marion Davies.

Tour Three covers one of the guest houses plus the "new wing" of the main house, with its 36

the Gothic Library

TOM MYERS PHOTOGRAPHY

luxurious bedrooms, sitting rooms, and marble bathrooms furnished with fine art. This tour also includes a short film detailing the extraordinary efforts involved in building the castle.

Gardeners will be moved to tears by **Tour Four** (Apr.–Aug. only), which includes a long stroll through the San Simeon grounds but does not go inside the castle itself. Realizing that all the rich topsoil here had to be manually carried up the hill makes the array of exotic plant life, including unusual camellias and some 6,000 rosebushes, all the more impressive—not to mention the fact that gardeners at San Simeon worked only at night because Hearst couldn't stand watching them. Also included on the fourth tour is the lower level of the elegant, 17-room Casa del Mar guesthouse (where Hearst spent much of his time), the recently redone underground Neptune Pool dressing rooms, the never-finished bowling alley, and Hearst's wine cellar. David Niven once remarked that, with Hearst as host, the wine flowed "like glue." Subsequently, Niven was the only guest allowed free access to the castle's wine cellar.

Evening Tours are two-hour adventures featuring the highlights of other tours—with the added benefit of allowing you to pretend to be some Hollywood celebrity, just arrived and in need of orientation. (Hearst himself handed out tour maps, since newcomers often got lost.) Docents dressed in period costume inhabit the rooms, play poker or pool, and show you around. It's worth it just to see the castle in lights. At last report, evening tours were offered on Fri. and Sat. nights Mar.–May and Sept.–Dec., but call for current details. December **Christmas at the Castle** tours are particularly festive.

Practical Hearst Castle

San Simeon is open daily except Thanksgiving, Christmas, and New Year's Day, with the regular two-hour tours leaving the visitors center area on the hour from early morning until around dusk. Tour schedules change by season and day of the week. Reservations aren't required, but the chance of getting tickets on a drop-in, last-minute basis is small. For current schedule information and reservations, call ReserveAmerica toll-free at 800/444-4445 and have that credit card handy. (For international ticket reservations, dial the U.S. extension then 1-880/444-4445.) Wheelchair-access tours of San Simeon are offered on a different schedule; call 805/927-2070 for reservations and information.

JULIA MORGAN: LETTING THE WORK SPEAK FOR ITSELF

Julia Morgan, San Simeon's architect, supervised the execution of almost every detail of Hearst's rambling 165-room pleasure palace. This 95-pound, teetotaling, workaholic woman was UC Berkeley's first female engineering graduate, and the first woman to graduate from the École des Beaux-Arts in Paris. Credited only after her death for her accomplishments, if acclaim came late for Morgan, it was partly her preference. She loathed publicity, disdained the very idea of celebrity, and believed that architects should be like anonymous medieval masters and let the work speak for itself.

Morgan's work with Hearst departed dramatically from her belief that buildings should be unobtrusive, the cornerstone of her brilliant but equally unobtrusive career. "My style," she said to those who seemed bewildered by the contradiction, "is to please my client." Pleasing her client in this case was quite a task. Hearst arbitrarily and habitually changed his mind, all the while complaining about slow progress and high costs. And she certainly didn't do the job for money, though Hearst and her other clients paid her well. Morgan divided her substantial earnings among her staff, keeping only about $10,000 annually to cover office overhead and personal expenses.

The perennially private Morgan, who never allowed her name to be posted at construction sites, designed almost 800 buildings in California and the West, among them the original Asilomar in Pacific Grove; the Berkeley City Club; the Oakland YWCA; and the bell tower, library, social hall, and gym at Oakland's Mills College. She also designed and supervised the reconstruction of San Francisco's Fairmont Hotel following its devastation in the 1906 earthquake. Other Hearst commissions included the family's Wyntoon retreat near Mount Shasta as well as the *Los Angeles Herald-Examiner* building.

Admission to each of the four San Simeon day tours is $10 adults, $5 children (ages 6–17). Evening tour rates are $20 adults, $10 children. A special brochure for international travelers (printed in Japanese, Korean, French, German, Hebrew, Italian, and Spanish) is available. With a little forethought (see Near San Simeon below), visitors can avoid eating the concession-style food here.

Adjacent to the visitors center is the Hearst Castle's giant-screened **National Geographic Theatre,** 805/927-6811, where at last report the larger-than-life *Hearst Castle—Building the Dream* and *Everest* were showing on the 70-foot by 52-foot screen. Call for current times and details (no reservations required).

For other information, contact: Hearst San Simeon State Historic Monument, 750 Hearst Castle Rd., San Simeon, CA 93452, 805/927-2020 or 805/927-2000, www.hearstcastle.org.

NEAR SAN SIMEON

San Simeon: The Beaches and the Town

Done with the display of pompous circumstance on the hill, head for the serene sandy beaches nearby for a long coast walk to clear out the clutter. Good ocean swimming. Nude sunbathers sometimes congregate at the north end of **William Randolph Hearst Memorial State Beach** across the highway from Hearst Castle, indulging in a healthy hedonism Hearst would absolutely hate, but otherwise it's a family-style stop with good picnicking, restrooms, and a public pier popular for fishing. Day-use fee: $2.

Another picnicking possibility, especially for whale-watchers, is **Piedras Blancas Lighthouse** just up the coast. The lighthouse, built in 1874, is now automated and off-limits to the public. Wonderful tidepools and good abalone diving are characteristics of the coast near here, at **Twin Creeks Beach,** but public access may be restricted, as the area seems to be turning into a seasonal home for a northern elephant seal colony. The beaches at **San Simeon State Park** farther south near Cambria are larger and rockier. The park features three separate day-use areas popular for fishing and picnicking, 70 primitive campsites, and 134 developed campsites near San Simeon Creek off San Simeon Creek Rd. (five miles

south of San Simeon on Hwy. 1). If you need to stretch your legs, take the pleasant three-mile **San Simeon Creek Trail,** starting from the Washburn Day Use Area. For park information, call 805/927-2035 or 805/927-2020.

The "town" of San Simeon is actually two tiny towns: the original Spanish-style, red-tile-roofed village built for Hearst employees, and "San Simeon Acres," the highway's motel row. The old **Sebastian's General Store,** 805/927-4217, in the real San Simeon is a state historic monument and a great picnic supply stop with old-time post office and more modern garden café. Quite casual and comfortable, with whaling implements on the wall. Party boats powered by **Virg's Fish'n,** 805/927-4676 or 805/927-4677, set out from the harbor Mar.–Oct. for fishing. Ask about whale-watching tours.

Cambria

Its borders blending into San Simeon about eight miles south of Hearst Castle, the artsy coastal town of Cambria now bears the Roman name for ancient Wales but was previously called Rosaville, San Simeon, and (seriously) Slabtown. In some

---

LIFE IN HARMONY

People like to start wedded life auspiciously by getting married at the chapel in Harmony, actually a converted wine and cheese shop. Over the years, this privately owned onetime dairy town has also grown into a laid-back artsy enclave, with pottery and glass-blowers' shops, an artists' studio, gift and T-shirt shop, and restaurant (shuttered at last report). As the story goes, Harmony (population 18, more or less) got its name in the 1890s when feuding neighbors put aside their differences to build a school; when it was finished, they called it Harmony Valley Schoolhouse. The old Harmony Valley Creamery, where none other than William Randolph Hearst once stopped for provisions on the way to his castle, is now an arts and crafts complex and restaurant.

If you're curious about life in Harmony, stop by to see what's new, now that the town has changed hands. Local life has been less harmonious since 1998 when the new owner, a Hollywood developer, began to unveil his plans for a 700-acre world peace theme park here.

ways, Cambria is becoming the Carmel of southern Big Sur, with its glut of galleries and other come-hither shops, but without the smog and crowds. Though the cliffs and No Trespassing signs across Santa Rosa Creek tend to slow people down, **Moonstone Beach** offers miles of walking, sea otters, sunsets, and good surfing.

Something of a tragedy for Cambria, and for everyone who loves this lovely town, is news that its breathtaking stands of Monterey pines are doomed, according to the experts—victims of a virulent fungus known as pine pitch canker, expected to wipe out 80 percent of the trees here over the next few decades. Cambria's forest of native Monterey pines is one of only three in California, five in the world. Since worried foresters fear spread of the disease elsewhere along the coast and eventually into the Sierra Nevada, do *not* pick up pine cones or other forest souvenirs to take home with you, since you may also be transporting this plague.

PRACTICAL SAN SIMEON AND VICINITY

San Simeon and the stretch of shoreline it dominates is so close to San Luis Obispo and Morro Bay that people often make day trips here from those communities to do the castle. For San Simeon visitors who have reserved four or five tours over a several-day period or who prefer more convenient accommodations and eateries, there are some decent choices near San Simeon and Cambria. For current information about local practicalities, contact the **San Simeon Chamber of Commerce,** 250 San Simeon Ave., Ste. 3-B, P.O. Box 1, San Simeon, CA 93452, 805/927-3500, or the **Cambria Chamber of Commerce,** 767 Main, Cambria, CA 93428, 805/927-3624.

Staying near San Simeon

The beachfront **Piedras Blancas Motel** seven miles north of Hearst's house on Hwy 1., 805/927-4202, boasts views of the castle on sunny days and often has vacancies when places closer to San Simeon are full. Premium. Another possibility is the remote **Ragged Point Inn,** 19019 Hwy. 1 (15 miles north of San Simeon), Ragged Point, 805/927-4502. Luxury. Well south of San Simeon and Cambria, **Cayucos** also has decent, less expensive motels.

From October or November into mid-spring, even the more expensive motels in San Simeon proper feature cheaper rates. Sometimes offering great bargains in the off-season is the **Silver Surf Motel,** 9390 Castillo Dr. (the frontage road parallel to the highway), 805/927-4661 or toll-free 800/621-3999 (reservations only), www.silversurfmotel.com. Moderate-Expensive. Also a bargain by San Simeon standards, and a particularly good deal in winter, is the **San Simeon Lodge,** 9520 Castillo Dr. (south of the monument), 805/927-4601, featuring basic but decent rooms (remodeled in 1997) with TV and phones. Moderate-Expensive. The nearby **El Rey Garden Inn,** 9260 Castillo Dr., 805/927-3998 or toll-free 800/821-7914, www.elreygardeninn.com, offers something close to luxury—large rooms with amenities (TV, movies, phones), some with gas fireplaces and refrigerators. Expensive. Both have heated swimming pools, and the good **Europa** restaurant is a bonus at the El Rey.

Staying in Cambria

Some Cambria accommodations are less pricey—and there are plenty of places to choose from. For cabins, try the **Cambria Pines Lodge,** 2905 Burton Dr., 805/927-4200 or toll-free 800/445-6868, where the facilities include an indoor pool, sauna, and whirlpool on a 25-acre spread. Rates include full breakfast. Moderate-Premium. The tiny **Bluebird Motel** just west of Burton Dr. at 1880 Main, 805/927-4634 or toll-free 800/552-5434, www.bluebirdmotel.com, offers creekside rooms and suites with fireplaces, in-room refrigerators, color TV, and VCRs. Moderate-Luxury.

ACCOMMODATIONS RATINGS

Accommodations in this book are rated by price category, based on double-occupancy, high-season rates. Categories used are:

Budget.	$35 and under
Inexpensive	$35-60
Moderate	$60-85
Expensive	$85-110
Premium	$110-150
Luxury	$150 and up

Other best bets include the **San Simeon Pines Seaside Resort,** 7200 Moonstone Beach Dr. (at Hwy. 1), 805/927-4648, woodsy and right across the street from Moonstone Beach, with heated pool, nine-hole par 3 golf, playground, croquet, and shuffleboard. Some cottage units feature wood-burning fireplaces. Moderate-Expensive. The small, smoke-free **White Water Inn** near Leffingwell Landing at 6790 Moonstone Beach Dr., 805/927-1066, refurbished in the mid-1990s, offers abundant amenities—VCRs and TVs, free movies, hair dryers, radios, in-room refrigerators, gas fireplaces, and continental breakfast delivered to your room—and some attractive special packages. Moderate-Premium.

For an air of English oceanside charm, consider the 60-room **Fogcatcher Inn** at 6400 Moonstone Beach Dr., 805/927-1400 or toll-free 800/425-4121, www.moonstonemgmt.com, with many amenities plus heated pool and whirlpool. Expensive-Luxury. Sometimes a good bargain, too, by local standards is the Fogcatcher's sister **Sea Otter Inn,** 6656 Moonstone Beach Dr., 805/927-5888 or toll-free 800/965-8347. Expensive-Premium.

Cambria also offers options for the bed-and-breakfast set, including the charming two-story 1870s **Olallieberry Inn** and cottage, 2476 Main, 805/927-3222, fax 805/927-0202, furnished with turn-of-the-20th-century antiques and offering nine rooms with private baths. Expensive-Luxury. The two-story early American **J. Patrick House Bed and Breakfast Inn,** 2990 Burton Dr., 805/927-3812 or toll-free 800/341-8258, is an intriguing log home and guest house. All rooms have private baths, most feature a wood-burning fireplace. Comfortable garden room, where breakfast and veggie hors d'oeuvres are served. Premium-Luxury.

Contact the chamber of commerce (see above) for more complete B&B listings.

Eating Well near Hearst Castle

Stop at **Sebastian's General Store** in San Simeon, 805/927-4217, to stock up on picnic supplies or enjoy burgers and such in the outdoor café. If you're here in winter, keep an eye out for the migrating monarch butterflies that flutter to these cypress and eucalyptus trees.

Most restaurants are in Cambria. Great for ethnic lunch or dinner, usually including some

vegetarian choices, is **Robin's** at 4095 Burton Dr., 805/927-5007. Reservations suggested on weekends, or call ahead for takeout. All-American **Linn's** at 2277 Main, 805/927-0371, is a best bet for soups, salads, sandwiches, and specialty pot pies. Open daily (except Christmas) for breakfast, lunch, and dinner. Or try **Grandma Porte's** across the street at 2282 Main St., 805/927-8519, also open for breakfast, lunch, and dinner daily, offering American standards plus some Mexican choices.

Casual but excellent for American fare from pastas to seafood, and famous for its fresh-baked breads and pastries, is the small dinners-only **Sow's Ear** restaurant at 2248 Main St. in Cambria, 805/927-4865. Diners *can* get a good hamburger for dinner at the English-style **Brambles Dinner House,** 4005 Burton Dr. in Cambria, 805/927-4716, but even better are the homemade soups, breads, and oakwood-broiled salmon. The Brambles is famous for its prime rib with Yorkshire pudding, excellent roast rack of lamb, and brandy ice cream for dessert. Reservations are almost essential, even at Sunday brunch.

The **Moonstone Beach Bar & Grill,** 6550 Moonstone Beach Dr., 805/927-3859, specializes in seafood and offers oceanfront dining alfresco (weather permitting) at lunch and dinner. Another possibility is the **Cambria Pines Restaurant** at the Lodge, 2905 Burton Dr., 805/927-4200, serving steak, seafood, pastas, and other upscale fare.

Canozzi's Saloon, 2226 Main, 805/927-8941, is a rusty old tavern and pool hall with odd signs and memorabilia hanging from the ceiling—*the* place for listening to live music and making the scene, Cambria-style, on Saturday night.

MORRO BAY AND VICINITY

The first thing visitors notice is the Rock, spotted by Cabrillo in 1542. Morro Reef has been a significant navigational landfall for mariners for more than three centuries and was noted in the diaries of Portolá, Crespi, and Costanso. (That wouldn't impress the native peoples, though; Chumash artifacts found here date to 4700 B.C.) Morro Rock is the last visible volcanic peak in the 21-million-year-old series of nine cones that stretch to San Luis Obispo; the chain is known as

Besides the rock, the coastal town of Morro Bay is noted for its giant chess board.

KIM WEIR

the **Seven Sisters** (one is submerged and one is out of line). Before extensive quarrying, this "Gibraltar of the Pacific" stood much higher than its current 576 feet and, until the 1930s, was an island at high tide. The height of the rock seems reduced even more by the proximity of the three 450-foot-tall power plant smokestacks jutting from the edge of the bay like giant gun barrels, part of the scenery since 1953.

Until the rise of tourism, commercial fishing, especially for abalone and albacore, was Morro Bay's major industry. But intrepid amateurs can try clam digging for geoducks (Washington clams) or some barehanded grunion snatching during full-moon high tides from March through August. Pier fishing is also good here on the city's three T-piers, north of the Embarcadero and opposite Morro Rock. Morro Bay also boasts a thriving nature-oriented tourism industry—and a kitsch- and gift-shop-oriented tourism industry, perfect for shopaholics. Or watch the boats in the bay from **Tidelands Park,** at the south end of the Embarcadero, or take a ride on the **Tiger's Folly II** replica river boat. Laid-back **Baywood Park** on the bay just a few miles south of Morro Bay is a better choice for those determined to avoid the crowds.

Thanks to a few local bars and the Morro Bay Chess Club, Morro Bay also has *culture.* The star in that department is the chess club's **giant outdoor chessboard,** especially eye-catching when demonstration tournaments are under way after noon on Saturday along the Embarcadero. With

each of the game's carved redwood pieces weighing between 18 and 30 pounds, playing chess here offers more than a mere mental workout.

For more information about local attractions, events, and practicalities, contact the **Morro Bay Chamber of Commerce,** 880 Main St., 805/772-4467 or toll-free 800/231-0592, and the **Los Osos/Baywood Park Chamber of Commerce,** 781 Los Osos Valley Rd., 805/528-4884.

Seeing and Doing Morro Bay

The entire town of Morro Bay, including Morro Rock, is a bird sanctuary and nature preserve in deference to the peregrine falcons, great blue herons, and other bird species that have selected the rock and vicinity as a rookery. The bay and adjacent mudflats create a fertile wetland, one of the most significant along the California coast for sheer number of resident bird species and one of the top 10 national bird-watching spots. Guns are banned throughout Morro Bay—the rock, the town, and the state park.

A multifaceted park dominating the entire bay area, **Morro Bay State Park** includes the mudflats, sand dunes on the spit, dual Morro Strand State Beach farther north, a natural history museum, adjacent golf course, and the **Los Osos Oaks State Reserve** (one of the few old stands of coast oaks remaining in the area) just inland from the bay on Los Osos Valley Road. The park's campgrounds and picnic areas seem like value-added bonuses. Eucalyptus trees shade the bay near park headquarters and attract monarch butterflies after the October bloom. A more interesting first stop for most people, though, is the park's excellent **Museum of Natural History** on Country Club Dr., 805/772-2694, www.mbspmuseum.org, which emphasizes the wildlife of the headlands and adjacent aquatic environments. It's open daily 10 A.M.–5 P.M., closed Thanksgiving, Christmas, and New Year's Day; free for campers, otherwise small admission.

Morro Bay State Park is open for day use sunrise to sunset daily. The park's day-use fee is $3 per vehicle (camping and museum admission extra). For camping and other park information, stop by the natural history museum (above) or call 805/772-2560 or 805/772-2694. To reserve campsites, call ReserveAmerica, toll-free 800/444-7275.

Just south of the sand spit is **Montaña de Oro State Park** ("Mountain of Gold"), its name particularly apt in spring when the hills are ablaze with yellow and orange wildflowers. Any time of year, 8,000-acre Montaña de Oro is a hiker's park. The seclusion here also means abundant wildlife: sea lions, harbor seals, and sea otters at sea; gray foxes, mule deer, bobcats, and sometimes even mountain lions on land. From certain points along the Bluff Trail, winter whale-watching is superb. The area's wild beauty stretches from the seven-mile shoreline of 50-foot bluffs and tidepools, surging surf, and sandy beaches inland to Valencia Peak (great ocean views looking north to Piedras Blancas, south to Point Sal) and up Islay Creek

to the waterfalls. South of the **Spooner's Cove** visitors center, part of the old ranch, is an old Chumash campsite. To get to Montaña de Oro, head west on Los Osos Valley Rd., then follow Pecho Valley Rd. south to the end. For basic information and to get oriented, stop by the natural history museum at Morro Bay State Park (see above) or call 805/528-0513 or 805/772-7434. Facilities are limited but picnic tables overlook the cove, and nearby is the valley **Islay Creek Campground,** 50 primitive, environmental, and hiker/biker sites, with pit toilets. Call for information.

Staying in Morro Bay

In addition to camping, Morro Bay offers comfy real-bed alternatives—most of these fairly reasonable. Close to the bay scene and a best bet is the tiny, two-story **Best Western Tradewinds Motel,** 225 Beach St. (at Market Ave.), 805/772-7376 or toll-free 800/628-3500, fax 805/772-2090, Moderate-Premium ($79 and up) in summer, though smaller rooms go for as low as $49 double in the off-season. All rooms have in-room refrigerators and coffeemakers and color TV with cable (free movies). Other midrange motel favorites include the **Breakers Motel,** 780 Market Ave. (at Morro Bay Blvd.), 805/772-7317 or toll-free 800/932-8899, fax 805/772-4771, with rates from $78, and **La Serena Inn,** 990 Morro Ave., 805/772-5665 or toll-free 800/248-1511, fax 805/772-1044, www.laserenainn.com. Both are Moderate-Expensive.

You'll know you're in Morro Bay when you see the three 450-foot-tall PG&E power plant smokestacks dominating the landscape.

KIM WEIR

Uptown for these parts is **The Inn at Morro Bay** a mile south of town outside the entrance to Morro Bay State Park, 805/772-5651 or toll-free 800/321-9566 for reservations, fax 805/772-4779, www.innatmorrobay.com, where attractive rooms are $99 and up—bay views come at a premium on summer weekends—though discounts and specials are possible. Expensive-Luxury.

Pleasant choices in Baywood Park include the 13-room **Back Bay Inn,** 1391 2nd St., 805/528-1233 or toll-free 877/330-2225, www.backbayinn.com, Premium-Luxury (continental breakfast included), and the 15-room **Baywood Bed & Breakfast Inn,** 1370 2nd, 805/528-8888, www.baywoodinn.com, Moderate-Luxury.

For more complete lodging listings, contact local chambers of commerce (see above).

Eating in Morro Bay

A local tradition is **Dorn's Original Breakers Cafe,** 801 Market St., 805/772-4415, with wonderful pecan waffles, buttermilk pancakes, and veggie omelettes for breakfast, an impressive Boston clam chowder and marinated seafood salads and various sandwiches at lunch. Generous seafood dinners are served with good views of the bay.

People could drown in the aquatic ambience around Morro Bay. Seafood places leap out all along the Embarcadero, many of them open for lunch and dinner and many featuring early-bird dinner specials. Very good and very popular is **Rose's Landing Restaurant,** 725 Embarcadero, 805/772-4441, on the waterfront overlooking the bay. Good specials, but come early or make reservations because people pack in here like sardines, probably because the bar is shaped like a boat. Also on the waterfront: the **Great American Fish Company,** 1185 Embarcadero, 805/772-4407, which specializes in mesquite-grilled seafood. The place for sushi and such is **Harada,** 630 Embarcadero, 805/772-1410. For pasta and vegetarian selections as well as seafood, jockey for a patio table at **Hoppe's Hip Pocket Bistro,** 901 Embarcadero, 805/772-5371.

For something a bit fancier at dinner—yet still casual—consider **Hoppe's Marina Square,** overlooking the bay at 699 Embarcadero, 805/772-5371, where the steak and seafood are served with continental flair. Or head for the popular **Paradise Restaurant** at the Inn at Morro Bay near Morro Bay State Park, 805/772-2743, for fine dining American style and an inviting Sunday brunch.

SAN LUIS OBISPO AND VICINITY

Before freeway arteries pulsed with California car traffic, when trips between San Francisco and Los Angeles took at least two days, north-south travelers naturally appreciated San Luis Obispo as the most reasonable midpoint stopover. So it's not surprising that San Luis Obispo gave birth to both the concept and the word "motel," a contraction of "motor hotel."

In 1925 when the Spanish colonial **Milestone Mo-tel** (now the Motel Inn) opened, it was the first roadside hostelry to call itself a motel. A sign at the entrance told travelers how to pronounce the new word, and Pasadena architect Arthur Heineman, who designed the place, even copyrighted it.

Playwright Sam Shepard uses motels as symbols of all that is déclassé, desolate, and depressing in the United States. Vladimir Nabokov vilified motels from a continental perspective in *Lolita:* "We held in contempt the plain whitewashed clapboard Kabins, with their faint sewerish smell or some other gloomy self-conscious stench and nothing to boast of. . . ." J. Edgar Hoover, former FBI director and self-styled arbiter of the nation's personal and political morality, attacked motels in 1940 as "assignation camps" and "crime camps" contributing to the downfall of America. From that perspective, then, seemingly innocent San Luis Obispo is where the downfall of America began.

Hoover's opinions aside, San Luis Obispo is a peaceful and pretty college town that has so far escaped the head-on collision with urban and suburban traffic under way in places such as Monterey and Ventura. **California State Polytechnic University** (Cal Poly) here is a major jewel in the community's crown, though the college is still snidely referred to as "Cow Poly" or "Cow Tech" in some circles. The Beef Pavilion, crops, swine, and poultry units do collectively clamor for center-stage attention on the campus just northeast of town, but the college is not just an agricultural school anymore. Cal Poly's architectural school is excellent, the largest in the country, as are the engineering and computer science departments. And since students here "learn by doing," there's almost always something fascinating doing on campus—particularly now that the impressive new $30 million **Performing Arts Center** has opened its opera house–style doors.

For more information about attractions and events throughout the county, contact: **San Luis Obispo County Visitors and Conference Bureau,** 1041 Chorro St., Ste. E, San Luis Obispo, CA 93401, 805/541-8000 or toll-free 800/634-1414, fax 805/543-1255, www.sanluisobispocounty.com. Alternatively, stop by or contact the adjacent **San Luis Obispo Chamber of**

interior of Mission
San Luis Obispo

TOM MYERS PHOTOGRAPHY

FOOTHILL BLVD.

To California State
Polytechnic University

SUPER 8

IZZY ORTEGA'S
MEXICAN RESTAURANT
AND CANTINA

VILLA
MOTEL

HOSTEL OBISPO

SAN LUIS
OBISPO

ADOBE
INN

BUONA
TAVOLA

AH LOUIS STORE
BULL AND
BEAR PIT

MISSION SAN LUIS
OBISPO DE TOLOSA

LOUISA'S
PLACE

MOTHER'S TAVERN

SAN LUIS OBISPO
COUNTY HISTORICAL
MUSEUM

Plaza

SAN LUIS OBISPO CHAMBER
OF COMMERCE

SAN LUIS OBISPO
ART CENTER

BIG SKY
CAFÉ

SLO BREWING COMPANY

GARDEN STREET INN

PETE'S SOUTHSIDE CAFÉ

Amtrak STATION

CAFÉ ROMA

HIGUERA ST.

MARSH ST.

PACIFIC ST.

PISMO ST.

ARCHER ST.

BUCHON ST.

GARDEN ST.

BROAD ST.

CHORRO ST.

MORRO ST.

CHURCH ST.

NIPOMO ST.

BEACH ST.

CARMEL ST.

EFF ST.

HIGH ST.

PRICE ST.

SOUTH ST.

SANTA BARBARA ST.

COTTAGE INN
BY THE SEA

THE
MADONNA
INN

MADONNA RD.

EL CAMINO REAL

S. HIGUERA ST.

0   0.5 mi
0   0.5 km

Morro
Bay

Los
Osos

LOS OSOS VALLEY RD.

FOOTHILL RD.

CALIFORNIA STATE
POLYTECHNIC
UNIVERSITY

Santa Lucia Range

Los Padres
National
Forest

San Luis
Obispo

EL CAMINO REAL

Montana
De Oro
State Park

Point Buchon

MAP AREA

BROAD ST.

SYCAMORE
MINERAL SPRINGS
RESORT

AVILA HOT
SPRINGS

Avila Beach

F. MCCLINTOCK'S
SALOON AND
DINING HOUSE

OLDE PORT INN/
HARFORD PIER

Avila State
Beach

EDNA RD.

PRICE CANYON RD.

ORCUTT RD.

LOPEZ DR.

Point San Luis

Shell Beach

Pismo Beach

SPLASH
CAFÉ

Arroyo
Grande

Pismo State
Beach

Grover
City

0   5 mi
0   5 km

© AVALON TRAVEL PUBLISHING, INC.

Commerce and Visitor Center, 1039 Chorro St., 805/781-2777, www.visitslo.com. The visitor center is open Tues.–Fri. 8 A.M.–5 P.M. and Sat.–Mon. 10 A.M.–5 P.M. The chamber also sells tickets for Hearst Castle tours at San Simeon up the coast, if you're thinking of heading that way and don't have reservations. For information about area arts events, contact the **San Luis Obispo County Arts Council,** 805/544-9251, www.sloartscouncil.org. For whatever else is happening here and in northern Santa Barbara County, pick up a copy of **New Times** magazine, www.newtimes-slo.com.

SEEING AND DOING SAN LUIS OBISPO

The creekside **Mission San Luis Obispo de Tolosa** downtown, founded by Father Junípero Serra in 1772 and still central to community life, was the fifth in the chain. Note the stars on the parish church ceiling—definitely different—and the mission's combination belfry and vestibule, another unique feature. The museum, once the priest's quarters, is worth a short stop for the arrowheads, baskets, Father Serra's vestments, and tangential trivia. The mission itself, at 751 Palm St. on the edge of the downtown Mission Plaza area between Chorro and Garden and Monterey and Higuera Sts., is open 9 A.M.–5 P.M. in summer, 10 A.M.–4 P.M. otherwise (closed Easter, Thanksgiving, Christmas, and New Year's Day). Small donation requested. Call 805/543-6850 for more information.

From the mission, San Luis Obispo's historic walking tour leads through parts of hip and homey downtown, past Victorians, adobes, and the old-time train depot. Court St. is the site of the old

---

TOURING THE COUNTY'S BOUNTY

The "Ag's My Bag" bumper stickers on cars and pick-up trucks you'll see throughout San Luis Obispo County don't lie; agriculture seems to be everybody's bag here. Local produce *is* local, and remarkably diverse because of the mild and varied climate. To find the best of the county's bounty, pick up pamphlets at the visitor bureau or chamber offices—or attend any of the eight weekly area farmers' markets.

The biggest and some say the best of these, a cross between a no-bargains-barred shopping spree and a street party, is San Luis Obispo's main event. The **San Luis Obispo Higuera Street Certified Farmers' Market,** 805/544-9570, is held in downtown San Luis Obispo every Thurs. 6:30–9:30 P.M., weather permitting, along the 600-900 blocks of Higuera (between Osos and Broad Streets). Show up early to find a parking place, since the whole county comes to the city on Thurs. evenings—the main reason area shops and restaurants are open late on this particular weeknight. On tap: live entertainment, arts, crafts, and good food in addition to fine fresh fruits, vegetables, and flowers.

Worth it, too, from late summer into early Nov., is the 13-mile **See Canyon apple tour** of the half-dozen 1900s-vintage orchards in the narrow canyon southwest of town. Apples grown here are not the kind usually found in supermarkets: old-time Arkansas Blacks, Splendors from Tasmania, and Gravensteins plus more modern "Jonalicious," New Zealand Galas, and the very tart Tohuku variety so popular in France. For tour details, inquire at the visitors bureau.

When you're done with apples, try some fruit of the vine. Together the **Edna Valley** and **Arroyo Grande Valley** comprise yet another upstart wine region just inland from the California coast; the small wineries here were first successful with chardonnay and pinot noir grapes. For a current tour map or other information, contact: **Edna Valley Arroyo Grande Valley Vintners,** 5825 Orcutt Rd., San Luis Obispo, CA 93401, 805/541-5868, fax 805/541-3934, www.thegrid.net/vintners. Some area wineries are not vintner association members, however, so be prepared to nose around.

North-county wineries are also well worth looking for. Another of California's newer small winery regions lies near **Paso Robles, Templeton,** and **Atascadero,** throughout the hills and valleys both east and west of Hwy. 101, a region where cabernet, chardonnay, merlot, syrah, and zinfandel grapes do well. As in Edna Valley and Arroyo Grande, most wineries here are small, family-run operations producing 5,000 or fewer bottles per year—casual and "country," as different from the now-big-business Napa and Sonoma county wine industries as well-broke cowboy boots are from Bruno Maglis. Many offer tours only with reservations, especially during the hectic autumn harvest season. For current regional wineries information, contact the **Paso Robles Vintners and Growers Association,** 622 12th St. in Paso Robles, 805/239-8463, fax 805/237-6439, www.pasowine.com.

Bull and Bear Pit, an early California "sporting" arena. The **San Luis Obispo County Historical Museum** at the far end of Mission Plaza in the old Carnegie library, 696 Monterey St., 805/543-0638, open Wed.–Sun. 10 A.M.–4 P.M., houses a collection of local memorabilia, including Chumash artifacts and settlers' glassware, antique clothes, even hair wreaths, also an extensive historical photo archive and research library. Just across the street is the **San Luis Obispo Art Center.** On the other side of the public bathrooms is the historic **Murray Adobe.** The **Ah Louis Store,** 800 Palm St., is all that remains of San Luis Obispo's once-thriving Chinatown. Established in 1874, Ah Louis's store was the county's first Chinese general store and the bank, counting house, and post office for the many Chinese employed by the Southern Pacific Railroad between 1884 and 1894 to dig eight train tunnels through the Cuesta Mountains.

Seeing and Doing San Luis Obispo Bay
Gentler than Big Sur's, the coastline near San Luis Obispo offers rocky terraces, sandy dunes, and a big-picture view of the Seven Sisters, volcanic peaks that saunter seaward from San Luis Obispo to "the rock" at Morro Bay. By car the coastal communities of Morro Bay, Avila Beach, and Pismo Beach are all less than 15 minutes away from San Luis Obispo.

The pier at **Port San Luis,** old Port Hartford and once a regular steamship stop, is now a favorite fishing spot. **Avila Beach** just east along the bay is a favorite surfers' beach town on the way to becoming trendy, its protected beaches tucked into the cove. (Try to ignore the oil tanks looming overhead.) Before leaving Avila Beach, do the hot springs. Relaxed, funky, and family-friendly **Avila Hot Springs,** also an RV and tent-camping resort at 250 Avila Beach Dr., 805/595-2359 or toll-free 800/332-2359 or 800/543-2359 for reservations, www.campgrounds.com, features a large freshwater swimming pool in addition to private step-down tiled hot mineral tubs in the original 1930s bathhouse and the hot outdoor pools. (Rent inner tubes and float in the warm pool.) Spa services are also available. The more uptown and historic **Sycamore Mineral Springs Resort,** 1215 Avila Beach Dr., 805/595-7302 or toll-free 800/234-5831 for reservations, www.smsr.com and www.sycamoresprings.com, offers pleasant

TOURING DIABLO CANYON

Since guards at the two-unit Diablo Canyon Nuclear Power Plant control the traffic flow here near Port San Luis, don't plan on walking in for a casual looksee. Years of antinuclear protest have made security serious business. Trouble was Diablo's middle name for 20 years, thanks to relentless antinuclear energy protesters. Critics of the plant, built just a few miles from the Hosgri offshore earthquake fault, have consistently attempted to shut down construction—then, later, the on-line plants—with lawsuits and civil disobedience.

In 1997, Pacific Gas & Electric (PG&E) agreed to pay $14 million to settle charges it had deliberately underreported damage to sealife at Diablo Canyon, the indirect result of the 2.5 billion gallons of seawater sucked into the plant each day.

Despite environmentalists and antinuke naysayers, PG&E promotes the plant as "solid as the Rock of Gibraltar," a good neighbor until the end of time; PG&E also hopes its rock is a rock-solid investment, with its total $5.8 billion construction price tag financed through Northern California customers' utility bills. Though both are now on-line, Diablo's first nuclear reactor set a nationwide performance record during its first year of operation, producing more than eight billion kilowatt-hours of electricity while operating at capacity 93 percent of the time.

How do local people feel about Diablo Canyon? You'll find both gung-ho support and absolute opposition but primarily, in the typically apolitical American tradition, a "let's-wait-and-see" attitude prevails.

The utility's pretty, Spanish-looking **PG&E Community Center** about 12 miles south of San Luis Obispo via Hwy. 101 at 6588 Ontario Rd. (exit at San Luis Bay Dr.) in Avila Beach, 805/546-5280, open 9 A.M.–5 P.M. daily, offers simple but flashy presentations on fission nuclear energy, also three-to four-hour **overlook tours** of the plant site by bus, including stops at the marine biology lab and a simulated control room. But if you want to hear what a nuclear-meltdown siren sounds like, you'll have to make reservations.

HIKING THE DIABLO COAST

The 10 miles of coast north of Port San Luis is pristine and rugged, home to sea lions, pelicans, and cormorants. The presence of the **Diablo Canyon Nuclear Plant** means this entire area has long been off-limits to coastwalkers for security reasons. But now the **Pecho Coast Trail** traverses several miles of this once-lost coast, from just north of Avila Beach to Point San Luis Lighthouse and the marine terrace just beyond. Before you strap on those hiking boots, though, pick up the phone and call 805/541-8735; the area is accessible on guided hikes only, and only by reservation.

motel-style hotel rooms, suites, and bed-and-breakfast stays—not to mention a swimming pool, volleyball courts, and the Gardens of Avila restaurant—in addition to hot mineral soaks, massage, facials, and other spa services. The very private lattice-screened redwood hot tubs, which rent by the hour 24 hours a day, are strategically scattered around the landscaped wooded hillside (hot tub reservations advised).

Shell Beach south of Pirate's Cove and north of Pismo Beach is a marine-terrace town with lots of antique shops and two wooden staircases leading to the rocky coast below. Primo is shoving off from Shell Beach for ocean kayaking, an adventure easily undertaken with help from **Central Coast Kayaks** on Shell Beach Rd., 805/773-3500.

Shell Beach segues into **Pismo Beach** proper, once a haute destination for 1930s celebrities, now a cleaned-up, family-friendly, and fairly affordable beach community. For more information about the area and its attractions, contact: **Pismo Beach Chamber of Commerce & Visitors Center,** 581 Dolliver, 805/773-4382, fax 805/773-6772, www.pismochamber.com. The six miles of shoreline from Pismo Beach to Oceano is primarily **Pismo State Beach,** dominated by the **Oceano Dunes State Vehicular Recreation Area** dune buggy heaven.

Oceano and vicinity, just south of Pismo Beach, have seen wilder days. Sneaky sand dunes advanced on the town's famous dance pavilion, cottages, and wharf years ago, destroying them all. The dunes here are the highest and whitest in the state, blocked from straying farther south by the Point Sal cliffs.

Inland from Oceano and the Pismo Beach area is **Arroyo Grande,** nothing but a stage stop in 1877, now an attractive village with Old West–style antique and other shops, some bed-and-breakfasts, and surrounding flower seed farms. For more information, contact: **Arroyo Grande Chamber of Commerce & Visitors Center,** 800 W. Branch, 805/489-1488, fax 805/489-2239, open weekdays 10 A.M.–5 P.M.

PRACTICAL SAN LUIS OBISPO

Staying in San Luis Obispo

Contact the visitors center in San Luis Obispo for area camping suggestions. San Luis Obispo also has a HI-AYH hostel, at a new location—**Hostel Obispo,** 1617 Santa Rosa St. (Hwy. 1), San Luis Obispo, CA 93401, 805/544-4678, fax 805/544-3142, www.hostelweb.com, with a per-bed rate of $15–17 for dorm beds, $37.50–40 for private rooms. Reservations accepted by mail or fax, with deposit (no credit cards). Extras here include laundry, bike rentals, on-site parking, and a garden and patio with barbecue. Hostel Obispo also offers group trips and hiking and biking "adventure tours." Budget.

Most San Luis Obispo motels are on or near Monterey St., including the local **Super 8,** 1951 Monterey St., 805/544-7895 or toll-free 800/800-8000 for reservations (nationwide), fax 805/546-7895, with summer double rates $55 and up. Inexpensive-Expensive. Also quite reasonable in the neighborhood: the small **Villa Motel,** 1670 Monterey (at Grand), 805/543-8071 or toll-free 800/554-0059, fax 805/549-4389, which also offers a heated pool and free breakfast. Inexpensive-Premium, with summer rates of $49 double and up, winter rates as low as $40 double. Weekly rates available. Quite inviting is the friendly Southwestern B&B-style **Adobe Inn,** 1473 Monterey, 805/549-0321 or toll-free 800/676-1588, fax 805/549-0383, www.adobeinns.com, with summer weekday rates $75 double, weekend rates $95, homemade breakfast included. (But off-season rates can be as low as $55—a real deal.) Moderate-Expensive.

More luxurious accommodations are available, too, particularly on Monterey St. and also on

WORTHWHILE NORTH OF SAN LUIS OBISPO

North of San Luis Obispo proper, Santa Margarita was once a small outpost of the mission, with a chapel, grain storage, and lodging rooms. The biggest thing around today, though, is tiny **Santa Margarita Lake,** which offers camping, picnicking, and fishing. For info, call 805/438-5485 or check www.centralcoast.com/santamargaritalake/. East via Hwy. 58 is the fascinating **Carrizo Plain Natural Area,** sometimes referred to as "California's Serengeti," much of the land now protected within a vast Nature Conservancy preserve. Though almost everything else in California has been endlessly exploited, the Carrizo Plain somehow missed out on the march of progress. The San Andreas Fault is on the plain's eastern edge, and the region is hot in summer and cold in winter. Yet the plain, once a prehistoric lake, was sacred to the Chumash, whose Great Spirits lived here—and shook the earth, when angered. Eight miles wide and 50 miles long, the Carrizo Plain preserves the last large remnant of the San Joaquin Valley's natural terrain, where sandhill cranes winter and some 600 pronghorn antelope roam native grasslands. The best time to come for a look is in late winter and early spring.

North via Hwy. 101 are **Atascadero** and **Paso Robles,** center of another notable California wine country. Still farther north on the main highway is sleepy little **San Miguel** with its fine old mission and, to the west, **Lake Nacimiento.** As the highway hums northward through the Salinas Valley, to the west lies **Lake San Antonio,** popular for bald eagle watching in winter.

Beyond Jolon, smack in the midst of Fort Hunter-Liggett, is **Mission San Antonio de Padua,** 831/385-4478, not the biggest nor most ravishingly restored mission, certainly not the most popular, but somehow the most evocative of Spanish California—well worth the detour.

For a simple yet special stay less than a half-mile away, consider the **Hacienda Guest Lodge,** 831/386-2900, the original ranch house designed for William Randolph Hearst by Julia Morgan, built in 1922. Later an officers club, the Hacienda is now a combination hotel, restaurant, bar, bowling alley with snack bar, and campground. Nothing fancy, but a tremendous value. A steak dinner is $10 or so. Rooms or suites with private baths start at $46 (Inexpensive); those with shared baths are $33 (Budget). Weather and road conditions permitting, from Fort Hunter-Liggett it's possible to take the backroads route, Nacimiento-Fergusson Rd., over the mountains to Big Sur.

Madonna Rd.; contact the visitors bureau for a current listing. For other affordable options, head for Pismo Beach, where bargains abound—especially in the off-season.

Some Memorable "Motor Hotels" and Inns

The **Motel Inn,** San Luis Obispo's first and original "mo-tel," closed some years back for historic renovation and eventual expansion. In the meantime the next best thing is right next door—the **Apple Farm Inn,** 2015 Monterey St., 805/544-2040 or toll-free 800/374-3705 for reservations, fax 805/546-9495, www.apple-farm.com. Behind the locally famous **Apple Farm Restaurant** is the rest of the ranch—in this case, a quaint three-story motel with contemporary country-inn airs. Rooms feature fireplaces, four-poster beds, and other period furnishings, even armoires. Equally pleasant but less expensive are the more motel-like rooms in the **Apple Farm Trellis Court,** adjacent. Inn rooms start at $169 in the high season, dropping to $149 in winter. Motel rooms start at $119 in summer, $99 at other times. Expensive-Luxury.

For a seaside retreat, head for Pismo Beach and the **Spyglass Inn,** 2705 Spyglass Dr., 805/773-4855 or toll-free 800/824-2612, fax 805/773-5298, www.spyglassinn.com (Expensive-Luxury), and **Cottage Inn by the Sea,** 2351 Price St., 805/773-4617 or toll-free 888/440-8400, www.cottage-inn.com (Luxury).

Fun for bed-and-breakfast fans: the 13-room **Garden Street Inn,** 1212 Garden St. in San Luis Obispo, 805/545-9802 or toll-free 800/488-2045, fax 805/545-9403, www.gardenstreetinn.com, an 1887 Italianate Queen Anne Victorian, was originally centerpiece of the local Mission Vineyard. Rooms and suites are individually decorated; Valley of the Moon commemorates the life and times of Jack London, Walden is a Thoreau tribute, and Amadeus remembers

JAMES DEAN DIED HERE

Rebels otherwise without a cause might spend a few minutes in Cholame (sho-LAMB), 27 miles east of Paso Robles on the way to Lost Hills via hustle-bustle Hwy. 46. At the onetime intersection of Highways 41 and 46 (the exact routing of the roads has since changed), actor James Dean met death at the age of 24. The star of only three movies—*East of Eden,* his trademark *Rebel Without a Cause,* and *Giant*— Dean, heading west into the blinding sun, died instantly when his speeding silver Porsche slammed head-on into a Ford at 5:59 P.M. on September 30, 1955.

And every September 30th since 1979, members of a Southern California car club trace the route of Dean's last road trip, starting in Van Nuys, during the annual en masse migration to Cholame on the James Dean Memorial Run—just about the ultimate experience for 1950s car enthusiasts.

But in front of Cholame's postage stamp–sized post office and outside the restaurant a half mile from the actual place Dean died, there's an oddly evocative stainless-steel obelisk in his memory, paid for by a businessman from Japan. The memorial is wrapped around a lone tree and landscaped with 9,000 pounds of imported Japanese gravel, a concrete bench, and engraved bronze tablets—a pilgrimage site for fans from around the world. (Inside, Dean fans can buy memorial T-shirts, sun visors, posters, and postcards. The proceeds go toward maintaining the monument.)

Seita Ohnishi's explanation etched on the tablets reads:

This monument stands as a small token of my appreciation for the people of America. It also stands for James Dean and other American Rebels. . . . In Japan, we say his death came as suddenly as it does to cherry blossoms. The petals of early spring always fall at the height of their ephemeral brilliance. Death in youth is life that glows eternal.

But in keeping with James Dean's own favorite words—from Antoine de Saint-Exupery, "What is essential is invisible to the eye"—what was important about Dean's life is not necessarily here.

Mozart. No phone, no TVs, so prepare to truly relax. Suites include extras such as hot tub bath/showers, private decks, separate bedrooms. Full breakfast is served every morning, wine and cheese every evening. Expensive-Luxury. Rooms start at $100, suites at $150, with a two-night minimum stay on weekends.

For something to write home about, consider **The Madonna Inn,** 100 Madonna Rd., San Luis Obispo, CA 93405, 805/543-3000 or toll-free 800/543-9666, fax 805/543-1800, www.madonnainn.com. One of the most unusual motels anywhere, the Madonna is noted for quirky "theme" rooms and suites, some with waterfalls and other dramatic elements, each one of the 109 rooms here unique. Some sample themes: the Daisy Mae Room, the Caveman Room, the Cloud Nine Suite, the Love Nest. You get the idea—immensely popular with newlyweds and couples tired of the same old anniversary celebration. This Madonna is getting a bit tired these days, too, but still, a stay here is *different.* Rooms are Premium-Luxury, with rates $127–310. Those who don't stay should satisfy their curiosity by wandering the halls and peeking into any open rooms.

Dining Downtown and Around

San Luis Obispo boasts more than 60 eateries, so look around—especially downtown, where delis, small cafés, and restaurants surround the plaza area. Good for breakfast is **Louisa's Place,** 964 Higuera St., 805/541-0227, a countertop-style café locally popular for its buckwheat pancakes and lunch specials. **Pete's Southside Cafe,** 1815 Osos St., 805/549-8133, is an outpost of the original Avila Beach Pete's all gussied up for more stylish times. But the fresh seafood is still fresh, the Mexican selections still good, and the atmosphere still bright and bustling. It's open for lunch and dinner, on Sun. for dinner only.

The **Big Sky Café,** 1121 Broad St., 805/545-5401, serves great Southwestern selections and other eclectic New American fare. Justifiably popular, too, is **Mother's Tavern,** 725 Higuera St., 805/541-3853, where the specialty is "California tavern food"—everything from burgers and steaks to pastas, salads, and sandwiches. Another hit at Mother's is the tavern's house band, the jump blues and swing band Sugar Daddy Swing Kings. So cool. The cool destination for the weekday "Happy Hour and a Half" is the old-brick **SLO Brewing Co.** downtown at 1119 Garden St. (between Higuera and Marsh Sts.), 805/543-1843, open for lunch and dinner daily (just noon–5 P.M. on Sunday). Brewpub fans believe the main attractions here are the Amber Ale, Pale Ale, and Porter—and at least one seasonal brew, on tap. Live entertainment later too, most nights.

Stylin' it in San Luis Obispo might include lunch or dinner at **Cafe Roma,** in a new location at Railroad Square near the train station, 1020 Railroad Ave., 805/541-6800, open Tues.–Fri. for lunch and Tues.–Sun. for dinner. Noted for its authentic northern Italian fare, Cafe Roma is one of San Luis Obispo's most popular fine food destinations. Also quite good, downtown next to the Fremont Theater, is **Buona Tavola,** 1037 Monterey St., 805/545-8000, also open for lunch and dinner.

A fun family-style place convenient to motel row is **Izzy Ortega's Mexican Restaurant and Cantina** next to the Holiday Inn at 1850 Monterey St., 805/543-3333, open daily 11:30 A.M. until at least 9 P.M. (bar open later). Colorful and cheerful with a party-hearty American attitude, Izzy's is one of San Luis Obispo's most popular restaurants. The food's quite good, and considerably more authentic than most Americanized Mexican. Try the shrimp or fish tacos, for example, the pork tamales, or the tasty bean soup. Entrées get more ambitious, including steak ranchero and broiled garlic shrimp. Children's menu available.

Another place to take the kids, especially if you can get them to pay: the original **F. McClintocks Saloon and Dining House,** 750 Mattie Rd. in Pismo Beach, 805/773-1892, open daily (after 3 or 4 P.M.) for dinner, and on Sunday from 9:30 A.M.–9 P.M., for "ranch breakfast," early supper, and dinner (closed some major holidays). Beef—aged, "hand-cut," and then barbecued over oak wood—is the secret to the success of this kicky outpost of commercialized mom-and-pop cowboy kitsch. (The gift shop overfloweth.) Everything here is pretty good, however. The machismo challenge, typically issued by men to men, is eating the oddest menu item—fried turkey nuts—without squawking. And if you like that sort of thing, come in mid-July for the Annual Mountain Oyster Feed, held out back. But kids are more impressed by the wait staff, who pour water by holding the pitcher at least two feet above the table—and never spill a drop. And don't miss the Birthday Picture Gallery. Or mosey on over to the other area F. McClintocks locations; there's one here in SLO at 686 Higuera St., 805/541-0686, and others in Paso Robles and Arroyo Grande.

The classic surfers' fuel center in Pismo Beach is the **Splash Café,** just a block from the pier at 197 Pomeroy Ave., 805/773-4653, where you can get a bread bowl full of wonderful New England–style clam chowder for under $5. A bit more stylish for seafood is the **Olde Port Inn,** in Avila Beach at Port San Luis's Pier #3, 805/595-2515. Well worth looking for in nearby Arroyo Grande is **Massimo's,** 640 Oak Park Blvd., 805/474-9211, where northern Italian is the specialty.

And if you're heading north from the area, **Villa Creek** in Paso Robles, 1144 Pine St., 805/238-3000, specializes in early Californian, and **McPhee's Grill** at 416 Main St. in Templeton, 805/434-3204, is known for its regional American.

SANTA MARIA AND LOMPOC

Santa Maria

This onetime ranch-country hitching post on the northern fringe of Santa Barbara County is quickly growing out into its flower fields, thanks in part to the proximity of Vandenberg Air Force Base. Built on sand flats, Santa Maria has an abundance of trees, unusually wide streets—originally to more easily reverse eight-mule wagon rigs—and one of the West's best repertory theater programs. Good times anytime are almost guaranteed by the fine **Pacific Conservatory of the Performing Arts,** which offers Shakespeare, musicals, and dramas. Performances are also held in Solvang (see below), but the troupe's headquarters are at the local Allan Hancock College, 800 S. College Dr. in Santa Maria, www.pcpa.org, 805/922-8313 or,

SANTA MARIA BARBECUE

Though Santa Maria is a difficult place for vegetarians to avoid feeling deprived, there are compensations—like the great Cajun fare at **Chef Rick's Ultimately Fine Foods,** in the Lucky Shopping Center at 4869 S. Bradley Rd., 805/937-9512. Or meat-eaters might want to track down some world-famous Santa Maria–style barbecue. Passed down from the days of the vaqueros, the meal traditionally includes delectable slabs of prime sirloin beef barbecued over a slow red-oak fire, then sliced as thin as paper and served with the chunky salsa cruda people drown it in. Also part of every traditional barbecue menu are pinquito beans (grown only in Santa Maria Valley), salad, toasted french bread with butter, and dessert—unquestionably the ultimate in California cowboy fare. Especially on Saturday, barbecue is the easiest meal to find in and around Santa Maria. The most authentic local version is served on weekends at local charity affairs of one sort or another, but several steakhouses serve it anytime.

The best of the Santa Maria barbecue bunch is the **Hitching Post,** open 5–9:30 P.M. at 3325 Point Sal Rd., 805/937-6151, in Casmalia, a tiny town southeast of Santa Maria. Another good bet, just north of Santa Maria, is **Jocko's,** 125 N. Thompson St. in Nipomo, 805/929-3686, a Santa Maria–style steakhouse also known for its spicy beans, open daily.

for tickets, toll-free 800/727-2123. Fairly new in the neighborhood is the two-hangar **Santa Maria Museum of Flight,** 3015 Airpark Rd., 805/922-8758, open Fri.–Sun. 9 A.M.–5 P.M. (until 4 P.M. in winter), which documents general flight history with both antique and model planes, with an emphasis on local contributions to aviation history. (Santa Maria was a basing station during World War II.) For broader local historical perspective, the **Santa Maria Valley Historical Museum** is downtown adjacent to the visitor bureau/chamber of commerce office at 616 S. Broadway, 805/922-3130, and is open Tues.–Sat. noon–5 P.M. A fascination here: the Barbecue Hall of Fame.

For more information about Santa Maria and vicinity, contact: **Santa Maria Visitor and Convention Bureau,** 614 S. Broadway, Santa Maria, CA 93454, 805/925-2403 or toll-free 800/331-3779, fax 805/928-7559, www.santamaria.com, which offers accommodations, food, and regional wine-tour information. Also pick up a copy of the *Walk Through History* local walking tour guide. For area camping and regional recreation information, contact the **Santa Lucia Ranger District** office of the Los Padres National Forest at 1616 N. Carlotti Dr. in Santa Maria, 805/925-9538, www.r5.fs.fed.us/lospadres.

Lompoc and Vicinity

Probably Chumash for "shell mound," Lompoc these days is a bustling military town amid flower fields that add bloom to the city's cheeks from

KIM WEIR

Mission La Purísima is the state's largest and only complete mission complex.

June through September. At **Vandenberg Air Force Base** just west of town—home of the 30th Space Wing, and the only U.S. military installation that launches unmanned government and commercial satellites in addition to intercontinental ballistic missiles (ICBMs)—evening launches create colorful sky trails at sunset. Free tours of Vandenberg, which might include a former space shuttle launch site, an underground missile silo, and a shipwrecked 1923 naval destroyer, are offered Wednesday at 10 A.M. (pending missions permitting). For details and reservations, call 805/606-3595.

La Purísima Mission State Historic Park is the area's main attraction. The largest mission complex in the state, now situated on 1,000 unspoiled acres about four miles east of Lompoc on Hwy. 246, Misión de la Concepción Purísima de María Santísima ("Mission of the Immaculate Conception of Most Holy Mary") was the 11th in California's chain of coastal missions when it was originally built in what is now downtown Lompoc in 1787. Now an impressive state historic park and California's only complete mission complex, La Purísima is open daily, May–Sept. 9 A.M.–6 P.M., otherwise 9 A.M.–5 P.M.;

IN SEARCH OF THE TEN COMMANDMENTS

The coastal dunes due west of Santa Maria provide habitat for California brown pelicans and the endangered least terns, though Cecil B. DeMille probably didn't think much about such things in 1923 when he built, and then buried, a dozen four-ton plaster sphinxes, four statues of Ramses the Magnificent, and an entire pharaonic city here—the original movie set for *The Ten Commandments*. Referred to as the dune that never moves, Ten Commandment Hill is now part of the Guadalupe-Nipomo Dunes Preserve and the first thing visitors see at the Guadalupe entrance.

This large coastal dunes preserve is part of the seemingly simple yet quite complicated and fragile Nipomo Dunes ecosystem, which stretches from Pismo Beach south to Vandenberg. Created by howling wind and enormous offshore swells, the seaward dunes are sizable parabola-shaped mounds of sharp-grained sand in almost perpetual motion. The more stable back dunes stand 200 feet tall and offer more hospitable habitat for the 18 endangered and rare endemic coastal scrub species counted to date by members of the California Native Plant Society. Among the most instantly impressive is the yellow-flowered giant coreopsis, which grows only on the Channel Islands and on the coast from Los Angeles north to the Nipomo Dunes.

Oso Flaco Lake to the north of Guadalupe is a surprising sparkling blue coastal oasis, actually a group of small lakes fringed by shrubs and surrounded by sand dunes (and the din from dune buggyists penned up just northward at the Oceano Dunes State Vehicular Recreation Area).

To the south is Mussel Rock, at 500 feet the tallest sand dune in California. Sit and watch the sunset while the surf spits and sputters across the sand. Or hike to Point Sal and Point Sal State Beach, a wonderfully remote stretch of headlands, rocky outcroppings, and sand (the treacherous surf is unsafe for swimming) just north of Vandenberg. (To get there, head west on the Brown Rd. turnoff three miles south of Guadalupe, and then take Point Sal Road.) Good whale-watching.

Though the preserve holdings started with 3,400 acres, including the critical central section relinquished by Mobil Oil Corporation, the preserve now embraces a total of 20,000 acres owned by The Nature Conservancy and various public agencies. The San Luis Obispo–based People for Nipomo Dunes led the dunes preservation effort with the idea of creating a Nipomo Dunes National Seashore, protected federally like Point Reyes to the north. The dunes are now recognized as a National Natural Landmark.

The preserve is accessible from Hwy. 101 in Santa Maria (via Hwy. 166) or from Hwy. 1 farther west near Guadalupe. There are two preserve entrances. To reach the Guadalupe entrance, from Guadalupe continue to the west end of W. Main Street. To reach the Oso Flaco Lake entrance, from Hwy. 1 about three miles north of Guadalupe turn left onto Oso Flaco Lake Road. The Oso Flaco Lake area is handicapped accessible, with a mile-long boardwalk. The preserve is open dawn to dusk 365 days each year. No overnight camping, dogs, or four-wheel drive vehicles are allowed.

For more information, stop by the Dunes Center, in downtown Guadalupe at 951 Guadalupe St. (Hwy. 1), 805/343-2455, www.dunescenter.org. The center is open Fri. 2–4 P.M. and on weekends noon–4 P.M.

$2 per vehicle day-use fee. Guided tours are available by appointment. For more information, contact: La Purísima Mission State Historic Park, 2295 Purisima Rd., 805/733-3713.

Stop by the **Lompoc Museum,** 200 S. H St., 805/736-3888, open afternoons Tues.–Sun., to review the city's pioneering prohibitionist history. And poke around town to appreciate the **Lompoc Valley Mural Project** (more than 60 and counting) and the city's unique Italian stone pines.

For more information about the area, contact the **Lompoc Valley Chamber of Commerce,** 111 S. I St., Lompoc, CA 93436, 805/736-4567, www.lompoc.com, which offers a "flower drive" brochure/map (routes also available on the website), events, and practical information.

Point Conception

Just below Vandenberg Air Force Base is the place California turns on itself. Point Conception, an almost inaccessible elbow of land stabbing the sea about 40 miles north of Santa Barbara, is the spot where California's coastal "direction" swings from north-south to east-west, the geographical pivotal point separating temperature and climate zones, northstate from southstate. A lone wind-whipped lighthouse teeters at the edge of every mariner's nightmare, California's Cape Horn.

Inaccessible by car, Point Conception can be reached by hikers from **Jalama Beach County Park** just south of Vandenberg (from south of Lompoc, take Jalama Rd. west from Hwy. 1). Some hike along the railroad right-of-way on the plateau—illegal, of course, so you've been warned—but with equal caution one can take the more adventurous route along the beach and cliffs to commune with startled deer, seals, sea lions, and whales offshore.

SOLVANG AND VICINITY

Solvang, "sunny meadow" or "sunny valley" in Danish, was founded in 1911 by immigrants from Denmark seeking a pastoral spot to establish a folk school. This attractive representation of Denmark is now a well-trod tourist destination in the otherwise sleepy Santa Ynez Valley, complete with Scandinavian-style motels, restaurants, shops, even windmills. Recent history has

Solvang's Danish history is evident in the architecture around town.

also had its impact here. Though national media always put former President Ronald Reagan's Western White House in Santa Barbara, it was actually closer to Solvang, off Refugio Road. The Reagans don't live at the ranch any more. But when they did, they made quite an impression. When Ron and Nancy arrived at the Solvang polls to vote, for example, SWAT teams took over the town.

In summer and on many weekends, tourists take over the town. To appreciate the authentic taste of Denmark here—and, surprisingly, the experience is largely authentic—come some other time. Yet there is a special compensation for those who do come in summer: **Summer Theaterfest** performances by the **Pacific Conservatory of the Performing Arts** in Solvang's 700-seat outdoor Solvang Festival Theatre. For current information, call the theatre at 805/922-8313 or try the website, www.pcpa.org. And about four miles from the Reagan ranch, the **Circle Bar B Guest Ranch,** 805/968-1113, www.circlebarb.com, stages dinner theater productions in an old barn (now a 100-seat theater) from May into Nov.; call for current information. For more information on attractions and events in and around Solvang, contact: **Solvang Conference and Visitors Bureau,** P.O. Box 70, Solvang, CA 93464, toll-free 800/468-6765, www.solvangusa.com, or the **Solvang Chamber**

SANTA BARBARA WINE COUNTRY

Santa Barbara County is premium wine country. The county's winemaking history reaches back more than 200 years, though small vineyards and wineries established since the 1970s and 1980s are responsible for the area's regional viticultural revival. The unusual east-west orientation of the Santa Ynez Mountains and associated valleys allows fog-laden ocean air to flow inland—creating dry summers with cool nights and warm days. Cabernet sauvignon, sauvignon blanc, pinot noir, chardonnay, and riesling are among the wine grapes that thrive here, though Rhône varietals are a new trend.

Yet when does a good thing become too much of a good thing?

This is a question asked more frequently here and elsewhere along the central coast, especially following a nearly successful local ballot initiative in fall 1998 that would have severely restricted local wine grape growers' ability to clear-cut native oaks and other vegetation to plant vineyards. Environmentalists, grape growers, and county planning officials are trying to come up with a collaborative solution to this particular problem, to avoid the possibility of another public—and vitriolic—political battle.

Most of Santa Barbara County's wineries—well over 50 and counting—are scattered throughout the Santa Ynez Valley, beyond San Marcos Pass northwest of Santa Barbara and southeast of Santa Maria.

Award-winning **The Gainey Vineyard,** 3950 E. Hwy. 246, P.O. Box 910, Santa Ynez, CA 93460, 805/688-0558, fax 805/688-5864, is noted for its cabernets, chardonnays, and pinot noirs. The contemporary 12,000-foot winery and tasting room and adjacent picnic area is open daily 10 A.M.–5 P.M. for tours and tasting. (Very informative tours.) The vineyard also sponsors a variety of evening concerts—popular regional jazz bands and the likes of Randy Newman—which sell out fast.

Almost everyone stops at the **Fess Parker Winery,** 6200 Foxen Canyon Rd. in Los Olivos, 805/688-1545 or toll-free 800/841-1104, fax 805/686-1130, www.fessparker.com, open for tasting and sales daily 10 A.M.–5 P.M. (closed Thanksgiving, Christmas, and New Year's Day) and for group tours only (by arrangement). Most popular here is syrah, which

tends to sell out almost instantaneously every year, and a very good chardonnay. And anyone with a yen for the good ol' days of 1950s television will have fun in the gift shop, featuring Davy Crockett "coonskin" caps and other Fess Parker TV-star memorabilia. On most weekends Parker is available in person to autograph wine bottles. Tours and admission to the gift shop are free, but there is a fee for tastings.

Also popular in Los Olivos is **Firestone Vineyard,** 5000 Zaca Station Rd., 805/688-3940, fax 805/686-1256, open daily 10 A.M.–5 P.M. for tasting (closed major holidays), tours also offered. Firestone was the first in the country to produce estate-grown wines. People go out of their way to pick up Firestone's award-winning cabernet sauvignon, though the winery is actually best known for Johannesburg riesling. Picnicking here is a pleasure, with picnic tables surrounding a fountain in the courtyard. Tastings and tours are free, but a fee is charged for groups of 15 or more.

Not far southeast of Santa Maria is the **Byron Vineyard and Winery,** located at 5230 Tepusquet Rd., 805/937-7288, named 1992 "Winery of the Year" by *Wine and Spirits* magazine and now owned by Robert Mondavi.

But with 50 or so member wineries in the local vintners' association—and major events such as the spring **Santa Barbara County Vintners' Festival,** the fall **Celebration of Harvest,** and other galas to help introduce them—it takes more than a few stops to fully appreciate the region. For a current winery map and guide, and for current events information, contact: **Santa Barbara County Vintners' Association,** P.O. Box 1558, Santa Ynez, CA 93460, 805/688-0881 or toll-free 800/218-0881, fax 805/686-5881, www.sbcountywines.com.

And the region's wineries don't begin or end in Santa Barbara County, thanks to the mild central coast climate. Small wineries also cluster farther north near San Luis Obispo—in the **Edna** and **Arroyo Grande Valleys**—and, more famously, north of San Luis Obispo near **Paso Robles** and **Templeton.** For more information, see San Luis Obispo and Vicinity.

of Commerce, P.O. Box 465, Solvang, CA 93464, 805/688-0701, www.solvangcc.com.

Seeing and Doing Solvang and Vicinity

A wander through Solvang offers thatched-roofed buildings with wooden roof storks, almost endless bakeries and gift shops, and surprises such as the **wind harp** near the **Bethania Lutheran Church,** where services are still conducted in Danish once each month. The **Wulff Windmill** on Fredensborg Canyon Rd. northwest of town is a historic landmark, once used to grind grain and pump water. For an appreciation of Danish culture, stop by the **Elverhøj Danish Heritage and Fine Arts Museum** on Elverjoy Way, 805/686-1211, an accurate representation of an 18th-century Danish farmhouse open Wed.–Sun. 1–4 P.M. Perfect for picnics: **Hans Christian Andersen Park** off Atterdag Rd., three blocks north of Mission Dr., complete with children's playground.

New in Solvang, open for tours by reservation only, is the free **Western Wear Museum,** 435 1st St., 805/693-5000 or 805/688-3388, 10 rooms of silver-screen cowboy regalia and other western wear themes; most fun for the kiddos is the "cowkids" room.

Mission Santa Inés just east of Solvang off Hwy. 246 (on Mission Dr.), 805/688-4815, www.missionsantaines.com, was established in 1804, the 19th of the state's 21 missions and the last in the region. Get a more complete story on the tour of this rosy-tan mission with its copper roof tiles, attractive bell tower, original murals, and decent museum. It's open daily; small donation requested. Bingo and such are the main attractions at the otherwise almost invisible **Santa Ynez Indian Reservation,** on the highway in Santa Ynez. More interesting for most folks is the **Santa Ynez Valley Historical Society Museum** on Sagunto St. in Santa Ynez, 805/688-7889, open Fri.–Sun. 1–4 P.M., a respectful look at local tradition. Also here is the **Parks-Janeway Carriage House,** with a restored collection of horse-drawn buggies, carriages, carts, and stagecoaches; at last report the carriage house was open during museum hours, and also open Tues.–Thurs. 10 A.M.–4 P.M.

Seeing and Doing the Santa Ynez Valley

Rancho San Fernando Rey near Santa Ynez is noteworthy as the birthplace of Palomino horses, one of the few "color" breeds, golden creatures descended from Arabian stock with flaxen manes and tails. Horse ranches, in fact, whether specializing in Arabians, American paints, quarter horses, thoroughbreds, Peruvian *paso finos* or other breeds, are big business in these parts. Monty Roberts of *The Man Who Listens to Horses* fame, is headquartered in the valley at 110-acre **Flag is Up Farms,** a thoroughbred racing and training ranch and event center.

Most Santa Ynez Valley back roads offer wonderful cycling, increasing numbers of small wineries, and sublime pastoral scenery. **Santa Barbara County wineries**—a cornucopia—are becoming big business, and a major regional attraction. For more on area wineries, see the special topic Santa Barbara Wine Country.

Nojoqui Falls County Park, www.sbparks.com, is about six miles south of Solvang on Alisal Rd., a beautiful bike ride from town but more easily accessible from Nojoqui Pass on Hwy. 101. The park itself includes 84 acres of oaks, limestone cliffs, and a sparkling 168-foot vernal (spring only) waterfall, in addition to hiking trails and picnic and playground facilities.

Los Olivos, once a stage stop at the end of a narrow-gauge railroad rolling down from the north, is now a tiny Western revival town seemingly transplanted from the Mother Lode. If the town looks familiar, it may be because its main street served as a set for TV series *Mayberry RFD.* Nowadays, the county's booming boutique wine trade is quite visible from here. Well worth a stop for wine aficionados is the **Los Olivos Wine & Spirits Emporium** on Grand Ave. south of town, 805/688-4409 or toll-free 888/729-4637 (SB-WINES), www.sbwines.com, which definitely purveys some of the area's finest. The main attraction in nearby **Ballard** is the Ballard School, a classic little red schoolhouse still used for kindergarten classes. **Los Alamos** off Hwy. 101 northwest of Buellton is another spot in the road experiencing a Western-style wine country renaissance.

Staying in and near Solvang

Quite basic but right in the middle of town is the 12-room **Viking Motel,** 1506 Mission Dr., 805/688-1337, fax 805/693-9499. Inexpensive-Premium ($42–125). The 14-room **Hamlet Motel,** 1532 Mission Dr., 805/688-4413 or toll-free 800/253-5033, fax 805/686-1301, also offers inexpensive rooms. Inexpensive-Luxury ($50–175).

SPECIAL SOLVANG-AREA STAYS

Since 1946 Solvang's 10,000-acre cattle ranch, **The Alisal Guest Ranch and Resort,** has become one of California's premier resorts—offering absolute peace and rustic luxury, with no phones, no television sets, and no radios. Though the "cottages" here are quite comfortable, the real appeal is out of doors: long hikes, wrangler-led horseback rides, tennis, horseshoes, shuffleboard, croquet, badminton, volleyball, pool, table tennis, swimming, and just lounging around the pool. The Alisal even has its own lake. But some come just for the exceptional 18-hole golf course here. And some come just to loaf in the mild climate—bestirring themselves only to head for the excellent ranch-house restaurant (breakfast and dinner are included; lunch is also available). The Alisal provides a children's program in summer. For summer, book six months in advance. Rates (two-night minimum) aren't affordable for most real cowpokes, though, at $375 and up. Luxury. For more information, contact: The Alisal Ranch, 1054 Alisal Rd., 805/688-6411 or toll-free 800/425-4725 for reservations, fax 805/688-2510, www.alisal.com.

Among other Solvang-area entries in the "very special stay" category is the historic Western-French

Fess Parker's Wine Country Inn in Los Olivos, formerly the Los Olivos Grand Hotel, a luxurious 21-suite turn-of-the-20th-century hostelry with rooms named after the Western artists or French impressionists whose works decorate the walls. The hotel's elegant but casual **Vintage Room** restaurant is open for lunch and dinner daily, breakfast on weekends. Luxury. Rooms, with gas fireplaces, are $175–400 and up, but inquire about discounts and off-season specials. For more information and reservations, contact: Fess Parker's Wine Country Inn, 2860 Grand Ave., P.O. Box 849, Los Olivos, CA 93441, 805/688-7788 or toll-free 800/446-2455, fax 805/688-1942, www.fessparker.com.

Quite nice, too, and also smack dab in the middle of Santa Barbara County wine country, is **The Ballard Inn,** 2436 Baseline Ave., Ballard, CA 93463, 805/688-7770 or toll-free 800/638-2466 for reservations, fax 805/688-9560, www.ballardinn.com, a contemporary two-story country inn with 15 rooms and all the amenities. Luxury, with rates $170–250. The inn offers breakfast cooked to order, afternoon hors d'oeuvres, and wine-tasting. The inn's dinner-only **Cafe Chardonnay** serves well-prepared fish, chicken, chops and other wine-enhancing possibilities.

Most lodgings in Solvang proper tend to be pricier, especially in summer. Weekend rates are often higher, too. The **Best Western Kronborg Inn,** 1440 Mission Dr., 805/688-2383 or toll-free 800/528-1234, fax 805/688-1821, features pleasant, newly redecorated rooms, refrigerators and coffeemakers in all rooms, color TV with cable, heated pool, and spa. Some "pet rooms" available, too. Moderate-Expensive ($60–95). **Inns of California,** 1450 Mission Dr., 805/688-3210, fax 805/688-0026, has comfortable rooms and a heated pool. Moderate-Luxury ($60–195).

Quite appealing in that Solvang style is the **Chimney Sweep Inn,** 1564 Copenhagen Dr., 805/688-2111 or toll-free 800/824-6444, fax 805/688-8824, which features individually decorated rooms, loft rooms, suites, and garden cottages. Complimentary Danish bakery breakfast. And there's a spa in the gazebo. Expensive-Luxury ($90 and up). Still a great value is **Country Inn & Suites,** 1455 Mission Dr., 805/688-2018 or toll-free 800/446-4000, fax 805/688-1156,

with attractive, spacious rooms, abundant amenities, and free country breakfast and "hospitality reception" refreshments and snacks daily. Premium ($128–148), but ask about specials.

Solvang's full-service hotel is the **Solvang Royal Scandinavian Inn,** 400 Alisal Rd., 805/688-8000 or toll-free 800/624-5572, fax 805/688-0761, featuring large rooms and heated pool. Moderate-Luxury, with summer rates of $99 and up ($79 and up in winter). An impressive newcomer is the 40-room **Petersen Village Inn,** 1576 Mission Dr., 805/688-3121 or toll-free 800/321-8985, fax 805/688-5732, featuring all the amenities, including European buffet breakfast and evening dessert buffet.

For more complete listings of accommodations, contact the local chamber of commerce or visitor bureau.

Eating in and near Solvang

Solvang's Danish bakeries are legendary, and many visitors manage to eat reasonably well without going much farther. The **Solvang Bakery,** 460 Alisal Rd., 805/688-4939, is one good choice. Farm-style breakfast places and pancake houses are also big around town. For truly sophisticated Solvang fare, the place is the **Brothers Restaurant** inside the Storybook Inn, 409 1st St., 805/688-9934. Always special for a fine dine is the **River Grill** at the Alisal Ranch, outside town at 1054 Alisal Rd., 805/688-7784.

Though the general consensus is that it's not as good as it used to be, now that it's become a restaurant chain, the original **Andersen's Pea Soup** is in nearby Buellton (you can't miss it on Hwy. 246, with its own Best Western motel). But Buellton won't disappoint. Best bet for breakfast, for miles around, is **Ellen's Danish Pancake House,** 272 Avenue of the Flags, 805/688-5312. For Mexican, the place is **Javy's Café,** 406 E. Hwy. 246, 805/688-7758. Buellton also boasts the sequel to the original Hitching Post barbecue palace and steakhouse in Casmalia (see the special topic Santa Maria Barbecue), the dinner-only **Hitching Post II,** 406 E. Hwy. 246, 805/688-0676.

Other great eating possibilities are scattered throughout surrounding vineyard country. The casual French country-style **Ballard Store** restaurant in block-long Ballard closed in late 1999, alas. But there are other possibilities, including the small **Cafe Chardonnay** in the Ballard Inn, 2436 Baseline Rd., 805/688-7770, open for dinner Wed.–Sun. nights. Reservations are advisable. Or head to Los Olivos.

About five miles north of Solvang on Hwy. 154 in Los Olivos is historic **Mattei's Tavern,** 805/688-4820, once a train depot and stage stop,

now a white-frame dinner house specializing in steak, seafood, and other hearty fare. It's open noon–3 P.M. for lunch too, Fri.–Sun. only. Reservations advisable. Or try the **Los Olivos Café,** 2798 Grand Ave., 805/688-7265, open daily for lunch and dinner. For something simple, stop by **Panino,** 2900 Grand Ave., 805/688-9304, for smoothies, any one of the 30-something sandwiches, and picnic supplies. Exceptional in these parts for fine dining is the elegant yet casual **Vintage Room** at Fess Parker's Wine Country Inn, 2860 Grand Ave., 805/688-7788, open for breakfast, lunch, and dinner.

As elsewhere in the Santa Ynez Valley, in Santa Ynez the tried-and-true bumps up against the new—though wine country sensibility is fast outpacing cowboy-style steak and eggs. Still going strong, though, for basic 1950s-style breakfast along with great burgers and fries is the **Longhorn Coffee Shop & Bakery,** 3687 Sagunto St., 805/688-5912. Also here is **Maverick Saloon,** 805/688-5841, kind of a country-western juke joint popular for line dancing and karaoke. At home in the same complex yet cultural and culinary worlds away is world-class **Trattoria Grappolo,** 805/688-6899, famous for its homemade pastas and wood-fired pizza. Other foodie destinations include the **Santa Ynez Feed & Grill,** 3544 Sagunto St., 805/693-5100, and **Vineyard House,** 3631 Sagunto, 805/688-2886.

Los Alamos also has its attractions, but still down-home and kicked-back, including **Charlie's,** 97 Den, 805/344-4404, and the fairly mellow biker tavern **Ghostriders,** 550 Bell, 805/344-2111.

SANTA BARBARA AND VICINITY

Santa Barbara is beautiful, rich, and proud of it. Though her past is somewhat mysterious—she goes by the name "Santa Teresa" in the works of mystery writers Ross MacDonald and Sue Grafton—her presence hints at natural luck almost as incredible as her beauty, cosmic beneficence only briefly perturbed by unavoidable misfortune. If she were a flesh-and-blood woman, she would sway down the brick sidewalks, her aristocratic nose pointed upward, a satisfied smile on her face.

But such easy grace is no accident, of course; Santa Barbara's beauty regime is strict. She insists that the facades of all buildings (including McDonald's) reflect the Spanish style she favors. Death, decay, or other disarray in her environment displeases her; the only time she curses is when she spits out the words "developer," "development," and "oil companies," these latter responsible for the 1969 oil spill that fouled 20 miles of her pristine beaches. Her most peculiar personality quirk is that she secretly believes she lives in Northern California, despite social intercourse with everything Southern Californian.

Santa Barbara is generous with her gifts, and she has everything: beautiful beaches and understated, stark chaparral slopes; colleges and universities; a celebrated arts and entertainment scene; fine restaurants (more restaurants per capita than any other U.S. city, in fact) and luxury resorts; trendy boutiques; antique shops. Though her sun shines brightest on celebrity residents—among them, in recent history, Cher, Julia Child, Michael Douglas, Jane Fonda, Steve Martin, Priscilla Presley, and John Travolta—she magnanimously allows the middle class to bask in her glow.

SEEING SANTA BARBARA: DOWNTOWN

Since the founding of **Mission Santa Barbara** in 1786 at the upper end of what is now Laguna St., the altar light has never been extinguished—and that's saying something. Originally a collection of simple adobes, Santa Barbara's "Queen of the Missions" and California's 10th

was subsequently all but flattened by the 1812 earthquake, the same year the town on the coastal plain below was all but swept away by a huge tidal wave. Another earthquake, in 1925, did its best to bring the mission down. Yet the Queen of the Missions still stands—indeed queenly, presiding over the city and sea with two massive squared towers, arcades, and domed belfries. The **museum** tells the mission's story with history displays, photographs, and a reconstructed kitchen. Self-guided tours are offered daily 9 A.M.–5 P.M., small admission fee (children under age 12 free). For details or more information, stop by the mission at 2201 Laguna St., call 805/682-4149, or try www.sbmission.org.

There's more historical Santa Barbara downtown, just down the hill. Get oriented at the **Santa Barbara Historical Society Museum,** 136 E. De La Guerra, 805/966-1601, an impressive regional history museum featuring everything from antique toys to vaquero-style saddles. The museum is free and open Tues.–Sat. 10 A.M.–5 P.M., Sun. noon–5 P.M. Guided tours are offered; call for details. The museum's adjacent 19th-century **Casa Covarrubias** and **Historic Adobe** also offer a peek into the past. (Museum docents can also tell you about the society's restored **Trussell-Winchester Adobe** and the 1862 Queen Anne **Fernald House,** located together at 412-414 W. Montecito St. and usually

---

SHAKIN' UP SANTA BARBARA STYLE

From the present-day perspective the earthquake of June 1925, which left the city in ruins, was the best thing that ever happened to Santa Barbara. During the city's reconstruction, a quickly formed architectural review board declared that new buildings in Santa Barbara would henceforth be Mediterranean in design and style, appropriate to the area's balmy climate and sympathetic to its Hispanic cultural heritage. The town's trademark old Spanish California adobe look—cream-colored stucco, sloping red-tile roofs, and wrought-iron grillwork—is a unified effect of fairly modern origin.

Santa Barbara's "Queen of the Missions"

KIM WEIR

open for guided tours on Sun. only, 2–4 P.M.) Nearby is the **Carriage and Western Arts Museum,** 129 Castillo St., 805/962-2353, at the north end of Pershing Park, open by donation Mon.–Sat. 9 A.M.–3 P.M. and 2–4 P.M. on Sunday. Most of Santa Barbara's other surviving adobes, now private residences or office buildings, are included on downtown's self-guided **Red Tile Walking Tour,** outlined in the visitor guide and also available on the website.

The walking tour's traditional starting point is the **Santa Barbara County Courthouse,** a must-see destination one block from State St. at Anapamu and Anacapa, 805/962-6464, an L-shaped Spanish-Moorish castle with spacious interiors decorated with murals, mosaics, ceramic Tunisian tile, and hand-carved wood—quite possibly the most beautiful public building anywhere in California. County supervisors meet in the Assembly Room, with its romantic four-wall historic mural created by a Cecil B. DeMille set designer, and sit in comfortable leather-covered, brass-studded benches and chairs under handmade iron chandeliers. The spectacular views of the city from the clock tower or the *mirador* balcony alone are worth the trip. The courthouse is open 8 A.M.–5 P.M. on weekdays, 9–5 on weekends and holidays, with free guided tours offered at 2 P.M. Mon.–Sat., also at 10:30 A.M. on Friday.

Across the street at 40 E. Anapamu St. sits the stunning Spanish-style **Santa Barbara Public Library,** 805/962-7653, with its grand Peake-Warshaw murals and both the Faulkner Gallery

and Townley Room art displays. It's open Mon.–Thurs. 10 A.M.–9 P.M., Fri. and Sat. 10 A.M.–5:30 P.M., and Sun. 1–5 P.M. Well worth a stop in the other direction is the unusual **Karpeles Manuscript Library,** 21 W. Anapamu, 805/962-5322, a free museum featuring an extensive collection of both original and facsimile manuscripts—music, letters, maps, illustrations, books, treaties, and such. It's open daily 10 A.M.–4 P.M., closed Thanksgiving and Christmas.

El Presidio de Santa Barbara State Historic Park, 123 E. Cañon Perdido St. (between Anacapa and Santa Barbara Sts.), 805/966-9719, an ambitious reconstruction, is now under way. The project was undertaken by the private Santa Barbara Trust for Historic Preservation to re-create the original 1782 Presidio Real, imperial Spain's last military outpost in California. Before restoration began, all that remained of the original presidio were two crumbling adobe buildings; one, El Cuartel, is Santa Barbara's oldest building and the second oldest in the state. Started in 1961, the project was expected to be completed by the year 2000. To date two buildings have been restored and five reconstructed.

Along with history, downtown offers its own perspectives on the history of art at the **Santa Barbara Museum of Art,** 1130 State St. (between Anapamu and Figueroa), 805/963-4364, www.sbmuseart.org, an outstanding regional museum that attracts impressive traveling exhibits. The permanent collection here boasts 19th-century impressionists including Chagall,

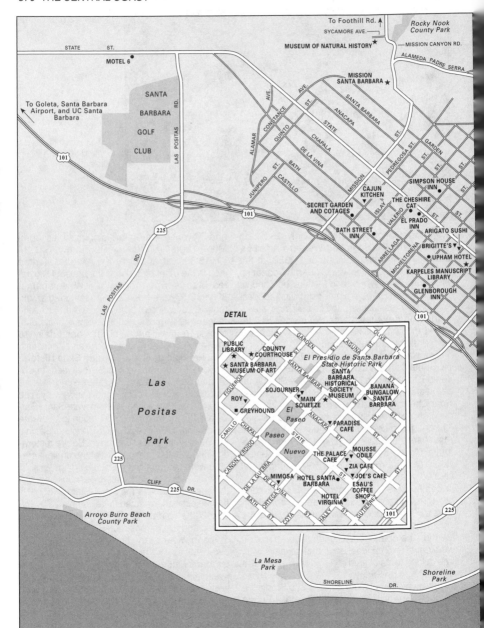

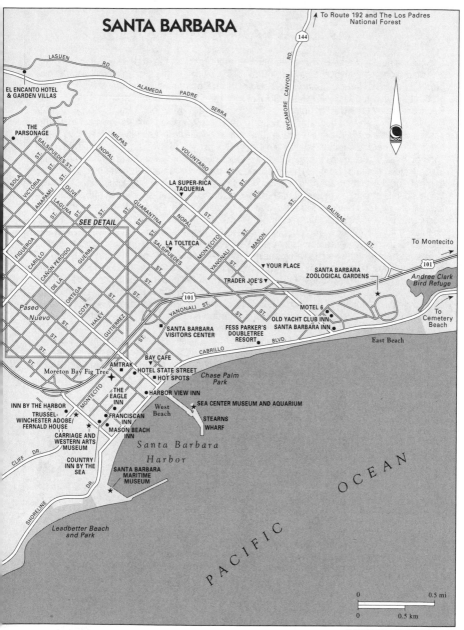

NATURAL SANTA BARBARA

The best of natural Santa Barbara and vicinity is on display at the exceptional **Santa Barbara Museum of Natural History** two blocks north of the mission at 2559 Puesta Del Sol Rd., 805/682-4711, www.sbnature.org. This Spanish-style cluster of buildings and courtyards includes excellent exhibits on the Chumash and other indigenous peoples, collections of fossils, geology displays, nature exhibits (including a busy beehive), even some original Audubon lithographs. In addition to the museum's classes on every natural history topic under the sun, there's a planetarium and observatory here, 805/682-3224, offering a popular Sunday afternoon program. The museum also sponsors a year-round schedule of films and special events—including **monarch butterfly tours** in January (by reservation) and the **Wine Festival** in August. On the way in or out, stop outside near the parking lot to appreciate the 72-foot-long skeleton of a blue whale, recently restored. The natural history museum is open 9 A.M.–5 P.M. daily (from 10 A.M. on Sun. and holidays), closed Thanksgiving, Christmas, and New Year's Day. Admission is $6 adults, $5 seniors and students (ages 13–17), and $4 children age 12 and

under, free on the first Sun. of every month. Nearby and perfect for an almost-country picnic is **Rocky Nook County Park.**

The 65-acre **Santa Barbara Botanic Garden,** 1212 Mission Canyon Rd., 805/682-4726, www.sbbg.org, is "dedicated to the study of California's native plants." Too many people miss this natural Santa Barbara treasure. Plants native to Santa Barbara and vicinity are the main event (don't miss the spectacular spring wildflowers) but cacti, other succulents, even redwoods are at home in the gardens here. Good gift shop—particularly popular with gardeners and plant lovers. Lectures, classes, trips, and special events are often scheduled, and docent-guided tours are offered daily at 2 P.M., also on Thurs., Sat., and Sun. at 10:30 A.M. Best, though, is showing up when nothing's going on and just wandering the grounds—a stroll that can easily become a brisk five-mile hike. The botanic garden is open daily 9 A.M.–sunset (gift shop open until 4 P.M. in winter, 5 P.M. in summer). Small admission (under age 5 free), and once you're in docent-guided tours are free, but donations and membership support are always appreciated.

You'll know you've found the Santa Barbara Museum of Natural History when you spot the whale skeleton.

KIM WEIR

Matisse, and Monet; O'Keeffe, Eakins, and other major American artists; and an eclectic assortment of classical antiquities, Asian art, photography, prints, and drawings. Good bookstore and on-site café. The museum is open Tues.–Sat. 11 A.M.–5 P.M. (until 9 P.M. on Thurs.) and Sun. noon–5 P.M. Docents guide free gallery tours at 1 P.M. Admission is $5 adults, $3 seniors, $2 students with ID and children ages 6–17. The museum is free to everyone, though, every Thurs. and on the first Sun. of every month (under age 6 always free).

Confusing the line between real and faux history are downtown's many stylish shops—art galleries galore and **Brinkerhoff Avenue,** famous for its antiques—and, now, two shopping centers. **El Paseo,** California's first shopping center and the originator of the city's distinctive architectural "look," is a clustered two-story collection of Spanish colonial revival shops built in the early 1920s around courtyards, fountains, and gardens (enter from State St., near De La Guerra). The stylish new **Paseo Nuevo** mission-style mall, anchored by Nordstrom and Ma-

cy's between State and Chapala Sts. and Ortega and Cañon Perdido, offers upscale shops and shopping. Particularly worthwhile here is the 4,500-square-foot **Contemporary Arts Forum,** 805/966-5373, an adventurous contemporary arts gallery and exhibition space often sponsoring traveling shows, other special exhibits, and lectures.

To the benefit of visitors and residents alike, Santa Barbara is generous with public parking downtown. Park in any of 10 various lots, and the first 90 minutes are free; the incorrigibly cheap could, conceivably, move their cars from lot to lot at precise intervals and stay downtown all day for free.

SEEING SANTA BARBARA: AROUND TOWN AND BEYOND

The **Moreton Bay Fig Tree** at Chapala and Montecito Sts. (where Hwy. 101 rolls by) is considered the nation's largest. Affectionately called "the old rubber tree" by some, though it pro-

EVENTFUL SANTA BARBARA

There's almost always something going on, starting in late February or early March (usually March) with the four-day **Santa Barbara International Film Festival,** with premieres and screenings of both international and U.S. films, followed by the city's three-month theater festival. Also in March comes the **Whale Festival & Week of the Whale,** and in April the **Santa Barbara County Vintners' Festival,** a spring wine aficionado and foodie fest.

Come in June for the **Big Dog Parade and Block Party** on State Street. Santa Barbara's **Fourth of July** celebration includes a parade downtown, fireworks along the waterfront, and parties all over town—including the Santa Barbara Symphony's free pops concert at the Santa Barbara Courthouse. August's **Old Spanish Days Fiesta** is a classy five-day celebration of the city's heritage with parades, carnival, rodeo, herds of horses, performances, other special events, and two colorful marketplaces—festive but dignified, a festival featuring plentiful freebies.

The elegant **Santa Barbara Concours d'Elegance** in September features spit-polished antique and classic cars, a winner's parade, and picnic. In

late September or early October comes the **Santa Barbara International Jazz Festival and World Music Beach Party** at Stearns Wharf. In October comes the Santa Barbara Vintners' Association **Celebration of Harvest,** another foodie and wine festival, this one also featuring dancing, exhibits, and storytelling.

Una Pastorella, a re-creation of the traditional shepherd's nativity play, is staged in December inside the Presidio Chapel, and the **Yuletide Boat Parade** lights up Stearns Wharf. Also show up for **Winterfest** at the Santa Barbara Botanic Garden.

For a complete calendar of events, contact the visitors bureau. To find out what's going on while you're in town—including the impressive array of area arts events and what might be hip or happening in local nightlife—pick up a current issue of the free **Santa Barbara Independent,** www.independent. com, published on Thursday each week and offering local news coverage and excellent arts and entertainment features, reviews, and calendar listings. The daily **Santa Barbara News-Press,** www.news-press.com, also features calendar listings and a special Friday *Scene* magazine insert.

duces neither rubber nor figs, this Australian native is large enough (they say) to shelter 10,000 people from the noonday sun. Street people and transient philosophers are attracted to its welcoming attitude, much to the rest of the community's chagrin.

Nearby is the Santa Barbara harbor area; the city's "bay" is little more than a curvaceous beach front. **Stearns Wharf,** 805/564-5518, at the foot of State St. and the oldest operating wharf on the West Coast, offers pier fishing, shops, and restaurants. Worthwhile here is the **Sea Center Museum and Aquarium,** 805/962-0885, a branch of the Santa Barbara Museum of Natural History open daily 10 A.M.–5 P.M. The emphasis here is on the marinelife of the Santa Barbara Channel, just offshore, with seawater tank exhibits, a computer learning center, and an outdoor "touch tank" for an up-close-and-personal introduction to underwater wonders (touch-tank exhibit open noon–4 P.M. every day except Wednesday). Small admission. Also worth a stop on the wharf, if you care to learn more about California's endlessly threatened natural environments, is **The Nature Conservancy Visitor Center,** 213 Stearns Wharf, 805/962-9111, open on weekdays noon–4 P.M., on Sat. and Sun. 11 A.M.–5 P.M.

To the east of the pier is pleasant **East Beach,** buffered from busy Cabrillo Blvd. by the manicured lawns, footpaths, and bike trails of expanded **Chase Palm Park,** which stretches along the north side of Cabrillo Blvd. from Garden St. to Calle César Chávez. At the east end of East Beach is **Cemetery Beach,** a popular nude beach (one of four in the area). Also reasonably secluded is Montecito's **Butterfly Beach,** below the Four Seasons Biltmore Hotel. West of Stearns Wharf is the municipal harbor, protected by a long stone breakwater, and **West Beach.** The promising new **Santa Barbara Maritime Museum,** 805/962-8404, www.sbmm.org, is situated at the harbor entrance, in the Waterfront Center. Pending unveiling of the museum's main exhibit hall, the "preview center" is open daily 10 A.M.–4 P.M. Farther west are **Leadbetter Beach** and **Shoreline Park,** also tiny **La Mesa Park** and **Arroyo Burro Beach,** popular for swimming and surfing.

Overlooking West Beach is the **Santa Barbara Zoological Gardens,** a onetime estate at 500 Niños Dr. (off E. Cabrillo Blvd.), 805/962-6310 (recorded) or 805/962-5339, www.santabarbarazoo.org, with more than 600 exotic animals in almost natural habitats—one of the best smaller zoos anywhere. Santa Barbara's zoo has an outstanding walk-through "aquatic aviary," a portholed Sealarium, and islands for squirrel monkeys and gibbons. Nocturnal Hall, a walk-in tropical aviary on the outside, houses nocturnal animals within. Also here: a peaceful picnic area, small botanic garden, farmyard, Wild West playground, and zany mini-trains. The zoo is open daily 10 A.M.–5 P.M., adults $7, children and seniors $5 (under age 2 free). The **Andree Clark Bird Refuge** is a landscaped 50-acre preserve of reclaimed marshland at the east end of E. Cabrillo Blvd. adjoining the zoo, with freshwater fowl, also bike trails and footpaths; if you really like to bike it, the paved **Cabrillo Bikeway** runs to the refuge from the harbor. Guided refuge tours are sometimes offered by the local Audubon Society chapter.

North and West of Santa Barbara

Just up the coast from Santa Barbara proper on a beautiful stretch of beachfront property in Goleta is the **University of California at Santa Barbara** campus. Bordered on two sides by the Pacific Ocean, miles of white-sand beaches, and a natural lagoon, the campus itself is a beauty. Noted for its comprehensive environmental studies program—one of the first of its kind in the nation—and its engineering, education, and scientific instrumentation programs, the university gained national attention in the late 1960s and early '70s for anti–Vietnam War activities in the adjacent "student ghetto" of **Isla Vista,** still jam-packed with stucco apartment buildings and bustling with student-oriented businesses and activities.

Diversions in nearby **Goleta** include the **South Coast Railroad Museum,** 300 N. Los Carneros Rd., 805/964-3540, featuring a restored 1901 Southern Pacific depot, antiques and artifacts, a 300-square-foot model railroad, miniature train rides for the kiddies, and handcar rides for older kids. Open Wed.–Sun. 1–4 P.M. Next door is the historic Victorian **Stow House,** 805/964-4407, open weekends only 2–4 P.M. from Feb. through Dec. (museum closed on rainy days), though the grounds are open year-round. Popular local events staged at Stow House include the annual **Goleta**

Valley Lemon Festival and the **Old-Time Fiddlers' Convention.** Another area attraction is the two-acre **Santa Barbara Orchid Estate,** 1250 Orchid Dr., 805/967-1284, www.sborchid.com, with more than 100 varieties on display (plants and cut flowers available for sale), an entire acre of them under glass.

Attractions along the coast north of Santa Barbara and Goleta include three spectacular state "beach" parks. Farthest north is **Gaviota State Park,** about 22 miles north of Goleta, a small beach area that also includes 3,000 associated acres of chaparral, campsites, picnic areas, hiking trails, and hike-in hot springs. Next down-coast and perhaps loveliest of all, just 12 miles north of Goleta, is breathtaking **Refugio State Beach,** a white-sand cove fringed by palm trees and protected from the pounding surf by a rocky point. Here are more campsites—just five facing the beach—plus a glorious group camp. Two miles south, connected by paved bike path to Refugio, is **El Capitan State Beach,** most popular for year-round camping. All three beaches are open daily dusk until dark for day use ($2 per vehicle fee). For current information on all three beaches, call 805/968-1033. For campground reservations—essential in summer and on weekends, prudent any time—call ReserveAmerica at toll-free 800/444-7275.

About 18 miles northwest of Santa Barbara, on the way to Solvang and Santa Ynez via Hwy. 154, is **Cachuma Lake,** the largest manmade lake in Southern California, a 3,200-acre, trout-stocked, oak woodland reservoir open for day use 6 A.M.–10 P.M. daily. Stop by the **Cachuma Nature Center** to get oriented. Also a county park, Cachuma is ripe for year-round recreation: boating, sailing, hiking, and swimming in pools (Memorial Day through Labor Day only). No "body contact" with the lake is allowed, since this is the city of Santa Barbara's primary water supply. Fishing is a year-round draw, as is bird-watching; more than 275 bird species have been spotted here. A major new attraction here is the two-hour **Eagle Cruise** led by the park's naturalist, offered only Nov. to Mar. When the bald eagles arrive for their own winter respite (fee, by reservation only). The lake has pleasant picnic areas and developed campsites for both tents and RVs, also group camps. Day use is $3.50 per vehicle, camping $12 and up. And a quarter will get you a three-minute hot shower. For more information, contact: Cachuma Lake Recreation Area, HC 58—Hwy. 154, Santa Barbara, CA 93105, 805/686-5054 (recorded) or 805/686-5050 for information, weekend events, and Fish Watch, 805/686-5055 (voice/TDD), www.sbparks.com.

Worth seeing, for dedicated back-roaders, is **Chumash Painted Cave State Historic Park** off Painted Cave Rd., with its characteristic black, red, and yellow pictographs. Gaze in through the iron grating now in place to discourage vandals, or call 805/968-3294 for tour information. Parking on the road's narrow shoulder accommodates only one or two cars (definitely no trailers or RVs).

South and East of Santa Barbara

The balmy beaches, yacht harbor, and wooded estates of **Montecito,** just south of Santa Barbara, seem tailor-made for the people behind commercial trademarks such as DuPont, Fleischmann, Pillsbury, and Stetson—and they were. Especially worth seeing in Montecito is surreal **Lotusland,** created by the flamboyant and independent Madame Ganna Walska, thwarted opera singer and compulsive marrier of millionaires. Here you'll find the world's finest private collection of cycads (relatives of pine trees that look like palms), also cacti and succulents, a luxuriant fern garden lacking only prehistoric dinosaurs, an eccentric "Japanese" garden, a fantastic aloe-and-abalone-shell "forest," weeping euphorbias, 20-foot-tall elephant's feet, lily and lotus ponds, bromeliads, orchids, and roses. Casual or drop-in garden tours are not possible, but the gardens are open by reservation to those interested in horticulture or botany. Make reservations for the two-hour tours ($10 per person, no children under age 12) by contacting the Ganna Walska Lotusland Foundation, 695 Ashley Rd., Santa Barbara, CA 93108, 805/969-3767. Because the house and gardens are in a residential area, there is an annual limit of 9,000 visitors (no drive-by lookie-loos, please; such voyeurism upsets the neighbors, and you can't see anything anyway). Beginning on or about Nov. 15, reservations are taken for the following year—and the entire year's tours are typically booked by Jan. 15.

If you miss Lotusland, don't miss **Casa del Herrero,** rich with Italian and Spanish antiquities.

George Fox Steedman's onetime estate, Casa del Herrero is open for guided 90-minute tours on Wed. and Saturday. The fee is $10 per person, children 10 and under not permitted. For details and reservations, call 805/969-9990.

The burg of **Summerland** just south along the coast is the site of California's first offshore oil drilling in the 1890s. The Spiritualists, a sect known for its séances and merriment, settled here first on former mission lands (thus the locals' derogatory nickname, "Spookville"). Most architectural evidence of Summerland's past was bulldozed during the 1925 construction of Hwy. 101 and 15 years later, when the highway became a freeway. Summerland offers a county park, a nice beach, and a boom in antique shops, restaurants, and bed-and-breakfast inns, but the town's most entertaining feature somehow disappeared in the last decade—the sign reading: Population 3,001, Feet Above Sea Level 280, Established 1870, Total: 5,151. Following Lillie Ave. east (it becomes Villa Real) leads to the **Santa Barbara Polo and Racquet Club,** where exhibitions and tournaments are scheduled on Sun., sometimes on Sat., spring through fall.

Carpinteria farther south on the way to Ventura was once a Chumash village. Cabrillo stumbled upon it in August of 1542, and Portolá later called it Carpinteria or "carpenter shop" because of the natives' industrious canoe-making. People say **Carpinteria State Beach,** a onetime bean field now complete with large campground and hiker/biker campsites, sports the "safest beach in the world" because the surf breaks 2,000 feet out from shore, beyond the reef, and there's no undertow. Other local attractions include the free **Carpinteria Valley Museum of History,** 956 Maple Ave., 805/684-3112 (free, but donations appreciated). Carpinteria's main streets also boast an abundance of antique shops.

For more information about Summerland and Carpinteria, call the **Carpinteria Valley Chamber of Commerce** at 805/684-5479 or toll-free 800/563-6900, www.carpcofc.com.

From south of Carpinteria, Hwy. 150 leads to Lake Casitas and to Ojai, made famous as a setting for Shangri-La in the movie *Lost Horizon.* For more information on these areas and the coast south of Carpinteria, see below.

ACCOMMODATIONS RATINGS

Accommodations in this book are rated by price category, based on double-occupancy, high-season rates. Categories used are:

Budget.	$35 and under
Inexpensive	$35-60
Moderate	$60-85
Expensive	$85-110
Premium	$110-150
Luxury	$150 and up

STAYING IN SANTA BARBARA

Santa Barbara is a popular destination year-round—a wonderful winter getaway when the rest of the nation is snowbound—but the "high season" is July and August, extending into balmy fall weekends, when warm weather coastal fog all but disappears. Most accommodation rates, fairly high any time, are highest in the summer, on weekends, and during major special events. If you plan to arrive in summer and are particular about where you'll be staying—an issue for budget travelers and families as well as the affluent—book your reservations many months, even a year, in advance. Though the practice has long been business as usual at area bed-and-breakfasts, increasingly even motels and hotels require a two-night minimum stay on weekends (three-night minimum on holiday weekends).

For help in sorting out the possibilities, try local no-fee booking agencies, including **Coastal Getaways,** 805/969-1258, **Central Coast Reservations,** toll-free 800/557-7898, and **Santa Barbara Hot Spots,** 805/564-1637 or toll-free 800/793-7666.

Campgrounds, Yurts, a Hostel, and a Monastery

Nearby **Los Padres National Forest** offers plenty of campgrounds. A complete campground listing and forest map, $2, is available at the National Forest headquarters in Goleta, 6755 Hollister Ave., Ste. 150, 805/968-6640, www.r5.fs.fed.us/lospadres; all are first-come, first-camped, with a two-week maximum stay. Closer to the ocean are the three developed state beach camp-

COWBOY-STYLE STAYS FOR FAMILIES

The **Circle Bar B Guest Ranch** at 1800 Refugio Rd. beyond Goleta, 805/968-1113, www.circlebarb.com, is a place the kids will get excited about—a genuine ranch dedicated to horseback rides (extra) and all kinds of family-appropriate fun, like hiking, picnicking, and diving into the neighborhood swimming hole. And the dinner theater does drama down at the barn, spring through fall. Accommodations, some cabin-style, are Western-themed and quite comfortable. Luxury, with high-season rates starting at $186 double (two-night minimum on weekends, three nights on holiday weekends). In summer, plan to book at least six weeks in advance on weekends, four weeks otherwise. The ranch is about three and a half miles inland from Refugio State Beach, via Refugio Rd., 20 miles north of Santa Barbara via Hwy. 101.

Just the basics for a campover-style stay but considerably less pricey is a stay at **Rancho Osos Stables & Guest Ranch,** 3750 Paradise Rd. in Santa Barbara, 805/683-5686 or toll-free 800/859-3640, adjacent to the Santa Ynez River and Los Padres National Forest. Overnight options at "Western Town" include colorful tongue-and-groove pine cabins complete with beds, coffeemaker, and small refrigerator or any of 10 Conestoga covered wagons circled around the campfire. Each wagon features electricity, hardwood floors, and four Army-style cots. Inexpensive, with cabins $46 a night, wagons $27. Hot showers, bathrooms, charcoal barbecue pits, and abundant picnic tables are nearby. Hearty meals are available on weekends at the on-site Chuck Wagon and nearby Stone Lodge Kitchen.

If money is no object and you and the li'l dogies will be moseyin' north, within easy reach is the luxurious **Alisal Guest Ranch and Resort** just outside Solvang, 805/688-6411 (for details, see Solvang and Vicinity).

grounds northwest of Santa Barbara—**Gaviota, Refugio,** and **El Capitan.** All are popular and quite nice, even for sunny winter camping (popular with snowbirds). For general information on all three, call 805/968-1033. Reserve campsites at all three—well-worn El Capitan is especially popular year-round—through ReserveAmerica, toll-free 800/444-7275; it's first-come, first-camped from Dec. through February. All offer sites with hot showers and flush toilets, some have RV hookups. Also within reasonable range of Santa Barbara is huge—262 total campsites, 126 with RV hookups—**Carpinteria State Beach** 12 miles southeast of Santa Barbara and just off Hwy. 101, 805/684-2811 or 805/968-3294, toll-free 800/444-7275 for reservations. Dogs (six-foot leash) are permitted at all of these state campgrounds for an extra $1 per day, but are not allowed on beaches or trails.

The biggest campground around is a bit farther away and inland via Hwy. 154: the county's very pleasant **Cachuma Lake Recreation Area,** with a total of almost 1,000 family and group campsites available on either a first-come or reservation basis, $12 and up (hookups extra). Cachuma offers tent, yurt, and RV camping. The fabric-covered yurts feature platform beds, electric lights and heating, lockable doors, and wood-framed screened windows. General camping amenities include hot showers, restrooms, fireplaces with grills, picnic tables, swimming pools (summer only), and nonswimming lake recreation opportunities. Primitive and hiker/biker campsites are less expensive. Dogs—on leashes—are welcomed, for a $1-per-day fee and current proof of rabies vaccination; pets are not allowed on trails. For current reservation information and other specifics, call 805/686-5054 or 805/686-5055, www.sbparks.org.

Santa Barbara also boasts a 60-bed **Banana Bungalow Santa Barbara,** 210 E. Ortega St., 805/963-0154 or toll-free 800/346-7835, fax 805/963-0184, www.bananabungalow.com, within an easy stroll of both the bus and train stations. Budget, with rates $16–22.

For a peaceful retreat, consider the **Mount Calvary Guest House** at 2500 Gibraltar Rd., 805/962-9855, www.mount-calvary.org, a palatial 1940s mountaintop Spanish-style villa with incredible vistas, great hiking access, plenty of comfortable spare bedrooms, and Benedictine monks happy to serve you. Moderate. Rates are $70 per person suggested donation (all meals included, on the American plan), with both single and double rooms (singles share an adjoining bath). Individuals—no partiers, please—are welcome for personal retreats.

In addition to the yurts available at Lake Cachuma, there's also the **White Lotus Foun-**

dation, 2500 San Marcos Pass, 805/964-1944, www.whitelotus.org, a yoga teaching institute that makes theirs available on a space available basis. Moderate ($70 couple per night).

Inexpensive-Moderate Motels and Hotels

Beyond hostels and such, finding inexpensive accommodations in Santa Barbara is a challenge. There's always Motel 6, which here isn't all that inexpensive. The **Motel 6 Santa Barbara,** 443 Corona Del Mar, 805/564-1392 or toll-free 800/466-8356 (nationwide), fax 805/963-4687, www.motel6.com, is close to the beach and downtown, newly renovated, and small, featuring the usual basic accommodations plus color TV and HBO, phones, free local calls. Very popular; for the summer-fall season, book at least six months in advance. Moderate, with rates $63–84, depending on the season (weekends in summer and fall are highest). If there's no room here, there's another Motel 6 downtown, 3505 State St., 805/687-5400, still another north of town near Goleta, and two more south of town near Carpinteria.

The once stately old hotels at the beach end of State St. are other low-end possibilities, though these are rapidly becoming boutique hotels. Of the rest, some places look better than they are, passing trains offer unwanted wake-up calls in the middle of the night, and it's a little sleazy here after dark (pack your street smarts). A best bet for an inexpensive stay, still, is the **Hotel State Street,** 121 State St., 805/966-6586, where high-season rates for clean rooms with shared baths are $50, with private baths $90 and up, continental breakfast included. Inexpensive-Expensive.

Mid-range Motels and Hotels

Most medium-priced motels here are pricey compared to similar accommodations elsewhere. But since this is Santa Barbara, who can complain? The following offer exceptional value, including good location, for the money.

Appealing and fairly affordable among Santa Barbara's burgeoning downtown boutique hotel roster is the 1926-vintage **Hotel Santa Barbara,** 533 State St. (at Cota), 805/957-9300 or toll-free 888/259-7700, fax 805/962-2412, www.hotelsantabarbara.com. Rooms are light, airy, and attractively decorated. An abundance of great restaurants are just a stroll away. Expensive-

Luxury ($99–209), but look for good seasonal specials.

Santa Barbara's newest downtown boutique, open since late 1999, is the very stylish Holiday Inn Express **Hotel Virginia,** just a hop and skip from the beach at 17 W. Haley St. (east of State St.), 805/963-9757 or toll-free 800/549-1700, fax 805/963-1747, www.hotelvirginia.com, listed on the National Register of Historic Places. Decor in this 1916-vintage, 61-room hotel emphasizes the spectacular Malibu and Catalina tilework now preserved and restored here—including the striking mosaic fountain in the lobby—and also showcases local art and artists. Rooms, decked out in a contemporary take on classic art-deco style, feature all the modern comforts, from state-of-the-art phones and data ports to hair dryers and in-room irons and ironing boards. A stay includes expanded continental breakfast. Luxury, with regular rates $159–199, though specials can drop the tab to as low as $99.

A classic in the Santa Barbara area is the historic blue-roofed **Miramar Hotel,** in Montecito at 1555 S. Jameson Ln., 805/969-2203 or toll-free 800/322-6983 for reservations (in California), fax 805/969-3163, www.sbmiramar.com. The Miramar was more tranquil in pre-freeway days but it's nonetheless still charming, perfect for unfussy families. Semitropical gardens and beachfront location add to the appeal. Expensive-Luxury. Regular rooms are $89 and up in summer, with cheaper, fairly spartan rooms closer to the thundering traffic, quieter ones clustered around the pool or along the 500-foot beachfront. Cottage and parlor suites with one, two, or three bedrooms (some have kitchens) start at $159. But even with a simple room you can enjoy the tennis and shuffleboard courts, the two swimming pools, the health spa, the on-site restaurants—and the beach.

The attractive 53-room **Franciscan Inn,** 109 Bath St. (just south of Hwy. 101), 805/963-8845, fax 805/564-3295, www.franciscaninn.com, offers high-season rates in the Expensive-Luxury range, $105–200, with tasteful decor and all the country-style comforts plus swimming pool and whirlpool, just a block from the beach. Almost half the rooms here have kitchenettes (extra).

Another find is **The Eagle Inn,** 232 Natoma Ave. (three blocks south of Hwy. 101, at Bath), 805/965-3586 or toll-free 800/767-0030, fax

805/966-1218, www.theeagleinn.com. Most rooms at this very attractive Spanish-style motel, a onetime apartment complex, are more like apartments, with full-stocked kitchens and the homey, well-kept kind of comfort that makes you want to stay longer than you'd planned. Even better is the fact that the Eagle Inn is only a block and a half from the beach. On-site laundry, cable TV, and free movies (no air-conditioning). Expensive-Luxury ($89–160), with off-season and weekday rates the real deal. For summer, book rooms by mid-May.

Also quite appealing and close to the beach is the **Inn by the Harbor,** 433 W. Montecito St., 805/963-7851 or toll-free 800/626-1986, fax 805/962-9428, www.sbhotels.com, a classic Mediterranean-style motel. Many units have kitchens. Expensive-Luxury ($102–168). See the website for the rundown on sister motels nearby.

A gussied-up motel done up in appealing country-French decor, well situated for a beach-oriented vacation, is the smoke-free 45-room **Country Inn by the Sea** two blocks south of Hwy. 101 at 128 Castillo St., 805/963-4471 or toll-free 800/455-4647, fax 805/962-2633, www.countryinnbythesea.com. Most rooms come with a balcony or patio plus color TV, VCRs, free movies. Continental breakfast. Extras include a small swimming pool, saunas, spa, and a nearby city park with tennis courts. Premium-Luxury ($149–209), though off-season and discounted rates drop down as low as $99.

Other good midrange possibilities include the **Coast Village Inn** in the center of Montecito at 1188 Coast Village Rd., 805/969-3266 or toll-free 800/257-5131, fax 805/969-7117, www.coastvillageinn.com, Premium-Luxury ($125–165), though specials drop to $89); the **El Prado Inn** downtown at 1601 State St., 805/966-0807 or toll-free 800/669-8979, fax 805/966-6502, www.elprado.com, Expensive-Luxury ($85–170); and the **Mason Beach Inn** just south of Hwy. 101 at 324 W. Mason St., 805/962-3203 or toll-free 800/446-0444, fax 805/962-1056, Expensive-Luxury ($85–195).

High-End Motels and Hotels

Lacking the history of other upscale area hotels but little else, 360-room **Fess Parker's Doubletree Resort,** previously the Red Lion Inn, is a luxurious Spanish-style resort motel across from the beach at 633 E. Cabrillo Blvd., 805/564-4333 or toll-free 800/879-2929, fax 805/564-4964, www.fpdtr.com. The huge resort motel, situated on 24 acres, features basketball and shuffleboard courts, a putting green, lighted tennis courts, exercise facilities, rental bikes, heated pool, sauna, and whirlpool. **Maxi's** restaurant is another mainstay. Rooms include all the usual comforts. Room rates starting at $195, but inquire about specials and seasonal discounts.

Also fronting the beach, adjacent to Stearns Wharf, is the 80-room **Harbor View Inn** just west of State St. at 28 W. Cabrillo Blvd., 805/963-0780 or toll-free 800/755-0222, fax 805/963-7967. Very attractive rooms feature the usual deluxe amenities plus in-room coffeemakers, refrigerators, safes, and color TV with cable. In addition to the swimming pool and whirlpool, there's a heated wading pool for the kiddos and bike and in-line skate rentals. On-site restaurant. Luxury, with high-season rates $180 and up (ocean-view rooms most expensive).

Though it's really just a spiffed-up Santa Barbara beach motel, dedicated foodies are drawn to the 71-room **Santa Barbara Inn,** 901 E. Cabrillo Blvd., 805/966-2285 or toll-free 800/231-0431, fax 805/966-6584, www.santabarbarainn.com. That's because after filling up on the fine California-French fare at **Citronelle,** chef Michel Richard's on-site restaurant, guests can just waddle right over to their rooms—or across the street to the beach—and rest until mealtime comes around again. Rooms here are spacious and attractive, with refrigerators, coffeemakers, and color TV with cable TV. Some have kitchens, some have air-conditioning. In addition to the heated pool and whirlpool, there's a sundeck on the 3rd floor. Luxury, with regular rates $219–309; discounts and off-season specials can drop the tab considerably. Weekly and monthly rates are available.

In 1928 the little tramp himself, Charlie Chaplin, and his later scandal-plagued partner Fatty Arbuckle established the **Montecito Inn,** 1295 Coast Village Rd., 805/969-7854 or toll-free 800/843-2017, fax 805/969-0623, www.montecitoinn.com, as a Hollywood hideout. These days an attractive and trendy small hotel with Mediterranean provincial style, the Montecito Inn features somewhat small rooms with all the usual amenities—no air conditioning, but there are ceiling fans—plus an attractive pool and spa area out back. Seven spacious new Mediterranean-style luxury suites feature bathrooms of Italian marble plus hot tubs; some suites have fireplaces. The inn sits close to the freeway, right in town—an easy stroll to most of Montecito's action. Luxury, with rates starting at $185.

Santa Barbara Area Bed-and-Breakfasts

Santa Barbara is a B&B bonanza—that phenomenon quite rare in and around Southern California. Many local bed-and-breakfasts and B&B-style inns are as reasonably priced as local motels, if not more so, and most offer reduced rates, specials, or packages for off-season and/or weekday stays. Many require a two-night minimum stay on weekends and/or a three-night stay over longer holiday weekends. Here as elsewhere, most bed-and-breakfasts are smoke-free—though you may be allowed to smoke on a terrace or patio, or on a nearby street corner.

Quite appealing and a great value by Santa Barbara standards is the **Secret Garden and Cottages,** 1908 Bath St., 805/687-2300, fax 805/687-4576, www.secretgarden.com, a collection of Craftsman-style cottages with most of the 11 rooms are named after particular birds. Weather permitting, breakfast is served out in the shady private garden. Premium-Luxury, with rates $115–225.

Near the beach is the award-winning **Old Yacht Club Inn,** 431 Corona Del Mar Dr., 805/962-1277 or toll-free 800/549-1676 (California) or 800/676-1676 (U.S.), fax 805/962-3989, www.oldyachtclubinn.com, actually once a yacht club, though this homey 1912 stucco Craftsman was built as a private home. Santa Barbara's first bed-and-breakfast, open since 1980, the Yacht Club's main house features yachting memorabilia and five rooms decorated in period furnishings of various moods. Four more rooms, all with private entrances, are available in the adjacent tile-roofed Hitchcock House. Just two blocks from the beach, the Yacht Club also provides bikes to tour the neighborhood. Fabulous breakfasts and famous Saturday night dinners (extra, by reservation). Premium-Luxury, with rates $110–190.

The gracious three-story Queen Anne **Bath Street Inn** is just south of Mission St. at 1720 Bath St., 805/682-9680 or toll-free 800/341-2284, fax 805/569-1281, www.travel-seek.com. Some of the 12 rooms, in the main house and summerhouse out back, feature fireplaces and whirlpool tubs; some also have in-room refrigerators and coffeemakers; one features a kitchen, whirlpool tub, and separate entrance. In addition to full breakfast, tea is served in the afternoon, wine in the evening. Expensive-Luxury, with rates $100–190 (20 percent discount Sun.–Thurs., summers and holiday weeks excepted).

Other bed-and-breakfast possibilities include the **Glenborough Inn,** 1327 Bath St., 805/966-0589 or toll-free 888/966-0589, fax 805/564-8610, www.silcom.com/~glenboro, actually a combination of five turn-of-the-20th-century homes and cottages with 14 rooms (Expensive-Luxury, $100–380); **The Parsonage,** 1600 Olive St., 805/962-9336, fax 805/962-9336, with six rooms in an 1892 Victorian (Premium-Luxury, $125–325); and **The Cheshire Cat,** 36 W. Valerio St. (at Chapala), 805/569-1610, fax 805/682-1876, www.cheshirecat.com, a collection of houses and cottages with rooms named after characters in Alice's adventures (Premium-Luxury, $140–350).

For those uncomfortable with the forced social intimacy of most bed-and-breakfast inns, the historic **Upham Hotel,** 1404 De La Vina St., 805/962-0058 or toll-free 800/727-0876, fax 805/963-2825, www.uphamhotel.com, offers a friendly alternative. Built in 1871 by Amasa Lincoln, a Boston banker who set sail for California to build himself a New England–style inn, these days the Upham is still more hotel than bed-and-breakfast. This Victorian hotel features 50 rooms and garden cottages on an acre of land in the heart of town, just a stroll from State Street. The Upham's primary eccentricity is in its guest register—an incongruous celebrity collection including Richard Nixon, Aldous Huxley, and Agatha Christie. Rooms in the main building are smallish but comfortable, with nice antique touches; more contemporary, more expensive rooms and suites are situated in various outbuildings and garden cottages. The fireplace-cozy lobby resembles an English parlor. The buffet breakfast can be taken indoors, out on the wraparound veranda, or out in the garden in an Adirondack chair. Wine and cheese are served in the evening. The on-site **Louie's** restaurant is quite good. Premium-Luxury ($140 and up).

Truly exceptional among Santa Barbara's bed-and-breakfast celebrities is the landmark **Simpson House Inn,** 121 E. Arrellaga St., 805/963-7067 or toll-free 800/676-1280, fax 805/564-4811, www.simpsonhouseinn.com. Centerpiece is the uncluttered 1874 Eastlake Italianate Victorian, exquisitely restored with period furnishings, Oriental rugs, and English lace. Other rooms are in a onetime barn—the 19th-century "barn suites," complete with authentic interior walls—and three separate garden cottages with stone fireplaces and English charm. The gardens here, an entire acre of horticultural adventure sculpted into various semi-private "outdoor rooms," are most charming of all. Full gourmet breakfast is served on the veranda or in the formal dining room, along with afternoon or evening hors d'oeuvres (including Santa Barbara County wines). Luxury, with rates $195–500.

Quite nice is the 16-room English country-style **Inn on Summerhill** south of Montecito at 2520 Lillie Ave. south of town in Summerland, 805/969-9998 or toll-free 800/845-5566, fax 805/565-9948, another award-winning bed-and-breakfast. This one boasts suite-style rooms with canopied beds and all the contemporary comforts—in-room refrigerators, hot tubs, color TV with cable and VCRs—plus full homemade breakfast and, come evening, hors d'oeuvres and dessert. Luxury, with rates $215 and up.

And if you're pushing farther on down the coast, a bed-and-breakfast gem along the way—particularly for fans of T. S. Eliot—is **Prufrock's Garden Inn,** 600 Linden Ave. in Carpinteria, 805/566-9696 or toll-free 877/837-6257, fax 805/566-9404, www.prufrocks.com. Premium-Luxury, with rates $120–250, but in the off-season weekday rates can drop quite a bit.

Luxury Hotels and Resorts

If money is no object—if this is a once-in-a-lifetime visit and you want something close to guaranteed bliss—*the* place is the **Four Seasons Biltmore Hotel** in the Montecito area at 1260 Channel Dr., 805/969-2261 or toll-free 800/332-3442 (U.S.) and 800/268-6282 (Canada), fax 805/969-4212, www.fourseasons.com. This vast but intimate tile-roofed 1927 resort, designed in "Spanish ecclesiastical" style with endless other Mediterranean details by architect Reginald Johnson, just oozes luxurious old-money charm.

Visitors could spend an entire stay just appreciating the craftsmanship, from the handmade decorative Mexican tiles and the irregular mission-style *ladrillos* (tile floors) to the massive oak doors at the hotel's entrance. Endless archways, stairways, low towers, fountains, loggias, and bougainvillea-draped walkways threaded through the lush 21-acre grounds make just finding your room an architectural adventure. Yet for all its understated elegance and luxury—and its Olympic-sized swimming pool, lighted tennis courts, kids program, excellent restaurants, multilingual staff, full conference and business facilities—a stay can be almost reasonable. And for sheer extravagance, nobody beats the Biltmore's Sunday brunch. Luxury. Regular high-season rates are $290–600, with larger ocean-view rooms and cottages most expensive; inquire about special packages and off-season specials.

Or head to the **San Ysidro Ranch,** in Montecito at 900 San Ysidro Ln. (at Mountain Dr.), 805/969-5046 or toll-free 800/368-6788, fax 805/565-1995, www.sanysidroranch.com. The ranch is an honorable member of the Relais at Châteaux international hotel association, one of the few in the United States, which explains its current exclusive cachet. But actor Ronald Colman owned the ranch in the 1930s, and in those rowdier years it was a popular Hollywood trysting place. One can still see why. These romantic cottages—the ultimate rooms with a view, scattered throughout some of Santa Barbara's most stunning gardens—are prized for their seclusion as well as their understated luxury. John and Jackie Kennedy honeymooned here, Laurence Olivier and Vivien Leigh were married here, and ink-stained scribes including Somerset Maugham and Sinclair Lewis hid out here to write. Winston Churchill wrote his memoirs here. Individually decorated rooms feature wood-burning fireplaces and endless little luxuries. The grounds include a swimming pool, wading pool, tennis courts, and stables. Horseback riding is immensely popular. You can also golf, with privileges at the nearby Montecito Country Club. If you can't afford to stay here, a special meal at the excellent California-style American **Stonehouse Restaurant** or the **Plow & Angel Bistro** at least gets you a look around (reservations highly recommended). Luxury. Cottage rooms start at $375 and luxury cottages top out at $3,750, with a two-night minimum stay on weekends, a three- or four-night minimum on holiday weekends.

Just as enchanting in its own way, and a tad less expensive, is the 10-acre hilltop **El Encanto Hotel & Garden Villas,** 1900 Lasuen Rd. (at Alameda Padre Serra), 805/687-5000 or toll-free 800/678-8946, fax 805/687-3903, www.nthp.org. This sprawling country inn, just a half-mile from the Santa Barbara Mission, once served as student and faculty housing for the original University of California at Santa Barbara campus; when the university headed north to Goleta in 1915, El Encanto was born. A charter member of the National Trust for Historic Preservation's Historic Hotels of America, El Encanto is a maze of tile-roofed Spanish colonial revival-style *casitas* and Craftsman-style cottages tucked in among the oaks and luxuriant hillside gardens. (Don't lose the map the staff give you when you check in; you'll definitely need it to find your way around.) Over the years El Encanto has welcomed endless celebrities and dignitaries, including Franklin Delano Roosevelt. But just about anyone will feel at home in these understated yet very pleasant lodgings. Many rooms feature wood-burning fireplaces, quite cheering on rain- or fog-chilled evenings. Some have refrigerators and kitchens. "View" rooms are higher on the hillside, some distance from the main building. El Encanto's amenities include a year-round solar- and gas-heated swimming pool, tennis courts and full-time tennis pro, library, and lounge. Views from the excellent on-site restaurant—open daily for breakfast, lunch, and dinner—and the hotel lobby overlook the city and the vast Pacific Ocean, a dazzling sight at sunset. Luxury, with rooms $239–419, cottage suites $379–1,200. Ask about off-season and midweek packages and specials.

EATING IN SANTA BARBARA

Farmers' Markets, Trader Joe's
The **Santa Barbara Downtown Certified Farmers' Market,** 805/962-5354, is the place to load up on premium fresh flowers, herbs, vegetables, fruits, nuts, honey, eggs, and other farm-fresh local produce. The market is held on the corner

---

COLD SPRING TAVERN

For something different on the San Marcos Pass route between Santa Barbara and the Solvang area, stop at **Cold Spring Tavern,** an old stagecoach stop at 5995 Stagecoach Rd. off Hwy. 154, 805/967-0066. The evocative Old West ambience here comes with some fairly sophisticated fare—such things as charbroiled quail—along with more traditional meat, potatoes, and biscuits with gravy. It's open daily for lunch and dinner, on weekends only for breakfast.

Ye Cold Spring Tavern, outside Santa Barbara, was once a stagecoach stop.

KIM WEIR

of Santa Barbara and Cota Sts. every Sat. 8:30 A.M.–12:30 P.M. The **Santa Barbara Old Town Certified Farmers' Market** (same phone) convenes along the 500-600 blocks of State St. on Tues., 4–7:30 P.M. in summer and 3–6:30 P.M. in winter. Other area farmers' markets are held in Goleta and Carpinteria on Thurs. afternoon, and in Montecito on Fri. morning; call for locations and current hours.

Though Santa Barbara has its share of gourmet delis—see food listings below—it also has a **Trader Joe's**, 29 S. Milpas St., 805/564-7878, which means just about anybody can afford to put together a stylish picnic dinner for the beach.

Inexpensive and Good

Even people who can't afford to sleep in Santa Barbara can find a good meal here. For "gourmet tacos," Santa Barbara's most famous dining destination is **La Super-Rica Taqueria**, 622 N. Milpas, 805/963-4940, an unassuming hole-in-the-wall and long-running favorite of chef Julia Child and appreciative fellow foodies. This mom-and-pop place serves the best soft tacos around—fresh house-made corn tortillas topped with chorizo, chicken, beef, or pork—and unforgettable seafood tamales. For Santa Barbara at its best, grab a taco and a cold beer and head for the patio—or head for the beach and a sunset picnic.

Also worth a takeout stop: **La Tolteca** restaurant and deli, 614-616 E. Haley, 805/963-0847, not real close to downtown but cheap—a tortilla-factory restaurant serving great homemade tamales, tostadas, tacos, and burritos (call for current hours).

Santa Barbara is a health-conscious city, and people from all walks of life tend to appreciate foods that'll do their bodies good. Been-there-forever **Sojourner**, 134 E. Cañon Perdido St., 805/965-7922, serves inexpensive vegetarian and vegan fare, from vegetable-rich homemade soups and black-bean stew to veggie lasagna. Also good for healthy and veggie basics, including juices and smoothies, is the **Main Squeeze** two doors down at 138 E. Cañon Perdido, 805/966-5365.

Super for inexpensive all-American breakfast is the people's favorite **Esau's Coffee Shop**, 403 State St., 805/965-4416, where everything is homemade, right down to the biscuits and home fries. It's open until 1 P.M. for breakfast and lunch (most people do breakfast).

The oldest place in town is reportedly **Joe's Cafe** and bar, 536 State St. (near Cota), 805/966-4638, a reasonably inexpensive local institution—marked by the eagle—that keeps shuffling around downtown. (Since Joe's is often mobbed, come at an off hour.) Check out the history on the walls while you enjoy excellent ravioli, steaks, fried chicken, sometimes-fresh swordfish, rainbow trout, and Santa Maria–style barbecue. Good pasta salads. *Big* meals, no desserts, and notoriously potent drinks. It's open for lunch and dinner daily.

Stylish Yet Affordable

Santa Barbara loves its restaurants served up with some style. The city's better restaurants also tend to cluster downtown, making many city blocks irresistible for foodies. For the best quiche in town, for example, head to **Mousse Odile**, 18 E. Cota St., 805/962-5393, actually a French deli serving breakfast, lunch, and dinner. The chocolate dessert mousse drives people wild. For California-style French bistro fare, the place is **Mimosa**, 700 De La Vina St., 805/682-2272, open for lunch weekdays only, for dinner nightly. For Thai, **Your Place**, 22 N. Milpas St., Ste. A, 805/966-5151, is a best bet. Fabulous and locally famous for sushi is **Arigato Sushi**, 11 W. Victoria St. #16, 805/965-6074.

For Southwestern, seek out the blue-corn tortillas and marvelous cheese *chiles rellenos* at the **Zia Cafe**, 532 State St., 805/962-5391, open daily for both lunch and dinner. **Roy**, 7 W. Carrillo, 805/966-5636, is famous for serving stylish and fresh California-style American at astonishingly low prices.

Fish, fish, fish—the ocean around here is still full of them, even after the Bay Cafe has had its way. The **Bay Cafe**, 131 Anacapa St., 805/963-2215, open for lunch and dinner daily, serves all kinds of charbroiled fish at dinner, from salmon to swordfish, plus the Bay's rendition of surf 'n' turf, paellas, and shrimp and other seafood pastas. At lunch, expect some of the same but also fish and chips, tostadas, crab melts, and seafood salad. Just about everything tastes better if you're sitting out on the patio.

Fun at breakfast, lunch, and dinner is the other-era **Paradise Café**, 702 Anacapa St., 805/962-4416, specializing in new renditions of predominantly all-American fare—eggs and omelettes, beefy burgers, and woodfire-grilled chicken, chops, fish, and steaks. But the Paradise Café is most famous for its steamed mussels—fresh from the Santa Barbara Channel, scraped off the legs of offshore oil rigs—and for the fact that it serves an exceptional selection of Santa Barbara County wines. Lively bar scene. Half the town shows up on Sun. (starting at 9 A.M.) for their killer breakfast/brunch. Breakfast is served only on Sunday.

Locally beloved for Cajun is the original **Cajun Kitchen,** 1924 De la Vina, Ste. A (near Mission St.), 805/965-1004. Those in the know say to show up early on Sat. morning—before everyone else gets there—for the unforgettable chile verde. There are Cajun Kitchens all over, elsewhere in town at 901 Chapala St., 805/965-1004, and also in Goleta and Carpinteria. **The Palace Cafe,** 8 E. Cota St. (at State), 805/966-3133, is Santa Barbara's other New Orleans niche, serving imaginative and exceptionally well-prepared fish, crawfish, "Cajun popcorn," and other Cajun-Creole and Caribbean fare. The menu changes nightly. It's open daily for lunch and dinner.

Busy **Brigitte's** California-style bistro at 1325 State St., 805/966-9676, serves everything one would expect—pizzas with pizzazz, refined pastas, grill specialties, grand salads—along with an impressive California wine list. For something simpler, stop by the associated bakery and deli adjacent for sandwiches, take-out salads, fresh-baked breads, and other bakery items.

Or try brunch at **Citronelle.** Santa Barbara's still all abuzz about Michel Richard's French restaurant at the Santa Barbara Inn, 901 Cabrillo Blvd., 805/963-0111, coastal sibling to the famous Citrus in Los Angeles. This attractive, upbeat, and airy oceanside bistro serves quiche Lorraine, eggs Benedict, and variations on more traditional American fare for brunch. Lunch and dinner selections include such choices as salmon fettuccine with saffron sauce, chicken ravioli, and Caesar salad with scallops. Wonderful appetizers and soups, exceptional California wine list, and unforgettable desserts—such as the famed chocolate hazelnut bar. It's open daily for lunch and dinner, for brunch on weekends, and sometimes for weekday breakfast; call for current details.

Then there's always **The Patio** at the Four Seasons Biltmore, 1260 Channel Dr., 805/969-2261, open daily for breakfast, lunch, and dinner.

Even if a stay at Santa Barbara's venerable Biltmore is impossible, almost anyone can swing a meal here—at least at The Patio, reasonably relaxed and quite good. A wonderful French, Mediterranean, or Italian buffet is served every evening. If money's no object, of course, the ultimate is dress-up dinner in the Biltmore's oceanview **La Marina** restaurant. Either choice offers an excuse to appreciate the lobby and explore the grounds of this stunning 1927 Spanish-Mediterranean hotel, exquisitely restored in 1987.

For more stylish dining options, head to Montecito, with many snazzy restaurants strung out along Coast Village Rd., the main drag—also home to the Fri. morning farmers' market—and many of them reasonably priced. For expensive fine dining, consider restaurants mentioned under Luxury Hotels and Resorts, above.

TRANSPORTATION AND INFORMATION

Santa Barbara Transportation

Many of the region's finest pleasures, including the Santa Barbara wine country and the lovely state beaches 20-plus miles north of town, can't be reached by public transit. Look in the telephone yellow pages or contact the local chamber of commerce or visitor bureau for car rental agencies.

To get around town without a car, **Santa Barbara Metropolitan Transit District** buses offer mainly commuter services but connect with most nearby destinations, including Goleta and Carpinteria. The transit center, 1020 Chapala St. at Cabrillo, is behind Greyhound. Call 805/683-3702 for current route and fare information, or try www.sbmtd.gov. But for many people the transit district's electric **Downtown-Waterfront Shuttles,** which run along State St. between Cabrillo Blvd. (at Stearns Wharf) and Sola St., 10:15 A.M.–6 P.M., and along the Waterfront (Cabrillo Blvd.) 10 A.M.–5:45 P.M. is all the assist needed; at last report the all-day fare was still just $.25. The less frequent morning and early evening service (times vary depending on the day) runs between the zoo on the east and the Arlington Theatre on the west. Also convenient in many cases is the **Santa Barbara Trolley,** 805/965-0353, which connects most of downtown's sights with destinations as far-flung as the Santa Barbara Mission and nearby botanic gardens with the waterfront, the zoo, and downtown Montecito. All routes start and end at Stearns Wharf. Pick up a current trolley schedule and route map; at last report all-day trolley fare was $3 adults, $2 children.

Greyhound, 34 W. Carrillo, 805/965-7551, offers good bus connections to and from L.A. and San Francisco. Even better than buses, though, is the opportunity Santa Barbara provides for traveling by train. The **Amtrak** station is downtown at 209 State St., 805/687-6848, with trains rolling south to Los Angeles and north to San Francisco; for current schedule and fare information, call toll-free 800/872-7245 or try the websites, www.amtrak.com or www.amtrakwest.com.

Limited air transport is available at the **Santa Barbara Municipal Airport** just north in Goleta at 601 Firestone Rd., 805/967-7111. But you can also arrange a ride to or from LAX with **Santa Barbara Airbus,** 805/964-7759. For prepaid reservations—usually the cheapest way to go—call toll-free 800/733-6354.

Santa Barbara Information

To request information before your trip, contact the **Santa Barbara Conference and Visitors Bureau,** 510 State St., Santa Barbara, CA 93101, 805/966-9222, fax 805/966-1728, www.santabarbaraca.com. For a copy of its comprehensive current visitor guide, call toll-free 800/927-4688—or download a PDF version from the website. (There's also a downtown parking map on the Web.) Or stop in for visitor information when you arrive. The visitors bureau sponsors two walk-in visitors centers: the **Santa Barbara Visitor Information Center,** 1 Garden St. (at Cabrillo Blvd., across from Chase Palm Park), 805/965-3021, open Mon–Sat. 9 A.M.–5 P.M. and Sun. 10 A.M.–5 P.M., and **Hot Spots,** 36 State St., 805/564-1637 or toll-free 800/793-7666; the lobby is open 24 hours, and there's an ATM here and a coffee machine. Among the informational offerings typically available: the current edition of the *Santa Barbara County Wineries* brochure and touring map and the *Antiques Map and Guide* for Santa Barbara, Montecito, and Summerland. Also pick up the *Red Tile Walking Tour* brochure (information and route also available on the website) and ask about bike rentals and such. People here are passionate about renting those "pedalinas," for example, for wheeling slowly along the beachfront bike path.

VENTURING VENTURA

Here's a thought to ponder while fueling that gas hog for a cruise from Santa Barbara to Ventura County, Los Angeles, and beyond. Scientists from USC now predict that rising sea levels caused by global warming will create havoc along much of the Ventura County coastline in the coming 50 years, with coastal military bases, power plants, harbors, hotels, businesses, and residential areas increasingly battered and left to bail out after major storms and associated floods. Because the coastal Oxnard Plain is so level, and so near sea level, the effects of global warming will be felt there sooner than elsewhere along the California coastline. By the year 2040, they say, sea level here will be permanently two feet higher than it is today. A 10-foot increase in sea level is "highly unlikely"—except during serious storms.

Road trippers not yet running on empty because of fossil-fuel guilt will find much to enjoy here along the coast north of Los Angeles.

The scenic route into Los Angeles County from the north is via the Pacific Coast Highway (PCH) to Malibu, though most people take the Ventura Freeway through the San Fernando Valley—one of L.A.'s most congested freeways. A more serene if roundabout inland alternative is Hwy. 126 through Piru, Fillmore, and Santa Paula; or take the Ronald Reagan Freeway, Hwy. 118, through Simi Valley.

Ventura County highlights include artsy Ojai, home to the annual Ojai Music Festival, and very Victorian Santa Paula, inland, home to the Santa Paula Union Oil Museum. Quite appealing along the coast is Ventura, with its San Buenaventura Mission and a welcoming old-fashioned downtown, state beach, and pleasant boat harbor—headquarters for Channel Islands National Park and point of departure for most park visitors. Fun for harbor hounds, too, is nearby Oxnard, with its downtown Heritage Square and historical museums.

VENTURA

RAMONA ST.

N. VENTURA AVE.

Ventura River

33

MISSION SAN BUENAVENTURA

ALBINGER ARCHAEOLOGICAL MUSEUM

CEDAR ST.

Grant Memorial Park

71 PALM RESTAURANT

NONA'S COURTYARD CAFÉ/ BELLA MAGGIORE INN

ORTEGA ADOBE

MAIN ST.

101

VENTURA COUNTY MUSEUM OF HISTORY AND ART

JONATHAN'S AT PEIRANO'S

Ventura County Fairgrounds

Surfer's Point

FIGUEROA

PALM ST.

OAK ST.

CALIFORNIA AVE.

CHESTNUT ST.

KALORAMA DR.

FIR ST.

VICTORIAN ROSE

POLI ST.

ROSARITO BEACH CAFÉ
Plaza Park

GREEK AT THE FISH COMPANY

VENTURA VISITORS AND CONVENTION BUREAU

VENTURA PIER

SANTA CLARA ST.

HEMLOCK ST.

E. THOMPSON BLVD.

SAN JON RD.

101

HARBOR

Ventura FWY.

HURST ST.

SANTA CRUZ ST.

CHRISMAN AVE.

MAIN ST.

NICHOLAS ST.

POLI ST.

FOOTHILL RD.

MAIN ST.

CATALINA ST.

CORONADO AVE.

S. SEWARD AVE.

San Buenaventura State Beach

PACIFIC OCEAN

SEAWARD AVENUE BUSINESS DISTRICT

SEWARD BLVD.

101

0   0.5 mi

0   0.5 km

Pierpont Bay

Ventura Harbor

HARBOR BLVD.

CHANNEL ISLANDS NATIONAL PARK VISITOR CENTER

SPINNAKER SEAFOOD BROILER

SPINNAKER DR.

Ventura Marina

Santa Clara River

Inset map

33

150

Ojai

150

River

Lake Casitas

33

Ventura

Santa Paula

126

SANTA PAULA UNION OIL MUSEUM

0   5 mi

0   5 km

101

To Santa Barbara

PACIFIC OCEAN

Ventura Harbor

MAP AREA

FOOTHILL RD.

TELEGRAPH RD.

126

OLIVAS PARK DR.

OLIVAS ADOBE

VICTORIA BLVD.

HARBOR BLVD.

101

232

SANTA CLARA AVE.

118

101

Camarillo

Oxnard

W. 5TH ST

CHANNEL ISLANDS BLVD.

OXNARD BLVD.

SAVIERS RD.

RICE AVE.

PLEASANT VALLEY RD.

34

LAS POSAS RD.

Channel Islands Harbor

Point Hueneme

HUENEME RD.

Port Hueneme

1

MOON

OJAI: SVELTE SHANGRI-LA

To the native Chumash peoples, Ojai (OH-hi) was the spiritual center of the world. Plenty of later arrivals shared similar beliefs, which is why the Krishnamurti Foundation and Library, the Krotona Institute of Theosophy and Library, Aldous Huxley's Happy Valley School, and so many other philosophical and religious icons have centered themselves in this lovely valley.

Southern California's newest religion, the quest for svelte health, is also reasonably well represented here—particularly at The Oaks at Ojai health spa downtown, sister to The Palms at Palm Springs.

The mountain-ringed Ojai Valley nests in the shadows of the Topatopa Mountains. According to local lore, Ojai means "the nest" in Chumash, though linguists say "moon" is the word's actual meaning; some residents now interpret the name of their spiritual nesting place as "valley of the nesting moon." Also according to local lore, Frank Capra set up his cameras at Dennison Grade east of town to shoot Ronald Coleman's first impressions of lush Shangri-La, the valley of eternal youth, for his 1937 film *Lost Horizons*—a film fact still in some dispute, since most of Capra's filming actually took place near Palm Springs.

But no one disputes the truth of Ojai's fabled "pink moment," that magical time close to sunset when the entire valley glows pink in the light of the waning sun—the community's most unifying spiritual event. Visitors can pay homage at least indirectly by signing on for a trip with **Pink Moment Jeep Tours**, 805/646-3227, which offers around-town tours as well as rugged backcountry jaunts.

For all its loveliness, in some ways Ojai is more event than destination—and that event is as famous as the pink moment. Ojai's three-day **Ojai Music Festival,** "the class act of all California music festivals" since the 1940s, is held either on the last weekend in May or in early June under the oaks at the Libbey Park Bowl. Along with the classics, the Ojai festival distinguishes itself by showcasing post–World War II works, including progressive and avant-garde compositions. For current schedule information or to buy tickets, contact: **Ojai Festi-**

vals, Ltd., 805/646-2053, fax 805/646-6037, www.ojaifestival.org.

For more information about the area, contact: **Ojai Valley Chamber of Commerce and Visitors Bureau,** 150 W. Ojai Ave., Ojai, CA 93023, 805/646-8126, www.the-ojai.org. For area hiking, camping, and other national forest information, stop by the **Ojai Ranger District Office** of Los Padres National Forest, 1190 E. Ojai Ave., 805/646-4348, www.r5.fs.fed.us/lospadres.

SANTA PAULA: BLAST FROM THE PAST

Like nearby Fillmore, Santa Paula is most famous for its delightful 19th-century downtown, both in its architecture and ambience. The Victorian-era buildings along well-manicured Main St., in other respects representing an antiquers' holiday, are constructed, uniquely, of weathered red brick and Sespe sandstone. Queen Anne and Victorian homes line nearby streets, blending here and there with Mediterranean and Craftsman styles. Yet Santa Paula offers its historic eccentricities; on the four-sided clock tower downtown, notice the bullet holes on the clock's north face, a distinguishing feature. Even the privately owned airport here is a surprise, a relic from the heyday of open-cockpit aviation; planes in the air on any weekend here comprise an ever-changing antique plane museum.

Still surrounded by orange and lemon groves and occasional oil derricks—and so far spared the indignities of suburban sprawl—Santa Paula was built from the wealth generated by the California oil boom of the late 1800s and the subsequent success of area agriculture. The free **Santa Paula Union Oil Museum,** 1001 E Main St. (10th and Main), 805/933-0076, open Wed.–Sun. 10 A.M.–4 P.M., tells part of the story. The museum store sells copies of the Santa Paula Historical Society's "Neighborhoods and Neighbors of the Past," which tells some of the rest by guiding visitors through historic residential neighborhoods. A drive through Santa Paula's surrounding citrus groves completes the tale. Ventura County is still California's largest lemon producer (California is the largest producer in the United States), and Santa Paula is the industry star. Santa Paula's Limoneira Co. is the county's largest lemon grower, with 40 percent of its crop—the most perfect oval fruit—exported to Hong Kong and elsewhere in Asia, where the lemons can fetch a price of $2 each.

For more information about the area, stop by the **Santa Paula Chamber of Commerce** at the historic train depot, 200 N. 10th St. (10th and Santa Barbara Sts.), 805/525-5561.

VENTURA: HOMETOWN ADVENTURES

Travelers on Hwy. 101 are typically in such a hurry to get either to or from Santa Barbara that they miss Ventura, still one of the most pleasant surprises along the coast north of Los Angeles. Its surrounding farmlands are fast being lost to the usual California housing developments and shopping centers, but historic downtown Ventura retains both its dignity and serenity. Stopping here is like visiting an old friend's oft-described hometown, since you'll feel like you've been here before.

For more information, contact: **Ventura Visitors and Convention Bureau,** 89 S. California St., Ste. C, Ventura, CA 93001, 805/648-2075 or toll-free 800/333-2989, fax 805/648-2150, www.ventura-usa.com.

Adventuring in Downtown Ventura
The centerpiece of Ventura's homey downtown Main St. business district is **Mission San Buenaventura,** 211 E. Main St., 805/643-4318, the ninth mission established in California and the last founded by Father Junípero Serra. Nearby is the very enjoyable **Ventura County Museum of History and Art,** 100 E. Main, 805/653-0323, www.vcmha.org, open Tues.–Sun. 10 A.M.–5 P.M. (closed major holidays). Beyond the excellent exhibits, the museum's gift shop is unusually fine. Admission is $4 adults, $3 seniors and AAA members, $1 children (under age 6 free). Nearby, at 113 E. Main, is the small but fascinating **Albinger Archaeological Museum,** 805/648-5823 or 805/658-4726, where an ongoing dig into one city block has unearthed artifacts from more than 3,500 years of coastal civilization; in 1974 and 1975 alone, more than 30,000 prehistoric, Chumash, Spanish, Mexican, American, and Chinese artifacts were unearthed. Admission is free. The Albinger museum is open Wed.–Sun 10 A.M.–4 P.M. in summer; call for current off-season hours.

A few blocks away is the simple **Ortega Adobe,** 215 W. Main St., 805/658-4726, the 19th-century birthplace of the Ortega chile and salsa company, the first commercial food concern of its kind in California and originator of both the chile fire-roasting and canning processes. More evocative of the days of the Mexican ranchos, however, is the two-story Monterey-style **Olivas Adobe** hacienda east of the harbor at 4200 Olivas Park Dr., 805/644-4346, once the main house of vast Rancho San Miguel. Grounds are open daily 10 A.M.–4 P.M.; the house is open weekends only 10 A.M.–4 P.M.

The visitors bureau can suggest more local attractions. But since Erle Stanley Gardner, prolific author of the Perry Mason mysteries, was once a notable local presence, consider taking the **Erle Stanley Gardner Tour** of Ventura. Suggested stops are included on the website, www.erlestanleygardner.com.

The Beach, the Pier, the Harbor
Not all of Ventura's pleasures are downtown, however—at least not right downtown. A popular surfing locale, Ventura also boasts fine two-mile-long **San Buenaventura State Beach,** within strolling distance of downtown, extended by miles and miles of beach access up and down the coast. The recently restored 1,958-foot-long **Ventura Pier,** just south of downtown and east of California St. off Harbor Blvd., reopened in 1993 after a seven-year renovation and unveiled anew in 2000 following the addition of a new octagonal extension, is the state's oldest and longest wooden pier. Still popular for fishing, the pier boasts a large restaurant, snack bar, the blowhole-like copper kinetic sculpture *Wavespout,* and lights that illuminate the beach after dark. West of the pier, at the end of Figueroa St., is **Surfer's Point,** one of the state's premier point breaks—a good place to watch longboard surfing.

South along the coast, past the beach-scene **Seaward Avenue Business District,** is relaxed **Ventura Harbor,** just off Harbor Boulevard. For information on the Channel Islands and permitted recreational activities, see Islands in Time: Channel Islands National Park, below.

Staying in Ventura

Stylish downtown is the historic **Bella Maggiore Inn,** 67 S. California St. (on the west side of California between Main and Santa Clara), 805/652-0277 or toll-free 800/523-8479, fax 805/648-5670. This three-story bed-and-breakfast hotel, built in 1924, has a breezy Mediterranean style—with fireplace, potted palms, and Italian chandeliers in the lobby, and shuttered windows, Capuan beds, ceiling fans, and fresh flowers in the graceful guest rooms. Moderate-Luxury, with rates $75–150. Weather permitting—and it usually is—breakfast is served outside, in the lovely interior courtyard. In fact **Nona's Courtyard Cafe** here, a snazzy little Californian with a Northern Italian accent, is reason enough to stay. Nona's is open daily for breakfast, Mon.–Sat. for lunch, and Fri., Sat., and Sun. for dinner.

Ventura's newest B&B is the **Victorian Rose,** 896 E. Main St., 805/641-1888, fax 805/643-1335, www.victorian-rose.com, a very Gothic onetime church where the five gorgeous guest rooms all feature private baths. Full breakfast included. Expensive-Premium, $99–145.

Ventura offers a number of surprising reasonable hotels and motels; for a complete listing, ask at the visitors bureau.

Eating in Ventura

Johnny's, 176 N. Ventura Ave., 805/648-2021, is famous for its burritos. People come from miles around just to sink their teeth into *chile verde* burritos, *chile relleno* burritos, and other intriguing possibilities. Another local draw is the **Rosarito Beach Café,** 692 E. Main St., 805/653-7343, where fresh fish is a main attraction. For more seafood at lunch or dinner, head to the harbor and the **Spinnaker Seafood Broiler,** Ventura Harbor Village, 1583 Spinnaker Dr., 805/339-0717, or the nearby **Greek at the Harbor,** 805/650-5350. Better yet is California-style **Eric Ericsson's Fish Company,** 668 Harbor Blvd., 805/643-4783.

Back downtown, quite fine is **Jonathan's at Peirano's,** 204 E. Main St., 805/648-4853, where the style is also Mediterranean. The **71 Palm Restaurant,** 71 N. Palm St., 805/653-7222, specializes in French classics.

ISLANDS IN TIME: CHANNEL ISLANDS NATIONAL PARK

Privately owned **Santa Catalina Island** is the only truly populated island among Southern California's eight Channel Islands. Populated by humans, that is. Many of the rest are inhabited by, or surrounded by, such rare, endangered, and endemic animals and plants—various whale and seal species, the island fox, the giant coreopsis "tree" (tree sunflowers), and the Santa Cruz Island ironweed among them—that biologists describe the Channel Islands, collectively, as North America's Galapagos.

San Miguel, Anacapa, Santa Cruz, and Santa Rosa Islands are seaward extensions of the east-west-trending Transverse Ranges (Santa Monica Mountains), and Santa Barbara, San Clemente, and San Nicolas are the visible ocean outposts of the Peninsular Range. Out-there **San Nicolas** and **San Clemente Islands,** property of the U.S. Navy, have rarely been visited. San Clemente has the unfortunate history of being used for bombing runs and military target practice. In the 1950s San Nicolas, inspiration for the book *Island of the Blue Dolphins,* was a top-secret post for monitoring submarines from the U.S.S.R. Since San Nicolas still contains ancient petroglyphs of dolphins, sharks, and whales, it's entirely appropriate that this same Cold War technology is now used to track the movements of migrating whales.

Islands in Time

The five northernmost Channel Islands are now included in Channel Islands National Park, 250,000 acres of isolated Southern California real estate set aside in 1980 by President Jimmy Carter for federal preservation. (Odd, by national park standards, is the fact that half these acres are below the ocean's surface.) With some planning, visitors can set out for San Miguel, Santa Rosa, Santa Cruz, Anacapa, and Santa Barbara Islands. Primitive camping is allowed on all five islands. Channel Islands National Park is also a national marine sanctuary and international biosphere preserve, an ecosystem protectorate including all five islands and a six-mile area surrounding each one.

The most westerly of the Channel Islands,

9,325-acre **San Miguel** is most famous for the thousands and thousands of seals and sea lions—up to 30,000 in summer, the population including the once-rare northern elephant seal—that bask in the sun at Bennett Point. Also notable for hikers are its giant coreopsis "trees" and ghostly caliche forests, the latter an odd moonscape of calcified plant fossils—a natural variation on sandcasting—of up to 14,000 years old. Primitive camping, hiking, beach exploration, and ranger-led hikes are the island's main attractions.

The national park system has owned 52,794-acre **Santa Rosa** since 1986. The island's main attractions aren't the usual tourist trappings, particularly some 2,000 archaeology sites (strictly off-limits) related to Chumash Indian and Chinese abalone fishing settlements. In addition to primitive camping and kayak beach camping, hiking, ranger-guided hikes, and vehicle tours are Santa Rosa's main attractions.

In 1997, preservationists finally took complete possession of 24-mile-long, 60,645-acre **Santa Cruz Island,** the largest of the eight Channel Islands. The Nature Conservancy owns 90 percent of the island and manages it as the **Santa Cruz Island Preserve,** to date a noticeably healthier ecosystem. But park officials are restoring damaged east-end habitats, long overgrazed by sheep, goats, and feral pigs, and the historic Gherini Ranch. The ranch will eventually become the human-oriented hub of the park's five islands. Already the park's primary draw, Santa Cruz is the most luxuriant of the Channel Islands. The island's curvaceous coastline boasts many natural harbors, bays, and popular dive spots, along with some spectacular sea caves. The landscape features 10 distinct plant communities, about 650 plant species scattered from pine forests, oak woodlands, and riparian streams and springs to meadows, sandy beaches, and dunes. More than 260 bird species have been spotted on and around the island, including the endemic Santa Cruz Island scrub jay, bigger and bluer than its mainland cousins.

Wind-whipped **Anacapa Island** is most accessible from the mainland, just 11 miles from Oxnard. Quite popular for day-trippers, 699-acre Anacapa is actually three distinct islands divided by narrow channels. **East Anacapa** is the usual human destination. Once ashore it's a quick 154 steps straight up to the bluff tops, where the meandering nature trail begins. Beyond the visitors center, standing vigil at the entrance to the Santa Barbara Channel, is the U.S. Coast Guard's restored, solar-powered **East End Lighthouse** and associated museum, open for public tours. Guided **kayak tours** are also popular here. On **Middle Anacapa** the stands of giant coreopsis ("tree sunflowers") are stunning when in bloom—on a clear day, their vibrant color is visible from the mainland. Craggy **West Anacapa,** the largest of the three, is off-limits to the public, protected as a brown pelican rookery and reserve.

Ever fantasized about being stranded on a desert island? Here's a possible destination. Unlike the lushly landscaped, socially sophisticated mainland city of the same name, 639-acre **Santa Barbara Island** is a piece of California in the raw. Smallest of the park's five islands, Santa Barbara has no trees, no natural beaches, and no fresh water. Its sheer cliffs rise abruptly from the sea. It's often windy and foggy in quick succession. Most popular with birders, divers, and kayakers, in warm weather Santa Barbara also attracts pinniped peerers, hikers, and campers. (Bring *everything,* including water.) A lonely 25 miles west of Catalina, a long, often choppy three hours from Ventura Harbor, Santa Barbara is most appreciated by avid island and/or wildlife aficionados.

Practical Channel Islands

For more information on the islands and permitted recreational activities, contact: **Channel Islands National Park Visitors Center,** 1901 Spinnaker Dr., Ventura, CA 93001, 805/658-5730, www.nps.gov/chis. The visitors center in Ventura Harbor is *the* stop for relevant books, maps, and a good general introduction to the history and natural history of the islands. For hiking permits for San Miguel Island, call 805/658-5711.

At last report primitive park campgrounds were available on all five islands. If you're planning to camp or hike (permits required), come prepared for anything—wind, in particular—because the weather can change abruptly. For current information, inquire at the park's visitors center; for camping permits—free, though there is a $2.50 reservation fee per campsite per day—are available by calling Biospherics, Inc., at toll-free 800/365-2267.

Unless you have your own boat, if you're shoving off from Ventura you'll be going via **Island Packer Cruises,** which offers the rare opportunity to get up close and personal with Channel Islands National Park. Since island access is limited, extra benefits of an Island Packer trip—some trips, anyway—include the chance to hike, snorkel, or kayak. Camping drop-offs can also be arranged. Whale-watching (Jan. through Mar.) is particularly popular, especially since whales, dolphins, seals, and sea lions favor the protected waters and abundant food supplies near the Channel Islands. But every season has its unique pleasures. For current information, contact: Island Packer Tours, 1867 Spinnaker Dr., Ventura, CA 93001, 805/642-7688 (recorded) or 805/642-1393, fax 805/642-6573, www.islandpackers.com.

If you're departing from Santa Barbara, the official Channel Islands trip concessionaire there is **Truth Aquatics,** 301 W. Cabrillo Blvd., Santa Barbara, CA 93101, 805/962-1127, fax 805/564-6754, www.truthaquatics.com.

Channel Islands Aviation offers day trip transportation, tours, and "drop-offs" to and from Santa Rosa Island (and Santa Catalina Island). For current information, contact: Channel Islands Aviation, 305 Durley Ave., Camarillo, CA 93010, 805/987-1301.

OXNARD AND VICINITY

One notices in Ventura County the immense impact of recent and continuing growth—subdivisions and commercial developments all but consuming the county's once sleepy, agricultural past. Oxnard, still known for its annual May **California Strawberry Festival,** was once known for its sugar beet, bean, and strawberry fields, along with mile after mile of citrus orchards and packing sheds. The vanishing fruit industry is memorialized at the stylized Oxnard Factory Outlet mall at Rice Ave. off Gonzales Road.

The center of civic pride downtown is impressive **Heritage Square,** a collection of immaculately restored, landmark historic local buildings and replicas now home to shops, law offices and such. A stroll away is the neoclassical **Carnegie**

Art Museum, 424 S. C St., 805/385-8179, which showcases local arts and artists Thurs.–Sun. (call for current hours, small admission), and the **Ventura County Gull Wings Children's Museum,** 414 W. 4th St., 805/483-3005, www.gullwingsmuseum4kids.org, open Wed.–Sun. 1–5 P.M. (small admission). Or head for the waterfront and Oxnard's surprisingly tony **Channel Islands Harbor,** where the **Ventura County Maritime Museum** at Fisherman's Wharf, 2731 S. Victoria Ave., 805/984-6260, open daily 11 A.M.– 5 P.M., offers an overview of maritime history, ship models, and ocean-themed artwork. Among the treasures collected here: a copy of the map of Anacapa Island drawn by James Whistler. Most appealing of all is **Oxnard State Beach,** broad and sandy, backed by dunes and comfortably weathered beach bungalows.

For more information about the area, contact: **Oxnard Convention & Visitors Bureau,** Heritage Square, 711 S. A St., Oxnard, CA 93030, 805/385-7545 or toll-free 800/269-6273, www.oxnardtourism.com. For harbor information, contact: **Channel Islands Harbor Visitor Center,** 3810 W. Channel Islands Blvd., Ste. G, Oxnard, CA 93035, 805/985-4852, www.channelislandsharbor.com.

Near Oxnard: Port Hueneme

The area's military-industrial development is most notable just south of Oxnard in and around Port Hueneme (wy-NEE-mee), about 60 miles north of L.A. and 40 miles south of Santa Barbara. A major military and civilian port—the only deep water port between San Francisco and Los Angeles—Hueneme is most noted for its **Point Mugu Naval Air Weapons Station,** at last report still a survivor of U.S. defense budget cuts. The **Naval Construction Battalion Center,** "Home of the Pacific Seabees," has been at home here since 1942. If naval history fans first stop at the Ventura Road gate for a visitor pass, the free **U.S. Navy Civil Engineer Corps/Seabee Museum** on the base at Ventura Rd. and Sunkist Ave., 805/982-5165, is well worth a visit—one of the finest military museums around. Open Mon.–Sat. 9 A.M.–4 P.M., Sun. 12:30–4:30 P.M. Free. Port Hueneme also boasts a small city history museum downtown next to the chamber of commerce.

TOM MYERS PHOTOGRAPHY

WELCOME TO L.A.

Scribes and small-screen prognosticators love to announce the death of Los Angeles. With every new disaster they do it again. Most recently L.A. was declared dead because of the nasty Northridge earthquake of 1994. In addition to demolishing entire neighborhoods and killing dozens of people, the quake snapped off major freeways, thereby desecrating the city's most cherished cultural symbol—spokes in the sacred wheel of Southern California life. Just months before that, Los Angeles seemed doomed because of raging wildfires and the winter mudslides that came in their wake. Before that the city was decimated by the demise of California's defense industry, coupled with the economic and social challenge of absorbing a seemingly endless stream of illegal immigrants. Not to mention riots related to the Rodney King police brutality case, and the Watts riots almost 30 years before that. Not to mention the smog.

The apocalyptic tendencies of Los Angeles—more accurately, our determination to place Los Angeles at the center of our fascinations with disaster and futuristic despair—are as well-represented in literature as in real life. Consider the nuclear holocaust in Thomas Pynchon's *Gravity's Rainbow*. The earthquake in *The Last Tycoon*. The riot in *The Day of the Locust*. And little-known classics such as Marie Corelli's strange 1921 romance *Secret Power,* in which L.A. is decimated by an atomic explosion, and Ward Moore's hilarious 1947 *Greener Than You Think,* in which the city is done in by bermuda grass. Movies have also made their contribution to the cult of L.A. Apocalypse, of course, *Blade Runner* most memorably.

Even so, in recent years L.A. has suffered from entirely too much dystopia, entirely too much rumination on the subject of utopia gone wrong. Entirely too much *reality.* And reality has never been the point here. Los Angeles, after all, is both the world's foremost fantasy factory and playground for America's most childlike narcissisms.

The lesson of Los Angeles is the lesson of the movies. Big faces on the big screen reassure us that "individual lives have scope and grandeur," in the words of California writer Richard Rodriguez. "The attention L.A. lavishes on a single face is as generous a metaphor as I can find for the love of God."

From a strictly secular point of view, the sun is also generous. In Los Angeles the sun always shines, on the degenerate and deserving alike. At last report this was still true.

LAND OF ENDLESS SUNSHINE

LOS ANGELES AS PLACE

As defined by the U.S. Census Bureau, the greater Los Angeles metropolitan area encompasses Los Angeles County, including the city of Los Angeles, and urban areas of adjacent Orange, Riverside, San Bernardino, and Ventura Counties. The total population of the five-county L.A. area—well over 15 million by now, and counting—exceeds the population of every state in the union except California, New York, and Texas. Taking in a total of 34,149 square miles, greater Los Angeles—with its abundance of computers, fax machines, and cellular phones—has more telephone area codes than any other region of the country.

Even Los Angeles proper is difficult to locate precisely. Its geographical boundaries are puzzling even to people who live here, which is why Angelenos have fairly vague notions of official local lines of demarcation. The writer Dorothy Parker once observed that Los Angeles amounted to "seventy-two suburbs in search of a city." She was correct, historically. In the latter years of the 19th century small cities sprang up throughout Los Angeles County, typically at the end of the city's famed trolley lines. Then came freeways and two-car garages and the dominance of L.A.'s automobility, trends that soon filled in the spaces between communities. Shortly after World War II the present-day tendency toward sprawl was well-established, with boundaries between L.A. the city and L.A. the county almost hopelessly blurred by exponential growth.

For the record, the present-day city of Los Angeles takes in 467 square miles, or almost one-tenth of Los Angeles County's 4,083-square-mile area; the city includes many apparently separate communities or districts such as Hollywood. Aside from the city of Los Angeles, there are numerous unincorporated areas known as Los Angeles—and 87 other incorporated cities within the county's borders—all of which are still considered "L.A." in a general sense.

Yet even the terms traditionally used to define L.A.'s relationship with itself—such as "city" or "downtown" or "suburbs"—have been largely abandoned by urban planners, who now conceive of L.A. as a series of "constellations" or urban villages comprising a metropolitan "galaxy."

Palm Trees and Feral Parakeets: Creating a New Ecology

The lushness of the Southern California landscape is as native as pink plastic lawn flamingos. Both the official city flower, the bird of paradise, and the official city tree, the Erythrina palm, are exotic imports. Except in rare areas, native plant species have long since lost out to domesticated plants in Los Angeles. Increasingly, native animal species that manage to survive in and around Los Angeles are forced to compete with humans and feral dogs and cats—even feral parakeets and parrots—for limited territory and food supplies.

a symbol of Southern California: the palm tree

ROBERT HOLMES/CALTOUR

GREATER LOS ANGELES

© AVALON TRAVEL PUBLISHING, INC.

SHAKY SOUTHSTATE GROUND

In many ways Los Angeles has challenged the very laws of nature and still lives to brag about it. Building itself upon a swarming underground snake pit of earthquake faults is L.A.'s first act of hubris, however unintentional. Though the San Andreas Fault is perhaps the world's most famous, Southern California actually features countless earthquake faults. More than 200 of these are capable of producing earthquakes of a magnitude greater than 6.0 on the Richter scale—two major new faults were recently discovered beneath downtown's high-rises—and no spot in Los Angeles County is more than 30 miles away from at least one of them. While Los Angeles has experienced more than 200,000 earthquakes in the past 100 years, only a handful have shaken things up enough to make the news.

As do other Californians, Angelenos live with a fairly constant if unacknowledged anxiety that the predicted "big one"—a massive earthquake, perhaps measuring 8.0 or 9.0 on the Richter scale—will hit here at some time within the next 50–100 years, causing death and destruction on an unimaginable scale. The recent Northridge earthquake, which struck in the early morning of January 17, 1994, a fortunate fact of timing that no doubt helped minimize the loss of human life, measured 6.7 on the Richter scale and brought down sections of nearby freeways and crippled large parts of the San Fernando Valley. To visualize what the "big one" might be like, keep in mind that the intensity of earthquakes increases by a factor of ten for every measured point—meaning that an 8.0 earthquake is 10 times more powerful than a 7.0 quake, for example.

While earthquake safety construction standards are taken seriously in California, and while "earthquake retrofitting" of older buildings, bridges, and freeways has been under way for quite some time, with every serious quake it becomes increasingly obvious that no amount of public earthquake and emergency preparedness will help much in a massive earthquake—an event that would disrupt communication, transportation, and water and electrical power supplies for lengthy periods. Even most Los Angeles residents, like people in the San Francisco Bay Area and other areas of quake-prone California, live in a state of denial about this fact. Few take even the most basic steps to safeguard their family's well-being in case of a major quake, such as setting aside functioning battery-operated flashlights and radios, extra blankets, and emergency water, food, and first aid supplies. Of those who are prepared, some also pack such provisions in their cars—since one never knows where or when an earthquake will hit.

In many ways Los Angeles has created, and is still creating, a new ecology, one dominated by introduced species of both plants and animals. Prominent among local plant immigrants are L.A.'s palm trees, none of which grow here naturally, though native palms do grow near Palm Springs and elsewhere in the low desert. Here as elsewhere in California native grasses were long ago replaced by introduced European species, and the L.A. landscape's native oaks, sycamores, alders, and shrubs are now far outnumbered by introduced species—camellias, azaleas, ferns, and exotic tropical and semi-tropical tree and shrub varieties—that thrive in the mild Mediterranean climate. Most vividly illustrating L.A.'s re-creation of itself as urban tropical forest in the animal kingdom are the impressive flocks of feral parakeets, representing several species and all domestic escapees or their descendants, which thrive throughout fruitful Los Angeles. Local ornithologists also estimate that at least 2,000 feral parrots are at home in Los Angeles, 1,000 in and around Pasadena alone. A flock of about 400 red-crowned parrots was spotted in 1995 in the San Gabriel Valley, for example, and red-crowned and lilac-crowned parrots have been spotted in the San Fernando Valley.

DUSTY PUEBLO DAYS

In the beginning there was "Los Angeles man," a mysterious area resident whose skeleton, unearthed in 1936, has been dated as 7,000 years old. In more recent times, from Malibu north lived the Chumash, a fairly sophisticated seafaring people who fished and traded along the coast and throughout the Channel Islands. But the first known residents of Los Angeles proper were the native Gabrieleño people, who had been pushed west onto this arid, drought-prone plain by more aggressive Shoshonean peoples who dominated territories to the east. Sometimes known as the Yang-Na, the name of their village near what is today downtown Los Angeles, the total local population has been estimated at about 5,000, scattered throughout the region in communities as large as 1,000 people. The Gabrieleño were here to welcome the first explorers to the Bahia de los Fumos or "Bay of the Fires" (or "Smokes"), so named by Portuguese explorer Juan Rodríguez Cabrillo from offshore in 1542. The "smokes" here were the Indian fires that created the landscape's notable and lingering brown haze—L.A.'s earliest smog.

But the first explorer to arrive in Los Angeles was Gaspar de Portolá, the Spanish governor of the Californias, while on his discovery mission of 1769–70. It would be 10 years before the Spanish availed themselves of the Gabrieleño's prime cottonwood- and alder-sheltered location along the river bank, one of the few spots where the Los Angeles River flowed year-round.

Los Angeles as place was officially founded in 1781, established by the Spanish as a supply center for Alta California and named after the L.A. River, which in turn was originally named after the festival of the Virgin corresponding to its date of discovery: El Pueblo de Nuestra Señora la Reina de los Angeles de Porciúncula, or "Town of Our Lady Queen of the Angels of Porciúncula." In the beginning Los Angeles was a dusty little pueblo of modest adobes scattered near the river. The city's first settlers were 44 villagers from the Spanish territory that later became Mexico's Sonora and Sinaloa Provinces— an entourage of blacks, Indians, and mestizos (people of mixed black, Indian, and Spanish ancestry) accompanied by two Spaniards. More than half of the new arrivals were children.

Though Los Angeles served as the capital of California briefly, in 1845, for the most part even the transfers of power between Spain and Mexico after Mexican independence and between Mexico and the United States after the Mexican-American War had little impact here. The Los Angeles area boasted vast ranchos and an early version of landed gentry, yet most of the Spanish missions and associated cultural enclaves were established elsewhere—along the coast, the region's primary transportation corridor. The 1849 discovery of gold near

SANTA ANA WINDS

Wherever you find yourself in the Los Angeles universe, things change when the Santa Ana winds blow from the northeast off the desert, typically between November and January. The atmosphere here becomes hot and dry and unbelievably irritating. The way Raymond Chandler described it in his short story "Red Wind," the dusty, desiccating Santa Ana winds "come down through the mountain passes and curl your hair and make your nerves jump and your skin itch. On nights like that every booze party ends in a fight. Meek little wives feel the edge of the carving knife and study the backs of their husbands' necks." This notable Southern California weather phenomenon, which reverses the usual cool west-to-east airflow off the ocean, also increases the danger of late fall wildfires and plays havoc with people's allergies. But don't let a blustery Santa Ana season put you off. Desert winds do have the beneficial effect of scrubbing the air clean throughout the entire Los Angeles Basin—which is why a December or January day can offer the most glorious scenic vistas in Southern California.

Sacramento in the north, and San Francisco's subsequent debut as California's center of wealth and power, created a temporary boom market for south-state beef but otherwise left Los Angeles to languish as a lawless frontier border town best known for murder, mayhem, and general anarchy.

In the devastating drought years of the 1860s the Spanish land grants came under American ownership, thanks to the U.S. judicial system, and cattle gave way to sheep, thanks to the great demand for wool during the Civil War era. Sheep gradually gave way to wheat and then orchards and vineyards and endless other agricultural crops as farmers discovered the profit potential of such a salubrious climate.

ORANGES, WATER, OIL– AND AUTOS EVERYWHERE

The coming of the railroads—first linking Los Angeles to San Francisco in 1871, and then directly to the rest of the United States via transcontinental railroad in 1876—set the stage for L.A.'s

an orange grove

TOM MYERS PHOTOGRAPHY

first, and subsequently unrelenting, boom years. As boosters and boosterism promoted the benefits to personal health and wealth offered by Southern California, the mass migration began.

There was a central idea behind the U.S. migration to Southern California—the belief that simple, healthful living amid gardens, orange groves, and the fellowship of good friends and neighbors could save civilization from the dehumanization and mindlessness of the industrial era. From the late 19th century well into the early 20th, Pasadena, Riverside, and countless other Southern California communities shaped themselves from such ideals. That idea came to be symbolized throughout the United States by the humble orange—by Southern California's endless orange groves.

Yet Southern California's endless self-promotion was limited by the landscape's semiarid nature. No matter how grand the gardens grew in Southern California, nothing could grow for long without water. And with the arrival of hordes of migrants, water was increasingly scarce. Just as Los Angeles was beginning to grow into a recognizable city, the severe Southern California drought of 1892–1904 threatened the city's fragile foothold at the edge of its own dream.

Enter William Mulholland, an Irish immigrant who came to America in 1878, a self-educated man who began his career in Los Angeles as a ditchdigger and ended it as the city's chief water engineer. As superintendent of the Los Angeles City Water Company, Mulholland was a conscientious steward of L.A.'s limited liquid resources, but even concerted conservation was not enough. By 1903 it was clear that L.A. would either have to stop growing altogether—certainly an unacceptable conclusion among L.A.'s well-invested business boosters—or find more water.

So Mulholland and his good friend Fred Eaton, former mayor of Los Angeles, set out to find more water—in the Owens Valley on the eastern side of the Sierra Nevada about 250 miles north of Los Angeles. Mulholland quickly figured that the Owens River could supply enough water to support a city of two million souls instead of 200,000. Thus the Los Angeles Aqueduct, "the most gigantic and difficult engineering project undertaken by any American city," was created—and William Mulholland became an overnight celebrity among the engineers of academe, self-educated immigrants everywhere, and civic boosters.

When in 1913 sweet Owens Valley water finally started flowing into the San Fernando Valley from Mulholland's ditch, an event for which 30,000–40,000 residents and a parade of dignitaries turned out, Mulholland said to the multitude: "There it is—Take it." And take it they did. They took it to transform the drought-parched landscape into a lush garden of palm trees, fruit trees, and roses that soon welcomed Hollywood—and which Hollywood soon shared with the world via the movies, attracting hundreds of thousands of new residents.

The landscape also sprouted oil wells. In 1892 Edward Doheny discovered oil at "Greasy Gulch,"

"REAL" LOS ANGELES

Outsiders' interpretations of Los Angeles—what everyone thinks they know about the place—are often seriously mistaken. For all its casual friendliness, Los Angeles is actually an aloof city, self-protective. One certainly experiences that truth on the freeways—so many millions of people, so oblivious to each other, every person moving through life in his own freewheeling, independent world. For all its fabled flamboyance and sometimes shameless public shenanigans, Los Angeles is in real life a very private place. "Real" L.A. is a private, not a public, domain—which is why finding it can be such a challenge for visitors. When L.A. isn't performing on its varied public stages—and L.A. in all its guises works long, hard hours—the city stays home with family and friends, or goes out to play, privately. Los Angeles tolerates its tourists as revenue enhancements—"tourist" a term that was invented here—but rarely invites them home or out on the town. Traditionally, the supremacy of individuality and the need for privacy follow Angelenos everywhere.

For all its vastness, or perhaps because of it, L.A. is also parochial and self-absorbed. "Family values" matter here because immediate family is almost all there is to anchor people in such a fast-paced, unrooted society. Even political battles in Los Angeles are largely fought on the neighborhood level. Yet such self-absorption has its price. While Southern California can't muster the political will to properly finance its public schools, libraries, and health-care services, Los Angeles is number one in the nation for plastic surgery: breast enhancements, liposuction, facelifts, nose and eyelid jobs. Fitness centers are also central to Southern California culture, as are psychiatrists and psychologists and sometimes outthere spiritual advisers.

For all its vast wealth, Los Angeles largely lacks the memorable monuments to grand ideas and idealism so typical of European and other American cities, be they cathedrals, museums, or public libraries. While exceptions to this rule can still be found downtown and in affluent communities including Beverly Hills and Pasadena, the most striking architecture in Los Angeles is private, not public. Rather than invest its billions in old-fashioned public betterment and enlightenment, L.A. spends its money on private pleasures—on great walled mansions and estates and, on a more modest scale out in the suburbs, on backyard barbecues, swimming pools, and all the other accoutrements of middle-class family living.

Parochial Los Angeles does seem improbable, given the city's social and cultural perch at the edge of both Mexico and the Pacific Rim. Yet even L.A.'s recent arrivals tend to settle into particular neighborhoods. Because of its insularity, until quite recently Los Angeles could imagine itself untouched by the multiethnic chaos that now defines it.

Rather than a melting pot, L.A. is a multicultural anthology in which every recent ethnic arrival has its own page, if not an entire separate chapter. Immigrants from more than 140 different nations live within Los Angeles County, including the largest populations of Armenians, Filipinos, and Koreans outside their respective nations and the largest U.S. populations of Cambodians, Iranians, and Japanese. Latin American immigrants—Guatemalans, Mexicans, and Salvadorans—dominate many chapters, as do third- and fourth-generation migrants from the U.S. Midwest. Still, the story lines rarely intersect.

This, says writer Richard Rodriguez, is as it has always been in Los Angeles—and in America. Thanks to Protestantism, he says, the 19th-century United States with its waves of new immigrants "became a country of tribes and neighborhoods more truly than a nation of solitary individuals. Then, as today, Americans trusted diversity, not uniformity." Yet, according to Rodriguez, "any immigrant kid could tell you that America exists. There *is* a culture. There is a shared accent, a shared defiance of authority, a shared skepticism about community." By extension, there is also a shared culture in Los Angeles.

A strikingly tolerant city, Los Angeles is also quite lively. National trendsetter in popular entertainment, lifestyle, style, and vocabulary, Los Angeles boasts more university graduates per capita than any other U.S. city. There are more colleges and universities here, a total of 176 at last count, than in the entire state of Massachusetts. But culture here doesn't always come with a university degree. Los Angeles is also the mural capital of the world, with a "collection" of more than 1,500 outdoor wall paintings displayed on storefronts (and sides), street corners, and alleyways throughout the county. Long characterized as culturally and intellectually vapid, Los Angeles is home to more actors, artists, dancers, filmmakers, musicians, and writers than any other city—at any time in the history of civilization.

After taking a good look around, even visitors soon realize that Los Angeles is not just a trip to Universal Studios or Disneyland anymore.

near what is now MacArthur Park. By 1897 there were more than 500 oil wells in and around downtown alone, although oil discoveries fanned out in all directions. Almost overnight California became the third-largest oil producing state in the nation. Wide open spaces and abundant local fuel supplies made far-flung Los Angeles a perfect testing ground for America's latest invention—the horseless carriage. Automobiles first took to the Los Angeles streets in 1897; by 1915 about 55,000 cars populated area roadways, and by 1927 L.A. was considered a "completely motorized civilization." Ever-inventive Los Angeles established the world's first gas station in 1912; built the West's first freeway in 1938–40, the Arroyo Seco Parkway (now known as the Pasadena Fwy. or the 110) from Pasadena into downtown; and installed the world's first parking meter in 1942.

HOLLYWOOD'S HEYDAY

To imagine Hollywood as a pious, prohibitionist utopia is more than most modern cinematic mythmakers could manage. Yet so it was, until moviemaking came to town. Technically the southstate's moving picture industry began in 1907 in Los Angeles, which Selig Studios chose for filming the outdoor scenes for *The Count of Monte Cristo*. But the distinction between Los Angeles and Hollywood as a film location was moot by 1911, in a sense, since in 1910 the small L.A. suburb of Hollywood surrendered its charter and became part of Los Angeles. In that same year David Wark Griffith, leading director of New York's Biograph film company, came west to Los Angeles with his wife, Linda, and his film troupe, including 17-year-old Mary Pickford, and installed them in the Hollywood Inn on Hollywood Blvd. for the winter-spring shooting season. Between January 20 and April 6, Griffith's troupe produced 21 films in distinct southstate settings—the first films shot entirely *in* Southern California—including *The Thread of Destiny* at Mission San Gabriel and *Ramona* in Ventura County. Griffith's disciple Mack Sennett arrived in 1912 to begin his Keystone comedies, star vehicles for the English vaudevillian Charlie Chaplin.

Still, Hollywood resisted Southern California's growing general affinity for film. But before the community could mobilize much protest against

LOS ANGELES AS DIVERSION

Unless one refuses to participate in the ongoing circus that is Los Angeles, it's almost impossible to avoid diversion here—starting with the family-focused theme parks scattered throughout Southern California. But L.A. offers much more to see and do, from exceptional museums to classic movie theaters, from live theater and concert performances to endlessly cool dance clubs. And the impressive Los Angeles parade of festivals and special community events could keep anyone entertained for a lifetime.

There are two primary approaches for experiencing Los Angeles arts and entertainment. The first is placing a major arts or entertainment performance (or community event) at the center of one's travel plans, and then planning everything else—where you'll stay and eat, what else you'll see and do—accordingly. The other is to grab a local newspaper—the L.A. *Weekly* or *New Times*, say, or the Thursday or Sunday Calendar sections of the *Los Angeles Times*—and see what strikes your fancy at the moment, a style of "planning" most Angelenos exercise frequently. Or, at least for major goings-on, call the **Los Angeles Convention and Visitors Bureau** 24-hour events line at 213/689-8822; a touch-tone menu allows callers to select from a five-language access menu, with events information available in English, French, German, Japanese, and Spanish.

the carousing, notoriously carefree movie people, they had already arrived. Within five years about 35 movie studios had relocated from the East and Midwest, creating overnight chaos on Hollywood's sleepy unpaved streets. But concerns about Hollywood's moral corruption proved to be no match for movie industry money, and by the Roaring '20s, Hollywood's stars glittered as national and international idols.

During the 1920s and '30s the stretch of Hollywood Blvd. between La Brea Ave. and Vine St. glittered with glitz, boasting magnificent movie theaters, notorious nightclubs (Hollywood invented the Flapper style), notoriously good restaurants, chic shops, and stylish hotels. By the mid-1920s the Hollywood movie business was the fifth-largest industry in the United States, generating 90 percent of the world's films and grossing about $1.5 billion per year.

But the emerging West Coast film industry reached far beyond Hollywood, right into the heart and mind of heartland America and, quite quickly, the world. Movies appealed to the elemental and universal human experience; to get the drift of the story lines, one did not need an Ivy League education. Soon Hollywood—Los Angeles—both created and interpreted national aspirations, and modern mass culture was born.

BARBIES AND BOMBERS: LOS ANGELES AFTER WORLD WAR II

For all of Southern California's earlier, more innocent glories, the modern middle-class myth of Los Angeles is largely the creation of the post–World War II era. And L.A. had rallied for the war effort in a big way, turning its entrepreneurial spirit to the task of building bigger and better aircraft and weaponry—the beginnings of Southern California's centrality to the U.S. defense and space technology industries. It's not by accident that Hughes Aircraft, McDonnell Douglas, Northrop, and Lockheed are practically neighborhood names in Los Angeles. Though the regional aerospace industry actually got its start in the first world war, during World War II Southern California produced one-third of America's warplanes. Military bases were

also a growth industry in and around Los Angeles; after passing through on the way to war in the Pacific theater, many soldiers decided to come back to L.A. to stay—a decision that fueled massive post-war suburban growth.

Yet for all their success in putting Los Angeles on the military-industrial map, the war years wrote particularly shameful chapters of American history, including the mass incarceration of L.A.'s Japanese-American citizens and Japanese immigrants in relocation camps—an event that disenfranchised and shattered entire families and communities. Also infamous were the "zoot suit riots" of 1943, during which uniformed U.S. servicemen took it upon themselves to beat bloody any young Mexican American, black, or Filipino males they found in the general vicinity of downtown—a rampage successfully stopped only by special order of the U.S. State Department.

Los Angeles in the 1950s and 1960s was, officially, a happy, homogenized, and sunny suburban existence, birthplace of the Barbie doll, the DC-3, and the Internet. Yet certain post-war chapters of L.A. history were also dark and frightening, early shadows cast by the Cold War, including local activities of the House Un-American Activities Committee. Such events successfully launched the national political career of young Richard Nixon, born and raised in Orange County just south of Los Angeles, but ended the

THE ARTS IN LOS ANGELES

For most of its short life Los Angeles has suffered a massive cultural inferiority complex. Helped along over the years by Johnny Carson's favorite late-night joke-"The difference between Los Angeles and yogurt is that yogurt has an active, living culture"—wags from New York and other points north and east have long enjoyed perpetuating it. One of the most cutting slurs came from the lips of architect Frank Lloyd Wright: "It's as if you tipped the United States up, so that all the commonplace people slid down there to Southern California."

But these days, vibrant and vital Los Angeles isn't listening to its detractors. With the city's growing wealth and sophistication and its large, diverse population has come exponential growth in both traditional and avant-garde arts. And in many areas

the local arts scene is inextricably entwined with L.A.'s new cutting-edge seat at the nation's culinary table, with stylish eateries an easy stroll or shuttle hop from major theaters and other performance venues.

Most of the city's major theaters and music venues are downtown, and most of its arts and cultural museums are either downtown or quite nearby; see that chapter for details. Pasadena is another major cultural destination; look to that chapter for more detailed suggestions. The Westside, including Santa Monica, Beverly Hills, and adjacent chi-chi sections of West Hollywood, is noted in particular for its impressive array of art galleries, though there are also a few don't-miss museums and other arts attractions; for more details, see relevant chapters.

careers of many actors, artists, and writers as a direct result of the Hollywood blacklist.

LOS ANGELES IN THE NEW AGE

Like the rest of the nation, most of Los Angeles remained fairly comatose, culturally speaking, throughout the 1950s. But that all changed in the 1960s as Southern California established itself as a high-tech and industrial center and the world's entertainment industry capital. In the 1960s messengers from L.A.'s ever-present spiritual fringe—rogue philosophers, faith-healers, and miscellaneous other true believers well established here since the city's early days of alternative cures for consumption (tuberculosis)—stepped forward to help create California's New Age along with wild-haired surfers, dope-smoking students, and fad-happy hipsters of all socioeconomic stripes.

But L.A.'s new age was not just dope and VW vans. Los Angeles awoke to sober new truths about itself in the 1960s, following the Watts riots of 1965—a firestorm of long-repressed racial rage ignited over a seemingly insignificant event, a six-day "incident" in which 34 people died. Sadly for Watts, the riots served primarily to end outside economic and social investment in some of L.A.'s poorest neighborhoods. In a sense, the incipient political messages of the 1960s weren't fully realized in Los Angeles until the 1970s, along with the next social sea change—the news that whites or "Anglos" were again a demographic minority in Los Angeles for the first time since the mid-1800s. Absorbing the full impact of this new reality, politically and socially, is proving to be a major challenge for Los Angeles.

The 1980s were watershed years for most of Los Angeles, especially in the period leading up to and immediately following the 1984 Olympic Games. (Los Angeles is the only city in the world to have hosted the Olympics twice; the first time was in 1932.) Suddenly Los Angeles, not New York, was the place to be—and continued to be that place, thanks to the city's newly vibrant architecture, arts, movie, music, and theater. That Los Angeles also came of age in a culinary sense, becoming one of the world's foremost destinations for fine food aficionados, also elevated the city's sense of itself.

Yet Los Angeles cannot forever evade its shadows, racism and poverty among the disenfranchised, a theme that emerged with a vengeance in the 1990s. Natural disasters grabbed their share of the headlines in these years—the Northridge earthquake, massive fires, mudslides—but social disasters had the most lasting impact. The racial rage that first ignited the Watts riots, having simmered almost silently for three decades, erupted again in full force when the videotape of Rodney King being "subdued" by Los Angeles Police Department officers was broadcast around the world. After the original acquittal of the officers, full-scale rioting ensued—throughout downtown L.A., Koreatown, Hollywood, and coming perilously close to Beverly Hills and other affluent Westside addresses. The riots again proved counterproductive, setting off racial backlash and sinking affected neighborhoods into deeper poverty. The acquittal of O. J. Simpson in the subsequent racially tinged murder case reinforced a self-righteous backlash, a development that seemed to offer little hope for more enlightened relations between the races.

Yet racial tension is not a black and white issue in Los Angeles. The question is much more complicated than that, given the vast numbers of African, Middle Eastern, Eastern European, South American, and Asian immigrants now at home in the region. For example, many segments of the white, black, and even Latino communities are outspoken these days against the social and economic impacts of ongoing illegal immigration on Los Angeles, which demonstrates what a racially and culturally loaded issue immigration has become.

As California writer Richard Rodriguez says, the birth of a new society—any birth—is traumatic. And Los Angeles is just now, at the beginning of the 21st century, being born. Now that the city has lost its "suburban innocence," that development certainly an improvement over past obliviousness, Los Angeles is beginning to create itself. While this new Los Angeles is "forming within the terror and suspicion and fear that people have of one another," as Rodriguez says, it's "better not to like one another than not to know the stranger exists."

PRACTICAL LOS ANGELES

GETTING INFORMED

To receive a comprehensive and current visitors guide, the glossy *Destination Los Angeles,* and other information before coming to Los Angeles, write to: **Los Angeles Convention and Visitors Bureau (LACVB),** 633 W. 5th St., Ste. 6000, Los Angeles, CA 90071, 213/689-8822, fax 213/624-1992, or call toll-free in the U.S. and Canada 800/228-2452 (24 hours a day). To get up to speed on the Internet, the address is www.lacvb.com. Visitors can also make hotel and rental car reservations through the LACVB's toll-free number. Other publications include a variety of popular "pocket guides" and the annual magazine-style *Festivals of Los Angeles* guide. To find out what else is going on around town, call the bureau's 24-hour events hot line at 213/689-8822; with a touch-tone phone, dial up current events information in English, French, German, Japanese, and Spanish.

Los Angeles also sponsors two separate walk-in visitor centers, both of which provide region-wide information—maps, brochures, calendars, information on foreign-language tours, shopping, dining, even listings of upcoming television tapings—much of it available in six languages, as well as multilingual personal assis-

tance. The LACVB's **Downtown Visitor Information Center,** 685 S. Figueroa St. (between Wilshire Blvd. and 7th St.), is open Mon.–Fri. 8 A.M.–5 P.M., and Sat. 8:30 A.M.–5 P.M. The satellite **Hollywood Visitor Information Center** is inside the historic Janes House at Janes Square, 6541 Hollywood Blvd. in Hollywood, and is open Mon.–Sat 9 A.M.–5 P.M. For visitor assistance by phone, call the LACVB at 213/689-8822.

Local chambers of commerce and visitor information bureaus also abound up and down the Los Angeles coast; all can be quite helpful. Contact any of them—listed in the following chapters—for visitor information in advance of, or during, your visit.

Local publications can be particularly helpful in introducing oneself to the wonders of Los Angeles. The local newspaper of record—California's newspaper of record, really—is the **Los Angeles Times,** distributed everywhere. Pick it up if only for the Sunday "Calendar" section, which lays out just about everything going on in town in the week ahead. The Thursday edition of the *Times* includes its "Calendar Weekend" pull-out section. Various cities also have local daily and/or weekly newspapers. Among magazines, **Los Angeles** is the slick "lifestyle" publication.

But to find out what's really hip and happenin', pick up alternative publications such as the **L.A.**

an omnipresent landmark of Los Angeles: the freeway

LOS ANGELES CVB/MICHELE & TOM GRIMM

STAY OUT OF THE WAY IN L.A.:
SOME RULES OF THE ROAD

People in Los Angeles measure distance not in miles but in minutes—meaning minutes by freeway, or drive time. Angelenos also chronically underestimate drive times. This peculiar form of bragging rights ultimately implies that a *true* Angeleno could actually get from Pasadena to Santa Monica in 15 minutes, though you'll soon realize that you won't. (Angelenos also typically blame traffic when they're late—an excuse almost everyone will accept.) When taking directions from locals, then, visitors would be wise to generously pad the alleged drive time—or to double-check it, with the aid of a good map.

In keeping with their underestimation of average drive times, Los Angeles drivers also grossly underestimate their travel speed. If the posted speed limit is 65 miles per hour, most Angelenos will drive 80 or 85—and actually believe themselves when they tell the California Highway Patrol officer they were only going 60.

Angelenos typically refer to local freeways by name, not number—which can be mighty confusing for neophytes, since the Hollywood Freeway (101) is also the Ventura Freeway, the Santa Monica Freeway (I-10) is also the San Bernardino Freeway, the Golden State Freeway (I-5) is also the Santa Ana Freeway, and the faithful north-south San Diego Freeway never actually arrives in San Diego (not until after it's become I-5). When Angelenos *do* mention freeway numbers instead of names they use "the" as a fairly pointless modifier, as in "the 405" and "the 110," so when you hear such phrases you'll at least know that the topic of freeways is under discussion. Fortunately for visitors, most maps list both freeway names and numbers.

Then there are those unique L.A. words or phrases that make no sense whatsoever to innocent tourists, such as "Sigalert," even if they are listed in the *Oxford English Dictionary*. A Sigalert, according to the *OED*, is "a message broadcast on the radio giving warning of traffic congestion; a traffic jam," though technically Sigalerts apply only to tie-ups of 30 minutes or more. The word itself pays homage to L.A. radio broadcaster Loyd Sigmon, whose breaking traffic-jam bulletins of the 1950s are the stuff of local legend.

More important than local lingo, however, is a clear understanding of the local rules of the road. Los Angeles drivers never signal their intention to change lanes on the freeway, for example—a sure mark of a tourist—because doing so only allows others an opportunity to fill that particular spot of road first. Yet if someone honks, rudely cuts you off—which probably wouldn't have happened if you hadn't signaled—or tailgates for revenge, do remain calm. Don't allow that middle finger to leave the steering wheel, either, since no amount of rude driving is worth getting rammed at 70 miles per hour (or worse).

Never drive in front of a BMW or behind a Volvo.

Be particularly generous to L.A. drivers—give them a wide berth—if it's "pouring down rain" (as measured in actual precipitation, a tenth of an inch or less) because most Angelenos have never seen rain. Those who have tend to use wet roadways as yet another technique to increase their overall speed, through the miracle of hydroplaning. Most L.A. drivers don't know the difference between headlight high beams and low beams, either, so don't bother trying to explain the concept. In Los Angeles, headlights are either on or off. Be grateful, when it's dark outside, if the car coming toward you has them on.

Weekly, not to mention countless 'zines that come and go faster than freeway traffic, available in coffeehouses, neighborhood restaurants, bookstores, and other popular hangouts. Particularly good, wherever you might find them: **Poetry Flash** and **Art Issues.**

Otherwise, the best local source of visitor information is the local telephone book, particularly if you seek a particular product or service. Pick the closest place with the right product and/or right price, since distances in Los Angeles can turn a simple errand into an all-day adventure.

GETTING THERE: BY FREEWAY

One self-guided Los Angeles tour that few visitors ever take, at least not intentionally, is a tour of local freeways—*every* local freeway. It wouldn't take all that long, either, if one drove a few miles on each. Depending upon local traffic, of course.

No, though Angelenos love their freeways they use them strictly to get wherever they're going. They've been doing it ever since 1940. And once visitors arrive by freeway, in either

TOURING L.A.

Los Angeles is a sprawling, spread-out place, a city that seems to extend beyond all landward horizons. Basic issues—like deciding what to see and do in this expansive world of possibilities, and figuring out how to get there—tend to confound first-time visitors. One perfectly legitimate way to "do" L.A., then, is by signing up for guided tours, thereby delegating the details to the hired help.

Guided Tours by Hearse, Trolley, Bus, and MTA

To tour the lives and lifestyles of L.A.'s rich and notorious, you can always stop for the latest editions of various "Maps to the Stars' Homes" hawked by Beverly Hills area entrepreneurs. Always more fun, though, was the **Grave Line Tours** guided postmortem tour of local fame, an enterprise launched in 1987. "Mourners" climbed into the Cadillac hearse and cruised the streets of Hollywood, Beverly Hills, and other Los Angeles neighborhoods to find out how, when, where, and sometimes why celebrities died. Since 1999 the classic Grave Line hearse tour has been offered by **Tourland,** 323/782-9652, www.tourlandusa.com. Tourland's **Oh Heavenly Tour** revisits the sometimes tawdry and twisted pasts of local celebrities by reservation only, though standby seating is sometimes available. Tours, which run about 2.5 hours, depart daily at 10 A.M. and 1 P.M. from the front of Ubon restaurant on the 1st floor of the Beverly Center on Beverly Boulevard. In addition, Tourland offers an evening **Haunted Hearse Tour,** which visits locales reportedly haunted by celebrities. The fee for each tour is $40 per person. For more conventional sightseeing, **Trollywood Tours,** 323/469-8184, offers one-hour Hollywood tours on a historic trolley car.

Architours promotes "architecture, art, and design as a cultural resource." Tours and special events emphasize culture, history, residential and public architecture, gardens and plazas, public and private art, and furniture and graphic design. For current details and reservations, contact: Architours, P.O. Box 8057, Los Angeles, CA 90008, 323/294-5821 or toll-free 888/627-2448, fax 323/294-5825, www.architours.com. Or try a quirky trip with **Googie Tours,** named for a defunct local coffee shop chain, which specializes in Southern California's fast-disappearing vernacular architecture. Tour stars include bowling alleys, cocktail lounges, coffee shops, motels, and fine-dining destinations such as the giant drive-through Donut Hole doughnut shop in La Puente. For information, contact: Googie Tours, P.O. Box 34787, Los Angeles, CA 90034, 323/980-3480.

Due to lack of funding, at last report the Social and Public Art Resource Center (SPARC) in Venice was no longer offering its immensely popular mural bus tours, which once roamed all over Los Angeles—but it's still possible to organize private group tours through SPARC ($200/hour, two-hour minimum) with at least two months' advance notice. For details, contact: SPARC, 310/822-9560, www.sparc murals.org. Still going but with a limited bus tour schedule ($25 per person, by advance reservation) is the **Mural Conservancy of Los Angeles** (MCLA), 818/487-0416 or 323/257-4544, www.lamurals.org. When the website is completely constructed, it will include maps to most L.A. mural sites—for do-it-yourselfers—as well as the existing indexes of murals and muralists.

Some of the neon lighting, dating to the 1920s, that made Los Angeles one of the world's flashiest

their personal or rental cars, they join in the same transportation rite.

Los Angeles is connected to itself and to the rest of the world by more freeways than any other city in America—a total of 16 major freeways and a large handful of lesser ones. Life on a Los Angeles freeway—any freeway—is life in the fast lane, a very fast lane. Noteworthy as the first freeway in Los Angeles, also the first freeway in the West, is the Pasadena Fwy., the 8.2-mile stretch of narrow-laned roadway still connecting Pasadena to downtown through the Arroyo Seco. The

freeway's first five miles opened for business on December 30, 1940, designed for cars traveling about 45 miles per hour. Of course no one called it a freeway in those days, though people did sometimes call it a "free way." One proposed name for L.A.'s first ode to automobility, which was known as the Arroyo Seco Parkway, was "stopless motorway," a phrase that somehow failed to seize the public's imagination.

But freeways themselves did.

Many Los Angeles freeway routes actually follow old footpaths once used by deer and native cities is now on display at the Museum of Neon Art (MONA) downtown; you can appreciate much of the rest at CityWalk outside Universal Studios, and still more abundantly along certain city streets. To see some of L.A.'s historic local lights in their neo-natural neon environments, sign on for the museum's after-dark **Neon Cruise** guided double-deck bus tour, an event usually offered every month for a fee of $45 per person. For current information, call the **Museum of Neon Art** at 213/489-9918, or check the museum's website—www.neonmona.org.—for a tour schedule.

For more local arts exposure, free guided, two-hour **Metro Art Project Tours** are also offered in L.A. For details, call 213/922-4278.

Guided Tours on Foot,
by Bike, via Skateboard
Guided walking tours are available in most areas of Los Angeles; contact visitor centers for current details. Now a long-running local institution, the **Los Angeles Conservancy** offers inexpensive and informative walking tours designed to interpret L.A.'s past, present, and future. The group offers 12 regular tours—in addition to occasional special tours—emphasizing historic areas and structures. These include **Little Tokyo, Pershing Square,** and **El Pueblo de Los Angeles** as well as **Union Station, City Hall,** and other landmark buildings. The **Broadway Theaters** tour, which allows visitors inside some of L.A.'s grand old movie theaters, is one of the Conservancy's most popular. The usual Conservancy tour fee is $8. All tours, typically one or two hours, start Saturday at 10 A.M. Reservations are required; you can reserve by phone or online. The Art Deco, Broadway Theaters, and Pershing Square tours are offered every Saturday. Others—including The Biltmore Hotel, Union Station, Little Tokyo,

Terra Cotta, Palaces of Finance, and Angelino Heights, in addition to miscellaneous special tours—are offered on a regular rotating schedule. No tours are offered on Thanksgiving, Christmas, or New Year's Day. For more information or reservations, contact: **Los Angeles Conservancy Tours,** 523 W. 6th St., Ste. 1216, Los Angeles, CA 90014, 213/623-2489, www.laconservancy.org.

Combining a walking tour with quick trips on the city's metro system and unique funicular railway, historian Greg Fischer's two-hour **Angel City Tours,** 310/470-4463, offer a facts-versus-fiction historical introduction to downtown L.A.

But why walk when you can run? **Off 'N Running Tours,** toll-free 800/523-8687, offers three- to eight-mile courses for fitness walkers and runners in Santa Monica, Beverly Hills, and downtown L.A.; the $45 per person fee includes a runner's breakfast and—for L.A. memorabilia—a T-shirt.

You can also bike it with the actor-guides of **L.A. Bike Tours, LLC,** 323/658-5890 or toll-free 888/775-2453, www.labiketours.com, whose motto is: Tour Buses Are for Couch Potatoes. Tours include mountain bike tours of Hollywood, Beverly Hills, Venice Beach/Santa Monica, and the Getty Center—bikes, helmets, lunches, snacks, and water included in the $20–55 per person price. For a little extra adventure, sign on for the two-day **Santa Barbara Coastal Adventure.** Or try a two- to four-hour tour of Santa Monica, Venice, and Marina del Rey by bicycle or roller blades, both offered by **Perry's Beach Café and Rentals,** 310/372-3138.

Spectator sports fans, how 'bout a behind-the-scenes baseball history tour? Dodger blue is on display at guided **Dodger Stadium Tours,** 323/224-1400 (tickets also available at the stadium gift shop), which include the clubhouse, press box, bullpen, dugout, and the new 8,000-square-foot museum.

---

peoples; the paths later became mission roads, stagecoach routes to the beach, paved roads, streetcar lines, and finally freeways. With the impressive tangle of roadway today—Los Angeles features 27 freeways, weaving in and out of each other like the strands of a giant, if loose, concrete yarn ball—it's almost impossible to imagine a footpath climbing sleepily up Sepulveda Pass, which the San Diego Fwy. dominates today.

The newest freeway in Los Angeles—most likely its last—is the 17-mile, eight-lane, east-west **Century Freeway,** also known as Inter-

state 105 or the Glenn Anderson Fwy., that stretches between Norwalk and El Segundo near LAX. The Century parallels the Santa Monica (10) and Artesia (91) Fwys., and connects four major north-south routes: the San Diego (405), Harbor (110), Long Beach (710), and San Gabriel River (605) Freeways. An alternate route from downtown to LAX, the Century's notable features include the elevated Green Line trolley tracks down the center median, traffic sensors, closed-circuit TV cameras (so Caltrans can see why traffic has slowed), and metered on-ramps.

Also quite modern is the new elevated section—the "transitway," for buses and carpoolers only—of the Harbor Fwy. (I-110) near downtown, just a few miles long but a harbinger of roadways to come, as Los Angeles builds and rebuilds its freeways to manage ever-increasing levels of traffic.

Yet other concerns tend to weave their way into local freeway lore. The area's shortest freeway—the Marina Fwy. (90), not even two miles long—was originally known as the Richard M. Nixon Fwy., for example, so named in 1971 by the California Assembly. But after the Watergate debacle, the state senate stripped Nixon of his freeway title in 1976.

Speeding Toward Freedom

The posted freeway speed in most areas of Los Angeles is 65 or 70 miles per hour (mph), sometimes faster, sometimes slower, depending upon local conditions. But speed is everything in L.A., another local metaphor for unlimited personal freedom. Even when 55 mph was the official speed limit here, almost no one paid any attention. And for newcomers and visitors, this can be a nerve-wracking fact of freeway life. Los Angeles drivers are typically good drivers, but people here drive fast—*very* fast, at least 70 or 75 mph when things are moving along well, though it's not uncommon for neophytes to be passed by locals zipping along at 80, 85, or 90. One must either "go with the flow," at least to an extent, to avoid the ire of fellow drivers—and to avoid becoming a traffic hazard or accident oneself—or stay in the right-hand lanes, stubbornly going the speed limit and contending with the constant distraction of cars jockeying for position as they merge on and off the freeway. Fast drivers have no problem with L.A.'s addiction to speed, but cautious drivers and slowpokes may be unnerved.

Beating the Rush

For years a local truism held that the Ventura Fwy. (Hwy. 101) through the San Fernando Valley was the world's busiest roadway, and L.A.'s busiest freeway. But this was never true, it turns out, despite what the *Guinness Book of World Records* says. Because car-counting meters on the Santa Monica (I-10) and San Diego (I-405) Fwys.—the actual record-breakers—were broken for almost five years, the entire world was

misinformed. Most nightmarish of all is the junction of the San Diego and Santa Monica, not far north of Los Angeles International Airport.

To avoid getting stuck in L.A.'s slow (but rarely stopped-dead) rush-hour freeway traffic, on weekdays avoid being on the road between peak commute hours, 6–10 A.M. and 3–7 P.M. Plan to set out on your sightseeing excursions mid-morning, enjoying lunch and dinner in the same general vicinity before getting back on the freeways. On weekends, avoid going in the same direction as "escape" and "return" traffic—leaving L.A. in all directions on Friday afternoons or evenings and returning late in the day on Sunday. Otherwise, get going early on weekends, and avoid stadiums and sports arenas before and after big games.

Avoiding traffic jams—knowing when to switch freeways, and when to exit freeways and take surface-street or connector road shortcuts—is something of an art in Los Angeles. Yet even visitors can play the game with the aid of a tutor, such as the popular *L.A. Shortcuts: The Guidebook for Drivers Who Hate to Wait*. For those who prefer to avoid freeways altogether—it's possible, even in Los Angeles—guides such as *Freeway Alternates* can help you do just that.

Don't ever misplace your map. Even native Los Angeles residents constantly refer to them, particularly the excellent, very detailed Thomas Bros. maps. Almost every car in Los Angeles has a Thomas Bros. guide to Los Angeles or Los Angeles/Orange County, if not San Diego or Riverside/San Bernardino, right there in the glove compartment, easily available when the need arises. And the need *will* arise, the minute you miss your first freeway change and need to figure out if there's another way to get where you're going without doubling back (sometimes there isn't). But such detailed maps cost money, not typically worth the investment if you'll only be here a week or two. If you're a AAA member, stock up on California, Southern California, and L.A. city or regional maps either before you come or as soon as you arrive. Or buy good road maps at local visitor bureaus and travel-oriented bookstores.

Basic Freeway Facts—and Safety

Despite increasingly congested freeways, the idea of carpooling didn't really begin to catch on in L.A. until the 1990s, when "carpool only" lanes—

THE FREEWAY MAZE:
UNTANGLING THE CONCRETE YARN BALL

High-Occupancy Vehicle (HOV) or "diamond lanes"—began to appear on local freeways, and when area employers started offering financial incentives to get people out of their cars. Even now, most vehicles on the road carry only one person. But HOV lanes, which require at least two occupants, are starting to work in Los Angeles—speeding up trip time in the diamond lane (usually the number one lane, closest to the freeway median) as well as the general flow of traffic. If you're driving solo on L.A.'s freeways, frustrated by a traffic slowdown, don't be tempted to dart into a diamond lane and cheat the system. Fines are stiff—close to $300, sometimes higher—and in the age of cellular phones, don't think an angry Angeleno stuck in traffic will hesitate to turn you in. Once you're pulled over by the California Highway Patrol (CHP), no excuse will get you off.

Given Los Angeles drivers' lust for speed, slower drivers—people going only 70 miles per hour, say—should stay in the center or center-right lanes if at all possible, allowing faster drivers plenty of room to move as they race toward their destinies. If you'll be traveling only a short distance on a particular freeway, and if traffic is heavy, stay in the freeway's right-hand lanes and avoid the frustration of maneuvering between lanes—assuming your upcoming exit will be to the right, of course. That's usually the case, particularly on L.A.'s newer freeways and interchanges, but some freeways feature surprising

(if you don't know about them) left-hand exits or traffic "splits." So study your road map carefully before setting off into unfamiliar territory—the Thomas Bros. guides include handy freeway entry and exit maps—and watch freeway signs carefully. If you're paying attention, you'll usually have plenty of time to prepare even for left exits. Familiarizing yourself with route maps ahead of time will also help in planning an instant emergency strategy, should you miss a key exit at some point. Also allow yourself extra travel time to avoid feeling pressured, a factor that may affect your concentration.

Most traffic congestion in Los Angeles is caused by "traffic incidents," not accidents, these varying from unexpected breakdowns to flat tires. To avoid being an incident, make sure your vehicle is road-ready before setting out. But should the unexpected occur, pull off to the right to park if at all possible, turn on your emergency blinkers or "flashers," and call for help from the nearest "call box." Numbered call boxes (yet another L.A. invention), no more than a mile apart (often closer) on the right shoulder of every area freeway, are not telephones; they can be used only for automobile emergencies. Once you explain your problem and your location (relative to the box), the operator will dispatch towing assistance—a service sometimes offered free by local authorities, but AAA or other towing service coverage is always handy.

GETTING THERE: BY BUS, BOAT, TRAIN, AND PLANE

By Bus, Boat, and Train

Greyhound, toll-free 800/231-2222, www.greyhound.com, is the primary commercial bus service into greater Los Angeles. Routes come from all directions—certainly wherever there's a freeway—and can deliver travelers, if not to the desired city, then at least as close as the nearest major transit center. The main L.A. Greyhound bus terminal is downtown. If you need to get to the coast and no one can meet you there—and Greyhound connections seem dubious—simply catch a local bus and complete the trip via the available mass-transit system. (Call to clarify local connections, once you devise your main bus route.) Alternative bus companies, including **Green Tortoise,** toll-free 800/867-8647, can also deliver travelers to Los Angeles.

Always a pleasure—harking back to Hollywood's golden era—is coming and going by train, a service provided these days by **Amtrak.** Stepping out into grand Union Station near downtown Los Angeles, where one can also make intercity train connections, is a delight even for the most jaded traveler. From Los Angeles, trains run to Santa Barbara and points farther north—a lovely trip, often following the coastline—as well as east across the desert. For Amtrak info and reservations, call toll-free 800/872-7245, www.amtrak.com. For more information on bus and train travel, see this book's introduction.

More unusual, but not *that* unusual, is arriving in Los Angeles by boat. Most major cruise ships dock at **Los Angeles Harbor** in San Pedro, or in adjacent Long Beach. Contact your travel agent to arrange a cruise-ship cruise to Los Angeles.

By Airplane

Most visitors, if they don't arrive by car, come by air. The largest airport in the region is **Los Angeles International Airport,** most commonly known by its unfortunately suggestive international handle, "LAX" (pronounced EL-AY-EX, however), and located near the coast just south of Marina del Rey and north of El Segundo, west of the San Diego Fwy. (I-405). This is the airport everybody loves to hate. But few hate it enough to try another airport, which is why traffic can be so nightmarish in the general vicinity.

To avoid the crush at LAX, even locals often use other regional airports, including the **Long Beach Airport,** 562/570-2600 (recorded) or 562/570-2619, www.ci.long-beach.ca.us; the **John Wayne Airport** in Orange County, 949/252-5200, www.ocair.com; the **Burbank/Pasadena/Glendale Airport,** 818/840-8840, www.bur.com, in the San Fernando Valley but convenient to Hollywood, Pasadena, and downtown; and the surprisingly busy **Ontario International Airport** serving San Bernardino and Riverside, 909/988-2700 or 909/937-1256 (Traveler's Aid of Ontario), www.lawa.org/ont.

Los Angeles International Airport

As writer Pico Iyer has observed, airports are "the new epicenters and paradigms of our dawning post-national age—not just the bus terminals of the global village but the prototypes, in some sense, for our polyglot, multicolored, user-friendly future." That's as good a general description as any for LAX, but Iyer points out that the airport is also a metaphor for L.A. itself, "a flat, spaced-out desert kind of place, highly automotive, not deeply hospitable, with little reading matter and no organizing principle."

What a welcome to L.A. Served by about 80 major airlines, Los Angeles International Airport handles about 54 million passengers each year, making this the fifth-busiest airport in the world. And while the idea seems insane, airport officials and some local politicians are pushing to expand airport business by about 60 percent by the year 2015—a likelihood none too popular with surrounding residents already beset by horrendous traffic, air pollution, and airplane noise. Since surrounding land is scarce, proposed new runways would be built out into Santa Monica Bay with an assist from massive landfill construction projects. If the idea of an endlessly bigger LAX, a $12 billion project, seems less than appealing, the only effective way travelers can express that opinion is by taking their business elsewhere—for a listing of other area airports, see above—and by further making that point in letters and phone calls to local officials. International visitors are almost destined to disembark here, however.

Even an unexpanded LAX can't help inventing and reinventing itself. These days LAX is busy improving itself yet again—adding a space-age veneer—including spiffing up its food service. The airport's Jetsonsesque "theme building" has become the otherworldly L.A. Encounter café, redesigned by Disney Imagineering and complete with lava lamps, a robotic maître d', and waiters in space suits. The futuristic menu, designed by local chefs John Sedlar and Patrick Glennon, includes "chocolate planetary orbs with Saturn rings" as the house dessert. But pay no attention to the restaurant's flight status video monitors—strictly fictitious, unless you're headed to Mars. Other airport food concessions include McDonald's, Wolfgang Puck's Express, the Daily Grill, and other trendy contenders. New, too, is the Rhino Chasers pub. Reasonably healthy food, from bran muffins to green salads and other vegetables, is available everywhere. Look for a variety of international cuisines in the International Terminal.

As in most monstrously large airports, once you arrive you follow airport signs to find parking, rental car agencies, and terminals—and pray you'll get to the right places on time. Pray, too, that no one breaks into your car if you leave it in the lots here. Because rates of vandalism tend to be high in the airport's far-flung B and C parking lots—though they are patrolled regularly by security guards—LAX users often opt for one of the many private guarded lots just west of the San Diego Fwy. (the 405) along Century Blvd.; various airport-area hotels also offer nonguest parking, for a price. That price—and the level of service provided—can vary greatly among private parking lots, so it pays to check out available options thoroughly.

All in all, it's much simpler to forget about driving and parking, if at all possible, and get a ride with **Super Shuttle,** 213/775-6600, 310/782-6600, or toll-free 800/554-3146 in Los Angeles County, www.supershuttle.com/lax. To make reservations from outside L.A. County, call 310/782-6600. There are many, many other shuttle services, of course—even flashier limo service, as well as regular cab service—so pick a carrier licensed by the Los Angeles Dept. of Airports. Some shuttles offer discounts for senior citizens and AAA members and on prepaid round-trips. Always make shuttle reservations at least 24 hours in advance. Many higher-end area hotels also offer airport shuttle service, either free or low-cost. For current LAX transit information, including public transit connections, try the websites: www.lawa.org/lax and www.quickaid.com/airports/lax.

LAX has eight domestic terminals and one international terminal, all of them connected by free shuttle buses. Restrooms, nursery rooms, basic business services, lockers, gift shops, restaurants, and bar/lounges are available in every terminal. For computerized visitor assistance in various languages, head to one of the airport's "QuickAID" touch-screen video terminals. Even better is LAX Traveler's Aid, which features a foreign language translation "link." To get away from the airport's bustle, head for the theme building or the palm-lined oasis in Terminal 5.

GETTING AROUND

Most visitors come to Los Angeles by car, or climb into a rental car immediately after arrival, and get around the way most Angelenos do— via the vast web of local freeways. Once you get here by freeway you're already getting around by freeway, so for a detailed introduction to that adventure see Getting There: By Freeway, above.

By MTA
The Los Angeles Metropolitan Transit Authority provides public bus service throughout Los Angeles County, with some routes more generously staffed—and more useful to visitors—than others. The city's MTA buses are the only reliable form of mass transit for city residents without cars, including large segments of L.A.'s working poor population and the elderly. When MTA raised bus fares in the mid-1990s, protests erupted in so many quarters, particularly from various public-interest groups and community organizations, that the preexisting general fare of $1.35 ($.90 with prepaid tokens) will continue at least for a while. Monthly MTA passes still cost $42, 15-day passes $21, and weekly passes $11. (Weekly and monthly passes run Sun.–Sat. and are also good for the local Metrorail subway system). On some bus routes, off-peak individual fares are just $.75. In addition, MTA agreed to beef up its bus service at least a bit—adding 150 or so buses.

For information on MTA routes and fares, call 213/626-4455 or toll-free 800/266-6883 (800/252-9040 TTY). Sometimes it seems as if no one will ever answer the phone, however, so for detailed regional bus route and schedule information, try the website: www.mta.net. And to buy passes, it's typically easier to stop by local **MTA Customer Centers,** at various locations.

See the website for a current listing of centers and other retail outlets—altogether some 750 possibilities, listed by community.

A variety of other local transit systems also serve greater Los Angeles; for current information on public transportation in Santa Monica, Long Beach, and other areas, see relevant sections in the following chapters; contact local visitors bureaus; or see the MTA website, www.mta.net, which provides handy transit "links" throughout Southern California.

By Metrorail and Metrolink

Los Angeles once boasted one of the world's most far-flung and efficient public transportation systems—the Pacific Electric Red Car electric trolley system that connected nearly every suburban or coastal L.A. community with each other and with downtown. The Red Cars, in fact, were largely responsible for L.A.'s sprawling growth pattern—more so than freeways, which came much later—since trolley transport made it convenient for people to get around even without cars. When the last of the Red Car trolley system was dismantled in 1961, L.A.'s congestion and smog problems quickly reached crisis proportions.

Los Angeles is once again looking to mass-transit trains and trolleys to solve its traffic problems, though at this point things aren't working quite as well as the old Red Cars did.

Operated by the Metropolitan Transit Authority (MTA) and built with generous amounts of federal funding, the new and multifaceted Los Angeles Metrorail system serves fairly limited areas of L.A. and Southern California, though original plans called for substantial regional expansion. Designed primarily for Los Angeles commuters of the professional class, it would seem, the system has suffered from cost overruns, dramatic construction delays, and the local and national humiliations of fraud and kickback allegations, federal investigations, and substantial recent funding cuts. Los Angeles itself seems almost evenly divided on the question of whether its modern mass-transit system has been worth it—and whether it will make any real difference in eliminating area traffic congestion. (Metrorail's ongoing disasters were publicly symbolized, in the mid-1990s, by the giant construction-related cave-in and sinkhole along Hollywood Boulevard.) A 1997 poll determined that, by a narrow majority, Los Angeles residents oppose the city's new subway system, including further construction, and doubt that it will ever serve parts of the city that most need it.

Metrorail's most vocal critics point out that the system was designed primarily for the convenience of more affluent commuters, that it rarely goes where many residents (and visitors) would like it to go, and that the money spent on Metrorail would have been better spent on improving the local bus system.

The MTA's **Red Line,** the city's subway, serves Union Station, downtown L.A., a short section of Wilshire Blvd., and Hollywood and North Hollywood; the line is now on its way into the San Fernando Valley—a construction process creating considerable local consternation—and will one day extend to the ocean, according to current plans. The MTA's **Blue Line** electric trolleys run 22 miles between Long Beach and downtown L.A., passing Watts Towers and other rarely-seen-by-tourists neighborhoods along the way. The Blue Line is linked to the recently opened east-west **Green Line** that connects Norwalk to El Segundo (but not nearby LAX; you'll have to lug your luggage onto an airport bus for that trip). For that utilitarian lapse in particular—and since El Segundo is no longer a major aerospace employment hub, thanks to U.S defense downsizing—the Green Line has been dubbed the "train to nowhere" in the local press. Scoring at least one point for convenience, however, the Blue Line stops just one block from the transit mall in downtown Long Beach.

The MTA's Metrolink commuter rail system, launched in 1992, is the fastest-growing commuter rail system in the nation. Metrolink "links" cities such as San Bernardino, Riverside, Lancaster, Oxnard, and Oceanside to Los Angeles. Though the entire system is far from entirely useful even for visitors, both Metrorail and Metrolink do offer the opportunity for unusual car-free day trips and around-town excursions.

Fares for the Metrorail system are the same as for MTA buses; for details, see By MTA, above. Fares for Metrolink trains vary according to distance traveled. For information on the Metrorail Red, Blue, and Green Lines, call MTA at 213/626-4455 or toll-free 800/266-6883, www.mta.net. For route and fare information for the Metrolink commuter trains, call toll-free 800/371-5465.

PASADENA CONVENTION AND VISITOR'S BUREAU

PASADENA AND VICINITY

Enthroned above an oak-studded arroyo in the shadow of the San Gabriel Mountains, Pasadena the place is actually an *idea*—the idea that simple, healthful living amid gardens, orange groves, and the fellowship of good neighbors can save civilization from the mass-production mindset of the industrial era. Pasadena represents the central idea that created Southern California. Described by acclaimed turn-of-the-20th-century astronomer George Ellery Hale as the "Athens of the West," Pasadena took root in agriculture and then grew its own golden age of arts and sciences.

CROWNED BY AGRICULTURE~ AND CULTURE

In the beginning there was Indiana, where the winters were cold and brutal. After the particularly harsh winter of 1872–73, a like-minded group of Indiana farmers sent schoolteacher and journalist Daniel M. Berry west by train to scout out a Southern California site for an agricultural paradise. Berry's choice was the western San

Gabriel Valley, where Ivy League–educated farmers already cultivated vineyards, orange groves, and roses in the sunshine and salubrious fresh air.

Berry and his fellows, who came to be known as the Indiana Colony, bought a 4,000-acre section of the San Pasqual Ranch, at the price of $6.31 per acre. The Indianans established themselves as the San Gabriel Orange Grove Association in 1875. They called their community Pasadena, a Chippewa word purported to mean "Crown of the Valley," and set about cultivating the good life.

Crowned by Upper-Crust Culture

Like the rest of Southern California, Pasadena grew rapidly during the real estate boom of the 1880s. In the wake of the settlers, the arrival of the railroad in 1885 brought bushels of well-heeled easterners eager to escape to a kinder climate—the beginning of Pasadena's long-running reputation as a choice West Coast winter vacation destination.

Many of Pasadena's wealthy winterers decided to stay on year-round, to soak up a full measure of

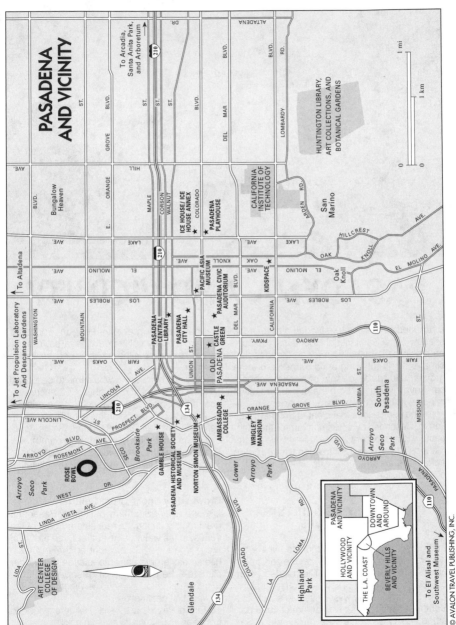

PASADENA AND VICINITY

© AVALON TRAVEL PUBLISHING, INC.

ORANGES AND CALIFORNIA CULTURE

As a symbol of the Southern California dream—a regional variation of the American dream, particularly "middle-class America's desire for a home and happy marriage and healthy children," according to historian Kevin Starr—the orange as icon of the good life was crated for wholesale consumption throughout the United States by advertising executives employed by the California Fruit Growers Exchange (known for its trademark "Sunkist" brand). Real estate sales campaigns in general, promoted by early L.A. power brokers and landowners—railroad barons such as Henry E. Huntington and Charles Nordhuff, and newspaper publishers such as Harrison Gray Otis of the *Los Angeles Times*—often emphasized the same theme, though the boosters' general credo was: "Big is Good, Bigger is Better, Biggest is Best." In parts of the country where winter meant blinding blizzards rather than blooming roses, the campaign wasn't a terribly hard sell.

Pasadena, in the San Gabriel Valley just east of downtown Los Angeles, would reap the richest rewards of California's orange era. Described by acclaimed turn-of-the-20th-century astronomer George Ellery Hale as the "Athens of the West," Pasadena took root in 1875 thanks to the San Gabriel Valley Orange Association and then grew its own golden age of arts and sciences. The arrival of the railroad in 1885 brought bushels of well-heeled easterners eager to escape to a kinder climate—the beginning of Pasadena's long-running reputation as a choice West Coast winter vacation destination. Many of Pasadena's wealthy winterers decided to stay on year-round, to soak up a full measure of sun and the scent of orange blossoms, and they soon built grand homes on the city's wide, wandering streets.

Thanks to the humble orange, the arts and all aspects of culture, not just horticulture, flourished in Pasadena, which made California's greatest contributions to the Arts and Crafts movement. Pasadena's Craftsman architecture—most popular from 1900 to 1940, and also fairly common elsewhere throughout Southern California—relied on an uncluttered, woodsy, nature-oriented approach that combined the sensibilities of a Swiss chalet with Japanese (sometimes Chinese) and Tudor touches. Emphasizing simplicity and harmony with nature, they stood as repudiation of all things Victorian.

Pasadena was in step with the march of progress throughout Southern California in other ways as well—most particularly with its annual Tournament of Roses Parade, the ultimate boosteristic beacon of the California good life. Where else, after all, could one find *roses* on New Year's Day?

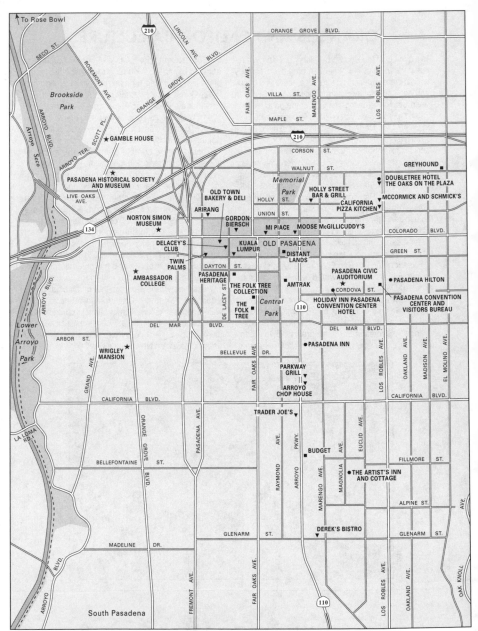

To Rose Bowl

SECO ST.

Brookside
Park

Arroyo Seco

ARROYO BLVD.

ROSEMONT AVE.

ARROYO TER. SCOTT PL.

★ GAMBLE HOUSE

LIVE OAKS AVE.

★ PASADENA HISTORICAL SOCIETY
AND MUSEUM

★ NORTON SIMON
MUSEUM

ARROYO BLVD.

Lower
Arroyo
Park

LA LOMA RD.

ARROYO BLVD.

210

LINCOLN AVE.

ORANGE GROVE BLVD.

134

ARBOR ST.

★ WRIGLEY
MANSION

GRAND AVE.

BELLEFONTAINE ST.

ORANGE GROVE BLVD.

MADELINE DR.

FREMONT AVE.

ORANGE GROVE BLVD.

FAIR OAKS AVE.

ORANGE GROVE BLVD.

VILLA ST.

MAPLE ST.

210

CORSON ST.

WALNUT ST.

Memorial
Park

HOLLY ST.

OLD TOWN
BAKERY & DELI

ARIRANG ★

GORDON-
BIERSCH

HOLLY STREET
BAR & GRILL

UNION ST.

MI PIACE

MOOSE McGILLICUDDY'S

DELACEY'S
CLUB

TWIN
PALMS ★

KUALA
LUMPUR

OLD PASADENA

DISTANT
LANDS

DAYTON ST.

★ AMBASSADOR
COLLEGE

PASADENA
HERITAGE

THE FOLK TREE
COLLECTION

THE
FOLK
TREE

Central
Park

DE LACEY ST.

DEL MAR BLVD.

BELLEVUE DR.

FAIR OAKS AVE.

CALIFORNIA BLVD.

PASADENA AVE.

TRADER JOE'S

RAYMOND AVE.

ARROYO PKWY.

AMTRAK

CORDOVA ST.

110

HOLIDAY INN PASADENA
CONVENTION CENTER
HOTEL

PASADENA CIVIC
AUDITORIUM ★

● PASADENA INN

DEL MAR BLVD.

PARKWAY
GRILL

ARROYO
CHOP HOUSE

BUDGET

MARENGO AVE.

MAGNOLIA AVE.

DEREK'S BISTRO

GLENARM ST.

South Pasadena

110

FILLMORE ST.

● THE ARTIST'S INN
AND COTTAGE

ALPINE ST.

GLENARM ST.

ORANGE GROVE BLVD.

MARENGO AVE.

LOS ROBLES AVE.

GREYHOUND

DOUBLETREE HOTEL
THE OAKS ON THE PLAZA

McCORMICK AND SCHMICK'S

CALIFORNIA
PIZZA KITCHEN

COLORADO BLVD.

GREEN ST.

● PASADENA HILTON

PASADENA CONVENTION
CENTER AND
VISITORS BUREAU

LOS ROBLES AVE.

OAKLAND AVE.

MADISON AVE.

EL MOLINO AVE.

CALIFORNIA BLVD.

EUCLID AVE.

LOS ROBLES AVE.

OAKLAND AVE.

OAK KNOLL AVE.

© AVALON TRAVEL PUBLISHING, INC.

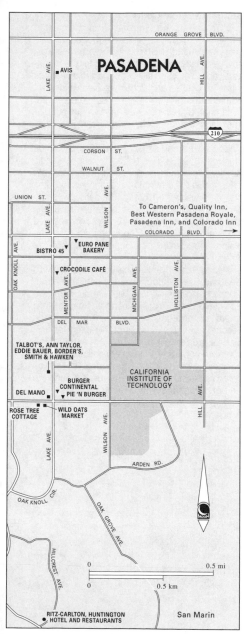

sun and the scent of orange blossoms. They soon built grand homes on the city's wide, wandering streets. Business tycoons and the heirs of industry included Adolphus Busch of St. Louis, Chicago's William J. Wrigley, and Henry E. Huntington. Prominent new citizens also included Mrs. James Garfield, widow of the assassinated president, and the children of John Brown, abolitionist martyr. Feminist writer Charlotte Perkins Gilman, once freed from the insanity behind "The Yellow Wallpaper," made her last home in Pasadena.

For writers and artists, Pasadena was a good choice. The arts and all aspects of culture, not just agriculture, flourished. Pasadena's genteel pursuit of history, literature, poetry, music, art, and the artistic aspects of horticulture created a heaven on earth for the upper middle-class liberal Protestants who made it their home.

THE CRAFTSMAN CROWN

By 1900 Pasadena's population was 10,000; within seven years it reached 30,000. The design and decorative demands of the city's well-to-do residents meant steady work for the country's finest artists and architects. It was no accident, then, that Pasadena soon became an architectural showcase. Many of its treasures still stand.

Most "Pasadena" of them all, ultimately, was the impact of the Arts and Crafts Movement, inspired by John Ruskin and William Morris in England but popularized throughout the United States by German immigrant Gustav Stickley, publisher of *The Craftsman* magazine and himself a Craftsman-style furniture designer.

Craftsman architecture, most popular from 1900 to 1940, relied on an uncluttered, woodsy, nature-oriented approach that combined the sensibilities of a Swiss chalet with Japanese (sometimes Chinese) and Tudor touches. In Pasadena these distinctive homes were sided with shakes or shingles, usually redwood, and built upon a foundation of boulders brought up from the Arroyo Seco; prominent chimneys also were built of arroyo stone. With wide porches supported by heavy tie beams, Craftsman houses typically featured roof supports that extended beyond the gable. Many included sleeping porches, to take full advantage of Southern California's mild weather.

Most important, though, the Craftsman approach was a repudiation of all things Victorian, including architecture and furnishings that were ornate, overly fussy, overstuffed. The Arts and Crafts movement instead emphasized simplicity and harmony with nature—integrating every element of interior design, including light and air, with the world outside, down to the last landscaping detail.

The Brothers Greene and Greene

The architectural achievements of brothers Charles Sumner Greene and Henry Mather Greene in Pasadena came to epitomize America's Arts and Crafts movement—pragmatic, functional design with aesthetic sensibility, a social statement made through architecture. "I seek till I find what is truly useful, and then I try to make it beautiful," Charles Greene once said.

The Greenes' oft-imitated style was reserved not just for a home's architecture. Greene and Greene also shared their design vision with talented craftspeople who created Tiffany stained-glass lamps, leaded-glass windows, furniture, light fixtures, rugs, and other interior and exterior items.

Yet Greene and Greene reserved their talents for the wealthy, contradicting core Arts and Crafts ideals. As historian Kevin Starr comments, a notable characteristic of a Greene and Greene home is its "cunning concealment" of servant staircases and other service features.

Bungalows Hold Court

The Greene brothers' unstinting commitment to quality workmanship—and their hope that their own work, though reserved for the rich, would set new, higher standards in housing for the masses—carried through in Pasadena's middle-class craze for Craftsman bungalows. Known for both quality construction and innovative style, the Craftsman represents Pasadena's most popular approach to domestic architecture.

Other popular area architects of the time included Alfred and Arthur Heineman, Sylvanus Marston, Louis B. Easton, and Frederick Louis Roehrig. Heineman, Heineman, and Marston were influential in the development of bungalow courts, many of which remain today. The bungalow court, originally designed to accommodate tourists, first appeared about 1910. The concept soon evolved into a fashionable form of apartment life, one combining the social benefits of group living with the privacy of single-family residences.

Also particularly influential during Pasadena's Arts and Crafts epoch was Ernest Batchelder, whose hand-carved tiles with almost medieval Southern California nature motifs can still be found in original local Craftsman homes. Batchelder's tiles were primarily used for fireplaces, rendered in earthy tones and left unglazed or finished with a very soft matte effect. Formerly, you could see Batchelder's work on public display in downtown Pasadena's Santa Fe Railroad Passenger Station, now closed.

SEEING AND DOING PASADENA

Surprisingly appealing, this self-satisfied city is so sure of its essential worth that it sees little need to primp and pimp for the almighty tourist dollar. Most famous as hometown for the annual New Year's Day Tournament of Roses Parade downtown and the afternoon Rose Bowl post-season college football game, Pasadena is otherwise low-key about its attractions, which are legion. Southern California boosterism played its part in Pasadena's past, but these days heavy-handed hype is notably absent. Pasadena simply *allows* one to enjoy its fairly civilized pleasures. And what a pleasure that is.

OLD PASADENA

The rudely reversed adage, in Angeleno lore, is that Pasadena is a nice place to live, but no one would want to *visit* there. The reinvigoration of Old Pasadena has changed all that. (The correct current promotional term, by the way, is "Old Pasadena," not "Old Town" or "Old Town Pasadena," a distinction largely lost even on native Pasadenans.) Once given over to harmless derelicts, pawn shops, and X-rated entertainment venues, Old Pasadena is now one of the liveliest street scenes in all of Southern California—a destination in its own right for tony trend-

setters and throngs of wannabes who stroll the streets in search of something new, something old, or something old that's been made new.

Old Pasadena's "center" lies at the intersection of Colorado Blvd. and Fair Oaks Ave., with most of the action on Colorado. The roughly 14-block district—defined by E. Holly and Union Sts. to the north, Green St. to the south, Pasadena Ave. to the west, and Arroyo Pkwy. to the east—keeps growing. The southern reach of Old Pasadena is fast approaching Del Mar, for example, with parking meters already in place.

To truly appreciate what's here, historically speaking, take a **Saturday morning walking tour** offered on the second Sat. of each month by Pasadena Heritage, $5 per person. For current information and reservations (required), call 626/441-6333, or check out www.pasadena-heritage.org.

Especially during the lunch hour and on Friday and Saturday nights, street parking is almost impossible to find in Old Pasadena. And if you do bulldoze your way into a metered space, the fee is a quarter per quarter-hour, with a two-hour total time limit. A better bet: reasonably convenient city parking lots.

THE ARROYO SECO

Pasadena's Arroyo Seco ("Dry River") is a steep-sided natural ravine stretching from the San Gabriel Mountains all the way into Los Angeles. Spanned by the recently restored, dramatically arched, and oddly curving 1913 **Colorado Street Bridge**, the arroyo has invited grand presence since early settlement days. Nearby, at 125 S. Grand Ave., is the original Vista del Arroyo Hotel, now the Ninth U.S. Circuit Court of Appeals. Farthest north, actually in La Cañada Flintridge, is the Cal Tech–affiliated Jet Propulsion Laboratory, the lead U.S. center for robotic exploration of the solar system, managed for NASA by the California Institute of Technology. Across the arroyo, adjacent to Glendale, is the Art Center College of Design. Then there's the Rose Bowl, a landmark amid the surrounding

---

ABOUT SMOG AND SUMMER WEATHER

The dazzling fresh air which drew early settlers, many of whom suffered respiratory ailments, is long gone. Given the lay of the land, otherwise welcome ocean breezes blow nearly all of L.A.'s smog east, smack dab into these foothills. The problem is particularly acute in summer. Trapped in the valley under a heat-induced inversion layer, the summer smog all but obliterates any view, even close up, of the neighboring San Gabriel Mountains. The simple act of opening one's eyes, not to mention breathing, can be mighty unpleasant during August, September, and sometimes October. Consider coming some other time.

public parklands, Brookside Park and Lower Arroyo Park, popular for hiking, biking, running, horseback riding, golfing, and swimming.

The Rose Bowl

The most famous sight in Pasadena is, of course, the Rose Bowl stadium, designed by Myron Hunt. This was the site of the nation's first post-season collegiate football championship game, in 1902. After Michigan stomped Stanford 49-0, it took 14 years for another West Coast team to agree to play. But by 1919 the contest was so popular—attracting 30,000 fans—that a stadium was needed. The original stadium, built in 1922, was open-ended and horseshoe-shaped. It was closed in 1928 for its first reconstruction and expansion, has been expanded and renovated several times since. For the most

impressive view of the stadium, look north from either the Foothill or Glendale Fwy. just before the Orange Grove exit.

The UCLA Bruins play their home games here, traditionally, and the Rose Bowl also hosts various special events throughout the year. Come on the second Sun. of every month for the famous **Rose Bowl Flea Market,** 323/560-7469, where astute antiquers can almost always find a treasure. The Rose Bowl, 991 Rosemont Blvd., 626/577-3100, is open Mon.–Fri. 9 A.M.–4 P.M. For $2—when no events are under way—come in through the Chrysler Court of Champions for a look-see.

The Art Center College of Design

The Art Center College of Design, across the Arroyo Seco at 1700 Lida St., 626/396-2200,

JACKIE ROBINSON: FROM SEGREGATION TO INTEGRATION

Pasadena's own Jackie Robinson faced insults and racism when he broke the color barrier and integrated Major League Baseball in 1947. He played his way into baseball's Hall of Fame and helped the Brooklyn Dodgers win five league championships and a World Series. His success, however, never dulled his memory of the first time he faced racial troubles. Robinson had learned about racism when he was a child growing up on Pepper St. in Pasadena.

His mother, three older brothers, and sister had moved from Georgia to Southern California when Robinson was an infant. One day when he was about eight years old, he was sweeping the sidewalk when a little neighbor girl shouted at him: "Nigger, nigger, nigger."

Within minutes, Robinson, the little girl, and her father were throwing rocks at each other. The girl's mother broke up the fight, but it was all part of a pattern that Robinson faced throughout his life. The all-white neighborhood was soon circulating a petition to force the Robinsons to move. The neighbors would call police and complain about noise. But the family remained united, and Robinson's mother told the neighbors that they did not frighten her. Robinson later credited his mother with teaching him strength in the face of adversity.

Sports became Robinson's outlet for his aggressiveness and his desire for competition. At John

Muir Technical School, he earned letters in baseball, basketball, football, and track. As quarterback, he led Pasadena Junior College to a perfect 11-0 season. At UCLA, he became the first athlete to earn letters in four sports.

After serving in World War II, Robinson was signed to a major league contract in the fall of 1945. But leading white players and baseball commentators called the signing a publicity stunt and claimed that no African American was good enough to play professional baseball with whites.

After the signing, the *Los Angeles Times* called Robinson the best all-around athlete of "his race" in Southern California. But Southern California's black newspaper, the crusading *California Eagle,* knew better. It called Robinson the best all-around athlete of any race in the nation. In 1947, Robinson was named Rookie of the Year and helped Brooklyn to the National League pennant.

During his 10-year career, Robinson saw hundreds of black players signed to major league teams. He had paved the way for integration of America's most popular game. Along the way he endured taunts from fans, jeers from fellow players, and constant mistreatment because his skin was black.

Throughout it all he remained calm and yet was known as a fiery competitor. Instead of throwing rocks at his tormentors, he let his dignity and great skills fight the hatred spawned by racism.

established in Los Angeles in 1930, is an internationally renowned arts and design school emphasizing the practical—the most basic practical consideration being post-college employment. The college's nine majors include advertising, illustration, environmental design, graphic design and packaging, photography, and filmmaking. Architect Craig Ellwood designed the college's current digs in 1977. The sleek, black, steel-and-glass rectangular box sits on a chaparral-covered hill and spans an adjacent ravine. The fine sculpture garden and striking views of the city still don't outshine the student work on display here. Galleries also feature revolving exhibits of national and internationally known artists and designers, working in various media. The **Williamson Gallery** is open to the public Tues.–Sun. noon–5 P.M., until 9 P.M. on Thurs., closed Mon. and holidays. Free campus tours are offered daily. To get here: Take Colorado Blvd. west to the Colorado St. Bridge. Turn right at San Rafael, which turns into Linda Vista. Follow Linda Vista north to Lida, turn left, and follow the signs.

THE GAMBLE HOUSE AND VICINITY

The Gamble House

If there's time for nothing else while in Pasadena, do visit the Gamble House. Pasadena's premier architectural showpiece, this is one of the finest examples of the finest moment in American domestic design—justifiably designated both a state and national historic landmark.

Architects Charles and Henry Greene designed this Japanese-influenced Craftsman as a winter home for David and Mary Gamble of Cincinnati, heirs to the Procter & Gamble fortune. No expense was spared in constructing this richly detailed 1908–1909 ode to simplicity. At a time when $5,000 would buy a very spacious house on a view lot, the Gambles spent $50,000 for this shingle-sided home graced with exotic hand-rubbed woods and inlays, leaded-glass windows, and the home's trademark oak-motif Louis Tiffany stained-glass door.

Now managed by the University of Southern California's School of Architecture, the Gamble House is meticulously maintained. Most astonishing, almost all of the original Greene and Greene furnishings and design details are still

here. Except for the rugs, everything was manufactured in the Greenes' own Pasadena studios.

The Gamble House, 4 Westmoreland Pl. (three blocks north of Colorado Blvd.), 626/793-3334, www.gamblehouse.org, is open for docent-led tours Thurs.–Sun. from noon to 3 P.M. (closed on major holidays). Tours begin every 15 minutes and typically last one hour. Admission is $5 for adults, $4 for seniors, $3 for students (with valid ID), and free for children 12 and under. Call to arrange group tours, offered by arrangement only. For something special, come during the Christmas season, when the house is decked out for the holidays—the only time visitors can take self-guided tours. Whenever you come, don't skip the Gamble House Bookstore in the onetime garage.

Near the Gamble House: Feynes Mansion

The **Pasadena Historical Society and Museum** is right in the neighborhood, inside the 1905 neoclassical Feynes Mansion, 470 W. Walnut St. (at N. Orange Grove Blvd.), 626/577-1660. Once home to the Finnish consul, the 18-room museum displays original 15th- and 16th-century European antiques alongside American paintings. In many ways the basement is more intriguing, with exhibits of historical photographs and memorabilia. The historical society's gift shop is also here—doing its part to assist the $2 million fundraising campaign for construction of the Pasadena History Center.

In a separate building on this lush four-acre estate is the **Finnish Folk Art Museum,** a replica of a 17th-century Finnish smokehouse and living room with antiquities from the collection of former Finnish Consul Y. A. Paloheimo.

The Pasadena Historical Society museums are open Thurs.–Sun. 1–4 P.M. for self-guided tours, $4 adults, $3 seniors and students, free for children under 12.

DOWNTOWN AGAIN

The California Institute of Technology

The original **Throop University,** founded in 1891, was at the corner of Fair Oaks and Green, still standing as part of the Castle Green. The four-year college evolved into the **Throop Polytechnic Institute** and emphasized training in the manual arts for all grades, heavily influenced by the Arts and Crafts movement philosophy. Polytechnic eventually split into two schools, the Hunt and Grey–designed Craftsman **Polytechnic School** preparatory at 1030 E. California Blvd. and the now world-renowned **California Institute of Technology** ("Cal Tech") at 1201 E. California Blvd., noted for its physics, engineering, and astronomy departments. This is the place Albert Einstein changed his mind about the nature of the cosmos, and where Carl Anderson discovered the positron. Cal Tech is the most selective undergraduate school in the nation, with 22 Nobel Prize laureates among its faculty and alumni.

Regular campus tours, geared toward students and prospective students, are offered during the school year Mon.–Fri. at 2 P.M., except during winter break or when it's raining. Even better is the free Cal Tech campus architectural tour, offered Sept.–Nov. and Jan.–June on the fourth Thurs. of the month. For information, call campus public relations at 626/395-6327. Also worth a stop: Cal Tech's well-known seismology facility, the **Earthquake and Media Center** and, during special events, the Cal Tech–affiliated **Jet Propulsion Laboratory,** specializing in National Aeronautics and Space Administration (NASA) research.

BUNGALOW HEAVEN

Always satisfying is a stroll through Pasadena's Bungalow Heaven neighborhood north of the Foothill Freeway (I-210), the area between Lake and Hill Aves. bordered on the north by Washington Blvd. and on the south by Orange Grove. Officially recognized as a local landmark district since 1989, here you'll find block after block of middle-class takes on the Craftsman theme. These "Model T"s of home design, some available by mail-order catalog, were marketable symbols of the California good life. A two-bedroom Pasadena bungalow that cost $2,000 in 1910 would set you back about $350,000 today, however. So the best way to appreciate the impressive interior workmanship is to take the annual neighborhood home tour, held on the last Sunday in April. For tickets and information, call the **Bungalow Heaven Neighborhood Association** at 626/585-2172.

Castle Green

Another Pasadena noteworthy, included on the National Register of Historic Places, Castle Green is all that remains of one of America's most prestigious resort hotels, **Hotel Green.** Built with the fortune Colonel G. G. Green made by hawking patent medicines, Castle Green, 50 E. Green St. (at Raymond), is the second of two hotel buildings once connected by the **Bridge of Sighs** promenade over Raymond Ave., the most desirable place in town from which to view the Rose Parade. (President Taft once stood here.) The first hotel building, originally the Hotel Webster, was built in 1890 and torn down in 1924, so now the promenade ends a bit abruptly.

The remaining six-story "castle," an apartment cooperative since 1926, was the original hotel's annex, constructed in 1899. Its architecture is an eccentric and extravagant interpretation of then-popular Spanish, Moorish, and Classical styles, with red-tiled roofs and turrets, towers, balconies, and verandas done in olive green, gold, and orange. The public rooms downstairs—the entry, main salon, card room, Moorish room, and downstairs ballroom—look much as they did originally and are rented out for special events and the occasional film crew.

Pasadena Civic Center

Inspired by the City Beautiful movement, Pasadena's regal Beaux Arts civic center is an intentionally striking symbol of civic pride, built in the 1920s. The three dominant public buildings are surrounded by a host of neoclassical commercial buildings downtown, all completed before the Great Depression.

Most striking is **Pasadena City Hall,** 100 N. Garfield Ave., with its crownlike dome and Italian Renaissance courtyard design, by John Bakewell Jr. and Arthur Brown Jr., who also created San Francisco's City Hall. The formal Italian/Spanish vernacular **Pasadena Central Library,** 285 E. Walnut St., was designed by Pasadena architect Myron Hunt, more famous for the Huntington estate in San Marino.

Now effectively cut off from the rest of the Civic Center by the Plaza Pasadena, the **Pasadena Civic Auditorium,** 300 E. Green St., is a venerable performance venue—an Italian Renaissance palace, known for its Pompeian revival interiors by artist Giovanni Smeraldi.

City Hall

The Pasadena Playhouse

The Spanish revival–style 1924 Pasadena Playhouse, the official State Theater of California since 1938, was founded by Gilmor Brown, who merged a traveling troupe with local amateur actors. Host to touring plays and musicals, and historic training ground for new Hollywood acting talent—including Conrad Bain, Katherine Helmond, Stacy Keach, and Stephanie Zimbalist—the playhouse was central to Los Angeles cultural life until the 1960s, when financial problems forced its closure. Another local star on the National Register of Historic Places, the Pasadena Playhouse was refinanced, carefully restored, and reopened in 1986.

Two theaters are on the premises, the main 700-seat auditorium and a smaller 99-seat house for Equity-waiver performances. The Pasadena Playhouse is downtown at 39 S. El Molino Ave. (between Colorado and Green). For information, call 626/792-8672; for tickets, call the box office at 626/356-7529 or toll-free 800/233-3123. Members of the **Pasadena Playhouse Alumni and Associates** offer behind-the-scenes tours, by appointment only. Special group tours can also be arranged.

ARTFUL, ENTERTAINING PASADENA

MUSEUM-QUALITY PASADENA

Norton Simon Museum

In 1974 Norton Simon rescued the floundering Pasadena Museum of Modern Art and set about creating one of the world's foremost art collections. And when you spot Rodin's *The Thinker* out on the lawn, you know what's inside has got to be good. There's more Rodin, of course, but the Norton Simon collection is richest in Picassos, Rembrandts—including *The Bearded Man in the Wide Brimmed Hat, Self-Portrait,* and *Titus*—and Goyas. An entire gallery of Degas, both paintings and sculptures, lines the curving staircase. The impressionist collection is vast, including also Cézanne, Matisse, Monet, Renoir, Lautrec, and van Gogh. Also here: Renaissance works by Raphael, Rubens, and Brueghel, ancient ivory, bronze, and stone sculptures from India and Southeast Asia. Don't miss the mu-

seum shop, with an exceptional selection of books, prints, and cards.

The Norton Simon Museum is near the Colorado St. Bridge at 411 W. Colorado Blvd., 626/449-6840, www.nortonsimon.org, and is open Thurs.–Sun. noon–6 P.M. Admission is $6 adults, $3 students and seniors, children under 12 free.

Pacific Asia Museum

Designed in 1924 by architects Mayberry, Marston, and Van Pelt as both gallery and home for Grace Nicholson, aficionado of Asian art, Pasadena's own northern Chinese Imperial Palace—included on the National Register of Historic Places—features a green tile roof, ceramic guard dogs to ward off evil spirits, and a peaceful central courtyard complete with bubbling brook and koi. (The garden is one of two authentic Chinese gardens in the United States.) Though the Pacific Asia Museum is the only

Norton Simon Museum

PASADENA CONVENTION & VISITORS BUREAU

Southern California museum specializing in the arts and crafts of Asia and the Pacific, most exhibits here are on loan from other museums or private collections. The bookstore/gift shop is worth a wander. Free lectures and workshops on Asian arts and culture are offered on the third Sat. of every month.

The Pacific Asia Museum, 46 N. Los Robles Ave. (at Colorado), 626/449-2742, www.pacific asiamuseum.org, is a block south of the Doubletree Hotel and is open Wed.–Sun., 10 A.M.–5 P.M. Admission is $5 adults, $3 seniors and students, children under 12 free.

Kidspace Museum

Kidspace is a children's museum founded by the Junior League of Pasadena in 1979 to encourage hands-on exploration by children—the perfect antidote after touring all the hands-off attractions in town. Housed in the onetime gymnasium of a former elementary school (now a continuation high school), Kidspace offers abundant opportunities for creative play without too many of the gee-whiz technoid special effects becoming so popular at children's museums. Exhibits include a child-size TV and radio station, talking robots, real uniforms to try on, and a hospital room with a soft-sculpture doll (complete with removable organs). Summer workshops are offered, and special events are held throughout the year at Kidspace, 390 S. El Molino (at California Blvd.), 626/449-9143. During the regular school year Kidspace is open only Wed.

2–5 P.M. and on weekends 12:30–5 P.M.; in summer and during school vacations, Mon.–Fri. 1–5 P.M. Admission is $5 for adults and children over age 2, $3.50 for seniors.

ENTERTAINING PASADENA

Theatrical Pasadena

Pasadena is a serious theater and concert city, attracting major regional, national, and international performers. The city's most prominent venue is the 1931 **Pasadena Civic Auditorium,** downtown at 300 E. Green St., where Natalie Cole's "Unforgettable" concert was filmed for PBS's *Great Performances.* Home to the **Pasadena Symphony** and former home of the annual Emmy Awards ceremony, the 2,961-seat Civic hosts performers such as Ray Charles, the American Ballet Theatre, and the Vienna Philharmonic. For current events information, call 626/793-2122. For tickets, call the box office at 626/449-7360.

Performances at Pasadena's most beloved theater, **Pasadena Playhouse,** tend toward the contemporary, with recent world premieres including "Same Time, Another Year" and "In the Moonlight." The season typically runs from Sept. to July, with ticket prices $12–40. For tickets, call 626/356-7529 or TicketMaster in Los Angeles, 213/365-3500.

Now that Pasadena's acoustically perfect Ambassador Auditorium at Ambassador College has closed shop, other schools are increasingly called upon to help fill the venue void. Concerts, dance performances, lectures, plays, and films are regularly scheduled at **Beckman Auditorium** and **Ramo Auditorium** on the Cal Tech campus. For information and tickets, call Cal

BOOSTERISM ON PARADE: THE TOURNAMENT OF ROSES

The only social artifact of Pasadena's past boosterism is now an international event. Every year on Jan. 1 Pasadena struts its stuff for the multitudes assembled along Colorado Blvd. and for a worldwide television audience of about 450 million. New Year's Day is the only time Pasadena as a destination is nearly impossible.

The **Tournament of Roses Parade** has been held here since 1890, when it was prosaically known as the "Battle of the Flowers" and featured Ben Hur–style chariot races, these followed in short order by ostrich races and (only once, in 1913) elephant and camel races.

Despite its fame, there's still something downhome and folksy about the Tournament of Roses Parade, with its high school marching bands and mounted sheriff's posses. But the real fascination is the fact that only "fresh plant material" can be used to decorate its fantastic floats. In the beginning, Pasadena loaded its horse-drawn creations with bushels and bushels of its own winter-grown roses—a scene undeniably appealing to snowbound easterners, making the event a major boon to local real estate sales. The scene is unbelievably sophisticated these days, with dedicated teams—

led by "floral directors"—creating mobile art using a palette of flowers, fresh greenery, vegetables, fruit rinds, beans, rice, seed pods, and dried tree bark. Since the flower artists can use no artificial chemicals or dyes, they make the most difficult colors (red, for instance) by resorting to exotic blends of spices.

In 1902 the first **Rose Bowl** post-season college football game was added to the day's festivities. Michigan stomped Stanford 49-0, and that West Coast humiliation was enough to retire football from the day's rosy agenda for 14 years. But football was a major passion by 1922, when the venerable Rose Bowl stadium was constructed.

For information on the Tournament of Roses Parade, the Rose Bowl, and associated before-and-after events, call 626/449-4100 or 626/449-7673 (ROSE), or try www.rosebowl.com. If you do come for the big day and want to book hotel rooms—at least a year in advance, and prices will be sky high—remember that when Jan. 1 falls on a Sunday, both the Rose Parade and Rose Bowl are scheduled for Jan. 2. This is Pasadena, after all, rooted in the Midwestern belief that it's a sin to so much as mow the lawn on a Sunday.

ROBERT HOLMES/CalTour

Tech's Office of Public Events, 626/395-4652. To find out what's going on at **Pasadena City College,** call 626/585-7123.

Comedy: The Ice House

The fun and funny Ice House, 24 N. Mentor Ave., 626/577-1894, is a fairly famous comedy club, where since opening night in 1960 the likes of Jay Leno, David Letterman, Steve Martin, Pat Paulsen, Lily Tomlin, and Robin Williams have made names for themselves. The **Ice House Annex** next door offers music acts, improv theater, and "one person" theater acts. Cover charge is $8.50 Sun.–Thurs. nights, $11.50–12.50 on Fri. and Sat. nights.

Making the Scene

Kevin Costner was once a major draw at the **Twin Palms** restaurant and nightclub, 101 W. Green St., 626/577-2567. After the divorce, Costner's ex-wife, Cindy, got sole custody of the place. While the Twin Palms has lost some of its movie star cachet, it's still quite glamorous. The restaurant fare is good, though some people come here to make the scene. Stars of the large patio bar are the—hey!—*twin palms.* Live music is on tap nightly after 9 P.M., except Mon., when comics take the stage. Cover charge varies.

Count on finding the more settled crowd mixed in with traveling business types at the **Ritz-Carlton, Huntington Hotel Lobby Lounge,** 1401 S. Oak Knoll Ave., 626/577-2867, an elegant bar featuring live entertainment. On Sat., count on show tunes 8–9 P.M., swing tunes 9 P.M.–midnight.

Otherwise, best bars include **Delacey's Club 41,** 41 S. DeLacey (between Colorado and Green), 626/795-4141, a 1920s-style saloon that's enjoyable for drinks and conversation if you can snag one of the high-walled booths. **McCormick and Schmick's Seafood Restaurant,** 111 N. Los Robles (at Union), 626/405-0064, is noted for its gorgeous Arts and Crafts interiors but is more famous for its happy hour, serving excellent appetizers to well-dressed professionals and the not-so-well-dressed crowd from City Hall. The nearby **Holly Street Bar & Grill,** 175 E. Holly (at Arroyo Pkwy.), 626/440-1421, offers a quiet, grown-up atmosphere for a similar crowd. Not feeling grown up? Then the place is **Moose McGillicuddy's** at 119 E.

WACKINESS ON PARADE: THE OCCASIONAL DOO DAH PARADE

It seems that for every action in California there's a reaction. Such is the case with Pasadena's Occasional Doo Dah Parade, which began in the 1970s as an almost spontaneous spoof of the city's long-running Tournament of Roses Parade. With no rules, no theme, and no beauty queens—but at least a few drag queens, not to mention other unusual personas—the Doo Dah is the antithesis of the sober, sunny, all-American image at the heart of the Tournament of Roses. An all-time favorite at the Doo Dah Parade, for example, is the stiffly starched and suited Synchronized Briefcase Drill Team, though the West Hollywood Cheerleaders are also immensely popular. Another recent entry: the Snake Sisters' Frida Kahlo Dreadfully Painful Memorial Art Walk in Homage to her Creative Genius and Superfluous Hair.

Among musical entries, the beloved Lounge Lizards don reptile costumes to croon Frank Sinatra tunes. For the big band sound, count on Snotty Scotty and the Hankies; Dred Zeppelin does Led Zeppelin to a reggae beat. The almost memorable Boring Men's Club, now defunct, was a past crowd pleaser, but the BBQ and Hibachi Marching Grill Team has since filled in admirably.

As fun and funny as the Doo Dah Parade is, its atmosphere is irreverent, almost intentionally tasteless, slightly unwholesome, and a bit wild. If you're concerned about your children being exposed to such raw and rough-edged community creativity, don't bring them—and don't allow them access to a Southern California television set on parade day. Like the Rose Parade, the Doo Dah has become so popular that it's now televised.

Originally staged as a Jan. 1 alternative to the Tournament of Roses, the Occasional Doo Dah Parade is now scheduled for the Sunday before Thanksgiving; the parade route winds through Old Pasadena.

For more information about the Occasional Doo Dah Parade and to submit proposed entries, call **The Light-Bringer Project,** at 626/440-7379. The Light-Bringer Project, an umbrella community arts organization, sponsors a variety of other intriguing events throughout the year.

A PARKING STRATEGY FOR SHOPPERS

For shoppers long on time and short on cash, the free Pasadena Area Rapid Transit (ARTS) Bus connects the South Lake shopping district, where parking is free, with Old Pasadena, where it isn't. Look for the clearly marked bus stops along South Lake, Green St., and Colorado Boulevard. Buses run every 15 minutes.

Colorado Blvd. (at Arroyo Pkwy.), 626/304-9955, providing *Northern Exposure* atmosphere, cheap well drinks, $2 beers, and theme nights for those in college or those who wish they still were. The food menu here leans heavily toward burgers.

SHOPPING AS ENTERTAINMENT

Shopping Old Pasadena

Inveterate shoppers find historic Old Pasadena quite appealing these days, with city blocks full of antique and specialty stores, art galleries, restaurants, and coffeehouses.

Del Mano, 517 S. Lake Ave. (near California Blvd.), 626/793-6648, offers some of the finest American-made arts and crafts, jewelry, and textiles you'll ever see.

Distant Lands, 62 S. Raymond Ave., 626/449-3220, is a specialty bookstore stocking a wide selection of books and videotapes about travel, domestic and international, and an impressively well-informed proprietor.

A bit off the boulevard along Fair Oaks but well worth finding is **The Folk Tree,** 217 S. Fair Oaks Ave., 626/795-8733, a small shop filled with reasonably priced folk art, clothing, and religious artifacts from Mexico and Central America. To the rear is an excellent contemporary folk art gallery. Next door is **The Folk Tree Collection,** 199 S. Fair Oaks, 626/793-4828, with furnishings, folk art, clothing, textiles, beads, and slightly more expensive artifacts from around the globe.

Shopping South Lake

Since the departure of The Gap and Banana Republic for hipper digs in Old Pasadena, the bankruptcy of the neighborhood's I. Magnin department store, and the arrival of Ross Dress for Less,

Pasadena's upscale old-money South Lake shopping district has been suffering an identity crisis. Local merchants are fighting the good fight to win back their former cachet, however, and are making headway. Anchoring the South Lake shopping district is a 250,000-square-foot Macy's and several smaller but well-known stores, including **Talbot's, Ann Taylor, Eddie Bauer, Smith & Hawken,** and the enormous **Borders Books and Music Store,** 475 S. Lake Ave., 626/304-9773, which took over the long vacant I. Magnin building.

At the south end of the district is the **Rose Tree Cottage,** 828 E. California Blvd. (at Lake), 626/793-3337, a Tudor-style bungalow court that has been converted into several shops. Stop for tea and scones and shop for English imports. Wander through other cottages to find antiques, herbal body treats, and needlepoint.

Next door is **Wild Oats Market,** 824 E. California Blvd. (at Lake), 626/792-1778, an excellent full-service natural/organic foods grocery store, including a juice bar, an oil bar, and deli. This squeaky-clean store also stocks an extensive selection of books, homeopathic herbs and vitamins, and natural beauty products. You can even get a massage here.

BARGAIN SHOPPERS' BONANZA: RESALE GLAD RAGS

Fueled by consumer desires to save money on high-end, quality clothing, an increasingly popular trend in Pasadena's glad rags trade is resale or "gently worn" clothing shops for women, and, to a lesser degree, men and children. Well-to-do women who buy designer couture or upscale sportswear to attend various charity functions can't be seen in the same outfit too often, after all. Just plain folks can benefit from this social fact of life by buying top-quality but used clothing at a fraction of the original price.

Several resale boutiques in Old Pasadena, all within easy walking distance of each other, sell not just fancy ball gowns but casual clothing and accessories as well: **Clothes Heaven,** 110 E. Union, 626/440-0929; **Bailey's Designer Resale for Men,** 109 Union, 626/449-0201, and **Bailey's Backstreet for Women,** 93 E. Union, 626/449-4101; and **Silent Partners,** 99 E. Union, 626/793-6877.

PRACTICAL PASADENA

STAYING IN PASADENA

Luxury Hotels

Pulling up to the **Ritz-Carlton, Huntington Hotel** is like arriving at the Huntington family's estate for the weekend, or so one can imagine. Touches of a 19th-century sensibility are everywhere, including fresh flowers, Oriental carpets, and British hunt club–era artwork. The staid but plush guest rooms feature fine furnishings and overstuffed armchairs, large closets, refrigerated honor bars, and three telephones, with the modern distraction of television discreetly tucked away in the armoire. The all-marble bathrooms are similarly sedate yet up to date, with hair dryers and thick terrycloth robes.

Once arrived at the Huntington, you might be tempted never to leave. Aside from the Olympic-size pool—the original and California's first—the hotel offers tennis courts, a fine fitness and exercise center, even spa and salon services. The hotel's restaurants are also enticing, from the formal signature restaurant, **The Georgian Room,** and men's-clubbish **The Grill,** to more relaxed **The Cafe and Terrace** (wonderful Sunday brunch). Especially popular with traditional Pasadenans is the **Lobby Lounge** for afternoon tea.

With its convenient central Southern California location, just minutes by freeway to downtown L.A. or the San Fernando Valley film and TV studios, the Huntington does a brisk convention and "business" business—typically great news for pleasure travelers, since weekend packages and Christmas-season rates here can be a bargain. Another plus is the exceptional service. Stop at the concierge desk, for example, to request the Ritz-Carlton's very helpful "how to get there" cards, which cover every imaginable southstate destination. For more information contact: **The Ritz-Carlton, Huntington Hotel,** 1401 S. Oak Knoll Ave., 626/568-3900. To make reservations, in the U.S. call toll-free 800/241-3333, www.ritzcarlton.com. Luxury. Room rates: $310–410, suites $495–2,500.

If the Ritz is just a bit too ritzy, try the 12-story **Doubletree Hotel** downtown at 191 N. Los Robles (at Walnut), 626/792-2727 or toll-free for reser-

---

THE HUNTINGTON HOTEL

Albert Einstein once stayed here. So did Theodore Roosevelt, Prince Philip and Princess Anne, even cosmetics queen Elizabeth Arden.

First known as the Wentworth Hotel, the Huntington was named by Civil War general M. C. Wentworth, who built it in 1906. The earliest days of this Oak Knoll landmark were difficult. Even during Pasadena's resort hotel heyday, it closed within months of opening, still unfinished. Henry E. Huntington bought it in 1911, completed construction, and hired William Hertrich, who landscaped his San Marino estate, to design the 23-acre grounds—including the still-thriving Horseshoe and Japanese gardens—before the hotel reopened for business in 1914. Despite fairly frequent changes in ownership over the years, it's been the Huntington Hotel ever since.

That the Huntington Hotel, the last of Pasadena's grand resorts, exists at all today is something of a miracle. Most of the hotel was closed in the 1980s because of seismic safety concerns, and it looked as if the grand old lady of Pasadena had presided over her last society gala. Then came the endlessly patient and persistent Ritz-Carlton people, who first tried to satisfy local preservationists' demands for total historic preservation. That was not possible, as it turned out, since the main hotel building was structurally unsound. Ritz-Carlton delivered the next best thing—an astonishingly accurate new version of the hotel's turn-of-the-century self with every conceivable modern amenity somehow incorporated, open for business since 1991.

Southern Californians love the Huntington Hotel—a statement on par with observing that the sun sets over the Pacific Ocean. If one's pocketbook permits, this stunning hotel is *the* place to stay in Pasadena.

ACCOMMODATIONS RATINGS

Accommodations in this book are rated by price category, based on double-occupancy, high-season rates. Categories used are:

Budget. . . . . $35 and under
Inexpensive $35-60
Moderate $60-85
Expensive $85-110
Premium $110-150
Luxury . . . . $150 and up

vations 800/222-8733, www.doubletree. com, located in the heart of downtown Pasadena. Within walking distance of Old Pasadena, great restaurants, and downtown arts and entertainment, the Doubletree features 360 very attractive rooms and suites, airy and contemporary, complete with wood-shuttered windows. Also here: an on-site restaurant (a *feast* for Sunday brunch) plus heated pool, sauna and whirlpool, complete fitness center. Airport van service is provided. If you drive, valet parking is optional. To park yourself—and avoid the occasional traffic jam at the entrance—drive around the corner and cruise into the shared hotel/public parking lot (underground); once parked, find the elevator that pops up in the hotel's lobby. As elsewhere, suites are substantially more expensive than rooms. Premium-Luxury. Rates: $139–179.

Other Downtown Hotels
Popular with conventioneers, of course, is the **Holiday Inn Pasadena Convention Center Hotel** downtown, 303 E. Cordova St., 626/449-4000 or toll-free for reservations 800/238-8000. It's two blocks south of Colorado via Marengo, adjacent to the Pasadena Convention Center and Civic Auditorium and across the street from the Plaza Pasadena shopping mall. The usual, plus pool and tennis courts. Expensive-Premium. Rates: $79–139.

Nearby is the **Pasadena Hilton,** a high-rise near the Pasadena Convention Center at 150 S. Los Robles, 626/577-1000, www.hilton.com, also especially amenable for business travelers. For reservations at this and other Hilton hotels, call toll-free 800/445-8667 (AAA members, call 800/916-2221). Premium. Rates: $109–139.

The Artists' Inn and Cottage
Near South Pasadena's Mission West antiques district, on Magnolia St. between Meridian and Fairview, The Artists' Inn is an 1895 Midwestern Victorian, once the centerpiece of a poultry farm. The place is now dressed in more artistic ambience, reminiscent of a visit to the Huntington or the Norton Simon Museum. Each room reflects either an artistic period or an artist's work—the soft colors of the "Impressionist," for example, the three-dimensional replication of "Van Gogh's Bedroom," and the works by Gainsborough, Reynolds, and Constable in "Eighteenth Century English." In addition to the four rooms in the main house, there are five suites in the cottage, most with fireplaces and hot tubs. All have private baths. Breakfast, everything homemade, is up to you—either full breakfast or something light. For more information and to make reservations, contact: The Artists' Inn, 1038 Magnolia St., 626/799-5668 or toll-free 888/799-5668, www.artistsinns.com. Expensive-Luxury. Rates: $110–205.

More Moderate Accommodations
Lower-priced accommodations are farther away from downtown—though keep in mind that all area room rates typically skyrocket around Jan. 1, when the Tournament of Roses is in full bloom.

Among better motel bets is the **Best Western Pasadena Royale,** 3600 E. Colorado Blvd. (two blocks west of Rosemead Blvd.), 626/793-0950, near Pasadena City College and just about as close to the Huntington Library, et al. as to downtown Pasadena. All rooms have cable TV, free movies, refrigerators; amenities include swimming pool, sauna, and whirlpool. Minisuites and suites are also available. Moderate to Expensive. Rates: $65–129. Nearby is the **Best Western Pasadena Inn,** with similar amenities and rates, 3570 E. Colorado Blvd. (just west of Rosemead), 626/796-9100. Both offer free continental breakfast and free local calls. For reservations at either—or at the similarly priced **Best Western Colorado Inn** at 2156 E. Colorado Blvd., 626/793-9339—call toll-free 800/528-1234. And ask about special discounts. There's also a quite nice **Quality Inn** in the same general vicinity at 3321 E. Colorado (at Madre), 626/796-9291, with basic rooms from $69, deluxe rooms with hot tub from $129. Expensive-Premium. For good family lodging elsewhere, try the

Pasadena Inn, 400 S. Arroyo Pkwy. (near California), 626/795-8401, a clean 62-unit motel with reasonable rates and recently renovated. There's a pool here, plus a Thai seafood restaurant. Moderate-Premium. Rates: $65–119.

EATING IN PASADENA

It's difficult to get a bad meal in Pasadena. The city boasts more than 250 restaurants, many of these concentrated in the Old Pasadena and Lake Ave. shopping districts. While Pasadena is not yet as trendy as West Hollywood or L.A.'s Westside, it's working on it. By the time you arrive some newer restaurants may be long gone, like so many tumbleweeds tossed aside by the Santa Ana winds. Most eateries listed here have passed the test of time, but call first or otherwise scout out the scene to avoid disappointment.

Cheaper Eats: Lake Avenue and Vicinity
Tiny **Euro Pane Bakery,** 950 E. Colorado Blvd., 626/577-1828, is a beloved local bakery with just several tables—*the* place for scrumptious cinnamon rolls, scones, croissants, specialty breads, and some wicked desserts (like those lemon bars). For lunch, stop by for simple yet stylish sandwiches.

Brought to you by the Parkway Grill people (see below), the **Crocodile Café,** 140 S. Lake Ave. (near Green), 626/449-9900, is something of a "people's Spago." Low-rent foodies congregate here for salads, pastas, pizzas from wood-burning ovens, and oakwood-grilled seafood, chicken, and other entrées, all in a crazed California-casual atmosphere. (Snag a spot out on the much quieter patio if at all possible.) Pizzas and pastas are always good; the grilled chicken sandwich is excellent. Get here early, though, because it's always crowded (no reservations) and there's almost always a wait—maddening when you're weak from hunger and it all smells so *good.* Service can be uneven. Another Crocodile Café is in Old Pasadena, 626/568-9310. To wrestle other Crocodiles, head for Burbank or Santa Monica.

Burger Continental, 538 S. Lake Ave. (near California), 626/792-6634, is a zany hole-in-the-wall burger joint and student hangout, just the place for a bargain-basement meal after upscale shopping. Owner Harry Hindoyan has presided over this Pasadena institution for more than 30 years. The extensive menu features Armenian specialties like kebabs and rice pilaf and just about everything else you can imagine, including American standards; if you can't decide, Harry's happy to make suggestions.

Just off Lake Ave. is **Pie 'N Burger,** 913 E. California Blvd. (at Lake), 626/795-1123, another place socialites and Cal Tech students are destined to blend—as American as pecan pie, though the burgers, fries, and milkshakes are the aristocrats here.

Cheaper Eats: Old Pasadena and Vicinity
South Pasadena's Trader Joe's—the first and original—has closed, but in Pasadena proper you can still easily pull together an instant picnic or replenish the road food stash. **Trader Joe's,** 613 S. Arroyo Pkwy., 626/568-9254, is a bargain gourmet store designed to "cater to the overeducated and the underpaid," in the words of the successful chain's founder Joe Coulombe. If that category fits, seek and find cheese, nuts, coffees, fresh juices, baked goods, selected wines and beer, plus a host of all-natural quick foods and assorted oddball essentials.

A best bet for breakfast is the **Old Town Bakery & Deli,** 166 W. Colorado Blvd. (near S. Pasadena Ave.), 626/793-2993. If you consider breakfast a variation on dessert, here you can choose hazelnut meringue cake with caramel filling.

For astonishing Malaysian specialties, such as spicy sweet *sambal* shrimp, curried eggplant filets, *asam laksa* noodles, and *rojak,* travel to **Kuala Lumpur,** 69 W. Green (near Pasadena), 626/577-5175, a clean, well-lighted, unassuming place. Closed Mondays.

If you've seen it and done it in Northern California, you'll know what to expect at the **Gordon Biersch** brewpub, One Colorado (41 Hugus Alley), 626/449-0052. The upscale brew is the real draw, so most customers care less about the beer hall fare, not bad at all—and not that expensive—if you stick to what's simplest. Well-selected appetizers or salad with soup of the day might get you out the door with some change to spare.

Near the Civic Center
A hot spot for Sunday brunch is indoor-outdoor **The Oaks on the Plaza** at the Doubletree Hotel, 191 N. Los Robles (at Walnut), 626/792-2727, where a shamelessly generous buffet spread—10 stations in all, offering French pas-

tries and omelettes, prime rib and sushi—includes champagne.

For something a bit lighter, look for **California Pizza Kitchen** nearby, at 99 N. Robles (at Union), 626/585-9020, with trademark eclectic toppings. In between is a branch of **McCormick & Schmick's**, 111 N. Los Robles (at Union), 626/405-0064, specializing in seafood but most noteworthy for its painstaking interior design, paying homage to Pasadena's Craftsman craftsmanship.

The people's choice for seafood, by the way, is family-run "always boneless" **Cameron's**, out toward Pasadena City College at 1978 E. Colorado Blvd. (at Berkeley), 626/793-3474. At a gawdawful early hour every day the proprietors set out for Long Beach/San Pedro, where they eyeball the day's catch before personally toting the best back to the Crown City. Fish doesn't get much fresher than that.

Fine and Fashionable

Always-packed **Mi Piace** is a chic New York–style café in Old Pasadena, 25 E. Colorado Blvd. (near Raymond), 626/795-3131, an Italian eatery as popular for its making-the-scene scene as its pizzas, pastas, fine pastries, and tiramisu. With Ol' Blue Eyes belting out some boisterous tunes, it's a good choice for late supper or after-theater dessert and cappuccino.

If you want something different, check out **Arirang,** an upscale authentic Korean barbecue in Old Pasadena, 114 W. Union (at Delacey), 626/577-8885, where patrons sizzle exotic variations on the themes of chicken, beef, and shrimp on the tabletop *hwaro.*

Looking for red meat in Pasadena? Try the **Arroyo Chop House,** 536 S. Arroyo Pkwy., 626/577-7463, which serves thick slabs of USDA prime-cut Midwestern aged beef steaks, big martinis, and big cigars (the latter only on the patio). Chow down, too, on the best Texas-style chili—better than the legendary chili at L.A.'s legendary Chasen's ever was—and other steakhouse selections. Prices are high, but portions are generous.

Very Fine and Fashionable

In the let's-do-the-town department, for Pasadenans the **Parkway Grill,** 510 S. Arroyo Pkwy. (at California), 626/795-1001, is the best restaurant in town—very California. Even after a successful decade-long run, the Parkway still serves fresh, cutting-edge fare, beautifully presented. Sometimes called "Spago of the East" for its similar open-kitchen approach and specialty oak-grilled pizzas and applewood-smoked free-range chicken (from Sonoma, no less), the Parkway is actually better—easier to get into, for one thing, and less expensive to boot. Graceful wood, brick, and stained-glass decor and exceptional, friendly service make the best even better. Open for lunch and dinner daily (semiformal attire at dinner). Sunday brunch is quite the treat, too. Excellent wine list. Reservations advisable.

The art-deco **Bistro 45** near the Pasadena Playhouse at 45 S. Mentor Ave., 626/795-2478, is one of the classiest kids in town, a Californian with a French accent. If dishes such as pan-roasted New Zealand elk with syrah-garlic sauce and pearl onion-apple compote or free-range veal with herbs, bacon, and sun-dried cherry sauce neither frighten nor offend you, this is the place.

Cornered in an unlikely mini-mall in a mostly residential district is **Derek's Bistro,** 181 E. Glenarm (at Marengo), 626/799-5252, where the menu changes frequently to include the freshest available ingredients. A fixed-price four-course dinner features appetizer, entrée, chef's selection of cheese and fruit, and dessert. One day's entrée selection might include Thai shrimp cakes on spicy Asian slaw with a savory caramel sauce, rack of lamb, venison in red pepper sauce, and superbly grilled fish. Cozy rooms, patio dining, and elegant service add appeal to this gem.

Or, for French/Japanese cuisine, head for South Pasadena and **Shiro,** 1505 Mission St. (near Fair Oaks), 626/799-4774, one of the best restaurants in Southern California, a quirky 1950s place where the food is allowed to be the main attraction. Chef Hideo Yamashiro's changing menu is the foodies' holy grail, so make reservations at least one week in advance. Most diners opt for the delectable catfish, which is garlanded with cilantro and served in a light Ponzu sauce.

GETTING ORIENTED, GETTING AROUND

Getting More Information

The best all-around source for current information on what to see and do in and around Pasadena is the very helpful **Pasadena Convention and Visitors Bureau,** 171 S. Los Robles Ave., 626/795-9311, www.pasadenavisitor.org. For pamphlets, guides, and other information related to local architecture and historic preservation efforts, contact **Pasadena Heritage,** 80 W. Dayton St., 626/793-0617, www.pasadenaheritage.org. Pasadena Heritage also sponsors a variety of walking tours and intriguing special events throughout the year.

The **Pasadena Star-News,** www.pasadena starnews.com, is the city's paper of record, with its free weekly "Cheers" entertainment section available throughout Old Pasadena. The free **Pasadena Weekly,** www.pasadenaweekly.com, also provides arts, entertainment, and restaurant listings.

Getting Here by Freeway

Freeways converge on Pasadena. The main drag coming from the east or west is the **Foothill Freeway** (I-210), with exits gracefully dumping people right downtown. Coming in from the San Fernando Valley is the **Ventura Freeway** (Hwy. 134). The **Pasadena Freeway** ("the 110") rolls up out of Los Angeles and into South Pasadena via the somewhat narrow Arroyo Seco roadway. Yet another local piece of history and California's first freeway, the Pasadena was originally known as the Arroyo Seco Parkway and completed in 1941.

A major local battle for several generations has been the attempt to stop CalTrans from extending the **Long Beach Freeway** (I-710) through South Pasadena to connect the Foothill and San Bernardino Fwys.—an "improvement" that will doom about 1,000 historic homes and cut into South Pasadena once again. Cities such as Sierra Madre want the link-up to improve foothill traffic flow; South Pasadenans and most Pasadenans, naturally enough, think one freeway dissection per community is more than enough. Even if locals manage to beat the freeway-building bureaucracy over this one—and they have managed to so far, for well over 40 years, partially because of the fact that South Pasadena is home to so many lawyers—CalTrans long ago acquired the project right-of-way, alas, so most of the buildings standing in the way of progress have been all but destroyed by intentional neglect.

Getting Here Other than by Car

Just 20 minutes away from downtown Pasadena is the **Burbank/Glendale/Pasadena Airport,** served by commuter lines at least from most major West Coast carriers, and it's a much more attractive alternative, budget-wise, to LAX now that it's served by Southwest Airlines. Though major hotels and some motels provide free shuttle service to and from the airport, **SuperShuttle,** 310/782-6600, serves this and all other major

DESCANSO GARDENS

To Pasadena's northwest, on the way to Glendale and the film industry's true home in the San Fernando Valley, is La Cañada Flintridge and 165-acre Descanso Gardens, onetime Rancho del Descanso ("Ranch of Rest")—the estate of *Los Angeles Daily News* owner and publisher E. Manchester Boddy.

Most famous here are the camellias, more than 100,000 plants representing about 600 species—the largest cultivated collection in the world. After building his 22-room Georgian colonial home in the oak forest here, Boddy was dismayed to discover that not much would grow on the grounds because of the soil's high acidity. Consultations with horticulturist J. Howard Asper convinced Boddy to try growing camellias, which thrived under similar conditions in eastern Asia's mountain valleys. The rest, as they say, is history. To fully appreciate

the camellia bloom, plan to come from January into March.

Fairly new is Descanso's five-acre International Rosarium, with 5,000–7,000 rose species and varieties arranged by "theme," these including the fascinating historic rose specimens of the California Mission Garden and the interplanted wonders of the White Garden. These displays are most impressive in spring and summer. Descanso Gardens also features a Bird Observation Station, built in conjunction with the Audubon Society.

Descanso Gardens is just south of Foothill Blvd. at 1418 Descanso Dr., 818/952-4400, www.descanso.com, and open daily (except Christmas) 9 A.M.–5 P.M. Admission is $5 adults, $3 seniors and students, $1 for children ages 5–12 (under 5 free). Call for current information on guided tram tours ($2).

southstate airports. **Airport Bus,** 714/938-8900 or toll-free 800/772-5299, offers nonstop service from LAX and John Wayne Airport to Pasadena hotels, but not the Burbank airport. If your travel plans are complicated, **Prime Time Shuttle,** toll-free 800/262-7433, connects Pasadena to the local airport and LAX, with connections also to cruise ships and Amtrak. Approximate fares to Pasadena airports are $16 from hotels, $25 from residences (or $20 for AAA members).

Glendale, about seven miles from Pasadena, has **Amtrak** service, with two trains daily. For information and reservations, call Amtrak toll-free at 800/872-7245 or try www.amtrak.com. Though everyone will wait until at least 2010 for the **Blue Line** Metrorail commuter train to open its Pasadena line, major-league mass transit is coming.

To come and go by bus, the **Greyhound** station is downtown at 645 E. Walnut St., 626/792-5116. Rent cars at **Avis,** 570 N. Lake Ave., 626/449-6122. Of the two local **Budget** car rental agencies, 626/449-0226 or toll-free 800/527-0700, the 750 S. Arroyo Pkwy. office is closest to downtown.

Getting Around: Public Transit

The **MTA** bus system, which services Pasadena, has headquarters at 1 Gateway Plaza, Los Angeles; call 213/626-4455 or toll-free 800/266-6883, or try www.mta.net, for current route and fare information. In addition, Old Pasadena and the South Lake shopping district are linked by the visitor-friendly Pasadena ARTS Bus shuttle system.

INTO THE MOUNTAINS: ANGELES NATIONAL FOREST

Where the Glendale Freeway ends in La Cañada Flintridge is where the **Angeles Crest Highway** (Hwy. 2) begins, snaking its way into Angeles National Forest via a busy residential boulevard, then up through scrubby foothills, and finally up into pines, firs, and brisk, truly blue skies.

If you drive strictly to get somewhere, after about 50 miles you'll end up in **Wrightwood,** a cabin-clustered resort area on the other side of the mountains. If you're heading into the woods for a respite, bring lunch and/or camping gear. Picnic areas and first-come, first-served public campgrounds abound, albeit packed in summer. (On peak weekends, when the forest is literally overwhelmed by families fleeing city heat, officials block key roadways at 11 A.M. or earlier to avoid absolute gridlock.) About 28 miles from La Cañada Flintridge is the **Chilao Visitor Center,** 626/796-5541, open daily, a worthwhile stop to gather both information and environmental insight.

Avoid the crowds and come in later fall, winter, or early spring, when the air is cleaner and the dry hills exchange their warm-weather straw for a green coat capped by snow. In many areas of Angeles National Forest hiking and backpacking are best in late winter and early spring, a time when the Sierra Nevada and other major West Coast mountain ranges are still snowed in. But if you're looking for snow play in winter you'll find it here—if you can find a place to park—along with nearly everyone else in Southern California. Small, family-friendly ski areas are here: **Mount Waterman, Kratka Ridge,** with its quaint single-seat chairlift to reach more challenging runs, and **Ski Sunrise,** with its spectacular desert views.

Road conditions permitting, essential is the five-mile detour to the **Mount Wilson Observatory,** 626/440-1136, owned by the Carnegie Institution of Washington. The observatory was established here in 1904, and by 1917 became the center of the world's astronomical universe with the help of both a 60-inch and 100-inch telescopes and galaxies of great scientists. Since World War II after-dark Los Angeles has become one gigantic night-light, so Mount Wilson's view of the heavens has dimmed somewhat. Important astrophysical research continues, however, solar astronomy in particular. The museum is open weekends from 10 A.M.–4 P.M., free admission. Tours are available weekends at 1 P.M. There are no restaurants or food service at the observatory, so you might want to pack a picnic lunch.

For more information on the area, including locations of ranger stations and district offices, campgrounds, picnic areas, hiking trails, and other forest attractions, contact **Angeles National Forest Headquarters,** 701 N. Santa Anita Ave., 626/574-5200. Day-use fees are now charged throughout the forest, so inquire if you plan to do anything other than drive through.

NEAR PASADENA

SOUTH PASADENA

South Pasadena is *very* Pasadena, but separate, a tightly knit small town with fine homes, wide and well-shaded streets, and one of the best public school systems in Southern California. South Pasadena is also a favored setting for the film industry, often a stand-in for Midwestern suburbs. No wonder it's one of the region's most desirable residential neighborhoods, even on TV and in the movies. The Spielberg-produced *Little Giants* was filmed here, for example, along with *thirtysomething* and countless other TV shows and made-for-TV movies.

Not being a typical tourist destination makes South Pasadena that much more appealing for exploration. The **Rialto Theater,** 1023 Fair Oaks, 626/799-9567, is one of the few cavernous old movie theaters not yet ruined by modern subdivision into miniplexdom. Stop in to see first-run art films as they were meant to be seen, on a *big* screen—all very appealing to the casual but well-to-do artistic community that lives in the area. **Mission West,** which takes in the 900- and 1000-numbered blocks along Mission St., is an unusually appealing historic shopping district featuring antique and specialty stores, an art gallery, and beloved **Buster's Ice Cream & Coffee Stop,** 1006 Mission (at Meridian), 626/441-0744.

SAN MARINO AND "THE HUNTINGTON"

San Marino is an exceptionally high-rent residential area hacked from the holdings of famed local robber baron—ahem, railroad and real estate tycoon—Henry E. Huntington in the 1920s and 1930s. San Marino is so exclusive that it lives by its own lights. People here, for example, take a dim view of reckless behavior such as allowing motorists to make right turns after stopping at red lights downtown—otherwise legal in California. So in San Marino it's against the law; you'll get a ticket if you're caught. San Marino has also outlawed all bars.

Understated opulence, at least the appearance of California-style "old money," is the community's keynote. To observe still more staid, serene, wealthy Californians—their homes, at least—explore the neighborhoods surrounding what remains of the original Huntington Estate. Cruising well-lit **St. Albans Road** during the somewhat ostentatious Christmas season is almost the ultimate in reverse slumming.

For ladies who lunch, of particular note in San Marino is **Julienne,** 2649 Mission St. (at Los Robles), 626/441-2299, a favorite of Julia Child whenever she's in town. It's also a real gem for breakfast. Or, at the adjacent takeout store, pick up everything a food lover could want for a seat-of-the-pants picnic. The Huntington doesn't permit picnics, alas; the best picnicking place close by is **Lacy Park,** 1485 Virginia Rd, $3 entrance fee for nonresidents. Call city hall for information at 626/300-0700.

The Huntington Library

One of the world's great research libraries, the Huntington emphasizes British and American history, literature, and art from the 11th century to modern times. Collected here are about 3.1 million manuscripts, 357,000 rare books, 321,000 reference volumes, and thousands of prints, photographs, and miscellany.

Inside the **Library Exhibition Hall,** open to the general public, are some of the Huntington's treasures, including John James Audubon's *The Birds of America,* an exceptional collection of early editions of Shakespeare, a Gutenberg Bible (circa 1450–55), and the illuminated Ellesmere manuscript of Chaucer's *The Canterbury Tales* (circa 1410). Popular favorites include letters and works from early American leaders such as Benjamin Franklin, Thomas Jefferson, George Washington, and Abraham Lincoln, along with first editions and manuscripts of Thoreau, Twain, Blake, Shelley, Wordsworth, and other literary lights. In addition to the permanent display, several changing exhibits from the collection are presented every year.

Technically part of the Huntington's impressive art array, the four galleries of the **Arabella D. Huntington Memorial Collection** are housed in the library's west wing—with Renaissance paintings and 18th-century French sculpture, tapestries, furniture, and sundry accessories of the era's cultured life.

Huntington Art Collection: Huntington Gallery
Housed in the baronial Beaux Arts residence designed for the family in 1910 by Myron Hunt and Elmer Grey, the Huntington Gallery is ded-

---

RAILROAD AND REAL ESTATE SPECULATION: THE HUNTINGTON FORTUNE

Nephew of Collis P. Huntington—he, president of the Southern Pacific Railroad and one of the "Big Four" credited with linking California to the rest of the nation by rail—Henry Edwards Huntington failed, upon his uncle's death in 1900, in his bid to become chief engineer of the family's railroad empire. But the younger Huntington soon made his own fortune by linking Los Angeles–area mass transit with real estate speculation, a career move capitalized by the sale of his Southern Pacific stock.

Starting with the failed remnants of the Los Angeles and Pasadena Railroad electric trolley system, Huntington's new **Pacific Electric Company** got its big red trolleys rolling in 1901. By 1910, when Huntington stepped down as the company's chief engineer and, ironically, Southern Pacific took over, the Pacific Electric had successfully connected downtown Los Angeles to more than 50 far-flung communities throughout Southern California, the first step toward suburbanization—a development that tripled the region's population. Huntington also succeeded in making an obscene profit, since he typically ran new trolley lines only into areas owned by his real estate partnerships. (One fellow land speculator was Harrison Gray Otis, then-publisher of the *Los Angeles Times*. It was really no surprise, then, to see trolley-related home developments praised in the pages of the *Times*.)

Henry Huntington inherited about $40 million upon his uncle's death in 1900 and earned another $30 million through his own railroad and real estate deals. When in 1913 he married his uncle's widow and only other heir, Arabella, he further compounded his fortune—though some would argue that she had compounded hers.

---

icated largely to 18th- and early 19th-century British art. The collection's most famous paintings are in the Main Gallery: the 1770 *Blue Boy,* by William Gainsborough, and, facing, the 1794 *Pinkie,* a portrait of young Sarah Barrett Moulton by Thomas Lawrence. (Pinkie died of tuberculosis within months of the portrait's completion; her brother, who owned the painting, grew up to become Elizabeth Barrett Browning's father.) Beyond the abundant displays of historic portraiture there is much more to see, including the exquisite 1782 bronze sculpture *Diana* by Jean-Antoine Houdon and Wedgwood ceramics.

Changing exhibits in the Huntington Gallery typically feature a thematic twist on more obscure treasures, be they Rembrandt etchings or the wild, wild visions of William Blake.

Huntington Art Collection: Scott Gallery
If more fascinated by American adventures in arts and crafts, allocate extra time for the Virginia Steele Scott Gallery of American Art north of the Huntington Gallery (just beyond the Shakespeare garden). Most of the painting collection spans the two centuries from the 1730s. Gilbert Stuart's *George Washington* is surely the most familiar face in the Portrait Gallery. Don't miss the stunning *Breakfast in Bed* by Philadelphia-born Mary Cassatt, in the Nineteenth-Century Gallery, and, in the Twentieth-Century Gallery, *Reflections* by Frank Benson, along with Walt Kuhn's *The Top Man.* The Main Gallery offers a brief historical overview of American art.

A fairly recent addition—well worth your time—is the impressive exhibit honoring Pasadena's part in the turn-of-the-20th-century revolution in home design and woodworking craftsmanship, particularly the contributions of architects Charles and Henry Greene.

The **Greene & Greene Center for the Study of the Arts and Crafts Movement in America,** in the Dorothy Collins Brown wing of the Steele Gallery, includes both the exhibit and the Greene & Greene Library, originally established by the Gamble House and University of Southern California in 1968. The library is open by appointment only; for information call 626/405-2225.

The Huntington Botanical Gardens
The impression is that of a public park, with people wandering throughout these 120 landscaped

acres in aimless but thorough appreciation. Though the expansive, eclectic gardens are themed—Australian, Japanese, jungle, subtropical, palm, rose, camellia—the overall idea is still the acquisitiveness of empire-building, since Henry Huntington was first and foremost a pragmatist. Most of the 14,000 species collected here, including the Chilean wine palm, represent plant families Huntington believed would further boost Southern California real estate and agricultural development. Since Huntington's day, however, the emphasis has changed. International species preservation—protecting endangered plants from Madagascar, for example—is now a high priority.

Visitor favorites include the Rose Garden, with 1,800–2,000 species, the meditative Japanese and Zen Gardens, and the spectacularly exotic Desert Garden—the largest outdoor grouping of mature cacti and succulents in the United States, about 4,000 species—that doesn't resemble any desert landscape.

The Practical Huntington
Though the fourth central aspect of the Huntington is actually its international research program, most visitors will be more attracted to **The Huntington Bookstore** in the entrance pavilion. The Huntington is Southern California's oldest book publisher; the scholarly list is available here. Also for sale—proceeds help finance the Huntington and its programs—are general-interest books, guides, cards and postcards, and high-quality reproductions.

Admission to the Huntington is free, by decree of Henry E. Huntington himself. Since the Huntington needs to generate substantial private funding to keep the institution up and running, however, a "voluntary donation" of $8.50 for adults, $7 seniors, and $5 for children and students is suggested (children under 12 admitted free).

The Huntington, 1151 Oxford Rd. (between Orlando and Euston) in San Marino, is open Tues.–Fri. noon–4:30 P.M. and 10:30 A.M.–4:30 P.M. on weekends. In the summer months of June through Aug. hours are 10:30 A.M.–4:30 P.M. Tues.–Sun. The museum is closed Mon. and major holidays. For current information call 626/405-2141 or check www.huntington.org; to arrange a school group tour, call 626/405-2127.

Videotaping and informal still photography are permitted throughout, but tripods and flash bulbs/flash attachments are not allowed inside the buildings. Picnics are not permitted on the grounds but food and refreshments are available at the **Rose Garden Cafe and Tea Room,** 626/683-8131.

HIGHLAND PARK: EL ALISAL ET ALIA

To fully appreciate the contrast between the aristocratic and democratic visions of the Golden State's golden age, if you tour the Huntington you also must visit Arroyo Seco. Visitable remnants of Pasadena's arroyo-culture roots are cultivated in Highland Park, an aging dream garden made that much more romantic by the surrounding area's poverty. Latino gang turf in recent years, Highland Park near the following attractions is typically safe for tourists during daylight.

El Alisal
Sliding downslope toward L.A. via the Pasadena Fwy., your first Arroyo Seco stop along the ravine's lower reaches is El Alisal, striking arroyo-stone home of Charles Fletcher Lummis. Described by Kevin Starr as the Arroyo Seco's "prophet of place," the Harvard-educated writer and editor Lummis branched out to embrace a self-consciously Southwestern sense of style, with Native American basketry and blankets as necessary accessories. Both blatant booster and provincial protector of the Southern California good life, Lummis landscaped fortress-like El Alisal with palms, succulents, and other desert plantlife. Also here: original and period furnishings, historical displays, photographs, and publications. Note the fireplace, designed by Mount Rushmore sculptor Gutzon Borglum.

Since the building also serves as headquarters of the **Historical Society of Southern California,** Lummis House docents are quite helpful, as are the books, periodicals, and pamphlets available here. El Alisal, 200 E. Ave. 43 (at Carlota Blvd.), 323/222-0546, is open only Fri.–Sun. noon–4 P.M. Free, though donations are greatly appreciated. Group tours are scheduled on Fri., by reservation only. To get here, from the Pasadena (110) Fwy. exit at Ave. 43, head east, and turn onto Carlota. Off-street parking is available near the entrance.

The Southwest Museum

Halfway up Mt. Washington, whose upper reaches are still home to a community of writers and artists, is another of Charles Fletcher Lummis's pet projects—the striking mission revival-style Southwest Museum. Opened in 1914, the Southwest is Southern California's finest collection of Native Americana, with art and artifacts presented in galleries on California, the Southwest, the Pacific Northwest, the Great Plains, and Northern Mexico. Though many aspects of the museum are renowned nationally and internationally, the Southwest's California basketry collection is particularly astonishing—the more so now that this art is all but lost. Proceeds from the gift shop help support the museum, its programs, and the maintenance of its treasures.

The Southwest Museum is just up the hill from El Alisal at 234 Museum Dr., 323/221-2164, www.southwestmuseum.org, open Tues.–Sun. 10 A.M.–5 P.M. (closed on major holidays). Admission is $5 adults, $3 seniors and students, $2 children ages 7–17 (under 7 free). If you happen to find yourself downtown near the Los Angeles County Museum of Art (LACMA), also see Southwest Museum exhibits at its **LACMA West** outpost.

Casa de Adobe, operated under Southwest's auspices nearby in Sycamore Grove Park, 4605 N. Figueroa St., 323/225-8653, was designed by Theodore Eisen and built in 1917, Eisen's imaginative representation of a Mexican-era rancho. At last report the Casa was closed for seismic retrofitting; call for current details.

If so much Southwestern exposure makes you hungry for a Mexican meal, been-there-forever **La Abeja** near the museum at 3700 Figueroa, 323/221-0474, serves the real thing, real cheap.

Heritage Square

If you do save historic structures from the wrecking ball of progress in Los Angeles, then the buildings have to go *somewhere.* One of those places is here in Heritage Square, just across the freeway from El Alisal et al. at 3800 Homer St. (off Ave. 43), where vanishing architectural species from the years 1865–1914 are penned up inside chain-link fencing. Most instantly impressive is the 1885 **Hale House,** with its wildly authentic color schemes. To get an idea of the ingenuity and determination it takes to move a building across the Los Angeles basin, study the **Palms Depot** photo documentary. Heritage Square is open to the public 11:30 A.M.–4:30

ARROYO CULTURE

In contrast to the Huntingtons' approach—the acquisition of European and East Coast perspective and style—arroyo culture found beauty in its own backyard, truth in transformative life lived at the edge of the vanishing western wilderness. In and around Pasadena's Arroyo Seco, a nativistic variant of the Arts and Crafts philosophy took root and flourished—the genesis of the Greene brothers' architectural creations for local gentry.

But arroyo culture did not concern itself with traditional notions of the genteel. Gentility, here, was a work in progress—"the spiritualization of daily life through an aestheticism tied to crafts and local materials," in the words of historian Kevin Starr, and "of pure, simple, democratic art," according to transplanted English preacher George Wharton James.

Arroyo Seco's aesthetic was most strikingly rendered in untamed, distinctly Southern California–style

craftsmanship in woodworking, metallurgy, and stone masonry, tile, pottery, and jewelry making. The Arroyo Seco's hands-on idealism was such a powerful philosophical influence in turn-of-the-20th-century California that both the local Throop Polytechnic Institute (forerunner of the much more theory-based California Institute of Technology) and Stanford University near San Francisco included crafts instruction as curriculum basics.

Bookishness, though, was more important, literature being the Arroyo Seco's most democratic art. Literary lights published by Charles Fletcher Lummis in his *Land of Sunshine* magazine included Jack London, Frank Norris, Robinson Jeffers, and Mary Austin—all of whom had moved on by the time Lummis died of a brain tumor at El Alisal in 1929, clutching the page proofs of *Flowers of Our Lost Romance,* his "best of" collection of essays.

P.M. on Sat., Sun., and most holidays, with tours typically offered every 45 minutes. Park inside the chain-link fence. Admission is $5 adults, $3 seniors and children 13–17, $2 children 7–12. But kick in more, if you can, because the Cultural Heritage Foundation of Southern California, Inc., 626/449-0193, can use all the help it can get.

THE ARBORETUM OF LOS ANGELES COUNTY

The Arboretum of Los Angeles County is the 127-acre remnant of Elias J. "Lucky" Baldwin's original 46,000 acres, bought in 1875, which soon became "Arcadia," a speculative real estate venture that rivaled any of land barons Henry Huntington and Harry Chandler. Chandler, in fact, bought and developed Baldwin's estate in 1936, minus this parcel.

Though the smog here is sometimes so thick one wonders how any plants survive, they do— and most of the 4,000 species represented seem to thrive. Historic on-site buildings include the 1840 Hugo Reid Adobe and the old Santa Anita Depot, a transportation boon that made millions for Lucky Baldwin. Baldwin's personal flamboyance lives on, too, in this patch of Arcadia, most notably in the fine frilly white Queen Anne "cottage" and outbuildings designed by architect A. A. Bennett, more famous for the state Capitol in Sacramento and Riverside's Mission Inn.

The Arboretum of Los Angeles County is just off the Foothill Fwy. (I-210) in Arcadia, at 301 N. Baldwin Avenue. Admission is $5 adults, $1 children ages 5–12 (under 5 free). Tram service is $2 per person until 3 P.M. For information on current hours and upcoming special events, call 626/821-3222, or check www.arboretum.org.

SANTA ANITA PARK

Horse ranching was once big business in these parts, so stumbling upon the illustrious Santa Anita racetrack out in the suburbs really isn't so strange. The original track, near here, was built by Lucky Baldwin in 1907, but Santa Anita as a public event got its start in 1934 as the vision of onetime minor league second baseman and credit dentist Charles H. "Doc" Strub. Snubbed by San Francisco, Strub sent his dream south. He gained the support of movie producer Hal Roach and, at a time when a loaf of bread cost a nickel, Strub spent the shocking sum of $1 million to build the grandest horse racing palace of them all. He stunned the racing world again by announcing Santa Anita's first-day $100,000 handicap. From the start Santa Anita attracted the best horses and riders, along with socialites, movie stars, and Depression-fatigued families, transforming the grifter's game into something respectable.

Santa Anita is still quite the scene, despite endless competition for Southern California's attention. The elite meet and greet in the private Turf Club upstairs. Best bet for just plain folks to fully appreciate horse racing's star qualities is near the valet parking booth, listening to the announcer rattle off the names of the rich and famous as their limos jockey for position. But even from the cheap seats you'll get a full-on view of the astonishing shadow-sculpted Sierra Madre just beyond the track.

Thoroughbred horse racing is a year-round event in California, the season at each track dictated both by climate and tradition. The race crowd is typically "back to the track" at Santa Anita by Christmas, and the season runs through April. The Oak Tree Racing Association also sponsors a month-long meet from early October into November. Admission is $4 (free for children under 17), parking $3. Post time is usually 12:30 or 1 P.M.

Santa Anita Park is just off the Foothill Fwy. (I-210) between Baldwin Ave. and Colorado Pl. (off Colorado St.); the entrance is at 285 W. Huntington Dr. at Colorado, in Arcadia. For more information, call the affiliated **Los Angeles Turf Club** at 626/574-7223, www.santaanita.com.

TOWARD THE DESERT: THE INLAND EMPIRE

Boosterism, that brand of civic self-promotion aimed at boosting local business, built contemporary Southern California. All but passé in Los Angeles, that philosophy is still embraced, unabashedly, in California's "Inland Empire" counties of San Bernardino and Riverside—the settlement bridge between the vastness of both L.A. and the California deserts.

Rivals in many ways, in at least one sense both the cities of Riverside and San Bernardino are absolutely in step. As society marches on, so do the suburbs—shimmering, mirage-like waves of vaguely Spanish-style red tile roofs stretching toward all horizons, threatening to landscape the desert with smog and other decidedly urban concerns.

RIVERSIDE: NAVEL OF THE INLAND EMPIRE

Riverside is home to the surviving Mother Tree—actually, Parent Tree—for much of the world's supply of seedless oranges now known as Washington navels, named for the characteristic "belly-button." Mother of California's orange industry—and, in a sense, mother of the Southern California myth—was Eliza Tibbets, who in 1873 planted the first two U.S. "bud sports" (mutant bud stock) of the Selecta orange that originated in Bahia, Brazil. The trees flourished, and the fruit was clearly superior to any other commercial orange variety of the day—in size, appearance, texture, and flavor. The fact that navel oranges were also seedless further enhanced their prospects as popular table fruit. Mother Tibbets's orange was originally christened the Riverside navel by the U.S. Department of Agriculture, but other Southern California citrus growers objected, vehemently, and campaigned for a name of more "national" scope. Thus navel oranges—and all their descendants—were named after the nation's father, George Washington.

One of the original two trees was acquired by Frank A. Miller, founder of the famed Mission Inn. With the hands-on assistance of President Teddy Roosevelt, Miller transplanted it to the inn's courtyard on May 8, 1903. That tree died in 1921, however, and was replaced by an 11-year-old descendant.

Ownership of Eliza Tibbets's surviving sport reverted to the city of Riverside in 1902, and the tree was transplanted to its current home on the corner of Arlington and Magnolia (across from the southeast corner of the Tibbets homestead). With help from a horticultural technique called "inarching," Riverside's **Parent Navel Orange Tree** has been revivified with new roots at least three times since.

For more information about regional attractions, special events, and practicalities, contact the **Riverside Visitor Center,** 3660 Mission Inn Ave. (Mission Inn Ave. and Main), 909/684-4636, www.riverside-chamber.com, or the **Riverside Convention Bureau** inside the convention

The Mission Inn started out as a clapboard-covered adobe.

KIM WEIR

91

60

MAIN ST.

215

ST.

SEE DETAIL

BUENA VISTA AVE.

River

ST.

MISSION BLVD.

MISSION INN AVE.

7TH

UNIVERSITY

AVE.

MT. RUBIDOUX DR.

9TH

MARKET

ST.

Mt. Rubidoux

14TH ST.

VINE ST.

Santa Ana

UNIVERSITY OF
CALIFORNIA AT
RIVERSIDE

★ UCR
BOTANICAL
GARDENS

To March
Field Museum

RIVERSIDE

MAGNOLIA

91

AVE.

Gage

Canal

PARENT NAVEL
ORANGE TREE ★

ARLINGTON AVE.

MADISON

ST.

HERITAGE
HOUSE ★

JEFFERSON

ST.

MAGNOLIA AVE.

ADAMS

ST.

91

0   0.75 mi

0   0.75 km

DUFFERIN AVE.

VANBUREN BLVD.

**California Citrus
State Historic Park**

Mockingbird
Canyon Lake

DETAIL

RAINCROSS SQUARE
CONVENTION CENTER ■

91

MAIN
STREET
PEDESTRIAN
MALL

ST.

ST.

ST.

AVE.

RIVERSIDE ART
MUSEUM
■ ★

FOX
THEATER ■

MISSION
INN ★

■ MUNICIPAL
AUDITORIUM

SANTA FE
RR DEPOT

RIVERSIDE
VISITOR CENTER ■

7TH ST.

★ RIVERSIDE
MUNICIPAL
MUSEUM

UNION
PACIFIC RR
DEPOT

UNIVERSITY   AVE.

SANTA FE

9TH

ST.

★ UCR MUSEUM OF
PHOTOGRAPHY

ST.

■ CITY HALL

MARKET

MAIN ST.

ORANGE

LEMON

LIME

VINE

SANTA FE

ST.

© AVALON TRAVEL PUBLISHING, INC.

center at 3443 Orange St., 909/222-4700 or toll-free 888/748-7733, www.riversidecb.com.

Seeing and Doing Riverside

Exploring the courtyards and labyrinthine byways of Riverside's famed **Mission Inn**, with its baroque arches, bell towers, and buttresses, endless odd angles, and occasional stairways to nowhere, is something like strolling through a three-dimensional M. C. Escher sketch. Finetune the mental picture by imagining the hotel's illustrious guests—presidents, kings, queens, and 20th-century celebrities, including Sarah Bernhardt, Booker T. Washington, Amelia Earhart, Humphrey Bogart, and Rin Tin Tin. The Carnegies, Rockefellers, Fords, Huntingtons, and other turn-of-the-20th-century industrialists considered the Mission Inn their personal West Coast retreat. Richard and Pat Nixon got married here (in the Presidential Suite, no less), as did Ronald and Nancy Reagan, who honeymooned here. John Steinbeck finished at least one of his novels here. And Will Rogers called the Mission Inn "the most unique hotel in America." So Southern Californians cheered the news that this grand old hotel, a national historic landmark, would reopen, finally, in the 1990s, after a $50 million facelift. For more information about the hotel and its attractions, contact: The Mission Inn, 3649 Mission Inn Ave., Riverside, CA 92501, 909/784-0300 or toll-free 800/843-7755 for reservations, www.missioninn.com.

Most of Riverside's historic sites and structures lie within the original one-square-mile downtown district along the Santa Ana River designated as "Riverside" by early orange growers of the Southern California Colony Association. Notable throughout downtown are Riverside's "raincross" street lamps—framed Spanish mission bells crowned by the double-armed Navajo raincross, a romantic marriage of mission and Indian history. Many noteworthy buildings are concentrated within several blocks of Mission Inn Ave. (7th Street). Across from the Mission Inn is the **Riverside Municipal Museum,** 3580 Mission Inn Ave. (at Orange), 909/782-5273, where the emphasis is on anthropology, history, and natural history. Another cultural and architectural find is the **Riverside Art Museum,** 3425 Mission Inn Ave. (at Lime), 909/684-7111, housed in the 1929 Young Women's Christian Associa-

tion (YWCA) building designed by noted California architect Julia Morgan. Next door (at Lemon) is the **Municipal Auditorium,** designed by Arthur Benton and G. Stanley Wilson, built in the late 1920s, and principal venue for the Riverside County Philharmonic.

Worth the trip from downtown is **Heritage House,** 8193 Magnolia Ave., 909/689-1333, just blocks beyond the Parent Navel Orange Tree, open for tours from Sept. through June (call for details). This outpost of Riverside's Victorian past is a special project of the Riverside Municipal Museum and one of the most authentic "museum houses" in California. Then there's **California Citrus State Historic Park,** 909/352-4098, carved into the remaining navel orchards and palm-lined old promenades of Riverside's Arlington Heights area—perfect for picnics or as a peaceful respite from freeway travel. To get here from the Riverside (91) Fwy., exit at Van Buren Blvd. and head south, just over a mile, to Dufferin Ave., then turn left. A giant orange marks the spot.

SAN BERNARDINO: BIRTHPLACE OF MCDONALD'S

Now a sprawling desert city of some 65 square miles, stretched out between old Route 66 and the Santa Ana River and invisibly sliced by the San Andreas Fault, San Bernardino was first an outpost of Mission San Gabriel and then settled, in the 1850s, by Mormons. This 4,000-acre spread, the state's first significant "irrigation colony," was once home to legendary lawman Wyatt Earp. In modern times San Bernardino is noteworthy as birthplace of both the Hell's Angels motorcycle club and the McDonald's fast-food restaurant chain.

For current information on San Bernardino and vicinity, contact the **San Bernardino Convention and Visitors Bureau,** downtown at 201 N. E St., Ste. 103, San Bernardino, CA 92401, 909/889-5998 or toll-free 800/867-8366. At last report, the visitors bureau also handled scheduling for guided **Redlands Historical Tours.** For a copy of the self-guided **Historic Redlands Driving Tour,** contact the **Redlands Chamber of Commerce** office (weekdays only) at 1 E. Redlands Blvd., 909/793-2546.

Seeing and Doing
San Bernardino and Vicinity

Golden arches and other fast fooderies now span the globe, but it all started here at the original McDonald Brothers restaurant downtown at 14th and E Streets. In the 1940s Maurice and Richard McDonald decided to phase out their carhops and offer "fast food." (A burger cost $.15, fries $.10, both promised within 20 seconds.) Ray Kroc, then based in the Midwest, worked as a milkshake machine salesman. To find out why the McDonald brothers bought so many machines, Kroc went west—and was so smitten with the concept that he bought the business in 1961, paying the McDonald brothers the then-princely sum of $1 million each. The rest is fast food history. And though the original McDonald Brothers restaurant is long-gone, since December 1998 a new facsimile McDonald's—a veritable museum—has stood in its place.

More fascinating, though, is natural history—particularly San Bernardino's prehistoric **Arrowhead,** emblazoned into a hillside six miles northeast

California Theatre, San Bernardino

ROBERT HOLMES/CALTOUR

of town near the original Arrowhead Hot Springs Hotel (now a Christian conference center). The Arrowhead measures 1,115 feet long and 396 feet wide, totaling about seven acres in size. Made of light gray granite and decomposed white quartz with a vegetative veneer of white sage and weeds, the Arrowhead is quite distinct from both surrounding geology and adjacent greasewood chaparral. Though the Cahuilla and other native peoples tell various stories to explain its creation, scientists speculate that the Arrowhead was created by water. Given the unusually thin soil layer, an unusually powerful cloudburst was all it took.

Downtown San Bernardino is renovating and revitalizing. If you have extra time, take a look around. But in many ways the San Bernardino area is more event than destination—a truism illustrated every spring when Southern California's **Renaissance Pleasure Faire** convenes at **Glen Helen Regional Park.** For current information and advance discount ticket sales (slightly cheaper), call toll-free 800/523-2473 or go to www.ren fair.com.

Generally more evocative of regional history, though, is **Redlands** just to the east, where the biggest thing going is the **San Bernardino County Museum,** 2024 Orange Tree Ln., 909/798-8570, a three-story parade of natural history, history, and art, including a hands-on "discovery hall" for children. Home to the only Lincoln memorial west of the Mississippi, the **Lincoln Memorial Shrine,** Redlands is also known for its exquisite Victorian neighborhoods. One of the most celebrated Victorian personalities is the 1897 **Kimberly Crest House and Gardens,** 1325 Prospect Dr., 909/792-2111, onetime family home of the Kimberly half of the Kimberly-Clark Corporation. It's closed during the suffocating month of August, but otherwise open for tours Thurs.–Sun. 1–4 P.M. (small admission). To tour more Victoriana—and the city boasts more than 300 citrus-era mansions—pick up the **Historic Redlands Driving Tour.**

INTO THE MOUNTAINS: BIG BEAR AND VICINITY

Big Bear Reclaims Its Bears

Fairly big news in Big Bear recently was big bears—grizzly bears. California hasn't had any grizzly bears, except on the state flag, since early settlers and hunters hounded the state's native species into extinction nearly a century ago. But grizzlies have returned to Big Bear, the result of this mountain resort community's all-out campaign to save a few Montana misfits from the death penalty. Big Bear's new bears—a mama grizzly with a lengthy federal rap sheet, plus the two cubs she has already led astray—had been on death row in Seattle pending the availability of a permanent bear-proof prison. In early 1996, Big Bear fundraising raised the $55,000 needed to build an appropriate den here.

There's more to Big Bear than bears, of course. Built around man-made Big Bear Lake high in the San Bernardino Mountains, this is a popular year-round L.A. getaway—a pine-scented village surrounded by vacation cabins and tall trees. Active diversions include downhill and cross-country skiing in winter and, in summer, swimming, fishing, horseback riding, hayrides, even carriage rides. For inveterate shoppers, Bear Valley has a dozen or so antique shops. There are also outdoor attractions, including **Big Bear Jeep Tours,** 909/878-5337.

Events and performances are scheduled year-round, but the biggest big deal is the two-week-long celebration of **Old Miners Days** in July, with everything from burro races and barbecues to log-rolling contests. For more information about Big Bear and vicinity, contact: **Big Bear Resort Association,** 630 Bartlett Rd., Big Bear Lake, CA 92315, toll-free 800/424-4232, www.bigbearinfo.com, also a visitor reservation service.

San Bernardino National Forest

With more than 810,000 acres, all within easy reach of greater Los Angeles, San Bernardino National Forest attracts more than six million visitors every year—earning it greater popularity, by the numbers, than any other national forest. Popular Southern California mountain resort areas, including Big Bear Lake and Lake Arrowhead, are included in the forest's northern section. For more detailed information and necessary wilderness permits, contact: San Bernardino National Forest headquarters, 1824 S. Commerce Center Circle, San Bernardino, CA 92408, 909/383-5588, www.r5.fs.fed.us/sanbernardino.

TOM MYERS PHOTOGRAPHY

DOWNTOWN
AND AROUND

With all due respect to Dorothy Parker and her historic quip about Los Angeles being "seventy-two suburbs in search of a city," these days there *is* a city here, even a downtown. Skyscrapers and a maze of frantic freeways have all but overshadowed its humble origins. Downtown Los Angeles was all of Los Angeles in the late 18th century, when this scruffy adobe outpost of Spanish empire was plopped down along the banks of the lazy Los Angeles River. Downtown Los Angeles today has that contemporary American look, with its dark, windy canyons of glass and steel surrounded, and intruded upon, by abject poverty. On weekdays scores of suits scurry along sidewalks going about the business of business. On weekends and after closing time, corporations close up shop and the heart of L.A. beats faster with the more exciting rhythms of performance art and panhandling.

City sans Suburbia

The city's long-running effort to revitalize downtown, to lure Angelenos back to this self-consciously contemporary "urban village" designed for shopping and other entertainments, has resulted in new luxury apartments and condominiums, trendy shops, new movie theaters, and restaurants. Residential buildings near the freeways boast signs of the times: "If You Lived Here You Would Be Home Now." But if you really lived in downtown Los Angeles you'd most likely either be homeless or a hopeless workaholic. In fact, in the shadows of towering office buildings, a group of 21 10-foot by 10-foot fiberglass domes that resemble golf balls make up **Dome Village,** providing transitional housing for the homeless outside the confines of traditional shelters and unsightly encampments.

A notable redevelopment focal point for visitors is 133-acre Bunker Hill, a once-funky neighborhood of grand but faded Victorians home to the urban poor before the houses were bulldozed to make way for upscale apartments and interconnected cultural attractions that now form an identifiable metropolitan center for Los Angeles. Pedestrian-friendly stairways, walkways,

GETTING UP TO SPEED DOWNTOWN

To get up to speed downtown, stop by or contact the **Los Angeles Convention and Visitors Bureau Downtown Visitor Center,** 685 S. Figueroa St. (between Wilshire Blvd. and 7th St.), 213/689-8822 or toll-free 800/228-2452, www.lacvb.com, open for walk-in assistance weekdays 8 A.M.–5 P.M. and Sat. 8:30 A.M.–5 P.M.

Another help in understanding what's up downtown is the Los Angeles Conservancy, www.laconservancy.org, which offers inexpensive and informative walking tours designed to interpret L.A.'s past, present, and future. The group offers 11 regular tours—in addition to occasional special tours—emphasizing historic areas and structures. These include **Little Tokyo, Pershing Square Landmarks,** and **Angeleno Heights** as well as **Union Station, Art Deco,** and other landmark buildings. The **Broadway Theaters** tour, which allows visitors inside some of L.A.'s grand old movie theaters, is one of the Conservancy's most popular.

The general Conservancy tour fee is $8. All tours, typically one or two hours, start Sat. at 10 A.M. Reservations are required. The Art Deco, Broadway Theaters, and Pershing Square Landmarks tours are offered every Saturday. Others—including the Biltmore Hotel, Union Station, Little Tokyo, Terra Cotta, and Palaces of Finance, in addition to miscellaneous special tours—are offered on a regular rotating schedule. No tours are offered on Thanksgiving, Christmas, or New Year's Day. For more information, contact: **Los Angeles Conservancy Tours,** 523 W. 6th St., Ste. 1216, 213/623-2489 or 213/430-4211 (event hot line), www.laconservancy.org.

and the newly refurbished Angels Flight railway link major destinations, the city's Central Library, the Museum of Contemporary Art, the Biltmore Hotel, and Pershing Square Park among them. Just blocks away are more local landmarks, including the Bradbury Building and the grand Grand Central Market.

Discovering Downtown

Downtown's slice of L.A. life is defined by tangled freeway angles and a jumble of zeros and ones—an area triangling both south and east from the junction of the Hollywood/Santa Ana Fwy. (Hwy. 101) and the Harbor/Pasadena Fwy. (the 110) in the north and, in the west, east from the junction of the Santa Monica (I-10) and the Harbor Freeways. As downtown trails off vaguely into a vast, seemingly abandoned warehouse district, its eastern "border" is established absolutely by the Los Angeles River, the unofficial boundary with East L.A., but perhaps more realistically by the railroad tracks along Alameda Street.

Most downtown attractions are concentrated in a much smaller area, however, within walking distance of the Los Angeles Civic Center—the largest government center outside Washington, D.C., they say—and the three-theater Performing Arts Center of L.A. County, formerly known as the Music Center. To the southwest, right next to the Museum of Contemporary Art (MOCA) is the new campus of the Colburn School of Performing Arts, a 55,000-square-foot facility complete with 420-seat chamber music hall. Other major downtown attractions include MOCA, the affiliated "Temporary Contemporary"—now a reasonably permanent fixture known as The Geffen Contemporary at MOCA—and the Museum of Neon Art.

Other notable landmarks beneath downtown's canopy of skyscrapers include the Los Angeles Public Library, also known as the Central Library; Los Angeles City Hall (a.k.a. *The Daily Planet* headquarters in the *Superman* TV series); the Bradbury Building; and Broadway's historic movie theaters. Broadway itself has become an attraction, the busiest Latino shopping district west of Chicago.

Well east of Broadway, near 3rd St. and Central Ave., is Little Tokyo, a busy Japanese-American cultural and shopping district. Other commercial downtown attractions include the Grand Central Market, the Flower Market (one of the nation's largest wholesale outlets), and the equally impressive Fashion District (formerly known as the Garment District). And if you're in town for a major convention—sometimes including national political conventions—the odds are you'll know your way around the ever-growing Los Angeles Convention Center, just off the Harbor Fwy. north of the Santa Monica Freeway. Brand new downtown, on Figueroa adjacent to the convention center, is the Staples Center, home court to the L.A. Lakers and

DOWNTOWN'S DASHING DASH

If planning an impromptu self-guided tour, keep in mind that getting around downtown sans car is fairly easy, at least during the day, thanks to the city's Downtown Area Shuttle Hop or **DASH minibuses**, 213/808-2273 or toll-free 800/266-6883, www.ladottransit.com. On weekends these magenta and silver buses loop through the area and stop every two or three blocks, connecting the Flower Market and Fashion District with the Financial District, Exposition Park, and various Metrorail stations. Looping north, DASH runs from the Central Library to the Grand Central Market, Little Tokyo, City Hall, Union Station, Olvera Street, Chinatown, and the Music Center. Fare is $.25 per "hop," no matter how far it takes you, which is a great deal no matter how you add it up. Weekday routes are different. Call or see the website for current route details.

And L.A.'s DASH shuttles now roam considerably farther afield—to Hollywood, Northridge, even Venice (summer only). For details, try the website or call 213, 310, 323, or 818/808-2273.

L.A. Clippers NBA teams, the L.A. Kings ice hockey franchise, and the L.A. Avengers Arena Football League team.

But the historic heart and soul of Los Angeles is just north of the downtown stretch of the Santa Ana Fwy. (Hwy. 101)—in tourist-friendly El Pueblo de Los Angeles, a historic district commemorating the city's official birth in 1781. Just east of El Pueblo is Union Station, L.A.'s grand art-deco train station and new central metropolitan transportation hub. Just north of El Pueblo is "New" Chinatown—as opposed, historically, to Old Chinatown, which was razed in the 1930s to make way for Union Station. Farther north—beyond the 110—is Elysian Park and beloved Dodger Stadium, where the L.A. Dodgers still star as the local boys of summer.

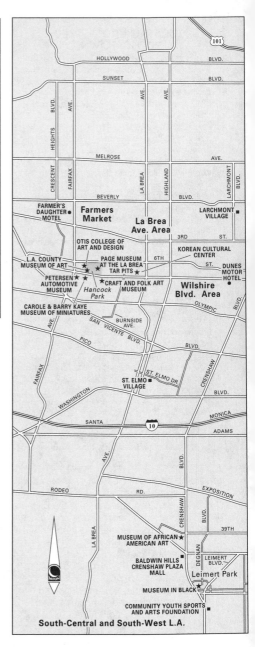

South-Central and South-West L.A.

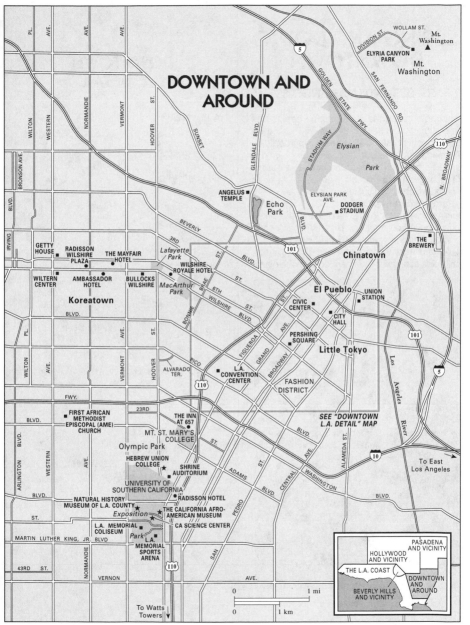

DOWNTOWN AND AROUND

© AVALON TRAVEL PUBLISHING, INC.

SEEING AND DOING DOWNTOWN

EL PUEBLO DE LOS ANGELES

Commemorating the city's humble beginnings at the junction of several worlds, **El Pueblo de Los Angeles Historic Monument** is bordered by Alameda, Arcadia, Ord, and Spring Sts.—and is situated somewhere near the city's birthplace. (The original 1781 pueblo was lost in 1815 to floods, which forced settlers to scramble to higher ground northwest of town.) Included within this 44-acre historic district are some of the oldest buildings in Los Angeles. The city's namesake church, finally completed by the Franciscans in 1822 and known today as the Old Plaza Church, still holds court on the northern edge of the plaza,

ROBERT HOLMES/CALTOUR

skyscraper with part of Alexander Calder's
Four Arches

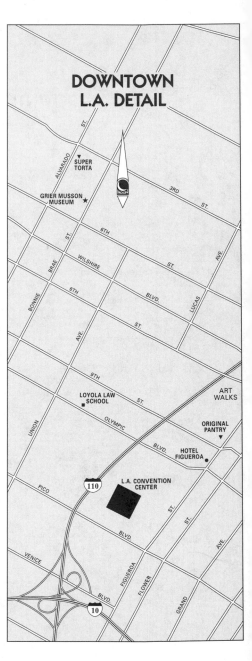

DOWNTOWN L.A. DETAIL

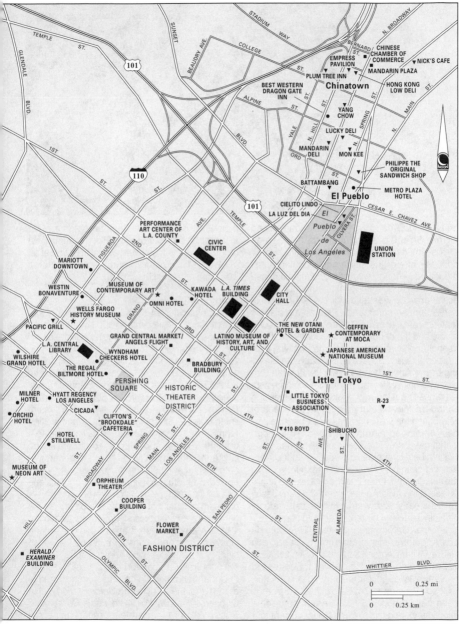

© AVALON TRAVEL PUBLISHING, INC.

El Pueblo's
Olvera Street

ROBERT HOLMES/CalTour

on N. Main Street. But the real action is along **Olvera Street,** a bright and bustling open-air 1930s-vintage marketplace dotted with historic adobes—one of the city's most popular tourist attractions. Though it wasn't always thus, these days the cultural color is fairly authentic, a particular draw on weekends for L.A.'s large Mexican-American community. The area's historic features, alas, are all but overwhelmed by commerce and the chaos of contemporary life. For a deeper appreciation, take a guided walking tour.

Special Olvera Street events include the **Blessing of the Animals** held every year on the Saturday before Easter, an event allowing hamsters to horses to get the nod from God; the weeklong **Cinco de Mayo** celebration held the week of May 5; and the pre-Christmas **Las Posadas** procession staged nightly from Dec. 16 through Christmas Eve. This Mexican Christmas celebration, held over nine consecutive nights, reenacts the search by Mary and Joseph for room at the inn. On Christmas Eve the procession finally arrives at the Avila Adobe, where the baby Jesus joins the party. Afterward, children celebrate by gleefully attacking piñatas filled with candy.

For more information, contact: El Pueblo de Los Angeles Historic Monument, Sepulveda House Visitor Center, 622 N. Main St., 213/628-1274. The Sepulveda House Visitor Center (and museum) is open Mon.–Sat. 10 A.M.–3 P.M. (closed Christmas Day), but Olvera Street is open daily 10 A.M.–8 P.M.; in summer, some shops stay open even later. Call for current tour schedules of various historic buildings and for information on free guided walking tours. At last report El Pueblo tours were offered Tues.–Sat. at 10 A.M., 11 A.M., noon, and 1 P.M. (excluding Thanksgiving and Christmas).

Union Station

This spectacular art-deco transportation palace, directly east of El Pueblo at 800 N. Alameda St. (at César E. Chávez Ave.), was built on the site of L.A.'s original Chinatown. The last of the grand American train stations, Union Station was built in 1939 by the Southern Pacific, Union Pacific, and Santa Fe Railroads. Its Spanish colonial revival style, the work of architects John and Donald Parkinson, blends Moorish influences with streamline moderne. Stepping inside the grand waiting room, where the wood-beamed ceiling rises to a dramatic 52 feet above polished marble floors, is like traveling back in time. Giant decorative archways at each end lead to serene courtyards landscaped with oaks, figs, and jacarandas along with Mexican fan palms and birds of paradise—a public embodiment of Southern California's private garden style, which was still inventing itself in the 1930s. Many of Union Station's original furnishings are intact and in fine form. Striking art-deco signs still point the way; heavy wooden chairs still offer travelers comfort and privacy.

Understandably, Union Station has starred in many films, these including *Union Station* (set in Chicago), *The Way We Were, Blade Runner,* and *Bugsy.* Yet L.A.'s grandest grande dame still

AMÉRICA TROPICAL

In summer of 1932 Mexican muralist David Alfaro Siqueiros began to paint a mural on the south side of Olvera Street's Italian Hall, a work he called *América Tropical.* Now undergoing a painstaking restoration by art conservators from L.A.'s Getty Conservation Institute, *América Tropical* depicts a tangle of ominously luxuriant vegetation surrounding a stylized pre-Columbian pyramid and totemic sculptures. But the artist's dramatic design finale—a crucified Indian lashed to a Christian cross clutched in the talons of an American eagle, and, just to the right, armed peasant revolutionaries posed on a rooftop as they take eagle-eyed aim at the predator—so outraged Depression-era L.A. civic leaders that this part of the mural was soon obliterated with white paint; within years the entire work was whitewashed.

Siqueiros, who found himself in Los Angeles during a period of California immigrant bashing, was soon deported from the United States.

Despite Siqueiros's less than rousing L.A. welcome, the artist is now considered one of *los tres grandes* among Mexico's muralists, keeping posthumous company with José Clemente Orozco and Diego Riviera. And, in one of those rich historical ironies, it turns out that L.A.'s early censorship greatly assisted his artistic legacy. Without the protection provided by such thick coats of white paint, *América Tropical* would have faded into absolute oblivion long ago. Just when restoration will be complete—and when the public will once again be able to view the mural—is uncertain, given the decades already committed to revivifying *América Tropical.*

---

presides over L.A. rail travel as home to **Amtrak** and, at the adjacent **Gateway Center,** both the **Metrorail Red Line** subway and the **Metrolink** regional commuter service. Well worth a peek: the impressive public art in the new transit center.

For the complete Union Station story, sign up for a Sat. walking tour with the Los Angeles Conservancy (see the special topic Getting up to Speed Downtown).

"New" Chinatown
Chinatown in Los Angeles certainly won't be mistaken for San Francisco's, but beyond the tourist traps it has authentic appeal—most particularly in the markets and the restaurants lining the streets. Events can be fun, too, including the major **Chinese New Year** celebration in late February or early March, the **Miss L.A. Chinatown Pageant,** the **Golden Dragon Parade,** and the **Chinese Moon Festival and Street Fair.**

Still considered "new" Chinatown, since L.A.'s original Chinatown was razed in the 1930s to make way for Union Station, the main drag here is N. Broadway; the district's general boundaries are created by César E. Chávez Ave. and Spring, Yale, and Bernard Streets. Making Chinatown still more fascinating these days is the fact that it's not just a reinvented Canton anymore. Home to 15,000 residents and still serving as the de facto cultural center for Chinese Americans living

throughout the L.A. area—particularly in East L.A.'s popular "Asian restaurant cities" south of Pasadena, including Alhambra, Monterey Park, San Gabriel, and very affluent San Marino—the neighborhood increasingly reflects the influence of more recent ethnic Chinese immigrants from Southeast Asia, the "Teo Chew" collectively known by longtime neighborhood residents as the Chiu Chou. Signs in Cambodian, Lao, Thai, and Vietnamese add to neighborhood business competition and communication confusion.

For more information about area attractions and businesses, contact: **Chinese Chamber of Commerce,** 977 N. Broadway, Ste. E, Los Angeles, 213/617-0396, www.lachinesechamber.org, which largely represents established Cantonese establishments.

Los Angeles Children's Museum
Strictly kids' stuff, this downtown museum offers hands-on arts, humanities, and science education for children ages 2–10. In **Club Eco,** kids create masterpieces from recyclables. In the **Recording Studio,** they become recording stars; in the **Video Zone,** TV news anchors. In **The Cave** they commune with lifelike dinosaur holograms. A huge pillow-filled room allows children to shed excess energy before settling down to focus on the kids-only exhibits here.

Los Angeles Children's Museum is located

inside the Los Angeles Mall at 310 N. Main St. (at Los Angeles St.), 213/687-8800, www.lacm.org. (The museum is looking for a new home, so be sure to call for current info before setting out.) During the school year, the museum caters to classroom groups and is open to the general public on weekends only, 10 A.M.–5 P.M. (closed Thanksgiving, Christmas, and New Year's Day). In summer, it's open to the public also Tues.–Fri. 11:30 A.M.–4 P.M., Sat.–Sun. 10 A.M.–5 P.M. Admission is $5, under age 2 free.

OTHER DOWNTOWN CULTURAL ATTRACTIONS

Los Angeles City Hall and the Civic Center

Now dwarfed by downtown high-rises, Los Angeles City Hall (1926–28) was until 1966 the tallest building in downtown L.A., the grand symbol of the city. Before 1957, earthquake building standards forbade all structures taller than 13 stories. The city's most notable exception, 27-story City Hall—designed by architects John C. Austin, John and Donald Parkinson, and Albert C. Martin, Sr., its interiors by Austin Whittlesey—was allowed only after L.A. voters approved its specific exception. And if you wonder why L.A.'s City Hall seems so *familiar,* the building was featured in the opening scenes of the popular 1950s TV series *Dragnet.* In addition to many other movie and TV roles, it also served as headquarters for *The Daily Planet* fictional news organization in the *Superman* television series.

Los Angeles City Hall is part of the Los Angeles Civic Center north of 1st St., at 200 N. Spring St. (between 1st and Temple), 213/485-2121, its "tourability" affected by ongoing restoration and budget-breaking seismic safety reconstruction. But do see the recently restored rotunda, featuring 23 spectacular ceramic tile panels. And take in the view from the top floor observation deck, which—despite subsequent skyscrapers—still presents a commanding view of downtown. Free 45-minute tours of City Hall are offered by reservation only (sometimes cancelled due to construction), weekdays at 11 A.M. and noon, or sign on for a guided Los Angeles Conservancy tour (see the special topic Getting up to Speed Downtown).

Latino Museum of History, Art, and Culture

A onetime Bank of America building on a dispirited stretch of Main St. one block south of City Hall at 112 S. Main St. (between 1st and 2nd Sts.), 213/626-7600, www.latinomuseum.org, is now home to one of L.A.'s newest museums—the long-promised Latino Museum of History, Art, and Culture, which opened in May 1998 after more than a decade of searching for a home and adequate funding. The museum celebrates Latino artistic, cultural, and historic achievements not just in Los Angeles but throughout the United States, the Americas, and the world. Beyond traditional exhibits, the museum also hosts art symposia, film festivals, and special cultural, educational, and other events. Recent exhibitions included *César E. Chávez: An American Leader* and *Dia de los Santos—Dia de los Muertos (Day of the Saints—Day of the Dead).* The museum is open daily 10 A.M.–4 P.M. except major holidays. Admission is free.

Travelers heading toward L.A.'s Westside shouldn't miss the **Museum of Latin American Art** in Long Beach, which opened its first wing in November 1996.

Los Angeles Times Building

The *Los Angeles Times* Building, 202 W. 1st St. (between Spring and Broadway), 213/237-5000, www.latimes.com, is easily identified by its stately clock tower. The Times-Mirror Corp. outgrew the original structure designed by Gordon Kaufmann in 1935, and the impressive moderne-style limestone structure was intermeshed in 1973 with a modern steel and glass addition by William Pereira and Associates—an interesting architectural hodgepodge, at any rate. Stop by the lobby to read the history of Los Angeles in headlines or take a free tour to peek in on the making of a great, if historically conservative, newspaper, from the newsroom to pressroom. The paper offers two different guided walk-through tours on weekdays—a free 45-minute stroll for individuals, couples, and school-age children through the "old plant" editorial offices (no reservations required, call for current time), and a group-oriented, reservations-only 45-minute tour of the new plant and its pressroom (times vary). Children must be over age 10 for either tour. Free parking is available at 213 S. Spring Street. Make tour reservations at least a week in advance.

RAILWAY TO HEAVEN

Care for some hands-on historical education with your downtown tour? The time-honored Bunker Hill **Angel's Flight** represents Old Los Angeles reborn. This soaring L.A. landmark—the city's most famous railway, an inclined funicular cable car system dating to 1901—recently flew back from the past. ("Funicular" refers to the fact that the two cars, one ascending and one descending, counterbalance each other along the three-track, 298-foot route.) In early 1996 Angel's Flight was officially resurrected, connecting the Red Line's Pershing Square subway station—the Fourth and Hill St. entrance—to the Water Court at California Plaza.

The original Angel's Flight, aptly called "the shortest railway in the world," departed from Third Street to connect the Hill St. business district with the once-fashionable Bunker Hill neighborhood. Dismantled and removed in 1969 for Bunker Hill redevelopment, the railway has been painstakingly refurbished and reconstructed. Included in the restoration project were the two orange and black cable cars—the Olivet and the Sinai, twin parallelograms with stair-stepped interiors—and the original

Beaux Arts classical revival station house and arched entryway.

Angels Flight is downtown—at 351 Hill St., on Hill between Third and Fourth Sts.—and operates daily 6:30 a.m.-10 p.m. Railway fare for the one-minute (one-way) ride is 25 cents per person. Ticket books (valid for one person only) are $1 for five rides. Official souvenirs are available at the top of the hill on Saturday and Sunday 10 a.m.-4 p.m. For current information, contact: **Angels Flight Railway Foundation,** P.O. Box 712345, Los Angeles, CA 90071, tel. (213) 626-1901. For additional information—or to request a mail-order merchandise catalog—call (213) 487-3716.

Last-Minute 2001 Update: On February 1, 2001, one of the two Angel's Flight cars broke lose and smashed into the other car in a freak accident, one in which one rider was killed and seven were injured. Preliminary investigation revealed that the railway's cable came off a spool, though what caused this to happen wasn't immediately clear. At last report the railway was closed pending necessary repairs, and planned to reopen.

Los Angeles Central Library

Still L.A.'s most astonishing public building even after two 1986 arson fires and subsequent reconstructive surgery, the beloved and strange Los Angeles Central Library is the 1926 masterwork of architect Bertram Goodhue, with an assist from Carleton M. Winslow, Sr. Centerpiece of this beaux arts–inspired landmark is the central book tower, topped by a pyramid of tiled mosaic sunbursts and, at the apex, a hand-held torch of knowledge. The search for knowledge is represented by the sphinx—and the bright rotunda, illuminated by a stunning globelike chandelier. Everywhere around, Goodhue's vision renders the ordinary quite extraordinary, an inventive adventure in art, history, religion, and portentous philosophy that is, architecturally, by turns Byzantine, Egyptian, and Spanish. Inimitably American, though, is the official beneficence and optimism suffusing Dean Cornwell's 1932 rotunda mural cycle, which depicts a fairy-tale version of California's colonization and multiethnic mixing. Also appreciate the library's restored fountains and gardens,

the largest of the latter complete with restaurant. Not to mention the library's new "modernist beaux arts" east wing—rather boring in comparison to Goodhue's contribution—designed by Hardy Holzman Pfeiffer Associates and named for former L.A. Mayor Tom Bradley. Bradley is also honored, if unofficially, by the three towering skyscrapers that now dwarf the Central Library, a clumsy collective homage to the chummy redevelopment relationships that financed library improvements.

The Los Angeles Public Library's Central Library, 630 W. 5th St. (between Flower and Grand), 213/228-7000, is open Mon.–Thurs. 10 A.M.–8 P.M., Fri.–Sat. 10 A.M.–6 P.M., and Sun. 1–5 P.M. Free guided tours are offered Mon.–Fri. at 12:30 P.M., Sat. at 11 A.M. and 2 P.M., and Sun. at 2 P.M. For library events information, call 213/228-7040, or check the library's website at www.lapl.org.

Pershing Square

The only park in downtown Los Angeles, Pershing Square was established in 1866 on a five-acre remnant of the original pueblo land grant. Bounded by 5th, 6th, Hill, and Olive Sts. and originally bordered by white picket fences, Pershing Square was once lush with banana trees, palms, and birds of paradise. By the 1930s it also accommodated evangelists, socialists, and other Angelenos sounding forth from figurative soapboxes.

This local free-speech tradition withered in the 1950s when the park was razed to plant, instead, an underground parking garage. The bleak urban badlands that quickly sprouted atop the garage soon became home to the homeless and, more insidiously, drug dealers and other shady characters. The destruction of Pershing Square by shortsighted civic leaders is not among L.A.'s finest accomplishments.

Yet in California even cities reserve the right to reinvent themselves—thus the latest "new" and newly improved Pershing Square. The first rush to clean it up came in 1984, when the Olympics came to town. That and subsequent efforts failed to thrive. But after a two-year, $14.7 million recreation, the new Pershing Square was unveiled in February of 1994. Its style suggesting a European plaza more than the wide-open urban grassland of American tradition, Pershing Square has distinct open-air "rooms," from performance area and statue garden park to stylized tidepool. Its bold colors and sleek contemporary whimsy—purple carillon tower, rose-colored walkways, canary yellow walls, even a faux earthquake fault line—seem strong enough to bridge the vast cultural gap, and the tiny geographical gap, between downtown's Latino and Anglo identities. To date, nothing else in Los Angeles has been that powerful.

The Biltmore Hotel

Backing up to Pershing Square is the Biltmore Hotel, the grandest of the grand old hotels in Southern California, designed by architects Schultze and Weaver and completed in 1923. Designated a Los Angeles Historical Cultural Landmark in 1969, the Biltmore had gotten a bit dowdy over the years. So Angelenos were understandably ecstatic about the grande dame's $40 million makeover in the late 1970s, a restoration that lovingly polished the hotel's marble, garish gold gilt, and crystal chandeliers. The Biltmore's magnificent painted ceilings were redone more recently. The hotel's wonders are abun-

dant. Secret details include the private elevator in the Presidential Suite—John F. Kennedy planned his successful 1960 presidential campaign from the Biltmore's lobby—and the baby grand piano in the Music Suite. Considerably more accessible for most of us are the stunning gold-gilt ceilings in the Galeria, adjoining the lobby, where Italian artist Giovanni Smeraldi symbolically re-created the city. Fans of the once popular *Murder, She Wrote* TV series will recognize the Biltmore's lobby, with an elaborate skylight and hand-painted carved wood ceilings, as a stand-in for miscellaneous ritzy hotels

GRAND CENTRAL MARKET

Here's the L.A. that defies the urban-cool stereotype. Yet the colorful Grand Central Market is so cool that everybody comes here, at least once in awhile. At lunchtime the goal is strictly satiation. Row after row of neon-lit food stalls feature some of the city's most authentic and least expensive Mexican food alongside endless other ethnic selections. Deciding what to buy, where, is something of a challenge; the best approach for first-timers is just to follow your nose as you shuffle through the sawdust. But you can find just about anything here—fresh produce, meat, and seafood, exotic herbs and spices. The Grand Central Market, 317 S. Market St. (between Broadway and Hill St. and 3rd and 4th Sts.), 213/624-2378, is open daily 9 A.M.–6 P.M., closed Thanksgiving and Christmas.

Grand Central Market

around the world. The lobby also starred in the movie *The Poseidon Adventure.* The public areas and restaurants of the Biltmore Hotel, 506 S. Grand Ave. (Grand at 5th), 213/624-1011 or toll-free 800/245-8673 for reservations, www.thebiltmore.com, are open to the public during reasonable business hours for impromptu self-guided tours. To truly appreciate what you're seeing, though, sign on for a Saturday tour with the Los Angeles Conservancy, 213/623-2489.

On Broadway
In fairly recent history Broadway between 1st and 9th Sts. has become the city's main Latino shopping district, one that offers considerably more—cheap stereos, bridal fashions, even immigration lawyers—than El Pueblo's tourist-oriented entertainments. Strolling this lively boulevard, studying the shop signs and listening in on passing conversations, may convince you that you've suddenly arrived in Mexico City, a fact that gives rise to the overall Angeleno tendency to describe the area as "third world." Stop at downtown's Grand Central Market, 317 S. Market St. (see sidebar for more detail) for a fascinating selection of authentic ethnic food and other wares.

Bradbury Building
This is one of L.A.'s notable architectural jewels, designed and built with guidance from a Ouija board, so be sure to stop by just to appreciate its sparkle. The modest five-story brick exterior of the 1893 Bradbury Building, 304 S. Broadway (at 3rd St.), 213/626-1893, gives no hint of the fantastic art-nouveau vision inside. The focal point of architectural draftsman George Herbert Wyman's inspiration is the small, open interior courtyard, almost frilly with elaborate wrought-iron grillwork yet grounded with rich, dark oak walls, old brick, and marble and tile floors. Balconies and open-cage elevators reach upward into a stunning glass atrium that fills the building with magical light. Modern movie buffs have seen this place before, as a rainy-day interior set in *Blade Runner.* The breathtaking first impression is well worth the trip. The Bradbury Building is open to the public (up to the 1st floor landing) daily 9 A.M.–5 P.M.

DOWNTOWN'S FASHION DISTRICT

Until recently known as the Garment District, L.A.'s Fashion District is a major center for garment manufacturing—both legal shops and sweatshops—and is a natural magnet for bargain shoppers. The district itself is generally defined as the area east of Main and west of San Pedro between 7th and 11th Streets. Serious shoppers will find the highest concentration of outlet stores on S. Los Angeles St. between 7th and 9th. Best bets include the **Cooper Building,** 860 S. Los Angeles St. (between 8th and 9th Sts.), 213/627-3754, with multiple floors and more than 80 stores filled with designer clothing, shoes, and linens offered at bargain-basement prices. Or try the **CaliforniaMart,** 110 E. 9th St. (at Main), 213/630-3710, the largest wholesale apparel center in the nation. Be prepared to pay for parking.

If wholesale shopping's your bag, there are other possibilities downtown. Extremely early risers and night owls enjoy the **Wholesale Flower Market,** at 742 Maple Ave. (between 7th and 8th Sts.), 213/627-2482, where the action begins daily at 3 A.M. as flower merchants begin picking through the colorful, fragrant bounty. Flowers and potted plants are available to the general public at a considerable discount. Other possibilities for truly adventurous shoppers: the city's **Jewelry District,** just south of Pershing Square and north of 7th St. (many outlets wholesale only), and the **Wholesale Toy District** in the midst of Skid Row just south of Little Tokyo and west of San Pedro Street.

Herald Examiner Building
Of particular interest to students of architecture, the *Herald Examiner Building,* 1111 S. Broadway (at 11th St.), was commissioned in 1912 by William Randolph Hearst. Julia Morgan, Hearst's architectural sidekick, designed this Spanish-style building to house Hearst's publishing empire. Hearst was so pleased with the results of their first collaboration that he hired Morgan to help create their joint masterpiece, the byzantine castle at Hearst's San Simeon "ranch."

PERFORMANCE L.A.

Los Angeles Concert Venues

The undisputed entertainment capital of the world, Los Angeles often poses as the world's live entertainment capital as well. One of the most famous concert venues in Los Angeles is the open-air **Hollywood Bowl** amphitheater in the Hollywood Hills, 323/850-2000, a popular venue for the Los Angeles Philharmonic Orchestra but most famous for its summer pops concerts; for detailed information, see the Hollywood and Vicinity chapter. The **John Anson Ford Theater** nearby, 323/461-3673, is famous for its summer Shakespeare as well as a variety of free summer concerts. Also immensely popular: the **Greek Theatre,** 323/665-1927.

Downtown, the Performing Arts Center's (formerly the Music Center's) **Dorothy Chandler Pavilion,** 213/972-7211, is home base for both the **Los Angeles Philharmonic Orchestra** and the immensely popular **Los Angeles Music Center Opera,** though other concerts and performances are often scheduled. Just south of town is the famed **Shrine Auditorium,** just west of Figueroa on W. Jefferson, 213/749-5123, where the annual Academy Awards ceremony is usually staged; it's also a popular concert venue.

Other major regional venues include the **Universal Amphitheatre** at Universal Studios, 818/777-3931; the **Santa Monica Civic Auditorium,** 310/458-8551; and the **Pasadena Civic Auditorium,** 626/793-2122.

Popular for big-deal yet intimate concerts and performances, from Sting to the Joffrey Ballet, is the grandly refurbished art-deco **Wiltern Theater,** 3790 Wilshire Blvd., 213/388-1400. The most stylish place around for musicals is Hollywood's art-deco **Pantages Theater** on Hollywood Blvd., 323/468-1770, also a smaller concert venue.

Local universities, particularly the University of California at Los Angeles and its **UCLA Center for the Performing Arts,** and even community colleges are other prime arts venues. The primary venue for UCLA is the **Wadsworth Theatre,** 310/825-2101, north of Wilshire Blvd. and just west of the San Diego (405) Fwy. on the grounds of the U.S. Veterans Administration complex in Westwood. UCLA's **Royce Hall,** a venerable on-campus venue, stages most major concerts and performances.

Los Angeles Theater Venues

Not quite ready to rival New York as an international theater destination, Los Angeles is nonetheless an increasingly serious U.S. contender. Greater L.A. stages about 1,100 theatrical productions annually, with an average of 21 openings each week. Particularly hot for alternative and "new" small theater

Little Tokyo

Just east of the Civic Center, along 1st St. between Main and Alameda, is the heart of Little Tokyo, cultural center for L.A.'s Japanese American community. Japanese immigrants first settled in the Los Angeles area more than 100 years ago, but the local community was devastated, overnight, when Japanese Americans were forcibly divested of their businesses, farms, homes, and neighborhoods and "relocated" in World War II–era internment camps throughout the West. After the war, many L.A.-area citizens of Japanese descent moved to the suburbs. But Little Tokyo rebounded; it remains a thriving—and growing—area cultural center. East 1st St. between Central Ave. and San Pedro St., listed on the National Register of Historic Places, is now protected as a National Historic Landmark.

For more information about the area, contact the **Little Tokyo Business Association,** 244 S. Pedro St., Ste. 303, Los Angeles, 213/620-0570. For tours of Little Tokyo, call 213/628-8268.

Japanese American National Museum

A 1990s museum exhibit here, *America's Concentration Camps: Remembering the Japanese American Experience,* reminded Americans about a chapter of U.S. history most would prefer to forget. But the World War II–era executive order that banished Japanese Americans living on the west coast—the majority of them U.S. citizens—to military relocation camps has not been forgotten in Southern California. Many California families so detained lost everything as a result—their homes, their land, their neighbors, their businesses and jobs—and have been struggling to rebuild their lives, and to understand, ever since.

productions these days is the greater Hollywood area—Hollywood (Hoho), West Hollywood (Weho), and North Hollywood (Noho)—though lively theatrical performances are staged all over town. Theater tickets are available through individual box offices, and also often through TicketMaster in L.A. at 213/365-3500 or Telecharge, toll-free 800/233-3123.

Starting with major-league theater, the **Performing Arts Center** on Grand Ave. downtown, formerly known as the Music Center, 213/972-7211, is the uptown theatrical showcase. The **Ahmanson Theatre** is the main stage for mainstream productions, and the trendsetting theater-in-the-round **Mark Taper Forum** is lauded for launching such original hits as *Angels in America, Children of a Lesser God,* and *Jelly's Last Jam.*

The **Shubert Theatre** in Century City, 310/201-1500 for tickets, is popular for musicals and long-running major productions such as *Sunset Boulevard,* which got its international start there. The onetime Westwood Playhouse on Le Conte Ave. in Westwood is now UCLA's **Geffen Playhouse,** 310/208-6500 or 310/208-5454 for the box office, most famous as the place Jason Robards and Nick Nolte got their respective show-biz starts; call for current program information. The historic **Pasadena Playhouse,** 626/792-8672 for information, 626/356-7529 or toll-free 800/233-3123 for tickets, features imports from New York as well as original local productions. Other popular theaters include the **Stella Adler Theater,** 6773 Hollywood Blvd., 323/655-8587 for tickets. Garnering many bouquets in recent years, on various local stages, is L.A.'s **Center Theatre Group.**

For summer-run weekend Shakespeare and such on a down-home neighborhood scale, head to Topanga Canyon and Will Geer's **Theatricum Botanicum,** 310/455-3723. Award-winning small or "alternative" theaters in Hollywood include actor-director Tim Robbins's equity-waiver **Actors' Gang,** 323/465-0566; the **Hudson Backstage Theater,** 1110 N. Hudson Ave., 323/769-5674; **Matrix Theater,** 7657 Melrose Ave., 323/852-1445; and West Hollywood's **Coast Playhouse,** 323/650-8507. Best bets farther west include the 99-seat **Santa Monica Playhouse,** 310/394-9779. For almost-sure-to-shock-mom-and-dad performance art, the place is **Highways** in Santa Monica, 310/453-1755, a venue so popular that potential performers must apply a year or more in advance.

Los Angeles also boasts a respectable number of ethnic theater venues, including the **Japan American Theatre** in Little Tokyo, 213/680-3700, which presents contemporary Japanese-American productions along with traditional Japanese theater.

The Japanese American National Museum, housed in a former Buddhist temple, emphasizes the history of Japanese in America in both permanent and special exhibits. The museum's newest feature is the 85,000-square-foot Pavilion of the Japanese American National Museum, adjacent, opened in early 1999. The most visible aspect of a $45 million expansion, designed by architect Gyo Obata, the new sandstone, granite, steel, and glass pavilion features interior cherry wood paneling, a grand staircase, and galleries with natural lighting. Don't miss the 90-foot-long "wall of water" in the garden.

The Japanese American National Museum, 369 E. 1st St. (at Central Ave.), 213/625-0414 or toll-free 800/461-5266, www.lausd.k12.ca.us/janm/, is open Tues.–Sun. 10 A.M.–5 P.M., with last admission at 4:30, but Thurs. 10 A.M.–8 P.M. (closed Thanksgiving, Christmas, and New Year's Day). Admission is $6 adults and $5 seniors, $3 college students with ID, and children ages 6–17. Free on Thurs. 5–8 P.M. and all day on the third Thurs. of every month. Call for current exhibit information.

Museum of Contemporary Art

Los Angeles is an international mecca for contemporary art and artists, with the post–World War II art world here defined, uniquely, by exposure to and creation of popular culture and the entertainment industry. The phenomenon is difficult to accommodate within museum walls, yet L.A. tries. Along with the 20th-century collections and exhibits at the Los Angeles County Museum of Art's Anderson Building, downtown's Museum of Contemporary Art (MOCA) on Grand Ave. at California Plaza is central to L.A.'s centrality on the world's easel.

NEON—L.A.'S SIGNATURE FLASH

If imitation is the sincerest form of flattery, just imagine how flattered Los Angeles is by the existence of Las Vegas and all that flashy neon.

The **Museum of Neon Art (MONA)** in L.A., open at its new downtown location since February of 1996, celebrates the city's love affair with neon lighting—a commercial art form that once decorated countless L.A. storefronts, theater marquees, and roof lines. The original fuel for L.A.'s signature flash was neon itself, a colorless, odorless gas that glows orangey-red when zapped by electricity, a fact of nature first discovered in France in 1898. (Other colors are created by other gases.) America's first neon signs, manufactured in France, were installed in 1923 at an L.A. Packard dealership.

Some of L.A.'s original tubular light show still shines, lighting up **Broadway** downtown, sections of **Wilshire Boulevard**, **Western Avenue** between Wilshire and 3rd St., **Alvarado Street** flanking MacArthur Park, and countless other streets. (For a fairly comprehensive map of restored Los Angeles neon, see the "neon map" on city's Department of Cultural Affairs website, www.culturela.org.) Other areas, such as **Melrose Ave.**, are at the forefront of the city's neo-neon renaissance, thanks in large part to citywide consciousness-raising credited to MONA and its founding artist Lili Lakich.

Downtown on the 1st floor of the Renaissance Tower, in Grand Hope Park on W. Olympic, the Museum of Neon Art (MONA) is the only permanent neon museum in the world. A stunning and electrically enigmatic likeness of the Mona Lisa—the museum's logo, designed by Lakich—marks the spot. The permanent collection at MONA includes an impressive array of classic L.A. neon and electric signs, dating from the 1920s. Changing exhibits—such as the museum's opening 1996 exhibition, *Electric Muse: A Spectrum of Neon, Electric, and Kinetic Sculpture*—emphasize neon as a contemporary art form. Head to **CityWalk** outside Universal Studios to appreciate more of the MONA collection, which includes the Richfield Eagle and the Melrose Theater sign.

For a still flashier appreciation of local lights, sign on for the museum's after-dark "Neon Cruise" L.A. bus tour, offered at least monthly, $40 per person. In addition to its neon tours, the museum offers introductory classes in neon design and technique four times each year.

The Museum of Neon Art is open Wed.–Sat. 11 A.M.–5 P.M. and Sun. noon–5 P.M. (closed Mon., Tues., and major holidays). On the second Thurs. of every month, the museum is also open 5–8 P.M.—and at that time admission is free to all. Otherwise admission is $5 adults, $3.50 seniors and students (children age 12 and under free). Call for current information on docent-led tours, current exhibits, neon art classes, and "Neon Cruise" tours. The museum's entrance is on Hope (at Olympic); during regular museum hours, free parking is available in the Renaissance Tower's garage on Grand just south of 9th Street.

For current exhibit and other information, and to make reservations for MONA's Neon Tours, contact: Museum of Neon Art (MONA), Renaissance Tower, 501 W. Olympic Blvd., 213/489-9918, fax 213/489-9932, www.neonmona.org.

When it opened in December 1986, already a celebrity among downtown redevelopment projects, MOCA was hailed as the tonic to revivify Los Angeles the cultural wasteland. Designed by acclaimed Japanese architect Irata Isozaki, the seven-level building—98,000 square feet of red sandstone and grand pyramidal skylights—takes an elegant and impressive (if all but underground) stand against downtown's skyline. Isozaki's first major U.S. work is a work of art in its own right, architecturally abstract but grounded in geometry and Eastern tradition.

What's inside, though, is predominantly Western. The museum's permanent collection boasts important works by Diane Arbus, Sam Francis, Franz Kline, Louise Nevelson, Claes Oldenburg, Jackson Pollock, Robert Raushenberg, Mark Rothko, Andy Warhol, and others. Both the museum's permanent collection and special exhibits showcase works created since the 1940s, including painting and sculpture, mixed media, environmental pieces, and performance art. Increasingly, MOCA's changing shows tend toward the hip and flashy L.A. art *event,* pop-culture and entertainment-industry shows Hollywood and the Westside will dress up and drive for. More cerebral topics, such as early 1997's "The Power of Suggestion: Narrative and Notation in Contemporary Drawing," also slip through the doors from time to time. MOCA's collection was bolstered in

1997 by a gift of 105 postwar artworks from the Lannan Foundation, greatly enriching the museum's 4,000-piece holding of postwar art.

In 1983, during early MOCA construction, a temporary museum outpost known as the Temporary Contemporary (or "TC") parked itself in an old police department garage near Little Tokyo at 152 N. Central Avenue. The TC has since become a seemingly permanent museum adjunct known as the **Geffen Contemporary at MOCA** (one same-day admission gets you into both) known for its adventuresome shows and performances.

For current exhibits, box office and other information, or to request a map and brochure by mail, contact: the Museum of Contemporary Art, 250 S. Grand Ave. (just south of 1st St.), 213/626-6222, www.moca.org. The museum is open Tues.–Sun. 11 A.M.–5 P.M. (until 8 P.M. on Thurs.), closed Thanksgiving, Christmas, and New Year's Day. Admission is $6 adults, $4 seniors (over age 65) and students with ID, free for children under age 12. On Thurs. evening, 5–8 P.M., admission is free. For parking, try the Performing Arts Center lot.

Performance Arts Center of L.A. County

This imposing performing arts center atop downtown's Bunker Hill is L.A.'s own Lincoln Center. Formerly known as the Music Center, the Performance Arts Center is composed of three separate theaters. The **Dorothy Chandler Pavilion,** named for the philanthropist wife of late *Los Angeles Times* publisher Otis Chandler, is the largest of the three, with seating for 3,250. The Chandler Pavilion's enormous marble lobby, lit with gigantic crystal chandeliers, has provided a glamorous photo-op backdrop for many Academy Awards ceremonies. The Pavilion is also a more permanent home for the L.A. Philharmonic, the Performing Arts Center Opera, and other worthies.

The **Ahmanson Theatre** is a 2,100-seat venue for popular performances, musicals, and plays, including L.A.'s run of *Phantom of the Opera* and *Kiss of the Spider Woman*. (Just in case you don't get a good seat, bring binoculars.)

The Center's **Mark Taper Forum** is an intimate 750-seat theater known for its adventurous and contemporary pre-Broadway premieres. *Zoot Suit, Children of a Lesser God, Jelly's Last Jam,* and *Angels in America* are among the hundreds of

THE DOWNTOWN WORLD OF DISNEY

Stalled for a decade in the planning and fundraising stages, official groundbreaking for the Walt Disney Concert Hall was scheduled for 1999—something of a new beginning. Construction of the concert hall's underground parking garage began in December 1992, but halted abruptly two years later due to cost overruns. Subsequent fundraising, earnest since 1996, raised almost 95 percent of monies needed for the $255 million venue.

The Disney Concert Hall, a long-awaited downtown landmark designed by L.A. architect Frank O. Gehry, has been through dozens of revisions since Gehry won the commission in 1988. The current design resembles sterling silver nun's caps caught in a tornado or perhaps, as the project's construction manager Jack Burnell has suggested, "the crash of a 747." But according to *Los Angeles Times* architecture critic Nicolai Ouroussoff, the new Gehry creation represents "a substantial victory against the commonplace and the mediocre." According to Ouroussoff, "the potential success of the project can be seen as a turning point in the city's cultural growth."

Recent additions to construction plans include administrative offices for the L.A. Philharmonic and a 200-seat performance space for the California Institute of the Arts. These new elements allowed Gehry to reconfigure the concert hall's design. The hall's curved exterior surfaces have been simplified, for one thing. The building's bowed facade now leans out over the curb line, providing a pedestrian canopy and stronger presence along the street's main access. Modifications to the interiors promise to be equally dramatic. Gehry has pulled the building's exterior "skin" away from the concert hall's interior, for example, creating a double-wall design with multilevel foyers in between. Audiences will scan the heavens through thin bands of skylights above, and natural light will illuminate the main lobby.

Still to be decided are the exact materials for constructing the building's dramatic exterior. At last report Gehry was considering stone for the building's base and titanium for the sweeping expanses of its giant metal plates.

by Karen Pollock

PUBLIC ART IN THE STREETS~
AND ON THE SUBWAYS

One of downtown's almost unsung wonders is the simple fact that, here, even the absolutely penniless can possess a wealth of art—public art, displayed out and about in sometimes surprising places. Many public art projects have been financed by developer fees associated with downtown's domineering high-rises, giving people on the ground something more entertaining to look at. Thus 30-foot-tall air raid alarms abandoned at Cold War's end have been transformed into giant yellow daffodils; even bike racks and office-building windows have become raw materials for artistic expression.

The corner of 7th and Figueroa Sts. sits on poetry, at least if you're looking at one of the granite benches. Among the miscellaneous Robert Creeley poems seated along 7th, accompanied by James Surls's etching of a rocking chair: "If I sit here/long enough/all will pass me by/one way or another." Another features five sets of eyes, with the words: "Human eyes/are lights to me/seated/in this stone"—all part of the **Poets' Walk Project** at Citicorp Plaza. But don't miss *Corporate Head* by sculptor Terry Allen, on the southeast corner of 7th and Figueroa. More than a few confused corporados have no doubt tried to offer aid and emergency assistance to this stranded bronze suit, his head hopelessly lost in the building itself.

At 8th and Figueroa is Andrew Leicester's sculpted futuristic courtyard with bat-wing gates, *Zanja Madre,* most famous in Hollywood circles as the subject of the artist's copyright infringement lawsuit against Warner Bros. over its use of the sculpture as a set design centerpiece for Gotham City in the film *Batman Forever.* Public art isn't necessarily *that* public.

Also worth a look downtown, before diving into the subway galleries: the 63-foot-tall *Four Arches* by Alexander Calder, 333 S. Hope St.; *Source Figure* by Robert Graham, atop the Bunker Hill steps; and Jonathan Borofsky's *Hammering Man,* on 9th between Main and Los Angeles Sts., and his *Molecule Man,* 255 E. Temple.

Though corporations sometimes work directly with individual artists on downtown public arts projects, the city's Cultural Affairs Department and downtown's Community Redevelopment Agency are the primary agents of artistic change. But L.A.'s Metropolitan Transportation Authority (MTA) has also gotten into the urban art act, offering its public art at its many Metrorail Red, Blue, and Green Line stations. You can see it all for $5, the price of an all-day fare. For more complete Metro arts information, or to take a guided tour, call 213/922-4278. For directions to the various Metro stations by car, bus, or train, call toll-free 800/266-6883 or try www.mta.net.

experimental productions that have established the Taper as a renowned innovative playhouse.

One day soon, the long-awaited Walt Disney Concert Hall will take wing here. Designed by architect Frank Gehry to dominate a full city block just west of the Dorothy Chandler Pavilion at 1st St. and Grand Ave., the Walt Disney Concert Hall has long been stalled by cost overruns. (Anyone with an extra $50 million in pocket change, deposit it here.)

For show and ticket information, call the Performing Arts Center, 135 N. Grand Ave. (at the corner of 1st St.), 213/972-7211, or check the website at www.performingartscenterla.com.

MID-WILSHIRE AND THE MIRACLE MILE

Wilshire Blvd. is among L.A.'s most historic thoroughfares. It predates even concrete, though not necessarily asphalt. This is the path native Shoshone peoples took to reach the sea—Spanish colonialists called it Camino Viejo, or "Old Road"—and to reach the now-famous La Brea Tar Pits, where they scooped up the sticky, petroleum-rich tar to caulk and waterproof their homes.

Though 16-mile Wilshire Blvd. continues west to the ocean—becoming a grand promenade through Beverly Hills and the Los Angeles Country Club before veering near UCLA and then jogging to Santa Monica—the following section covers the "mid-Wilshire" district, between the Harbor (110) Fwy. on the east and opulent Beverly Hills on the west.

WANDERING WEST ON WILSHIRE

At the edge of downtown, on Wilshire Blvd. between Figueroa and Beaudry, is a particularly good spot to view downtown L.A.'s oft-mentioned **four-level freeway interchange**—look north—and certainly a great photo opportunity for those who propose replacing the poppy as California's state flower with the concrete cloverleaf. For an intriguing side trip, just south and west is the **Loyola Law School,** 1441 Olympic Blvd., where the conversion from dreary warehouse to architectural phenomenon-cum-art collection was supervised by L.A.'s famed architect Frank Gehry.

MacArthur Park, on Wilshire between Alvarado and Park View, is 32 acres of rare plants and trees with lake and well-trodden children's play areas—yet not a particularly safe place for tourists, and decidedly dangerous after dark. But on the weekends neighborhood vendors sell crafts, sundries and jewelry made in Mexico from brightly colored wood-lacquered carts. Known as Westlake Park when the onetime marsh was claimed for the gentry in 1890, the park was renamed during World War II for General Douglas MacArthur. A statue of MacArthur stands at the park's southeast corner—and a statue of *Los Angeles Times* founder Harrison Gray Otis stands to the southwest, near Park View. The prestigious **Otis College of Art and Design**—originally the Otis Art Institute, long established at the north end of the park—is at least indirectly responsible for various contemporary artworks scattered throughout the park. *Clock Tower: A Monument to the Unknown,* fabricated from rusty found objects by George Herms, is dedicated to the old men who once played chess here. These days, though, Otis

Wilshire Boulevard, originally a Shoshone path to the sea

PUTTING WILSHIRE ON THE MAP

Wilshire Blvd., which meanders west from downtown to the Pacific Ocean, was named for H. Gaylord Wilshire (1861–1927), a somewhat eccentric socialist millionaire who meandered west to L.A. from Ohio to win (and lose) fortunes as a farmer, inventor, gold miner, and real estate developer. Considering renewed popular interest in healing magnets, keep in mind that Wilshire the man financed Wilshire the real estate venture with profits generated from an invention he called the I-on-a-co-a magnetic horse collar alleged to cure any ailment (including gray hair) by "magnetizing" the iron in the bloodstream. But it was the discovery of oil—vast underground pools of black gold—that put Wilshire Blvd. on the map. Edward Doheny was the first to strike it rich, accidentally digging into his own oil field with a garden shovel.

College is but a neighborhood memory. The school moved on, finding safer, more spacious digs elsewhere. The Los Angeles Board of Education hopes to transform the abandoned Otis campus into a much-needed elementary school, and the city planning commission may turn one of its dorms into a 400-bed correctional facility for minor offenders on work furlough.

"Los Angeles' Champs Elysées"
As recently as 1980 no lesser authority than the *Los Angeles Times* could boast that the two-mile stretch of Wilshire between MacArthur Park and Wilton Place was "Los Angeles' Champs Elysées." Those days are long gone. Most of the boulevard's art-deco icons are boarded up or otherwise gone for good, with only the homeless enjoying the fading historic scenery after dark. What large-scale corporate flight and drastically changing neighborhood demographics couldn't destroy, rioting looters in 1992 did—using the original Rodney King police-brutality verdicts as their excuse. (Given the well-publicized racial overtones of that case—and equally well-publicized tensions between the black and Korean communities, a subject given major play in the pages of the *Los Angeles Times*—perhaps it should have been no surprise that Koreatown businesses bore the brunt of the rampage. But it was still a surprise.) After

tearing up this section of Wilshire for the Metrorail subway, endlessly disruptive construction that put many surviving small businesses out of business, the city then decided to route the remainder of the rail line to the Westside from Western Ave. along Pico instead—virtually guaranteeing moribund future prospects for Wilshire.

Bullocks Wilshire, just east of Vermont Ave. (between Wilshire Pl. and Westmoreland) at 3050 Wilshire Blvd., was the city's premier department store during L.A.'s art-deco golden age. Known as I. Magnin Bullocks Wilshire before closing shop in 1993, this five-story masterpiece topped by a signature zigzag moderne copper-clad tower was L.A.'s initial link between cars and consumers. When it opened for business in 1929, Bullocks Wilshire was the first to successfully lure wealthy shoppers in shiny new cars out to the bean fields (literally) from fashionable downtown. The building is now owned by the Southwestern University School of Law, and the private law library and university offices now housed here are decked out in Bullocks Wilshire's original deco glory.

In the center of mid-Wilshire's Wilshire Center neighborhood, with its high-rises and immigrant-crowded housing, stands the old **Ambassador Hotel** at 3400 Wilshire—L.A.'s first grand resort hotel when it opened in 1921. The Ambassador reached stellar social heights during the heyday of Hollywood stars. The low point came in 1968, when presidential candidate Robert F. Kennedy was assassinated near the restaurant's kitchen. The aging hotel remained open for business until 1987, and preservationists have battled plans to demolish it—be the perpetrator developer Donald Trump or the city Board of Education—ever since. For current information on the hotel's status, contact the Los Angeles Conservancy, 213/623-2489, www.laconservancy.org.

Other art-deco icons have been successfully saved, including the classic Pellissier Building at the southeast corner of Wilshire and Western, now the stunning **Wiltern Center** with a 12-story tower and the lovingly restored **Wiltern Theatre.** Its deep turquoise terra-cotta facade embellished with dazzling zigzag moderne-style copper, the 2,300-seat Wiltern had been badly damaged by vandals before the building's restoration.

Just one block north of Wilshire at 605 S. Irving

Blvd. (at 6th St.) is the **Getty House,** built in 1921 in English half-timber style and the official residence of L.A.'s mayors—at least former Mayor Tom Bradley, who lived here for 16 years—since the home was donated to the city by the Getty Oil Company. Recently restored with $1.2 million in private contributions and the endless volunteer hours of L.A.-area designers, the Getty House now hosts foreign dignitaries, fundraising events, and official city functions, since Bradley's successor, Mayor Richard Riordan, has preferred living at his Brentwood estate.

Stretching from Wilshire to Beverly Blvd. and bounded on the east and west by Bronson and Highland Aves., respectively, is the rest of the leafy residential neighborhood of **Hancock Park,** one of the last elegant residential tracts developed in the Wilshire area and still home to respectable quantities of L.A.'s old and new money. Henry Hancock, who bought Rancho La Brea in 1860, discovered oil—the fluid foundation of the family's subsequent fortune—and in 1910 his son laid out subdivisions around the Wilshire Country Club. These mansion-rich neighborhoods housed the Crocker, Doheny, Huntington, and Van Nuys families, to name just a few of L.A.'s most prominent. Tours of area homes and buildings designed by Paul Revere Williams, the first African-American fellow of the American Institute of Architects, are typically offered in February—during Black History Month—by the Los Angeles Conservancy. (For general information on Conservancy tours, see the special topic Getting up to Speed Downtown.) Charming **Larchmont Village,** situated primarily on Larchmont Blvd. on a four-block stretch between 1st St. and Beverly Blvd., is the neighborhood's shopping district.

MIRACLE MILE MUSEUMS

Wilshire's Miracle Mile, between La Brea and Fairfax Aves., a somewhat self-promotional designation for the car-oriented 1920s shopping district built by A. W. Ross, is fast regaining its former glory. Between La Brea and Burnside, a historic district included on the National Register of Historic Places, are 19 elegant streamline and zigzag moderne survivors. Wilshire's expansive museum district—a must-do destination—begins here in Hancock Park (the park, not the neighborhood) at

the redundantly known La Brea Tar Pits (*la brea* means the tar) and associated George C. Page Museum. Next door is the Los Angeles County Museum of Art (LACMA), offering impressive collections, special shows, and endlessly popular Friday Night Jazz. Across the street is the fascinating Craft and Folk Art Museum. Fairly new to the neighborhood: the Carole and Barry Kaye Museum of Miniatures and the très-L.A. Petersen Automotive Museum.

Korean Cultural Museums

Though Koreatown is still recovering from Metrorail construction down Wilshire to Western—and from the ill-will so violently expressed during the 1992 Rodney King–related riots—well worth a stop for a general orientation is the **Korean American Museum,** located in a suite within the Wiltern Theatre building at 3780 Wilshire Blvd. (at Western), 213/388-4229, www.kamuseum.org. The Korean American Museum is dedicated to preserving Korean-American culture through educational activities and changing exhibitions (donations appreciated). There is no permanent collection, but exhibitions range from Korean family stories and malodorous kim chee to interactive exhibitions on Korean small businesses.

Another worthwhile stop is the **Korean Cultural Center,** along the Miracle Mile at 5505 Wilshire Blvd., 323/936-7141, www.kccla.org, open weekdays 9 A.M.–5 P.M. and Sat. 10 A.M.–1 P.M., closed Sun. and holidays. Through its various programs, the Korean Cultural Center introduces and supports Korean arts, history, and culture in America. Museum displays emphasize the Korean arts, from traditional to more contemporary forms. Of equal fascination, though, is the focus on the Korean immigrant experience—through photographs, letters, historical documents, and artifacts provided in large part by Susan Ahn, daughter of Chang Ho Ahn, who came to California in 1902 to lead an international movement to free Korea from Japanese rule. The museum is closed on all major U.S. holidays and on selective Korean national holidays; if in doubt, call ahead.

Page Museum at the La Brea Tar Pits

The main attractions here are the Pleistocene fossils—bones of sloths, saber-toothed cats, dire wolves, woolly mammoths, and prehistoric condors—plucked from L.A.'s famous La Brea

LA BREA AVENUE:
MELROSE FOR THE MORE SETTLED SET

La Brea between Wilshire and Santa Monica Blvds. could be classified as Melrose for the More Settled Set. (Since the two streets intersect, once you've taken the wild ride along mad, mad Melrose you can leap off here. Or vice versa.) During its heyday this wide, car-accommodating street overflowed with stylish car dealerships. Many of these neglected 1930s art-deco and Spanish-revival car palaces are flourishing in the neighborhood's rebirth as an upscale artsy enclave. Neighborhood attractions include good vintage clothing stores, unusual furniture and furnishings shops, and art and photography galleries. Best of all, La Brea boasts some of the city's most popular restaurants (reservations often mandatory) and one of L.A.'s best bakeries.

For glad rags, first stop is **American Rag Cie,** 150 S. La Brea Ave. (on the east side of La Brea, at 1st), 323/935-3154. American Rag's original claim to fame is retro clothing, both new and "gently used," though the glad-rag gallery has expanded to include a chic shoe emporium, stylish European fashions and accessories (for both men and women), and home furnishings. Just a few doors down is the terrific **Golyester,** 136 S. La Brea (between 1st and 2nd), 323/931-1339, with an outstanding collection of vintage and couture clothing from the 1930s and '40s plus antique textiles, all museum quality and offered at very reasonable prices. For hats, try **Drea Kadilak,** 463 S. La Brea (at 6th St.), 323/931-2051. If you've always hankered after one of those only-in-L.A. poured-on latex dresses, the place to look is **Syren,** just west of La Brea at 7225 Beverly Blvd. (near Formosa), 323/936-6693, which supplied the full-body rubber suits in the movie **Batman.**

Stylish antique and furniture shops—particularly near 6th St. and Beverly Blvd.—and art and photography galleries round out the neighborhood's shopping options. Check out **Mortise & Tenon,** 446 S. La Brea (one and a half blocks north of Wilshire), 323/937-7654, for its stylish handmade furniture, lighting, and accessories. Get out of your car and walk the neighborhood, just to see what's where, art-wise.

Hungry yet? Stop at the **La Brea Bakery,** 624 S. La Brea (near 6th St.), 323/939-6813, for the city's best breads and baked goods—such things as hearty whole-grain, walnut, and rye-currant bread, not to mention the scones, *fougassa,* and delectable pastries and desserts. Every morning well-heeled Angelenos join the "bread line" here quite happily, partaking in a local foodie tradition that gets particularly dramatic on weekends and before major holidays. The very popular California-style Mediterranean **Campanile** restaurant is right here, too—one of L.A.'s best restaurants, a relaxed bastion of well-being.

Quite good, at the more modest end of the expense spectrum, is **Flora Kitchen,** 460 S. La Brea, 323/931-9900, a casual café serving great salads, sandwiches, and specials. Half of the café seating is inside **Rita Flora** flower shop, where the aroma and arrangements are arresting. Immensely popular for Northern Italian is **Ca'Brea,** 346 S. La Brea (between 3rd and 4th Sts.), 323/938-2863, along with too-hip **Farfalla La Brea,** 143 N. La Brea (between 1st and 2nd Sts.), 323/938-2504. For French-Vietnamese, the place is **Mandalay,** 611 N. La Brea (north of Beverly Blvd. near Melrose, at Clinton), 323/933-0717. For more on where to eat in this and other Wilshire-area neighborhoods, see Practical Downtown (and Around).

Tar Pits, the largest fossil concentration ever discovered. Some of the pits are still open for active exploration, an urban aesthetic oddity complete with ersatz Ice Age mascots just outside the museum.

About 35,000–40,000 years ago, right here along what is now Wilshire Blvd., oil deposits rose from the earth's depths and collected in pools on the surface. The crude oil gradually thickened into sticky asphalt; when prehistoric California critters ambled down to this water-

ing hole, the goo got them. The remains of such unlucky animals—prey and predators alike—were first discovered in the early 1900s, and the bone harvest has continued ever since. Well over 100 tons of Ice Age fossils, more than 1.5 million vertebrate and another 2.5 million invertebrate fossils, have been recovered to date, representing more than 140 plant species and 420 species of animals, not counting birds and insects.

What was collected, and how, is the story told

La Brea Tar Pits

by the museum, which is hunkered down into the earth like a bunker; only the entrance and a frieze depicting life in prehistoric times are visible from the street. Exhibits include fossil reconstructions—whole skeletons of prehistoric mammoths, wolves, sloths, and birds—along with a glassed-in working paleontology lab (affectionately known as the "fishbowl") and short documentary films. Always the biggest hit with the kids: the "La Brea Woman" hologram, allowing bones to magically become flesh.

The Page Museum at the La Brea Tar Pits is in Hancock Park at 5801 Wilshire Blvd. (on the north side of the street, at Curson), 323/934-7243, www.tarpits.org. The museum is open Mon.–Fri. 9:30 A.M.–5 P.M., Sat.–Sun. 10 A.M.–5 P.M., closed major holidays. Two free tours are offered Wed.–Sun.; the first, at 1 P.M., explores Hancock Park, and the museum tour begins at 2 P.M. (To arrange tours for nonschool groups—reservations are required—call 323/857-6306.) Admission is $6 adults, $3.50 seniors and students with ID, $2 for children ages 5–10 (under 5 free), but free for everyone on the second Tues. of every month. All-day parking in the museum lot is $5 with museum validation, otherwise $7.50. Metered street parking is nearby, most feasible north of the park.

Los Angeles County Museum of Art

The well-endowed Los Angeles County Museum of Art in Hancock Park is typically known by its less than poetic abbreviation: LACMA. The largest county museum, LACMA is a collection of rather unremarkable buildings—"shopping mall architecture" one critic sniffed when it opened in 1965—surrounding a central courtyard. Yet neither the awkward acronym nor the architecture succeeds in keeping people away.

The remarkable art collected here will keep even a reluctant visitor busy for at least a half-day. The **Pavilion for Japanese Art** features the famed Shin'enkan painting collection as well as sculpture and ceramics. Galleries in the **Hammer Building,** home to often notable special exhibits, emphasize photography, drawings, and prints. The focus of the **Anderson Building** is 20th-century sculpture, painting, and special exhibits.

Do save time for the **Ahmanson Building,** home to most of the museum's eclectic but impressive collection—classical paintings, home furnishings and decorations, textiles, costumes, mosaics, silver, and ancient glass. Among its other treasures: the world's largest collection of Indian, Nepalese, and Tibetan art. The **Carter Gallery,** subdivided into four smaller rooms, successfully showcases 17th-century French paintings—one of the finest American collections, including *Magdalen with the Smoking Flame* by Georges de La Tour—English ceramics and European porcelain, 18th-century Italian sculpture and paintings, and 18th-century French paintings. The **Leo S. Bing Center** contains the 500-seat Bing Theater, venue for many film series, concerts, and public lectures. The museum also offers an art rental gallery, extensive art research library, and an excellent museum shop and on-site café.

The Los Angeles Museum of Art also includes the adjacent 1940s May Co. building at Wilshire and Fairfax—the best example of streamline moderne architecture, a post–art deco phenomenon, remaining in Southern California. Now known as **LACMA West,** since its $3 million renovation, the onetime department store is home to blockbuster exhibits such as *Van Gogh's Van Goghs.* Also intriguing at LACMA West is the satellite gallery space for L.A.'s venerable **Southwest Museum,** 323/933-4510, $6 admission, where exhibitions such as *Common Threads: Pueblo and Navajo Textiles* are always worth the time. (For more information on the Southwest Museum and its collection and programs, see Near Pasadena in the Pasadena and Vicinity chapter.)

Beyond its numerous special exhibits and events, the museum itself has become an event—thanks to its free **Friday Night Jazz** program in the central plaza, 5:30–8:30 P.M., which showcases L.A.'s best jazz artists in its ever-changing musical lineup. Occasional Sunday afternoon big-band concerts are also popular in summer.

The Los Angeles County Museum of Art (LACMA) is west of the Page Museum in Hancock Park, 5905 Wilshire Blvd. (at Ogden Dr.), 323/857-6000, www.lacma.org. The museum is open Mon., Tues., and Thurs. noon–8 P.M.; Fri. noon–9 P.M.; and on weekends 11 A.M.–8 P.M.

(closed on Wed. and major holidays). For tour information, call 323/857-6000. Admission is $7 adults, $5 seniors and students with ID, and $1 children ages 6–17 (age 5 and under free). On the second Tues. of each month, admission is free for everyone. Call 323/857-6010 for information on current and upcoming special exhibits, events, and jazz programs.

Craft and Folk Art Museum

Across the street from the Page Museum, the Craft and Folk Art Museum still features changing exhibits of ethnic, historic, and contemporary folk arts and crafts from around the world. Recent exhibitions included *Carnivale,* featuring carnival photographs and costumes; *Girls' Lowrider Bicycles;* and *Victoriana,* a look at both the romance and darker side of the 19th century. And, as one might imagine, the museum shop here is marvelous.

L.A.'s Craft and Folk Art Museum, 5814 Wilshire Blvd. (on the south side of Wilshire between Curson and Stanley Aves.), 323/937-4230, is open Tues.–Sun. 11 A.M.–5 P.M. (until 9 P.M. on Thursday). Admission is $3.50 adults, $2.50 seniors and students (age 12 and under free).

Carole & Barry Kaye Museum of Miniatures

Unless you're generally inspired by dollhouses, dollhouse-size furniture, and dollhouse-size scenes—poker-playing dogs, for example, a diorama of the O. J. Simpson trial, or a pint-size Louis Armstrong performing at the Hollywood

Los Angeles County Museum of Art

JEFF MYERS/TOM MYERS PHOTOGRAPHY

Bowl—L.A.'s miniatures museum won't be as worthwhile as the art and science enlightenment available just across the street in Hancock Park. One notable exception is the museum's **Eugene and Henry Kupjack Gallery,** displaying some of the finest examples of the genre. Eugene Kupjack, father of Henry, is most famous for his work on the **Thorne Rooms,** a 1930s project now part of the permanent collection at the Chicago Art Institute.

The Museum of Miniatures is directly across from LACMA at 5900 Wilshire Blvd., 323/937-7766, www.museumofminiatures.com. The museum is open Tues.–Sun. 10 A.M.–5 P.M. (Sun. from 11 A.M.–5 P.M.), closed major holidays. Admission is $7.50 adults, $6.50 seniors (60 and older), $5 ages 12–21, and $3 ages 3–11. Half-price validated parking is available directly below the museum every day but Sunday.

Petersen Automotive Museum

California couldn't live without the automobile, Americans assume. Los Angeles residents in particular live and breathe—or don't breathe—for their cars, it is also assumed. Cars in L.A. are like clothes in New York—the essential ingredient in presenting one's attitude and status to the world. Yet Californians actually own fewer vehicles, use less fuel, and drive fewer miles than the national average. Californians *do* love their cars, however, and the myth of unfettered geographic and social mobility that powers them. And L.A. *is* the only major U.S. city designed of, by, and for car culture.

Thus the appeal of the Petersen Museum, named after Robert Petersen, publisher of *Hot Rod* and *Motor Trend* magazines. This pop-arty paean to southstate automobility is not just another parking lot for antique cars. The Petersen, instead, acknowledges and incorporates almost every aspect of L.A.'s 20th-century car culture—from its oddball architecture and old gas stations to drive-in diners, L-shaped

strip malls (an L.A. first), and freeways. Upstairs are various cars presented as historical icons—including Greta Garbo's 1925 Lincoln—and works of art. It's all exceptionally well done. Past shows have included *The Lowriding Tradition,* examining L.A.'s lowrider culture as mobile folk art, and a feature on "woodies" and surf culture.

The Petersen Automotive Museum, 6060 Wilshire Blvd. (at Fairfax), 323/930-2277, www.petersen.org, is open Tues.–Sun. and "holiday Mondays" 10 A.M.–6 P.M., closed major holidays. Admission is $7 adults, $5 seniors (over age 62) and students with ID, $3 children ages 5–12 (under 5 free). To arrange guided tours, call 323/964-6346.

Farmers Market

An L.A. landmark since 1934, the Farmers Market ain't what it used to be. During the Depression farmers paid $.50 each day for the privilege of hawking produce from beat-up old trucks parked here. These days it's quite citified; vendors sell their wares from permanent stalls inside. But it's still casual, colorful, lively, and loud—one of those places kids can visit without constantly apologizing for themselves. You can find just about anything here—specialty foods, flowers, arts and crafts, clothing, jewelry—yet the food stands are the real draw. The **Kokomo** café, open at breakfast and lunch, is quite popular with show-biz types since CBS Studios' Television City is right next door. This is just the place to power down breakfast basics, hearty but hip burgers, and the best BLTs in town while waiting for some celebrity or pseudo-celeb to stroll by. Also here is the **Gumbo Pot,** a real deal for Cajun, serving the cheapest and best gumbo, jambalaya, and blackened redfish around.

The Farmers Market, 6333 W. 3rd St. (at Fairfax), 323/933-9211, is open Mon.–Sat. 9 A.M.–6:30 P.M. and Sun. 10 A.M.–5 P.M. (until later in summer) except on major holidays.

AROUND DOWNTOWN

EXPOSITION PARK

Directly south of the University of Southern California (USC) via Figueroa St. but otherwise not in the most inviting of neighborhoods is Exposition Park, originally an agriculture-oriented fairground established in 1872. The Southern California Agricultural Society organized fairs, carnivals, and eventually horse races here; but once gambling began, in the 1890s, saloons and houses of ill-repute soon followed. The 114-acre park was reclaimed for use by respectable people at the behest of Judge William Miller Bowen, who hoped to create a "landmark of worthwhile cultural significance." After the city and county of Los Angeles and the state of California jointly bought the land in 1910, work began on the park's first museum—the Natural History Museum of Los Angeles County.

But Judge Bowen's dream wasn't fully realized until 1932, when Los Angeles hosted the Olympics in Exposition Park, which explains the existence here of the Los Angeles Memorial Sports Arena and the Los Angeles Memorial Coliseum. (Many events were also held here during L.A.'s 1984 Olympics.) The Coliseum, seriously damaged in the 1994 Northridge earthquake, was recently home to the L.A. Raiders football team—repaired just in time for the Raiders' announcement that the football franchise was moving back to Oakland. Also still standing—and open, in summer, for public swimming—is the stunning Olympics-era **McDonald's Swim Stadium,** 213/740-8480, very carefully built out of beach sand. Impressive in peak season is the sunken **Exposition Park Rose Garden** at the park's north end at 900 Exposition Blvd., 213/763-3466, a popular site for weddings, with more than 20,000 rosebushes in at least 190 varieties. In Southern California, roses bloom from March to November. The garden is open daily 7 A.M.–5 P.M. Free.

Much more exposition than park even today, Exposition Park buildings house the jazzy new California Science Center, complete with new seven-story Imax theater; the venerable Natural History Museum of Los Angeles County; and the very appealing California Afro-American Museum, with its emphasis on both art and history.

Exposition Park is just south of USC, between Exposition and Martin Luther King Jr. Blvds. and Figueroa St. and Menlo Avenue. State Dr., with access to public parking lots, passes between the rose garden and the museums; take N. Coliseum Dr. to reach Memorial Coliseum, W. Coliseum Dr. to reach the Sports Arena. Entrance to the park is free, though fees are charged for parking and admission to some attractions.

California Science Center

Centerpiece of a $300 million master plan to spiff up Exposition Park, the dazzling new California Science Center is a 245,000-square-foot facility providing scientific "edutainment" for jaded Southern California kids already mesmerized by television, video games, and theme parks. Consider Tess, the 50-foot-tall animatronic "woman" whose bones, muscles, organs, and blood vessels are exposed to explain how the body works. More than 125 hands-on activities are included within the "World of Life," a contemporary biology expo, and the "Creative World," a technological exploration of computer technology, digital imaging, and other innovations. Here children can experience a simulated earthquake; strap themselves into a space docking simulator to retrieve a damaged satellite in zero gravity; watch you-are-there videotape of heart surgery as projected onto a dummy patient; simulate the experience of driving a car sober and then drunk; and watch antismoking videos while sitting in a coughing chair made of cigarette butts. There's plenty more, and plans for expansion are already in the works. It's fun and educational for the whole family and—with the exception of the 3-D movies in the Imax theater—the California Science Center is free.

The California Science Center, 700 State Dr. in Exposition Park, 213/744-7400, www.casciencectr.org, is open daily 10 A.M.–5 P.M. (closed major holidays). Museum admission is free. Parking is $5. Imax admission is $7.50 adults, $6 students with ID, $5.50 seniors, and

$4.75 children ages 4–12; theater times vary. Call for current exhibit and Imax information.

Natural History Museum of Los Angeles County

This is the largest and most popular museum in California, housed in a graceful 1913 Spanish Renaissance building boasting more than 30 galleries and halls. The museum collection includes more than 35 million specimens and artifacts, most of which come out of storage only for temporary exhibition. But what *is* on display can easily keep you occupied for an entire day—the uncannily real North American and African dioramas (veritable taxidermy theses), the prehistoric fossil and dinosaur exhibits, the rare "Megamouth" shark, the gem stones, the Times-Mirror Hall of Native American Cultures. A real hit with the kids is the museum's **Ralph M. Parsons Insect Zoo,** which comes complete with a "bioscanner" video camera for an up-close view of the "zoo" animals. A refrigerator door opens to reveal the critters' favorite foods—accompanied by a recorded kazoo rendition of "The worms crawl in, the worms crawl out." (Keep an eye on the family fridge once you get home.) There is always at least one special museum exhibit under way, too, such as *The Great Russian Dinosaurs* fossil show, *Pavilion of Wings* butterfly experience, and *Robot Zoo* exhibition on biomechanics.

For current special exhibit information, call the Natural History Museum, 900 Exposition Blvd., 213/763-3466, www.nhm.org. The museum offers a free guided tour daily at 1 P.M. June–Sept., weekends only Oct.–May. The museum is open daily, on weekdays 9:30 A.M.–5 P.M. and on weekends 10 A.M.–5 P.M. (closed major holidays). Admission is $8 adults, $5.50 seniors and students with ID, and $2 children ages 5–12. Group tour discounts available. Admission is free on the first Tues. of every month.

The California Afro-American Museum

Opened just in time for the 1984 Olympics and the Olympic Art Festival, the California Afro-American Museum is one of the loveliest buildings in Exposition Park, with airy galleries and a glass-roofed sculpture patio. Originally "dedicated to Afro-American achievements in politics, education, athletics, and the arts," the museum's ongoing emphasis is on the arts and art history—sculpture, paintings, photography, and multimedia exhibits. Recent shows have included a multimedia tribute to jazz genius Duke Ellington and an exhibit on black music in Los Angeles in the 1960s. Free admission. The museum is open Tues.–Sun. 10 A.M.–5 P.M. For current schedule and other information, contact: California Afro-American Museum, 600 State Dr., 213/744-7432, www.caam.ca.gov.

Los Angeles Memorial Coliseum and Sports Arena

Built in 1923, the L.A. Memorial Coliseum, 3911 S. Figueroa St., 213/748-6131, seats 91,000. It gained fame as a central venue for the 1932 Olympic Games, and took a bow again in the 1984 Olympics. While visiting the Coliseum, take note of Robert Graham's *Olympic Arch,* a work that created quite a stir when it was unveiled in 1984. The massive sculpture is topped with two headless bronze nudes—one male, one female—as symbolic representations of all athletes.

No longer home to the L.A. Raiders, who renamed themselves yet again and pulled up stakes for a rocky reunion in Oakland to the north, the Coliseum still hosts USC football games, soccer games, and other sports and special events. Should L.A. lure another National Football League franchise to town, it probably won't settle in here since the cost to outfit the Coliseum with sky boxes and other accoutrements of corporate sports is considered astronomical. The indoor **Los Angeles Sports Arena,** 3939 S. Figueroa St., 213/748-6131, built in 1958 as a companion to the Coliseum, seats 16,000. The Sports Arena regularly hosts USC basketball, conventions, car shows, an occasional concert, and the like.

BALDWIN HILLS, LEIMERT PARK, AND VICINITY

Most of South-Central/South-West L.A.'s most accessible attractions are concentrated in and around affluent Baldwin Hills and, just to the east, Leimert Park, soul of a thriving local arts community. Nearby highlights include the **First African Methodist Episcopal (AME) Church,** 2270 S. Harvard Blvd., 323/730-9180, designed by noted L.A. architect Paul Williams. The church is gospel music heaven—guests welcome on Sun. for 8 A.M., 10 A.M., and noon services—

"OUR TOWN" AND A TOWERING IMAGINATION

One of the world's finest folk art shrines, the elaborate walled complex known as **Watts Towers** at 1765 E. 107th St. in South-Central L.A., was built by Italian immigrant Simon Rodia. Working without helpers—without formal plans, for that matter, and without scaffolding, machinery, rivets, or bolts—from 1921 until 1954 Rodia labored in his free time to build what he called Nuestro Pueblo, or "Our Town." His walled town first consisted of his small home, a gazebo, a fountain, a fireplace, and a barbecue—all framed from discarded steel (old pipes and bedframes), slathered with cement, then decorated with broken bottle glass, seashells, and bits of broken tiles and dishes. Then Rodia expanded, adding the three eccentric Gothic-style spires, more fountains, a fishpond, birdbaths, even a covered porch—everything woven together with patterned pathways and elaborate arches.

Simon Rodia was not without detractors. During World War II, for example, some thought the towers were secret radio transmitters designed to aid the Japanese. Others believed the elaborate compound was actually a secret burial site for his wife. But Rodia's town was a monument to historic adventurers and explorers. One tower, for example, represents Marco Polo's ship.

Rodia, who earned his living as a mason and tilesetter, abandoned his masterpiece almost as soon as it was completed. He deeded the property to a neighbor and then vanished from the neighborhood without telling a soul why he was inspired to build his "town," or why he was leaving. Years later, Rodia was found living in Martinez, near San Francisco. He finally told at least part of the story. "I wanted to do something for the United States," he said. "Because I was raised here, you understand, because there are nice people in this country." Rodia's monument to the vastness of human potential is now a National Historic Landmark.

The Watts Towers sustained an estimated $2 million damage in the 1994 Northridge earthquake, and repairs were funded by the Federal Emergency Management Agency and a generous grant from American Express. Public tours of Watts Towers were suspended for years because of ongoing renovation and restoration work, but were scheduled to begin again in January 2001. Restoration is now expected to be completed in 2003. For current tour information, call the community-based **Watts Towers Art Center** next door to the towers, 213/847-4646. For additional information, contact: **Watts Towers of Simon Rodia State Historic Park,** c/o City of Los Angeles Department of Cultural Affairs, 1727 E. 107th St., Los Angeles, CA 90002, www.culturela.com. The Watts Towers complex is accessible by Metrorail's Blue Line; get off at the 103rd St. stop.

TOM MYERS PHOTOGRAPHY

founded in downtown L.A. by former slave Biddy Mason in 1872 and moved here in 1969. Not to mention the **Community Youth Sports and Arts Foundation**, 4828 Crenshaw Blvd., 323/294-8320, founded by Chilton Alphonse in 1983 to provide teenagers a constructive alternative to gangs and drugs, and the **Los Angeles Sentinel**, 3800 Crenshaw Blvd., 323/299-3800, one of the largest black-owned newspapers in the nation. And both Dulan's Restaurant on Crenshaw, something of a de facto community center famous for its Southern-style soul food, and elegant Harold & Belle's on Jefferson, known for its Cajun, Creole, and other specialties long before such fare became fashionable.

Various local tour companies can include other destinations on their itineraries, such as, farther east, the renowned **Watts Towers** and the adjacent **Watts Towers Art Center**, 1727 E. 107th St., 213/847-4646, the latter famous for its exceptional community arts workshops.

For cultural and historical tours of South-Central and South-West Los Angeles, custom tours, special-interest tours—to enjoy gospel music, say, or blues and jazz and other community arts—and tours combining other areas of the city, contact local companies. Valerie Holton's **Black L.A. Tours**, 3450 W. 43rd St., Ste. 108, 323/750-9267, specializes in historical and cultural tours, including tapings of popular TV shows. Her custom itineraries cover many of the places mentioned above and below—and then some. She can accommodate both small and large groups. **H. Weeks Tours**, 1421 S. Temple Ave., Compton, 310/603-2987, is another good bet. Hersley Weeks happily accommodates with custom-designed local tours, and he can also arrange longer bus tours to major L.A. tourist sights or to Las Vegas, the Grand Canyon, and various destinations en route. (For more suggestions, contact the L.A. Convention and Visitors Bureau.) In addition, during Black History Month in February, the local **Our Authors Study Club**, 323/758-4520, offers a major annual tour of L.A.'s black historical sights—an entourage of eight or more buses—in addition to sponsoring other community events throughout the year.

Baldwin Hills

The opening of Magic Johnson's dazzling **Magic Theatres** 12-screen movie complex, 323/290-5900, was big news in 1995 at the previously ailing **Baldwin Hills Crenshaw Plaza Mall**—the first first-run movie venture in the Crenshaw district, gratefully hailed by the community as both major cultural and economic investment by the famous former L.A. Lakers basketball star and his business partner Sony Pictures. Another major attraction at the mall itself, home to many black-owned small businesses, is the free **Museum of African American Art** on the 3rd floor of the Robinson's May building, 4005 S. Crenshaw Blvd. (at Martin Luther King, Jr. Blvd.), 323/294-7071. A large part of the museum's permanent collection comprises the art, art collection, and archives of noted Harlem Renaissance artist Palmer Hayden. Dedicated to preserving and promoting art by and about people of African descent, the museum sponsors several special exhibits each year; call for current show information. The museum is open Thurs.–Sat. 11 A.M.–6 P.M., Sun. noon–5 P.M. Admission is free, but donations are appreciated.

Leimert Park and Vicinity

Especially on weekends, the most intriguing place around is relaxed Leimert (le-MURT) Park, a neighborhood of black professionals just east of Baldwin Hills. Among the homes here is the longtime residence of **Ralph J. Bunche**, the first African American to win a Nobel Peace Prize. Leimert Park's Spanish-style homes, bungalows, and apartment buildings were designed in the late 1920s by Olmsted & Olmsted—an architectural firm headed by the sons of Frederick Law Olmsted, New York's Central Park planner. The neighborhood was named, prosaically, after developer Walter H. Leimert.

Leimert Park's "village" or commercial district—including the tiny triangular public park facing 43rd Pl., where impromptu conversations and performances convene—is centered along the one-block section of Degnan Blvd. between 43rd St. and 43rd Pl., several blocks east of Crenshaw Blvd. and just north of Vernon. To get here: If coming from Exposition Park or the Harbor Fwy. (I-10), head west via Martin Luther King Jr. Blvd. past Vermont and Western and then head southwest onto Leimert Blvd.; turn right onto either 43rd (Street or Place). From the Santa Monica Fwy. (I-10) head south on Crenshaw, past Exposition and Martin Luther King

Jr. for about 15 blocks, and then turn left onto either 43rd. From the west and the San Diego Fwy. (I-405), exit east at the Marina Fwy. (Hwy. 90) onto Slauson Blvd., continue east for almost two miles, and then head north into the Baldwin Hills via Stocker St.; four blocks past Crenshaw, turn right onto Degnan.

Food for the Soul: After seeing the Museum of African American Art at the mall (see above), the next tour stop should be Brian Breyé's free back-room **Museum in Black,** 4331 Degnan Blvd. (at Crenshaw Blvd.), 323/292-9528, with its gruesome collection of racist American memorabilia—thousands of horrifying mementos, from genuine baby shackles and slave manifests to "darkie" salt and pepper shakers—and, for sale up front, considerably more appealing African and African American crafts. (Call ahead for shop hours.) For more arts, crafts, and gift items, also well worth a stop is **Gallery Plus** next door at 4333 Degnan, 323/296-2398. Look for other fascinating shops in the immediate vicinity, including the **Dawah Book Shop and Fragrance Warehouse,** 4801 Crenshaw (near 48th St.), 323/299-0335, perhaps the most aromatic bookstore in the universe, featuring body oils and lotions, soaps, shampoos, and incense in addition to shelves stocked with history, science, and religion. Hot for jam sessions and poetry readings—and particularly popular with the hip-hop crowd—is the online **KAOS Network** coffeehouse and multimedia art scene at 4343 Leimert Blvd., 323/296-5717.

Food for the Body: Sooner or later one must minister to the stomach. A knockout for takeout—definitely not for vegetarians—is **Phillips Bar-B-Que,** 4307 Leimert Blvd. (two blocks east of Crenshaw Blvd.), 323/292-7613, where those in the know call in their orders to avoid the wait for delectable smoky pork ribs. For Southern-style soul food and community schmoozing, the place is **Dulan's,** 4859 Crenshaw Blvd., 323/296-3034—a relative of Marina del Rey's **Aunt Kizzy's Kitchen**—and famous for its fried catfish, chicken and dumplings, and other specialties, open for meals on Sun. only. Farther north, **Harold & Belle's,** 2920 W. Jefferson Blvd. (between Crenshaw and Arlington), 323/735-9023, offers the most upscale soul food in L.A. at both lunch and dinner—gargantuan portions of Creole and Cajun cuisine. Reservations a must. Another area favorite, now relocated some distance south, is the genuine Jamaican **Coley's Place,** 310 E. Florence (near La Brea) in Inglewood, 310/672-7474, where the fine fare includes shrimp St. James and other sumptuous seafood.

EAST LOS ANGELES: EL BARRIO

As poignantly depicted in the film *My Family (Mi Familia),* the Los Angeles River has long been the traditional boundary between downtown and East L.A.'s Mexican American community, El Barrio (The Neighborhood). But before L.A.'s downtown industrial expansion, from World War I through the 1920s, the city's Latino families rarely migrated far from their traditional "Sonoratown" neighborhoods surrounding the plaza at El Pueblo de Los Angeles. As Mexican Americans were shoved out of the city they largely moved north toward Elysian Park and across the river to the east and southeast, into Boyle Heights, Lincoln Heights, and Belvedere. Largely dependent on the city's original Pacific Electric trolley system, the earliest Latino citizens—who called themselves Mexicanos, or Mexicans, "Mexican American" being a post–World War II term—also migrated to areas served by public transit, including Watts, Long Beach, and Pasadena. But El Barrio in the undesirable lowlands of East L.A. was ultimately the preferred destination, since for a time at least families could establish homes, neighborhoods, and businesses without suffering segregation and the other forms of social ostracism that met them elsewhere in L.A.

Yet the overcrowded housing conditions and abject poverty in areas of downtown and East L.A. now beset by gang violence are not necessarily direct descendants of historically poor treatment of Mexican Americans and other Latinos in L.A. Certainly not entirely. The astonishing rates of recent Latino immigration into the community—both legal and illegal immigration—have created intense social and economic strains between "Americans" and "foreigners."

Touring East L.A.
East L.A. is one of the many separate "cities" that make up the whole of Los Angeles—this one the de facto Latin American capital of the

United States, its total estimated Latino population exceeded only by those of Guadalajara and Mexico City. **César E. Chávez Ave.**, the eastern extension of Macy St. formerly known as Brooklyn Ave., leads to "Little Mexico" and its restaurants and shops, though the flashiest introduction to East L.A. is via **Whittier Boulevard.** Or visit **El Mercado**, 3425 E. 1st St., 323/268-3451, a three-story marketplace overflowing with inexpensive pottery and glassware, clothing, produce, food stands, and mariachi music, open daily 10 A.M.–8 P.M. (until later on weekends). Yet these days "East L.A." also includes many areas west of the Los Angeles River, which explains why downtown's **Grand Central Market** is so popular with Latino shoppers. Another best bet is **Huntington Park** southeast of downtown, where **Pacific Blvd.** between Randolph and Florence has become a colorful, family-oriented Latino marketplace, particularly lively on weekends (free off-street parking provided in city lots).

But East L.A. is most famous for its vibrant murals—splashing color and culture as well as personal and political statements on available wall space—and for its South American and Mexican restaurants.

Striking out beyond the main drags, the markets, and the murals, try an eating tour. In L.A. even the most WASPish Westsiders take particular pride in knowing the best ethnic restaurants and cheap-eats places in town—which is why people from all over head to East L.A. for Mexican food. **El Tepayac Cafe**, 812 N. Evergreen Ave. (near César E. Chávez Ave.), 323/268-1960, is famous for its burritos—the biggest and the best, stuffed with various meat fillings, chile sauce, rice, beans, and guacamole. One makes a meal. Open daily 6 A.M.–9:45 P.M., on Fri. and Sat. until 11 P.M. Another possibility, beloved for its *taquitos*, is simple stucco **Ciro's**, 705 N. Evergreen Ave., 323/269-5104. A car-culture classic in East L.A.: **King Taco**, a 1950s-style drive-in at 2400 César E. Chávez (at Soto), 323/264-3940.

Pretty **La Parrilla**, 2126 César E. Chávez (at Chicago), 323/262-3434, is famous for its house-made tamales (fresh on the weekends) but most famous for its astonishingly fresh seafood. It's open daily for breakfast, lunch, and dinner. Top of the mark for foodies, though, is **La**

Serenata de Garibaldi, 1842 E. 1st St., 323/265-2887, open for lunch and dinner and a dazzling Sunday brunch. Try *gorditas* or fresh soup (served with rice and beans) at lunch. Seafood stars at dinner. Closed Monday.

DODGER STADIUM AND VICINITY

Just north of downtown are two geographic islands separated from downtown by L.A.'s "four-level interchange," where the San Bernardino, Pasadena, and Hollywood Fwys. intertwine themselves like thick concrete shoelaces. Tucked into long, deep ravines just beyond the freeways is an area rich with history, most easily separated into the Echo Park/Elysian Park and Highland Park/Eagle Rock neighborhoods. (For more on Highland Park, see Near Pasadena in the Pasadena and Vicinity chapter.) Home to L.A.'s first suburb and first public park, these gentle hills were originally the domain of native peoples who lived and hunted small game near the hillside springs. The area still has an almost rural feel, surprising so close to downtown. Small wood-frame homes from the late 1800s line the hillsides, the winding roads connecting them fringed by huge eucalyptus trees. The population is largely blue-collar Latino, although there is also a thriving artists' community drawn by both the affordable rents and the quaint, usually quiet surroundings.

Elysian Park and Dodger Stadium
Elysian Park was set aside for public use when Los Angeles was founded in 1781. The second-largest city park in L.A., 600-acre Elysian retains much of its natural chaparral, a landscape crisscrossed with hiking trails. At the central picnic area along Stadium Way are barbecue pits, a small manmade lake, and children's play area. The **Chávez Ravine Arboretum** protects 10 acres of rare trees. A recreation center offers basketball courts and volleyball. Despite the presence here of the **Los Angeles Police Academy** and shooting range—and the academy's cafeteria-style restaurant, open to the public—solo hikes into the more isolated areas of the park are not recommended. And after dark, forget it.

Hugging the slopes of Chávez Ravine is Dodger Stadium, 1900 Elysian Park Ave.,

SPORTING LOS ANGELES

The news in 1997 that **Los Angeles Dodgers** owner Peter O'Malley was planning to sell the city's National League baseball team, possibly to international media mogul Rupert Murdoch, was enough to send the entire region into fits of athletic apoplexy. At last report such evil deed had indeed been done, yet young boys and their fathers (and young girls and their mothers) still flock to Dodger Stadium in Chávez Ravine downtown, just off the Pasadena Freeway in Elysian Park, for the summer ritual of dugouts and Dodger 'dogs. For current info and tickets, call the Dodgers at 323/224-1400. For the latest news about the team, in five different languages no less, try www.dodgers.com. For American League ball, head for Anaheim in Orange County and the **Anaheim Angels,** formerly the California Angels, 714/634-2000.

Big news in Los Angeles is downtown's new **Staples Center,** 1111 S. Figueroa St., toll-free 877/305-1111 for general information or 213/742-7340 for tickets, www.staplescenter.com. Among the teams now calling the Staples Center home are the NBA's **Los Angeles Lakers,** a team still synonymous with Earvin "Magic" Johnson and Shaquille O'Neal, and the **Los Angeles Clippers.** The National Hockey League's **Los Angeles Kings** also get down at the Staples Center.

The oddest thing about sporting Los Angeles in 2000 is that the region lacks a national football franchise, since both the Los Angeles Rams and the Los Angeles Raiders (previously and subsequently the Oakland Raiders) packed up and left town in 1995. What to do? Since Los Angeles has always lived by the "If We Build It, They Will Come" sports philosophy, local discussion now centers on where to build a new football stadium to lure a new franchise. Local and regional boosters are salivating over the prospect of landing "the big one" for their own neighborhoods. Given the success of the Disney Company in regional sports—Disney's Mighty Ducks have made quite a splash in hockey at The Pond in Anaheim, and Disney is now part owner of the Anaheim Angels—some local wags think a new NFL expansion team here could be called the Lion Kings, perhaps housed in The Den.

While you wait for the return of the NFL, whenever and wherever that may be, there's always the Arena Football League and the **Los Angeles Avengers,** also part of the Staples Center sports stable (see above). And there's always collegiate football. The mythic L.A. teams are the **University of California at Los Angeles (UCLA) Bruins,** 310/825-2101, www.uclabruins.com (you can order tickets online) and the **University of Southern California (USC) Trojans,** 213/740-4672.

Other spectator sports abound throughout the region, from golf, tennis, beach volleyball, and surfing tournaments to thoroughbred racing; consult local newspapers for current offerings.

323/224-1400, www.dodgers.com, reached via the Pasadena Fwy. (the 110) and then Stadium Way. Dodger Stadium, home to the **Los Angeles Dodgers** since the team moved west from Brooklyn in 1969, offers 56,000 seats and almost as many parking spaces. Washing a few Dodger dogs down with cold beer on a summer afternoon has long been a form of high culture in L.A.—some sort of authentic culture, anyway, one that crosses all the city's usually well-drawn economic and ethnic lines.

Angelino Heights
The first suburb in Los Angeles, Angelino Heights just west of Dodger Stadium was built as a neighborhood for professionals, its stylish Victorian homes connected to downtown by a mile-long Pacific Electric trolley line. The homes here were built during California's real estate boom of the 1880s, when railroad passage from Kansas City dropped to as low as $1. Thousands of hopeful new residents soon arrived in sunny Southern California but, though they could afford passage, many could not sustain themselves once here. The big boom went bust and Angelino Heights, surrounded by less expensive homes, gradually deteriorated.

But in the 1970s residents of the 1300 block of **Carroll Avenue** decided to open their homes for tours—to raise money to restore the neighborhood to its former splendor. Eleven structures on this block (and others) are designated by the city of Los Angeles as cultural historical landmarks. Tours of Angelino Heights ($8 per person) begin at 10 A.M. on the first Sat. of every month, reservations required; call the Los Angeles Conservancy, 213/623-2489, www.laconservancy.org.

PRACTICAL DOWNTOWN (AND AROUND)

STAYING DOWNTOWN

Though Angelenos dash into downtown for the theater, musical performances, or the latest contemporary art show, the area is not typically on locals' lists of favorite destinations—largely because the social and economic gulf between affluence and abject poverty is so obvious, and so startling. Most people prefer to avoid having to notice. But for those unafraid of the downtown experience, quite decent inexpensive and moderately priced lodgings aren't difficult to find amid downtown's dour towers. In addition to glass-and-glamour accommodations, downtown also boasts one of Southern California's grandest old hotels. All high-end stays can be genuine bargains come weekends, when the suits depart, at least in the absence of major conventions. But inquire about hotel parking prices, which in some cases are exorbitant.

Less Expensive Accommodations

Best bets for budget travelers include the friendly and safe 250-room **Hotel Stillwell** opposite Chase Plaza at 838. S. Grand Ave. (between 8th and 9th Sts.), 213/627-1151 or toll-free 800/553-4774, www.stillwell-la.com. Rooms are quite basic but clean, with color TV, phone, air-conditioning, and private baths. East Indian and Asian art prints decorate the hallways and large lobby. Added bonuses: the tandoori breads, meat dishes, shrimp curry, vegetarian selec-

tions, and other specialties served at **Gill's Cuisine of India,** 213/623-1050, the restaurant in the back of the lobby (open for lunch and dinner, closed Sun.), as well as **Hank's American Grill,** the in-house bar and grill. Moderate-Expensive, with rooms $49–59, suites $75–95.

Also a bargain downtown: the **Orchid Hotel,** 819 S. Flower St., 213/624-5855. This 1920s flower, a real find, features clean, modern, quite basic rooms with in-house laundry and public parking nearby. Weekly rates available. Inexpensive. Rates: $38 double, $200 weekly. Right next door and also fairly friendly to the pocketbook is the **Milner Hotel,** 813 S. Flower St., 213/627-6981, where rates include breakfast. Moderate. Rates: $70–85.

Moderate Accommodations

A best bet in Chinatown is the 50-room **Best Western Dragon Gate Inn,** 818 N. Hill St. (at Alpine), 213/617-3077, toll-free 800/282-9999, www.dragongateinn.com, with all the usual plus in-room refrigerators, cable TV, free movies, and tea makers, not to mention the inexpensive on-site restaurants, Chinese herbalist shop and pharmacy, secured underground parking, and elevator to rooms. Children under 18 stay free. Moderate-Expensive, with rates $79–99. Also in Chinatown but adjacent to El Pueblo's Olvera Street and just a half-block from Union Station (and Metrorail) is the 82-room **Metro Plaza Hotel,** 711 N. Main St. (at César E. Chávez Ave.), 213/680-0200 or toll-free 800/223-2223, www.metroplazahotel.com, a comfortable motel featuring extras such as satellite TV (free movies), in-room refrigerators and microwaves, and phones in both the bedroom and bathroom. Moderate-Luxury, with rooms $69–85, suites $139–158.

More Expensive Accommodations

For an upscale yet reasonably cost-conscious European-style stay, consider the **Kawada Hotel** near the Civic Center at 200 S. Hill St., 213/621-4455 or toll-free 800/752-9232, www.kawada-hotel.com. Central to most of downtown's attractions yet popular with business types, the Kawada's rooms feature two phones, TV with

---

ACCOMMODATIONS RATINGS

Accommodations in this book are rated by price category, based on double-occupancy, high-season rates. Categories used are:

Budget.	$35 and under
Inexpensive	$35-60
Moderate	$60-85
Expensive	$85-110
Premium	$110-150
Luxury	$150 and up

VCR, and in-room refrigerators. Fun for those unafraid of earthquakes is the **Epicentre** quake-themed California-style restaurant downstairs, 213/625-0000, which serves lunch on weekdays, dinner nightly. The **Shockwave Café** is also a treat. Moderate-Premium, with standard rates $109–129 (weekend rates as low as $79).

The bloom may be off the neighborhood but not so 295-room **The Mayfair Hotel,** now a gracefully aging Best Western just west of most downtown action (and the Harbor Fwy.) at 1256 W. 7th St., between Figueroa and Union, 213/484-9789 or toll-free 800/528-1234. The Mayfair gathered bouquets for its Georgian grandeur in 1927 from *Architectural Digest,* and more recently received the community's Rose Award for Historic Preservation. Moderate-Luxury, with rates $70–280.

Downtown's most "L.A." midrange stay, though, is still the 285-room 1927 **Hotel Figueroa** across the street from the Staples Center and near the Convention Center at 939 S. Figueroa St. (south of 9th), 213/627-8971 or toll-free 800/421-9092, www.figueroahotel.com. Along with reasonable prices, the vaguely Spanish style here is much of the attraction—an appeal translated into a terra-cotta color scheme, hand-painted furniture in the very large guestrooms, tiled bathrooms, and ceiling fans almost everywhere. The lovely tiled lobby features a hand-painted ceiling but the balmy palm courtyard is more central, with graceful pool, spa, and bar. Two on-site restaurants add to the

Figueroa's convenience. Expensive-Luxury, with rates $98–165.

Luxury Accommodations

Grandest of the grand old Los Angeles landmark hotels, thanks to a $40 million facelift and a more recent makeover, **The Regal Biltmore Hotel** on S. Grand at 5th has been restored to its stylish 1923 supremacy. Details such as the stunning beamed ceiling—hand-painted by Italian artist Giovanni Smeraldi and now the oversoul of the hotel's new lounge—help create an ambience of classical luxury. So do imported Italian marble, plum velvet, **Bernard's** restaurant, and the Romanesque health spa. Even the pool is unbelievably beautiful, an elegant indoor art-deco ingenue that stole scenes in the movie *Bugsy.* For appetizing casual Italian, try in-house **Smeraldi's** restaurant. Downstairs is **Sai Sai,** for authentic Japanese. For more information or to make reservations, contact: The Regal Biltmore Hotel, 506 S. Grand Ave., 213/624-1011 or toll-free 800/245-8673, www.thebiltmore.com. Rates: $169–199, suites $300 and up.

Across from the Biltmore two stone sailing ships, the *Mayflower* and the *Santa Maria,* are chiseled into the stone facade of downtown's **Wyndham Checkers Hotel**—an elegant architectural reminder of its original 1927 incarnation as the Mayflower Hotel. To transform the Mayflower's tattered timbers into the luxurious 188-room Checkers boutique hotel took about $49 million, for starters. Now a boutique version

The Westin Bonaventure, with its futuristic style, shows up in many movies.

SALLY MYERS/TOM MYERS PHOTOGRAPHY

of the Biltmore, the Checkers Hotel imported intimate European ambience to downtown with fine art, exotic fabrics, and elegant antiques, everything polished with marble—along with every imaginable modern amenity. The hotel's restaurant, **Checkers,** is noted for its exceptional California cuisine. For more information and reservations, contact: Wyndham Checkers Hotel, 535 S. Grand Ave. (at 5th), 213/624-0000 or toll-free 800/996-3426, www.wyndham.com. Rates: $179–300, suites $400 and up.

Then there's the 35-story, 1,368-room **Westin Bonaventure,** John Portman's 1978 landmark hotel, the Buck Rogers–style futuristic fantasy with five mirrored cylindrical towers and multiple glass elevators that you've seen featured in so many movies—particularly popular with conventioneers. For more information and reservations, contact: Westin Bonaventure, 404 S. Figueroa (between 4th and 5th Sts.), 213/624-1000 or toll-free 800/228-3000, www.westin.com. Rates: $175–215, suites $200 and up.

Another sign that L.A. has arrived: the world-class **Omni Hotel** near downtown's Museum of Contemporary Art at 251 S. Olive St., 213/617-3300 or toll-free 800/442-5251, www.omnihotels.com, formerly an Inter-Continental and remembered by international media hounds as home-away-from-home for the jury in the original O. J. Simpson murder trial. The hotel includes the in-house **Grand Cafe,** workout room, heated swimming pool, steam room, and saunas. Rates: $175–210, suites $475 and up.

More Luxury Accommodations

The New Otani Hotel, star of downtown's Little Tokyo, blends elegant Japanese style with an all-American emphasis on convenience. In-room amenities include refrigerator, color TV, and kimonos. For the ultimate Zen experience, book a tatami suite with futon beds, *ofuro* baths, and first-class pampering. The hotel's rooftop **Garden in the Sky** offers a half-acre of Shinto serenity. Other Otani attractions: the exceptional **A Thousand Cranes** restaurant, a long-running star of L.A.'s cuisine scene; the American **Azalea Restaurant** and bar; and the convenience of on-site upscale shopping. For more information or to make reservations, contact: The New Otani Hotel, 120 S. Los Angeles St. (at 1st), 213/629-1200 or toll-free 800/252-0197, www.newotani.com.

Rates: $185–210, suites $475 and up.

Formerly the Los Angeles Hilton, and then the Omni Los Angeles Hotel and Centre, the 900-room **Wilshire Grand Hotel,** near the Convention Center at 930 Wilshire Blvd. (at Figueroa), 213/688-7777 or toll-free 888/773-2888, www.thewilshiregrand.com, is a financial district hotel catering to business travelers and conventioneers. Rates: $189–239, suites $375 and up.

Check out the deluxe and surprisingly intimate 469-room **Marriott Downtown,** at 333 S. Figueroa St. (near 6th St.), 213/617-1133 or toll-free 800/228-9297, www.marriott.com, where 14 stories of mirrored glass reflect upon four acres of landscaped grounds. Large guest rooms feature sofas, minibars, and marble baths, two-line phones, and morning newspapers and coffee. Other amenities: exercise facilities and heated pool, health club (fee), and the contemporary **Three Thirty Three** and other in-house restaurants. Also a plus: the never-crowded Laemmle four-plex movie theater right next door. Rates: $179–209, suites $249–350.

The sleek, glossy, and recently redone **Hyatt Regency Los Angeles,** 711 S. Hope St. (at 7th St.), 213/683-1234 or toll-free 800/233-1234, www.hyatt.com, in the heart of the financial district, also largely caters to business travelers—which makes it a best bet for weekenders. Aside from the tasteful underground lobby, which adjoins the Broadway Plaza shopping complex, every room offers a full wall of city views. Two floors of suites, known as The Regency Club, feature a private lounge, library, and VIP spa. Rates: $175–225, suites $250 and up. Weekend rates available.

STAYING AROUND DOWNTOWN

Staying South of Downtown

Best bet for an uptown hotel-style stay near the University of Southern California (USC) and Exposition Park is the 243-room **Radisson Hotel,** 3540 S. Figueroa St. (just west of the 110), 213/748-4141 or toll-free 800/244-7331, www.radisson.com. Premium-Luxury. Rates: $115–175. More intriguing alternatives nearby include bed-and-breakfasts. Five-room **The Inn at 657** is just a half-block west of Figueroa at 657 W. 23rd St., 213/741-2200 or toll-free

800/347-7512, www.patsysinn657.com. Suites at this tiny onetime 1948 home-cum-apartment complex include all the comforts of home. Among them: delightful and roomy rooms (three feature two bedrooms), color TV with VCR and cable, free local phone calls, stocked kitchens (in the four apartment-style units), free parking, even an outdoor spa. Full breakfast is served in the morning, snacks in the afternoon. The Inn at 657 is equally convenient to the Convention Center and downtown, too, just a dash away from the Downtown Area Short Hop (DASH) minibus stop. Premium. Rates: $110–125.

Staying on and along Wilshire

If you're doing Wilshire's museum row and can absorb Westside sticker shock, staying in West Hollywood or Beverly Hills is certainly convenient. But the area offers affordable options, including the **Dunes Motor Hotel** two blocks west of Crenshaw at 4300 Wilshire Blvd. 323/938-3616, toll-free 800/443-8637 in California, or toll-free 800/452-3863 from elsewhere in the U.S. Moderate. Rates: $59–79. A good bet closer to the museum action is the **Farmer's Daughter Motel** across from the Farmers Market at 115 S. Fairfax Ave. (near Beverly), 323/937-3930. Moderate-Expensive, with a summer rate of $71–95 (lower at other times).

For still more "real L.A." atmosphere, try the well-maintained 1924 **Chancellor Hotel** in Koreatown at 3191 W. 7th St., 213/383-1183. Primarily a residential hotel popular with young professionals and students, the Chancellor accommodates travelers on a space-available basis. The rates are a real deal since breakfast and dinner are included. Inexpensive, with rates $45.50–$54. Another art-deco classic even closer to downtown, near once-inviting MacArthur Park, is the Howard Johnson **Wilshire Royale Hotel,** 2619 Wilshire Blvd. (at Rampart), 213/387-5311, recently refurbished in contemporary style. Expensive-Premium, with rates $89–119. Still more stylish, though, is the **Oxford Palace Hotel** in Koreatown, six blocks south of Wilshire at 745 S. Oxford Ave. (between 7th and 8th Sts.), 213/389-8000. Basic amenities include in-room refrigerators, VCRs and movies, and breakfast. Luxury. High-season rates $175, and off-season rates $159. Inquire about specials and discounts.

EATING DOWNTOWN

Like accommodations, dining in downtown L.A. reflects the diversity of the population. Free meals for the skid row homeless are served within blocks of some of the most expensive meals in town. Gourmands can sample fine French, Italian, Californian, and nouvelle cuisine in the financial district—and Chinese (and Vietnamese) in Chinatown, Japanese in Little Tokyo, Mexican in El Pueblo, and working-class and ethnic American near the market districts.

People's Eats: El Pueblo and Vicinity

In honor of L.A.'s beginnings as El Pueblo de Los Angeles, if you find yourself anywhere near El Pueblo's Olvera Street stop for a sit-down meal at surprisingly good, surprisingly authentic **La Luz del Dia** ("The Light of Day"), 1 W. Olvera St., 213/628-7495, where specialties include *piccadillo* tacos, *carnitas,* and fresh cactus salad. (You can also find real Mexican in East L.A. and downtown, at the **Grand Central Public Market** on S. Broadway.) Best bet for *taquitos* is **Cielito Lindo,** on Olvera at César E. Chávez, 213/687-4391, the little shack next to the horse trough.

A classic one block north of Union Station is **Philippe the Original Sandwich Shop,** 1001 N. Alameda St. (at Ord), 213/628-3781, more than a place to grab a quick bite. Philippe's is a sociological phenomenon, a fragment of downtown history frozen in time. Most famous as the originator of the French-dipped sandwich—according to local lore, Philippe himself accidentally dropped a sandwich into gravy—Philippe's is also noted as home of the 10-cent cup of coffee. But be warned: during periods of rising coffee prices, a cup of Joe sometimes goes for 11 cents. The cavernous café is barnlike and basic, with sawdust floors and row upon row of shared chest-high tables and stools. Philippe's regular clientele includes escapees from downtown's glass canyons, fans and baseball players reel fortifying after a game at Dodger Stadium, and folks perennially down on their luck. No passing trend, Philippe's. At the end of a busy day, even the servers look as if they've been on their feet since the establishment first opened in 1908. So decide what you want, be it a beef, lamb, or pork dip, before you belly up to the endless counter, and be quick about it. Thousands are lining up behind you every day, hungry for a hit of Philippe's ripsnorting house mustard. After you're served, though, take your time. This is a perfect place for savoring a slice of L.A. life—and a slice of that cream pie. Philippe's is open daily 6 A.M.–10 P.M. With a sophisticated style and spirit inspired by its landmark location, **Traxx** at Union Station brings fine dining back to L.A.'s dazzling Spanish colonial art-deco train station. Both restaurant and bar, Traxx recaptures the glamour and excitement of the golden age of train travel while serving unmistakably contemporary and elegant meals. Traxx, on the main concourse of Union Station, 800 N. Alameda St., 213/625-1999, is particularly popular with local artists, downtown executives, and time-starved commuters who plug their laptops in at the bar.

People's Eats: Chinatown

In a sense, even L.A.'s "new" (post-1930s) Chinatown is no longer new. The contemporary Chinese migration is out toward the suburbs—to the clustered East L.A. cities of Alhambra, Monterey Park, Rosemead, and (for the very wealthy) San Marino and South Pasadena. Some of the best Chinese dim sum anywhere, for example, is served in East L.A. at well-known establishments that include the **Empress Pavilion, NBC Seafood Restaurant,** and the **Ocean Star Seafood Restaurant.**

Be that as it may, remnants of Chinatown's past culinary glory *do* survive in Chinatown—starting with the beef curry pies, shrimp dumplings, coconut sweet buns, and other delectable takeout available at **Hong Kong Low Deli,** 408 Bamboo Ln., 213/680-9827, a distant relative tucked into the alley behind the World War II–era Cantonese dining palace of the same name. (To find the place, look for the line of hungry customers.) You'll have to eat your meal elsewhere, but here you can easily gather up enough to gorge yourself for little more than pocket change. Hong Kong Low is open daily 7:30 A.M.–5 P.M. For the best Cantonese roast duck around, head for **Lucky Deli,** 706 N. Broadway (at Ord St.), 213/625-7847.

Another best bet for a quick bite in Chinatown is **Mandarin Deli,** 727 N. Broadway,

213/623-6054 (between Alpine and Ord Sts.), an inexpensive, clean, and popular place serving traditional noodle and dumpling dishes. Order the "handmade" noodles, and don't miss the marvelous fish dumplings. The Mandarin is open daily for lunch and dinner. There's another, more uptown Mandarin in Monterey Park at 728 S. Atlantic Blvd., 626/289-2891; you'll find them elsewhere around L.A., too. But this spartan noodle palace is the first and original.

For seafood, best bet is **Mon Kee,** 679 N. Spring St. (at Ord St.), 213/628-6717, serving the best Cantonese seafood in Chinatown at lunch and dinner daily. The food here is so good nobody cares about the minimal ambience. People's favorites include the crab in black bean sauce and chicken with scallops and snow peas. Expect to wait for a table. **Yang Chow,** 819 N. Broadway (between Alpine and College), 213/625-0811, is another best bet—in this case for Szechuan specialties, from slippery shrimp and *kung pao* chicken to *mu shu* anything. Another possibility, considerably more stylish and stylized, is the **Plum Tree Inn,** 937 N. Hill St. (at College), 213/613-1819, serving both Mandarin and Szechuan cuisines. Spicy Plum Tree beef and sweet and pungent shrimp are among the house favorites. If you like your food spicy, ask to order from the Chinese menu.

Then there's **Empress Pavilion,** 988 N. Hill St., Ste. 201 (at the mall on N. Hill between College and Bernard), 213/617-9898, pastel dim sum palace extraordinaire, open daily 9 A.M.–10 P.M., perfect for breakfast. If the kids have never been to Hong Kong, this huge Chinatown palace will give them the general idea. The Empress offers an astonishing number of items to choose from—you can't miss with a "gourmet selection" or specialty—but the dim sum selections, all quite good, are a great place to start. Or go for the seafood, something of a house specialty and usually perfectly prepared, such as the Maine lobster, Dungeness crab, and prawns with glazed walnuts. Killer crispy duck, too.

"New" new Chinatown is represented by some impressive places, including cuisine from other countries. For Cambodian, try **Battambang,** 648 New High St. (at Ord St.), 213/620-9015. And for more culinary surprises, wander the neighborhood.

People's Eats: Little Tokyo

The most enjoyable way to sample Little Tokyo is to wander rather aimlessly, if hungrily, through the various food courts. One possibility is **Japanese Village Plaza** between 1st and 2nd Streets. Another: **Weller Court**, 123 S. Ellison at Onizuka St., where you'll find everything from Japanese fast food to very elegant entrées.

One of the best and most elegant sushi bars around is **Shibucho** in Yaohan Plaza on the top floor, 333 S. Alameda St., 213/626-1184, which can also be quite reasonable. It's open for lunch Mon.–Sat., dinner daily. Hardly a people's palace but exceptional and surprising nonetheless: **A Thousand Cranes** at the New Otani Hotel, 120 S. Los Angeles St., 213/629-1200, where East and West blend deliciously at Sunday brunch.

Though the heyday has passed for the avant-garde restaurant and artsy club scene surrounding Little Tokyo—an era that boasted Gorky's, a hip Russian café, and café/clubs such as Troy—the neighborhoods bordering Little Tokyo are still a best bet for seeking outposts of the alternative, since they do pop up from time to time. Another of L.A.'s best sushi bars, **R-23** is an off-the-beaten-path Japanese restaurant that has remained one of the Loft District's best secrets for five years. Housed in a stunning industrial building minimally decorated with exposed brick and beams, vertical wood columns, and chairs made from cardboard, R-23 features a small menu and à la carte sushi. Best for a quick lunch: assorted *chirashi*, various high-quality sashimi resting atop a bowl of rice, with ginger and wasabi. If you can find your way here you'll find yourself doing lunch with escapees from City Hall and the hip Fashion District. L.A.-speak for "restaurant between 2nd and 3rd," R-23 is at 923 E. 3rd (at Alameda), 213/687-7178.

Other stylish alternatives to skid row have successfully taken root, too, such as **410 Boyd,** 410 Boyd St., 213/617-2491, beloved for its lobster club sandwich and lunch specials, and particularly popular with downtown loft-dwellers. Great place, but the neighborhood is definitely not recommended for the timid. Open for lunch Mon.–Fri., for both lunch and dinner Tues.–Fri.; secure parking.

People's Eats: Downtown and Around

Always reasonable—and always fun, given the setting—is sawdust-floored **Maddalena's Cucina** at downtown's own **San Antonio Winery,** 737 Lamar St. (off N. Main, just east of the L.A. River), 323/223-1401, open daily 10 A.M.–5 P.M.—the culinary outlet for a working winery in business here since 1916. Though it's a challenge to picture it these days, once—when L.A. boasted 20 wineries—this neighborhood was solidly Italian. The vineyards have long since been paved over, of course, and the San Antonio is the era's sole survivor. (The Riboli family now produces wines from grapes trucked in from elsewhere in California.) Take the tour, sample the wares. For downtown L.A., it's all a big surprise.

For coffee shop fans there's an L.A. classic nearby, tucked in among the railroad yards. Ham is the thing at **Nick's Cafe,** 1300 N. Spring St., 323/222-1450, famous for its ham and eggs breakfasts, ham omelettes, ham sandwiches, and just plain slabs o' ham. Sure, it's a working stiffs' breakfast and lunch stop—open from before dawn to 5 P.M. on weekdays, to 11:30 A.M. on Sat.—but it's meat and potatoes done right, cooked from scratch on the premises. Nick's is near the Police Academy, which explains all those regulation haircuts.

Another place most people are surprised to find in L.A., given the city's much-hyped hedonism, is **Clifton's "Brookdale" Cafeteria** downtown at 648 S. Broadway, 213/627-1673, built by Christian philanthropist Clifford E. Clifton. Throughout the Depression, Clifton's "Golden Rule Cafeterias" served ample portions of good, wholesome food to customers who paid what they could afford. But Clifton did more than feed the hungry huddled masses. He also attempted to elevate their spirituality and spirits—by building this strange six-level oasis, an ersatz redwood forest complete with babbling brook and waterfall. Clifton's is easy to find; just look for the street evangelists out front. On a chilly day, enjoy a hearty bowl of soup or chili with a side of cornbread.

Also très traditional downtown: the **Original Pantry,** 877 S. Figueroa St. (at 9th), 213/972-9279. Mayor Richard Riordan is the current owner of the restaurant and he and his circle of top L.A. businesspeople are often in residence. The Original has been open 24 hours a day, every day, since 1924—except for one much-publicized, politically scandalous day in November 1997, when the place was cited for health code violations and closed for a thorough cleaning. Even that event didn't dent the patient line of patrons outside on the sidewalk, waiting to get in—24 hours a day, every day, since 1924. Generous portions of good old-fashioned Americana—steaks, roast chicken, even macaroni and cheese—are the Original Pantry's specialties. Hearty bacon and egg breakfasts, accompanied by the best hash browns in town, propel Angelenos to get in line for more. The **Original Pantry Cafe**, now open next door, serves terrific hamburgers, sandwiches, and pastries from the Pantry's own bakery. You can expect an enormous meal.

Not to be missed if you're heading east toward Wilshire's museums is very purple **Super Torta** just north of MacArthur Park in a strip mall at 360 S. Alvarado St. (at Maryland), 213/413-7953, which serves a sumptuous Americanized version of the Mexican sandwich—your choice of meat with beans, guacamole, mayo, and jalapeños on the side—and even *horchata*, to wash it all down. If you're craving something from other locales, head for Koreatown and C & K Importing, the best-known ethnic market (Greek) in Los Angeles. Inside is **Papa Cristo's Taverna**, 2771 W. Pico (off Normandy), 323/737-2970, offering fab Greek grilled goodies—beef, lamb, or fish—served with creamy fried potatoes, a traditional salad, and pita bread. The garlicky *loukaniko* sausage, flavored with orange peel and simmered in wine, comes highly recommended. Eat in or take out. And such a deal.

If hunger assaults you somewhere south of Wilshire, the traditional USC student destination for Mexican food and margaritas is **El Cholo,** 1121 S. Western Ave. (between Pico and Olympic), 323/734-2773, open here since 1927. The taco tray delivers a do-it-yourself meal of tortillas, meats, beans, and sauces, though feel free to try anything. It's all good. In season—traditionally June to September—best bets include the green corn tamales and the salsa *verde* crab enchiladas.

More Uptown Downtown

If you're contemplating the Museum of Contemporary Art, also contemplate a scrumptious lunch or a light Thursday evening supper at Joachim Splichal's California-French **Patinette,** inside the museum at 250 S. Grand Ave. (near 2nd St.), 213/626-1178, serving surprising sandwiches and pasta salads, wine by the glass, and espresso.

Kissing cousin to the Contemporary's Patinette is **Café Pinot** in the garden near the Central Library at 700 W. 5th St. (at Flower), 213/239-6500. One of downtown's best eating events, Café Pinot is a sibling to Pinot Bistro in Studio City, Pinot Hollywood, and Pinot at the Chronicle in Pasadena—conceptual descendants, all, of Patina on Melrose, one of the city's best restaurants. What that pedigree brings you here is a Paris-style garden bistro serving wonderful roast chicken and other unforgettables at dinner, wonderful lunch specials and specialties. This place is perfect for a pre-theater meal, too, if you can get in by 6 P.M. Pinot is open weekdays only for lunch, 11:30 A.M.–2:30 P.M., and for dinner nightly from either 5 or 5:30 P.M., depending on the day (closed major holidays).

Uptown **Pacific Grill,** inside the Sanwa Bank building at 601 S. Figueroa St. (between 6th St. and Wilshire), 213/485-0927, serves contemporary American fare of all ethnic persuasions. Pacific Grill is open only for lunch on Mon.–Fri. 11 A.M.–2 P.M.

The Oviatt Building, an ersatz 1930s luxury ocean liner awash in rich woods, black marble, and burgundy velvet armchairs—is home to glamorous **Cicada,** at 617 S. Olive St. (between 6th and 7th Sts.), 213/488-9488, which took over the helm here, so to speak, when Rex, Il Ristorante closed following proprietor Mauro Vincenti's death. Owned by Stephanie and Bernie Taupin (he, Elton John's longtime songwriting partner), Cicada is Northern Italian and expensive. Free shuttle service to the music center makes this a popular pre-theater dinner spot.

For contemporary American on the company expense account, the place is **Bernard's** at the Biltmore Hotel, 506 S. Grand Ave. (at 5th), 213/612-1580, where the exquisite no-nonsense fare includes New York steak and chicken, lamb, and duck. Bernard's is open Tues.–Sat. for dinner.

Additional options for uptown dining downtown are mentioned under upscale hotel listings in Staying Downtown, above.

EATING AROUND WILSHIRE

Ethnic foodies, take note: Korean restaurants and shops abound in Koreatown, which skirts Wilshire Blvd. close to downtown. L.A.'s Korean

farmers market

TOM MYERS PHOTOGRAPHY

community is half a million strong, the largest anywhere outside Korea, which brings to mid-Wilshire an astonishing array of Korean bars, coffeehouses, restaurants, cafés, noodle houses, and elegant dining rooms. South of Wilshire along Pico and Olympic, stretching from downtown west to Fairfax Ave., are other surprising and distinct ethnic areas—Thai, Vietnamese, Taiwanese, Japanese, and Indonesian—blending at the edges with Central American and Mexican neighborhoods. Exploring along 8th and 9th Sts. is L.A.'s ultimate multicultural culinary adventure. Another dining destination, Fairfax Ave. between Pico and Wilshire, is becoming known for its Ethiopian restaurants. Kosher country begins just west of Fairfax, where Pico is becoming a Jewish "restaurant row." But Fairfax north of Wilshire, particularly between Beverly Blvd. and Melrose, marks the Fairfax district—L.A.'s traditional, now transitional, Russian-Jewish neighborhood, known for its Russian restaurants and kosher shops, groceries, and delis, including the famous 24-hour Canter's. Also in the neighborhood, at 3rd St., is the Farmers Market, where dozens of food stalls and simple restaurants attract all kinds of Angelenos (and buses of tourists). Prime-time for people-watching.

Korean People's Eats

Los Angeles food writer Jonathan Gold describes a bowl of Korean bean-curd stew like this: "Soon tofu looks less like food than a special effect from a Wes Craven movie, a heaving, bright-red mass in a superheated black cauldron that spurts geysers, spits like a lake of volcanic lava, and broadcasts a fine, red mist of chile and broth that tints anything within six inches a pale, lustrous pink. A network of bubbles forms on the surface of the stew and amalgamates into a throbbing, blood-colored froth that occasionally opens up like a cinematic portal to doom, revealing glistening white chunks bobbing within." If a close approximation of that experience appeals to you, **Beverly Soon Tofu,** 2717 W. Olympic Blvd., 213/380-1113, is the place to get it. Or try other Korean specialties—*mandoo* dumplings, for instance, both crispy fried or boiled versions—at **Ddo-Wa,** 3542 W. 3rd St., 213/387-1288. At **Shin Chon** 244 S. Oxford Ave., 213/384-2663, Korean beef soup *(sol-long-tang)* is the only thing on the menu. The bowl is bottomless. More upscale is **Sa Rit Gol** at 3189 W. Olympic Blvd., 213/387-0909, famous for pork barbecue, thin loin strips marinated in red chile sauce and then cooked on a tabletop grill. Intrigued but not quite willing to risk a full-fledged meal? Then consider **Sool In Nun Ma-Ool,** 2500 W. 8th St., 213/380-3346, an elegant drinking establishment that serves mini-meals such as leeks and oysters fried in egg batter, crisp mung-bean pancakes, and steamed tendon with scallion salad. The house specialty is something you won't find just anywhere—whole octopus, rubbed with chile paste and then grilled. To serve it, the waitress lifts the 'pus off the platter with tongs and then snips off pieces of tentacle with scissors.

Other People's Eats

If you're low on cash after doing museum row, head for the **Farmers Market,** 6333 W. 3rd St., on the north side of W. 3rd St. at Fairfax. The excellent **Gumbo Pot,** 323/933-0358, is among the choices here; the Cajun/Creole fare is almost a steal. The namesake gumbo is a mainstay, along with jambalaya, meatloaf, muffulettas, and catfish, chicken, shrimp, and oyster po' boys. Everything's available for takeout, too, so stop by to pack an unusual picnic. (For a Sierra Nevada or other brew, head to the beer bar nearby.) The Gumbo Pot is open Mon.–Sat. 8:30 A.M.–6:30 P.M., Sun. 10 A.M.–5 P.M., closed major holidays. Particularly entertaining at breakfast, because of its tendency to draw execs and even the occasional celeb from nearby CBS Television City, is the Farmers Market's **Kokomo,** 323/933-0773, a hip and happenin' café where such things as grilled cheese sandwiches and sweet-potato French fries manage to pass for health food. Those in the know say Kokomo also has the best BLT in town. Dinner served, too.

A real find nearby is **Fiddler's Bistro** at the Park Plaza Lodge motel, 6009 W. 3rd St. (at Martel), 323/931-8167, a coffee shop with Middle Eastern flair where the Greek fare is the best bet—and a low-budget opportunity to be a voyeur within the everydayness of the Hollywood scene. Entrées quite reasonable.

For kosher, try 24-hour **Canter's Delicatessen,** 419 N. Fairfax (between Beverly Blvd. and Melrose), 323/651-2030, a neighborhood fixture almost since time began. The food's just decent and the service often downright rude, but some folks also eat that up.

More People's Eats

Maurice's Snack 'n' Chat is an L.A. icon, this one south of Wilshire at 5549 W. Pico Blvd., 323/930-1795. A place frequented from time to time by Quincy Jones, Danny Glover, Whoopi Goldberg, and other celebs, this lively restaurant serves unpretentious soul food that gets there when it gets there—so you can chat even before you snack. The fare here is *not* what the doctor ordered—fried chicken, short ribs, black-eyed peas, yams, spoon bread, and down-home desserts, including peach cobbler and coconut cake—but it's tasty and the place is fun, so what

the heck. Make a reservation, BYOB, and plan on staying awhile. It's open for lunch and dinner daily. For a mid-Wilshire burger experience, head for **Mo' Better Meatty Meat Burger,** 5855 W. Pico Blvd., 323/938-6558. Some L.A. burger fanatics rate Mo' Better's best, but service can be slow—always a consideration if the kids are hungry and cranky. There's another Mo' Better on Melrose.

For real-thing Thai—and the choices are multiple in this neighborhood—try **Alisa,** 2810 W. 9th St., 213/384-7049, which is undistinguished except for the surprise Northern Thai "restaurant within a restaurant" **Chao Nue,** a rare find in L.A. Bring everyone you know, request "northern food," and order everything.

If hunger strikes while you're gallery-hopping along La Brea, one possibility is **Pink's Hot Dogs** north of Melrose at 711 N. La Brea, 323/931-4223 (no phone orders), justifiably famous for its chili dogs but increasingly popular for such things as chicken fajita burritos and chili-drenched tamales. Or stop by the cherubic and clean **Divine Pasta Co.,** 615 N. La Brea, 323/939-1148, where you can sit down to some of the city's best fresh pasta and sauce (served with salad). And if you're doing La Brea in the morning, line up with everyone else at the famed **La Brea Bakery,** 624 S. La Brea, 323/939-6813, for breakfast pastries to go or a bag full of specialty breads, including the wonderful sourdough black-olive.

Fancier Fare on and near La Brea

The La Brea Ave. area north of Wilshire sports more than its fair share of great midrange-and-more restaurants. For starters, try the **Authentic Cafe,** 7605 Beverly Blvd. (between Fairfax and La Brea), 323/939-4626, open daily for lunch and dinner. Tiny and terrifically popular, the Authentic Cafe is best known for tamales, nachos, new renditions of New Mexican standards, and somewhat Southwestern pastas and pizzas. Seemingly unrelated items appear on the menu, too, such as Chinese dumplings, other Asian dishes, and eclectic miscellany—which makes the Authentic Cafe as authentically Los Angeles as anyplace around. It's got a cappuccino bar, too. No reservations, so be prepared to wait.

Now that the semi-industrial City Restaurant at 180 S. La Brea has been recycled, **The Original**

Sonora Cafe, 323/857-1800, has transplanted its pretty pricey Southwestern self from downtown into that impressive space. It's open for lunch Mon.–Sat., for dinner daily.

But don't miss **Ca'Brea,** 346 S. La Brea (between 3rd and 4th), 323/938-2863. One of the most reasonably priced Northern Italian restaurants in Los Angeles, casual, stylish, and wildly popular Ca'Brea serves such things as baby-back ribs and beans, crab cakes, seafood pastas, and a wonderful fresh mozzarella salad. Daily specials bring new surprises, but count on fresh fish, pastas, soups, and salads. Ca'Brea is open weekdays only for lunch, Mon.–Sat. for dinner. Reservations always advisable. To meet a more uptown member of the same culinary family, frequently rated as L.A.'s best Italian, try **Locanda Veneta,** close to West Hollywood and Beverly Hills at 8638 W. 3rd St., 310/274-1893.

Hancock Park's Larchmont area also features some nice neighborhood eateries, these including an outpost of **Chan Dara,** 310 N. Larchmont Blvd., 323/467-1052, serving sophisticated Thai, and **Girasole Cucina Italiana,** 225 1/2 Larchmont, 323/464-6978, offering rustic, authentic Venetian cuisine (BYO alcoholic beverage).

Campanile

The ultimate neighborhood culinary destination is Campanile, 624 S. La Brea (between Wilshire and 6th St.), 323/938-1447. This onetime massage parlor, auto dealership, and Charlie Chaplin office building, a Moorish art-deco beauty complete with bell tower, has gone postmodern. Not the most expensive restaurant in Los Angeles nor the trendiest, Campanile is quite possibly the best. The fare here, from grilled chicken, lobster, and fresh fish dishes to sumptuous salads, is fairly simple yet superb, the atmosphere airy and unassuming, the prices quite reasonable. The real deal is breakfast—quite leisurely on a weekday, and always fortified by fresh baked goods from the associated and equally acclaimed La Brea Bakery, adjacent. Campanile is open daily for breakfast, weekdays only for lunch, and Mon.–Sat. for dinner (closed Thanksgiving and Christmas). Reservations are necessary for dinner.

ROBERT HOLMES/CALTOUR

HOLLYWOOD AND VICINITY
THE TRAPPINGS OF TINSELTOWN

"Strip away the phony tinsel in Hollywood and you'll find the real tinsel underneath," Oscar Levant once said of the world's supreme dream machine. Since then the phony tinsel has been stripped away, along with most of what might have been real. For a while it seemed the last few strands of authentic memorabilia had been all but buried by trash and trashy attractions.

Film aficionados flock here, pilgrims to a movieland mecca. Lured by the recollected romance of big-screen stars such as Marilyn Monroe and Lana Turner and the he-man heroism of the John Wayne western, people stumble off the tour bus onto the Hollywood Walk of Fame these days only to confront the gritty and grimy hard-eyed human conflagration of prostitution, porn palaces, and unapologetic poverty that is, now, Hollywood. Worldly wits foretold this turn of events. "It's hard to know where Hollywood ends and the DT's begin," W. C. Fields once said. Ditto for Oscar Wilde's general observation: "All of us are in the gutter, but some of us are looking up at the stars."

Tinseltown: The Place and the Idea
First and foremost, Hollywood is a place—a place that began its decline shortly after the peak of its prominence, during the Great Depression. During the past decades Hollywood successfully substituted one reel of illusion for another, dumping glued-on glamour for disaffection, desperation, and despair, right in step with the modern psyche.

But Hollywood is also an idea. If you prefer visiting the idea, a Hollywood Blvd. where everyone is clean-cut, courteous, and hopelessly happy, you can. You can go to Florida, for example. The Disney-MGM Studios theme park in Orlando features "Hollywood Boulevard as you've always imagined it to be." *That* Hollywood Blvd. features actors, animatronic actors, adoring crowds, various other artificial sights and sounds, and an admission price of well over $30. (On the other hand, the real Hollywood Blvd. is absolutely free and authentically eccentric.) Or you can visit CityWalk at Universal Studios, just up the hill. In the

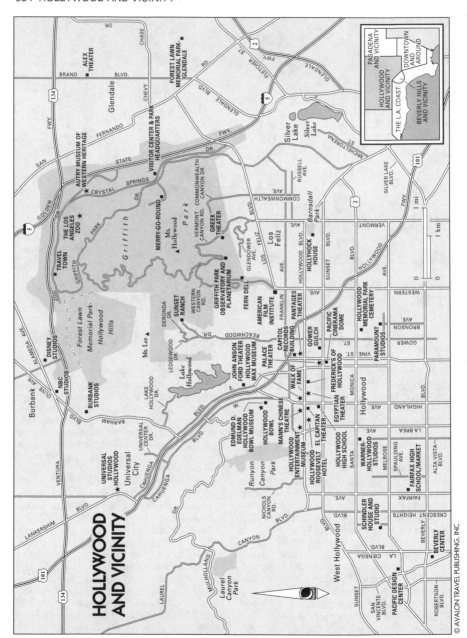

HOLLYWOOD AND VICINITY

© AVALON TRAVEL PUBLISHING, INC.

immediate vicinity, Hollywood the idea extends beyond Cahuenga Pass into the San Fernando Valley and, from the Hollywood flatlands, west into the fairly new city of West Hollywood. Coming soon: Hollywood's next installment, near the shores of the Pacific Ocean on L.A.'s Westside.

Tinseltown II: The Sequel

Hollywood is changing yet again—cleaning up its act, albeit laboriously, and getting ready for a new performance. In 1986 the Los Angeles City Council decided to help its Hollywood district, once referred to even by residents as a "Club Med for crime," glue some of its glamour back on with a 30-year, $922 million facelift affecting more than 1,000 acres—a project second only in scope to the massive downtown Bunker Hill redevelopment. Included in the price tag: housing for teenage runaways and otherwise homeless street people. In addition, a Hollywood Entertainment District was created in 1996, with property assessment funds earmarked for local security patrols, ongoing cleanup, and other civic improvements.

Symbolizing this snazzy, cleaned-up Hollywood is the Metro Red Line's new subway station, opened in 1999, a way station for the ride that whisks people between downtown and Hollywood and Vine in minutes. Symbols of Hollywood abound at the station. Bus shelters were constructed to look like cartoons of Mann's Chinese Theatre, a limousine, and the Brown Derby restaurant. Inside, stylized Southern California palm trees serve as columns and old film reels cover the ceiling.

Helping things along considerably is the fact that boom times are back—even in Hollywood— thanks to burgeoning international demand for entertainment industry "product." With total annual receipts in excess of $19 billion, Hollywood's export trade runs to at least $6 billion annually.

Most modern movie corporations abandoned Hollywood's first wave of building sites years ago, of course, but the new studios aren't all that far away. These days Tinseltown's true territory has vast but vague borders, starting somewhere on the far side of the Hollywood Hills in the sprawling San Fernando Valley. Hollywood's second wave includes the Disney, Warner Bros., and NBC studios in Burbank and the fairly new Manhattan Beach Studios in Manhattan Beach, entertainment industry outposts all undergoing major expansions. The tourist-oriented Universal Studios, on the cusp between old and new Hollywood in the Hollywood Hills, plans to double its size within the next few decades.

MAKING THE TINSELTOWN MYTH

To imagine Hollywood as a god-fearing, prohibitionist utopia is more than most modern Hollywood mythmakers can manage. Yet once the native Cahuenga people were dispensed with, so went the Cahuenga Valley. Scattered sheep ranches, small vegetable farms, and a few citrus groves defined the landscape in late 1887. That year, just before L.A.'s 1880s real estate boom went bust, Horace Henderson Wilcox and his wife, Daeida, bought up the area for a future subdivision. Active prohibitionists with utopian Midwestern ideals, the Wilcoxes cut the theoretical town from their own cloth—banning saloons and liquor stores and offering free land for church construction.

Hollywood's stolid sobriety was soon shattered, forever—because moviemaking came to town. In the beginning it was something of a bootleg business, in defiance of fees, royalties, and other efforts by Thomas Alva Edison and the Edison Company to control the new industry through the Motion Pictures Patents Company (known as "the Trust").

Technically the southstate moving picture industry began in 1907 in Los Angeles, which Selig Studios chose for filming the outdoor scenes for *The Count of Monte Cristo*. The first film companies to establish permanent Southern California studios selected Los Angeles, Santa Monica, and Santa Barbara—locations that shared the advantage of being close to Mexico, where film companies and crews could escape the Trust's attorneys, process servers, and thugs.

Hollywood resisted Southern California's growing general affinity for film. Before local morality mavens could mobilize much protest, however, those carousing carefree movie people had arrived. By 1916 about 35 movie studios had relocated from the East and Midwest, creating overnight chaos on Hollywood's sleepy unpaved streets. Not surprisingly, Hollywood boardinghouses shunned movie people. The Hollywood Hotel posted a "No Dogs or Actors" sign—a snub that reportedly caused actress Gloria Swanson to snarl: "We didn't even get top billing!" Los Angeles in general looked askance at Hollywood's glittery gypsies, shunning them socially. The Los Angeles Country Club was notorious for refusing membership to any and all actors. A classic Hollywood story features Victor Mature pulling bad reviews out of his pocket and telling club officials: "I'm no actor, and I can prove it."

Hollywood's "Conscientious Citizens" were indeed conscientious, and repeatedly petitioned the city to run film companies out of town. But moral concerns proved to be no match for movie industry money. By the Roaring '20s, Hollywood's stars glittered as national and international idols. Abundant cash and employment opportunity also changed the community's mind about the merits of the movies. They also changed the community; starry-eyed young people rushed the gates of Hollywood's Babylon, dreaming of stardom but settling for almost anything.

Accidental Purist: Cecil B. DeMille

Flamboyant director Cecil B. DeMille created the Hollywood of myth—almost an accidental result of his collaboration with fellow New Yorkers Jesse Lasky and Lasky's brother-in-law, Samuel Goldfish (later, Goldwyn), in the Jesse L. Lasky Feature Play Company. DeMille's directorial debut also resulted in Hollywood's first full-length film, The Squaw Man, more or less made in their studio—a barn—and adjacent orange grove at the dirt-road juncture of Selma and Vine.

If DeMille was almost an accidental director, Hollywood was his accidental destination. When C. B. (as he was called) set out from New York, he planned to shoot The Squaw Man in Flagstaff, Arizona. A dust storm foiled his filming schedule, so DeMille and company got back on the train and continued west. They ended up in Hollywood.

One could argue also that DeMille became Hollywood's accidental purist. Dogged by "accidents," disasters, threats, and at least one assassination attempt—"The first critic of a DeMille picture," the filmmaker reportedly quipped, while attributing such sabotage to the Trust—DeMille ultimately completed the film, a phenomenal six-reel success that led to many more.

DeMille also played a starring role in early Hollywood's cinematic subculture, becoming an enduring Southern California symbol—the heroic director all done up in jodhpurs, leather boots (to prevent rattlesnake bites), even holster and pistol. Others in DeMille's entourage exuded exuberance and creative extravagance, including Ina Claire, Geraldine Farrar, and Gloria Swanson, Wallace Berry and Walt Disney.

Film critics have blamed DeMille, father of the film spectacle (The Ten Commandments, Madame Satan, King of Kings), for demeaning and derailing the American film industry in its infancy. DeMille certainly did relish cinematic excess, the vulgarity of showmanship. But entertainment, not art, made money at the box office, and DeMille was the first to figure that out. So the year 1914, when Cecil B. DeMille decided to settle permanently in this sleepy L.A. suburb, "must be considered both the actual and symbolic founding of Hollywood," according to historian Kevin Starr.

SEEING AND DOING HOLLYWOOD

Hollywood proper is a not a city but a neighborhood district within the city of Los Angeles, further subdivided into two geographical areas: the flatlands and the hills. An industrial and residential hodgepodge inhabits the flats. Studios, soundstages, and businesses catering to the entertainment industry cluster along Hollywood, Sunset, and Santa Monica Blvds. in central Hollywood, along with run-down bungalows and small apartment buildings now home to recent immigrants from the Americas, Asia, and the Middle East. The neighborhood's cultural diversity is best reflected by the student population at Hollywood High School, where dozens of different native languages are spoken.

Some of Hollywood's fabled star quality not only survives but thrives in residential areas of the Hollywood Hills, particularly along the narrow streets of Nichols Canyon and Laurel Canyon. The eclectic cultural collection here is largely architectural, with the high-priced real estate mixing Moorish castles and Spanish-style haciendas, modest vine-covered cottages and ultramodern experiments in exhibitionism. Farther up in the hills, you can't miss Madonna's onetime home, a wildly striped maroon and yellow mansion not far from the Hollywood sign.

HOLLYWOOD BOULEVARD AND VICINITY

Vicinity of Hollywood and Vine

Look north into the hills from the intersection of Hollywood and Vine for the best downtown view of the landmark **Hollywood Sign,** the city's most famous symbol. In the foreground sits the landmark **Capitol Records Building,** 1750 N. Vine. In 1954, Nat King Cole and Johnny Mercer of Capitol Records proposed that the company's new headquarters be designed to resemble a giant stack of records with a stylus on top. So it was—and there it is, the world's first circular office building, by Welton Becket. Across the street, at 1735 N. Vine, is the **Palace Theater,** once home to *This Is Your Life,* Bing Crosby's *Hollywood Palace* show, and, later, *The Merv Griffin Show.* Look east to spot the spectacular 1929 **Pantages Theater,** 6233 Hollywood Blvd. (between Vine and Argyle Ave.), 323/468-1770, the first art-deco movie house in America. When Howard Hughes owned the theater in the 1950s, the Academy Awards were staged here. Also in the neighborhood, near Pantages Theater, is another real-Hollywood remnant—**Collectors Bookstore,** 6225 Hollywood Blvd., 323/467-3296, always a worthwhile stop for posters, photos, memorabilia, and books.

HOLLYWOOD COMING ATTRACTIONS

Even in Los Angeles, a town where theme parks increasingly interpret and create local culture, the logical place to start looking for Hollywood is still along famed Hollywood Boulevard—"Hollywood Bull" in the vernacular of 1930s-vintage hipsters. Most memorabilia-rich is the stretch between Vine St. on the east and, to the west, La Brea Ave.—about 13 city blocks roughly coinciding with the galaxy of stars' stars along the Hollywood Walk of Fame. Traditional here is the opportunity to buy classic tourist kitsch such as Hollywood beer-stein toothpick holders and gold lamé baseball caps. With Hollywood's makeover well under way, palm trees line the streets and public benches, a mixed blessing, are in place. The Hollywood Roosevelt Hotel, site of the first Academy Awards ceremony, has been grandly redone, along with some of Hollywood's spectacular old movie palaces, which once again host huge weekend crowds.

A Hollywood Boulevard stroll traditionally begins at the intersection of Hollywood and Vine, once the movie industry's much-romanticized heart. In mythic Hollywood, simply standing at Hollywood and Vine meant being besotted by celluloid celebrity—the producers, directors, stars, starlets, and sundry other celestials motoring by in their convertibles or sauntering into the nearby Brown Derby restaurant for a little deal making. But those days are long gone, as is the Derby. These days, the only stars in town are those memorialized on the sidewalk.

After shuffling along the Hollywood Walk of Fame and poking into Hollywood Boulevard's more garish tourist traps, the usual tourist visits Mann's Chinese Theatre and other historic movie venues, the new Hollywood Entertainment Museum, and the long-running Hollywood Studio Museum near the world-famous Hollywood Bowl amphitheater. Of lasting eccentric appeal: the Frederick's of Hollywood Lingerie Museum.

Some of Hollywood's most worthwhile sights are well beyond the usual loop—including the Hollywood Memorial Park Cemetery near Paramount Studios, Frank Lloyd Wright's spectacular Hollyhock House in Barnsdall Park (closed until 2003), and the Autry Museum of Western Heritage in 4,000-acre Griffith Park. Griffith Park also boasts a variety of family-friendly diversions, including the Los Angeles Zoo. Always interesting is the Silver Lake neighborhood.

Despite its more notorious neighborhoods, at least during daylight Hollywood is safe even for the most doe-eyed of innocent tourists—using reasonable caution, of course.

To get oriented to area attractions and Los Angeles in general, stop by the **Hollywood Visitors Bureau** inside the Janes House, 6541 Hollywood Blvd. (on the north side of the street, between Wilcox and Hudson), 323/461-9520. The tiny Victorian house, once a school attended by the children of Douglas Fairbanks, Charlie Chaplin, and other Hollywood heavies, is appropriately stranded in a minimall.

LOS ANGELES CVB/MICHELE & TOM GRIMM

the Capitol Records building

Hollywood Walk of Fame

Americans prefer their heroes and heroines down to earth, and Hollywood has been more than accommodating when it comes to memorializing movie stars. Here, you look down on them. You can even wipe your feet on fame, all along Hollywood Boulevard.

Hollywood Blvd. had been in decline almost since the beginning, certainly since the 1930s and the Great Depression, when studios and stars started leaving town. To recapture some of the glitz and glamour of bygone days, in the late 1950s the Hollywood Improvement Association launched the promotional Hollywood Walk of Fame—then a total of 2,518 coral-colored terrazzo stars outlined in brass and surrounded by squares of gray terrazzo. Walk of Fame stars extend one block north, south, and east from the intersection of Hollywood and Vine, but the dominant constellation shoots west about 12 blocks along both sides of the boulevard.

Just how celebrities make the final Walk of Fame cut, a decision made by the Hollywood

THE HOLLYWOOD SIGN

The huge "Hollywood" sign looming over the landscape from atop scrubby Mt. Lee is the city's universal symbol. The best pedestrian view is from Hollywood and Vine, looking north past the landmark Capitol Records Building. These fifty-foot-tall letters, fabricated from white sheet metal and originally outlined in 4,000 lights, advertised *Los Angeles Times* publisher Harry Chandler's adjacent 500-acre real estate development, a gated tract complete with castle towers, Black Forest cottages, and Ruritanian hunting lodges dubbed "Hollywoodland." The sign's maintenance was erratic, and abandoned altogether by 1939. The final bad-luck blow came in 1949 when the dilapidated "land" section tore loose and slid downhill to its doom. That same year, the Hollywood sign was deeded to the Hollywood Chamber of Commerce for the purposes of civic promotion.

This being Hollywood, the entire town eventually realized that a cosmetic makeover was long overdue. To raise the necessary cash to rebuild the sign, in 1978 local celebrities came to the rescue, donating $27,700 per letter. Hugh Hefner, for example, held a benefit at the Playboy Mansion for the sake of Y; Gene Autry paid for an L; and rocker Alice Cooper bought the last O in memory of Groucho Marx. But facelifts beget more facelifts. Thus in 1999, on QVC's *Extreme Shopping: Hollywood* show, an anonymous sponsor contributed another $100,000 to the Hollywood Sign Trust.

Chamber of Commerce's screening committee, is still one of those arcane mysteries—almost as puzzling as Academy Award winners. Why, for example, did hero dog Rin Tin Tin make the team but not King Kong? Why Mickey Mouse but not Donald Duck? Why the Beach Boys but not the Beatles? The process is otherwise quite straightforward. Assuming celebrities fit into one of Hollywood's stardom categories—theater, motion pictures, television, radio, recording—and otherwise pass muster, they fork over $15,000 to get their names walked on by the public.

New celebrities are regularly inducted into this earthy hall of fame, to great public fanfare. To find out who's next, and when, contact the **Hollywood Chamber of Commerce,** 7018 Hollywood Blvd., 323/469-8311, www.hollywoodcoc.org.

FREDERICK'S OF HOLLYWOOD LINGERIE MUSEUM

This, the original Frederick's of Hollywood, was started in 1946 by Frederick Mellinger, inspired by the popularity of the World War II–era Betty Grable pin-up. Unless you're underwear shopping, skip the crotchless panties and other merchandise displays and head upstairs to the lingerie museum, starring undergarments of the rich, famous, and sometimes voluptuous—Jayne Mansfield, Marilyn Monroe, and Mae West, Madonna, and Cher. (Though Madonna's black and gold bustier was ripped off during L.A.'s 1992 riot rampage, it later miraculously reappeared.) Drag queens, don't despair: unmentionables worn by Tony Curtis and Jack Lemmon in *Some Like It Hot* are also on display.

Frederick's, 6608 Hollywood Blvd., 323/466-8506, is free and open 10 A.M.–6 P.M. Mon.–Sat., noon–5 P.M. on Sunday.

Farther West on the Bull

The north side of Hollywood Blvd. between Cahuenga and Highland is known as **Booksellers' Row,** best bet for finding unusual and out-of-print books at a fair price. Most famous among the storefronts here is **Larry Edmonds Cinema Bookshop,** 6644 Hollywood Blvd. (three blocks east of Highland at Cherokee), 323/463-3273, open daily 10 A.M.–6 P.M. (closed on major holidays). A popular place even within "the industry," Larry Edmonds specializes in new and out-of-print books on film and theater—the world's largest collection—as well as movie memorabilia. The Marilyn Monroe and James Dean posters are always big sellers. **Musso & Frank Grill** across the way at 6667 Hollywood Blvd., 323/467-7788, is another Hollywood classic—the oldest restaurant in town, established in 1919.

Egyptian Theatre

Predecessor to Sid Grauman's more famous Chinese Theatre, the 1921 Egyptian Theatre hosted Hollywood's first movie premiere—the original 1922 screening of *Robin Hood.* Designed by architects Meyer and Holler in Egyptian revival style—all the rage in the 1920s, when King Tut's tomb was first unveiled—the aptly named Egyptian was once a stunning sight, a pre-Disneyland Disneyland fantasy. To enter, moviegoers wound through a courtyard bazaar lined with mummy cases, huge vases, banana palms, caged wild animals, and shops selling exotic wares. On opening night, a spear-carrying soldier paced the roofline; usherettes masqueraded as Cleopatra's handmaidens.

The historic Egyptian Theatre, 6712 Hollywood Blvd., 323/466-3456, is back—saved at long last from its long, slow destruction from modernization and from instantaneous damage inflicted by the 1994 Northridge earthquake. Restored to its original gaudy grandeur by American Cinematheque's determined $14.2 million campaign, this Hollywood landmark's "new" look includes a revivified 150-foot-deep exterior courtyard (sans caged animals), a state-of-the-art 650-seat auditorium that retains the ornate sunburst patterned ceiling, and a 1922 Wurlitzer organ to accompany silent film presentations.

The Egyptian Theatre is permanent home and headquarters of American Cinematheque, a nonprofit film center that presents classic,

---

HOLLYWOOD CITYPASS

For those planning to seriously see the sights in and around Hollywood, the local CityPass ticket book might be worth the investment. The Hollywood CityPass includes admission tickets to eight attractions—Universal Studios, the Egyptian Theatre, the Hollywood Entertainment Museum, the Museum of Television and Radio, the Petersen Automotive Museum, the Autry Museum of Western Heritage, the Museum of Tolerance, and the Reagan Presidential Library and Museum—and at last report cost $49.75 for an adult, $38 for children (age 3–11). Sure, that sounds steep—but in 2000 admission to Universal Studios alone was $41 for adults and $31 for children.

Conveniently for vacation planners, the Hollywood CityPass ticket book is undated and can be bought in advance. (Tickets are invalid, however, if removed in advance from the booklet.) The only limitation is, the CityPass is good only for 30 days, beginning with the first day of use.

For current information and to buy ticket books online, go to www.citypass.net. For recorded information, call 707/256-0490.

MONUMENTS TO THE MOVIES

Los Angeles is the best place in the world to go to the movies. Anyone anywhere can *get* movies—at the neighborhood multiplex, say, or at the video store. But L.A. is the land of grand movie theaters, single big-screen theaters that transform mundane human experience into myth in the larger-than-life Hollywood tradition. Though Los Angeles has been notably lax in saving its heritage—happily tearing down the past to make way for a more profitable future— many of its historic movie palaces survive. And a few relative newcomers expand the possibilities for movie fans and fanatics.

Visitors tend to think "Hollywood" when searching for a place-related synonym for the movies in L.A., but downtown Los Angeles is actually the city's movie theater capital. Or was. Broadway between 3rd and 9th Sts. is the largest registered district of historic movie theaters in the nation, the center of L.A.'s public cinematic display in the early 20th century. Many of the grandest grand old palaces on historic Broadway have become nightclubs, including the Mayan and the El Rey, and others have been converted into swap-meet venues, including the Arcade, the Cameo, and the Roxy. Other downtown movie icons have been bulldozed, the California and the Paramount among them; others, including the Million Dollar and United Artists, have become churches. The old Warner at 7th and Spring is now a jewelry market, and these days the spectacular Los Angeles is used as a set for film shoots and private parties.

But some are still open for business. Most notable among these is the lovingly restored 1911 French Renaissance **Orpheum,** 842 S. Broadway, the city's oldest operating movie theater—not to slight the rococo **Palace,** 630 S. Broadway, and the Spanish Renaissance **State,** 703 S. Broadway. Sadly for their determined owners, the neighborhood's changing character tends to discourage most moviegoers, particularly those from suburbia and the Westside. Another way to appreciate Broadway's movie places is on a walking tour with the nonprofit **Los Angeles Conservancy,** 213/623-2489, or www.laconservancy.org, which also sponsors a monthlong classic movie series, "The Last Remaining Seats," in various downtown theaters every June.

Mann's Chinese Theatre

Long after Broadway is finally bulldozed for a new crop of corporate skyscrapers, the famous Chinese Theatre in Hollywood will abide. Originally known as Grauman's Chinese Theatre, after owner and showman Sid Grauman, this elaborate impression of a Chinese temple was unveiled in 1927 with the premiere of Cecil B. DeMille's *King of Kings.* A 30-foot-tall dragon guards the huge pagoda-like entrance. Inside are more dragons and other Chinese motifs. The red lobby and auditorium are remarkably well preserved, just one reason why this is still one of L.A.'s best theaters. But if you do a movie here, be sure to see what's playing in the *main* theater, behind the courtyard, not in the two added-on shoeboxes—so you can see the theater. You can't miss Mann's Chinese Theatre at 6925 Hollywood Blvd. (near Highland Ave.) in Hollywood, 323/464-6266.

El Capitan Theatre

First opened in 1927 as a "legitimate" theater (for stage productions), El Capitan Theatre, 6838 Hollywood Blvd. (near Highland Ave.), 323/467-7674, was bought in 1941 by Paramount Pictures, transformed into a movie venue, and renamed the Paramount Theater. Its dazzling present-day reincarnation as the color-crazy El Capitan—dare we say reimagineered restoration?—financed by the Walt Disney Company, also made this the new Los Angeles debut theater for Walt Disney Productions. When it reopened for business in 1991, welcome improvements at El Capitan included bigger and better bathrooms as well as disabled access. But much of the glory here is pure grace, from El Capitan's outdoor box office, original lobby murals, and fabulously intricate ceiling to quaint opera boxes.

Egyptian Theatre

Restored to its original gaudy grandeur by the film organization American Cinematheque, the 1922 Egyptian Theatre, 6712 Hollywood Blvd., 323/466-3456, hosts a film series of classic, rare and unusual films, including a 55-minute documentary *Forever Hollywood,* which screens daily. The Egyptian, predecessor to Sid Grauman's more famous Chinese Theatre, hosted Hollywood's first movie premiere— the original 1922 screening of *Robin Hood.* Now that renovation is complete moviegoers are again able to wind their way to the theater through an exotic courtyard lined with banana palms, mummy cases, and other stylistic oddities.

Vista Theater

Something of a faded monument to Hollywood's glory, the Vista at 4473 Sunset Dr. (at Hollywood Blvd.) in East Hollywood, 323/660-6639, is a beloved neighborhood movie house—constructed on the site of Charlie Chaplin's very first movie studio, no less. And before the Egyptian reopened, the Vista's sphinxes were the only notable emblems of that particular movie-theater era. Every other row of seats has been removed, too, freeing extra leg room for enjoying French-language and other arty films as well as stellar Hollywood blockbusters. If the neighborhood makes you nervous, come for a matinee.

Showcase Theater

Hollywood also boasts the Showcase at 614 N. La Brea Ave. (one half block south of Melrose Ave.), 323/934-2944, once the Gordon Theater, preserved as a single-screen theater when it was rehabilitated in the 1980s. Famous for its Woody Allen premieres and similar fare, the Showcase also benefits from the fact that Pink's (as in hot dogs) is just a block away.

Silent Movie Showcase

Hollywood's eccentric, locally famous Silent Movie Showcase, 611 N. Fairfax Ave. (one half block south of Melrose Ave.), 323/655-2520, has been silent movie fans' (reportedly including Johnny Depp) holy grail since 1947. Now reopened following the tragic murder of its former proprietor, it is the only place to see the classics, with live organ accompaniment, almost any time.

Fine Arts Theater

Cecchi Gori got out the big Beverly Hills checkbook to finance a gloriously garish facelift for the art-deco Fine Arts Theater, 8556 Wilshire Blvd., 310/652-1330. Every bit as gaudy as Disney's El Capitan, the theater is a standout tribute to Hollywood even if the bill of fare shown here isn't always.

Bruin, Village, and National Theatres

Westwood is still one of Southern California's favorite destinations for moviegoers, with both large-

and small-screen theater stars. Dominating the big-screen department, historically speaking, are the neighboring Bruin and Village Theatres. The Bruin, at 948 Broxton Ave. (at Wayburn), 310/208-8998, is fairly modest by modern standards but the Village, at 961 Broxton (at Wayburn), 310/208-5576, with its landmark neon-lit tower, is one of L.A.'s great theaters—popular still for major movie premieres. A respected remnant of the Fox theater chain, slightly less foxy inside than out, the 1931 Spanish moderne Village is distinguished by its 70-foot screen and a superb sound system. Notice, too, the gold rush–themed frieze. To appreciate this theater in its totality, the best view is from the balcony—if it's open.

Crest Theater

Another find in Westwood, just south of Wilshire Blvd., is the art-deco Crest Theater, 1262 Westwood Blvd., 310/474-7866, reborn in recent years as an intimate and stylish venue for first-run and other films. Hollywood buffs in particular will appreciate the interior murals, showcasing street scenes from L.A.'s moviemaking golden age.

Other Fine Movie Houses

Still the artsy movie house in West Los Angeles, the **Nuart Theater,** 11272 Santa Monica Blvd. (one block west of the 405 Fwy.), 310/478-6379, screens the likes of *Antonio Gaudi* and *Woman in the Dunes.* But nothing beats the show down the coast at the weekends-only **Old Town Music Hall** revival house at 140 Richmond St. in downtown El Segundo, 310/322-2592, also a concert house. The after-show singalongs and fluorescent-painted pipe organ alone are worth the price of admission.

If you find yourself near Pasadena, the place for first-run art films on the big screen is the slightly fading **Rialto Theater** in South Pasadena at 1023 Fair Oaks Ave., 626/799-9567. And if you make the short trip west across the big water to Catalina, keep in mind that the spectacular art-deco **Casino** in Avalon, 310/510-0179, is another L.A. classic—the world's first theater designed specifically for "talking pictures," in fact.

rare, and unusual films, including new and experimental works. The theater is also open to the public for tours. For more information about the theater and about American Cinematheque, call the phone number listed above or try www.americancinematheque.com.

Hollywood Kitsch Museums

Unless you possess an insatiable appetite for California kitsch, lots of time, and a whole lot of extra cash, Hollywood Blvd.'s trio of tourist-kitsch museums is missable. Should any or all of the above describe your circumstances, the

Hollywood Wax Museum, 6767 Hollywood Blvd., 323/462-8860, is always popular. The museum is open 10 A.M.–midnight Thurs.–Sun., until 2 A.M. on Fri. and Sat. nights. Admission is $9.95 adults, $6.95 children, free for kids under age five. As if the free Hollywood sidewalk sideshow weren't entertaining enough, across the street is **Ripley's Believe It Or Not! Odditorium,** 6780 Hollywood Blvd., 323/466-6335, starring freaks, geeks, and original works such as the full-size portrait of Hollywood cowboy John Wayne fashioned from dryer lint. (To find this place, look for the large Tyrannosaurus rex on the roof.) The odditorium is open daily 10 A.M.–11 P.M. Admission is $8.95 adults, $5.95 children, free for kids under age five. The **Hollywood Guinness World Of Records Museum,** 6764 Hollywood Blvd., 323/463-6433, showcases fanaticism in general and world-class fanatics in particular. The World of Records is open Sun.–Thurs. 10 A.M.–midnight, until 2 A.M. on weekend nights, closed Monday. Admission is $14.95 adults, $8.95 children, free for kids under age five.

El Capitan Theatre

First opened in 1927 as a "legitimate" theater (for stage productions), El Capitan Theatre, 6838 Hollywood Blvd. (a half-block west of Highland), 323/467-7674, was purchased in 1941 by Paramount Pictures, transformed into a movie venue, and renamed the Paramount Theater. Its present-day reincarnation as El Capitan, with dazzlingly authentic interiors, made this the new debut theater for Walt Disney Productions. In addition to modern improvements such as earthquake safety features, bigger and better bathrooms, and access for the disabled, El Capitan's recently restored glories include its outdoor box office, original lobby murals, fabulously intricate ceiling, and quaint opera boxes. Worth a G or PG rest stop, no matter what's playing. And the "bargain matinees"—the first two shows of the day—make it almost a bargain.

Mann's Chinese Theatre and Vicinity

Most famous of all the famous Hollywood theaters, Mann's Chinese Theatre, 6925 Hollywood Blvd., 323/464-8111, was originally known as **Grauman's Chinese Theatre,** after owner-showman Sid Grauman. Grauman commissioned architects Meyer and Holler to construct this elaborate impression of a Chinese temple, unveiled in 1927 with the premiere of Cecil B. DeMille's *King of Kings*. The huge pagodalike entrance is guarded by a 30-foot-tall dragon. Inside, more dragons and other Chinese motifs populate the red lobby and the carpets, seats, walls, and ceilings of the auditorium. The original Chinese Theatre is surprisingly well-preserved, and still one of the best movie palaces in greater Los Angeles. But if you do see a movie here, for the genuine experience make sure the show is playing in the main theater behind the courtyard, not in the added-on shoeboxes up front.

A bigger draw than the theater itself is the courtyard. More than two million people come to mill around and study celebrity footprints in the concrete each year—the inspiration, no doubt, for the

Mann's Chinese Theatre

TOM MYERS PHOTOGRAPHY

later Walk of Fame. The impressions here, though, are highly individual—an imprint of Betty Grable's "million dollar legs"; the horseshoe prints of Trigger, Roy Rogers's legendary palomino steed; Jimmy Durante's schnozzola; Harpo Marx's harp; Donald Duck's webbed feet; and robotic treadmarks from both R2D2 and C-3PO of *Star Wars* fame.

Next door is the site of Hollywood's most visible redevelopment project, an open-air, four-story complex strategically located above the new Metrorail Red Line station that now links Hollywood with both downtown Los Angeles and Universal Studios. When completed, this shopping and entertainment complex will include 300,000 square feet of broadcast and music studios, entertainment venues, shops, and restaurants, with a grand staircase framing a view of the Hollywood sign. And the 3,300-seat auditorium that will soon bring the annual Academy Awards ceremony—and all those Oscars—back to Hollywood.

Hollywood Roosevelt Hotel

As tightly woven into the fabric of local history as the Chinese Theatre across the street, the lovely Spanish colonial Hollywood Roosevelt Hotel, 7000 Hollywood Blvd., is definitely worth a stop. This was the site of the somewhat disastrous first Academy Awards ceremony in 1927, Douglas Fairbanks presiding. In the glory days of the 1930s, the Roosevelt was *the* place to stay, but then Hollywood Blvd. slid straight downhill and took this dignified grande dame along for the ride. After a $35 million facelift and much fanfare, the Hollywood Roosevelt reopened in 1985.

An impromptu tour starts in the stunning art deco lobby, where piped-in vintage jazz accompanies you to the "museum" of movie memorabilia on the mezzanine. The Roosevelt's in-house supper club, **Cinegrill,** was a favorite of Marilyn Monroe, said to have favored the dark booth in the northwest corner. Don't miss the hotel's celebrated Olympic-size swimming pool in the courtyard, with a custom blue-squiggle bottom paint job by artist David Hockney. (When someone dives in, the entire pool shimmers.) Also well worth it: the courtyard's **Tropicana Bar.**

Hollywood Entertainment Museum

The 33,000-square-foot Hollywood Entertainment Museum at 7021 Hollywood Blvd. (at Sycamore), 323/465-7900, www.hollywoodmu-seum.com, actually pays homage to both old and new Hollywood, its timeline starting with silent films and film stars and ending with authentic *Star Trek* and *Cheers* sets.

The 15-foot-tall Goddess of Entertainment presides over the clean and stylish central gallery, cradling all of the entertainment arts—radio, television, film, and sound—in her arms. Every half-hour the big screen flashes the very entertaining six-minute high-speed retrospective *The Stuff That Dreams Are Made Of.* Also worth a look: the World War II–era mini-model of Hollywood; the museum's "Dream Merchants" audio exhibit, in which Walt Disney talks about animation, Tina Turner discusses sex appeal, and Orson Welles opines on the always troublesome artistic subject of money; and the "Back Lot" hodgepodge of props, costumes, and other movie memorabilia. Just beyond is an authentic set from the original *Star Trek* TV series. After sitting in Captain Kirk's chair you can examine Klingon masks and try to pass Trekkie trivia tests on video. Next stop is *Cheers,* or someplace that looks just like it, and then it's on to the gift shop.

The Hollywood Entertainment Museum is open daily 11 A.M.–6 P.M., closed Wednesday. Admission is $7.50 adults, $4.50 for seniors and students, $4 for children ages 5–12 (under 5 free). Parking is $2 with validation in the basement parking garage.

Also worth a stop for peeking into Hollywood's past—but usually open only on weekends—is the **Hollywood Studio Museum** near the Hollywood Bowl (see below), housed in Cecil B. DeMille's original moviemaking barn.

MORE HOLLYWOOD

Paramount Studios and Vicinity

Mae West once described herself as "the girl who works at Paramount all day and Fox all night." Her day job was at Paramount Studios, 5555 Melrose Ave., 323/956-4385, last of the major studios remaining in Hollywood—at home on the city's longest-running movie lot, built in 1917 for Peralta Studios. Paramount took over in 1926. Thousands of films have been produced at Paramount, which traces its heritage to *The Squaw Man* and the Jesse L. Lasky Feature Play Company—making this *the* time-honored

TOURING MOVIELAND

Spending time in Los Angeles includes the pleasure of unexpected celebrity sightings—at gas stations or drug stores, in restaurants and clubs, on the freeway or along a sidewalk in West Hollywood or Beverly Hills—and the sudden surprise of stumbling upon a film shoot. During on-location moviemaking, normal life in Los Angeles comes to a halt. Traffic is rerouted, landmark buildings "renamed," and entire neighborhoods redecorated and repopulated, if only for a few hours or days. For Angelenos it's all such a common occurrence that few pay much attention.

To increase your odds of discovering movieland on location, you need to know where to go. One possible spot on shoot-season weekdays is Paramount Ranch in Agoura Hills, famous for the repertoire of westerns shot here over the years—where *Dr. Quinn, Medicine Woman* was filmed—and now part of the Santa Monica Mountains National Recreation Area. Otherwise, the best plan of action is to

sidewalk in front of Mann's Chinese Theatre

make a plan. Find out what is being filmed, and where, on any given day at the **Los Angeles Film and Video Permit Office,** 7083 Hollywood Blvd., 5th Fl. in Hollywood, 323/957-1000, www.eidc.com, open weekdays 8 A.M.–6 P.M. The office provides a free "shoot sheet" for the day, and you can also download shoot sheets from the website. The shooting information includes the exact address of each filming location, along with the name of the production company, the movie or TV show, and the hours reserved for the shoot. Since you won't be allowed on private property, look for movies or TV shows (sometimes just scenes) being shot in public places. Even with plan in hand, don't be too disappointed if, upon your arrival, nothing's going on. Overnight the shoot may have been canceled, delayed until another date, or rescripted for another location. It happens. That's Hollywood.

You can also get someone else to show you around. **Hollywood Heritage** offers walking tours of historic Hollywood and its surviving monuments on the second Sat. of every month (at other times by reservation). For information, call 323/874-4005. Though a bit ghoulish for some tastes, the informative and highly entertaining **Oh Heavenly Tour** offers some sense of real-life Hollywood with a hearse ride through Movieland's past—particularly the places where movie stars and Hollywood movers and shakers have died. For current information and reservations (essential), call 323/782-9652.

For a close-up look at the workings of present-day Hollywood, head for the studios. In addition to the ongoing parade of possibilities that has transformed **Universal Studios** into a tourist diversion, several offer very informative public tours. And you can also sign up for a stint in the studio audience during the tapings of various TV shows.

Warner Bros. Studios VIP Tour

As almost the only tour, for decades Warner Bros. offered the best moviemaking tour in Hollywood. It still does. The two-hour Warner Bros. walkabout—through soundstages, prop rooms, set construction sites, and other peculiar places in the hardly glamorous backstage world of film—is quite good, the real deal. Unlike the Universal Studios tour, the VIP tour is far more personal, so expect to be educated and entertained. You'll most likely sit in on a live film shoot to boot.

ROBERT HOLMES/CALTOUR

Another reason to take the tour is the chance to visit the excellent new **Warner Bros. Museum,** well worth some extra time. (The museum is "doable" only on the tour.) On display here is an impressive selection of memorabilia and artifacts from the studio's animation and filmmaking history—everything from *Casablanca*'s piano, the real Maltese Falcon, and John Wayne's saddle to Jack Warner's personal address book. And find out just how little James Dean and his fellow actors were paid for their work in *Giant.*

To take the Warner Bros. VIP Tour, head for The Burbank Studios, 4000 Warner Blvd. in Burbank. For information and reservations—necessary at least a week in advance during the summer high season—call 818/954-1744. No tours are offered on Thanksgiving, Christmas, New Year's Day, or, usually, on other holidays that fall on a weekday. Golf-cart tours—with plenty of walking, so wear comfy shoes—are scheduled on the hour on weekdays, 9 A.M.–3 P.M. (last departure); in summer, tours are scheduled on the half hour 9 A.M.–4 P.M. often also offered on Sat. at 10 A.M. and 2 P.M. (call to verify). The per-person fee is $32, Visa and MasterCard accepted; no children under age 10 are allowed on studio tours. Free parking.

For free tickets to all Warner Bros. live audience TV shows, call Audiences Unlimited at 818/753-3470.

NBC Television Studios

Compared to the Warner Brothers tour, NBC's 70-minute tour isn't quite as much to write home about, but it is cheaper. You do get to poke into just about everything backstage, including *The Tonight Show* set. More fun for true TV junkies is lining up to land tickets for NBC shows taped before a live studio audience. The tour price is $7 adults, $3.75 for children ages 6–12, children under 5 free. Admission to live-audience NBC shows is free (advance tickets required). For information, call NBC at 818/840-3537 or 818/840-4444. NBC Studios, 3000 W. Alameda Ave. in Burbank, are closed on Thanksgiving, Christmas, and New Year's Day.

Paramount Studios

Head to Paramount Studios to tour the last major studio still in Hollywood. The tour involves two hours of walking (with no trams or golf carts), so be sure to wear comfortable shoes and bring a bottle of water. Adults and children ages 10 and older can take the guided Paramount Studios tour, scheduled every hour from 9 A.M. to 2 P.M. on weekdays only, for $15 per person (first-come basis). Tours start at the main gate, 5555 Melrose Ave. (nearby parking available). For current information call 323/956-4385 or 323/956-3036. Or opt to help populate the studio audience for popular TV shows, including *Frasier.*

Sony Pictures Studios

Once Columbia Pictures and MGM, Sony Pictures Studios in Culver City also offers a movieland walking working-studio tour of its past, present, and future—from *The Wizard of Oz* to *Men in Black* and beyond. The two-hour tour, $20 per person, wanders through soundstages and show sets, wardrobe departments, and "backdrop" artists' studios. There's a gift shop, of course, and you can even eat at the studio commissary. Sony Pictures is located at 10202 W. Washington Blvd. in Culver City. For tour reservations, call 323/520-8687.

Other Movieland Adventures

If you're poking around Hollywood's mean streets, be sure to stop at the **Hollywood Entertainment Museum,** 7021 Hollywood Blvd., 323/465-7900. To understand Hollywood's foundations, the place is the **Frederick's of Hollywood Lingerie Museum,** 6608 Hollywood Blvd., 323/466-8506.

As entertainment capital of the world, Hollywood is more than just the movies. The fascinating **Museum of Television and Radio** at 465 N. Beverly Dr. in Beverly Hills, 310/786-1000, is an unbelievably comprehensive collection of classic TV and radio programming—popular with researchers, of course, but well worth some time for popular media fans. For radio aficionados seeking more than entertainment, try the **Pacifica Radio Archives** at KPFK Radio, 3729 Cahuenga Blvd. W in North Hollywood, 818/506-1077, the oldest collection of public radio programming in the nation, with more than 40,000 documentary and historical tapes. For library access through the Internet: www.pacifica.org.

For more information on most of these attractions, see separate listings elsewhere in this chapter.

Hollywood institution. Thus, according to Hollywood lore, for good luck aspiring actors and actresses must hug the historic iron gate at Bronson and Marathon while chanting the Norma Desmond (Gloria Swanson) line: "I'm ready for my close-up, Mr. DeMille" and otherwise unloading some of the pathos of the 1950 *Sunset Boulevard,* filmed here. (Hug and chant at your own risk.) More pedestrian, by far, is the low-key two-hour Paramount Studios walking tour scheduled every hour from 9 A.M. to 2 P.M. on weekdays only, $15 per person (first-come basis). Children under 10 not admitted. Tours start at the main gate, 5555 Melrose Ave. (nearby parking available). Or opt to help populate the studio audience for popular TV shows, including *Frasier.* For current information call 323/956-4385 or 323/956-3036. For details on other Tinseltown studio tours, see the special topic Touring Movieland.

Hollywood Memorial Park Cemetery

Since perennial youth and beauty are Southern California's essential social standards, here the concept of eternal life takes on a strangely stagey, theatrical edge. It's no coincidence that the southstate boasts what Peter Theroux has called "the happiest cemeteries in the world," lushly landscaped afterlife theme parks. It's probably also no coincidence that most of them are near Hollywood.

A time-honored gem of the genre is right downtown—65-acre Hollywood Memorial Park Cemetery just north of Paramount Studios and east of Gower at 6000 Santa Monica Blvd. (south side), 323/469-1181, open daily 8 A.M.–5 P.M. (If you call and someone answers "Hollywood Forever," you've dialed the right number.) Here, some of Hollywood's immortals have taken their final rest. A map/guide to the gravestones is available at the gate.

Most spectacular of the stars' graves is that of **Douglas Fairbanks,** right next to the studio, with a view of the Hollywood Sign. Inside the entryway, the Fairbanks tomb is just beyond the lily pond. The sarcophagus, fronting a portrait portico and dramatic columns, is inscribed "Good Night Sweet Prince, and Flights of Angels Sing Thee to Thy Rest." Nearby is **Tyrone Power**'s grave, a useful marble bench inscribed with the same "Sweet Prince" sentiment plus a few more

thoughts from Shakespeare's *Hamlet.* Adjacent is the mausoleum of **Marion Davies,** William Randolph Hearst's mistress, inscribed "DOVRAS." Nearby is **Jayne Mansfield**'s memorial of pink granite. (Mansfield was famous for driving around town in her pink Cadillac.) Perhaps most peculiar is the full-size Atlas rocket replica marking the grave of **Carl Morgan Bigsby,** "symbolic of his pioneering work in graphic arts."

Most infamous over the years, though, has been **Rudolph Valentino**'s final rest, in unpretentious crypt No. 1205 inside the Cathedral Mausoleum—intended to be a temporary stay until a suitably dramatic personal monument could be constructed. Fancy digs or no, for many years a mysterious "Lady in Black," presumably a grieving love, appeared each year on the anniversary of Valentino's death to lay flowers at his grave—eventually unveiled as one of Hollywood's best post-career publicity stunts. Exposed, the lady visits no more.

Laid to rest in the cemetery's original Jewish section along with Las Vegas gangster **Bugsy Siegel** and actor/director **John Huston** is **Mel Blanc,** original voice for an astonishing array of Hollywood cartoon characters. His cemetery sign off? That old Warner Brothers standard: "That's all, folks!"

More on Santa Monica Boulevard

Other sights along Santa Monica Blvd. include the walls surrounding **Warner-Hollywood Studios** at Formosa Ave., historically home base for **United Artists** and, later, **Goldwyn Studios.** Across the street, at 7156 Santa Monica (two blocks west of La Brea), is the old **Formosa Cafe,** 323/850-9050, a traditional industry hangout and a virtual museum of on-the-walls movie memorabilia saved from progress only after a loud local fight.

At 1150 Highland Ave., just off Santa Monica, is one of L.A.'s great used-music stores, **Aron's Records,** 323/469-4700, specializing in used LPs and CDs but also carrying a vast selection of new CDs.

More on Sunset Boulevard

An experiment in 1950s futurism is the **Pacific Cinerama Dome,** impersonating a humongous golf ball at 6360 Sunset (near Vine), 323/466-3401. Once known as the best place in town to see "big movies" (70 mm blockbusters) on the theater's wrap-around wide screen, in the age of virtual reality and home video the Cinerama Dome here—the sole survivor of its era—no longer projects a viable vision of the future. Which is why the owner is turning it into yet another moneymaking multiplex. Fortunately, the city's preservation board has granted the Cinerama Dome's exterior "landmark" historic status.

Just down the street, the **Hollywood Athletic Club,** at 6525 Sunset, once held a pool, weight room, and gym, where stars such as Rudolph Valentino and Charlie Chaplin would work out and hide out with the all-male membership. It's now a restored local landmark, most recently a restaurant and nightclub, available for private parties and events.

The landmark **Hollywood High School,** 1521 Highland Ave., boasts dozens of graduates who later graduated to some notable role within "the industry," among them Lana Turner, Carol Burnett, Lawrence Fishburne, Judy Garland, Linda Evans, and John Ritter. These days most of the school's students are recent immigrants; like many public schools in Los Angeles—more than 80 native languages are spoken by the system's students—this school is a multilingual crazy-quilt of cultures representing almost every spot on the globe.

At Hollywood's end, at 1416 N. La Brea just south of Sunset, is **A&M Recording Studios,** once Charlie Chaplin's movie lot.

The most famous stretch of Sunset Blvd., the "Sunset Strip," begins in West Hollywood (see below).

SILVER LAKE, LOS FELIZ, AND VICINITY

Like the city of West Hollywood, Silver Lake is noted for its gay-ity. But the population here is actually quite diverse, with gays, lesbians, and a wide variety of cultural eccentrics sharing neighborhoods with residents of various ethnic persuasions—Guatemalan, Salvadorean, Honduran, Mexican—and a respectable number of well-rooted retirees. A low-rent refuge for punk rockers and other cultural misfits since the 1970s, the area's cultural fusion today is nearly impossible to categorize. Or describe. You'll have to ex-

perience it to understand it—or begin to understand it. In the view of many here, the fact that postcool, post-Westside artistic L.A. shares general territory with gangsters just makes it all the more cutting edge. Occasional nighttime gunplay keeps the Westside wimps away.

The district was named for Herman Silver, the city water and power commissioner who authorized the construction of namesake Silver Lake (west of Glendale Blvd.) in 1906. Hollywood arrived by the 1920s and '30s, when film stars including Fatty Arbuckle, Clark Gable, Judy Garland, and Gloria Swanson called the area home. Architects Rudolf Schindler and Richard Neutra took a shine to the neighborhood, too, which explains the impressive number of homes here that bear their architectural signatures. Over the years the beautiful people migrated west to Beverly Hills, Brentwood, and other Westside beauty spots, but their classy buildings still stand. One remaining Silver Lake star: the steep outdoor stairway featured in 1932's *The Music Box,* Stan Laurel and Oliver Hardy's Academy Award–winning comedy short, as well as in their 1927 *Hats Off.*

Aside from the ghosts of Laurel and Hardy, area attractions include Frank Lloyd Wright's spectacular Hollyhock House in Barnsdall Park; other architectural icons by Wright, Richard Neutra, Rudolph Schindler, and others; the posthip Vermont Ave. business district; and L.A.'s beloved Rockaway Records. Not to mention the wild nightclubs.

The Vermont Avenue and Silver Lake Scenes
Vermont Ave. forms the unofficial boundary between the Hollywood and Silver Lake districts, stretching north into Los Feliz. The stretch of Vermont between Hollywood Blvd. and Russell St. is also cutting-edge, commercially cool Los Angeles—an L.A. not created or interpreted by marketing directors, money managers, and the media. Proudly dubbed the "anti-Melrose" by its denizens—though the Melrose mayhem could be just around the corner, figuratively as well as literally—Vermont Ave.'s quirky business district includes shops such as the **Dresden Room,** 1769 N. Vermont (near Hollywood Blvd.), 323/665-4294, and **?Y Qui? (So What?),** 1770 N. Vermont, 323/664-0021, locally famous for its vintage toys and eccentric collection of cultural

remainders—such as "Welcome Back Kotter" dolls and Sharon Tate posters. Just down the street is also-out-there **Mondo Video A Go Go,** 1724 N. Vermont, 323/953-8896. Worth seeking out between tattoo and body-piercing shops is the **Skylight Bookstore,** local literary locus at 1818 N. Vermont Ave., 323/660-1175, at the onetime Chatterton's, the beloved neighborhood bookstore that closed when owner William Koki Iwamoto died.

But there's more to the Los Feliz/Silver Lake scene than Vermont Ave., including L.A.'s long-running independent **Rockaway Records,** 2395 Glendale Blvd. (near Fletcher), 323/664-3232, where the playlist includes an impressive selection of used CDs. In "downtown" Silver Lake, generally defined as the odd stretch just east of Vermont where Hollywood and Sunset Blvds. both funnel into Sunset, the center of the scene is **Ozzie Dots** vintage clothing at 4637 Hollywood Blvd., 323/663-2867 and, next door, **Soap Plant** 4633 Hollywood Blvd., 323/663-0122.

For local club information, see the special topic Clubbin' It.

Hollyhock House and Barnsdall Park

The American Institute of Architects has recognized Hollyhock House as one of the most significant structures of the 20th century—an official federal designation. Completed in 1921, this 6,200-square-foot Mayan temple of concrete and stucco, done in Frank Lloyd Wright's California Romanza style, is currently closed to the public for extensive renovation and restoration following major earthquake damage. But when Hollyhock House is open again for public tours, note that it is adorned inside and out with a stylized hollyhock motif—owner Aline Barnsdall's favorite flower. The astonishing living room, recently redone to reflect its original, highly unusual Craftsman concept, includes Wright's symmetrical oak sofas. Essentially room dividers fashioned into sofas with attached tables and then crowned by Arts and Crafts–style sculpture, the sofas surround the fireplace and its water-filled moat.

Wright had completed the main house and only two of the guest cottages when the owner called a halt to the project; in 1923 she donated what is now Barnsdall Park to the city of Los Angeles. Designated a historic cultural monument in 1963, Hollyhock House and the surrounding "arts park" are now operated by L.A.'s Department of Cultural Affairs. For current information, call 323/913-4157.

American Film Institute

The American Film Institute (AFI), 2021 N. Western Ave., was founded in 1965 with President Lyndon B. Johnson's signature on the National Foundation of the Arts and Humanities Act. The AFI's multiple mission includes preserving film and television heritage, identifying and training new talent, and increasing public recognition and understanding of "the moving image as art." Programs established to achieve these ends include AFI's **National Center for Film and Video Preservation,** its **Center for Advanced Film and Television Studies,** the **Louis B. Mayer Library,** and world-class film festivals held each year in New York, Washington, D.C., and (of course) Los Angeles. One of the largest and most prestigious film festivals in the country, the **Los Angeles International Film Festival** is scheduled during the last two weeks of October, screening almost 100 films at various venues throughout the city and drawing more than 40,000 participants. For current information about AFI, call 323/856-7707 or point your browser to www.afionline.org.

GRIFFITH PARK

Most famous for its main attractions, the Los Angeles Zoo and the Griffith Observatory and Planetarium, Griffith Park is a wonder—at 4,000 acres, the largest city park in the United States. The park was donated to the city of Los Angeles in 1896 by mining magnate Griffith J. Griffith (no relation to D. W. Griffith of Hollywood lore). Griffith had big plans for the park early on—including construction of the observatory, which came in the 1930s—but Los Angeles was reluctant to accept more of his largesse, at least during his lifetime, because of lingering scandal over Griffith's conviction and jail time for trying to murder his wife.

The park's sylvan attractions include hiking and horseback trails (stables, too), golf courses, tennis courts, soccer fields, a swimming pool, and a seemingly endless supply of picnic areas. Among the prettiest places for picnicking: the aptly named

*Griffith Observatory
and Planetarium*

Fern Dell, a shady glade along a spring-fed stream; small pathways wind around sparkling pools, waterfalls, and thousands of ferns.

Main attractions with kid appeal include the observatory, the zoo, and pony, stagecoach, and miniature train rides. The **merry-go-round** here is a piece of national history, complete with original organ and dazzling wooden horses with real horsehair tails—a 1926 Stillman Company carousel, one of the last ever built and one of the few still in operation. If younger kids need to run, climb, scream, and otherwise let off steam, head for the park's free Travel Town (see below), with tons and tons of kid-safe and climbable transport.

Though kids also like the Disneyfied exhibits at the fine Autry Museum of Western Heritage (see below), so do thinking adults. And even confirmed city slickers can take steeds out on leisurely trail rides from picturesque **Sunset Ranch** stables, on the park's eastern edge at 3400 N. Beachwood Dr., 323/469-5450. Popular even with Angelenos, Friday night "moonlight rides" climb up into the surrounding San Gabriel Mountains for breathtaking views of the sparkling lights (and smog) below. Also fun: special performances at the park's intimate **Greek Theater,** 2700 N. Vermont, 323/665-1927. An outdoor amphitheater nesting in the foothills, it hosts rock, pop, jazz, blues, country-western, and more from June through October. Pack a picnic along to put the tables outside to good use; just beyond the Doric columns you can buy box

suppers as well as beer and wine or you can bring your own.

Get oriented to the park's attractions and trails at the visitors center (free maps available). The park is technically open daily 5:30 A.M.–10 P.M.— the late hour to accommodate stargazers at the observatory—but roads and riding/hiking trails (except for the one leading to the observatory) are open only during daylight. Park admission is free, though various attractions and events within its boundaries charge separate admission. Griffith Park is just north of the Hollywood Fwy. (Hwy. 101) and south of the Ventura Fwy. (Hwy. 134), just west of the Golden State Fwy. (I-5). The park's main entry (at Crystal Springs Dr., which becomes Griffith Park Dr.) is reached from the south via Los Feliz Blvd., just off I-5, though you can also enter from Los Feliz at either Fern Dell Dr. or Vermont Avenue. For more information, contact the Ranger Station at 323/913-4688.

Griffith Observatory and Planetarium

The recently restored Griffith Observatory and Planetarium, a moderne classic poised just above the smoggy Los Angeles basin, was designed in 1935 by architects John C. Austin and F. M. Ashley. James Dean slashed it out here in *Rebel Without A Cause*. Even on a bad day, when smog-shrouded sights seem surreal, the view from the decks and walkways outside is impressive. On a clear day you really can see forever.

Exhibits in the **Hall of Science** include a seismograph that monitors Southern California's nearly constant earthquake activity. On clear nights (try winter) you can actually see something when you peek into the heavens through the observatory's twin refracting telescope, one of the world's largest. Particularly popular at the observatory's **Planetarium Theater** are the **Laserium** laser light shows, though informative astronomy programs are also offered.

The observatory is open 2–10 P.M. Tues.–Fri., 12:30–10 P.M. on weekends. In the summer months of June through Sept. the observatory is open every day from 12:30–10 P.M. Admission to Hall of Science exhibits (including the telescope) is free. The observatory's 12-inch telescope is available for night-sky viewing Tues.–Sun. 7–9:45 P.M. On clear days when the observatory is open, images from solar telescopes in the west dome are projected down to viewers on the main floor exhibit area. Children under age 5 aren't allowed to attend regular planetarium programs, but a special kids' show is scheduled every afternoon. Planetarium Theater admission is $4 adults, $3 seniors, and $2 children ages 5–12. Laserium admission is $9 adults, $8 seniors and children ages 5–12. The observatory sits in the heart of the park at 2800 Observatory Rd. (long and winding); enter the park from Vermont Avenue. For current observatory program information, call 323/664-1191 or look up www.griffithobs.org. For Laserium information, call 818/997-3624.

The Los Angeles Zoo

After a troubled decade, things are finally improving at the 113-acre Los Angeles Zoo, one of the nation's most prominent. Home to more than 2,000 animals in 75 simulated habitats, the L.A. Zoo includes exhibits arranged by general geographical region: North and South Americas, Africa, Australia, and Eurasia. At **Tiger Falls** the big cats lounge around near convincing but fake waterfalls and pools. The zoo's $4.5 million **chimpanzee exhibit** is the first phase of the much more ambitious **Great Ape Forest.** Other highlights: the **walk-through aviary** exhibiting about 50 exotic birds and Australia's **Koala House,** where the koalas on exhibit seem happy to hang out in the eucalyptus. In other animal pens "food toys" and other playthings help entertain animals who have yet to benefit much from zoo improvements.

A terrific state-of-the-art children's zoo, **Adventure Island,** offers touch-and-explore exhibits that teach children about animals, their habits, and their natural habitats. At the prairie dog exhibit, poke your head up from "underground" holes to see what the prairie dog sees; likewise, to see like a bee, try out the "bee head." Various gentle creatures tolerate petting, and the animal nursery allows human babies and their parents to coo over other species' new arrivals.

The entrance to the Los Angeles Zoo is at 5333 Zoo Dr. in Griffith Park. The zoo is open daily 10 A.M.–5 P.M., closed Christmas Day, and open until 6 P.M. in summer (July 1 to Sept. 4). General admission is $8.25 adults, $5.25 seniors, $3.25 children ages 2–12 (under 2 free). Walking the zoo's 113 acres can be exhausting, so take advantage of the tram if it's an issue—or get oriented on the **Safari Shuttle Tour.** Strollers and other special services are also available. For more information, call 323/644-6400 or 323/644-4200 or check www.lazoo.org.

Autry Museum of Western Heritage

America's legendary "singing cowboy" Gene Autry *(Back in the Saddle, Bells of Capistrano)* founded the Autry Museum, a fascinating collection of cowboy memorabilia. Credit Walt Disney Imagineering for museum exhibits scoring high in both content and entertainment value. Even the museum's guided-tour cassette is incredibly cool, narrated by hip cowboy crooner Willie Nelson. Autry's namesake is a very well-done general introduction to the colorful yet confusing heritage of the American West—sufficiently high-tech to hold the attention of generations raised by television sets yet thoughtful enough to be worth the electricity.

Sharing a parking lot with the Los Angeles Zoo, this fairly new addition to Griffith Park is dedicated to preserving the culture of the Old West, both real and imagined. **The Spirit of Imagination** exhibit, for example, allows the kids to view themselves (via video monitor) on horseback, being chased by cowboys and the William Tell Overture. Central to **The Spirit of Romance** is film footage of William F. ("Buffalo Bill") Cody performing in a 1902 Wild West Show. Even city slickers can appreciate the exquisite workmanship on hand-tooled silver-studded celebrity saddles, Annie Oakley's gold pistol, the Lone Ranger's spurs, and other examples of highfalutin cowboy high art. The real-life hardships of leaving home for a new life in the West is brought home by **The Spirit of Opportunity.** The museum's **Western Heritage Theater** screens westerns and documentaries, and sometimes presents live performances; stop at the information desk for theater schedules. Also on the premises: a family-friendly restaurant and an engaging gift shop.

The museum is open Tues.–Sun. 10 A.M.–5 P.M. (also on most Mon. holidays), Thurs. 10 A.M.–8 P.M. Admission is $7.50 adults, $5 seniors and students with ID, and $3 for children ages 2–12. The second Tues. of every month is free. Free parking. Free guided tours are offered only by reservation. For information on current and upcoming curated shows as well as special events, contact: Autry Museum of Western Heritage, 4700 Western Heritage Way, 323/667-2000, www.autry-museum.org.

Travel Town

At the north end of the park, at 5200 Zoo Dr., is Travel Town, 323/662-5874, an open-air museum dedicated to well-traveled transportation—and kids' inclination to climb all over same and *drive.* Unlike typical museums, here the displays—antique trains, planes, and automobiles—are designed to be used. Indoors, fire trucks, a circus animal wagon, and other vehicles beckon. Travel Town is open weekdays 10 A.M.–4 P.M., 10 A.M.–5 P.M. on weekends.

HOLLYWOOD BOWL AND VICINITY

Like almost every other star in town, this Hollywood landmark has had an expensive facelift—and now it's undergoing something of a "bottom lift," focusing this time on upgrading bathrooms and other fundamentals. No one complains, a rare thing in this city, because Los Angeles loves its Hollywood Bowl.

One of the world's most famous amphitheaters, the Hollywood Bowl in 1919 was known as Daisy Dell—simply a rough-cut stage set up in a natural "bowl" blessed with perfect acoustics, a venue popular for religious plays. Along came progress, alas. Determined to bend nature to its own design, soon thereafter L.A. County dynamited the area to make room for a new stage and 17,619 poured-concrete seats. The original sound quality was obliterated as a result; efforts to engineer a solution have never fully succeeded.

Perfect acoustics or no, this is one of L.A.'s favorite places, perfect for evening concerts—jazz, rock, pop, and classical. Though this is the summer home of the Los Angeles Philharmonic Orchestra, the Grateful Dead mounted the stage here, too, as did Bob Dylan, the Beatles, Mel Tormé, and Benny Goodman. And Miles Davis, Duke Ellington, Ella Fitzgerald, and Billie Holiday. And Aaron Copland, Vladimir Horowitz, Sergei Rachmaninoff, and Igor Stravinsky. The cheap seats offer some of the best views (bring seat cushions). The local concert custom is to come

Hollywood Bowl

SOME CLASSIC L.A. DRIVES

The Stars-to-Sea Highway

If you have an adventurous spirit and time to spare, the classic L.A. "view" tour is the "Stars-to-Sea Highway," 25-mile **Mulholland Drive** heading west from the Hollywood Fwy. (the 101) near Cahuenga Pass in the Hollywood Hills to Woodland Hills. For truly intrepid scenery seekers, the route continues out of the Santa Monica Mountains to the Pacific Ocean at Leo Carrillo State Beach and the Pacific Coast Hwy. (Hwy. 1) just east of the Ventura County line. (To do the entire route, which includes a fairly rugged unpaved section through Topanga State Park just southeast of Woodland Hills and other rough spots, a four-wheel-drive or other reasonably reliable, destruction-proof vehicle is advised.) Alternatively, take just half the trip by exiting in either direction from the San Diego Fwy. (the 405) north of Brentwood near Sepulveda Pass.

Notable just east of the Hollywood Fwy. is the lovely mission-style concrete "castle wall" and moat known as **Hollywood Reservoir**. Originally named Mulholland Dam when it was formally dedicated in 1925—to honor L.A.'s premier water engineer, William Mulholland, architect of the Los Angeles Aqueduct—the reservoir was quietly renamed after the St. Francis Dam disaster that soon doomed Mulholland's career and reputation. Yet Mulholland's namesake street remains unchanged.

Heading east to west, Mulholland Dr. snakes west along the ridge tops above Hollywood, offering both close-ups of some spectacular homes and breathtaking panoramas of the endless L.A. basin and the San Fernando Valley. At night, it's all absolutely dazzling, particularly from the **Mt. Olympus Overlook** about one mile west of the **Hollywood Bowl Overlook** (at Runyon Canyon Park's northern entrance). Both daytime and nighttime views are typically better—and, in a sense, less "breathtaking"—in winter and early spring, when the smog level is low.

At the junction of Mulholland Dr. and Topanga Canyon Blvd., Mulholland Dr. becomes "Hwy." but otherwise continues to slither west across the twisting spine of the Santa Monica Mountains, slicing through suburban sprawl and wilderness along the way. Most scenic is the eight-mile "outback" section between **Las Virgenes** and **Kanan Dume Roads,** which has starred as Australia, England, and other imaginary movie locales. Following the route all the way west eventually leads to the Pacific Ocean. Plan to pack a picnic lunch (or dinner) and head for remote, picturesque **Nicholas Canyon County Beach** south of Leo Carrillo State Beach.

Cheap Thrills

Another way to start a Mulholland Dr. sojourn—definitely a cheap thrill—is to begin your trip on **Dixie Canyon Ave.** just off Ventura Blvd. to the north in Sherman Oaks. At Dixie Canyon's suburban end, the road is wide and civilized, at least for a few blocks. But it soon descends wildly—hey, great views!—trying to decide, as its ruts, rattles, and rolls down the mountainside, whether it's merely a twisted and treacherous one-lane dirt road or a coyote path. (Not recommended for street cars, but definitely a possibility for off-roaders. And experienced mountain bikers.) The prospect of civilized transport, *paved road,* again presents itself at the intersection with Mulholland Drive.

Another cheap thrill starts in the Silver Lake neighborhood. From Glendale Blvd., head north on Alvarado into the hills above Echo Park to **Fargo St.**— L.A.'s steepest up-and-down thoroughfare—and create your own amusement ride. (Good brakes and steady nerves mandatory.) Adjacent **Baxter** is also good for a few gasps.

Urban adventurers with a preference for flatland might instead prefer the more thought-provoking sociological thrills associated with taking **Santa Monica Blvd., Sunset Blvd.,** or **Wilshire Blvd.** west from downtown.

On the Beach

By and large the Southern California coastal driving experience will not mirror any of those appealing escapist images used by TV car commercials to brainwash consumers. The success of the cars-are-freedom sales pitch is reflected, instead, in bumper-to-bumper traffic and the occasional sun- or celebrity-drunk yahoo determined to run others off the road. But a drive along L.A.'s stretch of the famed **Pacific Coast Hwy.** ("PCH," or Hwy. 1) can be a pleasure—especially on a nonsummer weekday—if you get out *early,* before the crazy people are out of bed.

But the point of driving PCH is not to escape the horrors of overpopulated urban life. The point is to immerse, wallow, or *drown* yourself in them. Since parking will be all but impossible in many coastal areas, you'll have plenty of time to work on it.

For a lightweight beach tour, begin amid the boat-groupie culture of **Marina del Rey,** the world's largest man-made harbor with associated upscale hotels and restaurants, and then work your way north through the tortured seaside eccentricities and spruced-up canals of **Venice** to open-minded **Santa Monica,** where at last report the middle-class still co-existed with the rich and famous and the occasional poor person. Heading north past **Pacific Palisades** and its swell seaside jogging park eventually leads to **Malibu,** where movie stars and other shy, affluent types apparently don't mind paying millions and millions of dollars for exclusive homes that periodically burn up in wildfires or, after the torrential rains that follow, slide down into the sea. Your reward, if you continue north to near **Ventura County,** is access to some of L.A.'s best "getaway" beaches.

A more serious—but more complicated—tour of the L.A. coastline starts in Long Beach far to the south, detouring from PCH to take in the heavy-industrial byways of sister port cities Wilmington and San Pedro on the way to the pleasant serenity of the Palos Verdes Peninsula. Once you roll down out of Rolling Hills, again stick to coastal roadways to tour the South Bay beaches and beach towns of Redondo Beach, Hermosa Beach, Manhattan Beach, and El Segundo, some quite semi-industrial. (Miniature oil derricks, even in people's backyards, are not particularly uncommon in this neck of the woods.) From El Segundo on into Playa del Rey, you can enjoy the endless aerial traffic coming and going from LAX.

---

early and picnic; many L.A. restaurants and delis offer Bowl-season picnic specials, made to order with one day's notice.

For historical perspective on the Hollywood Bowl, stop by the **Edmund D. Edelman Hollywood Bowl Museum,** fresh from a complete renovation and major expansion. The museum is open year-round, Tues.–Sat. 10 A.M. until showtime when there's entertainment at the bowl, 10 A.M.–4:30 P.M. otherwise. Admission is free. For more information, call 323/850-2058.

Practical Hollywood Bowl
Here's something only Angelenos typically know: Anyone can show up on most summer mornings at 9 or 9:30 A.M. to attend rehearsals for that evening's performance—free. No crowds, no parking headaches, and no problem grabbing the great seats. Bring your own coffee and croissants.

The Hollywood Bowl sits at the "intersection" of Highland Ave. (Hwy. 170) and the Hollywood Fwy. (Hwy. 101). The regular concert calendar starts in early July and runs through mid-Sept., but the grounds and picnic areas are open year-round (closed Christmas), sunrise to sunset. Access to the grounds is free, since this is a public park. Parking is free in the off-season, and, during concert season, free before 4 P.M. Since parking at the Bowl during performances is otherwise expensive and inconvenient, take one of the park-and-ride shuttles from around town. For more information: Hollywood Bowl, 2301 N. Highland Ave., 323/850-2000, www.hollywoodbowl.org.

Hollywood Studio Museum
Across bustling Highland Ave. from the Hollywood Bowl is the unassuming yellow barn that served as headquarters for Cecil B. DeMille during shooting for *The Squaw Man*—Hollywood's oldest existing studio building. DeMille rented the barn, known simply as the DeMille Barn or "the Barn" in these parts, and part of the surrounding orange grove for $25 per month. Later moved to what is now Paramount Studios, the decrepit old barn gathered cobwebs on Paramount's back lot until 1979. When the Hollywood Chamber of Commerce failed to put it to good use, Hollywood Heritage came to the rescue—restoring the barn and moving it to its present site.

Museum displays emphasize artifacts from the silent-movie era: historic motion-picture equipment and props dating from 1913 to the 1950s, a movie camera once belonging to Charlie Chaplin, and Cleopatra's 40-pound shield from the 1934 movie. Also here: a re-creation of DeMille's original office and miscellaneous furnishings from the Egyptian Theatre.

In 1996 the DeMille barn suffered a disastrous fire. Fortunately the building has been restored, and in 1999 Hollywood Heritage reopened the museum. At last report the Hollywood Studio Museum, 2100 N. Highland Ave., 323/874-2276, was open 11 A.M.–3:30 P.M. on weekends and at other times only by appointment. Admission is $4 adults, $2 seniors and children ages 5–12, children under 5 free. For the museum's current status, call Hollywood Heritage at 323/874-4005.

PRACTICAL HOLLYWOOD

STAYING IN HOLLYWOOD

"Living in Hollywood is like living in a lit cigar butt," irascible comic Phyllis Diller observed in the 1970s. Staying in Tinseltown a few days isn't so bad, though. Some areas are a bit dicey, true, and others astronomically expensive, but staying somewhere in or near Hollywood is feasible for just about everyone. The belly of the beast—Hollywood proper—features hostel options, definitely a boon for streetwise budget travelers. Even motel rooms here are more reasonably priced than those in more glamorous locales. Just steer clear of any establishment advertising hourly rates.

If you're in the market for upscale lodgings head to West Hollywood, which doesn't offer much else. In addition to WeHo's upmarket hotels, consider also Beverly Hills and vicinity—quite nearby, adjacent to West Hollywood—and other Westside possibilities. Since during the workweek swankier places often cater to business types with entertainment-industry expense accounts, weekend rates and special packages can be great deals.

Budget Bonanza: The Hollywood Hostels

For low cost and central location—right on the Hollywood Walk of Fame, close to West Hollywood and the club scene, reasonably close to Hollywood's little theater action—the **Hollywood International Hostel,** 6820 Hollywood Blvd. (between High and La Brea Aves.), 323/463-0797 or toll-free 800/750-6561, www.hollywoodhostel.com, can't be beat. Next to El Capitan Theatre and across from Mann's Chinese, the Hollywood International offers 40 rooms. Shared dorm space is the norm, two to four beds to a room, but private rooms are also available. Also here: a full kitchen, common areas (with game room, library, and TV with cable, satellite, and videos), laundry and storage facilities, even a sundeck and shuttle service (airport, bus, and train pickups, plus rides to the beach and major amusement parks). Free linens. Especially in summer students and out-of-state travelers get priority, so bring a passport and/or photo ID. Rates: $40 private room (maximum of two people), $15 dorm rooms. Breakfast included. Budget.

Fun and definitely above the Hollywood fray, the pleasant 250-bed **Banana Bungalow Hollywood Hotel and Hostel** features both private rooms (some with private bath) plus cheaper hostel-style accommodations. Facilities include full kitchen, laundry, library, weight room, arcade, basketball courts, pool, and sundeck, plus a store and café/restaurant. And color TV in every room. Free linens, breakfast, and parking. Free shuttle service to the beach, Disneyland, and Universal Studios, plus airport, train depot, and bus station pickup. Passport required (even for American travelers). Reservations advisable in summer. Dorm accommodations (four to six beds per bungalow) are $15–20. Budget. Private rooms start at $55. Inexpensive. Banana Bungalow is near the Hollywood Bowl (on the way to Universal Studios) in the Hollywood Hills, next to the Hollywood Fwy. about one mile north of Franklin Avenue. For more information, contact: Banana Bungalow Hollywood Hotel and Hostel, 2775 Cahuenga Blvd. W, Los Angeles, 323/851-1129 or toll-free 800/446-7835, www.bananabungalow.com.

Moderate to Expensive
Hollywood Stays: Off the Tourist Trail

The best bets for a midpriced overnight are motels a bit off the tourist trail, including smaller (cheaper) rooms at **Days Inn Hollywood,** 7023

ACCOMMODATIONS RATINGS

Accommodations in this book are rated by price category, based on double-occupancy, high-season rates. Categories used are:

Budget.	$35 and under
Inexpensive	$35-60
Moderate	$60-85
Expensive	$85-110
Premium	$110-150
Luxury	$150 and up

Sunset Blvd. (just east of La Brea), 323/464-8344 or toll-free 800/346-7723. Rates: $105 and up. Expensive. Not in the best neighborhood but closer to Griffith Park and within reasonable reach of Universal Studios is the recently renovated and quite comfortable **Ramada Limited Hollywood**, 1160 N. Vermont Ave., 323/660-1788 or toll-free 800/272-6232. In addition to standard rooms ($99 and up), suites with microwaves, refrigerators, and coffeemakers ($129 and up) can be a sweet deal for families or groups. Expensive-Premium. Then there's the quite nice, similarly priced **Best Western Hollywood Hills** right off the Hollywood Fwy. at 6141 Franklin Ave. (east of Vine), 323/464-5181, where many of the rooms come with microwaves. The on-site **Hollywood Hills Coffee Shop** shared some fame by association when its "Last Cappuccino Before 101" sign starred in *The Brady Brunch Movie*. Rates: $79 and up. Moderate-Expensive (more moderate in the off-season). This being California, all of the above come with a heated swimming pool and at least a few extra amenities.

Moderate to Expensive Hollywood Stays: In the Heart of Hollyweird
Also a pretty sweet deal for families or groups— if you don't mind the Hollyweird scene, and especially if you'll be staying awhile—is the **Hollywood Orchid Suites Hotel** near Mann's Chinese Theatre, just north of Hollywood Blvd. at 1753 N. Orchid Ave., 323/874-9678 or toll-free 800/537-3052. Suites here include kitchens, so you can cook (and eat) in. Rates: $79–109. Moderate-Expensive. Also in the heart of Hollyweird is the **Holiday Inn Hollywood,** 1755 N. Highland Ave, 323/850-5811 or toll-free 800/465-4329—but not for the faint of heart because the neighborhood is well, eccentric. The comfort level is fairly high, the decor decent standard-Holiday-Inn style, but the main attraction is the **Windows on Hollywood** revolving restaurant (dinner only) on the 23rd floor, which offers standard American cuisine and a view all the way to the San Bernardino Mountains on a clear night. Without a special discount standard high-season rates can be a bit stiff, though, so this isn't a midrange bargain unless you score a good weekend deal (sometimes possible). Rates: $129–229. Premium (and up).

Not in such an interesting setting but quite comfortable—and usually a much better deal—is the **Best Western Hollywood Plaza Inn** near the Hollywood Fwy., a half-mile north of Hollywood Blvd. at 2011 N. Highland Ave., 323/851-1800, or toll-free 800/445-4353. Rates: $89–119. Moderate-Premium (rates lower in the off-season).

Clarion Hollywood Roosevelt Hotel
This updated Hollywood classic holds revered rank in movie-industry mythology. On Hollywood Blvd. across the street from Mann's Chinese Theatre, the Hollywood Roosevelt was the setting of the first Academy Awards ceremony in 1927 (Douglas Fairbanks presiding) and the place Bill "Bojangles" Robinson taught Shirley Temple how to dance up the stairs. (Movie memorabilia and industry artifacts are on display on the mezzanine.) Meticulously restored to its original splendor after a $35 million facelift, the Hollywood Roosevelt is still Old Hollywood but hipper—with 40 movie-star "theme" suites and 65 ever-popular "cabana" bungalow-style suites surrounding the pool. The Olympic-size pool is itself a cultural landmark, painted by artist David Hockney. Do pop into the **Cinegrill** supper club here, one of Marilyn Monroe's favorite Old Hollywood haunts. Most rooms here are small but quite charming—and surprisingly reasonable, all things considered. Rates: $143–269. Premium-Luxury.

For more information, contact: Clarion Hollywood Roosevelt Hotel, 7000 Hollywood Blvd., 323/466-7000, or toll-free 800/950-7667 for reservations, www.hollywoodroosevelt.com.

EATING IN HOLLYWOOD

The best postdinner destination in all of Los Angeles is **Yamashiro,** the "castle on the hill" at 1999 N. Sycamore Ave. (off Franklin), 323/466-5125, a beautifully detailed 1913 Japanese mountain palace built by Asian art importers, the brothers Adolph and Eugene Bernheimer. A mansion surrounded by seven acres of glorious gardens, complete with 600-year-old pagoda, this was a star-happy club in Hollywood's golden age and now a stylish restaurant and bar. On a warm L.A. night, ask for a spot on the stunning indoor-outdoor garden patio to enjoy a drink—then drink in the most spectacular nighttime view of Los Angeles. Other good spots to drink in that Old Hollywood ambience include the **Formosa Cafe,** 7156 Santa Monica Blvd. (just west of La Brea), 323/850-9050, and the Raymond Chandleresque **Musso & Frank Grill,** 6667 Hollywood Blvd. (at Las Palmas Ave.), 323/467-7788.

Also "very Hollywood" for natural food folks is the weekly **Hollywood Farmers' Market** (certified), where produce, baked goods, and food stalls are accompanied by arts and crafts. The market is held Sun. 8:30 A.M.–2 P.M. at Ivar and Selma. Also try the **Melrose Weekend Market** at Fairfax High School (on the corner of Melrose and Fairfax), open Sun. 9 A.M.–5 P.M., small admission fee.

In restaurants as in nightclubs, many trendy "Hollywood" stars these days are actually in or near West Hollywood (see below) or just starting to constellate in and around North Hollywood.

Cheap Eats: Burgers and Such

Tommy's Original World Famous Hamburgers in Silver Lake at 2575 Beverly Blvd. (at Rampart), 213/389-9060, open 24 hours, is L.A.'s original Tommy's, yet another Tinseltown star. Tommy's serves "the world's only true chiliburger"—a meal that can stay with you for days, and a very spicy version at that. It's probably fitting that a Tommy's defector started **Jay's Jayburgers,** 4481 Santa Monica Blvd. (at Virgil), 323/666-5204, an immensely popular take-out shop serving much more civilized chiliburgers—restrained creations that won't wake you up at 2 A.M. Not only that, you can wash it down with genuine California sunshine—fresh-squeezed lemonade. **Pink's Hot Dogs,** 709 N. La Brea (at Melrose), 323/931-4223, is another fast-food chili icon. People (purportedly including stars like Kim Basinger and Winona Ryder) happily ignore the unhappy neighborhood to line up for the all-beef dogs drowning in all-beef chili.

People's Favorites: Ethnic Eats

Thai is big in these parts. The General's noodle soup—named for the very officially dressed fellow directing traffic in the lot on weekend afternoons—is one reason people throng around **Sanamluang Cafe,** 5176 Hollywood Blvd. (at Kingsley), 323/660-8006, open for late supper until 4 A.M. and everybody's favorite Thai noodle

shop. Wonderful for sit-down Thai at both lunch and dinner—at least before 9 P.M., when it becomes a noisier nightclub venue—is **Kruang Tedd,** 5151 Hollywood Blvd. (at Winona), 323/663-9988. **Jitlada** is an established local Thai star, a cozy family-run restaurant housed in a grungy minimall, 5233 1/2 Sunset Blvd. (at Howard), 323/667-9809, serving some of L.A.'s best—hot stuff. If you aren't familiar with spicy Thai food, let the staff guide your selection.

One of L.A.'s all-time favorites for Thai, still, is the original **Chan Dara** in Hollywood at 1511 N. Cahuenga Blvd. (at Sunset), 323/464-8585, open for dinner nightly, lunch on weekdays only. Everything here is done very well, from the satays to flaming barbecued chicken, pad Thai noodles, and panang curries. Another Chan Dara is just south at 310 N. Larchmont (near Hancock Park), 323/467-1052, yet another in West L.A. at 11940 W. Pico (between Bundy and Barrington), 310/479-4461.

For takeout, don't miss serene **Chamika Catering Sri Lankan Restaurant,** inside the onetime Big Weenies Are Better hot-dog stand at 1717 N. Wilcox (at Hollywood Blvd.), 323/466-8960, famous for its coconut-rich dishes and curries, unbelievably hot "deviled shrimp," and banana delight. (There are a few tables, if you prefer eating here.) To pack an international picnic basket, you could also start with an Armenian-style roast chicken to go from **Zankou Chicken,** 5065 Sunset Blvd. (at Normandy), 323/665-7842, which serves garlicky spit-roasted Armenian-Lebanese-style whole chickens. Or try popular **Moun of Tunis,** 7445 1/2 Sunset Blvd. (at Gardner, four blocks west of La Brea), 323/874-3333, where people line up to weep over the wickedly hot *harissa* and other Moroccan delicacies while sitting on floor cushions in exceptionally exotic surroundings.

People's Favorites: Melrose Avenue

For a taste of "historic" Melrose, try **Tommy Tang's,** a local favorite since 1982, at 7313 Melrose (near Fuller), 323/937-5733. There may be better Thai/sushi bars in L.A., but not many. And few could serve such theater. The crowd here is new-wave Fellini; on Tues. nights the waiters do it in drag. Open daily for lunch and dinner.

Among the worthiest neighborhood newcomers is the **Vienna Cafe,** 7356 Melrose (at Fuller),

323/651-3822, with a full Mediterranean café menu at breakfast, lunch, and dinner, and marvelous sandwiches, vegetarian selections, and bakery goods to go. **Chianti,** 7383 Melrose Ave. (between La Brea and Fairfax), 323/653-8333, is a very dark and romantic Old-World Northern Italian place with a knack for discretion even in seating arrangements (booths). More affordable, well-lit, and catering to a younger crowd is little sister **Chianti Cucina** adjacent (same address and phone), where the pastas and risottos are served with stylish simplicity.

Upscale Café Fare

Most of Hollywood's most stylish restaurants lie near Paramount and NBC Studios, within easy reach of folks with ready cash. Not all are horribly expensive, though, especially at breakfast or lunch. **Boxer,** 7615 Beverly Blvd. at Stanley (between Fairfax and La Brea), 323/932-6178, is a trendy storefront café serving box-shaped innovations to enthusiastic foodies—such things as tomato, beet, and avocado salad, and crusty pizza with caramelized onions, niçoise olives, roasted peppers, and garlic.

Long-running **Angeli Caffè,** 7274 Melrose Ave. (between Fairfax and La Brea), 323/936-9086, is a noisy, modern, and minimalist pizza and pasta joint catering to the hip and hungry at lunch and dinner. Still très cool for hanging out with the latest crop of young Hollywood stars and fashion models, at last report, was the inexpensive Italian **Caffè Luna,** 7463 Melrose Ave. (between Vista and Gardner), 323/655-8647. It's open until all hours, and always a good stop for a leisurely latte.

The French bistro **Les Deux Cafés,** 1638 N. Las Palmas Ave. (between Hollywood Blvd. and Selma Ave.), 323/465-0509, is/are one of those only-in-Hollywood kind of places, an exquisite and exquisitely relaxed fine foodery fashioned from a quaint onetime crack house attached, mid-parking lot, to the adjoining kitchen via an oddly lovely outdoor garden. Even the grease-pencil and mylar dining room menu is designed to change constantly, to take full advantage of the best and freshest produce, fish, and meats. Très L.A., also très cool. It's open daily for breakfast and lunch, Tues.–Sun. for dinner. Another possibility is the peaceful little oasis **Off Vine,** 6263 Leland (near

Vine parallel to Sunset, one block south), 323/962-1900, (lunch and dinner only), housed in a charming cottage with a romantic patio.

The stylish but casual French **Pinot Hollywood** bistro and its associated **Martini Lounge** and **Patinette** on-site bakery at 1448 N. Gower St. (at Sunset), 323/461-8800, are kissin' cousins to Joachim Splichal's other "Pinot"s—and to his acclaimed **Patina** (listed below). Some foodies consider Pinot Hollywood the Musso & Frank of the new century, what with its fatal attraction for Gower Gulch movie people and studio execs. The bakery opens at 7 A.M. for coffee, muffins, and such. The restaurant, patio, and sofa-stuffed lounge open for dinner Mon.–Sat., for lunch on weekdays.

Roscoe's House of Chicken and Waffles

Everybody loves this place, a mainstay of L.A.'s R&B crowd right in the heart of Hollywood at 1514 N. Gower St. (between Sunset and Hollywood Blvds.), 323/466-7453. Roscoe's is one of those classic Los Angeles dining experiences—a funky place in a funky neighborhood that manages to defy all trends, attracting L.A.'s upper crust, lower crust, and every kind of crust in between. The place delivers just what it promises, from morning till midnight—great Southern fried chicken with perfect waffles on the side. If you need vegetables, order some greens. Roscoe's also has places in the Mid-Wilshire district at 5006 W. Pico and at 106 W. Manchester in South-Central L.A.

Old Hollywood: Musso & Frank Grill

Musso & Frank, 6667 Hollywood Blvd. (three blocks west of Cahuenga Blvd.), 323/467-7788, is the last survivor of Old Hollywood, now that the original Chasen's is gone. William Faulkner, F. Scott Fitzgerald, Ernest Hemingway, and other literati hung out here while in town slumming for studio cash. But this is also a remnant of Raymond Chandler's imaginary Hollywood, a dark men's-clubby place outfitted with polished wood, red leather booths, and other stylish details circa 1919. Critics have described the cuisine as "simple food done well." Best bets: the grilled chops, famous chicken pot pie, and perennial breakfast menu. Not to mention the best martinis in town. It's open daily 11 A.M.–11 P.M., closed Christmas, Thanksgiving, and New Year's Day.

New Hollywood: Patina

Joachim Splichal's flagship French Californian at 5955 Melrose (between Highland and Vine), 323/467-1108, is one of L.A.'s best—famous for its imaginative yet substantial fare, starting with endless variations on the potato theme and ending with flawless desserts. Choosing one of the "tasting menus" eliminates the problem of what to order for an entrée. Premium. But children under age 10 eat here for free, so don't hesitate to bring the family if you're planning a truly special meal. Patina serves dinner nightly, lunch Tues.–Fri. only.

New Hollywood: Citrus

Chef Michel Richard started his L.A. sojourn with a wonderful West Hollywood pastry shop and catering biz—and though he no longer owns it, Michel Richard on S. Robertson Blvd. is still going strong, serving breads, cakes, and simple café fare, from omelettes and quiche to salads. But Richard's cheery Citrus, 6703 Melrose Ave. (at Citrus, a block west of Highland), 323/857-0034, is a bustling big-city French bistro included on all of L.A.'s "best restaurant" lists. Such things as crab coleslaw, Thai-spiced lobster, mesquite-smoked salmon, and superb desserts keep everyone coming back for more at both lunch (weekdays only) and dinner (every night but Sunday). Citrus is also quite expensive, however, so foodies on a budget will greatly appreciate the associated Bar Bistro.

EATING IN SILVER LAKE

Ever-popular Cha Cha Cha, 656 N. Virgil Ave. (just south of Melrose), 323/664-7723, is one of those places where the chi-chi go slumming. This terrific little Caribbean café, casual and cheery though in a fairly dicey neighborhood, is beloved for its empañadas, jerked chicken, Caribbean shrimp, and unusual pizzas. Reservations advisable at dinner. Valet parking suggested, to make sure your car's still around when you're ready to go.

At dinner-only Vida, 1930 Hillhurst Ave. (near Franklin), 323/660-4445, contemplate the very punny and fairly pricey entrées, such as "Okra Winfrey Creole Gumbo" and "Ty Cobb Salad." A neighborhood sibling, Fred 62, 1850 N. Vermont (at Franklin), 323/667-0062, serves 24-hour diner fare to a hip Silver Lake crowd.

Elegant dinner-only Mexico City, 2121 Hillhurst Ave. (near Los Feliz Blvd.) in Los Feliz, 323/661-7227, serves fine Mexican fare too few Americans have ever tasted, such as marinated pork or red snapper in a garlic and capers sauce. It serves many vegetarian options, too, including sweet green corn tamales and other appetizers, spinach enchiladas, and calabacitas poblanas (zucchini with cheese and chiles). Some say the area's best Mexican restaurant is long-running and romantic El Chavo, 4441 Sunset Blvd. (near Vermont) in Silver Lake, 323/664-0871, famous for its Sonora chicken and chicken mole. Yuca's Hut, 2056 N. Hillhurst in Los Feliz, 323/662-1214, is a people's favorite beloved for its burritos, carnitas, and such (closed Sunday). Netty's deli and café, 1700 Silver Lake Blvd., 323/662-8655, is the place for enjoying unusual Cajun, Californian, and Latin fusion.

Silver Lake's gay foodies tend to gravitate toward the Cobalt Cantina, 4326 Sunset Blvd. (at Fountain), 323/953-9991, with a local following lining up at the "shack"—originally home to the original L.A. Nicola—for the good soups and salads, roasted half-chickens, meatloaf, and corn tamales with sweet potatoes. The popular Martini Lounge is next door.

TINSELTOWN TRANSPORTATION AND INFORMATION

Arriving in Tinseltown by Metrorail and by Car

The Metrorail is a bit of a sore subject in L.A., as construction has been plagued by cost overruns, delays, and disasters. But progress is taking place: today the MTA's underground Metrorail Red Line provides connections between downtown and the communities of Hollywood, Long Beach, Redondo Beach, and Norwalk. The rail line now runs through (beneath) the Hollywood Hills to emerge in North Hollywood near Universal Studios. One-way tickets go for $1.35 and are available from coin-operated machines at rail stations. For Metrorail information, call 800/266-6883 within L.A. County or check www.mta.net.

From downtown L.A. and the Westside, it's reasonably easy to get to Hollywood and West

ROBERT HOLMES/CalTour

Hollywood by car via surface streets, **Wilshire, Santa Monica,** and **Sunset Blvds.** being the most obvious routes across the territory. But this being L.A., most people get around by freeway. As elsewhere throughout Southern California, the best freeway strategy on weekdays is to avoid peak commuter times if at all possible, setting out for a day's exploration at 9 or 10 A.M. and returning by 3 P.M.—or staying put until 7 P.M. or later, perhaps enjoying a leisurely evening meal while everyone else is stuck in traffic. Except at freeway bottlenecks and near major attractions (such as Universal Studios), weekend traffic is less horrifying.

From downtown, the **Hollywood Freeway (Hwy. 101)** quickly arrives in the heart of Hollywood and passes Universal Studios before descending into the San Fernando Valley, where it becomes the **Ventura Freeway (Hwy. 101)** heading west and the **Hollywood Freeway (Hwy. 170)** continuing north through North Hollywood.

The **Golden State Freeway (I-5)** skirts Hollywood east of Silver Lake and Griffith Park and slides down into the San Fernando Valley, traversing Glendale, Burbank, and Sun Valley before joining Hwy. 170. The massive L.A. traffic funnel manifests just north of the San Fernando Valley proper, as first I-405 (the San Diego Fwy.) and then I-5 and I-210 (the Foothill Fwy.) converge for the journey up and over the Tehachapis.

Something of a back-door route into Hollywood is provided by the **Glendale Freeway (Hwy. 2),** which meanders south from I-210 near La Cañada Flintridge to intersect the Ventura Fwy. (Hwy. 134 here) before pouring out onto Glendale Blvd. in Silver Lake. (Hwy. 2 resurrects itself as Santa Monica Blvd., nearby.) The dominant—and notably congested—thoroughfare traversing the territory from east to west is the **Ventura Freeway,** Hwy. 134 from Pasadena, which becomes Hwy. 101 near North Hollywood and Universal Studios.

Tinseltown by Air: The Burbank/Pasadena/Glendale Airport

Growing fast between the Golden State and Hollywood Fwys. and now officially known as the **Burbank/Pasadena/Glendale Airport,** 818/840-8847, this regional airport is popular with Angelenos, business travelers, and tourists trying to avoid the craziness at LAX. In addition to its multiple commuter services, its major carriers include Alaska, American, Southwest, and United Airlines.

Tinseltown Information

If you find yourself in the general vicinity anyway, Hollywood is a good general stop for Los Angeles visitor information. An outpost of the L.A. visitor bureau, the **Hollywood Visitor Information Center,** 6541 Hollywood Blvd., 213/689-8822, www.lacvb.com, is open Mon.–Sat. 9 A.M.–5 P.M. For information with a strictly local emphasis, and to find out when and where the next star will fall to earth along the Hollywood Walk of Fame, contact: **Hollywood Chamber of Commerce,** 7018 Hollywood Blvd., 323/469-8311, www.hollywoodcoc.org.

SEEING AND DOING WEST HOLLYWOOD

The distinction is largely lost on most visitors, but the hippest parts of "Hollywood"—the clubs, the famous bookstores, the best restaurants and hotels for spotting celebrities—are actually in West Hollywood. Affectionately called WeHo by its residents, West Hollywood is part of L.A.'s rather amorphous and affluent "Westside" but still a bit scruffy by Beverly Hills standards. If they're not hiding out in Beverly Hills, Bel-Air, or the Santa Monica area, some of the stars who star on West Hollywood's bold Sunset Strip billboards hang out with other tony industry trendoids in its hotels, power-lunch ghettos, designer shops, and fitness centers.

An unincorporated area of Los Angeles until cityhood was approved in late 1984, West Hollywood elected the nation's first predominantly gay city council—not too surprising since much of the motivation for cityhood grew out of alleged harassment toward the gay community by the Los Angeles Police Department (LAPD). One of the new mayor's first official acts was to ceremoniously remove the newly illegal "Fagots Stay Out" sign that had been hanging over the bar in Barney's Beanery for about 20 years. (In Hollywood mythology Barney's is best known as the place Janis Joplin beaned The Doors' Jim Morrison over the head with a bottle of Southern Comfort.) But West Hollywood's fantasy of becoming a "gay Camelot," which attracted international media attention, was, to a certain extent, delusional. The first disappointment came early, when the city's first mayor resigned after a $7,000 embezzlement conviction—and the city's gay coalition lost its majority on the city council. Soon thereafter the scourge of AIDS decimated the local community of gay activists. Though West Hollywood was among the first cities in the United States to extend health benefits to city employees' "domestic partners," two-thirds of city voters aren't gay.

Shaped cartographically like a handgun pointed due east down Santa Monica Blvd., West Hollywood covers just under two square miles and supports the highest population density of any city west of the Mississippi River. Families with children, the mainstay of most towns, make up a miniscule proportion of West Hollywood's population; about 75 percent of households here are "nonfamily." About 70 percent of residents are renters, which perhaps explains why rent control was also an early city council agenda item.

For information about the city of West Hollywood and its sights and attractions, contact: **West Hollywood Convention and Visitors Bureau,** 8687 Melrose Ave. (at the Pacific Design Center) in West Hollywood, 310/289-2525.

COMING ATTRACTIONS: WEST HOLLYWOOD

Centered along L.A.'s famous Sunset Strip, still renowned for its nightlife, West Hollywood boasts a lively street scene during daylight, too, when patrons pack coffeehouses, sidewalk cafés, bookstores, boutiques, and music shops. West Hollywood also teems with movie producers, music and publishing industry people, and agents—not to mention Warner Hollywood Studios, Geffen Records, and the Writers Guild of America West—which helps explain the Strip's two-mile stretch of bold "vanity billboards," some of the most overwhelming, far-out outdoor advertising you'll see anywhere. Other West Hollywood highlights include the monumental Pacific Design Center, its surrounding upscale designer district, and the gay business district along Santa Monica Avenue. West Hollywood's stylish eccentricities also extend east into L.A. along Melrose Ave., a once cutting-edge cultural destination that's now a notable commercial success. In the nearby Little Muscovy neighborhood, where a large population of Soviet Jews live, is the Schindler House and Studio, one of L.A.'s architectural landmarks.

SUNSET STRIP

From its intersection with poverty downtown near Olvera St., where the City of Angels was born, Sunset Blvd. winds northwest and then west for almost 25 miles, reaching land's end

CLUBBIN' IT

Los Angeles has its civilized corporate bars and reasonably civil coffeehouses. But supercool Los Angeles, the L.A. scene, is at home in the region's dance and music clubs.

In search of Los Angeles cool, the first place to look is in and around Hollywood, starting on Sunset Boulevard, a.k.a. the Sunset Strip—the historic convergence of hip since hep. In the 1920s, the neighborhood was known for its speakeasies and sometimes unspeakably shady characters. The fairly wild nightlife remains, these days with a cutting-edge cachet that comes with celebrity sanction. Don't end an exploration of Los Angeles nightlife in Hollywood, however. Cool clubs are all over Los Angeles, many serving less frenetic fun. To get up to speed on what's going on, pick up a current copy of the *L.A. Weekly,* known for its very cool, very comprehensive entertainment listings, or any number of free 'zines you'll find around town.

The Sunset Strip
The rusty old tin shack just up the hill from Sunset Blvd., **House of Blues** in West Hollywood at 8430 Sunset Blvd. (one block east of La Cienega), 323/848-5100, www.hob.com, looks as if it belongs anywhere but here. After you valet park the car, pretend you've just stepped off into the bayou—whatever gets you in the mood for blues, bluesy rock, jazz, gospel, reggae, zydeco, and more. The performance schedule is fairly eclectic, accommodating the varied celebrity performers that end up on stage. In a single week the likes of John Lee Hooker, King Crimson, and George Clinton might appear. You won't be disappointed if you come early for dinner, either. Ask for a table with a view and you'll look out over the Strip's snazzy neon. Still more stirring, spiritually speaking: gospel brunch on Sunday. Nightly show times vary, depending on whether single or double billing and/or early and late shows are scheduled. Call the box office for current show information or check schedules on the House of Blues website.

The cover charge at the House of Blues varies, but generally runs $20 and up. Gospel brunch runs $22–36, depending upon seating. Valet parking is steep ($8) and slow; you may do better at independent lots in the area. Gospel brunch (reservations required) is scheduled on Sundays. For 24-hour recorded show information, call 323/848-5100. For more details, reservations, and to order tickets, call

the box office at 323/848-5100, daily 9 A.M.–11 P.M.

Most famous of the newer clubs is the **Viper Room,** once known as the Central, 8852 Sunset Blvd. (near San Vicente), 310/358-1880, a popular "Hollywood brat pack" bar, dance club, and hangout most noted for the fact that Johnny Depp is co-owner. Very small, very hip, and very dark. On tap here: DJ nights (complete with disco ball) as well as live acts, everyone from Johnny Cash and Carol Channing to Beverly D'Angelo and Blue Martini, the Holy Barbarians, and the Imposters. The Viper is always a surprise. Full bar, over age 21 only.

Fun in a 1980s kind of way is **Key Club,** 9039 Sunset Blvd. (at Doheny), 310/274-5800, which took over the territory from Gazzarri's, in its last days proudly known as the Sunset Strip's oldest and sleaziest rock club. (Gazzarri's launched both Van Halen and Guns 'n' Roses.) The Key is a totally new gig, a three-story pleasure palace with low-tech-industrial looks and every imaginable high-tech toy, down to the video screens everywhere, even the tiny monitors mounted in the floor that give you a good view of the stage. In other words, this is yet another club trading in L.A. cool. The musical tenor ranges from country and rock to jazz and blues. The rockers give way to the dancers at around 11 P.M.

Most nights, the young, trendy, and "in the know" head to new venues like the **Cat Club,** 8911 Sunset Blvd. (at San Vicente), 310/657-0888, a rock 'n' roll bar with plush black booths and leopard print seating. Backed by Slim Jim Phantom, drummer for the Stray Cats, and a group of Sunset Strip club owners, the Cat charges no cover and offers no hassles getting in—and there's tons of parking out back. Just up the street, the beautiful people congregate in the **Sky Bar** at the Mondrian Hotel, 8440 Sunset Blvd., 323/650-8999, and the marvelous art deco Argyle Hotel nearby at 8358 Sunset Blvd. (at La Cienega Blvd.), 323/654-7100, where on Sat. nights the **Fenix** dining room is transformed into one of the hottest clubs in L.A.

Then there are the Sunset Strip's tried and true venues, including **The Roxy,** the top music club in L.A., in the middle of all the action at 9009 Sunset Blvd. (near Doheny), 310/276-2222. With its elegant art-deco interiors and sometimes eclectic combination of baby bands and big-time rockers on tour, The Roxy is also one of the best places around to come across rock stars—and entertainment industry

(continued on next page)

CLUBBIN' IT

(continued)

execs—in the audience. Talent attracts talent, after all. Since there's no age limit, The Roxy is also a magnet for young hipsters. Great sound.

Whisky A Go Go, 8901 Sunset Blvd. (at San Vicente), 310/535-0579, is another historic hot spot, prime-time for rock in the 1960s. Realistic scenes from Oliver Stone's film *The Doors* were shot here, of course, since Jim Morrison and company were asked not to come back to the Whisky after memorable misbehavior. The style these days runs to heavy metal, mosh pits, and such. With no age limit, the crowd is very young and very leather. Something of a spiritual match is **Coconut Teaszer,** 8117 Sunset (at Selma), 323/654-4773, once a DJed dance club, now a heavy-leather rock venue.

And there are always the comedy clubs. On the Strip is everybody's favorite, **The Comedy Store,** 8433 W. Sunset Blvd. (at La Cienega) in West Hollywood, 323/656-6225, though **The Improvisation,** 8162 Melrose Ave. (one and a half blocks west of Crescent Heights), 323/651-2583, and the very funny **Groundlings Theater,** 7307 Melrose (at Poinsettia), 323/934-9700, are also best bets.

Other Hollywood Clubs

The **Catalina Bar and Grill,** 1640 N. Cahuenga Blvd. (just off Hollywood Blvd.), 323/466-2210, is one of the best jazz clubs in the city, serving great seafood along with two shows nightly. Also pop into the elegant **Cinegrill** at the Hollywood Roosevelt Hotel, 7000 Hollywood Blvd., 323/466-7000, across from Mann's Chinese Theatre.

First famous as a 1960s folk-rock venue, **The Troubador** in West Hollywood at 9081 Santa Monica Blvd. (near Doheny), 310/276-6168, is the place where John Lennon scandalized the world by wearing a sanitary napkin on his head. Noted in the 1980s as a head-banging heavy metal/leather club, its fare these days is considerably more varied. Restaurant, three full bars, no age limit.

The **Lava Lounge,** 1533 N. La Brea (just above Sunset), 213/876-6612, takes cool to a whole new level with a retro-chic Hawaiian-style ambience, which some say inspired Quentin Tarantino's *Pulp Fiction.* Live bands play on the small corner stage with music ranging from blues, surf, lounge to rockabilly. Surfboard optional.

No time to get your nails done? Head on over to **Beauty Bar** at 1638 N. Cahuenga Blvd. (at Selma), 323/464-7676, and have a martini and a manicure for 10 bucks during happy hour on Thurs. and Friday. Like Beauty Bars in New York and San Francisco, this place evokes a 1960s beauty parlor ambience with fixtures salvaged from the Basque House of Style, a vintage salon in Bakersfield.

Other surprisingly comfortable neighborhood venues are at home in Hollywood and West Hollywood. For no-cover blues, jazz, and other cross-cultural surprises, the place is **Canter's Kibitz Room,** 419 N. Fairfax Ave. (at Beverly Blvd.), 323/651-2030. The fun **Genghis Cohen Cantina,** 740 N. Fairfax (at Melrose), 323/653-0640, a combination Chinese restaurant and top-notch acoustic/low-key rock venue, sometimes attracts some industry heavies along with the new talent. (Small cover charge.) **Molly Malone's Irish Pub,** 575 S. Fairfax Ave. (at 6th St.), 323/935-1577, is the place for rhythm and blues, rock, and Irish folk.

There's always North Hollywood—or "NoHo," to those in the know—up the hill near Universal Studios, if none of the other Hollywoods fill the bill. Hot NoHo nightspots include the seriously crowded **Blue Saloon,** 4657 Lankershim Blvd. (at Vineland Ave.), 818/766-4644, a straight-ahead beer hall also serving rock, rockabilly, and country. For jazz, the place here is **The Baked Potato,** 3783 Cahuenga Blvd. W, 818/980-1615, which also serves—surprise!—stuffed spuds. And even if it is at Universal Studios, **B. B. King's Blues Club** upstairs at CityWalk, 818/622-5464, serves up some of the all-time greats along with L.A.'s best, plus a great Gospel Sunday Brunch. Reservations advisable.

East Hollywood Clubs

Things change fast in Silver Lake's cutting-edge club scene, a fact complicated further by the proliferation of "concept" clubs that exist at other venues on certain nights of the week. So if none of the following remains true, head for Vermont Ave. and/or the W. Sunset Blvd. business district to find out what's going on.

At last report **Spaceland,** 213/833-2843, was still the preeminent dance and performance club in the neighborhood, premiering new local talent such as The Eels, Men of Porn, and The Snowmen, and attracting an endlessly varying audience—including, recently, "the industry" Spaceland—to its shows six nights a week (Mon.–Saturday). Ever-popular **Glaxa**

Studios, at 3707 Sunset, 323/663-5295, is a combination theater, music venue, and café. The **Garage,** 4519 Santa Monica Blvd. (at Virgil), 323/662-6802, once a gay cowboy bar called the Bunkhouse, now hosts live acts almost every night and the **Club Sucker** punk beer fest on Sun. from 4 or 5–8 P.M. And *the* place for drag is costume-themed **Dragstrip 66,** 323/669-1226, held on the second Sat. night of the month at **Rudolpho's,** 2500 Riverside Dr. (at Fletcher, just west of I-5). Sooner or later everyone goes to the **Dresden Room,** 1760 N. Vermont Ave. (near Franklin), 323/665-4294, just to hear Marty and Elayne's roof-ripping rendition of the Captain & Tenille's *Muskrat Love.*

Clubs Elsewhere
Don't miss **The Mint** midcity at 6010 Pico Blvd., 323/954-9630, in mint condition after an expansion and remodel. With great acoustics, and a rock, blues, and jazz clientele, The Mint also boasts a full bar and a relatively low cover charge. No age limit.

A best bet on the Westside on weekends is Santa Monica's **McCabe's Guitar Shop** nearby at 3101 Pico, 310/828-4497, which becomes a de facto coffeehouse on weekend nights, serving bluegrass, blues, folk, gospel, and other acoustic surprises (sometimes big names). If you're in Long Beach, the place is the **Blue Cafe** at 210 The Promenade, 562/983-7111, a long-running local blues venue with dance floor and, upstairs, pool tables.

Branford Marsalis and other bright lights regularly star on stage at the **Jazz Bakery** inside the old Helms Bakery in Culver City at 3233 Helms Ave., 310/271-9039; small café, too. **Fais Do-Do** in Culver City at 5257 W. Adams Blvd. (between La Brea and Fairfax), 323/954-8080, is another fine and friendly hangout, named Fais Do-Do after a Creole term for "time to put the little babies in bed and let the grownups play some music." At home in what first opened as a bank in 1912, it's now noted for cookin' up blues, jazz, and rock while the kitchen cooks up Cajun. Beer and wine, too.

The place in Leimert Park is **5th Street Dick's,** 3347 1/2 W. 43rd Pl., 323/296-3970, serving some of L.A.'s best jazz with home cooking and coffee. Just around the corner is **The World Stage,** 4344 Degnan Blvd., 323/293-2451, famous for its Thurs. night jams and world-class weekend performances.

at the comfortable community of Pacific Palisades. Along the way it connects many of L.A.'s famously segregated social extremes: illegal immigrants begging for work on street corners, teenage runaways trolling for tricks, the wealthy shoppers of Beverly Hills and Bel-Air. Midway down the Boulevard, in West Hollywood, is Sunset's most historic stretch—the mythic "Sunset Strip," less than two miles long and running along the base of the Hollywood Hills between Crescent Heights Blvd. to the east and Beverly Hills to the west. The Strip was known for its illicit casinos, gangsters, speakeasies, slumming movie stars, and general licentiousness in the 1930s and '40s; its clubs in those days included hot spots such as the Trocadero, Mocambo, and Ciro's. By the 1950s Las Vegas, with more neon and deeper pockets, was siphoning off the Strip's glitzy glamour and biggest talent, but the myth was maintained during the decline by Ed "Kookie" Byrnes and the faux freewheeling *77 Sunset Strip* TV show. In the 1960s flower children, bikers, and straight-ahead rock 'n' roll clubs invaded the Strip. So well established was the Sunset Strip's reputation

as a refuge from social norms that it made sense, in the 1970s, when gays began arriving in the general neighborhood—as did former Soviet citizens, then still moving into the fairly new ethnic enclave of Little Muscovy. But the Sunset Strip's final resurrection was financed by migrating music, television, and movie production companies and the upscale amenities they attracted.

These days the Strip's club scene is strong once again. Venerable venues such as the **Troubador,** the **Roxy,** and **Whisky A Go Go** still pack in the crowds, along with relative newcomers such as the **House of Blues,** a link in the Dan Akroyd–related chain, and Johnny Depp's **Viper Room.**

If you're not clubbin' it, consider strollin' it, especially easy to manage with a little help from West Hollywood's public **Sunset Shuttle,** 310/858-8000. As you drive east to west into the sea of celebrity faces magnified by vanity billboards, attractions include the 1927 **Château Marmont,** 8221 Sunset, famous "hideout" hotel for stumped screenwriters and movie stars. Other notable hotels include the striking art-deco **Argyle,** 8358 Sunset, the onetime St. James's Club private hotel and men's club known to Raymond Chandler fans as the Sunset Towers; the exclusive and hip **Sunset Marquis** just off Sunset at 1200 N. Alta Loma, popular with rock stars only in part because of the private recording studio; and **Wyndham Bel Age,** 1020 N. San Vicente.

Known more for its nightclubs, restaurants, and hotels, the Sunset Strip isn't so famous as a shopping destination. A few shops of particular interest in the neighborhood: **Book Soup,** 8818 Sunset Blvd. (between Laraby and Horn), 310/659-3110, a venerable locally owned L.A. bookstore and bistro specializing in literature and books on the entertainment industry, also famous for its international magazine and newspaper selection (and a best bet for book signings and celebrity spotting, some say); **Tower Records,** across the street at 8801 Sunset, popular PR venue for music celebs promoting new products (for classical music and videos, head for the annex across the street); and the **Virgin Megastore,** just beyond the Strip at 8000 Sunset (in Crescent Heights), 323/650-8666, where Hollywood's historic old Schwab's Drugstore once stood.

PACIFIC DESIGN CENTER

Despite apparently antithetical politics, West Hollywood is the place people from Beverly Hills and Bel-Air go to shop, dine, and otherwise divert themselves—a perfect locale for L.A.'s design district, the largest concentration of stylish showrooms in the country outside New York City. At its heart is the Pacific Design Center (PDC), a glossy beast affectionately known as the Blue Whale, with its colored-glass sidekick, the Green Hornet. (The third creature in the series—the red one, perhaps destined to be the Red Fox, Red Snapper, or Red-Tailed Hawk—has yet to be born. Or hatched.) Surrounded by a triangle of style-slick streets—La Cienega, Santa Monica, and Beverly Blvds.— the PDC boasts more than 200 top designer showrooms and 1.25 million square feet of spacious style. Once proudly aloof, exclusive, and open only to the trade, in recent years even the PDC has felt some pressure to open its doors to the bourgeoisie (and "discounted markup" retail sales). The result? A PDC somewhat friendlier to the more ordinary affluent and still trying to get

SCHINDLER HOUSE AND STUDIO

West Hollywood's only notable noncommercial attraction, this world-renowned modernist monument was designed by architect and Austrian immigrant Rudolf Schindler—a disciple of Frank Lloyd Wright—and built in 1921. And thanks to the largesse of Vienna's Museumangewandtekunst (MAK), or Museum of Applied Arts, the house has been renovated and preserved as a study center for experimental architecture. For all his brilliance, Rudolf Schindler was largely unappreciated—and underemployed—by Los Angeles. Most of his modest work can be seen in and around Silver Lake.

Inspired by the idea of airy North African desert camps, Rudolf Schindler built this radically modern two-family home at very low cost, using concrete, redwood, canvas walls, and floor-to-ceiling glass. The shared kitchen at the center served as the "pin" from which the minimalist pinwheel design spun outward into the outdoors. An Arts and Crafts innovation—sleeping porches—here evolved into open-air "baskets" on the roof. Revolutionary in construction as well as concept, Schindler's innovations included bare slab-tilt concrete wall panels and individual indoor "studios" in lieu of conventional living and dining rooms; the "living rooms," complete with fireplace, were outdoors.

The Schindler House and Studio, now open under the auspices of the MAK Center for Art and Architecture, is north of Melrose Ave. at 835 N. Kings Rd., 323/651-1510, www.makcenter. com, and open to the public Wed.–Sun. 11 A.M.–6 P.M., $5 admission. Guided tours are available Sat. and Sun. at 11:30 A.M. and at 12:30, 1:30, and 2:30 P.M.

in step with at-large L.A. The change hasn't revolutionized showroom admissions policies but it is reflected in the overall atmosphere, with public exhibits, events, and tours now offered in addition to people-friendly businesses such as cappuccino bars and cafés.

Most furnishings, fabrics, and art available at the PDC's private showrooms are for sale only to "the trade" (professional interior designers), though some shops do welcome interested amateurs for both browsing and buying. To get some idea of who has what and where it might be, public PDC tours are offered (weekdays at 10 A.M., at last report, arranged through the concierge). For more information, contact the Pacific Design Center, 8687 Melrose Ave. (at San Vicente Blvd.), 310/657-0800. For extra help, shops such as **L.A. Design Concepts,** 8811 Alden Dr., 310/276-2109, can negotiate purchases at PDC trade-only outlets for about 15 percent above list price.

If touring the PDC seems less than exciting, then tour the neighborhood. From the Whale and Hornet, "avenues of design" fan out in all directions. Both Robertson and La Cienega are famous for their art galleries and showrooms. Quite pleasant for window shopping is Robertson between Beverly Blvd. and Melrose—particularly appealing for an after-dinner stroll, when window displays shine forth.

MELROSE AVENUE AND AROUND

Melrose Avenue is très L.A. Imagine Venice Beach with a generous trust fund. Or Hollywood if it were backed up by a Beverly Hills bank account—casual and cheeky but unbelievably costly. Fashionably cheap. That's Melrose Avenue. This eclectic and entertaining neighborhood is prime time for people-watching. Coffeehouses, restaurants, and clubs abound. Shops sell antiques, used books, and vintage clothes, high-end arts, housewares, and L.A.-designer wear. Melrose seems too successful, too self-consciously cool, to be truly avant garde. But in L.A. one truth doesn't necessarily cancel out another. Judge for yourself.

To "do Melrose" right, wear good walking shoes and otherwise prepare to explore. Melrose Avenue is prominent in West Hollywood proper and extends east to Silver Lake, but "real Melrose" traditionally covers the distance between N. La Brea and Fairfax Avenues. This hipster heaven extends its reach all the time—to several blocks west of Crescent Heights Blvd., for example, and to the east as well—but what most people consider coolest are the 7200-7700 addresses, the nine-block stretch between Alta Vista Blvd. and Spaulding Avenue.

The emphasis at **Retail Slut,** 7308 Melrose, 323/934-1339, is vivid fashion for the young and the young at heart, from body-hugging knits to bold non-wallflower floral prints. The motto is: "If you don't know what it is, go ask your big sister." **Aardvark's Odd Ark,** 7579 Melrose (at Carson), 323/655-6769, is a recycled clothing store of long standing, just the place for finding a perfectly pitched loud Hawaiian shirt and 1950s bowling attire, and **Maya Jewelry,** 7452 Melrose (at Vista), offers an unbelievable selection of unusual yet affordable earrings and other items. For "antiques and weird stuff" try **Off the Wall,** 7325 Melrose, 323/930-1185, an assortment of cool finds like life-sized plastic cows and egg chairs. Always popular, too, is the **Wound and Wound Toy Co.,** 7374 Melrose, 323/653-6703, with a wonderful collection of—you guessed it—wind-up toys, music boxes, and more.

A fairly famous avenue resident is farther "up-town" on Melrose—**The Bodhi Tree** bookstore, 8585 Melrose, 310/659-1733, where actress Shirley MacLaine began her literary path to spiritual enlightenment among the New Age meditation, psychology, astrology, and music books. Being a public thoroughfare Melrose Ave. is always "open," though some of the more out-there Melrose neighborhoods are downright unappealing and/or unsafe after dark. Should you arrive on a Sunday before the shops open, stop off at the **Melrose Weekend Market** at Fairfax High School (on the corner of Melrose and Fairfax), for flea market finds including vintage 1940s-style Hawaiian shirts, California pottery, and cool records. This one has food and music too. Open 9 A.M.–5 P.M., small admission fee.

PRACTICAL WEST HOLLYWOOD

STAYING IN WEST HOLLYWOOD

Travelers looking to save money while looking here for L.A. design, art, and style trends may find better accommodations deals in Beverly Hills, believe it or not. But it's not true that only rock stars or music and movie execs can afford to stay in West Hollywood. Consider the very nice **Best Western Sunset Plaza Hotel** at 8400 Sunset Blvd., 323/654-0750, 323/656-4158, or toll-free 800/252-0645 in California, 800/421-3652 in the U.S. and Canada. Also a motel, the Sunset Plaza offers some apartment-style kitchen units. Plus it's within a crawdad's throw of the House of Blues, and boasts a heated swimming pool. Rooms and suites go for $135–225. Premium-Luxury.

Another reasonably priced option—by local standards—is the **Ramada Plaza Hotel** (formerly the Ramada West Hollywood), 8585 Santa Monica Blvd. (just west of La Cienega), 310/652-6400 or toll-free 800/845-8585. The place is right in step with the rest of West Hollywood, too (if you were worried), with even the postmodern exterior screaming "Hey, we're in style!" The futuristic sensibility travels from lobby into the guest rooms—the two-story "lofts" are coolest—without letting on that this is actually a stylish reincarnation of Hollywood's infamous Tropicana Motel, long beloved by degenerate rockers and L.A.'s artistic intelligentsia. Now that everything's spiffed up, expect to pay $145 and up (Premium-Luxury) for rooms, and $225 and up for suites (Luxury).

Good value is what you get at pleasant three-story **Grafton on Sunset,** a three-story boutique hotel just east of La Cienega at 8462 Sunset Blvd., 323/654-6470, which offers a galaxy of executive perks like VIP access to area clubs, same day laundry and dry cleaning service, and an outdoor Mediterranean garden. Rooms are $135–175, while suites start at $200. Premium-Luxury.

Otherwise, inquire about lower weekend rates and seasonal special packages at pricier places.

Château Marmont

All but out-shouted by the billboards and general chaos of the Sunset Strip, this serene French Normandy "château" has been famous since it first opened in 1929 as a haven for Hollywood celebrities. Once a residential castle for the likes of Errol Flynn, Greta Garbo, and Jean Harlow, and the place studios sent writers to "hole up" to finish movie scripts, in more recent years the Château Marmont gained unwelcome notoriety as the place John Belushi met his maker while on speedballs, that toxic concoction of cocaine and heroin. Still the best Hollywood-area choice for absolute privacy, and still a popular celebrity hideout, the Château Marmont specializes in reclusive luxury. The most coveted, and more expensive, are the bungalows near the pool. Child care, complimentary cell phones, full fitness center, and room service are available, though the understated dining room and **Bar Marmont** offer real Hollywood atmosphere. Rooms are $220–280, suites start at $335. Luxury. For information and reservations, contact: Château Marmont, 8221 W. Sunset Blvd., 323/656-1010 or toll-free 800/242-8328.

The Argyle

Until fairly recently the private St. James's Club, a British expatriate refuge renovated and refurbished in grand style in the 1980s at a cost of over $40 million, The Argyle is a 1931 art deco masterpiece now listed on the National Register of Historic Places—but it's a destination better known to mystery fans, and to Raymond Chandler's literary private eye, Philip Marlowe, as the **Sunset Towers.** Though rooms are a tad small by contemporary standards, they are stunning, with handcrafted Italian furniture (some feature gondola beds) and endless deco details. The Argyle includes all the usual comforts and deluxe amenities. And what views! Up here on top of the Hollywood world you can pretend to be a Hollywood player, which may explain why The Argyle starred in the film version of *The Player,* that slightly cynical Hollywood morality tale. Other main attractions: the hotel's Hollywood portrait collection, a wonderful book and video library (including all films ever shot here, quite a list), and the celebrated California-style French restaurant fenix. Its phonetically correct yet modest lower-cased presentation belies its reputation—and its classy Old Hollywood supper-club style. Expect to shell out $220–270 for a room, $300 and up for a suite. Luxury, but not that much more than expensive rooms at the Ramada. For more information, contact: The Argyle, 8358 Sunset Blvd., 323/654-7100 or toll-free 800/225-2637 for reservations, www.argylehotel.com.

Hotel Mondrian

Los Angeles is abuzz over the Mondrian all over again since a makeover by owner Ian Schrager, formerly of New York's Studio 54 and owner of New York's Royalton. The wildly playful exterior paint job, echoing namesake painter Piet Mondrian's geometric work, is long gone. The hotel's new stark sensibility was imported to Hollywood by French architect Philippe Starck; the result is self-consciously stylish and theatrical, the new Mondrian something of an outsiders' stagey reinterpretation of Hollywood's mythic see-and-be-seen scene. Enamored critics have lent the new Mondrian subtitles such as "Hotel Surreal," for its intentional distortions of scale—five-foot clay pots dwarf the outdoor dining area and freestanding 30-foot-tall "doors" marking the entrance also make visitors seem small—and its semi-futuristic obsession with white, light, and cool exhibitionistic *space.*

This may not be Tinseltown's idea of itself, but corporate types like it—and the Mondrian *is* right across the street from the House of Blues, itself a hip and high-concept outsiders' reinterpretation of a tin-roofed shack in the Louisiana bayou, so in that sense it fits right into the neighborhood. Rooms here are surprisingly inviting, with eat-in kitchens (harking back to its original incarnation as an apartment building) and all the comforts served up with some spectacular city views. The Sky Bar here is the ultimate scene. Rooms start at $240, and suites go all the way up to $2,600. Luxury. For more information and reservations, contact: Mondrian Hotel, 8440 Sunset Blvd., 323/650-8999 or toll-free 800/525-8029, www.mondrianhotel.com.

Sunset Marquis Hotel and Villas

This is where aging rock stars, sundry celebrities and pseudo celebs, music and movie industry execs, and other "real Hollywood" people stay, along with anyone else who can afford the freight. Just off the Sunset Strip in a quiet residential neighborhood, this onetime apartment building and surrounding "villas" (a collection of bungalows and homes) offer peace and privacy with California-style Mediterranean charm, mixed up here and there with '60s style. There's a $600,000 in-house recording studio here, too. The grounds have a flowing grace, with abundant greenery and exotic birds, swimming pools, sauna and health spa, hot tub, a koi pond, waterfall, and outdoor café, but the real sightseeing takes place in the **Whiskey Bar,** *the* star-watching watering hole. Suites start at $305, villas at $600. Luxury.

For more information, contact: Sunset Marquis Hotel and Villas, 1200 N. Alta Loma Rd., 310/657-1333 or toll-free 800/858-9758.

Wyndham Bel Age Hotel

Another onetime West Hollywood apartment building transformed into an elegant all-suites hotel, the recently renovated Bel Age just off the Sunset Strip is French provincial in style, classical in attitude—with carefully appointed suites, classical music, classy international fine art, and exquisite French-Russian fare in the acclaimed on-site **Diaghilev** restaurant here. For classic jazz and more casual continental fare, head to the hotel's **Club Brasserie.** Up on the roof you'll find a pool, garden, and hot tub. Suites are $240–500. Luxury. For more information, contact: Wyndham Bel Age Hotel, 1020 N. San Vicente Blvd., 310/854-1111. For reservations, in the United States and Canada call toll-free 800/996-3426.

"Le" Hotels and Hotel Sofitel

At one time six West Hollywood hotels sported "Le" in their titles to identify them as intimate upscale siblings of the L'Ermitage Hotel Group, onetime apartment buildings in quiet residential areas refashioned into elite retreats. Le Bel Age Hotel de Grande Classe is now a Wyndham hotel (see above), Le Mondrian Hotel de Grande Classe is now the Mondrian Hotel (see above), and Le Dufy is now a sophisticated Summerfield Suites (see below). Not usually inexpensive, these business-oriented hotels *can* be great bargains—with rates as low as $99—during the November–December holiday season and at other "off" business times.

The recently renovated all-suites **Le Montrose** (originally Le Valadon) near Beverly Hills, just south of Sunset Blvd. and east of Doheny at 900 Hammond St. (at Cynthia), 310/855-1115 or toll-free 800/776-0666, www.lemontrose.com, offers art-nouveau ambience, ample comforts, and extras such as mountain bikes and maps for neighborhood touring. Suites are $290–460. Luxury. Nearby is four-story **Le Rêve**, 8822 Cynthia St. (at Larrabe), 310/854-1114 or toll-free 800/835-7997, with country French demi-suites, junior suites, and executive suites, stunning rooftop "view" pool, and spa. Suites are $139–265. Premium-Luxury. Also popular with entertainment industry execs is the all-suites **Le Parc,** 733 Westknoll Dr., 310/855-8888 or toll-free 800/578-4837, www.leparcsuites.com, where each suite features a sunken living room, fireplace, kitchenette, wet bar, and separate bedrooms. Also here: a guests-only restaurant, tennis court (up on the roof), basketball hoops, workout room, pool, spa, and sundeck. Suites are $300–400. Luxury.

Sophisticated, recently renovated **Summerfield Suites Hotel,** formerly Le Dufy, 1000 Westmount Dr. (south of Sunset Blvd. near La Cienega and Santa Monica), 310/657-7400 or toll-free 800/833-4353, no longer features that French impressionist air. Understated contemporary style is accompanied by sunken living rooms, fireplaces, and kitchens or kitchenettes. Heated pool. Rates are $258–315. Luxury.

Facing the Beverly Center at the edge of West Hollywood proper is the ten-story California-style country French **Hotel Sofitel**, formerly Ma Maison Sofitel, 8555 Beverly Blvd., 310/278-5444, or toll-free 800/521-7772, www.sofitel.com, with pool, workout, and spa facilities, casual café, nice restaurant, every other imaginable amenity. Rack rates are $349–795, but inquire about specials. Luxury.

EATING IN WEST HOLLYWOOD

West Hollywood is a must-do destination for dedicated international foodies—a mythic L.A. restaurant locale. Long-running local restaurant celebrities include see-and-be-seen icons such as Diaghilev, Eclipse, fenix at the Argyle, and The Ivy. You get the idea. In and around West Hollywood famous and/or great restaurants outnumber parking spaces. At the hippest of the hip places, sometimes the stars and star-makers outnumber parking spaces.

WeHo People's Eats

West Hollywood's most famous diner these days is scruffy **Barney's Beanery,** 8447 Santa Monica Blvd. (one block east of La Cienega), 323/654-2287, infamous for its "celebrities out slumming" associations. Barney's offers a vast array of burgers and hot dogs, sandwiches, and omelettes, but most people come to play pool and to sample the impressive beer selection.

Cowboys and cowgirls are back in style at the countrified **Saddle Ranch Chop House,** 8371 Sunset Blvd., 323/822-3850, a nightclub and restaurant with an awesome mechanical bull. Munch on a plate of ribs or a burger, and order from the late-night menu until 1:15 A.M. The bar is an interesting place to stop for a soda or a shot of whiskey from a boot-shaped glass (the latter recommended if you'll be riding the bull later). The restaurant is usually packed.

Other popular and reasonably low-rent restaurants in West Hollywood include long-running **Jacopo's,** 8166 Sunset Blvd., 323/650-8128, which makes a good New York–style pizza (and delivers); **Poquito Mas** for Mexican, 8555 Sunset Blvd. (at La Cienega), 310/652-7008; and that "vernacular architecture" L.A. landmark **Tail o' the Pup,** 329 N. San Vicente Blvd., 310/652-4517, for hot dogs and such.

Rockin' Restaurants

It must confuse the tourists, what with the Hard Rock Café near soft-rock Beverly Hills in de facto West Hollywood and Planet Hollywood actually in Beverly Hills. But people find the way nonetheless. The **Hard Rock Café** at the Beverly Center, 8600 Beverly Blvd. (at La Cienega), 310/276-7605, is an entertaining and loud place to take the kids, but only if you don't mind paying almost $10 for a burger—not to mention the cost of T-shirts, the local signature Hard Rock lapel pin, and other tie-in merchandise. The hard-driving rock 'n' roll is the real draw, plus the wacky memorabilia and theme decor. Museum-quality exhibits here and elsewhere around the globe inspired Andy Warhol to call the Hard Rock the "Smithsonian of Rock 'n' Roll"; movie memorabilia rounds out the displays. The Hard Rock Café uses no food additives, preservatives, or polystyrene and recycles everything else—including leftover food, which is donated to local homeless charities. It's open daily 11:30 A.M.–midnight, until 12:30 A.M. on Fri. and Sat. nights, and closed Thanksgiving and Christmas. In Southern California there's another Hard Rock in Newport Beach, yet another in Universal City.

The rusty old tin shack just up the hill from Sunset Blvd. isn't typical in L.A., at least not in West Hollywood. But once you've valet-parked the car at the **House of Blues,** 8439 Sunset Blvd. (one block east of La Cienega), 323/848-5100, pretend you've stepped off into the bayou—whatever gets you in the mood for blues, bluesy rock, jazz, gospel, reggae, zydeco, and more. The Tinseltown link in the chain forged by Hard Rock founder Isaac Tigrett and "Blues Brother" Dan Ackroyd, Hollywood's House of Blues also serves "international peasant fare" at lunch, dinner, and Sunday brunch—Southern fried catfish, down-home barbecue, wood-fired peasant pizza, even Indian and Thai fare. For dessert, try the bourbon bread pudding. At dinner and at the immensely popular Sunday Gospel Brunch, reserving a table is the only way to get good seats. (Nightly show times vary, depending on single or double billings and/or early and late shows.) The high-energy gospel brunch (reservations required) is scheduled on Sun. and features fried catfish nuggets, smoked chicken with andouille potato hash, and cornbread. Call ahead for show times.

Casual Café Fare
Where to go near Beverly Hills and West Hollywood that's not celebrated, celebrity-hyped, and hyper-expensive? One place is **Kings Road Cafe,** 8361 Beverly Blvd. (at Kings Rd.), 323/655-9044. Tasty thin-crust pizzas and simple pastas are mainstays at this Italian-style café, but breakfast is also quite imaginative—at least 10 different egg dishes, such as eggs baked with goat cheese (served with toast made from house-baked bread) plus potato selections, oatmeal, risotto, scones and pastries, even fresh fruit. And the menu here keeps expanding, now that Kings Road has a full kitchen. It's open daily for breakfast, lunch, and dinner, closed major holidays.

The bustling sidewalk café credited with starting L.A.'s dim sum craze is **Chin Chin,** 8618 Sunset Blvd. (near La Cienega), 310/652-1818. It's open for lunch and dinner daily, late supper on weekends. Best bet for an imaginary and affordable trip to the Left Bank is **Le Petit Bistro,** 631 N. La Cienega (one block north of Melrose), 310/289-9797, where the simple fare—dishes such as roast chicken or eggplant and tomato tarts—is quite popular with people actually *from* France. It's open for lunch on weekdays only, for dinner nightly. Fancier, pricier, but also quite fun: the internationalist and romantic **Café La Bohème,** 8400 Santa Monica Blvd. (at Orlando), 323/848-2360. For Asian-French in the same price range, amazingly popular these days is relative newcomer **Jozu,** 8360 Melrose Ave. (at King's Rd.), 323/655-5600, serving such things as sautéed scallops with green curry sauce and crab-shrimp cakes with green papaya salad. Complimentary sake is served.

As elsewhere across America, the people's place to savor Wolfgang Puck's signature wood-fired pizzas and such is at the local **Wolfgang Puck Café,** 8000 Sunset Blvd. (near Crescent Heights), 323/650-7300.

More West Hollywood Fun
Long popular with the local gay crowd is the festive and hip **Marix Tex Mex Cafe,** 1108 N. Las Flores Dr. (at Santa Monica), 323/656-8800, known for its killer margaritas, superb fajitas, New Mexico–style chimichangas, chalupas, and chilaquiles. There's always a wait here, at lunch, dinner, or weekend brunch. There's another Marix near the beach in Santa Monica, but you'll wait there, too.

The Palm, 9001 Santa Monica Blvd. (between Robertson and Doheny), 310/550-8811, is a pricey California branch of the New York surf and turf joint. The sometimes boisterous men's club sensibility here is punctuated, on the walls, with caricatures of the famous and infamous who have enjoyed The Palm's huge steaks (with cottage fries), gigantic lobsters, and Maryland crab. Noted for noise, rude waiters, and an industry clientele.

For something considerably more romantic at dinner, try the often overlooked old **Trocadero,** 8280 Sunset Blvd. (near Harper), 323/656-7161, an emblem of Hollywood's Golden Age all jazzed up into an art-deco beauty boasting both California cuisine and big-band sounds. Or try quite reasonable **Talesai**, 9043 Sunset Blvd. (at Doheny), 310/275-9724, for elegant, upscale Thai conveniently close to the clubs. One of L.A.'s best.

Celebrity-Spotting Hot Spots

Regular folks can get short shrift at **The Ivy**, 113 N. Robertson Blvd. (between 3rd and Beverly), 310/274-8303, a popular spotlight-on-the-celebrities spot serving a West Hollywood version of American Cajun and Creole fare. It all seems casual enough—down to the intentionally tired upholstery—but appearances can be deceiving. "Power tables" are out on the garden patio and inside next to the fireplace. Once you turn your attention to the food here, you'll appreciate that the crab cakes, Caesar salads, and Cajun prime rib generally get rave reviews.

Social centerpiece of Hollywood powerbrokers is **Morton's**, a grown-up's star venue brought to you by Hard Rock Café co-founder Peter Morton. Now in minimalist digs at 8764 Melrose Ave. (at Robertson), 310/276-5205, Morton's showcases Hollywood ego-size T-bone steaks along with grilled veal chops, lamb, and swordfish and such. And Morton's famous lime-grilled chicken. It's open for lunch weekdays, for dinner every night but Sunday. On Mon. nights, the stars really shine.

At **Ago**, 8478 Melrose Ave., (at La Cienega), 323/655-6333, the owners—Robert De Niro, Tony and Ridley Scott, and Harvey and Bob Weinstein—are Hollywood stars of equal stature with the celebrity clientele. With help from restaurateur Agostino "Ago" Scinadri, here Hollywood serves up incredibly authentic Italian, and with none of the usual industry snobbery. This popular and not-too-pricey hot spot is beloved for its fine food, friendly service (no matter who you are), and lovely decor.

Other spots to spot at least the occasional star, star-to-be, or star wannabe include the swank French-Chinese **Chaya Brasserie**, 8741 Alden Dr. (near Robertson), 310/859-8833; the French-Vietnamese **Le Colonial**, 8783 Beverly Blvd. (at Robertson), 310/289-0660; the Italian **Madeo**, 8897 Beverly Blvd. (near Doheny), 310/859-4903; **Pane e Vino**, 8265 Beverly (at

Switzer), 323/651-4600; and the inventive Chinese **Yujean Kang's**, 8826 Melrose Ave. (between Robertson and Doheny), 310/288-0806. Also ask around, since restaurant fashions change as often as Hollywood hairstyles.

Fine Dining with or without Celebrities

Now back in the hands of original owners Gerard and Virginie Ferry, **L'Orangerie**, 903 N. La Cienega Blvd. (between Melrose and Santa Monica), 310/652-9770, is more than maintaining its reputation as one of L.A.'s best for French nouvelle cuisine—and as L.A.'s most romantic dining destination. The baby vegetable stew is always a hit. Like taking a quick trip to Versailles, L'Orangerie is very chic and très expensive. It's open Tues.–Fri. for lunch—power-lunching, usually—and Mon.–Sat. for dinner.

Le Chardonnay, 8284 Melrose Ave. (at Switzer), 323/655-8880, is also one of L.A.'s renowned beauties, a two-level art-nouveau dining room with mirrored walls, carved rosewood, and etched glass. Reflections from the glassed-in rotisserie make everything glow at this California-style French bistro—including the patrons. And they really light up when the food arrives, be it the grilled half-chicken with crispy pommes frites or Louisiana crab cakes. It's open weekdays only for lunch, Mon.–Sat. for dinner.

Named after Sergey Diaghilev, the 1920s Ballets Russes impressario, very elegant, very expensive dinner-only **Diaghilev** at the Wyndham Bel Age Hotel, 1020 N. San Vicente Blvd. (at Sunset), 310/854-1111, serves almost nouvelle Franco-Russian romance in grand style—with cozy loveseat-style seating, long-stemmed roses, and balalaika performances, caviar, flavored vodka cocktails, and chicken Kiev. And venison shish kebab. And tournedos Igor Stravinsky. And hazelnut-chestnut cake.

Formerly the former La Toque, chef Ken Frank seems to have found a fitting new home for his inspired California cuisine at the Argyle's art-deco **fenix at the Argyle**, 8358 Sunset Blvd. (near La Cienega), 323/654-7100, where the stars include seafood, fish, and steak with a Jack Daniels and pepper sauce. It's open Mon.–Sat. for breakfast, lunch, and dinner, for brunch on Sunday.

SEEING AND DOING "THE VALLEY"

Though the third wave of Southern California cinema seems destined to wash ashore near the Pacific Ocean on L.A.'s Westside, the San Fernando Valley is the present-day destination of Hollywood the idea. This is where most of Southern California's movie and television studios came, after all, when they abandoned Hollywood the place—to Burbank, Glendale, San Fernando, and a sea of stucco, shopping malls, and superheated summer smog.

Few people, even Angelenos, think of the Valley as "Los Angeles," but it is. It's been the entire suburban sector of the city since William Mulholland's earliest water engineering feats. Valley culture has been widely characterized, even locally, by Frank and Moon Unit Zappa's satirical 1982 "Valley Girl"—an ode to suburban shopping-mall speak in general, "Like, fer sure, totally," and to the Sherman Oaks Galleria in particular—but such white-bread social stereotypes no longer fit the San Fernando Valley. So it should come as no surprise that in 1999 the Galleria itself closed up shop for an ambitious two-year renovation that transformed the media-hyped mother of all malls into an office complex with movie theaters and sit-down restaurants. With the Sherman Oaks Galleria essentially gone for good, Valley culture is increasingly defined by the Latino, Asian, and other ethnic and immigrant populations, largely shoehorned into "inner city areas," which make up half the population. Regional cultural events include Glendale's annual only-in-L.A. **Blessing of the Cars,** during which a local priest anoints cars and prays for the safety of their drivers, and the equally unusual **Love Ride** motorcycle party, an annual muscular dystrophy benefit attracting more than 20,000 bikers. Much tamer: the very down-home **Granada Hills Christmas Parade** down Chatsworth Street. A bit more high-brow: the prestigious **Padua Hills Playwrights Festival and Workshop.**

Distanced from downtown L.A. politics and disaffected by overburdened schools, stand-still freeways, and other inadequate services, the San Fernando Valley loudly threatens secession. How that would work is a mystery, since L.A.'s Department of Water and Power controls the water, lifeblood of Southern California's seemingly endless growth. But in the wake of the 1994 Northridge earthquake centered here—the most destructive urban quake in U.S. history—reconstruction, recovery, and retrofitting are still primary local political concerns.

UNIVERSAL STUDIOS HOLLYWOOD

The third most popular tourist attraction in the United States, trailing only Disneyland and Disney World, Universal Studios Hollywood does have a certain universal appeal. This is especially true if visitors seek the abbreviated version of Hollywood and its historic impact—a family-friendly theme park on Hollywood themes. Universal Studios is also a genuine studio, however, established in 1915 by Carl Laemmle at this onetime chicken ranch. In the days before the "talkies," Laemmle let the public in to watch—cheering and jeering from nearby bleachers—and profited from it by charging a quarter admission and selling fresh eggs at all the exits. The end of the silent-picture era also ended public access, but in 1964 Universal Studios dusted off the tradition by offering its original "back lot" tram tour. Admission prices and cinematic sophistication have been increasing ever since, and Universal Studios the movie theme park just keeps growing. **Universal City**'s commercial "urbanopolis" spreads across 413 acres and already includes the **Universal Amphitheater,** an 18-screen **Cineplex** movie theater, hotels, multiple restaurants, and office space, everything linked by an abbreviated, commercialized collection of Los Angeles themes known as **CityWalk.**

Plenty else is here to see and do, but kids and childlike adults race first to the "rides." At least one major attraction is unveiled every two to three years. To get the most out of your admission investment arrive as early as possible—then *go* when the gates open, heading first to the most popular rides and other priority destinations. Lines get longer as the day goes on. Alternatively, in summer, head for popular attractions during the dinner hour. Summer is in some

Universal Studios Hollywood's "The E.T. Adventure"

COURTESY OF UNIVERSAL STUDIOS HOLLYWOOD

ways the worst time to come—huge crowds, long lines—but in other ways it's the best, since some shows and programs are seasonal, staged daily and/or frequently only in summer and on weekends.

Universal Studios Hollywood is open 8 A.M.–10 P.M. in summer (box office: 7:30 A.M.–5 P.M.) and 9 A.M.–6 P.M. at other times (box office: 8:30 A.M.–4 P.M.). Admission prices tend to increase regularly but at last report were $41 adults, $36 seniors (age 60 and older), $31 children (ages 3–11, under 3 free)—plus 2 percent L.A. municipal tax. Two-day admission tickets and season passes are also available. Cash and credit cards with ID (no personal checks) are accepted. Parking is extra: $8 for most vehicles, $9 for RVs.

For information on attractions, rides, and basic practicalities, contact: Universal Studios Hollywood, 100 Universal City Plaza in Universal City, 818/508-9600 (recorded message, in English and Spanish), www.universalstudios.com. Strollers, wheelchairs, and other special services and facilities are available. To get here: From the Hollywood Fwy. (Hwy. 101) between Hollywood and the San Fernando Valley take either the Universal Center Dr. or Lankershim Blvd. exits and go with the flow. From the Ventura Fwy. (Hwy. 134), exit at Cahuenga Blvd. and proceed south to the Lankershim Blvd. entrance.

The Rides

Always a must-do attraction is the **Backlot Tour,** a 45-minute ride that takes you behind the scenes of this particular moviemaking scene. The tram winds through 35 settings, from the Mummy's Tomb and the prehistoric jungle of *Lost World: Jurassic Park* to the Bates Motel featured in Alfred Hitchcock's *Psycho.* The fictional locations of popular TV shows are here too, from *Murder, She Wrote, Kojak,* and *Quantum Leap* to classics such as *McHale's Navy* and *Leave It To Beaver.* What you'll see when you're here depends on which sets are currently in use for filming.

Remember when James Cameron, Oscar-winning director of the Hollywood megahit *Titanic,* climbed up there on stage at the Academy Awards and declared himself King of the World? Well, the king has come down off his throne, at least long enough to create a major new attraction at Universal Studios. Cameron's futuristic film-based virtual adventure **Terminator 2: 3D,** a virtual sequel to *Terminator 2: Judgment Day,* is a 12-minute "giant format" combo of digital imaging technology and live action stunts.

In 1993 the Steven Spielberg–enhanced **Back to the Future—The Ride** made its debut. And it's no disappointment even now—a white-knuckle DeLorean ride from Doc Brown's Institute of Future Technology that blasts through the space-time continuum into futuristic Hill Valley and then snaps back into the Ice Age, free-falls into volcanoes, and faces off with dinosaurs. Then there's the tamer **E.T. the Extraterrestrial Adventure,** which takes star-bound bicyclists "home" with E.T. No doubt the hottest attraction is **Backdraft,** a simulated but very explosive warehouse fire.

Still the best thing going, though, is **Jurassic Park—The Ride,** adding a monstrously popular you-are-there element to some of the scarier scenes in Michael Crichton's novel and subsequent smash-hit movie. Sir Richard Attenborough, who played the park's creator in the movie, welcomes visitors via video at the gates of this Jurassic Park before guests climb onto river rafts and shove off for a tour. Early encounters with peaceable plant-eating dinosaurs in Herbivore Country offer no preparation for the demolished Land Rover later discovered dangling from a guardrail or the hole in the velociraptors' electrified fence. Or the terrifying Tyrannosaurus rex. Or for rafts suddenly careening over a waterfall, out of control, and plunging into nothingness at about 50 miles per hour. The finale of the 5.5-minute ride is so scary, in fact, that expectant mothers and people with cardiac conditions are advised to avoid Jurassic Park altogether. Parents and non-tall people, please note that riders must be at least 46 inches tall.

Beyond the Rides
Curious George Goes to Town is a new interactive playground, this one awash with water play. Live shows are also an integral part of the Universal Studios lineup. Movie-related revues don't always enjoy a long run, but action adventure does, including the always macho lineup of the **Wild, Wild, Wild West Stunt Show,** and the **Waterworld** live-action show, providing action and water-bound hijinks.

The **World of Cinemagic** is a comparatively cerebral demonstration of moviemaking magic—from the special effects in *Harry and the Hendersons* and *Back to the Future* to "The Magic of Alfred Hitchcock," which demonstrates just how the shower scene in *Psycho,* the "fall" from the Statue of Liberty in *Saboteur,* and other famously terrifying Alfred Hitchcock scenes were created.

Universal CityWalk: One-Stop Los Angeles
"What to do when you don't know what to do" is how CityWalk promotes itself these days. Perhaps it's the place to go when you don't know where else to go—L.A.'s L.A.-themed refuge from itself. Such was the consternation of critics when CityWalk first opened in 1993 as L.A.'s "idealized reality," a miniature mall-style Los Angeles concentrating simulated local culture into a few commercialized "city" blocks.

Before CityWalk opened its doors for business—the year after L.A.'s Rodney King–related riots—historian Kevin Starr, now state librarian, sounded the alarm about what it symbolized. "This sounds like the end of L.A. history," he said. "Los Angeles finally gives up on itself and creates an idealized version. Have we so lost L.A. as a real city that we need this level of social control for anything resembling the urban experience?"

But as much as critics decried CityWalk as plastic and pointless, it never entirely lived down to expectations. No matter how horrifying it is to contemplate the potential future represented by the mechanically reproduced "waves" at CityWalk's "beach," this poverty-free promenade did—and does—have a "real L.A." feel, understandably attractive to Angelenos battle-fatigued by the extra effort it takes just to live here. Among CityWalk's notable and worthwhile successes: the historic neon signage displayed by L.A.'s **Museum of Neon Art,** which now has its own real-city museum in downtown L.A.; the 350-seat **B. B. King Blues Club,** a genuinely great nightclub that serves up major-league blues artists and gospel breakfasts; and cultural oddities such as **Wizardz Magic Club and Dinner Theater,** where you can see a magic show, dine on a three-course meal, and have your fortune told. And among other benefits of CityWalk's recent expansion, nostalgia buffs really dig **Retro Rad,** with its impressive selection of retro-styled clothing and accessories.

So, you decide. Is this Los Angeles better than the real thing?

CityWalk is open daily, 11 A.M.–11 P.M. weekdays, 11 A.M.–midnight weekends, though some restaurants and nightspots stay open later. Admission is free. For current information, call 818/622-4455.

NORTH HOLLYWOOD AND THE NOHO ARTS DISTRICT

Right next door to Universal Studios and CityWalk is a slice of the real-life city both were created to avoid—North Hollywood. These days the neighborhood is undergoing a transformation, what with the arrival of the new Metrorail Red Line station on Lankershim Blvd. (at Chandler). Another shining neighborhood star is the new headquarters for the **Academy of Television Arts and Sciences** on Lankershim Blvd. (at Magnolia), featuring a 28-foot winged muse flying up from its outdoor fountain. Bohemian attitude got here first, though, with Lankershim Blvd. leading the way and Magnolia Ave. playing a supporting role in the development of the NoHo Arts District.

For information about Tinseltown north and the NoHo Arts District and vicinity, contact: **Universal City/North Hollywood Chamber of Commerce,** 5019 Lankershim Blvd. in North Hollywood, 818/508-5155, www.noho.org.

Seeing and Doing NoHo

Despite television's august organizational presence, live theater is *lively* in and around the NoHo neighborhood—at almost two dozen venues including **Actors Forum Theatre, American Renegade Theater, The Bitter Truth Theatre,** and **Deaf West Theatre,** not to mention the Equity playhouse performances at the historic **El Portal Theater** or the municipally owned **Lankershim Arts Center.**

Local night spots include the seriously cramped but seriously fun **Blue Saloon,** 4657 Lankershim Blvd. (near Riverside), 818/766-4644, a straight-ahead beer hall known for ear-blasting blues, rock, rockabilly, and country, and the small **Baked Potato,** 3787 Cahuenga Blvd., 818/980-1615, which serves up vintage jazz with a menu of 21 varieties of baked potato.

There's plenty more to explore in the neighborhood, too, including vintage clothing shops, coffeehouses, and ethnic eateries, as well as book and music stores. **Iliad Bookshop,** 4820 Vineland Ave. (at Camarillo), 818/509-2665, is among the best gently used bookstores around.

MID-VALLEY AND WEST

Mission San Fernando Rey de España

Why not use a little movie lore to lure the kids into a hands-on California history lesson? Some of Steve Martin's *L.A. Story* was filmed here, after all, as were dozens of other movies and *Dragnet* and *Gunsmoke* episodes. With four-foot-thick walls and named for King Ferdinand III of Spain, the 1797 Mission San Fernando is the largest adobe building in the United States. Mission San Fernando Rey de España, 15151 San Fernando Mission Blvd. in Mission Hills (two blocks east of Sepulveda Blvd.), 818/361-0186, is open daily 9

THE VALLEY'S CELEBRITY CEMETERIES

It's not your typical burial plot. **Forest Lawn Memorial Park** is more like a religious theme park—one that deals with the subject of death by avoiding it almost entirely, similar to youth-worshiping Los Angeles itself. Inspiration for both Jessica Mitford's book *The American Way of Death* and Evelyn Waugh's fictional country club for the dead in *The Loved One,* Forest Lawn is the final resting place of many southstate celebrities—Gracie Allen, George Burns, Nat King Cole, Walt Disney, W. C. Fields, Errol Flynn, Clark Gable, and Carole Lombard among them. Forest Lawn is also famous for its statuary and art replicas—in particular, dramatic presentations of a stained-glass *Last Supper,* and *Crucifixion* and *Resurrection* oil paintings. For more, stop in at the Forest Lawn Museum next to the Hall of Crucifixion-Resurrection. The self-guided tour brochure and map will show you around. Forest Lawn Memorial Park, 1712 S. Glendale Ave. in Glen-dale, 323/254-3131 or 818/241-4151, is open daily 8 A.M.–6 P.M.

A second Forest Lawn cemetery and park is just 10 minutes away by freeway in the Hollywood Hills west of Griffith Park, 323/254-7251 or 818/984-1711, this one with an "American liberty" statuary theme. There are at least three others—in **Covina Hills** to the east and in **Cypress** and **Sunnyside** farther south.

To truly tour the San Fernando Valley's cemetery scene, however, don't miss the **Los Angeles Pet Memorial Park** farther west in Calabasas at 5068 N. Old Scandia Ln., 818/591-7037, known as the "Happier Hunting Ground" in Waugh's *The Loved One.* Among celebrity pets buried there: Pete the ring-eyed pooch from "Our Gang," Humphrey Bogart's dog Droopy, Charlie Chaplin's cat Boots, Tonto's faithful steed Scout from *The Lone Ranger,* and Hopalong Cassidy's horse Topper.

KIM WEIR

Ronald Reagan, America's 40th president, still the star at the presidential library

A.M.–4:30 P.M., closed Thanksgiving and Christmas. Admission is $4 adults, $3 seniors, and $3 children ages 7–15 (under 7 free).

Ronald Reagan Presidential Library

Here's one won for the Gipper—an allusion better appreciated once you tour museum exhibits on Ronald Reagan's Hollywood days. Fans of former President Ronald Reagan—including "new" Republicans hoping to rewrite the U.S. Constitution, for whom the affable Ronald Reagan is founding father of America's resurrection—tend to love this place. Those who aren't Reagan enthusiasts, including those who view him as the Forrest Gump of modern American politics, may find the self-ovations on display here a bit excessive. In any case you can't help being saddened by the news that the most glorious memories of one of L.A.'s own, America's 40th president, are increasingly lost to him as Alzheimer's disease takes its relentless toll.

"Dutch" Reagan was born in Tampico, Illinois, and grew up in the white-clapboard town of Dixon. Once arrived in Tinseltown, he starred in an impressive string of B movies, from *Desperate Journey* and *Little Queen of Montana* to the chimp classic, *Bedtime for Bonzo*. But those were the Democratic years, when Reagan was a member of the Screen Actors Guild. Ronald Reagan became a Republican "in name as well as thought" at the age of 51. His surprisingly easy ascent to America's political summit began in 1960 when he campaigned for Richard M. Nixon; in 1964, he backed Barry Goldwater's presidential campaign. After a two-term dash through the California governorship Reagan arrived at the White House as 40th president of the United States. Most permanent exhibits here cover those years, including a section of the Berlin Wall, a replica of the Oval Office, and a recreation of the White House Cabinet Room. Don't even bother to ask about the Iran-Contra exhibit. There isn't one.

For more information, including current special exhibits and programs, contact: Ronald Reagan Presidential Library, 40 Presidential Dr. in Simi Valley, 805/522-8444, www.reagan.utexas.edu. Admission is $5 adults, $3 seniors, free for those under age 15. The library is open 10 A.M.–5 P.M., closed Thanksgiving, Christmas, and New Year's Day. To get here: From I-5 or 405, exit at Hwy. 118—the Ronald Reagan Fwy.—and head west. From the 118, exit at Madera Road S and continue three miles to Presidential Dr.; turn right. A Marie Callender's restaurant is now on-site, open 10 A.M.–5 P.M.

Los Encinos State Historic Park

If coming or going along the valley's southern edge, this is a place to stop for some peace or a picnic if the stop-and-go flow of the Ventura Fwy. starts making you crazy. This quiet five-acre park, named for its live oaks ("los encinos"), commemorates Gaspar de Portolá's expedition

GRANDMA PRISBEY'S BOTTLE VILLAGE

Grandma Prisbey started collecting her first cobalt-blue Milk of Magnesia bottles in 1956. But by the mid-1970s she had transformed thousands of them, along with car license plates, doll's heads, and old TVs, into an eccentric folk-art "village" including curving walls, wishing wells, the Shrine to All Faiths, Cleopatra's Bedroom, and the Pencil House. A wonder in the annals of American folk art, this particular creation represents the most time-involved art creation by any female in all of recorded history, according to Bottle Village enthusiasts. Grandma Prisbey died in 1988, and years of neglect and vandalism took their toll even before the 1994 Northridge quake shook down and damaged more of Grandma Prisbey's meandering masterpiece. Until recently Grandma Prisbey's Bottle Village, quite close to the Reagan Library, was scheduled for restoration with funds from a federal grant. But local Republican Representative Elton Gallegly declared preservation of the bottle empire a taxpayer boondoggle and successfully campaigned in early 1997 to cut off federal funds, suggesting instead that Grandma Prisbey's be bulldozed. The pro–Bottle Village people appealed the funding cut to no avail.

But all is not lost. As of late 1999 some $25,000 in grant funds had been received for minor repairs, and certain private parties have expressed an interest in helping with the estimated $500,000-plus price tag for total restoration. In the meantime, Grandma Prisbey's Bottle Village is viewable from the street at 4595 Cochran St. in Simi Valley. It's open to visitors for guided tours by appointment only (small donation requested); for $5, get your souvenir copy of Grandma Prisbey's own 1960 book about her project. For current information and visitor reservations, call Grandma Prisbey's Bottle Village at 805/583-1627.

through the neighborhood in 1769. The history of the land, which was once the heart of Vicente de la Osa's 4,460-acre Rancho del Encino, is told by a docent-led tour of period exhibits in the original nine-room "linear" adobe house here—a one-time "hospitality stop" along El Camino Real—and a self-guided tour of the grounds. The two-story French provincial Garnier House, now a visitors center and small museum, was built of native limestone by two Basque brothers who owned the ranch in 1872.

Los Encinos State Historic Park, 16756 Moorpark St. in Encino, 818/784-4849, is open Wed.–Sun. (except major holidays) 10 A.M.–5 P.M. Admission is free. Reservations are required for picnicking on weekends. Call for current guided tour schedule (small fee). To get here: From the Ventura Fwy. (101), exit at Balboa Blvd. and head south; turn east (left) onto Moorpark.

Leonis Adobe Museum and Vicinity

Despite the popularity of Spanish names for cities, streets, and chi-chi shopping districts, in Southern California it's difficult to find authentic remnants of California's rich history as part of Spain and Mexico. The Leonis Adobe is one such survivor, a humble early 19th-century mud-brick building remodeled into a gracious two-story Monterey-style home in 1879. For more Old California sensibility, explore the barn and barnyard and then compare and contrast the totality with the adjacent **Plummer House** Victorian and the Victorian garden on the other side of the restaurant. **Calabasas Creek Park** is also operated under museum auspices. For more information, contact: Leonis Adobe Museum, 23537 Calabasas Rd. in Calabasas, 818/222-6511, open Wed.–Sun. 1–4 P.M., closed Thanksgiving, Christmas, and New Year's Day.

Another respite, and vestige of the region's rural past, **Orcutt Ranch Horticultural Center** is a 25-acre outdoor "museum" in West Hills at 23600 Roscoe Blvd., 818/883-6641. The center is abloom with antique farm machinery and citrus orchards, roses, and other seasonal delights. For more outdoor access head to Agoura and the **Peter Strauss Ranch,** 818/597-1036, or, for longer hiking trails, the Santa Monica Mountains National Recreation Area's **Paramount Ranch** in **Agoura Hills,** 818/597-9192, where the TV show *Dr. Quinn, Medicine Woman* was filmed.

PRACTICAL VALLEY

STAYING IN THE VALLEY

The San Fernando Valley features the predictable tourist-type hotels—most noticeably the large and pricey **Sheraton Universal Hotel** at Universal Studios, 333 Universal Terrace Pkwy., 818/980-1212 or toll-free 800/325-3535 (internationally) for reservations, with regular rates starting at $279, and the more business-oriented **Universal City Hilton and Towers,** 555 Universal Terrace Pkwy., 818/506-2500 or toll-free 800/445-8667, with standard room rates of $150–185. Both are Luxury. Much more affordable options include the Banana Bungalow Hollywood hostel just down the hill near the Hollywood Bowl (see Staying in Hollywood, above). More interesting choices include those listed separately below.

Other good accommodations options are scattered throughout the San Fernando Valley; motels line lengthy stretches of Ventura Blvd. as it meanders west toward Calabasas. If you end up anywhere near Calabasas—while coming or going from Paramount Ranch in Agoura Hills or various other Santa Monica Mountains outings, for example—a perennial best bet is the **Country Inn** motel at 23637 Calabasas Rd., 818/222-5300 or toll-free 800/456-4000, where the amenities include breakfast. Weekend rates are $119, weekday rates $109. Expensive-Premium. In Mission Hills, you won't go wrong at the **Best Western Mission Hills Inn** at 106

ACCOMMODATIONS RATINGS

Accommodations in this book are rated by price category, based on double-occupancy, high-season rates. Categories used are:

Budget.	$35 and under
Inexpensive	$35-60
Moderate	$60-85
Expensive	$85-110
Premium	$110-150
Luxury	$150 and up

Sepulveda Blvd., 818/891-1771 or toll-free 800/352-5670, what with free breakfast and newspaper come morning—$73 double, with weekly rates available. Moderate. In Burbank, consider the fun **Safari Inn** (see listing below). Less expensive stays in Glendale, where motels tend to line the length of Colorado St. (east and west), include **The Chariot Inn,** 818/507-9600 or toll-free 800/458-4080, and the **Econo Lodge,** 818/246-8367 or toll-free 800/553-2666 (central reservations). Both are in the $45–70 range, Inexpensive-Moderate.

Sportsmen's Lodge Hotel

In general a family-friendly alternative to the towering tourist hotels at Universal Studios is the nearby Sportsmen's Lodge motel on Ventura Blvd. just a mile south of the Hollywood Freeway. Part of the appeal of this contemporary English-themed hostelry is strictly outdoors—particularly the expansive, lushly landscaped pines-and-palm-trees grounds complete with footbridges, waterfalls, and swans in the lagoon. The place also tries to live up to its country-manor image indoors, particularly at the semiformal **Caribou at the Lodge** wild game restaurant. Also here—great little on-site coffee shop, Olympic-size courtyard pool, spa, fitness center. Rooms are large yet simple, decked out in country pine, earth-bound colors, and the usual amenities. Free parking. Child-care services and monthly rates are available, along with free shuttle service to and from Universal Studios and the Burbank Airport. Standard rooms are $134, pool-view rooms $172, and suites $187–290. Premium-Luxury, but discounts and packages can lower the tariff considerably, particularly in the off-season.

For more information, contact: Sportsmen's Lodge Hotel, 12825 Ventura Blvd. in Studio City, 818/769-4700, www.slhotel.com. For reservations, call toll-free 800/821-8511.

The Safari Inn

This spirited and spunky motel, conveniently close to Warner Bros. Studios, is a favorite of entertainment industry people without big bucks or studio expense accounts. And it should be a favorite of just plain folks who find themselves in Burbank for whatever reason. Rooms are contemporary and quirky if otherwise fairly basic—the older rooms, in the original motel section, are the cheapest—and there's a good restaurant here, too. Free parking. The Safari is just over a mile southwest of the Golden State Fwy. (I-5) via Olive Avenue. Standard rooms are $89–109, deluxe rooms $109–129, and suites $129–159. Expensive-Premium. For more information, contact: The Safari Inn, 1911 W. Olive Ave. in Burbank, 818/845-8586. For reservations, call toll-free 800/782-4373.

EATING IN THE VALLEY

Eating in and around Universal Studios
Of course you'll end up at Universal Studios. CityWalk outside the gates offers the best eats. **Jody Maroni's,** 818/622-5639, serves sausages, about a dozen kinds including Italian and Mexican jalapeño. Then there's the **Hard Rock Café,** 818/622-7626, and the **Wolfgang Puck Café,** 818/985-9653, both serving the usual at lunch and dinner. And a couple dozen other possibilities.

Many worthwhile choices are reasonably close to Universal Studios. For an early-morning breakfast in Studio City, **DuPar's** coffee shop, 12036 Ventura Blvd. (at Laurel Canyon), 818/766-4437, is the hippest place around, what with the number of genuine Tinseltown action, actors, and actresses it attracts. (People have to get to work—early, in Hollywood—and they have to eat *somewhere* close to the studios.) A best bet in the casual-and-quite-good eclectic category for lunch or dinner is the immensely popular (and crowded) **Out Take Cafe,** 12159 Ventura Blvd. (near Laurel Canyon), 818/760-1111. Try the *vareniki,* or potato-filled ravioli, served with sour cream and caramelized onions. Or the chicken Vesuvio.

Another good bet is **Art's Deli,** 12224 Ventura Blvd. (at Laurel Canyon), 818/762-1221, beloved for its pastrami sandwiches. Or try the Valley's own **Killer Shrimp,** 4000 Colfax (at Ventura), 818/508-1570, serving only huge Gulf shrimp in simmered Cajun sauce—always best with the French bread cubes for dunking.

People's Eats in Burbank and Glendale
Barron's coffee shop, 4130 W. Burbank Blvd. (at Evergreen) in Burbank, 818/846-0043, is a local mainstay—a best bet for breakfast. Then there's circa-1946 **Chili John's,** 2018 Burbank Blvd., 818/846-3611, with its genuine U-shaped counter—a 24-seater—and famous groundsteak and chicken chilis. Not that you can't find more upscale style, especially near the Media Center—or up the hill in Studio City—like, for instance, **Au Bon Pain: Baker, Sandwich Maker,** 350 San Fernando Rd., 818/843-8946.

For inexpensive espresso, cappuccino, guava pastries, seafood sandwiches, and hot meat pies, the place is **Porto's Cuban Bakery** in Glendale at 315 N. Brand Blvd., 818/956-5996. For neighborhood Thai at either lunch or dinner, try **Indra,** 517 S. Verdugo Rd. (at Maple), 818/247-3176. If you're headed east to Pasadena—or just hungry for down-home Polish food at Prague prices—dance on into **Polka** just beyond Glendale at 4112 Verdugo Rd. (at York) in Eagle Rock, 323/255-7887, beloved for its kielbasa, *kotlet, golabki,* and *gulasz.* Polka is open daily for lunch and dinner.

People's Eats Elsewhere
North Hollywood's **Swasdee** in a strip mall across from the Thai Buddhist Temple, 8234 N. Coldwater Canyon Blvd., 818/997-9624, serves sizzling curries and other red-hot tastes of the real thing. And some folks say the best thin-crust pizza in L.A. is served forth from **Joe Peep's Pizzeria** near North Hollywood at 12460 Magnolia Blvd. in Valley Village, 818/506-4133.

But don't miss **Dr. Hogly Wogly's Tyler Texas Bar-B-Que,** 8136 N. Sepulveda Blvd. in Van Nuys, 818/780-6701, another mythic southstate dining destination—the kind of place people go hours out of their way to find. This funky Formica-clad café serves unforgettable ribs, beef brisket, Texas hot links, and chicken, everything smoked right here. No one walks away hungry at dinner, which comes with coleslaw (token vegetable), baked beans, macaroni salad, and a half-loaf of fresh-baked bread. Don't forget the pecan pie.

For hot dogs the place is **Rubin's Red Hot,** 15322 Ventura Blvd. (at Sepulveda) in Sherman Oaks, 818/905-6515, a Chicago-style drive-through and sit-down notable, too, for its El-track architecture. (You really can't miss it.) Not counting Joe Peep's fans, the general consensus is that the best around comes from **Paoli's Pizzeria** in Woodland Hills, 21020 Ventura Blvd., 818/883-4136, famous for its white-sauce and sausage pizzas.

Dining Destinations

Better restaurants aren't necessarily expensive. Witness the French **Café Bizou** in Sherman Oaks, 14016 Ventura Blvd. (between Hazeltine and Woodman), 818/788-3536. And the Venetian **Ca' del Sole** in North Hollywood, 410 Cahuenga Blvd., 818/985-4669, sibling to Ca' Brea, where even vegetarians leave with a satisfied smile. Don't forget the valley's colorful Caribbean **Cha Cha Cha,** 17499 Ventura Blvd. in Encino, 818/789-3600.

But cuisine can be quite dear. **Pinot Bistro,** 12969 Ventura Blvd. in Studio City, 818/990-0500, the first "concept" spinoff from Joachim

Splichal's California-French Hollywood star Patina, was quickly dubbed the valley's best by the *Los Angeles Times,* and "best new restaurant" by *Esquire* magazine. The concept is classy French bistro—checkered floor, dark wood, and fireplace—and the content is Parisian, too, featuring onion soup, pastas, and fish.

Saddle Peak Lodge between Calabasas and Malibu at 419 Cold Canyon Dr., 818/222-3888, is still the valley's special-event destination, a one-time mountain lodge with a rustic but elegant wilderness ambience. Saddle Peak is noted for serving perfectly prepared fresh American game—fish, fowl, and venison—and lots of it. Sunday brunch is a special treat. With such things as wild mushroom and onion pie on the appetizer menu, fixed-price entrées include crab cakes, the chef's omelette, fresh fish plate, and farm-style steak and eggs. Weather permitting, sit outside and take in the scenery, too. It's open daily for dinner and for brunch on Sunday.

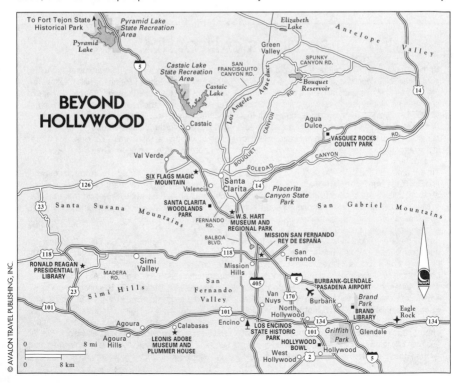

© AVALON TRAVEL PUBLISHING, INC.

Reservations required. The lodge is on Cold Canyon Dr. at Paiuma Rd. (nearest major intersection: Las Virgenes Rd. and Mulholland).

NORTH FROM TINSELTOWN: ESCAPE FROM L.A.

At the north end of the San Fernando Valley the San Diego, Golden State, Hollywood, and Foothill Fwys. all flow together to become I-5, a galloping freeway designed to funnel traffic up and out of the Los Angeles basin, over the Tehachapi Mountains, and eventually out into the arid San Joaquin Valley. Just north of this great convergence the Antelope Valley Fwy. (Hwy. 14) branches east toward Lancaster and Palmdale, the latter a technology and aeronautics oasis in the high desert where housing subdivisions have displaced most of the original Joshua trees.

Dominant in Valencia on I-5 is Six Flags Magic Mountain, a theme park most appreciated for its thrill-a-minute rides. Usually overlooked in the neighborhood is the **California Institute of the Arts,** or CalArts, an integrated arts college founded by Walt Disney. The five major departments here—art, music, film-video, dance, and theater—are well integrated, but CalArts is still most famous for its animation artists.

Farther along on I-5, attractions beyond Castaic Junction include **Castaic Lake** and **Pyramid Lake state recreation areas,** and fascinating **Fort Tejon State Historic Park.**

William S. Hart Museum and Regional Park

Amid all the usual signs of progress in the Santa Clarita Valley is this 253-acre Old West oasis, remnant of the vast rural acreage once owned by movie cowboy William S. Hart. Perfect for picnicking and family play, the park includes Hart's magnificent 1920s home, now the William S. Hart Museum, open for docent-guided tours. Classics of cowboy style collected here include Navajo rugs and works by Remington and Russell.

SIX FLAGS CALIFORNIA

Some people love roller coasters—people such as poet Peter Schjeldahl, who described in the pages of *Harper's* at least one spiritual benefit of his relationship with his Coney Island favorite: "It's important to ride the Cyclone many times, to comb out the distraction of terror—which gradually yields to the accumulating evidence that you are not dead." Hard to improve on the profundity of such a recommendation. And it's hard to miss, even from I-5, the mammoth Time Warner–affiliated **Six Flags Magic Mountain** and **Six Flags Hurricane Harbor** amusement parks, about 30 miles north of downtown L.A.

Magic Mountain, the first and original star here, specializes in not-so-cheap thrills—including 12 coasters and more than 100 rides in this 260-acre park. The latest addition is **Goliath,** which takes guests on a three-minute white-knuckle ride beginning with a near vertical 61-degree first drop and a series of intense turns and "zero gravity" drops. **Riddler's Revenge** is purported to be the world's tallest and fastest stand-up roller coaster. **Superman the Escape** launches from a 415-foot tower to reach speeds of 100 miles per hour. The looping two-minute **Batman The Ride** is in semi-industrial "Gotham City" along with the similarly themed circular **Acme Atom Smasher** and centrifugal-force **Gor-**

don Gearworks (look for the bathrooms at the Acme Atom Smasher Coolant Pump Facility). Other favorites include the three-looped, 188-foot-tall **Viper,** the **Ninja** with its enclosed, suspended train cars (the track is *above* you), **Flashback,** the dual-track **Colossus,** and the classic wooden **Psyclone.** If none of that proves that you're not dead there are other possibilities, including the **Dive Devil** skydiving bungee jump.

The faux tropical landscape and lagoons of Hurricane Harbor feature remnants of a lost civilization—could it be Los Angeles?—and more than a dozen water-play attractions, such as a wave pool, both tube and speed slides, and a pirate-themed kiddie play area.

Though closing hours vary, Six Flags California on Magic Mountain Pkwy. is open daily in summer at 10 A.M. (on weekends only during much of the year); call for current schedule information. At last report admission was $40.99 adults, $20.50 seniors, and $20.50 for children under 48 inches tall (free for age 2 and younger). Parking $7. There's an additional charge for some attractions, such as the Dive Devil. For current information, contact: Six Flags California, 818/367-5965 and 661/255-4849 (show and entertainment hot line), or 661/255-4136, www.sixflags.com.

The park is open daily 7 A.M.–sunset. The house, affiliated with the Los Angeles County Museum of Natural History, is open for 30-minute tours Wed.–Fri. 10 A.M.–12:30 P.M. and on weekends 11 A.M.–3:30 P.M. The museum is closed Thanksgiving, Christmas, and New Year's Day. For information, contact: William S. Hart Museum and Regional Park, 24151 N. San Fernando Rd. in Newhall, 661/254-4584. To get here from I-5, head east via Hwy. 126; from the Antelope Valley Fwy. (Hwy. 14), head northwest via Hwy. 126.

Placerita Canyon Park

The first gold discovered in California came out of Placerita Canyon, just north of L.A., in 1842, six years before James Marshall's much more famous find at Sutter's Mill in the Sierra Nevada foothills. The park features a pleasant picnic area, short self-guided nature trail, and a longer hiking route that highlights the lasting damage done by hydraulic mining technology. Placerita Canyon is most pleasant when it's green, in winter and spring. To get here: From I-5 exit at the Antelope Valley Fwy. (Hwy. 14, the route to Palmdale), continue several miles to Placerita Canyon Rd., then turn right. It's open daily 9 A.M.–5 P.M., closed Christmas. Free parking. For more information, contact: Placerita Canyon State and County Park, 19152 W. Placerita Canyon Rd. in Newhall, 661/259-7721.

Vasquez Rocks County Park

In the 1870s California's "Mexican Robin Hood," the bandit Tiburcio Vasquez, made a name for himself here—and finished making a name for himself here, after a shootout and chase with sheriff's deputies. (Vasquez escaped but was later captured and hanged.) In more recent history these twisted and surreal sandstone formations have starred in countless TV shows, westerns, and movies, including sci-fi spectaculars such as *Star Wars* in 1977, the 1979 *Star Trek* flick, and countless *Star Trek* TV episodes. L.A.'s Vasquez Rocks park is halfway to Palmdale near Agua Dulce on Escondido Rd. north of Hwy. 14, 661/268-0840, and is open daily dusk to dawn.

Santa Clarita Woodlands Park

The site of Chevron Oil's first well in the Newhall Oil Field is now included within one of L.A.'s newest parks, a lush and lovely "bridge" between the coastal Santa Monica Mountains (north slope

MUSEUM OF DEATH

With the recent opening of the Museum of Death in Hollywood, following its move from San Diego's Gaslamp Quarter, the aversion that Los Angeles has traditionally exhibited in the face of mortality seems to have, well, *died.* Or at least swooned into a temporary coma. Death is on the way to becoming cool in Los Angeles. Even here, it's fair to assume that the actual act of bidding adieu to life on earth is not notably more popular than it ever was. Yet as the museum's popularity testifies, the accessories and memorabilia of death and dying exert considerable fascination.

Among items in the extensive collection on display here are such treasures as letters and paintings by serial killers, graphic crime scene photos, and a baseball signed by Charles Manson, Mr. Helter-Skelter himself. The museum collection was inspired, in fact, by artworks requested by the owners from imprisoned serial killers. There's more, though, much more, from the working guillotine, embalming table, and vintage Vincent Price shrunken-head apple-sculpture kit to Tibetan funerary skulls and Heaven's Gate diorama.

For those interested in communing with mementos of life's ultimate transition, stop by the Museum of Death, 6340 Hollywood Blvd., Ste. 2 (entrance on Ivar), 323/466-8011, open daily noon–8 P.M. Admission is $7. For an introduction to an interesting but unrelated L.A. enterprise, visit www.citymorguegiftshop.com, where you can visit the online Cemetery of the Stars.

of the Santa Susana Mountains) and the inland San Gabriel Mountains. Here, migrating wildlife are granted at least the possibility of safe passage through one of L.A.'s fastest growing regions. Over 3,000 acres in total size, the park includes Rice, Wiley, and Towsley canyons, and the onetime oil town of Mentryville. Multiple hiking trails traverse the territory. The main entry to Santa Clarita Woodlands Park is at Towsley Canyon's Ed Davis Park, though all park trails are accessible from the Old Road, just off I-5. The park is open daily for day use only, from dawn to dusk. Starting at noon on the first and third Sun. of every month, docents show up at Mentryville to share the area's history.

For more information, contact **Ed Davis Park,** 661/255-2974, or the **Santa Monica Mountains Conservancy,** 310/589-3200.

BEVERLY HILLS AND VICINITY

Beverly Hills—or "BH," as irreverent Angelenos abbreviate it—is sister city to Cannes, France, which may help explain the astonishing number of French street names and other Old World affectations. Beverly Hills specializes in the retail sales of European, continental, and world-renowned everything. Despite its small-town suburban soul, BH is serious about maintaining its worldly image. Cachet saves the day in BH. When prestigious PaceWildenstein was getting ready to open its doors here in 1995, establish-

ing the city's new identity as L.A.'s high-end art center, 10 massive sculptures by Henry Moore were begged and borrowed from around the globe to celebrate the occasion and temporarily installed on the front lawn of Beverly Hills City Hall. But BH being BH—and considering the 15 obese Fernando Botero sculptures subsequently exhibited in Beverly Gardens Park—some wags couldn't resist observing that, *here* of all places, so many fat people so publicly displayed must surely be against the law.

SEEING AND DOING BEVERLY HILLS

Tourists are not exactly encouraged to drive around to stare, slack-jawed and speechless, at the city's most noted attractions: the splendid hillside palaces and mansions of the incredibly rich and sometimes famous. But you can—either on a tour, or on your own, after buying one of those cheesy "Maps to the Stars' Homes" hawked from street corners. Do be aware, however, that driving aimlessly through rich people's neighborhoods, especially in a derelict or dangerous-looking car,

will bring you to the attention of squads of private security guards and sometimes the local police. Beverly Hills, all six square miles of it, is a thoroughly policed and protected city.

For many, shopping is the other main BH attraction. Rodeo Drive is most famous, but most residents of Beverly Hills and Brentwood are more likely to shop almost-affordable Beverly Dr. (one block east of Rodeo Drive) and genuinely cutting-edge Beverly Boulevard.

For more information, and for assistance with hotel reservations and other practical matters, contact: **Beverly Hills Visitors Bureau,** 239 S. Beverly Dr., Beverly Hills, CA 90210, 310/248-1015 or toll-free 800/345-2210 (in California only), www.bhvb.org. If you'll be here only briefly, hop aboard the **Beverly Hills Trolley** for a 40-minute "Golden Triangle" tour of architecture and affluence. Tours leave on the hour between noon and 4 P.M., Tues.–Sat. in the off-season with extended hours in summer; meet at the corner of Rodeo Dr. and Dayton Way. For more information, call the City of Beverly Hills at 310/285-2438.

WELCOME TO THE WESTSIDE

The various cities and residential enclaves that comprise L.A. County's Westside—Beverly Hills, Bel-Air, Brentwood, Westwood, West L.A., Malibu, Pacific Palisades, Santa Monica, and Venice, for starters—are sometimes known, in more culturally diverse areas of town, as the "white-bread Westside."

This phrase refers to middle- and upper-class mores more than eating habits, of course, since health-conscious Westsiders typically prefer natural foods and whole grains. Relatively short on historical points of interest and big-time tourist attractions, the Westside compensates with great restaurants, art galleries, and shopping districts. (If it's hip, it's here.) A few fine museums, including the world-class Getty Center. Beaches for swimming, surfing, and seeing and being seen. Pleasant public parks and promenades. And hiking trails into what remains of L.A.'s coastal mountain wilderness.

According to the Westside myth, in Beverly Hills the streets are paved with jewels and jewelry stores. Exclusive Bel-Air, Brentwood, and Pacific Palisades are the toniest of the Westside's tony suburbs. The offspring of L.A.'s remarkably affluent live in Westwood, a collegiate metropolis adjacent to the University of California at Los Angeles (UCLA). In Malibu, celebrities and artsy eccentrics live on the beach and in the sylvan enclaves of Topanga Canyon. Then there's adjacent Santa Monica, beach city extraordinaire, where well-to-do homeowners, retirees, young families, and the homeless coexist peaceably—and where everyone else on the Westside comes to play. Next south is Venice, home to aging bohemians, young hipsters, street performers, and Muscle Beach. Less colorful but quieter West L.A. is a middle-class suburb packed with small single-family homes and condominiums.

Westside reality, however, is considerably more complicated. Long gone is the area's cherished cachet of semi-rural, small-town living. Population pressure—including the near impossibility of finding a parking space—is intense, and increasing. As liberal Santa Monica becomes increasingly intolerant of homelessness and the cutting-edge architecture of Venice a backdrop for gangsters, the indigent, and the elderly, inner-city teenagers have discovered the pleasures of hanging out in once-tony Westwood. Increased population has also increased the dangers of "natural disasters"—raging wildfires, mudslides, and earthquakes. Geologically speaking the area's bedrock is, at best, precarious. When the Really Really Big One hits on the Westside, the land beneath it will essentially liquefy.

Complicating the question of Westside identity still more is the fact that people don't agree on what is and isn't "Westside." Historically the divide between L.A.'s Eastside and Westside was established by the Los Angeles River. Yet according to the Los Angeles Police Department, L.A.'s Air Quality Management District, and public utilities such as Pacific Bell, the actual east-west border is La Cienega Blvd., a north-south thoroughfare that slices through West Hollywood and the far eastern section of Beverly Hills. Westside consumers, always on the lookout for stylish shopping opportunities, sometimes extend their neighborhood farther east, to increasingly fashionable La Brea Avenue.

Whatever the Westside's essential boundaries may be, the advent of the automobile made possible its mass settlement. The car also connects Westside communities to their most valuable assets: sunshine, balmy temperatures, and fresh air. The sun shines on everyone in L.A., rich and poor. But clean air—"air quality"—and the milder coastal climate come with a premium price tag. People on the Westside are united by their collective willingness to breathe deep while Pacific Ocean breezes suck up the smog—much of it generated here—and blow it inland to befoul foothill neighborhoods.

"Westside," then, is more state of mind than particular place. This is the Los Angeles of L.A.'s hedonistic imagination—a mental landscape of postcard-pretty palm trees, sporty convertibles, and luxurious private retreats close to crashing surf and white-sand beaches.

BASIC BEVERLY HILLS

The Golden Triangle

The triangular 20-block retail core of BH, north of Wilshire Blvd. and south of the intersection of Santa Monica Blvd. and Rexford Dr., is promoted as the "Golden Triangle." The visitor bureau's walking-tour brochure guides the hale and hearty past the major sights. You can also get a quickie overview via the Beverly Hills Trolley Tour.

Starting from the Beverly Hills Visitors Bureau on S. Beverly Dr., Golden Triangle highlights include the Spanish colonial **Artists and Writers Building,** 9501 Santa Monica Blvd. (at Rodeo Dr.), founded by Will Rogers and built in 1924 for use by Hollywood's writers, artists, and set designers—still in use today. Several blocks east on Little Santa Monica is the Litton Building at 375 N. Crescent Avenue. Onetime **Music Corporation of America (MCA)** headquarters, the building is a striking example of American Federal revival architecture, designed by noted L.A. architect Paul Williams and built in 1937. The east end pillars are survivors of Marion Davies's famous "Beach House," which also served as part-time residence of William Randolph Hearst. Across Little Santa Monica is a more contemporary local landmark—the 1950s space-age neon-lit **Unocal Gas Station,** 427 N. Crescent Dr., preserved against the ravages of progress. The soaring cantilevered three-cornered canopy, a brilliant beacon in the night, harks back to a time when America was as excited about the freedoms gained via cars (and gasoline) as it was about space travel.

Next stop is the impressive **Beverly Hills Civic Center** across Little Santa Monica on N. Crescent, where the stunning, recently restored 1932 Spanish Renaissance **Beverly Hills City Hall,** designed by architects William J. Gage and Harry Koerner, has long been the main attraction. Particularly wonderful at the civic center—and a tribute to the civic generosity of Beverly Hills—is the new mansionlike, vaguely Spanish baroque **Beverly Hills Public Library,** 444 N. Rexford Dr., 310/288-2220, spacious and splendid. Unlike other California libraries, ravaged by declining civic budgets, the Beverly Hills Public Library is open even on weekends, when working people are free to use it.

Another impressive public building, this one from another age, is the **Beverly Hills Post Office** on Santa Monica between Crescent and Cañon, a spectacular Italian Renaissance creation of terra-cotta and brick ablaze inside with murals and tiled mosaics. Then wander awhile along two-mile **Beverly Gardens Park.**

Back on Wilshire, east from Merv Griffin's Beverly Hilton Hotel, is the I. M. Pei–designed **Creative Arts Agency,** 9830 Wilshire Blvd., a major player in the highly competitive "agents" business. The neighborhood showstopper, though, is the 1928 Italian Renaissance **Regent Beverly Wilshire Hotel,** 9500 Wilshire Boulevard.

Museum of Television and Radio

"One Museum, Two Locations" is the way the Museum of Television and Radio in Beverly Hills explains its transcontinental kinship with

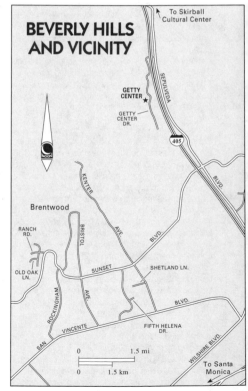

BEVERLY HILLS AND VICINITY

its New York twin, originally known as the Museum of Broadcasting and founded in 1973 by William S. Paley.

Designed by architect Richard Meier and open since March of 1996, the three-story, white steel-and-glass museum houses the total (duplicate) television and radio programming collection—about 100,000 programs spanning more than 75 years of broadcast history.

The museum is within BH's "Golden Triangle," 465 N. Beverly Dr. (at Little Santa Monica Blvd.), 310/786-1025, www.mtr.org. The museum is open Wed.–Sun. noon–5 P.M. (noon–9 P.M. on Thurs.) and closed July Fourth, Thanksgiving, Christmas, and New Year's Day. Suggested donation is $6 adults, $4 students and seniors, and $3 children (age 12 and under). Two hours free parking is available in the museum's underground garage with validation.

Academy of Motion Picture Arts and Sciences
Still without the equivalent of a Museum of Television and Radio to celebrate their arm of the entertainment industry, at least movie people have an uptown address. And the Academy of Motion Picture Arts and Sciences does more than just haul out all that glitz, glitter, and glib banter for the annual Academy Awards ceremony. It also has a swell theater at its headquarters here in Beverly Hills—the **Samuel Goldwyn Auditorium,** sometimes available for public screenings. Though this is not a museum, lobby exhibits are often worth a look-see. The Academy of Motion Picture Arts and Sciences is east of the Regent Beverly Wilshire Hotel at 8948 Wilshire Blvd., 310/247-3000.

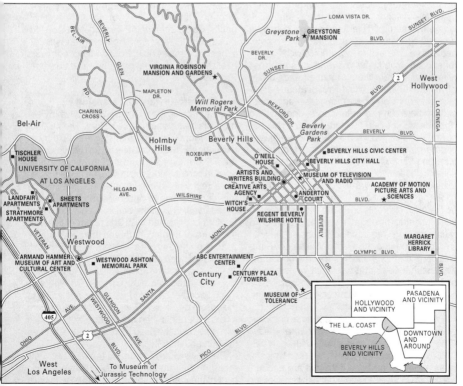

*Museum of
Television and Radio*

BEVERLY HILLS CONFERENCE & VISITORS BUREAU

Museum of Tolerance

Appropriate for children old enough to understand the historical depths of man's inhumanity, the Museum of Tolerance adopts a hands-on, high-tech approach in confronting bigotry and racism. The experience begins with a semi-formal tour. You know you're in for something different right from the start, when each group of visitors meets the Host Provocateur—a 10-foot-tall stack of video monitors—and must choose between two entry doors, one marked "Prejudiced," the other "Unprejudiced." The museum's very imaginative "Tolerancenter" engages visitors with more than 30 interactive displays, including "The Other America," a hate-group primer in the form of a wall map. Visitors move on to, and into, World War II's Holocaust, carrying photo passports of individual children affected by the Nazi reign of terror. As the tour continues—passing through a prewar Berlin café scene, through German discussions of "the final solution," and into the Hall of Testimony—the passports are updated. By the end you'll know what happened to that one child whose passport you carry. If the children ended up in the gas chambers, you'll also be able to imagine the horror of their last moments.

The Museum of Tolerance is just beyond Beverly Hills proper in Simon Wiesenthal Plaza, 9786 W. Pico Blvd. (at Roxbury Dr.), 310/553-8403, www.wiesenthal.com. The tour typically takes about 2.5 hours, but visitors are encouraged to stay longer, to see other exhibits. Call for current hours and tour information. Advance tickets are available through the museum or through TicketMaster. Tour tickets are $8.50 adults, $6.50 seniors (62 and older), $5.50 students with ID, and $3.50 children ages 3–12. Wheelchair accessible. Foreign-language tours available. Below-street parking (accessible from Pico) is free.

The Greystone Park and Mansion

The largest and most extravagant house in Beverly Hills has a scandalous history. The 46,000-square-foot Greystone Mansion was built by oil millionaire Edward L. Doheny Sr., implicated in the Teapot Dome scandal of the early 1920s after he contributed $100,000 to the private cause of Secretary of the Interior Albert Fall in exchange for secret leases to public-owned government oil reserves. Greystone became a gift to his son, Edward Jr., married man and father of five. But the younger Doheny had lived there less than a year when he and his secretary, Hugh Plunkett, were found dead in Doheny's bedroom. The family released a vague statement that Plunkett was "highly excited and nervous" and Doheny was trying to convince him to retire. But according to the gossip of the day, Doheny and Plunkett were lovers and, rather than risk the disgrace of public exposure, Doheny killed Plunkett and then turned the gun on himself.

Doheny's widow occupied the mansion until 1955, and eventually the city of Beverly Hills bought the mansion and adjacent hillside to build a reservoir, which now provides 50 percent of the city's water supply. The mansion, 905 Loma Vista Dr., 310/550-4654, is closed to the public, though the glorious 16-acre grounds are perfect for picnics (free) and open daily 10 A.M.–6 P.M.

Also fun for garden aficionados is the beaux arts–style **Virginia Robinson Mansion and Gardens,** 1008 Elden Way, 310/276-5367, tours available by appointment only, $7 ($4 seniors and students). Make your reservations at least one week in advance.

Rodeo Drive and Beverly Hills Shopping

If one's voyeuristic appetite for affluence can't be satisfied by touring well-manicured BH lawns and well-barred security gates, try upscale shopping. Or upscale window-shopping. For BH's most ostentatious displays, the time-honored destination is Rodeo Drive (pronounced ro-DAY-o, a deliberately correct, if somewhat affected, bow to proper Spanish pronunciation), particularly the stretch between

Bring the plastic if you shop in Beverly Hills.

Santa Monica and Wilshire Boulevards. For most people, the appeal is strictly vicarious—simply the desire to see where mythic star wardrobes were born. Especially in summer and on weekends, the streets are packed with camera-toting tourists just waiting for a chance to immortalize a frightful fashion mistake—spandex worn with fur, say—or document some major or minor star on film. What celebrities you do see in the neighborhood won't be visible for long. They tend to come early or at odd times, dash into exclusive shops, then dive back into their waiting limos (there's often a line of 'em, snaking around the block). Rather than schlep up and down Rodeo Drive dodging tourists, most people living in and around Beverly Hills are much more likely to shop along **Beverly Drive** just one block east of Rodeo, or ultrahip **Beverly Boulevard,** which segues into West Hollywood and similar great shopping along **Robertson Boulevard.** But if you must "do" Rodeo—and shops such as Cartier and Chanel—for window shopping, nighttime is the best time, when windows are lit and the glitz even more glittery.

BOPPING AROUND BEVERLY HILLS: CELEBRITY SIGHTS

Beverly Hills is L.A.'s most beloved tourist destination. Most people come here to see movie stars, which explains the hundreds and hundreds of outdated and inaccurate maps to the stars' homes sold each week. Real estate changes hands fast in this town, propelled in part by stars' rapidly changing fortunes. The only way to find out for sure who lives where is to research local property records—sometimes little help, in the case of corporate or otherwise hidden ownership—or the extremely inadvisable technique of knocking on doors to ask for autographs. (According to this theory, if the maid or butler says you need to contact such-and-such agency, assume you've got the right address. And if you're told so-and-so doesn't live there, that's probably the truth.)

But intentionally bothering people at home is always rude. The best way to see and appreciate movie and TV stars is to seek them out in their natural social habitats—at the restaurants, gal-

SHOP 'TIL YOU DROP

Shopping is a serious pursuit in Los Angeles, perhaps one reason L.A. is so popular with international travelers. For 88 percent of visitors from other lands, according to the U.S. Travel and Tourism Association, shopping is the preferred activity in the United States. But the region's sprawling malls, the magnets of local consumerism, are an outgrowth of Southern California car culture—the local preference for absolute mobility.

If you're doing the malls, seven-acre **Beverly Center** is centrally located just east of Beverly Hills and south of West Hollywood at 8500 Beverly Blvd., 310/854-0070, recognizable to movie addicts as the setting of the 1991 Woody Allen/Bette Midler movie *Scenes from a Mall* and home to a collection of more than 200 upscale shops and associated parking. Just across La Cienega is the **Beverly Connection,** another possibility, where the **Rexall Drugs** is locally known as the "drugstore to the stars." Then there's the **Century City Shopping Center** along Santa Monica Blvd. in Century City, 310/553-5300, a pleasant outdoor mall, and the glass-enclosed **Westside Pavilion** at Pico and Overland Blvds. in West L.A., 310/474-6255. Downtown offers the **Seventh Street Marketplace,** on S. Figueroa St. near the Hilton hotel, 213/955-7150. The most famous malls in L.A. proper—inspiration for Frank and Moon Unit Zappa's 1980s spoof *Valley Girls*—are in the San Fernando Valley, and include the **Glendale Galleria** in Glendale, 818/240-9481, and **Sherman Oaks Galleria** in Sherman Oaks, which ironically had to close due to lack of customers (it will reopen as a business center). The granddaddy of them all, though, is actually in Orange County—**South Coast Plaza,** 714/435-2000, just off the San Diego Fwy. (the 405) in Costa Mesa.

Increasingly, however, even Southern Californians are rejecting the malls—a fact of local life that sends various shopping centers into periodic fits of re-creation and remodeling on a more intimate scale. Shopping areas and districts are all the rage these days, at least among L.A.'s more affluent citizens, and you'll find dozens of these throughout greater Los Angeles. **Rodeo Drive** in Beverly Hills is L.A.'s most famous shopping destination, with stores so expensive and exclusive that they seem increasingly ridiculous even by local standards; most residents, after all, shop along Beverly Dr. and nearby Beverly Boulevard. Or on Melrose.

Now nearly as famous as Rodeo Drive, **Melrose Avenue** started as a fairly avant-garde youth-oriented rebellion against mass consumerism, in what was once a low-rent district just south of West Hollywood. Now Melrose, still hip but increasingly mainstream, is among the city's most commercial districts—though it still has its eccentricities.

"Melrose" was originally defined as the mile and a half of Melrose between La Brea and Crescent Heights, but now it extends into high-rent West Hollywood, its trendiness spreading south along **Robertson Boulevard,** the "decorator's row" of Beverly Hills, and also spilling south onto L.A.'s **Beverly Boulevard** and **W. 3rd Street.** And intersecting sections of both North and South **La Brea Avenue** also hold increasing local appeal for shopping and dining.

But trendier by far than Melrose—and at last report still L.A.'s post-hip, post-postmodern hangout and shopping destination—is **Vermont Avenue** in nearby Silver Lake, a fairly rough neighborhood on the eastern edge of Hollywood.

Other popular L.A. "destination streets," considerably more comfortable for most visitors and middle-class families, include **Old Pasadena** in downtown Pasadena and, in Santa Monica, the **Third Street Promenade, Main Street** near Venice, and **Montana Avenue.** Still up-and-coming and always surprising is **Abbott Kinney Boulevard** in Venice, a neighborhood still more neighborhood—albeit rough in surrounding areas—than tourist attraction.

The shopping experience at **CityWalk** outside Universal Studios is, sadly, probably a snapshot of our shared future—in L.A. and elsewhere—as the fear-driven middle class increasingly seeks entertainment, dining, and shopping opportunities in an absolutely safe, sanitized, and insular urban environment, the commercial equivalent of gated communities.

Most of L.A.'s unique and individual shops can be found in or near the shopping destinations and districts just mentioned; a few are specifically mentioned in the following chapters. But while poking around town in search of beautiful, odd, or unusual L.A. items to take home for family and friends, keep in mind that local museums boast some of the best general gift shops around. And museum shopping offers the added benefit of supporting local arts and cultural attractions.

leries, and clubs they're most likely to visit. Beverly Hills, West Hollywood, and nearby L.A. neighborhoods are thick with such places.

If you must peer at the well-protected homes of power and privilege, don't be obnoxious about it. Stay off people's lawns, don't climb through their trees, shrubs, and garbage cans, and resist poking your camera or camcorder lens in strangers' faces.

Touring Celebrity: Beverly Hills

Beverly Hills neighborhoods near triangular Will Rogers Memorial Park are star-studded. At 730 N. Bedford Dr. is the former **Lana Turner** home, where Turner's daughter stabbed her mother's lover Johnny Stompanato to death with a kitchen knife—a notorious Hollywood scandal ultimately judged as "justifiable homicide." Just west is Roxbury Dr., where the star roster includes the late **Jimmy Stewart** (918 Roxbury), **Lucille Ball** (1000 Roxbury, where she lived until her death in 1989), and **Peter Falk** (1004 Roxbury).

Pickfair, 1143 Summit Dr., the onetime mansion of **Mary Pickford** and **Douglas Fairbanks Sr.,** where Beverly Hills celebrity got its geographical start, was all but razed when **Pia Zadora** bought the place, tearing down all but one original room. Other onetime celebrity addresses include the retreat of silent screen cowboy **Tom Mix,** 1018 Summit, and **Charlie Chaplin**'s place, 1085 Summit.

Benedict Canyon is something of a bad-luck neighborhood. At 10048 Cielo Dr. (then numbered 10050), is the home where the followers of **Charlie Manson** murdered actress **Sharon Tate** and others during their helter-skelter 1969 killing spree. Just off Cielo at 1436 Bella Dr. is **Rudolph Valentino**'s onetime home, Falcon Lair, which he bought to escape his unrelenting fame and fawning fans. Valentino enjoyed his privacy for only a year before he died here in 1926. Down the hill at 1579 Benedict Canyon is original Superman **George Reeve**'s suicide site.

In the hills east of the canyons are the homes of Trousdale Estates, remnants of the old Doheny empire. **Elvis Presley**'s onetime mansion, at 1174 Hillcrest Dr., is a tourist favorite, as is Villa Rosa, 1187 Hillcrest, the **Danny Thomas** mansion where talk show host **Phil Donahue** and **Marlo Thomas** were married.

At 1011 N. Beverly Dr. is the onetime home of **Marion Davies,** mistress of **William Randolph Hearst** (Hearst died here in 1951). Other famous BH addresses include **Fred Astaire**'s onetime home, 1155 San Ysidro, and **John Barrymore**'s, 1400 Seabright Drive.

Touring Celebrity: Bel-Air

Among Bel-Air's more recognizable addresses is 750 Bel-Air Rd., where Jed, Granny, and the rest of the Clampett clan assembled to shoot episodes of the *Beverly Hillbillies* TV series. **Howard Hughes** once lived at 1001 Bel-Air Rd., property subsequently owned by **Zsa Zsa Gabor.** Famous residents of St. Cloud Rd. have included **Ronald and Nancy Reagan**—but only, according to local lore, after Nancy raised hell with the U.S. post office insisting that the original "666" street address be changed.

Notable addresses in the Holmby Hills area include **Jayne Mansfield**'s Pink Palace, 10100 Sunset Blvd., more recently owned by **Engelbert Humperdinck.** Look for **Hugh Hefner**'s infamous Playboy Mansion at 10236 Charing Cross Road. The former **Bing Crosby** family home, 594 S. Mapleton, is just blocks from the onetime home of **Humphrey Bogart** and **Lauren Bacall,** 232 S. Mapleton.

Touring Celebrity: Brentwood

Most recently notorious as the neighborhood where **O. J. Simpson**'s ex-wife **Nicole Brown Simpson** and **Ron Goldman** were murdered, Brentwood has attracted the media spotlight many times before. The unpretentious home at 12305 Fifth Helena Dr., for example, is where **Marilyn Monroe** died. Just around the corner and up the block, at 12216 Shetland Ln., is the house where **Raymond Chandler** lived and wrote detective novels during the 1940s. And in the 1930s and '40s actress **Joan Crawford** lived with her daughter Christina—who lived to tell about it in *Mommie Dearest*—at 426 N. Bristol. The childhood home of child star **Shirley Temple** is the European-style farmhouse at 231 N. Rockingham Road.

CENTURY CITY: MOVIE CITY

Formerly the back lot for Twentieth Century Fox Studios, Century City did not exist before 1961.

In the late 1920s Twentieth Century Fox was one of the most successful movie studios around, but by the mid-'50s television was cutting into the movie industry's audience. That fact, coupled with a series of box-office flops, shoved the studio into serious financial trouble. Desperate for money to keep the studio in business, executives realized that "location shooting" was the wave of the future in moviemaking—and that they could save their cinematic empire by developing the land upon which it stood. About 260 acres between Beverly Hills and West L.A. that once served as the back lot for Twentieth Century, some of the choicest real estate in Los Angeles, thus became Century City. Architect Welton Becket signed on to plan and design the glittery futuristic "city."

Now an upscale enclave of millions of square feet of office and commercial space, Century City is a very prestigious L.A. address—and still central to the film business, the place top entertainment-industry executives, accountants, and lawyers hang their hats. A 13-story triangular tower designed in 1975 by architect Minoru Yamasaki anchors the city at each end—the **ABC Entertainment Center** and **Century Plaza Towers.** Century City's future was clearly envisioned even at the opening of the first tower, in 1961. Actress Mitzi Gaynor snipped film footage, rather than the customary ribbon, at the dedication ceremony.

Between the towers is a below-street-level concourse of theaters, restaurants, and shops. The **Shubert Theatre,** 2020 Ave. of the Stars, 310/201-1500, is L.A.'s home for many Broadway plays and long-running musicals. Glenn Close had a very successful run here with *Sunset Boulevard.*

Another Century City draw is **Harry's Bar and American Grill,** 2020 Ave. of the Stars, 310/277-2333, an exact replica of Harry's Bar in Florence, Italy, made famous by Ernest Hemingway. Truly entertaining every year is the bar's festive **Imitation Hemingway Competition,** typically judged in March (grappa toasts included). Earnest entries from around the world, each including an obligatory promotional reference to Harry's, are judged by a dozen or so of L.A.'s most respected and most Hemingway-literate writers.

In L.A., the land of megamalls, the **Century City Shopping Center and Marketplace** along Santa Monica Blvd., 310/553-5300, is one of the most attractive and pleasant outdoor shopping malls around.

WESTWOOD VILLAGE: COLLEGIATE METROPOLIS

Westwood began as a section of the 1840 Rancho San Jose de Buenos Ayres land grant. The property changed hands many times before 1922, when the Janss Investment Company offered the Regents of the University of California a 200-acre parcel at a substantial discount. In 1929 the University of California at Los Angeles (UCLA)—then known simply as the Southern Branch of the University of California—opened its doors to students. And the Janss Company's surrounding development, charming Mediterranean-style Westwood Village, began to prosper.

The community partnership of UCLA and Westwood has been so successful that today Westwood boasts some of the most horrific traffic in Los Angeles; Westwood Blvd. at Wilshire is the busiest intersection in all of Los Angeles. Apartment buildings constructed to accommodate UCLA's record enrollment and high-rise residential and office complexes along Wilshire have pushed area "carrying capacity" to the breaking point.

Much of Westwood's original "village" charm has been lost to congestion and escalating land values that encourage, instead, high-volume chain stores, fast-food restaurants, and new banks and other quick-cash ATM outlets. Westwood's new appeal for inner-city teenagers looking for a late-night hangout has also challenged its long-running reputation as a mild-mannered middle-class cultural haven.

Yet Westwood still boasts the highest concentration of first-run movie theaters in the world. Beyond Hollywood Boulevard, this is L.A.'s most inviting—and exciting—place to do the movies. Blockbusters are premiered here regularly to take advantage of Westwood's huge old big-screen theaters with state-of-the-art sound systems—places such as **Village Theatre,** 961 Broxton Ave., 310/208-5576. For a genuine Southern California adventure, attend a movie in Westwood on opening night. About one-quarter of a premiere audience are people either involved in the production or special guests of the studio, while the rest are "real people" required to gauge audience reaction. Most premieres are scheduled for either Friday or Saturday night, when streets are blocked off to encourage a strolling fashion show amid the classic building facades.

Other commercial cultural attractions in Westwood include ever-popular and ever-growing **Rhino Records,** 1720 Westwood Blvd. (at Massachusetts), 310/474-8685, one of L.A.'s best for reggae, bluegrass, blues, rock, and jazz, whether mainstream or independent, domestic and imported, new or used.

UCLA: Berkeley's "Southern Branch"

It's ironic that the University of California at Los Angeles (UCLA) campus, 310/825-4321, www.ucla.edu, stood in for the UC Berkeley campus in the film *The Graduate.* When UCLA held its first classes as the "southern branch" of the original University of California campus at Berkeley, the 419-acre campus had just four buildings and 280 students. Today UCLA has grown to about 160 buildings and more than 35,000 students, the largest enrollment of any UC campus. Considered one of the finest research universities in the nation, UCLA is also lauded for its fine academic programs and as a major West Coast center for arts, culture, and cinema.

Bounded by Sunset Blvd. on the north, LeConte Ave. on the south, Hilgard Ave. on the east, and Gayley and Veteran Aves. on the west, UCLA still boasts its original four Italian Romanesque buildings from the late 1920s: **Powell, Royce, Haines** and **Kinsey Halls.** Powell is home to the Department of Film and Television's **Archive Research and Study Center,** where more than 25,000 films and TV episodes are preserved. (UCLA's **Melnitz Hall** often opens its doors for free screenings of the film school's collection.) Just across the well-manicured quadrangle from Powell is the campus symbol, Royce Hall, which includes a 1,850-seat performing-arts auditorium. Adjacent to Royce is the **Fowler Museum of Cultural History,** 310/825-4361, with permanent and changing exhibits on nonwestern cultures. It's open Wed.–Sun. noon–5 P.M., Thurs. until 8 P.M. Admission is $5 adult, $3 for seniors and students.

Among the loveliest places on campus is the **Franklin D. Murphy Sculpture Garden,** with five acres of lush landscaping and sculptures by Joan Miró, Henri Matisse, Henry Moore, and Auguste Rodin. Adjacent is the **Wight Art Gallery,** featuring contemporary and classics on display, and the **Grunwald Center for the Graphic Arts,** where the "works on paper" collection exceeds 35,000.

For sports fans—particularly Bruins fans— the **Morgan Center Hall of Fame** is a must-do destination. **Pauley Pavilion,** designed by Welton Becket and Associates, seats 12,545 and hosts UCLA Bruins basketball and various cultural events. Before big games, pick up ever-popular UCLA sweatshirts and other "Bearwear" selections at the **Ackerman Student Union** bookstore. The adjacent Gothic **Kerckhoff Hall,** home to student government offices and *The Daily Bruin* student newspaper, was designed by Royce Hall architects Allison and Allison in 1933 as a U.S. version of King Edward VII's Westminster chapel.

The **Center for Health Sciences** dominates the southern end of the UCLA campus—this the largest medical complex in the United States, home to the highly regarded **Schools of Medicine, Nursing, Dentistry, and Public Health.** Among the many health research institutes also housed here: the world-renowned **Jules Stein Eye Institute,** the **Jerry Lewis Center for Muscular Dystrophy,** and the **Neuropsychiatric Institute.**

Once you're done with a UCLA tour, the eight-acre **Mildred Mathias Botanical Gardens** on the southeastern edge of campus, with hundreds of species of trees and shrubs, make a pleasant escape.

UCLA Tours: The Bruin's-Eye View

To see what's where at UCLA, pick up a self-guided tour brochure at the on-campus **visitors center** or at the various campus entry kiosks. UCLA's **Campus Shuttle,** 310/206-2908, can get you around. Or sign up for a guided tour (reservations required), up to two hours long and scheduled on weekdays at 10:15 A.M. and 2:15 P.M., and on Sat. during regular semester session at 10:15 A.M. only. For more information, contact: **UCLA Campus Tours,** 310/825-8764. Then, assuming you've been able to find a place to park, spend some time poking into the shops and coffeehouses of Westwood, adjacent to the campus.

Armand Hammer Museum
of Art and Cultural Center

One of L.A.'s newer museums, the Armand Hammer Museum at 10899 Wilshire Blvd. (at Westwood), 310/443-7000, is built from the previously private collection of the increasingly controversial industrialist—a subject people here won't be inclined to discuss. Armand Hammer, former chair of Occidental Petroleum, was widely vilified throughout the L.A. art world when he reneged on his promise to leave his collection to the Los Angeles County Museum of Art. His namesake museum was hammered again in 1994, on a grander scale, when it decided to sell its Codex Hammer—Hammer's most prized possession, previously known as the Codex Leicester collection of original Leonardo da Vinci technical manuscripts—at auction, to the highest bidder. Microsoft's Bill Gates bought it, for $30.8 million.

Though the museum collection may expand dramatically someday, now that the Codex is gone "the Hammer" is noted for its thousands of Honoré Daumier sculptures and lithographs. The other real draw is the Hammer's world-class traveling exhibits. (Call for current shows.) The Hammer is open Tues.–Sat. 11 A.M.–7 P.M. (until 9 P.M. on Thurs.) and Sun. 11 A.M.–5 P.M., closed July Fourth, Thanksgiving, and Christmas. Admission is $4.50 adults, $3 students and seniors, $1 for UCLA students, and free for children under age 17. Parking is available at a discounted rate in the museum's underground parking garage.

CITIES ON A HILL—
THE GETTY AND VICINITY

Two new "cities" recently risen on the hills overlooking Sepulveda Pass, just off the San Diego Fwy. north of Brentwood and Bel-Air, are among L.A.'s most striking new cultural attractions. The $800 million Getty Center, one of the world's most remarkable arts facilities, finally opened its doors to the public in December 1997. Not far north of the Getty is the impressive $65 million Skirball Cultural Center, a three-winged modernist monument of pink granite, green slate, and curving stainless steel with visitor-friendly facilities including the extraordinary Skirball Museum of Jewish History and a children's Discovery Center. The two institutions occasionally offer joint collaborative exhibits, such as *Sigmund Freud: Conflict & Culture* in 2000.

The Getty Museum

Originally envisioned as a second location for Malibu's renowned J. Paul Getty Museum, "the Getty" has become considerably more—starting with six huge stone building complexes and gorgeous central garden on 110 terraced acres with panoramic views of the city, the sea, and surrounding mountains.

It is L.A.'s latest astonishment—architect Richard Meier's contemporary yet classic arts enclave, a 25-acre complex built of imported Italian travertine marble rising like a medieval castle above both city and sea on a ridge near Brentwood. "If God had the money," observed L.A. design critic Sam Hall Kaplan years before the Getty Center even opened its doors, "this is perhaps what he would do." The architectural

---

ROBERT IRWIN'S
CENTRAL GARDEN

Another Getty Center attraction is the 134,000-square-foot Central Garden near the museum, designed by "real-world" L.A. artist Robert Irwin—an intentionally self-conscious human-crafted garden reflecting upon the natural world as humanity has made it. Like a sculptor using both geometric and photosynthetic elements as "clay," Irwin has created a garden shaped like a huge handheld mirror, the overall image a severe and architectural landscape in winter yet soft, scented, and sensuous in summer. The mirror's "handle," roughly paralleled by a pathway, is created by an echo-chambered stream flanked by flowering plants and a canopy of trees. At stream's end, within a circular "natural" amphitheater, the stream becomes a shallow pool surrounded by a geometric maze of flowering azaleas—images of nature that seem to float on the water's surface. Irwin's garden won't be in full flower for at least a decade, since it will take at least that many years for the two main tree plantings—the sensuous crape myrtles and the London plane trees that will one day form a carefully clipped canopy above the stream—to achieve their intended effects. So in the meantime, just pull up one of the French café chairs and sit a spell. And enjoy.

statement, in his view, is that "this is a cultural institution here for the ages, not a passing indulgence, not a deconstructionist exercise by yet another narcissistic architect."

The Getty Center's centerpiece is its museum. Inside the two-story circular lobby are two small theaters for visitor orientation and a book and gift shop. Surrounding a central garden courtyard are the five museum pavilions—vast galleries that allow display of much more of the J. Paul Getty Museum's collection, including European sculptures, illuminated manuscripts from the Middle Ages and the Renaissance, photographs from its collection of more than 60,000, and a 15-room decorative arts section. Galleries are also highly interactive, with audio guides, multimedia computer stations, and expanded special-audience educational programs.

The previous showcase of the J. Paul Getty Trust was the original J. Paul Getty Museum in Malibu, an exact replica of a Roman villa. Now the museum's second campus, the Getty Villa has closed for renovation and reconfiguration, and is scheduled to reopen in the year 2002 as both the Getty Trust's museum of Greek and Roman antiquities and its "center for the display, conservation, and interpretation of ancient art in the broadest sense."

The Practical Getty

About 1.5 million visitors are expected to commune with the Old Masters and other elements of the Getty's art world here each year. They'll arrive at the hilltop palace after a five-minute electric monorail-style tram ride up the hill from the six-story underground parking garage at the west end of Getty Center Dr., just off the San Diego Fwy. (the 405) and N. Sepulveda Boulevard. The Getty Center is open to the public Tues. and Wed. 11 A.M.–7 P.M., Thurs. and Fri. 11 A.M.–9 P.M., and Sat. and Sun. 10 A.M.–6 or 7 P.M. (closed on Mon. and major holidays). Admission is free, though there is a $5 parking fee. Advance reservations (for parking) are required—except for college students with valid ID and for anyone arriving for the Getty's "reservation-free" evenings, Thurs. and Fri. after 4 P.M. Visitors arriving by bike, bus (MTA and Santa Monica buses serve the museum), or taxi also need no reservations. People planning to arrive by car and park elsewhere in nearby Brentwood are strongly discouraged, since this practice has caused considerable tension in the neighborhood. No pets are allowed, with the exception of trained guide and service animals.

In addition to its stunning new museum and ever-expanding museum collection, Getty Trust projects now housed at the Getty Center include its international arts conservation and restoration institute, its high-tech art history information institute, its research institute fellowships in art history and the humanities, and its education, grant, and museum management programs. Getty Center highlights also include a 450-seat auditorium, a 750,000-volume library with reading areas and a small exhibit area, and a restaurant, a cafeteria, and two cafés. Visitors can also pack a picnic and just enjoy the facilities—for free.

For information on special programs, current exhibits, and advance reservations, contact: Getty Center, 1200 Getty Center Dr., Los Angeles, CA 90049, 310/440-7300, www.getty.edu.

Beyond the Getty: Skirball Cultural Center

About two miles north of the Getty Center is the splendidly simple four-story Skirball Cultural Center, designed by Boston-based architect Moshe Safdie and named after Jack Skirball, a rabbi and producer of Alfred Hitchcock films. Various other museums and cultural monuments document the Jewish experience, but this one celebrates Jewish life—and Jewish-American life—in an effort to explain Jewish traditions, values, and vision. Yet the new Skirball Center is dedicated to full participation in L.A.'s efforts to "create a new paradigm for its cultural institutions." Part of the point here is interpreting the American-Jewish experience as it translates to the experience of all immigrants—an effort to strengthen the fabric of American society and its institutions.

The center itself is some institution—including the Skirball Museum of Jewish History, the hands-on children's Discovery Center, an education center with classrooms, plus auditorium, conference facilities, and a large outdoor courtyard for concerts and other events, altogether 125,000 square feet of buildings on a 15-acre site.

For information on current museum exhibits and other details, contact: Skirball Cultural Center, 2701 N. Sepulveda Blvd., 310/440-4500, www.skirball.org. The center is on N. Sepulveda

Blvd., on the west side of the San Diego Fwy. just south of Mulholland Dr.; from the 405, take the Skirball Center Dr./Mulholland Dr. exit and follow the signs, crossing Sepulveda Dr. into the center's south entrance. The museum is open Tues.–Sat. noon–5 P.M., Sun. 11 A.M.–5 P.M. (closed Monday). The Skirball is closed Thanksgiving, Christmas, and New Year's Day; call for other holiday closings. Admission is $8 adults, $6 seniors and students, free for children under age 12. The center is wheelchair accessible, and wheelchairs are available upon request. Facilities include **Zeidler's Cafe** (call 310/440-4515 for reservations) and the equally impressive **Audrey's Museum Store,** 310/440-4505.

WILDERNESS CITY: THE SANTA MONICA MOUNTAINS

One of the few east-west-trending mountain ranges in the United States, the Santa Monica Mountains extend upward from the sea as part of the Channel Islands and then eastward from Pacific Ocean beaches and tidepools to Mt. Hollywood in Griffith Park on the mainland, creating the geographical divide between the Los Angeles Basin and the San Fernando Valley.

The Santa Monica Mountains National Recreation Area, a 70,000-acre parkland pastiche created by Congress in 1978, protects much of the remaining open space in the Santa Monica Mountains—city, county, state, federal, private, and once-private lands and beaches—within a unified identity. Yet within that unity is great diversity. Maintaining separate boundaries are parks of long standing, including **Malibu Creek State Park,** 818/880-0367 or 818/880-0350; **Topanga State Park** in the Topanga Canyon watershed, 310/454-8212 or 818/880-0350; **Will Rogers State Historic Park** in Pacific Palisades, 310/454-8212; various public beaches; and attractions such as **Paramount Ranch, Peter Strauss Ranch,** and the fairly new **Streisand**

M*A*S*H AT MALIBU CREEK

Fans of the *M*A*S*H* television series, filmed at **Malibu Creek State Park,** will recognize the scenery—and enjoy posing for impromptu photos inside the junked jeep and ambulance parked in weeds along the Crags Road trail route. Much of the land now included in the park was owned by Twentieth Century Fox until the mid-1970s, so, naturally, many TV shows and movies have been filmed here over the years—and at adjacent **Paramount Ranch,** where TV series including *Dr. Quinn, Medicine Woman, The Rifleman,* and *Have Gun Will Travel* were shot at Western Town. Free and technical rock-climbing are also popular here.

Yet trails are the real draw. The short one-mile hike to Century Lake is an easy trek for the kids. (The old *M*A*S*H* set is one mile farther.) Starting at the parking lot, head west on Crags Road to Malibu Creek. Head right at the fork to reach the visitors center, for basic information and orientation. Cross the bridge here and continue up the road; at the crest, descend to the left. Man-made Century Lake, now something of a freshwater marsh, is quite inviting to ducks and other waterfowl. If the kids are still willing, backtrack toward the bridge and then take the Gorge Trail south to Rock Pool—yet another one of those Southern California sights that seems

vaguely familiar since you may have seen it before—in movies such as *Swiss Family Robinson.*

Six miles of the Backbone Trail also traverse the park. For inveterate hikers, Malibu Creek State Park also offers trail access to the city of Calabasas's **Lost Hills Park.** Other visitor draws include pleasant picnicking, a large campground, and the regional state park headquarters. The land's main claim to fame, however, is as the southernmost natural habitat of California's valley oak.

Parking lot hours are 8 A.M.–sunset, though the park itself is open 24 hours except in extreme fire danger or other emergency. Parking is $2 per vehicle. The visitors center is open limited hours, on weekends only. Call for information on nature walks and special activities. To get here: From the Ventura Fwy. (the 101) in Calabasas, head south on Las Virgenes Road three miles to the Mulholland Hwy. intersection. Continue south on Las Virgenes/Malibu Canyon Rd. another quarter-mile to the park's entrance. From Pacific Coast Hwy. (Hwy. 1), head north almost six miles on Malibu Canyon Road to the park entrance. For more information, contact: Malibu Creek State Park, 1925 Las Virgenes Rd. in Calabasas, 818/880-0367 or 818/880-0350, fax 818/880-6165.

Center for Conservancy Studies. Thanks to the Santa Monica Mountains Conservancy and other groups and individuals, land acquisitions continue to expand this national park—and the boundaries of individual parks within it—while extending the recreation area's trail system, popular with hikers, mountain bikers, and horseback riders. At last report, hikers, bikers, and equestrians were still battling over the issue of increasing mountain bike access to backcountry trails—to some an issue of overuse and abuse of trails as well as "machine-age encroachment," to others a question of equal rights for cyclists.

At the beaches summer is prime time, but the off-seasons offer at least the opportunity for solitude (and better beachcombing). Winter and spring, when the sky is blue and the hills are green, are the best seasons for exploring the mountains, which boast about 860 species of flowering plants in environments varying from grasslands, oak woodlands, and riparian sycamore and fern glades to coastal chaparral and craggy red-rock canyons. The only Mediterranean ecosystem protected by the National Park Service, the Santa Monicas have posed for TV and movie crews as Greece, Italy, France, Korea, the Wild West, and the antebellum South. Some areas are absolutely otherworldly; interplanetary film possibilities have yet to be fully explored here.

But because so much of the area is urban, surrounded by millions of people and bordered by two of the world's busiest freeways, and its attractions far-flung, finding one's way around in the Santa Monica Mountains can get complicated. To get oriented, stop by or contact the national park's visitor center and associated bookstore, (open daily 9 A.M.–5 P.M., closed Thanksgiving, Christmas, and New Year's Day). Along with maps and other helpful publications, the office offers a wonderful quarterly calendar of guided walks and other events, *Outdoors in the Santa Monica Mountains National Recreation Area,* also available online.

For more information, contact: **Santa Monica Mountains National Recreation Area** Visitor Center, 401 W. Hillcrest Dr., Thousand Oaks, CA 91360, 805/370-2301, www.nps.gov/samo. To get there from the Ventura Fwy. (Hwy. 101), exit at Lynn Rd. and continue north; turn east on Hillcrest; then turn left onto McCloud. The visitor center is the first driveway on the right. For information on area state parks, contact **California State Parks,** 1925 Las Virgenes Rd., Calabasas, CA 91302, 818/880-0350. Though associated state parks and beaches charge at least a nominal day-use fee, general access to national parks land is free.

Wildfires are a major threat to the park and its urban and suburban neighbors, so no fires are allowed within most park areas. Permission to explore environmentally sensitive areas, including **Cold Creek Canyon Preserve** near Topanga State Park, are by permit only, so docent-led hikes are usually the best way to go.

STAYING IN AND AROUND BEVERLY HILLS

Bankrolled by entertainment-industry wealth, together Beverly Hills and adjacent West Hollywood comprise L.A.'s premier hotel district; nearby Westwood and Bel-Air also offer uptown contenders, including the Hotel Bel-Air, one of the nation's most beloved luxury hotels. Yet serene Beverly Hills still has its surprises—including the fact that it can be less expensive to stay here than in wilder West Hollywood. (Besides, BH is that much closer to the beach.) Also look for reasonably priced accommodations in neighboring Westwood. As in other areas attractive to business travelers, inquire about discounts and holiday, seasonal, and/or weekend specials, which here can sometimes transform a pricey luxury stay into an unbelievable bargain.

STAYING IN BEVERLY HILLS

Reasonably Reasonable in BH
Not everything in Beverly Hills is outrageously expensive. One popular option is the **Beverly Terrace Motor Hotel** near the Pacific Design Center, one block from Melrose Ave. at 469 N. Doheny Dr. (near Santa Monica Blvd.), 310/274-8141. The 39 standard motel-style rooms are typically booked months in advance. Beyond the basics, enjoy the small pool, sundeck, free parking, and continental breakfast. Rates are $105–125. Premium. Another best bet in Beverly Hills is the brick colonial **Maison 140,** 140 S. Lasky Dr. (near Santa Monica Blvd.), 310/271-

ACCOMMODATIONS RATINGS

Accommodations in this book are rated by price category, based on double-occupancy, high-season rates. Categories used are:

Budget. . . . . $35 and under
Inexpensive $35-60
Moderate $60-85
Expensive $85-110
Premium $110-150
Luxury. . . . . $150 and up

2145 or toll-free 800/432-5444, a small, friendly hotel with European style and little extras such as continental breakfast and free parking. Who cares if the bathrooms are a bit small? Rooms are $140–180, a relative bargain. Premium-Luxury. If you *must* have opulence, just stroll through the neighborhood and eyeball the Peninsula Beverly Hills around the corner (and see other luxury hotel listings, below).

Possible Beverly Hills Deals
Once the Beverly Crest Hotel, the four-story, 48-room **Beverly Hills Inn,** 125 S. Spalding Dr., 310/278-0303 or, for reservations, toll-free 800/537-8483, isn't flashy yet is quite comfortable and convenient. Amenities include cable TV, free movies, in-room refrigerators, laundry and exercise facilities, saunas, pool, and coffee shop. Continental breakfast and parking included. Rates are $155–225. Luxury.

Even standard-brand stays are not entirely standard in and around Beverly Hills. The friendly, recently renovated **Holiday Inn Select Beverly Hills** just north of Pico Blvd. at 1150 S. Beverly Dr., 310/553-6561 or toll-free 800/465-4329 (worldwide), once a Ramada Inn, can still offer vacation value at a very convenient uptown address. All rooms feature coffeemakers and VCRs, color TVs, and both free and "fee" movies (making it easier to catch up on Tinseltown's tinsel while you're here). Beyond the usual motel amenities and the pool, a stay here includes free shuttle service and free use of a nearby fitness center. Rates run $149–190 for rooms, $300 for suites. Luxury.

Bargains are sometimes available at **Merv Griffin's Beverly Hilton Hotel,** fast becoming more than just another Hilton. Merv's Hilton, located at 9876 Wilshire Blvd. (at Santa Monica Blvd.), 310/274-7777 or toll-free 800/445-8667, is a pretty classy joint. Long gone are the dreary guest cubicles—in their stead are large, elegant rooms with terraces, color TVs, cable, movies, in-room coffeemakers, and honor bars. The elegant rooftop L'Escoffier restaurant is gone, but a spiffed-up **Trader Vic's** remains. **Griff's,** the new poolside restaurant, is a best bet for Sunday brunch. Rooms are $230–280 double, from $300 suite. Luxury.

If you've always fantasized about staying *on* Rodeo Drive, the 86-room **Luxe Hotel Rodeo Drive,** 360 N. Rodeo Dr., 310/273-0300 or toll-free 800/421-0545, recently renovated, features attractive rooms and the street's only sidewalk café—perfect for people-watching. Breakfast and free parking included. Rates are $255 and up. Luxury.

Particularly Good Value in BH

Some of the best BH stays lie just beyond the city limits. A bargain by Beverly Hills standards is the ever-popular **Beverly Plaza Hotel,** two blocks east of La Cienega at 8384 W. 3rd St., 323/658-6600 or toll-free 800/624-6835, www.beverly-plazahotel.com, just blocks away from the Beverly Center and otherwise well-situated for serious shopping. (The $10 per day taxi voucher helps, too.) Not to be confused with the Beverly Hills Plaza Hotel in nearby Westwood, the five-story, 98-room Beverly Plaza features simple, traditional, and tastefully decorated rooms amply stuffed with amenities. Standard here: cable TV, honor bars, and in-room refrigerators, plus exercise facilities, sauna, and pool. The wonderful Spanish-Mediterranean restaurant **Cava,** complete with tapas bar, is another draw. Rates are $149 and up, but inquire about discounts. Luxury.

The **Carlyle Inn,** near the design district one block south of Olympic Blvd. at 1119 S. Robertson Blvd., 310/275-4445 or toll-free 800/322-7595, www.carlyle-inn.com, appears to be a nondescript four-story stucco bunker. Yet inside hides a gracious little boutique hotel. The 32-room Carlyle features an interior courtyard, graceful lobby, lovely rooms, restaurant, fitness facilities, hot tub, and sundeck. Enjoy a full buffet breakfast, afternoon tea, wine in the evenings, and special extras—such as free shuttle service 6 A.M.–9 P.M. within a five-mile reach. All rooms have in-room coffeemakers, safes, and data ports as well as color TVs with cable. Rates of $130–165. Premium to Luxury.

The **Renaissance Beverly Hills** nearby, 1224 S. Beverwil Dr., 310/277-2800 or toll-free 800/421-3212, is the contemporary reincarnation of the old Beverly Hillcrest Hotel, once known for its 1960s kitsch. This Beverly has had a facelift in addition to a name change, and recently acquired a clever sophistication, making this one of the more affordable, attractive, and appealing "new" luxury hotels in town. All rooms at this 12-story beauty are large, with balconies, views, and the usual comforts. Other pluses here: pool, full fitness facilities, business suites with in-room faxes, good on-site restaurant, and around-town shuttle service. Rates are $198 and up, with special rates available. Luxury.

Another possibility: **The Radisson Beverly Pavilion,** 9360 Wilshire Blvd., 310/273-1400 or toll-free 800/441-5050, a small boutique-style hotel within walking distance of prime Beverly Hills shopping. Known for good service, its excellent on-site restaurant **Earth,** and stylish rooms—upper-floor rooms facing west come with sunset views—the Beverly Pavilion also provides a rooftop pool, sundeck, and the usual luxury amenities, including in-room refrigerators and hair dryers. Rates are $159–219. Luxury.

Beverly Hills Hotel

Even staid Beverly Hills was silly with excitement in the mid-1990s with the news that the mythic mission revival-style "Pink Palace" was ready to reopen after a $100 million renovation. Star of the original 1937 *A Star is Born* and of more recent films including *The Way We Were, California Suite,* and *American Gigolo,* for all its on-screen glory the Beverly Hills had needed some very basic rebuilding in addition to cosmetic improvements. Those tasks completed, the 194-room Beverly Hills Hotel is once again a favorite playground—no, elaborate stage set—for the rich, famous, and celebrity-conscious. Even if a stay here is ludicrous, consider a meal. Dining possibilities include the **Polo Lounge,** long renowned for its "power booths," favored uptown digs for Hollywood deal-making and once again fully plugged in. Also back in business is the **Fountain Coffee Shop,** still decked out in the hotel's trademark banana-leaf wallpaper. For romance, one of the best choices around is the art-deco ambience of the elegant California-style French **Polo Grill.**

The landmark pink stucco Beverly Hills Hotel is grandly situated on Sunset Boulevard above triangular Will Rogers Memorial Park (at Rodeo Drive), 9641 Sunset Blvd., 310/276-2251 or toll-free 800/283-8885, www.beverlyhillshotel.com. Historic bungalows and rooms are Luxury-Super

Luxury. Standard rooms start at a budget-breaking $325, while elaborate bungalows and suites top out at about $4,000. That's right—per night.

Regent Beverly Wilshire

In Beverly Hills one can also opt for Old World opulence. A good choice in that category, one of the city's finest hotels, is the Regent Beverly Wilshire, a posh circa-1928 Wilshire Blvd. landmark.

Start exploring in the lobby, a stunning display of antiques and elegant wood, glass, and marble, and soak up still more ambience in the **Lobby Lounge**—just the place for afternoon tea—**The Bar,** usually overflowing with agents and other entertainment industry types, and either the café or the elegant **Regent Dining Room.** Don't miss the lovely pool area, either, or the spa; the full gym is on the 2nd floor. The Beverly Wilshire's lavish $4,000-a-night presidential suite has hosted Elvis Presley and the late Japanese Emperor Hirohito, among many other international luminaries, though it's much more famous as home base for the cynical-businessman-meets-hooker-with-a-heart-of-gold movie romance *Pretty Woman.*

The Regent Beverly Wilshire sits at the foot of Rodeo Drive at 9500 Wilshire Blvd., 310/275-5200; for reservations within California, call toll-free 800/421-4354. "Standard" room rates are $365–540; suites range from $520 to a whopping $4,500. Here as elsewhere the tab is somewhat fluid, so ask about weekend specials.

Four Seasons Hotel Los Angeles

Another of L.A.'s best hotels—and one of its most attractive—the 16-story Four Seasons is another jewel in the impressive Canadian chain. This 285-room hotel features large rooms amply outfitted for either business or pleasure, with two TVs (one in the bathroom), two two-line telephones (and free mobile phones), a well-stocked honor bar, plus hair dryer, sumptuous terry robes, and other little luxuries. The inviting pool, exercise facilities, spa, and sundeck are on the 4th floor. Head for the lobby bar to be an entertainment industry social voyeur, to the café or swank **Gardens** restaurant for more substantial fare. Located in a quiet residential neighborhood. Room rates are $325–395, suites from $650, with various discounts usually available. Luxury. For more information or reservations, contact: Four Seasons Los Angeles, 300 S. Doheny Dr. (at Burton Way), 310/273-2222, www.fourseasons.com; for Four Seasons' central reservations service, call toll-free 800/332-3442.

Peninsula Beverly Hills

The Peninsula Beverly Hills is the epitome of discretion. Tucked into a quiet residential neighborhood, the contemporary French Renaissance palace and two-story villas serve as home-away-from-home for the classically, cautiously wealthy. Tasteful yet opulent rooms and suites feature marble floors, antique furnishings, fine fabrics, telephones with voice mail, TVs with VCRs, and

The Regent Beverly Wilshire Hotel presides over Rodeo Drive.

down comforters; refrigerators and minibars are discreetly tucked away behind French doors. Suites and villas come with individual security systems, fax machines, and CD players; some feature fireplaces, spa baths, and private patios. Full fitness and spa facilities are also available. Since the Peninsula Beverly Hills is sister to the Palace Hotel in Beijing and the Peninsula and the Kowloon in Hong Kong, it seems only fitting that the **Belvedere** here serves fine, formal French with Asian touches, though you can enjoy more casual fare at the lobby piano lounge. And if you need a lift somewhere, one of the hotel's Rolls-Royce fleet can drop you off.

For more information and reservations, contact: Peninsula Beverly Hills, 9882 Little Santa Monica Blvd., 310/273-4888 or toll-free 800/462-7899, www.peninsula.com. Deluxe rooms are $375–450, suites also available. Luxury.

L'Ermitage Beverly Hills
This luxury hotel is another of L.A.'s best, and it's also a darling of tech execs and entertainment people. Spacious guest rooms are appointed with guest cell phones that work as far away as San Diego and Palm Springs, high-speed Internet access and WEB TV, and "intelligent" in-room lighting and climate control systems that adapt to individual preferences. Other luxuries include L.A.'s largest rooftop pool, fitness facilities with a view, library, and tea lounge, not to mention free limousine service around Beverly Hills. Rooms are $330–475, suites $600 and up. Luxury. For more information or reservations, contact: L'Ermitage Beverly Hills, 9291 Burton Way, 310/278-3344 or toll-free 800/800-2113, www.lermitagehotel.com.

Le Meridien at Beverly Hills
Another excellent L.A. accommodation, the contemporary seven-story Le Meridien caters to business travelers and offers Asian style. Nondescript on the outside yet sleek, sophisticated, and charming inside, Le Meridien features a stylish Pacific Rim restaurant, **Pangaea,** fitness facilities, saunas, pool, and abundant all-business amenities. Generous rooms include sliding screens, fascinating desks, fully equipped phones, fax machines, in-room coffeemakers, refrigerators and honor bars, and complete entertainment set-ups: TV, VCR, CD player.

Techies will appreciate the bedside electronic "command center." Large bathrooms feature Japanese soaking tubs. Rooms start at $300, and suites are $345–1,800. Luxury. Free or valet parking.

For more information, contact: Le Meridien, 465 S. La Cienega, 310/247-0400, www.nikkohotels.com. For reservations, call toll-free 800/645-5624 or 800/645-5687.

STAYING IN BEL-AIR AND BRENTWOOD

Hotel Bel-Air
Beverly Hills and vicinity boasts glitzier and more ostentatious luxury hotels, but the Hotel Bel-Air is a world-class act—a stunningly beautiful 11-acre country château complete with creek, tiny lake with swans ("Swan Lake"), forested gardens, bougainvillea, birds of paradise, and the luxury of absolute serenity and solitude. This celebrated hideout for celebrities, royalty, and the reclusive rich, a hidden Mediterranean village with 92 tile-roofed bungalows, is also an immensely popular Southern California getaway for honeymoons, anniversaries, and other special occasions. (Here, affluence doesn't invariably translate into snobbery—a marvelous feature.) In the 1920s the hotel's main buildings were the real estate sales offices for the original Bel-Air development; hotel conversion came in the 1940s, with later buildings continuing the original style.

And the style here—terra-cotta tile floors, wood-burning fireplaces, handmade rugs, private patios and gardens, and endless understated luxuries—has attracted celebrities such as Grace Kelly and Gary Cooper, Howard Hughes, the Rockefellers, and the Kennedys. Marilyn Monroe's favorite bungalow has been converted into the Bel-Air's new health spa. More popular destinations, though, include the exceptional California-French restaurant, the Swan Lake dining terrace, and the fabulous pool (reserve a spot early). Rooms are $380–580, suites start at $650. Luxury.

For more information or reservations, contact: Hotel Bel-Air, 701 Stone Canyon Rd., 310/472-1211 or toll-free 800/648-4097, www.hotelbelair.com.

Brentwood Stays

Particularly convenient for business travelers is the **Summit Hotel Bel-Air** in Brentwood, just west of the San Diego Fwy. at 11461 Sunset Blvd., 310/476-6571 or toll-free 800/468-3541. Formerly a Radisson, this attractive two-story garden oasis features contemporary California style; large rooms with color TVs and VCRs, in-room coffeemakers, refrigerators, and honor bars; and tennis court, pool, and exercise facilities. Rooms are $139–165. Premium-Luxury.

Quite reasonable in Brentwood is the 20-room **Brentwood Motor Hotel** one mile west of the San Diego Fwy. at 12200 W. Sunset Blvd., 310/476-9981 or toll-free 800/840-3808, www. bmhotel.com, where recently renovated and re-decorated rooms feature cable TV, free movies, refrigerators, and coffeemakers. Rooms are $99–124. Expensive-Premium.

STAYING IN WESTWOOD AND CENTURY CITY

W Los Angeles

This elegant all-suites hotel, adjacent to UCLA and just a limo-stretch away from Beverly Hills, doesn't make a dazzling first impression. But the entertainment industry and other corporate client types are unperturbed, since the cold 15-story concrete facade is transformed, once inside, into warm and contemporary California suites featuring the usual luxuries, plus Ethernet laptop connections and Aveda toiletries. Not to mention two swimming pools, complete spa, and the outstanding **Mojo** restaurant. For more information or reservations, contact: W Los Angeles, 930 Hilgard Ave. (three blocks north of Wilshire Blvd.), 310/208-8765 or toll-free 800/421-2317, www.whotels.com. Rates in this all-suites property start at $239 for suites and $325 for penthouse suites. Luxury.

Other Westwood Stays

A more affordable alternative across the street from the Westwood Marquis (now the W) is three-story **Hilgard House,** 927 Hilgard Ave., 310/208-3945 or toll-free 800/826-3934, www.hilgardhouse.com. This small (47-room) European-style hotel on the eastern edge of UCLA offers quaint rooms with Queen Anne–style furnishings, window seats, refrigerators, color TVs with cable, and hot tub–equipped bathtubs (1st floor rooms only), breakfast and parking included. Room rates are $119–129, with special rates sometimes available. Premium. From here it's an easy stroll to Westwood Village restaurants and movie theaters and 10 minutes by van to the Getty Center.

Also quite comfortable and even more affordable: the quiet four-story, 80-room **Hotel del Capri** surrounded by high-rises at 10587 Wilshire Blvd., Los Angeles, CA 90024, 310/474-3511 or toll-free 800/444-6835, www.hoteldelcapri.com. Most of the 80 rooms feature fully equipped kitchenettes, whirlpool tubs, and color TVs with cable and free movies. Rooms are $100–110, suites $125–135. Premium. Free parking, pool, lovely gardens.

Then there's the **Beverly Hills Plaza Hotel,** 10300 Wilshire Blvd., 310/275-5575 or toll-free 800/800-1234, formerly the Beverly Hills Ritz Hotel and, before that, the Beverly Hills Comstock Hotel. The hotel is a snazzy and contemporary onetime apartment complex built around a central courtyard and pool; every suite but the studio suites features living room and kitchen, bathroom, and bedrooms—a very inviting setup for a longer stay. Rates start at $165 for a junior suite and soar to $495 for the penthouse suite. Luxury.

The 99-room **Century Wilshire Hotel,** 10776 Wilshire Blvd., 310/474-4506 or toll-free 800/421-7223, www.centurywilshirehotel.com, is another apartment building converted to a hotel, this one particularly popular with Europeans. Each suite features a fully equipped kitchenette, tiled bathroom, and English-style decor; extras include free parking, pool, and continental breakfast. Daily standard room rates are $95–115, suites $125–275, with weekly and monthly rates available. Premium-Luxury.

Other possible Westwood stays include the **Royal Palace Westwood** just north of Wilshire Blvd. at 1052 Tiverton Ave., 310/208-6677, www.royalpalacewestwood.com, a 36-unit apartment-style motel popular with visiting professors and featuring just the basics plus kitchenettes (rooms $80–125, Expensive-Premium), and the upscale 296-room **Doubletree Hotel** (formerly the Holiday Inn Westwood Plaza) close to UCLA and Westwood Village at 10740

Wilshire Blvd., 310/475-8711 or toll-free 800/472-8556 (rooms $185–219, with lower weekend and promotional rates, Premium-Luxury).

Best bets for a motel-style stay near Westwood include the **Best Western Westwood Pacific Hotel** a block west of the San Diego Fwy. at 11250 Santa Monica Blvd. (at Sawtelle Blvd.), 310/478-1400 or toll-free 800/528-1234. Room rates are $89–109. Expensive. And the all-suite **Best Western Royal Palace Inn and Suites** also near the freeway, just south of Pico Blvd. at 2528 S. Sepulveda Blvd., 310/477-9066 or toll-free 800/528-1234, where the basics include kitchenette and queen-size sleeper sofa (in addition to the bed). Room rates are $85–105. Expensive.

Westin Century Plaza Hotel

This is where Ronald Reagan usually stayed when he visited Los Angeles during his presidency. In fact, every president since Lyndon Baines Johnson has stayed here—as have miscellaneous international royalty—since the rooftop helipad is a major boon for the incessantly security-conscious. Designed in the mid-1960s by Minoru Yamasaki, the main body of this vast 20-story hotel has 724 rooms, each with three telephones, private wall vaults, stocked bars, and private balconies. Major benefits and other social events often whirl throughout the hotel. Most people are more entertained by the good restaurants here, the **Cafe Plaza,** the trendy **Breeze** restaurant, and the **Lobby Court** cocktail lounge. Room rates are $229–375, but this being a business-oriented hotel, look for specials and packages on weekends. Luxury.

For more information or reservations, contact: Westin Century Plaza Hotel and Tower, 2025 Ave. of the Stars, 310/277-2000 or 310/551-3300, toll-free 800/228-3000.

EATING IN AND AROUND BEVERLY HILLS

FAIRLY AFFORDABLE FARE

People's Eats in BH: Burgers and Such

Sooner or later everyone goes to **Hamburger Hamlet,** 122 S. Beverly Dr. (at Wilshire Blvd.), 310/274-0191, famous for its bacon cheeseburgers. The original Hamlet, on Bonner Dr. in West Hollywood, 310/278-4924, is now well past 50 years old, vinyl booths and all, but has had a facelift. For burgers and such served with self-conscious 1950s-style kitsch—and milkshakes made with Dreyer's ice cream—the place is campy **Ed Debevic's** diner, 134 N. La Cienega Blvd., 310/659-1952, open daily for lunch and dinner. For better 1950s fare, in this case with unmistakable New Wave flair (dig that fondue), even veggie options, the place is the new, improved **Cadillac Cafe** back again at 359 N. La Cienega Blvd., 310/657-6591, where it originally parked in the 1980s. For more predictable retro, there's always smallish **Johnny Rockets,** 474 N. Beverly Dr., 310/271-2222, where the fare runs to good malts, fries, juicy burgers, and general jocularity.

People's Eats in BH: Beyond Burgers

The place for fresh-baked bagels and other fundamentals is **The Nosh of Beverly Hills,** 9689 S. Santa Monica Blvd., 310/271-3730. But for sit-down breakfast consider the **Beverly Hills Breakfast Club** tucked into department store row at 9671 Wilshire Blvd. (at Roxbury Dr.), 310/271-8903, serving good french toast and omelettes or salads and sandwiches and open daily for breakfast and lunch.

Want to really save money for shopping Rodeo Drive? Then stop by the popular chain **Baja Fresh,** here situated across the street from Johnny Rockets at 475 N. Beverly Dr., 310/858-6690, and saluted for its freshly grilled healthy Mexican fare. Very inexpensive, tasty, and fresh.

Inexpensive Asian fare isn't easy to come by in Beverly Hills, but one possibility is **ABC Szechwan Chinese Restaurant,** 9036 Burton Way (at Doheny), 310/288-2182, where a four-course lunch will set you back less than $10. It's open for lunch Mon.–Sat., for dinner daily. Also unusual is the Japanese **Curry House,** 163 N. La Cienega Blvd. (one block north of Wilshire Blvd.), 310/854-4959, just a few doors down from the much more famous (and much, much more expensive) Matsuhisa. What's served here is an Americanized version of Japan's favorite curried dishes, as translated from the Indian originals through the English, including breaded pork cutlets, chicken, and

cruising BH

TOM MYERS PHOTOGRAPHY

battered shrimp, not to mention a number of other well-prepared entrées quite popular in Japan. Stay for coffee and dessert—particularly the tofu cheesecake. Takeout available. Validated parking in the adjacent lot.

For pizza, some say the best in town comes from actress Cathy "Raging Bull" Moriarty's **Mulberry Street Pizzeria,** 347 N. Cañon Dr. (at Dayton), 310/247-8998, famous for its thin-crust New York–style. Another people's favorite is tiny **Jacopo's,** 490 N. Beverly Dr. (at Little Santa Monica Blvd.), 310/858-6446, serving its own cheese-rich New York–style pizza (popular for takeout but Jacopo's delivers, too). **California Pizza Kitchen,** 207 S. Beverly Dr. (one block south of Wilshire Blvd.), 310/275-1101, colloquially known as the poor man's Spago, is another best bet. Wood-fired pizzas are the thing here, served up in exotic displays such as BLT or Thai chicken and in less unusual combos including tomato, garlic, and basil.

Richer People's Fare
Where you eat, more than what you eat, establishes social status in Beverly Hills. So many major movers and shakers frequent **Nate 'n' Al's,** 414 N. Beverly Dr. (near Little Santa Monica Blvd.), 310/274-0101, that you can almost make the BH scene—the Hollywood deal-making scene—just by strolling through the door of this, the world's largest deli. Nothing fancy about the food, though—just the basics: decent sandwiches, cheese blintzes, and such, fairly inexpensive.

Quite wonderful for takeout—definitely an eat-in dinner option if you've got a microwave or kitchenette handy—is stylish **Porta Via,** 424 N. Cañon Dr. (at Little Santa Monica Blvd.), 310/274-6534, where you can order everything from spectacular salads and wild mushroom-and-spinach lasagna to Italian sandwiches on house-made focaccia (seasonally changing menu). Offered in the A.M.: fresh-baked apple coffeecake, pear tarts, muffins, scones, and such.

At home in a former hardware store, **The Farm of Beverly Hills,** 439 N. Beverly Dr. (near Little Santa Monica Blvd.), 310/273-5578, is now a chic café whose chef is Ben Ford, son of Harrison. Wonderful sandwiches, salads, and desserts make this a great stop, after shopping or otherwise.

And there's always ever-popular **Il Fornaio,** 310 N. Beverly Dr. (at Dayton Way), 310/550-8330, open daily for breakfast, lunch, and dinner, where you can keep it fairly affordable by ordering carefully. You'll find plenty to choose from—fresh-baked breads, sandwiches, salads, pastas, rotisserie-roasted chicken, or just coffee and treats from the espresso bar. Even better, though, for a simple yet superb meal is **Il Pastaio,** 400 N. Cañon Dr. (at Brighton), 310/205-5444, a casual sibling to Santa Monica's famous Drago. Though the fresh pastas are the main attraction, the many distractions are worthy.

Stylish and catapulted to local stardom by the Silver Lake bohemian set is the elegant and colorful Indian **Bombay Palace,** 8690 Wilshire Blvd.

(two blocks east of Robertson), 310/659-9944, where the buffet lunch is a real deal. Vegetarians can have a fun, flavorful time, but Bombay Palace has something for everyone. Not in Beverly Hills proper but close enough is **Versailles**, 1415 S. La Cienega Blvd. (at Pico Blvd.), 310/289-0392, a hip and relaxed joint serving L.A.'s best Cuban food. The star here is the roast chicken, served whole or half, marinated in citrus vinegar, topped with raw onions, and stuffed with garlic cloves—crisp on the outside, juicy and flavorful on the inside—and served with fried plantains with black beans and white rice. If you're meandering south and then toward the coast, the original Versailles is south of Century City—and the Santa Monica Fwy.—in Culver City at 10319 Venice Blvd. (just west of Motor Ave.), 310/558-3168.

STYLISH AND EXPENSIVE FARE

Stylish, Somewhat Expensive Cafés

Fabulous for smoked fish, served as an accompaniment to eggs or as appetizers or presented as unusual sandwiches, is the chic **Barney Greengrass** café on the 5th floor of Barneys New York department store at 9570 Wilshire Blvd. (at Camden), 310/777-5877, a popular power breakfasting spot for industry agents working nearby. Another place to spy on the beautiful people is the **Armani Cafe** on the 3rd floor of Emporio Armani, 9533 Brighton Way, 310/271-9940, where light Northern Italian is the style.

Also quite pretty at lunch and dinner: the pricey Italian **Il Cielo**, 9018 Burton Way, 310/276-9990, one of the most romantic restaurants in Los Angeles.

But if you're pursuing great food more than style, the place is warm and welcoming **Trattoria Amici** at the Beverly Terrace Motor Hotel, 469 N. Doheny Dr., 310/858-0271, serving heaps of rustic Italian, from pizzas and pasta to grilled chicken. It's open for lunch Mon.–Fri., for dinner Mon.–Saturday. Also fun for Italian: hip yet refreshingly relaxed **Prego**, 362 N. Camden Dr. (a half block north of Wilshire Blvd.), 310/277-7346, a trattoria serving authentic Northern Italian, grilled specialties, sizzling pizzas hot out of the wood-fired oven, and pastas and salads.

For a stylish change-up, elegant **Gaylord**, 50 N. La Cienega (just north of Wilshire), 310/652-3838, serves traditional Indian fare carefully prepared by chefs trained at the original Gaylord in New Delhi. You can't miss with the nan bread and dishes such as mulligatawny soup and tandoori chicken—everything top-drawer.

Stylish, Somewhat Expensive Steakhouses and Such

For die-hard carnivores, BH's link in the New Orleans–based **Ruth's Chris Steak House** chain is a prominent presence. This restaurant, at 224 S. Beverly Dr. (between Olympic and Wilshire Blvds.), 310/859-8744, is particularly attractive for the genre, with posh semicircular leather booths and frosted-glass fixtures.

Men's-clubbish **The Grill on the Alley**, 9560 Dayton Way, 310/276-0615, is Southern California's original "Grill"—and proud papa of the Daily Grill chain. What you'd expect at such a manly restaurant is what you get: steaks, chops, fish, crab Louie, corn chowder, Hollywood's own cobb salad, and pecan pie. The Grill is open Mon.–Sat for both lunch and dinner.

Salmon, anyone? Something like a steakhouse for seafood, **McCormick and Schmick's**, 206 N. Rodeo Dr. (at Wilshire Blvd.), 310/859-0434, serves football-player portions of well-prepared seafood and fish in an attractive, relaxed setting. It's open daily for lunch and dinner. **Lawry's The Prime Rib**, 100 N. La Cienega Blvd. (just north of Wilshire Blvd.), 310/652-2827, is the place for—you guessed it—prime rib, tender and cut to order. It's open daily for dinner only.

Always fun after dinner is open-late **Kate Mantilini**, a painfully hip steakhouse at 9109 Wilshire Blvd. (at Doheny), 310/278-3699, named after a '40s female boxing promoter, where the doomsday architecture and the boisterous bar scene are often equally entertaining. Open daily for breakfast, lunch, and dinner until 2 A.M., which is when you are most likely to spot a celeb.

Still More Stylish, Still More Expensive

The new **Spago Beverly Hills**, 176 N. Cañon Dr., 310/385-0880, offers something considerably more elegant, and more expensive, than fans of the original Spago in West Hollywood might expect. Now that Puck's signature wood-fire baked pizzas and other favorites are widely available through the Wolfgang Puck Café and Wolfgang Puck Express chains—and now that Spago itself is becoming a nationwide chain—perhaps it was inevitable that Spago would restyle itself into something more uptown. At home on the former site of the Bistro Garden, the restaurant has been redesigned to accent natural lighting and to allow the indoor dining room to flow more gracefully into the garden setting. The new Spago is open for both lunch and dinner.

Lauded for its exceptional weekday happy hour, multilevel **Maple Drive,** 345 N. Maple Dr., 310/274-9800, is the rich person's idea of a neighborhood restaurant. Sampling the fare here, a selection of contemporary Mediterranean with California flair, is one way to see Beverly Hills through its own eyes. The tall-backed booths are where the celebs and the let's-make-a-dealers converge, but some prefer hovering around the maple bar. Maple Drive is open weekdays only for lunch—with happy hour 4–7 P.M., at last report, with well drinks served along with wonderful free fare—and Mon.–Sat. for dinner.

Another local magnet for the Hollywood power-lunch bunch is the Japanese-influenced **Matsuhisa,** 129 N. La Cienega Blvd., 310/659-9639, where the sushi is a unique art form and exotic seafood dishes are the other main attraction. It's open weekdays for lunch, nightly for dinner.

The Belvedere at the Peninsula Beverly Hills Hotel, 9882 Little Santa Monica Blvd. (at Wilshire), 310/788-2306, is another Hollywood power breakfast mecca. At other times expect sumptuous California Asian cuisine served to gorgeous diners in an equally gorgeous dining room. The menu includes low calorie "spa" dishes, too.

EATING IN BEL-AIR AND BRENTWOOD

Bel-Air Fare

For a friendly, inexpensive meal, the place in Bel-Air is tiny **Graziella** in the Glen Center at 2964 Beverly Glen Blvd., 310/475-7404, a best bet for light pastas and salads. Quite expensive and exceptional in the same general neighborhood is the ultra-romantic French **Four Oaks Restaurant,** a onetime speakeasy tucked away at 2181 N. Beverly Glen Blvd. (two lights north of Sunset Blvd.), 310/470-2265, open for Sunday brunch, for lunch Tues.–Sun., and for dinner every night. Patio dining, too, weather permitting.

And while we're discussing amore, the expensive and considerably more famous California-French fare at the **Hotel Bel-Air,** 701 Stone Canyon Rd., 310/472-1211, is without a doubt the neighborhood's most powerful draw. One of the most romantic places in L.A. for dinner, this is also an unforgettable choice at breakfast—try the lemon pancakes—and lunch. Reservations are always wise. Wander the lovingly tended grounds while you're here; the Hotel Bel-Air offers a civilized and sophisticated escape from L.A.'s harsher landscapes.

Brentwood Fare

The surfers' favorite South Bay takeout chicken joint now has an outlet in Brentwood—the wonderful Peruvian **El Pollo Inka,** a little piece of Machu Picchu at home in a faux-1950s diner in a strip mall at 11701 Wilshire Blvd. (at Barrington), 310/571-3334. El Pollo Inka is as famous for its green chile *aji* sauce as for its imaginative potatoes, wood fire-roasted chicken, and ice-cold Cuzquena beer. It's open daily for lunch and dinner, offering live music on weekends. A real deal.

Generally more "Brentwood" in style, though, is **A Votre Santé,** 13016 San Vicente Blvd. (at 26th St.), 310/451-1813, serving vegetarian and macrobiotic fare—a haven for those who don't do dairy or oil or sugar. A small eat-in area is filled with shiny people in spandex and sweats, but takeout is big business, too. Beyond the veggie burgers and wraps, the tabbouleh and hummus, dairyless corn chowder, salads, garden pastas, and fresh steamed vegetable dishes come highly recommended. It's open daily for breakfast, lunch, and dinner.

Fine dining in Brentwood is the bustling Italian **Toscana,** 11633 San Vicente Blvd. (one block east of Barrington), 310/820-2448, where the fine fare dances from pizza to steaks and game. It's a very popular industry hangout, so make reservations well in advance. Toscana is open for dinner daily, for lunch every day but Sunday. Good for celebrity-spotting—but every customer is treated like a star.

EATING IN CENTURY CITY

Family Fare

For affordable family fare—especially if those in your family have wildly different tastes—cruise the restaurant offerings in the Century City Marketplace, 10250 Santa Monica Blvd. (between Beverly Glen and Ave. of the Stars), the likes of New York–style **The Stage Deli** and **Houston's,** to retro burger joint **Johnny Rockets.** An intriguing choice is the **Tacone** stand, featuring a specialty devised here by Joachim Splichal of Patina—something like a handheld, cone-shaped taco shell. Ethnic-flavored fillings include such things as jerked shrimp with rice and black beans with shredded beef and rice.

Fancier Fare

Harry's Bar and American Grill inside the ABC Entertainment Center at 2020 Ave. of the Stars, 310/277-2333, is like a theme bar for expatriate Hemingway wannabes—an exact replica of the Harry's in Florence, Italy, a classy hideout of dark wood and brass. It's also the place to go before seeing a show at the Shubert. Harry's also serves good lunch, dinner, and after-theater fare—all-American burgers and steaks and Northern Italian specialties.

For fine dining, best bets beyond the Century City Plaza in Century City include the elegant yet relaxed French-Italian supper club **Lunaria,** 10351 Santa Monica Blvd., 310/282-8870, open for lunch on weekdays only, for dinner and jazz on Tues.–Sat. nights. **La Cachette,** 10506 Santa Monica, 310/470-4992, is a cozy romantic "hideaway." Owner/chef Jean-Francois Meteigner, formerly of the outstanding L'Orangerie, prepares classic French dishes with a California twist.

EATING IN AND AROUND WESTWOOD

Westwood is jammed with bars and restaurants, some quite memorable. On Westwood Blvd. south from Wilshire is L.A.'s "Little Persia," with an abundance of Iranian and other authentic bakeries, cafés, groceries, and shops. Good restaurants abound in nearby residential neighborhoods of West L.A., too, some of which are included in this section.

For good frozen nonfat yogurt, the place in Westwood is the **Bigg Chill,** 10850 W. Olympic Blvd., 310/475-1070. For connoisseur's coffee one possibility is **City Bean,** a "microroaster" at 10911 Lindbrook Dr., 310/208-0108.

People's Eats: Westwood and Vicinity

Definitely an L.A. classic, the **Apple Pan,** 10801 W. Pico Blvd. (at Glendon Ave., one block east of Westwood Blvd. in the shadow of the Westwood Pavilion), 310/475-3585, serves near-perfect burgers, cheeseburgers (topped with melted Tillamook cheddar), and thin-sliced Virginia ham sandwiches. Save room for the apple pie, the Apple Pan's claim to fame, though some people would kill for the banana cream—made with fresh bananas—or the chocolate, boysenberry, or pecan. No credit cards. It's open daily 11 A.M.–midnight, closed major holidays. If the Apple Pan is just too packed, other possibilities include classic **Marty's Hamburgers,** 10558 W. Pico Blvd., 310/836-6944, famous for its all-meat chiliburgers and foot-long hot dogs.

Another people's attraction along Pico is tiny **John O'Groats,** 10628 W. Pico Blvd. (a block west of Beverly Glen), 310/204-0692, a popular diner serving one of L.A.'s best inexpensive breakfasts and Scots-style specialties, including fish and chips, soups, and homemade biscuits. It's open daily for breakfast and lunch, Thurs.–Sat. only for dinner.

A popular collegiate hangout, complete with checkered tablecloths and Italian-style kitsch, **Lamonica's N.Y. Pizza,** 1066 Gayley Ave. (just off Wilshire), 310/208-8671, is designed to resemble a subway station and serves very good New York–style pizza by the slice.

For people's noodles, a best bet here is **Noodle Planet,** 1118 Westwood Blvd. (near Kinross), 310/208-0777, where first-rate pad Thai, yellow curry, Thai barbecue chicken, Vietnamese handroll, and such things as sticky rice with mango are all made with fresh, unprocessed ingredients. Head to West L.A. for inexpensive Japanese soul food, including **Ashai Ramen,** 2027 Sawtelle Blvd., 310/479-2231, beloved for noodles, dumplings, and pork pot stickers (closed Thursday). For some of L.A.'s best Japanese noodles, try **Yokohama Ramen,** 11600 Gateway Blvd. (at Barrington Ave.), 310/479-2321.

The most popular Mexican around is **La Salsa,** 11075 W. Pico Blvd. (at Sepulveda), 310/479-0919, famous for burritos and soft tacos and plenty of salsa choices. Wonderful for Iranian: **Shahrezad,** 1422 Westwood Blvd. (at Ohio), 310/470-3242. Other exotic possibilities include the more expensive dinner-only Moroccan **Koutoubia,** 2116 Westwood Blvd., 310/475-0729.

Fancier Fare

The pursuit of fancier fare in and around Westwood takes foodies on an international neighborhood journey, certainly appropriate given UCLA's worldly stature. The Italian **La Bruschetta,** 1621 Westwood Blvd. (at Massachusetts), 310/477-1052, was named after bread—Italian bread rubbed with garlic and olive oil and then grilled. This terrific neighborhood restaurant serves imaginative, reasonably priced pastas and exquisite seafood. It's open weekdays for lunch, Mon.–Sat. for dinner.

The Nuevo Latino **Mojo** at the W Hotel, 930 Hilgard Ave., 310/208-8765, is a complete turnaround from the stuffy Dynasty restaurant that once occupied this space. Things have lightened up all the way around now that local chef David Slatkin has taken over the space and turned it into a lively, younger scene. Sidle up to one of two bars—one drenched in red light, one in blue—and order a Cuban mojito (white rum, fresh mint, and lime mixed with sugar and crushed ice) or a Cuba libre. Signature dishes include beer-roasted clams, conch croquettes, and *ropa vieja* duck tamale. Reservations advisable.

TOM MYERS PHOTOGRAPHY

THE LOS ANGELES COAST

Beverly Hills may have the swank shopping districts and Brentwood the Getty Center, but coastal Los Angeles—the rest of L.A.'s Westside—has the sand. In some ways the only thing that connects the diverse communities of coastal L.A. is the beach, miles and miles of dazzling white sand, one of the most enduring symbols of the Southern California good life.

Santa Monica is L.A.'s beach city extraordinaire, where everyone else on the Westside comes to play. Just north is the strung-out stretch of beach known as Malibu, where celebrities and artsy eccentrics live both on the beach and in the sylvan enclaves of Topanga Canyon. Immediately south of Santa Monica is Venice,

home to aging bohemians, young hipsters, and street performers. Less colorful but quieter West L.A. is a middle-class suburb packed with small single-family homes and condominiums. On L.A.'s sociopolitical map the coastal Westside also includes Marina del Rey, Playa del Rey, the South Bay's stylish Palos Verdes Peninsula, and the very western working-port cities of Long Beach and San Pedro. A short boat ride west leads to fabled Santa Catalina Island and the tiny tourist town of Avalon. Also visible offshore on a clear day, seeming to bob in the blue Pacific Ocean like massive pieces of driftwood, are the lonely, lovely islands of Channel Islands National Park.

SANTA MONICA AND VICINITY

Santa Monica is the quintessential L.A. beach town, a distinction held since the early 1900s when the original Looff "pleasure pier" was the bayside beacon for long days of Southern California–style fun in the sun. But unlike other popular L.A. tourist destinations, Santa Monica is much more than

just a pretty face and a good time on the weekends—despite its place in L.A. literature as the barely disguised 1930s "Bay City" in Raymond Chandler's *Farewell My Lovely*. These days the city is considered politically "progressive," a rarity in Southern California. That tendency has

THE LOS ANGELES COAST

10
5
5
405
1

5

710

110
WESTERN AVE.

Long Beach
QUEEN MARY

AQUARIUM OF THE PACIFIC

Long Beach Harbor

Los Angeles Harbor

110

SANTA MONICA BLVD.
SEPULVEDA BLVD.
WILSHIRE
Beverly Hills
Century City
MUSEUM OF JURASSIC TECHNOLOGY
Culver City
SUNSET BLVD.

Torrance

PORTS O' CALL VILLAGE
San Pedro

Long Point

405
101

SKIRBALL CULTURAL CENTER
GETTY CENTER
Westwood
Brentwood
Pacific Palisades
Santa Monica
PALISADES PARK

Topanga
Topanga State Park

Mountains

27

J. PAUL GETTY MUSEUM

MALIBU CANYON RD.
TOPANGA CANYON BLVD.

1

Malibu

MULHOLLAND HWY.

Malibu Creek State Park

Santa

Monica

PACIFIC COAST HWY.

101

Leo Carrillo State Beach

Point Dume State Beach

Marina Del Rey
Venice
L.A. INTERNATIONAL AIRPORT
El Segundo

Santa

Monica

Bay

Manhattan Beach
Hermosa Beach
Redondo Beach

MANHATTAN BEACH BLVD.
TORRANCE BLVD.

405
1
1

Palos Verdes Estates
PALOS VERDES DR. N.
PALOS VERDES DR. S.
PALOS VERDES DR. W.
Point Vicente

PACIFIC

OCEAN

8 mi
8 km
0
0

PASADENA AND VICINITY
DOWNTOWN AND AROUND
HOLLYWOOD AND VICINITY
BEVERLY HILLS AND VICINITY
THE L.A. COAST

© AVALON TRAVEL PUBLISHING, INC.

translated into rent control—recently abolished, after significant local damage in the Northridge earthquake—and a trend toward liberal politicians that's still going strong. By Southern California standards the community is also atypical socially—movie stars and the just plain wealthy blended with a large expatriate British population, senior citizens, middle-class and low-income families, and poverty-stricken activists, artists, and street people. As odd as it seems in these days of escalating public intolerance, most everyone here gets along most of the time.

Most of Santa Monica's initial attractions are front and center, along or near the edge of Santa Monica Bay—the bay implied in the title of that insipid yet notoriously popular TV show *Baywatch,* which has since moved on to Hawaii. The city's own strand of sand is Santa Monica State Beach. On weekends and in summer an equal draw is the associated Santa Monica Pier—now including a 1922 carousel and a carnival of fun rides. But Santa Monica offers much, much more, including the nearby pleasures of Malibu, Venice, the Santa Monica Mountains National Recreation Area, and Will Rogers State Historic Park, wacky and world-class art galleries, imaginative shopping, and an unusual range of good accommodations and great restaurants—in every price category. Beach town or no, Santa Monica has it all.

For current information about "Bay City," contact: **Santa Monica Visitor Center,** 1400 Ocean Ave., Santa Monica, CA 90401, 310/393-7593, www.santamonica.com, which is in Palisades Park and open for drop-in assistance daily 10 A.M.–4 P.M. (until 5 P.M. in summer). Watch L.A.-area newspapers for Santa Monica special events, major ones scheduled on weekends and/or summer evenings, or call Santa Monica's 24-hour "Funshine Line," 310/393-7593.

AT THE BEACH

Chances are good that you'll recognize **Palisades Park,** even if you've never been there. Most people have seen it hundreds of times on TV and in the movies—the classic leisurely-L.A.-at-the-beach setting, where lovers stroll at sunset against a backdrop of swaying palms and rustling eucalyptus, and everybody's grandparents walk the poodle or gather on park benches to gossip and play friendly games of chess. This popular film location, a narrow 14-block-long strip of lawn, benches, and trees perched atop steep, eroding bluffs overlooking the Santa Monica Pier, the beach, and the Pacific Ocean, is often visitors' first stop, given the convenient location of the Santa Monica Visitor Center here. At the Senior Recreation Center, nearby at 1450 Ocean Ave., 310/458-8644, is Santa Monica's own **Camera Obscura,** a tourist attraction more popular in the 18th- and 19th-century United States than today. Perhaps the optical "illusion" created by a camera obscura—rendering reality so clearly—is simply too real in these days of virtual reality. (Ask for the key and see for yourself. Small fee.) An oddity that dates to Leonardo da Vinci's notebooks and 11th-century Arab scholarship, the Camera Obscura is composed of prisms, lenses, and mirrors installed in a darkened chamber that allows light in through an opening no larger than a pinhole. The camera then projects a reversed (upside-down) image of the outside world (in this case, a swath of the coastline) onto a white circular disk along the chamber's opposite wall.

Once reality has been virtually established, head for the beach. The good news is, the wide strand of dazzling white sand at **Santa Monica State Beach** is one of the busiest beaches around in summer—which is bad news if you're looking for privacy. It's also bad news if the ocean is temporarily off-limits because of pollution, an ongoing storm-drain and urban-waste disposal problem generated throughout L.A. and an issue that raises the ire of residents around Santa Monica Bay. (For the possibility of wide open spaces at the beach, head north beyond Malibu or south to the world-famous weirdness of Venice Beach, where most of the action is along the Boardwalk. For general beach information and a bay pollution update, see the special topic Life's a Beach.) A day at the beach includes the usual seeing-and-being-seen scene, sometimes a rousing round of beach volleyball, and performance artists—California clowns. Not to mention those overgrown lifeguard chairs-cum-musical instruments—let's call them "wind" instruments—installed as public art projects between the pier and Pico Boulevard. On a breezy day the aluminum pipes atop artist Douglas Hollis's 18-foot-tall *Singing Beach Chairs* catch the wind and make odd tunes.

LIFE'S A BEACH

Along with the cult of celebrity, palm trees, and fancy freeways lined with bright shiny cars, the beach is among L.A.'s most universal symbols. The beach—as in The Beach, the youthful social creation of 1950s Los Angeles—is all about sun-bleached attitude, arcane sports, superficial sexuality, and salt-water-scented steel guitar. And The Beach lives on today, with each youthful summer's new toast-brown crop happily packed into the stucco sameness of beachfront sardine cans. Pale imitations turn up in places such as Florida and Australia, but Los Angeles invented The Beach.

And so the slang phrase "Life's a Beach" takes on genuine meaning in Los Angeles County, where the sunny sands of L.A. lore now suffer a relentless assault of urban ills, all related to the southstate's relentless population growth. Too much traffic and too little parking. Garbage. Graffiti. Alcohol- and gang-related violence. Water pollution. Still a localized problem, ocean water pollution levels are generally decreasing because of improved sewage treatment facilities and greater citizen awareness about the effects of dumping toxic substances into sewers and storm drains. Yet if pollution is disappearing, in some places so is the sand—in a natural southward drift exacerbated by the construction of breakwaters and harbors and, inland, by damming the rivers and streams—and associated sediment flow—that would otherwise replenish the sand supply. These days, maintaining the bay's wide white beaches is additional engineering work.

Fun in the Sun

Santa Monica Bay, the shallow white sand-fringed coastal indentation harboring most of L.A. County's beaches, was once one of the world's richest fishing areas. Those days are long gone, after a half-century's relentless flow of industrial chemicals and other toxic wastes from land to sea. But the bay is slowly getting cleaner—clean enough that, in the 1990s, even porpoises returned. According to L.A.'s **Heal the Bay,** to swim safely avoid obvious pollution "problem areas" (usually posted as no-swim areas), steer clear of all storm drains (most of which are *not* signed or otherwise identified, so heads up), and don't swim for at least three days after a rainstorm. For the latest information on the environmental health of Santa Monica Bay's beaches, contact: Heal the Bay, 2701 Ocean Park Blvd., Ste.

150, Santa Monica, CA 90405, 310/581-4188, fax 310/581-4195, www.healthebay.org. A nonprofit coalition working to achieve fishable, swimmable, and surfable coastal waters—with pollution levels within standards set by the federal Clean Water Act—Heal the Bay publishes an **Annual Beach Report Card** for L.A. County's beaches, also available on the website, complete with maps and charts of both dry (summer) and wet weather pollution measurements. To support its work, Heal the Bay sponsors occasional fundraisers and community events and also sells T-shirts, sweatshirts, and other items. Go ahead and buy one. It's a very good cause.

But if alcohol—even beer or wine—is a central cause in your life, forget about enjoying it at the beach. It is illegal to drink alcohol on public beaches (and at city and county parks), a zero-tolerance policy that can get you booted off the beach and cost you $50 to boot if you're cited. The get-tough beach booze policy is in response to astronomical increases in alcohol-related assaults, drownings, and post-beach car wrecks. (And what lifeguards say is law at the beach. Unless you want to leave the beach earlier than planned, think twice before defying them.)

You can sunbathe, though. And swim, fairly safely where lifeguards are on duty. And surf, bodysurf, and boogie-board. And play very competitive beach volleyball. And picnic. Particularly north of Malibu and near the Palos Verdes Peninsula you can tidepool. Pier and surf fishing are permitted at most piers and many public beaches. Catches include spotfin and yellowfin croakers, corbina, and barred and walleyed perch. And you can run with the grunion, which come ashore to spawn on certain nights in March, June, July, and August. When the annual grunion runs are announced in local media, hundreds of people suddenly arrive after dark, flashlights in hand, ready to gather the slippery silver fish by hand—or try to. (For more on the annual grunion run, see the special topic Grunion Run Free, So Why Can't We? in the Orange County chapter.) Or you can watch sunsets, often spectacularly colorful given L.A.'s polluted air.

Deep-sea fishing expeditions—in search of barracuda, kelp bass, bonito, halibut, mackerel, rockfish, and sheepshead—and winter whale-watching excursions depart from Paradise Cove, Santa Monica, Marina del Rey, Redondo Beach, San Pedro, Long Beach and other spots along the coast. Contact local visitor bureaus and chambers of commerce for excursion boat suggestions.

Practical Considerations
Beach curfews are fairly standard, with beaches usually closed to the public at midnight–6 A.M.; some parking lots also close at midnight, though others close at sunset. No parking is allowed on most stretches of Pacific Coast Hwy. (PCH) 10 P.M.–6 A.M.; PCH parking is free, where you can find it. For public parking lots, available at many beaches, weekday rates range from $2 to $7 per day (rates usually higher on weekends). *Pay close attention to signs regarding parking restrictions* to avoid the unhappy experience of returning from a blissful day at the beach only to find that your car has been locked up for the night or, worse yet, towed and impounded. It'll be mighty expensive to get it out of car jail.

For general beach information, stop by or call the **Los Angeles County Department of Beaches and Harbors Visitor Information Center,** 4701 Admiralty Way in Marina del Rey, 310/305-9545 or 310/305-9546, fax 310/822-0119, http://beaches.co.la.ca.us. For questions about specific beaches, call **L.A. County Lifeguard Headquarters** at 310/577-5700. (Be patient if you're put on hold; rescues and other beach emergencies take precedence. And these folks do get busy, particularly in summer and on balmy weekends.) For general beach weather and tides (recorded), call 310/457-9701. For a beach-by-beach surf report, updated three times daily by L.A. County lifeguards (this is a revenue-generating service), call 900/844-9283. Make reservations for state park and beach campgrounds along the L.A. County coast, mentioned elsewhere in this chapter, through ReserveAmerica at toll-free 800/446-7275.

Santa Monica Pier and Pacific Park

Santa Monica's mild-mannered municipal pier and pleasure pier survived the usual ups and downs of tourist-town life largely unscathed until the 1970s, when civic warfare raged over the fate of the dilapidated piers, then slated for demolition by the Santa Monica City Council. The slow work of rebuilding the past began—an effort slowed still further by 1983's disastrous storms, which dismembered major sections of the pier. Work on the municipal pier was completed in 1990, including restoration of the two-story **Hippodrome** (with its 1922 Looff carousel, featured in *The Sting* and other films), the original arcades, and the old bumper cars. Much of the rest of the pier is lined with restaurants, fast fooderies, and curio shops. Fishing, once a favorite recreational activity at the pier, is no longer recommended because of bay pollution. Special events, including weekend **music concerts,** annual **Cirque du Soleil** performances, and multiple new amusements, now attract the crowds.

At the foot of the rebuilt and expanded pier complex is the new **children's playground** designed by Moore, Rubell, and Yudell, featuring an assortment of kiddie-style carnival rides and a huge dragon's head carved from river-washed granite that "snorts" a soothing, safe mist (water). Santa Monica's pier extension is Pacific Park, 310/260-8744, www.pacpark.com. Major attractions include an ocean-view roller coaster—the

five-story-tall **Santa Monica West Coaster**—and California's only giant ferris wheel, the **Pacific Wheel.** In addition to tamer rides for the kids, a thrill for adults is the **Sig Alert** bumper-car adventure. Other new pier attractions include the **UCLA Ocean Discovery Center,** 310/393-6149, an interactive aquarium-style education center with tidepool and "under the pier" marine life exhibits.

Admission to both the municipal pier and Pacific Park is free, but there is a charge for various attractions. Prices for most of the new Pacific Park amusement rides are in the $1–3 range, for example. The amusement park is open daily 10 A.M.–10 P.M. in summer, with an abbreviated schedule in winter.

MUSEUMS, ARTS, ARTSY SHOPS

Extremely hip Santa Monica claims its share of attractions from yesteryear, including the **Angel's Attic** museum of antique dollhouse miniatures, toys, trains, and dolls housed in a beautifully restored 19th-century Victorian at 516 Colorado Ave., 310/394-8331, open Thurs.–Sun. 12:30–4:30 P.M. Admission is $6.50 adults, $4 seniors, and $3.50 children under age 12. With reservations, you can enjoy tea, lemonade, and cookies on the veranda (for an additional $7.50 per person). The **California Heritage Museum,** 2612 Main St., 310/392-8537, open Wed.–Sun.

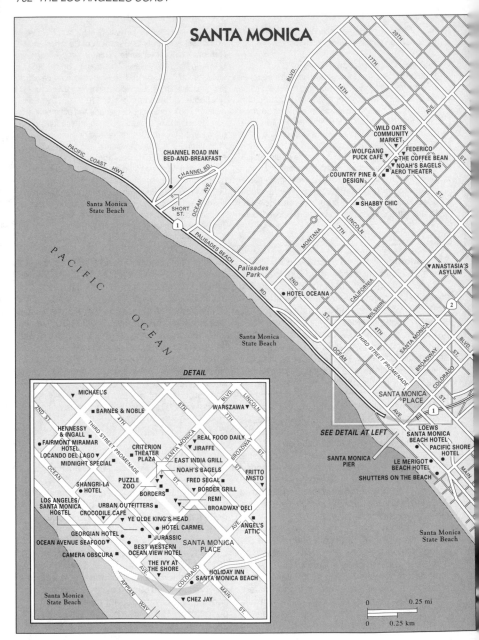

SANTA MONICA

PACIFIC COAST HWY

CHANNEL ROAD INN
BED-AND-BREAKFAST

CHANNEL RD.

Santa Monica
State Beach

SHORT
ST.

OCEAN AVE.

PALISADES BEACH

PALISADES BEACH RD.

Palisades
Park

P A C I F I C

O C E A N

Santa Monica
State Beach

WILD OATS
COMMUNITY
MARKET

WOLFGANG
PUCK CAFÉ

COUNTRY PINE &
DESIGN

FEDERICO
THE COFFEE BEAN
NOAH'S BAGELS
AERO THEATER

SHABBY CHIC

MONTANA

LINCOLN

7TH

2ND

CALIFORNIA

ANASTASIA'S
ASYLUM

HOTEL OCEANA

WILSHIRE

4TH

SANTA MONICA

BROADWAY

COLORADO

OCEAN

THIRD STREET PROMENADE

Santa Monica
State Beach

SANTA MONICA
PLACE

SEE DETAIL AT LEFT

LOEWS
SANTA MONICA
BEACH HOTEL

SANTA MONICA
PIER

LE MERIGOT
BEACH HOTEL

SHUTTERS ON THE BEACH

PACIFIC SHORE
HOTEL

MAIN

Santa Monica
State Beach

DETAIL

MICHAEL'S

BARNES & NOBLE

WARSZAWA

2ND ST.

THIRD STREET PROMENADE

4TH

6TH

LINCOLN

7TH

HENNESSY
& INGALL

FAIRMONT MIRAMAR
HOTEL

LOCANDO DEL LAGO

MIDNIGHT SPECIAL

CRITERION
THEATER
PLAZA

SANTA MONICA

REAL FOOD DAILY

JIRAFFE

EAST INDIA GRILL

NOAH'S BAGELS

FRED SEGAL

BROADWAY

FRITTO
MISTO

OCEAN

SHANGRI-LA
HOTEL

PUZZLE
ZOO

BORDERS

BORDER GRILL

REMI

BROADWAY DELI

LOS ANGELES/
SANTA MONICA
HOSTEL

URBAN OUTFITTERS

CROCODILE CAFÉ

YE OLDE KING'S HEAD

GEORGIAN HOTEL

HOTEL CARMEL

ANGEL'S
ATTIC

AVE.

OCEAN AVENUE SEAFOOD

CAMERA OBSCURA

JURASSIC

BEST WESTERN
OCEAN VIEW HOTEL

SANTA MONICA
PLACE

THE IVY AT
THE SHORE

COLORADO

HOLIDAY INN
SANTA MONICA BEACH

Santa Monica
State Beach

APPIAN WAY

MAIN ST.

CHEZ JAY

0   0.25 mi

0   0.25 km

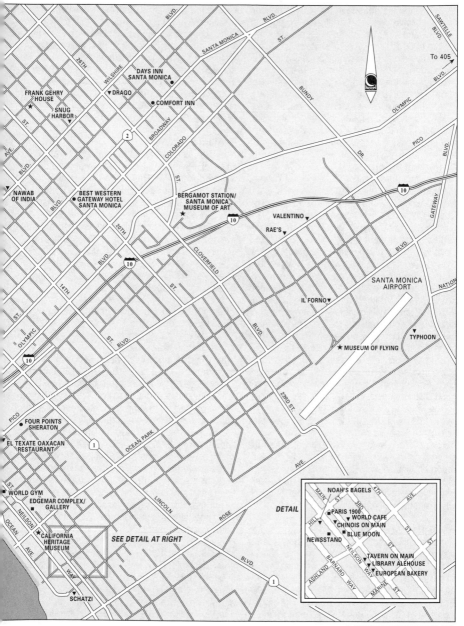

11 A.M.–4 P.M., is housed in an 1894 American colonial revival mansion designed by Sumner P. Hunt and later moved to the unlikely intersection of Ocean Park Ave. and Main. The home once belonged to Roy Jones, son of city founder John Jones. The 1st floor has been restored and furnished in typical Santa Monica style of three eras: the 1890s, the 1910s, and the 1920s. The 2nd floor serves as a gallery for historical exhibits and shows by contemporary local artists. The city's archives are also housed here. General admission is $3, students and seniors $2.

Museum of Flying

Airplane fans and fanatics will enjoy this colorful museum, starring the *New Orleans,* the first plane to fly around the world—one of two open-cockpit Douglas World Cruisers that made the trip in 1924. Douglas Aircraft Company planes are well represented throughout, in fact, which is only fitting since the museum sits on the site of the original Douglas Aircraft Company, precursor to McDonnell Douglas. Almost all planes here have been meticulously restored and are still flight-ready; video kiosks on the 1st floor, where most planes are displayed, show most of the planes in action. More history of flight awaits on the 2nd floor, largely dedicated to Donald Douglas memorabilia. The museum's theater, film and video archives, and the Donald Douglas library are on the 3rd floor. The museum also boasts a great little book and gift shop. For lunch and dinner, try the adjacent, very good **DC3 Restaurant,** 310/399-2323.

The Museum of Flying is at home in a hangar at 2772 Donald Douglas Loop N, on the north side of the Santa Monica Airport, one block south of Ocean Park Blvd. via 28th Street. The museum is open Wed.–Sun. 10 A.M.–5 P.M. At last report admission was $7 adults, $5 seniors and students with ID, and $3 for children ages 3–17. For more information, call 310/392-8822 or check www.museumofflying.com.

Santa Monica Museum of Art

Santa Monica cool extends to its arts scene, which succeeds in being as cutting edge—or just "edge," as they say in these parts—as any in Los Angeles. To start your personal search for edge art, try the Santa Monica Art Museum, 310/586-6488, previously at home in the Edgemar complex along Main St. and in new digs among various local edge galleries at Bergamot Station, 2525 Michigan Ave., Bldg. G-1. Call for information on current shows and events. At last report the museum was open Tues.–Sat. 11 A.M.–6 P.M. and for Friday night "salons," closed Sun. and Mon. and also Thanksgiving, Christmas, and New Year's Day. But call to verify hours, as well as current exhibit information, because the schedule is somewhat fluid. Admission is by suggested donation—$3 for most folks, $1 for artists.

Bergamot Station

Near the freeway and the intersection of 26th St. and Olympic Blvd., Bergamot Station—named for the old Red Car trolley station that stood here until the 1950s—at 2525 Michigan Ave., Bldg. G-2, 310/829-5854, is the city's latest cutting-edge arts locale. This contemporary but still fairly low-rent conglomeration of more than two dozen fine-arts galleries features almost six acres of "arts space." Bergamot Station is typically open Wed.–Sun. 11 A.M.–6 P.M. and Fri. 11 A.M.–10 P.M., but various galleries may schedule events at other times.

For a more comprehensive listing of local galleries, inquire at the visitors center—and pick up a current copy of the *L.A. Weekly.*

Third Street Promenade

When you're done with the public parade on and around the pier, try this one. Santa Monica's Third Street Promenade has become one of L.A.'s hottest "destination streets," an easygoing shopping and entertainment district just blocks from the beach. A pedestrian-only adventure, 3rd St. between Wilshire and Broadway is an intriguing mix of old and new Santa Monica, of kitsch and chic and chain stores, all decked out with palm trees, topiary sculpture, pushcart vendors, and street entertainers. Beyond the boutiques and funky stores here, diversions and entertainment along these three blocks include great bookstores, galleries, multiplex movie theaters, coffeehouses, and good restaurants.

Start with the bookstores. Long-running **Midnight Special,** 1318 3rd St. (between Arizona and Santa Monica), 310/393-2923, specializes in books and magazines and literature, politics, and poetry (regular readings scheduled). Equally revered **Hennessy & Ingall,** 1254 3rd (just north of Arizona), 310/458-9074, is *the* stop for

The Third St. Promenade is a mix of longtime local businesses and eclectic shops.

books and publications on architecture, art, and design. The chains are here, too. The neighborhood boasts a **Barnes & Noble,** 1201 3rd (at Wilshire), 310/260-9110, and a **Borders** bookshop, music store, and café at 1415 3rd (between Santa Monica and Broadway), 310/393-9290.

Equally fun, though, are the eccentricities of some of the truly eccentric shops—assuming they haven't been displaced by the chain-sponsored commerce rapidly increasing here. Always entertaining: the **Urban Outfitters** warehouse at 1440 3rd, 310/394-1404, stark in its ersatz post-Apocalypse decor and specializing in consumer goods for nonconsumers and **Jurassic**'s museum-grade fossils at 131 Broadway (at 2nd). One of the most intriguing toy stores around is **Puzzle Zoo,** 1413 3rd, 310/393-9201, where you might find the limited edition Goddess of the Sun Barbie and the Kasparov electronic chess partner.

Best for Third Street Promenade parking, by the way, are the various public lots along 4th,

reasonably inexpensive. But if you're just here for a quick stroll, the parking lot at Santa Monica Place is free for a stay under three hours (small flat fee in the evening).

Montana Avenue

Long considered one of Santa Monica's most stylish shopping streets, Montana Avenue between Lincoln Blvd. and 17th St. (near Brentwood north of Wilshire) is *very* Westside, an expensive blend of chic shops and nosh stops. **Federico,** 1522 Montana, 310/458-4134, is a long-running local favorite, selling Native American, Mexican, and silver jewelry. **Country Pine & Design,** 1318 Montana, 310/451-0317, is famous for its unique items for the home. **Shabby Chic,** 930 Montana, 310/453-0985, is a popular local furnishings shop. Stop at **The Coffee Bean** at 1426 Montana, 310/453-2093, for delicious coffee and baked goods. Or try the casual **Wolfgang Puck Café** at 1323 Montana Ave. (at 14th), 310/393-0290. And while you're in the neighborhood, see what's playing at the independent **Aero** theater, 1328 Montana, 310/395-4990, which starred in the movie *Get Shorty.*

Strolling Main Street

A stroll along Main always affords an intriguing introduction to the real Santa Monica and its unique cultural combination of chi-chi and cheap. Though Main stretches south from Pico Blvd. on the north to Rose Ave. in Venice Beach, particularly popular for shopping and dining is the area between Ocean Park and Rose, where the classic old-brick buildings attract both the trendy and the traditional. You'll know you've gone too far, and drifted south into eccentric Venice, once you see sculptor Jonathan Borofsky's clownish three-story-tall "ballerino" looming above Main like the crazed stage creation of some mad puppeteer—a huge ballerina's body, en pointe, crowned by a sad clown face complete with five-o'clock shadow.

To really find out what's going on, try **Newsstand,** 2726 Main St., 310/396-7722, boasting L.A.'s best selection of magazines and newspapers. Another hit is **Blue Moon,** 2717 Main, 310/450-7075, something of a French-styled *parfumerie* selling sunglasses on the side. **Paris 1900,** 2703 Main St., 310/396-0405, recycles the glad rags of the rich circa 1900–1930. Just down the way is cybersoul sister to Almost Paradise in Long Beach and Cyber Java in nearby Venice Beach, Santa Monica's own worldly **World Cafe,** 2820 Main, 310/392-1661 (www. worldcafela.com), where neon-lit hieroglyphics, Captain Nemo dining-room decor, and Mexican patio umbrellas set the stage for sophisticated drinks, snacks, and cyberchat.

Until recently home to the Santa Monica Museum of Art, the **Edgemar** complex along the 2400 block of Main was designed by Santa Monica architect Frank O. Gehry and built on the site of the old Edgemar Egg Company. Poke around here to find more galleries and shops and eateries.

VENICE: WESTSIDE BOHEMIA

Abbott Kinney had a dream. That dream became a vision, a utopian plan, then an obsession. What was Abbott Kinney's dream? He built an exotic

swimmers at Venice Beach

seaside resort here, patterned after the great Italian city (complete with canals), and he expected the grandeur of his creation to spark an early 20th-century American cultural renaissance and create an international image of Los Angeles as sophisticated Mediterranean city. Kinney's plans never quite succeeded. But in recent decades his vision has been revisited, as Venice has become one of L.A.'s avant-garde outposts of the arts and architecture. Yet, as in Kinney's day, the hedonistic eccentricities of Venice Beach and along its two-mile Ocean Front Walk are still the community's main attractions.

For some local events and referral information, call the **Venice Area Chamber of Commerce** at 310/396-7016. For current visitor information, call up Venice on the Internet at www.venice. net/chamber, or contact the L.A. visitor bureau at 213/689-8822, www.lacvb.com.

Abbott Kinney's Dream

After making his millions selling Sweet Caporal cigarettes, Abbott Kinney came to California to build his personal Venice. In 1904 Kinney bought 160 acres of marshland just south of Santa Monica for his "Venice of America" seaside resort. He drained the marsh, re-creating it as a canal-laced landscape, and then hired architect Norman F. Marsh to design Venice, patterned after its namesake Italian city. The first phase of Kinney's dream included an elaborate Italianate business district, its first first-class hotel—the St. Mark Hotel, patterned after St. Mark's Cathedral in Venice, Italy—and a grand 2,500-seat public auditorium out on the new pier. During the city's three-day opening gala, a veritable circus of enthusiasms, Sarah Bernhardt performed *Camille* during a black-tie performance out on the pier, backed by the Chicago Symphony Orchestra.

Yet Abbott Kinney soon concluded that most people were more interested in the pleasures of sun and surf than in high culture, and in 1907 he built a grand casino, soon followed by the world's largest amusement park. Abbott Kinney's Venice became a metaphor for what L.A. would become—a unique combination of popular and classical cultures. For all its successes, large and small, Abbott Kinney's dream seemed to depend on him, personally, for its continuing existence. After he died in 1920, Venice hit the skids—largely because of the demise of L.A.'s

DOING THE BEACH BY BIKE

What better way to see the beach, and the Los Angeles beach scene, than by bike? The **South Bay Bicycle Trail,** accessible at any point along the route, runs south from the white sand of Will Rogers State Beach along local beaches to Torrance, with a strategic inland detour only to bypass the harbor at Marina del Rey. Highlights along the way include the dazzling Santa Monica beach scene, wild and wacky Venice Beach, complete with in-line skaters run amok and muscle-bound Muscle Beach, and the tony trendiness of Marina del Rey's boating brigade. And the swaying palms, sun, sand, and fresh ocean air. Oh sure, a few ecstasy-assassinating intrusions await along the way, especially toward the South Bay, where the L.A. Department of Water and Power's power plant smokestacks and incessant LAX jet traffic detract from an otherwise postcard-perfect setting. But you can pull over to rest your angst at municipal piers and other key attractions, including Marina del Rey's boat harbor and the shop-happy King Harbor at the north end of Redondo Beach.

Since most people in greater Los Angeles don't make it to the beach until close to noon, early morning is a great time for a bike ride. (This being the beach side of a very urban area, avoid being on the bike path after dark.) The paved bike path runs a total distance of approximately 20 miles; even a biking beginner can make the one-way trip in two hours or less. Start early and stop for breakfast before heading back. Bike rental establishments are available all along the beachfront bike path.

electric trolley system and the increasing popularity of the automobile. (Venice's location, far from a major thoroughfare, put the resort at a competitive disadvantage for the tourist trade.) Then small oil wells and derricks dotted the landscape throughout Venice, petroleum-based goo blackened the canals and beaches, and the remaining tourists left town. Kinney's dream became a nightmare. Soon plagued by storms, fires, and political scandals, Venice residents voted in the 1920s to annex themselves to the city of Los Angeles. Most of the city's increasingly murky canals were filled in because of public health concerns. Abbott Kinney's dream died.

Of Arts and Eccentricities

In a style Abbott Kinney could never have imagined, the dream of Venice as cultural mecca did revive. Drawn to the community's relatively low rents and unique, vaguely European style—including the arched bridges over the canals—in the 1950s beatniks and other bohemians arrived to establish L.A.'s latest avant-garde enclave, quickly followed in the 1960s by Summer of Love devotees and in the 1970s by working artists. Many well-known L.A. artists have studios in Venice, lured by the (once) affordable rents, eccentric ambience, and proximity to the beach. In the 1980s Venice—certain parts of Venice— became a chi-chi address for cool-conscious Westsiders. The latter turn of events has spawned some interesting architectural styles as well. Though beset in recent years by seemingly uncontrollable gang violence and other urban ills, Venice still proudly parades its eccentricities. A community where million-dollar homes stand next to run-down shanties, Venice has even cleaned up its canals.

Ocean Front Walk and Venice Beach

Abbott Kinney's gaudy amusement park, the Coney Island of the West for two decades, is long gone. But its spirit lives on. Unless the kids have led a truly sheltered suburban life—or perhaps especially if they have—they'll probably enjoy the human zoo that Venice's Ocean Front Walk, known locally as the Venice Boardwalk, has exhibited in recent years. Watch 'em watch Rastafarians and bikini-clad babes on in-line skates blithely dodge bicyclists, baby strollers, and bug-eyed tourists. Robert Gruenberg, the Venice Boardwalk's famous chainsaw juggler, hung up his gas-powered Sears Craftsman in 1994, alas. But there's plenty more circus available here—roller-skating swamis, fire-eaters, palmists, and tarot card readers along with dancers, singers, and comedians. Sidewalk merchants sell T-shirts, sunglasses, hats, clothing, jewelry, crystals, and posters along the Venice Boardwalk, which stretches for two miles along Ocean Front Walk between Ozone Ave. and Washington Street. Venice's oceanfront promenade and pier have been undergoing major renovations—a $5.5 million project scheduled for completion in summer 2000—adding new entertainment areas, lighting, and even pagodas.

Once the kids are satiated with the street performance, nudge them on to Muscle Beach, "the pit" where muscle people get pumped on open-air weightlifting. (This Muscle Beach is no real relation to the original Muscle Beach of Jack LaLanne fame, just south of the Santa Monica Pier; old-timers say it was originally known as Mussel Beach—after those well-muscled bivalves.) Among the endless snack stands, best bet for meat lovers is **Jody Maroni's Sausage Kingdom,** 2011 Ocean Walk, 310/306-1995, famous throughout L.A. for its fabulous all-natural links—from sweet Italian to Yucatán chicken. But if the Boardwalk's crowded sidewalk cafés seem just too crowded, beat a retreat to the **Rose Cafe,** 220 Rose Ave., 310/399-0711, Venice's coolest coffeehouse, bakery, deli, and neighborhood café since almost forever. While in the neighborhood, die-hard shoppers should stop by **DNA Clothing Company,** 411 Rose, 310/399-0341, one of L.A.'s best outlet shopping spots, featuring top-drawer clothing and jeans for women and men at bargain-basement prices.

Then do the beach, which doesn't get nearly the attention—or crowds—as do the Venice Boardwalk or Santa Monica State Beach just north. Venice Beach is a *beautiful* beach, a broad belt of palm-dotted white sand stretching up the coast and down and out into the surf. The huge concrete **Venice Pier** at the foot of Washington Blvd.—still closed at last report, pending reconstruction—was a fairly unromantic contemporary creation that was quite popular with skaters and pier fishers.

Marina del Rey, Playa del Rey, and Playa Vista

Undeveloped coastal wetlands until 1968, when the county of Los Angeles set about the business of draining one of the coast's last remaining wetlands and building the largest man-made small-craft harbor in the world, Marina del Rey is largely boat harbor—and boats, boats, boats. When row after row of life-at-the-beach-themed apartment houses and condominiums were built here in the late 1960s and early '70s it was only natural, given the area's proximity to LAX, that planeloads of stewardesses, stewards, and other unattached airline employees would move in to share the neighborhood with the retirees and yachties—which won Marina del Rey its reputation as preferred port for swinging singles. Redevelopment plans—allowing 22-story high-rise "residential towers," apartment buildings, and hotels while ignoring the need for new parks and other genuine public access—will likely change the character of the neighborhood yet again.

For more information about the area, contact: **Los Angeles County Dept. of Beaches and Harbors,** Visitor Information Center, 4701 Admiralty Way, Marina del Rey, 310/305-9546, www.beaches.co.la.ca.us.

Just south of Marina del Rey and east of the beach, surrounding the intersection of Lincoln and

Ocean Front Walk eats

VIEW FROM THE EDGE:
THE MUSEUM OF JURASSIC TECHNOLOGY

If you bring the kids, prepare for possible whining. Prepare for the fact that they'll think you tricked them. They'll think you offered an afternoon in Jurassic Park (as in *Jurassic Park*—The Ride) when instead, you offered them something equally amazing from "real life"—a view of the world as seen from the edge of science.

The motto of West L.A.'s strange Museum of Jurassic Technology is "nature as metaphor." This particular metaphorical interpretation of the natural world is most intriguing. Half the exhibits are real— or seem to be—and the others are highly unlikely, from the mounted horns, spore-eating ants, and fruit-stone carvings to the superstitions exhibit. An enormous hit in 1996 was the exhibit of "microminiature" creations by Soviet-Armenian violinist Hagop Sandaldjian, including likenesses of Disney's Goofy and Snow White and the Seven Dwarfs, even Pope John Paul II, all mounted on sewing needles and visible only through microscopes. Some of Sandaldjian's works are still on display in the Churchy Marrin Annex, where at last report the main exhibit was **Garden of Eden on Wheels: Selected Collections from Los Angeles Area Mobile Home and Trailer Parks.** On exhibit in the Coolidge Pavilion, opened in September 1999, is **The World is Bound with Secret Knots: The Life and Works of Athanasius Kircher, S.J., 1602–1680.**

In the opinion of Lawrence Weschler, author of *Mr. Wilson's Cabinet of Wonder,* the Jurassic rekindles one's sense of wonder while undermining "the sense of the authoritative" normally extended to museums. But the museum's curator suggests you leave even that preconception at home. Wonder is as wonder does—metaphorically speaking.

The Museum of Jurassic Technology, in a nondescript storefront in Culver City's historic Palms District, on Venice Blvd. four blocks west of Robertson Blvd. (directly across from Bagley), is open Thurs. 2–8 P.M. (sometimes from noon) and Fri.–Sun. noon–6 P.M. (closed major holidays and the first Thurs. in May). Suggested donation is $4 adults, $2.50 children (under age 12 free), students, and seniors. For more information, contact: Museum of Jurassic Technology, 9341 Venice Blvd., Culver City, CA 90232, 310/836-6131, fax 310/287-2267, www.mjt.org.

Jefferson Blvds., is a surviving 1,000-acre section of the once-wildlife-rich **Ballona Wetlands,** owned at one time by billionaire Howard Hughes, who built his famous *Spruce Goose* here. The fate of the Ballona Wetlands—how much should be preserved or restored, how, and where—is an ongoing battle in one of L.A.'s latest development wars. **Playa Vista,** as this new city along the Westchester bluffs will be called, was slated to become the city's latest "Hollywood" if the new **Dreamworks SKG** film studio and other proposed commercial and residential developments proceeded as planned. Progress on the project was delayed when environmentalists protested the destruction of the area's wetlands. Dreamworks subsequently pulled out of the project.

STAYING IN SANTA MONICA AND VICINITY

Santa Monica and other coastal enclaves are typically well-booked and most expensive on weekends, though midweek and seasonal specials are possible. More significant, for true budget travelers and families, is the fact that in addition to the ubiquitous luxury options, Santa Monica and other coastal communities feature a variety of hostels and other inexpensive and midrange motel options.

LOW-RENT SANTA MONICA STAYS

The best bargain around is the 200-bed Hostelling International-American Youth Hostels **Los Angeles/Santa Monica Hostel**, 1436 2nd St. (between Santa Monica Blvd. and Broadway), 310/393-9913, www.hiayh.org or www.hostelweb.com/losangeles. This is a budget traveler's bonanza, even though prices here are a bit higher than in other area hostels. What you get for the difference is an exceptional value, just two blocks from the beach and pier and, in the other direction, one block from the lively Third Street Promenade. The Santa Monica International is at home in a four-story onetime town hall, an aged brick and dark wood building complete with historic common room (once a saloon), full-service travel store, laundry and kitchen, library, TV room, large open-air courtyard, bicycle storage, and lockers. Most of the rooms are dormitory style with two or four beds per room (linen rental, small extra fee), though private rooms are available for couples. Bathrooms are shared. Free airport shuttle service and organized area tours (extra) are also offered. This hostel is understandably popular, so make reservations (by phone, fax, or mail, with credit card confirmation) well in advance. Budget.

Venice, just blocks south of Santa Monica, offers other hostel-style accommodations. Also inquire at the visitor center for lower rent suggestions.

MIDRANGE SANTA MONICA STAYS

As elsewhere, midrange accommodations in Santa Monica comprise a somewhat confusing category. Most of the options listed here offer "moderate" prices throughout the year. Yet during the off-season or in slow years, and/or with the right discount or package deal, some of Santa Monica's "classic" and high-rent offerings can become quite affordable (see other listings below). It often pays to inquire. Many of the following offer student, senior citizen, AAA, and/or other discounts or specials.

Notable near the Beach
A notable deal by Santa Monica standards is the **Hotel Carmel** near the HI-AYH hostel at 201 Broadway (at 2nd St.), 310/451-2469, or toll-free 800/445-8695. This is one of Santa Monica's grande dames, well-preserved and still quite attractive after all these years, with lovely lobby and basic rooms with ceiling fans—a best bet for budget-conscious families bound for the beach. The Hotel Carmel is also a jump away from the Third Street Promenade's premier people-watching and shops, movie theaters, and restaurants. Though this is largely a families-and-couples kind of place, from mid-September through May the Hotel Carmel offers college students (with IDs) a hefty rate discount. Moderate-Premium, with rates $80–155.

Up on a hill three blocks inland from the ocean is the very comfortable 309-room **Four Points Sheraton**, 530 Pico Blvd., 310/399-9344 or toll-free 888/627-8532 for central reservations, www.fourpoints.com, featuring two heated pools, in-room coffeemakers and the usual comforts, even free airport shuttle service. Rates are

---

ACCOMMODATIONS RATINGS

Accommodations in this book are rated by price category, based on double-occupancy, high-season rates. Categories used are:

Budget. . . . . $35 and under
Inexpensive $35-60
Moderate $60-85
Expensive $85-110
Premium $110-150
Luxury . . . . $150 and up

Premium-Luxury ($139–175), sometimes dropping to Expensive in the off-season. For a similar deal close to the beach and pier, try the **Holiday Inn Santa Monica Beach,** 120 Colorado Blvd., 310/451-0676 or toll-free 800/465-4329 for central reservations, www.holidayinn.com, with swimming pool and the usual amenities. Luxury ($159–239).

Other possibilities include the **Best Western Ocean View Hotel,** 1447 Ocean Ave., 310/458-4888, or toll-free 800/452-4888. Premium ($139–259), but often Expensive in the off-season. And the 168-room **Pacific Shore Hotel** near both the beach and Main St. at 1819 Ocean Ave., 310/451-8711 or toll-free 800/622-8711, which features an exercise room, pool, sauna, hot tub, and sundeck. Some rooms have ocean views. Expensive-Luxury ($109–169).

Not near the Beach

Well away from the beach but fairly affordable—particularly in the off-season—and quite comfortable is the **Best Western Gateway Hotel Santa Monica,** 1920 Santa Monica Blvd., 310/829-9100 or toll-free 800/528-1234 (central reservations), www.bestwestern.com, which offers free beach shuttle service, full fitness facilities, and in-room video games among its many amenities. Premium ($109–139). Other possibilities in the same vicinity include the **Comfort Inn,** 2815 Santa Monica Blvd., 310/828-5517 or toll-free 800/228-5150, www.comfortinn.com, where a stay includes free morning newspaper and breakfast and amenities include in-room coffeemakers and refrigerators plus family-size heated pool, and the **Days Inn Santa Monica,** 3007 Santa Monica Blvd., 310/829-6333 or toll-free 800/591-5995, www.daysinn.com. Both are Expensive-Premium ($87–150).

CLASSIC SANTA MONICA STAYS

Santa Monica's 1939 **Shangri-La Hotel,** 1301 Ocean Ave. (at Arizona Ave.), 310/394-2791 or toll-free 800/345-7829, www.shangrila-hotel.com, is a local favorite, an art-deco ocean liner of a building looming large from a corner berth overlooking Palisades Park. Most of the tasteful rooms—successfully restored to their original deco glory, but with color TVs and cable—feature full kitchens and sundecks; most have ocean

views. Luxury ($145–420). Another art-deco gem, the historic eight-story **Georgian Hotel** near the pier at 1415 Ocean Ave., 310/395-9945 or toll-free 800/538-8147, www.georgianhotel.com, was lovingly restored to its 1933 ambience in 1993. Most of the 84 rooms and suites offer ocean views, along with contemporary comforts including coffeemakers, refrigerators, honor bars, and cable TV (free movies); some have microwaves. No air-conditioning, usually unnecessary here. Breakfast is served in the dining room every morning, afternoon tea and cocktails on the veranda. Lunch and dinner are also available. Luxury ($210–475).

Another likely spot to spot the occasional off-duty celebrity is the very cool **Hotel Oceana** a few blocks north of Wilshire at 849 Ocean Ave. (between Montana and Idaho Aves.), 310/393-0486 or toll-free 800/777-0758, www.hoteloceana.com. Tasteful rooms overlook the courtyard pool; others offer ocean views. Basic amenities include kitchens, in-room coffeemakers, microwaves, cable TV (free movies). Luxury ($250–600).

Channel Road Inn Bed-and-Breakfast

A real find for B&B fans, the Channel Road Inn just east of Pacific Coast Highway is just a mile or two north of the Santa Monica Pier and Third Street Promenade. The inn is an inviting shingle-sided 1910 colonial revival period piece moved to this site in the 1960s and transformed into a 14-room inn in the late 1980s. Most rooms and suites offer ocean views, some feature fireplaces, and all have private baths. Just a block from the beach, technically just beyond Santa Monica city limits, the inn also offers a friendly introduction to neighborhood life. Bikes are available if you feel like exploring, or soak up the ambience from the bayview hot tub. A good deal including full breakfast with home-baked muffins. For more information or reservations, contact: Channel Road Inn, 219 W. Channel Rd., 310/459-1920, www.channelroadinn.com. Luxury ($150–325).

MORE HIGH-RENT SANTA MONICA STAYS

Fairmont Miramar Hotel

Santa Monica's classic classy hotel is downtown's historic Miramar, "where Wilshire meets the sea," now a Fairmont, 101 Wilshire Blvd.,

310/576-7777 or toll-free 800/325-3535, www.fairmont.com. Onetime private mansion and Santa Monica playground for Hollywood stars including Humphrey Bogart, Greta Garbo, and Betty Grable, the Miramar still requires an entrance; visitors drive in through impressive wrought-iron gates and circle the huge Moreton Bay fig. Time and a $33 million restoration continue to transform the Miramar. The once-palatial grounds have been subdivided by progress, and the hotel's fabled courtyard bungalows, surrounding the lush jungle, pool, and patio just beyond the bright and spacious lobby, have been replaced with 31 snazzy new ones. Yet the Miramar abides, with a sophisticated international atmosphere both rarified and relaxed. The hotel's historic charms are most apparent in the older brick Palisades wing, overlooking Palisades Park, yet rooms in the more contemporary Ocean Tower come with almost aerial views. Amenities abound, including in-room safes, coffeemakers, and honor bars, color TVs with cable (free movies), countless little luxuries, a wonderful on-site restaurant, and full fitness facilities. Luxury, with rates $249 and up.

Le Merigot Beach Hotel

Santa Monica's newest upscale hotel, just a block from the beach at 1740 Ocean Ave., Le Merigot is a contemporary take on the city's art deco sensibilities, from the potted palms and blond woods in the lobby to the day-at-the-beach pastel colors and artful furnishings in the 175 guest rooms—some with views. Yet the attitude here is European—so L.A.—and extends to the hotel's **Cézanne** restaurant, **Café Promenade,** and **Le Troquet** bar. For more information or reservations, call 310/395-9700 or toll-free 877/637-4468, www.lemerigotbeachhotel.com. Luxury, with rates $279–459.

Loews Santa Monica Beach Hotel

Before Shutters opened its shutters onto the Santa Monica sands, the fairly new Loews Santa Monica Beach Hotel, 1700 Ocean Ave. (between Pico and Colorado), 310/458-6700 or toll-free 800/235-6397 (central reservations), www.loewshotels.com, had the notable distinction of being L.A.'s only beachfront hotel. Though this hotel isn't exactly *on* the beach, it's certainly close

enough. The stunning contemporary lobby, colored in soft tones of seafoam green, peach, and sand and accented by potted palms and bold wrought-iron grillwork and glass, somehow evokes L.A.'s most intriguing Victorian-era architecture, downtown L.A.'s famed Bradbury Building. The same general idea—inspiring skylit enclosures—carries over to the indoor-outdoor pool area overlooking the beach. Many of the hotel's 350 rooms and 35 one- and two-bedroom suites, luxuriantly decked out and featuring the usual amenities, overlook the beach. Other attractions include complete fitness facilities (personal trainers available), the adult-supervised Splash Club for vacationing families, the sophisticated French Provincial **Lavande** restaurant, 310/576-3181, and the casual **Ocean Cafe.** Luxury, with rates $310 and up.

Shutters on the Beach

Definitely on the beach, Shutters on the Beach, 1 Pico Blvd. (just off Ocean Ave.), 310/458-0030 or toll-free 800/334-9000, www.shuttersonthebeach.com, looms over the sand like an overgrown beach house—shutters and all—by design. Shutters, with its 198 rooms and suites right on the beach, was designed in the spirit of Southern California beach homes and resorts of the 1920s and 1930s. Otherwise, everything is cutting-edge contemporary, light, open, and vaguely reminiscent of plein-air watercolors. Rooms are small but attractive—note that some "partial view" rooms barely spy the sea—with the usual luxury amenities, marble bathrooms, and large hot tubs. Sliding shutter doors open onto private patios or balconies, providing the "shutters" of the hotel's name. Other pluses include two good on-site restaurants, the outstanding **One Pico,** 310/587-1717, and the casual café **Pedals,** both the **HandleBar** and an attractive lobby lounge, large pool and patio areas, spa, full fitness facilities—even a rental service for Santa Monica essentials, from bikes, in-line skates, and volleyball nets to swim fins and children's beach toys. Unfortunately for determined ocean swimmers, the hotel's beach sits at the mouth of the Pico-Kenter storm drain, with its attendant bacterial "danger" signs from time to time—so heads up if you actually brave the waters. Luxury, with rates $340 and up.

STAYING IN VENICE AND VICINITY

People's Stays: Venice Hostels

The **Cadillac Hotel**, 401 Ocean Front Walk (at Dudley), 310/399-8876, isn't the Cadillac of hotels. Venice isn't the Cadillac of beach towns, for that matter, and not a totally comfortable area after dark. But if the wild and wacky rush of Southern California humanity is your scene—peoplewatching from sidewalk cafés, dodging the in-line skaters and cheap trinket stalls on the way to the wide, wide expanse of white sand—then the artdeco Cadillac Hotel is one place to park yourself come nightfall. Most of the rooms (30) are private (just the basics), some with private bathrooms. Moderate-Expensive ($69–120). The remainder offer hostel-style dorm accommodations, with four beds to a room and bathrooms down the hall. Inexpensive. Other features: sundeck, sauna, gym, laundry and storage facilities, even a pool table. Free airport shuttle service.

Other nearby hostels run by InterClub include the **Venice Beach Hotel**, 25 Windward Ave., 310/392-3376, and the **Airport Hostel**, 2221 Lincoln Blvd., 310/305-0250, both of which offer dormitory-style and private rooms. Budget to Inexpensive.

Venice Beach House

The Venice Beach House is an L.A. rarity—a bed-and-breakfast. This one is a rarity among rarities, however, since this lovely, early 20th-century home also happens to be a graceful Craftsman bungalow just steps from the beach and a block from the Venice Canals. North of Washington Blvd. and west of Pacific Blvd. on one of Venice's "walk streets" (onetime canals, long since filled in), the Venice Beach House features nine well-appointed period rooms with antiques and wicker. The Pier Suite comes with a sitting room, fireplace, king-size bed, and ocean view; smaller, less expensive garden-view rooms share bathrooms. Expensive-Luxury. For reservations, contact: Venice Beach House, 15 30th Ave., Venice, CA 90291, 310/823-1966.

Other Venice Stays

Quite nice in Venice's motel category is the **Inn at Venice Beach** just two blocks from the beach at 327 Washington Blvd., 310/821-2557, toll-free 800/828-0688, or www.mansioninn.com. Expensive-Premium ($99–149). Fun and funky in Venice, with spacious and attractive rooms, is the **Marina Pacific Hotel and Suites** just a block from the beach and otherwise smack-dab in the middle of everything at 1697 Pacific Ave., 310/452-1111 or toll-free 800/421-8151, www.mphotel.com. Premium-Luxury ($119–169).

Staying in Marina del Rey

Reigning monarch of the South Bay hotel scene is **The Ritz-Carlton, Marina del Rey,** 4375 Admiralty Way, 310/823-1700 or toll-free 800/241-3333, www.ritzcarlton.com, which here serves as scenic backdrop for yachts and yachters. The usual ritzy amenities abound, thick terrycloth robes and every other imaginable comfort, plus full fitness and business facilities. The crisp, classic decor includes French doors in most rooms, opening out onto balconies overlooking the boat harbor. Dining options include the excellent **Terrace Restaurant** and the less formal **Pool Café.** Luxury.

More fun and much more affordable for most people, though, is the **Best Western Jamaica Bay Inn** on Mother's Beach at 4175 Admiralty Way, 310/823-5333 or toll-free 888/823-5333, www.bestwestern-jamaicabay.com, the only place around actually *on* the beach. (Because of harbor pollution, however, ocean swimming here is not advisable.) Rooms are large, with either terraces or balconies, and bathrooms are a bit small. Pleasant beachfront café. Expensive-Luxury ($89–189).

EATING IN SANTA MONICA AND VICINITY

PEOPLE'S EATS

People's Eats: Farmers' Markets
If you time things right, load up on fresh fruits, vegetables, fabulous flowers, and other essentials at the big-deal **Santa Monica Certified Farmers' Market,** held year-round at Arizona Ave. between 2nd and 3rd Sts. on Wed. 9:30 A.M.–2 P.M. (bring quarters for area parking meters) and on Sat. 8:30 A.M.–1 P.M. Also on Sat., there's an open-air Farmers' Market at the intersection of **Pico Blvd. and Cloverfield,** 8 A.M.–1 P.M. On Sun. there's still another, at **Victorian Heritage Square** at Ocean Park Blvd. and Main St., scheduled 9:30 A.M.–1 P.M., the fun here including pony rides and other kid's stuff.

Otherwise, for natural foods, cosmetics, and such, there's always the **Wild Oats Community Market,** 1425 Montana Ave. (at 15th St.), 310/576-4707, a link in the chain that genuine co-ops tend to disdain.

People's Eats near the Pier
A real deal for authentic Mexican is colorful **El Texate Oaxacan Restaurant,** 316 Pico Blvd. (at 4th St.), 310/399-1115, which at first glance looks something like a surfer bar. The treasure here is the wide selection of rich mole sauces, blends of roasted chiles, seeds, nuts, and spices so perfect with chicken (start with the *coloradito,* or "little red"). Entrées include enchiladas, *chiles rellenos, empañadas,* and pizzalike *clayudas* and *memelas.* If you're not in the mood for margaritas or beer, wash everything down with *tejate*—the traditional summer drink created from cornmeal, chocolate, and walnuts. El Texate is open daily 9 A.M.–11:30 P.M. Also always a people's favorite: the colorful **Crocodile Cafe,** 101 Santa Monica Blvd. (at Ocean), 310/394-4783, the onetime site of Santa Monica's dignified old-school French Belle-Vue restaurant. The terribly hip Crocodile is so popular that it's not the best choice if you'll need to be somewhere soon. Otherwise, the fare is usually worth the wait—especially for the money. Some appetizers, such as the chicken tacos, make a meal. Or order the

grilled romaine salad, dressed with yogurt and spicy pecans. Or the Santa Fe or "almost cheeseless" pizzas. And any of the desserts. It's open daily for lunch and dinner (until midnight). Full bar.

Numerous people's possibilities line the Third Street Promenade, an easy stroll from the beach. For an array of dining options, check out the food court at the **Criterion Theater Plaza,** 1315 3rd St., where nothing on any menu is more than $12 (most choices are much less). Among the stars here is **Wolfgang Puck Express,** 310/576-4770, for fast, reasonably priced pastas, pizzas, and salads. This and other fast food-eries here are open daily 11 A.M.–11 P.M.

People's Eats not near the Pier
A best bet for vegetarians, with the kitchen open into the wee hours seven days a week, is **Anastasia's Asylum,** 1028 Wilshire Blvd. (at 11th St.), 310/394-7113, a fun and funky art gallery/coffeehouse/restaurant serving tofu lasagna along with open-poetry nights. For organic vegetarian food, the place is **Real Food Daily,** 514 Santa Monica Blvd., 310/451-7544, fresh and unusually good, from *seitan* fajitas to vegetable sushi and eggless Caesar and Peruvian quinoa salads. Good desserts, too. It's open Mon.–Sat. for lunch and dinner. Exceptional vegetarian fare is available at **Nawab of India,** 1621 Wilshire Blvd. (at 17th St.), 310/829-1106, noted for its home-style Northern Indian lunch buffets (brunch buffet on weekends).

One of the best for all-American breakfast is **Rae's,** 2901 Pico Blvd. (at 29th St.), 310/828-7937, a real-deal 1950s diner where, most weekends, people are only too happy to line up and wait. (No credit cards.) Rae's is open daily for breakfast, lunch, and dinner. Or head to breakfast-anytime **Snug Harbor,** 2323 Wilshire Blvd. (between 23rd and 24th Sts.), 310/828-2991, where diner standards, including the dinner salad, are more sophisticated than you'd expect. Omelettes star at breakfast—available anytime—along with fresh-squeezed orange and grapefruit juices. Snug Harbor is open for breakfast, lunch, and dinner on weekdays, for breakfast and lunch only on weekends.

Given the endless possibilities along Main, one of the better choices is among the least expensive—attractive **Tavern on Main,** 2907 Main St. (at Ashland Ave.), 310/392-2772, serving contemporary ($5) takes on all-American standards in nouveau 1930s style. If you've been frugal while wandering Main, blow a few bucks at local sweets and dessert shops, including the nearby chocoholic shrine **European Bakery,** 2915 Main, 310/581-3525, famous for creating wonderful brownie biscotti, luscious cakes, and almost everything else in sight from Valrhona chocolate. For some after-dinner cheer, the **Library Alehouse,** 2911 Main, 310/314-4855, is a veritable library of Pacific Northwest microbrews on tap, where the various "taster specials" allow you to sample five three-ounce samples. (You can also "read" on the patio.) Some might prefer splurging on a Salty Dog—grapefruit juice and vodka served margarita style in a salt-rimmed glass. The place to get 'em is the **Galley,** 2442 Main, 310/452-1934, Santa Monica's oldest surviving dark bar and surf and turf restaurant.

A bit fancy for cheap-eats freaks but quite affordable for the genre is Italian **Il Forno,** 2901 Ocean Park Blvd. (between 29th and 30th Sts.), 310/450-1241, a best bet for antipasti, pastas, and pizza. It's noisy, friendly, reliable, and open weekdays only for lunch, Mon.–Sat. for dinner.

And there's a fabulous new Italian in town— **Fritto Misto,** 601 Colorado Ave. (at 6th St.), 310/458-2829, busy, unbelievably reasonable, and well worth the long waits. Owner Robert Kerr makes his own pasta, ravioli, and sausages fresh daily. House specialties include such things as "Atomic" pasta—two seared Cajun-seasoned chicken breasts served on a bed of chile linguine and tossed with peppers and onions in a chipotle cream sauce. Not to mention some marvelous vegetarian selections. Here, you can also create your own specialty by selecting pasta, sauce, and favorite add-ins. The wine list includes boutique wines listed at half the price other restaurants charge. Such a deal! Don't miss the delectable desserts. Open for lunch and dinner.

RICHER PEOPLE'S EATS

Richer People's Eats near the Pier

Almost always worth the dent in the pocketbook: **Ocean Avenue Seafood,** 1401 Ocean Ave. (at

Santa Monica Blvd.), 310/394-5669, a stylish yet classic oyster bar and seafood restaurant featuring modern art, pastel walls, dark wood paneling, and an indoor-outdoor bar. Classics such as the New England clam chowder, crab cakes, and blackened catfish are always available—but the ever-changing list of fish and fish dishes, usually offering more than two dozen choices on any given day, keeps everyone surprised. It's open daily for lunch and dinner (brunch on Sunday).

Even more expensive is **The Ivy at the Shore,** almost facing the pier from 1541 Ocean Ave. (at Colorado), 310/393-3113. This fashionable faux beach shack, complete with bamboo, breezy patio seating (glassed-in and heated on nippy evenings), and tropical-themed bar, is notable along palm-lined Ocean. Like its stylish older sibling near West Hollywood, this Ivy specializes in California-style adaptations of nononsense regional Americana—crab cakes, shrimp, and other seafood specialties, Cajun prime rib, Louisiana meatloaf, pizzas, and pastas. Simpler at lunch are the sandwiches and salads (don't forget the Maui onion rings). The Ivy's Caesar salad is famous throughout Los Angeles. Almost equally famous: delectable desserts. Ivy's is open daily for lunch and dinner (brunch on Sun.); closed major holidays.

Richer People's Eats near the Promenade

Start searching for possibilities where almost everyone else does, along the Third Street Promenade. Prime for people-watching—one of those only-in-L.A. places—is the spacious, light, and airy **Broadway Deli,** 1457 3rd St. (at Broadway), 310/451-0616, where the proprietors don't do a particularly good job with traditional New York deli standards. (But hey, this is California.) The Broadway does just about everything else, though, from superb French bistro fare to reinvented American comfort food, including macaroni and cheese and killer burgers. This is a fairly pricey place, but if you order judiciously you'll still be able to afford the gas—or plane fare—to get home. Espresso bar, fresh-baked breads and bagels, delightful desserts. Astonishing foodie shop, too, which you'll get to know well while you wait (no reservations). The Broadway Deli is open daily 7 A.M.–midnight, 8 A.M. until 1 A.M. on Fri. and Sat. nights.

But don't overlook dignified yet relaxed **Remi** also near Broadway, at 1451 3rd St. (near Broadway), 310/393-6545. Though cousin to New York's

Remi, this restaurant's influences come all the way from Venice—the one in Italy, not the eccentric upstart just down the beach. The jaunty nautical theme here launches all kinds of classics, such as grilled quail, roasted stuffed pork chops, rack of lamb, and some stunning seafood pastas. The perfect finish for a perfect meal: the house-made tiramisu. Remi is open daily for lunch and dinner (closed Christmas and New Year's Day). If Remi's not possible, other choices include **Locando del Lago,** 231 Arizona Ave. (between 2nd and 3rd Sts.), 310/451-3525, noted for dishes from Lombardy. The patio is also a plus.

One block east of the Promenade and well worth the detour is the flamboyant dinners-only **Border Grill,** 1444 4th St. (near Broadway), 310/451-1655. The bizarre and bright faux folk art–splashed walls serve as apt accompaniment to the stunning food served here—everything the creation of chefs Mary Sue Milliken and Susan Feniger, who apply their formal training in classical French cooking to the bold flavors of coastal Mexico and Central America. You can make a meal of the appetizers, the green corn tamales, the *panuchos* and *platano empañadas* stuffed with cheese and black beans, thereby keeping the total tab almost reasonable. Then again, you'd miss the entrées—such things as grilled skirt steak marinated with garlic, cilantro and cracked pepper, served with moros, avocado-corn relish and Roma tomatoes, sautéed rock shrimp with toasted *ancho* chiles, and marinated breast of chicken served with onion-orange salsa. And for dessert, how about a slice of Oaxacan chocolate cake? Full bar. The Border Grill is open nightly for dinner (closed major holidays).

Richer People's Eats Elsewhere

Culinary stars at the Santa Monica Airport include stylish California-style **DC-3** at the Museum of Flying, 2800 Donald Douglas Loop N (just off 28th St., south of Ocean Park Blvd.), 310/399-2323, which serves grilled seafood, chicken, and such, along with a hip and lively singles bar scene during happy hour and on weekends; live jazz some nights. Another high-flyer at the airport is the exotic Pacific Rim **Typhoon,** 3221 Donald Douglas Loop S (at Airport Ave.), 310/390-6565, where the "pilot's pillar" showcases the pilot's licenses of some of the famous and infamous who have flown in for the pan-Asian fare. Universal

favorites include Thai coconut chicken curry, Indonesian stir-fry, and fried catfish. Up on the roof, weather permitting, is the Asian beer garden.

Main St. has its own stars, including sophisticated California-style **Röckenwaggner** inside the Edgemar complex at 2435 Main (near Pico), 310/399-6504, the perfect choice for a special weekend brunch. The marinated mushroom salad is one of Chef Hans Röckenwaggner's signature dishes, along with the smoked salmon "short stack" and other exceptional fish and seafood. Röckenwaggner's is open for weekend brunch, lunch Tues.–Fri., and dinner daily.

Warszawa, 1414 Lincoln Blvd. (between Santa Monica Blvd. and Broadway), 310/393-8831, is the only Polish restaurant in town—and a very good one. In a onetime private home, Warszawa serves hearty dinners in four cozy lace-curtained rooms. Favorite dishes here include the thick pea soup with smoked ham, roast duckling stuffed with herbs, and hunter's stew with sausage, sauerkraut, beef, bacon, and dumplings. For dessert, try the cheesecake with brown sugar crust, the rum torte, or the chocolate cream walnut cake. Warszawa is open Tues.–Sun. for dinner.

Rich People's Eats

Known for its fine California cuisine, **JiRaffe,** 502 Santa Monica Blvd. (at 5th St.), 310/917-6671, is one of the Westside's most innovative and popular restaurants. The culinary creation of two talented L.A. chefs, Josiah Citrin and Raphael Lunetta, formerly of Jackson's in West Hollywood, JiRaffe serves such things as grilled smoked pork chops with wild rice, smoked bacon, apple chutney, and cider sauce, and whitefish with zucchini and artichokes, fava beans, and sugar snap peas.

Though there's plenty of competition these days, **Chinois on Main,** 2709 Main St. (between Hill and Ashland), 310/392-9025, is still one of L.A.'s best, and most popular, restaurants. One of the oldest L.A. offspring of celebrity chef Wolfgang Puck. Most of the "Chinois Classics" are still here, but the menu has also evolved into something simpler and lighter, with lovely vegetable-rich lo mein with soy, honey, and black bean sauce (lunch only) and seared scallops with a sauce of red onions, red wine, cream, and butter. Chinois is noisy, expensive, and sometimes a challenge for reservations—if it's important, try weeks in advance—but it's still one of the best shows in town.

If you can't get reservations at Chinois then try **Valentino**, 3115 W. Pico Blvd. (west of Bundy Dr.), 310/829-4313, the best Italian restaurant in L.A.; respectable restaurant critics say it's the best in the entire country. This casual, chic dining destination stars lobster cannelloni and other surprising pastas, osso buco, and fish, lamb, rabbit, and veal entrées. As important as the spectacular food is Valentino's wine list, one of the best anywhere—though it did suffer something of a setback when about 20,000 bottles of wine shattered in the 1994 Northridge earthquake. Valentino is open for dinner only, Mon.–Saturday. Very expensive. Reservations mandatory.

Drago, 2628 Wilshire Blvd. (at 26th St.), 310/828-1585, is Santa Monica's other dashing, elegant Italian, showcasing variations on Sicilian country fare—pastas and risottos, grilled fish and roasted quail. Excellent wine list. It's open for lunch on weekdays, for dinner every night. Reservations required.

Michael's, 1147 3rd St. (just beyond the Promenade), 310/451-0843, was Santa Monica's—and one of L.A.'s—original California cuisine scenes. Owner Michael McCarty, a Cordon Bleu chef, opened his restaurant here in 1979 at the brash age of 26—quickly "blowing L.A.'s mind" with his modern American cuisine. So many of L.A.'s great chefs and restaurant owners worked here at one time or another that in 1995 Michael's hosted a celebrity-chef reunion as a benefit for local museums—an immense success, with L.A.'s best manning personal cooking stations for the benefit of the assembled masses. Michael's is open Mon.–Fri. for lunch, Mon.–Sat. for dinner. Reservations wise. There's another **Michael's** in New York City.

For other fine dining possibilities, consider Santa Monica's upscale hotels.

EATING IN VENICE AND VICINITY

Eating in Venice

For all practical purposes the unincorporated Venice district of L.A. is the southern extension of Santa Monica—quite convenient if you've got wheels—and typically safe to explore if you stick to the main drags and don't hang out too late after nightfall.

If you're in or around Venice, the premier local people's place is the **Rose Cafe**, 220 Rose Ave. (at Main St.), 310/399-0711. Not the best restaurant in town and not one of the trendy beachfront venues, in many ways the Rose Cafe *is* Venice. This is where true Venetians hang out, along with an inordinate number of movie people at times and young execs. The style here is beach bohemian, coffee and pastries being the staff of life. For lunch and dinner, consider a salad or simple sandwich. The patio is the place to be.

Figtree's Cafe, right on the Venice Boardwalk at 429 Ocean Front Walk, 310/392-4937, is another locals' favorite for breakfast. (Get there early on weekends, by 9 A.M., and expect slow service; regulars are liable to nurse their cappuccinos and read the Sunday paper for hours.) Vegetarian dishes are a specialty. Try the wonderful polenta, the hearty French toast on thick-sliced raisin nut bread, or the satisfying Santa Fe omelette. Lunch and dinner fare includes pastas, burritos, tostadas, veggie stir-fry, and fresh fish. Figtree's is open daily for breakfast, lunch, and dinner.

A best bet among more expensive Venetian venues lives with Jonathan Borofsky's Emmett Kelly–faced dancer, the sad *Ballerina Clown en pointe* above the intersection of Rose and Main. Trendy **Chaya Venice**, 110 Navy St. (at Main), 310/396-1179, stars art-deco Asian decor, eclectic Franco-Japanese-California fare, and seafood—curried crab soup, spring rolls, even a sushi bar. It's open weekdays for lunch, Sun. for brunch, nightly for dinner. Even better, though, and a real find for frugal foodies, is **Joe's**, 1023 Abbott Kinney Blvd. (between Westminster and Broadway), 310/399-5811, where the California-French seafood stars at lunch (Tues.–Fri. only), Sun. brunch, and dinner. One of L.A.'s best restaurants, serving one of L.A.'s best Sunday brunches. Also fairly inexpensive and quite good for Thai is romantic **Siamese Garden** right on Venice's Grand Canal at 301 Washington Blvd. (near Strongs Dr.), 310/821-0098, open for lunch weekdays only, for dinner nightly.

Eating in Marina del Rey

Aunt Kizzy's Back Porch in the Villa Marina Shopping Center at 4325 Glencoe Ave. (between Washington Blvd. and Mindanao Way), 310/578-

1005, is not exactly what you'd expect in a Marina del Rey minimall. Aunt Kizzy's is a fantastic country-style soul food café serving crispy fried chicken, catfish, ribs, pork chops, and jambalaya, along with rice and red beans and Southern-style vegetables. Everything here is so good that people are willing to wait and wait to get in. Aunt Kizzy's is open daily for lunch 11 A.M.–4 P.M., for dinner 4–10 P.M. (closed Thanksgiving and Christmas).

If you just can't wait, another possibility is **Benny's Barbecue,** 4077 Lincoln Blvd. (near Washington), 310/821-6939, a take-out stand in the marina that's locally famous for dishing out fiery barbecued ribs, lamb shanks, L.A.'s best hot links, beans, and excellent coleslaw. Also beloved in these parts: **Killer Shrimp,** 523 Washington St. (at Ocean), 310/578-2293. You like the name? You'll like the place. An unassuming storefront in an ugly minimall that serves one item only: killer shrimp, flown in fresh daily from Louisiana, prepared in a lively sauce of beer, butter, garlic, secret herbs and spices, and served with crusty French bread just made for dipping.

Considerably more stylish and expensive is the California-style **Cafe del Rey,** 4551 Admiralty Way (at Bali Way), 310/823-6395, where the eclectic international fare runs from the very simple—pizzas, tasty burgers, niçoise salad—to the surprisingly imaginative. The café is open daily for lunch and dinner, also a good choice for Sunday brunch. Another fine-dining choice, especially if you're en route to LAX, is dinner-only **The Library** at the Los Angeles Renaissance Hotel, 9620 Airport Blvd. in Inglewood, 310/337-2800, famous for its exceptionally well-prepared seafood. For a dining *experience,* the place is **The Dining Room** at the Ritz-Carlton, 4375 Admiralty Way, 310/823-1700.

UP THE COAST: NORTH OF SANTA MONICA

Heading north from Santa Monica via the Pacific Coast Hwy. (PCH, or Hwy. 1) leads to the pleasures of Ventura, Santa Barbara, and San Luis Obispo Counties and, eventually, the famous Big Sur coast. Well worth exploring on this side of the L.A. County line are some of L.A.'s favorite residential hideouts—Pacific Palisades, Topanga Canyon, and Malibu—and some of its best beaches. Seeming almost as vast as the Pacific Ocean it looms above is the Santa Monica Mountains National Recreation Area, a crazy quilt of wilderness areas and preserves interspersed with outposts of suburbia. Many recreation area highlights, detailed in Wilderness City: The Santa Monica Mountains in the Beverly Hills chapter, are easily accessible from PCH north of Santa Monica.

PACIFIC PALISADES: AN OPTIMIST'S PARADISE

Like sections of Santa Monica and Malibu, Pacific Palisades perches atop high cliffs (palisades) overlooking the Pacific Ocean. The cliffs are famous for giving way during heavy rains, encouraging expensive homes to slip off their moorings and entire hillsides to slide away to sea—mudslides that inconveniently block the Pacific Coast Hwy. below. Otherwise the main event in this amazingly upmarket neighborhood just north of Santa Monica is the annual **Fourth of July parade**—an event in which members of the community's long-running **Optimist Club** march down the street, in close-order drill, in their underwear.

The existence of the Optimists is still central to community life, as is Swarthmore Ave., center of the low-key local business district. But Will Rogers State Historic Park is usually more celebrated—as are Gelson's grocery, a best bet for spotting local celebrities, and Mort's restaurant, *the* place to eat (celebs primarily hang on the wall). Celebrities are legion in Pacific Palisades. Ron and Nancy Reagan lived here before they moved to the White House in 1984, for example, and past mayors of Pacific Palisades include Chevy Chase, Dom DeLuise, Ted Knight, and Rita Moreno.

For current information on the area, contact: **Pacific Palisades Chamber of Commerce,** 15330 Antioch St., 310/459-7963.

UPLIFTERS CLUB: SOUTHSTATE BOHEMIANS

Harry Haldeman—grandfather of H. R. (Bob) Haldeman, a key player in ex-President Richard Nixon's infamous Watergate debacle—was a jovial plumbing supply businessman originally from Chicago, a man as passionate about hard liquor and Cuban cigars as conservative politics. Inspired by the example of San Francisco's exclusive Bohemian Club, in 1913 Haldeman and like-minded revelers recruited from the still-prestigious Los Angeles Athletic Club established the Uplifters Club—the name "The Lofty and Exalted Order of Uplifters" contributed by *The Wizard of Oz* author L. Frank Baum. Though the group's official motto was "to uplift art and promote good fellowship," the ability to lift up one's glass was also crucial. After Prohibition's nationwide alcohol ban went into effect in 1919, the group bought 120 acres of redwoods and eucalyptus groves in Rustic Canyon (below what would later become the Will Rogers ranch) and founded the Uplifters Ranch—a private retreat where captains of industry and a select group of talented friends could protect their sybaritic revelry from the long arm of the law.

The Uplifters' social centerpiece was its clubhouse, now part of the eight-acre **Rustic Canyon Recreation Center** and park on Latimer Rd., 310/454-5734, open to the public. Uplifting the grounds in the old days were tennis courts, a swimming pool, polo field, trapshooting range, outdoor amphitheater, and dormitories, all part of the wooded playground enjoyed by Walt Disney, Busby Berkeley, Harold Lloyd, Daryl F. Zanuck, and others among L.A.'s most privileged ranks. In 1922 members began to build rustic weekend and summer cabins on land leased from the Uplifters; many of these structures remain. The Uplifters Club dissolved more than 50 years ago but artists, writers, and actual and spiritual descendants of the Uplifters continue to live here.

To reach Rustic Canyon Recreation Center—and to take a respectful peek at this part of the Pacific Palisades past—head south from Sunset Blvd. via Brooktree Rd., which follows a tree-lined brook, to the old clubhouse at 600-700 Latimer Road. (Allow plenty of time to get lost. Both Latimer and Haldeman Rds., the Uplifters' main thoroughfares, are narrow, with no curbs or gutters, and largely unlighted at night.) A handful of cabins and lodges—all private residences, so don't trespass or otherwise be obnoxious—still stand, among them 31, 32, 34, 35, and 38 Haldeman and 1, 3, and 8 Latimer.

Seeing and Doing Pacific Palisades

The most popular local attraction lies well east along Sunset, near Brentwood—**Will Rogers State Historic Park,** 1501 Will Rogers State Park Rd. (just north of Sunset Blvd.), 310/454-8212. This 187-acre ranch estate is where noted cowboy humorist and philosopher Will Rogers lived from 1924 until his death in 1935. Rogers's ranch-style home, open daily for public tours, is also a museum; don't fail to appreciate the wraparound shower on the 2nd floor. The lush lawns and landscaped grounds, where the horsey set still plays polo matches on weekends, are also perfect for picnics, frisbee, and sunbathing.

Near the ocean end of Sunset is the **Self-Realization Fellowship Lake Shrine,** 17190 Sunset Blvd., 310/454-4114, which was used as a movie location before Paramahansa Yogananda, author of *Autobiography of a Yogi,* bought the 10-acre site in 1950. At the center of the shrine, dedicated to the universality of all religions and the exaltation of nature, is the picturesque, luxuriantly landscaped spring-fed lake. A small chapel shaped like a Dutch windmill, a golden-domed archway, a houseboat, and gazebos frame lake views and provide good photo ops. The shrine is open to the public for peaceful walks and meditation. Call for information.

Other Pacific Palisades sights are architectural. Most of the significant area architecture was influenced by John Entenza, editor and publisher of the trendsetting *Arts and Architecture* magazine, and his **Case Study House Project,** which encouraged prominent Southern California architects to experiment with new materials and styles. Noted "case study" houses include the landmark international-style **Eames House and Studio,** 203 Chautauqua Blvd., something like a three-dimensional Mondrian painting set in a meadow, designed by Charles Eames in 1947–49; the similar **Entenza House,** 205 Chautauqua Blvd., designed by Charles Eames and Eero Saarinen in 1949; and the international redwood-and-brick **Bailey House,** 219 Chautauqua, designed by Richard J. Neutra in 1946–48. Pacific Palisades features many other architectural gems, most of which are not visible from public streets.

MALIBU: SURFING CELEBRITY

Aside from an appreciation for Malibu's clean beaches, good surf, and aquamarine waters, the one thing that unites Malibu residents is the Pacific Coast Hwy., which here is a tenuous lifeline. Celebrated for its surfing, its celebrities, and its chic coastal cachet, Malibu most often makes it into the news as a disaster area for its almost predictable "natural" disasters, created by human incursions into an unstable, fire-adapted ecosystem. Whether or not wildfires have finished their occasional summer and fall windsprints to the sea, the rains begin—and the

THE GETTY VILLA

Beyond the surf and the stars, Malibu's most famous attraction is now the second location for the renowned **J. Paul Getty Museum,** the Getty Villa at 17985 Pacific Coast Hwy. in Malibu (between Sunset and Topanga Canyon Blvds.)—still closed at last report, though after remodeling it is expected to reopen soon as the Getty Center's classical antiquities exhibit and restoration center. Visit www.getty.edu/museum/villa.html for the latest update. (If you can't wait, head to Brentwood and the glorious new Getty Center, 310/440-7300, www.getty.edu. For details, see Cities on a Hill: The Getty and Vicinity in the Beverly Hills and Vicinity chapter.) The museum's collection of European paintings and drawings—Goya, Cézanne, van Gogh, Rembrandt, Renoir—along with illuminated manuscripts, American and European photography, home furnishings fit for French royalty, and European sculpture, bronzes, ceramics, and glass, are now installed at the Getty Center.

The 38-gallery Getty Villa is, and will be, perfect for the Getty classics, one of the finest U.S. collections of ancient Greek and Roman art and artifacts—sculptures and figurines, vases, mosaics, and paintings. When the museum reopens, expect special exhibits of ancient Asian and Eastern European art as well.

The Getty Villa is also a classic—a re-creation of the Villa dei Papiri, an ancient Roman country house with a view of the Bay of Naples. Even the Getty gardens, the trees, shrubs, and flowers, the statuary and outdoor wall paintings, represent those at the original villa of 2,000 years ago. Villa dei Papiri, thought to have belonged to Julius Caesar's father-in-law, was buried by the volcanic rubble of Mt. Vesuvius when the mountain erupted in A.D. 79. Discovered by treasure hunters and excavated during the 18th century, the reborn villa inspired Getty; the Getty Villa, completed in 1974, was constructed from excavation drawings.

The Getty Villa, to reopen soon to house the Getty collection of antiquities, is a re-creation of a Roman villa unearthed from the ashes of Pompeii.

KIM WEIR

mudslides, which may carry houses, carports, landscaped yards, sometimes streets and entire hillsides with them. If the Pacific Coast Hwy. is closed for days at a time, be it from behemoth bouncing boulders or mudslides, people here take it in stride. Building more houses here—and continually rebuilding them—is not particularly intelligent.

Yet try telling that to people in Malibu, who moved here to get away from it all. The fact that "it" had already arrived, in the forms of crushing urban crowds and nightmarish traffic, was a prime motivating factor for Malibu's incorpo- ration in 1990. During his one-year term as the city's "honorary mayor," actor Martin Sheen—current president of the United States on TV's *West Wing*—declared Malibu a nuclear-free zone and a refuge for the homeless. But since incorporation residents have drawn battle lines over growth-related issues.

Despite the definitive dot on most maps, Malibu as place has always been difficult to find. Though the star-studded Malibu Colony, the Malibu Pier, and several Malibu beaches have served as unofficial community signposts, in most people's minds "Malibu" was a rather vague

TOPANGA: MOUNTAINS THAT RUN INTO THE SEA

The equally indefinable inland and upland neighbor to Malibu is the laid-back burg of Topanga in mountainous Topanga Canyon, reached from PCH via Topanga Canyon Blvd. (Hwy. 27), increasingly a high-speed commuter thoroughfare. (The tailgaters' apparent message: Pull over or die.) Beyond the highway, the artsy community sprawls off in all directions—up tortured hillsides, down one-lane roads—within the canyon's 21-acre watershed. Famous for its mudslides, Topanga Canyon does shed water after heavy winter rains—which certainly explains the Chumash name, Topanga, roughly translated as "Mountains that Run into the Sea." Here, they often do. When hillsides aren't preoccupied with slip-sliding away, rustic cabins, lodges, standard-brand ranch homes, and more ambitious architectural adventures provide both physical and spiritual home for Topanga's people, predominantly actors, artists, musicians, poets, writers, and screenwriters. Topanga thrives on its artistic ambience and its community eccentricities—the roadside crystal stands and such—many of which hark back to the earliest inklings of the Age of Aquarius. Yet given the region's increasing suburban popularity, back-to-the-landers without 30-year-old roots would be financially challenged to plant themselves here today.

Most of Topanga the town is strung out along the highway about halfway between the San Fernando Valley and the Pacific Ocean. A popular stop for breakfast and lunch is **Willows,** 137 S. Topanga Canyon Blvd., 310/455-8788. You can also stop locally for supplies and deli sandwiches at places such as **Fernwood Market,** 446 S. Topanga Canyon Blvd., 310/455-2412, and **Froggy's Topanga Fresh Fish Market** (also a good restaurant), 1105 N.

Topanga Canyon Blvd., 310/455-1728.

Some classic Topanga neighborhoods and destinations, including the **Inn of the Seventh Ray** natural-foods restaurant, 310/455-1311, are tucked in among the creekside oaks and sycamores alongside Old Topanga Canyon Rd., which eventually intersects scenic Mulholland Highway. For books about the area and basic New Age supplies, stop by **The Spiral Staircase** next to the Inn of the Seventh Ray at 128 Old Topanga Canyon, 310/455-3370.

Another wonder in Topanga is **The Will Geer Theatricum Botanicum,** 1419 N. Topanga Canyon Blvd., 310/455-3723, a small, woodsy outdoor theater that remains part of the legacy of actor/philosopher Will Geer. The classically trained Geer eventually became one of the world's most beloved actors—baby boomers will remember him as Grandpa Walton on *The Waltons* TV series—yet his professional and personal lives were all but undone in the 1950s by his refusal to cooperate with the communist-hunting House Committee on Un-American Activities. "Blacklisted," or barred from working in Hollywood, Geer moved his family to Topanga Canyon and established a Shakespearean theater to showcase the talents of other blacklisted Hollywood talent. Along with theater tickets, he and his family also sold their homegrown vegetables. Will Geer's daughter, Ellen, has served as the theater's artistic director since 1979, the year after the actor's death. Call for current program information or check the theater's website at www.theatricum.com.

Easily accessible from Topanga is **Topanga State Park,** prime for hiking—in the absence of major storms and mudslides—especially in "the green months" of winter and early spring.

regional appellation taking in the 20-plus miles of Los Angeles County coastline between Topanga Canyon and Ventura County. But now Malibu has definite city limits, and an official 20-square-mile territory, stretching north from Topanga Canyon to Leo Carrillo State Beach at the Ventura County line.

The main attractions are Malibu's beaches—more than 20 miles of them. The beaches along the Malibu coastline are still reasonably clean, despite heavy recreational use and some local pollution problems, and provide some of the best surfing and ocean swimming in Southern California. Traffic on a summer day along the Pacific Coast Hwy. can be brutal and parking nearly impossible, however. Plan to arrive before the noontime "rush hour"—say, by 11 A.M., if not earlier—while parking places are still available. A second highway rush usually occurs between 4 and 5 P.M., when most people head home for dinner. If you're well supplied and willing to while away some time, the good news is that sunsets are fairly unpopulated and peaceful. Better yet, come in the off-season—spring, fall, and winter—when beaches can be quite balmy and pleasant yet much less crowded. The weather is moderate year-round. Barring the occasional storm, some of the finest beach days come in winter—though some spots are crowded on weekends during whale-watching season.

For current information about the area, contact: **Malibu Chamber of Commerce,** 23805 Stuart Ranch Rd., Ste. 100, 310/456-9025, www.malibu.org.

Malibu Pier

Start exploring Malibu at the 700-foot Malibu Pier, opened to the public with great fanfare and fireworks on July 4, 1945. The present-day pier replaced the 400-foot-long Rindge Pier, built here in 1903 so supplies could be delivered by boat. The pier area is particularly popular for fishing (tackle and bait available) and watching both surfers and sunsets. Surrounding the pier is Malibu Lagoon State Beach, which includes the Malibu estuary, the historic Adamson House and associated museum, and **Malibu Surfrider Beach,** one of the West Coast's most famous surfing beaches. Largely east of the pier (it feels "south") though the best breaks are to the west ("north"), Malibu Surfrider Beach has been cel-

ebrated in countless Frankie Avalon, Annette Funicello, and *Gidget* movies. More significantly, according to local lore, Surfrider is California's 1926 surfing birthplace. In summer perfect waves roll to shore at Surfrider day after day—an accident of ocean currents, upwellings, and winds that creates heaven for surfers, kayakers, and windsurfers but hell for those who dislike overcrowded beaches. Swimming and surfing aren't recommended here, since Heal the Bay regularly "flunks" Surfrider and adjacent beaches in its annual water quality survey. But surfers still come, since they have to go where the waves are. If you want to watch, the pier offers ringside railings for surfing voyeurs.

If you hunger for a bracing after-beach breakfast, head for the **PierView Cafe and Cantina,** 310/456-6962, on the beach just east of the pier. Or head for local shopping malls. Best bets for breakfast or weekend brunch—and later meals—include **Marmalade** in the Cross Creek Plaza, 310/317-4242, and, at Malibu Colony Plaza, both casual **Coogie's,** 310/317-1444, and uptown **Granita,** 310/456-0488, the latter sea-themed culinary adventure established by Wolfgang Puck and Barbara Lazaroff.

Malibu Lagoon State Beach

Malibu Lagoon offers an opportunity for impromptu bird-watching and nature appreciation, right off the highway. One of only two estuaries remaining within the boundaries of Santa Monica Mountains National Recreation Area, this small patch of marsh at the mouth of Malibu Creek serves as a natural fish nursery—and bountiful buffet for neighborhood and migrating shorebirds. (While visiting, stay on the boardwalks.) More than 200 species of birds use Malibu Lagoon as a migratory stopover. Nearby beach areas are popular for swimming, though water at the mouth of Malibu Creek is polluted—twice monthly, the lagoon is drained—and swimming is not recommended on those days. With its offshore reefs and kelp beds, the area is also popular with skin and scuba divers.

Also well worth exploring: the adjoining **Malibu Lagoon Museum** and the grand **Adamson House.** Chances are you'll never see the inside of local movie stars' homes, so amuse yourself, while touring Adamson House, with the knowledge that most celebrities would kill to own a place like this. Former home of Rhoda and Merritt Adamson—daughter and son-in-law of Frederick and May Rindge, who owned the vast Malibu Ranch in the early 1900s—this 1929 Spanish-Moorish beach house was designed by architect Stiles O. Clements, who took full advantage of the Rindge-owned Malibu Tile Company's exceptional craftsmanship. The stunning Adamson House, listed on the National Register of Historic Places, is rich with handcrafted teak, graceful wrought-iron work, and leaded-glass windows. But, inside and out, it is primarily a tile-setter's fantasy—a real-life museum-quality display of 1920s California tilework, richly colored geometric and animal-motif patterns worked into the walkways, walls, and lavish fountains. There's even a tiled outdoor dog shower. The museum adjacent, at home in the home's seven-car garage, chronicles area history with memorabilia, art, artifacts, and photographs.

Malibu Lagoon State Beach adjoins the Malibu Pier and includes famous Malibu Surfrider Beach (see above). Adamson House and the Malibu Lagoon Museum, 23200 Pacific Coast Hwy. (Hwy. 1), are one-quarter mile west of the Malibu Pier and 13 miles west of Santa Monica. The lagoon and Adamson House grounds are technically open 24 hours, though the adjacent county parking lot ($5 fee), shared with Surfrider Beach, is open daily 8 A.M.–5 P.M. only (side-street parking available early morning and evening). Another parking lot ($6) is one block north at Cross Creek Road. Beach, lagoon, and museum access are free. The Adamson House is open only for tours (one hour, small fee), usually offered Wed.–Sat. 11 A.M.–3 P.M. (last tour at 2 P.M.); the museum is open during the same hours. Reservations are required for groups of 12 or more and the museum closes on days with moderate to heavy rain—call ahead. For more information, call 310/456-8432.

MALIBU: THE COASTLINE

Beaches North of Malibu Colony

Last stop before the Ventura County line in the north is **Leo Carrillo State Beach,** typically

STAYING IN MALIBU

Malibu offers the main accommodations action north of Santa Monica. And Malibu is a bit short on inexpensive places to stay—on places to stay, period—which is just the way Malibu likes it. Beyond the area's state park campsites, the 30 fairly quaint but clean 1920s-vintage cabins of the **Topanga Ranch Motel** south of central Malibu, right across from the beach at 18711 Pacific Coast Hwy. (PCH), 310/456-5486, are among the area's more affordable options. Some units have kitchens; a few boast two bedrooms. Moderate ($60–85). The attractive 21-room **Casa Malibu Inn** right on the beach in "downtown" Malibu, 22752 PCH, 310/456-2219, features an inviting central courtyard, some rooms with kitchens and balconies. Expensive-Luxury ($95–329). Another possibility is the decent 16-room **Malibu Country Inn** motel north of Malibu proper at 6506 Westward Beach Rd. (at PCH), 310/457-9622, with a small swimming pool, in-room refrigerators and coffeemakers. Expensive-Luxury ($125–250), but somewhat less expensive in the off-season.

Since 1990, Malibu has boasted a seriously stylish small hotel right on the beach, complete with tile work and berber carpets—the **Malibu Beach Inn,** in the pink and snuggled onto a strip of beachfront near the pier at 22878 Pacific Coast Hwy., 310/456-6444 or toll-free 800/462-5428, www.malibubeachinn.com. Space here is too tight for so much as a swimming pool—but who needs a pool when the wide blue Pacific Ocean is in your front yard? Rooms are reasonably spacious, with the usual luxury amenities, small private balconies, and gas fireplaces (most rooms). Perfect for just hanging out: the motel's friendly Mediterranean-style terra-cotta-tiled patio hanging out over the rocky shore. Two-night minimum stay on weekends from May through October. Luxury ($169–249).

For a still quieter, still more serene weekend stay, room to retreat is often available for individuals at the Franciscan **Serra Retreat Center,** 3401 Serra Rd., P.O. Box 127, Malibu, CA 90265, 310/456-6631, or www.sbfranciscans.org, which offers regular group retreats at this scenic remnant of the original Topanga Malibu Sequit ranch, the spot where "Queen of Malibu" May Rindge started but never completed her hilltop mansion. Premium ($90–140) suggested per-day donation, which includes three substantial meals.

much less crowded than the "city beaches" closer to Malibu Colony, Santa Monica, and urban points south. Named for the actor who played Pancho in *The Cisco Kid* TV series, 1,600-acre Leo Carrillo features 1.5 miles of stupendous craggy coastline and both rocky and sandy beaches—the totality perfect for surfing, sailboarding, swimming, and, at low tide, tidepooling. A popular whale-watching spot in winter, Leo Carrillo is also good for scuba diving. (Riptides are a danger occasionally.) Inland, ranger-guided hikes are regularly scheduled, and, in summer, campfire programs. Pleasant picnicking, too (there's a store here). A pretty campground, across the highway, is set among the sycamores back from the beach, and there's another nearby at North Beach. For a spectacular ocean view with minimal effort, take the short trail up the hill from near the booth at the campground entrance. Leo Carrillo State Beach, 35000 Pacific Coast Hwy. (Hwy. 1), is 25 miles west of Santa Monica and about 15 miles from "downtown" Malibu. Leo Carrillo's main entrance is just east of Mulholland Hwy.'s intersection with the highway—a great drive, if you're out exploring. Day-use parking is $3 per vehicle; call for camping fees, which vary for developed, RV (self-contained), and hike/bike sites. The beach is open daily 8 A.M.–midnight. The visitor center is open daily in summer. For more information, call 805/488-5223. For camping reservations, a must in summer and on most weekends, call ReserveAmerica toll-free at 800/444-7275.

Next east is one of L.A.'s best-kept secrets, rumored to be the preferred beach escape for L.A.'s lifeguards on their days off—picturesque, pristine, and remote **Nicholas Canyon County Beach,** 34000 Pacific Coast Highway. Nicholas, a graceful quarter moon of sand curving around a small bay, is well-protected from highway noise and has no skate rentals, no snack stands—none of the usual L.A. beach chaos and clutter. Just peace, quiet, and a few kayakers and surfers. (And lifeguards and restrooms.) The **Robert H. Meyer Memorial State Beach,** next east at 33000 Pacific Coast Hwy., is actually a string of smaller state beaches tucked into a residential area: **El Pescador, La Piedra,** and **El Matador,** the lovely latter beach the most popular. As many as 10 episodes of *Baywatch* were once filmed here each year, but most people

come for the dramatic cliffs, rock formations, and caves along the sandy beach. (No lifeguards but picnic tables and portable toilets. Parking lot open 8 A.M.–sunset, fee.) Nearby is **El Sol State Beach,** difficult to find.

Trancas Beach at PCH and Guernsey Ave. is another residential-area beach, most accessible by walking from **Zuma Beach.** Zuma, 30000 Pacific Coast Hwy., was the location for a multitude of 1950s and 1960s surfing movies—the likes of *Deadman's Curve, Beach Blanket Bingo,* and *Back to the Beach*—but gathered even more fame in the 1970s, thanks to singer/songwriter Neil Young's album *Zuma.* Postcard-pretty if hardly private, Zuma's appeal is as fundamental as its endless expanse of white sand, rowdy beach volleyball, and children's playground. Popular with the rowdy surfing set. For all the fun and frolic, though, think safety. Riptides here have been known to drag up to 20 people at a time straight out to sea—keeping the lifeguards plenty busy. Access to the beach, open sunrise to sunset, is free but there is a fee to park in the *huge* lot. Locals avoid even that by jockeying for highway and street parking. Full services are available (lifeguards, restrooms, snack bars, and rental shops). Just below often-packed Zuma is clean, sandy, and equally popular **Westward Beach,** reached from Pacific Coast Hwy. via Westward Beach Rd. (limited free parking along the beach road). Or, park at Zuma and walk along the beach.

Continue on Westward Beach Rd. to reach the parking lot for busy **Point Dume State Beach,** whose sand neatly segues into Westward's. Point Dume once featured a vertical "point"—a rocky peak—in addition to its seaward point, until the former was flattened for a housing development. Reaching Point Dume's secluded series of sandy pocket beaches and rocky shores, scattered below impressive cliffs, requires a little walking. Small caves and tidepools abound throughout the 35-acre **Point Dume Natural Preserve,** where the rocky west face is popular with technical climbers. A stairway and hiking trail start at Westward Beach and climb to the headlands and the **Point Dume Whale Watch,** a popular series of sites for watching the midwinter migration of California gray whales—good for views any time. Look for California brown pelicans, California sea lions, and harbor seals on offshore rocks. Though it's not condoned as a nude beach officially, historically beach-in-the-buff enthusiasts have always hiked around the point or down the stairway from the headlands to the rocky north end of **Pirate's Cove** and its stunning beach, but winter storms often block access. Point Dume is a good swimming, sunbathing, and diving beach (for experienced divers), only fair for surfing; lifeguards, very clean restrooms, outdoor showers, and a soft drink vending machine provided. Parking at Point Dume is $3.

Point Dume adjoins pretty, private **Paradise Cove Beach.** But unless you're absolutely desperate to find a place to toss down the beach towel, the parking fee alone—$15—is enough to discourage most people from trying this tiny beach near the pier on Paradise Cove Road. (If you park on PCH and walk in, it'll cost you only $5. And the Sandcastle Restaurant validates parking.) But it is a quiet, family-friendly beach with rocky bluffs, caves, and tidepools to explore. At Pacific Coast Hwy. and Escondido Rd. is coastal access (highway parking only) for residential-area **Escondido Beach,** narrow, sandy, and empty, indeed fairly well hidden. Look for the Coastal Access signs. Actual "access" begins at a gate on the ocean side of the highway, which is unlocked 6:30 A.M.–6:30 P.M. daily, just north of Geoffrey's Restaurant in the 27400 "block" of the Pacific Coast Hwy.; the beach path starts at a stairwell between two houses. No lifeguard, no services.

Then there's very narrow **Dan Blocker State Beach,** named for the big, brawny actor better known as affable Hoss Cartwright on TV's long-running *Bonanza.* Dan Blocker extends from Malibu Rd. (at Pacific Coast Hwy.) to Corral Canyon Road. Most people head for the sandier southeast end, which can be packed; beach fans can find more privacy toward the less accessible, rockier end near the mouth of Corral Creek. Highway parking only, easy beach access. Popular for surf fishing and swimmers; lifeguards in summer and on busy weekends.

For those willing to brave the movie star–beach house obstacles along Malibu Rd., back in Malibu Colony both **Puerco Beach** and **Amarillo Beach** beckon (no lifeguards, bathrooms, or other services). Park on the north end of Malibu Rd., where it meets the highway, or

from the highway take Webb Way south to Malibu Rd., praying all the while for a parking spot. To reach Amarillo and points east, it's easiest to walk from Puerco.

Along the coast are a few decent stops for a meal with a view, including the **Paradise Cove Beach Café** at Paradise Cove, 310/457-2503, and **Geoffrey's** near Point Dume, 310/457-1519. If your beach explorations lead you far afield, don't forget the ever-popular **Neptune's Net** on PCH about a mile north of the Ventura County line, 310/457-3095, beloved for its down-home, no-frills funk. Best bet at lunch or dinner is the steamed shellfish. Pick your own lobsters or crabs right out of the fish tanks.

Beaches South of Malibu Colony

Beyond Malibu Lagoon State Beach and Malibu Surfrider Beach near the pier (see Malibu Pier and Malibu Lagoon listings above) is a string of difficult-to-reach residential-area sandy spots: **Carbon Beach,** 22200 Pacific Coast Hwy., just west of Carbon Canyon Rd.; **La Costa Beach,** 21400 PCH; **Las Flores Beach,** 20900 PCH; and **Big Rock Beach** (look for the big rock), 20600 PCH, just north of Carbon Canyon Road. The best way to reach all of these beaches—and watch the tides, so you don't get stranded—is by walking east from Malibu Surfrider Beach or west from Las Tunas. By contrast, rocky **Las Tunas Beach** next east, right on the highway, is very easy to reach but not all that pleasant because of the din of traffic. It's most popular with surf fishers and scuba divers; lifeguards in season, portable toilets. Bring water.

Topanga State Beach, easy to find along the 18700 "block" of Pacific Coast Hwy., a quarter-mile west of the J. Paul Getty Museum and a quarter-mile east of Topanga Canyon Blvd., is popular for swimming (if you don't mind dodging a few ocean rocks) and sunny picnics. On a clear day, from the bluffs here you can see Catalina Island. Sometimes you can also see dolphins just offshore, or passing whales. Mostly what you'll see at Topanga, though, are surfers and sailboats. The swells here are second only to those at Malibu Surfrider. The water quality is usually good, too, so in summer the beach can be quite crowded. The small parking lot (fee) is usually full by 11 A.M., or try to find a spot along the highway. Lifeguards, full services. Another good possibility is **Castle Rock Beach** across the highway from the Getty Museum, a pleasant sandy beach with easy access, parking lot (fee), portable toilets, lifeguards.

Will Rogers State Beach seems to stretch forever beneath the unstable palisades of Pacific Palisades—and this strand of sand does go on some distance, since from here to Redondo Beach it is interrupted only by the boat harbor at Marina del Rey. An excellent swimming beach—particularly toward the north, where water quality is usually best—Will Rogers is uncrowded, at least compared to teeming Santa Monica State Beach just south, because of limited parking. Surfing is fair. Facilities include playgrounds, picnic tables, volleyball nets, lifeguards, restrooms, the works.

DOWN THE COAST: SOUTH OF SANTA MONICA

SOUTH BAY BEACH CITIES

The strands of sand and beach towns south of Los Angeles International Airport (LAX) comprise L.A.'s "South Bay," the southern Santa Monica Bay. This is where the Beach Boys came of age—in Manhattan Beach—and where, in nearby Hermosa Beach and Redondo Beach, Southern California's middle-American surf culture got its biggest sendoff in the 1950s and '60s. But it all started in 1907 when George Freeth, billed as "the man who could walk on water," was imported to Redondo Beach by that ceaseless land-sales promoter Henry Huntington for a special "prove it" performance. Walking the offshore waves with the help of an eight-foot, 200-pound wooden surfboard, Freeth introduced the ancient Polynesian sport of kings to the neighborhood. You can tour the entire area from a bicycle seat, thanks to the 20-mile South Bay Bike Trail that runs from Will Rogers State Beach (north of Santa Monica) to Torrance Beach in the south. Or you can drive. Huge public parking lots abound along the South Bay's beaches.

Rising above the southernmost reach of Santa Monica Bay is the Palos Verdes Peninsula, a collection of affluent residential enclaves that separate L.A.'s surf cities and their semi-industrial inland neighbors from San Pedro and the Port of Los Angeles, next south, and Long Beach, home port of the RMS *Queen Mary,* the new Long Beach Aquarium of the Pacific, and other attractions. Next stop south of Long Beach is Orange County.

El Segundo and Manhattan Beach
El Segundo is sometimes also described as L.A.'s own Mayberry, U.S.A., for its insular Midwestern mores. Before the end of the Cold War and the rapid decline of Southern California's defense industry, no one much minded comments about "El Stinko," a reference to Playa del Rey's 144-acre Hyperion Waste Treatment Plant and its downwind influence here. And no one complained about the huge circa-1911 Chevron oil refinery just south. (The town was named for it. El Segundo means "The Second [One]" in Spanish, since Standard Oil's first refinery—this plant was Standard before it was Chevron—opened in Richmond, near San Francisco.) And no one seemed to hear the ear-rending racket from LAX jet traffic overhead. Everyone was too busy working—at Aerospace Corp., Hughes Aircraft, Northrop, Rockwell, and TRW. Not to mention Mattel Toys. Some of those jobs have disappeared, in L.A.'s new post-defense economy, but others have taken their place. These days El Segundo—conveniently near LAX, after all—is getting serious about attracting new industry and, closer to the beach, trendier and tourism-related businesses.

Chic Manhattan Beach, just south, already riding the latter wave, doesn't have such problems—which is why restaurants and businesses along the El Segundo side of the bustling, increasingly chi-chi Rosecrans Ave. corridor shamelessly advertise their address as "Manhattan Beach." At the beach—Manhattan State Beach, a continuation of the nearly seamless broad bay strand that starts north of Santa Monica—you'll find excellent swimming, lifeguards, both clean water and sand, the works. If you're driving, you'll find free parking along Vista del Mar to Highland, metered parking along most streets, and public lots close to attractive "downtown," at both 11th and 13th Streets. There's also a metered lot at 43rd Street. For fishing, try 900-foot **Manhattan Beach Pier** at the foot of Manhattan Beach Boulevard. You can also stroll **The Strand,** which here wanders past beachfront homes as it meanders south to Hermosa Beach.

For more information about the area, contact the **City of El Segundo,** 310/607-2249, www.elsegundo.org, and the **City of Manhattan Beach,** 310/802-5000, www.ci.manhattanbeach.ca.us.

Redondo Beach and Hermosa Beach

Redondo State Beach is the hot-weather hot spot in these parts, though nothing like this old resort town's turn-of-the-20th-century heyday. Still, at times it's almost as difficult to park your beach towel as it is your car. As elsewhere along L.A.'s South Bay, the two miles of beach here are wide and sandy. The **Redondo Beach Pier,** at the foot of Torrance Blvd., marks the beach's northern reaches. In 1988 storms and subsequent fires ravaged the 60-year-old wooden horseshoe-shaped pier, the most recent of many local pier incarnations—and the city rebuilt in grand style. Designed by Edward Beall, the new, nautically themed $11 million Redondo Beach Pier—complete with sail-like awnings—is a sturdy yet wondrous concrete creation, complete with 1,800 life-size etchings of marine life, including sharks, scuba divers, and whales. (Water quality near the pier is less than perfect, though.) **King Harbor** just north, along Harbor Dr. between Horondo and Beryl Sts., is the result of a massive redevelopment that cost Redondo Beach its historic downtown, replacing it with 50 acres of high-rise apartment buildings. King Harbor has its own piers, with restaurants, shops, and such, and also offers harbor cruises, sportfishing and winter whale-watching charters, and bike and other sports equipment rentals. Not to take a back seat to Long Beach, Redondo Beach even offers gondola rides at King Harbor, through **Gondola Amore,** 310/376-6977. The best surfing is just north, at Hermosa Beach, and well south of Redondo at Torrance Beach. Be that as it may, come to Redondo in August for the annual **Surf Festival.**

Head north from Redondo to Hermosa Beach, most famous as L.A.'s best for beach volleyball,

site of numerous competitions and championship matches. Hermosa Beach also features row upon row of at-the-beach apartments and the **Hermosa Beach Pier,** historically a fishing pier, which along with lower Pier Ave. had a $1.5 million facelift in early 1997 to create another L.A. "destination street." **The Strand** stroll here is quite pleasant, passing beach homes, restaurants, and shops. Not to be missed in the neighborhood is the independent **Nations! Travelstore,** 500-504 Pier Ave., 310/318-9915 or tollfree 800/546-8060, www.nationstravelmall.com, a combination bookstore, map and supply stop, and travel agency beloved for its exceptional product selection and customer service.

Head south from Redondo to Torrance Beach and then, for top-notch surfing, stroll to Malaga Cove below the bluffs. It's easier to get to the cove from the Palos Verdes Peninsula (see below).

For more information about the area, contact: **Redondo Beach Visitors Bureau,** 200 N. Pacific Coast Hwy., toll-free 800/282-0333 or 310/374-2171, www.redondo.org, and the **Torrance Visitors Bureau,** 3400 Torrance Blvd., 310/792-2343, www.torrnet.com.

PALOS VERDES PENINSULA

If you lived in paradise, wouldn't you want to keep it that way? The upper-class and uppermiddle-class communities atop Palos Verdes Peninsula are fairly exclusive, and largely proud of it—a sense of entitlement that, unfortunately, sometimes extends to local beaches. Demonstrating an international surfing phenomenon known as "localism," the feared Bay Boys of Palos Verdes—"trust-fund babies," according to a *Surfer* magazine editor—have long made it their business to keep nonlocals out of primo surf spots such as Lunada Bay, a stance that has led to verbal assaults and worse on more than one occasion, and an attitude that has led to significant lawsuits against Palos Verdes Estates. Whatever the absolute truth underlying such conflicts, it's clear that no one here wants the now-common California beach overcrowding problems and related traumas—trash, graffiti, violence—that are increasing all along the coast, particularly at the best surfing beaches.

Few such troubles perturb the Palos Verdes

Peninsula, which eons ago was one of the Channel Islands. Serious social problems here include the challenge of dodging horses and riders on public streets (equestrians have the right-of-way) and coping with the noise and effluence of the wild peacock flocks in Rolling Hills Estates and Palos Verdes Estates. The peninsula is home to several of L.A.'s most affluent communities—Rolling Hills is, officially, the wealthiest town in America, and its neighbors are also at the top of the list—and what its people value most is their privacy. Yet despite ongoing surf-turf wars the peninsula's parks, other public facilities, and businesses generally welcome visitors.

Though you must meander the peninsula's winding interior roads to get a close-up view of life here, most people are satisfied with a leisurely coastal drive. And, on a clear day, the views are spectacular. Starting in the north, from Pacific Coast Hwy. (Hwy. 1) head southwest on Palos Verdes Blvd., which soon becomes Palos Verdes Dr. W, then, at Hawthorne Blvd., Palos Verdes Dr. S; heading north on Palos Verdes Dr. E eventually leads to east-west Palos Verdes Dr. N, completing the bluff-top "perimeter" drive. But a true coastal tour would continue east along 25th St. into San Pedro, perhaps jogging south to Paseo del Mar and then east again to the Cabrillo Marine Aquarium.

To explore local features and natural history, sign on for one of the monthly guided hikes offered through the **Palos Verdes Peninsula Land Conservancy,** 310/541-7613, www.pvplc.

org. For more information about the area, contact: **Palos Verdes Peninsula Chamber of Commerce,** 310/377-8111, www.palosverdes. com/pvpcc.

San Pedro

With its hilly streets, ocean fog, views, and military installations, San Pedro is, some local wags say, L.A.'s own little San Francisco, complete with a miniature, but much friendlier, Mission District, along Pacific Street. (It's san PEE-dro, by the way, despite California's predilection elsewhere for correct Spanish pronunciation.) That perspective is a hard sell even in this semi-industrial port city, however.

If people find themselves in San Pedro, most head to the shops, restaurants, and other tourist diversions of **Ports O' Call Village** at the end of 6th St., 310/831-0287, a shopping mall in the style of a New England seaside village. But San Pedro has more intriguing features—including the **Port of Los Angeles** itself, which was created at a cost of $60 million between 1920 and 1940. The best way to get the big picture is on guided boat tours ($6–10) with **Spirit Cruises,** 310/548-8080, which depart from Ports O' Call. From the **World Cruise Terminal** and **Catalina Terminal** here, travelers depart on sea journeys near and far. A particularly impressive sight is soaring **Vincent Thomas Bridge,** which from the Harbor Fwy. (the 110) connects San Pedro (via Hwy. 47) to Terminal Island—Southern California's largest suspension bridge, built in 1963

San Pedro

(small toll on the return trip). **Terminal Island,** once known as Rattlesnake Island, was a vibrant resort destination earlier in this century, L.A.'s own Brighton Beach, complete with pleasure pier. Starting in 1906, it was also home to a close-knit village of Japanese-American fishermen and their families—an idyllic life ended forever with World War II–era Japanese internment in 1942. Terminal Island today, an uninviting diesel-scented jungle of canneries, loading cranes, and old warships, also includes a federal penitentiary.

Other significant San Pedro attractions include two seaworthy museums: the **Los Angeles Maritime Museum** at Berth 84 (at the foot of 6th St.), 310/548-7618, and the **S.S. Lane Victory Ship Museum** at Berth 94 (near the World Cruise Terminal), 310/519-9545, a onetime ammunition carrier, now a national historic landmark. Well worth a stop in nearby **Wilmington** are the **Banning Residence Museum,** 401 E. M St., 310/548-7777, the restored 1864 Greek Revival mansion of General Phineas Banning and a major interpretive center for 19th-century L.A. history, and the **Drum Barracks Civil War Museum,** 1052 Banning Blvd., 310/548-7509, the only remaining structure from the Civil War–era Camp Drum, where 7,000 troops were based. Both museums are open only for guided tours (call for times); donations greatly appreciated.

Definitely worth a stop, especially with tots in tow, is the **Cabrillo Marine Aquarium and Museum,** 3720 Stephen White Dr., 310/548-7562, open Tues.–Fri. noon–5 P.M. and on weekends 10 A.M.–5 P.M. (open on some "holiday" Mondays, closed Thanksgiving, Christmas). It's free—suggested donation is $2 adults, $1 children, and parking is $6.50—and full of educational opportunity, thus quite popular with school groups. But anyone can be a kid here. Housed in a contemporary Frank Gehry–designed building, the Cabrillo features 38 tanks now home to an abundance of Southern California sea life. Among the most popular exhibits: the "tidal tank," a veritable room with a view of a wave, and the shark tank. Other exhibits include a "touch tank" filled with sea anemones and starfish, and a whalebone graveyard. The aquarium also offers seasonal whale-watching tours and "grunion run" programs; call for current information. From here, set out for both **Cabrillo Beach** and 1200-foot **Cabrillo Pier,** just inside the breakwater.

Also worth a stop (though not open to the public) **Point Fermin Lighthouse** at the end of the breakwater at 807 Paseo del Mar—the only remaining wooden lighthouse on the Pacific Coast, shining forth here since 1874.

For more information about the area, contact: **San Pedro Peninsula Chamber of Commerce,** 390 W. 7th St., 310/832-7272, www.sanpedrochamber.com.

LONG BEACH: IOWA BY THE BAY GOES BIG TIME

Long Beach is the second-largest city in Los Angeles County, dwarfed only by L.A. itself, and the fifth-largest in the state. The city's history follows the fairly predictable Southern California course, from coastal wilderness and rangeland suburb of Spain and Mexico to extensive Midwestern settlement. The population of transplants from Iowa was once so dominant, in fact, that "Iowa picnics" became the most memorable community social gatherings during the Great Depression. Then came turn-of-the-20th-century seaside resort and booming port, regional oil development, and the monumental Long Beach earthquake that flattened downtown in 1933—the indirect impetus for downtown's then-new art deco style. Howard Hughes, the aviator and engineer later famous as the world's most eccentric billionaire, made history here in 1947 when he took his *Spruce Goose*—the world's largest airplane—for its first and only flight.

During and since World War II, but before the post–Cold War era of military downsizing, the U.S. Navy was central to Long Beach life, given the presence of the Long Beach Naval Station, Long Beach Naval Shipyard, and Boeing, Mc-Donnell Douglas, and other aviation and defense-related industry. Symbol of that past was the Iowa-class USS *Missouri,* America's last active battleship, host to Japan's formal surrender at the end of World War II and later recruit for offshore duty in the Persian Gulf during Operation Desert Storm. When "Mighty Mo" was finally decommissioned here in 1992, thousands and thousands turned out for the event. Both the naval station and shipyard have since been shut down. Yet the city is determined to recover from its defense-related economic losses. The Port of

Long Beach is the busiest cargo port on the West Coast, doing a brisk Pacific Rim trade, and promoting downtown and port-side tourism is also a major priority.

Long Beach is an astonishingly diverse community with large immigrant populations, recently gaining national notoriety as the first California city to adopt a uniforms-only public school dress code. Despite the city's pressing social problems, people visit Long Beach primarily because it's still apple-pie appealing, unassuming, and affordable, with clean air and coastal diversions, a spruced-up downtown, and a lively cultural scene. (Many also show up here on business; both the Long Beach Convention and Entertainment Center and the World Trade Center are downtown.) And some say there are more worthy breakfast, burger, and pie shops in Long Beach than anywhere else in L.A. County.

Though bad press from occasional outbreaks of gang warfare is a bane of Long Beach existence, visitors don't need to be overly concerned. (One area at high risk for violent crime is north of downtown, straddling the 710 between Hwy. 47 and Temple Ave., south of Pacific Coast Hwy. and north of 7th St.; another, well north of downtown, stretches between Long Beach Blvd. and Orange Ave., south of South St. and north of Del Amo Boulevard.) Reasonable precautions are prudent, of course, as in any urban area.

Special annual events well worth the trip include the **Toyota Grand Prix of Long Beach** in April—an event that transforms Shoreline Dr., Seaside Way, and other downtown streets into an international raceway—the **Cajun and Zydeco Festival** in June, and the long-running **Long Beach Blues Festival** in September.

The **Long Beach Freeway,** the 710, a major shipping corridor, delivers residents, visitors, and truckers alike right into downtown and/or the port district. Newcomers, heads up: Should you see a spectacular crash on six-lane **Shoreline Drive** in Long Beach, it's not always necessary to call 911. One of Hollywood's favorite filming sites for "freeway" disasters, Shoreline is regularly shut down for film shoots—20 or more times in an average year. (Don't worry. Actual traffic is routed around the action.) But in Long Beach, it's uniquely possible to get out—and stay out—of your car altogether, due to its excellent public transportation.

For more information about Long Beach and its attractions, contact: **Long Beach Convention and Visitors Bureau,** One World Trade Center, Ste. 300, Long Beach, CA 90831, 562/436-3645, or toll-free 800/452-7829, or www.go-longbeach.org.

Seeing and Doing Long Beach

The visitor action in Long Beach is downtown and nearby, on the waterfront. The famed **Pike Amusement Park**—where Southern California once entertained itself on the roller coaster and boardwalk, and where W. C. Fields, Buster Keaton, and other early film-industry icons made movies—once stood near the current site of the

The RMS Queen Mary *is one of the largest passenger ships ever built.*

TOM MYERS PHOTOGRAPHY

LONG BEACH AQUARIUM OF THE PACIFIC

The latest star brightening the Long Beach waterfront is the $100 million, 120,000-square-foot Long Beach Aquarium of the Pacific. The Aquarium of the Pacific features 550 species of aquatic life in three major galleries, these corresponding to the Pacific Ocean's three regions: **Southern California/Baja,** the **Tropical Pacific,** and the **Northern Pacific.** The Great Hall of the Pacific—the size of a football field, to represent the Pacific's vastness—offers an overview and a preview.

The aquarium first dips into the offshore waters of Southern California and the Baja Peninsula, from underwater kelp forests to bird's- and otter's-eye views of seals and sea lions frolicking in a facsimile Catalina Island environment. The interactive Kids' Cove here teaches the kiddos about other families' habits and habitats—in this case, those of marine animal families—and allows them to hike through whale bones, "hatch" bird eggs, and hide out with the hermit crabs. Then it's a quick splash south to Baja's Sea of Cortez and its sea turtles, skates, and rays. The Northern Pacific exhibits begin in the icy Bering Sea, where puffins nest near playful sea otters. This frigid sea shares other aquatic wealth, from schooling fish to giant octopuses and Japanese spider crabs. First stop in the Tropical Pacific is a peaceful lagoon in Micronesia, which sets the stage for the stunning 35,000-gallon Deep Reef exhibit—the aquarium's largest—with its vivid panorama of tropical sealife. If you time it right, you can watch divers feed the fish. Should you need feeding yourself, dive into the aquarium's **Café Scuba,** overlooking Rainbow Harbor. And to take home some specific memento of the Pacific Ocean, see what's on sale at the **Pacific Collections** gift shop.

Just off Shoreline Dr. at 100 Aquarium Way (follow the signs), the Aquarium of the Pacific is open daily 9 A.M.–6 P.M. (closed Christmas). At last report admission was $14.95 adults, $11.95 seniors (age 60 and older), and $7.95 children (ages 3–11). Group rates (for 20 or more) are available with advance reservations. For more information or to purchase advance tickets, call the aquarium at 562/590-3100 or check the website at www.aquariumofpacific.org.

---

huge Long Beach Convention and Entertainment Center. Though Hollywood subsequently stole the moviemaking spotlight, later Long Beach films have included *The Creature from the Black Lagoon, Corrina Corrina, Speed,* and the opening scenes to *Lethal Weapon.* And until quite recently TV's *Baywatch* was filmed here, too, at least in part.

Though the new **Long Beach Aquarium of the Pacific,** 562/590-3100, is the city's newest big attraction—and centerpiece of the $650-million Queensway Bay redevelopment project—the surrounding **Rainbow Harbor** resort complex is now home port for the tall ship **Californian,** toll-free 800/432-2201, www.californian.org, available for high-seas adventure sails when it's moored in Long Beach. For more boating, take a Venetian-style gondola ride through the Naples Island neighborhood with **Gondola Getaway,** 562/433-9595, where the basket of bread, cheese, and salami is provided—along with the "O Sole Mio"—but you'll have to bring your own vino. Still most famous in Long Beach, though, is the RMS **Queen Mary,** a floating cruise ship-cum-museum moored on the other side of Queensway Bridge featuring hotel rooms, restaurants, and shops, 562/435-3511 or toll-free 800/437-2934 (hotel reservations), www.queenmary.com. A new, also-tourable companion for the *Queen* is a retired Soviet submarine, Podvodnaya Lodka B-427, also known by the code name *Scorpion,* decommissioned in 1994. The gigantic golf ball–like geodesic dome nearby is the Queen Mary Seaport Dome, onetime home of Howard Hughes's *Spruce Goose,* now a popular moviemaking soundstage.

Looking out onto the Queen, from the downtown side of the bay, is the **Shoreline Village** shopping complex at 407 Shoreline Village Dr., 562/435-4093, complete with a 1906 **Charles Looff carousel** for the kiddos.

Or head for the wide white sandy beach. Or take a beachfront bike ride. Well worth a stop at the beach is the **Long Beach Museum of Art,** 2300 E. Ocean Blvd., 562/439-2119, www.lbma.org, where you get artistic beach views in addition to an eyeful of contemporary art, photography, and sculpture. The museum is scheduled to reopen, after renovation, in September 2000, and when it does will be open

Tues.–Sun. 11 A.M.–7 P.M. Admission is $5 adults, $4 students/seniors.

Other Long Beach attractions include the new **Museum of Latin American Art** close to downtown at 628 Alamitos Ave. (the northern extension of Shoreline Dr., south of 7th St.), 562/437-1689, www.molaa.com, the only U.S. museum with this exclusive artistic focus. This 1920-vintage 20,000-square-foot building houses the Robert Gumbiner Foundation collection of Latin American art, rotating contemporary exhibits, "La Galeria" gallery and store, and both performance area and research library. The museum is open Tues.–Sat. 11:30 A.M.–7:30 P.M., Sun. noon–6 P.M. Admission is $7 adults, $5 students and seniors, free for children 12 and under. Call for current exhibit information or check the museum website.

For an introduction to local history, stop by the **Historical Society of Long Beach Gallery and Research Center,** in the Breakers Building, 562/495-1210. Amateur historians should also explore two small outposts of early Southern California still at home in Long Beach. The seven-acre remnant of **Rancho Los Alamitos,** 6400 E. Bixby Hill Rd., 562/431-3541, offers free tours of the 1800-vintage adobe, later farm buildings, and lovely gardens Wed.–Sun. 1–5 P.M. (last tour starts at 4 P.M.). **Rancho Los Cerritos,** 4600 Virginia Rd., 562/570-1755, offers weekend-only guided tours of this 1844 Monterey-style adobe home and surrounding gardens—once the center of a 27,000-acre sheep ranch—which is also open to the public Wed.–Sun. 1–5 P.M. Admission to both homes is free. Closed on holidays.

Historians of California's future should visit **Little Cambodia** along Anaheim St., the largest Cambodian settlement outside Phnom Penh. For business, restaurant, and other information, call the **Cambodian Association of America,** 562/426-6002, or the **United Cambodian Community,** 562/433-2490.

Book lovers, don't miss family-run **Acres of Books,** 240 Long Beach Blvd. (at Maple), 562/437-6980, the nation's largest selection of used books, open here since 1934 and reported to be one of writer Ray Bradbury's favorites. Another historic local business is **Bert Grimms Tattoo Studio,** 22 S. Chestnut Pl. (at Ocean), 562/432-9304, where, according to local lore, gangsters Bonnie Parker and Pretty Boy Floyd got their skin ink. Prime-time for shopping is a 15-block stretch of 2nd St. in Belmont Shore and downtown's Pine Ave./Broadway district.

Staying in Long Beach

In the absence of a major downtown convention, and particularly in the off-season, Long Beach–area accommodations can be a relative bargain for families and budget travelers. The best bargain anytime, complete with panoramic ocean views and surrounding sports fields, park, and picnic areas, is the nearby 60-bed Hostelling International-American Youth Hostels **Los Angeles/South Bay Hostel** in Angel's Gate Park in San Pedro at 3601 S. Gaffey St., Bldg. 613, 310/831-8109, www.hostelweb.com, primarily dorm-style accommodations (groups welcome) though private rooms are available. The hostel features on-site kitchen and laundry, library, TV and VCR, and barbecue—and from here it's just a stroll to the beach. Dorm beds are $16 members, $18 non-members; private rooms $39 non-members, $42 members. Budget. Reservations essential in summer.

Other fairly inexpensive accommodations abound in Long Beach along or near Pacific Coast Highway. Here, though, the highway runs through some rough neighborhoods and—if you were expecting oceanfront views—doesn't get close to the coast until it reaches the Orange County line. Be that as it may, best bets include **Motel 6** on 7th St. near California State University at Long Beach, 562/597-1311 or toll-free 800/466-8356, www.motel6.com, with rates $54 double (Moderate), and **Super 8** across from the community hospital, 562/597-7701 with rates $66 double and up (Moderate-Expensive). Just south of PCH is the **Best Western of Long Beach,** 1725 Long Beach Blvd., 562/599-5555 or toll-free 800/528-1234 (central reservations), www.bestwestern.com, where a plus is the proximity of the Metrorail Blue Line across the street. Rates start at $89 double. Expensive.

Fairly basic but good choices closer to the beach and just a few blocks from the convention center include the **Inn of Long Beach,** 185 Atlantic Ave., 562/435-3791, innoflongbeach.com, from $79 double (Moderate), and the nearby **TraveLodge Convention Center,** 80 Atlantic Ave., 562/435-2471 or toll-free 800/578-7878, from $89 double (Expensive).

Keep in mind that high-end accommodations are sometimes quite reasonable in Long Beach,

camouflaged oil wells on a man-made island off Long Beach

TOM MYERS PHOTOGRAPHY

especially on weekends, during the holiday season, or with AAA, AARP, and other discounts. So inquire about discounts and packages at some of the nicest local hotels, including the **Hyatt Regency Long Beach** at Two World Trade Center (Ocean Ave. and Golden Shore St.), 562/491-1234, with rates $199–299 (Luxury); the **Renaissance Long Beach Hotel,** 111 E. Ocean Blvd. (at Pine), 562/437-5900, with rates $145–165 (Premium-Luxury); and the **Westin Long Beach,** 333 E. Ocean Blvd., 562/436-3000, with rates $119–199 (Premium-Luxury).

For something definitely different, consider an onboard overnight at the RMS *Queen Mary,* at 1126 Queen's Hwy., Pier J, 562/435-3511, www.queenmary.com, and sleep in a 1936-vintage oceanliner cabin. Special package deals include the Catalina Getaway, Paradise Package, and the Royal Romance Package. Rates are $125–400 (Deluxe-Luxury). For more ship information, see the general travel listing for the *Queen Mary,* above.

Long Beach also offers bed-and-breakfast choices, including the antique-rich **Lord Mayor's Inn Bed & Breakfast,** 435 Cedar Ave. (between 4th and 5th Sts.), 562/436-0324, www.lordmayors.com, the onetime home of Long Beach's first mayor, Charles Windham, elected in the early 1900s. Savory cinnamon rolls come with breakfast. Rates are $85–125 (Expensive-Premium).

Eating in Long Beach: Downtown

Increasingly stylish dining and shopping star downtown on and near Pine Ave. and along Belmont Shore's 2nd Street. Popular and good for fresh fish and seafood downtown is the **King's Fish House Pine Avenue,** 100 W. Broadway (at Pine), 562/432-7463, open for lunch and dinner daily, for breakfast on weekends. For classy Northern Italian, the place is grand **L'Opera,** 101 Pine (at 1st St.), 562/491-0066, open nightly for dinner, weekdays for lunch. Among the many other choices in the neighborhood: the see-and-be-seen **Alegria Cocina Latina,** 115 Pine (at 1st), 562/436-3388, where tapas star but gazpacho, sandwiches, salads, and substantial dinners are also on tap (the deli opens in the morning, too, for pastries and coffee). Live music nightly, and don't miss the Flamenco show. For a contemporary culinary escape to the islands of the Caribbean, try **Cha Cha Cha,** 762 Pacific Ave. (near 8th St.), 562/436-3900, open for lunch and dinner daily.

After dinner downtown, there's entertainment. Among downtown's most popular nightclubs: the **Blue Cafe,** 210 Promenade N (at Broadway), 562/983-7111, famous for its blues acts, billiards, and low ($5–10) cover charge; **Cohiba Club,** 144 Pine (at Broadway), 562/437-7700, for dancing to DJs and live bands; and **Jillian's,** 110 Pine (near Broadway), 562/628-8866, for billiards and dancing in The Vault.

If making the scene isn't your scene, the mellowest coffeehouse around is **The Library,** 3418 E. Broadway (at Redondo Ave.), 562/433-2393, which features plush couches and good paperbacks. Also here: banana-flavored cheesecake and baseball-sized blueberry muffins. And you can always go to the movies, at the large selection of screens downtown provided by AMC's **Pine Square 16,** 562/435-1335, one of Southern California's largest cinema complexes.

Eating in Long Beach: Near Belmont Shore
A classic Long Beach dining destination is lively **Small Cafe** (formerly Russell's) near Belmont Shore, 5656 E. 2nd St. (near Westminster), 562/434-0226, one of the southstate's best burger establishments. Some people come strictly for the pies with the mile-high meringues, including banana, chocolate, peanut butter, and sour cream. Another all-American burger destination is **Hof's Hut,** 4828 E. 2nd St. (at St. Joseph), 562/439-4775, where the Hofburger is the main attraction—not counting the snorkeler's fin dangling from the stuffed shark's mouth. For fancier American-style fare, the place is **Shenandoah Cafe,** 4722 E. 2nd (at Park), 562/434-3469.

A bit more international is **Provençe Boulangerie,** 191 Park Ave. (at 2nd St.), 562/433-8281, doing a brisk business in coffee, croissants, baguettes, wonderful breads, soup, and other simple wonders. Best for Italian is genuinely friendly **Christy's Italian Cafe,** 3937 E. Broadway

(at Termino Ave.), 562/433-7133. (If you're one of those cigar-sucking trendoids, the **Havana Cigar Club** is right next door.) For fabulous Indian food, the place is **Natraj,** 5262 E. 2nd St. (near La Verne Ave.), 562/930-0930, where the Mon.–Sat. lunch buffet and the all-you-can-eat Sunday brunch are particularly great deals. But the classic vegetarian hot spot in Belmont Shore is inexpensive **Papa Jon's Natural Market & Cafe,** 5006 E. 2nd St. (at Argonne Ave.), 562/439-1059, serving a great TLT—tofu, lettuce, and tomato sandwich—as well as broccoli sesame pasta, vegetable shepherd's pie, spinach lasagne, and veggie and tempeh burgers.

For eats at the beach try the **Belmont Brewing Company,** 25 39th Pl., near the end of Belmont Pier, 562/433-3891, where good food is served with respectable local brews—including the ever-popular dark Long Beach Crude. Also near the pier, overlooking the beach near the end of Termino (behind Yankee Doodles) is **Ragazzi Ristorante,** 562/438-3773, serving a nice selection of pastas, pizzas, and chicken and fish dishes. For big-time beefeaters, **555 East** at 555 E. Ocean Blvd. (near Atlantic), 562/437-0626, bills itself as an American Steakhouse and is generally considered the best in Long Beach.

CATALINA: 22 MILES ACROSS THE SEA

Thanks to one of those schmaltzy old songs, Santa Catalina Island's original location in the American imagination as "island of romance" was "twenty-six miles across the sea," though it's actually only 22 miles from San Pedro on the mainland. But romantic it was—first famous as the private fiefdom of William Wrigley Jr., of chewing gum fame, and as onetime spring training camp for his Chicago Cubs. The western pulp writer Zane Grey, whose "pueblo" now serves as a hotel, also loved Catalina. And the roster of movie stars and celebrities who have been here at one time or another, for one reason or another, would practically fill a book. Catalina even has its own movable movie memorabilia—a herd of buffalo, woolly chocolate-colored descendants of beasts originally imported in 1924 for the filming of *The Vanishing American.*

Yet all is not nostalgic. In its own way, quaint

Catalina also walks the cutting edge. To solve its ongoing water supply problems, for example, Catalina started up its own desalination plant to transform seawater into drinking water. Because unrestrained automobile traffic would clearly ruin the town, perhaps even sink the island, few cars are allowed on Catalina. Instead, if not on foot most people get around greater Avalon by golf cart—an appropriate local transportation. And most of the island is owned, and protected, by private trusts—which means that all but the most innocuous activities, such as eating and shopping, are strictly regulated. Hiking and biking are by permit only, for example, and camping in the interior is by reservation only.

Present-day Catalina, second largest of the Channel Islands at 48,438 acres, otherwise retains its charms—fresh air and mild climate, rugged open space, a healthy ocean environ-

TOM MYERS PHOTOGRAPHY

Santa Catalina Harbor

ment—because the island is relatively unpopulated. Avalon, the island's only town, boasts barely 3,000 souls. Southern California's version of a whitewashed Mediterranean hillside village perched above a balmy bay, Avalon is brushed with bright colors and stunning tiles—the most concentrated public and private displays of 1930s California tile work anywhere. Anchoring Avalon Bay on the north, just beyond the town's tiny bayside commercial district, is the spectacular Moorish Casino, the art-deco masterpiece built by William Wrigley, Jr., to house the first theater specifically designed for movies. Beyond Avalon the island's other primary visitor destination is remote Two Harbors, snuggled into the isthmus to the northwest.

The official island population may be miniscule but the unofficial head count can be astronomi-cal in summer and on "event" weekends. Crowds or no crowds, most folks manage only a day trip—taking in the ocean wind and waves on the way and then sampling the shops and the island's main "urban" sights before climbing back on the ferry to head home. (For day trips avoid Tues. and Wed., when the cruise ships dock.) One of California's small tragedies is the fact that so few visitors realize that on a longer stay Catalina offers *solitude,* a very rare Southern California commodity, and a wealth of other worthwhile pursuits.

For current details on transportation options, tours, special events, accommodations options and packages, and other practical information, contact: **Catalina Island Chamber of Commerce and Visitors Bureau,** P.O. Box 217, Avalon, CA 90704, 310/510-1520, www.catalina.com.

TOM MYERS PHOTOGRAPHY

ORANGE COUNTY

THE DIFFERENCE BETWEEN L.A AND ORANGE COUNTY

Sun-kissed Southern California rivals, Orange County and Los Angeles argue endlessly about whose neighborhood is most blessed—a full-blown feud evolved into advanced social sport, sometimes nasty, sometimes hilarious.

The differences between the two are difficult to grasp for those just passing through, though. Both feature sunny neighborhoods strung together by shopping centers and stressful freeways. Both have sped through the Southern California boom-bust cycles of agriculture, oil, land development, and aerospace. Both steal their water from elsewhere. Both have sandy beaches, bad neighborhoods, good neighborhoods, all of it high-priced. Both embrace an idealized self-image, disregarding uglier truths. And both believe the other is missing the best of all possible worlds.

Some say the spat started in the late 1800s, when Los Angeles County was almost as large as Ohio. Tired of taxation without representa-

tion, and bitter about their second-class status, residents of the Santa Ana Valley—modern-day Orange County—staged their first anti-tax rebellion by seceding from Los Angeles. Though often amicable, the post-break-up bickering continues to this day.

Urbane Angelenos point out that orange trees in Orange County are about as abundant as the seals at Seal Beach. (There are no seals at Seal Beach.) That high culture in Orange County is best represented by the John Wayne statue at the airport. That the entire county, in fact, is more G-rated than a Disney cartoon. That only Orange County could produce the likes of ex-President Richard Nixon, not to mention local politicians prone to stating publicly that men who support abortion rights are "women trapped in men's bodies . . . who are looking for an easy lay" as Representative Robert K. "B-1 Bob" Dornan of Garden Grove once said. (Dornan since lost his congressional seat to a Latina, Loretta Sanchez, a subject that still rankles.) That at its best Orange County exhibits a standard-brand and superficial beauty, at its worst, vapid nouveau-riche snobbery. That the FBI has identified

EVENTFUL ORANGE COUNTY

Among Orange County's more famous events is the astonishing **Pageant of the Masters** scheduled during July and August in Laguna Beach, with life imitating art imitating life in the form of *tableaux vivants,* or living pictures. The main annual events up the coast in Huntington Beach include the **Bluetorch Pro of Surfing,** (formerly known as the OP Pro) usually held in July, and the **U.S. Open of Surfing,** in August, the most well known among the multitude of local surfing competitions. The **Orange County Fair,** held at the fairgrounds in Costa Mesa, also comes in July.

But there's always something worth doing. Come at other times throughout the year to appreciate surprising aspects of local culture and community.

Whale-watching is a major draw in winter, particularly during January and February, with excursion boats departing from Newport Beach, Dana Point, and other coastal locales. Dana Point's popular **Festival of the Whales,** complete with film festival, street fair, and concert series, is held over several consecutive weekends from mid-February into early March. Unique in February is the **Tet Festival** in Westminster's Little Saigon, celebrating the Vietnamese New Year.

According to local legend the swallows return to Mission San Juan Capistrano every year on March 19—thus the annual **Festival de los Golondrinas** or The Swallows Festival in San Juan Capistrano, with **Swallows Day** now typically scheduled for the weekend closest to that mythic date. In late March and early April comes Mission San Juan Capistrano's **Mud Slinging Festival,** during which "children of all ages" (including politicians, appropriately enough) personally participate in renewing the adobe mud facades of the mission's historic buildings.

In April comes the **Spring Garden Tour** in Laguna Beach and, at the local Sawdust Festival grounds, Laguna's annual **Art Walk.** Another big deal in April is **A Night in Fullerton,** an all-out introduction to local art galleries and other downtown attractions, complete with convenient shuttle bus transport, not to mention the countywide **Imagination Celebration** for children, teenagers, and families. Also on tap for April: the popular **Temecula Balloon and Wine Festival** nearby, in Riverside County's Temecula Valley.

Garden Grove's historic **Strawberry Festival** in May celebrates the bygone days of gardens and groves, when the community was known as the strawberry capital of America. Also scheduled in May: the **Anaheim Children's Festival** and, in Costa Mesa, the annual **Highland Gathering and Festival** celebrating Scottish culture. In late June comes **A Taste of Orange County** held at the Irvine Spectrum in Irvine, a three-day sampling of local cuisine, wine, and music—blues, reggae, jazz, and country-western.

The high season for Orange County arts arrives in Laguna Beach in late June and early July—the beginning of the summer's continuing events in Laguna Canyon, including the juried **Art-A-Fair** show, the alternative arts **Sawdust Festival,** and the more traditional **Festival of Arts,** which includes the annual Pageant of the Masters performances. The annual mid-August **Pier Fest** in Huntington Beach celebrates the reconstructed Huntington Beach Pier, California's longest concrete municipal pier.

Autumn activities include the **Orange International Street Fair** in the city of Orange, the annual **Sand Castle and Sand Sculpture Contest** at Corona Del Mar State Beach, the **Tallships Festival** at the Orange County Marine Institute in Dana Point Harbor, and the **Wooden Ships Festival** in Newport Beach—all scheduled in September. The big event in October is the ghoulish, ghostly, and frightfully fun **Halloween Haunt** at Knott's Berry Farm—not recommended for children, who would probably prefer much less spooky **Camp Spooky.** Disneyland also gets into the act, with trick-or-treating at **Mickey's Halloween Treat.**

The holiday season officially begins in November, with **A Christmas Fantasy Parade** at Disneyland, the **Knott's Berry Farm Christmas Crafts Village,** and other crafts fairs. Traditional favorites in December include the **Christmas Boat Parade** in Newport Harbor and the Huntington Harbor **Cruise of Lights.**

For more information about these and other events, contact the Anaheim/Orange County Visitor and Convention Bureau, 714/765-8888, as well as local visitor bureaus.

Orange County as the capital of white-collar crime, and that when Orange County filed for bankruptcy in 1994, it entered the record books with the biggest municipal bankruptcy in U.S. history. That, all things considered, Orange County is little more than an emergency gasoline stop on the road to San Diego.

Indignant Orange County residents counter that people from Los Angeles are self-absorbed cultural elitists who live only to consume the latest fads in food, clothing, and thought. Behind all that anti-

Orange posturing, they say, Angelenos are just jealous—because Orange County, not L.A., now represents the quintessential Southern California lifestyle. Orange County has no smog. People in Orange County can still drop the tops on their convertibles and surf the freeways fast enough to get speeding tickets. They can go to the beach without getting caught in gang crossfire. And they aren't social hypocrites. People in Orange County, where beach-bleached blondes are the societal ideal, don't congratulate themselves on multicul-

turalism in the light of day and then retreat at night, in the L.A. style, to economically and ethnically segregated neighborhoods.

But according to T. Jefferson Parker in his entertaining essay "Behind the Orange Curtain," only one fundamental difference separates Los Angeles citizens from those who inhabit the Big Orange:

L.A. people all want to be someone else. Look at them, and, as Jim Harrison has written,

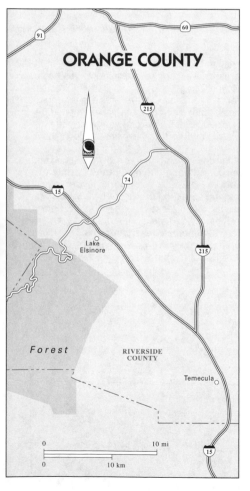

"see the folly whirling in their eyes." The waiters all want to be novelists; the novelists all want to be screenwriters; the screenwriters all want to direct; the directors all want to produce; the producers all want to keep the other guys relegated to net participation and guild minimums.

Now take Orange Countians. We know who we are. The blandly handsome, heavily mortgaged, marathon-running, aerospace department manager, driving to work in his Taurus, does not entertain dreams of movie making. He has weapons to build, a country to defend, a family to provide for. Or take the blond mall rat, age 16, eyes aflame with consumer fever. She doesn't secretly wish to be Michelle Pfeiffer. She actually has never heard of Michelle Pfeiffer. The loose-jawed surfer dude in Huntington Beach entertains not a single thought besides the next south swell, south being to his left, he's pretty sure, if he's facing the gnardical tubes of the Pacific, which he usually is.

People in L.A., Parker explains, "want to be someone else because they're miserable; people in Orange County are content to be who they are because they're happy. It's clear. People in L.A. can't face reality. We can."

Reality is complicated, of course. Orange County is whiter and wealthier than Los Angeles, still, but L.A. voters also sent Richard Nixon and Ronald Reagan to the White House. Orange County voters are more likely than Angelenos to oppose offshore oil-drilling and to support environmental action, but these days both regions are equally lathered over the issue of illegal immigration. And, all denial aside, Orange County does have smog, as well as nightmarish freeway congestion. But it also has culture with a capital "C," symbolized by the spectacular Performing Arts Center adjacent (you guessed it) to its most famous shopping mall.

Born into endless summer, freed from community by freeways, and taught to believe that here, life can be all things to all people, Orange County and Los Angeles are actually very much alike. But Los Angeles is older, more experienced. Like a village elder trying to atone for the folly of youth, the City of Angels seems more willing to acknowledge the shadow side of the sunny Southern California dream and to struggle to make peace with it.

PRACTICAL ORANGE COUNTY

Most cities in Orange County have visitor bureaus and/or chambers of commerce, many of these listed by locale below. Because Anaheim's Disneyland has been the main tourist attraction for decades, it's no accident that the best overall source for travel information is the **Anaheim/Orange County Visitor and Convention Bureau,** based at the Anaheim Convention Center, 800 W. Katella Ave., 714/765-8888. To request publications, call toll-free 888/598-3200. Call the **Visitor Information Hot Line,** 714/765-8888 ext. 9888, for timely recorded information on attractions, entertainment, and upcoming events. For fax-on-demand information, which requires a touch-tone phone, call the InfoFax number at toll-free 888/440-4405. For information via the Internet, the visitor bureau's address is www.anaheimoc.org. The visitor bureau also sponsors various promotions, sometimes including special discount coupons that come in handy (for example, a recent "Family Values" coupon book).

The newspaper of record is the *Orange County Register,* fast being outpaced by the highly competitive *Los Angeles Times,* which prints a special Orange County edition. The local *Daily Pilot,* now owned by the *Times,* is included with the *Times*'s home delivery.

Biggest and hippest of the alternative newspapers regionally has long been the *L.A. Weekly,* available at hip places countywide. In late 1995 the *Weekly* launched its *O.C. Weekly,* surely a sign that Orange County's arts, entertainment, and alternative political scene has come into its own. Other interesting free magazines and newspapers include *Entertainment Today,* and *The Sun* (the latter distributed in Seal Beach and Huntington Beach). The slick-paper lifestyle magazine, written more for residents than people just passing through, is *Orange Coast.*

Transportation by Air

Though LAX is Southern California's main international airport, the smaller regionals—John Wayne, Long Beach, Burbank, and Ontario—generally offer competitive fares and fewer hassles. Depending on where you're headed, regional flights may also let you avoid the freeway trip through L.A.—nightmarish during commute hours.

Inside Orange County's spiffy expanded and remodeled **John Wayne Orange County Airport,** 949/252-5200, John Wayne himself is there to greet you. (You can't miss him.) Along with various commuter services, airlines serving John Wayne include **Alaska, America West, American, Continental, Delta, Northwest, TWA,** and **United.** And it was a big, big deal in 1994 when no-frills **Southwest** added its name to the list.

Disney's California Adventure

SPORTING ORANGE COUNTY

Some sort of sports-franchise virus seems to be afflicting Southern California these days. Foreshadowing the Los Angeles loss—or, more appropriately, *return*—of the L.A. Raiders football team to Oakland, in 1995 Orange County lost its **Los Angeles Rams** pro football team to St. Louis. **Edison International Field of Anaheim** (formerly Anaheim Stadium) still hosts **Anaheim Angels** baseball games, however. For Angels ticket information, call 714/663-9000 or visit the Anaheim Angels website at www.angelsbaseball.com. For almost any stadium event, by the way, a popular pre- and post-game stop is **The Catch** restaurant right across the street, 714/978-3700, where fresh fish and Angus steaks are served in lively sports-bar style.

Also notable is the Disney Company's **Mighty Ducks of Anaheim** National Hockey League expansion team, 714/704-2500, part of the new NHL Pacific Division. Though some wags refer to the endeavor as the "Mighty Bucks," the Ducks nest at the area's newest sports stadium, the impressive **Arrowhead Pond of Anaheim** (known affectionately as "The Pond") across the street from Edison Field. The Ducks' season begins in early October and runs through April. For non-sports fans, right next door to the Pond is the **Stadium Promenade**, an entertainment complex complete with 25-screen movie theater, endless eateries, and a **Penske Racing Center** with full-size, full-motion, interactive Champ car simulators.

The John Wayne Airport is centrally located, technically in Santa Ana but also practically in Costa Mesa, Irvine, and Newport Beach. Easiest freeway access is from I-405. Also feasible is the Costa Mesa Fwy. (Hwy. 55), which connects I-5, the latter often a horrendous transition. If traveling Newport Bay area streets, another possibility is MacArthur Blvd. (Hwy. 73) from the coast, which delivers you right to the terminals.

Most car rental agencies have outposts at John Wayne. The cheapest but not most convenient means to and from the airport is public transit, **Orange County Transportation Authority (OCTA)** buses, 714/636-RIDE (636-7433), ext. 10 for route and fare information. If you go this route be sure to leave yourself *plenty* of time. Upmarket hotels (sometimes others)

offer free airport shuttles. Next-best bet: a commercial shuttle service such as **SuperShuttle**, toll-free 800/258-3826, which offers 24-hour door-to-door service.

Transportation by Train

The main Orange County stop for **Amtrak** is in the south, the striking **San Juan Capistrano Depot** in San Juan Capistrano, just west of Camino Capistrano at 26701 Verdugo St., 800/872-7245, open limited hours. Local OCTA buses (see Transportation by Bus, below) connect to Laguna Beach and San Clemente. Amtrak also stops at the pier in San Clemente—where you can catch Bus 91 south to the last stop, then take Bus 1 north along the coast. Amtrak also stops in Anaheim, Santa Ana, and Fullerton. Call Amtrak toll-free 800/872-7245 for route, fare, and reservation information, or check www.amtrak.com.

The first Orange County link in the periwinkle-and-white **Metrolink** Southern California mass transit system is at Fullerton, where the commuter trains made their debuts in March of 1994. The trains run on weekdays only; for current fare and schedule information, call toll-free 800/371-5465, or check www.metrolinktrains.com.

Transportation by Bus

Cars are king in Orange County, but you can get here and get around reasonably well by bus. The **Santa Ana Greyhound Station** is in the transit center just off the Santa Ana Fwy. (I-5), 1000 E. Santa Ana Blvd. at Santiago, toll-free 800/231-2222. In Santa Ana call 714/542-2115; in Anaheim, 714/999-1256. From Santa Ana, buses connect with L.A., Riverside, and San Diego as well as Santa Barbara, San Luis Obispo, and San Francisco. Greyhound can also get you to and from the coast, with very limited service to Laguna Beach and Huntington Beach. Local public transit expands bus travel options. **Orange County Transportation Authority (OCTA)** buses, 714/636-7433, ext. 10 for current schedule and fares, serve the entire county, albeit on a fairly limited basis. Daily start and end times vary by route, but on weekdays buses are available after 5 or 6 A.M. and run until 7 or 8 P.M. Weekend service starts later and ends earlier. If you're relying on buses, be sure to check current hours.

Transportation by Car

Two freeways—I-405, known as "the 405" or the San Diego Fwy. in local vernacular, and I-5, known hereabouts as the Santa Ana Fwy.—are Orange County's major north-south thoroughfares. Judicious use of other intersecting freeways will get you almost anywhere. Most Orange County freeways are now undergoing major reconstruction, however, to keep pace with general growth and traffic increases, so allow extra time in key locales (especially during commute hours).

Construction continues at I-5 and Hwy. 55, the Costa Mesa Fwy.; the 55 runs directly into downtown Newport Beach. If coming via the 405, take Hwy. 73, the Corona del Mar Fwy., *then* the 55. For more road construction headaches, head north to the junction of Hwy. 55 and Hwy. 91. The 55 connects Santa Ana, Tustin, and Orange with Hwy. 91, the Riverside Fwy., which in Orange County runs west-east from La Palma through the Anaheim/Fullerton area and on toward Corona in Riverside County.

The most notorious local freeway construction project has an unofficial title—"the Orange Crush," in the city of Orange at the intersection of I-5, Hwy. 57, and Hwy. 22. The Garden Grove Fwy., Hwy. 22, connects the 405 to the 55 just north of Santa Ana and Tustin as well as the southern end of Hwy. 57, the Orange Freeway. The Orange runs north through Placentia to intersect Hwy. 90, the Imperial Hwy., which connects Brea with Yorba Linda and Hwy. 91.

California's Pacific Coast Highway (PCH), or Hwy. 1, is Orange County's scenic route—running almost the entire length of the coastline before merging with I-5 just east of Dana Point in the south county. A multilane route most of the way, PCH is typically a slog—slowed like everything else in Southern California by too much traffic. And most people here do drive, usually one to a vehicle.

SEAL BEACH AND HUNTINGTON BEACH

SEAL BEACH AND VICINITY

Enticed by more famous Orange County beach towns, tourists tend to miss Seal Beach—a neat-as-a-pin neighborhood with a 1950s bohemian feel, an attractive downtown, and plenty of pompom palms. The beach itself is wide and sandy, offering a view of both ocean and the man-made offshore island featuring California's first offshore oil well, drilled in 1954.

Enjoy Main Street. The **Book Store,** 213 Main, 562/598-1818, is a classic in the used-book genre, an overwhelming hodgepodge of words in print. (Proprietor Nathan Cohen, a retired merchant seaman, may offer help in navigating the stacks.) With or without book in hand, stop nearby for ice cream or cappuccino; bikini shops and beach-style boutiques offer more expensive distractions. After the beach and a stroll on the **Seal Beach Pier,** to stay longer take in a movie at the landmark **Bay Theatre,** 562/431-9988, known for its eclectic and arty films.

If the beach scene here gets too crowded, just south are **Surfside Beach** and **Sunset Beach,** quieter areas with public beaches and lifeguard towers. (Stroll. Bike it. Take the bus. If driving, park along either North or South Pacific Aves., parallel to PCH.)

For a fine bike ride, the **bikeway** at Bolsa Chica State Beach, just south, begins at Warner and runs south all the way to Huntington State Beach, about five miles. Heading north by bike is not much fun, with cyclists competing with cars on PCH all the way to Belmont Shores (Long Beach).

For more information about the area, including exact dates for upcoming events, call the **Seal Beach Chamber of Commerce** at 562/799-0179 between 10 A.M. and 2 P.M. on weekdays or check www.sealbeachchamber.com.

Bolsa Chica State Beach and Reserve

Stretching south three miles from Seal Beach in the north to the Huntington Beach Pier, broad, sandy Bolsa Chica State Beach is in one sense an extension of what you'll find farther south at Huntington State Beach—thousands of paved parking places, restrooms with showers, fire rings, snack stands, and all. The primary differences? This is a better bet for beginning surfers than Huntington Beach. Also, Bolsa Chica offers 50 RV campsites. The main parking lot entrance is on PCH about 1.5 miles south of Warner Avenue. Day use (parking fee) is $3. For more information about Bolsa Chica, call 714/848-1566. To reserve a campsite—a necessity in summer—call ReserveAmerica toll-free at 800/444-7275 or check www.reserveamerica.com.

In many ways more fascinating than the beach is 1,100-acre Bolsa Chica Ecological Reserve across PCH. Not exactly pristine, Bolsa Chica is an ongoing oilfield restoration project; some areas are not open to the public. Bolsa Chica, one of the county's few remaining wetland tracts, provides seasonal habitat for more than 200 species of waterfowl and shorebirds, including the endangered California least tern. Amigos de Bolsa Chica, a local citizens' group, is responsible for preventing the total loss of Bolsa Chica to another marina and housing development. So shake that sand out of your shoes and stroll along the 1.5-mile loop trail, just to see what a little enlightened citizen action can do. For current information on guided walks, usually offered Sept. through Apr. on the first Sat. of the month starting at 9 A.M., call 714/897-7003.

Practical Seal Beach

If you think this laid-back, blast-from-the-past beach town is the perfect place to park yourself permanently, think again. At last report Seal Beach had Orange County's highest rents. And you won't find much here in the way of budget accommodations. (Try Huntington Beach instead.) If the 1850s are more your style than the 1950s, consider a stay at the two-story **Seal Beach Inn and Gardens,** a stylish and secluded 23-room bed-and-breakfast close to the beach at 212 5th St., 562/493-2416 or toll-free 800/443-3292, www.sealbeachinn.com. Guest rooms, some with kitchens, refrigerators, and whirlpool baths, are furnished with antiques and named after flowers—many of which you'll find here, part of the riot of color blooming forth from every container, cranny, and nook. There's a small swimming pool, too. Luxury, with rates $165–350.

Eating here is easier on the pocketbook. Head to the pier for bomber-size burgers and a view of the oil wells. *The* place forever—or at least since the Seal Beach Grand Old Opry House gave up the ghost—is flashy diner-style **Ruby's** at the end of the pier, 562/431-7829, where you'll find all kinds of patties, including chicken, turkey,

and veggie, plus great shakes and other tasty pleasures from the past. Breakfast is a best bet, too. And if you miss it here, Ruby's is almost an institution along the coast and elsewhere in Orange County.

The most popular all-around hangout in Seal Beach is **Hennessey's Tavern,** 140 Main, 562/598-4419, one of a small chain of Irish-style pubs serving breakfast, lunch, and dinner in addition to beer, here overflowing with surfers, hippies, country music, and the scent of suntan lotion. Best bet for breakfast, though, is the homey long-running **Harbor House Cafe** on PCH (at Anderson) just south of town in Sunset Beach, 562/592-5404, open 24 hours, famous for its omelettes, almost as famous for the gallery of movie stars on knotty-pine walls.

An unusual local landmark since 1930 and still offering homage to the good ol' stunt flying days is the **Glide 'er Inn,** 1400 PCH, 562/431-3022, where the reference is to aeronautics in general, biplanes in particular. Airplane memorabilia papers the walls, model planes serve as de facto mobiles, and seafood dominates the menu.

If seafood is your passion, though, **Walt's Wharf,** 201 Main, 562/598-4433, offers greater creativity with whatever's in season—such things as oak-grilled Chilean sea bass with roasted macadamia nuts. There's an oyster bar here, too, and a good selection of imported beers. Another good choice, for seafood and prime rib, not to mention great breakfasts, is the **Kinda Lahaina Broiler,** 901 Ocean Ave., 562/596-3864.

HUNTINGTON BEACH AND VICINITY

Surf City—Old and New

If you've tried to find Surf City on a California map, put an "X" right here, on the once-grungy blue-collar oil town of Huntington Beach. The city has long called itself "Surfing Capital of the World" and "Surf City." But now it's official. After some public skirmishes with Santa Cruz, that scrappy little surf city up north, Huntington Beach ended up with the Surf City trademark.

Surfers have dominated the local fauna since the 1920s. But surfing didn't become a social phenomenon even in Huntington Beach until the 1960s, when Bruce Brown of nearby Dana Point was knighted the "Fellini of foam" for *Endless Summer,* his classic surfing film, and Dick Dale, "King of the Surf Guitar," rode the same wave to the top of the pop music charts. (Dale's sound was a total Orange County creation, since even his guitar—a Fender Stratocaster—was a local invention, thanks to Leo Fender of Fullerton.) Then came the Beach Boys, who captured the national teenage imagination and catapulted surfing into the category of popular sport. But then came the Beatles. Almost overnight everyone—everyone except serious surfers—tuned into another wavelength, an entirely different cultural wave.

According to local lore, surfing was imported to Huntington Beach from Hawaii in 1907. In those days surfers were all but alone in the Orange County surf, riding 100-pound homemade redwood boards. But wood has long since given way to polyurethane, plain canvas swim trunks to neoprene wetsuits. And "mellow" has lost out to "aggro" (aggressive attitude, in the lingo) now that conditions are crowded and surfing is a multibillion-dollar international sports and fashion industry.

About seven million people do Huntington Beach every year, most just day tripping. It's tough to find the skurfy surf-rat bar scenes and seedy low-rent storefronts of yore, though. They're all but gone—replaced in the 1980s and '90s by a strategically redeveloped business and tourism district with a crisp California-Mediterranean style. But even with redevelopment, surfing is still the main event in Huntington Beach. Annual competitions include the **The Bluetorch Pro of Surfing** (formerly the OP Pro), usually held in late July, a famed stop on the Association of Surfing Professionals world tour and the largest surfing event on the U.S. mainland. But Bluetorch qualifier events are just the prelude to August's **U.S. Open of Surfing,** part of the World Surfing Championship tour. If battling the seriously surf-crazed crowds during big-time competition is an unappealing option, you'll find many smaller, more neighborly surfing events staged throughout the year.

For more information about Huntington Beach, contact: **Huntington Beach Conference and Visitors Bureau,** 417 Main St., toll-free 800/729-6232 (SAY-OCEAN) or 714/969-3492.

Huntington Beach Beaches and Pier

The city beach or **"Main Beach"** starts in the north at Goldenwest, saunters past the **Huntington Beach Pier**—itself a seaward extension of Main St.—and then meanders south, merging at Beach Blvd. (south of Main) with **Huntington State Beach.** The state beach stretches south another two miles to just beyond Brookhurst, at the Santa Ana River and Newport Beach border.

The pier area is Huntington's most famous and challenging surfing zone, but the state beach is the stuff of surfing movies—one of the widest, whitest expanses of sand you'll see this side of the Colorado Desert. A five-acre preserve along

Surf City

SALLY MYERS/TOM MYERS PHOTOGRAPHY

THE SURFRIDERS: SURFING GOES GREEN

You'd never guess it, to watch competitive young surfers duke it out for ocean elbow room, but surfing has *traditions,* concerns much more lasting than who gets there first, fastest, or with the most finesse.

One surfing tradition is caring about coastal waters and fighting environmental decline, whether from oil and sewage spills or impending development. Surfing is increasingly an endangered species, a development directly related to human activity as well as human efforts to correct the problem. Flood-control dams upriver, for example, prevent sand from flowing to sea to replenish beaches. The coastal breakwaters and jetties built to trap existing sand have the unfortunate side effect of aggravating sand erosion—the ocean continues to suck it out to sea—while destroying waves.

But even surfers were shocked in February of 1990 when the British Petroleum–chartered oil tanker *American Trader* impaled itself on its own anchor about a mile offshore. About 400,000 gallons of oil spilled, much of it scooped up or dispersed at sea but a substantial amount washing ashore to foul 15 miles of beaches and wetlands and kill seabirds from Anaheim Bay in L.A. County to the Newport Beach peninsula. In one of those ironies of fate—since Huntington Beach is still Orange County's main oil producer—most of the oil came ashore near Bolsa Chica and Huntington Beach. Along with the professional crews, hundreds of Orange County volunteers turned out to stop the oil and then to clean things up.

Since 1984 the Surfrider Foundation, which began in surf-happy Huntington Beach, has been on the front lines of the battle to protect the oceans and the coastline. Originally a handful of long-haired locals—the group began educating the public by spray painting storm drains with the message "Drains to Ocean," and it is still famous for its guerrilla theater—the Surfrider Foundation is now a national organization.

In addition to some notable national victories—including restoring natural dune habitat on the Outer Banks in North Carolina and, in Hawaii, successfully suing Honolulu for dumping raw sewage into Kailua Bay—the foundation is still at the forefront of the long-running local battle to forestall a housing subdivision at the Bolsa Chica wetlands.

For more information about the organization, or to join, contact: **Surfrider Foundation,** 122 S. El Camino Real #67, San Clemente, CA 92672, 949/492-8170, fax 949/492-8142, www.surfrider.org.

---

the river protects nesting sites for the California least tern. Across PCH from the state beach is 114-acre **Huntington Beach Wetlands,** a small preserve under the jurisdiction of the California Department of Fish and Game.

In summer, and on almost any hot-weather weekend, plan to arrive quite early to stake out territory for your beach towel. Aside from sunbathing, swimming, surfing, and just bummin' around, beaches around here are known for very serious volleyball. They're also popular for picnicking and the peaceable pursuit of surf fishing and cycling. Facilities include countless paved parking spaces, wheelchair access, restrooms with cold showers and dressing rooms, picnic tables, stores and snack stands, even fire rings for after-dark beach parties—the happening scene, especially near the pier. And the lifeguards mean it when they tell you to quit doing whatever you're doing. Parking lots are accessible from PCH at Magnolia, Newland, Huntington, and Main. For more beach information, call 714/848-1566.

The International Surfing Museum

Mandatory for any serious study of local history is a visit to Huntington Beach's International Surfing Museum, 411 Olive Ave., 714/960-3483. The spruced-up 1930s building itself offers hidden cultural history as the onetime location of Sam Lanni's acclaimed **Safari Sam's** nightclub—*the* local club scene until 1985, when Sam sauntered off to hunt new challenges. Among the oldies but goodies collected inside are vintage surfboards, of course, including Batman's board from the original movie; the cornerstone from the original 1903 pier; and the bust of Duke Kahanamoku once on display at the foot of the pier.

The museum is open noon–5 P.M., daily in summer and Wed.–Sun. in winter. Admission is $2 adults, $1 students, children under 6 free.

Staying in Surf City

Best for budget travelers is the very clean **Colonial Inn Youth Hostel,** housed in a circa-1903 three-story colonial at 421 8th St., 714/536-3315. Opt for a bed in one of three communal rooms ($16) or, for more privacy, get one of 14 double rooms with twin beds ($18 per person). Curfew here is 11 P.M., but you can rent a late key.

In other options, Huntington Beach offers more reasonably priced choices than most beach towns, but most of the better motel deals are inland along Beach Boulevard. Settle in at the **Comfort Suites,** for example, 16301 Beach Blvd. (at McDonald, one block west of I-405), toll-free 800/714-4040 or 714/841-1812, for $59 double. Inexpensive.

Comfortable, reasonable, and right across the highway from the beach is the small **Sun 'n' Sands Motel,** 1102 PCH (five blocks north of the pier, between Main and Goldenwest), 714/536-2543, with the basics plus pool and free movies, cable TV. Inexpensive-Moderate, with rates $59 and up in the summer season, from $45 otherwise (kids under 12 free).

For a different beach ambience, try the neat and neighborly **Sunset Bed and Breakfast,** 16401 PCH (at 25th St.), 562/592-1666. Inexpensive-Expensive, with summer rates $45–95, winter rates $45–85.

A central feature of downtown redevelopment is the upscale **Waterfront Hilton Beach Resort,** 21000 PCH, toll-free 800/822-7873 or 714/960-7873. Beyond the stunning lobby, with its waterfalls and tropical plants, the Mediterranean-style complex offers 12 stories of ocean-view rooms across from the beach and balmy palm landscaping, pretty pool area, tennis courts, and more. Premium-Luxury, with official rates $135 and up in summer, otherwise $115 and up, but ask about special discounts and packages.

Eating in Surf City: Locals' Favorites

Some of the local surf scene's most beloved hangouts survive, much to everyone's post-redevelopment relief. **The Sugar Shack,** 714/536-0355, still stands, for example, a funky little café at 213½ Main, the place *everybody* goes, for more than 25 years. The Shack serves surfer-sized breakfast starting at 6 A.M., juicy burgers and such at lunch and early dinner. If it's crowded, add your name to the waiting list—cleverly attached to the tree out front. Also everybody's favorite, wherever you find it in Orange County, along the southern L.A. coast, and elsewhere, is **Wahoo's Fish Tacos,** 120 Main St., 714/536-2050. A Wahoo's Fish of the Day or Banzai Burrito will fill you up just

fine—and deliciously—for under $5.

For healthy vegetarian, the place is **Mother's Market and Kitchen** next to the Newland House at 19770 Beach Blvd., 714/963-6667, where breakfast, lunch, and dinner are served daily, 9 A.M.–9:30 P.M. The market here is well worth a wander, too, selling fresh produce, kitchen gadgets, and natural cosmetics.

Popular with college students and the young local surf set, is boisterous, cool, and casual **Huntington Beach Beer Company,** 201 Main (at Walnut), 714/960-5343, where the specialty is pizza baked in a wood-fired oven. Sandwiches and salads are also on tap, everything washed down by brewskis such as Huntington Beach Blonde and Brick Shot Red. Quite the scene on Fri. and Sat. nights.

A popular locals' choice is the **Park Bench Cafe** in Huntington Central Park, 17732 Goldenwest (at Slater), 714/842-0775, especially enjoyable on a glorious sunny day—and most famous recently for the addition of its special Canine Cuisine menu, a bone tossed to patrons also visiting the neighborhood "bark park." Dogs and their people dine only on the perimeter of the patio, on the lawn. Breakfast and lunch are served daily except Mon. (closed). Another good bet here: **Breakfast in the Park,** 714/848-0690. Huntington Central Park is on both sides of Goldenwest, between Edwards and Gothard.

But don't miss **Tosh's Mediterranean Cuisine and Bakery,** 16871 Beach Blvd., 714/842-3315, where you can pack a special picnic basket or sit down for marvelous Greek and Turkish fare at either lunch or dinner (seafood and vegetarian selections also available). Very good value if you're ravenous, since bread, soup, and salad are served with meals. For good sushi and such, try **Matsu Japanese Restaurant, Steakhouse, and Sushi Bar** across from the Friendship Inn at 18035 Beach Blvd. (at Talbert), 714/848-4404.

For fancier yet casual dining, head over to **Studio Café,** 300 PCH, 714/536-8775, specializing in seafood and sea views. Other local restaurants get more attention. **Baci,** 18748 Beach Blvd. (at Ellis), 714/965-1194, is quite good—some say the best, locally—for Italian, and reasonably priced as well. The very good continental **Palm Court** restaurant at the Waterfront Hilton, 714/960-7873, is also quite popular—casual during the day but dress-up dining with a view come nightfall.

NEWPORT BEACH AND VICINITY

Postsuburbia seems to require constant investment in the supremacy of the new. In most parts of Southern California, for example, tradition dictates that at the first sign of aging either a bulldozer or cosmetic surgeon be called in. That said, even Orange County has history. And Newport Beach is a good place to start looking for it.

Now a nouveau-riche niche with a nautical theme, in the 1920s and '30s Newport Beach was the preferred seaside escape for the old-money minions from Los Angeles. (In California "old money," like all other things, is relative.) Henry E. Huntington made it all possible with the extension of the Pacific Electric Railroad to Newport Bay. And close-to-home adventure continued outward from Newport, the cat's meow being the ferryboat day trip to Catalina Island. Once the shallow harbor was dredged, landfill islands, yachting marinas, and summer homes starting popping up all over the place.

Famous former residents include John Wayne, Shirley Temple, even George Burns and Gracie Allen, Roy Rogers and Dale Evans. Celebrities come and go, though. In the end the truly astounding thing about Newport Beach is the price paid here for social status, reflected most obviously in the value of both real estate and boat slips. A million or two will buy little more than a modest beach bungalow with no yard, no parking, and no rest from the daily summer struggle with nightmarish tourist traffic. Some of the luxury yachts on display in Newport Harbor carry equally phenomenal price tags. And some people would sell their very souls just for the chance to drop anchor in one of the 10,000 slips here, *the* high-price, high-prestige California yacht harbor. Go figure.

Of course the *weather* is quite nice, year-round.

For those who track the ever-changing local identity of California's Hwy. 1, or Pacific Coast Hwy., as it slides south along the coast, here it's called West Coast Hwy. until it crosses the channel on the west side of the harbor at lower Newport Bay, and East Coast Hwy. on the east side. For more information on the area, contact the **Newport Beach Conference and Visitors Bureau,** 3300 W. Coast Hwy., Newport Beach, toll-free 800/942-6278 or 714/722-1611. To explore Newport on the Web, go to www.newportbeach-cvb.com.

SEEING NEWPORT BEACH

Despite its high-priced harbor and hotels, keep in mind that Newport Beach is still more residential area than tourist destination. The unmistakable aroma of money, money, money is often aloft on the sea breeze, but just plain folks still find plenty to do here. Newport Beach is just so darned *pleasant.*

Hold that thought when you're trapped in traffic on Pacific Coast Hwy. or desperately trying to snare a parking place.

Parking is such a nightmare, particularly near the college-student scene at Newport Pier, that touring the area on foot is truly a stress-reducing alternative. If hiking long urban distances isn't feasible, cycling might be—so bring bikes if you've got them, or plan to rent.

Exploring Newport Harbor from its watery underside isn't all that pleasurable, given the sheer numbers of boats and people. The exception to the rule is Corona del Mar State Beach, with offshore reefs worth exploring. Even better is Crystal Cove State Park between Newport and Laguna Beach, an underwater marine sanctuary with good diving. Laguna Beach is actually closer to Crystal Cove, but if you're based in Newport rent snorkeling or scuba gear (certification required for divers) at the **Aquatic Center,** 4537 W. Coast Hwy. (at Balboa), 949/650-5440.

The best way to tour Newport Harbor is by boat. Unusual is a one-hour gondola tour with **Gondola Company of Newport,** headquarters at Lido Marina Village, 3404 Via Oporto, Ste. 102B, 714/675-1212. For the classic harbor cruise—during which you'll find out just which celebrities lived where, et cetera—try **Catalina Passenger Service** and its *Pavilion Queen,* an ersatz river boat, and *Pavilion Paddy,* both docked at the Balboa Pavilion. In addition, CPS offers trips to and from Catalina Island as well as whale-watching tours. For current information call toll-free 800/830-7744 or 949/673-5245.

Most whale-watching and sportfishing tours also shove off from the pavilion. **Bongos Sportfishing Charters,** 2140 Newport Blvd., 949/673-2810, offers whale trips from just after Christmas through March and sportfishing year-round, as does **Newport Landing Sportfishing,** 309 Palm St., 949/675-0550. For information on private exclusive yacht charters, for total privacy and/or to accommodate large groups, contact the visitors bureau for referrals.

On the Balboa Peninsula

First and often last stop on a people's tour is the Balboa Peninsula, a long, arthritic finger of sand pointing south from **Newport Boulevard,** the seaward end of the line for the Costa Mesa (55) Freeway. You can also get here from the Coast Hwy. and **Balboa Boulevard.** Humanity is so well-established here, the entire harbor so sheltered from sea-driven storms, it's a surprise to discover that the peninsula is a geological newborn. The Balboa Peninsula didn't begin to exist until after 1825, a year of massive flooding that caused the

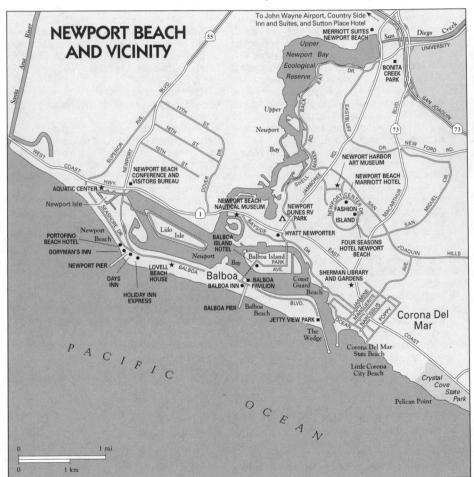

Santa Ana River to suddenly change course and deposit sand and sediments in the harbor.

The **Newport Pier**—about a half-mile past the highway at the ocean end of McFadden Pl., between 20th and 21st Sts.—was originally Mc-Fadden's Wharf, built in 1888 to accommodate the train from Santa Ana delivering produce and steamship passengers. **Newport Beach**—the actual beach by that name—stretches both west and east from the pier (this one constructed in the 1940s), which serves as madding-crowd central in summer and on most weekends.

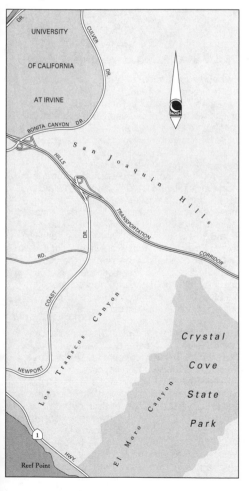

The most historic attraction at the Newport Pier is the **Newport Dory Fishing Fleet** adjacent. Hard at it since 1891, this is the only surviving dory fleet on the West Coast. Arrive by 10 A.M. to scoop up some of the day's catch, marketed in open-air stalls. For more information on the fleet and other aspects of Newport's harbor history, stop by the **Newport Beach Nautical Museum** at its new location in the Reuben E. Lee "river barge," 151 E. Coast Hwy., 949/673-7863, open Tues.–Sun. 10 A.M.–5 P.M.

A stroll to the Balboa Pier, which juts into the ocean from Balboa's Main St., two miles to the east, takes considerably longer—especially if you dawdle along the concrete boardwalk. Accompanied by landscaped lawn, bandstand, and palm trees, the Balboa Pier is the focal point for more placid pursuits. On most days **Balboa Beach** is relatively lonely and quiet, especially on the stretch toward the jetty. Even the ocean is quieter here, since the sandy beach falls away steeply and the waves seem to arrive from nowhere. Downcoast is the jetty, a rocky chin protecting the harbor mouth as it inhales and exhales sailboats. The angle formed between Balboa Beach and the jetty is known as **The Wedge,** internationally famous for its stupendous shore breaks, locally infamous for bone-breaking body-surfing, surfing, and swimming. (It's dangerous. No joke.) To get the big picture, head out to **Jetty View Park** at the tip of the peninsula.

As for **Balboa** proper, both the pier and the **Balboa Pavilion** at 400 Main St.—originally a bathhouse cum boathouse, now de facto loading dock for boat tours—were built in 1905 by Southern California developers working overtime to attract home buyers to this otherwise desolate sandspit. Not to be missed amid the surrounding shops and schlock is the reconstructed Balboa **Fun Zone** promenade along the bay, one of the few places left anywhere with genuine arcade-era pinball machines, skee ball, and such. For electronics addicts, video games are available. Adjacent to the pavilion is the three-car **Balboa Ferry,** for the trip to and from Balboa Island. Also worth appreciating is the lovely 1930 Spanish colonial **Balboa Inn** at the foot of the pier.

A still grander presence presides at W. Ocean Front and 13th St., back toward the Newport Pier—the concrete **Lovell Beach House.** Considered one of the finest American examples of

Balboa Beach

ROBERT HOLMES/CALTOUR

early modern architecture, it was designed in 1926 by Rudolph M. Schindler for health enthusiast Dr. Lovell. But Bauhaus is not *your* house, so don't bother the residents.

ORANGE COUNTY MUSEUM OF ART

Marooned in a business park near Fashion Island is the **Orange County Museum of Art,** originally known as the Newport Harbor Art Museum, 850 San Clemente Dr., 949/759-1122, www.ocma.net, nationally acclaimed in the late 1980s for its contemporary California art collection and cutting-edge special exhibits. One of its recent achievements was the traveling Anne Frank exhibit, with over 600 photographs. The museum's fortunes received another boost when it was announced that the Irvine Company was donating an adjoining library building for a proposed expansion project. Particularly striking outside are this museum's red "gem," a sculpture by Jonathan Borofsky, a rusting six-foot iron cube protruding from the building, and the outdoor sculptures. Particularly striking inside are the rotating exhibits—and here, even the permanent collection rotates. Stop for a bite at the Plein Air Café. The museum also has an outpost at the South Coast Plaza in Costa Mesa. The museum is open Tues.–Sun. 10 A.M.–5 P.M. (closed Monday). Admission is $5 adults, $4 students/seniors, free for children under 16.

Balboa Island and Vicinity

Not to be confused with Balboa Peninsula is Balboa Island just off the mainland, a buffed neighborhood of beach bungalows reached by car from W. Coast Hwy. and Marine Avenue. If you drive, though, you won't see much, because you'll never find a place to park. A better option—and much more fun—is coming over as a pedestrian on the nearly perpetual **Balboa Island Ferries,** 949/673-1070, a service shuttling people and automobiles (maximum capacity, three cars at a time) back and forth daily since the early 1900s. The ferries ($1 fare) run daily—from 6:30 A.M. to midnight Sun.–Thurs., until 2 A.M. on Fri. and Sat. nights—between Palm Ave. on the peninsula and Agate Ave. on the island.

Marine Ave. is the village boutiquery and business district, where one can also pursue simple pleasures—such as a world-famous "Balboa bar" (vanilla ice cream bars dipped in chocolate) from **Dad's,** or a frozen chocolate-dipped banana from **Sugar 'n' Spice.** *The* restaurant on Balboa Island is **Amelia's,** 311 Marine Ave., 949/673-6580, known for seafood, Italian specialties, and family-run atmosphere.

To eyeball James Cagney's onetime island estate, head west. That's it, just offshore at the end of Park—**Collins Isle,** sticking out from the west side of Balboa Island like a sandy little toe.

Like other private landfill islands scattered around the bay, **Lido Isle** to the harbor's far west—reached from the peninsula via Newport Blvd. and Via Lido—is an elite and elegant

THE BOWERS MUSEUM OF CULTURAL ART

That the largest museum in Orange County is dedicated to preserving the art and artifacts of the world's indigenous peoples is quite fitting, given the county's increasing cultural diversity.

Easily accessible from Newport Beach and reopened in 1992 after a four-year, $12 million facelift, the Bowers Museum of Cultural Art in Santa Ana is as expansive in scope as it is small in size. The appealing 1932 Spanish mission-style building downtown, complete with courtyard, was not only renovated but expanded, tripling exhibit space to more than 19,000 square feet. But the territory is still too tight for permanent display of the museum's 85,000-piece collection. So the Bowers Museum is known for its imaginative special shows, such as *African Icons of Power, Perú Before the Inca, Art of the Himalayas,* and *River of Gold: Pre-Columbian Treasures from Sitio Conte.* There's always a reason to come back.

Among permanent exhibits are *Arts of Native America*—art and artifacts from various North American cultures, including intricate beadwork from Plains cultures and exquisite Pomo basketry from Northern California—and *Realm of the Ancestors,* representations of the argonaut cultures of Southeast Asia and Pacific Oceania. Ancient stone art and ceramics of pre-Columbian Mexico and Central America are collected in *Vision of the Shaman, Song of the Priest.*

Also permanent is *California Legacies,* both tribute to Orange County's diverse cultural heritage and homage to the museum's humble beginnings as an odd collection of local memorabilia. (The museum's first show—recently repeated—was a collection of dolls donated by children.) Starting in the 1970s the Bowers Museum began to supplement its collection of regional ceramics and orange crate labels in an aggressive acquisitions program emphasizing pre-Columbian and Native American culture.

The museum's special evening and weekend events, such as "Spirits of the Rainforest" and "California Folk Art," are usually well worth the trip.

Family fun at the Bowers Museum centers around the **Kidseum,** an all-kid section opened in 1995 to "promote cultural understanding among the peoples of Africa, the Americas, and the Pacific Rim." Among the Kidseum's unique attractions: the storytelling room, the theater, the art laboratory, and exhibit space for children's art from around the world.

The Bowers Museum "partnership"—the institution is owned by the city of Santa Ana, managed and governed by a private, nonprofit Board of Governors, and financed with contributions from the private sector—also sponsors an impressive community education program. Unusual, too, is the Bowers's international cultural art travel program (members only).

Plan a stop at the museum shop for its unusually thoughtful array of books, jewelry, and one-of-a-kind art from around the world. Proceeds support the museum and its programs.

Practical Bowers

Do enjoy the Bowers Museum culinary offerings. New at the Bowers in late 2000, replacing David Wilhelm's Southwesternesque Topaz Café as the museum's social centerpiece, is **Tangata,** owned and operated by renowned L.A.-area restaurateurs Joachim and Christine Splichal, of Patina and Pinot fame—exceptional meals and memorable desserts, everything moderately priced. Chef Otto Guerra runs the restaurant and also supervises catering for special museum events. The indoor-outdoor Tangata is open for lunch Tues.-Sat. 11 a.m.–3 p.m. and for buffet brunch on Sunday (same hours)—the latter very popular and highly recommended. Brunch reservations are wise.

The Bowers Museum of Cultural Art, 2002 N. Main St., Santa Ana, CA 92706, on Main at 20th St., has free parking available in the adjacent lot (between 19th and 20th). Museum galleries are open Tues.–Fri. 10 A.M.–4 P.M., and Sat. and Sun. 10 A.M.–6 P.M. Kidseum galleries are open Sat. and Sun. 10 A.M.–4 P.M. Admission is $4 adults, $3 seniors/students, and $2 for children ages 5–12 (under 5 free). For general information call the Bowers Museum at 714/567-3600; for membership, 714/567-3688; for tours, 714/567-3680; for museum store information, 714/567-3643. For schedule information and reservations at the Tangata, call 714/550-0906.

Though the Orange, Garden Grove, and Costa Mesa Fwys. converge quite close to downtown Santa Ana, the easiest way to get to the Bowers Museum from the coast is via the 55 (the Costa Mesa Fwy.) then the Santa Ana Fwy. (I-5). From I-5 northbound, exit at 17th St. and head west four blocks to Main and turn north (right). If for some reason you're on I-5 southbound, exit at Main and turn right. (Call to verify directions; the details may change once freeway construction in the area is completed.) By bus, OCTA routes 51, 53, and 55 will get you to the Bowers.

residential enclave where potentially public lawn areas are designated "private" community parks.

Corona Del Mar and Vicinity

Gardeners enjoy the **Sherman Library and Gardens** in Corona del Mar. Here they get a thorough education in just what will grow, and grow well, in the onetime desert of Southern California. Just south of the harbor on the mainland at 2647 E. Coast Hwy. (at MacArthur Blvd.), 949/673-2261, the Sherman honors the "Pacific Southwest" in its specialized library and two-acre garden of desert and tropical plants. More tropicals, and a koi pond, are in the modern conservatory. Also here: a wheelchair-accessible "discovery garden" for the seeing-impaired. The gardens are open 10:30 A.M.–4 P.M. daily except major holidays, the library on weekdays only. Small admission. The Tea Garden restaurant here serves light lunch fare, pastries, beverages, but is open to the public only on Sat., Sun., and Mon. 11 A.M.–3 P.M.

Besides shops and shopping, the star attraction of Corona del Mar is half-mile-long **Corona Del Mar State Beach** at the mouth of Newport Harbor, operated by the city and framed by cliffs and the rocky jetty at the eastern harbor entrance. Offshore is crystal-clear azure ocean; underfoot, warm white sand; everywhere around, lush landscaping—the classic California postcard. It would be wonderful, too, if everyone else in Southern California weren't so determined to be here. To reach the parking lot and day-use facilities for the main beach, from the Coast Hwy. take Jasmine St. to Ocean Boulevard. Day use (parking) is $3, but for the privilege of paying it, be sure to get here early. Also hardly a secret is **Big Corona Beach** off Marguerite Ave., where one can just sit and watch the boats pass. The secluded cove at **Little Corona Beach,** with its **tidepool reserve** (visit at low tide), is reached via Ocean Blvd. (at Poppy).

Other Newport Beaches

Back in Newport is the only "secret" beach around, the small **Coast Guard Beach** at the Harbor Master Coast Guard Station. Here you'll find a relatively peaceful stretch of sand, safe swimming, volleyball nets (bring your own ball), and picnic tables. Park on the street. The Coast Guard Beach is off the 1900 block of Bayside Drive. To get here from the highway, take Jamboree toward Balboa Island and then turn left onto Bayside.

"Bay beaches" include just about any accessible patches of sand fringing Newport Bay. One with lifeguards, volleyball nets, restrooms, showers, and some wind protection is on the peninsula's Bay Ave. between 18th and 19th Streets. Look for others at Montero and 10th Sts., and at the end of every street on Balboa Island.

Upper Newport Bay Ecological Reserve

Visitors quickly appreciate why the Spanish called this place "Frog Swamp," since the Upper Newport Bay Ecological Reserve or "Back Bay"

*the marina at
Newport Beach*

ROBERT HOLMES/CalTour

is a brackish saltwater and freshwater marsh complete with cattails, pickleweed, and aromatic mudflats. The most frightening fact is that this very small preserve is the largest remaining unengineered estuary in Southern California. The Back Bay may be small but it is a marvel—an ecologically rich Pacific Flyway sanctuary that provides shelter to about 200 bird species and 20,000-30,000 birds during the year. Two endangered species, the light-footed clapper rail and Belding's savanna sparrow (found only in Southern California), can be spotted here, along with the California brown pelican, the California least tern, and the peregrine falcon.

Auto tour access (one-way only) is off lower Jamboree Rd.; turn onto Backbay Dr. at the Hyatt Newporter and keep going. Parking areas are scattered along the route—so even if you're driving, pick a spot, park, and get out to see the sights in person. Stop first at the **Newport Bay Naturalists office** on Shellmaker Island (600 Shellmaker Dr., just off Backbay Dr.), (949/640-6746, or check www.newportbay.org for maps, bird and plant checklists, and historical background. Guided discovery walks and walking tours are offered; contact the office for current details.

STAYING IN NEWPORT BEACH

Lower Rent Newport Stays

It's not cheap and the ambience leaves room for improvement, but **Newport Dunes RV Park** just off Jamboree Rd. at 1131 Back Bay Dr., 949/729-3863 or toll-free 800/288-0770, is close to the harbor action. It's also practically on the Back Bay, if you're hankering for a hike. It even

---

ACCOMMODATIONS RATINGS

Accommodations in this book are rated by price category, based on double-occupancy, high-season rates. Categories used are:

Budget.	$35 and under
Inexpensive	$35-60
Moderate	$60-85
Expensive	$85-110
Premium	$110-150
Luxury	$150 and up

---

has a small marina (rental boats available) and children's playground. But if you're going to play here, you'll pay: RVers and intrepid tent campers unpack themselves onto small concrete slabs—like sardines into a can—and pay $25 and up. Budget. Alternatives include state park campgrounds up and down the coast.

A pleasant motel on north-bound Newport Blvd. (where it becomes a one-way paralleling the 55 Fwy.) is less than a mile from the harbor and reasonably close to everything else—most notably the shops and restaurants at the Triangle Square complex, which is within easy walking distance. Rooms at the **Holiday Inn Express,** 2070 Newport Blvd., between 21st and Bay Ave., 949/631-6000, feature all the basics; some have microwaves and refrigerators. With the ocean so close by, who cares that it doesn't have a pool? Expensive, with standard rates starting at $99. The **Days Inn** adjacent, 2100 Newport Blvd., 949/642-2670, $59–89, has a pool.

One of the best deals in the entire county is just off the 405 Fwy.—the **Country Side Inn and Suites,** 325 S. Bristol St. in Costa Mesa (on S. Bristol at Red Hill Ave., on the west side of the street), toll-free 800/322-9992 or 714/549-0300. This well-appointed modern motel, within easy reach of the coast and all other major Orange County attractions, has country French bed-and-breakfast style. Amenities include in-room refrigerators and color TV with videocassette players. Some rooms and studio suites feature microwaves and whirlpools. Extras include full buffet breakfast and morning newspapers, plus two swimming pools, whirlpools, exercise facilities, coin laundry. Since the Country Side here does substantial "business" business, weekend rates are lowest—a real boon for pleasure travelers—starting at $89. Expensive-Luxury.

Higher Rent Newport Stays

The area's upmarket and luxury hotels generally do double-duty as both business and pleasure destinations, thus their locations—within easy reach of corporate business parks, major malls, and John Wayne Airport. Official rates are high; ask about specials and packages, especially for off-season weekends.

Top of the mark is the 19-story **Four Seasons Hotel Newport Beach** near Fashion Island, 690 Newport Center, toll-free 800/332-

SOUTH COAST PLAZA:
SHOPPING AS THE CENTER OF EVERYTHING

Consumerism as Culture

Think of it as a theme park for consumerism, this one attracting more than 20 million visitors each year and, in 1999, raking in an estimated $12.4 billion. The most notable diversion at Orange County's South Coast Plaza megamall in Costa Mesa is the mall itself. Unique in the neighborhood, though, are the sociocultural segues between art, commerce, entertainment, finance, and fine dining—Orange County's foremost foray into the culture of consumerism and consumerism as culture.

This being one of the largest-grossing retail centers in the United States, going to South Coast Plaza typically involves spending money. But rest assured that here commerce is not crass. The preferred promotional etiquette at South Coast Plaza is to refer the mall itself as a "retail center," its shoppers as "guests."

All in all, it's hard to imagine the landscape a few short decades ago, when it was just another Orange County lima bean field.

A New South Coast Plaza

As in other theme parks, the territory here is geographically subdivided. The center is three-story **South Coast Plaza at Bristol,** 3333 Bristol St. (between the 405 and Sunflower), 714/435-2000, www.southcoastplaza.com, with its multistory atriums and elegant decor and a surprising variety of shops anchored by Bullock's, Nordstrom, Macy's, Sears, and Robinsons-May. On the west end is **Jewel Court,** Orange County's version of Rodeo Drive, with upscale shops including Tiffany & Co., Emporio Armani, Louis Vuitton, Cartier, and Chanel. Centerpiece of **Carousel Court** on the mall's east end is— you guessed it—a turn-of-the-20th-century carousel, a fitting enticement for the Sesame Street General Store, Disney Store, GapKids, FAO Schwarz, and other attractions aimed at the younger set.

Then there's the single-level **South Coast Plaza Village** just east of the main mall at Sunflower and Bear Sts., where the Edwards Cinema complex is one notable diversion. Once known as Crystal Court, **South Coast Plaza at Bear,** north of the main mall at 3333 Bear St., includes an eclectic array, from Abercrombie & Fitch and Adrienne Vittadini to Victoria's Secret. There's also a kiddie carousel here, a new feature, this one with a King Arthur theme.

South of South Coast Plaza and Bristol is the **South Coast Plaza Town Center,** sometimes referred to as The Offices, an area bisected by Anton Blvd. and Town Center Dr.—a shimmering 96-acre orchard of bank and business office towers, visual and performing-arts venues, multiplex movie theaters, and inviting eateries.

Major changes at the mall in 1999 and 2000, announced as A New South Coast Plaza, include two new anchors for South Coast Plaza at Bear—a 42,000-square-foot Crate & Barrel Home Store, the chain's West Coast flagship, and a Macy's Home store. Also new is an elevated pedestrian walkway to connect the Bear and Bristol malls. At the main mall, Robinsons-May is expanding by 50,000 square feet. And a new 300,000-square-foot symphony hall designed by renowned architect Cesar Pelli, the **Segerstrom Center for the Arts** to be located next to South Coast Repertory, is coming soon.

Consuming Culture and *California Scenario*

The neighborhood's main action may be trafficking in commerce and consumer goods, but the main attraction is art—most of it in Town Center.

Almost perfectly hidden, wedged into the courtyard created by two black-glass business towers and the adjacent public parking lot, is an understated yet powerful exploration of the California myth—***California Scenario*** by the late Isamu Noguchi. This expansive "sculpture garden" offers much more than the term typically implies, staging separate but unified California themes with stunning directness and native-son humor. *Land Use,* for example, is a long, narrow chunk of concrete-colored granite dominating the crest of a landscaped knoll. A meandering stream flows from the tall *Water Source,* past *Desert Land,* to squat, stylized *Water Use.* Funniest of all, though, is *Spirit of the Lima Bean,* 15 dignified desert-colored boulders of decomposed granite piled up to honor South Coast Plaza's primary developers and benefactors, the Segerstrom family—perhaps only incidentally paying homage to the land's previous purpose.

California Scenario is tucked away behind the Great Western Bank Building, 3200 Park Center Dr. (off Anton Blvd.); parking is available in the adjacent public lot. The courtyard is open daily 8 A.M.–midnight. Appreciating Noguchi's art is absolutely free. For more information, call 714/435-2100.

Various other public sculptures—by **Henry Moore, Joan Miró, Alexander Calder, Claire Falkenstein,** and others—are scattered throughout the Town Center area, indoors and out. If you're too rushed to see them all after doing the mall, walk over to the performing arts center on Town Center Drive—take the pedestrian bridge that spans Bristol—for the stunning first-time impact of Richard Lippold's 60-foot-tall *Fire Bird,* a spectacular vision any time but especially after dark.

Also worthwhile in the arts department is the gallery inside **Bank of America,** 555 Anton. At South Coast Plaza proper, the **Laguna Art Museum** hosts a satellite gallery inside its shop at the mall's east end. Both are free.

Consuming Culture: Performance Arts

The post-modern **Orange County Performing Arts Center** hosts the Los Angeles Philharmonic and touring companies, including the American Ballet Theatre, the Joffrey Ballet, the New York City Ballet, and the New York City Opera, though popular musicals predominate. Near-perfect acoustics are the hallmark of the center's 3,000-seat Segerstrom Hall. Incidentally, the center's $73 million tab was picked up entirely through private donations. The performing arts center is on Town Center Dr. at Ave. of the Arts. Call 714/556-2787 for current performance information (recorded) or 714/556-2122 (administration). Or try the website, www.ocpac.org. Buy tickets for most performances through TicketMaster, 714/740-7878, though day-of-performance seats are often available.

Physically but not artistically overshadowed by the performing arts center is the Tony Award–winning **South Coast Repertory Theater,** 714/957-4033, www.scr.org. For tickets, call the box office at 714/708-5555. Started decades ago as a seat-of-the-pants repertory troupe, critical acclaim came along for South Coast Repertory with the brave decision to produce works by new playwrights, though not everything presented resembles avant-garde art. The Mainstage Theater here seats 507, the smaller Second Stage just 161, so call well in advance for current show schedule and reservations; last-minute tickets are scarce. Best bet for spur-of-the-moment attendance: matinees and midweek performances.

Eating at South Coast Plaza

There are dozens of dining options at South Coast Plaza. A best bet for families is the local **Ruby's** burgers-and-shakes outpost, at Bear St., 714/662-7829. For a change of pace head south to the Southwestern **El Torito Grill** in Town Center at 633 Anton Blvd. (at Bristol), 714/662-0798, where specialties such as red snapper fajitas keep the crowds coming back for more. Fun for sushi is **San Kai,** all but hidden away in a nondescript minimall at 3940 S. Bristol, 714/241-7115. This relaxed and unpretentious neighborhood-style Japanese restaurant, open for lunch and dinner, comes complete with sushi bar.

You won't go wrong with the California roll, but try San Kai's crunchy roll and spicy tuna handroll. Or the sautéed calamari.

Inside South Coast Plaza at Bristol, between Bullock's and the Bullock's men's store, is the **Wolfgang Puck Cafe,** 714/546-9653, a stylish but casual California cafe serving reasonably priced renditions of trademark Puck-style pizzas, pastas, and salads. In the Sears wing is the **Rainforest Café,** 714/424-9200, where the stylish casual fare comes with the ultimate in faux-environment dining. Justifiably popular is the casual **Gustaf Anders Back Pocket,** 714/668-1737.

For upper-crust pizza at lunch or before a show, the place is **Scott's Seafood Grill and Bar** at 3300 Bristol (at Anton), 714/979-2400. A Southern California link in the popular San Francisco–based chain, Scott's is considerably more famous for its seafood, its generous Sunday brunch, and its fixed-price pretheater menu.

Popular with patrons of the arts is David Wilhelm's dramatically elegant **Diva** near the performing arts center, 600 Anton (at Bristol), 714/754-0600, serving a contemporary California menu so exciting its audience keeps coming back for encores. The signature "ahi towers" here are meant to mimic neighborhood architecture. It's open for lunch weekdays only, for dinner nightly. Jazz several nights each week. Also drawing the stylish crowds these days is **Pinot Provence,** at the Westin Hotel, 686 Anton, 714/444-5900, a slice of life from the south of France and Joachim Splichal's only Orange County restaurant.

Practical South Coast Plaza

South Coast Plaza offers a multitude of "concierge services," including stroller and wheelchair loans, package checking, valet parking, and dinner or theater reservations. For assistance, stop by the concierge desk on the mall's first level, in the center near the carousel, or call 714/435-8571 or toll-free 800/782-8888. To find your way around, pick up a current South Coast Plaza Directory. Also request the mall's Address Book brochure and map. For other South Coast Plaza information, try the website, www.southcoastplaza.com.

Many area hotels offer free shuttle service to and from South Coast Plaza. If yours doesn't, a commercial shuttle bus service connects the three main shopping complexes—stops are shown in the directory and listed on the website—and the **Orange County Connection** "speed shuttle" makes the rounds between South Coast Plaza and Anaheim area (Disneyland), Long Beach area, and other hotels on a daily basis. Call 714/435-2000 or toll-free 800/782-8888 for current prices and schedules.

3442 or 949/759-0808, www.fourseasons.com, rated in 1994 by *Condé Nast Traveler* readers as one of the world's finest hotels. From the outside it looks like yet another too-tall, bewindowed box. Inside, though, it's elegant yet airy, all sand-beige and pastels. And those windows let in some grand views. Among the several restaurants here is **Pavilion,** where people dress up for the California-style American. The Four Seasons also boasts a complete business center, not to mention full conference and fitness facilities. Luxury, with rates $235–475.

Overlooking the Back Bay, **Marriott Suites Newport Beach,** 500 Bayview Circle (at Jamboree Rd.), toll-free 800/228-9290 or 949/854-4500, www.marriott.com, is primarily an upscale business-oriented hotel, quite welcoming on weekends for pleasure travelers. Pool, saunas, fitness facilities, and rental bikes make a weekend stay more than pleasant. Standard in-room amenities are almost too much, from two color TVs and two phones (with call waiting) to wet bar and refrigerator. Premium-Luxury, with rates $139–199 (children 18 and under free). And don't miss **The View** sushi bar.

From the outside the **Sutton Place Hotel** (formerly Le Meridien Newport Beach), 4500 MacArthur Blvd., toll-free 800/243-4141 or 949/476-2001, www.suttonplace.com, looks something like a squared-off cruise ship, this one with big windows on every deck. Inside, it's very contemporary, very Southern California, with all the expected amenities, including tennis courts, pool, and business center. Most beloved at Sutton Place is its French restaurant **Antoine,** one of Orange County's best in any category. Premium-Luxury, with rates $118–185. While Sutton Place is technically in Newport Beach, for all practical purposes it's a South Coast Plaza/John Wayne Airport hotel. Stay here to take advantage of weekend South Coast Repertory theater and/or Pageant of the Masters packages.

More convenient to Newport Harbor is the **Hyatt Newporter,** 1107 Jamboree Rd., toll-free 800/233-1234 or 949/729-1234, www.hyatt newporter.com, with spacious resort-style grounds and an amazing array of sports and fitness facilities—including access to the John Wayne Tennis Club. Luxury, with rates $169 and up. Lush, too, but less outdoorsy is the **New-port Beach Marriott Hotel and Tennis Club** near Fashion Island, 900 Newport Center Dr., toll-free 800/228-9290 or 714/640-4000, www.marriott.com. The "tennis club" refers to eight lighted tennis courts (extra). Golf is also available. Luxury, with rates $169 and up.

Anyone opting for a street-side room at the appealing 1930s Spanish-style **Balboa Inn,** by the Balboa Pier and Balboa Beach at 105 Main St., 714/675-3412, www.balboainn.com, also receives a free nightly live-jazz serenade from the Studio Cafe just across the way. The decor here is flowery country French. Each of the 34 rooms and 14 suites boasts a view of some sort (not necessarily the ocean), though the most pacifying peek at the Pacific is from the pool area. Seven rooms include an in-room spa, 10 have a fireplace. Continental breakfast is served in the lobby. Luxury, with rates from $169, from $145 in the off-season.

Newport Bed-and-Breakfast Inns

Newport Beach bed-and-breakfast inns deliver the most ocean ambience. Probably the best bet for romance—and not all that pricey if you opt for a cheaper room—is the two-story **Portofi-no Beach Hotel** on Balboa Peninsula just north of the pier, 2306 W. Ocean Front (at 23rd St.), 949/673-7030, www.portofinobeachhotel.com, with 15 rooms, four villas, and a "casa" that sleeps 10. The style here is upscale European, with decor running to antiques, armoires, and brass beds. Luxury, with rates $159–279 (weekly rates available), and children 16 and under stay free. Breakfast is included; there's also a restaurant on the premises.

For Victorian romance with frills, flounces, and French and American antiques, try the **Do-ryman's Inn** nearby, a dignified 1891 brick beauty across from the Newport Pier at 2102 W. Ocean Front, 949/675-7300. Every room features a fireplace and sunken marble hot tub, some have a four-poster bed with mirrored headboard. Besides breakfast, other goodies include a bottle of wine or champagne upon arrival, butter cookies and chocolates in the evening, a patio with a view, even a rooftop sundeck. Luxury, with rates $175–325.

The only place to stay out on Balboa Island (adults only) is the down-home 1925 **Balboa Is-land Hotel,** convenient to the ferry at 127 Agate

Ave., 949/675-3613. The three rooms here, two with a queen bed, one with a twin, share bathrooms. For breakfast, count on fresh fruit, muffins, and coffee. Moderate, with rates $85 in the high season, $65 otherwise.

EATING IN NEWPORT BEACH

Casual at Breakfast
You'll find no shortage of coffee-and-pastry stops in and around Newport Beach. For atmosphere à la Berkeley on Balboa Peninsula, try the **Alta Cafe Warehouse and Roasting Co.**, 506 31st St. (off Newport Blvd.), 949/675-0233. For croissants and great coffee, try **C'est Si Bon,** off the highway in Newport Beach at 149 Riverside, 949/645-0447, also in Corona del Mar at 3444 E. Coast Hwy., 949/675-0994.

As beloved in Orange County as Peet's is in Berkeley, **Diedrich's** is the native java hot spot. The closest Newport location for most folks is actually in Costa Mesa at 474 E. 17th St. (the extension of Westcliff Dr., near Irvine Ave.), 949/646-0323. There's another in Newport Beach proper, at 3601 Jamboree Rd., 949/833-9143, more convenient if you're heading out to the Back Bay. Seattle-based **Starbucks Coffee** is also established here, tucked into a little shopping center at 1128 Irvine Ave., 949/650-0369, and no doubt many more places by now, but the minimalist atmosphere is more conducive to takeout than hangout.

Funky for classic American breakfast is laid-back, low-key **Cappy's Cafe,** 5930 W. Coast Hwy., 949/646-4202. If you find yourself out on Balboa Island early in the day, try **Wilma's Patio,** 225 Marine, 949/675-5542. On the peninsula, consider **Britta's Cafe** two blocks from the Balboa Pavilion at 205 Main, 949/675-8146, though **Ruby's** at the end of the Balboa Pier has its charms. (For more on Ruby's, see below.)

Consider any of the area's upscale hotels for something more elegant in the morning.

Local Classics
The 1940s-style **Ruby's** out on Balboa Pier, 949/675-7829, is the first and original in this popular chain of boogying burger joints done in red, white, and polished chrome. Sitting on the roof for al fresco breakfast is a real treat at this one.

The original Ruby's is still going strong, but now there are Ruby's outposts all over Southern California. But the best bet for *fast* fast food—fresh burgers sans ambience—is **In-N-Out Burger,** closest here at 594 19th St. in Costa Mesa, toll-free 800/786-1000, where snap-to service comes with the employee profit-sharing plan.

Food snobs pooh-pooh the place, but for inexpensive and decent seafood *everybody* goes to **The Crab Cooker,** a lobster-red presence on the peninsula at 2200 Newport Blvd., 949/673-0100. Lunch and dinner specialties include Manhattan-style clam chowder, mesquite-grilled seafood and, yes, crab. As you can tell from a glance at the shuffling crowd on the sidewalk outside, no reservations are taken here (no credit cards either); add your name to the list and then join the line. Once you land a table, appreciate the ambience. A shark chained to the ceiling presides over the close-quarters decor: formica tables with quaint plastic breadstick and condiment containers, paper plates and placemats, even disposable silverware. At last report copies of the proprietor's 45 rpm single, "I Know Why The Fishes Cry," were still available for $1. There's another Crab Cooker in Tustin, 17260 E. 17th St., 714/573-1077.

Imaginative and Affordable
Virtually immune to tourist traffic is **Sabatino's Lido Shipyard Sausage Company,** 949/723-0645, tucked in among the boat shops and warehouses at 251 Shipyard Way, Cabin D on the Lido Peninsula—itself an opposable thumb on Balboa Peninsula, accessible via Lido Park Dr. just off Lafayette Ave. in Newport Beach. (Definitely tricky to find, so call for directions.) Sabatino's is open daily for lunch and dinner. The wonderful Sicilian sausages here date from an 1864 Sabatino family innovation, in which fat is removed from the meat and special goat's-milk cheese added in its stead. The result? Sausages, either mild or spicy, that are quite moist and incredibly tasty. Eat café-style outdoors, weather permitting, to fully appreciate the semi-industrial shipyard ambience, or indoors, where the atmosphere is also relaxed. At lunch you can't go wrong with any Sabatino's sausage sandwich or a Caesar salad, but the Sizzling Sausage Platter is a star attraction, served with pasta and bread (best with the giardiniera, or Italian-style olive relish). At dinner Sabatino's is also popular

for its pasta specialties and other traditional Italian dishes—chicken, fresh fish, and veal selections, not to mention a superb rack of lamb.

JACKshrimp, 2400 W. Coast Hwy. (near Tustin Ave.), 949/650-5577, is hot stuff, a jammin' jambalaya joint serving secret-recipe jambalaya and Louisiana-style shrimp specialties in a very casual atmosphere. Lunch is served only on Fri., 11:30 A.M.–2:30 P.M., dinner nightly.

The Golden Truffle, 1767 Newport Blvd. (between 17th and 18th, just before the 55 Fwy. begins in Costa Mesa), 949/645-9858, is as unassuming as it is exceptional, a French-Caribbean bistro serving specialties such as chianti braised lamb shank with noodles and Caribbean prime Angus skirt steak with soul slaw and fries. The Jamaican jerk chicken salad is nothing to shake a stick at either. The menu changes seasonally, featuring 15–20 specials every night. It's open Tues.–Sat. for lunch and dinner.

For healthy Mexican, the place is **La Fogata** near the Port Theater in Corona del Mar, 3025 E. Coast Hwy., 949/673-2211. In the same neighborhood and worth it for fancy Indian fare is **Mayur,** 2931 E. Coast Hwy., 949/675-6622, featuring seafood and other specialties, such as shrimp Vindaloo, shrimp tandoori, and chicken tikka Masala.

One of the area's best bets for Chinese is in Costa Mesa—the long-running **Mandarin Gourmet,** 1500 Adams Ave., 714/540-1937, is beloved for its traditional Peking duck, seafood dishes, and almost endless menu.

For exceptional French picnic fixings, try the **Pascal Epicerie,** 949/261-9041, adjacent to the famed restaurant of the same name on Bristol Street. For more information, see Fine Dining, below.

Higher-Priced Spreads

To dent the bankroll on behalf of the beefeater tradition, hoof it over to **Five Crowns,** 3801 Pacific Coast Hwy. (at Poppy) in Corona del Mar, 949/760-0331. This ersatz English manor is beloved by tourists and locals alike for its humongous portions of prime rib and other specialties. The filet mignon is excellent, tender enough to slice with a spoon. The tony New England–style **Yankee Tavern,** 333 Bayside Dr. in Newport Beach, 949/675-5333, adds dressed-down East Coast airs. Highlights include a tra-

A NEWPORT ROMANCE: VILLA NOVA

A Newport Beach favorite since the 1930s for romantic dress-up dining along the waterfront is Villa Nova, 3131 W. Pacific Coast Hwy. (near Newport Blvd.), 949/642-7880. This is the place, after all, where Joe DiMaggio took Marilyn Monroe on a blind date, and where Vincent Minelli proposed to Judy Garland. And how many places do you know that still have a piano bar?

Now open at a new location, since the original building perished in a fire a few years back, the very Italian Villa Nova is famous for its vast menu. Choosing is the hard part—from endless housemade pastas and gnocchi served with secret-recipe sauces "imported" from Abuzzi, Italy, to seafood, chicken, steak, veal, and various house specialties. Children's menu, too, and an impressive list of Californian, Italian, and French wines. Reservations definitely advisable.

ditional New England boiled dinner. The rest of the menu runs to beer-battered fish and chips, turkey meat loaf, and Yankee pot roast.

Tonier but most appreciated for its spectacular seafood is **21 Ocean Front** overlooking Newport Pier at 21 Ocean Front, 949/675-2566. One of the best bets around, though, is surprisingly relaxed **Bistro 201,** 3333 W. Pacific Coast Hwy., 949/631-1551.

Fine Dining, Dressed Up and Dressed Down

Genuine gastronomic adventure awaits in Newport Beach. Head to the south of France, for example, via one of Orange County's best restaurants. Serving Provençal in a rose garden of a bistro, **Pascal** at 1000 N. Bristol Ave. (near Jamboree), 949/752-0107, is just about everyone's favorite unstuffy French restaurant. Specialties include seared salmon fillet with watercress sauce and baby lamb rack with sweet garlic. Reservations definitely advised. Men: jacket required. You can also try Pascal to go—thanks to the dandy little take-out shop adjacent, 949/261-9041, which offers baguette sandwiches and such things as eggplant caviar, unusual salads, whole cooked chickens, and French ham and cheeses.

Another contender for favorite French restaurant is **Aubergine** on the Balboa Peninsula at 508 29th St., 949/723-4150, open Tues.–Sat. from 6 P.M. (reservations a must). For fancy-dress California cuisine at dinner or quite special Sunday brunch, **The Pavilion** at the Four Seasons Hotel near Fashion Island at 690 Newport Center Dr. (at Santa Cruz), 949/760-4920, is hard to beat. Orange County's most popular dress-up dining spot, though, seems to be Fashion Island's **The Ritz,** 880 Newport Center Dr. (at Santa Barbara), 949/720-1800, where you can expect traditional continental fare.

DOWN THE COAST: CRYSTAL COVE STATE PARK

South along the coast toward Laguna Beach is one of Orange County's genuine gems, Crystal Cove State Park, the largest remaining patch of coastal land still open to the general public. And what a patch it is—tidepools and sandy coves along more than three miles of shoreline, plus, on the other side of the highway, once-wooded El Moro Canyon in the San Joaquin Hills, a total of 2,791 acres owned until 1979 by the Irvine Company.

The beach here, open daily from 6 A.M. to sunset, is usually one of the loneliest around—a real draw when you've had enough of Orange County crowds. Offshore, to a depth of 120 feet, is one of the state's official "underwater parks," a prime scuba- and skin-diving locale. For more pedestrian aquatic explorations, study local tide tables and head for the tidepools. This low-tide adventure (don't touch) is usually better in winter, when the tides are more extreme because of the gravitational pull of both sun and moon. Access points to beach parking and facilities are at El Moro Canyon, Reef Point, Los Trancos, and Pelican Point.

Inland, some 23 miles of trails wind through the hills of El Moro Canyon, which is heaven for mountain bikers, hikers, and pikers on horseback. Climb on up, at least for the ocean views, or come along on park-sponsored interpretive walks or backcountry hikes—the latter often to places not otherwise open to the public.

Also fascinating is the *town* of **Crystal Cove,** seemingly unchanged since the 1920s and now included on the National Register of Historic Places. The 46 beachfront bungalows, originally built to house Irvine Company ranch hands, are scheduled to be made available for rent one day soon—a process delayed by the fact that current residents are (understandably) reluctant to leave their cheap oceanfront digs, and the fact that there has been some controversy over state park plans to "rehab" the town as a swank beach resort. Other park facilities are currently available, however, including fairly unobtrusive picnic areas and restrooms with showers.

The day-use fee at Crystal Cove is $3. For other park information, including if and when the cabins and campground will be available, contact: Crystal Cove State Park, 8471 Pacific Coast Hwy., Crystal Cove, 949/494-3539 or 949/492-0802.

LAGUNA BEACH AND VICINITY

THE ARTS, ARTISTS, AND ASSORTED OTHERS

Unlike most beach towns, laid-back Laguna Beach has tried to put a lid on the booming business of T-shirteries and other standards of the tourism trade—to little avail. It's hard to believe that this village of just under 30,000 attracts about three million tourists each year. Why do they come? Because Laguna Beach is lovely, for one thing, with a woodsy, small-town feel, white-sand beaches, and craggy coastal coves and outcroppings vaguely reminiscent of Big Sur. For another, because this artsy onetime artists colony has a quirky creative character.

Built on land never included within a land-grant rancho, since the days of early settlement Lagu-na Beach has gone its own way. And the town still cultivates its eccentricities. Chief among them is the odd and oddly compelling annual Pageant of the Masters presentation of *tableaux vivants,* "living pictures" allowing life to imitate art imitating life. Other oddities persist. Even in this uncharitable bottom-line age, for example, affluent Laguna Beach still tries to find room for artists, oddballs, and assorted others who don't fit the mass-produced American mold. Nonetheless, having money is almost a necessity here. Worthy civic intentions notwithstanding, bohemians have all but been replaced by BMWs and beach resorts.

Even this latest Laguna Beach lifestyle is threatened by success. The city's population has more than doubled in the past 10 years. With the arrival of tourist season every summer, the population doubles again. On summer weekends in particular, traffic can become hopelessly snarled—in town, and up and down the highway—with parking spaces nearly as precious as local real estate. And more people are on the way. Like waves from an inland sea, new residential developments roll toward Laguna Beach from the north, south, and east.

For more information about local attractions—including a listing of local galleries and shops—contact the **Laguna Beach Visitor Bureau and Chamber of Commerce,** 252 Broadway, Laguna Beach, toll-free 800/877-1115 (recorded) or 949/497-9229, www.lagunabeachinfo.org.

THE ART OF LAGUNA BEACH

Especially on a first-time trip to Laguna Beach, seeing the sights should be synonymous with attending the town's simultaneous Festival of the Arts and Pageant of the Masters, held together in July and August. The fine arts and crafts on display—all strictly local, displayed by artists and craftspeople from up and down the Orange County coast—*are* fine, the variety great: handmade musical instruments, furniture, sculpture, and scrimshaw. There's even a "junior art" division.

But the pageant is unlike anything you're likely to encounter anywhere else on earth—a living,

---

LAGUNA BEACH BASICS

If you plan to come or go from the east via Laguna Canyon Rd. (Hwy. 133), which connects Laguna Beach to the 405 inland—*be extra cautious.* This narrow two-lane highway has become Orange County's blood alley, its high accident rate attributed to too many people in too much of a hurry. The same caution holds for the alternative route inland, Laguna Canyon Rd. to El Toro Rd. to I-5. Aside from the coast highway, there are no other routes into Laguna Beach.

Once here, you'll need to orient yourself to Pacific Coast Hwy. Laguna Beach highway addresses north of Broadway are designated "North Coast Highway"; those south of town to Crown Valley Pkwy., "South Coast Highway."

Unless your vehicle is safely stored at a local motel or hotel, parking is a challenge. Metered parking (bring *lots* of quarters) is available on many streets. There are also various lots (try Ocean) where all-day parking runs around $8–10. If you're coming just for the Pageant of the Masters and associated arts festivals, *come early,* park in the large lots along Laguna Canyon Rd., and shuttle back and forth to town. Arrive by 10 A.M. and there should be no problem.

breathing tribute to the art world's old masters and ancient treasures, a carefully staged two-hour magic show that's been tickling everyone's fancy since the 1930s.

Pageant of the Masters and Other Festivals

The pageant's *tableaux vivants,* or living pictures, are large-scale sleight of hand or trompe l'oeil, literally, "fooling the eye." Whether the oversized artwork on display is Leonardo da Vinci's *Last Supper* (a pageant favorite), Renoir's *Grape Pickers at Lunch,* or Monet's *Women in the Garden,* on cue the costumed participants come on stage and freeze into the background frieze. Then—after the house goes dark and the stage lights come on—the entire audience gasps. Because

---

THE ART OF SHOPPING

Shopping is a serious local pastime, a primary local attraction. Laguna Beach is chock-full of shops, where you'll find the tackiest of tourist bric-a-brac as well as fine art and jewelry. Laguna Beach boasts 60–70 art galleries. Unlike special exhibits and collection displays at the local art museum, however, much of the gallery fare is far from cutting edge, in California or elsewhere. To be sure you're buying local art—to support the health and welfare of artists still managing to survive in high-rent Orange County—attend local arts and craft fairs. And when in doubt, don't hesitate to ask. Otherwise, to find out what's what and where it might be, pick up the current *Local Arts* guide, available in most shops.

For an introduction to Laguna Beach's Plein Air School, stop by **Redfern Gallery,** 1540 S. Coast Hwy., 949/497-3356. That's the specialty. **The Vladimir Solokov Studio Gallery** in the same complex, 714/494-3633, is a working studio specializing in bright-colored abstract and mixed media paintings. Nearby, at 1390 S. Coast, is the **Esther Wells Collection,** 949/494-2497, noted for its impressionistic watercolors (always some local art on display) as well as sculpture and jewelry.

To appreciate just how much disposable income some people have, stop by the **Sherwood Gallery,** 460 S. Coast Hwy., 949/497-2668, with its contemporary and pop art, sculpture (some kinetic), jewelry, and unusual furnishings.

---

there on stage, 50 times larger than life, is an uncanny reproduction of the real thing.

So there's really no need to traipse across the country to the Metropolitan, or cross oceans to the Louvre or Uffizi, when you can come to Laguna Beach.

It's not all high art, though. In the process of dazzling the crowds with impersonations of two- and three-dimensional reality, pageanteers also pose as sculptures, California orange-crate labels, hair combs and other jewelry, even postage stamps.

More than 250,000 people typically attend these events, so plan for lodgings in town and walk to the festival; it's only a few blocks from Main Beach. If you're here just for the day and driving, once parked, stay parked—then, if you're also heading downtown, walk. To find a parking place, arrive very early in the day. A shuttle bus service (small fee) runs between the area's summer festivals and the parking lots along Laguna Canyon Road.

The annual arts festival and pageant take place in July and August at Irvine Bowl Park, also known as the Festival of the Arts Pageant Grounds, 650 Laguna Canyon Road. The theater is the Irvine Bowl itself, a 2,500-seat theater nestled into the canyon hillside. Admission to the festival itself is $5. Pageant tickets start at $10 each and are generally sold out months in advance, but if you're lucky there may be cancellations on an appropriate performance night. For current information contact: **Festival of the Arts/Pageant of the Masters,** 650 Laguna Canyon Rd., Laguna Beach, 949/497-6582 for general information, toll-free 800/487-3378 to order tickets, or check www.pageanttickets.com.

Since the 1960s the **Sawdust Festival** has been the "alternative" Laguna Beach arts celebration, now a major-league crafts fair held more or less concurrently across the road at 935 Laguna Canyon Rd., 949/494-3030, www.sawdustartfestival.org. These days it's an "Auld Tyme Faire," in the ever-popular Renaissance style, with mimes, strolling minstrels, and plenty of ale. Also going on every summer: the juried **Art-A-Fair** festivities at 777 Laguna Canyon Rd., 949/494-4514, or check www.art-a-fair.com.

If slogging through the summer crowds seems unappealing, come some other time. Arts and crafts fairs of some sort are scheduled year-round, including the April **Art Walk Lunch** at the festival grounds (eat, then meet the artists) and the Sawdust Festival's **Winter Fantasy** from mid-November into December. During the rest of the year, crafts fairs are typically scheduled at least twice each month; call the visitors bureau at 949/497-9229 for information.

The Laguna Art Museum

These days Laguna Beach is hardly recognizable as "SoHo by the Sea." But at the turn of the century—the 20th century—scores of American artists arrived here determined to paint in the open air *(en plein air)* like the French impressionists and Hudson River School. The legacy of artists of The Plein Air School, including Joseph Kleitsch, William Griffith, and Frank Cuprien, has been lasting. Which explains the fact that, while other high school football teams identify themselves as "cougars" or "chargers," for example, the big bruisers here are known as the Laguna Beach High Artists—surely enough to strike fear into the heart of any opponent.

The hot pink Laguna Art Museum, 307 Cliff Dr. (at Coast Hwy.), 949/494-6531, www.lagunaartmuseum.org, has earned renown as the only Southern California art museum to focus exclusively on American art—contemporary California art in particular, along with avant-garde special shows. After a short-lived merger with the Orange County Museum of Art, the Laguna Art Museum is once again a local institution. At last report the museum was open Tues.–Sun. 11 A.M.–5 P.M., and until 9 P.M. the first Thurs. of the month (with free admission). Regular admission: $5 adults, $4 students, $3 children.

THE ART OF THE OUTDOORS: LAGUNA BEACH BEACHES AND PARKS

Main Beach and Vicinity

Main Beach is, well, the city's main beach, dominating the ocean side of downtown between the Laguna Art Museum and Hotel Laguna near Park Avenue. You'll know you've arrived when you spot the imposing glassed-in lifeguard tower, something of a local landmark. Most of the year you also can't miss the pick-up basketball players, almost as competitive as the volleyballers. A wooden boardwalk snakes along the beach, with its youngsters, oldsters, and in-line skaters. At this intriguing if tamer version of Muscle Beach in Venice, everybody and everything hangs out.

South of Main Beach, overseen by high-priced real estate, are Laguna's "street beaches." Sections of this slim one-mile strand of sand are known by the names of intersecting streets, from **Sleepy Hollow Lane** and **Thalia** to **Oak** and **Brooks.** Farther south still is half-mile **Arch Cove,** popular for sunbathing, its section again named after relevant streets (Bluebird Canyon, Agate, Pearl, etc.).

Since the coast (actually, the beach) is clear between Laguna Beach and South Laguna, you might find a completely private cove if you're willing to walk, surf-dodge, and rock-hop the distance—not advisable at high tide. For more on what you'll find if you're crazy enough to try it, see South Laguna Beaches and Aliso Pier, below.

More Laguna Beach Beaches

North of Main Beach, atop the bluffs along Cliff Dr., is the **Heisler Park** promenade, a fine place for lolling on the lawn, picnicking, and people-watching (public restrooms are here, too). Down

---

GREETERS CORNER

While wandering toward Main Beach, take note of Greeters Corner in **Main Beach Park** at the end of Forest Avenue. The statue in front of the **Greeters Corner Restaurant,** 329 S. Coast Hwy., 949/494-0361, commemorates the town's long tradition of greeters—and, in particular, Eiler Larsen. A Danish immigrant and World War I veteran, Larsen arrived in Laguna Beach in the 1930s to serve as "the Laguna greeter," a title (and unpaid job) he held for 30 years. An organized attempt to silence Larsen failed in 1959, once a local survey established that almost 90 percent of the citizenry wanted him to stay—and to continue waving and bellowing at passing cars.

Someone has served in the role of local greeter since the late 19th century, when Laguna Beach was known as Lagona—a variation of "Lagonas," a coastal territory named in the 1500s by local native peoples. In the 1880s, for example, Portuguese fisherman Joe Lucas would holler at passing stagecoaches.

GRUNION RUN FREE, SO WHY CAN'T WE?

It's a live sex show, yet almost innocent, even wholesome—and certainly educational. This particular procreation education usually begins after midnight. Sometimes shining small flashlights to show the way, people suddenly dash onto the beach, giggling and grabbing—for grunion, those silvery Southern California sexpots of the smelt persuasion.

Human voyeurs come down to the beach not only to watch the frenzied fish but also to catch them—literally—in the act. The hunt seems unsporting, since the grunion are, after all, deeply distracted. Without the aid of nets, window screens, kitchen sieves, and other illegal devices, however, grabbing grunion is actually a challenge. Grunion fisherfolk, optimistically armed with buckets as well as flashlights, can use only their bare hands. And grunion are slippery, like long, wriggling bars of soap. They're also rather sly. No matter what tide charts may say, grunion never show up exactly when and where they're predicted, sometimes skipping the days, hours, and locales people expect. Sometimes just a few roll in with the surf, sometimes thousands. Grunion seem to be more patient even than surfers, content to flip and flop around in the water as long as necessary, waiting for the right wave.

For many years the "grunion run," strictly a Southern California phenomenon, was thought to be some form of moonstruck romance. Much to the delight of local romantics, it was commonly believed that the fish swam ashore during spring and summer simply to fin-dance in the moonlight.

Scientists established in 1919, however, that nature was quite purposeful. The way it really works is this: After dark, near both the new and full moons but after high tide has started to recede, wave after wave of grunion surf onto local beaches. Each wave's "dance" takes 30 seconds or less. Females burrow into the sand, dorsal fin-deep, to lay their eggs (about 2,000 each) while the males circle seductively, fertilizing the roe. All parental responsibility thus discharged, the grunion catch the next wave and head back out to sea. About two weeks later, at the next moon-heightened high tide, the young'n' grunion hatch and are washed out into the big, big watery world.

Fairly remote beaches all along the coast, from Santa Barbara south, are good bets for the grunion grab. Prime possibilities in Orange County include dark stretches of beaches at or near Bolsa Chica, Huntington Beach, Laguna Beach, Dana Point, and San Clemente.

March through August are peak grunion-running periods. Grabbing grunion is against the law in April and May, however, to allow the species some spawning success. And anyone over age 16 must have a California fishing license—available at most local bait and sporting goods shops, along with tide charts, tall tales, and free advice.

---

below are two rocky coves with nice tidepools, **Picnic Beach** at the end of Myrtle St. and **Rockpile Beach** at the end of Jasmine.

Nearby are three inlets that manage to combine the best of the beach scene with the best of beach scenery: **Shaw's Cove, Fisherman's Cove,** and **Diver's Cove.** Needless to say, the area is beloved by locals and often crowded. The path down to Shaw's Cove is on Cliff Dr. at the end of Fairview; entrances to Fisherman's and Diver's Coves are close together on Cliff, in the 600 block.

Half-moon **Crescent Bay Beach** (entrance at Cliff and Circle Dr.) is quite enticing, and usually offers some privacy for sunning, swimming, and skin-diving. To reach **Crescent Bay Point Park** (great views) from Cliff Dr., turn left onto the highway and left again onto Crescent Bay Drive.

Special Beaches and a "Bark Park"

Popular for bodysurfing yet quite private by Laguna Beach standards, **Victoria Beach** is a local favorite. To get here, take Victoria Dr. from the highway and then turn right onto Dumond. Tiny fan-shaped **Moss Beach** at the end of Moss St. is one of the best around, well-protected for swimming, also popular for scuba diving. The three rocky fingers of **Wood's Cove** have helped create the pocket beaches here, plus providing a pounding-surf sideshow, great swimming, good scuba diving. (To get here, take the steps down from the intersection of Ocean Way and Diamond Street.) None of these beaches have public restrooms—the price of privacy—but at last report lifeguards were on duty, at least in summer.

If you bring Fido or Fifi along on this trip, you'll soon discover that dogs are not welcome at the beach (not to mention most other places). Laguna Beach offers some consolation, though. The city's Dog Park out on Laguna Canyon Rd., known by locals as the Bark Park, is one of very few public areas in Orange County where people can legally let their dogs run free. (Free in this case means "loose"; it actually costs $2 to use this well-fenced pooch park.) And if you're sans beast but bored, come out to the Bark Park anyway. Watching dogs and their people at play is cheap entertainment. Laguna Beach's Bark Park is sponsored by RUFF, "Rescuing Unwanted Furry Friends."

South Laguna Beaches and Aliso Pier

Several miles south of Laguna Beach proper is the area aptly known as South Laguna. The main attraction here is **Aliso Creek Beach Park** at the mouth of Aliso Creek. In the late 1800s Helena Modjeska—the Shakespearean actress for whom Orange County's Modjeska Canyon was named—camped out with her entourage here in the coastal wilderness to beat the summer heat. Though houses are now the dominant feature of the surrounding landscape, the first thing you'll really notice is the Aliso Pier, which looks like a gargantuan arrow about to be shot out to sea. But take time to explore the small sandy coves here and the rocky tidepools beyond. For relative privacy, head south; to commune with the college-age crowd, head north.

STAYING IN LAGUNA BEACH

"Inexpensive" and "expensive" are relative terms, but it's safe to say that nothing in Laguna Beach is truly inexpensive. If a low-rent stay is a must, hang your hat in Huntington Beach, or, if heading south, try camping or a cheap motel in Dana Point or the hostel in San Clemente.

Most Laguna Beach lodging rates go up for "the season" either in mid-June or on July 1—just in time for the local arts festivals—and then dive again in mid-September. If you're willing to miss the summer arts pageantry and attendant crowds, come in early June (it can be foggy) or just about any other time. For better value, look for establishments "close to" (not on) the beach and "near" (not in) town, and request a room at the lower end of the options range.

Less Expensive Laguna Options

Both Best Westerns offer good value even in summer, better value in the off-season. To make toll-free telephone reservations at any Best Western, call 800/780-7234 (U.S. and Canada). Closest to town is the **Best Western Laguna Brisas Spa Hotel**, 1600 S. Coast Hwy., toll-free 800/624-4442 or 949/497-7272, www.bestwestern.com, "just 58 steps from the beach." Half the rooms have an ocean view. All rooms include huge in-room whirlpools, cable TV, free movies, and refrigerators (the latter upon request). Continental breakfast is served. You'll find a coin laundry on the premises, along with heated pool, spa, and sundeck. Premium-Luxury, with rates $149 and up from June into early Sept., $129 and up otherwise, kids under 12 stay free (in your room). Senior and AAA discounts available. The attractive **Best Western Laguna Reef Inn** south of town at 30806 S. Coast Hwy., 949/499-2227, is Expensive—a straight $99 in the summer for one person ($10 for each extra person, kids 10 and under free), otherwise $69 and up in the off-season. Some units have kitchens, $15 extra. Continental breakfast.

In the motel category, you also can't go too far wrong at the 22-room **Best Inn**, 1404 N. Coast Hwy., toll-free 800/221-2222 for reservations, otherwise 949/494-6464, Expensive (basic rates $99 and up from mid-June through mid-Sept., otherwise $79 and up). And check www.bestinn.com for special discounts for seniors, government and the military.

More Expensive, More Ambience

There's something quite comforting about the predictability of motels, but other styles of accommodation offer more *romance*. Or something.

Two moderately expensive hotels offer both beach town ambience and convenient central location. The former Hotel San Maarten is now the **Holiday Inn Laguna Beach** across from the beach at 696 S. Coast Hwy., toll-free 800/228-5691 or 949/494-1001, www.holiday-inn.com. Breezy French Caribbean style enlivens the lobby—note the hand-painted ceiling, verdant nature scenes of birds, plants, and flowers—and the tropical courtyard, with its patio and pool. Rooms don't necessarily court the same flash but are reliably "Holiday Inn." Premium-Luxury. Regular rooms run $129–159 on weekdays in summer and $179–199 on weekends; rates are $109–139 at other times, continental breakfast included. Suites with kitchenettes and microwaves (some have in-room spas) are available. Also here, a restaurant and bar, plus free parking.

The local grande dame—and the only place around with a private beach—is the recently redone landmark **Hotel Laguna,** practically on Main Beach at 425 S. Coast Hwy., toll-free 800/524-2927 (in California only) or 949/494-1151, www.hotellaguna.com. Most rooms are modern, with ceiling fans and the basics, and some afford ocean views. Since the Hotel Laguna was Humphrey Bogart's favorite Laguna Beach hideaway, two suites—the **Bogart Suite** and **Bacall Suite**—get special treatment, complete with canopy beds. Premium-Luxury. Room rates run $110–250 in summer, $85–225 and up at other times, with free valet parking. On-site you'll find a spectacularly good seafood restaurant, **Claes Seafood, Etc.,** and **Le Bar,** for an ocean view with your cocktails.

Laguna Beach Bed-and-Breakfast Inns
Local bed-and-breakfast establishments also offer non-motel ambience. The **Carriage House Inn,** 1322 Catalina St., 949/494-8945, www.carriagehouse.com, is the historic colonial home once owned by film czar Cecil B. DeMille. In a residential neighborhood and all done up New Orleans style, the two-story Carriage House features a lushly landscaped brick courtyard and six one- and two-bedroom guest suites. All include a living room and private bathroom; all but one feature kitchens and refrigerators; some have in-room coffeemakers. Premium-Luxury. Basic rates year-round are $125–165 ($20 per additional person for the two-bedroom suites), weekly rates available. To get here: About one mile south of Laguna Beach turn east onto Cress St., go two blocks to Catalina, then turn left.

A long-running local favorite is the Mediterranean-style **Casa Laguna Inn** bed-and-breakfast at 2510 S. Coast Hwy., toll-free 800/233-0449 or 949/494-2996, www.casalaguna.com, an updated ode to 1930s California. Paths wander past the bell tower and courtyard and throughout the terraced gardens, connecting rooms and suites. Also here are a one-bedroom cottage with private ocean view, fireplace, and full kitchen, and the two-bedroom Mission House. Rooms are small, suites are spacious; some have views; and all are tastefully furnished with antiques and overhead fans. The pool has a view. Head to the library in the morning for continental breakfast; tea is served in the afternoon, wine and hors d'oeuvres in the evening. In July and Aug. there's a two-night minimum on weekends. Premium-Luxury. Peak weekend rates are $135–250, weekday rates $105–225. During the rest of the year, when rates run $105 and up (higher, again, on weekends), modest rooms here can be a best bet for budget romance.

A Family-Friendly Choice: Aliso Creek Inn
A nice set-up for families or traveling homebodies—and a good deal for just about anybody in the off-season—is the lovely **Aliso Creek Inn** in South Laguna at 31106 S. Coast Hwy., toll-free 800/223-3309 or 949/499-2271, www.alisocreek.com. Just a few hundred yards from the beach yet nestled into a steep-walled canyon, this relaxed 80-acre condo-style motel and resort complex offers a good selection of housekeeping units, from studios to one- and two-bedroom suites, all with kitchens, patios, sitting areas, color TV, free movies. Amenities include a pool, whirlpool, even a wading pool for the kids, not to mention the nine-hole golf course, restaurant, and bar. For those predictable practical family emergencies, there's a coin laundry. Free bonus: Aliso Creek itself, which meanders through the resort grounds on its way to the ocean. Luxury. From July 1 through Labor Day rates run $155–328. Otherwise, expect to pay $112–297. Meeting rooms are available.

High-End Hotels
If money is absolutely no object, consider heading south a short distance to Dana Point and the **Ritz-Carlton Laguna Niguel,** the south-state's most luxurious hotel resort. For details, see the special topic Ritz-Carlton Laguna Niguel.

Otherwise, if you plan to park yourself at the beach and don't care what it costs, *the* place in Laguna Beach is the light and airy **Surf & Sand Hotel** right on the beach south of town at 1555 S. Coast Hwy. (at Bluebird Canyon Dr.), toll-free 800/524-8621 for reservations or 949/497-4477, www.jcresorts.com. Rooms in the nine-story tower have the most breathtaking views, of course, but you won't go wrong elsewhere here, since most rooms are within 30 feet of the beach and include a private balcony looking out over the surf, surfers, and heated pool. Decor is tastefully understated in a day-at-the-beach palette, with sand-colored walls and raw-silk upholstery, shuttered windows and naked wood. The fun indoor-outdoor **Splashes** restaurant sits right on the beach. The art deco lounge is a choice spot for cocktails at sunset. Luxury. Rates run $310–425 from Memorial Day through Oct., with a two-night minimum stay in July and on June and Sept. weekends, and a three-day minimum in August. In other seasons prices start at $260, but if business is off you may be able to do better. Ask about specials and packages.

High-end hotels in Laguna Beach also include the fairly new, well-located, yet reasonably secluded **Inn at Laguna Beach** near Main Beach at 211 N. Coast Hwy., toll-free 800/544-4479 for reservations or 714/497-9722, fax 714/497-9972. Most rooms are fairly small but attractive, with abundant amenities. Many have a view, too, not to mention color TV/cable and VCRs. In-room continental breakfast is provided. Luxury. High-season rates, from July 1 through Labor Day, run $249–459. The Inn at Laguna Beach is an especially sweet deal in the off-season, when prices are $129 and up.

EATING IN LAGUNA BEACH

Beach Town Breakfast

Locals' choice for artsy minimalist breakfast is the very cool **Cafe Zinc**, 350 Ocean Ave. (at Forest), 949/494-6302, though on weekends be prepared to wait at the counter and to fight for a table. The morning repast here is as simple as a huge hot cappuccino with a muffin. The frittatas are also good, not to mention the huevos rancheros with papaya salsa. If you come late, order a salad and some homemade soup—very good here—and do lunch. No credit cards. Next door is the equally cool **Cafe Zinc Market,** where you can load up on bread and baked goods, salads, cookbooks, even sundry kitchen items.

The **Beach House Inn,** centrally situated between Main Beach and PCH behind Vacation Village at 619 Sleepy Hollow Ln., 949/494-9707,

is a Laguna Beach institution. This is the onetime home of Slim Summerstone, one of the original Keystone Cops. The ambience here is quite casual, and every table offers an ocean view—definitely a fine start for any day. The Beach House is best known for its lobster, steamed clams, and fresh fish specials, yet the all-American breakfast is also a best bet. Beloved locally for breakfast, especially al fresco, is **The Cottage,** 308 N. Coast Hwy., 949/494-3023. Another possibility is the **Laguna Village Cafe,** 577 S. Coast Hwy., 949/494-6344.

For a special see-and-be-seen Sunday brunch right on the beach, head to **Splashes** outside at the Surf & Sand Hotel, 1555 S. Coast Hwy. (at Bluebird Canyon Dr.), 949/497-4477. If it's foggy or cool, the food's just as good when served indoors.

Laguna Lunch

Many of the more upscale eateries around town also serve lunch, often a variation of the dinner menu but with smaller servings at lower prices. See the Dining Adventure listings below for possibilities.

Beloved here and elsewhere in Orange County is **Wahoo's Fish Taco,** 1133 S. Coast Hwy. (PCH about a mile south of Main Beach, between Oak and Brook Sts.), 949/497-0033. Also tops in the *very casual* cheap-eats fast-food category is **Taco Loco,** 640 S. Coast Hwy. (PCH between Cleo and Legion), 949/497-1635, where the ambience is asphalt-meets-the-sea-breeze and surfers scarf down fish tacos—such things as fresh lobster or mahi-mahi on blue corn tortillas—as quickly as possible. Vegetarians, don't despair. Taco Loco also serves a killer tofu burger.

For imaginative pizza, *the* place is **Z Pizza,** the original well south near Aliso Creek, 30902 S. Coast Hwy., 949/499-4949. Of course there's a **Ruby's** here (S. Coast Hwy. at Nyes), 949/497-7829, the nostalgic diner-style choice for burgers, shakes, fries, and all those other things we all know we shouldn't eat. Ditto for **Johnny Rockets,** at 190 S. Coast Hwy., 949/497-7252.

Late in the afternoon or before dinner, stop for a drink at **Las Brisas,** 361 Cliff Dr. (N. Coast Hwy.), 949/497-5434, a place still known among old-timers as the Victor Hugo Inn. The main reason to dawdle here, though, is to drink in the views—while considering the possibility that Orange County promoters haven't overhyped the "Riviera" angle after all.

Dining Adventures, Not Too Pricey
For intimate noshing, **Ti Amo,** 31727 S. Coast Hwy., 949/499-5350, is the perfect spot perched on a bluff overlooking the sea. The place has been lavishly decorated with sponge-painted walls and rich drapes. Entrées include paella, homemade pasta, and wonderful seafood. Or, create an appetizing light meal from several selections on the appetizer menu. Reservations wise at dinner.

If you're craving pasta at dinner, try the two-story **Sorrento Grille,** 370 Glenneyre St. (near Mermaid), 949/494-8686, an American bistro and "martini bar," though some people prefer the artier, quieter **Ristorante Rumari** (dinner only) on the highway between Center and Pearl, 949/494-0400, specializing in Northern Italian and Sicilian dishes, particularly fish. Another best bet is **Villa Romana Trattoria,** 303 Broadway, Ste. 101, 949/497-6220.

At 998 S. Coast Hwy. (just south of Thalia) is **Natraj,** 949/497-9197, the best bet for authentic Indian food—for many miles in any direction.

More Fine Dining Adventures
Five Feet refers to Laguna Beach's elevation. But this local hot spot at 328 Glenneyre, on the corner of Forest and Glenneyre, 949/497-4955, is actually more famous for fine nouvelle Chinese served up with pop art and pink neon. A must for first-timers: the catfish. It's open for dinner nightly, for lunch on Fri. only.

Tops in local hotel dining is **Claes Seafood, Etc.** at the Hotel Laguna, 425 S. Coast Hwy., 949/494-1151. The seafood, of course, is particularly spectacular. (It's also open daily for breakfast and lunch.) Or, drive south to Dana Point and **The Dining Room,** 949/240-2000, at the Ritz-Carlton Laguna Niguel for spectacular food in an equally stunning setting (semi-formal attire). The Ritz-Carlton also offers more casual fare at breakfast, lunch, and dinner in its **Terrace** restaurant, 949/240-5008—out on the terrace overlooking the ocean—and **Club Bar and Grill.** For more information, see the special topic Ritz-Carlton Laguna Niguel.

DANA POINT AND VICINITY

Before the Mast, Before the Hobie Cat
Given the modern-day dominance of subdivisions, shopping malls, and rush-hour traffic, one might forget that, before the United States claimed the territory, pioneers from Spain and the new nation of Mexico made their homes in a much quieter California. For a glimpse into that brave old world, pick up a copy of *Two Years Before the Mast,* published in 1840 by Richard Henry Dana, Jr. On leave from his studies at Harvard University to recover from measles-related afflictions, Dana put to sea onboard the *Pilgrim,* a small square-rigged Boston brig that delivered East Coast fineries to California in exchange for tanned cowhides carted over from the mission at San Juan Capistrano and other ports. San Juan Cove—now Dana Cove, which includes Dana Point Harbor, all within Capistrano Bay—was the only safe anchorage between

Dana Point: under the mast

RITZ-CARLTON LAGUNA NIGUEL

Just 10 miles south of Laguna Beach is Orange County's finest resort—a gem for those who can afford the price tag of pure getaway pleasure.

The Ritz-Carlton Laguna Niguel is a long, low château perched grandly on cliffs overlooking the ocean. The northern Monarch Bay Wing faces north toward Salt Creek Beach and an 18-hole par-70 golf course designed by Robert Trent Jones. The Dana Point Wing overlooks ocean, palm trees, and sunset scenery. Amenities here include four outdoor tennis courts, two heated pools with hot tubs, and a complete fitness center with exercise rooms, steam room, sauna, and massage. Once inside the lobby, guests are greeted by raw-silk wall coverings, French tapestries, Chinese horses, and art, art, art. This Ritz boasts an impressive hotel collection of American and British 19th-century art, not to mention crystal chandeliers (even in the elevators). All rooms have small private terraces, and are attractive and comfortable in the somewhat staid Ritz-Carlton style. Amenities include color TV, free movies, in-room honor bars and safes plus, in the bathrooms, hair dryers, an extra telephone, and thick terry bathrobes. As is typical at Ritz-Carlton hotels, 24-hour room service and other services are top drawer.

Casual meals, breakfast, lunch, and dinner, are served at the Ritz's **Terrace** café restaurant (outside on the terrace, overlooking the ocean). Another possibility is the **Club Grill and Bar,** which also serves live music in the evening. When cost is no object, **The Dining Room** is truly exceptional, one of the best restaurants in Orange County. And though a dressed-down dress code is otherwise strictly enforced in Dana Point and Laguna Beach, the Ritz-Carlton insists on some semblance of formality. Jackets and ties are required even in the bar, semiformal attire in The Dining Room.

The Ritz-Carlton Laguna Niguel is just off PCH at 33533 Ritz-Carlton Dr. in Dana Point, toll-free 800/241-3333 or 949/240-2000, www.ritzcarlton.com. Luxury, with room rates $395–575 per night in summer, from $295 otherwise. Suites start at $650. Ask about specials and packages.

San Diego and Santa Barbara. When Dana returned to Boston and an eventual career as a noted maritime attorney, he recalled the cove, with its rocky harbor and striking 200-foot cliffs, as "the only romantic spot in California."

More recently Dana Point has celebrated the grandeur of local surf, surfing, and surf-related innovations. Several times each year, when storms drove classic long-angled 30-foot waves around Dana Point from the west, hard-core surfers from far and wide assembled here to brave the "Killer Dana." Just like the local cattlehide trade, Killer Danas are history; harbor construction altered the offshore terrain. But to pay homage to those days of yore, stop by **Hobie Sports** in Lantern Bay Village, 24825 Del Prado, 949/496-2366, where rare and historic surfboards from the collection of Hobie Alter—local inventor of the foam-core surfboard and the Hobie Cat catamaran—are on display.

For more complete information about the area, including accommodation and restaurant suggestions, contact: **Dana Point Chamber of Commerce,** 24681 La Plaza, Ste. 120, Dana Point, 949/496-1555, www.danapoint-chamber.com.

Seeing and Doing Dana Point

A city only since 1989, Dana Point today combines boat harbor, beaches, and Boston saltbox condominium developments. This stylistic twist testifies to popular identification with Richard Henry Dana's East Coast origins yet is odd, given the area's more enduring Spanish and Mexican roots. To sample original local architectural styles, explore older streets, including Chula Vista, Ruby Lantern, Blue Lantern, El Camino Capistrano, and Santa Clara.

The cultural focal point for Dana Point is **Dana Point Harbor,** 949/496-6177, where breakwater construction began in 1966. Here, about 2,500 yachts bob and sway with the tides. The harbor also features a man-made island park—reached via Island Way—an inner breakwater created during the harbor's unusual cofferdam construction.

Though home port is now in Long Beach, Dana Point Harbor is a regular port for the Nautical Heritage Society's speedy topsail schooner *Californian,* the state's official tall ship, a re-creation of the first U.S. cutter to patrol the Pacific Coast during the bad and bawdy gold rush, the 1848 *C. W. Lawrence.* Public sails are offered from time to time; for more information, contact the **Nautical Heritage Society,** 1064 Calle Negocio, Unit B, San Clemente, CA 92673, 949/369-6773 or toll-free 800/432-2201, www.californian.org. Also here is the **Orange County Marine Institute,** 949/496-2274, noted for its educational and other programs, including nighttime "bioluminescence cruises."

Other harbor diversions include kayaking, canoeing, parasailing, fishing, sportfishing, whale-watching (in winter), and tidepooling. **Dana Wharf Sportfishing** on the harbor's eastern edge, 949/496-5794, handles sportfishing trips, whale-watching and other scenic excursions, and parasailing.

But don't miss Dana Point's **Doheny State Beach** just east of the harbor, donated to the state in the 1930s by L.A. oil man Edward Lawrence Doheny in honor of his son, Ned. The local surf made a bigger cultural splash, though, especially when Doheny made it into the lyrics of the Beach Boys' classic "Surfin' USA." Attractions beyond the broad white-sand beach include the annual grunion run (see the special topic Grunion Run Free, So Why Can't We? earlier in this chapter); the **marine life museum;** the **San Juan Creek Bike Trail** to San Juan Capistrano, which starts just north of the beach; and developed campsites and picnic areas. The entrance to Doheny State Beach is just off PCH at 25300 Dana Point Harbor Dr.; follow the signs. Day use is $3. For more information, call 949/496-6171. To reserve campsites through ReserveAmerica, call 800/444-7275. Also worth a wander is **Salt Creek Beach and Park** north of Dana Point proper, long noted for its good surfing and almost an adjunct to the Ritz-Carlton Laguna Niguel resort. On windy days you'll see hang gliders surf the thermals. And on a clear day you'll see Catalina Island.

San Juan Capistrano

A schmaltzy song started it all. The 1939 Leon Rene tune "When the Swallows Come Back to Capistrano" is responsible for the excited flutter here every year on March 19, St. Joseph's Day, when tourists flock to town to welcome the return of the cliff swallows from their annual Argentina migration. Identifiable by their squared-off cleft tails and propensity for nesting under overhangs and in other protected high-altitude spots, the swallows' first official return was in 1776—the year the United States became a nation and the year Father Junípero Serra established the mission. Serra recorded the event in his diary. Nowadays, though, on March 19 tourists typically far outnumber the swallows, which never did respect that particular day much anyway. (According to ornithologists, the swallows return in the spring, March 19 being close enough to the spring equinox, with "scouts" spotted quite early in March.) Modern life has created confusion for the mission's mythic swallows. Too many people and too much hubbub scare them off. As a result visitors are as likely to see cliff swallows nesting in the high arches of area

interior of Mission San Juan Capistrano

department stores as at the mission.

All that aside, San Juan Capistrano does what it can to help the swallows do their historical duty—by setting out a buffet of ladybugs and green lacewing larvae in the rose garden in March. It also plans most of its **Fiesta de las Golondrinas,** with parade, fun runs, and people dressed up in swallow costumes, for the week framing March 19. Putting local politicians and other volunteers to good use, the festivities culminate later in the month with a "mud-slinging" contest—with the mud and straw slapped onto old adobes to help preserve them.

Its crumbling church walls steadied by scaffolding and surrounded by very contemporary New World ambience, **Mission San Juan Capistrano** is not the most vigorous survivor of California's 21-mission chain. Yet it's impressive nonetheless. The **quadrangle,** with its storerooms and workshops for making clothing, candles, soap, and pottery, was the center of mission life. Today, exhibits, a 12-minute film, and museum displays (including the piano on which the famous swallow song was composed) tell the basic story. Most evocative, though—if you can imagine the scaffolding *desapareci-do*—are the ruins of the **Great Stone Church,** built in 1797 and destroyed by an earthquake in 1812. To get an exact idea of what the old church looked like, sans the patina of time, visit the Spanish Renaissance **New Church of Mission San Juan Capistrano** on Camino Capistrano, with its stunning interior murals and artwork. Next door—draped in spectacular color when the bougainvillea is in bloom, and still in use after all these years—is the mission's original **Serra Chapel,** the only one remaining in California in which Father Serra said mass. Capistrano's chapel, constructed in 1777, is also the oldest building standing in the Golden State. Mission San Juan Capistrano is on Camino Capistrano at Ortega Hwy. (Hwy. 74) and accessible either from PCH or I-5. Admission is $6 adults, $4 for seniors and children ages 3–12 (under 3 free). It's open daily 8:30 A.M.–5 P.M. Free guided tours are offered on Sun. at 1 P.M. Call 949/248-2048 for current information.

Not everything in the area is ancient. One of Orange County's hippest clubs is here—**The Coach House,** tucked into a warehouse at 33157 Camino Capistrano, 949/496-8930, known for good—sometimes great—live music acts. For the best seats, make dinner reservations. For more information on the area, contact: **San Juan Capistrano Chamber of Commerce,** 31781 Camino Capistrano, Ste. 306, San Juan Capistrano, 949/493-4700, www.sanjuanchamber.com.

San Clemente

This isn't much of a tourist town. The people of San Clemente prefer it that way—and you'll be glad, too, if peace and quiet have eluded you elsewhere. The well-guarded solitude of this red-tile-roofed Republican town was its primary appeal for ex-President Richard M. Nixon and his wife, Pat, who retreated here to La Casa Pacifica, the **Western White House,** overlooking the beach. The best view of Nixon's former estate, a palm-shrouded 25-acre compound, is from **San Clemente State Beach.** Otherwise, the most exciting scene around is at the **San Clemente Pier** adjoining the city beach, reached via Avenida Del Mar, where crewcut Marines from nearby Camp Pendleton cavort alongside civilians. For more information about the area, contact: **San Clemente Chamber of Commerce,** 1100 N. El Camino Real, 949/492-1131, www.scchamber.com.

INLAND ORANGE

DISNEYLAND AND VICINITY

The Happiest Place on Earth

Anyone who has been a child or had a child since Walt Disney first opened his Magic Kingdom in 1955 already knows most everything of import about Disneyland.

In Disneyland, stories have happy endings. And every performer on the 76-acre Disney stage—from Mickey Mouse and Donald Duck to the latest batch of lovable audio-animatronic creations—smiles, waves, and then smiles some more, as a matter of company policy. They don't call this "The Happiest Place On Earth" for nothing. In Disneyland, if the hero doesn't do it singlehandedly, then whiz-bang technological wizardry will save the day. In Disneyland, democracy equals capitalism. And capitalism automatically creates social justice.

In other words, Disneyland isn't real, though suburban America desperately wants to believe it is.

Real or not, Disneyland is as good as it gets, if what you're looking for is a clean, well-lighted, life-sized fantasy theater showcasing Mom, Pop, apple pie, and the American flag. It's also one of the few public places in socially subdivided Southern California where families play in public. For the middle class in particular, commercial enterprises such as Disneyland, Universal Studios, and regional malls have all but taken the places of downtown plazas and neighborhood parks.

Doing Disneyland

To make a conscious journey through this cartoon version of America's collective unconscious, consider Disneyland as an oversized map of psychic symbols. This territory is divided into eight distinct "lands," each with one overall theme but multiple attractions.

Though the Walt Disney Company cancelled plans to expand Disneyland into an international mega-resort—with a "Westcot" theme park, 4,600 new hotel rooms, new amphitheater, and two humongous parking structures—that goal may be achieved in increments. **Disney's California Adventure,** a separate 55-acre theme park adjacent to Disneyland, opened in February 2001. *This* California showcases Hollywood and the entertainment industry, the California beach scene, and outdoor California, along with a new hotel and other commercial features. It would be fair to count this as one large new land—Californialand. Disneyland is already planning yet another expansion here—a water park and amusement park incorporating the best rides now up and running at Disney ventures in Florida, Paris, and Tokyo—for a 78-acre site south of Katella Avenue. Elements of that "land" may open to the public as soon as 2003.

But of the lands in Disneyland proper, once "shoppe"ed out on **Main Street, U.S.A.,** from the Central Plaza wander straight ahead—through Sleeping Beauty's castle—into **Fantasyland** and then to **Mickey's Toontown,** both of these latter destinations mandatory for younger youngsters. To start exploring elsewhere, turn left to **Adventureland**—where the **Indiana Jones Adventure** still draws rave reviews and crowds—and **Frontierland/Rivers of America, Critter Country,** and **New Orleans Square.**

Turn right and you'll land in **Tomorrowland,** earning quite the visitor buzz these days. Walt Disney's original 1950s futurism had seemed terribly tired lately, considering the brave new worlds that have come along since, so Tomorrowland has had a conceptual and technical facelift. Particularly appealing is the new **Astro Orbitor,** inspired by 15th-century artist, futurist, and inventor Leonardo da Vinci. Or test drive the **Rocket Rods,** and visit **Innoventions** for a preview of futuristic technology hosted by that audio-animatronic wizard Mr. Tom Morrow. Still fun is the R2D2-introduced **Star Tours,** a fantastic voyage into virtual reality with stellar special effects and more than a few interstellar surprises.

Practical Disneyland

Though hours are subject to change, in summer the park is open 9 A.M.–midnight Sun. through Fri., until 1 A.M. on Sat. night. Otherwise, Disneyland is typically open 10 A.M.–6 P.M. on weekdays and 9 A.M.–midnight on weekends.

Bring plenty of money—what you'd like to spend and then some. At last report a one-day Disneyland "unlimited passport," covering park admission plus all attractions and rides, was $43 for adults (age 10 and over), with 10-year-olds defined as adults since May 2000, $41 for seniors, and $33 for children ages 3–9. (Children under age 3 get in free.) Three- and five-day, non-transferable "flex passports" are also available, but must be purchased in advance (try the website). Disneyland prices typically increase at least slightly every year. Guided tours, annual passes, and special packages are available.

But the price of admission is only the beginning. There's parking, too, and Disneyland doesn't allow you to pack in food or beverages, so expect to spend at least $25 per person for two meals and snacks. (The food tab can go much higher.) And the total cost of Mickey Mouse ears, miscellaneous T-shirts, and other Disneyland memorabilia may floor otherwise frugal fun lovers.

And while devil-may-care types arrive in Disneyland on a whim, most people (certainly most people with small children) *plan,* and plan carefully. Considering the investment of time, money, and emotional energy a trip to Disneyland requires—and since it matters what you'll see and do, and whether you'll enjoy it—it pays to make appropriate plans, including hotel or motel reservations, well in advance. A two- or three-day stay will allow you to see and do just about everything, much less stressfully than a whiz-bang one-day whirlwind tour.

But if your family can't afford the extra time or expense, do Disneyland in a day by accepting in advance that you won't accomplish everything—then set priorities. Making a whirlwind tour of Disneyland much more feasible is the free **Fastpass system,** available for at least some attractions, which allows visitors to reserve a particular "window of opportunity" for that attraction—cutting the otherwise interminable wait down to just a few minutes, thereby freeing people to do something else (other than stand in line) in the interim.

For more information, contact **Disneyland,** 1313 Harbor Blvd., P.O. Box 3232, Anaheim, CA 92803-3232, 714/781-4565, fax 714/781-1341, www.disneyland.com.

Near Disneyland

Just minutes from Disneyland in Buena Park is **Knott's Berry Farm,** the nation's first theme park. Originally famous for Cordelia Knott's fried chicken dinners and for its fresh berries—in particular Orange County's own boysenberries, a delectable cross between blackberries, raspberries, and loganberries that Walter Knott helped develop during the Depression—Knott's Berry Farm evolved into a family-run, family-friendly monument to America's pioneering spirit. It was only in 1968 that the family decided to fence the park and charge admission. Nowadays about five million people drop by each year to share the original Knott family dream. From attractions like **Ghost Town**—

Knott's Berry Farm

TOM MYERS PHOTOGRAPHY

Crystal Cathedral

ROBERT HOLMES/CALTOUR

Walter Knott's first and original outpost of wholesome, old-fashioned Old West fun—and other themed areas to radical rides like **HammerHead** and the **Supreme Scream,** Knott's offers family fun for all ages. A major Southern California attraction, come October, is Knott's **Halloween Haunt,** the best adult Halloween party *anywhere,* and **Knott's Scary Farm** for the kids. Very popular, so get your tickets early.

At last report park admission was $40 adults and $30 children (ages 3–11), seniors (age 60 and up), non-ambulatory, and expectant mothers. Or come after 4 P.M. on any day Knott's is open past 6 P.M. (in summer and on weekends) for just $16.95 (all ages). Annual passes are also available, along with substantial discounts for Southern California residents. Knott's is open every day but Christmas—in summer 9 A.M.–midnight (until 1 A.M. Sat. night) and in winter 10 A.M.–6 P.M. Mon.–Fri., 10 A.M.–10 P.M. on Sat., and 10 A.M.–7 P.M. Sun., though holiday hours may differ. The entire park may close during bad weather; if in doubt, call ahead. For more information, contact: Knott's Berry Farm, 8039 Beach Blvd., Buena Park, CA 90620, 714/220-5200 (taped information) or 714/220-5220 for special guest services, www.knotts.com.

Family-style amusement is a major industry in Buena Park, with various diversions strung out like Christmas lights along Beach Boulevard. One of the best is **Medieval Times,** an ersatz trip into the days of sword fights and knights in armor jousting on horseback. Show times at Medieval Times, 7662 Beach Blvd., 714/523-1100 or toll-free 800/899-6600, www.medievaltimes.com, vary depending on the day, so call for details. Reservations and an early arrival are advisable, too, since tour groups can pack the place. Another possibility is **Wild Bill's Wild West Dinner Extravaganza,** practically next door at 7600 Beach Blvd., 714/522-4611 or, for reservations, toll-free 800/883-1546, which offers the same family-oriented dinner-and-entertainment concept but with a country-western twang.

For current information on other nearby attractions and local practicalities, contact: **Buena Park Convention & Visitors Office,** 7711 Beach Blvd., Ste. 100, Buena Park, CA 90620, 714/562-3560, fax 714/562-3569, www.buena-park.com.

RICHARD NIXON LIBRARY

The Comeback Kid Comes Home

After his death in 1994, ex-President Richard Milhous Nixon finally came home—to the **Richard Nixon Library and Birthplace** in Yorba Linda. More than 40,000 people showed up to say goodbye to Orange County's most famous homeboy, including all five living U.S. presidents, heads of state, Watergate warrior G. Gordon Liddy, and immigrant Vietnamese shopkeepers from the Asia Garden Mall in nearby Westminster.

Some folks raised a ruckus when Richard Nixon was honored with a postage stamp.

For Nixon loyalists his funeral was a time of genuine grief. For his equally constant foes the day was also quite sad—because for all Nixon's brilliance in the political arena in the end he seemed a tragic figure.

The only American president ever forced by impending impeachment to resign from office, Richard M. Nixon personified the dark side of American politics yet never seemed to understand or accept any real responsibility for his fall. Those who knew him best, who were most familiar with the depths of that Nixonian darkness, have tried to understand. Some speculate that too much success, too soon, created a political persona ill prepared to handle defeat, let alone opposition. According to former Secretary of State Henry Kissinger, Richard Nixon was "a strange mixture of calculation, deviousness, idealism, tenderness, tawdriness, courage, and daring" and a man who wanted to be remembered for his idealism. Less widely quoted is another observation from Kissinger: "Think what this man could have done if anyone had ever loved him."

Nixon's World in Nixon's Words: The Nixon Library and Birthplace

Designated a California historical landmark in January 1995, the Richard Nixon Library and Birthplace first opened on July 19, 1990. The pageantry was nothing if not patriotic, with much speechifying, red, white, and blue balloons galore, and tens of thousands of well-wishers.

The $21 million price tag was equally impressive, making this the most expensive monument yet built in honor of presidents past. Unlike other presidential museums, funded at least in part by the government and subject to some degree of federal review, Nixon's is entirely self-supporting—a fact that threatened, early on, to embroil the institution in as much controversy as the ex-president himself. Before the Nixon Library even opened its doors, critics charged that Nixon and his employees would offer only a flattering spin on his life and times.

It's true that the Nixon Library—more accurately, museum—serves primarily to glorify its namesake rather than explain, let alone criticize. (With or without federal funding, the same can be said of all post-presidency memorials, however.) It's also true that the displays here are exceptionally well done, conceptually and technically. Exploring the place for yourself is well worth the side trip into Orange County's suburban hinterlands.

No matter how humbling his end, Richard Milhous Nixon's beginnings were humble indeed. He was born on January 9, 1913, in a tiny farmhouse built from a Sears Roebuck kit by his father, Frank. His mother, Hannah, named him after the English king Richard Plantagenet, "Richard the Lionhearted." (All the Nixon boys were named after English kings.)

Restored to its original simplicity at a cost of $400,000, the Nixon birthplace is definitely worth a stop after the museum tour. (On audio tape, Richard Nixon himself will guide you through.) Most of the modest furnishings are original, including the living room piano, Little Richard's violin, and the bed in which the future president was born, supplemented by a few period pieces and reproductions. The tiny kitchen comes complete with wood cooking stove, Hannah's cookbooks, and sundry everyday implements of domesticity. The attic room upstairs, shared by Richard Nixon and his three brothers, is typically off limits for visitors. But just imagine a barefoot, nine-year-old Richard Nixon scrambling upstairs to practice his accordion.

Practical Nixon Library

The Nixon Library and Birthplace is at the corner of Yorba Linda Blvd. and Eureka Avenue. For information (pre-recorded), including special exhibits and events, call 714/993-3393; on the Internet, try www.nixonfoundation.org. Otherwise, for information write: Richard Nixon Library and Birthplace, 18001 Yorba Linda Blvd., Yorba Linda, CA 92686 (fax 714/528-0544). The museum is open Mon.–Sat. 10 A.M.–5 P.M., Sun. 11 A.M.–5 P.M. Admission is $5.95 adults, $4.95 active military, $3.95 seniors, and $2 children ages 8–11 (under 7 free). Free parking.

If you're coming by car, both Hwy. 57 (the Orange Fwy.) and Hwy. 91 (the Riverside Fwy.) will get you here; both are also accessible from I-5. From Newport Beach and nearby coastal areas, the best option is heading inland via Hwy. 55, which merges into Hwy. 91 (then go east). From Hwy. 91, exit at Hwy. 90 (the Imperial Hwy.) and head north, exiting at Yorba Linda Blvd. and then heading west. From Hwy. 57, exit at Yorba Linda Blvd. and head east.

MADAME MODJESKA *IN AMERICA*

Susan Sontag's recent novel *In America* was inspired by Orange County's own Helena Modjeska, the noted 19th-century actress who renounced her European stage career and emigrated from Poland to the United States to start a utopian farming venture with her husband. In its fictionalized facts, the book parallels Modjeska's story. A star of the Warsaw stage married to the aristocratic Count Bozenta—in revolt against his family and dreaming of his own agricultural Eden—in 1876 Modjeska and her husband arrived in California with an accomplished entourage that included Henryk Sienkiewicz, who later won the Nobel Prize for literature.

In the book, as in real life, they all settled down in what was then the Wild West of Orange County— European overlords determined to wring both civilization and crops out of the wily Mexican-American wilderness.

And in the book, as in the course of actual events, none of the privileged Poles knew beans about farming. As Modjeska would later recall in her autobiography: "The most alarming feature of this bucolic fancy was the rapid disappearance of cash and the absence of even a shadow of income."

So Helena Modjeska resumed her career—and soon became one of the most accomplished actresses on the American stage during the golden age of theater.

"It felt like, an escapade; like leaving home; like telling lies—and she would tell many lies," reflects Sontag's protagonist as she arrives in San Francisco. "She was beginning again; she was rejoining her destiny, which conferred on her the rich sensation that she had never gone astray."

As Modjeska's star ascended in America, she crisscrossed the country in her own private railroad car and eventually played opposite Edwin Booth and Maurice Barrymore, the greatest actors of the day. She became Camille, and Ophelia. She was Nora in the premiere of Ibsen's *A Doll's House.* Yet her most famous role was Rosalind in Shakespeare's *As You Like It.*

Equally adept at besting the twists and turns of fate, in the 1880s the now wealthy Madame Modjeska and Count Bozenta returned to Orange County to build a more theatrical version of their earlier dream. The grand rambling home they built here, complete with a small stage extending out into the garden, was called Arden, as Modjeska later wrote, "because, like the Forest of Arden in *As You Like it,* everything that Shakespeare speaks of was on the spot—oak trees, running brooks, palms, snakes, even lions." She and the count lived here for 18 happy years, from 1888 to 1906.

Mountain lions still roam the Santa Ana Mountains, though they are not so common these days. And Modjeska's home still stands in a live oak grove on the banks of Santiago Creek, its original Forest of Arden—English yews, palms, white lilac, and crown of thorns—still thriving. Now a National Historic Landmark known as **Modjeska House Historical Park,** 25151 Serrano Rd. in Modjeska Canyon, about 10 miles east of Lake Forest via Santiago Canyon Rd., the estate is owned by the county of Orange.

The home and gardens are open to the public only for docent-guided tours—the canyon road is narrow, the area residential, and gawkers are discouraged— which at last report were offered by advance reservation only at 10 A.M. on the second and fourth Sat. of the month. Tour fee is $5. For more information and reservations, call 949/855-2028.

TOM MEYERS PHOTOGRAPHY

SAN DIEGO AND VICINITY
NORTHERN SAN DIEGO COUNTY

To discover San Diego County's northern coastline, exit the freeway and amble along the ocean. You can exit at Oceanside and head south to La Jolla for a coastal cruise. The street name changes in each community—becoming Carlsbad Blvd. in Carlsbad, for example, and Camino del Mar in Del Mar—so old Hwy. 101 is also known, prosaically, as County Road S21.

First stop for most people, just after the old highway separates from I-5, is Oceanside, with a nice pier and beach, urban adjunct to the sprawling Camp Pendleton U.S. Marine base. Just inland is Mission San Luis Rey, "King of the Missions." Farther north along the coast, just south of the county line, is San Onofre State Beach (san ON-uh-fray), technically in San Diego County but geopolitically more connected to San Clemente and other Orange County locales. An unavoidable feature of remote San Onofre is its mid-beach nuclear power plant, though the area also offers good spots for swimming and surfing.

South of Oceanside is Carlsbad, named after Karlsbad, Bohemia, for the similar mineral content in the local spring water, most famous these days as the home of Legoland. Next stop is Encinitas—including, technically, the communities of Leucadia, Cardiff-by-the-Sea, and Olivenhain. Encinitas is historically famous for its flower fields—poinsettias in particular, the downtown Self-Realization Fellowship, the Quail Botanical Gardens, San Elijo State Beach (and the area's various locals' beaches), and Leucadia's galleries and shops.

For a full measure of the simpler pleasures, stop in sunny Solana Beach, just north of Del Mar. Known for its celebrities and chic shopping, Del Mar is also home to the Del Mar Thoroughbred Club summer horse races—and the beach here is dandy. Torrey Pines Rd. leads south from Del Mar to La Jolla. Along the way are the Torrey Pines reserve, beach, and coastal lagoon, technically still part of the city of San Diego.

A thorough exploration of northern San Diego County also includes excursions inland to

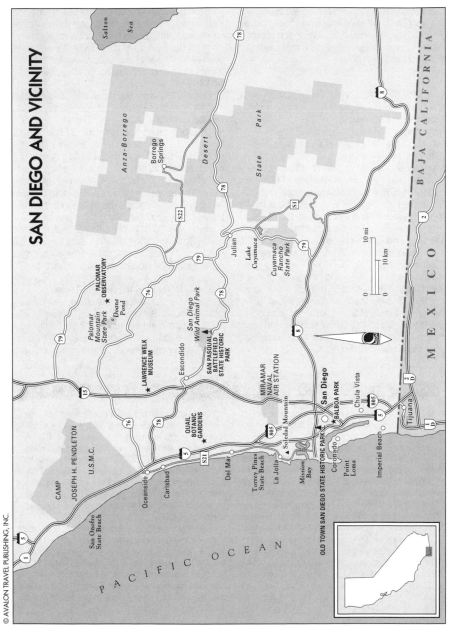

SAN DIEGO AND VICINITY

Escondido and vicinity, best known as home to the San Diego Wild Animal Park; the apple-pie American frontier town of Julian; and fabulous Anza-Borrego Desert State Park, most inviting in early spring.

SOUTH ALONG THE COAST

Oceanside and Vicinity
Immediately north of Carlsbad and almost a suburb of Camp Pendleton is Oceanside, with its own pier, a nice beach with largely crew-cut clientele, and an active, attractive harbor area. A local attraction is the **California Surf Museum,** 760/721-6876, www.surfmuseum.org, an eclectic, almost offhand display of surfboards with themed exhibits and zany gift shop. For more information about the area, call the **Oceanside Visitors and Conference Center** at 760/721-1101, or look them up online at www.oceanside chamber.com.

North of Oceanside and Camp Pendleton is **San Onofre State Beach.** The odd detail here is the **San Onofre Nuclear Power Plant,** about five miles south of San Clemente, serving as the Mason-Dixon line between north and south beaches though the two are connected by a public walkway along the seawall. The north is

known for excellent surfing, the south for good swimming and bodysurfing and its very nice "primitive" campground (for both tents and RVs, no hook-ups). It's open daily 6 A.M.–sunset. Day-use fee is $3 per vehicle, camping is extra. For more information about the beaches here, call 949/492-4872.

Historic **Mission San Luis Rey de Francia,** the "King of the Missions" at 4050 Mission Ave. in San Luis Rey, 760/757-3651, was founded in 1798 but not completed until 1815; in 1893 it became a Franciscan seminary. Wander the grounds of San Luis Rey, the state's largest but one of its less-visited missions, for an appreciation of early California culture—and the enduring wonder of adobe construction. Museum exhibits and displays reveal the rough reality of mission life. Mission San Luis Rey is four miles east of I-5 via Hwy. 76 (Mission Ave.) and is open Mon.–Sat. 10 A.M.–4:30 P.M., Sun. noon–4:30 P.M. for self-guided tours, closed major holidays. Admission is $4 adults, $1 children ages 8–14.

Carlsbad: Bracing for the Big Time
According to local lore, Carlsbad was named after Karlsbad, Bohemia, since its "waters" had a composition identical to the mineral waters of the Ninth Spa in what is now the Czech Republic. Little wonder, then, that the spa trade was

LEGOLAND CARLSBAD: A BIG-TIME SMALL WORLD

With over 40 rides, shows, and attractions on 128 acres of appealing parkland, Legoland Carlsbad offers a full and exciting day out for children and their families just 30 miles north of San Diego in Carlsbad.

Opened in 1999, Legoland Carlsbad is the world's second Lego-themed theme park, inspired by the original in Denmark. Like the first Legoland, this one is as expansive in scope as it is small in scale. For starters, there are fantastically detailed Lego models to admire, including 1:20 scale Lego brick reproductions of famous cities like San Francisco, Paris, and New York, each complete with moving vehicles and small-scale people scurrying about the streets. Also quite striking, and fun as educational tools, are replicas of favorite international landmarks; the Sydney Opera House, San Francisco's Alamo Square, New York's Empire State Building, and Mount Rushmore were built using over 30 million Lego bricks.

What sets Legoland apart from other California theme parks is its absence of white-knuckle rides. Rides and attractions here—including a driving school with cars, a gravity coaster, a mini excursion tour, and a DUPLO building area—appeal instead to the two-to-twelve-year-old crowd. Even the food differs from regular theme park fare, with a European twist. Expect fresh fruit, applesauce, salads, and breadsticks along with homemade pizzas, popcorn, and chicken sticks.

Legoland, 1 Lego Dr. (at Cannon Rd.), 760/918-5346, www.legolandca.com, is open daily 10 A.M. to dusk, which translates into 10 A.M.–5 P.M. in winter, 9 A.M.–9 P.M. in summer. Admission is $34 adults, $29 children (ages 3–16). Ask at the gate for special discounts for seniors (over 60). Parking, available in the adjacent lot, is $6. To get here from I-5, take the Cannon exit east.

by Pat Reilly

also hot here, beginning in the 1880s. You can see remnants and mementos of that era at the picturesque stone **Alt Karlsbad Haus,** now a gift shop and museum on Carlsbad Blvd. (closed at last report). Adjacent are the original wells, capped after World War II.

Present-day Carlsbad is best known as an affluent, family-friendly beach town-cum-San Diego bedroom community, populated by surfers, eccentrics, entrepreneurs, and high-technology firms. But this genuinely laid-back coastal escape exploded with hustle, bustle, and new business when the 128-acre **Legoland** children's theme park and affiliated resort opened here in 1999. Even now Carlsbad wows the crowds—every spring in particular, when tourists plow through surrounding **Carlsbad Ranch flower fields,** 760/431-0352, best for the ranunculus bloom, early Mar. through late Apr., and jam into California's largest street fair, the **Carlsbad Village Faire.**

Visitors attracted to homegrown pleasures can sunbathe and swim at the beach, stroll along the seawall (Carlsbad's beach promenade), explore local lagoons, and loll around in coffeehouses and the casual, sometimes eclectic restaurants and shops collected along Carlsbad Boulevard.

Lined with **antique shops** selling heavy silver jewelry, country quilts and estate furniture, the three blocks of State St. between Oak and Beech is an oasis of retro charm. Stroll over to **Aanteek Aavenue Mall,** 2832 State St., 760/434-8742, for an excellent variety of wares under one roof, including vintage china, glass, and jewelry. Find vintage wares at **Black Roads Antiques,** 2988 State St., 760/729-3032.

Wind-driven winter waves tend to batter Carlsbad-area beaches, so Carlsbad State Beach and others are typically closed in winter and spring. They're also typically rockier than the southstate stereotype. Of the two local state beaches, **Carlsbad State Beach** is usually the best bet for sandy sunbathing. Farther south on Carlsbad Blvd. (at Poinsettia Ln.) is **South Carlsbad State Beach,** popular for ocean swimming as well as its large bluff-top campground (reservations mandatory). Then there are Carlsbad's lagoons. South of Poinsettia along the shore is the quarter-mile interpretive walkway for **Batiquitos Lagoon,** now being revivified and reconnected with the ocean. For more information, call the Batiquitos Foundation at 760/943-7583. North of downtown is the **Buena Vista Lagoon,** with an Audubon Society nature center. Call the Audubon Society at 760/439-2473 or look up the Buena Vista chapter on www.audubon.org for information about scheduled birding and other events.

For more information about the community, contact the **Carlsbad Convention and Visitors Bureau** housed in the old Santa Fe Depot on Carlsbad Village Dr., 760/434-6093 or toll-free 800/227-5722. It's open Mon.–Fri. 9 A.M.–5 P.M., Sat. and Sun. 10 A.M.–2 P.M.

Quail Botanical Gardens

Known as "Flower Capital of the World," Encinitas is losing some floral ground to encroaching suburbia. Quail Botanical Gardens, a local horticultural star, is still going strong, however. Here you can wander 30 acres of canyon appreciating thousands of species: tropical and subtropical immigrants from Central and South America, Australia, Africa, and the Himalayas, as well as drought-resistant native plants.

Quail Botanical Gardens is closed the first Mon. of every month, otherwise open daily 9 A.M.–5 P.M. (closed Thanksgiving, Christmas, and New Year's Day). It offers general tours (free) every Sat. at 10 A.M. and free children's tours on the first Tues. of every month. (Group tours are offered only by appointment.) Admission is free on the first Tues. of every month, otherwise it's $5 adults, $4 seniors, $2 children ages 5–12 (under 5 free). For plant and gift shop purchases, come between 10 A.M. and 4 P.M. daily. Quail Botanical Gardens, 230 Quail Gardens Dr., Encinitas, 760/436-3036, www.qbgardens.com, is approximately 20 miles north of San Diego between Leucadia and Encinitas Boulevards. To get here from I-5, exit at Encinitas Blvd. and head east. Turn left (north) onto Quail Gardens Drive. The gardens are on the left.

Solana Beach

Solana means "sunny spot" in Español, and Solana Beach is still fun and funky in laid-back beach town style yet starting to try on civic phrases such as "chic" and "stylish." To sample the eclectic commercial side of this confusion, stroll the business district, more or less concentrated between Lomas Santa Fe Dr. to the north and Via de la Valle to the south, Old Hwy. 101 to the west, and Cedros Ave. to the east. Still, the beach in Solana Beach is the big thing, though finding a way down to it is something of a challenge. (Hint: Look for the "pillbox.")

STAYING ALONG THE COAST

Budget travelers, head to **Motel 6.** There's one in south Carlsbad at 750 Raintree Dr., toll-free 800/466-8356 or 760/431-0745, fax 760/431-9207. No surprises, and the price is right, $40 single, $46 double. Inexpensive. That price gets you basic rooms with color TV and cable, plus swimming pool and proximity to the beach. (If there's no room, there are two other Motel 6 choices in Carlsbad, and another two in adjacent Oceanside.) To get here from I-5: exit west at Poinsettia Ln., turn north on Avenida Encinas, then east (right) onto Raintree.

A decent choice in Oceanside is the **Days Inn,** 3170 Vista Way, toll-free 800/458-6064 or 760/757-2200, fax 760/757-2389. Rooms are nothing fancy but quite pleasant, with color TV, cable, and free movies. Special diversions include a children's playground, whirlpool, and exercise room plus (for a fee) access to the adjacent 18-hole golf course and lighted tennis courts. The motel is just a few miles from the Carlsbad beach. Moderate. Rates are $69–79, with weekly and monthly rates available.

In Carlsbad, a best bet for families is the very attractive, very popular **Best Western Beach View Lodge,** 3180 Carlsbad Blvd., toll-free 800/535-5588 or 760/729-1151, fax 760/434-5405, where

---

ACCOMMODATIONS RATINGS

Accommodations in this book are rated by price category, based on double-occupancy, high-season rates. Categories used are:

Budget.	$35 and under
Inexpensive	$35-60
Moderate	$60-85
Expensive	$85-110
Premium	$110-150
Luxury	$150 and up

---

all rooms have refrigerators, some have kitchens or kitchenettes. Expensive-Premium. There's also a heated pool, whirlpool, and sauna, with rates from $80–120. (Monthly rates available in the off-season.) Pricier but right on the beach is the **Best Western Beach Terrace Inn,** on the beach at 2775 Ocean St., toll-free 800/433-5415 or 760/729-5951, fax 760/729-1078. Most rooms have kitchens, many have ocean views. Premium-Luxury. Rates $119–189. Also popular and pricier still is the **Carlsbad Inn Beach Resort,** 3075 Carlsbad Blvd., toll-free 800/235-3939 or 760/434-7020, where the Old World meets the New World under the palm trees. Luxury. Rates $169–239. For the ultimate Carlsbad stay, head for **La Costa Resort and Spa** (see below).

Right next to I-5 but otherwise perfect for a more uptown stay is the **Country Inn,** 1661 Villa Cardiff Dr., Cardiff-by-the-Sea, toll-free 800/322-9993 or 760/944-0427, fax 760/944-7708, a stylish Old World–style motel with a pool, whirlpool, and bed-and-breakfast amenities—full breakfast and morning newspaper, fresh fruit, and afternoon refreshments. Moderate-Premium. A great deal, with rates $82–125.

The **Ocean Inn** in Encinitas at 1444 N. Hwy. 101 (between La Costa Ave. and Leucadia Blvd.), toll-free 800/546-1598 or 760/436-1988, fax 760/436-3921, is a best bet for a base camp, since from here it's just a five-minute walk to the beach. Rooms come with all the motel basics plus in-room refrigerators and microwaves—bring your own cookware and utensils—and color TV, cable, and video players; some feature in-room whirlpool tubs. Other pluses: on-site laundry and rental bikes. Moderate-Expensive. Rates start at $69 single, $79 double. Closest to the beach, though, is the relaxed **Moonlight Beach Hotel,** 233 2nd St., toll-free 800/323-1259 or 760/753-0623, with large rooms and kitchenettes. Moderate. Rates $56–76.

La Costa Resort and Spa

One of California's premier resort retreats, this one is luxurious but relaxed and low-key. Almost a self-contained city, this 400-acre spread comes complete with its own movie theater. Carlsbad's La Costa features world-class spa and fitness facilities, swimming pools, tennis courts, racquetball courts, and two PGA championship 18-hole golf courses. (Inquire about special golf and tennis packages.) To keep it simple, rent bikes here and cruise on down to the beach. Luxury. Rates $175–2,300. For more information call toll-free 800/854-5000 or 760/438-9111, fax 760/438-3758, or check out www.lacosta.com. To get here, drive two miles east of I-5 via La Costa Ave., and then continue north for a quarter-mile on El Camino Real.

EATING ALONG THE COAST

As might be expected, Carlsbad is rich with restaurants. Some okay choices: for southwestern, the **Coyote Bar & Grill** in the Village Faire Shopping Center at 300 Carlsbad Village Dr., 760/729-4695; for Mexican, **Fidel's Norte** near the beach scene at 3003 Carlsbad Blvd., 760/729-0903; for American, the **Pea Soup Andersen's** outpost at the Best Western Andersen's Inn, 850 Palomar Airport Rd., 760/438-7880.

For more bohemian atmosphere you can do better, though, at places such as **Kafana Coffee** at the beach, 3076 Carlsbad Blvd., 760/720-0074, which showcases live music every night in summer and on weekend nights in winter, and the **Pizza Port**, a pizza parlor-cum-surfer hangout at 571 Carlsbad Village Dr., 760/720-7007. For fine dining, the place is casual **Neimans** inside the grand Queen Anne mansion once owned by local "waters" promoter Gerhard Schutte, along the waterfront at 300 Carlsbad Village Dr., 760/729-4131. People come from miles around just for the Sunday brunch.

Rico's Taco Shop in the Target shopping center at 165-L S. El Camino Real in Encinitas, 760/944-7689, is a safe place to bring the kids even after a sand-in-their-shoes day at the beach—quick, casual, and quite good, if what you're looking for is health-conscious Mexican food. At lunch and dinner, the fish tacos and burritos, carne asada selections, and taquitos are hard to beat. Rico's is open daily 8 A.M.–9 P.M., closed holidays. For fancier fare, wander the **First Street** area in downtown Encinitas to see what's new and appetizing.

Ki's Juice Bar and Restaurant, 2591 S. Hwy. 101 (near Chesterfield) in Cardiff-by-the-Sea, 760/436-5236, is not strictly vegetarian—but if that's what you're looking for, this is where you'll find it. Everything here is fresh and healthy,

including organic seven grain cereal and tofu scramble at breakfast and veggie stir-fry, egg salad sandwiches, and Ki's salmon salad at lunch. Expect more of the same at dinner, plus pasta. Juice bar choices include fruit and ice cream smoothies—a chance to try a decent date shake—and fresh juices and blends, including orange and grapefruit, carrot and watermelon. Ki's serves food for the soul, too—live jazz on Fri. and Sat. nights (no cover with dinner). It's open Sun.–Thurs. 8 A.M.–9:30 P.M., Fri.–Sat. 8 A.M.–9 P.M., closed holidays. For a totally different take—steak and seafood and such—try the predictably good **Chart House**, nearby at 2588 S. Hwy. 101, 760/436-4044, and **The Beach House,** 2530 S. Hwy. 101, 760/753-1321.

The fare at **Solana Beach Brewery and Pizza Port,** 135 N. Hwy. 101 (at Lomas Santa Fe), 760/736-0370, includes good pizza and salads—simple, straightforward flavors intended to complement the local brew. Offerings here include Beacon's Bitter, 101 Nut Brown, Rivermouth Raspberry, and Sharkbite Red Ale. If you can't decide, ask for the "taster"—four four-ounce glasses, a sample of each. While you're sampling, the kids can visit the arcade area. The place is open daily 11 A.M.–midnight, closed major holidays. Another possibility: wood-fired pizzas from the **California Pizza Kitchen** in the Boardwalk mall, 437 S. Hwy. 1, 858/739-0999. The pizzas are out of the ordinary—popular choices include the BBQ Chicken Pizza with Gouda cheese, onions and barbecue sauce, the Thai Chicken Pizza with spicy peanut-ginger and sesame sauce, and the Vegetarian Pizza with Japanese Eggplant. Open Mon.–Sat. 11:30 A.M.–10 P.M., Sun. 11:30 A.M.–9 P.M. CPK also has outposts in La Jolla, 858/675-4424, and Carmel Mountain Ranch, 858/457-4222.

Two-story **Fidel's,** 607 Valley Ave. (near Stevens) in Solana Beach, 858/755-5292, is the place for Mexican food—and lots of it. A combination plate, with rice, beans, and entrées of your choice, should satisfy even the most boisterous beach appetite (children's plates available). If at all possible, grab a table out on the patio. There's another Fidel's on Carlsbad Blvd. in Carlsbad, 760/729-0903. Fidel's is open daily 11 A.M.–9:30 P.M., sometimes later on weekends, and closed Christmas. Reservations taken only for groups of eight or more.

INLAND FROM THE COAST: ESCONDIDO AND VICINITY

Escondido: Wine and Wild Animals

Escondido, which means "hidden" in Spanish, is far from invisible these days. Center of the vast inland territory north of San Diego and its suburbs, Escondido is home to the remarkable San Diego Wild Animal Park—where visitors "visit" Africa and Asia, and exotic animal and plantlife in open-air "natural" habitats, via monorail. Adjacent to this world tour of natural history is a monument to the hurried march of local history—the San Pasqual Battlefield State Historic Park. Here in 1846 a small band of "Californios," or California-born Mexican citizens, vanquished legendary scout Kit Carson and U.S. Army troops in one of the more infamous battles of the Mexican-American War. In more recent history Escondido has added high culture to its list of assets, with the $74 million California Center for the Arts, Escondido.

Radiating from Escondido like the spokes of a roughed-up wagon wheel are roads leading to other attractions—including the Lawrence Welk Resort, with its own theater for Broadway-style musical productions. Local vineyards and wineries are also a major draw, most particularly Deer Park Vintage Cars and Wines, famous also for its fabulous array of 1950s kitsch.

From Escondido, intrepid travelers can set out on multiple "loop" day trips—to Palomar Mountain State Park and the Palomar Observatory and then on to Julian, for example, or to Julian via Hwy. 78, and then on into Anza-Borrego or Rancho Cuyamaca State Parks before looping back. For more information on both, see below.

For more information on the region, contact: **San Diego North County Convention and Visitors Bureau,** 720 N. Broadway, Escondido 92025, toll-free 800/848-3336 or 760/745-4741, fax 760/745-4796 or www.sandiegonorth.com.

San Diego Wild Animal Park

The main modern-day attraction in San Pasqual Valley is the 2,200-acre San Diego Wild Animal Park, affiliated with the San Diego Zoo. Here, the collected endangered species are exhibited in their own wide open spaces, the separate habitats representing Asian plains, Asian marshlands and swamps, North Africa, South Africa, and East Africa. Hikers can hoof it into East Africa on the hilly 1.75-mile **Kilimanjaro Safari Walk,** with observation platforms that allow spying on the lions and elephants below. Cages are still cages, of course, no matter how aesthetic, so what you see here is far from "natural,"

TEMECULA VALLEY WINE COUNTRY

The best reason to visit Temecula Valley (teh-MEH-cyoo-lah), the area's premier wine-grape-growing region, is to personally sample the fruit of the vine—easily an all-day if not weekend-long task. With a climate similar to that of Southern France, the Temecula region specializes in premium varietals. Most wineries are spread out along Rancho California Rd. and are small, many offering wine-tasting and sales daily but limited tours. Come in May for the annual **Spring Passport Tasting,** in June for the ever-popular **Temecula Valley Balloon and Wine Festival.** The hot air (for the balloon rides) flows almost as fast as the fine wines.

First, though, stop off in **Old Town Temecula.** The false-front buildings here, along Front St. between Moreno and 3rd, are remnants of the town's dusty days at the edge of the frontier. Founded in 1882,

Temecula was a significant stop for the old Butterfield Stage and, later, a railroad station on the route connecting San Diego and San Bernardino. Also stop by the new, 7,200-square-foot **Temecula Valley Museum,** 28315 Mercedes St., in Sam Hicks Monument Park, 909/694-6480, open Tues.–Sat. 10 A.M.–5 P.M., Sun. 1–5 P.M. Exhibits chronicle area history, from the native Luise-o people and mission days to modern times. Free, but a $2 donation is requested.

For area information, contact the **Temecula Valley Chamber of Commerce** office, 27450 Ynez Rd., Ste. 124, Temecula, CA 92591, 909/676-5090, fax 909/694-0201, www.temecula.org. For current winery information, contact the **Temecula Valley Winegrowers Association,** P.O. Box 1601, Temecula, CA 92593, 909/699-3626 or toll-free 800/801-9463, fax 909/699-2353, www.temeculawines.org.

CONDOR RIDGE: BORN TO BE WILD

The world can be a dangerous place. And no one, certainly no nonhuman species, can keep all attendant hazards of the civilized world out of their neighborhood. The latest local symbol of this struggle is the California condor, *Gymnogyps californianus*, the powerful and primal vulture known to Native Americans as the thunderbird. The largest land bird in North America, until 10,000 to 12,000 years ago the California condor flew and foraged across the southern reaches of what is now the United States, from the Pacific to the Atlantic Oceans. Pre-Columbian hunters soon dispatched most of the mammoths and other large animals on whose carcasses the condor fed. By the time of early European exploration the species had retrenched along the North American coastline from British Columbia to Baja California; condors were sometimes observed feeding on beached whales. In more recent California history the California condor soared inland from the San Rafael Mountains to Sequoia National Park, protected from harm by the land's inaccessibility. Now most of the species' survivors live in protective custody—in "condorminium" cages at California zoos—because the condor's natural environment can no longer assure the bird's survival. Research suggests the precipitous recent decline of the condor was caused by lead shot and bullets, inadvertently consumed by feeding condors, in addition to the increasing incursions of civilization, in the form of power lines, antifreeze, and other hazards.

In 1987 the last wild California condors were captured and packed off as breeders for the captive breeding program, a last, fairly desperate attempt to save the species from extinction. For the coastal Chumash people—haunted by what they were witnessing—the condor round-up suggested the end of the condor, and the end of the condor signaled the end of the world, the "time of purification" when the earth would shake and all life would end then begin again.

Condor Ridge: Engaging Extinction

But the California condor hasn't yet disappeared. Though the species is still teetering on the edge of extinction, captive breeding and some success in releasing the birds into remote areas of their original range offer hope that the end of the world has been postponed. By mid-2000 85 condors had been released into the wild, and 49 were still thriving there.

To get up-close and personal with the California condor—not something likely to happen in nature—stroll through the San Diego Wild Animal Park's new **Condor Ridge** habitat.

A dozen species of rare and endangered North American animals are exhibited here, beginning with the endangered thick-billed parrots once thriving in the pines of Arizona, New Mexico, and northern Mexico. At the base of the pines here, darting among the shrubs, are western greater roadrunners. Next come the grasslands, where northern porcupines accompany the rare, steel-gray aplomado falcons. The prairies habitat is home to endangered black-footed ferrets, desert tortoises, black-tailed prairie dogs, western burrowing owls, American magpies, and western Harris hawks.

At the end of the trail is an observation deck and interpretive center concerning recovery efforts on behalf of the California condor and desert bighorn sheep, the latter observed here scrambling around on steep hillsides. Several California condors can also be seen, in their six-story cage.

in any meaningful sense. But here people are penned up, too—onboard the **Wgasa Bush Line** monorail, the park's main event. The five-mile monorail ride—sit on the right side if at all possible—traverses the prairies and canyonlands. Especially during summer heat, the best time to hop aboard is early evening, when the park's creatures are up and about and eating. Even better, in summer, are the after-dark treks, when all the park's a stage—lit by sodium-vapor lamps.

The kids will probably insist on extra time at **Nairobi Village,** the center of everything, complete with "petting kraal" (remarkably toddler-tolerant sheep and goats here); the interactive **Mombasa Lagoon** exhibit; the indoor **Hidden Jungle,** with tropical creatures not typically seen; the interactive **Lorikeet Landing,** an Australian rainforest where people can feed the nectar-loving birds all day long; and the long-running **Bird Show Amphitheater,** starring birds of prey and other performers. Exotic gardens here showcase more than 3,000 botanical specimens.

The park's most exotic activity—a must for photographers—is the **photo caravan tour,**

ROBERT HOLMES/CalTour

San Diego Wild Animal Park

which allows shutterbugs to get up close and personal from *inside* the animal compounds, snapping shots from an open-air truck. The tours run daily, and cost between $85–105, depending on the tour. For information and reservations, call 760/738-5049 or toll-free 800/934-2267. Family-friendly **Roar and Snore overnight campouts** are also offered, seasonally.

The San Diego Wild Animal Park is open daily from 9 A.M., with gates closing at 4 P.M. in winter and 6 P.M. in summer (grounds close an hour later). In summer, Thurs. through Sun. evenings are "Swamp Nights," with admission until 8 P.M. and the park itself open until 10 P.M. The park is open for extended hours at other times, too, for special events. At last report admission was $21.95 adults, and $14.95 children ages 3–11 (parking extra). A "combination pass," $38.35 adults, $23.15 children, also covers one day's admission to the San Diego Zoo (to use within five days of purchase). Wheelchairs and strollers are available for rent. To get here: exit I-15 in Escondido at Via Rancho Pkwy. and follow the

signs east; it's about six miles to the park. From I-5, exit at Hwy. 78 and head east to I-15; continue south on I-15, then exit east at Via Rancho Parkway. For current information (prerecorded), call the San Diego Wild Animal Park at 760/747-8702, TTY/TDD 760/738-5067, or check out www.sandiegozoo.org.

San Pasqual Battlefield State Historic Park
Near the San Diego Wild Animal Park is the battlefield park, with multiple historic sights and monuments. Even with the nice visitor center here, the social and territorial skirmishes leading to California statehood don't titillate visitors as much as the animal park. The area's roadside produce stands often do, however. Keeping in mind that more than half of the U.S. avocado crop comes from San Diego County, take in more of the area's agricultural riches by meandering north toward Pauma Valley, Pala, or Fallbrook via back roads.

Escondido-Area Wineries
Just north of the Lawrence Welk Resort is **Deer Park Vintage Cars and Wines,** 29013 Champagne Blvd. (old Hwy. 395), 760/749-1666, www.deerparkwinery.com. Adults will enjoy Deer Park's local chardonnay, plus the selection of award-winning red and white wines from its more famous Napa Valley winery. (Try the cabernet.) Also here are a great deli/gourmet market and very pleasant picnic area. Fun for the kids, too, is Deer Park's auto museum—spread throughout various buildings—which includes the world's largest collection of convertibles. Deer Park also displays an amazing antique radio and television collection. To take home some classic Americana, head for the gift shop. One-hour self-guided tours plus tasting are free; admission to the car museum is $6 adults, $4 seniors 55 and older, free for children under age 12. Deer Park is open daily 10 A.M.–5 P.M., until 6 P.M. in summer, closed Thanksgiving, Christmas, and New Year's Day.

The **Ferrara Winery,** 1120 W. 15th Ave. in Escondido, 760/745-7632, is a favorite wine stop. In honor of San Diego County's oldest winemaking and grape-growing family, the Ferrara enterprise has been designated a state historical point of interest. Of particular interest to travelers: the wonderful red wines, white wines, dry wines, and dessert wines. The tasting room also features fresh grape juice, wine marinades, and wine vinegars. All Ferrara grape products are crushed, aged and/or brewed, bottled, and sold only on the premises. Self-guided tours (15–20 minutes) and wine-tasting are free. The tasting room is open daily 10 A.M.–5 P.M., closed Christmas Day. To get here: From I-15 exit east at 9th Ave., turn south onto Upas, then west onto 15th.

Orfila Vineyards and Winery, 13455 San Pasqual Rd., toll-free 800/868-9463 or 760/738-6500, orfila.com, formerly Thomas Jaeger Vineyards, is a popular stop on Gray Line and other organized tours. Orfila's wine specialties include cabernet, merlot, chardonnay, and tawny port. The very pleasant picnic area here, overlooking vineyards and valley, is the site of many weddings and other celebrations. Custom gift baskets are available at the gift shop. Tours and tastings are free for individuals; for groups (fee) reservations are required. Orfila's is open daily 10 A.M.–6 P.M. One guided tour is offered daily, at 2 P.M., but visitors can take the self-guided tour any time. The winery is closed Thanksgiving, Christmas, and New Year's Day. To get here:

exit I-15 at Via Rancho Parkway. Follow the signs toward the San Diego Wild Animal Park, but turn right onto Pasqual Valley Rd. and continue one mile.

The **Bernardo Winery,** 13330 Paseo del Verano Norte, south of Escondido in the Rancho Bernardo area, 858/487-1866, www.bernardowinery.com, is one of the oldest continuously operating wineries in Southern California. The wine-tasting room, something of a general store, also features gourmet foods, olive oil, and private-label wines. Self-guided winery tours take about 10 minutes. Lunch is served in the patio dining room daily (except Mon.) 11 A.M.–3 P.M. The wine-tasting room is open daily 9 A.M.–5 P.M., gift shops 10 A.M.–5 P.M. (shops closed Mon.), and closed major holidays. To get here from I-15: exit at Rancho Bernardo Rd., turn north onto Pomerado Rd., then east onto Paseo del Verano Norte (just past the Oaks North Golf Club). Continue for 1.5 miles.

Palomar Mountain State Park

This mile-high park at the edge of the Cleveland National Forest offers a refreshing pine-scented change from the scrubbier foothills below. Aside from the fine conifers and oaks, the park's easy hikes, meadows, fishing pond, great campground, and just general remoteness are its main attractions. Visitors ascend from Hwy. 76 east of Pauma Valley via the "Highway to the Stars" (County Rd. S6), built for access to the famous Mount Palomar Observatory, which is just east of the park. The park is open for day use, sunrise to sunset, $2 per car. Campsites available. For more information, contact regional park headquarters: Cuyamaca Rancho State Park, 12551 Hwy. 79 in Descanso, 760/765-0755, www.cuyamaca.statepark.org, or call the park directly at 760/742-3462 (sometimes a recorded information message).

Mount Palomar Observatory

Something of a reluctant tourist attraction, the world-famous Mount Palomar Observatory was built in 1928 to take astronomical advantage of its elevation (6,100 feet), distance from coastal fog, and absence of urban light pollution. No longer boasting the world's largest reflecting telescope, this is still a serious research facility of the California Institute of Technology (Cal Tech) in

---

LAWRENCE WELK MUSEUM

The Lawrence Welk Resort north of town, just off I-15 at 8860 Lawrence Welk Dr., Escondido, 760/749-3448, is quite contemporary and well appointed, though in a sense it seems like something straight out of the 1950s. Most of Lawrence Welk's elderly fans come to his namesake resort to golf, swim, play tennis, just loaf, and take in a Broadway-style musical. Featuring stars from the long-running *Lawrence Welk Show,* the **Lawrence Welk Theater's** performance schedules include shows such as *Gotta Sing! Gotta Dance!, George M!, Mame,* and *A Welk Musical Christmas.* For a free look at memorabilia and a short lesson in television history, stop by the free **Lawrence Welk Museum** here. It's open daily 10:30 A.M.–5 P.M.

To get here: from I-15 northbound, exit at Deer Springs/Mountain Meadow Rd., turn right on Mountain Meadow, then left onto Champagne Boulevard. From I-15 southbound, exit at Gopher Canyon Rd., turn left (it becomes Old Castle Rd.), then right onto Champagne Boulevard.

Pasadena. Visitors can view the 200-inch Hale Telescope and study deep-space photos and other memorabilia. The observatory, 760/742-2119, astro.caltech.edu/observatories/palomar/, is open daily 9 A.M.–4 P.M.

For more excitement, consider taking the **Palomar Plunge,** the lazy person's observatory tour and cycling adventure—all downhill from Mount Palomar. The half-day trek costs $75 per person, including lunch at *the* place to eat on the mountain, the vegetarian **Mother's Kitchen.** If you're not camping, the place to stay in these parts is the **Lazy H Ranch,** down the mountain in Pauma Valley, 760/742-3669. For more information, contact: **Gravity Activated Sports,** 16220 Hwy. 76, P.O. Box 683, Pauma Valley, www.gasports.com, toll-free 800/985-4427.

Staying and Eating in the Escondido Area

Among inexpensive area stays: **Super 8,** 526 W. Washington Ave. (just west of Centre City Pkwy.), 760/747-3711. Inexpensive ($45 s, $55 d), and **Motel 6** off the parkway at 900 N. Quince St. (at Mission), 760/745-9252, $52 s/d. Inexpensive. The very nice **Best Western Escondido,** 1700 Seven Oakes Rd. east of I-15 (exit at El Norte Pkwy.), 760/740-1700, is a very good value, with rooms $79 and up. Expensive-Premium.

The undisputed star of local lodgings is south of town in the Rancho Bernardo area—the **Rancho Bernardo Inn,** 17550 Bernardo Oaks Dr., San Diego, toll-free 800/439-7529 or 858/675-8500, www.jcresorts.com, 265 acres of exquisite tile-roofed rooms, two restaurants, and exceptional resort facilities including a total of 108 holes of golf (45 on-site), tennis college, health spa, two swimming pools, rental bikes, the works. Luxury. Rates are $239 and up. If that's too rich for you, Rancho Bernardo boasts many other nice motels and hotels, most quite reasonably priced.

If you're in a hurry, fast fooderies abound. If you're freeway flyin', other choices concentrate along Centre City Pkwy., the I-15 business loop, including the **Fireside Grill & Deli,** 760/745-1931, for steaks and such, and **The Brigantine,** 760/743-4718, for seafood.

If you're looking for finer fare, **Sirino's,** 113 W. Grand Ave. (at Broadway), 760/745-3835, is locally famous for its French classics, quite the find in downtown Escondido. Nowadays Sirino's also offers Italian-style fare: pizzas, pastas, and salads perfect for a lighter meal. Whether you go Italian or French at dinner, be sure to leave room for delectable dessert. It's open for dinner Tues.–Sat., closed major holidays. Also quite good, just across the street, is **150 Grand** (fortunately, at 150 W. Grand), 760/738-6868.

The regional fine dining destination, though, is the elegant French **El Bizcocho** at the Rancho Bernardo Inn (see above), 858/675-8500.

INLAND FROM THE COAST: JULIAN AND VICINITY

The Apple-Pie Old West

This slice of apple-pie Americana, easily reached from either San Diego or Escondido, really does know its apples; small orchards climb the area's hillsides. Julian sprang to life as a hill-country mining town during Southern California's gold rush in the 1890s, and then declined into near ghost-town status until the area's affinity for apple growing was actively cultivated. Since then the town's Wild West character has been spruced up and tamed, as apples (also peaches and pears), fresh-squeezed apple cider, homemade apple pie, and the wistful American desire for simpler times have transformed tiny Julian into a major tourist draw. Bushels of visitors tumble into town during the desert's spring wildflower show, in summer, and for its **Apple Days** and **Fall Harvest Festival** celebrations—also peak seasons for local parking problems. Other main events in the fall include the **Julian Weed Show and Art Mart** and the ever-popular annual **Fiddle, Banjo, Guitar, and Mandolin Contest.**

Main attractions in Julian include the **Julian Pioneer Museum** just over a block south of Main at 2811 Washington St., 760/765-0227, memorializing the hardrock mining and hardscrabble living—as well as the lace curtains and high-button shoes—so prominent in this tiny town's past. It's open from Tues.–Sun. 10 A.M.–4 P.M. from Apr. through Nov., otherwise open only on weekends and national holidays (same hours) except New Year's Day, Thanksgiving, and Christmas. Admission is $1. The **Eagle Mining Company** is notable at the north end of C St., 760/765-0036—a rare opportunity to tour the inner workings of a gold mine. Dug into a mountainside, the old Eagle Mine and High Peaks Mine ceased commercial operation in 1942, but the mine tunnels and plenty of mining paraphernalia are still in place. Hourly tours are offered daily 10 A.M.–3 P.M., weather permitting, not counting time spent in the "rock shop." Come later in the day to dodge school tours. Admission is $7 adults, $3 children ages 6–15, $1 age 5 and under.

Another reason to tarry here—especially for intrepid desert and high-country explorers who prefer a bed to starry nights in a sleeping bag—is the town's proximity to both Anza-Borrego Desert State Park and Cuyamaca Rancho State Park.

For current information about the community, contact the **Julian Chamber of Commerce,** 2129 Main St., 760/765-1857 or visit the chamber's website at www.julianca.com.

Anza-Borrego Desert State Park

The largest state park in the contiguous United States, reaching south from the Santa Rosa Mountains almost to the Mexican border, Anza-Borrego Desert State Park consists of 600,000 acres of Colorado Desert. "Anza" refers to Juan Bautista de Anza, the Spanish captain who explored the area in 1774, establishing a viable land route from Mexico to California coastal settlements; "borrego" is Spanish for bighorn sheep. Some sights in this spectacular vastness can be appreciated from the road—the **Borrego Badlands,** the **Carrizo Badlands,** and the **Salton Sea** off in the distance—but other wonders, including **Borrego Palm Canyon, Hellhole Canyon,** and other palm oases, require the effort of a hike. In a good rain year, the park's spring wildflower bloom—usually starting in Mar., peaking in Apr.—can be spectacular.

An excellent **visitor center** near park headquarters, 760/767-4205, is the best place to start an Anza-Borrego exploration. Call the park's wildflower hot line, 760/767-4684, for peak spring wildflower bloom predictions. The park is open 24 hours and admission is free (except for the Palm Canyon Trail, where hikers are charged $5 at the gate); the visitor center is open daily 9 A.M.–5 P.M. For additional information—including campground details—contact the local state park headquarters at 200 Palm Canyon Dr., 760/767-5311.

Cuyamaca Rancho State Park

A high-country surprise on the edge of the desert east of San Diego, 25,000-acre Cuyamaca Rancho State Park (KWEE-uh-MACK-uh) features both lowland chaparral and fairly lush conifer and oak woodlands. As it's one of the few areas in Southern California with marked seasonal change, come for spring wildflowers, summer thunderstorms, fall colors, and, in winter, snow-dusted mountain peaks. Most of the area is designated as wilderness; camping, nature study, and serious hiking are the park's major attractions.

The park's 110 miles of hiking and horseback riding trails (backcountry camping allowed) lead to **Cuyamaca Peak,** the park's tallest at 6,512 feet; the less challenging **Stonewall Peak,** with kind switchbacks; and also wind through meadows and oak woodlands. In recent years, mountain lion attacks have become an increasing concern—so hike in groups and otherwise heed all recommended safety precautions.

Also of note: the 1870 **Stonewall Jackson Gold Mine** at the north end of the park, not particularly impressive but providing mute testimony to the area's gold-rush era, and the park museum. Housed, along with park headquarters, in the stone **Ralph M. Dyar Homestead,** the museum emphasizes the culture of the Kumeya'ay Indians who settled the area about 7,000 years ago.

The park is open for day use from sunrise to sunset ($2 per vehicle), and at least one campground is open year-round. Call for camping reservation information (seasonal). For more information, contact: Cuyamaca Rancho State Park, 12551 Hwy. 79 in Descanso, 760/765-0755, or visit www.cuyamaca.statepark.org.

Much of the rest of San Diego County's mountain wilderness is just to the east—the **Mount Laguna Recreation Area** in **Cleveland National Forest,** with still more hiking, camping, and picnicking potential. Though urbanites come east via I-8 and then amble north from Pine Valley via Laguna Mountain Rd., the area is also accessible from Julian. Instead of following Hwy. 79 to Cuyamaca, turn onto the **Sunrise Highway** (County Rd. S1) just before Lake Cuyamaca, and keep climbing for some of the county's most spectacular desert views.

Staying in and near Julian

Bed-and-breakfasts are the thing in these parts. *The* place since forever—the 1970s, actually—is the fine and funky old-time **Julian Hotel,** 2023

Main St., 760/765-0201, www.julianhotel.com, built during Julian's heyday by Albert and Margaret Robinson, freed slaves. Historical authenticity is the keynote here, since the hotel is listed on the National Register of Historic Places. Most rooms are small, with shared baths, though a one-room cottage, the honeymoon suite, and several rooms do feature private baths. Moderate-Luxury. Rates: $72–175 (two-night minimum stay on weekends).

Not part of the town's Wild West heritage but looking the part is the **Julian Lodge,** 2720 C St. (at 4th and C, a half-block south of Main), toll-free 800/542-1420 or 760/765-1420. This two-story wood frame hotel boasts modern amenities beneath its 19th-century charm, expressed in attractive period-style rooms (fairly small, as in the good ol' days). All rooms have cable TV but no phone; some have refrigerators and radios. A friendly fireplace beckons from downstairs in the breakfast parlor. And the conference room is not just for conferences—it turns into a good set-up for family stays, complete with a Murphy bed and rollaway cots. Moderate-Premium. Rates start at $74. Also new in the neighborhood, quite nice, and substantially more expensive is the **Orchard Hill Country Inn,** 2502 Washington St., 760/765-1700, www.orchardhill.com. Luxury. Rates are $160–265.

Shadow Mountain Ranch, beyond Julian proper at 2771 Frisius Rd., 760/765-0323, is a onetime cattle ranch and apple orchard refashioned into a country-style bed-and-breakfast inn. Accommodations are available in either the main house—two rooms with fireplaces and antiques—or in the ranch's four cottages, each with particular charms. Grandma's Attic is all wicker and lace, for example, and The Enchanted Cottage—atop a hill—has a potbellied stove and a view of the pines. For couples traveling together, Manzanita Cottage offers two bedrooms with separate entrances, a living room (complete with woodstove), and kitchen. Unique, though, is the Tree House, available only in the summer. Generous ranch-style breakfasts are included. Expensive-Premium. Rates are $90 and up, two-night minimum on weekends.

But if bed-and-breakfasts just aren't your style, plan to camp at either Cuyamaca Rancho or Anza-Borrego Desert State Parks (at least some campsites open year-round). Or beat a high-desert retreat to Borrego Springs in the midst of Anza-Borrego. **La Casa del Zorro** (see below) is the classiest act around, but another good choice is the frontier-style **Palm Canyon Resort** silhouetted against the stunning mountains at 221 Palm Canyon Dr. (near the park visitors center), Borrego Springs, toll-free 800/342-0044 in California or 760/767-5341. Rooms are spacious and quite attractive in subdued western style, with color TV, cable, and in-room coffeemakers and refrigerators. Also here are a swimming pool, whirlpool, and on-site restaurant and "saloon." Moderate-Premium. Rates start at $85 in the typical fall, winter, and spring travel season, at $60 in torrid summer heat. There's a Good Sam RV park here, too.

La Casa del Zorro Resort Hotel
One of those classic California desert resorts, La Casa del Zorro started out as an adobe ranch house, built in 1937. Since then, whitewashed adobe-style "casitas" have spread out over 32 tree-shaded acres. Rooms here are beautifully decorated and comfortable. Resort amenities include putting green, tennis courts, three swimming pools, rental bikes, and volleyball. (Childcare can be arranged.) Two good restaurants are also part of the complex. Moderate-Luxury. Room rates start at $85 for suites; the separate two- to four-bedroom "casitas" run $375 to $950 in season (substantially lower in summer), with a two-night minimum stay on weekends. For more information: La Casa del Zorro Resort Hotel, 3845 Yaqui Pass Rd., Borrego Springs, toll-free 800/824-1844 or 760/767-5323, www.lacasadelzorro.com.

Eating in and near Julian
Julian isn't known for its great restaurants. Popular for lunch, though, is **Mom's Apple Pies,** 760/765-2472, and for dinner, the **Julian Grill,** 760/765-0173. Except on weekends and holidays, the dining room at the Craftsman-style **Orchard Hill Country Inn** on Washington St. north of Main, 760/765-1420, is open to nonguests (call for reservations).

If a genuinely good meal is mandatory, get ready to drive—all the way to Borrego Springs, in the middle of Anza-Borrego Desert State Park. **La Casa del Zorro Restaurant** at the resort, 3845 Yaqui Pass Rd., 760/767-5323, is the place for dress-up dinners out in the desert, as well as a more casual breakfast and lunch. Dinner entrées include chicken *cordon bleu,* prime rib, scampi, Alaskan salmon, and vegetable curry. Lighter à la carte specials and the changing early bird specials are the real deals. La Casa del Zorro also offers a feast for the spirit—Old California ambience with candlelit whitewashed walls reminiscent of 1930s Palm Springs. The restaurant is open daily 7 A.M.–3 P.M., Fri. and Sat. 5–10 P.M., and on Sun. 4:30–10 P.M.

But don't miss **Dudley's Bakery,** 30218 Hwy. 78, an area institution near the junction with Hwy. 79 in Santa Ysabel, 760/765-0488 or toll-free 800/225-3348, open daily 8 A.M.–5 P.M. California history aficionados may stop in Santa Ysabel to peek into **Mission Asistencia de Santa Isabel,** a small 18th-century mission outpost reconstructed in more recent times. But everyone stops at Dudley's across the street before heading into the wilderness or back into the city. This is the place to load up on specialty breads—how about jalapeño loaf?—breakfast pastries, and other goodies. Dudley's offers deli fare, too.

GREATER SAN DIEGO

SAN DIEGO AS DISCOVERY

Captain Juan Rodríguez Cabrillo stepped out onto Point Loma, the tip of what is now San Diego Bay, and claimed the territory for Spain in 1542. His footfall has echoed through contemporary time as California's first and original point of discovery.

SAN DIEGO'S "PERFECT" CLIMATE

Just about everyone in San Diego will tell you the climate here is perfect. And so it usually is, if perfection is measured in the 60–70°F range in summer, in the mid-40s to mid-60s in winter. In late summer and fall, however, "Santa Anas" sometimes blow in—several-day events created by inland high pressure; in a reversal of the usual weather pattern, with winds blowing east, or inland, from the cool, moist coastal plain, desiccated desert winds blow west to the ocean. During strong Santa Ana conditions heat-wave mirages shimmer up and down the coastline, with temperatures reaching 100°F or higher; inland, grassland and wilderness wildfire danger becomes extreme. Milder Santa Anas, however, chase away the coastal fog and create wonderful dry weather and temperatures in the mid-80s, often sublime in October and November. What little rainfall there is along the coast and in the foothills—an average of 10–15 inches in a typical year—falls primarily from December into March.

The U.S. military discovered San Diego earlier this century and settled in for a long stay, drawn by the area's sublime weather, its fine natural port, and its high-flying wide open spaces.

Despite its straitlaced military tradition, San Diego is no longer a simple social montage of battleship gray and camouflage green, no longer a predictable bastion of conservatism. New people, new high-tech industries, and new ideas have moved in.

Visitors to San Diego discover, and rediscover, a salubrious endless summer of beaches and balmy breezes along with world-class enclaves of culture and equally surprising moderate prices. They discover San Diego's relaxed, casual approach to day-to-day life and find that, here, just about anyone can feel comfortable. The oldest city in California and the state's second largest, San Diego somehow still retains a simpler, small-town sensibility—beyond the freeway traffic, that is.

SEEING AND DOING SAN DIEGO

As predictable as the ocean tides, tourists tend to flow toward San Diego's major attractions: Sea World, the San Diego Zoo, and, in the north county, the San Diego Wild Animal Park. But San Diego—the sunny city, the county, and the endless sky and seashore—reveals its deeper nature only to those who take time to explore its neighborhoods and less advertised attractions.

Downtown's brightest light is Balboa Park, home of the San Diego Zoo and the most

WAR AT THE BORDER
IN A WORLD WITHOUT BORDERS

Globalization and "the global economy," those beloved buzzwords of international business, suggest that boundaries now have little meaning in matters of capital and commerce. This unfettered flow of finance, goods, and information, this brave new world without borders, clearly serves the interests of those who possess money, material wealth, and expertise—the winners of the globalization game in all nations. But in a world without economic borders, what becomes of the losers, the left-behind? Those displaced by the global economy seem doomed to wander across national borders, legally and otherwise, in search of work. In search of survival. Their fate is largely ignored by architects of the new one-world economy.

In California, the effects of immigration have reached phenomenal—some would say mythic—proportions. According to Rubén Martínez in "The Myth of Borders," published in 1996 by the *L.A. Weekly:* "There is no border; no matter how many walls and infrared goggles and moats and machine-gun turrets, there is no border—just history, and history is movement across the borders we imagine out of fear."

Yet just try telling that to most Californians—of all ethnicities—who increasingly feel besieged by "foreigners" in their own communities and who are baffled, culturally and politically, by the challenges of coping with such immense social change.

According to the federal Immigration and Naturalization Service (INS), by early 1997 the national surge in immigration totaled 24.6 million people, or 9.3 percent of the total U.S. population, the highest proportion since the 1930s. And the number of illegal immigrants nationwide had again reached five million—an increase of about 28 percent in four years, nearly the same peak levels reached before the sweeping Immigration Reform and Control Act (IRCA) amnesty program of a decade earlier.

California absorbs a disproportionate share of immigrants, legal and illegal. The Golden State now absorbs more than half of all legal immigrants annually. At least two million undocumented immigrants live in California, a number increasing by 100,000 each year. In Los Angeles County at least 40 percent of the population is foreign-born (compared to 11 percent in 1970). Latinos alone now account for over 28 percent of all California residents,

and are projected to reach 50 percent—representing the majority—by the year 2040. One in four Californians is foreign-born—more than eight million people—which is a simpler yet dramatic way to represent the impact of this new turn-of-the-century immigration boom on the Golden State.

Such is the statistical background for recent chapters in California political history that have earned banner headlines in newspapers nationwide—particularly the vitriolic political battle over Proposition 187, which denied public funding for education, health care, and other public services to illegal immigrants, and the surprisingly quick political backlash that removed Republican governor Pete Wilson from office and replaced him with a Democrat, Gray Davis.

San Diego has been ground zero in California for the federal government's long-running war against illegal border crossings from adjacent Mexico. And in the war over illegal immigration and Proposition 187, no place in California was more furious in its political fisticuffs than San Diego, sister city to Tijuana, Mexico. Tired of heavy illegal immigrant foot traffic in middle-class neighborhoods and traffic-dodging on area freeways, illegal shantytowns alongside tony suburbs, and overcrowded public schools and hospitals, conservative San Diego lost its cool. Ex-Mayor Roger Hedgecock, a radio talk show host opposed to "opening the trough for the whole Third World," helped fan the flames: "Jesus never said, 'Fork over your taxes because the government is going to take care of everyone in the world.'" To the chagrin of even Prop. 187 supporters, already a bit anxious over the measure's "police state" political potential, Republican state Senator William Craven proposed special "identification cards" for Latinos. After his office was inundated by angry protests, Craven said he meant to suggest identification cards only for individuals seeking state services.

On the other side of the fence, figuratively and sometimes literally, were anti–Prop. 187 forces, including the Catholic Church, college students, community activists, and the city of Tijuana, Mexico. The Tijuana City Council officially declared Governor Pete Wilson unwelcome in its town. Tijuana newspapers promoted a weekend boycott of San Diego businesses—underscoring just how economically interconnected the two cities, and the two nations, actually are. (The commerce issue did get some local attention, even among Prop. 187 supporters; according to the Greater San Diego Chamber of Commerce, cross-border commerce generates about $2 billion a year for San Diego.) And protesting students marched into an anti–Prop. 187 rally dressed as pilgrims to propose a "Mayflower Amendment" to send all European-Americans "back to Europe."

The fact is, immigration from Mexico to "El Norte" has gone on for so long—to the great benefit of California business, ever voracious for inexpensive labor—that in some regions of Mexico, particularly the impoverished north and west, the journey is now both a presumed right and rite of passage.

Disregarding the territorial claims of native peoples, in the beginning California and the rest of the U.S. Southwest *was* Mexico, the spoils of Mexico's war for independence from Spain. Though the new nation of Mexico inhabited the territory for just two decades, the "Californio" culture on both sides of what is now the U.S.-Mexican border had flourished for multiple generations. In that sense Mexican nationals and pro-immigrant activists are correct when they contend that "Anglos," a term generally referring to present-day white citizens of the United States, illegally invaded the territory. The ultimate result of the Mexican-American War waged between 1846 and 1848 was little more than a government-funded land grab—a touchy subject in U.S.-Mexico relations to this day.

The historical argument is generally a hard sell on this side of the border, though, particularly in areas—like San Diego—inundated by illegal immigrants.

Yet legally and otherwise, these days Mexico is coming home to California. And despite endless rhetoric and get-tough federal legislation to the contrary, the U.S. government has no real desire to end illegal immigration, and actually "protects the traffic in cheap Mexican labor," argues Wade Graham in the July 1996 *Harper's* article, "Masters of the Game." The reasons, he says, "are as old as our century-long thirst for cheap labor and as recent as today's currency-market fluctuations."

The truth about illegal immigration, Graham says, is that "until such time as U.S. law barring the employment of illegal aliens is enforced—or U.S. wages drop below those of the Third World—poor foreigners will continue to come here" because politicians have "neither the political security nor the will to alter this fact."

In other words, there will continue to be war at the border in this odd new world without borders. But as things stand, that war will never be won.

---

impressive concentration of world-class museums in any California city. Though new freeway interchanges make it more difficult to connect with the rest of downtown, the effort is worth it. The modern downtown mainstay is Horton Plaza, a stunning and stylish shopping mall disguised as a virtual city. Adjacent is San Diego's Gaslamp District, its Victorian buildings newly gussied-up and glittering with shops, restaurants, and nightlife.

Along the bay is the Embarcadero, offering a quick visual cruise of the city's maritime heart and military soul. Across the bay, reached by ferry or bridge, is Coronado, home of the historic Hotel Del Coronado, the North Island Naval Station, and neighborhoods of military retirees. Look for some astounding public art and the largely Latino Barrio Logan on the way to Coronado and in the shadow of the soaring San Diego–Coronado Bay Bridge.

Head uptown to Old Town San Diego, a state historic park where shopping and fairly commercial diversions attract most visitor interest. Technically, though, "uptown" is centered along Washington St. in artsy Hillcrest (from 1st to 5th Sts.), a San Diego version of San Francisco's Castro St.; eventually Washington becomes Adams Ave., "Antiques Row." Also worth exploring: the India Street Art Colony near Washington St. and "Little Italy," along India just north of Date Street. The Linda Vista and North Park neighborhoods, not far away, are home to San Diego's large Asian communities and to many of the city's most authentic (and least expensive) Asian restaurants.

Along the coast are San Diego's beach communities, from Ocean Beach, Mission Beach, and Pacific Beach to the distinct, and distinctly affluent, La Jolla and nearby Del Mar—all included within San Diego city limits.

BALBOA PARK

San Diego's cultural heart and soul, home to its renowned zoo, magnificent museums, and much of the city's thriving theater program, Balboa

PRACTICAL BALBOA PARK

If at all possible, spend at least two full days in Balboa Park. Entering the park is free, but the majority of its attractions—the zoo, most museums, the theater program—charge admission. The most economical option for touring the museums, typically, is the multiple-museum ticket—at last report, including admission to nine museums, $25—which is usually a bargain even if you won't be seeing them all. Most museums also offer a "free Tuesday" once each month, with some free on the first Tuesday of the month, others free on the second Tuesday, and so forth. Most museums are open daily from 10 A.M. to at least 4 P.M., but schedules can vary throughout the year; if your time in town is tight, call ahead to verify hours.

For more detailed information on the zoo, museums, and major attractions, see the listings in this chapter. For additional information on the park and its current programs and events, contact the very helpful **Balboa Park Information Center** in Balboa Park, inside the House of Hospitality at 1549 El Prado, 619/239-0512, open daily 9 A.M.–4 P.M.

If you're coming by car, the traditional entrance to Balboa Park is from downtown, heading east via Laurel St. and over the Laurel St. Bridge (the Cabrillo Bridge) spanning Hwy. 163. Once over the bridge, the street becomes El Prado, which soon becomes the park's primary pedestrian mall. Parking is a challenge on summer weekends, so come early in the day; you'll discover that the first lot, at Plaza de Panama, is almost always full. Continue south to find others. The other main route into the park, much more convenient if the zoo is your first or primary destination, is via Park Boulevard. From Hwy. 163, exit at Park Blvd.; from I-5, exit at Pershing Dr. and follow the signs.

Park is also an architectural and horticultural masterpiece. Unimaginatively known as City Park when its original 1,400 acres of chaparral and scrub brush were set aside by the city in 1868, Balboa Park began to develop its Spanish colonial revival character in preparation for the 1915–1917 Panama-California International Exposition, a massive cultural coming-out party sponsored by the city to celebrate the completion of the Panama Canal.

The elaborate exuberance of the original buildings, intended to be temporary, can be credited to New York architect Bertram G. Goodhue, who personally designed the Fine Arts Building, the California State Building (now the Museum of Man), and the Cabrillo Bridge along El Prado—the formal entrance into the park's beaux arts center. Goodhue also set the stage for other architects.

With the arrival of World War I and San Diego's sudden centrality to the war effort, the exhibition buildings were conscripted for service. In the 1920s, as the military settled into permanent San Diego quarters, the city wisely established the precedent that makes present-day Balboa Park possible—donating the exposition buildings to various nonprofit cultural institutions.

The development of Balboa Park's cultural

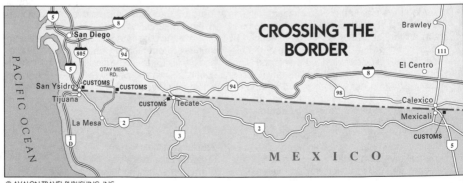

center continued with construction of the 1935 California-Pacific International Exposition, which added still more buildings, these by architect Richard Requa, with Aztec, Mayan, and Southwestern motifs.

Balboa Park Overview

San Diego's huge central park is lush and inviting, perfect for picnics and aimless ambling. Yet it's almost impossible to *be* aimless, given Balboa Park's astonishing array of attractions. Most visitors start at the San Diego Zoo, at the north end of the park just off Park Blvd.; the zoo can easily become a daylong adventure. Between the zoo and El Prado is the Spanish Village Art Center, studio space for artists and artisans who also sell their wares (open daily 11 A.M.–4 P.M., free). At the eastern end of El Prado begins Balboa Park's endless parade of museums. Fairly new ones, such as the Reuben H. Fleet Space Theater and Science Center and the Museum of Photographic Arts, stand beside longtime favorites, including the San Diego Natural History Museum, the San Diego Museum of Art, and the Museum of Man. Adjacent and just north, along Old Globe Way, is the rebuilt Old Globe Theatre—the original Shakespearean venue was torched in a 1978 arson fire—and the other two theaters of the Simon Edison Centre for the Performing Arts. Another don't-miss destination: the 1915 Botanical Building, with its lotus pond and impressive collection of tropical and subtropical plants.

Attractions south of El Prado include the Japanese Friendship Garden and the Spreckels Organ Pavilion with its 1914 Spreckels Organ featuring 4,445 pipes or 72 ranks. (Free con-

Balboa Park

ROBERT HOLMES/CALTOUR

certs are offered year-round on Sun. afternoons at 2 P.M. and, in July and Aug., on Mon. evenings at 8 P.M.) Still more museums farther south include the San Diego Automotive Museum and the excellent San Diego Aerospace Museum, as well as the Centro Cultural de la Raza, "the people's cultural center."

Museums along El Prado

Two blocks south of the zoo at 1875 El Prado, just off Park Blvd. near the fountain in Plaza de Balboa, the **Reuben H. Fleet Space Theater and Science Center** is ever popular. The main attraction here is the Omnimax theater, the world's first. Fun even for adults is the 9,500-square-foot science center, with dozens of well-done interactive and hands-on exhibits—such as Chinese resonant bowls and the Bernoulli Effect beachball. Don't miss the gift shop, with an unusually good selection of books, games, and toys. Theater admission varies, but is typically $6.50–11 for adults, $5.50–9 for seniors, and $5–8 for children ages 5–15. Center admission is free on the first Tues.

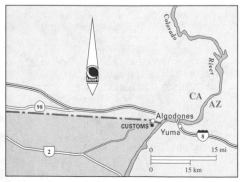

of every month, otherwise it's $6.50 adults, $5 for kids. The center is open Mon. and Tues. 9:30 A.M.–5 P.M.; Wed., Thurs., and Sun. 9:30 A.M.–7 P.M.; and Fri. and Sat. 9:30 A.M.–9 P.M. For current movie and other information, call 619/233-1233, or look up www.rhfleet.org.

The imposing **San Diego Natural History Museum** at 1788 El Prado chronicles the earth's wonders. Of the "all natural ingredients" on exhibit, kids most savor the live insect displays along with the dinosaur skeletons and other fossils. And just inside the main entrance, swinging from a 43-foot cable, the museum's Foucault Pendulum verifies that the planet is, in fact, rotating on its axis. Special traveling exhibits, films, lectures, and nature outings—including winter whale-watching tours—are also big draws. Museum admission is $7 adults, $6 seniors and active military, $5 children ages 6–17, free on the first Tues. of every month. Hours sometimes vary, but the museum is typically open daily 9:30 A.M.–4:30 P.M., closed on Thanksgiving, Christmas, and New Year's Day. For more information, call 619/232-3821, or check out www.sdnhm.org.

The **Museum of Photographic Arts** inside the Casa de Balboa, 1649 El Prado, focuses on both photography as art and the history of photographic arts—showcasing the works of well-known photographers such as Ansel Adams, Edward Weston, and Henri Cartier-Bresson along with those of newer artists. The museum sponsors six to eight special gallery exhibits each year. Don't miss the museum store, with fine prints, posters, calendars, cards, and the largest selection of photography books in the western United States. Admission is $6, free for museum members and children under age 12 accompanied by an adult. It's open daily 10 A.M.–5 P.M., closed on major holidays. For current and upcoming shows and other information, call 619/238-7559, or check out www.mopa.org.

Another prominent resident of Casa de Balboa at 1649 El Prado, the **Museum of San Diego History** features rotating thematic exhibits from the San Diego Historical Society's permanent collection plus national traveling exhibits—almost always something of interest, even for the kids. Also take time to take in at least one of the historical society's other local outposts—the **Junípero Serra Museum** in Old Town, for example, or the marvelous **Villa Montezuma/Jesse Shepard House** near the Gaslamp Quarter. The Museum of San Diego History is open Tues.–Sun. 10 A.M.–4:30 P.M., closed Thanksgiving, Christmas, and New Year's Day. Admission is free on the second Tues. of every month, otherwise $5 for adults; $4 for seniors, students, and active military; and $2 for children ages 6–17. For more information, call 619/232-6203.

Down in the Casa de Balboa basement at 1649 El Prado is the **San Diego Model Railroad Museum,** boasting the world's largest collection of mini-gauge trains—paradise for toy train lovers. The museum is open Tues.–Fri.—and the first Tues. of every month, when admission is free—11 A.M.–4 P.M., and on Sat. and Sun. 11 A.M.–5 P.M. Admission is free for children under age 15, otherwise $4 adults, $3 for students, seniors, and active military. For more information, call 619/696-0199 or check out www.sdmodelrailroadm.com. Casa de Balboa's **San Diego Hall of Champions Sports Museum,** 619/234-2544, is worth a stop for sports fans particularly interested in local heroes.

More Museums along El Prado

On the park's Plaza de Panama at 1450 El Prado, the **San Diego Museum of Art** is best known for its European Renaissance and Baroque paintings, including works by Goya, El Greco, Rubens, and Van Ruisdael, though the collection also includes Dalí, Matisse, O'Keeffe, and Toulouse-Lautrec. The cutting-edge contemporary California art in the Frederick R. Weisman Gallery alone is well worth the trip. Another draw here is the sculpture garden and, for lunch, the **Sculpture Garden Cafe.** Regular admission is $8 adults; $6 seniors, active military, and students (with ID); $3 children ages 6–17. Free admission on the third Tues. of every month. It's open Tues.–Sun. 10 A.M.–4:30 P.M. For current exhibits and other information, call 619/232-7931 or check www.sdmart.com.

Just east at 1500 El Prado, near the Lotus Pond, is the **Timken Museum of Art,** an intriguing collection dominated by lesser-known works of significant 18th- and 19th-century artists from both Europe and America. It's open Tues.–Sat. 10 A.M.–4:30 P.M., Sun. 1:30–4:30 P.M., closed Mon. and the month of September. Admission is free, with free guided tours offered Tues.–Thurs. 10 A.M.–noon. For more information call 619/239-5548 during regular museum hours.

OLD GLOBE THEATRE AND FRIENDS

First there was San Diego's Old Globe Theatre; dramatic outdoor Shakespeare productions were its original claim to fame. Now joining the 581-seat Old Globe are two more theaters in Balboa Park's performing arts center—the 225-seat **Cassius Carter Centre Stage** and the 612-seat **Lowell Davies Festival Theatre**. The performance calendar for this major-league regional repertory is full almost year-round.

The Old Globe and fellow theaters are in Balboa Park, near the Museum of Man, and reached via Park Blvd. and Old Globe Way. The regular theater season runs from January into June. The **Old Globe Festival**, showcasing Shakespeare, other classics, and modern works, both indoors and out, officially runs from July into September but summer shows can—and usually do—extend through November. No performances are scheduled on major U.S. holidays.

Advance ticket purchases are recommended. Admission varies, in the $23–42 range. For prerecorded ticket information, call 619/239-2255. For bargain same-day tickets to these and other area theaters, as well as to music and dance events, contact the **Times Arts Tix** ticket center at Horton Plaza, 619/497-5000, or check the San Diego Performing Arts League website at www.sandiegoperforms.com.

For current performance schedule and box office hours, contact the Old Globe Theatre, 619/231-1941, www.oldglobe.org.

After two distinguished decades in La Jolla, since the summer of 1996 the marvelous **Mingei International Museum of World Folk Art**—where the "art of the people, by the people, and for the people comes to the people"—has made its permanent home in Balboa Park's remodeled House of Charm at 1439 El Prado, an arrangement offering six times the museum's original space. Call for current exhibit information. At last report the Mingei was open Tues.–Sun. 10 A.M.–4 P.M., closed on all national holidays. Admission is $5 adults, $2 children. For more information, call 619/239-0003 or check www.mingei.org.

The grand **San Diego Museum of Man,** west of the Plaza de Panama at 1350 El Prado, under the California Tower, is striking enough from the outside. The anthropological collection here, one of the finest in the country, made its debut during the 1915 Balboa Park exposition. Expanded and updated over the years, exhibits chronicle human development but emphasize Mexican, Native American (particularly Southwestern), and South American societies. Egyptian artifacts are among recent acquisitions. The museum is open daily 10 A.M.–4:30 P.M., closed Thanksgiving, Christmas, and New Year's Day. Admission is $5 adults, $4.50 military and seniors, $3 children ages 6–17, free for children under age 6. It's free for everyone on the third Tues. of every month. For current program and other information, call 619/239-2001 or check www.museumofman.org.

Museums beyond El Prado

These days Balboa Park's exquisite art deco Ford Building—one of the finest remaining examples of its species in the United States, trimmed at night in blue neon—houses an equally impressive and artistic display of aeronautical history makers at the **San Diego Aerospace Museum and International Aerospace Hall of Fame.** Local history is represented by a replica of Charles Lindbergh's *Spirit of St. Louis,* and by a glider on loan from the National Air and Space Museum, first flown in 1883 near San Diego. Especially compelling: the ersatz aircraft carrier flight deck with its World War II–vintage planes. And there's much more. The aerospace museum is in the southern section of Balboa Park at 2001 Pan American Plaza, most easily reached via Park Blvd. and then President's Way. Admission is free on the fourth Tues. of the month, otherwise $8 adults, $6 seniors, $3 "juniors" ages 6–17, and free for children under 6 and active-duty military. It's open daily 10 A.M.–4:30 P.M., closed Thanksgiving and Christmas Day. For current exhibits and other information, call 619/234-8291 or check www.aerospacemuseum.org.

Nearby, at 2080 Pan American Plaza, the **San Diego Automotive Museum** inside the onetime Palace of Transportation is for car-loving kids of all ages. Classics and exotics—Hollywood's cars, roadsters, and an exceptional motorcycle collection—make up the permanent collection. Special shows and events—call for current program information—are often quite fun. Great gift shop. The museum is open daily 10 A.M.–4:30 P.M. (until 5:30 P.M. in summer),

HIGH-FLYING SAN DIEGO

The development of San Diego has been shaped more by its aerial history—commingled with U.S. military history—than by any other factor.

In the early days of aviation, the industry's pioneers took flight in San Diego to take full advantage of the superb flying weather. **Charles Lindbergh,** the first man to cross the Atlantic Ocean in an airplane, is perhaps the most famous of these fanatical flyboys. In 1927 Lindbergh commissioned San Diegan T. Claude Ryan to build a plane based on Ryan's M-1 design (with wings above the fuselage). Within months, after very few test flights, "Lucky Lindy" left San Diego in his *Spirit of St. Louis*—touching down only briefly on the East Coast before flying off into the history books.

The U.S. military has had a distinguished aerial history in San Diego as well, beginning with test flights made by Glen Curtiss from Coronado's **North Island Naval Station** in 1911. Special air shows and other public events are scheduled at North Island and—at least until its recent move east—at **Miramar Naval Air Station,** the real-life Top Gun, which preceded the movie of the same name.

To get up to speed on San Diego's high-flying history, visit the **San Diego Aerospace Museum** in Balboa Park.

last admission one-half hour before closing. It's closed Thanksgiving, Christmas, and New Year's Day. Admission is free on the fourth Tues. of every month, otherwise $7 adults, $6 seniors and active military, $3 children ages 6–15, free for children under 6. For current exhibits and other information, call 619/231-2886 or check www.sdautomuseum.org.

San Diego Zoo

The world-class San Diego Zoo sprang from very humble beginnings. Its original animals were chosen from those left behind by the Panama-California International Exposition. Now famous for its large exotic and endangered animal population and its lush, complex tropical landscape, the 100-acre San Diego Zoo is immensely popular—the city's top visitor draw, attracting more than three million people each year.

Part of the zoo's appeal is the near absence of prison-bar-style cages and pens. Most animals

here—the zoo refers to them as "captivating instead of captive"—are kept in naturally landscaped, moated enclosures, very large walkthrough aviaries, and other fairly innovative environments. Rarities among the zoo's 4,000 animals (800 species) include Australian koalas—the first exhibited outside Australia—New Zealand long-billed kiwis, Sichuan takins from China, wild Mongolian or Przewalski's horses—forerunners of all domesticated horses—and Komodo dragons from Indonesia. Special "guest animals" include

FUN NEAR BALBOA: HILLCREST AND VICINITY

Just north of Balboa Park and its fairly traditional ambience is Hillcrest, the one San Diego neighborhood noted for its eccentricities. This conservative city's gay district, centered along Washington and University Aves. between 1st and 5th, Hillcrest is also the place to sample the artsy bohemian life, San Diego–style—the small record and bookshops, eclectic art films, small theaters, and good casual restaurants. Redevelopment is the watchword here, though, as elsewhere in San Diego—so hurry, before it all gets too upscale and safely cool. For music classics and what's new internationally, spin into **Off The Record,** 3849 5th Ave. (at University), 619/298-4755. Some of San Diego's best independent bookstores are located in Hillcrest, including **Grounds for Murder,** 3940 4th St. (at Washington), 619/299-9500, which provides a vacation's worth of whodunits; **Bountiful Books,** 3834 5th Ave. between University and Robinson, 619/491-0664, which boasts more than 20,000 new, used, and rare titles; and **Fifth Avenue Books,** 3838 5th Ave. between University and Robinson, 619/291-4660, which offers collectible first editions. One of the best bookstores in town, though, is been-there-forever **Blue Door Books,** 3823 5th Ave. (at University), 619/298-8610, locally famous for the Lawrence Ferlinghetti poem the poet wrote in honor of the bookstore. The **Hillcrest Theater,** 3965 5th Ave., 619/299-2100, showing artsy independent and foreign films, is prominent at colorful **Village Hillcrest,** a neo-retro-looking contemporary complex at 5th and Washington. For coffee and philosophical conversation, *the* place is **The Coffee Bean & Tea Leaf** at 3865 5th Ave. (at University), 619/298-5908.

two giant pandas on loan from the People's Republic of China, Shi Shi and Bai Yun, who gave birth to a cub, Hua Mei, on August 21, 1999. The San Diego Zoo also boasts the world's largest collection of parrots and parrotlike birds.

The natural habitats—the **Polar Bear Plunge, Hippo Beach, Gorilla Tropics, Tiger River, Sun Bear Forest, Pygmy Chimps at Bonobo Road, African Kopje,** and **Australasia**—are most impressive, designed as distinct "bioclimatic zones" with characteristic combinations of plant and animal species. The free-flight **Scripps Aviary** is also quite the show, home to hundreds of exotic African birds. The **Children's Zoo**—where even the restrooms are designed for four-year-olds—is immensely appealing to "kids" of all ages, as is the **petting zoo.**

The zoo is open daily from 9 A.M. to dusk, which means entrance gates close at 4 P.M. from fall through spring and at 9 P.M. in summer (visitors can stay an hour longer). General admission, which includes admission to the Children's Zoo and all shows, is $18 adults, $8 for children ages 3–11, free for age 2 and under. Admission is free for everyone on October 3, Founder's Day, and free for children under age 12 during the entire month of October. For more information, contact the San Diego Zoo, 619/234-3153 (recorded) or 619/231-1515, www.sandiegozoo.org.

OLD TOWN SAN DIEGO

The old adobe survivors of Old Town San Diego, the state's most popular historic park, are intertwined with—and clearly outnumbered by—a wide variety of minimalls, gift shops, restaurants, and other commercial enterprises that now surround Old Town Plaza. But modern consumerism didn't doom Old Town's old-timers. It was fate, in the form of a devastating fire in 1872. Most of Old Town's surviving historic buildings, among the earliest outposts of early California settlement history, are clustered in the six-block area bounded by Juan St. on the north, Congress St. on the south, Wallace St. on the west, and Twiggs St. on the east.

Highlights of an Old Town history walk include the **Seeley Stables** at Calhoun and Twiggs Sts., 619/220-5442, Old Town San Diego's transportation center until the 20th century, now

Watch tortillas being made in Old Town.

a museum of horse-and-buggy rolling stock and western memorabilia. (Small admission.) On Mason at Calhoun is the 1829 **La Casa de Bandini,** center of the young city's social life during Mexican rule, and then after the Yankees arrived, the **Cosmopolitan Hotel.** The ground-floor rooms and walled gardens are now inhabited by a popular Mexican restaurant, **Casa de Bandini,** 619/297-8211, where strolling mariachi bands serenade diners on the patio.

A visit to adobe **La Casa de Estudillo,** 619/220-5422, on Mason St. between Calhoun and San Diego Ave., is a must. (Small admission includes admission to the Seeley museum, and vice versa.) Built in 1827 by Captain José M. Estudillo, commander of the presidio, this was one of the finest homes in Mexican California. Note the leather-tied beams, and the exquisite furnishings, from the Steinway spinet pianos to the blue Duncan Phyfe sofa and elegant Oriental rugs.

Well worth exploring: the 1847 **San Diego Courthouse,** the **Wells Fargo Museum,** the 1865 **Mason Street School,** and the local

SERRA MUSEUM AND THE MISSION

Most notable in **Presidio Park,** just up the hill from Old Town via Taylor St. and Presidio Dr., is the imposing mission revival-style **Junípero Serra Museum,** 2727 Presidio Dr., 619/297-3258, built in 1929, which many visitors mistake for San Diego's mission. Museum exhibits emphasize San Diego's Spanish period, including a fascinating furniture collection and artifacts from presidio excavations. Climb the museum tower for breathtaking panoramic views. The Junípero Serra Museum is open Fri.–Sun. 10 A.M.–4:30 P.M. Admission is $5 adults, $4 seniors, students and military, $2 children 6–17, free for kids age 6 and under. The presidio site, directly below the Serra museum, is a National Historic Landmark, where excavations have been ongoing since 1965.

Mission San Diego isn't the most exciting or evocative of California's 21 missions, but it is the first. First founded by Father Junípero Serra in 1769, atop what is now Presidio Hill, the mission was moved to this new location in 1774, a site that promised more water and improved agricultural prospects.

Wander the garden, stop by the museum, and visit the original chapel—California's first church—for a peek into the mission's past and present lives. To get to Mission San Diego, 10818 San Diego Mission Rd., from Presidio Park, follow Presidio Dr. down the hill and bear right onto Taylor; at the first light, turn left and merge onto I-8 (heading east). Exit at Mission Gorge Rd. and turn left; turn left again onto San Diego Mission Road. The museum and gardens are open daily 9 A.M.–5 P.M. Small admission. "Tote-a-tape" tours are available. For more information, call 619/281-8449.

ROBERT HOLMES/CALTOUR

Dental Museum. Inside the tiny **San Diego Union Newspaper Building** is a once-modern marvel of the journalism trade—an ancient Blickensderfer typewriter, complete with wood carrying case. Just outside Old Town proper is the **Mormon Battalion Visitors Center** at 2510 Juan St., 619/298-3317, free admission, which tells the story of the longest infantry march in history. Also worth a stop for history aficionados is the two-story brick 1857 **Whaley House Museum,** 2482 San Diego Ave., 619/298-2482, one of the few homes in the country ever declared by the U.S. government to be haunted. Admission $4 adults, $2 children.

The park itself is free, as is admission to most of its historic buildings, though a few other Old Town–area attractions charge admission. The park's historic buildings are open daily from 10 A.M. to at least 4 P.M., closed Thanksgiving, Christmas, and New Year's Day. Restaurants and some shops have extended hours. Free Old Town walking tours depart daily at 11 A.M. and 2 P.M. from the state park office—also the source for self-guided tour brochures, if you're lucky, as well as special event schedules and other current info. On the first Sat. of each month and every Wed., from 10 A.M.–1 P.M. in the Machado y Stewart Adobe, park staff and other local history buffs don period costumes to demonstrate various domestic arts and, next to La Casa de Bandini, the village smithy plies his trade. For more information contact: **Old Town San Diego State Historic Park,** 4002 Wallace St., San Diego, 619/220-5423.

DOWNTOWN SAN DIEGO

Until fairly recently San Diego was known as the city with no downtown, since even residents preferred to be anywhere but. All that has changed after more than two decades of serious redevelopment work that managed to preserve and polish, rather than destroy, what remained of the area's historic character. San Diego now has a lively, people-friendly downtown that segues quite neatly into the Embarcadero and the bay.

Downtown San Diego got its start in 1867, the day Alonzo Erastus Horton strolled off a sidewheel steamer onto the "New Town" wharf, at the foot of what is now 5th Street. Horton saw immediately that San Diego the city should be here, along the bay, not near the Old Town site chosen for security reasons by the Spanish. So Horton soon bought from the city 960 acres of "downtown" land for 27.5 cents an acre—a foolish outlay of $260 for jackrabbits, dust, and fleas, in the minds of lesser civic visionaries. The rest is downtown San Diego history.

EVENTFUL SAN DIEGO

With the sublime weather here, it's little wonder that so many San Diego events, among them open-air theater and street festivals, are staged outdoors. Unique or oddball local events can be the most fun, so while you're here ask around and study local newspapers. Museums, colleges, and universities also sponsor a variety of unusual activities.

Mid-December through mid-March is **whale-watching** season, when California gray whales make their northern migration. And in January, catch the **San Diego Marathon** as it winds 26.2 miles down the coast from Carlsbad. The ever-popular international **Festival of Animation,** staged in La Jolla at the Museum of Contemporary Art's Sherwood Auditorium, runs from mid-January through April; the *Sick and Twisted* short-subject collection is screened after midnight. Major San Diego spring events include the **Ocean Beach Kite Festival** in March; the **San Diego Crew Classic,** the **Downtown ArtWalk,** and the **Coronado Flower Show** in April; and the **Pacific Beach Block Party,** the Olympic-caliber **Del Mar National Horseshow,** and Old Town's **Cinco de Mayo** festivities in May.

In June, come for the **San Diego County Fair** at the fairgrounds in Del Mar, the **Mostly Mozart Festival** downtown in the Spreckels Theater, the annual **Ocean Beach Street Fair and Chili Cook-Off,** the **San Diego International Triathlon,** and the **Rock n' Roll Marathon.** Also in June, the **Twilight in the Park** summer concert series in Balboa Park begins, continuing through August. In July, the annual **San Diego Lesbian and Gay Pride Parade** is a huge draw, with a rally and festival well into the night. Also in July, **Sand Castle Days** at the Imperial Beach Pier is a big hit, fun in the sun along with serious competitive sand castle construction, along with the **Sizzling Summer Jazz Festival** on Coronado. The **Hillcrest Cityfest Street Fair** comes in August, along with the **Thundertub Regatta** at Mission Bay, part of America's Finest City Week festivities, and the immensely popular **San Diego Comic Convention** happens at the convention center. The convention pays homage to comic books, cartoon and comic art, and comic artists.

The biggest big deal in September is the Gaslamp Quarter's **Street Scene** fall food and music festival (sometimes scheduled in late August), while the **Adams Avenue Street Fair,** a right neighborly neighborhood block party, is much more laid-back. In October, when admission is free for children all month, **Zoo Founder's Day** makes a human zoo out of the San Diego Zoo. All kinds of Halloween fun—including the **Haunted Museum of Man** in Balboa Park, and an **Underwater Pumpkin Carving Contest** in La Jolla—round out the year's foremost month of fright. For animals on the march, head to El Cajon with kids in tow in November for the annual **Mother Goose Parade** or to the **Carlsbad Village Faire** in Carlsbad. Magical among the multitude of holiday events in December is **Christmas on El Prado** in Balboa Park and, along the bay downtown, the **San Diego Harbor Parade of Lights.**

DOWNTOWN SAN DIEGO

Balboa Park

SAN DIEGO ZOO

BALBOA PARK INN

TIMKEN MUSEUM OF ART

OLD GLOBE THEATER ★
★ SAN DIEGO MUSEUM OF ART

★ SAN DIEGO NATURAL HISTORY MUSEUM

★ REUBEN H. FLEET SPACE THEATER AND SCIENCE CENTER

CABRILLO BRIDGE

HOUSE OF CHARM

SAN DIEGO MUSEUM OF MAN

CASA DE BALBOA

SAN DIEGO AUTOMOTIVE MUSEUM

★ AEROSPACE MUSEUM

EMBARCADERO

LA PENSIONE

★ FIREHOUSE MUSEUM

LA PACIFICA HOTEL

MARITIME MUSEUM ★

HOLIDAY INN ON THE BAY

MUSEUM OF CONTEMPORARY ART

WESTGATE HOTEL

B ST. PIER

AMTRAK STATION

U.S. GRANT HOTEL

BROADWAY PIER

WYNDHAM EMERALD PLAZA

HORTON PLAZA

GASLAMP PLAZA SUITES

TUNA HARBOR

CHILDREN'S MUSEUM

EMBASSY SUITES

SEAPORT VILLAGE

HORTON GRAND HOTEL

HI-AYH METROPOLITAN HOSTEL

HYATT REGENCY SAN DIEGO

SAN DIEGO CONVENTION CENTER

VILLA MONTEZUMA/ JESSE SHEPARD HOUSE

Marina Park

San Diego Bay

Coronado

CORONADO TOLL BRIDGE

0   0.5 mi
0   0.5 km

© AVALON TRAVEL PUBLISHING, INC.

Horton Plaza rises out of old-fashioned downtown San Diego like a Mediterranean or Middle Eastern version of the Emerald City—a jumble of odd open-air plazas, tiled courtyards and fountains, sculptures, stairways, cupolas, and towers all splashed with bold colors and draped in fluttering banners. This architectural marvel, designed by Jon Jerde and presented to the world in 1985, is clearly not your run-of-the-mill shopping mall. Yet as a mall, anchored by Nordstrom, Macy's, Robinsons-May, and Mervyn's and stuffed to its ramparts with shops, restaurants, and movie theaters, it's a wild success. Particularly good reasons to start your downtown exploration here include the local visitor bureau's helpful **San Diego International Visitor Center,** at 11 Horton Plaza at the corner of 1st Ave. and F St., 619/236-1232; the **Horton Plaza Farmers' Market,** for uptown picnic fixings, good wines, and wonderful bakery goods; and the impressive **San Diego Repertory Theater Company,** with two stages here. Horton Plaza inhabits the entire downtown "block" between Broadway and G St. and 1st and 4th Avenues. Walk here or take the trolley or bus, if at all possible, since parking in the attached structures is often nonexistent. For more information, contact: Horton Plaza, 324 Horton Plaza, 619/238-1596 or toll-free 800/214-7467, www.horton-plaza.com.

Most of San Diego's venerable Victorian business buildings, constructed between the Civil War and World War I, are in the city's **Gaslamp Quarter,** the downtown area just east of Horton Plaza, between 4th and 6th Sts. and Broadway and L Street. Notorious for "nefarious activity" during decades of decline, the quarter has been undergoing a Renaissance of sorts—with historic hotels, new shops, art galleries, trendy restaurants, and nightclubs at the forefront of this particular downtown revival. To find out more, call the **Gaslamp Quarter Association,** 619/233-5227. For guided and self-guided historic tours, contact the **Gaslamp Quarter Foundation** headquarters, inside the William Heath Davis House at 410 Island (at 4th), 619/233-4692—the office is open weekdays 10 A.M.–4 P.M., Sat. 10 A.M.–4 P.M., Sun. noon–4 P.M.—or pick up a free brochure/map at area visitor information centers.

Other downtown draws include the **Children's Museum/Museo de los Niños of San Diego,** 200 W. Island Ave. (between Front and Union

Sts.), 619/233-5437, a seriously interactive educational funhouse open Tues.–Sun. 10 A.M.–4 P.M., closed Mon. and major holidays. Admission is $6 for adults and children age 3 and older, $3 for seniors. West of Horton Plaza, along Broadway at Kettner Dr., is the 1915 **Santa Fe Train Depot,** the city's Amtrak station these days, notably overshadowed by the 34-story **1 American Plaza** office tower. Part of the plaza is the downtown outpost of San Diego's **Museum of Contemporary Art,** 1001 Kettner Blvd. (at Broadway), 619/234-1001, www.mcasandiego.org, the museum's secondary locale housing part of the museum's 3,000 works. For more information on both museums, see La Jolla and Vicinity, below.

AROUND SAN DIEGO BAY

A superlative harbor, San Diego Bay begins at Point Loma, where Cabrillo stepped ashore. Its fairly narrow mouth is created by the "island" city of Coronado, which is connected to San Diego's South Bay area by a narrow isthmus of sand. This seemingly tenuous connection actually forms the long, protected bay.

Starting at Point Loma, major features along the bay's long inland curve include the **Cabrillo National Monument,** 1800 Cabrillo Memorial Dr. (the southern end of Cabrillo Memorial Dr., Hwy. 209), 619/557-5450, www.nps.gov/cabr, an impressive land's end complete with venerable lighthouse, whale-watching platform, excellent visitors center, bayside trails, even tidepools. Next come **Shelter Island** and **Harbor Island,** not natural islands but onetime shoals built into bayside real estate with the help of harbor dredging. Both are yachters' heavens, but Shelter Island's main claim to fame is as the harbor home of the America's Cup international sailing competitions, sponsored by the San Diego Yacht Club. Fronting San Diego Bay and increasingly integrated with most everyone's idea of "downtown" is the **Embarcadero,** a bayside walkway along Harbor Dr. that winds its way past an armada of vessels—some of them tour boats and cruise ships, others converted into gift shops and restaurants—and other harbor attractions.

Particularly noteworthy in the attractions category is the **San Diego Maritime Museum,** floating at the foot of Ash St., 1492 N. Harbor Dr.,

619/234-9153. Star of the show here is the three-masted *Star of India*—the oldest iron-hulled merchant ship still afloat, first launched from the Isle of Man in 1863 as the *Euterpe,* though the 1904 *Medea* and the 1898 ferry *Berkeley* are worth a peek. Admission is $6 adults ($12 for an entire family), $4 seniors and children ages 13–17, $2 children ages 6–12. About a half-mile south is the art deco **B Street Pier,** also known as the Cruise Ship Pier, local port for major cruise ship lines. Next south is the **Broadway Pier,** also known as the Excursion Pier, largely dedicated to sportfishing, whale-watching, and harbor tour companies. This is also the place to catch the San Diego–Coronado Ferry to Coronado Island.

Though San Diego's tuna fishing heyday is long gone, the next stop south is **Tuna Harbor,** headquarters for the American Tunaboat Association and also home to the very popular Fish Market restaurant and fresh-fish market. Navy ships may be tied up nearby; if so, on weekends they're usually open for tours.

Usually getting most of the neighborhood attention, though, is **Seaport Village,** a seafaring-themed shopping and restaurant development with turn-of-the-20th-century style. For children and nonshoppers, the best thing here goes 'round and 'round—the 1890 Looff Broadway Flying Horses Carousel, originally stabled at Coney Island. Worth a stroll nearby is the Embarcadero Marine Park North, a grassy public park angling out into the bay.

Seaport Village ends at the San Diego Marriott Hotel and Marina, though the walkway wanders on. The striking **San Diego Convention Center** at the foot of 5th, designed by Arthur Erickson and built by the Port of San Diego, is just beyond the hotel. With its fiberglass "sails" and wavelike walls, the convention center could only be confused with a choppy day at the America's Cup. South of the convention center is the Embarcadero Marina Park South and the stunning Coronado Bay Bridge. South of the bridge and east of I-5 begins the region's South Bay.

BEACH TOWNS AND BEACHES

Beyond downtown, starting north of Point Loma, are the oceanside communities of Ocean Beach, Mission Beach, and Pacific Beach. Still farther

Imperial Beach

ROBERT HOLMES/CALTOUR

north are the fairly exclusive and expensive communities of La Jolla and Del Mar, also included within San Diego's city limits.

Ocean Beach

Strung out along Sunset Cliffs Blvd. just north of Point Loma is Ocean Beach, "O.B." in locals' lingo. Just beyond the western end of the I-8 Fwy., Ocean Beach is San Diego's "farthest out" community—an unusual and unusually settled beach neighborhood with a hip (and hippie) history, an unusual collection of old-timers, surfers, young families, hipsters of all ages, and a smattering of ne'er-do-wells. To get a feel for the place, head for the **Ocean Beach Pier** (though beaches nearest the pier are sometimes unsavory) and stroll the **Newport Avenue** commercial district. Dog lovers, note that Ocean Beach's **Dog Beach** is one of only three in the county (along with Coronado and Del Mar) where canines can cavort sans leash. (Watch your step.) For more seclusion, head south to the cove beach at **Sunset Cliffs,** on the Point Loma peninsula—popular with locals and surfers, accessible at low tide and only via slippery sandstone pathways or from the stairways at the feet of Bermuda and Santa Cruz Avenues.

Mission Beach and Mission Bay

Next stop north, beyond the San Diego River, is Mission Beach—about 17 miles of ocean beach and boardwalk plus Mission Bay, onetime wetlands refashioned, in the 1960s, into a faux bay resort area with man-made beaches, hotels, motels, marinas, and condominiums. When passing through in 1542, Cabrillo himself called it a "false bay," since the outlet led straight into the swamp.

Inland, Mission Bay Park is largely "natural"— meaning, in this case, undeveloped—a park popular with San Diegans looking for open space and bracing saltwater breezes for jogging, walking, biking, kite-flying, and watersports. If you're interested in the view from the water but are without your own boat, get around via the **Harbor Hopper,** 858/488-2720, water taxi service or take a sunset cruise on the *Bahia Belle,* 858/488-0551, docked at the Bahia Hotel on West Mission Bay Drive.

Attractions along the ocean include both **South Mission** and **North Mission Beaches,** waterfront walkways, and grassy parks. The **Belmont Park** area, once an abandoned amusement park and boardwalk, now includes shops and shopping in addition to the historic **Giant Dipper** wooden roller coaster and equally venerable **The Plunge** swimming pool.

Sea World

People either love or hate Mission Bay's Sea World, an Anheuser-Busch entertainment park with an ocean animal theme. Those who love Sea World say it offers families the chance to see unusual or endangered sea life up close and personal, a positive experience that increases environmental awareness. Those who hate it point out that with friends such as these—and with an excellent aquarium just north, in La Jolla, not to mention San Diego County's exceptional zoos—the beleaguered and endangered creatures of the sea hardly need enemies.

The traditional star performers of the Sea World show, here and elsewhere, are **Shamu** the killer whale and **Baby Shamu,** actually stage names for a half-dozen or more individual whales. The aforementioned **Shamu Backstage** encounter is adjacent to Shamu Stadium; visitors view the whales through a 70-foot window in the 1.7 million gallon pool while waiting in line to touch them. And if that's not enough Shamu to-do, the kids can pose for pictures with an ersatz Shamu and Baby Shamu in two-acre **Shamu's Happy Harbor,** an active—and interactive— playground.

Increasingly, "encounter" and "interactive" are the watchwords at Sea World, because more than anything else, people want to touch—or almost touch—animals they would never see, even at a distance, in real life.

There's more to see and do at Sea World, open daily from at least 10 A.M. to dusk, from 9

Sea World

A.M. in summer (call for current summer schedule). As you might expect, the experience is expensive, with admission $40 adults, $30 children ages 3–11, plus food, high-priced mementos, and parking ($4 motorcycles, $7 cars, and $9 RVs). Behind-the-scenes tours, in addition to other educational activities and the dolphin interaction program, are available by arrangement. For more information, contact: Sea World, 1720 S. Shores Rd. in Mission Bay, 619/226-3901 for recorded information or 619/226-3815.

Pacific Beach
Hippest of all local beach towns these days is Pacific Beach or "P.B." in the local vernacular, where surf, surfers, skates, skaters, hip shops and just hangin' out define local culture. Most of the action is at the beach, at the **Lahaina Beach House** at 710 Oliver, 858/270-3888, at **Garnet Street** shops, and, after dark, at the **Society Billiard Café,** 1051 Garnet Ave., 858/272-7665, Unique here is the **Crystal Pier,** the only pier in California to include a hotel. Social historians and surf scene voyeurs can visit **Tourmaline Surfing Park** (Tourmaline St. at La Jolla Blvd.), the only stretch of local coastline dedicated exclusively to worshipers of the next wave, however grizzled they may be.

LA JOLLA AND VICINITY: SEASIDE SOPHISTICATION

Along the coast just north of Pacific Beach is the village of La Jolla, seven miles of sublime coastline that serves as San Diego's answer to the Riviera—a sophisticated red-tile-roofed Mediterranean image local commerce cultivates quite profitably, and one that attracts old-money minions as well as movie stars.

La Jolla (La HOY-yah, though people here say, simply, "the Village") means "jewel" in Spanish, or, according to local Native American tradition, "hole" or "cave." Both meanings are fitting. Hammered for eons by the relentless surf, the coastal bluffs beneath La Jolla's dazzling real estate are laced with caves, large and small, some explorable by land, some by sea. Other natural attractions are local beaches—including the infamous Windansea Beach, the top-notch but highly territorial surf scene described by Tom Wolfe in *The Pump House Gang*—and area

parks, including Torrey Pines State Reserve, sanctuary for about 6,000 very rare pine trees.

Not rare, however, is the human imperative to see, be seen, and make the scene—these, as well as shopping, are major pastimes in and around La Jolla's upmarket downtown. Any and all downtown adventures are best undertaken on foot, since finding a place to park can be all but impossible.

For more information about La Jolla, and for friendly practical assistance from the volunteer staff, contact the **La Jolla Town Council,** 7734 Herschel, La Jolla, 858/454-1444. Since La Jolla is technically part of the city of San Diego, information is also available from the International Visitor Information Center at Horton Plaza in downtown San Diego, 619/236-1232.

Seeing and Doing La Jolla
Primary location of San Diego's **Museum of Contemporary Art,** 700 Prospect, 858/454-3541, www.mcsandiego.org, this 1915 Irving Gill original

THE SCRIPPS LEGACY

Ellen Browning Scripps was half-sister of newspaper publisher Edward Wyllis Scripps, founder of the United Press (UP) newspaper syndicate. A respected journalist too, Ellen Browning Scripps also made millions in real estate—good fortune she shared with Southern California by founding Scripps College in Claremont and by endowing, with her brother, the Scripps Institution of Oceanography in La Jolla. Part of the genteel community of artists, writers, scientists, and just plain wealthy people that settled La Jolla at the turn of the 20th century, she was also a patron of architecture—in particular local architect Irving J. Gill, who designed her 1915 home, now San Diego's Museum of Contemporary Art, and various public buildings here.

In a sense the Scripps family's philanthropic contributions to the community set the stage for present-day La Jolla's cultural influence, with its renowned Salk Institute and the sprawling University of California at San Diego, which now includes the Scripps Institution of Oceanography, the Scripps-affiliated Stephen Birch Aquarium-Museum, and the nationally recognized La Jolla Playhouse theater program.

was once home to Ellen Browning Scripps. Traveling exhibits tend toward the provocative and cutting edge, as do shows from the post-1950s permanent collection. (Call for current program information.) A smaller museum branch in downtown San Diego, on Kettner Blvd. at Broadway, 619/234-1001, is also well worth a stop. Both museums are open Tues.–Sat. 10 A.M.–5 P.M., Sun. noon–5 P.M., closed Thanksgiving, Christmas, and New Year's Day. The La Jolla museum is also open Wed. night until 8 P.M. Admission is $4 for adults, $2 for seniors (ages 65 and older), military, and students (ages 12–18), and free for children under age 12. Both museums are free on the first Tues. and Sun. of every month.

The **Birch Aquarium at Scripps,** 2300 Expedition Way, 858/534-3474, www.aquarium.ucsd.edu, is the public information center for the University of California's renowned Scripps Institution of Oceanography. Exhibits include a replica of Scripps Canyon, the underwater valley just off the La Jolla coast, and an abundance of re-created marine habitats—a kelp forest, for example, and aquatic homes for creatures such as the bioluminescent "flashlight fish"—as well as displays on oceanography as science. Kids love the simulated submarine dive. The museum is open daily 9 A.M.–5 P.M. (last admission at 4:30 P.M.), closed on Thanksgiving and Christmas. Admission is $8.50 for adults, $7.50 for seniors (age 60 and older), $6 students, $5 for kids (ages 3–17). Parking is $3.

The Tony Award–winning **La Jolla Playhouse,** 2910 La Jolla Village Dr., 858/550-1010, was founded in 1947 by Gregory Peck and like-minded theater buffs. By producing original musicals and plays that subsequently made a name for themselves, such as *Big River, A Walk in the Woods,* The Who's *Tommy,* and various Neil Simon works, the La Jolla Playhouse has established itself in the past decades as one of the most innovative regional theaters in the country. The theater's performance season runs from May through October. Admission varies, but tickets are typically in the $25–40 range. For current program information, call 858/550-1010, or visit the playhouse website at www.lajollaplayhouse.com.

Seeing and Doing Natural La Jolla

La Jolla's aqua-blue ocean and adjacent beaches are beautiful but unbelievably popular. If personal space and peace are on your agenda, you won't find either here. Instead, head north along the coast. Nonetheless, one of La Jolla's jewels is **Ellen Browning Scripps Park** overlooking La Jolla Cove, a palm-lined promenade where everyone goes to see the sea scene (and be seen). Even children regularly dip into the Scripps legacy; a wonderful local diversion is the **Children's Pool** at the park's south end, with shallow waters and a curved beach protected by a seawall. In recent years, sea lions basking on **Shell Beach** just to the north have provided free entertainment.

South toward Pacific Beach is San Diego's surfing paradise, an area including mythic **Windansea Beach** and **Tourmaline Surfing Park.**

North from Children's Pool, starting offshore just south of Point La Jolla, is the **San Diego–La Jolla Underwater Park.** Most popular for skin diving and snorkeling is northern **La Jolla Cove.** Lining La Jolla Bay north of the cove are the town's famed **La Jolla Caves** (small admission), some of them accessible by a stairway starting at the La Jolla Cave and Shell Shop on Coast Boulevard. The best **tidepools** around are along the coast north of the Scripps Pier at the Scripps Institution of Oceanography on La Jolla Shores Dr., the former site of the Scripps aquarium. **La Jolla Shores beaches,** including those below residential areas, are among the best for swimming and sunbathing, along with Torrey Pines State Beach and Del Mar Beach farther north. Between La Jolla Shores and Torrey Pines is an almost inaccessible, unauthorized nude beach known as **Black's Beach,** best reached from Torrey Pines at low tide.

Torrey Pines State Reserve and Beach tells the story of endangered species that doesn't star human beings as the culprits. Protected in this small preserve are about 10,000 Torrey pines *(Pinus torreyana).* The rarest pine trees in the United States, these beautifully primeval, strange, and scraggly five-needle pines represent an Ice Age species endangered by too-specific climatic and soil needs. Get oriented at the attractive 1923 adobe-style visitors center, once a private lodge. Short and easy hiking trails wind through the semi-desert forests. Below the heavily eroded bluffs is **Torrey Pines State Beach,** one of the most beautiful in San Diego County. Adjacent, technically in Del Mar, is **Los Penasquitos Lagoon,** wetlands that serve as wildlife refuge and bird sanctuary, an area almost destroyed in the 1960s by the construction of the Pacific Coast Highway route here. Torrey Pines is north of La Jolla Village, just off N. Torrey Pines Road. To reach the preserve from I-5, exit at Genesee Ave. and head west. Turn north (right) onto N. Torrey Pines Road. To reach the beach from I-5, exit at Carmel Valley Rd. and head west. One parking lot is near the beach, another near the preserve's visitors center. Admission is free, but parking is $2 with a $1 discount for seniors. The beach is open daily, 8 A.M. to sunset; the visitor center is open 9 A.M. to sunset. For more information, contact Torrey Pines State Reserve and Beach, 858/755-2063, www.torreypine.org.

Del Mar: Where the Turf Meets the Surf
For Del Mar's surf, head for **Del Mar Beach.** To watch the sunset, locals and visitors alike gather up top, on the bluffs at the end of 15th Street. For Del Mar's turf, head to the fairgrounds. Del Mar is most famous for its elegant art deco Spanish colonial **Del Mar Race Track,** "Where the Turf Meets the Surf." Recently reconstructed, the track is the place for some serious thoroughbred racing from late July into mid-September. The show here has always been something of a star-studded affair. The Del Mar Thoroughbred Club was organized in the 1930s by entertainer Bing Crosby and some of his cronies, because Crosby wanted some of the glitz and glitter of glamour racing close to his home in Rancho Santa Fe. Admission to the Del Mar Race Track, 2260 Jimmy Durante Blvd. (Via de la Valle Rd. at Coast Blvd.), is $4 ($7 for grandstand seats). For more information, call 619/755-1141, or tap into current info via the Internet at www.dmtc.com.

CORONADO: CROWN OF THE BAY

Across from San Diego's Embarcadero is Coronado, an "island" connected to the mainland only by a sandy isthmus and by a sky-skimming arched bridge. A separate city reached from downtown San Diego either by ferry or via the San Diego–Coronado Bay Bridge, Coronado boasts the North Island U.S. Naval Air Station—Charles Lindbergh's departure point for his fa-

mous round-the-world flight—and, on the east, the U.S. Naval Amphibious Base, home for the elite Navy SEALS.

Not too surprisingly, the military has, in a sense, created the community here, a culture that revolves around the sound and fury of naval air technology and the needs and interests of retired naval officers and their families. Well-heeled tourists and celebrities are also well attended on Coronado, however, and have been for over a century. The local roll-call of fame includes Charles Lindbergh, the Duke and Duchess of Windsor, 14 U.S. presidents, and a dizzying number of stars from both the stage and the silver screen. The list also includes Frank Baum, who wrote *The Wizard of Oz* while living here. **The Wizard of Oz House** still stands, at 1101 Star Park Circle.

Getting around Coronado is fun (except on particularly hectic weekends), thanks to its walkable streets lined with trees and bungalows, its paved bike paths, and the **Coronado 904 Shuttle,** 619/233-3004, $1 fare. Getting to Coronado is even more fun, especially if you take the **Bay Ferry** from the Broadway Pier in San Diego to Coronado's Ferry Landing at 1st and B Streets. Ferries leave San Diego every hour on the hour 9 A.M.–9 P.M. Sun.–Thurs. (until 10 on weekend nights), and return from Coronado every hour on the half-hour, 9:30 A.M.–9:30 P.M. Sun.–Thurs. (until 10:30 P.M. on weekend nights). Ferry fare is $2 (pedestrians and bicyclists only), $.50 extra if you BYOB (bring your own bike). **San Diego Harbor Excursion water taxi,** 619/235-8294, travels to Ferry Landing Marketplace, the Hotel Del, and the Coronado Island Marriott from Seaport Village on the mainland.

It's also fairly exciting to drive over—like riding a rainbow, gliding up and then over the soaring arch of the **San Diego–Coronado Bay Bridge** (Hwy. 75). The toll is $1 heading into Coronado—free with two or more people in the car—and free returning to the mainland.

For more information about Coronado, contact the very helpful **Coronado Visitor Information** office, 1047 B Ave., Coronado, CA 92118, 619/437-8788, www.coronado.ca.us.

Seeing and Doing Coronado
Coronado's spectacular white-sand beaches are almost as revered as the Hotel Del. Just

HOTEL DEL:
THE VICTORIAN HEART OF LOCAL HISTORY

Coronado Island's historic centerpiece is the astonishing Hotel del Coronado—known affectionately as the "Hotel Del" or, simply, "the Del"—one of California's grand old hotels, built in 1888, a national historic landmark. When it opened, this sprawling barn-red-and-white Victorian, with its wood shingles, turrets, and cupolas, was the largest structure outside New York City to be lighted with electricity. (Thomas Edison himself officiated at the switch-on ceremony for the hotel's first Christmas tree.) Among other movies, the 1959 comedy *Some Like It Hot,* starring Tony Curtis, Jack Lemmon, and Marilyn Monroe, was filmed at the Hotel Del. Meander through the lobby and along dark-wood downstairs corridors, where photographs and other mementos tell the hotel's story, and stroll the gorgeous grounds. Fairly recent additions include the Craftsman-style **Duchess of Windsor Cottage.** Now a meeting hall, the cottage was onetime Coronado home of Wallis Warfield Spencer—the Duchess of Windsor after King Edward abdicated the English throne to marry her.

Guided tours of the Hotel del Coronado, at last report $10 per person, were being offered again starting in June 2000, following the hotel's $50 million restoration of its grand centerpiece, the Victorian building. Call the hotel at 619/435-6611, or try www.hoteldel.com, for details and reservations.

For the entire Coronado story, stop by the free **Coronado Historical Museum** on Loma Ave., 619/435-7242, open Wed.–Sat. 10 A.M.–4 P.M. and Sun. noon–4 P.M.

ROBERT HOLMES/CALTOUR

oceanward from the hotel is unbelievably broad **Coronado Beach,** typically uncrowded even in summer, since locals prefer beaches just north and south. On the island's bay side are several smaller, more protected beaches. **Silver Strand State Beach** extends the entire length of Coronado's sandy isthmus, with beaches on both sides of Silver Strand Blvd. (Hwy. 75), from near Hotel del Coronado to Imperial Beach. This popular family beach, great for swimming, was named for the small silver sea shells washed up along the shoreline.

Coronado's other present-day pleasures include sun, sand, sailing, windsurfing, 15 miles of shoreline bike paths—you can ride all the way to Imperial Beach—and specialty shopping along downtown Coronado's revitalized **Orange Avenue** and at the Seaport Village–like **Ferry Landing Marketplace.** In addition to its city pool, its 130-acre municipal golf course, its 18 parks, and its 18 public tennis courts, Coronado offers other diversions. **Gondola Cruises,** 619/429-6317, shoves off from the Loews Resort on Venetian-style tours of the Coronado Cays canals. Three-hour guided **Navy base tours** of North Island Naval Air Station are offered on Fri. by Old Town Trolley Tours, 619/298-8687. Or take a **Coronado Walking Tour,** 619/435-5892 or 619/435-5993. And you can always see what's playing at the **Coronado Playhouse** on Strand Way, 619/435-4856, or the **Lamb's Players Theatre** on Orange Ave., 619/437-0600.

STAYING IN SAN DIEGO

A pleasant surprise in San Diego is the range of surprisingly decent accommodation options, from dirt cheap to definitely expensive. You'd expect to find upscale hotels, inns, and resorts along the coast, downtown, and elsewhere. But the surprise is that prime visitor areas also feature hostels, very inexpensive hotels, and reasonably priced, pleasant motels. (For major deals—savings as much as 50 percent, in some cases—consider booking even resort accommodations through **San Diego Hotel Reservations,** toll-free 800/728-3227.) The following suggestions are arranged by general locale. For more choices, contact the local visitors bureau (see Practical San Diego, below). For bed-and-breakfast listings, contact the **Bed & Breakfast Guild of San Diego,** 619/523-1300, or the countywide **Bed & Breakfast Directory for San Diego,** 619/297-3130 or toll-free 800/619-7666.

While making travel plans, be aware of the city's all-out conventioneering—and be flexible about trip timing, if at all possible. San Diego's success at attracting major conventions and staging major events is great for the hotel business but bad news for savvy travelers suddenly unable to get a bargain rate.

STAYING IN AND AROUND OLD TOWN

In Old Town

Old Town San Diego offers some of the best lodging bargains around, including the all-suites **Best Western Hacienda Hotel Old Town.** Once a mission-style minimall, it's now a multilevel hillside motel—a quite clever renovation albeit a bit baffling at first, with multiple patios, passageways, stairways, terraces, and elevators to navigate. Wheelchair-accessible rooms are reached via elevators. Most rooms are smallish but quite adequate, with all the usual amenities plus ceiling fans, in-room coffeemakers, microwaves, and refrigerators. Great harbor views at night, especially from upper levels. Premium-Luxury. Rates are $145 and up in summer. The Hacienda Hotel Old Town is at 4041 Harney St.

(just off Juan), toll-free 800/888-1991 or 619/298-4707, www.bestwestern.com.

Depending on when you're coming—weekdays are usually the best deal any time but summer—other relative bargains in the neighborhood include the **Holiday Inn Hotel Old Town,** $118–189, right next to the freeway at 2435 Jefferson St. (exit I-5 at Old Town Ave.), toll-free 800/433-2131 or 619/260-8500; and the **Ramada Limited Old Town,** 3900 Old Town Ave., toll-free 800/451-9846 or 619/299-7400, where rooms ($129–159) include continental breakfast. Both are Premium-Luxury.

For a quick trip into Victorian San Diego, stay at the gracious two-story **Heritage Park Bed & Breakfast Inn,** the star of Heritage Park just above Old Town, 2470 Heritage Park Row, 619/299-6832, www.heritageparkinn.com. Eight rooms (some share a bath) and one suite make this 1889 Queen Anne most accommodating. Expensive-Luxury, with rates $100–235 (include breakfast and refreshments), with a two-night minimum on weekends; weekly and monthly rates are available. No smoking, no children under age 14.

Staying near Old Town:
Hotel Circle and Mission Valley

"Hotel Circle" refers to the low-priced and midrange motels that flank I-8 between Old Town and Mission Valley—not a bad location given the instant freeway access, assuming you have a car and don't mind doing the freeways to get around.

ACCOMMODATIONS RATINGS

Accommodations in this book are rated by price category, based on double-occupancy, high-season rates. Categories used are:

Budget.	$35 and under
Inexpensive	$35-60
Moderate	$60-85
Expensive	$85-110
Premium	$110-150
Luxury	$150 and up

downtown San Diego

Among the cheaper choices in the neighborhood is good old **Motel 6 Hotel Circle,** 2424 Hotel Circle N, 619/296-1612, or, for reservations at any Motel 6 nationwide, toll-free 800/466-8356, www.motel6.com. This one features a swimming pool and the usual basics for $45.99 and up. Inexpensive. A remarkable value for sporting types is the 20-acre **Quality Resort Mission Valley,** 875 Hotel Circle S, toll-free 800/362-7871 or 619/298-8281, www.qualityresort.com. Try to land a room away from the freeway noise, and then plunge into any of the three swimming pools (one's heated) or head to the adjacent tennis, racquetball, and health club facilities. Expensive-Luxury. Rooms here start at $99 in summer.

If you can't yet swing that trip to Hawaii, consider a stay at the very pleasant **Hanalei Hotel,** 2270 Hotel Circle N, toll-free 800/882-0858 or 619/297-1101, www.hanaleihotel.com, one of San Diego's Polynesian-themed sleep palaces. Since Hanalei is Hawaiian for "valley of the flowers," the lush tropical foliage fits—as do the extravagant summertime luaus staged in the courtyard and the appealing pool area. Premium-Luxury. Room rates start at $129 in summer, and $109 in the off-season.

STAYING IN AND AROUND DOWNTOWN

U. S. Grant Hotel

Downtown's most dignified and time-honored presence, the landmark U. S. Grant Hotel was built in 1910 by Ulysses S. Grant, Jr., son of the former Civil War general and U.S. president. After decades of decline mid-century, the 11-story U. S. Grant reopened in 1985 after an impressive $80 million renovation. Regular rooms are somewhat small but tastefully done in Queen Anne–style mahogany, even the armoire hiding the TV (cable provided; movies available). Luxury. Official room rates are $185–205 and up, but ask about off-season specials and packages. One of downtown's best restaurants is the **Grant Grill** here, 619/239-6806, surprisingly reasonable, serving breakfast, lunch, and dinner. Other facilities include exercise room (massage extra), business center, and conference rooms. The U. S. Grant, downtown at 326 Broadway, inhabits an entire city block. For more information, call 619/232-3121, or check www.grandheritage.com. For reservations, call toll-free 800/237-5029.

More Uptown Downtown Hotels

The 19-story **Westgate Hotel** is a classic modern American study in contrast—in this case, the contrast between somewhat formal Old World luxury and the ubiquitous, thoroughly modern downtown high-rise in which it hides. The theme of classical opulence continues through on-site restaurants and into the antique-furnished guest rooms, where bathrooms come with Italian marble and gold-plated fixtures. Luxury. Rates run $184–224, with considerable price flexibility; weekends are usually the best deal, with $150 the typical rate. The Westgate is at 1055 2nd Ave. (at C St.), 619/238-1818, fax

619/557-3737. For reservations, call toll-free 800/221-3802.

If you prefer more contemporary big-hotel ambience with the usual amenities plus an indoor pool and gym, another good choice downtown is the contemporary **Embassy Suites,** 601 Pacific Hwy. (at N. Harbor Dr.), 619/239-2400 or toll-free 800/EMBASSY. This is a better set-up for families, too, since all suites feature a separate bedroom plus conveniences like refrigerators, hairdryers, coffeemakers, and microwaves. All rooms have city or bay views. Full breakfast, as you like it (served in the restaurant), is included, along with free cocktails. Luxury. Rates run $189–300, with various discounts and specials often available.

The **Wyndham Emerald Plaza,** formerly the Pan Pacific Hotel, also caters to the business trade, but with swimming pool, full fitness facilities, and abundant other extras, it's quite comfortable for tourists who prefer a downtown base. Luxury. Rates are generally lowest on the weekend, too, sometimes starting at $129; ask about other discounts and specials. The Wyndham Emerald Plaza is at the Emerald Shapery Center (between Columbia and State), 400 W. Broadway, 619/239-4500, www.wyndham.com. For reservations, call toll-free 800/996-3426.

Horton Grand Hotel

A notable downtown presence is the genteel Horton Grand Hotel in the Gaslamp Quarter, on Island St. between 3rd and 4th. The ambience here is historic yet new, a neat trick achieved by building what amounts to a new hotel from the old-brick bones of two time-honored neighborhood hotels otherwise doomed by redevelopment. Rooms here are cozy, in the Victorian style, with neat touches such as gas fireplaces and TV sets cleverly tucked into the wall (behind a mirror). Premium-Luxury. Rates run $139–219, with various discounts and special packages often available. For more information, contact: Horton Grand Hotel, 311 Island Ave., 619/544-1886 or toll-free 800/542-1886, www.hortongrand.com.

Downtown Area Bed-and-Breakfasts

The friendly **Balboa Park Inn,** right across the street from Balboa Park, is a stylistic complement to the park's 1915 exposition architecture. All rooms at the inn—actually, four Spanish colonial homes interconnected by courtyards—are tasteful yet simple suites with either one or two bedrooms. Amenities vary (as does room decor) but include kitchens, fireplaces, patios, in-room whirlpools, and wet bars. The inn is on the north end of Balboa Park, and you can walk to park attractions. Expensive-Luxury. Rates start at $95 per night. For more information, contact: Balboa Park Inn, 3402 Park Blvd., 619/298-0823 or toll-free 800/938-8181, www.balboaparkinn.com.

Though a summertime stay often requires considerable advance booking, another great deal is the impeccably restored 1913 **Gaslamp Plaza Suites** just a block from Horton Plaza at 520 E St. (corner of 5th Ave.), 619/232-9500 or toll-free 800/874-8770, a time-share condo that also rents out rooms as available. The building itself, with a lovely lobby chiseled from marble and mosaic tiles, is San Diego's first high-rise, circa 1913, and listed on the National Register of Historic Places. The suites—larger ones feature a separate bedroom—are attractive, with various amenities, some including microwaves, refrigerators, coffeemakers, color TV, the works. Expensive-Luxury. Rates range from $93–200, depending on room size and amenities, and include continental breakfast—served on the roof, weather permitting. The view is free.

Best Downtown Bets on a Budget

A comfortable downtown budget hotel, on India St. at Date, residential-style **La Pensione** is contemporary and clean. Especially appealing if you'll be staying awhile—the general ambience here, plus on-site laundry, make that an attractive idea—each cozy room (two people maximum) features a private bath, a kitchenette with microwave and refrigerator, and adequate space for spreading out work projects or tourist brochures. Moderate. Daily rates are $60–80, single or double. Ask about weekly and monthly rates. For more information, contact: La Pensione, 1700 India St., 619/236-8000, www.lapensionehotel.com. For reservations, call toll-free 800/232-4683.

La Pacifica Hotel is another San Diego find—a well-located residential hotel with style, grace, and great rates (daily, weekly, monthly). This gem has a similar setup to La Pensione—private baths, kitchenettes with microwaves and refrigerators, telephone, color TV with cable.

Some rooms even have a harbor view. Other pluses: daily maid service, on-site laundry, bicycle storage, and nearby public parking. Moderate. In summer, rates start at $60 per day. La Pacifica is downtown on 2nd Ave., between Beech and Cedar. For more information, contact: La Pacifica Hotel, 1546 2nd Ave., 619/236-9292.

Definitely a bargain—one of those places where you'll find a bed even when conventioneers have taken every other place in town—is the landmark **Embassy Hotel** just north of Balboa Park at 3645 Park Blvd., 619/296-3141, these days primarily a residential home for the elderly. Inexpensive. Rooms, $54 per night, are fairly basic but quiet and roomy, with private bathrooms and in-room phones. Free laundry facilities. You can even eat with the residents, in the decent cafeteria-style dining room.

HI-AYH Metropolitan Hostel

The Metropolitan Hostel replaces downtown's Hostel on Broadway. On the corner of 5th Ave. and Market in the heart of the Gaslamp Quarter, the fully renovated Metropolitan features private and dorm rooms, a laundry, lockers, common kitchen, pool table, and rental bikes. Rates are $17–19 per person. For more information, contact: HI-AYH Metropolitan Hostel, 521 Market St., 619/525-1531, www.hiayh.org. Groups welcome. Children (under age 18) are welcome if accompanied by an adult. Reservations are essential in summer (through September). The office is open daily 7 A.M.–midnight.

BY THE BAY AND ALONG THE COAST

Near the Embarcadero

Downtown yet on the bay, adjacent to Seaport Village and a stone's throw from the convention center, is the stylish sky-high **Hyatt Regency San Diego** just off Harbor Dr., particularly popular with businessfolk and conventioneers—definitely a great choice if someone else is picking up the tab. Luxury. Regular room rates are $245–290, often lower on weekends. For more information, contact: Hyatt Regency San Diego, One Market Place (at Harbor Dr.), San Diego, 619/232-1234. For reservations, call toll-free 800/233-1234.

Also along the Embarcadero and almost affordable is the **Holiday Inn on the Bay,** 1355 N. Harbor Dr. (at Ash), 619/232-3861 or toll-free 800/465-4329, with large rooms and all the usual amenities. Premium-Luxury. Regular rates run $139–199, but inquire about off-season rates and other specials.

Shelter Island, Harbor Island, and Vicinity

Attractive Hawaii-like tropical landscape and the endless "tiki" on parade is the real appeal of **Humphrey's Half Moon Inn** on Shelter Island, making for comfortable California coastal kitsch complete with in-room refrigerators and coffeemakers. In the midst of San Diego's bustling boat harbor, Humphrey's provides a private boat dock, huge heated pool, and whirlpool spa; for

Stay minutes from the beach.

TOM MYERS PHOTOGRAPHY

tooling around, rental bikes are available; special events, such as the great outdoor jazz, folk, and easy-rock concerts in summer, keep everyone coming back. (For cool jazz—indoors—during the rest of the year, show up on Sun. and Mon. nights.) Luxury. High-season rates start at $169 or $179 depending on the view, with a two-night minimum on weekends from Memorial Day through Labor Day. For more information, contact: Humphrey's Half Moon Inn and Suites, 2303 Shelter Island Dr., 619/224-3411 or toll-free 800/345-9995, www.halfmooninn.com.

To spend substantially more, head for Harbor Island and the **Sheraton San Diego Hotel and Marina,** 1380 Harbor Island Dr., 619/291-2900 or toll-free 800/325-3535, www.sheraton.com, originally two separate Sheraton hotels, all recently redone and refashioned into one. Ongoing shuttle bus service connects the two high-rise towers, lower buildings, and various services and programs. Luxury. Regular rates start at $200.

Along the Coast and Mission Bay

Mission Beach, Mission Bay, and Pacific Beach are filled to the gills with resorts and large hotels, many quite pricey and, in summer, overrun by fellow travelers. But the coastal areas also offer some nice midrange motel-style stays; a motel sitting literally above the surf, on a pier; and several hostels. For more on inexpensive hostel stays, see below.

Mission Bay's classic family getaway is the lush and lovely **San Diego Paradise Point Resort,** a 44-acre island formerly the Princess Resort owned by Princess Cruises. The endless recreation here is the real draw—including paddleboats, water sports, five swimming pools, croquet, and volleyball. Rent bikes and cruise over to the beach, an easy few miles away, with or without the kids; in summer, the organized kids' program gives grown-ups a break, too. Luxury. Rates run $245–290 in summer. For more information, contact: San Diego Paradise Point Resort, 1404 W. Vacation Rd., 858/274-4630 or toll-free 800/344-2626, www.noble-househotels.com. Also on the upscale end of family-style fun is the 18-acre **San Diego Hilton Beach and Tennis Resort,** 1775 E. Mission Bay Dr., 619/276-4010 or toll-free 800/445-8667, www.hilton.com, offering both bungalows and high-rise rooms recently redone in modern mis-

sion style. Luxury. Summer rates are $205–335.

One of the best values around is the **Bahia Resort Hotel,** 998 W. Mission Bay Dr., 858/488-0551 or toll-free 800/576-4229, www.bahiahotel.com, semi-tropical and attractive, right across the street from a grassy park area and just a stroll from the beach. A bay beach and marina, where the paddle wheeler *Bahia Belle* is berthed (bay cruises, even dinner cruises, available), augment the backyard view from some rooms. Premium-Luxury. Rates are $129 and up, often discounted on a space-available basis. Also reasonable—and a reasonably good family setup, since some rooms feature kitchens or kitchenettes—is the very nice **Pacific Shores Inn** in Pacific Beach at 4802 Mission Blvd., toll-free 800/826-0715 (reservations only) or 858/483-6300, just 100 feet from the broad sandy beach. All rooms have HBO, some have kitchenettes, and continental breakfast is included. Premium-Luxury. Rates run $144–179, lower in the off-season.

The *classic* Pacific Beach stay, though, is right in the middle of the local action—out on the Crystal Pier, at the landmark 1930s **Crystal Pier Hotel,** 4500 Ocean Blvd., 858/483-6983 or toll-free 800/748-5894, actually a pier-long collection of motel-style cottages. The Crystal Pier Hotel features 26 white-and-blue cottages with kitchenettes and surf-view patios—nothing fancy but unique and immensely popular, a fact reflected in the price. Premium-Luxury, with rates $145–305. Make reservations well in advance for summer (three-day minimum stay in summer, two-night otherwise). Weekly and monthly rates are available in the off-season.

Budget-Travel Bonanza:
Three Coastal Hostels

Most surprisingly, San Diego boasts three hostels at, or very near, the beach. Bright yellow **Beach Banana Bungalow San Diego** is right at the beach—on Reed Ave. at Mission Blvd.—and right in the middle of the way-cool, way-young Pacific Beach scene. Accommodations are dormitory style, with four to eight beds per room. Budget. Rates run $16 for dormitory rooms, $20 for semi-private rooms. Breakfast and sand volleyball are included; laundry facilities and storage lockers are available. No reservations; show up by 11 A.M. to grab a bed. For more information, contact: Beach Banana Bungalow San Diego,

707 Reed Ave., 858/273-3060 or toll-free 800/546-7835, www.bananabungalow.com.

The newest place around is also the oldest—the 80-bed **Ocean Beach International Backpacker Hostel,** at home in the historic Hotel Newport in Ocean Beach, on Newport Ave. between Cable and Bacon just one block from the beach. Budget. Small but private "couples rooms," with two beds and a bathroom, cost $17–19. Most rooms are semi-private with four or six beds per room; most of these also have private bathrooms. (More bathrooms are in the hallways.) Rates are $15 per person semi-private, $17 private—including pastries for breakfast. For more information, contact: Ocean Beach International Backpacker Hostel, 4961 Newport Ave., 619/223-7873 or toll-free 800/339-7263, e-mail obihostel@aol.com.

The HI-AYH **Point Loma/Elliott Hostel,** is in a pleasant Point Loma residential neighborhood—close to the ocean but not particularly close to San Diego's other attractions. Yet this 60-bed hostel, on Udall St., off Voltaire between Warden and Poinsettia, is a reasonably good base for wanderings farther afield. Draws include full kitchen, a travel library, and baggage storage. The basic dormitory rate is $17 for nonmembers, $14 for members. Family rooms are also available. (Children under age 18 are welcome if accompanied by an adult.) Office hours are 8–11 A.M. and 5:30–11 P.M. For more information, contact: Point Loma/Elliott HI-AYH Hostel, 3790 Udall St., 619/223-4778, www.hiayh.org.

STAYING IN LA JOLLA AND DEL MAR

Affordable in La Jolla

As you'd guess in such exclusive neighborhoods, life can get quite pricey in La Jolla and adjacent Del Mar. Because parking space is also a local luxury, many establishments charge extra for parking; be sure to inquire. **La Jolla Town Council** volunteers, 858/454-1444, can be very helpful if you'd like some personal assistance in making local lodging arrangements.

Low-rent accommodations don't exist in and around upscale, conservative La Jolla. Quite decent midrange motels are available, however, including the **Holiday Inn Express** (previously the La Jolla Palms), 6705 La Jolla Blvd., 858/454-

7101 or toll-free 800/451-0358. About five long blocks south of downtown, an easy 20-minute walk, and close to world-famous "locals only" Windansea Beach, the Holiday Inn features large rooms, recently renovated, with all the basics plus a few extras, such as in-room coffeemakers, color TV, cable, and free movies. Some rooms here have full kitchens. Expensive-Luxury, with rates $89–149.

Nothing fancy, **La Jolla Cove Suites** is stylin' it circa the 1950s but still a sweet deal. Quite well-situated—right across the street from La Jolla Cove, as advertised—here you'll get the same views as the very rich at a much more reasonable price. You'll also get a full kitchen, so you can eat in anytime you want. Luxury. Rates run $165 and up in the summer, otherwise $125 and up. Find La Jolla Cove Suites at 1150 Coast Blvd., 858/459-2621 or toll-free 800/248-2683, www.lajollacove.com. And if there's no room here, there may be space at the **Shell Beach Apartment Motel,** 981 Coast Blvd., run by the same folks.

Usually more expensive but another great deal is the smoke-free **Prospect Park Inn,** a charming contemporary small motel with European hotel style. Squeezed onto a triangular lot at 1110 Prospect next to the grand La Valencia Hotel, it's too easily missed. Nice view from the patio up on the roof. High-season rates are Luxury—$150 and up for two, continental breakfast included—but ask about off-season specials. For reservations, call 858/454-0133 or toll-free 800/433-1609, www.prospectparkinn.com.

Affordable in Del Mar

A genuine gem in Del Mar, literally *on* the beach, is the minimalist **Del Mar Motel,** close to the racetrack and just a stroll into downtown at 1702 Coast Blvd., 858/755-1534 or toll-free 800/223-8449. Rooms come with refrigerators, color TV, and courtesy coffee; barbecue grills available. Premium-Luxury, with rates from $130 in the high season, starting at $85 otherwise.

Another good deal, between La Jolla and Del Mar, is **The Lodge at Torrey Pines,** 11480 N. Torrey Pines Rd., 858/453-4420 or toll-free 800/995-4507, www.lodgetorreypines.com, boasting one of the best "view" locations around and attractive motel-style rooms. Expensive-Luxury, with official rates $95–155, but look for discounts during the off-season.

Upmarket in and around La Jolla

La Jolla's oldest hotel is the still-dignified and fairly staid four-story **Grande Colonial,** close to everything downtown at 910 Prospect, 858/454-2181 or toll-free 800/829-1278, www.thegrandecolonial.com, with pool, restaurant, and full bar. Tea is served every afternoon. Luxury, with high season rates $229–429, low season rates $179–299. Ocean-view rooms are the more expensive.

Downtown's darling, though, is the historic **La Valencia Hotel,** 1132 Prospect (at Herschel), 858/454-0771 or toll-free 800/451-0772, www.lavalenciahotel.com. Art deco La Valencia, still pretty in pink, was one of those legendary Hollywood celebrity destinations in the 1930s and '40s—*the* place to be. And it still is, for those who can afford it. Luxury. Rates run $250 and up, with some of the cheaper rooms not all that stellar. The layout of this Mediterranean-style pleasure palace is stellar, however. "Street level" happens to be the 4th floor, with the floors below on the way down to the ocean, and the others above. Even the elevator is straight out of an old classic movie. Three restaurants—one with a 10th-floor view—a swimming pool and gardens terraced into the hillside, and a small spa are also modern classics.

For postmodern comforts, head for La Jolla's "Golden Triangle" east of I-5 and the neoclassical 400-room **Hyatt Regency La Jolla at Aventine,** designed by architect Michael Graves. The rooms here are large and airy—but not nearly as airy as the stunning atrium—and the associated health club is one of San Diego's best. Plenty of restaurants are on-site; it's also an easy stroll from here to the University Towne Centre, where you'll find more dining. Luxury. Regular rates run $215 and up, but weekend specials and other discounts can drop prices to $165, based upon availability. For more information, contact: Hyatt Regency La Jolla, 3777 La Jolla Village Dr., 858/552-1234 or toll-free 800/233-1234, www.hyatt.com.

Another best bet is the cliff-top **Hilton La Jolla Torrey Pines,** 10950 N. Torrey Pines Rd., 858/558-1500 or toll-free 800/774-1500, www.hilton.com, a subtle presence overlooking the ocean, and right next to a great municipal golf course and an excellent health club. Rooms are elegant and generous, with either a terrace or balcony and every imaginable luxury—including free Starbucks coffee, shirt press, and newspaper every morning. Luxury. Regular rates run $200 and up.

L'Auberge Del Mar Resort and Spa

Right in the middle of everything in Del Mar, this luxury resort with a hillside ocean view graces the site of the famed Hotel Del Mar, a playground for the Hollywood celebrity set from the 1920s through the 1940s. The architecture of this Victorian-style beach house mimics the original, and the lobby still serves as the resort's social center. Guest rooms are country French, with marble bathrooms and the usual luxury amenities. Also here: full European-style spa and fitness facilities—affordable, by separate fee, for just about anyone, if lodging at the hotel is a bit too rich—plus tennis courts, two pools, great restaurants. Best of all, it's only one block to the beach. Luxury. July, August, and September—race season at the Del Mar Race Track—is the high season, with rates $395 and up. Much lower rates are available at other times. L'Auberge Del Mar Resort and Spa is at 1540 Camino Del Mar, 858/259-1515 or toll-free 800/553-1336, www.laubergedelmar.com. To get here from I-5, head west on Del Mar Heights Rd. for one mile, then turn north onto Camino del Mar. The resort is one mile farther.

Resorts in Rancho Santa Fe

Often a real deal for a special-occasion escape is the **Inn at Rancho Santa Fe,** a San Diego classic with 20 acres of terraced gardens, vine-draped cottages, croquet courses, tennis courts, pool, exercise facilities, and on-site restaurant, with golf and horseback riding available nearby. Another perk here: daytime access to an inn-owned beach cottage in Del Mar. The inn's main building dates from 1923, and was originally built as a guesthouse for prospective real estate buyers after the Santa Fe Railroad's local experiment with eucalyptus trees failed. (Santa Fe had hoped eucalyptus would produce quality wood for railroad ties; instead, the trees grew up to produce shade for the very exclusive residential neighborhoods here.) Quiet and relaxed, it's not particularly oriented toward families though kids are welcome. Premium-Luxury, with rates $120 and up, discounts and other specials often available. To get here, exit I-5 at Lomas Santa Fe Dr. (Hwy. 58) and continue east four miles. For more information: Inn at Rancho Santa Fe, 5951 Linea del Cielo (at Paseo), 858/756-1131 or toll-free 800/843-4661, www.theinnatranchosantafe.com.

Privileged sibling to La Jolla's lovely La Valencia Hotel, the contemporary Old California–style **Rancho Valencia Resort,** near Del Mar in Rancho Santa Fe, has it all—red-tiled roofs, bougainvillea-draped walkways, fountains, romantic and luxurious suites tucked into the lush landscape, 18 tennis courts, exercise facilities, championship croquet lawn, pool, hot tubs, and sauna. You'll find an 18-hole golf course next door to this exclusive 40-acre playground. Luxury. Official rates are $425 and up, but ask about midweek and off-season specials. For more information: Rancho Valencia Resort, 5921 Valencia Circle, 858/756-1123 or toll-free 800/548-3664, www.ranchovalencia.com.

STAYING ON CORONADO

Staying on Coronado: Pricey
If planning to splurge while in the neighborhood, stay at least one night at the historic **Hotel del Coronado,** the bay's crowning glory. The legendary and eclectic Queen Anne "Hotel Del" features a classic dark-wood lobby, with a still-functioning birdcage elevator and a spectacular support-free formal dining room. Guest rooms in the original wooden section of the hotel, with its marvelous quirky corridors, boast all modern amenities yet a Victorian sensibility—all the more dazzling following the Hotel Del's $50 million renovation, completed in June 2000. Newer hotel units near the beach include the Ocean Towers, the California Cabanas, and the Beach House. And if you aren't sufficiently entertained by the hotel's grandeur and gorgeous grounds, then watch the hotel's closed-circuit TV, showing movie after movie filmed at the Hotel Del. Other amenities include wonderful on-site restaurants, from the stunningly Victorian Crown-Coronet dining room, complete with chandeliers designed by *Wizard of Oz* author Frank Baum, to the romantic Prince of Wales Grill and

the new Sheerwater (formerly the Ocean Terrace), serving California coastal cuisine. (For very Victorian High Tea, head for the Palm Court on Sun. afternoon.) Not to mention various business services, shopping, complete spa services (extra), and rental bikes, sailboards, and sailboats. Luxury. Summer room rates begin at $190, with a two-night minimum on weekends, though ask about packages and off-season deals. For more information, contact: Hotel del Coronado, 1500 Orange Ave., Coronado, CA 92118, 619/435-6611, www.hoteldel.com. For reservations, call toll-free 800/468-3533, fax 619/522-8262, or reserve online.

Another top choice is the 15-acre **Loews Coronado Bay Resort,** 4000 Coronado Bay Rd., 619/424-4000 or toll-free 800/235-6397, www.loewshotels.com, a lovely contemporary hotel with light and airy view rooms—every room has a view, be it of the ocean, the bay, or the marina (moor your own). All the usual luxuries, on-site restaurants, fitness and business facilities, even a kids' program are provided. Rates start at $195, but ask about specials. Luxury.

Also appealing in the pricier category is the **Coronado Island Marriott Resort,** formerly Le Meridien San Diego, 16 acres fronting the bay directly across from downtown, with lush landscaping, lagoons full of fish and flamingos, tennis courts, pools, health and fitness facilities, business services, and great restaurants. Rooms, suites, and villas, all with a balcony or patio, open onto either a bay or lagoon view. Luxury. Rates start at $230, but look for off-season specials and packages. The Coronado Island Marriott is at 2000 2nd St. (at Glorietta), 619/435-3000, fax 619/435-3032, www.marriotthotels.com.

Staying on Coronado: Not So Pricey
Thankfully for just plain folks and most families, Coronado also offers budget-friendlier choices, including the **Crown City Inn,** 520 Orange Ave. (between 5th and 6th), 619/435-3116 or toll-free 800/422-1173, www.crowncityinn.com. Every room at this attractive Mediterranean-style motel has a refrigerator, microwave, and coffeemaker, in-room modem hookup, ironing board and iron, plus color TV and cable with free movies. Heated pool, complimentary bikes, on-site laundry facilities. Even better, from here it's just a 10-minute walk to the beach. The **Crown City**

Bistro here is open for breakfast, lunch, and dinner and provides impressive room service. Expensive-Premium, with summer rates starting at $105 ($85 in the off-season). Ask about discounts and specials.

If there's no room at that inn, **La Avenida Inn,** 1315 Orange, 619/435-3191, and the **Best Western Suites Coronado Island,** 235 Orange, 619/437-1666 or toll-free 800/528-1234, are both good alternatives. Contact the Coronado visitors center, 619/437-8788, www.coronado.ca.us, for more suggestions.

EATING IN SAN DIEGO

IN OLD TOWN

The colorful **Old Town Mexican Cafe,** 2489 San Diego Ave. (at Congress), 619/297-4330, is famous for its humongous portions of just about every Mexican standard and a popular place for locals and tourists alike. And if the kids don't know how tortillas are made, here they can watch. It's open daily for both lunch and dinner.

But **Berta's Latin American Restaurant,** 3928 Twiggs St. (at Congress), 619/295-2343, ranges far beyond predictable Old Town south-of-the-border fare. High points of this Latin American tour include pastas, stews, Peruvian chicken with chiles and feta cheese, and seafood *vatapa* from Brazil—all good opportunities for the kids to move beyond tacos and burritos. The wine list is also international. You'll be pleasantly surprised by this friendly respite from the tourist hordes. In balmy weather, the patio is perfect. Berta's is open for lunch and dinner daily, 11 A.M.–10 P.M., closed major holidays.

California-style **Cafe Pacifica,** 2414 San Diego Ave. (between Arista and Linwood), 619/291-6666, a longstanding local choice for uptown dining in Old Town, specializes in seafood. Entrée choices change daily, but count on mesquite-grilled fresh fish selections served with house-made salsa, fruit chutney, or herbed sauces. For smaller appetites: fish tacos, crab cakes, and surprising salads and pastas. It's open for lunch Tues.–Fri. 11:30 A.M.–2 P.M., for dinner nightly 5:30–10 P.M.

IN AND AROUND DOWNTOWN

Uptown Downtown

Even for those who avoid shopping malls as a matter of principle, the **Panda Inn** at Horton Plaza, 619/233-7800, merits an exception. This wonderful Chinese restaurant is as elegant as it is inclusive, with an impressive list of Mandarin and Szechuan selections. From noodle dishes and twice-cooked pork to fresh seafood, nothing here disappoints. It's open daily 11 A.M.–10 P.M., until 10:30 P.M. on Fri. and Sat., closed Thanksgiving and Christmas.

Just across the street from hustle-bustle Horton Plaza, the **Grant Grill** at the venerable U. S. Grant Hotel, on Broadway between 3rd and 4th, 619/239-6806, is a sure bet for escaping the tourist hordes. The hotel's elegant, dignified, and historically correct decor lends a men's club sensibility to the surprisingly good food—from American standards at breakfast and good salads, sandwiches, and specials at lunch to steak and lobster dinners. Full bar. The Grant Grill is open daily 6:30–11 A.M. for breakfast, 11:30 A.M.–2 P.M. for lunch, and 5–10 P.M. for dress-up dinner (until 10:30 P.M. on weekends).

Rainwater's, 1202 Kettner (next door to the Santa Fe Depot), on the 2nd floor, 619/233-5757, is a very uptown downtown establishment and one of the best steakhouses around. Grilled seafood is also prominent on the menu. If you can manage dessert—and here, that's typically a challenge—locals swear by the hot-fudge sundaes. Rainwater's is also a popular lunchtime rendezvous for the suit and tie set. It's open Mon.–Fri. 11:30 A.M.–midnight, on Sat. 5–9 P.M., on Sun. 5–11 P.M. Call for holiday schedules (they vary from year to year).

The Gaslamp Quarter

Fio's, 801 5th Ave. (at F St.), 619/234-3467, is tried and true among the Gaslamp Quarter's trendy 5th Ave. restaurants—a cheery contemporary Italian place looking down on the fray from its seasoned-brick setting. This a very popular place, so reservations are advisable at dinner. It's open weekdays for lunch, nightly for dinner. Other excellent choices in the neighborhood: **Bella Luna,** with all those pretty moons, at 748 5th Ave. (between F and G), 619/239-3222, open daily for both lunch and dinner, and the stylish Tuscan **Trattoria La Strada,** 702 5th Ave. (at G), 619/239-3400, open nightly for dinner, weekdays only for lunch. More casual than its Italian neighbors, bistro-style **Osteria Panevino,** 722 5th Ave. (at G), 619/595-7959, open daily for lunch and dinner, serves wonderful vegetable focaccia, spinach ravioli, and pizzas.

Or, try another country. For tapas and other Spanish selections, head to very friendly **Tapas Picasso,** 3923 4th Ave. (between Washington and University), 619/294-3061, open nightly for dinner, Tues.–Fri. for lunch. Turn a corner and try yet another country. **Athens Market,** 109 W. F St. (at 1st Ave.), 619/234-1955, takes you on an ersatz sail through the Aegean—on weekend nights, an experience complete with Greek music, folk dancing, and belly dancers. Open daily for lunch and dinner. Reservations advisable. For coffee and after-dinner sweets, adjourn to the coffeehouse next door (open late).

Another shining light in downtown's Gaslamp Quarter is **Croce's,** 802 5th Ave. (at F St.), 619/233-4355, a noted jazz club named in honor of the late singer Jim Croce and operated by his family. The music continues, these days with a pretty jazzy dinner menu, too, on which imaginative international riffs include pastas, salads, and seafood entrées. Best of all, Croce's is open late every night—for dinner, 5 P.M.–midnight. The affiliated **Croce's West** in the same block, 619/233-6945, is another eat-out possibility, open every day at 7:30 A.M. for breakfast.

Not that the good ol' U.S. of A. can't be exotic. At the **Bayou Bar and Grill,** 329 Market St. (between 3rd and 4th), 619/696-8747, if you didn't know it was San Diego you'd swear you'd somehow stumbled into Louisiana, what with the ceiling fans and color scheme. Whether you choose seafood gumbo, another fresh fish dish, or rice and beans accompanied by homemade sausage, do leave room for dessert. Open daily for lunch and dinner.

And there are outposts of down-home Western exotica, such as the gussied-up **Dakota Grill and Spirits,** 901 5th (at E St.), 619/234-5554, specializing in "cowboy steak" and other surprises, and **Buffalo Joe's BBQ Grill and Saloon,** 600 5th (at F St.), 619/236-1616, where the 'cue is as good as the country-western.

Eateries on the Way to Hillcrest
Hob Nob Hill, just blocks from Balboa Park at 2271 1st Ave. (at Juniper), 619/239-8176, is a long-running neighborhood favorite—serving heaping helpings of all-American favorites, such as pot roast and fried chicken, at very reasonable prices. Breakfast here is one of the best deals in town, and on Sun. everyone shows up (reservations wise).

Also beyond the typical tourist definition of downtown, look for **Little Italy** along India St., just north of Date. The 1700 block of India is still the center of San Diego's historic Italian district, first settled more than 100 years ago by fishing families. Savory stops here include **Mimmo's Italian Village Deli & Bakery,** 619/239-3710, great for pizza; **Caffe Italia,** 619/234-6767, for sandwiches, coffee, and such; and a number of good delis and bakeries.

Farther north, in an area overrun with freeway on- and off-ramps, another section of India St. marks the turn-off to Hillcrest, with additional worthy (and inexpensive) eateries. An institution in San Diego, the original "uptown" **El Indio,** 3695 India St. (at Washington), 619/299-0333, is where locals go for Mexican. El Indio claims to have invented the term "taquito," so be sure to try a few. But save space for the killer fish tacos and cheese enchiladas, the burritos, the tostadas. Abundant vegetarian choices, everything inexpensive. And if you're in a hurry, call ahead for takeout. It's open daily from 7 A.M. The casual **Banzai Cantina,** 619/298-6388, specializing in imaginative Japanese-Mexican fare at both lunch and dinner, is another neighborhood celebrity. Stop by **Saffron,** 619/574-0177, for takeout.

Hot Stuff in Hillcrest
The **Corvette Diner Bar and Grill** in Hillcrest at 3946 5th Ave. (near Washington), 619/542-1001 or 619/542-1476, is one of San Diego's best bets for kids, a raucous rock-out joint complete with DJs and singing wait staff. They'll also like the burgers, shakes, and fries. A rollicking imitation of a 1950s-style diner, the Corvette is known, too, for its meatloaf and other baby-boomer-era comfort foods. Very popular, so expect to wait (no reservations taken). It's open daily from 11 A.M. Another hot spot for burgers is **Hamburger Mary's,** 308 University (at 3rd Ave.), 619/491-0400.

Best bet for pizza is **Pizza Nova** in the Village Hillcrest, 3955 5th Ave. (between Washington and University), 619/296-6682. Always cheap and also good is the down-to-earth Japanese **Ichiban** in Hillcrest at 1449 University, 619/299-7203. Another great Italian, this one popular for patio dining, is **Busalacchi's,** 3683 5th Ave. (at Pennsylvania), 619/298-0119.

Refreshingly, San Diego still doesn't entirely cotton to the faddish and overly fancy in food, which explains the popularity of casual yet cutting edge **Kemo Sabe,** 3958 5th Ave. (between Washington and University), 619/220-6802, with its imaginative and witty Mexican and multiethnic cuisine—"Mad About Moo" enchiladas, for example, starring moo shu pork. Then there's **Montanas,** "an American grill" at 1421 University (between Richmond and Normal), 619/297-0722, fueled by grilled everything and some incredible desserts. More chic in the usual sense is the exceptional **California Cuisine,** 1027 University Ave. (between 10th Ave. and University), 619/543-0790, closed on Mon. but otherwise serving lunch on weekdays, dinner nightly.

BY THE BAY AND ALONG THE COAST

Dining by the Bay

A local favorite is the **Fish Market,** 750 N. Harbor Dr. (near Broadway), 619/232-3474. Here, parents can enjoy good seafood—even with young children in tow—along with one of the best waterfront views in town. Most grownups go for the mesquite-grilled fish and seafood selections. Most kids are happy with fish and chips, though the children's menu also includes burgers and other American standards. There's a fish market downstairs, plus sushi and shellfish bars and a cocktail lounge. Upstairs is the dressier, more expensive **Top of the Market** dinner restaurant, 619/234-4867, also popular for self-indulgent Sunday brunch. The Fish Market is open daily from 11 A.M.

Another seafood hot spot is **Anthony's,** a popular local chain. The dress-up destination is **Anthony's Star of the Sea Room,** 1360 N. Harbor (at Ash), 619/232-7408, holding its own bayside with beautiful views and an even grander international seafood selection. A better bet by far, though, is **Sally's** at the Hyatt Regency, One Market Place (at Harbor Dr.), 619/687-6080, where the seafood is served Mediterranean style.

Of course, Coronado Island has its share of bayside bounty—including the elegant French **Chez Loma,** 1132 Loma (off Orange Ave.), 619/435-0661, set in an 1889 Victorian cottage and one of San Diego's most romantic restaurants in any category. For other suggestions, see On Coronado, below.

Coastal Cuisine: Ocean Beach, Mission Beach, Pacific Beach

San Diego's classic beach towns have their share of classic burger and taco joints—and a few surprises, such as **Machupicchu** in Ocean Beach, 4755 Voltaire St. (at Sunset Cliffs Dr.), 619/222-2656, which introduces the foods of Peru. The classic appetizer here: the *papas rellenas,* or spicy stuffed potatoes filled with three types of finely chopped meat and vegetables. For smaller appetites, try a few appetizers along with the special spinach soup—the latter a big hit with kids, believe it or not. Beer and wine available. It's open Wed.–Mon. for dinner, closed major holidays.

Also something of a surprise, and an Ocean Beach institution, is **The Belgian Lion,** a very fine dining destination at 2265 Bacon St. (near Lotus St.), 619/223-2700, specializing in traditional French fare and lighter seafood and fresh fish. It's open for dinner only, and only on Thurs., Fri., and Sat. nights. Reservations a must. For German at either lunch or dinner, head for **Kaiserhof,** 2253 Sunset Cliffs Blvd. (at W. Point Loma), 619/224-0606 (closed Monday).

IN LA JOLLA AND DEL MAR

Downtown La Jolla Jewels

If you're looking to pack a food-lover's picnic—a basket brimming with garden-fresh produce and fresh fruit—look no farther than **Chino's Vegetable Stand,** 6123 Calzada del Bosque, 858/756-3184. This vegetable stand supplies some of the best restaurants in California, including Berkeley's Chez Panisse. It's open Mon.–Sat. 10 A.M.–4 P.M., on Sun. 10 A.M.–1 P.M., closed Christmas Day.

If you've got teenagers in tow, you won't be able to avoid La Jolla's **Hard Rock Cafe,** 909 Prospect Ave. (at Fay), 858/454-5101, with good burger fare, the usual brain-scrambling blare, and rock memorabilia and mementos. For good coffee and a simple breakfast the place (packed on weekends) is the coffeehouse-style **Brockton Villa,** 1235 Coast Blvd. (near Prospect), 858/454-7393. Another locals' choice for a casual meal is

La Jolla cove

ROBERT HOLMES/CALTOUR

SamSon's deli, 8861 Villa La Jolla Dr., 858/455-1461, where you can count on great omelettes or lox plates at breakfast, great corned beef sandwiches at lunch, stick-to-your-ribs home-style dinners, and celebrity-kitsch decor anytime. It's open daily for breakfast, lunch, and dinner. For something more exotic, try the buffet lunch at the very good **Star of India,** 1000 Prospect (at Girard), 858/459-3355, a popular place. If you come for dinner, make reservations.

George's at the Cove, 1250 Prospect St. (near Ivanhoe), 858/454-4244, is at the top of La Jolla's seafood food chain, and as beloved for its contemporary American cuisine as for its spectacular local views. You'll have to dress up for the dining room (reservations), but not for either the **Cafe** or the **Terrace,** upstairs, which are more relaxed (no reservations taken, so be prepared for a wait). Simpler fare includes soups, salads, shellfish pastas, fish tacos, even seafood sausages. George's is open daily for lunch and dinner.

For fine dining, French sets the local standard. The excellent, expensive, and somewhat staid **Top o' the Cove,** 1216 Prospect St. (near Ivanhoe), 858/454-7779, a long-running local institution, serves classic French fare and romantic ambience with a view. **The Sky Room,** nearby at La Valencia Hotel, 1132 Prospect (at Herschel), 858/454-0771, is tiny (12 tables) and specializes in contemporary French and spectacular views of both sea and sky. La Valencia's continental **The Whaling Bar,** open for both lunch and dinner, is another option.

Inland La Jolla Jewels

Another dine-around destination is La Jolla's "Golden Triangle," rich real estate reared on biotechnology and other high-tech enterprise wedged into the triangle created by I-5, I-805, and Hwy. 52. The **Hops!** microbrewery at La Jolla's University Towne Centre (between Macy's and Robinson's May), 4353 La Jolla Village Dr., 858/587-6677, enlivens its shopping mall setting with high-test homemade beers—Brewer's Blonde, Red Moon Raspberry, Three-Peat Wheat, and Grateful Red ales plus Triangle India Pale Ale and Superstition Stout. The Brewmaster's Special changes. The food's also quite good—California-style bistro fare, wood-fired pizza and such, everything under $12. Patio dining available. It's open daily for lunch and dinner.

Other culinary attractions at and near University Towne Centre include the continental California-style **St. James Bar & Restaurant,** jazzing up a high-rise bank building at 4370 La Jolla Village Dr. (near Executive Way), 858/453-6650, with a menu including low-fat specialties high on flavor; and the Italian **Tutto Mare,** 4365 Executive Dr. (reached via Towne Centre Dr., north from La Jolla Village Dr.), 858/597-1188, where roasted seafood and seafood pastas star.

Center stage at the theatrical **Aventine Center** nearby, on University Center Ln., are a number of great restaurants, including the very stylish and fairly expensive **Cafe Japengo,** 858/450-3355, offering trendy Pacific Rim cuisine and sushi, and an extensive list of creative desserts.

Best Bets in and around Del Mar

Sbicca's in Del Mar, 215 15th St. (at Camino del Mar), 858/481-1001, is an inventive California bistro serving brunch—crepes, omelettes, *huevos rancheros,* and eggs Benedict—on weekends until 3 P.M. Count on healthy items like the free-range turkey burger, vegetable lasagna, or grilled ahi at lunch. For dinner, consider the salmon au poivre or the Asian-jalapeño flatiron steak. Hours vary, so call ahead.

Other best bets in Del Mar live in the Del Mar Plaza mall at 1555 Camino Del Mar (at 15th St.), including the 3rd-floor **Epazote,** 858/259-9966, serving California-style Mexican and southwestern cuisine; ever-popular northern Italian **Il Fornaio,** 858/755-8876; and **Pacifica Del Mar,** 858/792-0476, serving exotic California-style Cajun, Italian, Southwestern, and Pacific Rim fare. All are open daily for lunch and dinner, with dinner reservations advisable.

Downstairs from Pacifica Del Mar, the **Pacifica Breeze Café** serves breakfast, sandwiches, and dinners in the $7–10 range. And the bar draws a fun, trendy crowd on the weekends.

For dress-up dining in nearby Rancho Santa Fe, serving somewhat pricey but casual California-style American fare is **Delicias,** 6106 Paseo Delicias, 858/756-8000, open for lunch and dinner daily except Mon. and major holidays. At the top of the local food chain, though, is the fancy French **Mille Fleurs** just a stroll away at 6009 Paseo Delicias, 858/756-3085, open daily for lunch and dinner.

ON CORONADO

For fresh produce and flowers, show up on Tues. for the **Coronado Certified Farmers' Market,** 619/741-3763, held at the Ferry Market Landing, 1st St. and B Avenue. Microbrewery fans, you'll find Coronado's own at the **Coronado Brewing Company,** 170 Orange, 619/437-4452. For Pacific Rim–style Southwestern (reservations), the place is the **Chameleon Café,** 1301 Orange Ave., 619/437-6677. Delightful for French bistro fare is **Chez Loma,** near the history museum at 1132 Loma Ave. (at Orange), 619/435-0661.

Generally speaking, though, seafood is the thing in Coronado. For good seafood at lunch and dinner and a chance to appreciate America's Cup memorabilia, head for the **Bay Beach Cafe** at Ferry Market Landing, 619/435-4900. Another best bet for seafood—not to mention the macadamia nut pie—is **Pehoe's,** nearby at 1201 1st St., 619/437-4474, with bay views, patio tables, and a good Sunday brunch. For a bit of remodeled history with your seafood and steaks, **The Chart House** is at home in the Hotel del Coronado's onetime boathouse at 1701 Strand Way, 619/435-0155 (casual, children's menu, dinner only, reservations required).

If you're prepared to spend some real money, stars of the local fine dining scene tend to cluster at Coronado's luxury hotels. The elegant **Crown-Coronet Room** at the Hotel del Coronado serves an astonishing, excellent brunch banquet on Sunday—probably enough calories to fuel the entire naval air base for a week—but the hotel also offers more contemporary style, including the **Prince of Wales Grill** and **Sheerwater,** with spacious outside terraces and gigantic fireplaces. For more information or restaurant reservations, call the hotel at 619/435-6611. Other hotel hot spots include **Azzura Point** at Loews Coronado Bay Resort, 619/424-4000, and the charming **L'Escale** brasserie and jazzy **La Provence** at the Coronado Island Marriott, 619/522-3039.

PRACTICAL SAN DIEGO

VISITOR INFORMATION

For current visitor information, contact the multilingual **San Diego International Visitor Information Center,** 11 Horton Plaza in downtown San Diego, 619/236-1212. For information via the Internet, the address is www.sandiego.com.

If you're rolling into town on the spur of the moment, stop off at the **Mission Bay Visitor Information Center** on E. Mission Bay Dr. (exit I-5 at Clairemont), 619/276-8200, open daily, where you can get enough info to get you around.

The San Diego Union-Tribune is the local newspaper of record but not all that impressive a rag, though even a cursory read will give you some sense of just how conservative this city is. The Thursday "Night and Day" section is useful for figuring out what's going on, but all in all the weekly *San Diego Reader* is a better information source, particularly for entertainment and restaurant listings. Entertaining alternative publications pop up, too; look for them in hip bookstores, music shops, and cool coffeehouses.

SAN DIEGO TRANSPORT

Getting Here by Air
Everybody calls it Lindbergh Field, but the official name is the **San Diego International Airport,** just three miles northwest of downtown San Diego (closer to Harbor Island) near the bay, just off Harbor Drive. Served by all major U.S. carriers—including **America West, American, Continental, Delta, Northwest, Reno Air, TWA, United,** and including the ever-popular **Southwest Airlines.** The airport is also served by **Aeromexico,** and smaller commuter lines. You can't store anything at the airport (no lockers), but it is open 24 hours, with restaurants, snack stops, and ATMs. For general airport information, call 619/231-2100.

Getting Into Town from the Airport
By Bus: San Diego's Metropolitan Transit System (MTS) Route 992 provides service from the airport and downtown San Diego with stops outside each terminal. Buses run every 10 minutes during the week and every 15 minutes on weekends, though if you're traveling on a holiday be sure to check the holiday schedule. Fare is $2; for more information call 619/233-3004.

By Shuttle: One of the easiest ways to get where you're going is via shuttle. The 24-hour **Cloud 9 Shuttle,** 858/278-8877 or toll-free 800/9-SHUTTLE, is the most popular shuttle, and charges $6–10 to major points in the city.

By Taxi: Taxis line up outside the terminal and charge $7–10 for the trip downtown, usually a 5–10 minute ride.

Getting Here by Train
In many ways, the most civilized way to get here is by train. San Diego is easily reached by **Amtrak,** toll-free 800/872-7245 or 619/239-9021 for recorded information, www.amtrak.com, with daily trains coming and going from Los Angeles, Santa Barbara, and San Luis Obispo; you can also get to Solana Beach and other coastal San Diego County stops on one train or another.

The very attractive **Santa Fe Depot** downtown, 1050 Kettner Blvd. (at Broadway), is open all night; the ticket office is open daily 5 A.M.–9 P.M. The **San Diego Trolley** mass transit lines start here, too, making it quite easy to get around, at least between 5 A.M. and midnight.

Getting Here by Bus
The **Greyhound** bus station, open 24 hours, is downtown, just a few blocks east of the train station at 120 W. Broadway, toll-free 800/231-2222 or 619/239-3266. From here, L.A. is the major destination, though you can also trek east. Since the bus station is in an unsavory neighborhood, by San Diego standards, don't plan to walk the streets late at night—and keep an eye on your luggage. (Lockers are available.)

Getting Here by Car
Most people drive here—a fact quite obvious once you're on the local freeways, where traffic is typically nightmarish. The straight shot into downtown is provided by **I-5,** which dead-ends at

Santa Fe Depot

the Mexican border; I-5 is also the main thoroughfare for reaching San Diego beach towns, Old Town, and Coronado Island. Inland, **I-15** creates the city's de facto eastern edge; if you follow it north it'll eventually deliver you to Las Vegas. The area's major east-west freeway is **I-8,** which slithers in out of the desert and slides to a stop at Mission Bay (after crossing paths with both I-15 and I-5). Heads up. And good luck, especially when merging—or trying to merge.

Getting Around

San Diego's public **Metropolitan Transit System (MTS),** 619/685-4900 (recorded), also provides around-town bus service. Pick up a transit map at the visitor information center at Horton Plaza or call the MTS **Information Line,** 619/233-3004 or TTY/TDD 619/234-5005 (5:30 A.M.–8:30 P.M.), to figure out which bus will get you where. Another resource is the **Transit Store,** downtown at 449 Broadway (at 5th), 619/234-1060, where you can pick up free brochures, route maps, and schedules. This is also the place to buy a variety of passes: the **Day Tripper** pass, for example, buys all-day access to local buses, the trolley system, and the ferry to Coronado.

More fun by far is the **San Diego Trolley** mass transit system, 619/231-8549 for current route and fare information (recorded). For assistance call 619/233-3004, 619/234-5005 TTY/TDD. Several lines are now up and running—the **Old Town Line** from the Old Town

transit center to the Santa Fe Depot; the **South Line** to the U.S./Mexico border; the **East Line** serving the east-county cities of El Cajon, Lemon Grove, and La Mesa; and the **Bayside Line** through the Gaslamp Quarter and on to the convention center and Seaport Village. The recently completed **Mission Valley** extension extends to Qualcomm Stadium, and is a handy way to get to the park on game days. Trolleys run 5 A.M.–8 P.M. at least every 15 minutes, and every half-hour until midnight, though the schedule varies somewhat from line to line; call for current information, or pick up a schedule at the Transit Store on Broadway (see above). One-way trolley fares run $1–2, depending on how far you're going; before boarding, buy your ticket at the relevant transit center vending machines (carry exact change)—or buy a Day Tripper pass at the Transit Store.

If they didn't drive into town, to get farther faster most people "go local" and rent a car. San Diego is served by the usual car rental agencies—the visitors center can provide you with a current listing—and some allow their cars to be driven into Mexico. If you don't particularly care about appearances, save some money with **Rent-a-Wreck,** toll-free 800/535-1391 or 619/223-3300. Rent-a-Wreck even rents motor homes, along with new and used cars, trucks, and vans. Other options include **Avis,** toll-free 800/331-1212 or 800/331-2323 TDD, and **Payless Car Rental,** toll-free 800/PAYLESS.

THE DESERTS
LAND OF LOST BORDERS

California's desert is a rugged paint-box panorama of stone-faced mountains and lonely mesas. And sand. Mountains of sand, rivers of sand, valleys of sand, drifting plains of sand scoured white by sun, salt, and wind. Sage and creosotebush plateaus where tumbleweeds dodge prehistoric rock and rubble. Joshua trees, grizzled high-desert sentries as indifferent to hellish heat, high winds, and sudden snow as to any of humanity's higher hopes. Sweetwater palm oases ripe with songbirds and serpents. The fragile strength of spring wildflowers willing to accept, even celebrate, life in no-man's land.

California's desert is also space, time, and timelessness, the expansiveness of land without boundaries or any sense of limitation within very limiting natural laws. And air, and open-air attitudes. And sky, an enduring white-hot haze transmuted at dusk into cinnabar, sienna, and old gold. At night, on every horizon, the endless indigo sky contains all else.

In her 1903 *The Land of Little Rain,* California's desert-poet laureate Mary Austin described this "Country of Lost Borders" and the power of its night sky. "For all the toll the desert takes of a man it gives compensations," she wrote, "deep breaths, deep sleep, and the communion of the stars. . . . It is hard to escape the sense of mastery as the stars move in the wide clear heavens to risings and settings unobscured. They look large and near and palpitant; as if they moved on some stately service not needful to declare. Wheeling to their stations in the sky, they make the poor world fret of no account. Of no account you who lie out there watching, nor the lean coyote that stands off in the scrub from you and howls and howls."

GREATER PALM SPRINGS

THE DESERT RIVIERA

In the beginning was the desert—the wide and sandy Coachella Valley of the Colorado Desert, where Mount San Jacinto, the San Jacinto Mountains, and the scenic and steep Santa Rosa Mountains served as the scenic backdrop for scattered fan palm oases. The city of Palm Springs, still considered a "village" by locals, took its name from the Cahuilla people's sacred palm-shaded hot springs, atop which the Spa Hotel and Casino stands today.

Then came the movie stars. Palm Springs was renowned as a winter playground of the famous and the rich almost since its discovery by Hollywood in the 1920s. Aside from more sensible Cahuilla cultural traditions, the most fundamental history of Palm Springs is largely secret. This is the town, after all, where former President John F. Kennedy's illicit liaison with Marilyn Monroe purportedly took place, in March of 1962. The local attitude has always been that if movie stars, starlets, singers, dancers, rock stars, politicians, and just plain rich people want to get doped up, crazy drunk, or just plain crazy in reasonable privacy, then so what?

So what, indeed.

Then came everyone else. Since its early days the very idea of Palm Springs has influenced middle-class America's more innocent, more romantic ideals—many of these inspired by the thoughtful yet clearly promotional 1920 book *Our Araby: Palm Springs and the Garden of the Sun* by J. Smeaton Chase. Who wouldn't love a balmy valley surrounded by snow-covered peaks in winter, exotic desert, date gardens, and citrus and avocado groves? A place where the air is clean and the sun shines year-round? A place where, on Christmas Day, people sun themselves and frolic in swimming pools?

Who, indeed.

The Palm Springs Appeal

Greater Palm Springs has its peculiarities, including an excessive number of plastic surgeons, psychiatrists, and T-shirt shops. The area also has its charms—and an undeniable appeal. This sprawling rich people's retreat is also friendly to middle-income retirees, frugal sun-loving families, and a growing gay clientele. Though Easter week cruising and other once-riotous spring break celebrations were all but banned in the early 1990s, even college students are once again welcome. These days everyone but gang members from L.A. and Las Vegas are welcome in Palm Springs. And everything's cool—even under the influence of an incredible two million visitors per year.

There's plenty to do in and around Palm Springs, what with countless world-class golf

One day the elements will pound these boulders into desert sand.

KIM WEIR

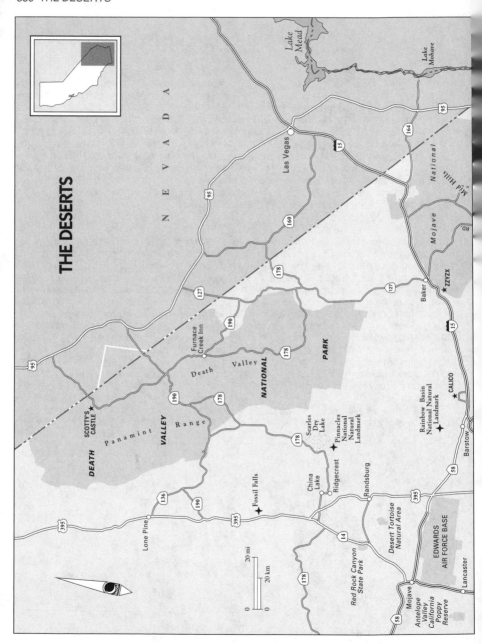

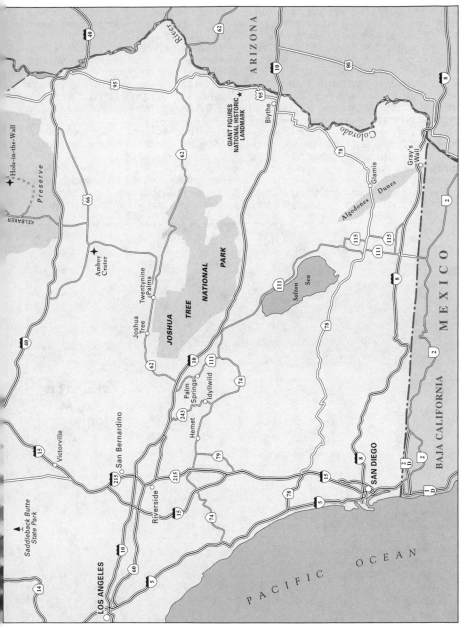

© AVALON TRAVEL PUBLISHING, INC.

and tennis resorts, swimming pools, cultural diversions, and shopping venues. Hot-spring spas, hikable canyons and mountains, botanical gardens and parks, museums, and almost endless outdoor activities connect the community to the region's unique natural history. The Coachella Valley is also still agricultural, or at least semi-agricultural, especially farther east in the less affluent communities of Coachella, Indio, and Thermal, where agricultural workers and many of the hotel industry's maids, gardeners, and restaurant employees live. Stopping at kitschy roadside produce stands and date groves is a pleasurable reprieve from garrulous glitz.

Best of all is the social acceptability of doing nothing, or next to nothing—a major attraction.

Unlike Los Angeles, with its hectic hipness, here no one will think less of you for just sitting around the pool reading a good book.

Winter is high season for Palm Springs tourism, also the peak season for spotting celebrities. Fall is the winter lead-in season, when the community's sociability comes out of heat-related hibernation. Spring is also party time. But you *can* enjoy summer here, despite the searing heat, thanks to moderating evening breezes, swimming pools, near-universal air-conditioning, and those nifty outdoor micro-misting systems. In fact, summer is the hot new season to do the town, with some businesses and attractions—even the Palm Springs Desert Museum—now open year-round. Better yet, summer prices are low and crowds are light.

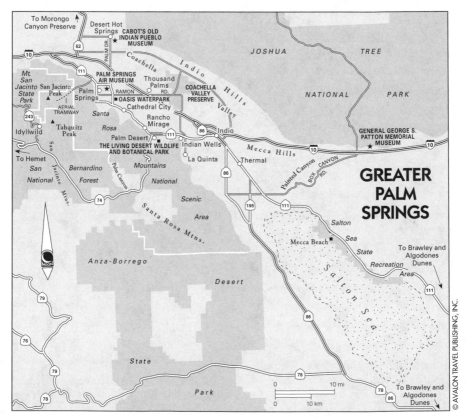

GREATER PALM SPRINGS

© AVALON TRAVEL PUBLISHING, INC.

THE CALIFORNIA DESERT: TWO BECOME ONE

California's 25 million acres of desert stretch east from Los Angeles and its edge cities into Nevada and Arizona, south into Mexico, and north to the Sierra Nevada foothills. Yet the Southern California desert is actually two distinct deserts—the low Colorado, which is the vast California extension of Mexico's Sonoran Desert, and the Mojave or high desert. Travelers heading north along the eastern Sierra Nevada traipse from the Mojave into the far western fringe of California's third desert—the Great Basin, the endless "sagebrush desert" of the West, which spreads into surrounding states from Nevada and extends also into Washington, Wyoming, Colorado, and New Mexico.

The Colorado Desert is desert as most people imagine it: a low-lying landscape of sand, undulating sand dunes, and stark mountains. It is hot in summer—an average of 120°F during the day—and mild and frost-free in winter. The Colorado is also very dry, with just a few inches of rain in an average year. For all its dessicated modesty, a secret flamboyance bursts into bloom after winters of above-average rainfall—almost embarrassing botanical excess. Yet the Colorado's plant and animal life is plentiful and quite diverse even during hard times. The two categories of primary Sonoran Desert "indicators" are trees of the legume (pea) family, such as the smoke tree and green-barked paloverde found in California, and giant cacti, such as the saguaro, that are not (because of insufficient summer rain). Unlike Great Basin flora, which have an evolutionary connection to arctic climates, plants of the Colorado Desert are tropical descendants—jungle plants that learned to live without water.

Most of the Mojave Desert (mo-HAW-vay), spreading north of the Colorado, ranges in elevation from 2,000 to 4,000 feet. It features one characteristic "indicator"—the striking Joshua tree, a giant yucca named by Mormons after the biblical Joshua, since its "arms" turned upward in supplication to heaven. In addition to other unique plant species, it shares many with both the Great Basin and Colorado Deserts. The presence or absence of Joshua trees helps determine the vague Coorado-Mojave boundary, an imaginary line that shimmers like a mirage between Indio near Palm Springs and Needles near the Nevada border. The transitional zone between the Colorado and Great Basin Deserts, the Mojave borrows seasonal extremes from each—being quite cold (sometimes snow-covered) in the winter, like the Great Basin, and hot in summer, like the Colorado.

For all their differences, the Colorado and the Mojave share a fundamental ecological fragility—a fact that at first strikes many visitors as odd or unbelievable, given the landscape's raw and rugged appearance and the well-honed survival skills of both animals and plants. Yet in such a dry climate with sparse, slow-growing vegetation, both major and seemingly minor disruptions leave lasting scars on the landscape—be they mining pits, off-road vehicle tracks, or old roads (some still marked by wagon-wheel ruts). And desert plants and animals, with so many specialized survival adaptations or requirements and sometimes vast territory needs, can suddenly face extinction with the loss of what might otherwise seem a minimal amount of habitat to housing and mall developments, golf courses, agriculture, and freeways.

OVERVIEW: GREATER PALM SPRINGS

Since Palm Springs is an attitude more than an easily definable place, it's not surprising that the entire Coachella Valley shares the city's mythic identity to some degree. Directly north of Palm Springs proper, for example, is Desert Hot Springs, atop the San Andreas fault—a geologic fact that explains why most of the valley's natural hot springs and historic health spas are here. But the Palm Springs cachet isn't confined to the valley's northwest side. Both new money and "new new" money have migrated down-valley into neighboring Coachella Valley communities retaining their fair share of celebrity.

Palm Springs the Village

Palm Springs proper, where the celebrity-watching and scandalous wild parties began, is like an aging movie star who's finally found the fountain of youth. Just years after being declared all but dead, not only is downtown still alive and kickin', it's *lively*, an inimitable mix of settled "old Palm Springs," with its historical sights, and increasingly hip "new Palm Springs" in its neighborhoods, restaurants, shops, and entertainment venues. Though prices are also increasing, this area is still the most central location for affordable accommodations. Stroll **Palm Canyon Drive** to appreciate the **Palm Springs Walk of Stars,** and follow downtown's new pedestrian- and bike-friendly one-mile **Heritage Trail** to see most of the sights.

For the dramatic "big picture" view of Palm Springs and vicinity, just outside town is the world-famous Palm Springs Aerial Tramway, which carts people straight up the face of Mount San Jacinto.

Major downtown attractions include the Palm Springs Desert Museum, a combination art, history, and natural history museum that also serves as a major area performance venue. For more historical perspective, head for the Village Green Heritage Center and adjacent Agua Caliente Cultural Museum Information Center. Fairly new is the Spa Hotel Casino, owned and operated by the Agua Caliente Band of Cahuilla Indians on the site of their original sacred palm spring. Newer still is the Palm Springs Air Museum, one of the world's largest collections of rare World War II–era aircraft. New in 2001: the National Big Band & Jazz Hall of Fame Museum.

South of downtown on Palm Canyon Dr. is long-running Moorten Botanical Garden, an impressive cactus and desert plant collection started more than 50 years ago by "Cactus Slim" Moorten and his wife. Beyond are the Cahuillas' Indian Canyons, tribal lands featuring some of the most striking natural palm oases and best hiking around.

Big doings in Palm Springs proper include the January **Nortel Palm Springs International Film Festival,** an event first launched in 1990 by then-mayor and late U.S. Congressman Sonny Bono, and the fairly new **Palm Springs International Shorts Film Festival** usually held in early August. During the traditional Palm Springs "season" the historic **Plaza Theatre,** recently restored to its original 1930s flash, hosts the fabulous **Fabulous Palm Springs Follies** vaudeville revue. **Palm Springs Village Fest**— with crafts, clothing, produce, food stands, and a Certified Farmers' Market—convenes along Palm Canyon Dr. on Thurs. evening year-round, 7–10 P.M., and look for free evening **Concerts in the Park,** blues and bluegrass to swing bands, in Sunrise Park on Ramon Road. Special events include the **Senior Softball World Series** in fall, the **Palm Springs Celebrity Golf Tournament** in December, and, substituting for spring break chaos, the annual **Palm Springs SunFest** during the weeks before and after Easter.

Greater Palm Springs

Just north of Palm Springs, almost astride the San Andreas fault, is Desert Hot Springs. Set apart from other Palm Springs–area resort cities both physically and socially, Desert Hot Springs is famous for its rejuvenating "waters"—hot mineral springs bubbling up from the ground, the main local draw since the 1930s. Hot Springs Park commemorates this "hot" local asset. The area's ritziest resorts are down-valley, east of Palm Springs on the way to La Quinta, but most hot springs spas—laid-back, sometimes historic shrines of healthy self-indulgence—are in Desert Hot Springs.

Just east of Palm Springs is Cathedral City, with most of the area's gay bars and craziest clubs. "Cat City," as locals call it, has a respectably renegade social history. During the 1920s and '30s, for example, Cat City was famous for its illicit gambling clubs and infamous for the very illegal—and very exclusive—Dunes Club casino.

Down valley and in the big money, Rancho Mirage is a major golf mecca, home to the annual **Nabisco Dinah Shore LPGA golf tournament.** It has been called the "playground of the presidents," and can claim one as a resident—Gerald Ford. Other famous residents include billionaire philanthropist Walter Annenberg, U.S. ambassador to Great Britain during Richard Nixon's presidency, and Nixon's ex-vice president, the late Spiro Agnew. Rancho Mirage is also noted for first-class medical facilities, including the Eisenhower Medical Center, the Barbara Sinatra Children's Center, and the now-famous Betty Ford Clinic.

Boasting the most golf courses in the Coachella Valley is Palm Desert farther down-valley, also famous for its country clubs, upscale shopping, and November **Golf Cart Parade.** Palm Desert's major natural attraction is its naturalistic zoo—The Living Desert Wildlife and

Botanical Park. Among the major annual events in Indian Wells, which boasts the area's highest per-capita income, are the **Bob Hope Chrysler Classic Golf Tournament** (played concurrently at other area courses as well), the **Newsweek Champions Cup** and **State Farm Evert Cup** tennis tourneys, and the annual **New Year's Jazz at Indian Wells** festivities. Fast-growing La Quinta was named for its namesake forebear—the elegant Spanish-style La Quinta Hotel, the only place for miles around when it was built in 1926, still going strong as the ritzy La Quinta Resort and Club.

The oldest city around is Indio at the southern end of the valley. Indio's attractions include date gardens and polo fields, the Coachella Valley Museum and Cultural Center, and two Indian gaming centers—Fantasy Springs Casino and Spotlight 29 Casino. Among fun annual events: the **National Date Festival,** part of the Riverside County Fair, and the **International Tamale Festival.**

DOWNTOWN AND AROUND

Palm Springs Desert Museum
This superb regional museum, downtown between Amado and Tahquitz Canyon, has benefited from Palms Springs–area wealth in general and its world-class private art collections in particular. Excellent dioramas and displays explore local natural history (kids love the live tarantula exhibit) and also showcase Palm Springs history and culture. The permanent art collection emphasizes both contemporary American and western Native American art; changing exhibits keep things lively. The museum's **Annenberg Theater** (separate admission) schedules dance, music, theater, and other performances and hosts an excellent film series. The Palm Springs Desert Museum also boasts a great museum store and an on-site café (the café open weekdays only).

The museum is open Tues.–Sun. 10 A.M.–5 P.M. (Fri. until 8 P.M.), closed Thanksgiving, Christmas, and New Year's Day. Hours are subject to change for selected special exhibits. Admission is $7.50 adults, $6.50 seniors (62 and over), and $3.50 children (6–17; age 5 and under free with adult). Free admission on the first Fri. of every month. For current exhibit information, call 760/325-0189 (recorded). For other information, contact: Palm Springs Desert Museum, 101 Museum Dr., Palm Springs, CA 92263, 760/325-7186, www. psmuseum.org.

Spa Hotel Casino
The newly renovated **Spa Hotel,** 100 N. Indian Canyon Dr., now owned and operated by the Agua Caliente Band of Cahuilla Indians, stands on the site of the hot-springs palm oases for which Palm Springs was named. These springs are the source of the hotel's famed

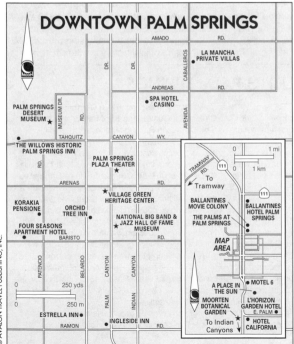

DOWNTOWN PALM SPRINGS

AMADO RD.

LA MANCHA PRIVATE VILLAS

CABALLEROS DR.

DR.

DR.

ANDREAS RD.

SPA HOTEL CASINO

AVENIDA

MUSEUM DR.

PALM SPRINGS DESERT MUSEUM

RD.

CANYON WY.

TAHQUITZ

THE WILLOWS HISTORIC PALM SPRINGS INN

RD.

PALM SPRINGS PLAZA THEATER ★

ARENAS RD.

★ VILLAGE GREEN HERITAGE CENTER

KORAKIA PENSIONE

ORCHID TREE INN

NATIONAL BIG BAND & ★ JAZZ HALL OF FAME MUSEUM

FOUR SEASONS APARTMENT HOTEL

BARISTO RD.

PATENCIO

BELARDO

CANYON

CANYON

0   250 yds

0   250 m

ESTRELLA INN ●

RAMON

INGLESIDE INN ●

PALM

INDIAN

RD.

TRAMWAY RD. (111)

To Tramway

0   1 mi

0   1 km

BALLANTINES MOVIE COLONY

(111)

BALLANTINES HOTEL PALM SPRINGS

THE PALMS AT PALM SPRINGS

MAP AREA

A PLACE IN THE SUN

MOTEL 6

MOORTEN BOTANICAL GARDEN

L'HORIZON GARDEN HOTEL E. PALM

To Indian Canyons

HOTEL CALIFORNIA

© AVALON TRAVEL PUBLISHING, INC.

hot mineral water "swhirlpool" soaks. Still hot news these days, though, is the adjacent Spa Hotel Casino, where pleasures run to video gaming, poker, and Spa 21 (similar to black-jack). The casino, which accommodates non-smokers, is downtown between Andreas Rd. and Tahquitz Canyon Way (enter the casino from Indian Canyon). It's open 365 days per year, 24 hours per day. For casino information call 760/323-5865 or toll-free 800/258-2946. For hotel information and reservations, call toll-free 800/258-2846. For spa information, call toll-free 888/293-0180.

Fabulous Palm Springs Follies

Vaudeville may be dead elsewhere, but in Palm Springs it's alive and kickin'—sky high, too, thanks to the Ziegfield Follies–style chorus line of the Fabulous Palm Springs Follies. All perform-ers, including the dancers, are at least "50 to 80 years young." The follies are staged at the his-toric 1930s **Palm Springs Plaza Theatre,** 128 S. Palm Canyon (100 Jack Benny Plaza), also home to the **Palm Springs Hollywood Muse-um.** (Museum admission is free with show ad-mission.) Follies tickets range from $35 to $65 or so, and the performance season runs from Nov. through May. Both matinee and evening perfor-mances are scheduled. For more information and tickets, call 760/327-0225, or point your browser to www.palmspringsfollies.com.

Village Green Heritage Center

What non–movie star history Palm Springs does have can be summed up in a very small amount of space. That space is right downtown at Village Green Heritage Center, 221 S. Palm Canyon Dr., where two historic homes and a facsimile 1930s general store are on display. The 1884 **McCallum Adobe** and **Cornelia White House,** built from old railroad ties in 1893, give present-day desert pilgrims a cleaned-up look at life in Palm Springs during its cowboy days. Though the Depression-era **Ruddy's General Store** has nothing to do with Palm Springs in particular, this small museum does offer an amazingly au-thentic look at the wares and the wherefores of the good ol' days of American shopping—in-cluding Prince Albert tobacco in a can (really). Though hours can change, all three museums are usually open at least Thurs.–Sun. 10 A.M.–4 P.M. Oct–June. Small admission donation.

In many ways more fascinating than the Vil-lage Green's official history are the tidbits of local

GOLFING PALM SPRINGS

Newcomers sometimes gasp at Palm Springs' gen-eral greenness, its greens, and its green. It does seem a bit garish. To justify the general atmosphere of excess, everyone eagerly explains that the Coachella Valley sits atop a massive underground lake. Even if the Colorado River Aqueduct were snipped tomorrow, they say, the valley's cities, agri-culture, and golf courses would stay green for at least 200 years.

So—water is abundant in and around Palm Springs, and so is world-class golf. All Palm Springs courses are way above par, designed by the likes of Robert Trent Jones, Jack Nicklaus, Gary Player, and Billy Casper. Most courses play through even in summer, though hot-season visitors should try for very early or very late (evening) tee times. And most are private and/or limited to resort guests, though at least limited public access is sometimes offered. Area standouts include the **Indian Wells Country Club** in Indian Wells, site of the Bob Hope Chrysler Classic; **PGA West** and the **La Quinta Resort Golf Club** in La Quinta; and the **Mission Hills North Golf Course** in Rancho Mirage.

Unlike other top-rated area golf courses, at which play is typically restricted to private club members and/or a resort's paying guests, the 18-hole **Tahquitz Creek Resort Golf Course** in Palm Springs is owned by the city of Palm Springs and available for the general public—including visitors. The 140-acre Tahquitz Creek course was designed by Ted Robin-son and is managed by Arnold Palmer Golf Man-agement in conjunction with the city's older public course. High-season green fees run $85 on week-ends, less during the week. Call for current rates (seasonal) and reservations. For more information, contact Tahquitz Creek Resort, 1885 Golf Club Dr. in Palm Springs, 760/328-1005, www.palmsprings.com/golf/tahquitz.html.

For information on other golf course options and availability, contact local visitor bureaus.

Native American culture on display at the adjacent **Agua Caliente Cultural Center Information Center**—Cahuilla basketry, cultural beliefs, ceremonial tradition, and plans for the cultural center and museum planned for Tahquitz Canyon near downtown. Since Tahquitz was the Cahuilla guardian spirit of the shamans, the location should prove propitious. Most of the year the information center, 219 S. Palm Canyon Dr., 760/323-0151, is open Thurs.–Sat. 10 A.M.–4 P.M. and Wed. and Sun. noon–3 P.M. It's open weekends only in summer, Fri.–Sun. noon–3 P.M.

National Big Band & Jazz Hall of Fame Museum

Palm Springs' jazzy new museum, a 16,000-square-foot venue at 296 S. Palm Canyon Dr., 760/320-3128 or toll-free 877/425-5633, is an event as much as a destination. Along with the exhibits, education center, and theater, the museum includes a dance floor, a bandstand with room for a 12- to 17-piece orchestra, the Java Jazz coffee lounge, and One Bourbon Street—an outdoor patio area with live entertainment. The museum is open Sun.–Wed. 10 A.M.–6 P.M., Thurs.–Sat. 10 A.M.–10 P.M. Admission is $12. You can't miss the place, especially after dark. Just look for the 17-foot water and fire saxophone out front.

Moorten Botanical Garden

Calling itself the "world's first cactarium," the Moorten Botanical Garden features more than 3,000 species of cacti and other desert plants in its circa-1938 arboretum and garden complex. Wander along the nature trail, where something is always in bloom. Exhibits are added regularly. Nursery-grown plants are available for sale. Small admission. It's open Mon.–Sat. 9 A.M.–4:30 P.M., Sun. 10 A.M.–4 P.M. Admission is $2 adults, $.75 for children ages 5–15. The garden is south of downtown on the way to Indian Canyons, on the west side of Hwy. 111 at the South/East Palm Canyon Dr. "split." For more information, contact: Moorten Botanical Garden, 1701 S. Palm Canyon Dr., 760/327-6555.

Palm Springs Air Museum

A fairly new museum in town, the $5 million Palm Springs Air Museum at the Palm Springs Regional Airport has a venerable starring cast.

One of the world's largest collections of World War II–vintage fighters and bombers still in flight form, the exhibits here include the rotating Robert J. Pond collection—everything from the Boeing B-17 Flying Fortress and Stearman PT-17 Kaydet to the Chance Vought F4U Corsair and the Russian Yakovlev YAK-11 Moose. Regular flight demonstrations are offered, of both the museum's planes and visiting aircraft. Other exhibits include rare, original combat photography, original artwork and murals, and video documentaries as well as artifacts, memorabilia, and uniforms. Admission is $7.50 adults, $6 seniors and military, $3.50 children ages 6–11 (under 6 free). The museum is open daily 10 A.M.–5 P.M., closed on Thanksgiving and Christmas Day. For more information, contact: Palm Springs Air Museum, 745 N. Gene Autry Trail, 760/778-6262, www.air-museum.org.

INDIAN CANYONS

The premier Palm Springs spot for hiking, picnicking, and up-close exploration of desert palm oases—best in spring and fall—the accessible San Jacinto Mountain canyons just beyond downtown Palm Springs are sacred lands of the Agua Caliente Band of Cahuilla Indians. "Indian Canyons" consist of the abundant plantlife, palm oases, and remote high-country scenery of **Andreas, Murray,** and **Palm Canyons.** Best bet for oasis lovers and distance hikers is Palm Canyon, with 3,000 native fan palms. **Tahquitz Canyon**—to date accessible by special permit only and future site of the Cahuilla people's Agua Caliente Cultural Museum—was Shangri-La in the classic 1937 film *Lost Horizon.*

The entrance to Indian Canyons is at the end of S. Palm Canyon Drive. At last report admission was $6 adults; $3.50 active military, students, and seniors; and $1 children (6–12), age 5 and under free. Group rates available. The canyons are usually open fall through spring 8 A.M.–5 P.M.; the summer schedule varies. Prices and hours are subject to change. For more information, contact: **Agua Caliente Band of Cahuilla Indians,** 760/325-3400 or toll-free 800/790-3398, http://aguacaliente.org. To tour by jeep, call 760/320-4600 or toll-free 877/269-5337. To tour on horseback, call **Smoketree Stables,** 760/327-1372.

Historic Cornelia White House offers a glimpse of life in Palm Springs during its cowboy days.

KIM WEIR

For still more World War II memorabilia, hit the freeway and head for Chiriaco Summit near the southern entrance to Joshua Tree National Park, where the star attraction is the **General George S. Patton Memorial Museum.**

Cabot's Old Indian Pueblo Museum

Aided by his faithful burro, Merry Christmas, and a pick and shovel, Cabot Yerxa took 20 years to build this eccentric, intentionally asymmetrical Hopi-style adobe in what is now Desert Hot Springs. The adobe, four stories tall, features 35 rooms, 150 windows, and walls two feet thick. These days the pueblo serves as an eclectic private museum, "trading post," and the town's pride and joy. Admission is $2.50 adults, $2 seniors, $1 children (16 and under). Cabot's, 67-616 E. Desert View Ave., 760/329-7610, is usually open Wed.–Sun. 10 A.M.–4 P.M. To get to Desert Hot Springs from the Palm Springs airport, head north on Gene Autry Trail.

Palm Springs Aerial Tramway

You might as well begin your area tour with the big picture. To get it, simply climb aboard the Palm Springs Aerial Tramway—and climb a vertical mile in under 15 minutes. Now a historic civil engineering landmark, "Crocker's Folly" took electrical engineer Francis Crocker 28 years to design and build. The views are spectacular, especially from the new 80-passenger Rotair tramcars from Switzerland, which slowly rotate to offer passengers "360 degrees of wow!" Once on top of the world—having traveled through five different climate zones, like driving between Mexico and Alaska—sit down for a meal at the station restaurant, picnic outdoors, or set off on a hike into **Mount San Jacinto State Park** or surrounding **San Bernardino National Forest** wilderness.

Tram cars leave at least every half hour. First car goes up at 10 A.M. weekdays, 8 A.M. weekends and holidays; last car goes up at 8 P.M. (9 P.M. during daylight saving time). The Tramway closes for two weeks in August. Admission is $19.65 adults, $17.65 seniors, and $12.50 children (5–12). "Ride 'n' Dine" tickets are extra. Group rates are available. To get here from downtown Palm Springs: head northwest via Hwy. 111, turn west onto Tramway Rd., and continue to the end (steep climb). For more information, call 760/325-1391 (recorded) or 760/325-1149, www.pstramway.com.

The Living Desert Wildlife and Botanical Park

This 1,200-acre spread, both innovative zoo and educational park, includes both desert plant and animal life on display in naturalistic settings. The **Indian Garden** explains how the Cahuilla people used native plants for medicine, food, clothing, and shelter. The 26,000-square-foot **Eagle Canyon** exhibits native wildlife, including mountain lions, bobcats, and golden eagles, and is also a breeding center for endangered species, including the cheetah, the fastest land animal on earth. Also new: the **Animal Wonders** live

DESERT ADVENTURING~BY JEEP

Even four-wheeling wannabes can do the desert's most adventurous back roads—by hitching a ride with Desert Adventures.

The flaming red Jeeps of this award-winning ecotour company take intrepid travelers into otherwise inaccessible areas of the Santa Rosa Mountains, scenic backdrop for Palm Springs and vicinity. Tour guides are knowledgeable and entertaining, providing a substantial introduction to local cultural and natural history, useful medicinal plants, and desert survival while tossing off tall tales and amusing trivia tidbits at every turn.

Back-road trips into Joshua Tree National Park— thrilling for desert adventurers of all ages—and other tour options are offered, all including pick-up and drop-off at area hotels. Also available through Desert Adventures: guided hiking tours, eco-hiking, and hosted barbecues.

Tours typically last from two to four hours (lunch included on longer trips), so bring your wide-brimmed hat, sunscreen, and jacket if you'll be out during early morning or evening. Also bring your camera. The price depends on the tour and the number of people on board, but most trips run $79–129 per person. Reservations are required.

For more information contact: **Desert Adventures Wilderness Jeep Tours**, 67-555 E. Palm Canyon Dr., Ste. A104, Cathedral City, CA 92234, 760/324-6530 (324-JEEP) or toll-free 888/440-6539 (440-JEEP), www.red-jeep.com.

---

animal show. Wander the park's six miles of trails or take a guided tram tour. Lucky visitors may spot bighorn sheep (an endangered species) scrambling around on the surrounding craggy hillsides. The native plant nursery here offers some intriguing desert plants for sale. Come in late October for the Living Desert's **Howl-O-Ween,** four days of carnival-style booths and costume contests. Other special events are scheduled year-round.

The Living Desert is in Palm Desert, about 1.5 miles south of Hwy. 111 at 47-900 Portola Ave. (near its intersection with Haystack Rd.), 760/346-5694, www.livingdesert.org. It's open 9 A.M.–5 P.M. from Sept. 1 through mid-June, and just 8 A.M.–1 P.M. in summer. Closed on Christmas. Admission is $7.50 adults, $6.50 seniors (62 and over), and $3.50 children (ages 3–12). Guided 50-minute tram tours are available, as well as group tours and special programs (by reservation).

STAYING IN PALM SPRINGS

Whatever you have in mind, it's here. Palm Springs offers an impressive array of historic lodgings—including a hotel built on the site of the city's namesake palm springs, and the desert resort that inspired Frank Capra's *It Happened One Night*—but budget travelers can also find some good choices. Motel 6 and other budget motels are hard to beat for frugal families, but special packages, off-season deals, and great children's programs sometimes make major area resorts quite competitive. For longer stays, apartment, condo, and home rentals are also options.

There's also the Palm Springs "resort spa" experience—once derogatorily called fat farms— for fighting the battle of the bulge in style and with dignity. For other "special interest" clientele, Palm Springs offers both clothing-optional (nudist or naturist) and gay- and lesbian-oriented hotels and resorts.

For help in sorting out available options—and in getting the best available deals for your particular needs—-contact both local visitor bureaus. In addition to fairly complete current listings, each also offers free toll-free reservations assistance.

BUDGET STAYS AND GOOD DEALS

A large, attractive, and well-located **Motel 6** sits right downtown at 660 S. Palm Canyon Dr., Palm Springs, CA 92262, 760/327-4200 or toll-free 800/466-8356, fax 760/320-9827, www. motel6.com, with weekend rates from $45 for

ACCOMMODATIONS RATINGS

Accommodations in this book are rated by price category, based on double-occupancy, high-season rates. Categories used are:

Budget	$35 and under
Inexpensive	$35-60
Moderate	$60-85
Expensive	$85-110
Premium	$110-150
Luxury	$150 and up

two (lower when business dries up in summer, higher on special-event weekends). Inexpensive. There's another on Hwy. 111 (E. Palm Canyon Dr.), 760/325-6129, another in **Rancho Mirage,** 760/324-8475, and still another in **Desert Hot Springs,** 760/251-1425.

The 17-room **Hotel California** motel, 425 E. Palm Canyon Dr., 760/322-8855, fax 760/323-0694, is a best bet for a budget stay and the basics, with rates as low as $49 in the off-season. High-season rates are $69 and up. Moderate-Premium. Some kitchen units are available.

A Place in the Sun, 754 San Lorenzo Rd., 760/325-0254 or toll-free 800/779-2254, fax 760/325-0254, is a very pleasant and unpretentious place to park oneself, old Palm Springs style. Offering a mix of studio and one-bedroom apartments (most with full kitchens), A Place in the Sun is smack dab in the middle of a private garden paradise (fruit trees included). Several blocks east of Palm Canyon via Mesquite Ave. and Random Rd., it's quiet here yet close (but not too close) to the hustle and bustle of downtown. And it features all the basic diversions: pool, whirlpool, putting green, and TV. Small pets are accepted ($10 fee), and a family plan is available year-round. High-season rates begin at $79. Moderate-Luxury.

A great choice for an apartment-style stay is the 11-unit **Four Seasons Apartment Hotel,** 290 San Jacinto Dr. (at Baristo), 760/325-6427, fax 760/325-0658. High-season rates are Premium-Luxury but drop as low as $70 at other times.

And at least in the summer, some rooms are quite reasonable at the very nice 1930s **Orchid Tree Inn,** 261 S. Belardo Rd., 760/325-2791 or toll-free 800/733-343, fax 760/325-3855. High-

season rates start at $125, but drop to $80 in the off-season. Moderate-Luxury.

Fairly inexpensive for a hot springs-spa vacation is the **Desert Hot Springs Spa Hotel,** 10-805 Palm Dr. in Desert Hot Springs, 760/329-6495 or toll-free 800/843-6053, fax 760/329-6915, http://dhsspa.com. This two-story motel complex offers the requisite palm-tree landscape and more than its share of Desert Hot Springs healing waters: four natural hot mineral pools, four hot mineral whirlpools, a sauna, even a wading pool for the kids. The rest of the spa treatment—body wraps, facials, and massage—is extra. High-season rates start at $69–79. Moderate-Expensive.

Palm Desert has its good values, too, particularly in the off-season—these including the **International Lodge** "studio condos" at 74-380 El Camino, 760/346-6161 or toll-free 800/874-9338 (reservations only), fax 760/568-0563, from $80 in winter, $55 in summer. Moderate-Premium.

HISTORIC STAYS

Stuck so long in the 1950s and 1960s, Palm Springs is discovering that styles recently considered passé are hip again. Notable is the **Ballantines Hotel Palm Springs,** 1420 N. Indian Canyon Dr., 760/320-1178. Plenty retro here in the 14 individual rooms and suites are the furnishings—Eames, Miller, Knoll, Lowey—the art, the B and 1950s classic movies, even the poolside scene. Dig that blue astroturf on the sundeck. New again in late 2000 was the **Ballantines Movie Colony,** 726 N. Indian Canyon Dr., 760/320-6340, a split-level 1937 Albert Frey–designed hotel with a total of 16 rooms (kitchens available). Danish House and Tiki House are among the three villas. For a preview of both hotels, see www.ballantineshotels.com. To make reservations at both, call toll-free 800/780-3454. Premium-Luxury.

Korakia Pensione, 257 S. Patencia Rd., 760/864-6411, fax 760/864-4147, was built in the 1920s by a Scottish artist whose visitors included both bohemians and dignitaries. Winston Churchill stayed here. Restored in 1989, this spectacular bed-and-breakfast villa is arty and colorful and still attracts a spirited crowd. Rooms at Korakia ("crows" in Greek) are distinctive and furnished with antiques; each features a kitchen and refrigerator, but no TV or phone (both are available upon request). Children are welcome on the family plan—sharing your room—but for this romantic trip into the past, it's usually best to leave the kids at home. Pool. Rates start at $119 (two-night minimum). Premium-Luxury. At last report Korakia, on Patencio (off Palm Canyon Dr.) between Arenas and Baristro, was closed in Aug. and September.

Winston Churchhill may have stayed at Korakia, but Albert Einstein was once a guest at **The Willows Historic Palm Springs Inn,** 412 W. Tahquitz Canyon Way, an elegant Mediterranean villa built in 1927 as the winter estate of Samuel Untermeyer, former U.S. Secretary of the Treasury. Now an exquisite eight room bed-and-breakfast, The Willows has its lore—including the rumor that Carole Lombard and Clark Gable honeymooned here. Luxury. For more information or reservations, call 760/320-0771 or toll-free 800/966-9597, or try www.thewillows-palmsprings.com.

In its heyday the **Estrella Inn,** 415 S. Belardo Rd., 760/320-4117 or toll-free 800/237-3687, www.estrella.com, one block west of Palm Canyon downtown, was renowned for the wild parties thrown by Clark Gable and Carole Lombard. And Bing Crosby was often a guest in this recently renovated 1930s motel-style hotel. In addition to regular guest rooms, the Estrella features 10 two-bedroom suites and four bungalows with private outdoor whirlpools. Three pools, whirlpools, volleyball court, shuffleboard, and lovely grounds complete the setting. Continental breakfast is included in the rates. Luxury (two-night minimum stay on weekends, three- or four-night minimum for holidays), but look for off-season deals. Weekly and monthly rates are also available.

The **Ingleside Inn,** 200 W. Ramon Rd. (at Bellardo), 760/325-0046 or toll-free 800/772-6655, www.inglesideinn.com, originally a private estate, was declared "one of the world's ten best hotels" by the TV show "Lifestyles of the Rich & Famous." This place is swell despite that fact. The Ingleside's hotel history began in 1935, its star clientele including Greta Garbo, Greer Garson, Elizabeth Taylor, and Salvador Dalí. This small full-service hotel is less restrictive these days. Rooms are individually decorated with antiques; all include a private whirlpool and sauna.

Suites and villas feature fireplaces and private terraces. High-season rates begin at $95 (two-night minimum on weekends) and are typically much higher—though summer rates drop. Expensive-Luxury.

The **Spa Hotel and Mineral Springs,** 100 N. Indian Canyon Dr. (at Tahquitz Canyon Dr.), Palm Springs, CA 92262, 760/325-1461 or toll-free 800/854-1279, www.spahotelandcasino.com, sits atop the hot springs for which Palm Springs was named. Owned and operated by the Agua Caliente Band of Cahuilla Indians, this 1960s-vintage spa hotel was completely renovated and redecorated in 1993, spiffed up even outside with lush landscaping and a striking salmon and teal paint job. Also improved: the sunken marble "swhirlpool" tubs and other full-service spa facilities, including the classic rooftop solarium for private sunbathing (clothing optional). Premium-Luxury. For spa information, call toll-free 888/293-0180.

La Quinta Resort and Club

For Old California romance and present-day celebrity appeal, the quintessential Palm Springs–area resort is the very elegant, very expensive La Quinta Resort and Club, 49-499 Eisenhower Dr. in La Quinta, 760/564-4111 or toll-free 800/854-1271, www.laquintaresort.com.

The La Quinta of today is a virtual city of simple yet simply stunning adobe-style "casitas." Legend has it that Irving Berlin was inspired to write "White Christmas," and Frank Capra the classic films *It Happened One Night* and *Lost Horizon,* while staying here. (Capra liked La Quinta so much, in fact, he moved in permanently. He and his wife lived at La Quinta until the end of their days.) In addition to the usual litany of illustrious Hollywood stars who sought desert refuge, La Quinta also hosted American business barons—the DuPonts, the Vanderbilts, the Gianninis (of Bank of America fame).

But in those days La Quinta boasted a mere 56 casitas. Today it has 640. The grounds alone, a 90-acre riot of annual color, bougainvillea vines, and evergreen lawns, require the attention of 40 full-time gardeners. Despite its immense size—with 25 swimming pools, 35 spas, 30 tennis courts, several restaurants, on-site shopping, children's center, 8,000-square-foot spa, and several affiliated world-class golf courses—

La Quinta is still surprisingly intimate. And popular with celebrities, who typically stay incognito. High-season rates start at $250. Luxury. If you don't mind the heat, summer rates can be a comparative bargain. Adding appeal are the resort's five great restaurants, including the four-star French-Mediterranean **Azur,** casual 1920s-style American **Morgans,** and, for authentic regional Mexican, the **Adobe Grill.**

Two Bunch Palms
Equally beloved but earthier is Two Bunch Palms, 67-425 Two Bunch Palms Trail in Desert Hot Springs, 760/329-8791 or toll-free 800/472-4334, www.twobunchpalms.com. This spot on the map was named (for its two bunches of palms) in 1907 by a U.S. Army Camel Corps survey team. One of those "secret" celebrity getaways everybody knows about, according to local lore even famed mobster Al Capone once hid out here in the 1930s, at a swank villa supposedly built for him—though some locals, including a former Palm Springs mayor, point out that Capone was in prison at the time.

Be that as it may, this *is* a great hideout. Simple bungalows and suite-style villas cluster around the lovely stone mineral pools, a main attraction. The full spa—massage, steam bath, and more—is among the best anywhere. Luxury, continental breakfast included (other meals available), spa services extra.

OTHER STYLISH STAYS

If money isn't an issue—and if you tire of the scenery elsewhere—there is no shortage of stylish stays throughout the Coachella Valley. Not particularly expensive though, by Palm Springs standards, is wonderful little **L'Horizon Garden Hotel,** 1050 E. Palm Canyon Dr. in Palm Springs, 760/323-1858 or toll-free 800/377-7855, www.lhorizonhotel.com, a walled garden enclosing seven buildings, each with two or three guest rooms (one with a kitchen/studio). Groups or extended families sometimes rent an entire building or two. The decor here is airy and contemporary. Each room has a private patio; some bathrooms feature a small, private atrium. Other attractions: a library, boccie ball, croquet, horseshoes, and loaner bicycles. Continental breakfast is delivered to your door along with the morning paper. Lunch can also be delivered, though plenty of restaurants are a stroll away. Premium-Luxury (two-night minimum on holiday weekends).

Need to evade celebrity hunters and the paparazzi, or just want to pretend you do? Try **La Mancha Private Villas,** 444 Avenida Caballeros in Palm Springs, 760/323-1773 or toll-free 800/255-1773, www.la-mancha.com. La Mancha is a state-of-the-art hideout, very secluded (security gates and all) as well as lovely and luxurious. Rooms here are actually private villas—from one-bedroom "casitas" to four-bedroom tennis villas with private tennis court, swimming pool, courtyard patio, and endless indoor comforts (the latter very expensive). Absolutely private restaurant and other top-drawer facilities. Premium-Luxury. La Mancha is about three-fourths of a mile east of Palm Canyon Dr., via Alejo Road.

Always elegant, in its trademark conservative style, is the **Ritz-Carlton, Rancho Mirage** up the hill at 68-900 Frank Sinatra Dr. in Rancho Mirage, 760/321-8282 or toll-free 800/241-3333, www.ritzcarlton.com. The view from the top of the hill here, which takes in almost the entire Coachella Valley, is stunning, particularly at sunset, but nothing is more surprising than the brazen (protected) bighorn sheep that come down out of the hills to graze the high-priced landscaping. Here, the Ritz-Carlton is a full-out resort, with a nine-hole on-site pitch and putt, preferred tee times at the Rancho Mirage Country Club, tennis courts—and a tennis program directed by U.S. Olympic Coach Tom Gorman—croquet, fitness center, pool, whirlpool spa, aerobics classes, and full-service health spa and salon. For folks who can't leave work at home, there's also a business center. And for folks who can't leave the kids at home, the **Ritz Kids** program provides endless activities and outings along with daycare and babysitters. Also here: great restaurants, lounge, and gift shops. Luxury, but summer rates can be a real deal.

RESORTING TO RESORTS

Golf Resorts
If families that play together really do stay together, then even the desert's most glorious golf sanctuaries now promote family values. The

main point of a resort vacation, of course, is that once you arrive you never need to leave—not a travel style that suits everyone.

A standout in this golf-and-kids getaway category is sprawling, 512-room **The Westin Mission Hills Resort** at Dinah Shore and Bob Hope Dr. in Rancho Mirage, 760/328-5955 or toll-free 800/335-3545, www.westin.com, quite contemporary, with an art-deco Moroccan sensibility. The three golf courses here include a Gary Player signature course (Mission Hills North) and a Pete Dye–designed course. The three swimming pool/spa complexes include a 60-foot waterslide. A 20-acre resort park and the Cactus Kids children's program cover just about everything else. And everywhere is that grand Southern California commitment to greening the desert, whether it wants to be green or not—the fountains and waterfalls here inspired by the region's natural oases and desert canyons. Luxury, with bargain summer rates. Inquire about specials and packages.

Another grand golf star is the **Hyatt Grand Champions Resort,** 44-600 Indian Wells Ln. in Indian Wells, 760/341-1000 or toll-free 800/233-1234 (reservations only), www.hyatt.com, with luxury accommodations, good restaurants, two "champion" Ted Robinson golf courses, 12 tennis courts (grass, clay, or hard surface)—the country's third largest tennis stadium—four swimming pools, health and fitness club. You name it. And for the kiddos, for a price: **Camp Hyatt** diversions from dawn to dusk. Peak golf-season rates are Luxury (golf extra).

Practically next door and similarly well-endowed is the **Renaissance Esmeralda Resort,** 44-400 Indian Wells Ln. in Indian Wells, 760/773-4444 or toll-free 800/468-3571, www.renaissancehotels.com. **Sirocco** here may be the best restaurant in the desert. Luxury, with room rates $250–300 in the fall and winter, dropping to $150 or so in summer.

Newest in the Indian Wells neighborhood and absolutely deluxe is the **Miramonte Resort,** 45000 Indian Wells Ln. in Indian Wells, 760/341-2200 or toll-free 800/237-2926, www.miramonteresort.com, a 226-room Tuscan Village with two swimming pools and every imaginable amenity, including on-site spa services. Though the Miramonte doesn't boast its own

golf courses or tennis courts, it does provide access to neighboring facilities. Call for details. Luxury.

For sheer unreality out in the desert, nothing beats huge **Marriott's Desert Springs Resort and Spa,** 74-855 Country Club Dr. in Palm Desert, 760/341-2211 or toll-free 800/228-9290, marriotthotels.com, with its indoor lagoon and eight-story atrium, pools, waterfalls, hanging gardens, indoor and outdoor lakes (boat tours available), golf courses, putting green, five swimming pools, 21 tennis courts, and endless other recreation facilities. Luxury. High-season rates run $250 but drop substantially in summer.

Resort Spas

The big-bucks buzz in Palm Springs lately has a French accent, what with the 1996 arrival of the region's newest ultraswank health spa, this one for both men and women. Now owned by Merv Griffin, **Merv Griffin's Resort Hotel and Givenchy Spa,** the first Givenchy outpost in the United States, is modeled after the spa at Trianon Palace in Versailles, France. At home at the revamped old Gene Autry Resort, 4200 E. Palm Canyon Dr. in Palm Springs, 760/770-5000 or toll-free 800/276-5000, www.merv.com/hotel/givenchy_spa, the spa's emphasis is on active and enjoyable exercise as well as refined and gentle body care. The key words here: *beauty, luxury,* and *voluptuousness.* Also served: very good, very healthful French food. Luxury. Ask about weekend packages and specials.

The long-running classic local health and fitness spa is **The Palms at Palm Springs,** 572 N. Indian Canyon Dr. (at Alejo) in Palm Springs, 760/325-1111 or toll-free 800/753-7256, www.palmsspa.com, which rates as one of the country's best by no lesser authority than *Condé Nast Traveler.* People typically stay a week or more, eating low-calorie meals and exercising, exercising, exercising; massages, manicures, and other spa services are available. Rooms are spacious and comfortable—and cheaper ($145 per person per day) if you're willing to share. Otherwise, rates begin at $210 per day (higher on weekends), all extras extra. Luxury.

Another time-honored alternative is **Two Bunch Palms** in Desert Hot Springs. For more information, see listing above.

EATING IN PALM SPRINGS

CHEAPER EATS

Fairly Inexpensive in Palm Springs

Unlike Palm Desert and Rancho Mirage, where community is defined by walled high-security compounds and empty streets, in Palm Springs people actually amble around and do things. And one of the things they do is eat.

Ever popular downtown is landmark **Louise's Pantry,** 124 S. Palm Canyon Dr. (between Tahquitz Canyon and Arenas), 760/325-5124. Breakfast is the real deal here, but people wait in line for burgers and milkshakes at lunch, and home-style meatloaf, pork chops, and fresh roasted turkey at dinner. Grab a booth, then let the kids sidle up to the Formica counter to peruse the pies. Since 1946, Louise's has been famous for its homemade cream pies—especially the banana split pie.

Palm Springs—the people's Palm Springs—is a coffee shop kind of town, favoring places with sunny attitudes and patios. It's just assumed that such places will serve generous helpings of good food at reasonable prices, as does **Bit of Country,** 418 S. Indian Canyon Dr., 760/325-5154, starting with hearty breakfasts. Open for breakfast and lunch.

A true local hot spot is **Elmer's Pancake and Steak House,** 1030 E. Palm Canyon, 760/327-8419, open daily for breakfast, lunch, and dinner. The Coachella Valley produces 95 percent of the dates consumed each year in the United States—so come to breakfast at Elmer's to polish off your share. The date-nut pancakes are great, as are the cheese blintzes. Elmer's specialty, though, is German pancakes. The only drawback to this place is its popularity; on weekends, the wait can be considerable.

Then there's **Las Casuelas—The Original,** 368 N. Palm Canyon (between Amado and Alejo), 760/325-3213, open for lunch and dinner. Kids like this place because it's cheerful and colorful. Parents like it for the same reasons, but also because the food at this Casuelas—at last count, there were three others in the area—is predictably good. The potent, pool-sized margaritas are another reason. Standards

include tacos, tostadas, enchiladas, and burritos, but try a homemade tamale. Beloved for its "wild coyote" margaritas and immensely popular for imaginative Southwestern is the **Blue Coyote Grill,** 445 N. Palm Canyon Dr., 760/327-1196, where you'll dive right into the tortilla soup and savor the enchiladas. Eat indoors or, weather permitting, outdoors.

And if you're hungry for all-American burgers and such, on the way into or out of Palm Springs you can't miss **The Wheel Inn** off I-10 in Cabazon, 909/849-7012, a gussied-up 24-hour truck stop famous for its humongous dinosaurs—the real reason the kids will want to stop here.

Inexpensive and
Almost Inexpensive Elsewhere

For south-of-the-border fare near Palm Springs, most authentic are some of the *taquerías* and tiny storefronts in and around Indio. Getting there from Palm Springs is some drive, however—so try **El Gallito Cafe,** 68-820 Grove St. in Cathedral City (two blocks south of Hwy. 111, via Cathedral Canyon Rd.), 760/328-7794, a popular local hangout with down-home decor—piñatas, funky paintings, and lit-up beer signs—and very good, inexpensive food. A real deal here is the "burrito especial."

The **Trader Joe's** chain, with an outpost here at 44-250 Town Center Way in Palm Desert, 760/340-2291, was once described by its founder, "Trader" Joe Coulombe, as catering to "the over-educated and underpaid." If that sounds relevant, stop by to stock up on baked goods, coffee, cheese, nuts, all-natural snacks, and assorted beers and wines. A little flashier in the neighborhood: L.A.'s popular all-American **Daily Grill,** 73-061 El Paseo, 760/779-9911. Pricier still, beloved for dinner by meat-eaters everywhere, is **Ruth's Chris Steak House,** 74-040 Hwy. 111, 760/779-1998. There's also a **Morton's of Chicago** in town, 74-880 Country Club Dr., 760/340-6865.

In La Quinta there's the **Beachside Cafe** in the Vons Shopping Center at 78-477 Hwy. 111, 760/564-4577. With the Salton Sea so far away, the most obvious question is: *What* beach? (It's on the wall, near the big beach umbrellas outside.) The fare is sunny and California-style,

DATE SHAKES AND OTHER DELICACIES

Few people in and around Palm Springs argue about how delectable a date milkshake tastes. They do quibble, however, over just which local enterprise makes the best date shakes—a blender brew of vanilla ice cream, milk, crystallized date sugar and, sometimes, chunks of fresh dates. You can get gussied-up dates in shops all around Palm Springs. Many specialize in the retail sale of dates—Medjools, Deglet Noors, Barhis, Black Abbadas, and honey dates—and date-related delicacies, such as marzipan-stuffed Medjools, date nut rolls, and chocolate date truffles.

The best place to go date hunting, though, is at the other end of the Coachella Valley, near Indio and Thermal—where most of the area's date palms are, and have been, since the first were imported from the Middle East in the late 1800s.

At **Oasis Date Gardens** just south of Thermal on Hwy. 111, the Laflin family has been growing dates—the oldest known domesticated fruit—since 1912. However, it wasn't until 1939 that the clan began growing the superb Medjool dates for which Oasis has become known. Attractions here include a retail shop and a small café serving thick, creamy, and truly delectable date shakes. It's a fun drive to Thermal—and, with a picnic under the palms, a relaxing half-day outing. Open daily 8:30 A.M.–5 P.M., closed on Easter and Christmas, Oasis Date Gardens is 1.5 miles south of Thermal at 59-111 Hwy. 111. For more information call 760/399-5665 or toll-free 800/827-8017, www.oasisdate.com.

Always popular in Indio is **Shields Date Gardens,** famous for its "Black Date" ice cream—rich vanilla swirled with date puree. This 1950s-vintage shop, starring Abdullah the mechanical camel, actually harks back to 1924. That's when the late E. Floyd Shields joined the local legion of date-growing pioneers. Shields narrates the aging but ever-popular *Romance and Sex Life of a Date* slide show, which is shown regularly. Shields Date Gardens is on the south side of Hwy. 111, just east of Jefferson St., at 80-225 Hwy. 111, Indio, CA 92201, 760/347-0996 or toll-free 800/414-2555, www.shieldsdates.com. The shop is open daily 8 A.M.–6 P.M. (closed on Christmas).

To do dates socioculturally, in mid-February come to the **National Date Festival** in Indio, part of the Riverside County Fair, where the theme since 1947 has been "1,001 Arabian Nights." The family-friendly fun here includes ostrich and camel racing—a species of California craziness hard to find elsewhere.

---

with fresh-baked pastries and breads—killer banana nut bread, delectable pies and cakes—homemade soups and imaginative salads. Fresh fish, too. Open daily 7 A.M.–9 P.M. Also a best bet: **Mario's on El Paseo,** 73-399 El Paseo, 760/346-0584, where the wait staff sings for your supper.

Devane's, 80-755 Hwy. 111 in Indio, 760/342-5009, is named after its owner, actor William Devane. This casual California-style joint serves some unusual salads and generous portions of pasta, great chicken, and seafood. But Devane's real claim to fame is its pizza. People drive here from all over the Coachella Valley just to get some, whether traditional pepperoni or vegetarian combinations. Full-service bar, too.

THE CUISINE SCENE

A dazzling fine-dining star downtown is **St. James at the Vineyard,** 265 S. Palm Canyon Dr., 760/320-8041, where the eclectic decor just about covers the map—the entire map of the world—as does the creative fare. From bouillabaisse Burmese and grilled Australian rack of lamb to the shrimp curry, come on in and prepare to be surprised.

Swingin' **Muriel's Supper Club,** 210 S. Palm Canyon Dr., 760/325-8839, is both dining destination and dance club. The daily changing dinner menu, emphasizing seasonal ingredients, might include George Banks sea scallops, pan seared blue prawns, or grilled elk medallions. Delectable desserts. The entertainment menu also changes constantly—both Eartha Kitt and the Cherry Poppin' Daddies have taken their bows here—but generally includes jazz, Latin jazz, salsa, and swing.

As hot with seniors as it is with its gay clientele, immensely popular **Shame on the Moon,** 69-950 Frank Sinatra Dr. in Rancho Mirage, 760/324-5515, is all but impossible to get into unless you book well in advance. Also a big hit is **The Left Bank** in Palm Springs proper, 150 E. Vista Chico Rd., 760/320-6116, a dinner-only French bistro.

Otani—A Garden Restaurant in downtown Palm Springs at 266 Avenida Caballeros, 760/327-6700, a relative of A Thousand Cranes in L.A., is the most beautiful shogun's palace in Palm Springs. Savvy diners don't even try to choose between the teppen-yaki and yakitori menus. Sushi lovers have a field day here (the California rolls are quite good). Tempura selections include calamari and clams. Early bird dinner specials are the real deal. Across from the convention center, three blocks east of Indian Canyon, Otani is open for dinner daily, lunch weekdays only, Sunday brunch.

Also fine for fancy dining in Palm Springs proper is romantic French **Le Vallauris,** 385 W. Tahquitz Canyon Way, 760/325-5059, open daily for both lunch and dinner.

Another favorite, for French-Mediterranean, is **The Dining Room** up the hill from the highway at the Ritz-Carlton, Rancho Mirage, 68-900 Frank Sinatra Dr., 760/321-8282. The Ritz-Carlton is a superb desert resort destination and—if you're in the mood for semiformal attire, formal atmosphere, and great food—a superb dinner destination. The menu includes three prix-fixe options and menu selections such as fresh black mussel soup with saffron and the house bouillabaisse. Full bar, excellent wine list. Reservations are highly recommended. For something more easygoing, consider one of the Ritz-Carlton's more casual dining options. Call for the current dinner schedule. Coming or going, perhaps you'll meet the Ritz-Carlton's regulars—bighorn sheep from the surrounding preserve grazing the flowerbeds.

For a stylistic change-up, there's **Palomino Euro Bistro,** 73-101 Hwy. 111 in Palm Desert, 760/773-9091. Stepping into a cutting-edge eatery with California style and European attitude usually costs plenty. Not so at uptown Palomino, one of the hippest places around. Beloved for its imaginative pizzas and pastas (wonderful coffee and desserts, too), this bistro is reasonably relaxed. For a horse of a different color, step up to the full-service bar for some house wine. From Iron Horse Vineyards, it carries the Palomino label. Palomino, on Hwy. 111 near Hwy. 74 (also known as Monterey Ave.), is usually open for dinner 6 P.M. to 10 P.M.; call for current schedule.

For French, consider **Cuistot** in Palm Desert's Galleria Centre at 73-111 El Paseo, one block south of Hwy. 111 between Ocotillo and Sage, 760/340-1000. Palm Springs has its venerated French restaurants, most of them quite classical and fairly formal. But Cuistot's "continental drift" combines Old World flavor with eclectic Californian attitude, with choices such as salmon with ginger-chervil sauce and duck in black currant and apricot sauce. Good wine list, full bar. Closed Mon. and in summer, at last report. Otherwise, it's open for lunch and dinner Tues.–Sat., dinner only on Sunday. Reservations are required, especially during the winter.

Another attraction in Indian Wells is excellent French **Le St. Germain,** 74-985 Hwy. 111, 760/773-6511, bistro-style sibling of the long-running local Le Vallauris: open nightly for dinner.

Then there's Mediterranean **Sirocco** just off Hwy. 111 at the Renaissance Esmeralda Resort, 44-400 Indian Wells Ln., 760/773-4444. Named for the hot Saharan wind, this premier dining establishment is something of an international oasis for food lovers. Sirocco's specialties include unique interpretations of standards, such as gazpacho and paella, and an exceptional wine list. Casual dining, reservations strongly advised. Sirocco regularly attracts celebrity chefs, so inquire about special events. At last report lunch was served on weekdays only, dinner every night, but call for current information on schedule and seasonal closings.

For other fine dining choices, consider other area luxury resorts.

TRANSPORTATION AND INFORMATION

Getting Here, Getting Around

San Gorgonio Pass, just northwest of Palm Springs, is such an effective wind funnel that local windshields are literally pitted and scarred by sand-blasting storms, particularly when Santa Anas blow hot off the desert. No wonder, then, that the region is such a productive power-generating windmill field—quite the striking scene. And you'll see it, too, especially driving. (If the setting looks familiar, this is the site of the opening scenes in *Rain Man,* with Tom Cruise and Dustin Hoffman.) By road, the primary route into the Coachella Valley from Los Angeles is I-10; heading into Palm Springs from the freeway, most folks take the Hwy. 111 cutoff through the

KIM WEIR

Hitch a ride on a covered wagon to sightsee

windmills. That route becomes one-way **Palm Canyon Dr.** heading south, which (1) loops around onto downtown's other central artery, one-way **Indian Canyon,** heading north and (2) continues, from the right-hand lanes, as E. Palm Canyon—still Hwy. 111, the main thoroughfare connecting the various valley towns. Most intersecting streets, shown on local maps, are usually well marked and visible. To avoid the often crushing traffic along Hwy. 111, use your map to plot alternative routes via the bigger cross-valley roads.

Most car rental agencies are at the airport (see below). Sans car, you can come via bus. There's a **Greyhound** terminal in downtown Palm Springs, 311 N. Indian Canyon Dr. (at Amado), 760/325-2053, and another in Indio, 760/347-5888, www.greyhound.com. **Amtrak** offers direct train service to Palm Springs—it's an undeveloped, unstaffed station, with all arrivals and departures between midnight and 5 A.M., at last report—so you can also come by train. The only trains stopping at this station are those of the *Sunset Limited,* which operates three days a

week between Los Angeles and Florida. The station is located on the Union Pacific (former Southern Pacific) Railroad tracks just south of I-10 west of Indian Ave., about 4 miles north of downtown Palm Springs. For current information on Amtrak trains, call toll-free 800/872-7245 or try amtrak.com or amtrakwest.com.

Palm Springs lacked airplane service until 1945, and what was available wasn't convenient even from Los Angeles until the 1950s. Flights here from any distance typically required so many transfers and "short hops" that it was all too tedious for most people's tastes. That fact of Palm Springs life is fast changing, even though some service is still "high-season" only. (Check with your travel agent or with the airlines.) At last report **Palm Springs Regional Airport,** at the out-there east end of Tahquitz Canyon Way, was well served by **American Airlines/American Eagle** and **Alaska Airlines.** American offers a Los Angeles hop and nonstop Chicago and Dallas/Ft. Worth service. Alaska offers nonstop San Francisco and Seattle service. Other carriers include **America West,** which offers jet service connecting to its hub in Phoenix, **Delta/Skywest** (Salt Lake City), **U.S. Airways/United Express** (Los Angeles), and **United Airlines** (Denver).

Palm Springs Area Information

For information about the city of Palm Springs, contact the **Palm Springs Visitor Information Center,** 2781 N. Palm Canyon Dr., Palm Springs, CA 92262, 760/778-8415 or toll-free 800/347-7746, fax 760/325-4335. In addition to providing all essential local information, the center also assists with motel, hotel, and resort reservations. For info via the Web, try www.palm-springs.org.

For information on the greater Palm Springs area—including, but not limited to, Palm Springs—contact **Palm Springs Desert Resorts Convention and Visitors Authority,** The Atrium, 69-930 Hwy. 111, Ste. 201, Rancho Mirage, CA 92270, 760/770-9000 or toll-free 800/417-3529, www.desert-resorts.com and (new website) www.palm-springsusa.com, which offers a 24-hour reservations service for hotels, golf, and other activities and services. The bureau also offers a visitor information desk at the Palm Springs Regional Airport. For 24-hour recorded information (message updated monthly), call 760/770-1992.

BEYOND PALM SPRINGS

Immediately south of the Coachella Valley is the rugged **Santa Rosa Mountains National Scenic Area,** a craggy collection of spires that seem to leap straight up out of the desert. Taking the spectacularly winding and scenic Palms to Pines Hwy. (Hwy. 74) south from Palm Desert and up into the Santa Rosa Mountains eventually leads to **Idyllwild,** a tiny resort town in the woods popular for its sweet mountain air and just general coziness. For current information about Idyllwild, call the local chamber of commerce at 909/659-3259 or try www.idyllwildchamber.com. The route leads to **Hemet,** site of the annual Ramona Pageant each spring. Roads soon spin off in all directions, like the spokes of a wagon wheel; Hwy. 79, for example, takes you to the wine country near Temecula and then on an extensive backcountry tour of San Diego County, including Julian and both Anza-Borrego and Cuyamaca State Parks.

Heading east from the Coachella via Hwy. 111 leads past the date groves of Indio and Thermal to the **Salton Sea,** which appears from a distance to be a massive desert mirage. But the Salton Sea is quite real—California's largest body of water, twice the size of Lake Tahoe and much saltier than the ocean. For more information about the **Salton Sea State Recreation Area,** call 760/393-3052 or 760/393-3059. Highway 111 leads to the vast Imperial Valley and its farm towns, a sandy breadbasket responsible for much of the delicate produce and fruit Americans enjoy in winter, and becomes yet another back-road route leading into Anza-Borrego (via Hwy. 78). East of the Imperial Valley, via Hwy. 78, is an almost endless sea of sand. Here are the intriguing **Algodones Dunes,** California's most extensive sand dune system—a natural national landmark; the **North Algodones Dunes Wilderness** is open for on-foot exploration only.

North and east from greater Palm Springs is the rest of California's desert, including its most famous natural attractions: Joshua Tree National Park, the new Mojave National Preserve, and Death Valley National Park.

THE RAMONA PAGEANT:
RACIAL INJUSTICE AS ROMANCE

Helen Hunt Jackson was an early activist on behalf of California's downtrodden native peoples. In despair that so few cared about the Indians' plight, Jackson decided to tell the story as a romance—an interracial romance. As she put it: "I am going to try to write a novel, in which will be set forth some Indian experiences in a way to move people's hearts. People will read a novel when they will not read serious books." The resulting *Ramona* was a national sensation when it was first published in 1884.

Jackson's story, about the beautiful young maiden Ramona and Alessandro, her Indian love, has been staged as an outdoor play since 1923. The remote Hemet-area locale is fitting, since the San Jacinto Valley was the setting for some of the novel's original scenes. Alessandro's murder, for example, was modeled after an all-too-true killing here in 1883. Though the story is the stuff of Hollywood movies—in 1959, showcasing the charms of Raquel Welch, the 1969 version starring Anne Archer—*Ramona* the novel became *Ramona* the play in 1923. It was dramatized by Garnet Holme, who also scripted the "Bracebridge Dinner" for Yosemite National Park's Ahwahnee Hotel Christmas celebration and Marin County's Mount Tamalpais *Mountain Play.*

Now the official California State Play, the Ramona Pageant is presented on select weekends each spring at the open-air **Ramona Bowl and Museum** in the rocky hills just south of Hemet. (Dress casually, wear a hat, and bring sunscreen.) Nothing much has changed over the years, except that the "cast of hundreds" often includes young girls in young-boy roles because of increasing lack of interest in the Y-chromosome crowd. The Ramona Pageant is staged each year over several consecutive weekends, typically mid-Apr. to May, matinee performances only. At last report ticket prices were $14–23. The Ramona Bowl is about three miles south of Florida Ave. via Girard. The museum is open weekends only, Jan.–May, 10 A.M.–4 P.M.

For more information, contact: **Ramona Pageant,** Ramona Bowl, 27400 Ramona Bowl Rd., Hemet, CA 92544, 909/658-3111 or toll-free 800/645-4465 for tickets and current information, or go to www.ramonapageant.com.

JOSHUA TREE NATIONAL PARK

Joshua trees, the kinetically kinky agaves for which this new national park is named, spooked early desert emigrants. Perhaps to express that anxiety they attached derogatory names and descriptions. But Mormon pioneers envisioned inspiration, perhaps even divine intervention, where others saw only grizzly grotesques. Thus the trees' given name, prompted by the Bible's Book of Joshua: "Thou shalt follow the way pointed for thee by the trees." Equally inspiring are Joshua Tree National Park's giant granite formations—eccentric arrangements of fat, khaki-colored stone as smooth and aesthetically well-rounded as Henry Moore sculptures.

The strange landscape here is solid and timeless yet in perpetual transition, the scenic backdrop for an endless juggling act. With airs both prehistoric and futuristic, the park embraces the Mojave and Colorado Deserts as it defines the weird no man's land connecting them. And connects visitors to this surreal and spacious landscape populated by expressive trees and serene stone—a holy place, its central shrine dedicated not to human idols but to the enduring wonders of everyday creation.

SEEING JOSHUA TREE

Seeing and doing Joshua Tree National Park requires some strategic planning, since the park's key features and diversions are fairly far-flung. If coming from the north, get oriented at the park's main **Oasis Visitor Center** on National Park Dr. (Utah Trail) in Twentynine Palms, just off Hwy. 62. Stroll the short nature trail through the native fan palms and mesquite of the adjacent **Oasis of Mara.** To the Serrano and Cheme-huevi peoples who called it home when explorers and settlers first passed through, this once well-watered oasis was known simply as *mara,* or "place of small springs and much grass."

Other northern attractions include the remote **Fortynine Palms Oasis** near Twentynine Palms, and the **Wonderland of Rocks** near **Indian Cove Campground,** geological magnet for hands-on mountaineers. Farther west, in the

Little San Bernardino Mountains near Yucca Valley, is the pleasant high-country **Black Rock Canyon Campground** area and, nearby, dirt-road access from the highway to **Covington Flat**—featuring the park's largest Joshua trees and wonderful picnicking—and **Eureka Peak.** The view from the peak, most spectacular in spring, takes in 10,000-foot **Mt. San Jacinto,** beyond Palm Springs to the southwest, and, directly west, Southern California's tallest, **San Gorgonio Mountain,** looming above its siblings at an elevation of 11,499 feet.

The central park includes a multitude of just-the-basics campgrounds—**Hidden Valley, Jumbo Rocks, Ryan, Belle,** and **White Tank**—and most of the park's major natural and historic attractions.

The short hike/scramble through surrealistic, stone-circled **Hidden Valley** also wanders into

Joshua trees are among the world's weirdest wildflowers.

KIM WEIR

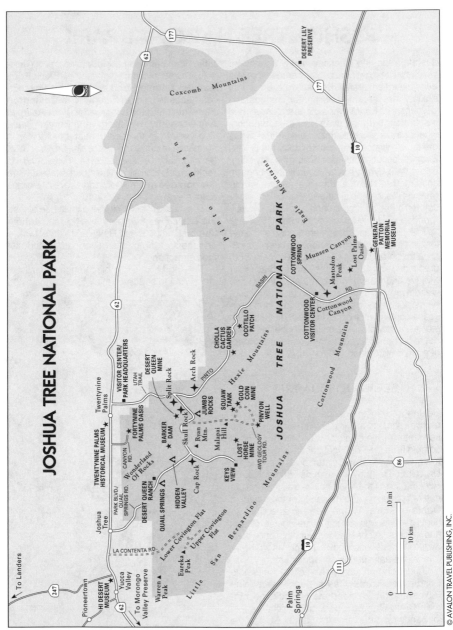

JOSHUA TREE NATIONAL PARK

© AVALON TRAVEL PUBLISHING, INC.

the dark side of local lore, since this was said to be the historic hideout and hidden grazing headquarters of the horse-rustling McHaney Gang during the late 1800s.

North of Hidden Valley is the southern jumble of the vast **Wonderland of Rocks,** scenic setting for the storied **Desert Queen Ranch** which can be seen only on guided tours. The serene Desert Queen is most infamous for the murder conviction of its owner Bill Keys, prospector, family man, and friend of Death Valley Scotty. For the best general on-foot introduction to the stony surroundings, hike the trail to **Barker Dam**— once associated with the Desert Queen, and one of the park's remaining "tanks" or artificial reservoirs. Equally pleasant for picnicking, if you're heading northwest, is **Quail Springs.**

South of Hidden Valley is the Joshua Tree wonderland of **Lost Horse Valley,** named for the **Lost Horse Mine**—the area's most successful gold mine, a claim purportedly "discovered" by prospector Johnny Lang (through Frank Diebold) while Lang was tracking his runaway horse. Farther south, and best for getting the indescribable big picture of the park, is mile-high **Keys View,** a vista sweeping the landscape from high to low— from San Gorgonio Mountain in the north to lonely Salton Sea in the south. The route south to Keys View begins at **Cap Rock,** a huge granite dome topped by a stone-brimmed baseball cap.

DESERT WILDERNESS: NEW NATIONAL PARKS

The California Desert Protection Act—passed by the U.S. Congress on October 8, 1994, and signed into law by President Clinton on October 31 of that year—protects the largest amount of wilderness ever set aside at one time, outside Alaska.

With the addition of 1.3 million acres, the former Death Valley National Monument became **Death Valley National Park**—at 3.3 million acres, the largest national park in the Lower 48 (Yellowstone, 2.2 million acres in Wyoming, is now second largest). The new **Joshua Tree National Park,** also previously a national monument, gained a few acres as well. And the East Mojave National Scenic Area previously managed by the U.S. Bureau of Land Management is now the 1.4 million-acre **Mojave National Preserve**—instead of the East Mojave National Park proposed by environmentalists—but nonetheless managed by the National Park Service.

Within these three new national parks, the California Desert Protection Act designated 39 new federal wilderness areas; 94 percent of Death Valley terrain, for example, is now protected as wilderness. The Act established 69 additional desert wilderness areas, totaling another 3.66 million acres, on nearby federal lands—largely BLM land but also national forests and wildlife refuges.

Aside from obvious turf and name changes, the primary effects of the California Desert Protection Act are philosophical and regulatory—eliminating mining, hunting, target practice, and widespread off-road vehicle use, among other long-running local traditions. (Regulated hunting is still allowed in the Mojave National Preserve and on nonwilderness BLM lands. Off-roading—whether with mountain bikes, dirt bikes dune buggies, or four-wheel drives—is still permitted on various state and federal lands.) Four-wheel-drive vehicles, motorcycles, and mountain bikes are still allowed even in national parks, but only on established gravel and dirt roadways. No vehicles are permitted "off-road" or in wilderness areas.

The most remarkable aspect of the California Desert Preservation Act is its emphasis on the cooperative "ecosystem management" of federal lands in the greater Mojave Desert. Altogether, 5.6 million acres of National Park Service lands—in Death Valley and Joshua Tree National Parks and in the Mojave National Preserve—and an additional 4 million acres of BLM wilderness are included in this effort to preserve natural and cultural resources across jurisdictional boundaries.

For detailed information on all 69 of the BLM's new desert wildernesses, contact the California Desert District Office, 6221 Box Springs Rd., Riverside, CA 92507, 909/697-5200, www.ca.blm.gov/cdd. For current information on the national parks, contact Joshua Tree National Park, 74485 National Park Dr., Twentynine Palms, CA 92277, 760/367-5500, www.nps.gov/jotr; Mojave National Preserve, 222 E. Main St., Ste. 202, Barstow, CA 92311, 760/733-4040, 760/326-6322, and 760/928-2572, www.nps.gov/moja; and Death Valley National Park, P.O. Box 579, Death Valley, CA 92328, 760/786-2331, www.nps.gov/deva.

DESERT QUEEN RANCH

Open to the public only for guided tours, the Desert Queen Ranch is like a well-preserved ghost town—this one preserving the memories of prospector and homesteader Bill Keys, his wife Frances, and their family and friends.

One of Teddy Roosevelt's fabled Rough Riders, William F. Keys worked as a bodyguard, sheriff, and cowboy before abandoning civilization altogether and picking his way across the California desert as a gold miner. If Keys imagined that desert life would be uncomplicated, his thinking was soon corrected. He was first arrested, along with Death Valley Scotty, for his involvement in the "Battle of Wingate Pass" ambush—a staged shootout aimed at preventing Scotty's actual gold mine, financier Albert Johnson of Chicago, from discovering he'd invested in a nonexistent mine. In 1943 he was arrested and convicted of manslaughter after gunplay with neighbor Worth Bagley. At the age of 64, Keys was sentenced to 12 years in San Quentin. His cause championed by mystery writer Erle Stanley Gardner, and his claims of self-defense ultimately bolstered by Bagley's ninth wife, Keys was freed in 1948 at age 69; he received a full pardon in 1956.

Bill Keys's ultimate achievement, of course, was the simple but gracious life he and his wife created for their family in the high desert. The ranch house and outbuildings are preserved by the park service much as the Keys family left them in the 1960s, from the original adobe barn built by the McHaney brothers to the schoolhouses, windmill, junked cars, and antique mining equipment scrounged from abandoned claims. The practical value of Joshua trees—crafted into sturdy corrals, fences, and gateposts—is also on display at the Desert Queen Ranch.

Guided tours of the Desert Queen Ranch, offered by the Joshua Tree Natural History Association, are offered daily Oct.–May, on weekdays at 10 A.M. and 1 P.M. and on weekends at 10 A.M., 1 P.M., and 3 P.M. In summer, tours are offered by reservation only. The cost is $5 per person. Buy tour tickets up to five months in advance by calling 760/367-5555, Mon.–Fri. 9 A.M.–5 P.M., or buy tickets at the Oasis Visitor Center.

East from Cap Rock is Ryan Campground, near remnants of the old Ryan Ranch; farther east, just before the turnoff to Sheep Pass Campground, is the rousing three-mile roundtrip trek to the top of **Ryan Mountain,** where the views are most dramatic at dawn and dusk.

Still farther east is broad **Queen Valley,** crowned on the north by the Queen Mountains and ending far to the south at intersecting Pleasant Valley. The ideal soils and elevations between Sheep Pass and Jumbo Rocks Campground support some of the park's most impressive forests of Joshua trees—thousands and thousands of them, pointing off in all directions. A short dirt road leads north to the ruins of the **Desert Queen Mine,** another historic Joshua Tree enterprise accompanied by murder, mysteries, and miscellaneous intrigues. The 18-mile **Geology Tour Rd.** loop shoots straight south through the valley to demonstrate key geological processes, intersecting the **California Riding and Hiking Trail** en route. Black **Malapai Hill** (a wannabe volcano), an impressive **balanced rock,** and the stunning stones surrounding **Squaw Tank** are tour highlights. To continue the loop, follow the road east toward the Hexie Mountains and the ruins of the **Gold Coin Mine** then south onto the clay Pleasant Valley playa (unwise after rain) and the trail to the onetime **Pinyon Well** gold camp.

Once back on paved road, next east is aptly named **Jumbo Rocks,** where the stone impersonations rival the best efforts of Joshua trees. Even nonhikers enjoy the quarter-mile interpretive stroll from the Jumbo Rocks Campground to the specter of **Skull Rock.** From here, the more adventuresome scramble north on Skull Rock Trail across the park road and through the silent stone canyons before returning to the campground entrance. Just east and north, across the highway from the **Live Oak Picnic Area,** is huge, neatly fractured **Split Rock** and its namesake picnic sites.

Pinto Basin Rd. ambles south past Belle Campground and nearby **Bread Loaf Rock** then White Tank Campground and its associated **Arch Rock** on the way to the **Cholla Cactus Garden** and **Ocotillo Patch**—clear indicators of the Colorado Desert. The road continues south through the stark basin, past its small sand dunes and on to **Cottonwood Spring,** where, beyond the small **visitors center,** camping, picnicking, and hiking are the main attractions. (Fresh water is available here, too.) Continuing south over Cottonwood Pass leads to the one-time site of World War II–era **Camp Young** and, just east along I-10, the **General Patton Memorial Museum** at **Chiriaco Summit.**

DOING JOSHUA TREE

For all its sacred detachment, Joshua Tree is quite sporting. Popular outdoor activities vary from campground loafing and leisurely hiking to biking and rock-climbing. Winter climbing in Joshua Tree, in fact, has achieved international stature, this being one of the few appropriate off-season spots in North America for "bouldering" and big wall climbing outdoors. The truly intrepid climb in other seasons, too. At last count there were 4,500 established park climbing routes. Mountain biking is also a draw, though at Joshua Tree the opportunity for outback biking adventures is limited to established (however tenuously) roads and four-wheel-drive routes. Also popular: bird-watching, botanizing, general nature study, and just staring up into the starry, starry night. For hiking, most Joshua Tree trails—

particularly interpretive loops—are family-friendly and fairly easy, but the park also serves up athletic challenge.

In addition to self-guided trails detailed under Seeing Joshua Tree, above, don't miss **Hidden Valley.** The surreal landscape, a giant stone fortification and gallery of human, animal, and abstract images autographed by ancient peoples with pictographs and petroglyphs, is circled by a fairly easy mile-long loop trail (though in some spots you'll have to scramble over and around boulders). Hidden Valley is also sublime at night—a prime location for watching stars, planets, and meteor showers.

The vigorous three-mile trudge up **Ryan Mountain** and back is a good workout with great eagle-eye views of surrounding valleys, most picturesque at sunrise and sunset. Also challenging among the park's shorter hikes, and a spring tradition for desert wildflower fans, is the three-mile roundtrip trek to **Fortynine Palms Oasis.** The half-day hike to **Lost Horse Mine** showcases remnants of the park's mining history—in this case, a ten-stamp mill and lonely foundations. For mining relics with a grand desert view—not to mention a shady cottonwood oasis—take the fairly challenging three-mile loop from the southern park's Cottonwood Spring to **Mastodon Peak,** an elephantine presence named for its animistic profile. Or use the Mastodon Peak walk as a warm-up for Lost Palms; the trails interconnect. Athletic aficionados of native fan palm oases set their lug soles on the rugged trail to **Lost Palms Oasis** and nearby **Munsen Canyon** (the latter requires a boulder scramble), an eight-mile roundtrip well worth the effort.

Also great for lung expansion is the six-mile roundtrip to Warren Peak via **Black Rock Canyon Trail** in the park's northwestern section, a trek that takes in cacti, Joshua trees, and piñon pines on the way to some inspiring views of the San Bernardino Mountains, the Little San Bernardinos, and Coachella Valley. Good for a one- to two-day walking workout is the 13-mile **Scout Trail** (still shown on some maps, stubbornly, as the Boy Scout Trail) along the western edge of the Wonderland of Rocks; this route also starts in the north, just south of the Indian Cove Ranger Station, and continues to Quail Springs. And 35 miles of the **California Riding and**

Hiking Trail traverse the park, from Covington Flat in the west to its eastern terminus near the junction of the main park road with Pinto Basin Road. It takes two to three days to hike the entire route, but you can turn it into multiple day trips by hopping on or off at Ryan Campground, the Geology Tour Rd., White Tank Campground, and other intersections along the way.

This and other vigorous treks, particularly in the Colorado Desert, are recommended only in winter and early spring, when temperatures are mild. Longer, more remote trails, including the California Riding and Hiking Trail, require backcountry registration as a safety precaution. For current trail information and conditions, contact park visitor centers or ranger stations.

PRACTICAL JOSHUA TREE

A Park Primer
Joshua Tree National Park, open year-round, is about 50 miles northeast of Palm Springs and 140 miles east of Los Angeles via I-10. Most visitors enter from the north, via Twentynine Palms Hwy. (Hwy. 62) and the desert highway towns of Joshua Tree or Twentynine Palms. Joshua Tree aficionados prefer entering from Hwy. 62 at the town of Joshua Tree, reaching the park's **West Entrance**—the most dramatic first impression—via Park Blvd./Quail Springs Road. For newcomers a proper introduction is offered just outside the park's **North Entrance** at the **Oasis Visitor Center** in Twentynine Palms (at the eastern edge of town; from Hwy. 62 follow the signs). Ask here about upcoming ranger-guided tours, walks, and campfire and stargazing programs, scheduled primarily in the fall and spring "interpretive season." Visitors also arrive from the Coachella Valley and I-10 in the south, heading north through Cottonwood Canyon to **Cottonwood Spring,** where there is another but smaller visitors center. All park visitors centers are open daily 8 A.M.–5 P.M. Park admission is $10 per vehicle per week. That fee includes a map/brochure and the current edition of the tabloid *Joshua Tree Journal,* which highlights local natural and cultural history and current park programs and regulations.

For current information, and to receive maps and other park information by mail, contact:

Joshua Tree National Park, 74485 National Park Dr., Twentynine Palms, CA 92277, 760/367-5500, www.nps.gov/jotr/home.html. For a current publications list, and to support park interpretative and preservation activities, contact the **Joshua Tree National History Association** at the same address. For additional California desert information, see www.californiadesert.gov.

When to Come, What to Bring, How to Behave
Fall and spring constitute prime time at Joshua Tree, the only seasons that invite all-day explorations. Officially, the park's interpretive seasons are mid-Oct. through mid-Dec. and mid-Feb. through May. The peak time to see the blooming desert, a phenomenon dependent on rainfall and temperature, is usually mid-Mar. through Apr.—a justifiably popular time to visit the park. Even the air sparkles.

Since summer is like a bake oven—reaching 115°F in the Colorado Desert—Joshua Tree's brisk winter temperatures sometimes surprise visitors. From Dec. through Feb. in the low desert, average daytime high temperatures range from 55 to 65°F and nighttime lows can drop below freezing. In the high desert, which includes most of the park's northern and central areas, temperatures typically run about 10 degrees cooler. April and May are balmy, with days in the 70s and 80s and nights averaging 40–50°F. (Though everything's much less green, temperatures are similar in Oct. and November.) Summer holds sway from June through Sept., 95–105°F during the day, 60–70 at night. Elevations within the park range from 1,000 to 6,000 feet, a fact which also affects area temperatures.

Though it can cook in summer, the season least attractive to visitors, sudden thunderstorms are not unusual. So come prepared for—and dress in layers for protection from—the cold in winter, and unobstructed sun and savage high winds in any season. Basic personal gear even in balmy seasons: broad-brimmed hat, broken-in hiking shoes or boots, T-shirts, shorts, long-sleeved shirts, long pants, longjohns, and a sweater or jacket.

It's tempting to toss sleeping bags right onto the ground for snoozing and late-night stargazing, but tents (and campers) offer better wind protection. If you plan to camp, bring everything—food, water, all essential supplies, even firewood. No collecting is allowed in the park, a prohibition that includes any and all downed plant matter.

Water is largely unavailable in Joshua Tree—in most campgrounds, along the road, and on the trail—so pack plenty. For drinking purposes alone, the recommendation is at least one gallon per person per day during hotter months. Water is available only in the park's "edge" areas: at Black Rock Canyon and Cottonwood Campgrounds, Indian Cove Ranger Station, and Oasis Visitor Center.

Absolutely no services or supplies are available within Joshua Tree National Park. Gasoline, groceries, and other supplies are available in greater Palm Springs, Yucca Valley, and the towns of Joshua Tree and Twentynine Palms.

Now that Joshua Tree is protected as a national park, attendance is up substantially—well over one million visitors annually, and counting—which means increasing strain on the park's campgrounds, limited visitor facilities, and personnel. Be respectful to other people and to the park—and remember that the rules and regulations exist to protect the park and its wonders for future generations.

While exploring, always bring more water than you think you'll need, never travel alone, and stay on established trails and roads. Given the park's vastness and extreme temperatures, getting lost can be deadly. Scofflaw four-wheelers and motorcyclists typically discover that off-limits old roads end in sand pits or steep-sided washes and discover themselves suddenly mired in immediate danger at worst, eventual embarrassment at best. The nearest hospital in the north is in the town of Joshua Tree, 26 miles from Jumbo Rocks; in the south, in Indio, 25 miles from Cottonwood Spring.

Camping at Joshua Tree

At Joshua Tree you feel the "bigness" of this big-sky country even in the campgrounds. Most campsites are tucked into and around towering granite boulders that offer protection from desert winds and provide some degree of soundproofing. Campfires—bring your own firewood—cast enchanting and eerie shadows onto boulder backdrops.

Camping is free (first-come, first-camped) yet spartan at the park's central campgrounds, which feature pit toilets, fire rings, and tables but no running water, no showers, and no electricity. These central campgrounds—**Jumbo Rocks, Hidden Valley,** and **Ryan**—tend to overflow with rock-climbers. Nearby **Belle** and **White Tank** campgrounds, on Pinto Basin Rd., were originally developed as "overflow" sites; White Tank is usually closed in summer.

Individual campsites at **Indian Cove Campground** and **Black Rock Canyon Campground,** $10 per night, and group sites at **Sheep Pass Group Camp,** $20–35 per night, are reservable through the National Park Reservation Service, toll-free 800/365-2267 or http://reservations.nps.gov.

Only Black Rock Canyon, Indian Cove, and Cottonwood Campgrounds have potable running water. Once a private campground, 4,000-foot Black Rock Canyon just outside Yucca Valley is perfect for campers who prefer to make mealtime a side trip to a local restaurant. In addition to drinking water, the 101-site campground here has flush toilets (but no showers) and an RV dump station—all the comforts of home, comparatively speaking. Ditto for 62-campsite Cottonwood Campground at Cottonwood Spring, $10 per night, which is first-come, first-camped (no reservations). At isolated Indian Cove Campground at the northern edge of the Wonderland of Rocks—near Hwy. 62 between the communities of Joshua Tree and Twentynine Palms—drinking water is available at the nearby ranger station.

There is a 14-day camping limit from fall through spring (Oct.–May), 30 days in summer. For more information about Joshua Tree campgrounds, contact park visitors centers.

Staying near Joshua Tree

Accommodations, food, and services are available in the nearby Morongo Basin towns of Twentynine Palms, Joshua Tree, and Yucca Valley. For information about what's available in towns bordering Joshua Tree, contact local chambers of commerce—**Twentynine Palms,** 6455-A Mesquite Ave. 760/367-3445, www.29chamber.com; **Joshua Tree Village,** 61325 Twentynine Palms Hwy. in Joshua Tree, 760/366-3723, www.desertgold.com/jtcc/jtcc.html; and **Yucca Valley,** 55569 Twentynine Palms Hwy. in Yucca Valley, 760/365-6323, www.yuccavalley.org.

Always a best bet in Twentynine Palms is

the **Best Western Garden Inn and Suites,** 71487 Twentynine Palms Hwy., 760/367-9141, fax 760/367-2584, with spring high-season rates $79 and up (Moderate-Premium) and extras including a heated swimming pool. Quite comfortable for a noncamping overnight is the **Circle C Lodge,** a motel at 6340 El Rey Ave., 760/367-7615, fax 760/361-0247; for reservations, call toll-free 800/545-9696. This attractive, intimate motel features just 11 rooms—all large, with kitchens—featuring cable TV, video players, and free movies. Best of all, after a day spent scrambling over rocks and around Joshua trees: the landscaped pool and whirlpool area plus outdoor barbecue and dining setup. Rates are $70–85. Moderate. The Circle C is 1.5 miles west of town via Hwy. 62, then one block north.

For something more out-there, quite fascinating are the four isolated and eccentric cabins offered at **Mojave Rock Ranch** ("Established Way Back") near Joshua Tree National Park. How many cabins, after all, are "elegantly rustic" and "cozy, funky, whimsical" at the same time? Yet hanging one's hat in the Mojave Desert does *not* mean abandoning creature comfort. All cabins at Mojave Rock Ranch feature a wood-burning stove or fireplace (firewood provided), fully equipped kitchen, private bathroom, unique decor (some combination of antique and eclectic), at least two bedrooms and two king-size beds (one also has a sleeping porch and a queen bed), and down comforters and pillows, linens, towels, and toiletries. Not to mention, for warm days, ceiling fans and evaporative coolers. Little extras include telephones with private numbers, stereo systems and CD players, satellite TV, outdoor barbecues or fire pits, and enclosed areas for dogs. For more information, contact: Mojave Rock Ranch, P.O. Box 552, Joshua Tree, CA 92252, 760/366-8455, fax 760/366-1996, www.mojaverockranch.com.

MOJAVE NATIONAL PRESERVE

Easily accessible from I-40 in the south and I-15 in the north, 1.4 million-acre Mojave National Preserve stretches east from Baker to Hwy. 95 and the Nevada border near Nipton. In deference to its freeway delimitation this sublime slice of desert life is affectionately known as "The Lonesome Triangle," though it was lonesome out here long before there were freeways.

In a sense, the entire area is a historic thoroughfare. Petroglyphs and other signs of early human habitation in the East Mojave date from at least 11,000 years ago. In more recent times native peoples, Mojave and Paiute traders alike, trekked back and forth across the desert to participate in California's earliest coastal commerce. The most credible predecessor of present-day freeways was created from this original Native American trading route—the Mojave Rd., first dubbed the Old Government Rd., which ran from Prescott, Arizona, to somewhere south of Los Angeles. But first came Spanish explorers, traveling to San Francisco from Mexico in 1776,

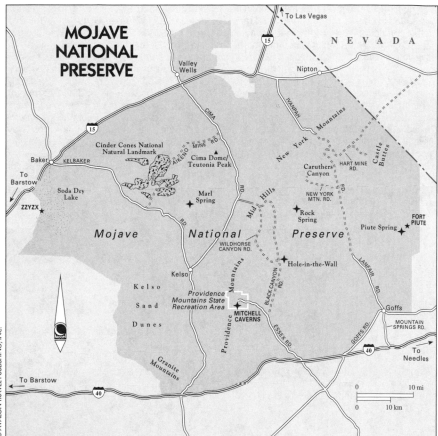

and Kit Carson, Jedediah Smith, and other early 19th-century American explorers and traders. This vast desert, more mountain than sand, also watered and sheltered stagecoaches and wagon trains and the lonely military outposts quickly built to protect them. The Mojave Rd. was also a freeway for camels. In one of the oddest chapters in the history of the West, from 1857 to 1860 Jefferson Davis attempted to introduce camels as desert-hardy American pack animals—a business venture that might have succeeded had it not been for impatient teamsters and the onrushing Civil War. Camels were already California history when Davis became president of the Confederacy.

Present-day signs of human habitation include shotgun shell casings, graffiti, mining mementos, rutted old roads, railroad tracks, and range cattle. Yet here the desert abides, an endless landscape of ancient mountains and youthful lava dotted with sand dunes and grasslands. As the western Mojave Desert is tamed by suburbs and military and space-age technology, the eastern Mojave is as lonely as ever—happy news for the city-weary. While it's possible to see, if not experience, most of the Mojave's main attractions in two to three days, it takes at least several days to shake off the side effects of urban worry and overscheduling—whatever it is that blinds people to the desert's graces. Stay a while.

Practical Mojave Preserve

The preserve ranges in elevation from 1,000 to 8,000 feet. Summer temperatures can exceed 100°F, which is why Oct. through May is the most popular time to come. Even in spring and fall be prepared for subfreezing temperatures and, in winter, snow. Popular activities include backpacking, hiking, camping, back-roads ambling, and stargazing. Legal game hunting is permitted, but no other gunplay (including target shooting).

Come prepared for anything, and bring everything. No services or gasoline and minimal water supplies are available within the preserve. Some roads are unpaved, or partially paved; high-clearance vehicles are recommended. You'll be on your own in very remote country, so be sure your vehicle is in good repair.

For more information about the area's attractions, recreation, hiking, and camping, contact: **Baker Information Center,** Mojave National Preserve, 72157 Baker Blvd., P.O. Box 241, Baker, CA 92309, 760/733-4040, www.nps.gov/moja—or stop by the center, conveniently located beneath the **World's Tallest Thermometer** adjacent to the Bun Boy restaurant in Baker. (Look up. You can't miss it.) Open daily. There's also the walk-in **Needles Information Center,** 707 W. Broadway in Needles (closed Monday). A park service information center is also at Hole-in-the-Wall, open daily from Nov. through Apr. at last report.

For basic campground information, see Mid Hills, Hole-in-the-Wall, and Vicinity, below; "no trace" backcountry camping—setting up camp at least a half-mile from a road and 1,000 feet back from any water source—is permitted throughout the preserve.

Mojave Desert ghost town

TOM MYERS PHOTOGRAPHY

THE ROAD TO ZZYZX

In 1944 Curtis Howe Springer, a colorful character in Mojave Desert history and the self-described "last of the old-time medicine men," established Zzyzx Mineral Springs. Here, 11 miles south of Baker at the end of 4.5-mile Zzyzx Road, on 12,000 acres of land that belonged to the U.S. government, Springer built his 60-room hotel, health spa, church, castle, and radio station. Ever the promoter, he chose the name "Zzyzx"—pronounced ZYE-Zix, to rhyme with "size six"—because he wanted his resort to be the last listing in the telephone book.

Neither a doctor nor Methodist minister, Springer claimed to be both. He solicited cash donations, over the radio, to cure ailments. And he sold his elixirs and potions internationally—until 1974, when he was arrested for unauthorized use of federal land and various violations of food and drug laws.

Since 1976, Zzyzx has served as the Desert Studies Center of the California State University system. Stop by the visitors center (unstaffed), and then wander the grounds and study exhibits to learn about the endangered Mojave chub (a fish) and other aspects of area natural history. For a picturesque view of dry Soda Lake and the mountains beyond, look east through the old bathhouse windows.

KIM WEIR

At Zzyzx Mineral Springs you can dip into the past of an old charlatan's desert resort, now part of the California State University system.

ALONG KELBAKER ROAD

Kelbaker Road introduces a few of the Mojave National Preserve's natural wonders. The route starts at I-15 near Baker and then meanders east and south for some 50 miles, eventually intersecting I-40, the preserve's southern boundary. Some sections of Kelbaker Road are unpaved to allow bighorn sheep to cross the road—they disdain pavement—but the route is typically passable even for passenger cars.

Kelbaker's first major sight: the Mojave Cinder Cones, also known as **Cinder Cones Natural National Landmark,** a very young volcanic formation atop older lava flows. (A side trip via Aiken's Mine Rd. takes you there.) About 35 miles from Baker is **Kelso,** where cottonwoods, palms, and the graceful **Kelso Depot** have long been the main attractions. Though the depot

was still dilapidated, at last report, and funding seemed somewhat dubious, plans to restore it as a visitors center were in the works.

Even before reaching Kelso, to the southwest you'll see the **Kelso Dunes,** wonderful for dune walks. The second tallest dune system in the California desert, rising some 600 feet to 700 feet above the desert floor and fanning out over 45 square miles, the isolated Kelso Dunes were created from fine wind-driven sand—golden rose quartz—blown down from the Mojave Sink in the northwest. To the southeast are the Providence Mountains, where the focal point of the **Providence Mountain State Recreation Area** is **Mitchell Caverns State Reserve.** Last stop before I-40: the stunning stone sculpture of the **Granite Mountains,** a desert research area reminiscent of Joshua Tree National Park. Among the protected species here is a cave-dwelling Venus hair fern—typically at home

DESERT SURVIVAL: BE PREPARED

Human survival in the desert is fairly easy to manage. Yet given the severity of the environment, it's also nothing to take for granted. In any season, never hike, bike, climb, or go four-wheeling alone. Be sure to let someone know where you're going and when you expect to arrive or return—a good idea even on highway trips.

First and foremost, plan your supply stops; beyond Palm Springs, best bets in the desert proper include Barstow and Ridgecrest. Basic readiness for desert travel includes a travel-worthy car—no known engine trouble, good tires and an inflated spare, tire chains, full tank of gas—along with accurate maps, extra water, extra food, extra clothing, blankets or sleeping bags, a fresh first-aid kit, and personal essentials (medications, extra eyeglasses, etc.). Basic emergency supplies include materials for makeshift shade and shelter (tarp or tube tent plus nylon cord), fire-starting and signaling supplies (waterproof matches or lighters, candles, safety flares, flashlight, signal mirrors, whistles), and both salty and high-energy foods.

If you'll be traveling on remote back roads, an extra five-gallon can of gasoline (carried outside the passenger compartment) *and* an emergency five-gallon can of water—beyond what you think you'll need—are also prudent. Also handy: tool kit and car repair manual, extra engine oil, carpet scraps (for traction if you get stuck), spare hoses and clamps, radiator stop-leak, tire repair kit and tire pump, jack pad (to support the tire jack in sandy soils), shovel, electrical tape, and baling or other sturdy wire.

In hot weather stay in the shade during the heat of the day, slow down—avoid overheating yourself—and drink plenty of water, even if you don't feel particularly thirsty. (By the time you do, you're on the way to dehydration.) Intense heat inspires heavy perspiration, which, in practical terms, means people need to drink at least one gallon of water per day. Wear a hat, sunglasses, and loose long pants and long-sleeved shirts to minimize sun exposure. Slather on the sunscreen. Wear (or at least carry) good sturdy shoes to protect your feet in case you'll need to walk any distance. When the ambient air temperature is 120°F or so, the temperature of the desert's surface is up to 40 percent higher.

Should you become stranded in the desert heat, even if within a few miles of a highway, remember the first rule of survival: Take care of yourself first. In other words, tend to basic survival needs before worrying about repairing your vehicle or otherwise seeking rescue. Stay with your vehicle and stay out of the sun (underneath your car if there's no other available shade). Wait until the day cools to work on the car or walk for help—if you must, and if you know where you're going. Even if you're hopelessly stuck, in most cases it's wiser to wait for help to come to *you*. Don't wander away from your car and get lost.

If stranded in cold weather, the same "personal survival first" rule applies. Dress warmly and stay dry to avoid hypothermia (a dangerous drop in body temperature). Build a fire if possible, wrap yourself in blankets or a sleeping bag, eat well, drink warm liquids, and move around—walk briskly, do jumping jacks—to maintain body temperature and circulation. Do *not* drink alcohol, which may make you feel warmer but actually lowers body temperature—starting with the heart, lungs, and other vital organs.

---

above 7,000 feet in the Sierra Nevada—trapped here since the end of the Ice Age.

MID HILLS, HOLE-IN-THE-WALL, AND VICINITY

Cima Dome

Cima Dome is the first thing visitors notice when approaching the preserve's central stone fortresses of Mid Hills and Hole-in-the-Wall, is actually much easier to see from a distance. Because of its perfect and gradual slope, under

foot it's all but invisible. Despite its proximity to the Mojave Cinder Cones, Cima does not share their volcanic history. This nearly symmetrical, 1,500-foot-tall mound of granitelike quartz monzonite, once a mass of molten rock, is a batholith 75 square miles in size (10 miles in diameter). Outcroppings of the original bedrock include **Teutonia Peak,** 5,755 feet tall; for up-close appreciation, scramble up the two-mile trail (marked) that starts just north of Sunrise Rock. Cima Dome also features one of the world's finest—and largest—forests of Joshua trees, a species distinct from those in Joshua

Tree National Park.

To get here: From I-15, exit south at Cima Rd. in Valley Wells and continue heading southeast about seven miles; follow the signed turnoffs.

Mid Hills and Hole-in-the-Wall

Named rather unimaginatively for their location midway between the New York and Providence Mountains, the mile-high Mid Hills serve cool, pine-scented mountain air with some grand desert views—the shimmering Kelso Dunes to the west, Cima Dome and the Pinto Mountains to the north. According to local lore, the rock outpost to the south known as Hole-in-the-Wall was named by a member of Butch Cassidy's outlaw gang, since it resembled his favorite Wyoming hideout. Another Hole-in-the-Wall attraction is the iron-ring-in-the-wall hand-holds for the short, steep trail into odd **Banshee Canyon,** a natural amphitheater.

For one of the best hikes around, take the eight-mile (one-way) **Mid Hills to Hole-in-the-Wall Trail,** which you can shorten to a three-mile loop at the cutoff (marked) and which is also convenient for car shuttles. Along the fairly rugged route: petroglyphs and a ceremonial Native American "birthing hole" (for spiritual, not actual, births). If you'd rather drive the distance, horseshoe-shaped **Wild Horse Canyon Rd.** meanders for 11 miles through the volcanic mesas and low-desert cactus land connecting Hole-in-the-Wall and Mid Hills—the nation's first official Back Country Byway, most scenic during spring wildflower season.

Marvelous **Mid Hills Campground,** tucked into the juniper and piñon pine at an elevation of 5,600 feet, can be downright cold—if not buried in sudden snow—during winter, sometimes also during the peak spring and fall camping season. Be prepared. The 26 campsites feature tables, fire rings, and pit toilets; as the road is a bit treacherous, RVs are not recommended. **Hole-in-the-Wall Campground,** with 37 campsites at 4,200 feet, is more RV friendly, with some pull-through campsites as well as dump station. Both campgrounds are $10 per night, first-come, first-camped, with a 14-day limit; both now feature potable water. But bring extra water if you can (supplies are limited) along with firewood, and anything else you think you'll need in the middle of nowhere. If preserve campgrounds are full, head for the BLM's **Afton Canyon Campground** west of Baker. By reservation only, group camping is available within the preserve at **Black Rock Canyon Group Campground.**

Mitchell Caverns State Reserve

Eons of calcium carbonate deposits created the graceful stone curtains, stalactites, and stalagmites at El Pakiva and Tecopa caves; these days, stairs and railings offer easy access. The limestone caves at Mitchell Caverns State Reserve, high on the craggy slopes of the Providence Mountains about 16 miles north of I-40 via Essex Rd., are the only Southern California caves developed for visitors. That fact makes them attractive to the occasional film crew. In 1990, for example, Oliver Stone filmed part of the Jim Morrison art-rock bio *The Doors* here.

Either before or after the guided tour, walk the short **Mary Beal Nature Trail** and—for the views—the more challenging **Crystal Spring Trail** up the canyon. Rock-climbing is also popular year-round. The park day-use fee is $2 per vehicle. Access to the caves is possible only on guided tours, which are offered from mid-Sept. through mid-June at 1:30 P.M. on weekdays, and at 10 A.M., 1:30 P.M., and 3 P.M. on weekends and state holidays. Tours are $3 adults, $1 children ages 6–17 (under 6 free). And no matter what the temperature may be outside, always bring a sweater or light jacket on cave tours; the temperature is a constant and cool 65°F.

The on-site visitors center here is staffed only part-time. So for more information and to arrange group tours, contact: **California Department of Parks and Recreation,** Mojave Desert Sector, 1051 W. Ave. M, Ste. 201, Lancaster, CA 93535, 805/942-0662, www.calparksmojave.com.

DEATH VALLEY NATIONAL PARK

To stargazers Death Valley is the closest thing to heaven in light-blinded Southern California. To rock hounds it's a timeless monument to very grounded geologic grandeur. To botanists and bird-watchers, it's a study in successful adaptation. Its vast spaces sprinkled with petroglyphs, ghost towns, mine ruins, and other enduring marks of human aspiration, to hikers and history buffs it's one endless discovery trail.

The essence of Death Valley, however, is its remoteness—and its aloof indifference to all things civilized.

Though this otherworldly landscape has been protected as a national monument since 1933, after decades of political wrangling California's astonishing Death Valley was re-created, as a national park, in 1994. With national park status came a near-doubling in size—that much more room to roam.

THE LAY OF THE LAND

Squeezed on all sides by bold, bare mountains, as the crow flies Death Valley extends about 90 miles from north to south; by road, following the valley's curves and canyons, the distance is 130 miles or more. Though the park boundaries are far more expansive, the valley itself measures less than a mile across at its narrowest point, about 10 miles at its widest. The nation's hottest, driest, and most dramatically desolate summer landscape, about 500 square miles of the valley floor lie below sea level. Not surprisingly, the lowest elevations in the United States are in Death Valley. Until the 1950s, Badwater was considered the lowest point in the United States, measured at 279 feet below sea level. More careful measurement revealed two lower spots in the park—one west-northwest of Badwater and the other north-northwest of Badwater, both measured at 282 feet below sea level. Death Valley's depths are all the more impressive when one considers that the highest point in the continental United States, Mount Whitney, is about 100 miles away, in the southern Sierra Nevada near Lone Pine.

In the south, Death Valley's floor is one vast and sandy salt flat, whitewashed over the eons by mineral deposits. This inhospitable landscape, this naturally toxic environment, is home to an astonishing array of alkali-adapted plants and animals. The Amargosa River ("bitter one," in Spanish) is the valley's one and only, an alkaline stream that flows south from Nevada, winds around the Black Mountains, and then heads north to percolate into oblivion. In the north, salt flats give way to sand dunes, white clay, and ghostly flatlands.

Surrounding the valley are more than 100 steep and narrow canyons, gorges, gulches, and washes leading up into colorful, craggy landscapes. At the mouths of many canyons are vast and sometimes stunning alluvial fans. Water-borne boulders blend with sand and gravel sediments—

the towering stalk of a century plant

KIM WEIR

"Badwater"), tainted by toxic concentrations of mineral salts.

Death Valley's Story: The Landscape

In many ways a Death Valley visit is also a trip through time, an exploration of an impressive open-air natural history museum narrated by the land itself. The landscape in Death Valley tells the story of the slow but dramatic passage of geologic time—a tale writ large here and flamboyantly illustrated by startling shapes and odd angles, everything brushed with vivid color and then etched by water and wind.

Death Valley's landscape began to emerge some 60 million years ago. Angry earthquakes re-created the Sierra Nevada—forcing the new granite blocks of that range up through the earth's crust where wild magma flows cemented them into place. This creative violence blew south, too; tiny fissures spread throughout the earth like the spindly threads of a spider's web. Rocked and rolled by the Sierra Nevada commotion, the molten rock of the inner earth broke through the earthquake faults here, too, rising and falling and tilting and twisting until the underground firestorm finally died out.

The stonefaced new landscape, later named the Mojave Block, covered 15,000 square miles. Time chipped away at it for the next 25 million years, eroding strong features into near oblivion and then feverishly creating them anew. During the next two million years, with the arrival of the Ice Age and the Pleistocene Epoch, Death Valley and the rest of the region rested.

As the ice receded, the land awakened. Rivers of ice-melt sliced through the stony landscape before racing to the sea or pooling into vast inland lakes. In a small corner of the Mojave Block, unrelenting erosion scoured out a deep but narrow trough almost 100 miles long from north to south, its low profile dramatized by resurging rocky ranges on both the east and west—the terrain we know today as Death Valley.

But Death Valley wasn't always dry, wasn't always a valley. Some 10,000 years ago it was a lake—actually, a series of lakes, separated by giant steps in time. (In recent history the large northern lake was posthumously named Lake Rogers, its large southern cousin, Lake Manly—after two heroes in early Death Valley settlement.) By 6,000 years ago the region's great

DEATH VALLEY AS TOURIST ATTRACTION AND PRESERVE

By the early 1900s wild Death Valley attracted its first tourists, who arrived by train. Motorized vehicles also gained a tirehold. Touring Death Valley by automobile was an adventure even in terms of simple mechanics, since the rugged roads repeatedly sacrificed tires, axles, and oil pans on the rocky altar of nature appreciation.

Early visitor facilities, including the Furnace Creek Inn, were owned and operated by the Pacific Borax Company—even for a time after 1933, when the valley gained national and international acknowledgment for its uniqueness, and a new level of protection, as Death Valley National Monument.

In late 1994 Death Valley's status was elevated again—to national park—with passage of the California Desert Protection Act. Along with Death Valley's new moniker came new land—an additional 1.3 million acres, for a total of almost 3.4 million acres (1,347,000 hectares), making this the largest national park outside Alaska. Onetime Bureau of Land Management (BLM) lands in Eureka Valley, Saline Valley, the Panamint Mountains, the northern Panamint Valley, Hunter Mountain, the Nelson Range, Greenwater Valley, and the Owlshead Mountains are now included in Death Valley National Park.

testimony to the power of water crashing down from the mountains.

The Panamint Range, from 6,000 to more than 11,000 feet in elevation, borders Death Valley on the west; the range's northern section is also known as the Cottonwood Mountains. On the east is the Amargosa Range, a stone-faced dirge composed of the Grapevine, Funeral, and Black Mountains. The equally optimistic Last Chance Range closes in on the valley from the northwest, the Owlshead Mountains from the southwest.

With the area's low rainfall—and keeping in mind that the potential evaporation rate here is about 150 inches per year—there's a surprising amount of water in Death Valley, provided by surrounding mountain springs. Furnace Creek visitor facilities sit astride a generous and historic freshwater spring, as does Scotty's Castle, though most of the valley's water is "bad" (as in lakes, including Death Valley's, had become mere puddles, the landscape watered only by streams and sweetwater springs. About 3,000 years ago the lakes, streams, and springs had all disappeared, the scenery taking on its contemporary salt-crusted characteristics. Then it rained again, the new deluge creating a 30-foot-deep lake. But by 2,000 years ago Death Valley's vast interior was once again bone-dry. Done with molten fire and water, for its further work time experimented with wind and intense dry heat.

The Land as Interpreter
Though the language of time is challenging to master, at Death Valley the land itself is a useful interpreter. The ancient lake shoreline is marked by terraces along the valley's walls, for example, and the work of big and boisterous rivers memorialized by monstrous alluvial fans. The vast salty bottomlands represent eons' worth of minerals washed down into the ancient lake from the mountains and then concentrated in one place, through evaporation. And the endlessly creative work of erosion and the adaptive evolution of plants and animals appears everywhere—on every mountain, in every canyon, atop every sand dune, even in streams flowing with toxic levels of minerals.

Death Valley Climate:
Warm, Hot, and Hotter
One glance at the desolate terrain convinces most people that Death Valley is a desert. Scientifically speaking, such classifications can be complicated, since "desert" does not apply to all hot, bleak landscapes nor to all areas of low precipitation. Death Valley is indeed a desert, however, for several official reasons. Its distance from the moderating effects of the California current virtually guarantees that cool Pacific Ocean air is well heated by the time it reaches the valley. Death Valley is also tucked away behind multiple rainshadows. Storms blowing in off the ocean must get up and over several major mountain ranges to reach the valley; few have any moisture left if and when they do arrive. Death Valley is also defined by stable subtropical high pressure, with the air descending and warming.

"Warming" is a euphemism. Winter is the traditional travel season here for good reason—extremely inhospitable summer temperatures.

Though winter is the "rainy season," not much rain falls; Death Valley's average annual rainfall is just 1.84 inches. What moisture does arrive often comes all at once. (Watch for flash flooding at all times after desert rainstorms.) In January of 1995, 2.59 inches of rain fell—the wettest month ever recorded in Death Valley—though record high rainfall came in 1913 and again in 1983, with annual totals of 4.54 inches.

The year 1913 was a record-breaker in terms of temperature, too, graced both with Death Valley's lowest recorded temperature—15°F, recorded in January—and highest temperature— 134°F, recorded on July 10, a temperature extreme expected only once every 650 years, according to weather experts. Average daytime winter temperatures are 60–70°F, summer

---

WILDFLOWERS: THE MOST EPHEMERAL DESERT BEAUTY

When first introduced to the California desert, neophytes typically see only sand, scrub brush, and an otherwise empty horizon of desolate mountain ranges. Yet California's Mojave and Colorado Deserts both boast an abundance of drought-adapted plant and animal life.

Most accessible for a natural history introduction is California's desert flora—more than 2,000 native species, including grasses, annuals, perennial herbs, shrubs, and trees. To appreciate desert plantlife at its most dazzling, visit during spring's ephemeral wildflower season. Dramatic desert-wide displays require early and fairly constant rain, through March—a rare phenomenon occurring only about once per decade. Because of local microclimates, some areas may put on a snazzy show in other years, however.

Popular areas to observe the desert flower frenzy—largely, but not exclusively, a Mojave Desert phenomenon—include the **Antelope Valley California Poppy Reserve** west of Lancaster; **Anza-Borrego Desert State Park** east of San Diego; **Death Valley National Park** southeast of the Sierra Nevada; the **Mojave National Preserve** in the high desert; and **Joshua Tree National Park** and other natural areas near **Palm Springs.** Call local parks for more information, including peak-bloom projections for a particular year. To avoid the wildflower-crazed crowds, arrive on a weekday.

temperatures 90–100°F. But white-hot misery is common enough in summer. In 1974 the park recorded 134 days when temperatures exceeded 100°F, and in 1994, 31 days over 120°F and 97 days over 110°F.

After scaring visitors silly with such statistics, people here typically soften the blow by saying: "But at least it's *dry* heat," meaning that the heat-related discomfort is much less severe than it would be in more humid climates. True enough, though summer perspiration rates can be astounding. (Drink water, drink water, drink water.) Dry heat or no, don't walk barefoot in and around Death Valley, particularly in summer. Ground temperatures generally exceed the ambient air temperature by about 40 percent; the highest ground temperature ever recorded here was 201°F, at Furnace Creek on July 15, 1972, on a day when the overall temperature was 128°F.

But Death Valley's extremist temperament shows in the winter, too. Though it rarely freezes here, it can get quite chilly during the November-to-March peak travel season; if you'll be camping out, come prepared for nighttime temperatures dipping into the 30s—not counting wind chill, which can make it feel much colder.

SEEING AND DOING DEATH VALLEY

You can do Death Valley in a day—if a tour of Scotty's Castle and an exhausting all-day road trip will assure you that you've "done it." Better by

far is a longer stay—a week to 10 days, if possible, or at least a long weekend—for in-depth exploration and more experiential memories.

Before setting out to discover Death Valley and vicinity, stop by the visitors center at Furnace Creek—then set priorities. Even with fairly few stops it can easily take an entire day just to get from one end of the valley to the other. Much more pleasant is charting, over a period of several days, various looping, long-distance road trips. With even minimal planning one can manage an early-morning hike, a pleasant picnic, and some leisurely sightseeing before heading back for a relaxed evening in the thrall of a Death Valley sunset.

"Big Picture" Viewpoints

Taking in Death Valley's stunning vistas from vantage points well above the valley itself—experiencing the "big picture"—is particularly spectacular at sunrise or sunset, when light and landscape are at their most dramatic. But getting the big picture involves mileage and, in some cases, shoe leather. Save at least some miles and time by stopping at the following panoramic (and semi-panoramic) "big picture" viewpoints on your way to or from elsewhere.

Just a few miles southeast of Furnace Creek via Hwy. 190, and therefore quite popular, is **Zabriskie Point.** The view here is toward the west—the Amargosa Range's yellow-clay hills, onetime lake-bottom sediments, and the towering Panamint Mountains beyond. It's a fairly

Zabriskie Point

easy downhill hike, about 2.5 miles, from here to Golden Canyon and then on to Badwater Road.

For another perspective on the grandeur of Death Valley, try mile-high **Dante's View,** a name inspired by purgatory's poetic description in *The Divine Comedy,* Dante Alighieri's classic 14th-century spiritual allegory. Just getting here, a 25-mile drive from the visitors center, is an awesome allegory on the true nature of time. Below the road's last steep, hairpin climb is a place to park one's excess baggage (in this case, hindrances such as motor homes and trailers) and slow down. At the overlook—at the edge of the visible world—comes the surprising sensation that time, human time, has stopped altogether.

Directly below is Badwater, an impressive puddle of same famous for its locale—near the lowest elevations in the continental United States—and connected to the green of Furnace Creek by a thin asphalt string. Directly across the valley, about a mile above one's head, is notched Telescope Peak, the most prominent presence in the Panamints; beyond to the northwest are the Sierra Nevada and triangular Mount Whitney (visible on a clear day), the highest point in the Lower 48. Between these highs and lows is almost everything else in Death Valley's careful crazy-quilt of color—nature at its most elemental. Most identifiable: the vast salt sink, at its blinding, Borax-bright whitest in summer, and the valley's immense and impressive alluvial fans, boulders bounced down out of the canyons by water and gravity and then neatly piled high by inertia.

Aguerreberry Point, just north of Emigrant Pass on the road to Wildrose, is a panoramic view looking east over Death Valley. For the best roadside view of the rugged Panamint Mountains, pull off at **Father Crowley Point** adjacent to Hwy. 190, on the edge of Rainbow Canyon. (To get here from the west and Hwy. 136, continue east for 21 miles on Hwy. 190. If coming from Death Valley, this viewpoint is about eight miles west of Panamint Springs.) Below in the Panamint Valley are the serene and sandy Panamint Dunes, supremely hikable. Look to the southeast for another view of Telescope Peak. Some say the best Death Valley view of all is from **Telescope Peak,** looking east from the summit—an experience you'll miss if uninspired by the idea of making the long-day's hike up from Wildrose Canyon (best in spring and fall).

The peak was named for the clarity and "up-closeness" of the view looking east, as if through a telescope. An easier climb, with great views of both east and west, is **Wildrose Peak** nearby.

IN AND AROUND FURNACE CREEK

Especially for first-time visitors, the best place to start a Death Valley adventure is at the **Death Valley National Park Visitor Center** at Furnace Creek. The museum introduces both the lay of the land—with a huge three-dimensional relief map, to scale—and the area's cultural and natural history. Park orientation programs are scheduled daily (film shown every half-hour from 8:30 A.M.–4 P.M., 10 A.M.–4 P.M. on Sun.), with special daytime talks, evening programs, and ranger-guided hikes throughout Death Valley offered from Oct. into April. The visitor center is also *the* place to stop for maps, books, and current road and trail information—the latter absolutely mandatory if you'll be leaving the blacktop behind, since conditions can change radically overnight. Other essential visitor facilities and services are nearby, so fill up on gas, emergency water, and trail snacks while in the neighborhood.

The Borax Story:
Memorabilia and Memorable Sights
The story of borax and related borates—essential ingredients in soaps and detergents, boric acid, photographic chemicals, porcelain enamel, solder, optical lenses, insulation, even antifreeze—is one of the world's less exciting tales. But Death Valley's contribution to borax mining mythology is legendary—the stuff of Hollywood legend, at any rate. Get the complete and unabridged borax story at the park's free **Borax Museum,** just north of the Furnace Creek Ranch entrance and southwest of the post office. The building itself, built in 1883 as a combination kitchen, office, and boarding house, was relocated here from its original site at the borax operations in Twenty-Mule Team Canyon. With historical photos and miscellaneous memorabilia—elegant Shoshone basketry, railroad schedules, prospecting tools, and very peculiar mining contraptions—the impacts of the local borax business, and mining in general, are well documented. But borax, too, is on display, an

astonishing collection of mineral samples. Out back is still more historical amazement—a virtual barnyard of wagons, buckboards, stagecoaches, and an oxen-shoeing rig keeping company with the original Greenwater **Chuckwalla** printing press, a Baldwin locomotive from the Death Valley Railroad, and the original 1880s 20-mule team barn from Mojave.

Two miles north of the visitor center are the remains of the **Harmony Borax Works,** where the interpretive quarter-mile path winds past an 1880s-vintage 20-mule team borax wagon, crumbling adobes, and antique equipment. Harmony was the "cottonball" borax processing center of the W. T. Coleman Company, Death Valley's first successful borax operation, established here in 1882. Harmony's most lasting contribution to borax mining history was the 20-mule team wagon rig—an innovation that allowed the mules, hitched in pairs, to pull two loaded borax wagons plus a 1,200-gallon water tank, a total load of 36.5 tons, from here across the desert to Mojave, some 180 rough and rugged miles distant.

It's a fairly easy, level five-mile hike from Harmony through the **Borax Haystacks** to the north, stacked by Chinese laborers to establish Harmony's mining claim—a sight most striking at sunrise.

East on Highway 190
The jaunt east from Furnace Creek via Hwy. 190 is perfect for a late afternoon tour. First stop is **Zabriskie Point,** with its panoramic view of the badlands below. (Bring camera and film.) Next stop, about two miles along, is the one-way side loop through **Twenty Mule Team Canyon,** a onetime mecca for borax mining and miners. The colorful undulating hills here were sculpted from mud—ancient lakebed sediments—that were folded, faulted, and uplifted before being smothered by lava flows. About five miles farther on is the turnoff to **Dante's View,** one of the park's most popular panoramic vistas and prime end-of-day destination for sunset seekers.

Before paved Dante's View Rd. jogs westward toward purgatory, unpaved **Furnace Creek Wash Rd.** shoots off to the southeast to **Greenwater Canyon** and its ridge-top petroglyphs (some damaged by modern-day cretins), other petroglyph sights, and the cholla-dotted landscape near what remains of the **Greenwater** copper mining camp.

Beyond the four-wheeling route into **Gold Valley,** the road eventually intersects Hwy. 178 east of Salsberry Pass near Shoshone.

Back on Hwy. 190 from Dante's View Rd., 19 miles to the east and outside the park is spot-in-the-road **Death Valley Junction,** known as Amargosa before becoming a de facto company town for the Tonopah and Tidewater Railroad. In the cooler months the hottest entertainment act around is staged at the **Amargosa Opera House,** a small theater included in the original **Amargosa Hotel** complex built by the Pacific Coast Borax Company in 1923–25.

HEADING SOUTH: BAD WATER, BETTER VIEWS

Heading due south from Furnace Creek via scenic Badwater Rd. (Hwy. 178) leads to **Badwater**—a desert pond of variable size not nearly as "bad" or as devoid of life as it might appear—and its surreal salt flat surroundings. On the way to Badwater but off the main road are other intriguing features, including hikable **Golden Canyon,** the one-way **Artists Palette** driving tour, the **Devil's Golf Course** salt formations, and the **Natural Bridge** stone arch shaped by ancient waterfalls.

Below Badwater the paved road continues south along the big toes of the Black Mountains—some notable alluvial fans—to the ruins of World War I–era **Ashford Mill,** then veers east to climb up and over Salsberry Pass and roll on to the tiny town of **Shoshone** just beyond the boundaries of Death Valley National Park—a total distance of over 70 miles from Furnace Creek. Some five miles south of Shoshone, via Hwy. 127, is **Tecopa Hot Springs,** a somewhat surreal snowbird hotspot; about 28 miles north of Shoshone is the one-actress town of **Death Valley Junction,** famous these days for its **Amargosa Opera House.**

Gravel-road adventure is also available in Death Valley's southern reaches. From Badwater Rd. near Artists Palette, **West Side Rd.** ambles southwest and then skirts the western edge of the valley before rejoining the paved road just north of Ashford Mill. Attractions along the way include the ruins of the failed **Eagle Borax Works** and the **Cinder Hill** cinder cone, in addition to four-wheel-drive roads into **Warm Springs** and other canyons. Another worthwhile four-wheel-drive route, starting just southeast of Ashford Mill, ambles south from Hwy. 178 along the Amargosa River to **Saratoga Spring**— a day-use destination that one can also reach, by better (unpaved) road, from Hwy. 127.

Golden Canyon and Artists Drive

If the ambient air temperature is tolerable, hike Golden Canyon in the late afternoon, when the sun's rays spin the sandy brown stone into gold—more accurately, warm-hued iron oxides. A 1.5-mile spur road leads to the parking lot; from there, hike right on in. At the end of the steep, narrow canyon, up the wash to the right, is aptly named **Red Cathedral** (also known as Cathedral Wall), a natural amphitheater created from an ancient, iron-capped Funeral Mountains alluvial fan—most dramatic in the late-day sun. Explore Golden Canyon's various side canyons for more colorful surprises and odd rock formations. The fairly gradual trail up through **Gower Gulch** leads to the scenic vistas of **Zabriskie Point**, though the hiking views are better—and the walking even easier—heading downhill. Happy hoofers can also hike to the base of **Manly Beacon**, a self-guided geology lesson.

Back on the main road heading south, ancient lake shorelines are visible in the basalt foothills of the Black Mountains. The flat point at the northern end is **Manly Terrace**, believed by archaeologists to be one of the first inhabited areas of Death Valley. Around the point to the east is **Mushroom Rock**, an apt name for an unusual lava formation once resembling a massive mushroom. The forces of erosion and vandalism have chipped away at that form; some say 'Shroom Rock now more closely resembles a well-known extraterrestrial film star.

Late afternoon is also the best time to dabble in **Artists Palette**, the next major attraction, where primary colors shade into badlands pastels. One-way, nine-mile Artists Dr. (enter at the south end) winds through mud hills splashed with mineral oxides and chlorides, lasting testament to nature's creativity.

Devil's Golf Course, Natural Bridge

About 10 miles south of the Artists Dr. exit is the short dirt spur leading to Devil's Golf Course. But even the devil might get mighty teed off if trying to whack a few across this ungodly salt-pocked landscape. These crusty salt spikes, from several inches to several feet tall, were created by evaporation and erosion. As the most recent lake receded more than 2,000 years ago, thick layers of salt crystals—here, almost pure table salt, or sodium chloride—sealed the lake-bottom sediments. Centuries of wind, rain, and heat have continued this creation. Wind and rain whittle the salt pinnacles, yet they continue to "grow"; in the presence of underground moisture, dissolved salts are drawn through capillary action back to the surface, where they recrystalize. When it's hot, the salt-

Old Scratch himself would find himself in the rough at this badlands golf course.

KIM WEIR

crystal crust breaks up anew—crackling, popping, and pinging.

Just two miles south on the main road and several steep dirt-road miles east, much quieter Natural Bridge is a short stroll up the canyon from the parking lot. This 50-foot-high formation—sculpted by a rushing waterfall—is a true Death Valley ancient, composed of sedimentary stone more than two million years old.

Badwater

Make way for the tour buses, because this is one place they all stop. Badwater is actually more famous for its longtime, if slightly inaccurate, billing as the lowest elevation in the Lower 48—the valley's two lowest points are actually a few miles away—and its earnest candidacy for hottest place on earth than for its "bad" water. How bad is bad? The water in the pool is not toxic, though it's none too tasty—the chemical equivalent of a very strong dose of Epsom salts. (Since Epsom salts are an effective laxative, sampling the water could prove quite distressing. Not recommended.) And it is capable of supporting life—soldier fly larvae, water beetles, water snails, algae, ditch grass, and (beyond the water's edge) pickleweed.

For some instant on-site perspective, look directly west across the valley to the Panamints' Telescope Peak—standing tall at an elevation of 11,049 feet but rising more than 11,300 feet above where you're standing.

HEADING NORTH: STOVEPIPES AND SCOTTY'S CASTLE

As you head north from Furnace Creek, three possible tour routes present themselves. Following Hwy. 190 as it snakes north and then southwest/west leads first to **Salt Creek**, one of the park's few remaining pupfish habitats, on the way to Stovepipe Wells Village, Death Valley's other primary visitor services center. Well before the village is the dirt-road turnoff to the lovely **Death Valley Sand Dunes** (picnic area), near the sand-proofed original **Stovepipe Well** for which this area is named. Farther west along the highway is **Devil's Cornfield,** the vaguely agricultural ambience created by 10-foot-tall arrowweed "stacks." Facilities at historic **Stovepipe Wells Village** include a pleasant Western-style motel, a fall-to-spring campground, restaurant

and saloon, general store, and gas station. Worth exploring near Stovepipe Wells Village: hikable **Mosaic Canyon** and, for four-wheelers, **Cottonwood** and **Marble Canyons.**

Alternatively, head northeast toward Daylight Pass Rd. (Hwy. 374) via **Beatty Cutoff** to reach the remains of **Keane Wonder Mill** and **Keane Wonder Mine** (dirt road and then foot trail) and the striking **Chloride Cliff** viewpoint at the end of the four-wheeling route to ghost town **Chloride City.** (A longer but much better road to Chloride City begins at the south side of the highway at the park's Hwy. 374 entrance.) East from the cutoff's junction with the highway and the **Hell's Gate** rest area/information stop, Hwy. 374 twists up and over Daylight Pass and down into the Amargosa Desert and **Beatty** in Nevada (gas, food, ranger station). More interesting attractions are en route, however, including the one-way (westward) dirt-road tour of Death Valley's **Titus Canyon** and the Nevada ghost towns of **Rhyolite,** where the beer-bottle adobe **Bottle House** still stands, and **Bullfrog.**

Heading north from Hwy. 190 past another information stop (just north of its junction with Hwy. 374) is **Death Valley North Hwy.,** which continues about 36 miles to grand **Scotty's Castle** and surrounding oasis, the park's most popular destination and tour (fee; gas available during the day).

From Scotty's Castle, take the road less traveled up narrow Grapevine Canyon via Hwy. 267 to reach spot-in-the-road Scotty's Junction (no services) in Nevada. Or continue west to nearby **Ubehebe Crater** for a quick geology lesson. A gravel road angles south from Ubehebe for some 20 miles through Racetrack Valley to **The Racetrack**—an odd and intriguing sun-blistered playa where stones "race" each other, though no one has actually seen the competition.

From near Ubehebe Crater, unpaved (and very rough) Death Valley Rd. snakes north into recently acquired park territory, eventually making its way up and over the Last Chance mountains. Make sure you've filled up on gas, water, and current weather and road information before setting out. The two most popular features north of Scotty's Castle are the **Eureka Dunes** in Eureka Valley and the clothing-very-optional hot springs in **Saline Valley** (actually more accessible from the west, via a very rough access road).

"DEATH VALLEY SCOTTY": A MAN AND HIS MYTH

A true celebrity among Death Valley's ever-quirky cast of characters, Walter "Death Valley Scotty" Scott has been memorialized as more colorful than even the desert's most garish sunset. And Death Valley Scotty ensured the world knew of his exploits, his self-promotional flair making him the darling of the Los Angeles press corps during the early 1900s.

After a youthful stint with Buffalo Bill Cody's Wild West Show, according to the myth, the Kentucky-born Scott headed west to Death Valley. In no time at all he laid claim to what he boasted was a fabulously rich gold mine, vaguely located in the south, somewhere near the modern ruins of Ashford Mill. All he lacked, subsequent backers were convinced, was sufficient capital to unearth this vast wealth. The myth itself proved to be a gold mine for Scott, despite his lasting inability to produce either the mine or its gold. As practiced prospector Pete Aguerreberry once put it, other people's pockets were all Death Valley Scotty ever mined.

And so it was, starting with Julian M. Gerard, conned into backing Scott's mining venture with the help of Ella Josephine McCarthy Milius Scott (Scotty's wife, known as "Jack") and two nuggets she'd brought west from Colorado. Death Valley Scotty's next benefactor was E. Burdon Gaylord, an L.A. mining engineer who in 1905 paid the freight for Scott's record-breaking cross-country train trip aboard the Coyote Special—a spectacularly successful publicity stunt for Gaylord, who was desperately seeking a buyer for his Death Valley mine, and for Walter Scott. The nation celebrated Death Valley Scotty's accomplishment, though he was merely a passenger aboard the Chicago-bound Coyote.

Scott's celebrity attracted the attention of Chicago financier Albert M. Johnson, who was soon convinced to back Scotty's nonexistent gold mining venture. Johnson headed west to examine the mine. Though the trip erupted in scandal and ended in arrests—an armed "ambush" near Wingate Pass had been arranged by Scott, to scare off the mine investigation—Johnson was not deterred. He and his wife became Death Valley Scotty's life-long benefactors, also putting up the money for elegant "Scotty's Castle" and other 1920s construction at Death Valley Ranch. Even Johnson's financial losses in the stock market crash of 1929, which introduced the Great Depression to Death Valley, failed to diminish their relationship. As to why he served as Death Valley Scotty's "gold mine" for so many years, in 1941 Johnson said it was because Scott was such a "swell companion," something money couldn't buy. "He repays me in laughs."

Aside from his enduring friendship with the Johnsons, Death Valley Scotty's most lasting accomplishment was the creation of a romantic 20th-century Western desert mythology—and his success in permanently placing that myth on the map of the nation's imagination.

By the time Death Valley Scotty died at the age of 81—in 1954, just six years after his good friend Albert Johnson passed on—his mythic persona had taken on a life of its own. Scotty had specified a fairly pedestrian message for his epitaph: *Here he is.* But those in charge of marking his memory instead inscribed: *I got four things to live by: Don't say nothing that will hurt anybody. Don't give advice—nobody will take it anyway. Don't complain. Don't explain.*

The fact that Death Valley Scotty consistently failed to live by such posthumous posturing is, in the realm of mythology, inconsequential.

Near Stovepipe Wells:
The Dunes, the Well

Until the Eureka Dunes and Panamint Dunes were added to the park's holdings in 1994, the Death Valley Sand Dunes were known as "the sand dunes," with little confusion. Covering roughly 25 square miles, these dunes are created—and constantly re-created—by crosswinds and eddies. Though most sand dunes migrate over time, this whirling wind-riffed sand is more or less stationary; major movement is "corrected" by seasonal changes in wind direction. Especially after heavy winter rains, spring wildflowers are a major draw. But a sandy stroll is a pleasure—and a challenge—any time temperatures are reasonably moderate. You'll find no trail, since shifting sands would soon obliterate any trace; here, you can blaze your own. You can even blaze a barefoot trail, if possible encounters with superheated sand, sidewinders, and thorns are no deterrent. (Carry shoes, just in case.) Distances are deceiving, so slather on the sunscreen and carry water.

The historic **Stovepipe Well** farther north along this road was named for the length of stovepipe once poked into the well here to prevent dune sand from choking off the water supply.

Mosaic and Other Area Canyons

Just west of Stovepipe Wells Village and then several miles south via unpaved road is dramatic **Mosaic Canyon,** popular for guided park service tours of the stunning polished stone "mosaics" for which it was named. As recently as the 1970s Mosaic Canyon featured unusual "whirlpools" and greater depth—even iron handrailings for precipitous passages—but heavy rains and accelerated erosion have silted things up considerably. Intrepid trekkers can make a challenging four- to five-mile hike out of excursions into side canyons.

Cottonwood Canyon beyond the Stovepipe Wells airstrip is immensely popular with four-wheelers—cottonwoods grow near a creek at the end of the road—but hikers use this road (and topo maps) to create longer looping routes through adjacent **LeMoigne** and **Marble** canyons.

The Titus Canyon Tour

This one-way dirt-road adventure through Titus Canyon begins at Hwy. 374 in the Nevada desert, the turnoff several miles south of Rhyolite and east of the park proper. Highlights of the dramatic 28-mile, two- to three-hour tour include the scant remains of **Leadfield,** a few tattered tin buildings built as props for Charles Courtney Julian's 1920s mining investment scam, the **When Rocks Bend** sign, petroglyphs at **Klare Spring,** and the canyon's narrow and steep stone-mosaic walls. The entire route is walkable, of course, but an immensely long trek requiring water caches and other forms of prudence. More popular with hikers is a round-trip walk starting from the canyon's Death Valley side; the road from the highway is two-way until the parking lot.

Because the road through Titus Canyon is very narrow, with very few turnouts, be sure your vehicle is up to the trip—gas, water, good tires—to avoid stranding yourself and others in the canyon; a stall during Easter Week, or on almost any busy spring weekend, could conceivably create a single-file parking lot.

Scotty's Castle and Gas House Museum

Toward the end of his days, Death Valley Scotty was perturbed that the expansive desert mansion

Elaborate as it is, Scotty's Castle stands unfinished.

KIM WEIR

named in his honor garnered more public attention than he did. "I'm the one-man circus," he reportedly said. "The castle is just the tail of my kite."

Some tail.

According to popular assumption in the 1920s and '30s, this vaguely Spanish tile-roofed mansion at Grapevine Springs was built with profits from Death Valley Scotty's fabled gold mine. But the gold mine never existed. And Death Valley Scotty had no money, aside from the sums he conned from various backers. The two-million-dollar castle complex, started in 1922 but never finished, was the brainchild and desert health retreat of Albert Mussey Johnson of Chicago, a millionaire insurance executive who became Scotty's most enthusiastic supporter. When the Johnsons wintered at the castle—entertaining guests including Will Rogers and Norman Rockwell while also offering tours of "Scotty's" castle to the public—Death Valley Scotty held court as if he owned the place, regaling his audiences with tall tales and dubious deeds. Though he sometimes stayed as a guest, Death Valley Scotty actually lived elsewhere—in his own cabin, several miles to the west.

These days, guides dressed in 1930s garb lead living history tours of the main house, also sharing anecdotes about and insights into the peculiar long-lived partnership between Death Valley Scotty and the Johnsons.

Centerpiece of the castle complex, officially known as Death Valley Ranch, is the 25-room main house with its immense Great Hall (de facto living room) and indoor waterfall, 18 fireplaces, music rooms, and guest suites. Elaborate tilework, wrought-iron accents, carved wooden doors, and beamed ceilings set the stage for exquisite Old World antiques, elaborate fakes (no original paintings here), and eccentric collectibles—the latter including the Welte-Mignon theater organ in the Upper Music Room. Either before or after the castle tour, wander the grounds (free) to appreciate other quirks and charms of the complex. The Gas House Museum exhibits artifacts from the Castle collection.

The 50-minute guided castle tours are offered daily, on the hour from 9 A.M. to 5 P.M.; each is limited to a maximum of 19 people. Tickets are sold here on a first-come basis, on the date of the tour only, and are $8 adults, $6 seniors, and $4 children (age 5 and under free); expect to wait. To improve the odds of landing tour tickets during busy times, arrive early—and be flexible about plans for the rest of the day. Late morning and early afternoon tours, for example, are easily sandwiched around a picnic (tables available) and a leisurely exterior tour of the grounds. Securing tickets for a late afternoon tour leaves the rest of the day open for excursions farther afield.

Ubehebe Crater

This notable upside-down cone eight miles from Scotty's Castle—800 feet deep, 450 feet across at bottom, and a half-mile wide at ground level—is still the subject of scientific quibbling. Formed by a massive volcanic steam explosion, Ubehebe Crater is assumed to be about 1,000 years old, though some say 4,000 to 10,000 years old and others contend that the crater is a mere 300 years old, like Little Hebe and similar smaller craters just south. Whenever Ubehebe blasted its way into existence, the force of creation was so intense that the colorful earth was sliced clean,

like a mega-layered cake. Examine those layers by taking the trail to the bottom. Another route circumnavigates the black perimeter before jogging on to Little Hebe.

The Racetrack

After a long, leisurely gravel-road sojourn up to a few stragglers and down again—the trip in can easily take a half-day—Racetrack Valley Rd. finally arrives at its surreal destination. One of the park's most mysterious features, the Racetrack hosts a "race" so slow that it's never been observed. What you do see here, though, are the racers—rocks seemingly tossed at random atop the fine-clay playa, their tracks indicating how far each contender has come. Some the size of baseballs, others boulders, the hardened competitors rest motionless and silent. Yet the sense that everything just moved—just *then,* when one's back was turned—is eerie, almost overwhelming. Scientists theorize that the race resumes with the arrival of strong winds on those rare days when the clay surface is just moist enough to become slick.

Eureka Sand Dunes

Eureka Sand Dunes National Natural Landmark, boasting California's tallest sand dune, is among the park's newly acquired attractions. Standing about 700 feet tall, Sand Mountain at the north end is notable, its ghostly pale sands a dramatic contrast to the Last Chance Range in the background. Like the Kelso Dunes in Mojave National Preserve, the dunes here "sing" when sand particles cascade from the summit—a rare sand dune feature and a real kick for the kids. Unusual also are the area's endemic plant species. Because of the hellacious summer heat, the dunes are best visited in late fall, winter, and early spring.

HEADING WEST: INTO THE PANAMINTS

Present-day park visitors can find their way west from Stovepipe Wells by virtually the same route early immigrants did—into the Panamint Mountains via the steep and deeply twisted **Wildrose Rd.** (Hwy. 178) along the alluvial fan and then into and out of Emigrant Canyon. Too treacherous for campers, trailers, and large RVs, the road continues from Emigrant for about 21 miles to the Wildrose ranger station and campground. Worthy side trips along the way include the mining ghost town of **Skidoo,** the site of short-lived **Harrisburg,** and **Aguerreberry Point,** with its spectacular sunset views of Death Valley below. At Wildrose, take **Mahogany Flat Rd.** (pavement, then dirt) for a still higher climb into Wildrose Canyon, a gain of 4,000 feet in a mere eight miles. On the left, after seven miles, are the imposing stone **Wildrose Canyon Charcoal Kilns,** beehivelike furnaces built by Chinese laborers for the task of transforming wood into charcoal. Popular for its stunning vistas is the vigorous 14-mile round-trip hike or backpack into the piñon pines atop **Telescope Peak,** best for wildflowers from May through July (snow and ice gear usually required for winter climbs). Easier and equally scenic is the eight-mile round-trip **Wildrose Peak** hike.

For some extra excitement on the way west, take winding **Wildrose-Trona Rd.** (gravel in places) down into the southern Panamint Valley. The route west from Stovepipe Wells via Hwy. 190 quickly leads up and over the Panamint Mountains and then down into the Panamint Valley before rolling on toward Lone Pine and the eastern slope of the Sierra Nevada. Reasonably accessible national park attractions include the **Panamint Dunes** (visible from Father Crowley Point) in the northern Panamint Valley, **Darwin Falls,** and **Lee Flat Joshua Tree Forest.** Intrepid travelers in search of solitude might seek the road less traveled past Lee Flat and on into **Saline Valley,** a wild wonderland equally accessible from near Lone Pine in the north.

STAYING AND EATING IN DEATH VALLEY

More than one million visitors make the desert trek to Death Valley each year, most of these arriving during the mild-weather winter season. So, without some strategy, don't be too surprised if there's no room at the inn—or at area campgrounds. Though Death Valley offers deluxe digs, due to an abundance of area campgrounds it's possible to do Death Valley on the cheap. For a current rundown on campgrounds—at least one has reservable sites—see the park's website.

Furnace Creek

As the human-centered hub of Death Valley, Furnace Creek is the park's most popular accommodations and restaurant option. Star of the show is the elegant and appropriately eccentric **Furnace Creek Inn,** snuggled into a hillside palm-tree oasis a mile south of the park visitors center. Originally part of Greenland Ranch, the 68-room hotel at Furnace Creek was built by the Pacific Coast Borax Company in 1927 as part of its package-tour railroad travel promotion. An adobe and stone villa with red-tiled roofs and lush landscaping, this onetime tourist lure is still some attraction. Decorated in pastel desert hues, most rooms feature fireplaces, ceiling fans, cable TV, refrigerators, and tiled bathrooms with whirlpool tubs. The Furnace Creek Inn also offers full fitness facilities, an 18-hole golf course (fee), horseback riding (fee), archery, tennis, spring-fed pool (heated naturally to 84°F), saunas, two restaurants, and lounge. This is an adult-oriented resort open only mid-Oct. through mid-May (closed after Mother's Day). Luxury, (two meals included). And the Furnace Creek Inn is *the* Death Valley dining destination, serving the best food for more than 100 miles in any direction.

A decent family-friendly choice year-round is the **Furnace Creek Ranch** motel, up the road near the visitors center. With comfortable, attractive motel rooms conveniently located near the middle of the park, Furnace Creek Ranch is quite popular with retirees, foreign tourists, and families—thus the playground, spring-fed pool, tennis courts, hayrides, and relatively inexpensive restaurants. High-season rates run $129 and up. Premium-Luxury. Less expensive cabin rooms are also available, as well as a small first-come, first-served campground ($20 per night for full hookups). For ranch-style fare, mosey on over to the **Wrangler Steak House,** which serves cafeteria-style breakfast and lunch by day—nothing fancy, just inexpensive and filling. Come nightfall it's a more ambitious Wrangler, specializing in steaks, chicken, and desert-style seafood.

For information about both the Furnace Creek Inn and the Furnace Creek Ranch, contact: **Furnace Creek Inn & Ranch Resort,** P.O. Box 1,

Death Valley, CA 92328; call 760/786-2345 or toll-free 800/236-7916 (central reservations); or try www.furnacecreekresort.com. To dial the Inn directly, call 760/786-2361.

Stovepipe Wells and Panamint Springs
Twenty-four miles from the maddening crowds, **Stovepipe Wells Village** in many ways offers the quintessential Death Valley stay. Launched in the lonesome desert as "Bungalow City" in 1926, this venerable 83-room motel features the basic modern comforts—sans TVs and telephones—along with steer-head light fixtures, oxen-yoke headboards, and other eccentric decorative touches that honor Death Valley's history. And it's still quiet and unhurried here. The fact that the water in some rooms is unsuitable for drinking (too saline) is no big deal for most people, since any sensible desert traveler should have an extra jug or two in the car anyway.

Amenities and associated facilities include a swimming pool, general store, restaurant (in summer, breakfast and dinner only) and the colorful Badwater Saloon—built with timbers from an old area mine. (Ranger station, gas station, campground, and airstrip nearby.) Moderate, the price depending on room size, water potability, and other details. For information and reservations call 760/786-2387 or contact the Furnace Creek Inn (above).

The newest resort destination *in* Death Valley is the **Panamint Springs Resort,** 775/482-7680, www.deathvalley.com, just inside the park's western boundary 48 miles east of Lone Pine and 31 miles west of Stovepipe Wells. The western-style facilities include 14 motel rooms (Moderate), campground with RV sites (full hookups $20) and tent sites ($10), store, and restaurant and bar. Pets welcome (deposit).

Staying near Death Valley
New in 1997, the 10-bed **HI-AYH Desertaire Hostel** is in Tecopa, just an hour drive from Death Valley. Rates are $12 per person per night. Budget. For more information, contact: HI-AYH Desertaire Hostel, 2000 Old Spanish Trail Hwy., P.O. Box 306, Tecopa, CA 92389, 760/852-4580 or toll-free 877/907-1265, www.hostelweb.com.

If you'll be attending a performance at Marta Becket's Amargosa Opera House, why not stay in her hotel? The **Amargosa Hotel** in Death Valley Junction, east of Death Valley at the junction of Hwys. 190 and 127, won't be mistaken for Death Valley's upmarket Furnace Creek Inn. But here you pay for a different kind of atmosphere, something simpler and probably more comfortable for artsy desert adventurers. Rooms here do have private bathrooms. The hotel is open for business only from Oct. through mid-May (closed after Mother's Day). Inexpensive-Moderate. For more information: Amargosa Hotel, P.O. Box 8, Death Valley Junction, CA 92328, 760/852-4441, fax 760/852-4138.

Motel accommodations are also available in a variety of towns within 50 to 150 miles of Death Valley, from Shoshone and Beatty to Ridgecrest, Lone Pine, and Independence. The visitors center can provide a complete listing. Or call the **Death Valley Chamber of Commerce,** in Shoshone, at 760/852-4524, www.deathvalley-chamber.org.

DEATH VALLEY INFORMATION AND ESSENTIALS

Death Valley Information
Among basic practical facts affecting Death Valley visitors: General park admission is $10 per vehicle ($20 for an annual pass) and $5 for hikers or bikers. All vehicles—including bicycles—must stay on established roads at all times. No target practice or other weapons use is allowed in the park. Collecting, damaging, or disturbing any park feature, be it plant, animal, or mineral, is strictly forbidden. Abandoned mine areas are designated for day use only. Pets must be leashed at all times. Backcountry hiking, backpacking, and camping are allowed in many areas, with no permits required; check with park rangers for current regulations. Considering the unforgiving nature of the terrain, it's prudent to complete a backcountry registration form (voluntary) before setting out on any independent trek.

The **Death Valley National Park Visitor Center** and museum at Furnace Creek is the essential all-purpose information stop. After an introduction to local history and natural history, inquire here about road, trail, and weather conditions—and about any special safety or other precautions deemed prudent for more obscure

GETTING SOME KICKS ON ROUTE 66

America's most famous roadway in the days before the interstate system, Route 66 once stretched west from Chicago, Illinois, to Santa Monica, California, sauntering through dozens of other cities and towns en route. Known also as the nation's "Mother Road" (thanks to John Steinbeck) and the "Main Street of America," the highway was immortalized in the popular imagination—a fact captured in music by Bob Troupe's "Route 66," performed by Nat King Cole and the King Cole Trio.

But even immortals have a short shelf-life in America. Route 66's days were numbered by 1956, when the U.S. Congress approved the Interstate Highway Program. Its official epitaph came in 1985, when the federal government "decertified" the 2,400-mile route as a national highway. Swaths of old Route 66 were paved over by faster freeways; some remnants were unofficially reassigned to scenic ghost town status.

In recent years America seems ready, again, to roll down its favorite highway, with new historical markers making it much easier to retrace the Mother Road. In California, the desert highway well beyond present population centers is most interesting; the route is all but lost from coastal Santa Monica through the streaming chaos of Los Angeles. But if coming from that direction, pick up old Route 66 in Pasadena. On Fair Oaks Ave. in South Pasadena, the **Fair Oaks Pharmacy** boasts an authentic soda-fountain interior transplanted here from Joplin, Missouri—a Route 66 shrine from the other end of the line. The main Pasadena route, though, passes through **Old Pasadena,** the city's vibrant historic district along Colorado Blvd.—the Rose Bowl parade route—before heading east and becoming Foothill Boulevard.

Surviving highlights along Foothill include the aging Mayan-Toltec **Aztec Hotel** in Monrovia, the down-home downtown surrounding **Claremont Colleges** in Claremont, the sadly seedy **Wigwam Motel** in Rialto (a sign here says: "Do It in a Tee Pee"), and the stunning **California Theater** in downtown San Bernardino.

In San Bernardino, Cajon Blvd. technically defines the route. The alternative way up and over Cajon Pass is I-15, which overlays much of the original road. Beyond the pass ribbons of old Route 66 are now called the **National Trails Highway.** In Barstow the route becomes Main Street. Beyond Barstow (off I-40) the National Trails Highway rolls almost all the way into Arizona.

To make a commemorative stop along Route 66, there are at least two choices. Victorville pays homage to America's Main Street at the **California Route 66 Museum** on D St. in the town's spruced-up downtown, 760/951-0436, http://califrt66museum.org. To get here, exit I-15 at D St. (Hwy. 118); the museum is on D between 5th and 6th. Barstow, too, has a Route 66 museum—the two-room **Mother Road Museum,** 681 N. 1st Ave., 760/255-1890, honoring the city's Route 66 highway history. The museum is housed in the newly rebuilt (from the original bricks) Santa Fe Railroad depot, **Casa del Desierto** ("House of the Desert"), which housed a Harvey House restaurant from 1911 through the 1950s.

trips and backcountry travel. Maps, books, hiking guides, and various other useful publications are available here. Ranger stations are at **Grapevine** (near Scotty's Castle), **Stovepipe Wells, Wildrose,** and **Beatty** (in Nevada).

For current park information, contact: **Death Valley National Park,** Death Valley, CA 92328, 760/786-2331, fax 760/786-2236, www.nps.gov/deva.

Death Valley Essentials

Get gasoline, water, and at least basic supplies at either Stovepipe Wells or Furnace Creek. Within the park, gas is also available at Scotty's Castle (during regular business hours only). Beyond the park, fuel stops include Shoshone (and Baker) to the southeast; Amargosa Valley (formerly known as Lathrop Wells) and Beatty in Nevada to the east; Trona (and Ridgecrest) to the southwest; and Lone Pine to the northwest.

Furnace Creek is also the place for just general gabbing, getting your hair done, getting towed (by AAA-affiliated service stations), going to church, grabbing a hot shower, gift and grocery shopping, and golfing 200 feet below sea level. Other Furnace Creek amenities and services include a 24-hour laundromat, full-service post office, swimming pools, horseback and carriage rides (seasonal), and guided Death Valley bus tours. For current information, refer to the tabloid *Death Valley Visitor Guide* distributed at park entrances.

NEAR DEATH VALLEY: BARSTOW AND VICINITY

A big city by Mojave Desert standards, present-day Barstow is the de facto desert crossroads—the place I-15, I-40, Hwy. 58, Hwy. 257, and the Union Pacific and Santa Fe Railroads converge. It's no real surprise that the town was named for the 10th president of the Santa Fe Railroad, William Barstow Strong, though it first made the map as a stop for cross-country wagon train expeditions. It was later a supply station for Death Valley adventurers. Barstow's historical heyday came during the gold and silver mining boom of the 1880s and '90s, when nearby Calico—now a gussied-up ghost town—was in its prime.

Conveniently situated halfway between Los Angeles and Las Vegas, these days Barstow is still the desert's central information, service, and supply stop. Barstow even has two factory outlet shopping malls. Aside from air-conditioned motels and restaurants—including the highly unusual McDonald's franchise here, housed in railroad cars—until recently Barstow's primary attraction was the **Mojave River Valley Museum,** 270 E. Virginia Way, 760/256-5452, open daily 11 A.M.–4 P.M. Newly rebuilt downtown, from the original bricks, is Barstow's classy Santa Fe Railroad depot, **Casa del Desierto** ("House of the Desert"), which housed a Harvey House restaurant from 1911 through the 1950s. For some idea of Harvey House's other-era significance, watch the 1946 Judy Garland film *Harvey Girls*. Barstow's Harvey House now houses the new two-room **Mother Road Museum,** 681 N. 1st Ave., 760/255-1890, commemorating the city's Route 66 highway history.

Calico Ghost Town 10 miles northeast of Barstow, just off I-15, 760/254-2122 or toll-free 800/862-2542, was a wild (and wildly successful) silver mining town born in 1881, wounded in 1893 when silver prices fell—and again in 1896 when borax faltered—and then finally declared dead and buried in 1907. Only old mine shafts, rusted railroad tracks, and a few faltering structures would stand in Calico today but for the intervention of Walter Knott (of Knott's Berry Farm fame) and his passion for ghost towns and Wild West lore. Knott, whose uncle made his fortune as a partner in the Silver King Mine, bought and began resurrecting the 60-acre Calico site in 1951. After restoring the few surviving original structures and reconstructing some of the rest, Knott gave Calico to the county in 1966.

The nearby **Calico Early Man Archaeological Site,** 760/256-5102, is one of the most important archaeological finds in North America, this the only continental dig directed by Dr. Louis S. B. Leakey—best known for his discoveries in East Africa's Olduvai Gorge—who worked here until his death in 1972. Scientists subsequently dated the calcium carbonate surrounding the encrusted artifacts as about 200,000 years old. The current speculation is that Calico Early Man may have been a now-extinct species, perhaps *Homo erectus* or *Homo sapiens neandertalensis*. Tour the excavation pits and stone-tool exhibits on either guided or self-guided tours—a chance for the kids to really "dig" the science of archaeology.

For more information about the area, contact the **Barstow Chamber of Commerce** at the Mercado Mall, 222 E. Main St., Ste. 216, P.O. Box 698, Barstow, CA 92312, 760/256-8617, www.barstowchamber.com.

OTHER HIGH DESERT HIGHLIGHTS

Ridgecrest

A shimmering mirage of concrete and condominiums, modern-day Ridgecrest sprang up out of the desert to keep company with the adjacent China Lake Naval Air Warfare Center, Weapons Division (NAWCWPNS). A major attraction here, in fact, is the **China Lake Exhibit Center,** 760/939-3105, where all species of naval warfare innovation are on display. Another draw is the small, excellent **Maturango Desert Museum,** also the Northern Mojave Visitor Center, 100 E. Las Flores Ave., 760/375-6900, with its excellent introductory natural history and history exhibits and visitor programs.

For Ridgecrest area visitor information, stop by the Maturango Desert Museum (open daily) or contact the **Ridgecrest Area Convention and Visitors Bureau,** 100 W. California Ave., Ridgecrest, CA 93555, 760/375-8202 or toll-free 800/847-4830, www.ridgecrest.ca.us/~racvb. For information about nearby Bureau of Land Management attractions, contact the local BLM office at 760/375-7125 or 760/384-5400.

Near Ridgecrest

Fans of *Star Trek V: The Final Frontier* and other sci-fi flicks will recognize this otherworldly landscape at **Trona Pinnacles**—500 tufa towers, some more than 140 feet tall, rising from the bone-dry Searles Lake basin. These are the finest examples of tufa towers in the United States. To get here from Ridgecrest, continue east of Ridgecrest via Hwy. 178 for 17 miles and turn right onto Pinnacles Rd.; you'll reach the pinnacles in 5.5 miles, but it's another mile or so to the parking area. The dirt road—slow going, washboardy sand, then gravel—is suited for passenger cars with good ground clearance. For more information call 760/375-7125.

Northwest from Ridgecrest and north of Little Lake, just off Hwy. 395 about 20 miles north of the Hwy. 14 junction, is another intriguing natural attraction—Fossil Falls, a section of the Owens River Gorge lava field where the lava "falls" were sculpted and smoothed by the once-rushing waters of the ancient river. To get here: Exit at Cinder Cone Rd., head east a half-mile; turn right and head south for about a quarter-mile on dirt road; then turn left (east again) and continue a half-mile to the parking lot. Paint blots mark the trailhead and the short trail.

Due south of Ridgecrest, **Randsburg,** a "living ghost town" with tired tin buildings and eccentric antique shops, is typically the focal point of the Mojave Desert's historic Rand Mining District—late-1800s gold mining territory named after the Witwatersrand of South Africa. The excellent **Randsburg Desert Museum** on Butte Ave., affiliated with the Kern County Museum in Bakersfield and open only on weekends and long-weekend holidays, 10 A.M.–5 P.M., tells the whole story. (The town is "open" daily.) A small shaded picnic area is adjacent to the museum.

The opening archaeological scenes of *Jurassic Park* and countless Westerns were filmed in 4,000-acre **Red Rock Canyon State Park,** 805/942-0662, something of a miniature Grand Canyon featuring some of the California desert's most unusual scenery. Though most people sightsee from the freeway—four-lane Hwy. 14 runs through Red Rock Canyon—stop at the visitors center for a proper introduction. On-foot exploration of these colorful "badlands"—a geologic transition zone between the Sierra Nevada and the Mojave Desert—is the main attraction (day-use fee $2), along with car camping (no reservations needed). To avoid the intense heat, visit any time but summer. Red Rock Canyon State Park is 25 miles northeast of Mojave on Hwy. 14. You can also get here from Randsburg, via two-lane desert Redrock-Randsburg Rd. straight across the desert—not advisable after rains, because of the danger of flash floods.

More Desert Highlights

Edwards Air Force Base boasts many test-flight firsts—breaking the sound barrier for the first time, firing rocket engines for the first time, and bringing the U.S. space shuttle back to earth for the first time. These and other

ROY ROGERS–DALE EVANS MUSEUM

Movie-cowboy kitsch displayed here includes Roy Rogers lunchboxes, comic books, and jigsaw puzzles. Most memorable, though, is Roy's famous palomino horse Trigger, co-star of countless TV shows and westerns. After Trigger died in 1963 he was stuffed—the museum prefers the term "mounted"—and then saddled up as if ready to hit the trail. Fresh from a million-dollar renovation, the museum now includes new exhibits, interactive video displays, and two theaters.

The Roy Rogers–Dale Evans Museum, 15650 Seneca Rd. in Victorville, 760/243-4547 (recorded) or 760/243-4548, www.royrogers.com ("the first cowboy in cyberspace"), is open daily 9 A.M.–5 P.M. (closed Easter, Thanksgiving and Christmas). Admission is $8 adults, $7 seniors and students, $5 children 6–12 (age 5 and under free). You can't miss it—"It's a big ol' fort sittin' out in the field." Even from I-15 you'll see the giant Trigger rearing up outside the fort.

Keep your ears peeled for news about ROGERSDALE, U.S.A., a huge entertainment and retail complex to be located somewhere in Southern California—near Temecula, at last report.

---

accomplishments are chronicled at the **Air Force Flight Test Center Museum,** 661/277-8050. Free tours of air base operations and of NASA's **Dryden Flight Research Center** (weekdays only), 661/276-3311, www.dfrc.nasa.gov.

The 1,740-acre **Antelope Valley California Poppy Reserve** is famous for its fabulous spring display of the California Poppy—the state flower—and other native wildflowers. Best visited during peak bloom, usually mid-Apr., the preserve features a picnic area and various short loop trails. Appreciate the state-of-the-art visitors center—dug into the hillside to conserve energy. Day-use fee is $2. The preserve is 15 miles west of Hwy. 14. on Lancaster Rd.—an extension of Lancaster's Ave. I. **Saddleback Butte State Park** 20 miles east of Lancaster is a 2,955-acre woodland preserve that suggests sights once common throughout Antelope Valley—even after the antelope disappeared. Stroll the short nature trail for an introduction to high-desert botany. Longer trails loop to the top of Saddleback Butte. Come in spring for wildflowers and the chance to spot a desert tortoise. Day-use fee is $2; camping (reservable) is also available. The park entrance is on E. Ave. J at 170th Street. For more information on both parks, call 661/724-1180 or try www.calparksmojave.com.

The fascinating **Antelope Valley Indian Museum** near Saddleback Butte State Park is housed in a handcrafted chalet literally carved into the bedrock of Piaute Butte. Artist Howard Arden Edwards started this homesteading project in 1928 and filled his new home with artifacts representing the native cultures of California and the Southwest. Anthropologist Grace Oliver bought the Edwards homestead in 1938 and—adding her own substantial collection to his—established this museum. Open weekends only, 11 A.M.–4 P.M., from late Sept. to mid-June for self-guided tours (small admission), the museum is on E. Ave. M between 170th and 150th Sts., 2.5 miles southwest of Saddleback Butte State Park. For more information, call 661/946-3055, contact the regional states parks office (above), or try www.avim.av.org.

BOOKLIST

The virtual "publisher of record" for all things Californian is the **University of California Press,** 2120 Berkeley Way, Berkeley, CA 94720, 510/642-4247 or toll-free 800/777-4726 and fax 800/999-1958 for orders, www.ucpress.edu, which publishes hundreds of titles on the subject—all excellent. Stanford University's **Stanford University Press,** 521 Lomita Mall, Stanford, CA 94305, 650/723-9434, fax 650/725-3457, www.sup.org, also offers some books of particular interest to Californiacs—especially under the subject categories of American Literature, California History, and Natural History—though in general these are books of academic interest.

Other publishers offering California titles, particularly general interest, history, hiking, and regional travel titles, include **Chronicle Books,** Division of Chronicle Publishing Co., 85 2nd St., 6th Fl., San Francisco, CA 94105, 415/537-3730 or toll-free 800/722-6657, www.chronbooks.com, and **Heyday Books,** 2054 University Ave., Ste. 400, P.O. Box 9145, Berkeley, CA 94709, 510/549-3564, fax 510/549-1889. **Foghorn Outdoors,** Avalon Travel Publishing, 5855 Beaudry St., Emeryville, CA 95608, 510/595-3664, fax 510/595-4228, www.foghorn.com, publishes a generous list of unusual, and unusually thorough, California outdoor guides, including Tom Stienstra's camping, fishing, and "getaways" guides. **Sierra Club Books,** 85 2nd St., 2nd Fl., San Francisco, CA 94105, 415/977-5500 or toll-free 888/722-6657 for orders, www.sierraclub.org/books, and **Wilderness Press,** 1200 5th St., Berkeley, CA 94704, 510/558-1666 or toll-free 800/443-7227 for orders, fax 510/538-1696, www.wildernesspress.com, are the two top publishers of wilderness guides and maps for California. Among their titles are some particularly handy for exploration of the San Francisco Bay Area. Particularly useful from the Sierra Club, for example, is Peggy Wayburn's *Adventuring in the San Francisco Bay Area.* Wilderness Press publishes some good regional hiking guides, including *East Bay Trails* and *North Bay Trails.*

Contact these and other publishers, mentioned below, for a complete list of current titles relating to California.

The following book listings represent a fairly basic introduction to books about California history, natural history, literature, recreation, and travel. The interested reader can find many other titles by visiting good local bookstores and/or state and national park visitor centers. As always, the author would appreciate suggestions about other books that should be included. Send the names of new candidates—or actual books, if you're either a publisher or an unusually generous person—for *Moon Handbooks: California's* booklist, not to mention possible text additions, corrections, and suggestions, to: Kim Weir, c/o Moon Handbooks, Avalon Travel Publishing, 5855 Beaudry St., Emeryville, CA 94608.

COMPANION READING, GENERAL TRAVEL

Abbey, Edward. *Desert Solitaire.* Ballantine Books, 1991. One of the classic books, a prose poem for seekers of solitude, inspired by Abbey's half year as a park ranger in Utah's Arches National Monument.

Austin, Mary. *Land of Little Rain.* Albuquerque: University of New Mexico Press, 1974. Originally published in 1903. Before it was likely that one would be such a person, Mary Austin was an ecologist, feminist, and mystic. The essays in *Land of Little Rain,* a classic of Southwestern literature, still reveal Austin to be something of a philosopher: "It is a question whether it is not better to be bitten by the little horned snake of the desert that goes sidewise and strikes without coiling than by the tradition of a lost mine." More than anything else Mary Austin was a superb writer, a writer utterly in love with the Owens Valley and the nearby deserts she called home for many years.

Austin, Mary, with a foreword by John Walton. *The Ford.* Berkeley: University of California Press, 1997. Appreciating Mary Austin's "bold and original mind" in reviewing this novel for the *New York Times,* Carey McWilliams also said: "Of her novels, *The Ford,* which deals with the battle for the water of the Owens Valley, [is] perhaps the best."

Baldy, Marian. *The University Wine Course.* San Francisco: The Wine Appreciation Guild, 1992. Destined to be a classic and designed for both instructional and personal use, this friendly book offers a comprehensive education about wine. *The University Wine Course* explains it all, from viticulture to varietals. And the lips-on lab exercises and chapter-by-chapter examinations help even the hopelessly déclassé develop the subtle sensory awareness necessary for any deeper appreciation of the winemaker's art. Special sections and appendices on reading (and understanding) wine labels, combining wine and food, and understanding wine terminology make it a lifelong personal library reference. Definitely "do" this book before doing the California wine country. For college wine appreciation instructors and winery personnel, the companion *Teacher's Manual for The University Wine Course* (1993) may also come in handy.

Bierce, Ambrose Gwinnet, wickedly illustrated by Gahan Wilson. *The Devil's Dictionary.* New York: Oxford University Press, 1998. According to *The Devil's Dictionary,* a saint is a "dead sinner revised and edited," and a bore is a "person who talks when you wish him to listen." The satiric aphorisms included herein earned Ambrose Bierce the nicknames Bitter Bierce and the Wickedest Man in San Francisco, though—considering his talent for heaving his witty pitchfork at any and all he happened to encounter in life—it's clear that Bierce was born way too soon. He would have a field day in contemporary California.

Bright, William O. *1,500 California Place Names: Their Origin and Meaning.* A revised version of the classic *1,000 California Place Names* by Erwin G. Gudde, first published in 1949. University of California Press, 1998. Though you also get the revised edition of Gudde's original masterpiece (see below), this convenient, alphabetically arranged pocketbook—now in an expanded and updated edition—is perfect for travelers, explaining the names of mountains, rivers, and towns throughout California.

Bronson, Po. *The Nudist on the Late Shift and Other True Tales of Silicon Valley.* New York: Random House, 1999. The extent that the technological innovations and inventions now streaming out of the San Francisco Bay Area's Silicon Valley are changing U.S.—and world—societies is all but impossible to chronicle. But Po Bronson gives it a go, bravely taking his readers on a personal nonfiction tour through the silicon heart of the beast. To sample Bronson's fiction, try *Bombardiers* and *The First $20 Million Is Always the Hardest.*

Browning, Peter. *Place Names of the Sierra Nevada.* Berkeley: Wilderness Press, 1991. Second ed. The first since Francis Farquhar's 1926 classic of the same title, the author used Farquhar's revision notes in addition to original source material to gather up this collection of lore.

Buckley, Christopher, and Gary Young, eds. *The Geography of Home: California's Poetry of Place.* Berkeley: Heyday Books, 1999. This contemporary anthology showcases the work of 76 California poets. In addition to multiple selections of each poet's work, the poets also talk about their history in California, and the state's influence on their poetry.

Cain, James. *Three Novels.* New York: Alfred A. Knopf, 1941. Los Angeles classics, all: *Double Indemnity, Mildred Pierce,* and *The Postman Always Rings Twice.*

Callenbach, Ernest. *Ecotopia.* Berkeley: Banyan Tree, 1975. Also worthwhile, from the perspective that northernmost Northern California belongs in its own utopian state, is Callenbach's *Ecotopia Emerging* (1981).

Chandler, Raymond. *The Big Sleep.* New York: Vintage Books, 1992. The first mystery writer to be initiated into the Library of America—the U.S.A.'s literary hall of fame—Raymond Chandler and his legacy have been all but put to sleep by successors who, including parodies such as the film *Dead Men Don't Wear Plaid.* But if one hasn't succumbed to today's trendy nihilism—if one understands that pain hurts and life matters—then *The Big Sleep,* first published in 1939, is still spellbinding and fresh. And Philip Marlowe, Chandler's alter ego and private-eye protagonist, is still the L.A. insider's outsider. (As James Wolcott puts it, to Marlowe the rich are risen scum.) Lesser works by Chandler include *Farewell, My Lovely, The Long Goodbye,* and *The Little Sister.*

Clappe, Louise Amelia Knapp Smith, with an introduction by Marlene Smithe-Baranzini. *The Shirley Letters from the California Mines, 1851–1852.* Berkeley: Heyday Books, 1998. A classic of California gold rush–era literature, and a vivid portrait of both the exuberance and brutality of life in that time—a tale told from a woman's perspective. An absolutely superb read.

Clark, Donald Thomas. *Monterey County Place Names: A Geographical Dictionary.* Carmel Valley, CA: Kestrel Press, 1991. This marvelous resource, meticulously researched and guaranteed to enlighten all who dip into it, is a gift from the UC Santa Cruz University Librarian, Emeritus. Also well worth searching for, though out of print at last report, is the author's *Santa Cruz County Place Names* (1986).

Dana, Richard Henry, Jr. *Two Years Before the Mast.* New York: New American Library, 1990. A classic of early California literature. After recovering from a bout with the measles, young Harvard man Richard Henry Dana sailed off to complete his convalescence— not as a privileged ship passenger but as a sailor. On August 14, 1834, he boarded the *Pilgrim* in Boston Harbor and was underway on what was to be the greatest adventure of his life. This realistic depiction of life on the high seas offers an accurate firsthand account of what it was like to see the California coastline for the first time—and to tie up in San Francisco *before* the gold rush. Some of the earliest written descriptions of California— and still an exceptional read.

Darlington, David. *The Mojave.* New York: Henry Holt & Co., 1996. Part history, part oral history, and part natural history, the sum total of this book is marvelous—the tale of the Mojave Desert writ almost as large as the otherworldly landscape itself.

Didion, Joan. *Run River.* New York: Vintage Books, 1994. First published in 1963, this is Sacramento native Joan Didion's best novel, some say, written when she was in her 20s. The action begins with a murder on the banks of the Sacramento River.

Drinkard, Michael. *Disobedience.* Berkeley: University of California Press, 1996. According to no lesser authority than the *New York Times Book Review:* "Orange groves are a metaphor for nothing less than creation and apocalypse in this sharply funny and affecting novel set in Redlands, California." An intriguing take on the myth of oranges.

Duane, Daniel. *Caught Inside: A Surfer's Year on the California Coast.* San Francisco: Northpoint Press, 1997. What would it be like to shuck the jive and live instead the inspired life of a surf rat? Duane decided to find out, and in the process he took a careful look at the quirks of surf culture and shared some appreciations of the coast's natural power.

Ellroy, James. *My Dark Places: An L.A. Crime Memoir.* New York: Alfred A. Knopf, 1996. Best known for his crime fiction, Ellroy this time is telling a real-life story. A lifetime after childhood, the author returns to the scene of his mother's murder in what he calls the "White Trash Heaven" of El Monte in the San Gabriel Valley—to unravel the mystery of that event, to understand the strange legacy of her life and death. This dark and disturbing memoir is the result, a writer's excavation of his own painful past.

Fitzgerald, F. Scott. *The Last Tycoon.* New York: Charles Scribner's Sons, 1940. The golden boy of American letters had a heck of a time as a screenwriter in Hollywood—people still say Tinseltown did him in—but, after this (unfinished) novel, there was never any question that he knew the place as well as his own skin. In this, the barely disguised story of MGM genius Irving Thalberg, Fitzgerald demonstrates his genius and supreme talent as a writer.

Fisher, M. F. K. *The Art of Eating.* Foster City, CA: IDG Books Worldwide, 1990. Reprint ed.

John Updike has called her "the poet of the appetites." According to the *Chicago Sun-Times,* "M. F. K. Fisher is to literary prose what Laurence Olivier is to acting." And that point is hard to argue. Often characterized as California's premier food writer, particularly after she settled into the Sonoma County wine country, Mary Frances Kennedy Fisher was actually a *writer*—one who understood that the fundamental human needs are food, love, and security. As Fisher put it, "When I write of hunger, I am really writing about love and the hunger for it, and warmth and the love of it . . . and it's all one." She wrote about hunger in more than 20 books and countless other essays, letters, and stories. Five of her most beloved book-length essays—*An Alphabet of Gourmets, Consider the Oyster, The Gastronomical Me, How to Cook a Wolf,* and *Serve It Forth*—are all included in this collection.

Gebhard, David. *The California Architecture of Frank Lloyd Wright.* San Francisco: Chronicle Books, 1997. Reprint ed. Accompanied by color photographs, architectural renderings, and floor plans, this book provides an analysis of 24 California buildings—public and private—designed by the noted American architect.

Gilbar, Steven, ed. *California Shorts.* Berkeley: Heyday Books, 1999. This wonderful collection of 20 short stories presents surprisingly different versions of the California experience—urban and rural, native and immigrant.

Gilbar, Steven. *Natural State: A Literary Anthology of California Nature Writing.* Berkeley: University of California Press, 1998. This hefty and dazzling collection includes many of the writers you'd expect—Gretel Ehrlich, M. F. K. Fisher, John McPhee, John Muir, Gary Snyder, and Robert Louis Stevenson—but also a few surprises, including Joan Didion, Jack Kerouac, and Henry Miller.

Gioia, Ted. *West Coast Jazz: Modern Jazz in California, 1945–1960.* Berkeley: University of California Press, 1998. Reprint edition.

Gudde, Erwin G. Edited by William O. Bright. *California Place Names: The Origin and Etymology of Current Geographical Names.* Berkeley: University of California Press, 1998. Did you know that *Siskiyou* was the Chinook word for "bobtailed horse," as borrowed from the Cree language? More such complex truths await every time you dip into this fascinating volume—the ultimate guide to California place names (and how to pronounce them). A revised and expanded fourth edition, building upon the masterwork of Gudde, who died in 1969.

Hamilton, Ian. *As Good as Their Words: Writers in Hollywood.* New York: Harper & Row, 1990. A primer on the literary world of Hollywood, including vignettes about the reluctant screenwriting lives of Chandler, Faulkner, and Fitzgerald. Aldous Huxley, on the other hand, loved writing for the silver screen—and was actually good at it.

Hammett, Dashiell. *The Maltese Falcon.* New York: Vintage Books, 1992. Reissue ed. More *noir* than even Humphrey Bogart, who starred in the Hollywood version of this classic mystery, Sam Spade is Dashiell Hammett's tough-as-nails San Francisco private dick. Also central to Hammett's *The Dain Curse* and *The Glass Key,* in this story Spade attempts to unravel the enigma of the Maltese Falcon, a solid-gold statuette originally crafted as a tribute to the Holy Roman Emperor Charles IV. While trying to find the falcon, Spade's partner is murdered, the coppers blame him for it, and the bad guys are determined to get him, too. Then, of course, there's also the beautiful redhead, who appears and just as mysteriously disappears. Whodunnit? And why? Other classic Hammett reads include *The Continental Op* and *The Thin Man.*

Hansen, Gladys. *San Francisco Almanac.* Second revised ed. San Francisco: Chronicle Books, 1995. Finally back in print after a too-long hiatus, this easy-to-use source for San Francisco facts was written by the city archivist. Contains a detailed chronology, maps, and bibliography. Also fun: what some famous people have said about San Francisco. Fascinating, too, is the author's *Denial of Disaster: The Untold Story & Unpublished Photographs of the San Francisco Earthquake*

& Fire of 1906, co-authored by Emmet Condon, 1989 (Cameron & Co.).

Hart, James D. *A Companion to California.* Berkeley: University of California Press. Revised and expanded, 1987 (OP). Another very worthy book for Californiacs to collect, if you can find it, with thousands of brief entries on all aspects of California as well as more in-depth pieces on subjects such as literature.

Herron, Don. *The Literary World of San Francisco and its Environs.* San Francisco: City Lights Books, 1985 (OP). A well-mapped "pocket guide" for do-it-yourself walking and driving tours to sites where literary lights shine in and around San Francisco, their homes and haunts. This is the companion guide to the excellent *Literary San Francisco* by Lawrence Ferlinghetti and Nancy J. Peters. Also by Herron: *The Dashiell Hammett Tour: A Guidebook.*

Hong Kingston, Maxine. *The Woman Warrior: Memoirs of a Girlhood Among Ghosts.* New York: Vintage Books, 1989. Reissue ed. Fictionalized memoir about growing up Chinese-American in Stockton, California. In China, ghosts are supernatural beings, but in California they become everyone who is not from China. This is an elliptical and powerful story about finding a place in American society, though still raising ire in some quarters for its representations of Chinese culture.

Houston, James D. *Californians: Searching for the Golden State.* Santa Cruz, CA: Otter B Books, 1992. 10th reprint ed. Good prose, good points in this collection of personal essays about Californians in their endless search for the meaning of their own dream.

Huxley, Aldous. *After Many a Summer Dies the Swan.* London: Chatto and Windus, 1939. As an expatriate in Southern California, Huxley never did entirely warm up to the place. But he understood it, as he so deftly demonstrated in this literary masterpiece, inspired by the larger-than-life life of William Randolph Hearst.

Jackson, Helen Hunt. *Ramona.* New York: New American Library, 1988. The author was an early activist on behalf of California's native peoples. Despairing that so few cared about the Indians' plight, Jackson decided to tell the story as a romance—an interracial romance. As she herself put it: "I am going to try to write a novel, in which will be set forth some Indian experiences in a way to move people's hearts. People will read a novel when they will not read serious books." The resulting *Ramona* was a national sensation when it was first published in 1884. It is the now the official California State Play, staged since 1923 at the annual outdoor Ramona Pageant near Hemet.

Jeffers, Robinson. *Selected Poems.* New York: Random House, 1965. The poet Robinson Jeffers died in 1961 at the age of 75, on a rare day when it actually snowed in Carmel. One of California's finest poets, sophisticated yet accessible, many of his poems pay homage to the beauty of his beloved Big Sur coast. Poems collected here are selections from some of his major works, including *Be Angry at the Sun, The Beginning and the End, Hungerfield,* and *Tamar and Other Poems.*

Kadohata, Cynthia. *In the Heart of the Valley of Love.* New York: Penguin Books, 1993. A new edition is published by the University of California Press. This gritty, stunning novel envisions a future Los Angeles in which almost nothing—food, water, clean air, education—is available to the multiethnic multitudes. Yet humanity abides. A beautifully written and inspiring, if disturbing, book.

Kael, Pauline, Herman J. Mankiewicz, and Orson Welles. *The Citizen Kane Book: Raising Kane.* New York: Limelight Editions, 1984 (OP). Includes an excellent essay on the classic American film—which one can't help wanting to see again, following a tour of Hearst's San Simeon palace—plus script and stills.

Kahrl, William. *Water and Power: The Conflict over Los Angeles' Water Supply in the Owens Valley.* Berkeley: University of California Press, 1982. Perhaps the best book available for anyone who wants to understand the politics of water and power in California, and how water and political power have transformed the state's economy and land.

Keithley, George. *The Donner Party.* New York: George Braziller, 1989. This deeply moving book tells the story of the Donner Party's tragic 19th-century trek to California in the form of a prose poem—the only poetry book ever featured as a Book of the Month Club selection.

Kerouac, Jack. *Subterraneans.* New York: Grove Press, 1989. Considered by some to be Kerouac's masterpiece and first published in 1958, this is a Beat exploration of life on the fringes, a novel largely set in the San Francisco Bay Area. Others, however, prefer *The Dharma Bums* (1958) and *Big Sur* (1962).

Kirker, Harold. *California's Architectural Frontier.* San Marino, CA: The Huntington Library, 1970 (OP). Perhaps more useful and easier to find is Kirker's 1991 *Old Forms on a New Land: California Architecture in Perspective.*

Kowalewski, Michael, ed. *Gold Rush: A Literary Exploration.* Berkeley: Heyday Books, 1998. This official companion guide to the PBS Special *The Gold Rush* commemorates the 150th anniversary of the California gold rush—and is, in the words of James D. Houston, "an extraordinary read."

Krutch, Joseph Wood. *The Desert Year.* Tucson: University of Arizona Press, 1985. Originally published in 1951, this classic by the noted naturalist describes his year in the desert. A good general companion for desert travel.

La France, Danielle, ed. *Berkeley! A Literary Tribute.* Berkeley: Heyday Books, 1997. Welcome to Berkeley's literary big leagues, with this collection of essays, memoirs, speeches, poetry, short stories, and letters featuring everyone from Jack Kerouac and Allen Ginsburg to Thomas Pynchon, from Jack London and Frank Norris to Ishmael Reed.

Le Guin, Ursula K. *Always Coming Home.* Unbelievably, this 1985 feminist/utopian novel

has long been out of print, though at last report it was scheduled for re-publication in late 2000. Ms. Le Guin gained fame as a science fiction writer, for novels including *The Left Hand of Darkness* and *The Dispossessed.* Her formal literary recognition includes the Hugo, Gandalf, Kafka, Nebula, and National Book awards. *Always Coming Home* is perhaps Le Guin's masterwork, and a special treat for those who love California—particularly Northern California, where the lay of the land happens to coincide with the geographical borders of the land she describes (and maps) in this imaginative exploration of "futuristic anthropology."

Le Guin, Ursula K. *Dancing at the Edge of the World: Thoughts on Words, Women, Places.* New York: Grove Press, 1989. This delightful collection of essays includes some rare sidelong glances into the soul of the northstate— and why not? The daughter of UC Berkeley anthropologist Alfred L. Kroeber and Ishi's biographer Theodora Kroeber, Le Guin offers a unique perspective on California as a place— then, now, and in the times to come. Particularly enjoyable in this context: "A Non-Euclidian View of California as a Cold Place to Be"; "The Fisherwoman's Daughter" (about, among other things, her mother); and "Woman/Wilderness."

London, Jack, ed. by Gerald Haslam. *Jack London's Golden State: Selected California Writings.* Berkeley: Heyday Books, 1999. The first major U.S. writer to use California as his base, Jack London has finally come home—so California can reclaim him. Included here are some of London's finest works, from *John Barleycorn: or Alcoholic Memoirs* and *Star Rover* to *Valley of the Moon,* along with journalism, short stories, and letters.

MacDonald, Ross. *The Moving Target.* New York: Alfred A. Knopf, 1967. In this, one of MacDonald's many Southern California intrigues, private dick Lew Archer encounters Los Angeles criminals at their most entertaining.

McNamee, Gregory, ed. *Sierra Club Desert Reader: A Literary Companion.* San Francisco: Sierra Club Books, 1995.

McPhee, John. *Assembling California.* New York: Noonday Press (Farrar, Straus and Giroux), 1993. If you didn't read it as excerpted in the *New Yorker,* here's your chance. The eclectic and indefatigable natural history writer here deconstructs California, tectonically speaking, as a cross-section of both human and geologic time. Who would have thought speculations about the geological underpinnings of the Golden State could be so fascinating?

Michaels, Leonard, David Reid, and Raquel Scherr, eds. *West of the West: Imagining California.* New York: HarperCollins Publishers, 1991. Though any anthology about California is destined to be incomplete, this one is exceptional—offering selections by Maya Angelou, Simone de Beauvoir, Joan Didion, Umberto Eco, Gretel Ehrlich, M. F. K. Fisher, Aldous Huxley, Jack Kerouac, Maxine Hong Kingston, Rudyard Kipling, Henry Miller, Ishmael Reed, Kenneth Rexroth, Richard Rodriguez, Randy Shilts, Gertrude Stein, John Steinbeck, Octavio Paz, Amy Tan, Gore Vidal, Walt Whitman, and Tom Wolfe.

Miller, Henry. *Big Sur and the Oranges of Hieronymus Bosch.* New York: W. W. Norton & Co., 1978. First published in 1958, the famed writer shares his impressions of art and writing along with his view of life as seen from the Big Sur coastline—the center of his personal universe in his later years, and the first real home he had ever found.

Mosley, Walter. *Devil in a Blue Dress.* New York: W. W. Norton & Co., 1990. Easy Rawlins, the reluctant private-eye hero of Walter Mosley's noir Los Angeles, reveals post–World War II truths from the perspective of Watts and South-Central Los Angeles. But beyond the plot—black detective takes job from white man to find a mysterious woman—the story of African American migration into Los Angeles is also told here, a depth of experience, and mistrust, grounded in the Deep South. Even after you've seen the movie (starring Denzel Washington as Easy Rawlins) and vicariously relived L.A.'s jazz club cultural heyday, you can follow Easy on more Los Angeles adventures in Mosley's *Black Betty, White Butterfly, A Red Death,* and *A Little Yellow Dog.*

Muir, John. *The Mountains of California.* Berkeley: Ten Speed Press, 1988. Very enjoyable facsimile reprint of the noted mountaineer's musings and observations.

Muir, John, ed. by Frederic Gunsky. *South of Yosemite: Selected Writings of John Muir.* Berkeley: Wilderness Press, 1988. The first collection of Muir's writings to explore what is now the Sequoia and Kings Canyon region fulfills the famed naturalist's dream of a book he intended to title *The Yosemite and the Other Yosemites.* This "Other Yosemite" anthology includes some of Muir's best work. To appreciate his complete works, find *John Muir: His Life and Letters and Other Writings* and *John Muir: The Eight Wilderness Discovery Books.*

Muscatine, Doris. *The University of California/Sotheby Book of California Wine.* Berkeley: University of California Press, 1984. A rather expensive companion but worthwhile for wine lovers.

Norris, Frank. *McTeague: A Story of San Francisco.* New York: New American Library, 1997. Reissue ed. The basis for the classic silent film *Greed,* Norris's novel is, in a way, the ultimate Western. First published in 1899, a retelling of an actual crime, *McTeague* tells the story of a dimwitted dentist and his greedy wife—all in all a bleak, lowbrow tour of life in San Francisco at the turn of the 20th century, ending with McTeague stumbling off into the desert.

Olmstead, R., and T. H. Watkins. *Here Today: San Francisco Architectural Heritage.* San Francisco: Chronicle Books, 1978 (OP).

Paddison, Joshua, ed. *A World Transformed: Firsthand Accounts of California Before the Gold Rush.* Berkeley: Heyday Books, 1999. According to popular California mythology, the Golden State was "born" with the onrushing change that came with the gold rush of 1848. But this collection of earlier California writings gathers together some intriguing earlier observations—from European explorers and visitors, missionaries, and sea captains—that reveal pre–gold rush California.

Parker, T. Jefferson. *Laguna Heat.* New York: St. Martin's Press, 1985. So, who says only L.A. does down and dirty whodunits? Orange County's own T. Jefferson Parker, in his best-selling national debut, certainly did Laguna Beach proud. And when you're done untangling this tale, there's always *Little Saigon, Pacific Beat,* and *Summer of Fear,* not to mention more recent works.

Reid, Robert Leonard, ed. *A Treasury of the Sierra Nevada.* Berkeley: Wilderness Press, 1983. Words by Mark Twain, Robert Louis Stevenson, Walt Whitman, and John Muir are included in this anthology, the first and only Sierra Nevada literary compilation.

Rice, Scott, ed. *It Was a Dark and Stormy Night: The Final Conflict.* New York: Penguin, 1992. An anthology of the best of bad fiction from San Jose State University's Bullwer-Lytton fiction contest.

Robertson, David. *A History of the Art and Literature of Yosemite.* Berkeley: Wilderness Press, 1984 (OP). A fully illustrated history and a thoughtful Yosemite travel companion.

Rodriguez, Richard. *Hunger of Memory: The Education of Richard Rodriguez.* New York: Bantam Books, 1983. California-born Rodriguez got into all kinds of trouble by suggesting, in this book, that affirmative action and bilingual education do a disservice to children of immigrants to the United States. He uses his own experience by way of illustration. As an intellectual biography of an immensely gifted writer, a longtime editor at San Francisco's Pacific News Service and frequent essayist on PBS's *The News Hour, Hunger of Memory* chronicles his education—when he starts school in Sacramento, knowing a sparse 50 words of English, and when he completes his formal studies in the elite reading room of the British Museum. He chronicles the high costs of social assimilation, including sadness at the increasing distance from his own family, but also exemplifies the freedoms that come with the mastery and love of language. Less controversial is Rodriguez's lyrical *Days of Obligation: An Argument with*

My Mexican Father, a fascinating extended essay on contemporary California—and much of the United States—as caught between optimism and pessimism, Protestantism and Catholicism, youth and old age.

Russack, Benjamin, ed. *Wine Country: A Literary Companion.* Berkeley: Heyday Books, 1999. This intriguing anthology includes stories from the Wappo Indians and early explorers as well as recognized literary figures—Robert Louis Stevenson, Jack London, Ambrose Bierce, Dorothy Bryant, Jessamyn West, among others—associated with the Napa and Sonoma Valleys.

Sale, Kirkpatrick. *Dwellers in the Land: The Bioregional Vision.* San Francisco: Sierra Club Books, 1985 (OP). One of the first books putting forth the bioregional philosophy, envisioning a world based not on political borders but on natural geographic regions.

Saroyan, William. *The Daring Young Man on the Flying Trapeze: And Other Stories.* New York: New Directions, 1997. Known for the *humanness* of his writings, Fresno's own William Saroyan won the Pulitzer Prize for his play *The Time of Your Life: A Comedy in Three Acts.* As befits one of the first writers in the 20th century to explore life in immigrant communities, the protagonists in "Daring Young Man"—a collection first published in 1934—are African, Armenian, Chinese, Jewish, and Irish immigrants. Also look for *Fresno Stories, The Human Comedy,* and *New Saroyan Reader.*

See, Carolyn. *Dreaming: Hard Luck and Good Times in America.* Berkeley: University of California Press, 1996. A bittersweet reevaluation of the American dream, presented as memoir. Also by See, and well worth a read: *Golden Days,* a provocative fictional look at life in 1970s and '80s L.A., as linked to an "iffy" future, and *Mother, Daughter.*

Sinclair, Upton. *Oil!* Berkeley: University of California Press, 1997. Reprise of the original 1927 edition, in which journalist and socialist gadfly Sinclair fictionally recreates the Signal

Hill oil fields of Long Beach and the Teapot Dome oil reserve scandals.

Snyder, Gary. *Turtle Island*. New York: W. W. Norton & Co., 1974. Titled with a Native American term for the entire North American continent, this Pulitzer Prize–winning 1975 poetry collection honors almost every aspect of that vast landscape. When the poem cycle *Mountains and Rivers Without End* was published in 1996, Snyder was awarded the Böllingen Poetry Prize and the *Los Angeles Times*'s Robert Kirsch Lifetime Achievement Award.

Southern, Terry. *Flash and Filigree*. New York: Grove Press, 1958. Just so you know what you're in for, Terry Southern was also the screenwriter for that hilarious cinematic celebration of apocalypse, *Dr. Strangelove: Or How I Learned to Love the Bomb*. No one else quite captures the banality of Los Angeles with such affectionate horror.

Stegner, Wallace Earle. *Angle of Repose*. New York: Penguin USA, 1992. Reprint ed. Wallace Stegner's Pulitzer Prize–winning novel, in which the disenchanted, wheelchair-bound historian Lyman Ward decides to write about the lives of his grandparents on the American frontier.

Stegner, Wallace Earle. Edited and with a preface from the author's son, Page Stegner. *Marking the Sparrow's Fall: Wallace Stegner's American West*. New York: H. Holt, 1998. This brilliant collection of Stegner's conservation writings traces his development as a Westerner—and as a Western writer—starting with his seemingly inauspicious beginnings as an avid reader, hunkered down in small-town libraries in places almost no one's ever heard of. The first collection of Stegner's work since the author's death in 1993, *Marking the Sparrow's Fall* includes 15 essays never before published, his best-known essays on the American West—including *Wilderness Letter*—and a little-known novella.

Stegner, Wallace Earle. *Where the Bluebird Sings to the Lemonade Springs: Living and Writing in the West*. New York: Penguin USA, 1993. Reprint ed. It's certainly understandable that, at the end of his days, Wallace Stegner wasn't entirely optimistic about the future of the West, bedeviled as it is, still, by development pressures and insane political decisions. In these 16 thoughtful essays, he spells out his concerns—and again pays poetic homage to the West's big sky and bigger landscapes. In the end, he remains hopeful that a new spirit of place is emerging in the West—and that within a generation or two we will "work out some sort of compromise between what must be done to earn a living and what must be done to restore health to the earth, air, and water."

Steinbeck, John. *Cannery Row*. New York: Penguin USA, 1993. Reprint ed. Here it is, a poem, a stink, a grating noise, told in the days when sardines still ruled the boardwalk on Monterey's Cannery Row. Also worth an imaginative side trip on a tour of the California coast is Steinbeck's *East of Eden,* first published in 1952, the Salinas Valley version of the Cain and Abel story. Steinbeck's classic California work, though, is still *The Grapes of Wrath*.

Stevenson, Robert Louis. *The Complete Short Stories of Robert Louis Stevenson: With a Selection of the Best Short Novels*. New York: Da Capo Press, 1998. It's hard to know where to start with Stevenson, whose California journeys served to launch his literary career. Da Capo's collection is as good a place as any.

Theroux, Peter. *Translating L.A.: A Tour of the Rainbow City*. New York: W. W. Norton & Co., 1994. Here, Paul Theroux's cousin takes the reader on an affectionate and quirky personal tour of Los Angeles as adopted hometown. Wearing the various hats of journalist, translator, and literacy tutor, Theroux visits earthquakes, mass transit, Beverly Hills, Hollywood, and Watts.

Thompson, Gary. *On John Muir's Trail*. Cohasset, CA: Bear Star Press, 1999. Includes all of the poems also published in Moon's *Northern California Handbook*. Copies are available directly from the publisher: Bear Star Press, 185 Hollow Oak Dr., Cohasset, CA 95973, 530/891-0360.

van der Zee, John, and Boyd Jacobson. *The Imagined City: San Francisco in the Minds of Its Writers.* San Francisco: California Living Books, 1980 (OP). Quotes about San Francisco pulled from the works—mostly fiction—of 37 writers, both widely known and locally celebrated. Accompanied by photos and a page-long biography of each author, as well as historical photographs.

Van Dyke, John C. *The Desert.* Layton, UT: Gibbs Smith Publishing, 1991. First published in 1901, this is Van Dyke's tale of his three-year solo trek through the desert landscapes of Arizona, California, and Mexico.

Wambaugh, Joseph. *The New Centurions.* Boston: Little, Brown, 1970. Los Angeles cops on patrol in East L.A.—a fictional look from a veteran of the Los Angeles Police Department.

Waugh, Evelyn. *The Loved One.* Boston: Little, Brown, 1948. Pet cemeteries and people cemeteries with that eternal touch—nobody denies death better than Los Angeles. And nobody writes about it better than Waugh.

West, Nathanael. *The Day of the Locust.* New York: New Directions, 1962. Before West and his wife were killed in a car accident, he published this surreal novel of L.A. apocalypse. This 1939 tale of terror premieres in Hollywood, naturally, but the story is about the troublesome troupes no longer needed by the silver screen.

WPA Guide to California: The Federal Writers Project Guide to 1930s California. New York: Pantheon Press (an imprint of Random House), 1984. The classic travel guide to California, first published during the Depression, is somewhat dated as far as contemporary sights but excellent as a companion volume and background information source.

Yogi, Stan, ed. *Highway 99: A Literary Journey through California's Great Central Valley.* Berkeley: Heyday Books, 1997. A regional bestseller, this wonderful collection of poetry, fiction, and nonfiction includes Joan Didion, Maxine Hong Kingston, David Mas Masumoto, Richard Rodriguez, Gary Snyder, John Steinbeck, and other California writers who either hailed from or explored the San Joaquin or Sacramento Valley.

HISTORY AND PEOPLE

Adams, Ansel, with Mary Alinder. *Ansel Adams: An Autobiography.* Boston: Bulfinch Press, 1990. A compelling, expansive, enlightening sharing of self by the extraordinary photographer—not coincidentally also a generous, extraordinary human being.

Anger, Kenneth. *Hollywood Babylon.* San Francisco: Straight Arrow Books, 1975. Along with Anger's sequel, this is the classic catalog of juicy gossip about Hollywood's glitterati.

Atherton, Gertrude. *My San Francisco, A Wayward Biography.* Indianapolis and New York: The Bobbs-Merrill Company, 1946. The 56th book—written at the age of 90—by the woman Kevin Starr has called "the daughter of the elite" whose career of historical fiction "document[ed] . . . itself . . . in a careless but vivid output. . . ." A delightfully chatty browse through the past, filled with dropped names and accounts of Atherton's own meetings with historic figures.

Balio, Tino. *Grand Design: Hollywood as a Modern Business Enterprise, 1930–1939.* Berkeley: University of California Press, 1995. Part of UC Press's History of the American Cinema series, *Grand Design* explores the development of the Hollywood system during the Great Depression.

Barlett, Donald L., and James B. Steele. *Empire: The Life, Legend and Madness of Howard Hughes.* New York: W. W. Norton & Co., 1979. He of obsessive habits and unclipped fingernails wasn't always a madman. Earlier, Hughes was a noted Hollywood gadfly-cum-empire builder. This is the definitive work on the man and his mission.

Bean, Lowell John, and Lisa J. Bourgeault. *The Cahuilla.* New York: Chelsea House Publishers, 1989. Part of Chelsea's Indians of North America Series, this book explores the culture and history of the native peoples near Palm Springs. From rock art, pottery, and other details of daily life to contemporary history, *The Cahuilla* is a good, very readable introduction.

Bonadio, Felice. *A. P. Giannini: Banker of America.* Berkeley: University of California Press, 1994. Fascinating biography of Amadeo Peter Giannini, son of Italian immigrants, ruthless financial genius, friend of "the people," and founder of San Francisco's own (at least at one time) Bank of America. This is the story of the man who was the first to extend credit to working stiffs, and who also shared the bank's wealth with bank employees.

Brady, Frank. *Citizen Welles.* New York: Scribner, 1989. One of the noted few in Hollywood's genius genre, even Orson Welles had a tough time of it in Tinseltown.

Bronson, William. *The Earth Shook, The Sky Burned: A Photographic Record of the 1906 San Francisco Earthquake & Fire.* San Francisco: Chronicle Books, 1997. Originally published by Doubleday, 1959. A San Francisco classic—just the book to tote home as a memento of your San Francisco vacation. This moving story of the city's 1906 earthquake and the four-day fire that followed includes more than 400 on-the-scene photographs.

Brownlow, Kevin. *Hollywood: The Pioneers.* New York: Alfred A. Knopf, 1979. The textbook of early Hollywood history, chronicling the era of silent films. Brownlow's trilogy also tells the story, in still more depth: *The Parade's Gone By, The War, the West, and the Wilderness,* and *Behind the Mask.*

Carnes, Mark C., ed. *Past Imperfect: History According to the Movies.* New York: Henry Holt & Co., 1995. Published under the aegis of the Society of American Historians, this historical peek into Hollywood's version of reality is offered via eclectic essays from about

60 writers, including Frances Fitzgerald, Stephen J. Gould, Antonia Fraser, Anthony Lewis, and Gore Vidal. *Past Imperfect* is as entertaining as it is educational.

Clarke, James Mitchell. *The Life and Adventures of John Muir.* San Francisco: Sierra Club Books (OP).

Cleland, Robert Glass. *From Wilderness to Empire: A History of California.* New York: Alfred A. Knopf, 1944 (OP).

Cleland, Robert Glass. *A History of California: The American Period.* Westport, CT: Greenwood Press, 1975. Originally published in 1922.

Cole, Tom. *A Short History of San Francisco.* Lagunitas, CA: Lexikos, 1986. Very accessible, thoroughly entertaining overview, with clean design and some great old photos and illustrations.

Dalton, David. *James Dean: The Mutant King.* San Francisco: Straight Arrow Books, 1974. Dean's cult has grown larger and more disaffected since the actor's violent death on the highway after completing only three films for Hollywood. This pulpy bio digs into the Dean legend.

Davis, Margaret Leslie. *Rivers in the Desert: William Mulholland and the Inventing of Los Angeles.* New York: HarperCollins, 1993 (published in paperback by HarperPerennial). The astonishing and meticulously researched story of how self-taught water engineer William Mulholland masterminded massive water supplies for present-day Los Angeles, told with admiration and respect. Davis sidesteps the temptation to demonize Mulholland with 20/20 hindsight, though she does acknowledge more pointed current criticisms. In her epilogue she also takes care to exonerate Mulholland for the grievous sins history had tarred him with— the St. Francis Dam disaster and the multitude of lives lost.

Davis, Mike. *City of Quartz: Excavating the Future in Los Angeles.* With photos by Robert

Morrow. New York: Vintage Books, 1992. Something of a surprise bestseller in Southern California, as historical dust-up *City of Quartz* takes issue with the idea of California as an innocent and sunny paradise lost. From the book's prologue: "The pattern or urbanization here is what design critic Peter Plagens once called 'the ecology of evil.' Developers don't grow homes in the desert—this isn't Marrakesh or even Tucson—they just clear, grade and pave, hook up some pipes to the artificial river (the federally subsidized California Aqueduct), build a security wall, and plug in the 'product.' With generations of experience in uprooting the citrus gardens of Orange County and the San Fernando Valley, the developers . . . regard the desert as simply another abstraction of dirt and dollar signs." And with that, he's just warming up. A must-read for anyone who loves Los Angeles—or even the idea of Los Angeles.

d'Azevedo, Warren. *Straight with the Medicine: Narratives of Washoe Followers of the Tipi Way.* Berkeley: Heyday Books, 1985 (OP). Cultural and spiritual insights shared by those involved in the peyote religious practices adopted in and around the eastern Sierra Nevada in the 1930s.

Dreyer, Peter. *A Gardener Touched with Genius: The Life of Luther Burbank.* Berkeley: University of California Press, 1985.

Ellison, William Henry. *A Self-Governing Dominion, California 1849–1860.* Berkeley: University of California Press, 1978.

Farquhar, Francis P. *History of the Sierra Nevada.* Berkeley: University of California Press, 1965.

Farquhar, Francis P., ed. *Up and Down California in 1860–1864: The Journal of William H. Brewer.* Berkeley: University of California Press, 1974. Reprint of 1966 edition.

Fogelson, Robert M. *The Fragmented Metropolis: Los Angeles, 1850–1930.* With a new foreword by Robert Fishman. Berkeley: University of California Press, 1993. This new UC Press edition of an urban history classic includes a new preface and updated bibliography.

Fradkin, Philip L. *A River No More: The Colorado River and the West.* Berkeley: University of California Press, 1996. Revised ed. It's not as if California is the only state that helps itself to the waters of the once mighty Colorado River. This, the definitive history, traces the tale from the river's headwaters in Wyoming's Rockies to the Arizona and California borders. Would there be any cities in the desert without the Colorado?

Frederick, David C. *Rugged Justice: The Ninth Circuit Court of Appeals and the American West.* With a foreword by U.S. Supreme Court Justice Sandra Day O'Connor. Berkeley: University of California Press, 1994. Now that the Republican U.S. Congress is trying to muzzle the independent and oft-overturned judicial voice of the West's Ninth Circuit Court—still half Democrat, half Republican, the only federal appeals court not yet dominated by party-line Republicans—what better time to read this colorful history?

Frémont, John Charles. *Memoirs of My Life.* New York: Penguin, 1984. Originally published in Chicago, 1887. The old Bearflagger himself tells the story of early California—at least some of it.

Friedrich, Otto. *City of Nets: A Portrait of Hollywood in the 1940s.* New York: Harper & Row, 1986. In 1939 provincial Hollywood almost went international, as expatriates from war-strafed Europe—the likes of Bertolt Brecht and Arthur Schoenberg—came to town. In one of the best books ever written about Tinseltown, Friedrich chronicles the following decade—a significant, substantive period for filmmaking.

Griswold del Castillo, Richard. *The Los Angeles Barrio, 1850–1890: A Social History.* Berkeley: University of California Press, 1980.

Gudde, Erwin G. *California Gold Camps.* Berkeley: University of California Press, 1975.

Guiles, Fred Lawrence. *Norma Jean: The Life of Marilyn Monroe.* New York: McGraw-Hill, 1969. The tragic life of Marilyn Monroe, studio creation, could have been scripted by Hollywood. Equally enlightening: *Legend: The Life and Death of Marilyn Monroe,* also by Guiles.

Gutiérrez, Ramon A., and Richard J. Orsi, eds. *Contested Eden: California Before the Gold Rush.* Berkeley: University of California Press, 1998. In this first volume of a projected four-part series, essays explore California before the gold rush.

Harlow, Neal. *California Conquered: The Annexation of a Mexican Province, 1846–1850.* Berkeley: University of California Press, 1982.

Hart, John. *Storm Over Mono: The Mono Lake Basin and the California Water Future.* Berkeley: University of California Press, 1996. While a fairly happy ending to the story is now being written on the pages of California newspapers, *Storm Over Mono* covers the fight to save Mono Lake as comprehensively as anyone. Illustrated with dozens of striking color photographs plus black-and-white photos, maps, and illustrations.

Harte, Bret. *The Writings of Bret Harte.* New York: AMS Press, 1903.

Heizer, Robert F. *The Destruction of the California Indians.* Utah: Gibbs Smith Publishing, 1974.

Heizer, Robert F., and Martin A. Baumhoff. *Prehistoric Rock Art of Nevada and Eastern California.* Berkeley: University of California Press, 1976.

Heizer, Robert F., and Albert B. Elsasser. *The Natural World of the California Indians.* Berkeley: University of California Press, 1980. As an adjunct to the rest of Heizer's work, this fact-packed volume provides the setting—the natural environment, the village environment—for California's native peoples.

Heizer, Robert F., and M. A. Whipple. *The California Indians.* Berkeley: University of California

nia Press, 1971. A worthwhile collection of essays about California's native peoples, covering general, regional, and specific topics—a good supplement to the work of A. L. Kroeber (who also contributed to this volume).

Hine, Robert V. *California's Utopian Colonies.* Berkeley: University of California Press, 1983.

Holiday, James. *The World Rushed In: The California Gold Rush Experience: An Eyewitness Account of a Nation Heading West.* New York: Simon and Schuster, 1981. Reprint of a classic history, made while new Californians were busy making up the myth.

Horton, Tom. *Super Span: The Golden Gate Bridge.* San Francisco: Chronicle Books, 1983. How the Golden Gate Bridge came to be, illustrated with anecdotes and photographs—a very compelling history of an inanimate object.

Houston, James, and Jeanne Houston. *Farewell to Manzanar.* New York: Bantam Books, 1983. A good goodbye to California's World War II internment of Japanese immigrants and American citizens of Japanese descent, a nightmarish experience that lives on in the cultural memory of Southern California's large population of Japanese Americans.

Hutchinson, W. H. *California: The Golden Shore by the Sundown Sea.* Belmont, CA: Star Publishing Company, 1988. The late author, a professor emeritus of history at CSU Chico known as Old Hutch to former students, presents a dizzying amount of historical, economic, and political detail from his own unique perspective in this analysis of California's past and present. Hutchinson saw the state from many sides during a lifetime spent as "a horse wrangler, cowboy, miner, boiler fireman, merchant seaman, corporate bureaucrat, rodeo and horse show announcer, and freelance writer."

Irons, Peter. *Justice at War: The Story of the Japanese-American Internment Cases.* Berkeley: University of California Press, 1993. Irons examines the internment of Japanese Americans and noncitizen immigrants in World War ll "relocation" camps as historical travesty in a brilliantly researched, beautifully written book.

Jackson, Helen Hunt. *Century of Dishonor: A Sketch of the U.S. Government's Dealings (with some of the Indian tribes).* Temecula, CA: Reprint Services, 1988. Originally published in Boston, 1881.

Jackson, Joseph Henry. *Anybody's Gold: The Story of California's Mining Towns.* San Francisco: Chronicle Books, 1970. A lively history back in print after a 30-year hiatus.

Kroeber, Alfred L. *Handbook of the Indians of California.* New York: Dover Publications, 1976 (unabridged facsimile version of the original work, *Bulletin 78* of the Bureau of American Ethnology of the Smithsonian Institution, published by the U.S. Government Printing Office). The classic compendium of observed facts about California's native peoples by the noted UC Berkeley anthropologist who befriended Ishi—but also betrayed him, posthumously, by allowing his body to be autopsied (in violation of Ishi's beliefs) then shipping his brain to the Smithsonian Institution.

Kroeber, Theodora. *Ishi in Two Worlds: A Biography of the Last Wild Indian in North America.* Berkeley: University of California Press, 1961. The classic biography of Ishi, an incredible 20th-century story—illustrating California's location at the edge of the wilderness well into the 20th century—well told by A. L. Kroeber's widow and also available in an illustrated edition. Also very worthwhile by Kroeber: *Inland Whale: California Indian Legends,* and, co-written with Robert F. Heizer, *Ishi the Last Yahi: A Documentary History.* That Ishi may not have been the last Yahi after all—see The Northern Mountains chapter for the latest twists in this tale—just makes the story all the more intriguing.

Lapsley, James T. *Bottled Poetry: Napa Winemaking from Prohibition to the Modern Era.* Berkeley: University of California Press, 1997. Though California's Napa Valley is now one of the world's premier wine regions, it was not always thus. This entertaining history explains how a collective post-Prohibition desire for excellence, in combination with promotional savvy, transformed the fate of the region and its wines.

Lennon, Nigey. *Mark Twain in California.* San Francisco: Chronicle Books, 1982. An entertaining, enlightened, easy-reading biography from a true lover of Samuel Clemens's writings as Mark Twain.

Lewis, Oscar. *The Big Four.* Sausalito, CA: Comstock Editions, 1982. Originally published in New York, 1938.

Margolin, Malcolm. *The Way We Lived.* Berkeley: Heyday Books, 1981. A wonderful collection of California native peoples' reminiscences, stories, and songs. Also by Margolin: *The Ohlone Way,* about the life of California's first residents of the San Francisco–Monterey Bay Area.

McDonald, Linda, and Carol Cullen. *California Historical Landmarks.* Sacramento, CA: California Department of Parks and Recreation, 1997. Revised ed. Originally compiled in response to the National Historic Preservation Act of 1966, directing all states to identify all properties "possessing historical, architectural, archaeological, and cultural value," this updated edition covers more than 1,000 California Registered Historical Landmarks, organized by category—sites of aboriginal, economic, or government interest, for example— and indexed by county. A wide variety of other publications is available from the Department of Parks and Recreation. To order, call toll-free 800/777-0369.

McWilliams, Carey, with a foreword by Lewis H. Lapham. *California, the Great Exception.* Berkeley: University of California Press, 1999. Historian, journalist, and lawyer Carey McWilliams, editor of *The Nation* from 1955 to 1975, stepped back from his other tasks in 1949 to assess the state of the Golden State at the end of its first 100 years. And while he acknowledged the state's prodigious productivity even then, he also noted the brutality with which the great nation-state of California dealt with "the Indian problem," the water problem, and the agricultural labor problem—all issues of continuing relevance to California today. McWilliams's classic work on the essence of California, reprinted with a new foreword by the editor of *Harper's* magazine, is a must-read for all Californians.

McWilliams, Carey. *Southern California Country: An Island Upon the Land.* New York: Duell, Sloan & Pierce, 1946. The classic of pre–World War II L.A. history, still the best in terms of placing the city's seeming peculiarities in their proper contexts.

Milosz, Czeslaw. *Visions from San Francisco Bay.* New York: Farrar, Straus & Giroux, 1982. Essays on emigration from the Nobel Prize winner in literature. Originally published in Polish, 1969.

Monroy, Douglas. *Thrown Among Strangers: The Making of Mexican Culture in Frontier California.* Berkeley: University of California Press, 1990.

Mungo, Ray. *Palm Springs Babylon: Sizzling Stories from the Desert Playground of the Stars.* New York: St. Martin's Press, 1993. It's tacky to pry into the private lives of Hollywood celebrities, politicians, and rich people, even when they're at play in Palm Springs. But Mungo does it so well—managing to spew out chapter after chapter of substantive local social history along with the snide asides (such as the caption for a photo of Sonny Bono: "Former Cher Bimbo Goes His Own Way"). All in all this book is a hoot—and you'll find out more about the sleazier side of Palm Springs than you ever wanted to know.

Murray, Keith A. *The Modocs and Their War.* Norman, OK: University of Oklahoma Press, 1976.

Nadeau, Remi. *City-Makers.* Garden City, NY: Doubleday, 1948. Hey, *Chinatown* fans. Here's the dark side of L.A. history in book form—the tale of the boosters, promoters, and sleazy business deals that together created present-day L.A., much to the detriment of the place and its people.

Perry, Charles. *The Haight-Ashbury: A History.* New York: Rolling Stone Press (an imprint of Random House), 1984. A detailed chronicle of events that began in 1965 and led up to the Summer of Love, with research, writing, and some pointed observations by the author, a *Rolling Stone* editor.

Pitt, Leonard. *Decline of the Californios: A Social History of the Spanish-Speaking Californians, 1846–1890.* Berkeley: University of California Press, 1966.

Powers, Stephen. *Tribes of California.* Berkeley: University of California Press, 1977.

Reisner, Marc. *Cadillac Desert: The American West and Its Disappearing Water.* New York: Penguin Books, 1993. Revised ed. Inspiration for the four-part PBS documentary of the same name, first broadcast in 1997, this is the contemporary yet classic tale of water and the unromantic West—a drama of unquenchable thirst and reluctant conservation, political intrigue and corruption, and economic and ecological disasters. How Los Angeles got its water figures prominently—the histories of William Mulholland and the Owens Valley as well as the Colorado River. A must-read book.

Ridge, John. *The Life and Adventures of Joaquin Murrieta.* Norman, OK: University of Oklahoma Press, 1986.

Riva, Maria. *Marlene Dietrich: By Her Daughter.* New York: Alfred A. Knopf, 1993. Marlene Dietrich was an alcoholic, bedridden ghost of a woman when she died. But that was no call for her daughter to betray her or the fond memories of their complex mother-daughter relationship. Though, as Riva puts it: "At the age of three, I knew quite definitely that I did not have a mother, that I belonged to a queen. Once that was settled in my head, I was quite content with my lot." Serious Dietrich fans must also read the definitive biography, *Marlene Dietrich: Life and Legend*, by Steven Bach (William Morrow, 1992).

Robertson, David. *West of Eden: History of Art and Literature of Yosemite.* Berkeley: Wilderness Press, 1984.

Robinson, W. W. *Land in California: The Story of Mission Lands, Ranchos, Squatters, Mining Claims, Railroad Grants, Land Scrip, Homesteads.* Berkeley: University of California Press, 1979.

Royce, Josiah. *California from the Conquest in 1846 to the Second Vigilance Committee in San Francisco 1856.* New York: AMS Press. Originally published in Boston, 1886.

Santa Barbara Museum of Natural History. *California's Chumash Indians.* San Luis Obispo, CA: EZ Nature Books, 1988. A fascinating overview of Chumash culture, innovation, trade, and tradition.

Saunders, Richard. *Ambrose Bierce: The Making of a Misanthrope.* San Francisco: Chronicle Books, 1984 (OP).

Sinclair, Upton. *American Outpost: A Book of Reminiscences.* Temecula, CA: Reprint Services, 1992.

Sinclair, Upton. *I, Candidate for Governor: And How I Got Licked.* Berkeley: University of California Press, 1994. Reprint of the original edition. This is a genuine treasure of California history—a first-person account of California's liveliest and most notorious gubernatorial race, in which California business employed Hollywood's tools to defeat muckraking journalist and socialist Democratic candidate Sinclair in the too-close-to-call 1934 campaign. Sinclair's platform was EPIC—End Poverty in California—and he almost got the chance to try. Though it's hard to imagine in the 21st century, at other times in its history—certainly during the Great Depression—California as place got seriously agitated over issues of social justice, giving the good ol' boys quite a scare.

Starr, Kevin. *Americans and the California Dream: 1850–1915.* New York: Oxford University Press, 1973. A cultural history, written by a native San Franciscan, former newspaper columnist, onetime head of the city's library system, professor and historian, and current California State Librarian. The focus on Northern California taps an impressively varied body of sources as it seeks to "suggest the poetry and the moral drama of social experience" from California's first days of statehood through the Panama-Pacific Exposition of 1915 when, in the author's opinion, "California came of age."

Starr, Kevin. *The Dream Endures: California Enters the 1940s.* New York: Oxford University Press, 1997. This, the fifth volume in Kevin Starr's impressive California history series, traces the history of the California good life—in architecture, fiction, film, and leisure pursuits—and how it came to define American culture and society. Chosen Outstanding Academic Book of 1997 by *Choice,* and one of the best 100 books of 1997 by the *Los Angeles Times Book Review.*

Starr, Kevin. *Endangered Dreams: The Great Depression in California.* New York: Oxford University Press, 1996. "California," Wallace Stegner has noted, "is like the rest of the United States, only more so." And so begins the fourth volume of Starr's imaginative and immense California history, in which the author delves into the Golden State's dark past—a period in which strikes and unions were forcibly suppressed, soup kitchens became social institutions, and both socialism and fascism had their day. The "therapy" that finally cured California involved massive transfusions of public capital in the form of public works projects. Yet some things don't change: San Francisco is still a strong union town, and Los Angeles barely tolerates unionism.

Starr, Kevin. *Inventing the Dream: California Through the Progressive Era.* New York: Oxford University Press, 1985. Second in Starr's respected series on California history, *Inventing the Dream* addresses Southern California's ascendancy in the late 19th and early 20th centuries.

Starr, Kevin. *Material Dreams: Southern California Through the 1920s.* New York: Oxford University Press, 1990. The third book in Starr's lively symbolic celebration of California history chronicles the most compelling period of explosive growth in Los Angeles—which the author affectionately calls "the Great Gatsby of American cities"—made possible by the arrival of water.

Stein, Ben. *Hollywood Days, Hollywood Nights.* New York: Bantam Books, 1988. Forget the fact that Stein was once a speechwriter for Richard Nixon. He also knows the mentality ("soul" too high-flown a phrase) of Hollywood, from paranoia to script punctuation, and is happy to share his secrets.

Steinbeck, John. *Working Days: The Journals of the Grapes of Wrath 1938–1941.* New York: Penguin, 1989. Less an explanation for *The Grapes of Wrath* than a portrait of a writer possessed—and therefore quite interesting.

Stevenson, Robert Louis. *From Scotland to Silverado.* Cambridge, MA: The Belknap Press of Harvard University Press, 1966. An annotated collection of the sickly and lovelorn young Stevenson's travel essays, including his first impressions of Monterey and San Francisco, and the works that have come to be known as *The Silverado Squatters.* Contains considerable text—marked therein—that the author's family and friends had removed from previous editions. A useful introduction by James D. Hart details the journeys and relationships behind the essays.

Stone, Irving. *Jack London: Sailor on Horseback.* New York: Doubleday, 1986. Originally published in Boston, 1938.

Stone, Irving. *Men to Match My Mountains.* New York: Berkeley Publishers, 1987. A classic California history, originally published in 1956.

St. Pierre, Brian. *John Steinbeck: The California Years.* San Francisco: Chronicle Books, 1983 (OP).

Stryker, Susan, and Jim Van Buskirk. *Gay by the Bay: A History of Queer Culture in the San Francisco Bay Area.* San Francisco: Chronicle Books, 1996. Chronicling the origin and evolution of lesbian, gay, bisexual, and transgender culture in San Francisco and environs, this book was published to coincide with the opening of the Gay and Lesbian Center—the first of its kind in this country—in the new San Francisco Public Library.

Turner, Frederick. *Rediscovering America.* New York: Penguin, 1985. A fascinating cultural history and biography of John Muir—the man in his time and ours—generally more interesting reading than much of Muir's own work.

Walton, John. *Western Times and Water Wars: State, Culture, and Rebellion in California.* Berkeley: University of California Press, 1992. Winner of both the Robert Park and J. S. Holliday Awards, Walton's compelling chronicle of the water wars between Los Angeles and the farmers and ranchers of the Owens Valley is a masterpiece of California history.

NATURE AND NATURAL HISTORY

Adams, Ansel. *Yosemite and the Range of Light.* Boston: Bulfinch Press, 1982. A coffee table photography art book—worth buying a coffee table for—from the master of Sierra Nevada photography.

Alden, Peter. *National Audubon Society Field Guide to California.* New York: Alfred A. Knopf, 1998. A wonderful field guide to some 1,000 of the state's native inhabitants, from the world's smallest butterfly—the Western Pygmy Blue—to its oldest, largest, and tallest trees. Well illustrated with striking color photography.

Alt, David, and Donald Hyndman. *Roadside Geology of Northern & Central California.* Missoula, MT: Mountain Press, 1999. Second edition. The classic glove-box companion guide to the northstate landscape is now revised—and expanded to include central regions.

Bailey, Harry P. *The Weather of Southern California.* Berkeley: University of California Press, 1966.

Bakker, Elna. *An Island Called California: An Ecological Introduction to Its Natural Communities.* Berkeley: University of California

Press, 1985. Expanded revised ed. An excellent, time-honored introduction to the characteristics of, and relationships between, California's natural communities. New chapters on Southern California, added in this edition, make *An Island* more helpful statewide.

Balls, Edward K. *Early Uses of California Plants.* Berkeley: University of California Press, 1962.

Barbour, Michael, Bruce Pavlik, Susan Lindstrom, and Frank Drysdale, with a foreword by Pulitzer Prize–winning California poet Gary Snyder. *California's Changing Landscapes: Diversity and Conservation of California Vegetation.* Sacramento: California Native Plant Society Press, 1993. Finalist for the Publishers Marketing Association's 1994 Benjamin Franklin Award in the Nature category, this well-illustrated, well-indexed lay guide to California's astonishing botanical variety is an excellent introduction. For more in-depth personal study, the society also publishes some excellent regional floras and plant keys.

Belzer, Thomas J. *Roadside Plants of Southern California.* Missoula, MT: Mountain Press, 1984. If as a nature lover you rarely venture far from the family car, this is the plant guide for you. From trees to cacti and wildflowers, the most likely roadside specimens are described in reasonable detail and illustrated with full-color photos.

Berry, William, and Elizabeth Berry. *Mammals of the San Francisco Bay Region.* Berkeley: University of California Press, 1959. Among other regional titles available: *Evolution of the Landscapes of the San Francisco Bay Region,* by Arthur David Howard; *Introduction to the Natural History of the San Francisco Bay Region,* by Arthur Smith; *Native Shrubs of the San Francisco Bay Region,* by Roxana S. Ferris; *Native Trees of the San Francisco Bay Region,* by Woodbridge Metcalf; *Rocks and Minerals of the San Francisco Bay Region,* by Oliver E. Bowen Jr.; *Spring Wildflowers of the San Francisco Bay Region,* by Helen Sharsmith; and *Weather of the San Francisco Bay Region,* by Harold Gilliam.

Blake, Tupper Ansel, and Peter Steinhart. *Two Eagles/Dos Aguilas: The Natural World of the United States–Mexico Borderlands.* Berkeley: University of California Press, 1994. One of those rare books well worth reading *and* displaying on the coffee table for everyone's appreciation. This award-winning book is a revelation, sharing its secrets through fine writing and stunning photography (color and black-and-white).

California Coastal Commission, State of California. *California Coastal Resource Guide.* Berkeley: University of California Press, 1997. This is the revised and expanded fifth edition of the California coast lover's bible, the indispensable guide to the Pacific coast and its wonders—the land, marine geology, biology—as well as parks, landmarks, and amusements. But for practical travel purposes, get the commission's *The California Coastal Access Guide,* listed under Enjoying the Outdoors below.

Carville, Julie Stauffer. *Hiking Tahoe's Wildflower Trails.* Renton, WA: Lone Pine Publishing, 1997. Reprint ed., previously published in 1990 as *Lingering in Tahoe's Wild Gardens.* A hiking guide offering 30 backcountry explorations and the 280 types of flowers you may find along the way (in late spring and summer).

Clarke, Charlotte Bringle. *Edible and Useful Plants of California.* Berkeley: University of California Press, 1977. With this book in hand, almost anyone can manage to make a meal in the wilderness—or whip up a spring salad from the vacant lot next door.

Cogswell, Howard. *Water Birds of California.* Berkeley: University of California Press, 1977.

Collier, Michael. *A Land in Motion: California's San Andreas Fault.* Berkeley: University of California Press, 1999. An intriguing geologic tour of the world's most famous fault, which runs the entire length of western California—and right through the San Francisco Bay Area. Wonderful photographs.

Crampton, Beecher. *Grasses in California.* Berkeley: University of California Press, 1974.

Dale, Nancy. *Flowering Plants of the Santa Monica Mountains: Coastal and Chaparral Regions of Southern California.* Santa Barbara: Capra Press, 1986. With 214 color photos, dozens of illustrations and maps, and suggested wildflower walks, this is an invaluable book to tuck into the daypack for anyone spending serious time in the Santa Monicas.

Dawson, E. Yale. *Cacti of California.* Berkeley: University of California Press, 1966.

Dawson, E. Yale, and Michael Foster. *Seashore Plants of California.* Berkeley: University of California Press, 1982.

DeSante, David, and Peter Pyle. *Distributional Checklist to North American Birds.* The most accurate and up-to-date information ever assembled on the abundance and status of birds north of Mexico—indispensable to serious birders—but hard to find. At last report, it was available through the Mono Lake Committee. For more information, see The Sierra Nevada chapter.

Duremberger, Robert. *Elements of California Geography.* Out of print but worth searching for. This is the classic work on California geography.

Ewing, Susan, and Elizabeth Grossman, eds. *Shadow Cat: Encountering the American Mountain Lion.* Seattle: Sasquatch Books, 1999. This engaging, highly partisan collection of essays explores the uneasy coexistence we humans have with *Felis concolor,* now that cougars are increasing in numbers and populating almost every area remaining to them.

Farrand, John, Jr. *Western Birds: An Audubon Handbook.* New York: McGraw-Hill Book Co., 1988. This birding guide includes color photographs instead of artwork for illustrations; conveniently included with descriptive listings. Though the book contains no range maps, the "Similar Species" listing helps eliminate birds with similar features.

Fitch, John. *Tidepool and Nearshore Fishes of California.* Berkeley: University of California Press, 1975.

Fitch, John E., and Robert J. Lavenberg. *California Marine Food and Game Fishes.* Berkeley: University of California Press, 1971.

Fix, David, and Andy Bezener. *Birds of Northern California.* Renton, WA: Lone Pine Publishing, 2000. This great new birding guide includes detailed, full-color illustrations of 328 birds found in Northern California along with other visual identification aids; range maps; complete bird descriptions; and lesser-known facts about each bird.

Fradkin, Philip L. *The Seven States of California: A Natural and Human History.* New York: Henry Holt & Co., 1995; subsequently published in paperback by the University of California Press. Both personal and historical exploration of California.

Fuller, Thomas C., and Elizabeth McClintock. *Poisonous Plants of California.* Berkeley: University of California Press, 1987.

Gaines, David. *Birds of Yosemite and the East Slope.* Berkeley: Artemisia Press, 1992. This comprehensive book describes the 343 species of birds in the Yosemite and Mono Lake regions, emphasizing their ecological relationships and survival status rather than serving as a birder's identification guide.

Gaines, David, and the Mono Lake Committee. *Mono Lake Guidebook.* Lee Vining, CA: Mono Lake Committee, 1989. *The* guidebook to Mono Lake and the eastern Sierra Nevada, now out in a new(er) edition, emphasizing the region's natural history.

Garth, John S., and J. W. Tilden. *California Butterflies.* Berkeley: University of California Press, 1986. At long last, the definitive field guide and key to California butterflies (in both the larval and adult stages) is available, and in paperback; compact and fairly convenient to tote around.

Geologic Society of the Oregon Country. *Roadside Geology of the Eastern Sierra Nevada.* Informative pamphlet-sized book including Devil's Postpile, Mono Lake, the White Mountains, and Yosemite, at last report available from the Mono Lake Committee (see The Sierra Nevada chapter).

Grillos, Steve. *Fern and Fern Allies of California.* Berkeley: University of California Press, 1966.

Grinnell, Joseph, and Alden Miller. *The Distribution of the Birds of California.* Out of print but worth looking for (try the Mono Lake Committee; see The Sierra Nevada chapter), this is the definitive California birder's guide—for those interested in serious study.

Hale, Mason, and Mariette Cole. *Lichens of California.* Berkeley: University of California Press, 1988.

Hall, Clarence A., Jr., ed. *Natural History of the White-Inyo Range, Eastern California.* Berkeley: University of California Press, 1991. This impressive 560-page tome covers all the natural wonders of the extraordinary landscape that rises up from the eastern edge of the Owens Valley—from native culture and the oldest living species on earth, the bristlecone pine, to hundreds of flowering plants and area fish, reptile, and bird species. Also well covered here: archaeology, geology, geomorphology, and meteorology.

Harris, Stephen. *Fire Mountains of the West: The Cascade and Mono Lake Volcanoes.* Missoula, MT: Mountain Press, 1988.

Hedgpeth, Joel W. *Introduction to Seashore Life of the San Francisco Bay Region and the Coast of Northern California.* Berkeley: University of California Press, 1969.

Hickman, Jim, ed. *The Jepson Manual: Higher Plants of California.* Berkeley: University of California Press (with cooperation and support from the California Native Plant Society and the Jepson Herbarium), 1993. At least 10 years in the making, *The Jepson Manual* is already considered the bible of California botany. The brainchild of both Jim Hickman and Larry Heckard, curator of the Jepson Herbarium, this book is a cumulative picture of the extraordinary flora of California, and the first comprehensive attempt to fit it all into one volume since the Munz *A California Flora* was published in 1959. The best work of almost 200 botanist-authors has been collected here, along with exceptional line drawings and illustrations (absent from the Munz flora) that make it easier to identify and compare plant species.

This book is the botanical reference book for a California lifetime—a hefty investment for a hefty tome, especially essential for serious ecologists and botanists, amateur and otherwise.

Hill, Mary. *California Landscape: Origin and Evolution.* Berkeley: University of California Press, 1984. An emphasis on the most recent history of California landforms. Also by Hill: *Geology of the Sierra Nevada.*

Hinton, Sam. *Seashore Life of Southern California.* Berkeley: University of California Press, 1988. Revised and expanded.

Houk, Walter, Sue Irwin, and Richard A. Lovett. *A Visitor's Guide to California's State Parks,* Sacramento, CA: California Department of Parks and Recreation, 1990. This large-format, very pretty book includes abundant full-color photography and brief, accessible basic information about the features and facilities of the state's parks and recreation areas. *A Visitor's Guide* is available at retail and online bookstores and at the state parks themselves.

Hunt, Charles B. *Death Valley: Geology, Ecology, Archaeology.* Berkeley: University of California Press, 1975.

Jaeger, Edmund C. *The California Deserts.* Palo Alto: Stanford University Press, 1965. Fourth ed. A true classic in natural history, first published in 1933, and a surprisingly poetic read. Example: "Let me have the delicious odors of the creosote bush and the saltbush when they are wetted with desert rains, look upon the endless variety and beauty of the clouds' far-flung forms, have the silence of the uninhabited mesas, and I am in a land enchanted."

Jaeger, Edmund C., and Arthur C. Smith. *Introduction to the Natural History of Southern California.* Berkeley: University of California Press, 1966. A must-have for the southstate naturalist's bookshelf.

Johnston, Verna R. *California Forests and Woodlands: A Natural History.* Berkeley: University of California Press, 1994. For beginning botany students, a very helpful general introduction to the plants, animals, and ecological relationships within California's varied types of forests.

Kaufman, Kenn. *Lives of North American Birds.* New York: Houghton Mifflin Co., 1997. Sponsored by the Roger Tory Peterson Institute. A bit bulky for a field guide but already considered a classic, this 674-page hardbound tome focuses less on identifying features and names and more on observing and understanding birds within the contexts of their own lives. Now, there's a concept.

Klauber, Laurence. *Rattlesnakes.* Berkeley: University of California Press, 1982.

Knute, Adrienne. *Plants of the East Mojave.* Cima, CA: Wide Horizons Press, 1991. A good botanical introduction to the plants of the Mojave National Preserve, well organized and easy to follow.

Latting, June, and Peter G. Rowlands, eds. *The California Desert: An Introduction to Natural Resources and Man's Impact. Volumes I and II.* June Latting Books, 1995 (distributed by the California Native Plant Society). This compendium includes just about everything known about California desert resources, a project unofficially started by June Latting in 1978 when the first Desert Conservation Area Advisory Committee meetings convened in Riverside. Published posthumously with the assistance of Peter Rowlands and June Latting's family, this is a must for any desert aficionado.

Leatherwood, Stephen, and Randall Reeves. *The Sierra Club Handbook of Whales and Dolphins.* San Francisco: Sierra Club Books, 1983.

Le Boeuf, Burney J., and Stephanie Kaza. *The Natural History of Año Nuevo.* Santa Cruz, CA: Otter B Books, 1985. Reprint ed. An excellent, very comprehensive guide to the natural features of the Año Nuevo area just north of Santa Cruz.

Lederer, Roger. *Pacific Coast Bird Finder.* Berkeley: Nature Study Guild, 1977. A handy, hip-pocket-sized guide to birding for beginners. Also available: *Pacific Coast Tree Finder* by Tom Watts, among similar titles. All "Finder" titles are now available through Wilderness Press.

McCauley, Jane, and the National Geographic Society staff. *National Geographic Society Field Guide to the Birds of North America.* Washington, D.C.: National Geographic Society, 1993. One of the best guides to bird identification available.

McConnaughey, Bayard H., and Evelyn McConnaughey. *Pacific Coast.* New York: Alfred A. Knopf, 1986. One of the Audubon Society Nature Guides. More than 600 color plates, keyed to region and habitat type, make it easy to identify marine mammals, shorebirds, seashells, and other inhabitants and features of the West Coast, from Alaska to California.

McGinnis, Samuel. *Freshwater Fishes of California.* Berkeley: University of California Press, 1985. Including a simple but effective method of identifying fish, this guide also offers fisherfolk help in developing better angling strategies, since it indicates when and where a species feeds and what its food preferences are.

McMinn, Howard. *An Illustrated Manual of California Shrubs.* Berkeley: University of California Press, 1939. Reprint ed. An aid in getting to know about 800 California shrubs, this classic manual includes keys, descriptions of flowering, elevations, and geographic distributions. For the serious amateur botanist, another title for the permanent library.

Miller, Crane S., and Richard S. Hyslop. *California: The Geography of Diversity*. Palo Alto, CA: Mayfield Publishing Company, 1999. Second ed.

Munz, Philip A. *California Desert Wildflowers*. Berkeley: University of California Press, 1962. A very useful and informative desert travel companion for wildflower aficionados, amateur and beginning botanists in particular. Entries are organized by flower color, so you don't have to do any "keying," and plants are listed first by common name. Line drawings illustrate each entry, and the book also includes 96 color photos.

Munz, Philip A. *A Flora of Southern California*. Berkeley: University of California Press, 1974. This hefty hardcover tome, 1,086 pages, should be more than enough to help any plant lover explore every square inch of unpaved Southern California.

Munz, Phillip A., and David D. Keck. *A California Flora and Supplement*. Berkeley: University of California Press, 1968. Until quite recently this was it, the California botanist's bible—a complete descriptive "key" to every plant known to grow in California—but quite hefty to tote around on pleasure trips. More useful for amateur botanists are Munz's *California Mountain Wildflowers, Shore Wildflowers,* and *California Desert Wildflowers,* as well as other illustrated plant guides published by UC Press. Serious amateur and professional botanists and ecologists are more than ecstatic these days about the recent publication of the *new* California plant bible: *The Jepson Manual,* edited by Jim Hickman. (For more information, see above.)

Neihaus, Theodore. *Sierra Wildflowers*. Berkeley: University of California Press, 1974.

Nilsson, Karen B. *A Wildflower by Any Other Name*. Yosemite National Park: Yosemite Association, 1994. This engaging book tells the story of pioneering Western naturalists whose names—Eschscholtz and Chamisso, for example—often define either genus or species in the Latin names of many native plants. In an age of mass-marketed information, this is a gold mine for serious botany students and trivia buffs alike.

Ornduff, Robert. *Introduction to California Plant Life*. Berkeley: University of California Press, 1974. An essential for native plant libraries, this classic offers a marvelous introduction to California's botanical abundance.

Orr, Robert T., and Roger Helm. *Marine Mammals of California*. Berkeley: University of California Press, 1989. Revised ed. A handy guide for identifying marine mammals along the California coast—with practical tips on the best places to observe them.

Orr, R. T., and D. B. Orr. *Mushrooms of Western North America*. Berkeley: University of California Press, 1979.

Pavlik, Bruce, Pamela Muick, Sharon Johnson, and Marjorie Popper. *Oaks of California*. Santa Barbara: Cachuma Press, 1991. In ancient European times, oaks were considered spiritual beings, the sacred inspiration of artists, healers, and writers since these particular trees were thought to court the lightning flash. Time spent with this stunning book will soon convince anyone that this truth lives on. Packed with photos and lovely watercolor illustrations, maps, even an oak lover's travel guide, this book celebrates the many species of California oaks.

Peterson, Roger Tory. *A Field Guide to Western Birds*. Boston: Houghton Mifflin Co., 1990. The third edition of this birding classic has striking new features, including full-color illustrations (including juveniles, females, and in-flight birds) facing the written descriptions. The only thing you'll have to flip around for are the range maps, tucked away in the back. Among other intriguing titles in the Peterson Field Guide series: *A Field Guide to Western Birds' Nests* by Hal Harrison.

Peterson, Victor. *Native Trees of the Sierra Nevada.* Berkeley: University of California Press, 1974.

Powell, Jerry. *California Insects.* Berkeley: University of California Press, 1980.

Raven, Peter H. *Native Shrubs of California.* Berkeley: University of California Press, 1966.

Raven, Peter H., and Daniel Axelrod. *Origin and Relationships of the California Flora.* Sacramento: California Native Plant Society Press, 1995. Reprint of the 1978 original, another title most appropriate for serious students of botany.

Rinehart, Dean, and Ward Smith. *Earthquakes and Young Volcanoes along the Eastern Sierra Nevada.* Palo Alto, CA: Genny Smith Books, 1982 (OP).

Robbins, Chandler, et al. *Birds of North America.* New York: Golden Books Publishing Co., 1983. A good field guide for California birdwatching.

Roos-Collins, Margit. *The Flavors of Home: A Guide to the Wild Edible Plants of the San Francisco Bay Area.* Berkeley: Heyday Books, 1990. Just the thing to help you whip up a fresh trailside salad, a botanical essay, field guide, and cookbook all in one.

Schmitz, Marjorie. *Growing California Native Plants.* Berkeley: University of California Press, 1980. A handy guide for those interested in planting, growing, and otherwise supporting the success of California's beleaguered native plants.

Schoenherr, Allan A. *A Natural History of California.* Berkeley: University of California Press, 1992. With introductory chapters on ecology and geology, *A Natural History* covers California's climate, geology, soil, plant life, and animals based on distinct bioregions, with almost 300 photographs and numerous illustrations and tables. An exceptionally readable and well-illustrated introduction to California's astounding natural diversity and drama

written by an ecology professor from CSU Fullerton, this 700-plus page reference belongs on any Californiac's library shelf.

Schoenherr, Allan A. and C. Robert Feldmeth. *A Natural History of the Islands of California.* Berkeley: University of California Press, 1999. A comprehensive introduction to California's Año Nuevo Island, Channel Islands, Farallon Islands, and the islands of San Francisco Bay—living evolutionary laboratories with unique species and ecological niches.

Starker, Leopold A. *The California Quail.* Berkeley: University of California Press, 1985. This is the definitive book on the California quail, its history and biology.

Stebbins, Robert. *California Amphibians and Reptiles.* Berkeley: University of California Press, 1972.

Storer, Tracy I., and Robert L. Usinger. *Sierra Nevada Natural History: An Illustrated Handbook.* Berkeley: University of California Press, 1989. The indispensable, all-in-one natural history companion volume, compact and packable, for appreciating and understanding Sierra Nevada.

Wallace, David Rains. *The Klamath Knot.* San Francisco: Sierra Club Books, 1983. Worthwhile and readable natural history of California's Klamath Mountains.

Weeden, Norman. *A Sierra Nevada Flora.* Berkeley: Wilderness Press, 1996. Fourth ed. Perhaps *the* definitive field guide to Sierra Nevada plants, this one includes trees, shrubs, and ferns in addition to wildflowers. Complete, accurate, and quite compact, with hundreds of illustrations.

Whitley, Stephen. *A Sierra Club Naturalist's Guide to the Sierra Nevada.* New York: Random House, 1982. Another excellent resource, perfect for backpackers and hikers as well as drive-by nature lovers.

Williams, H., and G. H. Curtis. *The Sutter Buttes of California: A Study of Plio-Pleistocene Vol-*

canism. Berkeley: University of California Press, 1979 (OP).

Wilson, Lynn, Jim Wilson, and Jeff Nichols. *Wildflowers of Yosemite.* Berkeley: The Sierra Press (distributed by Wilderness Press), 1994. A useful guide to most of the wildflowers common to Yosemite and the central Sierra Nevada, with descriptions in everyday English, color photographs, and species-specific road and trail wildflower tours.

Wiltens, James. *Thistle Greens and Mistletoe: Edible and Poisonous Plants of Northern California.* Berkeley: Wilderness Press, 1988 (OP). How to eat cactus and pinecones and make gourmet weed salads are just a few of the fascinating and practical facts shared here about common northstate plants.

ENJOYING THE OUTDOORS: RECREATION, TOURS, TRAVEL

Arce, Gary. *Defying Gravity: High Adventure on Yosemite's Walls.* Berkeley: Wilderness Press, 1995. So you need a little inspiration before you scale the heights? Here it is—a collection of adventurous climbers' stories, from early Yosemite climbing tales to more contemporary accounts of the park's classic climbs.

Bakalinsky, Adah. *Stairway Walks in San Francisco.* Berkeley: Wilderness Press, 1998. Third revised ed. This updated San Francisco classic offers 27 neighborhood walks connecting San Francisco's 200-plus stairways, choreographed by a veteran city walker and walking tour guide.

Brant, Michelle. *Timeless Walks in San Francisco: A Historical Walking Guide.* Berkeley: Brant, 1996.

Brown, Anne Marie. *Foghorn Outdoors: California Waterfalls—Your Key to Accessing the State's Most Spectacular Falls.* Emeryville, CA: Avalon Travel Publishing, 2000. Second ed. This trail guide points the way for thorough enjoyment of some 225 California waterfalls, whether you prefer to get there via hike, bike, backpack, or drive.

California Coastal Commission, State of California. *The California Coastal Access Guide.* Berkeley: University of California Press, 1997. Fifth revised ed. According to the *Oakland Tribune,* this is "no doubt the most comprehensive look at California's coastline published to date." A must-have for serious Californiacs.

California Coastal Conservancy, State of California. *San Francisco Bay Shoreline Guide.* Berkeley: University of California Press, 1995. This is it, the definitive guide to the entire 400-mile Bay Trail shoreline route, from its piers to its paths and parks. Comprehensive and user-friendly, with full-color maps and illustrations.

Cassady, Jim, and Fryar Calhoun. *California White Water: A Guide to the Rivers.* Berkeley: North Fork Press, 1995. Third revised ed. Also available: *California River Maps* and *White Water Guides.*

Clark, Jeanne L. *California Wildlife Viewing Guide.* Helena, MT: Falcon Press, 1996. Second ed. This revised and expanded guide tells you where to go for a good look at native wildlife, and what to do once you're there. Color photos, overview maps.

Coale, Jim. *Canoeing the California Highlands: A Quiet Water Guide to Paddler's Paradise.* Berkeley: Wilderness Press, 1998. This guide takes readers to more than 120 serene and scenic canoeing spots, from the southern Sierra Nevada to the Klamath Mountains in the far north. Both short trips and adventure treks are included, along with paddle-in camping suggestions. Now all you need are a two-wheel-drive vehicle, canoe, paddles, and life vests.

Collins, Andrew. *Fodor's Gay Guide to Los Angeles and Southern California.* New York: Fodor's, 1997.

Culliney, John, and Edward Crockett. *Exploring Underwater.* San Francisco: Sierra Club Books, 1980.

Cutter, Ralph, et al. *Sierra Trout Guide.* Portland, OR: Frank Amato Publications, 1991. Expanded and revised, this is a comprehensive introduction to High Sierra trout fishing.

Darvil, Fred, Jr., M.D. *Mountaineering Medicine and Backcountry Medical Guide.* Berkeley: Wilderness Press, 1998. 14th revised ed. Written specifically for mountaineers, this small manual is indispensable for all outdoorsfolk and wilderness travelers.

Dirksen, Diane J. *Recreation Lakes of California.* Port Angeles, WA: Recreation Sales Publishing, 1999. 12th ed. A very useful guide to the multitude of recreation lakes in California, complete with general maps (not to scale) and local contact addresses and phones. A worthwhile investment for boaters and fisherfolk.

Doss, Margot Patterson. *New San Francisco at Your Feet.* New York: Grove-Atlantic Press, 1990. One of a series of popular Bay Area walking guides by the same author, including: *The Bay Area at Your Feet,* 1987 (Lexikos); *There, There: East San Francisco Bay at Your Feet* (OP); and *A Walker's Yearbook: 52 Seasonal Walks in the San Francisco Bay Area,* (OP).

Fein, Art. *L.A. Musical History Tour: A Guide to the Rock and Roll Landmarks of Los Angeles.* London: Faber and Faber, 1990.

Felzer, Ron. *High Sierra Hiking Guide to Hetch Hetchy.* Berkeley: Wilderness Press, 1983 (OP). Other High Sierra Hiking Guides by Felzer include *Mineral King* and *Devil's Postpile.*

Fong-Torres, Shirley. *San Francisco Chinatown: A Walking Tour.* San Francisco: China Books, 1991. Definitely an insider's guide to Chinatown, escorting visitors through the neighborhood almost step by step while filling in fascinating details about the history and culture of the Chinese in California. Fong-Torres also includes a culinary education, even abundant recipes for simple and authentic Chinese cuisine. For information on "Wok Wiz" culinary tours led by the author and her staff, see this book's San Francisco chapter. And buy *In the*

Chinese Kitchen with Shirley Fong-Torres, 1993 (Pacific View Press).

Forée, Rebecca Poole, et al., eds. *Northern California Best Places.* Seattle: Sasquatch Books, 1998. Third ed. This compilation of detailed restaurant and accommodation reviews offers some entertaining insights as well as good local guidance in most price categories— always a plus.

Foster, Lynne. *Adventuring in the California Desert: The Sierra Club Travel Guide to the Great Basin, Mojave, and Colorado Desert Regions of California.* San Francisco: Sierra Club Books, 1997. Revised and updated ed. So, you wanna do the desert? This book is the best overall guide for figuring out where to go, when, and how. Out-there desert hikes are the book's obvious strength. But along with such sage advice you'll also find out plenty about desert history and natural history.

Freeman, Jim. *California Steelhead Fishing.* San Francisco: Chronicle Books, 1984 (OP). An outdoor bible for California fisherfolk, with firsthand tips on how and where to fish for steelhead. Also by Freeman, if you can find it somewhere: *California Trout Fishing.*

Gayot, André, ed. *The Best of Los Angeles and Southern California.* Los Angeles: Gault Millau, 2001. Updated every three to four years. The bible for what to see and do, where to shop, and where to eat in L.A. and Southern California. Even Angelenos always have a copy on hand.

Gebhard, David, and Robert Winter. *Los Angeles: An Architectural Guide.* Layton, UT: Gibbs Smith, 1994. This is the Baedeker for devotees of Los Angeles architecture, encyclopedic in scope, though you may find the error quotient a bit high, even by everything-always-changes L.A. standards. Also worth it, from the same authors, with a broader reach: *A Guide to Architecture in Los Angeles and Southern California.*

Gersg-Young, Marjorie. *Hot Springs and Hot Pools of the Southwest.* Berkeley: Aqua Thermal Access (distributed by Wilderness Press), 1998. Revised and updated ed. A useful guide to California's commercial as well as unimproved (natural) yet accessible hot springs, including those in Arizona, Nevada, New Mexico, Texas, and Baja Mexico.

Gleeson, Bill. *Back Road Wineries of California*. San Francisco: Chronicle Books, 1994. Revised ed. Also by Gleeson: *Weekends for Two in Northern California* (1995).

Green, David. *Marble Mountain Wilderness*. Berkeley: Wilderness Press, 1980 (OP). Also by Green: *A Pacific Crest Odyssey*.

Greenwald, John A. *Saddleback Sightseeing in California: A Guide to Rental Horses, Trail Rides, and Guest Ranches*. Baldwin Park, CA: Gem Guides Book Co., 1992. For modern-day dudes and dudettes, everything from hourly rental riding opportunities to guest ranch riding and pack trips is included here.

Hart, John. *Walking Softly in the Wilderness: The Sierra Club Guide to Backpacking*. San Francisco: Sierra Club Books, 1998. Third reprint ed. Also by Hart: *Hiking the Bigfoot Country* and *Hiking the Great Basin*.

Hosler, Ray. *Bay Area Bike Rides*. San Francisco: Chronicle Books, 1994. Second ed. More than 50 bike rides throughout the greater Bay Area—all the way to Napa and Sonoma Counties—useful for both mountain bikers and touring cyclists.

Jardine, Ray. *The Pacific Crest Trail Handbook: Innovative Techniques and Trail Tested Instruction for the Long Distance Hiker*. Berkeley: Adventure Lore Press, 1992 (OP). The author and his wife have hiked the entire 2,500-mile route between Mexico and Canada *twice,* so the information included here—on everything from equipment and clothing to mosquitoes, ticks, and bears—is all a serious hiker needs to know. Also by Jardine—and still available, at last report—is *Beyond Backpacking: Ray Jardine's Guide to Lightweight Hiking.*

Jeneid, Michael. *Adventure Kayaking: Trips from the Russian River to Monterey*. Berkeley: Wilderness Press, 1998. Tired of fighting that freeway traffic around the Bay Area? Try a kayak. Under decent weather conditions—and with an experienced kayaker to clue you in—you can get just about everywhere. If you'll be shoving off a bit farther south, try *Adventure Kayaking: Trips from Big Sur to San Diego,* by Robert Mohle (1998).

Jenkins, J. C., and Ruby Johnson Jenkins. *Exploring the Southern Sierra: East Side*. Berkeley: Wilderness Press, 1992. Third ed. Originally titled *Self Propelled in the Southern Sierra, Volume 1*. This guide includes 150 adventures in one of the state's remaining sanctuaries of solitude. Includes a four-color foldout map. Also by the Jenkins' (also retitled): *Exploring the Southern Sierra: West Side* (1995).

Keator, Glenn. *Complete Garden Guide to the Native Shrubs of California*. San Francisco: Chronicle Books, 1994. California's native plants are under siege just about everywhere in the Golden State—so help nature out by stashing some natural biological diversity in your own backyard. More than 500 native shrub species are listed here, some beautifully represented by turn-of-the-20th-century line drawings.

Kegan, Stephanie, and Elizabeth Pomada. *Fun Places to go with Children in Southern California*. San Francisco: Chronicle Books, 1997. Sixth ed. As important as finding a place to eat with kids is finding appropriate places to take them before and after meals.

Kirkendall, Tom, and Vicky Springs. *Bicycling the Pacific Coast*. Seattle: The Mountaineers, 1998. Third ed. A very good, very practical mile-by-mile guide to the tricky business of cycling along the California coast (and north).

Koenig, David. *Mouse Tales: A Behind-the-Ears Look at Disneyland*. Irvine, CA: Bonaventure Press, 1994. Disneyland is still one of Koenig's happiest places on earth, but that doesn't mean there aren't unofficial tales to tell—unsavory stories such as labor and discrimination disputes, gang fights, stabbings, shootings, a full-tilt riot, accidents, and of course lawsuits. And then there was the time the Yippies—Youth International Party antiwar activists—flew the Viet Cong flag over Tom Sawyer Island and turned Monsanto's Adventure through Inner Space into a potsmoking den of druggy iniquity. Too much like real life, sure, and more than the average reader would care to know about Disneyland, but a good read nonetheless.

Larson, Lane, and Peggy Larson. *Caving.* San Francisco: Sierra Club Books, 1982.

Libkind, Marcus. *Ski Tours in Lassen Volcanic National Park.* Berkeley: Bittersweet Enterprises (distributed by Wilderness Press), 1989. This tour-by-tour guide includes options for beginners and accomplished cross-country skiers. Special features are highlighted; topo maps and mileage logs included. Libkind has also written four Ski Tours in the Sierra Nevada guides, covering *Lake Tahoe; Carson Pass, Bear Valley, and Pinecrest; Yosemite, Kings Canyon, Sequoia, and Vicinity;* and *East of the Sierra Crest.*

Lindsay, Lowell, and Diana Lindsay. *The Anza-Borrego Desert Region: A Guide to the State Park and Adjacent Areas.* Berkeley: Wilderness Press, 1998. Fourth ed. This guide will take you wherever you want to go—responsibly, whether on foot or in four-wheel drive—and bring you back amazingly well-informed about the life and lore of this immense and lovely desert.

Linkhart, Luther. *The Trinity Alps: A Hiking and Backpacking Guide.* Berkeley: Wilderness Press, 1994. Third ed.

Lorentzen, Bob. *The Hiker's Hip Pocket Guide to the Mendocino Coast.* Mendocino, CA: Bored Feet Publications, 1998. Third ed. This easy-to-follow hiking guide now includes 100 more miles of trails. Coverage includes all Mendocino area state parks, Jackson State Forest, Sinkyone Wilderness State Park, and little-known coastal access points. Also by Lorentzen: *The Hiker's Hip Pocket Guide to*

the *Mendocino Highlands, The Hiker's Hip Pocket Guide to the Humboldt Coast,* and *The Hiker's Hip Pocket Guide to Sonoma County.*

Lorentzen, Bob, and Richard Nichols. *Hiking the California Coastal Trail, Volume One: Oregon to Monterey.* Mendocino, CA: Bored Feet Publications, 1998. The first comprehensive guide to the work-in-progress California Coastal Trail, America's newest and most diverse long-distance trail. Published in conjunction with Coastwalk—which receives a hefty percentage of the proceeds, to support its efforts to complete the trail—this accessible guide describes 85 sections of the California Coastal Trail's northern reach. Keep an eye out, too, for *Hiking the California Coastal Trail, Volume Two: Monterey to Mexico,* tentatively scheduled for publication in 1999.

Margolin, Malcolm. *East Bay Out.* Berkeley: Heyday Books, 1988. Second revised ed. Published with the cooperation and sponsorship of the East Bay Regional Parks District, this excellent guide focuses as much on the *feeling* as the facts of the East Bay's remaining wildlands, also urban parks and diversions. Highly recommended.

McConnell, Doug, with Jerry Emory and Stacy Gelken. *Bay Area Backroads.* San Francisco: Chronicle Books, 1999. Day trips and more throughout the greater Bay Area—and beyond—brought to you by the host of the San Francisco Bay Area's most popular local television show.

McKinney, John. *Coast Walks: 150 Adventures Along the California Coast.* Santa Barbara: Olympus Press, 1999. The new edition of McKinney's coast hiking classic contains plenty of new adventures, from Border Field State Park at the Mexican Border north to Damnation Creek and Pelican Bay. Along the way, you'll also learn about local lore, history, and natural history—a bargain no matter how you hike it. Maps and illustrations.

McKinney, John. *Day Hiker's Guide to California State Parks.* Santa Barbara: Olympus Press,

2000. All you need to know to stretch your legs *and* see the sights in the Golden State's hikable parks and recreation areas.

McKinney, John. *Day Hiker's Guide to Southern California*, Santa Barbara: Olympus Press, 1998. Second revised ed. Out in new, updated form in May 1998, McKinney's Southern California hiking guide covers it all, from beach to desert badlands. Helpful maps (to scale) and black-and-white photos.

McMillon, Bill, and Kevin McMillon. *Best Hikes With Children: San Francisco's North Bay.* Seattle: The Mountaineers, 1992. Also consider the McMillons' hiking guides to the South Bay and Sacramento.

Mitchell, Linda, and Allen Mitchell. *California Parks Access.* Berkeley: Cougar Pass Publications, 1992 (distributed by Wilderness Press). A very useful guide to national and state parks in California for visitors with limited mobility. Both challenges and wheelchair-accessible features are listed. Accessible appendixes are helpful, too.

Morey, Kathy. *Hot Showers, Soft Beds, and Dayhikes in the Sierra Nevada: Walks and Strolls Near Lodgings.* Berkeley: Wilderness Press, 1996. You say the ol' bones are getting too creaky to spend too many nights on the cold, hard ground? Well, so be it. With this handy guide for companionship, you can still enjoy the spectacular strolls available throughout the Sierra Nevada. Collected here are 120 great day hikes, complete with trailhead directions and thorough route descriptions.

National Register of Historic Places, Early History of the California Coast. Washington, D.C.: National Conference of State Historic Preservation Officers, 1997. Map. This fold-out introduction to the California coast serves as a travel itinerary with 45 stops illustrating the coast's earliest settlement and culture.

Neumann, Phyllis. *Sonoma County Bike Trails.* Second ed. Penngrove, CA: Penngrove Publications, 1999. Third revised ed. The long-running, ever-popular cycling guide to Sonoma County. Also available: *Marin County Bike Trails.*

Niesen, Thomas M. *Beachcomber's Guide to California Marine Life.* Houston: Gulf Publishing Co, 1994.

Olmsted, Gerald W. *The Best of the Sierra Nevada.* New York: Crown Publishers, Inc., 1991 (OP). Still a fascinating and useful guidebook and companion volume, especially generous with history, natural history, and outback recreational information.

Ostertag, Rhonda, and George Ostertag. *California State Parks: A Complete Recreation Guide.* Seattle: The Mountaineers, 1995. Moving from north to south, this readable companion serves as a good general introduction to the state parks—and guide to what to do while you're there, with an emphasis on hikes. Here California is divided into six regions. Helpful maps, some entertaining photos.

Parr, Barry. *San Francisco and the Bay Area.* Oakland: Compass American Guides, 1999. Fifth ed. With its dazzling prose and impressive intellectual intimacy, Parr's general guide to The City and vicinity is one of the best available—enjoyable, too, even for California natives, as companion reading.

Perry, John, and Jane Greverus Perry. *The Sierra Club Guide to the Natural Areas of California.* San Francisco: Sierra Club Books, 1997. Second ed. A just-the-facts yet very useful guide to California's public lands and parks—a book to tuck into the glove box. Organized by regions, also indexed for easy access.

Pitcher, Don. *Berkeley Inside/Out.* Berkeley: Heyday Books, 1989 (OP). The definitive general guide to Berkeley, featuring an abundance of practical facts and insider insights as well as Malcolm Margolin's "Historical Introduction."

Pomada, Elizabeth. *Fun Places to Go with Children in Northern California.* San Francisco:

Chronicle Books, 1997. Eighth ed. This long-running guide is based on the premise that, as important as it is to find a comfortable place to eat with kids, equally important is finding appropriate places to take them before and after meals. For aficionados of California's Victorian homes and buildings, the author's *Painted Ladies* series, co-authored with Michael Larsen, is also quite charming.

Rae, Cheri, ed. *Death Valley: A Guide. The 1938 WPA Guide Updated for Today's Traveler.* Santa Barbara: Olympus Press, 1991. Originally written and compiled by the Federal Writers' Project of the Works Progress Administration of Northern California, and published as part of the WPA's American Guide Series by Houghton Mifflin Co., Boston, 1939. For enlightenment, entertainment, and the surprising historical perspective of a mere half-century or so, this book is hard to beat as a general interest guide to Death Valley.

Rae, Cheri, and John McKinney. *Mojave National Preserve: A Visitor's Guide.* Santa Barbara: Olympus Press, 1999. A good introduction to the preserve itself, and particularly its hiking trails.

Rizzo, David "Dr. Roadmap." *Freeway Alternates.* Baldwin Park, CA: Gem Guides Book Co., 1990. So, you plan to get around Southern California without venturing onto the fearsome freeways? It can be done—and this book shows you how.

Roberts, Brian, and Richard Schwadel. *L.A. Shortcuts: The Guidebook For Drivers Who Hate To Wait.* Los Angeles: Red Car Press, 1989. Hey, road warriors. Here's another book that'll help you master the mysteries of L.A. driving. This one does indeed offer some great L.A. shortcuts—making it possible to get from Burbank to Los Feliz without freeways, for example, avoid crazed surface streets on the way to Hollywood, and take the "back door" route into Dodger Stadium. And with this book you get just the basics—brief descriptions of what you're doing plus maps—so you won't get slowed down by history, social issues, shopping, etc.

Roper, Steve. *The Climbers' Guide to the High Sierra.* New York: Random House, 1995. Also by Roper: *The Climbers' Guide to Yosemite Valley.*

Rowell, Galen, ed. *The Vertical World of Yosemite: A Collection of Writings and Photographs on Rock Climbing in Yosemite.* Berkeley: Wilderness Press, 1974; re-released in 1991. An inspiration to climbers everywhere, Rowell's first book, back in print with a new introduction, shares the Yosemite mountain high in the words of 14 climbers. Abundant astounding photographs, some color.

Rusmore, Jean. *The Bay Area Ridge Trail: Ridgetop Adventures Above San Francisco Bay.* San Francisco: Wilderness Press, 1998. This update of the original edition offers abundant adventures for hikers, bikers, and horseback riders, along 38 completed segments of this in-progress trail. Includes area maps, trailhead directions, and complete trail descriptions.

Rusmore, Jean, et al. *Peninsula Trails: Outdoor Adventures on the San Francisco Peninsula.* Berkeley: Wilderness Press, 1999. This updated third edition covers all parks and open-space preserves from Fort Funston south to Saratoga Gap. Also by Rusmore, and Frances Spangle: *South Bay Trails: Outdoor Adventures Around the Santa Clara Valley.*

Schad, Jerry. *Afoot and Afield in San Diego County.* Berkeley: Wilderness Press, 1998. Third ed. Well-written, informative hiking guide offering a wide variety of hikes (rated for difficulty) along the coast and inland both in mountainous areas and desert. Also by Jerry Schad: *Afoot and Afield in Los Angeles County* (2000) and *Afoot and Afield in Orange County* (1996).

Schad, Jerry. *California Deserts.* Helena, MT: Falcon Press, 1997. Second ed. A good out-and-about guide to the desert, from the Mojave to Death Valley. Lots of lore, lots of hikes.

Schaffer, Jeffrey. *Hiking the Big Sur Country: The Ventana Wilderness.* Berkeley: Wilderness Press, 1988. Other good hiking and backpacking guides by this prolific pathfinder include: *The Carson-Iceberg Wilderness; Desolation Wilderness and the South Lake Tahoe Basin; Lassen Volcanic National Park; The Pacific Crest Trail Volume 1: California; The Tahoe Sierra;* and *Yosemite National Park.*

Schifrin, Ben. *Emigrant Wilderness and Northwestern Yosemite.* Berkeley: Wilderness Press, 1990.

Selters, Andy, and Michael Zanger. *The Mt. Shasta Book: A Guide to Hiking, Climbing, Skiing, and Exploring the Mountain and Surrounding Area.* Berkeley: Wilderness Press, 2001. Second ed.

Silverman, Goldie. *Backpacking with Babies and Small Children.* Berkeley: Wilderness Press, 1998. Third ed. Everything adventurous parents need to know, or consider, before heading to the woods with youngsters in tow.

Soares, Marc J. *Best Coast Hikes of Northern California: A Guide to the Top Trails from Big Sur to the Oregon Border.* San Francisco: Sierra Club Books, 1998. There's something for everyone here—75 scenic trails, organized north to south, suited for all skill levels (including mention of those that allow dogs). Also well worth it from Soares: *75 Year-Round Hikes in Northern California* and *100 Classic Hikes in Northern California,* the latter coauthored with John R. Soares.

Socolich, Sally. *Bargain Hunting in the Bay Area.* San Francisco: Chronicle Books, 2000. The ultimate shop-til-you-drop guide, now in its 13th edition, including discount stores, outlets, flea markets, and the year's best sales.

Stanton, Ken. *Great Day Hikes in & around Napa Valley.* Mendocino, CA: Bored Feet Publications, 1997. Updated edition. There's more to do in the Napa Valley than eat and sample fine wines—like hiking. This engrossing guide, combining detailed trail information with local history and lore, leads readers to 16 separate destinations and along some 40 trails.

Stevens, Barbara, and Nancy Conner. *Where on Earth: A Guide to Specialty Nurseries and Other Resources for California Gardeners.* Berkeley: Heyday Books, 1999. Fourth ed. Ever wondered where to get that unusual color of iris or that exotic azalea, or where to find the state's best native plant nurseries? Wonder no more. California gardeners won't be able to live for long without *this* essential resource.

Stienstra, Tom. *Foghorn Outdoors: California Camping—The Complete Guide to More Than 1,500 Campgrounds in the Golden State.* Emeryville, CA: Foghorn Outdoors, 2001. Twelfth ed. This is undoubtedly the ultimate reference to California camping and campgrounds, public and private. Every single one is in here. Also included here are Stienstra's "Secret Campgrounds," an invaluable list when the aim is to truly get away from it all. In addition to a thorough practical introduction to the basics of California camping—and reviews of the latest high-tech gear, for hiking and camping comfort and safety—this guidebook is meticulously organized by area, starting with the general subdivisions of Northern, Central, and Southern California. Even accidental outdoorspeople should carry this one along at all times.

Stienstra, Tom. *Foghorn Outdoors: California Fishing.* Emeryville, CA: Foghorn Outdoors, 1999. This is it, *the* guide for people who think finding God has something to do with strapping on rubber waders or climbing into a tiny boat; making educated fish-eyed guesses about lures, ripples, or lake depths; and generally observing a strict code of silence in the outdoors. As besieged as California's fisheries have been by the state's 30 million-plus population and the attendant devastations and distractions of modern times, fisherfolk can still enjoy some world-class sport in California. This tome contains just about everything novices and masters need to know to figure out what to do as well as where and when to do it.

Stienstra, Tom. *Foghorn Outdoors: Easy Camping in Northern California.* Emeryville: Foghorn Outdoors, 1999. Second ed. A great guide for beginning campers, detailing 100 easily accessible campgrounds and cabin getaways.

Also worthwhile from Stienstra: *Foghorn Outdoors: California Recreational Lakes and Rivers* and *Foghorn Outdoors: California Wildlife* (among others).

Sunderland, Bill. *Fly Fishing the Sierra Nevada.* Aguabonita Books, 1999. A must-have for High Sierra fly fishers, this book is something of a road guide to fine fishing—taking fisherfolk along major highways to all the essential turnoffs and best streams.

Sunderland, Bill, and Dale Lackey. *California Blue Ribbon Trout Streams.* Portland, OR: Frank Amato Publications, 1998. Second revised ed. This great angling guide includes world-class fishing sites accessible by car plus all the particulars, including best baits, flies, and lures.

Tejada-Flores, Lito. *Backcountry Skiing.* San Francisco: Sierra Club Books, 1981.

Unterman, Patricia, *Patricia Unterman's Food Lover's Guide to San Francisco.* San Francisco: Chronicle Books, 1997. Now out in an updated second edition, this is a marvelous guide to gustatory bliss by the Bay—written by the *San Francisco Examiner* food critic, also owner of the Hayes Street Grill—includes cheese shops, coffee emporiums, and favorites cafés and restaurants.

Varney, Philip. *Southern California's Best Ghost Towns: A Practical Guide.* Norman, OK: University of Oklahoma Press, 1990. For anyone intrigued by the vastness of California's deserts, particularly those empty areas once home to human enterprise, this book is a treasure. Lively, informative histories combine with photographs and maps to take you there. The large-format presentation of this book is its only drawback—an awkward, impractical size to pack along.

Wach, Bonnie. *San Francisco as You Like It: 20 Tailor-Made Tours for Culture Vultures, Shopaholics, Neo-Bohemians, Fitness Freaks, Savvy Natives, and Everyone Else.* San Francisco: Chronicle Books, 1998. A hefty helping of more than the usual tourist fare, from The Politically Correct and Avant-Garde Aunts tours to Current and Former Hippies, and Queer and Curious. And a good time will be had by all.

Wallis, Michael. *Route 66: The Mother Road.* New York: St. Martin's Press, 1990. Worthwhile purchase for those obsessed with the almost vanished two-lane visage of the Mother Road, ol' Route 66 from Illinois to California. Though *Route 66* is a bit heavy on diners and waitresses and anti-interstatism, what is also here is the species memory of what it was like to take that lonely road west—accompanied by hang-on-the-door canvas water bags to make sure you and yours didn't die before you'd arrived.

Wayburn, Peggy. *Adventuring in the San Francisco Bay Area.* San Francisco: Sierra Club Books, 1999. Third ed. A fine guide to outdoor activities in the nine Bay Area counties, as well as the islands of the bay. Appendices list frequent and occasional bird visitors, as well as California state parks, environmental organizations, and nature classes, all with addresses and phones.

Weintraub, David, with a foreword by Galen Rowell. *East Bay Trails: Outdoor Adventures in Alameda and Contra Costa Counties.* Berkeley: Wilderness Press, 1998. This complete and up-to-date guide to Alameda and Contra Costa Counties is particularly useful for hikers, but also offers out-there guidance for mountain bikers and equestrians.

Weintraub, David. *North Bay Trails: Outdoor Adventures in Marin, Napa, and Sonoma Counties.* Berkeley: Wilderness Press, 1999. Once you get there, this substantial guide to North Bay trails will help you get around.

White, Michael C. *Snowshoe Trails of Tahoe.* Berkeley: Wilderness Press, 1998. Snap on those snowshoes and hike Tahoe trails in winter. This guide takes you on 43 of the Tahoe area's best snowshoe trips, from easy jaunts to all-day workouts. Includes trailhead directions and detailed trip descriptions.

Whitnah, Dorothy L. *Point Reyes*. Berkeley: Wilderness Press, 1997. Third revised ed. A very good and comprehensive guide (with an introduction by John Carroll) including trails, campgrounds, and picnic areas.

Winnett, Thomas, and Melanie Findling. *Backpacking Basics*. Berkeley: Wilderness Press, 1994. Fourth ed. All you need to know about going the distance on foot—with an emphasis on getting (and staying) in shape, the principles of low-impact camping, and how to save money on just about everything you'll need.

Winnett, Thomas, and Kathy Morey. *Guide to the John Muir Trail*. Berkeley: Wilderness Press, 1998. Very worthwhile, also co-authored by Winnett: *Sierra North: 100 Back-Country Trips* (1997) and *Sierra South: 100 Back-Country Trips* (1993).

Zagat Survey, ed. *Los Angeles/Southern California Restaurants*. New York: Zagat Survey. An eater's survey of the best and most beloved southstate dining destinations in Los Angeles and beyond (Orange County, Palm Springs, San Diego, Santa Barbara), annually updated.

Zagat Survey, ed. *San Francisco/Bay Area Restaurants*. New York: Zagat Survey. This annually updated collection, a compilation of "people's reviews" of regional restaurants, is a fairly reliable guide to what's hot and what's not in San Francisco and surrounding Bay Area destinations.

ABOUT THE AUTHOR

Kim Weir is a California native. She is also a journalist and writer. A curious generalist by nature, Weir is most happy when turning over rocks—literally and figuratively—or poking into this and that to discover what usually goes unnoticed. She lives in Northern California.

Weir's formal study of environmental issues began at the University of California at Santa Barbara and continued at California State University, Chico, where she studied biology and earned a bachelor's degree in environmental studies and analysis. Since all things are interconnected, as a journalist Weir covered the political environment and the natural and unnatural antics of politicians. Before signing on with Moon Publications, she held an editorial post with a scholarly publishing company. She has also served as communications director for the Faculty Association of California Community Colleges (FACCC).

Weir is a member of the Society of American Travel Writers (SATW). Her award-winning essay on ecotourism was published in the 1993 international *American Express Annual Review of Travel.* She is also a graduate student, a member of the initial class of the new California State University consortium MFA in Creative Writing program.

U.S.~METRIC CONVERSION

1 inch = 2.54 centimeters (cm)
1 foot = .304 meters (m)
1 yard = 0.914 meters
1 mile = 1.6093 kilometers (km)
1 km = .6214 miles
1 fathom = 1.8288 m
1 chain = 20.1168 m
1 furlong = 201.168 m
1 acre = .4047 hectares
1 sq km = 100 hectares
1 sq mile = 2.59 square km
1 ounce = 28.35 grams
1 pound = .4536 kilograms
1 short ton = .90718 metric ton
1 short ton = 2000 pounds
1 long ton = 1.016 metric tons
1 long ton = 2240 pounds
1 metric ton = 1000 kilograms
1 quart = .94635 liters
1 US gallon = 3.7854 liters
1 Imperial gallon = 4.5459 liters
1 nautical mile = 1.852 km

To compute celsius temperatures, subtract 32 from Fahrenheit and divide by 1.8. To go the other way, multiply celsius by 1.8 and add 32.

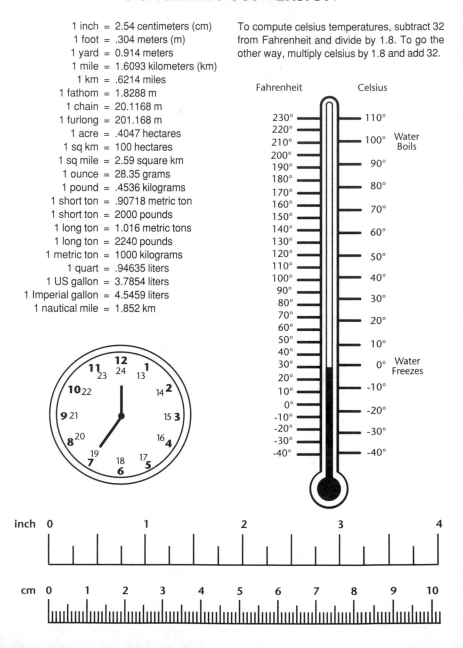

ACCOMMODATIONS

RESTAURANTS

GENERAL INDEX

**AVALON
TRAVEL**
p u b l i s h i n g

How far will our travel guides take you? As far as you want.

Discover a rhumba-fueled nightspot in Old Havana, explore prehistoric tombs in Ireland, hike beneath California's centuries-old redwoods, or embark on a classic road trip along Route 66. Our guidebooks deliver solidly researched, trip-tested information—minus any generic froth—to help globetrotters or weekend warriors create an adventure uniquely their own.

And we're not just about the printed page. Public television viewers are tuning in to Rick Steves' new travel series, Rick Steves' Europe. On the Web, readers can cruise the virtual black top with Road Trip USA author Jamie Jensen and learn travel industry secrets from Edward Hasbrouck of The Practical Nomad. With Foghorn AnyWare eBooks, users of handheld devices can place themselves "inside" the content of the guidebooks.

In print. On TV. On the Internet. In the palm of your hand.
We supply the information. The rest is up to you.

Avalon Travel Publishing
Something for everyone

www.travelmatters.com

Avalon Travel Publishing guides are available at your favorite book or travel store.

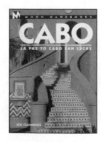

FOGHORN OUTDOORS guides are for campers, hikers, boaters, anglers, bikers, and golfers of all levels of daring and skill. Each guide focuses on a specific U.S. region and contains site descriptions and ratings, driving directions, facilities and fees information, and easy-to-read maps that leave only the task of deciding where to go.

"Foghorn Outdoors has established an ecological conservation standard unmatched by any other publisher."
~Sierra Club

WWW.FOGHORN.COM

TRAVEL SMART guidebooks are accessible, route-based driving guides focusing on regions throughout the United States and Canada. Special interest tours provide the most practical routes for family fun, outdoor activities, or regional history for a trip of anywhere from two to 22 days. Travel Smarts take the guesswork out of planning a trip by recommending only the most interesting places to eat, stay, and visit.

"One of the few travel series that rates sightseeing attractions. That's a handy feature. It helps to have some guidance so that every minute counts."
~San Diego Union-Tribune

CiTY·SMaRT™ guides are written by local authors with hometown perspectives who have personally selected the best places to eat, shop, sightsee, and simply hang out. The honest, lively, and opinionated advice is perfect for business travelers looking to relax with the locals or for longtime residents looking for something new to do Saturday night.

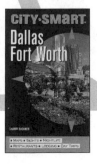

Will you have enough stories to tell your grandchildren?

Yahoo! Travel

DO YOU YAHOO!?